ENCYCLOPAEDIA
JUDAICA

ENCYCLOPAEDIA JUDAICA

SECOND EDITION

VOLUME 22
THEMATIC OUTLINE AND INDEX

Fred Skolnik, *Editor in Chief*
Michael Berenbaum, *Executive Editor*

MACMILLAN REFERENCE USA
An imprint of Thomson Gale, a part of The Thomson Corporation

IN ASSOCIATION WITH
KETER PUBLISHING HOUSE LTD., JERUSALEM

Detroit • New York • San Francisco • New Haven, Conn. • Waterville, Maine • London

ENCYCLOPAEDIA JUDAICA, Second Edition

Fred Skolnik, *Editor in Chief*
Michael Berenbaum, *Executive Editor*
Shlomo S. (Yosh) Gafni, *Editorial Project Manager*
Rachel Gilon, *Editorial Project Planning and Control*

Thomson Gale
Gordon Macomber, *President*
Frank Menchaca, *Senior Vice President and Publisher*
Jay Flynn, *Publisher*
Hélène Potter, *Publishing Director*

Keter Publishing House
Yiphtach Dekel, *Chief Executive Officer*
Peter Tomkins, *Executive Project Director*

Complete staff listings appear in Volume 1

LIBRARY OF CONGRESS CATALOGING-IN-PUBLICATION DATA

Encyclopaedia Judaica / Fred Skolnik, editor-in-chief ; Michael Berenbaum, executive editor. -- 2nd ed.
  v. cm.
  Includes bibliographical references and index.
  Contents: v.1. Aa-Alp.
  ISBN 0-02-865928-7 (set hardcover : alk. paper) -- ISBN 0-02-865929-5 (vol. 1 hardcover : alk. paper) -- ISBN 0-02-865930-9 (vol. 2 hardcover : alk. paper) -- ISBN 0-02-865931-7 (vol. 3 hardcover : alk. paper) -- ISBN 0-02-865932-5 (vol. 4 hardcover : alk. paper) -- ISBN 0-02-865933-3 (vol. 5 hardcover : alk. paper) -- ISBN 0-02-865934-1 (vol. 6 hardcover : alk. paper) -- ISBN 0-02-865935-X (vol. 7 hardcover : alk. paper) -- ISBN 0-02-865936-8 (vol. 8 hardcover : alk. paper) -- ISBN 0-02-865937-6 (vol. 9 hardcover : alk. paper) -- ISBN 0-02-865938-4 (vol. 10 hardcover : alk. paper) -- ISBN 0-02-865939-2 (vol. 11 hardcover : alk. paper) -- ISBN 0-02-865940-6 (vol. 12 hardcover : alk. paper) -- ISBN 0-02-865941-4 (vol. 13 hardcover : alk. paper) -- ISBN 0-02-865942-2 (vol. 14 hardcover : alk. paper) -- ISBN 0-02-865943-0 (vol. 15: alk. paper) -- ISBN 0-02-865944-9 (vol. 16: alk. paper) -- ISBN 0-02-865945-7 (vol. 17: alk. paper) -- ISBN 0-02-865946-5 (vol. 18: alk. paper) -- ISBN 0-02-865947-3 (vol. 19: alk. paper) -- ISBN 0-02-865948-1 (vol. 20: alk. paper) -- ISBN 0-02-865949-X (vol. 21: alk. paper) -- ISBN 0-02-865950-3 (vol. 22: alk. paper)
  1. Jews -- Encyclopedias. I. Skolnik, Fred. II. Berenbaum, Michael, 1945-
    DS102.8.E496 2007
    909'.04924 -- dc22
                                                                    2006020426

ISBN-13:

978-0-02-865928-2 (set)
978-0-02-865929-9 (vol. 1)
978-0-02-865930-5 (vol. 2)
978-0-02-865931-2 (vol. 3)
978-0-02-865932-9 (vol. 4)
978-0-02-865933-6 (vol. 5)
978-0-02-865934-3 (vol. 6)
978-0-02-865935-0 (vol. 7)
978-0-02-865936-7 (vol. 8)
978-0-02-865937-4 (vol. 9)
978-0-02-865938-1 (vol. 10)
978-0-02-865939-8 (vol. 11)
978-0-02-865940-4 (vol. 12)
978-0-02-865941-1 (vol. 13)
978-0-02-865942-8 (vol. 14)
978-0-02-865943-5 (vol. 15)
978-0-02-865944-2 (vol. 16)
978-0-02-865945-9 (vol. 17)
978-0-02-865946-6 (vol. 18)
978-0-02-865947-3 (vol. 19)
978-0-02-865948-0 (vol. 20)
978-0-02-865949-7 (vol. 21)
978-0-02-865950-3 (vol. 22)

This title is also available as an e-book
ISBN-10: 0-02-866097-8
ISBN-13: 978-0-02-866097-4
Contact your Thomson Gale representative for ordering information.
Printed in the United States of America
10 9 8 7 6 5 4 3 2 1

TABLE OF CONTENTS

Introduction to the Thematic Outline

5

Thematic Outline

7

•

Introduction to the Index

277

Abbreviations of the Index

281

Index

283

INTRODUCTION TO THE THEMATIC OUTLINE

The outline presented here is intended to provide a general view of the conceptual scheme of the *Encyclopaedia*. It is divided into five parts: I. *History*; II. *Religion*; III. *Jewish Languages & Literature*; IV. *Jews in World Culture*; V. *Women*. To show the conceptual components of the *Encyclopaedia*'s coverage, each of these general parts is subdivided into a variety of sections and sub-sections. The categories used in this outline are intended to be heuristic and thereby serviceable in guiding users through the *Encyclopaedia*. Because the rubrics used as section headings are not necessarily mutually exclusive, certain entries in the *Encyclopaedia* are listed in more than one section.

I. HISTORY

A. ANCIENT PERIOD

1. BIBLE   p. 7
2. TALMUD   p. 19
3. SECOND TEMPLE AND LATE ROMAN PERIODS   p. 26

B. MEDIEVAL & MODERN PERIOD

1. GENERAL HISTORY   p. 34
   a. **Antisemitism**   p. 35
   b. **Demography**   p. 36
   c. **Economic History**   p. 36
   d. **Zionism**   p. 37
2. REGIONAL HISTORY
   a. **Israel, Land and State of**   p. 39
   b. **Byzantium**   p. 61
   c. **Muslim Lands (incl. Islam)**   p. 61
   d. **Asia and Africa**   p. 67
   e. **Western Europe**   p. 68
      1. England & British Commonwealth   p. 68
      2. France, Luxembourg & Belgium   p. 78
      3. Germany & Austria   p. 86
      4. Italy   p. 101
      5. Netherlands   p. 105
      6. Scandinavia   p. 107
      7. Spain & Portugal   p. 108
      8. Switzerland   p. 111
   f. **Eastern Europe**   p. 111
      1. Bulgaria, Albania & Armenia   p. 111
      2. Czechoslovakia   p. 112
      3. Greece   p. 115
      4. Hungary   p. 115
      5. Poland   p. 119
      6. Romania   p. 125
      7. Russia & Former Soviet Union   p. 127
      8. Yugoslavia   p. 135
   g. **United States**   p. 136
   h. **Canada**   p. 171
   i. **Latin America**   p. 173
3. HOLOCAUST HISTORY   p. 175

II. RELIGION

A. JEWISH

1. JEWISH LAW   p. 187
2. JEWISH RITUAL & OBSERVANCE   p. 188
3. JEWISH THOUGHT & PHILOSOPHY   p. 192
4. RABBINICS   p. 194
5. KABBALAH & JEWISH MYSTICISM   p. 214
6. HASIDISM   p. 217

B. OTHER

1. CHRISTIANITY   p. 218
2. ISLAM (see MUSLIM LANDS)
3. KARAITES   p. 220
4. MARRANOS   p. 221
5. SAMARITANS   p. 222

III. JEWISH LANGUAGES & LITERATURE

A. JEWISH LANGUAGES   p. 222

B. JEWISH LITERATURE   p. 223

C. HEBREW LITERATURE   p. 223

D. YIDDISH LITERATURE   p. 228

IV. JEWS IN WORLD CULTURE

A. ART   p. 232

1. ARCHITECTURE   p. 233
2. CARTOONING   p. 233
3. PAINTING   p. 234

THEMATIC OUTLINE

I. HISTORY

A. ANCIENT PERIOD

1. BIBLE

Main Surveys
ARCHAEOLOGY
BIBLE
HISTORY

General Entries
AARONIDES
ABADDON
ACROSTICS
AGRICULTURAL LAND-MANAGEMENT METHODS AND
    IMPLEMENTS IN ANCIENT EREZ ISRAEL
AGRICULTURE
AKEDAH
ALLEGORY
ALTAR
AM HA-AREZ
ANCIENT OF DAYS
ANGELS AND ANGELOLOGY
ANOINTING
ARCHAEOLOGISTS
ARCHITECTURE AND ARCHITECTS
ARCHIVES
ARIEL
ARK OF MOSES
ARK OF NOAH
ARK OF THE COVENANT
AZAZEL
BAAL WORSHIP
BAHUR
BALANCE
BANNER
BARRENNESS AND FERTILITY
BDELLIUM
BELIAL
BIBLE CODES
BITUMEN
BREAD
BURNING BUSH
CANAAN, CURSE OF
CENSUS
CHEESE
CHERUB
CHIEFTAIN
CITY
CITY OF REFUGE
CONCUBINE
CONGREGATION
COOKING AND BAKING

COPPER SERPENT, THE
CORVÉE
COSMETICS
COVENANT
CRAFTS
CROWNS, DECORATIVE HEADDRESSES AND WREATHS
CULT
CULT PLACES, ISRAELITE
CUPBEARER
DAY OF THE LORD
DEATH, KISS OF
DECALOGUE
DEEP, THE
DEMONS, DEMONOLOGY
DIVINATION
DOLMENS
DOOR AND DOORPOST
DREAMS
DRUNKENNESS
EARTH
EARTHQUAKE
ECSTASY
ELDER
EMBALMING
EPHOD
ETHICS
EUNUCH
EUPHEMISM AND DYSPHEMISM
EXILE, ASSYRIAN
EXILE, BABYLONIAN
FAMINE AND DROUGHT
FIRE
FISH AND FISHING
FLAG
FLESH
FLOOD, THE
FODDER
FOOD
GENEALOGY
GEZER CALENDAR
GOD, NAMES OF
GOG AND MAGOG
GOLDEN CALF
GROVES, SACRED
HAPAX LEGOMENA
HAZAK
HEBREW BOOK TITLES
HIGH PRIEST
HISTORIOGRAPHY
HOLINESS CODE
HOST OF HEAVEN
HUNTING

I. HISTORY
A. ANCIENT PERIOD
1. Bible
GENERAL ENTRIES (*continued*)

IDOLATRY

IMPALEMENT

INCENSE AND PERFUMES

IR HA-NIDDAHAT

ISRAEL

ISRAEL, KINGDOM OF

JACHIN AND BOAZ

JACOB, BLESSING OF

JEALOUSY

JESHURUN

KEDUSHAH

KING, KINGSHIP

KIPPER

LABOR

LACHISH OSTRACA

LANDMARKS

LEPROSY

LETTERS AND LETTER-WRITERS

LEVITICAL CITIES

LOTS

LOVE

MAGIC

MANNA

MATRIARCHS

MENE, MENE, TEKEL, U-FARSIN

MENORAH

MESHA STELE

MILK

MILLSTONE

MISHMAROT AND MAAMADOT

MOLOCH, CULT OF

MOON

MOSES, BLESSING OF

MYTH, MYTHOLOGY

NAMES

NASI

NATIONS, THE SEVENTY

NEHUSHTAN

NETHERWORLD

NOACHIDE LAWS

NOMADISM

NUMBERS, TYPICAL AND IMPORTANT

OILS

ORDEAL

ORDEAL OF JEALOUSY

OSSUARIES AND SARCOPHAGI

OSTRACA

PARABLE

PARADISE

PHOENIX

PILLAR

PILLAR OF CLOUD AND PILLAR OF FIRE

PLAGUES OF EGYPT

POETRY

POISON

POOR, PROVISION FOR THE

POTTERY

POVERTY

PRECIOUS STONES AND JEWELRY

PRIESTLY VESTMENTS

PRIESTS AND PRIESTHOOD

PROPHETS AND PROPHECY

PROSTITUTION

PROVERB

PURITY AND IMPURITY, RITUAL

RAIN

RED HEIFER

RIGHT AND LEFT

ROD OF AARON

ROD OF MOSES

SALT

SCEPTER

SCRIBE

SEA, SONG OF THE

SEMITES

SEPTUAGINT

SERVANT OF THE LORD

SHEKEL

SHEWBREAD

SHIPS AND SAILING

SIGNS AND SYMBOLS

SILOAM (OR SHILOAH) INSCRIPTION

SIN

SOAP

STRANGERS AND GENTILES

SUN

SUNDIAL

TABERNACLE

TABLETS OF THE LAW

TANAKH

TARGUM

TARTAN

TEKHELET

TEMPLE

THRONE

THUNDER AND LIGHTNING

TIKKUN SOFERIM

TITHE

TOMBS AND TOMBSTONES

TREASURE, TREASURY

TRIBES, THE TWELVE

UGARITIC

URIM AND THUMMIM

VULGATE

WAR AND WARFARE

WATCHERS

WEIGHTS AND MEASURES

WELLS

WIDOW

WISDOM; WISDOM LITERATURE

WOOD

WORSHIP

WRITING

I. HISTORY
A. ANCIENT PERIOD
1. Bible
BIBLICAL FIGURES (*continued*)

ASENATH
ASHER
ASHERAH
ASHIMA
ASHTORETH
ATHALIAH
BAAL-BERITH
BAALIS
BAASHA
BALAAM
BALAK
BARAK
BARUCH
BARZILLAI
BATH-SHEBA
BELSHAZZAR
BELTESHAZZAR
BENAIAH
BEN-HADAD
BENJAMIN
BETHUEL
BEZALEL
BILHAH
BITHIAH
BIZTHA
BOAZ
CAIN
CALEB, CALEBITES
CAMBYSES
CANAAN
CHEDORLAOMER
CHEMOSH
COZBI
CUSH
CUSHAN-RISHATHAIM
CYRUS
DAGON
DAN
DANIEL
DARIUS I
DARIUS THE MEDE
DATHAN AND ABIRAM
DAVID
DAVID, DYNASTY OF
DEBORAH
DELILAH
DINAH
DOEG
EBER
EGLON
EHUD
ELAH
ELASAH
ELDAD AND MEDAD
ELEAZAR

ELHANAN
ELI
ELIASHIB
ELIEZER
ELIHU
ELIJAH
ELIMELECH
ELIPHAZ
ELISHA
ELISHAH
ELISHEBA
ELKANAH
ELNATHAN BEN ACHBOR
EN-DOR, WITCH OF
ENOCH
ENOSH
EPHRAIM
EPHRON
ER
ESARHADDON
ESAU
ESTHER
ETHAN
ETHBAAL
EVE
EVIL MERODACH
EZRA
GAAL
GAD
GAD
GAD
GEDALIAH
GEHAZI
GEMARIAH
GERSHOM
GERSHON, GERSHONITES
GESHEM, GASHMU
GIDEON
GOIIM
GOLIATH
GOMER
HABAKKUK
HADAD
HAGAR
HAGGAI
HAM
HAMAN
HAMMURAPI
HAMOR
HANANIAH SON OF AZZUR
HANNAH
HAVILAH
HAZAEL
HEBER
HEMAN
HEZEKIAH
HEZIR
HIEL
HILKIAH
HIRAM

HOPHNI AND PHINEHAS
HOPHRA
HOSHEA
HULDAH
HUR
HUSHAI THE ARCHITE
ICHABOD
IMMANUEL
ISAAC
ISAIAH
ISH-BOSHETH
ISHMAEL
ISHMAEL
ISSACHAR
ITHAMAR
ITTAI
JAAZANIAH
JABAL
JABIN
JACOB
JAEL
JAIR
JANNES AND JAMBRES
JAPHETH
JAVAN
JEDAIAH
JEDUTHUN
JEHOAHAZ
JEHOAHAZ
JEHOASH
JEHOIACHIN
JEHOIADA
JEHOIAKIM
JEHOIARIB
JEHORAM
JEHORAM
JEHOSHAPHAT
JEHU
JEHU
JEPHTHAH
JEREMIAH
JEROBOAM
JEROBOAM II
JESHUA
JESSE
JETHRO
JEZEBEL
JOAB
JOASH
JOCHEBED
JOHANAN
JOKTAN
JONATHAN
JONATHAN
JOSEPH
JOSHUA
JOSIAH
JOTHAM
JOTHAM
JUBAL

JUDAH
KETURAH
KISH
KOHATH AND KOHATHITES
KORAH
LABAN
LAMECH
LEAH
LEMUEL
LEVI
LOT
MAACAH
MACHIR
MAHER SHALAL HASH BAZ
MAHLON AND CHILION
MANASSEH
MANASSEH
MARDUK
MELCHIZEDEK
MENAHEM
MEPHIBOSHETH
MERAB
MERNEPTAH
MERODACH
MERODACH-BALADAN
MESHA
METHUSELAH
MICA
MICAH
MICAIAH
MICAIAH
MICHAEL AND GABRIEL
MICHAL
MIRIAM
MITHREDATH
MORDECAI
MOSES
NAAMAH
NAAMAN
NABAL
NABONIDUS
NABOTH
NADAB
NAHASH
NAHOR
NAHSHON
NAHUM
NAOMI
NAPHTALI
NATHAN
NAZIRITE
NEBUCHADNEZZAR
NEBUZARADAN
NECO
NEHEMIAH
NEPHILIM
NERGAL-SHAREZER
NIMROD
NOAH
OBED

I. HISTORY
A. ANCIENT PERIOD
1. Bible
BIBLICAL FIGURES (*continued*)

OBED-EDOM
OG
OHOLIAB
OMRI
ONAN
ONKELOS AND AQUILA
OREB AND ZEEB
ORPAH
OTHNIEL
PALTI
PASHHUR
PATRIARCHS, THE
PEKAH
PEKAHIAH
PENINNAH
PEREZ
PHARAOH
PHINEHAS
POTIPHAR
POTI-PHERA
PUT
PUTIEL
QUEEN OF SHEBA
RAB-SARIS AND RAB-MAG
RAB-SHAKEH
RACHEL
RAHAB
RAMSES
RAPHAEL
REBEKAH
RECHAB AND BAANAH
REGEM-MELECH
REHOBOAM
REHUM
REPHAIM
RESHEPH
REUBEN
REZIN
RIMMON
RIZPAH
SAMSON
SAMUEL
SANDALFON
SARAH
SARGON II
SAUL
SENNACHERIB
SERAIAH
SERAPH
SETH
SETI I
SHADRACH, MESHACH, ABED-NEGO
SHALLUM
SHALMANESER III
SHALMANESER V

SHAMGAR
SHAMMAH
SHAPHAN
SHAREZER
SHEALTIEL
SHEBA BEN BICHRI
SHEBNAH
SHEM
SHEMAIAH
SHESHBAZZAR
SHIMEI
SHIPHRAH AND PUAH
SHISHAK
SHULAMMITE
SIHON
SIKKUTH AND CHIUN
SIMEON
SISERA
SO
SOLOMON
SOLOMON, SERVANTS OF
SUCCOTH-BENOTH
TABEEL, THE SON OF
TAMAR
TAMMUZ
TEMA
TEMAN
TERAH
TERAPHIM
TIBNI
TIGLATH-PILESER III
TIRHAKAH
TUBAL-CAIN
URIAH
URIEL
UZZAH
UZZIAH
VASHTI
ZADOK
ZEBAH AND ZALMUNNA
ZEBULUN
ZECHARIAH
ZECHARIAH
ZECHARIAH
ZECHARIAH
ZEDEKIAH
ZEDEKIAH
ZELOPHEHAD
ZEPHANIAH
ZERAH
ZERAH THE CUSHITE
ZERUBBABEL
ZIBA
ZILPAH
ZIMRI
ZIMRI
ZIPPORAH

PLACES AND PEOPLES
ABEL SHITTIM

ABEL, AVEL
ABEL-BETH-MAACAH
ABEL-MAUL
ABEL-MEHOLAH
ACHOR, VALLEY OF
ACHSHAPH
ACHZIB
ACRE
ADAM
ADORAIM
ADULLAM
AHLAB
AI
AKKAD
ALALAKH
ALMON
ALMON-DIBLATHAIM
AMALEKITES
AMMON, AMMONITES
AMORITES
ANAB
ANAHARATH
ANATHOTH
ARAM, ARAMEANS
ARAM-DAMASCUS
ARARAT
ARGOB
ARNON
AROER
ASHDOD
ASHKELON
ASHKENAZ
ASHTAROTH, ASHTEROTH-KARNAIM, KARNAIM
ATAROTH
AVVIM
AZEKAH
AZNOTH-TABOR
AZOR
BAALAH
BAAL-GAD
BAAL-HAZOR
BAAL-MEON
BAAL-PERAZIM
BAAL-ZEPHON
BABEL, TOWER OF
BABYLON
BABYLONIA
BAHURIM
BASHAN
BEER
BEEROTH
BEERSHEBA
BENE-BERAK
BESOR, BROOK OF
BET AGLAYIM
BET(H)-ANATH
BET(H)-CHEREM
BET(H)-DAGON
BET(H)-EDEN
BET(H)-EL

BET(H)-HARAM
BET HARODON
BET(H)-HORON
BETHLEHEM
BET(H) LEHEM (Ha-Gelilit)
BET(H)-NIMRAH
BET(H)-REHOB
BET(H)-SHEAN
BET(H)-SHEMESH
BET(H)-SHITTAH
BET YERAH
BET(H)-ZUR
BEZEK
CABUL
CALNEH
CANAAN, LAND OF
CAPHTOR
CARMEL
CARMEL, MOUNT
CHALDEA, CHALDEANS
CHEBAR
CHERITH
CHINNERETH
COZEBA
CUSH
CUTH, CUTHAH
DAMASCUS
DAN
DEBIR
DOBRATH
DOR
DOTHAN
EBEN-EZER
EBLA
EDOM
EDREI
EGLON
EGYPT
EGYPT, BROOK OF
EKRON
ELAM
EL-AMARNA
ELATH
ELEALEH
ELTEKEH
EMAR
EN-DOR
EN-GANNIM
EN-HAROD
EN-RIMMON
EN-ROGEL
EPHRATH
EPHRON
ERECH
ESHTAOL
ESHTEMOA
ETAM
EUPHRATES
EZION-GEBER
GALILEE

MAMRE
MA'ON
MARESHAH
MARI
MEDES AND MEDIA
MEGIDDO
MEMPHIS
MERON
MEROZ
MESHECH
MESOPOTAMIA
MEUNITES
MICHMASH
MIDIAN, MIDIANITES
MIGDOL
MINNITH
MISREPHOTH-MAIM
MIZPEH; MIZPAH
MOAB
MOLADAH
MORESHETH-GATH
MORIAH
MOUNT OF OLIVES
MOZA, (HA-) MOZAH
NAHALAL
NAVEH
NEBAIOTH
NEBO
NEGEV
NETOPHAH
NILE
NINEVEH
NOB
NUZI
ONO
OPHEL
OPHIR
OPHRAH
PADDAN-ARAM
PARAH, PERATH
PARAN
PARVAIM
PATHROS
PEKOD
PELLA
PENUEL
PERGAMUM
PERIZZITES
PHILISTINES
PHOENICIA, PHOENICIANS
PI-HAHIROTH
PISGAH
PITHOM
PUNON
QUE
RABBAH
RABBATH-AMMON
RAFA
RAMAH
RAMAT RAHEL

RAMOTH
RAMOTH-GILEAD
RAMSES
RECHABITES
RED SEA
REHOB
REHOBOTH
REHOV, TEL
REPHAIM
REPHIDIM
RESEN
RIBLAH
RIMMON-PEREZ
RODANIM
RUMAH OR ARUMAH
SABEA
SALCHAH
SAMARIA
SEIR, MOUNT
SENAAH
SEPHARAD
SEPHARVAIM
SHAALBIM
SHA'AR HA-GOLAN
SHARUHEN
SHECHEM
SHEPHELAH
SHIHIN
SHIHOR, SHIHOR-LIBNATH
SHILOAH, SILOAM
SHILOH
SHIMRON
SHINAR
SHUNEM
SHUSHAN
SIDON
SIN, WILDERNESS OF
SINAI
SINAI, MOUNT
SOCOH OR SOCO
SODOM AND GOMORRAH
SOREK, VALLEY OF
SUCCOTH
SUMER, SUMERIANS
TAANACH
TABOR, MOUNT
TADMOR
TAMAR
TAPPUAH
TARSHISH
TEKOA
TEMA
THEBES
THEBEZ
TIGRIS
TIMNA
TIMNAH
TIMNATH-HERES
TIRZAH
TOB

I. HISTORY
A. ANCIENT PERIOD
1. Bible
PLACES AND PEOPLES (*continued*)

TRANSJORDAN
TYRE
UGARIT
UR
UZ
UZAL
WADI AL-NATTUF
WILDERNESS
ZAMZUMMIM
ZANOAH
ZAPHON
ZAREPHATH
ZARETHAN
ZEMARAIM
ZERED
ZEREDAH
ZIKLAG
ZION
ZIPH
ZOAN
ZORAH

FLORA AND FAUNA
ALGUM
ALMOND
ANIMALS OF THE BIBLE AND TALMUD
APPLE
BALSAM
BARLEY
BAY TREE
BEAR
BEE
BEHEMOTH
CALAMUS, SWEET
CAMEL
CAPER
CAROB
CASTOR-OIL PLANT
CAT
CATTLE
CEDAR
CENTIPEDE
CHAMELEON
CHICKEN
CINNAMON
CORAL
CORIANDER
COTTON
CRANE
CRIMSON WORM
CROCODILE
CUCUMBER
CYPRESS
DEER
DOG

DOVE
DYE PLANTS
EAGLE
EBONY
ELEPHANT
FENNEL
FIG
FLAX
FLEA
FLOWERS
FLY
FOX
FRANKINCENSE
FROG
GALBANUM
GARLIC
GAZELLE
GECKO
GNAT
GOAT
GOOSE
GRASSHOPPER
GULL
HARE
HAWK
HEMLOCK
HENNA
HONEY
HOOPOE
HORNET
HORSE
HYRAX
HYSSOP
IBEX
IVORY
JACKAL
JUNIPER
KITE
LAUDANUM
LEECH
LEEK
LENTIL
LEOPARD
LEVIATHAN
LION
LIZARD
LOCUST
MANDRAKE
MELON
MILLET
MOLE
MOTH
MOUSE
MULBERRY
MUSHROOMS
MYRRH
MYRTLE
NIGHTINGALE
NUT
OAK

OLEANDER

OLIVE

ONAGER

ONION

ORACH

OSTRICH

OWL

PALM

PAPYRUS

PARTRIDGE

PIG

PINE

PISTACHIO

PLANE TREE

PLANTS

PLUM

POMEGRANATE

POPLAR

QUAIL

RAT

RAVEN

REED

ROCKET

ROSE

SAFFRON

SCORPION

SHEEP

SILK

SKINK

SNAKE

SORGHUM

SPARROW

SPICES

SPIDER

SPIKENARD

STORAX

STORK

SWIFT

SYCAMORE

TAHASH

TAMARISK

TEREBINTH

THISTLES AND THORNS

TORTOISE

TRAGACANTH

TURTLE DOVE

VEGETABLES

VINE

VULTURES

WEEDS

WHEAT

WILD BULL

WILLOW

WOLF

WORM

WORMWOOD

Biblical Scholars

AHARONI, YOHANAN

AINSWORTH, HENRY

ALBRIGHT, WILLIAM FOXWELL

ALT, ALBRECHT

ANDREWES, LANCELOT

ASTRUC, JEAN

BADE, WILLIAM FREDERIC

BAETHGEN, FRIEDRICH WILHELM ADOLPH

BAUDISSIN, WOLF WILHELM, GRAF VON

BAUER, HANS

BAUMGARTEL, ELISE J.

BAUMGARTNER, WALTER

BECK(IUS), MATTHIAS FRIEDRICH

BEEK, MARTINUS ADRIANUS

BEN-ASHER, AARON BEN MOSES

BEN-ASHER, MOSES

BEN-NAPHTALI, MOSES BEN DAVID

BENTZEN, AAGE

BENZINGER, IMMANUEL

BERGSTRAESSER, GOTTHELF

BERTHOLET, ALFRED

BLEEK, FRIEDRICH

BONFRERE, JAQUES

BUDDE, KARL FERDINAND REINHARD

BUHL, FRANZ PEDER WILLIAM MEYER

BUTTENWIESER, MOSES

CASSUTO, UMBERTO

CHEYNE, THOMAS KELLY

COCCEIUS, JOHANNES

COLENSO, JOHN WILLIAM

COOK, STANLEY ARTHUR

COOKE, GEORGE ALBERT

CORNILL, CARL HEINRICH

CROWFOOT, JOHN WINTER

DAVIDSON, SAMUEL

DEL MEDICO, HENRI E.

DELITZSCH, FRIEDRICH

DEUTSCH, EMANUEL OSKAR

DIEZ MACHO, ALEJANDRO

DILLMANN, AUGUST

DOTHAN, TRUDE

DRIVER, SAMUEL ROLLES

DUBNO, SOLOMON BEN JOEL

DUHM, BERNHARD

DUPONT-SOMMER, ANDRE

EERDMANS, BERNARDUS DIRKS

EHRLICH, ARNOLD BOGUMIL

EICHHORN, JOHANN GOTTFRIED

EISSFELDT, OTTO

ERMAN, JOHANN PETER ADOLF

EWALD, HEINRICH GEORG AUGUST

FEIGIN, SAMUEL ISAAC

FINKELSTEIN, JACOB JOEL

FISHBANE, MICHAEL

FRANKFORT, HENRI

FRYMER-KENSKY, TIKVA

GALLING, KURT

GARSTANG, JOHN

GEDDES, ALEXANDER

GELB, IGNACE JAY

GESENIUS, HEINRICH FRIEDRICH WILHELM

GEVIRTZ, STANLEY

I. HISTORY

A. ANCIENT PERIOD

1. Bible

BIBLICAL SCHOLARS (*continued*)

GINSBERG, HAROLD LOUIS

GINSBURG, CHRISTIAN DAVID

GORDIS, ROBERT

GORDON, CYRUS HERZL

GRAF, KARL HEINRICH

GREENBERG, MOSHE

GREENFIELD, JONAS CARL

GRESSMANN, HUGO

GRUENBERG, SAMUEL

GUNKEL, HERMANN

GUTHE, HERMANN

HALLO, WILLIAM

HARAN, MENAHEM

HELD, MOSHE

HENGSTENBERG, ERNST WILHELM

HITZIG, FERDINAND

HOELSCHER, GUSTAV

HOSCHANDER, JACOB

HOTTINGER, JOHANN HEINRICH

HRABANUS MAURUS

HUPFELD, HERMANN CHRISTIAN KARL

ILGEN, KARL DAVID

JACOB BEN HAYYIM BEN ISAAC IBN
    ADONIJAH

JACOB, BENNO

JAMPEL, SIGMUND

JEREMIAS, ALFRED

JIRKU, ANTON

KALISCH, MARKUS MORITZ

KAUFMANN, YEHEZKEL

KAUTZSCH, EMIL FRIEDRICH

KEIL, KARL FRIEDRICH

KENYON, KATHLEEN MARY

KIRKPATRICK, ALEXANDER FRANCIS

KITTEL, RUDOLF

KUENEN, ABRAHAM

KUGEL, JAMES

LA PEYRERE, ISAAC

LANDSBERGER, BENNO

LEIBOWITZ, NEHAMA

LEUSDEN, JOHANN

LEVENSON, JON

LEVINE, BARUCH

LEWY, JULIUS

LIGHTFOOT, JOHN

LODS, ADOLPHE

LOEWE, JOEL (BRILL)

LOEWISOHN, SOLOMON

LOISY, ALFRED FIRMIN

LOWTH, ROBERT

MACALISTER, ROBERT ALEXANDER STEWART

MAHLER, EDUARD

MALAMAT, ABRAHAM

MARGOLIS, MAX LEOPOLD

MARTI, KARL

MAZAR, BENJAMIN

MEINHOLD, JOHANNES FRIEDRICH

MEYER, EDUARD

MICHAELIS, JOHANN DAVID

MILGROM, JACOB

MOWINCKEL, SIGMUND OLAF PLYTT

NATHAN, MORDECAI

NICHOLAS DE LYRE

NOTH, MARTIN

NOWACK, WILHELM GUSTAV HERMANN

ORLINSKY, HARRY MEYER

PARROT, ANDRE

PEDERSEN, JOHANNES

PELLICANUS (Rubeaquensis), CONRAD

PETRIE, SIR WILLIAM MATTHEW FLINDERS

PFEIFFER, ROBERT HENRY

POPPER, WILLIAM

RAD, GERHARD VON

REUSS, EDUARD

ROSENMUELLER, ERNST FRIEDRICH KARL

ROWLEY, HAROLD HENRY

RYSSEL, VICTOR

SANDMEL, SAMUEL

SARNA, NAHUM

SCHAEFFER, CLAUDE F. A.

SEELIGMANN, ISAC LEO

SEGAL, MOSES HIRSCH (ZEVI)

SELLIN, ERNST

SHAPIRO, DAVID S.

SMEND, RUDOLPH

SMITH, SIR GEORGE ADAM

SMITH, JOHN MERLIN POWIS

SMITH, WILLIAM ROBERTSON

SPEISER, EPHRAIM AVIGDOR

STEUERNAGEL, CARL

TADMOR, HAYIM

TALMON, SHEMARYAHU

TAVUS, JACOB BEN JOSEPH

THEODORE OF MOPSUESTIA

TIGAY, JEFFREY

TORREY, CHARLES CUTLER

TUR-SINAI (Torczyner), NAPHTALI HERZ (Harry)

TYNDALE, WILLIAM

VATKE, WILHELM

VAUX, ROLAND DE

VOLZ, PAUL

VRIEZEN, THEODORUS CHRISTIAAN

WALTON, BRYAN

WEILL, RAYMOND

WEINGREEN, JACOB

WEISS, MEIR

WELLHAUSEN, JULIUS

WETTE, DE, WILHELM MARTIN LEBERECHT

WIENER, HAROLD MARCUS

WINCKLER, HUGO

WOOLLEY, SIR CHARLES LEONARD

YEIVIN, SHEMUEL

ZIMMERLI, WALTHER

2. TALMUD

MAIN SURVEYS

MISHNAH

TALMUD, BABYLONIAN

TALMUD, JERUSALEM

GENERAL ENTRIES

ACADEMIES IN BABYLONIA AND EREZ ISRAEL

AGGADAH

AHERIM

ALEF

ALLEGORY

ALLUF

ALPHABET, HEBREW, IN MIDRASH, TALMUD, AND
    KABBALAH

AM HA-AREZ

AMORA

AMORAIM

ANDROGYNOS

ANGELS AND ANGELOLOGY

ANOINTING

ARK OF THE COVENANT

BAHUR

BARRENNESS AND FERTILITY

BAT KOL

BEI AVIDAN

BEI-RAV

BET HILLEL AND BET SHAMMAI

BREAD

CAPTIVES, RANSOMING OF

CHEESE

CHURCH FATHERS

COSMETICS

CROWNS, DECORATIVE HEADDRESSES AND
    WREATHS

DEMONS, DEMONOLOGY

DESKARTA

DIVINATION

DREAMS

DRUNKENNESS

EARTH

EGGS

ELDER

EUPHEMISM AND DYSPHEMISM

EVEN SHETIYYAH

FIRE

FISH AND FISHING

FLESH

FLOOD, THE

GEMARA

GENEALOGY

GOD, NAMES OF

GREEK AND LATIN LANGUAGES, RABBINICAL
    KNOWLEDGE OF

HAVER, HAVERIM

HAVER IR

HEBREW BOOK TITLES

HERMENEUTICS

IDOLATRY

INCENSE AND PERFUMES

JEALOUSY

KABBALAH

KALLAH, MONTHS OF

KEZAZAH

LABOR

LEKET, SHIKHHAH, AND PEAH

LEPROSY

LUZ OF THE SPINE

MAGIC

MAHOZA

MAR

MATA MEHASYA

MISHMAROT AND MA'AMADOT

MNEMONICS

MOON

NAMES

NARESH

NEHUTEI

OILS

PARABLE

PESHAT

PILPUL

PITTUM HA-KETORET

POVERTY

PRECIOUS STONES AND JEWELRY

PROFANITY

PROSBUL

PROSTITUTION

PROVERBS, TALMUDIC

PUMBEDITA

RAIN

RESH KALLAH

RIGHT AND LEFT

SALT

SEA, SONG OF THE

SHAS

SHEKANZIB

SOAP

SUN

SURA

SYNAGOGUE

TALMID HAKHAM

TALMUD

TALMUD, BURNING OF

TALMUD, MUSICAL RENDITION

TALMUD AND MIDDLE PERSIAN
    CULTURE

TANNA, TANNAIM

TEN MARTYRS, THE

THUNDER AND LIGHTNING

TIGRIS

TITLES

USHA, SYNOD OF

WEIGHTS AND MEASURES

WINE

WRITING

ZAKEN MAMRE

ZUGOT

I. HISTORY
A. ANCIENT PERIOD
2. Talmud (*continued*)

Talmudic Literature
Orders and Tractates
ARAKHIN
AVODAH ZARAH
AVOT
BAVA BATRA
BAVA KAMMA
BAVA MEZIA
BEKHOROT
BERAKHOT
BEZAH
BIKKURIM
DEMAI
DEREKH EREZ
EDUYYOT
ERUVIN
GITTIN
HAGIGAH
HALLAH
HORAYOT
HULLIN
KALLAH
KELIM
KERITOT
KETUBBOT
KIDDUSHIN
KILAYIM
KINNIM
KODASHIM
MA'ASEROT
MA'ASER SHENI
MAKHSHIRIN
MAKKOT
MASSEKHET
MEGILLAH
ME'ILAH
MENAHOT
MIDDOT
MIKVAOT
MINOR TRACTATES
MOED
MOED KATAN
NASHIM
NAZIR
NEDARIM
NEGAIM
NEZIKIN
NIDDAH
OHOLOT
ORLAH
PARAH
PEAH
PESAHIM
ROSH HA-SHANAH
SANHEDRIN

SEMAHOT
SHABBAT
SHEKALIM
SHEVI'IT
SHEVU'OT
SOFERIM
SOTAH
SUKKAH
TA'ANIT
TAMID
TEMURAH
TERUMOT
TEVUL YOM
TOHOROT
TOHOROT
UKZIN
YADAYIM
YEVAMOT
YOMA
ZAVIM
ZERA'IM
ZEVAHIM

Other Literature
AGGADAT BERESHIT
AVOT DE-RABBI NATHAN
AVOT NEZIKIN
BARAITA, BERAITOT
BARAITA DE-MELEKHET HA-MISHKAN
BARAITA DE-NIDDAH
BARAITA OF 32 RULES
BOOK OF LIFE
DEUTERONOMY RABBAH
ESTHER RABBAH
EXODUS RABBAH
GENESIS RABBAH
LAMENTATIONS RABBAH
LEVITICUS RABBAH
MEGILLAT SETARIM
MEGILLAT TA'ANIT
MEGILLAT YUHASIN
MEKHILTA DEUTERONOMY
MEKHILTA OF R. ISHMAEL
MEKHILTA OF R. SIMEON BEN YOHAI
MIDRESHEI AGGADAH
MIDRESHEI HALAKHAH
PESIKTA DE-RAV KAHANA
POLEMICS AND POLEMICAL LITERATURE
RUTH RABBAH
SEDER OLAM
SIFRA
SIFREI DEUTERONOMY
SIFREI HA-MINIM
SIFREI NUMBERS
SIFREI ZUTA DEUTERONOMY
SIFREI ZUTA NUMBERS
SONG OF SONGS RABBAH
TANHUMA YELEMMEDENU
TOSEFTA

Amoraim and Tannaim

ABBA
ABBA BAR AHA
ABBA BAR AVINA
ABBA BAR KAHANA
ABBA BAR MARTA
ABBA BAR MEMEL
ABBA BAR ZAVDA
ABBA BAR ZEMINA
ABBA BEN ABBA HA-KOHEN
ABBA BENJAMIN
ABBA GURYON OF SIDON
ABBA HILKIAH
ABBAHU
ABBA KOHEN BARDELA
ABBA OF AKKO
ABBA OSHAYA (Hoshaya) OF TIRIAH
ABBA SAUL
ABBA SAUL BEN BATNIT
ABBAYE
ABBAYE KASHISHA
ABBA YOSE BEN DOSTAI
ABBA YOSE BEN HANIN (Johanan)
ADDA BAR AHAVAH
AHA
AHA BAR HANINA
AHA BAR RAV
AHA BEN JACOB
AHAI
AHAI BEN JOSIAH
AIBU
AKAVYAH BEN MAHALALEL
AKIVA
ALEXANDRI
AMEIMAR
AMMI BAR NATHAN
AMRAM
AMRAM HASIDA ("The Pious")
ANAN
ASHI
ASSI
ASSI, RAV
AVDAN
AVDIMI BAR HAMA
AVDIMI OF HAIFA
AVIA
AVIMI
AVIMI BEN ABBAHU
AVIN
AVINA
AVIRA
AVTALYON
AZARIAH
AZARIAH
BAR HEDYA
BAR KAPPARA
BEBAI
BEBAI BAR ABBAYE
BENAAH

BEN AZZAI, SIMEON
BEN BAG BAG
BEN HE HE
BENJAMIN BEN JAPHET
BEN KALBA SAVUA
BEN PETURA (Ben Peturi, Ben Peturin)
BEN STADA
BEN ZOMA, SIMEON
BERECHIAH
DANIEL HAYYATA
DIMI
DIMI OF NEHARDEA
DOSA BEN HARKINAS
DOSTAI BEN JUDAH
DOSTAI BEN YANNAI
ELEAZAR BEN ARAKH
ELEAZAR BEN AZARIAH
ELEAZAR BEN DAMMA
ELEAZAR BEN HANANIAH BEN HEZEKIAH
ELEAZAR BEN JUDAH OF BARTOTA
ELEAZAR BEN MATYA
ELEAZAR BEN PARTA
ELEAZAR BEN PEDAT
ELEAZAR BEN SHAMMUA
ELEAZAR BEN SIMEON
ELEAZAR BEN YOSE I
ELEAZAR BEN YOSE II
ELEAZAR BEN ZADOK
ELEAZAR HA-KAPPAR
ELEAZAR HISMA
ELEAZAR OF MODI'IN
ELIEZER BEN HYRCANUS
ELIEZER BEN JACOB
ELIEZER BEN YOSE HA-GELILI
ELISHA BEN AVUYAH
GAMALIEL (HA-ZAKEN), RABBAN
GEBIHA OF BE-KATIL
GIDDAL
HAGGAI
HAGGAI OF SEPPHORIS
HALAFTA
HALAFTA BEN SAUL
HAMA (of Nehardea)
HAMA BAR BISA
HAMA BAR HANINA
HAMNUNA
HANA BAR HANILAI
HANA BEN BIZNA
HANAN THE EGYPTIAN
HANANIAH (Hanina)
HANANIAH (Hanina) BEN HAKHINAI
HANANIAH (Hanina) BEN TERADYON
HANANIAH (Hanina) OF SEPPHORIS
HANINA (Hananiah)
HANINA BAR HAMA
HANINA (Hinena) BAR-PAPA (Pappi)
HANINA BEN ABBAHU
HANINA BEN ANTIGONUS
HANINA BEN DOSA

I. HISTORY
A. ANCIENT PERIOD
2. Talmud
AMORAIM AND TANNAIM (*continued*)

HANINA BEN GAMALIEL
HANINA SEGAN HA-KOHANIM
HELBO
HEZEKIAH
HIDKA
HILLEL
HILLEL
HILLEL (II)
HISDA
HIYYA
HIYYA BAR ABBA
HIYYA BAR AVIN
HOSHAIAH, RAV
HUNA
HUNA BEN AVIN HA-KOHEN
HUNA BEN JOSHUA
HUNA BEN NATHAN
HUNA OF SEPPHORIS
HUNYA OF BETH-HORON
HUZPIT HA-METURGEMAN
IDI
IDI BAR AVIN
ILAI
ILAI
ILFA
ISAAC
ISAAC BAR JOSEPH
ISAAC BAR RAV JUDAH
ISAAC BEN AVDIMI
ISAAC BEN ELEAZAR
ISAAC NAPPAHA
ISHMAEL BEN ELISHA
ISHMAEL BEN JOHANAN BEN BEROKA
ISHMAEL BEN YOSE BEN HALAFTA
JACOB
JACOB BEN AHA
JACOB BEN IDI
JACOB BEN KORSHAI (Kodshai)
JEREMIAH BEN ABBA
JOHANAN BEN BEROKA
JOHANAN BEN GUDGADA
JOHANAN BEN HA-HORANIT
JOHANAN BEN NAPPAHA
JOHANAN BEN NURI
JOHANAN BEN TORTA
JOHANAN BEN ZAKKAI
JOHANAN HA-SANDELAR
JONAH
JONATHAN
JONATHAN BEN AMRAM
JONATHAN BEN ELEAZAR
JOSEPH BEN HIYYA
JOSHUA
JOSHUA BEN HANANIAH
JOSHUA BEN HYRCANUS

JOSHUA BEN KORHA
JOSHUA BEN LEVI
JOSHUA BEN PERAHYAH
JOSHUA HA-GARSI
JOSIAH
JOSIAH
JUDAH
JUDAH III
JUDAH IV
JUDAH BAR EZEKIEL
JUDAH BAR ILAI
JUDAH BAR SHALOM (ha-Levi)
JUDAH BAR SIMEON
JUDAH BEN BATHYRA I
JUDAH BEN BAVA
JUDAH BEN DOSOTHEOS
JUDAH BEN GERIM
JUDAH BEN HIYYA
JUDAH BEN NAHAMANI (Nahman)
JUDAH BEN PEDAYA (Padah)
JUDAH BEN SHAMMUA
JUDAH BEN TABBAI
JUDAH BEN TEMA
JUDAH HA-NASI
KAHANA
LEVI
LEVI BEN SISI
MANI
MAR BAR RAV ASHI
MAR BAR RAVINA
MARI BEN ISSUR
MATTIAH BEN HERESH
MATTNAH
MEIR
MEREMAR
NAHMAN BAR RAV HUNA
NAHMAN BEN ISAAC
NAHMAN BEN JACOB
NAHUM OF GIMZO
NAHUM THE MEDE
NAKDIMON BEN GURYON
NATHAN HA-BAVLI
NEHEMIAH
NEHORAI
NEHUNYA BEN HA-KANAH
NITTAI OF ARBELA
OSHAIAH RABBAH
PAPA
PAPI
PAPPUS BEN JUDAH
PHINEHAS BEN HAMA HA-KOHEN
PHINEHAS BEN JAIR
RABBA BEN MATNAH
RABBAH BAR BAR HANA
RABBAH BAR HANA
RABBAH BAR HUNA
RABBAH BAR NAHAMANI
RABBAH BEN AVUHA
RABBAH BEN SHILAH
RABBAH TOSFAAH

RAV

RAVA

RAVINA

REHUMEI

REUBEN BEN STROBILUS

SAFRA

SAMUEL

SAMUEL BEN NAHMAN

SAMUEL BEN SHILAT

SAMUEL HA-KATAN

SHAMMAI (Ha-Zaken)

SHELA

SHEMAIAH

SHESHET

SHILA OF KEFAR TAMARTA

SIMEON BAR YOHAI

SIMEON BEN ABBA

SIMEON BEN ELEAZAR

SIMEON BEN GAMALIEL I

SIMEON BEN GAMALIEL II (of Jabneh)

SIMEON BEN HALAFTA

SIMEON BEN JEHOZADAK

SIMEON BEN JUDAH HA-NASI

SIMEON BEN LAKISH

SIMEON BEN MENASYA

SIMEON BEN NANAS

SIMEON BEN NETHANEL

SIMEON BEN PAZZI

SIMEON BEN SHETAH

SIMEON HA-PAKULI

SIMEON HA-TIMNI

SIMEON OF MIZPAH

SIMLAI

SYMMACHUS BEN JOSEPH

TANHUM BEN HANILAI

TANHUM BEN HIYYA

TANHUMA BAR ABBA

TARFON

UKBA, MAR

ULLA I

YANNAI

YESHEVAV THE SCRIBE

YOSE

YOSE BAR HANINA

YOSE BEN AKAVYAH

YOSE BEN AVIN

YOSE BEN DORMASKOS

YOSE BEN HALAFTA

YOSE BEN JOEZER OF ZEREDAH

YOSE BEN JOHANAN HA-TANNA OF JERUSALEM

YOSE BEN JUDAH

YOSE BEN KIPPAR

YOSE BEN KISMA

YOSE BEN MESHULLAM

YOSE BEN ZIMRA

YOSE HA-GELILI

YOSE HA-KOHEN

YUDAN

ZADOK

ZECHARIAH BEN AVKILUS

ZE'EIRA

ZE'IRI (ben Hinna)

Biblical Figures and Subjects

AARON

ABIATHAR

ABIGAIL

ABIMELECH

ABISHAG THE SHUNAMMITE

ABISHAI

ABNER

ABRAHAM

ABSALOM

ACHAN

ADAM

ADONIJAH

AGAG

AHAB

AHIMELECH

AHITHOPHEL THE GILONITE

ALTAR

AMALEKITES

AMASA

AMAZIAH

AMMON, AMMONITES

AMNON

AMON

AMORITES

AMRAM

ASA

ASAHEL

ASAPH

ASHER

BABEL, TOWER OF

BALAAM

BARUCH

BATH-SHEBA

BELSHAZZAR

BENJAMIN

BETHUEL

BEZALEL

BILHAH

BOAZ

CAIN

CALEB, CALEBITES

CHERUB

COPPER SERPENT, THE

DAN

DANIEL

DATHAN AND ABIRAM

DAVID

DEBORAH

DELILAH

DINAH

DOEG

EDOM

ELDAD AND MEDAD

ELI

ELIEZER

ELIHU

I. HISTORY
A. ANCIENT PERIOD
2. Talmud
BIBLICAL FIGURES AND SUBJECTS (*continued*)

ELIJAH

ELIPHAZ

ELISHA

ELKANAH

EN-DOR, WITCH OF

ENOCH

ENOSH

EPHRAIM

ESAU

ESTHER

EVE

EZEKIEL

EZRA

GAD

GARDEN OF EDEN

GEHAZI

GIBEONITES AND NETHINIM

GIDEON

GOLDEN CALF

GOLIATH

HAGAR

HAM

HAMAN

HANANIAH SON OF AZZUR

HANNAH

HEZEKIAH

HOSEA, BOOK OF

HULDAH

HUR

HUSHAI THE ARCHITE

ISAAC

ISAIAH

ISHMAEL

ISRAEL, KINGDOM OF

ISSACHAR

ITHAMAR

JABNEH

JACOB

JACOB, BLESSING OF

JAEL

JAIR

JAPHETH

JEHOIACHIN

JEHOIADA

JEHOIAKIM

JEHORAM

JEPHTHAH

JEREMIAH

JEROBOAM

JERUSALEM

JESSE

JESUS

JETHRO

JEZEBEL

JOAB

JOB, BOOK OF

JOCHEBED

JONAH, BOOK OF

JONATHAN

JOSEPH

JOSHUA

JOSIAH

JOTHAM

JUDAH

KETURAH

KOHATH AND KOHATHITES

KORAH

LABAN

LAMECH

LEAH

LEVI

LOT

MALACHI, BOOK OF

MANASSEH

MANASSEH

MANNA

MEPHIBOSHETH

MERODACH-BALADAN

MICAH

MICHAEL AND GABRIEL

MICHAL

MIDIAN, MIDIANITES

MIRIAM

MORDECAI

MOSES

NAAMAN

NABAL

NABOTH

NADAB

NAHSHON

NAOMI

NATIONS, THE SEVENTY

NAZIRITE

NEBUCHADNEZZAR

NEBUZARADAN

NEHEMIAH

NEPHILIM

NETHERWORLD

NIMROD

NINEVEH

NOAH

OG

ORPAH

OTHNIEL

PATRIARCHS, THE

PENINNAH

PEREZ

PHARAOH

PHILISTINES

PLAGUES OF EGYPT

POTIPHAR

PROPHETS AND PROPHECY

PSALMS, BOOK OF

QUEEN OF SHEBA

RACHEL

RAHAB
REBEKAH
RED HEIFER
RED SEA
REHOBOAM
REUBEN
ROD OF AARON
ROD OF MOSES
RUTH, BOOK OF
SAMSON
SAMUEL
SANDALFON
SARAH
SAUL
SENNACHERIB
SETH
SHEBA BEN BICHRI
SHEM
SHIMEI
SHISHAK
SIMEON
SINAI, MOUNT
SODOM AND GOMORRAH
SOLOMON
TABERNACLE
TABLETS OF THE LAW
TAMAR
TERAH
TRIBES, THE TWELVE
TUBAL-CAIN
URIAH
URIM AND THUMMIM
VASHTI
WELLS
WILDERNESS
ZECHARIAH
ZECHARIAH
ZEDEKIAH
ZELOPHEHAD
ZERAH THE CUSHITE
ZERUBBABEL
ZIMRI
ZIPPORAH

Other Figures
ABBA GULISH
ABBA KOLON
ABBA UMANA
ADMON BEN GADDAI
AGRAT BAT MAHALATH
AHASUERUS
ALEXANDER THE GREAT
ANTONINUS PIUS
APOSTOMOS
AVIN THE CARPENTER
BAITOS BEN ZONIN
BAVA BEN BUTA
BEN TEMALYON
BERURYAH
CYRUS

DAMA, SON OF NETINA
EGLON
ELISHA BAAL KENAFAYIM
HABBAR, HABBAREI
HADRIAN, PUBLIUS AELIUS
HOMA
HONI HA-ME'AGGEL
HOVAH
IMMA SHALOM
ISSUR GIYYORA
JUDITH
KAMZA AND BAR KAMZA
MAHLON AND CHILION
MARTHA
MERCURY
MICAIAH (Micah)
NATHAN DE-ZUZITA RESH GALUTA
PAPPUS AND JULIANUS
PHINEHAS
RACHEL
RAPHAEL
TABI
TITUS, FLAVIUS VESPASIANUS
YALTA

Flora and Fauna
ALGUM
ANIMALS OF THE BIBLE AND TALMUD
ANT
APE
APPLE
ASS
BALSAM
BAT
BAY TREE
BEAR
BEE
BEET
BEHEMOTH
BOX
BROOM
CABBAGE
CALAMUS, SWEET
CAMEL
CAPER
CAROB
CASTOR-OIL PLANT
CAT
CEDAR
CHICKEN
CINNAMON
CORIANDER
COTTON
CUMIN
DEER
DOG
DOVE
EAGLE
ELEPHANT
FENNEL

I. **HISTORY**
  A. ANCIENT PERIOD
    2. Talmud
      Flora and Fauna (*continued*)

FIG
FLAX
FLEA
FRANKINCENSE
GALBANUM
GARLIC
GAZELLE
GOURD
GRASSHOPPER
HEMP
HENNA
HERBS, MEDICINAL
HOOPOE
HORNET
HORSE
HYSSOP
IVY
JACKAL
JUJUBE
KITE
KOI
LEECH
LEEK
LEGUMES
LENTIL
LEOPARD
LETTUCE
LEVIATHAN
LIZARD
LOCUST
LOUSE
MALLOW
MASTIC
MELON
MILLET
MOUSE
MULBERRY
MULE
MUSHROOMS
MUSTARD
MYRRH
MYRTLE
NUT
OLEANDER
OLIVE
ONAGER
ONION
ORACH
OSTRICH
PALM
PAPYRUS
PARTRIDGE
PEACH
PEACOCK
PEAR

PELICAN
PEPPER
PHEASANT
PIG
PINE
PISTACHIO
PLANTS
PLUM
POMEGRANATE
POPLAR
QUAIL
QUINCE
RADISH
RAT
RAVEN
REED
RICE
ROCKET
ROSE
SAFFRON
SHEEP
SILK
SNAKE
SORGHUM
SPARROW
SPICES
SQUILL
SUMAC
SYCAMORE
TEREBINTH
TORTOISE
TURTLE DOVE
VEGETABLES
VINE
VULTURES
WHEAT
WILD BULL
WILLOW
WOLF
WORM

3. SECOND TEMPLE AND LATE ROMAN PERIODS
  Main Surveys
  HISTORY

  General Entries
  ABOMINATION OF DESOLATION
  ABSALOM, MONUMENT OF
  AGORANOMOS
  AGRICULTURAL LAND-MANAGEMENT METHODS AND
      IMPLEMENTS IN ANCIENT EREZ ISRAEL
  AGRICULTURE
  ALABARCH
  ANGARIA
  ANGLO-ISRAEL ARCHAEOLOGICAL SOCIETY
  ANTICHRESIS
  APOCALYPSE
  APOCRYPHA AND PSEUDEPIGRAPHA
  ARCHAEOLOGISTS
  ARCHAEOLOGY

ARCHISYNAGOGOS

ARCHITECTURE AND ARCHITECTS

ARCHON

ARNONA

ASS WORSHIP

AURUM CORONARIUM

BOETHUSIANS

BOULE

CART AND CHARIOT

CIRCUSES AND THEATERS

CISTERN

COINS AND CURRENCY

CRAFTS

CRUCIFIXION

CYNICS AND CYNICISM

DAVID, DYNASTY OF

DEAD SEA SECT

DEMONS, DEMONOLOGY

DIASPORA

DIONYSUS, CULT OF

EMPEROR WORSHIP

EPICUREANISM

ESSENES

ETHNARCH

FISCUS JUDAICUS

GERUSIA

GLADIATOR

GREEK AND LATIN LANGUAGES, RABBINICAL
   KNOWLEDGE OF

GREEK LITERATURE, ANCIENT

GYMNASIUM

HASMONEAN BET DIN

HASMONEANS

HASSIDEANS

HELLENISM

HELLENISTIC JEWISH LITERATURE

HERODIANS

HEVER HA-YEHUDIM

HIGH PRIEST

HISTORIOGRAPHY

HOLY CONGREGATION IN JERUSALEM

JEW

JUDEAN DESERT CAVES

LETTERS AND LETTER-WRITERS

LOGOS

LOTS

MACCABEE

MAGIC

MAIUMAS

MENORAH

MIKVEH

MIN

MONEY CHANGERS

MOSES

NAG HAMMADI CODICES

NASH PAPYRUS

NASI

NICANORS GATE

OIL OF LIFE

ONYCHA

OSSUARIES AND SARCOPHAGI

PALESTINE

PAPYRI

PESHER

PHARISEES

PILGRIMAGE

PILLAR

POTTERY

PRIESTS AND PRIESTHOOD

PROCURATOR

QUMRAN

SADDUCEES

SAMARITANS

SANHEDRIN

SECTS, MINOR

SEEKERS AFTER SMOOTH THINGS

SELEUCID ERA

SEREKH

SHEKEL

SHIPS AND SAILING

SICARII

SOFERIM

SONS OF LIGHT

SYNAGOGUE

SYNAGOGUE, THE GREAT

TAX GATHERERS

TEACHER OF RIGHTEOUSNESS

TEMPLE

TEMPLE MOUNT

THERAPEUTAE

TITHE

TITUS, ARCH OF

TOMBS AND TOMBSTONES

TOPARCHY

USHA, SYNOD OF

WAR AND WARFARE

WORSHIP

XENOPHON OF LAMPSACUS

YAHAD

ZADOKITES

ZEALOTS AND SICARII

ZENO, PAPYRI OF

Literature

ABRAHAM, APOCALYPSE OF

ABRAHAM, OTHER BOOKS OF

ABRAHAM, TESTAMENT OF

ACRO, PSEUDO-

ADAM, OTHER BOOKS OF

ADAM AND EVE, BOOK OF THE LIFE OF

AELIAN (Claudius, Aelianus)

AHIKAR, BOOK OF

ALEXANDRIAN MARTYRS, ACTS OF

ARISTEAS, LETTER OF

BARUCH, APOCALYPSE OF

BARUCH, BOOK OF

BARUCH, GREEK APOCALYPSE OF

BARUCH, REST OF THE WORDS OF

BEL AND THE DRAGON

BEN SIRA, WISDOM OF

I. HISTORY
A. ANCIENT PERIOD
3. Second Temple and Late Roman Periods
LITERATURE (*continued*)

COPPER SCROLL
DAMASCUS, BOOK OF COVENANT OF
DANIEL, BOOKS OF
DEAD SEA SCROLLS
DISCIPLINE, MANUAL OF
ENOCH
ENOCH, ETHIOPIC BOOK OF
ENOCH, SLAVONIC BOOK OF
ESTHER, ADDITIONS TO THE BOOK OF
EZEKIEL, APOCRYPHAL BOOKS OF
EZRA, APOCALYPSE OF
EZRA, GREEK BOOK OF
HABAKKUK, PROPHECY OF
HISTORIA AUGUSTA
ISAAC, TESTAMENT OF
JACOB, TESTAMENT OF
JEREMIAH, EPISTLE OF
JOB, TESTAMENT OF
JOSEPH AND ASENATH
JOSIPPON
JUBILEES, BOOK OF
JUDITH, BOOK OF
LAMECH, BOOK OF
LEVI, TESTAMENT OF
MACCABEES, FIRST BOOK OF
MACCABEES, SECOND BOOK OF
MACCABEES, THIRD BOOK OF
MACCABEES, FOURTH BOOK OF
MANASSEH, PRAYER OF
MOSES, ASSUMPTION OF
MURABBAAT SCROLLS
NAPHTALI, TESTAMENT OF
NOAH, BOOKS OF
PATRIARCHS, TESTAMENTS OF THE TWELVE
PHILO
PROPHETS, LIVES OF THE
PSALMS, APOCRYPHAL
ROMAN LITERATURE
SCROLL OF ANTIOCHUS
SEVENTY SHEPHERDS, VISION OF
SIBYL AND SIBYLLINE ORACLES
SOLOMON, PSALMS OF
SOLOMON, TESTAMENT OF
SOLOMON, WISDOM OF
SONG OF THE THREE CHILDREN AND THE PRAYER OF
    AZARIAH
SUSANNA AND THE ELDERS
TEMPLE SCROLL
THANKSGIVING PSALMS
TOBIT, BOOK OF
WAR SCROLL

PLACES AND PEOPLES
ABILENE
ACRA

ACRABA
ACRE
ADASA
ADIABENE
ADORAIM (Adora)
AELIA CAPITOLINA
AGRIPPINA
AIJALON
AKHBAREI
ALAMAH
ALEXANDRIA
AMANA
AMMATHA
ANTHEDON
ANTIOCH
ANTIPATRIS
ANTONIA
APAMEA
APHEK
APOLLONIA
ARABA
ARAD
ARADUS
ARBATTA
ARCHELAIS
ARETHUSA
ARPAD
ASARAMEL
ASHKELON
ASSUR
ATHRIBIS
AVEDAT
AZMON
BABYLONIA
BANIAS
BASHAN
BATHYRA
BE-HOZAI
BENE-BERAK
BERENIKE
BET(H)-ANATH
BET(H)-CHEREM
BET GUVRIN
BETHANY
BETHAR
BET(H)-HARAM (Haran)
BETHBASI
BETHLEHEM
BETHLEPTEPHA
BET(H)-HORON
BETHPHAGE
BETHSAIDA
BETHULIA
BET(H)-MAON
BET NETOFAH
BET(H)-SHEAN
BET SHEARIM
BET YERAH
BET ZEKHARYAH
BET(H)-ZUR

BIRIYYAH
BITHYNIA
BORSIPPA
BOSPHORUS, KINGDOM OF
BOZRAH
BUTNAH
CABUL
CAESAREA
CAESAREA IN CAPPADOCIA
CAPERNAUM
CAPITOLIAS
CAPPADOCIA
CARCHEMISH
CARIA
CARMEL, MOUNT
CARTHAGE
CHALCIS
CHORAZIN
CILICIA
COELE-SYRIA
COMMAGENE
CTESIPHON
CYRENE
DAMASCUS
DECAPOLIS
DELOS
DIBON
DIUM
DOBRATH
DOK
DOR
DURA-EUROPOS
EDESSA
EDOM
EGYPT
EIN FASHKHAH
EIN KEREM
ELASA
ELEPHANTINE
ELUSA
EMESA
EMMAUS
EN-GEDI
EPHESUS
EVEN HA-TOIM
GADARA (Gadar, Gader)
GALATIA
GALILEE
GAMALA
GAZA
GEBA
GERASA
GERIZIM, MOUNT
GEZER
GINNOSAR, PLAIN OF
GISCALA
GOFNAH
HAGRONIA
HALHUL
HAMMAT-GADER (Geder)

HAMMATH
HAPHARAIM
HAR HA-MELEKH
HEBRON
HERODIUM (Herodion)
HESHBON
HIERAPOLIS
HORONAIM
HULEH
HUZAL
HYRCANIA
JABNEH
JAFFA
JAPHIA
JAZER
JERICHO
JERUSALEM
JEZREEL, VALLEY OF
JORDAN
JOTAPATA
JUDEA
KABRITHA
KEFAR AKKO
KEFAR GAMALA
KEFAR HANANYAH
KEFAR HATTIN
KEFAR NEBURAYA
KEFAR OTNAY
KEFAR SHIHLAYIM
KEILAH
KENATH
KERAK OR CHARAX
KIDRON
KINNERET, LAKE
KITTIM
LAODICEA
LEGIO
LEONTOPOLIS
LYDDA (Lod)
LYDIA, LYDIANS
MACEDONIA
MACHAERUS
MACHPELAH, CAVE OF
MADABA, MEDEBA
MAGDALA
MAMPSIS
MAʾON
MARESHAH
MASADA
MERON
MESENE
MICHMASH (Michmas)
MILETUS
MODIʾIN (Modiʾim)
MOUNT OF OLIVES
MOZA, (HA-) MOZAH
NAARAH (Naaran)
NABATEANS
NABLUS
NAIN

I. HISTORY
A. ANCIENT PERIOD
3. Second Temple and Late Roman Periods
PLACES AND PEOPLES (*continued*)

NARBATA
NAVEH
NEGEV
NEHAR PEKOD
NEHARDEA
NISIBIS
NIZZANAH
ONIAS, TEMPLE OF
ONO
OSROENE
PAMPHYLIA
PARAH, PERATH
PEKI'IN
PELLA
PERSIA
PETRA
PHAROS
PHASAELIS
PHOTIS
PHRYGIA
RABBATH-AMMON
RAFA
RAMAT HA-GOLAN
RAMAT RAHEL
RECHABITES
REHOBOTH
SABEA
SAFED
SAMARIA
SARDIS
SARTABA
SELEUCIA
SENNABRIS
SEPPHORIS
SHALEM
SHECHEM
SHEPHELAH
SHILOAH, SILOAM
SHILOH
SHION
SHIVTAH
SHUNEM
SHUSHAN
SICHAR
SIDON
SIKHNIN
SINAI
SPARTA
SUSITA
SYRIA
TABGHA
TABOR, MOUNT
TADMOR
TAMAR
TEKOA

TIBERIAS
TIMNATH-HERES
TIRAT ZEVI
TRACHONITIS
TRANSJORDAN
TUNIS, TUNISIA
TYRE
TYRE, LADDER OF
TYRE OF THE TOBIADS
USHA
WADI DALIYA
WESTERN WALL
ZAPHON
ZAREPHATH
ZEREDAH
ZION
ZIPH
ZOFIM

Biographies
ABBA SIKRA
ABSALOM
AGATHARCHIDES OF CNIDUS
AGRIPPA I
AGRIPPA II
AGRIPPA, CAIUS JULIUS
AGRIPPA, MARCUS VIPSANIUS
ALARIC II
ALBINUS, LUCCEIUS
ALCIMUS
ALEXANDER
ALEXANDER BALAS
ALEXANDER THE FALSE
ALEXANDER THE GREAT
ALEXANDER LYSIMACHUS
ALEXANDER OF APHRODISIAS
ALEXANDER POLYHISTOR
ALEXANDER SON OF ARISTOBULUS II
ALEXANDER THE ZEALOT
ALEXANDRA
ALEXANDRA
ALEXAS
ALITURUS (Alityros)
AMMIANUS MARCELLINUS
ANAN, SON OF ANAN
ANAN BEN SETH
ANANIAS AND HELKIAS
ANANIAS BEN NEDEBEUS
ANANIAS OF ADIABENE
ANANIAS SON OF ZADOK
ANDRONICUS SON OF MESHULLAM
ANILAEUS AND ASINAEUS
ANTIGONUS
ANTIGONUS II
ANTIGONUS OF CARYSTUS
ANTIGONUS OF SOKHO
ANTIOCHUS
ANTIPAS, HEROD
ANTIPATER II
ANTIPATER

ANTONINUS PIUS
ANTONIUS DIOGENES
ANTONIUS JULIANUS
APION
APOLLONIUS
APOLLONIUS MOLON
APPIAN OF ALEXANDRIA
APULEIUS, LUCIUS
ARCHELAUS
ARDAVAN
AREIOS I
ARES
ARETAS
ARISTEAS
ARISTOBULUS I
ARISTOBULUS II
ARISTOBULUS III
ARISTOBULUS
ARISTOBULUS
ARISTOBULUS OF PANEAS
ARISTON OF PELLA
ARMILUS
ARRIAN
ARTAPANUS
ARTAXERXES
ARTEMION
ASINIUS POLLIO, GAIUS
ASMODEUS
ATHRONGES
AUGUSTUS
AVTINAS
AZIZ
BACCHIDES
BAGOHI
BANUS
BAR GIORA, SIMEON
BAR KOKHBA
BASSUS, LUCILIUS
BATHYRA, SONS OF
BEN LAANAH
BEN SIRA, SIMEON BEN JESUS
BEN ZIZIT HA-KASSAT
BERENICE
BEROSUS
BET GARMU
BET ZERIFA
CAECILIUS OF CALACTE
CAESAR, SEXTUS JULIUS
CAIAPHAS, JOSEPH
CALIGULA, CAIUS CAESAR AUGUSTUS
CALLISTHENES
CAPITO, MARCUS HERENNIUS
CARACALLA, MARCUS AURELIUS
    ANTONINUS
CASSIUS LONGINUS
CELSUS
CELSUS, AULUS CORNELIUS
CENSORINUS
CESTIUS GALLUS
CHAEREMON

CHARAX OF PERGAMUM
CHARES
CHOERILOS OF SAMOS
CICERO, MARCUS TULLIUS
CLAUDIAN (Claudius Claudianus)
CLAUDIUS
CLAUDIUS IOLAUS (Julius)
CLEARCHUS OF SOLI
CLEODEMUS MALCHUS
CLEOMEDES
CLEOPATRA
CLEOPATRA OF JERUSALEM
CONON I
CONON II
COPONIUS
COSTOBAR
CRASSUS, MARCUS LICINIUS
CRINAGORAS OF CARYSTUS
CUMANUS VENTIDIUS
CYPROS
CYPROS
DAMASCIUS
DAMOCRITUS
DEMETRIUS
DEMETRIUS
DEMETRIUS I SOTER
DEMETRIUS II
DEMETRIUS III
DIO CASSIUS
DIO CHRYSOSTOM
DIOCLETIAN, CAIUS VALERIANUS
DIODORUS OF SICILY
DIODOTUS-TRYPHON
DIOGENES LAERTIUS
DIOS
DIOSCORIDES PEDANIUS
DOMITIAN
DORIS
DOROTHEUS
DRUSILLA
ELEAZAR
ELEAZAR BEN ANANIAS
ELEAZAR BEN DINAI
ELEAZAR BEN HARSOM
ELEAZAR BEN JAIR
ELEAZAR BEN MATTATHIAS
ELEAZAR BEN SIMEON
ELIONAEUS, SON OF CANTHERAS
EMPEDOCLES
EPICTETUS
ERATOSTHENES OF CYRENE
EUHEMERUS
EUPOLEMUS
EUTROPIUS
EZEKIEL THE POET
FADUS, CUSPIUS
FELIX, ANTONIUS
FESTUS, PORCIUS
FLACCUS, AVILLIUS AULUS
FLACCUS, VALERIUS

I. HISTORY
A. ANCIENT PERIOD
3. Second Temple and Late Roman Periods
BIOGRAPHIES (continued)

FLAVIUS, CLEMENS
FRONTO, MARCUS CORNELIUS
FULVIA
GABINIUS, AULUS
GALEN (Galenus), CLAUDIUS
GEBINI
GESSIUS FLORUS
GLAPHYRA
GORGIAS
HADRIAN, PUBLIUS AELIUS
HANAMEL (Hananel)
HANNAH AND HER SEVEN SONS
HAURAN
HECATAEUS OF ABDERA
HELENA
HELIODORUS
HELLADIUS OF ANTINOUPOLIS
HERACLES
HERACLITUS
HERMIPPUS OF SMYRNA
HERMOGENES
HEROD
HEROD I
HEROD II
HERODIAS
HERODOTUS
HEROD PHILIP I
HEZEKIAH
HEZEKIAH, THE HIGH PRIEST
HOLOFERNES
HOMER
HONORIUS FLAVIUS
HORACE, QUINTUS HORATIUS FLACCUS
HYPSICRATES OF AMISUS
HYRCANUS II
HYRCANUS, JOHN (Johanan)
ISHMAEL BEN PHIABI (PHABI) II
IZATES II
JACOB BEN SOSAS (Susa)
JADDUA (Jaddus)
JANNES AND JAMBRES
JANUARIUS
JASON
JASON OF CYRENE
JOEZER, SON OF BOETHUS
JOHANAN BEN JEHOIADA
JOHANAN THE HASMONEAN
JOHN THE ESSENE
JOHN OF GISCALA
JONATHAN BEN ANAN
JONATHAN BEN UZZIEL
JONATHAN THE HASMONEAN
JONATHAN SON OF ABSALOM
JOSEPH
JOSEPH AND AZARIAH BEN ZECHARIAH

JOSEPH BEN ELEM
JOSEPH OF GAMALA
JOSEPHUS FLAVIUS
JOSHUA, SON OF SAPPHAS
JOSHUA, SON OF SETH
JOSHUA BEN DAMNAI
JOSHUA BEN GAMLA
JOSHUA BEN PHABI
JUDAH, SON OF ZIPPORAI
JUDAH THE GALILEAN
JUDAH MACCABEE
JULIAN THE APOSTATE
JULIUS ARCHELAUS
JULIUS CAESAR
JULIUS FLORUS
JULIUS SEVERUS
JUSTIN
JUSTUS OF TIBERIAS
JUVENAL
KETIA BAR SHALOM
KIMHIT
LAETUS
LAMECH
LAMPON AND ISIDOROS
LIES, MAN OF
LIES, PROPHET OF
LION OF WRATH
LIVY
LUCAN (Marcus Annaeus Lucanus)
LUCIAN OF SAMOSATA
LUCUAS
LYSANIAS
LYSIAS
LYSIMACHUS OF ALEXANDRIA
MACROBIUS, AMBROSIUS
MANETHO
MARCUS AURELIUS ANTONINUS
MARIAMNE
MARKAH
MARSUS, C. VIBIUS
MARTIAL
MASTEMA
MATTATHIAS
MATTATHIAS BEN SIMEON
MATTHIAS BEN THEOPHILUS
MAXIMUS, MAGNUS CLEMENS
MEGASTHENES
MELEAGER OF GADARA
MENAHEM THE ESSENE
MENAHEM SON OF JUDAH
MENANDER OF EPHESUS
MENANDER OF LAODICEA
MENELAUS
MNASEAS OF PATARA
MONOBAZ
MUCIANUS, CAIUS LICINIUS
MURASHUS SONS
NERO
NERVA
NICANOR

NICARCHUS
NICHOLAS OF DAMASCUS
NIGER OF PEREA
NUMENIUS
NUMENIUS OF APAMEA
OBEDAS
ODENATHUS AND ZENOBIA
OENOMAUS OF GADARA
ONIAS
OVID
PAUSANIAS
PERSIUS
PETRONIUS, PUBLIUS
PETRONIUS ARBITER, GAIUS
PHASAEL
PHERORAS
PHILIP OF BATHYRA
PHILO (The Elder)
PHILO OF BYBLOS
PHILODEMUS
PHILOSTRATUS
PHINEHAS
PHINEHAS BEN SAMUEL
PLINY THE ELDER
PLUTARCH
POLEMON II
POLEMON OF ILIUM
POLYBIUS OF MEGALOPOLIS
POMI(S), DE
POMPEIUS TROGUS
POMPEY (Gnaeus Pompeius Magnus)
POMPONIUS MELA
PONTIUS PILATE
POPPAEA, SABINA
PORPHYRY
POSIDONIUS
PSEUDO-LONGINUS
PSEUDO-PHOCYLIDES
PSEUDO-SCYLAX
PTOLEMY
PTOLEMY
PTOLEMY
PTOLEMY THE BIOGRAPHER
PTOLEMY THE GEOGRAPHER
PTOLEMY MACRON
PTOLEMY OF CHENNOS
PTOLEMY OF MENDE
PYTHAGORAS
QUADRATUS, UMMIDIUS CAIUS
QUIETUS, LUSIUS
QUINTILIAN (Marcus Fabius Quintilianus)
QUINTILIUS VARUS
QUIRINIUS, P. SULPICIUS
ROMAN EMPERORS
RUFUS OF SAMARIA
RUTILIUS NAMATIANUS
SABINUS
SALOME
SALOME ALEXANDRA
SANBALLAT

SELEUCUS IV PHILOPATOR
SENECA THE ELDER
SENECA THE YOUNGER
SEVERUS, ALEXANDER
SEVERUS, SEPTIMIUS
SEXTUS EMPIRICUS
SHAPUR
SILAS
SILIUS ITALICUS, TIBERIUS CATIUS
    ASCONIUS
SILVA, FLAVIUS
SIMEON BEN BOETHUS
SIMEON THE HASMONEAN
SIMEON THE JUST
SIMEON SON OF ONIAS I
SOLINUS, CAIUS JULIUS
SOSIUS, GAIUS
STATIUS, PUBLIUS PAPINIUS
STRABO
SUETONIUS
TACITUS
TATTENAI
TETRARCH
TEUCER OF CYZICUS
THALLUS
THEMISTIUS
THEODOSIUS
THEODOSIUS I
THEODOSIUS II
THEODOSIUS OF ROME
THEODOTUS
THEOPHILUS
THEOPHILUS
THEOPHRASTUS OF ERESOS
THEUDAS
THRASYLLUS OF MENDES
TIBERIUS JULIUS ALEXANDER
TIBULLUS, ALBIUS
TIMAGENES OF ALEXANDRIA
TIMOCHARES
TINNEIUS RUFUS
TITANS
TITUS FLAVIUS VESPASIANUS
TOBIADS
TRAJAN, MARCUS ULPIUS
ULPIAN
VALERIUS GRATUS
VALERIUS MAXIMUS
VARRO, MARCUS TERENTIUS
VENTIDIUS, PUBLIUS (Bassus)
VESPASIAN, TITUS FLAVIUS
VIRGIL
VITRUVIUS, POLLO
WICKED PRIEST
YANNAI, ALEXANDER
ZADOK
ZADOK THE PHARISEE
ZAMARIS
ZENODORUS
ZOPYRION

I. HISTORY (*continued*)

B. MEDIEVAL & MODERN PERIOD

1. GENERAL HISTORY

Main Entries

ANTISEMITISM
COMMUNITY
ECONOMIC HISTORY
EDUCATION, JEWISH
HISTORY
WOMAN

General Entries

ADVERTISING
AGE AND THE AGED
AGRICULTURE
AGUDAT ISRAEL
ALLIANCE ISRAELITE UNIVERSELLE
AMENITIES, COMMUNAL
ANTHROPOLOGY
ANUSIM
APOSTASY
ARCHAEOLOGISTS
ARCHITECTURE AND ARCHITECTS
ARCHIVES
ASSIMILATION
AUTOGRAPHS
AUTONOMISM
AUTONOMY
AUTONOMY, JUDICIAL
AVELEI ZION
BADGE, JEWISH
BADHAN
BANKING AND BANKERS
BARBARIANS
BARON DE HIRSCH FUND
BATLANIM
BEGGING AND BEGGARS
BERLIN, CONGRESS OF
BETH JACOB SCHOOLS
BLACK DEATH
BLINDNESS
BOOKS
BOOK TRADE
BROKERS
BUND
CANDLE TAX
CAPTIVES, RANSOMING OF
CARDS AND CARDPLAYING
CENSORSHIP
CHARITY
CHESS
CHOLENT
CHRONOLOGY
CLASSICAL SCHOLARSHIP, JEWS IN
COINS AND CURRENCY
COMMUNISM
COMMUNITY TOKENS

CONFERENCES
CONSTRUCTION
CONTRACTORS
COOKBOOKS
COOPERATIVES
COURT JEWS
CRAFTS
CRIME
CRIMINOLOGY
CRYPTO-JEWS
DEMOGRAPHY
DIAMOND TRADE AND INDUSTRY
DISPUTATIONS AND POLEMICS
DIVORCE
DRESS
DRUNKENNESS
DYEING
EDUCATION
ELDER
EMANCIPATION
EPISCOPUS JUDAEORIUM
EPITAPHS
EUROPE
EUROPEAN COMMUNITY, THE
EXILARCH
EXPULSIONS
FAMILY
FEDERATIONS OF COMMUNITIES, TERRITORIAL
FINANCES, AUTONOMOUS JEWISH
FLAG
FOOD
FORGERIES
FOUNDATIONS
FRANK, JACOB, AND THE FRANKISTS
FRATERNAL SOCIETIES
FREEMASONS
FUR TRADE AND INDUSTRY
GABBAI
GALUT
GAMES
GENEALOGY
GENIZAH
GEOGRAPHY
GHETTO
GUILDS
HAPSBURG MONARCHY
HAREDIM
HASKALAH
HE-HALUTZ
HEP! HEP!
HERALDRY
HEVRA (Havura) KADDISHA
HEVRAH, HAVURAH
HISTORIANS
HISTORIOGRAPHY
HOSPITALS
HUMOR
INFORMERS
INQUISITION

INSURANCE
INTERNATIONAL CONFERENCE OF JEWISH
    COMMUNAL SERVICE
JEWISH AGENCY
JEWISH-CHRISTIAN RELATIONS
JEWISH IDENTITY
JEWISH QUARTER
JEWISH TELEGRAPHIC AGENCY
JOURNALISM
JUDAISM
JUDAIZERS
LABOR
LANDSMANNSCHAFTEN
LAWYERS
LEAGUE OF NATIONS
LEATHER INDUSTRY AND TRADE
LIBERALISM
LIBRARIES
LIVESTOCK, TRADE IN
MACCABI WORLD UNION
MAGEN DAVID
MANUSCRIPTS, HEBREW
MAP MAKERS
MEDINAH
MEMORBUCH
MENTAL ILLNESS
MESSIANIC MOVEMENTS
METALS AND MINING
MIGRATIONS
MILITARY SERVICE
MINORITY RIGHTS
MINTMASTERS AND MONEYERS
MIXED MARRIAGE, INTERMARRIAGE
MOTION PICTURES
MUSEUMS
NAMES
NASI
NEO-FASCISM
NEO-NAZISM
NEW LEFT
NEWSPAPERS, HEBREW
NUMERUS CLAUSUS
NUMISMATICS
OATH MORE JUDAICO.
OLYMPIC GAMES
ORPHAN, ORPHANAGE
ORT
OZE (OSE)
PARNAS
PETROLEUM AND OIL PRODUCTS
PHILANTHROPY
PHILOSOPHY
PINKAS
PLETTEN
POLITICS
POPULATION
PRESS
PRINTING, HEBREW
PROSTITUTION

PSYCHOLOGY
PUBLIC RELATIONS
PUBLISHING
RADANIYA
SALONS
SAMBATYON
SAN REMO CONFERENCE
SCOUTING
SEAL, SEALS
SELF-DEFENSE
SELF-HATRED, JEWISH
SEPHARDIM
SERVI CAMERAE REGIS
SETTLEMENT HOUSES
SHABBETAI ZEVI
SHADKHAN
SHELUHEI EREZ ISRAEL
SHIPS AND SAILING
SHTADLAN
SHTETL
SICK CARE, COMMUNAL
SLAVE TRADE
SOCIALISM
SOCIALISM, JEWISH
SOCIETIES, LEARNED
SOCIOLOGY
SPORTS
STAMPS
STUDENTS' MOVEMENTS, JEWISH
SUMPTUARY LAWS
SYNAGOGUE
TALMUD, BURNING OF
TANZHAUS
TAXATION
TELEVISION AND RADIO
TEN LOST TRIBES
THEATER
TITLES
TITLES OF NOBILITY
TRAVELERS AND EXPLORERS
UNITED NATIONS
UNIVERSITIES
VIENNA, CONGRESS OF
VITAL STATISTICS
WANDERING JEW
WORLD CONFERENCE OF JEWISH ORGANIZATIONS
WORLD JEWISH ASSOCIATIONS
WORLD JEWISH CONGRESS
WORLD SEPHARDI FEDERATION
WRITING
YIHUS

a. Antisemitism
MAIN SURVEYS
ANTISEMITISM

GENERAL ENTRIES
BLOOD LIBEL
BOYCOTT, ANTI-JEWISH

I. HISTORY
B. MEDIEVAL & MODERN PERIOD
1. General History
a. Antisemitism
GENERAL ENTRIES (continued)

DISCRIMINATION
ELDERS OF ZION, PROTOCOLS OF THE LEARNED
HOST, DESECRATION OF
NARA
NEO-NAZISM
NUMERUS CLAUSUS
OZON
RACE, THEORY OF
ROZWOJ
STUERMER, DER

BIOGRAPHIES
ABRAHAM A SANCTA CLARA
CARBEN, VICTOR VON
CHIARINI, LUIGI
CHRISTIANI, PABLO
CODREANU, CORNELIU ZELEA
COSTA DE MATTOS, VICENTE DA
CUZA, ALEXANDER C.
DARQUIER DE PELLEPOIX, LOUIS
DAUDET, LEON
DECKERT, JOSEPH
DLUGOSZ, JAN
DRUMONT, EDOUARD-ADOLPHE
EISENMENGER, JOHANN ANDREAS
ENDLICH, QUIRIN
ENDRE, LASZLO
ESTE, JOÃO BAPTISTA DE
FARINACCI, ROBERTO
FETTMILCH, VINCENT
FOLIGNO, HANANEL (DA)
FRIES, JAKOB FRIEDRICH
FRITSCH, THEODOR
GHILLANY, FRIEDRICH WILHELM
GOUGENOT DES MOUSSEAUX, HENRI
GRAES, ORTWIN VAN DE
GRATTENAUER, KARL WILHELM FRIEDRICH
HUNDT-RADOWSKY, HARTWIG VON
IGNATYEV, COUNT NIKOLAI PAVLOVICH
ISTOCZY, GYOZO
JELENSKI, JAN
LAGARDE, PAUL ANTON DE
LUEGER, KARL
LUTOSTANSKI, HYPPOLITE
MARR, WILHELM
MAURRAS, CHARLES
MICZYNSKI, SEBASTIAN
MOJECKI, PRZECLAW
ONODY, GEZA
PREZIOSI, GIOVANNI
PROUDHON, PIERRE JOSEPH
ROHLING, AUGUST
SCHOENERER, GEORG VON
SESSA, KARL BORROMAEUS ALEXANDER
SKARGA, PIOTR
STOECKER, ADOLF
SZALASI, FERENC
VALLAT, XAVIER
VOGELSANG, KARL VON

b. Demography
MAIN SURVEYS
DEMOGRAPHY
MIGRATIONS
MIXED MARRIAGE, INTERMARRIAGE
POPULATION
STATISTICS
VITAL STATISTICS

c. Economic History
MAIN SURVEYS
ECONOMIC HISTORY

GENERAL ENTRIES
ADVERTISING
BANKING AND BANKERS
BEGGING AND BEGGARS
BOOK TRADE
BROKERS
CANDLE TAX
CHEMICAL CRAFTS AND INDUSTRIES
CONSTRUCTION
CONTRACTORS
COOPERATIVES
COURT JEWS
CRAFTS
DEPARTMENT STORES
DIAMOND TRADE AND INDUSTRY
DYEING
FINANCES, AUTONOMOUS JEWISH
FOUNDATIONS
FUR TRADE AND INDUSTRY
GLASS
GUILDS
INSURANCE
LABOR
LEATHER INDUSTRY AND TRADE
LIVESTOCK, TRADE IN
MARKET DAYS AND FAIRS
METALS AND MINING
MONEYLENDING
PEDDLING
PETROLEUM AND OIL PRODUCTS
PUBLIC RELATIONS
PUBLISHING
RAILROADS
SALT TRADE AND INDUSTRY
SECONDHAND GOODS AND OLD CLOTHES, TRADE IN
SPICE TRADE
STOCK EXCHANGES
SUGAR INDUSTRY AND TRADE
TAILORING
TAXATION

TEXTILES
TOBACCO TRADE AND INDUSTRIES
TRADE AND COMMERCE
WINE AND LIQUOR TRADE

d. Zionism

MAIN SURVEYS
ZIONISM

GENERAL ENTRIES
BALFOUR DECLARATION
BASLE PROGRAM
BENEI MOSHE
BERIHAH
BETAR
BILTMORE PROGRAM
BILU
BLAU-WEISS
BNEI AKIVA
DEMOCRATIC FRACTION,
EMUNAH
FARBAND
GENERAL ZIONISTS
GORDONIA
HA-NOAR HA-IVRI-AKIBA
HAOLAM
HA-POEL HA-MIZRACHI
HA-SHAHAR
HA-SHOMER HA-ZAIR
HA-TIKVAH
HE-HALUTZ
HE-HAVER
HELSINGFORS PROGRAM
HIBBAT ZION
IHUD HABONIM
JEWISH AGENCY
JEWISH COLONIAL TRUST
JEWISH COLONIZATION ASSOCIATION
JEWISH NATIONAL FUND
JEWISH STATE PARTY
JUEDISCHER VERLAG
KATTOWITZ CONFERENCE
KEREN HAYESOD
KHARKOV CONFERENCE
LANGUAGE WAR (SPRACHENKAMPF)
MAURITIUS
MINSK CONFERENCE
MIZRACHI
ODESSA COMMITTEE
PETROGRAD CONFERENCE
POALEI ZION
REVISIONISTS, ZIONIST
SAN REMO CONFERENCE
SELBSTEMANZIPATION
SYKES-PICOT TREATY
TERRITORIALISM
TORAH VA-AVODAH
UGANDA SCHEME
VATICAN
WELT, DIE

WIZO
YOUTH ALIYAH
Z.S. (Zionist Socialists)
ZEIREI ZION
ZIONIST COMMISSION
ZIONIST CONGRESSES
ZIONIST ORGANIZATION OF AMERICA (Z.O.A.)
ZIONIST SOCIALIST WORKERS PARTY (S.S.)

BIOGRAPHIES
ABELES, OTTO
AHAD HA-AM
ALKALAI, JUDAH BEN SOLOMON HAI
ALLOUCHE, FELIX NISSIM SAIDOU
BARUCH, JOSEPH MARCOU
BATO, LUDWIG YOMTOV
BEIN, ALEXANDER
BEN-YEHUDA, ELIEZER
BERLIAND, SHLOMO MEIR
BERNSTEIN-KOGAN (Cohen), JACOB
BIERER, RUBIN
BIRNBAUM, NATHAN
BLUMEL, ANDRE
BLUMENFELD, KURT YEHUDAH
BODENHEIMER, MAX ISIDOR
BOEHM, ADOLF
BOROCHOV, BER (Dov)
BRANDT, BORIS (Baruch)
BRODETSKY, SELIG
BRUCK, GRIGORI
BUCHMIL, JOSHUA HESHEL
BUXBAUM, NATHAN
CARPI, LEONE
CHASANOWICH, JOSEPH
CHASANOWICH, LEON
COHEN, ISAAC KADMI
COHEN, ISRAEL
COWEN, JOSEPH
DE LIEME, NEHEMIA
DEEDES, SIR WYNDHAM
DON-YAHIA, YEHUDAH LEIB
DUGDALE, BLANCHE ELIZABETH CAMPBELL
EDELSTEIN, JACOB
EDER, MONTAGUE DAVID
EHRLICH, JACOB
EISLER, EDMUND MENAHEM
ELIASBERG, MORDECAI
FARBSTEIN, DAVID ZEVI
FASTLICHT, ADOLFO
FEIWEL, BERTHOLD
FINKELSTEIN, CHAIM
FINKELSTEIN, NOAH
FISCHER, JEAN
FITCH, LOUIS
FRIEDEMANN, ADOLF
FRIEDMANN, DESIDER
FRISCH, DANIEL
GASTER, MOSES
GELBER, NATHAN MICHAEL
GELLMAN, LEON

I. HISTORY
B. MEDIEVAL & MODERN PERIOD
1. General History
d. Zionism
BIOGRAPHIES (*continued*)

GESANG, NATHAN-NACHMAN
GOLDBERG, BORIS
GOLD BERG, ISAAC LEIB
GOLDBLOOM, JACOB KOPPEL
GOLDHAMMER-SAHAWI, LEO
GOLDMAN, PAUL L.
GOLDMANN, NAHUM
GOLDSTEIN, ALEXANDER
GOLDSTEIN, ANGELO
GOODMAN, PAUL
GORDON, AHARON DAVID
GOTTHEIL, GUSTAV
GOTTLIEB, YEHOSHUA
GREENBERG, HAYYIM
GREENBERG, LEOPOLD JACOB
GROSS, NATHAN
GROSSMAN, MEIR
GRUENBAUM, YIZHAK
GRUNBERG, ABRAHAM
HALPRIN, ROSE LURIA
HANTKE, ARTHUR (Menahem)
HARKAVI, YIZHAK
HARTGLAS, MAXIMILIAN MEIR APOLINARY
HECHLER, WILLIAM HENRY
HELLMAN, JACOB
HERBST, KARL
HERLITZ, GEORG
HERMANN, LEO
HERRMANN, HUGO
HERZL, THEODOR
HESS, MOSES
HICKL, MAX
HODESS, JACOB
HOFFMANN, JACOB
HORODISCHTSCH, LEON
IDELSON, ABRAHAM
ISH-KISHOR, EPHRAIM
JABOTINSKY, VLADIMIR (Ze'ev)
JACOBSON, VICTOR
JAFFE, BEZALEL
JAFFE, LEIB
JARBLUM, MARC
JASINOWSKI, ISRAEL ISIDORE
KAHN, FRANZ
KALEF, YEHOSHUA
KALISCHER, ZEVI HIRSCH
KATZENELSON, NISSAN
KATZNELSON, BERL (Beeri)
KESSLER, LEOPOLD
KIRSHBLUM, MORDECAI
KISCH, FREDERICK HERMANN
KITRON (KOSTRINSKY), MOSHE
KLARMAN, YOSEF
KLEE, ALFRED

KLUMEL, MEIR
KOKESCH, OZER
KOMOLY, OTTO
KORKIS, ABRAHAM ADOLF
LANDAU, SAUL RAPHAEL
LANDAU, SHEMUEL HAYYIM
LANDAUER, GEORG
LEVIN, SHMARYA
LEWINSKY, ELHANAN LEIB
LEWITE, LEON
LICHT, ALEXANDER
LICHTHEIM, RICHARD
LINDHEIM, IRMA LEVY
LIPSKY, LOUIS
LOEWE, HEINRICH (Eliakim)
MACCOBY, HAYYIM ZUNDEL
MANDELSTAMM, MAX EMMANUEL
MARMOREK, ALEXANDER
MOTZKIN, LEO (Aryeh Leib)
NATONEK, JOSEPH
NEUMANN, EMANUEL
NEWLINSKI, PHILIPP MICHAEL
NISSENBAUM, ISAAC
NORDAU, MAX
NUROCK, MORDECHAI
PASMANIK, DANIEL
PINSKER, LEON (Judah Leib)
REICH, LEON
REVUSKY, ABRAHAM
RINGEL, MICHAEL
ROMANO, MARCO
RONAI, JANOS
ROTENSTREICH, FISCHEL
RUFEISEN, JOSEPH
RUPPIN, ARTHUR
SACHER, HARRY
SALZ, ABRAHAM ADOLPH
SCHACH, FABIUS
SCHACHTEL, HUGO-HILLEL
SCHALIT, ISIDOR
SCHAPIRA, HERMANN (Zevi-Hirsch)
SCHECHTMAN, JOSEPH B.
SCHENK, FAYE L.
SCHLESINGER, AKIVA JOSEPH
SCHLOESSINGER, MAX
SCHOENFELD, JOSEPH
SCHOOLMAN, BERTHA S.
SCHWARZBART, ISAAC IGNACY
SHRAGAI, SHLOMO ZALMAN
SHREIER, FEIWEL
SILVER, ABBA HILLEL
SIMON, JULIUS
SIMON, SIR LEON
SOKOLOW, NAHUM
SOMMERSTEIN, EMIL
STAND, ADOLF
STEINER, HANNAH
STRICKER, ROBERT
SYKES, SIR MARK
SYRKIN, NACHMAN

TAUBES, LOEBEL
THON, OSIAS (Jehoshua)
TIOMKIN, VLADIMIR (Ze'ev)
TORCZYNER, JACQUES
TRIETSCH, DAVIS
TSCHLENOW, JEHIEL (Yefim Vladimirovich)
USSISHKIN, ABRAHAM MENAHEM MENDEL
VAN VRIESLAND, SIEGFRIED ADOLF (Zadok)
WARBURG, OTTO
WEISGAL, MEYER WOLF
WEIZMANN, CHAIM
WELTSCH, ROBERT
WERNER, SIEGMUND
WILENSKY, YEHUDAH LEIB NISAN
WOLFFSOHN, DAVID
WORLD LABOR ZIONIST MOVEMENT
WORTSMAN, YECHESKIEL CHARLES
YOFFE, ALTER
ZIPPER, GERSHON
ZISSU, ABRAHAM LEIB
ZLATOPOLSKY, HILLEL
ZLOCISTI, THEODOR
ZUCKERMAN, BARUCH

2. REGIONAL HISTORY

a. Israel, Land and State of
MAIN SURVEYS
ISRAEL, LAND OF
ISRAEL, LAND OF – CLIMATE
ISRAEL, LAND OF – FLORA AND FAUNA
ISRAEL, LAND OF – GEOGRAPHICAL SURVEY
ISRAEL, LAND OF – GEOLOGY
ISRAEL, LAND OF – HISTORY
ISRAEL, LAND OF – PHYSIOGRAPHY
ISRAEL, STATE OF – ALIYAH, ABSORPTION AND
    SETTLEMENT
ISRAEL, STATE OF – ARAB POPULATION
ISRAEL, STATE OF – CULTURAL LIFE
ISRAEL, STATE OF – DEFENSE FORCES
ISRAEL, STATE OF – ECONOMIC AFFAIRS
ISRAEL, STATE OF – EDUCATION
ISRAEL, STATE OF – GOVERNANCE
ISRAEL, STATE OF – HEALTH
ISRAEL, STATE OF – HISTORICAL SURVEY
ISRAEL, STATE OF – HUMAN GEOGRAPHY
ISRAEL, STATE OF – LABOR
ISRAEL, STATE OF – LEGAL AND JUDICIAL SYSTEM
ISRAEL, STATE OF – POLITICAL LIFE AND PARTIES
ISRAEL, STATE OF – POPULATION
ISRAEL, STATE OF – RELIGIOUS LIFE AND
    COMMUNITIES
ISRAEL, STATE OF – WELFARE AND SOCIAL
    SECURITY

GENERAL ENTRIES
AGRICULTURE
AISH HATORAH
ALIYAH

ARCHAEOLOGISTS
ARCHAEOLOGY
ARCHIPHERECITES
ARCHITECTURE AND ARCHITECTS
ARMISTICE AGREEMENTS, ISRAEL-ARAB
ART
BI-NATIONALISM
COINS AND CURRENCY
COMMUNITY TOKENS
COOPERATIVES
CRIME
CRUSADES
DECLARATION OF INDEPENDENCE, ISRAEL
DEW
EARTHQUAKE
ENTEBBE RAID
EREZ ISRAEL
FLAG
GULF WAR
HALUKKAH
HAMAS
HA-TIKVAH
HIGH COMMISSIONER FOR PALESTINE
HIZBOLLAH
HOLY PLACES
HOREV COMMISSION
ILLEGAL IMMIGRATION
INDEPENDENCE DAY, ISRAEL
INTIFADA
ISRAEL PRIZE
ITINERARIES OF EREZ ISRAEL
ITINERARIUM ANTONINI
ITINERARIUM HIEROSOLYMITANUM OR
    ITINERARIUM BURDIGALENSE
KAHAN COMMISSION
KIBBUTZ FESTIVALS
KNESSET
LAVON AFFAIR
LEBANON WAR
MABARAH
MACCABIAH
MANDATE FOR PALESTINE
MAPS OF EREZ ISRAEL
MOSHAV
MOSHAV SHITTUFI
NATIONAL PARKS IN ISRAEL
NATURE RESERVES IN ISRAEL
NEW LEFT
OLEI HA-GARDOM
PALESTINE
PALESTINE, INQUIRY COMMISSIONS
PALESTINE, PARTITION AND PARTITION PLANS
PALESTINE LIBERATION ORGANIZATION
PALESTINIAN AUTHORITY
PATRIA
PILGRIMAGE
PRESIDENT OF ISRAEL
PROJECT RENEWAL
RISHON LE-ZION
SAINT JAMES CONFERENCE

I. HISTORY
B. MEDIEVAL & MODERN PERIOD
2. Regional History
a. *Israel, Land and State of*
GENERAL ENTRIES *(continued)*

SALT
SHEKEL
SHELUHEI EREZ ISRAEL
SINAI CAMPAIGN
SIX-DAY WAR
STOCKADE AND WATCHTOWER
SYKES-PICOT TREATY
TEMPLERS
TRAVELERS AND TRAVELS TO EREZ ISRAEL
UNSCOP
VANUNU AFFAIR
WAR OF INDEPENDENCE
WHITE PAPERS
YOM HA-ZIKKARON
YOM KIPPUR WAR

FLORA AND FAUNA

ACACIA
ALGUM
ALMOND
ANIMALS OF THE BIBLE AND TALMUD
ANT
ANTELOPE
APPLE
ASS
BALSAM
BARLEY
BAT
BEANS
BEAR
BEE
BEET
BITTERN (Heron)
BOX
BROOM
BUFFALO
BUZZARD
CABBAGE
CALAMUS, SWEET
CAMEL
CAPER
CAROB
CASTOR-OIL PLANT
CAT
CATTLE
CEDAR
CENTIPEDE
CHAMELEON
CINNAMON
CITRUS
CORAL
CORIANDER
COTTON
CRANE

CRIMSON WORM
CROCODILE
CUCUMBER
CUMIN
CYPRESS
DEER
DOG
DOVE
DYE PLANTS
EAGLE
EBONY
ELEPHANT
FENNEL
FIG
FLAX
FLEA
FLOWERS
FLY
FOX
FRANKINCENSE
FROG
GALBANUM
GARLIC
GAZELLE
GECKO
GNAT
GOAT
GOOSE
GOURD
GULL
HARE
HAWK
HEMLOCK
HEMP
HERBS, MEDICINAL
HONEY
HOOPOE
HORNET
HORSE
HYENA
HYRAX
HYSSOP
IBEX
IVORY
IVY
JACKAL
JUJUBE
JUNIPER
KITE
LAUDANUM
LEECH
LEEK
LEGUMES
LENTIL
LEOPARD
LETTUCE
LEVIATHAN
LION
LIZARD
LOCUST

LOUSE
MALLOW
MANDRAKE
MASTIC
MELON
MILKWEED
MILLET
MOLE
MONITOR
MOTH
MOUSE
MULBERRY
MULE
MUSHROOMS
MUSTARD
MYRRH
MYRTLE
NIGHTINGALE
NUT
OAK
OLEANDER
OLIVE
ONAGER
ONION
ORACH
OSTRICH
OWL
PALM
PAPYRUS
PARTRIDGE
PEACH
PEACOCK
PEAR
PELICAN
PEPPER
PHEASANT
PIG
PINE
PISTACHIO
PLANE TREE
PLANTS
PLUM
POMEGRANATE
POPLAR
QUAIL
QUINCE
RADISH
RAT
RAVEN
REED
RICE
ROCKET
ROSE
SAFFRON
SCORPION
SHEEP
SILK
SKINK
SNAKE
SORGHUM

SPARROW
SPICES
SPIDER
SPIKENARD
SQUILL
STORAX
STORK
SUMAC
SWIFT
SYCAMORE
TAHASH
TAMARISK
TARES
TEREBINTH
THISTLES AND THORNS
TORTOISE
TRAGACANTH
TURTLE DOVE
VEGETABLES
VINE
VULTURES
WEEDS
WHEAT
WILD BULL
WILLOW
WOLF
WORM
WORMWOOD

Places
ABU AWEIGILA
ABU GHOSH
ADULLAM REGION
AIJALON
ARABAH
ARBEL
AVELIM OR OVELIM
BANIAS
BASHAN
BET NETOFAH
BETHAR
CARMEL, MOUNT
DEAD SEA
EN-DOR
GERIZIM, MOUNT
GESHER BENOT YAAKOV
GILBOA
GINNOSAR, PLAIN OF
HAMMAT-GADER (Geder)
HAMMATH (Tiberias)
HECHAL SHLOMO
HEFER PLAIN
HERMON, MOUNT
HULEH VALLEY
JABBOK
JEZREEL, VALLEY OF
JORDAN
JOTABAH
KINNAROT, VALLEY OF
KINNERET, LAKE

I. HISTORY

B. MEDIEVAL & MODERN PERIOD

2. Regional History

a. *Israel, Land and State of*

PLACES (*continued*)

KISHON
LATRUN
MAALEH AKRABBIM
MACHPELAH, CAVE OF
MEIR BAAL HA-NES, TOMB OF
MIKVEH ISRAEL
MOUNT OF OLIVES
NEGEV
ONO
RAIN
RAMAT HA-GOLAN
RED SEA
SHEPHELAH
SINAI
SODOM AND GOMORRAH
SOREK, VALLEY OF
TABOR, MOUNT
TIMNA
WESTERN WALL
YARKON
YARMUK
ZION

COMMUNITIES

ABU GHOSH
ACRE
ADAMIT
AFIKIM
AFULAH
ALFEI MENASHE
ALLONEI ABBA
ALLONEI YIZHAK
ALLONIM
ALMAGOR
ALMAH
ALUMMOT
AMAZYAH
AMIR
AMIRIM
AMMIAD
AMMINADAV
ANATHOTH
APHEK
APOLLONIA
ARA
ARABA
ARAD
ARARA
ARIEL
ARRABA
ARTAS
ASHDOD
ASHDOT YAAKOV
ASHKELON

ATAROT
ATHLIT
AVIGDOR
AVIHAYIL
AYANOT
AYYELET HA-SHAHAR
AZOR
BALFOURIYYAH
BAQA AL-GHARBIYYA; BAQA AL-SHARQIYYA
BARKAI
BAT HEFER
BAT SHELOMO
BAT YAM
BEERI
BEER ORAH
BEEROT YIZHAK
BEERSHEBA
BEER TOVIYYAH
BEER YAAKOV
BEIT JANN
BEIT JIMAL
BEN SHEMEN
BENE-BERAK
BENEI AISH
BENEI DAROM
BENEI DEROR
BENEI ZION
BEROR HAYIL
BET ALFA
BET(H)-ARABAH
BET(H)-DAGON
BET(H)-EL
BET ESHEL
BET GUVRIN
BET HA-EMEK
BET HALEVI
BET HANAN
BETHANY
BET HERUT
BET HILLEL
BETHLEHEM
BET (Bayt) IKSA
BET KESHET
BET(H) LEHEM (Ha-Gelilit)
BET MEIR
BET NEHEMYAH
BET OREN
BET OVED
BET(H)-SHEAN
BET SHEARIM
BET(H)-SHEMESH
BET(H)-SHITTAH
BET YANNAI
BET YEHOSHUA
BET YERAH
BET YIZHAK
BET YOSEF
BET ZAYIT
BET ZERA
BINYAMINAH

BIRANIT
BIRIYYAH
BITAN AHARON
BIZZARON
BOZRAH
CAESAREA
DABBURIYYA
DAFNAH
DALIYAT AL-KARMIL
DALIYYAH
DALTON
DAN
DEGANYAH
DEIR AL-BALAH
DIMONAH
DOBRATH
DOR
DOROT
EFRAT
EILAT
EILON
EILOT
EIN FASHKHAH
EIN GEV
EIN HA-EMEK
EIN HA-HORESH
EIN HA-MIFRAZ
EIN HA-NAZIV
EIN HA-SHELOSHAH
EIN HA-SHOFET
EIN HOD
EIN IRON
EIN KEREM
EIN SHEMER
EIN VERED
EIN YAHAV
EIN ZEITIM
EIN ZURIM
ELAD
ELATH
ELYASHIV
EMMAUS
EN-GEDI
EN-HAROD
ESHTAOL
ESHTEMOA
EVEN YEHUDAH
EVEN YIZHAK
EVRON
EYAL
FASSUTA
FURAYDIS, AL-
GA'ATON
GALILEE
GALON
GAN HAYYIM
GANNEI TIKVAH
GANNEI YEHUDAH
GAN SHELOMO
GAN SHEMUEL

GAN SHOMRON
GAN YAVNEH
GAT
GAZIT
GEDERAH
GELIL YAM
GESHER
GESHER HA-ZIV
GEULEI TEIMAN
GEULIM
GEVA
GEVARAM
GEVAT
GEVIM
GEVULOT
GEZER
GIBBETHON
GINNEGAR
GINNOSAR
GISCALA
GIVAT ADA
GIVATAYIM
GIVAT BRENNER
GIVAT HA-SHELOSHAH
GIVAT HAYYIM
GIVAT HEN
GIVAT SHMUEL
GIVAT ZE'EV
GOFNAH
GUSH ETZYON
GUSH KATIF
HA-BONIM
HADERAH
HADID
HAFEZ HAYYIM
HA-GOSHERIM
HAIFA
HALHUL
HAMADYAH
HA-MAPIL
HANITAH
HA-OGEN
HA-ON
HAREL
HA-SOLELIM
HAZER, HAZERIM
HAZEVAH
HAZOR (ha-Gelilit)
HAZOR ASHDOD
HA-ZORE'A
HA-ZORE'IM
HEBRON
HEFZI BAH
HELEZ
HEREV LE-ET
HERUT
HERZLIYYAH
HIBBAT ZION
HOD HA-SHARON
HOGLAH

I. HISTORY
B. MEDIEVAL & MODERN PERIOD
2. Regional History
a. Israel, Land and State of
COMMUNITIES (continued)

HOLON
HUKOK
HULATAH
HULDAH
HULEH
HURFAYSH
ILANIYYAH
JABNEEL
JAFFA
JENIN
JERICHO
JERUSALEM
JERUSALEM, LEGAL ASPECTS
JOKNEAM
JOTAPATA
KABRI
KADIMAH
KAFR KAMA
KAFR QASIM
KARMIEL
KARMIYYAH
KARNEI SHOMRON
KAZIR HARISH
KAZRIN
KEFAR AZAR
KEFAR BARAM
KEFAR BARUKH
KEFAR BIALIK
KEFAR BILU
KEFAR BLUM
KEFAR DAROM
KEFAR EZYON
KEFAR GAMALA
KEFAR GIDEON
KEFAR GILADI
KEFAR GLICKSON
KEFAR HABAD
KEFAR HA-HORESH
KEFAR HA-MACCABI
KEFAR HANANYAH
KEFAR HA-NASI
KEFAR HA-RO'EH
KEFAR HASIDIM
KEFAR HATTIN
KEFAR HAYYIM
KEFAR HESS
KEFAR HITTIM
KEFAR JAWITZ
KEFAR KANNA
KEFAR KISCH
KEFAR MALAL
KEFAR MANDI
KEFAR MASARYK
KEFAR MENAHEM

KEFAR MONASH
KEFAR MORDEKHAI
KEFAR NETTER
KEFAR PINES
KEFAR ROSH HA-NIKRAH
KEFAR RUPPIN
KEFAR SAVA
KEFAR SHEMARYAHU
KEFAR SYRKIN
KEFAR SZOLD
KEFAR TAVOR
KEFAR TRUMAN
KEFAR URIYYAH
KEFAR VITKIN
KEFAR VRADIM
KEFAR WARBURG
KEFAR YASIF
KEFAR YEHEZKEL
KEFAR YEHOSHUA
KEFAR YONAH
KHAN YUNIS
KINNERET
KINNERET
KIR HARESETH
KIRYAT ANAVIM
KIRYAT ATA
KIRYAT BIALIK
KIRYAT EKRON
KIRYAT GAT
KIRYAT-HAROSHET
KIRYAT MALAKHI
KIRYAT MOTZKIN
KIRYAT ONO
KIRYAT SHEMONAH
KIRYAT TIVON
KIRYAT YAM
KISSUFIM
KOKHAV YAIR
LACHISH REGION
LAHAVOT HA-BASHAN
LAVI
LEHAVIM
LOHAMEI HA-GETTAOT
LYDDA
MA'AGAN MIKHAEL
MA'ALE ADUMIM
MA'ALEH HA-HAMISHAH
MA'ALOT TARSHIHA
MA'ANIT
MA'AS
MA'BAROT
MAGHAR, AL-
MAHANAYIM
MAJDAL AL-SHAMS
MAJD AL-KURUM
MAKKABIM-RE'UT
MANARAH
MA'OZ HAYYIM
MASSADAH
MASSUOT YIZHAK

MA'YAN BARUKH
MA'YAN ZEVI
MAZKERET BATYAH
MAZLI'AH
MEI AMMI
ME'IR SHEFEYAH
MEITAR
MENAHEMIYYA
MERHAVYAH
MERON
MESILLAT ZION
MESILLOT
METULLAH
MEVASSERET ZION
MIGDAL
MIGDAL HA-EMEK
MI'ILYA
MIKHMORET
MISGAV AM
MISHMAR HA-EMEK
MISHMAR HA-NEGEV
MISHMAR HA-SHARON
MISHMAR HA-YARDEN
MISHMAROT
MIZPAH
MIZPEH RAMON
MIZRA
MODI'IN
MOLEDET
MOZA, (HA-) MOZAH
NA'AN
NABLUS
NAHALAL
NAHALAT YEHUDAH
NAHAL OZ
NAHARIYYAH
NAVEH
NAZARETH
NEGBAH
NEHALIM
NEHORAH
NE'OT MORDEKHAI
NESHER
NES ZIYYONAH
NETA'IM
NETANYAH
NETIV HA-LAMED-HE
NETIVOT
NEVATIM
NEVEH EITAN
NEVEH YAM
NEZER SERENI
NIR AM
NIR DAVID
NIR EZYON
NIRIM
NIZZANAH
NIZZANIM
OFAKIM
OMER

OR AKIVA
ORANIT
OR HA-NER
OROT
OR YEHUDAH
PARDES HANNAH-KARKUR
PARDESIYYAH
PEKI'IN
PETAH TIKVAH
PORIYYAH
QUNAYTIRA, AL-
RA'ANANNAH
RAFA
RAMA, AL-
RAMALLAH
RAMAT DAVID
RAMAT GAN
RAMAT HA-KOVESH
RAMAT HA-SHARON
RAMAT HA-SHOFET
RAMAT RAHEL
RAMAT RAZIEL
RAMAT YISHAI
RAMAT YOHANAN
RAMAT ZEVI
RAMLEH
RAMOT HA-SHAVIM
RAMOT MENASHEH
RAMOT NAFTALI
REGAVIM
REGBAH
REHOVOT
REKHASIM
REVADIM
REVIVIM
RIHANIYYA, AL-
RISHON LE-ZION
RISHPON
ROSH HA-AYIN
ROSH PINNAH
RUHAMAH
SA'AD
SAFED
SALCHAH
SARID
SASA
SAVYON
SEDEH BOKER
SEDEH ELIYAHU
SEDEH NAHUM
SEDEH NEHEMYAH
SEDEH WARBURG
SEDEH YAAKOV
SEDEROT
SEDOT YAM
SHAALBIM
SHA'AREI TIKVAH
SHAAR HA-AMAKIM
SHA'AR HA-GOLAN
SHADMOT DEVORAH

I. HISTORY
B. MEDIEVAL & MODERN PERIOD
2. Regional History
a. *Israel, Land and State of*
COMMUNITIES (*continued*)

SHAMIR
SHARONAH
SHAVEI ZION
SHE'AR YASHUV
SHEFARAM
SHEFAYIM
SHELOMI
SHELUHOT
SHIVTAH
SHOHAM
SHOMRAT
SHORESH
SHOVAL
SHUNEM
SIKHNIN
SUSITA
TAANACH
TAL SHAHAR
TAYYIBA, AL-
TEKOA
TEKUMAH
TEL ADASHIM
TEL AVIV-JAFFA
TEL HAI
TEL KAZIR
TEL MOND
TEL YIZHAK
TEL YOSEF
THEBEZ
TIBERIAS
TIRA, AL-
TIRAT HA-CARMEL
TIRAT ZEVI
TIVON
TUL KARM
UDIM
URIM
USHA
USIFIYYA
YAD HANNAH
YAD MORDEKHAI
YAGUR
YAKUM
YAMMIT REGION
YARDENAH
YARKONAH
YAVNEH
YAVNEH
YEDIDYAH
YEHI'AM
YEHUD
YEROHAM
YESODOT
YESUD HA-MA'ALAH

YIZREEL
YOTVATAH
ZAREPHATH
ZIKHRON YAAKOV
ZOFIT
ZORAH
ZORAN
ZUR MOSHE
ZUR YIGAL

ORGANIZATIONS
AHDUT HA-AVODAH
AHDUT HA-AVODAH-POALEI ZION
AMIDAR
A.S.A.
BAR-ILAN UNIVERSITY
BENEI BINYAMIN
BEN-GURION UNIVERSITY OF THE NEGEV
BEN-ZVI INSTITUTE
BERIT HA-BIRYONIM
BERIT SHALOM
BETH HATEFUTSOTH
BEZALEL
BILU
BNEI AKIVA
CAMERI
CANAANITES
DEMOCRATIC MOVEMENT FOR CHANGE
EGGED
EL AL
ELITZUR
EL-YAM
EMUNAH
EZ HAYYIM
FARMERS FEDERATION OF ISRAEL
FRIENDSHIP LEAGUES WITH ISRAEL
GADNA
GAHAL
GEDUD HA-AVODAH
GHETTO FIGHTER'S HOUSE
GUSH EMUNIM
HABIMAH
HAGANAH
HAIFA, UNIVERSITY OF
HAIFA MUNICIPAL THEATER
HA-KIBBUTZ HA-ARZI HA-SHOMER HA-ZAIR
HA-KIBBUTZ HA-DATI
HA-KIBBUTZ HA-MEUHAD
HAMASHBIR HAMERKAZI
HA-NO'AR HA-OVED VE-HA-LOMED
HA-OVED HA-ZIYYONI
HAPOEL
HA-POEL HA-MIZRACHI
HA-POEL HA-ZAIR
HA-SHOMER
HA-TENU'AH LE-MA'AN EREZ ISRAEL HA-
    SHELEMAH
HEBREW UNIVERSITY OF JERUSALEM
HERUT MOVEMENT
HEVRAT HA-OVEDIM

HIEROSOLYMITANISCHE STIFTUNG
HISTADRUT
HISTADRUT HA-OVEDIM HA-LE'UMMIT
HITAHDUT
IHUD HA-KEVUZOT VE-HA-KIBBUTZIM
INDEPENDENT LIBERAL PARTY
IRGUN ZEVAI LEUMMI
ISRAEL ACADEMY OF SCIENCES AND HUMANITIES
ISRAEL CHAMBER ORCHESTRA
ISRAEL EXPLORATION SOCIETY
ISRAEL LABOR PARTY
ISRAEL MUSEUM
ISRAEL PHILHARMONIC ORCHESTRA
JERUSALEM INSTITUTE FOR ISRAEL STUDIES
JERUSALEM PUBLISHING HOUSE, THE
JEWISH AGENCY
JEWISH BRIGADE GROUP
JEWISH LEGION
KACH
KADOORIE
KETER PUBLISHING HOUSE
KIBBUTZ MOVEMENT
LEO BAECK INSTITUTE
LIBRARY, JEWISH NATIONAL AND UNIVERSITY
LIKUD
LOHAMEI HERUT ISRAEL (Lehi)
MACCABI
MAGEN DAVID ADOM
MAHAL
MALBEN
MAPAI
MAPAM
MEKOROT WATER COMPANY
MERETZ
MO'EZET HA-PO'ALOT
NAHAL
NATIONAL RELIGIOUS PARTY
NETUREI KARTA
NILI
OHEL
PALESTINE ECONOMIC CORPORATION
PALESTINE EXPLORATION FUND
PALESTINE OFFICE
PALMAH
PEACE MOVEMENTS, RELIGIOUS
PEACE NOW
PEEL COMMISSION
PICA
PO'ALEI AGUDAT ISRAEL
RAFI
ROCKEFELLER MUSEUM
SCHECHTER INSTITUTE OF JEWISH STUDIES, THE
SCHOCKEN INSTITUTE
SHAS
SHINUI
SOLEL BONEH
TAHAL
TARBUT
TEACHERS ASSOCIATION IN ISRAEL
TECHNION, ISRAEL INSTITUTE OF TECHNOLOGY

TEL AVIV UNIVERSITY
TNUVA
TSOMET
ULPAN
VA'AD HA-PEKIDIM VE-HA-AMARKALIM
VA'AD LE'UMMI
VA'AD PEKIDEI EREZ ISRAEL BE-KUSHTA
WEIZMANN INSTITUTE OF SCIENCE
WRITERS ASSOCIATION IN ISRAEL
YAD VASHEM
ZIM

PUBLICATIONS
AHDUT HA-AVODAH
AL HA-MISHMAR
BUSTENAI
DAVAR
DO'AR HA-YOM
DVIR
GILYONOT
GLOBES
GOLDENE KEYT, DI
HAARETZ
HA-BOKER
HA-LEVANON
HA-MODI'A
HA-PO'EL HA-ZA'IR
HAVAZZELET
HA-ZOFEH
JERUSALEM POST
JERUSALEM REPORT
MAARIV
TARBIZ
UJ KELET
YATED NEEMAN
YEDIOTH AHARONOTH

BIOGRAPHIES
Academic Life
ADAR, ZVI
AHARONI, YOHANAN
ALCALAY, REUVEN
ALLON, GEDALYA
AMIR, MENACHEM
AMIRAN, DAVID
AMITSUR, SAMSON ABRAHAM
ANKORI, ZEVI
ARIELI, YEHOSHUA
ARNON, ABRAHAM
ARUSI, ABRAHAM BEN MOSES HA-LEVI
ASHTOR, ELIYAHU
AUERBACH, ELIAS
AUMMANN, ROBERT J.
AVIGAD, NAHMAN
AVINERI, SHLOMO
AVINERI, YITZHAK
AVIRAM, JOSEPH
AVITZUR, SHMUEL
AVI-YONAH, MICHAEL
AVRUNIN, ABRAHAM

I. HISTORY
B. MEDIEVAL & MODERN PERIOD
2. Regional History
a. Israel, Land and State of
Biographies
Academic Life (continued)

AYALON, DAVID
BACHI, ROBERTO
BAER, GABRIEL
BAER, YITZHAK
BANETH
BAR-DAROMA, HAYYIM ZE'EV
BAR-HILLEL, YEHOSHUA
BAR-YOSEF, OFER
BAUER, YEHUDA
BEIN, ALEXANDER
BEINART, HAIM
BEIT-HALLAHMI, BENJAMIN
BEN-ARIEH, YEHOSHUA
BENAYAHU, MEIR
BEN-DAVID, JOSEPH
BEN-DOR, IMMANUEL
BEN HAYYIM, ZE'EV
BEN-SASSON, HAIM HILLEL
BEN-SHAKHAR, GERSHON
BENTWICH
BENVENISTI, DAVID
BEN-YEHUDA, ELIEZER
BEN-YEHUDAH, BARUKH
BERGER-BARZILAI, JOSEPH
BERGMAN, SAMUEL HUGO
BERGMANN, JUDAH
BIALOBLOCKI, SAMUEL SHERAGA
BILLIG, LEVI
BIRAN, AVRAHAM
BLAU, JOSHUA
BLEJER, MARIO ISRAEL
BONDY, RUTH
BONFIL, ROBERT
BONNE, ALFRED ABRAHAM
BRASLAVI (Braslavski), JOSEPH
BRAVERMAN, AVISHAY
BRAWER, ABRAHAM JACOB
BRAWER, MOSHE
BRINKER, MENACHEM
CHOURAQUI, ANDRE
CHURGIN, PINKHOS
CONFINO, MICHAEL
CORCOS, DAVID
DALESKI, HILLEL
DAN, JOSEPH
DAVID D'BETH HILLEL
DE VRIES, BENJAMIN
DIAMANT, PAUL JOSEPH
DINUR, BENZION
DORON, ABRAHAM
DOTAN, ARON
DOTHAN, MOSHE
DOTHAN, TRUDE

DRAPKIN, ABRAHAM
DRAPKIN, ISRAEL
DVORZETSKY, MARK MEIR
EISENSTADT, SAMUEL NOAH
ELON, AMOS
ELON, MENACHEM
EPSTEIN, CLAIRE
EPSTEIN, JACOB NAHUM
ESTORI (ISAAC BEN MOSES) HA-PARHI
ETTINGER, SHMUEL
ETZIONI, AMITAI WERNER
EVEN SHEMUEL, JUDAH
EVEN-SHOSHAN, AVRAHAM
FAITLOVITCH, JACQUES
FEINBERG, NATHAN
FEUERSTEIN, REUVEN
FINKELSTEIN, ISRAEL
FISH, HAREL (HAROLD)
FRANKEL, YA'AKOV
FRANKENSTEIN, CARL
FREIMANN, ABRAHAM HAYYIM (Alfred)
FRIEDLAENDER, SAUL
FRIEDMAN, SHAMMA
FRIEDMANN, DANIEL
FUKS, ALEXANDER
FUNKENSTEIN, AMOS
GAON, MOSES DAVID
GARTNER, LLOYD P.
GAVISON, RUTH
GOITEIN, SHLOMO DOV (Fritz)
GOLDMAN, ELIEZER
GOLDSCHMIDT, ERNST DANIEL
GOPHNA, RAM
GOSHEN-GOTTSTEIN, MOSHE
GOTTLIEB, EPHRAIM
GRAJEWSKY, PINCHAS
GRANOTT, ABRAHAM (Granovsky)
GROSSMAN, AVRAHAM
GULAK, ASHER
GUTMAN, ISRAEL
GUTMANN, JOSHUA
HABERMANN, ABRAHAM MEIR
HADDAD, EZRA
HAKHAM, SIMON
HALPERN, ISRAEL
HARAN, MENAHEM
HAREL, MENASHEH
HEINEMANN, YIZHAK
HELD, MOSHE
HELFMAN, ELHANAN
HERLITZ, GEORG
HEYD, URIEL
HIRSCHBERG, HAIM ZEW
HOROWITZ, ISRAEL ZEEV
IDEL, MOSHE
KADDARI, MENAHEM ZEVI
KAHANA, ABRAHAM
KAHANE, ISAAK (Yizhak Ze'ev)
KAHNEMAN, DANIEL
KATZ, ELIHU

KATZ, ISRAEL
KATZ, JACOB
KAUFMANN, YEHEZKEL
KAZNELSON, SIEGMUND
KEMPINSKY, AHARON
KIEL, YEHUDA
KISTER, MEIR J.
KLAR, BENJAMIN MENAHEM
KLAUSNER, ISRAEL
KLAUSNER, JOSEPH GEDALIAH
KLEIN, SAMUEL
KLEINMANN, MOSHE
KOOK, SAUL HONE BEN SOLOMON ZALMAN
KORIAT, ASHER
KRAUS, PAUL ELIEZER
KUTSCHER, EDWARD YECHEZKEL
LANDAU, JACOB M.
LAPIDOT, RUTH
LEIBOWITZ, NEHAMA
LEIBOWITZ, YESHAYAHU
LEWY, YOHANAN
LIEBERMAN, SAUL
LIEBMAN, CHARLES (YESHAYAHU)
LIPSCHUETZ, ELIEZER MEIR
LISSAK, MOSHE
LOEWINGER, DAVID SAMUEL
LUNCZ, ABRAHAM MOSES
MAHLER, RAPHAEL
MAISELS, MOSES HAYYIM (Misha)
MALAMAT, ABRAHAM
MANHEIM, BILHAH
MANI, EZRA
MARGALIOT, MORDECAI
MAYER, LEO ARY
MAZAR, AMIHAI
MAZAR, BENJAMIN
MELAMED, EZRA ZION
MOREH, SHMUEL
MUNTNER, ALEXANDER SUESSMAN
NAVON, DAVID
NEUMANN, ERICH
NOY, DOV
OLSVANGER, IMMANUEL
ORMIAN, HAYYIM
PATINKIN, DON
PERI, HIRAM (Heinz)
PIAMENTA, MOSHE
PINES, NOAH
PINES, SHLOMO (Solomon)
PLESSNER, MARTIN (Meir)
POSNER, AKIVA BARUKH (Arthur)
POZNANSKI, EDWARD
PRAWER, JOSHUA
PRESS, YESHAYAHU
PROBST, MENAHEM MENDEL
RABAN, AVNER
RABIN
RAND, YAAKOV
RAVITZKY, AVIEZER
RIEGER, ELIEZER

RIVLIN, ELIEZER
RIVLIN, JOSEPH JOEL
ROSÉN, HAIIM B.
ROTENSTREICH, NATHAN
ROTH, LEON
SAFRAI, SHMUEL
SALOMON, GAVRIEL
SARFATTI, GAD
SCHAECHTER, JOSEPH
SCHALIT, ABRAHAM CHAIM
SCHAPIRO, ISRAEL
SCHIRMANN, JEFIM (Hayyim)
SCHMELZ, USIEL OSCAR
SCHOLEM, GERSHOM GERHARD
SCHWABE, MOSHE (Max)
SCHWADRON (SHARON), ABRAHAM
SCHWARZ, YEHOSEPH
SEGAL, MOSES HIRSCH (ZEVI)
SERMONETA, JOSEPH BARUCH
SHACHAR, ARIE
SHAHAR, SHULAMIT
SHILOH, YIGAL
SHMUELI, EPHRAIM
SHOHAM, SHLOMO-GIORA
SHOHETMAN, BARUCH
SHUVAL, JUDITH
SILBERNER, EDMUND
SIMON, AKIBA ERNST
SIMONSOHN, SHLOMO
SOMEKH, SASSON
SPERBER, DANIEL
SPIEGEL, NATHAN
STEKELIS, MOSHE
STERN, EPHRAIM
STERN, MENAHEM
SUKENIK, ELIEZER LIPA
TADMOR, HAYIM
TALMON, JACOB LEIB
TALMON, SHEMARYAHU
TARTAKOWER, ARIEH
TA-SHMA, ISRAEL MOSES
TCHERIKOVER, VICTOR (Avigdor)
TELLER, ISRAEL
TISHBY, ISAIAH
TUR-SINAI (Torczyner), NAPHTALI HERZ (Harry)
URBACH, EPHRAIM ELIMELECH
URMAN, DAN
USSISHKIN, DAVID
VILNAY, ZEV
WALLENSTEIN, MEIR
WARBURG, GAVRIEL REUBEN
WEIL, GOTTHOLD
WEISS, ABRAHAM
WEISS, MEIR
WERBLOWSKY, RAPHAEL JUDA ZWI
WERTHEIMER, SOLOMON AARON
WIGODER, GEOFFREY
WINNINGER, SOLOMON
WIRSZUBSKI, CHAIM
WISE, GEORGE SCHNEIWEIS

I. HISTORY
B. MEDIEVAL & MODERN PERIOD
2. Regional History
a. *Israel, Land and State of*
BIOGRAPHIES
Academic Life (continued)

WISTRICH, ROBERT
WIZEN, MOSHE AHARON
WORMANN, CURT
YAARI, ABRAHAM
YAARI, MENAHEM
YADIN, YIGAEL
YAHUDA, ABRAHAM SHALOM
YARON, REUVEN
YAVETS, ZVI
YEFET, SARAH
YEIVIN, ISRAEL
YOVEL, YIRMIYAHU
ZAND, MICHAEL
ZULAY, MENAHEM

Art
ABSALON
AGAM, YAACOV
AMISHAI-MAISELS, ZIVA
APPELBAUM, MOSHE
ARDON, MORDECAI
ARIKHA, AVIGDOR
AROCH, ARIE
ASCHHEIM, ISIDOR
ATAR, HAIM
AVNI, AHARON
BACON, YEHUDA
BAERWALD, ALEX
BAR-AM, MICHA
BARASCH, MOSHE
BEERI, TUVIA
BEN-ZVI, ZEEV
BERGNER, YOSSL (Yosef L.)
BERNSTEIN, MOSHE
BEZEM, NAPHTALI
BLUM, LUDWIG
BOGEN, ALEXANDER
BROWN, AIKA
CASTEL, MOSHE ELAZAR
COHEN, ELISHEVA
COHEN GAN, PINHAS
DANZIGER, ITZHAK
DAVID, JEAN
ELHANANI, ABA
ELHANANI, ARYEH
ENGELSBERG, LEON
FEIGIN, DOV
FIMA
FRENKEL (FRENEL), ITZHAK
GAD, DEVORAH
GAMZU, HAYYIM
GARBUZ, YAIR
GARDOSH, KARIEL (Charles; "Dosh")

GERSHUNI, MOSHE
GIDAL, TIM
GROSS, MICHAEL
GRUNDMAN, ZWI
GUTMAN, NAHUM
HABER, SHAMAI
HALEVY, YOSEF
IDELSON, BENJAMIN
JANCO, MARCEL
KADISHMAN, MENASHE
KAHANA, AHARON
KARAVAN, DANI
KARMI, DOV
KAUFMANN, RICHARD
KLARWEIN, JOSEPH
KRAKAUER, LEOPOLD
KUPFERMAN, MOSHE
LAVIE, RAFFI
LEVANON, MORDECAI
LIFSCHITZ, URI
LISHANSKY, BATYA
LITVINOVSKY, PINHAS
MAIROVICH, ZVI
MANDL, SAADIA
MANSFELD, ALFRED
MELNIKOFF, AVRAHAM
MERZER, ARIEH
MOKADY, MOSHE
MOREH, MORDECAI
MOSKOVITZ, SHALOM
NARKISS, BEZALEL
NARKISS, MORDECHAI
NEIMAN, YEHUDAH
NIKEL, LEA
OFEK, AVRAHAM
OFIR, ARIE
PALDI, ISRAEL
PALOMBO, DAVID
PANN, ABEL
PINS, JACOB
RAPAPORT, NATHAN
RATNER, YOHANAN
RAU, HEINZ
RECHTER
REZNIK, DAVID
RUBIN, REUVEN
RUBINGER, DAVID
SAFDIE, MOSHE
SCHATZ, BORIS
SCHUMACHER, GOTTLIEB
SEBBA, SHALOM
SHARON, ARYEH
SHEMI, MENAHEM
SHEMI, YEHIEL
SIMA, MIRON
STEINHARDT, JAKOB
STEMATSKY, AVIGDOR
STERNSCHUSS, MOSHE
STREICHMAN, YEHEZKIEL
TAGGER, SIONA

TALPIR, GABRIEL JOSEPH
TEVET, NAHUM
TICHO, ANNA
TUMARKIN, IGAEL
ULLMAN, MICHA
WEILL, SHRAGA
WOLPERT, LUDWIG YEHUDA
YASKI, AVRAHAM
ZARITSKY, YOSSEF
ZVIA

Literature
ADELMAN, URI
AGMON, NATHAN
AGNON, SHMUEL YOSEF
ALFES, BENZION
ALMOG, RUTH
ALONI, NISSIM
ALTERMAN, NATHAN
AMICHAI, YEHUDA
AMIR, AHARON
AMIR, ANDA
AMIR, ELI
APPELFELD, AHARON
ARICHA, YOSEF
ASHMAN, AHARON
AVIDAN, DAVID
AVIGUR-ROTEM, GABRIELA
AVINOAM, REUVEN
AVI-SHAUL, MORDEKHAI
BALLAS, SHIMON
BARASH, ASHER
BARON, DEVORAH
BARTOV, HANOCH
BAR-YOSEF, YEHOSHUA
BAT-MIRIAM, YOKHEVED
BEER, HAIM
BEILINSON, MOSHE
BEJERANO, MAYA
BEN-AMITAI, LEVI
BEN-AMOTZ, DAHN
BEN-GAVRIEL, MOSHE YA'AKOV
BEN-NER, YITZHAK
BEN-YEHUDA, HEMDAH
BEN YEHUDA, NETIVA
BEN YIZHAK, AVRAHAM
BEN-ZION, S.
BERNSTEIN, ORI
BIALIK, HAYYIM NAHMAN
BRENNER, JOSEPH HAYYIM
BROD, MAX
BROIDES, ABRAHAM
BROIDO, EPHRAIM
BURLA, YEHUDA
CARMI, T.
CASTEL-BLOOM, ORLY
CHOMSKY, DOV
DAYAN, YAEL
DOR, MOSHE
ELMALEH, ABRAHAM

EVER HADANI
EYTAN, RACHEL
FEYGENBERG, RAKHEL
FINBERT, ELIAN-J.
FRANKEL, NAOMI
FRIEDMANN, DAVID ARYEH
GALAI, BINYAMIN
GELDMAN, MORDECHAI
GILBOA, AMIR
GILEAD, ZERUBAVEL
GINZBURG, SIMON
GOLDBERG, LEA
GORDON, SAMUEL LEIB
GOURI, HAIM
GREENBERG, URI ZEVI
GROSSMAN, DAVID
GUR, BATYA
GURFEIN, RIVKA
HABIBI, EMIL
HACOHEN, MORDECAI BEN HILLEL
HAEZRAHI, YEHUDA
HALKIN, SIMON
HAMEIRI, AVIGDOR
HAREVEN, SHULAMIT
HAZAZ, HAYYIM
HENDEL, YEHUDIT
HOFFMANN, YOEL
HOROWITZ, YAAKOV
HOURVITZ, YA'IR
JAFFE, ABRAHAM B.
KABAK, AARON ABRAHAM
KADARI, SHRAGA
KAHANA-CARMON, AMALIA
KAMSON, YAAKOV (Jacob) DAVID
KANIUK, YORAM
KARNI, YEHUDA
KARU, BARUCH
KATZIR, JEHUDIT
KENAN, AMOS
KENAZ, YEHOSHUA
KERET, ETGAR
KIPNIS, LEVIN
KISHON, EPHRAIM
KLAUSNER, JOSEPH GEDALIAH
KOVNER, ABBA
KRAFT, WERNER
KRAUS, OTA
KURZWEIL, BARUCH
K. ZETNIK
LACHOWER, YERUHAM FISHEL
LAMDAN, YIZHAK
LAOR, YITZHAK
LAPID, SHULAMIT
LEVIN, HANOCH
LIEBRECHT, SAVYON
MATALON, RONIT
MEGGED, AHARON
MEITUS, ELIAHU
MICHAEL, SAMI
MIRON, DAN

I. **HISTORY**
   B. MEDIEVAL & MODERN PERIOD
      2. **Regional History**
         a. Israel, Land and State of
           Biographies
              Literature (continued)

MIRSKY, AARON
MISHOL, AGI
MOSSINSOHN, YIGAL
OFEK, URIEL
OREN, RAM
OREN, YIZHAK
ORLAND, YAAKOV
ORLEV, URI
ORPAZ AVERBUCH, YIZHAK
OVSAY, JOSHUA
OZ, AMOS
PAGIS, DAN
PENN, ALEXANDER
PINCAS, ISRAEL
RAAB, ESTHER
RAGEN, NAOMI
RAHEL
RATOSH, YONATHAN
RAVIKOVITCH, DALIA
REICH, ASHER
RIMON, JACOB
RUEBNER, TUVIA
SADAN, DOV
SADEH, PINHAS
SERI, DAN BENAYA
SHABTAI, AHARON
SHABTAI, YAAKOV
SHAHAM, NATHAN
SHAHAR, DAVID
SHAKED, GERSHON
SHALEV, MEIR
SHALEV, YITZHAK
SHALEV, ZERUYA
SHALOM, SHIN
SHAMI, YITZHAK
SHAMIR, MOSHE
SHENHAR, YITZHAK
SHIMONI (Shimonovitz), DAVID
SHIMONI, YOUVAL
SHLONSKY, ABRAHAM
SHOFMAN, GERSHON
SILMAN, KADISH YEHUDA LEIB
SIVAN, ARYE
SMILANSKY, MEIR
SMILANSKY, MOSHE
SMOLI, ELIEZER (Smoler)
SOBOL, YEHOSHUA
SOMECK, RONNY
STEINBERG, JACOB
STERN, NOAH
STRAUSS, ARYEH LUDWIG
STREIT, SHALOM
STURMANN, MANFRED

SUSSMAN, EZRA
SVERDLIK, ODED
TABIB, MORDEKHAI
TALPIR, GABRIEL JOSEPH
TAMMUZ, BENJAMIN
TCHERNOWITZ-AVIDAR, YEMIMAH
TEMKIN
TEVET, SHABBETAI
TIDHAR, DAVID
TOCHNER, MESHULLAM
TSALKA, DAN
TWERSKY, YOHANAN
UKHMANI, AZRIEL
UNGERFELD, MOSHE
WALLACH, YONA
WEINBERG, ZEVI ZEBULUN
WERSES, SAMUEL
WIESELTHIER, MEIR
WOYSLAWSKI, ZEVI
YAARI, YEHUDAH
YALAN-STEKELIS, MIRIAM
YEHOSHUA, AVRAHAM B.
YEIVIN, YEHOSHUA HESCHEL
YERUSHALMI, RINA
YESHURUN, AVOT
YIZHAR, S.
YONATHAN, NATHAN
YZRAELY, YOSSI
ZACH, NATHAN
ZARCHI, ISRAEL
ZELDA (MISHKOVSKY)
ZEMACH, SHLOMO
ZMORA, YISRAEL

Music
ABILEAH, ARIE
ADLER, ISRAEL
ADMON, YEDIDYAH
AGADATI, BARUCH
AHARON, EZRA
ALDEMA, GIL
ALEXANDER, HAIM
AMIRAN, EMANUEL
ARBATOVA, MIA
ARGOV, ALEXANDER (SASCHA)
AROM, SIMHA
ARONOVICH, YURI MIKHAYLOVICH
ATZMON, MOSHE
AVENARY, HANOCH
AVIDOM, MENAHEM
AVNI, TZEVI
BARDANASHVILI, YOSEF
BARENBOIM, DANIEL
BAYER, BATHIA
BEER, RAMI
BEN-HAIM, PAUL
BEN-HAIM, YIGAL
BEN-SHABETAI, ARI
BERGEL, BERND
BERTINI, GARY

BERTONOFF, DEBORAH
BOEHM, YOHANAN
BOSCOVITCH, ALEXANDER URIYAH
BRAUN (BROWN), ARIE
BRAUN, YEHEZKIEL
BRONFMAN, YEFIM
CHURGIN, BATHIA
COHEN MELAMED, NISSAN
COHEN, YARDENA
DA-OZ, RAM
DAUS, AVRAHAM
DE PHILIPPE, EDIS
DORFMAN, JOSEPH
EDEN-TAMIR
EHRLICH, ABEL
ENGEL, JOEL (Yuli Dimitriyevich)
EVEN-OR, MARY
FEIDMAN, GIYORA
FISHER, DUDU
FLEISCHER, TSIPPI
FRIED (-BISS), MIRIAM
GELBRUN, ARTUR
GERSON-KIWI, EDITH (Esther)
GESHURI, MEIR SHIMON
GILBOA, JACOB
GOLDSTEIN, RAYMOND
GOLINKIN, MORDECAI
GRADENWITZ, PETER EMANUEL
GRAZIANI, YIZHAK
HAJDU, ANDRE
HARRAN, DON
HERSTIK, NAPHTALI
HIRSH, NURIT
HIRSHBERG, JEHOASH
HOLDHEIM, THEODOR
INBAL, ELIAHU
JACOBI, HANOCH (Heinrich)
JAFFE, ELI
KADMAN, GURIT
KALICHSTEIN, JOSEPH
KARACZEWSKI, HANINA
KATZ, RUTH
KOPYTMAN, MARK RUVIMOVICH
LAKNER, YEHOSHUA
LEEF, YINAM
LERER, JOSHUA
LERER, SHMUEL
LEVI, LEO
LEVI, YOEL
LEVI-AGRON, HASIA
LEVI-TANNAI, SARA
LIFSHITZ, NEHAMAH
MAAYANI, AMI
MANOR, EHUD
MEDINA, AVIHU
MEHTA, ZUBIN
MINTZ, SHLOMO
MIRON, ISSACHAR
NAHARIN, OHAD
NARDI, NAHUM

NATRA, SERGIU
NAVON, ISAAC ELIYAHU
NIKOVA, RINA
NOY, MEIR
OLIVERO, BETTY
ORDMAN, JEANETTE
ORGAD, BEN ZION
OVED, MARGALIT
PANOV, VALERY
PARTOS, OEDOEN
PELLEG, FRANK
PERLMAN, ITZCHAK
RAN, SHULAMIT
RODAN, MENDI
RONLY-RIKLIS, SHALOM
SALMON, KAREL (Karl Salomon)
SALZMAN, PNINA
SCHIDLOWSKY, LEON
SEGAL, URI
SETER, MORDECHAI
SHAHAM, GIL
SHALLON, DAVID
SHELEM, MATTITYAHU
SHEMER, NAOMI
SHERIFF, NOAM
SHILOAH, AMNON
SHLONSKY, VARDINA
SHMUELI, HERZL
SMOIRA-COHN, MICHAL
SOBOL, MORDECHAI
STERN, MOSHE
STERNBERG, ERICH WALTER
TAL, JOSEF
TALMON, ZVI
TAUBE, MICHAEL
WILENSKY, MOSHE
YAMPOLSKY, BERTA
YELLIN-BENTWICH, TELMA
ZEFIRA, BRACHAH
ZEHAVI, DAVID
ZEIRA, MORDECHAI
ZUKERMAN, PINCHAS
ZUR, MENAHEM

Popular Culture
ALBERSTEIN, HAVA
ALMAGOR, GILA
ARAD, YAEL
ARGOV, ZOHAR
ARNOLD, PAULA
ARTZI, SHLOMO
BAKRI, MUHAMMAD
BANAI FAMILY
BAR, SHLOMO
BARUCH, ADAM
BEN, ZEHAVA
BEN-AVI, ITHAMAR
BERKOWITZ, MICKEY
BERNSTEIN-COHEN, MIRIAM
BRODY, TAL

BAR-YEHUDAH, ISRAEL
BAUM, MENAHEM MENDEL BEN AARON OF
    KAMENETZ
BECKER, AHARON
BEER, ISRAEL
BEGIN, MENAHEM
BEGIN, ZE'EV BINYAMIN
BEHAR, NISSIM
BEILIN, YOSSI
BEINISCH, DORIT
BEJERANO
BELKIND
BEN-AHARON, YIZHAK
BEN-AMI, OVED
BEN DOV, YAAKOV
BEN-ELIEZER, BINYAMIN
BEN ELIEZER, MOSHE
BEN-GURION, DAVID
BEN-HORIN, ELIAHU
BEN-ISRAEL, RUTH
BENJAMIN OF TIBERIAS
BEN-NATAN, ASHER
BEN-PORAT, MIRIAM
BEN PORAT, MORDECAI
BENTOV, MORDEKHAI
BENTWICH
BEN-YOSEF, SHELOMO
BEN-ZVI, IZHAK
BEN-ZVI, RAHEL YANAIT
BEN-ZVI, SHLOMO
BERAB, JACOB BEN HAYYIM
BERENSON, ZVI
BERLIGNE, ELIYAHU MEIR
BERMAN, ADOLF ABRAHAM
BERMAN, SIMEON
BERNSTEIN, PEREZ
BET-ZURI, ELIAHU
BEYTH, HANS
BIRAM, ARTHUR (Yizhak)
BLAU, AMRAM
BLAU, MOSHE
BOGALE, YONA
BOGER, HAYYIM
BRILL, JEHIEL
BURG, AVRAHAM
BURG, YOSEF
BUSEL, JOSEPH
CARLEBACH, EZRIEL
CARMEL, MOSHE
CAROL, ARYEH
COHEN, ELI
COHEN, GE'ULAH
COHEN, SHLOMO
COHN, HAIM
COHN-REISS, EPHRAIM
COMAY, MICHAEL SAUL
CHELOUCHE
CHIZHIK
DAGAN, AVIGDOR
DANIN, YEHEZKEL

DANKNER, AMNON
DAYAN
DAYAN, MOSHE
DAYAN, YAEL
DERI, ARYEH
DICKENSTEIN, ABRAHAM
DINITZ, SIMCHA
DISKIN, MORDEKHAI
DISKIN, MOSES JOSHUA JUDAH LEIB
DISSENTCHIK, ARIE
DIWAN, JUDAH BEN AMRAM
DIZENGOFF, MEIR
DOBKIN, ELIYAHU
DOLGIN, SIMON ARTHUR
DORI, YA'AKOV
DREZNER, YEHIEL DOV
DULZIN, ARYE LEIB
DUSHKIN, ALEXANDER MORDECHAI
EBAN, ABBA (Aubrey)
EHRLICH, SIMHA
EISENBERG, AHARON ELIYAHU
EISENBERG, SHOUL
EITAN, RAPHAEL ("Raful")
ELATH, ELIAHU
ELAZAR, DAVID
ELAZARI-VOLCANI, YIZHAK
ELDAD, ISRAEL
ELIACHAR, MENACHE
ELIAV, ARIE LOVA
ELIAV, BINYAMIN
ELIYAHU, MORDECHAI
ELON, BINYAMIN
ELON, MENACHEM
ELYASHAR, JACOB SAUL BEN ELIEZER JEROHAM
ENGLARD, YITZHAK
EPSTEIN, IZHAC
ESHKOL, LEVI
ETTINGER, AKIVA JACOB
EVENTOV, YAKIR
EVRON, EPHRAIM
EYTAN, WALTER
FARBSTEIN, JOSHUA HESCHEL
FEINBERG
FEINSTEIN, HAYYIM JACOB HA-KOHEN
FEINSTEIN, MEIR
FELMAN, AHARON LEIB
FELLER, SHNEYUR ZALMAN
FISCHER, STANLEY
FOERDER, YESHAYAHU (Herbert)
FRANCO, AVRAHAM
FREIER, RECHA
FRUMKIN, ARYEH LEIB
FRUMKIN, ISRAEL DOV
GALIL, UZIA
GALILI, ISRAEL
GEDALIAH OF SIEMIATYCZE
GERI, JACOB
GILADI, ISRAEL
GINOSSAR, ROSA
GISSIN, AVSHALOM

I. HISTORY
B. MEDIEVAL & MODERN PERIOD
2. Regional History
a. Israel, Land and State of
BIOGRAPHIES
Public & Economic Life (continued)

GLIKIN, MOSHE
GLUECKSOHN, MOSHE
GLUSKA, ZEKHARYAH
GLUSKIN, ZEEV
GOLDBERG, ISAAC LEIB
GOLOMB, ELIYAHU
GORDON, AHARON DAVID
GRAJEWSKI, ELIEZER ZALMAN
GRANOTT, ABRAHAM (Granovsky)
GROSSMAN, YIZHAK DAVID
GRUENBAUM, YIZHAK
GRUNER, DOV
GUBER, RIVKA
GUR, MORDECAI (Motta)
GUTMANN, DAVID MEIR
GVATI, CHAIM
HABIBI, EMIL
HACOHEN, DAVID
HAKIM, ELIAHU
HALPERIN, YEHIEL
HALPERN, GEORG GAD
HAMMER, ZEVULUN
HANKIN, YEHOSHUA
HARARI (Blumberg), HAYYIM
HAREL, YISRAEL
HARMAN (Herman), AVRAHAM
HARZFELD, AVRAHAM
HATOKAI, ALDIN
HAUSDORF, AZRIEL ZELIG
HAUSNER, GIDEON
HAVIV, AVSHALOM
HAVIV-LUBMAN, AVRAHAM DOV
HAZAN, YAʾAKOV
HAZANI, MIKHAʾEL YAʾAKOV
HECHT, REUBEN
HELPERN, MICHAEL
HERMANN, LEO
HERZOG, CHAIM
HESHIN, SHNEUR ZALMAN
HILLEL, SHELOMO
HISIN, HAYYIM
HOLZBERG, SIMCHAH
HOOFIEN, ELIEZER SIEGFRIED
HOREV, AMOS
HOROWITZ, DAVID
HOS, DOV
HURVITZ, ELI
HURWITZ, YIGAL
IDELOVITCH, DAVID
IDELSON, BEBA
IRAQI, SHALOM JOSEPH
ISRAEL
ISRAELI, BENZION

ITZIK, DALIA
JAFFE, BEZALEL
JAFFE, MAURICE ABRAHAM
JAGLOM, RAYA
JOFFE, ELIEZER LIPA
JOFFE, HILLEL
JOSEPH, DOV
JOSEPHTHAL, GIORA
KAHANA, KALMAN
KAHANE, MEIR
KALIR, AVRAHAM
KAPLAN, ELIEZER
KAPLANSKY, SHELOMO
KASHANI, ELIEZER
KASZTNER, REZSO RUDOLF
KATZ, SHMUEL
KATZAV, MOSHE
KATZENELSON, YOSEF
KATZIR, EPHRAIM
KATZNELSON, BERL (Beeri)
KATZNELSON, RAHEL
KATZNELSON, REUBEN
KATZNELSON, SHULAMIT
KESSAR, ISRAEL
KHOUSHI, ABBA
KIRSCHENBAUM, MORDECAI
KITRON (KOSTRINSKY), MOSHE
KLARMAN, YOSEF
KOHN, LEO
KOL, MOSHE
KOLLEK, THEODORE (Teddy)
KORMAN, EDWARD R.
KRAUSE, ELIYAHU
KRINITZI, AVRAHAM
KUBOVY (Kubowitzki), ARYEH LEON
LAHAT, SHLOMO ("Chich")
LANDAU, ANNIE
LANDAU, DAVID
LANDAU, MOSHE
LANDAUER, GEORG
LAPID, TOMI
LAPIN, ISRAEL MOSES FISCHEL
LASKOV, HAYYIM
LAUFBAHN, YITSHAK
LAUTMAN, DOV
LAVI, SHELOMO
LAVON, PINHAS
LEHMANN, SIEGRIED
LEVI, MOSHE
LEVI, SAID BEN SHALOM
LEVI, SHABBETAI
LEVIEV, LEV
LEVIN, YIZAK MEIR
LEVITT, ESTHER
LEVONTIN, ZALMAN DAVID
LEVY, DAVID
LEWIN-EPSTEIN, ELIAHU ZEEV
LEWINSKY, YOM TOV
LIBAI, DAVID
LIPKIN-SHAHAK, AMNON

LISHANSKY, YOSEF
LIVNAT, LIMOR
LIVNI, TZIPI
LOCKER, BERL
LOEWENSON, JEAN (Hans)
LOPOLIANSKY, URI
LOTAN, GIORA
LOURIE, ARTHUR
LUDVIPOL, ABRAHAM
LURIE, JOSEPH
LURIE, TED
LURIE, ZVI
LUZ, KADISH
MAGIDOR, MENACHEM
MAIMON, ADA
MAIMON, YAACOV
MAISEL-SHOHAT, HANNAH
MAKLEFF
MAOR, GALIA
MARGALIT, DAN
MARGOLIN, ELIEZER
MARGOLIN, JULIJ
MARGOLIS-KALVARYSKI, HAIM
MARMORI, HANOCH
MAZUR, ELIYAHU
MAZUZ, MENI
MAZZUVAH
MEEROVITCH, MENACHE
MEIR, GOLDA
MEIR BEN HIYYA ROFE
MELCHIOR, MICHAEL
MERIDOR, DAN
MESHEL, YERUHAM
METMAN-COHEN, YEHUDAH LEIB
MEYUHAS, YOSEF BARAN
MILEYKOWSKY, NATHAN (Netanyahu)
MILO, RONI
MINZ, BENJAMIN
MIZRAHI, HANINAH
MODAI, YIZHAK
MOFAZ, SHAUL
MOLLER, HANS AND ERICH
MOSES, SIEGFRIED
MOSSINSON, BENZION
MOZES
MUYAL, AVRAHAM
NADAV, ZEVI
NADDAF, ABRAHAM HAYYIM
NAFTALI, PEREZ (Fritz)
NAKAR, MEIR
NAMIR, MORDEKHAI
NAMIR, ORA
NAVON, JOSEPH
NAVON, YITZHAK
NEBENZAHL, ITZHAK ERNST
NEEMAN, YUVAL
NEIPRIS, JOSEPH
NETANYAHU, BINYAMIN
NETTER, CHARLES
NIEGO, JOSEPH

NIMRODI
NIR-RAFALKES, NAHUM
NISSAN, AVRAHAM
NISSIM, MOSHE
NOVOMEYSKY, MOSHE
NUROCK, MORDECHAI
OFER, AVRAHAM
OFNER, FRANCIS-AMIR
OLMERT, EHUD
OLSHAN, ISAAC
OSSOWETZKY, O. YEHOSHUA
PA'IL, MEIR
PATT, GIDEON
PEARLMAN, MOSHE
PERES, SHIMON
PERETZ, AMIR
PERI, YA'AKOV
PERLMAN, SAMUEL
PERSITZ, SHOSHANAH
PEVZNER, SAMUEL JOSEPH
PINCUS, LOUIS ARIEH (Louis Abraham)
PINKAS, DAVID ZVI
POLLACK, ISRAEL
PORUSH, MENAHEM & MEIR
PROPPER, DAN
PUKHACHEWSKY, MICHAEL ZALMAN
RAAB, JUDAH
RABBI BINYAMIN
RABIN, YIZHAK
RABINOVICH, ITAMAR
RABINOWITZ, LOUIS ISAAC
RABINOWITZ, YEHOSHUA
RAGER (IJO), ITZHACK
RAKOWSKI, PUAH
RAMON, HAIM
RAMON, ILAN
RAPHAEL, GIDEON
RAPHAEL, YIZHAK
RAZIEL, DAVID
RECANATI, ABRAHAM SAMUEL
REIK, HAVIVAH (Emma)
REMEZ, MOSHE DAVID
RIVLIN
RIVLIN, YOSEF YIZHAK
ROKACH, ELEAZAR
ROKACH, SHIMON
ROSEN, JOSEPH A.
ROSEN, PINHAS
ROSEN, SHELOMO
ROSENBAUM, SEMYON (Shimshon)
ROSENBLUM, HERZL
ROSENFELD, SHALOM
ROTEM, CVI (Zvi)
RUBINSTEIN, AMNON
RUPPIN, ARTHUR
RUTENBERG, PINHAS (Piotr)
SADEH, YIZHAK
SALOMON, JOEL MOSES
SAMUEL BEN SAMSON
SANBAR (Sandberg), MOSHE

I. **HISTORY**

  B. MEDIEVAL & MODERN PERIOD

    2. **Regional History**

      a. *Israel, Land and State of*

        BIOGRAPHIES

          Public & Economic Life (continued)

SAPIR, ELIYAHU
SAPIR, JOSEPH
SAPIR, PINHAS
SARID, YOSSI
SARUM, ABRAHAM
SASSON, ELIYAHU
SCHILLER, SOLOMON
SCHNITZER, SHMUEL
SCHOCKEN
SCHUB, MOSHE DAVID
SENATOR, DAVID WERNER
SHAHAL, MOSHE
SHALEM, SAMUEL
SHALEV, AVNER
SHALOM, SILVAN
SHALTIEL, DAVID
SHAMGAR, MEIR
SHAMIR, YITZHAK
SHAPIRA, ABRAHAM
SHAPIRA, HAYYIM MOSHE
SHAPIRA, YESHAYAHU
SHAPIRO, YA'AKOV SHIMSHON
SHARANSKY, NATAN (Anatoly)
SHARETT, MOSHE
SHARON, ARIEL ("Arik")
SHAZAR, SHNEUR ZALMAN
SHEETRIT, MEIR
SHEINKIN, MENAHEM
SHEMTOV, VICTOR
SHENKAR, ARIE
SHERF, ZEEV
SHILOAH, REUBEN
SHITRIT, BEHOR SHALOM
SHOCHAT, ISRAEL
SHOCHAT, MANIA WILBUSHEWITCH
SHOHAT, AVRAHAM BEIGA
SHOHAT, ELIEZER
SHOMRON, DAN
SHOSTAK, ELIEZER
SHURER, HAIM
SHWED, GIL
SILBERG, MOSHE
SIMHONI, ASSAF
SIMON, ARYEH
SMOIRA, MOSHE
SNEERSOHN, HAYYIM ZEVI
SNEH, MOSHE
SOLIELI, MORDECAI (Max)
SPITZER, MOSHE
SPRINZAK, JOSEPH
STAMPFER, JEHOSHUA
STERN, AVRAHAM (Yair)
STURMAN, HAYYIM

SUPRASKY, YEHOSHUA
SUSSMAN, YOEL
SWET, GERSHON
SZENES, HANNAH
SZOLD, HENRIETTA
TABENKIN, YIZHAK
TABIB, AVRAHAM
TAMIR, SHMUEL
TARIF, AMIN
TCHERNOWITZ, SAMUEL
TEHOMI, ABRAHAM
TEKOAH, YOSEF
THON, YAAKOV YOHANAN
TOLKOWSKY, SHEMUEL
TOUROFF, NISSAN
TRUMPELDOR, JOSEPH
TSABAN, YAIR
TSUR, JACOB
TURNER, YAAKOV
UZAN, AHARON
UZIEL, BARUCH
VALERO
VAN LEER, LIA
VAN VRIESLAND, SIEGFRIED ADOLF (Zadok)
VARDI, MOSHE
VITKIN, JOSEPH
VON WEISL, ZE'EV (Wolfgang)
WALKOMITZ, SIMHAH HAYYIM
WARHAFTIG, ZERAH
WEINSHALL
WEISGAL, MEYER WOLF
WEISS, YAACOV
WEITZ, NAPHTALI
WEIZMAN, EZER
WEIZMANN, CHAIM
WERTHEIMER, STEF
WILBUSCHEWITZ
WITKON, ALFRED
YA'ACOBI, GAD
YA'ALON, MOSHE
YAARI, MEIR
YADIN, YIGAEL
YADLIN, AHARON
YAHIL, CHAIM
YARIV, AHARON
YARON, ZEVI
YASSKY, HAIM N.
YAVIN, HAYYIM
YAVNEELI, SHEMUEL
YELLIN
YELLIN-MOR, NATHAN
YESHAYAHU, ISRAEL
YINNON, MOSHE
YUDKOVSKY, DOV
ZADOK, HAIM JOSEPH
ZAMIR, YITZHAK
ZE'EVI, REHAVAM
ZEID, ALEXANDER
ZEMER, HANNAH
ZERUBAVEL, JACOB

ZISLING, AHARON
ZOREF, ABRAHAM SOLOMON ZALMAN
ZUR, ZEVI
ZURI (Zuri-Szezak), JACOB SAMUEL
ZUTA, HAYYIM ARYEH

Religion
BEKACHE, SHALOM
EPSTEIN HA-LEVI, MOSES JEHIEL
FAITUSI, JACOB BEN ABRAHAM
FINKEL, ELIEZER JUDAH
FRANCO, MOSES
FRANK, ZEVI PESAH
FRENKEL, IZHAK YEDIDIAH
GALANTE, MOSES BEN JONATHAN (II)
GOLINKIN, DAVID
GOREN, SHLOMO
GRUENHUT, ELEAZAR (Lazar)
HACOHEN, RAPHAEL HAYYIM
HADAYAH, OVADIAH
HADUTA BEN ABRAHAM
HA-LEVI, EZEKIEL EZRA BEN JOSHUA
HALEVI, HAYYIM DAVID
HALEVI, JOSEPH ZEVI BEN ABRAHAM
HAMEIRI, MOSHE
HAMMER, REUVEN
HARLAP, JACOB MOSES BEN ZEBULUN
HERZOG, ISAAC
HIRSCHENSOHN
HOROWITZ, SAUL HAYYIM BEN ABRAHAM HA-LEVI
IBN JAMIL, ISAAC NISSIM
ISRAELI, SHAUL
KASOVSKY, CHAYIM YEHOSHUA
KOOK, ABRAHAM ISAAC
KOOK, ZEVI JUDAH BEN ABRAHAM ISAAC HA-
  KOHEN
LAU, ISRAEL MEIR
LEVI BEN HABIB (Ralbah)
LEVIN, ARYEH
LEVY, JUDAH BEN MENAHEM
MAIMON, JUDAH LEIB
MALIK AL-RAMLI
MALKHI, MOSES
MALKHI, MOSES BEN RAPHAEL MORDECAI
MASHASH, SHLOMO
MEIR, JACOB
MENAHEM BEN MOSES HA-BAVLI
MENAHEM MENDEL OF SHKLOV
MEYUHAS, MOSES JOSEPH MORDECAI BEN
  RAPHAEL MEYUHAS
MEYUHAS, RAPHAEL MEYUHAS BEN SAMUEL
MODAI, HAYYIM
NATHAN BEN ABRAHAM I
NATHAN BEN ABRAHAM II
NATHAN OF GAZA
NAVON, JONAH BEN HANUN
NAVON, JONAH MOSES BEN BENJAMIN
NAZIR, MOSES HA-LEVI
NERIAH, MOSHE ZEVI
NISSIM, ISAAC

OUZIEL, BEN-ZION MEIR HAI
PANIGEL, RAPHAEL MEIR BEN JUDAH
PARDES, ELIYAHU
PARDO, MOSES BEN RAPHAEL
PORATH, ISRAEL
RABINOWITZ-TEOMIM, ELIJAH DAVID BEN
  BENJAMIN
RAPAPORT, DAVID HA-KOHEN
RICHIETTI, JOSEPH SHALLIT BEN ELIEZER
RISKIN, SHLOMO
RUBIO, MORDECAI
SALANT, SAMUEL
SARNA, EZEKIEL
SCHWARZ, YEHOSEPH
SHAPIRA, ABRAHAN ELKANA KAHANA
SONNENFELD, JOSEPH HAYYIM BEN ABRAHAM
  SOLOMON
STEINSALTZ, ADIN
SUZIN, SOLOMON MOSES
TOLEDANO, JACOB MOSES
TOLEDO, MOSES DE
UNTERMAN, ISSER YEHUDA
URI BEN SIMEON OF BIALA
VITAL, HAYYIM BEN JOSEPH
WALDENBERG, ELIEZER JUDAH
YIZHAKI, DAVID
YOSEF, OVADIAH
ZE'EVI, ISRAEL BEN AZARIAH
ZEVIN, SOLOMON JOSEPH
ZOLTY, YAACOV BEZALEL

Science
AARONSOHN
ABIR (Abramovitz), DAVID
ADLER, SAUL AARON
AGMON, SHMUEL
AHARONI, ISRAEL
AHARONOV, YAKIR
AMIRA, BINYAMIN
AMITSUR, SAMSON ABRAHAM
APELOIG, YIZHAK
ARNON, ISAAC
ARNON, RUTH
ASCHNER, MANFRED
ASHBEL, DOV
AVIDOV, ZVI
AVIV, HAIM
BEN-ABRAHAM, ZVI
BENTOR, JACOB
BERENBLUM, ISAAC
BERGMANN, ERNST DAVID
BERGMANN, FELIX ELIEZER
BERNSTEIN, JOSEPH
BIRK, YEHUDITH
BOBTELSKY, MORDEKHAI (Max)
BODENHEIMER, FREDERICK SIMON
BONDI, ARON
CEDAR, CHAIM
CHET, ILAN
COHEN, YIGAL RAHAMIM

I. HISTORY
B. MEDIEVAL & MODERN PERIOD
2. Regional History
a. Israel, Land and State of
BIOGRAPHIES
Science (continued)

DEMALACH, YOEL

DE VRIES, ANDRE

DORON, HAIM

DOSTROVSKY, ARYEH

DOSTROVSKY, ISRAEL

DUVDEVANI, SHMUEL

DVORETSKY, ARYEH

EFRAT, YAACOV

ELDAR, REUVEN

ELIAKIM, MARCEL

ERLIK, DAVID

EVENARI, MICHAEL

FARKAS, LADISLAUS (Wilhelm)

FEIGENBAUM, ARYEH

FEINBRUN-DOTHAN, NAOMI

FEINGOLD, DAVID SIDNEY

FEKETE, MICHAEL

FODOR, ANDOR

FRAENKEL, ABRAHAM ADOLF

FROHMAN, DOV

FURSTENBERG, HILLEL (Harry)

GINSBURG, DAVID

GOLDBERG, ALEXANDER

GOLDBERG, EMANUEL

GOLDBLUM, NATAN

HAAS, GEORG

HALBERSTAEDTER, LUDWIG

HALEVY, ABRAHAM

HALPERIN, HAIM

HALPERN, LIPMAN

HANANI, HAIM

HARARI, HAYYIM

HARARI, OVADIAH

HAREL, DAVID

HA-REUBENI, EPHRAIM

HERSHKO, AVRAM

HESTRIN, SHLOMO

HESTRIN-LERNER, SARAH

HIRSHBERG, YEHUDAH

JAMMER, MAX

JAMMER, MOSHE

JORTNER, JOSHUA

KAGAN, HELENA

KARPLUS, HEINRICH

KATZIR, AHARON

KATZIR, EPHRAIM

KEDEM, ORA

KLIGLER, ISRAEL JACOB

KOGAN, ABRAHAM

KORINE, EZRA

KURREIN, MAX

LEEUW, AVRAHAM DE

LEIBOWITZ, JOSHUA O.

LEVINE, RAPHAEL

LEVITZKI, ALEXANDER

LIBAI, AVINOAM

LIFSON, SHNEIOR

LOW (Lev), WILLIAM ZE'EV

MECHOULAM, RAPHAEL

MENDELSSOHN, HEINRICH

MER, GIDEON

MICHAELSON, ISAAC CHESAR

MILLER, LOUIS

MIROWSKI, MICHEL

NE'EMAN, YUVAL

NEUFELD, HENRY

OLITZKI, ARYEH LEO

OLLENDORFF, FRANZ

OPPENHEIMER, HILLEL (Heinz) REINHARD

PADEH, BARUCH

PEKERIS, CHAIM LEIB

PICARD, LEO

PNEULI, AMIR

PRYWES, MOSHE

RABIN, MICHAEL OSER

RACAH, GIULIO (Yoel)

RACHMILEWITZ, MOSHE

RAGER, BRACHA

RAHAMIMOFF, RAMI

RAM, MOSHE

RAMOT, BRACHA

RAYSS, TSCHARNA

REICHERT, ISRAEL

REIFENBERG, ADOLF

REINER, MARKUS

REVEL, MICHEL

ROM, YOSEF

ROSEN, MOSHE

SACHS, LEO

SALITERNIK, ZVI

SAMBURSKY, SAMUEL

SELA, MICHAEL

SHALON, RAHEL

SHEBA, CHAIM

SHECHTMAN, DAN

SHELAH, SAHARON

SHIFTAN, ZEEV

SIMON, ERNST

SINGER, JOSEF

SONDHEIMER, FRANZ

SOSKIN, SELIG EUGEN

STEIN, RICHARD

STEIN, YEHEZKIEL

STEINBERG, AVRAHAM

STOLLER, SAMUEL

SUSSMAN, ABRAHAM

TABOR, HARRY ZVI

TALMI, IGAL

VAN DER HOEDEN, JACOB

VOET, ANDRIES

VROMAN, AKIVA

WAHL, ISAAK

WALLACH, MOSHE (Moritz)

WERTHEIMER, CHAIM ERNST
WILCHEK, MEIR
WILLNER, ITAMAR
WINIK, MEIR
WINNIK, HENRY ZVI
WOOLF, MOSHE
YONATH, ADA
ZAIZOV, RINA
ZARCHIN, ALEXANDER
ZIV, JACOB
ZOHARY, MICHAEL

b. Byzantium
MAIN SURVEYS
BYZANTINE EMPIRE

GENERAL ENTRIES
CIRCUS PARTIES
CONSTANTINOPLE
KOILA

BIOGRAPHIES
BASIL I
CONSTANTINE VII PORPHYROGENITUS
HERACLIUS
JUSTINIAN I
LEO III (the Isaurian)
LEO VI, THE WISE
MANUEL I COMNENUS
MICHAEL II
MICHAEL VIII (Palaeologus)

c. Muslim Lands (incl. Islam)
MAIN SURVEYS
ARAB WORLD
EGYPT
IRAN
IRAQ
ISLAM
LEBANON
LIBYA
MOROCCO
OTTOMAN EMPIRE
SYRIA
TUNIS, TUNISIA
TURKEY
YEMEN

GENERAL ENTRIES
ABBASIDS
AGGADAH
AGHLABIDS
AHL AL-KITĀB
ALAWIDS
ALMOHADS
ALMORAVIDES
ARAB LEAGUE
ARABIC LANGUAGE
ĀSHŪRĀ
AYYUBIDS

BAHUZIM
BERBERS
BOYCOTT, ARAB
BRETHREN OF SINCERITY, EPISTLES OF
CAIRO TRIAL
CALIPH
CAPITULATIONS
DAMASCUS AFFAIR
DHIMMA, DHIMMI
DOENMEH
ESCHATOLOGY
EXILARCH
FATIMIDS
FIQH
GENIZAH, CAIRO
GHETTO
HADITH
HAFSIDS
HAMAS
HANĪF
HIMYAR
HIZBOLLAH
HUD
IBĀDĪS
ISRAELITE
JADĪD AL-ISLĀM
JEWISH AND ISLAMIC LAW
JIHĀD
KAKHYA
KALĀM
KARIYAH, AL-
KHARĀJ AND JIZYA
KIERA
KORAN
MAMLUKS
MERINIDS
MILLET
MULUK AL-TAWA'IF
MUQADDIM
MUSTAʿRAB, MUSTAʿRABS
NAGID
OMAR, COVENANT OF
ORIENTAL LITERATURE
ORIENTALISTS
OZAR HATORAH
PALESTINE LIBERATION ORGANIZATION
PALESTINIAN AUTHORITY
QAYNUQĀ, BANŪ
QURAYZA, BANŪ
SAʾDIS
SARRĀF
SATRAP
SELJUKS
SIJILL
SUFISM
UMAYYADS
WATTASIDS
YAHŪD
ZIRIDS
ZIYANIDS

I. HISTORY
B. MEDIEVAL & MODERN PERIOD
2. Regional History
c. *Muslim Lands (incl. Islam)* (*continued*)

BIBLE IN ISLAM

AARON
ABRAHAM
ADAM
BALAAM
BENJAMIN
CAIN
CANAAN
DANIEL
DAVID
ELIJAH
ELISHA
ENOCH
EVE
EZEKIEL
EZRA
GOLIATH
HAMAN
ISAAC
ISAIAH
ISHMAEL
JACOB
JEREMIAH
JERUSALEM
JETHRO
JOB, BOOK OF
JONAH, BOOK OF
JOSEPH
JOSHUA
KORAH
LOT
MIRIAM
MOSES
NEBUCHADNEZZAR
NIMROD
NOAH
PHARAOH
POTIPHAR
QUEEN OF SHEBA
SAMUEL
SAUL
SETH
SOLOMON
TERAH

COMMUNITIES

ABADAN
ADEN
AFGHANISTAN
AGADIR
AHWAZ
AKABA
AKRA
ALEPPO
ALEXANDRIA

ALGERIA
ALGIERS
AMADIYA
AMASIYA
AMRAN
ANKARA
ANTIOCH
ARABIA
ARCILA
ATLAS
AYDIN
AZEMMOUR
BĀB AL-ABWĀB
BAGHDAD
BAHREIN
BALKH
BA'QŪBA
BASRA
BAYHAN
BAYRAMIC
BEIRUT
BENGHAZI
BILBEIS
BONE
BOUGIE
BURSA
BUSHIRE
CAIRO
CANAKKALE
CASABLANCA
CONSTANTINE
DAMANHŪR
DAMASCUS
DAMAVAND
DAMIETTA
DAMĪRA
DEBDOU
DEHOK
DEMNAT
DHAMĀR
DIYALA
DJERBA
DRA
DUMUH
EDESSA
EDIRNE
EL-ARISH
EMESA
EZINE
FAIYUM
FEZ
GABÈS
GALLIPOLI
GAZA
GAZA STRIP
GILAN
HABBĀN
HABIL
HADRAMAUT
HAMADAN

HAYDAN
HEJAZ
HERAT
HILLA
HĪRA
HIT
HONEIN
HORMUZ
IRBIL
ISFAHAN
ISKENDERUN
ISTANBUL
IZMIR
IZMIT
JAZIRAT IBN ʾUMAR
JORDAN, HASHEMITE KINGDOM OF
JUBAR
JUBAYL
KAIROUAN
KASHAN
KAWKABĀN
KAZVIN
KERMAN
KERMANSHAH
KHANAQIN
KHAYBAR
KHURASAN
KIRKUK
KOILA
KURDISTAN
LAPSEKI
LAR
MAHALLA AL-KUBRA
MANAKHA
MANISSA
MANSURA
MARDIN
MARRAKESH
MAWZA
MĀZANDARĀN
MEDINA
MEKNÈS
MERSIN
MESHED
MINYAT ZIFTA
MOCHA
MOGADOR
MOSUL
MZAB
NAHRAWĀN
NAJRĀN
NEHARDEA
NEHAVEND
NISHAPUR
NISIBIS
OFRAN
ORAN
PAKISTAN
PERSIA
PORT SAID

QALʾAT HAMMĀD
QASR IBN HUBAYRAH
RAHBAH, AL-
RAQQA AL-
RIZAIEH
ROSETTA
RUWANDIZ
SADAH
SAFI
SALÉ-RABAT
SANʾA
SANANDAJ
SARUJ
SAUDI ARABIA
SHARAB
SHARM-EL-SHEIKH, TIRAN ISLAND, AND TIRAN
    STRAITS
SHIBĀM
SHIRAZ
SHUSHAN
SHUSHTAR
SIDON
SIJILMASSA
SOUS
SULEIMANIYA (AL-)
SUNBAT
TABRIZ
TADEF
TANGIER(S)
TANTA
TAYMA
TEHERAN
TLEMCEN
TOKAT
TRANSJORDAN
TRIPOLI
TRIPOLI
TUAT
TYRE
ʾUKBARĀ
WASIT
YARĪM
YEZD

Biographies

AARON BEN AMRAM
AARON BEN BATASH
AARON OF BAGHDAD
ABBAS I
ABBAS II
ʾABD AL-HAQQ AL-ISLĀMĪ
ABD AL-MĀLIK IBN MĀRWAN
ABDALLAH IBN SABĀʾ
ABDALLAH IBN SALĀM
ABDALLAH, YUSEF
ABDUL MAJID
ABDULLAH IBN HUSSEIN
ABRAHAM BEN ISAAC HA-KOHEN BEN AL-FURAT
ABRAHAM BEN NATHAN
ABU AL-MUNAJJA SOLOMON BEN SHAYA

I. HISTORY
B. MEDIEVAL & MODERN PERIOD
2. Regional History
c. *Muslim Lands (incl. Islam)*
BIOGRAPHIES (*continued*)

ABU 'ISĀ, ISAAC BEN JACOB AL-ISFAHĪN-Ī

ABU SA'D AL-TUSTARĪ

ADANI, MAHALAL

ADANI, SAMUEL BEN JOSEPH (Yeshua)

ADJIMAN

AKBAR THE GREAT (Moghul)

ALASHKAR, SOLOMON

ALATON, ISHAK

ALCEH, MATILDE

AL-GHARĪD AL-YAHŪDĪ

ALI IBN SAHL IBN RABBĀN AL-TABARĪ

ALNAKAR, ABRAHAM BEN JOSEPH

ALROY, DAVID (Menahem)

ALLOUCHE, FELIX NISSIM SAIDOU

AMINA

AMRAM

ANGEL, SHEMAYAHU

ARAFAT, YASSER

ASAD, HAFIZ AL-

ASHKENAZI, BEHOR

ASHKENAZI, JONAH BEN JACOB

ASHKENAZI, SOLOMON

ASHRIKI, MORDECAI

ASSEO, DAVID BEN ISAAC

AVEMPACE

AVERROES

AVICENNA

AZANCOT

BABAI BEN FARHAD

BABAI IBN LUTF

BACRI

BALI, RIFAT

BARAZANI, ASENATH

BARUCH BEN SAMUEL

BASRI, MEER

BATALYAWSĪ, ABU MUHAMMAD ABDALLAH IBN MUHAMMAD IBN AL-SĪD AL-

BATTAT, REUBEN

BAYAZID II

BELISHA

BENAROYA, AVRAM

BENAYAH

BENCHIMOL

BENGALIL

BENIDER

BEN-KIKI

BENOLIEL

BENSUSAN

BENVENISTE, MOSES

BENWAISH, ABRAHAM

BENZAMERO

BEN ZAQEN

BERGEL

BESSIS, ALBERT

BESSIS, JESHUA

BONASTRUC, ISAAC

BOUCHARA

BOUZAGLO, DAVID

BRUDO, ABRAHAM BEN ELIJAH

BUSNACH

BUSTANAI BEN HANINAI

BUZAGLO

CABESSA (Cabeca, Cabecao)

CAMONDO (De)

CANSINO

CAPSALI, MOSES BEN ELIJAH

CARASSO, EMMANUEL

CARMONA, BEKHOR ISAAC DAVID

CASTRO, ABRAHAM

CATTAN

CATTAUI

COHEN, JUDAH

COHEN, LEVI-ABRAHAM

CORCOS

CORCOS, DAVID

CORCOS, STELLA

CHALOM, MARCEL

CHOURAQUI

CHRIQUI

DANIEL BEN HASDAI

DANIEL, MENAHEM SALIH

DANON, ABRAHAM

DARMON

DARWISH, SHALOM

DAYYAN

DELMAR

DELOUYA

EDREHI, MOSES BEN ISAAC

ELDAD HA-DANI

ELEAZAR BEN JACOB HA-BAVLI

ELIAS, JOSEPH

EMANUEL

EMRANI

EPHRAIM BEN SHEMARIAH

ESCAPA, JOSEPH BEN SAUL

EZEKIEL BEN REUBEN MANASSEH

FĀRĀBĪ, ABU NASR MUHAMMAD, AL-

FARHI

FARHI, MORIS

FRANCO, GAD

FREHA BAT AVRAHAM OF MOROCCO

FRESCO, DAVID

GABBAI

GALANTE, ABRAHAM

GALIPAPA, ELIJAH MEVORAKH

GARIH, ÜZEYIR

GEREZ, JOSEF HABIB

GHAZĀLĪ, ABU HAMID MUHAMMAD IBN MUHAMMAD AL-TUSĪ AL-

GHERON, YAKKIR MORDECAI BEN ELIAKIM

GHEZ

GOZLAN, ELIE

HABIB, MOSES BEN SOLOMON IBN

HABSHUSH, SHALOM BEN YAHYA

HAGIZ

HAJJAJ, DANIEL

HAKAM, AL-

HĀKIM BI-AMR ALLAH, AL-

HALEVA, ISHAK

HA-LEVI, EZEKIEL EZRA BEN JOSHUA

HA-LEVI, SASSON BEN ELIJAH BEN MOSES

HALFON, ABRAHAM

HALFON BEN NETHANEL HA-LEVI ABU SAID (Dimyati)

HAMON

HANDALI, ESTHER

HARARI, SIR VICTOR RAPHAEL

HASAN, ABU ALI JEPHETH IBN BUNDĀR

HASDAI

HASSAN

HATCHWELL, SOL (Suleika)

HIBAT ALLAH, ABU AL-BARAKĀT (NATHANEL) BEN
    ALI (ELI) AL-BAGHDĀDĪ

HIBAT ALLAH, IBN JUMAY' IBN ZAYN

HIBSHUSH, HAYYIM

HOZIN, ZEDAKAH BEN SAADIAH

HUBES, ROZET

HUSSEIN

HUSSEINI, HĀJJ (Muhammad) AMIN

IBN ABĪ AL SALT

IBN AL-BARQŪLĪ

IBN KILLIS, ABU AL-FARAJ YA'QŪB IBN YŪSUF

IBN SAHL, ABU ISHĀQ IBRĀHĪM

IBRAHIM IBN SAHL AL-ANDALŪSI AL-ISRA'ILI (Abu
    Ishak)

IBRĀHĪM PASHA

IRAQI, SHALOM HA-KOHEN (al-Usta)

ISCANDARI

JACOB BEN HAYYM TALMID

JACOB BEN ZEMAH BEN NISSIM

JAVETZ, BARZILLAI BEN BARUCH

JAVID BEY, MEHMED

JIZFĀN, JUDAH BEN JOSEPH

JOSEPH BEN AHMAD IBN HASDAI

JOSEPH BEN PHINEHAS

JOSEPH HAYYIM BEN ELIJAH AL-HAKAM

JOSEPH ROSH HA-SEDER

JOSHUA BEN ABRAHAM MAIMUNI

JOSIAH BEN JESSE

JUDAH HA-PARSI

KA'B AL-AHBĀR

KA'B AL-ASHRAF

KA'B BEN ASAD

KABIR, ABRAHAM SALIH AL-

KADOORIE

KADOORIE, SASSON

KAFAH, YIHYE BEN SOLOMON

KAFAH, YOSEF

KĀHINA

KALAI, SAMUEL BEN MOSES

KAMHI, JAK V.

KANETI, SELIM

KARASU, ALBERT

KAREH, SOLOMON

KASABI, JOSEPH BEN NISSIM

KAZIN, JUDAH BEN YOM TOV

KAZIN, RAPHAEL BEN ELIJAH

KEMAL MUSTAFA (ATATURK)

KHOMEINI

KIMHI, SOLOMON BEN NISSIM JOSEPH DAVID

KINDĪ, ABU YŪSUF YA'QŪB IBN ISHAQ AL-

KOHEN, ALBERT

KOHEN, SAMI

KORAH, AMRAM IBN YAHYA

KORAH, SHALOM BEN YIHYE

KRISPIN, JOSHUA ABRAHAM

KUFA

KUHAYL, SHUKR SĀLIM

KUWAITI, SALEH

LANIADO, ABRAHAM BEN ISAAC

LANIADO, RAPHAEL SOLOMON BEN SAMUEL

LANIADO, SAMUEL BEN ABRAHAM

LANIADO, SOLOMON BEN ABRAHAM

LAPAPA, AARON BEN ISAAC

LAWĀNI, DAUD

LEV (Lab; Leb), JOSEPH BEN DAVID IBN (Maharival)

LEVI, MARIO

LEVY-BACRAT, ABRAHAM BEN SOLOMON

LEYON, AVRAM

LONGO, SAADIAH

LUMBROSO

MACNIN

MADMŪN BEN JAPHETH BEN BUNDĀR

MAGHREBI-MAARAVI

MALCHI, ESPERANZA

MANSŪR (al-)

MANSURAH, SAADIAH BEN JUDAH

MANSURAH, SHALOM BEN JUDAH

MARHAB AL-YAHŪDĪ IBN AL-HĀRITH

MĀSHĀ'ALLAH B. ATHAN

MASHAIRI, AL-

MASHASH, SHLOMO

MASLI'AH ŞALIH

MASNUT, SAMUEL BEN NISSIM

MA'TUK, SULAYMAN BEN DAVID

MAYMERAN

MELAMED, RAHAMIM REUVEN

MELAMED, SIMAN TOV

MENASCE, DE

MENDA, ELIEZER

MENDES

MESHWI AL-'UKBARĪ

MEVORAKH BEN SAADIAH

MĪKHĀ'ĪL, MURAD

MIRIAM BAT BENAYAH OF YEMEN

MIZRAHI, ASHER

MIZRAHI, DAVID BEN SHALOM

MIZRAHI, ELIJAH

MOLCHO, DAVID EFFENDI ISAAC PASHA

MONZON, ABRAHAM

MORDECAI BEN JUDAH HA-LEVI

MOSES BEN LEVI

MOSES BEN MEVORAKH

MOSSERI

MOYAL, ESTHER

I. HISTORY
B. MEDIEVAL & MODERN PERIOD
2. Regional History
c. *Muslim Lands (incl. Islam)*
Biographies (*continued*)

MUBĀRAK, MUHAMMAD HUSNI SAʿID
MUBASHSHIR BEN NISSI HA-LEVI
MUBASHSHIR BEN RAV KIMOI HA-KOHEN
MUHAMMAD
MUHAMMAD ALI
NĀDER SHAH
NAEH, BARUKH BEN MENAHEM
NAHON
NAHOUM, HAIM
NAHRAI BEN NISSIM
NAHUM, AARON SASSON BEN ELIJAH
NAHUM, ELIEZER BEN JACOB
NAJAR
NAJĪB AL-DAWLA
NARBONI
NASSER, GAMAL ABDUL
NATHAN BEN ISAAC HA-KOHEN HA-BAVLI
NATRONAI BEN HAVIVAI (Zavinai)
NAWI
NETHANEL BEN AL-FAYYUMI
NETHANEL BEN ISAIAH
NETIRA
NEUMARK, EPHRAIM
NISSIM, ABRAHAM HAYYIM
NOM, IBRAHIM
OBADYA, ABRAHAM
OMAR IBN AL-KHAṬṬĀB
PAHLAVI, MOHAMMAD REZA SHAH
PAHLAVI, REZA SHAH
PALACHE
PALACHE, HAYYIM
PALTIEL
PARIENTE
PARIUM
PASSI, DAVID
QAZZĀZ, MANASSEH BEN ABRAHAM IBN (AL-)
RABĪ IBN ABI AL-HUQAYQ
RACCAH, MASʾŪD BEN AARON
RASHID AL-DAWLA (al-Din)
RENASSIA, YOSSEF
ROSANES
ROSANES, JUDAH BEN SAMUEL
ROTE
RYVEL
SAʿADI, JUDAH BEN SOLOMON
SAADIAH
SAADIAH BEN JOSEPH HA-LEVI
SAʿD AL-DAWLA AL-SAFĪ IBN HIBBATALLAH
SADAT, MUHAMMED ANWAR AL-
SAHLAN BEN ABRAHAM
SAʿĪD IBN HASAN
SALADIN
SĀLIH, ABRAHAM
SALIH IBN YAHYA IBN JOSEPH

SALIH, YAHYA BEN JOSEPH (MAHARIS)
SAMAMA (Shemama), NESSIM
SAMAUʾAL BEN JUDAH IBN ʿABBAS (ibn Yahya al-Magribi)
SAMBARI, JOSEPH BEN ISAAC
SAMRA, DAVID
SAMUEL BEN ALI
SAMUEL BEN AZARIAH
SAMUEL BEN DANIEL ABU RABĪʿA HA-KOHEN
SAMUEL BEN HANANIA
SAMUEL BEN HOPHNI
SAMUEL IBN ADIYA (al-Samawal ben Gharid ben Adiya)
SANU, YAQUB (James)
SAPHIR, JACOB
SARFATY
SARMAD, MUHAMMAD SAʿID
SASSON, AARON BEN JOSEPH
SASSOON, SIR EZEKIEL
SCIALOM, DAVID DARIO
SEBAG
SEFIRAH, SAADIAH BEN JOSEPH
SELIM I
SELIM II
SERERO
SERERO, SAUL
SEROR
SERUSI
SERUYA
SEVERUS
SHAHIN
SHAKI, ISAAC
SHAMOSH, YIZHAK
SHASHU, SALIM
SHAUL, ANWAR
SHEIKH, ABRAHAM BEN SHALOM HA-LEVI AL-
SHEMARIAH BEN ELHANAN
SHIMON, JOSEPH BEN JUDAH IBN
SHINAH, SELMAN
SHINDOOKH, MOSES BEN MORDECHAI
SHOLAL, ISAAC HA-KOHEN
SHOLAL, NATHAN (Jonathan) HA-KOHEN
SIBONI
SID, SAMUEL IBN
SITBON
SOLAL
SOLOMON BEN ELIJAH HA-KOHEN
SOLOMON BEN HASDAI
SOMEKH, ABDALLAH BEN ABRAHAM
SONCINO
SONCINO, JOSHUA
STORA
SUAREZ
SULEIMAN I (the Magnificent)
SUMBAL, SAMUEL
SUSAN, ISSACHAR BEN MORDECAI
TABRIZI, MAHOMET ABU-BEKR-AT-BEN MAHOMET
TAM IBN YAHYA, JACOB BEN DAVID
TANUJI
TANUJI, ISHMAEL HA-KOHEN

TANUJI, JOSEPH BEN SHALOM HA-KOHEN
TARAGAN, BEN-ZION
TETUAN
UKBA, MAR
UMAYYA IBN ABI AL-SALT
UZAN
VALENSI
VENTURA, MICHON (Moses)
WAHB IBN MUNABBIH
WANNEH, ISAAC BEN ABRAHAM
WAQQĀSA
WUHSHA AL-DALLALA
YIHYE, ISAAC HA-LEVI
YUDGHAN (Yehudah)
YULY
YŪSUF AS'AR YATH'AR DHŪ NUWĀS
　(MASRUQ)
ZAKHO
ZECHARIAH AL-DĀHIRI
ZECHARIAH BEN BARACHEL
ZECHARIAH BEN SOLOMON-ROFE
ZILKHA
ZILKHA, NAIM
ZONANA
ZUTA
ZUTRA, MAR

Scholars
AYALON, DAVID
BAER, GABRIEL
BILLIG, LEVI
BRUNSCHVIG, ROBERT
BURCKHARDT, JOHANN LUDWIG
CAZES, DAVID
GOITEIN, SHLOMO DOV (Fritz)
GOLDENTHAL, JACOB
GOLDZIHER, IGNAZ (Isaac Judah)
HEYD, URIEL
HIRSCHFELD, HARTWIG
HOROVITZ, JOSEF
KISTER, MEIR J.
LANDAU, JACOB M.
LEVI DELLA VIDA, GIORGIO
LEWIS, BERNARD
MANN, JACOB
MAYER, LEO ARY
MOREH, SHMUEL
MUELLER, DAVID HEINRICH
PIAMENTA, MOSHE
ROMAN, JACOB BEN ISAAC
ROSENTHAL, FRANZ
SOMEKH, SASSON
STERN, SAMUEL MIKLOS
STILLMAN, NORMAN
WEIL, GOTTHOLD
WEIL, GUSTAV

d. Asia and Africa
Main Surveys
AFRICA

ASIA
CHINA
INDIA
JAPAN

General Entries
AFRICAN JEWISH CONGRESS
BAYUDAYA
BENE ISRAEL
BENE MENASHE
BETA ISRAEL
HOUSE OF ISRAEL COMMUNITY
IBO
LEMBA
MAKUYA
MONGOLS
TUTSI
ZAKHOR

Communities
AHMADNAGAR
ALIBAG
ASIA MINOR
BENARES
BOMBAY
BURMA
CALCUTTA
CALICUT
CANTON
CEYLON (Sri Lanka)
CHENNAMANGALAM (Chennotty)
CRANGANORE
ERNAKULAM
ETHIOPIA
GOA
HANGCHOW
HARBIN
HONG KONG
INDONESIA
KAIFENG
KASHMIR
KENYA
KOBE
KOCHI
MADAGASCAR
MADRAS
MALAYSIA
MANCHURIA
MONGOLIA
NAGASAKI
NINGPO
NINGSIA
PEKING
PHILIPPINES
POONA
SHANGHAI
SINGAPORE
SURAT
THAILAND
TIENTSIN

LEICESTER
LIMERICK
LINCOLN
LIVERPOOL
LONDON
MANCHESTER
MAURITIUS
MELBOURNE
NEWCASTLE-UPON-TYNE
NORTHAMPTON
NORWICH
NOTTINGHAM
OUDTSHOORN
OXFORD
PENZANCE
PERTH
PLYMOUTH
PORT ELIZABETH
PORTSMOUTH
PRETORIA
ROCHESTER
SALISBURY
SCOTLAND
SHEFFIELD
SOUTH WEST AFRICA
SOUTHAMPTON
STAMFORD
SUNDERLAND
SWANSEA
SYDNEY
TASMANIA
WALES
WARWICK
WINCHESTER
WORCESTER
YORK
ZAMBIA
ZIMBABWE

ORGANIZATIONS
AGUDAT HA-SOZYALISTIM HA-IVRIM
ANGLO-JEWISH ASSOCIATION
BOARD OF DEPUTIES OF BRITISH JEWS
BRITISH ISRAELITES
CENTRAL BRITISH FUND
INSTITUTE OF JEWISH AFFAIRS
JEWISH HISTORICAL SOCIETY OF
    ENGLAND
JEWS COLLEGE
JEWS' TEMPORARY SHELTER
MACCABEANS, ORDER OF ANCIENT
PALESTINE EXPLORATION FUND
UNITED SYNAGOGUE
WIENER LIBRARY

PUBLICATIONS
HA-MEORER
JEWISH CHRONICLE
JEWISH WORLD
ZEIT, DIE

BIOGRAPHIES
Academic Life
ABRAHAMS, ABRAHAM
ABRAHAMS, ISRAEL
ADLER, ELKAN NATHAN
AINSWORTH, HENRY
ALDERMAN, GEOFFREY
ALEXANDER, SAMUEL
BACON, ROGER
BALOGH, THOMAS, BARON
BARNETT, LIONEL DAVID
BAUMAN, ZYGMUNT
BAUMGARTEL, ELISE J.
BELOFF, MAX
BERLIN, SIR ISAIAH
BERNARD, EDWARD
BEVAN, EDWYN ROBERT
BLISS, FREDERICK JONES
BOGDANOR, VERNON
BOSHAM, HERBERT DE
BRONOWSKI, JACOB
BUECHLER, ADOLF
CASTELL, EDMUND
CESARANI, DAVID
CHEYNE, THOMAS KELLY
CHOTZNER, JOSEPH
COHEN, CHAPMAN
COHEN, RUTH LOUISA
COHN, NORMAN
COHN-SHERBOK, DAN
COLENSO, JOHN WILLIAM
COOK, STANLEY ARTHUR
COOKE, GEORGE ALBERT
COSTA ATHIAS, SOLOMON DA
COWEN, ZELMAN
COWLEY, SIR ARTHUR ERNEST
CROOL, JOSEPH
CROWFOOT, JOHN WINTER
CUDWORTH, RALPH
DAICHES, DAVID
DANBY, HERBERT
DAUBE, DAVID
DAVIDSON, SAMUEL
DEUTSCHER, ISAAC
DEVONS, ELY
DRIVER, SAMUEL ROLLES
DUSCHINSKY, CHARLES (Jacob Koppel)
EINZIG, PAUL
ELIAS, NORBERT
ELKIN, ADOLPHUS PETER
ELTON, GEOFFREY RUDOLPH
ETHERIDGE, JOHN WESLEY
FERDINAND, PHILIP
FILIPOWSKI, ZEVI HIRSCH
FINCH, SIR HENRY
FINLEY, SIR MOSES
FISHMAN, WILLIAM
FORTES, MEYER
FOX, CHARLES
FRANKEL, SALLY HERBERT

TRIVETH, NICHOLAS (Trivetus)
TYNDALE, WILLIAM
ULLENDORF, EDWARD
VAN PRAAGH, WILLIAM
VERMES, GEZA
WAKEFIELD, ROBERT (Wakfeldus)
WALSTON, SIR CHARLES
WALTON, BRYAN
WASSERSTEIN, BERNARD
WEINGREEN, JACOB
WEISS, JOSEPH G.
WIENER, HAROLD MARCUS
WINTER, PAUL
WISTRICH, ROBERT
WITTGENSTEIN, LUDWIG
WOLF, ABRAHAM
WOLF, LUCIEN
WOOLLEY, SIR CHARLES LEONARD
ZELLICK, GRAHAM
ZIMMERN, SIR ALFRED

Art
ABRAHAMS, IVOR
AMSHEWITZ, JOHN HENRY
AUERBACH, FRANK
BARLIN, FREDERICK WILLIAM
BENNETT, SALOMON YOM TOV
BLACK, SIR MISHA
BOMBERG, DAVID
BRYER, MONTE
CARO, SIR ANTHONY
CASSAB, JUDY
COHEN, BERNARD
COHEN, HAROLD
COOPER, ALEXANDER
COSTA, CATHERINE DA
DANIELS, ALFRED
DAVIS, HENRY DAVID
DUVEEN
DUVEEN, JOSEPH, LORD
ELKAN, BENNO
EPSTEIN, SIR JACOB
EZEKIEL, ABRAHAM EZEKIEL
FEIBUSCH, HANS
FOX, EMANUEL PHILIPS
FREEDMAN, BARNETT
FREUD, LUCIAN
GAMES, ABRAM
GERTLER, MARK
GLUCK, HANNAH
GOMBRICH, SIR ERNST
HANSON, NORMAN LEONARD
HART, SOLOMON ALEXANDER
HERMER, MANFRED
HILLMAN, DAVID
INLANDER, HENRY
KAHAN, LOUIS
KANTOROWICH, ROY
KEMPF, FRANZ MOSHE
KESTLEMAN, MORRIS

KIBEL, WOLF
KOENIG, GHISHA
KORMIS, FRED
KOSSOFF, LEON
KOTTLER, MOSES
KRAMER, JACOB
LANGDON, DAVID
LASDUN, DENYS
LE ROITH, HAROLD HIRSCH
LIPSHITZ, ISRAEL LIPPY
MENINSKY, BERNARD
MEYEROWITZ, HERBERT VLADIMIR
NEMON, OSCAR
OPPE, ADOLPH
RABIN, SAM
RIE, DAME LUCIE
ROGERS, CLAUDE MAURICE
ROSENBERG, EUGENE
ROTHENSTEIN (WILLIAM), MICHAEL
ROTHENSTEIN, SIR WILLIAM
SALAMAN
SCHOTTLANDER, BERNARD
SCHOTZ, BENNO
SOLOMON, SIMEON
SOLOMON, SOLOMON JOSEPH
SONNABEND, YOLANDA
STERN, IRMA
SUTTON, PHILIP
SZIGETI, IMRE
TOPOLSKI, FELIKS
TOWNE, CHARLES
UHLMAN, FRED
ULLMANN, ERNEST
VINCZE, PAUL
VOGEL, KAREL
WALD, HERMAN
WEISZ, VICTOR ("Vicky")
WERTHEIMER, ASHER
WILSON, "SCOTTIE"
WOLMARK, ALFRED
ZEC, PHILIP
ZIEGLER, ARCHIBALD
ZVIA

Literature
AARONSON, LAZARUS LEONARD
ABSE, DANNIE
AGUILAR, GRACE
ALVAREZ, ALFRED
BARON, JOSEPH ALEXANDER
BERGNER, HERZ
BLAKE, WILLIAM
BOAS, FREDERICK SAMUEL
BROOKNER, ANITA
BROWNING, ROBERT
BYRON, GEORGE GORDON, LORD
CECIL, HENRY
CHARLES, GERDA
CHAUCER, GEOFFREY
COHEN, JOHN MICHAEL

I. HISTORY
  B. MEDIEVAL & MODERN PERIOD
    2. Regional History
      e. Western Europe
        1) England & British Commonwealth
          BIOGRAPHIES
            Literature (*continued*)

CUMBERLAND, RICHARD
DAVIDSON, LIONEL
DICKENS, CHARLES
D'ISRAELI, ISAAC
ELIOT, GEORGE
ELLMANN, RICHARD
EMANUEL, WALTER LEWIS
FALK, BERNARD
FARHI, MORIS
FARJEON, BENJAMIN LEOPOLD
FEINSTEIN, ELAINE
FISCH, HAROLD
FRAM, DAVID
FRANKAU
GEORGE, WALTER LIONEL
GERSHON, KAREN
GLANVILLE, BRIAN LESTER
GOLDHAR, PINCHAS
GOLDING, LOUIS
GOLLER, IZAK
GORDIMER, NADINE
GORDON, SAMUEL
GROSS, JOHN JACOB
HALL, OWEN
HAMBURGER, MICHAEL
HENRY, EMMA
HUDSON, STEPHEN
JACOB, NAOMI ELLINGTON
JACOBSON, DAN
JACOBSON, HOWARD
JHABVALA, RUTH PRAWER
JOSIPOVICI, GABRIEL
KATZ, MENKE
KERSH, GERALD
KINROSS, ALBERT
KOPS, BERNARD
KROOK, DOROTHEA
LANDAU, JUDAH LOEB (Leo)
LEAVIS, QUEENIE DOROTHY
LEE, SIR SIDNEY
LEFTWICH, JOSEPH
LEVERSON, ADA
LEVERTOV, DENISE
LEVINSON, OLGA
LEVY, AMY
LEVY, BENN WOLFE
LEWIS, LEOPOLD DAVIS
LIBERMAN, SERGE
LITVINOFF, EMANUEL
LYONS, ALBERT MICHAEL NEIL
MANKOWITZ, WOLF
MARCUS, FRANK

MARLOWE, CHRISTOPHER
MARTIN, DAVID
MERRICK, LEONARD
MEYERSTEIN, EDWARD HARRY WILLIAM
MIKES, GEORGE
MILLIN, SARAH GERTRUDE
MILTON, JOHN
MULLER, ROBERT
NASSAUER, RUDOLF
PINTER, HAROLD
PINTO, VIVIAN DE SOLA
PYE, JAEL HENRIETTA
RAPHAEL, FREDERIC
RAPHAEL, JOHN N.
RODKER, JOHN
ROSENBERG, ISAAC
RUBENS, BERNICE
RUBENS, PAUL ALFRED
RUBINSTEIN, HAROLD FREDERICK
SASSOON, SIEGFRIED LORRAINE
SCOTT, SIR WALTER
SHAFFER, SIR PETER
SHAKESPEARE, WILLIAM
SHULMAN, MILTON
SILKIN, JON
SINCLAIR, CLIVE
SPIELVOGEL, NATHAN
STEINER, GEORGE
STERN, BERTHA GLADYS
STRAUS, RALPH
STRAUSS, GUSTAVE LOUIS MAURICE
SUTRO, ALFRED
SYMONS, JULIAN
TARN, NATHANIEL
WALEY, ARTHUR
WATEN, JUDAH
WESKER, ARNOLD
WOLFE, HUMBERT
ZANGWILL, ISRAEL

Music
ABRAHAM, GERALD
AGUILAR, EMANUEL ABRAHAM
BARNETT, JOHN
BARNETT, JOHN FRANCIS
BART, LIONEL
BENEDICT, SIR JULIUS (Isaac)
BRAHAM, JOHN
COHEN, HARRIET
COWEN, SIR FREDERIC HYMEN
CRANKO, JOHN
DU PRE, JACQUELINE
ESPINOSA, EDOUARD
FRANKEL, BENJAMIN
HASKELL, ARNOLD LIONEL
HESS, DAME MYRA
ISSERLIS, STEVEN
JACOBS, ARTHUR (David)
KENTNER, LOUIS
LEIGH, ADELE

LEONI, MYER
MARKOVA, ALICIA
NATHAN, ISAAC
RAMBERT, DAME MARIE
ROLL, MICHAEL
ROSENTHAL, HAROLD (David)
RUSSELL (Levy), HENRY
SADIE, STANLEY (John)
SALAMAN
SAMUEL, HAROLD
SCHWARZ, RUDOLF
SOLOMON
TERTIS, LIONEL
WASSERZUG (Lomzer), HAYYIM
WILLIAMS, CHARLES

Popular Culture
ABRAHAMS
ALEXANDER, MURIEL
BALCON, SIR MICHAEL
BARNA, VICTOR
BERGMANN, RICHARD
BERGNER, ELIZABETH
BERKOFF, STEVEN
BERMANT, CHAIM ICYK
BLOOM, CLAIRE
BLUMENFELD, RALPH DAVID
BROOK, PETER STEPHEN PAUL
BROTHERS, RICHARD
BUXTON, ANGELA
CASTRO, JACOB DE
COLLINS, LOTTIE
DELFONT, BERNARD
ELLIS, VIVIAN
EPSTEIN, BRIAN
FELDMAN, MARTIN
FLANAGAN, BUD
FRANKEL, WILLIAM
GINGOLD, HERMIONE
GOLDSMITH, LEWIS
GOLOMBEK, HARRY
GRADE, LEW, BARON
GUNSBERG, ISIDOR
HANBURY, LILY
HANRAY, LAWRENCE
HARVEY, LAURENCE
HOWARD, LESLIE
ISAACS, SIR JEREMY
JACKSON, HARRY
JAMES, DAVID
JAMES, SIDNEY
JAY, ALLAN
KAY, BARRY
KNOPFLER, MARK
KORDA, SIR ALEXANDER
KOSSOFF, DAVID
LAWRENCE, GERALD
LION, LEON M.
LIPZIN, KENI
LOM, HERBERT

MANNHEIM, LUCIE
MENDOZA, DANIEL
MIESES, JACQUES (Jacob)
MILLER, MARTIN RUDOLF
MILTON, ERNEST
MITCHELL, YVONNE
MOSHINSKY, ELIJAH
NEILSON, JULIA
NEWTON-JOHN, OLIVIA
NORSA, HANNAH
PROOPS, MARJORIE
REEVE, ADA
REISZ, KAREL
RENE, ROY
SACHS, ANDREW
SACHS, LEONARD
SAVILLE, VICTOR
SCHACH, LEONARD LAZARUS
SCHLESINGER, JOHN
SELLERS, PETER
SLOMAN, HENRY (Solomon)
SOFAER, ABRAHAM
SOLOMONS, JACK
STEINITZ, WILHELM
SUZMAN, JANET
SYLVIA, SARAH
TEITELBAUM, ABRAHAM
TZELNIKER, MEIR
ULLMAN, TRACEY
VAUGHAN, FRANKIE
ZUKERTORT, JOHANNES

Public & Economic Life
AARON OF LINCOLN
AARON OF YORK
ABRAHAMS, ABRAHAM
ABRAHAMS, GERALD
ABRAHAMS, SIR LIONEL
ADOLPHUS
ALBU, SIR GEORGE
ALEXANDER
ALEXANDER, BERNARD
ALEXANDER, MORRIS
ALLENBY, EDMUND HENRY HYNMAN,
  VISCOUNT
AMERY, LEOPOLD STENNETT
ASHENHEIM
ATTLEE, CLEMENT RICHARD, EARL
AVIDA, YEHUDA LEIB
BAGRIT, SIR LEON
BALFOUR, ARTHUR JAMES, EARL OF
BARD, BASIL JOSEPH ASHER
BARNATO, BARNEY
BARNETT, JOEL BARON
BARON, BERNHARD
BAROU, NOAH
BAUME, PETER
BEARSTED, MARCUS SAMUEL, FIRST
  VISCOUNT
BEDDINGTON

GOLLANCZ, SIR VICTOR
GOMPERTZ
GOODMAN, PAUL
GORDON, LORD GEORGE
GRANT, BARON ALBERT
GRAUMANN, SIR HARRY
GREEN, PHILIP
GREENBERG, LEOPOLD
GREENBERG, LEOPOLD JACOB
GUEDALLA, HAIM
GUTNICK
HAHN, KURT
HAMBURGER, SIR SIDNEY
HAMLYN, PAUL, BARON
HARRIS, SIR DAVID
HARRIS, SIR PERCY
HART
HART, DANIEL
HASSAN, SIR JOSHUA (Abraham)
HATRY, CLARENCE CHARLES
HEILBRON, ROSE
HENOCHSBERG, EDGAR SAMUEL
HENRIQUES
HENRY, MICHAEL
HENRY OF WINCHESTER
HERBSTEIN, JOSEPH
HORE-BELISHA, LESLIE LORD
HORT, ABRAHAM
HOWARD, MICHAEL
HUGH OF LINCOLN
HYAMSON, ALBERT MONTEFIORE
ISAAC OF SOUTHWARK
ISAACS, SIR ISAAC ALFRED
ISAACS, NATHANIEL
ISH-KISHOR, EPHRAIM
JACOBS, LAZARUS
JACOBS, SIMEON
JACOBSON, NATHAN
JACOBSON, SYDNEY
JAFFE, SIR OTTO
JANNER, LORD BARNETT
JESSEL, SIR GEORGE
JOEL, SIR ASHER
JOEL, SOLOMON BARNATO ("Solly")
JOSCE OF YORK
JOSEPH
JURNET OF NORWICH
KAGAN, JOSEPH, BARON
KAHN, RICHARD FERDINAND, LORD
KALLENBACH, HERMANN
KALMS, SIR (HAROLD) STANLEY, BARON
KARMINSKI, SIR SEYMOUR EDWARD
KASRILS, RONNIE
KAUFMAN, SIR GERALD
KAYE, SIR EMMANUEL
KENTRIDGE, MORRIS
KENTRIDGE, SIR SYDNEY
KIMCHE, JON
KISCH
KISSIN, HARRY, BARON

KOPELOWITZ, LIONEL
KUPER, SIMON MEYER
LANDA, ABRAM
LANDA, MYER JACK
LANGERMANN, MAX
LASKI
LASKI, HAROLD JOSEPH
LAUTERPACHT, SIR HERSCH
LAWSON
LEIBLER, ISI JOSEPH
LEITNER, GOTTLEIB
LEON, ANTHONY JAMES
LEVENE, PETER, BARON
LEVER, NORMAN HAROLD
LEVEY, BARNETT
LEVIN, NATHANIEL WILLIAM
LEVIN SMITH, SIR ARCHIBALD
LEVY, SIR ALBERT
LEVY, BENJAMIN
LEVY, SIR DANIEL
LEVY, JOSEPH LANGLEY
LEVY, MICHAEL ABRAHAM, BARON OF MILL
    HILL
LEWIS, SIR GEORGE
LEWIS, HYMAN
LEWIS, SAMUEL
LICORICIA OF WINCHESTER
LINCOLN, TREBITSCH
LINDO
LITTMAN, JOSEPH AARON
LLOYD GEORGE, DAVID
LOPES
LOVELL, LEOPOLD SOLOMON
LOW
LOWY, FRANK
LYONS, SIR JOSEPH
MACCOBY, HAYYIM ZUNDEL
MAGNUS
MAGNUS, SOLOMON WOLFF
MAISELS, ISRAEL AARON
MANCROFT
MANDELSON, PETER
MANNHEIM, HERMANN
MARKS, HARRY HANANEL
MARKS, SAMUEL
MARKS, SIMON BARON
MARRE, ALAN, SIR
MATALON, ELI
MAXWELL, ROBERT
MAYER, SIR ROBERT
MEDINA, SIR SOLOMON DE
MEINERTZHAGEN, RICHARD HENRY
MENDES
MERTON
MEYERSTEIN, EDWARD WILLIAM
MICHAELIS, SIR ARCHIE
MICHAELIS, SIR MAX
MIKARDO, IAN
MILLETT, SIR PETER, BARON
MILLIN, PHILIP

I. HISTORY
B. MEDIEVAL & MODERN PERIOD
2. Regional History
e. Western Europe
1) England & British Commonwealth
BIOGRAPHIES
Public & Economic Life (continued)

MINC, HILARY

MISHCON, VICTOR, BARON

MOCATTA

MONASH, SIR JOHN

MOND

MONTAGU

MONTAGU, LILY

MONTEFIORE, JOSEPH BARROW

MONTEFIORE, JOSHUA

MONTEFIORE, JUDITH

MONTEFIORE, SIR MOSES

MONTEFIORE, SEBAG-MONTEFIORE

MOONMAN, ERIC

MORRIS, HENRY HARRIS

MORRIS, NATHAN

MOSENTHAL

MOSER, JACOB

MOSER, SIR CLAUDE

MOSES, MARCUS

MOSS, CELIA AND MARION

MYER, SIDNEY BAEVSKI

MYERS, SIR ARTHUR MELZINER

MYERS, ASHER ISAAC

MYERS, SIR MICHAEL

NATHAN

NATHAN, DAVID

NATHAN, HARRY LOUIS, BARON

NATHAN, JOSEPH EDWARD

NATHAN, MANFRED

NATHAN, MULLA IBRAHIM

NAVARRO, ABRAHAM

NICHOLAS, EDWARD

NORDEN

OCHBERG, ISAAC

OLIPHANT, LAURENCE

OPPENHEIM, LASSA FRANCIS LAWRENCE

OPPENHEIM, SALLY BARONESS

OPPENHEIMER, SIR ERNEST

PACIFICO, DAVID

PAIVA, JACQUES

PALGRAVE

PATTERSON, JOHN HENRY

PHILLIPS, SIR LIONEL

PHILLIPS, MARION

PICCIOTTO

POLACK, JOEL SAMUEL

PORTER, SIR LESLIE

PRATT, RICHARD

PRYNNE, WILLIAM

PULVERMACHER, OSCAR

PULZER, PETER G.J.

RACHMAN, PETER

RAISMAN, SIR ABRAHAM JEREMY

RAPHAEL, ALEXANDER

RATHBONE, ELEANOR

RAYNE, SIR MAX, BARON

READING

READING, FANNY

RIFKIND, SIR MALCOLM

ROBSON, WILLIAM ALEXANDER

RODRIGUES, BARTHOLOMEW

ROSENBLUM, SIGMUND GEORGIEVICH

ROTHSCHILD

ROTHSCHILD, JAMES ARMAND DE

ROTHSCHILD, NATHANIEL CHARLES JACOB,
    FOURTH BARON ROTHSCHILD

SAATCHI, CHARLES

SACHER, HARRY

SALMON

SALMON, ALEXANDER

SALMON, CYRIL BARNET, BARON

SALOMONS, SIR DAVID

SALOMONS, SIR JULIAN EMANUEL

SAMUDA, JOSEPH

SAMUEL, EDWIN, SECOND VISCOUNT

SAMUEL, HAROLD, BARON SAMUEL OF
    WYCH CROSS

SAMUEL, HERBERT LOUIS, FIRST VISCOUNT

SAMUEL, HOWARD

SAMUEL, SIR SAUL

SAMUEL, SYDNEY MONTAGU

SAMUEL, WILFRED SAMPSON

SAMUELSON, SIR BERNHARD

SASSOON

SASSOON, VIDAL

SCHLESINGER, ISIDORE WILLIAM

SCHOMBERG

SCHON, FRANK

SCHUSTER

SCHWARZ, HARRY

SCOTT, CHARLES PRESTWICH

SEGAL, SAMUEL, BARON

SELDEN, JOHN

SELIG, PHINEAS

SELIGMAN, HERBERT SPENCER

SHERMAN, ARCHIE

SHILL, LOUIS

SHINWELL, EMANUEL, BARON

SHORT, RENEE

SIEFF, ISRAEL MOSES, BARON

SIEFF, REBECCA

SILBERMANN, ABRAHAM MORITZ

SILKIN, LEWIS, FIRST BARON

SILVERMAN, SIDNEY

SIMON

SIMON, SIR JOHN

SIMON, SIR LEON

SLATER, OSCAR

SLOVO, JOE

SMORGON

SMUTS, JAN CHRISTIAAN

SOLOMON

SOLOMON
SOLOMON, BERTHA
SOMEN, ISRAEL
SONNTAG, JACOB
SOSKICE, SIR FRANK
SOUTHWOOD, JULIUS SALTER ELIAS, FIRST
    VISCOUNT
SPEYER, SIR EDGAR
SPIELMAN (-N)
STEIN, LEONARD
STERLING, SIR JEFFREY
STERN
STERN, SIR FREDERICK CLAUDE
STERN, PHILIP COHEN
STERNBERG, SIR SIGMUND
STORRS, SIR RONALD
STRAUSS, GEORGE RUSSEL, BARON
SUGAR, SIR ALAN
SUGERMAN, SIR BERNARD
SUZMAN, HELEN
SYKES, SIR MARK
SYMONDS, PAUL
TAYLOR, SIR PETER MURRAY
THATCHER, MARGARET
THORN, SIR JULES
TOLAND, JOHN
TONNA, CHARLOTTE E.
TRASKE, JOHN
TUCK, RAPHAEL
VAN OVEN
VOGEL, SIR JULIUS
WAGG
WALEY
WARBURG, FREDERIK
WARBURG, SIR SIEGMUND
WARREN, SIR CHARLES
WAY, LEWIS
WEDGWOOD, JOSIAH CLEMENT, FIRST
    BARON
WEIDENFELD, GEORGE, BARON
WEINSTOCK, SIR ARNOLD, BARON
WEIZMANN, CHAIM
WELENSKY, SIR ROY (Roland)
WERTH, ALEXANDER
WIGODER, BASIL THOMAS, BARON
WILSON, SIR CHARLES WILLIAM
WILSON, HAROLD
WINGATE, ORDE
WOLFENSOHN, JAMES D.
WOLFF, GUSTAV
WOLFSON, SIR ISAAC
WOOLF, SIR HARRY, BARON
WORMS, DE
WYNN, SAMUEL
XIMENES, SIR DAVID
XIMENES, SIR MORRIS
YARROW, SIR ALFRED
YOUNG, DAVID IVOR, BARON YOUNG OF
    GRAFFHAM
YOUNG, STUART

Religion
ABELSON, JOSHUA
ABENDANA, JACOB BEN JOSEPH
ABRAHAMS
ABRAHAMS, ISRAEL
ABRAMSKY, YEHEZKEL
ADLER, HERMANN
ADLER, MICHAEL
ADLER, NATHAN MARCUS
APPLE, RAYMOND
ARTOM
BOTEACH, SHMUEL
BRASCH, RUDOLPH
BRODIE, SIR ISRAEL
CASPER, BERNARD MOSES
COHEN, FRANCIS LYON
DANGLOW, JACOB
DAVIS, ALEXANDER BARNARD
ELIJAH MENAHEM BEN MOSES
EPSTEIN, ISIDORE
FERBER, ZEVI HIRSCH
GAON, SOLOMON
GOLLANCZ, SIR HERMANN
GRONER, DOVID YITZCHOK
GRUNFELD, ISIDOR
GRYN, HUGO
HARRIS, CYRIL KITCHENER
HERTZ, JOSEPH HERMAN
HERZOG, ISAAC
HIRSCHEL, SOLOMON
HYAMSON, MOSES
JACOB BEN JUDAH OF LONDON
JACOBS, LOUIS
JAKOBOVITS, IMMANUEL
JOSEPH, MORRIS
KAHANA, KOPPEL
LEVI, JOHN SIMON
MARGOLIOUTH, MOSES
MATTUCK, ISRAEL ISIDOR
MAYBAUM, IGNAZ
MELDOLA, RAPHAEL
MONTEFIORE, CLAUDE JOSEPH GOLDSMID
MOSES BEN YOM-TOV
NATHAN, ABRAHAM
NIETO, DAVID
NIETO, ISAAC
ORNSTEIN, ABRAHAM FREDERICK
PERLZWEIG, MAURICE L.
PORUSH, ISRAEL
RABINOWITZ, JOEL
RABINOWITZ, LOUIS ISAAC
ROBERT OF READING
ROMAIN, JONATHAN A.
ROSENBAUM, MORRIS
SACKS, JONATHAN HENRY
SCHIFF, DAVID TEVELE
SCHONFELD, VICTOR
SILVA, JOSHUA DA
SINGER, SIMEON
SOLA, DE

I. HISTORY
B. MEDIEVAL & MODERN PERIOD
2. Regional History
e. Western Europe
1) England & British Commonwealth
BIOGRAPHIES (*continued*)

Science
ANDRADE, EDWARD NEVILLE DA COSTA
AYRTON, HERTHA
BACHARACH, ALFRED LOUIS
BARNETT, SIR LOUIS EDWARD
BERNAL, JOHN DESMOND
BLOK, ARTHUR
BODMER, SIR WALTER
BONDI, SIR HERMANN
BRAUDE, ERNEST ALEXANDER
BRENNER, SYDNEY
BRODETSKY, SELIG
CARVALLO, JULES
CHAIN, SIR ERNST BORIS
COHEN, HENRY BARON
COHEN, JULIUS BEREND
COHEN, SIR PHILIP
COPISAROW, MAURICE
COSTA, EMANUEL MENDES DA
FINLAY-FREUNDLICH, ERWIN
FINNISTON, SIR HAROLD MONTAGUE (Monty)
FOX, SIR JOHN JACOB
FRANKLIN, ROSALIND ELSIE
FREUD, ANNA
FRIEDLANDER, KATE
FRISCH, OTTO ROBERT
FROHLICH, HERBERT
GABOR, DENNIS
GAUNSE, JOACHIM
GOLDSTEIN, RICHARD FRANK
GOLDSTEIN, SIDNEY
GUTTMANN, SIR LUDWIG
HART, ERNEST ABRAHAM
HEILBRON, SIR IAN MORRIS
JOSEPHSON, BRIAN DAVID
KALNITSKY, GEORGE
KATZ, SIR BERNARD
KLEIN, MELANIE REIZES
KLUG, AARON
KORNBERG, HANS LEO
KREBS, SIR HANS ADOLF
KROTO, SIR HAROLD W.
LACHMANN, SIR PETER JULIUS
LEVINSTEIN, HERBERT
LEVY, HYMAN
LEWIS, SIR AUBREY JULIAN
LEWKOWITSCH, JULIUS
LOCKSPEISER, BEN, SIR
LOEWE, FRITZ PHILIPP
MARGULES, MAX
MELDOLA, RAPHAEL
MENDELSSOHN, KURT ALFRED GEORG
MILLER, EMANUEL

MORDELL, LOUIS JOEL
NEUBERGER, ALBERT
NOSSAL, SIR GUSTAV
ORENSTEIN, ALEXANDER JEREMIAH
PEIERLS, SIR RUDOLF ERNST
PENN, JACK
PEPPER, JOSEPH
PERUTZ, MAX FERDINAND
POLANYI, MICHAEL
QUASTEL, JUDAH HIRSCH
RAPHAEL, RALPH ALEXANDER
ROSENHEAD, LOUIS
ROSENHEIM, MAX (Leonard), BARON
ROSENHEIM, OTTO
ROTBLAT, SIR JOSEPH
ROTH, KLAUS FRIEDRICH
ROTH, SIR MARTIN
ROTHSCHILD, NATHANIEL MAYER VICTOR,
    LORD
SALAMAN, REDCLIFFE NATHAN
SCHRIRE, VELVA
SCHUSTER, SIR ARTHUR
SEMON, SIR FELIX
SIMON, SIR FRANCIS EUGENE
SINGER, CHARLES JOSEPH
STENGEL, ERWIN
SYLVESTER, JAMES JOSEPH
TABOR, DAVID
TABOR, HARRY ZVI
TOBIAS, PHILLIP VALLENTINE
TOLANSKY, SAMUEL
VANE, SIR JOHN R.
VOGEL, ARTHUR ISRAEL
WEISS, JOSEPH JOSHUA
WINSTON, ROBERT, BARON
WOLFF, CHARLOTTE
YOUNG, ALEC DAVID
YUDKIN, JOHN
ZUCKERMAN, SOLLY, LORD

2) France, Luxembourg & Belgium
MAIN SURVEYS
BELGIUM
FRANCE
FRENCH LITERATURE

GENERAL ENTRIES
ALLIANCE ISRAELITE UNIVERSELLE
ASSIMILATION
FINALY CASE
FRENCH REVOLUTION
JEWISH STUDIES
PASTOUREAUX
SAINT-SIMONISM
SANHEDRIN, FRENCH

COMMUNITIES
AGDE
AGEN
AIX-EN-PROVENCE

ALBI
ALES
ALSACE
AMMERSCHWIHR
ANGERS
ANGOULEME
ANJOU
ANTWERP
APT
ARLES
AUVERGNE
AUXERRE
AVIGNON
BAIGNEUX-LES-JUIFS
BAR-LE-DUC
BAYONNE
BEAUCAIRE
BEDARRIDES
BELFORT
BENFELD
BERGHEIM
BESANÇON
BEZIERS
BIARRITZ
BIDACHE
BISCHHEIM
BLOIS
BORDEAUX
BOULAY
BOURG-EN-BRESSE
BOURGES
BRAY-SUR-SEINE
BRESSE
BRITTANY
BRUSSELS
BURGUNDY
CADENET
CAEN
CAPESTANG
CARCASSONNE
CARPENTRAS
CASTELSARRASIN
CAVAILLON
CHÂLONS-SUR-MARNE
CHALON-SUR-SAÔNE
CHAMBERY
CHAMPAGNE
CHARLEVILLE
CHARTRES
CHÂTEAU-LANDON
CHÂTEAU-THIERRY
CHINON
CLERMONT-FERRAND
CLUNY
COLMAR
COMTAT VENAISSIN
CORBEIL
CREMIEU
DAMPIERRE-DE-LAUBE
DAUPHINE

DIGNE
DIJON
DRAGUIGNAN
DREUX
ENSISHEIM
EPERNAY
ÉTAMPES
ETTENDORF
EVREUX
FALAISE
FOIX
FONTAINEBLEAU
FORCALQUIERS
FRANCHE-COMTÉ
GASCONY
GEVAUDAN
GHENT
GRENOBLE
GUEBWILLER
HAGUENAU
HAVRE, LE
HEGENHEIM
HYÈRES
INGWILLER
ISLE-SUR-LA-SORGUE, L'
JOIGNY
JUNGHOLZ
LANGUEDOC
LIÉGE
LILLE
LIMOGES
LIMOUX
LODEVE
LONS-LE-SAUNIER
LORRAINE
LUNEL
LUNEVILLE
LUXEMBOURG
LYONS
MÂCON
MANOSQUE
MANS, LE
MARSEILLES
MELUN
METZ
MONTELIMAR
MONTEREAU
MONTPELLIER
MORHANGE
MULHOUSE
NANCY
NANTES
NARBONNE
NEVERS
NICE
NIMES
NYONS
OBERNAI
ORANGE
ORLEANS

I. HISTORY
B. MEDIEVAL & MODERN PERIOD
2. Regional History
e. *Western Europe*
2) France, Luxembourg & Belgium
COMMUNITIES (*continued*)

PAMIERS
PARIS
PERPIGNAN
PEYREHORADE
PHALSBOURG
POITIERS
POITOU
PONTOISE
POSQUIERES
PROVENCE
PROVINS
PUY (-EN -VELAY), LE
RAMERUPT
RHEIMS
RIBEAUVILLE
ROCHELLE, LA
ROSENWILLER (Rosenweiler)
ROSHEIM
ROUEN
ROUFFACH
ROUSSILLON
SAINT-DENIS
SAINTES
SAINT-GILES
SAINT-JEAN-DE-LUZ
SAINT-PAUL-TROIS CHATEAUX
SAINT-REMY-DE-PROVENCE
SAINT-SYMPHORIEN-DOZON
SARREGUEMINES
SAVERNE
SAVOY
SELESTAT
SENLIS
SENS
SERRES
SISTERON
SOISSONS
SOULTZ (Sulz)
STRASBOURG
TARASCON
THIONVILLE
TOUL
TOULON
TOULOUSE
TOURAINE
TOURS
TRETS
TREVOUX
TROYES
VALENCE
VALREAS
VERDUN
VERDUN-SUR-GARONNE

VESOUL
VIENNE
VILLEFRANCHE-DE-CONFLENT
VITRY (-en-Perthois)

ORGANIZATIONS
ACTION FRANCAISE
ASSEMBLY OF JEWISH NOTABLES
CENTRE DE DOCUMENTATION JUIVE
    CONTEMPORAINE
COMITE DES DELEGATIONS JUIVES
CONSISTORY
LES COLLOQUES DES INTELLECTUELS JUIFS DE
    LANGUE FRANCAISE
MUSEE D'ART ET DE HISTOIRE DU JUDAISME
SEMINAIRE ISRAELITE DE FRANCE
SOCIETE DES ETUDES JUIVES
UNION GENERALE DES ISRAELITES DE FRANCE
    (U.G.I.F.)

PUBLICATIONS
CROIX, LA
REVUE DES ETUDES JUIVES
UNIVERS ISRAELITE

BIOGRAPHIES
Academic Life
ABEL, LOUIS FELIX
ABELARD, PETER
ADLER, ALEXANDRE
AFTALION, ALBERT
ALKAN, ALPHONSE
AMADO LEVY-VALENSI, ELIANE
ANCHEL, ROBERT
ARON, RAYMOND
ARON, ROBERT
ATTALI, JACQUES
BADINTER, ELIZABETH
BASCH, VICTOR GUILLAUME
BEGIN, EMILE-AUGUSTE
BENDA, JULIEN
BENRUBI, ISAAC
BENSOUSSAN, GEORGES
BENVENISTE, EMILE
BERGSON, HENRI LOUIS
BLOCH, CAMILLE
BLOCH, GUSTAVE
BLOCH, JULES
BLOCH, MARC
BLUMENKRANZ, BERNHARD
BODIN, JEAN
BONALD, LOUIS GABRIEL AMBROISE,
    VICOMTE DE
BONFRÈRE, JAQUES
BREAL, MICHEL
BRUNSCHVICG, LEON
BRUNSCHVIG, ROBERT
CAHEN, ISIDORE
CAQUOT, ANDRE
CHALIER, CATHERINE

CLERMONT-GANNEAU, CHARLES
COHEN, GUSTAVE
COHEN, MARCEL
COHEN, ROBERT
COHN, ALBERT
DANIEL-ROPS, HENRI
DARMESTETER, ARSENE
DEPPING, GEORGES-BERNARD
DERENBURG
DERRIDA, JACQUES
DIDEROT, DENIS
DIDI-HUBERMAN, GEORGES
DRAI, RAPHAEL
DUPONT-SOMMER, ANDRE
DURKHEIM, EMILE
EISENMANN, LOUIS
ERLANGER, PHILIPPE
FINKIELKRAUT, ALAIN
FOURIER, FRANCOIS MARIE CHARLES
FRANCK, ADOLPHE
FREY, JEAN BAPTISTE
FRIEDMANN, GEORGES
GAFFAREL (Gaffarellus), JACQUES
GENEBRARD, GILBERT
GHIRSHMAN, ROMAN
GINSBURGER, ERNEST
GLOTZ, GUSTAVE
GOLDMANN, LUCIEN
GOTTSCHALK, MAX
GREGORY OF TOURS
GUERIN, VICTOR
GURVITCH, GEORGES
HALBWACHS, MAURICE
HALEVY, ELIE
HALEVY, JOSEPH
HALEVY, MEYER ABRAHAM
HALPHEN
HALPHEN, LOUIS
HAUSER, HENRI
HOLBACH, PAUL HENRI DIETRICH, BARON D'
HOURWITZ, ZALKIND
ISAAC, JULES MARX
JANKELEVITCH, VLADIMIR
KAHN, LEON
KASPI, ANDRE
KOJEVE, ALEXANDRE
KRIEGEL, ANNIE
LA BOETIE, ETIENNE DE
LA PEYRERE, ISAAC
LAMBERT, MAYER
LE FÈVRE DE LA BODERIE, GUY
LEON, XAVIER
LÉVI, SYLVAIN
LÉVI ALVARÈS, DAVID
LEVI BEN ABRAHAM BEN HAYYIM
LEVINAS, EMMANUEL
LÉVI-PROVENÇAL, EVARISTE
LEVI-STRAUSS, CLAUDE
LÉVY, ARTHUR
LÉVY, BENNY

LÉVY-BRUHL, LUCIEN
LÉVY, ISIDORE
LÉVY, PAUL
LODS, ADOLPHE
LOISY, ALFRED FIRMIN
MAES, ANDREAS
MAUSS, MARCEL
MERCIER, JEAN
MONTESQUIEU, CHARLES LOUIS DE
    SECONDAT, BARON DE LA BREDE ET DE
MOPSIK, CHARLES
MORIN, EDGAR
MUNK, SOLOMON
NATHAN, MORDECAI
NEHER, ANDRÉ
OPPERT, JULES JULIUS
OUAKNIN, MARC-ALAIN
PALLIÈRE, AIMÉ
PARAF, PIERRE
PARROT, ANDRÉ
PASCAL, BLAISE
PEREIRE, EMILE (Jacob) and ISAAC
PERELMAN, CHAIM
PERROT, JEAN
PLANTAVIT DE LA PAUSE, JEAN
POLIAKOV, LÉON
POSENER, GEORGES HENRI
POSTEL, GUILLAUME
RABBINOWICZ, ISRAEL MICHEL
RAOUL GLABER
RAUH, FREDERIC
REINACH
RENAN, ERNEST
REVAH, ISRAEL SALVATOR
ROUSSEAU, JEAN JACQUES
RUEFF, JACQUES
SACY, ANTOINE ISAAC SILVESTRE DE
SALVADOR, JOSEPH
SAULCY, LOUIS FELICIEN DE JOSEPH
    CAIGNART
SCALIGER, JOSEPH JUSTUS
SCHEID, ELIE
SCHUHL, PIERRE-MAXIME
SCHWAB, MOISE
SCHWARTZENBERG, ROGER-GERARD
SCHWOB, MARCEL
SEPHIHA, HAIM VIDAL
SLOUSCHZ, NAHUM
SPERBER, DAN
STEIN, HENRI
STRAUSS-KAHN, DOMINIQUE
TRIGANO, SHMOUEL
URI, PIERRE EMMANUEL
VAJDA, GEORGES
VAUX, ROLAND DE
VEIL, LEWIS (Daniel) COMPIÉGNE DE
VIDAL-NAQUET, PIERRE
VINCENT, LOUIS HUGUES
VOGÜÉ, CHARLES EUGENE MELCHOIR,
    COMTE DE

PEREC, GEORGES
PORTO-RICHE, GEORGES DE
PROUST, MARCEL
RACINE, JEAN
SACHS, MAURICE
SARRAUTE, NATHALIE
SCHEINERT, DAVID
SCHULSINGER, JOSEPH
SCHWARZ-BART, ANDRÉ
SEE, EDMOND
SPERBER, MANES
SPIRE, ANDRE
SUARES, ANDRE
THARAUD, JEROME AND JEAN
THEMANLYS, PASCAL
VERCORS
VIGÉE, CLAUDE
WEILL, ALEXANDRE ABRAHAM
ZOLA, EMILE

Music
ALKAN (Morhange), CHARLES HENRI-VALENTIN
BABILÉE, JEAN
BLOCH, ANDRE
BLUM, RENÉ
BRÉVAL, LUCIENNE
CHAGRIN, FRANCIS
COLONNE, JULES (Judah) EDOUARD
DAVID, ERNEST
DUKAS, PAUL
ERLANGER, CAMILLE
GEDALGE, ANDRE
HALÉVY, JACQUES (François) FROMENTAL
    ÉLIE
JONAS, EMILE
LEVY
LÉVY, LAZARE
MACHABEY, ARMAND
MILHAUD, DARIUS
OFFENBACH, JACQUES
ROLAND-MANUEL
ROSENTHAL, MANUEL (Emmanuel)
TUGAL, PIERRE
WALDTEUFEL, EMIL
WIENER, JEAN
WOLFF, ALBERT LOUIS
WORMSER, ANDRÉ (Alphonse-Toussaint)

Popular Culture
AIMÉE, ANOUK
BACRI, JEAN-PIERRE
BARBARA
BAUR, HARRY
BERNHARDT, SARAH
BERNSTEIN, OSIP SAMOILOVICH
BLOWITZ, HENRI GEORGES STEPHANE
    ADOLPHE OPPER DE
BOBER, ROBERT
DARMON, PIERRE
ELKABBACH, JEAN-PIERRE

EPSTEIN, JEAN
HELD, ANNA
HIRSCH, ROBERT PAUL
JANOWSKI, DAVID MARKELOVICH
KORENE, VERA
LANZMANN, CLAUDE
LELOUCH, CLAUDE
LINDER, MAX
MACIAS, ENRICO
MARCEAU, MARCEL
MNOUCHKINE, ALEXANDRE
MOATI, SERGE
OURY, GERARD
RACHEL
SIGNORET, SIMONE
TARTAKOVER, SAVIELLY GRIGORYEVICH

Public & Economic Life
ABBA MARI BEN ISAAC OF ST. GILLES
AGOBARD
ALCAN, ALKAN
ALPHONSE OF POITIERS
ALTARAS, JACQUES ISAAC
ANSPACH, PHILIPPE
ANTOINE, NICOLAS
ASHKENAZI, LEON
ATTALI, BERNARD
BADINTER, ROBERT
BAIL, CHARLES-JOSEPH
BAMBERGER, EDOUARD-ADRIEN
BARRÉS, AUGUSTE MAURICE
BÉDARRIDE, ISRAÉL (Isaiah)
BEER-BING, ISAIAH
BERNHEIM, LOUIS
BERR, JACOB
BERR (de Turique), MICHEL
BERR ISAAC BERR DE TURIQUE
BEUGNOT, AUGUSTE ARTHUR
BIGART, JACQUES
BISCHOFFSHEIM
BLEUSTEIN-BLANCHET, MARCEL
BLOCH, PIERRE
BLUM, LEON
BLUMEL, ANDRE
BOKANOWSKI, MAURICE
BOURGEOIS, JEAN
BROGLIE, VICTOR-CLAUDE, PRINCE DE
CALMER, MOSES ELIEZER LIEFMANN
CASSIN, RENÉ SAMUEL
CERFBERR, HERZ
CERFBERR, MAXIMILIEN-CHARLES
    ALPHONSE
CHARLEMAGNE
CHARLES IV
CHARLES V
CHARLES VI
CHILDEBERT I
CITROËN, ANDRÉ GUSTAVE
CLERMONT-TONNERRE, COUNT STANISLAS
    DE

I. HISTORY
B. MEDIEVAL & MODERN PERIOD
2. Regional History
e. Western Europe
2) France, Luxembourg & Belgium

BIOGRAPHIES

Public & Economic Life (continued)

CLOOTS, JEAN BAPTISTE DU VAL-DE-GRACE,
    BARON DE
CLOTHAIRE II
COHEN, ISAAC KADMI
COHEN, JOSEPH
COLBERT, JEAN BAPTISTE
COPE, JEAN-FRANCOIS
CREHANGE, ALEXANDRE
CREMIEUX, ISAAC ADOLPHE
CUKIERMAN, ROGER
DANIEL, JEAN
DARMON, AMRAM
DARQUIER DE PELLEPOIX, LOUIS
DASSAULT, DARIUS PAUL
DASSAULT, MARCEL
DAUDET, LEON
DAVIN DE CADEROUSSE
DEUTSCH DE LA MEURTHE, HENRI
DEUTZ, SIMON
DRACH, PAUL-LOUIS-BERNARD (David)
DRAY, JULIEN
DREYFUS, ALFRED
DRUMONT, EDOUARD-ADOLPHE
DU BARTAS, GUILLAUME DE SALLUSTE
EICHTHAL, GUSTAVE D'
ELKANN, JEAN-PAUL
ENNERY, JONAS D'
ERLANGER, MICHEL
ERRERA, PAUL JOSEPH
FABIUS, LAURENT
FISCHER, JEAN
FITERMAN, CHARLES
FOULD
FURTADO, ABRAHAM
GAMZON, ROBERT
GINIEWSKI, PAUL
GIROUD, FRANCOISE
GOBINEAU, JOSEPH ARTHUR, COMTE DE
GOUDCHAUX, MICHEL
GOUGENOT DES MOUSSEAUX, HENRI
GRADIS
GRANDVAL (Hirsch-Ollendorf), GILBERT
    YVES EDMOND
GRÉGOIRE, HENRI BAPTISTE
GRESH, ALAIN
GRUMBACH, SALOMON
GUNZBURG, NIKO
GUTT, CAMILLE
HAMON, LEO
HYMANS, PAUL
JAURÈS, JEAN LEON
JAVAL

JOHN II ("The Good")
JUSTER, JEAN
KAHN, ALBERT
KAHN, JEAN
KAHN, LOUIS
KARPEL, HERMAN
KLEIN, THEODORE (Theo)
KLOTZ, LOUIS-LUCIEN
KOENIGSWARTER
KOUCHNER, BERNARD
KRASUCKI, HENRI
KRIEGEL-VALRIMONT, MAURICE
LAMBERT, AIMÉ
LAMBERT, RAYMOND RAOUL
LANG, JACK
LANGALLERIE, PHILIPPE GENTIL DE
LAVAL, PIERRE
LAZARD
LAZAREFF, PIERRE
LAZURICK, ROBERT
LECACHE, BERNARD
LEHMANN, LEONCE
LEVAILLANT, ISAIE
LEVEN, NARCISSE
LEVY
LEVY, ABRAHAM EUGENE
LÉVY, RAPHAEL
LEVY, SAM SAADI
LOUIS
LUSTIGER, JEAN-MARIE ARON
LYON-CAEN, CHARLES LÉON
MACHAUT, DENIS DE
MALESHERBES, CHRETIEN GUILLAUME DE
    LA-MOIGNON DE
MANDEL, GEORGES
MANESSIER DE VESOUL
MARITAIN, JACQUES
MAURRAS, CHARLES
MAYER, DANIEL
MAYER, RENÉ
MENDES-FRANCE, PIERRE
MEYER, LEON
MIRABEAU, HONORE GABRIEL RIQUETI,
    COMTE DE
MIRES, JULES ISAAC
MOCH, JULES
MOCH, JULES SALVADOR
NAPOLEON BONAPARTE
NAQUET, ALFRED JOSEPH
NATHAN, VENGUESSONE
NETTER, CHARLES
NEVEJEAN, YVONNE
NOSTRADAMUS (Michel de Nostre-Dame)
OSIRIS, DANIEL ILLFA
OULIF, CHARLES NARCISSE
PEREIRE, JACOB RODRIGUES
PHILIP
PICARD, EDMOND
PLANTIN, CHRISTOPHE
PRISCUS

PROUDHON, PIERRE JOSEPH
PULCELINA OF BLOIS
RAPPOPORT, CHARLES
RAYNAL, DAVID
REINACH
ROEDERER, COUNT PIERRE LOUIS
ROTHSCHILD
ROTHSCHILD, BARON EDMOND JAMES DE
ROTTEMBOURG, HENRI
ROULEAU, ERIC (Elie Rafoul)
SCHILLER, ARMAND
SCHRAMECK, ABRAHAM
SCHUMANN, MAURICE
SEE
SEE, LEOPOLD
STERN, JACQUES
TORRES, HENRY
TOUSSENEL, ALPHONSE
VALABRÈGUE, MARDOCHÉE GEORGES
VALLAT, XAVIER
VEIL, SIMONE
VENEZIANI, EMMANUEL FELIX
VIBERT OF NOGENT
VIGENERE, BLAISE DE
WAHL, JACQUES HENRI
WIENER, ERNEST EDOUARD
WORMSER, OLIVIER BORIS
ZAY, JEAN

Religion
ABBA MARI BEN ELIGDOR
BEBE, PAULINE
BODO
ELIEZER OF TOUL
FARHI, DANIEL
FARHI, GABRIEL
HAYYIM BEN HANANEL HA-KOHEN
HIRSCHLER, RENE
ISIDOR, LAZARE
JACOB BEN MOSES OF BAGNOLS
JACOB OF MARVEGE
JACOB OF ORLEANS
JACOB OF PONT-SAINTE-MAXENCE
JONATHAN BEN DAVID HA-KOHEN OF LUNEL
JOSEPH BEN ASHER OF CHARTRES
JOSEPH BEN BARUCH OF CLISSON
JOSEPH BEN MOSES OF TROYES
JOSEPH HAZZAN BEN JUDAH OF TROYES
JUDAH BEN ISAAC (Sir Leon of Paris)
JUDAH BEN MOSES HA-DARSHAN
JUDAH BEN NATHAN
KAHN, ZADOC
KAPLAN, JACOB
KARA, JOSEPH
KARMI (Cremieux)
KIMHI, DAVID
KIMHI, JOSEPH
KLEIN, SALOMON WOLF
KOKHAVI, DAVID BEN SAMUEL
KRYGIER, RIVON

LATTES, ISAAC BEN JACOB
LATTES, JUDAH
LEHMANN, JOSEPH
LEVI BEN GERSHOM (Ralbag)
LÉVI, ISRAEL
LÉVY, ALFRED
LÉVY, ISAAC
LÉVY, SAMUEL
LIBER, MAURICE
LOEB, ISIDORE
LUBETZKY, JUDAH
MANOAH OF NARBONNE
MEIR BEN ISAAC OF TRINQUETAILLE
MEIR BEN SAMUEL OF RAMERUPT
MEIR BEN SIMEON HA-ME'ILI
MEIRI, MENAHEM BEN SOLOMON
MENAHEM BEN HELBO
MESHULLAM BEN JACOB OF LUNEL
MESHULLAM BEN MOSES
MESHULLAM BEN NATHAN OF MELUN
MOSES BEN ABRAHAM OF PONTOISE
MOSES BEN JACOB OF COUCY
MOSES BEN JOSHUA OF NARBONNE
MOSES OF EVREUX
NETHANEL OF CHINON
NISSIM BEN MOSES OF MARSEILLES
OVADIA, NISSIM
PEREZ BEN ELIJAH OF CORBEIL
PROVENÇAL, JACOB BEN DAVID
RASHI (Solomon ben Isaac)
REUBEN BEN HAYYIM
SAMSON BEN ABRAHAM OF SENS
SAMSON BEN ISAAC OF CHINON
SAMSON BEN JOSEPH OF FALAISE
SAMSON BEN SAMSON OF COUCY
SAMUEL BEN DAVID
SAMUEL BEN MEIR (Rashbam)
SAMUEL BEN SOLOMON OF FALAISE
SAMUEL OF EVREUX
SCHLETTSTADT, SAMUEL BEN AARON
SHEMAIAH OF TROYES
SIMEON BEN SAMUEL OF JOINVILLE
SINZHEIM, JOSEPH DAVID BEN ISAAC
SIRAT, RENE SAMUEL
SITRUK, JOSEPH
SOLOMON BEN ABRAHAM OF
    MONTPELLIER
SOLOMON BEN JUDAH "OF DREUX"
SOLOMON BEN JUDAH OF LUNEL
SOLOMON BEN MEIR
TAM, JACOB BEN MEIR
TIBBON, IBN (Tibbonids)
TOUATI, CHARLES
TREVES, JOHANAN BEN MATTATHIAS
ULLMANN, SALOMON
VAEZ, ABRAHAM
WARSCHAWSKI, MAX
WEILL, MICHEL AARON
WORMS, AARON
YOM TOV OF JOIGNY

I. HISTORY
B. MEDIEVAL & MODERN PERIOD
2. Regional History
e. *Western Europe*
2) France, Luxembourg & Belgium
BIOGRAPHIES (*continued*)

Science
ABRAHAM BEN SOLOMON OF SAINT MAXIMIN
ATLAN, HENRI
BARUK, HENRI
BERNHEIM, HIPPOLYTE
BESREDKA, ALEXANDER
BONFILS, IMMANUEL BEN JACOB
CHARPAK, GEORGES
COHEN TANNOUDJI, CLAUDE
EPHRUSSI, BORIS
ERRERA, LEO
GERHARDT, CHARLES FREDERIC
GOLDSCHMIDT, HERMANN
HADAMARD, JACQUES SALOMON
HAVA OF MANOSQUE
ISAAC BEN TODROS
JACOB, FRANÇOIS
LEVY, LUCIEN
LIPPMANN, GABRIEL
LIPSKI, ABRAHAM
LWOFF, ANDRE MICHEL
MEYERSON, EMILE
MICHEL-LÉVY, AUGUSTE
MINKOWSKI, EUGENE
MOISSAN, HENRI
SCHWARTZ, LAURENT
SIMON, PIERRE
STEG, ADOLPHE
STERN, ERICH
WEIL, R. ADRIENNE
WIDAL, FERNAND

3) Germany & Austria
MAIN SURVEYS
AUSTRIA
GERMAN LITERATURE
GERMANY

GENERAL ENTRIES
AGRARIAN LEAGUE
ARMLEDER
HASIDEI ASHKENAZ
JUDENPFENNIGE
IUDEX JUDAEORUM
LEIBZOLL
MAGDEBURG LAW
OPFERPFENNIG
SCHUTZJUDEN
TOLERANZPATENT
WIENER GESERA

COMMUNITIES
AACHEN

AHLEM
AHRWEILER
ALTENSTADT
ALTONA
ALZEY
AMBERG
ANDERNACH
ANHALT
ANSBACH
ARNSTADT
ASCHAFFENBURG
ASHKENAZ
AUGSBURG
AURICH
BACHARACH
BADEN
BADEN BEI WIEN
BAIERSDORF
BAMBERG
BAVARIA
BAYREUTH
BERG
BERLIN
BIELEFELD
BINGEN
BOCHUM
BONN
BOPPARD
BRANDENBURG
BREISACH
BREMEN
BRUCHSAL
BRUNSWICK
BURGENLAND
CARINTHIA
CHEMNITZ
CLEVES
COBURG
COCHEM
COLOGNE
CONSTANCE
COTTBUS
DARMSTADT
DEGGENDORF
DEUTSCHKREUTZ
DEUTZ
DORTMUND
DRESDEN
DUEREN
DUESSELDORF
DUISBURG
DYHERNFURTH
EINBECK
EISENSTADT
EMDEN
ENDINGEN
ERFURT
ESSEN
ESSLINGEN
ETTLINGEN

FLOSS
FRANKFURT ON THE MAIN
FRANKFURT ON THE ODER
FREIBURG IM BREISGAU
FRIEDBERG
FUERTH
FULDA
GELNHAUSEN
GELSENKIRCHEN
GEMEN
GIESSEN
GLUECKSTADT
GOERLITZ
GOETTINGEN
GOSLAR
GOTHA
GRAZ
HAGEN
HAGENBACH
HALBERSTADT
HALLE
HAMBURG
HAMELN
HANAU
HANOVER
HEIDELBERG
HEIDINGSFELD
HEILBRONN
HESSE
HILDESHEIM
HOHENAU
HOHENEMS
HOHENZOLLERN
HOMBURG
INGOLSTADT
INNSBRUCK
JEBENHAUSEN
JUDAESAPTAN
JUDENBURG
JUELICH
KAISERSLAUTERN
KARLSRUHE
KASSEL
KEMPEN
KIEL
KISSINGEN
KITZINGEN
KLAGENFURT
KLOSTERNEUBURG
KOBLENZ
KOENIGSBERG
KORNEUBURG
KREFELD
KREMS
KREUZNACH
LANDAU
LANDSHUT
LAUINGEN
LEIPZIG
LINDAU

LINZ
LIPPE (-Detmold)
LUEBECK
LUENEBURG
MAGDEBURG
MAINZ
MANNHEIM
MARBURG
MATTERSDORF (Mattersburg)
MECKLENBURG
MEININGEN
MEISSEN
MEMMINGEN
MERGENTHEIM
MERSEBURG
MINDEN
MOSBACH
MUEHLHAUSEN
MUENSTER
MUNICH
NASSAU (-Usingen)
NAUHEIM
NIEDERSTETTEN
NOERDLINGEN
NORDHAUSEN
NUREMBERG
OETTINGEN
OFFENBACH
OFFENBURG
OLDENBURG
OPPENHEIM
OSNABRUECK
PADERBORN
PALATINATE
PASSAU
PFORZHEIM
POMERANIA
PRUSSIA
PULKAU
RAVENSBURG
RECKLINGHAUSEN
REGENSBURG
REUTLINGEN
REXINGEN
ROEDELHEIM
ROTHENBURG OB DER TAUBER
SAARBRUECKEN
SALZBURG
SAXONY
SCHLESWIG-HOLSTEIN
SCHNAITTACH
SCHWEINFURT
SEESEN
SHUM
SILESIA
SOEST
SPANDAU
SPEYER
STENDAL
STRAUBING

I. HISTORY
B. MEDIEVAL & MODERN PERIOD
2. Regional History
e. *Western Europe*
3) Germany & Austria
COMMUNITIES (*continued*)

STUTTGART
STYRIA
SULZBACH
TALHEIM
TAUBERBISCHOFSHEIM
TESCHEN
THURINGIA
TRIER
TUEBINGEN
TYROL
UEBERLINGEN
ULM
VIENNA
VILLINGEN
VORARLBERG
WANDSBECK
WARENDORF
WEINHEIM
WESTPHALIA
WETZLAR
WIENER NEUSTADT
WIESBADEN
WOLFENBUETTEL
WOLFSBERG
WORMS
WUERTTEMBERG
WUERZBURG
WUPPERTAL
XANTEN
ZERBST
ZWICKAU

ORGANIZATIONS
AKADEMIE FUER DIE WISSENSCHAFT DES
    JUDENTUMS
ALLIANZ, ISRAELITISCHE, ZU WIEN
BLAU-WEISS
CENTRAL-VEREIN DEUTSCHER
    STAATSBUERGER JUEDISCHEN GLAUBENS
CHRISTIAN SOCIAL PARTY
CHRISTIAN-SOCIAL PARTY. GERMAN
CONSERVATIVE PARTY, GERMAN
DEUTSCHER PALAESTINA-VEREIN
DEUTSCH-ISRAELITISCHER GEMEINDEBUND
ESRA
GESELLSCHAFT DER FREUNDE
GESELLSCHAFT ZUR FOERDERUNG DER
    WISSENSCHAFT DES JUDENTUMS
HE-HALUTZ
HEIMWEHR
HILFSVEREIN DER DEUTSCHEN JUDEN
HOCHSCHULE FUER DIE WISSENSCHAFT DES
    JUDENTUMS

INSTITUTUM JUDAICUM DELITZSCHIANUM
ISRAELITISCH-THEOLOGISCHE LEHRANSTALT
JUEDISCHE FREISCHULE
JUEDISCHER FRAUENBUND
JUEDISCHER KULTURBUND
JUEDISCHER VERLAG
JUEDISCH-LITERARISCHE GESELLSCHAFT
JUEDISCHE VOLKSPARTEI
JUEDISCH-THEOLOGISCHES SEMINAR,
    BRESLAU
KADIMAH
KARTELL-CONVENT DER VERBINDUNGEN
    DEUTSCHER STUDENTEN JUEDISCHEN
    GLAUBENS
KARTELL JUEDISCHER VERBINDUNGEN
LANDJUDENSCHAFT
NATIONALRAT
OESTERREICHISCHE NATIONALBIBLIOTHEK
PARLAMENTSKLUB, JUEDISCHER
REICHSBUND JUEDISCHER FRONTSOLDATEN
SCHUTZBUND, REPUBLIKANISCHER
SONCINO GESELLSCHAFT DER FREUNDE DES
    JUEDISCHEN BUCHES
STUDENTS' FRATERNITIES, GERMAN
SWABIAN LEAGUE
UNION, OESTERREICHISCH ISRAELITISCHE
VERBAND DER DEUTSCHEN JUDEN
VERBAND DER VEREINE FUER JUEDISCHE
    GESCHICHTE UND LITERATUR
VERBAND NATIONAL-DEUTSCHER JUDEN
VEREIN FUER KULTUR UND WISSENSCHAFT
    DES JUDENTUMS
VEREIN ZUR ABWEHR DES ANTISEMITISMUS
VEREINIGUNG FUER DAS LIBERALE JUDENTUM
    IN DEUTSCHLAND
VOLKSPARTEI, JUEDISCHE
ZENTRALRAT DER JUDEN IN DEUTSCHLAND
ZENTRALSTELLE DER FUERSORGE FUER
    KRIEGSFLUECHTLINGE
ZENTRAL-WOHLFAHRTSTELLE DER
    DEUTSCHEN JUDEN

PUBLICATIONS
ALLGEMEINE ZEITUNG DES JUDENTHUMS
ASEFAT HAKHAMIM
C.V.-ZEITUNG
HA-EMET
HA-MAGGID
HA-ME'ASSEF
HA-SHAHAR
HE-HALUTZ
ISRAELIT, DER
ISRAELITISCHES FAMILIENBLATT
JESCHURUN
JUDE, DER
JUEDISCHE PRESSE
JUEDISCHE RUNDSCHAU
KEREM HEMED
KOHELETH MUSSAR
MENORAH

MONATSSCHRIFT FUER GESCHICHTE UND
    WISSENSCHAFT DES JUDENTUMS
NEUZEIT, DIE
OESTERREICHISCHES CENTRAL-ORGAN FUER
    GLAUBENSFREIHEIT, CULTUR, GESCHICHTE
    UND LITERATUR DER JUDEN
PHILO VERLAG
SULAMITH
ZUKUNFT

BIOGRAPHIES

Academic Life

ABICHT, JOHANN GEORG
ADLER, GEORG
ADORNO, THEODOR W.
ALBERTUS MAGNUS
ALT, ALBRECHT
ALTMANN, ALEXANDER
ARENDT, HANNAH
ARNHEIM, HEYMANN
ARONIUS, JULIUS
ASCHAFFENBURG, GUSTAV
ASCHER, SAUL
ASHER, DAVID
AVE-LALLEMANT, FRIEDRICH CHRISTIAN
    BENEDICT
BAER, SELIGMAN ISAAC
BAER, YITZHAK
BAETHGEN, FRIEDRICH WILHELM ADOLPH
BAUMGARDT, DAVID
BAUMGARTEN, EMANUEL MENDEL
BECHER, SIEGFRIED
BECK, MICHAEL
BEER, MAX
BEER, PETER (Perez)
BENDAVID, LAZARUS (Eleazar)
BENFEY, THEODOR
BENJACOB, ISAAC
BEN ZE'EV, JUDAH LEIB
BENZINGER, IMMANUEL
BERGSTRAESSER, GOTTHELF
BERLINER, ABRAHAM
BERNFELD, SIEGFRIED
BIALOBLOTZKY, CHRISTIAN HEINRICH
    FRIEDRICH
BIRNBAUM, NATHAN
BISCHOFF, ERICH
BLEEK, FRIEDRICH
BLOCH, ERNST
BLOCH, JOSEPH
BLOGG, SOLOMON BEN EPHRAIM
BLUMENFELD, WALTER
BODENSCHATZ, JOHANN CHRISTOPH GEORG
BOESCHENSTEIN, JOHANN
BOHL (Bohlius), SAMUEL
BONDY, CURT
BONN, MORITZ JULIUS
BORCHARDT, LUDWIG
BRANN, MARCUS
BRAUNTHAL, JULIUS

BREITHAUPT, JOHANN FRIEDRICH
BRESSLAU, HARRY
BRILL, ABRAHAM ARDEN
BRILLING, BERNHARD
BRUNNER, CONSTANTIN
BRUNSWIG, ALFRED
BUDDE, KARL FERDINAND REINHARD
BUEDINGER, MAX
BUHLER, CHARLOTTE
CALLENBERG, JOHANN HEINRICH
CAPITO, WOLFGANG FABRICIUS
CARO, GEORG MARTIN
CASSEL, DAVID
CASSEL, PAULUS STEPHANUS (Selig)
CASSIRER, ERNST
COHEN, ARTHUR
COHEN, HERMANN
COHN, GUSTAV
COHN, JONAS
COHN, LEOPOLD
CORNILL, CARL HEINRICH
DALMAN, GUSTAF HERMANN
DANZ, JOHANN ANDREAS
DAVID, MARTIN
DAVIDSOHN, ROBERT
DELITZSCH, FRANZ (Julius)
DELITZSCH, FRIEDRICH
DESSAU, HERMANN
DESSOIR, MAX
DEUTSCH, EMANUEL OSKAR
DILLMANN, AUGUST
DUBISLAV, WALTER ERNST OTTO
DUEHRING, KARL EUGEN
DUHM, BERNHARD
ECKHART, MEISTER
EHRENBERG, VICTOR LEOPOLD
EICHHORN, JOHANN GOTTFRIED
EISLER, RUDOLF
EISSFELDT, OTTO
ELBOGEN, ISMAR
ENGELMANN, SUSANNE CHARLOTTE
ERMAN, JOHANN PETER ADOLF
ESCHELBACHER, JOSEPH
EUCHEL, ISAAC ABRAHAM
EWALD, HEINRICH GEORG AUGUST
FAGIUS, PAULUS
FICHTE, JOHANN GOTTLIEB
FORSTER, JOHANN (Forsthemius)
FRANKFURTER, SOLOMON FRIEDRICH
FRANKL, PINKUS FRITZ (Pinhas)
FRAUENSTAEDT, JULIUS
FREIMANN, ARON
FREIMANN, JACOB
FRENSDORFF, FERDINAND
FRENSDORFF, SOLOMON
FREUDENTHAL, JACOB
FRIEDJUNG, HEINRICH
FRIEDLAENDER, MORITZ
FRIEDLAENDER, OSKAR EWALD
FRIEDRICHSFELD, DAVID

I. HISTORY
  B. MEDIEVAL & MODERN PERIOD
    2. Regional History
      e. Western Europe
        3) Germany & Austria
          BIOGRAPHIES
           Academic Life (continued)

FRIES, JAKOB FRIEDRICH
FUERST, JULIUS
GALLING, KURT
GANS, EDUARD
GEIGER, ABRAHAM
GEIGER, BERNHARD
GEIGER, LAZARUS (Eliezer Solomon)
GEIGER, MORITZ
GELBER, NATHAN MICHAEL
GESENIUS, HEINRICH FRIEDRICH WILHELM
GHILLANY, FRIEDRICH WILHELM
GOLDENTHAL, JACOB
GOLDSCHEID, RUDOLF
GOLDSCHMIDT, LAZARUS
GOLDSCHMIDT, RICHARD HELLMUTH
GOLDSTEIN, JULIUS
GOMPERZ, THEODOR
GRAETZ, HEINRICH
GRAF, KARL HEINRICH
GRESSMANN, HUGO
GRUENBAUM, MAX
GRUENHUT, MAX
GRUNWALD, MAX
GUMPLOWICZ, LUDWIG
GUNKEL, HERMANN
GUTHE, HERMANN
GUTTMANN, JACOB
GUTTMANN, JULIUS
HALLO, WILLIAM
HANAU, SOLOMON ZALMAN BEN JUDAH
    LOEB HA-KOHEN
HEGEL, GEORG WILHELM FRIEDRICH
HEICHELHEIM, FRITZ MORITZ
HEIDENHEIM, WOLF (Benjamin Ze'ev)
HEINEMANN, FRITZ
HEINEMANN, JEREMIAH
HELLER, HERMANN
HELLER, JOSEPH ELIJAH
HELLER, THEODOR
HENGSTENBERG, ERNST WILHELM
HEPPNER, ARON
HERDER, JOHANN GOTTFRIED
HERZ, MARCUS
HERZFELD, ERNST EMIL
HERZOG, DAVID
HEYMANN, FRITZ
HILDESHEIMER, HIRSCH
HIRSCH, JULIUS
HIRSCH, MENDEL
HIRSCHFELD, GUSTAV
HIRSCHFELD, HEINRICH OTTO
HOELSCHER, GUSTAV

HOENIGSWALD, RICHARD
HORKHEIMER, MAX
HOROVITZ, JOSEF
HOROVITZ, SAUL
HRABANUS MAURUS
HUPFELD, HERMANN CHRISTIAN KARL
HUSSERL, EDMUND GUSTAV ALBRECHT
ILGEN, KARL DAVID
ISAACSOHN, SIEGFRIED
ITELSON, GREGOR
JEREMIAS, ALFRED
JERUSALEM, KARL WILHELM
JERUSALEM, WILHELM
JIRKU, ANTON
JOEL, KARL
JOST, ISAAC MARCUS
KAHLE, PAUL ERNST
KANT, IMMANUEL
KANTOROWICZ, ERNST HARTWIG
KASTEIN, JOSEF
KATZ, DAVID
KAUFMANN, DAVID
KAUFMANN, FELIX
KAUFMANN, FRITZ
KAUTZSCH, EMIL FRIEDRICH
KAYSERLING, MEYER (Moritz)
KEIL, KARL FRIEDRICH
KELLNER, LEON
KIRCHHEIM, RAPHAEL
KITTEL, RUDOLF
KLEMPERER, VICTOR
KOEBNER, RICHARD
KRACAUER, ISADOR
KRACAUER, SIEGFRIED
KRAUSS, FRIEDRICH SALAMO
KRAUSS, SAMUEL
KRONER, RICHARD
KRUG, WILHELM TRAUGOTT
LAGARDE, PAUL ANTON DE
LANDAUER, GUSTAV
LANDAUER, MEYER HEINRICH HIRSCH
LANDAUER, SAMUEL
LANDSBERGER, BENNO
LANDSHUT, SIEGFRIED
LANDSHUTH, ELIEZER (Leser)
LASK, EMIL
LASSON, ADOLF
LAZARUS, MORITZ
LEBRECHT, FUERCHTEGOTT
LEHMANN-HAUPT, CARL FRIEDRICH
LESSING, THEODOR
LEVISON, WILHELM
LEWIN, KURT ZADEK
LEWKOWITZ, ALBERT
LEWY, JULIUS
LIDZBARSKI, MARK (Abraham Mordechai)
LIEBERMANN, FELIX
LIEBERT, ARTHUR
LIEBMANN, OTTO
LIPMANN, OTTO

LOEWE, JOEL (BRILL)
LOEWE, VICTOR
LOEWENTHAL, EDUARD
LOEWITH, KARL
LOEWY, EMANUEL
LOWE, ADOLPH
LUSCHAN, FELIX VON
MAIMON, SOLOMON
MANNHEIM, KARL
MARCK, SIEGFRIED
MARCUS, AARON
MARCUS, ERNST
MARKUS, LUDWIG
MARX, KARL HEINRICH
MAUTNER, KONRAD
MAYER, GUSTAV
MEINHOLD, JOHANNES FRIEDRICH
MEISL, JOSEPH
MENDELSSOHN
MENDELSSOHN, MOSES
METZGER, ARNOLD
MEYER, EDUARD
MICHAELIS, JOHANN DAVID
MISES, LUDWIG EDLER VON
MITTWOCH, EUGEN
MOMMSEN, THEODOR
MUELLER, DAVID HEINRICH
MUENSTER, SEBASTIAN
MUENSTERBERG, HUGO
MYNONA
NACHOD, OSKAR
NAFTALI, PEREZ (Fritz)
NELSON, LEONHARD
NEUBAUER, JACOB (Jekuthiel)
NIETZSCHE, FRIEDRICH WILHELM
NOELDEKE, THEODOR
NOTH, MARTIN
NOWACK, WILHELM GUSTAV HERMANN
NUSSBAUM, ARTHUR
NUSSENBLATH, TULO
OBERMEYER, JACOB
OLSHAUSEN, JUSTUS
OPPENHEIMER, FRANZ
OPPERT, GUSTAV SALOMON
OTTENSOSSER, DAVID
OTTO, RUDOLPH
PELLICANUS (Rubeaquensis), CONRAD
PERLBACH, MAX
PERLES
PHILIPPSON
PICK, HAYYIM HERMANN
PINNER, FELIX
PISTORIUS (de Nida), JOHANNES
POLOTSKY, HANS JACOB
POPPER, JOSEF (Lynkeus)
POPPER, SIR KARL RAIMUND
PRIBRAM, ALFRED FRANCIS
RAD, GERHARD VON
RECKENDORF, HERMANN SOLOMON
REICH, WILHELM

REICHENBACH, HANS
REINACH, ADOLF
REUSS, EDUARD
RICHTER, ELISE
RICHTER, RAOUL
RIESS, LUDWIG
ROEHRICHT, REINHOLD
ROSENMUELLER, ERNST FRIEDRICH KARL
ROSENTHAL, LESER
ROSIN, DAVID
RUEHS, CHRISTIAN FRIEDRICH
RYSSEL, VICTOR
SAALSCHUETZ, JOSEPH LEWIN
SACHS, MICHAEL
SALFELD, SIEGMUND
SALOMON, ALICE
SALOMON, GOTTFRIED
SAMTER, ERNST
SATANOW, ISAAC
SCHEFTELOWITZ, ISIDOR
SCHELER, MAX FERDINAND
SCHELLING, FRIEDRICH WILHELM JOSEPH
SCHICK, CONRAD
SCHICKARD, WILHELM (Guillielmus)
SCHOEPS, HANS JOACHIM
SCHUBERT, KURT
SCHUDT, JOHANN JAKOB
SCHUERER, EMIL
SCHWAB, HERMANN
SELLIN, ERNST
SELZ, OTTO
SIEVERS, EDUARD
SIMMEL, GEORG
SIMSON, BERNHARD VON
SIMSON, PAUL
SMEND, RUDOLPH
SOMBART, WERNER
SPANIER, ARTHUR
SPATH, JOHANN PETER
SPITZER, HUGO
STEIN, ARTHUR
STEIN, EDITH
STEIN, LUDWIG
STEINSCHNEIDER, MORITZ
STEINTHAL, HERMANN HEYMANN
STERN, ALFRED
STERN, FRITZ
STERN, MORITZ
STERN, WILLIAM
STERNBERG, KURT
STERN-TAEUBLER, SELMA
STEUERNAGEL, CARL
STOBBE, OTTO
STRACK, HERMANN LEBERECHT
STRAUSS, LEO
SUEDFELD, GABRIEL
SULZBACH, ABRAHAM
SULZBACH, WALTER
TAEUBLER, EUGEN
THIEME, KARL

I. HISTORY
B. MEDIEVAL & MODERN PERIOD
2. Regional History
e. *Western Europe*
3) Germany & Austria
####### BIOGRAPHIES
Academic Life (*continued*)

THOMSEN, PETER
TRAUBE, LUDWIG
VATKE, WILHELM
VELTWYCK, GERARD
VOLZ, PAUL
WACHSTEIN, BERNHARD
WAGENSEIL, JOHANN CRISTOPH
WAHLE, RICHARD
WAISMANN, FRIEDRICH
WALZER, RICHARD RUDOLF
WARBURG, ABY MORITZ
WATZINGER, CARL
WEIDENREICH, FRANZ
WEIGAND, THEODOR
WEIL, ERIC
WEININGER, OTTO
WELLHAUSEN, JULIUS
WELTSCH, FELIX (Baruch)
WENDLAND, PAUL
WERTHEIMER, JOSEPH, RITTER VON
WERTHEIMER, MAX
WETTE, DE, WILHELM MARTIN LEBERECHT
WINCKLER, HUGO
WINTERNITZ, MORITZ
WITTGENSTEIN, LUDWIG
WOLF, GERSON
WOLF, JOHANN CHRISTOPH
WORMS, ASHER ANSHEL
WRESCHNER, ARTHUR
WUENSCHE, AUGUST KARL
ZEDNER, JOSEPH
ZOLLSCHAN, IGNAZ
ZUCKERMANN, BENEDICT
ZUNZ, LEOPOLD

Art
ABRAMSON
ADLER, FRIEDRICH
ARON
BARTHOLDY, JACOB
BENDEMANN, EDUARD JULIUS FRIEDRICH
BENDIX, BENEDICT HEINRICH
BIRNBAUM, MENACHEM
BLAU, TINA
BLOCH, MARTIN
CASSIRER, PAUL
COHN-WIENER, ERNST
EISENSTAEDT, ALFRED
ELKAN, BENNO
FLECHTHEIM, ALFRED
FRANK, JOSEF
FREUND, GISELE

FREUNDLICH, OTTO
GODAL, ERIC
GRUNDIG, LEA AND HANS
HALLO, RUDOLF
HEARTFIELD, JOHN
HEINE, THOMAS THEODOR
HENSCHEL BROTHERS
HERLINGEN, AARON WOLF
HIRSCHFELD-MACK, LUDWIG
KAHNWEILER, DANIEL-HENRY
KATZ, HANNS LUDWIG
KAUFMANN, OSKAR
KIRSCHSTEIN, SALLI
KIRSZENBAUM, JESEKIEL DAVID
KRESTIN, LAZAR
LEVY, RUDOLF
LIEBERMANN, MAX
LILIEN, EPHRAIM MOSES
LISMANN, HERMANN
MAGNUS, EDUARD
MEIDNER, LUDWIG
MENDELSOHN, ERIC
MESSEL, ALFRED
NUSSBAUM, FELIX
NUSSBAUM, JAKOB
OPPENHEIM, MORITZ DANIEL
OPPENHEIMER, JOSEPH
ORLIK, EMIL
OSBORN, MAX
RINGL & PIT (STERN, GRETE; ROSENBERG
    AUERBACH, ELLEN)
SALOMON, CHARLOTTE
SALOMON, ERICH
SEGAL, ARTHUR
STRNAD, OSKAR
STRUCK, HERMANN
TRIER, WALTER
URY, LESSER
WOLF, GUSTAV
WOLLHEIM, GERT
WOLPERT, LUDWIG YEHUDA
ZADIKOW, ARNOLD

Literature
ADLER, HERMANN
ADLER, PAUL
AICHINGER, ILSE
ALTENBERG, PETER
AMERY, JEAN
ANDERS, GUNTER
AUERBACH, ERICH
AUERNHEIMER, RAOUL
AUSLAENDER, ROSE
AVIGDOR BEN SIMHAH HA-LEVI OF GLOGAU
BAB, JULIUS
BECKER, JUREK
BEER, MICHAEL
BEER-HOFMANN, RICHARD
BEN-CHORIN, SHALOM
BENJAMIN, WALTER

BERENDSOHN, WALTER A.
BERG, LEO
BERMANN, RICHARD ARNOLD
BETTAUER, HUGO
BIEBER, HUGO
BLUMENTHAL, OSKAR
BORCHARDT, RUDOLF
BRAUN, FELIX
BROCH, HERMANN
BRUCKNER, FERDINAND
CALE, WALTER
CELAN, PAUL
DOEBLIN, ALFRED
DOMIN, HILDE
DONATH, ADOLPH
EHRENSTEIN, ALBERT
EINSTEIN, CARL
ELOESSER, ARTHUR
FEUCHTWANGER, LION
FRANK, BRUNO
FRANKL, LUDWIG AUGUST
FRANZOS, KARL EMIL
FRIED, ERICH
FRIEDELL, EGON
FRISCH, EFRAIM
FULDA, LUDWIG
GEIGER, LUDWIG
GOETHE, JOHANN WOLFGANG VON
GOLDSTEIN, MORITZ
GOLL, CLAIRE
GRONEMANN, SAMUEL (Sami, Sammy)
GUMPERT, MARTIN
GUNDOLF, FRIEDRICH
GUTZKOW, KARL FERDINAND
HAAS, WILLY
HABE, HANS
HASENCLEVER, WALTER
HEILBORN, ERNST
HEIMANN, MORITZ
HEINE, HEINRICH
HERMANN, GEORG
HERMLIN, STEPHAN
HESSEL, FRANZ
HEYM, STEFAN
HEYMANN, WALTHER
HEYSE, PAUL
HILDESHEIMER, WOLFGANG
HILSENRATH, EDGAR
HIRSCHFELD, GEORG
HITZIG, JULIUS EDUARD
HOCHHUTH, ROLF
HOCHWAELDER, FRITZ
HOFMANNSTHAL, HUGO VON
HOLITSCHER, ARTHUR
HOLLAENDER
HONIGMANN, BARBARA
JACOB, HEINRICH EDUARD
JACOBOWSKI, LUDWIG
JELINEK, ELFRIEDE
KAHANE, ARTHUR

KALEKO, MASHA
KALISCH, DAVID
KAUFMANN, FRITZ MORDECAI
KAYSER, RUDOLF
KERR, ALFRED
KESTEN, HERMANN
KLEIN, JULIUS LEOPOLD
KOESTLER, ARTHUR
KOLMAR, GERTRUD
KOMPERT, LEOPOLD
KOREFF, DAVID FERDINAND
KORNFELD, PAUL
KRAMER, THEODOR
KRAUS, KARL
KROJANKER, GUSTAV
KUH, EPHRAIM MOSES
LANDSBERGER, ARTHUR
LASKER-SCHUELER, ELSE
LAZARUS, NAHIDA RUTH
LEONHARD, RUDOLF
LESSING, GOTTHOLD EPHRAIM
LEWALD, FANNY
LIPINER, SIEGFRIED
LISSAUER, ERNST
LORM, HIERONYMUS
LOTHAR, ERNST
LOTHAR, RUDOLF
LUBLINSKI, SAMUEL
LUDWIG, EMIL
MANN, THOMAS
MARCUSE, LUDWIG
MARGUL-SPERBER, ALFRED
MAUTHNER, FRITZ
MEHRING, WALTER
MEYER, RICHARD MORITZ
MOMBERT, ALFRED
MOSENTHAL, SALOMON HERMANN
MUEHSAM, ERICH
NADEL, ARNO
NEUMANN, ALFRED
NEUMANN, ROBERT
PAULI, JOHANNES
PERUTZ, LEO
PICARD, JACOB
POLGAR, ALFRED
REHFISCH, HANS JOSE
REICH-RANICKI, MARCEL
ROBERT, LUDWIG
RODA RODA, ALEXANDER
RODENBERG, JULIUS
ROESSLER, CARL
ROTH, JOSEPH
RUBINER, LUDWIG
SACHS, NELLY
SALTEN, FELIX
SAPHIR, MORITZ (Moses) GOTTLIEB
SCHERLAG, MARK
SCHILLER, FRIEDRICH VON
SCHNITZLER, ARTHUR
SCHWIEFERT, PETER

I. **HISTORY**
   B. MEDIEVAL & MODERN PERIOD
      2. **Regional History**
         e. *Western Europe*
            3) Germany & Austria
               BIOGRAPHIES
                  Literature (continued)

                  SEGHERS, ANNA
                  STERNHEIM, CARL
                  STRICH, FRITZ
                  SUESSKIND VON TRIMBERG
                  SUSMAN, MARGARETE
                  TOLLER, ERNST
                  TORBERG, FRIEDRICH
                  TREBITSCH, SIEGFRIED
                  TUCHOLSKY, KURT
                  URY, ELSE
                  VAN HODDIS, JAKOB
                  VIERTEL, BERTHOLD
                  WALDEN, HERWARTH
                  WALDINGER, ERNST
                  WASSERMANN, JAKOB
                  WEISS, ERNST
                  WEISS, PETER
                  WERFEL, FRANZ
                  WIHL, LUDWIG
                  WINDER, LUDWIG
                  WOLF, FRIEDRICH
                  WOLFENSTEIN, ALFRED
                  WOLFSKEHL, KARL
                  WOLFSOHN-HALLE, AHARON
                  ZUCKERMANN, HUGO
                  ZUCKMAYER, CARL
                  ZWEIG, ARNOLD
                  ZWEIG, STEFAN

                  Music
                  ABRAHAM, OTTO
                  ADLER, GUIDO
                  BEDA
                  BEER, AARON
                  BEKKER, PAUL
                  BIE, OSCAR
                  BIRNBAUM, EDUARD
                  BLECH, LEO
                  BRUELL, IGNAZ
                  DAVID, FERDINAND
                  DESSAU, PAUL
                  DEUTSCH, OTTO ERICH
                  EISLER, HANNS
                  FISCHOFF, JOSEPH
                  GEIRINGER, KARL
                  GERNSHEIM, FRIEDRICH
                  GOLDSCHMIDT, HUGO
                  HELLER, STEPHEN
                  HENLE, MORITZ
                  HERZ, HENRI (Heinrich)
                  HILLER, FERDINAND
                  HINRICHSEN

                  HOLLAENDER
                  JACOBSTHAL, GUSTAV
                  JADASSOHN, SALOMON
                  JAPHET, ISRAEL MEYER
                  KINSKY, GEORG LUDWIG
                  KOHN, MAIER
                  KOLISCH, RUDOLF
                  LEICHTENTRITT, HUGO
                  LEVI, HERMANN
                  LIPSCHITZ, SOLOMON BEN MOSES
                  LUCCA, PAULINE
                  MARX, ADOLF BERNHARD
                  MENDEL, HERMANN
                  MENDELSSOHN, ARNOLD
                  MENDELSSOHN, FELIX (Jakob Ludwig Felix)
                  MENDELSSOHN HENSEL, FANNY CAECILIE
                  MEYER, ERNST HERMAN
                  MEYERBEER, GIACOMO
                  MOTTL, FELIX JOSEF
                  NADEL, ARNO
                  OCHS, SIEGFRIED
                  SACHS, CURT
                  SCHLESINGER
                  SCHOENBERG, ARNOLD
                  SCHOENE, LOTTE
                  SILBERMANN, ALPHONS
                  STERN, JULIUS
                  STRAUSS, JOHANN
                  SULZER, SOLOMON
                  ULLMAN, VIKTOR
                  UNGER, MAX
                  WAGNER, RICHARD
                  WALTER, BRUNO
                  WEILL, KURT
                  WOLFF, HERMANN

                  Popular Culture
                  ABARBANELL, LINA
                  BARNAY, LUDWIG
                  BARNOWSKY, VIKTOR
                  BERGMANN, RICHARD
                  BERGNER, ELIZABETH
                  BRAHM, OTTO
                  CHRONEGK, LUDWIG
                  DAWISON, BOGUMIL
                  DESSOIR, LUDWIG
                  DEUTSCH, ERNST
                  GIEHSE, THERESE
                  GRANACH, ALEXANDER
                  HOMOLKA, OSCAR
                  JESSNER, LEOPOLD
                  KOLISCH, IGNAZ VON
                  KORTNER, FRITZ
                  LANG, FRITZ
                  LUX, STEFAN
                  MARLE, ARNOLD
                  MASSARY, FRITZI (Friedrike Massarik)
                  MIESES, JACQUES (Jacob)
                  OPHUELS, MAX
                  PALLENBERG, MAX

LABAND, PAUL
LADENBURG
LAEMEL, SIMON VON
LANDAU, EUGEN
LANDAU, JACOB
LANDSBERG, OTTO
LASKER, EDUARD
LASSALLE (LASSAL), FERDINAND
LEHMANN, BEHREND
LEHMANN, EMIL
LEICHTER, KAETE PICK
LEIDESDORFER
LEMLEIN, ASHER
LEOPOLD I
LEVI, BEHREND
LEVI, PAUL
LICHTHEIM, RICHARD
LIPPOLD
LOEWE, HEINRICH (Eliakim)
LOEWE, LUDWIG AND ISIDOR
LOEWENSTEIN, KURT
LORJE, CHAIM
LUEGER, KARL
LUSTIG, MOSES
LUTHER, MARTIN
LUXEMBURG, ROSA
MAGNUS, MARCUS
MARIA THERESA
MARR, WILHELM
MARX, KARL
MAXIMILIAN
MELANCHTHON, PHILIPP
MELCHIOR, CARL
MENDELSSOHN
MENDELSSOHN-VEIT-SCHLEGEL, DOROTHEA
MERTON
MERZBACHER
MERZBACHER, GOTTFRIED
MESSEL
METTERNICH, PRINCE KLEMENS WENZEL VON
MEYER, PAULUS (Pawly)
MICHAEL, HEIMANN JOSEPH HAYYIM
MICHEL, JUD
MODEL, MARX
MOND
MORAWITZ, KARL RITTER VON
MORGENSTERN, LINA
MOSER, MOSES
MOSES, SIEGFRIED
MOSSE
MOSSNER, WALTHER VON
MUELLER-COHEN, ANITA
MUHR, ABRAHAM
NACHMANN, WERNER
NACHOD, JACOB
NATHAN, PAUL
NEUMEYER, ALFRED
NEUMEYER, KARL
NIEBUHR, KARSTEN
OESTERREICHER, TOBIAS VON

OFNER, JULIUS
OLLENDORFF, FRIEDRICH
OPPENHEIM
OPPENHEIM
OPPENHEIM, LASSA FRANCIS LAWRENCE
OPPENHEIMER, JOSEPH BEN ISSACHAR
 SUESSKIND
OPPENHEIMER, KARL
OPPENHEIMER, SAMUEL
OSIANDER, ANDREAS
PAPPENHEIM, BERTHA
PERNERSTORFER, ENGELBERT
PHILIPPSON
PICK, ALOIS
PICK, HAYYIM HERMANN
POPPER, SIEGFRIED
PREUSS, HUGO
RABINOWICH, SARAH
RATHENAU, EMIL
RATHENAU, WALTHER
REDLICH, JOSEPH
REUTER, PAUL JULIUS, BARON VON
RIEGNER, GERHART
RIESSER, GABRIEL
RIESSER, JACOB
RINDFLEISCH
ROCKER, RUDOLF
RODE, WALTHER
ROSENBERG, ARTHUR
ROSENBERG, LUDWIG
ROSENTHAL, PHILIPP
ROTHSCHILD
RUDOLF I (of Hapsburg)
RUMPLER, EDUARD
SCHACH, FABIUS
SCHACHTEL, HUGO-HILLEL
SCHAEFFER, HANS
SCHALIT, ISIDOR
SCHAPIRA, HERMANN (Zevi-Hirsch)
SCHLEIERMACHER, FRIEDRICH
SCHLESINGER
SCHLESINGER, KARL
SCHMID, ANTON VON
SCHOCKEN
SCHOCKEN, SALMAN
SCHOENERER, GEORG VON
SCHOLEM, WERNER
SCHOTTLAENDER, BENDET (Benedict)
SEETZEN, ULRICH JASPER
SEIPEL, IGNAZ
SERING, MAX
SESSA, KARL BORROMAEUS ALEXANDER
SHLOM THE MINTMASTER
SICHROVSKY, HEINRICH VON
SIMON, HEINRICH
SIMON, JAMES
SIMSON, MARTIN EDUARD VON
SINGER, PAUL
SMOL (Samuel)
SOMARY, FELIX

I. HISTORY
   B. MEDIEVAL & MODERN PERIOD
      2. Regional History
         e. Western Europe
            3) Germany & Austria
                BIOGRAPHIES
                   Public & Economic Life (continued)

SOMMER, EMIL VON
SONNEMANN, LEOPOLD
SONNENFELS, ALOYS VON
SPEYER
SPIEGEL, PAUL
SPITZER, KARL HEINRICH
SPRINGER, AXEL
STAHL, FRIEDRICH JULIUS
STAHL, HEINRICH
STAUB, HERMANN
STEIN, BARON KARL VOM ZUM
STEINBACH, EMIL
STEUSS, DAVID
STOECKER, ADOLF
STRECKFUSS, ADOLF FRIEDRICH KARL
STRICKER, ROBERT
STRISOWER, LEO
STROUSBERG, BETHEL HENRY
SYNGALOWSKI, ARON
TEKA
THEBEN (MANDL), JACOB KOPPEL
TIETZ
TODESCO, HERMANN
TREITSCHKE, HEINRICH VON
TRIETSCH, DAVIS
TRITHEMIUS, JOHANNES (Tritheim)
ULLSTEIN
UNGER, JOSEF
VAN DAM, HENDRIK GEORGE
VARNHAGEN, RAHEL
VEIT
VEIT, MORITZ
VEITH, JOHANN EMANUEL
VOGELSANG, KARL VON
WARBURG
WARBURG, MAX
WASSERMANN, OSKAR
WEICHMANN, HERBERT
WENCESLAUS IV
WERTHEIM
WERTHEIMER, SAMSON
WETZLAR VON PLANKENSTERN
WIDMANSTETTER, JOHANN ALBRECHT
    (Widmanstadius, Lucrecius)
WINKLER, LEO (Judah)
WOLF, FRUMET
WOLFF, BERNHARD
WOLFF, JEANETTE
WOLFF, THEODOR
WRONSKY, SIDDY
WUNDERLICH, FRIEDA
YORK-STEINER, HEINRICH ELCHANAN

ZLOCISTI, THEODOR

Religion
ADLER
ADLER, LAZARUS LEVI
ADLER, SAMUEL
BLOCH, PHILIPP
BRUNA, ISRAEL BEN HAYYIM
DEUTSCH, IGNAZ
DEUTSCH, ISRAEL
DIENEMANN, MAX
DUEREN, ISAAC BEN MEIR
EGER, AKIVA BEN MOSES GUENS
EGER, AKIVA BEN SIMHAH BUNIM
EGER, SAMUEL (Perez Sanwel) BEN JUDAH
    LOEB
EHRENTREU, HEINRICH
EINHORN, DAVID
ELIEZER BEN NATHAN OF MAINZ
EPPENSTEIN, SIMON
EPSTEIN, JEHIEL MICHAL BEN ABRAHAM
    HA-LEVI
ETTLINGER, JACOB
FORMSTECHER, SOLOMON
FRAENKEL, DAVID BEN NAPHTALI HIRSCH
FREUDENTHAL, MAX
GLOGAU, JEHIEL MICHAEL BEN ASHER
    LEMMEL HA-LEVI
GUEDEMANN, MORITZ
HAGOZER, JACOB AND GERSHOM
HAHN, JOSEPH BEN MOSES
HAHN, JOSEPH YUSPA BEN PHINEHAS
    SELIGMANN
HALBERSTADT, ABRAHAM BEN MENAHEM
    MENKE
HALBERSTADT, MORDECAI
HAMBURG, ABRAHAM BENJAMIN (Wolf)
HAMBURGER, JACOB
HAYYIM (Eliezer) BEN ISAAC "OR ZARUA"
HAYYIM BEN JEHIEL HEFEZ ZAHAV
HAYYIM JUDAH BEN HAYYIM
HAYYIM PALTIEL BEN JACOB ("Tola'at")
HEILBUT, ELEAZAR LAZI BEN JOSEPH BEN
    LAZI
HEILPRIN, SAMUEL HELMANN BEN ISRAEL
HERXHEIMER, SALOMON
HERZFELD, LEVI
HESS, MENDEL
HILDESHEIMER, AZRIEL (Israel)
HILDESHEIMER, MEIR
HIRSCH, SAMUEL
HOESCHEL (Joshua) BEN SAUL
HOFFMAN, JACOB
HOFFMANN, DAVID ZEVI
HOLDHEIM, SAMUEL
HOROVITZ, JACOB
HOROVITZ, MARCUS
HOROWITZ, ISAAC HA-LEVI BEN JACOB JOKEL
HOROWITZ, LAZAR BEN DAVID JOSHUA
    HOESCHEL

HOROWITZ, ZEVI HIRSCH BEN PHINEHAS HA-
LEVI
ISSERLEIN, ISRAEL BEN PETHAHIAH
JACOB BEN YAKAR
JACOB OF VIENNA
JAMPEL, SIGMUND
JOEL BEN ISAAC HA-LEVI
JONAS, REGINA
JOSEPH BEN JOSHUA MOSES OF FRANKFURT
JUDAH BEN KALONYMUS BEN MEIR
JUDAH BEN KALONYMUS BEN MOSES OF MAINZ
JUDAH LEIB BEN ENOCH ZUNDEL
KALONYMUS
KAMINKA, ARMAND (Aaron)
KANN, MOSES
KARGAU, MENAHEM MENDEL BEN NAPHTALI
HIRSCH
KIRSCHSTEIN, MORITZ
KISCH, ALEXANDER
KLAUSNER, ABRAHAM
KLEY, EDUARD (Israel)
KOHN, ABRAHAM
KRONER, THEODOR
LAZA OF FRANKFURT
LEHMANN, MARCUS
LEWIN, ADOLF
LIPSCHUTZ, ISRAEL BEN GEDALIAH
LOEWENSTEIN, LEOPOLD
MANNHEIMER, ISAAC NOAH
MAYBAUM, IGNAZ
MEKLENBURG, JACOB ZEVI
MENAHEM BEN JACOB
MENAHEM OF MERSEBURG
MESHULLAM ZALMAN HA-KOHEN
MEYER, SELIGMANN
MINTZ, MOSES BEN ISAAC
MOELLIN, JACOB BEN MOSES (Maharil)
MORDECAI BEN HILLEL HA-KOHEN
MUNK
NOBEL, NEHEMIAH ANTON
OPPENHEIM, BEER BEN ISAAC
OPPENHEIM, JOACHIM
POPPERS, JACOB BEN BENJAMIN HA-KOHEN
PRIJS, JOSEPH
PROTESTRABBINER
RABBINER-SEMINAR FUER DAS ORTHODOXE
JUDENTUM
RIEGER, PAUL
RITTER, IMMANUEL HEINRICH
ROSENHEIM, JACOB
ROSENTHAL, LUDWIG A.
SACHS, MICHAEL
SALOMON, GOTTHOLD
SAMSON BEN ELIEZER
SAMSON HA-NAKDAN
SAMUEL BEN KALONYMUS HE-HASID OF SPEYER
SAMUEL BEN NATRONAI
SCHMIEDL, ADOLF ABRAHAM
SELIGMANN, CAESAR
SIMEON BAR ISAAC

SIMHAH BEN SAMUEL OF SPEYER
SOLOMON BEN SAMSON
SONDERLING, JACOB
SPITZER, SOLOMON
STADTHAGEN, JOSEPH
STEINHARDT, JOSEPH BEN MENAHEM
STEINHARDT, MENAHEM MENDEL BEN
SIMEON
STERN, SIGISMUND
SUTRO, ABRAHAM
TAGLICHT, DAVID ISRAEL
THEODOR, JULIUS
TYRNAU, ISAAC
VOGELSTEIN
WEIL, JACOB BEN JUDAH
WEIL, NETHANEL BEN NAPHTALI ZEYI
WESEL, BARUCH BENDET BEN REUBEN
WEYL, MEIR BEN SIMHAH
WINTER, JACOB

Science
ABEL, EMIL
ABRAHAM, KARL
ABRAHAM, MAX
ADLER, ALFRED
ALBU, ISIDOR
ARCO, GEORG WILHELM ALEXANDER HANS,
GRAF VON
ARONS, LEO
ASCHERSON, PAUL FRIEDRICH AUGUST
ASKENASY, EUGEN
ASKENASY, PAUL
AUERBACH, LEOPOLD
BAEYER, ADOLF VON
BAGINSKY, ADOLF ARON
BAMBERGER, EUGEN
BAMBERGER, HEINRICH VON
BARANY, ROBERT
BECHHOLD, JACOB HEINRICH
BEER, WILHELM
BENEDIKT, MORITZ
BERENDT, GOTTLIEB MICHAEL
BERL, ERNST
BERNSTEIN, JULIUS
BERSON, ARTHUR JOSEPH STANISLAV
BESSELS, EMIL
BILLROTH, THEODOR
BLANCKENHORN, MAX
BLAU, FRITZ
BLOCH, IWAN
BORN, MAX
BREDIG, GEORGE
BRESLAU, ERNST
BREUER, JOSEPH
BUCKY, GUSTAV
CANNSTADT, KARL FRIEDRICH
CANTOR, MORITZ BENEDICT
CARO, HEINRICH
CARO, NIKODEM
COHN, BERTHOLD

I. HISTORY
B. MEDIEVAL & MODERN PERIOD
2. Regional History
e. Western Europe
3) Germany & Austria
BIOGRAPHIES
Science (*continued*)

COHN, FERDINAND JULIUS
COHN, FRITZ
COHN, LASSAR
COHNHEIM, JULIUS
CONRAD, VICTOR
COURANT, RICHARD
CREIZENACH, MICHAEL
DEMBER, HARRY L.
DESSAUER, FRIEDRICH
DEUTSCH, FELIX
DONATH, EDUARD
EDINGER, LUDWIG
EDINGER, TILLY
EHRENFEST, PAUL
EHRLICH, PAUL
EINSTEIN, ALBERT
EISENSTEIN, FERDINAND GOTTHOLD
EISSLER, KURT R.
EITINGON, MAX
EMBDEN, GUSTAV
FEDERN, PAUL
FENICHEL, OTTO
FINKELSTEIN, HEINRICH
FRANCK, JAMES
FRANK, ALBERT RUDOLPH
FRANKEL, HEINRICH WALTER
FRANKENTHAL, KATE
FRANKL, VIKTOR E.
FREUD, ANNA
FREUD, SIGMUND
FREUND, MARTIN
FRIEDEMANN, ULRICH
FRISCH, OTTO ROBERT
FROEHLICH, ALFRED
GOLDSCHMIDT, GUIDO
GOLDSCHMIDT, HANS
GOLDSCHMIDT, RICHARD BENEDICT
GOLDSCHMIDT, VICTOR
GOLDSTEIN, EUGEN
GOLDSTEIN, KURT
GOTTLIEB, BERNHARD
GRUEN, ADOLF
GRUENSTEIN, NATHAN
GUMPERT, MARTIN
HAAS, FRITZ
HABER, FRITZ
HALBERSTAEDTER, LUDWIG
HANNOVER, RAPHAEL LEVI
HARTMANN, HEINZ
HAUSDORFF, FELIX (Paul Mongre)
HEIDENHAIN, RUDOLF
HENLE, JACOB

HENSEL, KURT
HERTZ, GUSTAV
HERZOG, REGINALD OLIVER
HIRSCH, AUGUST
HIRSCH, RACHEL
HIRSCHBERG, JULIUS
HIRSCHFELD, MAGNUS
HITSCHMANN, EDWARD
HOFF, HANS
HOFFER, WILLI
HURWITZ, ADOLF
JACOBI, KARL GUSTAV JACOB
JACOBI, MORITZ (Moses) HERMANN
JACOBSON, PAUL HEINRICH
JADASSOHN, JOSEF
JELLINEK, KARL
KOREFF, DAVID FERDINAND
KRISTELLER, SAMUEL
KRONECKER, LEOPOLD
LADENBURG, ALBERT
LANDAU, EDMUND
LANDSTEINER, KARL
LASSAR, OSCAR
LESS, EMIL
LIEBEN, ADOLPH
LIEBEN, ROBERT VON
LIEBERMANN, CARL THEODOR
LILIENTHAL, OTTO
LIPPMANN, EDMUND OSKAR VON
LIPPMANN, EDUARD
LIPSCHITZ, RUDOLF OTTO SIGISMUND
LOEW, MORITZ
LOEWE, FRITZ PHILIPP
LOEWI, OTTO
LONDON, FRITZ
LUNGE, GEORG
MAGNUS, HEINRICH GUSTAV
MAGNUS, PAUL WILHELM
MAGNUS, RUDOLPH
MA'OR KATAN
MARCKWALD, WILLY
MARCUS, SIEGFRIED
MEITNER, LISE
METCHNIKOFF, ELIE
MEYER, HANS JOHANNES LEOPOLD
MEYER, RICHARD JOSEPH
MEYER, VICTOR
MEYERHOF, MAX
MEYERHOF, OTTO
MICHAELIS, LEONOR
MINKOWSKI, HERMANN
MUNK, HERMANN
NEUBERG, GUSTAV EMBDEN CARL
NEUBURGER, MAX
NEUGEBAUER, OTTO
NOETHER
OPPENHEIM, HERMANN
OPPENHEIM, PAUL LEO
OPPENHEIMER, CARL
PAGEL, JULIUS LEOPOLD

PANETH, FRIEDRICH ADOLF

PICK, ALOIS

PICK, ERNST PETER

PINNER, ADOLF

PLAUT, HUGO CARL

PRAGER, RICHARD

PREUSS, JULIUS

PRINGSHEIM, HANS

RANK, OTTO

REIK, THEODOR

REMAK

ROMBERG, MORITZ HEINRICH

ROSENBUSCH, KARL HARRY FERDINAND

ROSENHEIM, ARTHUR

ROTHSCHILD, FRIEDRICH SALOMON

RUEDENBERG, REINHOLD

SACHS, JULIUS

SACKUR, OTTO

SAKEL, MANFRED JOSHUA

SALOMON-CALVI, WILHELM

SCHILDER, PAUL FERDINAND

SCHLESINGER, GEORG

SCHOENBERG, ALEXANDER JULIUS WILHELM

SCHOENHEIMER, RUDOLPH

SCHWARZSCHILD, KARL

SEMON, RICHARD WOLFGANG

SENATOR, HERMANN

SIMON, SIR FRANCIS EUGENE

SORAUER, PAUL KARL MORITZ

SPIEGEL-ADOLF, MONA

SPIRO, KARL

STEINACH, EUGEN

STEKEL, WILHELM

STERN, OTTO

STILLING, BENEDICT

STRASBURGER, EDUARD

STRAUS, RAHEL

STRAUSS, BENNO

STRAUSS, EDUARD

SUESS, EDUARD

TANDLER, JULIUS

TAUSK, VIKTOR

TOEPLITZ, OTTO

TRAUBE, ISIDOR

TRAUBE, LUDWIG

TRAUBE, MORITZ

TRAUBE, WILHELM

UNNA, PAUL GERSON

VALENTIN, GABRIEL GUSTAV

WALLACH, OTTO

WALLICH

WARBURG, OTTO

WARBURG, OTTO HEINRICH

WASSERMANN, AUGUST VON

WEIDNER, PAULUS

WEIGERT, CARL

WEIGERT, FRITZ

WIGNER, EUGENE P.

WILLSTAETTER, RICHARD

WOLFF, CHARLOTTE

WORMS, ASHER ANSHEL

ZUCKERKANDL, EMIL

4) Italy

MAIN SURVEYS

ITALIAN LITERATURE

ITALY

GENERAL ENTRIES

COLLEGIO RABBINICO ITALIANO

DIENCHELELE

FINZI-NORSA CONTROVERSY

GORNI

MONTI DI PIETÀ

MORTARA CASE

RIVISTA ISRAELITICA

VESSILLO ISRAELITICO, IL

COMMUNITIES

ACQUI

AGRIGENTO

ALESSANDRIA

ALGHERO

AMALFI

ANCONA

APULIA

AQUILA

AQUILEIA

AREZZO

ASCOLI PICENO

ASTI

BARI

BASSANO

BENEVENTO

BERGAMO

BOLOGNA

BOLZANO

BOZZOLO

BRESCIA

BRINDISI

CAGLIARI

CALABRIA

CAPUA

CASALE MONFERRATO

CATANIA

CATANZARO

CENTO

CESENA

CHIERI

CIVIDALE

COMO

CONEGLIANO

CORSICA

COSENZA

CREMONA

CUNEO

FAENZA

FANO

FERRARA

FINALE EMILIA

I. HISTORY
B. MEDIEVAL & MODERN PERIOD
2. Regional History
e. Western Europe
4) Italy

COMMUNITIES (*continued*)

FLORENCE
FORLI
FOSSANO
FRIULI-VENEZIA GIULIA
GAETA
GENOA
GORIZIA
IMOLA
ISTRIA
LECCE
LEGHORN
LODI
LOMBARDY
LUCCA
LUGO
MALTA
MANTUA
MARSALA
MERANO
MESSINA
MILAN
MODENA
MONCALVO
NAPLES
ORIA
ORVIETO
OSTIA
OTRANTO
PADUA
PALERMO
PARMA
PAVIA
PERUGIA
PIACENZA
PIEDMONT
PIOVE DI SACCO
PISA
POMPEI
RAVENNA
RECANATI
REGGIO DI CALABRIA
REGGIO EMILIA
RIMINI
RIVA (di Trento)
ROME
ROVIGO
SABBIONETA
SALERNO
SALUZZO
SAN DANIELE DE FRIULI
SAN MARINO
SAN NICANDRO
SARDINIA

SENIGALLIA
SICILY
SIENA
SIPONTO
SPOLETO
SYRACUSE
TARANTO
TRANI
TRAPANI
TRENT
TREVISO
TRIESTE
TURIN
TUSCANY
URBINO
VENICE
VENOSA
VERCELLI
VERONA
VICENZA
VITERBO
VITTORIO VENETO

BIOGRAPHIES

AARON OF PESARO
ABRABANEL
ABRABANEL, BENVENIDA
ABRAHAM BEN HAYYIM, THE DYER
ABRAHAM BEN ISAAC BEN GARTON
ADELKIND, ISRAEL CORNELIUS
ALATINO
ALATRI, SAMUEL
ALATRINI (Alatrino)
ALDO MANUZIO
ALMAGIA, ROBERTO
ALMANSI
ALMANZI, JOSEPH
AMBRON, SHABBETAI ISAAC
ANCONA
ANCONA, CESARE D'
ANCONA, MARIO
ANCONA, VITO D'
ARBIB
ARPA, ABRAMO DALL'
ARTOM
ARTOM, CESARE
ASCARELLI, DEBORAH
ASCARELLI, TULLIO
ASCOLI
ASCOLI, ETTORE
ASCOLI, GRAZIADIO ISAIA
ASSEMANI
AZEGLIO, MASSIMO TAPARELLI, MARCHESE D
AZULAI
BACHI, ARMANDO
BACHI, RICARDO
BAK
BALMES, ABRAHAM BEN MEIR DE
BARTOLOCCI, GIULIO
BARUCH, JACOB BEN MOSES HAYYIM

BARZILAI
BASEVI
BASSANI, GIORGIO
BASSANO
BEDARIDA, GUIDO
BELFORTE, SOLOMON
BEMPORAD, AZEGLIO
BEMPORAD, ENRICO
BENEVENTO, IMMANUEL BEN JEKUTHIEL
BENJAMIN NEHEMIAH BEN ELNATHAN
BERNHEIMER, CARLO
BLAYER, PIETRO
BOCCACCIO, GIOVANNI
BOLAFFI, MICHELE
BOLAFFIO, LEONE
BOMBERG, DANIEL
BONAVENTURA, ENZO JOSEPH
BORGHI, LAMBERTO
BOZECCO (Bozecchi), BENJAMIN BEN JUDAH
BRAGADINI
BRUNETTI, ANGELO
CAGLI, CORRADO
CALIMANI, SIMHA BEN ABRAHAM
CAMERINI, EUGENIO SALOMONE
CAMMEO, FEDERICO
CANTARINI
CANTONI, ALBERTO
CANTONI, LELIO (Hillel)
CANTONI, RAFFAELE
CAPON, AUGUSTO
CAPSALI, ELIJAH
CARPI, LEONE
CASSUTO, UMBERTO (Moses David)
CASTELLAZZO, MOSES DA
CASTELLI, DAVID
CASTELNUOVO, ENRICO
CASTELNUOVO-TEDESCO, MARIO
CASTIGLIONI, HAYYIM (Vittorio)
CATTANEO, CARLO
CIVITA, DAVIT (David)
COEN, ACHILLE
COEN, GRAZIADIO VITA ANANIA
COHEN
COLOGNA (DE), ABRAHAM VITA
COLOMBO, SAMUEL
COLOMBO, YOSEPH
COLON, JOSEPH BEN SOLOMON (Maharik)
COLORNI, VITTORE
COLUMBUS, CHRISTOPHER
CONAT, ABRAHAM BEN SOLOMON
CONCIO, JOSEPH BEN GERSON
CONEGLIANO
CONSIGLI(O), AVTALYON (Ottavio) BEN SOLOMON
CORCOS, VITTORIO
DA VERONA, GUIDO
DANTE ALIGHIERI
DATO, MORDECAI BEN JUDAH
DE BENEDETTI, ALDO
DE ROSSI, GIOVANNI BERNARDO
DEBENEDETTI, GIACOMO

DEL BANCO, ANSELMO (Asher Levi Meshullam)
DELLA SETA, ALESSANDRO
DELLA TORRE, LELIO (Hillel)
DEL MONTE, CRESCENZO
DEL VECCHIO
DEL VECCHIO, SHABBETAI ELHANAN BEN ELISHA
DESSAU, BERNARDO
DI GARA, GIOVANNI
DIENNA, AZRIEL BEN SOLOMON
DIRINGER, DAVID
DISEGNI, DARIO
DONATI, ENRICO
DONATI, LAZZARO
DONNOLO, SHABBETAI
EGIDIO DA VITERBO
ELIJAH BEN SHABBETAI BEER
ELIJAH OF LA MASSA
ELIJAH OF PESARO
ENRIQUES, PAOLO
ERRERA, CARLO
FALCO, MARIO
FANO
FANO, GUIDO ALBERTO
FARINACCI, ROBERTO
FIGO, AZARIAH
FINZI
FINZI, GIUSEPPE
FIORENTINO, SALOMONE
FOA
FOA, RAIMONDO
FOLIGNO, HANANEL (DA)
FORMIGGINI, ANGELO FORTUNATO
FORTI, BARUCH UZZIEL BEN BARUCH
FORTI, JACOB RAPHAEL HEZEKIAH BEN
    ABRAHAM ISRAEL
FRANCES, JACOB BEN DAVID
FRANCHETTI, RAIMONDO
FRIZZI, BENEDETTO
FUBINI, GUIDO
FUBINI, MARIO
GABBAI
GALLICO
GENTILI
GERSHON, ISAAC
GHIRONDI, MORDECAI SAMUEL BEN BENZION
    ARYEH
GINZBURG, NATALIA
GIOVANNI MARIA
GIUSTINIANI, AGOSTINO (Pantaleone)
GIUSTINIANI, MARCO ANTONIO
GRAZIANO, ABRAHAM JOSEPH SOLOMON BEN
    MORDECAI
GUASTALLA, ENRICO
GUGLIELMO DA PESARO
GUIDACERIO, AGACIO
GUNZENHAUSER, JOSEPH BEN JACOB
HALFANUS
IBN YAHYA, GEDALIAH BEN JOSEPH
IMBONATI, CARLO GIUSEPPE (Imbonatus)
IMMANUEL (ben Solomon) OF ROME

I. HISTORY
  B. MEDIEVAL & MODERN PERIOD
    2. Regional History
      e. Western Europe
        4) Italy
          BIOGRAPHIES (*continued*)

ISAAC BEN JACOB MIN HA-LEVIYYIM
ISHMAEL BEN ABRAHAM ISAAC HA-KOHEN
JAGEL, ABRAHAM BEN HANANIAH DEI GALICCHI
JARE
JEDIDIAH (AMADIO) BEN MOSES OF RECANATI
JERAHMEEL BEN SOLOMON
JESI, SAMUEL
JOEL, OTTO J.
JOHN OF CAPUA
JOSEPH HA-KOHEN
JOSHUA BOAZ BEN SIMON BARUCH
LATTES
LATTES, ABRAHAM BEN ISAAC
LATTES, DANTE
LATTES, ISAAC JOSHUA
LERMA, JUDAH BEN SAMUEL
LEVI, BENEDETTO
LEVI, CARLO
LEVI (GRAZIADIO), DAVID
LEVI, DORO
LEVI, EUGENIO
LEVI, GIORGIO RENATO
LEVI, GIULIO AUGUSTO
LEVI, GIUSEPPE
LEVI, MARIO GIACOMO
LEVI, PAOLO
LEVI, PRIMO
LEVI-BIANCHINI, ANGELO
LEVI-CIVITA, TULLIO
LEVI DELLA VIDA, GIORGIO
LEVI-MONTALCINI, RITA
LEVI-PEROTTI, GIUSTINA
LIUZZI
LOLLI, EUDE
LOMBROSO, CESARE
LOPEZ, SABATINO
LORIA, ACHILLE
LUZZATTI, LUIGI
LUZZATTO
LUZZATTO, EPRRAIM
LUZZATTO, GINO
LUZZATTO, ISAAC
MAGINO, MEIR
MALACHI BEN JACOB HA-KOHEN
MALVANO, GIACOMO
MANETTI, GIANNOZZO
MANIN, DANIELE
MANTINO, JACOB BEN SAMUEL
MARGULIES, SAMUEL HIRSCH
MARINI, SHABBETHAI HAYYIM (Vita)
MARLI, SAMUEL (RAPHAEL) BEN MAZLIAH
MASSARANI, TULLO
MASSARANO, JACCHINO OR ISACCHINO

MAYER, SALLY
MEIR BEN EPHRAIM OF PADUA
MICHELSTAEDTER, CARLO
MILANO, ATTILIO
MINZ, ABRAHAM BEN JUDAH HA-LEVI
MINZ, JUDAH BEN ELIEZER HA-LEVI
MITHRIDATES, FLAVIUS
MODENA, ANGELO
MODENA, AVTALYON (da)
MODENA, FIORETTA DI
MODENA, LEONE (Judah Aryeh)
MODIGLIANI, AMEDEO
MODIGLIANI, VITTORIO EMANUELE
MOMIGLIANO, ARNALDO DANTE
MOMIGLIANO, ATTILIO
MOMIGLIANO, FELICE
MONDOLFO, RODOLFO
MORAVIA, ALBERTO
MORPURGO
MORPURGO, GIUSEPPE
MORPURGO, RACHEL
MORPURGO, SALOMONE
MORPURGO, SAMSON BEN JOSHUA MOSES
MORTARA, LODOVICO
MORTARA, MARCO
MOSCATI, SABATINO
MOSES OF PALERMO
MUSOLINO, BENEDETTO
MUSSAFIA, ADOLFO
MUSSOLINI, BENITO
NATHAN, ERNESTO
NATHAN BEN JEHIEL OF ROME
NEPPI, HANANEL (Grazziadio)
NORZI
NORZI, JEDIDIAH SOLOMON RAPHAEL BEN
    ABRAHAM
NUNES VAIS
OLIVETTI
OLMO, JACOB DANIEL BEN ABRAHAM
ORVIETO, ANGIOLO
OTTOLENGHI
OTTOLENGHI, GIUSEPPE
OTTOLENGHI, JOSEPH BEN NATHAN
OTTOLENGHI, MOSES JACOB
PACIFICI, ALFONSO
PACIFICI, RICCARDO
PAGNINI, SANTES (Xanthus Pagninus)
PAPERNA, ABRAHAM BARUCH
PAPO, SAMUEL SHEMAIAH
PARDO, JOSEPH
PARENZO
PASTA, GUIDITTA
PERGOLA, RAPHAEL DE LA
PERREAU, PIETRO
PESARO, ABRAMO
PICO DELLA MIRANDOLA, GIOVANNI
PIPERNO BEER, SERGIO
PISA, DA
PITIGRILLI
POLACCO, VITTORIO

PONTECORVO, BRUNO
PORTALEONE
PORTALEONE, ABRAHAM BEN DAVID II
PORTO
PORTO, ABRAHAM MENAHEM BEN JACOB HA-
    KOHEN
PORTO-RAFA, MOSES BEN JEHIEL HA-KOHEN
PREZIOSI, GIOVANNI
PROVENÇAL, ABRAHAM BEN DAVID
PROVENÇAL, DAVID BEN ABRAHAM
PROVENÇAL, MOSES BEN ABRAHAM
PUGLIESE, EMANUELE
PUGLIESE, UMBERTO
RABBA, MENAHEM
RAPHAEL, MARK (Marco)
RASSEGNA MENSILE DI ISRAEL, LA
RAVA, MAURIZIO
RECANATI
REGGIO, ISACCO SAMUEL
REUVENI, DAVID
REVERE, GIUSEPPE PROSPERO
RIETI
RIETI, MOSES BEN ISAAC DA
ROGERS, ERNESTO
ROMANELLI, SAMUEL AARON
ROMANIN JACUR, LEONE
ROMANIN, SAMUELE
ROMANO, JUDAH BEN MOSES BEN DANIEL
ROSSELLI
ROSSI, MADAMA EUROPA DE
ROSSI, SALAMONE DE
SABA, UMBERTO
SACERDOTE, DAVID
SACERDOTI, ANGELO-RAPHAEL CHAIM
SAMEGAH, JOSEPH BEN BENJAMIN
SANGUINETTI, AZARIAH HAYYIM
SARAVAL
SARAVAL, JACOB RAPHAEL BEN SIMHAH JUDAH
SARAVAL, JUDAH LEIB
SARFATI
SCHANZER, CARLO
SCHIFF, HUGO
SEGRE
SEGRE, ARTURO
SEGRE, BENIAMINO
SEGRE, CORRADO
SEGRE, EMILIO GINO
SEGRE, GINO
SEGRE, JOSHUA BENZION
SEGRE, ROBERTO
SEGRE, SALVATORE
SERENI, ANGELO PIERO
SERENI, ENZO HAYYIM
SERVI, FLAMINIO (Ephraim)
SESSO, SALAMONE DA
SFORNO, OBADIAH BEN JACOB
SIERRA, SERGIO JOSEPH
SILANO
SINIGAGLIA
SINIGAGLIA, LEONE

SIXTUS OF SIENA
SOAVE, MOISE
SONCINO
SONNINO, SIDNEY
SULLAM, SARA COPPIO
SVEVO, ITALO
TEDESCHI
TEDESCHI (Tedesco), MOSES ISAAC BEN SAMUEL
TERNI, DANIEL BEN MOSES DAVID
TERRACINI, BENVENUTO ARON
TERRACINI, UMBERTO ELIA
TIVOLI, SERAFINO DA
TOAFF
TRABOT
TREMELLIUS, JOHN IMMANUEL
TREVES, EMILIO
TREVES, JOHANAN BEN JOSEPH
VALABREGA, CESARE
VENTURA, RUBINO
VITERBO, CARLO ALBERTO
VITTA, CINO
VIVANTE, CESARE
VIVANTI, DAVID ABRAHAM
VIVANTI CHARTRES, ANNIE
VOLLI, GEMMA
VOLTERRA
VOLTERRA, EDOARDO
VOLTERRA, MESHULLAM BEN MENAHEM DA
VOLTERRA, VITO
WOLLEMBORG, LEONE
YAISH, BARUCH BEN ISAAC IBN
ZEVI, BRUNO
ZIFRONI, ISRAEL BEN DANIEL
ZOLLER, ISRAEL

5) Netherlands
MAIN SURVEYS
DUTCH LITERATURE
NETHERLANDS, THE

GENERAL ENTRIES
FELIX LIBERTATE

COMMUNITIES
AMSTERDAM
HAGUE, THE

BIOGRAPHIES
ABENDANA, ISAAC SARDO
ABENDANA, JACOB BEN JOSEPH
ABRAHAM, SAMUEL
ABRAHAM BAR JACOB
ALTING, JACOBUS
AMELANDER, MENAHEM MANN BEN SOLOMON
    HA-LEVI
ANDRADE, VELOSINO JACOB DE
ASSCHER, ABRAHAM
ASSER
ATHIAS, JOSEPH AND IMMANUEL
BEEK, MARTINUS ADRIANUS

I. **HISTORY**
  B. MEDIEVAL & MODERN PERIOD
    2. **Regional History**
      e. *Western Europe*
        5) Netherlands
          BIOGRAPHIES (*continued*)

BELINFANTE
BELINFANTE, ISAAC BEN ELIAH COHEN
BENVENISTE, IMMANUEL
BERGH, VAN DEN
BERLIJN, ANTON (Aron Wolf)
BLANKENSTEIN, MARCUS VAN
BOAS
BOAS, HENRIETTE
BOUWMEESTER, LOUIS FREDERIK JOHANNES
BRANDON, OHEB ISAAC
BREGSTEIN, MARCEL HENRI
BRUGGEN, CARRY VAN
CACERES, ABRAHAM
CAMPEN (Campensis), JOHANNES VAN
CAMPEN, MICHEL HERMAN VAN
CASTRO TARTAS, DAVID DE
CITROEN, ROELOF PAUL
COCCEIUS, JOHANNES
COHEN, BENJAMIN
COHEN, DAVID
COHEN, ERNST JULIUS
CORREA, ISABEL REBECCA DE
COSTA, ISAAC DA
COSTA, URIEL DA
CUNAEUS (Van der Cun), PETRUS
DA COSTA, JOSEPH MENDES
DAVIDS, AARON ISSACHAR (Bernard) BEN NAHMAN
DE CHAVES, AARON
DE KLERK, MICHEL
DE LIEME, NEHEMIA
DICKER-BRANDEIS, FREDERIKE
DOZY, REINHART PIETER ANNE
DRUSIUS, JOHANN CLEMENS
DUQUE, SIMON DAVID
EERDMANS, BERNARDUS DIRKS
ELKERBOUT, BEN
ELTE, HARRY
EMPEREUR, CONSTANTIN L'
ERASMUS OF ROTTERDAM
ERPENIUS, THOMAS
FRANK, ANNE
FRANKFORT, HENRI
FRANKFURTER, MOSES
FRIEDE, SHALOM
GANS, MOZES ("Max")
GASKELL, SONJA
GODEFROI, MICHAEL HENRI
GOUDEKET, MAURITS
GOUDSMIT, JOEL EMANUEL
GROTIUS, HUGO
HAAN, JACOB ISRAEL DE
HAAN, MEIJER DE
HARTOG, LEVIE DE

HEIJERMANS, HERMAN
HERTZVELD-HIJMANS, ESTELLA
HERZBERG, ABEL JACOB
HEYMANS, GERARDUS F.
HILLESUM, JEREMIAS
HIRSCHEL, LEVIE (Louis)
HOND, MEIJER DE
HORODISCH, ABRAHAM
ISRAELS, JOZEF
JACOBS, ALETTA
JITTA, DANIEL JOSEPHUS
JONG, LOUIS DE
KANN, JACOBUS HENRICUS
KLEEREKOPER, ASSER BENJAMIN
KOENIGSWARTER
KUENEN, ABRAHAM
LARA, ISAAC COHEN DE
LEEUW, JACOB BEN HAYYIM (Heymann) DE
LEHREN
LEMANS, MOSES
LEUSDEN, JOHANN
LIMBURG, JOSEPH
LIPSCHUTZ, SOLOMON BEN MORDECAI
LOEWENSTAMM
LOGGEM, MANUEL VAN
MAARSEN, ISAAC
MANASSEH BEN ISRAEL
MEIJER, JACOB
MEIJERS, EDUARD MAURITS
MENDELS, MAURITS
MEYER, JONAS DANIEL
MINCO, MARGA
MIRANDA, SALOMON RODRIGUES DE
MONTEZINOS, DAVID
MORTEIRA, SAUL LEVI
MULDER, SAMUEL ISRAEL
MULISCH, HARRY
MUSSERT, ANTON ADRIAAN
NIEROP, VAN
ONDERWIJZER, ABRAHAM BEN SAMSON HA-
  KOHEN
OPPENHEIM, JACQUES
ORNSTEIN, LEONARD SALOMON
PALACHE, JUDAH LION
PEREIRA DE PAIVA, MOSES
PINTO, DE
PINTO, ISAAC DE
POLAK, GABRIEL ISAAC
POLAK, HENRI
POLAK, LEONARD
PRAAG, SIEGFRIED EMANUEL VAN
PRESSER, JACOB
PRINS, LIEPMAN PHILIP
PROOPS
QUERIDO, ISRAEL
RELAND, ADRIAN (Hadrian)
REMBRANDT VAN RIJN
REVESZ, GEZA
ROEST, MEIJER MARCUS
ROSENBERG, LAZAR

SANDBERG, WILLEM JACOB
SARPHATI, SAMUEL
SCHULTENS, ALBRECHT
SCHUSTER, AARON
SEELIGMANN, ISAC LEO
SEELIGMANN, SIGMUND
SOLA, DE
SPATH, JOHANN PETER
SPINOZA, BARUCH DE
SUASSO
SURENHUIS, WILHELM (Guilielmus)
SURGUN, ISAAC
TEMPLO, JACOB JUDAH (ARYEH) LEON
TIRADO, JACOB
URI BEN AARON HA-LEVI
VAN DER HOEDEN, JACOB
VAN RAALTE, EDUARD ELLIS
VAN VRIESLAND, VICTOR EMANUEL
VISSER, LODEWIJK ERNST
VOS, ISIDOR H. J.
VRIEZEN, THEODORUS CHRISTIAAN
VROMAN, LEO
WAGENAAR, LION
WAGNER, SIEGFRIED
WEINREB, FRIEDRICH
WERTHEIM, ABRAHAM CAREL
WIJNKOOP, DAVID

6) Scandinavia
MAIN SURVEYS
DENMARK
FINLAND
NORWAY
SCANDINAVIAN LITERATURE
SWEDEN

COMMUNITIES
COPENHAGEN
MALMO
OSLO
STOCKHOLM

BIOGRAPHIES
ABRAHAMS, NICOLAI CHRISTIAN LEVIN
ADLER, DAVID BARUCH
ASLAKSSEN, CORT (Aslacus, Conrad)
BALLIN, JOEL
BALLIN, MOEGENS
BALLIN, SAMUEL JACOB
BENDIX, VICTOR EMANUEL
BENKOW, JO (Josef Elias)
BENTZEN, AAGE
BERNADOTTE, FOLKE
BESEKOW, SAMUEL
BOHR, NIELS HENRIK DAVID
BORCHSENIUS, POUL
BORGE, VICTOR
BRANDES, CARL EDVARD
BRANDES, GEORG
BRANDES, LUDWIG ISRAEL

BRICK, DANIEL
BUHL, FRANZ PEDER WILLIAM MEYER
COHEN, EMIL WILHELM
COHN, CILLA CYPORA
COHN, GEORG ARYE
EDELMANN, RAPHAEL
EIBESCHUETZ, SIMON AARON
EITINGER, LEO S.
ELKAN, SOPHIE
EMSHEIMER, ERNST
FEIGENBERG, MEIR
FISCHER, JOSEF
FOIGHEL, ISI
FRAENKEL, LOUIS
FRIEDMANN, JANE
GLUECKSTADT, ISAAC HARTVIG
GOLDSCHMIDT, HEINRICH JACOB
GOLDSCHMIDT, MEIR ARON
GOLDSCHMIDT, VICTOR MORITZ
GONDOR, FERENC
GOTEBORG (Gothenburg)
GRANDITSKY, PALLE
GRUENBAUM, HENRY
HAMBRO, JOSEPH
HANNOVER, ADOLPH
HECKSCHER, ELI FILIP
HEDEGARD, OSKAR DAVID LEONARD
HERTZ, HENRIK (Heyman)
HURWITZ, STEPHAN
ISAAC, AARON
ISENSTEIN, KURT HARALD
JACOBSEN, ARNE EMIL
JACOBSON, LUDVIG LEVIN
JAKOBSON, MAX
JAKUBOWSKI, JACKIE
JOSEPHSON
KAUFMANN, HANNE
KLEIN, GEORGE
LAMM, MARTIN
LEVERTIN, OSCAR IVAR
LEVIN, POUL THEODOR
LEVY, LOUIS
MANNHEIMER, THEODOR
MELCHIOR
MELCHIOR, MARCUS
MELCHIOR, MICHAEL
MEYER, LUDWIG BEATUS
MEYER, TORBEN LOUIS
MOTTELSON, BENJAMIN R.
MOWINCKEL, SIGMUND OLAF PLYTT
MUNK, KAJ
NARROWE, MORTON
NATHANSEN, HENRI
NATHANSON, MENDEL LEVIN
OPPENHEJM, RALPH GERSON
PEDERSEN, JOHANNES
QUISLING, VIDKUN ABRAHAM LAURITZ
RUBENSON, ROBERT
RUBIN, EDGAR
SALOMON, GESKEL

I. **HISTORY**
   B. MEDIEVAL & MODERN PERIOD
      2. Regional History
         e. Western Europe
            6) Scandinavia
               BIOGRAPHIES (*continued*)

               SALOMON, JULIUS
               SALOMONSEN, CARL JULIUS
               SCHUCK, JOHAN HENRIK EMIL
               SIESBY, GOTTLIEB ISASCHAR
               SIMONSEN, DAVID JACOB
               TAU, MAX
               TYCHSEN, OLAUS GERHARD (Oluf)
               VALENTIN, HUGO MAURICE
               WARBURG, KARL JOHAN
               WARRENS, ROSA
               WERGELAND, HENRIK ARNOLD
               WOLFF, ABRAHAM ALEXANDER
               YSANDER, TORSTEN
               ZACHARIAS, JOHN

            7) Spain & Portugal
               MAIN SURVEYS
               PORTUGAL
               SPAIN
               SPANISH AND PORTUGUESE LITERATURE

               GENERAL ENTRIES
               ADELANTADOS
               ALBORAYCOS
               ANUSIM
               ARRABY MOOR
               AUTO DA FÉ
               BARCELONA, DISPUTATION OF
               BERUREI AVERAH
               CALATRAVA
               CONVERSOS
               CRYPTO-JEWS
               INQUISITION
               LIMPIEZA DE SANGRE
               RAB DE LA CORTE
               TORTOSA, DISPUTATION OF

               COMMUNITIES
               AGRAMUNT
               AGUILAR DE CAMPÓO
               ALAGÓN
               ALBA DE TORMES
               ALBARRACÍN
               ALCALÁ DE HENARES
               ALCAÑIZ
               ALCOLEA
               ALJAMA
               ALMAGRO
               ALMERIA
               ASTORGA
               AVILA
               AZORES
               BADAJOZ

               BALAGUER
               BARBASTRO
               BARCELONA
               BAZA
               BEJA
               BELMONTE
               BESALU
               BIEL
               BRAGANZA
               BRIVIESCA
               BUITRAGO
               BURGOS
               BURRIANA
               CADIZ
               CALAHORRA
               CALATAYUD
               CANARY ISLANDS
               CARMONA
               CARRION DE LOS CONDES
               CARTAGENA (Cartageni)
               CASTELO BRANCO
               CASTELLÓN DE LA PLANA
               CASTROJERIZ
               CEA
               CERVERA
               CEUTA
               CIUDAD REAL
               CIUDAD RODRIGO
               COCA
               COIMBRA
               CORDOBA
               CORUNNA
               COVILHA
               CUENCA
               CHAVES
               CHILLON
               DAROCA
               DENIA
               DUEÑAS
               ECIJA
               ELCHE
               ELVIRA
               ESCALONA
               ESTELLA
               EVORA
               FARO
               FRAGA
               FUNES
               GERONA
               GRANADA
               GUADALAJARA
               GUADALUPE
               HARO
               HERRERA DE PISUEGRA
               HÍJAR
               HUESCA
               HUETE
               IBIZA AND FORMENTERA
               ILLESCAS
               JACA

JAEN
JÁTIVA
JEREZ DE LA FRONTERA
LAGOS
LEIRIA
LEON
LERIDA
LISBON
LUCENA
LLERENA
MADRID
MAJORCA
MÁLAGA
MAQUEDA
MEDINA DE POMAR
MEDINA DEL CAMPO
MEDINACELI
MÉRIDA
MINORCA
MIRANDA DE EBRO
MONCORVO
MONTCLUS
MONTIEL
MONZÓN
MURCIA
MURVIEDRO
NÁJERA
OCANA
OLMEDO
OPORTO
ORENSE
ORIHUELA
PALENCIA
PALMA, LA
PAMPLONA
PECHINA
PLASENCIA
SAHAGÚN
SALAMANCA
SANTA COLOMA DE QUERALT
SANTARÉM
SARAGOSSA
SEGORBE
SEGOVIA
SEPÚLVEDA
SETUBAL
SEVILLE
SICILY
SIGÜENZA
SORIA
TALAVERA DE LA REINA
TARAZONA
TARRAGONA
TARREGA
TAUSTE
TERUEL
TOLEDO
TOMAR
TORTOSA
TRUJILLO

TUDELA
VALENCIA
VALMASEDA
VALLADOLID
VICH
VILA REAL
VILLADIEGO
VILLAFRANCA DEL PANADÉS
VITORIA
ZAMORA

Biographies

ABENMENASSE
ABENSUR
ABENVIVES
ABNER OF BURGOS
ABOAB
ABRABANEL, ABRAVANEL
ABRAHAM EL-BARCHILON
ABRAHAM OF BEJA
ABRAHAM OF SARAGOSSA
ABRAHAO, COJE
ABU AL-FADL HASDAY
ABUDARHAM
ABULAFIA
ABULAFIA, SAMUEL BEN MEIR HA-LEVI
ABULAFIA, SAMUEL HA-LEVI
AFFONSO
ALCONSTANTINI
ALFONSO
ALFONSO DE ESPINA
ALFONSO DE OROPESA
ALFONSO OF ZAMORA
ALFONSUS BONIHOMINIS (Buenhombre)
AL-MANSUR AL-YAHUDI
ALMOSNINO
ALTARAS
ALVAREZ GATO, JUAN
AMADOR DE LOS RIOS, JOSE
AMZALAK, MOSES BENSABAT
ANTONIO
ARAGÃO, FERNÃO XIMENES DE
ARDUT
ARIAS MONTANO, BENITO
ARRAGEL, MOSES
AT(H)IAS
AUB, MAX
AVENDAUTH
AVILA, DE
AVILA, PROPHET OF
BAENA, JUAN ALFONSO DE
BARRIOS, DANIEL LEVI (Miguel) DE
BENARUS, ADOLFO
BENJAMIN (BEN JONAH) OF TUDELA
BENOLIEL, JOSEPH (Jose)
BENREMOKH
BENSAUDE
BENVENISTE
BENVENISTE, ABRAHAM
BENVENISTE, ISAAC BEN JOSEPH

I. HISTORY
  B. MEDIEVAL & MODERN PERIOD
    2. Regional History
      e. Western Europe
        7) Spain & Portugal
          BIOGRAPHIES (*continued*)

            BENVENISTE, SAMUEL
            BENVENISTE, SHESHET BEN ISAAC BEN JOSEPH
            BENVENISTE DE PORTA
            BENZAMERO
            BIBAGO, ISAAC
            BONJORN, BONET DAVI(D)
            BONSENYOR, JUDAH (Jafuda)
            BOTAREL, MOSES BEN ISAAC
            BRANDÃO, AMBRÓSIO FERNANDES
            CANTERA BURGOS, FRANCISCO
            CARRASCON, JUAN
            CASTRO QUESADA, AMERICO
            CAVALLERIA, DE LA
            CERVANTES SAAVEDRA, MIGUEL DE
            CHARLES V
            CHAVES
            CORDOBA, ALONSO FERNANDEZ DE
            COSTA DE MATTOS, VICENTE DA
            COTA DE MAGUAQUE, RODRIGO DE
            CRESCAS
            CRESQUES ABRAHAM
            CRESQUES DE VIVERS
            DESMAESTRE, JONAH
            DIEZ, MACHO ALEJANDRO
            ECIJA, JOSEPH (Yucaf) DE
            ELEAZAR
            ENRIQUEZ GOMEZ, ANTONIO
            ENRIQUEZ, ISABEL
            ESCUDERO, LORENZO
            FALAQUERA
            FALAQUERA, NATHAN BEN JOEL
            FERDINAND AND ISABELLA
            FERNANDES VILLAREAL, MANOEL
            FERRIZUEL, JOSEPH HA-NASI
            FLORETA CA NOGA OF ARAGON
            FOREIRO, FRANCISCO
            GALIPAPA, HAYYIM BEN ABRAHAM
            GALIPAPA, MAIMON
            GAMA, GASPAR DA
            GAVISON (Gavishon)
            GEDALIAH, JUDAH
            GERONDI, ISAAC BEN JUDAH
            GERONDI, JACOB BEN SHESHET
            GERONDI, MOSES BEN SOLOMON DESCOLA
            GERONDI, SAMUEL BEN MESHULLAM
            GERONDI, SOLOMON BEN ISAAC
            GIKATILLA, ISAAC IBN
            GIKATILLA, JOSEPH BEN ABRAHAM
            GIKATILLA, MOSES BEN SAMUEL HA-KOHEN
            GODINEZ, FELIPE
            GOLLUF, ELEAZAR
            GRACIAN, SHEALTIEL BEN SOLOMON
            HABIBA, JOSEPH

            HAMON
            HANOKH BEN MOSES
            HASSAN
            HASSAN IBN (Mar) HASSAN
            HAYYIM BEN SAMUEL BEN DAVID OF TUDELA
            HAYYUN, ABRAHAM BEN NISSIM
            HAYYUN, JOSEPH BEN ABRAHAM
            HISDAI IBN SHAPRUT
            HUARTE DE SAN JUAN, JUAN
            IBN ABBAS, JUDAH BEN SAMUEL II
            IBN ALFAKHAR
            IBN BIKLARISH, JUNAS (Jonah) BEN ISAAC
            IBN DAUD, ABRAHAM BEN DAVID HALEVI
            IBN HASAN, JEKUTHIEL BEN ISAAC
            IBN JANAH, JONAH
            IBN JAU, JACOB
            IBN MIGASH, JOSEPH BEN MEIR HA-LEVI
            IBN MUHAJIR, ABRAHAM BEN MEIR
            IBN SAID, ISAAC
            IBN SHOSHAN
            IBN VERGA, SOLOMON
            IBN WAQAR
            IBN ZADOK, SOLOMON
            IBRAHIM IBN YAQUB OF TORTOSA
            ISRAELI, ISAAC BEN JOSEPH
            ISRAELI, ISRAEL
            JACOBSON, KURT
            JEHOSEPH HA-NAGID
            JEWESS OF TOLEDO
            JOHN
            JONAH BEN ABRAHAM GERONDI
            JOSEPH BEN JUSTU OF JAEN
            JUAN DE CIUDAD
            JUDAH BEN BARZILLAI AL-BARGELONI
            KAMNIEL, ABU AL-HASAN MEIR IBN
            LABI, SOLOMON (IBN)
            LA GUARDIA, HOLY CHILD OF
            LEON, LUIS DE
            LEVY
            LORKI, JOSHUA
            MAIMI, SIMON
            MANUEL I
            MARTÍNEZ DE OVIEDO, GONZALO
            MARTÍNEZ, FERRANT
            MARTINI, RAYMOND
            MELAMED, MEIR
            MENAHEM BEN JACOB IBN SARUQ
            MILLAS VALLICROSA, JOSE MARIA
            MONTORO, ANTON DE
            MOSES BEN HANOKH
            MOSES HA-KOHEN OF TORDESILLAS
            NAHMIAS, IBN
            NAHMIAS, JOSEPH BEN JOSEPH
            NAVARRO
            NIFOCI, ISAAC
            NISSIM BEN REUBEN GERONDI
            OHEV BEN MEIR HA-NASI
            ORABUENA
            OROBIO DE CASTRO, ISAAC (Balthazar)
            PABLO DE SANTA MARIA (el Burguense)

MORAVSKY KRUMLOV
MOST
NACHOD
NITRA
NOVE MESTO NAD VAHOM
NOVE ZAMKY
NOVY BOHUMIN
NOVY BYDZOV
NOVY JICIN
OLOMOUC (Olmuetz)
OPAVA
OSOBLAHA
PEZINOK
PIESTANY
PILSEN
POBEZOVICE NA SUMAVE
POHORELICE (Pohrlitz)
POLNA
PRAGUE
PRESOV
PROSTEJOV
ROUDNICE NAD LABEM
SLOVAKIA
SOBEDRUHY
TABOR
TACHOV (Tachau)
TEPLICE (Teplice-Sanov)
TOPOLCANY
TREBIC (Trebitsch)
TRENCIN (Trencsin)
TREST
TRNAVA
TURNOV
UDLICE
UHERSKE HRADISTE
UHERSKY BROD
USOV
USTEK
USTI NAD LABEM
VOTICE
YEDINTSY
ZATEC

Biographies

ABELES, SIMON (Simele)
ASKENAZY, LUDVIK
BAK
BASS, SHABBETAI BEN JOSEPH
BASSEVI OF TREUENBERG (Treuenburg), JACOB
BAUM, OSCAR
BEER, SAMUEL FRIEDRICH
BERGEL, JOSEPH
BONDY, BOHUMIL (Gottlieb)
BONDY, FILIP
BONN, HANUS
BOR, JOSEF
BRECHER, GIDEON
BRETHOLZ, BERTHOLD
BROD, MAX
CZECH, LUDWIG

DAGAN, AVIGDOR
D'ELVERT, CHRISTIAN RITTER VON
DEMETZ, PETER
DEUTSCH, ALADAR
DOBRUSCHKA, MOSES
DOBRUSCHKA-SCHOENFELD
DOSTAL, ZENO
EDELSTEIN, JACOB
EHRENFELD, NATHAN
EIDLITZ, LEOPOLD
EISLER, EDMUND MENAHEM
EISLER, MORITZ
EISNER, PAVEL (Paul)
ELIEZER BEN ISAAC
ELIJAH OF PRAGUE
FEDER, RICHARD
FEIGL, BEDRICH (Friedrich)
FEUERSTEIN, BEDRICH
FIRT, JULIUS
FISCHER
FISCHER, CAROLUS (Karl)
FISCHER, OTOKAR
FLEISCHMANN, GISI
FORMAN, MILOS
FRANKL-GRUEN, ADOLF ABRAHAM
FRIEDER, ARMIN
FRITTA
FRÝD, NORBERT (Nora)
FUCHS, ALFRED
GAL, FEDOR
GALSKY, DESIDER
GELLNER, FRANTIŠEK
GLASER, EDUARD
GOLDFLAM, ARNOST
GOLDSTEIN, ANGELO
GOLDSTUECKER, EDUARD
GOTTLIEB, FRANTIŠEK
GROSMAN, LADISLAV
GRUENWALD, MORITZ
GUTFREUND, OTTO
GUTTMANN, ROBERT
HAAS, HUGO
HAAS, LEO
HAAS, SOLOMON BEN JEKUTHIEL KAUFMANN
HELLER, YOM TOV LIPMANN BEN NATHAN HA-LEVI
HOCK, SIMON (Sinai)
HOFFMANN, CAMILL
HOSTOVSKY, EGON
ILLOWY (Illovy)
JACOB BEN ABRAHAM SOLOMON
JACOBUS APELLA VICEDOMINUS
JAKOBOVITS, TOBIAS
JAKOBSON, ROMAN
JEITELES
JELLINEK, HERMANN
JOEL, RAPHAEL
JOSEPH BEN ISAAC HA-LEVI
JUSTITZ, ALFRED
KAFKA, BRUNO ALEXANDER

I. HISTORY
  B. MEDIEVAL & MODERN PERIOD
    2. Regional History
      f. Eastern Europe
        2) Czechoslovakia
          Biographies (*continued*)

KAFKA, FRANTIŠEK
KAFKA, FRANZ
KAHN, FRANZ
KAPPER, SIEGFRIED (Vitezslav)
KARA, MENAHEM BEN JACOB
KAREL, RUDOLF
KARPELES, GUSTAV (Gershon)
KAUDER, SAMUEL JUDAH BEN DAVID
KISCH
KISCH, EGON ERWIN
KISCH, GUIDO
KLEMPERER, GUTMANN (Gumper)
KLIMA, IVAN
KNIEZA, EMIL
KOHEN
KOHN, JINDRICH
KOHN, SALOMON
KOHN, THEODOR
KOLMAN, ARNOST (Ernest)
KORNFELD, AARON BEN MORDECAI BAER
KRAUS, FRANTIŠEK R.
KRAUS, IVAN
KRAUS, OSKAR
KRAUS, OTA
KUGEL, HAYYIM
KUH, DAVID
KULKA, ERICH
LANDAU, MOSES
LANDSOFER, JONAH BEN ELIJAH
LANGER, FRANTIŠEK
LANGER, JIŘÍ MORDECHAI
LAUB, GABRIEL
LEDA, EDUARD
LEDERER, ABRAHAM
LEDERER, FRANCIS
LICHTENSTADT, ABRAHAM AARON
LICHTENSTADT, BENJAMIN WOLF BEN JUDAH
LIEBEN, KOPPELMANN
LIEBEN, SALOMON
LIEBEN, SALOMON HUGO
LISTOPAD, FRANTIŠEK
LOEBL, EUGEN
LOEW-BEER
LOEWENSTEIN, NATHAN
LOEWISOHN, SOLOMON
LONDON, ARTUR
LUSTIG, ARNOST
MAHLER, ARTHUR
MARGULIES, EMIL
MASARYK, JAN GARRIGUE
MASARYK, THOMAS GARRIGUE
MEISEL, MORDECAI (MARCUS, MARX) BEN SAMUEL
MILLER, MARTIN RUDOLF

MUELHAUSEN, YOM TOV LIPMANN
MUSIL, ALOIS
OLBRACHT, IVAN
ORNEST, OTA
ORTEN, JIŘÍ
OSTRAVA
PASCHELES, WOLF
PAVEL, OTA
PETHAHIAH OF REGENSBURG
PETSCHEK
PICK, JIRI ROBERT
PLACZEK, ABRAHAM
POLAČEK, KAREL
POLAK, JACOB EDUARD
POPPER
PREMYSL OTTOKAR II
PROSTITZ, ISAAC BEN AARON
QUETSCH, SOLOMON
RAKOUS, VOJTECH
RETI, RICHARD
ROTTOVA, INNA
RUDOLF II
RUFEISEN, JOSEPH
SALUS, HUGO
SCHMOLKA, MARIE
SCHORSCH, GUSTAV
SHAHOR
SICHER, GUSTAV
SIDON, KAROL EFRAIM
SIMONE, ANDRE
SINGER, LUDVIK
SPIEGEL, LUDWIG
SPITZER, JURAJ
STEIN, AUGUST
STEINER, HANNAH
STEINER-PRAG, HUGO
STEINHERZ, SAMUEL
STRANSKY, JAROSLAV
SZOBEL, GEZA
TELLER, ISSACHAR BAER
TEWELES, JUDAH
THIEBERGER, FRIEDRICH
TIGRID, PAVEL
TREBITSCH, ABRAHAM
UHDE, MILAN
UTITZ, EMIL
VOGEL, KAREL
VOHRYZEK, JOSEF
VOSKOVEC, GEORGE
VRCHLICKY, JAROSLAV
WEBER, KOLOMAN
WEIL, JIŘÍ
WEINBERGER, JAROMIR
WEINER, RICHARD
WEINMANN, JACOB
WEISS, JIŘÍ
WESSELY, WOLFGANG
WINTER, GUSTAV
ZELENKA, FRANTIŠEK
ZEYER, JULIUS

ZIDEK, PAVEL

3) Greece
MAIN SURVEYS
GREECE
GREEK LITERATURE, MODERN

GENERAL ENTRIES
ROMANIOTS

COMMUNITIES
ARTA
ATHENS
CANEA
CHALCIS
CHIOS
CORFU
CORINTH
CRETE
CUOMOTINI
CYPRUS
DIDYMOTEIKHON (Didymotica)
DRAMA
EPIRUS
IOANNINA
KASTORIA
KAVALLA
KORONE
KOS
LARISSA
MODON
NAUPAKTOS
PATRAS
PHLORINA
RETHYMNON
RHODES
SALONIKA
SERRAI
SPARTA
THEBES
TRIKKALA (Trikala)
VEROIA
VOLOS
XANTHI
ZANTE

BIOGRAPHIES
AFIA, AARON
ALHANATI, DAVID
ALMOSNINO, MOSES BEN BARUCH
ARDITI, ALBERT JUDAH
BALBO, MICHAEL BEN SHABBETAI COHEN
BELLELI, LAZARUS MENAHEM
BEN-AROYA, AVRAHAM
BENSANCHI, MENTESH (Mordecai)
CAIMIS, JULIUS
CAIMIS, MOISIS
DALVEN, RACHEL
ELAZAR, YAAKOV
ELIYIA, JOSEPH

ESTROSA, DANIEL
FRANCO, MOSES
HAYYIM (Ben) SHABBETAI (Maharhash)
IBN ARDUT, HAYYIM JOSEPH BEN AZRIEL HA-KOHEN
IBN YAHYA, GEDALIAH BEN TAM
ISTRUMSA (Istrusa), HAYYIM ABRAHAM
JABEZ
JOSEPH DAVID (Salonika)
KALA'I, MORDECAI BEN SOLOMON
KAPUZATO, MOSES HA-YEVANI
KORETZ, ZVI
LEVI, ABRAHAM BEN JOSEPH
LEVI (Bet ha-Levi), ISAAC BEN SOLOMON
LEVI, JACOB BEN ISRAEL
LEVI (Bet ha-Levi), SOLOMON BEN ISAAC
LEVI, SOLOMON BEN ISAAC (II)
MAESTRO, YAAKOV
MALKHI, EZRA BEN RAPHAEL MORDECAI
MATSAS, JOSEPH
MATSAS, NESTORAS
MOISSIS, ASHER
MOLHO, ISAAC RAPHAEL
MOTAL, ABRAHAM BEN JACOB
NEHAMA, JOSEPH
NOVITCH, MIRIAM
PERAHYAH, AARON BEN HAYYIM ABRAHAM HA-KOHEN
PERAHYAH, HASDAI BEN SAMUEL HA-KOHEN
QUERIDO, JACOB
RAZON, JACKO
RECANATI, ABRAHAM SAMUEL
RECANATI, LEON
ROMANUS I LECAPENUS
SALEM, EMMANUEL RAPHAEL
SCHIBY, BARUCH
SCIAKI, JOSEPH
TEKINALP, MUNIS (Kohen, Moiz)
ZARCO, JUDAH

4) Hungary
MAIN SURVEYS
HUNGARIAN LITERATURE
HUNGARY

GENERAL ENTRIES
ARROW CROSS PARTY
BEN CHANANJA
EGYENLOSEG
IZRAELITA MAGYAR IRODALMI TÁRSULAT (IMIT)
LANDESRABBINERSCHULE
MAGYAR ZSIDO SZEMLE
MULT ÉS JÖVÖ
PRAEFECTUS JUDAEORUM
STATUS QUO ANTE
UJ KELET

COMMUNITIES
ABONY

I. HISTORY
B. MEDIEVAL & MODERN PERIOD
2. Regional History
f. Eastern Europe
4) Hungary

COMMUNITIES (*continued*)

ALBERTI-IRSA
ASZOD
BAJA
BALASSAGYARMAT
BÉKÉSCSABA
BELED
BERETTYÓUJFALU
BODROGKERESZTUR
BONYHAD
BUDAPEST
DEBRECEN
EGER
ESZTERGOM
GYONGYOS
GYOR
HODMEZOVASARHELY
KAPOSVAR
KECSKEMET
KISVARDA
KOSZEG
MAKO
MISKOLC
NAGYKANIZSA
NYIREGYHAZA
PAKS
PAPA
PECS
PESTSZENTERZSEBET
SATORALJA UJHELY
SOPRON
SZEGED
SZEKESFEHERVAR
SZOLNOK
SZOMBATHELY
TISZAESZLAR
VAC
VESZPREM

BIOGRAPHIES
ACSÁDY, IGNÁC
ACZÉL, TAMÁS
ADAM, LAJOS (Louis)
ADLER, MORITZ
ÁGAI, ADOLF
AKIVA BEN MENAHEM HA-KOHEN OF OFEN
ALCONIÈRE, THEODORE
AMIGO
AUER, LEOPOLD
BACHER, WILHELM
BAKY, LASZLO
BALÁZS, BÉLA
BALLAGI, MOR
BÁNÓCZI

BARACS, KÁROLY
BARNA, VICTOR
BATO, LUDWIG YOMTOV
BAUMGARTEN, SANDOR
BAUMHORN, LIPOT
BECK, KARL ISIDOR
BECK, WILLY
BENJÁMIN, LÁSZLO
BEREGI, ARMIN BENJAMIN
BEREGI, OSZKAR
BÉRENY, RÓBERT
BERNSTEIN, BELA
BETTELHEIM
BETTELHEIM, SAMUEL
BIHARI, ALEXANDER
BIRÓ, LAJOS
BLAU, LUDWIG LAJOS
BLUM, AMRAM BEN ISAAC JACOB
BOHM, HENRIK
BOKROS-BIRMAN, DEZSÖ (Desiderius)
BRAND, JOEL JENÖ
BREYER, JULIUS (Gyula)
BROD, DOVIDL
BRÓDY, HEINRICH (Hayyim)
BRÓDY, LÁSZLÓ
BRÓDY, LILI
BRÓDY, SÁNDOR
BRÓDY, ZSIGMOND
BRUCK, LAJOS
BRUCK, MIKSA
BUECHLER, ALEXANDER
CHAROUSEK, RUDOLPH
CHORIN, AARON
CSERGÓ, HUGO
CSERMELY, GYULA
CZOBEL, BELA
DEAK, FERENCZ
DENES, BELA
DÉRY, TIBOR
DEUTSCH, DAVID BEN MENAHEM MENDEL
DEUTSCH, ELIEZER HAYYIM BEN ABRAHAM
DEUTSCH, JUDAH JOEL
DÓCZY, LAJOS
DUKES, LEOPOLD (Judah Loeb)
DUSCHINSKY, JOSEPH ZEVI BEN ISRAEL
EGER, SIMHAH BUNIM BEN MOSES
EHRENFELD
EHRENFELD, SAMUEL BEN DAVID ZEVI
EHRENREICH, HAYYIM JUDAH BEN KALONYMUS
EINHORN, IGNAZ
EISLER, MATYAS
ELEK, ARTUR
EMÓD, TAMAS
ENDRE, LASZLO
ENGEL, JOZSEF
ENGELMANN, GABRIEL
EÖTVÖS, BARON JÓZSEF
EPPLER, SANDOR
FALK, MIKSA
FALUDY, GYÖRGY

FEJÉR, LEOPOLD
FEJTÖ, FRANÇOIS
FELEKY, GÉZA
FENICHEL, SAMUEL
FÉNYES, ADOLF
FENYŐ, LÁSZLÓ
FENYŐ, MIKSA
FERENCZI, SÁNDOR
FISCHER, ANNIE
FISCHER, GYULA
FISCHER, MORITZ VON
FLEISCHER, JUDAH LOEB
FÖLDES, JOLÁN
FRANKEL, LEO
FRANKL, ADOLF
FRENK, BEER (Issachar Dov)
FREUND, VILMOS
FRIED, AARON
FRIEDMAN, DÉNES
FRIEDMANN, ABRAHAM
FRIEDMANN, MORITZ
FUCHS, MOSES ZEVI
FUST, MILAN
GÁBOR, ANDOR
GÁBOR, IGNÁC
GELLÉRI, ANDOR ENDRE
GELLÉRT, OSZKÁR
GERÖ, ERNÖ
GISZKALAY, JÁNOS
GLASNER, MOSES SAMUEL
GLUECK, ABRAHAM ISAAC
GOITEIN, BARUCH BENEDICT
GOLDBERGER, IZIDOR
GOLDZIHER, IGNAZ (Isaac Judah)
GRISHABER, ISAAC
GROSS, HEINRICH (Henri)
GRUENFELD, JUDAH
GRUENHUT, ELEAZAR (Lazar)
GRUNVALD, PHILIP (Fulop)
GRUNWALD, AMRAM
GRUNWALD, JUDAH
GUENZLER, ABRAHAM
GUTTMANN, MICHAEL (Mihály)
HAJDU, MIKLOS
HAJNAL, ANNA
HAJÓS, ALFRÉD
HATVANY-DEUTSCH
HAVAS, GÉZA
HÁY, GYULA (Julius)
HAZAI, SAMU
HEGEDÜS, ARMIN
HELLER, BERNAT
HELLER, JUDAH
HELTAI, JENŐ
HERTZKA, THEODOR
HEVESI, LAJOS (Ludwig)
HEVESI, SÁNDOR
HEVESI, SIMON
HIRSCHLER, IGNAC
HIRSCHLER, PÁL

HOROVITZ, LEOPOLD
HOROWITZ, SHRAGA FEIVEL HA-LEVI
HUGÓ, KÁROLY
IGNOTUS, HUGÓ
ILLÉS, BÉLA
ISTOCZY, GYÖZÖ
IVANYI-GRUNWALD, BÉLA
JAKAB, DEZSŐ
JAMBOR, FERENC-IOSEF
JÁSZI, OSZKÁR
JEREMIAH BEN ISAAC
JOAB BEN JEREMIAH
JONATHAN BEN JACOB
JOSEPH SOLOMON ZALMAN BEN MEIR
JUNGREIS, ASHER ANSHEL
KACZÉR, ILLÉS
KÁDAR, JÁN
KAHANA, JEHIEL ZEVI BEN JOSEPH MORDECAI
KAHANA, NAHMAN
KARÁCSONY, BENÖ
KARDOS, ALBERT
KARDOS, LÁSZLÓ
KARINTHY, FERENC
KÁRMÁN, MÓR
KATZ, MENAHEM
KAUFMANN, ISIDOR
KECSKEMÉTI, ÁRMIN
KECSKEMÉTI, GYORGY
KECSKEMÉTI, LIPOT
KELEN, IMRE
KELETI, ÁGNES
KEMÉNY, SIMON
KERTÉSZ, ANDRE
KERTÉSZ, IMRE
KERTÉSZ, ISTVAN
KESZI, IMRE
KISS, JÓZSEF
KITTSEE, HAYYIM BEN ISAAC
KITTSEE, JEHIEL MICHAEL BEN SAMUEL
KLEIN, MORITZ
KLEIN, SAMUEL SHMELKA
KLEIN, WILHELM
KÓBOR, TAMÁS
KOHLBACH, BERTALAN
KOHN, SAMUEL
KOHUT
KOMÁROMI CSIPKÉS, GYÖRGY
KOMLÓS, ALADÁR
KOMOLY, OTTÓ
KOMOR, ANDRAS
KONRÁD, GYÖRGY
KÖRMENDI, FERENC
KORNFELD, ZSIGMOND
KOSSUTH, LAJOS
KRAUSS, JUDAH HA-KOHEN
KRAUSZ, ZSIGMOND
KUN, BÉLA
KUNFI, ZSIGMOND
KUNSTADT, ISAAC (Ignaz) BEN ELIEZER LIPMAN
LAJTA, BÉLA

I. **HISTORY**
  B. MEDIEVAL & MODERN PERIOD
    2. Regional History
      f. Eastern Europe
        4) Hungary
          Biographies (*continued*)

LAKATOS, LÁSZLÓ
LÁNCZY, GYULA
LÁNCZY, LEÓ
LANDAU, NATHAN
LASZLO, PHILIP ALEXIUS DE LOMBOS
LEIMDOERFER, DAVID
LENGYEL, JÓZSEF
LENGYEL, MENYHÉRT (Melchior)
LENKEI, HENRIK
LÉVAI, JENÖ
LICHTENSTEIN, HILLEL BEN BARUCH
LOEW, IMMANUEL
LOEW, LEOPOLD (Lipot)
LOEWENTHAL, JOHANN JAKOB
LOEWINGER, DAVID SAMUEL
LOEWY, ISAAC
LUKÁCS, GEORG (Gyorgy)
MAHLER, EDUARD
MAJOR, ERVIN
MAKAI, EMIL
MALNAI, BELA
MARCZALI, HENRIK
MARKOVITS, RODION (Jakab)
MARTON, ERNÖ JECHEZKEL
MENDEL
MÉRAY, TIBOR
MEZEI, MÓR
MEZEY, FERENC
MEZŐFI, VILMOS
MODERN, JUDAH
MOHÁCSI, JENÖ
MOHOLY-NAGY, LÁSZLÓ
MOLNÁR, ÁKOS
MOLNÁR, FERENC
MUENZ, MOSES BEN ISAAC HA-LEVI
MUNKÁCSI, BERNÁT
MUNKÁCSI, ERNÖ
NAGY, ENDRE
NAGYBACZONI-NAGY, VILMOS
NAMÉNYI, ERNEST (Ernö)
NATONEK, JOSEPH
NÉMETH, ANDOR
ÓNODY, GÉZA
ORMÓDY, BERTALAN
OSVÁT, ERNÖ
PALÁGYI, LAJOS
PALÁGYI, MENYHERT (Melchior)
PAP, KÁROLY
PATAI, JÓZSEF
PÉCHI, SIMON
PERLES, ISAAC MOSES
PERLMUTTER, IZSAK
PLAUT, HEZEKIAH FEIVEL

POLLAK, MIKSA
POLLAK, MOSES HA-LEVI
QITTNER, ZSIGMUND
RADNÓTI, MIKLOS
RADÓ, ANTAL
RÁKOSI, MÁTYÁS
RAPOPORT, BENJAMIN ZEEV WOLF HA-KOHEN
  BEN ISAAC
REICH, IGNAC
REICH, KOPPEL (Jacob)
REICHARD, PIROSKA
RÉVÉSZ, BÉLA
REVICZKY, IMRE
RICHTMANN, MOZES
RÓNAI, JÁNOS
ROSENBAUM, MOSES HAYYIM LITS
ROSENTHAL, NAPHTALI
RÓZSAVÖLGYI, MÁRK
SALAMON, ERNO
SÁNDOR, PÁL
SCHEIBER, ALEXANDER
SCHICK, MOSES BEN JOSEPH
SCHILLER-SZINESSY, SOLOMON MAYER
SCHIPER, IGNACY (Yizhak)
SCHLESINGER, AKIVA JOSEPH
SCHOENFELD, JOSEPH
SCHREINER, MARTIN (Mordechai)
SCHWAB, LÖW
SCHWARTZ, ABRAHAM JUDAH HA-KOHEN
SCHWARTZ, JOSEPH HA-KOHEN
SCHWARTZ, PHINEHAS (Pinhas) SELIG HA-
  KOHEN (Sigmund)
SCHWEITZER, EDUARD VON
SCHWERIN-GOETZ, ELIAKIM HA-KOHEN
SEIBER, MÁTYÁS GYÖRGY
SHAG, ABRAHAM
SIDON, SIMEON
SILBERSTEIN, DAVID JUDAH LEIB
SILBERSTEIN-ÖTVÖS, ADOLF
SIMON, JOSEPH
SIMON, TAMÁS
SINGER, ABRAHAM
SINGER, JOSEPH
SINGER, PESAH
SOMLYÓ, ZOLTÁN
SOMOGYI, BELÁ
SONNENFELD, SIGISMUND
SPIRO, GYÖRGY
STEIN, ELIEZER LIPMAN
STERN, JOSEPH
STERN, MENAHEM
STERN, SAMUEL MIKLOS
SZABÓ, IMRE
SZABOLCSI, BENCE
SZABOLCSI, LAJOS
SZABOLCSI, MIKSA
SZALASI, FERENC
SZÁNTÓ, GYÖRGY
SZÁNTÓ, SIMON
SZEKELY, EVA

SZENDE, PÁL
SZENDE, STEFAN
SZENES, BÉLA
SZENES, ERZSI
SZENES, HANNAH
SZÉP, ERNŐ
SZERB, ANTAL
SZERENCSÉS, IMRE (Fortunatus)
SZILÁGYI, GÉZA
SZILARD, LEO
SZOMORY, DEZSŐ
SZTÓJAY, DÖME
TABAK, SOLOMON LEIB
TABOR (Tabori), PAUL
TABORI, GEORGE
TENNENBAUM, JACOB
TURÓCZI-TROSTLER, JÓZSEF
UJVÁRI, PETER
ULLMANN, ADOLPH
ULMAN, ABRAHAM
UNGAR, JOEL OF RECHNITZ
VADÁSZ, LIPÓT
VÁGÓ, JÓZSEF
VÁGÓ, LÁSZLÓ
VALYI, PETER
VAMBERY, ARMINIUS (Vamberger, Hermann)
VÁNDOR, LAJOS
VÁRNAI, ZSENI
VAS, ISTVÁN
VÁZSONYI, VILMOS
VEIGELSBERG, LEO
VENETIANER, LAJOS (Ludwig)
VÉSZI, ENDRE
VÉSZI, JOZSEF
VIHAR, BÉLA
VOGEL, SIMON
WAHRMANN, ISRAEL
WAHRMANN, MORITZ
WEINER, LEO
WEISS, JOSEPH MEIR
WEISS, MANFRED
WEISZ, MAX
WELLESZ, JULIUS
WERTHEIMER, EDUARD VON
ZELK, ZOLTAN
ZIEGLER, IGNAZ
ZIPSER, MAJER
ZÖLD, MÁRTON
ZSIGMOND, EDE
ZSOLDOS, JENÖ
ZSOLT, BÉLA

5) Poland

Main Surveys

LITHUANIA
POLAND
POLISH LITERATURE

General Entries

AGRICULTURE

AGUDDAT AHIM
ARENDA
HALLER'S ARMY
JABLONNA
KOROBKA
MORGENTHAU COMMISSION
SAMUEL COMMISSION
STEIGER TRIAL
UGODA

Communities

ALEKSANDROW LODZKI
AUGUSTOW
BEDZIN
BELCHATOW
BELZYCE
BIALA
BIALA PODLASKA
BIALYSTOK
BIELSKO
BIELSK PODLASKI
BILGORAJ
BOCHNIA
BOJANOWO
BRESLAU
BRODY
BRZEG
BRZESC KUJAWSKI
BRZEZINY
BUCHACH
BUSK
BYDGOSZCZ
BYTOM
CHECINY
CHELM
CHMIELNIK
CHORZOW
CHRYZANOW
CIECHANOW
CRACOW
CZESTOCHOWA
DABROWA GORNICZA
DROGOBYCH (Drohobycz)
DZIALOSZYCE (Dzialoshitz)
ELBLAG (Elbing)
GABIN
GALICIA
GDANSK (Danzig)
GLIWICE
GLOGAU
GNIEZNO
GORA KALWARIA
GORLICE
GORZOW WIELKOPOLSKI
GOSTYNIN
GRAJEWO
GREAT POLAND
GRODZISK MAZOWIECKI
GRODZISK WIELKOPOLSKI
GROJEC

I. HISTORY
B. MEDIEVAL & MODERN PERIOD
2. Regional History
f. Eastern Europe
5) Poland
COMMUNITIES (*continued*)

HALICZ
HRUBIESZOW
INOWROCLAW
IZBICA LUBELSKA
JANOW LUBELSKI
JAROSLAW
JASLO
JEDRZEJOW
JONAVA
JURBARKAS (Jurburg)
KALISZ
KALUSZYN
KALVARIJA
KATOWICE
KAUNAS
KEDAINIAI
KELME
KIELCE
KLODAWA
KOCK (Kotsk)
KOLBERG
KOLO
KONIN
KONITZ
KONSKIE (Konsk)
KONSKOWOLA
KORNIK
KOZIENICE (Kozenitsy)
KOZLE
KRASNIK
KRASNYSTAW
KRETINGA
KROSNO
KROTOSZYN
KRYNKI
KRZEPICE
KUPISKIS (Kupiskiai; Kupishki)
KUTNO
KYBARTAI
LANCUT
LASK
LEBORK
LECZNA
LECZYCA
LEGNICA
LELOW
LESKO
LESSER POLAND
LESZNO
LEZAJSK
LIPNO
LODZ

LOMZA (Lomzha; Lomzhe)
LOSICE (Lositsy)
LOWICZ
LUBACZOW
LUBARTOW
LUBLIN
LUBRANIEC
LUKOW
LUTOMIERSK
LYCK
MAKOW MAZOWIECKI
MARIJAMPOLE
MEMEL
MIEDZYRZEC PODLASKI
MIELEC
MINSK MAZOWIECKI
MLAWA (Mlwa; Mlava)
NAROL
NASIELSK
NOWY DWOR MAZOWIECKI
NOWY SACZ
OLESNICA
OLKUSZ
OPATOW
OPOCZNO
OPOLE LUBELSKIE
OSTROLEKA (Ostrolenka)
OSTROW MAZOWIECKA
OSTROWIEC (Ostrowiec Swietokrzyski)
OSWIECIM (Auschwitz)
OTWOCK
OZORKOW
PABIANICE
PANEVEZYS (Panevezhis)
PARCZEW
PEREMYSHLYANY
PIASECZNO
PINCZOW
PIOTRKOW (Piotrkow-Trybunalski)
PLOCK
PLONSK
PLUNGE
POZNAN
PRZEDBORZ
PRZEMYSL
PRZEWORSK
PRZYSUCHA
PRZYTYK
PULAWY
PULTUSK
RADOM
RADOMSKO
RADYMNO
RADZYMIN
RADZYN (Radzyn-Podlaski)
RASEINIAI
RAWICZ (Rawitsch)
ROKISKIS
ROPCZYCE (Ropshits)

ROZWADOW
RYMANOW
RYPIN
RZESZOW
SAKIAI (Shakyai, Shakay)
SAMBOR
SAMOGITIA
SANDOMIERZ
SANOK
SEDUVA
SIAULIAI
SIEDLCE
SIEMIATYCZE
SIERADZ
SIERPC
SKARZYSKO-KAMIENNA
SKIERNIEWICE
SKUODAS
SOCHACZEW
SOKOLKA
SOKOLOW PODLASKI
SOSNOWIEC (Sosnovets)
SREM
STASZOW
STETTIN
STOPNICA
STRYKOW
SUWALKI
SWIDNICA
SZCZEBRZESZYN
SZCZERCOW
SZYDLOWIEC
TARNOBRZEG
TARNOGROD (Tarnograd)
TARNOW
TAURAGE
TELSIAI (Telshi; Telschen)
TOMASZOW LUBELSKI
TOMASZOW MAZOWIECKI
TORUN
TROKI
TRZCIANKA
TYKOCIN
TYSZOWCE
UKMERGE
UTENA
VILKAVISKIS
VILNA
VIRBALIS
WARSAW
WEGROW
WIELICZKA
WIELUN
WISLICA
WLOCLAWEK
WLODAWA
WODZISLAW
WOLBROM
WOLOMIN

WRONKI
WYSZKOW
WYSZOGROD
ZABLUDOW
ZABRZE
ZAGARE
ZAMBROW (Zambrov)
ZAMOSC
ZARASAI
ZAWIERCIE
ZDUNSKA-WOLA
ZELECHOW
ZELOW
ZGIERZ (Zgerzh)
ZHMERINKA
ZMIGROD NOWY
ZUELZ
ZWOLEN
ZYCHLIN
ZYRARDOW

ORGANIZATIONS

CENTOS
COUNCIL OF FOUR LANDS
COUNCILS OF THE LANDS
ENDECJA (Endeks)
FOLKSPARTEI (POLAND)
GORDONIA
HA-NOAR HA-IVRI-AKIBA
HE-HALUTZ
JEWISH HISTORICAL INSTITUTE, WARSAW
JEWISH SOCIAL DEMOCRATIC PARTY
MAHZIKE HADAS
MINORITY BLOC
NARA
OZON
PPS
ROZWOJ
SEJM
SHOMER ISRAEL
TOZ
VILNA TROUPE

PUBLICATIONS

BEOBACHTER AN DER WEICHSEL
CHWILA
HA-ASIF
HA-BOKER
HA-KARMEL
HALICZ
HA-MIZPEH
HAYNT
HA-ZEFIRAH
HA-ZOFEH
IZRAELITA
JAFFE
JEKELES
MOMENT, DER
NASZ PRZEGLAD

I. HISTORY

B. MEDIEVAL & MODERN PERIOD

2. Regional History

f. Eastern Europe

5) Poland

PUBLICATIONS (continued)

NOWY DZIENNIK

BIOGRAPHIES

Academic Life

ASKENAZY, SIMON
ATLAS, ELEAZAR
BALABAN, MEIR (Majer)
BISLICHES, MORDECAI LEIB
BODEK, JACOB
BORNSTEIN, HAYYIM JEHIEL
BUBER, SOLOMON
BUCHNER, ABRAHAM
CHAJES, SAUL
CHARNA, SHALOM YONAH
CHATZKELS, HELENE
CHWISTEK, LEON
DEMBITZER, HAYYIM NATHAN
DICKSTEIN, SZYMON
EDELMANN, SIMHAH REUBEN
FEINSTEIN, ARYEH LOEB
FRENK, EZRIEL (Azriel) NATHAN
FRIEDBERG, BERNARD
FRIEDMAN, PHILIP
GLUSK, ABRAHAM ABBA
GOLDBERG, BAER (DOV) BEN ALEXANDER
GOLDBERG, BORIS
GOLDBLUM, ISRAEL ISSER (Isidore)
GOLDENBERG, BAERISH
GORDON, JACOB
HALBERSTAM, SOLOMON (Zalman) HAYYIM
HALEVY, ISAAC
HANDELSMAN, MARCELI
HERSCHBERG, ABRAHAM SAMUEL
HURWITZ, JUDAH BEN MORDECAI HA-LEVI
HURWITZ, PHINEHAS ELIJAH
ILNAE, ELIEZER ISAAC
JAWITZ, ZEEV
KALECKI, MICHAL
KAMENETZKY, ABRAHAM SHALOM
KATZ, BENZION
KATZENELLENBOGEN, ZEVI HIRSH (Naphtali)
KIRSCHBAUM, ELIEZER SINAI
KOTARBINSKA, JANINA
KRESSEL, GETZEL
KROCHMAL, ABRAHAM
KROCHMAL, NACHMAN
LAUTERBACH, ASHER ZELIG
LIPSCHITZ, JACOB HA-LEVI
MAGGID-STEINSCHNEIDER, HILLEL NOAH
MANASSEH BEN JOSEPH OF ILYA
MARK, BERNARD (Berl)
MARK, YUDEL
MICZYNSKI, SEBASTIAN

MIESES, FABIUS
MIESES, MATTHIAS
MOHR, ABRAHAM MENAHEM MENDEL
NUSSBAUM, HILARY (Hillel)
OBERMANN, JULIAN JOEL
PELTIN, SAMUEL HIRSH
PINELES, HIRSCH MENDEL BEN SOLOMON (Shalosh)
PLUNGIAN (Plungiansky), MORDECAI
POSNANSKI
RABBINOWITZ, SAUL PHINEHAS
REICHERSON, MOSES
REIFMANN, JACOB
RUBIN, SOLOMON
SACHS, SENIOR
SCHAFF, ADAM
SCHOENHACK, JOSEPH
SCHORR, JOSHUA HESCHEL
SCHULMAN, KALMAN
SHATZKES, MOSES AARON
SIMCHONI (Simchowitz), JACOB NAFTALI HERTZ
STEIN, EDMUND MENAHEM
TCHERIKOWER, ELIAS
TRUNK, ISAIAH
TUGENDHOLD, JACOB
TYKOCINSKI, HAYYIM
WETTSTEIN, FEIVEL HIRSCH
ZAMENHOF, LUDWIK LAZAR
ZHITLOWSKY, CHAIM

Art

CENTERSZSWER, STANISLAWA
FEUERRING, MAXIMILIAN
GOTTLIEB, MAURYCY
HIRSHENBERG, SAMUEL
PILICHOWSKI, LEOPOLD

Literature

ADALBERG, SAMUEL
BEHR, ISSACHAR FALKENSOHN
BIEGELEISEN, HENRYK
BRANDSTAETTER, ROMAN
BRANDYS, KAZIMIERZ
BRAUN, MIECZYSLAW
BRZECHWA, JAN
DRZEWIECKI, HENRYK
FELD, ISAAC
FELDMAN, WILHELM
GORSKA, HALINA
GRAY, MARTIN
GRYDZEWSKI, MIECZYSLAW
GRYNBERG, HENRYK
HEMAR, MARIAN
HERTZ, BENEDYKT
JASIENSKI, BRUNO
JASTRUN, MIECZYSLAW
JUNOSZA, KLEMENS
KLACZKO, JULIAN (Judah)
LEC, STANISLAW JERZY

LESMIAN, BOLESLAW
MICKIEWICZ, ADAM
MORGENSTERN, SOMA
NOWACZYNSKI, ADOLF
ORZESKOWA (Orzesko), ELIZA
PEIPER, TADEUSZ
ROZEWICZ, TADEUSZ
RUDNICKI, ADOLF
SCHULZ, BRUNO
SLONIMSKI, ANTONI
STANDE, STANISLAW RYSZARD
STERN, ANATOL
STRYJKOWSKI, JULJAN
SZENWALD, LUCJAN
TUWIM, JULIAN
WAT, ALEXANDER
WAZYK, ADAM
WINAWER, BRUNO
WITTLIN, JOZEF
WOROSZYLSKI, WIKTOR
WYGODZKI, STANISLAW

Music

ALTSCHUL, JOSEPH
BERGSON, MICHAEL
SZERMAN, PINCHAS
WEINTRAUB, SOLOMON
WIENIAWSKI, HENRI

Popular Culture

FORD, ALEXANDER
KAMINSKI
KIRSZENSTEIN-SZEWINSKA, IRENA
MOREWSKI, ABRAHAM
POLANSKI, ROMAN
ROTBAUM, JACOB
RUBINSTEIN, AKIVA
SAMBERG, ISAAC (Aizik)
SATZ, LUDWIG
TURKOW

Public & Economic Life

DLUGOSZ, JAN
FEDERBUSCH, SIMON
FORTIS, ABRAHAM ISAAC
GOLDMAN, BERNARD
GORDON, ABRAHAM
GORDON, DAVID
GOTTLIEB, HEINRICH
GOTTLIEB, HIRSCH LEIB
GOTTLIEB, YEHOSHUA
GRABSKI, STANISLAW
GRAEBER, SCHEALTIEL EISIK
GROSS, NATHAN
GROSSER, BRONISLAW
GRUENBAUM, YIZHAK
HARTGLAS, MAXIMILIAN MEIR APOLINARY
HAUSNER, BERNARD
HERSCH, PESACH LIEBMAN
HERZBERG-FRAENKEL, LEO

HIRSCHHORN, SAMUEL
HIRSZOWICZ, ABRAHAM
HOROWITZ, SAMUEL BEN ISAIAH ARYEH
    LEIB HA-LEVI
JELENSKI, JAN
JOGICHES, LEON
JOSELEWICZ, BEREK
JOSKO
JOZEFOWICZ
KAHNSHTAM, AHARON
KALLIR, MEIER
KATZ-SUCHY, JULIUSZ
KIRSCHBRAUN, ELIJAH
KLUMEL, MEIR
KOLISCHER, HEINRICH
KON, FELIKS
KOPELSON, ZEMAH
KORCZAK, JANUSZ
KORKIS, ABRAHAM ADOLF
KOSCIUSZKO, TADEUSZ
KOVNER, ABBA
KRONENBERG
LACHS, MANFRED
LANDAU, LEIB
LANDAU, SHEMUEL HAYYIM
LEKERT, HIRSCH
LELEWEL, JOACHIM (Ignacy)
LEVIN, YIZAK MEIR
LEWIN, GERSHON
LEWITE, LEON
LEWKO, JORDANIS
LIBER, MARC
LIEBERMAN, HERMAN
LIEBERMANN, AARON SAMUEL
LILIENBLUM, MOSES LEIB
LITAUER, JAN JAKUB
LITWAK, A.
LONDON, SOLOMON ZALMAN BEN MOSES
    RAPHAEL
LUTOSTANSKI, HYPPOLITE
MAYZEL, MAURYCY
MEISELS, DOV BERUSH
MENAHEM MENDEL BEN ISAAC
MIESIS, JUDAH LEIB
MIKHALEVICH, BEINISH
MILL, JOSEPH SOLOMON (John)
MOJECKI, PRZECLAW
MOND, BERNHARD STANISLAW
MOTKE HABAD
MUSZKAT, MARION (Max)
MUTNIK, ABRAHAM
NACHMANOVICH (Nachmanowicz)
NATANSON, LUDWIK
NEUFELD, DANIEL
ORGELBRAND, SAMUEL
OSTROPOLER, HERSHELE
PAWLIKOWSKI, JOZEF
PESAHSON, ISAAC MORDECAI
PIATTOLI, SCIPIONE
PILSUDSKI, JOZEF

I. HISTORY
B. MEDIEVAL & MODERN PERIOD
2. Regional History
f. Eastern Europe
5) Poland
BIOGRAPHIES

Public & Economic Life (continued)

PINES, MEYER ISSER
PLOTNICKA, FRUMKA
POPPER-BOZIAN, WOLF
PORTNOY, JEKUTHIEL (Noah; Yuzef)
POTOCKI, VALENTINE
PROHOVNIK, ABRAHAM
PRYLUCKI, NOAH
PRYLUCKI, ZEVI HIRSCH
PRYSTOR, JANINA
RAKOWSKI, PUAH
RAWNITZKI, YEHOSHUA HANA
REICH, LEON
REINMANN, SALOMON
RINGEL, MICHAEL
ROMM
ROSEN, MATHIAS
ROSENTHAL, PAVEL (Pinhas)
ROSMARYN, HENRYK
ROTENSTREICH, FISCHEL
RUMKOWSKI, CHAIM MORDECHAI
SALZ, ABRAHAM ADOLPH
SAWICKI, JERZY
SCHENIRER (Schnirer), SARAH
SCHRENZEL, MOSES
SCHUSSHEIM, AARON LEIB
SCHWARZBART, ISAAC IGNACY
SHABAD, ZEMAH
SHULMAN, VICTOR
SLAWOJ-SKLADKOWSKI, FELICJAN
SLUCKI, ABRAHAM JACOB
SLUTZKI, DAVID
SMOLAR, HERSH
STAND, ADOLF
STYBEL, ABRAHAM JOSEPH
SUROWIECKI, WAWRZYNIEC
SZER, SEWERYN
SZERESZEWSKI, MOSES DAVID
SZYR, EUGENIUSZ
TAMARES, AARON SAMUEL
TAUBES, LOEBEL
THON, ALBERT
THON, OSIAS (Jehoshua)
TREPPER, LEOPOLD
WEICHERT, MICHAEL
WILENSKY, YEHUDAH LEIB NISAN

Religion
DREYZL, LEAH
EISENSTADT, MEIR (Maharam Esh)
EISENSTADT, MENAHEM ZEVI
ENGEL, JOSEPH BEN JUDAH

ETTINGER, MORDECAI ZE'EV BEN ISAAC
    AARON SEGAL
EZEKIEL FEIVEL BEN ZE'EV WOLF
FALK, JOSHUA BEN ALEXANDER HA-KOHEN
FEIGENBAUM, ISAAC HA-KOHEN
GESUNDHEIT, JACOB BEN ISAAC
GOMBINER, ABRAHAM ABELE BEN HAYYIM
    HA-LEVI
HANOKH ZUNDEL BEN JOSEPH
HARIF HA-LEVI
HOROWITZ, ABRAHAM BEN ISAIAH
HOROWITZ, ISAIAH BEN JACOB HA-LEVI
HOROWITZ, PHINEHAS BEN ISRAEL HA-LEVI
HOROWITZ, SARAH REBECCA RACHEL LEAH
ISAAC BEN BEZALEL OF VLADIMIR
ISAAC BEN SAMUEL HA-LEVI
JOEL BEN MOSES GAD
JOSEPH BEN MORDECAI GERSHON HA-
    KOHEN OF CRACOW
JOSEPH BEN MOSES OF KREMENETS
JOSEPH BEN MOSES PHINEHAS
JOSEPH SAMUEL BEN ZEVI OF CRACOW
JOSHUA HOESCHEL BEN JOSEPH OF
    CRACOW
JUDAH BEN NISSAN
KAHANA, SOLOMON DAVID
KLEPFISH, SAMUEL ZANVIL
KOWALSKY, JUDAH LEIB
KRENGEL, MENAHEM MENDEL
KRISTIANPOLLER
LEWYSOHN, ABRAHAM
LICHTSTEIN, ABRAHAM BEN ELIEZER
    LIPMAN
LICHTSTEIN, ABRAHAM JEKUTHIEL
    ZALMAN BEN MOSES JOSEPH
LIPSCHITZ, SOLOMON ZALMAN
LUBLIN, MEIR BEN GEDALIAH
MAISEL, ELIJAH HAYYIM
MALAKH, HAYYIM BEN SOLOMON
MARGOLIES, ISAAC BEN ELIJAH
MEHLSACK, ELIAKIM BEN JUDAH HA-
    MILZAHGI
MEISELS, DAVID DOV
MEISELS, DOV BERUSH
MESHULLAM PHOEBUS BEN ISRAEL SAMUEL
MICHAELSON, EZEKIEL ZEVI BEN ABRAHAM
    HAYYIM
MORDECAI BEN NAPHTALI HIRSCH OF
    KREMSIER
MOSES BEN ISAIAH KATZ
PERLMUTTER, ABRAHAM ZEVI
PLOTZKI, MEIR DAN OF OSTROVA
POLLACK, JACOB BEN JOSEPH
RAPOPORT, ABRAHAM BEN ISRAEL JEHIEL
    HA-KOHEN
RAPOPORT, SOLOMON JUDAH LEIB
REIZES (Reizeles)
ROSANES, ZEVI HIRSCH BEN ISSACHAR
    BERISH

ROZIN (Rosen), JOSEPH
RUBINSTEIN, ISAAC
SAMUEL BEN URI SHRAGA PHOEBUS
SCHMELKES, GEDALIAH BEN MORDECAI
SCHOR, EPHRAIM SOLOMON (THE ELDER)
    BEN NAPHTALI HIRSCH
SCHORR, MOSES (Mojzesz)
SHALOM SHAKHNA BEN JOSEPH
SHAPIRA, MEIR
SHIFRAH OF BRODY
SHRAGAI, SHLOMO ZALMAN
SIRKES, JOEL
SLONIK, BENJAMIN AARON BEN ABRAHAM
SOCHACZEW, ABRAHAM BEN ZE'EV NAHUM
    BORNSTEIN OF
TRUNK, ISRAEL JOSHUA
WEINGARTEN, JOAB JOSHUA
ZEMBA, MENAHEM
ZUENZ, ARYEH LEIB BEN MOSES

Science
CALAHORA
DICKSTEIN, SAMUEL
HIRSZFELD, LUDWIK
INFELD, LEOPOLD
MARMOREK, ALEXANDER
PARNAS, YAKUB KAROL
STEINHAUS, HUGO DYONIZY
STERN, ABRAHAM JACOB

6) Romania
MAIN SURVEYS
ROMANIA
ROMANIAN LITERATURE

GENERAL ENTRIES
ADAM
AGRICULTURE
C.D.E. (Comitetul Democratic Evreiesc)
EGALITATEA
HASEFER
IRON GUARD
LUMINA
REVISTA CULTULUI MOZAIC

COMMUNITIES
ALBA IULIA
ARAD
BACAU
BAIA-MARE
BANAT
BARLAD
BENDERY
BEZIDUL NOU
BISTRITA (Bistritz)
BORSA
BOTOSANI
BRAILA
BRASOV

BUCHAREST
BUHUSI
BUKOVINA
BURDUJENI
BUZAU
CAMPULUNG MOLDOVENESC
CAREI
CLUJ
CONSTANTA
CRAIOVA
DARABANI
DEJ
DOROHOI
FAGARAS
FALTICENI
FOCSANI
GALATI (Galatz)
GERTSA
GURA-HUMORULUI
HARLAU
HUSI
IZMAIL
JASSY
KALARASH
KAUSHANY
LUGOJ (Lugos)
MARGHITA (Margit(t)a)
MIHAILENI
MOINESTI
MOLDOVENESC
NASAUD
NASNA
ORADEA (Oradea Mare)
ORSOVA
PASCANI
PIATRA-NEAMT (Piatra)
PLOESTI
RADAUTI (Radautz)
REBREANU
REGHIN (Reghinul Săsesc)
REZINA (Rezinz)
ROMAN
RYSHKANY
SALONTA
SATU-MARE
SEINI
SIBIU
SIGHET
SIMLEUL-SILVANIEI
SIRET
SOROKI (Soroca)
STEFANESTI
SUCEAVA
SULITA
TALMACIU
TARGU-MURES
TELENESHTY (Telenesti)
TIMISOARA
TIRASPOL

I. HISTORY

B. MEDIEVAL & MODERN PERIOD

2. Regional History

f. Eastern Europe

6) Romania

COMMUNITIES (*continued*)

TIRGU NEAMT
TIRGU-FRUMOS
TRANSYLVANIA
TURDA
VAD RASHKOV
VASLUI
VATRA DORNEI
VISEUL DE SUS
ZGURITSA (Zgurita)

BIOGRAPHIES

ADELSTEIN-ROZEANU, ANGELICA
ADERCA, FELIX
ANTONESCU, ION
ANTONESCU, MIHAI
AXELRAD, AVRAM
BALTAZAR, CAMIL
BALLY, DAVICION
BALLY, ISAAC DAVID
BANUȘ, MARIA
BARANGA, AUREL
BARASCH, JULIUS (Judah)
BENADOR, URY
BENJAMIN II (Israel Joseph)
BERLIAND, SHLOMO MEIR
BLANK, MAURICE
BLECHER, MARCEL
BOGDAN, CORNELIU
BONCIU, H.
BRAHAM, RANDOLPH L.
BRAUNER, HARRY
BRESLASU, MARCEL
BROCINER, JOSEPH
CAJAL, NICOLAE
CALIN, VERA
CĂLUGĂRU, ION
CARMILLY-WEINBERGER, MOSHE
CARP, HORIA (Jehoshua)
CARP, PAULA
CASSIAN, NINA
CELAN, PAUL
CILIBI, MOISE
CODREANU, CORNELIU ZELEA
CORNEA, PAUL
COSAȘU, RADU
CROHMALNICEANU OVID S.
CUZA, ALEXANDER C.
DAN, SERGIU
DOBROGEANU-GHEREA, CONSTANTIN
DOMINIC, ALEXANDRU
DORIAN, DOREL
DORIAN, EMIL
DUDA, VIRGIL

EBNER, MEIR (Mayer)
FELLER, SHNEYUR ZALMAN
FERARU, LEON
FILDERMAN, WILHELM
FONDANE, BENJAMIN
FURTUNĂ, ENRIC
GALACTION, GALA
GASTON-MARIN, GHEORGHE
GHELERTER, LUDWIG LITMAN
GRAUR, ALEXANDRU
GRAUR, CONSTANTIN
GRUENBERG, KARL
GURIAN, SORANA
HAIMOVICI, MENDEL
HALEVY, MEYER ABRAHAM
HASKIL, CLARA
HEFTER, ALFRED (Hidalgo)
IACOBESCU, D.
IONESCO, EUGENE
IOSIFESCU, SILVIAN
ISER, JOSIF
ISOU, ISIDORE
JANCO, MARCEL
JUSTER, GEORGE
LAVI, THEODOR
LAZAR, SAMSON
LĂZĂREANU, BARBU
LECCA, RADU
LIPPE, KARPEL
LUCA, B.
LUDO, ISAC IACOVITZ
MAIORESCU, GEORGE TOMA
MAXY, MAX HERMAN
MILIAN, MAXIMIN
MIRODAN, ALEXANDRU
MONDA, VIRGILIU
MUGUR, FLORIN
NEMTEANU, BARBU
NIEMIROWER, JACOB ISAAC
PANĂ, SAȘA
PAUKER, ANA
PELTZ, ISAC
PINELES, SAMUEL
POPPER, JULIUS
PORUMBACU, VERONICA
PROBST-KRAID, RIZA
PSANTIR, JACOB
RELGIS, EUGEN
ROMAN-RONETTI, MOISE
ROSEN, MOSES
RUDICH, MAYER
SAFRAN, ALEXANDER
SAFRAN, BEZALEL ZE'EV
SAFRAN, JOSEPH
SAINEANU, LAZAR
SANIELEVICI, HENRIC
SCHWARZFELD
SEBASTIAN, MIHAIL
SEMILIAN, SAVIN SOLOMON
SERBU, IERONIM

SERGHI, CELLA
SEVER, ALEXANDRU
SILVIU, GEORGE
SIMA, HORIA
SOARE, IULIA
SPINA, GERI
STERN, ADOLPHE
STEUERMAN, ADOLF RODION
SULITEANU, GISELA
TELLER, ZEVI LAZAR
TERTULIAN, NICOLAE
TOMA, A.
TRIVALE, ION
TZARA, TRISTAN
VEREA, ADRIAN
VICOL, ADRIAN
VORONCA, ILARIE
WALD, HENRI
WECHSLER, MAX
WEISS, AURELIU
ZISSU, ABRAHAM LEIB

7) Russia & Former Soviet Union
Main Surveys
RUSSIA
RUSSIAN LITERATURE

General Entries
AGRICULTURE
ASSIMILATION
CANTONISTS
COSMOPOLITANS
CRIMEAN AFFAIR
DOCTORS' PLOT
DUMA
GERY
HAIDAMACKS
JEWISH STUDIES
KAZYONNY RAVVIN
KHAZARS
KRIMCHAK LANGUAGE
KRIMCHAKS
MAY LAWS
MOUNTAIN JEWS
PALE OF SETTLEMENT
PETROGRAD CONFERENCE
POGROMS
REFUSENIKS
SARKIL

Communities
ABKHAZIYA (AUTONOMOUS SOVIET SOCIALIST
   REPUBLIC)
ALEKSANDRIYA
ALEKSANDRIYA
ANANYEV
ANAPA
ARCHANGEL
ARMENIA
ARTEMOVSK

ASHKHABAD
ASTRAKHAN
ATAKI
ATIL
AZERBAIJAN
BAKHCHISARAI
BAKU
BALANJAR
BALTA
BAR
BARANOVICHI
BATUMI
BAUSKA
BELARUS
BELAYA TSERKOV
BELGOROD-DNESTROVSKI
BELORUSSIA
BELTSY
BELZ
BERDICHEV
BERDYANSK
BEREGOVO
BERESTECHKO
BEREZA
BEREZHANY
BEREZINO
BEREZOVKA
BERSHAD
BESSARABIA
BIROBIDZHAN
BIRZAI
BIRZULA
BOBROVY KUT
BOBRUISK
BOGUSLAV
BOJAN
BOLEKHOV (Bolechow)
BORISLAV
BORISOV
BRAILOV
BRASLAV
BRATSLAV
BREST-LITOVSK
BRICEVA
BRICHANY
BRYANSK
BUKHARA
BYKHOV
CAUCASUS
CHERKASSY
CHERNIGOV
CHERNOBYL
CHERNOVTSY
CHORTKOV
CHUDNOV
CHUFUT-KALE
COURLAND
CRIMEA
DAUGAVPILS
DAVID-GORODOK

LYAKHOVICHI
LYUBOML
MAKAROV
MARCULESTI
MEDZIBEZH (Medzibozh)
MELITOPOL
MERV
MEZHIRECH (Mezhirichi)
MINSK
MIR
MOGILEV
MOGILEV-PODOLSKI
MOLDOVA (Moldavia)
MOLODECHNO
MONASTYRISKA
MOSCOW
MOSTISKA
MOZYR
MSTISLAVL
MUKACHEVO
NADVORNAYA (Nadworna)
NEMIROV
NESVIZH
NEZHIN
NIKOLAYEV
NOVAYA USHITSA
NOVGOROD-SEVERSK
NOVOGRUDOK
NOVOSELITSA
NOVOZYBKOV
NOVY DVOR
NOVY OLEKSINIEC
ODESSA
OLESKO
OLGOPOL
OLYKA
OMSK
ORDZHONIKIDZE
OREL
ORGEYEV (Orhei)
ORSHA
OSHMYANY
OSTROG (Ostraha)
OSTRYNA
OVRUCH
OZERY
PALANGA
PAVLOGRAD
PAVOLOCH
PEREYASLAV-KHMELNITSKI
PERVOMAISK
PINSK
PIRYATIN
POCHEP
PODGAITSY
PODKAMEN
PODOLIA
PODVOLOCHISK (Podwloczyska)
POGREBISHCHENSKI (Pogrebishche)
POLONNOYE

POLOTSK
POLTAVA
PRILUKI
PROSKUROV
PRUZHANY
RADOMYSHL
RADOSHKOVICHI (Radoszkowice)
RADUN
RADZIWILLOW
RECHITSA
REZEKNE (Rezhitsa)
RIGA
ROGACHEV
ROGATIN
ROMNY
ROSTOV
ROVNO
ROZDOL
RUZHANY
SADAGORA
SAMANDAR (Khazar)
SAMARKAND
SARATOV
SARNY
SASOV
SATANOV
SEKIRYANY
SEVASTOPOL
SHARGOROD
SHCHEDRIN
SHEPETOVKA
SHKLOV
SHPOLA
SIBERIA
SIMFEROPOL
SKALAT
SKIDEL
SKOLE
SKVIRA
SLAVUTA
SLONIM
SLUTSK
SMELA
SMOLENSK
SMORGON (Smorgonie)
SNYATYN
SOKAL
STANISLAV
STARODUB
STARO-KONSTANTINOV
STOLBTSY
STOLIN
STOROZHINETS
ST. PETERSBURG
STRY (Stryj)
SUBCARPATHIAN RUTHENIA
SVISLOCH
TADZHIKISTAN
TAGANROG
TALLINN

I. HISTORY
B. MEDIEVAL & MODERN PERIOD
2. Regional History
f. *Eastern Europe*
7) Russia & Former Soviet Union
COMMUNITIES (*continued*)

TALNOYE
TARNOPOL
TARTU
TARUTINO
TASHKENT
TIFLIS
TLUMACH (Tlumacz)
TOLSTOYE
TOMASHPOL
TOMSK
TORCHIN (Torczyn)
TUCHIN
TUKUMS
TULCHIN
TURKA
TYSMENITSA (Tysmienica)
UFA
UKRAINE
UMAN
UZBEKISTAN
UZHGOROD
VAD RASHKOV
VALEA-LUI-VLAD
VASILKOV
VELIZH
VENTSPILS
VERKHNEUDINSK
VINNITSA
VISHNEVETS
VITEBSK
VIZHNITSA
VLADIMIR VOLYNSKI
VLADIVOSTOK
VOLHYNIA
VOLKOVYSK
VOLOZHIN
VOLPA
VORONEZH
VOZNESSENK
VYSOKOYE
YALTA
YAVOROV
YEFINGAR
YEVPATORIYA
ZABOLOTOV
ZALESHCHIKI
ZAPOROZHE
ZASTAVNA
ZBARAZH
ZBOROV
ZELVA (Zelwa)
ZHDANOV
ZHIDACHOV

ZHITOMIR
ZHMERINKA
ZHOLKVA
ZHURAVNO
ZLATOPOL
ZOLOCHEV
ZOLOTONOSHA
ZVENIGORODKA

ORGANIZATIONS
AM OLAM
ANTI-FASCIST COMMITTEE, JEWISH
BENEI MOSHE
DECEMBRISTS
DEPUTIES OF THE JEWISH PEOPLE
FOLKSPARTEI
HE-HALUTZ
INDEPENDENT JEWISH WORKERS PARTY
JEWISH SOCIALIST WORKERS PARTY
JEWISH SOCIETY FOR HISTORY AND
    ETHNOGRAPHY
KOMZET
NES ZIYYONAH
NEW ISRAEL
OCTOBRISTS
ODESSA COMMITTEE
SOCIETY FOR THE ATTAINMENT OF FULL CIVIL
    RIGHTS FOR THE JEWISH PEOPLE IN RUSSIA
SOCIETY FOR THE PROMOTION OF CULTURE
    AMONG THE JEWS OF RUSSIA
UNION OF THE RUSSIAN PEOPLE
UNITED JEWISH SOCIALIST WORKERS PARTY
VOZROZHDENIYE
YEKOPO
YEVREYSKI KOMISSARIAT
YEVSEKTSIYA
ZIONIST SOCIALIST WORKERS PARTY

PUBLICATIONS
EYNIKEYT
HA-MELIZ
HA-SHILOAH
HA-YOM
MORIAH
RAZSVET
SOVETISH HEYMLAND
VOSKHOD

BIOGRAPHIES
Academic Life
ABRAMOWICZ, DINA
ADMONI, VLADIMIR GRIGORYEVICH
AGURSKY, MIKHAIL
AMUSIN, JOSEPH
ANISIMOV, ILYA SHERBATOVICH
BERLIN, ISRAEL
BERLIN, MOSES
BERSHADSKI, SERGEY ALEXANDROVICH
BOGORAZ, VLADIMIR GERMANOVICH
BORISOV, ANDREY YAKOVLEVICH

BOROVOY, SAUL YAKOVLEVICH
BRAUDO, ALEXANDER ISAYEVICH
BUCHBINDER, NAHUM
CHORNY, JOSEPH JUDAH
CHWOLSON, DANIEL
DEBORIN, ABRAM MOISEYEVICH
DUBNOW, SIMON
EDELMANN, ZEVI HIRSCH
ELKIND, ARKADI DANILOVICH
FRANK, SEMYON LYUDVIGOVICH
GALANT, ELIAHU (IIya) VLADIMIROVICH
GAPONOV, BORIS (Dov)
GINSBURG, SAUL
GOLDSTEIN, SALWIAN
GORDIN, JACOB
GRANDE, BENZION MOISEEVICH
GURLAND, HAYYIM JONAH
HARKAVY, ALBERT (Abraham Elijah)
HERZENSTEIN, MIKHAIL YAKOVLEVICH
HESSEN, JULIUS ISIDOROVICH
HORODEZKY, SAMUEL ABBA
HOROWITZ, HAYYIM DOV
ISRAELSOHN, JACOB IZRAILEVICH
JOCHELSON, VLADIMIR (Waldemar)
KAHANA, DAVID
KATZENELSON, JUDAH LEIB BENJAMIN
KIRZHNITZ, ABRAHAM
KLATZKIN, JACOB
KOIGEN, DAVID
KOKOVTSOV, PAUL KONSTANTINOVICH
LEKHNO, DAVID
LEONTOVICH, FEDOR
LESTSCHINSKY, JACOB
LEVIN (Lefin), MENAHEM MENDEL
LEVIN, MAKSIM GRIGORYEVICH
LEVINSOHN, ISAAC BAER
LIBERMAN, YEVSEY GRIGORYEVICH
LOTMAN, YURI MIKHAILOVICH
LOZINSKI, SAMUEL
LURIA, ALEXANDER ROMANOVICH
LURIA, DAVID BEN JACOB AARON
MAGGID, DAVID
MANDELSTAMM, BENJAMIN
MANDELSTAMM, LEON
MAREK, PESACH (Piotr)
MARGOLIN, MOSES
MARKEL-MOSESSOHN, MIRIAM
MARKON, ISAAC DOV BER
MARSHAK, SAMUEL YAKOVLEVICH
MINOR, SOLOMON ZALMAN (Zalkind)
MITIN, MARK BORISOVICH
NEKLYUDOV, NICOLAI ADRIANOVICH
NEVAKHOVICH, JUDAH LEIB
NIKITIN, VICTOR
ORSHANSKI, ILYA (Elijah) GRIGORYEVICH
OSTROGORSKI, MOSES
PEREFERKOVICH, NEHEMIAH
PINSKER, SIMHAH
POSENER, SOLOMON
RABINOVICH, YEHUDAH LEIB (Leon)

RABINOWITZ, ZEVI HA-COHEN
RAFFALOVICH, ARTHUR GERMANOVICH
RUBINSTEIN, SERGEY LEONIDOVICH
SHESTOV, LEV
SLATKINE, MENAHEM MENDEL
SOLOVIEV, VLADIMIR
SOSIS, ISRAEL
STANISLAVSKY, SIMON JUDAH
STERNBERG, LEV YAKOVLEVICH
SUBBOTIN, ANDREY PAVLOVICH
VARGA, YEVGENI SAMOILOVICH
VINNIKOV, ISAAC N.
VOLYNSKI, AKIM LEVOVICH
VYGOTSKI, LEV SEMYONOVICH
WARSHAWSKY, ISAAC
WEISSENBERG, SAMUEL ABRAMOVICH
WIENER, SAMUEL
WILENSKY, MICHAEL
WUNDERBAR, REUBEN JOSEPH
ZAND, MICHAEL
ZEITLIN (Zeitlis), JOSHUA
ZEITLIN, WILLIAM (Zeev)
ZHIRMUNSKY, VIKTOR MAKSIMOVICH

Art
AIZENBERG, NINA
ALTMAN, NATHAN
ANTOKOLSKI, MARK (Mordecai)
ASKNAZI, ISAAC LVOVICH
AXELROD, MEYER
BAKST, LEON
CHAPIRO, JACQUES
GRILICHES, AVENIR
GUENZBURG, ILYA YAKOVLEVICH
JUDIN, SAMUEL
KAPLAN, ANATOLI LVOVICH
KUZKOVSKI, JOSEPH
LEVITAN, ISAAC ILITCH
LISSITZKY, EL (Lazar)
NEIZVESTNY, ERNST
PAOVLOTZKY, RAUL
PASTERNAK, LEONID OSIPOVICH
PEVSNER, ANTON AND NAUM NEHEMIA
  (Gabo)
RABIN, OSCAR
RYBACK, ISSACHAR
SEROV, VALENTIN
SOUTINE, CHAIM
TATLIN, VLADIMIR E.
ZHITNITSKI, MARK

Literature
AGURSKY, SAMUEL
AIKHENVALD, YULI ISAYEVICH
AIZMAN, DAVID YAKOVLEVICH
ALDANOV, MARK
ALIGER, MARGARITA YOSIFOVNA
ALTAUZEN, YAKOV MOYSEYEVICH
ANTOKOLSKI, PAVEL GRIGOREVICH
AVERBAKH, LEOPOLD LEONIDOVICH

I. HISTORY
B. MEDIEVAL & MODERN PERIOD
2. Regional History
f. Eastern Europe
7) Russia & Former Soviet Union
BIOGRAPHIES
Literature (continued)

BAAZOV, HERZL
BABEL, ISAAC EMMANUILOVICH
BAGRITSKI, EDUARD GEORGIYEVICH
BELINKOV, ARKADII VIKTOROVICH
BELOV, A.
BEN-ADIR
BEN-AMMI, MORDECAI
BILL-BELOTSERKOVSKI, VLADIMIR NAUMOVICH
BOGROV, GRIGORI ISAAKOVICH
BRIK, OSIP MAKSIMOVICH
BRODSKI, YOSIF
BYADULYA-YASAKAR, ZMITROK
CHAKOVSKI, ALEXANDER BORISOVICH
CHERNY, SASHA
DANIEL, M.
DANIEL, YULI MARKOVICH
DOLMATOVSKI, YEVGENI ARONOVICH
DOMALSKY, I.
DUBNOW-ERLICH, SOPHIA
EHRENBURG, ILYA GRIGORYEVICH
EICHENBAUM, BORIS MIKHAILOVICH
FEYGENBERG, RAKHEL
FRIEDLAENDER, SOLOMON JUDAH
FRUG, SHIMON SHMUEL
GALICH, ALEXANDR ARKADYEVICH
GEKHT, SEMEN GRIGOREVICH
GERSHENZON, MIKHAIL OSIPOVICH
GILELS, EMIL GRIGORYEVICH
GINSBURG, EVGENIA SEMIONOVNA
GODINER, SAMUEL NISSAN
GOLODNY, MIKHAIL
GORDON, SHMUEL
GORKI, MAXIM
GORSHMAN, SHIRA
GRANIN, DANIEL ALEKSANDROVICH
GROSSMAN, LEONID PETROVICH
GROSSMAN, VASILI SEMYONOVICH
GUKOVSKY, GRIGORY ALEKSANDROVICH
ILF, ILYA
ILIN, M.
INBER, VERA MIKHAILOVNA
ISBAKH, ALEXANDER ABRAMOVICH
KANNEGISER, LEONID AKIMOVICH
KANOVICH, GRIGORY
KASSIL, LEV ABRAMOVICH
KAVERIN, BENJAMIN ALEKSANDROVICH
KAZAKEVICH, EMMANUIL GENRIKHOVICH
KHODASEVICH, VLADISLAV FELITSIANOVICH
KIPEN, ALEKSANDR ABRAMOVICH
KIRSANOV, SEMYON ISAAKOVICH
KIRSHON, VLADIMIR MIKHAILOVICH
KNUT, DOVID

KOROLENKO, VLADIMIR GALAKTIONOVICH
KOZAKOV, MIKHAIL EMMANUILOVICH
KRYMOV, YURI
KUSHNER, ALEKSANDER SEMENOVICH
LERNER, JOSEPH JUDAH
LESKOV, NIKOLAY SEMYONOVICH
LEVANDA, LEV (Leo; Yehudah Leib) OSIPOVICH
LIBEDINSKI, YURI NIKOLAYEVICH
LIVSHITS, BENEDIKT KONSTANTINOVICH
LUNTS, LEV NATANOVICH
MAMISTABOLOB, ABRAHAM
MANDELSHTAM, NADEZHDA YAKOVLEVNA
MANDELSHTAM, OSIP EMILYEVICH
MINSKI, NIKOLAI MAXIMOVICH
NADSON, SEMYON YAKOVLEVICH
NOTOVICH, OSIP KONSTANTINOVICH
NUSINOV, ISAAC
OSIPOVICH, NAHUM
PARNAKH, VALENTIN YAKOVLEVICH
PASTERNAK, BORIS LEONIDOVICH
RABINOVICH, OSIP ARONOVICH
SELVINSKI, ILYA LVOVICH
SHKLOVSKI, ISAAC VLADIMIROVICH
SLONIM, MARC
SLONIMSKI, MIKHAIL LEONIDOVICH
SLUTSKI, BORIS ABRAMOVICH
SOBOL, ANDREY MIKHAILOVICH
SVETLOV, MIKHAIL
SVIRSKI, ALEXEY IVANOVICH
TUR BROTHERS
TYNYANOV, YURI NIKOLAYEVICH
UTKIN, JOSEPH PAVLOVICH
WENGEROFF, PAULINE
WENGEROFF, SEMYON AFANASYEVICH
YAHUDI, YUSUF
YEVTUSHENKO, YEVGENI ALEXANDROVICH
YUSHKEVICH, SEMYON SOLOMONOVICH

Music
ABELIOVICH, LEV MOYSSEYEVICH
ABRASS, OSIAS (Joshua)
ALSHVANG, ARNOLD ALEKSANDROVICH
ARONOVICH, YURI MIKHAYLOVICH
BABIN, VICTOR
BACHMANN, JACOB
BARSHAI, RUDOLPH
BELY, VICTOR ARKADYEVICH (Aronovich)
BEREGOVSKI, MOSHE
BLUMENTHAL, NISSAN,
BRODSKY, ADOLF
BRUSSILOVSKY, YEVGENI GRIGORYEVICH
CHAGY, BERELE
CHERNIAVSKY
DAVYDOV, KARL YULYEVICH
DUNAYEVSKI, ISAAC OSIPOVICH
EIFMAN, BORIS
ENGEL, JOEL (Yuli Dimitriyevich)
GEROVICH, ELIEZER MORDECAI BEN ISAAC
GLIÈRE, REINHOLD MORITZEVICH

GNESIN, MIKHAIL FABIANOVICH
KOGAN, LEONID BORISSOVICH
KROSHNER, MIKHAIL YEFIMOVICH
LAMM, PAVEL ALEKSANDROVICH
LIFSHITZ, NEHAMAH
LITINSKI, GENRIKH ILYICH
MESSERER, ASAF MIKHAILOVICH
MINKOWSKI, PINCHAS
NOWAKOWSKI, DAVID
OISTRAKH, DAVID FEDOROVICH
PANOV, VALERY
PLISETSKAYA, MAYA
RUBINSTEIN, IDA
SLONIMSKY, SERGEI MIKHAILOVICH
SPIVAKOVSKY, TOSSY
STEINBERG, MAXIMILIAN OSSEJEVICH
TSFASSMAN, ALEXANDER NAUMOVICH
VEINBERG, MOISSEY SAMUILOVICH
VEPRIK, ALEXANDER MOISEYEVITCH
WEINBERG, JACOB
ZHITOMIRSKI, ALEXANDER MATVEYEVITCH

Popular Culture
ABRAMOWITZ, BINA
BERNSTEIN, OSIP SAMOILOVICH
BOLESLAVSKI, ISAAC
BOTVINNIK, MIKHAIL
BRONSTEIN, DAVID
DONSKOY, MARK SEMENOVICH
EISENSTEIN, SERGEI MIKHAILOVICH
FLOHR, SALO
FRIED, LAZAR
GOLDENBURG, SAMUEL
GOMELSKY, ALEXANDER
GOROKHOVSKAYA, MARIA
GRANOVSKY, ALEXANDER
GUZIK, HANNA
KALIK, MIKHAIL
KASPAROV, GARY
KORCHNOY, VIKTOR LVOVICH
KRISS, GRIGORY
LEONIDOV, LEONID MIRONOVICH
LOYTER, EFRAIM BARUKHOVICH
MIKHOELS, SOLOMON
MOSCOVITCH, MAURICE
NIMZOVITCH, AARON
RAYKIN, ARKADI ISAAKOVICH
RUNITSCH, OSSIP
SLUTSKAYA, IRINA
TAL, MIKHAIL
VERTOV, DZIGA

Public & Economic Life
ABRAMOVICH, ROMAN ARKADYEVICH
ABRAMOWITZ, GRIGORI
ABRAMOWITZ, RAPHAEL
ACOSTA, JOAN D
ALEXANDER
AMSTERDAM, ABRAHAM MEIR
ARONSON, GRIGORI

ASHANSKI, ABEL-AARON ITSKOVICH
AXELROD, LUBOV
AXELROD, PAVEL BORISOVICH
AZARKH, RAISA MOYSEYEVNA
AZEFF, ZEVNO FISHELEVICH
BAKST, NICOLAI (Noah) IGNATYEVICH
BAKUNIN, MIKHAIL ALEKSANDROYICH
BARATZ, HERMANN (Hirsch)
BARBASH, SAMUEL
BARZILAI, YEHOSHUA
BEILIS, MENAHEM MENDEL
BELKOWSKY, ZEVI HIRSCH (Grigori)
BEREZOVSKY, BORIS ABROMOVICH
BERMANN, VASILI (Ze'ev Wolf)
BERNSTEIN, NATHAN OSIPOVICH
BERNSTEIN-KOGAN (Cohen), JACOB
BIENSTOK, JUDAH LEIB
BIKERMAN, JOSEPH
BLIOKH, IVAN STANISLAVOVICH
BLUMENFELD, EMANUEL
BLUMENFELD, HERMANN FADDEYEVICH
BOGROV, DMITRI
BONNER, ELENA GEORGIEVNA
BOROCHOV, BER (Dov)
BORODIN, MICHAEL MARKOVITSCH
BRAFMAN, JACOB
BRAMSON, LEON (Leonty)
BRANDT, BORIS (Baruch)
BRAUN, ABRAHAM
BRODSKI
BRUCK, GRIGORI
BRUTZKUS, BORIS DOV
BRUTZKUS, JULIUS
BUCHMIL, JOSHUA HESHEL
BULAN
BUNIN, HAYYIM ISAAC
CATHERINE II
CHMIELNICKI, BOGDAN
DAN, FYODOR ILYICH
DASHEWSKI, PINHAS
DENIKIN, ANTON IVANOVICH
DERZHAVIN, GABRIEL ROMANOVICH
DEUTSCH, LEO (Lev Grigoryevich)
DIMANSTEIN, SIMON
DISKIN, CHAIM
DOBIN, SHIMON (Shimoni)
DRAGUNSKI, DAVID ABRAMOVICH
DUBIN, MORDECAI
DUBNOW, ZE'EV
DYMSHYTS, VENIAMIN E.
EFRON, ILYA
EHRLICH, EUGEN
EICHENBAUM (Gelber), JACOB
EISENSTADT, ISAIAH (Isay)
EISMANN, MOSES
ELIASBERG, MORDECAI
ESTHER
FEINBERG, DAVID
FOMIN, YEFIM MOISEYEVICH
FRIEDLAND

I. HISTORY
B. MEDIEVAL & MODERN PERIOD
2. Regional History
f. Eastern Europe
7) Russia & Former Soviet Union
BIOGRAPHIES
Public & Economic Life (continued)

FRIEDMAN, NAPHTALI
FRUMKIN, BORIS MARKOVICH
FUENN, SAMUEL JOSEPH
GAMARNIK, YAN BORISOVICH
GELFOND (Gelfand), ALEXANDER
　　LAZAREVICH (Israel)
GERSHUNI, GRIGORI ANDREYEVICH
GOLDBERG, ISAAC LEIB
GOLDBERG, J. B.
GOLDENBERG-GETROITMAN, LAZAR
GOLDENWEISER, ALEXANDER
　　SOLOMONOVICH
GOLDSTEIN, ALEXANDER
GOLITSYN, COUNT NIKOLAI NIKOLAYEVICH
GOTS
GOZHANSKY, SAMUEL
GRULEV, MIKHAIL VLADIMIROVICH
GRUNBERG, ABRAHAM
GRUSENBERG, OSCAR OSIPOVICH
GUENZBURG
GUENZBURG
GUREVICH, MOSHE
GUSEV, SERGEI IVANOVICH
GUSINSKY, VLADIMIR ALEXANDROVICH
HELFMAN, HESSIA MEYEROVNA
HESSEN, JOSEPH VLADIMIROVICH
HORODISCHTSCH, LEON
HOROWITZ, AARON JUDAH LOEB (Leon)
IGNATYEV, COUNT NIKOLAI PAVLOVICH
JASINOWSKI, ISRAEL ISIDORE
JOFFE, ADOLPH ABRAMOVICH
JOSEPH
KAGANOVICH, LAZAR MOISEYEVICH
KAHAN, BARUCH MORDECAI
KAMENEV, LEV BORISOVICH
KATKOV, MIKHAIL NIKIFOROVICH
KATZENELSON, NISSAN
KAUFMAN, AVRAHAM YOSIFOVICH
KHODORKOVSKY, MIKHAIL BORISOVICH
KOL'TSOV, MIKHAIL
KOSSOVSKY, VLADIMIR
KOSTOMAROV, NIKOLAI IVANOVICH
KREININ, MEIR
KREISER, JACOB GRIGORYEVICH
KREMER, ARKADI (Aaron, Alexander)
KRUSHEVAN, PAVOLAKI
KULISHER
KUPERNIK; ABRAHAM
KURSKY, FRANZ
LANDAU, ADOLPH
LANDAU, GREGORY ADOLFOVICH
LARIN, YURI

LASERSON, MAX
LATZKY-BERTHOLDI, JACOB ZE'EV WOLF
　　(Wilhelm)
LENIN, VLADIMIR ILYICH
LESTSCHINSKY, JOSEPH
LEVIN, EMANUEL
LEVIN, SHMARYA
LEVINE, EUGENE
LEVIN-SHATZKES, YIZHAK
LIPMAN, LEVI
LITVINOV, MAXIM MAXIMOVICH
LOZOVSKI, SOLOMON ABRAMOVICH (Dridzo)
LUBARSKY, ABRAHAM ELIJAH
LVOVICH, DAVID
MANDELBERG, AVIGDOR (Victor)
MANDELSTAMM, MAX EMMANUEL
MANEVICH, LEV YEFIMOVICH
MARGOLIN, ARNOLD
MARTOV, JULIUS
MAZEH, JACOB
MEDEM, VLADIMIR
MEISEL, NOAH
MEKHLIS, LEV ZAKHAROVICH
MINOR, OSIP S. (Joseph)
MINTZ, PAUL
MORDOVTSEV, DANIIL LUKICH
MORDVINOV, NICOLAI SEMIONOVICH
MORGULIS, MANASSEH (Mikhail)
MYSH, MICHAEL
NAIDITSCH, ISAAC ASHER
NATANSON, MARK
NEVZLIN, LEONID
NICHOLAS
NISSELOVICH, LEOPOLD (Eliezer)
NOTKIN, NATA
NOVOMEYSKY, MOSHE
NOVOSILTSEV, NICOLAI NIKOLAYEVICH
NUDEL, IDA
NUROCK, MORDECHAI
OBADIAH
OLGIN, MOSHE J.
PASSOVER, ALEXANDER
PAUL I
PERETZ, ABRAHAM
PERGAMENT, OSIP YAKOVLEVICH
PETLYURA, SIMON
PINSKER, LEON (Judah Leib)
PLEHVE, VYACHESLAV KONSTANTINOVICH
　　VON
POBEDONOSTSEV, KONSTANTIN PETROVICH
POLYAKOV
PORTUGALOV, BENJAMIN OSIPOVICH
RADEK, KARL
RAFES, MOSES
RATNER, MARC BORISOVICH
REVUSKY, ABRAHAM
ROSENTHAL, LEON (Judah Leib)
SCHATZ-ANIN, MAX
SCHWARZ, SOLOMON
SHARANSKY, NATAN (Anatoly)

SHEFTEL, MIKHAIL
SHMUSHKEVICH, YAACOV
SILBERFARB, MOSES
SLIOZBERG, HENRY
SLONIMSKI, LEONID ZINOVYEVICH
SPEYER, BENJAMIN
STALIN, JOSEPH VISSARIONOVICH
STEINBERG, ISAAC NAHMAN
STERN, BEZALEL
STERN, GRIGORI
STIEGLITZ
SVERDLOV, YAKOV MIKHAILOVICH
SYRKIN, JOSHUA (Grigory)
SYRKIN, MOSES NAHUM SOLOMONOVICH
TARNOPOL, JOACHIM HAYYIM
TEITEL, JACOB
TEMKIN, ASHER
TIOMKIN, VLADIMIR (Ze'ev)
TROTSKY, LEV DAVIDOVICH
TSHEMERISKI, ALEXANDER (Solomon)
UVAROV, SERGEY SEMYONOVICH
VARSHAVSKI, ABRAHAM
VINAWER, MAXIM
VOZNITSYN, ALEXANDER ARTEMYEVICH
WALDMANN, ISRAEL
WEINRUB, MATVEY
WEINSTEIN, AARON
WEIZMANN
WITTE, SERGEY YULYEVICH, COUNT
YAKIR, YONAH
YAROSLAVSKY, YEMELYAN
ZAK, ABRAM
ZAM, ZVI HERZ
ZASLAVSKY, DAVID
ZEDERBAUM, ALEXANDER
ZEITLIN, HILLEL
ZEMLYACHKA (Zalkind), ROZALIYA
    SAMOYLOVNA
ZINOVIEV, GRIGORI YEVSEYEVICH
ZLATOPOLSKY, HILLEL
ZUCKERMANN, ELIEZER
ZUNDELEVITCH, AARON

Religion
ABU 'IMRĀN AL-TIFLĪSĪ
EPSTEIN, BARUCH HA-LEVI
JEWNIN, ABRAHAM JONAH
LILIENTHAL, MAX (Menahem)
MASKILEISON, ABRAHAM BEN JUDAH LEIB
MOSES OF KIEV
OLSCHWANGER, ISAAC WOLF
RABINOWICH (Rabinowitsch), ELIYAHU
    AKIVA
ROSEN, JOSEPH BEN ISAAC
SCHLIEFER, SOLOMON
SERL BAS JACOB BEN WOLF KRANZ
SILBERSTEIN, SOLOMON JOSEPH
VOLOZHINER, HAYYIM BEN ISAAC
VOLOZHINER, ISAAC BEN HAYYIM
WIERNIKORSKI, JUDAH

YOFFEY
ZIRELSON, JUDAH LEIB

Science
ABELMANN, ILYA SOLOMOVITCH
ABRAMOWITZ, EMIL
ALFEROV, ZHOREZ I.
BAKST, NICOLAI (Noah) IGNATYEVICH
CYON, ELIE DE
FRANK, ILJA MIKHAILOVICH
FREIDLINA, RAKHIL KHATSKELEVNA
FRENKEL, JACOB ILICH
FROLKIS, VLADIMIR VENIAMIOVICH
FRUMKIN, ALEKSANDR NAUMOVICH
GELFAND, IZRAIL MOISEVICH
GELFOND, ALEKSANDR OSIPOVICH
GINZBURG, VITALY LAZAREVICH
GRINBERG, ALEKSANDER ABRAMOVICH
GUREVICH, MIKHAIL IOSIFOVICH
GURWITSCH, ALEXANDER GAVRILOVICH
JOFFE, ABRAHAM FEODOROVICH
KABACHNIK, MARTIN IZRAILOVICH
KANTOROVICH, LEONID
KAZARNOVSKI, ISAAC ABRAMOVICH
LANDAU, LEV DAVIDOVICH
LIPKIN, YOM TOV LIPMAN
LOEWINSON-LESSING, FRANZ YULYEVICH
MANDELSHTAM, LEONID ISAAKOVICH
PIROGOV, NIKOLAI
RABINOVICH, ISAAK MOSEYEVICH
ROGINSKI, SIMON ZALMANOVICH
SAMOILOVICH, RUDOLPH LAZAREVICH
STERN, LINA SOLOMONOVNA
TALMUD, DAVID L.
TAMM, IGOR YEVGENYEVICH
VEKSLER, VLADIMIR
ZELDOVICH, YAKOV BORISOVICH
ZENKEVICH, LEV ALEKSANDROVICH
ZILBER, LEV ALEKSANDROVICH

8) Yugoslavia
   MAIN SURVEYS
   YUGOSLAVIA
   YUGOSLAV LITERATURE

   COMMUNITIES
   ADA
   BANJA LUKA
   BELGRADE
   DUBROVNIK
   LJUBLJANA
   MARIBOR
   MONASTIR
   NIS
   NOVI SAD
   OCHRIDA
   OSIJEK (Eszek)
   RIJEKA
   SARAJEVO
   SENTA

I. HISTORY
B. MEDIEVAL & MODERN PERIOD
2. Regional History
f. *Eastern Europe*
8) Yugoslavia
COMMUNITIES (*continued*)

SKOPLJE (Skopje)
SOMBOR
SPLIT
SUBOTICA
TRAVNIK
VARAZDIN
VINKOVCI
ZAGREB
ZEMUN
ZENICA
ZRENJANIN

BIOGRAPHIES
ALBAHARI, DAVID
ALBALA, DAVID
ALCALAY, ISAAC
ALKALAI, DAVID
ALKALAJ, ARON
BARUH, BORA
BIHALJI MERIN, OTO
DAVIČO, HAJIM S.
DAVIČO, LUJO
DAVIČO, OSCAR
DAVID, FILIP
DEBRECENJI, JOZEF
DOHANJ, JULIJE
ERLICH, VERA STEIN
EVENTOV, YAKIR
FELDMAN, MIROSLAV
FINCI, ELI
FREIBERGER, MIROSLAV SALOM
GLID, NANDOR
GOTTLIEB, HINKO
HABILLO, ELISHA
HAJIM, JISRAEL
HERMAN, OSKAR
IVANJI, IVAN
JUN-BRODA, INA
KADELBURG, LAVOSLAV
KAMHI, LEON
KIŠ, DANILO (Daniel)
KONFINO, ZAK
LEBOVIČ, DJORDJE
LEVI, MORITZ
LICHT, ALEXANDER
LIVNI, HILLEL
LOEWENTHAL, ZDENKO
MANDL, SAADIA
NAHMIJAS, DANILO
NAJMAN, JULIJA
OFNER, FRANCIS-AMIR
PAPO, IZIDOR JOSEF
PIJADE, MOSA

ROMANO, SAMUEL
ROTEM, CVI (ZVI)
SAMOKOVLIJA, ISAK
ŠINKO, ERVIN
TIŠMA, ALEKSANDAR
VAJS, ALBERT

g. United States
MAIN SURVEYS
AMERICA
UNITED STATES LITERATURE
UNITED STATES OF AMERICA

GENERAL ENTRIES
AGRICULTURE
ART
ASSIMILATION
BLACK-JEWISH RELATIONS IN U.S.
CEMETERY
CHOIRS
CONSERVATIVE JUDAISM
FAMILY, AMERICAN JEWISH
GALVESTON PLAN
HISTORIOGRAPHY
HOSPITALS
JEWISH STUDIES
LABOR
LOEB-LEOPOLD CASE
NEW LEFT
NEWSPAPERS, HEBREW
PITTSBURGH PLATFORM
POLLARD AFFAIR
RABBINICAL TRAINING, AMERICAN
RECONSTRUCTIONISM
REFORM JUDAISM
ROSENBERG CASE

COMMUNITIES
AKRON
ALABAMA
ALASKA
ALBANY
ALBUQUERQUE
ANN ARBOR
ARIZONA
ARKANSAS
ATLANTA
ATLANTIC CITY
AUSTIN
BALTIMORE
BERGEN COUNTY
BIRMINGHAM
BOSTON
BRIDGEPORT
BROWARD COUNTY
BUFFALO
CALIFORNIA
CAMDEN
CHARLESTON
CHARLOTTE

I. HISTORY
B. MEDIEVAL & MODERN PERIOD
2. Regional History
g. *United States*
COMMUNITIES (*continued*)

TOLEDO
TRENTON
TUCSON
UNION COUNTY
UTAH
UTICA
VERMONT
VINELAND
VIRGINIA
VIRGIN ISLANDS
WASHINGTON
WASHINGTON, D.C.
WEST VIRGINIA
WESTCHESTER COUNTY
WILKES-BARRE AND KINGSTON
WILMINGTON
WISCONSIN
WORCESTER
WYOMING
YOUNGSTOWN

ORGANIZATIONS
AMERICA-ISRAEL CULTURAL FOUNDATION
AMERICAN ACADEMY FOR JEWISH RESEARCH
AMERICAN ASSOCIATION FOR JEWISH EDUCATION
AMERICAN COUNCIL FOR JUDAISM
AMERICAN GATHERING OF JEWISH HOLOCAUST
    SURVIVORS
AMERICAN ISRAEL PUBLIC AFFAIRS COMMITTEE
    (AIPAC)
AMERICAN JEWISH ARCHIVES
AMERICAN JEWISH COMMITTEE
AMERICAN JEWISH CONFERENCE
AMERICAN JEWISH CONGRESS
AMERICAN JEWISH HISTORICAL SOCIETY
AMERICAN SEPHARDI FEDERATION
AMERICAN SOCIETY FOR JEWISH MUSIC
AMERICAN ZIONIST MOVEMENT (AZM)
AMIT: MIZRACHI WOMEN'S ORGANIZATION OF
    AMERICA
ANTI-DEFAMATION LEAGUE
ASSOCIATION FOR JEWISH STUDIES
BALTIMORE HEBREW UNIVERSITY
B'NAI B'RITH
BOARD OF DELEGATES OF AMERICAN ISRAELITES
BONDS, STATE OF ISRAEL
BRANDEIS UNIVERSITY
BRANDEIS-BARDIN INSTITUT
BRITH ABRAHAM
CENTER FOR JEWISH HISTORY
CENTRAL CONFERENCE OF AMERICAN
    RABBIS
CITY OF HOPE NATIONAL MEDICAL CENTER
CLAL

COALITION FOR THE ADVANCEMENT OF JEWISH
    EDUCATION
CONFERENCE OF PRESIDENTS OF MAJOR
    AMERICAN JEWISH ORGANIZATIONS
CONFERENCE ON JEWISH SOCIAL STUDIES
CONGRESS FOR JEWISH CULTURE
COUNCIL OF JEWISH FEDERATIONS AND WELFARE
    FUNDS
DROPSIE UNIVERSITY
EDAH
EMMA LAZARUS FEDERATION OF JEWISH
    WOMEN'S CLUBS
ETHICAL CULTURE
FARBAND
FREE SONS OF ISRAEL
GRATZ COLLEGE
HADASSAH, THE WOMENS ZIONIST
    ORGANIZATION OF AMERICA
HAVURAH
HEBREW COLLEGE
HEBREW IMMIGRANT AID SOCIETY
HEBREW THEOLOGICAL COLLEGE
HEBREW UNION COLLEGE-JEWISH INSTITUTE OF
    RELIGION
HE-HALUTZ
HERZLIAH HEBREW TEACHERS' INSTITUTE
HILLEL
HISTADRUT IVRIT OF AMERICA
INDUSTRIAL REMOVAL
INSTITUTE OF SOUTHERN JEWISH LIFE
INSTITUTE OF TRADITIONAL JUDAISM, THE
INTERNATIONAL ASSOCIATION OF JEWISH
    GENEOLOGICAL SOCIETIES
INTERNATIONAL LADIES GARMENT WORKERS
    UNION
ISRAEL POLICY FORUM
JEWISH AGRICULTURAL SOCIETY
JEWISH BOOK COUNCIL
JEWISH CAMPING
JEWISH COMMUNAL SERVICE ASSOCIATION OF
    NORTH AMERICA
JEWISH COUNCIL ON PUBLIC AFFAIRS
JEWISH CULTURAL RECONSTRUCTION
JEWISH EDUCATION SERVICE OF NORTH AMERICA
JEWISH LABOR COMMITTEE
JEWISH MUSEUM
JEWISH PUBLICATION SOCIETY OF AMERICA
JEWISH SOCIALIST VERBAND
JEWISH TEACHERS' SEMINARY AND PEOPLE'S
    UNIVERSITY
JEWISH THEOLOGICAL SEMINARY OF AMERICA,
    THE
JEWISH WAR VETERANS OF THE UNITED STATES
    OF AMERICA
LABOR ZIONIST ALLIANCE (AMEINU)
LAURA AND ALVIN SIEGAL COLLEGE OF JUDAIC
    STUDIES
LEAGUE FOR ISRAEL, THE AMERICAN JEWISH
    MAGNES MEMORIAL MUSEUM
MENORAH ASSOCIATION AND MENORAH JOURNAL

NATIONAL CONFERENCE ON SOVIET JEWRY
NATIONAL COUNCIL OF JEWISH WOMEN
NATIONAL FEDERATION OF TEMPLE SISTERHOODS
NATIONAL FOUNDATION FOR JEWISH CULTURE
NATIONAL HAVURAH COMMITTEE
NATIONAL JEWISH CENTER FOR IMMUNOLOGY
NATIONAL JEWISH DEMOCRATIC COUNCIL
NATIONAL MUSEUM OF AMERICAN JEWISH
    HISTORY
NATIONAL YIDDISH BOOK CENTER
NEW ISRAEL FUND
PIONEER WOMEN
POALEI AGUDAT ISRAEL
PROGRESSIVE JEWISH ALLIANCE
RABBINICAL ALLIANCE OF AMERICA
RABBINICAL ASSEMBLY
RABBINICAL COUNCIL OF AMERICA
RECONSTRUCTIONIST RABBINICAL COLLEGE
REPUBLICAN JEWISH COALITION
SIMON WIESENTHAL CENTER
SKIRBALL CULTURAL CENTER
SPERTUS INSTITUTE OF JEWISH STUDIES
STUDENT STRUGGLE FOR SOVIET JEWRY
SYNAGOGUE COUNCIL OF AMERICA, THE
TIKKUN
TORAH UMESORAH
TOURO COLLEGE
UNION OF COUNCILS FOR JEWS IN FORMER
    SOVIET UNION
UNION OF ORTHODOX JEWISH CONGREGATIONS
    OF AMERICA
UNION OF ORTHODOX RABBIS OF THE UNITED
    STATES AND CANADA
UNION OF REFORM JUDAISM
UNION OF SEPHARDIC CONGREGATIONS
UNITED JEWISH COMMUNITIES
UNITED STATES HOLOCAUST MEMORIAL MUSEUM
UNITED SYNAGOGUE OF AMERICA
UNIVERSITY OF JUDAISM
VAAD HA-HATZALAH
WOMEN'S LEAGUE FOR CONSERVATIVE JUDAISM
WORKMEN'S CIRCLE
YESHIVA UNIVERSITY
YESHIVAS CHOVEVEI TORAH
YIDDISHER KULTUR FARBAND
YOUNG ISRAEL, THE NATIONAL COUNCIL OF
YOUNG JUDAEA
ZIONIST ORGANIZATION OF AMERICA (Z.O.A.)

PUBLICATIONS
AMERICAN HEBREW, THE
AMERICAN ISRAELITE
AMERICAN JEWESS
ARBEITER-ZEITUNG
ARTSCROLL
COMMENTARY
DIE DEBORAH
JEWISH DAILY FORWARD
JEWISH DAY
JEWISH MESSENGER, THE

JEWISH MORNING JOURNAL
JEWISH QUARTERLY REVIEW
JEWISH WOMAN, THE
LILITH
MENORAH ASSOCIATION AND MENORAH JOURNAL
MIDSTREAM
MORNING FREIHEIT
TIKKUN
TSUKUNFT

BIOGRAPHIES
Academic Life
ABELSON, HAROLD HERBERT
ABRAHAMSEN, DAVID
ABRAM, MORRIS BERTHOLD
ABRAMOVITZ, MOSES
ABRAMOWICZ, DINA
ACKERMAN, NATHAN WARD
ADELSON, HOWARD LAURENCE
ADLER, CYRUS
ADLER, FELIX
ADLER, MORTIMER JEROME
ADLER, SELIG
ADLERBLUM, NIMA
AGUS, IRVING ABRAHAM
AIKEN, HENRY DAVID
AKERLOF, GEORGE
ALEXANDER, FRANZ
ALMOND, GABRIEL ABRAHAM
ALTMAN, OSCAR LOUIS
APTER, DAVID ERNEST
ARENDT, HANNAH
ARNSTEIN, WALTER LEONARD
ARROW, KENNETH JOSEPH
ASKOWITH, DORA
AUERBACH, CARL, A.
AUSUBEL, DAVID PAUL
AUSUBEL, NATHAN
BAILYN, BERNARD
BAKAN, DAVID
BAMBERGER, FRITZ
BAND, ARNOLD
BARDIN, SHLOMO
BARON, SALO (Shalom) WITTMAYER
BASKIN, JUDITH
BAUMGARDT, DAVID
BECKER, GARY STANLEY
BEER, GEORGE LOUIS
BELL, DANIEL
BENARDETE, MAIR JOSE
BENDIX, REINHARD
BENEDEK, THERESE F.
BEN-HORIN, MEIR
BERENBAUM, MICHAEL
BERGER, DAVID
BERGSON, ABRAM
BERKOVITS, ELIEZER
BERKSON, ISAAC BAER
BERNARD, JESSIE
BERNSTEIN, HARRY

I. HISTORY
B. MEDIEVAL & MODERN PERIOD
2. Regional History
g. United States
BIOGRAPHIES
Academic Life (continued)

BERNSTEIN, SIMON
BESSO, HENRY
BETTELHEIM, BRUNO
BIALE, DAVID
BICKERMAN, ELIAS JOSEPH
BIDNEY, DAVID
BIEBER, MARGARETE
BILDERSEE, ADELE
BIRNBAUM, PHILIP
BLACK, MAX
BLAU, JOSEPH LEON
BLAU, PETER MICHAEL
BLOCH, HERBERT
BLONDHEIM, DAVID SIMON
BLOOM, SOLOMON FRANK
BLOOMFIELD, LEONARD
BLOOMFIELD, MAURICE
BLUM, JEROME
BOAS, FRANZ
BOAS, GEORGE
BOKSER, BARUCH
BOORSTIN, DANIEL J.
BORAH, WOODROW WILSON
BOSKOFF, ALVIN
BOYARIN, DANIEL
BRODSKY, STANLEY L.
BRONFENBRENNER, MARTIN
BROUDY, HARRY SAMUEL
BROWNING, CHRISTOPHER
BRUNER, JEROME
BUHLER, CHARLOTTE
BUNZEL, RUTH LEAH
BUTLER, JUDITH
BUTTENWIESER, MOSES
CAHNMAN, WERNER J.
CALABRESI, GUIDO
CANTOR, NORMAN FRANK
CAPLAN, HARRY
CARLEBACH, ELISHEVA
CARMILLY-WEINBERGER, MOSHE
CHAZAN, ROBERT
CHEIN, ISIDOR
CHERNISS, HAROLD
CHESLER, PHYLLIS
CHOMSKY, NOAM AVRAM
CHOMSKY, WILLIAM
CHOPER, JESSE
COHEN, BOAZ
COHEN, GERSON D.
COHEN, I. BERNARD
COHEN, MORRIS RAPHAEL
COHEN, NAOMI W.
COHEN, NATHAN EDWARD

COHEN, SAUL BERNARD
COHEN, SHAYE J.D.
COHEN, WILBUR JOSEPH
COLEMAN, EDWARD DAVIDSON
COLM, GERHARD
COSER, LEWIS A.
COSER, ROSE LAUB
CREMIN, LAWRENCE ARTHUR
DAVIDSON, ISRAEL
DAVIS, DAVID BRION
DAVIS, MOSHE
DAVIS, NATALIE ZEMON
DAWIDOWICZ, LUCY
DEINARD, EPHRAIM
DELOUGAZ, PIERRE PINCHAS
DENMARK, FLORENCE LEVIN
DEUTSCH, GOTTHARD
DIAMOND, SIGMUND
DIESENDRUCK, ZEVI
DIMITROVSKY, CHAIM ZALMAN
DINER, HASIA
DINITZ, SIMON
DONIGER, WENDY
DORFF, ELLIOT N.
DORFMAN, JOSEPH
DRACHSLER, JULIUS
DUBERMAN, MARTIN
DUKER, ABRAHAM GORDON
DWORKIN, RONALD
EATON, JOSEPH W.
ECKARDT, ROY A.
EDMAN, IRWIN
EDWARDS, PAUL
EFROS, ISRAEL ISAAC
EHRLICH, ARNOLD BOGUMIL
EISEN, ARNOLD
EISENSTADT, ABRAHAM SELDIN
EISENSTEIN, JUDAH DAVID
ELAZAR, DANIEL J.
EMBER, AARON
EMERY, RICHARD WILDER
ENDELMAN, TODD
EPSTEIN, ABRAHAM
EULAU, HEINZ
EZEKIEL, MORDECAI JOSEPH BRILL
FABRICANT, SOLOMON
FARBER, MARVIN
FEIGIN, SAMUEL ISAAC
FEIGL, HERBERT
FEILER, ARTHUR
FEIS, HERBERT
FELDMAN, LOUIS
FELLNER, WILLIAM JOHN
FERNBERGER, SAMUEL
FEUER, LEWIS SAMUEL
FILLER, LOUIS
FINE, REUBEN
FINE, SIDNEY
FINER, HERMAN
FINKEL, JOSHUA

FINKELSTEIN, JACOB JOEL
FISCHEL, WALTER JOSEPH
FISCHER, LOUIS
FISCHER, STANLEY
FISHBANE, MICHAEL
FISHMAN, JOSHUA AARON
FLEXNER
FLEXNER, ABRAHAM
FLUSSER, DAVID
FOX, MARVIN
FREEDMAN, JAMES
FREIDUS, ABRAHAM SOLOMON
FRIED, MORTON HERBERT
FRIEDLAENDER, ISRAEL
FRIEDMAN, LEE MAX
FRIEDMAN, MILTON
FRIEDMAN, SHAMMA
FRYMER-KENSKY, TIKVA
GANDZ, SOLOMON
GARTNER, LLOYD P.
GAY (Froehlich), PETER JACK (Joachim)
GELB, IGNACE JAY
GERSHOY, LEO
GEVIRTZ, STANLEY
GILBERT, FELIX
GILBERT, MILTON
GILLIGAN, CAROL
GILLMAN, NEAL
GINOTT, HAIM G.
GINSBERG, HAROLD LOUIS
GINSBURG, NORTON SIDNEY
GINZBERG, ELI
GINZBERG, LOUIS
GITIN, SEYMOUR
GLATZER, NAHUM NORBERT
GLAZER, NATHAN
GLOCK, CHARLES
GLUECK, NELSON
GLUECK, SHELDON
GOFFMAN, ERVING
GOITEIN, SHLOMO DOV (Fritz)
GOLB, NORMAN
GOLDBERG, HARVEY
GOLDENWEISER, ALEXANDER ALEXANDROVICH
GOLDENWEISER, EMANUEL ALEXANDROVICH
GOLDIN, JUDAH
GOLDMAN, ERIC FREDERICK
GOLDMAN, HETTY
GOLDMAN, MARTIN
GOLDSMITH, RAYMOND WILLIAM
GOODENOUGH, ERWIN RAMSDELL
GOODMAN, NELSON
GOODMAN, PAUL
GOOR, YEHUDAH
GORDIS, ROBERT
GORDON, CYRUS HERZL
GORDON, MILTON M.
GORNICK, VIVIAN
GOTTHEIL, RICHARD JAMES HORATIO
GOTTSCHALK, LOUIS REICHENTAL

GOTTSCHALL, MORTON
GOULD, SAMUEL BROOKNER
GRAYZEL, SOLOMON
GREEN, ARTHUR
GREENBERG, JOSEPH
GREENBERG, MOSHE
GREENFIELD, JONAS CARL
GREENSTONE, JULIUS HILLEL
GROSS, CHARLES
GURALNIK, DAVID
GURWITSCH, AARON
GUTMANN, AMY
GUTTMACHER, MANFRED
GUTTMAN, LOUIS
HABER, SAMUEL L.
HABER, WILLIAM
HADAS, MOSES
HALKIN, ABRAHAM SOLOMON
HALLE, MORRIS
HALPERN, BENJAMIN
HAMEROW, THEODORE STEPHEN
HANDLIN, OSCAR
HANFMANN, GEORGE MAXIM ANOSSOV
HARRIS, MARVIN
HARRIS, ZELLIG SABBETAI
HARRISSE, HENRY
HARTMAN, GEOFFREY
HAUPT, PAUL
HAUSER, PHILIP MORRIS
HEILBRUN, CAROLYN G.
HEILPRIN
HELLER, HAYYIM
HELLMAN, CLARISSE DORIS
HENRY, JULES
HERBERG, WILL
HERSKOVITS, MELVILLE JEAN
HEXTER, JACK H.
HILBERG, RAUL
HIMMELFARB, GERTRUDE
HIRSCHMAN, ALBERT OTTO
HOFSTADTER, RICHARD
HOOK, SIDNEY
HOSCHANDER, JACOB
HOSELITZ, BERTHOLD FRANK
HURWITZ, SAMUEL JUSTIN
HUSIK, ISAAC
HYMAN, HAROLD MELVIN
HYMAN, PAULA E.
INKELES, ALEX
INSDORF, ANNETTE
JACOBSON, ANNA
JANOWITZ, MORRIS
JANOWSKY, OSCAR ISAIAH
JASNY, NAUM
JASTROW
JONAS, HANS
JOSEPH, SAMUEL
JOSEPHSON, MATTHEW
JUSTMAN, JOSEPH
KABAKOFF, JACOB

I. HISTORY
B. MEDIEVAL & MODERN PERIOD
2. Regional History
g. United States
BIOGRAPHIES
Academic Life (continued)

KAGAN, SOLOMON ROBERT
KAHLER, ERICH
KAHN, ALFRED JOSEPH
KAHNEMAN, DANIEL
KALLEN, HORACE MEYER
KANDEL, ISAAC LEON
KANTOR, JACOB ROBERT
KANTOROWICZ, ERNST HARTWIG
KAPLAN, ABRAHAM
KARPF, MAURICE JOSEPH
KATSH, ABRAHAM ISAAC
KATZ, DANIEL
KATZ, SOLOMON
KATZ, STEVEN T.
KAUFMANN, FELIX
KAUFMANN, WALTER
KELLER, MORTON
KEMPNER, ROBERT MAX WASILII
KEYSERLING, LEON H.
KIRCHHEIMER, OTTO
KLEIN, LAWRENCE ROBERT
KOBRIN, SOLOMON
KOFFKA, KURT
KOHN, HANS
KOHS, SAMUEL CALMIN
KOMAROVSKY, MIRRA
KONVITZ, MILTON RIDVAS
KRAMER, SAMUEL NOAH
KRAUS, MICHAEL
KRIEGER, LEONARD
KRIPKE, SAUL
KRIS, ERNST
KRISTELLER, PAUL OSKAR
KRISTOL, IRVING
KUBLIN, HYMAN
KUGEL, JAMES
KUHN, THOMAS S.
KUZNETS, SIMON
LAMM, NORMAN
LANDES, DAVID SAUL
LANDES, RUTH
LANGER, LAWRENCE
LAZARSFELD, PAUL F.
LAZEROWITZ, MORRIS
LEA, HENRY CHARLES
LEAF, HAYIM
LEHMANN, KARL
LEHRMAN, DANIEL
LEISERSON, WILLIAM MORRIS
LENGYEL, EMIL
LEON, HARRY JOSHUA
LERNER, ABBA PETACHJA
LERNER, GERDA

LERNER, MAX
LERNER, RALPH
LESLAU, WOLF
LEVENSON, JON
LEVENSON, JOSEPH RICHMOND
LEVIAS, CASPAR
LEVIN, A. LEO
LEVIN, NORA
LEVINE, BARUCH
LEVY, HARRY LOUIS
LEVY, LEONARD WILLIAMS
LEVY, MARION JOSEPH, JR.
LEWIN, KURT ZADEK
LEWIS, OSCAR
LIBOWITZ, SAMUEL NEHEMIAH
LICHTENSTEIN, WALTER
LIEBERMAN, MYRON
LIEBERMAN, SAUL
LIPSET, SEYMOUR MARTIN
LIPTZIN, SOL
LOEWENSTEIN, KARL
LOPEZ, ROBERT SABATINO
LORGE, IRVING
LOWE, ADOLPH
LOWE, ELIAS AVERY
LOWIE, ROBERT HARRY
LUBIN, ISADOR
LUBIN, SIMON JULIUS
MACHLUP, FRITZ
MAIER, JOSEPH
MAISELS, MOSES HAYYIM (Misha)
MALACHI, ELIEZER RAPHAEL
MALKIEL, YAKOV
MALLER, JULIUS BERNARD
MALTER, HENRY
MANDELBAUM, DAVID GOODMAN
MANN, JACOB
MANUEL, FRANK EDWARD
MARCUS, JACOB RADER
MARCUS, JOSEPH
MARCUS, RALPH
MARCUS, RUTH BARCAN
MARCUSE, HERBERT
MARGET, ARTHUR W.
MARGOLIS, MAX LEOPOLD
MARKOWITZ, HARRY M.
MARSCHAK, JACOB
MARWICK, LAWRENCE
MARX, ALEXANDER
MASLOW, ABRAHAM H.
MAXIMON (Maximowski), SHALOM DOV BER
MAYER, ARNO JOSEPH
MEDNICK, MARTHA TAMARA SCHUCH
MENES, ABRAM
MERTON, ROBERT C.
MERTON, ROBERT KING
MEYER, MICHAEL
MEYERHOFF, HANS
MILGRAM, STANLEY
MILGROM, JACOB

MISES, LUDWIG EDLER VON
MODIGLIANI, FRANCO
MONIS, JUDAH
MOORE, GEORGE FOOT
MORENO, JACOB
MORGENSTERN, OSKAR
MORGENTHAU, HANS JOACHIM
MORRIS, RICHARD BRANDON
MORTON, LOUIS C.
MOSSE, GEORGE L.
MYERHOFF, BARBARA
NADLER, MARCUS
NAGEL, ERNEST
NASATIR, ABRAHAM PHINEAS
NATHAN, ROBERT ROY
NAUMBURG, MARGARET
NEISSER, HANS PHILIPP
NELSON, BENJAMIN
NEMOY, LEON
NETANYAHU, BENZION
NEUGARTEN, BERNICE L.
NEUSNER, JACOB
NEWMAN, AUBREY
NUSSBAUM, ARTHUR
OKO, ADOLPH S.
OPLER, MARVIN KAUFMANN
OPLER, MORRIS EDWARD
ORLINSKY, HARRY MEYER
OSCHINSKY, LAWRENCE
OSTROLENK, BERNHARD
PAP, ARTHUR
PASSOW, AARON HARRY
PATAI, RAPHAEL
PEIXOTTO, JESSICA BLANCHE
PERLBERG, ABRAHAM NATHAN
PERLMAN, JACOB
PERLMANN, MOSHE
PETEGORSKY, DAVID
PFEFFER, LEO
PFEIFFER, ROBERT HENRY
PINSON, KOPPEL S.
PIPES, RICHARD EDGAR
POLANYI, KARL
POMERANTZ, SIDNEY IRVING
POPPER, WILLIAM
POWDERMAKER, HORTENSE
PRIBRAM, KARL
PUTNAM, HILARY
RADIN, PAUL
RAISZ, ERWIN J.
RAPPAPORT, ARMIN H.
RAPPAPORT, ROY
RATNER, SIDNEY
RAZRAN, GREGORY
REDL, FRITZ
REICH, ROBERT BERNARD
REICH, WILHELM
REINHARZ, JEHUDA
REVEL, BERNARD
RIESMAN, DAVID

RISCHIN, MOSES
RIVKIN, ELLIS
RIVKIND, ISAAC
RIVLIN, HARRY N.
ROBACK, ABRAHAM AARON
ROBINSON, EDWARD
ROBISON, SOPHIA
RODELL, FRED M.
RODIN, JUDITH
ROHEIM, GEZA
ROSE, ARNOLD MARSHALL
ROSENBACH, ABRAHAM SIMON WOLF
ROSENBAUM, JONATHAN
ROSENTHAL, ERICH
ROSENTHAL, FRANZ
ROSENTHAL, JUDAH
ROSENTHAL, WILLIAM
ROSKIES, DAVID
ROSTOW, EUGENE VICTOR
ROSTOW, WALT WHITMAN
ROWE, LEO STANTON
RUBINOW, ISAAC MAX
RUDAVSKY, DAVID
SACHAR, ABRAM LEON
SACHS, HANNS
SACHS, JULIUS
SAHLINS, MARSHALL
SALOMON, ALBERT
SAMUELSON, PAUL ANTHONY
SANDMEL, SAMUEL
SAPIR, EDWARD
SARNA, JONATHAN
SARNA, NAHUM
SAXON, DAVID STEPHEN
SCHAECHTER, MORDKHE
SCHAFER, STEPHEN
SCHAPIRO, JACOB SALWYN
SCHAPPES, MORRIS U.
SCHARFSTEIN, ZEVI
SCHEFFLER, ISRAEL
SCHEINDLIN, RAYMOND
SCHIFFMAN, LAWRENCE
SCHOLES, MYRON
SCHRECKER, PAUL
SCHWARTZ, ANNA JACOBSON
SELIGMAN, EDWIN ROBERT ANDERSON
SEMMEL, BERNARD
SHANKS, HERSHEL
SHAPIRO, DAVID S.
SHAPIRO, HAROLD
SHAPIRO, HARRY LIONEL
SHARFMAN, ISAIAH LEO
SHATZKY, JACOB
SHEFFER, HENRY M.
SHILS, EDWARD
SHUB, DAVID
SHULIM, JOSEPH ISIDORE
SHULVASS, MOSES AVIGDOR
SIMON, HERBERT ALEXANDER
SINGER, MILTON B.

I. HISTORY
B. MEDIEVAL & MODERN PERIOD
2. Regional History
g. United States
BIOGRAPHIES

Academic Life (continued)

SKLARE, MARSHALL
SKOSS, SOLOMON LEON (Zalman Leib)
SLAVSON, SAMUEL RICHARD
SLONIMSKY, HENRY
SMELSER, NEIL JOSEPH
SMITH, JOHN MERLIN POWIS
SMITH, JONATHAN
SMITH, MORTON
SNYDER, LOUIS LEO
SOLOW, ROBERT MERTON
SONNE, ISAIAH
SORKIN, MICHAEL
SOVERN, MICHAEL IRA
SPEISER, EPHRAIM AVIGDOR
SPIEGEL, SHALOM
SPIEGELBERG, HERBERT
SPIER, LESLIE
SPIRO, MELFORD ELLIOT
SPITZER, LEO
SPOEHR, ALEXANDER
STARR, JOSHUA
STEIN, HERBERT
STERN, BERNHARD JOSEPH
STERN, FRITZ
STIGLITZ, JOSEPH
STILES, EZRA
STILLMAN, NORMAN
STRAUSS, LEO
SULZBACH, WALTER
SWADESH, MORRIS
SZAJKOWSKI, ZOSA
TANNENBAUM, FRANK
TAUBENSCHLAG, RAPHAEL
TAUSSIG, FRANK WILLIAM
TAX, SOL
TCHERNOWITZ, CHAIM
TEC, NECHAMA
TIGAY, JEFFREY
TITIEV, MISCHA
TOBACH, ETHEL
TOBY, JACKSON
TORREY, CHARLES CUTLER
TREFOUSSE, HANS LOUIS
TRIBE, LAWRENCE H.
TRUNK. ISAIAH
TUCHMAN, BARBARA WERTHEIM
TUMIN, MELVIN MARVIN
TWERSKY, ISADORE
UNGER, IRWIN
VINER, JACOB
WALZER, MICHAEL
WAXMAN, MEYER
WECHSLER, DAVID

WECHSLER, HERBERT
WEINBERG, GLADYS DAVIDSON
WEINBERG, SAUL S.
WEINREICH, URIEL
WEINRYB, BERNARD DOV SUCHER
WEISBERGER, BERNARD ALLEN
WEISS, ALBERT PAUL
WEISS, PAUL
WEISS-ROSMARIN, TRUDE
WERNER, HEINZ
WHITE, HARRY D.
WHITE, MORTON GABRIEL
WIENER, PHILIP PAUL
WIERUSZOWSKI, HELENE
WIRTH, LOUIS
WISCHNITZER, MARK
WISSE, RUTH
WOLF, ERIC ROBERT
WOLFE, ALAN
WOLFE, BERTRAM DAVID
WOLFF, WERNER
WOLFSON, ELLIOT
WOLFSON, HARRY AUSTRYN
WOLFSON, THERESA
WUNDERLICH, FRIEDA
YERUSHALMI, YOSEF HAYIM
YOUNG, JAMES
YOUTIE, HERBERT CHAYYIM
ZEICHNER, OSCAR
ZEITLIN, SOLOMON

Art
ABRAMOVITZ, MAX
ADLER, DANKMAR
ADLER, SAMUEL M.
AGREST, DIANA
ALSCHULER, ALFRED
ARBUS, DIANE NEMEROV
ARNOLD, EVE
ARONSON, DAVID
AVEDON, RICHARD
BAIZERMAN, SAUL
BARNET, WILL
BASKIN, LEONARD
BENN, BEN
BEN-ZION (Weinman)
BERENSON, BERNARD
BERNSTEIN, THERESA
BING, ILSE
BLOOM, HYMAN
BLUME, PETER
BOLOTOWSKY, ILYA
BOROFSKY, JONATHAN
BOURKE-WHITE, MARGARET
BRENNER, VICTOR
BREUER, MARCEL (Lajos)
BRUNNER, ARNOLD
BUNSHAFT, GORDON
CAPA, CORNELL
CAPA, ROBERT

CARVALHO, SOLOMON NUNES
CHAST, ROZ
CHICAGO, JUDY
CRUMB, ROBERT
CSUPO, GABOR (and Irene Klasky)
DAVIDSON, JO
DINE, JIM
EIDLITZ (Abraham Moses), ZERAH BEN MEIR
EILSHEMIUS, LOUIS
EISENMAN, PETER D.
EISENSTAEDT, ALFRED
EISNER, WILL
EIZENBERG, JULIE
ELDER, WILL
ELISOFON, ELIOT
ERWITT, ELLIOTT
ETTINGHAUSEN, RICHARD
ETTLINGER, MARION
EZEKIEL, MOSES JACOB
FEIFFER, JULES
FERBER, HERBERT
FLEISCHER, MAX
FRANK, ROBERT
FRANKENTHALER, HELEN
FREED, JAMES INGO
FRELENG, I. J.
FRIEDLANDER, LEE
FURST, MORITZ
GANDELSONAS, MARIO
GEHRY, FRANK O.
GIKOW, RUTH
GOLDBERG, BERTRAND
GOLDBERG, RUBE
GOLDIN, NAN
GOLDWATER, JOHN
GOLUB, LEON
GOODMAN, PERCIVAL
GORLIN, ALEXANDER
GOTTLIEB, ADOLPH
GREENBERG, CLEMENT
GROPPER, WILLIAM
GROSS, CHAIM
GUTMANN, JOSEPH
HALSMAN, PHILIPPE
HAMMER, ARMAND
HARKAVY, MINNA
HIRSCH, JOSEPH
HIRSCHFELD, AL
HIRSHFIELD, MORRIS
JACOBI, LOTTE
KAHN, ALBERT
KAHN, ELY JACQUES
KAHN, LOUIS I.
KALMAN, TIBOR
KANE, BOB
KANE, GIL
KANOVITZ, HOWARD
KATZ, ALEX
KERTESZ, ANDRE
KIESLER, FREDERICK JOHN

KIRBY, JACK (Kurtzberg)
KITAJ, R. B.
KLINE FRANZ
KOLB, LEON
KRASNER, LEE
KRUGER, BARBARA
KURTZMAN, HARVEY
LAPIDUS, MORRIS
LASANSKY, MAURICIO
LASSAW, IBRAM
LAZARUS, MEL
LEE, STAN
LEIBOVITZ, ANNIE
LEVINE, JACK
LEVITT, HELENE
LEWITT, SOL
LIBESKIND, DANIEL
LICHTENSTEIN, ROY
LIPCHITZ, JACQUES (Chaim Jacob)
LIPTON, SEYMOUR
LOUIS, MORRIS
LOZOWICK, LOUIS
MANSO, LEO
MARGO, BORIS
MARGOULIES, BERTHA
MARIL, HERMAN
MARK, MARY ELLEN
MARYAN
MEIER, RICHARD
MENDELSOHN, ERIC
MENKES, ZYGMUNT
MEYEROWITZ, JOEL
MOÏSE, THEODORE SYDNEY
MOSLER, HENRY
MYERS, MYER
NADELMAN, ELIE
NEUTRA, RICHARD JOSEPH
NEVELSON, LOUISE
NEWMAN, ARNOLD
NEWMAN, BARNETT
NEWTON, HELMUT
OLITSKI, JULES
OPPER, FREDERICK BURR
PANOFSKY, ERWIN
PEARLSTEIN, PHILIP
PENN, IRVING
PLACHY, SYLVIA
POLSHEK, JAMES
RATTNER, ABRAHAM
RAY, MAN
REDER, BERNARD
REISS, LIONEL
RIVERS, LARRY
ROSE, HERMAN
ROSENBERG, HAROLD
ROSENTHAL, MAX
ROTHKO, MARK
ROTHSTEIN, IRMA
RUBIN, GAIL
SAITOWITZ, STANLEY

I. **HISTORY**
  B. MEDIEVAL & MODERN PERIOD
    2. Regional History
      g. United States
        BIOGRAPHIES
          Art (continued)

SCHAMES, SAMSON
SCHANKER, LOUIS
SCHAPIRO, MEYER
SCHINDLER, RUDOLPH M.
SCHOR, ILYA
SCHWARTZ, FREDERIC
SCHWARTZ, MANFRED
SEGAL, GEORGE
SELIGMANN, KURT
SERRA, RICHARD
SEYMOUR, DAVID
SHAHN, BEN
SHUSTER, JOE
SIEGEL, JERRY
SIMON, SIDNEY
SISKIND, AARON
SOYER, MOSES
SOYER, RAPHAEL
SPERO, NANCY
SPIEGELMAN, ART
SPIRO, EUGEN
STEIG, WILLIAM, SHREK
STEINBERG, SAUL
STERN, ROBERT A.M.
STERNE, HEDDA
STERNE, MAURICE
STIEGLITZ, ALFRED
STRAND, PAUL
TEWI, THEA
TIGERMAN, STANLEY
TWORKOV, JACK
WALKOWITZ, ABRAHAM
WEBER, MAX
WEEGEE
WILSON, SOL
WINOGRAND, GARRY
ZORACH, WILLIAM
ZUCKER, JACQUES

Literature
ABRAMS, MEYER
ADAMS, HANNAH
ADLER, RENATA, ESSAYIST
ALTER, ROBERT B.
ANGOFF, CHARLES
ANTIN, MARY
APPLE, MAX
ASIMOV, ISAAC
AUSLANDER, JOSEPH
AUSTER, PAUL
BAUM, VICKI
BEHRMAN, SAMUEL NATHANIEL
BELLOW, SAUL

BERCOVICI, KONRAD
BERCOVITCH, SACVAN
BLANKFORT, MICHAEL S.
BLOOM, HAROLD
BODENHEIM, MAXWELL
BRINIG, MYRON
BRODY, ALTER
BRONER, ESTHER M.
BRUSTEIN, ROBERT SANFORD
BUKIET, MELVIN JULES
BUSCH, CHARLES
CAHAN, ABRAHAM
CAHAN, JUDAH LOEB (Lewis)
CALISHER, HORTENSE
CHABON, MICHAEL
CHAYEFSKY, PADDY
CHODOROV, EDWARD
CHODOROV, JEROME
COHEN, ARTHUR A.
COHEN, ROSE GOLLUP
COURNOS, JOHN
DAHLBERG, EDWARD
DAVENPORT, MARCIA
DE CASSERES, BENJAMIN
DEUTSCH, BABBETTE
DOCTOROW, EDGAR LAWRENCE
ELKIN, STANLEY
EPHRON, NORA
EPSTEIN, LESLIE
EPSTEIN, MORRIS
EPSTEIN, SEYMOUR
FADIMAN, CLIFTON
FALK, MARCIA
FAST, HOWARD MELVIN
FEARING, KENNETH
FELDMAN, IRVING
FERBER, EDNA
FIEDLER, LESLIE AARON
FINEMAN, IRVING
FISH, STANLEY
FRANK, WALDO DAVID
FRANKEN, ROSE
FRANKS, BILHAH ABIGAIL LEVY
FREEMAN, JOSEPH
FRIEDLAND, ABRAHAM HYMAN (Hayyim)
FRIEDMAN, BRUCE JAY
FUCHS, DANIEL
GABRIEL, GILBERT W.
GAMORAN, MAMIE
GASSNER, JOHN
GELBER, JACK
GINSBERG, ALLEN
GLANZ-LEYELES, AARON
GLASS, MONTAGUE MARSDEN
GLUCK, LOUISE
GOLD, HERBERT
GOLD, MICHAEL
GOLDBERG, ISAAC
GOLDEN, HARRY LEWIS
GOLDMAN, WILLIAM

GOLDSTEIN, REBECCA

GOODMAN, ALLEGRA

GREEN, GERALD

GREENBERG, JOANNE

GREENBERG, SAMUEL BERNARD

GROSSMAN, ALLEN

HALPER, ALBERT

HARRIS, MARK

HART, MOSS

HECHT, BEN

HELLER, JOSEPH

HELLINGER, MARK

HELLMAN, LILLIAN FLORENCE

HINDUS, MAURICE GERSCHON

HIRSCH, ERIC DONALD

HOBSON, LAURA Z.

HOLLANDER, JOHN

HOROVITZ, ISRAEL

HOWE, IRVING

HURST, FANNIE

IGNATOW, DAVID

ISAACS, JACOB

ISAACS, SUSAN

JAFFE, RONA

JONG, ERICA

JUDAH, SAMUEL BENJAMIN HELBERT

KALMAN, MAIRA

KANIN, GARSON

KAPLAN, JOHANNA

KAUFMAN, BEL

KAUFMAN, GEORGE SIMON

KAZIN, ALFRED

KELLERMAN, FAYE

KELLERMAN, JONATHAN

KEMELMAN, HARRY

KINGSLEY, SIDNEY

KLEPFISZ, IRENA

KOBER, ARTHUR

KOCH, KENNETH

KOMROFF, MANUEL

KOPIT, ARTHUR

KOSINSKI, JERZY

KRAMER, LARRY

KRAMM, JOSEPH

KRANTZ, JUDITH

KREYMBORG, ALFRED

KRONENBERGER, LOUIS

KUNITZ, STANLEY JASSPON

KUSHNER, TONY

LAURENTS, ARTHUR

LAWSON, JOHN HOWARD

LAZARUS, EMMA

LEVERTOV, DENISE

LEVIANT, CURT

LEVIN, HARRY

LEVIN, IRA

LEVIN, MEYER

LEWISOHN, LUDWIG

LIEBERMAN, ELIAS

LISITZKY, EPHRAIM E.

LOWENTHAL, MARVIN

MAILER, NORMAN

MALAMUD, BERNARD

MALTZ, ALBERT

MAMET, DAVID

MILLER, ARTHUR

MOISE, PENINA

NATHAN, GEORGE JEAN

NEMEROV, HOWARD

NEUGEBOREN, JAY

NISSENSON, HUGH

ODETS, CLIFFORD

OLSEN, TILLIE

OPPEN, GEORGE

OPPENHEIM, JAMES

ORNITZ, SAMUEL BADISCH

OSTRIKER, ALICIA SUSKIN

OZICK, CYNTHIA

PALEY, GRACE

PARKER, DOROTHY

PERELMAN, SIDNEY JOSEPH

PHILLIPS, WILLIAM

PINSKY, ROBERT

PLAIN, BELVA

PODHORETZ, NORMAN

POTOK, CHAIM

POUND, EZRA LOOMIS

PROSE, FRANCINE

RAGEN, NAOMI

RAHV, PHILIP

RAND, AYN

RAPHAELSON, SAMSON

REZNIKOFF, CHARLES

RICE, ELMER LEOPOLD

RICH, ADRIENNE

ROBBINS, HAROLD

ROSEN, NORMA

ROSENFELD, ISAAC

ROSENFELD, PAUL

ROSS, LILLIAN

ROSTEN, LEO CALVIN

ROTH, HENRY

ROTH, PHILIP MILTON

RUKEYSER, MURIEL

SALINGER, JEROME DAVID

SAMPTER, JESSIE ETHEL

SAMUEL, MAURICE

SCHISGAL, MURRAY

SCHULBERG, BUDD WILSON

SCHWARTZ, DELMORE

SCHWARZ, LEO WALDER

SEGAL, ERICH

SEID, RUTH

SERLING, ROD

SHAPIRO, KARL JAY

SHAW, IRWIN

SHELDON, SIDNEY

SHEVELOVE, BURT

SHULMAN, MAX

SIMON, KATE

I. HISTORY
B. MEDIEVAL & MODERN PERIOD
2. Regional History
g. United States
BIOGRAPHIES

Literature (*continued*)

SIMON, NEIL
SINGER, HOWARD
SKLAREW, MYRA
SOLOTAROFF, THEODORE
SONTAG, SUSAN
SPEWACK, BELLA
SPIEGELMAN, ART
SPINGARN
STEELE, DANIELLE
STEIN, GERTRUDE
STEIN, JOSEPH
STERN, STEVE
STINE, R. L.
STONE, IRVING
SUSANN, JACQUELINE
TAYLOR, SIDNEY
TOBENKIN, ELIAS
TRILLIN, CALVIN, ESSAYIST
TRILLING, DIANA
TRILLING, LIONEL
TUROW, SCOTT
UNTERMEYER, LOUIS
URIS, LEON
WALLACE, IRVING
WALLANT, EDWARD LEWIS
WASSERMAN, DALE
WASSERSTEIN, WENDY
WEIDMAN, JEROME
WELLER, MICHAEL
WEST, NATHANAEL
WOLFERT, IRA
WOUK, HERMAN
YARMOLINSKY, AVRAHM (Abraham)
YEZIERSKA, ANZIA
ZUKOFSKY, LOUIS

Music
ABRAVANEL, MAURICE (DE)
ADLER, LARRY (Lawrence)
ADLER, RICHARD
AMRAM, DAVID
ARLEN, HAROLD
AVSHALOMOV, JACOB
AX, EMMANUEL
BABBITT, MILTON
BABIN, VICTOR
BACHARACH, BURT
BAUER, MARION EUGENIE
BELL, JOSHUA
BENDIX, OTTO
BERGER, ARTHUR VICTOR
BERK, FRED
BERLINSKI, HERMAN

BERNSTEIN, LEONARD
BINDER, ABRAHAM WOLF
BLITZSTEIN, MARC
BLOOMFIELD-ZEISLER, FANNY
BOLM, ADOLPH RUDOLPHOVICH
BORIS, RUTHANNA
BRAILOWSKY, ALEXANDER
BRONFMAN, YEFIM
BROOK, BARRY SHELLEY
BROWNING, JOHN
CHASINS, ABRAHAM
CHUJOY, ANATOLE
CHURGIN, BATHIA
COHEN, JACOB RAPHAEL
COHEN, SELMA JEANNE
CONRIED, HEINRICH
COPLAND, AARON
DIAMOND, DAVID
DIAMOND, LOUIS KLEIN
DICHTER, MISHA
EISENSTEIN, JUDITH KAPLAN
ELLSTEIN, ABRAHAM (Abe)
FARBER, VIOLA
FELDMAN, MORTON
FIEDLER, ARTHUR
FLEISHER, LEON
FOGELBERG, DAN
FOSS, LUKAS
FREED, ISADORE
FRIEDMAN, DEBORAH LYNN
FUCHS, LILLIAN
GANCHOFF, MOSES
GEIRINGER, KARL
GERBER, MAYNARD
GIDEON, MIRIAM
GLASS, PHILIP
GLUCK, ALMA
GOLDMAN, EDWIN FRANKO
GOODMAN, BENNY
GOTTSCHALK, LOUIS MOREAU
GOULD, MORTON
GRAF, HERBERT
GRAFFMAN, GARY
GREENBERG, NOAH
GRUENBERG, LOUIS
HALPRIN, ANN
HAMMERSTEIN
HAYDEN, MELISSA
HERRMANN, BERNARD
HESKES, IRENE
HOROWITZ, VLADIMIR
HUROK, SOLOMON
ISTOMIN, EUGINE
JACOBI, FREDERICK
KALIB, SHALOM
KATZ, ISRAEL
KAYE, NORA
KENT, ALLEGRA
KERN, JEROME DAVID
KIDD, MICHAEL

KIRCHNER, LEON
KIRSTEIN, LINCOLN
KLEMPERER, OTTO
KOLISCH, RUDOLF
KOSTELANETZ, ANDRE
LANG, PEARL
LAPSON, DVORA
LEAR, EVELYN
LEFKOWITZ, DAVID
LEVINE, JAMES
LEVY, MARVIN DAVID
LEWENTHAL, RAYMOND
LEWITZKY, BELLA
LIEBERSON, GODDARD
LIEBLING, ESTELLE
LIST, GEORGE
LOESSER, FRANK
LOEWE, FREDERICK
LOWINSKY, EDWARD
LUBIN, ABRAHAM
LUBOSHUTZ
MANNES
MANNES, LEOPOLD
MASLOW, SOPHIE
MENDELSON, JACOB BEN-ZION
MENKEN, ALAN
MERRILL, ROBERT
MILLER, MITCH
MILSTEIN, NATHAN
MLOTEK, CHANA
NEWMAN, ALFRED
NULMAN, MACY
ORENSTEIN, ARBIE
OVED, MARGALIT
PEERCE, JAN
PERAHIA, MURRAY
PERLMAN, ITZCHAK
PETERS, ROBERTA
PLAMENAC, DRAGAN
PREVIN, ANDRE (George)
PUTTERMAN, DAVID
QUELER, EVE
RASKIN, JUDITH
REICH, STEVE
REISENBERG, NADIA
RESNIK, REGINA
RINGER, ALEXANDER
ROBBINS, JEROME
ROCHBERG, GEORGE
RODGERS, MARY
RODGERS, RICHARD
ROGERS, BERNARD
ROMBERG, SIGMUND
ROSE, LEONARD
ROSENBAUM, SAMUEL
ROSS, HERBERT
RUDEL, JULIUS
RUDOLF, MAX
SCHACHTER, CARL
SCHIFRIN, LALO

SCHLAMME, MARTHA
SCHUMAN, WILLIAM HOWARD
SCHWARTZ, STEPHEN
SECUNDA, SHOLOM
SERKIN, PETER
SHAPERO, HAROLD
SHARLIN, WILLIAM
SHAW, ARTIE
SIEGMEISTER, ELIE
SILLS, BEVERLY (Belle Silverman)
SLATKIN, LEONARD
SLONIMSKY, NICOLAS
SOKOLOW, ANNA
SONDHEIM, STEPHEN
SPECTOR, JOHANNA
SPIVACKE, HAROLD
SPIVAKOVSKY, TOSSY
STARER, ROBERT
STARK, EDWARD
STENN (STEEN), REBECCA
STERN, ISAAC
STYNE, JULE
SZIGETI, JOSEPH
TAMIRIS, HELEN
TARUSKIN, RICHARD
TAUBE, MOSHE
TEMIANKA, HENRI
THOMAS, MICHAEL TILSON
TISCHLER, HANS
TOCH, ERNST
TOUREL, JENNIE
TUCKER, RICHARD
TURECK, ROSALYN
VOLPE, ARNOLD
WALDMAN, LEIBELE
WALLENSTEIN, ALFRED
WEILL, KURT
WEINBERG, JACOB
WEINBERGER, JAROMIR
WEINER, LAZAR
WEINSTOCK, HERBERT
WEISGAL, ABBA JOSEPH
WEISGALL, HUGO
WEISSER, ALBERT
WEISSER, JOSHUA
WERNER, ERIC
WINTERNITZ, EMANUEL
WOHLBERG, MOSHE
YASSER, JOSEPH
ZEMACH, BENJAMIN
ZILBERTS, ZAVEL
ZIMBALIST, EFREM
ZUKOFSKY, PAUL

Popular Culture
ABARBANELL, LINA
ABBOTT, BUD
ABEL, ELIE
ABRAMOWITZ, BINA
ABRAMS, CAL

I. HISTORY
B. MEDIEVAL & MODERN PERIOD
2. Regional History
g. United States
BIOGRAPHIES
Popular Culture (continued)

ABRAMSON, JESSE
ACE, GOODMAN
ADAMS, FRANKLIN PIERCE
ADLER
ADLER, HARRY CLAY
ADLER, POLLY
ADLER, STELLA
ALBERT, MARV
ALBERT, MILDRED
ALCOTT, AMY
ALDRICH, ROBERT
ALEXANDER, JASON
ALLEN, MEL
ALLEN, WOODY,
ALPERT, HERB
ANTHONY, JOSEPH
ARATON, HARVEY
ARCEL, RAY
ARCHERD, ARMY
ARKIN, ALAN W.
ARONSON, BORIS
ARUM, ROBERT
ASNER, EDWARD
ATTELL, ABRAHAM WASHINGTON
AUERBACH, RED (Arnold Jacob)
AVNET, JON
AXELROD, ALBERT
AXELROD, GEORGE
AZENBERG, EMANUEL
BACALL, LAUREN
BAER, MAX (Maximilian Adelbert)
BAKSHI, RALPH
BALABAN, BARNEY
BALIN, MARTY
BARA, THEDA
BARR, ROSEANNE
BARRIS, CHUCK
BELASCO, DAVID
BEN-AMI, JACOB
BENJAMIN, RICHARD
BENNETT, MICHAEL
BENNY, JACK
BENSON, ROBBY
BERENSON, SENDA
BERG, GERTRUDE
BERG, JACKIE "KID"
BERG, MOE
BERGEN, POLLY
BERGER, ISAAC
BERGMAN, ALAN & MARILYN
BERGMAN, ANDREW
BERGNER, ELIZABETH

BERKOW, IRA
BERLE, MILTON
BERLIN, IRVING
BERMAN, PANDRO S.
BERMAN, SHELLEY
BERNARDI, HERSCHEL
BERNHARD, SANDRA
BERNSTEIN, ALINE
BERNSTEIN, ELMER
BERNSTEIN, HERMAN
BERNSTEIN, SID
BERNSTEIN, THEODORE
BETTMAN, GARY
BIKEL, THEODORE MEIR
BIMSTEIN, WHITEY
BISHOP, JOEY
BLANC, MEL
BLANK, LEON
BLAU, HERBERT
BLOCK, HERBERT LAWRENCE ("Herblock")
BLOOMGARDEN, KERMIT
BLUM, WALTER
BOCK, JERRY
BOGDANOVICH, PETER
BOONE, RICHARD
BORGE, VICTOR
BOUDREAU, LOU
BOZYK, MAX
BRECKER BROTHERS
BRENNER, TEDDY
BRICE, FANNY
BRODER, DAVID SALZER
BRODERICK, MATTHEW
BRODY, JANE
BROOKS, ALBERT
BROOKS, MEL
BROOKS, RICHARD
BROOKS, JAMES L.
BROTHERS, JOYCE
BROWN, LAWRENCE H.
BRUCE, LENNY
BRUCKHEIMER, JERRY
BUCHWALD, ART
BULOFF, JOSEPH
BURNS, GEORGE
BURROWS, ABE
BURSTEIN
BURSTYN, MIKE
BUTTONS, RED
CAAN, JAMES
CAESAR, SID
CAHN, SAMMY
CANTOR, EDDIE
CAPP, AL
CARNOVSKY, MORRIS
CARTER, NELL
CHESS, LEONARD AND PHIL
CHETWYND, LIONEL
CHOPRA, JOYCE
CLAYBURGH, JILL

CLURMAN, HAROLD
COBB, LEE J.
COEN, JOEL & ETHAN
COHEN, ALEXANDER H.
COHEN, ELLIOT ETTELSON
COHEN, NATALIE
COHEN, SASHA
COHN, HARRY
COHN, LINDA
COLEMAN, CY
COMDEN, BETTY
COOPER, JACKIE
COPELAND, LILLIAN
COPPERFIELD, DAVID
CORWIN, NORMAN LEWIS
COSELL, HOWARD
CRYSTAL, BILLY
CUBAN, MARK
CUKOR, GEORGE
CURTIS, JAMIE LEE
CURTIS, TONY
CURTIZ, MICHAEL
DA SILVA, HOWARD
DANGERFIELD, RODNEY
DANIEL, DAN
DARVAS, LILI
DASSIN, JULES
DAVID, LARRY
DAVIS, AL
DAVIS, AL "BUMMY"
DAVIS, SAMMY JR.
DEMILLE, CECIL
DEREN, MAYA
DIAMOND, I.A.L.
DIAMOND, NEIL
DILLER, BARRY
DONATH, LUDWIG
DONEN, STANLEY
DOUGLAS, KIRK
DOUGLAS, MELVYN
DOUGLAS, MICHAEL
DREYFUSS, BARNEY
DREYFUSS, RICHARD
DYLAN, BOB
ELFMAN, DANNY
ELLIOT, "MAMA" CASS
ELMAN, ZIGGY
EPSTEIN, ALVIN
EPSTEIN, CHARLOTTE
EPSTEIN, JULIUS J. AND PHILIP G.
EVANS, ROBERT
FAIN, SAMMY
FALK, PETER
FEATHER, LEONARD
FEINMAN, SIGMUND
FELDSHUH, TOVAH
FIELDS, DOROTHY
FIELDS, JACKIE
FINE, REUBEN
FISCHLER, STAN

FISHER, CARRIE
FISHER, EDDIE (Edwin)
FLAM, HERB
FLECK, BELA
FLEISCHER, NATHANIEL STANLEY
FLEISHER, LARRY
FORD, HARRISON
FOREMAN, CARL
FORMAN, MILOS
FOX, WILLIAM
FRANKENHEIMER, JOHN MICHAEL
FRANKLIN, SIDNEY
FREED, ALAN
FREED, ARTHUR
FRIEDKIN, WILLIAM
FRIEDMAN, BENJAMIN (Benny)
FRIEDMAN, KINKY
FRIEDMAN, THOMAS
FRIENDLY, FRED W.
FROHMAN
FULLER, SAMUEL MICHAEL
FUNT, ALLEN
GABEL, MAX
GABLER, MILTON
GABOR, JOLIE, MAGDA, ZSA ZSA, EVA
GAINES, WILLIAM M.
GARFIELD, JOHN (Jules)
GARFUNKEL, ART
GAYLORD, MITCHELL
GEFFEN, DAVID
GERSHWIN, GEORGE
GERSTEN, BERTA
GETZ, STAN
GIBBS, TERRY
GILBERT, BRAD
GILBERT, MELISSA
GILLMAN, SID
GLICKMAN, MARTIN IRVING
GLOBUS, YORAM
GODDARD, PAULETTE
GOLAN, MENACHEM
GOLDBERG, MARSHALL "BIGGIE"
GOLDBLUM, JEFF
GOLDEN, JOHN
GOLDENBERG, CHARLES "BUCKET"
GOLDSTEIN, JENNIE
GOLDSTEIN, RUBY
GOLDWYN, SAMUEL
GOODRICH, FRANCES AND HACKETT, ALBERT
GORCEY, LEO
GORDON, MAX
GORDON, MICHAEL
GORDON, SID
GOREN, CHARLES HENRY
GOTTLIEB, EDWARD
GOULD, ELLIOT
GRAHAM, BILL
GRANZ, NORMAN
GRAZER, BRIAN
GREEN, ABEL

I. HISTORY

   B. MEDIEVAL & MODERN PERIOD

      2. Regional History

         g. United States

           Biographies

             Popular Culture (*continued*)

GREEN, ADOLPH

GREEN, SHAWN

GREENBERG, HENRY BENJAMIN

GREENE, LORNE

GREENE, SHECKY

GREENSPAN, BUD

GREY, JOEL

GROSSFELD, ABRAHAM ISRAEL

GRUNFELD, ERNIE

GRUNWALD, HENRY ANATOLE

GUBER, PETER

GUGGENHEIM, CHARLES

GUTHRIE, ARLO

HACKETT, BUDDY

HALBERSTAM, DAVID

HALL, MONTY

HALMI, ROBERT

HAMLISCH, MARVIN

HAMMERSTEIN

HARBURG, E.Y. (Edgar "Yip")

HARMATZ, WILLIAM

HARNICK, SHELDON

HARRIS, BARBARA

HARRIS, JED

HARRIS, SAM HENRY

HARRISON, LESTER

HART, KITTY CARLISLE

HART, LORENZ

HAWN, GOLDIE

HEAD, EDITH

HECKERLING, AMY

HEINE-HEIMOWITZ, MORRIS

HENRY, BUCK

HENTOFF, NAT

HERMAN, JERRY

HERSH, SEYMOUR

HERSHEY, BARBARA

HERSHKOWITZ, VICTOR

HERSKOVITZ, MARSHALL AND ZWICK, EDWARD

HEWITT (Horowitz), DON

HILLER, ARTHUR

HIRSCH, JUDD

HOFFMAN, DUSTIN

HOLLANDERSKY, ABRAHAM ("Abe the Newsboy")

HOLLIDAY, JUDY

HOLMAN, NATHAN

HOLTZMAN, KENNETH DALE

HOLZMAN, WILLIAM (RED)

HOROWITZ, ISRAEL ALBERT

HOUDINI, HARRY

HOUSEMAN, JOHN

HOWARD, MOE, SHEMP AND CURLY (Three Stooges)

HUGHES, SARAH

IAN, JANIS

IRVING, AMY

IRVING, JULES

ISAACS, EDITH JULIET

IZENBERG, JERRY

JACOBS, HIRSCH

JACOBS, BERNARD B.

JACOBS, JAMES LESLIE

JACOBS, JOE

JACOBS, MICHAEL STRAUSS

JACOBY, OSWALD

JAFFE, SAM

JAFFEE, IRVING

JAGLOM, HENRY

JAMES, HARRY

JESSEL, GEORGE ALBERT

JOEL, BILLY

JOLSON, AL

KAEL, PAULINE

KAHN, MADELINE

KAHN, ROGER

KALICH, BERTHA

KANE, CAROL

KANIN, FAY

KARAN, DONNA

KARFF, MONA MAY

KARP, MAX AND SOPHIE

KASDAN, LAWRENCE

KASHDAN, ISAAC

KATZ, MICKEY

KATZENBERG, JEFFREY

KATZMAN, SAM

KAUFMAN, ANDY

KAUFMAN, BORIS

KAUFMAN, PHILIP

KAVNER, JULIE

KAYE, DANNY

KAZAN, LAINIE

KEITEL, HARVEY

KEMPNER, AVIVA

KESSEL, BARNEY

KESSLER, DAVID

KING, ALAN

KING, CAROLE

KING, LARRY

KLEIN, ANNE

KLEIN, CALVIN

KLEIN, MANNIE

KLUGMAN, JACK

KOLTANOWSKI, GEORGE

KONITZ, LEE

KOPPETT, LEONARD

KOPPLE, BARBARA

KORNHEISER, TONY

KOUFAX, SANFORD (Sandy)

KRAMER, STANLEY E.

KRASNA, NORMAN

KRAYZELBURG, LENNY

KRESSYN, MIRIAM

KUBRICK, STANLEY

KUDROW, LISA

LACY, STEVE

LAEMMLE, CARL

LAHR, BERT (Irving Lahrheim)

LAMARR, HEDY

LANDAU, MARTIN

LANDESMAN, ROCCO

LANDIS, JOHN

LANDON, MICHAEL

LANG, FRITZ

LANSING, SHERRY

LASKER, EMANUEL

LASKY, JESSE L.

LASSER, LOUISE

LAUREN, RALPH

LAVIN, LINDA

LAWRENCE, STEVE AND GORME, EYDIE

LE ROY, MERVYN

LEACHMAN, CLORIS

LEAR, NORMAN

LEBEDEFF, AARON

LEBOW, FRED

LEDERER, ESTHER PAULINE

LEHMAN, ERNEST

LEIBER, JERRY AND STOLLER, MIKE

LEONARD, BENNY

LEONTOVICH, EUGENIE

LERNER, ALAN JAY

LESTER, RICHARD

LEVANT, OSCAR

LEVENE, SAM

LEVENSON, SAM

LEVIEN, SONYA

LEVIN, BERNARD

LEVINE, JOSEPH E.

LEVINSKY, BATTLING (Barney Lebrowitz)

LEVINSON, BARRY

LEVY, MARV

LEWIS, JERRY

LEWIS, SHARI

LEWIS, TED (Kid)

LIEBERMAN, NANCY

LIEBLING, A.J.

LIPSYTE, ROBERT MICHAEL

LITVAK, ANATOLE (Michael)

LITWACK, HARRY

LOEW, MARCUS

LORRE, PETER

LORTEL, LUCILE

LOUIS-DREYFUS, JULIA

LUBITSCH, ERNST

LUKAS, PAUL

LUMET, SIDNEY

LYONS, LEONARD

MALTIN, LEONARD

MANILOW, BARRY

MANKIEWICZ, HERMAN

MANKIEWICZ, JOSEPH LEO

MANN, ABBY

MANN, DANIEL

MANN, DELBERT

MANN, HERBIE

MANNE, SHELLY

MARTIN, TONY

MARX BROTHERS

MASON, JACKIE

MATLIN, MARLEE

MATTHAU, WALTER

MAY, ELAINE

MAYER, LOUIS BURT

MAYSLES, ALBERT AND DAVID PAUL

MAZURSKY, PAUL

MEDVED, MICHAEL

MENDES, SAM

MENKEN, ADAH ISAACS

MERCHANT, LARRY

MERRICK, DAVID

MESSING, SHEP

MEYERS, NANCY JANE

MEZZROW, MILTON (Mezz)

MICHAELS, ALAN RICHARD

MICHAELS, LORNE

MIDLER, BETTE

MILLER, MARVIN

MIRISCH BROTHERS

MIX, RONALD

MODELL, ARTHUR B.

MOGULESKO, SIGMUND (Zelig)

MONROE, MARILYN

MOONVES, LES

MORRIS, ERROL

MORRIS, WILLIAM

MOSBACHER, EMIL JR.

MOSTEL, ZERO

MUNI, PAUL

MURRAY, ARTHUR

MYERS, LAWRENCE E. (Lon)

NAZIMOVA, ALLA

NEUWIRTH, BEBE

NEVINS, SHEILA

NEWMAN, PAUL

NEWMAN, RANDALL STUART

NICHOLS, MIKE

NIMOY, LEONARD

NORELL, NORMAN

OCHS, PHILIP DAVID

OVITZ, MICHAEL

PAKULA, ALAN

PALMER, LILLI

PALTROW, GWYNNETH

PAPP, JOSEPH

PARKER, SARAH JESSICA

PASTERNAK, JOSEPH

PATINKIN, MANDY

PATKIN, MAX

PAUL, GABRIEL HOWARD

PENN, ARTHUR

PENN, SEAN

PERRY, FRANK

PERSOFF, NEHEMIAH

I. HISTORY

B. MEDIEVAL & MODERN PERIOD

2. Regional History

g. United States

BIOGRAPHIES

Popular Culture (continued)

PICON, MOLLY
PIKE, LIPMAN E. (Lip)
PODOLOFF, MAURICE
POLLACK, SYDNEY
POLLIN, ABE
POMUS, DOC
POVICH, SHIRLEY
PREMINGER, OTTO LUDWIG
PRINCE, HAROLD
RADNER, GILDA
RAFELSON, ROBERT
RAMONE, JOEY
RANDALL, TONY
REDSTONE , SUMNER
REED, LOU
REESE, JIMMIE
REINER, CARL
REINER, ROB
REINHARDT, MAX
REINSDORF , JERRY
REISER, PAUL
RESHEVSKY, SAMUEL HERMAN
RICH, BUDDY
RICHARDS, MARTIN
RICKLES, DON
RITT, MARTIN
RITZ BROTHERS
RIVERS, JOAN
ROBERTS, TONY
ROBINSON, EDWARD G.
RODNEY, RED
ROSE, BILLY
ROSE, MAURICE
ROSEN, ALBERT LEONARD
ROSENBLOOM, CARROLL
ROSENBLOOM, MAX ("Slapsie")
ROSS, BARNEY
ROSSEN, ROBERT
ROTH, DAVID LEE
ROTH, MARK
RUDIN, SCOTT
RUDNER, RITA
RUDOLPH, MARVIN ("Mendy")
RYDER, WINONA
SAHL, MORT
SAKS, GENE
SALITA, DMITRI
SALTZMAN, HARRY
SAMPRAS, PETE
SANDLER, ADAM
SAPERSTEIN, ABRAHAM M. ("Abe")
SARACHEK, BERNARD (Red)
SAVITT, RICHARD

SCHAAP, RICHARD
SCHACHT, ALEXANDER
SCHARY, DORE
SCHAYES, ADOLPH (Dolph)
SCHECKTER, JODY
SCHENKER, JOEL W.
SCHNEIDER, ALAN (Abram Leopoldovich)
SCHNEIDER, MATHIEU
SCHWARTZ, MAURICE
SCHWIMMER, DAVID
SEDAKA, NEIL
SEDRAN (Sedransky), BARNEY
SEGAL, GEORGE
SEINFELD, JERRY
SELDES, MARIAN
SELIG, ALLAN H. ("Bud")
SELZNICK
SEYMOUR, JANE
SHAMSKY, ARTHUR LOUIS
SHANDLING, GARY
SHAPIRO, ESTHER
SHATNER, WILLIAM
SHAWN, DICK
SHEAN, AL
SHEARER, NORMA
SHER, SIR ANTHONY
SHERMAN, ALEXANDER ("Allie")
SHERMAN, ALLAN
SHERRY, LAWRENCE AND NORMAN BURT
SHORE, DINAH (Francis Rose)
SHUBERT
SHUSTER, JOE
SIDNEY, SYLVIA
SIEGEL, JERRY
SILVER, JOAN MICKLIN
SILVER, RON
SILVERMAN, SIME
SILVERS, PHIL
SIMMONS, GENE
SIMON, CARLY
SIMON, PAUL FREDERIC
SINGER, BRYAN
SKULNIK, MENASHA
SOBEL, BERNARD
SODERBERGH, STEVEN
SOLOMON, HAROLD
SONNENFELD, BARRY
SORKIN, AARON
SPECTOR, PHIL
SPELLING, AARON
SPELLMAN, FRANK
SPIEGEL, SAMUEL P.
SPIELBERG, STEVEN
SPITZ, MARK
STAR, DARREN
STARK, ALBERT ("Dolly")
STEIN, JULES
STERN, BILL
STERN, DAVID
STERN, HOWARD

STERNBERG, JOSEF VON
STILLER, BEN
STILLMAN, LOUIS
STONE, OLIVER
STONE, PETER
STONE, STEVE
STRASBERG, LEE
STREISAND, BARBRA
STRICK, JOSEPH
STROHEIM, ERICH VON
STRUG, KERRI
SUSSKIND, DAVID
TANENBAUM, SIDNEY HAROLD
TAYLOR, ELIZABETH
TAYMOR, JULIE
THALBERG, IRVING GRANT
THOMASHEFSKY, BESSIE
THOMASHEFSKY, BORIS
TOBACK, JAMES
TODD, MIKE
TORME, MEL
TUCKER, SOPHIE
ULLMAN, TRACEY
WALD, JERRY
WALETZKY, JOSH
WALLACH, ELI
WANAMAKER, SAM
WARFIELD, DAVID
WARNER
WASSERMAN, LEW
WEBB, JACK
WEIN, GEORGE
WEINSTEIN, HARVEY AND BOB
WEISSLER, BARRY AND FRAN
WEST, MAE
WESTHEIMER, RUTH
WILDER, BILLY
WILDER, GENE
WILPON, FRED
WINGER, DEBRA
WINKLER, HENRY
WINKLER, IRWIN
WINSTON, STAN
WINTERS, SHELLEY
WISE, ROBERT EARL
WISEMAN, FREDERICK
WOLPER, DAVID LLOYD
WOOLF, BOB
WYLER, WILLIAM
WYNN, ED
WYNN, KEENAN
YARROW, PETER
YOUNGMAN, HENNY
ZASLOVSKY, MAX
ZIEGFELD, FLORENZ
ZIMBALIST, EFREM
ZINNEMANN, FRED
ZORN, JOHN
ZUCKER, DAVID
ZUCKER, JEFF

ZUKOR, ADOLPH

Public & Economic Life

ABBELL, MAXWELL
ABELSON, PAUL
ABRAHAM
ABRAHAMS, ISAAC
ABRAMS, CHARLES
ABRAMS, ELLIOTT
ABRAMS, FLOYD
ABRAMS, ROBERT
ABRAMSON, JERRY EDWIN
ABZUG, BELLA
ACKERMAN, GARY
ADAMS, ARLIN MARVIN
ADAMS, JOHN
ADLER, ELMER
ADLER, EMANUEL PHILIP
ADLER, JULIUS OCHS
ADLER, MAX
ALEXANDER, ABRAHAM
ALEXANDER, BEATRICE
ALEXANDER, MOSES
ALLEN, ISAAC
ALLEN, PAUL
ALSCHULER, SAMUEL
ALTER, ELEANOR (Breitel)
ALTHEIMER, BENJAMIN
ALTMAN, BENJAMIN
ALTSCHUL, FRANK
ALTSCHUL, LOUIS
AMATEAU, ALBERT JEAN
AMERICAN, SADIE
AMRAM, DAVID WERNER
AMSTERDAM, BIRDIE
AMTER, ISRAEL
ANNENBERG, WALTER H.
ANSORGE, MARTIN
APPELMAN, HARLENE
ARONSON, ARNOLD
ARVEY, JACOB M.
ATRAN, FRANK Z.
AUERBACH, BEATRICE FOX
BAAR, EMIL
BACHARACH
BACHARACH, ISAAC
BACHE
BACKER, GEORGE
BAERWALD, PAUL
BAKER, EDWARD MAX
BALLMER, STEVEN
BAMBERGER, LOUIS
BAMBERGER, SIMON
BARNERT, NATHAN
BARONDESS, JOSEPH
BARRON, JENNIE LOITMAN
BARSHEFSKY, CHARLENE
BARSIMSON, JACOB
BARUCH
BAUM, MORTON

I. HISTORY
B. MEDIEVAL & MODERN PERIOD
2. Regional History
g. United States
BIOGRAPHIES
Public & Economic Life (continued)

BAZELON, DAVID L.

BEAME, ABRAHAM DAVID

BECKELMAN, MOSES W.

BECKER

BECKER, EDWARD ROY

BEDACHT, MAX

BEHAR, NISSIM

BEHRMAN, MARTIN

BEILENSON, ANTHONY

BELMONT, AUGUST

BENDERLY, SAMSON

BENESCH, ALFRED ABRAHAM

BENJAMIN, JUDAH PHILIP

BEN-VENISTE, RICHARD

BERG, PHILIP

BERGER, MEYER

BERGER, SAMUEL R.

BERGER, VICTOR

BERKLEY, ROCHELLE

BERKLEY, WILLIAM R.

BERMAN, HOWARD

BERMAN, JULIUS

BERNAYS, EDWARD

BERNBACH, WILLIAM

BERNHEIM, ISAAC WOLFE

BERNHEIMER, CHARLES SELIGMAN

BERNSTEIN, CARL

BERNSTEIN, LUDWIG BEHR

BERNSTEIN, ZALMAN CHAIM

BERNSTEIN, ZVI HIRSCH

BETTMANN, BERNHARD

BIALKIN, KENNETH

BICKEL, ALEXANDER M.

BIEN, JULIUS

BIJUR, NATHAN

BILLIKOPF, JACOB

BINSWANGER, ISIDORE

BISGYER, MAURICE

BITTELMAN, ALEXANDER

BLACK, ALGERNON

BLACKSTONE, WILLIAM E.

BLANK, ARTHUR

BLAUSTEIN

BLAUSTEIN, DAVID

BLITZER, WOLF

BLOCH

BLOCH, CLAUDE

BLOCK, H&R

BLOCK, PAUL

BLOOM, BENJAMIN SAMUEL

BLOOM, SOL

BLOOMBERG, MICHAEL

BLOOMINGDALE

BLUESTONE, JOSEPH ISAAC

BLUHDORN, CHARLES

BLUMENBERG, LEOPOLD

BLUMENFIELD, SAMUEL

BLUMENTHAL, GEORGE

BLUMENTHAL, JOSEPH

BLUMENTHAL, JOSEPH

BLUMENTHAL, WERNER MICHAEL

BOESKY, IVAN

BOGEN, BORIS DAVID

BOLTEN, JOSHUA B.

BONDI, AUGUST

BONDI, JONAS

BONDY, MAX

BOOKBINDER, HYMAN H.

BORINSTEIN, LOUIS J.

BOSCHWITZ, RUDOLPH ELI

BOTEIN, BERNARD

BOXER, BARBARA

BOYAR, LOUIS H.

BRANDEIS, LOUIS DEMBITZ

BREITEL, CHARLES

BRENNER, ROSE

BRENTANO

BRESLAW, JOSEPH

BRESSLER, DAVID MAURICE

BREYER, STEPHEN GERALD

BRIN, SERGEY

BROAD, ELI

BROIDO, LOUIS

BRONFMAN, EDGAR MILES

BROWN, BENJAMIN

BROWN, DAVID ABRAHAM

BROWN, HAROLD

BRUCKMAN, HENRIETTA

BUCHALTER, LOUIS ("Lepke")

BUERGENTHAL, THOMAS

BURNS, ARTHUR FRANK

BUSH, GEORGE HERBERT WALKER

BUSH, GEORGE WALKER

BUSH, ISIDOR

BUSH, SOLOMON

BUTTENWIESER

BUTZEL

CAHN, EDMOND NATHANIEL

CALOF, RACHEL

CANTOR, ERIC

CANTOR, JACOB AARON

CARDIN, BENJAMIN L.

CARDIN, SHOSHANA

CARDOZO

CARDOZO, BENJANIN NATHAN

CARNEGIE, HATTIE

CARTER, JAMES EARL (Jimmy)

CARTER, VICTOR M.

CELLER, EMANUEL

CERF, BENNETT ALFRED

CHAIKIN, SOL

CHERTOFF , MICHAEL

CHIPKIN, ISRAEL

CHUDOFF, EARL
CLINTON, WILLIAM JEFFERSON
COHEN
COHEN, ALFRED MORTON
COHEN, BENJAMIN VICTOR
COHEN, FANNIA M.
COHEN, H. RODGIN
COHEN, JOHN SANFORD
COHEN, MARY MATILDA
COHEN, PHILIP MELVIN
COHEN, WILLIAM S.
COHEN, WILLIAM WOLFE
COHN, MORRIS MANDEL
COHON, GEORGE
COLE, KENNETH
CONE
COPPERSMITH, SAMUEL
COWEN, PHILIP
CROWN, HENRY
CUBAN, MARK
CULLMAN
CUTLER, BRUCE
CUTLER, HARRY
DA COSTA, ISAAC
D'AMATO, ALPHONSE
DARMSTADT, JOSEPH
DAROFF, SAMUEL H.
DASH, SAMUEL
DAVIDSON, WILLIAM
DAVIS, ABEL
DAVIS, MARVIN H.
DAVIS, SUSAN
DE CORDOVA, JACOB
DE HAAS, JACOB
DE LA MOTTA, JACOB
DE LEON
DE LEON, DANIEL
DE LUCENA
DELL, MICHAEL
DEMBITZ, LEWIS NAPHTALI
DERSHOWITZ, ALAN M.
DEUTCH, JOHN M.
DEUTSCH, BERNARD SEYMOUR
DICKSTEIN, SAMUEL
DININ, SAMUEL
DITTENHOEFER, ABRAM JESSE
DORPH, SHELDON
DREBEN, SAM
DREXLER, MILLARD (Mickey)
DROPSIE, MOSES AARON
DUBINSKY, DAVID
DUSHKIN, ALEXANDER MORDECHAI
DYCHE, JOHN ALEXANDER
EINSTEIN, LEWIS
EISENHOWER, DWIGHT DAVID
EISENMAN, CHARLES
EISNER, MARK
EISNER, MICHAEL DAMMANN
EIZENSTAT, STUART
ELCAN, MARCUS

ELIAS, ELI
ELKUS, ABRAM ISAAC
ELLENSTEIN, MEYER C.
ELLINGER, MORITZ
ELLISON, LAWRENCE J.
ELLSBERG, DANIEL
ELLSBERG, EDWARD
ENGEL, ELIOT L.
EPSTEIN, JUDITH
ETTENBERG, SYLVIA
ETTING
EVANS, ELI
EVANS, JANE
EZEKIEL, JACOB
FACTOR, MAX
FAIRSTEIN, LINDA
FALK
FARKAS, RUTH
FEINBERG, ABRAHAM
FEINBERG, KENNETH
FEINBERG, ROBERT
FEINGOLD, RUSSELL
FEINSTEIN, DIANNE
FEINSTONE, MORRIS
FEITH, DOUGLAS J.
FELDHEIM, PHILIPP
FELDMAN, HERMAN
FELDMAN, SANDRA
FELLER, ABRAHAM HOWARD
FELS
FERKAUF, EUGENE
FILENE
FINEMAN, HAYYIM
FINKELSTEIN, ARTHUR
FISCHEL, ARNOLD
FISCHEL, HARRY
FISHER, DONALD
FISHER, MAX M.
FISHMAN, JACOB
FLEISCHMANN, JULIUS
FLEISHER
FLEXNER
FOREMAN, MILTON J.
FORMAN, PHILLIP
FORTAS, ABE
FOXMAN, ABRAHAM
FRAENKEL, OSMOND K.
FRANK, BARNEY
FRANK, ELI
FRANK, JEROME
FRANK, LEO MAX
FRANK, RAY
FRANKEL, HIRAM D.
FRANKEL, LEE KAUFER
FRANKEL, MARVIN E.
FRANKEL, MAX
FRANKEL, SAMUEL BENJAMIN
FRANKENTHALER, GEORGE
FRANKFURTER, FELIX
FRANKS, DAVID

I. HISTORY

B. MEDIEVAL & MODERN PERIOD

2. Regional History

g. United States

BIOGRAPHIES

Public & Economic Life (continued)

FRANKS, DAVID SALISBURY
FRANKS, JACOB
FRANKS, JACOB
FREIBERG LIST
FREUND, ERNST
FREUND, PAUL ABRAHAM
FREUND-ROSENTHAL, MIRIAM KOTTLER
FRIEDAN, BETTY
FRIEDENBERG, ALBERT MARX
FRIEDENBERG, SAMUEL
FRIEDENWALD
FRIEDLANDER, ISAAC
FRIEDLANDER, WALTER
FRIEDMAN, HERBERT A.
FRIEDSAM, MICHAEL
FRIEND, HUGO MORRIS
FRIENDLY, HENRY JACOB
FRISCH, DANIEL
FROST, MARTIN
FUCHSBERG, JACOB D.
FULD, STANLEY HOWELLS
GADOL, MOISES
GAER, FELICE
GAMORAN, EMANUEL
GANS, BIRD STEIN
GARMENT, LEONARD
GELB, ARTHUR
GELLMAN, LEON
GEORGE, MANFRED
GERSHOVITZ, SAMUEL
GERSONI, HENRY
GERSTLE, LEWIS
GERTZ, ELMER
GIMBEL
GINGOLD, PINCHAS M.
GINSBERG, EDWARD
GINSBERG, MITCHELL I.
GINSBURG, RUTH JOAN BADER
GITLOW, BENJAMIN
GLICKMAN, DANIEL
GLUCKSMAN, HARRY L.
GOLD, BENJAMIN
GOLDBERG, ARTHUR JOSEPH
GOLDBERG, JEANNETTE MIRIAM
GOLDIN, DANIEL SAUL
GOLDMAN
GOLDMAN, EMMA
GOLDMAN, MAYER CLARENCE
GOLDMAN, MOSES HA-KOHEN
GOLDMAN, PAUL L.
GOLDMANN, SIDNEY
GOLDMARK
GOLDSCHMIDT, NEIL EDWARD

GOLDSMITH, HORACE WARD
GOLDSMITH, SAMUEL ABRAHAM
GOLDSTEIN, ABRAHAM SAMUEL
GOLDSTEIN, FANNY
GOLDSTEIN, JUDAH JAMISON
GOLDWASSER, ISRAEL EDWIN
GOLDWATER
GOLDWATER, SIGMUND SCHULZ
GOMEZ
GOMPERS, SAMUEL
GOODHART, ARTHUR LEHMAN
GOODMAN, ANDREW
GOODMAN, ARNOLD ABRAHAM, LORD
GOTSFELD, BESSIE GOLDSTEIN
GOTTESMAN
GOULD, MILTON S.
GRANT, LEE
GRANT, ULYSSES SIMPSON
GRATZ
GRATZ, REBECCA
GREENBAUM, EDWARD SAMUEL
GREENBERG, HAYYIM
GREENBERG, MAURICE
GREENBLATT, ALIZA
GREENE, HAROLD
GREENEBAUM
GREENFIELD, ALBERT MONROE
GREENSPAN, ALAN
GREENSTEIN, HARRY
GROSSINGER, JENNIE
GROSSMAN, STEVEN
GROVE, ANDREW S.
GRUBER, RUTH
GRUENBERG, SIDONIE MATSNER
GRUENING, ERNEST HENRY
GUGGENHEIM
GUINZBURG, HAROLD KLEINERT
GUZIK, JACOB
HACKENBURG, WILLIAM BOWER
HAHN, MICHAEL
HALLGARTEN
HALPRIN, ROSE LURIA
HAMMER, ARMAND
HANDLER, MILTON
HANDLER, RUTH MOSKO
HARBY, ISAAC
HARBY, LEVI MYERS
HARDMAN, JACOB BENJAMIN
HARMAN, JANE
HARRIS, LOUIS
HART, ABRAHAM
HART, BERNARD
HART, EMANUEL BERNARD
HART, EPHRAIM
HART, ISAAC
HART, MYER
HARTOGENSIS, BENJAMIN HENRY
HASSENFELD, SYLVIA
HAUSER, RITA
HAY, JOHN MILTON

HAYES, ISAAC ISRAEL
HAYS
HAYS, ARTHUR GARFIELD
HAYS, DANIEL PEIXOTTO
HELD, ADOLPH
HELLERSTEIN, ALVIN K.
HELLMAN, ISAIAS WOLF
HELMSLEY, LEONA
HENDRICKS
HENRY, JACOB
HENSHEL, HARRY D.
HERLANDS, WILLIAM BERNARD
HERSTEIN, LILLIAN
HERTZ, EMANUEL
HEYDENFELDT, SOLOMON
HILLMAN, BESSIE ABRAMOWITZ
HILLMAN, SIDNEY
HILLQUIT, MORRIS
HIMMELSTEIN, LENA
HIRSCH, SOLOMON
HIRSCHMANN, IRA ARTHUR
HIRSHHORN, JOSEPH HERMAN
HOCHMAN, JULIUS
HOENLEIN, MALCOLM
HOFFMAN, CHARLES ISAIAH
HOFFMAN, JEFFREY
HOFFMAN, JULIUS JENNINGS
HOFFMAN, PHILIP E.
HOLBROOKE, RICHARD CHARLES
HOLLZER, HARRY AARON
HOLTZMAN, ELIZABETH
HONOR, LEO L.
HORNER, HENRY
HOROWITZ, LOUIS J.
HUMPHREY, HUBERT H.
HURWICH, LOUIS
HURWITZ, HENRY
HYMAN, JOSEPH C.
ICAHN, CARL
INDYK, MARTIN
ISAACS
ISAACS, ISAIAH
ISAACS, JOSEPH
ISAACS, NATHAN
ISRAEL, STEVE
JACKSON, SOLOMON HENRY
JACOBS, FRANCES WISEBART
JACOBS, IRWIN
JACOBS, ROSE GELL
JACOBS, SOLOMON
JACOBSON, EDWARD (Eddie)
JAFFA
JAVITS, JACOB KOPPEL
JEFFERSON, THOMAS
JESSELSON, LUDWIG
JOACHIMSEN, PHILIP J.
JOEL, RICHARD
JOHNSON, LYNDON BAINES
JONAS, JOSEPH
JONAS, NATHAN S.

JORDAN, CHARLES HAROLD
JOSEPHSON, MANUEL
JOSEPHTAL, LOUIS MAURICE
JUDAH
KAHANE, MEIR
KAHN, ALEXANDER
KAHN, BERNARD
KAHN, DOROTHY C.
KAHN, FLORENCE PRAG
KAHN, JULIUS
KAHN, OTTO HERMANN
KALB, BERNARD
KALB, MARVIN
KALIKOW, PETER
KAMPELMAN, MAX M.
KANE, IRVING
KANEV, ISAAC
KANN, PETER R.
KANTOR, MICKEY
KAPLAN, LOUIS LIONEL
KAR-BEN/LERNER
KARMAZIN, MEL
KARSEN, FRITZ
KATZ, LABEL A.
KAUFMAN, IRVING R.
KAYE, JUDITH
KEMPNER, HARRIS
KENNEDY, JOHN FITZGERALD
KIMMEL, SIDNEY
KIRSTEIN, LOUIS EDWARD
KISSINGER, HENRY ALFRED
KLAPPER, PAUL
KLEIN, JULIUS
KLEIN, MORTON
KLEIN, PHILIP
KLUTZNICK, PHILIP MORRIS
KNEFLER, FREDERICK
KNOPF, ALFRED A.
KNOPF, BLANCHE WOLFE
KOBLER, FRANZ
KOCH, EDWARD IRVING
KOENIGSBERG, MOSES
KOHL, HERBERT
KOHLER, MAX JAMES
KOPELMAN, ARIE
KOPPEL, TED
KOPPLEMANN, HERMAN PAUL
KORNFELD, JOSEPH SAUL
KOSNER, EDWARD
KOZINSKI, ALEX
KRAFT, LOUIS
KRAUS, ADOLF
KRAVIS, HENRY
KRAVITCH, PHYLLIS A.
KRISTOL, WILLIAM
KROCK, ARTHUR
KROSS, ANNA
KRULEWITCH, MELVIN LEVIN
KUHN-LOEB
KUNIN, MADELEINE MAY

I. HISTORY
B. MEDIEVAL & MODERN PERIOD
2. Regional History
g. United States
BIOGRAPHIES
Public & Economic Life (continued)

KUNSTLER, WILLIAM
KUNZ, JOSEF LAURENZ
KURSHEEDT, ISRAEL BAER
KURTZER, DANIEL CHARLES
LA GUARDIA, FIORELLO HENRY
LADEJINSKY, WOLF ISAAC
LANSKY, MEYER
LANTOS, TOM
LASKER
LAUDER, ESTÉE
LAUDER, RONALD
LAURENCE, WILLIAM L.
LAUTENBERG, FRANK
LAUTERBACH, EDWARD H.
LAWRENCE, DAVID
LAWTON, SAMUEL T.
LAZARD
LAZARUS
LEAVITT, MOSES A.
LEFKOWITZ, LOUIS
LEFRAK, SAMUEL J.
LEHMAN
LEHMAN, HERBERT HENRY
LEHMAN, IRVING
LEHMAN, WILLIAM
LEIBER, JUDITH
LEIBOWITZ, SAMUEL SIMON
LEIDESDORF, SAMUEL DAVID
LEIPZIGER, HENRY M.
LELYVELD, JOSEPH
LEMKIN, RAPHAEL
LERNER, MICHAEL
LESLIE, ROBERT L.
LEVI, EDWARD H.
LEVIN, CARL
LEVIN, LEWIS CHARLES
LEVIN, RICHARD
LEVIN, SANDER
LEVIN, THEODORE
LEVIN-SHATZKES, YIZHAK
LEVINSON, SALMON OLIVER
LEVITAN, SOLOMON
LEVITT
LEVITT, ARTHUR SENIOR AND JR.
LEVY, AARON
LEVY, AARON
LEVY, ALBERT J.
LEVY, ASSER
LEVY, CHAPMAN
LEVY, HAYMAN
LEVY, JEFFERSON MONROE
LEVY, JONAS PHILLIPS
LEVY, MOSES

LEVY, MOSES
LEVY, MOSES ELIAS
LEVY, NATHAN
LEVY, URIAH PHILLIPS
LEW, JACOB
LEWIN, NATHAN
LEWIS, ANTHONY
LEWIS, PETER B.
LEWIS, SAMUEL ALEXANDER
LEWISOHN
LICHT, FRANK
LIEBERMAN, JOSEPH
LIEBMANN, ESTHER SCHULHOFF ARON AND JOST
LILIENTHAL, DAVID ELI
LIMAN, ARTHUR
LINCOLN, ABRAHAM
LINDHEIM, IRMA LEVY
LINGLE, LINDA
LINOWITZ, SOL MYRON
LIPPMANN, WALTER
LIPSKY, LOUIS
LIT
LITTAUER, LUCIUS NATHAN
LIVERIGHT, HORACE BRISBIN
LOEB, JAMES
LONDON, MEYER
LOPEZ, AARON
LOURIE, NORMAN VICTOR
LOVESTONE, JAY
LOW, MINNIE
LOWENSTEIN, ALLARD KENNETH
LOWENSTEIN, SOLOMON
LOWEY, NITA
LOWN, PHILIP W.
LURIE, HARRY LAWRENCE
LYONS, EUGENE
MACK, JULIAN WILLIAM
MACKLOWE, HARRY
MADISON, JAMES
MAGNES, JUDAH LEON
MAGNIN, MARY ANN COHEN
MALKIEL, THERESA SERBER
MALSIN, LANE BRYANT
MANDEL, MARVIN
MANN, FREDERIC RAND
MANN, THEODORE R.
MARCOSSON, ISAAC
MARCUS, BERNARD
MARCUS, DAVID DANIEL
MARCUS, STANLEY
MARGARETEN, REGINA
MARGOLIN, ARNOLD
MARGOSHES, SAMUEL
MARIX, ADOLPH
MARKEL, LESTER
MARKS, HAYMAN
MARKS, MARCUS M.
MARSHALL, LOUIS
MASSELL, SAM JR.
MATZ, ISRAEL

MAYER, LEOPOLD
MAYER, LEVY
MAZER
MAZUR, JAY
MCDONALD, JAMES GROVER
MEARS, OTTO
MEDALIE, GEORGE ZERDIN
MEED, BENJAMIN
MEED, VLADKA
MEIER, JULIUS
MELTON, FLORENCE ZACKS
MELTON, SAMUEL MENDEL
MENKEN
MESSINGER, RUTH
MEYER, ANNIE NATHAN
MEYER, BARON DE HIRSCH
MEYER, EUGENE
MEYERHOFF, HARVEY
MEYERHOFF, JOSEPH
MICHAEL, JAKOB
MICHAEL, MOSES
MICHELSON, CHARLES
MIKVA, ABNER J.
MILKEN, MICHAEL
MILL, JOSEPH SOLOMON (John)
MILLER, LOUIS E.
MILSTEIN
MINIS
MINOW, NEWTON NORMAN
MINSKY, LOUIS
MOÏSE, ABRAHAM
MONSKY, HENRY
MONTOR, HENRY
MORDECAI, ALFRED
MORDECAI, JACOB
MOREEL, BEN
MORGENTHAU
MORRIS, NELSON
MORSE, DAVID ABNER
MORSE, LEOPOLD
MORWITZ, EDWARD
MOSES, MYER
MOSES, RAPHAEL J.
MOSES, ROBERT
MOSKOWITZ, HENRY
MOSS, JOHN
MYERS, GUSTAVUS
MYERS, MORDECAI
MYERS, MOSES
MYERS, SAMUEL
MYERSON, BESS
NAAR, DAVID
NADLER, JERROLD
NAGLER, ISADORE
NATHAN
NATHAN, MAUD
NAUMBURG
NELSON, LOUIS
NEUBERGER, RICHARD LEWIS
NEUMANN, EMANUEL

NEUMANN, HENRY
NEWHOUSE, SAMUEL IRVING
NEWMAN, ISIDORE
NEWMAN, JON O.
NEWMAN, PAULINE
NEWMARK
NEWMYER, ARTHUR GROVER
NILES, DAVID K.
NIXON, RICHARD MILHAUS
NIZER, LOUIS
NOAH, MORDECAI MANUEL
NONES, BENJAMIN
NORMAN, EDWARD ALBERT
NOVAK, ROBERT
NOVY, JIM
OCHS
OHRBACH
OPPENHEIMER, FRITZ E.
ORTENBERG, ARTHUR
OTTINGER, ALBERT
PACHECO, RODRIGO BENJAMIN MENDES
PACHT, ISAAC
PACKMAN, JAMES JOSEPH
PADWAY, JOSEPH ARTHUR
PALEY, WILLIAM SAMUEL
PAM, HUGO
PANKEN. JACOB
PARNIS, MOLLIE
PAT, JACOB
PATRICOF, ALAN
PEARL, DANIEL
PEARLSTINE, NORMAN
PEIXOTTO
PEIXOTTO, JUDITH
PEKARSKY, MAURICE
PEKELIS, ALEXANDER HAIM
PEMBER, PHOEBE YATES
PERELMAN, RONALD O.
PERLE, RICHARD N.
PERLMAN, ALFRED EDWARD
PERLMAN, HELEN HARRIS
PERLMAN, SELIG
PERSKY, DANIEL
PESOTTA, ROSE
PFORZHEIMER, CARL HOWARD
PHILADELPHIA, JACOB
PHILLIPS
PHILLIPS, PHILIP
PHILLIPS, REBECCA MACHADO
PHILLIPSON, IRVING JOSEPH
PILCH, JUDAH
PINANSKI, ABRAHAM
PINNER, MORITZ
PINTO, ISAAC
PISCO, SERAPHINE
POGREBIN, LETTY COTTIN
POLACHEK, VICTOR HENRY
POLIER, SHAD
POLLACK, MILTON
POLLAK, WALTER HEILPRIN

I. HISTORY
B. MEDIEVAL & MODERN PERIOD
2. Regional History
g. United States
BIOGRAPHIES
Public & Economic Life (continued)

POLYKOFF, SHIRLEY
POMERANTZ, FRED
POSNER, RICHARD A.
POTOFSKY, JACOB SAMUEL
PRAGER, DENNIS
PRESSMAN, LEE
PRITZKER
PROSKAUER, JOSEPH MEYER
PULITZER, JOSEPH
RABB, MAXWELL MILTON
RABINOFF, GEORGE W.
RABINOWICZ, OSKAR K.
RABINOWITZ, LOUIS MAYER
RADIN, MAX
RATNER, BRUCE
RATNER, LEONARD
RATSHESKY, ABRAHAM CAPTAIN
RAUH, JOSEPH L.
RAYNER, ISIDOR
RAYNOR, BRUCE
RAZOVSKY, CECILIA
REAGAN, RONALD WILSON
REDLICH, NORMAN
REE, HARTVIG PHILIP
REESE, MICHAEL
REHINE, ZALMA
REINHARDT, STEPHEN R.
REMNICK, DAVID
RENDELL, EDWARD
RESNIK, JUDITH
REVSON, CHARLES HASKELL
RIBICOFF, ABRAHAM A.
RICE, ISAAC LEOPOLD
RICE, JAMES P.
RICE, JOSEPH MAYER
RICH
RICH, MARC
RICHARDS, BERNARD GERSON
RICHMAN, JULIA
RICKOVER, HYMAN GEORGE
RIEGELMAN, HAROLD
RIFKIND, SIMON HIRSCH
RIKLIS, MESHULAM
RIVERA, JACOB RODRIGUEZ
RIVLIN, ALICE MITCHELL
ROBINSON, JACOB
ROBINSON, NEHEMIAH
ROCKER
RODKINSON, MICHAEL LEVI
ROHATYN, FELIX G.
ROOSEVELT, FRANKLIN DELANO
ROOSEVELT, THEODORE
ROSE, ALEX

ROSE, ERNESTINE POTOVSKY
ROSE, MAURICE
ROSEN, CARL
ROSENBERG, ABRAHAM
ROSENBERG, ABRAHAM HAYYIM
ROSENBERG, ANNA MARIE LEDERER
ROSENBERG, JAMES NAUMBURG
ROSENBLATT, BERNARD ABRAHAM
ROSENBLATT, SOL ARIEH
ROSENBLOOM, SOLOMON
ROSENBLUM, FRANK
ROSENDALE, SIMON WOLFE
ROSENFELD, SAMUEL
ROSENMAN, SAMUEL IRVING
ROSENSAFT, JOSEF
ROSENSOHN, ETTA LASKER
ROSENTHAL, ABRAHAM MICHAEL
ROSENTHAL, BENJAMIN
ROSENTHAL, HERMAN
ROSENTHAL, IDA COHEN
ROSENWALD
ROSEWATER, EDWARD
ROSS, DENNIS B.
ROSS, STEPHEN
ROSTOW, EUGENE VICTOR
ROSTOW, WALT WHITMAN
ROTHBERG, SAMUEL
ROTHENBERG, MORRIS
ROTHSCHILD, WALTER N.
ROTHSTEIN, ARNOLD
RUBIN, ROBERT
RUBIN, SAMUEL
RUBINSTEIN, HELENA
RUBY, JACK
RUDIN
RUDMAN, WARREN BRUCE
RUEF, ABRAHAM
RUKEYSER, MERRYLE STANLEY
SABAN, HAIM
SABATH, ADOLF JOACHIM
SABSOVICH, H. L.
SACHS
SAFIRE, WILLIAM
SAKOWITZ, BERNARD
SALIT, NORMAN
SALOMON, HAYM
SALTZMAN, MAURICE
SALVADOR
SALZMAN, WILLIAM
SAMUEL, RALPH E.
SAND, LEONARD
SANDERS, BERNARD
SAPIRO, AARON
SAPIRSTEIN-STONE-WEISS
SARASOHN, KASRIEL HERSCH
SARNOFF, DAVID
SATINSKY, SOL
SCAASI, ARNOLD
SCHAKOWSKY, JANICE
SCHANBERG, SYDNEY

SCHECHTMAN, JOSEPH B.

SCHECK, BARRY

SCHENK, FAYE L.

SCHEUER, JAMES

SCHIFF, ADAM

SCHIFF, DOROTHY

SCHIFF, JACOB HENRY

SCHLESINGER, BENJAMIN

SCHLOSSBERG, JOSEPH

SCHMIDT, SAMUEL MYER

SCHNEIDER, IRVING

SCHOOLMAN, BERTHA S.

SCHORR, DANIEL L.

SCHOTTLAND, CHARLES IRWIN

SCHRADER, ABE

SCHULTZ, DUTCH

SCHULTZ, HOWARD

SCHUSTER, MAX LINCOLN

SCHUSTERMAN, CHARLES AND LYNN

SCHWAB, JOSEPH J.

SCHWARTZ, DAVID

SCHWARTZ, FELICE NIERENBERG

SCHWARTZ, JOSEPH J.

SCHWARZBERG, SAMUEL BENJAMIN

SCHWIMMER, ROSIKA

SEASONGOOD

SEGAL, BERNARD GERARD

SEGAL, LOUIS

SEIXAS

SELDES, GEORGE

SELEKMAN, BENJAMIN M.

SELIGMAN

SELIGSBERG, ALICE LILLIE

SELTZER, LOUIS BENSON

SEMAN, PHILIP LOUIS

SENIOR, MAX

SHALOM, ISAAC I.

SHANKER, ALBERT

SHAPERO, NATE S.

SHAPIRO, EZRA Z.

SHAPIRO, IRVING SAUL

SHAPIRO, ROBERT

SHAPIRO, SAMUEL HARVEY

SHAPP, MILTON J.

SHAVELSON, CLARA LEMLICH

SHAW, BENJAMN

SHEFTALL

SHEINDLIN, JUDITH

SHEINKMAN, JACOB

SHER, NEAL

SHETZER, SIMON

SHIPLACOFF, ABRAHAM ISAAC

SHRODER, WILLIAM J.

SHULMAN, HARRY

SIEBERT, MURIEL

SIEGEL, BENJAMIN ("Bugsy")

SIEGEL, MARK

SIGMAN, MORRIS

SILBERBERG, MENDEL

SILVER, EDWARD S.

SILVER, HAROLD M.

SILVERSTEIN, LARRY

SIMON

SIMON, JOSEPH

SIMON, NORTON

SIMONS, JAMES

SIMSON

SINGER, ISIDORE

SINGER, ISRAEL

SLAWSON, JOHN

SLOMOVITZ, PHILIP

SLOSS, MARCUS CAUFFMAN

SOBELOFF, ISIDOR

SOBELOFF, SIMON ERNEST

SOFAER, ABRAHAM

SOKOLOF, PHIL

SOLARZ, STEPHEN JOSHUA

SOLIS-COHEN

SOLOMON, EZEKIEL

SOLOMON, HANNAH GREENEBAUM

SOLOMONS, ADOLPHUS SIMEON

SONNEBORN, RUDOLF GOLDSCHMIDT

SONNENFELDT, HELMUT

SONNENSCHEIN, ROSA

SOROS, GEORGE

SPANEL, ABRAM NETHANIEL

SPECTER, ARLEN

SPEYER

SPIEGEL, DORA

SPIELVOGEL, CARL, AD, AMBASSADOR

SPITZER, ELIOT

SPORKIN, STANLEY

SQUADRON, HOWARD MAURICE

STACHEL, JACOB

STARK, LOUIS

STEIMER, MOLLY

STEIN, HERMAN D.

STEINEM, GLORIA

STEINGUT

STEINHARDT, LAURENCE ADOLF

STEINHARDT, MICHAEL

STERN, ELIZABETH

STERN, HORACE

STERN, JULIUS DAVID

STERN, LEONARD

STERN, LOUIS

STERN, MAX

STERNE, SIMON

STOKES, ROSE PASTOR (Wieslander)

STONE, DEWEY

STONE, I.F. (Isidore Feinstein)

STONE, JULIUS

STONE, RICHARD BERNARD

STRASSFELD, SHARON

STRAUS

STRAUS, ROGER JR.

STRAUSS, LEVI

STRAUSS, LEWIS LICHTENSTEIN

STRAUSS, ROBERT SCHWARTZ

STROOCK

ACKERMAN, PAULA
ADAMS, THEODORE
ADLER, JOSEPH
ADLER, LIEBMANN
ADLER, MORRIS
ADLER, SAMUEL
AGUS, JACOB BERNARD
ALBUM, ZVI SHIMON
ALPER, MICHAEL
ALPERSTEIN, AVRAHAM
ANGEL, MARC
ARONOWITZ, BENJAMIN
ARONSON, DAVID
ARZT, MAX
ASH, AVRAHAM J.
ASHER, JOSEPH
ASHINSKY, AARON MORDECAI HALEVI
AVRUTICK, ABRAHAM
AZUBY, ABRAHAM
BAAR, HERMAN
BACKMAN, JULES
BAMBERGER, BERNARD JACOB
BARISHANSKY, RAPHAEL
BARNSTON, HENRY
BARON, JOSEPH LOUIS
BAUM, SHEPARD
BAUMOL, JOSHUA
BEERMAN, LEONARD
BELKIN, SAMUEL
BENJAMIN, RAPHAEL
BERGER, ELMER
BERKOWITZ, HENRY
BERMAN, MORTON MAYER
BERMAN, MYRON
BERNSTEIN, LOUIS
BERNSTEIN, PHILIP SIDNEY
BESDIN, MORRIS J.
BESSER, CHASKEL O.
BETTAN, ISRAEL
BETTELHEIM, ALBERT (Aaron) SIEGFRIED
BLANK, SHELDON HAAS
BLEICH, J. DAVID
BLOCH, CHAIM
BLOCH, ELIJAH MEYER
BLOCH, JOSHUA
BLUMENTHAL, AARON
BOHNEN, ELI AARON
BOKSER, BEN ZION
BOROWITZ, EUGENE
BOSNIAK, JACOB
BOTEACH, SHMUEL
BRAUDE, MAX A.
BRAUDE, WILLIAM GORDON
BRESLAU, ISADORE
BRICKNER, BALFOUR
BRILL, ISAAC
BRONSTEIN, HERBERT
BROWN, SAUL PARDO
BROWNE, EDWARD B.M.
BROWNE, LEWIS

BUNIM, IRVING
BURSTEIN, ABRAHAM
CALISCH, EDWARD NATHAN
CANTOR, BERNARD
CARLEBACH, SHLOMO
COFFEE, RUDOLPH I.
COHEN, ARMOND
COHEN, HENRY
COHEN, JACK
COHEN, JACOB XENAB
COHEN, JOSEPH ISAAC
COHEN, MORTIMER JOSEPH
COHEN, SEYMOUR J.
COHN, ELKAN
COHON, SAMUEL SOLOMON
COOK, SAMUEL
CRESSON, WARDER
CRONBACH, ABRAHAM
CURRICK, MAX COHEN
CHANOVER, HYMAN
CHARLOP, YECHIEL
CHAVEL, CHARLES (Dov) BER
CHAZAN, ELIAHU
CHIEL, ARTHUR
CHIEL, SAMUEL
DAVIDSON, DAVID
DAVIDSON, MAX DAVID
DOLGIN, SIMON ARTHUR
DONIN, HAYIM HALEVY
DRACHMAN, BERNARD
DRESNER, SAMUEL
DREYFUS, STANLEY
DROB, MAX
DWORKIN, ZALMAN (Lubavitch)
ECKMAN, JULIUS
EHRENREICH, BERNARD
EICHHORN, DAVID M.
EICHLER, MENAHEM
EILBERG, AMY
EINHORN, DAVID
EISENDRATH, MAURICE NATHAN
EISENSTADT, BENZION
EISENSTEIN, IRA
ELFENBEIN, ISRAEL
ELIASSOFF, HERMAN
ELZAS, BARNETT ABRAHAM
ELLENSON, DAVID HARRY
ENELOW, HYMAN (Hillel Gershom)
EPSTEIN, CHAIM FISCHEL
EPSTEIN, GILBERT
EPSTEIN, HARRY
EPSTEIN, LOUIS M.
ETTELESON, HARRY
FALK, JOSHUA
FEDERBUSCH, SIMON
FEIBELMAN, JULIAN BECK
FEINBERG, LOUIS
FEINSTEIN, MOSES
FELDMAN, ABRAHAM JEHIEL
FELSENTHAL, BERNHARD

I. HISTORY
B. MEDIEVAL & MODERN PERIOD
2. Regional History
g. United States
BIOGRAPHIES
Religion (continued)

FEUER, LEON ISRAEL

FEUERLICHT, MORRIS M.

FEUERSTEIN

FINEBERG, SOLOMON ANDHIL

FINESHRIBER, WILLIAM HOWARD

FINK, JOSEPH L.

FINKELSTEIN, LOUIS

FINKELSTEIN, SHIMON

FLEISCHER, CHARLES

FRANKLIN, LEO MORRIS

FREEHOF, SOLOMON BENNETT

FRIEDERMAN, ZALMAN JACOB

FRIEDMAN, THEODORE

FRISCH, EPHRAIM

GEFFEN, JOEL

GEFFEN, TOBIAS

GELB, MAX

GIFTER, MORDECAI

GINZBERG, LOUIS

GITTELSOHN, ROLAND BERTRAM

GLASER, JOSEPH

GLAZER, SIMON

GOLD, HENRY RAPHAEL

GOLD, WOLF (Zeev)

GOLDENSON, SAMUEL HARRY

GOLDFARB, ISRAEL

GOLDFEDER, FISHEL

GOLDIN, HYMAN ELIAS

GOLDMAN, ISRAEL

GOLDMAN, SOLOMON

GOLDSTEIN, HERBERT S.

GOLDSTEIN, ISRAEL

GOLDSTEIN, SIDNEY EMANUEL

GOLINKIN, DAVID

GOLINKIN, MORDECHAI YAAKOV

GOLINKIN, NOAH

GOODBLATT, MORRIS

GORDON, ALBERT I.

GORDON, HAROLD

GOTTHEIL, GUSTAV

GOTTSCHALK, ALFRED

GREENBERG, IRVING

GREENBERG, LOUIS

GREENBERG, SIDNEY

GREENBERG, SIMON

GREENWALD, JEKUTHIEL JUDAH (Leopold)

GRODZINSKI, ZVI HIRSCH

GRUENEWALD, MAX

GRYN, HUGO

GUTHEIM, JAMES KOPPEL

GUTTMANN, ALEXANDER

HABERMAN, JOSHUA

HAILPERIN, HERMAN

HALIVNI, DAVID WEISS

HALPERN, HARRY

HAMMER, REUVEN

HARLOW, JULIUS

HARRIS, MAURICE

HARRISON, LEON

HAUPTMAN, JUDITH

HEILPRIN, PHINEHAS MENAHEM

HELLER

HELLER, BERNARD

HERSCHER, URI

HERSHMAN, ABRAHAM M.

HERTZBERG, ARTHUR

HIER, MARVIN

HIGGER, MICHAEL

HIRSCH, EMIL GUSTAVE

HIRSCH, RICHARD

HIRSHENSON, HAYIM

HOCHEIMER, HENRY

HOFFMAN, LAWRENCE I.

HOROWITZ, PINCHAS

HURWITZ, SHMARYA LEIB

HYAMSON, MOSES

ISRAEL, EDWARD LEOPOLD

ISSERMAN, FERDINAND MYRON

JACOB, WALTER

JACOBS, GEORGE

JOSEPH, JACOB

JOSPE, ALFRED

JUNG, LEO

KADUSHIN, MAX

KAHN, ROBERT

KAMENETSKY, YAAKOV

KAMINETSKY, JOSEPH

KAPLAN, ARYEH

KAPLAN, MORDECAI MENAHEM

KARP, ABRAHAM J.

KAUVAR, CHARLES ELIEZER HILLEL

KELMAN, WOLFE

KIEVAL, HERMAN

KIRSHBLUM, MORDECAI

KLAUSNER, ABRAHAM

KLAVAN, ISRAEL

KLEIN, EDWARD E.

KLEIN, ISAAC

KLEIN, PHILIP

KLENICKI, LEON

KOBER, ADOLF

KOGEN, DAVID

KOHLER, KAUFMANN

KOHN, EUGENE

KOHN, JACOB

KOLATCH, ALFRED

KONVITZ, JOSEPH

KORN, BERTRAM WALLACE

KOTLER, AARON

KRAUSKOPF, JOSEPH

KREITMAN, BENJAMIN

KRONISH, LEON

KURTZ, VERNON

KUSHNER, HAROLD
KUSHNER, LAWRENCE
LANDESMAN, ALTER
LANDMAN, ISAAC
LAUTERBACH, JACOB ZALLEL
LAZARON, MORRIS SAMUEL
LEESER, ISAAC
LEHRMAN, IRVING
LEIPZIGER, EMIL WILLIAM
LELYVELD, ARTHUR JOSEPH
LEVI, SAMAUEL GERSON
LEVIN, JUDAH L
LEVINGER, LEE JOSEPH
LEVINTHAL
LEVITSKY, LOUIS MOSES
LEVY, CLIFTON HARBY
LEVY, FELIX ALEXANDER
LEVY, JOSEPH LEONARD
LICHTENSTEIN, TEHILLA
LIEBER, DAVID
LIEBMAN, JOSHUA LOTH
LIFSHITZ, DAVID
LILIENTHAL, MAX (Menahem)
LIPMAN, EUGENE JAY
LOEWENSTEIN, BERNHARD
LOOKSTEIN, HASKELL
LOOKSTEIN, JOSEPH HYMAN
LYONS, JACQUES JUDAH
MAGNES, JUDAH LEON
MAGNIN, EDGAR FOGEL
MALEV, WILLIAM S.
MALINO, JEROME
MALTER, HENRY
MANDELBAUM, BERNARD
MANISCHEWITZ, HIRSCH
MARCUS, JACOB RADER
MARGOLIES, MOSES SEBULUN
MARGOLIS, GAVRIEL ZEV
MARK, JULIUS
MARTIN, BERNARD
MASLIANSKY, ZVI HIRSCH
MATLIN, MOSHE
MATT, C. DAVID
MATTUCK, ISRAEL ISIDOR
MENDES
MENDLOWITZ, SHRAGA FEIVEL
MERZBACHER, LEO
MEYER, MARTIN ABRAHAM
MIELZINER, MOSES
MIHALY, EUGENE
MILLER, IRVING
MILLER, ISRAEL
MILLGRAM, ABRAHAM
MINDA, ALBERT
MINKIN, JACOB SAMUEL
MIRSKY, SAMUEL KALMAN
MORAIS, SABATO
MORGENSTERN, JULIAN
MOSES, ADOLPH
MOSES, ISAAC S.

MOWSHOWITZ, ISRAEL
NADICH, JUDAH
NAROT, JOSEPH
NEULANDER, ARTHUR
NEUMAN, ABRAHAM AARON
NEUMARK, DAVID
NEWFIELD, MORRIS
NEWMAN, LOUIS ISRAEL
NOVAK, DAVID
NOVECK, SIMON
NUSSBAUM, MAX
NUSSBAUM, PERRY
OFFNER, STACY
OLAN, LEVI
OLITZKY, KERRY
OSTFELD, BARBARA
PARDES, SHMUEL
PARIS, HAILU
PARZEN, HERBERT
PETEGORSKY, DAVID
PETUCHOWSKI, JAKOB JOSEF
PHILIPSON, DAVID
PILCHIK, ELY EMANUEL
PLAUT, W. GUNTHER
POLISH, DAVID
POOL, DAVID DE SOLA
PORATH, ISRAEL
POUPKO, BERNARD
POZNANSKI, GUSTAVUS
PREIL, ELAZAR MEYER
PRESSMAN, JACOB
PRIESAND, SALLY
PRINZ, JOACHIM
RABINOWITZ, STANLEY
RACKMAN, EMANUEL
RADIN, ADOLPH MOSES
RAISIN, JACOB ZALMAN
RAISIN, MAX
RAPHALL, MORRIS JACOB
REGNER, SIDNEY
REINES, ALVIN
RICE, ABRAHAM JOSEPH
RISKIN, SHLOMO
ROSENAU, WILLIAM
ROSENBAUM, JONATHAN
ROSENBERG, ISRAEL
ROSENBLATT, SAMUEL
ROTH, JOEL
ROTHSCHILD, JACOB M.
ROUTTENBERG, MAX JONAH
RUBENOVITZ, HERMAN H.
RUBENSTEIN, RICHARD LOWELL
RUDERMAN, DAVID
RUDERMAN, JACOB ISAAC
RUDIN, A. JAMES
RUDIN, JACOB PHILIP
SAMFIELD, MAX
SANDROW, EDWARD T.
SAPERSTEIN, DAVID
SAPERSTEIN, HAROLD

I. HISTORY
B. MEDIEVAL & MODERN PERIOD
2. Regional History
g. United States
BIOGRAPHIES
Religion (continued)

SAR, SAMUEL
SARACHEK, JOSEPH
SASSO, SANDY
SCHAALMAN, HERMAN
SCHACHTER, HERSCHEL
SCHACHTER, JACOB J.
SCHACTER-SHALOMI, ZALMAN
SCHANFARBER, TOBIAS
SCHECHTER, ABRAHAM ISRAEL
SCHECHTER, MATHILDE
SCHECHTER, SOLOMON (Shneur Zalman)
SCHEINFELD, SOLOMON ISAAC
SCHERMAN, NOSSON
SCHINDLER, ALEXANDER M.
SCHINDLER, SOLOMON
SCHNEEBERGER, HENRY WILLIAM
SCHORSCH, ISMAR
SCHULMAN, SAMUEL
SCHULWEIS, HAROLD
SCHWAB, SHIMON
SCHWARTZMAN, SYLVAN D.
SCHWARZSCHILD, STEVEN SAMUEL
SEGAL, BERNARD
SEIGEL, JOSHUA
SHANKMAN, JACOB K.
SHAPIRO, ALEXANDER
SHAPIRO, RAMI
SHUBOW, JOSEPH
SHULMAN, CHARLES E.
SIEGEL, MORTON
SIEGEL, SEYMOUR
SILBER, SAUL
SILBERSTEIN, SOLOMON JOSEPH
SILVER, ABBA HILLEL
SILVER, DANIEL J
SILVER, ELIEZER
SILVERMAN, IRA
SILVERMAN, JOSEPH
SILVERMAN, MORRIS
SILVERSTEIN, ALAN
SILVERSTONE, GEDALYAH
SIMON, ABRAM
SIMON, CARRIE OBENDORFER
SIMON, RALPH
SIVITZ, MOSHE
SOBEL, RONALD
SOLOMON, ELIAS L.
SOLOVEICHIK, AARON
SOLOVEICHIK, MOSHE
SOLOVEITCHIK, JOSEPH DOV
SONDERLING, JACOB
SPERO, SHUBERT
STAMPFER, JOSHUA

STEINBACH, ALEXANDER ALAN
STEINBERG, MILTON
STEINBERG, PAUL
STERN, CHAIM
STERN, JACK
STERN, MALCOLM HENRY
STERNSTEIN, JOSEPH PHILIP
STOLZ, JOSEPH
STRASSFELD, MICHAEL
SZOLD, BENJAMIN
TEITELBAUM, AARON
TEITZ, PINCHAS (Mordecai)
TELUSHKIN, NISSAN
TENDLER, MOSES D.
TEPLITZ, SAUL
TEUTSCH, DAVID
TRACHTENBERG, JOSHUA
TUSKA, SIMON
VOORSANGER, JACOB
VORSPAN, MAX
WAGNER, STANLEY M.
WASHOFSKY, MARK
WASKOW, ARTHUR
WAXMAN, MORDECAI
WECHSLER, JUDAH
WEINBERGER, MOSHE
WEINSTEIN, JACOB
WEISS, AVI
WEISS, SAMSON
WIENER, MAX
WINE, SHERWIN
WISE, ISAAC MAYER
WISE, JONAH BONDI
WISE, STEPHEN SAMUEL
WOLF, ALFRED
WOLF, ARNOLD J.
WOLPE, DAVID J.
WOLSEY, LOUIS
YOFFIE, ERIC
YUDELOVITZ, ABRAHAM A.
ZARCHI, ASHER LIPPMAN
ZELDIN, ISAIAH
ZELIZER, NATHAN
ZIMMERMAN, SHELDON
ZLOTOWITZ, MEIR
ZLOTOWITZ, BERNARD
ZOLA, GARY P.

Science
ABRAHAMS, ISAAC
ABT, ISAAC ARTHUR
ADLER, CHARLES
ALTSCHUL, AARON MEYER
ANFINSEN, CHRISTIAN B.
ANGRIST, ALFRED ALVIN
ARNON, DANIEL ISRAEL
ATLAS, DAVID
AXEL, RICHARD
AXELROD, JULIUS
BACHER, ROBERT FOX

BALINT, MICHAEL
BALTIMORE, DAVID
BAUER, SIMON HARVEY
BENACERRAF, BARUJ
BENDER, MORRIS BORIS
BENIOFF, HUGO
BENZER, SEYMOUR
BERG, PAUL
BERL, ERNST
BERLINER, EMILE
BETHE, HANS ALBRECHT
BIKERMAN, JACOB JOSEPH
BLOCH, FELIX
BLOCH, HERMAN SAMUEL
BLOCH, KONRAD
BLUMBERG, BARUCH SAMUEL
BODANSKY, OSCAR
BODIAN, DAVID
BOGORAD, LAWRENCE
BOHM, DAVID
BOROWITZ, SIDNEY
BORSOOK, HENRY
BROWN, HAROLD
BROWN, HERBERT C.
BROWN, MICHAEL STUART
BUCKY, GUSTAV
BUERGER, LEO
CALVIN, MELVIN
CHARGAFF, ERWIN
COHEN, ELIZABETH D. A.
COHEN, HARRY
COHEN, PAUL JOSEPH
COHEN, PHILIP PACY
COHEN, SEYMOUR STANLEY
COHEN, STANLEY
COHEN, STANLEY N.
COHN, EDWIN JOSEPH
COOPER, LEON N.
CORI, GERTY THERESA
CROHN, BURRILL BERNARD
DAMESHEK, WILLIAM
DAVIDOFF, LEO MAX
DAVIDSOHN, ISRAEL
DE LEE, JOSEPH B.
DEUTSCH, FELIX
DEUTSCH, HELENE
DISCHE, ZACHARIAS
DJERASSI, CARL
DORFMAN, RALPH ISADORE
DRESSLER, WILLIAM
DROSDOFF, MATTHEW
DRUCKER, DANIEL CHARLES
DUSHMAN, SAUL
EDELMAN, GERALD MAURICE
EDINGER, TILLY
EINHORN, MAX
EINHORN, MOSES
EINSTEIN, ALBERT
ELION, GERTRUDE BELL
EPSTEIN, PAUL SOPHUS

ERIKSON, ERIK HOMBERGER
ERLANGER, JOSEPH
ESTERMANN, IMMANUEL
FAJANS, KASIMIR
FALK, KAUFMAN GEORGE
FELD, JACOB
FEUER, HENRY
FEYNMAN, RICHARD PHILLIPS
FISCHER, EDMOND
FISHBEIN, MORRIS
FISHBERG, MAURICE
FISHMAN, WILLLAM HAROLD
FLEISCHER, MICHAEL
FOLKMAN, JUDAH
FONDILLER, WILLIAM
FRANCK, JAMES
FRANK, PHILIPP
FRANZBLAU, ABRAHAM NORMAN
FREUDENTHAL, ALFRED MARTIN
FRIEDENWALD
FRIEDMAN, JEROME ISAAC
FRIEND, CHARLOTTE
FROEHLICH, ALFRED
FROMM, ERICH
FROMM-REICHMANN, FRIEDA
FUNK, CASIMIR
FURCHGOTT, ROBERT F.
GARLOCK, JOHN HENRY
GASSER, HERBERT SPENCER
GELL-MANN, MURRAY
GILBERT, WALTER
GILMAN, ALFRED G.
GINSBURG, JEKUTHIEL
GLASER, DONALD ARTHUR
GLAUBER, ROY J.
GLICK, DAVID
GOLD, HENRY RAPHAEL
GOLDBERGER, JOSEPH
GOLDMARK, PETER CARL
GOLDSTEIN, JOSEPH LEONARD
GOLDSTEIN, KURT
GOMBERG, MOSES
GOULD, STEPHEN JAY
GREEN, DAVID EZRA
GREENACRE, PHYLLIS
GREENBERG, DAVID MORRIS
GREENGARD, PAUL
GREENSTEIN, JESSE PHILIP
GRINKER, ROY RICHARD SR.
GROSS, DAVID J.
GROSSMAN, MORTON IRVING
GRUNBAUM, ADOLF
GUTENBERG, BENO
GUTMAN, ALEXANDER B.
GUTTMACHER, ALAN F.
HANDLER, PHILIP
HARRIS, MILTON
HART, JOEL
HARTMANN, HEINZ
HASSID, WILLIAM ZEV

I. HISTORY
B. MEDIEVAL & MODERN PERIOD
2. Regional History
g. United States
BIOGRAPHIES
Science (continued)

HAUPTMAN, HERBERT A.

HAURWITZ, BERNHARD

HAYS, ISAAC

HECHT, SELIG

HEEGER, ALAN J.

HEIDELBERGER, MICHAEL

HELPERN, MILTON

HEYMAN, MOSES DAVID

HIRSCHFELD, ISADOR

HOFFMANN, ROALD

HOFSTADTER, ROBERT

HOLLANDER, FRANKLIN

HORWITZ, H. ROBERT

HORWITZ, PHINEAS JONATHAN

HYDE, IDA HENRIETTA

HYMAN, LIBBIE HENRIETTA

ISAACS, JACOB

ISRAEL, EDWARD

JACOBI, ABRAHAM

JAFFE, LEONARD

JANOWITZ, HENRY D.

JUDA, WALTER

KANDEL, ERIC R.

KANNER, LEO

KANTROWITZ, ADRIAN

KANTROWITZ, ARTHUR

KAPLAN, JOSEPH

KARDINER, ABRAM

KARLE, JEROME

KATZ, ISRAEL

KAUFMAN, JOYCE JACOBSON

KITSEE, ISADOR

KLEMPERER, PAUL

KLINE, NATHAN S.

KOHN, WALTER

KOLLER, CARL

KOPLIK, HENRY

KORNBERG, ARTHUR

KRIM, MATHILDE

KUBIE, LAWRENCE

LAND, EDWIN H.

LANDSTEINER, KARL

LANGER, ROBERT

LEDEEN, HYMAN

LEDERBERG, JOSHUA

LEDERER, JEROME F.

LEDERMAN, LEON MAX

LEE, DAVID M.

LEES, LESTER

LEFSCHETZ, SOLOMON

LEVENE, PHOEBUS AARON THEODOR

LEVINE, PHILIP

LEVINSON, ABRAHAM

LEVY, LOUIS EDWARD

LEWI, MAURICE J.

LIPMAN, JACOB GOODALE

LIPMANN, FRITZ ALBERT

LITMAN, SAMUEL

LOEB, JACQUES

LOEB, LEO

LOEB, MORRIS

LOEWENSTEIN, RUDOLPH MAURICE

LOEWI, OTTO

LOWDERMILK, WALTER CLAY

LURIA, SALVADOR EDWARD

MACHT, DAVID

MACHTA, LESTER

MAHLER, MARGARET

MALZBERG, BENJAMIN

MANDELBROT, BENOIT

MARCUS, RUDOLPH ARTHUR

MASSERMAN, JULES HYMAN

MASTER, ARTHUR M.

MENDEL, LAFAYETTE BENEDICT

MESELSON, MATTHEW

MICHELSON, ALBERT ABRAHAM

MILLMAN, JACOB

MOTTELSON, BENJAMIN R.

MULLER, HERMAN JOSEPH

MUSHER, SIDNEY

NAGIN, HARRY S.

NAMIAS, JEROME

NATHANS, DANIEL

NEUGEBAUER, OTTO

NEUMANN, JOHANN (Johnny) LUDWIG VON

NIRENBERG, MARSHALL WARREN

NUNBERG, HERMAN

OLAH, GEORGE

OPPENHEIMER, J. ROBERT

OSHEROFF, DOUGLAS DEAN

PEKERIS, CHAIM LEIB

PENZIAS, ARNO ALLAN

PERL, MARTIN

PERLSTEIN, MEYER A.

PERLZWEIG, WILLIAM ALEXANDRE

PINCUS, GREGORY GOODWIN

PINKEL, BENJAMIN

POLITZER, H. DAVID

PRESS, FRANK

PRESSMAN, DAVID

PRUSINER, STANLEY B.

PTASHNE, MARK

RABI, ISIDOR ISAAC

RABINOWITCH, EUGENE

RACKER, EFRAIM

RADO, SANDOR

RAPAPORT, DAVID

RAPPAPORT, HENRY

REDLICH, FREDERICK C.

REIK, THEODOR

RESNIK, JUDITH

RICHTER, BURTON

RIGLER, LEO GEORGE

RITTENBERG, DAVID
RODBELL, MARTIN
ROSE, IRWIN
ROSEN, FRED
ROSEN, SAMUEL
RUBIN, MORTON JOSEPH
SABIN, ALBERT BRUCE
SACHS, BERNARD
SAGAN, CARL EDWARD
SALK, JONAS EDWARD
SANDGROUND, JACK HENRY
SCHALLY, ANDREW V.
SCHAWLOW, ARTHUR L.
SCHICK, BELA
SCHILDER, PAUL FERDINAND
SCHLESINGER, FRANK
SCHMERLING, LOUIS
SCHWARTZ, MELVIN
SCHWINGER, JULIAN SEYMOUR
SELDIN, HARRY M.
SEQUEYRA, JOHN DE
SERBIN, HYMAN
SHAPIRO, ASCHER HERMAN
SHEAR, MURRAY JACOB
SHEDLOVSKY, THEODORE
SILVERMAN, ALEXANDER
SILVERMAN, LESLIE
SILVERSTEIN, ABE
SLEPIAN, JOSEPH
SOBOTKA, HARRY HERMAN
SPIEGEL-ADOLF, MONA
SPIEGELMAN, SOL
SPITZ, RENE A.
SPORN, PHILIP
STEIN, WILLIAM HOWARD
STEINBERG, MARTIN R.
STEINBERGER, JACK
STENT, GUNTHER SIEGMUND
STERN, ARTHUR C.
STERN, KURT GUNTER
STERN, OTTO
STIEGLITZ, JULIUS OSCAR
STROMINGER, JACK
SURE, BARNETT
SZASZ, THOMAS STEPHEN
SZILARD, LEO
SZWARC, MICHAEL
TARSKI, ALFRED
TELLER, EDWARD
TEMIN, HOWARD MARTIN
TENENBAUM, JOSEPH L.
TISCHLER, MAX
TOCH, MAXIMILIAN
ULAM, STANISLAW MARCIN
VARMUS, HAROLD ELIOT
WAKSMAN, SELMAN ABRAHAM
WALD, GEORGE
WATTERS, LEON LAIZER
WECHSLER, ISRAEL
WEIL, JOSEPH

WEINBERG, STEVEN
WEINHOUSE, SIDNEY
WEISENBURG, THEODORE H.
WESTHEIMER, FRANK HENRY
WEXLER, HARRY
WHITE, ROBERT MAYER
WIENER, ALEXANDER S.
WIENER, NORBERT
WIESNER, JEROME BERT
WIESNER, JULIUS VON
WIGNER, EUGENE P.
WINSTEIN, SAUL
WINTROBE, MAXWELL MYER
WISE, LOUIS ELSBERG
WOLBERG, LEWIS ROBERT
WOLF, ABNER
WOLMAN, ABEL
YALOW, ROSALYN SUSSMAN
ZACHARIAS, JERROLD REINACH
ZAMENHOF, STEPHEN
ZARISKI, OSCAR
ZIFF, MORRIS
ZILBOORG, GREGORY
ZIMMERMAN, HARRY M.
ZUCROW, MAURICE JOSEPH

h. Canada
MAIN SURVEYS
AMERICA
CANADA
CANADIAN LITERATURE

GENERAL ENTRIES
AGRICULTURE
B'NAI B'RITH CANADA
CANADIAN JEWISH CONGRESS
JEWISH IMMIGRANT AID SERVICES OF CANADA

COMMUNITIES
ALBERTA
ATLANTIC CANADA
BRITISH COLUMBIA
CALGARY
EDMONTON
HAMILTON
MANITOBA
MONTREAL
ONTARIO
OTTAWA
QUEBEC
SASKATCHEWAN
TORONTO
VANCOUVER
WINNIPEG

BIOGRAPHIES
ABELLA, ROSALIE SILBERMAN
ABRAMOWITZ, HERMAN
ADASKIN, MURRAY
ANHALT, ISTVAN

I. HISTORY
B. MEDIEVAL & MODERN PERIOD
2. Regional History
h. Canada
BIOGRAPHIES (*continued*)

ANSELL, DAVID ABRAHAM
APPLEBAUM, LOUIS
ARNOLD, ABE
ASPER, ISRAEL H.
AVIDA, YEHUDA LEIB
AZRIELI, DAVID
BARRETT, DAVID
BAYEFSKY, ABA
BECKER, LAVY M.
BELKIN, SIMON
BELZBERG, SAMUEL
BENNETT, ARCHIE (Aaron Baehr)
BENNETT, AVIE
BERCOVITCH, PETER
BERNSTEIN, HAROLD JOSEPH
BLANKSTEIN, CECIL N.
BORENSTEIN, SAM
BORNSTEIN, ELI
BOROVOY, ALAN
BOSCO, MONIQUE
BRANDEAU, ESTHER
BRANDSTAEDTER, MORDECAI DAVID
BRONFMAN
CAISERMAN, HANANE MEIER
CAISERMAN-ROTH, GHITTA
CAPLAN, ELINOR
CARR, JUDY FELD
CASS, SAMUEL
COHEN, HIRSH
COHEN, LEONARD
COHEN, LYON
COHEN, MATT
COHEN, MAXWELL
COHEN, MORRIS ABRAHAM
COHEN, NATHAN
COTLER, IRWIN
CROLL, DAVID ARNOLD
CRONENBERG, DAVID
CHERNEY, BRIAN
CHERNIACK, SAUL
DAN, LESLIE
DAVID
DAVIS, MORTIMER
DE SOLA
DENBURG, CHAIM
DIAMOND, JACK
DIAMOND, JACK
DONALDA, PAULINE
DUNKELMAN, BENJAMIN
DUNKELMAN, ROSE
ELBERG, YEHUDA
EZRIN, HERSCHEL
FEDERMAN, MAX
FEINBERG, ABRAHAM L.

FELDER, GEDALIAH
FINESTONE, SHEILA
FITCH, LOUIS
FRANKLIN, SELIM
FREEDMAN, HARRY
FREEDMAN, SAMUEL
FREIMAN
FRENKEL, VERA
FRUM
FURIE, SYDNEY J.
GELBER
GERSHMAN, JOSHUA
GILBERT, INA
GIVENS, PHILIP S.
GLICK, IRVING SRUL
GOFFMAN, ERVING
GOLD, PHILIP
GOLDBLOOM FAMILY
GOLDSTEIN, ELYSE
GORDON, JACOB
GORDON, NATHAN
GOTLIEB, ALLAN
GRAFSTEIN, JERAHMIEL S.
GRAUBART, Y. L.
GRAY, HERBERT ESER
GRAY, MORRIS ABRAHAM
GREENE, LORNE
GROSSMAN, ALLAN AND LARRY
HALPERN, JACK
HALL, MONTY
HARRIS, SYDNEY
HART, AARON
HART, BENJAMIN
HART, CECIL M.
HART, EZEKIEL
HART, SAMUEL
HAYES, SAUL
HEAPS, ABRAHAM ALBERT
HEICHELHEIM, FRITZ MORITZ
HERSCHORN, JOSHUA (She'ea) HALEVY
HERZOG, SHIRA
HILLER, ARTHUR
HIRSCH, JOHN STEPHEN
HIRSCHPRUNG, PINHAS
HOROWITZ
ISKOWITZ, GERSHON
JACOBS, SAMUEL WILLIAM
JACOBS, SOLOMON
JOSEPH
JOSEPH, NORMA BAUMEL
JUDAH
KAGE, JOSEPH
KAHANOVITCH, ISRAEL ISAAC
KANEE, SOL
KAPLAN, ROBERT P.
KAPLANSKY, KALMEN
KATTAN, NAIM
KAYFETZ, BEN
KLEIN, ABRAHAM MOSES
KOFFLER, MURRAY

KREISEL, HENRY
KUPER, JACK
LAMBERT, PHYLLIS
LANDSBERG, MICHELLE
LANTOS, ROBERT
LASKIN, BORA
LASTMAN, MEL
LAYTON, IRVING
LENKINSKY, LOUIS
LEVI, SAMAUEL GERSON
LEVINE, LES
LEVINE, NORMAN
LEWIS, DAVID
LEWIS, STEPHEN
LITTMAN, SOL
LUFTSPRING, SAMMY
MANDEL, ELI
MARMUR, DOW
MARRUS, MICHAEL
MATAS, DAVID
MAYNARD, FREDELLE BRUSER
MAZE, IDA
MICHAELS, ANNE
MICHAELS, LORNE
MIRANSKY, PERETZ
MIRVISH, ED/DAVID
MORAWETZ, OSCAR
MORGENTALER, HENRY
MUHLSTOCK, LOUIS
NATHAN, HENRY
NEMETZ, NATHAN
NEWMAN, PETER C.
NICHOLS, JACK
ORLIKOW, DAVID
OSHRY, EPHRAIM
PACHTER, CHARLES
PETEGORSKY, DAVID
PHILLIPS, LAZARUS
PHILLIPS, NATHAN
PLAUT, W. GUNTHER
POLANYI, JOHN
PRICE, ABRAHAM
RANKIN, HARRY
RAPHAEL, WILLIAM
RASKY, HARRY
RASMINSKY, LOUIS
REICHMANN
REISMAN, HEATHER
RHINEWINE, ABRAHAM
RICHLER, MORDECAI
ROBACK, LEAH
ROBIN, REGINE
ROME, DAVID
ROSE, FRED
ROSENBERG, LOUIS
ROSENBERG, STUART E.
ROSENBERG, YEHUDAH YUDEL
ROSENFELD, FANNY
ROTENBERG, MATTIE
ROTHSCHILD, KURT

ROTHSCHILD, ROBERT PHINIAS
RUBENSTEIN, LOUIS
SACK, BENJAMIN G.
SAFDIE, MOSHE
SAFDIE, SYLVIA
SALSBERG, JOSEPH B.
SAMUEL, SIGMUND
SCHEUER, EDMUND
SCHILD, EDWIN
SCHLESINGER, JOE
SCHULTZ, SAMUEL
SCHWARTZ, GERALD
SEGAL, ESTHER
SEGAL, HUGH
SEGAL, JACOB ISAAC
SHAPIRO, BERNARD J.
SHARP, ISADORE NATANIEL
SHATNER, WILLIAM
SHERMAN, JASON
SHTERN
SHUCHAT, WILFRED
SIEGEL, IDA LEWIS
SINGER, YVONNE
SLONIM, REUBEN
SOLA, ABRAHAM DE
SPECTOR, NORMAN
SPRACHMAN
STEIN, JANICE
STEINBERG
STEINFELD, JJ
STERN, HARRY JOSHUA
TANENBAUM
TORGOV, MORLEY
TREPMAN, PAUL
UNGERMAN, IRV
VAN PAASSEN, PIERRE
VEINER, HARRY
WADDINGTON, MIRIAM (Dworkin)
WASSERMAN, DORA AND BRYNA
WAXMAN, AL
WAYNE AND SHUSTER
WEIDER, BEN
WEIDMAN, HIRAM
WEINZWEIG, HELEN
WEINZWEIG, JOHN
WILDER, HERTZ
WISEMAN, ADELE
WISEMAN, SHLOIME
WOLFE
WOLOFSKY, HIRSH
WOSK
YUDIKA
ZIPPER, YA'AKOV
ZNAIMER, MOSES
ZOLF

i. **Latin America**
Main Surveys
AMERICA
ARGENTINA

I. HISTORY

B. MEDIEVAL & MODERN PERIOD

2. Regional History

i. Latin America

MAIN SURVEYS (continued)

BRAZIL
CUBA
LATIN AMERICA
MEXICO
SPANISH AND PORTUGUESE LITERATURE

GENERAL ENTRIES

AGRICULTURE
A.M.I.A.
DAIA
FESELA
GENEALOGY
LAJSA (LATIN AMERICAN JEWISH STUDIES
    ASSOCIATION)

COMMUNITIES

BAHIA
BARBADOS
BOLIVIA
BUENOS AIRES
CARACAS
CARIBBEANS, SPANISH-PORTUGUESE NATION
    OF THE: LA NACION
CAYENNE
COLOMBIA
CORDOBA
CORO
COSTA RICA
CURACAO
CHILE
DOMINICAN REPUBLIC
ECUADOR
EL SALVADOR
ENTRE RÍOS
GUATEMALA
GUIANA
HAITI
HAVANA
HONDURAS
IQUITOS
JAMAICA
LIMA
MENDOZA
MONTEVIDEO
NICARAGUA
PANAMA
PARAGUAY
PERU
PORTO ALEGRE
PUERTO RICO
RECIFE
RIO DE JANEIRO
ROSARIO
SANTA FE

SÃO PAULO
SURINAME
TUCACAS
URUGUAY
VENEZUELA

BIOGRAPHIES

AGUINIS, MARCOS
ALPERSOHN, MARCOS
ANGEL, AARON
ARBELL, MORDECHAI
AVNI, HAIM
BAITLER, ZOMA
BARYLKO, JAIME
BEHAR, LEON
BEIDERMAN, BERNARDO
BELKIN, ARNOLD
BENZAQUEN, SAADIA
BERAJA, RUBEN
BERDICHEVSKY, SCHER
BERGER, MEIR
BERLINER, ISAAC
BERMAN BERMAN, NATALIO
BLAZKO, MARTIN
BLEJER, DAVID
BLIS, DAVID
BRENER, PYNCHAS
BRIE, LUIS HARTWIG
BURLE-MARX, ROBERTO
CARVAJAL
COHEN GELLERSTEIN, BENJAMIN
COHEN, JOSEPH ISAAC
CONSTANTINER, JAIME
CONSTANTINI, HUMBERTO
CZENSTOCHOWSKI, WALTER
CHAMUDES REITICH, MARCOS
CHEHEBAR, ITZHAK
CHOCRON, ISAAC
DE SOLA, JUAN BARTOLOMÉ
DELVALLE, MAX SHALOM
DELVALLE LEVI MADURO, ERIC
    ARTURO
DINES, ALBERTO
DOUDTCHITZKY, DINORA
DUJOVNE, LEON
EICHELBAUM, SAMUEL
ELNECAVE, DAVID
ESPINOZA, ENRIQUE
FAIVOVICH HITZCOVICH, ANGEL
FASTLICHT, ADOLFO
FEIERSTEIN, RICARDO
FEIGL, FRITZ
FELDMAN, SHIMSHON SIMON
FINGERMAN, GREGORIO
FINKELSTEIN, CHAIM
FLORENTIN, MEVORAH
FREIFELD, ABRAHAM
FUTORANSKY, LUISA
GAMUS GALLEGOS, PAULINA
GELMAN, JUAN

GERCHUNOFF, ALBERTO
GESANG, NATHAN-NACHMAN
GLANTZ, JACOBO
GLANTZ, MARGO
GOERITZ, MATHIAS
GOLDEMBERG, ISAAC
GOLDMAN, AHARON
GOLDMAN, MOISES
GOLOBOFF, GERARDO MARIO
GRINSPUN, BERNARDO
GROBART, FAVIO
GRUNBERG, CARLOS M.
HANNEMANN, PABLO
HARF, HANNS
HARF, SUSE HALLENSTEIN
HARKAVI, YIZHAK
HERDAN, KURT LUCIAN
HOCHSCHILD, MAURICIO
ISAACS, JORGE
ISAACSON, JOSE
JOSEPH, HENRY
KAMENSZAIN, TOBIAS
KAPLAN, ISAAC
KAPLAN, SENDER
KITRON (Kostrinsky), MOSHE
KLABIN
KLEIN, ALBERTO
KLENICKI, LEON
KOCH, ADELHEID LUCY
KOSICE, GYULA
KOVADLOFF, SANTIAGO
KOZER, JOSE
LAFER, HORACIO
LASANSKY, MAURICIO
LERNER, JAIME
LEVI, RINO
LEVY, ROBERT
LEVY, SION
LIACHO, LAZARO
LIBEDINSKY, TSCHORNE MARCOS
LISPECTOR, CLARICE
LIWERANT, DANIEL
MADURO, RICARDO
MALDONADO DA SILVA, FRANCISCO
MENDELSON, JOSE
MEYER, MARSHALL
MILEVSKY, AHARON
MILSTEIN, CESAR
MINDLIN, HENRIQUE
MIRELMAN
MUÑIZ-HUBERMAN, ANGELINA
NAJDORF, MIGUEL
NAJNUDEL, LEON
NASSY, DAVID DE ISAAC COHEN
NIERMAN, LEONARDO
NORONHA, FERNAO DE
NUDELMAN, SANTIAGO I.
OSTROWER, FEYGA
OTTA, FRANCISCO
PECAR, SAMUEL

PEKERMAN, JOSÉ
PIZARNIK, ALEJANDRA
PORZEKANSKI, TERESA
RABINOVICH, JOSE
RAFALIN, DAVID SHLOMO
RAFFALOVICH, ISAIAH
RAUCH, EDUARDO
RAWET, SAMUEL
RESNICK, SALOMON
ROSENBERG, MOISHE
ROSENCOF, MAURICIO
ROSENMANN-TAUB, DAVID
ROVINSKY, SAMUEL
ROZENMACHER, GERMAN
SAFRA
SAJAROFF, MIGUEL
SASLAVSKY, LUIS
SATANOWSKI, MARCOS
SATZ, MARIO
SCLIAR, MOACYR
SCHAPIRA, DAVID
SCHAULSON BRODSKY, JORGE
SCHAULSON NUMHAUSER, JACOBO
SCHIFRIN, LALO
SCHLESINGER, GUILLERMO
SEGALL, LAZAR
SELIGSON, ESTHER
SEROUSSI, ELIAS
SHUA, ANA MARIA
SINGERMAN, BERTA
SITTEON DABBAH, SHAUL DAVID
SNEH, SIMJA
SOURASKY
STEIMBERG, ALICIA
STEINBRUCH, AARÃO
STERN, HANS
SVERDLIK, ODED
SWARSENSKY, HARDI (Bernhard)
SZERYNG, HENRYK
TARNOPOLSKY, SAMUEL
TEITELBOIM VOLOSKY, VOLODIA
TEUBAL, EZRA
TIEMPO, CÉSAR
TIMERMAN, JACOBO
TOKER, ELIAHU
TOPOLEVSKY, GREGORIO
TURKOW, MARK
VERBITZKY, BERNARDO
WALD, ARNOLD
WECHSLER, ELINA
WEISER-VARON, BENNO
WOLF, RICHARD RIEGEL (Subirana y Lobo)
YAGUPSKI, MAXIMO
YARCHO, NOE (Noah)
ZITNITSKY, PINCAS LAZARO

3. HOLOCAUST HISTORY
Main Surveys
HOLOCAUST

I. HISTORY
B. MEDIEVAL & MODERN PERIOD
3. Holocaust History (continued)

GENERAL ENTRIES
ART
AUSCHWITZ
AUSCHWITZ BOMBING CONTROVERSY
AUSCHWITZ CONVENT
AUSCHWITZ TRIALS
BABI YAR
BADGE, JEWISH
BELZEC
BERGEN-BELSEN
BERMUDA CONFERENCE
BERNHEIM PETITION
BITBURG CONTROVERSY
BOYCOTT, ANTI-NAZI
BUCHENWALD
CAMPS
CHELMNO
CHILDREN'S LITERATURE
DACHAU
DEATH MARCHES
DENAZIFICATION
DISPLACED PERSONS
DRANCY
EUROPA PLAN
EUTHANASIA – T-4 PROGRAM
EVIAN CONFERENCE
FACING HISTORY AND OURSELVES
FINAL SOLUTION
FORCED LABOR
FOSSOLI
GASSING
GENOCIDE CONVENTION
GESTAPO
GHETTO
GURS
HAAVARA
HOLOCAUST, RESCUE FROM
HOLOCAUST, THE
HOLOCAUST DENIAL
HOLOCAUST REMEMBRANCE DAY
HOLOCAUST RESCUERS, JEWISH
IRVING V. LIPSTADT
JUDENRAT
JUDENREIN
KAPO
KIDDUSH HA-HAYIM
KINDERTRANSPORT
KISTARCSA
KOLDYCHEVO (Koldyczewo) CAMP
KRIMCHAKS
KRISTALLNACHT
MADAGASCAR PLAN
MAJDANEK
MALINES
MAUTHAUSEN
MUSELMANN

NATIONAL SOCIALISM
NATZWEILER-STRUTHOF
NAZI-DEUTSCH
NAZI MEDICAL EXPERIMENTS
NINTH FORT
NUREMBERG LAWS
PARTISANS
PLASZOW
PONARY (Paneriai)
RAVENSBRUECK
REFUGEES
REPARATIONS, GERMAN
RESTITUTION AND INDEMNIFICATION
RIGHTEOUS AMONG THE NATIONS
RSHA
SACHSENHAUSEN ORANIENBURG
SCHACHT PLAN
SOBIBOR
SONDERKOMMANDO, JEWISH
SS AND SD
ST. LOUIS, VOYAGE OF
STUERMER, DER
STUTTHOF
THERESIENSTADT
TRANSNISTRIA
TREBLINKA
U.S. ARMY AND THE HOLOCAUST
VUGHT
WALDHEIM AFFAIR
WANNSEE CONFERENCE
WAR CRIMES TRIALS
WESTERBORK

COMMUNITIES
AACHEN
ABONY
ADA
AHLEM
AHRWEILER
AIX-EN-PROVENCE
ALBA IULIA
ALBANIA
ALBERTI-IRSA
ALEKSANDRIYA
ALEKSANDRIYA
ALEKSANDROW LODZKI
ALESSANDRIA
ALGERIA
ALISTAL
ALSACE
ALTENSTADT
ALZEY
AMBERG
AMSTERDAM
ANANYEV
ANAPA
ANDERNACH
ANHALT
ANSBACH
ANTWERP

ARAD
ARNSTADT
ARTEMOVSK
ASCHAFFENBURG
ASZOD
ATHENS
AUGSBURG
AUGUSTOW
AURICH
AUSTERLITZ
AUSTRIA
BACAU
BADEN
BADEN BEI WIEN
BAIA-MARE
BAJA
BAKHCHISARAI
BALASSAGYARMAT
BALTA
BAMBERG
BANJA LUKA
BANSKA BYSTRICA
BAR
BARANOVICHI
BARDEJOV
BARLAD
BAR-LE-DUC
BAUSKA
BAVARIA
BAYONNE
BAYREUTH
BECHYNE (Bechin)
BEDZIN
BEKESCSABA
BELAYA TSERKOV
BELCHATOW
BELED
BELFORT
BELGIUM
BELGOROD-DNESTROVSKI
BELGRADE
BELTSY
BELZ
BELZYCE
BENDERY
BENEŠOV (Beneschau)
BENFELD
BERDICHEV
BERDYANSK
BEREGOVO
BERESTECHKO
BERETTYOUJFALU
BEREZA
BEREZHANY
BEREZINO
BEREZOVKA
BERLIN
BERSHAD
BESANÇON
BEZIDUL NOU

BIALA PODLASKA
BIALYSTOK
BIELEFELD
BIELSKO
BIELSK PODLASKI
BILGORAJ
BINGEN
BIRZAI (Birzhi)
BIRZULA
BISTRITA (Bistritz)
BOBROVY KUT
BOBRUISK
BOCHNIA
BOCHUM
BODROGKERESZTUR
BOGUSLAV
BOJAN
BOLEKHOV (Bolechow)
BOLOGNA
BOLZANO
BONYHAD
BOPPARD
BORDEAUX
BORISLAV
BORISOV
BORSA
BOSKOVICE (Boskowitz)
BOTOSANI
BOULAY
BOURG-EN-BRESSE
BRAILA
BRAILOV
BRANDYS NAD LABEM
BRASLAV
BRASOV
BRATISLAVA
BRATSLAV
BRECLAV
BREISACH
BREMEN
BRESLAU
BREST-LITOVSK
BREZNICE
BRICEVA
BRICHANY
BRNO
BRODY
BRUCHSAL
BRUNSWICK
BRUSSELS
BRYANSK
BRZEG
BRZESC KUJAWSKI
BRZEZINY
BUCHACH
BUCHAREST
BUCOVICE
BUDAPEST
BUDYNE NAD OHRI
BUHUSI

I. HISTORY
B. MEDIEVAL & MODERN PERIOD
3. Holocaust History
COMMUNITIES (*continued*)

BUKOVINA
BULGARIA
BURDUJENI
BURGENLAND
BUSK
BUZAU
BYDGOSZCZ
BYKHOV
BYTOM
BZENEC
CAMPULUNG MOLDOVENESC
CARLSBAD
CESKA LIPA
CESKE BUDEJOVICE
CHAMBON-SUR-LIGNON
CHEB
CHECINY
CHELM
CHEMNITZ (Karl-Marx-Stadt)
CHERKASSY
CHERNIGOV
CHERNOBYL
CHERNOVTSY
CHMIELNIK
CHORTKOV
CHORZOW
CHRYZANOW
CHUDNOV
CIECHANOW
CLEVES
CLUJ
COBURG
COCHEM
COLMAR
COLOGNE
CONSTANCE
CONSTANTA
COTTBUS
CRACOW
CRAIOVA
CZECHOSLOVAKIA
CZESTOCHOWA
DABROWA GORNICZA
DARABANI
DARMSTADT
DAUGAVPILS
DAVID-GORODOK
DEBRECEN
DEGGENDORF
DEJ
DENMARK
DERAZHNYA
DEUTSCHKREUTZ
DEUTZ
DIJON

DISNA
DIVIN
DNEPROPETROVSK
DOKSHITSY (Dokszyce)
DOLGINOVO (Dolhinow)
DOLINA
DOLNI KOUNICE
DOLNI KUBIN
DOMBROVENI
DONETSK
DOROHOI
DORTMUND
DRAMA
DRESDEN
DROGOBYCH (Drohobycz)
DRUYA
DUBNO
DUBOSSARY
DUBROVNIK
DUBROVNO
DUEREN
DUESSELDORF
DUISBURG
DUNAJSKA STREDA
DUNAYEVTSY
DYATLOVO
DZIALOSZYCE (Dzialoshitz)
EGER
EINBECK
EISENSTADT
EMDEN
EPERNAY
ERFURT
ESSEN
ESSLINGEN
ESTONIA
ESZTERGOM
ETTLINGEN
FAGARAS
FALESHTY
FALTICENI
FERRARA
FLORENCE
FOCSANI
FONTAINEBLEAU
FRANCE
FRANKFURT ON THE MAIN
FRANKFURT ON THE ODER
FREIBURG IM BREISGAU
FRIEDBERG
FUERTH
FULDA
GABIN
GADYACH
GAISIN
GALANTA
GALATI (Galatz)
GDANSK (Danzig)
GELSENKIRCHEN
GENOA

GERMANY
GERTSA
GIESSEN
GLINYANY
GLIWICE
GLOGAU
GLUBOKOYE
GLUSSK
GNIEZNO
GOERLITZ
GOETTINGEN
GOLCUV JENIKOV
GOLOVANEVSK
GOMEL
GORA KALWARIA
GORIZIA
GORKI
GORLICE
GORODENKA
GORODOK
GORODOK (Grodek Wilenski)
GORZOW WIELKOPOLSKI
GOSLAR
GOSTYNIN
GOTHA
GRAJEWO
GRAZ
GREECE
GRENOBLE
GRODNO
GRODZISK MAZOWIECKI
GRODZISK WIELKOPOLSKI
GROJEC
GURA-HUMORULUI
GYONGYOS
GYÖR
HAGEN
HAGUE, THE
HALBERSTADT
HALICZ
HALLE
HAMBURG
HAMELN
HANAU
HANOVER
HARLAU
HEIDELBERG
HEIDINGSFELD
HEILBRONN
HERMANUV MESTEC
HESSE
HILDESHEIM
HLOHOVEC
HODMEZOVASARHELY
HODONIN
HOHENAU
HOHENEMS
HOHENZOLLERN
HOLESOV
HOMBURG

HRANICE
HRUBIESZOW
HUMENNE
HUNCOVCE
HUNGARY
HUSI
ILINTSY
ILYA
INGWILLER
INNSBRUCK
INOWROCLAW
IOANNINA
ITALY
IVANCICE
IVANOVO
IVYE
IZBICA LUBELSKA
IZMAIL
IZYASLAV
JABLONEC NAD NISOU
JANOW LUBELSKI
JAROSLAW
JASLO
JASSY
JAUNIJELGAVA
JEBENHAUSEN
JEDRZEJOW
JEKABPILS
JELGAVA
JEMNICE
JEVICKO
JIHLAVA
JINDRICHUV HRADEC
JONAVA
JUDENBURG
JUELICH)
JURBARKAS (Jurburg)
KADAN
KAISERSLAUTERN
KALARASH
KALININDORF
KALINKOVICHI
KALISZ
KALUSH
KALUSZYN
KALVARIJA
KAMENETS-PODOLSKI
KAMENKA-BUGSKAYA (Strumilovskaya)
KANEV
KAPOSVAR
KARASUBAZAR
KARLSRUHE
KASEJOVICE
KASSEL
KASTORIA
KATOWICE
KAUNAS
KAUSHANY
KAVALLA
KAZATIN

I. HISTORY
B. MEDIEVAL & MODERN PERIOD
3. Holocaust History
COMMUNITIES (*continued*)

KECSKEMET
KEDAINIAI
KELME
KEMPEN
KERCH
KHARKOV
KHERSON
KHMELNIK
KHOROL
KHOTIN
KHUST
KIEL
KIELCE
KIEV
KILIYA
KIROVOGRAD (Kirovo)
KISHINEV
KISSINGEN
KISVARDA
KITZINGEN
KLAGENFURT
KLATOVY (Klattau)
KLETSK
KLINTSY
KLODAWA
KOBLENZ
KOBRIN
KOCK (Kotsk)
KOENIGSBERG
KOIDANOVO
KOJETIN (Kojetein)
KOLIN
KOLO
KOLOMYYA (Kolomea; Kolomyja)
KOMARNO
KOMARNO
KONIN
KONOTOP
KONSKIE (Konsk)
KONSKOWOLA
KORETS
KOROSTEN
KORSUN-SHEVCHENKOVSKI
KOS
KOSICE
KOSOV
KOSOVA HORA
KOSZEG
KOTOVSKOYE
KOVEL
KOZIENICE (Kozenitsy)
KOZLE
KRASLAVA
KRASNIK
KRASNODAR

KRASNOYE
KRASNYSTAW
KREFELD
KREMENCHUG
KREMENETS
KREMS
KRETINGA
KREUZNACH
KRICHEV
KRIVOI ROG
KRIVOYE OZERO
KROMERIZ
KROSNO
KROTOSZYN
KRUSTPILS
KRYNKI
KRZEPICE
KUPISKIS (Kupiskiai; Kupishki)
KURSK
KUTNO
KUTY
KYBARTAI
KYJOV
LACHVA (Lachwa)
LANCUT
LANDAU
LANDSHUT
LARISSA
LASK
LATVIA
LAZNE KYNZVART
LECZNA
LECZYCA
LEGHORN
LEGNICA
LEIPZIG
LELOW
LEOVO (Leova)
LEPEL
LESHNEV
LESKO
LESZNO
LETICHEV
LEZAJSK
LIBEREC
LIDA
LIEGE
LIEPAJA
LILLE
LINZ
LIOZNO
LIPKANY
LIPNIK NAD BECVOU
LIPNO
LIPOVETS
LIPPE (-Detmold)
LIPTOVSKY MIKULAS
LITHUANIA
LITIN
LITOMERICE

LODZ
LOMZA (Lomzha; Lomzhe)
LOSICE (Lositsy)
LOSTICE
LOUNY
LOWICZ
LUBACZOW
LUBARTOW
LUBAVICH
LUBLIN
LUBNY
LUBRANIEC
LUCENEC
LUDZA
LUEBECK
LUENEBURG
LUGANSK
LUGO
LUGOJ (Lugos)
LUKOW
LUNEVILLE
LUTOMIERSK
LUTSK
LUXEMBOURG
LVOV (Lemberg)
LYADY
LYAKHOVICHI
LYCK
LYONS
LYUBOML
MAGDEBURG
MAINZ
MAKAROV
MAKO
MAKOW MAZOWIECKI
MANNHEIM
MANS, LE
MANTUA (Mantova)
MARCULESTI
MARGHITA (Margit(t)a)
MARIBOR
MARIENBAD
MARIJAMPOLE
MARSEILLES
MATTERSDORF (Mattersburg)
MEDZIBEZH (Medzibozh)
MEININGEN
MELITOPOL
MEMEL
MEMMINGEN
MERGENTHEIM
MERSEBURG
METZ
MEZHIRECH (Mezhirichi)
MICHALOVCE
MIEDZYRZEC PODLASKI
MIELEC
MIHAILENI
MIKULOV
MILAN

MINDEN
MINSK
MINSK MAZOWIECKI
MIR
MIROSLAV
MISKOLC
MLADA BOLESLAV
MLAWA (Mlwa; Mlava)
MODENA
MOGILEV
MOGILEV-PODOLSKI
MOINESTI
MOLODECHNO
MONASTIR
MONASTYRISKA
MONTPELLIER
MORAVIA (Morava)
MORAVSKE BUDEJOVICE
MORAVSKY KRUMLOV
MOSBACH
MOSTISKA
MOZYR
MSTISLAVL
MUEHLHAUSEN
MUENSTER
MUKACHEVO
MULHOUSE
MUNICH
NACHOD
NADVORNAYA (Nadworna)
NAGYKANIZSA
NANCY
NANTES
NAROL
NASAUD
NASIELSK
NASNA
NAUHEIM
NEMIROV
NESVIZH
NEZHIN
NICE
NIEDERSTETTEN
NIKOLAYEV
NIS
NITRA
NOERDLINGEN
NORDHAUSEN
NORWAY
NOVAYA USHITSA
NOVE MESTO NAD VAHOM
NOVE ZAMKY
NOVGOROD-SEVERSK
NOVI SAD
NOVOGRUDOK
NOVOSELITSA
NOVOZYBKOV
NOVY BOHUMIN
NOVY BYDZOV
NOVY DVOR

I. **HISTORY**
  B. MEDIEVAL & MODERN PERIOD
   3. Holocaust History
    COMMUNITIES (*continued*)

NOWY DWOR MAZOWIECKI
NOWY SACZ
NUREMBERG
NYIREGYHAZA
ODESSA
OETTINGEN
OFFENBACH
OFFENBURG
OLDENBURG
OLESKO
OLESNICA
OLGOPOL
OLKUSZ
OLOMOUC (Olmuetz)
OLYKA
OPATOW
OPAVA
OPOCZNO
OPOLE LUBELSKIE
OPPENHEIM
ORADEA (Oradea Mare)
ORDZHONIKIDZE
OREL
ORGEYEV (Orhei)
ORSHA
ORSOVA
OSHMYANY
OSIJEK (Eszek)
OSLO
OSNABRUECK
OSTRAVA
OSTROG (Ostraha)
OSTROLEKA (Ostrolenka)
OSTROWIEC (Ostrowiec Swietokrzyski)
OSTROW MAZOWIECKA
OSTRYNA
OSWIECIM (Auschwitz)
OTWOCK
OVRUCH
OZERY
OZORKOW
PABIANICE
PADERBORN
PADUA
PAKS
PALANGA
PALATINATE
PANEVEZYS (Panevezhis)
PAPA,
PARCZEW
PARIS
PARMA
PASCANI
PAVLOGRAD
PAVOLOCH

PECS
PEREMYSHLYANY
PEREYASLAV-KHMELNITSKI
PERVOMAISK
PESTSZENTERZSEBET
PEZINOK
PFORZHEIM
PHLORINA
PIASECZNO
PIATRA-NEAMT (Piatra)
PIESTANY
PILSEN
PINCZOW
PINSK
PIOTRKOW (Piotrkow-Trybunalski)
PIRYATIN
PISA
PLOCK
PLOESTI
PLONSK
PLUNGE
POBEZOVICE NA SUMAVE
POCHEP
PODGAITSY
PODKAMEN
PODOLIA
PODVOLOCHISK (Podwloczyska)
POGREBISHCHENSKI (Pogrebishche)
POHORELICE (Pohrlitz)
POLAND
POLNA
POLONNOYE
POLOTSK
POLTAVA
POMERANIA
PORTUGAL
POZNAN
PRAGUE
PRESOV
PRILUKI
PROSKUROV
PROSTEJOV
PRUZHANY
PRZEDBORZ
PRZEMYSL
PRZEWORSK
PRZYSUCHA
PRZYTYK
PULAWY
PULTUSK
RADAUTI (Radautz)
RADOM
RADOMSKO
RADOMYSHL
RADOSHKOVICHI (Radoszkowice)
RADUN
RADYMNO
RADZIWILLOW
RADZYMIN
RADZYN (Radzyn-Podlaski)

RASEINIAI
RAVENSBURG
RAWICZ (Rawitsch)
REBREANU
RECHITSA
RECKLINGHAUSEN
REGENSBURG
REGHIN (Reghinul Săesc)
REUTLINGEN
REXINGEN
REZEKNE (Rezhitsa)
REZINA (Rezinz)
RIGA
RIJEKA
ROGACHEV
ROGATIN
ROKISKIS
ROMAN
ROMANIA
ROME
ROMNY
ROPCZYCE (Ropshits)
ROSHEIM
ROSTOV
ROUDNICE NAD LABEM
ROUEN
ROVNO
ROZDOL
ROZWADOW
RUSE
RUSSIA
RUZHANY
RYMANOW
RYPIN
RYSHKANY
RZESZOW
SAARBRUECKEN
SADAGORA
SAINT-DENIS
SAKIAI (Shakyai, Shakay)
SALONIKA
SALONTA
SALZBURG
SAMBOR
SAMOGITIA
SANDOMIERZ
SANOK
SARAJEVO
SARNY
SARREGUEMINES
SASOV
SATANOV
SATORALJA UJHELY
SATU-MARE
SAVERNE
SAXONY
SCHNAITTACH
SCHWEINFURT
SEDUVA
SEESEN

SEINI
SEKIRYANY
SELESTAT
SERRAI
SEVASTOPOL
SHARGOROD
SHCHEDRIN
SHEPETOVKA
SHKLOV
SHPOLA
SIAULIAI
SIBIU
SIEDLCE
SIEMIATYCZE
SIENA
SIERADZ
SIERPC
SIGHET
SILESIA
SIMFEROPOL
SIMLEUL-SILVANIEI
SIRET
SKALAT
SKARZYSKO-KAMIENNA
SKIDEL
SKIERNIEWICE
SKOLE
SKOPLJE (Skopje)
SKUODAS
SKVIRA
SLAVUTA
SLONIM
SLUTSK
SMELA
SMOLENSK
SMORGON (Smorgonie)
SNYATYN
SOCHACZEW
SOEST
SOKAL
SOKOLKA
SOKOLOW PODLASKI
SOMBOR
SOPRON
SOROKI (Soroca)
SOSNOWIEC (Sosnovets)
SPAIN
SPANDAU
SPEYER
SPLIT
SREM
STANISLAV
STARODUB
STARO-KONSTANTINOV
STASZOW
STEFANESTI
STENDAL
STETTIN
STOLBTSY
STOLIN

I. HISTORY
B. MEDIEVAL & MODERN PERIOD
3. Holocaust History
COMMUNITIES (*continued*)

STOPNICA

STOROZHINETS

STRASBOURG

STRAUBING

STRY (Stryj)

STRYKOW

STUTTGART

STYRIA

SUBCARPATHIAN RUTHENIA

SUCEAVA

SULITA

SULZBACH

SUWALKI

SVISLOCH

SWEDEN

SWIDNICA

SWITZERLAND

SZCZEBRZESZYN

SZCZERCOW

SZEGED

SZEKESFEHERVAR

SZOLNOK

SZOMBATHELY

SZYDLOWIEC

TABOR

TACHOV (Tachau)

TAGANROG

TALHEIM

TALLINN

TALNOYE

TARGU-MURES

TARNOBRZEG

TARNOGROD (Tarnograd)

TARNOPOL

TARNOW

TARTU

TARUTINO

TAUBERBISCHOFSHEIM

TAURAGE

TELENESHTY (Teleneşti)

TELSIAI (Telshi; Telschen)

TESCHEN

THIONVILLE

THURINGIA

TIMISOARA

TIRASPOL

TIRGU-FRUMOS

TIRGU NEAMT

TLUMACH (Tlumacz)

TOLSTOYE

TOMASHPOL

TOMASZOW LUBELSKI

TOMASZOW MAZOWIECKI

TOPOLCANY

TORCHIN (Torczyn)

TORUN

TOULOUSE

TOURS

TRANSYLVANIA

TRAVNIK

TREBIC (Trebitsch)

TRENCIN (Trenčín)

TREST

TRIER

TRIESTE

TRIKKALA (Trikala)

TRIPOLI

TRNAVA

TROKI

TROYES

TRZCIANKA

TUCHIN

TUEBINGEN

TUKUMS

TULCHIN

TUNIS, TUNISIA

TURDA

TURIN

TURKA

TURNOV

TYKOCIN

TYROL

TYSMENITSA (Tyśmienica)

TYSZOWCE

UDLICE

UHERSKE HRADISTE

UHERSKY BROD

UKMERGE

ULM

UMAN

USOV

USTI NAD LABEM

UTENA

UZHGOROD

VAC

VAD RASHKOV

VALEA-LUI-VLAD

VASILKOV

VASLUI

VATRA DORNEI

VELIZH

VENICE

VENTSPILS

VERCELLI

VEROIA

VERONA

VESZPREM

VIENNA

VILKAVISKIS

VILLINGEN

VILNA

VINNITSA

VIRBALIS

VISEUL DE SUS

VISHNEVETS

VITEBSK
VIZHNITSA
VLADIMIR VOLYNSKI
VOLHYNIA
VOLKOVYSK
VOLOS
VOLPA
VORONEZH
VOTICE
VOZNESSENK
VYSOKOYE
WARENDORF
WARSAW
WEGROW
WEINHEIM
WESTPHALIA
WIELICZKA
WIELUN
WIENER NEUSTADT
WIESBADEN
WISLICA
WLOCLAWEK
WLODAWA
WODZISLAW
WOLBROM
WOLFENBUETTEL
WOLOMIN
WORMS
WRONKI
WUERTTEMBERG
WUERZBURG
WUPPERTAL
WYSZKOW
WYSZOGROD
XANTEN
YALTA
YAVOROV
YEDINTSY
YEFINGAR
YEVPATORIYA
YUGOSLAVIA
ZABLUDOW
ZABOLOTOV
ZABRZE
ZAGARE
ZAGREB
ZALESHCHIKI
ZAMBROW (Zambrov)
ZAMOSC
ZAPOROZHE
ZARASAI
ZASTAVNA
ZATEC
ZAWIERCIE
ZBARAZH
ZBOROV
ZDUNSKA-WOLA
ZELECHOW
ZELOW
ZELVA (Zelwa)

ZEMUN
ZERBST
ZGIERZ (Zgerzh)
ZGURITSA (Zgurita)
ZHDANOV
ZHIDACHOV
ZHITOMIR
ZHMERINKA
ZHOLKVA
ZHURAVNO
ZILINA
ZLATOPOL
ZMIGROD NOWY
ZNOJMO (Znaim)
ZOLOCHEV
ZOLOTONOSHA
ZRENJANIN
ZVENIGORODKA
ZWICKAU
ZWOLEN
ZYCHLIN
ZYRARDOW

ORGANIZATIONS

ASSOCIATION OF HOLOCAUST ORGANIZATIONS
CENTRE DE DOCUMENTATION JUIVE CONTEMPORAINE
CONFERENCE ON JEWISH MATERIAL CLAIMS
    AGAINST GERMANY
COUNCIL OF JEWS FROM GERMANY
FORTUNOFF VIDEO ARCHIVES OF HOLOCAUST
    TESTIMONY
INTERNATIONAL TRACING SERVICE
JEWISH SUCCESSOR ORGANIZATIONS
JUEDISCHER KULTURBUND
MEMORIAL FOUNDATION FOR JEWISH CULTURE
MORESHET
MUSEUM OF JEWISH HERITAGE
OFFICE OF SPECIAL INVESTIGATIONS (OSI)
REICHSVEREINIGUNG
REICHSZENTRALE FUER JUEDISCHE AUSWANDERUNG
SURVIVORS OF THE SHOAH VISUAL HISTORY
    FOUNDATION
UNION GENERALE DES ISRAELITES DE FRANCE (U.G.I.F.)
UNITED RESTITUTION ORGANIZATION
UNITED STATES HOLOCAUST MEMORIAL MUSEUM
UNRRA
WAR REFUGEE BOARD
YAD VASHEM
ZENTRALE STELLE DER LANDESJUSTIZVERWALTUNGEN

BIOGRAPHIES

ANIELEWICZ, MORDECAI
ARAD, YITZHAK
ATLAS, JECHEZKIEL
BAK, SAMUEL
BARASH, EPHRAIM
BECCARI, ARRIGO
BENOIT, PIERRE-MARIE
BIELSKI, TUVIA, ASAEL, AND ZUS
BRAND, JOEL JENO

LANGER, LAWRENCE
LANZMANN, CLAUDE
NOVITCH, MIRIAM
YOUNG, JAMES

II. RELIGION

A. JEWISH

1. JEWISH LAW
   MAIN SURVEYS
   HALAKHAH
   MISHPAT IVRI

   GENERAL ENTRIES
   ABDUCTION
   ABORTION
   ACQUISITION
   ADMISSION
   ADOPTION
   ADULTERY
   AGENCY
   AGUNAH
   APOSTASY
   APOTROPOS
   APPEAL
   ARBITRATION
   ARTIFICIAL INSEMINATION
   ASMAKHTA
   ASSAULT
   ASSIGNMENT (OF DEBT)
   ATTORNEY
   AUTHORITY, RABBINICAL
   AUTOPSIES AND DISSECTION
   AV BET DIN
   BANISHMENT
   BET DIN AND JUDGES
   BETROTHAL
   BIGAMY AND POLYGAMY
   BLINDNESS
   BLOOD-AVENGER
   BLOODGUILT
   BRIBERY
   BUSINESS ETHICS
   CAPITAL PUNISHMENT
   CAPTIVES, RANSOMING OF
   CASTRATION
   CHASTITY
   CHILD MARRIAGE
   CHILDREN
   CITY OF REFUGE
   CIVIL MARRIAGE
   CLEVES GET
   CODIFICATION OF LAW
   COLLATIO LEGUM MOSAICARUM ET ROMANORUM
   COMPOUNDING OFFENSES
   COMPROMISE
   CONCUBINE
   CONDITIONS

CONFESSION
CONFISCATION, EXPROPRIATION, FORFEITURE
CONFLICT OF LAWS
CONFLICT OF OPINION
CONSERVATION
CONSUMER PROTECTION
CONTEMPT OF COURT
CONTRACT
DAMAGES
DAYYAN
DEAF-MUTE
DETENTION
DINA DE-MALKHUTA DINA
DISINTERMENT
DIVINE PUNISHMENT
DIVORCE
DOMICILE
DOWRY
ECOLOGY
EMBRYO
EVIDENCE
EXECUTION (CIVIL)
EXTRADITION
EXTRAORDINARY REMEDIES
FINES
FIRSTBORN
FLOGGING
FORGERY
FRAUD
GAMBLING
GENTILE
GERAMA AND GARME
GEZERTA
GIFT
HA'ANAKAH
HAFKA'AT SHE'ARIM
HAMEZ, SALE OF
HASKAMAH
HASSAGAT GEVUL
HAZAKAH
HEFKER
HEKDESH
HEREM
HEREM BET DIN
HEREM HA-IKKUL
HEREM HA-YISHUV
HEREM SETAM
HOMICIDE
HUMAN DIGNITY AND FREEDOM
IMPRISONMENT
IMPRISONMENT FOR DEBT
INCEST
INFORMERS
INSULT
INTERPRETATION
JERUSALEM
JEW
JEWISH AND ISLAMIC LAW, A COMPARATIVE REVIEW
KARET
KETUBBAH

II. RELIGION
A. JEWISH
1. Jewish Law
GENERAL ENTRIES (*continued*)

LABOR LAW
LAW AND MORALITY
LAW OF RETURN
LEASE AND HIRE
LEGAL MAXIMS
LEGAL PERSON
LEVIRATE MARRIAGE AND HALIZAH
LIABILITY
LIEN
LIMITATION OF ACTIONS
LOAN
LOST PROPERTY
MA'ARUFYA
MA'ASEH
MAINTENANCE
MAJORITY RULE
MAMRAM
MAMZER
MARITIME LAW
MARRIAGE
MARRIAGE, PROHIBITED
MATRIMONIAL PROPERTY
MAZRANUT
MEDIATION
MEDICINE AND THE LAW
MEHILAH
MILITARY LAW
MINHAG
MISTAKE
MIXED MARRIAGE, INTERMARRIAGE
MONEYLENDING
NOACHIDE LAWS
NUISANCE
OATH
OBLIGATIONS, LAW OF
ONA'AH
ONES
OPPRESSION
ORAL LAW
ORPHAN, ORPHANAGE
OWNERSHIP
PARAPET
PARENT AND CHILD
PARTNERSHIP
PENAL LAW
PERJURY
PIKKU'AH NEFESH
PLANNING AND CONSTRUCTION
PLEAS
PLEDGE
POLICE OFFENSES
PRACTICE AND PROCEDURE
PROPERTY
PROSELYTES
PUBLIC AUTHORITY

PUNISHMENT
RANSOM
RAPE
REBELLIOUS SON
RIGHTS, HUMAN
SALE
SEPARATION OF POWERS
SERVITUDES
SEVARAH
SEXUAL OFFENSES
SHALISH
SHETAR
SHI'BUDA DE-RABBI NATHAN
SHOMERIM
SIKARIKON
SLANDER
SLAVERY
SORCERY
STRANGERS AND GENTILES
SUCCESSION
SUICIDE
SURETYSHIP
TAKKANOT
TAKKANOT HA-KAHAL
TALION
TAXATION
TECHNOLOGY AND HALAKHAH
TEMPLE MOUNT
THEFT AND ROBBERY
TORTS
TRADITION
TRANSPLANTS
UNJUST ENRICHMENT
VALUES OF A JEWISH AND DEMOCRATIC STATE
VIRGIN, VIRGINITY
VOWS AND VOWING
WEIGHTS AND MEASURES
WIDOW
WILLS
WITNESS
WOMAN
YEUSH
YUHASIN

2. JEWISH RITUAL & OBSERVANCE
MAIN SURVEYS
HALAKHAH

GENERAL ENTRIES
ABLUTION
ABOMINATION
ADAR
ADAR, THE SEVENTH OF
ADASS JESHURUN, ADASS JISROEL
ADDIR BI-MELUKHAH
ADDIR HU
ADLOYADA
ADON OLAM
ADONAI, ADONAI, EL RAHUM VE-HANNUN
AFIKOMAN

AHAVAH RABBAH; AHAVAT OLAM

AHOT KETANNAH

AKDAMUT MILLIN

AL HA-NISSIM

AL HET

AL TIKREI

ALEINU LE-SHABBE'AH

AMARKAL

AMEN

AMIDAH

AMULET

ANIM ZEMIROT

ANINUT

ANNA BE-KHO'AH

ANNA BE-KORENU

APAM

ARBA AMMOT

ARBA KOSOT

ARK

ART

ARVIT

ASHAMNU

ASHKAVAH

ASHREI

ATTAH EHAD

ATTAH HORETA LADA'AT

ATTAH ZOKHER

AUFRUFEN

AUTHORITY, RABBINICAL

AV

AV HA-RAHAMIM

AV, THE FIFTEENTH OF

AV, THE NINTH OF

AVERAH

AVI AVI

AVINU MALKENU

AVINU SHE-BA-SHAMAYIM

AVODAH

AZAZEL

AZERET

AZHAROT, AZHARAH

BAKI

BAKKASHAH

BA-MEH MADLIKIN

BAR MITZVAH, BAT MITZVAH

BAREKHI NAFSHI

BAREKHU

BARNACLE GOOSE MYTHS

BARRENNESS AND FERTILITY

BARUKH

BARUKH SHE-AMAR

BARUKH SHEM KEVOD MALKHUTO LE-OLAM VA-ED

BARUKH SHE-PETARANI

BATH, BATHING

BEARD AND SHAVING

BEDIKAT HAMEZ

BE-MOZA'EI MENUHAH

BENEDICTIONS

BENSHEN

BERAH DODI

BIMAH

BIRKAT HA-MINIM

BIRKAT HA-TORAH

BIRTH

BIRTH CONTROL

BIRTHDAY

BITTUL HA-TAMID

BLASPHEMY

BLEMISH

BLESSING AND CURSING

BLESSING OF CHILDREN

BLOOD

BREASTPLATE

BRIDEGROOMS OF THE LAW

BURIAL

CALENDAR

CALENDAR REFORM

CANDLES

CASTRATION

CATACOMBS

CELIBACY

CEMETERY

CHILDREN'S SERVICES

CHOIRS

CIRCUMCISION

COFFIN

COMMANDMENTS, THE 613

CONFESSION OF SINS

CREMATION

DAVID

DAY AND NIGHT

DAY OF ATONEMENT

DAYYEINU

DEATH

DESECRATION

DEW, PRAYER FOR

DIETARY LAWS

DISINTERMENT

DUKHAN

EGGS

EGLAH ARUFAH

EHAD MI YODE'A

EIN KE-ELOHENU

EL MALE RAHAMIM

EL MELEKH NE'EMAN

EL MELEKH YOSHEV

EL NORA ALILAH

ELI ZIYYON VE-AREHA

ELIJAH, CHAIR OF

ELIJAH, CUP OF

ELUL

ERUV

ESHET HAYIL

ESTHER, FAST OF

ETROG

EVER MIN HA-HAI

FASTING AND FAST DAYS

FESTIVALS

FIRST FRUITS

FIRZOGERIN

II. RELIGION
A. JEWISH

2. Jewish Ritual & Observance

GENERAL ENTRIES (*continued*)

II. RELIGION
A. JEWISH
2. Jewish Ritual & Observance
General Entries (*continued*)

USURY
VEIL
WINE
YA'ALEH VE-YAVO
YAD
YAH RIBBON OLAM
YAHRZEIT
YAKNEHAZ
YAMIM NORA'IM
YEKUM PURKAN
YEZIV PITGAM
YIGDAL
YISHTABBAH
YIZKOR
YOM KIPPUR KATAN
YOZEROT
ZEMIROT
ZIDDUK HA-DIN
ZIKHRONOT
ZIZIT
ZUR MI-SHELO

3. JEWISH THOUGHT & PHILOSOPHY
Main Surveys
PHILOSOPHY, JEWISH

General Entries
ABRAHAM
ADAM
AFTERLIFE
AKEDAH
ANGEL OF DEATH
ANGELS AND ANGELOLOGY
ANI MA'AMIN
ANIMALS, CRUELTY TO
ANTHROPOMORPHISM
ANTINOMIANISM
APIKOROS
APOLOGETICS
ARTICLES OF FAITH
ASCETICISM
ASTROLOGY
ATOMISM
ATONEMENT
BEATITUDE
BELIEF
BODY AND SOUL
BUSINESS ETHICS
CATEGORIES
CAUSE AND EFFECT
CHARITY
CHASTITY
CHILDREN
CHIROMANCY
CHOSEN PEOPLE

COMMANDMENTS, REASONS FOR
COMPASSION
CONSERVATION
CONSERVATIVE JUDAISM
COSMOLOGY
COVETOUSNESS
CREATION AND COSMOGONY
DEATH
DECALOGUE
DEREKH EREZ
DOMESTIC PEACE
DREAMS
DUALISM
DUTY
EMANATION
EMOTIONS
ESCHATOLOGY
ETHICAL CULTURE
ETHICAL LITERATURE
ETHICS
ETIQUETTE
EUTHANASIA
EVIL EYE
EVOLUTION
EXISTENTIALISM
FEAR OF GOD
FORGIVENESS
FORM AND MATTER
FREEDOM
FREE WILL
FRIENDSHIP
GALUT
GEMILUT HASADIM
GILGUL
GOD
GOD, NAMES OF
GOOD AND EVIL
HASIDEI ASHKENAZ
HASIDIM, SEFER
HATRED
HEART
HEMDAT YAMIM
HERESY
HERMETIC WRITINGS
HOMOSEXUALITY
HONOR
HOSPITALITY
HUMILITY
HUNTING
HYGIENE
IMITATION OF GOD
INCLINATION, GOOD AND EVIL
INGATHERING OF THE EXILES
INTELLECT
JOY
JUDAISM
JUSTICE
KALAM
KEDUSHAH
KELAL YISRAEL

KENESET YISRAEL
KIDDUSH HA-SHEM AND HILLUL HA-SHEM
KING, KINGSHIP
KISS AND KISSING
LAMED VAV ZADDIKIM
LASHON HA-RA
LESBIANISM
LIFE AND DEATH
LOGIC
LOGOS
LOVE
MAIMONIDEAN CONTROVERSY
MAN, THE NATURE OF
MARRIAGE
MERCY
MESSIAH
METAPHYSICS
METATRON
MICROCOSM
MIRACLE
MONOTHEISM
MOSES
MUSAR MOVEMENT
NATURE
NEOLOGY (Neologism)
NEO-ORTHODOXY
NEOPLATONISM
NESHAMAH YETERAH
OLAM HA-BA
ONANISM
ORTHODOXY
PARADISE
PARENTS, HONOR OF
PEACE
PIETY AND THE PIOUS
PLATO AND PLATONISM
PRAYER
PRESENCE, DIVINE
PROPHETS AND PROPHECY
PROSELYTES
PROVIDENCE
RAINBOW
REDEMPTION
REMNANT OF ISRAEL
REPENTANCE
RESURRECTION
REVELATION
REWARD AND PUNISHMENT
RIGHTEOUSNESS
RU'AH HA-KODESH
SABBATH
SATAN
SEX
SHEKHINAH
SICK, VISITING THE
SIN
SKEPTICS AND SKEPTICISM
SON OF MAN
SOUL
SOUL, IMMORTALITY OF

SPACE AND PLACE
STOICISM
SUBSTANCE AND ACCIDENT
SUFFERING
THEOCRACY
THEOLOGY
THRONE OF GOD
TIME AND ETERNITY
TORAH
TRUTH
VENGEANCE
VISIONS
WISSENSCHAFT DES JUDENTUMS
WORD
ZEDAKAH
ZEKHUT AVOT
ZODIAC

Biographies

ABBA MARI ASTRUC BEN MOSES BEN JOSEPH OF
    LUNEL
ABBAS, JUDAH BEN SAMUEL IBN
ABRABANEL, ISAAC BEN JUDAH
ABRABANEL, JUDAH
ABRAHAM BAR HIYYA
ABRAHAM BEN JUDAH LEON
ABRAHAM BEN MOSES BEN MAIMON
ABULRABI, AARON
AKNIN, JOSEPH BEN JUDAH BEN JACOB IBN
ALAMI, SOLOMON
ALBALAG, ISAAC
ALBO, JOSEPH
ALCONSTANTINI, ENOCH BEN SOLOMON
ALCORSONO, JUDAH BEN JOSEPH
ARAMA, ISAAC BEN MOSES
ARISTOTLE
ARUNDI, ISAAC (Ibn)
ASCHER, SAUL
ASHKENAZI, SAUL BEN MOSES HA-KOHEN
ATLAS, SAMUEL
BAECK, LEO
BAHYA (Pseudo)
BAHYA BEN JOSEPH IBN PAQUDA
BERKOVITS, ELIEZER
BIBAGO, ABRAHAM BEN SHEM TOV
BONAFOS, MENAHEM BEN ABRAHAM
BOROWITZ, EUGENE
BREUER, ISAAC
BUBER, MARTIN
CRESCAS, HASDAI
DELMEDIGO, ELIJAH BEN MOSES ABBA
DELMEDIGO, JOSEPH SOLOMON
DONNOLO, SHABBETAI
DURAN, PROFIAT (Profayt)
DURAN, SIMEON BEN ZEMAH (Rashbaz)
FACKENHEIM, EMIL LUDWIG
FALAQUERA, SHEM TOV BEN JOSEPH
FORMSTECHER, SOLOMON
GABIROL, SOLOMON BEN JUDAH, IBN
GEIGER, ABRAHAM

II. RELIGION
A. JEWISH

3. Jewish Thought & Philosophy
BIOGRAPHIES (*continued*)

GHĀZALĪ, ABU HAMID MUHAMMAD IBN MUHAMMAD
    AL-TŪSĪ AL-
GOLDBERG, OSCAR
GOLDMAN, ELIEZER
GUTTMANN, JULIUS
HABILLO, ELIJAH BEN JOSEPH
HARTMAN, DAVID
HESCHEL, ABRAHAM JOSHUA
HILLEL BEN SAMUEL (of Verona)
HIRSCH, SAMSON (Ben) RAPHAEL
HIRSCH, SAMUEL
HIWI AL-BALKHI
HOLDHEIM, SAMUEL
IBN DAUD, ABRAHAM BEN DAVID HALEVI
IBN EZRA, ABRAHAM
IBN EZRA, MOSES BEN JACOB
IBN KAMMŪNA, SAʿD IBN MANSŪR
IBN SHEM TOV, ISAAC BEN SHEM TOV
IBN SHEM TOV, JOSEPH BEN SHEM TOV
IBN SHEM TOV, SHEM TOV BEN JOSEPH BEN SHEM
    TOV
IMAGINATION
ISRAELI, ISAAC BEN SOLOMON
JABES, EDMOND
JAGEL, ABRAHAM
JEDAIAH BEN ABRAHAM BEDERSI (ha-Penini)
JUDAH BEN ELEAZAR
JUDAH HALEVI
JUDAH LOEW BEN BEZALEL (Maharal)
KAPLAN, MORDECAI MENAHEM
KASPI, JOSEPH BEN ABBA MARI IBN
KATZ, JOSEPH BEN ELIJAH
KELLERMANN, BENZION
KOOK, ABRAHAM ISAAC
LEIBOWITZ, YESHAYAHU
LEON, MESSER DAVID BEN JUDAH
LEVI BEN ABRAHAM BEN HAYYIM
LEVI BEN GERSHOM (Ralbag)
LEVINAS, EMMANUEL
LUZZATTO, SAMUEL DAVID
LYOTARD, JEAN FRANCOIS
MAIMONIDES, MOSES
MALKAH, JUDAH BEN NISSIM IBN
MANN, ABRAHAM AARON OF POSNAN
MATKAH, JUDAH BEN SOLOMON HA-KOHEN
MENDELSSOHN, MOSES
MOSES BEN JOSEPH HA-LEVI
MOSES BEN JOSHUA OF NARBONNE
MOSES BEN JUDAH NOGA
MUKAMMIS, DAVID IBN MARWAN AL-RAQI AL-
    SHIRAZI AL-
NAGARI, MOSES BEN JUDAH
NISSIM BEN MOSES OF MARSEILLES
PHILO JUDAEUS
POLLEGAR, ISAAC BEN JOSEPH IBN

RAWIDOWICZ, SIMON
ROSENSTOCK-HUESSY, EUGEN
ROSENZWEIG, FRANZ
ROSSI, AZARIAH (Bonaiuto) BEN MOSES DEI
ROTENSTREICH, NATHAN
SAADIAH (Ben Joseph) GAON
SCHECHTER, SOLOMON (Shneur Zalman)
SCHWARZSCHILD, STEVEN SAMUEL
SCHWEID, ELIEZER
SHALOM, ABRAHAM BEN ISAAC BEN JUDAH BEN
    SAMUEL
SHEMARIAH BEN ELIJAH BEN JACOB
SIMON, AKIBA ERNST
SOLOMON BEN JUDAH OF LUNEL
SPINOZA, BARUCH DE
STEINHEIM, SALOMON LUDWIG
WOLFSON, HARRY AUSTRYN
ZADDIK, JOSEPH BEN JACOB IBN
ZAMOSC, ISRAEL BEN MOSES HALEVI
ZARZA, SAMUEL IBN SENEH
ZERAHIAH BEN ISAAC BEN SHEALTIEL (GRACIAN)

4. RABBINICS
GENERAL ENTRIES
ACADEMY ON HIGH
AHARONIM
BAʾALEI TESHUVAH
BET (Ha-) MIDRASH
CHIEF RABBI, CHIEF RABBINATE
CLEVES GET
CODIFICATION OF LAW
DARSHAN
DERASH
DIVINATION
EZ HAYYIM
GAON
GEMATRIA
HAGGAHOT
HAKHAM
HAKHAM BASHI
HALAKHAH
HALAKHIC PERIODICALS
HASIDEI UMMOT HA-OLAM
HASIDIM
HAVER, HAVERIM
HEDER
HERMENEUTICS
KOLEL
LANDESRABBINERSCHULE
LANDRABBINER
MAʾAMAD (Mahamad)
MAGGID
MITNAGGEDIM
NEOLOGY (Neologism)
NEO-ORTHODOXY
NETUREI KARTA
ORAL LAW
PARDES
PILPUL
POSEKIM

PREACHING
RABBANITES
RABBI, RABBINATE
RABBINER-SEMINAR FUER DAS ORTHODOXE
   JUDENTUM
RABBINICAL ALLIANCE OF AMERICA
RABBINICAL ASSEMBLY
RABBINICAL CONFERENCES
RABBINICAL COUNCIL OF AMERICA
RABBINICAL SEMINARIES
RABBINICAL TRAINING, AMERICAN
REBBETZIN
RISHON LE-ZION
RISHONIM
SAVORA, SAVORAIM
SCRIBE
SEMIKHAH
SIYYUM
SLOBODKA YESHIVAH
SOFERIM
STUDY
SYNODS
TALMID HAKHAM
YESHIVOT
YOKE
ZADDIK

Rabbinic Literature
CHAPBOOKS
ECCLESIASTES RABBAH
ETHICAL LITERATURE
GENESIS RABBATI
GEONIC LITERATURE
HAGGAHOT MAIMUNIYYOT
HA-HINNUKH
HAKDAMAH
HALAKHOT GEDOLOT
HALAKHOT KEZUVOT (*Ketu'ot*)
HALAKHOT PESUKOT
HA-PARNAS, SEFER
HASSAGOT
HEBREW BOOK TITLES
HEMDAT YAMIM
HIDDUSHIM
HOMILETIC LITERATURE
KOL BO
KUNTERES
LA'AZ
ME-AM LO'EZ
MIDRASH ASERET HA-DIBBEROT
MIDRASH HA-GADOL
MIDRASH LEKAH TOV
MIDRASH PROVERBS
MIDRASH SAMUEL (*Shemuel*)
MIDRASH TEHILLIM
MIDRASH VA-YISSAU
MIDRASHIM, SMALLER
MIDRESHEI AGGADAH
MINHAGIM BOOKS
MISHNAT HA-MIDDOT

MIVHAR HA-PENINIM
NUMBERS RABBAH
ORHOT HAYYIM
ORHOT ZADDIKIM
PERI-EZ-HAYYIM
PESIKTA RABBATI
PIRKEI DE-RABBI ELIEZER
POLEMICS AND POLEMICAL LITERATURE
RABBINICAL LITERATURE
RESPONSA
SEFER HA-MA'ASIM LI-VENEI EREZ YISRAEL
SEFER HA-NEYAR
SEFER HA-YASHAR
SHA'AREI SHEVUOT
SUPERCOMMENTARIES ON THE PENTATEUCH
TANNA DE-VEI ELIYAHU
TARGUM SHENI
TOHOROT HA-KODESH
TOLEDOT YESHU
TOSAFOT
YALKUT (ha-) MAKHIRI
YALKUT SHIMONI
ZERUBBABEL, BOOK OF

Biographies
Geonim
  AARON BEN JOSEPH HA-KOHEN SARGADO
  ABBA
  ABIATHAR BEN ELIJAH HA-KOHEN
  ABRAHAM BEN N... HA-BAGHDADI
  ABRAHAM BEN NATHAN
  ABRAHAM GAON
  AHA OF SHABHA
  ALBARADANI, JOSEPH
  AL-BAZAK, MAZLIAH BEN ELIJAH IBN
  ALI BEN ZECHARIAH
  AMRAM BEN SHESHNA (Amram Gaon)
  AZARIAH BEN SOLOMON
  BEN ALAN, JOSHUA
  DANIEL BEN AZARIAH
  DANIEL BEN ELEAZAR BEN NETHANEL HIBAT
    ALLAH
  DAVID BEN DANIEL
  DAVID BEN JUDAH
  DAVID BEN ZAKKAI
  DOSA BEN SAADIAH
  DUNASH IBN TAMIM
  ELHANAN BEN HUSHIEL
  ELHANAN BEN SHEMARIAH
  ELIJAH BEN SOLOMON HA-KOHEN
  EPHRAIM BEN SHEMARIAH
  HAI BAR RAV DAVID GAON
  HAI BEN NAHSHON
  HAI BEN SHERIRA
  HANANEL BEN HUSHIEL
  HANINA (Ahonai) KAHANA BEN HUNA
  HEFEZ BEN YAZLIAH
  HEZEKIAH BEN DAVID
  HUSHIEL BEN ELHANAN (of Kairouan)
  IBN ABITUR, JOSEPH BEN ISAAC

II. RELIGION
A. JEWISH
4. Rabbinics
BIOGRAPHIES
Geonim (*continued*)

ISAAC
ISRAEL BEN SAMUEL HA-KOHEN
JACOB BEN DUNASH BEN AKIVA
JACOB HA-KOHEN BAR MORDECAI
JOSEPH BAR ABBA
JOSEPH BAR HIYYA
JOSEPH BEN JACOB BAR SATIA
JOSIAH BEN AARON HE-HAVER
JUDAH BEN JOSEPH OF KAIROUAN
KOHEN-ZEDEK BAR IVOMAI (bar lkhumai)
KOHEN ZEDEK OF PUMBEDITA (bar Joseph)
MOSES KAHANA BEN JACOB
MUBASHSHIR BEN NISSI HA-LEVI
MUBASHSHIR BEN RAV KIMOI HA-KOHEN
NAHSHON BAR ZADOK
NATHAN BEN ABRAHAM I
NATHAN BEN ABRAHAM II
NATRONAI BAR NEHEMIAH
NEHEMIAH BAR KOHEN ZEDEK
NETHANEL BEN MOSES HA-LEVI
NISSI BEN BERECHIAH AL-NAHRAWANI
NISSIM BEN JACOB BEN NISSIM IBN SHAHIN
PALTOI BAR ABBAYE
PIRKOI BEN BABOI
RABBAH
SAADIAH (Ben Joseph) GAON
SAMUEL BEN ALI
SAMUEL BEN DANIEL ABU RABIʿA HA-KOHEN
SAMUEL BEN HOPHNI
SAR SHALOM BEN BOAZ
SAR SHALOM BEN MOSES HALEVI
SHEMARIAH BEN ELHANAN
SHERIRA BEN HANINA GAON
SIMEON BAR ISAAC
SIMONA
SOLOMON BEN JUDAH
YEHUDAI BEN NAHMAN (Yehudai Gaon)
ZADOK (ISAAC) BAR MAR YISHI (ASHI)
ZEMAH BEN HAYYIM
ZEMAH BEN PALTOI
ZEMAH ZEDEK BEN ISAAC

Rishonim
AARON BEN JACOB HA-KOHEN OF LUNEL
AARON BEN JOSEPH HA-LEVI
AARON BEN MESHULLAM OF LUNEL
AARON OF NEUSTADT
ABBA MARI BEN ELIGDOR
ABBAS, MOSES BEN SAMUEL
ABENAFIA, JOSEPH
ABOAB, ISAAC I
ABOAB, ISAAC II
ABRAHAM BEN AZRIEL
ABRAHAM BEN DAVID MAIMUNI

ABRAHAM BEN DAVID OF POSQUIÈRES (Rabad)
ABRAHAM BEN ISAAC OF MONTPELLIER
ABRAHAM BEN ISAAC OF NARBONNE
ABRAHAM BEN MAZHIR
ABRAHAM BEN NATHAN HA-YARHI ("of Lunel")
ABRAHAM BEN SAMUEL HE-HASID (of Speyer)
ABRAHAM BEN SAMUEL OF DREUX
ABRAHAM BEN SOLOMON
ABUDARHAM
ABUDARHAM, DAVID BEN JOSEPH
ABULAFIA, MEIR
ABZARDIEL, MOSES
ADANI, DAVID BEN AMRAM
ADANI, DAVID BEN YESHA HA-LEVI
ADANI, SAADIAH BEN DAVID (Saʾid ibn Daud)
ADONIM BEN NISAN HA-LEVI
ADRET, SOLOMON BEN ABRAHAM (Rashba)
AGHMATI, ZECHARIAH BEN JUDAH
AHITUB BEN ISAAC
ALAMANI, AARON HE-HAVER BEN YESHUʾAH
ALBALIA, BARUCH BEN ISAAC
ALBALIA, ISAAC BEN BARUCH
AL-BARGELONI, ISAAC BEN REUBEN
ALDUBI, ABRAHAM BEN MOSES BEN ISMAIL
ALEXANDER SUSLIN HA-KOHEN OF FRANKFURT
ALFASI, ISAAC BEN JACOB (Rif)
ALGUADES (Alguadez), MEIR
ALI BEN AMRAM
AL-MADARI, JUDAH HA-KOHEN BEN ELEAZAR HE-
   HASID
AL-NAKAWA, ISRAEL BEN JOSEPH
AMRAM OF MAINZ
ANAN BEN MARINUS HA-KOHEN
ANATOLI, JACOB BEN ABBA MARI BEN SAMSON
ANATOLI BEN JOSEPH
ANAU
ANAV, BENJAMIN BEN ABRAHAM
ANAV, JEHIEL BEN JEKUTHIEL BEN BENJAMIN HA-
   ROFE
ANAV, JUDAH BEN BENJAMIN HA-ROFE
ANAV, ZEDEKIAH BEN ABRAHAM
ASHER BEN JEHIEL (Rosh)
ASHER BEN MESHULAM HA-KOHEN OF LUNEL
ASHER BEN SAUL
ASHKENAZI, DAN
ASTRUC HA-LEVI
AVIGDOR BEN ELIJAH HA-KOHEN
BAHYA BEN ASHER BEN HLAVA
BAMBERG, SAMUEL BEN BARUCH
BARUCH BEN ISAAC OF ALEPPO
BARUCH BEN ISAAC OF REGENSBURG
BARUCH BEN ISAAC OF WORMS
BARUCH BEN SAMUEL OF ALEPPO
BARUCH BEN SAMUEL OF MAINZ
BEKHOR SHOR, JOSEPH BEN ISAAC
BEN MEIR, AARON
BENJAMIN BEN SAMUEL HA-LEVI
BONAFED, DAVID BEN REUBEN
BONAVOGLIA, MOSES DE MEDICI
BONDAVIN, BONJUDAS (Bonjusas)

BONFILS, JOSEPH BEN SAMUEL

BRUNA, ISRAEL BEN HAYYIM

CANPANTON, ISAAC BEN JACOB

CANPANTON, JUDAH BEN SOLOMON

CRESCAS, ASHER (Bonan) BEN ABRAHAM

DANIEL BEN JEHIEL OF ROME

DANIEL BEN SAADIAH HA-BAVLI

DANIEL BEN SAMUEL IBN ABI RABI HA-KOHEN

DAVID BEN ABRAHAM MAIMUNI

DAVID BEN DANIEL

DAVID BEN HEZEKIAH

DAVID BEN JOSHUA MAIMUNI

DAVID BEN LEVI OF NARBONNE

DAVID BEN SAADIAH

DAVID BEN SAMUEL

DAVID BEN SAUL

DAVID BEN ZAKKAI II

DAVID IBN HAJJAR

DHAMARI, MANSUR SULEIMAN

DHAMARI, SAID BEN DAVID

DUEREN, ISAAC BEN MEIR

DURAN, SIMEON BEN ZEMAH (Rashbaz)

DURAN, SOLOMON BEN SIMEON

DURAN, ZEMAH BEN SOLOMON

ELEAZAR BEN JUDAH OF WORMS

ELEAZAR BEN MOSES HA-DARSHAN OF WUERZBURG

ELHANAN BEN ISAAC OF DAMPIERRE

ELHANAN BEN YAKAR

ELIEZER BEN ISAAC OF WORMS

ELIEZER BEN JOEL HA-LEVI OF BONN

ELIEZER BEN NATHAN OF MAINZ

ELIEZER BEN SAMUEL OF METZ

ELIEZER BEN SAMUEL OF VERONA

ELIEZER OF BEAUGENCY

ELIEZER OF TOUL

ELIEZER OF TOUQUES

ELIJAH BEN JUDAH OF PARIS

ELIJAH MENAHEM BEN MOSES

ELIJAH OF LA MASSA

EPHRAIM BEN ISAAC (of Regensburg)

EPHRAIM BEN JACOB OF BONN

EPHRAIM IBN AVI ALRAGAN

EZRA BEN ABRAHAM BEN MAZHIR

EZRA OF MONTCONTOUR

GABBAI, MOSES BEN SHEM-TOV

GAGIN, HAYYIM

GALIPAPA, HAYYIM BEN ABRAHAM

GATIGNO

GERONDI, MOSES BEN SOLOMON DESCOLA

GERONDI, SAMUEL BEN MESHULLAM

GERONDI, ZERAHIAH BEN ISAAC HA-LEVI

GERSHOM BEN JUDAH MEOR HA-GOLAH

GERSHOM BEN SOLOMON

GERSHON BEN SOLOMON OF ARLES

GRACIAN, SHEALTIEL BEN SOLOMON

HABIBA, JOSEPH

HANANEL BEN SAMUEL

HANOKH BEN MOSES

HAYYIM BEN HANANEL HA-KOHEN

HAYYIM (Eliezer) BEN ISAAC "OR ZARUA"

HAYYIM BEN JEHIEL HEFEZ ZAHAV

HAYYIM BEN SAMUEL BEN DAVID OF TUDELA

HAYYIM PALTIEL BEN JACOB ("Tola'at")

HEZEKIAH BEN JACOB

HEZEKIAH BEN MANOAH

HILLEL BEN ELIAKIM

HILLEL OF ERFURT

IBN BALAM, JUDAH BEN SAMUEL

IBN EZRA, ABRAHAM

IBN GAON, SHEM TOV BEN ABRAHAM

IBN GHAYYAT

IBN MIGASH, JOSEPH BEN MEIR HA-LEVI

IBN PLAT, JOSEPH

IBN SHUAIB, JOSHUA

ISAAC BAR DORBELO

ISAAC BAR ISRAEL IBN AL-SHUWAYK

ISAAC BEN ABBA MARI OF MARSEILLES

ISAAC BEN ABRAHAM

ISAAC BEN ABRAHAM OF NARBONNE

ISAAC BEN ASHER HA-LEVI

ISAAC BEN ELIEZER

ISAAC BEN JACOB HA-LAVAN OF PRAGUE

ISAAC BEN JOSEPH OF CORBEIL (Semak)

ISAAC BEN JUDAH OF MAINZ

ISAAC BEN MEIR (Ribam)

ISAAC BEN MELCHIZEDEK OF SIPONTO

ISAAC BEN MENAHEM THE GREAT

ISAAC BEN MERWAN HA-LEVI

ISAAC BEN MORDECAI (Ribam)

ISAAC BEN MOSES OF VIENNA

ISAAC BEN SAMUEL OF DAMPIERRE

ISAAC BEN SHESHET PERFET (Ribash)

ISAAC BEN TODROS OF BARCELONA

ISAAC FROM OURVILLE

ISAAC OF CHERNIGOV

ISAAC OF EVREUX

ISAIAH BEN ELIJAH DI TRANI

ISAIAH BEN MALI DI TRANI

ISRAEL BEN JOEL (Susslin)

ISRAELI, ISRAEL

ISRAEL OF BAMBERG

ISRAEL OF KREMS

ISSERLEIN, ISRAEL BEN PETHAHIAH

JACOB BEN ASHER

JACOB BEN MOSES OF BAGNOLS

JACOB BEN NETHANEL BEN (AL-) FAYYUMI

JACOB BEN SAMSON

JACOB BEN YAKAR

JACOB OF CORBEIL

JACOB OF MARVEGE

JACOB OF ORLEANS

JACOB OF PONT-SAINTE-MAXENCE

JACOB OF VIENNA

JAMA, SAMUEL

JEHIEL BEN JOSEPH OF PARIS

JEROHAM BEN MESHULLAM

JESSE BEN HEZEKIAH

JOEL BEN ISAAC HA-LEVI

JONAH BEN ABRAHAM GERONDI

JONATHAN BEN DAVID HA-KOHEN OF LUNEL

II. RELIGION
A. JEWISH
4. Rabbinics
BIOGRAPHIES
Rishonim (continued)

JOSEPH BEN BARUCH OF CLISSON
JOSEPH BEN JUSTU OF JAEN
JOSEPH BEN MOSES OF TROYES
JOSEPH HAZZAN BEN JUDAH OF TROYES
JOSEPH ROSH HA-SEDER
JOSHUA BEN ABRAHAM MAIMUNI
JUDAH BEN ASHER
JUDAH BEN BARZILLAI AL-BARGELONI
JUDAH BEN ISAAC (Sir Leon of Paris)
JUDAH BEN KALONYMUS BEN MEIR
JUDAH BEN KALONYMUS BEN MOSES OF MAINZ
JUDAH BEN MOSES HA-DARSHAN
JUDAH BEN NATHAN
JUDAH BEN SAMUEL HE-HASID
KALONYMUS
KIMHI, DAVID
KIMHI, JOSEPH
KIMHI, MORDECAI
KIMHI, MOSES
KIRIMI, ABRAHAM
KOKHAVI, DAVID BEN SAMUEL
LATTES, ISAAC BEN JACOB
LATTES, JUDAH
LEVI BEN GERSHOM (Ralbag)
MACHIR BEN JUDAH
MAIMON BEN JOSEPH
MAIMONIDES, MOSES
MANOAH OF NARBONNE
MATTATHIAS HA-YIZHARI
MAZLI'AH BEN SOLOMON HA-KOHEN
MEIR BEN BARUCH HA-LEVI
MEIR BEN BARUCH OF ROTHENBURG (Maharam)
MEIR BEN ISAAC OF TRINQUETAILLE
MEIR BEN ISAAC SHELIAH ZIBBUR
MEIR BEN SAMUEL OF RAMERUPT
MEIR BEN SIMEON HA-MEILI
MEIRI, MENAHEM BEN SOLOMON
MENAHEM BEN AARON IBN ZERAH
MENAHEM BEN HELBO
MENAHEM BEN JACOB
MENAHEM BEN SOLOMON
MENAHEM OF MERSEBURG
MESHULLAM BEN JACOB OF LUNEL
MESHULLAM BEN KALONYMUS
MESHULLAM BEN MOSES
MESHULLAM BEN NATHAN OF MELUN
MORDECAI BEN HILLEL HA-KOHEN
MOSES BEN ABRAHAM OF PONTOISE
MOSES BEN JACOB OF COUCY
MOSES BEN JOSEPH BEN MERWAN LEVI
MOSES BEN YOM-TOV
MOSES HA-DARSHAN
MOSES HA-KOHEN OF TORDESILLAS
MOSES OF EVREUX

MOSES OF KIEV
MOSES OF PAVIA
MOSKONI, JUDAH LEON BEN MOSES
MUELHAUSEN, YOM TOV LIPMANN
NAHMANIDES
NAHMIAS, JOSEPH BEN JOSEPH
NAJAR
NATHAN BEN JEHIEL OF ROME
NATRONAI BAR HILAI
NETHANEL BEN AL-FAYYUMI
NETHANEL BEN ISAIAH
NETHANEL OF CHINON
NISSIM BEN REUBEN GERONDI
OFFICIAL, NATHAN BEN JOSEPH AND JOSEPH
PERAHYAH BEN NISSIM
PEREZ BEN ELIJAH OF CORBEIL
PETTER BEN JOSEPH
RASHI (Solomon ben Isaac)
REUBEN BEN HAYYIM
SAMSON BEN ABRAHAM OF SENS
SAMSON BEN ELIEZER
SAMSON BEN ISAAC OF CHINON
SAMSON BEN JOSEPH OF FALAISE
SAMSON BEN SAMSON OF COUCY
SAMUEL BEN DAVID
SAMUEL BEN KALONYMUS HE-HASID OF SPEYER
SAMUEL BEN MEIR (Rashbam)
SAMUEL BEN NATRONAI
SAMUEL BEN SOLOMON OF FALAISE
SAMUEL OF EVREUX
SARDI, SAMUEL BEN ISAAC
SCHLETTSTADT, SAMUEL BEN AARON
SHALOM BEN YIZHAK OF NEUSTADT
SHEMAIAH OF TROYES
SHIMON, JOSEPH BEN JUDAH IBN
SIKILI, JACOB BEN HANANEL
SIMEON BEN SAMUEL OF JOINVILLE
SOLOMON BEN ABRAHAM OF MONTPELLIER
SOLOMON BEN ELIJAH HA-KOHEN
SOLOMON BEN JUDAH "OF DREUX"
SOLOMON BEN MEIR
SOLOMON BEN SAMSON
SOLOMON BEN SAMUEL
TAKU, MOSES BEN HISDAI
TAM, JACOB BEN MEIR
TAMAKH, ABRAHAM BEN ISAAC HA-LEVI
TANHUM BEN JOSEPH HA-YERUSHALMI
TREVES, JOHANAN BEN MATTATHIAS
TYRNAU, ISAAC (Tyrna)
VIDAL, CRESCAS
VIDAL YOM TOV OF TOLOSA
WEIL, JACOB BEN JUDAH
YOM TOV BEN ABRAHAM ISHBILI (Ritba)
ZECHARIAH BEN BARACHEL
ZECHARIAH BEN SOLOMON-ROFE
ZERAHIAH BEN ISAAC HA-LEVI

Aharonim
AARON BEN DAVID COHEN OF RAGUSA
AARON BEN ISAAC BENJAMIN WOLF

AARON BEN MEIR BRISKER
AARON BEN SAMUEL
AARON SAMUEL BEN MOSES SHALOM OF KREMENETS
AARON SAMUEL BEN NAPHTALI HERZ HA-KOHEN
AARONSOHN, MOSES
ABBAS, MOSES JUDAH BEN MEIR
ABENDANAN
ABENSUR, JACOB
ABIOB, AARON
ABITBOL
ABOAB, JACOB BEN SAMUEL
ABOAB, SAMUEL BEN ABRAHAM
ABOAB DA FONSECA, ISAAC
ABRAHAM ABELE BEN ABRAHAM SOLOMON
ABRAHAM ABUSCH (Lissa) BEN ZEVI HIRSCH
ABRAHAM BEN AVIGDOR
ABRAHAM BEN BENJAMIN ZEEV BRISKER
ABRAHAM BEN DANIEL
ABRAHAM BEN ELIJAH OF VILNA
ABRAHAM BEN ISAAC HA-KOHEN OF ZAMOSC
ABRAHAM BEN MORDECAI HA-LEVI
ABRAHAM BEN MOSES HA-KOHEN HA-SEPHARDI
ABRAHAM HAYYIM BEN GEDALIAH
ABRAHAMS
ABRAHAMS, ISRAEL
ABRAHAM ZEVI BEN ELEAZAR
ABRAMOWITZ, DOV BAER
ABRAMSKY, YEHEZKEL
ABRAMSON, SHRAGA
ABSABAN, SOLOMON
ABTERODE, DAVID BEN MOSES ELIAKIM
ABUKARA, ABRAHAM BEN MOSES
ABULAFIA, HAYYIM BEN DAVID
ABULAFIA, HAYYIM BEN JACOB (I)
ABULAFIA, HAYYIM BEN JACOB (II)
ABULAFIA, HAYYIM NISSIM BEN ISAAC
ABULAFIA, ISAAC
ABULAFIA, ISAAC BEN MOSES
ABULAFIA, JACOB BEN SOLOMON
ABULKER
ABYAD, YIHYA BEN SHALOM
ACOSTA, ISAAC (Yshak)
ADAMS, THEODORE
ADARBI, ISAAC BEN SAMUEL
ADENI, SOLOMON BAR JOSHUA
ADLER, HERMANN
ADLER, JOSEPH
ADLER, NATHAN BEN SIMEON HA-KOHEN
ADLER, NATHAN MARCUS
ADLER, SHALOM BEN MENAHEM
ADRET, MOSES IBN
AGUILAR, MOSES RAPHAEL D
AKLAR, MORDECAI BEN RAPHAEL
AKRISH, ISAAC BEN ABRAHAM
ALASHKAR, JOSEPH BEN MOSES
ALASHKAR, MOSES BEN ISAAC
ALBA, JACOB DI
ALBECK
ALBELDA, MOSES BEN JACOB
ALBUM, ZVI SHIMON

ALCALAY, ISAAC
ALEGRE, ABRAHAM BEN SOLOMON
ALFALAS, MOSES
ALFANDARI (Alfanderi)
ALFANDARI, AARON BEN MOSES
ALFANDARI, JACOB
ALFANDARI, SOLOMON ELIEZER BEN JACOB
ALFASI
ALGAZI
ALGAZI (Nissim), SOLOMON BEN ABRAHAM
ALGAZI, SOLOMON BEN ABRAHAM
ALHAYK, UZZIEL BEN MORDECAI
ALKALAI, ABRAHAM BEN SAMUEL
ALKALAI, JUDAH BEN SOLOMON HAI
ALMOSNINO, MOSES BEN BARUCH
ALPERSTEIN, AVRAHAM
ALSHEIKH, RAPHAEL BEN SHALOM
ALSHEIKH, SHALOM BEN JOSEPH
ALSHEKH, MOSES
ALTMANN, ADOLF
ALTSCHUL (-ER; Perles)
ALTSCHULER, DAVID
AMARILLO, HAYYIM MOSES BEN SOLOMON
AMARILLO, SOLOMON BEN JOSEPH
AMIEL, MOSHE AVIGDOR
AMIGO, ABRAHAM
AMRAM, NATHAN BEN HAYYIM
ANASCHEHON
ANAU
ANAU, PHINEHAS HAI BEN MENAHEM
ANGEL, MARC
ANGEL, MEIR BEN ABRAHAM
ANKAWA, RAPHAEL BEN MORDECAI
ANSELM HA-LEVI
ANTIBI
ANTIBI, ABRAHAM BEN ISAAC
APTOWITZER, VICTOR
ARAMA, MEIR BEN ISAAC
ARDIT
ARDIT, EPHRAIM BEN ABRAHAM
ARIELI, YIZHAK
ARIPUL, SAMUEL BEN ISAAC
AROLLIA, ISAAC BEN MOSES
ARONOWITZ, BENJAMIN
ARONSON, SOLOMON
ARTOM, ELIA SAMUELE
ARYEH JUDAH LEIB BEN EPHRAIM HA-KOHEN
ARYEH LEIB BEN ELIJAH
ARYEH LEIB BEN SAMUEL ZEVI HIRSCH
ASAEL, HAYYIM BEN BENJAMIN
ASH
ASH, AVRAHAM J.
ASHER, ABRAHAM BEN GEDALIAH IBN (Aba)
ASHER, JOSEPH MICHAEL
ASHER ANSCHEL BEN ISAAC OF PRZEMYSL
ASHINSKY, AARON MORDECAI HALEVI
ASHKENAZI, ABRAHAM BEN JACOB
ASHKENAZI, BEZALEL BEN ABRAHAM
ASHKENAZI, ELIEZER BEN ELIJAH THE PHYSICIAN
ASHKENAZI, GERSHON

BLOCH, MOSES
BLOCH, SAMSON BEN MOSES
BLUM, AMRAM BEN ISAAC JACOB
BONAFOUX, DANIEL BEN ISRAEL
BONAN
BONDI
BONDY, FILIP
BONFILS, JOSEPH BEN ELIEZER
BORDJEL
BORGIL, ABRAHAM BEN AZIZ
BOSHAL, MOSES BEN SOLOMON
BOSKOWITZ, BENJAMIN ZEEV (Wolf) HALEVI
BOSKOWITZ, HAYYIM BEN JACOB
BOTEACH, SHMUEL
BOTON, ABRAHAM BEN JUDAH DE
BOTON, ABRAHAM BEN MOSES DE
BOTON, HIYYA ABRAHAM BEN AARON DI
BOTON, JACOB BEN ABRAHAM DI
BOTON, MEIR BEN ABRAHAM DI
BRACH, SAUL
BRAUDE, MARKUS (Mordekhai Ze'ev)
BRESLAU, ARYEH LOEB BEN HAYYIM
BRESLAU, JOSEPH MOSES BEN DAVID
BREUER, JOSEPH
BREUER, MORDECHAI
BREUER, RAPHAEL
BREUER, SOLOMON
BRICKNER, BARNETT ROBERT
BRIEL, JUDAH BEN ELIEZER
BRILL, AZRIEL
BRILL, ISAAC
BRISZK
BRODA
BRODA, ABRAHAM BEN SAUL
BRODY, SOLOMON ZALMAN BEN ISRAEL
BROIDA, SIMHAH ZISSEL BEN ISRAEL
BRUDO, ABRAHAM BEN ELIJAH
BRUELL
BRUELL, JACOB
BUENO, ISAAC ABRAHAM
BUKARAT, ABRAHAM BEN SOLOMON HA-LEVI
BULA, RAPHAEL MOSES
BULAT, JUDAH BEN JOSEPH
BURLA
CALAHORA, JOSEPH BEN SOLOMON
CALAHORRA, ISRAEL SAMUEL BEN SOLOMON
CANTARINI, ISAAC VITA HA-KOHEN
CAPSALI, ELIJAH
CAPSALI, MOSES BEN ELIJAH
CAPUSI, HAYYIM
CARIGAL, RAPHAEL HAYYIM ISAAC
CARLEBACH, JOSEPH
CARLEBACH, SHLOMO
CARMI, JOSEPH JEDIDIAH
CARMILLY-WEINBERGER, MOSHE
CARMOLY, ELIAKIM
CARMOLY, ISSACHAR BAER BEN JUDAH LIMA
CARO, ISAAC BEN JOSEPH
CARO, JOSEPH BEN EPHRAIM
CARO, JOSEPH HAYYIM BEN ISAAC

CARVALHO, MORDECAI BARUCH
CASE, JOSEPH BEN ABRAHAM
CASES
CASES, BENJAMIN BEN DAVID
CASTELLO, ABRAHAM ISAAC
CASTELNUOVO, MENAHEM AZARIAH MEIR
   (Menahem Hayyim) BEN ELIJAH
CASTIGLIONI, HAYYIM (Vittorio)
CASTRO, JACOB BEN ABRAHAM
CHAJES, GERSHON BEN ABRAHAM
CHAJES, HIRSCH (Zevi) PEREZ
CHAJES, ISAAC BEN ABRAHAM
CHAJES, ZEVI HIRSCH
CHARLOP, YECHIEL
CHAVEL, CHARLES (Dov) BER
CHAZAN, ELIAHU
CHEHEBAR, ITZHAK
CHELM, SOLOMON BEN MOSES
CIECHANOW, ABRAHAM BEN RAPHAEL LANDAU
   OF
COEN, GRAZIADIO VITA ANANIA
COHEN, DAVID (Ha-Nazir)
COHEN, HIRSH
COHEN, JOSEPH ISAAC
COHN, MESHULLAM ZALMAN BEN SOLOMON
COLOGNA (DE), ABRAHAM VITA
COLOMBO, SAMUEL
COLON, JOSEPH BEN SOLOMON (Maharik)
COMA, HERZ
COMTINO, MORDECAI BEN ELIEZER
CONFORTE, DAVID
CORCOS, HEZEKIAH MANOAH HAYYIM THE
   YOUNGER
CORIAT
CORONEL, NAHMAN NATHAN
COVO
CULI, JACOB
CURIEL, ISRAEL BEN MEIR DI
DAHAN
DAICHES
DAINOW, ZEVI HIRSCH BEN ZEEV WOLF
DANGOOR, EZRA SASSON BEN REUBEN
DANIEL BEN PERAHYAH HA-KOHEN
DANZIG (Danziger), ABRAHAM BEN JEHIEL MICHAL
DAVID BEN ARYEH LEIB OF LIDA
DAVID BEN HAYYIM OF CORFU
DAVID BEN MANASSEH DARSHAN
DAVID (Tevele) BEN NATHAN OF LISSA
DAVID BEN SAMUEL HA-LEVI (Taz)
DAVID BEN SHIMEON
DAVID BEN SOLOMON IBN ABI ZIMRA (Radbaz)
DAVID OF MAKOW
DAVIDS, AARON ISSACHAR (Bernard) BEN NAHMAN
DEL BENE, ELIEZER DAVID BEN ISAAC
DEL BENE, JUDAH ASAHEL BEN DAVID ELIEZER
DEL VECCHIO
DEL VECCHIO, SHABBETAI ELHANAN BEN ELISHA
DELLA TORRE, LELIO (Hillel)
DESSLER, ELIJAH ELIEZER
DEUTSCH, ALADAR

II. RELIGION
A. JEWISH
4. Rabbinics
BIOGRAPHIES
Aharonim (continued)

DEUTSCH, DAVID BEN MENAHEM MENDEL
DEUTSCH, ELIEZER HAYYIM BEN ABRAHAM
DEUTSCH, IGNAZ
DEUTSCH, ISRAEL
DEUTSCH, JUDAH JOEL
DIENNA, AZRIEL BEN SOLOMON
DISEGNI, DARIO
DISKIN, MOSES JOSHUA JUDAH LEIB
DIWAN, JUDAH BEN AMRAM
DOLGIN, SIMON ARTHUR
DONIN, HAYIM HALEVY
DON-YAHIA, YEHUDAH LEIB
DRABKIN, ABRAHAM
DRACHMAN, BERNARD
DUCKESZ, EDUARD (Yecheskel)
DUENNER, JOSEPH ZEVI HIRSCH
DURAN
DURAN, SIMEON BEN SOLOMON (ben Simeon)
DUSCHAK, MORDECAI (Moritz)
DUSCHINSKY, JOSEPH ZEVI BEN ISRAEL
DUWAYK
EDELS, SAMUEL ELIEZER BEN JUDAH HA-LEVI
    (Maharsha)
EGER, AKIVA ("The Younger") BEN MOSES GUENS
EGER, AKIVA BEN SIMHAH BUNIM ("The Elder")
EGER, SAMUEL (Perez Sanwel) BEN JUDAH LOEB
EGER, SIMHAH BUNIM BEN MOSES
EGER, SOLOMON BEN AKIVA
EGOZI
EHRENFELD
EHRENFELD, NATHAN
EHRENFELD, SAMUEL BEN DAVID ZEVI
EHRENPREIS, MARCUS (Mordecai)
EHRENREICH, HAYYIM JUDAH BEN KALONYMUS
EHRENTREU, HEINRICH
EIDLITZ, LEOPOLD
EISENSTADT, ABRAHAM ZEVI HIRSCH BEN JACOB
EISENSTADT, BENZION
EISENSTADT, MEIR (Maharam Esh)
EISENSTADT, MENAHEM ZEVI
EISENSTADT, MOSES ELEAZAR
EISENSTADTER, MEIR BEN JUDAH LEIB
EISLER, MATYAS
ELBAZ
ELIAKIM GOETZ BEN MEIR
ELIASBERG, MORDECAI
ELIEZER BEN MANASSEH BEN BARUCH
ELIEZER BEN MEIR HA-LEVI OF PINSK
ELIEZER BEN SAMSON
ELIJAH BEN BENJAMIN HA-LEVI
ELIJAH BEN HAYYIM
ELIJAH BEN KALONYMUS OF LUBLIN
ELIJAH BEN LOEB OF FULDA

ELIJAH BEN SOLOMON ABRAHAM HA-KOHEN OF
    SMYRNA
ELIJAH BEN SOLOMON ZALMAN ("Vilna Gaon")
ELIJAH OF PRAGUE
ELISHA BEN ABRAHAM
ELISHA HAYYIM BEN JACOB ASHKENAZI
ELIYAHU, MORDECHAI
ELMALEH
ELYASHAR, JACOB BEN HAYYIM JOSEPH
ELYASHAR, JACOB SAUL BEN ELIEZER JEROHAM
EMDEN, JACOB
EMMANUEL, ISAAC SAMUEL
ENGEL, JOSEPH BEN JUDAH
ENGELMANN, GABRIEL
ENOCH BEN ABRAHAM
EPHRAIM BEN JACOB HA-KOHEN
EPHRAIM SOLOMON BEN AARON OF LUNTSHITS
    (Leczyca)
EPHRATI, DAVID TEVELE BEN ABRAHAM
EPSTEIN, ABRAHAM
EPSTEIN, ABRAHAM MEIR BEN ARYEH LEIB
EPSTEIN, BARUCH HA-LEVI
EPSTEIN, CHAIM FISCHEL
EPSTEIN, ISIDORE
EPSTEIN, JEHIEL MICHAL BEN AARON ISAAC HALEVI
EPSTEIN, JEHIEL MICHAL BEN ABRAHAM HA-LEVI
EPSTEIN, MOSES MORDECAI
EPSTEIN HA-LEVI, MOSES JEHIEL
ESCAPA, JOSEPH BEN SAUL
ESTROSA, DANIEL
ETTINGER, MORDECAI ZEEV BEN ISAAC AARON
    SEGAL
ETTLINGER, JACOB
EULENBURG, ISAAC BEN ABRAHAM MOSES ISRAEL
EYBESCHUETZ, JONATHAN
EYLENBURG, ISSACHAR BAER BEN ISRAEL LEISER
    PARNAS
EZEKIEL FEIVEL BEN ZEEV WOLF
EZRA BEN EZEKIEL HA-BAVLI
FAITUSI, JACOB BEN ABRAHAM
FALK, JACOB JOSHUA BEN ZEVI HIRSCH
FALK, JOSHUA
FALK, JOSHUA BEN ALEXANDER HA-KOHEN
FARISSOL, ABRAHAM BEN MORDECAI
FEDER, RICHARD
FEDERBUSCH, SIMON
FEIGENBAUM, ISAAC HA-KOHEN
FEINSTEIN, MOSES
FELDER, GEDALIAH
FERBER, ZEVI HIRSCH
FEUCHTWANG, DAVID
FEUERSTEIN
FIGO, AZARIAH
FINKEL, ELIEZER JUDAH
FINKEL, NATHAN ZEVI BEN MOSES
FINKELSTEIN, SHIMON
FISCHELS, MEIR BEN EPHRAIM
FISCHER, JOSEF
FLECKELES, ELEAZAR BEN DAVID

FORTI, BARUCH UZZIEL BEN BARUCH
FRAENKEL, DAVID BEN NAPHTALI HIRSCH
FRAENKEL-TEOMIM, BARUCH BEN JOSHUA
    EZEKIEL FEIWEL
FRANCES, ISAAC
FRANCO, MOSES
FRANK, MENAHEM MENDEL
FRANK, ZEVI PESAH
FRANKEL, ZACHARIAS
FRANKFURTER, MOSES
FRANKL, ADOLF
FRANKL-GRUEN, ADOLF ABRAHAM
FREIBERGER, MIROSLAV SALOM
FREIMANN
FREIMANN, JACOB
FRENKEL, IZHAK YEDIDIAH
FREUDEMANN, SIMHAH
FREUND, SAMUEL BEN ISSACHAR BAER
FRIED, AARON
FRIEDERMAN, ZALMAN JACOB
FRIEDLAND, NATAN
FRIEDMANN, ABRAHAM
FRIEDMANN, DAVID BEN SAMUEL
FRIEDMANN, MEIR
FRUMKIN, ARYEH LEIB
FUCHS, MOSES ZEVI
FULD, AARON BEN MOSES
FUNK, SOLOMON
GABBAI IZIDRO (Ysidro), ABRAHAM
GAGIN, HAYYIM ABRAHAM BEN MOSES
GAGIN, SHALOM MOSES BEN HAYYIM ABRAHAM
GALANTE
GALANTE, JEDIDIAH BEN MOSES
GALANTE, MOSES BEN JONATHAN (II)
GALIPAPA, ELIJAH MEVORAKH
GANSO, JOSEPH
GANZFRIED, SOLOMON BEN JOSEPH
GAON, SOLOMON
GARMISON, SAMUEL
GASTER, MOSES
GATIGNO
GEDALIAH, JUDAH BEN MOSES
GEDALIAH OF SIEMIATYCZE
GEDILIAH, ABRAHAM BEN SAMUEL
GEFFEN, TOBIAS
GELBHAUS, SIGMUND (Joshua Samuel)
GENNAZANO, ELIJAH HAYYIM BEN BENJAMIN OF
GENTILI
GERSHON, ISAAC
GESUNDHEIT, JACOB BEN ISAAC
GHERON, YAKKIR MORDECAI BEN ELIAKIM
GHEZ
GHIRON
GIFTER, MORDECAI
GINSBURGER, ERNEST
GLASNER, MOSES SAMUEL
GLAZER, SIMON
GLOGAU, JEHIEL MICHAEL BEN ASHER LEMMEL
    HA-LEVI

GLUECK, ABRAHAM ISAAC
GOITEIN, BARUCH BENEDICT
GOLD, WOLF (Ze'ev)
GOLDBERGER, IZIDOR
GOLDIN, HYMAN ELIAS
GOLDMAN, AHARON
GOLDSTEIN, HERBERT S.
GOLINKIN, MORDECHAI YAAKOV
GOMBINER, ABRAHAM ABELE BEN HAYYIM HA-
    LEVI
GORDON, ELIEZER
GORDON, JACOB
GOREN, SHLOMO
GOSLAR, NAPHTALI HIRSCH BEN JACOB
GOTA, MOSES ZERAHIAH BEN SHNEUR
GOTTLIEB, JEDIDIAH BEN ISRAEL
GRAJEWSKI, ARYEH LEIB
GRAJEWSKI, ELIEZER ZALMAN
GRAUBART, Y. L.
GRAZIANO, ABRAHAM JOSEPH SOLOMON BEN
    MORDECAI
GREENWALD, JEKUTHIEL JUDAH (Leopold)
GRISHABER, ISAAC
GRODZINSKI, HAYYIM OZER
GRODZINSKI, ZVI HIRSCH
GROSS, HEINRICH (Henri)
GROSSBERG, MENASSEH
GROSSMAN, YIZHAK DAVID
GRUENFELD, JUDAH
GRUENHUT, ELEAZAR (Lazar)
GRUENWALD, MORITZ
GRUNFELD, ISIDOR
GRUNWALD, AMRAM
GRUNWALD, JUDAH
GRUNWALD, MAX
GUEDEMANN, MORITZ
GUENZIG, EZRIEL (Azriel)
GUENZLER, ABRAHAM
GUNZBERG, ARYEH LEIB BEN ASHER
GURLAND, HAYYIM JONAH
GUTTMACHER, ELIJAH
GUTTMANN, ALEXANDER
GUTTMANN, MICHAEL (Mihčdly)
HAAS, SOLOMON BEN JEKUTHIEL KAUFMANN
HABIB, HAYYIM BEN MOSES BEN SHEM TOV
HABIB, MOSES BEN SOLOMON IBN
HABILLO, ELISHA
HABSHUSH, SHALOM BEN YAHYA
HACOHEN, MORDECAI
HACOHEN, RAPHAEL HAYYIM
HADAYAH, OVADIAH
HAGIZ, JACOB (Israel)
HAHN, JOSEPH BEN MOSES
HAHN, JOSEPH YUSPA BEN PHINEHAS SELIGMANN
HAKIM, SAMUEL BEN MOSES HA-LEVI IBN
HALBERSTADT, ABRAHAM BEN MENAHEM MENKE
HALBERSTADT, MORDECAI
HALBERSTAM, ISAAC BEN HAYYIM
HALEVA, ISHAK

II. RELIGION
A. JEWISH
4. Rabbinics
BIOGRAPHIES
Aharonim (continued)

HALEVI, EZEKIEL EZRA BEN JOSHUA
HALEVI, HAYYIM DAVID
HALEVI, JOSEPH ZEVI BEN ABRAHAM
HA-LEVI, SASSON BEN ELIJAH BEN MOSES
HALEVY, MEYER ABRAHAM
HALFON, ABRAHAM
HAMBURG, ABRAHAM BENJAMIN (Wolf)
HAMBURGER, JACOB
HAMEIRI, MOSHE
HANDALI, JOSHUA BEN JOSEPH
HANNELES, JUDAH LEIB BEN MEIR
HANOKH ZUNDEL BEN JOSEPH
HARARI
HARIF
HARIF HA-LEVI
HARLAP, JACOB MOSES BEN ZEBULUN
HAVER
HAYYIM (Ben) SHABBETAI (Maharhash)
HAYYIM BEN BEZALEL
HAYYIM JUDAH BEN HAYYIM
HAYYOT, MENAHEM MANISH BEN ISAAC
HAYYUN, ABRAHAM BEN NISSIM
HAYYUN, JOSEPH BEN ABRAHAM
HAZZAN
HAZZAN, ISRAEL MOSES BEN ELIEZER
HEILBRONN, JACOB BEN ELHANAN
HEILBRONN, JOSEPH BEN DAVID OF ESCHWEGE
HEILBUT, ELEAZAR LAZI BEN JOSEPH BEN LAZI
HEILPERN (Raphael), YOM TOV LIPMAN BEN ISRAEL
HEILPRIN, JEHIEL BEN SOLOMON
HEILPRIN, PHINEHAS MENAHEM
HEILPRIN, SAMUEL HELMANN BEN ISRAEL
HEILPRUN, ELIEZER LEIZER BEN MORDECAI
HELLER, ARYEH LEIB BEN JOSEPH HA-KOHEN OF STRY
HELLER, JEHIEL BEN AARON
HELLER, JOSHUA BEN AARON
HELLER, JUDAH
HELLER, YOM TOV LIPMANN BEN NATHAN HA-LEVI
HELLER, ZEVI HIRSCH
HENKIN, JOSEPH ELIJAH
HEPPNER, ARON
HERSCHORN, JOSHUA (She'ea) HALEVY
HERZFELD, LEVI
HERZOG, DAVID
HERZOG, ISAAC
HESCHEL, ABRAHAM JOSHUA BEN JACOB
HEZEKIAH BEN DAVID DA SILVA
HIER, MARVIN
HILDESHEIMER, AZRIEL (Israel)
HILDESHEIMER, MEIR
HILEWITZ, ALTER
HILLEL BEN NAPHTALI ZEVI (Herz)
HILLMAN, SAMUEL ISAAC
HIRSCH, MARKUS

HIRSCH, SAMSON (Ben) RAPHAEL
HIRSCHENSOHN
HIRSCHLER, PAL
HIRSCHLER, RENE
HIRSCHPRUNG, PINHAS
HIRSHENSON, HAYIM
HIYYA ROFE
HOECHHEIMER, MOSES BEN HAYYIM COHEN
HOESCHEL (Joshua) BEN SAUL
HOFFMAN, JACOB
HOFFMANN, DAVID ZEVI
HOLLANDER, ISAIAH BEN AARON
HOROVITZ, JACOB
HOROVITZ, MARCUS
HOROWITZ
HOROWITZ, ABRAHAM BEN ISAIAH
HOROWITZ, ABRAHAM BEN SHABBETAI SHEFTEL
HOROWITZ, ARYEH LEIB BEN ELEAZAR HA-LEVI
HOROWITZ, ARYEH LEIB BEN ISAAC
HOROWITZ, DAVID JOSHUA HOESCHEL BEN ZEVI
    HIRSCH HA-LEVI
HOROWITZ, ISAAC HA-LEVI BEN JACOB JOKEL
HOROWITZ, ISAIAH BEN ABRAHAM HA-LEVI
HOROWITZ, ISAIAH BEN JACOB HA-LEVI
HOROWITZ, ISAIAH BEN SHABBETAI SHEFTEL
HOROWITZ, JACOB BEN ABRAHAM
HOROWITZ, JACOB JOKEL BEN MEIR HA-LEVI
HOROWITZ, LAZAR BEN DAVID JOSHUA HOESCHEL
HOROWITZ, MESHULLAM ISSACHAR BEN ARYEH
    LEIB HA-LEVI
HOROWITZ, MOSES BEN JUDAH
HOROWITZ, PHINEHAS BEN ISRAEL HA-LEVI
HOROWITZ, PHINEHAS BEN ZEVI HIRSCH HA-LEVI
HOROWITZ, SAMUEL SHMELKE OF NIKOLSBURG
HOROWITZ, SAUL HAYYIM BEN ABRAHAM HA-
    LEVI
HOROWITZ, SHRAGA FEIVEL HA-LEVI
HOROWITZ, ZEVI HIRSCH BEN HAYYIM ARYEH
    LEIBUSH HA-LEVI
HOROWITZ, ZEVI HIRSCH BEN JOSHUA MOSES
    AARON HA-LEVI
HOROWITZ, ZEVI HIRSCH BEN PHINEHAS HA-LEVI
HOROWITZ, ZEVI JOSHUA BEN SAMUEL SHMELKE
HOZIN, ZEDAKAH BEN SAADIAH
HUEBSCH, ADOLPH
HURVITZ, JOSEPH YOZEL
HURWITZ, SHMARYA LEIB
HUTNER, ISAAC
HYAMSON, MOSES
HYAMSON, NATHAN
HYMAN, AARON
IBN ARDUT, HAYYIM JOSEPH BEN AZRIEL HA-
    KOHEN
IBN DANAN, SAADIAH BEN MAIMUN
IBN EZRA, JOSEPH BEN ISAAC
IBN EZRA, SOLOMON BEN MOSES
IBN HABIB, JACOB BEN SOLOMON
IBN HAYYIM, AARON (ben Abraham)
IBN HAYYIM, AARON
IBN JAMIL, ISAAC NISSIM

IBN MUSA, HAYYIM BEN JUDAH

IBN SHOSHAN, DAVID

IBN SHUAIB, JOEL

IBN VERGA, JOSEPH

IBN YAHYA, DAVID BEN JOSEPH

IBN YAHYA, DAVID BEN SOLOMON

IBN YAHYA, GEDALIAH BEN DAVID

IBN YAHYA, GEDALIAH BEN JOSEPH

IBN YAHYA, JOSEPH BEN DAVID

IBN ZUR, JACOB BEN REUBEN

IGRA, MESHULLAM (Moses) BEN SAMSON

ILLOWY, BERNARD

ISAAC BEN ABRAHAM DI MOLINA

ISAAC BEN ABRAHAM OF POSEN

ISAAC BEN BEZALEL OF VLADIMIR

ISAAC BEN JACOB MIN HA-LEVIYYIM

ISAAC BENJAMIN WOLF BEN ELIEZER LIPMAN

ISAAC BEN NOAH KOHEN SHAPIRA

ISAAC BEN SAMSON HA-KOHEN

ISAAC BEN SAMUEL HA-LEVI

ISAIAH HASID FROM ZBARAZH

ISAIAH MENAHEM BEN ISAAC

ISCANDARI

ISHMAEL BEN ABRAHAM ISAAC HA-KOHEN

ISIDOR LAZARE

ISRAEL

ISRAEL, YOM TOV BEN ELIJAH

ISRAEL BEN BENJAMIN OF BELZEC

ISRAEL BEN SAMUEL OF SHKLOV

ISRAELI, SHAUL

ISRAEL ISSERL BEN ISAAC SEGAL

ISRAEL MEIR HA-KOHEN (Hafez Hayyim)

ISRAEL MOSES BEN ARYEH LOEB

ISSACHAR BAER BEN SOLOMON ZALMAN (Klazki)

ISSACHAR BAER BEN TANHUM

ISSACHAR BERMAN BEN NAPHTALI HA-KOHEN

ISSAR JUDAH BEN NEHEMIAH OF BRISK

ISSERLES, MOSES BEN ISRAEL (Rema)

ISTRUMSA (Istrusa), HAYYIM ABRAHAM

ITALIENER, BRUNO

JABEZ, JOSEPH BEN HAYYIM

JACOB, BENNO

JACOB BEN AARON OF KARLIN

JACOB BEN ABRAHAM SOLOMON

JACOB BEN BENJAMIN ZEEV

JACOB BEN EPHRAIM NAPHTALI HIRSCH OF LUBLIN

JACOB BEN JUDAH OF LONDON

JACOB BEN MORDECAI OF SCHWERIN

JACOB BEN NISSIM IBN SHAHIN

JACOB ISAAC BEN SHALOM

JACOB JOSEPH OF OSTROG

JACOB (Jakob) OF BELZYCE

JACOB SAMSON OF SHEPETOVKA

JAFFE, MORDECAI-GIMPEL

JAFFE, SAMUEL BEN ISAAC ASHKENAZI

JAFFE-MARGOLIOT, ISRAEL DAVID

JAKOBOVITS, IMMANUEL

JAVETZ, BARZILLAI BEN BARUCH

JEHIEL MICHAEL (Michel) BEN ABRAHAM MEIR OF CIFER

JEHIEL MICHAEL (Michel) BEN JUDAH LEIB HE-HASID

JELLIN, ARYEH LOEB BEN SHALOM SHAKHNA

JELLINEK, ADOLF

JENER, ABRAHAM NAPHTALI HIRSCH BEN MORDECAI

JEREMIAH BEN ISAAC

JERUSALIMSKI, MOSES NAHUM BEN BENJAMIN

JESHUA BEN JOSEPH HA-LEVI

JESURUN, ISAAC BEN ABRAHAM HAYYIM

JEWNIN, ABRAHAM JONAH

JIZFAN, JUDAH BEN JOSEPH

JOAB BEN JEREMIAH

JOEL, DAVID HEYMANN

JOEL, MANUEL

JOEL BEN MOSES GAD

JOFFEN, ABRAHAM

JOLLES, ZECHARIAH ISAIAH

JONATHAN BEN ABRAHAM ISAAC

JONATHAN BEN JACOB

JONATHAN BEN JOSEPH OF RUZHANY

JOSEPH, JACOB

JOSEPH BEN ELIJAH OF ZASLAW

JOSEPH BEN ISSACHAR BAER OF PRAGUE

JOSEPH BEN JOSHUA MOSES OF FRANKFURT

JOSEPH BEN MORDECAI GERSHON HA-KOHEN OF CRACOW

JOSEPH BEN MORDECAI HA-KOHEN

JOSEPH BEN MOSES

JOSEPH BEN MOSES (Ashkenazi), DARSHAN OF PRZEMYSLANY

JOSEPH BEN MOSES OF KREMENETS

JOSEPH BEN MOSES PHINEHAS

JOSEPH BEN ZADDIK

JOSEPH BEN ZE'EV WOLF HA-LEVI

JOSEPH DAVID (Salonika)

JOSEPH HAYYIM BEN ELIJAH AL-HAKAM

JOSEPH MAMAN AL-MAGHRIBI

JOSEPH SAMUEL BEN ZEVI OF CRACOW

JOSEPH SOLOMON ZALMAN BEN MEIR

JOSHUA BEN MORDECAI FALK HA-KOHEN

JOSHUA HOESCHEL BEN JACOB

JOSHUA HOESCHEL BEN JOSEPH OF CRACOW

JOSPE, ALFRED

JUDAH ARYEH LEIB BEN DAVID

JUDAH BEN ELIEZER

JUDAH BEN JACOB HA-KOHEN

JUDAH BEN MOSES OF LUBLIN

JUDAH BEN NISSAN

JUDAH HASID (Segal) HA-LEVI

JUDAH LEIB BEN ENOCH ZUNDEL

JUDAH LEIB BEN HILLEL OF SCHWERSENZ

JUDAH LOEW BEN BEZALEL (Maharal)

JUNG, LEO

JUNGREIS, ASHER ANSHEL

KAATZ, SAUL

KADOORIE, SASSON

KAEMPF, SAUL ISAAC

KAFAH, YIHYE BEN SOLOMON

KAFAH, YOSEF

II. RELIGION
A. JEWISH
4. Rabbinics
BIOGRAPHIES
Aharonim (*continued*)

KAHANA, ABRAHAM ARYEH LEIB BEN SHALOM
  SHAKHNA
KAHANA, JACOB BEN ABRAHAM
KAHANA, JEHIEL ZEVI BEN JOSEPH MORDECAI
KAHANA, KALMAN
KAHANA, NAHMAN
KAHANA, SOLOMON DAVID
KAHANEMAN, JOSEPH ("Ponevezer Rav")
KAHANOV, MOSES NEHEMIAH
KAHANOVITCH, ISRAEL ISAAC
KAHN, ZADOC
KALA'I, MORDECAI BEN SOLOMON
KALAI, SAMUEL BEN MOSES
KALISCHER, JUDAH LEIB BEN MOSES
KALISCHER, ZEVI HIRSCH
KALLIR, ELEAZAR BEN ELEAZAR
KALMANOWITZ, ABRAHAM
KAMELHAR, JEKUTIEL ARYEH BEN GERSHON
KAMENETSKY, YAAKOV
KANIEVSKY, JACOB ISRAEL
KANN, MOSES
KAPLAN, ALEXANDER SENDER BEN ZERAH HA-KOHEN
KAPLAN, JACOB
KAPUZATO, MOSES HA-YEVANI
KARA, JOSEPH
KARA, MENAHEM BEN JACOB
KAREH, SOLOMON
KARELITZ, AVRAHAM YESHAYAHU (Hazon Ish)
KARFUNKEL, AARON BEN JUDAH LEIB HA-KOHEN
KARGAU, MENAHEM MENDEL BEN NAPHTALI HIRSCH
KARMI (Cremieux)
KASABI, JOSEPH BEN NISSIM
KASHER, MENAHEM
KASOVSKY, CHAYIM YEHOSHUA
KASPI, NETHANEL BEN NEHEMIAH
KATTINA, JACOB
KATZ, MENAHEM
KATZ, REUVEN
KATZBURG, DAVID ZEVI
KATZENELLENBOGEN
KATZENELLENBOGEN, DAVID TEVEL
KATZENELLENBOGEN, MEIR BEN ISAAC
KAUDER, SAMUEL JUDAH BEN DAVID
KAZIN, JUDAH BEN YOM TOV
KAZIN, RAPHAEL BEN ELIJAH
KECSKEMETI, ARMIN
KECSKEMETI, LIPOT
KIMHI, JACOB BEN SAMUEL
KIMHI, RAPHAEL ISRAEL BEN JOSEPH
KIMHI, SOLOMON BEN NISSIM JOSEPH DAVID
KIRSHBLUM, MORDECAI
KITTSEE, HAYYIM BEN ISAAC
KITTSEE, JEHIEL MICHAEL BEN SAMUEL
KLATZKIN, ELIJAH BEN NAPHTALI HERZ

KLATZKO, MORDECAI BEN ASHER
KLAUSNER, ABRAHAM
KLAUSNER, ZEVI HIRSCH
KLAVAN, ISRAEL
KLEIN, MORITZ
KLEIN, PHILIP
KLEIN, SALOMON WOLF
KLEIN, SAMUEL SHMELKA
KLEMPERER, GUTMANN (Gumper)
KLEPFISH, SAMUEL ZANVIL
KLUGER, SOLOMON BEN JUDAH AARON
KOENIGSBERGER, BERNHARD (Barukh)
KOERNER, MOSES BEN ELIEZER PHOEBUS
KOHEN, ELEAZAR BEN ZEEV WOLF
KOHEN, RAPHAEL BEN JEKUTHIEL SUESSKIND
KOHN, PINCHAS
KOHN, SAMUEL
KOIDONOVER, AARON SAMUEL BEN ISRAEL
KOIDONOVER, ZEVI HIRSCH
KOLIN, SAMUEL BEN NATHAN HA-LEVI
KONVITZ, JOSEPH
KOOK, ZEVI JUDAH BEN ABRAHAM ISAAC HA-
  KOHEN
KOPPELMAN, JACOB BEN SAMUEL BUNIM
KORNFELD, AARON BEN MORDECAI BAER
KORNIK, MEIR BEN MOSES
KOTLER, AARON
KOWALSKY, JUDAH LEIB
KRAMER, MOSES BEN DAVID, OF VILNA
KRANZ, JACOB BEN WOLF (Maggid of Dubno)
KRAUSS, JUDAH HA-KOHEN
KREMNITZER, JOHANAN BEN MEIR
KRENGEL, MENAHEM MENDEL
KRISPIN, JOSHUA ABRAHAM
KRISTIANPOLLER
KROCH, JACOB LEIB BEN SHEMAIAH
KROCHMAL, MENAHEM MENDEL BEN ABRAHAM
KRONIK, MOSES BEN AKIVA
KRYGIER, RIVON
LAMPRONTI, ISAAC HEZEKIAH BEN SAMUEL
LANDAU, ELEAZAR BEN ISRAEL
LANDAU, EZEKIEL BEN JUDAH
LANDAU, ISAAC ELIJAH BEN SAMUEL
LANDAU, ISRAEL JONAH BEN JOSEPH HA-LEVI
LANDAU, JACOB
LANDAU, LEIBUSH MENDEL
LANDAU, NATHAN
LANDSOFER, JONAH BEN ELIJAH
LANIADO, ABRAHAM BEN ISAAC
LANIADO, RAPHAEL SOLOMON BEN SAMUEL
LANIADO, SAMUEL BEN ABRAHAM
LANIADO, SOLOMON BEN ABRAHAM
LAPAPA, AARON BEN ISAAC
LAPIDOT, ALEXANDER MOSES
LATTES, ABRAHAM BEN ISAAC
LATTES, BONET
LATTES, ISAAC JOSHUA
LAU, ISRAEL MEIR
LAWANI, DAUD
LEESER, ISAAC

LEEUW, JACOB BEN HAYYIM (Heymann) DE

LEHMANN, JOSEPH

LEHMANN, MARCUS

LEIBOWITZ, BARUCH BER

LEMBERGER, MOSES BEN AARON

LEON

LEON, MESSER JUDAH BEN JEHIEL

LEONE, LEON (Judah) DI

LERNER, MAYER BEN MORDECAI OF ALTONA

LEV (Lab; Leb), JOSEPH BEN DAVID IBN (Maharival)

LEVI

LEVI, ABRAHAM BEN JOSEPH

LEVI, BENEDETTO

LEVI (Bet ha-Levi), ISAAC BEN SOLOMON

LEVI, ISRAEL

LEVI, JACOB BEN ISRAEL

LEVI, MORITZ

LEVI, SOLOMON BEN ISAAC

LEVI (Bet ha-Levi), SOLOMON BEN ISAAC

LEVI BEN HABIB (Ralbah)

LEVIN, JUDAH LEIB

LEVIN, ZEVI HIRSCH (-el) BEN ARYEH LOEB

LEVY, ALFRED

LEVY, ISAAC

LEVY, JACOB

LEVY, JUDAH BEN MENAHEM

LEVY, SAMUEL

LEVY, SION

LEWIN, AARON BEN NATHAN OF RZESZOW

LEWIN, BENJAMIN MANASSEH

LEWIN, JOSHUA HESHEL BEN ELIJAH ZEEV HA-LEVI

LEWIN, JUDAH LEIB

LEWIN, LOUIS

LEWINSTEIN, JOSEPH BEN ABRAHAM ABUSH

LEWY, ISRAEL

LEWYSOHN, ABRAHAM

LEWYSOHN, YEHUDI LEIB LOUIS

LIBER, MAURICE

LIBSCHITZ, BARUCH MORDECAI BEN JACOB

LICHTENSTADT, BENJAMIN WOLF BEN JUDAH

LICHTENSTEIN, HILLEL BEN BARUCH

LICHTSTEIN, ABRAHAM BEN ELIEZER LIPMAN

LICHTSTEIN, ABRAHAM JEKUTHIEL ZALMAN BEN
    MOSES JOSEPH

LIFSHITZ, DAVID

LIMA, MOSES BEN ISAAC JUDAH

LIPKIN (Salanter), ISRAEL BEN ZEEV WOLF

LIPSCHITZ, SOLOMON ZALMAN

LIPSCHUETZ

LIPSCHUETZ, BARUCH ISAAC BEN ISRAEL

LIPSCHUETZ, GEDALIAH BEN SOLOMON ZALMAN

LIPSCHUETZ, HILLEL ARYEH LEIB BEN ZEEV DOV

LIPSCHUETZ, ISRAEL BEN ELIEZER

LIPSCHUTZ, ELIEZER BEN SOLOMON

LIPSCHUTZ, ISRAEL BEN GEDALIAH

LIPSCHUTZ, SOLOMON BEN MORDECAI

LISSER, JOSHUA FALK

LOEB, ISIDORE

LOEBEL, ISRAEL

LOEW, ELEAZAR

LOEWENSTAMM

LOEWENSTEIN, LEOPOLD

LOEWY, JACOB EZEKIEL BEN JOSEPH

LOLLI, EUDE

LONDON, JACOB BEN MOSES JUDAH

LOOKSTEIN, JOSEPH HYMAN

LOPIAN, ELIJAH

LORBEERBAUM, JACOB BEN JACOB MOSES OF LISSA

LUBETZKY, JUDAH

LUBLIN, MEIR BEN GEDALIAH

LURIA

LURIA, DAVID BEN JUDAH

LURIA, SOLOMON BEN JEHIEL (Maharshal)

LUZZATTO, JACOB BEN ISAAC

LUZZATTO, SAMUEL DAVID

LUZZATTO, SIMONE BEN ISAAC SIMHAH

LYONS, JACQUES JUDAH

MAARSEN, ISAAC

MAIMI, SIMON

MAIMON, JUDAH LEIB

MAISEL, ELIJAH HAYYIM

MALACHI BEN JACOB HA-KOHEN

MALBIM, MEIR LOEB BEN JEHIEL MICHAEL

MALCA

MALKHI, EZRA BEN RAPHAEL MORDECAI

MALKHI, MOSES

MALKHI, MOSES BEN RAPHAEL MORDECAI

MANI

MANISCHEWITZ, HIRSCH

MANSURAH, SAADIAH BEN JUDAH

MANSURAH, SHALOM BEN JUDAH

MARGALIOT, REUBEN

MARGOLIES, ISAAC BEN ELIJAH

MARGOLIES, MOSES SEBULUN

MARGOLIOT, MOSES BEN SIMEON

MARGOLIOTH

MARGOLIOTH, EPHRAIM ZALMAN BEN MENAHEM
    MANNES

MARGOLIOTH, JACOB

MARGOLIOTH, JUDAH LOEB

MARGOLIS, GAVRIEL ZEV

MARGULIES, SAMUEL HIRSCH

MARINI, SHABBETHAI HAYYIM (Vita)

MARLI, SAMUEL (RAPHAEL) BEN MAZLIAH

MARMORSTEIN, ARTHUR

MASHASH, SHLOMO

MASKILEISON, ABRAHAM BEN JUDAH LEIB

MASLI'AH SALIH

MASNUT, SAMUEL BEN NISSIM

MAT, MOSES

MATLIN, MOSHE

MATTERSDORF, JEREMIAH BEN ISAAC

MAYBAUM, SIGMUND

MEDINA, SAMUEL BEN MOSES DE

MEDINI, HAYYIM HEZEKIAH BEN RAPHAEL
    ELIJAH

MEHLSACK, ELIAKIM BEN JUDAH HA-MILZAHGI

MEIR, JACOB

MEIR BEN ELIJAH

MEIR SIMHAH HA-KOHEN OF DVINSK

II. RELIGION
A. JEWISH
4. Rabbinics
BIOGRAPHIES
Aharonim (continued)

MEISEL, MOSES BEN MORDECAI
MEISELS, DAVID DOV
MEISELS, DOV BERUSH
MEKLENBURG, JACOB ZEVI
MELAMED, RAHAMIM REUVEN
MELAMED, SIMAN TOV
MELCHIOR, MARCUS
MELCHIOR, MICHAEL
MELDOLA
MELDOLA, RAPHAEL
MELTZER, ISSER ZALMAN
MENAHEM BEN MOSES HA-BAVLI
MENAHEM MENDEL OF SHKLOV
MENDES
MENDES
MENDLOWITZ, SHRAGA FEIVEL
MESHULLAM PHOEBUS BEN ISRAEL SAMUEL
MESHULLAM ZALMAN HA-KOHEN
MEYER, SELIGMANN
MEYUHAS, MOSES JOSEPH MORDECAI BEN RAPHAEL
    MEYUHAS
MEYUHAS, RAPHAEL MEYUHAS BEN SAMUEL
MICHAELSON, EZEKIEL ZEVI BEN ABRAHAM HAYYIM
MILEVSKY, AHARON
MILLER, ISRAEL
MINTZ, MOSES BEN ISAAC
MINZ, ABRAHAM BEN JUDAH HA-LEVI
MINZ, JUDAH BEN ELIEZER HA-LEVI
MIRSKY, SAMUEL KALMAN
MIZRAHI, DAVID BEN SHALOM
MIZRAHI, ELIJAH
MODAI, HAYYIM
MODENA, LEONE (Judah Aryeh)
MODERN, JUDAH
MOELLIN, JACOB BEN MOSES (Maharil)
MOHILEWER, SAMUEL
MONZON, ABRAHAM
MORDECAI (Mokhiah) BEN HAYYIM OF EISENSTADT
MORDECAI BEN JUDAH HA-LEVI
MORDECAI BEN NAPHTALI HIRSCH OF KREMSIER
MORPURGO, SAMSON BEN JOSHUA MOSES
MORTARA, MARCO
MORTEIRA, SAUL LEVI
MOSCATO, JUDAH BEN JOSEPH
MOSES BEN DANIEL OF ROHATYN
MOSES BEN HANOKH
MOSES BEN ISAIAH KATZ
MOSES BEN JACOB OF KIEV
MOSES ESRIM VE-ARBA
MOSES ISAAC
MOSES ZEEV BEN ELIEZER OF GRODNO
MOTAL, ABRAHAM BEN JACOB
MOWSHOWITZ, ISRAEL
MUELLER, JOEL

MUENZ, ELEAZAR BEN ARYEH LEIB
MUENZ, MOSES BEN ISAAC HA-LEVI
MUNK
MURMELSTEIN, BENJAMIN
MUSSAFIA, BENJAMIN BEN IMMANUEL
MUSSAFIA, HAYYIM ISAAC
NAHON
NAHOUM, HAIM
NAHUM, ELIEZER BEN JACOB
NAJARA
NATHAN OF GAZA
NATHANSON, JOSEPH SAUL
NATONEK, JOSEPH
NAVON, EPHRAIM BEN AARON
NAVON, JONAH BEN HANUN
NAVON, JONAH MOSES BEN BENJAMIN
NAWI
NAZIR, MOSES HA-LEVI
NEPPI, HANANEL (Grazziadio)
NERIAH, MOSHE ZEVI
NEUDA, ABRAHAM
NIEMIROWER, JACOB ISAAC
NIETO, DAVID
NIETO, ISAAC
NISSENBAUM, ISAAC
NISSIM, ISAAC
NOBEL, NEHEMIAH ANTON
NORZI
NORZI, JEDIDIAH SOLOMON RAPHAEL BEN
    ABRAHAM
NUNES VAIS
OBERNIK, JUDAH
OLIVEYRA, SOLOMON BEN DAVID DE
OLMO, JACOB DANIEL BEN ABRAHAM
OLSCHWANGER, ISAAC WOLF
ONDERWIJZER, ABRAHAM BEN SAMSON HA-KOHEN
OPPENHEIM, BEER BEN ISAAC
OPPENHEIM, DAVID
OPPENHEIM, DAVID BEN ABRAHAM
OPPENHEIM, HAYYIM
OPPENHEIM, JOACHIM
ORNSTEIN, JACOB MESHULLAM BEN MORDECAI
    ZEEV
OSHRY, EPHRAIM
OTTOLENGHI, JOSEPH BEN NATHAN
OUZIEL, BEN-ZION MEIR HAI
OVADIA, NISSIM
OVCHINSKI, LEVI
PACIFICI, RICCARDO
PALACHE, HAYYIM
PANET, EZEKIEL BEN JOSEPH
PANIGEL, ELIYAHU MOSHE
PANIGEL, RAPHAEL MEIR BEN JUDAH
PAPO, SAMUEL SHEMAIAH
PARDES, ELIYAHU
PARDES, SHMUEL
PARDO
PARDO, DAVID SAMUEL BEN JACOB
PARDO, JOSEPH
PARDO, MOSES BEN RAPHAEL

PARIS, HAILU

PARNAS, HAYYIM NAHMAN

PERAHYAH, AARON BEN HAYYIM ABRAHAM
HA-KOHEN

PERAHYAH, HASDAI BEN SAMUEL HA-KOHEN

PERELMANN, JEROHMAN JUDAH LEIB BEN SOLOMON
ZALMAN

PEREZ, JUDAH BEN JOSEPH

PEREZ BEN MOSES OF BRODY

PERGOLA, RAPHAEL DE LA

PERLA, JEROHAM FISCHEL BEN ARYEH ZEVI

PERLES, ISAAC MOSES

PERLES, MOSES MEIR BEN ELEAZAR

PERLHEFTER, ISSACHAR BEHR BEN JUDAH MOSES

PERLMUTTER, ABRAHAM ZEVI

PESANTE, MOSES BEN HAYYIM BEN SHEM TOV

PINES, YEHIEL MICHAEL (Michal)

PINHEIRO, MOSES

PINNER, EPHRAIM MOSES BEN ALEXANDER SUSSKIND

PINTO

PLACZEK, ABRAHAM

PLAUT, HEZEKIAH FEIVEL

PLOTZKI, MEIR DAN OF OSTROVA

POLACHEK, SOLOMON

POLLACK, JACOB BEN JOSEPH

POLLAK, MIKSA

POLLAK, MOSES HA-LEVI

POPPERS, JACOB BEN BENJAMIN HA-KOHEN

PORATH, ISRAEL

PORGES, MOSES BEN ISRAEL NAPHTALI

PORGES, NATHAN

PORTO, ABRAHAM MENAHEM BEN JACOB HA-KOHEN

PORTO-RAFA, MOSES BEN JEHIEL HA-KOHEN

PORUSH, ISRAEL

POSNER, DAVID BEN NAPHTALI

POSNER, SOLOMON ZALMAN BEN JOSEPH

POUPKO, BERNARD

PRATO, DAVID

PREIL, ELAZAR MEYER

PRIJS, JOSEPH

PRIMO, SAMUEL (Judah)

PROSSNITZ, JUDAH LEIB BEN JACOB HOLLESCHAU

PROSSTITZ, DANIEL

PROVENÇAL, DAVID BEN ABRAHAM

PROVENÇAL, MOSES BEN ABRAHAM

PUKHOVITSER, JUDAH LEIB

QUERIDO, JACOB

QUETSCH, SOLOMON

RABBA, MENAHEM

RABBINOVICZ, RAPHAEL NATHAN NATA

RABINOVICH, ISAAC JACOB

RABINOWICH (Rabinowitsch), ELIYAHU AKIVA

RABINOWITZ, SAMUEL JACOB

RABINOWITZ-TEOMIM, ELIJAH DAVID BEN BENJAMIN

RACCAH, MASUD BEN AARON

RACKMAN, EMANUEL

RAGOLER, ABRAHAM BEN SOLOMON

RAGOLER, ELIJAH BEN JACOB

RANSCHBURG, BEZALEL BEN JOEL

RAPAPORT, DAVID HA-KOHEN

RAPHALL, MORRIS JACOB

RAPOPORT

RAPOPORT, ABRAHAM BEN ISRAEL JEHIEL HA-
KOHEN

RAPOPORT, BENJAMIN ZEEV WOLF HA-KOHEN BEN
ISAAC

RAPOPORT, SAMUEL

RAPPAPORT, ISAAC BEN JUDAH HA-KOHEN

RATH, MESHULLAM

RATNER, DOV BAER

REGGIO, ISACCO SAMUEL

REICH, KOPPEL (Jacob)

REINES, ISAAC JACOB

REISCHER, JACOB BEN JOSEPH

REIZES (Reizeles)

RENASSIA, YOSSEF

RESNICK, ZVI (HIRSH) YOSEF HAKOHEN

RICE, ABRAHAM JOSEPH

RICHIETTI, JOSEPH SHALLIT BEN ELIEZER

RISIKOFF, MENAHEM (MENDEL) HACOHEN

RISKIN, SHLOMO

RIVKES, MOSES BEN NAPHTALI HIRSCH

ROKEAH, ELAZAR BEN SHMELKE

ROSANES, JUDAH BEN SAMUEL

ROSANES, ZEVI HIRSCH BEN ISSACHAR BERISH

ROSEN, JOSEPH BEN ISAAC

ROSEN, MOSES

ROSENAK, LEOPOLD

ROSENBAUM, MOSES HAYYIM LITS

ROSENBERG, ISRAEL

ROSENBLATT, MORDECAI BEN MENAHEM

ROSENBLATT, SAMUEL

ROSENTHAL, NAPHTALI

ROZIN (Rosen), JOSEPH

ROZOVSKI, PINHAS

RUBINSTEIN, ISAAC

RUBIO, MORDECAI

RUDERMAN, JACOB ISAAC

RUELF, ISAAC

SAADIAH BEN JOSEPH HA-LEVI

SACERDOTI, ANGELO-RAPHAEL CHAIM

SAFRAN, ALEXANDER

SAFRAN, BEZALEL ZEEV

SAFRAN, JOSEPH

SAGIS

SALANT, JOSEPH SUNDEL BEN BENJAMIN BENISH

SALANT, SAMUEL

SALIH, ABRAHAM

SALIH, YAHYA BEN JOSEPH (MAHARIS)

SALIH IBN YAHYA IBN JOSEPH

SALVENDI, ADOLF

SAMEGAH, JOSEPH BEN BENJAMIN

SAMUEL BEN AVIGDOR

SAMUEL BEN DAVID MOSES HA-LEVI

SAMUEL BEN JACOB OF KELMY

SAMUEL BEN URI SHRAGA PHOEBUS

SANGUINETTI, AZARIAH HAYYIM

SAPORTA, HANOKH

SAR, SAMUEL

SARAVAL

II. RELIGION

A. JEWISH

4. Rabbinics

BIOGRAPHIES

Aharonim (*continued*)

SARAVAL, JACOB RAPHAEL BEN SIMHAH JUDAH

SARAVAL, JUDAH LEIB

SARFATY

SARNA, EZEKIEL

SASPORTAS, JACOB

SASSON, AARON BEN JOSEPH

SCHACHTER, HERSCHEL

SCHACHTER, JACOB J.

SCHACTER-SHALOMI, ZALMAN

SCHEIBER, ALEXANDER

SCHEINFELD, SOLOMON ISAAC

SCHERMAN, NOSSON

SCHICK, ABRAHAM BEN ARYEH LOEB

SCHICK, BARUCH BEN JACOB

SCHICK, MOSES BEN JOSEPH

SCHIFF, DAVID TEVELE

SCHIFF, MEIR BEN JACOB HA-KOHEN

SCHILLER-SZINESSY, SOLOMON MAYER

SCHLESINGER, AKIVA JOSEPH

SCHLIEFER, SOLOMON

SCHMELKES, GEDALIAH BEN MORDECAI

SCHMELKES, ISAAC JUDAH

SCHONFELD, VICTOR

SCHOR, ALEXANDER SENDER BEN EPHRAIM ZALMAN

SCHOR, EPHRAIM SOLOMON (THE ELDER) BEN
    NAPHTALI HIRSCH

SCHORR, ABRAHAM HAYYIM BEN NAPHTALI ZEVI
    HIRSCH

SCHORR, MOSES (Mojzesz)

SCHUECK, JENO

SCHULHOF, ISAAC

SCHUSTER, AARON

SCHWAB, LOW

SCHWAB, SHIMON

SCHWABACHER, SIMEON ARYEH

SCHWARTZ, ABRAHAM JUDAH HA-KOHEN

SCHWARTZ, JOSEPH HA-KOHEN

SCHWARTZ, PHINEHAS (PINHAS) SELIG HA-KOHEN
    (SIGMUND)

SCHWARZ, ADOLF (Aryeh)

SCHWARZ, YEHOSEPH

SCHWERIN-GOETZ, ELIAKIM HA-KOHEN

SEFER HUKKEI HA-TORAH

SEFIRAH, SAADIAH BEN JOSEPH

SEGAL, GEDALIAH BEN ELIEZER

SEGRE

SEGRE, JOSHUA BENZION

SEGRE, SALVATORE

SEIGEL, JOSHUA

SERERO

SERERO, SAUL

SEROR

SERVI, FLAMINIO (Ephraim)

SFORNO, OBADIAH BEN JACOB

SHABBETAI BEN MEIR HA-KOHEN (Shakh)

SHAG, ABRAHAM

SHAKI, ISAAC

SHALOM, ABRAHAM (Salonika)

SHALOM SHAKHNA BEN JOSEPH

SHAPIRA, ABRAHAN ELKANA KAHANA

SHAPIRA, ELIJAH BEN BENJAMIN WOLF

SHAPIRA, JOSHUA ISAAC BEN JEHIEL

SHAPIRA, MEIR

SHAPIRO, ARYEH LEIB BEN ISAAC

SHAPIRO, SAUL BEN DOV

SHATZKES, MOSES

SHKOP, SIMEON JUDAH

SHREIER, FEIWEL

SHVADRON, SHALOM MORDECAI BEN MOSES

SIBONI

SICHER, GUSTAV

SID, SAMUEL IBN

SIDON, SIMEON

SIERRA, SERGIO JOSEPH

SILBER, SAUL

SILBERSTEIN, DAVID JUDAH LEIB

SILBERSTEIN, SOLOMON JOSEPH

SILVA, JOSHUA DA

SILVER, ELIEZER

SILVERSTONE, GEDALYAH

SIMHAH BEN SAMUEL OF SPEYER

SINGER, ABRAHAM

SINGER, PESAH

SINGER, SIMEON

SINIGAGLIA

SINZHEIM, JOSEPH DAVID BEN ISAAC

SIRAT, RENE SAMUEL

SIRILLO, SOLOMON BEN JOSEPH

SIRKES, JOEL

SITRUK, JOSEPH

SITTEON DABBAH, SHAUL DAVID

SIVITZ, MOSHE

SLONIK, BENJAMIN AARON BEN ABRAHAM

SOCHACZEW, ABRAHAM BEN ZE'EV NAHUM
    BORNSTEIN OF

SOFER

SOFER, HAYYIM BEN MORDECAI EPHRAIM FISCHEL

SOFER, MOSES

SOLA, ABRAHAM DE

SOLOVEICHIK

SOLOVEICHIK, AARON

SOLOVEICHIK, HAYYIM

SOLOVEICHIK, ISAAC ZEEV HA-LEVI

SOLOVEICHIK, JOSEPH BAER OF VOLOZHIN

SOLOVEICHIK, MOSHE

SOLOVEITCHIK, JOSEPH DOV

SOMEKH, ABDALLAH BEN ABRAHAM

SONCINO, JOSHUA

SONNENFELD, JOSEPH HAYYIM BEN ABRAHAM
    SOLOMON

SOROTZKIN, ZALMAN BEN BEN-ZION

SPEKTOR, ISAAC ELHANAN

SPERO, SHUBERT

SPITZER, SAMUEL

SPITZER, SOLOMON

STADTHAGEN, JOSEPH

STEIN, ELIEZER LIPMAN

STEIN, ISAAC

STEINHARDT, JOSEPH BEN MENAHEM

STEINHARDT, MENAHEM MENDEL BEN SIMEON

STEINSALTZ, ADIN

STERN, GERSHON

STERN, JOSEPH

STERN, JOSEPH ZECHARIAH

STERN, MENAHEM

STRASHUN, MATHIAS (Mattityahu)

STRASHUN, SAMUEL BEN JOSEPH

SUSAN, ISSACHAR BEN MORDECAI

SUZIN, SOLOMON MOSES

TABAK, SOLOMON LEIB

TAENZER, ARNOLD (Aaron)

TAGLICHT, DAVID ISRAEL

TAM IBN YAHYA, JACOB BEN DAVID

TANHUM BEN ELIEZER

TANUJI, ISHMAEL HA-KOHEN

TANUJI, JOSEPH BEN SHALOM HA-KOHEN

TAUBES, AARON MOSES BEN JACOB

TAUBES, HAYYIM ZEVI

TEDESCHI

TEITELBAUM, AARON

TEITZ, PINCHAS (MORDECAI)

TELUSHKIN, NISSAN

TEMPLO, JACOB JUDAH (ARYEH) LEON

TENNENBAUM, JACOB

TEOMIM, AARON BEN MOSES

TEOMIM, ARYEH LEIB

TEOMIM, JOSEPH BEN MEIR

TERNI, DANIEL BEN MOSES DAVID

TEWELES, JUDAH

THEODOR, JULIUS

TIKTIN

TIKTINSKI

TOAFF

TOLEDANO

TOLEDANO, JACOB MOSES

TOLEDO, MOSES DE

TOUATI, CHARLES

TRABOT

TRANI, JOSEPH BEN MOSES

TRANI, MOSES BEN JOSEPH

TREBITSCH, NEHEMIAH (Menahem Nahum)

TREVES

TREVES, JOHANAN BEN JOSEPH

TRUNK, ISRAEL JOSHUA

TYKOCINSKI, JEHIEL MICHEL

UCKO, SIEGFRIED (Sinai)

ULLMANN, SALOMON

ULMAN, ABRAHAM

UNGAR, JOEL OF RECHNITZ

UNTERMAN, ISSER YEHUDA

URI BEN SIMEON OF BIALA

UZIEL

UZIEL, ISAAC BEN ABRAHAM

VAEZ, ABRAHAM

VENETIANER, LAJOS (Ludwig)

VENTURA, MOISE

VITAL, DAVID BEN SOLOMON

VITERBO, JEHIEL HAYYIM

VIVANTI, DAVID ABRAHAM

VOLOZHINER, HAYYIM BEN ISAAC

VOLOZHINER, ISAAC BEN HAYYIM

VORST, LOUIS J.

WAGENAAR, LION

WAGNER, STANLEY M.

WAHRMANN, ISRAEL

WALDENBERG, ELIEZER JUDAH

WALKIN, AARON

WARSCHAWSKI, MAX

WASSERMAN, ELHANAN BUNIM

WEBER, KOLOMAN

WEIL, NETHANEL BEN NAPHTALI ZEYI

WEILL, MICHEL AARON

WEINBERG, JEHIEL JACOB

WEINER, ANTHONY D.

WEINGARTEN, JOAB JOSHUA

WEISS, AVI

WEISS, ISAAC HIRSCH

WEISS, ISAAC JACOB

WEISS, JOSEPH MEIR

WEISS, SAMSON

WEISSMANDEL, MICHAEL DOV

WEISZ, MAX

WELLESZ, JULIUS

WESEL, BARUCH BENDET BEN REUBEN

WEYL, MEIR BEN SIMHAH

WIEDENFELD, DOV

WIERNIKORSKI, JUDAH

WILDMANN, ISAAC EISIK

WILLOWSKI, JACOB DAVID BEN ZEEV

WILNA, JACOB BEN BENJAMIN WOLF

WOGUE, LAZARE ELIEZER

WOHLGEMUTH, JOSEPH

WOLFF, ABRAHAM ALEXANDER

WORMS, AARON

WURZBURGER, WALTER S.

XIMENES, SOLOMON MORDECAI

YIHYE, ISAAC HA-LEVI

YIZHAKI, DAVID

YOFFEY

YOSEF, OVADIAH

YUDELOVITZ, ABRAHAM A.

ZACUTO, ABRAHAM BEN SAMUEL

ZAHALON

ZARCHI, ASHER LIPPMAN

ZECHARIAH AL-DAHIRI

ZECHARIAH MENDEL BEN ARYEH LEIB

ZE'EVI, ISRAEL BEN AZARIAH

ZEMBA, MENAHEM

ZEVI HIRSCH OF NADWORNA

ZEVIN, SOLOMON JOSEPH

ZIMMELS, HIRSCH JACOB

ZIPSER, MAJER

ZIRELSON, JUDAH LEIB

ZOLTY, YAACOV BEZALEL

II. RELIGION
A. JEWISH
4. Rabbinics
BIOGRAPHIES
Aharonim (continued)

ZOMBER, DOV BAER
ZOREF, JOSHUA HESHEL BEN JOSEPH
ZUCKER, MOSHE
ZUCKERMANDEL, MOSES SAMUEL
ZUENZ, ARYEH LEIB BEN MOSES

Conservative Rabbis
ABRAMOWITZ, HERMAN
ADLER, MORRIS
AGUS, JACOB BERNARD
ARONSON, DAVID
ARZT, MAX
BERMAN, MYRON
BETTELHEIM, ALBERT (Aaron) SIEGFRIED
BLUMENTHAL, AARON
BOHNEN, ELI AARON
BOKSER, BEN ZION
BOSNIAK, JACOB
BURSTEIN, ABRAHAM
CANTOR, BERNARD
CASS, SAMUEL
CHANOVER, HYMAN
CHIEL, ARTHUR
CHIEL, SAMUEL
COHEN, ARMOND
COHEN, MORTIMER JOSEPH
COHEN, SEYMOUR J.
DAVIDSON, MAX DAVID
DRESNER, SAMUEL
DROB, MAX
EICHLER, MENAHEM
EILBERG, AMY
EPSTEIN, GILBERT
EPSTEIN, HARRY
EPSTEIN, LOUIS M.
FEINBERG, LOUIS
FINKELSTEIN, LOUIS
FRIEDMAN, THEODORE
GEFFEN, JOEL
GELB, MAX
GINZBERG, LOUIS
GOLDFEDER, FISHEL
GOLDMAN, ISRAEL
GOLDMAN, SOLOMON
GOLDSTEIN, ISRAEL
GOLINKIN, DAVID
GOODBLATT, MORRIS
GORDON, ALBERT I.
GREENBERG, LOUIS
GREENBERG, SIDNEY
GREENBERG, SIMON
HAILPERIN, HERMAN
HALPERN, HARRY
HAMMER, REUVEN

HARF, HANNS
HARLOW, JULIUS
HAUPTMAN, JUDITH
HERSHMAN, ABRAHAM M.
HERTZBERG, ARTHUR
HIGGER, MICHAEL
KARP, ABRAHAM J.
KAUVAR, CHARLES ELIEZER HILLEL
KELMAN, WOLFE
KIEVAL, HERMAN
KLEIN, ISAAC
KOGEN, DAVID
KOHN, JACOB
KREITMAN, BENJAMIN
KURTZ, VERNON
KUSHNER, HAROLD
LEHRMAN, IRVING
LEVI, SAMAUEL GERSON
LEVITSKY, LOUIS MOSES
LIEBER, DAVID
MALEV, WILLIAM S.
MANDELBAUM, BERNARD
MATT, C. DAVID
MEYER, MARSHALL
MINKIN, JACOB SAMUEL
MORAIS, SABATO
NADICH, JUDAH
NEULANDER, ARTHUR
NOVECK, SIMON
PARZEN, HERBERT
PRESSMAN, JACOB
RABINOWITZ, STANLEY
ROTH, JOEL
ROUTTENBERG, MAX JONAH
RUBENOVITZ, HERMAN H.
SANDROW, EDWARD T.
SARACHEK, JOSEPH
SCHECHTER, SOLOMON (Shneur Zalman)
SCHILD, EDWIN
SEGAL, BERNARD
SHAPIRO, ALEXANDER
SHUBOW, JOSEPH
SHUCHAT, WILFRED
SIEGEL, SEYMOUR
SILVERMAN, MORRIS
SILVERSTEIN, ALAN
SIMON, RALPH
SLONIM, REUBEN
SOLOMON, ELIAS L.
STAMPFER, JOSHUA
STEINBERG, MILTON
STERNSTEIN, JOSEPH PHILIP
TEPLITZ, SAUL
WAXMAN, MORDECAI
WOLPE, HOWARD ELLIOT
ZELIZER, NATHAN

Reform Rabbis
AARON, ISRAEL
AARONSOHN, MICHAEL

ADLER, LAZARUS LEVI
ADLER, LIEBMANN
ASHER, JOSEPH
AUB, JOSEPH
AUERBACH, ISAAC LEVIN
BACKMAN, JULES
BAMBERGER, BERNARD JACOB
BARNSTON, HENRY
BARON, JOSEPH LOUIS
BEBE, PAULINE
BEERMAN, LEONARD
BENJAMIN, RAPHAEL
BERGER, ELMER
BERKOWITZ, HENRY
BERLIN, SAUL BEN ZEVI HIRSCH LEVIN (Saul Hirschel)
BERMAN, MORTON MAYER
BERNSTEIN, PHILIP SIDNEY
BETTAN, ISRAEL
BLANK, SHELDON HAAS
BLOCH, JOSHUA
BLOCH, PHILIPP
BRASCH, RUDOLPH
BRAUDE, WILLIAM GORDON
BRICKNER, BALFOUR
BRICKNER, BARNETT ROBERT
BRONSTEIN, HERBERT
BROWNE, EDWARD B.M.
BROWNE, LEWIS
CALISCH, EDWARD NATHAN
CHORIN, AARON
COFFEE, RUDOLPH I.
COHEN, HENRY
COHEN, JACOB XENAB
COHN, ELKAN
COHON, SAMUEL SOLOMON
CRONBACH, ABRAHAM
CURRICK, MAX COHEN
DAVIDSON, DAVID
DIENEMANN, MAX
DREYFUS, STANLEY
EHRENREICH, BERNARD
EICHHORN, DAVID M.
EINHORN, DAVID
EINHORN, IGNAZ
EISENDRATH, MAURICE NATHAN
ELIASSOFF, HERMAN
ELLENSON, DAVID HARRY
ELZAS, BARNETT ABRAHAM
ENELOW, HYMAN (Hillel Gershom)
EPPENSTEIN, SIMON
ETTELESON, HARRY
FARHI, DANIEL
FARHI, GABRIEL
FEIBELMAN, JULIAN BECK
FEINBERG, ABRAHAM L.
FELDMAN, ABRAHAM JEHIEL
FELSENTHAL, BERNHARD
FEUER, LEON ISRAEL
FEUERLICHT, MORRIS M.

FINEBERG, SOLOMON ANDHIL
FINESHRIBER, WILLIAM HOWARD
FINK, JOSEPH L.
FISCHER, GYULA
FRANKL, PINKUS FRITZ (Pinhas)
FRANKLIN, LEO MORRIS
FREEHOF, SOLOMON BENNETT
FREUDENTHAL, MAX
FRIEDER, ARMIN
FRISCH, EPHRAIM
GEIGER, ABRAHAM
GLASER, JOSEPH
GOLDENSON, SAMUEL HARRY
GOLDSTEIN, ELYSE
GOLDSTEIN, SIDNEY EMANUEL
GORDON, NATHAN
GOTTHEIL, GUSTAV
GOTTSCHALK, ALFRED
GOUDEKET, MAURITS
GRYN, HUGO
GUTHEIM, JAMES KOPPEL
HABERMAN, JOSHUA
HARRIS, MAURICE
HARRISON, LEON
HELLER
HERXHEIMER, SALOMON
HESS, MENDEL
HIRSCH, EMIL GUSTAVE
HIRSCH, RICHARD
HIRSCH, SAMUEL
HOCHEIMER, HENRY
HOFFMAN, LAWRENCE I.
HOLDHEIM, SAMUEL
ISRAEL, EDWARD LEOPOLD
ISSERMAN, FERDINAND MYRON
JACOB, WALTER
JOSEPH, MORRIS
KAHN, ROBERT
KLEIN, EDWARD E.
KLEIN, GOTTLIEB
KLENICKI, LEON
KLEY, EDUARD (Israel)
KOBER, ADOLF
KOHLBACH, BERTALAN
KOHLER, KAUFMANN
KOHN, ABRAHAM
KORN, BERTRAM WALLACE
KRAUSKOPF, JOSEPH
KRONISH, LEON
KUSHNER, LAWRENCE
LANDMAN, ISAAC
LAUTERBACH, JACOB ZALLEL
LAZARON, MORRIS SAMUEL
LEIMDOERFER, DAVID
LEIPZIGER, EMIL WILLIAM
LELYVELD, ARTHUR JOSEPH
LEVINGER, LEE JOSEPH
LEVY, CLIFTON HARBY
LEVY, FELIX ALEXANDER
LEVY, JOSEPH LEONARD

ANTHROPOMORPHISM

ANTINOMIANISM

BAAL SHEM

CHIROMANCY

COMMANDMENTS, REASONS FOR

DAVID

DEMONS, DEMONOLOGY

DEVEKUT

DIBBUK

EIN-SOF

ELIJAH

EMANATION

ESCHATOLOGY

ETHICAL LITERATURE

GEMATRIA

GILGUL

GOD

GOD, NAMES OF

GOLEM

HIBBUT HA-KEVER

JERUSALEM

MAGGID

MEDITATION

MENORAH

MERKABAH MYSTICISM

MICHAEL AND GABRIEL

PROVIDENCE

RAPHAEL

RAZIEL

REDEMPTION

SABBATH

SACRIFICE

SAMAEL

SANDALFON

SEFIROT

SHIUR KOMAH

SONG, ANGELIC

SOUL, IMMORTALITY OF

USHPIZIN

WORLDS, THE FOUR

Kabbalistic Literature

AZILUT

BAHIR, SEFER HA-

IGGERET HA-KODESH

KANAH AND PELIYAH, BOOKS OF

MA'AREKHET HA-ELOHUT

RAZA RABBA, SEFER

RAZIEL, BOOK OF

RAZIM, SEFER HA-

TEMUNAH, THE BOOK OF

TOLEDOT HA-ARI

ZOHAR

Biographies

AARON BERECHIAH BEN MOSES OF MODENA

AARON SELIG BEN MOSES OF ZOLKIEW

ABI-HASIRA

ABRAHAM BEN ALEXANDER OF COLOGNE

ABRAHAM BEN ELIEZER HA-LEVI (ha-Zaken)

ABRAHAM BEN ELIEZER HA-LEVI BERUKHIM

ABRAHAM BEN ISAAC (Gerondi)

ABRAHAM BEN ISAAC OF GRANADA

ABRAHAM BEN ISRAEL OF BRODY

ABRAHAM BEN JEHIEL MICHAL HA-KOHEN

ABRAHAM BEN SIMEON OF WORMS

ABULAFIA, ABRAHAM BEN SAMUEL

ABULAFIA, TODROS BEN JOSEPH HA-LEVI

ADADI, ABRAHAM HAYYIM BEN MASOUD HAI

ADANI, MIZRAHI SHALOM

AKIVA BAER BEN JOSEPH

ALBAZ, MOSES BEN MAIMON

ALBOTINI, JUDAH BEN MOSES

ALCASTIEL, JOSEPH

ALDABI, MEIR BEN ISAAC

ALEMANNO, JOHANAN BEN ISAAC

ALEXANDER SUSSKIND BEN MOSES OF GRODNO

ALFANDARI, HAYYIM BEN ISAAC RAPHAEL

ALGAZI, ISRAEL JACOB BEN YOM TOV

ALGAZI, YOM TOV BEN ISRAEL JACOB

ALKABEZ, SOLOMON BEN MOSES HA-LEVI

ALMOSNINO, JOSEPH BEN ISAAC

AMARILLO, AARON BEN SOLOMON

ANGEL, BARUCH

ANKAWA, ABRAHAM BEN MORDECAI

ARHA, ELIEZER BEN ISAAC

ARZIN, JOSEPH BEN JACOB

ASHER BEN DAVID

ASHKENAZI, MALKIEL

ASHLAG, YEHUDAH

ATTAR, HAYYIM BEN MOSES (IBN)

ATTIA, SHEM-TOV

AYLLON, SOLOMON BEN JACOB

AZIKRI, ELEAZAR BEN MOSES

AZRIEL OF GERONA

AZULAI

AZULAI, ABRAHAM BEN ISRAEL

AZULAI, ABRAHAM BEN MORDECAI

AZULAI, HAYYIM JOSEPH DAVID

AZULAI, MASUD

BACHARACH, NAPHTALI BEN JACOB ELHANAN

BARAZANI, SAMUEL BEN NETHANEL HA-LEVI

BARUCH

BARUCH (ben Abraham) OF KOSOV

BASHIRI, YAHYA

BASILEA, SOLOMON AVIAD SAR-SHALOM

BAVLI, MENAHEM BEN MOSES

BENAMOZEGH, ELIJAH BEN ABRAHAM

BENJAMIN, ISRAEL

BENJAMIN, MOSES

BENJAMIN BEN ELIEZER HA-KOHEN VITALE OF REGGIO

BIKAYAM, MEIR BEN HALIFA

BRANDWEIN, YEHUDAH ZEVI

BUSAL, HAYYIM BEN JACOB OBADIAH DE

BUZAGLO, SHALOM BEN MOSES

CARO, JOSEPH BEN EPHRAIM

CASTELLAZZO

CHOTSH, ZEVI HIRSCH BEN JERAHMEEL

CORDOVERO, GEDALIAH BEN MOSES

CORDOVERO, MOSES BEN JACOB

II. RELIGION
A. JEWISH
5. Kabbalah & Jewish Mysticism
BIOGRAPHIES (*continued*)

CUENQUE (Cuenca), ABRAHAM BEN LEVI
DATO, MORDECAI BEN JUDAH
DAVID BEN ABRAHAM HA-LAVAN
DAVID BEN JUDAH HE-HASID
DELACRUT, MATTATHIAS BEN SOLOMON
ELIASHOV, SOLOMON BEN HAYYIM
ELIEZER FISCHEL BEN ISAAC OF STRZYZOW
ELIJAH BEN RAPHAEL SOLOMON HA-LEVI
ELIJAH PHINEHAS BEN MEIR
EPSTEIN, ARYEH LEIB BEN MORDECAI
ERGAS, JOSEPH BEN EMANUEL
EYBESCHUETZ, JONATHAN
EZRA BEN SOLOMON
FALK, SAMUEL JACOB HAYYIM
FANO, MENAHEM AZARIAH DA
FORTI, JACOB RAPHAEL HEZEKIAH BEN ABRAHAM ISRAEL
FRANK, JACOB, AND THE FRANKISTS
GABBAI, MEIR BEN EZEKIEL IBN
GALANTE, ABRAHAN BEN MORDECAI
GALANTE, MOSES BEN MORDECAI
GALATINUS, PIETRO (Petrus) COLUMNA
GALLICO, ELISHA BEN GABRIEL
GEDALIAH HA-LEVI
GERONDI, JACOB BEN SHESHET
GIKATILLA, JOSEPH BEN ABRAHAM
GIORGIO, FRANCESCO
GORDON, JEKUTHIEL BEN LEIB
GRUENHUT, DAVID BEN NATHAN
HABILLO, DAVID
HAGIZ, MOSES
HALFAN, ELIJAH MENAHEM
HAMIZ, JOSEPH BEN JUDAH
HANNOVER, NATHAN NATA
HARIRI
HART, JACOB
HAYON, NEHEMIAH HIYYA BEN MOSES
HAYYAT, JUDAH BEN JACOB
HAYYIM ABRAHAM RAPHAEL BEN ASHER
HAYYIM BEN ABRAHAM HA-KOHEN
HAZKUNI, ABRAHAM
HERRERA, ABRAHAM KOHEN DE
HOROWITZ, ISAIAH BEN ABRAHAM HA-LEVI
HOROWITZ, JACOB BEN ABRAHAM
HOROWITZ, SAMUEL SHMELKE OF NIKOLSBURG
HOROWITZ, SHABBETAI SHEFTEL BEN AKIVA
HOROWITZ, ZEVI HIRSCH BEN JOSHUA MOSES AARON
    HA-LEVI
IBN GAON, SHEM TOV BEN ABRAHAM
IBN MOTOT. SAMUEL BEN SAADIAH
IBN SHEM TOV, SHEM TOV
IBN WAQAR, JOSEPH BEN ABRAHAM
IDEL, MOSHE
ISAAC BEN JACOB HA-KOHEN
ISAAC BEN SAMUEL OF ACRE
ISAAC THE BLIND

ISAIAH BEN ABRAHAM
ISRAEL BEN JONATHAN FROM LECZYCA
ISRAEL HARIF OF SATANOV
JACOB BEN JACOB HA-KOHEN
JACOB DAVID BEN ISRAEL ISSAR
JACOB KOPPEL BEN MOSES OF MEZHIRECH
JACOB NAZIR
JAFFE, ISRAEL BEN AARON
JAFFE, MORDECAI BEN ABRAHAM
JAMAL, SULAYMAN
JEHIEL MICHAEL (Michel) BEN ELIEZER
JOLLES, JACOB ZEVI BEN NAPHTALI
JONAH, MOSES
JOSEPH BEN SHALOM ASHKENAZI
JOSEPH DELLA REINA
JOSEPH IBN SHRAGA
JOSEPH IBN TABUL
JOSEPH ISSACHAR BAER BEN ELHANAN
JOSEPH JOSKE BEN JUDAH JUDEL OF LUBLIN
JOSEPH MOSES BEN JEKUTHIEL ZALMAN
JOSHUA IBN NUN
JUDAH BEN YAKAR
JUDAH LEIB BEN BARUCH
KARA, AVIGDOR BEN ISAAC
KATZ, NAPHTALI BEN ISAAC (ha-Kohen)
KHALAZ, JUDAH BEN ABRAHAM
KNORR VON ROSENROTH, CHRISTIAN
KORAH, HAYYIM BEN JOSEPH
KORAH, YIHYE BEN SHALOM
LABI, SIMEON
LANDAUER, MEYER HEINRICH HIRSCH
LARA, HIYYA KOHEN DE
LATIF, ISAAC BEN ABRAHAM IBN
LEON, ISAAC DE
LIPSCHUTZ, SHABBETAI BEN JACOB ISAAC
LOANZ, ELIJAH BEN MOSES
LONZANO, ABRAHAM BEN RAPHAEL DE
LONZANO, MENAHEM BEN JUDAH DE
LURIA, ISAAC BEN SOLOMON (Ha-Ari)
LURIA, JEHIEL BEN ISRAEL ASHKENAZI
LUZZATTO, MOSES HAYYIM (Ramhal)
MAHALALEL BEN SHABBETAI HALLELYAH
MARCUS, AARON
MENAHEM ZIYYONI
MEYUHAS, ABRAHAM BEN SAMUEL
MOLCHO, SOLOMON
MOLITOR, FRANZ JOSEPH
MOSES BEN MENAHEM GRAF
MOSES BEN SHEM TOV DE LEON
MOSES BEN SOLOMON BEN SIMEON OF BURGOS
MUELLER, ERNST
NAHMANIDES
NAHMAN OF KOSOV
NAVON, BENJAMIN MORDECAI BEN EPHRAIM
NEHEMIAH HA-KOHEN
NETHANEL BEN MESHULLAM HA-LEVI
ORNSTEIN, MORDECAI ZEEV BEN MOSES
OSTROPOLER, SAMSON BEN PESAH
OTTOLENGO, SAMUEL DAVID BEN JEHIEL
PINTO, JOSIAH BEN JOSEPH

POPPERS, MEIR BEN JUDAH LOEB HA-KOHEN
RECANATI, MENAHEM BEN BENJAMIN
REGGIO, ABRAHAM BEN EZRIEL
REUBEN HOESHKE BEN HOESHKE KATZ
REUCHLIN, JOHANNES
RICCHI, RAPHAEL IMMANUEL BEN ABRAHAM HAI
RICIUS, PAULUS (Rici)
ROVIGO, ABRAHAM BEN MICHAEL
RUNKEL, SOLOMON ZALMAN
SABA, ABRAHAM BEN JACOB
SAHULA, MEIR BEN SOLOMON ABI
SAMUEL BEN ELIEZER OF KALVARIJA
SANDZER, HAYYIM BEN MENAHEM
SARUG (Saruk), ISRAEL
SCHOLEM, GERSHOM GERHARD
SHABBETAI ZEVI
SHARABI, SHALOM
SHEPHATIAH BEN AMITTAI
SPIRA, NATHAN NATA BEN SOLOMON
TAITAZAK, JOSEPH
TAYYIB, ISAAC BEN BENJAMIN
TEMERLS, JACOB BEN ELIEZER
TISHBY, ISAIAH
UCEDA, SAMUEL BEN ISAAC
VALLE, MOSES DAVID BEN SAMUEL
VIDAS, ELIJAH BEN MOSES DE
VIGENERE, BLAISE DE
VITAL
VITAL, HAYYIM BEN JOSEPH
VITAL, SAMUEL BEN HAYYIM
WANNEH, ISAAC BEN ABRAHAM
WORMSER, SECKEL (Isaac Loeb)
YAKHINI, ABRAHAM BEN ELIJAH
YIZHAKI, ABRAHAM BEN DAVID
ZACUTO, MOSES BEN MORDECAI
ZAYYAH, JOSEPH BEN ABRAHAM IBN
ZEMAH, JACOB BEN HAYYIM

6. HASIDISM

MAIN SURVEYS
HASIDISM

GENERAL ENTRIES
ADMOR
BA'AL SHEM
CHABAD
DAVID-GORODOK
ETHICAL LITERATURE
SEFER HA-HAYYIM
ZAVA'AT RIBASH

BIOGRAPHIES
AARON BEN MOSES HA-LEVI OF STAROSIELCE
AARON OF ZHITOMIR
ABRAHAM BEN ALEXANDER KATZ OF KALISK
ABRAHAM BEN DOV OF MEZHIRECH (ha-Malakh)
ABRAHAM DOV BAER OF OVRUCH
ABRAHAM GERSHON OF KUTOW
ABRAHAM JOSHUA HESCHEL OF APTA (Opatow)

ADAM BA'AL SHEM
ADEL (Ba'al Shem Tov)
ALEKSANDROW
APTA, MEIR
ARYEH JUDAH LEIB (the "Mokhiah") OF POLONNOYE
ARYEH LEIB OF OZAROW
ARYEH LEIB OF SHPOLA
ARYEH LEIB SARAHS
BARUCH BEN JEHIEL OF MEDZIBEZH
BELZ
BERNARD, HAYYIM DAVID
BOBOV
DAVID OF TALNA
DOV BAER OF MEZHIRECH
DWORKIN, ZALMAN (Lubavitch)
DYNOW, ZEVI ELIMELECH
EGER, JUDAH LEIB OF LUBLIN
ELIEZER BEN JACOB HA-LEVI OF TARNOGROD
ELIMELECH OF LYZHANSK
EPSTEIN, ISAAC BEN MORDECAI
EPSTEIN, KALONYMUS KALMAN OF CRACOW
GORA KALWARIA
GRONER, DOVID YITZCHOK
HALBERSTAM
HANOKH OF ALEKSANDROW
HAYYIM BEN SOLOMON TYRER OF CZERNOWITZ
HAYYIM HAIKL BEN SAMUEL OF AMDUR
HOROWITZ, PINCHAS
HOROWITZ, SAMUEL SHMELKE OF NIKOLSBURG
ISRAEL BEN ELIEZER BA'AL SHEM TOV
ISRAEL BEN PEREZ OF POLOTSK
ISSACHAR DOV BAER BEN ARYEH LEIB OF ZLOCZOW
IZBICA-RADZYN
JACOB ISAAC HA-HOZEH MI-LUBLIN
JACOB JOSEPH BEN ZEVI HA-KOHEN KATZ OF
    POLONNOYE
JEHIEL MEIR (LIFSCHITS) OF GOSTYNIN
JEHIEL MICHAEL (Michel) OF ZLOCZOW
JOSEPH MOSES OF SALOSITZ
KALLO, YIZHAK ISAAC (of Taub)
KAMENKA, ZEVI HIRSCH OF
KARLIN
KAZIMIERZ
KOBRIN, MOSES BEN ISRAEL POLIER OF
KOIDANOV
KORETS, PHINEHAS BEN ABRAHAM ABBA SHAPIRO
    OF
KOTSK, MENAHEM MENDEL OF
KOZIENICE, ISRAEL BEN SHABBETAI HAPSTEIN
LACHOWICZE, MORDECAI BEN NOAH OF
LAWAT, ABRAHAM DAVID BEN JUDAH LEIB
LEINER, GERSHON HANOKH BEN JACOV
LELOV (Lelow)
LEVI ISAAC BEN MEIR OF BERDICHEV
LIPSCHUTZ, ARYEH LEIB
LUDOMIR, MAID OF
LUNIETZ, GEDALIAH BEN ISAAC OF
LYUBESHOV
MARCUS, AARON
MARGOLIOUTH, MEIR OF OSTRAHA (Ostrog)

II. RELIGION
A. JEWISH
6. Hasidism
BIOGRAPHIES (*continued*)

MEIR JEHIEL HA-LEVI OF OSTROWIEC
MEISELS, UZZIEL BEN ZEVI HIRSCH
MENAHEM MENDEL OF PEREMYSHLANY
MENAHEM MENDEL OF VITEBSK
MESHULLAM FEIVUSH HELLER OF ZBARAZH
MODZHITZ
MORDECAI OF NESKHIZ
MOSES HAYYIM EPHRAIM OF SUDYLKOW
MOSES LEIB OF SASOV
MOSES SHOHAM BEN DAN OF DOLINA
NAHMAN OF BRATSLAV
NAHMAN OF HORODENKA
PEREMYSHLYANY, MEIR BEN AARON LEIB OF
PRZEDBORZ
PRZYSUCHA, JACOB ISAAC BEN ASHER
RADOMSKO, SOLOMON HA-KOHEN RABINOWICH OF
RADOSHITSER, ISSACHAR BAER
RADZYMIN
RAPHAEL OF BERSHAD
ROPSHITSER, NAPHTALI ZEVI
ROTH, AARON
RUZHIN, ISRAEL
RYMANOWER, MENAHEM MENDEL
RYMANOWER, ZEVI HIRSH
SAFRIN, ISAAC JUDAH JEHIEL
SAVRAN (Bendery)
SCHNEERSOHN
SCHNEERSOHN, ISAAC
SCHNEERSOHN, MENACHEM MENDEL
SHABBETAI BEN ZEVI HIRSCH OF RASZKOW
SHAPIRA
SHAPIRA, KALONYMOUS KALMAN
SHAPIRA, YESHAYAHU
SHNEUR ZALMAN OF LYADY
SIMHAH BEN JOSHUA OF ZALOZHTSY
SIMHAH BUNEM OF PRZYSUCHA
SLONIM
SPINKA, JOSEPH MEIR WEISS OF
STERNBERG, SARAH FRANKEL
STERNHARZ, NATHAN
STRELISK, URI BEN PHINEHAS OF
STRETYN, JUDAH ZEVI HIRSCH (Brandwein) OF
TEITELBAUM
TWERSKI, JACOB ISRAEL
TWERSKY
VIZHNITZ
WAHRMANN, ABRAHAM DAVID BEN ASHER ANSCHEL
WALDEN, AARON BEN ISAIAH NATHAN
WARKA
ZADOK HA-KOHEN RABINOWITZ OF LUBLIN
ZE'EV WOLF OF ZHITOMIR
ZEVI HIRSCH FRIEDMAN OF LESKO
ZHIDACHOV
ZUSYA OF HANIPOLI
ZWEIFEL, ELIEZER

B. OTHER

1. CHRISTIANITY
MAIN SURVEYS
CHRISTIANITY
CHURCH, CATHOLIC
PROTESTANTS

GENERAL ENTRIES
ABRAHAM'S BOSOM
ALBIGENSES
ANTICHRIST
APOSTLE
ARMAGEDDON
ARTHURIAN LEGENDS
BAPTISM, FORCED
BIBLE SOCIETIES
BULLS, PAPAL
CARNIVAL
CATECHUMENS, HOUSE OF
CHRISTIAN SCIENCE CHURCH
CHURCH COUNCILS
CIVILTA CATTOLICA, LA
CRUSADES
DEMONS, DEMONOLOGY
DOMUS CONVERSORUM
ECCLESIA ET SYNAGOGA
EXCERPTA VALESIANA
FRANCISCANS
GNOSTICISM
HUSSITES
INQUISITION
INSTITUTUM JUDAICUM DELITZSCHIANUM
ISAIAH, ASCENSION OF
ISAIAH, MARTYRDOM OF
JESUITS
JEWISH-CHRISTIAN RELATIONS
LATERAN COUNCILS III, IV
MANICHAEISM
NAZARETH
NEW CHRISTIANS
NEW TESTAMENT
PASSSOVER
PILGRIMAGE
REFORMATION
SERMONS TO JEWS
SOLOMON, ODES OF
SOMREI SABAT
TITHES, CHURCH
VATICAN
WANDERING JEW

BIBLE
AARON
ABRAHAM
ADAM
CAIN
DAVID
EVE
GOLDEN CALF

ISAAC
JERUSALEM
JEZEBEL
JONAH, BOOK OF
JOSHUA
MELCHIZEDEK
MOSES
NOAH

Biographies

ALCUIN
ALEXANDER
ALEXANDER, MICHAEL SOLOMON
ALEXANDER OF HALES
ALEXEYEV, ALEXANDER
AMBROSE
AMULO
ANACLETUS II, PETER PIERLEONE
ANDREW OF SAINT-VICTOR
ANSELM OF CANTERBURY
AQUINAS, THOMAS
ARBUES, PEDRO DE
ARNALDO OF VILLANOVA
AUGUSTINE
AVITUS
BAR HEBRAEUS, JOHANAN
BARRUEL, AUGUSTIN
BARTH, KARL
BASHUYSEN, HEINRICH JACOB VAN
BASNAGE, JACQUES CHRISTIAN (Basnage de Beauval)
BATE, JULIUS
BAUER, BRUNO
BEA, AUGUSTIN
BENEDICT
BERNARD OF CLAIRVAUX
BERNARDINO DA FELTRE
BERNARDINO DA SIENA
BERTHOLD OF FREIBURG
BERTHOLD OF REGENSBURG (Ratisbon)
BONIFACE
BORROMEO, CARLO
BOSSUET, JACQUES BENIGNE
BOUDIN, JEAN-FRANCOIS
BRUNNER, SEBASTIAN
BUCER, MARTIN
BUDNY, SZYMON
BUGENHAGEN, JOHANN
BURCHARD OF WORMS
BURCHARDUS DE MONTE SION
CALIXTUS
CALVIN, JOHN
CAPISTRANO, JOHN (Giovanni) OF
CARBEN, VICTOR VON
CHIARINI, LUIGI
CHRISTIANI, PABLO
CHURCH FATHERS
CLEMENT
CLEMENT OF ALEXANDRIA
CRISPIN, GILBERT (Gislebertus)
CUSA, NICHOLAS OF

DAMIAN, PETER (Petrus Damiani)
DIONYSIUS VAN RYCKEL
DOMENICO GEROSOLIMITANO
DOMINICANS
DONIN, NICHOLAS
DUNS SCOTUS, JOHN
ECKHART, MEISTER
EGIDIO DA VITERBO
ELHANAN
ELIANO, GIOVANNI BATTISTA
ERASMUS OF ROTTERDAM
EUGENIUS
EUSEBIUS
FABRI, FELIX
FERRER, VICENTE
FIOGHI (Fiocchi), FABIANO
FLORUS OF LYONS
FULBERT OF CHARTRES
GELASIUS I
GRATIAN (Franciscus Gratianus)
GREGORY
HADRIAN I
HEBRAISTS, CHRISTIAN
HELENA AUGUSTA
HILDEBERT OF LAVARDIN
HILDUIN
HIRSCHENSOHN-LICHTENSTEIN, JEHIEL ZEVI
    HERMANN
HONORIUS
HOOGSTRAATEN, JACOB
INNOCENT
ISIDORE OF SEVILLE
IVO (Ives) OF CHARTRES
JACOB OF KEFAR SAKHNAYYA (Sama)
JEROME
JESUS
JOHN THE BAPTIST
JOHN CHRYSOSTOM
JOHN PAUL II
JOHN XXII
JOHN XXIII
JONA, GIOVANNI BATTISTA
JUDAS
JULIUS III
JUSTIN MARTYR
KOBIELSKI, FRANCISZEK ANTONI
KOLLONITSCH, LEOPOLD
LEÃO, GASPAR DE
LEO
LEVERTOFF, PAUL PHILIP
LUSTIGER, JEAN-MARIE ARON
LUTHER, MARTIN
MARGARITA, ANTON
MARTIN
MELITO OF SARDIS
MOROSINI, GIULIO
NEANDER, AUGUST
NICHOLAS
NIEBUHR, REINHOLD
NIGRI, PETRUS

II. RELIGION
B. OTHER
1. Christianity
BIOGRAPHIES (*continued*)

NOLA, ELIJAH BEN MENAHEM DA
OBADIAH, THE NORMAN PROSELYTE
ODO OF CAMBRAI
ODO OF CHATEAUROUX
ODO OF SULLY
OLESNICKI, ZBIGNIEW
ORIGEN
OROSIUS, PAULUS
PABLO DE SANTA MARIA (el Burguense)
PAUL IV
PAUL VI
PAUL OF TARSUS
PETER OF BLOIS
PETER OF CLUNY
PFEFFERKORN, JOHANNES (Joseph)
PIERLEONI
PIUS X
PIUS XI
PIUS XII
POPES
PORCHETUS SALVAGUS
QUARESMIUS, FRANCISCUS
RABINOVICH, JOSEPH
RAMON LULL
RATISBONNE BROTHERS
RAYMOND DE PENAFORTE
RUDOLPH
RUEDIGER (Hutzmann)
SIMON, RICHARD
SIXTUS IV
SULPICIUS SEVERUS
TILLICH, PAUL
WOLFF, JOSEPH

2. ISLAM (SEE MUSLIM LANDS)

3. KARAITES
MAIN SURVEYS
KARAITES

BIOGRAPHIES
AARON BEN ELIJAH
AARON BEN JOSEPH HA-ROFE
AARON BEN JUDAH KUSDINI
ABRAHAM BEN JOSIAH TROKI
ABRAHAM BEN JOSIAH YERUSHALMI
ABRAHAM BEN JUDAH BEN ABRAHAM
ABU AL-FARAJ HARUN IBN AL-FARAJ
AFENDOPOLO, CALEB BEN ELIJAH
AGA
ALFASI, DAVID BEN ABRAHAM
ALI IBN SULEIMAN
AL-TARAS, SIDI IBN

ANAN BEN DAVID
AZARIAH BEN ELIYAH
BABOVICH, SIMHAH BEN SOLOMON
BALI ABRAHAM BEN JACOB
BALI, MOSES BEN ABRAHAM
BASHYAZI (Bashyatchi)
BASĪR, JOSEPH BEN ABRAHAM HA-KOHEN HA-ROʾEH AL-BEGHI
BEIM, SOLOMON BEN ABRAHAM
BEN ZUTA ABU AL-SURRĪ
BENJAMIN BEN ELIJAH
BENJAMIN BEN ELIJAH DUWAN
DANIEL BEN MOSES AL-QŪMISĪ
DARI, MOSES BEN ABRAHAM
DAVID BEN BOAZ
DAVID BEN HUSSEIN, ABU SULEIMAN
DAVID BEN JOSHUA
DAVID BEN SOLOMON
ELIJAH BEN AARON BEN MOSES
ELIJAH BEN ABRAHAM
ELIJAH BEN BARUCH THE ELDER
EZRA BEN NISAN
FARAJ, MURAD
FIRKOVICH, ABRAHAM (Even Reshef)
FIRUZ
GIBBOR, JUDAH BEN ELIJAH
HADASSI, JUDAH (ha-Avel) BEN ELIJAH
HASAN (Hussein) BEN MASHIʾAH
IBN AL-HĪTĪ, DAVID BEN SEʾADEL
IBN FADANJ (Fadanq)
IBN SÁQAWAYH (Sakuyah; Saquyah)
ISAAC BEN SOLOMON
ISAIAH BEN UZZIAH HA-KOHEN
ISHMAEL OF ʿUKBARA
ISRAEL (ben Samuel?) HA-DAYYAN HA-MAʾARAVI
JACOB BEN REUBEN
JACOB BEN SIMEON
JAPHETH AL-BARQAMANI
JAPHETH BEN DAVID IBN SAGHIR
JAPHETH BEN ELI HA-LEVI
JESHUA BEN JUDAH
JOSEPH BEN NOAH
JOSEPH BEN SAMUEL BEN ISAAC RODI
JOSIAH BEN SAUL BEN ANAN
JUDAH BEN ELI (Elan)
KALAI, SAMUEL BEN JOSEPH
KALFA, ISAAC BEN JOSEPH
KAZAZ, ELIJAH
KIRKISANI, JACOB AL-
KUKIZOW
LABANOS
LEONOVICH
LEVI BEN JAPHETH
LUZKI, ABRAHAM BEN JOSEPH SOLOMON
LUZKI, JOSEPH SOLOMON BEN MOSES
LUZKI, SIMHAH ISAAC BEN MOSES
MALINOVSKI, JOSEPH BEN MORDECAI
MARZOUK, MOSHE
MENAHEM BEN MICHAEL BEN JOSEPH
MORDECAI BEN NISAN

MOSES BEN ELIJAH HA-LEVI
MOSES BEN ELIJAH PASHA
MOSES BEN SAMUEL OF DAMASCUS
NAHAWENDI, BENJAMIN BEN MOSES AL-
NISSI (Nissim) BEN NOAH
PIGIT, SAMUEL BEN SHEMARIA
POKI, JUDAH BEN ELIEZER CHELEBI
SAHL BEN MAZLI'AH HA-KOHEN ABU AL-SURRI
SAHL IBN FADL
SALMON BEN JEROHAM
SAMUEL BEN DAVID
SAMUEL BEN MOSES AL-MAGHRIBI
SAUL BEN ANAN
SHAPSHAL (Szapszal) SERAYAH
SOLOMON BEN AARON (of Troki)
SULTANSKY, MORDECAI BEN JOSEPH
TAWRIZI, JUDAH MEIR BEN ABRAHAM
TOBIAS BEN MOSES HA-AVEL (Or ha-Matik)
TROKI, ISAAC BEN ABRAHAM
ZEPHANIAH BEN MORDECAI
ZERAH BEN NATHAN OF TROKI

4. MARRANOS
GENERAL ENTRIES
CHUETAS
MARRANO
MARRANO DIASPORA
NEW CHRISTIANS

BIOGRAPHIES
ABENAES, SOLOMON
ABENATAR MELO, DAVID
ABENDANA
ABENDANA, ISAAC
ABOAB, IMMANUEL
ABOAB, ISAAC DE MATTATHIAS
ACOSTA, CHRISTOBAL
AGUILAR, DIEGO D'
ALEMAN, MATEO
ALVARES
AMES
ANTUNES
ARIAS, JOSEPH SEMAH
ASSUMPÇÃO, DIOGO DA
AZEVEDO
BARGAS, ABRAHAM DE
BARRASSA, JACOB
BARROS BASTO, ARTURO CARLOS DE
BELMONTE
BERNAL
BRUDO, MANUEL
BUENO
CACERES, FRANCISCO DE
CARDOSO
CARDOZO, ABRAHAM MIGUEL
CARDOZO, ISAAC
CASTRO
CASTRO, DE
CASTRO, PEDRO DE

CASTRO SARMENTO, JACOB (Henrique) DE
CASTRO TARTAS, ISAAC DE
CORONEL CHACON, SIR AUGUSTIN
COUTINHO
CURIEL
CHIRINO
DIAS, LUIS
ENRIQUEZ BASURTO, DIEGO
FARIA, FRANCISCO DE
FONSECA, DANIEL DE
GOMEZ DE SOSSA, ISAAC
GRANADA, GABRIEL DE
HOMEM, ANTONIO
JESURUN
JESURUN, REUEL
JUAN DE ESPANA
JUAN DE VALLADOLID
LAGUNA, DANIEL ISRAEL LOPEZ
LAMEGO
LOBATO
LOPEZ, RODERIGO
LOPEZ ROSA
MACHADO
MALDONADO DE SILVA, FRANCISCO
MENDES, DIOGO
MESQUITA
MONTEZINOS, ANTONIO DE
NASI, GRACIA
NASI, JOSEPH
NUÑEZ
NUÑEZ, HECTOR
OLIVER Y FULLANA, NICOLAS DE
ORTA, GARCIA DE
PAZ, DUARTE DE
PENSO DE LA VEGA, JOSEPH
PINA, JACOB (Manuel) DE
PINEDA, JUAN DE
PINTO DELGADO, JOAO (Mosseh)
PRADO, JUAN (Daniel) DE
PYRRHUS, DIDACUS
ROBLES, ANTONIO RODRIGUES
ROCAMORA, ISAAC DE
RODRIGUES, DIONISIUS (Diniz)
ROJAS, FERNANDO DE
SANCHEZ, ANTONIO NUNEZ RIBEIRO
SENIOR, SOLOMON
SILVA, RODRIGO MENDEZ DA
SILVA, SAMUEL DA
SILVEYRA, MIGUEL DE
SOLIS
TEIXEIRA, PEDRO
TEIXEIRA DE SAMPAIO, ABRAHAM SENIOR (Diego)
TEIXEIRA PINTO, BENTO
TORRE, ALFONSO DE LA
TREVINO DE SOBREMONTE, TOMAS
USQUE, ABRAHAM
USQUE, SAMUEL
USQUE, SOLOMON
VITORIA, FRANCISCO DE
ZACUTUS LUSITANUS

II. RELIGION
B. OTHER (*continued*)

5. SAMARITANS
MAIN SURVEYS
SAMARITANS

GENERAL ENTRIES
AL-ASĀTĪR
DUSTAN
GERIZIM, MOUNT

BIOGRAPHIES
ABU AL-FAT
ABU AL-HASAN OF TYRE
AMRAM DARAH
BABA RABBAH

III. JEWISH LANGUAGES & LITERATURE

A. JEWISH LANGUAGES
MAIN SURVEYS
ALPHABET, HEBREW
HEBREW GRAMMAR
HEBREW LANGUAGE
LINGUISTIC LITERATURE, HEBREW
MASORAH
PRONUNCIATIONS OF HEBREW
PROSODY, HEBREW
SEMITIC LANGUAGES
YIDDISH LANGUAGE

GENERAL ENTRIES
ABBA
ABBREVIATIONS
ABRACADABRA
ABRECH
ABU
ACADEMY OF THE HEBREW LANGUAGE
ACROSTICS
AKKADIAN LANGUAGE
AKKUM
ALEF
ARAMAIC
ASH
AYIN
BAAL HA-BAYIT
BET
BRIT IVRIT OLAMIT
DALET
FRANCOS (Franji)
GIMMEL
GREETINGS AND CONGRATULATIONS
HAKETIA
HAPAX LEGOMENA
HE
HET
JEWISH LANGUAGES
JUDEO-ARABIC

JUDEO-ARABIC LITERATURE
JUDEO-FRENCH
JUDEO-GREEK
JUDEO-ITALIAN
JUDEO-PERSIAN
JUDEO-PROVENCAL
JUDEO-TAT
KAF
KOF
LADINO
LAMED
MASORETIC ACCENTS
MEDINAH
MEM
MIZRAYIM
NAMES
NEO-ARAMAIC
NOTARIKON
NUN
OKHLAH VE-OKHLAH
PE
RESH
SADE
SAMEKH
SHALOM ALEIKHEM
SHIN
TAV
TET
UGARITIC
VAV
YOD
ZAYIN

SCHOLARS
ABRAHAM HA-BAVLI
ALCALAY, REUVEN
ALMOLI, SOLOMON BEN JACOB
AUERBACH, ISAAC EISIG BEN ISAIAH
AVE-LALLEMANT, FRIEDRICH CHRISTIAN BENEDICT
AVINERI, YITZHAK
AVRUNIN, ABRAHAM
BAER, SELIGMAN ISAAC
BARANOWICZ, DAVID ELIEZER
BAR-ASHER, MOSHE
BARDACH, ISRAEL (Isaac hen ftayyim Moses)
BARTH, JACOB
BEN HAYYIM, ZEEV
BEN ZEEV, JUDAH LEIB
BEN-ASHER, AARON BEN MOSES
BEN-ASHER, MOSES
BEN-NAPHTALI, MOSES BEN DAVID
BEN-YEHUDA, ELIEZER
BLAU, JOSHUA
BUCHNER, ZE'EV WOLF BEN DAVID HA-KOHEN
BURSTEIN, ISRAEL
CAMPEN (Campensis), Johannes Van
CASTELL, EDMUND
DOTAN, ARON
EVEN-SHOSHAN, AVRAHAM
GOSHEN-GOTTSTEIN, MOSHE

HARKAVY, ALEXANDER
HAYYUJ, JUDAH (Jahah) BEN DAVID
IBN BARUN, ABU IBRAHIM ISAAC BEN JOSEPH IBN
    BENVENISTE
IBN JANAH, JONAH
IBN QURAYSH, JUDAH
IBN YASHUSH, ISAAC ABU IBRAHIM
JACOB BEN HAYYIM BEN ISAAC IBN ADONIJAH
JACOB KOPPEL BEN AARON SASSLOWER
JEKUTHIEL BEN JUDAH HA-KOHEN
JOSEPH BEN DAVID HA-YEVANI
KADDARI, MENAHEM ZEVI
KUTSCHER, EDWARD YECHEZKEL
LARA, DAVID BEN ISAAC COHEN DE
LERNER, HAYYIM ZEVI BEN TODROS
LEVITA, ELIJAH (Babur)
LIFSHITS, SHIYE-MORDKHE
MANI, EZRA
MENAHEM BEN JACOB IBN SARUQ
MORAG, SHLOMO
MORDELL, PHINEHAS
MOSES BEN HA-NESIAH
PLANTAVIT DE LA PAUSE, JEAN
POLOTSKY, HANS JACOB
SAMSON HA-NAKDAN
SARFATTI, GAD
SCHAECHTER, MORDKHE
SCHNEIDER, MORDECAI BEZALEL
SCHULMANN, ELIEZER
STEINBERG, JOSHUA
WARSHAWSKY, ISAAC
WEINREICH, URIEL
WIZEN, MOSHE AHARON
YALON, HANOCH
YEIVIN, ISRAEL
ZAMENHOF, LUDWIK LAZAR
ZAND, MICHAEL

B. JEWISH LITERATURE
MAIN SURVEYS
LITERATURE, JEWISH

GENERAL ENTRIES
ANIMAL TALES
BIBLIOGRAPHY
BIBLIOPHILES
BIBLIOTHEQUE NATIONALE
BIOGRAPHIES AND AUTOBIOGRAPHIES
BOOKS
CHILDREN'S LITERATURE
DIBBUK
ENCYCLOPEDIAS
ETHICAL LITERATURE
FABLE
FESTSCHRIFTEN
FOLKLORE
GOLEM
KALILA AND DIMNA
MANUSCRIPTS, HEBREW

PARABLE
PRINTING, HEBREW
SCIENCE FICTION AND FANTASY, JEWISH
WANDERING JEW

BIBLE IN JEWISH LITERATURE
ABRAHAM
ABSALOM
ADAM
AKEDAH
ATHALIAH
BABEL, TOWER OF
BALAAM
BELSHAZZAR
BIBLE – IN THE ARTS
CAIN
CHERUB
DANIEL
DAVID
DEBORAH
ELIJAH
ESTHER
EZEKIEL
GIDEON
HEZEKIAH
ISAAC
ISAIAH
JACOB
JEPHTHAH
JEREMIAH
JERUSALEM
JOB, BOOK OF
JONAH, BOOK OF
JOSEPH
JOSHUA
LAMENTATIONS, BOOK OF
MOSES
NEBUCHADNEZZAR (Nebuchadrezzer)
NOAH
PSALMS, BOOK OF
RACHEL
RUTH, BOOK OF
SAMSON
SAMUEL
SAUL
SODOM AND GOMORRAH
SOLOMON
SONG OF SONGS
TEMPLE

C. HEBREW LITERATURE

1. MEDIEVAL
    MAIN SURVEYS
    POETRY

    GENERAL ENTRIES
    ABRAHAM
    ALEXANDER THE GREAT

III. JEWISH LANGUAGES & LITERATURE
C. HEBREW LITERATURE
1. Medieval
GENERAL ENTRIES (*continued*)

ALLEGORY
APOCRYPHA AND PSEUDEPIGRAPHA
AZ ROV NISSIM
BEN HA-MELEKH VE-HA-NAZIR
BEN SIRA, ALPHABET OF
BIOGRAPHIES AND AUTOBIOGRAPHIES
BODLEIAN LIBRARY
COLOPHON
DANIEL, VISION OF
DERASHOT HA-RAN
ELIJAH
ELIJAH, APOCALYPSE OF
EXEMPLA OF THE RABBIS
EXEMPLUM
FICTION, HEBREW
FOUR CAPTIVES, THE
HAGIOGRAPHY
INCUNABULA
INSTITUTE FOR THE RESEARCH OF MEDIEVAL
    HEBREW POETRY
LETTERS AND LETTER-WRITERS
MAGIC
MAQAMA
MEKIZE NIRDAMIM
MOSES, CHRONICLES OF
MUSAR HASKEL
NAJARA, ISRAEL BEN MOSES
NEVU'AT HA-YELED
PARABLE
PARODY, HEBREW
PEREK SHIRAH
PIYYUT
PURIM-SHPIL
TRANSLATION AND TRANSLATORS
UZZA AND AZA'EL
WILLS, ETHICAL

BIOGRAPHIES
AARON HAKIMAN
ABBASI, JACOB BEN MOSES IBN
ABI ZIMRA, ISAAC MANDIL BEN ABRAHAM
ABRAHAM BEN HALFON
ABRAHAM BEN HILLEL (Ben Nissim) OF FOSTAT
ABRAHAM BEN SHABBETAI HA-KOHEN (Zante)
ABRAHAM BEN SOLOMON OF TORRUTIEL
ABRAHAM OF SARTEANO
ABULAFIA, EZEKIEL DAVID BEN MORDECAI
ABULAFIA, TODROS BEN JUDAH HA-LEVI
ABUN (Abuna, Bun)
ACAN, MOSES DE TARREGA
AHIMAAZ BEN PALTIEL
AL-AVANI, ISAAC
ALHADIB, ISAAC BEN SOLOMON BEN ZADDIK
AL-HARIZI, JUDAH BEN SOLOMON
ALI (ben David)

ALTARAS, JOSEPH
ALVAN BEN ABRAHAM
ALVAREZ GATO, JUAN
AMITTAI
AMITTAI BEN SHEPHATIAH
ARCHIVOLTI, SAMUEL
ARYEH JUDAH HARRARI (ha-Yarbi)
AVIGDOR, ABRAHAM
BEDERSI, ABRAHAM BEN ISAAC
BENJAMIN BEN AZRIEL
BENJAMIN BEN HIYYA (Jehiel)
BENJAMIN BEN ZERAH
BERECHIAH BEN NATRONAI HA-NAKDAN
BONAFED, SOLOMON BEN REUBEN
CASPI, SAUL
DAVID BEN AARON IBN HASSIN (Hussein)
DAVID BEN MESHULLAM OF SPEYER
DE PIERA, MESHULLAM BEN SOLOMON
DE PIERA, SOLOMON BEN MESHULLAM
DUNASH BEN LABRAT
ELEAZAR BEN HALFON HA-KOHEN
ELEAZAR BEN JACOB HA-BAVLI
ELIJAH BEN ELIEZER PHILOSOPH HA-
    YERUSHALMI
ELIJAH BEN SHEMAIAH
ELIJAH CHELEBI HA-KOHEN OF ANATOLIA
EZOBI, JEHOSEPH BEN HANAN BEN NATHAN
FARISSOL, JACOB BEN HAYYIM (Comprat; Vidal)
FRANCES, IMMANUEL BEN DAVID
FRANCES, JACOB BEN DAVID
GABIROL, SOLOMON BEN JUDAH, IBN
GALIPAPA, MAIMON
GALLEGO, JOSEPH SHALOM
GERONDI, ISAAC BEN JUDAH
GERONDI, SOLOMON BEN ISAAC
GIKATILLA, ISAAC IBN
GIKATILLA, MOSES BEN SAMUEL HA-KOHEN
HARIZI, ABU ISAAC ABRAHAM
HISDAI IBN HISDAI, ABU AL-FADL
IBN AL-RABIB, ABRAHAM
IBN ALTABBAN, LEVI BEN JACOB
IBN AL-TAQANA, MOSES
IBN BARZEL, JOSEPH
IBN BILIA, DAVID BEN YOM-TOV
IBN EZRA, ISAAC
IBN EZRA, MOSES BEN JACOB
IBN GHAYYAT
IBN HABIB, MOSES BEN SHEM TOV
IBN HASDAI, ABRAHAM BEN SAMUEL HA-LEVI
IBN KAPRON, ISAAC
IBN KHALFUN, ISAAC
IBN MAR SAUL, ISAAC BEN LEVI
IBN PAQUDA, DAVID BEN ELEAZAR
IBN SAHL, JOSEPH BEN JACOB
IBN SASSON, SAMUEL BEN JOSEPH
IBN SHUWAYK, ISAAC BEN ISRAEL
IBN ZABARA, JOSEPH BEN MEIR
IBN ZABARRA, JUDAH
IBN ZAKBEL, SOLOMON
IMMANUEL (ben Solomon) OF ROME

ISAAC

ISAAC BEN ABRAHAM HA-GORNI

ISAAC BEN HAYYIM BEN ABRAHAM

ISAAC BEN JUDAH

ISAAC BEN JUDAH HA-SENIRI

ISSACHAR, SIMHAH

JACOB BEN ELEAZAR

JACOB BEN JUDAH

JACOB BEN NAPHTALI

JACOB HA-KATAN

JOAB THE GREEK (Ha-Yevani)

JOHANAN BEN JOSHUA HA-KOHEN

JOSEPH BAR NISSAN

JOSEPH BEN ASHER OF CHARTRES

JOSEPH BEN ISRAEL

JOSEPH BEN JACOB

JOSEPH BEN KALONYMUS HA-NAKDAN I

JOSEPH BEN SHESHET IBN LATIMI

JOSEPH BEN SOLOMON OF CARCASSONNE

JOSEPH BEN TANHUM YERUSHALMI

JOSEPH BEN UZZIEL

JOSHUA

JOSHUA BEN ELIJAH HA-LEVI

JOSIPHIAH THE PROSELYTE

JUDAH BEN ISAAC IBN SHABBETAI

JUDAH BEN MENAHEM OF ROME

JUDAH HALEVI

JUDAH HA-LEVI BEI-RABBI HILLEL

KALAI, JOSEPH BEN JACOB

KALLIR, ELEAZAR

KALONYMUS BEN KALONYMUS

LEONTE (Judah) BEN MOSES

MATTATHIAS

MEIR BEN ELIJAH OF NORWICH

MEIR BEN SAMUEL OF SHCHEBRESHIN

MERECINA OF GERONA

MEVORAKH HA-BAVLI

MOSES BEN JOAB

MOSES NATHAN

OHEV BEN MEIR HA-NASI

PHINEHAS BEN JACOB HA-KOHEN (Kafra)

PHINEHAS BEN JOSEPH HA -LEVI

ROSSENA, DANIEL BEN SAMUEL OF

SAADIAH

SAHULA, ISAAC BEN SOLOMON ABI

SAMUEL HA-SHELISHI BEN HOSHANA

SANTOB DE CARRION

SHABAZI, SHALEM

SHE'ERIT HA-HAZZAN

SILANO

SIMEON BEN MEGAS HA-KOHEN

SOLOMON BEN JUDAH HA-BAVLI

SOLOMON SULIMAN BEN AMAR

SOMMO, JUDAH LEONE BEN ISAAC

YANNAI

YEHUDI BEN SHESHET

YOM TOV OF JOIGNY

YOSE BEN YOSE

ZARKO (Zarka), JOSEPH BEN JUDAH

ZEBIDAH

2. MODERN

MAIN SURVEYS

HEBREW LITERATURE, MODERN

GENERAL ENTRIES

ALLEGORY

BIKKUREI HA-ITTIM

DAVID

HA-ASIF

HA-TEKUFAH

JERUSALEM

KIRJATH SEPHER

LETTERS AND LETTER-WRITERS

MOZNAYIM

PARODY, HEBREW

BIOGRAPHIES

ADELMAN, URI

AESCOLY, AARON ZEEV

AGMON, NATHAN

AGNON, SHMUEL YOSEF

AHAD HA-AM

AKAVYA, AVRAHAM ARYEH LEIB

ALFES, BENZION

ALMANZI, JOSEPH

ALMOG, RUTH

ALONI, NISSIM

ALTERMAN, NATHAN

AMICHAI, YEHUDA

AMIR, AHARON

AMIR, ANDA

AMIR, ELI

ANOKHI, ZALMAN YIZHAK

APPELFELD, AHARON

ARICHA, YOSEF

ASHER, ISAIAH BEN MOSES HA-LEVI

ASHMAN, AHARON

AVIDAN, DAVID

AVIGUR-ROTEM, GABRIELA

AVINOAM, REUVEN

AVI-SHAUL, MORDEKHAI

BACHER, SIMON

BADER, GERSHOM (Gustav)

BALLAS, SHIMON

BARASH, ASHER

BARON, DEVORAH

BARTOV, HANOCH

BAR-YOSEF, YEHOSHUA

BASSAN, ABRAHAM HEZEKIAH BEN JACOB

BAT-MIRIAM, YOKHEVED

BAVLI, HILLEL

BE'ER, HAIM

BEHAK, JUDAH

BEILIN, ASHER

BEILINSON, MOSES ELIEZER

BEILINSON, MOSHE

BEJERANO, MAYA

BEN YEHUDA, NETIVA

BEN YIZHAK, AVRAHAM

BEN-AMITAI, LEVI

III. JEWISH LANGUAGES & LITERATURE
C. HEBREW LITERATURE
2. Modern
Biographies (continued)

BEN-AMOTZ, DAHN

BENJACOB, ISAAC

BEN-NER, YITZHAK

BEN-YEHEZKIEL, MORDEKHAI

BEN-YEHUDA, HEMDAH

BEN-ZION, S.

BERDYCZEWSKI, MICHA JOSEF

BERGSTEIN, FANIA

BERKOWITZ, YITZHAK DOV

BERNSTEIN, ORI

BERSHADSKY, ISAIAH

BERTINI, K. AHARON

BIALIK, HAYYIM NAHMAN

BICK, JACOB SAMUEL

BIRKENTHAL, DOV BER

BIRSTEIN, YOSSEL

BLANK, SAMUEL LEIB

BLOCH, SAMSON HA-LEVI (Simson)

BOSAK, MEIR

BRAININ, REUBEN

BRANDSTAEDTER, MORDECAI DAVID

BRAUDES, REUBEN ASHER

BRAUNSTEIN, MENAHEM MENDEL

BRENNER, JOSEPH HAYYIM

BRESSELAU, MEYER ISRAEL

BRILL, JOSEPH

BROIDES, ABRAHAM

BROIDO, EPHRAIM

BURLA, YEHUDA

CAHAN, YAAKOV

CARMI, ISAIAH HAI BEN JOSEPH

CARMI, T.

CASTEL-BLOOM, ORLY

CHOMSKY, DOV

CHURGIN, YAAKOV YEHOSHUA

COHEN, ISRAEL

COHEN, SHALOM BEN JACOB

DAGON, BARUKH (Asher David)

DAYAN, YAEL

DOLITZKI, MENAHEM MENDEL

DOR, MOSHE

DRUYANOW, ALTER (Asher, Avraham Abba)

DYKMAN, SHLOMO

EHRENKRANZ, BENJAMIN (Wolf) ZEEB

EICHENBAUM (Gelber), JACOB

ELISHEVA

ELMALEH, ABRAHAM

EPSTEIN, ABRAHAM

EPSTEIN, ZALMAN

ERTER, ISAAC

EVER HADANI

EYTAN, RACHEL

FAHN, REUBEN

FEDER, TOBIAS

FEIERBERG, MORDECAI ZE'EV

FEINSTEIN, MOSES

FEITELSON, MENAHEM MENDEL

FERNHOF, ISAAC

FEYGENBERG, RAKHEL

FICHMAN, JACOB

FISCHMANN, NAHMAN ISAAC

FRAENKEL, FAIWEL

FRANCO-MENDES, DAVID

FRANKEL, NAOMI

FREHA BAT AVRAHAM OF MOROCCO

FRIEDBERG, ABRAHAM SHALOM

FRIEDLAND, ABRAHAM HYMAN (Hayyim)

FRIEDMANN, DAVID ARYEH

FRISCHMANN, DAVID

GALAI, BINYAMIN

GELDMAN, MORDECHAI

GILBOA, AMIR

GILEAD, ZERUBAVEL

GINZBURG, SIMON

GNESSIN, URI NISSAN

GOLDBERG, LEA

GOLDENBERG, SAMUEL LEIB

GOLDIN, EZRA

GORDON, JUDAH LEIB

GORDON, SAMUEL LEIB

GOREN, NATAN

GOTTLIEB, JACOB

GOTTLOBER, ABRAHAM BAER

GOURI, HAIM

GREENBERG, URI ZEVI

GROSSMAN, DAVID

GUENZBURG, MORDECAI AARON

GUR, BATYA

GURFEIN, RIVKA

HABAS, BRACHA

HACOHEN, MORDECAI BEN HILLEL

HA-EFRATI, JOSEPH

HAEZRAHI, YEHUDA

HALKIN, SIMON

HAMEIRI, AVIGDOR

HAMENAHEM, EZRA

HAMON, AARON BEN ISAAC

HAREVEN, SHULAMIT

HAZAZ, HAYYIM

HENDEL, YEHUDIT

HILLELS, SHELOMO

HOFFMANN, YOEL

HOGA, STANISLAV

HOROWITZ, YAAKOV

HOURVITZ, YA'IR

HURWITZ, SAUL ISRAEL

IMBER, NAPHTALI HERZ

JAFFE, ABRAHAM B.

KABAK, AARON ABRAHAM

KADARI, SHRAGA

KAHANA-CARMON, AMALIA

KAMINER, ISAAC

KAMSON, YAAKOV (Jacob) DAVID

KANIUK, YORAM

KAPLAN, PESAH

KARIV, AVRAHAM YIZHAK

KARNI, YEHUDA

KARU, BARUCH

KATZ (Benshalom), BENZION

KATZENELSON, BARUCH

KATZENELSON, ITZHAK

KATZIR, JEHUDIT

KENAANI, DAVID

KENAN, AMOS

KENAZ, YEHOSHUA

KERET, ETGAR

KESHET, YESHURUN

KIMHI, DOV

KINDERFREUND, ARYEH LEIB

KIPNIS, LEVIN

KISHON, EPHRAIM

KLAUSNER, JOSEPH GEDALIAH

KOHEN-ZEDEK, JOSEPH

KOVNER, ABBA

KOVNER, ABRAHAM URI

KURZWEIL, BARUCH

K. ZETNIK

LACHOWER, YERUHAM FISHEL

LAMDAN, YIZHAK

LANDAU, JUDAH LOEB (Leo)

LAOR, YITZHAK

LAPID, SHULAMIT

LEBENSOHN, ABRAHAM DOV

LEBENSOHN, MICAH JOSEPH

LEIBL, DANIEL

LENSKI, HAYYIM

LETTERIS, MEIR (Max)

LEVI, JOSHUA JOSEPH BEN DAVID

LEVIN, ALTER ISAAC

LEVIN, HANOCH

LEVIN, JUDAH LEIB

LEVNER, ISRAEL BENJAMIN

LEVONTIN, JEHIEL JOSEPH

LEWINSKY, ELHANAN LEIB

LICHTENBAUM, JOSEPH

LIEBRECHT, SAVYON

LIPSON, MORDEKHAI

LISITZKY, EPHRAIM E.

LUBOSHITZKI, AARON

LUIDOR, JOSEPH

MANDELKERN, SOLOMON

MANNE, MORDECAI ZEVI

MAPU, ABRAHAM

MARKSON, AARON DAVID

MATALON, RONIT

MEGGED, AHARON

MEITUS, ELIAHU

MELTZER, SHIMSHON

MENDELSOHN, FRANKFURT MOSES

MEZAH (SEGAL) JOSHUA HA-LEVI

MICHAEL, SAMI

MICHALI, BINYAMIN YIZHAK

MIRON, DAN

MIRSKY, AARON

MISHOL, AGI

MOHR, MEIR

MORPURGO, RACHEL

MOSSINSOHN, YIGAL

NATHANSON, BERNHARD (Dov Baer)

OFEK, URIEL

OMER, HILLEL

OREN, RAM

OREN, YIZHAK

ORLAND, YAAKOV

ORLEV, URI

ORPAZ AVERBUCH, YIZHAK

OVSAY, JOSHUA

OZ, AMOS

PAGIS, DAN

PAPERNA, ABRAHAM JACOB

PAPPENHEIM, SOLOMON

PATAI, JOZSEF

PENN, ALEXANDER

PENUELI, SHEMUEL YESHAYAHU

PERL, JOSEPH

PERSKI, JOEL DOV BAER

PINCAS, ISRAEL

POMERANTZ, BERL

POZNANSKY, MENAHEM

PREIL, GABRIEL JOSHUA

RAAB, ESTHER

RABINOVITZ, ALEXANDER SISKIND

RABINOWITZ, ELIAHU WOLF

RABINOWITZ, YAAKOV

RABINOWITZ, ZINA

RAHEL

RALL, YISRAEL

RATOSH, YONATHAN

RAVIKOVITCH, DALIA

REGELSON, ABRAHAM

REICH, ASHER

REUVENI, AHARON

RIBALOW, MENACHEM

RIMON, JACOB

RIMON, JOSEPH ZEVI

RODIN, ELISHA

ROKEAH, DAVID

ROMANELLI, SAMUEL AARON

ROSEN, ABRAHAM

ROSENFELD, AHARON

ROSENZWEIG, GERSON

RUEBNER, TUVIA

SACKLER, HARRY

SADAN, DOV

SADEH, PINHAS

SALKINSON, ISAAC EDWARD (Eliezer)

SCHAPIRA, NOAH

SCHATZ, ZEVI

SCHORR, NAPHTALI MENDEL

SCHUR, ZEV WOLF (William)

SCHWARTZ, ABRAHAM SAMUEL

SENED, ALEXANDER

SERI, DAN BENAYA

SHAANAN, AVRAHAM

SHABTAI, AHARON

KULTUR-LIGE
MAYSE-BUKH
MELOKHIM BUKH
PARIZ UN VIENE
SHMUEL BUKH
SOVETISH HEYMLAND
SWEATSHOP POETRY
THEATER
TOPLPUNKT
TSUKUNFT
VIDVILT
YIDDISH THEATER, FOLKSBIENE
YIDISHE SHTIME
YIDISHER KEMFER
YIDISHES TAGEBLAT
YIVO INSTITUTE FOR JEWISH RESEARCH
YUNGE, DI
YUNGMAN, MOSHE
YUNG VILNE
ZE'ENAH U-RE'ENAH

Biographies

AARON BEN SAMUEL
ABRAMOVITSH, SHOLEM YANKEV (Mendele Mokher Seforim)
ABTSHUK, AVRAHAM
ADLER, JACOB
ALPERSOHN, MARCOS
ALTMAN, MOISHE
ALTSCHUL, MOSES BEN HANOKH
ANSHEL OF CRACOW
AN-SKI, S.
ASCH, SHOLEM
ASHENDORF, ISRAEL
AUERBACH, EPHRAIM
AUERBAKH, ROKHL
AUSLAENDER, NAHUM
AXELROD, SELIK
AXENFELD, ISRAEL
AYALTI, HANAN J.
BAAL-MAKHSHOVES
BASMAN BEN-HAYIM, RIVKE
BASS, HYMAN B.
BASSIN, MOSES
BEIDER, CHAIM
BERGELSON, DAVID
BERGER, LILY
BERGNER, HERZ
BERINSKI, LEV
BERKOWITZ, YITZHAK DOV
BERLINER, ISAAC
BERNSTEIN, IGNATZ
BIALOSTOTZKY, BENJAMIN JACOB
BICKEL, SOLOMON
BICKELS-SPITZER, ZVI
BILETZKI, ISRAEL HAYYIM
BIMKO, FISHEL
BIRNBAUM, SOLOMON ASHER
BIRSTEIN, YOSSEL
BLUM, ELIEZER

BOMZE, NAHUM
BORAISHA, MENAHEM
BOTOSHANSKY, JACOB
BOVSHOVER, JOSEPH
BRAININ, REUBEN
BRESCH (Bres), JUDAH LOEB (Leo) BEN MOSES NAPHTALI
BRODER, BERL
BRODERZON, MOYSHE
BRYKS, RACHMIL
BUBLICK, GEDALIAH
BUCHWALD, NATHANIEL
BURSZTYN, MICHAL
CAHAN, JUDAH LOEB (Lewis)
CALOF, RACHEL
CHAGALL, BELLA ROSENFELD
CHARNEY, DANIEL
CHMELNITZKI, MELECH
CORALNIK, ABRAHAM
DANIEL, M.
DEMBLIN, BENJAMIN
DER NISTER
DIK, ISAAC MEIR
DILLON, ABRAHAM MOSES
DINESON, JACOB
DLUZHNOWSKY, MOSHE
DOBRUSHIN, YEKHEZKEL
DOLITZKI, MENAHEM MENDEL
DROPKIN, CELIA
DYMOV, OSSIP
EDELSTADT, DAVID
EHRENKRANZ, BENJAMIN (Wolf) ZEEB
EINHORN, DAVID
ELBERG, YEHUDA
EMIOT, ISRAEL
ENTIN, JOEL
EPSTEIN, MELECH
ERIK, MAX
ESSELIN, ALTER
ESTRAIKH, GENNADY
ETTINGER, SOLOMON
FALKOWITSCH, JOEL BAERISCH
FEFER, ITZIK
FEIGENBAUM, BENJAMIN
FEINBERG, LEON
FELZENBAUM, MICHAEL
FEYGENBERG, RAKHEL
FININBERG, EZRA
FOX, CHAIM-LEIB
FRAM, DAVID
FRIEDMAN, JACOB
FUCHS, ABRAHAM MOSHE
FUKS, LAJB
FURMAN, YISROEL
GEBIRTIG, MORDECAI
GILBERT, SHLOMO
GINZBURG, ISER
GISER, MOSHE DAVID
GLANTZ, JACOBO
GLANZ-LEYELES, AARON

III. JEWISH LANGUAGES & LITERATURE
D. YIDDISH LITERATURE
BIOGRAPHIES (*continued*)

GLASMAN, BARUCH
GLATSTEIN, JACOB
GLICK, HIRSH
GLUECKEL OF HAMELN
GODINER, SAMUEL NISSAN
GOLDBERG, ABRAHAM
GOLDBERG, BEN ZION
GOLDFADEN, ABRAHAM
GOLDHAR, PINCHAS
GOLDIN, EZRA
GOLOMB, ABRAHAM
GORDIN, ABBA
GORDIN, JACOB
GORDON, MIKHL
GORDON, SHMUEL
GORELIK, SHEMARYA
GORIN, BERNARD
GORSHMAN, SHIRA
GOTTESFELD, CHONE
GOTTLIEB, JACOB
GOTTLOBER, ABRAHAM BAER
GRADE, CHAIM
GREENBERG, ELIEZER
GREENBLATT, ALIZA
GROPER, JACOB
GROSS, NAPHTALI
GROSS-ZIMMERMANN, MOSHE
GRYNBERG, BERL
GURSHTEIN, AARON
GUTMAN, CHAIM
HAIMOWITZ, MORRIS JONAH
HALKIN, SHMUEL
HALPERN, MOYSHE-LEYB
HARENDORF, SAMUEL JACOB
HARKAVY, ALEXANDER
HARSHAV, BENJAMIN
HEILPERIN, FALK
HELLER, BUNIM
HERMAN, DAVID
HERSHELE
HIRSCHBEIN, PERETZ
HIRSCHKAHN, ZEVI
HOFFER, YEHIEL
HOFSTEIN, DAVID
HORONTCHIK, SIMON
HOROWITZ, BER
HURWITZ, CHAIM (Haykl)
ICELAND, REUBEN
IGNATOFF, DAVID
IMBER, SAMUEL JACOB
ISAAC BEN ELIAKIM OF POSEN
IZBAN, SHMUEL
JANOVSKY, SAUL JOSEPH
JOFFE, JUDAH ACHILLES
JUSTMAN, MOSHE BUNEM
KACYZNE, ALTER

KACZERGINSKY, SZMERKE
KAGANOWSKI, EFRAIM
KAHAN, SALOMON
KALMANOVITCH, ZELIG
KAPLAN, PESAH
KARPINOVITSH, AVROM
KASSEL, DAVID
KATZ, ALEPH
KATZ, DOVID
KATZ, MENKE
KATZ, MOSES
KATZENELENBOGEN, URIAH
KATZENELSON, BARUCH
KATZENELSON, ITZHAK
KAZDAN, HAYYIM SOLOMON
KERLER, DOV-BER
KERLER, YOYSEF
KHARIK, IZI (Itzhak)
KIPNIS, ITZIK
KOBRIN, LEON
KOENIG, LEO
KOENIGSBERG, DAVID
KORN, RACHEL HARING
KOTIK, YEKHESKL
KRANTZ, PHILIP
KULBAK, MOYSHE
KURTZ, AARON
KUSHNIROV, AARON
KVITKO, LEIB
LANDAU, ALFRED
LANDAU, ZISHE
LAPIN, BERL
LATTEINER, JOSEPH
LEE, MALKE
LEHRER, LEIBUSH
LEIBL, DANIEL
LEIVICK, H.
LERER, YEHIEL
LEV, ABRAHAM
LIBIN, Z.
LICHT, MICHAEL
LIEBERMAN, CHAIM
LIESSIN, ABRAHAM
LINETZKY, ISAAC JOEL
LITVAKOV, MOSES
LITVIN, A.
LITVINE, M.
LOCKER, MALKE
LUDWIG, REUBEN
LURIA, NOAH
LUTZKY, A.
MAGIDOV, JACOB
MALACH, LEIB
MANGER, ITZIK
MANI-LEIB (Brahinsky)
MANN, MENDEL
MARGOLIN, ANNA
MARINOFF, JACOB
MARKISH, PERETZ
MARMOR, KALMAN

MASTBAUM, JOEL
MAYZEL, NACHMAN
MAZE, IDA
MEDRES, ISRAEL
MENDELSOHN, SHELOMO
MENDELSON, JOSE
MESTEL, JACOB
MILLER, SHAYE
MINKOFF, NAHUM BARUCH
MIRANSKY, PERETZ
MOLODOWSKY, KADIA
MUKDONI, A.
MYER, MORRIS
NADIR, MOYSHE
NAIDUS, LEIB
NEUGROESCHEL, MENDEL
NEUMANN, YEHESKEL MOSHE
NIGER, SHMUEL
NISSENSON, AARON
NOMBERG, HERSH DAVID
OLEVSKI, BUZI
OLITZKY
OPATOSHU, JOSEPH (Joseph Meyer Opatovsky)
ORLAND, HERSHL
ORNSTEIN, LEO
OSHEROWITCH, MENDL
OYVED, MOYSHE
PAPIERNIKOV, JOSEPH
PERETZ, ISAAC LEIB
PERLE, JOSHUA
PERLOV, YITSKHOK
PERSOV, SHMUEL
PINSKI, DAVID
PREGER, JACOB
RABINOVICH, JOSE
RABON, ISRAEL
RABOY, ISAAC
RASHKIN, LEYB
RAVITCH, MELECH
RAZUMNI, MARK
REBECCA BAT MEIR TIKTINER
REISEN, ABRAHAM
REJZEN, ZALMAN
RESSLER, BENJAMIN
REZNIK, LIPE
RIVKIN, BORUCH
ROCHMAN, LEIB
ROGOFF, HARRY (Hillel)
ROLNICK, JOSEPH
ROSENBLATT, H.
ROSENFARB, CHAVA
ROSENFELD, JONAH
ROSENFELD, MORRIS
ROSSIN, SAMUEL
RUBIN, HADASSAH
RUBINSTEIN, JOSEPH
SALKIND, JACOB MEIR
SANDLER, BORIS
SAPHIRE, SAUL
SCHAECHTER-GOTTESMAN, BEYLE

SCHNAPPER, BER
SCHWARTZ, ISRAEL JACOB
SCHWARZBARD, SHOLEM (Samuel)
SCHWARZMAN, ASHER
SEGAL, ESTHER
SEGAL, JACOB ISAAC
SEGALOWITCH, ZUSMAN
SELIKOVITCH, GEORGE (Getzel)
SFARD, DAVID
SHAKESPEARE, WILLIAM
SHALOM ALEICHEM
SHAMRI, ARIE
SHAPIRO, LAMED
SHAYEVITSH, SIMKHA-BUNEM
SHEKHTMAN, ELYE
SHMERUK, CHONE
SHOMER
SHPIGLBLAT, ALEKSANDER
SHRAYBMAN, YEKHIEL
SHTERN, ISRAEL
SHTIF, NOKHEM
SHULNER, DORA
SHUMIATCHER-HIRSCHBEIN, ESTHER
SIEMIATYCKI, CHAIM
SIMON, SHLOME
SINGER, ISAAC BASHEVIS
SINGER, ISRAEL JOSHUA
SPECTOR, MORDECAI
SPIEGEL, ISAIAH
SPIVAK, ELYE
STEIMAN, BEYNUSH
STEINBARG, ELIEZER
STENCL, ABRAHAM NAHUM
STERNBERG, JACOB
STRIGLER, MORDECAI
SUTZKEVER, ABRAHAM
TABACHNIK, ABRAHAM BER
TASHRAK
TEIF, MOSHE
TEITSH, MOYSHE
TENENBAUM, JOSHUA
TEPPER, KOLYA
TKATCH, MEIR ZIML
TOLUSH
TRUNK, YEHIEL YESHAIA
TSANIN (YESHAYE), MORDKHE
TUNKEL, JOSEPH
TUSSMAN, MALKA
ULIANOVER, MIRIAM
VEINGER, MORDECAI
VERGELIS, AARON
VINCHEVSKY, MORRIS
WALDMAN, MOSHE
WARSHAVSKY, YAKIR
WARSHAWSKI, MARK
WARSZAWSKI, OSER
WEINPER (Weinperlech), ZISHE
WEINREICH, MAX
WEINSTEIN, BERISH
WEISSENBERG, ISAAC MEIR

BASILICA
CEREMONIAL OBJECTS
HANUKKAH LAMP
ICONOGRAPHY
ILLUMINATED MANUSCRIPTS, HEBREW
MENORAH
NEW YEAR'S CARDS
PAPER-CUTS
PAROKHET AND KAPPORET
PASSSOVER
PEWTER PLATES
PORTAL
SABBATH
SYNAGOGUE
TAGIN
TOMBS AND TOMBSTONES
TORAH ORNAMENTS

1. ARCHITECTURE
Biographies
ABRAMOVITZ, MAX
ADLER, DANKMAR
AGREST, DIANA
ALDROPHE, ALFRED-PHILIBERT
ALSCHULER, ALFRED
BAERWALD, ALEX
BAUMGARTEN, SANDOR
BAUMHORN, LIPOT
BLACK, SIR MISHA
BLANKSTEIN, CECIL N.
BOHM, HENRIK
BREUER, MARCEL (Lajos)
BRUNNER, ARNOLD
BRYER, MONTE
BUNSHAFT, GORDON
DAVIS, HENRY DAVID
DE KLERK, MICHEL
DIAMOND, JACK
EIDLITZ (Abraham Moses), ZERAH BEN MEIR
EISENMAN, PETER D.
EIZENBERG, JULIE
ELHANANI, ABA
ELHANANI, ARYEH
ELTE, HARRY
FEUERSTEIN, BEDRICH
FRANK, JOSEF
FREED, JAMES INGO
FREUND, VILMOS
GAD, DEVORAH
GANDELSONAS, MARIO
GEHRY, FRANK O.
GOERITZ, MATHIAS
GOLDBERG, BERTRAND
GOODMAN, PERCIVAL
GORLIN, ALEXANDER
GRUMBACH, ANTOINE
HAJOS, ALFRED
HANSON, NORMAN LEONARD
HEGEDUS, ARMIN
HERMER, MANFRED

IDELSON, BENJAMIN
JACOBSEN, ARNE EMIL
JAKAB, DEZSO
KAHN, ALBERT
KAHN, ELY JACQUES
KAHN, LOUIS I.
KANTOROWICH, ROY
KARMI, DOV
KAUFMANN, OSKAR
KAUFMANN, RICHARD
KIESLER, FREDERICK JOHN
KLARWEIN, JOSEPH
KRAKAUER, LEOPOLD
LAJTA, BELA
LAMBERT, PHYLLIS
LAPIDUS, MORRIS
LASDUN, DENYS
LE ROITH, HAROLD HIRSCH
LERNER, JAIME
LEVI, RINO
LIBESKIND, DANIEL
MALNAI, BELA
MANDL, SAADIA
MANSFELD, ALFRED
MEIER, RICHARD
MENDELSOHN, ERIC
MESSEL, ALFRED
MEYER-LEVY, CLAUDE
MINDLIN, HENRIQUE
NEUTRA, RICHARD JOSEPH
PERSITZ, ALEXANDRE
POLSHEK, JAMES
PONTREMOLI, EMMANUEL
QITNER, ZSIGMUND
RATNER, YOHANAN
RAU, HEINZ
RECHTER
REZNIK, DAVID
ROGERS, ERNESTO
ROSENBERG, EUGENE
SAFDIE, MOSHE
SAITOWITZ, STANLEY
SCHINDLER, RUDOLPH M.
SCHUMACHER, GOTTLIEB
SCHWARTZ, FREDERIC
SHARON, ARYEH
STERN, ROBERT A.M.
STRNAD, OSKAR
TIGERMAN, STANLEY
VAGO, JOZSEF
VAGO, LASZLO
YASKI, AVRAHAM
ZELENKA, FRANTISEK
ZEVI, BRUNO

2. CARTOONING
Biographies
BLOCK, HERBERT LAWRENCE ("Herblock")
CAPP, AL
CHAST, ROZ

IV. JEWS IN THE WORLD

A. ART

2. Cartooning

BIOGRAPHIES (*continued*)

CRUMB, ROBERT
CSUPO, GABOR (and Irene Klasky)
EISNER, WILL
ELDER, WILL
ELISOFON, ELIOT
FEIFFER, JULES
FLEISCHER, MAX
FRELENG, I. J.
GARDOSH, KARIEL (Charles; "Dosh")
GODAL, ERIC
GOLDBERG, RUBE
GOLDWATER, JOHN
GROPPER, WILLIAM
HIRSCHFELD, AL
KANE, BOB
KANE, GIL
KELEN, IMRE
KIRBY, JACK (Kurtzberg)
KURTZMAN, HARVEY
LANGDON, DAVID
LAZARUS, MEL
LEE, STAN
OPPER, FREDERICK BURR
SHUSTER, JOE
SIEGEL, JERRY
SPIEGELMAN, ART
STEIG, WILLIAM, SHREK
STEINBERG, SAUL
TIM
TRIER, WALTER
WEISZ, VICTOR ("Vicky")
ZEC, PHILIP

3. PAINTING

BIOGRAPHIES

ABERDAM, ALFRED
ABRAHAMS, IVOR
ABSALON
ADLER, JANKEL (Jacob)
ADLER, JULES
ADLER, MORITZ
ADLER, SAMUEL M.
ADLIVANKIN, SAMUIL
AGAM, YAACOV
AIZENBERG, NINA
ALCONIERE, THEODORE
ALECHINSKY, PIERRE
ALTMAN, NATHAN
ALVA, SIEGFRIED
AMSHEWITZ, JOHN HENRY
ANCONA, VITO D'
ANISFELD, BORIS
APPELBAUM, MOSHE
ARDON, MORDECAI
ARIKHA, AVIGDOR

AROCH, ARIE
ARONSON, DAVID
ASCHHEIM, ISIDOR
ASKNAZI, ISAAC LVOVICH
ATAR, HAIM
ATLAN, JEAN
AUERBACH, FRANK
AVNI, AHARON
AXELROD, MEYER
BACHI, RAPHAEL
BACON, YEHUDA
BAITLER, ZOMA
BAK, SAMUEL
BAKST, LEON
BALLIN, JOEL
BALLIN, MOEGENS
BARCINSKY, HENRYK
BARLIN, FREDERICK WILLIAM
BARNET, WILL
BARUH, BORA
BAYEFSKY, ABA
BECK, WILLY
BEERI, TUVIA
BELKIN, ARNOLD
BENDEMANN, EDUARD JULIUS FRIEDRICH
BENN
BENN, BEN
BEN-ZION (Weinman)
BERENY, ROBERT
BERGNER, YOSSL (Yosef L.)
BERLEWI, HENRYK
BERNSTEIN, MOSHE
BERNSTEIN, THERESA
BEZEM, NAPHTALI
BIHARI, ALEXANDER
BIRNBAUM, MENACHEM
BIRNBAUM, URIEL
BLAU, TINA
BLOCH, MARTIN
BLOOM, HYMAN
BLUM, LUDWIG
BLUME, PETER
BOGEN, ALEXANDER
BOLOTOWSKY, ILYA
BOMBERG, DAVID
BORENSTEIN, SAM
BORNFRIEND, JACOB
BORNSTEIN, ELI
BRAUNER, ISAAC
BRAUNER, VICTOR
BRAZ, OSIP
BRAZER, ABRAM
BRODSKII, ISAAK
BROWN, AIKA
BRUCK, LAJOS
BRUCK, MIKSA
BUDKO, JOSEPH
CAGLI, CORRADO
CAHN, MARCELLE
CAISERMAN-ROTH, GHITTA

CARO-DELVAILLE, HENRI	HAAS, LEO
CARVALHO, SOLOMON NUNES	HALEVY, YOSEF
CASSAB, JUDY	HALTER, MAREK
CASTEL, MOSHE ELAZAR	HART, SOLOMON ALEXANDER
CASTELLAZZO, MOSES DA	HAYDEN, HENRI
CENTERSZSWER, STANISLAWA	HENSCHEL BROTHERS
CHAGALL, MARC	HERDAN, KURT LUCIAN
CHAPIRO, JACQUES	HERLINGEN, AARON WOLF
CHICAGO, JUDY	HERMAN, JOSEF
CITROEN, ROELOF PAUL	HERMAN, OSKAR
COEN, GIUSEPPE	HILLMAN, DAVID
COHEN, BERNARD	HIRSCH, JOSEPH
COHEN, HAROLD	HIRSCHFELD-MACK, LUDWIG
COHEN GAN, PINHAS	HIRSHENBERG, SAMUEL
COOPER, ALEXANDER	HIRSHFIELD, MORRIS
CORCOS, VITTORIO	HOROVITZ, LEOPOLD
COSTA, CATHERINE DA	IBN HAYYIM, JOSEPH
CZOBEL, BELA	INLANDER, HENRY
DANIELS, ALFRED	ISER, JOSIF
DAVID, JEAN	ISKOWITZ, GERSHON
DE CHAVES, AARON	ISRAELS, JOZEF
DELAUNAY-TERK, SONIA	IVANYI-GRUNWALD, BELA
DICKER-BRANDEIS, FREDERIKE	JANCO, MARCEL
DINE, JIM	JUSTER, GEORGE
DONATI, ENRICO	JUSTITZ, ALFRED
DONATI, LAZZARO	KADISHMAN, MENASHE
EILSHEMIUS, LOUIS	KAHAN, LOUIS
ENGELSBERG, LEON	KAHANA, AHARON
ESTEVENS, DAVID	KANOVITZ, HOWARD
EZEKIEL, ABRAHAM EZEKIEL	KARAVAN, DANI
FEIBUSCH, HANS	KARS, JIRI
FEIGL, BEDRICH (Friedrich)	KATZ, ALEX
FENYES, ADOLF	KATZ, HANNS LUDWIG
FEUERRING, MAXIMILIAN	KAUFMANN, ISIDOR
FIMA	KEMPF, FRANZ MOSHE
FOX, EMANUEL PHILIPS	KESTLEMAN, MORRIS
FRAENCKEL, LIEPMANN	KIBEL, WOLF
FRANKENTHALER, HELEN	KIKOINE, MICHEL
FREEDMAN, BARNETT	KIRSCHSTEIN, SALLI
FRENKEL (Frenel), ITZHAK	KIRSZENBAUM, JESEKIEL DAVID
FREUD, LUCIAN	KISLING, MOISE
FREUNDLICH, OTTO	KITAJ, R. B.
FRIEDLAENDER, JOHNNY	KLEIN, YVES
FRITTA	KLINE FRANZ
GARBUZ, YAIR	KOLNIK, ARTHUR
GERSHUNI, MOSHE	KOPF, MAXIM
GERTLER, MARK	KOPPEL, HEINZ
GIKOW, RUTH	KOSSOFF, LEON
GILBERT, INA	KRAMER, JACOB
GLUCK, HANNAH	KRASNER, LEE
GOLUB, LEON	KRAYN, HUGO
GOTTLIEB, ADOLPH	KRESTIN, LAZAR
GOTTLIEB, MAURYCY	KUPFERMAN, MOSHE
GROSS, MICHAEL	KUZKOVSKI, JOSEPH
GRUNDIG, LEA AND HANS	LASZLO, PHILIP ALEXIUS DE LOMBOS
GRUNDMAN, ZWI	LAVIE, RAFFI
GUSTON, PHILIP	LEVANON, MORDECAI
GUTMAN, NAHUM	LEVINE, JACK
GUTTMANN, ROBERT	LEVITAN, ISAAC ILITCH
HAAN, MEIJER DE	LEVY, RUDOLF

IV. JEWS IN THE WORLD
A. ART
3. Painting
Biographies (*continued*)

LEVY-DHURMER, LUCIEN
LICHTENSTEIN, ROY
LIEBERMANN, MAX
LIFSCHITZ, URI
LISMANN, HERMANN
LISSITZKY, EL (Lazar)
LITVINOVSKY, PINHAS
LOEVENSTEIN, FEDOR
LOUIS, MORRIS
LOZOWICK, LOUIS
MAGNUS, EDUARD
MAIROVICH, ZVI
MANE-KATZ
MANSO, LEO
MARCOUSSIS (Marcous), LOUIS
MARGO, BORIS
MARIL, HERMAN
MARYAN
MAXY, MAX HERMAN
MEIDNER, LUDWIG
MENINSKY, BERNARD
MENKES, ZYGMUNT
MILICH, ADOLPHE
MINTCHINE, ABRAHAM
MODIGLIANI, AMEDEO
MOHOLY-NAGY, LASZLO
MOISE, THEODORE SYDNEY
MOKADY, MOSHE
MONDZAIN, SIMON
MOPP
MOSKOVITZ, SHALOM
MOSLER, HENRY
MUHLSTOCK, LOUIS
MUTER (Mutermilch), MELA
NADELMAN, ELIE
NEIMAN, YEHUDAH
NEWMAN, BARNETT
NICHOLS, JACK
NIERMAN, LEONARDO
NIKEL, LEA
NUSSBAUM, FELIX
NUSSBAUM, JAKOB
OFEK, AVRAHAM
OLITSKI, JULES
OPPENHEIM, MORITZ DANIEL
OPPENHEIMER, JOSEPH
ORLIK, EMIL
OTTA, FRANCISCO
PACHTER, CHARLES
PAILES, ISAAC (Jacques)
PALDI, ISRAEL
PANN, ABEL
PAOVLOTZKY, RAUL
PASCIN, JULES
PASTERNAK, LEONID OSIPOVICH

PEARLSTEIN, PHILIP
PERLMUTTER, IZSAK
PICART, BERNARD
PILICHOWSKI, LEOPOLD
PISSARRO, CAMILLE
PRESSMANE, JOSEPH
PROBST-KRAID, RIZA
RABIN, OSCAR
RABIN, SAM
RAPHAEL, WILLIAM
RASKIN, SAUL
RATTNER, ABRAHAM
RAY, MAN
REDER, BERNARD
REISS, LIONEL
REMBRANDT VAN RIJN
RIVERS, LARRY
ROGERS, CLAUDE MAURICE
ROSE, HERMAN
ROSENBERG, LAZAR
ROSENTHAL, MAX
ROTHENSTEIN, SIR WILLIAM
ROTHKO, MARK
RUBIN, REUVEN
RYBACK, ISSACHAR
SAFDIE, SYLVIA
SALAMAN
SALOMON, CHARLOTTE
SALOMON, GESKEL
SCHAMES, SAMSON
SCHANKER, LOUIS
SCHATZ, BORIS
SCHOR, ILYA
SCHWARTZ, MANFRED
SEBBA, SHALOM
SEGAL, ARTHUR
SEGALL, LAZAR
SELIGMANN, KURT
SEROV, VALENTIN
SHAHN, BEN
SHEMI, MENAHEM
SIMA, MIRON
SIMON, SIDNEY
SOLOMON, SIMEON
SOLOMON, SOLOMON JOSEPH
SOUTINE, CHAIM
SOYER, MOSES
SOYER, RAPHAEL
SPERO, NANCY
SPIRO, EUGEN
STEINER-PRAG, HUGO
STEINHARDT, JAKOB
STEMATSKY, AVIGDOR
STERN, IRMA
STERNE, HEDDA
STERNE, MAURICE
STREICHMAN, YEHEZKIEL
STRUCK, HERMANN
SUTTON, PHILIP
SZALIT-MARCUS, RACHEL

SZOBEL, GEZA
SZYK, ARTHUR
TAGGER, SIONA
TATLIN, VLADIMIR E.
TICHO, ANNA
TIVOLI, SERAFINO DA
TOPOLSKI, FELIKS
TOWNE, CHARLES
TWORKOV, JACK
UHLMAN, FRED
ULLMANN, ERNEST
URY, LESSER
VARLIN (Guggenheim, Willy)
WALKOWITZ, ABRAHAM
WEBER, MAX
WEILL, SHRAGA
WILSON, "SCOTTIE"
WILSON, SOL
WOLF, GUSTAV
WOLLHEIM, GERT
WOLMARK, ALFRED
ZAK, EUGENE
ZARITSKY, YOSSEF
ZHITNITSKI, MARK
ZIEGLER, ARCHIBALD
ZUCKER, JACQUES

4. PHOTOGRAPHY
Biographies
ARBUS, DIANE NEMEROV
ARNOLD, EVE
AVEDON, RICHARD
BAR-AM, MICHA
BING, ILSE
BOURKE-WHITE, MARGARET
BRENNER, FREDERIC
CALLE, SOPHIE
CAPA, CORNELL
CAPA, ROBERT
CARVALHO, SOLOMON NUNES
EISENSTAEDT, ALFRED
ERWITT, ELLIOTT
ETTLINGER, MARION
FRANK, ROBERT
FREUND, GISELE
FRIEDLANDER, LEE
GIDAL, TIM
GOLDIN, NAN
HALSMAN, PHILIPPE
HEARTFIELD, JOHN
IZIS
JACOBI, LOTTE
KAGAN, ELIE
KERTESZ, ANDRE
LEIBOVITZ, ANNIE
LEVITT, HELENE
MARK, MARY ELLEN
MEYEROWITZ, JOEL
NEWMAN, ARNOLD
NEWTON, HELMUT

PENN, IRVING
PLACHY, SYLVIA
RINGL & PIT (STERN, GRETE; ROSENBERG AUERBACH,
    ELLEN)
RUBIN, GAIL
RUBINGER, DAVID
SALOMON, ERICH
SEYMOUR, DAVID
SISKIND, AARON
STIEGLITZ, ALFRED
STRAND, PAUL
VISHNIAC, ROMAN
WEEGEE
WINOGRAND, GARRY

5. SCULPTURE
Biographies
ANTOKOLSKI, MARK (Mordecai)
ARONSON, NAUM LVOVICH
ASTRUC, ZACHARIE
BAIZERMAN, SAUL
BASKIN, LEONARD
BEER, SAMUEL FRIEDRICH
BEN-ZVI, ZEEV
BERNSTEIN-SINAIEFF, LEOPOLD
BLAZKO, MARTIN
BLOC, ANDRE
BOKROS-BIRMAN, DEZSO (Desiderius)
BOROFSKY, JONATHAN
CARO, SIR ANTHONY
DA COSTA, JOSEPH MENDES
DANZIGER, ITZHAK
DAVIDSON, JO
EHRLICH, GEORG
ELKAN, BENNO
ENGEL, JOZSEF
EPSTEIN, SIR JACOB
ETROG, SOREL
EZEKIEL, MOSES JACOB
FEIGIN, DOV
FERBER, HERBERT
FREIFELD, ABRAHAM
FRENKEL, VERA
GLICENSTEIN, ENRICO
GLID, NANDOR
GORDON, WILLY
GROSS, CHAIM
GUENZBURG, ILYA YAKOVLEVICH
GUTFREUND, OTTO
HABER, SHAMAI
HANNEMANN, PABLO
HARKAVY, MINNA
ISENSTEIN, KURT HARALD
KOENIG, GHISHA
KOGAN, MOYSE
KORMIS, FRED
KOSICE, GYULA
KOTTLER, MOSES
KREMEGNE, PINCHAS
LASSAW, IBRAM

B. LITERATURE

1. BULGARIAN LITERATURE
   Main Surveys
   BULGARIAN LITERATURE

   Biographies
   PETROV, VALERY
   WAGENSTEIN, ANGEL

2. CZECHOSLOVAK LITERATURE
   Main Surveys
   CZECHOSLOVAK LITERATURE

   Biographies
   ASKENAZY, LUDVIK
   BONN, HANUS
   BOR, JOSEF
   DAGAN, AVIGDOR
   DOSTAL, ZENO
   EISNER, PAVEL (Paul)
   FISCHER, OTOKAR
   FRÝD, NORBERT (Nora)
   GELLNER, FRANTIŠEK
   GOLDFLAM, ARNOST
   GOLDSTUECKER, EDUARD
   GOTTLIEB, FRANTIŠEK
   GROSMAN, LADISLAV
   HOFFMANN, CAMILL
   HOSTOVSKY, EGON
   KAFKA, FRANTIŠEK
   KAPPER, SIEGFRIED (Vitezslav)
   KLIMA, IVAN
   KNIEZA, EMIL
   KOHN, SALOMON
   KRAUS, FRANTIŠEK R.
   KRAUS, IVAN
   KRAUS, OTA
   LANGER, FRANTIŠEK
   LANGER, JIŘÍ MORDECHAI
   LAUB, GABRIEL
   LEDA, EDUARD
   LISTOPAD, FRANTISEK
   LUSTIG, ARNOST
   OLBRACHT, IVAN
   ORNEST, OTA
   ORTEN, JIRI
   PAVEL, OTA
   PICK, JIŘÍ ROBERT
   POLACEK, KAREL
   RAKOUS, VOJTECH
   ROTTOVA, INNA
   SALUS, HUGO
   SIDON, KAROL EFRAIM
   SPITZER, JURAJ
   UHDE, MILAN
   VOHRYZEK, JOSEF
   VRCHLICKÝ, JAROSLAV
   WEIL, JIŘÍ
   WEINER, RICHARD

ZEYER, JULIUS

3. DUTCH LITERATURE
   Main Surveys
   DUTCH LITERATURE

   Biographies
   BRUGGEN, CARRY VAN
   CAMPEN, MICHEL HERMAN VAN
   CORREA, ISABEL REBECCA DE
   COSTA, ISAAC DA
   DE LIMA, JOSEPH SUASSO
   HAAN, JACOB ISRAËL DE
   HEIJERMANS, HERMAN
   HERTZVELD-HIJMANS, ESTELLA
   HERZBERG, ABEL JACOB
   LOGGEM, MANUEL VAN
   MINCO, MARGA
   MULISCH, HARRY
   PRAAG, SIEGFRIED EMANUEL VAN
   QUERIDO, ISRAËL
   VAN VRIESLAND, VICTOR EMANUEL
   VROMAN, LEO

4. ENGLISH LITERATURE
   Main Surveys
   ENGLISH LITERATURE
   SOUTH AFRICAN LITERATURE
   UNITED STATES LITERATURE

   General Entries
   CHILDREN'S LITERATURE

   Biographies
   AARONSON, LAZARUS LEONARD
   ABSE, DANNIE
   ADAMS, HANNAH
   AGUILAR, GRACE
   ALTER, ROBERT B.
   ALVAREZ, ALFRED
   ANGOFF, CHARLES
   ANTIN, MARY
   APPLE, MAX
   ASIMOV, ISAAC
   AUSLANDER, JOSEPH
   AUSTER, PAUL
   BARON, JOSEPH ALEXANDER
   BAUM, VICKI
   BEHRMAN, SAMUEL NATHANIEL
   BELLOW, SAUL
   BERCOVICI, KONRAD
   BERCOVITCH, SACVAN
   BLAKE, WILLIAM
   BLANKFORT, MICHAEL S.
   BLOOM, HAROLD
   BOAS, FREDERICK SAMUEL
   BODENHEIM, MAXWELL
   BRINIG, MYRON
   BRODY, ALTER
   BRONER, ESTHER M.

IV. JEWS IN THE WORLD
B. LITERATURE
4. English Literature
BIOGRAPHIES (*continued*)

JONG, ERICA
JOSIPOVICI, GABRIEL
JUDAH, SAMUEL BENJAMIN HELBERT
KALMAN, MAIRA
KANIN, GARSON
KANOVICH, GRIGORY
KAPLAN, JOHANNA
KARMEL, ILONA
KAUFMAN, BEL
KAUFMAN, GEORGE SIMON
KAZIN, ALFRED
KELLERMAN, FAYE
KELLERMAN, JONATHAN
KEMELMAN, HARRY
KERSH, GERALD
KINGSLEY, SIDNEY
KINROSS, ALBERT
KLEIN, ABRAHAM MOSES
KLEPFISZ, IRENA
KOBER, ARTHUR
KOCH, KENNETH
KOESTLER, ARTHUR
KOMROFF, MANUEL
KOPIT, ARTHUR
KOPS, BERNARD
KOSINSKI, JERZY
KRAMER, LARRY
KRAMM, JOSEPH
KRANTZ, JUDITH
KREISEL, HENRY
KREYMBORG, ALFRED
KRONENBERGER, LOUIS
KROOK, DOROTHEA
KUNITZ, STANLEY JASSPON
KUSHNER, TONY
LAURENTS, ARTHUR
LAWSON, JOHN HOWARD
LAYTON, IRVING
LAZARUS, EMMA
LEAVIS, QUEENIE DOROTHY
LEE, SIR SIDNEY
LEFTWICH, JOSEPH
LEVERSON, ADA
LEVERTOV, DENISE
LEVIANT, CURT
LEVIN, HARRY
LEVIN, IRA
LEVIN, MEYER
LEVINE, NORMAN
LEVINSON, OLGA
LEVY, AMY
LEVY, BENN WOLFE
LEWIS, LEOPOLD DAVIS
LEWISOHN, LUDWIG
LIBERMAN, SERGE
LIEBERMAN, ELIAS
LITVINOFF, EMANUEL
LOWENTHAL, MARVIN
LYONS, ALBERT MICHAEL NEIL

MAILER, NORMAN
MALAMUD, BERNARD
MALTZ, ALBERT
MAMET, DAVID
MANDEL, ELI
MANKOWITZ, WOLF
MARCUS, FRANK
MARLOWE, CHRISTOPHER
MARTIN, DAVID
MAYNARD, FREDELLE BRUSER
MERRICK, LEONARD
MEYERSTEIN, EDWARD HARRY WILLIAM
MICHAELS, ANNE
MIKES, GEORGE
MILLER, ARTHUR
MILLIN, SARAH GERTRUDE
MILTON, JOHN
MOÏSE, PENINA
MULLER, ROBERT
NASSAUER, RUDOLF
NATHAN, GEORGE JEAN
NEMEROV, HOWARD
NEUGEBOREN, JAY
NISSENSON, HUGH
ODETS, CLIFFORD
OLSEN, TILLIE
OPPEN, GEORGE
OPPENHEIM, JAMES
ORNITZ, SAMUEL BADISCH
OSTRIKER, ALICIA SUSKIN
OZICK, CYNTHIA
PALEY, GRACE
PARKER, DOROTHY
PERELMAN, SIDNEY JOSEPH
PHILLIPS, WILLIAM
PINSKY, ROBERT
PINTO, VIVIAN DE SOLA
PLAIN, BELVA
PODHORETZ, NORMAN
POTOK, CHAIM
POUND, EZRA LOOMIS
PROSE, FRANCINE
PYE, JAEL HENRIETTA
RAGEN, NAOMI
RAHV, PHILIP
RAND, AYN
RAPHAEL, FREDERIC
RAPHAEL, JOHN N.
RAPHAELSON, SAMSON
REZNIKOFF, CHARLES
RICE, ELMER LEOPOLD
RICH, ADRIENNE
RICHLER, MORDECAI
ROBBINS, HAROLD
RODKER, JOHN
ROSEN, NORMA
ROSENBERG, ISAAC
ROSENFELD, ISAAC
ROSENFELD, PAUL

IV. JEWS IN THE WORLD
B. LITERATURE
4. English Literature
BIOGRAPHIES (*continued*)

ROSS, LILLIAN
ROSTEN, LEO CALVIN
ROTH, HENRY
ROTH, PHILIP MILTON
RUBENS, BERNICE
RUBENS, PAUL ALFRED
RUBINSTEIN, HAROLD FREDERICK
RUKEYSER, MURIEL
SALINGER, JEROME DAVID
SAMPTER, JESSIE ETHEL
SAMUEL, MAURICE
SASSOON, SIEGFRIED LORRAINE
SCHISGAL, MURRAY
SCHULBERG, BUDD WILSON
SCHWARTZ, DELMORE
SCHWARZ, LEO WALDER
SCOTT, SIR WALTER
SEGAL, ERICH
SEID, RUTH
SERLING, ROD
SHAFFER, SIR PETER
SHAKESPEARE, WILLIAM
SHAPIRO, KARL JAY
SHAW, IRWIN
SHELDON, SIDNEY
SHEVELOVE, BURT
SHULMAN, MAX
SHULMAN, MILTON
SILKIN, JON
SIMON, KATE
SIMON, NEIL
SINCLAIR, CLIVE
SINGER, HOWARD
SKLAREW, MYRA
SOLOTAROFF, THEODORE
SONTAG, SUSAN
SPEWACK, BELLA
SPIEGELMAN, ART
SPIELVOGEL, NATHAN
SPINGARN
STEELE, DANIELLE
STEIN, GERTRUDE
STEIN, JOSEPH
STEINER, GEORGE
STEINFELD, JJ
STERN, BERTHA GLADYS
STERN, STEVE
STINE, R. L.
STONE, IRVING
STRAUS, RALPH
STRAUSS, GUSTAVE LOUIS MAURICE
SUSANN, JACQUELINE
SUTRO, ALFRED
SYMONS, JULIAN

TARN, NATHANIEL
TAYLOR, SIDNEY
TOBENKIN, ELIAS
TORGOV, MORLEY
TRILLIN, CALVIN, ESSAYIST
TRILLING, DIANA
TRILLING, LIONEL
TUROW, SCOTT
UNTERMEYER, LOUIS
URIS, LEON
WADDINGTON, MIRIAM (DWORKIN)
WALEY, ARTHUR
WALLACE, IRVING
WALLANT, EDWARD LEWIS
WASSERMAN, DALE
WASSERSTEIN, WENDY
WATEN, JUDAH
WEIDMAN, JEROME
WEINZWEIG, HELEN
WELLER, MICHAEL
WESKER, ARNOLD
WEST, NATHANAEL
WOLFE, HUMBERT
WOLFERT, IRA
WOUK, HERMAN
YARMOLINSKY, AVRAHM (Abraham)
YEZIERSKA, ANZIA
ZANGWILL, ISRAEL
ZUKOFSKY, LOUIS

5. FRENCH LITERATURE
MAIN SURVEYS
CANADIAN LITERATURE (French)
FRENCH LITERATURE

BIOGRAPHIES
ABECASSIS, ELIETTE
AREGA, LEON
ARGENS, JEAN BAPTISTE DE BOYER
BENICHOU, PAUL
BERL, EMMANUEL
BERNARD, TRISTAN
BERNSTEIN, HENRI-LEON
BERRI, CLAUDE
BLANCHOT, MAURICE
BLOCH, JEAN-RICHARD
BLOCH-MICHEL, JEAN
BLOY, LEON
BOBER, ROBERT
BOSCO, MONIQUE
CHATEAUBRIAND, FRANÇOIS RENÉ, VICOMTE DE
CIXOUS, HELENE
CLAUDEL, PAUL
COHEN, ALBERT
CREMIEUX, BENJAMIN
CROISSET, FRANCIS DE
DUVERNOIS, HENRI
EYDOUX, EMMANUEL
FEJTO, FRANCOIS

6. GERMAN LITERATURE
MAIN SURVEYS

BIOGRAPHIES

IV. JEWS IN THE WORLD
B. LITERATURE
6. German Literature
BIOGRAPHIES (*continued*)

FRANKL, LUDWIG AUGUST

FRANZOS, KARL EMIL

FRIED, ERICH

FRIEDELL, EGON

FRISCH, EFRAIM

FULDA, LUDWIG

GEIGER, LUDWIG

GOETHE, JOHANN WOLFGANG VON

GOLDSTEIN, MORITZ

GOLL, CLAIRE

GOLL, YVAN

GRONEMANN, SAMUEL (Sami, Sammy)

GUMPERT, MARTIN

GUNDOLF, FRIEDRICH

GUTZKOW, KARL FERDINAND

HAAS, WILLY

HABE, HANS

HASENCLEVER, WALTER

HAY, GYULA (Julius)

HEILBORN, ERNST

HEIMANN, MORITZ

HEINE, HEINRICH

HERMANN, GEORG

HERMLIN, STEPHAN

HESSEL, FRANZ

HEYM, STEFAN

HEYMANN, WALTHER

HEYSE, PAUL

HILDESHEIMER, WOLFGANG

HILSENRATH, EDGAR

HIRSCHFELD, GEORG

HITZIG, JULIUS EDUARD

HOCHHUTH, ROLF

HOCHWAELDER, FRITZ

HOFMANNSTHAL, HUGO VON

HOLITSCHER, ARTHUR

HOLLAENDER

HONIGMANN, BARBARA

HUGO, KAROLY

JACOB, HEINRICH EDUARD

JACOBOWSKI, LUDWIG

JELINEK, ELFRIEDE

KAFKA, FRANZ

KAHANE, ARTHUR

KALEKO, MASHA

KALISCH, DAVID

KARPELES, GUSTAV (Gershon)

KAUFMANN, FRITZ MORDECAI

KAYSER, RUDOLF

KERR, ALFRED

KESTEN, HERMANN

KLEIN, JULIUS LEOPOLD

KOLMAR, GERTRUD

KOMPERT, LEOPOLD

KOREFF, DAVID FERDINAND

KORNFELD, PAUL

KRAFT, WERNER

KRAMER, THEODOR

KRAUS, KARL

KROJANKER, GUSTAV

KUH, EPHRAIM MOSES

LANDSBERGER, ARTHUR

LASKER-SCHUELER, ELSE

LAZARUS, NAHIDA RUTH

LEONHARD, RUDOLF

LESSING, GOTTHOLD EPHRAIM

LEWALD, FANNY

LIPINER, SIEGFRIED

LISSAUER, ERNST

LORM, HIERONYMUS

LOTHAR, ERNST

LOTHAR, RUDOLF

LUBLINSKI, SAMUEL

LUDWIG, EMIL

MANN, THOMAS

MARCUSE, LUDWIG

MARGUL-SPERBER, ALFRED

MAUTHNER, FRITZ

MEHRING, WALTER

MEYER, RICHARD MORITZ

MOMBERT, ALFRED

MORGENSTERN, SOMA

MOSENTHAL, SALOMON HERMANN

MUEHSAM, ERICH

NADEL, ARNO

NEUMANN, ALFRED

NEUMANN, ROBERT

PAULI, JOHANNES

PERUTZ, LEO

PICARD, JACOB

POLGAR, ALFRED

REHFISCH, HANS JOSE

REICH-RANICKI, MARCEL

ROBERT, LUDWIG

RODA RODA, ALEXANDER

RODENBERG, JULIUS

ROESSLER, CARL

ROTH, JOSEPH

RUBINER, LUDWIG

SACHS, NELLY

SALTEN, FELIX

SAPHIR, MORITZ (Moses) GOTTLIEB

SCHERLAG, MARK

SCHILLER, FRIEDRICH VON

SCHNITZLER, ARTHUR

SCHWIEFERT, PETER

SEGHERS, ANNA

STERNHEIM, CARL

STRICH, FRITZ

STURMANN, MANFRED

SUESSKIND VON TRIMBERG

SUSMAN, MARGARETE

TABORI, GEORGE

12. RUSSIAN LITERATURE

Main Surveys

Biographies

IV. JEWS IN THE WORLD
B. LITERATURE
12. Russian Literature
BIOGRAPHIES (*continued*)

RABINOVICH, OSIP ARONOVICH
SELVINSKI, ILYA LVOVICH
SHKLOVSKI, ISAAC VLADIMIROVICH
SLONIM, MARC
SLONIMSKI, MIKHAIL LEONIDOVICH
SLUTSKI, BORIS ABRAMOVICH
SOBOL, ANDREY MIKHAILOVICH
SVETLOV, MIKHAIL
SVIRSKI, ALEXEY IVANOVICH
TUR BROTHERS
TYNYANOV, YURI NIKOLAYEVICH
UTKIN, JOSEPH PAVLOVICH
WENGEROFF, SEMYON AFANASYEVICH
YEVTUSHENKO, YEVGENI ALEXANDROVICH
YUSHKEVICH, SEMYON SOLOMONOVICH

13. SCANDINAVIAN LITERATURE
MAIN SURVEYS
SCANDINAVIAN LITERATURE

BIOGRAPHIES
ABRAHAMS, NICOLAI CHRISTIAN LEVIN
ELKAN, SOPHIE
GOLDSCHMIDT, MEIR ARON
KAUFMANN, HANNE
LEVERTIN, OSCAR IVAR
LEVIN, POUL THEODOR
LEVY, LOUIS
MUNK, KAJ
NATHANSEN, HENRI
SCHUCK, JOHAN HENRIK EMIL
WARBURG, KARL JOHAN
WARRENS, ROSA
WERGELAND, HENRIK ARNOLD

14. SPANISH AND PORTUGUESE LITERATURE
MAIN SURVEY
SPANISH AND PORTUGUESE LITERATURE

BIOGRAPHIES
AGUINIS, MARCOS
CERVANTES SAAVEDRA, MIGUEL DE
CONSTANTINI, HUMBERTO
COSTA, URIEL DA
COTA DE MAGUAQUE, RODRIGO DE
CHOCRON, ISAAC
DINES, ALBERTO
EICHELBAUM, SAMUEL
ENRÍQUEZ, ISABEL
ENRÍQUEZ GÓMEZ, ANTONIO
ESPINOZA, ENRIQUE
FEIERSTEIN, RICARDO
FUTORANSKY, LUISA
GELMAN, JUAN
GERCHUNOFF, ALBERTO

GLANTZ, MARGO
GODÍNEZ, FELIPE
GOLDEMBERG, ISAAC
GOLOBOFF, GERARDO MARIO
GRUNBERG, CARLOS M.
ISAACS, JORGE
ISAACSON, JOSE
KOVADLOFF, SANTIAGO
KOZER, JOSE
LAGUNA, DANIEL ISRAEL LOPEZ
LEÓN, LUIS DE
LIACHO, LÁZARO
LISPECTOR, CLARICE
MUÑIZ-HUBERMAN, ANGELINA
PECAR, SAMUEL
PIZARNIK, ALEJANDRA
RABINOVICH, JOSE
RAWET, SAMUEL
RIBEIRO DOS SANTOS, ANTONIO
ROSENCOF, MAURICIO
ROSENMANN-TAUB, DAVID
ROVINSKY, SAMUEL
ROZENMACHER, GERMAN
SATZ, MARIO
SCLIAR, MOACYR
SELIGSON, ESTHER
SHUA, ANA MARIA
SILVA, ANTÓNIO JOSÉ DA
SNEH, SIMJA
STEIMBERG, ALICIA
SVERDLIK, ODED
TARNOPOLSKY, SAMUEL
TIEMPO, CÉSAR
TOKER, ELIAHU
VERBITZKY, BERNARDO
WECHSLER, ELINA

15. YUGOSLAV LITERATURE
MAIN SURVEYS
YUGOSLAV LITERATURE

BIOGRAPHIES
ALBAHARI, DAVID
DAVIČO, OSCAR
DAVID, FILIP
DEBRECENJI, JOZEF
FELDMAN, MIROSLAV
GOTTLIEB, HINKO
IVANJI, IVAN
JUN-BRODA, INA
KIŠ, DANILO (Daniel)
KONFINO, ZAK
LEBOVIČ, DJORDJE
NAHMIJAS, DANILO
NAJMAN, JULIJA
ROMANO, SAMUEL
SAMOKOVLIJA, ISAK
ŠINKO, ERVIN
TIŠMA, ALEKSANDAR

C. MUSIC & DANCE

MAIN SURVEYS

DANCE
MUSIC

GENERAL ENTRIES

AMERICAN SOCIETY FOR JEWISH MUSIC
BATSHEVA AND BAT-DOR DANCE COMPANIES
BEN SIRA, WISDOM OF
BIBLE – IN THE ARTS
CANTATAS AND CHORAL WORKS, HEBREW
CANTILLATION
CHOIRS
DIBBUK
HASIDISM
HA-TIKVAH
HAZZAN
HORAH
INBAL DANCE THEATER
ISRAEL CHAMBER ORCHESTRA
LADINO
MAQAM
ORGAN
RECORDS, PHONOGRAPH
SHTAYGER
SOCIETY FOR JEWISH FOLK MUSIC
TALMUD, MUSICAL RENDITION
TANZHAUS

COMMUNITIES

AFRICA, NORTH: MUSICAL TRADITIONS
ALEPPO
AMSTERDAM
FRANKFURT ON THE MAIN
GREECE
INDIA
IRAN, MUSICAL TRADITION
IRAQ
ITALY
KARAITES
KURDISTAN
SAMARITANS
TURKEY
YEMEN
YUGOSLAVIA

RITUAL

ADDIR HU
ADON OLAM
AHOT KETANNAH
ALEINU LE-SHABBEAH
AMEN
AMIDAH
AVODAH
BAKKASHAH
EL MALE RAHAMIM
HALLELUJAH
KADDISH
KOL NIDREI

LEKHAH DODI
MA'OZ ZUR
MASORETIC ACCENTS (MUSICAL RENDITION)
MI-SINAI NIGGUNIM
NUSAH
YIGDAL
ZEMIROT

BIBLE IN MUSIC

ABRAHAM
ABSALOM
ADAM
AKEDAH
ATHALIAH
BABEL, TOWER OF
BELSHAZZAR
CAIN
COSTA, URIEL DA
DANIEL
DAVID
DEBORAH
ELIJAH
ESTHER
EZEKIEL
GIDEON
HABAKKUK
HASMONEANS
HEROD I
HEZEKIAH
ISAAC
ISAIAH
JACOB
JEPHTHAH
JEREMIAH
JERUSALEM
JOB, BOOK OF
JOEL
JONAH, BOOK OF
JOSEPH
JOSHUA
LAMENTATIONS, BOOK OF
MOSES
NEBUCHADNEZZAR (Nebuchadrezzer)
NOAH
PSALMS, BOOK OF
RACHEL
SAMSON
SAMUEL
SAUL
SCROLLS, THE FIVE
SODOM AND GOMORRAH
SOLOMON
SONG OF SONGS

BIOGRAPHIES

ABELIOVICH, LEV MOYSSEYEVICH
ABER, ADOLF
ABILEAH, ARIE
ABRAHAM, GERALD

IV. JEWS IN THE WORLD
C. MUSIC & DANCE
BIOGRAPHIES (*continued*)

ABRAHAM, OTTO
ABRASS, OSIAS (Joshua)
ABRAVANEL, MAURICE (DE)
ACHRON, JOSEPH
ACKERMAN, SHABTAI
ADASKIN, MURRAY
ADLER, GUIDO
ADLER, HUGO CHAIM
ADLER, ISRAEL
ADLER, LARRY (Lawrence)
ADLER, RICHARD
ADMON, YEDIDYAH
AGADATI, BARUCH
AGUILAR, EMANUEL ABRAHAM
AHARON, EZRA
ALDEMA, GIL
ALEXANDER, HAIM
ALGAZI, ISAAC BEN SOLOMON
ALGAZI, LEON (Yehudah)
AL-GHARĪD AL-YAHŪDĪ
AL-HARIZI, JUDAH BEN SOLOMON
ALKAN (Morhange), CHARLES HENRI-VALENTIN
ALMAN, SAMUEL
AL-MANSŪR AL-YAHŪDĪ
ALPERT, HERB
ALSHVANG, ARNOLD ALEKSANDROVICH
ALTER, ISRAEL
ALTSCHUL, JOSEPH
ALTSCHULER, MODEST
AMAR, LICCO
AMIRAN, EMANUEL
AMRAM, DAVID
ANCERL, KARL
ANCONA, MARIO
ANHALT, ISTVÁN
ANTHEIL, GEORGE
APEL, WILLI
APPLEBAUM, LOUIS
ARBATOVA, MIA
ARGOV, ALEXANDER (Sascha)
ARGOV, ZOHAR
ARIE, RAFAEL
ARLEN, HAROLD
AROM, SIMHA
ARONI (Aharoni), TSVI
ARONOVICH, YURI MIKHAYLOVICH
ARPA, ABRAMO DALL
ARTZI, SHLOMO
ASHKENAZY, VLADIMIR DAVIDOVICH
ATZMON, MOSHE
AUER, LEOPOLD
AVENARY, HANOCH
AVIDOM, MENAHEM
AVNI, TZEVI
AVSHALOMOV, AARON
AVSHALOMOV, JACOB

AX, EMMANUEL
BABBITT, MILTON
BABILÉE, JEAN
BABIN, VICTOR
BACHARACH, BURT
BACHAUER, GINA
BACHMANN, JACOB
BACON, HIRSCH LEIB
BACON, ISRAEL
BACON, SHLOMO REUVEN
BACON, YIDEL
BAER, ABRAHAM
BAGLEY, DAVID
BAR, SHLOMO
BARDANASHVILI, YOSEF
BARENBOIM, DANIEL
BAR-ILAN, DAVID
BARMAS, ISSAY
BARNEA, EZRA
BARNETT, JOHN
BARNETT, JOHN FRANCIS
BARSHAI, RUDOLPH
BART, LIONEL
BAUER, JACOB
BAUER, MARION EUGENIE
BAYER, BATHIA
BEDA
BEER, AARON
BEER, RAMI
BEIMEL, JACOB
BEKKER, PAUL
BELL, JOSHUA
BELLISON, SIMEON
BELY, VICTOR ARKADYEVICH (Aronovich)
BENATZKY, RALPH
BENDIX, OTTO
BENDIX, VICTOR EMANUEL
BENEDICT, SIR JULIUS (Isaac)
BEN-HAIM, PAUL
BEN-HAIM, YIGAL
BEN-SHABETAI, ARI
BEREGOVSKI, MOSHE
BERGEL, BERND
BERGER, ARTHUR VICTOR
BERGGRÜN, HEINRICH
BERGSON, MICHAEL
BERK, FRED
BERLIJN, ANTON (Aron Wolf)
BERLIN, IRVING
BERLINSKI, HERMAN
BERNSTEIN, ABRAHAM MOSHE
BERNSTEIN, ELMER
BERNSTEIN, LEONARD
BERTINI, GARY
BERTONOFF, DEBORAH
BIE, OSCAR
BINDER, ABRAHAM WOLF
BIRNBAUM, ABRAHAM BAER
BIRNBAUM, EDUARD
BLANES, JACOB

BLANTER, MATVEY ISAAKOVICH

BLAUSTEIN, ABRAHAM

BLECH, LEO

BLINDMAN, YERUHAM

BLITZSTEIN, MARC

BLOCH, ANDRE

BLOCH, CHARLES

BLOCH, ERNEST

BLOCH, ROSINE

BLOOMFIELD-ZEISLER, FANNY

BLUM, RENÉ

BLUMENFELD, FELIX MIKHAYLOVICH

BLUMENTHAL, NISSAN,

BODANZKY, ARTHUR

BODKY, ERWIN

BOEHM, YOHANAN

BOGHEN, FELICE

BOLAFFI, MICHELE

BOLM, ADOLPH RUDOLPHOVICH

BORGE, VICTOR

BORIS, RUTHANNA

BOROVSKY, ALEXANDER

BOSCOVITCH, ALEXANDER URIYAH

BOTSTEIN, LEON

BOUZAGLO, DAVID

BRAHAM, JOHN

BRAILOWSKY, ALEXANDER

BRANDON, OHEB ISAAC

BRANT, HENRY DREYFUS

BRAUDO, YEVGENI MAXIMOVICH

BRAUN (BROWN), ARIE

BRAUN, YEHEZKIEL

BRAUNER, HARRY

BRECHER, GUSTAVE

BRECKER BROTHERS

BRÉVAL, LUCIENNE

BROD, DOVIDL

BROD, MAX

BRODER SINGERS

BRODSKY, ADOLF

BRONFMAN, YEFIM

BROOK, BARRY SHELLEY

BROWNING, JOHN

BRUELL, IGNAZ

BRUSSILOVSKY, YEVGENI GRIGORYEVICH

BUCHWALD, THEO

BUKOFZER, MANFRED

BURLE MARX, WALTER

CACERES, ABRAHAM

CAHN, SAMMY

CAREGAL, HAYYIM MOSES BEN ABRAHAM

CARLEBACH, SHLOMO

CARP, PAULA

CASTELNUOVO-TEDESCO, MARIO

CERVETTO, JACOB BASEVI

CHAGRIN, FRANCIS

CHAGY, BERELE

CHASINS, ABRAHAM

CHERKASSKY, SHURA

CHERNEY, BRIAN

CHERNIAVSKY

CHUJOY, ANATOLE

CHURGIN, BATHIA

CIVITA, DAVIT (David)

COHEN, HARRIET

COHEN, JACOB RAPHAEL

COHEN, LEONARD

COHEN, SELMA JEANNE

COHEN, YARDENA

COHEN MELAMED, NISSAN

COLEMAN, CY

COLONNE, JULES (Judah) EDOUARD

COMISSIONA, SERGIU

CONRIED, HEINRICH

CONSOLO, FEDERICO

COOPER, EMIL ALBERTOVICH

COPLAND, AARON

COSTA, SIR MICHAEL

COWEN, SIR FREDERIC HYMEN

CRANKO, JOHN

DA PONTE, LORENZO

DAMARI, SHOSHANA

DAMROSCH

DANTO, LOUIS

DA-OZ, RAM

DAUS, AVRAHAM

DAVIČO, LUJO

DAVID, ERNEST

DAVID, FERDINAND

DAVID, SAMUEL

DAVYDOV, KARL YULYEVICH

DE PHILIPPE, EDIS

DESSAU, PAUL

DEUTSCH, MORITZ

DEUTSCH, OTTO ERICH

DIAMOND, DAVID

DICHTER, MISHA

DI-ZAHAV, EPHRAIM

DOBROVEN, ISSAY ALEXANDROVICH

DONALDA, PAULINE

DORATI, ANTAL

DORFMAN, JOSEPH

DRESDEN, SEM

DU PRÉ, JACQUELINE

DUKAS, PAUL

DUNAYEVSKI, ISAAC OSIPOVICH

DUQUE, SIMON DAVID

DUSHKIN, SAMUEL

EDEL, YIZHAK

EDEN-TAMIR

EHRLICH, ABEL

EIFMAN, BORIS

EINSTEIN, ALFRED

EISENSTEIN, JUDITH KAPLAN

EISLER, HANNS

ELLSTEIN, ABRAHAM (Abe)

ELMAN, MISCHA

EMSHEIMER, ERNST

ENGEL, JOEL (Yuli Dimitriyevich)

EPHROS, GERSHON

IV. JEWS IN THE WORLD
C. MUSIC & DANCE
Biographies (continued)

ERLANGER, CAMILLE
ESHEL, YITZHAK
ESPINOSA, EDOUARD
EULENBURG, ERNST
EVEN-OR, MARY
FALL, LEO
FANO, GUIDO ALBERTO
FARBER, VIOLA
FEIDMAN, GIYORA
FEINBERG, SAMUEL YEVGENYEVICH
FEINSINGER, JOSHUA
FELDMAN, MORTON
FEUERMANN, EMANUEL
FIEDLER, ARTHUR
FISCHER, ANNIE
FISCHOFF, JOSEPH
FISHER, DUDU
FITELBERG, GRZEGORZ (Gregor)
FLEISCHER, TSIPPI
FLEISHER, LEON
FLESCH, CARL
FOGELBERG, DAN
FOSS, LUKAS
FRANKEL, BENJAMIN
FREED, ISADORE
FREEDMAN, HARRY
FRIED (-BISS), MIRIAM
FRIEDE, SHALOM
FRIEDLAENDER, MAX
FRIEDMAN, DEBORAH LYNN
FRIEDMAN, KINKY
FRIEDMANN, ARON
FRIEDMANN, MORITZ
FROMM, HERBERT
FUCHS, LILLIAN
GABRIELOVITCH, OSIP SOLOMONOVICH
GANCHOFF, MOSES
GANTMAN, JUDAH LEIB (LEO)
GASKELL, SONJA
GEBIRTIG, MORDECAI
GEDALGE, ANDRE
GEIRINGER, KARL
GELBRUN, ARTUR
GERBER, MAYNARD
GERNSHEIM, FRIEDRICH
GEROVICH, ELIEZER MORDECAI BEN ISAAC
GERSON-KIWI, EDITH (Esther)
GESHURI, MEIR SHIMON
GETZ, STAN
GIBBS, TERRY
GIDEON, MIRIAM
GILBOA, JACOB
GILÈLS, EMIL GRIGORYEVICH
GIOVANNI MARIA
GLANZ, LEIB
GLASS, PHILIP

GLICK, IRVING SRUL
GLIÈRE, REINHOLD MORITZEVICH
GLUCK, ALMA
GNESIN, MIKHAIL FABIANOVICH
GODOWSKY, LEOPOLD
GOLDBERG, SZYMON
GOLDFARB, ISRAEL
GOLDMAN, EDWIN FRANKO
GOLDMARK, KARL
GOLDSCHMIDT, HUGO
GOLDSTEIN, JOSEF
GOLDSTEIN, RAYMOND
GOLINKIN, MORDECAI
GOLSCHMANN, VLADIMIR
GOODMAN, BENNY
GOTTSCHALK, LOUIS MOREAU
GOULD, MORTON
GRADENWITZ, PETER EMANUEL
GRAF, HERBERT
GRAFFMAN, GARY
GRAZIANI, YIZHAK
GREENBERG, NOAH
GREENBLATT, ELIYAHU
GRUENBERG, LOUIS
GUGLIELMO DA PESARO
GUSIKOW, JOSEPH MICHAEL
HAENDEL, IDA
HAHN, REYNALDO
HAINOVITZ, ASHER
HAJDU, ANDRÉ
HALÉVY, JACQUES (Francois) FROMENTAL ÉLIE
HALPRIN, ANN
HAMDI, LEVI BEN YESHUAH
HAMMERSTEIN
HARRAN, DON
HASKELL, ARNOLD LIONEL
HASKIL, CLARA
HAST, MARCUS
HAUBENSTOCK-RAMATI, ROMAN
HAUSER, EMIL
HAYDEN, MELISSA
HEIFETZ, JASCHA
HEILLMANN, YITZHAK
HELLER, STEPHEN
HEMAN
HEMSI, ALBERTO
HENLE, MORITZ
HENSCHEL, SIR GEORGE (Isidor Georg)
HERRMANN, BERNARD
HERSCHMAN, MORDECHAI
HERSKOVITS, BELA
HERSTIK, NAPHTALI
HERTZKA, EMIL
HERZ, HENRI (Heinrich)
HERZOG, GEORGE
HESKES, IRENE
HESS, DAME MYRA
HILLER, FERDINAND
HINRICHSEN
HIRSH, NURIT

HIRSHBERG, JEHOASH
HOLDHEIM, THEODOR
HOLLAENDER
HORENSTEIN, JASCHA
HORNBOSTEL, ERICH MORITZ VON
HOROWITZ, VLADIMIR
HUBERMAN, BRONISLAW
HUROK, SOLOMON
IBN ABĪ AL SALT
IDELSOHN, ABRAHAM ZVI
INBAL, ELIAHU
ISSERLIS, STEVEN
ISTOMIN, EUGENE
JACOBI, ERWIN R.
JACOBI, FREDERICK
JACOBI, GEORG
JACOBI, HANOCH (Heinrich)
JACOBS, ARTHUR (David)
JACOBSTHAL, GUSTAV
JADASSOHN, SALOMON
JADLOWKER, HERMANN
JAFFE, ELI
JANOWSKI, MAX
JAPHET, ISRAEL MEYER
JASSINOWSKY, PINCHAS
JOACHIM, JOSEPH
JOCHSBERGER, TZIPORAH
JONAS, EMILE
JUDAH BEN ISAAC
KADMAN, GURIT
KAHN, ERICH ITOR
KAISER, ALOIS
KALIB, SHALOM
KALICHSTEIN, JOSEPH
KALMAN, EMMERICH (Imre)
KARACZEWSKI, HANINA
KAREL, RUDOLF
KARLINER, BARUCH
KARMON, ISRAEL
KARNIOL, ALTER YEHIEL
KATCHEN, JULIUS
KATZ, ISRAEL
KATZ, MINDRU
KATZ, RUTH
KATZ, SHOLOM
KAYE, NORA
KENT, ALLEGRA
KENTNER, LOUIS
KERN, JEROME DAVID
KERTESZ, ISTVAN
KESTENBERG, LEO
KIDD, MICHAEL
KINSKY, GEORG LUDWIG
KIPNIS, ALEXANDER
KIPNIS, MENAHEM
KIRCHNER, LEON
KIRSCHNER, EMANUEL
KIRSTEIN, LINCOLN
KLEMPERER, OTTO
KLETZKI, PAUL

KOGAN, LEONID BORISSOVICH
KOHN, MAIER
KOLISCH, RUDOLF
KOLODIN, IRVING
KOPYTMAN, MARK RUVIMOVICH
KORNGOLD, ERICH WOLFGANG
KORNITZER, LEON
KOSHETZ, NINA
KOSTELANETZ, ANDRE
KOUSSEVITZKY, MOSHE
KOUSSEVITZKY, SERGE
KOWALSKI, MAX
KRAUS, GERTRUD
KRAUS, LILI
KRAUS, MOSHE
KREIN, ALEXANDER ABRAMOVICH
KREISLER, FRITZ
KREMER, ISA
KRIPS, JOSEF
KROSHNER, MIKHAIL YEFIMOVICH
KURTH, ERNEST
KURZ, SELMA
KUWAETI, SALEH
KWARTIN, ZAVEL
LACHMANN, ROBERT
LAKNER, YEHOSHUA
LAMM, PAVEL ALEKSANDROVICH
LANDOWSKA, WANDA
LANG, PEARL
LAPSON, DVORA
LAVRY, MARC
LEAR, EVELYN
LEBERT, SIGMUND
LEEF, YINAM
LEFKOWITZ, DAVID
LEIBOWITZ, RENE
LEICHTENTRITT, HUGO
LEIGH, ADELE
LEINSDORF, ERICH
LEONI, MYER
LERER, JOSHUA
LERER, SHMUEL
LERT, ERNST
LEVI-AGRON, HASIA
LEVI, HERMANN
LEVI, LEO
LEVI, YOEL
LEVINE, JAMES
LEVINSON, ANDRE
LEVI-TANNAI, SARA
LEVITSKY, MISCHA
LEVY
LEVY, LAZARE
LEVY, MARVIN DAVID
LEWANDOWSKI, LOUIS
LEWENTHAL, RAYMOND
LEWITZKY, BELLA
LHEVINNE, JOSEF
LICHINE, DAVID
LIEBERMANN, ROLF

IV. JEWS IN THE WORLD
C. MUSIC & DANCE
BIOGRAPHIES (continued)

LIEBERSON, GODDARD
LIEBLING, ESTELLE
LIFSHITZ, NEHAMAH
LIGETTI, GYORGI
LIPSCHITZ, SOLOMON BEN MOSES
LISSA, ZOFIA
LIST, EMANUEL
LIST, GEORGE
LITINSKI, GENRIKH ILYICH
LIUZZI, FERNANDO
LOCKSPEISER, EDWARD
LOESSER, FRANK
LOEWE, FREDERICK
LOEWENSTEIN-STRASHUNSKY, JOEL DAVID
LONDON, GEORGE
LOURIE, ARTHUR (Vincent)
LOVY, ISRAEL
LOWINSKY, EDWARD
LUBIN, ABRAHAM
LUBOSHUTZ
LUCCA, PAULINE
MAAYANI, AMI
MAAZEL, LORIN
MACHABEY, ARMAND
MAHLER, GUSTAV
MAJOR, ERVIN
MAJOR, JULIUS (Gyula, Jacob)
MALAVSKY, SAMUEL
MALOVANY, JOSEPH
MANDEL, SHELOMOH
MANNES
MANNES, LEOPOLD
MANOR, EHUD
MARKOVA, ALICIA
MARX, ADOLF BERNHARD
MASLOW, SOPHIE
MASSARANO, JACCHINO OR ISACCHINO
MATZENAUER, MARGARETE
MAYER, SIR ROBERT
MAYKAPAR, SAMUIL MOYSEYEVICH
MEDINA, AVIHU
MEDVEDEV, MIKHAIL
MEHTA, ZUBIN
MEISELS, SAUL
MENDEL, ARTHUR
MENDEL, HERMANN
MENDELSON, JACOB BEN-ZION
MENDELSON, SOLOMON
MENDELSSOHN, ARNOLD
MENDELSSOHN, FELIX (Jakob Ludwig Felix)
MENDELSSOHN HENSEL, FANNY CAECILIE
MENKEN, ALAN
MENUHIN, HEFZIBAH
MENUHIN, YEHUDI
MERRILL, ROBERT
MESSERER, ASAF MIKHAILOVICH

METZGER, OTTILIE (Metzger-Latterman)
MEYER, ERNST HERMAN
MEYERBEER, GIACOMO
MILHAUD, DARIUS
MILLER, BEN-ZION
MILLER, MITCH
MILNER, MOSES MICHAEL
MILSTEIN, NATHAN
MINKOWSKI, PINCHAS
MINTZ, SHLOMO
MIRON, ISSACHAR
MIZRAHI, ASHER
MLOTEK, CHANA
MOISEIWITSCH, BENNO
MONTEUX, PIERRE
MORAWETZ, OSCAR
MOROGOWSKI, JACOB SAMUEL
MOSCHELES, IGNAZ
MOSZKOWSKI, MORITZ
MOTTL, FELIX JOSEF
MULLER, BENJAMIN
NACHEZ, TIVADAR
NADEL, ARNO
NAHARIN, OHAD
NARDI, NAHUM
NATHAN, ISAAC
NATRA, SERGIU
NAUMBOURG, SAMUEL
NAVON, ISAAC ELIYAHU
NE'EMAN, YEHOSHUA LEIB
NETTL, PAUL
NEWMAN, ALFRED
NIKOVA, RINA
NOWAKOWSKI, DAVID
NOY, MEIR
NULMAN, MACY
OBADIAH, THE NORMAN PROSELYTE
OCHS, SIEGFRIED
OFFENBACH, ISAAC
OFFENBACH, JACQUES
OISTRAKH, DAVID FEDOROVICH
OLIVERO, BETTY
ORDMAN, JEANETTE
ORENSTEIN, ARBIE
ORGAD, BEN ZION
ORMANDY, EUGENE
OSTFELD, BARBARA
OVED, MARGALIT
OYSHER, MOISHE
PANOV, VALERY
PARTOS, OEDOEN
PASTA, GUIDITTA
PAULY, ROSA
PEERCE, JAN
PELLEG, FRANK
PERAHIA, MURRAY
PERGAMENT, MOSES
PERLMAN, ITZCHAK
PETERS, ROBERTA
PIATIGORSKY, GREGOR

PINCHERLE, MARC
PINCHIK, PIERRE
PISK, PAUL AMADEUS
PLAMENAC, DRAGAN
PLISETSKAYA, MAYA
POLACHEK, SENDER
POLLACK, EGON
POLLAK, ZALMAN
POLLINI, BERNHARD
POPPER, DAVID
PORGES, HEINRICH
POSTOLSKY, SHALOM
PRESSLER, MENAHEM
PREVIN, ANDRE (George)
PRUEWAR, JULIUS
PUTTERMAN, DAVID
QUELER, EVE
RABINOVICH, HAIM BEN ZION
RABINOVICZ, PINCHAS
RADZYNSKI, JAN
RAISA, ROSA
RAMBERT, DAME MARIE
RAN, SHULAMIT
RAPPAPORT, JACOB
RASKIN, JUDITH
RATHAUS, KAROL
RAVINA, MENASHE
RAVITZ, SHELOMO
RAZUMNI, EPHRAIM ZALMAN (Solomon)
REDLICH, HANS FERDINAND
REICH, STEVE
REINER, FRITZ
REISENBERG, NADIA
REIZENSTEIN, FRANZ
REMENYI, EDUARD
RESNIK, REGINA
RÉTI, RUDOLF
RICARDO, DAVID
RIETI, VITTORIO
RINGER, ALEXANDER
RIVLIN, SHELOMO ZALMAN
ROBBINS, JEROME
ROCHBERG, GEORGE
RODAN, MENDI
RODGERS, MARY
RODGERS, RICHARD
RODZINSKY, ARTUR
ROGERS, BERNARD
ROITMAN, DAVID
ROLAND-MANUEL
ROLL, MICHAEL
ROMANOS MELODOS
ROMBERG, SIGMUND
RONLY-RIKLIS, SHALOM
ROSE, ARNOLD JOSEF
ROSE, LEONARD
ROSEN, CHARLES
ROSENBLATT, JOSEF
ROSENFELD, ABRAHAM ISAAC JACOB
ROSENSTOCK, JOSEPH

ROSENTHAL, HAROLD (David)
ROSENTHAL, MANUEL (Emmanuel)
ROSENTHAL, MORIZ (Maurycy)
ROSOWSKY, SOLOMON
ROSS, HERBERT
ROSSI, MADAMA EUROPA DE'
ROSSI, SALAMONE DE
ROTHMUELLER, AARON MARKO
ROZSAVOLGYI, MARK
RUBIN, RUTH
RUBINSTEIN, ANTON GRIGORYEVICH
RUBINSTEIN, ARTUR
RUBINSTEIN, IDA
RUDEL, JULIUS
RUDINOW, MOSHE
RUDOLF, MAX
RUSSELL (Levy), HENRY
SACERDOTE, DAVID
SACHS, CURT
SADAI, YIZHAK
SADIE, STANLEY (John)
SAINT-LEON, ARTHUR MICHEL
SALAMAN
SALMON, KAREL (Karl Salomon)
SALZMAN, PNINA
SAMBURSKY, DANIEL
SAMINSKY, LAZARE
SAMUEL, HAROLD
SANDERLING, KURT
SANDLER, JACOB KOPPEL
SCHACHTER, CARL
SCHAECHTER-GOTTESMAN, BEYLE
SCHALIT, HEINRICH
SCHENKER, HEINRICH
SCHIDLOWSKY, LEON
SCHIFF, ANDRAS
SCHIFRIN, LALO
SCHILLINGER, JOSEPH
SCHINDLER, KURT
SCHLAMME, MARTHA
SCHLESINGER
SCHMIDT, JOSEPH
SCHNABEL, ARTHUR
SCHNEIDER, ALEXANDER
SCHOENBERG, ARNOLD
SCHOENE, LOTTE
SCHORR, BARUCH
SCHORR, FRIEDRICH
SCHREKER, FRANZ
SCHUBERT, LIA
SCHULHOF, MOSHE
SCHULHOFF, JULIUS
SCHULLER, GUNTHER
SCHUMAN, WILLIAM HOWARD
SCHWARTZ, STEPHEN
SCHWARZ, RUDOLF
SECUNDA, SHOLOM
SEGAL, URI
SEIBER, MATYAS GYORGY
SENDREY, ALFRED

IV. JEWS IN THE WORLD
C. MUSIC & DANCE
BIOGRAPHIES (*continued*)

SERKIN, PETER
SERKIN, RUDOLF
SETER, MORDECHAI
SEVITZKY, FABIEN
SHAHAM, GIL
SHALLON, DAVID
SHAPERO, HAROLD
SHARETT, YEHUDAH
SHARLIN, WILLIAM
SHAW, ARTIE
SHELEM, MATTITYAHU
SHEMER, NAOMI
SHERIFF, NOAM
SHESTAPOL, WOLF
SHILOAH, AMNON
SHLONSKY, VARDINA
SHMUELI, HERZL
SHULSINGER, BEZALEL
SIEGMEISTER, ELIE
SILBERMANN, ALPHONS
SILLS, BEVERLY (Belle Silverman)
SINGER, GEORGE
SINGER, JOSEF
SINGER, KURT
SINIGAGLIA, LEONE
SIPRUTINI, EMANUEL
SIROTA, GERSHON
SLATKIN, LEONARD
SLONIMSKY, NICOLAS
SLONIMSKY, SERGEI MIKHAILOVICH
SMOIRA-COHN, MICHAL
SOBOL, MORDECHAI
SOKOLOW, ANNA
SOLOMON
SOLTI, GEORG
SONDHEIM, STEPHEN
SPECTOR, JOHANNA
SPIVACKE, HAROLD
SPIVAK, NISSAN
SPIVAKOVSKY, TOSSY
STARER, ROBERT
STARK, EDWARD
STEIN, ERWIN
STEINBERG, MAXIMILIAN OSSEJEVICH
STEINBERG, WILLIAM
STENN (STEEN), REBECCA
STERN, ISAAC
STERN, JULIUS
STERN, MOSHE
STERNBERG, ERICH-WALTER
STEUERMANN, EDWARD
STOLYARSKI, PETER SOLOMONOVICH
STRAKOSCH, MAURICE
STRANSKY, JOSEF
STRAUS, OSCAR
STRAUSS, JOHANN

STUTSCHEWSKY, JOACHIM
STYNE, JULE
SULITEANU, GISELA
SULZER, SOLOMON
SUSSKIND, WALTER
SZABOLCSI, BENCE
SZELL, GEORGE
SZERMAN, PINCHAS
SZERYNG, HENRYK
SZIGETI, JOSEPH
TAL, JOSEF
TALMON, ZVI
TAMIRIS, HELEN
TANSMAN, ALEXANDER
TARUSKIN, RICHARD
TAUBE, MICHAEL
TAUBE, MOSHE
TAUBE, SAMUEL BARUCH
TAUBER, RICHARD
TAUSIG, KARL
TEMIANKA, HENRI
TERTIS, LIONEL
THALBERG, SIGISMUND
THOMAS, MICHAEL TILSON
TISCHLER, HANS
TOCH, ERNST
TOUREL, JENNIE
TSFASSMAN, ALEXANDER NAUMOVICH
TUCKER, RICHARD
TUGAL, PIERRE
TURECK, ROSALYN
ULLMAN, VIKTOR
UNGAR, BENJAMIN
UNGER, MAX
VALABREGA, CESARE
VARDI, ARIEH
VEINBERG, MOISSEY SAMUILOVICH
VEPRIK, ALEXANDER MOISEYEVITCH
VICOL, ADRIAN
VIGODA, SAMUEL
VINAVER, CHEMJO
VOGEL, WLADIMIR
VOLPE, ARNOLD
WAGHALTER, IGNATZ
WAGNER, RICHARD
WALDMAN, LEIBELE
WALDTEUFEL, EMIL
WALLENSTEIN, ALFRED
WALTER, BRUNO
WASSERZUG (Lomzer), HAYYIM
WEILL, KURT
WEINBERG, JACOB
WEINBERGER, JAROMIR
WEINER, LAZAR
WEINER, LEO
WEINSTOCK, HERBERT
WEINTRAUB, SOLOMON
WEINZWEIG, JOHN
WEISGAL, ABBA JOSEPH
WEISGALL, HUGO

WEISSBERG, JULIA LAZAREVNA

WEISSENBERG, ALEXIS

WEISSER, ALBERT

WEISSER, JOSHUA

WEISSMANN, ADOLF

WELLESZ, EGON JOSEPH

WERNER, ERIC

WERTHEIM, ROSALIE MARIE

WIENER, JEAN

WIENIAWSKI, HENRI

WILENSKY, MOSHE

WILLIAMS, CHARLES

WINTERNITZ, EMANUEL

WITTGENSTEIN, PAUL

WOHLBERG, MOSHE

WOLFF, ALBERT LOUIS

WOLFF, HERMANN

WOLFSOHN, JULIUSZ

WOLFSTHAL, CHUNE

WOLPE, STEFAN

WORMSER, ANDRÉ (Alphonse-Toussaint)

YAMPOLSKY, BERTA

YASSER, JOSEPH

YELLIN-BENTWICH, THELMA

ZALUDKOWSKI, ELIJAH

ZEFIRA, BRACHAH

ZEHAVI, DAVID

ZEIRA, MORDECHAI

ZEMACH, BENJAMIN

ZHITOMIRSKI, ALEXANDER MATVEYEVITCH

ZILBERTS, ZAVEL

ZIMBALIST, EFREM

ZUKERMAN, PINCHAS

ZUKOFSKY, PAUL

ZUR, MENAHEM

D. SCIENCE
Main Surveys
CHEMISTRY

COMPUTER SCIENCE

ENVIRONMENTAL SCIENCES

LIFE SCIENCES

MATHEMATICS

MEDICINE

PHYSICS

PSYCHIATRY

General Entries
AERONAUTICS, AVIATION, AND ASTRONAUTICS

ALCHEMY

NOBEL PRIZES

TECHNOLOGY AND HALAKHAH

1. BIOLOGY
General Entries
GENETIC ANCESTRY, JEWISH

Biographies
ABIR (ABRAMOVITZ), DAVID

ABULAFIA, SAMUEL HA-LEVI

AHARONI, ISRAEL

ALTMAN, SIDNEY

ALTSCHUL, AARON MEYER

ANFINSEN, CHRISTIAN B.

ARNON, DANIEL ISRAEL

ARNON, ISAAC

ARNON, RUTH

ARTOM, CESARE

ASCHERSON, PAUL FRIEDRICH AUGUST

ASCHNER, MANFRED

ASHBEL, DOV

ASIMOV, ISAAC

ASKENASY, EUGEN

ATLAN, HENRI

AUERBACH, LEOPOLD

AVIV, HAIM

AXELROD, JULIUS

BALTIMORE, DAVID

BERG, PAUL

BLOCH, MARCUS (Mordecai) ELIEZER

BODENHEIMER, FREDERICK SIMON

BODMER, SIR WALTER

BOGORAD, LAWRENCE

BRESSLAU, ERNST

CEDAR, CHAIM

COHEN, STANLEY N.

COHEN, YIGAL RAHAMIM

COHN, FERDINAND JULIUS

CHET, ILAN

DUVDEVANI, SHMUEL

EDINGER, TILLY

EIG, ALEXANDER

ENRIQUES, PAOLO

EPHRUSSI, BORIS

ERRERA, LEO

EVENARI, MICHAEL

EZEKIEL, MOSES

FAHN, ABRAHAM

FEINBRUN-DOTHAN, NAOMI

GILBERT, WALTER

GOLDSCHMIDT, RICHARD BENEDICT

GOULD, STEPHEN

GURWITSCH, ALEXANDER GAVRILOVICH

HAAS, FRITZ

HAAS, GEORG

HABERLANDT, GOTTLIEB

HAFFKINE, WALDEMAR MORDECAI

HALEVY, ABRAHAM

HA-REUBENI, EPHRAIM

HORWITZ, H. ROBERT

HYMAN, LIBBIE HENRIETTA

JACOB, FRANCOIS

LEDERBERG, JOSHUA

LURIA, SALVADOR EDWARD

LWOFF, ANDRE MICHEL

MAGNUS, PAUL WILHELM

MARMOREK, ALEXANDER

MENDELSSOHN, HEINRICH

MESELSON, MATTHEW

IV. JEWS IN THE WORLD
D. SCIENCE
1. Biology
BIOGRAPHIES (*continued*)

METCHNIKOFF, ELIE
OPPENHEIMER, HILLEL (Heinz) REINHARD
PINCUS, GREGORY GOODWIN
RAGER, BRACHA
RAYSS, TSCHARNA
REICHERT, ISRAEL
ROTHSCHILD, NATHANIEL MAYER VICTOR, LORD
SACHS, JULIUS
SACHS, LEO
SEMON, RICHARD WOLFGANG
SORAUER, PAUL KARL MORITZ
SPIEGELMAN, SOL
STEINACH, EUGEN
STENT, GUNTHER SIEGMUND
STRASBURGER, EDUARD
VARMUS, HAROLD ELIOT
WAKSMAN, SELMAN ABRAHAM
WALD, GEORGE
WARBURG, OTTO
WIESNER, JULIUS VON
ZENKEVICH, LEV ALEKSANDROVICH
ZILBER, LEV ALEKSANDROVICH
ZOHARY, MICHAEL

2. CHEMISTRY
GENERAL ENTRIES
CHEMICAL CRAFTS AND INDUSTRIES
CHEMISTRY

BIOGRAPHIES
ABEL, EMIL
ASKENASY, PAUL
BACHARACH, ALFRED LOUIS
BAEYER, ADOLF VON
BAMBERGER, EUGEN
BECHHOLD, JACOB HEINRICH
BERGMANN, ERNST DAVID
BERGMANN, FELIX ELIEZER
BERGMANN, MAX
BERL, ERNST
BERNSTEIN, HAROLD JOSEPH
BIKERMAN, JACOB JOSEPH
BIRK, YEHUDITH
BLAU, FRITZ
BLOCH, HERMAN SAMUEL
BLOCH, KONRAD
BLOCH, MOSES RUDOLPH
BOBTELSKY, MORDEKHAI (Max)
BODANSKY, OSCAR
BORSOOK, HENRY
BRAUDE, ERNEST ALEXANDER
BROWN, HERBERT C.
CALVIN, MELVIN
CARO, HEINRICH
CARO, NIKODEM

CHAIN, SIR ERNST BORIS
CHARGAFF, ERWIN
CIECHANOVER, AARON J.
COHEN, ERNST JULIUS
COHEN, JULIUS BEREND
COHEN, SIR PHILIP
COHEN, PHILIP PACY
COHEN, SEYMOUR STANLEY
COHEN, STANLEY
COHN, EDWIN JOSEPH
COHN, LASSAR
COHN, MILDRED
COPISAROW, MAURICE
DEUEL, HANS ERWIN
DISCHE, ZACHARIAS
DJERASSI, CARL
DONATH, EDUARD
DORFMAN, RALPH ISADORE
DREYFUS BROTHERS
DROSDOFF, MATTHEW
DUSHMAN, SAUL
EDELMAN, GERALD MAURICE
EHRLICH, PAUL
ELIEL, ERNEST LUDWIG
EMBDEN, GUSTAV
FAJANS, KASIMIR
FALK, KAUFMAN GEORGE
FARKAS, LADISLAUS (Wilhelm)
FEIGL, FRITZ
FEINGOLD, DAVID SIDNEY
FEUER, HENRY
FISCHER, EDMOND
FISHMAN, WILLLAM HAROLD
FLEISCHER, MICHAEL
FODOR, ANDOR
FOX, SIR JOHN JACOB
FRANK, ALBERT RUDOLPH
FREIDLINA, RAKHIL KHATSKELEVNA
FREUND, MARTIN
FRUMKIN, ALEKSANDR NAUMOVICH
FUNK, CASIMIR
GERHARDT, CHARLES FREDERIC
GINSBURG, DAVID
GLICK, DAVID
GOLDBERG, ALEXANDER
GOLDSCHMIDT, GUIDO
GOLDSCHMIDT, HANS
GOLDSCHMIDT, HEINRICH JACOB
GOLDSTEIN, RICHARD FRANK
GOMBERG, MOSES
GREEN, DAVID EZRA
GREENBERG, DAVID MORRIS
GREENSTEIN, JESSE PHILIP
GRINBERG, ALEKSANDER ABRAMOVICH
GRUEN, ADOLF
GRUENSTEIN, NATHAN
HABER, FRITZ
HALPERN, JACK
HANDLER, PHILIP
HARRIS, MILTON

HASSID, WILLIAM ZEV
HEIDELBERGER, MICHAEL
HEILBRON, SIR IAN MORRIS
HERSHKO, AVRAM
HERZOG, REGINALD OLIVER
HESTRIN, SHLOMO
HEVESY, GEORGE CHARLES DE
HIRSHBERG, YEHUDAH
HOFFMANN, ROALD
JACOBSON, KURT
JACOBSON, PAUL HEINRICH
JELLINEK, KARL
JOLLES, ZVI ENRICO
JORTNER, JOSHUA
KABACHNIK, MARTIN IZRAILOVICH
KALNITSKY, GEORGE
KATZIR, AHARON
KATZIR, EPHRAIM
KAUFMAN, JOYCE JACOBSON
KAZARNOVSKI, ISAAC ABRAMOVICH
KEDEM, ORA
KHARASCH, MORRIS SELIG
KLUG, AARON
KOLTHOFF, IZAAK MAURITS
KORNBERG, ARTHUR
KORNBERG, HANS LEO
KREBS, SIR HANS ADOLF
KROTO, SIR HAROLD W.
LADENBURG, ALBERT
LEVENE, PHOEBUS AARON THEODOR
LEVI, GIORGIO RENATO
LEVI, MARIO GIACOMO
LEVINE, RAPHAEL
LEVINSTEIN, HERBERT
LEVITZKI, ALEXANDER
LEVY, LOUIS EDWARD
LEWKOWITSCH, JULIUS
LIEBEN, ADOLPH
LIEBERMANN, CARL THEODOR
LIPMAN, JACOB GOODALE
LIPMANN, FRITZ ALBERT
LIPPMANN, EDMUND OSKAR VON
LIPPMANN, EDUARD
LOEB, JACQUES
LOEB, MORRIS
LUNGE, GEORG
MARCKWALD, WILLY
MARCUS, RUDOLPH ARTHUR
MECHOULAM, RAPHAEL
MELDOLA, RAPHAEL
MENDEL, LAFAYETTE BENEDICT
MEYER, HANS JOHANNES LEOPOLD
MEYER, RICHARD JOSEPH
MEYER, VICTOR
MEYERHOF, OTTO
MEYERSON, EMILE
MICHAELIS, LEONOR
MOISSAN, HENRI
MOND
MUSHER, SIDNEY

NEUBERG, GUSTAV EMBDEN CARL
NEUBERGER, ALBERT
NIRENBERG, MARSHALL WARREN
OLAH, GEORGE
OPPENHEIMER, CARL
PANETH, FRIEDRICH ADOLF
PARNAS, YAKUB KAROL
PERLZWEIG, WILLIAM ALEXANDRE
PERUTZ, MAX FERDINAND
PINNER, ADOLF
POLANYI, JOHN
POLANYI, MICHAEL
PRINGSHEIM, HANS
PTASHNE, MARK
QUASTEL, JUDAH HIRSCH
RABINOWITCH, EUGENE
RACKER, EFRAIM
RAPHAEL, RALPH ALEXANDER
RAPKINE, LOUIS
RAZIN, AHARON
REICHINSTEIN, DAVID
REICHSTEIN, TADEUS
REIFENBERG, ADOLF
RITTENBERG, DAVID
RODBELL, MARTIN
ROGINSKI, SIMON ZALMANOVICH
RONA, PETER
ROSE, IRWIN
ROSENHEIM, ARTHUR
ROSENHEIM, OTTO
SACKUR, OTTO
SCHIFF, HUGO
SCHMERLING, LOUIS
SCHOENBERG, ALEXANDER JULIUS WILHELM
SCHOENHEIMER, RUDOLPH
SELA, MICHAEL
SHAPIRO, BENJAMIN
SHARON, NATHAN
SHEAR, MURRAY JACOB
SHEDLOVSKY, THEODORE
SILVERMAN, ALEXANDER
SIMON, ERNST
SOBOTKA, HARRY HERMAN
SONDHEIMER, FRANZ
SPIEGEL-ADOLF, MONA
SPIRO, KARL
STEIN, WILLIAM HOWARD
STERN, KURT GUNTER
STIEGLITZ, JULIUS OSCAR
STRAUSS, EDUARD
STROMINGER, JACK
SURE, BARNETT
SYRKIN, YAKOV KOVOVICH
SZWARC, MICHAEL
TALMUD, DAVID L.
TISCHLER, MAX
TOCH, MAXIMILIAN
TRAUBE, ISIDOR
TRAUBE, MORITZ
TRAUBE, WILHELM

IV. JEWS IN THE WORLD
D. SCIENCE

2. Chemistry
BIOGRAPHIES (*continued*)

VOET, ANDRIES
VOGEL, ARTHUR ISRAEL
WALLACH, OTTO
WARBURG, OTTO HEINRICH
WEIGERT, FRITZ
WEINHOUSE, SIDNEY
WEISS, JOSEPH JOSHUA
WERTHEIMER, CHAIM ERNST
WESTHEIMER, FRANK HENRY
WILLNER, ITAMAR
WILLSTAETTER, RICHARD
WINSTEIN, SAUL
WINTERSTEIN, ALFRED
WISE, LOUIS ELSBERG
YONATH, ADA
ZAMENHOF, STEPHEN

3. ENGINEERING (INCL. INVENTORS)
Biographies

ADLER, CHARLES
ARCO, GEORG WILHELM ALEXANDER HANS, GRAF
    VON
BERLINER, EMILE
BLOK, ARTHUR
CARVALLO, JULES
COHEN, MORRIS
DRUCKER, DANIEL CHARLES
FELD, JACOB
FONDILLER, WILLIAM
FREUDENTHAL, ALFRED MARTIN
FROHMAN, DOV
GAUNSE, JOACHIM
GOLDBERG, EMANUEL
GOLDMARK, PETER CARL
GUREVICH, MIKHAIL IOSIFOVICH
HARARI, OVADIAH
HEYMAN, MOSES DAVID
ISAACS, JACOB
JAFFE, LEONARD
JUDA, WALTER
KATZ, ISRAEL
KITSEE, ISADOR
KURREIN, MAX
LAND, EDWIN H.
LEDEEN, HYMAN
LEDERER, JEROME F.
LEES, LESTER
LEEUW, AVRAHAM DE
LIBAI, AVINOAM
LIEBEN, ROBERT VON
LILIENTHAL, OTTO
LIPSKI, ABRAHAM
LITMAN, SAMUEL
LOCKSPEISER, BEN, SIR
MAGINO, MEIR

MARCUS, SIEGFRIED
MICHEL-LEVY, AUGUSTE
MILLMAN, JACOB
NAGIN, HARRY S.
OLLENDORFF, FRANZ
PINKEL, BENJAMIN
RABINOVICH, ISAAK MOSEYEVICH
RAM, MOSHE
REINER, MARKUS
RESNIK, JUDITH
ROM, YOSEF
RUEDENBERG, REINHOLD
SAMOILOVICH, RUDOLPH LAZAREVICH
SCHLESINGER, GEORG
SCHWARZ, DAVID
SERBIN, HYMAN
SHALON, RAHEL
SHAPIRO, ASCHER HERMAN
SHECHTMAN, DAN
SILVERMAN, LESLIE
SILVERSTEIN, ABE
SINGER, JOSEF
SLEPIAN, JOSEPH
SPORN, PHILIP
STRAUSS, BENNO
WEIL, JOSEPH
WEIL, R. ADRIENNE
WIESNER, JEROME BERT
WOLMAN, ABEL
YOUNG, ALEC DAVID
ZARCHIN, ALEXANDER
ZIV, JACOB
ZUCROW, MAURICE JOSEPH

4. GEOLOGY
Biographies

ANCONA, CESARE D
BEN-ABRAHAM, ZVI
BENIOFF, HUGO
BENTOR, JACOB
BERENDT, GOTTLIEB MICHAEL
BLANCKENHORN, MAX
COHEN, EMIL WILHELM
GOLDSCHMIDT, VICTOR
GOLDSCHMIDT, VICTOR MORITZ
LOEWINSON-LESSING, FRANZ YULYEVICH
OPPENHEIM, PAUL LEO
PICARD, LEO
ROSENBUSCH, KARL HARRY FERDINAND
SALOMON-CALVI, WILHELM
SHIFTAN, ZEEV
SUESS, EDUARD
VROMAN, AKIVA

5. MEDICINE & PHYSIOLOGY
General Entries

ANATOMY
ARTIFICIAL INSEMINATION
AUTOPSIES AND DISSECTION
BLINDNESS
BLOODLETTING

GENETIC DISEASES IN JEWS
HERBS, MEDICINAL
HYGIENE
MEDICINE AND THE LAW
SICKNESS
TAY-SACHS DISEASE
TRANSPLANTS

Biographies

ABRAHAM BEN SOLOMON OF SAINT MAXIMIN
ABRAHAM, KARL
ABRAHAMS, ISAAC
ABRAMOWITZ, EMIL
ABT, ISAAC ARTHUR
ACKORD, ELIAS
ADAM, LAJOS (Louis)
ADLER, ALFRED
ADLER, SAUL AARON
ALBU, ISIDOR
ALI IBN SAHL IBN RABBAN AL-TABARI
ALTSCHUL, EMIL
AMATUS LUSITANUS
ANGRIST, ALFRED ALVIN
ARDUT
ASAPH HA-ROFE
ASTRUC, SAUL HA-KOHEN
AXEL, RICHARD
BAKST, NICOLAI (Noah) IGNATYEVICH
BALINT, MICHAEL
BALLIN, SAMUEL JACOB
BAMBERGER, HEINRICH VON
BÁRÁNY, ROBERT
BARNETT, SIR LOUIS EDWARD
BARUK, HENRI
BENACERRAF, BARUJ
BENCHETRIT, AARON
BENDER, MORRIS BORIS
BENEDIKT, MORITZ
BENEVENUTUS GRAPHEUS HIEROSOLYMITANUS
BENZER, SEYMOUR
BERENBLUM, ISAAC
BERNHEIM, HIPPOLYTE
BERNSTEIN, JULIUS
BERNSTEIN, NATHAN OSIPOVICH
BESREDKA, ALEXANDER
BESSELS, EMIL
BILLROTH, THEODOR
BLOCH, IWAN
BLUMBERG, BARUCH SAMUEL
BODIAN, DAVID
BRENNER, SYDNEY
BREUER, JOSEPH
BROWN, MICHAEL STUART
BUCKY, GUSTAV
BUERGER, LEO
CALAHORA
CANNSTADT, KARL FRIEDRICH
COHEN, ELIZABETH D. A.
COHEN, HARRY
COHEN, HENRY BARON

COHNHEIM, JULIUS
CORI, GERTY THERESA
CYON, ELIE DE
DAMESHEK, WILLIAM
DAVIDOFF, LEO MAX
DAVIDSOHN, ISRAEL
DE LEE, JOSEPH B.
DE VRIES, ANDRE
DEUTSCH, FELIX
DEUTSCH, HELENE
DIAMOND, LOUIS KLEIN
DONNOLO, SHABBETAI
DORON, HAIM
DOSTROVSKY, ARYEH
DRESSLER, WILLIAM
EDINGER, LUDWIG
EINHORN, MAX
EINHORN, MOSES
EISSLER, KURT R.
EITINGER, LEO S.
EITINGON, MAX
ELDAR, REUVEN
ELIAKIM, MARCEL
ELIJAH BEN SHABBETAI BEER
ELION, GERTRUDE BELL
ERIKSON, ERIK HOMBERGER
ERLANGER, JOSEPH
ERLIK, DAVID
FALAQUERA, NATHAN BEN JOEL
FARAJ BEN SOLOMON (Salim) DA AGRIGENTO
FEDERN, PAUL
FEIGENBAUM, ARYEH
FENICHEL, OTTO
FERENCZI, SÁNDOR
FINKELSTEIN, HEINRICH
FISHBEIN, MORRIS
FISHBERG, MAURICE
FLORETA CA NOGA OF ARAGON
FOLKMAN, JUDAH
FRANKENTHAL, KATE
FRANKL, VIKTOR E.
FRANZBLAU, ABRAHAM NORMAN
FREUD, ANNA
FREUD, SIGMUND
FRIEDEMANN, ULRICH
FRIEDENWALD
FRIEDLANDER, KATE
FRIEND, CHARLOTTE
FRIGEIS, LAZARO DE
FROEHLICH, ALFRED
FROLKIS, VLADIMIR VENIAMIOVICH
FROMM, ERICH
FROMM-REICHMANN, FRIEDA
FURCHGOTT, ROBERT F.
GARLOCK, JOHN HENRY
GASSER, HERBERT SPENCER
GILMAN, ALFRED G.
GOLD, HENRY RAPHAEL
GOLD, PHILIP
GOLDBERGER, JOSEPH

IV. JEWS IN THE WORLD
D. SCIENCE
5. Medicine & Physiology
BIOGRAPHIES (*continued*)

GOLDBLUM, NATAN
GOLDSTEIN, JOSEPH LEONARD
GOLDSTEIN, KURT
GOTTLIEB, BERNHARD
GREENACRE, PHYLLIS
GREENGARD, PAUL
GRINKER, ROY RICHARD SR.
GROSSMAN, MORTON IRVING
GRUBY, DAVID
GUMPERT, MARTIN
GUTMAN, ALEXANDER B.
GUTTMACHER, ALAN F.
GUTTMANN, SIR LUDWIG
HAJEK, MARKUS
HALBERSTAEDTER, LUDWIG
HALPERN, LIPMAN
HANNOVER, ADOLPH
HART, ERNEST ABRAHAM
HART, JOEL
HARTMANN, HEINZ
HAVA OF MANOSQUE
HAYS, ISAAC
HEIDENHAIN, RUDOLF
HELPERN, MILTON
HENLE, JACOB
HESTRIN-LERNER, SARAH
HIRSCH, AUGUST
HIRSCH, RACHEL
HIRSCHBERG, JULIUS
HIRSCHFELD, ISADOR
HIRSCHFELD, MAGNUS
HIRSCHLER, IGNAC
HIRSZFELD, LUDWIK
HITSCHMANN, EDWARD
HOFF, HANS
HOFFER, WILLI
HOLLANDER, FRANKLIN
HORWITZ, PHINEAS JONATHAN
HYDE, IDA HENRIETTA
IBN BIKLĀRISH, JUNAS (Jonah) BEN ISAAC
ISAAC BEN TODROS
JACOBI, ABRAHAM
JACOBSON, LUDVIG LEVIN
JADASSOHN, JOSEF
JANOWITZ, HENRY D.
KAGAN, HELENA
KANDEL, ERIC R.
KANNER, LEO
KANTROWITZ, ADRIAN
KAPOSI, MORITZ
KARDINER, ABRAM
KARPLUS, HEINRICH
KATZ, SIR BERNARD
KISCH, BRUNO ZECHARIAS
KLEIN, GEORGE

KLEIN, MELANIE REIZES
KLEMPERER, PAUL
KLIGLER, ISRAEL JACOB
KLINE, NATHAN S.
KOCH, ADELHEID LUCY
KOLLER, CARL
KOPLIK, HENRY
KOREFF, DAVID FERDINAND
KORINE, EZRA
KRIM, MATHILDE
KRISTELLER, SAMUEL
KRONECKER, HUGO
KUBIE, LAWRENCE
LACHMANN, SIR PETER JULIUS
LANDAU, LEOPOLD
LANDSTEINER, KARL
LANGER, ROBERT
LASSAR, OSCAR
LEIBOWITZ, JOSHUA O.
LEVI, GIUSEPPE
LEVI-MONTALCINI, RITA
LEVINE, PHILIP
LEVINSON, ABRAHAM
LEWI, MAURICE J.
LEWIS, SIR AUBREY JULIAN
LOEB, LEO
LOEWENSTEIN, RUDOLPH MAURICE
LOEWI, OTTO
MACHT, DAVID
MAGNUS, RUDOLPH
MAHLER, MARGARET
MAIMONIDES, MOSES
MALZBERG, BENJAMIN
MA'OR KATAN
MARCUSE, MOSES
MASIE, AARON MEIR
MASSERMAN, JULES HYMAN
MASTER, ARTHUR M.
MER, GIDEON
MEYERHOF, MAX
MICHAELSON, ISAAC CHESAR
MILLER, EMANUEL
MILLER, LOUIS
MILSTEIN, CESAR
MINKOWSKI, EUGENE
MIROWSKI, MICHEL
MORGENTALER, HENRY
MULLER, HERMAN JOSEPH
MUNK, HERMANN
NASSY, DAVID DE ISAAC COHEN
NATHANS, DANIEL
NEUFELD, HENRY
NOSSAL, SIR GUSTAV
NUNBERG, HERMAN
OLITZKI, ARYEH LEO
OPPENHEIM, HERMANN
ORENSTEIN, ALEXANDER JEREMIAH
PADEH, BARUCH
PAGEL, JULIUS LEOPOLD
PAPO, IZIDOR JOSEF

PENN, JACK
PERLSTEIN, MEYER A.
PICK, ALOIS
PICK, ERNST PETER
PLAUT, HUGO CARL
POLAK, JACOB EDUARD
POLITZER, ADAM
PRESSMAN, DAVID
PREUSS, JULIUS
PRUSINER, STANLEY B.
PRYWES, MOSHE
RACHMILEWITZ, MOSHE
RADO, SANDOR
RAHAMIMOFF, RAMI
RAHBAR, SAMUEL
RAMOT, BRACHA
RANK, OTTO
RAPAPORT, DAVID
RAPPAPORT, HENRY
REDLICH, FREDERICK C.
REIK, THEODOR
REMAK
REVEL, MICHEL
RIGLER, LEO GEORGE
ROMBERG, MORITZ HEINRICH
ROSEN, FRED
ROSEN, SAMUEL
ROSENHEIM, MAX (Leonard), BARON
ROTH, SIR MARTIN
ROTHSCHILD, FRIEDRICH SALOMON
SABIN, ALBERT BRUCE
SACHS, BERNARD
SAKEL, MANFRED JOSHUA
SALAMAN, REDCLIFFE NATHAN
SALITERNIK, ZVI
SALK, JONAS EDWARD
SALOMONSEN, CARL JULIUS
SANDGROUND, JACK HENRY
SCHALLY, ANDREW V.
SCHICK, BELA
SCHILDER, PAUL FERDINAND
SCHRIRE, VELVA
SCIALOM, DAVID DARIO
SELDIN, HARRY M.
SEMON, SIR FELIX
SENATOR, HERMANN
SEQUEYRA, JOHN DE
SHEBA, CHAIM
SIMON, PIERRE
SPITZ, RENE A.
STARKENSTEIN, EMIL
STEG, ADOLPHE
STEIN, RICHARD
STEIN, YEHEZKIEL
STEINBERG, AVRAHAM
STEINBERG, MARTIN R.
STEKEL, WILHELM
STENGEL, ERWIN
STERN, ARTHUR C.
STERN, ERICH

STERN, LINA SOLOMONOVNA
STILLING, BENEDICT
STRAUS, RAHEL
SZASZ, THOMAS STEPHEN
TANDLER, JULIUS
TARNOPOLSKY, SAMUEL
TAUSK, VIKTOR
TELLER, ISSACHAR BAER
TEMIN, HOWARD MARTIN
TENDLER, MOSES D.
TENENBAUM, JOSEPH L.
TOBIAS, PHILLIP VALLENTINE
TRAMER, MORITZ
TRAUBE, LUDWIG
UNNA, PAUL GERSON
VALENTIN, GABRIEL GUSTAV
VAN DER HOEDEN, JACOB
VANE, SIR JOHN R.
VORONOFF, SERGE
WALLACH, MOSHE (Moritz)
WASSERMANN, AUGUST VON
WATTERS, LEON LAIZER
WECHSLER, ISRAEL
WEIDNER, PAULUS
WEIGERT, CARL
WEISENBURG, THEODORE H.
WIDAL, FERNAND
WIENER, ALEXANDER S.
WINNIK, HENRY ZVI
WINSTON, ROBERT, BARON
WINTROBE, MAXWELL MYER
WOLBERG, LEWIS ROBERT
WOLF, ABNER
WOLFF, CHARLOTTE
WOOLF, MOSHE
WORMS, ASHER ANSHEL
YALOW, ROSALYN SUSSMAN
YUDKIN, JOHN
ZACUTUS LUSITANUS
ZAIZOV, RINA
ZIFF, MORRIS
ZILBOORG, GREGORY
ZIMMERMAN, HARRY M.
ZONDEK
ZUCKERKANDL, EMIL
ZUCKERMAN, SOLLY, LORD

6. PHYSICS & MATHEMATICS (INCL. ASTRONOMY & METEOROLOGY)
BIOGRAPHIES
ABELMANN, ILYA SOLOMOVITCH
ABRAHAM, MAX
ABRAHAM BAR HIYYA
AGMON, SHMUEL
AHARONOV, YAKIR
ALFEROV, ZHOREZ I.
AMIRA, BINYAMIN
AMITSUR, SAMSON ABRAHAM
ANDRADE, EDWARD NEVILLE DA COSTA
ARONS, LEO

IV. JEWS IN THE WORLD

D. SCIENCE

6. Physics & Mathematics (incl. Astronomy & Meteorology)

BIOGRAPHIES (continued)

ATLAS, DAVID
AYRTON, HERTHA
BACHER, ROBERT FOX
BAGINSKY, ADOLF ARON
BAUER, SIMON HARVEY
BEER, WILHELM
BEMPORAD, AZEGLIO
BERNAL, JOHN DESMOND
BERNSTEIN, JOSEPH
BERSON, ARTHUR JOSEPH STANISLAV
BESICOVITCH, ABRAM SAMOILOVITCH
BETHE, HANS ALBRECHT
BLOCH, FELIX
BOHM, DAVID
BOHR, NIELS HENRIK DAVID
BONDI, SIR HERMANN
BONFILS, IMMANUEL BEN JACOB
BONJORN, BONET DAVI(D)
BORN, MAX
BOROWITZ, SIDNEY
BREDIG, GEORGE
BRODETSKY, SELIG
BROWN, HAROLD
CANTOR, MORITZ BENEDICT
CHARPAK, GEORGES
COHEN TANNOUDJI, CLAUDE
COHEN, PAUL JOSEPH
COHN, BERTHOLD
COHN, FRITZ
COHN, TOBIAS BEN MOSES
CONRAD, VICTOR
COOPER, LEON N.
COURANT, RICHARD
CREIZENACH, MICHAEL
CROHN, BURRILL BERNARD
DEMBER, HARRY L.
DE-SHALIT, AMOS
DESSAU, BERNARDO
DESSAUER, FRIEDRICH
DICKSTEIN, SAMUEL
DOMNINUS OF LARISSA
DOSTROVSKY, ISRAEL
DVORETSKY, ARYEH
EHRENFEST, PAUL
EINSTEIN, ALBERT
EISENSTEIN, FERDINAND GOTTHOLD
EPSTEIN, PAUL SOPHUS
ESTERMANN, IMMANUEL
FEJER, LEOPOLD
FEKETE, MICHAEL
FEYNMAN, RICHARD PHILLIPS
FINLAY-FREUNDLICH, ERWIN
FINNISTON, SIR HAROLD MONTAGUE (Monty)
FRAENKEL, ABRAHAM ADOLF
FRANCK, JAMES

FRANK, ILJA MIKHAILOVICH
FRANK, PHILIPP
FRANKEL, HEINRICH WALTER
FRANKLIN, ROSALIND ELSIE
FRENKEL, JACOB ILICH
FRIEDMAN, JEROME ISAAC
FRISCH, OTTO ROBERT
FROHLICH, HERBERT
FUBINI, GUIDO
FURSTENBERG, HILLEL (Harry)
GABOR, DENNIS
GANS, DAVID BEN SOLOMON
GELFAND, IZRAIL MOISEVICH
GELFOND, ALEKSANDR OSIPOVICH
GELL-MANN, MURRAY
GINSBURG, JEKUTHIEL
GINZBURG, VITALY LAZAREVICH
GLASER, DONALD ARTHUR
GLASHOW, SHELDON LEE
GLAUBER, ROY J.
GOLDSCHMIDT, HERMANN
GOLDSTEIN, EUGEN
GOLDSTEIN, SIDNEY
GROSS, DAVID J.
GUTENBERG, BENO
HADAMARD, JACQUES SALOMON
HAIMOVICI, MENDEL
HANANI, HAIM
HANNOVER, RAPHAEL LEVI
HARARI, HAYYIM
HAREL, DAVID
HASSAN IBN (Mar) HASSAN
HAUPTMAN, HERBERT A.
HAURWITZ, BERNHARD
HAUSDORFF, FELIX (Paul Mongre)
HECHT, SELIG
HEEGER, ALAN J.
HENSEL, KURT
HERTZ, GUSTAV
HOFSTADTER, ROBERT
HURWITZ, ADOLF
IBN SAʿĪD, ISAAC
INFELD, LEOPOLD
ISRAEL, EDWARD
ISRAELI, ISAAC BEN JOSEPH
JACOBI, KARL GUSTAV JACOB
JACOBI, MORITZ (Moses) HERMANN
JAMMER, MAX
JAMMER, MOSHE
JOFFE, ABRAHAM FEODOROVICH
JOSEPHSON, BRIAN DAVID
KANTOROVICH, LEONID
KANTROWITZ, ARTHUR
KAPLAN, JOSEPH
KARLE, JEROME
KARMAN, THEODORE VON
KOGAN, ABRAHAM
KOHN, WALTER
KORN, ARTHUR
KRONECKER, LEOPOLD

LANDAU, EDMUND
LANDAU, LEV DAVIDOVICH
LEDERMAN, LEON MAX
LEE, DAVID M.
LEFSCHETZ, SOLOMON
LESS, EMIL
LEVI-CIVITA, TULLIO
LEVITSKY, JACOB
LEVY, HYMAN
LEVY, LUCIEN
LICHTENFELD, GABRIEL JUDAH
LIFSON, SHNEIOR
LIPKIN, YOM TOV LIPMAN
LIPPMANN, GABRIEL
LIPSCHITZ, RUDOLF OTTO SIGISMUND
LOEW, MORITZ
LOEWE, FRITZ PHILIPP
LOEWY, MAURICE
LONDON, FRITZ
LOW (Lev), WILLIAM ZE'EV
MACHTA, LESTER
MAGNUS, HEINRICH GUSTAV
MANDELBROT, BENOIT
MANDELSHTAM, LEONID ISAAKOVICH
MARGULES, MAX
MĀSHĀ'ALLAH B. ATHAN
MEITNER, LISE
MENDELSSOHN, KURT ALFRED GEORG
MICHELSON, ALBERT ABRAHAM
MINKOWSKI, HERMANN
MORDELL, LOUIS JOEL
MOTTELSON, BENJAMIN R.
NAMIAS, JEROME
NE'EMAN, YUVAL
NEUGEBAUER, OTTO
NEUMANN, JOHANN (Johnny) LUDWIG VON
NOETHER
OPPENHEIMER, J. ROBERT
ORNSTEIN, LEONARD SALOMON
OSHEROFF, DOUGLAS DEAN
PAULI, WOLFGANG
PEIERLS, SIR RUDOLF ERNST
PEKERIS, CHAIM LEIB
PENZIAS, ARNO ALLAN
PEPPER, JOSEPH
PERL, MARTIN
PIROGOV, NIKOLAI
POLITZER, H. DAVID
PONTECORVO, BRUNO
PRAGER, RICHARD
PRESS, FRANK
PRIGOGINE, ILYA
RABI, ISIDOR ISAAC
RABIN, MICHAEL OSER
RACAH, GIULIO (Yoel)
REINES, FREDERICK
RICHTER, BURTON
ROSEN, MOSHE
ROSENHEAD, LOUIS
ROTBLAT, SIR JOSEPH

ROTENBERG, MATTIE
ROTH, KLAUS FRIEDRICH
RUBENSON, ROBERT
RUBIN, MORTON JOSEPH
SAGAN, CARL EDWARD
SAMBURSKY, SAMUEL
SCHAWLOW, ARTHUR L.
SCHLESINGER, FRANK
SCHUR, ISSAI (Isaiah)
SCHUSTER, SIR ARTHUR
SCHWARTZ, LAURENT
SCHWARTZ, MELVIN
SCHWARZSCHILD, KARL
SCHWINGER, JULIAN SEYMOUR
SEGRÈ, BENIAMINO
SEGRÈ, CORRADO
SEGRÈ, EMILIO GINO
SHELAH, SAHARON
SIMON, SIR FRANCIS EUGENE
STEINBERGER, JACK
STEINHAUS, HUGO DYONIZY
STERN, ABRAHAM JACOB
STERN, OTTO
SYLVESTER, JAMES JOSEPH
SZILARD, LEO
TABOR, DAVID
TABOR, HARRY ZVI
TALMI, IGAL
TAMM, IGOR YEVGENYEVICH
TARSKI, ALFRED
TELLER, EDWARD
TEPPER, MORRIS
THRASYLLUS OF MENDES
TOEPLITZ, OTTO
TOLANSKY, SAMUEL
ULAM, STANISLAW MARCIN
VEKSLER, VLADIMIR
WEIL, ANDRE
WEINBERG, STEVEN
WEISSKOPF, VICTOR F.
WEXLER, HARRY
WHITE, ROBERT MAYER
WIENER, NORBERT
WIGNER, EUGENE P.
WILCHEK, MEIR
ZACHARIAS, JERROLD REINACH
ZACUTO, ABRAHAM BEN SAMUEL
ZARISKI, OSCAR
ZELDOVICH, YAKOV BORISOVICH

7. OTHER
Biographies
AVIDOV, ZVI
BONDI, ARON
COSTA, EMANUEL MENDES DA
DEMALACH, YOEL
EFRAT, YAACOV
GRUNBAUM, ADOLF
HALPERIN, HAIM
LOWDERMILK, WALTER CLAY

IV. JEWS IN THE WORLD
D. SCIENCE
7. Other
BIOGRAPHIES (*continued*)

NEUBURGER, MAX
PNEULI, AMIR
SINGER, CHARLES JOSEPH
SLONIMSKI, HAYYIM SELIG
SOSKIN, SELIG EUGEN
STOLLER, SAMUEL
SUSSMAN, ABRAHAM
WAHL, ISAAK
WINIK, MEIR

V. WOMEN
MAIN SURVEYS
WOMAN

GENERAL ENTRIES
AGGADAH
ANUSIM
ASCETICISM
BANKING AND BANKERS
BARRENNESS AND FERTILITY
BIRTH
COOKBOOKS
DOMESTIC PEACE
DOMESTIC VIOLENCE
FEMINISM
HALUKKAH
HASIDISM
HISTORIANS
HISTORIOGRAPHY
LESBIANISM
LETTERS AND LETTER-WRITERS
ORPHAN, ORPHANAGE
PROSTITUTION
PSYCHOLOGY
REBBETZIN
SALONS
SHEKHINAH
SHTETL
SOCIALISM
SOCIOLOGY
STUDY
THEOLOGY

WOMEN IN BIBLE
ABIGAIL
ABISHAG THE SHUNAMMITE
ASENATH
ATHALIAH
BATH-SHEBA
BILHAH
DEBORAH
DELILAH
ELISHEBA

EN-DOR, WITCH OF
ESTHER
EVE
HAGAR
HANNAH
HULDAH
JAEL
JEZEBEL
JOCHEBED
KETURAH
LEAH
MAACAH
MERAB
MICHAL
MIRIAM
NAAMAH
NAOMI
PENINNAH
RACHEL
RAHAB
REBEKAH
RIZPAH
SARAH
SHIPHRAH AND PUAH
SHULAMMITE
TAMAR
VASHTI
ZILPAH
ZIPPORAH

WOMEN IN TALMUD AND SECOND TEMPLE PERIOD
BERURYAH
CLEOPATRA OF JERUSALEM
CYPROS
DORIS
HANNAH AND HER SEVEN SONS
HERODIAS
HOMA
HOVAH
IMMA SHALOM
JUDITH
MARTHA
SALOME
SALOME ALEXANDRA
YALTA

WOMEN IN JEWISH RITUAL
AUFRUFEN
BAR MITZVAH, BAT MITZVAH
BLOOD
CANDLES
DIETARY LAWS
ESHET HAYIL
FESTIVALS
FIRZOGERIN
HAGGADAH, PASSOVER
HALLAH
HEAD, COVERING OF THE
KADDISH

NEW MOON
NIDDAH
PASSSOVER
PRAYER
SEMIKHAH
SHEHITAH
SYNAGOGUE
TKHINES

ORGANIZATIONS
AMIT: MIZRACHI WOMEN'S ORGANIZATION OF AMERICA
BNAI BRITH WOMEN
EMMA LAZARUS FEDERATION OF JEWISH WOMEN'S CLUBS
EMUNAH
HADASSAH, THE WOMENS ZIONIST ORGANIZATION OF
   AMERICA
HEVRAH, HAVURAH
INTERNATIONAL COUNCIL OF JEWISH WOMEN
INTERNATIONAL LADIES GARMENT WORKERS UNION
JUEDISCHER FRAUENBUND
NATIONAL COUNCIL OF JEWISH WOMEN
NATIONAL FEDERATION OF TEMPLE SISTERHOODS
WIZO
WOMEN'S LEAGUE FOR CONSERVATIVE JUDAISM

PUBLICATIONS
AMERICAN JEWESS
DIE DEBORAH
JEWISH WOMAN, THE
LILITH

BIOGRAPHIES
Academic Life
ABRAMOWICZ, DINA
ADLERBLUM, NIMA
ARENDT, HANNAH
ASKOWITH, DORA
BADINTER, ELIZABETH
BASKIN, JUDITH
BAUMGARTEL, ELISE J.
BENEDEK, THERESE F.
BERNARD, JESSIE
BIEBER, MARGARETE
BILDERSEE, ADELE
BOAS, HENRIETTE
BONDY, RUTH
BUHLER, CHARLOTTE
BUNZEL, RUTH LEAH
BUTLER, JUDITH
CALIN, VERA
CARLEBACH, ELISHEVA
CHALIER, CATHERINE
CHATZKELS, HELENE
CHESLER, PHYLLIS
COHEN, NAOMI W.
COHEN, RUTH LOUISA
COSER, ROSE LAUB
DALVEN, RACHEL
DAVIS, NATALIE ZEMON
DAWIDOWICZ, LUCY

DENMARK, FLORENCE LEVIN
DINER, HASIA
DONIGER, WENDY
DOTHAN, TRUDE
ENGELMANN, SUSANNE CHARLOTTE
EPSTEIN, CLAIRE
ERLICH, VERA STEIN
FRYMER-KENSKY, TIKVA
GAVISON, RUTH
GILLIGAN, CAROL
GOLDMAN, HETTY
GORNICK, VIVIAN
GUGGENHEIM-GRUENBERG, FLORENCE
GUTMANN, AMY
HEILBRUN, CAROLYN G.
HELLMAN, CLARISSE DORIS
HERSCH, JEANNE
HIMMELFARB, GERTRUDE
HIMMELWEIT, HILDEGARD
HYMAN, PAULA E.
INSDORF, ANNETTE
JACOBSON, ANNA
JAHODA, MARIE
JOSEPH, NORMA BAUMEL
KOMAROVSKY, MIRRA
KOTARBINSKA, JANINA
KRIEGEL, ANNIE
LANDES, RUTH
LAPIDOT, RUTH
LEIBOWITZ, NEHAMA
LERNER, GERDA
LEVIN, NORA
MANHEIM, BILHAH
MARCUS, RUTH BARCAN
MARKEL-MOSESSOHN, MIRIAM
MEDNICK, MARTHA TAMARA SCHUCH
MEYER, ANNIE NATHAN
MYERHOFF, BARBARA
NAUMBURG, MARGARET
NEUGARTEN, BERNICE L.
NOVITCH, MIRIAM
PEIXOTTO, JESSICA BLANCHE
PORZEKANSKI, TERESA
POWDERMAKER, HORTENSE
PRINGLE, MIA
RAJAK, TESSA
RICHTER, ELISE
ROBISON, SOPHIA
RODIN, JUDITH
RUTLAND, SUZANNE
SALOMON, ALICE
SCHWARTZ, ANNA JACOBSON
SHAHAR, SHULAMIT
SHUVAL, JUDITH
STEIN, EDITH
STEIN, JANICE
STERN-TAEUBLER, SELMA
TEC, NECHAMA
TOBACH, ETHEL
TUCHMAN, BARBARA WERTHEIM

V. WOMEN

BIOGRAPHIES

Academic Life (*continued*)

WEIL, SIMONE
WEINBERG, GLADYS DAVIDSON
WEISS-ROSMARIN, TRUDE
WIERUSZOWSKI, HELENE
WIEVIORKA, ANNETTE
WISSE, RUTH
WOLFSON, THERESA
WUNDERLICH, FRIEDA
YEFET, SARAH

Art

AGREST, DIANA
AIZENBERG, NINA
AMISHAI-MAISELS, ZIVA
ARBUS, DIANE NEMEROV
ARNOLD, EVE
BERNSTEIN, THERESA
BING, ILSE
BLAU, TINA
BOURKE-WHITE, MARGARET
CAISERMAN-ROTH, GHITTA
CALLE, SOPHIE
CASSAB, JUDY
CENTERSZSWER, STANISLAWA
CHICAGO, JUDY
COHEN, ELISHEVA
COSTA, CATHERINE DA
DAVIDSON, JO
DELAUNAY-TERK, SONIA
DICKER-BRANDEIS, FREDERIKE
EIZENBERG, JULIE
FRANKENTHALER, HELEN
FRENKEL, VERA
FREUND, GISELE
GAD, DEVORAH
GIKOW, RUTH
GILBERT, INA
GLUCK, HANNAH
GOLDIN, NAN
GRUNDIG, LEA AND HANS
HARKAVY, MINNA
JACOBI, LOTTE
KOENIG, GHISHA
KRUGER, BARBARA
LAMBERT, PHYLLIS
LEIBOVITZ, ANNIE
LEVITT, HELENE
LISHANSKY, BATYA
MARGOULIES, BERTHA
MARK, MARY ELLEN
MUTER (Mutermilch), MELA
NEVELSON, LOUISE
NIKEL, LEA
ORLOFF, CHANA
OSTROWER, FEYGA
PLACHY, SYLVIA

RIE, DAME LUCIE
RINGL & PIT (Stern, Grete; Rosenberg Auerbach, Ellen)
ROTHSTEIN, IRMA
RUBIN, GAIL
SAFDIE, SYLVIA
SALOMON, CHARLOTTE
SINGER, YVONNE
SONNABEND, YOLANDA
SPERO, NANCY
STERN, IRMA
STERNE, HEDDA
SZALIT-MARCUS, RACHEL
TAGGER, SIONA
TEWI, THEA
TICHO, ANNA
ZVIA

Literature

ABECASSIS, ELIETTE
ADAMS, HANNAH
ADLER, RENATA
AGUILAR, GRACE
AICHINGER, ILSE
ALIGER, MARGARITA YOSIFOVNA
ALMOG, RUTH
AMIR, ANDA
ANTIN, MARY
ASCARELLI, DEBORAH
AUERBAKH, ROKHL
AUSLAENDER, ROSE
AVIGUR-ROTEM, GABRIELA
BANUS, MARIA
BARON, DEVORAH
BASMAN BEN-HAYIM, RIVKE
BAT-MIRIAM, YOKHEVED
BAUM, VICKI
BEJERANO, MAYA
BEN-YEHUDA, HEMDAH
BEN YEHUDA, NETIVA
BERGER, LILY
BERGSTEIN, FANIA
BOSCO, MONIQUE
BRONER, ESTHER M.
BROOKNER, ANITA
BRUGGEN, CARRY VAN
CALISHER, HORTENSE
CALOF, RACHEL
CASSIAN, NINA
CASTEL-BLOOM, ORLY
CHAGALL, BELLA ROSENFELD
CHARLES, GERDA
CIXOUS, HELENE
COHEN, ROSE GOLLUP
COHN, CILLA CYPORA
CORREA, ISABEL REBECCA DE
DAVENPORT, MARCIA
DEUTSCH, BABBETTE
DOMIN, HILDE
DROPKIN, CELIA
DUBNOW-ERLICH, SOPHIA

ELISHEVA

ELKAN, SOPHIE

ENRIQUEZ, ISABEL

EPHRON, NORA

EYTAN, RACHEL

FALK, MARCIA

FEINSTEIN, ELAINE

FERBER, EDNA

FEYGENBERG, RAKHEL

FOA, ESTHER EUGENIE REBECCA

FRANKEL, NAOMI

FRANKEN, ROSE

FRANKS, BILHAH ABIGAIL LEVY

FREHA BAT AVRAHAM OF MOROCCO

FUTORANSKY, LUISA

GAMORAN, MAMIE

GERSHON, KAREN

GINSBURG, EVGENIA SEMIONOVNA

GINZBURG, NATALIA

GLUCK, LOUISE

GLUECKEL OF HAMELN

GOLDBERG, LEA

GOLDSTEIN, REBECCA

GOLL, CLAIRE

GORDIMER, NADINE

GORSHMAN, SHIRA

GORSKA, HALINA

GREENBERG, JOANNE

GREENBLATT, ALIZA

GUR, BATYA

GURFEIN, RIVKA

GURIAN, SORANA

HABAS, BRACHA

HAJNAL, ANNA

HAREVEN, SHULAMIT

HARRY, MYRIAM

HELLMAN, LILLIAN FLORENCE

HENDEL, YEHUDIT

HENRY, EMMA

HERTZVELD-HIJMANS, ESTELLA

HOBSON, LAURA Z.

HONIGMANN, BARBARA

HURST, FANNIE

INBER, VERA MIKHAILOVNA

ISAACS, SUSAN

JACOB, NAOMI ELLINGTON

JAFFE, RONA

JELINEK, ELFRIEDE

JHABVALA, RUTH PRAWER

JONG, ERICA

JUN-BRODA, INA

KAHANA-CARMON, AMALIA

KALEKO, MASHA

KALMAN, MAIRA

KAPLAN, JOHANNA

KARMEL, ILONA

KATZIR, JEHUDIT

KAUFMAN, BEL

KELLERMAN, FAYE

KLEPFISZ, IRENA

KOLMAR, GERTRUD

KORN, RACHEL HARING

KRANTZ, JUDITH

KROOK, DOROTHEA

LANGFUS, ANNA

LAPID, SHULAMIT

LASKER-SCHUELER, ELSE

LAZARUS, EMMA

LAZARUS, NAHIDA RUTH

LEE, MALKE

LEVERSON, ADA

LEVERTOV, DENISE

LEVINSON, OLGA

LEVI-PEROTTI, GIUSTINA

LEVY, AMY

LEWALD, FANNY

LIEBRECHT, SAVYON

LISPECTOR, CLARICE

LOCKER, MALKE

MANDELSHTAM, NADEZHDA YAKOVLEVNA

MARGOLIN, ANNA

MATALON, RONIT

MAYNARD, FREDELLE BRUSER

MAZE, IDA

MERECINA OF GERONA

MICHAELS, ANNE

MILLIN, SARAH GERTRUDE

MINCO, MARGA

MISHOL, AGI

MOISE, PENINA

MOLODOWSKY, KADIA

MORPURGO, RACHEL

MUÑIZ-HUBERMAN, ANGELINA

NAJMAN, JULIJA

NEMIROWSKY, IRENE

OLSEN, TILLIE

ORZESKOWA (Orzesko), ELIZA

OSTRIKER, ALICIA SUSKIN

OZICK, CYNTHIA

PALEY, GRACE

PARKER, DOROTHY

PIZARNIK, ALEJANDRA

PLAIN, BELVA

PORUMBACU, VERONICA

PORZEKANSKI, TERESA

PROSE, FRANCINE

PYE, JAEL HENRIETTA

RAAB, ESTHER

RABINOWITZ, ZINA

RAGEN, NAOMI

RAHEL

RAND, AYN

RAVIKOVITCH, DALIA

REBECCA BAT MEIR TIKTINER

RICH, ADRIENNE

ROBIN, REGINE

ROSEN, NORMA

ROSENFARB, CHAVA

ROSS, LILLIAN

ROTTOVA, INNA

V. WOMEN
BIOGRAPHIES
Literature (continued)

RUBENS, BERNICE
RUBIN, HADASSAH
RUKEYSER, MURIEL
SACHS, NELLY
SAMPTER, JESSIE ETHEL
SARRAUTE, NATHALIE
SEGAL, ESTHER
SEGHERS, ANNA
SEID, RUTH
SELIGSON, ESTHER
SHALEV, ZERUYA
SHUA, ANA MARIA
SHULNER, DORA
SHUMIATCHER-HIRSCHBEIN, ESTHER
SIMON, KATE
SKLAREW, MYRA
SOARE, IULIA
SONTAG, SUSAN
SPEWACK, BELLA
STEELE, DANIELLE
STEIMBERG, ALICIA
STEIN, GERTRUDE
STERN, BERTHA GLADYS
SULLAM, SARA COPPIO
SUSANN, JACQUELINE
SUSMAN, MARGARETE
SZENES, ERZSI
TAYLOR, SIDNEY
TCHERNOWITZ-AVIDAR, YEMIMAH
TRILLING, DIANA
TUSSMAN, MALKA
ULIANOVER, MIRIAM
URY, ELSE
VIVANTI CHARTRES, ANNIE
WADDINGTON, MIRIAM (DWORKIN)
WARRENS, ROSA
WASSERSTEIN, WENDY
WECHSLER, ELINA
WEINZWEIG, HELEN
WENGEROFF, PAULINE
WISEMAN, ADELE
YALAN-STEKELIS, MIRIAM
YERUSHALMI, RINA
YEZIERSKA, ANZIA
YUDIKA
ZELDA (MISHKOVSKY)
ZYCHLINSKA, RAJZEL

Music & Dance
ARBATOVA, MIA
BACHAUER, GINA
BAUER, MARION EUGENIE
BAYER, BATHIA
BERTONOFF, DEBORAH
BLOCH, ROSINE
BLOOMFIELD-ZEISLER, FANNY

BOGHEN, FELICE
BORIS, RUTHANNA
BREVAL, LUCIENNE
CARP, PAULA
CHURGIN, BATHIA
COHEN, HARRIET
COHEN, SELMA JEANNE
COHEN, YARDENA
DE PHILIPPE, EDIS
DONALDA, PAULINE
DU PRÉ, JACQUELINE
EDEN-TAMIR
EISENSTEIN, JUDITH KAPLAN
EVEN-OR, MARY
FARBER, VIOLA
FISCHER, ANNIE
FLEISCHER, TSIPPI
FRIED (-BISS), MIRIAM
FRIEDMAN, DEBORAH LYNN
FUCHS, LILLIAN
GASKELL, SONJA
GERSON-KIWI, EDITH (Esther)
GIDEON, MIRIAM
GIOVANNI MARIA
GLUCK, ALMA
HAENDEL, IDA
HALPRIN, ANN
HASKIL, CLARA
HAYDEN, MELISSA
HAZZAN
HESKES, IRENE
HESS, DAME MYRA
HIRSH, NURIT
JOCHSBERGER, TZIPORAH
KADMAN, GURIT
KATZ, RUTH
KAYE, NORA
KENT, ALLEGRA
KOSHETZ, NINA
KRAUS, GERTRUD
KRAUS, LILI
KREMER, ISA
KURZ, SELMA
LANDOWSKA, WANDA
LANG, PEARL
LAPSON, DVORA
LEAR, EVELYN
LEIGH, ADELE
LEVI-AGRON, HASIA
LEVI-TANNAI, SARA
LEWITZKY, BELLA
LIEBLING, ESTELLE
LIFSHITZ, NEHAMAH
LISSA, ZOFIA
LUCCA, PAULINE
MARKOVA, ALICIA
MASLOW, SOPHIE
MATZENAUER, MARGARETE
MENDELSSOHN HENSEL, FANNY CAECILIE
MENUHIN, HEFZIBAH

METZGER, OTTILIE (Metzger-Latterman)
MLOTEK, CHANA
NIKOVA, RINA
OLIVERO, BETTY
ORDMAN, JEANETTE
OSTFELD, BARBARA
OVED, MARGALIT
PASTA, GUIDITTA
PAULY, ROSA
PETERS, ROBERTA
PLISETSKAYA, MAYA
QUELER, EVE
RAISA, ROSA
RAMBERT, DAME MARIE
RAN, SHULAMIT
RASKIN, JUDITH
REISENBERG, NADIA
RESNIK, REGINA
RODGERS, MARY
ROSSI, MADAMA EUROPA DE'
RUBIN, RUTH
RUBINSTEIN, IDA
SALZMAN, PNINA
SCHAECHTER-GOTTESMAN, BEYLE
SCHLAMME, MARTHA
SCHOENE, LOTTE
SCHUBERT, LIA
SHEMER, NAOMI
SHLONSKY, VARDINA
SILLS, BEVERLY (Belle Silverman)
SMOIRA-COHN, MICHAL
SOKOLOW, ANNA
SPECTOR, JOHANNA
STENN (STEEN), REBECCA
SULITEANU, GISELA
TAMIRIS, HELEN
TOUREL, JENNIE
TURECK, ROSALYN
WEISSBERG, JULIA LAZAREVNA
WERTHEIM, ROSALIE MARIE
YAMPOLSKY, BERTA
YELLIN-BENTWICH, THELMA
ZEFIRA, BRACHAH

Popular Culture
ABARBANELL, LINA
ADELSTEIN-ROZEANU, ANGELICA
ADLER, POLLY
ADLER, STELLA
AIMÉE, ANOUK
ALBERSTEIN, HAVA
ALBERT, MILDRED
ALCOTT, AMY
ALEXANDER, MURIEL
ALMAGOR, GILA
ARAD, YAEL
ARNOLD, PAULA
BACALL, LAUREN
BARA, THEDA
BARBARA

BARR, ROSEANNE
BEN, ZEHAVA
BERENSON, SENDA
BERG, GERTRUDE
BERGEN, POLLY
BERGMAN, ALAN & MARILYN
BERGNER, ELIZABETH
BERNHARD, SANDRA
BERNHARDT, SARAH
BERNSTEIN, ALINE
BERNSTEIN-COHEN, MIRIAM
BLOOM, CLAIRE
BRICE, FANNY
BRODY, JANE
BROTHERS, JOYCE
BUXTON, ANGELA
CARTER, NELL
CHOPRA, JOYCE
CLAYBURGH, JILL
COHEN, NATALIE
COHEN, SASHA
COHN, LINDA
COLLINS, LOTTIE
COMDEN, BETTY
COPELAND, LILLIAN
CURTIS, JAMIE LEE
DAMARI, SHOSHANA
DARVAS, LILI
DEREN, MAYA
ELLIOT, "MAMA" CASS
EPSTEIN, CHARLOTTE
FRIEDMANN, JANE
GABOR, JOLIE, MAGDA, ZSA ZSA, EVA
GERSTEN, BERTA
GIEHSE, THERESE
GILBERT, MELISSA
GINGOLD, HERMIONE
GODDARD, PAULETTE
GOLDSTEIN, JENNIE
GOODRICH, FRANCES AND HACKETT, ALBERT
GOROKHOVSKAYA, MARIA
GUZIK, HANNA
HADDAD, SARIT
HANBURY, LILY
HARRIS, BARBARA
HART, KITTY CARLISLE
HAWN, GOLDIE
HAZA, OFRA
HEAD, EDITH
HECKERLING, AMY
HELD, ANNA
HELDMAN, GLADYS
HENDEL, NEHAMA
HERSHEY, BARBARA
HOLLIDAY, JUDY
HUGHES, SARAH
IAN, JANIS
IRVING, AMY
ISAACS, EDITH JULIET
KAEL, PAULINE

V. WOMEN

BIOGRAPHIES

Popular Culture (*continued*)

KAHN, MADELINE
KALICH, BERTHA
KANE, CAROL
KANIN, FAY
KARAN, DONNA
KARFF, MONA. MAY
KARP, MAX AND SOPHIE
KAVNER, JULIE
KAZAN, LAINIE
KELETI, AGNES
KEMPNER, AVIVA
KING, CAROLE
KIRSZENSTEIN-SZEWINSKA, IRENA
KLEIN, ANNE
KONIG, LEA
KOPPLE, BARBARA
KORENE, VERA
KRESSYN, MIRIAM
KUDROW, LISA
LAMARR, HEDY
LANSING, SHERRY
LASSER, LOUISE
LAVIN, LINDA
LAWRENCE, STEVE AND GORME, EYDIE
LEACHMAN, CLORIS
LEDERER, ESTHER PAULINE
LEIBOWITZ, KEREN
LEONTOVICH, EUGENIE
LEVIEN, SONYA
LEWIS, SHARI
LIEBERMAN, NANCY
LORTEL, LUCILE
LOUIS-DREYFUS, JULIA
MANNHEIM, LUCIE
MATLIN, MARLEE
MAY, ELAINE
MENKEN, ADAH ISAACS
MERON, HANNA
MEYERS, NANCY JANE
MIDLER, BETTE
MITCHELL, YVONNE
MONROE, MARILYN
NAZIMOVA, ALLA
NEILSON, JULIA
NEUWIRTH, BEBE
NEVINS, SHEILA
NEWTON-JOHN, OLIVIA
NORSA, HANNAH
PALMER, LILLI
PALTROW, GWYNNETH
PARKER, SARAH JESSICA
PATINKIN, MANDY
PICON, MOLLY
PORAT, ORNA
PROOPS, MARJORIE
RACHEL

RADNER, GILDA
RAINER, LUISE
RIVERS, JOAN
ROSENFELD, FANNY
ROTH-SHACHAMOROV, ESTHER
ROVINA, HANNA
RUDNER, RITA
RYDER, WINONA
SELDES, MARIAN
SEYMOUR, JANE
SHAPIRO, ESTHER
SHEARER, NORMA
SHORE, DINAH
SIDNEY, SYLVIA
SIGNORET, SIMONE
SILVER, JOAN MICKLIN
SIMON, CARLY
SINGERMAN, BERTA
SLUTSKAYA, IRINA
STREISAND, BARBRA
STRUG, KERRI
SUZMAN, JANET
SYLVIA, SARAH
TAYLOR, ELIZABETH
TAYMOR, JULIE
THOMASHEFSKY, BESSIE
TUCKER, SOPHIE
WASSERMAN, DORA AND BRYNA
WEIGEL, HELENE
WEISSLER, BARRY AND FRAN
WEST, MAE
WESTHEIMER, RUTH
WINGER, DEBRA
WINTERS, SHELLEY
ZOHAR, MIRIAM

Public & Economic Life

ABELLA, ROSALIE SILBERMAN
ABRABANEL, BENVENIDA
ABZUG, BELLA
ACKERMAN, PAULA
ALEXANDER, BEATRICE
ALIAV, RUTH
ALONI, SHULAMIT
ALTER, ELEANOR (Breitel)
AMERICAN, SADIE
AMSTERDAM, BIRDIE
APPELMAN, HARLENE
AUERBACH, BEATRICE FOX
AZARKH, RAISA MOYSEYEVNA
BADT-STRAUSS, BERTHA
BALABANOFF, ANGELICA
BARRON, JENNIE LOITMAN
BARSHEFSKY, CHARLENE
BEER, RACHEL (Richa)
BEINISCH, DORIT
BEN-ISRAEL, RUTH
BEN-PORAT, MIRIAM
BEN-ZVI, RAHEL YANAIT
BERKLEY, ROCHELLE

BONNER, ELENA GEORGIEVNA
BORCHARDT, LUCY
BOXER, BARBARA
BRANDEAU, ESTHER
BRENNER, ROSE
BRUCKMAN, HENRIETTA
CAPLAN, ELINOR
CARDIN, SHOSHANA
CARNEGIE, HATTIE
CARR, JUDY FELD
COHEN, FANNIA M.
COHEN, GE'ULAH
COHEN, MARY MATILDA
CORCOS, STELLA
CURRIE, EDWINA
DAVIS, SUSAN
DAYAN, YAEL
DREIFUSS, RUTH
DUGDALE, BLANCHE ELIZABETH CAMPBELL
DULCEA OF WORMS
DUNKELMAN, ROSE
EPSTEIN, JUDITH
ESTERKE OF OPOCZNO
ESTHER
ETTENBERG, SYLVIA
EVANS, JANE
FAIRSTEIN, LINDA
FARKAS, RUTH
FEINSTEIN, DIANNE
FELDMAN, SANDRA
FERRIS, IRIS
FINESTONE, SHEILA
FISCHER, RUTH
FISHELS, ROIZEL OF CRACOW
FLEISCHMANN, GISI
FRANK, ANNE
FRANK, RAY
FREIER, RECHA
FREUND-ROSENTHAL, MIRIAM KOTTLER
FRIEDAN, BETTY
FUERTH, HENRIETTE
GAER, FELICE
GAMUS GALLEGOS, PAULINA
GANS, BIRD STEIN
GINOSSAR, ROSA
GINSBURG, RUTH JOAN BADER
GIROUD, FRANCOISE
GOLDBERG, JEANNETTE MIRIAM
GOLDMAN, EMMA
GOLDSCHMIDT, HENRIETTE
GOLDSCHMIDT, JOHANNA SCHWABE
GOLDSTEIN, FANNY
GOTSFELD, BESSIE GOLDSTEIN
GRATZ, REBECCA
GROSSINGER, JENNIE
GRUBER, RUTH
GRUENBERG, SIDONIE MATSNER
GUBER, RIVKA
HALPRIN, ROSE LURIA
HANDALI, ESTHER

HANDLER, RUTH MOSKO
HARMAN, JANE
HASSENFELD, SYLVIA
HAUSER, RITA
HAUTVAL, ADELAIDE
HEILBRON, ROSE
HELFMAN, HESSIA MEYEROVNA
HELMSLEY, LEONA
HERSTEIN, LILLIAN
HERZ, HENRIETTE
HERZOG, SHIRA
HILLESUM, ETTY
HILLMAN, BESSIE ABRAMOWITZ
HIMMELSTEIN, LENA
HOLTZMAN, ELIZABETH
IDELSON, BEBA
ITZIK, DALIA
JACOBS, ALETTA
JACOBS, FRANCES WISEBART
JACOBS, ROSE GELL
JAGLOM, RAYA
KAHN, DOROTHY C.
KAHN, FLORENCE PRAG
KANDLEIN OF REGENSBURG
KARMINSKI, HANNAH
KATZNELSON, RAHEL
KATZNELSON, SHULAMIT
KAYE, JUDITH
KLARSFELD, BEATE AUGUSTE
KLEIN, GERDA WEISSMAN
KNOPF, BLANCHE WOLFE
KORCZAK-MARLA, ROZKA
KRAVITCH, PHYLLIS A.
KROSS, ANNA
KUNIN, MADELEINE MAY
LANDAU, ANNIE
LAUDER, ESTÉE
LEIBER, JUDITH
LEICHTER, KAETE PICK
LEVITT, ESTHER
LICORICIA OF WINCHESTER
LIEBMANN, ESTHER SCHULHOFF ARON AND JOST
LINDHEIM, IRMA LEVY
LINGLE, LINDA
LIVNAT, LIMOR
LIVNI, TZIPI
LOW, MINNIE
LOWEY, NITA
LUBETKIN, ZIVIA
LUXEMBURG, ROSA
MAGNIN, MARY ANN COHEN
MAIMON, ADA
MALCHI, ESPERANZA
MALKIEL, THERESA SERBER
MALSIN, LANE BRYANT
MAOR, GALIA
MARIA THERESA
MEIR, GOLDA
MELTON, FLORENCE ZACKS
MENDELSSOHN-VEIT-SCHLEGEL, DOROTHEA

V. WOMEN

BIOGRAPHIES

Public & Economic Life (continued)

MESSINGER, RUTH
MONTAGU, LILY
MONTEFIORE, JUDITH
MORGENSTERN, LINA
MOSS, CELIA AND MARION
MUELLER-COHEN, ANITA
MYERSON, BESS
NAMIR, ORA
NATHAN, MAUD
NATHAN, VENGUESSONE
NEVEJEAN, YVONNE
NEWMAN, PAULINE
NUDEL, IDA
OPPENHEIM, SALLY BARONESS
PAPPENHEIM, BERTHA
PARNIS, MOLLIE
PAUKER, ANA
PEIXOTTO, JUDITH
PEMBER, PHOEBE YATES
PERLMAN, HELEN HARRIS
PERSITZ, SHOSHANAH
PESOTTA, ROSE
PHILLIPS, REBECCA MACHADO
PISCO, SERAPHINE
PLOTNICKA, FRUMKA
POGREBIN, LETTY COTTIN
POLYKOFF, SHIRLEY
PRYSTOR, JANINA
PULCELINA OF BLOIS
RABINOWICH, SARAH
RAKOWSKI, PUAH
RATHBONE, ELEANOR
RAZOVSKY, CECILIA
READING, FANNY
REEVE, ADA
REIK, HAVIVAH (Emma)
REISMAN, HEATHER
RESNIK, JUDITH
RICHMAN, JULIA
RIVLIN, ALICE MITCHELL
ROBACK, LEAH
ROSE, ERNESTINE POTOVSKY
ROSENBERG, ANNA MARIE LEDERER
ROSENSOHN, ETTA LASKER
ROSENTHAL, IDA COHEN
RUBINSTEIN, HELENA
SARAH OF TURNAVO
SCHAKOWSKY, JANICE
SCHENIRER (Schnirer), SARAH
SCHENK, FAYE L.
SCHIFF, DOROTHY
SCHMOLKA, MARIE
SCHOOLMAN, BERTHA S.
SCHWARTZ, FELICE NIERENBERG
SCHWIMMER, ROSIKA
SELIGSBERG, ALICE LILLIE

SENDLER, IRENA
SHAVELSON, CLARA LEMLICH
SHEINDLIN, JUDITH
SHORT, RENEE
SIEBERT, MURIEL
SIEFF, REBECCA
SIEGEL, IDA LEWIS
SOLOMON, BERTHA
SOLOMON, HANNAH GREENEBAUM
SONNENSCHEIN, ROSA
SPIEGEL, DORA
STEIMER, MOLLY
STEINEM, GLORIA
STEINER, HANNAH
STERN, ELIZABETH
STOKES, ROSE PASTOR (Wieslander)
STRASSFELD, SHARON
SUZMAN, HELEN
SYRKIN, MARIE
SZENES, HANNAH
SZOLD, HENRIETTA
THATCHER, MARGARET
TONNA, CHARLOTTE E.
TRIGERE, PAULINE
UDIN, SOPHIE
VARNHAGEN, RAHEL
VEIL, SIMONE
VON FURSTENBERG, DIANE
WACHNER, LINDA
WALD, LILLIAN
WALTERS, BARBARA
WASSERMAN-SCHULTZ, DEBBIE
WEIGEL, CATHERINE
WOLF, FRUMET
WOLFF, JEANETTE
WRONSKY, SIDDY
WUHSHA AL-DALLALA
WUNDERLICH, FRIEDA
ZEMER, HANNAH
ZEMLYACHKA (Zalkind), ROZALIYA
    SAMOYLOVNA

Religion
ABERLIN, RACHEL
BACHARACH, EVA
BARAZANI, ASENATH
BAS-TOVIM, SARAH
BEBE, PAULINE
BERLIN, RAYNA BATYA
DREYZL, LEAH
EILBERG, AMY
FRANK, EVA
GOLDSTEIN, ELYSE
HAUPTMAN, JUDITH
HOROWITZ, SARAH REBECCA RACHEL LEAH
ISSERLEIN, ISRAEL BEN PETHAHIAH
JONAS, REGINA
LAZA OF FRANKFURT
LICHTENSTEIN, TEHILLA
LUDOMIR, MAID OF

MIRIAM BAT BENAYAH OF YEMEN
MODENA, FIORETTA DI
OFFNER, STACY
OSTFELD, BARBARA
PRIESAND, SALLY
RASHI
SASSO, SANDY
SCHECHTER, MATHILDE
SERL BAS JACOB BEN WOLF KRANZ
SHIFRAH OF BRODY
SIMON, CARRIE OBENDORFER
STERNBERG, SARAH FRANKEL

Science

ARNON, RUTH
AYRTON, HERTHA
BIRK, YEHUDITH
COHEN, ELIZABETH D.A.
COHN, MILDRED
CORI, GERTY THERESA
DEUTSCH, HELENE
EDINGER, TILLY
ELION, GERTRUDE BELL
FEINBRUN-DOTHAN, NAOMI
FLORETA CA NOGA OF ARAGON
FRANKENTHAL, KATE
FRANKLIN, ROSALIND ELSIE
FREIDLINA, RAKHIL KHATSKELEVNA
FREUD, ANNA

FRIEDLANDER, KATE
FRIEND, CHARLOTTE
FROMM-REICHMANN, FRIEDA
GREENACRE, PHYLLIS
HAVA OF MANOSQUE
HESTRIN-LERNER, SARAH
HIRSCH, RACHEL
HYDE, IDA HENRIETTA
HYMAN, LIBBIE HENRIETTA
KAGAN, HELENA
KAUFMAN, JOYCE JACOBSON
KLEIN, MELANIE REIZES
KOCH, ADELHEID LUCY
KRIM, MATHILDE
LEVI-MONTALCINI, RITA
MAHLER, MARGARET
MEITNER, LISE
RAMOT, BRACHA
RAYSS, TSCHARNA
ROTENBERG, MATTIE
SHALON, RAHEL
SPIEGEL-ADOLF, MONA
STERN, LINA SOLOMONOVNA
STRAUS, RAHEL
WEIL, R. ADRIENNE
WOLFF, CHARLOTTE
YALOW, ROSALYN SUSSMAN
YONATH, ADA
ZAIZOV, RINA

INTRODUCTION TO THE INDEX

Creating a comprehensive book index for a work with the scope and depth of the *Encyclopaedia Judaica (EJ)* is a worthy challenge for any team of indexers. This is especially true because of the ambitious standard set by the first edition's index by Prof. Raphael Posner. I am confident that users of the second edition's index will agree that this index has risen to that challenge for a new generation of users.

A good reference index is not a concordance, a mere listing of every instance in which a person or a place is mentioned in print. An index's purpose is to help the user find relevant information as quickly and easily as possible. To do this, the index must do two things well. It must point a user toward those places where useful information is to be found. And it must gather those pointers in a single, easily found place, so that a user need not search here and there about the index, gathering references as if on a scavenger hunt of arcana. An index that does both of these things will help a user to quickly and confidently find all of the relevant information about a topic.

To create this index a large team of indexers from around the globe has read and re-read essays, seeking to ensure that our coverage of terms, themes, and concepts is both comprehensive and useful. Many headings and subheadings have been consolidated to ensure that all of the significant information about a topic or an aspect of a topic has been gathered in a single place.

We have consulted frequently with the first edition's index as we built the index for the second edition. The valuable *See* and *See Also* cross-references created by Prof. Posner for the first edition have been carried over wherever possible, and enhanced with additional references for the many new topics that appear in the second edition. We have also incorporated many of the first edition's headings and subheadings in the second edition's index. Great thanks are due to the help provided by that singular reference. Users will find two other avenues for accessing information in this edition as described below: the thematic outline and the online e-book version of this reference.

THE THEMATIC OUTLINE

An index is not a thematic outline, nor is a thematic outline an index. Instead, the two tools are designed to work together. The thematic outline that precedes this introduction arranges all the entries under logically structured main categories. It is an excellent tool for researchers seeking an overview of the encyclopedia's coverage. The alphabetical index is an excellent tool for researchers seeking specific information. Using the two together can greatly enhance any research effort. A reader who finds an essay of interest in the thematic outline would be well served to check the index for a sense of the encyclopedia's specific coverage of the topic. A user of the index who finds a topic of interest would be well served to consult the thematic outline for a handy overview of that topic's place in the encyclopedia.

Where practical the structure of the index's headings and subheadings has been coordinated with the thematic outline to help users move smoothly from one to the other. I strongly encourage readers and researchers alike to use both tools.

SEARCHING THE E-BOOK VERSION OF ENCYCLOPAEDIA JUDAICA

A print index is designed to be a complete and independent reference source for that print edition, and this is the case with the index for *Encyclopaedia Judaica*. However, it is worth noting that this second edition of *Encyclopaedia Judaica* will be released in both a print and an e-book format available as part of the Gale Virtual Reference Library. Many purchasers of this edition will have access to both versions of the encyclopedia. Electronic references provide search tools that simply can not exist in the printed version of a book. A user seeking additional ways to search the *Encyclopaedia Judaica* would do well to consult the electronic version.

Every effort has been made to use both the index and the thematic outline to enhance the searchability of the electronic version of this reference. In the e-book version page references in the index and main entries in the thematic version are hyperlinked to the entry and page to which they refer. Users who scroll to the end of an essay in the e-book version will see a list of the indexing terms that point to the essay. In those terms at the bottom, page references that point to other essays are hyperlinked to those essays to provide users with direct access to other information on a topic.

For general searching of the e-book version of *Encyclopaedia Judaica*, headings from the print index are included in the keyword search. Should a concept or name appear nowhere in either the thematic outline or the index, or should a user wish to conduct an exhaustive search for *all* mentions of a name or a concept, a convenient full-text search of the entire *Encyclopaedia Judaica* is available for the e-book.

CONVENTIONS OF THE INDEX

Alphabetization: This index is sorted letter-by-letter to reflect the arrangement of essays in the encyclopedia itself. To find headings the user should search alphabetically as if there are no spaces between words. Diacritical marks such as "Ḥ" or "ā" are ignored for sorting purposes. The sort stops at the period, comma, colon, and semi-colon punctuation marks. Words that break at those marks will sort above words that carry through, e.g. Rubin, Solomon comes before Rubiner, Ludwig.

Numbers, including Roman numerals, will appear at the top of lists. Parenthetical modifiers are not included in the sorting. Initial articles in both English and foreign languages – e.g. the, a, der, or la – are ignored for sorting purposes.

Page References: The volume number precedes the page reference the first time that the volume number is used, e.g. 8:123, 157 or 12:15-27, 145. Bolded page references refer to a main essay on a topic, e.g. Lee, Stan, 12:**598** or Kirby, Jack, 12:**183-184.**

Italicized page references refer to an image or map, e.g. A (letter), 1: *207* or Israel (ancient), 10: *101*. Page references followed by an italicized *t* indicate a table or genealogical chart, e.g. Kibbutz festivals, 12:120*t* or Rothschild family, 17:488*t*. Color inserts have been identified by the volume to which they belong, e.g. *Maus* (Spiegelman), vol. 2: color insert or Mint, vol. 16: color insert.

Person Names: Person names with surnames are generally inverted and appear as they have been listed in their main essay in the encyclopedia, e.g. Kane, Bob, 11:760-761. Person names consisting of forenames only are in natural order as Caecilius of Calacte, 4:331-332. Where advisable – especially with names containing *bar, ben,* or *ibn* – a *See* cross-reference has been created from the alternate inversion. *See* references have also been created for

alternate names, so that all of the page references for a person are gathered under a single heading.

Work Names: Titles of works such as novels, newspapers, monographs, and other longer works have been italicized, e.g. *Diary of a Young Girl* (Frank), or *The Spirit* (comic strip). Short works such as poems, short stories, or songs appear in quote marks, e.g. "Frailach in Swing" (Elman).

Most work names have received a parenthetical qualifier to distinguish them from similarly titled works, e.g. *Sefer ha-Musar* (Aknin) and *Sefer ha-Musar* (Kaspi). Books of the Bible appear in this format: Exodus, Book of.

In the case of works known by both foreign-language and English-language titles, the language of original publication has generally been preferred, with *See* references pointing to that name, from the English-language variant.

Place Names: Most place names have received a modifier to specify their location, e.g. Fort Michilimackinac (MI) or Eshtemoa (ancient Israel). Modifiers generally favor the current place unless a place name is only relevant within the context of its ancient location, e.g. Jahaz (Moab). Postal abbreviations for states and provinces have been used for place names within the U.S. and Canada, e.g. NY for New York and QC for Quebec. A list of geographic and other abbreviations used in the index follows this introduction.

Term Selection, Inversions and Natural Word Order: The terms selected for headings and subheadings in this index reflect the terms and concepts used in the essays themselves and seek to replicate them as closely as possible. Wherever practical, concept terms appear in natural word order, e.g. "Jewish philosophy" instead of "Philosophy, Jewish". *See* references have been created from the inverted term in many cases to avoid confusion and direct the user to the correct term.

ACKNOWLEDGMENTS

Finally, in addition to thanking Prof. Posner for the guidance provided by the index for the first edition, great thanks are due to Trish Yancey of Factiva and her team of indexers. They worked many long hours to create this index and bring it to a successful and timely conclusion. I would also like to thank the many Thomson Gale editors and staff members who have contributed to this index, especially indexing specialists Lynne Maday, Amy Jerome, and Cathy Fisher, without whose help this index would simply not exist.

John Magee
Manager, Book and Database Indexing
Thomson Learning

ABBREVIATIONS OF THE INDEX

The following standard abbreviations have been used in this index.

AB	Alberta
AK	Alaska
AL	Alabama
AS	American Samoa
AR	Arkansas
AZ	Arizona
BC	British Colombia
B.C.E	Before Common Era
c.	century
CA	California
CO	Colorado
CT	Connecticut
d.	died
DC	District of Columbia
DE	Delaware
fl.	flourished
FL	Florida
FM	Federated States of Micronesia
GA	Georgia
GU	Guam
HI	Hawaii
IA	Iowa
ID	Idaho
IL	Illinois
IN	Indiana
Inc.	Incorporated
Jr.	Junior
KS	Kansas
KY	Kentucky
LA	Louisiana
Ltd.	Limited
MA	Massachusetts
MB	Manitoba
MD	Maryland
ME	Maine
MH	Marshall Islands
MI	Michigan
MN	Minnesota
MO	Missouri
MP	Northern Mariana Islands
MS	Mississippi
MT	Montana
NB	New Brunswick
NC	North Carolina
ND	North Dakota
NE	Nebraska
NH	New Hampshire
NJ	New Jersey
NL	Newfoundland and Labrador
NM	New Mexico
NS	Nova Scotia
NT	Northwest Territories
NU	Nunavut
NV	Nevada
NY	New York
OH	Ohio
OK	Oklahoma
ON	Ontario
OR	Oregon
PA	Pennsylvania
PE	Prince Edward Island
PR	Puerto Rico
PW	Palau
QC	Quebec
RI	Rhode Island
SC	South Carolina
SD (Nazi intelligence unit)	Sicherheitsdienst
SD (place)	South Dakota
SK	Saskatchewan
Sr.	Senior
SS	Schutzstaffel
TN	Tennessee
TX	Texas
U.K.	United Kingdom
UN	United Nations
U.S.	United States of America
USSR	United Soviet Socialist Republics
UT	Utah
v.	versus in legal citations
VA	Virginia
VI	Virgin Islands
vol.	volume
vs.	versus
VT	Vermont
WA	Washington
WI	Wisconsin
WV	West Virginia
WW I	World War I
WW II	World War II
WY	Wyoming
YT	Yukon

INDEX

Page numbers in bold indicate main entries. Page numbers in italic indicate illustrations or maps. A "t" following a page number indicates a table or chart. References to color inserts include the pertinent volume number. Please see the "Introduction to the Index" for a full explanation of the conventions used in this index.

9/11 attacks. *See* September 11, 2001 terrorist attacks

23 Contratos Comercials Escritos por Los Judios de Toldeo en Los Siglos XIII Y XIV: Edicion Completa y Estudio Linguistico de los Datos Judeo-arabes Andalusies (Ferrando), 18:471

The 28th Day of Elul (Elman), 9:407

29 mois et quelques jours (Elkabbach), 6:356

1939 White Paper, 10:203

A

A (letter), 1:*207*, 2:5

Aachen (Germany), 1:**207**

De Aanslag. See The Assault

Aargau (Switzerland), 1:**207–208**

Aaron (biblical figure), 1:**208–211**
  ancient paintings, 6:53–54
  artwork, 14:542
  Eleazar (High Priest), 6:298
  Elisheba, 6:354
  golden calf, 6:618
  mediation by, 13:719
  Miriam, 14:311–312
  Moses, 14:523–531, 535
  rod of, 17:365

Aaron, House of. *See* Aaronides

Aaron, Israel, 1:**211**

Aaron, Judah, 15:474

Aaron, Sons of. *See* Aaronides

Aaron ben Abraham Safarty, 18:55

Aaron ben Amram, 1:**211–212**, 11:425

Aaron ben Asher, 13:649–650

Aaron ben Batash, 1:**212**, 16:346

Aaron ben David Cohen of Ragusa, 1:**212**, 6:38

Aaron ben Elijah, 1:**212–213**

Aaron ben Elijah ha-Kohen, 2:24

Aaron ben Gershon Elmali, 6:363

Aaron ben Isaac Benjamin Wolf, 1:**213**

Aaron ben Israel Broda, 4:193

Aaron ben Jacob ha-Kohen of Lunel, 1:**213–214**, 12:405

Aaron ben Jeshua. *See* Abu al-Faraj Harun ibn al-Faraj

Aaron ben Jeshu'a. *See* Abu al-Faraj Harun ibn al-Faraj

Aaron ben Jonah, 6:34

Aaron ben Joseph ha-Kohen Sargado, 1:**214**

Aaron ben Joseph ha-Levi, 1:**214–215**, 14:463

Aaron ben Joseph ha-Rofe, 1:213, **215–216**

Aaron ben Joshua ibn Alamani. *See* Alamani, Aaron he-Ḥaver ben Yeshu'ah

Aaron ben Judah Kosdani. *See* Aaron ben Judah Kusdini

Aaron ben Judah Kusdini, 1:**216**

Aaron ben Judah of Constantinople. *See* Aaron ben Judah Kusdini

Aaron ben Mashiah, 11:555

Aaron ben Meir. *See* Ben Meir, Aaron

Aaron ben Meir Brisker, 1:**216**

Aaron ben Meshullam of Lunel, 1:**216**

Aaron ben Moses ha-Levi of Starosielce, 1:**216–217**

Aaron ben Reuben Elmaleh, 6:364

Aaron ben Samuel, 1:**217**

Aaron ben Samuel (of Hergerhausen), 1:**217**

Aaron ben Senton. *See* Aaron ben Batash

Aaron ben Senton-ben Shem Tov. *See* Aaron Ben Batash

Aaron ben Solomon Duran, 6:56

Aaron Berechiah ben Moses of Modena, 1:**217**, 14:407

Aaron fil Josce of York. *See* Aaron of York

Aaron Ḥakiman, 1:**217**

Aaron ha-Levi of Barcelona. *See* Aaron ben Joseph ha-Levi

Aaronides, 1:**217–219**, 218*t*

Aaron Isaac. *See* Isaac, Aaron

Aaron Menahem Mendel, of Radzymin, 17:61

Aaron of Baghdad, 1:**219**

Aaron of Barcelona. *See* Aaron ben Joseph ha-Levi

Aaron of Copenhagen. *See* Aaron Simeon ben Jacob Abraham of Copenhagen

Aaron of Kremenets. *See* Aaron Samuel ben Moses Shalom of Kremenets

Aaron of Lincoln, 1:**219**

Aaron of Lunel (12/13th c.). *See* Aaron ben Jacob ha-Kohen of Lunel

Aaron of Lunel (13/14th c.). *See* Aaron ben Meshullam of Lunel

Aaron of Neustadt, 1:**219–220**

Aaron of Nicomedia. *See* Aaron ben Elijah

Aaron of Pesaro, 1:**220**

Aaron of Ragusa. *See* Aaron ben David Cohen of Ragusa

Aaron of Starosielce. *See* Aaron ben Moses ha-Levi of Starosielce

Aaron of York, 1:**220**

Aaron of Zhitomir, 1:**220**

Aaron of Zolkiew. *See* Aaron Selig ben Moses of Zolkiew

Aaron Samuel ben Moses Shalom of Kremenets, 1:**220**

Aaron Samuel ben Naphtali Herz ha-Kohen, 1:**220**

Aaron Selig ben Moses of Zolkiew, 1:**220–221**

Aaron Setzer. *See* Aaron ben Elijah ha-Kohen

Aaron Simeon ben Jacob Abraham of Copenhagen, 1:**221**

Aaronsohn, Aaron, 1:**221–222**, 223, 6:736, 15:267–268

Aaronsohn, Alexander, 1:222

Aaronsohn, Michael, 1:**223**

Aaronsohn, Moses, 1:**223–224**

Aaronsohn, Sarah, 1:222–223, 15:267–268

Aaronsohn family, 1:**221–223**

Aaronson, Lazarus Leonard, 1:**224**

Aaron the Elder. *See* Aaron ben Joseph ha-Rofe

Aaron the Great. *See* Perlov, Aaron ben Jacob

Aaron the Second, 11:810

Aaron the Younger. *See* Aaron ben Elijah

Aaron with Tablet (Reder), 17:156

Aaron Wolff Schreiber of Gewitsch. *See* Herlingen, Aaron Wolff of Gewitsch

Ab, Ninth of. *See* Av, the Ninth of

Aba. *See* Asher, Abraham ben Gedaliah Ibn

Abadan (Iran), 1:**224**

Abaddon, 1:**224**

Abaelard, Peter. *See* Abelard, Peter

Abaelardus, Petrus. *See* Abelard, Peter

Abag. *See* Gottlober, Abraham Baer

Abailard, Pierre. *See* Abelard, Peter

Abandoned Property. See Rekhush Natush

The Abandonment of the Jews: America and the Holocaust (Wyman), 9:420

Abarbanel, Isaac, 7:360

Abarbanell, Lina, 1:**224**

Abazardiel. *See* Abzardiel, Moses

Abazardiel, Moses. *See* Abzardiel, Moses

Abba, 1:**224–225**

Abba (3rd-4th centuries), 1:**225**

Abba (4th-5th centuries), 1:**225**

Abba (8th century), 1:**225**

Abba Arikha. *See* Rav

Abba bar Aḥa, 1:**225**

Abba bar Avina, 1:**225–226**

Abba bar Hanna. *See* Rabbah bar Ḥana

Abba bar Huna. *See* Rabbah bar Huna

Abba bar Kahana, 1:**226**

Abba bar Marta, 1:**226**

Abba bar Memel, 1:**226**

Abba bar Minah. *See* Abba bar Avina

Abba bar Zavda, 1:**226–227**

Abba bar Zemina, 1:**227**

Abba bar Zevina. *See* Abba bar Zemina

Abba bar Zimna. *See* Abba bar Zemina

Abba bar Zimona. *See* Abba bar Zemina

Abba ben Abba ha-Kohen, 1:**227**

Abba ben Aivu. *See* Rav

Abba ben Dostai. *See* Abba Yose ben Dostai

Abba Benjamin, 1:**227**

Abba Dan. *See* Avdan

Abba Gulish, 1:**227**

Abba Guryon of Sidon, 1:**227–228**

Abba Ḥilkiah, 1:**228**

Abba Hoshaya of Tiriah. *See* Abba Oshaya of Tiriah

Abbahu, 1:**228–229**, 18:594

Abbahu de-Shemu'el. *See* Abba ben Abba ha-Kohen

Abba Isi ben Ḥanin. *See* Abba Yose ben Ḥanin

Abba Kohen Bardela, 1:**229**

Abba Kolon, 1:**229**

Abba Mari Astruc, 1:302, 422, 12:697

Abba Mari ben Eligdor, 1:**229**

Abba Mari ben Isaac of St. Gilles, 1:**230**

Abba Mari ben Moses ben Joseph Astruc of Lunel, 1:**230**, 2:530

Abba of Acre. *See* Abba of Akko

Abba of Akko, 1:**230**

Abba of Sidon. *See* Abba Guryon of Sidon

Abba Oshaya of Tiriah, 1:**230–231**

Abbas, Judah ben Samuel ibn, 1:**231**

Abbas, Mahmoud, 10:252, 15:595, 600

Abbas, Moses ben Samuel, 1:**231–232**

Abbas, Moses Judah ben Meir, 1:**232**

Abbas, Samuel, 3:683

Abba Sakkara. *See* Abba Sikra

Abba Saul, 1:**232**

Abba Saul ben Batnit, 1:**232**

Abba Shaul Heisinovitch. *See* Aḥimeir, Abba

Abbas I, 1:**231**

Abbasi, Jacob ben Moses ibn, 1:**232–233**

Abbasids, 1:**233–234**, 4:364, 10:14–15, 11:155

Abbas II, 1:**231**

Abba Sikra, 1:**234–235**

Abba Umana, 1:**235**

Abbaye, 1:**235–236**

Abbaye Kashisha, 1:**236**

Abbaye the Elder. *See* Abbaye Kashisha

Abba Yose ben Dosai. *See* Abba Yose ben Dostai

Abba Yose ben Dostai, 1:**236**

Abba Yose ben Hanan. *See* Abba Yose ben Ḥanin

Abba Yose ben Ḥanin, 1:**236**

Abba Yose ben Johanan. *See* Abba Yose ben Ḥanin

Abba Yudan. *See* Avdan

Abbell, Maxwell, 1:**236**

Abbing, Justine. *See* Bruggen, Carry van

Abbott, Bud, 1:**236–237**

Abbott, William. *See* Abbott, Bud

Abbreviations, 1:**237–240**

'Abd al-Ḥaqq al-Islāmī, 1:**240**

Abdallah, Yusef, 1:**240**

Abdallah ibn Sabā', 1:**240–241**

Abdallah ibn Salāam, 1:**241**

'Abd al-Malik, 14:497

Abd al-Mālik Māwan, 1:**241**

Abde. *See* Avedat

'Abdin, Sheikh, 15:596

Abdon, 1:**241**, 11:565

Abduction, 1:**241–243**

   domicile of minors and, 5:742

Mortara case, 14:513

'Abduh, Muhammad, 10:93–94

Abdullah (King of Saudi Arabia), 18:78

Abdullah (King of Transjordan). *See* Abdullah ibn Hussein

Abdullah ibn Hussein, 1:**243–244**, 11:404

Abdullah II (King of Jordan), 11:405

Abdullah Yacoub. *See* Querido, Jacob

Abdul Mejid I, 1:**244**

Abécassis, Eliette, 1:**244–245**

Abed-Nego. *See* Shadrach, Meshach, Abed-Nego

Abedroth, David ben Moses Eliakim. *See* Abterode, David ben Moses Eliakim

Abeilard, Peter. *See* Abelard, Peter

Abel (ancient Israel). *See* Abel-Beth-Maacah (ancient Israel)

Abel (biblical figure), 1:**245**, 291, 4:340–342, 18:319

Abel, Avel, 1:**245**

Abel, Elie, 1:**245**

Abel, Emil, 1:**245**

Abel, Louis Felix, 1:**246**

Abelard, Peter, 1:**246**

Abel-Beth-Maacah (ancient Israel), 1:**246–247**

Abele Poswoler. *See* Abraham Abele ben Abraham Solomon

Abeles, Otto, 1:**247**

Abeles, Simele. *See* Abeles, Simon

Abeles, Simon, 1:**247**

Abeliovich, Lev Moysseyevich, 1:**247**

Abella, Rosalie Silberman, 1:**247–248**

Abel-Maim (ancient Israel). *See* Abel-Beth-Maacah (ancient Israel)

Abelman, Jonathan. *See* Jonathan ben Abraham Isaac

Abelmann, Ilya Solomovich, 1:**248**

Abel-Maul (ancient Israel), 1:**248**

Abel Mayin. *See* Abel-Beth-Maacah

Abel-Meholah (ancient Israel), 1:**248**, 6:350

Abel Shittim (ancient Israel), 1:**248**

Abelson, Harold Herbert, 1:**248–249**

Abelson, Joshua, 1:**249**

Abelson, Paul, 1:**249**

Abenabez, Moses. *See* Abbas, Moses ben Samuel

Abenabez, Moses ben Samuel. *See* Abbas, Moses ben Samuel

Abenaes, Solomon, 1:**249–250**

Abenafia, Joseph, 1:**250**, 15:581

Abenaish, Solomon. *See* Abenaes, Solomon

Abenalaza. *See* Eleazar

Abenalazar. *See* Eleazar

Abenardut family. *See* Ardut family

Abenatar family. *See* Atar family

Abenatar Melo, David, 1:**250**

Abenavez, Moses. *See* Abbas, Moses ben Samuel

Abenavez, Moses ben Samuel. *See* Abbas, Moses ben Samuel

Aben-Ayesh. *See* Abenaes, Solomon

Aben-Ayesh, Solomon. *See* Abenaes, Solomon

Abenbenist. *See* Benveniste

Abenbenist family. *See* Benveniste family

Abendana, David, 1:250

Abendana, Isaac, 1:**250**

Abendana, Isaac Sardo, 1:**251**

Abendana, Jacob ben Joseph, 1:**251**

Abendana family, 1:250

Abendanan, Maimon, 1:251

Abendanan, Saadiah. *See* Ibn Danan, Saadiah ben Maimun

Abendanan, Samuel, 1:251

Abendanan, Saul, 1:251–252

Abendanan, Solomon, 1:251

Abendanan family, 1:**251–252**

Abengalel family. *See* Bengalil family

Abenmenasse, Judah, 1:252

Abenmenasse, Samuel, 1:252

Abenmenasse family, 1:**252**

Abensur, Jacob, 1:**252–253**

Abensur, Louis. *See* Abensur, Jacob

Abensur family, 1:**252**

Abenvives family, 1:**253**

Abenyaex, Solomon. *See* Abenaes, Solomon

Aben-Yuly. *See* Yuly family

Aben-Yuly family. *See* Yuly family

Abenzardel, Moses. *See* Abzardiel, Moses

Aber, Adolf, 1:**253**

Aberdam, Alfred, 1:**253**, 15:649

Aberdeen (Scotland), 1:**253–254**

Aberdeen Bible, 3:679

Abergel family. *See* Bergel family

Aberle, Reb. *See* Nathan, Abraham

Aberlin, Rachel, 1:254

Abe Schrader Corp., 18:166, 167

Abe the Newsboy. *See* Hollandersky, Abraham

Abgar of Edessa, 3:599

Abgar V (King of Adiabene), 15:506

Ab-Ḥisda Azzuri. *See* Abu al-Hasan of Tyre

Abi-Afeta Ban ab-Ḥisdah. *See* Abu al-Fat

Abiatar family. *See* Atar family

Abiathar, 1:**254–255**, 2:132, 18:755

Abiathar ben Elijah ha-Kohen, 1:**255**, 18:770

Abichabod. *See* Ichabod

Abicht, Johann Georg, 1:**255**

ʾAbid, Ezra Menasheh, 15:473

Abiezer, 1:**255**

Abiezer the Anathothite, 1:255

Abigail, 1:**256**

Abi-Ḥasira, Jacob II ben Masoud, 1:256

Abi-Ḥasira family, 1:256

Abihazira family, 18:572–573

Abihu, 1:**256–257**, 14:721–722

Abijah, 1:**257**, 542

Abijam. *See* Abijah

Abileah, Arie, 1:257

Abilene (Syria), 1:257

Abimelech (King of Gerar), 1:**257–258**
    Abraham, 1:282
    Jotham, 11:465
    Judges, Book of, 11:564
    See also Ahimelech

Abimelech (King of Philistines), 16:55

Abimelech (son of Gideon), 1:258

Abimelechn (Ruler of Shechem), 3:5–6

Abinadab, 1:**258–259**

Abinnaxim family. *See* Abenmenasse family

A Bintl Blumen (Shalom Aleichem), 18:381

Abiob, Aaron, 1:259

Abir, David, 1:259

Abiram, 5:**440**

Abishag the Shunammite, 1:259, 413

Abishai, 1:**260**

Abishʿa Scroll, 15:754–755

Abitbol, Amor ben Solomon, 1:260

Abitbol, Saul Jeshua ben Isaac, 1:260

Abitbol family, 1:**260**

Abi Zimra, David ben Solomon ibn. *See* David ben Solomon ibn Abi Zimra

Abi Zimra, Isaac Mandil ben Abraham, 1:260

Abkhaz Autonomous Soviet Socialist Republic. *See* Abkhaziya

Abkhaziya (Georgia), 1:**261**, *261*

Ablution, immersion, 1:**261–263**

Abner, 1:**263–264**
    David and, 5:447
    Joab as murderer of, 11:339
    Palti, 15:607

Abner bar Ner ha-Sharoni. *See* Bashiri, Yaḥya

Abner of Burgos, 1:**264–265**, 15:562, 16:87

Aboab, Immanuel, 1:**265–266**, 2:267

Aboab, Isaac da Fonseca. *See* Aboab da Fonseca, Isaac

Aboab, Isaac de Mattathias, 1:**268**

Aboab, Isaac I, 1:**266–267**, 686

Aboab, Isaac II, 1:**267–268**

Aboab, Jacob ben Samuel, 1:**268**

Aboab, Mattathias. *See* Aboab, Isaac de Mattathias

Aboab, Samuel ben Abraham, 1:**268–269**

Aboab da Fonseca, Isaac, 1:**269**
    Amsterdam, 2:109
    as bibliophile, 3:683

Aboab family, 1:**265**, 267t

Aboaf family. *See* Aboab family

L'abolition (Badinter), 3:50

Abomination, 1:**269–270**

Abomination of Desolation, 1:270

Abony (Hungary), 1:270

Abortion, 1:**270–273**, 10:288, 14:488

Aboulker family. *See* Abulker family

About the Fifth Year. See Fun Finften Yor

A Boyden (Shalom Aleichem), 18:385

Abrabanel, Benvegnita. *See* Abrabanel, Benvenida

Abrabanel, Benvenida, 1:274, **275–276**

Abrabanel, Bienvenita. *See* Abrabanel, Benvenida

Abrabanel, Isaac ben Judah (1437-1538), 1:**276–279**, 12:519, 16:90
    articles of faith, 2:531
    biblical exegesis and study, 3:643, 662
    biography of, 3:706
    Derekh Emunah and, 3:571
    Ḥasidei Ummot ha-Olam, 8:389
    Joshua, Book of, 11:444
    moneylending, 14:440

Abrabanel, Isaac ben Samuel, 1:274

Abrabanel, Jacob, 1:274

Abrabanel, Jacob ben Samuel, 1:274

Abrabanel, Joseph, 1:274

Abrabanel, Judah (fl. 1310), 1:274–275

Abrabanel, Judah (fl. 1535), 10:791

Abrabanel, Judah (of Córdoba). *See* Abrabanel, Judah (fl. 1310)

Abrabanel, Judah (son of Samuel of Seville), 1:275

Abrabanel, Judah ben Isaac, 1:274

Abrabanel, Judah ben Isaac (c. 1460-c. 1523), 1:274, **279–280**, 11:379, 16:90

Abrabanel, Judah ben Samuel, 1:274

Abrabanel, Samuel (1473-1547), 1:274–275, 276

Abrabanel, Samuel (of Seville), 1:274–275

Abrabanel family (Italy), 1:**274**, 7:84
Abrabanel family (Spain), 1:**274–275**, 275t
Abracadabra, 1:**280**
Abraham, 1:**280–288**
   Abimelech and, 1:257
   Abraham's bosom, 1:316, 317
   adoption, 1:415
   in the aggadah, 1:283–284
   Akedah, 1:555–560
   angels announcing birth of Isaac, vol. 7: color insert
   Apocalypse of, 1:288–289
   in the arts, 1:287–288
   biblical, 1:281, 281–282
   Christian tradition, 1:285
   Eliezer, 6:322
   Ephron, 6:461–462
   as ethical ideal, 6:532
   historicity of, 9:165, 15:747
   interpretations, 16:62, 63
   Islamic tradition, 1:286
   Jewish philosopher, 1:284–285
   Laban and, 12:406–407
   Mamre (Israel), 13:442
   medieval Hebrew literature, 1:286–287
   Melchizedek and, 14:11
   oak of Abraham in Hebron, 15:357
   other books of, 1:290
   as Patriarch, 15:689–691
   Philistines and, 16:55
   sacrifice of Isaac, vol. 8: color insert
   Sarah, 18:46, 47
   Testament of, 1:291
Abraham, Abele ben Abraham Solomon, 1:**291**
Abraham, Abraham, 1:288, 5:588
Abraham, Apocalypse of. See Apocalypse of Abraham
Abraham, David, 1:**289**
Abraham, Gerald, 1:**289–290**
Abraham, Karl, 1:**290**
Abraham, Louis. *See* Pincus, Louis Arieh
Abraham, Max, 1:**290**
Abraham, other books of, 1:**290**
Abraham, Otto, 1:**290–291**
Abraham, Samuel, 1:**291**
Abraham, Testament of. See Testament of Abraham
Abraham Aaron ben Shalom Broda, 4:193
Abraham Abele ben Abraham Solomon, 1:291

Abraham Abusch ben Zevi Hirsch, 1:**291–292**
Abraham Abusch Lissa. *See* Abraham Abusch ben Zevi Hirsch
Abraham a Sancta Clara, 1:**292**
Abraham Axelrod. *See* Abraham ben Alexander of Cologne
Abraham bar Hayya. *See* Abraham bar Hiyya
Abraham bar Hiyya, 1:**292–294**, 2:618, 13:673, 16:82
   emanation, 6:373
   gilgul, 19:37
   language of, 8:659
   soul, immortality of, 19:37
Abraham bar Jacob, 1:**294**, 2:122
Abraham ben Abraham. *See* Potocki, Valentine
Abraham ben Alexander Katz of Kalisk, 1:**294**
Abraham ben Alexander Katz of Kalisz. *See* Abraham ben Alexander Katz of Kalisk
Abraham ben Alexander of Cologne, 1:**294**
Abraham ben Aryeh Loeb Hayyim ha-Kohen of Mogilev, 11:412
Abraham ben Avigdor, 1:**295**
Abraham ben Axelrad of Cologne. *See* Abraham ben Alexander of Cologne
Abraham ben Azriel, 1:**295**, 11:423, 18:603
Abraham ben Benjamin Ze'ev Brisker, 1:**295**
Abraham ben Daniel, 1:**295–296**
Abraham ben David Maimuni, 1:**296**
Abraham ben David of Posquières, 1:**296–298**, 4:772, 11:426
Abraham ben Dov of Mezhirech, 1:**298**
Abraham ben Eliezer ha-Levi, 1:**298–299**, 11:428
Abraham ben Eliezer ha-Levi Berukhim, 1:**299**
Abraham ben Elijah of Vilna, 1:**299**, 3:610
Abraham ben Halfon, 1:**299–300**
Abraham ben Hasdai, 11:541
Abraham ben Hayyim, 1:**300**
Abraham ben Hayyim, dei Tintori. *See* Abraham ben Hayyim, the Dyer
Abraham ben Hayyim, the Dyer, 1:**300**
Abraham ben Heilprin. *See* Abraham ben Hayyim
Abraham ben Hillel of Fostat, 1:**300**
Abraham ben Hisdai, 11:555
Abraham ben Hiyya ha-Nasi, 2:624, 6:399
Abraham ben Isaac, 1:**300–301**, 547–548, 6:325–326

Abraham ben Isaac ben Garton, 1:**301**
Abraham ben Isaac Gerondi. *See* Abraham ben Isaac
Abraham ben Isaac ha-Kohen al-Furat, 1:**301**
Abraham ben Isaac ha-Kohen of Zamość, 1:**301**
Abraham ben Isaac of Granada, 1:**301–302**
Abraham ben Isaac of Montpellier, 1:**302**
Abraham ben Isaac of Narbonne, 1:**302–303**, 11:483, 484
Abraham ben Israel of Brody, 1:**303**
Abraham ben Jacob. *See* Abraham bar Jacob
Abraham ben Jehiel (12th c.), 2:136
Abraham ben Jehiel Michal ha-Kohen, 1:**303**
Abraham ben Joseph Elmaleh, 6:364
Abraham ben Joseph of Lissa, 1:**303**
Abraham ben Josiah Troki, 1:**303**
Abraham ben Josiah Yerushalmi, 1:**303–304**
Abraham ben Judah ben Abraham, 1:**304**
Abraham ben Judah Elmalik, 6:363
Abraham ben Judah Leon, 1:**304**
Abraham ben Maimon. *See* Abraham ben Moses ben Maimon
Abraham ben Mazhir, 1:**304**
Abraham ben Mordecai ha-Levi, 1:**304**
Abraham ben Moses ben Maimon, 1:**304–308**
   Abraham ben Hillel of Fostat, 1:300
   Bilbeis, letter to Jews of, 3:697
   Islamic influence on, 11:267
   Judeo-Arabic literature and, 11:536–537
   Sufism and, 11:542–543
Abraham ben Moses ha-Kohen ha-Sephardi, 1:**308**
Abraham ben Naphtali Tang. *See* Abrahams, Abraham
Abraham ben Nathan (11th-12th centuries), 1:**308–309**
Abraham ben Nathan (c. 1025), 1:**309**
Abraham ben Nathan ha-Baghdadi, 1:**309**
Abraham ben Nathan ha-Yarhi, 1:**309**, 2:133
Abraham ben Nisssim of Fostat. *See* Abraham ben Hillel of Fostat
Abraham ben Samuel Feivush. *See* Hayyim ben Samuel Feivush
Abraham ben Samuel he-Hasid, 1:**309**, 3:683
Abraham ben Samuel of Dreux, 1:**310**

Abraham ben Shabbetai, 3:697

Abraham ben Shabbetai ha-Kohen, 1:310

Abraham ben Sherira, 11:418

Abraham ben Simeon of Saint Maximin, 1:310

Abraham ben Simeon of Worms, 1:310

Abraham ben Solomon, 1:310, 11:538

Abraham ben Solomon of Torrutiel, 1:311, 11:427

Abraham ben Solomon Zalman Broda, 4:193

Abraham ben Yashar. See Abu Sa'd al-Tustarī

Abraham ben Yoske of Leszno. See Abraham ben Joseph of Lissa

Abraham de Porto. See Alvarez, Fernando

Abraham de Toledo. See Toledo, Abraham de

Abraham Dov Baer of Ovruch, 1:311

Abraham El-Barchilon, 1:311

Abraham family, 1:288

Abraham fil' Deulecresse, 15:312

Abraham Gaon, 1:311

Abraham Gershon of Kutow, 1:311–312, 8:395

Abraham Guer of Cordova. See Escudero, Lorenzo

Abraham ha-Bavli, 1:312

Abraham ha-Levi, 1:312

Abraham Ḥayyim ben Gedaliah, 1:312

Abraham he-Ḥasid. See Abraham ben Hillel of Fostat

Abraham he-Ḥasid of Cairo, 4:77

Abraham he-Ḥaver. See Abraham ben Hillel of Fostat

Abrahami, Ẓevi. See Abramowitz, Grigori

Abrahamites, 1:312, 15:323

Abraham Joshua Heschel of Apta, 1:312–313

Abraham Joshua Heschel of Opatow. See Abraham Joshua Heschel of Apta

Abraham Judaeus Bohemus, 1:313

Abraham Lincoln Brigade, Spanish civil war, 15:218

Abraham Maimuni. See Abraham ben Moses ben Maimon

Abraham of Apta. See Abraham Joshua Heschel of Apta

Abraham of Beja, 1:313

Abraham of Bohemia. See Abraham Judaeus Bohemus

Abraham of Brody. See Abraham ben Israel of Brody

Abraham of Cologne. See Abraham ben Alexander of Cologne

Abraham of Dreux. See Abraham ben Samuel of Dreux

Abraham of Fostat. See Abraham ben Hillel of Fostat

Abraham of Granada. See Abraham ben Isaac of Granada

Abraham of Hamburg. See Nathan, Abraham

Abraham of Kalisk. See Abraham ben Alexander Katz of Kalisk

Abraham of Lissa. See Abraham ben Joseph of Lissa

Abraham of Mezhirech. See Abraham ben Dov of Mezhirech

Abraham of Miropolye. See Abraham ben Isaac of Montpellier

Abraham of Narbonne. See Abraham ben Isaac of Narbonne

Abraham of Ovruch. See Abraham Dov Baer of Ovruch

Abraham of Posquières. See Abraham ben David of Posquières

Abraham of Ragola. See Ragoler, Abraham ben Solomon

Abraham of Ragoler. See Ragoler, Abraham ben Solomon

Abraham of Sancta Clara. See Abraham a Sancta Clara

Abraham of Saragossa, 1:313

Abraham of Sarteano, 1:313–314

Abraham of Theomanaria, 11:474

Abraham of Torrutiel. See Abraham ben Solomon of Torrutiel

Abraham of Vilna. See Abraham ben Elijah of Vilna

Abraham of Worms. See Abraham ben Simeon of Worms

Abrahams, Abraham (Author), 1:315

Abrahams, Abraham (Scholar), 1:315

Abrahams, Abraham Isaac, 1:315

Abrahams, Adolphe, 1:314

Abrahams, Barnett, 1:314

Abrahams, Gerald, 1:315

Abrahams, Harold Maurice, 1:314–315

Abrahams, I., 11:313

Abrahams, Isaac, 1:315

Abrahams, Israel (Rabbi), 1:316

Abrahams, Israel (Scholar), 1:315–316

Abrahams, Ivor, 1:316

Abrahams, Joseph, 1:314

Abrahams, Lionel, 1:316

Abrahams, Nicolai Christian Levin, 1:316

Abrahams, Sidney, 1:314

Abrahams, Solly. See Abrahams, Sidney

Abraham's bosom, 1:316–317

Abrahamsen, David, 1:317

Abraham Seneor. See Seneor, Abraham

Abrahams family (Athletes), 1:314–315

Abrahams family (Scholars), 1:314

Abrahamson, Abe, 4:267

Abrahamson, Otto. See Brahm, Otto

Abraham & Straus (A. & S.), 1:288, 5:588

Abraham the Pious. See Abraham ben Hillel of Fostat

Abraham Ẓevi ben Eleazar, 1:317

Abrahão, Coje, 1:317

Abram. See Abraham

Abram, Morris Berthold, 1:317–318, 4:124

Abram Bonet Avigdor. See Avigdor, Abraham

Abramovich, Bernat, 4:91

Abramovich, Roman Arkadyevich, 1:318

Abramovitsh, Sholem Jacob. See Abramovitsh, Sholem Yankev

Abramovitsh, Sholem Yankev, 1:318–322, 3:691, 8:693, 18:367–368, 21:345–346

Abramovitz, David. See Abir, David

Abramovitz, Max, 1:323

Abramovitz, Moses, 1:323

Abramowicz, Dina, 1:323–324

Abramowitz, Bina, 1:324

Abramowitz, Dov Baer, 1:324

Abramowitz, Emil, 1:324

Abramowitz, Grigori, 1:324–325

Abramowitz, Herman, 1:325

Abramowitz, Raphael, 1:325, 16:348

Abramowitz, Rein. See Abramowitz, Raphael

Abrams, Cal, 1:325–326

Abrams, Calvin Ross. See Abrams, Cal

Abrams, Charles, 1:326

Abrams, Elliott, 1:326–327

Abrams, Floyd M., 1:327

Abrams, Meyer H., 1:327

Abrams, Robert, 1:327–328, 12:602, 15:224

Abramsky, Yeḥezkel, 1:328

Abramson, Abraham, 1:328

Abramson, Jacob, 1:328

Abramson, Jerry Edwin, 1:328

Abramson, Jesse, 1:328–329

Abramson, Shraga, 1:329

Abramson family, 1:328

Abrass, Joshua. See Abrass, Osias

Abrass, Osias, 1:329

Abravanel, Maurice. See Abravanel, Maurice de

Abravanel, Maurice de, 1:**329**

Abravanel family (Spain). *See* Abrabanel family (Spain)

Abravaniel family (Spain). *See* Abrabanel family (Spain)

Abrech, 1:**329–330**

Abrek. *See* Abrech

A Briv tsu a Gutn Fraynd (Shalom Aleichem), 18:381

Abruzzi, Duke D'. *See* Tepper, Kolya

Absaban, Solomon, 1:**330**

Ab Sʾad, 6:231

Absalom (biblical figure), 1:**330–331**
    Ahimazz, 1:543
    Ahithophel the Gilonite, 1:545
    Amasa, 2:32
    Amnon, 2:87
    David and, 5:447–448, 450, 451
    Tamar and, 19:494
    tomb of Absalom, vol. 10: color insert

Absalom (name), 1:**331–332**

Absalom, monument of, 1:**332**

Absalom and Achithophel (Dryden), 1:331

Absalon, 1:**332**

Abse, Dannie, 1:**332–333**

Absolon (Makai), 9:604

Absolute idealism, 18:119–120

Absolute rule based on mercantile economy, 15:449

Absolution. *See* Forgiveness

Absorption in Israel. *See* Aliyah

The Absorption of Immigrants (Eisenstadt), 5:295, 6:271

Abstinence. *See* Fasting and abstinence

Abt, Isaac Arthur, 1:**333**

Abterode, David ben Moses Eliakim, 1:**333**

Abterode, Solomon, 1:333

Abtshuk, Avraham, 1:**333**

Abtshuk, Avrom. *See* Abtshuk, Avraham

Abu, 1:**333**

Abu Aaron, 18:460

Abu Aaron ben Samuel ha-Nasi. *See* Aaron of Baghdad

Abu Alafia family. *See* Abulafia family

Abualefia family. *See* Abulafia family

Abū al-Faḍl Dāʾūd ibn Abī al-Bayān Suleimān al-Isrāʾīlī. *See* David ben Solomon

Abu al-Faḍl Hasday, 1:**333–334**

Abu al-Faraj. *See* Bar Hebraeus, Johanan

Abu al-Faraj Harun ibn al-Faraj, 1:**334**, 11:425

Abu al-Fat, 1:**334**, 2:105

Abu al-Hasan. *See* Ibn al-Taqana, Moses

Abu al-Hasan of Tyre, 1:**335**

Abu Ali al-Hussein ibn ʾAbdallah ibn Sīnā. *See* Avicenna

Abu Ali Hasan ibn Bundar, 1:387

Abual-Munā ibn abi Naṣr al-Kohen al-ʾAṭṭār, 11:536

Abu al-Munajjā Solomon ben Shaya, 1:**335**

Abu al Rabi, Aaron. *See* Abulrabi, Aaron

Abu al-Walid Muhammad Ibn Rushd. *See* Averroes

Abu-ʾAmr. *See* Ibn Sahl, Joseph ben Jacob

Abu Aweigila (Sinai), 1:**335**

Abu ʿAweiqila (Sinai). *See* Abu Aweigila (Sinai)

Abu Bakr Muhammad ibn Yahya ibn Fajja. *See* Avempace

Abucarat, Abraham. *See* Bukarat, Abraham ben Solomon ha-Levi

Abucarat, Abraham ben Solomon ha-Levi. *See* Bukarat, Abraham ben Solomon ha-Levi

Abudaram family. *See* Abudarham family

Abudaran family. *See* Abudarham family

Abudarham, David ben Joseph, 1:**336**

Abudarham family, 1:**335–336**

Abudarhan family. *See* Abudarham family

Abudarhen family. *See* Abudarham family

Abudiente, Gideon. *See* Gideon, Samson

Abu Ghosh, 1:**336**

Abu Harun. *See* Ibn Ezra, Moses ben Jacob

Abu Ibrahim. *See* Ibn Khalfun, Isaac

Abū Ibrāhīm ibn Kastār. *See* Ibn Yashush, Isaac Abu Ibrahim

Abu I-Khayr family. *See* Abulker family

Abu ʿImram Mūsā al-Ẓafārānī. *See* Abu ʿImrān al-Tiflīsī

Abu ʿImrān al-Tiflīsī, 1:**336**

Abu Isā, Isaac ben Jacob al-Iṣfahīnī, 1:**337**

Abu ʿĪsā, 15:786

Abū Isḥāq. *See* Ibrahim ibn Sahl al-Andalusī al-Israʾili

Abu Isḥaq Abraham ibn ʿta, 11:727

Abu Isḥāq Ibrahim ibn ʿAṭāʾ. *See* Abraham ben Nathan (c. 1025)

Abū Isḥāq Kaʿb al-Aḥbār. *See* Kaʿb al-Aḥbār

Abu Jaʿfar Muhammad al-Ṭabarï, 3:668–669

Abukara, Abraham ben Moses, 1:**337**

Abukara, Jacob ben Elijah, 1:337

Abukarat, Abraham. *See* Bukarat, Abraham ben Solomon ha-Levi

Abukarat, Abraham ben Isaac ha-Levi, 4:257

Abukarat, Abraham ben Solomon ha-Levi. *See* Bukarat, Abraham ben Solomon ha-Levi

Abulaffia family. *See* Abulafia family

Abulafia, Abraham ben Samuel, 1:**337–339**, 11:607–608, 15:249–250
    allegories, 1:667
    approach to meditation, 13:761–762

Abulafia, Ezekiel David ben Mordecai, 1:**339**

Abulafia, Ḥayyim, 3:695

Abulafia, Ḥayyim ben David, 1:**339**

Abulafia, Ḥayyim ben Jacob I, 1:**339**

Abulafia, Ḥayyim ben Jacob II, 1:**339–340**

Abulafia, Ḥayyim Nissim ben Isaac, 1:**340**

Abulafia, Hezekiah. *See* Abulafia, Ezekiel David ben Mordecai

Abulafia, Isaac ben Moses, 1:**340**, 516–517

Abulafia, Issachar, 4:270

Abulafia, Jacob ben Solomon, 1:**340–341**

Abulafia, Meir, 1:**341–342**, 341*t*, 6:176

Abulafia, Meir ben Todros ha-Levi, 13:652

Abulafia, Samuel ben Meir ha-Levi, 1:**343**

Abulafia, Samuel ha-Levi, 1:**343**

Abulafia, Todros, 16:117, 267

Abulafia, Todros ben Joseph ha-Levi, 1:**343–344**, 18:327

Abulafia, Todros ben Judah ha-Levi, 1:**344–345**

Abulafia family, 1:**337**

Abulefia family. *See* Abulafia family

Abu l-Fahm. *See* Ibn Altabban, Levi ben Jacob

Abulfahm, Levi. *See* Ibn Altabban, Levi ben Jacob

Abulker, Isaac ben Samuel, 1:**345**

Abulker family, 1:**345**

Abulrabi, Aaron, 1:**345–346**

Abu Manṣūr al-Daimari, 11:538

Abun, 1:**346**

Abuna. *See* Abun

Abū Naṣ. *See* Fārābī, Abū Naṣr Muḥammad al-

Abu Nazzara. *See* Sanū', Yaʿqub

Abu Naẓẓāra. *See* Sanū', Yaʿqub

Abu Saad,. *See* Ibn Ezra, Isaac

Abū Saʿd al-Tustarī, 1:**346**

Abū Saʿd ben Sahl al-Tustari. *See* Abu Saʿd al-Tustarī

Abu Sahl. *See* Dunash Ibn Tamim

Abu Saʾid. *See* Ben-Asher, Aaron ben Moses

Abu Saʾid. *See* Levi ben Japheth

Abu Saʾīd ben Boaz. *See* David ben Boaz

Abu Saʾid Ḥalfon ha-Levi of Damietta, 11:493

Abusch Frankfurter. *See* Abraham Abusch ben Ẓevi Hirsch

Abu Suleiman al-Qūmisī. *See* David al-Qumisì

Abu Suleiman Dāʾūd ibn Ibrahim Al-Fāsī. *See* Alfasi, David ben Abraham

Abu Suleiman ibn Muhagir. *See* David ibn Hajjar

Abu Yaʾqūb al-Baṣīr. *See* Baṣīr, Joseph ben Abraham ha-Kohen Haroʾeh al-

Abu Yaʿq̄ub Yūsuf ibn Nūh. *See* Joseph ben Noah

Abū Yeshaʾ. *See* Fārābī, Abū Naṣr Muḥammad al-

Abu Zakariyyā Yaḥyā. *See* Ibn Balʾam, Judah ben Samuel

Abu-Zikri. *See* Zuta

Abwehrverein. *See* Verein Zur Abwehr des Antisemitismus

Abyaḍ Yiḥya ben Shalom, 1:**346**

Abysmal Reflections (Barasch), 3:135

Abyssinia. *See* Ethiopia

Abzardiel, Moses, 1:**346**

Abzug, Bella Savitzky, 1:**346**–**347**, 15:224

Açac de Çalema, 3:688

Acacia, 1:**347**

Academias morales de las musas (Enríquez Gomez), 6:446

Academic Sports Association (A.S.A), 2:**541**

Academicus. *See* Hersch, Pesach Liebman

Academies in Babylonia and Ereẓ Israel, 1:**347**–**351**

Academy for Jewish Religion, 17:28

Academy for Jewish Scholarship. *See* Akademie Fuer Die Wissenschaft Des Judentums

Academy for the Hebrew Language, 8:573

Academy of Motion Picture Arts and Sciences, 11:763

Academy of the Hebrew Language, 1:**351**–**353**, 3:388, 18:724

Academy on High, 1:**353**–**354**

Açan, Moses de Tarrega, 1:**354**

Açan, Moses de Zaragua. *See* Açan, Moses de Tarrega

Accents of the Torah. *See* Masorah vocalization

Acchabaron (Galilee). *See* Akhbarei (Galilee)

Accident and substance. *See* Substance and accident

Acco. *See* Acre (Israel)

Accounting for Genocide (Fein), 9:416, 418

Acculturation. *See* Assimilation

Ace, Goodman, 1:**354**

Ace, Jane, 1:**354**

Achan, 1:**354**, 355

Achbor, 1:**355**

"Achdut" club, 18:125

Acher. *See* Elisha ben Avuyah

Achish, 1:**355**, 5:447

Achor, valley of (ancient Israel), 1:**355**

Achron, Joseph, 1:**355**–**356**

Achsah, 1:**356**

Achshaph (ancient Israel), 1:**356**

Het Achterhuis. See Diary of a Young Girl

Achzib (ancient Israel), 1:**356**–**357**

Ackerman, Gary, 1:**357**

Ackerman, Nathan Ward, 1:**357**

Ackerman, Paula Herskovitz, 1:**357**–**358**, 18:278

Ackerman, Shabtai, 1:**358**

The Ackerman Institute for Family Therapy, 1:357

Ackord, Elias, 1:**358**

Acorns, vol. 16: color insert

Acosta, Christobal, 1:**358**–**359**

Acosta, Gabriel. *See* Costa, Uriel da

Acosta, Isaac, 1:**359**

Acosta, Joan D', 1:**359**

Acosta, Uriel da. *See* Costa, Uriel da

Acosta, Yhsak. *See* Acosta, Isaac

Acqui (Italy), 1:**359**

Acquisition, 1:**359**–**363**, 12:568

The Acra, 1:**363**–**364**

Acraba (ancient Israel), 1:**364**

Acre (Israel), 1:**364**–**368**, *366*, 11:693, 14:778

Acre-Tyre Plain (Israel), 10:111

Acro, pseudo-, 1:**368**

The Acrophile. See Ha-Yored le-Maʾalah

Acrostics, 1:**368**–**369**, 385

Acsády, Ignác, 1:**369**

Acta Isidori et Lamponis, 1:635, 12:453–454

L'Action catholique (newspaper), 4:403

Action Française, 1:**369**–**370**

L'Action française, 1:369, 370

Act of Faith. *See* Auto da Fé

Actors, 5:341–342

    Aimée, Anouk, 1:550

    Alexander, Jason, 1:623

    Alexander, Muriel, 1:624

    Aliturus, 1:660

    Almagor, Gila, 1:678

    Barnowsky, Viktor, 3:170

    Benjamin, Richard, 3:358

    Benny, Jack, 3:358–359

    Benson, Robby, 3:378

    Beregi, Oszkár, 3:408

    Berg, Gertrude, 3:415

    Bergen, Polly, 3:419–420

    Bergner, Elisabeth, 3:430

    Berkoff, Steven, 3:438

    Berman, Shelley, 3:464–465

    Bernardi, Herschel, 3:468–469

    Bernhard, Sandra, 3:473

    Bernhard, Sarah, 3:473–474

    Bernstein-Cohen, Miriam, 3:486

    Besekow, Samuel, 3:494

    Bouwmeester, Louis Frederik Johannes, 4:107

    Brice, Fanny, 4:177

    Broderick, Matthew, 4:195

    Brooks, Albert, 4:209

    Brooks, Mel, 4:209–210

    Buloff, Joseph, 4:278

    Burns, George, 4:298

    Burstyn, Mike, 4:301

    Busch, Charles, 4:303

    Caan, James, 4:329

    Carnovsky, Morris, 4:486–487

    Carter, Nell, 4:498

    Chronegk, Ludwig, 4:695

    Clayburgh, Jill, 4:752

    Cobb, Lee J., 4:764

    Cooper, Jackie, 5:205

    Crystal, Billy, 5:315

    Curtis, Jamie Lee, 5:342

    Curtis, Tony, 5:342–343

    Da Silva, Howard, 5:439

    Dessoir, Ludwig, 5:605

    Deutsch, Ernst, 5:622

    Donath, Ludwig, 5:748

    Douglas, Kirk, 5:764–765

    Douglas, Melvyn, 5:765

    Douglas, Michael, 5:765

    Einstein, Arik, 6:263

    England, 5:58, 6:716, 11:76

    Ford, Harrison, 7:125

Actors, *continued*
    Hanbury, Lily, 8:318
    Hanray, Lawrence, 8:330–331
    Harris, Barbara, 8:362
    Hawn, Goldie, 8:473–474
    Hershey, Barbara, 9:45
    Hirsch, Judd, 9:126
    Hirsch, Robert Paul, 9:129
    Hoffman, Dustin, 9:307–308
    Holliday, Judy, 9:322–323
    Homolka, Oscar, 9:516
    Howard, Leslie, 9:572
    Howard, Moe, Shemp, and Curly, 9:572–573
    Huarte de San Juan, Juan, 9:575
    Israel, 10:821
    Jaffe, Sam, 11:69
    Lahr, Bert, 12:439–440
    Lamarr, Hedy, 12:442
    Landon, Michael, 12:473
    Lasser, Louise, 12:503
    Lavin, Linda, 12:532
    Lawrence, Gerald, 12:545
    Leachman, Cloris, 12:563
    Lederer, Francis, 12:597
    Leonidov, Leonid Mironovich, 12:648
    Leontovich, Eugenie, 12:649
    Levant, Oscar, 12:678
    Levene, Sam, 12:679
    Levey, Barnett, 12:682
    Matlin, Marlee, 13:679–680
    Matthau, Walter, 13:687
    Mazursky, Paul, 13:709
    Menken, Adah Isaacs, 14:48
    Mitchell, Yvonne, 14:369
    Mogulesko, Sigmund, 14:418
    Morewski, Abraham, 14:486
    Moscheles, Ignaz, 14:516
    Neilson, Julia, 15:66
    Neuwirth, Bebe, 15:125–126
    Persoff, Nehemiah, 15:793
    Picon, Molly, 16:147
    Polanski, Roman, 16:326
    Rachel (Felix, Eliza Rachel), 17:50
    Radner, Gilda, 17:55
    Rainer, Luise, 17:74
    Randall, Tony, 17:90–91
    Reeve, Ada, 17:162
    Reiner, Carl, 17:205–206
    Reiner, Rob, 17:206–207
    Rickles, Don, 17:292
    Rieser, Paul, 17:212
    Ritt, Martin, 17:345
    Roberts, Tony, 17:354

    Robinson, Edward G., 17:355
    Rodensky, Shemuel, 17:363
    Roessler, Carl, 17;367
    Rovina, Hanna, 17:501
    Rubinstein, Ida, 17:517
    Rudner, Rita, 17:523
    Runitsch, Ossip, 17:529
    Schottlaender, Bendet, 18:165
    Schwimmer, David, 18:195
    Segal, George, 18:246
    Seldes, Marian, 18:259
    Sellers, Peter, 18:271–272
    Seymour, Jane, 18:332–333
    Shatner, William, 18:420
    Sher, Sir Anthony, 18:461
    Signoret, Simone, 18:568
    Silver, Ron, 18:585–586
    Singerman, Berta, 18:640–641
    Sloman, Henry, 18:675
    Sofaer, Abraham, 18:740
    Yiddish
        Ben-Ami, Jacob, 3:316
        Dzigan, Shimon, 6:80
        Kalich, Bertha, 11:734
        Lebedeff, Aaron, 12:589
        Satz, Ludwig, 18:76
Actors' Equity Association, 18:586
Acts of Alexandrian Martyrs. *See* Alexandrian Martyrs, Acts of
Acts of Pilate, 15:394
Acts of the Alexandrine Martyrs. See Acta Isidori et Lamponis
Acts of the Apostles, 15:190
Acts of the Pagan Martyrs. *See* Alexandrian Martyrs, Acts of
Acts of Thomas, 15:394
Actuality and Potentiality. *See* Form and matter
ACWA. *See* Amalgamated Clothing Workers of America (ACWA)
Aczél, Tamás, 1:**370**
Ada (Austria), 1:**370**
Adāb al-Falāsifa (Ḥunain), 1:657
Adabberah va-Yirvaḥ Li (Kariv), 11:808
Adad. *See* Hadad
Adadah. *See* Aroer (Israel)
Adadi, Abraham Ḥayyim ben masoud Ḥai, 1:**370**
Adah, 1:**370–371**
Adalberg, Samuel, 1:**371**
Adam, 1:**371–376**
    aggadic literature, 1:372–373
    in the arts, 1:375–376
    biblical literature, 1:371
    Eve and, 6:572–573

    Islamic legend, 1:374–375
    medieval philosophy, 1:373–374
    Seth and, 18:319
    symbolism of, 16:106, 107
Adam (ancient Israel), 1:**376**
Adam (journal), 1:**376–377**
Adam (Sobol), 18:702
Adam (sculpture, Epstein), 6:471
Adam, Lajos, 1:**377**
Adam, Louis. *See* Adam, Lajos
Adam, other books of, 1:**377**
Adamah le-Lo Ẓel (Sened), 18:288
Adam and Eve, Book of the Life of. See Book of the Life of Adam and Eve
Adam Ba'al Shem, 1:**378**, 3:9
Adam Elyon. *See* Adam Kadmon
Adam ha-Kohen. *See* Lebensohn, Abraham Dov
Adamit (Israel), 1:**378**
Adam Kadmon, 1:**378–379**, 11:645
Adam Kadmon (Herrera), 9:40–41
"Adam mi-Yisrael" (Hazaz), 8:493
Adams, Arlin Marvin, 1:**379–380**
Adams, Franklin Pierce, 1:**380**
Adams, Hannah, 1:**380**
Adams, John, 1:**380**
Adams, Theodore L., 1:**380–381**
Adani. *See* Dahan Family
Adani, David ben Amram, 1:**381**
Adani, David ben Yesha ha-Levi, 1:**381**
Adani, Mahalal, 1:**381**, 389
Adani, Mahallal ben Shalom ben Jacob. *See* Adani, Mahalal
Adani, Mizraḥi Shalom, 1:**381**
Adani, Saadiah ben David, 1:**381**
Adani, Sa'id ibn Daud. *See* Adani, Saadiah ben David
Adani, Samuel ben Joseph, 1:**381–382**
Adani, Samuel ben Yeshua. *See* Adani, Samuel ben Joseph
Adani, Shalom Jacob. *See* Adani, Mahalal
Adani, Solomon. *See* Adeni, Solomon bar Joshua
Adar, 1:**382**
Adar, seventh of, 1:**382–383**
Adar, Zvi, 1:**383**
Adarbi, Isaac ben Samuel, 1:**383**, 15:537
Adarique, Isaac, 4:257
Adar symbolism, vol. 2: color insert
Adasa (ancient Israel) l, 1:**383**
Adas Israel Anshe Poilen (Ontario), 8:304
Adaskin, Murray, 1:**384**
Adass Jeshurun, Adass Jisroel, 1:**384**

Adath Israel (Cincinnati), 7:705
Adato, Solomon, 16:346
Adda bar Ahavah, 1:**384–385**
Addams, Jane, 18:320
Adderet Eliyahu (Bashyazi), 3:**198,**
  11:800
Adderet Eliyahu (Elijah), 6:339
"Addir bi-Melukhah," 1:**385**
"Addir Hu," 1:**385**
Addison, Lancelot, 6:180
Additional service. *See* Musaf
*Addresses to the German Nation. See
  Reden an die deutsche Nation*
  (Fichte)
Addu. *See* Hadad
Ad Eilat (Shamir), 18:392
Adel, 1:**385**
Adelaide (Australia), 1:**385–386**
Adelantado. *See* Adelantados
Adelantados, 1:**386**
Adelantatus. *See* Adelantados
Adelbert, Maximilian. *See* Baer, Max
Adelkind, Cornelio, 15:641
Adelkind, Israel Cornelius, 1:**386,** 4:52
Adelman, A. *See* Tashrak
Adelman, Uri, 1:**386**
Adelson, Howard Laurence, 1:**386**
Adelstein, Angelica. *See* Adelstein-
  Rozeanu, Angelica
Adelstein-Rozeanu, Angelica, 1:**386–
  387**
Aden (Saudi Arabia), 1:381–382, **387–
  389,** 5:681
Adenantado. *See* Adelantados
Adenauer, Konrad, 1:**390**
Adeni, Solomon bar Joshua, 1:**390,**
  14:329
Aderca, Felix, 1:**390–391**
Aderca, Froim Zeilig. *See* Aderca, Felix
AdeReT. *See* Rabinowitz-Teomim,
  Elijah David ben Benjamin
Adhan, Solomon, 5:379
Adiabene (Mesopotamia), 1:**391–392,**
  3:27, 10:823, 14:447
Adiabene family
  Ananias of Adiabene, 2:129
  Josephus' *Jewish Antiquities* on,
    11:440
Adieu Babylone (Kattan), 4:425
Adir. *See* Deinard, Ephraim
Adi the Arab, 15:377
Adjiman, Abraham, 1:392
Adjiman, Baruch, 1:392
Adjiman, Eliya, 1:392
Adjiman, Isaiah, 15:542
Adjiman, Meir, 15:542
Adjiman, Yeshaya, 1:392

Adjiman family, 1:**392**
ADL (Anti-Defamation League). *See*
  Anti-Defamation League (ADL)
Adler. See Der Keneder Adler
Adler, Abraham, 8:504
Adler, Alexandre, 1:**394**
Adler, Alfred, 1:**394–395,** 5:302, 6:160–
  161
Adler, Celia, 1:394
Adler, Chaim, 18:735
Adler, Charles, 1:**395**
Adler, Cyrus, 1:**395,** 5:172
  American Jewish Committee, 2:54,
    55
  American Jewish Historical
    Society, 2:58, 59
  Dropsie College, 6:25
  Jewish Quarterly Review, 11:313
  Jewish Theological Seminary,
    6:197, 11:328, 329
Adler, Dankmar, 1:**395–396**
Adler, David Baruch, 1:**396**
Adler, Elkan Nathan, 1:392, **396**
  as bibliophile, 3:684
  Eleazar ben Jacob ha-Bavli, 6:302
  Judeo-Persian manuscripts
    collected by, 11:558
Adler, Elmer, 1:**396**
Adler, Emanuel Philip, 1:**396,** 11:468
Adler, Felix, 1:392, **396–397,** 407,
  4:122
Adler, Frances, 1:394
Adler, Friedrich (designer), 1:**397**
Adler, Friedrich (labor leader), 1:**397,**
  16:340–341, 18:705, 712
Adler, Georg, 1:**397**
Adler, Guido, 1:**397–398**
Adler, Harry Clay, 1:**398**
Adler, Herbert Marcus, 1:392
Adler, Hermann (poet), 1:**398–399**
Adler, Hermann (rabbi), 1:392, **398,**
  11:417
Adler, Hermann Naphtali. *See* Adler,
  Hermann (rabbi)
Adler, Hugo Chaim, 1:**399**
Adler, Isaac, 1:392
Adler, Israel, 1:**399**
Adler, Jacob (actor), 1:392–393, 393*t*
Adler, Jacob (artist). *See* Adler, Jankel
Adler, Jacob (poet), 1:**399–400**
Adler, Jankel, 1:**400–401,** 4:87
Adler, Joseph, 1:**401**
Adler, Jules, 1:**401,** 3:695
Adler, Julia, 1:394
Adler, Julius Ochs, 1:**401**
Adler, Larry, 1:**401–402**
Adler, Lazarus Levi, 1:**402**

Adler, Liebman, 1:**402**
Adler, Luther, 1:394
Adler, Marcus, 1:392
Adler, Marcus Nathan, 1:392
Adler, Max, 18:705
Adler, Max (Philanthropist), 1:**402**
Adler, Max (Socialist), 1:**402–403,**
  18:729
Adler, Michael, 1:**403**
Adler, Mordechai. *See* Adler, Marcus
Adler, Moritz, 1:**403**
Adler, Morris, 1:**403,** 12:411
Adler, Mortimer Jerome, 1:**403–404**
Adler, Naphtali. *See* Adler, Hermann
  (rabbi)
Adler, Nathan, 4:58
Adler, Nathan ben Simeon ha-Kohen,
  1:392, **404–405**
Adler, Nathan Marcus, 1:392, **405,**
  6:415
  Jews' College, 11:332
  Schiller-Szinessy, Solomon Mayer
    and, 18:134
Adler, Nettie, 1:392
Adler, Paul, 1:**405**
Adler, Pearl. *See* Adler, Polly
Adler, Polly, 1:**405–406**
Adler, Rachel, 6:755, 756, 16:111–112
Adler, Renata, 1:**406**
Adler, Richard, 1:**406–407**
Adler, Samuel (1809-1891), 1:392,
  407, 15:199
Adler, Samuel M. (1898-1979), 1:**407**
Adler, Sara, 1:393–394
Adler, Saul Aaron, 1:**407–408**
Adler, Selig, 1:**408**
Adler, Shalom ben Menahem, 1:**408**
Adler, Shulamit. *See* Aloni, Shulamit
Adler, Stella, 1:394, **408–409**
Adler, Victor, 1:**409,** 4:137, 16:340,
  18:705
Adlerblum, Nima, 1:**409**
Adler family (Frankfurt, Germany),
  1:**392,** 393*t*
Adler family (U.S.), 1:**392–394**
Adler Planetarium and Astronomical
  Museum, 1:402
Adler-Rudel, Salomon, 1:**409–410**
Adlivankin, Samuil, 1:**410**
Adloyada, 1:**410,** vol. 6: color insert
Ad Mashber (Halkin), 8:736–737
Administrative Behavior (Simon),
  18:611
The Admiral's Log Vol. 1 and Vol. 2
  (Moreel), 14:483
Admission, 1:**410–411,** 5:191
Admon, Yedidyah, 1:**411**

Admon ben Gaddai, 1:**412**

Admoni, Vladimir Grigoryevich, 1:**412**

Admonition. *See* Rebuke and reproof

Admonition and chastisement. *See* Rebuke and reproof

Admor, 1:**412**

Adolphus, Jacob, 1:412

Adolphus, John, 1:412

Adolphus, John Leycester, 1:412

Adolphus, Joy. *See* Adolphus, Simhah

Adolphus, Meir. *See* Adolphus, Michael

Adolphus, Michael, 1:412

Adolphus, Moses, 1:412

Adolphus, Simhah, 1:412

Adolphus family, 1:**412**

Adonai, 7:674–675

Adonai, Adonai, El Raḥum ve-Ḥannun, 1:**412**

Adoni-Bezek, 1:**413**, 414

Adonijah, 1:259, **413**, 18:755

Adonim. *See* Dunash Ibn Tamim

Adonim ben Nisan ha-Levi, 1:**413**

Adonim ha-Levi. *See* Dunash ben Labrat

Adoniram, 1:**413**

Adonis. *See* Tammuz (Sumerian-Babylonian fertility god)

Adonis (Sivan), 18:647

Adoni-Zedek, 1:**413–414**

Adon Olam, 1:*414*, **414–415**

Adoption, 1:**415–420**, 6:693
  biblical, 1:415–416
  Halakhah, 1:417–418
  Israel, 1:418–419

Adoraim (ancient Israel), 1:**420**

Adoram. *See* Adoniram

Adorno, Theodor W., 1:**420**, 18:739

Ad quaestiones et obiecta Judaei cuiusdam Responsio (Calvin), 4:376–377

Adrakhta, writ of, 6:592–593

Adrammelech (deity), 1:**421**, 2:126

Adrammelech (son of Sennacherib), 1:**421**

Adret, Moses ibn, 1:**421**

Adret, Solomon ben Abraham, 1:**421–423**, 8:449
  Aaron ben Joseph ha-Levi and, 1:215
  Abba Mari ben Moses ben Joseph Astruc of Lunel and, 1:230
  allegorical interpretation of scripture, 3:645
  amulets, 2:121
  Anatoli, Jacob ben Abba Mari ben Samson, 2:132

codification, 4:774
  mistakes, 14:368–369
  moneylending, 14:439

Adrian I. *See* Hadrian I (pope)

Adrianople (Turkey). *See* Edirne (Turkey)

Adriel, 1:**423**

Adullam (ancient Israel), 1:**423–424**

Adullam Region (ancient Israel), 1:**424**

Adultery, 1:**424–427**
  abortion, 1:272
  bigamy and polygamy, 3:691–694
  bitter water ordeal, 11:374
  Joseph and Potiphar's wife, 11:407, 411, 413
  ordeal of jealousy, 15:462–463
  as sexual offense, 18:329
  Talmud, 4:582
  water of bitterness, 15:462

Adult Jewish Education (AJE), 4:15

Advances in Petrography in Russia. See Uspekhi petrografii v Rossii (Loewinson-Lessing)

Adventures of an Economist (Modigliani), 14:411

The Adventures of Augie March (Bellow), 3:300, 301

The Adventures of Mr. Ionel Lacusta Termidor. See Aventurile domnului Ionel Lăcusta Termidor

Adverbs in Hebrew, 8:585–586

Adversus Judaeorum inveteratum duritiam (Peter of Cluny), 16:15–16

Advertising, 1:**427–429**, 3:471, 4:315, 5:329, 12:496

Advertising, misrepresentation, 5:188

Aegidius da Viterbo. *See* Egidio Da Viterbo

Aelana. *See* Akaba (Jordan)

Aelfric of Eynsham, 3:611

Aelia Capitolina, 1:*429*, **429**, 11:152

Aelian, 1:**429**

Aeltestenrat, Kovno, 6:358–359

Der aelteste Prophetismus (Sellin), 18:272

Aeon (Mombert), 14:430

Aerojet Engineering Corporation, 11:812

Aeronautics, 1:**429–430**
  Brodetsky, Selig, 4:196
  Hoffman, Jeffrey, 9:308
  Kármán, Theodore Von, 11:811–812
  Lees, Lester, 12:600
  Lilienthal, Otto, 13:17
  Rom, Yosef, 17:373
  Rumpler. Eduard, 17:529

Schwarz, David, 18:189
  Silverstein, Abe, 18:588

Aeronomy, 11:776

Aescoly, Aaron Ze'ev, 1:**430–431**

Aesopian fables, 6:666, 667, 669

Afam. *See* Apam

Afarayim. *See* Hapharaim (Ancient Israel)

Afarsemon. *See* Balsam

Afendopolo, Caleb ben Elijah, 1:**431**

Afer, Constantinus. *See* Africanus

Affirmative action and quotas, 3:737

Affonso, 1:**431–432**

Affonso Henriques, King of Portugal, 1:431

Affonso II, King of Portugal, 1:431

Affonso III, King of Portugal, 1:431

Affonso IV, King of Portugal, 1:431

Affonso V, King of Portugal, 1:431–432

Afforestation, 6:452

Afghanistan, 1:*432*, **432–433**
  Jewish quarters, 11:312
  Judeo-Persian language in, 11:548

Afia, Aaron, 1:**433**

Afike Jehuda, 1:**433**

Afikim (Israel), 1:**433–434**

Afikoman, 1:**434**

Aflalo, Moses, 14:499

AFL-CIO. *See* American Federation of Labor

Afonso. *See* Affonso

Afriat, Judah, 15:391

Africa, 1:**434–437**, *435*
  African Jewish Congress, 1:440–441
  community organization and structures, 5:108, 115*t*, 119*t*
  foreign policy and relations with Israel (state), 10:257–258, 259, 260, 262, 263, 264, 265
    technical and economic assistance, 10:221, 266
  House of Israel community, 9:569–570
  Jewish settlement, 1:434–437
  languages, biblical translations, 3:601–602, 637
  Lemba, 12:636–637
  See also North Africa; South Africa

African Americans, antisemitism and, 2:231–232, 238

African Jewish Congress (AJC), 1:**440–441**

Africanus, 6:159

Afro. *See* Ephron (town, Israel)

Afro-Asian Institute, 18:709

Aftalion, Albert, 1:**441**

After All is Said and Done. See Nokh Alemen

After Auschwitz (Rubenstein), 9:392–393, 17:271–272, 511

After Emancipation (Ellenson), 6:360

Afterlife, 1:**441–442**
    beatitude, 3:237–240
    body and soul, concept of, 4:31
    embalming, 6:390
    existence, 14:34
    Mishnah, 14:323
    Netherworld, 15:110–112
    philosophy of, 13:447–448
    See also Eschatology; Olam ha-ba

After the Fall (Miller), 14:252

After the Tradition: Essays on Modern Jewish Writing (Alter), 2:18

Afulah (Israel), 1:**442–443**

Aga, Benjamin, 1:443

Aga, Samuel ben Abraham, 1:443

Die Agadah der Palaestinensischen Amoraeer (Bacher), 1:460

Die Agadah der Tannaiten (Bacher), 1:460

Agadati, Baruch, 1:**443–444**

Agadir (Morocco), 1:**444**

Aga family, 1:**443**

Agag, 1:**444–445**, 2:29, 30, 31

Ágai, Adolf, 1:**445**

Against Appion (Josephus), 11:440

Against the Apocalypse: Responses to Catastrophe in Modern Jewish Culture (Roskies), 9:415

Agam, Yaacov, 1:**445**

Agar, Emile. *See* Gary, Romain

Agatharchides of Cnidus, 1:**445–446**

Agatstein, Mieczyslaw. *See* Jastrun, Mieczyslaw

Agbara *v.* Agbara, 5:135–136

Agde (France), 1:**446**

Age and the aged, 1:**446–449**, 5:568–570, 12:417

Agen (France), 1:**449**

Agency, 1:**449–454**, 15:425

Agenda 21 (sustainable development plan), 6:453

The Age of Capital (Howbsbawm), 9:299

The Age of Empire (Howbsbawm), 9:299

The Age of Extremes (Howbsbawm), 9:299

The Age of Revolution (Howbsbawm), 9:299

Age of the earth, 15:498

Age of the Ghetto (Italy), 10:800–801

Aggadah (Alexander Suslin ha-Kohen of Frankfurt), 1:630

Aggadah or Haggadah, 1:**454–464**
    Aaron, 1:210
    Abba Bar Kahana, 1:226
    Abiathar, 1:254–255
    Abigail, 1:256
    Abilmelech, 1:257–258
    Abishag the Shunammite, 1:259
    Abishai, 1:260
    Abner, 1:264
    Aboab, Isaac I, 1:266
    Abraham, 1:283–284
    Abraham, Testament of, 1:291
    Abraham's bosom, 1:317
    Absalom, 1:331
    academies, 1:348
    Achan, 1:354
    Adam, 1:372–373, 374–375
    Adonijah, 1:413
    Adret, Solomon ben Abraham, 1:423
    Agag, 1:445
    Aggadat Bereshit, 1:464
    Ahab, 1:524
    Ahasuerus, 1:538, 14:479
    Ahimelech the Hittite, 1:545
    Ahithophel the Gilonite, 1:545
    'Alef, 1:607–608
    Alexander the Great, 1:626–627
    allegorical interpretation of scripture in, 3:643–644
    Amalekites, 2:30–31
    Amasa, 2:33
    Amaziah, 2:36
    Ammonites, 2:86
    Amon, 2:88
    amoraim, 2:94
    Amram, 2:103
    anthropomorphism, 2:190
    Antoninus Pius, 2:248–249
    Apocalypse of Baruch, 3:184–185
    Ark of the Covenant, 2:468–469
    Asa, 2:540–541
    Ashburnham Pentateuch, 1:463
    Asher, 2:560
    Balaam, 3:80
    Baruch, 3:182
    Bath-Sheba, 3:212
    Belshazzar, 3:306
    Benjamin, tribe of, 3:**356**
    Bethsaida (Israel), 3:536
    Bilhah in, 3:698
    Bithiah in, 3:729

Boaz, 4:22–23

Cain, 4:340

Caleb, Calebites, 4:354

calligraphy, modern Hebrew, 4:366–367

cherub, cherubim, 4:600–601

Chilion, 13:361–362

Christian illustrated manuscripts, 1:463

Church Fathers, 4:721

commentaries, 11:69

copper serpent, 5:214–215

David, 5:451–453

day and night, 5:486–487

Deborah, 5:518–519

Delilah, 5:539

Dinah, 5:669

doctrines, 1:458–459

Doeg, 5:730

Edom, 6:156–157

eggs, 6:219–620

Eglon (King), 6:222

Egyptians, 16:28–29

Eldad and Medad, 6:293

Eleazar ben Azariah, 6:299–300, 300–301

Eleazar ben Ḥarsom, 6:301–302

Eleazar ben Pedat, 6:306–307

Eleazar ben Simeon, 6:308

Eleazar ben Yose I, 6:308

Eleazar ben Zadok, 6:309

Eleazar ha-Kappar, 6:309

Eleazar Ḥisma, 6:309–310

Eleazar of Modi'in, 6:310

Eli, 6:317

Eliakim Goetz ben Meir, 6:318

Eli and Hannah, 6:317

Eliezer, 6:322

Eliezer ben Hyrcanus, 6:322–325

Elihu, 6:331

Elijah, 6:333–334

Eliphaz, 6:350

Elisha, 6:351

Elkanah, 6:357

Enoch, 6:442

Enosh, 6:445

Ephraim, 6:*456*, 456–457

Esau, 6:487–488

Esther, 6:*516*, 14:479

Esther Rabbah, 6:519–520

Eve, 6:573

evolution in, 6:587

Ezekiel, 6:644–645

Ezra, 6:653

fire, 7:43–44

Aggadah or Haggadah, *continued*
the Flood, 7:83
folkloristic, 1:455–456
Gabriel, 14:168
Gad, 7:330
Garden of Eden, 7:388–389
Gehazi, 7:411–412
Gehenna, 15:111–112
geography, 7:489–490
Gibeonites, 7:585
Gideon, 7:587–588
God, 7:660–661
golden calf, 7:700–701
Goliath, 7:738
Hadrian, 8:194
Hagar, 8:206
Ham, 8:290
Haman, 8:294
Hananiah son of Azzur, 8:317
Ḥanina bar Ḥama, 8:321–322
Ḥanina ben Dosa, 8:323
Hannah and birth of Samuel,
8:324–325
heart references, 8:509–510
Hebrew manuscripts, 13:489
Ḥelbo, 8:780
Hezekiah, 9:89
historical, 1:457–458
Hosea, Book of, 9:558
Huldah, 9:581
Hur, 9:623
Hushai the Archite, 9:640
hymns, 1:385
intention of act, 11:58–59
Isaac, 10:33
Isaiah, Book of, 10:73
Ishmael (son of Abraham), 10:81–
82
Islamic, 1:463
Israel, Kingdom of, 10:741
Issachar, 10:767
Ithamar, 10:817
Jacob, 11:20–22, 27
Jair, 11:73
Japeth, 11:86
Jehoiachin, 11:107
Jehoiada, 11:108
Jehoiakim, 11:109
Jehoram (King of Israel), 11:110
Jephthah, 11:123
Jeremiah, 11:133
Jeroboam I, 11:140–141
Jerusalem, 11:211–213, 226
Jesse, 11:243
Jethro, 11:252

Jezebel in, 11:334
Joab, 11:339
Job, 11:356–357
Jochebed, 11:360–361
Jonah, Book of, 11:390
Jonathan (son of Saul), 11:395–
396
Joseph, 11:411–412
Joseph ben Judah Engel, 6:409
Josephus' *Jewish Antiquities* and,
11:438
Joshua, 11:443
Joshua ben Levi, 11:453–454
Josiah, 11:459
Jotham, 11:466
Jubilees, Book of, 11:473
Judah, 11:477–478
Judah Loew ben Bezalel, influence
of, 11:507
Kabbalah, influence on, 11:669–
671
kabbalists' interpretations of,
11:669–670
Kamẓa and Bar Kamẓa, 11:758
Kohath and Kohathites, 12:257
Korah, 12:298–299
Krochmal, Nachman, 12:368
Laban, 12:406–407
Lamech, 12:445
Leah, 12:567
leprosy, 12:653
Levi, 12:683–684
Lot, 13:216
Mahlon, 13:361–362
Malachi, Book of, 13:423
Manasseh (King), 13:453
Manasseh (tribe), 13:452
manna, 13:478–479
methods, 1:456–457
Micaiah (son of Imlah), 14:165
Michael (angel), 14:168
Michah (prophet and book),
14:163
Michal, 14:172
Midian, Midianites, 14:181–182
Miriam, 14:311–312
Mishnah, 14:322–323
moon, 14:467–468
Mordecai (5th c. B.C.E.), 14:479
Moses, 14:534, 538
Mount Sinai, 18:627–629
mushrooms, 14:636
Naaman, 14:713–714
Nabal, 14:715–716
Naboth, 14:720
Nadab and Abihu, 14:721–722

Naomi, 14:773
Nashon, 14:757
Nebuchadnezzar, 15:49–50
Nebuzaradan, 15:52
Nedarim, 15:53–54
Nehemiah (5th c. B.C.E.), 15:61
Netherworld, 15:111–112
niddah, 15:257
Nimrod, 15:269
Nineveh, 15:272
Noah, 15:288
Og, 15:391–392
Orpah, 15:482
Othniel, 15:515
Passover, Dayyeinu, 5:496
patriarchs and matriarchs, 15:691
Peninnah, 15:726
Perez, 15:769
Philistines, 16:55
Phinehas, 16:114–115, 115
Phinehas ben Ḥama ha-Kohen,
16:116
pigs, 16:150–151
Pirkei de Rabbi Eliezer, 16:182–183
Pollegar, Isaac ben Joseph ibn,
16:359
Potiphar, 16:419–420
pre-Middle Ages, 13:88–89, 91–93
Queen of Sheba, 16:765
Rabbah bar bar Ḥana, 17:8
Rachel, 17:48
Rahab, 17:66–67
Rea Sea, 17:160–161
Rebekah, 17:137–138
Rehoboam, 17:192
religious impact of Bible and,
3:661, 662
Reuben, 17:246
rod of Aaron, 17:365
rod of Moses, 17:366
Ruth, Book of, 17:595
Samael, 17:715
Samson, 17:750
Samuel, 17:755–756
Sarah, 18:46–47
Saul, 18:80–81
Sennacherib, 18:290
Seth, 18:319
Sheba ben Bichri, 18:428
Shem, 18:453
Shimei, 18:480
Sihon, 15:391–392
Simeon, 18:592
Simeon ben Gamaliel II, 18:596
Simeon ben Jehozadak, 18:597

Simeon ha-Timni, 18:601

Sodom and Gomorrah, 18:738–739

Solomon, 18:759–760

sources of, 1:454–455

structure and style, 1:457

studies and scholarship, 1:460–463

sun, 19:313–314

synagogues, 19:364

Tabernacle, 19:423–424

Tablets of the Law, 19:425

Tamar, 19:493–494

Terah, 19:645–646

32 rules, 3:129

Thummim, 20:423

Titus, Flavius Vespasianus, 19:744

Tower of Babel, 3:20–21

Tubal-Cain, 20:166

twelve tribes, 20:140

Uriah, 20:421

Urim, 20:423

Vashti, 20:479

Venice edition, 8:214–215

in vernacular, *Mayse-Bukh*, 13:702–703

wells, 21:7

wilderness, 21:61

witch of En-Dor, 6:405

women in, 1:459–460

Zebulon, 10:767

Zechariah, 21:481, 482, 485–486

Zedekiah, 21:489

Zelophehad, 21:502

Zerah the Cushite, 21:513

Zerubbabel, 21:517

Zimri, 21:536

Zipporah, 21:639

See also Midrash

Aggadat Arba Kosot (Pappenheim), 8:687, 15:618

Aggadat Aseret Harugei Malkhut, 7:10

Aggadat Bereshit, 1:**464**

Aggadat Desheh (song), 6:263

Aggadat Eikhah. See Lamentations Rabbah

Aggadat Proverbs. See Midrash Proverbs

Aggadat Samuel. See Midrash Samuel

Aggadat Shir ha-Shirim, 14:187

Aggadat Tehillim. See Midrash Tehillim

Aggadic Midrash. See Midrash Aggadah

Aggav karka, 1:362

Aggide. See Akkad (Sumer)

Aggudath Harabbonim. See Union of Orthodox Rabbis of the United States and Canada

Aghlabids, 11:726–727

Aghlabids dynasty, 1:**464–465**

Aghmati, Zechariah ben Judah, 1:**465**

Agmon, Nathan, 1:**465**, 8:716, 11:441

Agmon, Shmuel, 1:**465**

Agnes Jordan (Hirschfeld), 9:137

Agnon, Shmuel Yosef, 1:**465–469**, 8:696–697, 698–699, 11:217

Agnon's Alef Bet. See Sefer ha-Otiyyot

Agobard, 1:**469**, 2:124, 3:121, 13:296

Agorah series of coins, 5:55

Agoranomos, 1:**469–470**

Agram. See Zagreb (Croatia)

Agramunt (Spain), 1:**470**

Agranat, Shimon, 1:**470**

Agranat Commission, 6:289

Agranium. See Hagronia (Mesopotamia)

Agrarian League, 1:**470**

Agrat Bat Mahalath, 1:**470–471**, 5:575

Agrest, Diana, 1:**471**

Agricultural arendas, 2:422–423

Agricultural festivals, 5:167

Agricultural land-management methods and implements in ancient Erez Israel, 1:**471–486**

  agronomy, 6:290

  field boundaries, 1:474–476

  hoeing, weeding, harvesting, 1:484–485

  implements, installations, 1:482–483

  irrigation, 1:481–482

  land-management, 1:472–474

  manuring procedures, 1:479–480

  plowing, 1:483–484

  Raab, Judah, 17:5–6

  shape and size, 1:476–479

  Solomon, 18:757

  sowing, planting, 1:484

  terracing, 1:474

  topographical influence, 1:472

  winnowing, 1:485–486

Agriculture, 1:**486–502**

  Abel, 1:245

  Agrarian League, Germany, 1:470

  agronomy

    Elazari-Volcani, Yizhak, 6:290

    Rosen, Joseph A., 17:428

  American-Jewish Joint Agricultural Corporation, 2:60

  Am Olam, 2:87–88

  Argentina, 6:448–449

  Babylon, 1:493–494

  Birobidzhan, 3:717–720

  in Bolivia, 4:48

Bondi, Aron, 4:57

Brazil, 4:145–146

Broward County, FL, 4:212–213

Brown, Bejamin, 4:214

Brutzkus, Boris Dov, 4:228

Canada, 1:500, 4:399, 407

citriculture, 4:737–738

commandments concerning, 5:82*t*

Dagon, god of, 5:378

drought, 6:**707–708**

economic history, 6:96–97, 100–101, 102, 132–133

economic history, and employment in, 6:132–134

Erez Israel, 1:471–486

Europe

  Jewish Colonization Association, 11:286

  modern, 1:497–499

fig cultivation, 7:18

five species, 7:66

flax, 7:69–70

flowers, 7:89–91

Halperin, Haim, 8:283

Israel, 1:486–490, 6:543

  aliyah, First, 10:357–358, 480–482

  aliyah, Fourth, 10:199

  aliyah, Second, 10:358–359

  aliyah and absorption of immigrants, 10:342, 527–529, 528*t*

  animal distribution and, 10:142–143

  Arab, 10:713

  Arab labor, 10:195

  Arab population, 10:485–486

  Baron de Rothschild settlements, 11:9

  citrus culture, 6:750

  continuous from ancient times in Peki'in, 15:716–717

  cooperatives, 5:209–210

  Demalach, Yoel, 5:548

  development projects in foreign nations, 10:267

  education, 10:668–669

  employment trends, 10:557–558

  Erfat, Yaacov, 6:216

  Farmers' Federation of Israel, 6:718

  Israel Prize, 10:760

  Jewish Agency, 11:259

  Lavi, Shelomo, 12:531

  Levitt, Esther, 12:743

Agriculture, *continued*

    performance, 10:530–531

    population of Sharon region, 10:378

    rural planning, 10:368–369

    schools, 13:788

    self-sufficiency, 10:222

    settlement beyond Green Line, 10:361–366

  Joseph's agrarian measures in Egypt, 11:409, 410

  Lachish region, 12:422–423

  Latin America, 1:500–501

  lease and hire, 12:572

  leket, shikhḥah, and pe'ah, 12:631–632

  Middle Ages, 1:494–497

  mixed species, 14:385–387

  Moab, 14:400

  modern period, 12:427

  movements, Esra, 6:509

  nomadism/seminomadism and, 15:294, 295

  olive cultivation, 15:406–407

  Oppenheimer, Hillel, 15:448

  organizations, Esra, 6:509

  ORT, 15:488–492

  Ottoman period, 10:174, 183

  Palestine, 10:201, 204, 206

    Arab, 10:710–711

    Byzantine-Muslim period, 1:492–493

    downturn, 10:502–503

    economic affairs, 10:506–511

    employment in, 10:495–496

    Hasmonean period, 1:490

    Histadrut and, 10:595

    land purchases by Jews, 10:488

    leaders, 13:765

    Mishnaic and Talmudic period, 1:490–492

    mixed farming strategy, 10:491–942, 508–509, 510–511

    Reichert, Israel, 17:199–200

    restructuring of, 10:496

    Second Temple period, 1:490

    post World War II, 10:506–507

  population, farm output and land possession, 10:483t

  Ra-anannah, 17:6

  research, 6:574

  Romania, 4:177–178

  Russia, 4:177–178

  schools

    Beit Jamāl, 3:272

    Mikveh Israel, 14:222

  Second Aliyah, 10:483–485

  Smilansky, Moshe, 18:687

  U.S., 1:499–500

    Morgenthau, Henry, Jr., 14:489

    settlement of Jews, 11:262

  USSR regime projects, 17:544–545

  water supply constraints, 10:531–532

  See also Agricultural land-management methods and implements in ancient Ereẓ Israel; Botany; Moshavim

Agrigento (Italy), 1:**502**

Agrippa, Caius Julius, 1:**503–504**

Agrippa, Marcus Julius. *See* Agrippa II

Agrippa, Marcus Vipsanius, 1:**504**

Agrippa I, 1:**502–503**, 502t–503t, 9:199

  Caligula, Caius Caesar Augustus, 4:363

  Capito, Marcus Herennius, 4:451

  Drusilla (daughter), 6:28

  Jonathan ben Anan, 11:396

  Josephus' *Jewish Antiquities* on, 11:440

  Julius Archelaus and, 11:574

  Justus of Tiberias and, 11:581–582

Agrippa II, 1:**503**

  Anan, son of Anan, 2:126

  Bethsaida (Israel), 3:536

  Drusilla (wife), 6:28, 394

  Eleazar ben Ananias, 6:299

  Juvenal on, 11:582

Agrippias. *See* Anthedon (Hellenistic city)

Agrippina (ancient Israel), 1:**504**

Agrob. *See* Trachonitis (Palestine)

Agro-Joint. *See* American Jewish Joint Agricultural Corporation

Agron (Saadia Gaon), 8:653, 13:31–32

Agron, Gershon, 1:**504**

Agronim, 12:672–673

Agronsky, Gershon. *See* Agron, Gershon

Agudat ha-Soẓyalistim ha-Ivrim, 1:**504–505**, 18:704

Agudath Harabbonim. *See* Union of Orthodox Rabbis of the United States and Canada

Agudath Israel of America, 18:181

Agudat Israel, 1:**505–508**

  Bar-Ilan University, 3:153

  Birnbaum, Nathan, 3:715

  Blau, Amram, 3:742

  Blau, Moshe, 3:744

  Bloch, Joseph Leib, 3:763

  Dubin, Mordecai, 6:31

  education, Jewish, 6:184

  Halévy, Isaac, 8:270

  Latvia, 12:522

  Levin, Yiẓḥak Meir, 12:714

  Lieben, Salomon, 12:803

  Poland

    Kirschbraun, Elijah, 12:188

  Schwab, Hermann, 18:179

  Silver, Eliezer, 18:585

  U.S. branch, 18:585

  zionism and, 14:15

  See also Po'alei Agudat Israel

Aguddat Aḥim, 1:**508**

Aguddat ha-Koremim, 8:470

Aguddat ha-Soẓyalistim ha-Ivrim. *See* Agudat ha-Soẓyalistim ha-Ivrim

Aguilar, Diego D', 1:**508–509**

Aguilar, Emanuel Abraham, 1:**509**

Aguilar, Grace, 1:**509**

Aguilar, Moses Raphael D', 1:**509–510**

Aguilar de Campóo (Spain), 1:**509–510**

Aguilar Samuda, Joseph d'. *See* Samuda, Joseph d'Aguilar

Aguinis, Marcos, 1:**510**, 16:350

A Gumsucker on the Tramp (Spielvogel), 19:109

Agunah, 1:**510–520**

  annullment issues, 1:514–517

  avoidance of precautions, 1:512–513

  Benjamin Ze'ev Ben Mattathias of Arta, 3::364

  Chmielnicki massacres, 9:72

  civil marriage, 4:746–748

  concubine, 5:135

  definition, 1:510–511

  divorce, 5:711–719

  Epstein, Louis M., 6:475

  feminism and, 6:753

  husband death, proof of, 1:511–512

  Israel, 1:513, 517–520

  Judah ben Bava, 11:484

  Kahana, Solomon David, 11:712

  ketubbah, 12:97

  Sasson, Aaron ben Joseph, 18:67–68

  Slonik, Benjamin Aaron ben Abraham, 18:675

  takkanot, 19:440, 443–444, 450–452

  Tevul Yom, 19:658

  witnesses, 21:120, 124

Agunot, 4:656, 5:173, 18:169, 21:206–207

Agur (biblical figure). *See* Solomon (biblical figure)

Agur (Landau), 8:444

Agur (son of Jakeh), 1:**521**

Agursky, Mikhail, 1:**520**

Agursky, Samuel, 1:**520–521**

Agus, Irving Abraham, 1:**521**

Agus, Jacob B., 1:**521–522**

Aḥa (Babylonian scholar). *See* Aḥai (Babylonian scholar)

Aḥa (Palestinian amora), 1:**522**

Ahab (King of Israel), 1:**522–525**, *523*, 9:176

    Elijah, 6:331–332, 335–336

    Jezebel and, 11:333–334

    at Jezreel, 11:334

    Moab, 14:402

Ahab (son of Kolaiah), 1:**525**

Aḥa bar Ḥanina, 1:**525**

Aḥa bar Rav, 1:**525**

Aḥa ben Jacob, 1:**525**

Aḥad ha-Am, 1:**525–529**, 3:561–562, 8:692–693, 10:682, 683

    biblical exegesis and study, 3:647

    on blood libel, 3:778

    Brenner, Joseph Ḥayyim, 4:160

    Dubnow, Simon, 6:34

    Ehrenpreis, Marcus, 6:240

    encyclopedias, 6:400

    Ha-Shiloaḥ, 8:381

    Hebrew vocabulary, 8:675

    Judaism, on essence of, 11:512

    Minsk Conference, 14:297

    Montefiore, Claude Joseph Goldsmid, 14:456

    Moses, 14:537

    Nordau, Max, 15:298

    Odessa Committee, 15:382

    soul, immortality of, 19:38

    translations of writings of, 18:613–614

Aḥai (Babylonian scholar), 1:**529**

Aḥai (Palestinian amora). *See* Aḥa (Palestinian amora)

Aḥai ben Josiah, 1:**529**

Aḥai of Shabḥa. *See* Aḥa of Shabḥa

Ahalan Ḥaver (Ziblin), 18:206

Ahamant. *See* Rabbath-Ammon (Ancient Israel)

Aḥa of Shabḥa, 1:**529–531**

Aḥarei ha-Ḥagim (Kenaz), 12:75

'Aḥarit ha-yamim. *See* Eschatology

Aharon, Ezra, 1:**531**

Aharoni. *See* Mazeh, Jacob

Aharoni, Israel, 1:**531**

Aharoni, Yoḥanan, 1:**531–532**, 2:329, 330, 371, 11:523, 524

Aḥaronim, 1:**532–537**

    eighteenth century, 1:534–535

    informers, 9:785

    mishpat Ivri, 14:340

    nineteenth century, 1:535–536

    seventeenth century, 1:532–534

    sixteenth century, 1:532

Aharonov, Yakir, 1:**537**

Aharonovitch, Yosef, 1:**537–538**, 4:159

Aharonovitz, Joseph. *See* Aharonovitch, Yosef

Aharonowitz, Isaac. *See* Arnon, Isaac

Aharonowitz, Zalman. *See* Aran, Zalman

Ahasuerus, 1:**538**, 18:215, 216, 333

    Biztha, 3:730

    Mordecai, 14:478–479

    See also Wandering Jew

Ahasuerus-Xerxes, 1:**538**, 18:216

Ahasver. *See* Wandering Jew

Ahavah ba-Ta'anugim (Moses), 14:552–553

Ahavah Rabbah, 1:**538–539**

Ahavah Zarah (Barash), 3:136

Ahavat David (Fleckeles), 7:71

Ahavat David (Franco-Mendes), 6:399

Ahavat Olam, 1:**538–539**

Ahavat Ẓiyyon (Mapu), 18:202

Ahaz, 1:**539**, 2:88, 9:179–180

    Edom, 6:155

    eschatology, 6:491

Ahaziah, 1:**539–540**

Ahaziah (son of Ahab, king of Israel), 1:539, 9:177

Ahaziah (son of Jehoram, king of Judah), 1:539–540

Aḥdut ha-Avodah (periodical), 1:**540**, 8:382, 18:425

Aḥdut ha-Avodah ha-Historit (Shapiro), 1:540

Aḥdut ha-Avodah-Po'alei Zion, 8:341

Aḥdut ha-Avodah-Po'alei Zion, 1:**540–541**

A héber nyelv elemi tankönyve (Ballagi), 3:91

Ahenakew, David, 18:65

Aḥer. *See* Elisha ben Avuyah

Aḥerim, 1:**541**

Ahḥad ha-Am, 8:726–727

Ahijah, 1:**541**

Ahijah the Shilonite, 1:**542**, 18:758

Ahikam, 1:**542**, 6:287, 18:398

Ahikar, 1:542, 543

Ahikar, Book of, 1:**542–543**, 542*t*

Ahilot, 15:394

Aḥim (Barash), 3:136

Ahimaaz (father-in-law of Saul), 1:**543**

Ahimaaz (son of Zadok), 1:**543**

Ahimaaz (son-in-law of Solomon), 1:**543**

Aḥimaaz, 15:607

Ahimaaz, Chronicle of, 5:691

Ahimaaz ben Paltiel, 1:**543–544**, 543*t*, 3:706, 8:653

Ahimaaz chronicle. *See Megillat Yuḥasin*

Ahiman, 1:**544**

Aḥimeir, Abba, 1:**544**

Ahimelech (son of Abiathar), 1:**545**

Ahimelech (son of Ahitub), 1:**544**

Ahimelech the Hittite, 1:**545**

Aḥio, 1:258, 259

Aḥisefer publishing house, 18:374

Ahithophel the Gilonite, 1:**545**

Ahitub, 1:**545–546**

Aḥitub ben Isaac, 1:**546**

Aḥitub ben Isaac, 15:581

Aḥituv ve-Ẓalmon (Mattathias), 13:685–686

Ahlab (Canaan), 1:**546**

Ahl al-Kitāb, 1:**546**

'Aḥlamah, 16:477

Ahlem (Germany), 1:**547**

Ahlwardt, Hermann, 1:**547**

Aḥmad Khān, Sayyid, Sir, 10:94

Ahmadnagar (India), 1:**547**

AHO (Association of Holocaust Organizations). *See* Association of Holocaust Organizations (AHO)

Ahonai ben Kahana ben Huna. *See* Ḥanina ben Kahana ben Huna

Aḥot Ketannah (Abraham ben Isaac), 1:300, **547–548**

Ahrne, Mariane, 18:93

Ahrweiler (Germany), 1:**548**

Ahwaz (Persia), 1:**548**

Ai (ancient Israel), 1:**548–549**

Aiath. *See* Ai (Ancient Israel)

Aibu (3rd-4th c.), 1:**549**

Aibu (father of Rav), 1:**549**

Aibu (grandson of Rav), 1:**549**

Aibu (son of Rav), 1:**549**

Aichinger, Ilse, 1:**549**

AIDS/HIV, 15:227–228

AIef, Beit, Gimmel, Dalet. *See* Druyanow, Alter

Aijah. *See* Ai (Ancient Israel)

Aijalon (ancient Israel), 1:**549–550**

Aijalon (territory of Zebulun), 1:**550**

Aiken, Henry David, 1:**550**

Aikhenvald Yuli Isayevich, 1:**550**

AIKO, 19:649–650

Aila. *See* Elath (Israel)

Aimée, Anouk, 1:**550**

Ain. *See* En-Rimmon (ancient Israel)

Ainsworth, Henry, 1:**550–551**

AIPAC (American Israel Public Affairs Committee). *See* American Israel Public Affairs Committee (AIPAC)

Airborne Warning and Control System (AWACS) aircraft, 2:52

Aircraft, 5:439–440

Airplane hijackings, 6:282–283, 447–448

AIS. *See* Association for Jewish Studies

Aish HaTorah, 1:**551**, 3:680

Aiskowitz, Goodman. *See* Ace, Goodman

Ai T'ien, 1:**551–552**, 11:726

Aix-en-Provence (France), 1:**552**

Aix-la-Chapelle. *See* Aachen (Germany)

Aizenberg, Nina, 1:**553**

Aizman, David Yakolevich, 1:**553**

AJA (American Jewish Archives). *See* American Jewish Archives (AJA)

AJA (Anglo-Jewish Association). *See* Anglo-Jewish Association (AJA)

AJC (African Jewish Congress), 1:**440–441**

AJC (American Jewish Committee). *See* American Jewish Committee (AJC)

AJCongress (American Jewish Congress). *See* American Jewish Congress (AJCongress)

AJOP (Association for Jewish Outreach Professionals and Programs), 3:7

AJPC (American Jewish Periodical Center). *See* American Jewish Periodical Center (AJPC)

Ajzersztejn, Rivka. *See* Robin, Régine

Akaba (Jordan), 1:**553**, 6:287

Akademie Fuer Die Wissenschaft Des Judentums, 1:**554**

Akasi, Jacob. *See* Abbasi, Jacob ben Moses ibn

Akasi, Jacob ben Moses ibn. *See* Abbasi, Jacob ben Moses ibn

Akavya, Avraham Aryeh Leib, 1:**554**

Akavyah ben Mahalalel, 1:**554**, 5:760–761, 6:215

Akbara (Galilee). *See* Akhbarei (Galilee)

Akbar Abū al-Fatḥ Jalāl al-Dīn Muhammad. *See* Akbar the Great

Akbar the Great, 1:**554–555**

Akbon, 3:16

Akdamut Millin (Meir ben Isaac Shli'aḥ Ẓibbur), 1:**555**, 13:784

Akedah, 1:**555–560**

Akedah illustration (Prais), vol. 2: color insert

Akedat Yizhak (Arama), 2:531

Akerlof, George A., 1:**560**

A Khasene on Klezmer (Shalom Aleichem), 18:384

Akhbarei (Galilee), 1:**560–561**

Akhbar Marcus ben Samuel. *See* Meisel Mordecai ben Samuel

Akhbar Marx ben Samuel. *See* Meisel Mordecai ben Samuel

Akhbar Mordecai ben Samuel. *See* Meisel Mordecai ben Samuel

akhchisarai (Ukraine), 3:**72**

Akhenaten. *See* Akhenaton

Akhenaton, 1:**561**, 2:41, 6:284

Akhen Ḥaz-Am (Bialik), 3:562

Akhetaton (Egypt). *See* El-Amarna (Egypt)

Akhshaf. *See* Achshaph (ancient Israel)

Akhshav u-ve-Yamim Aḥerim (Amchai), 2:71

Akhzar mi-Kol ha-Melekh (Aloni), 1:687

Akhzar mi-kol ha-Melekh (Shamir), 8:720

Akiba. *See* Ha-No'ar Ha-Ivri-Akiba

Akirov, Alfred, 1:**561–562**

Akiva, 1:**562–563**

   Bible text treated as binding authority by, 3:584–585

   biblical exegesis and study, 3:641

   Dosa ben Harkinas, 5:760–761

   Eduyyot, 6:215

   Eleazar ben Shammua, 6:307

   hermaneutics, 9:28

   Johanan ben Torta and, 11:373

   Johanan ha-Sandelar and, 11:377

   Joshua ben Hananiah, 11:450, 451

   Joshua ha-Garsi, 11:455

   Lag ba-Omer and, 12:436, 15:421

   Otiyyot De R. Akiva, 14:188

   Pappus ben Judah, 15:619

   Simeon ha-Timni, 18:602

Akiva Baer ben Joseph, 1:**563**

Akiva ben Jacob Frankfurter, 7:76

Akiva ben Joseph. *See* Akiva

Akiva ben Menahem ha-Kohen of Ofen, 1:**563–564**

Akka, 3:23, 6:535

Akkad (Sumer), 1:**564**, *564*

Akkadian language, 1:**564–569**, 565*t*, 3:216, 8:621, 622, 624, 647

   El-Amarna letters, 6:284–285

   Epic of Atrahasis, 7:81

   Mesopotamia, 14:87

   in Mishnaic Hebrew, 8:647

   Semitic languages and, 18:282

Akkerman. *See* Belgorod-Dnestrovski (Ukraine)

Akkerman (Ukraine). *See* Belgorod-Dnestrovski

Akko. *See* Acre (Israel)

Akkum, 1:**569**

Die Akkumulation des Kapitals (Luxemburg), 13:277

Akkush. *See* Achish

Aklar Mordecai ben Raphael, 1:**569**, 11:557

Aknin, Joseph ben Judah ben Jacob ibn, 1:**569–570**, 3:645, 6:173, 11:535–536

Akra. *See* The Acra

Akra (Iraq), 1:**570–571**, 3:138

Akrish, Isaac ben Abraham, 1:**571**

Akron (OH), 1:**571**

Aksai, Jacob ben Moses ibn. *See* Abbasi, Jacob ben Moses ibn

Aktion Petliura, 13:291

Aktion Reinhard, 3:309–311, 9:85

Akzin, Benjamin, 1:**571–572**

Alabama (U.S.), 1:**572–573**, *573*, 573*t*, 15:134–135

   See also names of specific cities in Alabama

Alabarch, 1:**573–574**

Alagón (Spain), 1:**574**

Alais. *See* Elasa (Israel)

Alais (France). *See* Alès (France)

Al-'Āl, 6:298

Alalach. *See* Alalakh

Alalah. *See* Alalakh

Alalakh (Turkey), 1:**574**

Alamah (Gilead), 1:**575**

Alamani, Aaron he-Ḥaver ben Yeshu'ah, 1:**575**

A'lā Mawdūdī, Abū al-, 10:94–95

Alami, Solomon, 1:**575**

Al-Andalus. *See* Spain, cultural and social life, Moorish

Al 'Aqīda al-Rafī 'a (Ibn Daud), 9:662, 663

Al-Aqsa Intifada (2000), 15:595, 599, 600

Al Arba'a Sippurim (Shaked), 18:367

A la Recherche du temps perdu (Proust), 16:635

Alaric II, 1:**575**

Alarko Holdings, 1:**578**

Alasa. *See* Elasah

Al-Asad al-Mahalli. *See* Jacob ben Isaac

Āl-Asāṭīr, 1:**576**

Alashiya. *See* Cyprus

Alashkar, Joseph ben Moses, 1:**576**

Alashkar, Moses ben Isaac, 1:**515**, **576–577**, 6:233

Alashkar, Solomon, 1:**577**, 15:523

Alaska (U.S.), 1:*577*, **577–578**, 577t

Alatini family. *See* Alatino family

Alatino, Azriel Bonaiuto. *See* Alatino, Azriel Pethahiah

Alatino, Azriel Pethahiah, 1:578

Alatino, Moses Amram, 1:578

Alatino family, 1:**578**

Alaton, Ishak, 1:**578**

Alatri, Samuel, 1:**578–579**

Alatrini, Isaac ben Abraham, 1:**579**

Alatrini, Johanan Judah ben Salomon, 1:579

Alatrini family, 1:**579**

Alatrino family. *See* Alatrini family

Alatzar. *See* Eleazar

Al-Avani, Isaac, 1:**579**

Alawid dynasty, 1:**579–581**, 14:497–499

'Alawiyyūn dynasty. *See* Alawid dynasty

Alazar. *See* Eleazar family

Alazar, Don Mair, 6:298

Alazar, Mosse, 6:298

Alazar, Todros, 6:298

Alba, Jacob di, 1:**581**

Alba Bible, 3:636

Alba Carolina (Transylvania). *See* Alba Iulia (Transylvania)

Alba de Tormes (Spain), 1:**581**

Albahari, David, 1:**581**

Alba Iulia (Transylvania), 1:**581–582**

Albala, David, 1:**582**

Albalag, Isaac, 1:**582–583**, 2:160, 461, 16:87

    allegorical interpretation of scripture, 3:645

    soul, immortality of, 19:37

Albala-Levy, Ana, 11:469

Albalia, Baruch ben Isaac, 1:**583**

Albalia, Isaac ben Baruch, 1:**583–584**

Al-Balideh, Moses. *See* Balideh, Moses

Albania, 1:584, **584**, *584*

Albany (NY), 1:**584–586**

Albaradani, Joseph, 1:**586**

Al-Bargeloni, Isaac ben Reuben, 1:**586**, 6:158

Al-Bargeloni, Judah. *See* Judah ben Barzillai al-Bargeloni

Albarracín (Spain), 1:**587**

al-Baṣīr, Joseph ben Abraham ha-Kohen Haro'eh. *See* Baṣir, Joseph ben Abraham ha-Kohen Haro'eh al-

Albategnius, 4:62

Al-Bathaniyya. *See* Bashan region (Israel)

Albaz, Moses ben Maimon, 1:**587**, 6:290

Al-Baẓak, Maẓli'aḥ ben Elijah ibn, 1:**587**

Albeck, Ḥanokh, 1:587, 3:126, 14:325–326

Albeck, Shalom, 1:302, 587–588

Albeck family, 1:**587–588**

Albelda, Moses ben Jacob, 1:**588**

Albenzubron. *See* Gabirol, Solomon ben Judah, ibn

Alberstein, Hava, 1:**588**

Albert, Marv, 1:**588–589**

Albert, Mildred Elizabeth Levine, 1:**589**

Alberta (Canada), 1:**589–591**

Albert Einstein Archives (Hebrew University), 6:262

Alberti-Irsa (Hungary), 1:**591**

Albertirsa (Hungary). *See* Alberti-Irsa (Hungary)

Albert-Lazard, Albert, 2:517

Albert Shanker Institute (Washington, D.C.), 18:397

Albertus Denis. *See* Denis, Albertus

Albertus Magnus, 1:**591**

Albert V (Holy Roman Emperor), 11:337

Albi (France), 1:**591–592**

Albigenses, 1:**592–593**, 3:629

Albinus, 2:126, 129

Albinus, Lucceius, 1:**593**

Albinus Flaccus. *See* Alcuin

al-Bīra. *See* Ramallah (Palestine)

Albo, Joseph, 1:**593–595**, 2:267, 618–619, 16:89–90

    Adam, 1:374

    allegorical interpretation of scripture, 3:645

    articles of faith, 2:531

    commandments, reasons for, 5:88

    freedom of thought, 7:227

    inclination, good and evil, 9:757

    Maimonides' essential principles of Judaism, 11:513

    moneylending, 14:439–440

    on peace, 15:702

    revelation, 17:257

    soul, immortality of, 19:37–38

    Torah, 20:41, 43, 45

    vegetarianism, 5:165

Albom, Mitch, 4:125

Alboraycos, 1:**595**

Albotini, Judah ben Moses, 1:**595–596**

Albrecht, Bruno. *See* Katzmann, Friedrich

Albright, William Foxwell, 1:**596**, 2:374, 378, 8:621, 13:60

    biblical archaeology of, 3:650, 654

    Joshua, Book of, 11:447, 448

Albu, George, 1:**596**

Albu, Isidor, 1:**596**

Album, Simon Hirsch, 1:**596–597**

Albuquerque (NM), 1:**597–598**

Albutaini, Judah. *See* Albotini, Judah ben Moses

Albutaini, Judah ben Moses. *See* Albotini, Judah ben Moses

Alcalá de Henares (Spain), 1:**598**

Alcalaj, Isaac. *See* Alcalay, Isaac

Alcalay, Isaac, 1:**598**

Alcalay, Reuven, 1:**598**

Alcama. *See* Aljama

Alcan, Félix, 1:**599**

Alcan, Michel, 1:**599**

Alcan, Moÿse, 1:**599**

Alcan family, 1:**599**

Alcañiz (Spain), 1:**599**

Alçar ben Alazrach Eleazar, 6:298

Alcastiel, Joseph, 1:**599**

Alcay, Albert, 4:91

Alceh, Matilde, 1:**599**

Alchemy, 1:**599–603**

Alcimus, 1:**603**

Alcohol and drunkenness, 6:**26–28**, 14:58

    Bronfman family liquor business (Seagram's), 4:205–206

    contemporary U.S., 6:704

    etiquette, 6:539

    Noah, 15:288, 289, 290

Alcolea (Aragon), 1:**603**

Alcolea de Cinca (Aragon). *See* Alcolea (Aragon)

Alconière, Theodore, 1:**603**

Alconstantini, Bafi'el. *See* Alconstantini, Baḥya

Alconstantini, Baḥi'el. *See* Alconstantini, Baḥya

Alconstantini, Baḥya, 1:**604**

Al-Constantini, Enoch ben Solomon, 1:**604**

Alconstantini, Moses, 1:604

Alconstantini, Solomon, 1:604

Alconstantini family, 1:**604**

Alcorsono, Judah ben Joseph, 1:**604–605**

Alcott, Amy, 1:**605**

Alcuin, 1:**605**

Aldabi. *See* Abulrabi, Aaron

Aldabi, Aaron. *See* Abulrabi, Aaron

Aldabi, Meir ben Isaac, 1:**605**, 6:399

Aldanov, Mark, 1:**605–606**

Aldema, Gil, 1:**606**

Alderman, Geoffrey, 1:**606**

ALDJR. *See* American League for the Defense of Jewish Rights

Al-Doji, Menahem. *See* Alroy, David

Aldo Manuzio, 1:**606**

Aldrich, Robert, 1:**606–607**

Aldrophe, Alfred-Philibert, 1:**607**

Aldubi, Abraham ben Moses ben Ismail, 1:**607**

Alduin. *See* Hilduin

Aldus Manutius. *See* Aldo Manuzio

Al-Dustān. *See* Dustan

Alechinsky, Pierre, 1:**607**

ʾAlef, 1:**607–608**

Alef (periodical), 2:78

Alegre, Abraham ben Solomon, 1:**608**

Aleichem, Sholem, 1:321

Aleinu le-Shabbeʾaḥ, 2:76

    apologetics, 2:267

Aleinu le-Shabbeʾaḥ, 1:**608–610**, 608t

Aleksander Jagiellonczyk, 1:**610**

Aleksandriya (Kirovograd district, Ukraine), 1:**610**

Aleksandriya (Rovno district, Volhynia, Ukraine), 1:**610**

Aleksandrov, Hillel, 11:322

Aleksandrow dynasty, 1:**610–611**, 8:423, 424

Aleksandrow Lodzki (Poland), 1:**611**

Alemán, Mateo, 1:**611**

Alemanno, Johanan ben Isaac, 1:**611–613**

Alemeth (territory of Benjamin). *See* Almon (territory of Benjamin)

Aleph Zadik, 4:14

Aleppo (Syria), 1:**613–617**, 3:399

    Aleppo Jews in Israel, 10:296

    bakkashot, 3:73

    capitulations, 4:452

    Francos of, 4:451

    Kaẓin, Judah ben Yom Tov, 12:45

    Sitteon Dabbah, Shaul David, 18:646–647

Aleppo Codex, 4:173

Alès (France), 1:**617**

Alessandra Tornimparte. *See* Ginzburg, Natalia

Alessandria (Italy), 1:**617–618**

Ale Verk: Yubileum Oysgabe (Shalom Aleichem), 18:385

Ale Verk fun Shalom Aleichem (Shalom Aleichem), 18:383

Alexander (c. 36-37 B.C.E.), 1:**618–619**, 618t

Alexander (Hassid dynasty). *See* Aleksandrow dynasty

Alexander (King of Poland), 11:462

Alexander (popes), 1:**619–620**

Alexander (Russian czars), 1:**620–621**

Alexander (Son of Aristobulus II), 1:**629–630**, 629t

Alexander, A., 3:614

Alexander, Abraham, 1:**621**

Alexander, Abraham, Senior. *See* Alexander, Abraham

Alexander, Alexander, 1:**621**

Alexander, Beatrice, 1:**621–622**

Alexander, Bernard, 1:**622**

Alexander, E., 16:138

Alexander, Franz, 1:**622**

Alexander, Haim, 1:**622–623**

Alexander, Heinz. *See* Alexander, Haim

Alexander, James, 15:196

Alexander, Jason, 1:**623**, 15:228

Alexander, Jeffrey, 18:730–731

Alexander, Judah Leib. *See* Alexander, Levy

Alexander, Kobi, 1:**623**

Alexander, Levy, 1:**621**

Alexander, M., 6:451

Alexander, Michael Solomon, 1:**623–624**

Alexander, Morris, 1:**624**, 16:349

Alexander, Moses, 1:**624**

Alexander, Muriel, 1:**624**

Alexander, Samuel, 1:**624–625**

Alexander, Tiberius Julius. *See* Severus, Alexander

Alexander I (czar), 1:620

    blood libel and, 3:779

    Pale of Settlement under, 15:577

Alexander II (pope), 1:619

Alexander II (czar), 1:620, 9:235, 17:534

    emancipation, 6:383–384

    Judaizers under, 11:522

    Levanda, Lev Osipovich, 12:677

    numerus clausus, 15:343

    Pale of Settlement under, 15:578

Alexander III (czar), 1:620–621, 16:373

    blood libel and, 3:779

    emancipation, 6:384

    laws restricting Jews, 13:701–702

    numerus clausus, 15:343

Alexander III (pope), 1:619

Alexander IV (czar), 16:373

Alexander IV (pope), 1:619

Alexander V (pope), 1:619

Alexander VI (pope), 1:619, 16:374

Alexander VII (pope), 1:619–620, 16:376

Alexander Balas, 1:**625**, 11:398

Alexander family, 1:**621**

Alexander Lysimachus, 1:**627**

Alexander Nevsky (motion picture), 6:274

Alexander of Aphrodisias, 1:**628**

Alexander of Hales, 1:**628–629**

Alexander of Macedonia, 7:13

Alexander Polyhistor, 1:**629**

Alexander's Department Store, 15:226

Alexandersohn, Jonathan, 18:195

Alexander Suslin ha-Kohen of Frankfurt, 1:**630**, 11:424

Alexander Susskind ben Moses of Grodno, 1:**630–631**

Alexander the False, 1:**625**

Alexander the Great, 1:**625–627**, 3:25, 26, 18:602

    influence of, 6:554

    Josippon, 11:462

Alexander the Zealot, 1:**631**

Alexander Yannai. *See* Yannai, Alexander

Alexandra (daughter of Aristobulus II), 1:**631**, 631t

Alexandra (daughter of Hyrcanus II), 1:**631**, 631t

Alexandrah. *See* Alexandri

Alexandrai. *See* Alexandri

Alexandra Salome. *See* Salome Alexandra

Alexandretta (Turkey). *See* Iskenderun (Turkey)

Alexandri, 1:**631–632**

Alexandria (Egypt), 1:**632–635**, 633, 14:28

    Anatoli ben Joseph, 2:133

    Andronicus son of Meshullam, 2:145

    Angel, Aaron, 2:146

    beliefs of Jewish community, 2:456

    community organization and structures, 5:101

    Jews, 1:434–435, 6:228–230

    temporary expulsion of Jews from, 4:326

Alexandrian Martyrs, Acts of, 1:**635–636**

Alexandrium (Jordan Valley). *See* Sarṭaba (Jordan Valley)

Alexandros. *See* Alexandri; Yannai, Alexander

Alexandrovich, Sergei, 14:517

Alexandrovsk. *See* Zaporozhe (Ukraine)

Alexas, 1:**636**

Alexenicer, Jose, 16:349

Alexeyev, Alexander, 1:**636**

Alez (France). *See* Alès (France)

"*Alfa Beta of Ben Sira*", 7:12

Al-Fakhar. *See* Ibn Alfakhar

Alfalas, Moses, 1:**636**

Alfandari, Aaron ben Moses, 1:**637**

Alfandari, Elijah ben Jacob, 1:637

Alfandari, Ḥayyim (Rabbenu), 1:637

Alfandari, Ḥayyim (the Elder), 1:637

Alfandari, Ḥayyim ben Isaac Raphael, 1:**637–638**

Alfandari, Isaac Raphael, 1:637

Alfandari, Jacob, 1:**638**

Alfandari, Joseph, 1:637

Alfandari, Obadiah, 1:636–637

Alfandari, Solomon Eliezer ben Jacob, 1:340, **638**

Alfandaric family. *See* Alfandari family

Alfandari family, 1:**636–637**

Alfandary, Solomon ben Ḥayyim, 1:637

Alfandrec family. *See* Alfandari family

al-Faraj, Abu. *See* Abu al-Faraj

Alfas, Benzion. *See* Alfes, Benzion

Alfasi, David ben Abraham, 1:**638–639**

　dictionary for Hebrew and biblical Aramaic, 13:31

　Judeo-Arabic literature and, 11:532

Alfasi, Isaac ben Jacob, 1:**639–641**, 4:770, 779

　Abraham ben David of Posquières, 1:297

　in Fez, Morocco, 7:6

　halakhah, 8:257

　Joseph ben Justu of Jaén, 11:423

　Judah ben Barzillai al-Bargeloni, 11:483

　Montpelier (France), 14:463

　Nissim ben Reuben Gerondi, 15:281

Alfasi, Masʿud Raphael, 1:638

Alfasi, Solomon ben Masʿud Raphael, 1:638

Alfasi family, 1:638

Al-Fayyumi, Saadiah. *See* Saadiah Gaon

Alfei Menasheh (Samaria), 1:**641**

Alferov, Zhores I., 1:**641**

Alfes, Benzion, 1:**641–642**

Alfes' Story. *See* Ma'aseh Alfes

Alfieri, Vittorio, 10:788

Alfonsìn, Raul, 2:442, 443

Alfonso. *See* Affonso

Alfonso (Spanish kings), 1:**642**

Alfonso I (King of Aragon), 1:642

Alfonso II (King of Aragon), 1:642

Alfonso IV (King of Aragon), 6:91

Alfonso V (King of Aragon), 1:642, 18:44

Alfonso VI (King of Castile and Leon), 1:642

Alfonso VII (King of Castile and Leon), 1:642, 18:570

Alfonso VIII (King of Castile), 1:642, 11:255

Alfonso X, King of Castile, 1:343, 642, 18:327

Alfonso XI (King of Castile and Leon), 1:642

Alfonso de Espina, 1:**642**

Alfonso de la Cavallería, 15:375

Alfonso de Oropesa, 1:**643**

Alfonso de Spina. *See* Alfonso de Espina

Alfonso D'espina. *See* Alfonso de Espina

Alfonso of Burgos. *See* Abner of Burgos

Alfonso of Valladolid. *See* Abner of Burgos

Alfonso of Zamora, 1:**643**

Alfonsus Bonihominis, 1:**643**

Alfonsus Buenhombre. *See* Alfonsus Bonihominis

Alfred J. Kahn Doctoral Fellowship, 11:719

Alfred the Great, 3:611

Al-Furaydis. *See* Furaydis, Al- (Israel)

Algazi, Abraham ben Moses, 1:643

Algazi, Ḥayyim ben Abraham, 1:643

Algazi, Ḥayyim ben Menahem, 1:643

Algazi, Isaac ben Abraham, 1:643–644

Algazi, Isaac ben Solomon, 1:**644**

Algazi, Israel Jacob ben Yom Tov, 1:**644**

Algazi, Judah, 1:644

Algazi, Leon, 1:**644–645**, 12:661

Algazi, Moses ben Abraham, 1:643

Algazi, Moses ben Joseph, 1:644

Algazi, Nissim. *See* Algazi, Solomon ben Abraham (1610?-c.1683)

Algazi, Nissim Jacob Ben Ḥayyim Solomon, 1:643

Algazi, Solomon, 4:103

Algazi, Solomon ben Abraham (1610?-c.1683), 1:**645**, 18:345

Algazi, Solomon ben Abraham (1673-1762), 1:**645**

Algazi, Yehudah. *See* Algazi, Leon

Algazi, Yom Tov ben Israel Jacob, 1:**645**

Algazi family, 1:**643–644**

Algemeyne Entsiklopedye (encyclopedia), 6:399

Algemeyne Ilustrirte Entsiklopedye (Goldblatt), 6:399

Algemeyner Yidisher Arbeter Bund in Lite, Poyln un Rusland. *See* Bund

Di Algemeyne Yidishe Entsiklopedye (Lurie, Horowitz), 6:399

Algeria, 1:**645–652**, *646*, 650*t*, 2:322–323, 14:712

　Abulker family, 1:345

　amulets, 2:123

　antisemitism, 1:649–651, 4:533

　　Algiers, 1:653–654

　assimilation, 1:648

　Azubib family, 2:772–773

　Bone, 4:61

　Bougie, 4:105

　Busnach, Naphtali ben Moses, 4:316

　community organization and structures, 5:105, 108, 110, 111–112, 118*t*

　Draï, Raphaël, 6:7

　French immigration, 7:163

　Gozlan, Elie, 8:21–22

　Holocaust, 1:649

　immigration to Israel from, 10:523

　Israel (State), 1:651

　Jews

　　dress, 6:14

　　French rule, 1:648–649

　　modern, 1:649–651

　　music, 1:440

　　Muslim rule, 1:645–648

　Oran, 15:459–460

　synagogue architecture, 19:375

Al-Gharīd al-Yahūdī, 1:**652**

Al-Ghazālī, 11:539, 541

Alghero (Sardinia), 1:**652**

Algiers (Algeria), 1:**652–654**

　Duran, Simeon ben Simeon, 6:61

　Duran, Simeon ben Solomon, 6:58

　Duran family, 6:56

Algonquin Round Table, 1:380

Algorithms, 5:129–131

Alguades, Don Meir, 15:562

Alguades, Meir, 1:**654**

Alguadez, Meir. *See* Alguades, Meir

Algum, 1:**654**

Al ha-Bikkoret ha-Yoẓeret (Fichman), 7:8

Alḥadib, Isaac ben Solomon ben Ẓaddik, 1:**654**

Al Ha-Ḥalomot (Shaḥar), 18:363

Al-Ḥākim

　ghetto created by, 11:312

Al-Ḥākim, *continued*
  Jubayl, 11:473
Al ha-Mishmar (newspaper), 1:**655**
Alhanati, David, 1:**655**
Al ha-Nissim, 1:**655**, 2:75
Al-Ḥarizi, Judah, 15:655
Al-Ḥarizi, Judah ben Solomon, 1:579, **655–657**, 6:173, 8:660, 9:591
  Edessa, 6:147
  Joseph ben Baruch of Clisson and, 11:419
  Joseph ben Tanḥum Yerushalmi, 11:427
  on Josiah ben Jesse, 11:460
  as Orientalist, 15:471
Al-Ḥasan (Mulay of Morocco), 14:499
Alhayk, Uzziel ben Mordecai, 1:**657**
Al Ḥet (prayer), 1:**658**
al-Ḥira. *See* Ḥīra (Persia)
Ali, 1:240–241, **658**
Aliama. *See* Aljama
Aliav, Ruth, 1:**658**
Alibag (India), 1:**658**
Ali ben Amram, 1:**659**
Ali ben David. *See* Ali
Ali ben Zechariah, 1:**659**
Alien Love. See Ahavah Zarah
Aliens Act of 1905, 1:**659**
Alien slaves. *See* Slavery
Aliger, Margarita Yosifovna, 1:**659**
Ali ibn Sahl ibn Rabbān al-Ṭabarī, 1:**659–660**
Ali ibn Suleiman, 1:**660**
Alī Jandubī, 1:439–440
Alik ve-ha-Kallaniyyot (Shamir), 18:392
Alilot Akavyah (Burla), 4:295
Alimony, 4:748
Al-Iscandari family. *See* Iscandari family
Alistál (Slovakia), 1:**660**
Al-Istibsar (Basir), 3:200
Aliturus, 1:**660**
Alityros. *See* Aliturus
Aliyah, 1:**660–661**, 10:346, 481*t*
  1948-Six-Day War, 10:339–345
  by 1958, 10:223
  1980s and 1990s, 10:239, 241, 243, 263, 264
  1982-1992, 10:350, 352–353
  1993-2002, 10:353–354
  American Jewish Committee, 2:55
  American Joint Distribution Committee, 2:62–63
  Amidar, 2:76–77
  Churchill White Paper and, 10:336

education and, 10:343, 344, 526, 657, 658, 668
Ethiopians, 10:631
Fifth, 10:201, 496, 498
First, 1:660, 10:180, 193–194, 273, 282, 357–358, 480–482, 522–523
Fourth, 10:199–201, 337, 489–490, 523–524
Hasidic, 8:395
of Holocaust survivors, 10:215
Horev Commission, 9:525
housing, 10:526–527, 527
illegal post World War II, 10:467
illegal pre World War II, 10:499–500
Israel (state), 10:329–373, 334*t*, 341*t*, 342*t*, 344*t*, 345*t*, 347*t*, 349*t*, 351*t*, 352*t*, 354–366, 358*t*
  1880–1948, 10:333–339, 334*t*
  post 1980s settlements and housing, 10:365–366
  1982-1992, 10:345*t*, 347*t*, 350–353, 351*t*
  1993-2002, 10:345*t*, 347*t*, 351*t*, 353–354
  absorption methods, 10:340–345
  building and construction of housing, 10:354–355
  from Bukhara, 4:263
  from Bulgaria, 4:273–274
  from Bushire, 4:306
  difficulties, 10:330
  health services, 10:675
  ingathering of exiles, 10:339–340
  introduction, 10:329
  from Iran, 10:11–12, 11*t*, 20
  land ownership, 10:371–372, 527
  land reclamation, 10:372–373
  motives for aliyah, 10:329–330
  post-1948, 10:339–354, 341*t*, 355–357, 360–361
  post-Six Day War, 10:344*t*, 345–350, 345*t*, 347*t*, 349*t*, 361–365
  pre-WW I settlements and housing, 10:357–359, 358*t*
  public housing, 10:355
  regional and settlement planning, 10:370–371
  rural development, 10:366–370
  from Russia, 17:558, 569–571, 570*t*, 571*t*, 572, 573, 579
  Second Temple period to Ḥibbat Zion or 1880s, 10:330–333

teshuvah, 3:572
urbanization, 10:366–370
Israel Defense Forces role, 10:467–468
Law of Return, 10:215, 414–415, 626
musicians, 10:688, 689
non-Jewish, 10:636
of North African Jews, 10:223–224
of Oriental Jews, 10:215, 223–224, 226, 235–236
Palestine (Mandate)
  housing and settlements, 10:354
Palestine Office, 15:595
partisan groups after WW II, 15:668
post-Holocaust problems, 10:216
Second, 10:180–181, 194–196, 282, 334–335, 358–359, 482–485, 523
  Histadrut and, 10:606
Six-Day War to 1982, 10:345–350
Soviet Jews, 10:631–632
  burial and, 10:638
from Soviet Union, 10:346, 348–349
of Soviet Union Jews, 10:235, 453
theater and, 10:688
Third, 10:199, 335, 489, 510, 523
from West, 10:344–345
women and, 6:754
during World War II, 10:339
Youth Aliyah, 10:338, 343–344
See also Migrations; Torah, reading of; Youth Aliyah movement
Aliyah Bet. *See* Illegal immigration
Aliyyat Yeladim va-No'ar. *See* Youth Aliyah
Aljama, 1:**661**
Al-Jazair (Algeria). *See* Algiers (Algeria)
Al-Jazā'ir. *See* Algeria
Al-Kabbir. *See* Attar, Judah ben Jacob Ibn
Alkabez, Solomon ben Moses ha-Levi, 1:**662–663**, 662*t*
Alkabri, Joseph. *See* Ferrizuel, Joseph ha-Nasi
Alkaḥi, Mordekhai, 1:**663**, 6:22
Alkalai, Abraham ben Samuel, 1:**663**
Alkalai, David, 1:**663**
Alkalai, Judah ben Solomon Ḥai, 1:**663–664**, 11:308, 21:540–541
Alkalai, Y., redemption, 17:155
Alkalaj, Aron, 1:**664**
Alkalaj, Isaac. *See* Alcalay, Isaac

Alkan, Alphonse, 1:**664**

Alkan, Charles Henri-Valentin, 1:**665**

Alkan family. *See* Alcan family

Al-Khaḍir, 14:539

al-Khalil. *See* Hebron (Israel)

al-Kirkisāni, Abu Yūsuf Yaʾqūb, 11:790

Al-Kitāb al-Kāfi (Abu al-Faraj), 1:334

Al-Kitāb al-Mushtamil (Abu al-Faraj), 1:334

Al-Kufa. *See* Kufa (Iraq)

Al-Kūfa (Iraq). *See* Kufa (Iraq)

Alkvit, B. *See* Blum, Eliezer

Allah Karim (Orloff-Arieli), 8:718

Allaman Oglou. *See* Ashkenazi, Solomon

All But My Life (Weissman), 4:631

Allegeine Juedische Kolonisations-Organisation. *See* AIKO

Allegorical interpretation of Bible, 3:641, 643–645, 660, 665

Allegories, 1:373–374, **665–667**

Allemania. *See* Germany

Allen, Gracie, 4:298

Allen, Isaac, 1:**667**

Allen, Isaac A., 15:205

Allen, Lewis. *See* Reed, Lou

Allen, Mel, 1:**667–668**

Allen, Paul G., 1:**668–669**

Allen, Woody, 1:**669–670**, 12:503

Allenby, Edmund Henry Hynman, 1:222, **670**, 2:393

Allenby, George, 11:305

Allende, Salvador, 4:644

Allgemeine Zeitung des Judentums (periodical), 1:**670–671**

All God's Children: A Jew Speaks (Cohen), 5:9

Alliance, David (Lord), 11:820

L'Alliance avec la nature (Chalier), 4:562

Alliance Israelite Universelle, 1:**671–675**, 673t

    Alkalai, Judan ben Solomon Ḥai, 1:664

    American Joint Distribution Committee, 2:62

    Anglo Jewish Association, 2:162

    archives, 2:409

    assimilation, 9:237–238

    Benas, Baron Louis, 3:319

    Bigarte, Jacques, 3:694

    Board of Delegates of American Israelites, 4:19

    boycott, anti-Nazi, 4:110

    Brafman, Jacob, 4:116

    Cahen, Isidore, 4:337

Carvallo, Jules, 4:503

Cassin, René Samuel, 4:509

Cazès, David, 4:533

    education, Jewish, 6:183–184, 185, 213–214

    founding, 7:158

    France, 7:166–167

    Hirsch, Baron Maurice de, 9:127

    language, 12:482

    League of Nations, 12:565

    Lehmann, Léonce, 12:615

    Libya, 12:793

    Loeb, Isidore, 13:160

    Morocco, 14:500, 502–503, 504, 505–507

    Mortara case, 14:513

    in Ottoman empire, 6:149, 15:530, 542

    philanthropy, 16:43

    social organization, 9:245

Alliance Israélite Universelle, 18:722

Alliance of German Jews. *See* Verband der Deutschen Juden

Allianz, Israelitische zu Wien, 1:**675**

Allium cepa. *See* Onions

All My Sons (Miller), 14:251

Allon, Gedalya, 1:**675**

Allon, Yigal, 1:**675–676**

    Palmaḥ, 15:604

    settlements beyond Green Line and, 10:362, 364, 440, 441

Allon Bakhut (Benjamin), 3:360

Allonei Abba (Israel), 1:**676–677**

Allonei Yitzḥak (Israel), 1:**677**

Allonim (Israel), 1:**677**

Allouche, Felix Nissim S'Aidou, 1:**677**

All Rivers Run to The Sea (Wiesel), 9:401

"All the news that's fit to print" slogan, 15:375–376

All the Presidents' Men (motion picture), 15:572

Alluf, 1:**677**

Allweiss, Solomon. *See* Alva, Siegfried

Alma (Sobol), 18:702, *702*

Al-Madari, Judah ha-Kohen ben Eleazar he-Ḥasid, 1:**677**

Al-Madari, Judah ha-Kohen ben Eliezer he-Ḥasid. *See* Al-Madari, Judah ha-Kohen ben Eleazar he-Ḥasid

Al-Maghar. *See* Maghar, al- (Israel)

Almagià, Roberto, 1:**677–678**

Almagor (Israel), 1:**678**

Almagor, Gila, 1:**678**

Almagro (Spain), 1:**678**

Almah (Israel), 1:**678**

Alm al Fath. *See* Ibn Shuwayk, Isaac ben Israel

al-Maʾmūn, 6:603–604

Alman, Samuel, 1:**678–679**

Almansi, Dante, 1:**679**

Almansi family, 1:**679**

Al-Mansura (Egypt). *See* Mansura (Egypt)

Al-Mansurah (Egypt). *See* Mansura (Egypt)

Al-Manṣūr al-Yahūdī, 1:**679**

al-Mansur Ibn Abi ʾAmir. *See* Manṣūr

Almanzi, Joseph, 1:**679**

Almanzi family. *See* Almansi family

Almanzor. *See* Manṣūr

Al-Mawjib. *See* Arnon

Almemar, 3:701

Almería (Spain), 1:**680**

Almog. *See* Algum

Almog, Ruth, 1:**680**

Almog, Yehuda, 1:**680–681**, 8:293

Almogi, Yosef Aharon, 1:**681**

Almohades, 4:105

Almohad persecutions, 6:5

Almohads, 1:**681–682**, 684, 11:757

    conquering of Tunisia, 11:727

    Morocco, 14:494–495

    Omar, Covenant of, 15:417–418

    Sijilmassa (Morocco), 18:572

Almoli, Solomon ben Jacob, 1:**682**, 6:399

Almon (territory of Benjamin), 1:**682**

Almond, 1:**683**, vol. 16: color insert

Almond, Gabriel Abraham, 1:**683**

Almon-Diblathaim (Moabite plain), 1:**683**

Almoravids, 1:**681**, **684**, 18:572

Almosnino, Abraham, 1:**684**, 18:451

Almosnino, Isaac Ḥasdai, 1:**685**

Almosnino, Joseph ben Isaac, 1:**685**

Almosnino, Moses, 15:540, 541, 16:109

Almosnino, Moses ben Baruch, 1:**685**

Almosnino family, 1:**684–685**, 684t

Almsgiving. *See* Charity

al-Muʾallima, 2:17

Al-Mudari, Judah ha-Kohen ben Eleazar he-Ḥasid. *See* Al-Madari, Judah ha-Kohen ben Eleazar he-Ḥasid

Almug. *See* Algum

Al-Muhtawi (Basir), 3:200

al-Mukammaṣ, ibn Marwān al-Rāqi. *See* Mukammis, ibn Marwān al-Rāqi al-Shirazi al-

Al-Mukhā) (Yemen). *See* Mocha (Yemen)

Almuli, Jesse, 4:103

Almuli, Solomon ben Jacob. *See* Almoli, Solomon ben Jacob

Al-Mundari, Judah ha-Kohen. *See* Al-Madari, Judah ha-Kohen ben Eleazar he-Ḥasid

Al-Mundari, Judah ha-Kohen ben Eleazar he-Ḥasid. *See* Al-Madari, Judah ha-Kohen ben Eleazar he-Ḥasid

Al-Munqidh min al-Ḍalāl (al-Ghazālī), 7:571

Al-Muqtadir (caliph), 11:425

Al-Muwaḥḥidūn. *See* Almohads

Al-Muwaḥḥidūn. *See* Almohads

al-Naḥ'āwendī, Benjamin ben Moses. *See* Naḥ'āwendī, Benjamin ben Moses al-

Al-Nahrawani, Nissi ben Berechiah. *See* Nissi ben Berechiah al-Nahrawani

Alnakar, Abraham ben Joseph, 1:**685–686**

Al-Nakawa, Israel ben Joseph, 1:266, **686**

Al-Nuqra. *See* Bashan region (Israel)

Aloni, Nissim, 1:**687**, 8:723

Aloni, Shulamit, 1:**687**

Alonso de Espina. *See* Alfonso de Espina

Alonso Fernandez de Cordoba. *See* Córdoba, Alonso Fernandez de

Alonso of Cartagena, 15:563

Alouf, Yehoshua, 1:**687–688**

Al-Palas, Moses, 15:572–573

Al-Palas family. *See* Palache family

Alper, Michael, 1:**688**

Alperovitz *v.* Mizrahi, 5:197–198

Alpersohn, Marcos, 1:**688**

Alpersohn, Mordecai. *See* Alpersohn, Marcos

Alperstein, Avraham Eliezer ben Yeshaya, 1:**688**

Alpert, Herb, 1:**688–689**

Alphabet
acrostics, 1:368–369
Nun, 15:344
Pe, 15:700

Alphabet, Hebrew. *See* Hebrew alphabet

Alphabetizing compositions. *See* Acrostics

Alphabet of Ben Sira, 3:**375–376**, 6:667, 7:12, 11:427, 454, 13:19, 170

Alphonse of Poitiers, 1:**730**, 7:150

Al-Pumbedita. *See* Pumbedita (Babylonia)

al-Qānūn fī al-Ṭibb (Avicenna), 2:728–729, vol. 8: color insert

Al-Qirqisānī, Jacob, 11:532

Al-Quds. *See* Jerusalem (Israel)

al-Queda
Morocco, 14:505
Saudi Arabia support of, 18:77–78

al-Qūmisī, Daniel ben Moses. *See* Daniel ben Moses al-Qūmisī

al-Qūmisī, David. *See* David al-Qumisì

Al-Rāa. *See* Rāma, al- (Israel)

Alrabi. *See* Abulrabi, Aaron

Alrabi, Aaron. *See* Abulrabi, Aaron

Al-Ragil, Moses. *See* Arragel, Moses

Al-Raḥbah. *See* Raḥbah, al- (Mesopotamia)

al-Raqqa. *See* Raqqa (Mesopotamia)

Al-Rashid (Mulay of Morocco), 14:497

Al-Reuti family. *See* Rote family

Al-Roḥi, David. *See* Alroy, David

Alroy (Disraeli), 5:699

Alroy, David, 2:**5–6**

al-Rueti. *See* Rote family

Al-Ruha. *See* Edessa (Turkey)

Al-Sab'uni. *See* Siboni family

Alsace (France), 2:**6–9**, *7*
Bischheim, 3:724
Joseph ben Gershon of Rosheim, 11:420–421
linguistic assimilation, 8:436

Al Saf Beit ha-Midrash (Bialik), 3:562

Al-Salt. *See* Salt

Al-Sam, 2:79

Al-Samaw'al al-Maghribī, 3:669

Al-Samawal ben Ghārid Ablaq. *See* Samuel ibn 'Ādiyā

Alsari. *See* Fuerst, Julius

Alsatian rite, 2:6

Alsbacher Ethical Testament, 4:755

Alschuler, Alfred S., 2:**9–10**

Alschuler, Samuel, 2:10

al-Shaharastānī, 6:65–67

Alsheikh, Raphael ben Shalom, 2:10

Alsheikh, Shalom ben Joseph, 2:10

Alshekh, Hayyim, 2:10, 11

Alshekh, Moses, 2:**10–11**

Al Shelosha Maḥzot (Shaked), 18:367

Alshvang, Arnold Aleksandrovich, 2:11

Alsingari, Solomon. *See* Solomon Suliman ben Amar

Alsókubin (Slovakia). *See* Dolni Kubin (Slovakia)

Alt, Albrecht, 2:**11**, 3:658
Joshua, Book of, 11:446, 447, 449
moneylending, 14:436–437
Noth, Martin, 15:315

Altabet, Mark A., 6:450–451

al-Tabib, Yahya ibn Suleiman. *See* Zechariah ben Solomon-Rofe

Al-Tal. *See* Bethsaida (Israel)

Altalena, 20:660

Altalena (ship), 3:261, 346

Al-Tamiz (Basir), 3:200

Altaras, David ben Solomon, 2:16–17

Altaras, Jacques Isaac, 2:**17**

Altaras, Joseph, 2:**17**

Altaras, Moses, 2:16

Altaras, Nissim, 2:**17**

Altaras, Solomon, the Elder, 2:16

Altaras, Solomon, the Younger, 2:17

Al-Tarās, Sīdī ibn, 2:**17**

Al Targum Rav Sa'adyah la-Torah (Zucker), 21:674–675

Altars, 2:**11–16**, 16:515
Joshua, Book of, 11:448–449
Moses, 2:29

Altauzen, Dzhek Moyseyevich. *See* Altauzen, Yakov Moyseyevich

Altauzen, Yakov Moyseyevich, 2:**17**

Al-Tayyah, Moses. *See* Ibn al-Taqana, Moses

Alt-Breisach (Germany). *See* Breisach; Breisach (Germany)

Al Tehi ka-Avotekha (Duran), 6:56–57, 13:112

Al-Tell. *See* Bethsaida (Israel)

Altenberg, Peter, 2:**17**

Altenstadt (Germany), 2:**17–18**

Alter, Abraham Mordecai, 7:761

Alter, Eleanor B., 2:**18**

Alter, Isaac Meir, 18:604

Alter, Israel, 2:**18**, 7:761

Alter, Judah Aryeh Leib, 7:761

Alter, Mendele, 15:561

Alter, Robert B., 2:**18**, 3:624, 15:358

Alter, Victor, 2:**18**, 6:481

Alterman, Nathan, 2:**19–20**, 8:720, 18:761

Alternate history (counterfactual thought), 18:206

Alternate history literature, 18:201

Al-Tha'labī, 3:669

Altheimer, Benjamin, 2:**20**

Al tikrei, 2:**20**

Alting, Jacobus, 2:**20–21**

Altman, Aryeh, 2:**21**

Altman, Benjamin, 2:**21**, 15:203

Altman, Moishe, 2:**21**

Altman, Morris, 15:203

Altman, Nathan, 2:**21–22**

Altman, Oscar Louis, 2:**22**

Altman, Sidney, 2:**22**, 4:593, 13:9

Altman Foundation, 2:21

Altmann, Adolf, 2:**22–23**

Altmann, Alexander, 2:**23**, 4:125, 16:69, 70

Altneuland (Herzel), 18:202

Alt-Ofen (Hungary). *See* Obuda (Hungary)

Altona (Germany), 2:**23–24**, 8:296

Altschul, Aaron ben Moses Meir Perles, 2:24

Altschul, Aaron Meyer, 2:**25**

Altschul, Abraham ben Isaac Perles, 2:24

Altschul, Abraham Eberle, 2:24

Altschul, Eleazar ben Abraham Ḥanokh Perles, 2:24

Altschul, Eliakim ben Ze'ev Wolf, 2:24

Altschul, Emil, 2:**25**

Altschul, Frank, 2:**25**

Altschul, Gottschalk ben Ze'ev Wolf. *See* Altschul, Eliakim ben Ze'ev Wolf

Altschul, Ḥanokh ben Moses, 2:24

Altschul, Isaac, 2:24

Altschul, Joseph, 2:**25**

Altschul, Judah Aaron Moses ben Abraham Ḥanokh, 2:24

Altschul, Louis, 2:**25–26**

Altschul, Moses, 2:24

Altschul, Moses ben Ḥanokh, 2:**26**

Altschul, Moses Meir ben Isaac Eleazar Perles, 2:24

Altschul, Naphtali Hirsch ben Asher, 2:24

Altschul, Ze'ev Wolf ben Dov Baer, 2:24

Altschuler, Aaron ben Moses Meir Perles. *See* Altschul, Aaron ben Moses Meir Perles

Altschuler, Abraham ben Isaac Perles. *See* Altschul, Abraham ben Isaac Perles

Altschuler, David, 2:**26**, 3:643

Altschuler, Eleazar ben Abraham Ḥanokh Perles. *See* Altschul, Eleazar ben Abraham Ḥanokh Perles

Altschuler, Gottschalk ben Ze'ev Wolf. *See* Altschul, Eliakim ben Ze'ev Wolf

Altschuler, Hillel, 3:643

Altschuler, Isaac. *See* Altschul, Isaac

Altschuler, Judah Aaron Moses ben Abraham Ḥanokh. *See* Altschul, Judah Aaron Moses ben Abraham Ḥanokh

Altschuler, Modest, 2:**26**

Altschuler, Moses Meir ben Isaac Eleazar Perles. *See* Altschul, Moses Meir ben Isaac Eleazar Perles

Altschuler, Naphtali Hirsch ben Asher. *See* Altschul, Naphtali Hirsch ben Asher

Altschuler, Ze'ev Wolf ben Dov Baer. *See* Altschul, Ze'ev Wolf ben Dov Baer

Altschuler family. *See* Altschul family

Altschul family, 2:**24–25**

Alttestamentliche Studien (Eerdmans), 6:215–216

Altusky, Hirsch, 2:48

Al-Tustarī. *See* Sahl ibn Faḍl

Alukah, 5:572

Alummot (Israel), 2:**26**

'Aluqah. *See* Alukah

Al-Usta. *See* IrĀQĪ, Shalom ha-Kohen

Alva, Siegfried, 2:**26**

Al-Valensi. *See* Valensi family

Alvan ben Abraham, 2:**27**

Alvares, Daniel Cohen Henriques, 2:27

Alvares, Duarte Henriques, 2:27

Alvares, Isaac, 2:27

Alvares, Isaque, 2:27

Alvares, Nuño, 4:121

Alvares, Samuel Dios-Ayuda, 2:27

Alvares Correa family, 2:27

Alvares de Tavara, Manuel. *See* Zacutus Lusitanus

Alvares family, 2:**27**

Alvarez, Alfred, 2:**27**

Alvarez, Antonio, 2:**27**

Alvarez, Daniel Cohen Henriques. *See* Alvares, Daniel Cohen Henriques

Alvarez, Duarte Henriques. *See* Alvares, Duarte Henriques

Alvarez, Fernando, 2:**27**

Alvarez, Isaac. *See* Alvares, Isaac

Alvarez, Martin. *See* Bueno, Ephraim Hezekiah

Alvarez, Rodrigo, 2:**27**

Alvarez, Samuel Dios-Ayuda, 2:27

Alvarez Delcon, Garcia. *See* Alvares, Samuel Dios-Ayuda

Alvarez Delcón, Garcia. *See* Alvares, Samuel Dios-Ayuda

Alvarez family. *See* Alvares family

Álvarez Gato, Juan, 2:**27**

Alvaro, Paolo, 4:30

Alvarus of Córdoba. *See* Alvaro, Paolo

Al-Yamani a-Rabbānī. *See* Adani, Saadiah ben David

Al-Yasaʾ. *See* Elisha

Alyasaʾ. *See* Elisha

Al-Yazid (Mulay of Morroco), 14:497–498

Alypius of Antioch, 2:82

Alyussani, Isaac ben Levi. *See* Ibn Mar Saul, Isaac ben Levi

Alzey (Germany), 2:**27**

Am, Ma'akhal Melakhim (Laor), 12:488

Am, Ma'akhal Melakhim (Laor), 18:206

AMaD. *See* Dik, Isaac

Amadio ben Moses of Recanati. *See* Jedidiah ben Moses of Recanati

Amadio ben Moses of Rimin. *See* Jedidiah ben Moses of Recanati

ʾAmadiya (Kurdistan), 2:**27–28**, 3:138

Amado Lévy-Valensi, Eliane, 2:**28**

Amador de los Rios, Jose, 2:**28**

A magyar birodalom története (Acsády), 1:369

A magyar jobbágyság történte (Acsády), 1:369

Amalek, 2:**28–31**, 33

Amalekites, 1:444–445, 2:**28–31**, 18:79

Amalfi (Italy), 2:**31**

Amalgamated Clothing Workers of America (ACWA), 4:608–609, 9:117, 118, 12:411, 18:144

Potofsky, Jacob Samuel, 16:420–421

Sheinkman, Jacob, 18:438

Amana (Syria), 2:**31**

Amanah (Syria), 2:**31**

Amar, David, 16:346

Amar, Licco, 2:**31**

Amarillo, Aaron ben Solomon, 2:**31–32**

Amarillo, Ḥayyim Moses ben Solomon, 2:**32**

Amarillo, Moses, 2:**31**

Amarillo, Solomon ben Joseph, 2:**32**, 4:102

Amarkal, 2:**32**

Amarna tablets, 8:621–622, 9:623–624

Amarot Tehorot (Eliezer ben Jacob ha-Levi of Tarnogrod), 6:326

Amasa, 2:**32–33**

Amasai, 2:32

Amasiya (Turkey), 2:**33**

Amateau, Albert Jean, 2:**33–34**

Amatus Lusitanus, 2:**34–35**, 135

Amaw, 2:30

A Mayse mit a Grinhorn (Shalom Aleichem), 18:388

Amaziah, 2:**35–36**, 97, 98, 6:155, 156, 15:357

The Amazing Adventures of Kavalier and Clay (Chabon), 4:555

Amazing Stories (periodical), 18:197

Amazyah (Israel), 2:**36**

Amazyahu (Shemariah ben Elijah ben Jacob), 18:457

Amberg (Germany), 2:**36**

Le ambizioni sbagliate (Moravia). *See Wheel of Fortune* (Moravia)

Ambron, Ezekiel, 2:37

Ambron, Sabbato Isaac, 2:37

Ambron, Shabbetai Isaac, 2:**36–37**

Ambrose, 2:**37**, 4:720, 9:206

Ambrose of Milan. *See* Ambrose

Ambrosian Bible, 3:678

Ameimar, 2:**37–38**

Ameinu. *See* Labor Zionist Alliance

Amelander, Menahem Mann ben Shlomo, 2:108

Amelander, Menahem Mann ben Solomon Ha-Levi, 2:38

Amen, 2:**38–39**, 3:192, 6:365

Amenhotep III. *See* Amenophis III

Amenities, communal, 2:**39–40**, 6:95

Amenities of Literature (D'Israeli), 5:702

Amenophis III, 2:**40–41**

Amenophis IV. *See* Akhenaton

America, 2:**41–46**, *42, 43, 44, 45,* 107

Jewish settlement in, Jewish Immigrant Aid Services of Canada, 11:299–300

Judah Loew ben Bezalel on, 11:507

See also Canada; Latin America; United States

La America (newspaper), 7:332

America-Israel Cultural Foundation, 2:**46–47**

America-Israel Culture House (NY), 2:46

American, Sadie, 2:**47**

American Abstract Artists, 4:50

American Academy for Jewish Research, 2:**47**, 18:723

American Association for Jewish Education, 2:**47–48**, 6:196

See also Jewish Education Service of North America

The American College (Flexner), 7:78

American Communist Party, 3:247, 5:98, 13:232

American Council for Judaism, 2:**48**

American Ethical Union. *See* Ethical culture

American Examiner (periodical), 2:49

American Exceptionalism, 13:232

American Families of Jewish Descent (Stern), 19:214

American Federation of Labor, 12:411

American Foreign Policy Between the Wars (Adler), 1:408

American Foundation for AIDS Research (Amfar), 5:56

American Gathering of Jewish Holocaust Survivors, 2:**48–49**

American Graffiti, 6:21

American Greetings Corporation, 18:39

American Hebrew (periodical), 2:**49**, 4:214, 5:255

American history

Bailyn, Bernard, 3:68–69

Boorstin, Daniel J., 4:79

Sarna, Jonathan Daniel, 18:58–59

American Indians. *See* Native Americans

American Israelite (periodical), 2:**50**, 6:320

American Israel Public Affairs Committee (AIPAC), 2:**50–52**, 18:462

The American Jew: A Zionist Analysis (Halpern), 8:283

American Jewess (periodical), 2:**53**

American Jewish Archives (AJA), 2:**53–54**, 407, 9:161–162, 425

An American Jewish Bibliography (Rosenbach), 17:432

American Jewish Committee (AJC), 2:**54–56**, 5:90–91

Adler, Cyrus, 1:395

Bijur, Nathan, 3:695

Fineberg, Solomon Andhil, 7:26

Loeb, Morris, 13:161

Slawson, John, 18:673

American Jewish Conference, 2:**56**, 14:451

American Jewish Congress (AJCongress), 2:**56–58**

Bikel, Theodore Meir, 3:696

Black-Jewish relations in U.S. and, 3:735

boycotts, anti-Nazi, 4:111

minority rights, 14:289

Pam, Hugo, 15:608

American Jewish family, 6:**695–707**

American Jewish Historical Society, 2:**58–59**, 9:160, 18:723

Adler, Cyrus, 1:395

American Sephardi Federation, 2:64

Center for Jewish History, 4:542

founding, 9:161

Holocaust, 9:425

Karp, Abraham J., 11:815

American Jewish Joint Agricultural Corporation (Agro-Joint), 2:60, 3:718

American Jewish Joint Distribution Committee (JDC), 2:**59–64**, 3:434, 7:19, 9:245, 490, 11:719, 20:256–257

Asociación Mutual Israelista Argentina, 2:71

Baerwald, Pau, 3:55

education, Jewish, 6:186

France, 7:163

Haber, Samuel L., 8:175

Holocaust rescues

funding, 13:700

Hyman, Joseph, 9:650

Jordan, Charles Harold, 11:403

Latvia, 12:521

Leavitt, Moses, 12:577

Romania, 7:19

Slovak Jews, aid to, 18:684

The American Jewish League for Israel, 12:**563–564**

American Jewish Periodical Center (AJPC), 2:54

American Jewish Publication Society. *See* Jewish Publication Society

American Jewish World Service, 14:123

American Jewish Year Book (periodical), 2:56

American League for the Defense of Jewish Rights (ALDJR), 4:110–111

American literature. *See* Canadian literature; United States literature

The American Negro: A Study in Racial Crossing (Herskovits), 9:46

American Palestine Fund, Inc., 2:46

American Pastoral (Roth), 20:295–296

American Pop (Bakshi), 3:74

The American Princess. See Ha-Nesikhah ha-Amerikait

American Professors for Peach, 13:75

American Psychiatry Association, 11:766

American Psychoanalytic Association, 13:169

American Red Cross, 18:773

American Revolution, 2:43–44

Bush, Solomon, 4:305

New York City and, 15:197–198

American Sephardi Federation (ASF), 2:**64–65**, 4:542

Americans for Democratic Action, 2:653

Americans no Iewes, or Improbabilities that the Americans Are of that Race (L'Estrange), 14:460

American Society for Jewish Music (ASJM), 2:**65**

Americans of Jewish Descent (Stern), 2:54

American Youth and the Holocaust study, 9:449

American Zionist Committee for Public Affairs, 2:50

American Zionist Council (AZC)

American Israel Public Affairs Committee, 2:50

American Zionist Movement, 2:65

American Zionist Emergency Council, 2:65, 6:773, 18:584, 21:607

American Zionist Federation, 2:65

American Zionist Medical Unit (AZMU), 2:60, 8:186

American Zionist Movement (AZM), **2:65**

Americas. *See* America

Amerika – heute und morgen (Holitscher), 9:321

Das amerikanische Wirtschaftswunder (Hirsch), 9:126

Améry, Jean, **2:65–66**

Amery, John, 2:66

Amery, Julian, Baron Amery of Lustleigh, 2:66

Amery, Leopold Charles Maurice Stennett, 2:66

Amery, Leopold Charles Mauritz. *See* Amery, Leopold Charles Maurice Stennett

Ames family, **2:66**

Amfar (American Foundation for AIDS Research), 5:56

Am ha-arez, **2:66–70**

AMIA (Asociación Mutual Israelita Argentina), **2:70–71,** 11:754

Amichai, Yehuda, **2:71–72,** 8:703, 704, 11:217

Amici Israel association, 4:712

Amidah, **2:72–76**
    Al ha-Nissim, 1:655, 2:75
    Al Ḥet, 1:658
    Anenu, 2:75
    Arvit, 2:537
    Attah, Eḥad, 2:645
    benedictions, 3:331–332
    Berakhot, 3:399–400
    Birkat ha-Minim, 3:711–712
    Book of Life, 4:69
    festivals, 6:770
    Jerusalem, 11:214
    kedushah, 2:74
    Kerovah, 12:**88**
    kerovah, 12:88
    laborer, 12:410
    liturgy, 13:131–132, 135–136
    Maimon ben Joseph, 13:371
    Maimonides, Moses, 13:384
    min, 2:72, 74, 75, 14:280
    minḥah, 2:72, 74, 75, 14:302
    Ne'ilah, 2:72, 76, 15:65
    prayers for rain, 13:601
    priestly blessing, 16:510–511
    proselytes, 16:589
    resurrection, 17:240–241

Shemoneh Esreh, 18:458

Shofarot, 18:508

syogogues, 19:353, 362

Amidar, **2:76–77**

Amiel, Barbara, 11:467

Amiel, Moshe Avigdor, 2:**77**

Amiel - Rabbi Emanuel Rackman Program for Practical Rabbinics, 17:30

Amiens, Viscomte D'. *See* Calmer, Moses Eliezer Liefmann

Amieth. *See* Almon (territory of Benjamin)

Amigo, Abraham, 2:**77**

Amigo, Isaac, 2:77

Amigo, Joseph Meir, 2:77

Amigo, Meir, 2:**77**

Amigo family, 2:**77**

Amina, **2:77–78,** 11:555, 556

Aminoff, Abraham, 11:557

Amintū (widow), 6:66

Amir (Israel), 2:**78**

Amir, Aharon, 2:**78,** 4:393

Amir, Anda, 2:**78**

Amir, Eli, 2:**78**

Amir, Menahem, **2:78–79**

Amir, Yigal, 10:246–247

Amira, Binyamin, 2:**79**

Amiran, David, 2:**79**

Amiran, Emanuel, 2:**79**

Amiran, Ruth, 2:79, 329, 330, 371

Amir Faysal, 10:17

Amirim (Israel), 2:**79**

Amishai-Maisels, Ziva, **2:79–80**

AMIT (Mizrachi Women's Organization of America), 2:**80**

Amit, Meir, 2:**80**

Amital, Yeḥudah, 15:703

Amitay, Morris J., 2:51, 52

Amitsur, Samson Abraham, **2:80–81**

Amittai, 2:**81**

Amittai ben Avida Ahizedek. *See* Caro, David

Amittai ben Shephatiah, 2:**81,** 4:184

Amittai of Oria, 15:470

Amlander, Menahem. *See* Amelander, Menahem Mann ben Solomon Ha-Levi

Amman (ancient Israel). *See* Rabbath-Ammon (ancient Israel)

Amman (Jordan), 11:404
    See also Rabbath-Ammon (ancient Israel)

Ammatha (ancient city), 2:**81**

Ammatu. *See* Ammatha (ancient city)

Ammatus. *See* Ammatha (ancient city)

Ammerschweier (France). *See* Ammerschwihr (France)

Ammerschwihr (France), **2:81–82**

Ammi'ad, 2:**82**

Ammianus Marcellinus, 2:**82,** 11:573

Ammi bar Nathan, 2:**82,** 11:478–479

Amminadab (Ammonite king), 2:85

Amminadav (Israel), 2:**83**

Amminadbi (Ammonite king). *See* Amminadab (Ammonite king)

Ammon and Ammonites, 2:83, **83–87**
    alphabet, Hebrew, 1:694*t,* 695
    Amalekites, 2:29
    conquest of, 11:122–123
    David and, 5:450
    inscriptions and seals, 3:657
    Jotham and, 11:465
    Moab, 14:399

Ammudei ha-Avodah (Landshuth), 12:476–477

Ammudei ha-Golah (Corbeil), 4:773

Ammudei Lashon (Loewe), 13:166

Ammudei Sheva (Aaron Selig ben Moses of Zolkiew), 1:221

Ammud ha-Esh (Barash), 3:136

Ammundei Gavra (Segal), 18:246

Amnon (son of David), 2:**87,** 19:494

Amnon of Mainz, 2:**87**

Am Olam, **2:87–88**

Amon, 2:**88,** 9:181

Among Friends: Who We Like, Why We Like Them and What We Do with Them (Pogrebin), 16:278

Among Lions. See Be-Tokh Leva'im

Among People. See Vlyudjakh

Among the Nations. See Silbermann

Amora, **2:88–89**
    academies, 1:349–350
    Dimi, 5:662
    Dimi of Nehardea, 5:662–663
    Levi, 12:684
    Levi ben Sisi, 12:702–703

Amoraic period
    Bible, interpretation of, 9:817–818
    legal maxims, 12:603
    Samael, 17:714
    Satan, 18:72–73
    sevarah, 18:323
    Takkanot, 19:446

Amoraim, 2:88, **89–95,** 89*t,* 91, 92
    academies, 1:349–351
    aggadah, 1:455–458, 459, 462, 464, 2:94
    Alexandri, 1:631–632
    aliyah of, 10:330
    Babylonian, 10:40–41, 11:135–136, 708
    baraitot, 3:124–126

Amoraim, *continued*
 Benjamin ben Japheth, 3:361
 codification of law, 4:768
 controversy restrictions, 5:157
 Eleazar ben Pedat, 6:306–307
 Eleazar ben Yose II, 6:308–309
 halakhah, 2:89, 94, 8:252–256
 Ḥama Bar Bisa, 8:291
 Ḥama Bar Ḥanina, 8:291
 Ḥama of Nehardea, 8:291
 Hamnuna, 8:310
 Hamnuna Saba, 8:310
 Hamnuna Zuta, 8:310
 Ḥana Bar Ḥanilai, 8:313
 Ḥana ben Bizna, 8:313
 Ḥanina Bar Papa, 8:322
 Ḥanina ben Abbahu, 8:322
 Ḥisda, 9:144
 Ḥiyya, 9:295–296
 Ḥiyya bar Abba, 9:295–297
 Ḥiyya bar Avin, 9:297
 Hoshaiah, Rav, 9:559
 Ḥunya of Beth-Horon, 9:622
 Jerusalem Talmud, 2:93, 95,
  19:483–485
 Ketuvim cited by, 3:579
 law and morality, 12:536–537, 539
 legal maxims, 12:603–604
 liturgy, 13:131
 Mishnah, 14:320–321
 Mishnaic Hebrew of, 8:649–650
 mishpat Ivri, 14:337, 340
 Palestinian, 11:30, 32–33
  Isaac Nappaḥa, 10:52
 savora, 18:85
 Sheshet, 8:313, 18:466
 Simeon ben Abba, 18:594
 Simeon ben Jehozadak, 18:597
 Simeon ben Lakish, 18:597–598
 Simeon ben Pazzi, 18:599
 Simlai, 18:606
 tannaim, 19:505
Amorite language, 8:621, 622, 625
Amorites, 2:95–97
 Adoni-Zedek, 1:414
 Anath, 2:131
 defeat of, 11:72
 Mari, 2:131
 Phoenicia, 16:120
Amorkesos, 11:464
Amos, 2:97–103
 book, 2:98–100
 eschatology in, 6:490
 prophecies, 2:100–103
 prophet, 2:97–98, 101–103

Amos Studies (Morgenstern), 14:486
Un amour amaldroit (Bosco), 4:425
Amphibians, 7:297
Amphictyonic hypothesis, 3:654, 658
Amram (14th c.), 2:103–104
Amram (Babylonian amoraim), 2:103
Amram (father of Aaron, Moses, and
 Miriam), 2:103, 14:311–312, 523,
 526
Amram, David, 2:104
Amram, David Werner, 2:104
Amram, Mordecai. *See* Hirsch,
 Markus
Amram, Nathan ben Ḥayyim, 2:104
Amram, Werner David, 2:104
Amram ben Sheshna, 2:104–105
 Amidah, 2:73, 75
 angels, 2:158
Amram Darah, 2:105
Amram Gaon. *See* Amram ben
 Sheshna
Amram Ḥasida, 2:105
Amram I, 2:103
Amram II, 2:103
Amram of Mainz, 2:106
Amran (Yemen), 2:106
Am Rande der Zeit (Bab), 3:14
Amraphel, 2:106
Am Roked (Kadman), 11:700
Amschelberg (Bohemia). *See* Kosová
 Hora (Bohemia)
Amshewitz, John Henry, 2:106
Amshinov, Jacob David of, 20:651
Amshinov dynasty, 20:651
Amsterdam (Netherlands), 2:106–120,
 116
 1795-1870, 2:110–111, 6:749
 1870-1940, 2:113–115
 pre-1795, 2:106–110, 117
 Aboab da Fonseca, Isaac, 1:269
 bankers, moneylending, 3:114
 community leaders
  seventeenth century, 15:759
 diamond trade and industry, 5:635
 post-1945, 2:116–120
 Holocaust, 2:115–116, 18:11
 Meyer, Jonas Daniel, 14:147
 printing, publishing, 7:207, 16:533
 Sarphati, Samuel, social projects
  by, 18:60
 seals, use of, 18:227
 Sheluḥei Ereẓ Israel, 18:449
 ties with Cochin (India), 15:759
 See also The Netherlands
Amsterdam, Birdie, 2:120–121
Amsterdam editions, Haggadah, 8:215

Amsterdam Joodsche Raad, 2:599
Amsterdam School (architectural
 movement), 5:534
Amtaḥ binyamin, 3:9
Amtchislav (Belarus). *See* Mstislavl
 (Belarus)
Amuladi (king of Kedar), 14:403
Amulets, 2:121–123
 ba'al shem, 3:9
 birth amulet, vol. 7: color insert
 birth customs and folklore, 3:721,
  722
 Judeo-Persian, 11:554
 Samaritan, 2:123–124
 See also Magic
A mulher que escrevu a Bíblia
 (Moacyr), 18:207
Amulo, 2:124
Amunhotpe, Nebmare. *See* Amenophis
 III
Amurru. *See* Amorites
Amusin, Joseph, 2:124, 11:321
Am va-Sefer (Brit Ivrit Olamit), 4:189
Amzalak, Ḥayyim, 2:124
Amzalak, Moses Bensabat, 2:124–125
Anab, 2:125
Anacharsis. *See* Cloots, Jean Baptiste
 du Val-de-Grâce
Anacletus II, 2:125, 16:148, 373
Anaharath, 2:125
Anak, Anakim, 1:544, 2:125–126
Anakim. *See* Anak, Anakim
*An American Testament: A Narrative
 of Rebels and Romantics* (Freeman),
 7:228
Anammelech, 2:126
Anan (Babylonian scholar), 2:126
Anan (high priest). *See* Anan ben Seth
Anan, son of Anan, 2:126–127
Anan ben David, 2:127–128
 Judeo-Arabic literature and,
  11:532
 Karaites historical development,
  11:787–789
Anan ben Marinus ha-Kohen, 2:128
Anan ben Seth, 2:128–129
 biblical commentaries by, 3:641
 biography of, 3:706
Ananel the Babylonian. *See* Hanamel
Ananiah ben Azariah (groom), 6:312
Ananias and Helkias, 2:129
Ananias ben Nedebeus, 2:129, 6:299
Ananias of Adiabene, 2:129
Ananias son of Zadok, 2:130
Ananiev (Ukraine). *See* Ananyev
 (Ukraine)
Ananites, 2:127–128, 11:787

Ananiyyim. *See* Ananites

Ananus, son of Seth. *See* Anan ben Seth

Ananyev (Ukraine), 2:**130**

Anapa (Russia), 2:**130**

Anarchism, 3:75, 18:709–710

Anarchisms, 16:13

Anaschehon, Joseph, I, 2:130

Anaschehon, Joseph, II, 2:130

Anaschehon, Meir, II, 2:130

Anaschehon family, 2:**130–131**

Anaschichun family. *See* Anaschehon family

Anashikon, Meir. *See* Anaschehon, Meir, II

Anath, 2:**131**, 3:11, 12

Anathema. *See* Blessing and cursing

Anat Hoffman *v.* Jerusalem Municipal Council, 5:128

Anathoth (Israel), 2:131, **132**

Anatol ben Joseph, 15:581

Anatoli. *See* Anatoli ben Joseph

Anatoli, Jacob ben Abba Mari ben Samson, 2:**132–133**, 3:645, 12:698, 16:86

    Judah ha-Nasi and, 11:501

Anatolia. *See* Asia Minor

Anatoli ben Joseph, 2:**133**

Anatomy, 2:**133–135**, 13:721–722

    See also Medicine

Anatomy of the Auschwitz Death Camp (Gutman & Berenbaum), 9:420

Anatomy of the Auschwitz Death Camp (Van Pelt), 9:415

Anatomy of the SS State (Jacobesen), 9:416

Anau, Phinehas Ḥai ben Menahem, 2:**136–137**

Anau family, 2:136, **136**

Anav. *See* Anab

Anav, Abraham ben Jacob, 2:136

Anav, Benjamin ben Abraham, 2:**137**

Anav, Jehiel ben Jekuthiel ben Benjamin ha-Rofe, 2:**137–138**

Anav, Judah ben Benjamin ha-Rofe, 2:**138**

Anav, Moses ben Abraham, 2:136

Anav, Nathan ben Jehiel. *See* Nathan ben Jehiel of Rome

Anav, Salvatore, 2:136

Anav, Zedekiah ben Abraham, 2:136, **138–139**

Anav family. *See* Anau family

Anbar. *See* Pumbedita (Babylonia)

Anĉerl, Karel, 2:**139**

Ancestral guilt, inheriting, 21:498

Ancestral merit, inheriting, 21:497–498

Anchel, Robert, 2:**139**

Anchetatorul apatic. See The Apathetic Interrogator

Anchor Bible, 3:616–617

Ancient Aramaic. *See* Aramaic, ancient

The Ancient Economy (Finley), 7:39

The Ancient Melodies of the Liturgy of the Spanish and Portuguese Jews (de Sola), 18:751

Ancient of Days, 2:**139–140**

Ancient Order of Maccabeans. *See* Order of Ancient Maccabeans

Ancona (Italy), 2:**140–141**

    Paul IV, 15:531–532

    Paul VI, 15:695

Ancona, Alessandro, 2:141–142

Ancona, Cesare D', 2:**142**

Ancona, Mario, 2:142

Ancona, Paolo, 2:142

Ancona, Sansone, 2:142, 16:345

Ancona, Vito D', 2:**142–143**

Ancona family, 2:**141–142**

Ancyra. *See* Ankara (Turkey)

Andalusian poetry, 1:438–439, 6:47–48

Anderle von Rinn. *See* Andrew of Rinn

Andernach (Germany), 2:**143**

Anders, Guenther, 2:**143**

Andersch, Alfred, 2:65

Anderson, Gilbert Maxwell, 14:570

Anderson, Paul, 18:93

And He Is Different. See Ve-Hu Aḥer

And It Came to Pass (Bialik), 18:761

Andrada, Salvador d', 15:195

Andrade, Abraham, 4:83

Andrade, Edward Neville da Costa, 2:**143–144**

Andrade, Velosino Jacob de, 2:**144**

Andreas. *See* Lucuas

Andreas of Rinn. *See* Andrew of Rinn

Andreas of Saint-Victor. *See* Andrew of Saint-Victor

Andrewes, Lancelot, 2:**144**, 3:613

Andrew of Rinn, 2:**144**

Andrew of Saint-Victor, 2:**144–145**, 4:96

Andreyev (Poland). *See* Jedrzejow (Poland)

Androgynos, 2:**145**

Andronicus II (Byzantine emperor), 4:327

Andronicus son of Meshullam, 2:**145**

And Stars Remain (Epstein and Epstein), 6:474

"And the Angels Sing" (Elman), 6:365

And the Crooked Shall be Made Straight (Robinson), 9:415

Anello, Solomon, 1:502

Anenu, 2:75

Aner, Eshkol, and Mamre, 2:**145**

Anes. *See* Ames family

Añes, Dunstan. *See* Añes, Gonsalvo

Añes, Francisco, 2:66

Añes, George, 2:66

Añes, Gonsalvo, 2:66

Añes, Jacob, 2:66

Añes, Sarah, 2:66

Añes, William, 2:66

Añes family. *See* Ames family

Anfei Ereẓ (Silver), 18:585

Anfinsen, Christian Boehmer, 2:**145–146**, 4:592–593, 13:10

Angaria, 2:**146**

Angel, Aaron, 2:**146–147**

Angel, Baruch, 2:**147**

Angel, Marc D., 2:**147**

Angel, Meir ben Abraham, 2:**147**

Angel, Shemayahu, 2:**147**

Angelo, Aaron Vita di, 17:297

Angel of Death, 2:**147–150**

The Angel of Death. *See* Mengele, Josef

Angels and angelology, 2:**150–161**

    Abaddon, 1:224

    Abraham

        announcement of birth of Isaac, vol. 7: color insert

        Apocalypse of, 1:288–289

        Testament of, 1:291

    Adam, 1:372

    "Addir bi-Melukhah," 1:385

    Amen, 2:39

    amulets, 2:121, 122

    Apocalypse, 2:257

    Apocrypha, 2:152–156

    Balaam, 3:78

    Belial, 3:289–290

    Bible, 2:150–152

    cherub and cherubim, 2:150, 4:600–601

    Daniel ben Moses al-Qūmisī, 5:428

    Daniel's dream, 5:421

    Dead Sea Scrolls, 5:502–503

    death, angel of, 2:147–150

    vs. demons, 5:573–574

    Elimelech of Lyzhansk, 6:348

    Enoch, Ethiopic Book of, 6:443

    Gabriel, 2:152, 153, 5:421, 14:167–169

    host of heaven, 9:566–567

    idolatry, 9:710

    Jacob and, 11:18, 19

        in art, 11:23–24

Angels and angelology, *continued*
  Jerusalem Talmud, 19:484
  Jewish philosophy, 2:159–161
  Karaites, 11:789
  liturgy, 2:158
  logos, 2:159, 13:174–175
  magic, 13:342–345, 347–348, 350, 352
  Maimonides, 2:160, 13:390
  manna, 13:478
  Manual of Discipline, 5:676–677
  Metatron, 14:132–134
  Michael, 2:152, 14:167–169
  Midrash, 2:156–158
  modern period, 2:161
  Moses, 14:534–536, 539
  mysticism, 2:158–159
  nature of man, 13:446, 448, 450
  Philo (the Elder), 16:58
  prayer, 16:459
  providence, 16:648–649
  Raphael, 17:93–94
  Sadducees, 17:655
  Samael, 17:715
  Samson, 17:749
  Sandalfon, 18:10
  Sefer ha-Razim, 17:130
  Solomon, 18:760
  Solomon, Testament of, 18:768
  song, angelic, 19:14
  Talmud, 2:156–158
  Uriel, 20:421–422
  visions, 20:543–545
  watchers, 20:688
  See also Nephilim; Satan
The Angels Are Coming. See Malakhim Ba'im
Angels in America (Kushner), 15:227
Angelus, Theodore Ducas, 6:463
The Angel with the Trumpet. See Der Engel mit der Posaune
Angers (France), 2:**161,** 175
Anghelov, Dimitur, 4:276
Angicaymal. *See* Ernakulam
Anglican Church
  Alexander, Michael Solomon, 1:623–624
  Israel (state), 10:640
  Jewish relations, 11:281
  See also World Council of Churches (WCC)
Anglo-American Committee of Enquiry Regarding the Problems of European Jewry and Palestine (1946), 3:703, 15:584–585, 586
Anglo-Boer War. *See* Boer War

Anglo-Israel Archaeological Society, 2:**161–162**
Anglo-Israeli theory, 4:188
Anglo-Jewish Association (AJA), 2:**162,** 3:319, 353, 6:415, 419, 12:565
Anglo-Jewish Historical Exhibition (1887), 11:292, 14:626
Anglo-Palestine Bank, 3:180, 10:513, 514, 547, 586, 587
Anglo-Saxon Federation of America, 4:188
Angoff, Charles, 2:**162**
Angora. *See* Ankara (Turkey)
Angoulême (France), 2:**162–163**
Angrist, Alfred Alvin, 2:**163**
Anhalt (Germany), 2:**163**
Anhalt, István, 2:**163–164**
Anielewicz, Mordecai, 2:**164**
Anilaeus and Asinaeus, 2:**164–165,** 3:27, 11:440
Ani Ma'amin, 2:**165**
Animales feroces (Chocrón), 4:657
Animal Liberation (Singer), 18:640
Animals, 2:168*t*–171*t*
  in art
    bulls, bronze figures, vol. 1: color insert
    calf, ivory figure, vol. 1: color insert
    fish, paper cut, vol. 2: color insert
    Jonah and the whale, illustration, vol. 1: color insert
    leopard, mosaic, vol. 1: color insert
    lion, seal, vol. 1: color insert
    lionness and cub, mosaic, vol. 1: color insert
    monkey, bronze figure, vol. 1: color insert
    ram, mosaic, vol. 1: color insert
    sacrificial animals, painting, vol. 1: color insert
    scarab seals, 18:225
    sculpture, 18:222
    Taurus the Bull, mosaic, vol. 1: color insert
    Tiberias reliefs, vol. 1: color insert
  of the Bible and Talmud, 2:166–172, 12:696–697
  blemished, 3:749–750
  bull symbolism, 18:570
  Commandments, the 613, 5:75–76, 78, 80–84
  concern for, 5:165–166

  cruelty to, 2:165–166
  damages from, 2:751–752
  dietary laws, 5:650–659
  Elephantine Temple, 6:312–313
  fables, 6:666–669
  fasting, 6:721
  firstborn, 7:45–46
  goats, 5:488, 492–493
  hides, 12:574–577
  homicidal, bloodguilt of, 3:774
  vs. human life ethics, 5:168–169
  Ir ha-Niddaḥat, 10:28–29
  Israel, 10:143
  leopards, 12:649
  lions, 5:418
  lion symbolism, 18:570
  Mishnah, 14:324
  mixed species, 14:385–387
  moles, 14:425
  nature of man, 13:448
  nevelah, 15:129
  Noah, 15:287–288
  Parah, 15:630
  prehistoric Israel, 10:142
  prohibited, hare, 8:347–348
  proverbs, 16:647
  ritual purity and impurity, 16:746–747
  sacrifices, 17:639–649
  Sheḥitah, 18:434–437
  soul, 19:34
  terefah, 19:647
  torts, 20:63–66
  tribal representations, 11:26
  See also specific animals and classes of animals
The Animals' Collection (Kalonymus ben Kalonymus). *See Iggeret Ba'alei Ḥayyim*
Animal slaughtering, commandments concerning, 5:76*t*–77*t*
Animal tales, 2:**173–174,** 15:622
Anim Zemirot, 2:**174**
Aninut, 2:**174,** 14:587
Anise, vol. 16: color insert
Anisfeld, Boris, 2:**174–175**
Anisimov, Ilya Sherbatovich, 2:**175**
Ani ve-Shimon u-Moise ha-Kattan (Banai), 3:106
Anjou (France), 2:**175**
Ankara (Turkey), 2:**175–176**
Ankawa, Abraham ben Mordecai, 2:**176,** 13:24
Ankawa, Raphael ben Mordecai, 2:**176**
Ankori, Zevi, 2:**176–177**
Anman. *See* Rosenthal, Pavel

Anman, P. Rol. *See* Rosenthal, Pavel

Anna Akhmatova (Eichenbaum), 6:246

Annaba (Algeria). *See* Bone (Algeria)

Anna be-Kho'ah, 2:**177**

Anna be-Korenu, 2:**177**

Annaeus Seneca. *See* Seneca the Elder

Annals. See Kitāb al-Tarīkh

Ann Arbor (MI), 2:**177–178**

Anna Teller (Seid), 18:253

L'Année Sociologique (periodical), 6:63–64

Anne Frank: The Whole Story, 9:440

Annenberg, Walter H., 2:**178–179**, 6:25–26, 11:468

Annenberg Research Institute for Judaic and Near Eastern Studies, 6:25–26

Annita (King of Kuššar), 9:291

The Ann Landers Encyclopedia (Lederer), 12:596

Annotations (Ainsworth), 1:550–551

Annulment, 1:514–517, 518, 520

Anointing, 2:**179–180**, 15:395–396

Anokhi, Zalman Yizḥak, 2:**180**

"The Anonymous" (13th c.). *See* Jacob ha-Katan

Another Language (Franken), 7:202

An San. *See* Chao Ch'eng

Ansbach (Germany), 2:**180**, 7:144

Ansell, David Abraham, 2:**180–181**

Anselm ha-Levi, 2:**181**

Anselm of Canterbury, 2:**181**

Anshei Knesset ha-Gedolah. *See* Synagogue, The Great

Anshel ha-Levi. *See* Anselm ha-Levi

Anshel of Cracow, 2:**181**

An-Ski, S., 2:**181–182**, 11:694, 17:98
    The Dybbuk, 8:179
    Justman, Moshe Bunem, 11:581

An-Ski collections, 2:**182–183**

Ansorge, Martin Charles, 2:**183–184**

Anspach, Philippe, 2:**184**

Antaka (Turkey). *See* Antioch (Turkey)

Antakya (Turkey). *See* Antioch (Turkey)

Antebi, Albert, 2:**184**

Antebi, Avraham. *See* Antebi, Albert

Antelope, 2:**184–185**

Anthedon (Hellenistic city), 2:**185**

Anthologie juive des orgines á nos jours (Fleg), 7:72

Anthony, Joseph, 2:**185**

Anthropocentrism, 5:164

Anthropodicy
    Job as, 11:355–356

Anthropology, 2:**185–188**
    Boas, Franz, 4:21–22

Bunzel, Ruth Leah, 4:285
    cultural materialism, 8:363
    Elkin, Adolphus Peter, 6:359
    Erlich, Vera Stein, 6:481
    Fortes, Meyer, 7:133
    Harris, Marvin, 8:363
    Herskovits, Melville Jean, 9:46
    Landes, Ruth, 12:468–469
    Levin, Maksim Grigoryevich, 12:710
    Levi-Strauss, Claude, 12:730
    Lévy-Bruhl, Lucien, 12:756–757
    Lewis, I. M., 12:765
    Lewis, Oscar, 12:766
    Lowie, Robert Harry, 13:236–237
    Luschan, Felix von, 13:270
    Montagu, Montague Francis Ashley, 14:452
    Polányi, Karl, 16:326–327
    race, theory of, 17:45–47
    Radin, Paul, 17:54–55
    Rappaport, Roy, 17:100
    Róheim, Géza, 17:369–370
    Sapir, Edward, 18:37
    Schapera, Isaac, 18:107
    Seligman, Charles Gabriel, 18:266
    Shapiro, Larry Lionel, 18:405–406
    Singer, Milton B., 18:639

Anthropomorphic God, 11:516

Anthropomorphism, 1:213, 379, 2:**188–192**, 7:659, 11:730

Antibi, Abraham ben Isaac, 2:192, **192–193**

Antibi, Jacob, 2:192

Antibi family, 2:**192**

Antichresis, 2:**193**

Antichrist, 2:**193–194**, 474–475

Anti-Christian Polemics. *See* Polemics and polemical literature

Anti-Defamation League (ADL), 2:**194–195**, 9:245
    American Israel Public Affairs Committee, 2:52
    Arab propaganda, 2:194
    Foxman, Abraham, 7:142
    history of, 4:14

Anti-Dictator. See Discours de la servitude volontaire

Anti-Fascist Committee, Jewish, 2:**196–197**

Antigonus, 11:414, 13:299

Antigonus I, 2:**197**

Antigonus II, 2:**197–198**, 9:197

Antigonus Mattathias, 8:446–447

Antigonus of Carystus, 2:**198**

Antigonus of Sokho, 2:**198**

Anti-Israel Arab boycott, 4:111–113

Anti-Jewish boycotts, 4:**109–110**, 9:328, *461. See also antisemitic political parties and organizations; Antisemitism; Boycotts*

Anti-Jewish Decrees. *See* Antisemitism

Antilles, Netherlands. *See* Netherlands Antilles

Antimony, 14:128

Antin, Mary, 2:**198–199**

Anti-Nazi boycotts, 4:**110–111**, 111*t*

Antinomianism, 1:231, 2:**199–201**, 18:353

Antioch (Turkey), 2:*201*, **201–202**

Antiochene school, 3:665–666

Antioch on the River Chrysorrhoas. *See* Gerasa (Jordan)

Antiochus (ancient Israel). *See* Banias (ancient Israel)

Antiochus, Scroll of. *See* Scroll of Antiochus

Antiochus I, 2:202

Antiochus II, 2:202, 5:422

Antiochus III, 2:202–203, 3:26, 9:192, 193, 13:295

Antiochus IV, 2:203, 9:193, 194
    blood libel and, 3:775
    Eleazar, 6:298
    Jason and, 2:203, 11:90
    Jerusalem and, 11:148
    Nicholas of Damascus on, 15:252
    Scroll of Antiochus, 18:213–214

Antiochus V, 2:203

Antiochus VII, 2:203, 18:601

Antiochus IX, 2:203–204

Antiochus Cyzicenus. *See* Antiochus IX

Antiochus dynasty, 2:**202–204**

Antiochus Epiphanes. *See* Antiochus IV

Antiochus Eupator. *See* Antiochus V

Antiochus III, 4:781

Antiochus Sidetes. *See* Antiochus VII

Antiochus Soter. *See* Antiochus I

Antiochus the Great. *See* Antiochus III

Antiochus Theos. *See* Antiochus II

Antipas. *See* Antipater II

Antipas, Herod, 2:*204*, **204**, 9:39
    fortification of Sepphoris, 18:306
    John the Baptist and, 11:381

Antipater
    Joseph (son), 11:414
    Julius Caesar and, 11:574

Antipater I, 2:**204–205**, *205*

Antipater II, 2:*205*, **205**

Antipatris (Palestine), 2:**205–206**

Antiphonal Psalmody. *See* Music

Antiphony I (Brant), 4:130

Antiproton, 18:252

Antiquities of the Jews. See Jewish Antiquities

Antisemitism, 2:**206–246**, *215*, 14:41–142

    Abbas I, 3:15

    Abbasids, 1:234

    Abbas II, 1:231, 3:15

    Abd al-Ḥaqq al-Islāmī, 1:240

    Abraham a Sancta Clara, 1:292

    Aden, 1:388, 389, 5:681

    Afghanistan, 1:433

    Africa, 1:436

    Agobard, 1:469, 2:124

    Ahlwardt, Hermann, 1:547

    Alaric II, 1:575

    Algeria, 1:649–651, 4:533

        Algiers, 1:653–654

    Alliance Israelite Universelle, 1:671–675

    American Jewish Committee, 2:55–56

    American Jewish Congress, 2:57–58

    Amran, 2:106

    Amsterdam, 2:106, 115–166, 119

    Amulo, 2:124

    Andrew of Rinn, 2:144

    Anglo-Saxon Federation of America, 4:188

    Anti-Defamation League, 2:194–196

    in antiquity, 2:206–209

    anti-sheḥitah movements and, 18:435

    Apion, 2:256

    Arab countries, 2:225–226, 236

    Argentina

        Buenos Aires, 4:253–254

        DAIA, 5:379–380

    Asia-Pacific region, 2:238–239

    Austria, 2:*217*, 219, 4:224, 16:340

        Carinthia, 4:480

        Charles VI of Hapsburg, 4:576–577

        Christian Social Party, 4:694

        Deckert, Joseph, 5:528

        Eisenstadt, 6:268–269

        references in Catholic literature, 18:168

        Schoenerer, Georg von, 18:156–157

        Seipel, Ignaz on, 18:255

    Babylonia

        Sasanid dynasty, 3:29–30

    badges, Jewish, 3:45–48

        Austria, 2:689

        Belgium, 2:250

        Boniface IX, 4:63

        England, 3:45

        France, 2:6, 81, 3:45–46, 47

        Germany, 3:46–47, 450

        Italy, 2:137, 140, 292, 3:46, 47, 12:506

        Netherlands, 2:115

        Spain, 6:91

    Basil I, decrees of, 18:460–461

    Battle of Cable Street, 3:215

    Belgium, 2:234, 16:144

    Bernheim Petition, 3:475–476

    of Billroth, Theodor, 3:699

    Birobidzhan, interest in, 3:719

    Bischhoff, Erich, 3:724

    Black Code of 1685, 8:240

    Black Death and, 3:731–734, *732–733*, 15:94–95

    Blake, William, 3:737

    blood libel and, 3:775, 776, 778, 779, 17:163

    Bloomberg, Michael, on, 3:782

    B'nai Brith, 4:14, 15

    Board of Delegates of American Israelites, 4:19

    Bohemia, 1:312, 4:39, 41

    Bonald, Louis de, 4:55

    Boniface VIII, 4:63

    boycotts, 4:109–110

    Brafman, Jacob, 4:116–117

    Brazil, 4:148–150, 151, 16:407, 18:31–32, 33

    British West Indies, 4:473, 474

    Brunner, Sebastian, 4:224

    Bucer, Martin, 4:237

    Bukhara (Uzbekistan), 4:261–262

    Bulgaria, 4:271–273

    Byzantine empire, 4:325–326

    Calvin, John, 17:163

    Canada, 4:18, 91, 186, 394–395, 396–397, 402, 403–404, 408–409, 415–416, 422, 423

        Ahenakew, David, 18:65

        Alberta, 1:590

        Scheuer, Edmund on, 18:124

    caricatures of Jews, 4:477–479

    carnival customs, 4:486

    Carthage, 4:499

    Catholic Chuch

        Second Vatican Council on, 11:380

    Catholic Church, 4:710–711, 712, 713–714, 716–717

        Calixtus III, 4:365

        censorship, 4:540

        Church Fathers, 4:719–721

        La Civiltà Cattolica, 4:748–749

        Clement, 4:752–753

        Clement VIII, 2:140

        Crusades, 2:162, 5:310–315

        Dominicans, 5:745–746, 17:126–127

        Paul IV, 2:140

    Caucasus, 4:527

    Chamberlain, Houston Stewart, 4:563

    Chiarini, Luigi, 4:607

    Chile, 4:643

    Christianity, 2:106, 124, 239, 4:685, 690, 713

        early period, 2:209–210

        Melito of Sardis, 14:13

    Cicero, Marcus Tullius, 4:725

    circuses, 4:735

    Colombia, 4:475

    "cosmopolitans," 5:232

    Coudenhove-Kallergi, Heinrich von, 5:238

    Crimean affair, 5:301

    Cuba, 5:319–321

    Cuza, Alexander C., 5:345

    Czechoslovakia, 2:229, 5:360–361, 363, 13:600

        in literature, 5:365–366

        Slánský Trial, 18:665–666

        pre WW II, 5:356

    Czech Republic, 4:534–535

        Carlsbad, 4:482

        Ceska Lipa, 4:552

        Ceske Budejovice, 4:552

        Cheb, 4:585–586

        Chomutov, 4:666

        Miroslav, 14:314

    Damascus Affair, 5:399–401

    Denmark, 5:584

    development of, 9:238, 10:36, 821

    Diaspora, 2:207–209

    discrimination and, 5:679–681

    Dubrovnik (Croatia), 6:38–39

    Dutch literature and, 6:68–69

    early Islam, 2:210

    early postwar period, 2:224–225

    economic history, 6:103–129, 134–138

    effect on Jewish philosophy, 16:92

    Egypt, 6:234–235

        Alexandria, 1:632, 634, 635–636, 6:229–230

        Arab rule, 6:230–232

        Cairo, 4:343–344, 345

modern period, 6:234–236
Ottoman Turks, 6:232–234
Roman era, 6:228–229, 16:28
Eichmann, Adolf Otto, 6:248
Eisenmenger, Johann Andreas,
6:268
Eleazar ben Judah of Worms,
6:303–304
emancipation period, 2:214–223
England, 6:410, 418, 423, 425, 426,
427
Canterbury, 4:435–436
London, 13:182
Enlightenment period, 2:213–214
Erasmus of Rotterdam, 6:477
Evian Conference, 6:576–577
expulsions, German, 7:523
expulsions and, 6:625
Filderman, Wilhelm, 7:19
Ford, Henry, 18:39
former Communist nations,
11:282
France, 2:6–9, 221–223, 238, 4:82
Action Française, 1:369–370
Agde, 1:446
Agen, 1:449
Aix-en-Provence, 1:552
Albi, 1:591–592
Alphonse of Poitiers, 1:730
Bergheim, 3:427
Béziers, 3:559
Blois, 1:609
Cadenet, 4:331
Caen, 4:332, 460–461, 515
Carcassonne, 4:460–461
Carpentras, 4:493–494
Castelsarrasin, 4:515
Châlons-sur-Marne, 4:563
Chalon-sur-Saône, 4:563
Chambéry, 4:564
Champagne, 4:565
Charles II, King of France,
1:310
Charles IV, 4:575
Charles VI, 4:576
Chateaubriand, François
René, 4:582–583
Chinon, 4:651
Clermont-Ferrand, 4:755
Cluny, 4:763
Draguignan, 6:6–7
Dreyfus affair, 6:18–19, 26
Drumont, Edouard-Adolphe,
6:26
Ensisheim, 6:447
French Revolution, 7:252–255

Lyons, 1:469
Morhange, 14:491
Pastoureaux, 15:685
Provence, 1:592, 16:638
Savoy, 18:86
Third Republic, 7:158
twentieth century, 3:378,
5:438, 441, 7:167–168,
13:692
Galicia
Lvov, 4:724
Germany, 2:215, 215–216, 217,
218–219, 238, 4:540, 546, 7:624,
12:436
Agrarian League, 1:470
Berlin, 3:445, 447, 448–451
Calwer, Richard, 4:378
Carben, Victor von, 4:460
Charles IV, 4:575
Chemnitz, 4:593–594
Christian Social Party, 4:695
Cleves, 4:759
Coburg, 4:764
Cochem, 4:765
Delitzsch, Friedrich, 5:540–
541
Einbeck, 6:255
Emden, 6:392
Erfurt, 6:478
Essen, 6:509
Esslingen, 6:514
Fulda, 7:309
German Conservative Party,
5:177
Hamburg, 8:296
Hanover, 8:330
Heidingsfeld, 8:764
Kristallnacht, 12:362–363
medieval, 5:436
Mommsen, Theodor, 14:431
Mosbach, 14:515
Nuremberg laws, 15:348–350
Saxony, 18:88
Unified Germany, 7:543
Greece
Chalcis, 4:561
Chios, 4:651
Haidamacks, 8:233–234
Hapsburg dominions, 2:219
Hep! Hep!, 8:811–812
Herzl, Theodor, 9:55
Hungary, 1:369, 377, 2:217, 219–
220, 4:540, 9:612, 618–619,
10:786
Ada, 1:370
Alberti-Irsa, 1:591

literature, 9:604–605
informers, 9:780–786
interreligious societies to fight,
11:278–279
inter-war period, 2:223–224
Iran, 10:12–13
Hamadan, 8:292–293
Iraq, 5:681, 10:18–19, 20–21
Ḥilla, 9:107–108
Ireland, 10:26–27
Irving v. Lipstadt, 10:30–32
Islam
dhimma, dhimmi, 5:631–632
Israel, 2:206–207
Istanbul (Ottoman period), 10:778
Italy, 2:140, 4:382, 445, 10:799–
801, 803–805, 807, 808–809,
810–811, 812, 813
Acqui, 1:359
Alessandria, 1:618
Bergamo, 3:418
Bologna, 4:49
Brescia, 4:163
Calabria, 4:348
Capistrano, John of, 4:445
Capua, 4:457
carnival celebrations, 4:486
Casale Monferrato, 4:504
Catania, 4:523
Catanzaro, 4:523
Cesena, 4:551–552
Chieri, 4:615
Fascist regime, 6:716–717
Franciscan order, 3:469
Palermo, 15:581
Rome, 4:523–524
Japan, 2:240–242, 11:81, 85,
18:289
Jewish identity and, 11:293, 297,
299
Jewish image, 7:511–513
Jewish labor and, 12:411
John Paul II on, 11:384
Josephus on, 11:438, 440
Justin Martyr, 11:580
of Juvenal, 11:582
Latin America, 2:46, 235, 238,
12:511
League of Nations, 12:565
Lenin, Vladimir Ilyich, 5:92–94
Libya, 5:681
Lithuania
Aleksander Jagiellonczyk,
1:610
Brest-Litovsk, 4:168–170
liturgy
Kol Nidrei, 12:277

Antisemitism, *continued*
  Luther, Martin, 17:163–164
  Majorca
       Chuetas, 4:707–708
  Masaryk, Thomas Garrigue and,
       13:600
  medals indicating, 13:714, 715*t*,
       716
  Middle Ages, 2:211–212, 476–477,
       477, 6:555–556
       agriculture, Jewish, 1:494
       Dulcea of Worms, 6:44
       France, 4:460, 563
       Hugh of Lincoln, 9:579
  modern
       1970s, 2:233–238
       1980s, 2:238–242
       1990s, 2:242–244
       2000s, 2:244–245
       origins of, 6:544
  Mojecki, Przeclaw, 14:423
  Morocco, 14:499, 501, 502–503
       Casablanca, 4:503, 504
  Moses, 14:531–532
  New Zealand, 15:244–245
  Nietzsche, Friedrich Wilhelm,
       7:512, 15:262
  Nordau, Max, 15:298
  in Norway, 15:308–309, 310
  oaths more Judaico or
       Juramentum Judaeorum,
       15:364–365
  Ónody, Géza, 15:434
  OZON, 15:558
  Palestinian Authority, 2:328
  Paraguay, 15:630
  in partisan movement, 15:666
  Peru, 15:795–796
  pogroms, 16:279–282
  Poland, 1:508, 2:*217*, 220, 229,
       4:445, 540, 5:97–98, 11:102,
       12:594–595, 16:300–305, 317–
       318, 321, 322–323
       Aleksander Jagiellonczyk,
            1:610
       Bialystok, 3:567
       Breslau, 18:319
       Checiny, 4:586
       Chelm, 4:588
       Chmielnicki, Bogdan, 4:654–
            656
       Chmielnik, 4:656, 657
       Chryzanow, 4:707
       Ciechanow, 4:725
       Cracow, 5:261–262
       Dmowski, Roman, 5:723–724
       Endecja party, 6:402–403,
            11:740

  Kalisz, 11:740
       Legnica, 12:610
       literature, 16:335–338
       Mlawa, 14:395–396
       nineteenth century, 11:117–
            118
       Pilsudski, Józef, 16:163–164
       Rozwój, 17:505–506
       Samuel Commission, 17:775
       Skarga, Piotr, 18:657
  political participation and, 16:339
  Portugal, 1:431–432, 18:28–29
       Lisbon, 13:79–80
  Protestants, 16:631, 633
  *Protocols of the Learned Elders of
       Zion*, 6:297
  Prussia
       Calmanson, Jacob, 4:374
  Rathenau, Walther, 17:111
  Reformation, 2:212–213
  refutations, 6:688
  Rindfleisch, 17:334–335
  Rohling, August, 17:370
  Roman Empire, 4:486, 12:453–
       454, 17:374–375
  Romania, 2:*217*, 220–221, 5:433–
       434, 8:474, 11:91, 92, 17:382,
       383, 396
       Campulung Moldovenesc,
            4:390
       Cluj, 4:762
       Codreanu, Corneliu Zelea,
            4:781
       Focsani, 7:93
       Iron Guard, 10:29–30
       Siret, 18:643
       Slonim, 18:676
  Rosenberg, Alfred, 17:434–435
  Ruehs, Christian Friedrich, 17:526
  Russia, 2:*217*, 221–222, 4:525, 540,
       9:238
       1970s, 17:569
       1980s, 17:572–573
       Alexander, 1:620–621
       cantonists, 4:437–439
       Eliasberg, Mordecai, 6:319
       Moscow, 14:517–518, 520–
            521
       post-WW II, 17:553–554,
            556, 558
       Russian Federation, 17:583–
            586
       USSR regime, 17:543
       WW II, 17:547–549
  Saint Louis incident, 5:320
  Sardinia, 18:53
       Alghero, 1:652

  Cagliari, 4:335
       Schnitzler, Arthur on, 18:152
       science fiction and fantasy,
            18:201–202
  Sephardim and, 18:301–302
  Serbia
       Ada, 1:370
  Slovakia, 18:683, 684
       Dunajska Streda, 6:46
  socialism and, 18:704, 705, 707,
       708, 710–711
  South Africa, 2:238
  Spain, 2:213, 4:519
       Aguilar de Campóo, 1:509–
            510
       Alba de Tormes, 1:581
       Albarracín, 1:587
       Alfonso X, 1:642
       Almohads, 1:681
       Cádiz, 4:331
       Calahorra, 4:350
       Calatayud, 4:351–352
       Carmona, 4:485
       Carrion de los Condes, 4:496
       Cartagena, 4:496–497, 497
       Castellón de la Plana, 4:514
       Castile, 1:643
       Castrojeriz, 4:518–519
       Cea, 4:534
       Cervera, 4:550–551
       Chillón, 4:645
       Ciudad Real, 4:745
       Ciudad Rodrigo, 4:745
       Coca, 4:764–765
       Écija, 6:91
       Elvira, 6:371
       Escalona, 6:488
       Estella, 6:514–515
       Madrid, 13:333
       Majorca, 13:412–414
       medieval, 5:437
       Miranda de Ebro, 14:310
       Segovia, 18:250
       Seville, 18:327
       Tarragona, 19:521
  St. Eustatius, 4:472
  Stalin, Joseph, 5:96, 99
  Swedish literature, 18:92
  Switzerland
       Berne, 3:471
       Endingen and Lengnau, 6:404
  Syria, 4:495–496, 5:681
       Aleppo, 1:614, 615, 616,
            4:587
  Der Talmudjude (Rohling), 17:370
  Transylvania
       Alba Iulia, 1:582

Turkey
  Edessa, 6:148–150
U.K., 2:233, 237
  Aliens Act of 1905, 1:659
  Samuel Commission, 17:775
Ukraine, 20:235–236, 238, 244–245
  Aleksandriya, 1:610
  Bratslav, 4:134
  Cherkassy, 4:594–595
  Chernigov, 4:596
  Chernobyl, 4:597
  Chernovtsy, 4:597–599
  Chudnov, 4:708
  Ehrlich, Eugen, 6:243
  Haller's Army, 8:281
  Yekaterinoslav, 5:724–725
Uman massacre, 20:244–245
United Nations, 20:268–269
Uruguay, 20:426
U.S., 2:214, 223, 229–233, 237, 238, 20:387–394
  1920s-1930s, 6:697
  Alabama, 1:573
  Birmingham, 3:713
  Black-Jewish relations in, 3:736
  Boston, 4:99
  Civil War, 2:44, 8:34–35
  dance, 5:414
  Detroit (MI), 5:610–611
  efforts to combat, 15:716
  Frank, Leo, 7:192–193
  Global Anti-Semitism Review Act of 2004, 4:305
  Montana, 14:454
  North Carolina, 15:303
  Orange County, 15:462
  Westchester County, 21:22
USSR, 2:226–229, 235–236, 4:65, 16:320–321
  Broadsky, Joseph, trial of, 4:198
  dance, 5:415
  doctors' plot, 5:728–729
  literature, 5:427
Venezuela, 4:474–475, 20:497–498
  Curaçao, 4:471
Wagner, Richard, 20:595
Wiener Gesera, 21:50
Yemen, 18:6
See also Blood libel; Communism; Emancipation; Neo-Nazism; Numerus clausus
Antisemitism, its History and Causes (Lazare), 12:558

Antisemitism and the Christian Mind (Davies), 4:684
L'Antisémitismeé son histoire et ses causes (Lazare), 12:558
Anti-semitizm w Swietle Cyfr (Alter), 2:18
Anti-sheḥitah movements, 18:435
Antisthenes, 2:459
Anti-Trinitarians, 4:249–250
Anti-Zionism
  1970s, 2:236–237
  1980s, 2:239–240
  1990s, 2:243–244
  Berger, Elmer, 3:424
  Blau, Amram, 3:742
  Brach, Saul, 4:116
  Brazil, 4:151
  Dragunski, David Abramovich, 6:7
  Dubnow, Simon, 6:35–37
  Montefiore, Claude Joseph Goldsmid, 14:455
  Norway, 15:308–309
Antloifers (Bryks), 4:230
Antoine, Nicolas, 2:246
Antokolski, Mark, 2:246–247
Antokolski, Mordecai. See Antokolski, Mark
Antokolski, Pavel Grigorevich, 2:247
Antonescu, Ion, 2:247
Antonescu, Mihai, 2:247
Antonia (fortress in Jerusalem), 2:247–248
Antonin Collections, 13:494–495
Antoninus Pius, 2:248–249
Antonio, 2:249
Antonius Diogenes, 2:249
Antonius Julianus, 2:249
Ants, 2:184
Antschel, Paul. See Celan, Paul
Antuñes family, 2:249
Antwerp (Belgium), 2:249–251, 3:281–282, 5:635
Anusim, 2:251–254, 3:121
  Aklar Mordecai ben Raphael, 1:569
  Bibago, Isaac, 3:571
  Jewish identity and, 9:223, 11:294–295
  new Muslims, 11:58
  Paul IV, 9:226
  Portuguese communities, 6:588
  Uzbekistan, 4:259
In Anxiety. See In Umru (Litvakov)
L'an zéro de l'Allemagne (Morin), 14:492
Apam, 2:254
Apamea (Turkey), 2:254, 587

Apartheid, 7:762
The Apathetic Interrogator (Duda), 6:40
Apel, Willi, 2:254
Apeloig, Yitzhak, 2:254–255
Apes, 2:254
Apfelboym, Maurycy. See Appelbaum, Moshe
Aphek, 2:205, 255, 6:85
Aphraates, 4:720
Aphrahat, 3:599
Aphrodite (opera, Erlanger), 6:480
Apikoros, 2:255–256, 9:20
Apikoros Sleuth (Majzels), 4:424
Apion, 2:256, 3:775
'Apiru, 15:748
Apiryon Asah Lo (Solomon ben Aaron), 18:769
Apocalypse, 2:256–258
  of Abraham, 1:288–289
  Apocalypse of Baruch, 3:184–185
  Apocalypse of Elijah, 6:337
  apocrypha, 6:495–498
  Bloch, Joshua, on, 3:764
  Daniel, Vision of (13c.), 5:426
  Daniel and, 5:418, 420–421, 423–424, 6:494–495
  Dead Sea Scrolls, 6:498–500
  Elijah, 6:333
  Greek Apocalypse of Baruch, 3:186
  Isaiah, Book of, 10:66–67
  See also Eschatology
Apocalypse of Abraham, 1:288–289
Apocalypse of Adam, 14:728–729
Apocalypse of Baruch, 3:184–186
Apocalypse of Elijah, 6:337
Apocalypse of Isaiah
  Deutero-Isaiah, 6:493
  eschatology, 6:491, 494
Apocalypsis Moysis. See Book of the Life of Adam and Eve
Apocalyptic esotericism. See Kabbalah
Apocalyptic literature
  Abraham ben Eliezer ha-Levi, 1:298
  Assumption of Moses, 14:544–545
  Beck(ius) Matthias Friedrich, 3:250
  Enoch, 6:441–445
  ingathering of the exiles, 9:786
  Joel, Book of, 11:361–362
  Judah Halevi, 11:495
  Judas (Christian writer), 11:523
  medieval, 7:10–11
  modern biblical criticism and, 3:654–655

Apocalyptic literature, *continued*
    Moses, 14:533
    mysticism in, 11:590
    olam ha-ba, 15:399–400
    paradise in, 15:628
    Persian influence, 6:495
    Samael, 17:714
    Testaments of the Twelve
      Patriarchs, 15:692
    See also Apocalypse; Eschatology
Apocrypha, 2:*258*, **258–261**
    Abraham, Testament of, 1:291
    angels in, 2:152–156
    Apocalypse of Elijah, 6:337
    Assumption of Moses, 14:544–545
    astrology, 2:615–616
    astronomy, 2:621
    Book of the Life of Adam and Eve,
      1:377–378
    Davidic Messiah, 14:111–112
    devil in, 13:668–669
    dualism, 6:30
    folklore, 7:96–97
    halakhah, 8:255
    Hebrew fiction, 7:11–12
    Hellenistic literature, 7:659
    Jacob, Testament of, 11:29
    Jeremiah, Epistle of, 11:135
    Jewish censorship, 4:540–541
    Jewish literature, 13:85–86
    Joseph and Asenath, 11:418
    Jubilees, Book of, 13:668–669
    Kahana, Abraham, 11:710
    labor, 12:409
    Lamech, 12:444–445
    magic, 13:343–344
    Martyrdom of Isaiah, 10:76
    New Testament, 15:191
    Prayer of Manasseh, 13:453–454
    pre-Middle Ages, 13:85–86
    providence, 16:648–649
    Psalms of Solomon, 18:766–767
    Rest of the Words of Baruch,
      3:187–188
    Sabbath, 17:618
    Sifrei ha-Minim, 18:564
    Temple destruction, 10:144
    Ten Lost Tribes, 19:639
    Testaments of the Twelve
      Patriarchs, 15:691–693
    Tobit, 6:691
    Wisdom of Ben Sira, 3:376–378
    Wisdom of Solomon, 18:768–769
Apocryphal Ezra. *See* Ezra, Greek
    Book of
Apocryphal literature
    Abraham, other books of, 1:290

Abraham, Testament of, 1:291
Adam, other books of, 1:377
Adam and Eve, Book of, 1:377–
    378
    afterlife, 1:441
    Apocalypse of Abraham, 1:288–289
    Book of Baruch, 3:185–186
    Enoch, 6:441–442
    Enoch, Ethiopic Book of, 6:442–
      444
    Enoch, Slavonic Book of, 6:444–
      445
    eschatology, 6:495–498
    Esther, additions to the Book of,
      8:294
    God, names of, 7:676–677
    Lamech, Book of, 12:445
    Maccabees, Book of, 8:325, 331
    magic, 13:343–344
    prayer, 16:458
    Rest of the Words of Baruch,
      3:187–188
    Susanna and the Elders, 19:326–
      327
    Tobit, Book of, 20:12–14
The Apocryphon of John, 14:729
Apodictic legal formulation, in Book
    of the Covenant, 4:68
Apollinaris of Hierapolis, 4:719
Apollonia (Israel), 2:**261–262**
Apollonius, 2:**262**
Apollonius Molon, 2:**262**, 14:532
Apologetic literature. *See* Apologetics
Apologetics, 2:**262–269**
    Christianity, 2:263–264
    eighteenth century, 2:268
    Hellenism, 2:262–263
    Luzzatto, Simone ben Isaac
      Simḥah, 13:287–288
    medieval, 2:264–268
    Midrash, 2:263
    nineteenth century, 2:268–269
    Philo Verlag, 16:114
    Talmud, 2:263
    twentieth century, 2:269
Apologia (Pico della Miraondola),
    16:146–147
The Apologia (Jedaiah ben Abraham
    Bedersi), 11:101
Apologia David altera (Ambrose), 2:37
Apologie des Juifs (Hourwitz), 8:439
*An Apology for the Honourable Nation
    of the Jews, and all the Sons of Israel*
    (Nicholas), 15:252
Apostasy, 1:209, 2:**269–277**
    Abdallah ibn Salāam, 1:241
    Abner of Burgos, 1: 264–265

Alboraycos, 1:595
Alexander, Michael Solomon,
    1:623
Alexeyev, Alexander, 1:636
Alfonso of Zamora, 1:643
Bernays, Michael, 3:470
Bourges, 4:106
Brafman, Jacob, 4:116
Brandstaetter, Roman, 4:128
Carben, Victor von, 4:460
Cassel, Paulus Stephanus, 4:508
Christiani, Pablo, 4:673
Christianity, 2:270–272, 4:677
Christian Science Church, 4:694
Chwolson, Daniel, 4:724
Dawlah, Rashid al-, 8:292
Diaspora, 2:274–275
Donin, Nicholas, 5:750
eighteenth century, 2:271–272
Elisha ben Avuyah, 6:352–354
Fioghi, Fabiano, 7:41
folklore, 2:277
Frank, Jacob, 7:187–189
Gamaliel ben Pedahzur, 7:366
Gans, Eduard, 7:377
Ginsburg, Christian David, 7:610
golden calf, 1:209, 14:525, 528,
    530, 535–536
Halévy, Daniel, 8:269
Hellenism, 2:269–270
Hermanus Quondam Judaeus,
    9:25
Hirschensohn-Lichtenstein, Jehiel
    Ẓevi Hermann, 9:136
informers revealed by, 9:780
Islam, 2:270, 275
Jewish law, 2:275–277, 12:543–544
Jona, Giovanni Battista, 11:387
Juan de Espagña, 11:472
from Judaism to Christianity
    Buedinger, Max, 4:251
    Carben, Victor von, 4:460
    Domus Conversorum, 5:747
    Drach, Paul-Louis-Bernard,
      6:5–6
    Ehrlich, Arnold Bogumil,
      6:242–243
    Eliano, Giovanni Battista,
      6:318
    Elias Le Eveske, 6:320
    Engelberg, Ḥayyim of, 6:409
    Este, João Baptista de, 6:514
    Hermanus Quondam
      Judaeus, 9:25
    Hirschensohn-Lichtenstein,
      Jehiel Ẓevi Hermann, 9:136

John XXII on, 11:379
Julian III on, 11:574
Levertoff, Paul Philip, 12:681
Mithridates, Flavius, 14:370
Morosini, Giulio, 14:508
in Ottoman empire, 15:531
Pablo de Santa Maria,
15:562–563
Vineam sorce of Nicholas III,
15:249
from Judaism to Islam
Bābāī ben Farhād, Judeo-
Persian poetry of, 11:556
Jewish identity and, 11:295
in Ottoman empire, 15:531
Klaczko, Julian, 12:209
Kraus, Karl, 12:341
Lorki, Joshua, 13:192–193
Lothar, Ernst, 13:216
Margarita, Anton, 13:522
Margoliouth, Moses, 13:528
Maritain, Raïssa, 13:546
Marranos, 2:271
medieval Germany, 16:25–26
Mendelssohn-Veit-Schlegel,
Dorothea, 14:41
Mithridates, Flavius, 14:370–371
Monis, Judah, 14:444
Neander, August, 15:47
nineteenth century, 2:272
Nola, Elijah ben Menachem da,
15:294
Nuñez, Henrique, 15:345
Pasternak, Boris Leonidovich,
15:684
Pasternak, Boris Leonidovich,
2:272–273
Pauli, Johannes, 15:695–696
Petrus Alfonsi, 16:21
Pfefferkorn, Johannes, 16:25–26
Pitigrilli, 16:188
Provence (France), 16:638
Rabinovich, Joseph, 17:37
Ratisbonne brothers, 17:111–112
Reformation period, 2:271
Reuter, Paul Julius, Freiherr von,
17:249
Ricardo, David, 17:282
Ricius, Paulus, 17:292
Rosenstock-Huessy, Eugen,
17:450–451
Rufeisen, Oswald, 2:273, 274
Sa'id ibn Hasan, 17:668
Salkinson, Isaac Edward, 17:691–
692
Samau'al ben Judah ibn 'Abbās
al-Maghribī, 17:741–742

Schereschewsky, Samuel Isaac
Joseph, 18:122
Schumann, Maurice, 18:175
Seneor, Abraham, 18:288–289
Shabbetai Ẓevi, 18:348–350, 351
Sixtus of Siena, 18:656
Spain
Alcañiz, 1:599
Stahl, Friedrich Julius, 19:156–157
Stein, Edith, 19:176
Trebitsch, Arthur, 20:124
Trebitsch, Siegfried, 20:124
twentieth century, 2:272–273
Vambery, Arminius, 20:470
Veith, Johann Emanuel, 20:491
Weidner, Paulus, 20:699
Weininger, Otto, 20:722
Wolff, Joseph, 21:144–145
Žídek, Pavel, 21:527
Zoller, Israel, 21:666
See also Conversion; Forced
conversion
The Apostate (Molnár), 14:427
Apostles, 2:**277–278**
Apostolic Age, 2:278
Apostomos, 2:278
Apoteke, 12:815–816
Apotropos, 2:**278–283**
Apparel industry. *See* Clothing and
textiles industry; Fashion industry
Apparition. *See* Divination
Appeals, 2:**283–284**
Appeals of Communism (Almond),
1:683
Appearance of a Man (Backer), 3:40
Appel, Judah Leib, 2:**284–285**
Appelbaum, Moshe, 2:**285**
Appelboym, Maurycy. *See* Appelbaum,
Moshe
Appelfeld, Aharon, 2:**285–286**, 8:704,
705
Appelman, Harlene, 2:**286–287**
Apphus. *See* Jonathan the Hasmonean
Appian of Alexandria, 2:**287**
Appion, 11:440
Appiryon Asah Lo (Troki), 11:792
Apple, Max, 2:**287**
Apple, Raymond, 2:**287–288**
Applebaum, David, 18:775
Applebaum, Louis, 2:**288**
Applebaum, Maurycy. *See* Appelbaum,
Moshe
Apple blossoms, vol. 16: color insert
Apples, 2:**287**
Appleton's New American Cyclopaedia,
8:768

Appobalsamon. *See* Balsam
Apprenticeship of Duddy Kravitz
(motion picture), 6:21
The Apprenticeship of Duddy Kravitz
(Richler), 4:423–424
*L'Apprenti sorcier. See The Sorcerer's
Apprentice*
*Approaches to Auschwitz: The
Holocaust and Its Legacy*
(Rubenstein & Roth), 9:418
Apt (France), 2:**288**
Apta (Poland). *See* Opatow
Apta, Meir, 2:**288**
Apter, David Ernest, 2:**288–289**
Aptheker, Haim. *See* Atar, Haim
Aptowitzer, Avigdor. *See* Aptowitzer,
Victor
Aptowitzer, Victor, 2:**289**
Aptrod, David. *See* Abterode, David
ben Moses Eliakim
Aptrod, David ben Moses Eliakim. *See*
Abterode, David ben Moses Eliakim
Apuleius, Lucius, 2:**289**
Apulia (Italy), 2:**289–291**
Apulum (Transylvania). *See* Alba Iulia
(Transylvania)
'Aqedah. *See* Akedah
An Aquarius. See Vodnář
Aquila, 15:**433–434**
Greek translation of Bible by,
3:585, 597, 601
Targum Onkelos and, 3:590
Aquila (Italy), 2:**291**
Aquileia (Italy), 2:**291**
Aquinas, Thomas, 2:**291–292**, 6:50
Aquino, Benigno S., 18:752
Aquino, Corazon, 18:752
"A.R.". *See* Rothstein, Arnold
'Ara (Canaan), 2:**292**
al -'Araba. *See* The Arabah
Araba (Israel), 2:**292–293**
The Arabah, 2:**293**, 10:122–123
Arabarch. *See* Alabarch
Arab boycott, 4:**111–113**, 10:22, 256
Arabia, 2:**293–296**, *294*, 15:259
See also Saudi Arabia
Arabian Peninsula. *See* Arabia
Arabic and Judeo-Arabic
Bible translations
ancient, 3:603–605
modern, 3:627
Arabic language, 2:**296–299**, *297*,
8:658–659
Abu, 1:333
Ammonites, 2:84
Blau, Joshua, 3:743–744
commentaries in, 11:86–87

Arabic language, *continued*
  Dunash ibn Tamim, 6:48–49
  Hebrew, influence on, 8:658–665
  Hebrew translations, 2:132
    Al-Ḥarizi, Judah ben
      Solomon, 1:655–657
  in Mishnaic Hebrew, 8:647–648
  Moreh, Shmuel, 14:484
  nouns, 8:556
  Semitic languages and, 18:283
  sentence syntax, 8:602
  Skoss, Solomon Leon, 18:662
  translations from Hebrew, 8:734
  See also Judeo-Arabic language
Arabic Literary Society, 6:318
Arabic literature, 4:170–171, 10:734–
  737, 15:472–473
  See also Judeo-Arabic literature
Arabishce Syntax (Reckendorf), 17:146
Arab-Israeli conflict
  Arab League, 2:300
  Arab world, 2:305–309, 310–311,
    328
  bi-nationalism, 3:702–703
  Holocaust art imagery, 2:520–521
  peace negotiations, 4:760–761
Arab-Israeli peace negotiations, 4:760–
  761
Arab-Israel War (1948)
  Jordan, 11:404
Arabists
  Dozy, Reinhart Pieter Anne, 5:772
  Heller, Bernát, 8:793–794
Arab League, 2:**299–300**, 6:145, 12:580
Arab League Council, boycott against
  Palestine, 4:111–112
Arab Legion, 1:243–244, 11:178–179
*Arab Literature under the Shadow of
  War* (Ballas), 3:92
Arab nationalism, 1:244, 10:196, 271–
  272, 279–281
Arab period
  Egypt
    Alexandria, 1:634
  Israel, land of, 10:*157*, 157–161
Arab population
  Gaza Strip
    after Six-Day war, 10:717–718
    Egyptian control, 10:303, 717
  Israel (state), 10:278, 485–486,
    521–522, 679, 712–739
    1948–67, 10:712–715
    1970s, 10:719–721
    1980s to mid-1990s, 10:721–
      728
    1995 to 2005, 10:728–733

  in administered territories,
    10:239, 241–242
  Arab refugees, 10:256, 267–
    271
  arts and popular culture,
    10:733–734
  Bedouin, 10:737–739
  demography, 10:485–486,
    521–522
  farming, and urbanization,
    10:485–486
  Gaza Strip, 10:303, 717
  health services, 10:679
  Jordanian Rule, 1948–67,
    10:715–717
  post-Six-Day War, 10:231,
    232, 717–719
  refugee problem, 10:256
  refugees and, 10:256
  Six-Day War and, 10:231, 232
  standard of living, 10:224–
    225
  voting by, 10:250–251
  Palestine (Mandate), 10:710–712,
    712*t*
  West Bank
    after Six-Day war, 10:717–718
    Jordanian control, 10:715–
      717
  See also Palestinians
Arab Revolt (1936-1939), 10:277, 338,
  18:753
Arab world, 1945-2006, 2:**300–328**
  Algeria, 2:322–323
  Arab-Israeli conflict, 2:305, 306–
    309, 310–311, 328
  Bombay, Arabic Jews in, 4:51
  caricatures of Jews, 4:479
  democracy, 2:326–328
  demography, 2:328
  discrimination and, 5:681
  Egypt, 2:300, 307–308, 309–311,
    326–327
  Egyptian-Israeli peace, 2:311–313
  Fertile Crescent, 2:300, 301
  foreign policy and relations with
    Israel (state), 10:264, 12:546
  globalization, 2:324–326
  Hashemite Kingdom of Jordan,
    2:301
  inter-Arab politics, 2:301–304,
    309–310
  Iran-Iraq war, 2:313
  Iraq, 2:301, 326–328
  Islamists, 2:324–325, 326
  Israel, 2:313–316, 317–320, 320–
    324, 475–476
  Jordan, 2:305, 316–320

  Lebanon, 2:301, 313, 314
  Maghreb, 2:300, 320–324
  Morocco, 2:306, 314, 320–322,
    326, 327
  musical influence of, 14:696
  Nasserists, 2:325–326
  Operation Peace for Galilee, 2:313
  Oslo Accords, 2:316–320
  Palestine, 2:301, 302–303, 317–320
  Palestine Liberation Organization,
    2:304–305, 313, 317
  Palestinian Authority, 2:300, 301,
    320, 326
  Sudan, 2:300–301
  Syria, 2:302–303, 306, 317–320
  Tunisia, 2:323–324
  Yemen, 2:304
  See also Middle East; Near East
Arab world, pre-1945
  Abbasids, 1:233–234
  blood libel in, 3:780
Arad (Israel), 2:**328–331**
  archaeology, 2:371
  Eliashib (name), 6:320
  excavations, 5:335
  stone altar at, 2:12
Arad (Romania), 2:**331**
Arad, Ron, 2:**331–332**
Arad, Yael, 2:**332**
Arad, Yitzhak, 2:**332**
Arad ostraca, 3:656
Arad Program, 21:614
Aradus (Syria), 2:**332**
Arafat, Musa, 15:600
Arafat, Yasser, 2:309, **332–335**
  agreements signed with, 10:245,
    246
  Bush, George W., 4:305
  death of, 15:595
  Al -Fataḥ and, 10:279–280
  Intifada (second), 10:251
  Oslo Accords, 10:245
  Palestine Liberation Organization
    and, 15:590, 593, 594, 595
  Palestinian Authority and, 15:596,
    597, 598, 599, 600
  Wye Plantation Agreement, 10:249
Aragão, Fernão Ximenes de, 2:**335**
Aragon (medieval Spain)
  Alconstantini family, 1:604
  conversion in, 5:437
  Eleazar family, 6:298
Aragon, Louis, 3:763
Aragon Synagogue, 11:828
Arakhim u-Derakhim (Dinur), 5:672
Arakhin, 2:**335–337**

Aram. *See* Mar (term of respect)

Aram (Syria)

Ahab, 1:523

Ahaz, 1:539

Aram-Damascus, 2:359–360, 8:485–486

Arama, Isaac, 2:160, 531, 6:726

Abraham, 1:285

allegorical interpretation of scripture, 3:645

Bibago, Abrahem ben Shem Tov, 3:571

exile, meaning of, 7:360

Ḥasidei Ummot ha-Olam, 8:389

Maimonides' essential principles of Judaism, 11:513

Moses, 14:537

Arama, Isaac ben Moses, 2:**339–341**

Arama, Meir ben Isaac, 2:**341–342**

Arama, Moses, 2:274

Aramaic Documents of the Fifth Century B.C. (Driver), 6:22

Aramaic language, 2:**342–359**, 344*t*, 345*t*, 8:647–648, 669–670

alphabet, Hebrew, 1:694*t*, 695–697, 706, 709*t*

Amorites, 2:96

ancient, 2:342, 343–346, 345*t*

Chaldean language, 4:561, 562

classical, 2:356

Daniel, Book of, 5:424

Dead Sea scrolls, 8:635

decline in importance of, 3:641

European languages and, 2:356

He, letter, 8:506

Hebrew, spoken, 2:357

Hebrew grammar, influence on, 8:573

Hebrew influenced by, 11:301

Jewish languages, as element in, 11:302

Job, Aramaisms in book of, 11:351

Jonah, Aramaisms in book of, 11:389

Judah ha-Nasi on, 11:503

Judeo-Persian grammars, 11:554

Lamentations Rabbah, 12:452

late, 2:343, 348–357, 350*t*

Eastern, 2:352–357, 353*t*, 355*t*

Western, 2:348–349

Levi, Testament of, 12:694–695

middle, 2:342–343, 347–348

in Mishnaic Hebrew, 8:647–648

Mishnaic Hebrew and, 2:356

Neo-Aramaic, 15:70–72

New Testament and, 15:192

official, 2:343–347, 345

parts of Bible composed in, 3:581

proverbs, 16:647

Scroll of Antiochus, 18:214

Semetic languages and, 18:282, 284

translations of Bible, ancient

CPA, 3:600

Judith, Book of, 11:567

Onkelos, 15:433–434

Peshitta (Syriac Aramaic), 3:599–601

Samaritan Bible, 3:599, 652

targumim, 3:588–594

Aramaic literature

Abraham ben Daniel, 1:295

Aḥa of Shabḥa, 1:530

Akdamut Millin, 1:555

Āl-Asāṭīr, 1:576

The Jewish War (Josephus), lost Aramaic version of, 11:436

Josippon, 11:462

Sefer ha-Mitzvot, 2:127

Die aramaischen Texte vom Toten Meer (Beyer), 18:470

Aram and Arameans, 2:**337–339**, *338*

Aramatha. *See* Ramoth-Gilead (ancient Israel)

Aram-Damascus, 2:**359–360**

Aramean kingdom, 2:489

Arameans

Chaldeans, 4:561

Laban, 12:406

Pekod, 15:717

Les Araméens (Dupont-Sommer), 6:51

Aram Zoba. *See* Aleppo

Aram-Ẓoba (Syria). *See* Aleppo (Syria)

Aram-Ẓova (Syria). *See* Aleppo (Syria)

Aran, Zalman, 2:**360**

Aranha, Oswaldo, 4:153

Aranne, Zalman, 10:224

'Arʾara (Israel), 2:**360**

Ararat, 2:**360–361**

Ararat (NY), 15:291

Araton, Harvey, 2:**361**

Araunah, 2:**361**

The Aravah. *See* The Arabah

Aravot. *See* Hoshanot

Arazi, Yehuda, 2:**361–362**

Arbaʾah Kinyanim (Canpanton), 4:432

Arbaʾah minim. See Four species

Arbaʾah Turim. See Even Shetiyyah

Arbaʾah Turim (Jacob ben Asher), 4:307, 8:552, 11:30

Arba Ammot, 1:360, 2:**362**

Arba kosot, 2:**362**

Arba Panim (Ephraim ben Isaac). *See Four Aspects* (Ephraim ben Isaac)

Arba Shitot, 11:729

Arbatova, Mia, 2:**362–363**

Arbatta, 2:**363**

Arbeh. *See* Locusts

Das Arbeitende EretzYisrael (periodical), 18:425

Arbeiter Ring. *See* Workmen's Circle

Arbeiter-Zeitung (newspaper), 2:**363**, 12:625

Arbeit macht frei mi-Toitland Europa, 8:723

Arbeitslager. *See* Camps, concentration and extermination

Die Arbeitslosen von Marienthal (Lazarsfeld), 12:559–560

Arbel (Israel), 2:**363–364**

Arbela (Israel). *See* Arbel (Israel)

Arbell, Mordecai, 2:**364**

Arbeter Ring. *See* Workmen's Circle

Arbib, Isaac ben Arroyo. *See* Arollia, Isaac ben Moses

Arbib family, 2:**364**

Arbil (Iraq). *See* Irbil (Iraq)

Arbitration, 1:249, 2:**364–368**

Arbol de Diana (Pizarnik), 16:209

Arbués, Pedro de, 2:**368**

Arbus, Diane, 2:**368–369**, 16:125

Arcel, Ray, 2:**369**

Archa, 2:**369–370**, 14:442

Archaeologists, 2:125, **370–372**

Aharoni, Yoḥanan, 1:531–532

Albright, William Foxwell, 1:596

Ben-Dor, Immanuel, 3:328

Dothan, Trude, 5:764

Finkelstein, Israel, 7:33–34

Frankfort, Henri, 7:204

Herzfeld, Ernst Emil, 9:53

Hirschfeld, Gustav, 9:137

Kempinsky, Aharon, 12:**73**

Lawrence, Thomas Edward, 12:546

Lehmann, Karl, 12:615

Levi, Doro, 12:687

Mazar, Amihai, 13:705

Mazar, Benjamin, 13:705–706

Moscati, Sabatino, 14:515

Petrie, Sir William Matthew Flinders, 16:18–19

Raban, Avner, 17:6

Ramoth-Gilead, 17:88

Reifenberg, Adolf, 17:203

Reinach, Solomon, 17:205

Saulcy, Louis Felicien de Joseph Caignart, 18:83

Schaeffer, Claude F.A., 18:102–103

Schumacher, Gottlieb, 18:175

See also specific names

Archaeology, 2:**372–397**, *373*
  Achzib, 1:356
  Ai, 1:548–549
  Alalakh, 1:574
  altars, 2:12, 14
  animal reliefs at Tiberias (3rd c. B.C.E.), vol. 10: color insert
  archaeological periods, 2:380–397
      Bronze Age, 2:384–387, 12:420–421
      Byzantine, 2:391
      Chalcolithic, 2:383–384
      Crusader, 2:392
      Hellenistic, 2:388–390
      Iron Age, 2:387–388
      Islamic, 2:391–392
      Ottoman, 2:392–393
      Persian, 2:388
      prehistoric, 2:381–383
      Roman, 2:390–391
  Assyria and Mesopotamia, 14:92–93
  Babylon, 3:24
  Banias, 3:109
  Bar Kokhba, 3:160–162
  bas relief of menorah (3rd c.), vol. 14: color insert
  Beersheba, 3:256–257
  Bet She'arim amphitheater (8th c.), vol. 14: color insert
  Bible and, 11:77
  biblical criticism and, 3:650, 652, 654
  bone-reaping hook (10th millenium B.C.E.), vol. 10: color insert
  Bar'am Synagogue remains, Golan Heights (3rd c.), vol. 14: color insert
  Butnah, 4:318
  capital, Corinthian (4th-3rd c. B.C.E.), vol. 10: color insert
  capital from Kazerin synagogue (3rd-5th c.), vol. 14: color insert
  capital from Philistine city, vol. 10: color insert
  Christian history, 7:174–175
  chronology, 4:704–705
  Copper scroll, 5:213–214
  Della Seta, Alessandro, 5:541
  Delos (Greece), 5:545
  dolmens, 5:736–737
  Dura-Europos, 6:51–55
  economic history, 6:95–96
  Edom, 6:152
  Ein Fashkhah, 6:255–256

  Ein Gedi, vol. 10: color insert
  Ekron, 6:281–282
  Elam, 6:283–284
  El-Amarna, 6:284–285
  El-Amarna letters, 6:284–285
  Elephantine, 6:311–314
  Elusa, 6:370–371
  Emar, 6:386–390
  Emmaus, 6:395–396
  En-Gedi, 6:406–407
  Eshtaol, 6:507
  "Galilean" Mona Lisa (3rd c.), vol. 14: color insert
  gateway decoration, Jerusalem (19th c.), vol. 10: color insert
  Gezer, 7:569
  gibeah, geba, 7:580–582
  glass, 7:628–632
  Golan, 17:79–80
  Hammath, 8:307
  Hanfmann, George Maxim Anossov, 8:320
  Ḥazor, 8:498–500
  Herat, 9:7
  history of research in Israel, 2:377–379
  household objects (2nd c. B.C.E.), vol. 10: color insert
  household objects, Golan Heights (3rd-5th c.), vol. 14: color insert
  Israel
      Caesarea, 4:333–334
      Epstein, Claire, 6:469
      Israel Exploration Society, 10:750
      Jerusalem, 18:126–127
      Misrephoth-Maim, 14:364
  Judean Desert caves expeditions, 11:523–525
  Kazerin, Golan Heights, vol. 14: color insert
  Lachish ostraca, 12:421–422
  Loewy, Emanuel, 13:172
  Madaba mosaic map, 13:329–330
  Mamshit, vol. 10: color insert
  Masada, vol. 14: color insert
  methods and approaches, 2:372, 374–377
  mikveh, 14:227–228
  Mizpeh, 14:388
  mizrah of ancient synagogues, 16:421–426
  Moab, 14:399, 400, 403
  Modi'in, 14:412
  Moloch, cult of, 14:427–428
  Murabba'at scrolls, 14:616–617

  Nash papyrus, 14:783–784
  Old City, Jerusalem, vol. 10: color insert
  origins of Israel and Israelites, 2:379–380
  ossuaries, 15:506–507
  ostraca, 15:508–509
  Oven Cave, Carmel Cave, and River Cave (Israel), vol. 10: color insert
  Palestine
      seals, 18:226
  Palestine Exploration Fund, 15:589
  Philistines, 7:619
  pillars, 16:159–161
  pottery, 16:421–426
  Rabbath-Ammon, 17:11
  Ramat Raḥel, 17:82
  sarcophagi, 15:506–507
  Sepphoris, 18:307
  Shaalbim, 18:334
  Sha'ar ha-Golan, 18:336
  Shechem, 18:430
  Shivta (4th-6th c.), vol. 14: color insert
  Shuqba Cave, 20:593
  Sinai, 14:528
  Solomon, 18:755, 757–758
  Spain
      Elche, 6:292
  synagogue at Tiberias, vol. 10: color insert
  synagogue pavement (5th-6th c.), vol. 14: color insert
  Syria
      Ebla, 6:85–87
  Tel Hazor, vol. 10: color insert
  Tell al-Qīdāh, 8:498–499
  Tel Reḥov, 17:193–195
  tombs of Absalom, Zechariah, and the Hezir family, vol. 10: color insert
  underwater, 17:6
  Wadi al-Naṭṭuf, 20:593
  Wadi Dāliya, 20:593
  wine press (2nd c.), vol. 10: color insert
Archaeology and the Religion of Israel (Albright), 1:596
The Archaeology of Palestine (Albright), 1:596
The Archaeology of the United Monarchy: An Alternative View (Finkelstein), 7:34
Archagathus. *See* Caecilius of Calacte
Archangel (Russia), 2:**397**
Archeion. *See* Archives

Archelais (Jordan Valley), 2:**397**
Archelaus, 2:**397–398**, 3:110, 4:455, 11:367
Archeologists. *See* Archaeologists
Archeology. *See* Archaeology
Archer, Armand. *See* Archerd, Army
Archerd, Army, 2:**398**
Archipherecites, 2:**398**
Archisynagogos, 2:**398**, 4:163
Architecture and architects, 2:**399–402**
  Abramovitz, Max, 1:323
  Agrest, Diana, 1:471
  Almoravids, 1:684
  Baerwald, Alex, 3:54
  basilica, 3:199
  biblical influence, 3:673
  bimah, 3:701–702
  Black, Sir Misha, 3:731
  Blankstein, Cecil, 3:740
  Brazil
    Lerner, Jaime, 12:657–658
  Breuer, Marcel, 4:172
  Brunner, Arnold, 4:224
  Brutzkus, David Anatol, 4:228–229
  Bryer, Monte, 4:229
  Bunshaft, Gordon, 4:284–285
  Canada, 12:442–443
  Denmark, 11:52
  door and doorpost, 5:752–753
  Dutch
    De Klerk, Michel, 5:534–535
  Eidlitz, Leopold, 3:740
  Elḥanani, Aba, 6:316
  Elḥanani, Aryeh, 6:316
  Elte, Harry, 6:369
  England
    Rosenberg, Eugene, 17:435–436
  France
    Aldrophe, Alfred-Philibert, 1:607
    Persitz, Alexandre, 15:792
  Frank, Josef, 7:192
  Gehry, 7:412
  Germany
    Mendelsohn, Eric, 14:29–30
  Hanson, Norman Leonard, 8:331
  Hegedüs, Armin, 8:755
  Hellenistic Jewish, 8:789–790
  historians of
    England, 16:23
  Hungary, 11:73, 12:440
    Baumhorn, Lipót, 3:222
  Israel, 10:701–704, 702–704
    Karmi, Dov, 11:813

    Rachter, Ya'akov, 17:144–145
    Ratner, Yohanan, 17:113
    Rau, Heinz, 17:115
    Rechter family, 17:144–145
  Italy
    Rogers, Ernesto, 17:368
  Kantorowich, Roy, 11:771–772
  Kaufmann, Richard, 12:32–33
  Lambert, Phyllis, 12:442–443
  Lapidus, Morris, 12:491
  Lasdun, Sir Denys, 12:494
  Levi, Rino, 12:692
  Neutra, Richard Joseph, 15:125
  Palestine (Mandate), 10:701–702
  Palestine (Ottoman), 10:701
  Phoenician, 16:123
  photography, 16:126
  pillars, 16:159–161
  Schindeler, Rudolph M., 18:137
  Sebestyén, Artur, 8:755
  Sharon, Aryeh, 18:417–418
  Solomon, 18:757–758
  South Africa
    Hermer, Manfred, 9:29
    Le Roith, Harold Hirsch, 12:659
  Sterk, Izidor, 8:755
  synogogue, 11:722, 16:160–161, 19:364–383
  Tower of Babel, 3:19, 20–21
  U.K., 5:481, 12:494
  U.S.
    Adler, Dankmar, 1:395–396
    Eisenman, Peter, 6:267
    Eizenberg, Julie, 6:280
    Freed, James Ingo, 7:224
    Koning, Hendrick, 6:280
    Lapidus, Morris, 12:491
    Lerner, Ralph, 12:659
    Libeskind, Daniel, 12:782
    Meier, Richard, 13:774
    Schwartz, Frederic, 18:184
  See also specific locations
Archives, 2:**402–418**
  Archives de la Planete, 11:718
  Archives of Jewish resistance, 3:569
  Archives of Traditional Music, 13:83
  biblical period, 2:402–405
  The Central Archives for the History of the Jewish People, 2:413–414
  Central Zionist Archives, 2:414
  Diaspora, 2:406–410
  Holocaust period, 2:410–413, 9:362

  Israel, 2:414–417
  Middle Ages, 2:405–406
  post-biblical period, 2:405
  Rabbi Moses Nahum Yerushalimsky Collection, 18:155
Archivolti, Samuel, 2:**418**
Archivo Urbino, 2:409
Arch of Titus, 14:51, 19:**743**
Archon, 2:**418–419**
Archpresbyter, 2:**419**, 6:320, 411
Arcila, 2:**419**
Arco, Georg Wilhelm Alexander Hans, Graf Von, 2:**419**
Ard-al-Birka. *See* Benjamin, Walter
Ardashir (Armenia), 2:**419–420**
Ardavan, 2:**420**
Ardeal. *See* Transylvania
Ardit, Ephraim ben Abraham, 2:**420**
Ardit, Solomon, 3:695
Ardit family, 2:**420**
Arditi, Albert Judah, 2:**420–421**
Arditi, Benjamin, 4:276
Arditi, Eliezer, 4:276
Ardon, Mordecai, 2:**421**, 8:743
Ardut family, 2:**421**
Aréga, Léon, 2:**421**
Areios (King of Sparta), 15:431
Areios I, 2:**421–422**
Arenda, 2:**422–423**, 16:296–297
Arendt, Hannah, 2:143, **423–424**, 16:109, 18:736
  Eichmann in Jerusalem, 6:251–252
  Judenrat institution, 11:527
Arendt, Otto, 2:**424**
Arens, Moshe, 2:**424–425**
Areopolis. *See* Rabbath-Moab (ancient Israel)
Ares, 2:**425**
Aretas, 2:**425**
Arethusa (Judea), 2:**425**
Areus. *See* Areios I
Areus I. *See* Areios I
Arezzo (Italy), 2:**425–426**
Argens, Jean Baptiste de Boyer, 2:**426**
Argentina, 2:**426–450**, *428, 446t*
  pre-1840, 2:426
  1840-1890, 2:427
  1890-1918, 2:427–431
  1918-1930, 2:431–433
  1930-1946, 2:433–437
  1946-1968, 2:437–440
  1968-2005, 2:437–448
  agriculture, Jewish, 1:501, 11:775
  Brie, Luis Hartwig, 4:181
  cooperatives, 5:206

Argentina, *continued*
Daia, 5:379–380
education, Jewish, 6:211–212, 7:33
Entre Ríos, 6:448–449
Finkelstein, Chaim, 7:33
Fondo Communal of Clara, 11:775
immigration to, 11:286–287
Jewish community, 3:398–399, 11:754
Jewish settlement in, 2:46
Jewish writers, 19:90
journalism, 11:469, 12:513–514, 16:496
legal status, 2:427
literature
Aguinis, Marcos, 1:510
Alpersohn, Marcos, 1:688
Constantini, Humberto, 5:182
Eichelbaum, Samuel, 6:245
Espinoza, Enrique, 6:509
Liacho, Lázaro, 12:773
poetry, 8:111, 115, 16:209
Rozenmacher, Germán, 17:503
Satz, Mario, 18:76
Sneh, Simja, 18:697
twentieth century, 6:732–733
Meyer, Marshall T., 14:148
Moisesville, 7:709
Nazi fugitives, 6:250, 15:76–77
philanthropy, 16:42
politics, 16:350
relations with Israel, 2:448–450
Zionism, 12:206–207, 21:593
Argintar, Virginia, 15:605
Argob, 2:450
Argonautica (Flaccus), 7:66
Argosi da Silva, Phinehas Hananiah. *See* Loeb, Baruch
Argov, Alexander, 2:451
Argov, Zohar, 2:451
Argumentation and dialectic. *See* Disputations and polemics
Arḥa, Eliezer ben Isaac, 2:451
Arhangelsk (Russia). *See* Archangel (Russia)
Arias, Joseph Semah, 2:451–452
Arias Montano, Benito, 2:452
Aricha, Yosef, 2:452
Aridor, Yoram, 2:452–453
Arie, Rafael, 2:453
Ariel, 2:453
Ariel (Israel), 2:453–454
Ariel, Dov, 2:454
Ariel, Joseph, 2:454

Arieli, Yehoshua, 2:454
Arieli, Yiẓḥak, 2:454
Arieti. *See* Rieti family
Arikha, Avigdor, 2:454–455
Arimanon. *See* Ramoth-Gilead (ancient Israel)
Ari Noḥem (Modena), 14:409
Arioch, 2:455
Aripul, Samuel ben Isaac, 2:455
Arish, El-. *See* El-Arish (Egypt)
Arison, Shari, 2:455
Arison, Ted, 2:455
Arisoteikhem, 8:278
Aristeas, 2:456
Job, Testament of, 11:359
religious impact of Bible on Hellenistic Judaism and, 3:660
Aristeas, Letter of, 2:456–457, 4:73
Aristides of Athens, 4:719
Aristobulus (brother of Agrippa), 2:458–459
Aristobulus (son of Herod), 1:618–619, 2:458
Aristobulus I (King of Judea), 2:457, 8:446, 9:195
Aristobulus II (King of Judea), 2:457–458, 11:574
Aristobulus III (high priest), 2:458
Aristobulus of Paneas, 2:459–460, 16:74–75
allegorical interpretation of scripture, 3:644, 660
Moses, 14:531
The Aristocrat. *See* Samuel ben Ali
Ariston of Pella, 2:460, 4:719
Aristotelianism, 2:460–462, 16:78, 83, 84, 88, 106–107
Aaron ben Elijah, 1:212–213
Alexander of Aphrodisias, 1:628
allegorical interpretation of scripture and, 3:644, 645
beatitude, 3:238–240
Bibago, Abraham ben Shem Tov, commentator on, 3:570–571
commentaries by Ibn Shem Tov, Joseph ben Shem Tov, 9:690–691
cosmology, 5:231
Crescas critique, 5:285–287
emanation, 6:373, 374
God, attributes of, 7:667
Ḥibat Allah criticism, 9:93
Ibn Daud, Abraham ben David Halevi, 9:663–665
Ibn Gabirol, 7:324–325
imagination and, 9:736
immortality of the soul, 1:442

Maimonides, 16:85
matter and form, 7:324–325
miracles, 14:307–308
modern biblical study, as precursor of, 3:648
nature, 15:34–35
space and place, 19:66
See also Aristotle
Aristotle, 2:460–462
Alexander of Aphrodisias, 1:628
body and soul, concept of, 4:31
Bonafed, Solomon ben Reuben, 4:54
categories, 4:524–525
on categories of beings, 4:524–525
Clearchus of Soli, 4:752
Islamic interpretation, 6:709–710
Judah ben Eleazar on, 11:485
Judah Halevi on, 11:498
Judah Loew ben Bezalel on, 11:507
Levi Ben Gershom on, 12:698–699
moneylending, 14:437
Philo Judaeus and, 16:62
platonism, 16:226–227
See also Aristotelianism
Arithmetic. *See* Mathematics
Arizona (U.S.), 2:463, **463**
Ark, 2:463–464
ceremonial objects, 4:547–548
dancing before, 5:409
Moses, 14:527, 529
Ner Tamid, 15:88
ritual opening, 16:16–17
Ark, the Aphod, and the "Tent of Meeting" (Morgenstern), 14:486
Arkān al-islām. *See* Islam
Arkansas (U.S.), 2:465, **465**
Arkansas Jewish Assembly, 2:465
Arkhangelsk. *See* Archangel (Russia)
Arkin, Alan W., 2:466
Ark of Moses, 2:469, vol. 8: color insert
Ark of Noah, 2:469
Ark of Testimony. See Aron ha-Edut
Ark of the Covenant, 2:466–469, *468*
Abinadab and, 1:258–259
ancient paintings, 6:53–54
Arlen, Harold, 2:469–470
Arles (France), 2:470–471
Arlosoroff, Chaim, 2:471–472
Arluck, Hyman. *See* Arlen, Harold
Armageddon, 2:472
Armed and Dangerous: My Undercover Struggle Against Apartheid (Kasrils), 11:825–826

Armed forces. *See* Military service
Armenia, 2:**472–474**
Armenian Bible, 3:602–603
Armenian Church
   Israel (state), 10:644
Armenian Church in Israel, 10:639,
   642
Armilus, 2:**474–475**
Armistice agreements, Israel-Arab,
   2:**475–476**, 8:741
   See also Sinai Campaign
Armiya. *See* Jeremiah
Armleder, 2:6, **476–477**, *477*, 3:31,
   4:79
*Armonim, Tavasim u-Petakim mi-
   Shamayim* (Sened), 18:288
*Armonium, Tavasim, u-Petakim mi-
   Shamayim* (Sened), 18:288
Arms (weapons), 5:198–200, 439
Arms, Coats of. *See* Heraldry
Armstrong, Louis, 4:112
Army service. *See* Military service
Arnaldo of Villanova, 2:**477**
Arnd ben Isaac. *See* Aaron ben Isaac
   Benjamin Wolf
Arnd ben Isaac Benjamin Wolf. *See*
   Aaron ben Isaac Benjamin Wolf
Arndt, Adolf, 2:**477**, 12:551
Arndt, Ernst Moritz, 2:**477–478**
Arnheim, Fischel, 2:**478**, 16:344
Arnheim, Heymann, 2:**478**
Arnold, Abe, 2:**478**
Arnold, Eve, 2:**478–479**
Arnold, Paula, 2:**479**
Arnold Levenberg (Pinski), 16:175–176
Arnold of Vilanova. *See* Arnaldo of
   Villanova
Arnoldovich, Mikhail. *See* Milner,
   Moses Michael
Arnon, 2:**479**
Arnon, Abraham, 2:**480**
Arnon, Daniel Israel, 2:**480**
Arnon, Isaac, 2:**480**
Arnon, Ruth, 2:**480–481**, 15:313
Arnona, 2:**481**
Arnstadt (Germany), 2:**481**
Arnstein, Julius (Nick), 4:177
Arnstein, Walter Leonard, 2:**483**
Arnsteiner family. *See* Arnstein family
Arnstein family, 2:**481–482**, 482*t*
Arnswalde, Moses. *See* Philippson,
   Moses
Aroch, Arie, 2:**483**, 10:696
Aroer (Israel), 2:**483–484**
Arollia, Isaac ben Moses, 2:**484**
Arom, Simha, 2:**484**
Aron, Esther. *See* Liebmann, Esther
   Schuloff Aaron

Aron, Isa, 6:201
Aron, Leo, 2:**486**
Aron, Raymond, 2:**484–485**, 18:730
Aron, Robert, 2:**485**
Aron Czenstochower. *See* Syngalowski,
   Aron
Aron family, 2:**484**
Aron ha-Edut (Aboab), 1:267
Aron ha-Edut (Alcorsono), 1:604–605
Aroni, Tsvi, 2:**485**
Aronid, Moses, 3:570
Aronius, Julius, 2:**485–486**
Aron Kodesh. *See* Ark
Aronova ljubav (Šinko), 18:641
Aronovich, Yuri Mikhaylovich, 2:**486**
Aronowitz, Benjamin, 2:**486**
Arons, Leo, 2:**486**
Aronsohn, Z. I. *See* Anokhi, Zalman
   Yiẓḥak
Aronson, Arnold, 2:**486–487**, 3:736
Aronson, Boris, 2:**487**
Aronson, David (painter), 2:**488**
Aronson, David (rabbi), 2:**487–488**
Aronson, Grigori, 2:**488**
Aronson, Max. *See* Anderson, Gilbert
   Maxwell
Aronson, Naum, 2:**488**
Aronson, Solomon, 2:**488–489**
Aroti, Isaac, 17:476
Aroti family. *See* Rote family
Arouet, François-Marie. *See* Voltaire
Around the World. See Arum der Velt
Arpa, Abramo Dall', 2:**489**
Arpad, 2:**489**
Arquivo Histórico Judaico Brasileiro,
   18:33
'Arrāba (Israel), 2:**489**
Arraby Moor, 2:**489–490**
Arragel, Moses, 2:**490**, 3:636
Arrapha archives, 2:404
Ar-Reuti family. *See* Rote family
Arrian, 2:**490**
Arricha de Tolvens. *See* Hollaender,
   Victor
Arrow, Kenneth Joseph, 2:**490**
Arrow Cross Party, 2:**491**, 3:75
Arrowsnake. *See* Kippod
Arrow's paradox, 2:**490**
Arroyo, Isaac ben (Arbib), 2:364
Arrueti, Joseph, 17:476
Arrueti, Juce. *See* Arrueti, Joseph
Arrueti family. *See* Rote family
Arsacid dynasty, 3:26
Arshawsky, Arthur. *See* Shaw, Artie
Arsur. *See* Apollonia (Israel)
Arta, 2:**521**

Artabanus. *See* Ardavan
Artafernes. *See* Holofernes
Artamonov, Mikhail, 11:321
Art and artists, 2:**491–521**
   Abraham ben Jacob, 2:122
   Absalom, 1:331
   Agadati, Baruch, 1:443–444
   Akedah, 1:559–560
   Alechinsky, Pierre, 1:607
   Amshewitz, John Henry, 2:106
   anthropomorphism, 2:191
   antiquity to 1800, 2:491–492
      after the fall of Jerusalem,
         2:493–494
      biblical period, 2:492–493,
         502–503
      crafts, 2:496
      early Christian art and, 2:494
      funerary, 2:497
      illuminated manuscripts,
         2:495–496, 497–498
      Islam, 2:495
      museums and collections,
         2:498–499
      new developments, 2:498–499
      Northern Europe, 2:495
      printed book, 2:497
      Renaissance period, 2:496
      ritual, 2:496–497
      Roman Empire, 2:494–495
      Sanctuary and First Temple
         Period, 2:492–493
      Second Temple Period, 2:493
   Auerbach, Frank, 2:654
   Balaam, 3:81
   Bezalel Academy of Arts and
      Design, 3:557
   Bibles, illuminated, 3:678–679
   Bible's impact on, 3:673–674
   Brazil, 4:152
   Burle-Marx, Roberto, 4:296
   Cain, images of, 4:341–342
   calligraphy, Hebrew, 4:366–367
   "Canaanites," 4:393
   Canada
      Caiserman-Roth-Ghitta, 4:347
      Iskowitz, Gershon, 10:87
      Raphael, William, 17:95–96
   caricatures of Jews, 4:477–479, 499
   cartoonists and cartoons, 4:499–
      501
   Cassab, Judy, 4:507
   ceremonial, 2:525–526
   ceremonial objects, 4:547–549
   cherub, cherubim, 4:601
   Chicago, Judy, 4:612

Art and artists, *continued*
childbirth amulets, 2:122
Christian
Abraham, 1:287
Adam, 1:375–376
Elijah, 6:336
Herod I, 9:37–38
collectors and dealers, 2:523–524
collectors of ritual art, 4:548–549
crafts, 5:263–272, 16:123
Cubists, 15:648
Czechoslovakia, 6:734–735
Dada, 11:77–78
Daniel in, 5:418–419
David in, 5:456–457
Deborah and, 5:519
Dibbuk, 5:644
Dicker-Brandeis, Frederike, 5:646
Dine, Jim, 5:669–670
Dura-Europa paintings, 6:52–55
in Eastern Europe, 2:507–509
ecclesia et synagga, 6:88
Ehrlich, Georg, 6:243–244
Eilshemius, Louis M., 6:255
Ein Hod, 6:257–258
Estevens, David, 6:515
Esther, representation of, 6:516–517
expressionism, Meidner, Ludwig, 13:773–774
Ezekiel in, 6:645–646
Fauvists, 15:648
Ferber, Herbert, 6:759
Fima, Efraim, 7:20–21
folklore, 7:103
Fox, Emanuel Philips, 7:140
Fraenckel, Liepmann, 7:142
France
Adler, Jules, 1:401
Cahn, Marcelle, 4:338
Calle, Sophie, 4:365
Caro-Delvaille, Henri, 4:492
Chagall, Marc, 4:556–557
Chapiro, Jacques, 4:568
Ecole de Paris artists, 2:517
Modigliani, Amedeo, 14:411
Picart, Bernard, 16:144–145
Frankenthaler, Helen, 7:203–204
Freedman, Barnett, 7:224
Germany
Abramson family, 1:328
Adler, Friedrich, 1:397
Cassirer, Paul, 4:510
Schottlander, Bernard, 18:166
Segal, Arthur, 18:244

Gottlieb, Adolph, 8:9
Gottlieb, Maurycy, 8:13
Gross, Michael, 8:96
Grundig, Hans, 8:111
Grundig, Lea, 8:111
Grundman, Zwi, 8:111–112
Guggenheim, Peggy, 8:124
Guston, Philip, 8:149
Gutman, Nahum, 8:152–153
Gutmann, Joseph, 8:154
Guttmann, Robert, 8:159
Haan, Meijer De, 8:164–165
Haggadot, illuminated, 4:76, 8:210–214
Ḥanukkah lamps, 8:334–335
Hayden, Henri, 8:474–475
Hellenism, 2:493, 8:789–790
Henschel brothers, 8:811
heraldry, 9:6–7
Herdan, Kurt Lucian, 9:9
Herman, Josef, 9:24
Herman, Oskar, 9:24
Hildesheimer, Wolfgang, 9:105
Hillman, David, 9:117
Hirsch, Joseph, 9:126
Hirschfeld, Al, 9:136
Hirschfeld-Mack, Ludwig, 9:139
historians and critics, 2:524–528
Holocaust
ghettos and camps, 2:515, 516–519, 3:41
influence of, 2:519–521
Hungary, 10:821, 12:505
Alconière, Theodore, 1:603
Laszlo, Philip Alexius de Lombos, 12:505
Perlmutter, Izsák, 15:780
Schoeffer, Nicolas, 18:155
iconography, 9:703–706
illuminated amulets, 2:122–123
illuminated manuscripts, Hebrew, 9:734–735
illustrated books, 4:75–76
Isaac (patriarch), 10:34–35
Isaiah, Book of, 10:*74–75*
Isaiah's prophecies in, 10:74–75
Islamic
Abraham, 1:287
historians of, 6:545
Israel, 10:695, 696–698, 699–700, 701
Agam, Yaacov, 1:445
Arab population, 10:733–734
artworks, 10:695–701
Castel, Moshe Elazar, 4:511–512

galleries and museums, 10:697–698, 704, 757–758
Janco, 11:77–78
Lavie, Raffi, 12:532
Sebba, Shalom, 18:231
Israel Arab, 10:734
Israëls, Jozef, 10:765
Italy
Cagli, Corrado, 4:335
Castellazzo, Moses da, 4:513
Corcos, Vittorio, 5:218
Jacob in, 11:23–24
Jephthah in, 11:123
Jeremiah in, 11:134
Jerusalem in, 11:224–228
Jewish
Abraham, 1:287–288
Abraham bar Jacob, 1:294
Adam, 1:376
Adler, Jacob, 1:400–401
Adler, Samuel M., 1:407
Jewish school of Paris, 15:647–648
Jewish themes in, 14:49
Job in, 11:358
Joel, Book of, 11:362
Jonah, Book of, 11:391
Joseph as portrayed in, 11:412–413
Josephus and, 11:441–442
Joshua as portrayed in, 11:444
Judah Maccabee in, 11:511
Judith, Book of, 11:568
Kahana, Aharon, 11:710
Kanovitz, Howard, 11:767
Karavan, Dani, 11:803–804
Katz, Alex, 12:8–9
Katz, Hans Ludwig, 12:**11–12**
Kaufmann, Isidor, 12:**32**
Kempf, Franz Moshe, 12:**73**
kettubot, illuminated, 12:97–98
Kirszenbaum, Jesekiel David, 12:190
Kistling, Moise, 12:201
Kitaj, R. B., 12:205–206
Klein, Yves, 12:226
Lamentations, Book of, 12:*447*, 450
Lasansky, Mauricio, 12:494
Lassaw, Ibram, 12:502–503
Lavie, Raffi, 12:532
Lifschitz, Uri, 13:11
Lilien, Ephraim Moses, 13:14
lion, image of, 13:62
Mandelshtam, Osip Emilyevich, 13:463–464
medals, 13:713–717

menorah in, 14:53–54
Merzer, Arieh, 14:**74**
Mesopotamia, 14:92
Middle Ages
    Absalom, 1:331
    Creation, 5:279–280
modern
    defined, 2:500–504
    Ereẓ Israel, 2:509–513
Moholy-Nagy, László, 14:419–420
Moïse, Theodore Sydney, 14:421–422
Mokady, Moshe, 14:423
Mondzain, Simon, 14:435
Montparnasse school of art, 15:647, 648, 649
Mopp, 14:469
Moses, 14:539–540, 541–542
murals, Mexico, 3:296
Nebuchadnezzar, 15:51
Neiman, Yehudah, 15:66
Neoromanticism, 15:648
"New Figuration," 13:11
Newman, Barnett, 15:145–146
Noah in, 15:289–290
Palestine (Ottoman), 10:695
paper-cuts, 15:615–616
Paris school, 15:647–651
Passover and Seder in, 15:682–683
pewter plates, 16:24
Phoenicia, 16:123
pillar motif, 16:160
poetic cinema, 11:734
Poland
    Barcinsky, Henryk, 3:146
    Centerszwer, Stanisława, 4:543
    Halter, Marek, 8:286–287
    Le Witt, Jan, 12:769
    Pilichowski, Leopold, 16:159
portal, 16:402
portraits, of Jews, 16:408
psalms, 16:678
Rachel in, 17:48–49
Rattner, Abraham, 17:114–115
Ray, Man, 17:126
Reder, Bernard, 17:155–156
Reiss, Lionel, 17:212–213
Rembrandt van Rijn, 17:215–216
Renaissance, 3:411
Rivers, Larry, 17:347
Rogers, Claude Maurice, 17:368
Rose, Herman, 17:426
Rosenberg, Isaac, 17:436–437
Rosenberg, James Naumburg, 17:437

Rosenberg, Lazar, 17:437–438
Rosenmann-Taub, David, 17:449
Rosenthal Maz, 17:455–456
Rothenstein, Michael, 17:486
Russia
    1970s, 17:566
    Aizenberg, Nina, 1:553
    Levitan, Isaac Ilitch, 12:732
    Rabin, Oscar, 17:33–34
    Raskin, Saul, 17:107–108
    Serov, Valentin, 18:314
Ruth, Book of, 17:595–596
Sabbath, 17:621–622
Salome, 17:694
Samson, 17:750–752
Samuel, 17:756
Saul, 18:81–82
Scroll of Esther, 18:218–220, *219*
Segall, Lasar, 18:248–249
Sima, Miron, 18:590
Simon, Sidney, 18:**617**
Singer, Yvonne, 18:640
Solomon, 18:761–762, 761–763
Solomon, Simeon, 18:767
Solomon, Solomon Joseph, 18:767–768
spice box, Havdallah, 8:467–468
Surrealists, 15:648
synagogue destruction, 19:356–357
Titus, Flavius Vespasianus, 19:744–745
tombstones, 20:35–36
Tower of Babel, 3:21
U.K.
    Costa, Catherine da, 5:233
    Rabin, Sam, 17:34
    Rie, Dame Lucie, 17:293
    Schotz, Benno, 18:166
    twentieth century, 6:729, 14:48
U.S., 2:513–516
    Carvalho, Solomon Nunes, 4:502
    Lewitt, Sol, 12:769–770
    New York City, 15:221
    Pearlstein, Philip, 15:706
    Peixotto, George da Maduro, 15:713–714
    Reder, Bernard, 17:155–156
    Reiss, Lionel, 17:212–213
    San Diego, 18:14
    Sarasota, 18:50–51
    Schames, Samson, 18:106
    Schanker, Louis, 18:106–107
    Schor, Ilya, 18:162
    Schwartz, Manfred, 18:186

Segal, George, 18:246
Seligmann, Kurt, 18:267–268
Serra, Richard, 18:314
Shahn, Ben, 18:365–366
twentieth century, 14:49
USSR
    Adlivankin, Samuil, 1:410
Western Europe, 2:504–507
Yemen, 21:309
See also Painters and painting; Sculpture; *specific artists*
The Art and Craft of Judging: The Opinions of Judge Learned Hand (Shanks), 18:397
Artapan. *See* Ardavan
Artapanus, 2:**521–522**
    Moses, 14:531, 532
    religious impact of Bible on Hellenistic Judaism and, 3:660
Arṭas, 2:**522**
Artaxata (Armenia). *See* Ardashir (Armenia)
Artaxerxes, 2:**522–523**, 6:659
Art collectors and art dealers, 2:**523–524**
    Duveen, Joseph, 6:73
    Duveen, Joseph Joel, 6:73
    Flechtheim, Alfred, 7:70–71
    Hirshhorn, Joseph Herman, 9:143
    Schocken, Salman, 18:154–155
Artemion, 2:**524**
Artemovsk (Ukraine), 2:**524**
Artephius, 1:602
Art historians and art critics, 2:**524–528**
    Barasch, Moshe, 3:135
    Berenson, Bernard, 3:411
    Bersohn, Matthias, 3:489
    Brookner, Anita, 4:208
    Didi-Huberman, Georges, 5:647
    Donath, Adolph, 5:747–748
    Erlanger, Philippe, 6:481
    Greenberg, Clement, 8:67–68
    Hallo, Rudolph, 8:282
    Rosenberg, Harold, 17:436
    Schapiro, Meyer, 18:109–110
Arthurian legends, 2:**528–529**
Artichoke, 20:488
Articles of faith, 2:165, **529–532**, 11:789
Artificial insemination, 2:**532–533**
Artisans. *See* Crafts
Artis Cabbalisticae, hoc est reconditae theologiae et philosophiae Scriptorum Tomus I (Pistorius), 16:187
Artists International Association, 3:731
Art Music. *See* Music

The Art of Biblical Poetry (Alter), 16:256

The Art of Educational Research, Its Problems and Procedures (Abelson), 1:248

Artom, Cesare, 2:**534**

Artom, Elia Samuele, 2:**534**

Artom, Emanuele, 15:668

Artom, Isaac, 16:345

Artom, Meir, 15:581

Artom family, 2:**533**

Arts and the Man (Edman), 6:150

ArtScroll, 2:**534–535**, 18:123

ArtScroll/Mesorah series, 18:123, 21:644–645

Artuković, Andrija, 15:698

Artzi, Shlomo, 2:**535**

Artzi, Yitzhak, 2:**535–536**

Aruba (Netherlands Antilles), 4:472

Aruck, Hyman. *See* Arlen, Harold

Aruck ha-shalem (Kohut, Alexander), 12:266

Aruety, Abraham. *See* Aruety, Habran

Aruety, Habran, 17:476

Aruety family. *See* Rote family

Arugat ha-Bosem (Abraham ben Azriel), 1:295, 18:772

Arukh (Nathan ben Jehiel), 11:74, 12:405, 13:43

Arukh ha-Shulḥan (Epstein), 6:473

Arukh la-Ner. *See* Ettlinger, Jacob

Arum, Robert, 2:**536**

Arumah (Canaan). *See* Ruma (Canaan)

Arumah (Galilee). *See* Ruma (Galilee)

Arum der Velt (Hirschbein), 9:133

Arum Vokzal (Bergelson), 3:419

Arundi, Isaac, 2:**536**

Arusi, Abraham, 2:106

Arusi, Abraham ben Moses Ha-Levi, 2:**536**

Arvey, Jacob M., 2:**536–537**

Arvic. *See* Judeo-Arabic

Arvit, 2:72, 75, **537–538**, 13:305

Aryan, Semitic races, 17:46–47

Aryeh. *See* Judah ben Isaac (1166-1224)

Aryeh Judah Harari, 2:**538**, 14:463

Aryeh Judah Leib ben Ephraim ha-Kohen, 2:**538**

Aryeh Judah Leib of Polonnoye, 2:**538**

Aryeh Leib ben Asher. *See* Gunzberg, Aryeh Leib ben Asher

Aryeh Leib ben Elijah, 2:**538**

Aryeh Leib ben Joseph ha-Kohen. *See* Heller, Aryeh Leib ben Joseph Ha-Kohen of Stry

Aryeh Leib ben Samuel Ẓevi Hirsch, 2:**538–539**

Aryeh Leib of Oẓarów, 2:**539**

Aryeh Leib of Shpola, 2:**539**

Aryeh Leib Sarahs, 2:**539**

Aryeh Leibush Bolekhover. *See* Aryeh Leib ben Elijah

Arzhak, Nikolai. *See* Daniel, Yuli Markovich

Arẓi Ha-Shomer ha-Ẓa'ir. *See* Kibbutz Arẓi Ha-Shomer ha-Ẓa'ir

Arzila. *See* Arcila

Arzin, Joseph ben Jacob, 2:**539–540**

Arzt, Max, 2:**540**

Asa, 2:**540–541**, 3:13, 9:175

A.S.A. (Academic Sports Association), 2:**541**

Asad, Hafez al-, 2:**541–542**

al-Asad al-Maḥallī. *See* Jacob ben Isaac

Asael, Ḥayyim ben Benjamin, 2:**542**

Asaf. *See* Asaph ha-Rofe

Aṣāf ben Barakhyā, 18:761

Asaf ha-Levi Ish Yerushalayim. *See* Levin, Alter Isaac

Asahel, 1:264, 2:**542**

'Asā'-i Pīrān (Brudo), 4:221

Asaph, 2:**542–543**

Asaph ben Berechiah. *See* Asaph ha-Rofe

Asaph ha-Rofe, 2:**543–544**

Asaph ha-Yarhoni. *See* Asaph ha-Rofe

Asaph ha-Yehudi. *See* Asaph ha-Rofe

Asaphites. *See* Asaph

Asaph Judaeus. *See* Asaph ha-Rofe

Asarah batlanim. *See* Batlanim

Asarah harugei ha-malkhut (Emrāni). *See The Ten Martyrs of the Kingdom* (Emrāni)

Asarah harugei malkhut. *See The Ten Martyrs*

Asarah ha-rugei malkhut. *See The Ten Martyrs*

Asarah Ma'amarot (Abraham ben Benjamin Ze'ev Brisker), 1:295

Asarah Ma'amarot (Elijah ben Baruch), 6:338

Asaramel, 2:**544**

Asbili, Yom Tov. *See* Yom Tov ben Abraham Ishbili

Ascalon (Israel). *See* Ashkelon (Israel)

Ascama, 2:**545**

Ascamot. *See* Ascama

Ascandarani, Joseph ben Abraham, 10:79

Ascandarani family. *See* Iscandari family

Ascarelli, Deborah. *See* Ascarelli, Devora

Ascarelli, Devora, 2:**545**, 7:50

Ascarelli, Tullio, 2:**545**

Ascending and descending numbers, 15:337

Ascension of Isaiah, 10:**75–76**

The Ascent of Man (Bronowski), 4:207

Ascent to Heaven (Rudnicki), 9:410

Asceticism, 2:**545–550**, 3:155, 6:532

    Abraham ben Moses ben Maimon, 1:307–308

    fasting, 6:720, 722

    philosophical analysis of, 16:81

    Sefer ha-Nezirim (Fraenkel), 7:144

    See also Nazirite

Asch, Sholem, 2:**550–551**, 11:412, 12:660–661, 14:541

Aschaffenburg (Germany), 2:**551–552**

Aschaffenburg, Gustav, 2:**552**

Ascher, Saul, 2:**552**

Ascherson, Paul Friedrich August, 2:**552**

Aschheim, Isidor, 2:**552**

Aschner, Manfred, 2:**553**

Ascoli, Ettore, 2:**553–554**

Ascoli, Graziadio Isaia, 2:**554**

Ascoli family, 2:**553**

Ascoli Piceno (Italy), 2:**554**

Asefat Ḥakhamim (Israel Isserl ben Isaac Segal), 10:753

Asefat Ḥakhamim (journal), 2:**554–555**

Asefat ha-Nivḥarim, 10:392–393

Asenapper, 2:**555**

Asenath, 2:**555**, 11:418

Asenov, Dragomir, 4:276

Aseret ha-Dibbrot. *See* Decalogue

Aseret Yemai Teshuvah. *See* Ten Days of Penitence

Aseret yemei teshuvah. *See* Ten Days of Penitence

ASF. *See* American Sephardi Federation (ASF)

Asfi (Morocco). *See* Safi (Morocco)

Asgnedau. *See* Asmodeus

Ash (abbreviation), 2:**555**

Ash, Abraham, 2:555

Ash, Abraham ben Joseph, 2:555–556

Ash, Abraham Joseph, 1:223, 2:555, **556**

Ash, Joel Ben Meir Jospeh, 2:556

Ashamnu, 2:**556**, 8:493

Asham Talui (Segrè), 18:252

Ashanski, Abel-Aaron Itskovich, 2:**556**

Ash'arite Kalām, 16:77

Ash'ariyya, 11:729–730

Ashartu (Emarite deity), 6:387

Asha'yā, Najīb, 15:473

Ashbel, Dov, 2:**556–557**

Ashburnham Pentateuch, 1:463, 3:674, 675

Ashdod (Israel), 2:**557–558**, 11:715–716

Ashdot Ya'akov (Israel), 2:**558**

Ashendorf, Israel, 2:**558**

Ashenheim, Louis, 2:558

Ashenheim, Neville Noel, 2:**558–559**

Ashenheim family, 2:**558–559**

Asher (son of Jacob), 2:*559*, **559–560**

Asher, Abraham, 2:**560**

Asher, Abraham ben Gedaliah Ibn, 2:**560**

Asher, Adolph. *See* Asher, Abraham

Asher, ben Jehiel, 2:32, 6:174

Asher, David, 2:**560**

Asher, Isaiah ben Moses ha-Levi, 2:**561**

Asher, Joseph, 2:**561**

Asher, Joseph Michael, 2:**561**

Asherah, 2:**562**, 3:656, 6:332

Asher Anshel ben Isaac of Przemyśl, 2:**562**

Asher Barash Bio-Bibliographical Institute, 18:724

Asher ben David, 2:**563**

Asher ben Jehiel, 2:**563–564**, 4:772, 773, 779, 18:574
    fines and damages, 7:29
    halakhah, 8:257

Asher ben Meshullam ha-Kohen of Lunel, 2:**564–565**

Asher ben Saul, 2:**565**, 4:653

Asherim, 3:656

Asher of Cracow. *See* Anshel of Cracow

Ash family, 2:**555–556**

Ashi, 2:**565–566**

Ashima, 2:**566**

Ashinsky, Aaron Mordecai Halevi, 2:**566**

Ashkanasy, Maurice, 2:**566–567**

Ashkavah, 2:**567**

Ashkelon (Israel), 2:**567–569**, 11:772, 15:263

Ashkelon onions, 15:433

Ashkenaz (biblical name), 2:**569**

Ashkenaz (Jewish settlement, NW Europe), 2:107, 472, **569–571**, *570*
    Akdamut Millin, 1:555
    Aleinu le-Shabbe'aḥ, 1:609–610
    alphabet, Hebrew, 1:705*t,* 706, 716*t,* 717*t,* 718
    Amsterdam, 2:106–108, 110, 114, *116,* 117, 6:41
        emancipation, 6:749

Schuster, Aaron, 18:177

amulets, 2:122

An-Ski collections, 2:182–183

arts, Sabbath, 17:620–621

betrothal customs and, 3:541

Bible cantillation, 13:658–664, 663–664

birth customs and folklore, 3:721–722

Caracas (Venezuela), 4:459–460

Caribbean, 4:477

Caucasus, 4:527–528

Chernovtsy (Ukraine), 4:597

Chile, 4:638, 640, 641, 643

Cuba, 5:317–318

demography, 5:571

domestic violence, Middle Ages, 5:740

Dutch literature and, 6:69

economic history, modern, 6:118–119

Eleazar ben Judah of Worms, 6:303–305

Eleazar ben Moses ha-Darshan of Wuerzburg, 6:305

El Male Raḥamim (funeral prayer), 6:364–365

England, 6:414–415
    Elhanan ben Yakar, 6:316
    London, 12:747, 13:180–181

Europe, 1:521, 9:211–212, 222

evil eye folk beliefs, 6:585

Halakhah, 6:41

Ḥanukkah, 13:496–497

hymns, 1:385, 414–415, 6:259–260

illuminated Hebrew Bibles, 3:678

influence of Meir ben Baruch of Rothenburg, 13:781–782

Israel (state), 10:294
    religious schools, 10:632–633
    tensions with other edot, 10:298–299, 300

Istanbul (Ottoman period), 10:774, 775, 777–778

Jacob Saul ben Eliezer Jeroham Elyashar, 6:371–372

Jerusalem
    nineteenth century, 11:172–173
    seventeenth century, 11:164

Kaddish, 11:697

kolel, 12:273

Latin America, 12:510–511

literature
    fiction, 7:14
    folk, *Mayse-Bukh,* 13:702–703
    ḥasidic, 1:219, 6:529–531

liturgy, 13:134
    Mi-Sinai Niggunim, 14:363–364
    shtayger, 18:522–523

Mexican leaders, 6:748

Montreal (Canada), 14:463–464

morbidity statistics, 18:546

Pale of Settlement, 18:602

Palestine (Ottoman), 10:294, 619–621

population, 18:300

post-Holocaust aliyah, 10:215

pre-French Revolution, 7:253

rabbis, dress, 6:15

renewal of Jerusalem community, 14:24–25

Sarajevo, 18:48

Seattle (WA), 18:229

Sefer ha-Ḥayyim, 18:239–240

Simferopol, 18:602

similarities to Sephardim, 18:295–296

traditional cookery style, 7:118

U.K., 18:129

See also Germany

Ashkenazi, Abraham ben Jacob, 2:**571–572**

Ashkenazi, Abraham Nathan ben Elisha Hayyim. *See* Nathan of Gaza

Ashkenazi, Asher Judah ben Nathan. *See* Weidner, Paulus

Ashkenazi, Azariah Ḥayyim, 6:354

Ashkenazi, Azriel. *See* Gunzenhauser, Azriel

Ashkenazi, Bahur ben Asher ha-Levi. *See* Levita, Elijah

Ashkenazi, Beḥor, 2:**572**, 16:346

Ashkenazi, Berman. *See* Issachar Berman ben Naphtali ha-Kohen

Ashkenazi, Bezalel ben Abraham, 2:**572–573**, 13:262

Ashkenazi, Dan, 2:**573**

Ashkenazi, David, 4:190

Ashkenazi, Eliezer Baruch. *See* Meyer, Paulus

Ashkenazi, Eliezer ben Elijah the Physician, 2:**573**

Ashkenazi, Eliezer Isaac. *See* Eliezer ben Isaac

Ashkenazi, Feibush. *See* Joel ben Simeon

Ashkenazi, Gershon, 2:**574**, 14:472

Ashkenazi, Hakham Zevi, 6:21

Ashkenazi, Jacob. *See* Temerls, Jacob ben Eliezer

Ashkenazi, Jacob ben Isaac, 3:611

Ashkenazi, Jehiel ben Israel. *See* Luria, Jehiel ben Israel Ashkenazi

Ashkenazi, Jonah ben Jacob, 2:**574**

Ashkenazi, Joseph, 2:**574–575**

Ashkenazi, Joseph ben Jacob. *See*
Gunzenhauser, Joseph ben Jacob

Ashkenazi, Joseph ben Shalom. *See*
Joseph ben Shalom Ashkenazi

Ashkenazi, Judah ben Joseph, 2:**575**

Ashkenazi, Judah ben Simeon, 2:**575**

Ashkenazi, Judah Samuel, 2:**575**

Ashkenazi, Leon, 2:**575–576**

Ashkenazi, Malkiel, 2:**576**

Ashkenazi, Meir ben Benjamin Wolf,
2:**576**

Ashkenazi, Menahem. *See*
Bekemoharar, Menahem ben Isaac
Ashkenazi

Ashkenazi, Mordecai ben Isaac Kohen,
2:**576**

Ashkenazi, Moses David, 2:**576–577**

Ashkenazi, Naphtali ben Joseph, 2:**577**

Ashkenazi, Nissim Abraham ben
Raphael, 2:**577**

Ashkenazi, Samuel Jaffe ben Isaac,
2:**577**

Ashkenazi, Saul ben Moses ha-Kohen,
2:**577**

Ashkenazi, Shalom, of Neustadt, 4:269

Ashkenazi, Solomon, 2:**577–578**, 9:7,
15:541, 16:345–346

Ashkenazi, Ẓevi Hirsch ben Jacob,
2:**578–579**, 8:477, 478

Ashkenazim. *See* Ashkenaz (Jewish
settlement, NW Europe)

Ashkenazy, Vladimir Davidovich,
2:**579**

Ashkhabad, 2:**579**

Ashlag, Judah Leib, 11:679

Ashlag, Yehudah, 2:**579–580**, 4:128

Ashman, Aharon, 2:**580**, 8:715

Ashmedai. *See* Asmodeus

Ashmedai (opera, Tal), 18:762–763

Ashor (groom), 6:312

Ashrei, 2:**580**

Ashriki, Mordecai, 2:**580–581**

Ashtamker, Benjamin Samson, 15:474

Ashtar. *See* Ashtoreth

Ashtaroth (biblical city), 2:**581**

Ashtor, Eliyahu, 2:**581**

Ashtoreth, 2:131, **581–582**, 3:11

Ashtumker, B. S. *See* Ashtamker,
Benjamin Samson

ʾĀshūrāʿ, 2:**582**

Ashurbanipal, 14:91, 403

Ashurbanipal library, 2:404

Asia, 2:**582–586**, 583, 585t, 586

  agriculture, 12:427

  aliyah and absorption, Israel,
    10:341t

  foreign policy and relations
    with Israel, 10:264–265, 265

  technical and economic
    assistance, 10:221

  Middle Ages, Jewish education,
    6:176

Asia Minor, 2:**586–587**, 587, 3:729

Asia Minor Agreement. *See* Sykes-
Picot Agreement

Asian communities, 5:115t, 120t

Asian Socialist Conference, 18:709

Asia-Pacific region, 2:238–239

Di Asife (Shalom Aleichem), 18:381

Asila. *See* Arcila

Asimov, Isaac, 2:**588**

Asinaeus and Anilaeus, 2:**164–165**,
11:440

Asinius Pollio, Gaius, 2:**588**

ASJM. *See* American Society for
Jewish Music

Askama. *See* Ascama

Askelon (Israel). *See* Ashkelon (Israel)

Askenasy, Eugen, 2:**588**

Askenasy, Paul, 2:**588–589**

Askenazy, Simon, 2:**589**

Aškenazy, Ludvík, 2:**589**

Askhabad. *See* Ashkhabad

Asknazi, Isaac Lvovich, 2:**589**

Askowith, Dora, 2:**590**

Aslakssen, Cort, 2:**590**

Asmakhta, 2:**590–592**, 7:27

Asmodeus, 2:**592–593**

Asmussen, J. P., Judeo-Persian
literature, 11:558

Asner, Edward, 2:**593**

Asochis (Galilee). *See* Shiḥin (Galilee)

Asociación Israelita de Beneficencia,
17:423

Asociación Israelita Sefaradi La
Fraternidad, 3:262

Asociación Mutual Israelita Argentina
(AMIA), 2:**70–71**

Asophon. *See* Zaphon

Aspamia. *See* Spain

Aspects of Judaism (Montefiore),
14:455

Asper, Israel H., 2:**593–594**

Asper, Izzy. *See* Asper, Israel H.

Asper family, 11:470

Asqanu. *See* Ashkelon (Israel)

Assa. *See* Assi

Assaf, Michael, 2:**594**

Assaf, Simha, 2:**594–595**, 9:160

Assault, 2:**595–598**

The Assault (Mulisch), 6:71

Asscher, Abraham, 2:**599**

Assemani family, 2:**599**

Assembly. *See* Congregations

Assembly, Sukkot. *See* Hakhel

Assembly of Jewish Notables, 2:8,
599–602, *600*, 7:155, 8:439, 9:231,
18:641–642

Assembly of Sages (journal). *See*
Asefat Ḥakhamim (journal)

Asseo, David, 2:**602**

Asser, Carel, 12:552

Asser, Moses, 12:552, 16:345

Asser, Tobias, M. C., 2:114, 12:552

Asser family, 2:112, **602**

Asses, 2:**594**

  Balaam, 3:78

  worship, 2:**615–616**

Assessment. *See* Damages

Asset lien, 12:812–817

Assi, 2:**603**

  Ammi ben Nathan and, 2:82

  Amram I, 2:103

  Judah III, 11:478

Assi, Rav, 2:**603**, 18:598

Assideans. *See* Hassideans

Assignment of debt, 2:**603–605**

Assimilation, 2:**605–613**

  Aguddat Aḥim, 1:508

  Algeria, 1:648

  antiquity and Middle ages, 2:605–
    606

  Bohemia, 4:40–41

  Buchner, Abraham, 4:243

  Byk, Emil, 4:323–324

  Canada, 4:420

  Čechů-Židů, Svaz, 4:534–535

  communism and, 5:91–96

  Enlightenment period, 2:606–607

  Germany

    Berlin, 3:446

    Central-Verein Deutscher
      Staatsbuerger Juedischen
      Glaubens, 4:546

  Halakhah

    technology, 19:573

  Haskalah and, 8:434, 439–440

  Hungary, 9:611, 618

  Kook, Abraham Isaac, 12:291

  late nineteenth and twentieth
    centuries, 2:607–608, 9:283–284

  linguistic, 8:436–437

  literature

    Poland, 6:748

  Orthodox Judaism and, 15:493–
    494, 496, 498

  Peru, 15:794, 797

  Poland, 4:318, 16:302

    Czartoryski, Prince Adam
      Jerzy, 5:351–352

Eisenbaum, Antoni, 6:265
political participation and, 16:339
Russia
  1970s, 17:564–566
  post-WW II, 17:553
  USSR regime, 17:544
Shomer Israel, 18:518
surnames, establishment of, 14:768
U.S., 2:608–611, 6:695–696, 698–700
USSR, 2:611–613
Western countries, 2:611
Associated Artists of Revolutionary Russia, 4:197
Association for Defense against Antisemitism. *See* Verein Zur Abwehr des Antisemitismus
Association for Friendship and Cultural Ties with Israel, 14:520
Association for Jewish Demography and Statistics, 18:724
Association for Jewish Outreach Professionals and Programs (AJOP), 3:7
Association for Jewish Studies (AIS), 11:318
Association for Jewish Studies (AJS), 2:**613–614**
Association for Medieval Judeo-Arabic, 3:744
Association for Psychoanalytic Medicine (APM), 11:804
Association for the Diffusion of Religious Knowledge, 6:205
  See also Jewish Religious Education Board
Association of Activists and Friends of Soviet Jewish Culture, 14:520
Association of Holocaust Children (Poland), 2:64
Association of Holocaust Organizations (AHO), 2:614–615, **614–615**
Association of Israel. *See* Agudat Israel
Association of Jewish 6th Formers, 6:428
Association of Jewish Libraries, 12:785
Association of Reform Rabbis of New York and Vicinity, 18:586
Associations. *See specific society or association*
Association Vidas Largas for the Defense and Promotion of the Judeo-Spanish Language and Culture, 18:306
Assumpção, Diogo da, 2:**615**
Assumptio Moysis. See Assumption of Moses
Assumption of Moses, 14:533, **544–545**

Assur (Iraq), 2:404, **615**
Ass worship, 2:**615–616**
Assyria
  Ahaz, 1:539
  Akkadian language, 1:565
  Ammonites, 2:85–86
  Arameans, 2:337
  archives, 2:403
  Esarhaddon, 6:486
  Hammurapi, 8:309–310
  Haran, 8:343–344
  Haurina, 8:461
  Megiddo, 13:767
  Mesopotamia, 14:87–88
  Moab, 14:402–403
  Nineveh, 15:271–272
  Phoenicia, 16:121–122
  rebellions, 2:489
  Sargon II, 18:56
  Shalmaneser III, 18:375–376
Assyrian exile, 6:**607–608**, 9:*180*
Assyriology, 15:471
  archaeological excavations, 14:92–93
  Finkelstein, Jacob Joel, *7:34*
  Hallo, William, 8:282
  Landsberger, Benno, 12:475–476
  Lewy, Julius, 12:771
  Oppenheim, Ḥayyim, 15:445
  Oppert, Jules Julius, 15:452
  Pick, Ḥayyim Hermann, 16:146
Astarte, 2:581–582
Astarté. *See* Ashtoreth
Asti (Italy), 2:**616**
Astorga (Spain), 2:**616**
Astrakhan (Russia), 2:**616**
Astrological chiromancy, 4:653–654
Astrology, 2:**616–620**, 21:646–647
  Abraham bar Ḥiyya, 1:293
  Cresques de Vivers, 5:288
  divination and, 5:705
  Nostradamus, 15:314
  Paltiel, 15:607
  theories of Ibn Ezra, Abraham ben Meir, 9:670–671
Astronautics. *See* Aeronautics
Astronomy, 2:**620–626**
  Abraham bar Ḥiyya, 1:293
  Albalia, Isaac ben Baruch, 1:583
  Alḥadib, Isaac ben Solomon ben Zaddik, 1:654
  Anatoli, Jacob ben Abba Mari ben Samson, 2:132
  Apocrypha, 2:621
  Beer, Wilhelm, 3:254
  Bemporad, Azeglio, 3:312

Bible, 2:620–621
Cleomedes, 4:753
Comtino, Mordecai ben Eliezer, 5:132–133
Delacrut, Mattathias ben Solomon, 5:535
Dunash ibn Tamim, 6:48–49
Ḥassān ibn Ḥassān, 8:454
Hoffman, Jeffrey, 9:308
Ibn Daud, Abraham ben David Halevi, 9:662–665
Ibn Sahl, Joseph ben Jacob, 9:689
Israeli, Isaac ben Joseph, 10:751
Jonathan ben Joseph of Ruzhany, 11:398
Judeo-Arabic literature on, 11:531
Judeo-Persian, 11:554
Lattes, Bonet, 12:518–519
Levi Ben Gershom, 12:698, 701
Loew, Moritz, 13:164
Loewy, Maurice, 13:172
Maimonides, Moses, 13:395
Māshā'Allah ben Athaň, 13:600
measurement, 13:674
Middle Ages, 2:622–625
modern times, 2:625–626
Nieto, David, 15:261
Nifoci, Isaac, 15:262
physics and, 16:132–133, 141
Renaissance, 2:625–626
Schickard, Wilhelm, 18:128
Schlesinger, Frank, 18:140
Schwarzschild, Karl, 18:193
Shesh-Kenafayim, 4:62
Talmud and Midrash, 2:621–622
Astrophysics, 16:141
Astruc, Elie-Aristide, 2:**626–627**
Astruc, Jean, 2:**627**, 3:646, 649
Astruc, Mardochee, 11:560
Astruc, Saul ha-Kohen, 2:**627**, 4:56
Astruc, Zacharie, 2:**627**
Astruc de Noves. *See* Abba Mari ben Eligdor
Astruc ha-Levi, 2:**627**
Asveiros. *See* Quintilius Varus
Asylum
  altars as, 2:13, 15
  cities, 4:742–744, *743*
  See also Refugees
Aszód (Hungary), 2:**627–628**
Aszod, Judah ben Israel, 2:**628**
Atair (Mombert), 14:430
Ataki (Moldavia), 2:**628–629**
Atar, Haim, 2:**629**
Atar, Moses, 16:346
Atar family, 2:**629**

Atarot (Israel), 2:**629**

Ataroth (biblical settlements), 2:**629–630**

Ataturk. *See* Kemal Mustafa

Atavism, 13:178

Ateret Baḥurim (Ehrenfeld), 6:239

Atfah, 2:468

Athaliah, 2:**630,** 9:177, 11:107–108

Athanasius
    Syro-Hexapla, 3:601
    on Zenobia, 15:377

Atheism, 7:670

Athens (Greece), 2:**630–632,** 9:340

Athens and Jerusalem (Shestov), 18:467

Athias, David, 4:82

Athias, Immanuel, 2:**632–633**

Athias, Jacob Ḥayyim, 4:82

Athias, Joseph, 2:109, **632–633**

Athias, Solomon da Costa. *See* Costa Athias, Solomon da

Athias family. *See* Atias family

Athletics. *See* Sports

Athlit (Israel), 1:221, 2:**633–634,** *634*

At Home in America: Second Generation (Moore), 9:152–153

Athribis (Egypt), 2:**634**

Athronges, 2:**634**

Atias family, 2:**632**

Atil (Turkey), 2:**634–635**

Atirat. *See* Asherah

Atlan, Henri, 2:**635**

Atlan, Jean, 2:**635**

Atlanta (GA), 2:**635–639,** 7:502, 13:667–668

Atlantic (vessel), 15:689

Atlantic Canada, 2:**639–641**

Atlantic City (NJ), 2:**641**

Atlantic Jewish Council, 2:640

Atlas (mountains), 2:**641–642**

Atlas, David, 2:**642**

Atlas, Eleazar, 2:**642–643**

Atlas, Jechezkiel, 2:**643,** 15:667

Atlas, Samuel, 2:**643**

Atlas of Israel (Amiran), 2:79

Atlas of the Historical Geography of the Holy Land (Smith), 18:688

Atlas Shrugged (Rand), 17:90

Atmospheres (Ligeti), 13:12

Atmospheric sciences, 6:449–450

Atom bomb. *See* Nuclear physics

Atomic Energy Commission, 13:16, 18:587

Atomism, 1:213, 2:**643–644**

Aton cult, 1:561, 2:41

Atonement, 2:**644**
    fasting, 6:719, 720, 722

forgiveness, 7:127–129
    Kipper, 12:180–183
    See also Day of Atonement

Atran, Frank Z., 2:**644–645**

Attachment to God. *See* Devekut

Attah, Eḥad, 2:**645**

Attah Beḥartanu, 2:75

Attah Horeta Lada'at, 2:**645**

Attah Zokher, 2:**645**

Attal, Jacob, 14:499

Attali, Bernard, 2:**645**

Attali, Jacques, 2:**645**

Attar, Ḥayyim ben Moses, 2:**645–646**

Attar, Judah ben Jacob Ibn, 2:**646**

Attar family. *See* Atar family

Attell, Abe. *See* Attell, Abraham Washington

Attell, Abraham Washington, 2:**646–647**

At the Depot. See Arum Vokzal

At the End of Days. See Be-Kez ha-Yamim

At the Gate (Molodowsky), 14:430

Attia, Isaac ben Isaiah, 2:**647**

Attia, Shem Tov, 2:**647**

Attias, Jean-Christophe, 11:326

Attik yomaya. *See* Ancient of Days

Attlee, Clement Richard, Earl, 2:**647–648**

Atto di Fede. *See* Auto da Fé

Attorneys, 2:**648**
    Belgium
        Picard, Edmond, 16:144
    Canada
        Bercovitch, Peter, 3:401
        Freedman, Samuel, 7:225
        human rights, 13:670–671
        Matas, David, 13:670–671
    Dash, Samuel, 5:438–439
    Denmark
        Hurwitz, Stephan, 9:633
    France
        Berr, Michel, 3:487
        Beugnot, Auguste Arthur, 3:555
    Germany
        Hollaender, Ludwig, 9:321–322
    Greece
        Alhanati, David, 1:655
        Herzog, Chaim, 9:67–68
        Hessen, Joseph Vladimiovich, 9:78
    Israel
        Akzin, Benjamin, 1:571–572
        Attorney General, 13:709
    Israel (State)
        Shapiro, Ya'akov Shimshon, 18:408

Latvia
    Mintz, Paul, 14:301–302
Lauterbach, Edward H., 12:529
Poland
    Lemkin, Raphael, 12:637–638
    Lieberman, Herman, 12:804
Polish
    Berenson, Leon, 3:411–412
Russia
    Pergament, Osip Yakovlevich, 15:770
    Slonimski, Leonid Zinovyevich, 18:679
Sawicki, Jerzy, 18:86
Scheck, Barry, 18:116
scholars
    Ben-Israel, Ruth, 3:353
    David, Martin, 5:464
Sciaki, Joseph, 18:197
South Africa
    Alexander, Morris, 1:624
    de Vries, M., 5:629–630
    Morris, Henry Harris, 14:510
    Solomon, Bertha, 18:764
Turkey
    Franco, Gad, 7:177
U.S.
    Abrams, Floyd M., 1:327
    Abrams, Robert, 1:327–328
    Bacher, Eduard, 3:36
    Benesch, Alfred Abraham, 3:340
    Benjamin, Judah Philip, 3:357–358
    Ben-Veniste, Richard, 3:384–385
    Berman, Julius, 3:463
    Bialkin, Kenneth J, 3:565–566
    Chertoff, Michael, 4:599–600
    Dershowitz, Alan M., 5:600
    Deutsch, Bernard Seymour, 5:621
    Dittenhoefer, Abram Jesse, 5:702
    Dworkin, Ronald, 6:74–75
    Fraenkel, Osmond K., 7:145
    Frankel, Hiram D., 7:196–197
    Frankenthaler, Alfred, 7:203
    Frankenthaler, George, 7:203
    Herlands, William Bernard, 9:22–23
    Hertz, Emanuel, 9:47
    Hoffman, Charles Isaiah, 9:307
    Hoffman, Philip E., 9:309–310
    Lefkowitz, Louis, 12:602

Lehmann, Emil, 12:615

Leibowitz, Samuel Simon, 12:622

Levi, Edward H., 12:687

Lewin, Nathan, 12:761–762

Lieberman, Joseph, 12:804–805

Mayer, Levy, 13:699

Medalie, George Zerdin, 13:713

Morse, David Abner, 14:512–513

Pfeffer, Leo, 16:25

Sapiro, Aaron, 18:39

Schiff, Adam, 18:128–129

Segal, Bernard Gerard, 18:245

Shanks, Hershel, 18:397

Shapiro, Robert, 18:407–408

Shapiro, Samuel Harvey, 18:408

Shetzer, Simon, 18:471

Sloss, Marcus Cauffman, 18:680

See also specific attorneys

Atwood, Margaret, 15:563

Atzmon, Moshe, 2:**648–649**

Aub, Joseph, 2:**649**

Aub, Max, 2:**649**

Auckland (New Zealand), 2:**649**

Audoin. *See* Hilduin

Auer, Leopold, 2:**649–650**

Auerbach, Abraham ben Selig Avi'ezri, 2:**652**

Auerbach, Arnold Jacob. *See* Auerbach, "Red"

Auerbach, Beatrice Fox, 2:**652**

Auerbach, Berthold, 2:**653**, 13:193

Auerbach, Carl A., 2:**653**

Auerbach, Elias, 2:**653–654**

Auerbach, Ellen Rosenberg, 17:336–337

Auerbach, Ephraim, 2:**654**

Auerbach, Erich, 2:**654**

Auerbach, Frank, 2:**654**

Auerbach, Isaac Eisig ben Isaiah, 2:**654–655**

Auerbach, Isaac Levin, 2:**655**

Auerbach, Israel, 2:**655**

Auerbach, Jacob, German translation of Bible, 3:631

Auerbach, Judith, 18:733

Auerbach, Leopold, 2:**655**

Auerbach, Meir ben Isaac, 2:**655–656**

Auerbach, Menahem Mendel, 2:650

Auerbach, Moses, 2:**652**

Auerbach, Nathan of Satanov, 2:650

Auerbach, Philipp, 2:**656**

Auerbach, "Red," 2:**656–657**

Auerbach, Walter, 17:337

Auerbach, Ẓevi Benjamin, 1:302

Auerbach family, 2:**650–652**, 2 :*651*

Auerbakh, Rachel. *See* Auerbakh, Rokhl

Auerbakh, Rokhl, 2:**657**

Auernheimer, Raoul, 2:**657**

Aufrichtig, Marv Philip. *See* Albert, Marv

Aufrufen, 2:**657**

Aufruf zum Mißtrauen (Aichinger), 1:549

Augsburg (Germany), 2:**657–658**

Augury. *See* Divination

August III. *See* Frederick Augustus II (King of Saxony)

Augustine, 2:**658–659**, 4:720, 9:205–206

Augustow (Poland), 2:**659**

Augustus, 2:**659–660**

   Diaspora, 5:640

   Egyptian Jews, 6:228–229

Augustus III. *See* Frederick Augustus II (King of Saxony)

Auman, Yisrael. *See* Aumman, Robert J.

Aumman, Robert J., 2:**660**

Au nom de l'autre, sur l'antisémitisme qui vient (Finkielkraut), 7:36

Auranitis. *See* Hauran (Syria)

Aurelia Esbus. *See* Heshbon (ancient Israel)

Aurelius, Marcus. *See* Marcus Aurelius Antoninus

Aurich (Germany), 2:**660**

Aurum Coronarium, 2:**661**

Auscha. *See* Ustek (Czech Republic)

Auschwitz (town; Poland). *See* Oswiecim

Auschwitz Bombing Controversy, 2:**673–674**

Auschwitz concentration camp, 2:**661–673**, *671*, 5:358, 9:337–338, 430, 13:159–160

   aerial view, vol. 9: color insert

   child survivors, 9:*488*

   crematorium, 2:663, 664, 667

   gas chambers, 2:664–665, 667

   historiography, 9:420

   Hoess, Rudolf, 9:304–306

   infrastructure, 2:661

   John Paul II's visit to, 11:384

   knowledge of, 2:670

   liberation, 2:672

   living conditions, 2:662–663

   main camp and fence, vol. 9: color insert

   medical experimentation, 2:669–670, 14:47

   orchestras, 14:698

   photographs, 9:*481–482, 488*

   population, 2:662

   Ravensbrueck concentration camp and, 17:121

   selection of prisoners, 2:669, 9:*482*

   transports to, 2:662, 666, 670, 9:*479*

   working conditions, 2:663–664

Auschwitz Convent, 2:**674–675**, 11:384

Auschwitz trials, 2:**676**

Aus der Petersburger Bibliothek (Solomon ben Aaron), 18:769

Aus drei Jahrtausenten (Baeck), 3:51

Ausdruckstanz dance, 5:412–413

Ausgewaehlte Dedicte (Bab), 3:14

Aus Halb-Asien (Franzos), 7:219

Auslaender, Nahum, 2:**677**

Auslaender, Rose, 2:**677**

Auslander, Joseph, 2:**677**

Auspitz, L. A., 3:687

Auspitz, Rudolph, 16:340

Auspitz family, 2:**677–678**

Aussig. *See* Usti Nad Labem

Auster, Daniel, 2:**678**

Auster, Paul, 2:**678**

Austerlitz (Czech Republic), 2:**678–679**

Austerlitz, Friedrich, 16:340

Austin (TX), 2:**679–680**

Australia, 2:**680–688**, *681, 682t*

   antisemitism, 2:687

   cultural and social life

      assimilation, 2:611

      communal centers, 14:7–8

      community organization and structures, 5:108, 110, 119t

      community organizations, 2:686–687

      ḥud Habonim, 9:717t, 719

      journalism in, 11:470

      libraries, 12:786

      literature, 6:717, 12:781

      museums, 14:634

      newspapers, 16:487

      Sephardi Jews, 2:681–682

      synagogues, 2:685–686

   defense, Australia and New Zealand Army Corps, 14:432

   early twentieth century, 2:682–683

   education, 2:685, 6:207–208

   foreign relations with Israel, 2:687

   government officials

      Baume, Peter, 3:220–221

Australia, *continued*
  Cass, Moses Henry, 4:506–507
  Einfeld, Sydney, 6:256
  Isaacs, Sir Isaac Alfred, 10:54–55
  Jews in public life, 2:680–681, 687, 12:619–620
  laws and legal systems
    criminals, 5:480
    law, 11:55, 12:548
    WW II war crimes trials, 20:646–647
    Zionism, 21:580–581
  mid to late twentieth century, 2:684
  nineteenth century, 2:680–681, 14:456
  political theories, parties and organizations, 12:456–457, 749, 16:339–340, 18:706
  population, 2:682t, 683–684
  synagogues, 2:685–686
Australia-Israel Review (periodical). *See The Review* (periodical)
The Australian Aborigines (Elkin), 6:359
Australian Association for Jewish Studies, 2:685
Australian Jewish News (newspaper), 2:686
Australian Victories in France in 1918 (Monash), 14:432
Australian Writers: The Face of Literature (Kahan), 11:708
Austria, 2:**688–702,** 689, 692t, 12:547–548
  1980s, 2:698–699
  1990s and after, 2:699–701
  antisemitism, 2:*217,* 219, 691, 701, 4:224, 5:736 (*See also* Austria-Hungary; *specific cities; specific rulers*)
    badges, Jewish, 2:689
    Carinthia, 4:480
    Charles VI of Hapsburg, 4:576–577
    Eisenstadt, 6:268–269
    references in Catholic literature, 18:168
    Waldheim Affair, 20:602–604
  Counter Reformation-nineteenth century, 2:689–690
  cultural and social life
    archives, 2:408
    community, nature of, 5:110
    journalism, 11:466–467
    libraries, 12:786

  museums, 14:627
  Oesterreichische Nationalbibliothek, 15:384
  seals, use of, 18:227
  economic affairs
    publishing, 16:715–716
    reparations, 6:280–281
  education
    contributions to general, 6:160–161
    Jewish education, 6:177–179, 181–182
  foreign policy and affairs
    Israel, 2:698, 701–702
    Jerusalem, 11:168–169
    reparations, 6:280–281
  Holocaust, 2:693–695
    archives, 2:408
    documentation, resource centers, 9:428
    Dzialoszyce, 6:80
    Ehrlich, Jacob, 6:244
    Sephardim, 18:301
    Styria, 19:279
    Tyrol, 20:220
    war crimes trials, 20:642–643
    Wiener Neustadt, 21:51
  laws and legal systems, 12:548–549
    Code of Regulations Concerning the Jews, 7:342
    emancipation, 6:375, 380, 7:175
    Hapsburg monarchy, 8:342–343
    Middle Ages, 10:820
    war crimes trials, 20:642–643
  Middle Ages, 2:688–689, 10:820
  nineteenth century, 2:690–692, 692t
  political theories, parties and organizations
    Berihah, 3:434
    Blau-Weiss, 3:747
    Christian Social Party, 4:694
    Ehrlich, Jacob, 6:244
    Juedischer Parlamentsklub, 15:652
    Nationalrat, 15:26
    Zionism, 2:691–692
  politicians
    Byk, Emil, 4:323–324
    Ehrlich, Jacob, 6:244
    Heimwehr, 8:770
    Leichter, Kaethe Pick, 12:625
    Pernerstorfer, Engelbert, 15:780–781
    Seipel, Ignaz, 18:254–255

    post-WW I, 2:692–693
    post-WW II, 2:695–698
Austria-Hungary
  antisemitism, anti-Jewish boycotts, 4:109
  laws and legal systems
    emancipation, 12:778–779, 18:683
    Toleranzpatent, 20:29
  political theories, parties and organizations, 16:338, 340–341
    liberalism, 12:778–779
    Oesterreichische-Israelitische Union, 20:249
    Po'alei Zion, 16:245
    Volkspartei, Juedische, 20:574
    Zionism, 21:581–582
  population, 16:395
  printing, publishing, 16:536–537
  resistance and rescue
    Jewish participation in military service, 14:241–242
    pogrom self-defense, 18:263
    self-defense, 18:263
Ausubel, David Paul, 2:**702–703**
Ausubel, Nathan, 2:703
An Authentic Account of the Late Expedition to Bulam (Montefiore), 14:456
The Authoritarian Personality (AJC), 2:56
Authorities. *See* Reshut
Authority, public. *See* Public authority
Authority, rabbinical, 2:**703–705**
  Landrabbiner, 12:474
  Noachide laws, 15:285–286
The Author of Himself. See Mein Leben (Reich-Ranicki)
Autism, early infantile, 11:766
Autobiographies. *See* Biographies and autobiographies
Autobiography of an Adventurer (Lincoln), 13:27
Autocritique (Morin), 14:492
Auto da Fe (Canetti). *See Die Blendung*
Auto da Fé, 2:**705–706,** 18:45
Autoemancipation (Pinsker), 9:247, 11:700, 16:173
Autographs, 2:**706**
Automobile racing, 19:134
Autonomism, 2:**706–707,** 6:37, 7:56
Autonomy, 2:**707–710**
  Diaspora, 5:642
  duty, 6:72, 12:562
  Lesser Poland, 12:664
  Poland, 16:303

Autonomy, judicial, 2:**710–711,**
14:341–344, 16:735–736

Autopsies and dissection, 2:**711–713,**
15:567

Autour du monde fellowships, 11:718

Auvergne (France), 2:**713**

Auxerre (France), 2:**713**

Av, 2:**713–714**

Av, the fifteenth of, 2:**714**

Av, the ninth of, 2:**714–716,** 7:120,
12:446, 13:661–662
    See also Kinah

Avadenka, Lynne, 4:372

Avahu. *See* Abbahu

Avar. *See* Lead

Avazim. *See* Hussites

Av Bet Din, 2:**716–717**

Avco Corporation, 11:772

Avdan, 2:**717**

Avdat I. *See* Obedas I (Arabian king)

Avdat II. *See* Obedas II (Arabian king)

Avdimai of Haifa. *See* Avdimi of Haifa

Avdima of Haifa. *See* Avdimi of Haifa

Avdimi Bar Ḥama, 2:**717**

Avdimi Naḥta. *See* Dimi

Avdimi of Haifa, 2:**717**

Avedah. *See* Lost property

Avedat (Negev), 2:**717–719,** *718*

Avedon, Richard, 2:**719–720,** 16:126

Avel. *See* Abel

Avé-Lallemant, Friedrich Christian
    Benedict, 2:**720**

Avelei Zion, 2:**720–721,** 5:428

Avelim (Israel), 2:**721**

Avelut. *See* Mourning

Avempace, 2:**721–722**

Avenarius. *See* Gabirol, Solomon ben
    Judah, ibn

Avenary, Hanoch, 2:**722,** 8:504

Avendauth, 2:**722**

Avendeath. *See* Avendauth

Avendeuth. *See* Avendauth

Avenger. *See* Blood-avengers

Aventurile domnului Ionel Lăcusta
    Termidor (Aderca), 1:391

Averah, 2:**722**

Averbakh, Leopold Leonidovich,
    2:**722–723**

Avernas de Gras, Baron of. *See* Suasso,
    Antonio Lopez

Averroes, 2:**723–726**
    Albalag, Isaac, 1:582–583
    Alexander of Aphrodisias, 1:628
    allegorical interpretation of
        scripture, 3:645
    angels and, 2:160

categories, 4:524–525
    commentaries by Ibn Shem Tov,
        Joseph ben Shem Tov, 9:690,
        691
    Crescas, Hasdai, 2:266
    Levi Ben Gershom on, 12:698–699

Av ha-Raḥamim, 2:**726**

Avia, 2:**726**

Aviad, Yeshayahu, 2:**726**

Avi'asaf (Eliezer ben Joel ha-Levi of
    Bonn), 6:327

Aviation. *See* Aeronautics

Avi Avi, 2:**726–727**

Avicenna, 2:160, **727–729,** 4:529,
    19:284

Avicenna's Canon. See al-Qānūn fī
    al-Ṭibb

Avida, Yehuda Leib, 2:**729,** 3:611

Avidan. *See* Avdan

Avidan, David, 2:**729–730,** 18:204

Avidom, Menahem, 2:**730**

Avidov, Zvi, 2:**730–731**

Avigad, Naḥman, 2:371, **731,** 11:524

Avigdor (Israel), 2:**731**

Avigdor, Abraham, 2:**731–732**

Avigdor, Abram Bonet. *See* Avigdor,
    Abraham

Avigdor, Bonet Ben Meshullam Ben
    Solomon. *See* Avigdor, Abraham

Avigdor, Jacob, 15:527, 537

Avigdor ben Elijah ha-Kohen, 2:**732**

Avigdor ben Isaac Kara. *See* Kara,
    Avigdor ben Isaac

Avigdor ben Joseph Ḥayyim, 2:**732–**
    733

Avigdor ben Simḥah ha-Levi of
    Glogau, 2:**733**

Avignon (France), 2:**733–734**

Avigur, Shaul, 2:**734–735**

Avigur-Rotem, Gabriela, 2:**735**

Avi ha-Ezri. See My Father Is My Help

Aviḥayil, 2:**735**

Avikhavod. *See* Ichabod

Ávila (Spain), 2:**735–736**

Avila, De family, 2:**736**

Avila, Eliezer ben Samuel ben Moses
    De, 2:**736**

Avila, prophet of, 2:**736**

Avila, Samuel ben Moses, 2:**736–737**

Avimi, 2:**737**

Avimi ben Abbahu, 2:**737**

Avin, 2:**737**

Avina, 2:**737–738**

Avineri, Shlomo, 2:**738**

Avineri, Yitzhak, 2:**738**

Avinoam, Reuven, 2:**738–739**

Avin the Carpenter, 2:**738**

Avinu Malkenu (prayer), 2:**739–740**

Avinu She-ba-Shamayim, 2:**740**

Avira, 2:**740**

Aviram, Joseph, 2:**740**

Avi-Shaul, Mordekhai, 2:**740,** 8:719

Avitus, 2:**741**

Avitzur, Shmuel, 2:**741**

Aviv, Haim, 2:**741**

Avi-Yitzhak, Dan, 2:**741**

Avi-Yonah, Michael, 2:371, **741–742**

Avlona. *See* Valona (Albania)

Avnei Derekh (Luz), 13:278

Avnei Kodesh (Elbaz), 1:260

Avnei Nezer (Sochaczew), 18:704

Avnei Shayish (Abitbol), 1:260

Avnei Yehoshu'a (Falk), 8:735

Avnei Zikkaron (Firkovich), 7:44

Avner. *See* Rosenfeld, Aharon

Avnery, Uri, 2:**742–743,** 4:393

Avnet, John, 2:**743**

Avni, Aharon, 2:**743**

Avni, Haim, 2:**743**

Avni, Tzevi, 2:**743–744**

Avnimos ha-Gardi, 15:383

Avodah, 2:**744–745**

Avodah Zarah, 2:**745–746**

Avodat ha-Bore (Akiva Baer ben
    Joseph), 1:563

Avodat ha-Kodesh (Adret), 1:423

Avodat ha-Levi (Aaron ben Moses ha-
    Levi of Starosielce), 1:216

Avodat ha-Tamid (Habillo), 8:179

Avodat Massa (Joseph ben Saul
    Escapa), 6:488

Avodat Yisrael (Baer), 3:53

Avot, 6:526
    commentaries, 12:714, 18:602

Avot (tractate), 2:**746–750**

Avot de-Rabbi Nathan, 2:**750–751,**
    13:719
        See also Nathan Ha-Bavli

Avot de-Rabbi Nathan (Schechter),
    18:113

Avot nezikin, 2:**751–753**

Avriel, Ehud, 2:**753**

Avrunin, Abraham, 2:**753–754**

Avrutick, Abraham N., 2:**754**

Avshalomov, Aaron, 2:**754**

Avshalomov, Jacob, 2:**754**

Avtalyon, 2:**754–755**
    biblical exegesis and study, 3:641
    God fearers as ancestors of, 11:293
    Shemaiah (1st c. B.C.E.), 18:456

Avtinas family, 2:**755**

Avudama of Haifa. *See* Avdimi of
    Haifa

Avun. *See* Avin

Avvim, 2:**755**

AWACS (Airborne Warning and Control System) aircraft, 2:52

The Awakening of Word Lore: From the Masorah to the Beginnings of Hebrew Lexicography. See Min ha-Masorah el Reshit ha-Milona'ut ha-Irvit

Ax, Emanuel, 2:**755**

Axel, Richard, 2:**755–756**, 13:10–11

Axelrad, Adolf. *See* Axelrad, Avram

Axelrad, Avram, 2:**756**

Axelrod, Albert, 2:**756**

Axelrod, Albie. *See* Axelrod, Albert

Axelrod, Esther. *See* Axelrod, Lubov

Axelrod, George, 2:**756**

Axelrod, Julius, 2:**756–757**, 13:10

Axelrod, Lubov, 2:**757**

Axelrod, Meyer, 2:**757**

Axelrod, Pavel Borisovich, 2:**757–758**, 16:348

Axelrod, Selik, 2:**758**

Axenfeld, Israel, 2:**758**, 9:593

Axiomatik der relativistischen Raum-Zeit-Lehre (Reichenbach), 17:199

Ayalah. *See* Horowitz, Aaron Judah Loeb

Ayalon, Ami, 2:**758–759**

Ayalon, David, 2:**759**

Ayalti, Hanan J., 2:**759**

Ayaluna. *See* Aijalon

Ayanot, 2:**759**

Ayash family, 2:**759–760**

Aydan, David, 2:**760**

Aydin (Turkey), 2:**760**

Ayelet Ha-Shaḥar (newspaper). *See* Jutrzenka

Ayil Meshullash (Elijah ben Solomon Zalman), 6:343, 345

'Ayin, 2:**760**

Ayin, Hillel. *See* Omer, Hillel

Ayin be-Ayin (Mohr), 14:420

Ayllon, Solomon ben Jacob, 2:**760–761**, 8:477, 478
    Joseph della Raina legend, 11:428
    Sheluḥei Erez Israel, 18:451

Ayna (ancient Israel). *See* Ai (ancient Israel)

Aynzamlung (Shamri), 18:395

Ayrton, Hertha, 2:**761**

Ayyal, Ayyalah. *See* Deer

Ayyalon. *See* Aijalon

al-Ayyam (newspaper), 15:597

Ayyash family. *See* Ayash family

Ayyelet ha-Shaḥar, 2:**761**

Ayyubid dynasty, 2:**761–762**

Ayzik Sheftl (Pinski), 16:175

Azancot family, 2:**762**

Azar. *See* Rabinovitz, Alexander Siskind

Azarch, Abraham. *See* Granovsky, Alexander

Azardel, Moses. *See* Abzardiel, Moses

Azarel (Pap), 15:614

Azariah (Book of Daniel), 5:418, 419

Azariah (first c. C.E.), 2:**762**

Azariah (fourth c. C.E.), 2:**762**

Azariah ben Eliyah, 2:**762**

Azariah ben Solomon, 2:**762–763**

Azariah ben Zechariah, 11:**418**

Azarkh, Raïsa Moyseyevna, 2:**763**

Azat Yehoshu'a (Shapira), 18:401

Azazel, 2:**763–764**, 5:573

Azazel rites, 5:492–493

AZC. *See* American Zionist Council

Azeff, Yevno Fishelevich, 2:**764**, 18:707

Azeglio, Massimo Taparelli, Marchese D', 2:**765**

Azekah (Israel), 2:**765**

Az ember tragédiája (Madách), 9:603

Azemmour (Morocco), 2:**765**

Azenberg, Emanuel, 2:**765–766**

Azerbaijan, 2:**766–767**
    Messianic movement in, 6
    Persia, 2:76
    See also Mountain Jews

Azeret, 2:**767**

Azevedo, Moses Cohen D', 2:**768**

Azevedo family, 2:**767**

Azharot (Isaac ben Reuben al-Bargeloni), 6:158

Azharot, Azharah, 2:**768**

Azikri, Eleazar ben Moses, 2:**768–769**

Azilut, 2:**769–770**, 6:374

Aziz, 2:**770**

'Azīz al-, 6:724

Aziz ben Jonah Naim. *See* Naim, Aziz ben Jonah

Azizus (King of Emesa), 6:28

AZJ (periodical). *See Allgemeine Zeitung Des Judentums* (periodical)

Azkari, Eleazar ben Moses. *See* Azikri, Eleazar ben Moses

AZM. *See* American Zionist Movement

Azmon (Israel), 2:**770**

AZMU (American Zionist Medical Unit), 2:60, 8:186

Aznoth-Tabor (Israel), 2:**770**

Azor (Israel), 2:**770–771**

Azores, 2:**771**

Azrach, Abraham, 8:33

Azrail. *See* Angel of Death

Azrieli, David, 2:**771**

Azriel of Gerona, 2:**771–772**, 13:761

Azriel of Shklov. *See* Israel ben Samuel of Shklov

Az Rov Nissim, 2:**772**

A zsidókról (Ballagi), 3:91

Azubib, Joseph ben Nehorai, 2:**772**

Azubib, Saadiah ben Nehorai, 2:272

Azubib family, 2:**772–773**

Azuby, Abraham, 2:**773**

Az új keresztény (Ujvári), 20:232

Azulai (Castilian family), 2:*773*, **773**

Azulai (Italian family), 2:**773**

Azulai, Abraham ben Israel, 2:**774**

Azulai, Abraham ben Mordecai, 2:**774**

Azulai, Ḥayyim Joseph David, 2:77, **774–775**, 3:572, 4:21, 104, 117, 7:16
    Adeni, Solomon bar Joshua, 1:390
    bibliography of, 3:681, 682
    Jacob ben Ḥayyim Joseph Elyashar, 6:371
    Joshua ben Nun, 11:457

Azulai, Mas'ud, 2:**775**

Azzabim (Brenner), 4:160

B

B (letter), 3:5, 4:5

Ba (3rd-4th centuries). *See* Abba (3rd-4th centuries)

Ba (4th-5th centuries). *See* Abba (4th-5th centuries)

Ba Ahmad (Sultan of Morocco), 14:499–500

Baal. *See* Baal worship

Baalah, 3:**5**

Ba'alat ha-Armon (Goldberg), 8:721

Baal-Berith, 3:**5–6**

Ba'al berit milah. *See* Sandak

Ba'alei Asufot (Lattes), 12:519

Ba'alei Mikra. *See* Karaites

Ba'alei Shem. *See* Ba'al Shem

Ba'alei teshuvah, 3:**6–7**

Baal-Gad (ancient Israel), 3:**7**

Ba'al ha-Bayit, 3:**7**

Baal-Hadad. *See* Rimmon

Ba'al ha-Kelim. *See* Laniado, Samuel ben Abraham

Ba'al ha-Kenafayim, 4:62

Ba'al ha-Ma'amarim. *See* Bachrach, Jacob Ben Moses

Ba'al ha-Turim. *See* Jacob ben Asher

Baal Hazor (ancient Israel), 3:**7**

Ba'al he-Arukh. *See* Nathan ben Jehiel of Rome

Baalis (King of Ammon), 2:86, 3:**8**

Baal-Makhshoves, 3:**8**

Baal-Meon (Transjordan), 3:**8**

Baal-Perazim, 3:**8–9**

Ba'al Shem, 3:**9**, 12:466

Ba'al Shem of Bingen. *See* Adam Ba'al Shem

Ba'al Shem of London. *See* Falk, Samuel Jacob Ḥayyim

Ba'al Shem Tov. *See* Israel ben Eliezer Ba'al Shem Tov

Ba'al Shem Tov family, 10:*744*

Baal T'fillah (Baer), 3:52

Ba'al ve-Ishah (Shalev), 18:373

Baal worship, 3:5, 6, **9–12**
    Elijah, 6:331–332, 335
    extermination of, 11:113
    Jezebel, 1:524

Baal-Zephon (Egypt), 3:**13**

Baanah. *See* Rechab and Baanah

Baar, Emil N., 3:**13**

Baar, Herman, 3:**13**

Baasa. *See* Baasha

Baasha, 2:85, 3:**13**

Baaz. *See* Jachin and Boaz (sanctuary pillars)

Baazov, Herzl, 3:**14**

Baazov, Meir, 3:**14**

Bab, Julius, 3:**14**

Babad, Joseph ben Moses, 3:**15**

Babad, Simeon, 3:**15**

Babad family, 3:**14**

Baba ha-Gadol. *See* Baba Rabbah

Babai ben Farhad, 3:**15**

Bābāī ben Farhād, 11:556

Babai ben Luṭf, 3:**15**

Bābāī ben Luṭf of Kashan, 11:555

Bāb al-Abwāb (Caucasus), 3:**16**
    See also Derbent (Caucasus)

Babalikashvili, Nisan, 11:322

Baba Rabbah, 3:**16**

Babatha, 11:524

Babbitt, Milton, 3:**16–17**

Babel, Isaac Emmanuilovitch, 3:**17–19**, 15:380

Babel, Nathalie, 3:18, 19

Babel, Tower of, 3:**19–21**, 4:94

Babilée, Jean, 3:**21**

Babin, Victor, 3:**21–22**

Babi Yar (Kuznetsov), 9:405

Babi Yar (Ukraine), 3:**22–23**, 9:430

"Babi Yar" (Yevtushenko), 3:22, 18:685–686, 21:327

Babovich, Simḥah ben Solomon ben Nahamu, 3:**23**, 7:44, 11:793

Bábszinház (Bródy), 4:201

Babylon (Mesopotamia), 3:**23–24**
    alphabet, Hebrew, 1:698–699, 701*t*, 706, 707, 712*t*

Geonim, 7:380–384, 383*t*, 384*t*

host of heaven, and practices in, 9:567

Sura and Pumbedita, 7:380–384

Tower of Babel, 3:19

See also Exilarch; Nebuchadnezzar

Babylonia, 3:**24–30**
    Abba, 1:225
    academies, 1:347–351, *350*
        alluf, 1:677
        Kairouan, 11:726–727
    agriculture, 1:493–494
    Akkadian language, 1:565–566
    Ammonites, 2:85–86
    amoraim, 2:*89*, 89–95, *91*, 11:708, 12:702–703
    Anilaeus and Asinaeus, 2:164–165
    archives, 2:403, 404
    Borsippa, 4:94
    crowns and wreaths, 5:308
    diaspora, 9:203–204
    education, 6:163–169
    Elam, 6:283
    ethics, 6:535
    exile, 3:25, 6:**608–611**, 9:*180*, 186, 21:488–489
        economic history, 6:98–99
        education during, 6:163
        eschatology, 6:492–493
        Jewish identity and, 11:292
        return from, 6:658, 659
    Hammurapi, 8:309–310
    Jewish community, 3:27–29
    Judeo-Arabic literature in, 11:530–531
    magical prayers, 11:594
    Middle Ages
        education, Jewish, 6:172–173
    Moab, 14:403
    moneylending, 14:438
    monogamy, 14:448
    Nebuchadnezzar, 15:48–49
    Nehardea, 15:59–60
    Nehar Pekod, 15:60
    Neḥutei, 15:65
    population, 16:386
    Rabbinic academies, 3:27–28
    Shalmaneser V, 18:376
    shekel weights, 18:439
    See also Exilarch; Iraq; Mesopotamia; Nebuchadnezzar

Babylonian, the. *See* Nathan Ha-Bavli

Babylonian Aramaic, 2:353–356, 353*t*, 355*t*

Babylonian brothers (Anilaeus and Asinaeus), 11:440

Babylonian dialect. *See* Akkadian language

Babylonian Empire. *See* Babylonia

Babylonian Masorah system, 13:630–633
    contamination of, 13:618
    notations, 13:619–620
    terminology, 13:617–618
    tonal meanings, 13:624
    Torah divisions, 13:607, 609–610
    written symbols, 13:616

Babylonian supralinear punctuation, 3:591

Babylonian Talmud, 5:429, 11:741–742, 13:91, 19:**470–481**, 472*t*, 473*t*
    Aggadah of the Bavli, 19:478–479
    am ha-areẓ, 2:68, 69
    Amidah, 2:76
    amoraim, 2:89, 93, 94, 95, 11:136
    Arakhin, 2:336–337
    Ashi's authorship, 2:565–566
    astrology, 2:617
    baraita, 3:125
    Bava Batra, 3:223–224
    Bava Kamma, 3:224–226
    Bava Metẓia, 3:226–227
    Bavli, 19:470, 475–478
    biblical orthography, 13:612
    commentators
        Rashi, 17:104–105
    Dikdukei Soferim, variant readings of, 17:31
    Eleazar ben Parta, 6:305
    Eliezer ben Hyrcanus, 6:325
    Elisha ben Avuyah, 6:352–354
    Eruvin (tractate), 6:485–486
    Ḥama Bar Bisa, 8:291
    history of interpretation, 19:479–481
    Jacob ben Korshai, 11:34
    Jesus in, 11:249–250
    Johanan ben Nappaḥa, 11:370–372
    Kallah, 11:741–742
    laws and legal systems
        divine punishment, 5:709
    maẓanut in, 13:708
    Megillah, 13:768
    Me'ilah, 13:**775**
    Menaḥ, 14:**27–28**
    Mishnah, 14:328
    mishpat Ivri, 14:337, 346
    mistakes, 14:367
    Niddah, 15:258–259
    prolongation of life, 13:744
    proverbs, 16:647
    rabbinic literature, 19:475–477

Babylonian Talmud, *continued*
Rav, as founder of, 17:117
redaction, 9:206
Resh Lakish, 18:597–598
Samuel, as founder of, 17:117
Semaḥot, 18:273
Sugya, 19:470–475
on Targum Onkelos, 3:590
tractates, 13:667
Babylonische Wanderung (Doeblin), 5:729–730
Bacall, Lauren, 3:30
Bacau (Romania), 3:30–31
Bacchides, 3:31
Bathbasi, siege of, 18:601
Elasa, 6:287
Jonathan the Hasmonean, 11:398
Bacchus. *See* Dionysus, cult of
Bacculus, 13:674
Bach, Aaron J., 14:446
Bach, Carl Philipp Emanuel, 14:542
Bacharach (Germany), 3:31
Bacharach, Abraham Samuel ben Isaac, 3:32
Bacharach, Alfred Louis, 3:32
Bacharach, Benjamin, 3:32, 33
Bacharach, Burt, 3:32
Bacharach, Ephraim Gumbrecht, 3:32
Bacharach, Eva, 3:32–33
Bacharach, Gottschalk of, 3:32
Bacharach, Harry, 3:32, 33
Bacharach, Ḥavvah. *See* Bacharach, Eva
Bacharach, Isaac, 3:32, **33**
Bacharach, Israel, 3:32
Bacharach, Jacob, 3:32
Bacharach, Jair Ḥayyim ben Moses Samson, 3:**33–34**, 6:628, 13:676
Bacharach, Judah Loeb ben Aaron, 3:32
Bacharach, Menachem, 3:32
Bacharach, Moses Samson ben Abraham Samuel, 3:**34**
Bacharach, Naphtali ben Jacob Elhanan, 3:**34–35**
Bacharach, Simon. *See* Bacher, Simon
Bacharach, Tobias ben Joseph Solomon, 3:32
Bacharach family (Europe), 3:**31–32**
Bacharach family (U.S.), 3:32
Bachauer, Gina, 3:**35**
Bache, Jules Semon, 3:**35–36**
Bache family, 3:**35–36**
Bacher, Eduard, 3:**36**
Bacher, Robert Fox, 3:**36**
Bacher, Simon, 3:**36**

Bacher, Wilhelm, 3:**36–37**
aggadah, 1:460
Judeo-Persian literature, 11:558
Bacherach (Germany). *See* Bacharach (Germany)
Bacherach family. *See* Bacharach family
Bachi, Armando, 3:**37**
Bachi, Raphael, 3:**37**
Bachi, Riccardo, 3:**37–38**
Bachi, Roberto, 3:**38**, 18:735
Bachman, Jacob, 3:**38**
Bachrach, Israel, 3:**39**
Bachrach, Jacob ben Moses, 3:**38–39**
Bachrach, Judah ben Joshua Ezekiel, 3:**39**
Bachrach, Moses ben Isaiah Menahem, 3:**39**
Bachrach family. *See* Bacharach family
Bachrich family. *See* Bacharach family
Bârlad (Moldavia). *See* Barlad (Moldavia)
Back, Samuel, 3:**39**
Backer, George, 3:**39–40**
Backman, Jules, 3:**40**
Backofen, Jacob. *See* Reischer, Jacob ben Joseph
BackRub, 4:183
"Back to God" telecast, 11:723
Bacon, Hirsch Leib, 3:**40**, 8:504
Bacon, Isaac, 8:504
Bacon, Israel, 3:**40**
Bacon, Roger, 2:144, 3:**40–41**
Bacon, Shlomo Reuven, 3:**41**
Bacon, Yehuda, 3:**41**
Bacon, Yidel, 3:**41**
Bacrat, Abraham ben Solomon. *See* Levy-Bacrat, Abraham ben Solomon
Bacri, David Coen, 3:**41**
Bacri, Jacob Coen, 3:**42**
Bacri, Jean-Pierre, 3:**42**
Bacri, Joseph Coen, 3:**41–42**
Bacri family, 3:**41**
Bacteriology. *See* Medicine
Baculus Jacobi. *See* Jacob's staff
Bacău (Romania). *See* Bacau (Romania)
Badajoz (Spain), 3:**42**
Badè, William Frederick, 3:**43**
Baden (Germany), 3:**43**, 43–44, 6:363
antisemitism, 9:466
Frederick I, 7:220–221
Baden-Baden (Germany), 9:466
Baden Bei Wien (Austria), 3:**44**
Baden-Durlach (Germany), 3:43, 44
Bader, Gershom, 3:**44–45**

Bader, Gustav. *See* Bader, Gershom
Badge of Shame. *See* Jewish badges
Badges, Jewish. *See* Jewish badges
Badḥan, 3:**48**
Badhav, Isaac ben Michael, 3:**48–49**
Bad Homburg (Germany). *See* Homburg (Germany)
Badiḥi, Yaḥya ben Judah, 3:**49**
Badinter, Elizabeth, 3:**49**
Badinter, Robert, 3:**49–50**
Bādīs (King of Granada), 11:111
Bad Kissingen. *See* Kissingen (Germany)
Bad Koenigswart. *See* Lazne Kynzvart (Czech Republic)
Bad Kreuznach (Germany). *See* Kreuznach (Germany)
Bad Mergentheim. *See* Mergentheim (Germany)
Bad Nauhuheim. *See* Nauheim (Germany)
Bad Nauheim. *See* Nauheim (Germany)
Badt, Hermann, 3:**50**
Badt-Strauss, Bertha, 3:**50**
Baeck, Leo, 3:**50–51**, 11:513
Baeck, Samuel, 3:**52**
Baehr, Aaron. *See* Bennett, Archie
Baena, Juan Alfonso de, 3:**52**
Baena, Juan de. *See* Pineda, Juan de
Baer, Abraham, 3:**52**
Baer, Buddy, 3:53
Baer, Fritz. *See* Baer, Yitzhak
Baer, Gabriel, 3:**52**
Baer, Issachar. *See* Jeiteles, Berthold
Baer, Issachar Falkensohn. *See* Behr, Issachar Falkenstein
Baer, Jacob Henry. *See* Baer, Buddy
Baer, Max, 3:**52–53**
Baer, Max Jr., 3:53
Baer, Seligman Isaac, 3:**53**, 13:653
German translation of Bible by, 3:631
printed editions of Hebrew Bible, 3:587–588
Baer, Simeon Akiva. *See* Akiva Baer ben Joseph
Baer, Yitzhak, 3:**53–54**, 9:160–161
"Ba-Erev" (Feierberg), 6:731
Baer Frankfurter. *See* Joseph Issachar Baer ben Elhanan
Ba'er Heitev. *See* Isaiah ben Abraham
Ba'er Heitev (Isaiah ben Abraham), 10:76–77
Baerwald, Alex, 3:**54**
Baerwald, Moritz, 3:**54–55**
Baerwald, Paul, 3:**55**

Baethgen, Friedrich Wilhelm Adolph, 3:**55**

Baeyer, Adolf Von, 3:**55**

Bag. *See* Goldberg, Baer ben Alexander

Ba Gad (Alfalas), 1:636

Les Bagages de Sable (Langfus), 12:482

Bagely, David, 3:**59–60**

Baghdad (Iraq), 3:**55–59**, 10:15

 Aaron ben Amram and, 1:211

 Aaron Ḥakiman and, 1:211

 Abbasid dynasty, 1:234

 bar mitzvah, 3:165–166

 demography, 10:16

 exilarchate and, 6:605

 exilarchs, 5:466–467, 469

 ḥakham bashi, 8:268

 Jewish quarter, 11:312

 Kazin, Raphael ben Elijah, 12:45

 Netira, 15:113

 Ottoman conquest of, 15:525

 philanthropy in, 11:36–37

Baghdadali, Ezekiel hen Joseph Nissim Menahem. *See* Gabbai, Ezekiel ben Joseph Nissim Menahem

Baghdadli. *See* Gabbai, Ezekiel ben Joseph Nissim Menahem

Baginsky, Adolf Aron, 3:**59**

Bagliar, Joseph, 15:523

Bagoti, 3:**60**

Bagrit, Leon. *See* Bagrit, Sir Leon

Bagrit, Sir Leon, 3:**60**

Bagritski, Eduard Georgiyevitch, 3:**60**

BaḤ. *See* Sirkes, Joel

Bahá'í, 10:650

 Hamadan, 8:293

 holy places in Israel, 9:501, *502*

Ba-Ḥanuto shel Mar Lublin (Agnon), 1:467

Bahaṭ, 16:478

Bahia (Brazil), 3:**60–62**

Bahir, Sefer ha-. *See* Sefer ha-Bahir

Bahlul, Daniel ben Judah, 3:63

Bahlul, Eleazar, 3:64

Bahlul, Samuel, 3:64

Bahlul family, 3:**63–64**

Bahrain (Middle East), 3:**64**

Baḥur, 3:**64**

Baḥur (Levita), 12:731

Baḥurim (Israel), 3:**64**

Baḥur yeshivah, 3:7

Baḥuzim, 3:**64**

Baḥya, 3:**65**

Baḥya ben Asher ben Ḥlava, 3:**65–66**, 645

Baḥya ben Joseph Ibn Paquda, 3:66–67, **66–67**, 6:527–528, 16:81, 106, 198, 489*t*

 beatitude, 3:237

Bible narratives, 7:14

 commandments, reasons for, 5:86–87

 Divine attributes, 19:283–284

 duty, 6:72

 education, 6:173

 free will, 7:231

 God, attributes of, 7:667

 God, nature of, 7:661, 662

 Judeo-Arabic literature and, 11:534, 539

 repentance, 17:222

Baia-Mare (Romania), 3:**67**

Baiersdorf (Germany), 3:**67–68**

Baiersdorf, Samson Solomon, 3:**68**

Baigneux-Les-Juifs (France), 3:**68**

Bail. *See* Suretyship

Bail, Charles Joseph, 3:**68**

Bailees. *See* Shomerim

Bailyn, Bernard, 3:**68–69**

Bairam Ali. *See* Merv (ancient city)

Baitler, Zoma, 3:**69**

Baito Anaia. *See* Bet-Anath (Israel)

Baitos ben Zonin, 3:**69**

Baizerman, Saul, 3:**69**

Baja (Hungary), 3:**69–70**

Bajaya (Algeria). *See* Bougie (Algeria)

Bajjana (Spain). *See* Pechina (Spain)

Bak, Gerson, 3:70

Bak, Israel, 3:71, 8:466

Bak, Jacob, 3:70

Bak, Joseph, 3:70

Bak, Judah, 3:70

Bak, Moses, 3:70

Bak, Nisan, 3:71

Bak, Samuel, 3:71

Bakan, David, 3:72

Bakehouses, communal, 2:39

Bak family (Ashkenazi), 3:70

Bak family (Israel), 3:71

Bakhmut (Ukraine). *See* Artemovsk (Ukraine)

Baki, 3:72

Baking. *See* Cooking and baking

Baking and cooking. *See* Cooking and baking

Bakkashah, 1:438, 439, 617, 3:**72–73**

Bakker-Nort, Betsie, 16:345

Bakl, Mania, 2:87

Bakri. *See* Bacri family

Bakri, Mohammed, 3:73

Bakshi, Ralph, 3:**73–74**

Bakshi-Doron, Eliahu, 3:74

Bakst, Leon, 3:74

Bakst, Nicolai Ignatyetvich, 3:**74–75**

Bakst, Noah. *See* Bakst, Nicolai Ignatyetvich

Baku (Azerbaijan), 3:**75**

Bakunin, MIkhail Aleksandrovich, 3:**75**

Baky, Lázló, 3:**75–76**

Balaam, 3:**76–81**, 11:250–251, 14:401, 528, 536, 545

"The Balaam Pericope," 3:76, 77

Balaban, Barney, 3:**81**

Balaban, Majer. *See* Balaban, Meir

Balaban, Meir, 3:**81–82**

Balabanoff, Angelica, 3:**82–83**

Balabanov, Angelica, 18:713

Balādhurī, 15:419

Balaguer (Spain), 3:**83**

Balak, 3:77, **83**, 14:401

Balance, 3:**83**

Balance à trois (Babilée), 3:21

Balanjar (Caucasus), 3:**83–84**

Balansi, Isaac ben David, 3:679

Balassagyarmat (Hungary), 3:**84**

Baláz, Béla, 3:**84**

Balbo, Michael ben Shabbetai Cohen, 3:**84–85**

Balcon, Michael. *See* Balcon, Sir Michael

Balcon, Sir Michael, 3:**85**

Bal-Dimyen. *See* Shtif, Nokhem

Balearic Islands, 9:795

Balfour, Arthur James, Earl of, 3:**85**, 6:42

Balfour Declaration, 3:**85–89**, 4:722, 6:417, 430, 9:249, 13:148, 20:747

 American Jewish Committee, 2:55

 American Jewry and, 2:45

 Amery, Leopold Charles Maurice Stennet, 2:66

 Biltmore Program and, 3:700

 Churchill White Paper, 10:198

 Frank, Ẓevi Pesaḥ, 7:196

 Montefiore, Claude, 2:162

 Nordau, Max, 15:298

 Ottoman empire and, 15:544–545

 Palestine Inquiry Commissions, 15:582

 Palestine Liberation Organization, 15:591

 San Remo Conference and, 18:26

Balfouriyyah, 3:**90**

Bali, Abraham ben Jacob, 3:**90**

Bali, Moses ben Abraham, 3:**90**

Bali, Rifat, 3:**90**

Balideh, Moses, 3:**90**

Balin, Marty, 3:**90–91**

Baline, Israel. *See* Berlin, Irving

Balint, Michael, 3:**91**

Balkans

 community, nature of, 5:110–111

Balkans, *continued*
  Congress of Berlin, 3:453–454,
    6:381–382
  eighteenth-early nineteenth
    century
      education, Jewish, 6:183–184
  emancipation, 6:381
  Ladino newspapers, 16:495
  Middle Ages
    agriculture, Jewish, 1:495
Balkan Wars (1912-1913), 18:315
Balkh, 3:**91**
Ballagi, Mór, 3:**91**, 632
Ballarat (Australia), 3:**92**
Ballas, Dalia. *See* Itzik, Dalia
Ballas, Shimon, 3:**92**, 15:473
Ballet, 5:412
  choreographers, 13:667
    Eifman, Boris, 6:253
    Lewitzky, Bella, 12:770
    Lichine, David, 12:795–796
    Schubert, Lia, 18:168–169
  Espinosa, Edouard, 6:508
  European, 5:444, 12:479
  Hayden, Melissa, 8:475
  Levinson, Andre, 12:722–723
  Ordman, Jeanette, 15:463
  Plisetskaya, Maya, 16:238
Ballin, Albert, 3:**92–93**
Ballin, Joel, 3:**93**
Ballin, Moegens, 3:**93**
Ballin, Samuel Jacob, 3:**93**
Ballmer, Steve, 3:**93–94**
Bally, Davicon, 3:**94**
Bally, Isaac David, 3:**94**
Balm. *See* Balsam
Balm (plant), vol. 16: color insert
Balmes, Abraham ben Meir de, 3:**94–
  95**, 13:42–43
Balmes, Abraham de, 3:**94**, 4:52
Balm for the Body (Falaquera). *See*
  Zori ha-Guf
Balogh, Thomas, Baron, 3:**95**
Balsam, 3:**95–96**, 15:396
Balshazzar, 5:420
Balta (Ukraine), 3:**96**
Baltassar. *See* Belteshazzar
Baltazar, Camil, 3:**96**
Baltic states
  emancipation, 6:385
  Latvia, 12:520–524
Baltimore (MD), 3:**97–100**
  Baltimore Ravens football team,
    14:407
  Meyerhoff, Harvey, 14:151–152
  pioneer Jews, 6:542–543

Baltimore, David, 3:**100**, 13:9
Baltimore Bargain House, 3:98
Baltimore Hebrew University (MD),
  3:98, **100–101**, 11:776
Balyash family. *See* Palache family
Bamah. *See* Cult Places, Israelite
Bamberg (Germany), 3:**101**, 778
Bamberg, Israel of. *See* Israel of
  Bamberg
Bamberg, Samuel ben Baruch, 3:**101–
  102**
Bamberger, Bernard Jacob, 3:**102**
Bamberger, Edouard-Adrien, 3:**102**
Bamberger, Eugen, 3:**102**
Bamberger, Fritz, 3:**102**
Bamberger, Heinrich Von, 3:**103**
Bamberger, Isaac Dov ha-Levi. *See*
  Bamberger, Seligmann Baer
Bamberger, Louis, 3:**103**, 6:513
Bamberger, Ludwig, 3:**103**, 725, 726,
  12:778, 16:344
Bamberger, Moses Loeb, 3:104
Bamberger, Moses Loeb II, 3:104
Bamberger, Moses Loeb III, 3:104
Bamberger, Nathan, 3:104
Bamberger, Seckel (1863-1934), 3:104
Bamberger, Seckel Isaac, 3:104
Bamberger, Selig, 3:104
Bamberger, Seligmann Baer, 3:**103**,
  15:493
Bamberger, Simon, 3:**105**
Bamberger, Simon Simḥ, 3:104
Bamberger, Simon Simḥ II, 3:104
Bamberger, Simon Simḥ III, 3:104
Bamberger, Solomon, 3:104
Bamberger, Solomon Memaḥem,
  3:104
Bamberger family, 3:104
Bambus, Willy, 3:**105**
Ba-Meh Madlikin, 3:**105**
Ba-Mishol ha-Ẓar (Kabak), 11:584
Banai, Ehud, 3:106
Banai, Evyatar, 3:106
Banai, Gavri, 3:106, 8:206–207
Banai, Meir, 3:106
Banai, Orna, 3:106
Banai, Yossi, 3:105–106
Banai, Yuval, 3:106
Banai family, 3:**105–106**
Bana'im, 18:232
Banat (Romania), 3:**106–107**
Band, Arnold, 3:**107**
  Agnon, Shmuel Yosef, 1:468
  on Jewish studies, 11:317–318
Bandera, Stefan, 4:86
Bandes, Louis E. *See* Miller, Louis E.

Bandman, Daniel, 14:454
Banet, Aber, 3:107
Banet, Fradl, 3:107
Banet, Jacob, 3:107
Banet, Johanan, 3:107
Banet, Mordecai ben Abraham, 3:**107–
  108**, 4:156
Banet, Mordecai ben Yom Tov, 3:107
Banet, Naphtali ben Mordecai, 3:**108**
Banet family, 3:**107**
Baneth, David Hartwig, 3:108
Baneth, Eduard Ezekiel, 3:108
Baneth, Ezekiel ben Jacob, 3:**108–109**
Baneth family, 3:**108**
  See also Banet family
Banias (ancient Israel), 3:**109**, 9:40
Banishment, 3:**109–111**
Banja Luka, 3:**111**
Bank Hapoalim, 10:579, 587, 590, 601
Banking and bankers, 3:**111–119**
  Aaron ben Amram, 1:211–212
  Abbasid dynasty, 1:234
  antiquity, 3:111
  Benwaish, Abraham, 3:386
  Bischhoffsheim family, 3:724–725
  Blank, Maurice, 3:739
  Blumenthal, George, 4:12
  Blum Pasha, 4:7
  Boas family, 4:20–21
  in Bologna, 4:48
  Borovoy, Saul, 4:92
  brokers, 4:203–204
  Camondo family, 4:382
  cooperatives, 5:206
  Credit Mobilier, 15:759
  Denmark
    Adler, David Baruch, 1:396
  Dreyfus family, 6:18
  economic history, 6:103, 107, 113
  Egypt
    Harari, Sir Victor Raphael,
      8:345
  England, 6:411–413
    Benas, Baron Louis, 3:319
  Europe
    Jewish Colonization
      Association, 11:286
    Mendelsohn and Co., 14:31
  Fraenkel, Louis, 7:145
  Germany
    Bamberger, Ludwig, 3:103
    Itzig, Daniel, 10:818–819
    Riesser, Jacob, 17:296
  Hallgarten family, 8:281
  Hambros, 8:295

Holocaust restitution, 6:280–281,
18:637
Israel
Dickenstein, Abraham, 5:645–
646
Hoofien, Eliezer Sigried,
9:521
Levontin, Zalman David,
12:744–745
Mizrachi, 14:391–392
Italy
Forlì, 7:129–130
monti di pietà, 14:461
Ravenna, 17:120
Rieti family, 17:296–297
Jewish Colonial Trust, 11:**285**
Kaskel family, 11:822
Ladenburg, Wolf Hayum, 12:427
Lánczy, Léo, 12:456
Landau, Eugen, 12:459
Luzzatto family, 18:10
Middle Ages
the caliphate, 3:111–112
Conversos, 3:113–114
Holy Roman Empire, 3:114
Italy, 3:114, 10:778–799, 16:6
merchants, 3:112
moneylenders, 3:112–113
women bankers, 3:115
Morawitz, Karl Ritter von, 14:478
Netherlands
Lehren family, 12:616–617
in New York City, 15:203, 225–
226
nineteenth and twentieth
centuries, 3:115
merchant bankers, 3:115–116
Russia and Eastern Europe,
3:116–117
Scandinavia and the
Netherlands, 3:117
U.S., 3:117–119, 15:761
Oppenheim family, 15:443
Orvieto, 15:500
in Ottoman empire, 15:525, 532–
533, 542
Padua, 15:566
in Parma, 15:652–653
Poland
Lewko, Jordanis, 12:770
Raisman, Sir Jeremy, 17:75
Rathenau, Walther, 17:110–111
Ratshesky Abraham Captain,
17:114
Ravay, Joseph, 17:119
Recanati, Leon, 17:141–142
role and influence of Jewish
bankers, 3:119

Rosen, Mathias, 17:429
Rosenbloom, Solomon, 17:442–
443
Rothschild, Nathaniel Charles
Jacob, 17:494
Rothschild Bank, 16:20
Russia
Barbash, Samuel, 3:140
Horodischtsh, Leon, 9:528
ṣarrāf, 18:61
Turkey
Carmona, Bekhor Isaac
David, 4:486
U.K.
Cassel, Ernest Joseph, 4:508
U.S., 3:117–119
Becker family, 3:244
Belmont, August, 3:301
Lazard family, 12:558
Lehman, Herbert Henry,
12:613–614
Levitan, Solomon, 12:732
See also Financiers; Moneylending;
Obligations, law of
Bank Leumi le-Israel, 3:180, 10:547,
579, 587, 590
Bank notes, Israeli, 5:55
See also Coins and currency
Bank of Israel (BOI), 5:54, 7:55–56,
10:551–553, 570–573, 579, 581–586,
590
The Bankrupts (Glanville), 6:438
Banners, 3:**119–120**
Banning. *See* Ḥerem
Bannus, ascetic, 2:547–548
Bánóczi, József, 3:120
Bánóczi, Lázló, 3:120
Bánóczi family, 3:**120**
Banon, Jacob, 16:346
Banska, Bystrica (Slovakia), 3:**120**
Bántomlács (Romania). *See* Talmaciu
(Romania)
Banū al-Aghlab. *See* Aghlabids dynasty
Banu Hafs. *See* Hafsids
Banu- Marin. *See* Merinids
Banus, 3:**120**
Banus, Maria, 3:**120–121**
Banū Sa'd family. *See* Sa'dis family
Banu Wattas. *See* Wattasid dynasty
Banu Ziyan. *See* Ziyanid dynasty
Banya Luka. *See* Banja Luka
Baptism, 11:381
Baptism, forced. *See* Forced Baptism
Bāqā al-Gharbbiyya (Israel), 3:**122–
123**
Bāqā al-Sharqiyya (Israel), 3:122–123
Ba'qūba (Iraq), 3:**123**

Bar (Ukraine), 3:**123**
Bar, Shlomo, 3:**123**
Bara, Theda, 3:**123–124**
Baracs, Károly, 3:**124**
Bar-Adon, Pesah, 11:524
Baraita (of *Sifra*), 18:561
Baraita, Baraitot, 3:**124–128**, 21:523
Midreshei Halakhah, 14:196
Sifra, 18:561
Baraita de-Melekhet ha-Mishkan, 3:**128**
Baraita de-Niddah, 3:**128–129**, 15:256
Baraita de-Rav Adda (Adda bar
Ahavah), 1:384
Baraita of 32 Rules, 3:**129**, 6:329
Baraita of 49 Rules. See Mishnat ha-
Middot
Barak (biblical figure), 3:**129–130**,
8:361, 9:170, 11:563–564
Barak, Aharon, 3:**130–131**, 14:358–
359, 362, 20:466–468
Barak, Ehud, 3:**131–132**, 266, 10:250
American Israel Public Affairs
Committee, 2:51
government of, 10:459–460, 459*t*
Palestinian Authority and, 15:599
Sharansky, Natan and, 18:412
Sharon, Ariel and, 18:417
Shas (political party) and, 18:419
Bar-am, Micha, 3:**132**
Baram, Moshe, 3:**132**
Baram, Uzi, 3:**133**
Baranga, Aurel, 3:**133**
Baranovichi (Belarus), 3:**133–134**
Baranowicz, David Eliezer, 3:**134**
Baranowicze (Belarus). *See*
Baranovichi (Belarus)
Bárány, Robert, 3:**134**
Barasch, Julius, 3:**134–135**, 6:399
Barasch, Moshe, 3:**135**
Barasch Judah. *See* Barasch, Julius
Barash, Asher, 3:**135–137**
Barash, Ephraim, 3:**137**, 568, 569
Bar-Asher, Moshe, 3:**137**
Baratz, Hermann, 3:**137–138**
Baratz, Hirsch. *See* Baratz, Hermann
Baratz, Joseph, 3:**138**
Barazani, Asenath, 3:**138**, 15:525
Barazani, Moshe, 3:**138**
Barazani, Samuel ben Nethaniel Ha-
Levi, 3:**138–139**
Barbados (Caribbean), 2:41, 3:**139**,
4:473
Barbara, 3:**139–140**
Bar bar Huna. *See* Rabbah bar Huna
Barbarians, 3:**140**
Barbarossa. *See* Frederick I (Holy
Roman Emperor)

Barbary States. *See* Africa
Barbash, Samuel, 3:**140**
Barbastro (Spain), 3:**140**, 14:466–467
Barbie, Klaus, 13:297
Barbie, Nikolaus. trial of, 3:**141**
Barbie dolls, 8:320
Barby, Meir ben Saul, 3:**141–142**
Barcelona (Spain), 3:**142–145**, 146, 17:127
Barcelona, Disputation of. *See* Disputation of Barcelona
Barcelona, Isaac ben Reuben of. *See* Al-Bargeloni, Isaac ben Reuben
Barcinsky, Henryk, 3:**146**
Barczinsky, Henoch. *See* Barcinsky, Henryk
Bard, Basil Joseph Asher, 3:**147**
Bardach, Israel, 3:**147**
Bardaki, Isaiah ben Issachar Ber, 3:**147**
Bardanashvilli, Josef, 3:**147**
Bar-Daroma, Ḥayyim Ze'ev, 3:**147–148**
Bardejov (Slovakia), 3:**148**
Bar Derora. *See* Liebermann, Aaron Samuel
Bardin, Shlomo, 3:**148–149**, 4:124
Bardiya, 4:379
Bar 'Ebhraya, Johanan. *See* Bar Hebraeus, Johanan
Bareheadedness. *See* Head, covering of
Barekhi nafshi, 3:**149**
Barekhu, 3:**149**
Barenboim, Daniel, 3:**149–150**, 6:51
Bārforush (Iran), 13:704–705
Bargas, Abraham de, 3:**150**
Bargeloni, Judah ben Barzillai al-. *See* Judah ben Barzillai al-Bargeloni
Barghuti, Marwan, 15:600
Bar Giora, Simeon, 3:**150–151**, 11:383
Bar-Giora society, 8:382
Bar Hebraeus, Johanan, 2:17, 3:**151**, 599
Bar Hediya, 3:**151–152**
Bar-Hillel, Yehoshua, 3:**152**
Bar Hiyya, Abraham, 2:618
Bari (Italy), 3:**152**
Bar-Ilan, David, 3:**153**
Bar-Ilan, Meir, 3:**153**, 8:497, 14:390–392
Bar-Ilan Responsa Project, 5:131–132
Bar-Ilan University, 3:**153–154**, 14:391
Barishansky, Raphael, 3:154
Barit, Jacob, 3:**154–155**
Barjanski, Alexander, 18:762
Bar-Josef, Ofer, 3:**193**
Bar-Josef, Yehoshua, 3:**193**
Bar-Josef, Yosef, 3:193

Barkai (Israel), 3:**155**
Bar Kalba Savu'a. *See* Ben Kalba Savu'a
Bar Kappara, 3:**155–156**, 18:597–598
    Judah ha-Nasi, 3:156, 11:504
    parodies of, 15:655
Barkat, Reuven, 3:156
Bar Kochba Association, 3:156
Bar Kokhba (d. 135), 3:**156–162**, 9:202
    Bethar, 3:527–528
    letters, 12:669–670
Bar Kokhba revolt, 3:*158*, 158–162, *159*, 18:573, 20:628
    Ben Kosebat letters, 14:617
    coinage, 5:50–51
    Israel (ancient), 10:148–151
    Julius Severus, 11:575
    Lag ba-Omer and, 12:437
    Palestine (Roman), 10:148–151
Bar Kokhva (Halkin), 8:275
Bar Kozeva. *See* Bar Kokhba
Bar Kozevah. *See* Bar Kokhba
Barlaam and Josaphat. *See* Ben ha-Melekh ve-ha-Nazir
Barlach, Ernst, 15:289
Barlad (Moldovia), 3:**162**
Bar-le-Duc (France), 3:**162**
Bar-Lev, Haim, 3:**162–163**
Barley, 3:**163**, 7:93, vol. 16: color insert
Barlin, Frederick William, 3:**163**
Barlow, Samuel, 8:366
Barmas, Issay, 3:**163–164**
Bar Mitzvah, Bat Mitzvah, 3:**164–167**, 11:778, 13:139
    Barukh she-petarani, 3:192
    haftarah, 8:198–200
    mitzvot, 14:372
    photographs of, 16:128, vol. 3: color insert
Barna, Victor, 3:**167**
Barnacle Goose myths, 3:**167**
Barnard, Christaan, 18:168
Bar-Nash. *See* Schapira, Noah
Barnato, Barney, 3:**167–168**, 11:365, 377, 16:349
Barnay, Ludwig, 3:**168**
Barnea, Ezra, 3:**168**
Barnea, Nahum, 3:**168**
Barnert, Nathan, 3:**168**, 15:686
Barnet, Dov Ber. *See* Ross, Barney
Barnet, Jacob, 3:**318**
Barnet, Will, 3:**169**
Barnett, Bernhard. *See* Beer, Bernhard
Barnett, Charles, 16:349
Barnett, Joel, Baron, 3:**169**

Barnett, John, 3:**169**
Barnett, John Francis, 3:**169**
Barnett, Lewis Edward. *See* Barnett, Sir Lewis Edward
Barnett, Lionel David, 3:**169**
Barnett, Richard David, 2:371, 3:**169–170**
Barnett, Sir Lewis Edward, 3:**170**
Barnett, Zerah, 3:**170**
Barnowsky, Viktor, 3:**170**
Barnston, Henry, 3:170
Baron, Bernhard, 3:**171**
Baron, David. *See* Pinter, Harold
Baron, Devorah, 3:**171**
Baron, Joseph Alexander, 3:**171–172**
Baron, Joseph Louis, 3:**172**
Bar-On, M. Y., 15:662
Baron, Salo Wittmayer, 3:**172–173**
    American Academy for Jewish Research, 2:47
    American Jewish Historical Society, 2:59
    Blau, Joseph Leon, 3:743
    Jewish studies in American universities, 11:317
Baron, Shalmo Wittmayer. *See* Baron, Salo Wittmayer
Baron d'Auvernas le Gras. *See* Suasso, Antonio Lopez
Baron de Hirsch Fund, 3:**173**, 695
Barondess, Joseph, 3:**173**, 15:205
Baroness Oppenheim-Barnes. *See* Oppenheim, Sally
Baron Taylor of Gosforth. *See* Taylor, Sir Peter Murray
Baron von Sparzenstein. *See* Ricius, Paulus
Baroque period
    Italian literature, 10:791–792
    Lamentations, Book of, 12:450
Baroto. *See* Beirut
Baroto (Lebanon). *See* Beirut
Barou, Noah, 3:**173–174**
Barouch, André, 16:346
Bar Pada. *See* Judah ben Pedaya
Barr, Roseanne, 3:**174**
Barranquilla (Colombia), 5:62–63
Barrassa, Jacob, 3:**174**
Barrenness and fertility, 2:532–533, 3:**174–175**, 6:692
Barrés, Auguste Maurice, 3:**175**
Barrett, David, 3:**175–176**, 4:186–187, 187, 16:341
Barrios, Daniel Levi De, 3:**176–177**, 6:69
Barrios, Miguel de, 6:446
Barris, Chuck, 3:**177**

Barron, Jennie, 3:**177**

Barron, Milton, 18:733

Barros Basto, Arturo Carlos de, 3:**177–178,** 15:441

Barroso, Gustavo, 4:149–150

Barruel, Augustin, 3:**178**

Barshai, Rudolf, 3:**178**

Barshefsky, Charlene, 3:**178–179**

Barsimon, Jacob, 3:**179,** 15:195

Bart, Lionel, 3:**179**

Barter. *See* Ḥalifin

Bartfa (Slovakia). *See* Bardejov (Slovakia)

Bartfeldt (Slovakia). *See* Bardejov (Slovakia)

Barth, Aharon, 3:**180**

Barth, Eliezer, 3:**180**

Barth, Jacob, 3:**179**

Barth, Karl, 3:**180,** 651

Bartholdy, Jacob, 3:**180**

Bartolocci, Giulio, 2:37, 3:**180–181,** 681, 8:514

Bartov, Hanoch, 3:**181,** 8:704

Bar Tuvia. *See* Fraenkel, Faiwel

Bar Tuviah. *See* Fraenkel, Faiwel

Baruch (kabbalists), 3:**182–183**

Baruch (scribe), 3:**181–182**

Baruch, Adam, 3:**184**

Baruch, Apocalypse of. See Apocalypse of Baruch

Baruch, Bernard, 3:**183–184**

Baruch, Book of, 3:**185–186,** 11:129, 131–132

Baruch, Franziska, 4:369

Baruch, Greek Apocalypse of. See Greek Apocalypse of Baruch

Baruch, Jacob ben Moses Ḥayyim, 3:**186–187**

Baruch, Joseph Marcou, 3:**187,** 4:276

Baruch, Judah, 15:542

Baruch, Kosman ben Josef, 2:38

Baruch, Loeb. *See* Boerne, Ludwig

Baruch, Paul. *See* Bekker, Paul

Baruch, Rest of the Words of. See Rest of the Words of Baruch

Baruch, Simon, 3:**183**

Baruch Ashkenazi, 3:83

Baruch ben David Yavan, 3:**188**

Baruch ben Isaac Mitrani, 6:149

Baruch ben Isaac of Aleppo, 3:**188**

Baruch ben Isaac of Regensburg, 3:**188**

Baruch ben Isaac of Worms, 3:**189**

Baruch ben Jehiel of Medzibezh, 3:**189**

Baruch ben Samuel, 3:**189–190**

Baruch ben Samuel of Aleppo, 3:**190**

Baruch ben Samuel of Mainz, 3:**190**

Baruch ben Samuel of Pinsk, 8:474

Baruch family, 3:**183–184**

Baruch of Arezo, 18:354

Baruch of Greece. *See* Baruch ben Samuel of Aleppo

Baruch (ben Abraham) of Kosov, 3:**190–191**

Baruch of Medzibezh. *See* Baruch ben Jehiel of Medzibezh

Baruch Shei'aḥ Togarmi, 3:**182–183**

Baruch the Kabbalist, 3:**182–183**

Baruch the Sephardi. *See* Baruch ben Samuel of Aleppo

Baruh, Armand, 4:276

Baruh, Bora, 3:**191**

Baruh, Victor, 4:276

Baruj Spinoza (Dujovne), 6:43

Baruk, Henri, 3:**191**

Barukh, 3:**191**

Barukh ben Isaac, 1:613

Barukh she-Amar, 3:**191–192**

Barukh Shem, 18:454

Barukh shem kevod malkhuto le-olam va-ed, 3:**192**

Barukh she-petarani, 3:**192**

Barukh Spinoza u-Zemanno (Sokolow), 18:749

Barukh Ta'am (Fraenkel-Teomim), 7:145

Bar-Yehudah, Israel, 3:**192–193**

Barylko, Jaime, 3:**193**

"Bar Yoḥai Nimshaḥta Ashrekha" (Labi), 12:408

Bar-Yosef, Rivka, 18:737

Bar-Yosef, Y., 8:720

Barzel. *See* Iron

Barzilai, Giuseppe, 3:**194**

Barzilai, Salvatore, 3:**194**

Barzilai, Yehoshua, 3:**194**

Barzilai family, 3:**194**

Barzilay, Isaac E., 2:47

Barzillai (biblical figures), 3:**194**

Barzillai of Abel-Meholah, 3:**194**

Barzillai the Gileadite, 3:**194,** 18:755

Basal. *See* Basle (Switzerland)

Basar. *See* Flesh

Basar va-Dam. *See* Flesh

Basar va-Dam (Shenhar), 18:459

Basch, Henry, 15:677

Basch, Jacob, 15:676

Basch, Victor Guillaume, 3:**194–195**

Baschko, Ẓevi Hirsch ben Benjamin, 3:**195**

Baseball, 1:325–326, 19:134–136

Allen, Mel, 1:667–668

Berg, Moe, 3:416–417

Boudreau, Lou, 4:105

Daniel, Dan, 5:425

Dreyfuss, Barney, 6:20–21

Green, Shawn David, 8:66–67

Greenberg, Henry Benjamin, 8:69–70

Holtzman, Kenneth Dale, 9:498

Patkin, Max, 15:688

Paul, Gabriel Howard, 15:695

Pike, Lipman Emanuel, 16:152

Reese, Jimmie, 17:162

Reinsdorf, Jerry, 17:210

Rosen, Albert Leonard, 17:427

Schacht, Alexander, 18:98–99

Selig, Allan H., 18:265

Shamsky, Arthur Louis, 18:395

Sherry, Lawrence, 18:465

Sherry, Norman Burt, 18:465

Basevi, Abraham, 3:**195**

Basevi, Abramo, 3:**195**

Basevi, Emanuele, 3:**195**

Basevi, Gioacchino, 3:**195**

Basevi, James Palladio, 3:**195**

Basevi, Joseph, 3:**195**

Basevi, Maria. *See* Disraeli, Maria

Basevi, Naphtali. *See* Basevi, Nathan

Basevi, Nathan, 3:**195**

Basevi, Nathanel, 3:**195**

Basevi Cervetto. *See* Basevi family

Basevi Cervetto, Jacob. *See* Cervetto, Jacob Basevi

Basevi della Gondola. *See* Basevi family

Basevi family, 3:**195–196**

Bash. *See* Basevi family

Bashan (Israel). *See* Bozrah (Israel)

Bashan region (Israel), 3:*196*, **196–197,** 10:130, 131, 11:814

Bashevi, Maria. *See* Disraeli, Maria

Bashevis, Isaac. *See* Singer, Isaac Bashevis

Bashiri, Yahya, 3:**197**

Bashrav (Ehrlich), 6:242

Bashyazi, Moses, 3:**198**

Bashyazi family, 3:**197–198**

Basic Black with Pearls (Weinzweig), 20:729

Basic Law: Freedom of Occupation of 1992, 14:359–360

Basic Law: Human Dignity and Freedom of 1992, 14:359–360

Basilea, Solomon Aviad Sar-Shalom, 3:**199**

Basil I (Byzantine emperor), 3:**198–199,** 4:327

Basilica, 3:**199**

Baṣīr, Joseph ben Abraham ha-Kohen Haro'eh al-, 3:**200,** 11:425, 532, 790

Basketball, 19:136–138
  announcing, 7:638
  Berenson, Senda, 3:412
  Berkowitz, Mickey, 3:440
  Brody, Tal, 4:202, 14:392
  Brown, Herb, 4:215
  Brown, Lawrence H., 4:215
  Dallas Mavericks, 5:326
  Gottlieb, Edward, 8:10–11
  Grunfeld, Ernie, 8:112
  Harrison, Lester, 8:366
  Holman, Nathan, 9:323–324
  Holzman, William "Red," 9:503–504
  Klein, Ralph, 12:225
  Lieberman, Nancy Elizabeth, 12:805–806
  Litwack, Harry, 13:142
  Mizrachi, Shimon, 14:392
  Podoloff, Maurice, 16:253
  Reinsdorf, Jerry, 17:210
  Rosen, Yehoshua, 17:431
  Rudolph, Marvin, 17:525
  Saperstein, Abraham M., 18:34
  Saracheck, Bernard, 18:40–41
  Schayes, Adolph, 18:112
  Sedran, Barney, 18:237
Basket tax, 5:242
Baskin, Judith, 3:**200–201**
Baskin, Leonard, 3:**201**
Basle (Switzerland), 3:**201–202**
Basle Program, 3:**202–203**, 15:298
Basman, Ben-Hayim, Rivke, 3:**203–204**
Basnage, de Beuval. *See* Basnage, Jacques Christian
Basnage, Jacques Christian, 3:**204**, 16:629
Basola, Moses ben Mordecai, 2:141, 3:**204–205**
Basola, Moses II, 3:204–205
Basola, Moses III, 3:204–205
Basque language, 3:636
Basra (Iraq), 3:**205–206**
Baṣri, Meer, 3:**206**, 15:473
Bass, Hyman B., 3:**206**
Bass, Shabbetai ben Joseph, 3:**206**, 681, 6:77–78
Bassan, Abraham Hezekiah ben Jacob, 3:**206–207**
Bassan family. *See* Bassano family
Bassani, Giorgio, 3:**207**, 10:794
Bassani, Marco. *See* Bassani, Mordecai
Bassani, Mordecai, 3:**207**, 208
Bassani family. *See* Bassano family
Bassano (Italy), 3:**207–208**
Bassano, Isaiah ben Israel Hezekiah, 3:208

Bassano, Israel Benjamin, 3:208
Bassano family, 3:**208**
Bassermann, Albert, 4:118
Bassevi of Treuenberg, Jacob, 3:**208–209**, 4:39, 9:6
Bassin, Moses, 3:**209**
Bassin, Moyshe. *See* Bassin, Moses
Bassista, Shabbetai ben Joseph. *See* Bass, Shabbetai ben Joseph
Bassola, Moses ben Mordecai. *See* Basola, Moses ben Mordecai
Bassora (Iraq). *See* Basra (Iraq)
Bassus, Lucilius, 3:**209**
Basta. *See* Baza (Spain)
Basta (Spain). *See* Baza (Spain)
Bastard. *See* Mamzer
Bas Tovim, Sarah, 3:**209**, 7:50
Batalyawsi, Abu Muhammad Abdallah Ibn Muhammad Ibn Al-Sid Al-, 3:**210**
Batanea. *See* Bashan region (Israel)
Bat Avin (Abraham Dov Baer of Ovruch), 1:311
Bat-Dor Dance Company. *See* Batsheva and Bat-Dor dance companies
Bate, Julius, 3:**210**
Ba-Teva (Solodar), 18:754
Bath (England), 3:**210**
Bath, bathing, 3:**210–211**
  See also Mikveh
Bat Ḥefer, 3:**211**
Bath-Sheba, 1:545, 3:**211–212**, 5:452–453, 457, 458, 18:755
Bathyra (Syria), 3:**212**
Bathyra, sons of, 3:**212**
Batista, Fulgencio, 5:323
Bat Kol, 3:**213**
Batlanim, 3:**213**
Batman (comic strip), 11:760–761
Batman (motion picture), 6:315
Bat-Miriam, Yokheved, 3:**213–214**
Bat Mitzvah. *See* Bar Mitzvah, Bat Mitzvah
Bato, Ludwig Yomtov, 3:**214**
Baton Rouge (LA), 13:224
Bats, 3:**209–210**
Bat Shelomo, 3:**214**
Bat-Sheva. *See* Basevi family
Batsheva and Bat-Dor dance companies, 3:**214–215**
Battat, Reuben, 3:**215**
Battei ha-Nefesh ve ha-Lḥashim (Levi), 12:697
The Battiad (Mendes), 6:437
Battle of al-Qaṣr al-Kabīr of 1578. *See* Battle of the Three Kings of 1578

Battle of Cable Street (England), 3:**215**
Battle of the Three Kings of 1578, 14:497
Battleship Potemkin (motion picture), 6:274
Batumi (Georgia), 3:**215**
Bat yaʿanah, 15:550
Bat Yam (Israel), 3:**215–216**, vol. 21: color inserts
Baudissin, Wolf Wilhelm, Graf von, 3:**216**
Bauer, Bruno, 3:**216**, 9:232
Bauer, Felice, 11:704–705
Bauer, Hans, 3:**216**, 13:58
Bauer, Jacob, 3:**217**
Bauer, Lina. *See* Morgenstern, Lina
Bauer, Marion Eugenie, 3:**217**
Bauer, Otto, 3:**217**, 16:340, 18:705, 715, 729
Bauer, Simon Harvey, 3:**218**
Bauer, Yehudah, 3:**218–219**
Bauernfreund, Jakub. *See* Bornfriend, Jacob
Bauhaus, 4:172, 14:420
Baum, Father Gregory, 4:681
Baum, Herbert, 3:**219**
Baum, Menaḥem ben Aaron of Kamenetz, 3:**219**
Baum, Morton, 3:**220**, 15:220
Baum, Oscar, 3:**220**
Baum, Shepard, 3:**220**
Baum, Vicki, 3:**220**
Bauman, Zygmunt, 3:**220**
Baumann, Gustav, 3:769
Baumann, Isaac, of Hesse-Cassel, 3:769, 16:349
Baumann, Kurt, 11:570
Baume, Erne. *See* Baume, Peter
Baume, Peter, 3:**220–221**
Baumgardt, David, 3:**221**
Baumgartel, Elise J., 3:**221**
Baumgarten, Emanuel Mendel, 3:**221–222**
Baumgarten, Jean, 11:325
Baumgarten, Sandor, 3:**222**
Baumgartner, Hieronymus, 4:70
Baumgartner, Walter, 3:**222**
Baumhorn, Lipót, 3:**222**
Baumol, Joshua, 3:**222**
Baur, Ferdinand Christian, 15:191
Baur, Harry, 3:**223**
Bauska (Latvia), 3:**223**
Bava Batra (tractate), 1:341, 3:**223–224**
Bava ben Buta, 3:**224**
Bava Kamma, 3:28, 224–226, 6:397
Bava Metzia, 3:**226–227**

Bava(h) Rabbah. *See* Baba Rabbah

Bavaria (Germany), 3:*228*, **228–229**
    Landshut, 12:476
    Lauingen, 12:526
    revolution (1918), 6:276

Bavli, Hillel, 3:**230**, 8:736

Bavli, Menahem ben Moses, 3:**230**

Bavli v. Rabbinical Court of Appeals, 14:362

Baxa, Karel, 9:120

Bayahu, Jonathen ben, 3:160

Bayard, Herbert, 11:468

Bay Area Jewish Healing Center, 6:254

Bayazid II, 3:**230**

Bay di Taykhn fun Mazovye (Bursztyn), 4:203

Bayefsky, Aba, 3:**230–231**

Bayer, Bathja. *See* Bayer, Batya

Bayer, Batya, 3:**231**

Bayhan (Saudi Arabia), 3:**231**

Bayit le-Adam Eḥad (Orpaz), 15:483

Bayit va-Gan. *See* Bat Yam (Israel)

Baym Dnieper (Bergelson), 3:419

Baym Toyer (Molodowsky). *See* At the Gate (Molodowsky)

Bay Nakht Oyfn Altn Mark (Perets), 21:347

Bayne, ben Joseph ibn Paquda. *See* Baḥya ben Joseph Ibn Paquda

Bayonne (France), 3:**231–232**

Bayramic, 3:**232**

Bayreuth (Germany), 3:**232–233**

Bayside Land Corporation Ltd., 15:588

Bayt al-Maqdis. *See* Jerusalem (Israel)

Baytalsky, Mikhail Davidovich. *See* Domalsky, I.

Bayt Jann. *See* Beit Jann

Bay Tree, 3:**233**

Bayudaya, 3:**233**, 11:521

Bay Zikh (journal), 21:354

Baza (Spain), 3:**233**

Bazelon, David L., 3:**233–234**, 12:556

Bazín (Slovakia). *See* Pezinok (Slovakia)

A Bazini zsidók (Biró), 9:604

Bazīrkān, 6:233

BBYO (B'nai B'rith Youth Organization), 4:14–15

Bdellium, 3:**234**

Bé, Guillaume le. *See* Le Bé, Guillaume

Bea, Augustin, 3:**234**, 11:380

Beackon, Derek, 6:426

Beaconsfield, Benjamin Disraeli, Earl of. *See* Disraeli, Benjamin

Beadle. *See* Shammash

Beame, Abraham David, 3:**234–235**, 15:215, 216, 224

Beans, 3:**235**

Bear, 3:**235**

Bear, Jacob, 6:451

Beard and shaving, 3:**235–236**

Bearing Witness teacher training program, 9:454

Bearsted, Marcus Richard Samuel, Third Viscount, 3:237

Bearsted, Marcus Samuel, First Viscount, 3:**236–237**

Bearsted, Walter Horace Samuel, Second Viscount, 3:237

Beati misericordes (Morpurgo), 14:509

Beating. *See* Floggings

Beatitude, 3:**237–241**

The Beatles (musical group), 6:468, 12:666

Beaucaire (France), 3:**241**

Beautiful Gate. *See* Nicanor's gate (Jerusalem)

Beautiful Losers (Cohen), 4:423, 5:25

Beauty and the environment, 5:168

Bebai, 3:**241**

Bebai Bar Abbaye, 3:**241**

Bebe, Pauline, 3:**241–242**

Beber, Sam, 4:14

Bebuquin oder die Dilettanten des Wunders (Einstein), 6:263

Beccari, Arrigo, 3:**242**

Bech(ius), Matthias Friedrich, 3:**243**

Becha (Kirovograd district, Ukraine). *See* Aleksandriya (Kirovograd district, Ukraine)

Becher, Sigfried, 3:**242**

Bechhold, Jacob Heinrich, 3:**242**

Bechin (Bohemia). *See* Bechyne (Bohemia)

Bechtolsheim, Andy, 4:183

Bechyne (Bohemia), 3:**242–243**

Beck, Balthazar, 4:472

Beck, Karl Isidore, 3:**243**

Beck, Michael, 3:**243**

Beck, Willy, 3:**243**

Beckelman, Moses W., 3:**244**

Becker, Aharon, 3:**244**

Becker, Edward Roy, 3:**244–245**

Becker, Gary Stanley, 3:**245**

Becker, Ham G., 3:**244**

Becker, Harry, 15:304

Becker, Helen. *See* Tamiris, Helen

Becker, Howard, 18:734

Becker, James Herman, 3:**244**

Becker, Julius, 3:**245**

Becker, Jurek, 3:**245–246**

Becker, Lavy M., 3:**246**

Becker family, 3:**244**

Becket, Thomas, 4:96

Beckett, Samuel, 3:742–743

Bécsi Magyar Ujság (newspaper), 8:282

Beda, 3:**246–247**

Bedacht, Max, 3:**247**

Bedarida, Guido, 3:**247**

Bédarride, Israél, 3:**247**

Bédarrides (France), 3:**247**

Bedbugs (Sinclair), 18:632

Beddington, Alfred Henry, 3:**248**

Beddington, Claude, 3:**248**

Beddington, Edward Henry Lionel, Sir, 3:**248**

Beddington, Henry Beddington, 3:**248**

Beddington, Henry Moses, 3:**248**

Beddington, John Louis "Jack," 3:**248**

Beddington, Maurice, 3:**248**

Beddington, William Richard, 3:**248**

Beddington family, 3:**248**

Bede, English translation of Bible, 3:611

Bedeken, 3:48

Bedek ha-Bayit (Aaron ben Joseph ha-Levi), 1:215

Bedek ha-Bayit (Caro), 8:444

Bedersi, Abraham ben Isaac, 3:**248**, 16:117, 267–268

Bedersi, Jedaiah ha-Penini. *See* Jedaiah ben Abraham Bedersi

Bedford (England), 3:**248–249**

Bedikat Ḥamez, 3:**249**

Bedil. *See* Tin

Bedouins, 10:737–739
    Ishmaelites as, 10:85
    Israel (state), 10:737–739

Bedzin (Poland), 3:**249–250**

Bee, 3:**250**

Be-Ein Ḥazon, 17:236

Be-Ein Mattarah (Bershadsky), 3:489

Beek, Martinus Adrianus, 3:**250**

Beekeeping, 3:250

Be-Emẓa ha-Roman (Bartov), 3:181

Beer (Israel), 3:**250**

Beer, Aaron, 2:76, 3:**250–251**

Beer, Bernhard, 3:**251**, 6:11, 12:615

Beer, George Lucas, 3:**251**

Be'er, Haim, 3:**251–252**

Beer, Israel, 3:**252**

Beer, Jacob Liebmann. *See* Meyerbeer, Giacomo

Beer, Max, 3:**252**

Beer, Michael, 3:**253**

Beer, Moses. *See* Beer, Max

Be'er, Orah, 3:**256**

Beer, Peter, 3:**253**

Beer, Rachel, 3:**253**

Be'er, Rami, 3:**254**

Beer, Richa. *See* Beer, Rachel

Beer, Samuel Friedrich, 3:**254**, 18:223

Beer, Wilhelm, 3:**254**

Be'er Avraham (Weinberg), 18:677

Beer-Bing, Isaiah, 3:**254**, 703

Be-Ereẓ Gezerah (Almog), 1:680

Be'er ha-Golah (Bezalel), 9:225

Beer-Hoffman, Richard, 3:**254–255**

Be'eri (Israel), 3:**255**

Beeri, Tuvia, 3:**255**

Beerman, Leonard, 3:**255–256**, 13:204

Be'er Mayim Ḥayyim (Ḥayyim), 8:481

Be'er Moshe (Epstein), 6:476

Be'erot, Yiẓḥak, 3:**256**

Beeroth (ancient Israel), 3:**256**, 17:142–143

Beersheba (Israel), 2:371, 3:**256–258**

Be'er Toviyyha, 3:**258**

Be'er Ya'akov, 3:**258**

Beet, 3:**258**

Be-Fardes ha-Ḥasidut (Buber), 8:416–417

Befejezetlen mondat, 5:600–601

Before, During and After (Halbreich), 9:413

Begging and beggars, 3:**258–260**, 6:690

Beghi, Elijah Afdah. *See* Beghi, Elijah Afidah

Beghi, Elijah Afidah, 3:**260**, 11:546

Beghi, Joseph ben Moses, 3:**260**

Beghi, Moses ben Benjamin, 3:**260**

Beghi family, 3:**260**

Bégin, Emile Auguste, 3:**261**

Begin, Menaḥem, 3:**261–262**, 9:283, 17:264–267

    American Israel Public Affairs Committee, 2:51

    governments of, 10:444–448, 445t, 447t

    Lebanese War and, 10:240, 12:583

    Likud, 13:13

    as prime minister, 10:238–239

    Schindler, Alexander M. and, 18:135–136

    settlements beyond Green Line and, 10:363–364

Begin, Ze'ev Binyamin, 3:**262**

Begun, Yosef, 14:520

Behak, Judah, 3:**262**

Beham, Barthel, 4:70

Beham, Hans Sebald, 4:70

Behar, Bucha, 4:276

Behar, Leon, 3:**262–263**

Behar, Nissim, 2:184, 3:**263**

Beharav, Dmitri. *See* Bogrov, Dmitri

Behavioral psychology. *See* Psychology

Behavior finance theories, 11:725

Behemoth, 3:**263**

Behem *v.* the Rabbinical Hight Court of Appeals, 5:138–139

Beḥinat ha-Dat (Delmedigo), 2:531

Beḥinat ha-Dat (Delmedigo, Elijah ben Moses Abba), 5:542

Behind the Door. See Dietro la porta

Behind the Polish-Soviet Break (Brody), 4:200

Beḥinot, 11:634–635

Behold a Great Image, 16:127–128, 129

Behold the Man (Moorcock), 18:199

Be-Ḥozai, 3:**263**

Behr, Issachar Falkenstein, 3:**263–264**

Behrein. *See* Bahrain (Middle East)

Behrend, Jacob Friedrich, 3:**264**, 12:551

Behrends, Leffmann, 3:**264**, 8:330, 13:253

Behrens, Leffman. *See* Behrends, Leffmann

Behrman, Martin, 3:**264**

Behrman, Samuel Nathaniel, 3:**264–265**

Bei Avidan, 3:**265**

Beider, Chaim, 3:**265**

Beiderman, Bernardo, 3:**265**

Beihan. *See* Bayhan (Saudi Arabia)

Beijing (China). *See* Peking (China)

Beilenson, Anthony Charles, 3:**265–266**

Beilin, Arkadi, 3:75

Beilin, Asher, 3:**266**

Beilin, Yossi, 3:**266–267**

Beilinson, Moses Eliezer, 3:**267**, 13:260

Beilinson, Moshe, 3:**266**

Beilis, Menahem Mendel, 3:**267–268**

Beilis blood libel trial (Kiev), 12:780

    Duma, 6:45

    Nicholas II and, 15:250

Beim, Solomon ben Abraham, 3:**268**

Beimel, Jacob, 3:**268**

Bein, Alexander, 3:**268**

Beinart, Haim, 3:**268–269**

Bein ha-Metim u-vein ha-Ḥayyim (Sened), 18:288

Bein ha-Meẓarim. *See* Three weeks

Bein ha-Shemashot. *See* Twilight

Beinisch, Dorit, 3:**269**

Bein Mayim le-Mayim (Brenner), 4:160

Bein Ẓeḥok le-Dema (Shaked), 18:367, 368

Bei-Rav, 3:**269**

Beirav, Jacob. *See* Berab, Jacob

Beirav, Jacob ben Ḥayyim. *See* Berab, Jacob ben Ḥayyim

Beirut, 3:**269–271**, 12:587–589

Beisan. *See* Bet(h)-Shean (Israel)

Beis HaMidrash LaTorah. *See* Hebrew Theological College

Beit, Alfred. *See* Beit, Sir Alfred

Beit, Sir Alfred, 3:**271**

Beit Abraham (Abraham ben Isaac ha-Kohen of Zamość), 1:301

Beit Aharon (Aaron ben Samuel), 1:217

Beit Aharon (Abiob), 1:259

Beit Avraham (Abraham ben Josiah Troki), 1:303

Beit Avraham (Weinberg), 18:677

Beit-El. *See* Pisa, da, family

Beit Eshel. *See* Bet Eshel (Israel)

Beit Gubrin. *See* Bet Guvrin (Israel)

Beit ha-Beḥira (Ha-Meiri), 8:667

Beit ha-Beḥirah (Meiri), 13:786

Beit ha-Levi: Novellae on the Talmud, 102 responsa and sermons (Soloveichik), 18:776

Beit-Hallahmi, Benjamin, 3:**271–272**

Beit ha-Oẓar (Abraham ben Josiah Troki), 1:303

Beit ha-Oẓar (Joseph ben Judah Engel), 6:409

Beit Hashoah Museum of Tolerance, 9:451

Beit Hillel (Lipschuetz), 13:73

Beit Jamāl, 3:**272**

Beit Jann, 3:**272**

Beit Leḥem Yehudah (Modena), 14:409

Beit Mo'ed (Rabba), 17:7

Beitraege zur aelteren deutschen Wirtschafts-und Verfassungsgeschichte (Caro), 4:487

Beitraege zur Einleitung in das Alte Testament (Wette de), 21:30

Beitraege zur Geographie Palaestinas (Hildesheimer), 9:105

Beitraege zur geschichte und Literatur im geonaeischen Zeitalter (Eppenstein), 6:465

Beit T'Shuva, 13:210

Beit Tzvi school, 11:736

Beit Ya'ar ha-Levanon. *See* House of the Forest of Lebanon

Beit Yehudah (Levinsohn), 12:721

Beit Yehudah (Modena), 14:409

Beit Yisrael (Falk), 6:686

Beit Yosef (Caro), 1:532, 4:489–490, 776, 778, 779, 8:257, 14:481

Beja (Portugal), 3:**272**

Beja, Isaac ben Moses, 3:**272**

Bejerano, Bejerano, 3:**272**

Bejerano, Bekhor Ḥayyim ben Moses, 3:272–273
Bejerano, Maya, 3:273
Bejerano, Moshe, 3:272
Bejerano, Shimon, 3:272
Bejerano family, 3:272
Bejski report, 2:453
Bekache, Shalom, 3:273
Békécsaba (Hungary), 3:274–275
Bekemoharar, Joseph Raphael ben Mordecai, 3:274
Bekemoharar, Menahem (III), 3:274
Bekemoharar, Menahem ben Isaac Ashkenazi, 3:273
Bekemoharar, Menahem (II) ben Mordecai, 3:274
Bekemoharar, Menahem (IV) R. Mordecai Simeon, 3:274
Bekemoharar, Mordecai ben Menahem, 3:273–274
Bekemoharar, Mordecai (II) ben Menahem, 3:274
Bekemoharar, Mordechai Simeon ben Nissim Solomon, 3:274
Bekemoharar, Raphael, 3:274
Bekemoharar, Yom Tov, 3:274
Bekemoharrar family, 3:273–274
Békessy, János. See Habe, Hans
Be-Keẓ ha-Yamim (Hazaz), 8:493
Bekher. See Camels
Bekhor. See Firstborn
Bekhorot, 3:275–276
Bekhor Shor, Joseph ben Isaac, 3:276–277, 642
Bekker, Balthasar, 2:21, 15:191
Bekker, Paul, 3:277
Beklemishev, Yuri Solomonovich. See Krymov, Yuri
Be-Kolar Eḥad (Hazaz), 8:494
Bel. See Marduk
Belachatow (Poland), 3:279
Belair (Satan). See Belial
Belais(h), Abraham ben Shalom, 3:277, 16:346
Bel and the Dragon, 3:277
Belarus, 3:277–278
    cultural and social life
        community archives, 2:408
        Karaites, 4:130
        literature, 4:323
        Lithuanian Jewry, 13:121
        museums, 14:630
    Holocaust
        Baranovichi, 3:134
        Bereza, 3:413–414
        Bobruisk, 4:24–25
        Borisov, 4:86

Braslav, 4:130–131
Bykhov, 4:324
David-Godorok, 5:473–474
Dolginovo, 5:735
Druya, 6:28–29
Dubrovno, 6:39
Dyatlovo, 6:75
Ilya, 9:736
Ivanovo, 10:821
Ivye, 10:822
Kobrin, 12:244
Koidanovo, 12:267
Krichev, 12:356
Lachva, 12:426
Lepel, 12:650
Lida, 12:802
Lyakhovichi, 13:293
Minsk, 14:293–297
Mir, 14:304–305
Mogilev, 14:417
Molodechno, 14:429
Mozyr, 14:592–593
Mstislavl, 14:593
Nazi occupation, 11:735–736
Novogrudok, 15:321
Novy Dvor, 15:323–324
Orsha, 15:487
Oshmyany, 15:502–503
Ostryna, 15:514–515
Ozery, 15:557
Pinsk, 16:172
Polotsk, 16:361
Pruzhany, 16:657
Radoshkovichi, 17:59
Radun, 17:59
Rechitsa, 17:144
Rogachev, 17:367–368
Shchedrin, 18:426
Skidel, 18:658
Slonim, 18:676–677
Slutsk, 18:685
Stolbsty, 19:234
Stolin, 19:234
Svisloch, 19:334
Vitebsk, 20:560
Volkovysk, 20:573–574
Volpa, 20:578
Vysokoye, 20:590
Zelva, 21:502
    See also Belorussia (Russia); specific cities
Belasco, David. See James, David
Belaya Tserkov (Ukraine), 3:278–279
Belaya Vezha, Sarkil (Khazaria)
Beled (Hungary), 3:279

Belev, Alexander, 3:279
Belfast (Ireland), 3:280, 11:68
Belfort (France), 3:280
Belforte, Solomon, 3:280
Belgium, 3:280–287, 281, 14:625
    antisemitism, 2:234
    cultural and social life
        literature, 5:305
        museums, 5:305
        newspapers, 16:487
    demography, 4:227
    early postwar years, 3:284–285
    emancipation, 6:378
    Holocaust, 3:282–283, 9:339
        Antwerp, 2:250
        badges, Jewish, 2:250
        Brussels, 4:227
    leather industry and trade, 12:576
    literature, 18:118
    Middle Ages, 3:280–281
    modern period
        community life, 3:285
        interfaith relations, 3:285
        politics, 3:285
        relations with Israel, 3:286–287
        remembering the Holocaust, 3:286–287
    resistance, 3:282–283
Belgorod-Dnestrovski (Ukraine), 3:287–288
Belgrade (Serbia), 3:288–289, 14:629
Belgrado, David Fernando, 3:289
Belial, 3:289–290
Beliar. See Belial
Belief, 3:290–294, 6:682–683
Beli Kokhav (Burla), 4:295
Belinas. See Banias (ancient Israel)
Belinfante, Aron, 3:295
Belinfante, Ary, 3:295
Belinfante, Elijah Hezekiah, 3:294
Belinfante, Emilie Josephine, 3:295
Belinfante, George, 3:295
Belinfante, Isaac, 3:295
Belinfante, Isaac ben Eliah Cohen, 3:295
Belinfante, Jacob Cohen, 3:295
Belinfante, Joseph Cohen, 3:294
Belinfante, Josephus Justus, 3:295
Belinfante, Judith, 3:295
Belinfante, Maurits Ernst, 3:295
Belinfante, Meir Ḥayyim, 3:294
Belinfante, Moses Cohen, 2:112, 3:295
Belinfante, Saddik, 3:294
Belinfante, Sara, 3:295
Belinfante family, 3:294–295

Belinkov, Arkhadii Viktorovich, 3:**295–296**

Belinson, Moses Eliezer. *See* Beilinson, Moses Eliezer

Belinson, Moses Eliezeri. *See* Beilinson, Moses Eliezer

Belisha, Barrow, 3:**296**

Belisha, Isaac, 3:**296**

Belisha, Moses, 3:**296**

Belisha, Solomon, 3:**296**

Belisha family, 3:**296**

Belize (Central America), 4:476

Belkin, Arnold, 3:**296**

Belkin, Samuel, 3:**296**, 15:498

Belkin, Simon, 3:**296–297**

Belkind, Israel, 3:**297**

Belkind, Meir, 3:**297**

Belkind, Na'aman, 3:**297**, 15:268

Belkind, Shimshon, 3:**297**

Belkind family, 3:**297**, 297t

Belkowsky, Ẓevi Hirsch, 3:**297–298**

Bell, Daniel, 3:**298**

Bell, Francis Henry Dillon. *See* Bell, Sir Francis Henry Dillon

Bell, Joshua, 3:**299**

Bell, Sir Francis Henry Dillon, 3:**299**

The Bellarosa Connection (Bellow), 3:300

Belleli, Lazarus Menahem, 3:**299**

Belleli, Vito, 15:689

Bellinson, Simeon, 3:**299–300**

Bellis (Russia), 3:778, 779

Bellow, Saul, 3:**300–301**, 9:595–596, 20:293–294

Bellum Civile (Lucan), 13:247

Belmain. *See* Ibleam (Israel)

Belmont, August, 3:**301**, 15:200

Belmonte, 3:**302**

Belmonte, Francisco Isaac, 3:302

Belmonte, Isaac Nuñez, 3:302, 16:344–345

Belmonte, Jacob Abraham, 3:302

Belmonte, Jacob Israel, 3:302

Belmonte, Manuel, 3:302

Belmonte, Moses, 3:302

Belmonte family, 3:**302**

Belmonte Science Laboratory for Youth, 8:743

Beloff, Max, Baron, 3:**302–303**

Belogorsk (Ukraine). *See* Karasubazar (Ukraine)

Belorussia (Russia), 3:**303–305**
  agriculture, Jewish, 1:498
  education, Jewish, 6:188
  Holocaust, 17:597–598
  See also Belarus

Belov, A., 3:**305–306**

The Beloved and the Pleasant or The Black Youth. See Ha-Neʿehovim ve-ha-Neʿimim oder der Shvartse Yungermantshik

Belshazzar, 7:32

Belshazzar (biblical figure), 1:538, 3:**306–307**

Belteshazzar (biblical figure), 3:**307**, 5:419

Beltsy (Moldova), 3:**307**

Bely, Viktor Arkadyevich, 3:**307–308**

Belz (Ukraine), 3:**308**

Belz, Aaron, 3:**308**

Belzberg, Samuel, 3:**309**

Belzec concentration camp, 3:**309–312**, 9:336, 343, 430, 11:751, 754, 13:239, 244

Belzer, Nissi. *See* Spivak, Nissan

Belzer Ḥasidim, 8:423, 428–429

Belz ḥasidic dynasty, 3:**308–309**

Belzyce (Poland), 3:**312**

Be-Mehoza Yisadeti et Medinat ha-Yehudim (Gose), 18:206

Be-Mifneh ha-Dorot (Dinur), 5:672

Be-Moaz'ei Menuḥa, 3:**312**

Bemporad, Azeglio, 3:**312**

Bemporad, Enrico, 3:**312–313**

Ben, Zehava, 3:**313**

Bena'ah, 3:**313**

Ben-Abraham, Zvi, 3:**313**

Benacerraf, Baruj, 3:**313–314**, 13:11

Ben-Adir, 3:**314**

Benador, Ury, 3:**314**

Benadov, Haim, 4:276

Ben-Aharon, Yitzḥak, 3:**314–315**

Benaiah (3rd c.). *See* Bena'ah

Benaiah (biblical figure), 3:**315**

Benaim, Jacob Ḥayyim, 3:**315**, 4:104

Benaim, Joseph, 3:**315**

Benaim, Moses, 3:**315**

Benaim, Raphael Ḥayyim, 3:**315**

Benaim family, 3:**315**

Ben ʾAlān, Joshua, 3:**315**

Ben'ālan, Joshua, 3:**315**

Ben-ami, Jacob, 3:**316**

Ben-ami, Oved, 3:**316**

Ben-Amitai, Levi, 3:**316**

Ben Ammi (Ben-Zion), 3:392

Ben-Ammi, Mordecai, 3:**316–317**

Ben-Amotz, Dahn, 3:**317**

Benamozegh, Elijah ben Abraham, 3:**317**, 15:602

Benardete, Mair José, 3:**318**

Benares (India), 3:**318**

Ben-Arieh, Yehoshua, 3:**318**

Benário, Olga, 4:149

Ben-Aroya, Avraham, 3:**318–319**

Benaroya, Avram, 3:**319**

Benaroya, Mois, 4:276

Benarus, Adolfo, 3:**319**

Benas, Baron Louis, 3:**319**

Benas, Bertram Benjamin Baron, 3:**319**

Benas, Henriette. *See* Goldschmidt, Henriette

Ben-Asher, Aaron ben Moses, 3:**319–320**

Ben-Asher, Moses, 3:**321**

Ben Asher's Creed: A Study of the History of the Controversy (Dotan), 5:762–763

Ben Asher system (Hebrew grammar), 3:588, 11:117

Benatar family. *See* Atar family

Benatzky, Ralph, 3:**312**

Ben-avi, Ithamar, 3:**322**

Ben-Avigdor. *See* Shalkovich, Abraham Leib

Benayah, Ben Merjaz, 3:**322**

Benayah, Miriam, 3:**322**

Benayah family, 3:**322**

Benayahu, Meir, 3:**322**

Benazareff, David, 14:503

Benazerat, David, 16:346

Ben Azzai, Simeon, 3:**322–323**, 8:391, 18:601

Ben Bag Bag, 3:**323**

Benbassa, Esther, 11:326

Ben Chananjah, 3:**323**

Benchetrit, Aaron, 3:**323**

Benchimol, Abraham, 3:**324**

Benchimol, Ḥayyim, 3:**324**

Benchimol family, 3:**324**

Ben-Chorin, Schalom, 3:**324**

Benda, Julien, 3:**324–325**

Bendahan, Jacob, 5:379

Bendahan, Joseph, 5:379

Bendahan, Joseph Nissim, 5:379

Bendahan, Maimon, 5:379

Bendahan, Moses, 5:379

Ben David (Modena), 14:409

Bendavid, Eleazar. *See* Bendavid, Lazarus

Ben-David, Joseph, 3:**325**, 18:735

Bendavid, Lazarus, 3:**325**, 11:569

Bendek, Therese F., 3:**329**

Bendell, Herman, 16:124

Bendemann, Eduard Julius Friedrich, 3:**325–326**

Bendemman, Felix, 3:**326**

Bendemman, Rudolf, 3:**326**

Bender, Alfred Philip, 3:**326**

Bender, Morris Boris, 3:**326**

Benderly, Samson, 3:98, **326–327,**
11:271–272, 15:208

    Bureau of Jewish Education (New
York, NY), 6:194–195

    summer camps, 6:199–200

Bendery (Romania), 3:**327**

Bendery dynasty. *See* Savran dynasty

Bendin (Poland). *See* Bedzin (Poland)

Bendix, Benedict Heinrich, 3:**327**

Bendix, Otto, 3:**327**

Bendix, Reinhard, 3:**327–328**

Bendix, Victor Emanuel, 3:**328**

Bendor, Ariel, 20:468

Ben-dor, Immanuel, 3:**328**

Ben Dov, Yaakov, 3:**328**

Bene-Berak, 3:**328–329**, 11:715–716,
742

Benedict (popes), 3:**329–330**

Benedict, Isaac. *See* Benedict, Sir Julius

Benedict, Julius. *See* Benedict, Sir
Julius

Benedict, Sir Julius, 3:**330**

Benedict VIII (pope), 3:329, 16:372

Benedict XII (pope), 3:329, 16:374

Benedict XIII (antipope), 3:329, 4:74,
13:193, 14:467

Benedict XIII (pope), 4:277, 15:609,
16:374, 20:62

    Pablo de Santa Maria, 15:562

    papal bulls, 3:330

Benedict XIV, 2:144, 3:122, 330

Benedict XV (pope), 16:377

Benedict XVI (pope), 16:378

Benedict ben Moses of Lincoln, 3:**330**

Benedict family. *See* Banet family

Benedictions, 1:538–539, 3:**330–333**,
13:131–132, 14:492

Benedict le Puncteur of Oxford,
15:554

Benedikt, Moritz (journalist), 3:**333**

Benedikt, Moritz (neurologist), 3:**333**

Bene Ephraim, 3:**334**

Beneficencia, 6:140–141

Benefield, 3:**342**

Bene hanevi'im, 6:168

Benei Aish (Israel), 3:**334**

Benei Arav (Smilansky), 18:687

Benei Binyamin, 1:222, 3:**334**

Benei Darom (Israel), 3:**334**

Benei Deror (Israel), 3:**334**

Benei ha-Ir, 12:605

Benei Moshe, 1:526, 3:**334–335**

Benei Moshe League, 12:666

Bene Israel, 3:**335–339**

    India, 1:658, 3:356–357

Israel (state), 10:226, 298

    Italy, 4:50

Benei Zion (Israel), 3:**339**

Benei Zion Society, founder Mazeh,
Jacob, 13:706

Ben-Eleizer, Binyamin, 3:**339–340**

Ben Eleizer, Moshe, 3:**340**

Bene Menashe, 3:**340**

Ben Erezve-Shamayim (Sackler), 8:736

Benesch, Alfred Abraham, 3:**340**

Beneschau (Bohemia). *See* Benešov
(Bohemia)

Benešov (Bohemia), 3:**340–341**

Benet, Ezekiel ben Jacob. *See* Baneth,
Ezekiel ben Jacob

Benet, Mordecai ben Abraham. *See*
Banet, Mordecai ben Abraham

Benet, Naphtali ben Mordecai. *See*
Banet, Naphtali ben Mordecai

Benet family. *See* Banet family

Benet Mikra, 3:662

Benevento (Italy), 3:**341**

Benevento, Immanuel ben Jekuthiel,
3:**341**

Benevenutus Grapheus
Heirosolymitanus, 3:**341**

Benevolent societies. *See* Charity;
Philanthropy

Ben-Ezer, Judah. *See* Raab, Judah

Benfey, Theodor, 3:**342**

Bengalil, Abraham, 3:**342**

Bengalil, Joseph, 3:**342**

Bengalil, Samuel, 3:**342**

Bengalil family, 3:**342**

Ben-Gavriel, Moshe Ya'akov, 3:**342**

Benghazi (Libya), 3:**342–343**, 12:791

Bengis, Selig Reuben, 3:**343–344**

Ben-Gurion, David, 3:**344–348**, 9:50

    Adenauer, Konrad, 1:390

    Aliav, Ruth, 1:658

    Blood for Trucks offer, 4:120

    declaration of independence,
Israel, 5:529–530

    Eichmann trial, 6:250

    Eldad, Israel, 6:292

    Eshkol, Levi, 6:506

    governments of

        first, 10:429, 429*t*

        second, 10:430, 430*t*

        third, 10:430–431, 431*t*

        fourth, 10:431, 431*t*

        seventh, 10:433, 433*t*

        eighth, 10:434, 434*t*

        ninth, 10:435–436, 435*t*

        tenth, 10:436–437, 436*t*

    Histadrut and, 10:595, 597, 600

Jewish identity, what constitutes,
11:298

Jewish Legion, 11:303, 305

    Lavon and, 10:225, 12:533–534

    resignation (1953), 10:217

    resignation (1960), 10:225

    Sharett, Moshe and, 18:412–413

    State of Israel Bonds, 4:58

Ben-Gurion, Paula, 3:**344**

Ben Gurion University of the Negev,
3:**348–349**

Ben-Hadad (Kings), 1:523, 3:**349–350**,
6:350

Ben-Hadad I, 3:349

Ben-Hadad II, 3:349–350

Ben-Hadad III, 3:350

Ben-Haim, Paul, 3:**350–351**

Ben-Haim, Yigal, 3:**351**

Ben Ḥakhinai. *See* Hananiah ben
Ḥakhinai

Ben ha-Melekh Ve-ha-Nazir, 3:351,
6:667

Benhamu, Shlomo, 2:71

Ben Hanila. *See* Tanḥum ben Ḥanilai

Ben Harosh, Moshe. *See* Bar-Asher,
Moshe

Ben Ḥayyim, Ze'ev, 3:**351–352**, 13:615

Ben He He, 3:**352**

Ben Horin, Eliyahu, 3:**352**

Ben Horin, Meir, 3:**352**

Benichou, Paul, 3:**352–353**

Benider, Abraham, 3:**353**

Benider, Jacob, 3:353

Benider family, 3:**353**

Benioff, Hugo, 3:**353**

Benisch, Abraham, 3:**353**, 614

Ben-Israel, Ruth, 3:**353**

Benista, Zehava. *See* Ben, Zehava

Benjacob, Isaac, 3:**353–354**, 682

Benjamin (biblical figure, tribe), 3:*354*,
354–356

    Anathoth, 2:132

    Jabesh-Gilead and, 11:6

    Jacob's blessing, 11:27

    Judges, Book of, 11:565–566

    Mizpeh, 14:388

Benjamin, Baruch ben Israel, 3:**356**

Benjamin, Baruch Tzion, 3:**356–357**

Benjamin, Ernest Frank, 3:**357**

Benjamin, Israel, 3:208, **357**

Benjamin, Israel Joseph. *See* Benjamin
II

Benjamin, Judah Philip, 3:**357–358**,
12:555

    American Jewish Archives, 2:53

    on slavery, 3:734

Benjámin, László, 3:**357–358**

Benjamin, Lewis Saul. *See* Melville, Lewis

Benjamin, Moses, 3:**358**

Benjamin, Raphael, 3:**358**

Benjamin, Richard, 3:**358**

Benjamin, Walter, 3:**359**

Benjamin, Yehoshua, 3:**360**

Benjamin and Vladka Meed Registry of Jewish Holocaust Survivors, 2:49, 20:276

Benjamin ben Aaron of Zalozce, 3:**360**

Benjamin ben Azriel, 3:**360**

Benjamin ben Eliezer ha-Kohen Vitale of Reggio, 3:**360–361**, 18:354

Benjamin ben Elijah, 3:**361**

Benjamin ben Elijah Duwan, 3:**361**

Benjamin ben Ḥiyya, 3:**361**

Benjamin ben Japheth, 3:**361**

Benjamin ben Jehiel, 2:136

Benjamin ben Moses Naḥ'āwendī. *See* Naḥ'āwendī, Benjamin ben Moses al-

Benjamin ben Solomon ha-levi, 3:**361**

Benjamin Ben Zerah, 3:**362**

Benjamin II, 3:**356**, 6:147

Benjamin Nehemia Ben Elnathan, 3:**362**, 9:157

Benjamin of Brody, 3:**362**

Benjamin of Cambridge, 3:**362**

Benjamin of Tiberias, 3:**362**, 4:326

Benjamin of Tudela, 2:108, 3:**362–364**, 363

    'Amadiya, 2:27–28

    on Bingen, 3:704

    Borsippa, 4:94

    on Brindisi, 4:184

    Byzantine empire, Jewish communities in, 4:327

    Daniel ben Jehiel, 2:136

    on Drama (Greek city), 6:7

    dyeing, 6:76

    Egypt, 6:231

    French scholars, 6:174, 13:258

    on functions of rabbinate, 18:275

    Hamadan, 8:292

    on Jewish quarters, 11:310

    Jubayl, 11:473

    Lunel (France), 13:258

    Modon, 14:412–413

    on Palermo, 15:580

    Patras, 15:688

Benjamin Ze'ev Ben Mattathias of Arta, 3:**364**

Ben Jonah of Tudela. *See* Benjamin of Tudela

Ben Kalba Savu'a, 3:**365**

Ben Karshook's Wisdom (Browning), 4:218

Ben-Kiki, Eleasar, 3:**365**

Ben-Kiki, Reuben, 3:**365**

Ben-Kiki family, 3:**365**

Ben Kosebat letters, 14:617

Benkow, Jo, 3:**365**

Ben Kozevah. *See* Bar Kokhba

Ben Koziva. *See* Bar Kokhba

Ben La'anah, 3:**365**

Ben Malca, Jacob ben Joseph, 13:429–430

Ben Malca, Khalifa, 13:430

Ben Malca family. *See* Malca family

Ben Mar David of Narbonne. *See* Moses ben Joshua of Narbonne

Ben Meir, Aaron, 3:**366**

Benn, 3:**366**

Benn, Ben, 3:**366–367**

Ben-Naphtali, Jacob ben David. *See* Ben-Naphtali, Moses ben David

Ben-Naphtali, Moses Ben David, 3:**367**

Ben-Naphtali System, 13:644, 650

Ben-Natan, Asher, 3:**367**

Ben-Natan, Shemu'el. *See* Pevzner, Samuel Joseph

Ben Naẓer, 15:377

Bennett, Archie, 3:**368**

Bennett, Avie. J., 3:**368**

Bennett, Michael, 3:**369**

Bennett, Salomon Yom Tov, 3:**369**

Benny, Jack, 3:**369–370**

Benoit, Pierre-Marie, 3:**370–371**

Benoliel, 3:**371**

Benoliel, Eliezer, 3:**371**

Benoliel, Joseph, 3:**371**, 8:243

Benoliel, Judah, 3:**371**, 14:499

Ben Paltiel, Ahimaaz, 8:666

Ben Petura, 3:**371**

Ben Peturi. *See* Ben Petura

Ben Peturin. *See* Ben Petura

Ben-Porat, Miriam, 3:**371–372**

Ben-Porat, Mordekhai, 3:**372**

Benremokh, Abraham ben Ḥayyim, 3:372

Benremokh, Ḥayyim ben Shem Tov, 3:372

Benremokh, Saul Ben Shem Tov, 3:372

Benremokh, Shem Tov, 3:372

Benremokh, Yamin, 3:372

Benremokh family, 3:**372**

Benremokh, Solomon, 3:372

Benrubi, Isaac, 3:**372–373**

Bensanchi, Mentesh, 3:**373**

Bensanchi, Mordecai. *See* Bensanchi, Mentesh

Ben-Sasson, Haim Hillel, 3:**373**, 9:153, 161

Bensaude, 3:**373**

Bensaude, Abraham, 3:373

Bensaude, Elias, 3:373

Bensaude, Joaquim, 3:373

Bensaude, José, 3:373

Bensaude, Solomon, 3:373

Ben Sender, Ephraim Moses. *See* Cilibi Moïse

Ben Senton-Ben Shem Tov. *See* Aaron ben Batash

Ben-Shabetai, Ari, 3:**373–374**

Ben Shachar *v.* Yosef Machlev, 5:138

Ben-Shakhar, Gershon, 3:**374**

Benshalom, Benzion. *See* Katz, Benzion (1907-1968)

Ben Shemen, 3:**374**

Benshen, 3:**374**

Ben Simeon, Raphael Aaron, 3:**374–375**

Ben Sira, Alphabet of. See Alphabet of Ben Sira

Ben Sira, Simeon ben Jesus, 3:**376**

    Elijah, 6:333

    Joseph ben Uzziel, grandson of, 11:427

    on labor, 12:409

    on tripartite canon, 3:576, 579

    See also Alphabet of Ben Sira

Ben Sira, Wisdom of (Apocrypha), 3:**376–378**

Benson, Robby, 3:**378**

Bensoussan, Georges, 3:**378**

Ben Ṣtada, 3:**378**

Ben Ṣtara. *See* Ben Stada

Bensusan, 3:**379**

Bensusan, Levy. *See* Bensusan

Bensusan, Nathan Levi, 3:379

Bensusan, Samuel Levy, 3:380

Ben Susan, Y., 3:605

Ben Temalyon, 3:**380**

Bentor, Jacob, 3:**380**

Bentov, Mordekhai, 1:655, 3:**381–382**, 702

Bentwich, Herbert, 3:381

Bentwich, Joseph, 3:381

Bentwich, Norman De Mattos, 3:381

Bentwich family, 3:**381**

Bentzen, Aage, 3:**381–382**

Benvenist, Adzay, 3:382

Benvenist, Ḥayyim ben Israel. *See* Benveniste, Ḥayyim ben Israel

Benveniste, Abraham (18th c.), 3:382

Benveniste, Abraham (1406-1454), 3:**382**, 6:176

Benveniste, Emile, 3:**382**

Benveniste, Ḥayyim ben Israel, 1:637, 3:**382–383**, 4:102, 18:344–345

Benveniste, Immanuel, 3:**383**

Benveniste, Isaac Ben Joseph, 3:**383**

Benveniste, Joseph Ben Moses De Segovia, 3:**383–384**

Benveniste, Joshua Raphael Ben Israel, 3:**384**

Benveniste, Judah ben Abraham, 3:382

Benveniste, Manoel. *See* Benveniste, Immanuel

Benveniste, Moses, 3:**384**, 4:102, 15:541, 678

Benveniste, Nissim, 3:382

Ben-Veniste, Richard, 3:**384–385**

Benveniste, Samuel, 3:**385**

Benveniste, Sheshet Ben Isaac Ben Joseph, 3:**385**

Benveniste De Porta, 3:**385**

Benveniste family, 3:**382**

Benveniste Ibn Benveniste, 3:382

Benvenisti, David, 3:**386**

Benvist family. *See* Benveniste family

Benwaish, Abraham, 3:**386**

Ben-Yehezki'el, Mordekhai, 3:**386**

Ben-Yehuda, Eliezer, 3:**386–388**, 8:671–673, 675, 10:683, 704–705

Ben-Yehuda, Hemdah, 3:**388**

Ben Yehuda, Netiva, 3:**388–389**

Ben-Yehudah, Barukh, 3:**389**

Ben Yizḥak, Avraham, 3:**389**

Ben-Yosef, Shelomo, 3:**390**

Ben Yukhid (Ben-Ammi), 3:316

Benzamero, 3:**390**

Benzamero, Aaron, 3:390

Benzamero, Abraham, 3:390

Benzamero, Abraham ben Meir, 3:390

Benzamero, David, 3:390

Benzamero, Ephraim, 3:390

Benzamero, Isaac II, 3:390

Benzamero, Judah, 3:390

Benzamero, Judah ben Ephraim, 3:390

Benzamero, Meir, 3:390

Benzamero, Moses, 3:390

Benzamero, Moses II, 3:390

Benzamero, Sliman, 3:390

Benzamero, Solomon, 3:390

Benzamero, Solomon II, 3:390

Ben Zaqen, 3:**390**

Ben Zaqen, Isaac ben Vidal, 3:390

Ben Zaqen, Jacob ben Samuel, 3:390

Ben Zaqen, Joseph, 3:390

Ben Zaqen, Leon, 3:390, 16:346

Ben Zaqen, Samuel, 3:390

Ben Zaqen family, 3:**390**

Benzaquén, Saadia, 3:**390–391**

Ben Ze'ev, Judah Leib, 3:**391**, 15:658

Ben Zekunim (Abulafia), 1:339

Benzer, Seymour, 3:**391**, 13:11

Benzinger, Immanuel, 3:**391–392**

Ben-Zion, 3:**392**, 4:50

Ben-Zion, S., 3:**392–393**

Ben Zita, Abu Al-Surri. *See* Ben Zuta, Abu Al-Surri

Ben Zizit Ha-Kasat, 3:**393**

Ben Zoma, Simeon, 3:**393**, 18:601

Ben Zuta, Abu Al-Surri, 3:**393**

Ben-Zvi, Izhak, 3:**393–395**, 4:189, 14:430

    Arad, 2:330

    Jewish Legion, 11:303, 305

Ben-Zvi, Rahel Yanait, 3:**395**, 6:260

Ben-Zvi, Shlomo, 3:**395**

Ben-Zvi, Zeev, 3:**395**, 18:223

Ben-Zvi Institute, 18:724

Ben Zvi Institute for the Study of the Jewish Communitities of the East, 3:**395–396**

Beobachter An Der Weichsel, 3:**396**

Beograd (Serbia). *See* Belgrade (Serbia)

Be-Olam she-Shaka 1884-1914 (Dinur), 5:672

Beon. *See* Baal-Meon

Be-Ovoyn Oves (Dineson), 5:671

Berab, Jacob, 3:**397–398**, 18:276

Berab, Jacob, I, 18:376

Berab, Jacob ben Ḥayyim, 3:**398**

Berachia, 3:406

Berah Dodi, 3:**391**

Beraja, Ruben Ezra, 3:**398–399**

Berakhah, Isaac, 3:**399**

Berakh Moshe (Adret), 1:421

Berakhot (tractate), 3:330–333, **399–400**

Berats, 8:245–246

Berbers, 3:**400–401**, 11:530, 14:493, 496

    See also Sijilmassa (Morocco)

Berchenko, Israel. *See* Galili, Israel

Bercovici, Konrad, 3:**401**, 14:541

Bercovitch, Peter, 3:**401**, 16:341

Bercovitch, Sacvan, 3:**401–402**

Bercu Haimovici. *See* Bonciu, H.

Berdichev, 3:**402–405**

Berdichevsky Scher, Jose, 3:**403**

Berdugo, 3:**403–404**

Berdugo, Jacob ben Mordecai, 3:404

Berdugo, Jekuthiel Ḥayyim ben Elisha, 3:404

Berdugo, Joseph, 3:404

Berdugo, Joshua ben Jacob, 3:404

Berdugo, Judah ben Joseph, 3:403

Berdugo, Maimon, 3:403

Berdugo, Mordecai ben Joseph, 3:403

Berdugo, Moses ben Abraham, 3:403

Berdugo, Raphael, 3:403

Berdugo, Solomon ben Daniel, 3:404

Berdugo, Yaḥya, 3:403

Berdyansk (Ukraine), 3:**404**

Berdyczewski, Immanuel bin Gorion, 3:406

Berdyczewski, Micha Josef, 3:**404–406**, 4:159, 8:726–727, 11:412, 12:424

Berechiah, 3:**406**

Berechiah ben Isaac ha-Levi, 7:550

Berechiah ben Natronai ha-Nakdan, 3:**406–407**, 6:437, 667–668, 15:554

Berechiah Berakh ben Eliakim Getzel, 3:**407**

Berechiah Berakh ben Isaac Eisik, 3:**407**

Berechiah family, 11:727

Beregi, Ármin Bengamin, 3:**407**

Beregi, Oszkár, 3:**408**

Beregovo (Ukraine), 3:**408**

Beregovski, Moshe, 3:**408**

Beregovskii, Moses, 11:322

Berek son of Yosel. *See* Joselewicz, Berek

Berele Bunes. *See* Issachar Baer ben Tanḥum

Berenbaum, Michael, 3:**408–409**

Berenblum, Isaac, 3:**409**

Berend Lehmann Museum, 8:263

Berendsohn, Walter A., 3:**409–410**

Berendt, Gottlieb Michael, 3:**410**

Berenguer, Ramon, 20:60–61

Berenice, 3:**410–411**, 11:582

Berenice (daughter of Agrippa I), 1:503, 3:**410–411**

Berenice (daughter of Salome), 3:**410**, 410t

Berenike (Egypt and Israel), 3:**411**

Berenson, Bernard, 3:**411**, 6:73

Berenson, Leon, 3:**411–412**, 12:553

Berenson, Zvi, 3:**412**

Berenson (Abbott), Senda (Valvrojenski), 3:**412**

Berenstein, Issachar Baer, 6:685

Berény, Róbert, 3:**412**

Bereshit-Nāmeh (Shāhin), 18:365

Beresht Zuta, 14:189

Berestechko (Ukraine), 3:**412–413**

Beresteczko (Ukraine). *See* Berestechko (Ukraine)

Berettyóújfalu (Hungary), 3:**413**

Bereza (Belarus), 3:**413–414**

Bereza Kartuska (Belarus). *See* Bereza (Belarus)

Berezhany (Ukraine), 3:**414**

Berezino (Belarus), 3:**414**

Berezovka (Ukraine), 3:**414**

Berezovsky, Boris Abramovich, 3:**414–415**

Berg (Germany), 3:**415**

Berg, Gertrude (Edelstein), 3:**415**

Berg, Jackie "Kid" (Judah Berman), 3:**415–416**

Berg, Karen, 3:417–418

Berg, Leo, 3:**416**

Berg, Moe (Morris), 3:**416–417**

Berg, Morris. *See* Berg, Moe

Berg, Paul, 3:**417**, 13:9

Berg, Philip (Gruberger), 3:**417–418**, 13:205

Bergamo (Italy), 3:**418**

Berge, Meere und Giganten (Doeblin), 5:729–730

Bergel, Bernd, 3:**418**

Bergel, Joseph, 3:**418**

Bergel family, 3:**418**

Bergelson, David, 3:**418–419**

Bergen, Polly, 3:**419–420**

Bergen-Belsen (Germany), 3:**420–422**, 632, 676

Bergen-Belsen concentration camp, 9:342, 369–370, 17:131
    Bitburg Controversy, 3:728
    John XXIII on, 11:380
    SS and SD
        burial of prisoners, 9:*487*
    survivors, 9:*487*

Bergen County (NJ), 3:**422–423**

Berger, Arthur Victor, 3:**423–424**

Berger, David, 3:**424**

Berger, Elmer, 3:**424**

Berger, Isaac ("Ike"), 3:**424–425**

Berger, Lili, 3:**425**

Berger, Meir, 3:**425**

Berger, Meyer, 3:**425**

Berger, Samuel R. (Sandy), 3:**425**

Berger, Sandy. *See* Berger, Samuel R.

Berger, Victor, 3:**426**, 18:708

Berger-Barzilai, Joseph, 3:**426**

Berggrün, Heinrich, 3:**426**

Bergh, Daniel Van Den, 3:**426**

Bergh, George Van Den, 3:**427**

Bergh, Robert Van Den, 3:**427**

Bergh, Samuel Van Den, 3:**427**, 16:345

Bergh, Sidney James Van Den, 3:**427**, 16:345

Bergh, Simon Van Den, 3:**426–427**

Bergh, Van Den, 3:**426–427**

Bergh, Zadok Van Den, 3:**426**

Bergheim (France), 3:**427**

Bergman, Alan, 3:**427**

Bergman, Andrew, 3:**427–428**

Bergman, Judah. *See* Berg, Jackie "Kid"

Bergman, Lawrence, 14:464

Bergman, Marilyn, 3:**427**

Bergman, Samuel Hugo, 3:**428–429**, 12:788

Bergmann, Ernst David, 3:**429**

Bergmann, Felix Eliezer, 3:**429**

Bergmann, Judah, 3:**429–430**

Bergmann, Max, 3:**430**

Bergmann, Richard, 3:**430**

Bergner, Elisabeth, 3:**430**

Bergner, Herz, 3:**430**

Bergner, Hinde, 17:123

Bergner, Yosef. *See* Bergner, Yossl

Bergner, Yossl, 3:**431**

Bergner, Zejharye Khone. *See* Ravitch, Melech

Bergner, Zekharye Khone. *See* Ravitch, Melech

Bergreen, Morris, 18:660

Bergson, Abram, 3:**431–432**

Bergson, Henri, 3:**431**

Bergson, Henri Louis, 3:**432–433**

Bergson, Joseph, 3:**431**

Bergson, Michael, 3:**431**, **433**

Bergson (Berkson) family, 3:**431**

Bergstein, Fania, 3:**433**

Bergstraesser, Gotthelf, 3:**433**, 13:58

Bergtheil, Jonas, 3:**433**, 16:349

Berihah, 3:**433–436**, 9:381

Berinski, Lev, 3:**436**

Berit Avraham (Horowitz), 9:532

Berit Emet (Caro), 4:487

Berit ha-Biryonim, 3:**436**

Berit ha-Olamit shel Torah va-Avodah, 14:391

Berit Menuhah (Abraham ben Isaac of Granada), 1:301–302

Berit milah. See Circumcision

Berit Shalom, 3:**436–437**, 702, 703, 13:269

Berit Trumpeldor. *See* Betar

Berk, Fred, 3:**437**, 5:414

Berkeley (CA)
    New Left, 15:142
    University of California, 15:358

Berkelhammer, Wilhelm, 15:326

Berkley, Rochelle, 3:**437**

Berkley, William R., 3:**437**

Berkman, Alexander, 18:710

Berkoff, Steven, 3:**438**

Berkovits, Eliezer, 3:**438–439**, 9:399–400

Berkow, Ira, 3:**439–440**

Berkowicz, Joseph, 3:**440**, 11:406

Berkowicz, Józef. *See* Berkowicz, Joseph

Berkowicz, Michael, 3:689

Berkowitz, Henry, 3:**440**, 6:192

Berkowitz, Mickey, 3:**440**

Berkowitz, Yitzhak Dov, 3:**440–442**, 8:717–718

Berkson, Isaac Baer, 3:**442**

Berkson family. *See* Bergson family

Berl, Emmanuel, 3:**442**

Berl, Ernst, 3:**442**

Berle, Milton, 3:**442–443**, 15:221

Berlewi, Henryk, 3:**443–444**

Berliand, Shlomo Meir, 3:**444**

Berligne, Eliyahu Meir, 3:**444**

Berlijn, Anton, 3:**444**

Berlin (Baline), Irving (Israel), 3:**455–456**

Berlin (Germany), 3:**444–453**, 7:349, 16:535
    17th-18th centuries, 3:445–447
    19th and 20th centuries, 3:447–452
        Aaron ben Isaac Benjamin Wolf and, 1:213
        antisemitism, 3:445, 447, 448–451
        assimilation, 3:446
        badges, Jewish, 3:450
        Black Death, 3:445
        displaced persons (DP), 3:451
        East Berlin, 3:452
        Hebrew printing industry, 3:452
        Holocaust memorials, 6:267, 9:431, vol. 9: color insert
        Host, desecration of, 3:445
        Jewish Museum, 4:13
        Juedische Freischule, 3:446, 447, 11:569
        Kristallnacht, 3:449
        Liebmann family, 12:810–811
        Middle Ages, 3:444–445
        museums, 14:628
        Orthodox Judaism, 3:448
        population statistics, 3:451*t*
        Reform Judaism, 3:448
        reunification, 3:452
        Zionist movement, 3:448

Berlin, Aryeh Loeb ben Abraham Meir, 3:**453**

Berlin, Congress of. *See* Congress of Berlin

Berlin, Daniel. *See* Itzig, Daniel

Berlin, David ben Judah Loeb. *See* Berlin, David ben Loeb

Berlin, David ben (Judah) Loeb, 3:**454**

Berlin, Hayyim, 3:**455,** 14:517

Berlin, Irving, 3:**455–456,** 4:177, 14:571

Berlin, Isaiah, 3:**456**

Berlin, Isaiah ben Judah Loeb (Pick, Isaiah), 3:**456–457**

Berlin, Israel, 3:**457**

Berlin, Meir. *See* Bar-Ilan, Meir

Berlin, Moses, 3:**457**

Berlin, Naphtali Ẓevi Judah (ha-Neẓiv), 3:**457–458,** 18:776

Berlin, Noah Ḥayyim Ẓevi Hirsch, 3:**458–459**

Berlin, Rayna Batya, 3:**459**

Berlin, Saul ben Ẓevi Hirsch Levin, 3:**459–460,** 7:126

Berlin-Al-exanderplatz (Doeblin), 5:729–730

Berlin Chantiers: Essair sur les passés fragiles (Robin), 17:354

Berliner, Abraham, 3:**460**

Berliner, David, 9:135

Berliner, Emile, 1:430, 3:**460–461,** 17:149

Berliner, Isaac, 3:**461**

Berlinger, Mendel. *See* Berle, Milton

Berlin Junction (Serra), 18:314

Berlin Memorial to the Murdered Jews of Europe, 6:267

Berlinski, Herman, 3:**461**

Berman, Aaron Levi, 7:143

Berman, Adof Abraham, 3:**461,** 16:347

Berman, Adolfo, 16:349

Berman, Howard Lawrence, 3:**461–462**

Berman, Issachar, 7:143

Berman, Jacob, 3:**462,** 16:347

Berman, Jakub, 3:**462–463**

Berman, Judah Loeb, 7:143

Berman, Julius, 3:**463**

Berman, Morton Mayer, 3:**463–464**

Berman, Myron R., 3:**464**

Berman, Pandro S., 3:**464**

Berman, Pauline, 15:476

Berman, Saul, 6:142

Berman, Shelley, 3:**464**

Berman, Simeon, 3:**465**

Berman Ashkenazi. *See* Issachar Berman ben Naphtali ha-Kohen

Berman Berman, Natalio, 3:**465**

Bermann, Adolf. *See* Kóbor, Tamás

Bermann, Richard Arnold, 3:**465**

Bermann, Vasili, 3:**466**

Bermant, Chaim Icyk, 3:**466**

Bermbach, William, 3:**471**

Bermuda Conference, 3:**466**

Bernadotte, Count, 11:178

Bernadotte, Folke, 3:**466–467,** 10:210, 211, 212

Bernadotte Rescue Operation
Oppenhejm, Ralph Gerson, 15:451
Ravensbrueck concentration camp and, 17:121

Bernal, Abraham, 3:**467**

Bernal, Edward, 3:**467–468**

Bernal, Jacob, 3:**467**

Bernal, Jacob Israel, 3:**467**

Bernal, John Desmond, 3:**467**

Bernal, Marco, 3:**467**

Bernal, Ralph, 3:**467**

Bernal family, 3:**467**

Bernal-Osborne, Ralph, 3:**467**

Bernard, Ḥayyim David, 3:**468**

Bernard, Ḥayyim Dov. *See* Friedberg, Bernard

Bernard, Jessie, 2:610, 3:**468,** 18:736

Bernard, Rosine. *See* Bernhardt, Sarah

Bernard, Tristan, 3:**468**

Bernardi, Herschel, 3:**468–469**

Bernardino da Feltre, 3:**469,** 4:48, 163, 14:461
Brescia, 4:163
Padua, 15:566
Pavia, 15:698

Bernardino da Siena, 3:**469**

Bernard of Clairvaux, 2:125, 3:**469,** 9:214–215

Bernays, Edward L., 3:**470–471**

Bernays, Isaac ben Jacob, 3:**469–470**

Bernays, Jacob, 3:**470**

Bernays, Michael, 3:**470**

Bernays, Paul Isaac, 3:**470**

Bernays family, 3:**469–470**

Bernbach, William, 1:428

Berne (Switzerland), 3:**471–472,** 688, 4:225

Bernfeld, Siegfried, 3:**472,** 6:161

Bernfeld, Simon, 3:**472,** 9:160

Bernhard, Emil. *See* Cohn, Emil Moses

Bernhard, Georg, 3:**472–473**

Bernhard, Sandra, 3:**473**

Bernhardt, Sarah, 3:**473–474,** 14:570

Bernhart (Hoffmann), 9:312

Bernheim, Franz, 12:565

Bernheim, Gilles, 3:**474**

Bernheim, Hippolyte, 3:**474**

Bernheim, Isaac Wolfe, 3:**474**

Bernheim, Louis, 3:**475**

Bernheimer, Carlo, 3:**475**

Bernheimer, Charles Seligman, 3:**475**

Bernheim Petition, 3:**475–476,** 18:580

Bernstein, Abraham Moshe, 3:**476**

Bernstein, Aline, 3:**476**

Bernstein, Arnold, 3:**476**

Bernstein, Aron David, 3:**476–477**

Bernstein, Aryeh Leib, 3:**477**

Bernstein, Béla, 3:**477,** 15:355

Bernstein, Carl, 3:**477–478,** 11:468

Bernstein, Charles, 20:300

Bernstein, Deborah, 18:736–737

Bernstein, Eduard, 3:**478,** 16:344, 18:705, 729

Bernstein, Elmer, 3:**478**

Bernstein, Fritz. *See* Bernstein, Perez

Bernstein, Harold Joseph, 3:**478–479**

Bernstein, Harry, 3:**479**

Bernstein, Henri-Leon, 3:**479**

Bernstein, Henry, 11:568

Bernstein, Herman, 2:49, 3:**479**

Bernstein, Ignatz, 3:**479**

Bernstein, Issachar ber, 3:**477**

Bernstein, Issachar Berush ben Aryeh Loeb, 3:**480**

Bernstein, Jacob Naphtali Herz, 3:**480**

Bernstein, Joseph, 3:**480**

Bernstein, Julius, 3:**480**

Bernstein, Karl, 12:553

Bernstein, Leonard, 3:**480–481,** 12:451

Bernstein, Louis, 3:**481–482**

Bernstein, Luca. *See* Luca, B.

Bernstein, Ludwig Behr, 3:**482**

Bernstein, Meyer Yefimiovich. *See* Medvedev, Mikhail

Bernstein, Morris Louis. *See* Louis, Morris

Bernstein, Moshe, 3:**482**

Bernstein, Nathan Osipovitch, 3:**482–483**

Bernstein, Ori, 3:**483**

Bernstein, Osip Samoilovich, 3:**483**

Bernstein, Perez (Fritz), 3:**483**

Bernstein, Philip. *See* Hugó, Károly

Bernstein, Philip Sidney, 3:**435, 483–484**

Bernstein, Sid, 3:**484**

Bernstein, Sidney Lewis, 3:**484**

Bernstein, Simon, 3:**484**

Bernstein, Theodore M., 3:**484–485**

Bernstein, Theresa, 3:**485**

Bernstein, Zalman Chaim, 3:**485**

Bernstein, Zvi Hirsch, 3:**485–486**

Bernstein-Cohen, Jacob. *See* Bernstein-Kogan, Jacob

Bernstein-Cohen, Miriam, 3:**486**

Bernstein-Kogan, Jacob, 3:**486**

Bernstein-Namierowski, Lewis. *See* Namier, Sir Lewis

Bernstein-Sinaieff, Leopold, 3:**486**

Beroea. *See* Veroia

Beror Ḥayil (Israel), 3:**486**

Berosus (Berossus), 3:**486–487,** 15:287

Berr, Jacob, 3:**487**

Berr (de Turique), Michel, 3:**487–488**

Berr Isaac Berr de Turique, 3:**488,** 8:437, 439, 13:194

Bershad (Ukraine), 3:**488**

Bershadski, Sergey Alexandrovich, 3:**488–489**

Bershadsky, Isaiah, 3:**489**

Bersin, Alan, 18:15

Bersohn, Matthias, 3:**489**

Berson, Arthur Joseph Stanislav, 1:430, 3:**489–490**

Berstein, Marver H., 4:124

Berthold of Freiburg, 3:**490**

Berthold of Ratisbon. *See* Berthold of Regensburg

Berthold of Regensburg, 3:**490,** 775

Bertholet, Alfred, 3:**490**

Bertig, Mordecai. *See* Gebirtig, Mordechai

Bertini, Gary, 3:**490–491**

Bertini, K. Aharon, 3:**491**

Bertinoro, Obadiah ben Abraham Yare, 3:*491,* **491–492,** 14:329, 15:581

Bertonoff, Deborah, 3:**492**

Berurei Averah/Averot, 3:**492**

Beruryah, 3:**492–493**

Berytus (Lebanon). *See* Beirut

Besalú (Spain), 3:**493**

Besançon (France), 3:**493–494**

Besara (Israel). *See* Bet She'arim (Israel)

Besdin, Morris J., 3:**494**

Besdin, Samuel, 3:**494**

Besekow, Samuel, 3:**494**

Besem. *See* Balsam

BeShT. *See* Israel ben Eliezer Ba'al Shem Tov

Besicovitch, Abram Samoilovitch, 3:**494–495**

Besor, Brook of (Israel), 3:**495**

Besredka, Alexander, 3:**495**

Bessarabia
  Holocaust
    Dombroveni, 5:738
    Kaushany, 12:37
    Khotin, 12:117–118
    Kiliya, 12:154
    Kishinev, 12:199
    Sekiryany, 18:256–257
    Vad Raskov, 20:457
    Valea-Lui-Vlad, 20:459
    Yedintsy, 21:292–293

Bessarabia (Moldova), 3:**495–498,** *496,* 5:738

Bessels, Emil, 3:**498**

Besser, Chaskel O., 3:**498**

Bessin, Hyman, 15:517

Bessis, Albert, 3:**498–499,** 16:346

Bessis, Jeshua, 3:**499**

Besso, Henry, 3:**499**

Best, Werner, 5:582

The Best and the Brightest (Halberstam), 8:265

Bestiality, 18:329

Bestimmung, Heimat and Alter der synagogalen Poesie (Edelmann), 6:143

"Best interest of the child" concept, 15:639–640

The Best of Everything (Jaffe), 11:68–69

The Best Use of Economic Resources (Kantorovich), 11:771

Besztercebánya (Slovakia). *See* Banska, Bystrica (Slovakia)

Bet, 3:**499**

Bet Aglayim (Israel), 3:**499**

Beta Israel, 3:**499–509**
  Eldad ha-Dani, 6:294
  history of, 3:499–502, 503–509
  Israel, and immigration and absorption of Ethiopian Jews of, 3:507, 508–509
  Italy, and conquest of, 3:504–505
  leadership of, 3:504, 505
  legends and, 3:499
  missionaries and, 3:503–504
  organization of, 3:502
  study of, 6:677–678

Bet Alfa (Israel), 3:**509**

Bet Alpha synagogue, 2:371

Bet-Anath (Israel), 2:131, 3:**509–510**

Bet Aniyya (Israel). *See* Bethany (Israel)

Betar, 3:**510–511**
  Anielewicz, Mordecai, 2:164
  Begin, Menahem, 3:261
  Eliav, Binyamin, 6:321
  Jabotinsky, Vladimir, 11:10–11
  Jewish State Party, 11:315, 316
  Kahane, Meir, 11:715

Bet-Arabah (Israel), 3:**511**

Bet Berl Teachers Training College, 18:618

Bet-Cherem (Israel), 3:**511–512**

Bet-Dagon (Israel), 3:**512**

Bet din and judges, 3:**512–524,** 5:495
  Amsterdam, 2:107
  authorization for rabbinical court decisions by Israel, 3:520
  civil law in, 3:520–521
  dayyanim appointments and status, 3:522–523
  defined, 3:512–513

Ehrlich, Arnold Bogumi, 6:243
  in Europe, 3:515
  extralegal remedies in capital cases, 6:631–632
  High Courts and, 3:521
  Israel (state), 3:516–524
  of Judah ha-Nasi, 11:502–503
  judgments of, 3:523
  jurisdiction law, 3:517–520
  Middle Ages, 3:514–515
  origins of, 3:513–514
  procedural rules and, 3:522
  and refusal, writ of, 3:520–521
  in Russia, 3:515
  structure of, 3:521–522
  Talmudic period, 3:514
  See also Judges and judiciary

Bet-Eden (Syria), 3:**524**

Bet-El (Israel), 3:**524–526**
  Ai, 1:548
  Jacob and, 11:18, 19–20
  temple, 2:97–100

Bet El Kabbalists, 11:621

Bet Eshel (Israel), 3:**526**

Bet Garmu family, 3:**526**

Bet Gufnin. *See* Gofnah

Bet Guvrin (Israel), 3:**526–527**

Beth Adam decision, 17:174–175

Bet ha-Emek (Israel), 3:**527**

Bet ha-Levi (Israel), 3:**527,** 12:685

Bet ha-Midrash (Jellinek), 14:539

Bet Ḥanan (Israel), 3:**527**

Bet Hananyah (Israel). *See* Bethany (Israel)

Beth-Anath (Israel). *See* Bet-Anath (Israel)

Bethany (Israel), 3:**527**

Bethar, 3:**527**

Bet-Haram (Israel), 3:**528–529**

Bet Ḥarodon (Israel), 3:**529**

Beth-Baal-Meon. *See* Baal-Meon

Bethbasi (Israel), 3:**529**

Beth-Cherem (Israel), 6:260

Beth-Dagon (Israel). *See* Bet-Dagon (Israel)

Beth Din of America, 13:188

Bethe, Hans Albrecht, 3:**529**

Beth-Eden (Syria). *See* Bet-Eden (Syria)

Beth-El (Israel). *See* Bet-El (Israel)

Beth El: Ehrentempel verdienter ungarischer Israeliten (Reich), 17:196

Beth-El Mountains (Israel), 10:115

Bethel-Sharezer. *See* Sharezer

Bet Ḥerut (Israel), 3:**529**

Beth Hamedrash Heshaim, 6:204

Beth-Haram (Israel). *See* Bet-Haram (Israel)

Beth-Haran (Israel). *See* Bet-Haram (Israel)

Beth Hatefutsoth, 3:**529–530**

Beth Hayeled School (New York, NY), 6:197

Bet Hillel (Israel), 3:**530**

Bet Hillel and Bet Shammai, 3:**530–533**

   creation, 5:275–276

   halakhah, approach to, 6:486, 8:255

   ḥallah, 8:278

   Ḥanukkah lamp, 8:333

   hefker, 8:753–755

   marriage, 8:255, 21:324

   on New Year, 15:193

   on non-Jewish women and niddah, 15:256–257

   praising the bride, 8:247–248

   resurrection, 17:242

   Second Temple period, 1:348

   on Shema reading, 18:454

Beth Jacob Congregation, 13:200

Beth Jacob schools, 3:**533**, 12:455, 18:121

Bethlehem (Israel), 3:**533–535**

   See also Ephrath

Bethleptepha (Israel), 3:**535**

Beth-Meon. *See* Baal-Meon

Beth Mikra (periodical), 18:724

Bet(h)-Horon (Israel), 3:**535**

Bethphage (Israel), 3:**536**

Bethsaida (Israel), 3:**536**

Beth Shalom (Philadelphia), 5:29

Bethuel, 3:**536–537**

Bethulia (Israel), 3:**537**

Bet (Bayt) Iksa (Israel), 3:**537**

Bet Keshet (Israel), 3:**537**

Bet(h) Leḥem (Ha-Gelilit) (Israel), 3:**537**

Bet(h)-Maon (Israel), 3:**537**

Bet Meir (Israel), 3:**537**

Bet (ha)-Midrash, 3:**537–538**

Bet Neḥemyah (Israel), 3:**538**

Bet Netofah (Israel), 3:**538**

Bet(h)-Nimrah (Israel), 3:**538–539**

Be-Tokh Levaʿim (Dolitzki), 5:735–736

Betomarsea (Israel), 13:407

Bet Oren (Israel), 3:**539**

Bet Oved (Israel), 3:**539**

Bet Porat (Joseph ben Judah Engel), 6:409

The Betrayal (Kreisel), 4:424

Bet(h)-Rehob (Israel), 3:**539**

Betrothal, 3:**539–541**

Bet Shammai. *See* Bet Hillel and Bet Shammai

Bet Shammai school, 18:394

Bet(h)-Shean (Israel), 3:**541–547**

Bet She'arim (Israel), 3:**547–548**

Bet(h)-Shemesh (Israel), 3:**548–550**, *549*

Bet(h)-Shittah (Israel), 3:**550**

Bettan, Israel, 3:**550**

Bettauer, Hugo, 3:**550–551**

Bettelheim, Aaron Siegfried. *See* Bettelheim, Albert Siegfried

Bettelheim, Albert Siegfried, 3:**551**

Bettelheim, Bruno, 3:**551–552**

Bettelheim, Karl, 3:**551**

Bettelheim, Lipot Leopold Meyer Leb, 3:**551**

Bettelheim, Loeb, 3:**551**

Bettelheim, Moses, 3:**551**

Bettelheim, Samuel, 3:**552**

Bettelheim family, 3:**551**

Better Generation (Balin), 3:91

Bettman, Gary, 3:**552**

Bettman, Gilbert, 15:393

Bettmann, Bernhardt, 3:**552**

The Betty Bacharach Home for Afflicted Children (NJ), 3:32, *33*

Bet-Unyaki, 3:**729**

Between Earth and Heaven. See Ben Erezve-Shamayim

Between the Calendars (Ben Yehuda), 3:389

Between the Dead and the Living (Sened). *See Bein ha-Metim u-vein ha-Ḥayyim* (Sened)

Between Two Worlds (weekly column), 6:259

Between Worlds: The Paintings and Drawings of Samuel Bak from 1946-2001, 3:71

Bet Yannai (Israel), 3:**552**

Bet Yehoshu'a (Israel), 3:**552–553**

Bet Yeraḥ (Israel), 3:*553*, **553–554**

Bet Yizḥak (Israel), 3:**554**

Bet Yosef (Israel), 3:**554**

Bet Zayit (Israel), 3:**554**

Bet Zayyada (Israel). *See* Bethsaida (Israel)

Bet Zekharyah (Israel), 3:**554**

Bet Zera (Israel), 3:554, **554**

Bet Ẓerifa family, 3:**554–555**

Bet Zevul (Ḥalap), 8:358

Bet(h)-Zur (Israel), 3:**555**

Bet-Ẓuri, Eliahu, 3:**555**

Beugnot, Auguste Arthur, 3:**555**

Be'ur ha-Gra (Elijah ben Solomon Zalman), 6:345

Be'urim Ḥadashim (Lebensohn), 12:590

Be'ur Inyan Shenei Kavvim (Provençal, Moses), 16:636

Beuthen (Germany). *See* Bytom (Germany)

Bevan, Edwyn Robert, 3:**555–556**

Be-Veito ba-Midbar (Shalev), 18:372

Bevin, Ernest, 3:**556**, 6:430

Bey, Cattaui, 16:346

Be-Yishuv shel Ya'ar (Hazaz), 8:492

Beyond Criticism (Shapiro), 18:406

Beyond the river, 6:551–552

Beyond the River Lethe. See Me-Ever Nehar ha-Lethe (Lenski)

Beyrouth (Lebanon). *See* Beirut

Beyth, Hans, 3:**556**

Beẓah (Aaron ben Joseph ha-Levi), 1:215

Beẓah (tractate), 3:**556**

Bezalel, 3:**557**

Bezalel, Cecil. *See* Roth, Cecil

Bezalel Academy of Arts and Design (Jerusalem), 3:**557**, 4:75, 10:653, 695, 696, 13:14, 18:110, 111

Bezalel Ashkenazi, 11:163

Bezalel ben Moses ha-Kohen, 3:**557–558**

Bezalel ben Solomon of Kobryn, 3:**558**

Bezalel National Art Museum. *See* Israel Museum

Bezalel style, 2:510

Bezek (Israel), 1:413, 3:**558**

Bezek Law, 13:145

Bezem, Naftali, 3:**558**

Bezidul Nou (Romania), 3:**558–559**

Béziers (France), 3:**559–560**

Bezprozvany, Hyman B. *See* Bass, Hyman B.

Bezruč, Petr, 5:366

Bezusy entuziast (Altauzen), 2:17

Bi'ah marriage, 4:747

Biala. *See* Zuelz

Biala (Poland), 3:**560**, 689

Biale, David, 3:**560**

Biale dynasty, 8:422

Bialeh, Ẓevi Hirsch ben Naphtali Herz, 3:**560–561**

Bialik, Ḥayyim Naḥman, 2:21, 3:**561–565**, 8:725, 727–728, 9:412, 15:380

   aggadah, 1:460

   children's literature, 4:621

   Dvir publishing firm, 6:74

   Hebrew language, 8:675

   influence on Fichman, Jacob, 7:8–9

   Judeo-Persian poetry of, 11:558

Bialik, Ḥayyim Naḥman, *continued*
  Lachower, Yeruḥam Fishel, 12:424
  Moriah publishing house, 14:491,
    17:126
  piyyut, language of, 8:652
  Rawnitzki, Yehoshua Ḥana, 17:126
  Shalom Aleichem and, 18:384
  Solomon, 18:761
  translation of *Julius Caesar,* 18:370
Bialkin, Kenneth J., 3:**565–566**, 728
Bialloblotzky, Christian Heinrich
  Friedrich. *See* Bialoblotzky,
  Christian Heinrich Friedrich
Bialoblocki, Samuel Sheraga, 3:**566**
Bialoblotzky, Christian Heinrich
  Friedrich, 3:**566**
Bialostozky, Benjamin Jacob, 3:**566**
Biała Podlaska (Poland), 3:**560**
Bialystok (Poland), 3:137, **567–570,**
  567*t, 568*
  Holocaust, 16:312–313
  partisans, 15:666, 667
  pogrom (1906), 6:45
Biarritz (France), 3:**570**
Biazi *v.* Levi, 5:127
Bibago, Abrahem ben Shem Tov,
  3:**570–571,** 11:472
Bibas, Abraham, 3:571
Bibas, Ḥayyim, 3:571
Bibas, Joseph, 3:571
Bibas, Judah, 3:572
Bibas, Samuel, 3:572
Bibas, Shem Tov, 3:571
Bibas family, 3:**571–572**
Bible, 3:**572–679,** 13:446–448
  allegories, 1:665, 16:74–75, 106
  altars in, 2:12–13
  Alt School or Alt-Noth trend, 2:11
  anatomy, 2:133
  angels, 2:150–152
    Angel of Death, 2:148–149
    cherubim, 4:600
    Gabriel, 14:167–169
    Michael, 14:167–169
    Raphael, 17:93
    Raziel, 17:128–129
    Uriel, 20:421–422
  animals, 2:166–167, 168*t–171t,*
    12:696–697
    amphibia, 2:172
    animal tales, 2:173
    antelope, 2:184–185
    ants, 2:184
    apes, 2:254
    birds, 2:171–172
    camels, 4:380–381

    cattle, 4:526–527
    deer, 5:530–531
    eagles, 6:81
    fish, 2:172
    horses, 9:546
    invertebrates, 2:172
    mammals, 2:167–171, 12:649
    owls in, 15:550
    ravens, 17:119
    red heifer, 17:156–157
    reptiles, 2:172
    sheep, 18:431
  anointing, 2:179–180
  apocalyse, 2:257
  Arabia, 2:293
  Arad, 2:328–329
  Aramaic, 2:343–345
  Aram and Arameans, 2:337, 338,
    339
  Ararat, 2:361
  archaeology, 2:380, 11:77
  in the arts, 3:669–679
    fine art, 3:673–674
    music, 3:672–673
  astrology, 2:615–616
  astronomy, 2:620–621
  atonement, 2:644
  Bethlehem (Israel), 3:533–534
  blindness in, 3:753–754
  breast as heart, 8:508–509
  bribery, 4:175
  candles, 4:429
  canon, 3:574–583
    Armenian, 3:603
    Christian, 3:574, 666
    contents of, 3:576
    definition and use of concept,
      3:574–575
    definitive canon, 11:10
    Hellenistic, 3:579, 579*t*
    languages of, 3:582–583
    New Testament, 15:190–191
    number of books in, 3:580
    order of books, 3:579*t,* 580–
      582, 580*t,* 581*t,* 582*t*
    order of books in, 3:579*t,*
      580–582, 580*t,* 581*t,* 582*t*
    process of canonization,
      3:575–576
    significance of, 3:575
    tripartite, 3:576–579
  capital punishment, 4:445–446
  carts and chariots, 4:497
  castration, 4:516–517
  cause and effect, relation between,
    4:529

  celibacy, 4:537
  census, 4:541–542
  Chaldeans, 4:561–562
  charity, 4:569
  chastity, 4:581
  Christianity
    allegorical interpretation of
      scripture in, 3:643
    biblical exegesis and study,
      Jewish influence on, 3:648
    canon, 3:574, 666
    religious impact of Bible on,
      3:663–667
    Septuagint and, 3:596–597
    translations, modern, 3:611,
      625
  cloth and clothing, 6:12
    dyeing, 6:76, 77
    sha'atnez, 18:336
  commentaries
    Alshekh, Moses, 2:10–11
    early Christian, 11:143
    German, 13:775–776, 15:718–
      719
    Italian, 5:441
    Italy, 6:717
    Kara, Joseph, 11:783–784
    Kara, Menahem ben Jacob,
      11:784
    Karaite, 5:428
    Kirimi, Abraham, 12:185
    la'az in, 12:405–406
    Laniado, Abraham ben Isaac,
      12:484
    Laniado, Samuel ben
      Abraham, 12:485
    Latif, Isaac B. Abraham ibn,
      12:506–507
    Levi Ben Gershom, 12:699
    Me-Am Lo'ez, 13:710–711
    medieval France, 7:153
    medieval Spain, 6:681
    medieval Syria, 13:603
    Philo Judaeus, 16:60, 61–62
    Sforno, Obadiah ben Jacob,
      18:333–334
  concordances and dictionaries
    glossaries, 3:605–606, 628
  criticism, 2:627
    Davidson, Samuel, 5:477
    development of, 15:744
    Hitzig, Ferdinand, 9:293–294
    Hupfeld, Hermann Christian
      Karl, 9:622
    Ilgen, Karl David, 9:721
    Jacob, Benno, 11:25
    Jeremias, Alfred, 11:136

Pedersen, Johannes, 15:711–
712
Perles, Felix, 15:776
Perles, Joseph, 15:776
Protestant, 5:477, 16:26–27
Smend, Rudolph, 18:686–687
curses, power of, 3:752
Damascus Keter (13th c.), vol. 7:
color insert
day and night in, 5:486–488
death, 2:148, 5:510–511
burial customs, 4:291–292
cemeteries, 4:538
debt recovery in, 6:590–591
deep, the, 5:530
deists and, 5:533–534
demons, demonology, 5:572–573
desecration, 5:601
dew, 5:629–630
divination, 5:704–705
divorce, 5:710–711
door and doorpost, 5:752–753
dowries, 5:768
dreams, 6:8–9
drunkenness, 6:26–27
dysphemisms, 6:550
ebony, 6:88
ecology, 6:92–93
education, 6:159, 12:621–622
Emar cuneiform discoveries,
6:386–390
emotions, 6:396
environmental responsibility,
6:449, 454
ethics in, 6:531–534
euphemisms, 6:549–550, 13:616
evil eye in, 6:584, 585
evil speech, 12:495
exegesis and study, 3:640–656,
9:814–821
allegorical interpretation,
3:641, 643–645, 660, 665
Alshekh, Moses, 2:10, 11
archaeological influence on,
3:650, 652, 654
Ben-Asher, Aaron ben Moses,
3:319–320
Bendavid, Lazarus, 3:325
Bozecco, Benjamin ben
Judah, 4:113–114
Breuer, Mordecai, 4:172–173
Breuer, Raphael, 4:173
Buber, Martin, 4:231, 235
Budde, Karl Ferdinand
Reinhard, 4:249
Buhl, Franz Peder William
Mayer, 4:256

Buttenweiser, Moses, 4:319
Dubno, Solomon ben Joel,
14:486
Duhm, Bernhard, 6:42–43
Dupont-Sommer, André, 6:51
Eerdmans, Bernardus Dirks,
6:215–216
Eissfeldt, Otto, 6:278
Eliezer of Beaugency, 6:330
in France, 3:642
French commentators, 3:642
Hebrew manuscripts, 13:488
homiletic commentary, 3:641,
660–662
Ibn Ezra, Abraham ben Meir,
9:666–669
Judaism, development of
concept of, 11:517
in Judeo-Persian, 11:551
La Peyrère, Isaac, 12:488–489
Levenson, Jon D., 12:679–680
Levine, Baruch, 12:717
literal commentary, 3:641,
642
Middle Ages, 13:94–95
modern critical studies,
3:648–656
modern Jewish exegesis,
3:645–648, 663
Morgenstern, Julian, 14:486
pardes as mnemonic for
types of, 15:632
philological commentary,
3:642
philosophical commentary,
3:643
philosophical methodology
applied to, 16:72–73, 74–75
Postillae Perpetuae of
Nicholas de Lyre, 15:251
pre-Middle Ages, 13:87–88
rabbinic literature, 3:641–643,
660–662
Rosenmueller, Ernst Friedrich
Karl, 17:449
Rosenthal, Judah, 17:454
Sarna, Nahum M., 18:59
Solieli, Mordecai, 18:753
Spanish commentators, 3:642
synthetic commentary, 3:642–
643
Talmudic literature, 3:640–
641, 660–663
by women, 3:663
fables, 6:666–667
family in, 6:690–693
fasting, 6:719–721, 722–723
fictional stories from, 7:11

friendship, 7:289–290
Gemara
order of books in, 3:581
religious impact of, 3:662
grammar, 8:554–558, 576–577
ḥamez, 8:302
Hapax Legomena, 8:337
hatred, 8:458
Havilah, 8:470
Hebrew manuscripts, 13:488
Hexateuch, 11:446
history of, 3:583–586
homicide, 6:220–221, 9:506–507
homosexuality, 9:516
honor, 9:519
hospitality, 9:561
host of heaven, 9:566–567
human dignity and freedom,
9:586–587
as human document, 16:93
humility, 9:589–590
humor, 9:590
hunting, 9:621
hygiene, 9:647–648
iconography, 9:703–704, *704*
idolatry, 9:710–712
illuminated or illustrated, 3:674–
679
imitation of God, 9:737–738
imprisonment, 5:606, 9:743
imprisonment for debt, 9:748
inaccuracies, Abd al-Ḥaqq
al-Islāmī on, 1:240
incest, 9:755
inclination, good and evil, 9:756–
757
Islam
allegorical interpretation of
scripture in, 3:644
art of, 3:674
Bible translations in Arabic
and Judeo-Arabic, 3:603–
605, 627
exegesis and study stimulated
by rise of, 3:641
religious impact on, 3:667–
669
tales, 10:754
jealousy in, 11:98
Jerusalem in, 11:208–211
Jewish identity in, 11:292–293
Josephus' *Jewish Antiquities* and,
11:438
Josiah's discovery of "Book of the
Torah," 11:457–458
joy, concept of, 11:470–471
Jubilees, Book of, 11:473, 474

Bible, *continued*
  Judaism during biblical period, development of, 11:514–515
  kapparot custom, 11:782
  Karaites and Karitism, 11:785–786
  kiss of death, 5:513
  labor and laborers, 12:408–409, 410
  laws and legal systems
    judges in, 5:495
    justice, terms for, 11:578
    labor laws, 12:411–412
    law of evidence, 6:577, 578, 579
    legal maxims, 12:603
    morality and law, 12:535
    prohibitions in and penal law, 15:720
    shomerim, 18:513–514
    as source of law, 14:337
    taxation, 19:534
  leprosy, 12:650–653
  letters and letter writers, 12:668–669
  literature influenced by
    Danish, 18:89
    Dante, 10:788
    Dutch, 6:67–68
    Egyptian, 6:225–226
    English, 6:432–434
    Hungarian, 9:602–604
    Italian, 10:787–788
    musical intonation, 13:656–664
    Norwegian, 18:90–91
    Russian, 17:587–588
    Swedish, 18:90–91
  logos, 13:174
  lots, 13:217–219
  love, 13:227–229
  Maimonides, Moses, 13:392
  manna, 13:478
  Mari (Mesopotamia), 13:537–541
  marriages, 12:725, 13:563–564, 565
  mashal proverbs, 16:640–642
  mathematics in, 13:671
  Matriarchs, 4:562–563
  medicine in, 13:720–722
  miracles, 14:305–306, 309
  mishmarot and ma'amadot, 14:317–318, 319
  mitzvah, 14:372
  moneylending, 14:436–437
  monogamy, 14:447–448
  monotheism, 14:448–450
  names for
    Bible as a whole, 3:574

    in Hellenistic Judaism, 3:660
    Jewish sensitivities regarding, 3:608
    sections and individual books, 3:576
  naturalistic explanations, 15:280
  nature of man, 13:446–448
  nomadism in, 15:294–295
  oaths in, 15:358–360
  oils in, 15:395–396
  olam ha-ba in, 15:400
  "Old Testament," 15:190, 191
  Oral Law and, 15:455
  parables, 15:620–621
  paradise in Eden narrative, 15:623–627
  parody in, 15:654
  peace, concept of, 15:700–701
  perjury in, 15:772
  Philo Liber Antiquitatum Biblicarum, 16:58–59
  physical format, 4:71–76
  places named in, 6:568–569
  printing, 2:633
  proverbs, 16:647
  providence, 16:648
  psychiatry, 16:684
  psychology, 16:687
  punishment, 16:734–735, 736–737
  purity and impurity, ritual, 16:746–750
  reading
    al tikrei, 2:20
    mnemonics, 13:619, 14:397
    vocalizations, 13:611
  related materials, 3:656–658
  religious impact, 3:659–669
    Christianity, 3:663–667
    Islam, 3:667–669
    Judaism, 3:659–663
  sacrifices, 17:643
  Satan, 18:72
  sederim, 18:235
  shofar, 18:506–507
  signs and symbols, 18:568–570
  sin, 18:621–624
  sociology of, 3:658–659
  Tabernacle, 19:418–423
  taking of life in, 13:743
  Tanakh, 19:499
  texts and editions
    evolution of text, 3:583–586
    Hebrew editions, printed, 3:586–588
    polyglots, 3:588, 613, 636, 13:56

  Thanksgiving Psalms, 5:507, 19:668
  theology, 19:694–695
    anthropomorphism, 2:188–189
    deism, 5:533–534
    eschatology, 6:489–495
    particularism in, 11:514–515
    universalism in, 11:514–515
  throat as heart, 8:509
  translations, ancient, 3:588–606, 12:405–406
    Aquila, 15:433–434
    Arabic and Judeo-Arabic, 3:603–605
    Aramaic, 3:588–594, 599–601, 600, 652
    Armenian, 3:602–603
    Egyptian (Coptic), 3:602
    Ethiopic, 3:601
    glossaries, 3:605–606, 12:406
    Greek, 3:595–598, 13:87
    Hungariand, 10:829
    Judeo-Persian, 11:552–553
    Karaite, 3:604–605
    Latin, 3:598, 11:142–143
    Onkelos, 15:433–434
    Peshitta, 3:599–600
    Saadiah Gaon, 3:603–604, 605, 17:612–613
    Samaritan, 3:599, 652
    Septuagint, 18:307
    sharh, 3:605
    Syriac, 3:599–601
  translations, modern, 3:606–640
    aesthetics of, 3:609
    Arabic, 3:627
    Basque, 3:636
    Catalan, 3:627
    Celtic, 3:636–637
    Danish, 3:627
    Dutch, 3:627–628
    English, 2:144, 633, 3:611–627, 18:688
    faithfulness to original text in, 3:606–608, 621, 625, 628
    feminist sensitivities regarding, 3:608
    Finnish, 3:628
    French, 3:628–629
    German, 3:629–632, 4:231, 235, 7:509, 14:36–37, 39, 15:719
    Greek, 3:636
    Hebrew, 2:633
    Hungarian, 3:632

Icelandic, 3:632–633

on Internet, 3:637

Italian, 3:633

Jewish languages, 3:609–611

Jewish sensitivities regarding, 3:608

Judeo-Italian, 11:547

Judeo-Persian, 11:557

Lithuanian, 3:636

Maltese, 3:636

name of God, 3:608–609

neo-Aramaic, 15:70–72

non-European languages, 3:637

Norwegian, 3:633

Provençal, 3:629

Romanian, 3:633

Romanish, 3:633

Slavonic, 3:634–636

Spanish, 2:490, 3:636

Swedish, 3:636

transmission of, 13:606–612

methods of writing, 13:606–609, 787

writing instruments, 4:73

Urim and Thummim, 5:704

wisdom as female, 16:105

women in

charitable work, 16:46

niddah, 15:254

stereotypes of, 16:105–106

Yiddish language, 2:108

zeal in, 11:98

See also Bible scholars; Pentateuch; *specific books, people and places of the Bible*

The Bible and the Image, the History of Photography in the Holy Land 1839-1899 (Nir), 16:127

The Bible as it Was (Kugel), 1:461

"Bible as Literature" movement, 3:655

Bible codes, 3:**679–680**

The Bible in Spain (Borrow), 13:80

Bible Project (Yerushalmi), 8:722

Bible scholars

Aharoni, Yoḥanan, 1:531–532, 2:329, 330, 371, 11:523, 524

Ainsworth, Henry, 1:550–551

Albright, William Foxwell, 1:596, 2:374, 378, 8:621, 13:60

biblical archaeology, 3:650, 654

Joshua, Book of, 11:447, 448

Alt, Albrecht, 2:11, 3:658

Joshua, Book of, 11:446, 447, 449

moneylending, 14:436–437

Noth, Martin, 15:315

Andrewes, Lancelot, 2:144, 3:613

Astruc, Jean, 2:627, 3:646, 649

Badè, William Frederick, 3:43

Baudissin, Wolf Wilhelm, Graf von, 3:216

Bauer, Hans, 3:216, 13:58

Baumgartel, Elise J., 3:221

Baumgartner, Walter, 3:222

Bech(ius), Matthias Friedrich, 3:243

Beek, Martinus Adrianus, 3:250

Ben-Asher, Aaron ben Moses, 3:319–320

Ben-Asher, Moses, 3:312, 320

Ben-Naphtali, Moses Ben David, 3:367

Bentzen, Aage, 3:381–382

Benzinger, Immanuel, 3:391–392

Bergstraesser, Gotthelf, 3:433, 13:58

Bertholet, Alfred, 3:490

Bleek, Friedrich, 3:747–748

Bonfrère, Jacques, 4:62–63

Budde, Karl Ferdinand Reinhard, 4:249

Buhl, Franz Peder William Meyer, 4:256, 11:343, 344

Buttenwieser, Moses, 4:319

Cassuto, Umberto, 3:647–648, 650, 4:510–511, 9:161

Cheyne, Thomas Kelly, 4:606

Cocceius, Johannes, 4:765

Colenso, John William, 5:57

Colombo, Samuel, 5:64

Cook, Stanley Arthur, 5:200

Cooke, George Albert, 5:203

Cornill, Carl Heinrich, 5:224

Crowfoot, John Winter, 5:307, 15:589

Davidson, Samuel, 5:477

Delitzsch, Friedrich, 5:540–541, 8:470

Del Medico, Henri E., 5:542

Deutsch, Emanuel Oskar, 5:622

Diez Macho, Alejandro, 5:659

Dillmann, August, 5:661–662

Dothan, Trude, 5:764

Driver, Samuel Rolles, 6:22, 15:554

Dubno, Solomon ben Joel, 6:34, 8:436, 440

Amsterdam, 2:108

biblical exegesis and study of, 3:646

as bibliophile, 3:684

Mendelssohn, Moses, 2:108

Duhm, Bernhard, 6:42–43

Dupont-Sommer, André, 6:51

Eerdmans, Bernardus Dirks, 6:215–216

Ehrlich, Arnold Bogumil, 3:647, 6:242–243

Eichhorn, Johann Gottfried, 3:646, 649, 6:247

Eissfeldt, Otto, 6:278

Erman, Johann Peter Adolph, 6:482

Ewald, Heinrich Georg August, 3:649, 6:589

Feigin, Samuel Isaac, 6:734

Finkelstein, Jacob Joel, 7:34

Fishbane, Michael, 4:125, 7:60

Frankfort, Henri, 3:651, 7:204

Frymer-Kensky, Tikva, 7:303

Galling, Kurt, 7:350

Garstang, John, 7:391, 8:499

Geddes, Alexander, 7:408

Gelb, Ignace Jay, 7:417–418

Gesenius, Heinrich Friedrich Wilhelm, 7:562, 13:57–58, 15:753

Gevirtz, Stanley, 7:567

Ginsberg, Harold Lewis, 7:609–610

English translations of Bible, 3:621, 622

Job, Book of, 11:343, 344, 346, 351, 352, 353, 355

Ugaritic language and biblical exegesis, 3:652

Ginsburg, Christian David, 3:588, 7:610–611

Gordis, Robert, 7:764, 11:343, 353

Gordon, Cyrus Herzl, 7:767

Graetz, Heinrich, 8:26–29

Graf, Karl Heinrich, 8:29, 16:630

Greenberg, Moshe, 8:72–73

Greenfield, Jonas Carl, 8:79

Gressman, Hugo, 8:87

Gruenberg, Samuel, 8:107

Gunkel, Hermann, 3:650–651, 8:137

Guthe, Hermann, 8:150

Hallo, William, 8:282

Haran, Menahem, 8:344

Held, Moshe, 8:781

Heller, Ḥayyim, 8:794

Hengstenberg, Ernst Wilhelm, 8:807

Hirschler, Pál, 9:140

Hitzig, Ferdinand, 9:293–294

Hoelscher, Gustav, 9:302, 11:442

Hoffmann, David Ẓevi, 9:310–311

Hoschander, Jacob, 9:547

Hottinger, Johann Heinrich, 9:568

Bible scholars, *continued*
Hrabanus Maurus, 9:573
Hupfeld, Hermann Christian Karl, 9:622
Ilgen, Karl David, 9:721
Jacob, Benno, 11:25
Jacob ben Ḥayyim ben Issac ibn Adonijah, 4:52, 11:32, 13:620–621
Jampel, Sigmund, 11:77
Jeremias, Alfred, 3:651, 11:136
Jirku, Anton, 11:337–338
Kalisch, Markus Moritz, 11:736
Kaufmann, Yeḥezkel, 12:33
Job, Book of, 11:347
Joel, Book of, 11:362
Jonah, Book of, 11:388
Joshua and book of Joshua, 11:442, 449
Kautzsch, Emil Friedrich, 12:37
Keil, Karl Friedrich, 12:67
Kenyon, Dame Kathleen Mary, 11:201, 12:80
Kirkpatrick, Alexander Francis, 12:186–187
Kittel, Rudolf, 12:207
Kuenen, Abraham, 12:378–379
Kugel, James L., 1:461, 12:379–380
Landsberger, Benno, 12:475–476
La Peyrère, Isaac, 3:649, 12:488–489
Lauterbach, Asher Zelig, 12:529
Leibowitz, Neḥama, 3:625, 12:621–622
Leusden, Johann, 12:675
Levenson, Jon D., 12:679–680
Levine, Baruch, 12:717
Lewy, Julius, 12:771
Lightfoot, John, 13:13, 59
Lods, Adolphe, 3:658, 13:155
Loewe, Joel, 13:166
Loewisohn, Solomon, 8:440, 687, 13:171
Loisy, Alfred Firmin, 13:176
Lowth, Robert, 3:646, 737, 13:237
Macalister, Robert Alexander Stewart, 2:377, 13:315, 15:589
Mahler, Eduard, 13:360
Malamat, Abraham, 13:425–426
Margolis, Max Leopold, 3:614, 13:529–530
Marti, Karl, 13:581–582
Mazar, Benjamin, 2:371, 3:547, 9:159, 13:705–706
Meinhold, Johannes Friedrich, 13:775
Meyer, Eduard, 9:159, 14:146

Michaelis, Johann David, 8:515, 14:169
Milgrom, Jacob, 14:233
Morgenstern, Julian, 14:486
Mowinckel, Sigmund Olaf Plytt, 3:651, 14:590
Nathan, Mordecai, 15:10–11
Neubauer, Adolf, 15:115
Nicholas de Lyre, 8:512
Noth, Martin, 2:11, 3:651, 15:315
Joshua, Book of, 11:446, 447, 449
sociology of Bible and, 3:658
Nowack, Wilhelm Gustav Hermann, 15:324
Orlinsky, Harry Meyer, 2:47, 3:614, 621, 622, 15:478
Parrot, André, 15:664
Pedersen, Johannes, 3:651, 658, 659, 15:711–712
Pellicanus, Conrad, 15:696, 718–719
Petrie, Sir William Matthew Flinders, 15:589, 16:18–19
Pfeiffer, Robert Henry, 16:26–27
Popper, William, 16:380
Rad, Gerhard von, 17:52
Reuss, Eduard, 17:249
Rosenmueller, Ernst Friedrich Karl, 17:449
Rowley, Harold Henry, 17:502–503
Ryssel, Victor, 17:603
Sandmel, Samuel, 18:16
Sarna, Nahum M., 4:125, 18:59
Schaeffer, Claude F.A., 18:102–103
Seeligmann, Isac Leo, 18:238–239
Segal, Moses Hirsch (Zevi), 8:355, 574, 640–641, 13:59, 14:330, 18:247–248
biblical exegesis and study, 3:647
modern biblical exegesis by, 3:650
Sellin, Ernst, 18:272
Shapiro, David S., 18:404
Smend, Rudolph, 6:278, 18:239, 686–687
Smith, John Merlin Powis, 18:688
Smith, Sir George Adam, 18:687–688
Smith, William Robertson, 3:658, 18:689
Solieli, Mordecai, 18:753
Speiser, Ephraim Avigdor, 9:159, 294–295, 19:94–95
Steuernagel, Carl, 19:224
Tadmor, Hayim, 19:431

Talmon, Shemaryahu, 19:469
Tavus, Jacob ben Joseph, 3:609, 11:552, 19:531
Theodore of Mopsuestia, 3:599, 648, 666, 19:692
Tigay, Jeffrey H., 19:719
Torrey, Charles Cutler, 20:59–60
Tur-Sinai, Naphtali Herz, 20:204–205
biblical exegesis and study, 3:647
Job, Book of, 11:343, 344, 346, 351, 352
Tyndale, William, 3:611, 612, 619, 20:212
Vatke, Wilhelm, 3:649, 20:486
Vaux, Roland de, 20:487
Volz, Paul, 20:580
Vriezen, Theodorus Christiaan, 20:588
Walton, Bryan, 13:56, 20:614
Weill, Raymond, 20:714
Weingreen, Jacob, 20:721
Weiss, Meir, 20:735
Wellhausen, Julius, 6–7, 16:630, 21:6–7
Eissfeldt, Otto, 6:278
on incense altar, 2:14
modern biblical crticism and, 3:648, 649–650
Wette, de, Wilhelm Martin Leberecht, 21:30
Wiener, Harold Marcus, 21:47
Winckler, Hugo, 3:651, 21:79–80
Woolley, Sir Charles Leonard, 21:212
Yeivin, Shemuel, 21:298
Zimmerli, Walther, 21:534
Bible societies, 3:**680–681**
Biblia Hebraica Leningradensia (Dotan), 5:762–763
Bibliander, Theodor, 3:**681**
Biblia Polyglotta, 2:452
Biblia Regia. See Biblia Polyglotta
Biblia Sacra hebraice, chaldaice graece et latine (Plantin), 16:219
Biblical Aramaic, 2:343–345
Biblical archaeology, 3:650, 652, 654
Biblical Archaeology Review (periodical), 18:397
Biblical criticism, 3:648–656
Aaron ben Elijah, 1:212
Aaronides in, 1:218–219
Abba Mari ben Moses ben Joseph Astruc of Lunel, 1:230
Abrabanel, Isaac ben Judah, 1:276–279
Abraham, 1:283

Abraham ben Moses ben Maimon, 1:305–306

Abraham ben Solomon, 1:310

Adar, Zvi, 1:383

Ainsworth, Henry, 1:550–551

Albelda, Moses ben Jacob, 1:588

Albright, William Foxwell, 1:596

Alcuin, 1:605

Alemanno, Johann ben Isaac, 1:611

Ali ibn Suleiman, 1:660

archaeological influence and evidence, 3:650, 652

Baudissin, Wolf Wilhelm, Graf von, 3:216

"biblical theology" movement, 3:651–652

Calvin, John, 4:376–377

Castelli, David, 4:513–514

Castro Quesada, Americo, 4:519

Celsus, 4:537–538

Cheyne, Thomas Kelly, 4:606–607

Cocceius, Johannes, 4:765

Coèn, Graziadio Vita Anania, 4:781

Cornill, Carl Heinrich, 5:224

Costa, Uriel da, 5:234–235

early modern period, development in, 3:648–649

Ehrlich Arnold Bogumil, 6:242–243

Eleazar ben Judah of Worms, 6:303–305

form criticism, 3:650–651

Hitzig, Ferdinand, 9:293–294

Ḥiwi al-Balkhi, 9:295

La Peyrère, Isaac, 12:488–489

later twentieth century developments in, 3:652–656

Meyer, Eduard, 14:146

nineteenth and early twentieth century developments in, 3:649–651

Smend, Rudolph, 18:686–687

Biblical imagery, 2:502–503

Biblical Interpretations in Ancient Israel (Fishbane), 7:60

Biblical literature

    Aaron, 1:208–210

    Aaronides, 1:217–219, 218*t*

    abomination, 1:269–270

    abortion, 1:270–271

    Abraham, 1:*281*, 281–282

    Absalom, 1:330

    Achan, 1:354

    Achbor, 1:355

    acrostics, 1:368–369

Adam, 1:371–372

adoption, 1:415–416

adultery, 1:423–424, 423–425

afterlife, 1:441

age and the aged, 1:446–447

Ahaziah, 1:539

Ai, 1:548–549

aims and purposes, 4:700–702

alchemy, 1:599–600

algum, 1:654

Baal worship, 3:12

banishment, 3:110

barrenness and fertility, 3:175

belief, faith, 3:290–291

benedictions, 3:331–332

Cain, 4:340

capital punishment, 4:445–446

carts, 4:497

cedar, 4:535

chariots, 4:497

children's, 4:619

choral singing, 4:658–659

chosen people doctrine, 4:669–670

Chronicles, book of, 4:695–704, 695*t*

circumcision, 4:730–731

cities, 4:739–741, 742–744

city of refuge, 4:742–744, *743*

community structure, 5:101

compassion, 5:122–123

compounding offenses, 5:123

compromise, 5:124, 125

concubines, 5:133–134

confession of sins, 5:148–149

confiscation, expropriation, forfeiture, 5:150–151

congregation, 5:158–160

conservation, 5:164–166

contractual ties, 5:190

conversion, laws of, 16:587–589

copper scroll, 5:213–214

copper serpent, 5:214–215

corvée labor, 5:226

cosmogony, 5:273–280

Covenant, 5:249–253

covetousness, 5:254

crafts, 5:263–264

creation, 5:273–280

cremation, 5:281

Crete, 5:289

crocodiles, 5:304–305

crowns, 5:307–308

crucifixion, 5:309–310

cult sacrifices, 5:330–333

Damascus, 5:390–391

Dead Sea scrolls and, 5:503–504

divine presence, 16:481–484

drama, German, 7:509–510

dualism, 6:30

earth in, 6:82

Edom and Esau, 6:488

El, name of God, 7:672–674

Elam, 6:283–284

Elath, 6:287

Eldad and Medad, 6:293

elders, 6:294–296

elephants, 6:310–311

Eli, 6:317

Eliezer, 6:322

Elijah, 6:332–333

embalming, 6:390

emotions, 6:396

En-Gedi, 6:407

environment and beauty, 5:168

Ephod, 6:455–456

Ephraim, 6:456–457

Erez Israel agriculture, 1:472–473

Esau, 6:487, 488

eschatology

    Dead sea scrolls, 6:498–500

    post-exilic prophets, 6:492–495

    pre-exilic prophets, 6:490–492

fire, 7:43–44

firstborn, 7:45–46

first fruits, 7:48–49

fish and fishing, 7:58–59

flogging, 7:78

flora, 7:90–91

forgiveness, 7:127–128

fruit trees, 5:166–167

Gaza, 7:399

geneology, 8:290

Genesis, book of, 7:440–447, 441*t*, 447*t*

Gideon, 7:586–588, *587*

Gilead, 7:600–601

Gilgal, 7:601–602

glass, 7:629

goats, 7:651–652

God, 3:290, 7:652–658

Gog and Magog, 7:683–684

Golan, 17:78–79

golden calf, 7:700

Goliath, 7:738–739

good and evil, 7:752

Habakkuk, 8:171–172

Biblical literature, *continued*

haftarah, 8:198–200

Hagar, 8:205–206

Haggai, 8:222–223

hagiography, 8:224–226

hakhel, 8:247

hakkafot, 8:250

Hannah and birth of Samuel, 8:324–325

hassegat gevul, 8:448–449

hatred, ill-will, 8:458

ḥerem, 9:10–11

hermaneutics, 9:25–29

Hezekiah, 9:87–90

historiography, 9:153–154

Hittites, 9:292–293

Holiness code, 9:318–320, 12:738–740

human rights, 17:312–313

hunting, 5:166

Jubilee, 5:166

Kings, Kingship, 12:167–168

lamentations, 14:586–587

land management, 1:472–486

law and morality, 12:535

Leviathan, 12:696–697

Levi ben Gershom commentaries, 12:699

Levirate marriage and ḥaliẓa, 12:725

locust plague, 6:494

masorah vocalization, 7:475–476

mourning, 14:585–586

mules, 14:609–610

music, 14:640–642

mythical influences, 14:711

Naḥmanides commentary, 14:740–741

plagues of Egypt, 6:494, 16:210–214, 211t

planning and construction, laws of, 16:215–216

plants and products of plants, 16:220t–225t

poetry, 16:254–262

police offenses, 16:331–332

pomegranates, 16:364

poor, provision for, 16:371–372

poverty, 16:427

prayer, 16:456–458

prayer, women's role in, 16:460

precious stones and jewelry, 16:475–478, 476t

primogeniture, 19:284

prostitution, 16:625–626

ransom, 17:91–92

Rashi, 17:101–106, 102t

Rea Sea, 17:160

Rebekah, 17:137–138

rebellious son, 17:138–139

rebuke and reproof, 17:139–140

redemption, 17:151–152

red heifer, 17:156–157

reeds, 17:161

Reifmann, Jacob, 17:203–204

remnant of Israel, 17:217

repentance, 17:221

Rephaim, 17:224

Resheph, 17:226

resurrection, 17:240–241

Reuben, 17:244–246, *245*

revelation, 17:253–254

reward and punishment, 17:269–270

right and left, 17:301

righteousness, 17:307–308

Rome and Esau, 6:488

Rowley, Harold Henry, 17:502–503

sabbatical year, 5:166

shemittah and yovel, 6:454

Song of Songs, 19:14–19

son of man, 19:25

sorcery, 19:27

Sotah (tractate), 19:32–33

soul, 19:33–34

soul, immortality of, 19:35

sources of, 4:699–700

strangers and gentiles, 19:241–242

suffering, 7:656

suicide, 19:295–296

sukkah, 19:297–298

Sukkot, 19:299–300

Sumerian influence, 19:311–312

supercommentaries, 19:315–316

suretyship, 19:317–318

sustainable development, 6:454

theodicy, 7:656

tombs and tombstones, 20:33, 34

trade and commerce, 20:79–81

treasure, treasury, 20:122–123

truth, 20:162

Tu Bi-Shevat, 20:167

twelve tribes, 20:137–140

unjust enrichment, 20:413–414

usury, 20:437–438

veil, 20:490

vine, 20:536–537

virginity, 20:539–540

visions, 20:543–544

vows and vowing, 20:585–586

waste disposal, 5:167

weights and measures, 20:700–701

widows, 21:40–42

wilderness, 21:60

willow, 21:65

wisdom literature, 21:95–98

witness, 21:115

wood, 21:210

yoke, 21:381

Zadok, 21:439–441

Zaken Mamre, 21:446

Zechariah, 21:482–486

zekhut avot, 21:497

Zephaniah, 21:511–512

See also Eschatology; Haggadah, Passover; Prophets and prophecy

Biblical Myth and Legend in Jewish Education (Fineberg), 7:26

Biblical Myth and Rabbinic Mythmaking (Fishbane), 7:60

Biblical period

liturgy, 13:131

sculpture, 18:222

ships and sailing, 18:486–487

Biblical scholars. *See* Bible scholars

"Biblical theology" movement, 3:651–652

Bibliography, 3:**681–683**

Bass, Shabbetai ben Joseph, 3:206

Benjacob, Isaac, 3:353–354

Bernard, Edward, 3:467–468

Chajes, Saul, 4:559–560

Cowley, Sir Arthur Ernest, 5:256

Deutsch, Otto Erich, 5:625

encyclopedias, 6:401–402

Freidus, Abraham Solomon, 7:236

Freimann, Aron, 7:237–238

Habermann, Abraham Meir, 8:176–177

Heilprin, Jehiel Ben Solomon, 3:681, 8:768–769

Herschel, Levie, 9:134–135

Neubauer, Adolf, 15:115

Polak, Gabriel Isaac, 16:286

Rapoport, Solomon Judah Leib, 17:99

Roan, Jacob ben Isaac, 17:374

Roest, Meijer Marcus, 17:367

Rosenthal, Leser, 17:455

Schapiro, Israel, 18:108–109

Seeligmann, Sigmund, 18:239

Slatkine, Menahem Mendel, 18:666–667

Bibliography of Jewish Music (Sendrey), 18:287

Bibliophiles, 3:**683–685**

Adler, Elkan Nathan, 1:396

Adler, Elmer, 1:396

Almanzi, Joseph, 1:679

Baracs, Károly, 3:124

Beer, Bernhard, 3:251

Benoliel, Joseph, 3:371

Horodisch, Abraham, 9:527–528

Montezinos, David, 14:460

Mortara, Marco, 14:513

Rosenbach, Abraham Simon Wolf, 17:431–432

Rosenthal, Leser, 17:455

Simonsen, David Jacob, 18:618

Biblioteca di studi sociali (Mondolfo), 14:435

Bibliotheca Americana Vetustissima (Harrisse), 8:366

Bibliotheca Historica Italo-Judaica (Milano), 14:232

Bibliotheca Magna Rabbinica (Bartolocci), 2:37, 3:181

Bibliotheca Sancta ex praecipuis Catholicae Ecclesiae auctoribus collecta (Sixtus of Siena), 18:656

Bibliothèque Nationale (France), 3:**685**, 11:558

Biblisches Organon, 9:137

Bîrlad (Moldavia). *See* Barlad (Moldovia)

Bick, Jacob Samuel, 3:**685**, 4:199

Bickel, Alexander M., 3:**685**

Bickel, Solomon, 3:**686**

Bickels-Spitzer, Zvi, 3:**686**

Bickerman, Elias Joseph, 3:**686**, 18:217

Biculturalism, 6:698

Bidache (France), 3:**686**

Biden, Louis H., 2:49

Bidermanas, Izrael. *See* Izis

Bidner, Zelig. *See* Ben Horin, Eliyahu

Bidney, David, 3:**686–687**

Bie, Oscar, 3:**687**

Bieber, Hugo, 3:**687**

Bieber, Margarete, 3:**687**

Biedermann, Michael Lazar, 3:**687**

Biegeleisen, Henryk, 3:**688**

Biegeleisen-Żelsazowski, Bronislaw, 3:688

Biel (Spain), 3:**688**

Biel (Switzerland), 3:**688**

Bielefeld (Germany), 3:**688**

Bielski, Asael, 3:**688–689**

Bielski, Tuvia, 3:**688–689**, 9:496

Bielski, Zus, 3:**688–689**

Bielsko (Poland), 3:**689**

Bielsk Podlaski (Poland), 3:**689–690**

Bien, Julius, 3:**690**

Bienenfeld, Franz Rudolf, 3:**690**

Bienenstock, Max, 3:**690**

Bienstok, Judah Lieb, 3:**690–691**

Bienveniste family. *See* Benveniste family

Bierer, Rubin, 3:**691**, 11:699

Bi-Fero'a Pera'ot be-Yisrael (Eismann), 6:276

Bigamy and polygamy, 3:**691–694**, 6:693, 15:539

   Bulgarian Romaniots, 4:269

   concubines, 5:135

   Gershom ben Judah Me'or ha-Golah, 7:552

   Ḥaliẓah in Ashkenaz, 12:727

   See also Monogamy

Bigart, Jacques, 3:**694–695**

Bigdei ha-Melekh ha-Ḥadashim (Aloni), 1:687

Bigman, Stanley, 18:733

Bihalji, Pavle, 3:695

Bihalji Merin, Oto, 3:**695**

Bihari, Alexander, 3:**695**

Bijur, Nathan, 2:49, 3:**695**

Bikayam, Meir ben Ḥalifa, 3:**695**

Bikel, Theodore Meir, 3:**696**

Bikerman, Jacob Joseph, 3:**696**

Bikerman, Joseph, 3:**696**

Bikhowsky, Elizaveta. *See* Elisheva

Bikkurei ha-Ittim, 3:**696–697**, 8:688, 12:460

Bikkurei Yehudah (Don-Yaḥia), 5:752

Bikkur ḥolim. *See* Sicknesses, sick, visiting the

Bikkurim (tractate), 3:**697**

Bikszad dynasty, 8:425

Bilam (Shoham), 8:716

Bilbeis (Egypt), 3:**697**

Bilbū,Yaʾqūb, 15:473

Bilder aus dem juedischen Familienleben (Mosenthal), 14:521–522

Bildersee, Adele, 3:**697–698**

Biletzki, Israel Ḥayyim, 3:**698**

Bilgoraj (Poland), 3:**698**

Bilhah, 1:415, 3:**698**

Bill-Belotserkovski, Vladimir Naumovich, 3:**698–699**

Billiards, 19:138

Billig, Levi, 3:**699**

Billikopf, Jacob, 3:**699**

Billings (MT), 14:454

Bill of Rights (U.S.), 2:42

Billroth, Theodor, 3:**699**

Bills & Contracts From Lucena (Rivlin), 18:471

Billy Bathgate (Doctorow), 5:728

Bilsky, Moses, 15:516

Biltmore Program, 3:**699–700**

   American Jewish Committee, 2:55

   bi-nationalism and, 3:703

Bilu, 3:**700–701**, 6:37

Bimah, 3:**701–702**

Bimetallism, in currency, 2:424

Bimko, Fishel, 3:**702**

Bimstein, "Whitey," 3:**702**

Binah la-Ittim (Hart), 8:370

Binah le-Ittim (Figo), 7:18–19

Bi-nationalism, 3:**702–703**

Binder, Abraham Wolf, 3:**703**, 8:503

Binder, Alexander. *See* Pană, Saşa

Bineter family. *See* Banet family

Binet family. *See* Banet family

Bin-Forion, Micha Josef. *See* Berdyczewski, Micha Josef

Bing, Abraham, 3:**704**

Bing, Albert, 3:**704**

Bing, Ilse, 3:**704**

Bing, Isaac ben Samuel, 3:**704**

Bing, Joseph, 3:704

Bing, Seligmann, 15:442

Bing, Solomon, 3:704

Bingen (Germany), 3:703, **704–705**

Bingen, Jacques, 15:668

Bing family, 3:**703–704**

Bingham, Theodore A., 6:193, 15:209

Bin-Gorion, Micha Josef. *See* Berdyczewski, Micha Josef

Binswanger, Isidore, 3:**705**

Bintel Brief, 6:696–697, 15:210, 16:503–504, 20:325–326

Binyamin, Rabbi. *See* Rabbi Binyamin

Binyaminah (Israel), 3:**705**

Binyamin ben Mishael. *See* Amina

Binyamin Ze'ev. *See* Herzl, Theodor

Binyamin Ze'ev (Benjamin), 3:364

Binyan Ari'el (Loewenstamm), 13:167–168

Binyan Av (Bakshi-Doron), 3:74

Binyan av rule, 9:26–27

Binyan ha-Bayit (Altschuler), 2:26

Binyan Shelomo (Hanau), 8:318

Binyan Shelomo le-Ḥokhmat Beẓalel (Adeni), 1:390

Binyan Ẓiyyon (Freimann), 7:237

Biochemistry, 13:10

   Canada

      Fishman, William Harold, 7:65

   France

      Rapkine, Louis, 17:97

   Germany

      Ehrlich, Paul, 6:244

      Embden, Gustav, 6:390–391

      Meyerhof, Otto, 13:10, 14:151

      Michaelis, Leonor, 14:169

Biochemistry, *continued*
  Neuberg, Gustav Embden Carl, 15:116
  Oppenheimer, Carl, 15:447
  Pringsheim, Hans, 16:528
  Warburg, Otto Heinrich, 20:633
  Hungary
    Rona, Peter, 17:418
  Israel
    Ciechanover, Aaron J., 4:725
    Fodor, Andor, 7:94
    Hershko, Avram, 4:593, 9:45, 13:10
    Hestrin, Shlomo, 9:79
    Katzir, Aharon, 12:22
    Katzir, Ephraim, 12:22–23, 13:10
    Levitzki, Alexander, 12:744
    Razin, Aharon, 17:130
    Sela, Michael, 13:11, 18:257
    Shapiro, Benjamin, 18:404
    Sharon, Nathan, 18:418
    Simon, Ernst, 6:161, 18:611
    Wertheimer, Chaim Ernst, 21:16
  Poland
    Parnas, Yakub Karol, 15:654
  Portugal
    Jacobson, Kurt, 11:55
  Switzerland
    Winterstein, Alfred, 21:92
  U.K.
    Chain, Sir Ernest Boris, 4:558
    Cohen, Sir Philip, 5:31
    Klug, Aaron, 4:593, 12:233, 13:9
    Kornberg, Hans Leo, 12:311–312
    Krebs, Hans Adolf, 12:347, 13:10
    Neuberger, Albert, 15:116
    Perutz, Max Ferdinand, 15:798
    Quastel, Judah Hirsch, 16:761–762
    Rosenheim, Otto, 17:448
  U.S.
    Berg, Paul, 3:417
    Bodansky, Oscar, 4:27
    Borsook, Henry, 4:95
    Calvin, Melvin, 4:377–378, 13:10
    Chargaff, Erwin, 4:568
    Cohen, Philip Pacy, 5:31, 13:10
    Cohen, Seymour Stanley, 5:34, 13:9
    Cohen, Stanley, 5:36
    Cohn, Edwin Joseph, 5:40
    Cori, Gerty Theresa, 5:223
    Dische, Zacharias, 5:676
    Dorfman, Ralph Isadore, 5:756
    Edelman, Gerald Maurice, 6:142
    Fischer, Edmond, 7:53, 13:10
    Funk, Casimir, 7:310
    Glick, David, 7:636
    Green, David Ezra, 8:66
    Greenberg, David Morris, 8:68
    Greenstein, Jesse Philip, 8:81
    Handler, Milton, 8:319
    Handler, Philip, 8:319
    Hassid, William Zev, 8:455
    Heidelberger, Michael, 8:762–763, 13:11
    Kalnitsky, George, 11:747
    Kornberg, Arthur, 12:311, 13:9
    Langer, Robert S., 12:481
    Levene, Phoebus Aaron Theodor, 12:679
    Lipmann, Fritz Albert, 13:68
    Nirenberg, Marshall Warren, 13:9, 15:273–274, 476
    Perlzweig, William Alexandre, 15:780
    Ptashne, Mark Stephen, 13:9, 16:693
    Rabinowitch, Eugene, 17:40
    Racker, Efraim, 17:51
    Rittenberg, David, 13:10, 17:345–346
    Rodbell, Martin, 13:10, 17:362
    Shear, Murray Jacob, 18:427
    Sobotka, Harry Herman, 18:703
    Stein, Wililam Howard, 19:182
    Stern, Kurt Gunter, 19:213
    Strominger, Jack, 13:11, 19:260
    Sure, Barnett, 19:317
    Weinhouse Sidney, 20:722
    Zamenhof, Stephen, 21:451
Biodiversity, 5:164
Bioengineering, 11:772
Bioethics
  Draï, Raphaël, 6:7
  France, 6:716
Biographies and autobiographies, 3:**705–709**
  as exempla, 6:599
Heilprin, Jehiel Ben Solomon, 8:768
Historia Augusta, 9:151
Italian Renaissance, 7:15
Josephus' *The Life,* 11:440
leaders of modern hasidic movements, 11:751–752
Luftspring, Sammy, 13:253
Lukacs, Georg, 13:253
rabbis, of, 11:751–752
Biological plant protection, 6:452
Biology
  Austria
    Marmorek, Alexander, 13:556–557
  Belgium
    Arnon, Isaac, 2:480
  Canada
    Altman, Sidney, 2:22, 4:593, 13:9
  France
    Atlan, Henri, 2:635
    Jacob, François, 11:27–28
    Lwoff, Andre Michel, 13:9, 293
  Germany
    Aschner, Manfred, 2:553
    Auerbach, Leopold, 2:655
    Cohn, Ferdinand Julius, 5:41, 13:7
    Edinger, Tilly, 6:147–148
    Haberlandt, Gottlieb, 8:176
    Sorauer, Paul Karl Moritz, 19:27
    Steinach, Eugen, 19:182–183
  Horwitz, H. Robert, 9:546–547
  Israel
    Arnon, Ruth, 2:480–481, 15:313
    Aviv, Haim, 2:741
    Chet, Ilan, 4:605–606, 6:452
    Cohen, Yigal Rahamim, 5:38
    Rager, Bracha, 17:65
  Italy
    Artom, Cesare, 2:534
    Levi-Montalcini, Rita, 12:706
  Romania
    Sanielevici, Henric, 18:24
  Russia
    Gurwitsch, Alexander Gavrilovich, 8:142
    Haffkine, Waldemar Mordecai, 8:196
    Metchnikoff, Elie, 14:134
    Zenkevich, Lev Aleksandrovich, 21:508–509

Zilber, Lev Aleksandrovich, 21:530
U.K.
    Bodmer, Walter, 4:29–30
    Rothschild, Nathaniel Mayer Victor, Lord, 17:491, 494
U.S.
    Altschul, Aaron Meyer, 2:25
    Anfinsen, Christian Boehmer, 2:145–146, 4:592–593, 13:10
    Arnon, Daniel Israel, 2:480
    Asimov, Isaac, 2:588
    Axelrod, Julius, 2:756–757, 13:10
    Baltimore, David, 3:100
    Berg, Paul, 3:417, 13:9
    Bogorad, Lawrence, 4:36
    Gilbert, Walter, 4:593, 7:598, 13:9
    Gould, Stephen Jay, 8:18–19
    Horwitz, H. Robert, 9:546, 13:9
    Luria, Salvador Edward, 13:9, 267–268
    Meselson, Matthew, 13:9, 14:74
    Pincus, Gregory Goodwin, 16:165
    Rose, Irwin, 17:426
    Spiegelman, Sol, 13:9, 19:107–108
    Stent, Gunther Siegmund, 13:9, 19:202
    Varmus, Harold Eliot, 20:477
    Waksman, Selman Abraham, 20:599
    Wald, George, 13:10, 20:600
    See also Life sciences
Biophysics, 13:12
Biow, Milton H., 1:428, 3:428
Bira family. See Adolphus family
Biram, Arthur, 3:709–710
Biran, Avraham, 3:710
Biranit (Israel), 3:710
Birbaum, Nathan. See Burns, George
Birck, Sixtus, 18:761
Birds, 2:171–172
    barnacle geese, 3:167
    buzzards, 4:323
    doves, 5:768
    eagles, 6:81
    hoopoes, 9:522
    peacocks, 15:704
    pelicans, 15:717–718
    pheasants, 16:32–33
Birds' Head Haggadah, 8:212–213

Birds of Shade (Seri). See Zipporei Zel (Seri)
Biriyyah (Israel), 3:710–711, 6:264
Birk, Alm, 16:343
Birk, Yehudith, 3:711
Birkat ha-Levanah. See Blessing of the Moon
Birkat ha-mazon. See Grace after meals
Birkat ha-Minim, 3:711–712
    Amidah, 2:74
    Jewish identity and, 11:294
    luz of the spine, 13:279
Birkat ha-Torah, 3:712
Birkat Shemu'el (Leibowitz), 12:620
Birkenau concentration camp, 3:421, 9:430, 481–482, 488
Birkenstadt, Ger Shon Ben Abraham. See Chajes, Gershon ben Abraham
Birkenstadt, Gershon Ben Abraham. See Chajes, Gershon ben Abraham
Birkenthal, Dov Ber, 2:268, 3:712
Birmingham (AL), 3:712–713
Birmingham (England), 3:713–714
Birmingham, Steven, 15:227
Birnbaum, A. H., 15:475
Birnbaum, Abraham Baer, 3:714
Birnbaum, Eduard, 2:25, 3:714
Birnbaum, Ferdinand, 6:161
Birnbaum, Jacob, 3:716
Birnbaum, Menachem, 3:714
Birnbaum, Nathan (1864-1937), 3:714–716, 11:699, 18:257
Birnbaum, Nathan (1896-1996). See Burns, George
Birnbaum, Philip, 3:716
Birnbaum, Pierre, 11:326
Birnbaum, Solomon Asher, 3:716
Birnbaum, Uriel, 3:716–717
Birnboim, Moses Joseph, 3:717
Biró, Lajos, 3:717
Birobidzhan (Russia), 3:717–720
Birobidzhan (USSR), 3:718, 719
The Birobidzhan Affair (Emiot), 6:395
Der Birobidzhaner Inyen (Emiot). See The Birobidzhan Affair (Emiot)
Birobidzhan Jewish Musical Chamber Theater, 14:520
Birs Nimrud (Iraq), 4:94
Birstein, Yossel, 3:720
Birth, 3:720–723
    abortion, 1:271–272
    amulets, vol. 7: color insert
    astrology, 2:617, 619
    birthdays, 3:723
    celebrations, dance, 5:411
    Commandments, 5:75

folklore, 7:100, 103, 106, 109–110
    impurity period, 12:737–738
    Lilith, 13:17–19
    niddah, 15:256–258
    rites and rituals
        Sholem Zokhor, 18:512–513
    sacrifice following, 17:640–641
    vital statistics, 20:551t–552t, 556–557
The Birth and Growth of Religion (Moore), 14:469
Birth certificate, Chinese, vol. 20: color insert
Birth control, 3:723
    Judith, wife of Rabbi Ḥiyya, and, 11:566
    onanism, 15:426–427
    See also Barrenness and fertility
Birthdates, 3:721
Birthday celebrations, 3:723–724
The Birthday Party (Pinter), 16:177
Birth defects, 1:272
The Birth of Energy (sculpture, Epstein), 6:471
The Birth of Europe (Lopez), 13:189–190
Birthright Israel, 7:137
Birthrights
    Jacob, 11:18, 21, 27
    Jacob and Esau, 6:487–488
    Manasseh and Ephraim, 6:456, 457, 11:20
Birzai (Lithuania), 3:724
Birzula (Ukraine), 3:724
Bisa, 15:501
Bischheim (France), 3:724
Bischhoff, Erich, 3:724
Bischhoffsheim, Amalia, 3:725
Bischhoffsheim, Ellen Odette, 3:725
Bischhoffsheim, Henry Louis, 3:725
Bischhoffsheim, Raphael, 3:724–725
Bischhoffsheim, Raphael Jonathan, 3:725
Bischhoffsheim, Raphael Louis, 3:725
Bischhoffsheim family, 3:724–725, 725t
Bischofsheim on the Tauber (Germany). See Tauberbischofsheim (Germany)
Bisenz (Czech Republic). See Bzenec (Czech Republic)
Bisgyer, Maurice, 3:725
Bi-Shevilei Musar (Benamozegh), 3:317
Bishop, Joey, 3:726
"Bishop of the Jews." See Episcopus Judaeorum

Bisliches, Mordecai Leib, 3:**726**

Bismarck, Otto von, 3:**726**
  Bleichroeder, Gerson von,
    relationship with, 3:726, 748
  Blowitz, Henri Georges Stephane
    Adolphe Opper de, as
    interviewer of, 3:784
  Lasker, Eduard, 12:497

Bistrita (Romania), 3:**727**

Bistritski, Nathan. *See* Agmon, Nathan

Bitan Aharon (Israel), 3:**727**

Bitburg Controversy, 3:**727–728**

Bithiah, 3:**729**

Bithynia (Asia Minor), 3:**729**

Bitola (F.Y.R. of Macedonia). *See*
  Monastir (F.Y.R. of Macedonia)

Bitolj (F.Y.R. of Macedonia). *See*
  Monastir (F.Y.R. of Macedonia)

Bittelman, Alexander, 3:**729**

Het bittere kruid (Minco). *See Bitter
  Herbs* (Minco)

Bitter Herbs (Minco), 6:71

Bitterns, 3:**729**

Bitter water ordeal, 11:374, 15:462

Bittul ha-Tamid, 3:**729–730**

Bitumen, 3:**730**

Biur (Mendelssohn), 6:34, 8:437

Biurists, 3:631

*Bi-Ymei Milhamah u-Mahpekhah
  1914-21* (Dinur), 5:672

Biztha, 3:**730**

Bizza and pesharah, 5:124

Bizzaron (Israel), 3:**730**

Black, Algernon David, 3:**730**

Black, Conrad, 11:467

Black, Fischer, 18:159–160

Black, Max, 3:**730–731**

Black, Misha. *See* Black, Sir Misha

Black, Sir Misha, 3:**731**

Black Americans. *See* African
  Americans

Blackbirds of 1928, 7:17

The Black Book. See Cartea Neagra

Black Box (Amos Oz), 15:555

Black Canopy. See Huppah Shehorah
  (Ratosh)

Black Death, 3:**731–734**, *732*, 9:215–
  216
  antisemitism, 15:94–95
  Brussels, 4:226
  France, 7:151
    Alsace, 2:6
    Franche-Comté, 7:172
    Lorraine, 13:194
    Nyons, 15:356
    Obernai, 15:368
    Sèlestat, 18:260

Seres, 18:316
  Germany, 4:63, 5:60
    Ansbach, 2:180
    Bacharach, 3:31
    Berlin, 3:445
    Bingen, 3:704
    Bonn, 4:63
    Boppard, 4:79
    Brandenburg, 4:125, 126
    Breisach, 4:167
    Bruchsal, 4:219
    Brunswick, 4:226
    Bytom, 4:324
    Dresden persecutions, 6:10
    Dueren, 6:41
    Duisberg, 6:43
    Frankfurt on the Main, 7:208
    Fulda, 7:309
    Juelich, 11:572
    Kaiserslautern, 11:728
    Landau, 12:457
    Landshut, 12:476
    Lauingen, 12:526
    Lueneburg, 13:253
    Noerdlingen, 15:293
    Nordhausen, 15:299
    Nuremberg, 15:346
    Offenbach, 15:386
    Offenburg, 15:387
    Oldenburg, 15:401
    Osnabrueck, 15:505
    Palatinate, 15:575
    Passau, 15:677
  Italy
    Parma, 15:652
  Lag ba-Omer associated with,
    15:421
  Luxembourg, 13:275
  Oppenheim, 15:442
  Spain
    Barcelona, 3:143
    Dueñas, 6:40
    Lérida, 12:654–655
    Sargossa, 18:42–43
  Switzerland
    Berne, 3:471
    Lucerne, 13:249

*Black Form Dedicated to the Missing
  Jews* (Lewitt), 12:769–770

Black Hundreds, 15:250

Black-Jewish relations in United
  States, 3:**734–737**
  affirmative action and numerus
    clausus, 15:343
  Butzel, Fred M., 4:320
  Goodman, Benny, 15:220

Passover and Seder, significance
    of, 15:681–682
  See also Civil rights movement;
    New York City

Black Jews
  India, supporters, 6:741
  United States, 11:520, 521

Black Judaizing movements, 1:437

*Black Mountain: An Exploration of
  Community* (Duberman), 6:31

Black Panther movement (Israel),
  10:442

Black Saturday, 8:204

Blackstone, William E., 3:**737**

Blair, Tony, 6:432, 12:753

Blake, William, 3:**737–738**
  Bronowski, Jacob, 4:207
  Moses, 14:542

Blanc, Mel, 3:**738**

Blanchot, Maurice, 3:**738**

Blanckenhorn, Max, 3:**738**

Blanes, Jacob, 3:**738**

Blank, Aristide, 3:**739**

Blank, Arthur M., 3:**739**

Blank, Leon, 3:**739**

Blank, Maurice, 3:**739–740**

Blank, Samuel Leib, 3:**740**

Blank, Sheldon Haas, 3:**740**

Blankenstein, Marcus van, 3:**740**

Blankenstein, Solomon. *See* Schiller,
  Solomon

Blankfort, Michael S., 3:**740**

Blankstein, Cecil, 3:**740**

Blanter, Matvey Isaakovich, 3:**740–741**

Blaser, Isaac, 3:**741**

Blasphemy, 3:**741–742**, 5:79*t*

Blass, Simcha, 6:452

Blatas, Arbit, 15:649

Blatt, Joseph, 15:397

Blau, Amram, 3:**742**, 744

Blau, Bruno, 3:**742**

Blau, Fritz, 3:**742**

Blau, Herbert, 3:**742–743**

Blau, Joseph Leon, 3:**743**

Blau, Joshua, 3:**743–744**

Blau, Ludwig Lajos, 3:**744**

Blau, Moshe, 3:**744**

Blau, Peter Michael, 3:**744–745**

Blau, Pinchas, 3:**744**

Blau, Tina, 3:**745**

Blaubaum, Elias, 3:**745**

Der blaue Reiter, 4:139

Blaustein, Abraham, 3:**746**

Blaustein, David, 3:**746**

Blaustein, Jacob, 2:55, 3:**745–746**

Blaustein, Louis, 3:98, 745

Blaustein family, 3:**745–746**

Blaustein Philanthropic Group, 3:746

Blau-Weiss, 3:**746–747**, 8:385, 11:721, 12:466

Blayer, Pietro, 3:**747**

Blazko, Martin, 3:**747**

Blech, Leo, 3:**747**

Blecher, Marcel, 3:**747**

The Bleeding Man (painting, Mopp), 14:470

Bleek, Friedrich, 3:**747–748**

Bleich, J. David, 3:**748**

Bleichroeder, Gerson von, 3:726, 748

Bleichroeder, Samuel, 3:748

Bleichroeder family, 3:748

Blejer, David, 3:**748–749**, 16:349

Blejer, Mario Israel, 3:**749**

Blemishes, 3:**749–750**

Blendenish (Altman), 2:21

Die Blendung (Canetti), 4:431

Blessé (Morhange), 14:491

Blessedness. *See* Beatitude

Blessing and cursing, 3:330–333, **750–752**

    Berakhot, 3:400

    blasphemy, 3:741–742

    children, blessing of, 3:752

    in colophons, 5:65–67

    grace after meals, 8:22–23, 18:489

    grace before meals, 8:24

    oaths, relationship to curses, 15:358, 462

    ordeal and curses, 15:462

Blessing of children, 3:752

Blessing of the Moon, 14:**468**

Bleter far Yidishe Demografye, Statistik un Ekonomik, 4:228

Bleustein-Blanchet, Marcel, 3:**752–753**

Blick, Elsa. *See* Triolet, Elsa

Blíženci (Dostál), 5:762

Blindman, Yeruḥam, 3:**753**

Blind man and lame parable, 6:647

Blindness, 3:**753–756**, *754*, 7:86

Bliokh, Ivan Stanislavovich, 3:**756**

Blis, David, 3:**756–757**

Bliss. *See* Beatitude

Bliss, Frederick Jones, 3:**757**, 15:589

Blitz, Jekuthiel ben Isaac, 3:610

Blitzer, Wolf, 3:**757**

Blitzkrieg, 9:332–333

Blitzstein, Marc, 1:224, 3:**757**

Blobel, Paul, 3:22

Bloc, André, 3:**757–758**

Bloch, Adolfo, 11:469

Bloch, André, 3:**758**

Bloch, Annette, 3:769

Bloch, Camille, 3:**758**

Bloch, Chaim Isaac, 3:**758–759**

Bloch, Charles (ḥazzan), 3:**759**

Bloch, Charles (publisher), 3:758

Bloch, Claude, 3:**759**

Bloch, Darius Paul. *See* Dassault, Darius Paul

Bloch, Dora, 6:448

Bloch, Edward, 3:758

Bloch, Edward H., 3:758

Bloch, Elijah Meyer, 3:**759**

Bloch, Ernest, 3:**759–760**, 4:661–662, 18:762

Bloch, Ernst, 3:**760–761**

Bloch, Felix, 3:**761**

Bloch, Gustave, 3:**761**

Bloch, Ḥayyim Isaac ben Ḥanokh Zundel ha-Kohen, 3:**761**

Bloch, Henry Wollman, 3:768

Bloch, Herbert, 3:**761–762**, 5:302, 18:732

Bloch, Hermann, 3:**762**

Bloch, Herman Samuel, 3:**762**

Bloch, Hyman Morris, 3:**762**

Bloch, Issachar Baer ben Samson, 3:**762**

Bloch, Iwan, 3:**762–763**

Bloch, Jean-Richard, 3:**763**

Bloch, Joseph, 3:**763**, 18:705

Bloch, Joseph Leib, 3:**763**

Bloch, Joseph Samuel, 3:**763–764**, 16:340

Bloch, Joshua, 3:**764**

Bloch, Jules, 3:**764**

Bloch, Konrad, 3:**765**, 13:10

Bloch, Marc, 3:**765**, 18:730

Bloch, Marcus Eliezer, 3:**765**

Bloch, Martin, 3:**766**

Bloch, Mattathias ben Benjamin Ze'ev Ashkenazi, 3:**766**

Bloch, Maurice. *See* Bloch, Sir Maurice

Bloch, Mór. *See* Ballagi, Mór

Bloch, Moses, 3:**766**

Bloch, Moses Rudolph, 3:**766–767**

Bloch, Philipp, 3:**767**

Bloch, Richard, 3:**768–769**

Bloch, Rolf, 3:**767**

Bloch, Rosine, 3:**767**

Bloch, Sam, 2:48, 49

Bloch, Samson ben Moses, 3:**767**

Bloch, Samson ha-Levi, 3:**767–768**

Bloch, Samson the Ḥasid. *See* Bloch, Samson ben Moses

Bloch, Sir Maurice, 3:**766**

Bloch Editores, 11:469–470

Bloch family, 3:758

Blochman family, 18:14

Bloch-Michel, Jean, 3:**768**

Block, Herbert Lawrence, 3:**769**

Block, H&R, 3:**768–769**

Block, Joseph Samuel, 4:712

Block, Paul, 3:**769**, 11:468

Block 23/ Mikhtavim mi-Nes Ẓiyyonah (Kenan), 12:**75**

Bloemfontein (South Africa), 3:**769–770**

Blogg, Solomon ben Ephraim, 3:**770**

Blois (France), 3:**770**

Blok, Arthur, 3:**770**

Blonde on Blonde (Dylan), 6:78

Blondes, David, 3:**770–771**, 779

Blondheim, David Simon, 3:**771**, 12:405

Blondheim, Solomon Hillel, 3:771

Blondzhende Shtern (Shalom Aleichem), 18:384

Blood, 3:**771–772**

    altars and, 2:12, 13–14

    Brazil, colonial, 4:143

    cult, 5:331

    in folk medicine, 7:111

    Judaizers, 11:520

    menstrual, 2:135, 3:772, 776

    niddah, 15:253–258

    Passover, 15:679

    plagues of Egypt, 16:212–213

    sheḥitah, 18:434

    virginal, 15:255

Blood-avengers, 3:**772–773**

Blood-for-trucks negotiations, 6:250

Blood for Trucks offer, 4:120, 9:490–491

Blood from the Sky (Rawicz), 9:411

Bloodguilt, 3:**773–774**, 4:68

Blood Harvest. *See* Shtol un Ayzn

Bloodletting, 3:**774**

Blood libel, 3:**266–267**, **774–780**, *777*

    Aleppo (Syria), 1:615

    Alexeyev, Alexander, 1:636

    Alfonso X, King of Castile, 1:642

    Alfonso de Espina, 1:642

    Amasiya (Turkey), 2:33

    Andrew of Rinn, 2:144

    antisemitism and, 3:776, 778, 779, 17:163

    apologetics, 2:267

    Arab countries, 3:780

    Austria, 2:144

    Beilis, 6:45, 15:250

    Beirut, 3:270

    Benedict XIV, 3:330

Blood libel, *continued*
  Berne (Switzerland), 3:471
  Biel, 3:688
  Bielsk Podlaski, 3:689
  Bloch, Joseph Samuel, 3:764
  in Blois, 3:770
  Blondes, David, 3:770, 779
  Boleslav V, 4:45
  Bourgeois, Jean, 4:106
  Bristol, England, 4:185
  Bruna, Israel ben Ḥayyim, 4:222
  Buna, Israel ben Ḥayyim, 7:222
  Bursa, 4:300
  Bury St. Edmunds, 4:302
  Canterbury Tales, 4:584
  Catholic Church, 3:776, 778, 779,
    4:710–712, 17:163
  Christians accused of, 3:775, 776
  La Civiltà Cattolica, 4:748–749
  Classical period, 3:774–775
  Clement XII, 16:376
  Clement XIII, 4:753, 16:376
  Clement XIV, 3:778, 4:753, 16:376
  Clement XIII, 4:753
  Council of the Lands, 5:244
  Damascus Affair, 5:399–401
  Damocritus, 5:403
  defined, 3:774
  Donin, Nicholas, 5:750
  Dubossary (Moldova), 6:38
  Dubrovnik (Croatia), 6:38
  Eastern Europe, 3:778
  Elijah of Prague, 6:347
  Endingen libel, 6:403–404
  England, 3:775
        London, 6:410
        Northampton, 15:301
        Norwich, 15:312
  France, 4:105
        Blois, 7:150
        Boulay, 4:105
        Bourgeois, Jean, 4:106
        Lévy, Raphaël, 12:754
        Paris, 15:643
        Troyes, 20:157
        Valréas, 20:466
  Frankist movement, 7:185–188,
    191
  Frederick II of Hohenstaufen,
    7:222
  Germany, 4:79
        Boppard, 4:79
        Endingen, 6:403–404
        Fulda, 7:222, 309
        Pforzheim, 16:27

  Ravensburg, 17:121
  thirteenth century, late,
    17:334–335
  Velhartice, 3:778
  Hilsner Case, 9:119–120
  Istanbul (Ottoman period), 10:778
  Italy, 10:798
        Brescia, 4:163
        Rome, 17:414
        Trent, 3:469, 15:566
  Izmir (Turkey), 10:827
  Joseph ben Gershon of Rosheim,
    11:420, 421
  Kalisz, Statute of, 4:45
  Kolin (Czech Republic), 12:273
  Levinsohn, Isaac Baer on, 3:779
  Machaut, Denis de, 15:643–644
  Majorca (Spain), 13:410, 414
  Malta, 13:436
  map of sites in Europe, 3:777
  Meyer, Paulus, 14:149
  Middle Ages, 3:775–776, 9:214
  modern period, 3:776–780
  Olkusz (Poland), 15:408
  Ónody, Géza, 15:434
  origins of, 3:774–775
  Orléans and Blois communities,
    15:476
  Ottoman empire, 15:529–531
  Passover, association with, 3:775–
    776, 778
  Pezinok (Slovakia), 16:24
  prohibitions on consuming blood,
    3:772
  Raphaël Levy, 12:**754**
  refutations of, 3:776, 778, 779
  Rohling, August, 3:764, 778
  Rudolf I, 17:524
  Russia, 3:778–780, 18:51
        Polna, 3:779, 15:352
        Velizh, 3:779, 14:483, 20:492–
          493
  Sandomierz (Poland), 18:17
  Sochaczew, 18:703
  Spain, 12:438
  Der Stuermer, 19:275
  Tirgu Neamt (Romania), 19:730–
    731
  Tiszaeszlar (Hungary), 3:778, 779,
    4:246, 15:355, 19:735
  Volhynia (Ukraine), 20:571
  Volos (Greece), 20:574
  See also Damascus Affair
Blood on the Tracks (Dylan), 6:78
Blood revenge, 6:691
Blood Simple (motion picture), 4:782

*The Bloody Countess. See La condesa
  sangrienta*
Bloom, Benjamin Samuel, 3:**780**
Bloom, Claire, 3:**780–781**
Bloom, Harold, 3:**781**
Bloom, Hyman, 3:**781**
Bloom, Robert, 1:577–578
Bloom, Sol, 3:**782**
Bloom, Solomon Frank, 3:**782**
Bloomberg, Abe, 16:349
Bloomberg, Michael R., 3:**782,** 15:224,
  226, 238
Bloomberg LP, 3:782
Bloomfield, Leonard, 3:**783**
Bloomfield, Maurice, 3:**783**
Bloomfield, Meyer, 15:205
Bloomfield-Zeisler, Fanny, 3:**783**
Bloomgarden, Kermit, 3:**783**
Bloomgarden, Yehoash Solomon. *See*
  Yehoash
Bloomingdale, Alfred S., 3:**784**
Bloomingdale, Benjamin, 15:203
Bloomingdale, Emanuel Watson, 3:**784**
Bloomingdale, Hiram C., 3:**784**
Bloomingdale, Joseph Bernhardt,
  3:**784,** 15:203
Bloomingdale, Lyman Gustavus,
  3:**783–784,** 15:203
Bloomingdale, Samuel Joseph, 3:**784**
Bloomingdale family, 3:**783–784,** 5:588
Bloomingdale's Department Store,
  3:**784,** 15:203, 226
*The Bloudy Tenet of Persecution for
  Cause of Conscience Disgust*
  (Williams), 9:227–228
Blowitz, Henri Georges Stephane
  Adolphe Opper de, 3:**784**
Bloy, Léon, 3:**784**
Blue Army. *See* Haller's Army
Bluestone, Joseph Isaac, 4:**5–6**
Die Bluete des Chaos (Mombert),
  14:430
Bluhdorn, Charles G., 4:**6**
Blum, Amram ben Isaac Jacob, 4:**6**
Blum, Ben-Zion, 4:**6**
Blum, Eliezer, 4:**6–7**
Blum, Isaac Jacob, 4:**6**
Blum, Jerome, 4:**7**
Blum, Judah Zevi, 4:**6**
Blum, Julius, 4:**7**
Blum, Léon, 4:**7–8,** 11:467, 16:343,
  18:705
Blum, Ludwig, 4:**8**
Blum, Moses Nahum, 4:**6**
Blum, René, 4:**8**
Blum, Walter, 4:**8–9**
Blumberg, Baruch Samuel, 4:**9,** 13:9

Blumberg, Ḥayyim. *See* Harari, Ḥayyim

Blume, Peter, 4:**9**

Blumel, André, 4:**9–10**

Blumenberg, Leopold, 4:**10**

Blumenfeld, Aharon. *See* Roman-Ronetti, Moïse

Blumenfeld, Dov Ber, 4:199

Blumenfeld, Emanuel, 4:**10**

Blumenfeld, Felix Mikhaylovich, 4:**10**

Blumenfeld, Hermann Fadeevich, 4:**10–11,** 12:554

Blumenfeld, Kurt Yehudah, 4:**11**

Blumenfeld, Ralph David, 4:**11,** 11:467

Blumenfeld, Walter, 4:**11**

Blumenfeld alleys, 4:**11**

Blumenfield, Samuel, 4:**11**

Blumenkranz, Bernhard, 4:**11,** 11:324

Blumenthal, Aaron H., 4:**12**

Blumenthal, Albert, 15:224

Blumenthal, David, 4:12

Blumenthal, George, 4:**12**

Blumenthal, I.D., 4:579

Blumenthal, Joseph (1834-1901), 4:**12,** 15:211

Blumenthal, Joseph (1897-1990), 4:**12**

Blumenthal, Nissan, 4:**12–13**

Blumenthal, Oskar, 4:**13**

Blumenthal, Werner Michael, 4:**13**

Blumenthal family, 15:303

Blumlein, Aaron. *See* Aaron of Neustadt

Blutiker Shptas (Shalom Aleichem), 18:388

Bluwstein, Rahel. *See* Raḥel

B'nai B'rith, 4:**13–18**

    America, 2:43

    American Jewish Archives, 2:53

    American Jewish Conference, 2:56

    Anti-Defamation League, 2:194, 195

    Bien, Julius, 3:690

    Bisgyer, Maurice, 3:725

    B'nai B'rith Girls, 4:14

    B'nai B'rith Hillel Foundation, 12:635

    B'nai B'rith Women, 4:14, 17

    B'nai B'rith Youth Organization (BBYO), 4:14–15

    boycotts, anti-Nazi, 4:111

    Canada, 14:466

    Hillel, 9:111–112

    Hillel Foundation, 9:725, 16:724

    Independent Order of True Sisters, 4:220

    Jewish settlement in America and, 2:43

    New York City, 15:198

    publishing, 16:724

    San Diego, 18:13

    Wexler, William Abe, 21:32

Bnei Akiva, 4:**18–19,** 492–493, 14:391, 15:87

Board of Delegates of American Israelites, 4:**19–20**

Board of Deputies of British Jews, 2:408, 4:**20,** 12:565

    Anglo-Jewish Association, 2:162

    Fisher, Samuel, Baron Fisher of Camden, 7:64

Boas, Abraham, 4:20

Boas, Abraham Tobias, 1:385, 4:21

Boas, A.T. *See* Boas, Abraham Tobias

Boas, Franz, 2:185–186, 4:**21–22,** 13:236–237, 18:731

Boas, Frederick Samuel, 4:22

Boas, George, 4:22

Boas, Harold, 4:21

Boas, Henriette, 4:22

Boas, Hyman, 4:20

Boas, Isaac Herbert, 4:21

Boas, Simon, 4:20

Boas, Tobias, 4:20–21

Boas family, 4:**20–21**

Boaz, 1:416, 4:**22–23**

Boaz and Jachin (sanctuary pillars). *See* Jachin and Boaz (sanctuary pillars)

Bobe-Mayse, 4:**23**

Bober, Robert, 4:**23**

Bobov, 4:**23–24**

Bobover Ḥasidim, 8:424, 15:230–231

Bobrovy Kut (Ukraine), 4:**24,** 11:735

Bobruisk (Belarus), 4:**24–25**

Bobtelsky, Mordekhai, 4:**25**

Boca Raton (FL), 15:605

Boccaccio, Giovanni, 4:**25,** 10:789

Bochnia (Poland), 4:**25–26**

Bochum (Germany), 4:**26**

Bock, Jerry, 4:**26,** 8:360

Bodansky, Meyer, 4:**27**

Bodansky, Oscar, 4:**27**

Bodanzky, Arthur, 4:**27**

Bodek, Jacob, 4:**27**

Bodenheim, Maxwell, 4:**27**

Bodenheimer, Frederick Simon, 4:**27**

Bodenheimer, Max Isidor, 4:**27–28**

Bodenschatz, Johann Christoph Georg, 4:**28,** 18:605

Bodenstein, Charlotte. *See* Schoene, Lotte

Bodian, David, 4:**28**

Bodies That Matter: On the Discursive Limits of "Sex" (Butler), 4:317

Bodin, Jean, 4:**28–29,** 9:227

Bodky, Erwin, 4:**29**

Bodleian Library, 4:**29**

Bodley, Sir Thomas, 4:**29**

Bodley, Thomas. *See* Bodley, Sir Thomas

Bodmer, Johann Jacob, 15:289, 18:761

Bodmer, Sir Walter, 4:**29–30**

Bodmer, Walter. *See* Bodmer, Sir Walter

Bodo, 4:**30,** 6:14

Bodrogkeresztúr (Hungary), 4:**30**

Body and soul, 4:**30–31**

Boehm, Adolf, 4:**31**

Boehm, Yohanan, 4:**31–32**

Boehmisch-Leipa (Czech Republic). *See* Ceska Lipa (Czech Republic)

Boerne, Ludwig, 4:**32**

Boer War, 3:769

Boeschenstein, Johann, 4:**32**

Boesing (Slovakia). *See* Pezinok (Slovakia)

Boesky, Ivan Frederick, 4:**33**

Boethus, ben Zonin. *See* Baitos

Boethusians, 2:198, 4:**33–34,** 358

Boetticher, Paul Anton de. *See* Lagarde, Paul de

Bogale, Yona, 3:505, 4:**34**

Bogart, Humphrey, 3:30

Bogaty, Jacob, 11:116

Bogdan, Corneliu, 4:**34**

Bogdanor, Vernon, 4:**34**

Bogdanovich, Peter, 4:**34–35**

Bogen, Alexander, 4:**35**

Bogen, Boris David, 2:59, 4:**35,** 728

Boger, Ḥayyim, 4:**35**

Boghen, Felice, 4:**36**

Bogorad, Lawrence, 4:**36**

Bogoraz, Vladimir Germanovich, 4:**36,** 11:361

Bogrov, Dmitri, 4:**36–37**

Bogrov, Grigori Isaakovich, 4:**37,** 12:457

Boguslav (Ukraine), 4:**37**

Bohemia, 4:**37–41,** *38*

    Abrahamites, 1:312

    conferences, 5:145–146

    equality, 7:173

    fur trade, 7:313

    Holocaust

        Kosová Hora, 12:321

    Holocaust Period, 5:358–359

    Jewish population, 4:40*t*

    Landesjudenschaft, Boehmische, 12:469

    laws controlling Jewish population, 6:689–690

Bohemia, *continued*
  leather industry and trade,
    12:575–576
  peddling in, 15:709
  scholars, 9:298
  textiles, 19:663–664
  See also Czechoslovakia
Bohemia (newspaper), 11:704
Bohem Zaddik (Perl), 15:774
Bohl, Samuel, 4:**41**
Bohm, David, 4:**41–42**
Böhm, Henrik, 4:**42**
Böhm, Tomas, 18:93
Bohnen, Eli Aaron, 4:**42**
Bohóc (Bródy), 4:201
Bohor, Jisrael. *See* Hajim, Jisrael
Bohr, Niels Henrik David, 4:**42**
Bohybryszcze. *See* Pogrebishchenski
Boingo (music group). *See* Oingo
  Boingo (music group)
Bojan (Ukraine), 4:**42–43**
Bojanowo (Poland), 4:**43**
Bokanowski, Maurice, 4:**43**, 16:343
Boker Avraham (Cardozo), 4:464,
  18:353
Boker shel Shotim (Ben-Ner), 3:368
Boker Yizrah (Kamelhar), 11:751
Bokher, Elye. *See* Levita, Elijah
Bokros-Birman, Dezsö, 4:**43**
Bokser, Baruch M., 4:**43–44**
Bokser, Ben Zion, 4:**44**
Bolaffi, Ezekiel. *See* Abulafia, Ezekiel
  David ben Mordecai
Bolaffi, Giulio, 15:668
Bolaffi, Hezekiah David ben Mordecai.
  See Abulafia, Ezekiel David ben
  Mordecai
Bolaffi, Michele, 4:**44**
Bolaffio, Leone, 4:**44**
Bolechów (Poland). *See* Bolekhov
Bolechów (Ukraine). *See* Bolekhov
  (Ukraine)
Bolekhov (Ukraine), 4:**44–45**
Boleslavski, Isaac, 4:**46**
Boleslav V, 4:**45**
Bolivia, 4:**46–48**
Bolm, Adolph Rudolphovich, 4:**48**
Bologna (Italy), 4:**48–50**
Bolotowsky, Ilya, 4:**50**
Bolshaya Seidemenukha. *See*
  Kalinindorf
*The Bolshevik Revolution, its Rise and
  Meaning* (Litvinov), 13:141
Bolshevik theory, 5:92–94
Bolshevism in American Labor Unions
  (Dyche), 6:76
Bolten, Joshua B., 4:**50**

Bolten, Seymour, 4:50
Bolzano (Italy), 4:**50–51**
Bolzen (Italy). *See* Bolzano (Italy)
Bombay (India), 3:335–338, 4:**51–52**
Bomberg, Daniel, 4:**52**, 8:514
  Adelkind, Israel Cornelius, 1:386
  early printed editions of Hebrew
    Bible, 3:587
  Targum Yerushalmi II, 3:592
Bomberg, David, 4:**52–53**
*The Bombing of Auschwitz: Should the
  Allies Have Attempted It?*, 9:420
Bom Retiro (São Paulo, Brazil), 18:31
Bomze, Nahum, 4:**53**
Bona (Algeria). *See* Bone (Algeria)
Bonacosa, Jacob, 15:566
Bonafed, David ben Reuben, 4:**53**
Bonafed, Solomon ben Reuben, 4:**53–
  54**
Bonafos, Menahem B. Abraham, 4:**54–
  55**
Bonafoux, Daniel ben Israel, 4:**55**,
  18:352–353
En Bonafoux del'Argentière. *See* Kaspi,
  Joseph ben Abba Mari ibn
Bonaiuoto, Isaac Levi, 2:409
Bonald, Louis Gabriel Ambroise,
  Vicomte de, 4:**55**
Bonan, David, 4:**55–56**
Bonan, Hayyim Mordecai, 4:**55**
Bonan, Isaac, 4:**55**
Bonan, Mas'ud, 4:**55**
Bonan family, 4:**55–56**
Bonaparte, Napoleon. *See* Napoleon
  Bonaparte
Bonastruc, Isaac, 4:**56**, 6:58
Bonaventura, Arnaldo, 4:**56**
Bonaventura, Enzo Joseph, 4:**56**
Bonavoglia, Moses de' Medici, 4:**56**
Bonciu, H., 4:**56**
Bondavin, Bonjudas, 4:**56–57**
Bondi, Abraham ben Yom Tov, 4:**57**
Bondi, Aron, 4:**57**
Bondi, August, 3:734, 4:**57**
Bondi, Elijah ben Selig, 4:**57**
Bondi, Hermann. *See* Bondi, Sir
  Hermann
Bondi, Isaac, 15:199
Bondi, Jonas, 4:**58**
Bondi, Nehemiah Feivel, 4:**57**
Bondi, Simeon ben Isaac, 4:**57**
Bondi, Sir Hermann, 4:**57–58**
Bondi, Yom Tov ben Abraham, 4:**57**
Bondi family, 4:**57**
Bonds
  of indebtedness, 5:154–155

  sale of, 2:604
  State of Israel, 4:**58–59**, *59*
Bondy, Bohumil, 4:**59–60**
Bondy, Curt, 4:**60**, 6:160
Bondy, Filip, 4:**60**, 129
Bondy, Gertrud, 4:**60**
Bondy, Gottlieb. *See* Bondy, Bohumil
Bondy, Jonah, 4:**57**
Bondy, Max, 4:**60**
Bondy, Ruth, 4:**60–61**
Bondy, Samuel, 4:**57**
Bondy family. *See* Bondi family
Bone (Algeria), 4:**61**
Bone, Sir Muirhead, 4:52
Bone-reaping hook (10th millenium
  B.C.E.), vol. 10: color insert
Bonet, Jacob, 4:**63**
Bonfil, Robert, 4:**61–62**
Bonfils, Immanuel ben Jacob, 4:**62**,
  13:674
Bonfils, Joseph ben Eliezer, 4:**62**
Bonfils, Joseph ben Samuel, 2:175,
  4:**62**, 8:488, 14:438
Bonfrère, Jacques, 4:**62–63**
Boniface IX, 4:**63**, 16:374
Boniface popes, 4:**63**
Boniface VIII, 4:**63**, 16:373
Bonjorn, Bonet Davi, 4:**63**
Bonjorn, David Bonet. *See* Bonjorn,
  Bonet Davi
Bonjusas. *See* Bondavin, Bonjudas
Bonn (Germany), 4:**63–64**
Bonn, Hanuš, 4:**64**
Bonn, Moritz Julius, 4:**64–65**
Bonn, Moses, 2:24
Bonné, Alfred Abraham, 4:**65**
Bonner, Elena Georgievna, 4:**65**
Bono, David, 4:77
Bonsenyor, Astruc ben Judah, 4:**65**
Bonsenyor, Judah, 4:**65**
Bonte family. *See* Bondi family
Bonyhád (Hungary), 4:**66**
*The Boof of Morality. See Sefer ha-
  Musar* (Kaspi)
*The Book and the Sword: A Life of
  Learning in the Shadow of
  Destruction* (Halivni), 8:275
Bookbinder, Hyman H., 4:**66–67**
Bookbinding, 2:496, 4:**73–75**
*Book of Adam and Eve. See Book of the
  Life of Adam and Eve*
*The Book of Argument and Proofs in
  Defense of the Despised Faith*
  (Halevi). *See Kitāb al-Hujja wa
  al-Dalīl fi Nasr al-Dhalī* (Halevi)
*The Book of Blessings: New Jewish
  Prayers for Daily Life, the Sabbath,
  and the New Moon Festival* (Falk),
  13:138

Book of Brightness. See Sefer ha-Bahir

The Book of Daniel (Doctorow), 5:728

The Book of Degrees (Falaquera). *See Sefer ha-Ma'alot*

Book of Delights. See Sefer Sha'ashu'im

Book of Doctrines and Beliefs (Gaon), 11:730

Book of Enoch, 14:132–133

Book of Festivals (Lewisnsky), 6:74

The Book of God: A Response to the Bible (Josipovici), 6:439

Book of Intercalation. See Sefer ha-Ibbur

Book of Jashar (aggadic work). *See Sefer ha-Yashar*

Book of Jashar (poetic source book), **4:69**

The Book of Jokes and Witticisms (Druyanow), 6:29

Book of Jubilees. See Jubilees, Book of

Book of Life, **4:69–70**

Book of Lights and Watch Towers (al-Kirkisănĭ), 6:230

Book of Magical Secrets. See Sefer ha-Razim

"The Book of Minute Research." *See Kitāb al-Tashwīr* (Ibn Janāah, Jonah)

Book of Miracles…, An Historical Account of the Ten Tribes Settled Beyond the River Sambatyon in the East (Edrehi)

Book of Miracles… (Edrehi). *See An Historical Account of the Ten Tribes Settled Beyond the River Sambatyon in the East* (Edrehi)

Book of Nahum, 14:758

Book of Opinions and Beliefs (Saadiah Gaon), 16:78–79

Book of Prayers (Calisch), 4:364

Book of Precepts. See Sefer ha-Mitzvot

Book of Principles. See Sefer ha-Ikkarim

Book of Principles (Albo). *See Sefer ha-Ikkarim* (Albo)

Book of Raziel. *See Raziel, Book of*

The Book of Redemption. See Sefer ha-Maasiyyot

Book of Remembrance (Ephraim ben Jacob of Bonn), 6:460

The Book of Riddles (Gikatilla). *See Sefer ha-Meshalim*

"Book of Righteousness, The". *See Sefer ha-Yashar*

Book of Roots. See Sefer ha-Shorashim

The Book of Routes (Ibn Khurdadhbah), 6:106

The Book of Ruth and Esther (Pissarro), 16:187

Book of Secrets. See Sefer ha-Razim

Book of Songs. See Kitāab al-Aghānī

Book of Stories. See Mayse-Bukh

Book of Stories (Nissim). *See Sefer ha-Maasiyyot*

"Book of the Commandments." *See Sefer ha-Mitzvot*

Book of the Cook. See Kitāb al-Tabbākh

Book of the Covenant, **4:67–69,** 6:616–617

"Book of the Dead" (Egyptian), 6:534–535

Book of the Druggist. See Kitāb al-Tabbākh

Book of the Five Substances (treatise), 6:397

The Book of the Great Secret. See Raza Rabba; Sefer Raza Rabba

"Book of the Laws of the Torah, The." *See Sefer Ḥukkei ha-Torah*

Book of the Life of Adam and Eve, 1:**377–378,** 15:394

Book of the Living. *See Book of Life*

Book of the Microcosm. See Sefer ha-Olam ha-Katan

Book of the Paths of Peace (Mendelssohn). *See Sefer Netivot ha-Shalom* (Mendelssohn)

The Book of the Sacred Magic of Abra-Melin, 11:667

Book of the Secret. See Sefer ha-Sod (Kaspi)

Book of the Secrets of Enoch. *See Enoch, Slavonic Book of*

The Book of the Seeker (Falaquera). *See Sefer ha-Mevakesh*

The Book of the Soul (Falaquera). *See Sefer ha-Nefesh*

Book of the Stones of Joshua. See Avnei Yehoshu'a

Book of the Wars of the Lord, **4:70**

Book of the Wars of the Lord (Reuben). *See Sefer Milhamot Adonai* (Reuben)

Book of Travels. See Sefer ha-Massa'ot

Book of Treasure (Emrāni), 6:398

Book of Victory (Emrāni), 6:398

Book of Wisdom (Eleazar ben Judah of Worms), 6:304

Book of Zerubbabel, 21:**517–518**

Bookplates, **4:70–71**

Books, **4:71–76**

    art in, 2:497–498

    in Bibliothèque Nationale, 3:685

    burning, 9:328

    chapbooks, 4:568

    collectors of, 3:683–685

    illuminated

        Maḥzor, 13:363–365

    Warsaw ghetto, 9:472

    See also Illuminated manuscripts; Printing; Publishing

Books and Fates. See Knihy a osudy

Books of the Bible. *See specific books by name.*

Books of the Chronicles of the Kings of Judah and Israel, 4:**76–77,** 9:154

Book trade, 4:**77–78**

    Brentano family, 4:162–163

    Horodisch, Abraham, 9:527–528

    Rosenbach, Abraham Simon Wolf, 17:431–432

Boone, Richard, 4:**78–79**

Boorstin, Daniel J., 4:**79**

Boorstin, Ḥannah Cohn, 15:572

Booz. *See Jachin and Boaz (sanctuary pillars)*

Bopp, F., 4:155

Boppard (Germany), 4:**79**

Bor, Josef, 4:**79**

Borah, Woodrow Wilson, 4:**80**

Boraisha, Menahem, 4:**80**

Borchardt, Georg. *See Hermann, Georg*

Borchardt, Lucy, 4:**80**

Borchardt, Ludwig, 2:371, 4:**80–81**

Borchardt, Rudolf, 4:**81**

Borchsenius, Poul, 4:**81**

Bordeaux (France), 4:**81–83**

"Bordeaux Itinerary." *See Itinerarium Hierosolymitanum*

The Border (Feinstein), 6:440, 741

Borders, decorative, in books, 4:75

Border Street (Ford), 9:440

Bordjel, Abraham, 4:**83**

Bordjel, Elijah Ḥai I, 4:**84**

Bordjel, Elijah Ḥai II, 4:**84**

Bordjel, Nathan I, 4:**83**

Bordjel, Nathan II, 4:**84**

Bordjel family, 4:**83–84**

Borenstein, Sam, 4:**84**

Borge, Victor, 4:**84–85**

Borgenicht, Louis, 15:205

Borghi, Lamberto, 4:**85,** 6:161

Borgil, Abraham ben Aziz, 4:**85,** 270

Borinstein, Louis J., 4:**85**

Boris, Ruthanna, 4:**85**

Borislav (Ukraine), 4:**85–86**

Borisov (Belarus), 4:**86**

Borisov, Andrey Yakovlevich, 4:**86**

Borisovich, Rudolf. *See Barshai, Rudolf*

Bormann, Martin, 4:**87**

Born, Max, 4:**87,** 15:193

Bornfriend, Jacob, 4:**87**

Bornstein, Eli, 4:**87–88**

Bornstein, Ḥayyim Jehiel, 4:**88**

Borochov, Ber, 4:**88–90**, 18:717

Borodavka, Isaac, 4:**91**

Borodin, Michael Markovitsch, 4:**91**

Borofsky, Jonathan, 4:**91**

Boro Park (NYC), 15:203, 213, 217, 223, 231–232

Borovoy, A. Alan, 4:**91–92**

Borovoy, Saul, 4:**92**

Borovsky, Alexander, 4:**92**

Borowitz, Abram Solman. *See* Burrows, Abe

Borowitz, Eugene B., 4:**92–94**

Borowitz, Sidney, 4:**94**

Borowski, Tadeusz, 9:412

Borromeo, Carlo, 4:**94**

Borşa (Romania). *See* Borsa (Romania)

Borsa (Romania), 4:**94**

Borscht Belt (NY), 15:221, 241

Borsippa (Bablyonia), 4:**94**

Borsook, Henry, 4:**95**

Boryslaw (Ukraine). *See* Borislav; Borislav (Ukraine)

Bosak, Meir, 4:**95**

Boschwitz, Rudolph Eli, 4:**95**

Bosco, Monique, 4:**95–96**, 425

Boscovitch, Alexander Uriyah, 4:**96**

Bosem. *See* Balsam

Boshal, Moses ben Solomon, 4:**96**

Bosham, Herbert de, 4:**96**, 8:512

Boskoff, Alvin, 4:**97**, 18:732

Boskovice (Czech Republic), 4:**97**

Boskowitz (Czech Republic). *See* Boskovice (Czech Republic)

Boskowitz, Benjamin Ze'ev ha-Levi, 4:**98**

Boskowitz, Ḥayyim ben Jacob, 4:**98**

Bosna-Serai (Bosnia-Herzegovina). *See* Sarajevo (Bosnia-Herzegovina)

Bosnia. *See* Bosnia-Herzegovina

Bosnia-Herzegovina, Travnik, 20:122

Bosniak, Jacob, 4:**98**

Bosnian War (1992-1994), Jewish refugees, 18:49

Bosor. *See* Boẓrah (Trachonitis)

Bosphorus, kingdom of. *See* Kingdom of Bosphorus

Bossuet, Jacques Benigne, 4:**99**

Bostal, Moses. *See* Boshal, Moses ben Solomon

Boston (MA), 4:**99–101**, 13:664

  ḥasidism, 9:541

    Horowitz, Pinchas David ha-Levi, 9:541

  New England Holocaust Memorial, vol. 9: color insert

Boswell: a Modern Comedy (Elkin), 6:359

Botanical medicine. *See* Medicine

Botany

  Acosta, Christobal, 1:358–359

  Austria

    Fahn, Abraham, 6:676

    Wiesner, Julius von, 21:55–56

  Belgium

    Errera, Léo, 6:483

  Duvdevani, Shmuel, 6:73

  dye plants, 6:77

  Eig, Alexander, 6:253

  Germany

    Ascherson, Paul Friedrich August, 2:552

    Askenasy, Eugen, 2:588

    Magnus, Paul Wilhelm, 13:357

    Sachs, Julius, 17:635

    Strasburger, Eduard, 13:7, 19:245–246

    Warburg, Otto, 20:632–633

  Halevi, Abraham H., 8:269

  Ha-Reubeni, Ephraim, 8:353

  India

    Ezekiel, Moses, 6:648

  Israel, 6:676, 739

    Duvdevani, Shmuel, 6:73

    Evenari, Michael, 6:573–574

    Feinbrun-Dothan, Naomi, 6:739

    Halevy, Abraham H., 8:269

    Ha-Reubeni, Ephraim, 8:353

    Rayss, Tscharna, 17:128

    Reichert, Israel, 17:199–200

    Zohary, Michael, 21:664

  mixed species, 14:385–387

  Oppenheimer, Hillel, 15:448

  Reichert, Israel, 17:199–200

  Russia

    Eig, Alexander, 6:253

  See also specific plants

Botarel, Moses ben Isaac, 4:**101**, 11:613

Boteach, Shmuel, 4:**101**

Botein, Bernard, 4:**101–102**

Both Sides Now (Slonim), 18:678

Boton, Abraham ben Judah di, 4:**102**

Boton, Abraham ben Moses de, 4:**102**

Boton, Ḥiyya Abraham ben Aaron di, 4:**102**

Boton, Jacob ben Abraham di, 4:**102–103**

Boton, Meir ben Abraham di, 4:**103**

Botosani (Romania), 4:**103**

Botoshansky, Jacob, 4:**103–104**

Botstein, Leon, 4:**104**

Botswana, 6:371

  See also South Africa

Botticelli, Sandro, 14:542

Botvinnik, Mikhail, 4:**104**, 207

Bouchara, Abraham, 4:104

Bouchara, Isaac, 4:104

Bouchara, Jacob Raphael, 4:104

Bouchara family, 4:**104–105**

Boudin, Jean-François, 4:**105**

Boudreau, Lou, 4:**105**

Bougie (Algeria), 4:**105**

Bou-Hallais, 15:391

Boulay (France), 4:**105**

Boule, 4:**105–106**

Les boulevards de ceinture (Modiano). *See* Circle Line Boulevards (Modiano)

Boundaries, 1:474–476

Boundary stones, moving, 8:448–450, 12:473

Bourassa, Henri, 4:397

Bourel, Dominique, 11:325

Bourg-en-Bresse (France), 4:**106**

Bourgeois, Jean, 4:**106**

Bourges (France), 4:**106**

Bourke-White, Margaret, 4:**106–107**

Bourla, Yehuda. *See* Burla, Yehuda

Boussidan, Ya'akov, 4:372–373

Bouwmeester, Louis Frederik Johannes, 4:**107**

Bouzaglo, David, 4:**107**

Bove-Bukh (Levita), 4:**107–108**, 15:651

Bovo D'Antona, 4:23

Bovshover, Joseph, 4:**108**, 18:370

Bowling (tenpin), 17:483–484, 19:138

Bowman-Birk Inhibitor (BBI), 3:711

Box (flora), 4:**108**

Boxer, Barbara, 4:**108**

Boxer, Oswald, 4:145

Boxing, 3:52–53, 19:138–139

  Baer, Max, 3:52

  Berg, Jackie "Kid," 3:415–416

  Bimstein, Morris "Whitey," 3:702

  Brenner, Teddy, 4:162

  Davis, Al "Bummy," 5:479

  Fields, Jackie, 7:17–18

  Fleischer, Nathaniel Stanley, 7:74

  Hollandersky, Abraham, 9:322

  Leonard, Benny, 12:647

  Levinsky, Battling, 12:720

  Lewis, Ted, 12:767

  Luftspring, Sammy, 13:253

  Mendoza, Daniel, 14:45

  Newark (NJ), 6:512

Razon, Jacko, 17:130–131

Rosenbloom, Max Everitt "Slapsie Maxie," 17:442

Ross, Barney, 17:468–469

Solomons, Jack, 18:773

Boyar, Louis H., 4:108–109

Boyarin, Daniel, 1:461, 4:109, 15:358

Boyarin, Mordkhe. *See* Litvine, M.

Boycotts

anti-Jewish, 4:109–110, 9:328, *461*

anti-Nazi, 4:110–111, *111t*

Arab, 4:111–113

movements, Bohemia, 4:41

See also antisemitic political parties and organizations

Boycott Sabbath, 5:61

Der Boym fun Lebn (Rosenfarb), 4:427

The Boys of Summer (Kahn), 11:724

Boystk (Latvia). *See* Bauska (Latvia)

Bozecco, Benjamin ben Judah, 4:113–114

Bozrah (Israel), 4:115, 6:152, 8:260

Boẓrah (Bashan), 4:*114*, 114–115

Boẓrah (Edom), 4:115

Boẓrah (Trachonitis), 4:115

Bozyk, Max, 4:115

Bozyk, Rose, 4:115

Bozzolo (Italy), 4:116

Braak, Menno ter, 6:69

Braatbard, Avraham Haim, 2:38

Brabanel family. *See* Abrabanel family

Brach, Saul, 4:116

Brack, Viktor, 4:387

Bradford (England), 4:116

Bradlow, Henry, 3:769

Brafman, Jacob, 4:116–117

Bragadini, Alvise, 4:117, 15:641

Bragadini, Giovanni, 4:117

Bragadini family, 4:117

Braganza (Portugal), 4:117

Bragin, Abraham

on Birobidzhan, 3:718

Braham, John, 4:117

Braham, Randolph Louis, 4:118

Brahinsky, Mani Leib. *See* Mani Leib

Brahm, Otto, 4:118

Brăila (Romania). *See* Braila (Romania)

Braila (Romania), 4:118

Braille, 3:*754*

Brailov (Ukraine), 4:118–119

Brailowsky, Alexander, 4:119

"The Brain." *See* Rothstein, Arnold

"Brain, The". *See* Rothstein, Arnold

Brainin, Joseph, 4:119

Brainin, Reuben, 4:119, 8:726

Brampton, Edward. *See* Brampton, Sir Edward

Brampton, Sir Edward, 4:120

Bramson, Leon, 4:120

Bramson, Leon (Leonty), 16:348

Branche francaise de la Jewish Trust Corporation for Germany, 11:327

Branco, João Rodrigues de Castelo. *See* Amatus Lusitanus

Brand, Joel, 9:122

Brand, Joel Jenö, 4:120–121

Brandão, Edward. *See* Brampton, Sir Edward

Brandão, Ambrósio Fernandes, 4:121, 143

Brandeau, Esther, 4:121

Brandeis, Adolph, 4:121

Brandeis, Frederika, 4:121, 122

Brandeis, Jonas L., 15:415

Brandeis, Louis Dembitz, 4:121–124, 20:328, 21:606

American Jewish Congress, 2:57

Breslau, Isadore, 4:166

Frankfuter, Felix, 7:205

on Jewish Legion, 11:305

labor movement and, 15:205

U.S. Supreme Court, 12:556

Brandeis, Pavel, 5:646

Brandeis an der Elbe (Czech Republic). *See* Brandys nad Labem (Czech Republic)

Brandeis-Bardin Institute, 4:124

Brandeis Camp Institute, 3:148–149

Brandeis University, 4:124–125

American Jewish Historical Society, 2:58

Fox, Marvin, 7:141

Jewish studies at, 11:317, 319

Levine, Baruch, 12:717

Shapero, Harold, 18:397

Brandenburg (Germany), 4:125–126

Brandes, Carl Edvard, 4:126

Brandes, Georg, 4:126–127, 7:38

Brandes, Ludwig Israel, 4:127

Brandes, Reuben Asher, 8:691

Brandon, David Henry, 15:610

Brandon, Edward. *See* Brampton, Sir Edward

Brandon, Jacques-Emile-Edouard, 2:505

Brandon, Oheb Isaac, 4:127

Brandstaedter, Mordecai David, 4:127

Brandstaetter, Roman, 4:127–128

Brandt, Boris, 4:128

Brandt, Willy, 3:757, 4:128

Brandwein, Yehuda Ẓevi, 4:128–129

Brandys, Kazimierz, 4:129

Brandys nad Labem (Czech Republic), 4:129

Brann, Marcus, 4:129, 14:433

Brant, Henry Dreyfuss, 4:129–130

Brant Shpigl (Altschul), 2:26

Brasch, Rudolph, 4:130

Brash, Henry, 7:87

Brasil, País do futuro (Zweig), 17:338

Braslav (Belarus), 4:130–131

Braslav Ḥasidim, 8:425

Braslavi, Joseph, 4:131

Braslavski, Joseph. *See* Braslavi, Joseph

Braslaw (Belarus). *See* Braslav (Belarus)

Braşov (Romania), 4:131

Brassavola, 2:34

Brassó (Romania). *See* Braşov (Romania)

Bratcher, Robert G., 3:619

Bratislava (Slovakia), 4:131–134, *132t*, 18:682, 684

Bratslav (Ukraine), 4:134

Braude, Ernest Alexander, 4:134

Braude, Jacob, 4:135

Braude, Markus, 4:135

Braude, Max A., 4:135

Braude, Mordecau Ze'ev. *See* Braude, Markus

Braude, Mordekhai Ze'ev. *See* Braude, Markus

Braude, William Gordon, 4:135–136

Braudes, Reuben Asher, 4:136

Braudo, Alexander Isayevich, 4:137

Braudo, Yevgeni Maximovich, 4:137

Braun, Abraham, 4:137

Braun, Adolf, 4:137

Braun, Arie, 4:137

Braun, Felix, 4:137–138

Braun, Gyozo. *See* Barna, Victor

Braun, Heinrich, 4:137

Braun, Lily, 4:137

Braun, Mieczyslaw, 4:138

Braun, Sergei. *See* Braun, Abraham

Braun, Yehezkiel, 4:138

Brauner, Harry, 4:138–139

Brauner, Isaac, 4:139

Brauner, Victor, 4:139, 15:648

Brauner, Wincenty. *See* Brauner, Isaac

Braunschweig (Germany). *See* Brunswick (Germany)

Braunstein, Menahem Mendel, 4:139–140

Braunstein, Mieczyslaw. *See* Braun, Mieczyslaw

Braunthal, Julius, 4:140, 16:341, 18:705

Braverman, Avishay, 4:140

Braverman, Nahum, 13:202
Brawer, Abraham Jacob, 4:**140**
Brawer, Moshe, 4:**140–141**
Bray-sur-Seine (France), 4:**141**
Braz, Osip, 4:**141**
Brazda, 7:25
Brazer, Abram, 4:**141–142**
Brazil, 4:**142–154**
   Aboab da Fonseca, Isaac, 1:269
   agricultural settlements in, 4:145–146
   agriculture, Jewish, 1:501
   Alvares Correa family, 2:27
   antisemitism, 4:148–150, 151, 16:407, 18:31–32, 33
   anti-Zionist movement, 4:151
   architecture, 2:400, 12:657–658, 692
   Bahia new Christians, 3:60–61
   Brandão, Ambrósio Fernandes, 4:121, 143
   cemeteries, 18:31
   Colonial period, 4:142–143
   communism, 4:149
   community leaders, 6:735
   community life and social organization in, 4:146–148
   Crypto-Jews in, 4:143
   as Dutch colony, 4:144
   education, 4:148, 152, 18:32, 33
   education, Jewish, 6:212
   hospitals, 18:31
   immigration to, 11:287
   independence, 4:144–145
   Inquisition, 4:142, 143, 9:796–797
   interfaith relations, 4:151–152
   Jewish organizations, 18:31, 33–34
   Jewish settlement in, 2:41, 46, 4:469, 470–471
   journalism, 11:469–470, 12:514, 16:496
   Levi-Strauss, Claude, 12:730
   literature, 4:152
      Dines, Alberto, 5:670–671
      Rawet, Samuek, 17:124
      Scliar, Moacyr, 18:207
   migrations, 18:30, 31, 32
   modern period, 4:145–150, 12:436
   New Christians, 4:142–144
   Noronha, Fernão de, 15:301
   political participation of Jews in, 4:148, 150–151, 153
   politics, 16:350
   population statistics, Jewish, 4:142, 146*t*, 153, 154
   as Portuguese colony, 4:142–144
   Portuguese translations of Bible, 3:633
   post-WW II, 4:150–151
   relations with
      Israel (state), 4:153–154
   Sephardim, 18:31
   settlements, 4:*142*
   synagogues, 18:33
   terrorism in, 4:153
   twenty-first century, 4:152–153
   Tzvi Migdal traffic network, 4:147–148
   universities, 18:33
   urban immigration, 4:146
   Vargas regime, 4:148–150
   Zionism, 18:32, 21:593–594
   Zionist movement, 4:148, 150–151
Bread, 1:434, 4:**154–155**, 7:115, 8:277–278
   Ḥallah, 7:118
   Lodz ghetto, 9:*470*
   shewbread or showbread, 18:473–474
   See also Manna; Shewbread or showbread
Bread and Salt (Bursztyn). *See Broyt mit Zalts*
Bread of affliction. *See* Matzah
Break Glass in Case of Fire. See Rómpase en case de incendio
Breaking New Ground (Levi), 12:693
Breaking Point (Presser), 9:409
Breaking Ranks (Podhoretz), 16:251
The Breaks of the Game (Halberstam), 8:265
Bréal, Michel, 4:**155–156**
Breastplates, 4:**156**, 16:512, 20:52
Brecher, Gideon, 4:**156**
Brecher, Gustav, 4:**156**
Brecker, Michael, 4:156
Brecker, Randy, 4:156
Brecker Brothers, 4:**156**
Breclav (Czech Republic), 4:**156–157**
Bredig, George, 4:**157**
Bregstein, Marcel Henri, 4:**157**
Bregstein, Philo, 4:157
Breidenbach, Julius, 4:157
Breidenbach, Moritz, 4:157
Breidenbach, Wolf, 4:**157**, 15:386
Breisach (Germany), 4:**157**
Breitel, Charles, 4:**157–158**
Breithaupt, Johann Friedrich, 4:158
Breitner, Hugo, 4:**158**, 16:341, 18:705
Breman Museum, 2:638
Bremen (Germany), 4:**158**
Brenendike Likht. See Burning Lights
Brener, Pynchas, 4:**158**
Brenner, Frédéric, 4:**158–159**
Brenner, Joseph Ḥayyim, 4:**159–161**, 8:301, 696, 728, 13:254
Brenner, Rose, 4:**161**
Brenner, Sydney, 4:**161–162**, 13:9
Brenner, Teddy, 4:**162**
Brenner, Uri, 15:604
Brenner, Victor, 4:**162**
Brentano, Arthur, 4:**162–163**
Brentano, August, 4:162
Brentano, Lowell, 4:163
Brentano, Simon, 4:162, 163
Brentano family, 4:**162–163**
Bresch, Judah Loeb ben Moses Naphtali, 4:**163**
Bresch, Leo, 3:610
Brescia (Italy), 4:**163**
Breshis-Inmitn (Lutzky), 13:275
Breslasu, Marcel, 4:**163–164**
Breslau (Poland), 4:**164–165**, 7:200–201, 18:578–580
Breslau, Aryeh Loeb ben Ḥayyim, 4:**165–166**
Breslau, Isadore, 2:47, 4:166
Breslau, Joseph Moses ben David, 4:**166**
Breslaw, Joseph, 4:**166–167**
Bresliska, Marcel. *See* Breslasu, Marcel
Bresnitz-Lokschan (Czech Republic). *See* Breznice; Breznice (Czech Republic)
Bresse (France), 4:**167**
Bresselau, Meyer Israel, 4:**167**
Bresslau, Ernst, 4:**167**
Bresslau, Harry, 4:**167–168**
Bresslau, Helena, 4:167
Bressler, David Maurice, 4:**168**
Brest Kuyavsk (Poland). *See* Brzesc Kujawski (Poland)
Brest-Litovsk (Lithuania), 4:**168–170**, 18:775
Bretagne (France). *See* Brittany (France)
Bretholz, Berthold, 4:**170**
Brethren of Sincerity, Epistles of. See Epistles of Brethren of Sincerity
Breton, André, 4:139
Breton language, biblical translations into, 3:637
Breuer, Isaac, 4:**171**
Breuer, Joseph (1842-1925), 4:**171**
Breuer, Joseph (1882-1980), 4:**171–172**, 18:180
Breuer, Marcel, 4:**172**
Breuer, Mordechai, 4:**172–173**
Breuer, Raphael, 4:**173**

Breuer, Solomon, 4:**173**

Breuerer family, 4:79

Bréval, Lucienne, 4:**174**

Bréviaire de la haine (Poliakov), 9:415–421

Breyer, Julius, 4:**174**

Breyer, Stephen Gerald, 4:**174–175,** 12:556–557

Breyter, Isaac, 16:349

Brezin (Poland). *See* Brzeziny (Poland)

Brezinka (Poland). *See* Birkenau concentration camp

Breznice (Czech Republic), 4:**175**

Březnice (Czech Republic). *See* Breznice; Breznice (Czech Republic)

Briar, vol. 16: color insert

Briar Rose (Yolen), 18:200

Bribery, 4:**175–177**

Brice, Fanny, 4:**177**

Briceni (Moldova). *See* Brichany (Moldova)

Briceva (Ukraine), 4:**177–178**

Brichany (Moldova), 4:**178**

Brick, Daniel, 4:**178**

Brickner, Balfour, 4:**178–179**

Brickner, Barnett Robert, 4:**179**

Bridal Canopy. See Hakhasat Kallah

Bridegrooms of the Law, 4:**179–180**

Bridge (card game). *See* Cards and cardplaying

Bridgeport (CT), 4:**180**

Brie, Luis Hartwig, 4:**181**

Brief aan mijn moeder (Meijer). *See Letter to My Mother* (Meijer)

The Brief Travels of Benjamin the Third, Kitser Masoes Binyomen Hashlishi

Brieg (Poland). *See* Brzeg (Poland)

Briel, Judah ben Eliezer, 4:**181**

Brietel, Charles, 2:18

Brifnshteler, 6:187

The Brigade. See Piẓei Bagrut

The Brigegroom Cometh (Frank), 7:195

Bright, John, 3:651

Bright, Myron, 15:304

Brighton (England), 4:**181**

Brighton Beach (NYC), 15:230, 231

Brik, Osip Maksimovich, 4:**181**

Brill, Abraham Arden, 4:**181–182**

Brill, Azriel, 4:**182**

Brill, Isaac Lipa, 4:**182**

Brill, Jehiel, 4:**182–183,** 8:267

Brill, Joel, 8:724

Brill, Joseph, 4:**183,** 15:662

Brill, Samuel Loew, 4:**182**

Brill Building songwriters, 18:234

Brilling, Bernhard, 4:**183**

Brin, Sergey, 4:**183–184**

Brindisi (Italy), 4:**184**

Bringing It Back Home (Dylan), 6:78

Brinig, Myron, 4:**184**

Brinker, Menachem, 4:**184–185**

Brisac. *See* Ensheim, Moses

Brisbane (Australia), 4:**185**

Briscoe, Benjamin, 16:343

Briscoe, Robert, 4:**185,** 6:33, 16:343

Brisk (Lithuania). *See* Brest-Litovsk; Brest-Litovsk (Lithuania)

Brisk de Koyavi (Poland). *See* Brzesc Kujawski (Poland)

Brisker, R' Ḥayyim. *See* Soloveichik, Ḥayyim

Brisker, Yehudah. *See* Haezrahi, Yehuda

Bristol (England), 4:**185–186**

Briszk, Mordecai ben Joshua, 4:**186**

Briszk, Nathan Ẓevi ben Joshua, 4:**186**

Briszk family, 4:**186**

Britain. *See* United Kingdom

Brith Abraham, 4:**186**

British Art, 5:429

British Columbia (Canada), 4:**186–188**

British Commonwealth. *See* United Kingdom

British Guiana. *See* Guiana

British Israelite movement, 4:211

British Israelites, 3:670, 4:**188**

British Israel World Federation, 4:188

British literature

    Daniel in, 5:418

    Davidson, Lionel, 5:476

    Jacobson, Howard, 11:53–54

    Leavis, Queenie Dorothy, 12:577

    Leveen, Jacob, 12:678

    Leverson, Ada, 12:680–681

    Levertov, Denise, 12:681–682

    Raphael, Chaim, 17:94

    Raphael, Frederic, 17:94

    Rubens, Bernice, 17:510

    Sassoon, Siegfried Lorraine, 18:71

    Shaffer, Peter, 18:361

    twentieth century, 6:716

    See also English literature

British Museum

    Miscellany, 3:678

    Samaritan amulets, 2:123

British West Indies, 4:473–474

Brit Ivrit Olamit, 4:**188–189**

Brittan, Leon, Baron, 4:**189**

Brittan, Sir Samuel, 4:189

Brittany (France), 2:175, 4:**189,** 7:150

Briviesca (Spain), 4:**189–190**

Briyo ve-Zimro (fiction), 4:**190**

Brno (Czech Republic), 4:**190–191**

Broad, Eli, 4:**191**

Broad, Max, 18:377

Broad bean blossoms, vol. 16: color insert

Broad Foundation, 4:191

Broadway Heartbeat (Sobel), 18:699

Broadway theater (New York City, NY), 15:220, 227–228

    Burrows, Abe, 4:299

    Fields, Dorothy, 7:17

    Kanin, Garson, 11:763

    Lahr, Bert, 12:439–440

    Landesman, Rocco, 12:470

Broch, Hermann, 4:**191–192**

Brociner, Andrei, 4:192

Brociner, Joseph, 4:**192**

Brociner, Marco, 4:192

Brociner, Mauriciu, 4:192

Brod, Dovidl, 4:192

Brod, Max, 4:**192–193,** 11:705, 12:480

Broda, Aaron, 4:193

Broda, Abraham, 4:166

Broda, Abraham ben Saul, 4:**194**

Broda, Benjamin, 4:193

Broda, Dov Ber, 4:193

Broda, Ḥayyim, 4:193

Broda, Joseph, 4:193

Broda, Moses, 4:194

Broda family, 4:**193–194**

Brodavka, Isaac. *See* Borodavka, Isaac

Broder, Berl, 4:**194**

Broder, David Salzer, 4:**194–195**

Broderick, Matthew, 4:**195,** 15:652

Broder Singers, 4:194, **195,** 19:678

Brodersohn, Mario, 16:350

Broderzon, Moyshe, 4:**195–196**

Broderzon, Sheyne Miriam, 4:195–196

Brodetsky, Selig, 4:**196**

Brodie, Israel. *See* Brodie, Sir Israel

Brodie, Sir Israel, 4:**196,** 6:419, 11:332

Brodski, Abraham, 4:197

Brodski, Arieh Leibush, 4:197

Brodski, Eliezer, 4:197

Brodski, Israel, 4:197

Brodski, Meir, 4:196–197

Brodski, Samuel, 4:197

Brodski, Yosif. *See* Brodsky, Joseph

Brodski family, 4:**196–197**

Brodskii, Isaak, 4:**197**

Brodsky, Adolf, 4:**197–198**

Brodsky, Joseph, 4:**198**

Brodsky, Stanley L., 4:**198**

Brodsky Quartet, 4:197

Brody (Ukraine), 4:**198–200**
Brody, Adrien, 16:210
Brody, Alter, 4:**200**
Brody, Ḥayyim. *See* Brody, Heinrich
Brody, Heinrich, 4:**200**
Brody, Heinrich (Ḥayyim), 6:302
Brody, Jane E., 4:**200–201**
Bródy, László, 4:**201**
Bródy, Lili, 4:**201**
Brody, R., 2:47
Bródy, Sándor, 4:**201**
Brody, Solomon Zalman ben Israel,
  4:**201**
Brody, Tal, 4:**202**
Bródy, Zsigmond, 4:**202**
Broglie, Victor-Claude, Prince de,
  4:**202**
Broida, Simḥah Zissel ben Israel,
  4:**202**, 13:190–191
Broides, Abraham, 4:**202–203**
Broido, Ephraim, 4:**203**
Broido, Louis, 4:**203**
Broido, Lucy Kaufmann, 4:203
The Broken Branch (Vamos), 16:148–
  149
*Broken Millstones. See Reḥayim
  Shevurim*
Brokerage, 1:451
Brokers (economics), 4:**203–204**
Bromberg (Poland). *See* Bydgoszcz
  (Poland)
Bromet, H.L., 16:345
Broner, Esther M., 4:**204**, 15:682
Bronfenbrenner, Martin, 4:**204–205**
Bronfman, Aileen Mindel, 4:205–206
Bronfman, Charles Rosner, 4:206
Bronfman, Edgar Miles, 4:**206**
Bronfman, Sam, 4:205, 346, 407, 408,
  422, 423, 14:464
Bronfman, Yefim, 4:**206–207**
Bronfman family, 4:**205–206**
Bronice forest (Ukraine), 6:23–24
Bronowski, Jacob, 4:**207**
Bronstein, David, 4:**207**
Bronstein, Herbert, 4:**207–208**
Bronstein, Lev. *See* Trotsky, Lev
  Davidovich
Bronze Age
  Arad, 2:329–330
  archaeology, 2:384–387, 12:420–
    421
  architecture, 2:399
  Finkelstein, Israel, 7:33–34
Brook, Barry Shelley, 4:**208**
Brook, Peter Stephen Paul, 4:**208**
Brookner, Anita, 4:**208–209**, 6:439

Brooks, Albert, 4:**209**
Brooks, James L., 4:**209**
Brooks, Mel, 4:**209–210**, 15:228
Brooks, Richard, 4:**210**
Broom (flora), 4:**210**
Brooten, Bernadette, 4:125
Bross, Jacob, 4:**211**
Brother Daniel case, 11:298
The Brotherhood. *See* Aguddat Aḥim
Brothers
  ona'ah and, 15:425
Brothers. See Aḥim
Brothers, Joyce, 4:**211**
Brothers, Richard, 4:188, **211**
The Brothers Ashkenazi (Singer),
  18:637
Brothers' role, 6:692, 693
Brotzlewsky, Haim. *See* Bar-Lev, Haim
Broudy, Harry Samuel, 4:**211–212**
Broughton, Hugh, 4:**212**
Broun, Kenneth, 6:62
Broward County (FL), 4:**212–213**, 7:88
Brown, Aika, 4:**214**
Brown, Arie. *See* Braun, Arie
Brown, Benjamin, 4:**214**, 14:446
Brown, David Abraham, 4:**214**
Brown, General George S., 2:51
Brown, H. Maurine. *See* Neuberger,
  H. Maurine
Brown, Harold, 4:**214**
Brown, Herbert C., 4:**214–215**, 593
Brown, John, 4:57
Brown, Larry. *See* Brown, Lawrence H.
Brown, Lawrence H., 4:**215**
Brown, Michael Stuart, 4:**215–216**,
  13:10
Brown, Saul Pardo, 4:**216**
Browne, Edward B. M., 4:**216–217**
Browne, Lewis, 4:**217**
Browning, Christopher R., 4:**217**
Browning, John, 4:**217–218**
Browning, Robert, 4:**218**, 6:436
Brownsville (NY), 12:469
Brown v. Board of Education (1954),
  18:700
Broyt mit Zalts (Bursztyn), 4:203
Bruce, Lenny, 4:**218–219**
Bruchsal (Germany), 4:**219**
Bruck, Grigori, 4:**219**
Bruck, Lajos, 4:**219**
Bruck, Miksa, 4:**219**
Bruckheimer, Jerry, 4:**219–220**
Bruckman, Henrietta, 4:**220**
Bruckner, Ferdinand, 4:**220**
Brudo, Abraham ben Elijah, 4:**220**
Brudo, Manuel, 4:**220–221**

Bruecke und Tuer (Simmel), 18:607
Bruell, Adolf, 4:221
Bruell, Ignaz, 4:**221**
Bruell, Jacob, 4:**221–222**
Bruell, Nehemiah, 3:682, 4:221
Bruell family, 4:221
Bruenn (Czech Republic). *See* Brno;
  Brno (Czech Republic)
Bruex (Czechoslovakia). *See* Most
  (Czechoslovakia)
Bruggen, Carry van, 4:**222**, 6:70
Bruller, Jean. *See* Vercors
Brumlik, Micha, 16:344
Brun, Antoinette, 7:22–23
Bruna, Israel ben Ḥayyim, 4:**222**,
  7:222
Bruner, Jerome Seymour, 4:**222–223**
Brunetti, Angelo, 4:**223**
Brunner, Alois, 4:**223–224**
Brunner, Arnold, 4:**224**
Brunner, Constantin, 4:**224**
Brunner, John, 14:434
Brunner, Jožef. *See* Debrecenji, Jožef
Brunner, Sebastian, 4:**224**
Brunschvicg, Leon, 4:**224–225**, 15:674
Brunschvig, Georges, 4:**225**
Brunschvig, Robert, 4:**225**
Brunswick (Germany), 4:**225–226**
Brunswig, Alfred, 4:**226**
Brusa (Anatolia). *See* Bursa (Anatolia)
Brussels (Belgium), 4:**226–227**
Brussilovsky, Yevgeni Grigoryevich,
  4:**227–228**
Brustein, Robert Sanford, 4:**228**
Brutal Mandate (Lowenstein), 13:235
Brutzkus, Boris Dov, 4:**228–229**
Brutzkus, David Anatol, 4:228–229
Brutzkus, Julius, 4:**229**
Bryansk (Russia), 4:**229**
Bryer, Monte, 4:**229**
Bryks, Rachmil, 4:**229–230**
Brzechwa, Jan, 4:**230**
Brzeg (Poland), 4:**230**
Brzeg Dolny (Poland). *See*
  Dyhernfurth (Poland)
Brześć. *See* Bresch, Judah Loeb ben
  Moses Naphtali
Brześć, Leyb. *See* Bresch, Judah Loeb
  ben Moses Naphtali
Brzesc Kujawski (Poland), 4:**230**
Brzeżany (Ukraine). *See* Berezhany
  (Ukraine)
Brzeziny (Poland), 4:**230–231**
Buber, Martin, 4:**231–236**, 7:666,
  8:416–417, 16:98, 109–110
  Bar Kochba Association, 3:156

on Bible, 4:231, 235
bi-nationalism promoted by, 3:703
biography, 4:231–232
Borowitz, Eugene B., 4:92
Brod, Max, 4:192
Centenary of, 4:235
disputations and polemics, 5:698–699
Existentialism, 6:612
free will, 7:233
German translation of Bible by, 3:631
good and evil, 4:233, 7:754
Ḥasidism, 4:231, 234, 8:416–417
I and Thou, 4:231, 232–233, 234
impact on education, 6:161
on Judaism, 4:234
Der Jude, 4:231, 11:523
Landauer, Gustav, 12:467
miracles, 14:309
Moses, 14:538
mysticism of, 4:234
nature, 15:35
philosophy of, 4:232–233
redemption, 17:154
repentance, 17:223–224
Rosenzweig, Franz, 4:231, 233, 235, 17:460
on Shekhinah, 18:442
socialism of, 4:231, 235
theology of, 4:233–234
Torah, 20:43–44
truth, 20:162
Zionism of, 4:231, 234–235
Buber, Solomon, 4:**236**, 12:452, 16:12
Bubis, Ignatz, 4:**236–237**, 16:344
Bublick, Gedaliah, 4:**237**
Bucer, Martin, 4:**237**, 376
Buchach (Ukraine), 4:**237–238**
Buchalter, "Lepke." *See* Buchalter, Louis
Buchalter, Louis, 4:**238**
Buchanan, Claudius, 4:**238–239**
Bucharest (Romania), 3:135, 4:**239–241**, 239t
Buchbinder, Nahum, 4:**241**
Buchenwald concentration camp, 4:**241–242**, 11:812, 15:246, 18:99
Buchholz, Carl August, 4:**242**, 13:252
Buchmil, Joshua Heshel, 4:**242–243**
Buchner, Abraham, 4:**243**, 8:436, 15:352
Buchner, Ze'ev Wolf ben David ha-Kohen, 4:**243**
Buchwald, Art, 4:**243**
Buchwald, Naftule. *See* Buchwald, Nathaniel

Buchwald, Nathaniel, 4:**243**
Buchwald, Theo, 4:**244**
Buchwald Martyn. *See* Balin, Marty
Buckley, William F., 3:728
Bucky, Gustav, 4:**244**
Bucovice (Czech Republic), 4:**244**
București (Romania). *See* Bucharest (Romania)
Bucurie (Banus), 3:121
Buczacz (Ukraine). *See* Buchach (Ukraine)
Buda community, 4:**244–245**
Budapest (Hungary), 4:**244–249**, 246t, 9:341, 12:470
Budapesti tavasz (Karinthy), 11:808
Budde, Karl Ferdinand Reinhard, 4:**249**
Budge, E.A.W., 2:123
Budin (Czech Republic). *See* Budyně Nad Ohří (Czech Rebulic)
Budko, Joseph, 4:70, **249**
Budnaeus, Simon. *See* Budny, Szymon
Budny, Szymon, 4:**249–250**
Buduilu, king of Ammon, 2:85
Budyně Nad Ohří (Czech Rebulic), 4:**250**
Buechelin, Paul. *See* Fagius, Paulus
Buechler, Adolf, 4:**250–251**
Buechler, Alexander, 4:**251**
Buedinger, Max, 4:**251**
Buehler, Josef, 4:**251–252**
Buelow, Bernhard von, 9:57–58, 59
Bueno, Ephraim Hezekiah, 4:252
Bueno, Isaac Abraham, 4:**252**
Bueno, Joseph, 4:252
Bueno de Mesquita, Benjamin, 4:252
Bueno de Mesquita, David, 4:252
Bueno de Mesquita, Isaac, 4:252
Bueno de Mesquita, Jacob, 4:252
Bueno de Mesquita, Joseph, 4:252
Bueno de Mesquita family. *See* Bueno family
Bueno family, 4:252
Buenos Aires (Argentina), 2:439, 4:**252–254**, 11:754
Buergenthal, Thomas, 4:**254**
Buerger, Leo, 4:**254**
Buerger's disease, 4:254
Bueschenthal, Lippmann Moses, 18:761
Bueshel, Ben Zion. *See* Orgad, Ben Zion
Buffalo (NY), 4:**254–255**, 7:30–31
Buffaloes, 4:**255–256**
Bugenhagen, Johann, 4:**256**
Buhl, Franz Peder William Meyer, 4:**256**, 11:343, 344

Buhler, Charlotte, 4:**256**
Buhler, Karl, 4:256
Buhuşi (Romania). *See* Buhusi (Romania)
Buhusi (Romania), 4:**256–257**
Building. *See* Architecture and architects; Construction
Building and construction, 9:538
Building a Philosophy of Education (Broudy), 4:211–212
Buitrago (Spain), 4:**257**
Bukarat, Abraham ben Solomon ha-Levi, 4:**257**
Bukhara (Uzbekistan), 4:**257–265**, *258*, 20:447
    aliyah from, 4:263
    anusim, 4:259
    communities of Jews
        Israel (state), 10:297
    costumes, 4:263–264
    Jewish community, 4:257–258
    Judeo-Persian literature in, 11:556–557
    literature, 4:262–263
    music-dance, 4:264
    New York City, Russian Jewish community in, 15:230
    Russian regime in, 4:259–261
    Soviet Union rule over, 4:261–262
Bukhārāī, Khāja, 11:555
Buki ben Yogli. *See* Katzenelson, Judah Leib Benjamin
Bukiet, Melvin Jules, 4:**265**
Bukofzer, Manfred, 4:**265**
Bukovina (Romania), 4:**265–266**, 6:87–88
Bukrat, Abraham ben Solomon ha-Levi. *See* Bukarat, Abraham ben Solomon ha-Levi
Bula, Raphael Moses, 4:**266**
Bula, Solomon, 4:266
Būlān (Khazar king), 4:**266–267**
Bulat, Judah ben Joseph, 4:**267**, 6:399
Bulawayo (Zimbabwe), 4:**267**
Bulgaria, 4:**267–275**, *268*
    ancient period, 4:267–268
    anti-Jewish policies, 4:271–273
    antisemitism, 4:271–273
    Byzantine and Bulgar rule, 4:268–269
    communal organization in, 4:270
    Communism in, 4:273–274
    Congress of Berlin, 3:454
    education in, 4:270
    Holocaust, 6:7, 9:339
        deportation policy, 4:271–273
        Ruse, 17:530–531

Bulgaria, *continued*

    Sephardim, 18:301

    immigration to Israel from, 4:273–274

    independence, period following, 4:269–270

    Jewish participation in military service, 14:245

    journalism in, 4:270–271

    Ladino newspapers, 16:495

    language, 3:634, 4:275

    Law to Protect the Nation, 19:172

    Nikopol, 15:266

    partisans, 15:668

    population, Jewish, 4:*268*

    population statistics, 4:271*t*

    post-WW II, 4:273–275

    pre-WW II, 4:267–271

    rabbis and scholars, 4:270

    relations with

        Israel (state), 4:275

    restitution of Jews in, 4:273

    Sarah of Turnovo, influence of, 18:47

    settlements, 4:*268*, 271*t*

    Sofia, 18:745

    Turkish rule, 4:269

    WW II, 4:271–273

    Zionism, 11:733, 21:582–583, *583*

    Zionism in, 4:270

Bulgarian literature, 3:671, 4:270–271, **275–277**, 16:21

    Canetti, Elias, 4:430–431

    Petrov, Valeri, 4:276

    Wagenstein, Angel Raymond, 20:594

Bullae. *See* Seals

Bulletin of the Jewish University of Moscow (periodical), 14:520

Bullfighter from Brooklyn: An Autobiography of Sidney Franklin (Franklin), 7:216

Bullfighting, 7:216, 19:139

Bull of July 12, 1555, Papal, 2:140

Bulls, papal. *See* Papal bulls

Buloff, Joseph, 4:**278**

Bun. *See* Abun; Avin

Buna labor camp, 17:130–131

Bunche, Ralph, 2:475

Bund, 4:137, **278–284**, 18:715–716

    establishment of, 9:245

    1907 to 1917, 4:281

    Abramowitz, Raphael, 1:325

    Agudat Israel, 1:505

    Alter, Victor, 2:18

    Argentina, 2:430, 445

communism, 4:281–282

    Comintern and, 5:96–97

    Lenin, Vladimir Ilyich, 12:639

    Trotsky, Lev Davidovich, 20:157

    Yevsektsiya and, 21:326

Duma, 6:45

Eisenstadt, Isaiah, 6:270

Erlich, Henryk, 6:481

establishment of, 4:280–281

Esther (1880-1943), 6:518

Gozhansky, Samuel, 8:21

Gurevich, Moshe, 8:140

Independent Jewish Workers Party, 9:770–771

Jewish socialism, 18:715–716

Kopelson, Zemah, 12:294

leaders

    Hersch, Pesach Liebman, 9:42

    Medem, Vladimir, 13:717

    Zygelbojm, Samuel Mordecai, 21:696–697

Leivik, H., 12:629

Lekert, Hirsch, 12:630

Lewis, David, 12:764

Liber, Marc, 12:775

Liessin, Abraham, 12:819

Lithuania, 13:121

Litwak, A., 13:142

Lodz Bakers Union, 6:32

Mill, Joseph Solomon, 14:250

Mutnik, Abraham, 14:705

origins of, pre-Bund, 4:278–279

pioneers

    Kremer, Arkadi, 12:353

    Pesahson, Isaac Mordecai, 16:6

Poland, 4:282–283

Rafes, Moses, 17:63

Russia, 17:537–538

    Belorussia, 3:304

    Bobruisk, 4:25

    Borisov, 4:86

Russian Revolution and aftermath, 4:281–282

self defense, 18:262

socialism and, 18:707

Tshemeriski, Alexander, 20:165

Uruguay, 20:425

Warsaw (Poland), 20:668–669, 673

Workmen's Circle, 21:214–215

Zhitlowsky, Chaim, 21:523

Zionism and, 4:278, 279, 280, 281

Bund der Landwirte. *See* Agrarian League

Bunderker, S. R., 15:474

Bundes Bruder, 4:13

Bund hymn, 2:182

Bundle of Letters. See Bintel Brief

Bunem, Simhah, 20:651

Bunim, Irving M., 4:**284**

Bunin, Hayyim Isaac, 4:**284**

Bunshaft, Gordon, 4:**284–285**

Bunzel, Ruth Leah, 2:186, 4:**285**

Bunzi, George, 4:285

Bunzi, Hugo, 4:285

Bunzi, Max, 4:285

Bunzi, Moritz, 4:285

Bunzi family, 4:285

Burchard of Worms, 4:285

Burchardt, Hermann, 4:**285–286**, 8:621

Burchardus de Monte Sion, 4:**286**

Burchstein, Raisa. *See* Raisa, Rosa

Burckhardt, Johann Ludwig, 4:**286**

Burden of proof, 18:323

Burdujeni (Romania), 4:**286**

Bureau of Jewish Education (New York, NY), 6:194–195

Burg, Avraham, 4:**286–287**

Burg, Avrum. *See* Burg, Avraham

Burg, Menke. *See* Burg, Meno

Burg, Meno, 4:**287**

Burg, Yosef, 4:**287–288**

Burgel family. *See* Bordjel family

Burgenland (Austria), 4:**288–289**, *289*

Burgin, Nellie Paulina. *See* Bergen, Polly

Burgon, Dean, 3:664

Burgos (Spain), 4:*289*, **289–290**

el Burguense. *See* Pablo de Santa Maria

Burgundy (France), 4:**290–291**

Burhān Nizām Shah, 1:547

Burial customs, 4:**291–294**, 782–783

    aliyah and, 10:329

    Altschul, Emil, 2:25

    aninut, 2:174

    archaeology

        religious interpretations and, 10:631

    Ash, Abraham, 2:555

    ashkavah, 2:567

    coffins, 4:783

    vs. cremation, 5:281

    David, 5:453

    death, 5:510

    demons, demonology, 5:576

    dolmens and, 5:736–737

    epitaphs, 6:464

    gemilut Hasadim, 7:428

    hakkafot, 8:250

Hebron (Israel), 8:744, 745
ḥibbut ha-kever, 9:94
Holocaust, mass graves, 9:369
husband's obligation, 9:636
impalement punishment and, 9:742
Israel (state), 10:637–638
Jerusalem, 11:202, 203–204, 210
keri'ah, 12:84–85
kitel, 12:206
likkut aẓamot, 13:13
Mendelssohn, Moses, 14:37
Moses, 14:526, 529–530, 536
niddui and ḥerem, 9:15
organ transplantation and, 13:747
in ossuaries, 15:506–507
Palestine (Ottoman), 10:620
Phinehas, 16:114–115
priests, 16:525
purity and impurity, ritual, 16:753
requirements, 14:37
rites against Angel of Death, 2:149
Samaritans, 17:732
in sarcophagi, 15:506–507
Sefer Torah, 18:242
suicides, 19:295
tallit, 19:466
Tobit, Book of, 20:12
See also Cemeteries; Funerals
Burla, Israel Jacob, 4:294
Burla, Jacob Hai ben Judah, 4:295
Burla, Joseph Nissim ben Ḥayyim, 4:294
Burla, Judah Bekhor ben Israel Jacob, 4:294
Burla, Yehuda, 4:295–296, 11:500
Burla family, 4:294–295
Burle-Marx, Roberto, 4:296
Burle Marx, Walter, 4:296
Burleski, elegii, difiramby v presrennoy prose (Slonimsky), 18:680
Burma, 4:296, 296–297
Burnaya zhizn Lazika Roytshvantsa (Ehrenburg). *See The Stormy Life of Lazik Roitschwantz* (Ehrenburg)
Burning (execution method). *See* Capital punishment
Burning bush, 4:297–298, 6:613, 14:524, 527, 535
Burning Lights (Chagall), 4:556
Burns, Arthur Frank, 4:298
Burns, George, 4:298–299
Burnstein, George. *See* London, George
Burnsun, George. *See* London, George
Burriana (Spain), 4:299

Burrows, Abe, 4:299
Burrows, James, 4:299
Bursa (Anatolia), 4:300–301
Bursa (Asia Minor)
    Ottoman empire, first Jewish community to come under protection of, 15:520
Burschenschaften. *See* Student's fraternities, German
Burstein, Abraham, 4:301
Burstein, Israel, 4:301
Burstein, Pesach, 4:301
Burstein, Pinchas. *See* Maryan
Burstein, Reuven. *See* Barkat, Reuven
Burstein family, 4:301
Burstyn, Mike, 4:301
Bursztyn, Michal, 4:302
Burton, Montague. *See* Burton, Sir Montague
Burton, Sir Montague, 4:302
Burton, Tim, 6:315
Bury St. Edmunds (England), 4:302
Busaglo, Shalom ben Moses. *See* Buzaglo, Shalom ben Moses
Busal, Ḥayyim ben Jacob Obadiah de, 4:302–303
Busch, Charles, 4:303, 303
Busch, Isidor. *See* Bush, Isidor
Busel, Hayyuta, 4:303
Busel, Joseph, 4:303
Bush, burning, 4:297–298
Bush, George Herbert Walker, 4:303–304
    American Israel Public Affairs Committee, 2:51, 52
    Boschwitz, Rudolph Eli, 4:95
Bush, George Walker, 4:304–305
    American Israel Public Affairs Committee, 2:52
    Bolten, Joshua B., 4:50
    Palestinian Authority and, 15:599–600
Bush, Isidor, 4:305, 15:384
Bush, Solomon, 4:305
Bushehr (Persian Gulf). *See* Bushire (Persian Gulf)
Bushire (Persian Gulf), 4:306
Business. *See* Industrialists; Trade and commerce
Business ethics, 4:306–315
    competition, 4:312–315
    historic sources, 4:307–309
    individual and corporate responsibilities, 4:308–312
    Israel, state of, 4:315
    wealth, role of, 4:306–307
Busk (Ukraine), 4:315–316

Busnach, Naphtali, 4:316
Busnach, Naphtali ben Moses, 4:316
Busnach family, 4:316
Buṣr al-Ḥarīrī. *See* Boẓrah (Trachonitis)
Bustanai, 15:419
Bustanai ben Ḥaninai, 4:316–317
Bustenai (journal), 4:317
Butcher of Lyons, 3:141
Butcher Shop (Segal), 18:246
Butelbroit, Israel. *See* Giladi, Israel
Butler, Benjamin Franklin, 4:19
Butler, Judith, 4:317, 18:733, 736
Butnah (Israel), 4:318
Butrymowicz, Mateusz, 4:318
Butschowitz (Czech Republic). *See* Bucovice
Buttenweiser, Benjamin Joseph, 4:318–319
Buttenweiser, Helen Lehman, 4:319
Buttenwieser, Joseph Leon, 4:318–319
Buttenwieser, Moses, 4:319
Buttenwieser family, 4:318–319
Buttons, Red, 4:319–320
Butzel, Fred M., 4:320
Butzel, Henry M., 4:320, 12:556
Butzel, Leo M., 4:320
Butzel, Magnus, 4:320
Butzel, Martin, 4:320
Butzel, Martin L., 4:320
Butzel family, 4:320
Butzer, Martin. *See* Bucer, Martin
Buxbaum, Nathan, 4:320
Buxton, Angela, 4:320–321
Buxtorf, Johannes (1564-1629), 3:681, 4:321
Buxtorf, Johannes (1599-1664), 2:21, 4:321–322
Buxtorf family, 3:587, 4:77
Buzagli, Shalom ben Moses. *See* Buzaglo, Shalom ben Moses
Buzaglio, Shalom ben Moses. *See* Buzaglo, Shalom ben Moses
Buzaglo, Abraham, 4:322
Buzaglo, Joseph, 4:322
Buzaglo, Shalom ben Moses, 4:322
Buzaglo family, 4:322
Buzar-Kasbadji, Nadya, 1:440
Buzău (Romania). *See* Buzau (Romania)
Buzau (Romania), 4:322
Buzzards, 4:323
Byadulya-Yasakar, Zmitrok, 4:323
Byblos (Lebanon). *See* JUBAYL
Bydgoszcz (Poland), 4:323, 16:308
By Herself (Kabak). *See* Levaddah

Býk, Beran a Váhy (Dostál), 5:762
Byk, Emil, 4:**323–324**
Bykhov (Belarus), 4:**324**
Byron, George Gordon, Lord, 4:**324**
By the Rivers of Mazovia (Bursztyn).
　See Bay di Taykhn fun Mazovye
Bytom (Germany), 4:**324**
*By Words Alone: The Holocaust in
　Literature* (Ezrahi), 9:414
Byzantine Empire, 2:391, 4:**324–328,**
　325
　　Bulgaria ruled by, 4:268–269
　　circus parties, 4:735–736
　　Constantine VII Porphyrogenitus,
　　　5:181
　　Egypt
　　　Alexandria, 1:634
　　Greece
　　　Salonika, 17:699–700
　　Heraclius, 9:5–6
　　Israel (ancient), 10:156
　　Justinian I, 11:579–580
　　Karaism, 11:791
　　Leo III, 12:642
　　Leo VI, 12:642
　　Masada (Israel), 13:599
　　medicine, 13:725
　　Michael II, 14:165
　　Michael VIII Palaeologus, 14:165
　　population, medieval, 16:386
　　pottery, 16:426
　　trade, 1:386
Byzantine Kabbalah, *Kanah and
　Peliyah,* 11:759
Byzantium (Turkey). *See*
　Constantinople (Turkey)
Bzenec (Czech Republic), 4:**328**

C

C (letter), 4:*329,* 5:5
C. V. *See* Central-Verein Deutscher
　Staatsbuerger Juedischen Glaubens
CAA. *See* Creative Artists Agency
Caan, James, 4:**329**
Caballeria family, de la. *See* Cavalleria
　family, de la
Cabbage, 4:**329**
Cabeça family. *See* Cabessa family
Cabeçáo family. *See* Cabessa family
Caberet, 9:442
Cabessa, Abraham, 4:329–330
Cabessa family, 4:**329–330**
Cabildo, Abierto, 2:427
Cables (motion picture), 6:263
Cabor. *See* Cabul (Israel)
Cabul (Israel), 4:**330**

Caceres, Abraham, 2:119, 4:**330**
Caceres, Daniel de, 4:330–331
Caceres, Diego Garcia de, 4:636
Caceres, Francisco de, 4:330–331
Caceres, Jacob de. *See* Caceres, Simon
　de
Caceres, Simon de, 4:331, **331,** 637
Cacophysms, 6:551
Cadenet (France), 4:**331**
Cádiz (Spain), 4:**331**
Caecilius of Calacte, 4:**331–332**
Caedmon, English translation of Bible,
　3:611
Caen (France), 4:**332**
Câeres, Leonor de, 4:501
Caesar, Sextus Julius, 4:**332**
Caesar, Sid, 4:**332–333**
Caesarea (ancient Israel). *See* Banias
　(ancient Israel)
Caesarea (Cappadocia), 4:**335**
Caesarea (Israel), 4:**333–335,** 16:385
Caesarea Philippi. *See* Banias (ancient
　Israel)
Caesarius of Arles, 4:721
Caesarius of Heisterbach, 3:775
Cafersi. *See* Kefar Yasif (Upper
　Galilee)
Caffa. *See* Feodosiya (Ukraine)
The Cage (Sender), 4:631
Cagli, Corrado, 4:**335**
Cagliari (Sardinia), 4:**335**
Cahan, Abraham, 4:**335–336,** 15:210,
　20:280–281
　　Jewish Daily Forward, 16:503–504,
　　　20:325–326
　　use of Yiddish in speeches, 18:719
Cahan, Judah Loeb, 4:**336**
Cahan, Yaakov, 4:**336–337,** 8:715
Cahen, Isidore, 4:**337**
Cahen, Samuel, 3:629
CAHJP (The Central Archives for the
　History of the Jewish People). *See*
　The Central Archives for the
　History of the Jewish People
Cahn, Aaron, 15:415
Cahn, Edmond Nathaniel, 4:**337–338,**
　12:556
Cahn, Marcelle, 4:**338**
Cahn, Moïse. *See* Crohmălniceanu,
　Ovid S.
Cahn, Sammy, 4:**338**
Cahnman, Werner J., 4:**338–339,**
　18:733
Cahun, Lémon, 2:8
Caiaphas, Joseph, 4:**339**
Caïmis, Julius, 4:**339**
Caimis, Moisis, 4:**339–340**

Caimont. *See* Jokneam (Israel)
Cain, 1:245, 4:**340–342,** 12:444–445,
　18:319
Caine, Thomas Henry Hall, 6:436
Cairo (Egypt), 4:*342,* **342–346,** *343,*
　11:312, 14:300
　　See also Genizah, Cairo
Cairo Genizah. *See* Genizah, Cairo
Cairo trial, 4:**346**
Caiserman, Hanane Meier, 4:205, **346**
Caiserman-Roth, Ghitta, 4:**347**
Caius Julius Caesar Actanianus. *See*
　Augustus
Caius Suetonius Tranquillas. *See*
　Suetonius
Caius Suetonius Tranquillus. *See*
　Suetonius
Cajal, Nicolae, 4:**347,** 8:379–380
CAJE (Coalition for the Advancement
　of Jewish Education), 4:**763–764**
Cajetan of Berchem-Haimhausen,
　4:658
Calabrese, Joseph Vital. *See* Vital,
　Joseph
Calabresi, Guido, 4:**347–348**
Calabria (Italy), 4:**348**
Calahora, Aaron, 4:349
Calahora, David, 4:349
Calahora, Israel Samuel ben Solomon.
　See Calahorra, Israel Samuel ben
　Solomon
Calahora, Joseph ben Solomon, 4:**349**
Calahora, Mattathias, 4:349
Calahora, Solomon, 4:348–349
Calahora family, 4:**348–349**
Calahorra (Spain), 4:**349–350**
Calahorra, Israel Samuel ben
　Solomon, 4:**350**
Calahorra family. *See* Calahora family
Calamus, sweet, 4:**350–351**
Calatayud (Spain), 4:**351–352**
Calatrava, 4:**352**
Calculation of the Courses of the Stars.
　*See Ḥeshbon Mahalekhot ha-
　Kokhavim*
Calcutta (India), 4:**352–353**
Caldwell, Erskine, 4:107
Calé, Walter, 4:**353**
Caleb (biblical figure), 14:525
Calebites, 1:356, 4:**353–354**
Calendar reform, 4:**359–360**
Calendars, 4:88, **354–359**
　　Abraham bar Ḥiyya, 1:293
　　Abudarham's tables, 1:336
　　Adar, 1:382–383
　　Akavya, Avraham Aryeh Leib,
　　　1:554

Apocrypha, 2:259
Babylon, 3:27, 28
Baraita de-Rav Adda, 1:384
bet din rulings, 3:515, 10:146
Bornstein, Ḥayyim Jehiel, 4:88
Cohn, Berthold, 5:40
dating, 4:705
Day of Atonement, 5:488
Dead Sea Scrolls, 5:502, 503, 505
duration of day, 6:586
Dustan, 6:66
Enoch, Ethiopic Book of, 6:443
Filipowski, Ẓevi Hirsch, 7:20
Gezer, 7:569
Hahn, Joseph Yuspa ben Phinehas
    Seligmann, 8:231
Hillel II, 9:110
Holiness Code, 9:320
Isaac ben Solomon, 10:49–50
Iyyar, 10:823
Johanan ben Zakkai, 10:146
Jubilees, Book of, 11:474
Karaites, 11:798
Kornik, Meir ben Moses, 12:314
leap year, 12:567
lunar, 2:128
Marḥeshvan, 13:533
*Me-ha-Ibbur u-Minyan ha-
    Shanim,* 3:39
Meshwi al-ʿUkbarī, 14:80
Mesopotamia, 14:90
Nahshon Bar Zadok, 14:757
New Moon, 15:150–151
New Year, 15:193
Nieto, David, 15:261
pages in illuminated Spanish
    Hebrew Bibles, 3:677
physics and, 16:132–133
reform of, 4:**359–360**
Saadiah Gaon, 17:606, 607
Samaritans, 17:732–733
Seder Olam, 18:235–236
Seleucid era, 18:260
Sivan, 18:647
Slonimski Ḥayyim, 18:679
Tykocinski, Jehiel Michel, 20:212
year, 21:**291–292**
See also New Moons; *specific
    months*
Calf, golden. *See* Golden calf
Calgary (Canada), 1:589–591, 4:**360–
361**
Calicut (India), 4:**361**
Calid Hebraeus. *See* Khalid ben Jasikhi
California (U.S.), 2:43, 4:**361**, **361–363**
    Orange County, 15:460–462

Pacht, Isaac, 15:563
    Palm Springs and desert area,
        15:606
    See also specific California cities
Caligula, Caius Caesar Augustus,
    1:502, 4:**363**, 451, 6:229, 397, 9:199
Calimani, Simḥah ben Abraham, 4:**363**
Calimani, Simone. *See* Calimani,
    Simḥah ben Abraham
Calin, Vera, 4:**363–364**
Caliph, 3:111–112, 4:**364**
Caliphate. *See* Caliph
Calisch, Edward Nathan, 4:**364**
Calisher, Hortense, 4:**365**
Calisthenics. *See* Gymnastics
Calixtus (popes), 4:**365**
Calixtus II (pope), 4:277, 365, 16:372–
    373
Calixtus III, 4:365, 16:374
Calle, Sophie, 4:**365**
Callenberg, Johann Heinrich, 4:**366**
Calligraphy, modern Hebrew. *See*
    Modern Hebrew calligraphy
Calligraphy and writing masters,
    4:**373–474**
        See also Modern Hebrew
            calligraphy; Writing
Callinicum, synagogue destruction,
    2:37
Callisthenes, 4:**374**
Call It Sleep (Roth), 17:481–482
Call me Sammy (Luftspring), 13:253
Calmanson, Jacob, 4:**374**
Calmanson, Jacques. *See* Calmanson,
    Jacob
Calmer, Antoine Louis Isaac Calmer,
    4:374
Calmer, Moses Eliezer Liefmann,
    4:**374**
Calmeyer, Hans-Georg, 4:**374–375**
Calneh (Mesopotamia), 4:**375**
Calneh (Syria), 4:**375**
Calno (Syria). *See* Calneh (Syria)
Caló, Eugenio, 15:668
Calof, Rachel Bella Kahn, 4:**375–376**
Calsena (Spain). *See* Pechina (Spain)
Călugăru, Ion, 4:**376**
Calumny. *See* Slander
Calvin, John, 4:**376–377**, 14:440–441,
    17:163
Calvin, Melvin, 4:**377–378**, 13:10
Calvinism, 4:376–377, 12:675
Calvinist Bibles, 3:612–613
Calwer, Richard, 4:**378**
Cambridge (England), 4:**378–379**,
    7:477–478
    Genizah, Cairo, 11:548, 549, 558

Cambridge University (England),
    4:378–379
Cambridge Yiddish Codex, 4:**379**
Cambyses, 4:**379**
Camden (NJ), 4:**379–380**
Camels, 4:**380–381**, 7:93
Cameri, 3:696, 4:**381**
Camerini, Donato, 15:653
Camerini, Eugenio Salomone, 4:**381**
Camerino, Manuele da, 14:461
Cameri Theater, 10:686, 687–688
Cammeo, Federico, 4:**381–382**, 12:552
Camondo, Abraham-Behor, 4:382
Camondo, Abraham de, 10:781,
    15:527
Camondo, Abraham-Salomon, 4:382
Camondo, Isaac de, 4:382
Camondo, Moïse de, 4:382
Camondo, Nissim de, 4:382
Camondo, Solomon, 15:542
Camondo de family. *See* Camondo
    family
Camondo family, 4:**382**
Campanton, Isaac ben Jacob. *See*
    Canpanton, Isaac ben Jacob
Camp David Accords, 6:236, 10:238,
    259, 20:398
        Kach on, 11:693
        settlements beyond Green Line,
            10:364
Campen, Johannes van, 4:**383**
Campen, Michel Herman van, 4:**383**
Campensis. *See* Campen, Johannes van
Campensis, Transislanus. *See* Campen,
    Johannes van
Campfire (motion picture), 4:535, 536
Camping, Jewish. *See* Jewish camping
Camp of National Unity. *See* OZON
Camp of National Unity (Obóz
    Zjednoczenia Narodowego). *See*
    OZON
Camps
    concentration and extermination,
        4:**383–390**, 9:336 (*See also
        specific camps*)
            administration and structure,
                4:388–389
            art and artists, 2:516–519
            Belzec, 3:309–312
            Bergen Belsen, 3:420–422
            Bitburg Controversy, 3:727–
                728
            Buchenwald, 4:241–242
            Chelmno, 4:589–590
            Cueno (Italy), 5:338–339
            Czech Republic,
                Theresienstadt, 19:703

Camps, *continued*

Dachau, 5:375–376

death camps and killing centers, 4:385–387

death marches from, 5:513–515, *514*, 9:342, *515*

death statistics, 4:390

Drancy (France), 6:7

establishment of, 9:288–299

euthanasia program, 4:384–385

evacuation, 4:389–390

forced labor, 7:122–124

Gurs, 8:141

kapos, 11:781

liberation, 9:342–343

locations of, 4:*389*

Lublin (Poland), 16:310

Majdanek (Poland), 13:407–408

Malines (Belgium), 13:431–432

Mauthausen, 13:692–693

medical experiments, 4:387–388, 5:376, 14:47

Natzweiler-Struthof, 15:36

Ohdruf, 9:*486*

pre-WW II, 4:383–384

prison labor program, 4:385

psychological trauma of survivors, 3:551, 6:279

Skarzysko-Kamienna (Poland), 18:657

Sobibor, 15:707, 18:700–701

tracing services, 9:813–814

types of, 4:383

Ukraine, Lvov, 13:291–292

Wobbelin, survivors, 9:*486*

WW II, 4:384

educational and recreational (*See also* Jewish camping)

Achvah, 6:199–200

Brandeis-Bardin Institute, 4:124

Kawaga, 6:241

Massad, 6:200

Pennsylvania, 15:729

Ramah, 6:200, 542

Yavneh, 6:200

Campulung Moldovenesc (Romania), **4:390**

Câmpulung Moldovenesc (Romania). *See* Campulung Moldovenesc (Romania)

Campus Maximus Legionis. *See* Legio (ancient Israel)

Cana. *See* Kefar Kanna (Israel)

Canaan (son of Ham), 4:**390–391**, *391*

Canaan, Land of, 4:**391–393**, *392*

Adoni-Bezek, 1:413

Anaharath, 2:125

Ashdod, 2:557

Asherah, 2:562

borders, 6:236

Canaanite-Phoenician script, 1:689, 691

Chedorlaomer, 4:587

conquest and settlement in Book of Judges, 9:169–170, 11:562

demons, demonology, 5:572, 573

economic history, 6:96

elders, 6:295

Genesis, Book of, 7:445–446

Hadad, 8:184

Hebrew language, 8:621

ḥerem, 9:10–13

invasion of, 2:106

Jerusalem, 11:144–145

Joshua's conquest and settlement of, 9:167–169, 11:442, 446–447

Judah, tribe of, 11:475, 477

language, 18:281

Libnah, 12:783

Megiddo, 13:**766–767**

peoples driven out of, 11:99

Phoenicia, 16:118–124

priesthood, 16:153

Samaritan chronology, 17:719

Semitic languages, 18:281

spies from Kadesh-Barnea, 11:698

Tell Arad, 2:328–329, 330

Twelve Tribes, 20:138, 139

Ugaritic, 20:229

war and warfare, 20:621, 622

weights and measures, 20:700, 703

Canaanite Myths and Legends (Driver), 6:22

"Canaanites," 1:413, 2:78, 4:**393**

Canada, 4:**393–421**, 5:108, 110, 119*t*

1960 -1990, 4:410–411, 423

Abella, Rosalie Silberman, 1:247–248

abortion, 14:488

Abramowitz, Herman, 1:325

acculturation, Scheuer, Edmund on, 18:124

agriculture, Jewish, 1:500

antisemitism, 4:91, 186, 394–395, 396–397, 402, 403–405, 408–409, 414–416, 422, 423

Alberta, 1:590

Scheuer, Edmund on, 18:124

architecture, 12:442–443

art

Bayefsky, Aba, 3:230

Iskowitz, Gershon, 10:87

Levine, Les, 12:719

assimilation, 4:420

Atlantic, 2:639–641

B'nai Brith Canada, 4:17–18

B'nai B'rith Canada, 4:14

Borenstein, Sam, 4:84

Borovoy, A. Alan, 4:91–92

British Colombia, 4:186–188

Caplan, Elinor, 4:454

civil rights, 4:408–409

clothing industry, 4:396, 401–402, 405

community leaders, 6:663–664, 728

Bennett, Archie, 3:368

Bercovitch, Peter, 3:401

community organization, Montreal, 14:466

courts, 12:499–500

demographics, Montreal, 14:464–465

economics, 4:412–413

education, 4:397, 402, 403, 409, 419–420

Montreal, 14:465–466

education, Jewish, 6:208–210, 209*t*

film, 12:486

government officials, 6:663–664

Phillips, Lazarus, 16:56

Phillips, Nathan, 16:56–57

Hillel, 4:17

history, 4:394–396

Holocaust, 4:18, 408, 419, 423

response to, 9:370

immigration, 4:404–405, 411

Jewish Colonization Association, 11:287

industrialists

Bronfman, Edgar Miles, 4:206

Davis, Mortimer B., 5:481

Lastman, Melvin Douglas, 12:503–504

Israel (State), 4:415–416, 419

Israel, and relations with, 4:420–421

Jewish community leaders, 11:51

Jewish farm colonies, 18:64–65

Jewish Immigrant Aid Services of Canada, 11:299–300

Jewish immigration to, 2:41, 46

Jewish studies in, 11:316–319

Joseph family, 11:415

journalism, 11:470, 12:474–475

Judah family, 11:479

Judaism, 4:416–417

labor, 4:400, 406–407

labor union activities, 4:401–402, 405

laws and legal systems, 12:549, 14:488

Levi, Samuel Gershon, 12:692–693

libraries, 12:786

map, 4:394

migrations, 4:395, 398, 408, 410, 411, 414–415, 421–422

museums, 14:634

music, 1:384

newspapers, 16:487–488

Ontario, 15:434–436

Orthodox Judaism, rabbis, 6:745–746

Ottawa, 15:516–517

Pachter, Charles, 15:563

philanthropy, 5:481, 16:42

Dan, Leslie L., 5:408

political history, 4:401–402, 405–406, 413–415, 420–421

political participation, 16:341–342

Belkin, Simon, 3:296–297

politicians

Cherniack, Saul Mark, 4:595

Lewis, David, 12:764

Lewis, Stephen, 12:767

Segal, Hugh, 18:246–247

population statistics, Jewish, 4:393, 394, 394t, 402–403, 405–406, 412t, 413t

Quebec issue, 14:466

socialism, 18:706

social organization, 4:393–394, 394, 397–400, 402, 403, 405, 413, 417–419, 419–420, 423

trade and commerce, 4:394–395

Vancouver, 4:187, 188

WW II, 4:407–408, 409–410, 422–423, 423

WW II war crimes trials, 20:646

Yiddish education, 6:189

youth movements, ḥud Habonim, 9:717t, 718

Zionism, 21:583–585

zionism, 4:410

Zionist movement, 4:400–401, 406–407, 408, 421–423

See also specific Canadian cities and provinces

Canadian Constitutional Law (Laskin), 12:500

Canadian Council for Israel and Jewish Advocacy (CIJA), 4:418

The Canadian Eagle. See Der Keneder Adler

Canadian Jewish Congress (CJC), 3:296–297, 4:187, 346, 402, 403, 407, 418, **421–423**, 11:300, 716, 761–762, 14:466

Canadian Jewish News (newspaper), 4:419

Canadian Jewish Standard (periodical), 6:50

Canadian literature, 4:**423–428**

biblical influence, 3:672

Jewish contribution, 4:413

Layton, Irving, 12:557–558

Levine, Norman, 12:719

Maynard, Fredelle Bruser, 13:702

Richler, Mordecai, 17:288

Roskies, David G., 17:467–468

Sherman, Jason, 18:464–465

Canadian Medicine Aid Programme (CAN-MAP), 5:408

Canadian Security Intelligence Service, 11:779

Canakkale (Turkey), 4:**428**, 12:491

Çanakkale (Turkey). *See* Canakkale (Turkey)

Cananaite language, 8:621–625

Canano, 2:34, 35

Canary Islands (Spain), 4:**428–429**, 9:798–799

See also New Granada

Canatha. *See* Kenath (ancient city)

Cancioniero de Baena (Baena), 3:52

Candelabrum. *See* Ḥanukkah lamp

Candia, 3:84

Candles, 4:**429–430**

Candles in the Wind. See Svechi na vetru (Kanovich)

Candlestick of Light. See Menorat ha-Ma'or

Candle tax, 4:**430**

Candlewicks (Esselin), 6:509

Cane, Mark, 6:450

Canea (Crete), 4:**430**

Canetti, Elias, 2:65, 4:**430–431**

CAN-MAP (Canadian Medicine Aid Programme), 5:408

The Cannibal Galaxy (Ozick), 15:558

Cannibalism, 6:707

Cannstadt, Karl Friedrich, 4:**431**

Canoeing, 19:139

The Canonization of the Synagogue Service (Hoffman), 9:309

Canon of Medicine. See al-Qānūn fī al-Ṭibb

Canpanton, Isaac ben Jacob, 4:**431–432**, 12:644

Canpanton, Judah ben Solomon, 4:**432**

Cansino, Abraham, 4:432

Cansino, Jacob, 4:432

Cansino family, 4:**432**, 432t

Cantarini, Angelo di Grassin, 4:433

Cantarini, Isaac Vita ha-Kohen, 4:**433**

Cantarini, Leone di Simone, 4:433

Cantarini family, 4:**433**

Cantatas and choral works, Hebrew. *See* Hebrew cantatas and choral works

Cantera Burgos, Francisco, 4:**435**

Canterbury (England), 4:**435**, 435–436

The Canterbury Tales (Chaucer), 3:775–776, 4:584

Cantheras, Simeon. *See* Simeon ben Boethus

Cantheras, Simeon ben Boethus. *See* Simeon ben Boethus

A Canticle for Leibowitz (Miller), 18:199

Canticle of Canticles. *See* Song of Songs

Canticum Canticorum. *See* Song of Songs

Cantillation, 4:**436**, 8:627, 10:815, 13:656–664

Canton (China), 4:**436**

Cantoni, Alberto, 4:**436–437**

Cantoni, Hillel. *See* Cantoni, Lelio

Cantoni, Lelio, 4:**437**

Cantoni, Raffaele, 4:**437**, 7:85

Cantonists, 4:**437–439**

Finland, 7:37

forced baptism, 3:122

Moscow, 14:517

residence rights of, 15:579

Cantor, Bernard, 4:**439**

Cantor, Eddie, 4:**439**

Cantor, Eric, 4:**439–440**

Cantor, Jacob A., 15:211

Cantor, Jacob Aaron, 4:**440**

Cantor, Moritz Benedict, 4:**440**

Cantor, Norman Frank, 4:**440–441**

Cantorial Anthology (Ephros), 6:462

Cantors. *See* Ḥazzanim

Cantors Assembly of the United States, 8:504–505

CanWest Capital, 18:184

CanWest Global Communications, 18:184

Capa, Cornell, 4:**441**

Capa, Robert, 4:441, **441–442**, 16:126

Caparcotnei. *See* Kefar Otnay (ancient city)

The Cape Argus (newspaper), 18:763

Cape Board of Jewish Education, 6:210

Caper (flora), 4:**442–443**

Capernaum (Israel), 4:*443*, **443**, 9:500

Capestang (France), 4:**443**

Cape Town (South Africa), 4:**444–445**, 14:634–635

Caphtor (Middle East), 4:**445**

Capillary-electrometer, 13:70

Capistrano, Giovanni. *See* Capistrano, John of

Capistrano, John of, 4:**445**, 12:610, 15:566, 18:578

Capital punishment, 4:**445–451**, 9:507, 12:537
    abortion, 1:271
    autonomy, judicial, 2:711
    Babylonia, 3:28
    Badinter, Robert, 3:50
    biblical literature, 4:445–446
    bloodguilt, 3:774
    Commandments, 5:78
    confession, 5:147
    cremation, 5:281
    defenses against, 13:5–6, 15:720–723
    divine punishment, 5:708, 709
    extraordinary remedies, 6:331, 332
    flogging, 7:78
    ḥazakah in cases of, 8:489
    impalement, 9:742
    imprisonment, 9:743
    informers, 9:784
    Inquisition, 9:790
    Israel (State), 4:448–451
    Joseph David on, 11:428
    karet, 11:806–807
    Leibowitz, Samuel Simon, 12:622
    nasi, 4:614
    Noachide laws, violations of, 15:286, 287
    Parthnia, 4:601
    Sadducees, 17:655
    Spain, 19:75
    Talmud, 4:446–448
    Talmudic literature, 5:606
    witness, 21:116
    zaken mamre, 21:446

Capito, Marcus Herennius, 4:**451**

Capito, Wolfgang Fabricius, 4:**451**

Capitolias (Middle East), 4:**451–452**

Capitulations, 4:**452–454**, 9:501, 15:524, 533

Caplan, Elinor, 4:**454**

Caplan, Harry, 4:**454**

Caplin, Alfred Gerald. *See* Capp, Al

Capnio. *See* Reuchlin, Johannes

Capnion. *See* Reuchlin, Johannes

Capon, Augusto, 4:**454**

Capp, Al, 4:**454–455**

Cappadocia (Asia Minor), 4:**455**

Capsali, Elijah, 3:683, 4:163, **455–456**, 9:225, 15:534

Capsali, Moses ben Elijah, 4:**456**, 5:106–107, 10:775, 14:393–394, 15:534, 536

Captives, ransoming of, 4:**456–457**

Capua (Italy), 4:**457–458**

Capucci, Hilarion, 20:483

Capusi, Ḥayyim, 4:**458**

Caquot, André, 4:**458**, 11:326

Cara, Avigdor ben Isaac. *See* Kara, Avigdor ben Isaac

Caracalla, Marcus Aurelius Antoninus, 4:**458–459**, 9:203, 204

Caracas (Venezuela), 4:**459–460**

Caraffa, Cardinal Giovanni Pietro. *See* Paul IV (pope)

Caraffa, Giovanni Pietro. *See* Paul IV (pope)

Carasso, Emmanuel, 4:**460**, 15:543–544

Caravita, Joseph ben Abraham, 3:586

Carben, Victor von, 4:**460**

Carcassona family, 1:652

Carcassone (France), 4:**460–461**

Carchemish (Syria), 4:**461**

Cardiff (Wales), 4:**461–462**

Cardin, Benjamin Louis, 4:**462**

Cardin, Shoshana Shoubin, 4:**462–463**

Cardinal Numbers (Shelah), 18:445

Cardiology. *See* Medicine

Cardoso, Abraham Michael. *See* Cardozo, Abraham Miguel

Cardoso, Abraham Miguel. *See* Cardozo, Abraham Miguel

Cardoso, Fernando. *See* Cardozo, Isaac

Cardoso, Isaac. *See* Cardozo, Isaac

Cardoso, Isaac Nuñes, 4:463

Cardoso, Jacob, 4:463

Cardoso family, 4:**463**

Cardozo, Aaron Nuñez, 4:**464**

Cardozo, Abraham Miguel, 1:637, 4:55, 463, **464–466**, 12:791, 15:538, 18:347, 352, 353

Cardozo, Albert Jacob, 4:463, 15:199, 200

Cardozo, Benjamin Nathan, 4:**466**, 12:556, 611

Cardozo, David Nuñez, 4:463

Cardozo, Ernest Abraham, 4:463

Cardozo, Fernando. *See* Cardozo, Isaac

Cardozo, Isaac Nuñes, 4:463, **466–467**
    apologetics, 2:267

Enríquez, Isabel, 6:446

Cardozo, Jacob Nuñez, 4:463

Cardozo, Michael Hart IV, 4:463–464

Cardozo family (ex-Marranos). *See* Cardoso family

Cardozo family (U.S.), 4:**463–464**, 463t

Cards and cardplaying, 4:**467–468**, 7:371, 11:57

Caregal, Ḥayyim Moses ben Abraham, 4:**468**

Carei (Romania), 4:**468**

Carei-Mare (Romania). *See* Carei (Romania)

The Caretaker (Pinter), 16:177

Cargo Ships El-Yam Ltd., 6:371

Caria (Asia Minor), 4:**468**

Caribbean
    agriculture, Jewish, 1:501
    Jewish settlement, 2:41, 12:508
    museums, 14:634
    See also The Spanish-Portuguese Nation of the Caribbean: La Nacion

Caricatures, 4:**477–479**, 499

Carigal, Raphael Ḥayyim Isaac, 4:**479**

Carinthia (Austria), 4:**480**

Carl-Blumenkranz, Malla, 4:371

Carlebach, Elisheva, 4:**480**

Carlebach, Ezriel, 4:**480**, 15:326

Carlebach, Joseph, 4:**481**

Carlebach, Shlomo, 4:**481–482**, 13:203, 15:234

Carlebach family, 4:481t

Carlosburg (Transylvania). *See* Alba Iulia (Transylvania)

Carlsbad (Czech Republic), 4:**482–483**, 13:254

Carlson, Gerald, 15:79

Carmel (Israel), 4:**483**

Carmel, Moshe, 4:**483**

Carmel, Mount (Israel). *See* Mount Carmel (Israel)

Carmel Cave (Israel), vol. 10: color insert

Carmel Coast Plain (Israel), 10:111

Carmel College, 6:206, 211

Carmelite monks, 6:336, 8:235

Carmi, Charney. *See* Carmi, T.

Carmi, Isaiah Ḥai ben Joseph, 4:**484**

Carmi, Joseph Jedidiah, 4:**484**

Carmi, T., 4:**484**, 8:703

Carmilly-Weinberger, Moshe, 4:**485**

Carmoly, Eliakim, 4:**485**
    as bibliophile, 3:684
    forgeries, 7:126

Carmoly, Issachar Baer ben Judah Lima, 4:**485**

Carmona (Spain), 4:**485–486**

Carmona, Bekhor Isaac David, 4:**486**

Carmona, Daniel, 16:346

Carnegie, Hattie, 4:**486**, 15:30

Carnival (pre-Lenten period), 4:**486**

Carnival Overture (composition, Morawetz), 14:478

Carnivals, 1:410, 7:371

Carnovsky, Morris, 4:**486–487**

Caro, Anthony. *See* Caro, Sir Anthony

Caro, David, 4:**487**

Caro, Georg Martin, 4:**487–488**

Caro, Heinrich, 4:**488**

Caro, Isaac ben Joseph, 4:**488**

Caro, Joseph ben Ephraim, 2:10, 4:**488–491**, 8:480
  Absaban, Solomon, 1:330
  Aḥaronim, 1:532
  Bedek ha-Bayit, 8:444
  on bimah, 3:701
  at Biriyyah, 3:710
  business ethics, 4:307
  codification, 4:775–780
  fines and damages, 7:29
  halakhah, 8:257
  Laniado, Abraham Ben Isaac, 12:484
  Lev, Joseph Ben David Ibn, 12:676
  Maggid Meisharim
    autobiographical elements in, 3:706–707
    printing of, 3:704
  Mordacai ben Hillel ha-Kohen, 14:481
  on onanism, 15:427
  Shulḥan Arukh, 18:529–530

Caro, Joseph Ḥayyim ben Isaac, 4:**491–492**

Caro, Nikodem, 4:**492**

Caro, Sir Anthony, 4:**487**, 18:223

Carob, 4:**492**, 7:93, vol. 16: color insert

Caro-Delvaille, Henri, 4:**492**

Carol, Aryeh, 4:**492–493**

Carp, Horia, 4:**493**

Carp, Jehoshua. *See* Carp, Horia

Carp, Matatias, 4:493

Carp, Paula, 4:**493**

Carpathia. *See* Subcarpathian Ruthenia

Carpathian Ruthenia. *See* Subcarpathian Ruthenia

Carpatho-Russia. *See* Subcarpathian Ruthenia

Carpatho-Ukraine. *See* Subcarpathian Ruthenia

Carpentras (France), 4:105, **493–495**, 13:259

Carpet pages in Hebrew illuminated manuscripts, 3:675–678

Carpi, Leone, 4:**495**, 544

Carr, Judy Feld, 4:**495–496**

Carrascon (Texeda), 4:496

Carrascon, Juan, 4:**496**

Carregal, Raphael Ḥayyim Isaac. *See* Carigal, Raphael Ḥayyim Isaac

Carr-Gottstein, Inc., 1:577

Carrion de Los Condes (Spain), 4:**496**

Carta esperanzada a un General (Aguinis), 1:510

Cartagena (Spain), 4:**496–497**

Cartaphilus. *See* Wandering Jew

Las cartas que no llegaron (Rosencof), 17:444

Cartea Neagra (Carp), 4:493

Carter, Jimmy, 4:**497–498**, 6:280, 12:656

Carter, Nell, 4:**498**

Carter, Victor M., 4:**498–499**

Cartesian approach, to New Testament, 15:191

Carthage (North Africa), 4:**499**
  amulets, 2:123
  Phoenician colonization, 16:122

Cartigena. *See* Cartagena (Spain)

Cartography. *See* Map makers

Cartoonists and cartoons, 4:**499–501**
  Amshewitz, John Henry, 2:106
  Bakshi, Ralph, 3:73–74
  Block, Herbert Lawrence, 3:769
  Capp, Al, 4:454–455
  caricatures, 4:477–479
  Chast, Roz, 4:581
  Crumb, Robert, 5:310
  Csupo, Gabor, 5:315–316
  Eisner, WIll, 6:277–278
  Elder, Will, 6:296–297
  Elisofon, Eliot, 6:354–355, 16:126
  Feiffer, Jules, 6:733
  Fleischer, Max, 7:73
  Freleng, Isadore "Friz", 7:238
  Gardosh, Kariel, 7:389
  Godal, Eric, 7:678
  Goldberg, Rube, 7:696
  Goldwater, John L., 7:734
  Gropper, William, 8:94
  Hirschfeld, Al, 9:136
  Kane, Bob, 11:760–761
  Kane, Gil, 11:761
  Kelen, Imre, 12:68
  Kirby, Jack, 12:183–184, 598
  Klasky, Arlene, 5:315–316
  Kurtzman, Harvey, 6:296, 12:395
  Langdon, David, 12:479

  Lazarus, Mel, 12:**561**
  Lee, Stan, 12:598
  Lurie, Ranan Raymond, 13:270
  Opper, Frederick Burr, 4:499, 15:451
  Shuster, Joe, 18:536
  Siegel, Jerry, 18:555
  Spiegelman, Art, 4:500–501, 19:107
  Steig, William, 19:173–174
  Steinberg, Saul, 15:225, 19:189–190
  Tim, 19:724
  Trier, Walter, 20:144
  Weisz, Victor, 20:741
  Zec, Philip, 21:481

Carts and chariots, 4:**497**, 11:592

Carvajal, Abraham Israel, 4:**502**

Carvajal, Antonio Fernandez. *See* Carvajal, Abraham Israel

Carvajal, Luis de, 4:501

Carvajal family, 4:**501–502**, 501*t*

Carvajal y de la Cueva, Luis de, 4:501

Carvalho, Emanuel N., 6:190

Carvalho, Mordecai Baruch, 4:**502**

Carvalho, Solomon Nunes, 4:**502**, 16:125

Carvallo, Jules, 4:**502–503**

Casa, Joseph ben Abraham. *See* Case, Joseph ben Abraham

Casablanca (Morocco), 4:**503–504**

Casablanca (motion picture), 6:474

Casa dei catecumeni. *See* Catechumens, house of

Casale Monferrato (Italy), 4:**504–505**

Case, Joseph ben Abraham, 4:**505**

The Case for Auschwitz: Evidence from the Irving Trial (Van Pelt), 9:420

The Case for the Chosen People (Plaut), 16:228

The Case of Professor Körner. See Případ profesora Körnera

The Case of Sergeant Grischa (Zweig), 21:694

Casès, Benjamin ben David, 4:**505**

Cases family, 4:**505**

Casimir III, 4:**505**, 6:515

Casimir IV, 4:445

Casius (Egypt), 3:13

Caspari, C. P., 3:633

Caspary, Eugen, 4:**505–506**

Casper, B. M., 11:378

Casper, Bernard Moses, 4:**506**

Caspi, Joseph, 2:461

Caspi, Joseph ben Abba Mari. *See* Kaspi, Joseph ben Abba Mari ibn

Caspi, Matti, 4:**506**

Caspi, Saul, 4:**506**

Cass, Frank, 4:**506**

Cass, Mama. *See* Elliot, "Mama" Cass

Cass, Moses Henry, 4:**506–507**

Cass, "Moss" Henry. *See* Cass, Moses Henry

Cass, Samuel, 4:407–408, **507**

Cassab, Judy, 4:**507**

Cassel. *See* Kassel (Germany)

Cassel, David, 4:**507–508**

Cassel, Ernest Joseph. *See* Cassel, Sir Ernest Joseph

Cassel, Paulus Selig. *See* Cassel, Paulus Stephanus

Cassel, Paulus Stephanus, 4:**508**

Cassel, Sir Ernest Joseph, 4:**508,** 16:346, 17:70

Casseres, Abraham. *See* Caceres, Abraham

Casseres, Joseph. *See* Caceres, Francisco de

Casseres, Joseph de. *See* Caceres, Francisco de

Cassian, Nina, 4:**508**

Cassin, Matilde, 7:85

Cassin, René Samuel, 4:**508–509**

Cassirer, Ernst, 2:370, 4:**509–510**

Cassirer, Paul, 4:**510**

Cassius, Dio. *See* Dio Cassius

Cassius Longinus, 4:**510**

Cassuto, Moses David. *See* Cassuto, Umberto

Cassuto, Nathan, 7:85

Cassuto, Umberto, 3:647–648, 650, 4:**510–511,** 9:161

Castel, Moshe Elazar, 4:**511–512**

Castel-Bloom, Orly, 4:**512–513**

Castelfranco, Joseph ben Samuel, 4:163

Castell, Edmund, 4:**513**

Castellazzo, Jehiel ben Moses Saks da, 4:513

Castellazzo, Moses, 4:513

Castellazzo, Moses da, 4:**513**

Castellazzo, Simeon, 4:513

Castellazzo family, 4:**513**

Castelli, David, 3:633, 4:**513–514**

Castello, Abraham Isaac, 4:**514**

Castellón de la Plana (Spain), 4:**514**

Castellum Beleismum. *See* Ibleam (Israel)

Castellum Dok. *See* Dok (Israel)

Castelnuovo, Enrico, 4:**514**

Castelnuovo, Menahem Azariah Meir ben Elijah, 4:**515**

Castelnuovo, Menahem Ḥayyim ben Elijah. *See* Castelnuovo, Menahem Azariah Meir ben Elijah

Castelnuovo-Tedesco, Mario, 4:**515**

Castelo Branco (Portugal), 4:**515**

Castelo Branco, João Rodrigues de. *See* Amatus Lusitanus

Castelo Branco, Juan Rodrigues de. *See* Amatus Lusitanus

Castelsarrasin (France), 4:**515**

Castiglioni, Camillo, 4:**515–516**

Castiglioni, Ḥayyim, 4:**516**

Castiglioni, Vittorio. *See* Castiglioni, Ḥayyim

Castile, 1:343, 346, 13:248, 18:589

Castilian rite. *See* Liturgy

Casting of lots. *See* Lots

"Castle of the Carmel" (Israel). *See* Tirat ha-Karmel (Israel)

Castor. *See* Gamzon, Robert

Castoria (Greece). *See* Kastoria (Greece)

Castor-oil plant, 4:**516**

Castration, 4:**516–517,** 18:330

    See also Barrenness and fertility

Castro, Abraham, 4:**517–518,** 15:523

Castro, Aida de, 15:610

Castro, Bendito de, 4:518

Castro, David Henriques de, 4:517

Castro, de, family, 4:**518,** 13:728

Castro, Ezekiel de. *See* Castro, Pedro de

Castro, Fidel, 5:323–325

Castro, Herbert de, 15:610

Castro, Jacob ben Abraham, 4:**518**

Castro, Jacob de, 4:**518**

Castro, Moses Woodrow de, 4:517

Castro, Orobio de. *See* Orobio de Castro, Isaac

Castro, Pedro de, 4:**518**

Castro, Rodrigo de, 4:518

Castro family, 4:**517**

Castrojeriz (Spain), 4:**518–519**

Castro Quesada, Americo, 4:**519**

Castro Sarmento, Henrique de. *See* Castro Sarmento, Jacob de

Castro Sarmento, Jacob de, 4:**519–520,** 13:728

Castro Tartas, David de, 2:109, 4:**520**

Castro Tartas, Isaac de, 4:**520–521**

Catacombs, 3:673, 4:**521–522**

Catalan language, Bible translation, 3:627

Catalogo real de Espana (Silva), 18:583

Catalogus Librorum Hebraeorum in Bibliotheca Bodleiana (Steinschneider), 19:198

Catalyst (organization), 18:183–184

Catania (Sicily), 4:**523**

Catanzaro (Italy), 4:**523**

Catapulte. *See* Eydoux, Emmanuel

Catch-22 (Heller), 8:795

Catechism, Jewish. *See* Articles of faith; Belief

Catechism for Younger Children (Leeser), 6:190

Catechumens, 4:94

    house of, 3:122, 4:**523–524**

        in Bologna, 4:48

        Borromeo, Carlo, 4:94

        Julian III, 11:574

        Mortara case, 14:513

Catedrala. *See The Cathedral*

Categories (Aristotle), 4:**524–525**

Categories of beings, 4:**524–525**

Catenary theory, 11:242

Caterpillar. *See* Worms

Cathar. *See* Albigenses

Catharism, 1:592

The Cathedral (Duda), 6:40

Catherine II (empress of Russia), 4:**525,** 15:577

Catholic Bibles

    canon of, 3:666

    English translations, 3:625

        early modern, 3:612–613

        post-WW II, 3:614–621

    German, 3:630–631

    translation issues for Catholics, 3:606, 612, 617–618, 629

Catholic Church, 4:687–690, **709–715**

    Agobard, 1:469

    Albigenses, 1:592

    antisemitism, 2:231

        blood libel, 3:776, 778, 779, 4:710–712, 17:163

        Calixtus III, 4:365

    Bible, meaning of, 3:664

    Brazil, 4:151–152

    bulls, papal, 4:277–278

    Canada, 4:397

    Catholic-Jewish relations, 12:567, 16:323, 20:379

        Nostra aetate, 4:687–690

    censorship, 4:539–540

    Chile, 4:638

    church councils, 4:715–719

    church fathers, 4:719–721, 41:285

    Civiltà Cattolica, La, 4:748–749

    Colombia, 5:62

    Deckert, Joseph, 5:528

    Desecration of the Host, 9:565–566

    forced baptism, 3:121–122

    Franciscans, 7:173–175, 10:640

    Holocaust, response to, 9:370–375, 402

Holocaust education, 9:453–454

Israel and, 10:640, 642, 644, 11:277, 280

Italy, 10:809, 811

Jewish relations with, 3:234, 4:680, 9:374–375, 11:275–277, 279–281, 282, 18:777

Lateran Councils III, IV, 4:716–717, 6:14, 12:505–506

Middle Ages, 4:710–711

modern, 4:711–713

"New Jerusalem," 11:219

Nostra Aetate, 11:380, 15:695

orders and movements

    Dominicans, 5:745–746, 17:126–127

    Ecumenical Movement, 4:714–715

    Franciscans, 10:640

    Jesuits, 11:245

    Judaizers, 11:520–523

popes, 16:372–378

post-World War I, 4:713–714

Renaissance and Counter-Reformation, 4:711

Roman Empire, 4:709–710

under Roman Empire, 4:709–710

theologians, Duns Scotus, John, 6:50

tithes, 19:739–740

U.S., 4:713–715

usury, 2:554, 3:112, 20:437–443

Vatican councils, 4:687–689

See also Crusades; Forced conversion

Catholic Monarchs. *See* Ferdinand and Isabella of Spain

Cato, Gavin, 15:228

Cats, 4:**521**

Catskill Honeymoon (Yiddish musical), 4:115

Cattails, vol. 16: color insert

Cattan, Henry, 11:233

Cattan, Jacob, 4:525

Cattan, Joseph ben Samuel, 4:525

Cattaneo, Carlo, 4:**525–526**

Cattan family, 4:**525**

Cattaui, Georges, 4:526

Cattaui, Jacob, 4:526

Cattaui, Joseph Aslan, 4:526, 16:346

Cattaui, Moses, 4:526

Cattaui, René, 4:526

Cattaui family, 4:**526**

Cattle, 4:**526–527**

    bull symbolism, 18:570

    ecology, and rearing small, 6:93

    livestock, trade in, 13:144–145

mixed species, 14:385–387

"Cattle Rancher's Field" (Israel). *See* Sedeh Boker (Israel)

Cauca. *See* Coca (Spain)

Cauca (Spain). *See* Coca (Spain)

Caucasus, 4:**527–528**

Causani. *See* Kaushany (Moldova)

Cause and effect, relation between, 4:**528–529**

Causse, A., 3:658

Cavaillon (France), 4:**529–530**

Cavalleria, Alfonso de la, 4:532, 18:45

Cavalleria, Bonafos de la, 4:531

Cavalleria, Don Benveniste de la, 15:562

Cavalleria, Ferdinand de la. *See* Cavalleria, Bonafos de la

Cavalleria, Gaspar de la. *See* Cavalleria, Judah de la

Cavalleria, Judah Benveniste de la, 4:531

Cavalleria, Judah de la, 4:530, 18:42

Cavalleria, Orovida de la, 4:530–531

Cavalleria, Pedro de la, 4:531–532, 18:45

Cavalleria, Salomon de la, 3:688, 4:531

Cavalleria, Solomon de la. *See* Cavalleria, Salomon de la

Cavalleria, Tolosana de la, 4:531

Cavalleria, Vidal de la, 4:530, 18:43, 44

Cavalleria, Vidal Joseph de la, 4:531

Cavalleria family, de la, 4:**530–532**, 532*t*, 18:43

Cave of Machpelah, 8:744

Cave of Treasures, 1:377

Caves, Judean Desert. *See* Judean Desert caves

Cavid Bey, Mehmed. *See* Javid Bey, Mehmed

Cayenne (French Guyana), 4:**532–533**

Caylar, Crescas du, 3:610

Cazalet, Edward, 4:**533**

Cazalet, Victor Alexander, 4:533

Cazès, David, 4:**533**

CBF. *See* Central British Fund

CBS, 1:406, 14:469

CCAR. *See* Central Conference of American Rabbis

CCAR Journal: A Reform Jewish Quarterly, 7:31

CCJP (Committee on the Church and the Jewish People), 16:630, 631–632

C.D.E., 4:**533–534**

CDJC. *See* Centre de Documentation Juive Contemporaine

Cea (Spain), 4:**534**

Cech, Thomas, 2:22, 4:593

Čech, Svatopluk, 5:365–366

Čechů-Židů, Svaz. *See* Svaz čechů-Židů

Cecil, Henry, 4:**535**

Cedar, 4:**535**, vol. 16: color insert

Cedar, Chaim, 4:**535**, 13:9

Cedar, Joseph, 4:**535–536**

Cedars of Lebanon Hospital, 13:196

CEJ (Centro de Estudios Judaicos), 4:641

Cejwin Camps, 18:161

Celan, Paul, 4:**536–537**

Celebi. *See* Chelebi

Celery, 20:488

LA Celestina (Rojas), 17:371

Celibacy, 4:**537**, 18:329

Cellali gangs, 2:33

Cell biology, 13:**10**

Celler, Emanuel, 4:**537**

Cellulose acetate rayon, 6:20

Celsus, 4:**537–538**, 5:689–690

Celsus, Aulus Cornelius, 4:538

Celtic languages, translations of Bible, 3:636–637

Cemeteries, 4:**538–539**

    Béziers, 3:559

    Bordeaux, 4:82

    Brazil, 18:31

    Chile, 4:638

    disinterment and, 5:682

    Genizah and, 7:460

    kever avot, 12:99–100

    location, 16:215

    Mount of Olives, 14:584–585

    Muiderberg, 2:107

    photographs of, 16:129

    Prague, vol. 7: color insert

    suicides, 19:295

    tombs, 20:32

    washing hands, 1:263

    See also Burial customs

Cencio Savelli. *See* Honorius III (pope)

Ceneda. *See* Vittorio Veneto (Italy)

Censorinus, 4:**539**

Censorship, 4:**539–541**

    Aleinu le-Shabbe'aḥ, 1:609

    Alexander of Hales, 1:629

    Avodah Zarah, 2:746

    biblical influence on music and, 3:672–673

    Dominicans, 5:745

    gemilut ḥasadim, 7:428

    hakhnasat kallah, 8:247

    ḥalukkah, 8:287, 289

    haskamah, 8:444

    heresy, 9:21

Censorship, *continued*
  ḥevra kaddisha, 9:81
  Ḥibbut ha-Kever, 9:94
  honor, reward of, 9:519
  Inquisition and, 5:739
  interest on loans, 12:606
  Mapu, Abraham, 13:505
  monti di pietà, 14:461
  offensive books, 7:227
  orphan, 15:484, 485
  Pe'ah, 15:705
  pletten, 16:237
  poor, provision for, 16:371–372
  Purim, 16:742
  ransom of captives, 4:456
  Talmud, 19:481
  tax, 19:535, 540
  tokens, 5:121–122
  wills, 21:69
  yeshivot, 21:317
Censorship and Freedom of Expression in Jewish History (Carmilly-Weinberger), 4:485
Census, 4:**541–542**
The Centaur in the Garden (Moacyr), 18:207
Center for Advanced Holocaust Studies, 20:277
Center for Jewish Art, 2:527
Center for Jewish History, 2:64, 410, 4:**542–543**
Center for Jewish Immigration. *See* Reichszentrale Fuer Juedische Auswanderung
Center for the Study of Judeo-Arabic Culture and Literature at the Ben-Zvi Institute, 7:480, 11:797
Centerszwer, Stanisława, 4:**543**
Centerszwerowa, Stanisława. *See* Centerszwer, Stanisława
Centipede, 4:**543**
Cento (Italy), 4:**543–544**
Centos, 4:**544**
Central Agency for the Care of War Refugees. *See* Zentralstelle der Fuersorge Fuer Kriegsfluechtlinge
Central Agency of Jewish Education (Argentina), 2:71
Central Agency of the Ministries of Justice of the States. *See* Zentrale Stelle der Landesjustizverwaltungen
Central Archives for Research on the History of Jews in Germany, 2:407
The Central Archives for the History of the Jewish People (CAHJP), 2:406, 413–414, 9:160, 161
Central Archives for the Jewish People, 9:427

Central Association of German Citizens of Jewish Faith. *See* Central-Verein Deutscher Staatsbuerger Juedischen Glaubens
Central Bank of Cooperative Institutions in Palestine, 15:588
Central Board of Education (Argentina), 6:211
Central British Fund (CBF), 4:**544–545**
Central Committee for the Relief of Jewish War Sufferers. *See* YEKOPO
Central Conference of American Rabbis (CCAR), 4:**545–546**
  American Jewish Archives, 2:53
  Bronstein, Herbert, 4:208
  Fink, Joseph Lionel, 7:30
  Franklin, Leo, 7:215
  Freehof, Solomon Bennett, 7:227–228
  Lipman, Eugene Jay, 13:67
  Mielziner, Moses, 14:205–206
  Silverman, Joseph, 18:586
  Simon, Abram, 18:609
Central Council of Jewish Religious Education, 6:206
Central Council of Jewish Social Services, 6:428
Central Council of Jews in Germany. *See* Zentralrat der Juden in Deutschland
Centrale Arbeiders Verzekeringsbank, 5:538
Central Europe
  eighteenth and nineteenth centuries, economic and social development, 9:233–234
  Hebrew literature, publishing, 16:721–722
  informers, 9:782
  Landrabbiner, 12:474
  textiles, 19:663
  See also Europe
Central Government Archives of Literature and Art (Moscow), 11:766
Centralization of cult, Josiah, reforms of, 11:458
Central Mountain Massif (Israel), 10:114–117
Central Negev Highlands (Israel), 10:113
Central Office of the Ministries of Justice of the Laender. *See* Zentrale Stelle der Landesjustizverwaltungen
Central-Organ. See Oesterreichisches Central-Organ Fuer Glaubensfreiheit, Cultur, Geschichte und Literatur der Juden

Central Sephardic Jewish Community of America, 18:302–303
Central Union of the Jewish Communities (Slovakia), 5:360
Central-Verein Deutscher Staatsbuerger Juedischen Glaubens, 4:**546–547,** 9:245, 16:114
Central-Vereins-Zeitung. See C.V.-Zeitung (newspaper)
Central Welfare Organization of German Jews. *See* Zentralwohlfahrtstelle der Deutschen Juden
Central Yiddish School Organization, 6:188
Central Zionist Archives (CZA), 2:407, 414, 9:427
Centre de Documentation Juive Contemporaine, 2:411, 4:**547,** 9:428, 18:147–148, 723
Centro de Estudios Judaicos (CEJ), 4:641
Centro Israelita, 5:318, 321
Centuria (Lusitanus), 2:34, 35
Century of Jewish Life (Elbogen), 6:291
Ceramics. *See* Pottery
Cereals. *See* Five species
Ceremonial art, 2:525–526
Ceremonial objects, 1:397, 4:**547–549**
  Esther scroll and case (19th c.), vol. 15: color insert
  Ḥanukkah lamp (6th c. En-Gedi), vol. 18: color insert
  Havdalah candle holder (18th c.), vol. 15: color insert
  Havdalah candles (20th c.), vol. 15: color insert
  mezuzah cases (19th-20th c.), vol. 15: color insert
  oil lamp (5th-6th c.), vol. 15: color insert
  Sabbath table covering (19th c.), vol. 18: color insert
  seder set (18th-19th c.), vol. 18: color insert
  spice box and Havdalah cup (19th c.), vol. 15: color insert
  sukkah decorative paper cutting (19th c.), vol. 18: color insert
  tallit and accessories (20th c.), vol. 18: color insert
  tevah (18th c.), vol. 15: color insert
  Torah binders (19th-20th c.), vol. 15: color insert
  Torah case (18th c.), vol. 18: color insert
  Torah case and finial (18th c.), vol. 18: color insert
  Torah scroll and case (19th c.), vol. 15: color insert

Torah shrine wall painting (3rd c.), vol. 18: color insert

Cerf, Bennett Alfred, 4:**549,** 13:143

Cerfberr, Herz, 2:7–8, 3:724, 4:**550**

Cerfberr, Maximilien-Charles Alphonse, 4:**550**

Cerfberr family, 13:194

Cerfberr of Bischheim. *See* Cerfberr, Herz

Cernǎu (Ukraine). *See* Chernovtsy (Ukraine)

Cernǎui (Ukraine). *See* Chernovtsy (Ukraine)

Cernauti. *See* Chernovtsy (Ukraine)

Cernǎuţi (Ukraine). *See* Chernovtsy (Ukraine)

Cervantes Saavedra, Miguel de, 4:**550**

Cervera (Spain), 4:**550–551**

Cervera Bible, 3:677, 11:430

Cervetto, Jacob Basevi, 3:195, 4:**551**

Cervetto, James, 3:195

Cesarani, David, 4:**551**

Cesena (Italy), 4:**551–552**

Ceska Lipa (Czech Republic), 4:**552**

Česká Lípa (Czech Republic). *See* Ceska Lipa (Czech Republic)

Ceske Budejovice (Czech Republic), 4:**552**

České Budějovice (Czech Republic). *See* Ceske Budejovice (Czech Republic)

Český Těšín (Teschen). *See* Teschen (Silesia)

Cestius Gallus, 3:150, 4:**552–553,** 6:307

Cetatea-Alba. *See* Belgorod-Dnestrovski (Ukraine)

Cetatea-Albǎ (Ukraine). *See* Belgorod-Dnestrovski (Ukraine)

Ceuta (Morocco), 4:**553**

Ceylon, 4:**553**

Chabad, 4:**553–555,** 8:349

    Aaron ben Moses ha-Levi of Starosielce and, 1:216–217

    death of Menachem Schneersohn, 13:201

    Epstein, Isaac ben Mordecai, 6:470

    Judah Leib ben Baruch, 11:506

    Lubavich, 13:240

    Nezhin, 15:246

Chabad Ḥasidism. *See* Chabad

Chabad-Lubavitch, 2:611, 3:6

    Argentina, 2:447, 448

    Australia, Groner, Dovid Yitzchok, 8:93–94

    Rutgers University, 15:132

    Schneersohn, Menachem Mendel, 18:148–149

    U.S., 8:398

Chabon, Michael, 4:**555**

Chacon, Sir Augustin Coronel. *See* Coronel Chacon, Sir Augustin

Chadic languages, 18:280–281

Chaeremon, 4:**555–556**

Chafetz, Janet Saltzman, 18:736

Chagall, Bella Rosenfeld, 4:**556**

Chagall, Marc, 4:**556–557**

    Altman, Nathan, 2:21

    biblical influence, 3:674

    Cubism, 15:648

    La Ruche, 15:649

    Noah in painting of, 15:290

Chagrin, Francis, 4:**557**

Chagy, Berele, 4:**557**

Chaikin, Sol C., 4:**557–558**

Chaimov, Yakub, Judeo-Persian literature, 11:557

Chain, Ernest Boris. *See* Chain, Sir Ernest Boris

Chain, Sir Ernest Boris, 4:**558**

"The Chain of Tradition" (Ibn Yaḥya). *See* Shalshelet ha-Kabbalah

Chair of Elijah, 6:**337–338**

Chajes, Gershon ben Abraham, 4:**558**

Chajes, Hirsch Perez, 4:**558–559**

Chajes, Isaac ben Abraham, 4:**559**

Chajes, Saul, 4:**559–560**

Chajes, Ẓevi Hirsch, 4:**560**

Chajes, Ẓevi Perez. *See* Chajes, Hirsch Perez

Chajn, Leon, 4:**560**

Chakovski, Alexander Borisovich, 4:**560–561**

Chalcis (Greece), 1:503, 4:**561,** 13:299

Chalcis (Lebanon), 4:**561**

The Chalcolithic Culture of the Golan (Epstein), 6:469

Chalcolithic period, 2:383–384

Chaldeans, 4:**561–562**

Chalfan family. *See* Halfanus family

Chalier, Catherine, 4:**562–563,** 16:111

Challenger space shuttle, 7:6

Challenges and Responses (Simon), 18:616

Chalom, Marcel, 4:**563**

Chalomot, 6:212

Châlons-sur-Marne (France), 4:**563**

Chalons-sur-Saône (France), 4:**563**

Chamberlain, Houston Stewart, 4:**563–564**

Chamberlain, Joseph, 4:**564**

Chamberlain, Neville, 4:**564**

Chamber of Commerce of New York, 18:620

Chamber of Hewn Stone, 1:348, 18:602

The Chamber Theater. *See* Cameri

Chambéry (France), 4:**564**

Chambon-sur-Lignon (France), 4:**564–565**

Chameau. *See* Hammel, Shimon

Chameleon, 4:**565**

Champagne (France), 4:**565**

Chamudes Reitich, Marcos, 4:**565,** 642–643, 11:469

The Changelings (Seid), 18:253

Channel Islands (U.K.), 4:**565–566**

Chanover, Hyman, 4:**566**

Chanting, 4:659

Chants religieux (Lovy), 13:232

Chanukah. *See* Ḥanukkah

Chao Ch'eng, 4:566

Chao Ch'eng-Chi, 4:566

Chao family, 4:**566–568,** 567t

Chao Kuang-Yü, 4:566

Chao Ying-Ch'eng, 4:566–567

Chao Ying-Kun, 4:568

Chao Ying-Tou, 4:567

Chapbooks, 4:**568,** 6:335

Chapel Hill Kehillah, 6:62

Chapiro, Jacques, 4:**568**

Chaplaincy, 14:247–248

    Board of Delegates of American Israelites, 4:19, 7:51

    hospitals and, 9:564–565

    military

        Bohnen, Eli Aaron, 4:42

        Breslau, Isadore, 4:166

    U.S.

        Coffee, Rudolph Isaac, 4:782

        Dreyfus, Stanley A., 6:20

        Fischel, Arnold, 7:51

        hospitals and, 9:564–565

    See also National Jewish Welfare Board

Chaplin, Saul, 4:338

Chapoval, 15:650

Characene. *See* Mesene (ancient geographic location)

Charax. *See* Kerak (ancient city)

Charax of Pergamum, 4:**568**

Charbona, M. S. *See* Steinschneider, Moritz

Charenton, Enguerrand, 14:542

Chares, 4:**568**

Chargaff, Erwin, 4:**568**

Chariots. *See* Carts and chariots

Charity, 4:**569–575**

    age and the aged, 1:447, 448

    beggars, 3:259

    Boston institutions, 4:100

    Commandments, 5:77

Charity, *continued*
death, 5:512
domicile and obligation, 5:741
Eleazar ben Judah of Bartota,
6:303
Fasting and abstinence, 10:91
finances, autonomous Jewish,
7:23–24
fines, 7:27–28
firstborn redemption, 7:46
gambling and gamblers, 7:367, 368
Me'ot ḥittim, 14:60
rise of benevolent societies, 16:38–
39
Savannah institutions, 18:84
Schenectady institutions, 18:120
Seattle institutions, 18:229
Segal, Gedaliah ben Eliezer, 18:246
See also Philanthropy
Charlemagne, 3:598, 4:**575,** 7:147,
11:220
Charles, Gerda, 4:**577**
Charles II (King of England), 6:413
Charles II (King of France), 1:310,
2:124
Charles III. *See* Charles VI of
Hapsburg
Charles IV (Holy Roman Emperor),
4:**575**
Black Death, protection of Jews
during, 3:733
Jihlava, Jews of, 11:337
Charles IV (King of Bavaria), 15:346,
347
Charles IV (King of France), 4:**575**
Charles V (Holy Roman Emperor),
4:**576,** 11:420
Charles V (King of France), 4:**576,**
7:151, 11:379, 14:424
Charles VI (King of France), 4:**576,**
7:151–152, 15:643
Charles VI of Hapsburg, 14:474–475
Charles VI of Hapsburg, 4:**576–577**
Charles IX (King of France), 15:314
Charles Alexander (duke of
Wuerttemberg), 15:449
Charles and Lynn Family Foundation,
18:178–179
Charles of Luxembourg. *See* Charles
IV (Holy Roman Emperor)
Charles the Bald. *See* Charles II (King
of France)
Charleston (SC), 4:**577–578,** 19:61
Charles William Ferdinand, Duke of
Brunswick, 4:226
Charleville (France), 4:**578**
Charlop, Yechiel Michel, 4:**578**
Charlotte (NC), 4:**579**

Charlotte County (FL), 12:**598–599**
Charna, Shalom Yonah, 4:**579–580**
Charney, Carmi. *See* Carmi, T.
Charney, Daniel, 4:**580**
Charoset. *See* Ḥaroset
Charousek, Rudolph, 4:**580**
Charpak, Georges, 4:**580**
Charred Journal (paintings) (Louis),
13:222
Chartres (France), 4:**580**
Chasanowich, Joseph, 4:**580–581**
Chasanowich, Leon, 4:**581**
Chasbi. *See* Achzib (ancient Israel)
Chasins, Abraham, 4:**581**
Chaskalson, Arthur, 4:**581**
Chasman, Rose Ann, 4:372
Chast, Roz, 4:**581**
Chastisement. *See* Rebuke and reproof
Chastity, 4:**581–582**
Chateaubriand, François René,
Vicomte de, 4:55, **582–583,** 14:540
Château-Landon (France), 4:**583**
Château-Thierry (France), 4:**583**
Chatham (England), 4:**583**
Chattanooga Times, 1:398
Chatzkels, Helene, 4:**583–584**
Chaucer, Geoffrey, 3:775, 4:**584**
Chavel, Charles Ber, 4:**584**
Chavel, Dov Ber. *See* Chavel, Charles
Ber
Chaves (Portugal), 4:**584**
Chaves family, 4:**584**
Chaweriem (de Vries). *See* Friends (de
Vries)
Chayefsky, Paddy, 4:**584–585**
Chayl Masorti, 18:588
Chazan, Eliyahu Simcha, 4:**585**
Chazan, Robert, 2:47, 4:**585**
Chazen, Jerome, 15:492
Cheb (Czech Republic), 4:**585–586**
Chebar (Mesopotamia), 4:**586**
Checiny (Poland), 4:**586–587**
Chedorlaomer, 4:**587,** 11:698
Cheese, 4:**587**
Chehebar, Isaac, 4:**587**
Chein, Isidor, 4:**587–588**
Chekov, Anton, 4:141
Chelebi, 6:233
Chelebi, Abraham. *See* Brudo,
Abraham ben Elijah
Chelm (Poland), 4:**588–589,** 12:662
Chelm, Solomon ben Moses, 4:**589,**
6:34
Chelmaxioms (Mandelbaum), 20:300–
301
Chelm literature, humor and, 9:592

Chelmno concentration camp, 4:**589–
590,** 9:337, *485,* 13:159
Chelouche, Avraham, 4:590
Chelouche, Yosef Eliyahu, 4:590
Chelouche family, 4:**590**
Chemeriski, Alexander. *See*
Tshemeriski, Alexander
Chemical crafts and industries, 4:**591–
592**
Chemistry, 4:**592–593**
Austria
Abel, Emil, 1:245
Berl, Ernst, 3:442
Blau, Fritz, 3:742
Donath, Eduard, 5:748
Goldschmidt, Guido, 7:717
Gruen, Adolf, 8:105
Lieben, Robert von, 12:802–
803
Lippmann, Eduard, 13:70
Meyer, Hans Johannes
Leopold, 14:147
Paneth, Friedrich Adolf,
15:611
Spiegel-Adolf, Mona, 19:107
Brazil, Feigl, Fritz, 6:735
Canada
Bernstein, Harold Joseph,
3:478–479
Halpern, Jack, 8:285
Marcus, Rudolph Arthur,
4:593, 13:515
Polanyi, John C., 16:326
Czechoslovakia
Bloch, Moses Rudolph,
3:766–767
Goldschmidt, Heinrich Jacob,
7:718
France
Gerhardt, Charles Frederic,
7:506–507
Meyerson, Emile, 14:153
Moissan, Henri, 14:422
Germany
Askenasy, Paul, 2:588–589
Baeyer, Adolf von, 3:55
Bamberger, Eugen, 3:102
Bechhold, Jacob Heinrich,
3:242
Bergmann, Max, 3:430
Bredig, George, 4:157
Caro, Heinrich, 4:488
Caro, Nikodem, 4:492
Ehrlich, Paul, 6:244–245
Frank, Albert Rudolph, 7:178
Freund, Martin, 7:264
Gruenstein, Nathan, 8:109

Haber, Fritz, 8:174–175

Herzog, Reginald Oliver, 9:70

Hevesy, George Charles de, 9:80

Jacobson, Paul Henrich, 11:55

Jellinek, Karl, 11:121

Ladenburg, Albert, 12:427

Liebermann, Carl Theodor, 12:808

Lippmann, Edmund Oskar von, 13:70

Lunge, Georg, 13:259

Marckwald, Willy, 13:511

Meyer, Richard Joseph, 14:149

Meyer, Victor, 14:150

Pinner, Adolf, 16:169

Rosenheim, Arthur, 17:448

Sackur, Otto, 17:639

Schoenberg, Alexander Julius Wilhelm, 18:155

Schoenheimer, Rudolf, 18:157–158

Spiro, Karl, 19:120

Strauss, Eduard, 19:252

Traube, Isidor, 20:112

Traube, Moritz, 20:112

Traube, Wilhelm, 20:112

Wallach, Otto, 4:592, 20:610–611

Weigert, Fritz, 20:700

Willstaetter, Richard, 4:592, 21:75–76

Hungary, Hevesy, George Charles de, 9:80

Israel

Bergmann, Ernst David, 3:429

Birk, Yehudith, 3:711

Bobtelsky, Mordekhai, 4:25

Farkas, Ladislaus, 6:717–718, 16:137–138

Feingold, David Sidney, 6:739

Ginsburg, David, 7:611

Goldberg, Alexander, 7:690

Hirshberg, Yehudah, 9:142

Jortner, Joshua, 11:405

Kedem, Ora, 12:50

Levine, Raphael, 12:719–720

Mechoulam, Raphael, 13:711–712

Reifenberg, Adolf, 17:203

Shapiro, Benjamin, 18:404

Sharon, Nathan, 18:418

Willner, Itamar, 21:64

Yonath, Ada, 21:392–393

Italy

Jolles, Zvi Enrico, 11:386

Levi, Giorgio Renato, 12:688

Levi, Mario Giacomo, 12:690

Schiff, Hugo, 18:130

Netherlands

Cohen, Ernst Julius, 5:14

Kolthoff, Izaak Maurits, 12:280–281

Russia

Freidlina, Rakhil Khatskelevna, 7:141, 235–236

Frumkin, Aleksandr Naumovich, 7:300–301

Grinberg, Aleksander Abramovich, 8:88

Kabachnik, Martin Izrailovich, 11:583

Kazarnovski, Isaac Abramovich, 12:44

Reichinstein, David, 17:200

Roginski, Simon Zalmanovich, 17:369, 18:369

Syrkin, Yakov Kovovich, 19:400

Talmud, David L., 19:483

Switzerland

Deuel, Hans Erwin, 5:612

Drefus brothers, 6:20

Reichstein, Tadeus, 17:201–202

synthetic polymers, 8:364

U.K.

Bacharach, Alfred Louis, 3:32

Bard, Basil Joseph Asher, 3:147

Braude, Ernest Alexander, 4:134

Cohen, Julius Berend, 5:25

Copisarow, Maurice, 5:212

Fox, John Jacob, 7:141

Franklin, Rosalind Elise, 7:215

Goldstein, Richard Frank, 7:731–732

Heilbron, Sir Ian Morris, 8:765

Kroto, Harold Walter, 12:373

Levinstein, Herbert, 12:723

Lewkowitsch, Julius, 12:770–771

Meldola, Raphael, 14:12

Mond family, 14:434–435

Raphael, Ralph Alexander, 17:95

Sondheimer, Franz, 19:14

Vogel, Arthur Israel, 20:566

Weiss, Joseph Joshua, 20:734

U.S.

Bauer, Simon Harvey, 3:218

Berl, Ernst, 3:442

Bikerman, Jacob Joseph, 3:696

Bloch, Herman Samuel, 3:762

Bloch, Konrad, 3:765, 13:10

Brown, Herbert C., 4:214–215, 593

Brown, Michael Stuart, 4:215–216

Djerassi, Carl, 5:722

Drosdoff, Matthew, 6:26

Dushman, Saul, 6:65

Eliel, Ernest Ludwig, 6:322

Fajans, Kasimir, 6:679

Falk, Kaufman George, 6:686

Feingold, David Sidney, 6:739

Feuer, Henry, 6:773

Fleischer, Michael, 7:73

Gomberg, Moses, 7:746

Harris, MIlton, 8:364

Hoffman, Roald, 9:311–312

Hoffmann, Roald, 9:311–312

Kalnitsky, George, 11:747

Kaufman, Joyce Jacobson, 12:29–30

Kharasch, Morris Selig, 12:104

Langer, Robert S., 12:481

Levy, Louis Edward, 12:752

Lipman, Jacob Goodale, 13:67

Loeb, Jacques, 13:7, 160

Loeb, Morris, 13:161

Mendel, Lafayette Benedict, 14:29

Musher, Sidney, 14:636

Olah, George A., 4:593, 15:599

Rose, Irwin, 17:426

Schmerling, Louis, 18:145

Shear, Murray Jacob, 18:427

Shedlovsky, Theodore, 18:430–431

Silverman, Alexander, 18:586

Stieglitz, Julius Oscar, 19:225–226

Szwarc, Michael, 19:412

Tischler, Max, 19:733

Toch, Maximilian, 20:14

Voet, Andries, 20:566

Westheimer, Frank Henry, 21:27–28

Winstein, Saul, 21:90

Chemistry, *continued*
    Wise, Louis Elsberg, 21:100
Chemnitz (Germany), 4:**593–594**
Chemosh, 4:**594,** 14:400
Chemosh-halta (king of Moab), 14:403
Chennai (India). *See* Madras (India)
Chennamangalam (India), 4:**594**
Chennotty (India). *See* Chennamangalam (India)
Chęciny (Poland). *See* Checiny (Poland)
Cherethites, 16:54–55
Cherith, 4:**594**
Cherkassky, Shura, 4:**594**
Cherkassy (Ukraine), 4:**594–595**
Cherli Ka-Cherli (Horowitz), 8:722
Chermela. *See* Carmel (Israel)
Cherney, Brian, 4:**595**
Cherniack, Saul Mark, 4:**595**
Cherniak, Nathalie. *See* Sarraute, Nathalie
Cherniavsky, Alexander, 4:**595**
Cherniavsky, Jan, 4:**595**
Cherniavsky, Leo, 4:**595**
Cherniavsky, Michael, 4:**595**
Cherniavsky family, 4:**595**
Chernigov (Ukraine), 4:**596**
Chernin, Velvl. *See* Chernin, Vladimir
Chernin, Vladimir, 11:324
Cherniss, Harold Fredrik, 4:**596–597**
Chernobyl (Ukraine), 4:**597**
Chernobyl dynasty, 8:420
Chernomorski, Benzion. *See* Israeli, Benzion
Chernovtsy (Ukraine), 4:**597–599**
Cherny, Sasha, 4:**599**
Chersonese Jewish community, 5:299
Chertoff, Michael, 4:**599–600**
Cherub and cherubim, 2:150, 4:**600–601**
Chervonoarmeisk. *See* Radziwillow (Ukraine)
Cheshin, Mishael, 9:73–74
Chesler, Phyllis, 4:**601–602**
Chess, 1:315, 4:**602–605,** 7:371
    Boleslavski, Isaac, 4:46
    Botvinnik, Mikhail, 4:104
    Breyer, Julius, 4:174
    Bronstein, David, 4:207
    Charousek, Rudolph, 4:580
    Fine, Reuben, 7:25
    Flohr, Salo, 7:80
    Gunsberg, Isidor, 8:137
    Horowitz, Israel Albert, 9:537
    Karff, Mona May, 11:807

Kashdan, Isaac, 11:820–821
Kasparov, Gary, 11:823
Lasker, Emanuel, 12:497
masters
    France, 11:80
    Russia, 3:483, 11:823
    U.S., 11:807, 820–821
    women, 11:807
Mieses, Jacques, 14:206
Nimzovitch, Aaron, 15:270
Réti, Richard, 17:244
Rubinstein, Akiva, 17:515
U.S. women's champion, 11:807
Chess, Leonard, 4:**605**
Chess, Phil, 4:605
Chess Records, 4:605
Chet, Ilan, 4:**605–606,** 6:452
Chetwynd, Lionel, 4:**606**
Chevalier von Geldern. *See* Geldern, Simon von
Der Chevalier von Geldern (Heymann), 9:**86**
Chevreshuls, 2:111
Cheyne, Thomas Kelly, 4:**606**
Chezib. *See* Achzib (ancient Israel)
Chiang Kai-Shek, 4:91
Chiarini, Luigi, 4:243, **607**
Chicago (IL), 4:**607–612**
    Alschuler, Alfred S., 2:9–10
    Congregation Anshe Shalom, 18:576
    Hebrew Theological College, 8:738–739, 18:576
    Levin, Meyer, 12:711–712
    Maxwell Street Settlement House, 13:233
Chicago, Judy, 4:**612**
Chicago Seven trial, 9:309
Chich. *See* Lahat, Shlomo
Chicken, 4:**613**
Chicken Soup (Kalman), 11:745–746
Chickpeas, 12:611
Chief rabbi and rabbinate, 4:**613–614,** 14:352–353
Chieftains, 4:**614**
Chiel, Arthur Abraham, 4:**614–615**
Chiel, Samuel, 4:**615**
Chiera. *See* Kiera
Chieri (Italy), 4:**615**
Child, Rebellious. *See* Rebellious son
Child abduction, 1:242–243
Childbirth
    ablution, 1:263
    amulets, 2:122
    niddah and, 15:256
Childebert I, 4:**615**

Childhood. See Detstvo
Childhood and Society (Erikson), 6:479
Childlessness. *See* Barrenness and fertility
Child marriage, 4:**616–617,** 16:355
Child of Our Time (Castillo), 9:409
Child of the Shadow (Grynberg), 9:404
Child Psychiatry (Kanner), 11:766
Children, 4:**617–618**
    adoption, 1:417–419, 6:693
    "best interest of the child" concept, 15:639–640
    birth rate, U.S., 6:698–699, 702–703
    blessing of, 3:**752**
    cantonists, 4:437–439
    care of, OZE, 15:556
    contemporary relationship to grandparents, 6:703–704
    contemporary U.S. Jewish family, 6:701
    corporal punishment, 15:640
    Day of Atonement observance by, 5:488
    domestic violence and, 5:739
    education, general, 6:159–161
    education, Jewish, 6:162–214
        honey and, 9:517–518
        Torah, 6:170
    Familiants Laws, 6:689–690
    fasting, 6:720
    funerals, 4:293
    Germany, Bergen-Belsen, 3:421
    Holocaust, 6:755, 16:318
        Auschwitz survivors, 9:369
        custody, 7:22–23
        Kindertransport, 9:369, 12:160–161
        Lodz ghetto, 9:*469, 470, 476, 477*
        Theresienstadt ghetto, 9:*473*
        Warsaw ghetto, 9:*468, 469*
    of Holocaust survivors, 9:382–387
    Immanuel sign, and name for still unborn male, 9:736–738
    of immigrants, 6:696
    importance of, 6:692
    Lag ba-Omer and, 12:437
    one parent not Jewish, 15:637–638
    orphans and orphanages, 15:483–487
    parental rights and obligations, 15:635–640
    psychology of, 17:158
    Russian seizure for compulsory military service, 15:250, 265
    sacrifice of, 2:84

status under Jewish law, 15:635
See also Custody of children;
Maintenance, parental
obligation of; Parents
Children and Youth Aliyah. *See* Youth
Aliyah
Children God (Russell), 18:200
The Children of Israel of the New
Testament, 17:37
Children of My Spirit. *See Yaldei Ruḥi*
The Children of Sanchez (Lewis),
12:766
Children of the Ghetto (Zangwill),
21:456
*Children of the Holocaust:
Conversations with Sons and
Daughters of Survivors* (Epstein),
9:414
*Children of the Shadow. See Yaldei
ha-Ẓel*
Children's Haggadah (Silbermann),
18:577
Children's literature, 2:78, **4:618–636**
Amir, Anda, 2:78
Czech, 4:635
Dutch, 4:634
English, 4:631–634
French, 4:634
German, 4:634
Grininke Beymelekh (periodical),
8:767
Haskalah movement, 4:620–621
Hebrew, 4:619–628, 627t
Kaplan, Pesaḥ, 11:779
Kipnis, Levin, 12:179
Heilperin, Falk, 8:767–768
Holocaust, 4:625, 626, 627, 630–
631, 633, 15:477
Hungarian, 4:635
Israel, 6:575
Italian, 4:634
journals of literary criticism, 8:733
Ladino, 4:629–630
Latin American, 4:635
military narrative, 4:625–626
Ofek, Uriel, 15:386
poetry, 4:627
Polish, 4:635
Romanian, 4:634–635
Russian, 4:635
Serbo-Croatian, 4:635
Steig, William, 19:173–174
translations, 8:734
U.S., 4:628, 629, 632–633
Kar-Ben Publishing, 11:804
Yiddish, 4:628–629, 18:616–617
Moysheles Kinderyorn
(Kassel), 11:827

Children's services, **4:636**
Children Who Hate (Redl), 17:158
Childs, Brevard, 3:653, 654
Chile, **4:636–645**, *637*
colonial period, 4:636–637
contemporary period, 4:640–641
Israeli relations, 4:643–645
Jewish political figures, 4:642
Jewish publishing, 4:641–642
journalism, 11:469, 12:514, 755
Judaizers in, 11:521
Libedinsky Tschorne, Marcos,
12:775
migrations to, 4:638, 639–640
modern period, 4:637–639
1990-2006, 4:643
Otta, Francisco, 15:516
politicians, 6:678
Chamudes Reitich, Marcos,
4:565
Faivovich Hitzcovich, Angel,
6:678
Schaulson Brodsky, Jorge,
18:111–112
Schaulson Numhauser,
Jacobo, 18:112
prisons, 6:8
Zionism, 21:594
Chileab. *See* Daniel (biblical figure)
Chiliah-Noua. *See* Kiliya (Moldova)
Chilia-Nova. *See* Kiliya (Moldova)
Chilion. *See* Mahlon and Chilion
Chillón (Spain), **4:645**
Chilperic, 4:615
Chilperic (Merovingian king), 15:643
Chilton, Nola, 8:721
Chim. *See* Seymour, David
China, 4:*645*, **645–651**, 646t
birth certificate, vol. 20: color
insert
diplomats, Ho Feng-Shan, 9:306
early Jewish history, 4:645–646
foreign policy and relations with
Israel, 10:264
historians, 12:680
Israeli relations, 4:647–651
Jews of
Ai T'ien, 1:551–552
dress, 6:14
Joseph, Saul Abdallah, 11:417
Kaifeng, 15:474
modern Jewish communities,
4:646–647
museums, 14:635
Ningpo, 15:272
Ningsia, 15:272

ORT, 15:489
publishing, Hebrew, Shanghai,
18:396
translations of Bible, 3:637
Chinnereth (Israel), **4:651**
Chinnereth, Sea of. *See* Kinneret, Lake
Chinneroth (Israel). *See* Chinnereth
(Israel)
Chinon (France), **4:651**
Chios (Greece), **4:651–652**
Chipkin, Israel, 2:47, **4:652**
Chiquatilla, Joseph. *See* Gikatilla,
Joseph ben Abraham
Chiquatilla, Moses. *See* Gikatilla,
Moses ben Samuel ha-Kohen
Chiquitilla, Isaac ibn. *See* Gikatilla,
Isaac ibn
Chirino, Alonso, 4:652
Chirino, Diego de Valera, 4:652
Chirino, Juan Garcia, 4:652
Chirino, Sebastian, 4:652
Chirino family, **4:652**
Chiromancy, **4:652–654**
Chisinau. *See* Kishinev (Moldova)
Chiun. *See* Sikkuth and Chiun
Chizbatron, 15:389
Chizhik, Barukh, 4:654
Chizhik, Efrayim, 4:654
Chizhik, Hannah, 4:654
Chizhik, Sarah, 4:654
Chizhik family, **4:654**
Chizhik, Yiẓhak, 4:654
Chlenov, Michael, 11:324
Chmelnitzky, Melech, **4:654**
Chmielewski, Karl, 20:588
Chmielnicki, Bogdan, **4:654–656**
Chmielnicki massacres
agunot issue, 9:72
Bar, 3:123
Bloch, Matthias ben Benjamin
Ze'ev Ashkenazi, 3:766
Bogrov, Grigori Isaakovich, 4:37
Bohemia, 4:39
Borovoy, Saul, 4:92
Bratslav, 4:134
Brest-Litovsk, 4:168
Bykhov, 4:324
Dubno, 6:33
Jewish refugees, 11:738–740
Joshua Hoeschel ben Jacob, 11:455
Judah Leib ben Enoch Zundel
and, 11:506
memoirs associated with, 3:707
Nezhin, 15:246
in Novgorod-Seversk, 15:319
Olyka, 15:412

Chmielnicki massacres, *continued*
  in Ostrog, 15:511
  Yeven Mezulah, 8:327
Chmielnik (Poland), 4:**656–657**
Chmiel the Wicked. *See* Chmielnicki, Bogdan
The Chocolate Soldier (Strauss), 14:427
Chocrón, Isaac, 4:**657**
Chodorov, Edward, 4:**657–658**
Chodorov, Jerome, 4:657, 658, **658**
Chodorow, Nancy, 18:733
Chodova Plana (Bohemia), 4:**658**
Chodowiecki, Daniel N., 4:70
Chodziesner, Gertrud. *See* Kolmar, Gertrud
Choerilos of Samos, 4:**658**
Chofetz Chaim Yeshiva, 17:30
Choice, free. *See* Free will
"A Choice of Pearls." *See* MivḤar ha-Peninim
Choirs, 4:**658–664**, 12:758, 14:679–681
Chojnice (Poland). *See* Konitz (Poland)
Cholent, 4:**664**, 7:119
Cholera. *See* Medicine
Chomsky, Dov, 4:**664**
Chomsky, Noam Avram, 4:**664–665**, 13:60
Chomsky, William, 4:**665–666**
Chomutov (Bohemia), 4:**666**
Choper, Jesse H., 4:**666**
Chopra, Joyce, 4:**666**
Chora, 6:227–228
Choral singing. *See* Choirs
Choral Works (Derrida, Eisenman), 6:267
Choral works, Hebrew. *See* Hebrew cantatas and choral works
Chorazin (Galilee), 4:**666–667**, 667
Choreb, oder Versuche ueber Jissroels Pflichten in der Zerstreung (Hirsch), 9:129–130
Choreography. *See* Dance
Chorin, Aaron, 2:331, 4:**667–668**
Chorin, Abraham
  on Oral Law, 15:456
  Orthodox Judaism and, 15:494
Chorny, Joseph Judah, 4:**668**
Chortkov (Ukraine), 4:**668–669**
Choruses. *See* Choirs
A Chorus Line (Bennett), 3:369
Chorzów (Poland), 4:**669**
Chosen people, 3:292, 4:**669–672**, 682–684
  Aleinu le-Shabbe'aḥ, 1:609
  denial of as heresy, 9:20
  Genesis, Book of, 7:446

Judah Halevi, 11:495
Julian the Apostate, 11:573
kiddush ha-Shem, 12:143
Pentatuech, 15:733
providence, 16:648
Remnant of Israel, 17:217
Zangwill, Israel, 21:455
The Chosen People in America: A Study in Jewish Religious Identity (Eisen), 6:265
Chotsh, Ẓevi Hirsch Ben Jerahmeel, 4:**672**
Chotzner, Joseph, 4:**672**
Chouraqui, André, 3:629, 4:**672–673**
Chouraqui, Elijah, 4:672
Chouraqui, Isaac, 4:672
Chouraqui, Saadiah, 4:672
Chouraqui family, 4:**672**
Chrestomathia aethiopica (Dillmann), 5:661–662
Chriqui, Abraham-Ḥayyim Delevante, 4:673
Chriqui, Joseph Mas'ud, 4:673
Chriqui, Mordecai, 4:673, 14:499
Chriqui family, 4:**673**
Christchurch (New Zealand), 4:**673**
Christiana pietas, 4:278
Christian V (King of Denmark and Norway), 15:305
Christian Friends of Israel, 11:82
Christian Front movement, 4:99
Christian Hebraists. *See* Hebraists, Christian
Christiani, Pablo, 1:310, 3:145, 4:**673**
Christian Identity movement, 15:79
Christianity, 4:**673–694**
  Aaron, 1:210–211
  Abbahu, 1:229
  Abelard, Peter, 1:246
  Abrabanel, Isaac ben Judah, 1:278
  Abraham, 1:285, 287
  Abraham, Apocalypse of, 1:288, 289
  Abraham's bosom, 1:317
  Adam, 1:374, 375, 377
  amen, 2:38, 39
  Antichrist, 2:193–194
  antinomianism, 2:199–200
  Antioch, 2:202
  anti-popes, 2:125
  antisemitism, 2:209–210, 239, 4:690, 692
    Holocaust, 4:685
    medieval, 6:556
  apologetics, 2:263–264
  apostasy, 2:270, 271, 272

  archaeology, 2:391
  badges, Jewish and, 3:45
  barbarians, 3:140
  Bible codes, use of, 3:680
  Birkat ha-Minim, 3:711–712
  Bithynia, 3:729
  blood libel and, 3:775, 776
  Bodin on, 4:28–29
  Bohemia, Hussites, 9:644–645
  Bonafed, Solomon ben Reuben, 4:54
  Bonfil, Robert, 4:61–62
  Boyarin, Daniel, 4:109
  brokers, 4:203
  Buber on, 4:234
  Cain, 4:340–341
  Calvinism, 4:376–377
  cantonists, 4:437–439
  carnival, 4:486
  catacombs, 4:521
  catechumens, 4:94
  Catholic attitudes, 4:687–690
  Celsus, 4:537–538
  censorship, 4:539–540
  Church Councils, 4:715–719
  Church Fathers, 4:719–721
  criticism of Jewish sexism, 6:752
  Daniel prefiguring Jesus, 5:418
  David, 5:454, 460
  dialogue, Jewish-Christian, 4:93, 12:673
  disputations and polemics, 5:686–690, 691
  Dutch Reform Church, 2:144
  ecclesia et synagoga, 6:88
  election of, 4:682–684
  Episcopus Judaeorum, 6:463
  in Ethiopia, 6:537–538
  Eve and, 6:573
  Ezra IV and, 6:654–655
  holy places in Israel, 9:500–501, 502
  and Host, desecration of, 9:565, 565–566
  Isaac (patriarch), 10:33–34
  Isaiah, Book of, 10:73
  Islam and, 1:546, 3:668
  Israel (state), 10:638–646
  Italy, Catholic-Jewish relations, 10:811
  Jerusalem in, 11:218–222
    arts, 11:225–226
    as Christian center, 11:152
    sects, 11:164–165
  Jesus, 4:675–676, 681–682
  Jewish attitudes, 4:678–679

Jewish identity, 11:293–294

Jewish popes, 2:125, 140

Jews, attitudes towards, 4:720–721, 9:205–206, 205–207

Jews and Judaism, 4:677–678, 679–687

Jezebel in, 11:334

Job and, 11:342, 357, 358, 360

John the Baptist, 11:380–381

Jonah, Book of, 11:390

Josephus and, 11:439–440, 441

Joshua and, 11:443

Josippon on, 11:462

Judaism

    development of concept of, 11:515

    influence of, 11:519

    relationship to, 3:663–664, 6:91–92, 9:22, 375–376, 417, 12:505–506

    split from, 4:674–675

Judaizers within, 11:520

Julian the Apostate and, 11:573–574

Kabbalah influences, 11:671–673, 16:146–147

Leibowitz, Yeshayahu, 12:624

liturgy and rituals, 4:676–677, 688

Marrano diaspora, 13:561

medieval Jewish view of believers of, 13:787

Messiah, sermons on, 7:308

Middle Ages

    ecclesia et synagoga, 6:88

    economic history, 6:108–114

missionaries, 2:181, 4:238–239

    during Ottoman period, 10:176–177

mission to the Jews, 4:677, 684–685

Montefiore, Claude Joseph Goldsmid, 14:455

Moses, 14:538

Naḥmanides views, 14:745

Nietzsche, Friedrich Wilhelm, 15:262

as Noachide religion, 15:284

Noah in, 15:288, 289

as official religion of Roman Empire, 10:154

Omar, Covenant of, 15:416–419

Ottoman empire, Christian-Jewish tensions in, 15:530

Palestinian Christian Aramaic, 2:351–352

Paul of Tarsus and, 15:696–697

Philo Judaeus and, 16:62, 64

pilgrimages, 16:156–157

primitive, 18:161

Protestant attitudes, 4:690–693

Reformation, 17:163–165

Roman Empire during, restrictions on Jews in, 6:555

separation from, 10:147

Testaments of the Twelve Patriarchs, 15:691

theology, 6:59–60

tithes, church, 19:739–740

view of Isaiah, Book of, 10:71–72, 74

Zionism and Israel, 4:685–686, 8:750

Zionist movement and millenarianism, 3:737

See also Catholic Church; Frankist movement; Hebraists, Christian; Inquisition; Reformation

Christian-Jewish relations. *See* Jewish-Christian relations

Christian literature

    aggadah, 1:463

    Balaam, 3:80–81

    Baruch, Rest of the Words of, 3:187–188

    beliefs about Jews, 3:180

    Belshazzar, 3:306–307

    creation hierarchy, 5:165

    Elijah, 6:336

    Emmaus, 6:395–396

    Epistle of Barnabas, 4:719

    golden calf, 7:700

    Greek Apocalypse of Baruch, 3:186

    Hannah and her seven sons, 8:325

    messianism, 6:496–497

    Odes of Solomon, 18:765–766

    Wandering Jew, 20:616–617

Christianowitch, Alexandre, 1:440

Christian Palestinian Aramaic (CPA) translation of Bible, 3:600

Christian Phalange, 11:713–714

Christians, Maronite, 7:617

Christians and Jews: a Psychoanalytic Study (Loewenstein), 13:169

Christians and Jews in Germany: Religion, Politics and Ideology in the Second Reich (Tal), 9:417

Christian Science Church, 4:**694**

Christian Socialist Workingmen's Union (Germany), 16:630–631

Christian Social Party (Austria), 2:693, 4:**694,** 13:252

Christian Social Party (Germany), 4:**695**

Christian Typography, 9:89

Christian Zionism, 21:621–622

Christ in the Synagogue (Aaronson), 1:224

Christlichsoziale Partei. *See* Christian Social Party

Christoph, Ernst Friedrich. *See* Sauckel, Fritz

Christopher, Warren, 15:598

Christ Stopped at Eboli (Levi), 12:686

Chronegk, Ludwig, 4:**695**

The Chronicle of Ahimaaz. See Megillat Aḥima'aẓ

The Chronicle of the Lodz Ghetto (Dubroszycki), 9:419

Chronicle of the Persecution of the Jews. See Kroniek der Jodenvervolging

Chronicles, Book of, 4:**695–704,** 695t

    Aaronides and, 1:218–219

    Abijah, 1:257

    author, 4:703

    Books of the Chronicles of the Kings of Judah and Israel, 4:76–77

    canon, 4:695–696

    composition, 4:702–703

    contents, 4:695t, 696–699

    Joseph ben Ḥiyya, 11:421

    mishmarot and ma'amadot, 14:317–318

    purpose, 4:700–702

    satan, 18:72

    sources, 4:699–700

    Spinoza, Baruch de, 19:118

    targum to, 3:594

Chronicles of Jeremiah. See Rest of the Words of Baruch

Chronicles of Moses, 14:**545–546**

Die Chronik des deutschen Dramas (Bab), 3:14

Chronography, 4:705–706

Chronology, 4:**704–707**

    Demetrius (Greco-Jewish writer), 5:549, 17:235, 18:235

    Holocaust, 9:344–352

        1932-1935, 9:344

        1936-1938, 9:344–346

        1938-1940, 9:346–347

        1941-1942, 9:347–349

        1943-1945, 9:349–351

        1946-2000, 9:351–352

    Jewish history, 9:254–280t

    rabbinical literature, 17:22

    Seder Olam, 18:235–236

Chrysography, 4:73

Chrysorhoas. *See* Amanah (Syria)

Chrysostom. *See* John Chrysostom

Chryzanow (Poland), 4:**707–708**

Chrzanów (Poland). *See* Chryzanow (Poland)

Chuadit, 11:560

Chudnick, Robert. *See* Rodney, Red

Chudnik, Robert. *See* Rodney, Red

Chudnov (Ukraine), 4:**708**

Chudoff, Earl, 4:**708**

Chuetas, 4:**708–709**

Chufut-Kale (Crimea), 3:72, 4:**709,** 5:299

Chugerman, Daniel. *See* Mann, Daniel

Chujoy, Anatole, 4:**709**

Chukar partridges, 15:673

The Chumash, 3:623

Church, Catholic. *See* Catholic Church

Church, Greek Orthodox. *See* Greek Orthodox Church

Church, Protestant. *See* Protestants

Church and Synagogue. *See* Ecclesia et synagoga

Church Councils, 4:**715–719**
    attitude toward Jews, 4:716–719
    Basle, 3:201, 4:716, 717
    Elvira, 4:716, 6:371
    Paris, 4:716, 717, 15:642
    Zamora, 4:717, 21:451

Church Fathers, 1:285, 4:**719–721,** 753
    Herodians, theories on, 9:38
    Julian the Apostate and, 11:574

Churchill, Sir Winston Leonard Spencer, 2:66, 4:**722–723,** 20:750

Churchill, Winston. *See* Churchill, Sir Winston Leonard Spencer

Churchill White Paper, 10:198, 336, 497, 21:36–37

Church music. *See* Music

Church of the East, 3:599

Church of the East, Peshitta used by, 3:600

Church of the Holy Sepulcher (Jerusalem), 11:153–154

Church Slavonic language, 3:634

Churgin, Bathia, 4:**723**

Churgin, Pinkhos, 3:153, 4:**723**

Churgin, Ya'akov Yehoshua, 4:**723–724**

Chust. *See* Khust (Ukraine)

The Chute (Halper), 8:283

La Chute de la Maison Usher (motion picture), 6:473

Chwat, Szymon. *See* Wat, Alexander

Chwatt, Aaron. *See* Buttons, Red

Chwila (newspaper), 4:**724**

Chwistek, Leon, 4:**724**

Chwolson, Daniel, 3:779, 4:**724–725**

Cibo, Giovanni Battista. *See* Innocent

Cicero, Marcus Tullius, 4:**725**
    Cartesian method applied to works of, 15:191

Ciceruacchio. *See* Brunetti, Angelo

Cicurel, Salvador, 4:345

Cidellus. *See* Ferrizuel, Joseph Ha-Nasi

Ciechanover, Aaron J., 4:593, 725, **725,** 13:10

Ciechanover, Joseph, 15:589

Ciechanow (Poland), 4:**725–726,** 16:308–309

Ciechanow, Abraham ben Raphael Landau of, 4:726

Cieszyn (Teschen). *See* Teschen (Silesia)

Cigarette smoking, 5:329

CIJA (Canadian Council for Israel and Jewish Advocacy), 4:418

Cilibi Moïse, 4:**726**

Cilicia (Asia Minor), 4:**726–727**

Cincinnati (OH), 4:**727–730,** 6:738, 14:632, 15:392–393, 18:228

Cincinnati Haggadah, 8:213

Cincinnati Royals, 8:366

Cinema. *See* Motion pictures

Cinnamon, 4:730

Cinque storie ferraresi (Bassani), 3:207

La cintura di castita (Pitigrilli), 16:188

Ciocchi del Monte, Giovanni Maria. *See* Julius III (pope)

La Ciociara (Moravia). *See* Two Women (Moravia)

Circassians, 10:647

Circle Center Mall (Indianapolis), 18:608

Circle Line Boulevards (Modiano), 14:410

Circumcision, 2:40, 4:**730–735,** 8:227–228
    Abraham, 1:282, 283
    Ammonites, 2:84
    astrological influence, 2:620
    banquets celebrating, 18:321
    birthdate for purposes of, 3:721
    ceremonial objects, 4:548
    costume for infant, vol. 7: color insert
    dance, 5:411
    Elijah's chair, 6:337–338
    embroidered cushion, vol. 7: color insert
    first in Durban (South Africa), 6:62
    instrument set, vol. 7: color insert
    mohel performing rite, vol. 7: color insert
    Morocco, 1:439
    Nunberg, Herman, on psychology of, 15:344–345
    practical Kabbalah, 11:668
    Samaritans, 3:16, 17:730

sandak, 18:10
    sign of covenant, 5:249
    Zipporah circumcising her sons, 14:535, 21:639

Circuses, 4:**735,** 736
    See also Theater

Circus parties, 4:**735–736**

Cirta (Algeria). *See* Constantine (Algeria)

Cisjordan Mountains (Israel), 10:112

Cisneros, Cardinal Ximenes de, 3:587

Cisterns, 4:736

Cities, 4:**738–741**
    elders, 6:294–295
    Joshua, Book of, 11:447–448, 448, 12:733–734
    of Judah, 11:476, 477
    planning, 5:168
    of refuge, Joshua, Book of, 11:447, 448

"Cities of the Plain." *See* Sodom and Gomorrah (ancient cities)

Citizenship of Jews
    Fichte, Johann Gottlieb, 7:9–10
    New York City, colonial period, 15:196

Citizenship rights, 11:720

Citroën, André Gustave, 4:**736–737**

Citroen, Roelof Paul, 4:**737**

Citron, vol. 16: color insert

Citrus, 4:**737–738**

Citrus growers (FL), 18:51

Citrus-growers' Association. *See* Pardes

City, Levitical. *See* Levitical cities

The City and the Fullness Thereof. See Ir u-Melo'ah

The City and the People (Baizerman), 3:69

City College of New York, 4:19

City of Culture of Galicia (Santiago de Compostela, Spain), 6:267

City of David. *See* Jerusalem (Israel)

The City of David - A Guide to Biblical Jerusalem (Shanks), 18:397

City of God (Doctorow), 5:728

City of Hope National Medical Center, 4:**741–742,** 13:196

City of refuge, 4:**742–745,** 743, 16:216

City of Refuge. See Ir Miklat

Ciudad Real (Spain), 4:**745**

Ciudad Rodrigo (Spain), 4:**745**

The Civic Culture (Almond and Verba), 1:683

Cividale (Italy), 4:**745–746**

Civilization, influence of Judaism on, 11:519–520

The Civilizing Process (Elias), 6:319
Civil law conflicts, 5:154
Civil marriage, 4:**746–748**
Civil rights
> Board of Delegates of American
> > Israelites, 4:19–20
> Canada, 4:408–409
> France, French Revolution, 7:254–
> > 255
> Germany, 4:546
> husband and wife obligations,
> > 9:634, 635–638
> Israel (State), Aloni, Shulamit,
> > 1:687
> The New Israel Fund, 15:138–139
> Russia, Duma, 6:45–46
> women, 4:409
> *See also* Emancipation; New Left
Civil rights movement (U.S.), 2:486–
> 487
> Anti-Defamation League, 2:194,
> > 195
> Baltimore, 3:100
> Jewish artists, 2:515
> Jewish involvement
> > Alabama, 1:573
> > Birmingham, 3:713
> > Black-Jewish relations and,
> > > 3:734–735
> > Brickner, Balfour, 4:178–179
> > Polier, Shad, 16:332–333
> > Polish, David, 16:334
> leaders
> > Dershowitz, Alan M., 5:600
> > Herstein, Lillian, 9:47
> > Mississippi, 14:365
> > Nussbaum, Perry, 15:353–354
> > Polier, Shad, 16:332–333
> > Polish, David, 16:334
La Civiltà Cattolica, 4:**748–749**
Civil War (Spain), 15:218
Civil War (U.S.), 2:44–45, 465
> antisemitism, 8:34–35
> Benjamin, Judah Philip, 3:357–358
> Blumenberg, Leopold, 4:10
> Board of Delegates of American
> > Israelites, 4:19
> Louisiana, 13:223–224
> New York City and, 15:200
Civita, Davit, 4:**749**
Cixous, Hélenè, 4:**749**
CJC. *See* Canadian Jewish Congress
> (CJC)
CJF (Council for Jewish Federations).
> *See* Council of Jewish Federations
> and Welfare Funds
Claiborne, Liz, 15:**492–493**

Claims. *See* Pleas
Claims Conference. *See* Conference on
> Jewish Material Claims Against
> Germany
Clairvoyance and prediction, 16:571
CLAL (National Jewish Center for
> Learning and Leadership), 4:**749–
> 750**
*Clarification of the Fundamentals of
> Faith. See Risālat al-ibānah fi uṣūl
> al-diyānah*
Clarion (UT), 20:444
Class conflict
> medieval Spain, 18:42
> San Francisco, 18:19
Class Factors in the National Question
> (Borochov), 4:90
Classical education, 1:403–404
Classical history
> Bloch, Gustave, 3:761
> Bloch, Herbert, 3:761–762
> Leon, Harry Joshua, 12:644
Classical scholarship
> Hadas, Moses, 8:185
> Jews in, 4:**750–751**
> Lewy, Yoḥanan, 12:771–772
Classici del ridere (Formiggini), 7:131
Clauberg, Karl, 17:121
Claudel, Paul, 4:**751**
Claudia (Franken), 7:201
Claudian, 4:**751–752**
Claudius, 1:502, 635–636, 4:**752,** 6:229,
> 12:453–454
Claudius Aelianus. *See* Aelian
Claudius Claudianus. *See* Claudian
Claudius Iolaus, 4:**752**
Claudius Julius. *See* Claudius Iolaus
Clayburgh, Jill, 4:**752**
Cleanliness
> ritual (*See* Purity and impurity,
> > ritual)
> *See* Hygiene
Clearchus of Soli, 4:**752**
> on Jewish identity, 11:293
> Judea as term, use of, 11:523
Clejan, Vera. *See* Calin, Vera
Clement (popes), 4:**752–753**
Clement I (pope), 3:574
Clement III (antipope), 4:752
Clement III (pope), 4:752
Clement IV (pope), 4:277, 752–753
Clement V (pope), 16:374
Clement VI (pope), 4:277, 16:374
> Black Death and, 3:731, 733
> Molcho, Solomon, 14:424
Clement VII (pope), 4:753, 16:375

Clement VIII (pope), 4:753, 16:375–
> 376
> Ancona, 2:140
> antisemitism, 2:140
Clement VIII (pope), 4:49, 753
Clement IX (pope), 16:376
Clement X (pope), 4:753
Clement XII (pope), 4:753, 16:376
Clement XIII (pope), 4:753, 16:376
Clement XIV (pope), 4:753, 16:377
> Ambron, Ezekiel, 2:37
> blood libel, 3:778, 4:753
Clement of Alexandria, 2:459, 4:720,
> **753**
Clement VI (pope), 4:752–753
Cleodemus Malchus, 4:**753**
Cleomedes, 4:**753**
Cleopatra, 4:**754**
Cleopatra I, 4:**754**
Cleopatra II, 4:**754**
Cleopatra III, 2:129, 4:**754**
Cleopatra of Jerusalem, 4:**754**
Cleopatra VII, 4:**754**
Clermont-Ferrand (France), 4:**754–755**
Clermont-Ganneau, Charles, 4:**755,**
> 15:589
Clermont-Tonnerre, Count Stanislas
> de, 4:**755**
Cleve (Germany). *See* Cleves
> (Germany)
Cleveland (OH), 4:**755–759**
> Benesch, Alfred Abraham, 3:340
> Cleveland Browns football team,
> > 14:407
> Laura and Alving Siegal College of
> > Judaic Studies, 12:526
> Shapiro, Ezra Z., 18:405
> Silver, Abba Hillel, 18:583–584
> Silver, Daniel Jeremy, 18:584
Cleveland Federation of Jewish
> Charities, 3:72
Cleveland Jewish News, 11:761
Cleves (Germany), 4:**759–760**
Cleves get, 1:221, 291–292, 4:**760**
Clinical Cardiology (Dressler), 6:17
Clinton, William Jefferson, 4:**760–761**
> American Israel Public Affairs
> > Committee, 2:52
> Block, Herbert Lawrence, 3:769
> Lerman, Miles, 12:656
> Supreme Court appointments,
> > 12:556
Clipper (Chocrón), 4:657
Cloots, Jean Baptiste du Val-de-Grâce,
> Baron de, 4:**761**
Clore, Charles. *See* Clore, Sir Charles
Clore, Sir Charles, 4:**761**

Close Encounters of the Third Kind
   (motion picture), 6:21
Clotaire II, 4:**761–762**
Clothar. *See* Clotaire II
Clothing. *See* Dress
Clothing and textiles industry, 20:327–
   328
   Baltimore, 3:97
   Bialystok, 3:567
   Canada, 4:396, 401–402
   Chicago, 4:608–609
   Drexler, Millard S., 6:17–18
   Dreyfus Brothers, 6:20
   Elias, Eli, 6:318
   Elkann, Jean-Paul, 6:358
   Kalir, Avraham, 11:736
   labor unions, 6:32
   Lodz, 13:156
   Loew-Beer family, 13:164
   Moller, Hans and Erich, 14:426–
      427
   New York City, 15:202–205, 204t,
      213
   North Carolina, 15:302
   ona'ah, personal apparel not
      subject to, 15:425
   Ottoman empire, 15:532
   Passaic-Clifton, 15:676
   Rosen, Carl, 17:427
   Rosenthal, Ida, 17:454
   Schrader, Abe, 18:166–167
   Schwartz, David, 18:183
   secondhand goods, 18:231–232
   See also Dress; Fashion industry;
      Silk
"The Clown Prince of Baseball." *See*
   Schacht, Alexander
CLSA. *See* Commission on Law and
   Social Action
Cluj (Romania), 4:**762–763**
Cluny (France), 4:**763**
Clurman, Harold, 4:**763**
Coalition for the Advancement of
   Jewish Education (CAJE), 4:**763–
   764**
Coalition on the Environment and
   Jewish Life, 6:449
Coats of arms. *See* Heraldry
Cobb, Lee J., 3:783, 4:**764**
Coburg (Germany), 4:**764**
Coca (Spain), 4:**764–765**
Coca, Imogene, 4:332
Coca-Cola formula heksher, 7:411
Cocceius, Johannes, 4:**765**
Cochem (Germany), 4:**765**
Cochin (India). *See* Kochi (India)
Code of Hammurapi
   blindness in, 3:753

concubines, 5:133–134
Code of Nehemiah, 6:661–662
Code of Regulations Concerning the
   Jews, 7:342
Codes of Jewish law. *See* Codification
   of Law
Codex Neofiti I, 3:591
Codex Reuchlinianus of the Prophets,
   13:642
Codices, 4:71, 72
Codification of law, 4:**765–781**
   Abraham ben David of
      Posquières, 1:297
   Abraham ben Isaac of Narbonne,
      1:302
   Alfasi, Isaac ben Jacob, 4:770
   Alkalai, Abraham ben Samuel,
      1:663
   Benveniste, Ḥayyim ben Israel,
      3:382–383
   Caro, Joseph ben Ephraim, 4:489–
      490, 775–780
   Danzig, Abraham ben Jehiel
      Michal, 5:432
   Geonic period, 4:768–769
   Isserles, Moses ben Israel, 4:777–
      778
   Jacob ben Asher, 4:774–775
   Jewish law, 4:766–767
   literary forms, 4:768, 773–774
   Maimonides, 4:770–773, 774–775,
      776, 777, 778
   Mishnah, 4:767–768
   mishpat Ivri, 14:338
   non-Jewish law, 4:766
   See also Laws and legal systems
Codreanu, Corneliu Zelea, 4:**781**
Coele-Syria, 4:**781**
Coelostat, 13:70
Coen, Achille, 4:**781**
Coen, Ethan, 4:**781–782**
Coen, Giuseppe, 4:**781**
Coèn, Graziadio Vita Anania, 4:**781**
Coen, Joel, 4:**781–782**
Coercion. *See* Duress
Coffee, Rudolph Isaac, 4:**782**
Coffins, 4:293, **782–783**
Cogan, M., 11:362
Cogitant religious society, 13:170
Cognitive psychology, 4:222
Cohabitation, Sexual. *See* Sex
Cohan, Charles S., 14:454
Cohen, Aaron, 15:302
Cohen, Aaron ben David, of Ragusa,
   4:77
Cohen, Abby Joseph, 15:225
Cohen, Abraham, 3:713, 5:8

Cohen, Aharon, 3:702
Cohen, Albert, 5:8
Cohen, Albert K., 5:302
Cohen, Alexander H., 5:**8–9**
Cohen, Alexandra Pauline. *See* Cohen,
   Sasha
Cohen, Alfred Morton, 5:9
Cohen, Andrew. *See* Cohen, Sir
   Andrew
Cohen, Armond E., 5:9
Cohen, Arthur (England), 5:**10**
Cohen, Arthur (Germany), 5:**10**
Cohen, Arthur A., 5:**10**, 9:396
Cohen, Barrow E., 15:198
Cohen, Barry, 5:**10**
Cohen, Benjamin, 5:**10–11**
Cohen, Benjamin Victor, 5:**11**
Cohen, Bernard, 5:**11**
Cohen, Boaz, 5:**11–12**
Cohen, Chapman, 5:**12**
Cohen, David, 17:13
Cohen, David (1883-1967), 5:**12–13**
Cohen, David (1887-1972), 5:**13**
Cohen, Edward, 16:340
Cohen, Eli, 5:**13–14**
Cohen, Elisheva, 5:**14**
Cohen, Elizabeth. *See* Comden, Betty
Cohen, Elizabeth D.A. Magnus, 5:**14**
Cohen, Ellen Naomi. *See* Elliot,
   "Mama" Cass
Cohen, Elliot Ettelson, 5:**14**
Cohen, Elliot T., 5:90
Cohen, Emil Wilhelm, 5:**14**
Cohen, Erik, 18:735
Cohen, Ernst Julius, 5:**14**
Cohen, Esperance, 15:473
Cohen, Fannia, 5:**15**
Cohen, Felix, 5:29
Cohen, Francis Lyon, 5:**15**
Cohen, Gerson D., 5:**15–16**, 11:330–
   331
Cohen, Geulah, 5:**16–17**
Cohen, Gustave, 5:**17**
Cohen, H. Rodgin, 5:**21**
Cohen, Haim, 20:468
Cohen, Harold, 5:**17**
Cohen, Harold Edward, 16:340
Cohen, Harold Leopold, 5:**6–8**
Cohen, Harriet, 5:**17**
Cohen, Harry, 5:**17**
Cohen, Henry, 5:**17–18**
Cohen, Henry, Baron, 5:**18**
Cohen, Henry Isaac, 16:340
Cohen, Hermann, 5:**18–20**, 6:611–612,
   7:665–666, 668–669, 16:96–97
   Anhalt, 2:163

duty, 6:72–73
free will, 7:233
good and evil, 7:754
Kantian ethical imperative and, 11:770
nature, 15:35
redemption, 17:154
Ruʾaḥ ha-Kodesh, 17:509
soul, immortality of, 19:38
truth, 20:162
Cohen, Hirsh, 5:20–21
Cohen, I. Bernard, 5:21
Cohen, Isaac Kadmi, 5:21
Cohen, Israel (England), 5:21–22
Cohen, Israel (Israel), 5:22
Cohen, Israel I., 5:5
Cohen, Jack. See Cohen, Sir John Edward
Cohen, Jack Joseph, 5:22–23
Cohen, Jacob I. (1744–1823), 5:5
Cohen, Jacob I. (1789–1869), 5:5–6
Cohen, Jacob Raphael, 5:23, 15:475
Cohen, Jacob Xenab, 5:23
Cohen, Job, 16:345
Cohen, John Edward. See Cohen, Sir John Edward
Cohen, John Michael, 5:24
Cohen, John Sanford, 5:24
Cohen, Joseph, 5:24
Cohen, Joseph H., 15:205
Cohen, Joseph Isaac, 5:24–25
Cohen, Joshua I, 5:6
Cohen, Judah, 5:25
Cohen, Judy. See Chicago, Judy
Cohen, Julius Berend, 5:25
Cohen, Leo, 4:276
Cohen, Leonard, 4:423, 5:25–26
Cohen, Levi-Abraham, 5:26
Cohen, Levi Barent, 5:6
Cohen, Lionel Leonard, Baron, 5:26
Cohen, Lionel Louis, 5:6, 16:342
Cohen, Louis Samuel, 5:6
Cohen, Ludwig. See Coser, Lewis A.
Cohen, Lyon, 5:26, 11:300
Cohen, Marcel, 5:26
Cohen, Mary Matilda, 5:26–27
Cohen, Matt, 4:424, 5:27
Cohen, Maxwell, 5:27–28
Cohen, Mendes (1831-1915), 5:6
Cohen, Mendes I. (1796-1879), 5:6
Cohen, Michael, 4:182
Cohen, Morris, 5:28
Cohen, Morris Abraham, 5:28
Cohen, Morris Raphael, 5:28–29, 12:556
Cohen, Mortimer Joseph, 5:29

Cohen, Moses Isaac, 4:267
Cohen, Naomi Wiener, 5:29–30, 9:152
Cohen, Naphtali. See Neyrac, Pierre
Cohen, Natalie, 5:30
Cohen, Nathan, 5:30
Cohen, Nathan Edward, 5:30–31
Cohen, Paul Joseph, 5:31
Cohen, Peter, 15:225
Cohen, Philip. See Cohen, Sir Philip
Cohen, Philip Melvin, 5:31
Cohen, Philip Pacy, 5:31, 13:10
Cohen, Robert, 5:31–32
Cohen, Robert Waley. See Cohen, Sir Robert Waley
Cohen, Rose Gollup, 5:32
Cohen, Ruth Louisa, 5:32–33
Cohen, Sam, 18:706
Cohen, Samuel. See Cahn, Sammy; Cohen, Simon
Cohen, Samuel Herbert, 5:33, 16:340
Cohen, Samuel Myers, 15:197
Cohen, Samuel Raphael. See Cohen, Marcel
Cohen, Sasha, 5:33
Cohen, Saul Bernard, 5:33–34
Cohen, Selma Jeanne, 5:34
Cohen, Seymour J., 5:34
Cohen, Seymour Stanley, 5:34, 13:9
Cohen, Shalom ben Jacob, 3:696, 5:35, 8:688
Cohen, Shaye J.D., 5:35
Cohen, Shlomo, 5:35
Cohen, Simon, 5:35–36, 11:333
Cohen, Sir Andrew, 5:9
Cohen, Sir John Edward, 5:23
Cohen, Sir Philip, 5:31, 13:10
Cohen, Sir Robert Waley, 5:32
Cohen, Stanley, 5:36
Cohen, Stanley N., 5:36, 13:9
Cohen, Toviah. See Cohn, Tobias ben Moses
Cohen, Wilbur Joseph, 5:36–37
Cohen, William Howard. See Cosell, Howard
Cohen, William S., 5:37
Cohen, William Wolfe, 5:37–38
Cohen, Yardena, 4:96, 5:38
Cohen, Yigal Rahamim, 5:38
Cohen, Ẓevi Hirsch. See Hirschkahn, Ẓvi
Cohen ben Maknin family. See Macnin family
Cohen family (England), 5:6, 7t
Cohen family (Italy), 5:5
Cohen family (Liverpool, England), 5:6–8, 588

Cohen family (U.S.), 5:5–6
Cohen Gan, Pinchas, 5:38–39, 10:697, 699
Cohen Gellerstein, Benjamin, 5:39
Cohen Henriques, Jacob. See Henriques, Jacob Cohen
Cohen Ibn Sūsā. See Bensusan
Cohen Lobato family. See Lobato family
Cohen Melamed, Nissan, 5:39
Cohen-Tannoudji, Claude, 5:39
Cohen-Tanoudjis. See Tanuji family
Cohn, Albert, 5:39–40
Cohn, Arthur, 5:39
Cohn, Arye. See Cohn, Georg
Cohn, Berthold, 5:40
Cohn, Cilla Cypora, 5:40
Cohn, Edwin Joseph, 5:40
Cohn, Elkan, 5:40–41
Cohn, Emil. See Ludwig, Emil
Cohn, Emil Moses, 5:41
Cohn, Fannia M., 18:713
Cohn, Ferdinand Julius, 5:41, 13:7
Cohn, Fritz, 5:41–42
Cohn, Georg, 5:42
Cohn, Gustav, 5:42
Cohn, Haim, 5:42–43, 14:358
Cohn, Harry, 5:43, 14:571
Cohn, Heinrich. See Conried, Heinrich
Cohn, Herman. See Alconière, Theodore
Cohn, Hermann. See Cohn, Haim
Cohn, Jonas, 5:43, 6:160
Cohn, Lassar, 5:43
Cohn, Leopold, 5:43
Cohn, Linda, 5:43
Cohn, Manfred. See George, Manfred
Cohn, Marcus, 5:39
Cohn, Meshullam Zalman ben Solomon, 5:44
Cohn, Mildred, 5:44, 13:10
Cohn, Morris Mandel, 5:44
Cohn, Norman, 5:44
Cohn, Oscar, 5:44
Cohn, Paul. See Cornea, Paul
Cohn, Roy, 15:215
Cohn, Tobias ben Moses, 5:44–45, 6:399, 13:729, 15:541
Cohn-Bendit, Daniel, 5:45
Cohn family, 5:39
Cohnheim, Julius, 5:45
Cohn-Reiss, Ephraim, 5:45–46
Cohn-Sherbok, Dan, 5:46
Cohn-Wiener, Ernst, 5:46
Cohon, George A., 5:46

Cohon, Samuel Solomon, 5:**46–47**

Coimbra (Portugal), 5:**47**

Coins and currency, 5:**47–55**
bimetallism, 2:424
Byzantine, 1:386
commemorative, 13:716
community tokens as, 5:121–122
dina de-malkhuta dina, and value of, 5:666
Ephraim, Veitel Heine, 6:459
Ḥezi, 18:440
Israel, 5:54–55
judenpfennige, 11:525
Judin, Samuel, 11:566
mintmasters and moneyers, 14:298–301
perutah, 18:439–440
revi'a, 18:440
shekel, 18:439–440
Talmudic literature, 5:51t, 52t
value of, 20:441
Zionism, 18:440
See also Numismatics

Coit, Stanton, 18:320

Coitus interruptus, 15:426–427

COJO. *See* World Conference of Jewish Organizations

Colbert, Jean Baptiste, 5:**56**

Colby, Mary, 15:442

Colchester (England), 5:**56**

The Cold Crematorium. See Hladni krematorijum

Cole, Kenneth, 5:**56**

Coleman, Cy, 5:**56–57**

Coleman, Edward Davidson, 5:**57**

Coleman, George W., 15:266

Colenso, John William, 5:**57**

Coleridge, Samuel Taylor, 6:436

Collateral. *See* Suretyship

Collatio Legum Mosaicarum et Romanarum, 5:**57**

Colleagues Theater Company, 6:467

"Collected Sayings". *See* Tanya

Collected Stories (Babel), 3:19

Collected Works (Entin), 6:448

Colleges. *See* Universities

Collegio Rabbinico Italiano, 5:**57–58**

Collins, Hyman Henry, 5:**58**

Collins, Lottie, 5:**58**

Les Colloques des Intellectuels Juifs de Langue Français, **12:661–662**

Colm, Gerhard, 5:**58**

Colmar (France), 5:**58–59**

Colocasia, 20:488

Cologna, Abraham Vita, 5:**59**

Cologne (Germany), 5:*59*, **59–62**, 311, 312

Colombia, 5:*62*, **62–64**
Caribbean, Spanish-Portuguese Nation of the: La Nacion, 4:475
immigration, 5:63
Zionism, 21:594

Colombo, Samuel, 5:**64**

Colombo, Yoseph, 5:**64**

Colon, Joseph ben Solomon, 4:456, 5:**64–65**, 12:462, 646, 14:440, 481

Colonial America
Levy, Nathan, 12:754
New York City in, 15:194–197

Colonia Lucia Septimia Severa Diospolis, 13:294

Colonne, Judah. *See* Colonne, Jules Edouard

Colonne, Jules Edouard, 5:**65**

Colophon, 2:404, 5:**65–67**

Colophon (periodical), 1:396

Colorado (CO), 5:**67–68**, *68*

Colorni, Vittore, 5:**68–69**, 12:552

Colors (periodical), 11:746

Columbia Broadcasting System (CBS), 11:812

Columbia Records, 12:809

Columbia University (NY), 15:343

Columbus (OH), 5:**69–70**

Columbus, Christopher, 5:**70–71**, 13:675
Jews accompanying, 2:41
Sánchez, Gabriel, 18:9
Santangel, Luis de, 18:28

Column. *See* Pillars

Coma, Herz, 5:**71**

Comay, Michael Saul, 5:**71**

Comden, Betty, 5:**71–72**

Come, My Beloved. See Lekhah Dodi

Comedia famosa de Aman y Mordochay (Lara), 12:493

Comedians
Allen, Woody, 1:669–670
Barr, Roseanne, 3:174
Benny, Jack, 3:369–370
Berman, Shelley, 3:464–465
Bernhard, Sandra, 3:473
Brooks, Albert, 4:209
Brooks, Mel, 4:209–210
Bruce, Lenny, 4:218–219
Burns, George, 4:298
Buttons, Red, 4:319–320
Caesar, Sid, 4:332–333
Cantor, Eddie, 4:439
Castro, Jacob de, 4:518
Flanagan, Bud, 7:69
Hackett, Buddy, 8:183
Howard, Moe, Shemp, and Curly, 9:572–573
King, Alan, 12:162–163
Levenson, Sam, 12:680
Lewis, Jerry, 12:765
Opper, Frederick Burr, 15:451
Ostropoler, Herschele, 15:512–513
Rickles, Don, 17:292
Rivers, Joan, 17:347
Rosten, Leo Calvin, 17:474
Rudner, Rita, 17:523
Seinfeld, Jerry, 18:254
Shandling, Garry, 18:395–396
Shawn, Dick, 18:424
Shean, Al, 18:427
Silvers, Phil, 18:588
Skulnik, Menasha, 18:662
See also Humor

Comediennes. *See* Comedians

"Come Out, Come Out" (song, Miron), 14:313

Comic and Sequential Art (Eisner), 6:278

Comic books and strips
Eisner, Will, 6:277–278
Elder, Will, 6:296
Jewish cartoonists, 4:499–500
Kane, Bob, 11:760–761
Kane, Gil, 11:761
Kirby, Jack, 12:183–184
Kurtzman, Harvey, 12:395
Lee, Stan, 12:598
Shuster, Joe, 18:536
Siegel, Jerry, 18:555
See also Cartoonists and cartoons

Comics. *See* Comedians

Coming from Behind (Jacobson), 11:53–54

Coming of Post-Industiral Society (Bell), 3:298

Comintern, 5:96–100

Comissiona, Sergiu, 5:**72**

Comité des Delegations Juives, 5:**72–73**

Comité Representativo de las Entidades Judías (CREJ), 4:640

Comitetul Democrat Evreiesc, Jewish Democratic Committee. *See* C.D.E.

Comitiano, Mordecai. *See* Comtino, Mordecai ben Eliezer

Commagene (Mesopotamia), 5:**73**

Commandments
the 613, 5:**73–85**, 74t–84t (*See also* Midrash Aseret Ha-Dibberot)
Askenazi-Hasidic ranking of, 6:529
binding nature of, 16:93–94
Decalogue given, 6:616
duties of limbs vs. duties of heart, 16:81

ethical, 6:534

Ha-Ḥinnukh, 8:230

Ḥanokh of Aleksandrow, 8:329

Judah Halevi on, 11:499

Kabbalistic symbolic approach to, 6:530

Muslim, 10:88

piety is result of adherence to, 16:83

religious fulfillment of, 6:528

source of, 16:85–86

spiritual, 6:527–528

reasons for, 5:**85–90**

Commandments, Ten. *See* Decalogue

Commemorative coins, 5:55

Commentaries on the Bible. *See* Bible

Commentario delle leggi sulla guistizia amministrativa (Cammeo), 4:382

Commentary (periodical), 2:56, 5:14, **90–91,** 16:251, 18:734

Commentary on the Torah (Friedman), 3:624

Commentary on the Torah (Rashi), 1:345–346

Commerce. *See* Trade and commerce

Comme si c'était fini (Aréga), 2:421

La Commission Française des Archives Juifs, 2:408–409

Commission on Law and Social Action (CLSA), 2:57–58

Committee for Open Debate on the Holocaust, 20:380

The Committee for the Formation of the Hebrew Youth. *See* "Canaanites"

Committee of Jewish Delegations. *See* Comité des Delegations Juives

Committee on Army and Navy Religious Activities (CANRA), 14:248

Committee on Jewish Education (New York, NY), 6:193–194

Committee on Jewish Law and Standards, 5:173, 174

Committee on Military Affairs, 11:720

Committee on the Church and the Jewish People (CCJP), 16:630, 631–632

Common origin theories, Japanese and Jews, 11:84–85

Communal amenities, 2:**39–40,** 5:60

Communal enactment. *See* Takkanot ha-Kahal

Communal organizations

eighteenth and nineteenth centuries, Europe, 9:235–236

Latin America, 12:510–512

letters and letter writers, 12:672

Middle Ages, Europe, 9:224

in Odessa, 15:379

orphans and orphanages, 15:484, 486–487

Communal Regulations. *See* Devekut

Communauté Sépharade du Québec, 14:465

Communications

Halakhah, technology, 19:573

wireless, 11:47–48

Communism, 5:**91–101**

Agursky, Samuel, 1:520

anti-Zionism, 5:99–100

Baum, Herbert, 3:219

Bittelman, Alexander, 3:729

Bolshevik era, 5:92–94

Brazil, 4:149

Bulgaria, 4:273–274

Bund and, 4:281–282

Canada, 4:406

C.D.E., 4:533–534

Comintern, 5:96–98

Dimanstein, Simon, 5:662

Eisler, Gerhart, 6:275

Filderman, Wilhelm, 7:19

Hungarian literature and, 9:606–607

Hungary and, 9:611–612

Iraq, 10:19

Israeli, 5:99–100

Jewish Socialist Verband, 11:314

Lakatos, Imre, 12:440

Lenin, Vladimir Ilyich, 5:92–94, 12:639–640

Mitin, Mark Borisovich, 14:371

Morning Freiheit (newspaper), 14:492–493

New York City labor movement and, 15:214

Oppen, George, 15:442

partisans, 15:668

Pauker, Ana, 15:694

relationship of Jews to, 6:744–745

Romania, 4:241

Rosenbergs and, 15:215

secession from the party, 5:99

Soviet era, 5:94–96

world communist movement, 5:96–99

Communist-Futurist (ComFut) Association., 2:22

Communist Party (United States). *See* American Communist Party

Communist Party of Germany (KPD), 13:277

The Communist Party vs. the CIO (Kampelman), 11:758

Community, 5:**101–121**

Africa, 5:108, 110, 115*t,* 116*t,* 119*t*

Basle, 3:201–202

Batlanim, 3:213

Brazil, 4:146–148, 146*t*

business ethics and, 4:311–312

Canada, Montreal, 14:466

eighteenth and nineteenth centuries

religious and cultural differentiation, 9:237

religious reform, 9:238

England, 6:421, 427–429

Europe, 5:108–111, 115*t,* 116*t,* 117*t*

Germany, 5:109–110

Fuerth, 7:307

Hungary, 9:610–611, *611,* 618, 619

Buda, 4:245

Pest, 4:246

intermarriage, 10:809, 14:374–376, 378–379, 381–382

Iraq

Baghdad, 3:58

Basra, 3:205–206

Israel's influence upon, 5:121

Italy, 10:806, 809

Sicily, 18:542

Landesjudenschaft, Boehmische, 12:469

Landjudenschaft, 12:471–472

landsmannschaften, 12:477

Latin America, 5:113–114, 115*t,* 116*t,* 120*t*

majority rule, 13:415

Middle Ages, 5:102–108

cultural and spiritual life, 9:211–212, 218–220

economic and social patterns, 9:215

education, 9:220–221

education, Jewish, 6:176–177

ḥerem ha-Yishuv, 9:18–19

leadership, 9:210–211, 217–218

into the Millennium, 9:283–284

modern period, economic history, and role of, 6:125–126

Muslim countries, 5:103–105, 118*t*

Ottoman Empire, 5:106–108

Palestine (Mandate), 10:391–393, 392*t*

population numbers, 5:115*t,* 116*t*

post-World War II changes, 5:114–121, 117*t*

public relations, 16:712–713

Russia, 17:574, 577–579

Community, *continued*
  Russian Federation, 17:580–581
    Moscow, 14:520
  shammash, 18:395
  sixteenth and seventeenth
    centuries
      education, 9:224
      policies and aims, 9:225–227
      religious toleration, 9:225–
        227
      social confrontations, 9:225–
        227
  Spain
    Huesca, 9:578
    Majorca, 13:411
    Saragossa, 18:41
    Seville, 18:326
  theft and robberies, 19:690
  Ukraine, Lvov, 13:288–290
  U.S., 5:112–113, 115t, 116t, 119t
    Baltimore (MD), 3:97–100,
      98
    Chicago (IL), 4:607–612
    Cincinnati (OH), 4:727–730
    Cleveland (OH), 4:755–759
    Columbus (OH), 5:69–70
    Los Angeles (CA), 13:196–
      197
    Saint Louis (MO), 17:673
    San Diego (CA), 18:13–14
  See also Kelal Yisrael; *specific cities
    and countries*
*Community and Polity: The
  Organizational Dynamics of
  American Jewry* (Elazar), 6:289
Community tokens, 5:**121–122**
Como (Italy), 5:**122**
Comparative Education (Kandel),
  11:760
Comparative religion
  Emar texts, 6:386–390
  Flusser, David, 7:91
  Otto, Rudolph, 15:518
Comparative Social Problems
  (Eisenstadt), 6:271
Comparative tables of masorah in
  illuminated Spanish Hebrew Bibles,
  3:677
Compassion, 5:**122–123**
  See also Mercy
*The Compendium for the Servants of
  the Lord. See Kifayat al-abidin*
*Compendium grammatices linguae
  hebraeae* (Spinoza), 13:56
*Complete Dictionary of Ancient and
  Modern Hebrew* (Ben-Yehuda),
  3:387–388
Composers
  Abrass, Osias, 1:329, *329*

Achron, Joseph, 1:355–356
Adaskin, Murray, 1:384
Adler, Hugo Chaim, 1:399
Adler, Richard, 1:406–407
Admon, Yedidyah, 1:411
Adorno, Theodor W., 1:420
Alberstein, Hava, 1:588
Aldema, Gil, 1:606
Alexander, Haim, 1:622–623
Algazi, Isaac ben Solomon, 1:644
Algazi, Leon, 1:644–645
Alkan, Charles Henri-Valentin,
  1:665
Alman, Samuel, 1:678–679
Alpert, Herb, 1:688–689
Babbitt, Milton, 3:16–17
Babin, Victor, 3:21–22
Bacharach, Burt, 3:32
Bachmann, Jacob, 3:38
Bardanashvilli, Josef, 3:147
Barnett, John Francis, 3:169
Bauer, Marion Eugenie, 3:217
Beer, Aaron, 3:250–251
Bely, Victor Arkadyevich, 3:307–
  308
Benatzky, Ralph, 3:321
Bendix, Victor Emanuel, 3:328
Benedict, Sir Julius, 3:330
Ben-Haim, Paul, 3:350–351
Ben-Shabetai, Ari, 3:373–374
Bergel, Bernd, 3:418
Berggrün, Heinrich, 3:426
Bergman, Alan, 3:427
Bergman, Marilyn, 3:427
Berlinski, Herman, 3:461
Bernstein, Elmer, 3:478
Bernstein, Leonard, 3:480–481
Bertini, Gary, 3:490–491
Brant, Henry Dreyfuss, 4:129–130
Braun, Yehezkiel, 4:138
Brecher, Gustav, 4:156
Brod, Max, 4:192–193
Bruell, Ignaz, 4:221
Brussilovsky, Yevgeni
  Grigoryevich, 4:227–228
Caceres, Abraham, 4:330
Castelnuovo-Tedesco, Mario,
  4:515
Cervetto, Jacob Basevi, 4:551
Chagrin, Francis, 4:557
Chagy, Berele, 4:557
Chasins, Abraham, 4:581
Cherney, Brian, 4:595
Coleman, Cy, 5:56–57
Consolo, Federico, 5:180
Copland, Aaron, 5:212

Costa, Sir Michael, 5:234
Cowen, Sir Frederic Hymen, 5:255
David, Samuel, 5:464
Dessau, Paul, 5:604
Diamond, David, 5:632
Dobroven, Issay Alexandrovich,
  5:726
Dorati, Antal, 5:755
Dorfman, Joseph, 5:756
Dukas, Paul, 6:43
Dunayevski, Isaac Osipovich, 6:49
Edel Yizhak, 6:142
Ehrlich, Abel, 6:242
Eisler, Hanns, 6:275
Elfman, Danny, 6:314–315
Ellis, Vivian, 6:361
Ellstein, Abraham, 6:363
Erlanger, Camille, 6:480
Fall, Leo, 6:688
Fano, Guido Albert, 6:708–709
Feldman, Morton, 6:747
Fischhoff, Joseph, 7:56–57
Fleischer, Tsippi, 7:74
Fogelberg, Dan, 7:94
Foss, Lukas, 7:134–135
Frankel, Benjamin, 7:196
Freed, Isadore, 7:224
Freedman, Harry, 7:224–225
Hamlisch, Marvin, 8:305–306
Harnick, Sheldon, 8:360–361
Haubenstock-Ramati, Roman,
  8:460
Herman, Jerry, 9:23
Hermann, Bernard, 9:41
Herz, Henri, 9:51
Hirsh, Nurit, 9:141–142
Holdheim, Theodore, 9:317
Israel, 13:758
Jadassohn, Salomon, 11:57
Japhet, Israel Meyer, 11:85
Kaiser, Alois, 11:728
Kalman, Emmerich, 11:745
Karaczewski, Hanina, 11:785
Karel, Rudolph, 11:805
Karliner, Baruch, 11:810
Kuweiti, Salah, 12:400
Lakner, Yehoshua, 12:441–442
Lavry, Marc, 12:534–535
Leef, Yinam, 12:600
Lefkowitch, Henry, 17:150
Lefkowitz, David, 12:601–602
Leibowitz, René, 12:622
Leichtentritt, Hugo, 12:625
Lerner, Alan Jay, 12:656–657
Levant, Oscar, 12:678

Leviev, Manos, 4:264

Levistky, Mischa, 12:742

Lévy, Lazare, 12:752

Levy, Marvin David, 12:753

Lewandowski, Louis, 12:758

Liebermann, Rolf, 12:808–809

Lieberson, Goddard, 12:809

Liebling, Estelle, 12:809–810

Ligeti, Gyorgy, 13:12–13

Litinski, Genrikh Ilyich, 13:129

Liuzzi, Fernando, 13:143

Loesser, Frank, 13:162

Loewe, Frederick, 13:164

Lourie, Arthur, 13:226

Maykapar, Samuil Moyseyevich, 13:701

Mendelssohn, Arnold, 14:**32**

Mendelssohn, Felix, 14:**32–33**

Menken, Alan, 14:48–49

Meyerbeer, Giacomo, 14:150

Milhaud, Darius, 14:234

Milner, Moses Michael, 14:257–258

Miron, Issachar, 14:313–314

Morawetz, Oskar, 14:477–478

Moscheles, Ignaz, 14:516

musical theater, Yiddish, 19:680

Nathan, Isaac, 15:9

Natra, Sergiu, 15:32

Newman, Alfred, 15:145

Pergament, Moses, 15:770

Pisk, Paul Amadeus, 16:186

Radzynski, Jan, 17:61–62

Ran, Shulamit, 17:89

Rathaus, Karol, 17:109

Ravina, Menashe, 17:123

Ravitz, Shelomo, 17:124

Razumni, Ephraim Zalman, 17:133

Reich, Steve, 17:198

Reizenstein, Franz, 17:213

Réti, Rudolf, 17:244

Rieti, Vittorio, 17:298

Rivlin, Shelomo Zalman, 17:351

Rochberg, George, 17:357

Rodgers, Mary, 17:363–364

Rodgers, Richard, 17:364

Rogers, Bernard, 17:368

Roitman, David, 17:370

Roland-Manuel, 17:372

Romanos Melodos, 17:405

Romberg, Sigmund, 17:406

Rosenbaum, Samuel, 17:433

Rosenblatt, Josef, 17:441

Rosenmann-Taub, David, 17:449

Rosenthal, Manuel, 17:455

Rosowsky, Solomon, 17:468

Rossi, Salamone de', 17:473–474

Rothmueller, Aaron Marko, 17:487

Rózsavölgyi, Márk, 17:505

Rubens, Paul Alfred, 17:510

Rubinstein, Anton Grigoryevich, 17:516

Russell, Henry, 17:531

Sabzanov, Yahiel, 4:264

Sandler, Jacob Koppel, 18:16

Schalit, Heinrich, 18:104

Schidlowsky, Leon, 18:128

Schindler, Kurt, 18:136

Schnittke, Alfred, 18:151–152

Schorr, Baruch, 18:162–163

Schreker, Franz, 18:167–168

Schulhoff, Julius, 18:171–172

Schuller, Gunther, 18:172

Schuman, William Howard, 18:175

Schwartz, Stephen, 18:187

Secunda, Sholom, 18:233–234

Sedaka, Neil, 18:234

Seiber, Mátyás György, 18:253

Seter, Mordecai, 18:318

Shapero, Harold, 18:397–398

Sharett, Yehudah, 18:413

Shaw, Artie, 18:423

Shelem, Mattityahu, 18:445–446

Shemer, Naomi, 18:457

Sheriff, Noam, 18:462–463

Singer, George, 18:634

Sinigaglia, Leone, 18:641

Slonimsky, Sergei Mikhailovich, 18:680

Udakov, Solomon, 4:264

See also Musicians and dancers

Compounding offenses, 5:**123–124**

Comprado, Vidal Farissol. *See* Farissol, Jacob ben Ḥayyim

Comprat, Jacob Vidal Farissol. *See* Farissol, Jacob ben Ḥayyim

Compromise, 5:**124–129**

Compsus b. Compsus, 11:758

Compulsion (Levin), 12:712

Compulsion of another. *See* Duress

Compulsory baptism. *See* Forced baptism

Computer science, 5:**129–132**

Ellison, Lawrence J., 6:361–362

Jacobs, Irwin M., 11:47–48

ORT, 15:491

Pnueli, Amir, 16:243

Comrad Arthur. *See* Zygelbojm, Samuel Mordecai

Comrade of the Rabbis. *See* Ḥanina

Comtat Venaissin (France), 5:**132,** 7:121

La Comtesse de Chalis (Lévy), 12:746

Comtino, Mordecai ben Eliezer, 5:**132–133,** 11:783, 13:674–675

Comunidad Israelita Sefaradi, 18:313

Comverse USA, 1:623

Conat, Abraham ben Solomon, 5:**133**

Conat, Estellina, 5:133

Concentration camps. *See* Camps, concentration and extermination

Concentration Camp Survivors in Norway and Israel (Eitinger), 6:279

The Concept of God after Auschwitz (Jonas), 9:397

Concerned Jewish Students, 21:613

Concerning Intercalation and the Calendar. See Me-ha-Ibbur u-Minyan ha-Shanim

Concerning Jewish Affairs: the Emigration Question (Eismann), 6:276

Concerning the Jews (Alexander Polyhistor), 1:629

Concerto for Harp and Orchestra (composition, Morawetz), 14:478

Concerto for Spy and Orchestra (Adelman), 1:386

Concessions. *See* Arenda

Conciliador (Manasseh Ben Israel), 18:295

Concio, Joseph ben Gerson, 5:**133**

Conclusiones cabalisticae secundum opinionem propriam (Pico della Mirandola), 16:146–147

Concubines, 5:**133–136**

Conder, Claude Regnier, 5:**136,** 15:589

La condesa sangrienta (Pizarnik), 16:209

Conditions, legal, 5:**136–139**

Condorcet, un intellectuel en politique (Badinter), 3:49

Conductors

Algazi, Leon, 1:644–645 (*See also* Musicians and dancers)

Altschuler, Modest, 2:26

Barshai, Rudolf, 3:178

Benedict, Sir Julius, 3:330

Bernstein, Leonard, 3:480–481

Bertini, Gary, 3:490–491

Botstein, Leon, 4:104

Brant, Henry Dreyfuss, 4:129–130

Brecher, Gustav, 4:156

Buchwald, Theo, 4:244

Cooper, Emil Albertovich, 5:205

Costa, Sir Michael, 5:234

Cowen, Sir Frederic Hymen, 5:255

Conductors, *continued*
  Dobroven, Issay Alexandrovich, 5:726
  Dorati, Antal, 5:755
  Fitelberg, Grzegorz, 7:65
  Fleisher, Leon, 7:76
  Hermann, Bernard, 9:41
  Hiller, Ferdinand, 9:115
  Horenstein, Jascha, 9:525
  Inbal, Eliahu, 9:752
  Lavry, Marc, 12:534–535
  Leibowitz, René, 12:622
  Leinsdorf, Erich, 12:627
  Levi, Hermann, 12:688
  Levi, Yoel, 12:695
  Levine, James, 12:718
  Monteux, Pierre, 14:460
  Rodan, Mendi, 17:361–362
  Rodzinsky, Artur, 17:366
  Ronald, Sir Landon, 17:531
  Ronly-Riklis, Shalom, 17:419
  Rosenstock, Joseph, 17:450
  Rosenthal, Manuel, 17:455
  Rudel, Julius, 17:519
  Rudolf, Max, 17:524
  Schreker, Franz, 18:167–168
  Schwarz, Rudolf, 18:190
  Segal, Uri, 18:248
  Sendrey, Alfred, 18:287
  Sevitzky, Fabien, 18:329
  Shallon, David, 18:375
  Singer, George, 18:634
  Slatkin, Leonard, 18:666
  Solti, Sir Georg, 18:781
Cone, Caesar, 5:139
Cone, Claribel, 5:139
Cone, Etta, 5:139
Cone, Herman, 5:139
Cone, Moses and Caesar, and Cone Mills (NC), 15:302, 303
Cone, Moses Herman, 5:139
Cone family, 5:**139**
Conegliano (Italy), 5:**139–140**
Conegliano, Abraham Joel, 5:140
Conegliano, Carlo Angelo, 5:140
Conegliano, Emanuel. *See* Da Ponte, Lorenzo
Conegliano, Israel, 5:140, 15:541
Conegliano, Judah, 5:140
Conegliano, Solomon, 5:140
Conegliano family, 5:**140**
Conference of Jewish Charities. *See* The Jewish Communal Association of North America
Conference of Presidents of Major American Jewish Organizations, 4:462, 5:**140–143**, 9:304
  American Gathering of Jewish Holocaust Survivors, 2:49

Mizrachi Women's Organization of America, 2:80
Conference of the Workmen's Circle, 6:189
Conference on Jewish Material Claims Against Germany, 5:**143–145**, 7:124
  American Gathering of Jewish Holocaust Survivors, 2:49
  American Joint Distribution Committee, 2:62
  education, Jewish, 6:186
  See also Kent, Roman R.
Conference on Jewish Social Studies, 3:743, 5:**145**, 18:723
Conferences, 5:**145–147**
  See also names of specific conferences
Confession (Bakunin), 3:75
Confession of sins, 1:658, 5:**148–149**
  Abba bar Avina, 1:226
  Amidah, 2:75, 76
  Commandments, the 613, 5:75t
  Day of Atonement, 5:489, 490, 491, 493
  death, 5:511, 512, 513
  fasting and abstinence, 6:721
  forgiveness, 7:127
  Naḥman of Bratslav, 14:750
  Ne'ilah, 15:65
  repentance, 17:222
  sacrifice, 17:640
  seliḥot, 18:268, 269
Confessions, 5:**147–148**, 489
Confessions (Heine), 14:540
The Confessions of Zeno (Svevo), 19:334
Confino, Michael, 5:**150**
Confirmation. *See* Bar Mitzvah, Bat Mitzvah
Confirmation ceremony, 3:204
Confiscation, expropriation, forfeiture, 5:**150–151**
Conflagratio Sodomae (Saurius), 18:739
Conflict between Paganism and Christianity in the Fourth Century (Momigliano), 14:431
Conflict of laws, 5:**151–157**
  autonomy, judicial, 2:710–711
  civil marriage, 4:748
  foreign law applicability, 5:155–156
  indebtedness, 5:153–154
  Jewish, non-Jewish lawsuits, 5:155
  ketubbah bond, 5:154–155
  labor law, 5:153–154
  lawsuits, 5:155
  marriage and divorce, 5:152–153

  mishpat Ivri, 14:347
  wills, 5:156
Conflict of opinion, 5:157–158, **157–158**
The Conflict of the Church and the Synagogue (Parkes), 4:679–680
The Conformist (Bertolucci), 9:442
Conforte, David, 5:**158**, 11:728, 15:534
  Angel, Baruch, 2:147
  bibliography of, 3:681
Confusión de Confusiones (Penso de la Vega), 15:730
Confutazioni alle Saette del Gionata del Benetelli (Morpurgo), 14:510
Congregation of Notre Dame de Sion. *See* Sisters of Zion
Congregations, 5:**158–160**
  Congregation Beth Israel (Houston), 3:170
  Congregation Emanu-El (CA), 2:561
  Congregation Yeshuat Israel (Newport, RI), 15:153
  Holy Congregation in Jerusalem, 9:498–499
  Sisters of Zion, 17:111–112
Congresses of National Minorities, 6:88
Congress for Jewish Culture, 5:**160–161**
Congressional representatives
  Bacharach, Isaac, 3:33
  Beilenson, Anthony Charles, 3:265–266
  Berger, Victor, 3:426
  Berkley, Rochelle, 3:437
  Berman, Howard Lawrence, 3:461
  Cantor, Eric, 4:439–440
  Cardin, Benjamin Louis, 4:462
  Celler, Emanuel, 4:537
  Chudoff, Earl, 4:708
  Dickstein, Samuel (1885-1954), 5:646
  Engel, Eliot L., 6:408
  Frank, Barney, 7:179
  Holtzman, Elizabeth J., 9:497–498
  Kahn, Florence Prag, 11:720
  Kahn, Julius, 11:721–722
  Lantos, Tom, 12:486–487
  Lehman, William, 12:614
  Levin, Lewis Charles, 12:710
  Levin, Sander, 12:713
  Lowey, Nita Melnikoff, 13:235–236
  Morse, Leopold, 14:513
  Neuberger, H. Maurine, 15:116
  Sanders, Bernard, 18:11–12

San Diego, 18:15

Schakowsky, Janice D., 18:104

Scheuer, James H., 18:124–125

Schiff, Adam, 18:128–129

Solarz, Stephen, 18:752

Congressional representatives (U.S.)

  Ackerman, Gary, 1:357

Congress Monthly (periodical), 2:58

Congress of Argentinian Jewry, 2:430

Congress of Berlin, 3:**453–454**, 6:375, 381–382

Congress of Vienna, 9:232, 13:255, 20:**523–524**

Coniah. *See* Jehoiachin (King of Judah, 6th c. B.C.E.)

Conian. *See* Conegliano family

Conical seals, 18:226

Coningsby (Disraeli), 5:700

Conjeturas Sagradas (Acosta), 1:359

Conjoint Foreign Committee. *See* Anglo-Jewish Association (AJA)

Conjugations in Hebrew, 8:587–589

Conn, Catherine. *See* Hart, Kitty Carlisle

Connecticut (U.S.), 5:*161*, **161–162**

  Bridgeport, 4:180

  Judah family, 11:479–480

  Norwalk and Westport, 15:304–305

Conon I, 5:**162**

Conon II, 5:**162**

The Conquerer (Reder), 17:156

Conquest of Canaan. *See* Canaan, Land of

Conrad, Victor, 5:**162–163**

Conradus Aslacus Bergensis. *See* Aslakssen, Cort

Conried, Heinrich, 5:**163**

Consanguinity, 6:691–692

Conscription

  Amsterdam, 2:110

  Angaria, 2:146

  cantonists, 4:437–439

  of labor, 12:409

  See also Military service

Consecration. *See* Hekdesh

Consejos y documentos al rey don Pedro. See Proverbios morales

Conservation, 5:**163–171**

Conservative Judaism, 5:**171–177**, 20:350, 365–366

  Agus, Jacob B., 1:521–522

  angels, 2:161

  Argentina, 2:439, 447

  Canada, 4:410, 416

    Montreal, 14:465

  contemporary, 11:519

converts, 5:176, 16:593

dietary laws and, 5:658

education, Jewish, 6:198

gender equality, 6:753

halakhah and concept of Judaism, 11:518–519

ḥazzanim, 8:505

Israel (state), 10:628–629, 636

Jewish Theological Seminary, 11:328–331

Kaplan, Mordecai Menahem, 11:777, 779

ketubbot, 12:97

liturgy, 8:359

Maḥzor for Rosh Hashanah and Yom Kippur, 8:359

mixed marriage, intermarriage, 14:376–377, 381

niddah, 15:257

Oral Law, 15:457–458

periodicals, 11:241

prayers

  Hazkarat neshamot, 8:497

  morning benedictions, 14:492

  prayer books, 16:466–467

Rabbinical Assembly, 6:23, 15:120, 17:20

rabbinical training

  The Institute of Traditional Judaism, 17:26

  Jewish Theological Seminary of America, 17:25–26

  Union of Traditional Judaism, 17:26

  Ziegler School of Rabbinic Studies at the Univ. of Judaism, 17:26

rabbis

  Abramowitz, Herman, 1:325

  Adler, Morris, 1:403

  Agus, Jacob B., 1:521–522

  Aronson, David, 2:487–488

  Arzt, Max, 2:540

  Berman, Myron R., 3:464

  Bettelheim, Albert Siegfried, 3:551

  Blumenthal, Aaron H., 4:12

  Bohnen, Eli Aaron, 4:42

  Bokser, Ben Zion, 4:44

  Bosniak, Jacob, 4:98

  Burstein, Abraham, 4:301

  Cantor, Bernard, 4:439

  Cass, Samuel, 4:507

  Chanover, Hyman, 4:566

  Chiel, Arthur Abraham, 4:614–615

  Chiel, Samuel, 4:615

Cohen, Armond E., 5:9

Cohen, Mortimer Joseph, 5:29

Cohen, Seymour J., 5:34

Davidson, Max David, 5:477

Dresner, Samuel Hayim, 6:11–12

Drob, Max, 6:22–23

Eichler, Menahem Max, 6:247

Eilberg, Amy, 6:253–254

Epstein, Gilbert, 6:469–470

Epstein, Harry H., 6:470

Epstein, Louis M., 6:475

Feinberg, Louis, 6:738

Finkelstein, Louis, 7:34–35

Friedman, Theodore, 7:284

Geffen, Joel, 7:410–411

Gelb, Max, 7:418

Ginzberg, Louis, 7:613–614

Goldfeder, Fishel, 7:705

Goldman, Israel, 7:712

Goldman, Solomon, 7:713–714

Goldstein, Israel, 7:729

Golinkin, David, 7:739

Goodblat, Morris, 7:754–755

Gordon, Albert I., 7:766–767

Greenberg, Louis, 8:71

Greenberg, Sidney, 8:73

Greenberg, Simon, 8:73–74

Hailperin, Herman, 8:238–239

Halpern, Harry, 8:284

Hammer, Reuven, 8:308

Harf, Hanns, 8:354

Harlow, Julius, 8:359

Hauptman, Judith, 8:461

Hershman, Abraham M., 9:46

Hertzberg, Arthur, 9:49

Higger, Michael, 9:98

Karp, Abraham J., 11:815

Kauvar, Charles Eliezer Hillel, 12:37–38

Kelman, Wolfe, 12:71

Kieval, Hayyim, 12:153

Klein, Isaac, 12:222

Kogen, David, 12:256

Kohn, Jacob, 12:263

Kreitman, Benjamin Zvi, 12:350–351

Kurtz, Vernon H., 12:394

Kushner, Harold S., 12:396–397

Lehrman, Irving, 12:617–618

Levi, Samuel Gershon, 12:692–693

Conservative Judaism, *continued*

Levitsky, Louis Moses, 12:742

Lieber, David, 12:803–804

Malev, William S., 12:431

Mandelbaum, Bernard, 13:459–460

Matt, C. David, 13:684–685

Mayer, Marshall T., 14:148

Minkin, Jacob Samuel, 14:281

Morais, Sabato, 14:471

Nadich, Judah, 14:724–725

Neulander, Arthur H., 15:120

Noveck, Simon, 15:318

Parzen, Herbert, 15:674

Pressman, Jacob, 16:506–507

Rabinowitz, Stanley, 17:41–42

Roth, Joel, 17:482

Routtenberg, Max Jonah, 17:499

Rubenovitz, Herman H., 17:509–510

Sandrow, Edward T., 18:17–18

Sarachek, Joseph, 18:41

Schechter, Solomon, 18:113–114

Schild, Edwin, 18:132–133

Segal, Bernard, 18:244–245

Shapiro, Alexander M., 18:403–404

Shubow, Joseph Shalom, 18:528–529

Shuchat, Wilfred G., 18:529

Siegel, Seymour, 18:556

Silverman, Morris, 18:587

Silverstein, Alan, 18:588

Simon, Ralph, 18:616

Slonim, Reuben, 18:677–678

Solomon, Elias Louis, 18:764

Stampfer, Joshua, 19:160

Steinberg, Milton, 19:188–189

Sternstein, Joseph Philip, 19:223

Teplitz, Saul I., 19:644–645

Waxman, Mordecai, 20:690–691

Wolpe, Howard, Eliot III, 21:154–155

Zelizer, Nathan, 21:500–501

Schechter, Solomon, 18:113–114

Siddur Sim Shalom, 8:359

South Africa, 19:45

United Synagogue (London), 20:404–405

United Synagogue of America, 18:244

United Synagogue of Conservative Judaism, 20:405–406

University of Judaism, 20:411–413

U.S., 2:45

Bergen County (NJ), 3:423

growth, 6:698

New York City, 15:218

Philadelphia, 16:35, 36, 37

Saint Louis, 17:671–672

San Francisco, 18:19

San Gabriel-Pomona Valleys, 18:21

summer camps, 11:272–273

women

cantors, 8:505

gender equality, 6:753

Kaddish recitation by, 11:698

lesbianism, 12:661

prayer, role in, 16:461

separation of, in synagogues, 13:771

Women's League for Conservative Judaism, 21:209–210

See also Masorti

Conservative Judaism (periodical), 6:11

Conservative Party, German. *See* German Conservative Party

Consideration in contracts, 5:190–191

Consideratio reponsionis judaicae ad viginti tres quaestiones, 4:765

Consigli, Avtalyon ben Solomon, 5:**177–178**

Consigli, Ottavio. *See* Consigli, Avtalyon ben Solomon

Consistent empiricism. *See* Logical positivism

Consistoire. *See* Consistory

Consistory, 5:*178,* 178–180, 7:155

Consolaçam as Tribulaçoens de Israel (Usque), 9:156, 225, 18:295, 20:433–434

Consolo, Federico, 5:**180**

Consonants in Hebrew, 8:560–565

La conspiracion de los idiotas (Aguinis), 1:510

Constance (Germany), 3:43, 5:**180**

Constanta (Romania), 5:**180–181**

Constantine (Algeria), 5:**181,** 6:7

Constantine I the Great (Roman emperor)

Aelia Capitolina, 11:152

crucifixion abolished, 4:326, 5:309

Greece, 8:45

"The New Jerusalem," 11:219

Constantine VII Porphyrogenitus, 5:**181,** 15:364

Constantiner, Jaime, 5:**181–182**

Constantini, Humberto, 5:**182**

Constantinople (Turkey), 5:**182–183**

Adjiman family, 1:392

conquest by Ottoman empire, 15:521–522

Fourth Crusade, 4:327

halukkah, 8:287

printing, publishing, 16:536

See also Istanbul (Turkey)

Constellation. See Sozvezdiye

Constitutional law, 12:407

Constitutio pro Judaeis, 3:122

Construction, 5:**183–184,** 264–265, 12:602, 742–743, 16:**215–219**

Construction and building, 18:752–753

Construction Studies: On the Construction of the Golden Chain (Erik), 6:479

Consumer protection, 5:**184–189**

Consumer's League, 15:10

Contemplation, 13:761

Contemporary English Version (Bible), 3:621

Contemporary Jewish Documentation Center, 9:428

Contemporary Jewry (journal), 18:734

Contempt of court, 5:**189**

The Contender (Lipsyte), 13:76

Continuous revelation, 15:494

Contraception. *See* Birth control

Contract law, 5:**189–198**

Asmakhta, 2:590–592

breach and compensation, 5:195

conditions, legal, 5:136, 137, 138, 139

consideration, 5:190–191

customs, influence of, 5:192–193

Elephantine Papyri, 6:312–313

embryos, 6:392

gifts, 7:591

illegal contracts, 5:193–194

imprisonment for debt, 9:748, 749

interpretation of, 9:823–824

labor law, 12:412–419

lease and hire, 12:568–574, 569, 571–573

loans, 13:149, 151

maintenance, 13:399, 400

marriage, 9:638, 13:564, 571, 575, 576

Mishpat Ivri, 14:334, 342, 345, 347, 348, 356

mistakes, 14:367–369, 369

obligations, 5:190, 191–192, 192–193, 15:369, 370, 372–373, 373–374, 374

ona'ah, contracting out of, 15:424

partnerships, 15:669, 671

performance, 5:194–195

servant, 12:412–415

stipulation, 5:193

suretyship, 19:318, 321, 322

usury, 20:438, 439, 440, 443

Contractors, 5:**198–200**

Contractors and suppliers, court, 5:246–248

Contracts. *See* Contract law

A Contract with God (Eisner), 6:277–278

Contra la Verdad no hay Fuerça (Barrios), 18:295

Contra perfidiam Judaeorum (Peter of Blois), 16:15

The Control of Fire (Brentano), 4:162

Controversialists, Spanish, 4:496

Controversy. *See* Conflict of opinion

The Controversy between the Karaites and the Rabbanites (Elijah ben Abraham), 6:338

The Conventional Lies of Our Civilization. See Die Conventionellen Luegen der Kulturmenschheit

Die Conventionellen Luegen der Kulturmenschheit (Nordau), 15:297

Conversion

    Abdallah ibn Salām, 1:241

    abductions, Mortara case, 14:513

    ablution, 2:262

    Abner of Burgos, 1:264

    Alboraycos, 1:595

    Bourges, 4:106

    Brzesc Kujawksi, 4:230

    to Christianity

        Boerne, Ludwig, 4:32

        Bogrov, Grigori Isaakovich, 4:37

        Bonafed, Solomon ben Reuben, 4:53–54

        Bonjorn, Davi Bonet, 4:63

        Bossuet, Jacques Benigne, 4:99

        Catholic Church, 4:710–711

        Dialogi... in quibus judaeorum opiniones... confutanur (Petrus Alfonsi), 16:21

        Draguignan, 6:6

        Levertoff, Paul Philip, 12:681

        Lustiger, Jean-Marie Aron, 13:271

        Raymond de Penaforte, 17:127

    Dutch literature and, 6:70

    Holy Cross Day (Browning), 4:218

    Italy, 1930s, 10:803

    Izates, 1:391

to Judaism, Roman period, 10:795–796, *796*

laws of, 12:544–545, 16:587–589

    medieval Spain, 5:437

        Maimonides ethical teachings and, 6:528

    officials, 14:6

    sermons to Jews, 18:312–313

    See also Crypto-Jews; Forced conversion; Proselytes

Conversion from Judaism. *See* Apostasy

Conversion to Judaism. *See* Proselytes

Conversos, 3:**52,** 4:645, 5:**200**

    banking, moneylending, 3:113–114, 18:9

    Barcelona, 3:144

    Burgos, 4:290

    Canary Islands, 4:428–429

    Carvajal, Luis de, 4:501

    Castro Quesada, Americo, 4:519

    Cervantes Saavedra, Miguel de, 4:550

    Ciudad Real, 4:745

    communities, 13:760

    France, 7:153

    Huesca, 9:578

    Jesuits and, 11:245

    Juan de Ciudad, 11:472

    Lagos, 12:437

    La Palma, 15:603

    Lima (Peru), 13:20

    Mexico, 14:138–139

    Móntoro, Antón de, 14:462

    Orobio de Castro, Isaac, 15:481–482

    Portugal, 4:469

    Santangel family, 18:28

    Spain, 1:611, 9:209

        Alboraycos, 1:595

        Almagro, 1:678

        Barbastro, 3:140

        Cádiz, 4:331

        Calatayud, 4:351–352

        Calatrava Order, 4:352

        Castile, 1:643

        Ciudad Real, 4:745

        Córdoba, 5:218–219

        Écija, 6:91

        Guadalupe, 8:116

        Herrera de Pisuegra, 9:41

        Lérida, 12:654–655

        Madrid, 13:333

        Majorca, 13:413

        Ocaña, 15:375

        Orihuela, 15:474

        Palencia, 15:577

        Palermo, 15:581

        Saragossa, 18:43–44, 45

        Seville, 18:328

        Toledo, 18:57–58

    See also Marranos; New Christians

Conversos on Trial (Beinart), 3:269

Converts. *See* Proselytes

Convocation. *See* Congregations

Cook, Samuel, 5:**200**

Cook, Stanley Arthur, 5:**200**

Cookbooks, Jewish. *See* Jewish cookbooks

Cooke, George Albert, 5:**203**

Cooking and baking, 5:**203–204**

    Jewish style, 7:117–118

    Passover, 15:681

    utensils, 5:203

Coonskin (Bakshi), 3:74

Cooper, Alexander, 5:**204**

Cooper, Emil Albertovich, 5:**205**

Cooper, Jackie, 5:**205**

Cooper, John, Jr. *See* Cooper, Jackie

Cooper, Leon N., 5:**205**

Cooper, Morris, 4:213

Cooperatives, 5:**205–211,** 9:147–148

    See also Kibbutz movement

Copé, Jean-François, 5:**211**

Copeland, Lillian, 5:**211**

Copenhagen (Denmark), 5:**211–212,** 7:54

Copenhagen, Aaron Simeon, 4:760

Coper, Hans, 17:293

Copisarow, Maurice, 5:**212**

Copland, Aaron, 5:**212,** 15:220

Coponius, 5:**212–213**

Copper, 14:125, 127

Copperfield, David, 5:**213**

Copper scroll, 5:**213–214,** 505

Copper serpent, 5:**214–215,** 8:480

    Moses, 14:528

    Nehushtan, 15:64

Coppersmith, Sam, 5:**215**

Coptic Church, Israel, 10:639

Coptic language, 3:602, 18:280

Copulas, 8:602, 612–613

Copyright law, 8:450–451, 453

Coqui, Adolphe, 16:349

Corach, Carlos, 16:350

Coral, 5:**215**

Coralnik, Abraham, 4:111, 5:**216**

Corbeil (France), 5:**216**

Corbin, Solange, 4:436

Corcos, Abraham, 14:499

Corcos, David, 5:**217**

Corcos, Hezekiah Manoah Ḥayyim the Younger, 5:**217**

Corcos, Joshua, 5:216

Corcos, Stella, 5:**217**

Corcos, Tranquillo Victor. *See* Corcos, Hezekiah Manoah Ḥayyim the Younger

Corcos, Vittorio, 5:**218**

Corcos family, 5:**216–217**, 16:346

Córdoba (Argentina), 5:**219**

Córdoba (Spain), 5:**218–219**

Córdoba, Alonso Fernandez de, 4:75, 5:**219–220**

Cordova (Spain). *See* Córdoba (Spain)

Cordova, Abraham Guer de. *See* Escudero, Lorenzo

Cordovero, Gedaliah ben Moses, 5:**220**, 13:188, 18:451

Cordovero, Moses ben Jacob, 4:128, 5:**220–221**, 11:616

    Abraham ben Isaac of Granada, 1:301

    Alkabeẓ, Solomon ben Moses ha-Levi, 1:662

    Joseph della Raina legend, 11:428

Core Knowledge Foundation, 9:125

Corfu (Greece), 5:**221–223**

Cori, Gerty Theresa, 5:**223**, 13:10

Coriander, 5:**223**, vol. 16: color insert

Coriat, Abraham, 5:223

Coriat, Isaac, 5:223

Coriat, Judah, 5:223

Coriat, Nissim, 5:223

Coriat, Samuel, 5:223

Coriat, Solomon, 5:223

Coriat family, 5:**223**

Corinth (Greece), 5:**223–224**

Corinthian Gate. *See* Nicanor's gate (Jerusalem)

Corky's Brother (*Neugeboren*), 15:119

Corn. *See* Five species

Cornea, Paul, 5:**224**

Corneal transplants, 20:106–107

Corneas, grafting of, 3:755

Cornforth, John Warcup, 3:765

Cornill, Carl Heinrich, 5:**224**

Coro (Venezuela), 5:**224–225**

Coron (Greece). *See* Korone (Greece)

Coronel, Fernando Nuñez. *See* Seneor, Abraham

Coronel, Fernando Peréz. *See* Melamed, Meir

Coronel, Naḥman Nathan, 4:252, 5:**225**

Coronel Chacon, Augustin. *See* Coronel Chacon, Sir Augustin

Coronel Chacon, Sir Augustin, 5:**225**

Corporal punishment of children, 15:640

Corporation, legal person, 12:**604–608**

Corpses

    anatomy, 2:133–134

    ritual impurity, *Oholot*, 15:394

    See also Burial customs

Corpus inscriptionum hebraicarum (Chwolson), 4:724–725

Corpus Inscriptionum Judaicarum (Frey), 6:464

Correa, Isabel de, 5:225, 225, 15:408

Correa, Rebecca. *See* Correa, Isabel de

Correction. *See* Rebuke and reproof

The Correct Syllogism. See Ha-Hekkesh ha-Yashar (Gershom)

Correspondence. *See* Letters and letter writers

Corriere Israelitico (newspaper), 12:519

Corsica (Mediterranean), 5:**225**

Corsono, Judah. *See* Alcorsono, Judah ben Joseph

Cortes, Fernando, 2:41

Coruniya. *See* Corunna

Corunna (Spain), 5:**225–226**

Corvée, 5:**226**

Corwin, Norman Lewis, 5:**226–227**

Cos (Greece). *See* Kos (Greece)

Cosaşu, Radu, 5:**227**

Cosel (Poland). *See* Kozle (Poland)

Cosell, Howard, 5:**227–228**

Cosenza (Italy), 5:**228**

Coser, Lewis A., 5:**228**, 18:709

Coser, Rose Laub, 5:**228–229**, 18:736

Cosigner. *See* Suretyship

Cosman, I., 3:631

Cosmas of Prague, 4:37

Cosmetics, 5:**229–231**

    Lauder, Estée, 12:525

    Max Factor & Company, 6:674–675

    Rubinstein, Helena, 17:517

Cosmic cycles. *See* Sabbatical Year and Jubilee

Cosmogony in the Bible, 1:278, 5:**273–280**

Cosmology, 5:**231–232**

    biblical, 5:486–488

    emanation and creation, 6:372–374

    matter and form, 7:324–326

    physics and, 16:141

Cosmopolitans, 5:**232**

Cossack massacres. *See* Chmielnicki, Bogdan

Costa, Alvaro da, 5:232

Costa, Anthony, 5:232

Costa, Catherine da, 5:**233**

Costa, Emanuel Mendes da, 5:**233**

Costa, Isaäc da, 2:112, 5:**233–234**, 6:70

Costa, James Lopes da. *See* Tirado, Jacob

Costa, Michael. *See* Costa, Sir Michael

Costa, Sir Michael, 5:**234**

Costa, Uriel da, 5:**234–235**, 11:294

Costa Athias, Solomon da, 5:**235**

Costa de Mattos, Vincente da, 5:**235**

Costa family, 5:**232**, 9:6

Costa Rica, 4:475, 5:**235–237**

Costello, Lou, 1:236–237

Costobar, 5:**237**

The Cost of Accidents: A Legal and Economic Analysis (Calabresi), 4:348

Costume. *See* Dress

Cota de Maguaque, Rodrigo de, 5:**237**

Cothino family. *See* Coutinho family

Cotinio family. *See* Coutinho family

Cotinsio family. *See* Coutinho family

Cotler, Irwin, 5:**237**, 14:464, 16:341

Cottbus (Germany), 5:**237–238**

Cotton, 5:**238**

Cotton, Jack, 5:**238**

The Cotton Genesis, 3:674, 675

Cottonseed Oil. *See* Castor-oil plant

Coudenhove-Kalergi, Heinrich von, 5:**238**

Coudenhove-Kalergi, Richard Nicholas von, 5:238

Coughlin, Charles E., 4:99, 713–714, 15:215

Council for Jewish Federations (CJF). *See* Council of Jewish Federations and Welfare Funds

Council of Education and Culture (Brazil), 6:212

Council of Four Lands, 5:**238**, 239–240, 6:144, 686, 11:739–740

    Abraham ben Ḥayyim, 1:300

    Abraham ben Isaac ha-Kohen of Zamość, 1:301

    Abraham ben Joseph of Lissa, 1:303

    Isaiah Menahem ben Isaac, 10:78

    Kamenets-Podolski, 11:753

    See also Council of the Lands

Council of Israeli Organizations, 13:199

Council of Jewish Communities, 5:360

Council of Jewish Federations and Welfare Funds, 4:463, 5:**238–239**, 11:761, 13:269, 20:257

Council of Jews from Germany, 5:**239**, 12:642

Council of Lithuania, 4:457

Council of Settlements of Judea, Samaria, and Gaza, 8:353
Council of the Lands, 5:**239–245**, *241*, 13:242, 245
  autonomy, 2:708–709
  Brest-Litovsk, 4:169
  Brody, 4:199
  captives, ransoming of, 4:457
  elder, 6:296
  fines, 7:28
  imprisonment for debt, 9:750
  Jaroslaw, 11:88
  jurisdiction of, 3:515
  Kalisz, 11:739
  Lesser Poland, 12:664
  Lutsk (Ukraine), 13:273
  Lvov (Ukraine), 13:289
  market days and fairs, 13:550
  Poland, 16:296, 297, 298, 299, 300
  ransoming of captives, 4:457
  Samogitia, 17:747
  shtadlan, 18:522
  Slonik, Benjamin Aaron ben Abraham, 18:675
  sumptuary laws, 19:313
  takkanot, 19:449
  taxation, 19:533
  taxes, 7:23
  Vilna, 20:529
  Volhynia, 20:571, 572
  See also Council of Four Lands
Council of Thirty, 3:142–143
Council of Trent. *See* Trent (Italy)
Councils of Christians and Jews (CCJs), 11:281
Counter-Enlightenment, 14:39
Counterfactual thought (alternate history), 18:206
Counter-Reformation
  in Bologna, 4:48
  in Rome, 17:413
The Countess Maritza (Kalman), 11:745
Courant, Richard, 5:**245**
Courland (Latvia), 5:**245–246**, 15:694
Cournos, John, 5:**246**
Cours de thermodynamique (Lippmann), 13:70
Court jesters, 1:359
Court Jews, 5:**246–248**
  Ansbach, 2:180
  Baruch ben David Yavan, 3:188
  Bassevi of Treuenberg, Jacob, 3:208–209
  Behrends, Leffmann, 3:264
  Behrens, Leffman, 8:330

Breidenbach, Wolf, 4:157
  coinage, 14:300
  diamond trade and industry, 5:635
  economic history, 6:120–121
  Eichthal-Seligmann family, 6:252
  Fraenkel, Elkan, 7:144
  Germany, 4:63, 6:42, 7:526, 13:69
  Hamon, Moses, 8:311–312
  Haskalah, 8:435, *435*, 9:*237*
  Informers, 9:781
  Lehmann, Behrend, 8:263, 12:614–615
  Lichtenstadt, Abraham Aaron, 12:797–798
  Liebmann, Esther Schulhoff Aaron, 12:810–811
  Liebmann, Jost, 12:810–811
  Lippe, 13:69
  mintmasters and moneyers, 14:300
  Model, Marx, 14:406–407
  moneylending, 14:441
  Oppenheimer, Joseph ben Issachar Suesskind, 15:449
  Oppenheimer, Samuel, 15:450–451
  in Ottoman empire, 15:541–542
  railroads, 17:69
  Schlesinger family, 18:139
  Smol of Derenburg, 18:690
  Spain, 19:69–75, 78, 79
Court rabbi. *See* Rab de la Corte
Courts
  community, 5:495
  Labor, 12:415–419
  majority rule, 13:415
  See also Bet din and judges; Supreme Court
Courts, Jewish. *See* Bet din and judges
Coutinho, Francisco de Sousa, 5:248
Coutinho, Gonsalvo Lopes, 5:249
Coutinho, Henriquez, 5:249
Coutinho, Lourença, 5:249
Coutinho, Moses ben Abraham Mendes, 5:248
Coutinho, Sebastian, 5:248
Coutinho family, 5:**248–249**
Couty, Rabba, 15:196
Covenant, 5:**249–253**, 8:375, 15:732–733, 734, 750
  Abraham and David, 5:251–252
  adoption, 1:417
  Borowitz, Eugene B., 4:93
  chosen people doctrine, 4:669–670
  Decalogue, 5:521, 525
  Ezekiel, 5:638, 640, 643
  forgiveness of sin, 7:127–128
  in Genesis, 7:445–446

Holiness Code, 9:318, 319
  Hosea, Book of, 9:547, 548, 549, 550, 551, 554, 558
  idolatry, 9:712
  Israel, 5:249–251
  kings and kingship, 12:164, 165, 168
  Mari, 13:539
  Moses, 14:528–529
  Noah, 15:287
  oaths, 15:359, 360
  Pentateuch, 15:732, 733, 734, 735, 737, 738, 739, 743, 744, 745, 746, 750
  prophetic literature, 5:252–253
  prophets and prophecy, 16:567, 568, 579, 580
  sin, 18:622
  Sinai, 6:616–617, 618, 623
  sukkot, 19:299, 300
Covenant of Blood: Circumcision and Gender in Rabbinic Judaism (Hoffman), 9:309
Covenant of Omar, 9:209, 14:444, 15:**416–419**, 18:271
  Jewish quarters, 11:312
The Covenant of Rest. See Berit Menuḥah
Covenant of Shechem, Joshua, Book of, 11:449
Coverdale, Miles, 3:612
Cover-up: the Army's Secret Investigation of the Massacre at My Lai 4 (Hersch), 9:44
Covetousness, 5:**254**
Covilhā (Portugal), 5:**254**
Covington, Harold, 15:79
Covo, Elijah, 5:254
Covo, Isaac ben Hezekiah Joseph, 5:254
Covo, Isaac ben Joseph Hezekiah, 5:254–255
Covo, Jacob Hananiah, 5:255
Covo, Jacob Joseph, 5:255
Covo, Joseph ben Shemaiah, 5:254
Covo, Joseph Hezekiah ben Isaac, 5:254
Covo, Judah (d. 1636), 5:254
Covo, Judah (d. 1907), 5:255
Covo, Raphael Asher, 5:255
Covo, Raphael Ḥayyim Abraham, 5:254
Covo family, 5:**254–255**
Cowen, Frederick Hymen. *See* Cowen, Sir Frederic Hymen
Cowen, Joseph, 5:**255**
Cowen, Philip, 5:**255**
  The American Hebrew, 2:49

Cowen, Philip, *continued*
  American Jewish Historical
    Society, 2:59
Cowen, Sir Frederic Hymen, 5:**255**
Cowen, Zelman, 5:**255–256**, 16:340
Cowley, Arthur Ernest. *See* Cowley, Sir
  Arthur Ernest
Cowley, Sir Arthur Ernest, 5:**256**
Cows. *See* Cattle
Cows, red. *See* Red heifers
Cozbi, 5:**256**
Cozeba (ancient Israel), 5:**256**
Crachuneşti family. *See* Kretchnif
  family
Crackpot (Wiseman), 4:424
Cracow (Poland), 5:**256–263**, 260,
  261*t*
  archives, 2:408
  Austrian era, 5:260–261
  Epstein, Kalonymus Kalman of
    Cracow, 6:474–475
  Fishel family, 7:61–62
  Holocaust, 5:262–263, 16:311
  Polish era, 5:259–260
  printing, 5:261
  post WW I, 5:260–261
Crafts, 5:**263–272**, 269*t*
  artistic, 2:496
  biblical period, 5:263–264
  bootmaking, 12:631
  dress, 6:16, 17
  freemasons, 7:228
  Greece, 8:49, 50
  guilds, 8:128–129
  ḥazakah, 8:490
  ḥerem ha-yishuv, 9:18
  Israel (ancient), 9:185
  Israel (land of), 10:148, 154, 159,
    160, 170
  Israel (Mandate), 10:711
  Israel (State), 10:696
    1880-1948, 10:192
    vs. agriculture, 10:557, 558,
      559
    Bezalel School of Arts and
      Crafts, 10:653
    in early settlement, 10:606
    education, 10:604, 654
    Histadrut and, 10:597
    vs. manufacturing, 10:503,
      504
    Notre Dame of Jerusalem
      Center, 10:643
    Samaria, 10:381
    Schatz, Boris, 10:695
    West Bank, 10:718
  Kenite, 12:76

Middle Ages, 5:265–269
modern period, 5:269–272, 270*t*,
  271*t*, 272*t*
Phoenicians, 16:123
Talmudic period, 5:264–265
Wadi al-Naṭṭūf, 20:593
Yemen, 21:305, 306, 307, 309
craftsmen. *See* Guilds
Craiova (Romania), 5:**272**
Cranach, Lucas, 14:542
Crane, C. R., 15:582
Cranes, 5:**272**
Cranganore (India), 5:**272–273**
Cranko, John, 5:**273**
Cranz, August Friedrich, 14:37–38
Crassus, Marcus Licinius, 5:**273**
Crato, Prior of. *See* Antonio
Crawford College, 6:211
Creation
  Abrabanel, Isaac ben Judah, 1:278
  Abraham bar Ḥiyya, 1:292, 293
  Aristobulus on, 2:459
  attitudes towards, 5:163–165
  Bet Shammai, Bet Hillel, 5:275–
    276
  biblical cosmogony, 5:273–280
  cause and effect, 4:528–529
  Crescas' view, 5:278–279
  emanation and, 6:374
  in Genesis, 7:445–446, 447*t*
  Gerondi formulation, 7:549
  God in, 7:653–654
  Ḥasidic ideas, 8:408
  hierarchy in, 5:165–166
  hymns to, 15:760
  interpretations, Philo Judaeus,
    16:61–62
  Jewish Aristotelianism, 2:461
  Karaite view of, 14:737
  Levi ben Gershom view, 12:699–
    700
  Maimonides, Moses, 13:390
  Maimonides view, 2:461, 5:278
  Mesopotamia, 5:274–275
  modern thought, 5:279
  neoplatonic view, 5:277–278,
    10:752
  philosophical analysis of, 16:72–
    73, 75, 82, 85, 88
  Rabbinical literature, 5:275–277
  See also Evolution
Creation and the Persistence of Evil
  (Levenson), 12:679
Creative Artists Agency (CAA), 15:549
Credence clause (shetar), 18:468
Credit and creditors
  Court Jews, 5:246–248

merchants, 16:298–299
See also Obligations, law of
Crédit Mobilier, 15:759, 17:69
Creditor. *See* Moneylending
Credit unions, 7:20
Créhange, A. Ben-Baruch, 3:629
Créhange, Alexandre, 5:**280**
Creizenach, Michael, 5:**280–281**,
  15:457
CREJ (Comité Representativo de las
  Entidades Judías), 4:640
Cremation, 5:**281**
Crematorium, 9:*484*
Crémieu (France), 5:**281–282**
Crémieux, A., 12:550, 15:529
Crémieux, Adolphe. *See* Crémieux,
  Isaac Adolphe
Crémieux, Benjamin, 5:**282**
Crémieux, Isaac Adolphe, 5:**282–283**,
  12:678, 777, 16:343
Crémieux Decree, 15:459, 460
Crémieux family. *See* Karmi family
Cremin, Lawrence Arthur, 5:**283**
Cremona (Italy), 5:**283–284**, 13:177
Creolized languages, 11:302
Crescas (Elisha ben Abraham ben
  Benveniste ben Elisha), 3:677
Crescas (name), 5:**284**
Crescas, Abraham. *See* Cresques,
  Abraham
Crescas, Asher ben Abraham, 5:**284**
Crescas, Ḥasdai ben Judah, 1:304,
  2:618–619, 3:240, 5:**284–288**, 16:89
  angels, 2:160
  apologetics, 2:266
  Aristotelianism, 2:461, 462
  articles of faith, 2:530
  Averroism, 2:266, 725
  beatitude, 3:240
  commandments, reasons for, 5:88
  cosmology, 5:232
  creation, 5:278–279
  Crescas' Critique of Aristotle
    (Wolfson), 21:149
  free will, 7:232
  God, attributes of, 7:667
  Ḥasidei Ummot ha-Olam, 8:389
  Maimonides, critique of, 5:285,
    287
  Or Adonai, 5:285–287
  Ravitzky, Aviezer, on, 17:124
  resurrection, 17:243
  revelation, 17:257
  Sargossa (Spain) community,
    18:43
  skeptics and skepticism, 18:658
  soul, immortality of, 19:37

space and place, 19:67
    Torah, 20:40–41, 42–43, 45
Crescas, Ḥasdal, 4:101
Crescas' Critique of Aristotle
    (Wolfson), 21:149
Cresques, Abraham, 5:**288**
Cresques, Judah, 5:**288**
Cresques de Vivers, 5:**288**
Cress, 20:488
Cresson, Warder, 5:**288–289**
Crete (Greece), 5:*289*, **289–291**, 15:526
Cretensis, Elijah. *See* Delmedigo, Elijah
    ben Moses Abba
Cricket, 19:140
Criers and Kibitzers, Kibitzers and
    Criers (Elkin), 6:359
Crimchak language, 11:302
Crime, 5:**291–298**
    abduction, 1:241–243
    adultery, 1:424–427
    assault, 5:595–598
    Australia, 5:480
    bribery, 4:175–177
    Buchalter, Louis, 4:238
    criminology, 5:301–304
    Diaspora, 5:292–293
    extradition, 6:626
    forgery, 7:126–127
    fraud, 7:219–220
    homicide, 9:506–507
    homosexuality, 9:516
    immigrant population, 5:294–295
    imprisonment and, 9:744–745
    incest, 9:755–756
    Israel, 5:291–292, 293–298, 293*t*,
        294*t*
    law, 14:347
    mental illness, 14:58, 59
    mobsters, 5:479, 12:485–486, 504
    ones in, 15:428
    Palestine, 5:293, 293*t*
    perjury, 15:772–773
    police offenses, 16:331–332
    rape, 17:93
    sexual offenses, 18:329–332
    slavery, 18:667–670
    theft and robberies, 19:686–691
    U.S., 5:291, 292
    See also War crimes trials
Crime, Its Causes and Conditions
    (Lombroso), 13:178
Crimea (Russia), 5:**298–301**, *299*
    Abdul Mejid I, 1:244
    Aga family, 1:443
    education, Jewish, 6:176
    Jewish settlement, 12:493–494

Karaites, 11:792
Crimean affair, 5:**301**
Crimes, War. *See* War crimes trials
The Criminal, the Judge and the Public.
    See Der Verbrecher und seine Richter
Criminal law. *See* Penal Law
The Criminal Man. See L'Uomo
    delinquente (Lombroso)
Criminal Registry and Rehabilitation
    of Offenders Act of 1981, 14:360
Criminal Sentences: Law without Order
    (Frankel), 7:197
Criminology, 5:**301–304**, 14:59
    Amir, Menahem, 2:78–79
    Beiderman, Bernardo, 3:265
    Brodsky, Stanley L., 4:198
    Dinitz, Simon, 5:671–672
    Drapkin, Abraham S., 6:8
    Drapkin, Israel, 6:8
    fines in Jewish law, 7:27
    Hitzig, Julius Eduard, 9:294
    Hurwitz, Stephan, 9:633
    Radzinowicz, Sir Leon, 17:60
    Schafer, Stephen, 18:103
Crimson worm, 5:**304**
Crinagoras of Carystus, 5:**304**
Crisis in English Poetry (Pinto), 16:179
Crispin, Gilbert, 5:**304**
    Anselm of Canterbury, 2:181
    disputations and polemics, 5:691
Cristaler, Aaron, 14:445
Cristall, Abe, 6:150
Cristãos-Novos. *See* Crypto-Jews
Cristo si è fermato a Eboli (Levi),
    12:686
Critica Hebraica (Bate), 3:210
Critical and Exegetical Commentary on
    Judges (Moore), 14:469
Critical idealism, 2:643
Critique of Pure Reason (Kant), 11:769
Croatia
    antisemitism, 6:38–39
    Holocaust, 9:340
        Dubrovnik, 6:39
        Rijeka, 17:332–333
        Split, 19:126
        Zagreb, 21:444
    language, biblical translation,
        3:635
    Osijek, 15:503–504
Crocodiles, 5:**304–305**
Crohmălniceanu, Ovid S., 5:**305**
Crohn, Burrill Bernard, 5:**305**
Crohn's disease, 5:**305**
Croisset, Francis de, 5:**305**
La Croix (newspaper), 5:**305**

Croll, David Arnold, 5:**305–306**
Cromwell, Oliver, 5:**306**
    Manasseh ben Israel, 6:413
    Palache family, 15:573
Cronbach, Abraham, 5:**306**
Cronenberg, David, 5:**306**
Crónica de los Reyes Católicos
    (Chirino), 4:652
Crool, Joseph, 5:**307**
Crops, doubtfully tithed. *See* Demai
Cross, Frank, 3:618, 653, 655, 11:448
Crossbreeding of sheep, 13:8
The Crossing of the Jabbok. See
    Ma'avar Yabbok (Aaron Berechiah
    ben Moses of Modena)
Cross-staff, 13:674
The Crotonian Noon. See Krotonsky
    polden (Livshits)
Crowds and Power. See Masse und
    Macht
Crowfoot, Grace Mary, 5:**307**
Crowfoot, John Winter, 5:**307**, 15:589
Crown, Henry, 5:**307**
Crown Heights incident (NY), 3:737,
    20:377–378
Crown of the Law. See Keter Torah
Crowns, 5:**307–309**
Crowns, Torah, 20:52
The Crucible (Miller), 14:251–252
Crucifixion, 5:**309–310**
Crucifix libels, 15:554
Cruelty to animals, 2:**165–166**
Cruez (Austria). *See* Deutschkreutz
    (Austria)
Crumb, Robert, 5:**310**
The Crusaders (Heym), 9:85
Crusades, 2:392, 4:710, 5:**310–315**
    aliyah during, 10:331
    antisemitism, 2:162
    archaeology, 2:392
    Bratislava, 4:131
    Brittany, 4:189
    Bulgaria, 4:269
    Byzantine Empire, 4:327
    Erez Israel map (11th c.), vol. 13:
        color insert
    first, 5:310–312, 9:210
    fourth, 4:327
    France, 7:150
    genizah records, 7:468
    Germany, 7:519–520
        Bonn, 4:63
        Boppard, 4:79
    Haifa, 8:234–235
    holy places in Israel and, 9:501
    Israel, land of, 10:161–165, *163*

Crusades, *continued*
Italy, antisemitism, 3:469
Jaffa and, 11:61–62
Jericho and, 11:139
Jerusalem and, 11:157–159
Kalonymus family, 11:747–749
liturgy, influence on, 5:314
martyrs' suicide, 5:313–314
Omer, recollection during, 15:422
Palestine during, 16:16
papal response to, 5:313
Pastoureaux, 15:685
Samaritans, 17:723–724
second, 5:312
significance of, 5:313–315, 9:213–214, 216–217
third, 5:312–314
La Cruz Invertida (Aguinis), 1:510
Crying Girl (Lichtenstein), vol. 4: color insert
Cryptography, 5:131
Crypto-Jews, 5:**315**
Aboab, Immanuel, 1:265
Andalusia, 11:58
Anusim, 2:253
Bolivia, 4:46–47
Brazil, 4:143
Buenos Aires, 4:252
Cervantes Saavedra, Miguel de, 4:550
Chile, 4:636–637, 638
Chuetas, 4:708–709
England, Carvajal, Abraham Israel, 4:502
France, 4:82
Jamaica, 11:75
Jewish identity and, 11:294–295
Latin America, 12:507–508
new Muslims, 11:58
Peru, 13:20–21, 15:793–794
Portugal, 3:178, 302, 18:190
Braganza, 4:117
Setubal, 18:320
U.S., 16:57
See also Conversos; New Christians
Crystal, Billy, 5:**315**
Crystal Night. *See* Kristallnacht
A császár dajkája (Molnár). *See The Emperor's Nurse* (Molnár)
Csergő, Hugo, 5:**315**
Csermely, Gyula, 5:**315**
Csupo, Gabor, 5:**315–316**
Ctesiphon (Mesopotamia), 5:**316**
Cuando digo Magdalena (Steimberg), 19:175

Cuba, 5:**316–326**
antisemitism, 5:319–320
Batista regime, 5:319, 320, 323
Blis, David, 3:756–757
Castro regime, 5:323–325
colonial period, 5:316
economy, 5:318–319
education, 5:321, 324–325
emigration to Miami, 5:324, 14:161
Grobart, Fabio, 8:89
immigration, 5:316–318, 319–320
Israel, relations with, 5:325–326
Jewish communities in, 2:46
journalism, Kaplan, Sender Meyer, 11:780
Republican period, 5:317–323
Saint Louis incident, 5:320, 19:228–229
teenagers playing board game, vol. 5: color insert
Zionist movement, 5:321–323
Cuban, Mark, 5:**326**
Cubism, 4:338, 11:725, 15:648
Cubits, 1:360, 362, 20:701–702
Cucumber, 5:**327**
Cudworth, Ralph, 5:**327**
Cuéllar, Moshe, 4:257
Cuenca (Spain), 5:**327–328**
Cuenque, Abraham Ben Levi, 5:**328**
Cuidad, Juan de, 3:571
Cuisines et dépendances (Bacri), 3:42
Cuker, Jakub. *See* Zucker, Jacques
Cukierman, Antek. *See* Zuckerman, Itzhak
Cukierman, Roger, 5:**328**
Cukor, George, 5:**328**
Cul-de-sac (Polanski), 16:326
Çulema, Don. *See* Ibn Zadok, Solomon
Culi, Jacob, 5:**328–329**, 12:432, 13:710
Culi, Jacob ben Meir, 15:540
Cullman, Dorothy, 5:330
Cullman, Edgar M., Sr., 5:330
Cullman, Howard S., 5:330
Cullman, Joan Paley, 5:330
Cullman, Joseph F., 5:329
Cullman, Joseph F., II, 5:329
Cullman, Joseph F., III, 5:329
Cullman, Lewis B., 5:330
Cullman family, 5:**329–330**
Cult places, Israelite, 5:**333–337**
Bamah, 5:335–336
Bet YHWH, 5:333–334
Mikdash, 5:334–335
Mizbe'ah, 5:336–337

Cults, 1:561, 5:**330–333**, 6:704–705
animal sacrifices, 5:330–332
Ephod, 6:455–456
grain offerings, 5:332–333
modern biblical criticism and, 3:651–652
Moon, 14:467
Moses, 14:529
other offerings, 5:333
The Cultural Contradictions of Capitalism (Bell), 3:298
Cultural Literacy: What Every American Needs to Know (Hirsch), 9:125
Cultural Literacy Foundation. *See* Core Knowledge Foundation
Cultural materialism, 8:363
Cultural Zionism. *See* Zionism
Culture and intellectual life. *See* specific countries and cultures
Culture and Mental Disorders (Eaton, Weil), 6:84
"Culture League". *See* Kultur-Lige
Cultus, modern biblical criticism and, 3:654
Cum am devenit huligan (Sebastian), 18:231
Cumanus. *See* Cumanus Ventidius
Cumanus Ventidius, 1:631, 5:**337**, 11:396
Cumberland, Richard, 5:**337**
Cumin, 5:**337–338**, vol. 16: color insert
Cum nimis absurdum, 3:46, 4:278, 15:695
Cunaeus, Petrus, 5:**338**
Cuneiform
Ebla site (Syria), 6:85
El-Amarna letters, 6:284–285
Emar texts, 6:386–390
law
Book of the Covenant's similarity to, 4:67–68
Finkelstein, Jacob Joel, 7:34
Mesopotamia, 14:93–97
Oppert, Jules Julius, 15:452
Cuneo (Italy), 5:**338–339**
Cunin, Baruch Shlomo, 13:201
The Cunning of History (Rubenstein), 17:511
Cuomotini (Greece), 5:**339–340**
Cupbearer, 5:**340**
Cup of Elijah, 6:338
Curaçao (Venezuela), 5:**340–341**
Ashkenaz, 2:107
Goudeket, Maurits, 8:16
Jewish settlement in, 2:41, 4:471–472, 12:508

libraries, 12:786

See also De Sola family

The Cure (Levitin), 18:200

Curiel, Abigail, 5:341

Curiel, Israel ben Meir di, 5:**341**

Curiel, Jacob, 5:341

Curiel, Moses, 5:341

Curiel, Solomon, 5:341

Curiel family, 5:**341**

Curiosities of Literature (D'Israeli), 5:702

Curran, Edward Lodge, 15:215

Currency. *See* Coins and currency

Currick, Max Cohen, 5:**341–342**

Currie, Edwina, 5:**342**

Curse of Canaan (son of Ham), 4:**391**

Cursing. *See* Blessing and cursing

Cursing God. *See* Blasphemy

Cursos Religiosos Israelitas, 18:141

Curtain of Torah Ark. *See* Parokhet and Kapporet

Curtis, Jamie Lee, 5:**342**

Curtis, Tony, 5:**342–343**

Curtiz, Michael, 5:**343**, 14:571–572

Cusa, Nicholas of. *See* Nicholas of Cusa

Cush (Africa), 5:**343–344,** 14:525, 526, 532

Cush (son of Ham), 5:**344**, 8:290

Cushan-Rishathaim, 5:**344**

Cushitic languages, 18:280

Custodian. *See* Apotropos

Custody of children

in Israeli law, 15:638

in Jewish law, 15:636–637

Custom and halakhah, 1:309, 8:254

acquisition, 1:362

labor law, 12:412, 413

Customs. *See* Minhag

Cuth, Cuthah, 5:**344–345**

Cutheans. *See* Samaritans

Cutinho family. *See* Coutinho family

Cutler, Bruce, 5:**345**

Cutler, Harry, 5:**345**

Cutner, Solomon. *See* Solomon (pianist)

Cut-outs. *See* Paper-cuts

Cuza, Alexander, C., 5:**345**

CV. *See* Central-Verein Deutscher Staatsbuerger Juedischen Glaubens

C.V.-Zeitung (newspaper), 5:**346**

Cyaxares (King of Media), 13:718

Cyberdémocraties: Traversées Fugitives (Robin), 17:354

Cycling, 19:140

Cylinder seals, 18:225

Cynics and cynicism, 5:**346**, 15:383

Cyon, Elie de, 5:**346**

Cypress, 5:**346–347**

Cyprian of Carthage, 3:598, 4:720

Cypros (mother of Herod), 5:**347**

Cypros (wife of Agrippa I), 5:347*t*

Cyprus, 5:**347–349,** *348*

Cyrenaica (Libya). *See* Cyrene (Libya)

Cyrene (Libya), 5:**349–350,** 12:*789,* 789–790, 13:249–250

Cyril and Methodius, 3:634

Cyril II (Greek Orthodox patriarch), 11:167

Cyrus (emperor of Persia), 3:25, 4:379, 5:**350–351,** 6:610, 658

CZA (Central Zionist Archives). *See* Central Zionist Archives (CZA)

Czacki, Tadeusz, 5:**351**

Czaczkes, Samuel Josef. *See* Agnon, Shmuel Yosef

Czarniecki, Stefan, 5:**351**

Czartoryski, Prince Adam Jerzy, 5:**351–352**

Czech, Ludwig, 5:**352**, 18:705

Czechanower. *See* Ciechanow, Abraham ben Raphael Landau of

Czechanower, Abraham ben Raphael Landau. *See* Ciechanow, Abraham ben Raphael Landau of

The Czech Memorial Scrolls, 5:**352–353**

Czechoslovakia, 5:**353–364,** *354*

antisemitism, 2:229, 13:600

Slánský Trial, 18:665–666

pre WW II, 5:356

archives, 2:408

Arts, 6:734–735

Blau-Weiss, 3:747

Bohemia, 4:37–41

Čechů-Židů, Svaz, 4:534

communal history, 5:354

communal organizations, postwar, 5:360

community, nature of, 5:110

cooperatives, 5:206

cultural life, pre WW II, 5:356

declared nationality, 5:355*t*

demography, 5:353–354, 353*t*, 359

economic life, pre WW II, 5:355–356

education, early twentieth century, 5:355

emigration and exile (1938-1945), 5:356–357

He-Ḥalutz, 8:760

Holocaust, 5:357–359, 9:340

Tachov, 19:429

Israel, relations with, 5:361–362

Jews in public life, postwar, 5:360–361

language, Bible translated into, 3:634

medicine, 12:803

newspapers, 16:489

oil industry development, 16:20

political affiliation, 5:354–355

population, 16:393

printing and publishing, 16:536, 717

renewal of Jewish life, 5:362–363

Slovak Jewry, history, 5:363–364

WW II refugees, 20:740

WW II war crimes trials, 20:643

Zionism, 21:585–586

See also Bohemia; Czech Republic; *specific cities*

Czechoslovak literature, 5:**364–369**

antisemitism in literature, 5:365–367

Baum, Oscar, 3:220

biblical influences, 3:671–672, 5:365

Brod, Max, 4:192–193

children's, 4:635

communist influence, 5:368–369

Dagan, Avigdor, 5:377–378

Demetz, Peter, 5:550–551

Dostál, Zeno, 5:762

Eisner, Pavel, 6:277

Fischer, Otokar, 7:54–55

Hostovský, Egon, 9:567–568

Jewish characters and themes, 5:365

Jewish contribution to, 5:367–368

Kapper, Siegfried, 11:782

Klíma, Ivan, 12:231

Langer, Frantisel, 12:479–480

Langer, Jiří Mordechai, 12:480

Laub, Gabriel, 12:525

Leda, Eduard, 12:595–596

Lustig, Arnost, 13:270

poetry

Gottlieb, František, 8:11–12

Kapper, Siegfried, 11:782

Langer, Jiří Mordechai, 12:480

Listopad, Frantisek, 13:83

Pick, Jiří Robert, 16:146

Poláček, Karel, 16:285

Rakous, Vojtěch, 17:76

Uhde, Milan, 20:230–231

Vohryzek, Josef, 20:568–569

Vrchlicky Jaroslav, 20:587–588

Czechoslovak literature, *continued*
　Weiner, Richard, 20:720
　Zeyer, Julius, 11:412
Czechoslovak Zionist Federation, 11:721
Czech Republic, 5:**369–370**
　antisemitism
　　Carlsbad, 4:482
　　Ceska Lipa, 4:552
　　Ceske Budejovice, 4:552
　　Cheb, 4:585–586
　　Chomutov, 4:666
　Boskovice, 4:97
　Brandys nad Labem, 4:129
　Breclav, 4:156–157
　Breznice, 4:175
　Brno, 4:190
　Čechů-Židů, Svaz, 4:534–535
　concentration and extermination camps, Theresienstadt, 19:703
　ghettos, Theresienstadt, 19:701–703
　Holocaust
　　Brno, 4:190
　　Cheb, 4:586
　　Chodova Plana, 4:658
　　Chomutov, 4:666
　　documentation, resource centers, 9:428–429
　　Edelstein, Jacob, 6:145
　　Jablonec Nad Nisou, 11:8
　　Jemnice, 11:121
　　Jevicko, 11:253
　　Jihlava, 11:337
　　Jindrichuv Hradec, 11:337
　　Klatovy, 12:212
　　Kojetin, 12:269
　　Kolin, 12:273
　　Kromeriz, 12:369
　　Kyjov, 12:402
　　Mikulov, 14:223
　　Miroslav, 14:314
　　Moravske Budejovice, 14:477
　　Moravsky Krumlov, 14:477
　　Nachod, 14:721
　　Pilsen, 16:163
　　Pobezovice na Sumave, 16:249
　　Pohorelice, 16:282
　　Polna, 16:360
　　Prague, 16:453–454
　　Prostejov, 16:625
　　Roudnice nad Labem, 17:497
　　Tabor, 19:426
　　Theresienstadt, 6:145
　　Trebic, 20:124

　　Trest, 20:134
　　Turnov, 20:203–204
　　Udlice, 20:224
　　Uherske Hradiste, 20:231
　　Uhersky Brod, 20:231
　　Usov, 20:433
　　Usti nad Labem, 20:437
　　Votice, 20:585
　　Zatec, 21:462
　　Znojmo, 21:646
　Jihlava, 11:337
　Jindrichuv Hradec, 11:337
　Klatovy, 12:212
　Lazne Kynzvart, 12:562–563
　libraries, 12:786
　Mikulov, 14:223
　museums, 14:628–629
　Novy Bohumin, 15:323
　Novy Bydzov, 15:323
　Novy Jicin, 15:324
　Olomouc, 15:411
　Osoblaha, 15:505–506
　Ostrava, 15:509–510
　Sobedruhy, 18:699
　WW II, Theresienstadt, 19:701–703
　Zionist movement, Brod, Max, 4:192–193
　See also Czechoslovakia
Czenstochowski, Walter, 5:370
Czerniak, Moshe, 5:370–371
Czerniakow, Adam, 5:**371–372**, 11:526–527, 775
Czernowitz (Ukraine). *See* Chernovtsy (Ukraine)
Czernowitz Yiddish Language Conference, 5:372
Czerny family. *See* Shaḥor family
Czestochowa (Poland), 5:**372–373**
　Frank, Jacob, 7:188–189
Czobel, Béla, 5:373
Czortków. *See* Chortkov (Ukraine)
Czortków (Ukraine). *See* Chortkov (Ukraine)
Czyz, Lazer Shmuel. *See* Chess, Leonard

D

D (letter), 5:375, 6:5
Daalmann, Marius. *See* Eloesser, Arthur
Dabbūriyya, 5:**375**
Dabrowa Gornicza (Poland), 5:375
Dachau (Germany), 5:**375–376**, *376*
Dachau concentration camp, 5:375–376, 9:328

Da Costa, Isaac, 5:**376–377**
D'Acosta, Joan. *See* Acosta, Joan D'
Da Costa, Joseph Mendes, 5:**377**
Da Costa, Uriel. *See* Costa, Uriel da
Da Costa Athias, Solomon. *See* Costa Athias, Solomon da
Dada movement, 11:77–78, 20:221
Dafina. *See* Cholent
Dafnah (Israel), 5:**377**
Dafter. See Defter
Dagan, Avigdor, 5:**377–378**
Dagan, Gedeon, 6:451
Dagan ve-Oferet (Shaḥam), 18:363
Dagestanis, in Israel, 10:297
　See also Mountain Jews
Dagim Metim Be-Yafo (Seri), 18:310
Dagon, 5:**378**, 6:387
Dagon, Barukh, 5:**378–379**
D'Aguilar, Diego, 2:77
D'Aguilar, Moses Raphael, 18:297
D'Aguilar, Moses Raphael, 3:683, 4:144
Dahan, Gilbert, 11:325
Dahan, Masʿud, 5:379
Dahan, Saadiah, 5:379
Dahan, Solomon, 5:379
Dahan family, 5:**379**
Dahir al-'Amr, 1:339
Dahl, Basil. *See* Bovshover, Joseph
Dahlberg, Edward, 5:**379**
DAIA, 2:433–434, 5:**379–380**
Daiaghilev Company, 5:412
Daiches, David, 5:**381**
Daiches, Israel Ḥayyim, 5:380
Daiches, Loeb Hirsh Aryeh Ẓevi ben David, 5:380
Daiches, Salis, 5:381, 6:147
Daiches, Samuel, 5:380–381
Daiches family, 5:**380–381**
Daighilev Company, 5:412
Daily Mail (newspaper). *See Do'ar Ha-Yom* (newspaper)
Daily Telegraph (newspaper), 12:546–547
Dainow, Ẓevi Hirsch ben Ze'ev Wolf, 5:**381**
Dairy products, 7:117
　cheese, 4:587
　milk, 14:249
　Shavuot, 7:119–120
Daleski, Hillel, 5:**381–382**
Dalet, 5:**382**
The Daleth Effect (Harrison), 18:199
Dāliya. See Wadi Dāliya
Dāliyat al-Karmil (Israel), 5:**382**
Daliyyah (Israel), 5:**382**, 10:694

Dallas (TX), 5:**382–383**

Dallas Holocaust Musuem, 9:436

Dallas Mavericks, 5:326

Dalman, Gustaf Hermann, 2:11, 5:**383–384,** 13:59

Dalmanutha. *See* Magdala (Israel)

Dalsheimer, Helen, 3:99

Dalton (Upper Galilee), 5:**384**

Dalven, Rachel, 5:**384**

Daly, Charles P., 9:161

Dama, Son of Netina, 5:**384–385**

Damage, evidentiary, 7:504

Damages, 5:**385–389**

    assault, 2:595, 596, 598

    Avot Nizikin, 2:751–753

    business ethics and, 4:313

    Civil Wrongs Ordinance (Israel), 5:389

    divorce, Samaritan, 17:732

    fines, 7:27–29

    forgiveness for, 7:129

    Halakhah le-Moshe mi-Sinai, 8:258

    labor law, 12:414, 415, 416, 418

    Mishnah, 14:324

    oaths, 15:361

    ransom, 17:91

    rape, 17:93

    See also Obligations, law of

Damanhūr (Egypt), 5:**389–390**

Damari, Shoshana, 5:**390**

Damascius, 5:**390**

Damascus (Syria), 5:**390–397,** *394*

    Abraham ben Mazhir, 1:304

    Ahab, 1:522–523

    altar of main temple, 2:12

    Aram-Damascus, 2:359–360

    artwork, 5:394*i*

    blood libel in, 3:780

    Geonim, 7:386

Damascus, Book of Covenant of, 5:**397–399**

Damascus Affair, 2:192, 5:**399–401**

    Alkalai, Judah ben Solomon Ḥai, 1:663–664

    Jewish converts and, 16:630

    New York City, reaction in, 15:199

    Noah, Mordecai Manuel, 15:291

    other blood libels in Ottoman empire and, 15:529

Damascus Document, 5:**502–503,** 11:787

Damascus Keter, 3:676, 677

Damasus I (pope), 3:598, 666

D'Amato, Alfonse, 15:225

    See also Finkelstein, Arthur

D'Amato, Alfonse M., 5:**401–402**

Damavand (Iran), 5:**402**

Dameshek, William, 5:**402**

Damian, Peter, 5:**402**

Damietta (Egypt), 5:**402–403**

Damīra (Egypt), 5:**403**

Dammesek. *See* Damascus (Syria)

The Damned (Visconti), 9:442

Damn Yankees (musical), 1:406

Damocritus, 5:**403**

Dampierre-De-L'aube (France), 5:**403**

Damrosch, Frank Heino, 5:**403–404**

Damrosch, Leopold, 5:**403–404**

Damrosch, Walter Johannes, 5:**403–404**

Damrosch family, 5:**403–404**

Damwa. *See* Dumuh (Egypt)

Dan (biblical city), 3:109, 5:**404–405**

Dan (biblical figure), 3:698, 5:*405,* **405–407**

Dan (river), 11:401

Dan (tribe), 5:406–407, 11:565–566

Dan, Fyodor Ilyich, 5:**407,** 16:348

Dan, Joseph, 5:**407–408**

Dan, Leslie L., 5:**408**

Dan, Sergiu, 5:**408**

Danby, Herbert, 5:**408,** 15:554

Danby, Michael, 5:**408,** 18:706

Dance, 5:**409–416**

    Agadati, Baruch, 1:443–444

    Babilée, Jean, 3:21

    Batsheva and Bat-Dor dance companies, 3:214–215

    Bennett, Michael, 3:369

    Berk, Fred, 3:437

    Bertonoff, Deborah, 3:492

    of Bukharan Jews, 4:264

    Chujoy, Anatole, 4:709

    Cohen, Selma Jeanne, 5:34

    Cranko, John, 5:273

    Guglielmo Da Pesaro, 8:126

    Halprin, Ann, 8:286

    horah, 9:523–524

    Inbal Dance Theater, 9:752

    Israel Arab, 10:734

    Kibbutz Contemporary Dance Company, 3:254

    Lang, Pearl, 12:479

    Lapson, Dvora, 12:492

    Levi-Agron, Hassia, 12:695

    Levinson, Andre, 12:722–723

    Levi-Tannai, Sara, 12:732–733

    Lewitzky, Bella, 12:770

    Lichine, David, 12:795–796

    Ordman, Jeanette, 15:463

    Oved, Margalit, 15:548–549

    Rambert Dame Marie, 17:84

    rituals, 8:286

    Robbins, Jerome, 17:353–354

    Ross, Herbert, 17:469

    Rubinstein, Ida, 17:517

    Schubert, Lia, 18:168–169

    Sokolow, Anna, 18:747

    U.S., twentieth century, 6:713, 13:602–603

    Uzbekistan, 4:264

    See also Musicians and dancers; *specific types of dance*

The Dance of Genghis Cohen (Gary), 9:411

Dancers. *See* Musicians and dancers

D'Ancona. *See* Ancona family

D'Ancona, Alessandro. *See* Ancona, Alessandro D'

D'Ancona, Cesare. *See* Ancona, Cesare D'

D'Ancona, Hedy, 16:345

D'Ancona, Paolo. *See* Ancona, Paolo D'

D'Ancona, Sansone. *See* Ancona, Sansone D'

D'Ancona, Vito. *See* Ancona, Vito

D'Ancona family. *See* Ancona family

Dandan-Uiliq letter, 11:548, 549, 552, 12:669

Dane, Maxwell, 1:428

Dangerfield, Rodney, 5:**417**

Dangling Man (Bellow), 3:301

Danglow, Jacob, 5:**417**

Dangoor, Ezra Sassoon ben Reuben, 3:59, 5:**417**

Daniel (biblical figure), 5:**417–419,** *420*

    eschatology, 6:494–495

    mene, mene, tekel, u-farsin and, 14:45–46

    Shadrach, Mishach, Abed-Nego, 18:361

    vision of, 5:426

Daniel, Book of, 5:418, **419–425**

    abomination of desolation, 1:269

    Abraham ben Samuel of Dreux, 1:310

    angels, 2:152, 153

    Daniel A, 5:419–420, 421, 422, 424

    Daniel B, 5:420–421, 422, 423–424

    modern biblical criticism and, 3:655

    pesher and raz, 16:9

Daniel, Books of (Apocryphal), 5:**425**

Daniel, Dan, 5:**425**

Daniel, Ezra Menahem, 5:426, 16:346

Daniel, Jean, 5:**425–426**

Daniel, Leon, 4:277

Daniel, Leone de Ser. *See* Romano, Judah ben Moses ben Daniel

Daniel, M., 5:**426**

Daniel, Menaham Salih, 5:**426**, 16:346

Daniel, Vision of, 5:**426**

Daniel, Yitzhak, 21:258

Daniel, Yuli Markovich, 5:**426–427**

Daniel ben Azariah, 5:**427**, 6:341, 606

Daniel ben Eleazar ben Nethanel Ḥibbat Allah, 5:**427**

Daniel ben Ḥasdai, 3:56, 5:**427**

Daniel ben Jehiel of Rome, 2:136, 5:**428**

Daniel ben Moses al-Qūmisī, 2:128, 5:**428**, 11:532, 789

Daniel ben Peraḥyah ha-Koen, 5:**428**

Daniel ben Saadiah ha-Bavli, 5:**429**

Daniel ben Samuel ibn Abī Rabī', 5:**429**

Daniel ben Samuel of Rossena. *See* Rossena, Daniel ben Samuel of

Daniel Deronda (Eliot), 6:349, 435, 12:746

Danielevitz, Hersh. *See* Herschele

Daniel ha-Bavli. *See* Daniel ben Saadiah ha-Bavli

Daniel Ḥayyata, 5:**429**

Daniel ibn al Amshata. *See* Daniel ben Saadiah ha-Bavli

Daniel ibn al-Amshata. *See* Daniel ben Saadiah ha-Bavli

Danielillo, 4:496

Daniel Ish Hamudot. *See* Liebermann, Aaron Samuel

The Daniel Jazz (Lindsay), 5:419

Daniel-Rops, Henri, 5:**429**

Daniels, Alfred, 5:**429**

Daniel Shafranov (Kabak), 11:584

Daniel Sieff Research Institute. *See* Weizmann Institute of Science

Daniilovich, Issur. *See* Douglas, Kirk

Danin, Yeḥezkel, 5:**430**

Danish literature, 18:89–90
Brandes, Carl Edward, 4:126
Brandes, Georg, 4:126
Hertz, Henrik, 9:48
Levin, Pul Theodor, 12:712
Levy, Louis, 12:752
Nathansen, Henri, 15:18

Danish West Indies. *See* Virgin Islands

Dankner, Amnon, 5:**430**

Dankner, Oved. *See* Ben-Ami, Oved; Ben-ami, Oved

Danneberg, Robert, 16:341

Danner, Blythe, 15:608

Danny le rouge. *See* Cohn-Bendit, Daniel

Danny the Red. *See* Cohn-Bendit, Daniel

Danon, Abraham, 5:**430**

La Danse devant l'Arche (Franck), 7:176

Dante Alighieri, 5:**430–431**, 10:788, 789

Dante's Equation (Jensen), 18:200

Danto, Louis, 5:**431**

Danz, Johann Andreas, 5:**431–432**

Danzig. *See* Gdansk (Poland)

Danzig (Poland), 16:308

Danzig, Abraham ben Jehiel Michal, 5:**432**, 12:459

Danziger, Abraham ben Jehiel Michal. *See* Danzig, Abraham ben Jehiel Michal

Danziger, Isaac Menahem, 1:611

Danziger, Itzhak, 5:**432**

Danziger, Jarahmeel Israel Isaac, 1:611

Danziger, Judah Moses Tiehberg, 1:611

Danziger, Yitzhak, 18:223

Danziger family. *See* Aleksandrow dynasty

Danzius, Johann Andreas. *See* Danz, Johann Andreas

Da-Oz, Ram, 5:**433**

Da Pisa. *See* Pisa, da, family

Da Ponte, Lorenzo, 5:140, **433**, 12:688

Dappim Yeushalmiyyim (Gouri), 8:20

Dar, 16:478

Dar, Avraham, 4:346

Dar'ā. *See* Edrei (Transjordan)

Darabani (Romania), 5:**433–434**

Dār al-Baiḍā (Morocco). *See* Casablanca (Morocco)

Darash Moshe (Albelda), 1:588

Darband. *See* Bāb al-Abwāb (Caucasus)

Darda'im movement, 11:703

Dardanelles (Turkey). *See* Canakkale (Turkey)

Dar el Beida. *See* Casablanca (Morocco)

Dar'ī, Moses ben Abraham, 5:**434**

Da Rieti. *See* Rieti family

da Rieti. *See* Rieti family

Darius (Persian kings), 5:**434–435**

Darius I (King of Persia), 3:25, 4:379, 5:**434–435**, 6:658

Darius III Codomanus (King of Persia), 5:435

Darius II Nothus (King of Persia), 5:435

Darius the Mede, 5:420, 422, **435**

Dark Ages. *See* Middle Ages

Darkah shel Torah (Pineles), 16:166

Darkhei Ha-Aggadah (Heinemann), 1:461, 462

Darkhei Ha-Aggadah ve-Ha-Midrash (Fraenkel), 1:461, 462

Darkhei ha-Talmud (Canpanton), 4:431, 432

Darkhei Hora'ah (Eliasberg), 6:319

Darkhei Moshe (Isserles), 4:777, 10:770

Darkhei No'am (Alkalai), 1:663–664

Darkhei No'am (Mordecai ben Judah ha-Levi), 14:481

Darkhei Taharah (Eliyahu), 6:355

Darkhei Ẓiyyon (Porges), 16:401

Dark Shops Street (Modiano), 14:410

The Dark Side of Camelot (Hersch), 9:44

Darling, John. *See* Dar, Avraham

Darmesek. *See* Damascus (Syria)

Darmesteter, Arsène, 3:771, 5:**435**

Darmesteter, James, 5:435

Darmon, Amram, 5:**436**

Darmon, Pierre, 5:**436**

Darmon, Victor, 14:499

Darmon family, 5:**435–436**

Darmstadt (Germany), 5:**436–437**

Darmstadt, Joseph, 5:**437**

Darmstadt Haggadah, 8:213

Darnel. *See* Tares

Daroca (Spain), 5:**437**

Daroff, Samuel H., 5:**437–438**

Darom, Abraham S. *See* Drapkin, Abraham S.

Darquier de Pellepoix, Louis, 5:**438**

Darrow, Clarence, 8:478, 13:162

Darshan, 5:**438**, 6:669
See also specific Darshan

Darshan (Moses Isaac). *See* Moses Isaac

Darshan, Joseph. *See* Calahora, Joseph ben Solomon

Darshan Zaken. *See* Lewinsky, Elhanan Leib

Dartmouth College (NH), 7:225, 15:136

Darvas, Lili, 5:**438**

Darwīsh, Shalom, 5:**438**, 15:473

Dash, Samuel, 5:**438–439**

Dashewski, Pinḥas, 5:**439**

Da Silva, Antonio Jose, 4:143

Da Silva, Hezekiah, 1:645

Da Silva, Howard, 5:**439**

Da Silva, luiz Inácio Lula, 4:153

Daskarta (Iraq). *See* Deskarta (Iraq)

Dassault, Darius Paul, 5:**439**

Dassault, Marcel, 5:**439–440**

Dassin, Jules, 5:**440**

Data, data collection. *See* Statistics

Datafernes. *See* Holofernes
Dates and date palms, 15:602–603, vol. 16: color insert
Date tree. *See* Palms
Dathan, 5:**440**
Dating, chronological, 4:704–706
Da Tivoli, Serafino. *See* Tivoli, Serafino da
Dato, Mordecai ben Judah, 5:**440–441,** 11:547
Daube, Dave, 15:397
Daube, David, 5:**441**
Daube, Sam, 15:397
Da'ud, Sultana, 1:440
Daudet, Léon, 5:**441**
Daugavpils (Latvia), 5:**441–442,** 12:520, 18:262
Daughters. *See* Women
Dauphiné (France), 5:**442–443,** 7:152
Daus, Avraham, 5:**443**
Davan, Abraham. *See* Vaez, Abraham
Davar (newspaper), 5:**443**
Davar Davur (Pigit), 16:151
Davenport, Marcia, 5:**443–444**
Da Verona, Guido, 5:**444**
Davey, Jocelyn. *See* Raphael, Chaim
Daviĉo, Hajim S., 5:**444**
Daviĉo, Lujo, 5:**444**
Daviĉo, Oscar, 5:**444**
David (biblical figure), 5:**444–458**
 Abigail and, 1:255
 Abinadab and, 1:259
 Abishai and, 1:260
 Abner, 1:263–264
 Absalom, 1:330
 Achish, 1:355
 Adonijah, 1:413
 Adoniram, 1:413
 adoption, 1:417
 Adullam, 1:423
 Aggadah, 5:451–453
 Ahimazz, 1:543
 Ahimelech, 1:544, 545
 Ahithophel the Gilonite, 1:545
 alchemy, 1:600
 Bath-Sheba, 3:211–212
 biblical texts compared, 5:445
 census, 4:541, 542
 Chronicles, Book of, 4:699–701
 dance, 5:409
 Edom, 6:154
 Elhanan, 6:315
 genealogy, 5:446–447, 454, 459, *461*
 Goliath, 6:226
 government of, 5:450–451

historical evidence, 5:445
historiography, 9:153–154
Jerusalem and, 11:145–146
Joab and, 11:338–339
Jonathan and, 11:395–396
kingdom, 9:172–173
Merab, 1:423
Messiah and, 11:247
modern literature, 5:454–455
name, 5:446
as Patriarch, 15:689
Philistines and, 16:53, 54–55, 18:79
physical strength, 5:453
Psalms, Book of, 14:387, 16:668–669
Rabbinical criticism, 5:452–453
reign, 4:697–698
rise to kingship, 5:448–449
Saul and, 9:172, 18:80–81
scholar and poet, 5:453
Sheba ben Bichri and, 18:428
shield of, 2:123
Solomon, 18:755
sons, 5:418
state builder, 5:449–451
Tamar and, 19:493–494
wars of, 5:*448, 449, 450*
youth, 5:445, 447
David, Benjamin, 16:343
David, dynasty of, 5:446, **459–463,** *461*
 exilarchate and, 6:601, 603, 605, 606
 opponents of, 5:453
 Pharisees and, 5:453
 restoration, 5:453
 Syrian, 5:495
David, Ernest, 5:**463,** 15:243
David, Ferdinand, 5:**463**
David, Filip, 5:**463**
David, House of. *See* David, dynasty of
David, Ismar, 4:371–372
David, Jean, 5:**463**
David, Joseph, 2:32, 5:**463**
David, Larry, 5:**463–464,** 15:228
David, Martin, 5:**464**
David, Percival, 18:71
David, Samuel, 5:**464**
David, Sassoon Jacob, 18:71
David Abu Suleiman al-Qumisì. *See* David al-Qumisì
David Alfasi. *See* Alfasi, David ben Abraham
David al-Qumisì, 5:**428**
David ben Aaron ibn Ḥassin, 5:**464**

David ben Aaron ibn Hussein. *See* David ben Aaron ibn Ḥassin
David ben Abraham, 11:537
David ben Abraham Alfasi. *See* Alfasi, David ben Abraham
David ben Abraham ha-Lavan, 5:**464,** 11:612
David ben Abraham Maimuni, 5:**464–465**
David ben Amram Adani. *See* Adani, David ben Amram
David ben Aryeh Leib of Lida, 5:**465**
David ben Azariah, 6:606
David ben Boaz, 5:**465–466,** 11:532
David ben Daniel, 1:255, 11:473
David ben Daniel (11th c.), 5:**466,** 6:231
David ben Daniel (13th c.), 5:**466**
David ben Eliezer ibn Pakuda. *See* Ibn Paquda, David ben Eleazar
David ben Hasan. *See* David ben Hussein
David ben Hass̄n. *See* David ben Hussein
David ben Hayyim of Corfu, 5:**466**
David ben Hezekiah, 5:**466–467**
David ben Hussein, Abu Suleiman, 5:**467**
David ben Joseph Abudarham. *See* Abudarham, David ben Joseph
David ben Joseph ben Ezra, 6:654
David ben Joshua, 5:**467**
David ben Joshua Maimuni, 5:**467**
David ben Judah, 5:**467**
David ben Judah, Messer Leon. *See* Leon, Messer David ben Judah
David ben Judah He-Hasid, 6:261
David ben Judah he-Hasid, 5:**467–468**
David ben Levi of Narbonne, 5:**468**
David ben Manasseh Darshan, 5:**468**
David ben Menahem ha-Kohen, 3:611
David ben Meshullam of Speyer, 5:**468**
David ben Nathan of Lissa, 5:**468–469**
David ben Saadiah, 5:**469**
David ben Sa'del al-Hīti, 11:537
David ben Samuel, 5:**469**
David ben Samuel ha-Levi, 5:**469–470,** 18:338–339
David ben Saul, 5:**470,** 18:770
David ben Shimeon, 5:**470**
David ben Solomon, 5:**470,** 11:536
David ben Solomon Ben Abi Zimra. *See* David ben Solomon ibn Abi Zimra
David ben Solomon ibn Abi Zimra, 5:**470–472,** 6:233, 11:513
David ben Yom Tov. *See* Ibn Bilia, David ben Yom Tov

David ben Zakkai I, 5:**472,** 15:278

David ben Zakkai II, 5:**472**

David ben Zimra, 2:40

David D'Beth Hillel, 5:**472–473,** 8:292

David de Caderousse. *See* Davin de Caderousse

David family (Canadian), 5:**458–459**

David Frischmann - poète (Slouschz), 18:681

David-Gorodok (Poland), 5:**473–474**

David ha-Dayyan. *See* David ibn Hajjar

David ha-Lavan. *See* David ben Abraham ha-Lavan

David ha-Nasi. *See* David ben Boaz

Davidhof, Karl Yulyevich. *See* Davydov, Karl Yulyevich

David ibn Bilia. *See* Ibn Bilia, David ben Yom Tov

David ibn Hajjar, 5:**474**

David ibn Pakuda. *See* Ibn Paquda, David ben Eleazar

Davidman, Lynn, 18:736

Davidoff, Abraham. *See* Davis, Al "Bummy"

Davidoff, Hyman, 16:349

Davidoff, Leo Max, 5:**474**

David of Lida. *See* David ben Aryeh Leib of Lida

David of Makow, 5:**474**

David of Minzburg, 11:489

David of Narbonne. *See* David ben Levi of Narbonne

David of Oxford, 15:552

David of Speyer. *See* David ben Meshullam of Speyer

David of Talna, 5:**474–475**

Davidovich. *See* Lvovich, David

David Reuveni. *See* Reuveni, David

Davids, Aaron Issachar ben Naḥman, 5:**475**

David Schwartz Foundation, 18:183

Davidsohn, Bogumil. *See* Dawison, Bogumil

Davidsohn, Hans. *See* Van Hoddis, Jakob

Davidsohn, Israel, 5:**475**

Davidsohn, Robert, 5:**475**

Davidson, Avram, 18:204

Davidson, Cecelia. *See* Razofsky, Cecilia

Davidson, Cecilia. *See* Razofsky, Cecilia

Davidson, David, 5:**475**

Davidson, Israel, 5:**475–476,** 6:438

Davidson, Jo, 5:**476**

Davidson, Lionel, 5:**476**

Davidson, Max David, 5:**477**

Davidson, Samuel, 5:**477**

Davidson, Thomas, 15:207

Davidson, William, 5:**477–478**

Davies, Philip, 3:659

D'Avigdor family, 5:**478,** 478t

D'Avigdor Goldsmid. *See* D'Avigdor family

D'Avigdor-Goldsmid family. *See* D'Avigdor family

D'Avila. *See* Avila, De family

Davin de Caderousse, 5:**478**

Davis, Abel, 5:**478–479**

Davis, Al, 5:**479**

Davis, Al "Bummy," 5:**479**

Davis, Alexander Barnard, 5:**479**

Davis, David, 3:713

Davis, David Brion, 5:**479–480**

Davis, Edmund. *See* Davis, Sir Edmund

Davis, Edward, 5:**480**

Davis, Ernest Hyam. *See* Davis, Sir Ernest Hyam

Davis, Henry David, 5:**481**

Davis, James. *See* Hall, Owen

Davis, Marvin H., 5:**481**

Davis, Mortimer B., 5:**481**

Davis, Moshe, 5:**481–482**

Davis, Natalie Zemon, 5:**482,** 9:152

Davis, Sammy, Jr., 4:26, 5:**482–483**

Davis, Sir Edmund, 5:**480**

Davis, Sir Ernest Hyam, 5:**480–481**

Davis, Susan A., 5:**483**

Davydov, Karl Yulyevich, 5:**483**

Dawidgródekó (Poland). *See* David-Gorodok (Poland)

Dawidowicz, Lucy, 5:**483,** 9:152

Dawidsohn, Hayyim, 5:**483–484**

Dawidsohn, Joseph, 5:**484**

Dawison, Bogumil, 5:**484**

Dawlah, Rashid al-, 8:292

Dawn. See Razsvet (journal)

Dawn of Dusk? (Heller), 8:793

The Dawn of Hebrew Linguistics. See Or Rishon be-Ḥokhmat ha-Lashon

The Day (newspaper). *See Jewish Day* (newspaper)

Dayan, Assaf, 5:**484**

Dayan, Moshe, 3:347, 5:**485–486,** 10:363–364

Dayan, Yael, 5:**486**

Day and night, 5:**486–488**

Dayan family, 5:**484**

Dayaukku (Median leader), 13:717–718

Day Lewis, Cecil, 15:289

Day-Morning Journal. *See Jewish Morning Journal*

Day of Atonement, 5:**488–493**

   Al Ḥet, 1:658

   Amidah, 2:72, 75

   Anna be-Korenu, 2:177

   Avodah, 2:744–745

   El Nora Alilah, 6:366

   fasting, 6:719–720, 722, 723

   foods for before and after, 7:120

   Kol Nidrei, 12:276–278

      text, 13:785

   Ne'ilah, 15:65–66

   post-exilic establishment of, 15:743

   sacrifices, 17:647

   Samaritans, 17:730

Day of the Lord, 2:100, 101, 5:**494,** 6:491

   See also Eschatology

Dayr al-Balah (Israel). *See* Deir al-Balaḥ (Israel)

The Days Before (Agnon), 11:216

Day schools

   Argentina, 6:211–212

   Australia, 6:207–208

   Brazil, 6:212

   Canada, 6:208–210

   Cuba, 5:321

   Latin America, 12:512–513

   Mexico, 6:213

   North Africa, 6:213–214, 214

   South Africa, 6:210–211

   United Kingdom, 6:206–207

   United States, 6:191, 198, 201–202

      Monmouth County (NJ), 14:447

   Uruguay, 6:212–213

The Days of Bruce (Aguilar), 1:509

Days of Destruction and Revolt (Lubetkin), 13:241

The Days to Come (Chilton, Sobol), 18:702

Dayton (OH), 5:**494–495**

Dayyan (Hebrew judge), 5:**495**

   Elijah of La Massa, 6:346–347

   Eliyahu, Mordecai, 6:355

   Lichtstein, Abraham Ben Eliezer Lipman, 12:800

Dayyan family, 5:**495**

Dayyanim

   Algiers, 6:56, 61

   Amsterdam, 2:107, 110

   Hungary, 11:711

Dayyeinu, 5:**496**

Dayyena, Azriel. *See* Dienna, Azriel ben Solomon

D'Azevedo family. *See* Azevedo family

D.B. Adler and Co., 1:396

DC Comics, 11:761

Dead Fish in Jaffa (Seri). *See Dagim Metim Be-Yafo* (Seri)

Dead Hours. See Sha'ot Metot

The Dead of the Desert. See Metei Midbar

Dead Sea (Israel), 5:*496*, **496–498,** 10:123

    Jordan River and, 11:401–402

    Novomeysky, Moshe, commercial exploitation by, 15:322

    tourist area, vol. 21: color insert

Dead Sea Region. See Ḥevel Yam ha-Melaḥ

Dead Sea scrolls, 5:**498–506,** vol. 21: color insert

    am ha-areẓ, 2:67

    Amidah, 2:73

    Anan, son of Anan, 2:127

    Anan ben David, 2:128

    Aramaic, 2:347–348

    biblical manuscripts and, 5:503–504

    calligraphy, Hebrew, 4:370

    copper scroll, 5:213–214, 505

    demons in, 5:573–574

    Dupont-Sommer, André, 6:51

    eschatology, 6:498–500

    Essenes, 6:510–511

    flags, 7:68

    Flusser, David, 7:91

    forgeries, 7:126

    gnosticism, 7:651

    halakhah, 19:633–634

    Isaiah scroll, 8:635–636

    Jewish literature, 5:505

    Jubilees, Book of, 11:474

    Judean Desert caves, 5:498–499, 11:523–525

    Karaites, 11:786–787, 796

    Khirbat Mird (West Bank) and, 5:505

    Khirbat Qumran and, 5:500–501

    Kittim, 5:208

    language, orthography, and spelling in, 5:499–500, 8:634–639

    Lies, Man of, 12:818–819

    Lies, prophet of, 12:819

    Lilith, 13:18–19

    Man of Lies, 12:818

    materials, 5:500

    Murabbaʿat scrolls, 14:616–617

    Naphtali, testament of, 14:775

    New Testament and, 15:192

    Noah, Books of, 15:290

Oral Law, 15:456

    Qumrān and, 5:498–499

    research on, 5:501–502

    Ru'aḥ ha-Kodesh, 17:508

    Samuel, Book of, 17:758

    sectarian writings of Qumran scrolls, 5:502–503

    Shapira fragments, 18:402–403

    Shrine of the Book at the Israel Museum, vol. 14: color insert

    Sons of Light, 19:25–26

    Sukenik, E. L., 2:371, 378

    Teacher of righteousness, 19:568–570

    tefillin, 19:579–560

    Temple scroll, 19:633

    Testaments of the Twelve Patriarchs and, 15:692

    texts

        biblical criticism affected by, 3:652

        copper scroll, 5:505

        Damascus, Book of Covenant of, 5:397–398

        English translations of Bible influenced by, 3:617, 622

        Greek language in, 3:596

        history of Bible text and, 3:583–584

        Isiah scroll, vol. 14: color insert

        Manual of Discipline, 5:676–679

        Pesher, 16:9–10

        printed editions of Hebrew Bible and, 3:588

        seekers after smooth things, 18:238

        Testament of Naphtali, 14:775

        Thanksgiving Psalms, 19:667–669

        tripartite canon referred to in, 3:577

    War Scroll, 20:675–676

    Wicked Priest, 21:**38–39**

    writings and, 5:505

    Yadin, Yigael, 21:265

    yaḥad, 21:268

    Zadokites, 21:442

    See also Essenes; Qumran

Dead Sea sect, 2:153–154, 5:**506–508,** 6:29–30

    calendar, 4:359

    dualism, 1:29–30

    eschatology, 6:498–500

    kipper, 12:183

    modes of life, 5:507–508

Oral Law, 15:456

    redemption, 17:152

    Teacher of Righteousness, 19:568–570

    tefillin, 19:579–560

    Temple scroll, 19:633

    views, 5:506–507

    See also Essenes

The Deaf Man. See Der Toyber

Deaf-mute people, 5:**508–510,** *509*

    education of, 15:759

    finger spelling, 1:727

    Johanan ben Gudgada, 11:369

Deák, Ferencz, 5:**510**

"Dear Abby." *See* Friedman, Pauline Esther

Death, 5:**510–513**

    of Aaron, 1:209–210

    agunah, 1:510–512

    Altschul, Emil, 2:25

    Angel of, 2:147–150

    Bible, 2:148

    conversion or threat of, 15:721–722

    dignity, with, 18:616

    ethical wills, 13:783

    Keri'ah, 12:84–85

    kiss of (*See* Kiss of death)

    life and death, 13:6

    memorial lights, 14:18

    moment of, 13:750–751

    mourning texts, *Semaḥot,* 18:273–274

    necrologies, *Memorbuch,* 14:17–18

    resurrection, and, 13:6

    rites and rituals, shofar, 18:507

    sheloshim, 18:446

    See also Life and death; Netherworld

The Death and Life of Dith Pran (Schanberg), 18:106

Death camps. *See* Camps, concentration and extermination

Death in the Rain. See Mavet ba-Geshem

Death Is Called Engelchen (Kadar), 11:695

Death marches, 5:**513–515,** *514, 515*

The Death of a Red Republic. See Moartea unei republici roşii

Death of a Salesman (Miller), 14:251

Death of a Son (Silkin), 18:580–581

The Death of Virgil (Broch). *See Der Tod des Vergil*

Death penalty. *See* Capital punishment

De aventu Messiae, 1:643

De Avila family. *See* Avila, De family

De Barrio. *See* Bonjorn, Bonet Davi
DeBartolo Realty Corporation, 18:608
Debdou (Morocco), 5:**516**
De Benedetti, Aldo, 5:**516**
Debenedetti, Giacomo, 5:**516–517**
Debir (Israel), 5:**517**
Debir (King), 5:**517**, 6:221
Deborah, 5:**517–519**
    Jabin and, 11:7–8
    Judges, book of, 11:561, 563–564
Deborah (Mosenthal), 14:521
Deborah, Golda, and Me: Being Female and Jewish in America (Pogrebin), 16:278
Deborah organization, 2:118
Deborin, Abram Moiseyevich, 5:**519–520**
Debrecen (Hungary), 5:**520**
Debrecenji, Jožef, 5:**520**
De Brito. *See* Abendana family
Debs, Eugene D., 15:277, 278
Debt lien. *See* Liens and debts
Debts. *See* Liens and debts
Debussy: His Life and Mind (Lockspeiser), 13:154
Decalogue, 5:**520–526**, 522t, 526t
    Eshkol ha-Kofer (Hadassi), 8:188–189
    fiction, *Midrash Aseret ha-Dibberot*, 7:12
    given, 6:616
    J (YHWH) source of Torah, 15:736
    Moses, 14:525, 528–529
    parents, honoring, 15:641
    similarity of, to treaties of ancient era, 15:744–745, 751
    Tablets of the Law, 19:425
de Camondo family. *See* Camondo family
De Campo, Johannes. *See* Campen, Johannes van
de Campo, Transislanus. *See* Campen, Johannes van
Decapolis, 4:451, 5:**526–528**, 527
De Casseres, Benjamin, 5:**528**
Decastro, Jacob. *See* Castro, Jacob de
DeCastro, Leon, 2:452
De Castro, Manoel Mendes, 4:144
de Castro family. *See* Castro, de, family
de Castro Tartas, David. *See* Castro Tartas, David de
Decembrists, 5:**528**
De Chaves, Aaron, 5:**528**
De Chinese fluitspeler (Loggem), 13:172–173

Decimal system, 15:333
Deciphering Mysteries. See Zafenat Pane'ah
Decision, rules of, 5:157–158
Deckert, Franz, 3:764
Deckert, Joseph, 5:**528**
Declaration Nostra Aetate, 4:687–690
Declaration of Independence, Israel, 5:**528–529**, 18:211
Declaration of Principles (1885), 17:168–169
Declaration of Principles (1993). *See* Oslo Accords (1993)
Deconstructionism, 3:655, 5:598–599
Decorative borders in books, 4:75
De Cordova, Jacob, 5:**529–530**
Decorporatization, 5:114–115
Decrees, legal. *See* Takkanot
Décret infâme of March 17, 1808. *See* Infamous decree of March 17, 1808
De Die Natali (Censorinus), 4:539
De douuă mii de ani (Sebastian), 18:231
Deed. *See* Shetar
Deed, Acquisition by. *See* Acquisition
Deedes, Sir Wyndham, 5:**530**
Deedes, Wyndham. *See* Deedes, Sir Wyndham
The deep, 5:**530**
Deer, 5:**530–531**
La défaite de la pensée (Finkielkraut), 7:36
Defamation. *See* Slander
Defects. *See* Blemishes
Defense. *See* Practice and procedure
Defense, Jewish self-. *See* Self-defense
Defense literature. *See* Apologetics
Defenses of the Imagination: Jewish Writers and Modern Historical Crisis (Alter), 2:18
Defter (Darah), 2:105, 3:16
Defus ha-Almanah ve-ha-Aḥim ROmm, 17:418
Deganyah (Israel), 3:138, 5:**531**, 20:659
de Gaulle, Charles, 4:509, 7:164, 169
Degel. *See* Banners
Degel maḥaneh Efraim (Moses), 14:557
Degeneration (Nordau). *See* Entartung
Deggendorf (Germany), 5:**531–532**, 12:476
De Groot, Hugo. *See* Grotius, Hugo
de Groot, Huig. *See* Grotius, Hugo
De Haan, Jacob Israël. *See* Haan, Jacob Israël De
De Haas, Jacob, 4:122, 5:**532**
De Hirsch, Maurice, 2:429, 11:285–286, 287

Dehok (Iraq), 5:**532**
Deidesheimer, Philip, 14:454
Deinard, Ephraim, 5:**532**, 15:661
Deioces. *See* Dayaukku (Median leader)
Deir al-Balaḥ (Israel), 5:**532–533**
Deir 'Alla inscriptions, 3:78–80
Deir 'Alla texts, 3:76, 78–80, 656, 657
Dei Rossi, Azariah ben Moses. *See* Rossi, Azariah ben Moses dei
Deir Yassin (Israel), 15:571, 20:656
Deism, 7:671–672
Deists, 5:**533–534**
Deities. *See specific gods and godesses*
Dej (Romania), 5:**534**
De Jong, Louis (Loe). *See* Jong, Louis De
De Joodse Wachter (newspaper), 16:492
De Jure Belli ac Pacis (Grotius), 9:227
De Jure Naturali et Gentium (Selden), 18:258
Dekabrists. *See* Decembrists
Dekel. *See* Palms
Dekker, Maurits, 6:70
De Klerk, Michel, 5:**534–535**
Delacroix, Eugene, 1:438
Delacrut, Mattathias ben Solomon, 5:**535**
De la division du travail social (Durkheim), 6:64
De la Mar family. *See* Delmar family
De La Motta, Jacob, 5:**535**
Delasem, 4:49
Delatot, Neḥoshet (Hazaz), 8:493–494
De Lattes, Bonet. *See* Lattes, Bonet
Delaunay-Terk, Sonia, 5:**535**, 15:648
Delaware (U.S.), 5:**535–536**, 536
Del Banco, Anselmo, 5:**536–537**
Del Banco, Vita, 5:**537**
Del Bene, Eliezer David Ben Isaac, 5:**537**
Del Bene, Judah Asahel ben David Eliezer, 5:**537**
De Lee, Joseph B., 5:**537**
Delegación de Asociaciones Israelitas Argentinas. *See* DAIA
Delegazione Assistenza Emigrati Ebrei, 3:370–371, 7:484
De Lemos, Henriette. *See* Herz, Henriette
De Leon, Daniel, 3:173, 5:**538**, 18:708
De Leon, David Camden, 5:**537**
De Leon, Edwin, 5:**537–538**
De Leon, Thomas Cooper, 5:**537–538**
De Leon family, 5:**537–538**
Delevante. *See* Chriqui family

Delevante family. *See* Chriqui family

Delfont, Bernard, Lord, 5:**538**

De Lieme, Nehemia, 5:**538–539**, 18:613

Delilah, 5:**539**

De Lima, Joseph Suasso, 5:**539**

Delitzsch, Franz, 5:**539–540**, 16:630, 17:370

    Einhorn, David (Reform rabbi), 6:258

    Hebrew version of New Testament produced by, 3:681

    pan-Babylonianism of, 3:651

    printed editions of Hebrew Bible, 3:588, 622

Delitzsch, Friedrich, 5:**540–541**, 8:470

Delitzsch, Julius. *See* Delitzsch, Franz

Deliver Us From Error (al-Ghazālī), 7:571

Dell, Edmund, 5:**541**

Dell, Michael S., 2:679–680, 5:**541**

Della Seta, Alessandro, 2:370, 5:**541**

Della Torre, Hillel. *See* Della Torre, Lelio

Della Torre, Lelio, 3:633, 5:**541–542**

Delmar, Abraham, 5:**542**

Delmar, Joseph, 5:**542**

Delmar, Mas'ūd, 5:**542**

Delmar, Mordecai, 5:**542**

Delmar family, 5:**542**

Delmar-Lebhar, Shalom, 5:**542**

Del Medico, Henri E., 5:**542**

Delmedigo, Elijah ben Moses Abba, 2:531, 5:**542–543**, 16:90

Delmedigo, Joseph Solomon, 3:35, 5:**543–544**, 13:675–676, 677, 16:91

    alchemy, 1:603

    Joseph ben Shalom Ashkenazi, 11:426

Del Monte, Crescenzo, 5:**544**

De Lonzano, Menahem. *See* Lonzano, Menahem ben Judah de

Delos (Greece), 5:**544–545**

Delougaz, Pierre Pinchas, 2:371, 5:**545**

Delouya, Issac, 5:545

Delouya, Jacob, 5:545

Delouya, Jaki, 5:545

Delouya, Judah, 5:545

Delouya, Meir (c. 1625), 5:545

Delouya, Meir (c. 1780), 5:545

Delouya, Mordecai ben Isaac, 5:545

Delouya, Moses, 5:545

Delouya family, 5:**545**

De Loya. *See* Delouya family

De Lucena, Abraham Haim, 5:545–546

De Lucena, Samuel, 5:545–546

De Lucena family, 5:**545–546**

Delvalle, Max Shalom, 5:**546**, 16:349–350

Delvalle, Max Sḥalom, 15:610

Delvalle Levi Maduro, Eric Arturo, 5:**546**

Del Vecchio, Abraham ben Shabbetai, 5:546

Del Vecchio, Samuel Mahalalel, 5:546

Del Vecchio, Shabbetai el-Hanan ben Elisha, 5:546

Del Vecchio, Solomon David ben Moses, 5:546

Del Vecchio, Solomon Moses, 5:546

Del Vecchio family, 5:**546**

D'Elvert, Christian Ritter von, 5:**547**

Delyon, Isaac, 20:308

De Lyre, Nicholas. *See* Nicholas de Lyre

Demai, 5:**547–548**

Demalach, Yoel, 5:**548**

Demanjuk case, 20:644–645

Dember, Harry L., 5:**548**

Dembitz, Lewis Naphtali, 5:**548**

Dembitzer, Ḥayyim Nathan, 5:**548**

Demblin, Benjamin, 5:**548**

Dembo, Isaac, 5:**549**

De Medico Hebraeo Enarratio Apologetica (de Pomis), 14:440

Demetrius (Greco-Jewish writer), 5:**549**

    Moses, 14:532

    religious impact of Bible on Hellenistic Judaism and, 3:660

Demetrius (Jewish notable of Alexandria), 5:**549**

Demetrius II, 5:**550**, 9:194, 11:399

Demetrius III Eukarios Theos Philopater Soter, 5:**550**

Demetrius I Soter, 1:603, 5:**549–550**, 9:194, 11:398–399

Demetz, Peter, 5:**550–551**

Demikovsky, Jules. *See* Olitski, Jules

Demille, Cecil B., 5:**551**

Demjanjuk, Ivan. *See* Demjanjuk, John

Demjanjuk, Jan, 15:388

Demjanjuk, John, 5:**551–552**, 18:462

Demnat (Morocco), 5:**552**

Demnate (Morocco). *See* Demnat (Morocco)

Democracy and Assimilation (Drachsler), 6:6

Democratic Education (Gutmann), 8:153

Democratic Fraction, 5:**552–553**, 13:14

    Minsk Conference, 14:297

    Sheinkin, Menahem, 18:437

Democratic Movement for Change (DMC), 5:**553**

Demography, 5:**553–572**

    about Jewish, 5:554

    Association for Jewish Demography and Statistics, 18:724

    Belgium, 4:227

    Brutzkus, Boris Dov, 4:228

    Canada, Montreal, 14:464–465

    characteristics of populations, 5:568–572

        age composition, 5:568–570, 569*t*

        origin groups (edot), 5:570–572

        sex, 5:570

    Chicago, 4:609–610

    Drachsler, Julius, 6:6

    England, 6:420, 422–423

    Iran, 10:10, *10*, 10*t*, 12–13

    Iraq, 10:15–16, 16*t*

    Israel (state), 5:554, 560, 562, 10:373–387

        Arab population, 10:485–486, 521–522

        Coastal Plain, 10:373, 375–383

        distribution of population, 10:374–375

        introduction, 10:373–374

        Mount Hermon, 10:386

        Negev, 10:384–386

        Rift Valley, 10:383–384

    Italy, 10:*804*, 804*t*, 805–806, 807

    Latin America, 12:512

    Lestschinsky, Jacob, 12:666

    marriage and divorce rates, 20:554–556, 554*t*, 555*t*, 558–559

    Morocco, 14:501, 504, 505

    Palestine (Mandate), economic affairs, 10:496–500, 497*t*, 498*t*, 499*t*

    post-WW II, USSR, 17:555*t*, 571–572

    Rosenberg, Louis, 17:438

    Russia, 17:580

        1881-1917: Second Phase, 17:537*t*, 539

        1970s, 17:569

        1980s, 17:571–572, 571*t*

        post-WW II, 17:554–556, 554*t*, 555*t*, 557

        USSR regime, 17:545–546, 545*t*, 546*t*

    Samaritans, 17:726–727

    size and geographical distribution, 5:554–568, 564*t*, 565*t*, 566*t*

        dispersion and concentration, 5:562–568

Demography, *continued*
> geographic shifts, 5:554–562, 554t, 556t, 557t, 559t, 560–561t
> urbanization and, 5:565–567, 567t
> vital statistics, 20:550–559
> *See also* Population
Demography, Jewish. *See specific countries*
Demons and demonology, 1:470–471, 5:**572–578**, 13:17
> abracadabra, 1:280
> Agrat Bat Mahalath, 1:470–471
> amulets, 2:121–122
> Angel of Death, 2:147–150
> Azazel, 2:763–764
> Ben Temalyon, 3:380
> demon king, 2:592–593
> Kabbalah, 5:575–577
> netherworld, 15:110–112
> Samael, 17:714–715
> Solomon, testament of, 18:769
> *Testament of Solomon*, 18:768
> visions, 20:544–545
> *See also* Satan
Demotika (Greece). *See* Didymoteikhon (Greece)
Demsky, Issur Danielovich. *See* Douglas, Kirk
Denazification, 5:**578–579**
Denburg, Chaim, 5:**579**
Dénes, Béla, 5:**579**
Denia (Spain), 5:**579**
De Nicols *v.* Curlier, 5:156–157
De Nida, Johannes. *See* Pistorius, Johannes
Denikin, Anton Ivanovich, 5:**580**
Denis, Albertus, 5:**580**
Denis the Carthusian. *See* Dionysius van Ryckel
Denkmaeler der Tonkunst in Oesterreich (publication), 1:398
Denmark, 5:**580–585**, *581*
> banking and bankers, Adler, David Baruch, 1:396
> bible translated into Danish, 3:627–628
> chief rabbis, Melchior, Marcus, 14:10–11
> emancipation, 6:377
> Foighel, Isi, 7:94
> Holocaust, 9:341–342
> Jewish literature, 18:90
> journalism in, 11:467, 12:752
> librarians, Edelmann, Raphael, 6:143
> libraries, 12:786
> museums, 14:627
> newspapers, 16:502
> prominent families, Melchior, 14:10
> theater, 6:734
Denmark, Florence Levin, 5:**586**
Denouncers. *See* Informers
Dentistry
> Gottlieb, Bernhard, 8:10
> Seldin, Harry M., 18:259–260
Denver (CO), 5:**586–587**
> Kauvar, Charles Eliezer Hillel, 12:37–38
> philanthropy in, 11:46–47
Denying the Holocaust: The Growing Assault on Truth and Memory (Lipstadt), 9:494, 10:30, 31
De-oraita vs De-rabbanan, 8:253–254, 14:335–336
De'ot ha-Philosofim (Falaquera), 6:399, 681
De Palatio family. *See* Palache family
Department of Jewish Matters and Deportation (Germany), 6:248–251
Department stores, 5:**587–589**
> Bamberger, Louis, 3:103
> Bloomingdale's, 3:784, 5:588
> Filene, 7:19–20
> in New York City, 15:203, 226
> *See also* specific stores
De Pass, Aaron, 5:589
De Pass, Alfred, 5:589
De Pass, Daniel, 5:589
De Pass, Elias, 5:589
De Pass, Spence, and Company, 5:589
De Pass family, 5:589
De Paz. *See* Buzaglo, Joseph
De Philippe, Edis, 5:589
De Piera, Meshullam ben Solomon, 5:**589–590**
De Piera, Solomon ben Meshullam, 1:231, 5:**590–591**
De Pinto. *See* Pinto, de, family
de'Pomi, David. *See* Pomi, David de'
De Porta, Benveniste. *See* Benveniste De Porta
Deportations
> Armenia, 2:474
> artists, 2:518
> Austria, 2:693–695
> Belgium, 2:250
> Brunner, Alois, 4:223
> Bulgaria, 4:271–273
> documentation of, 2:520
> Germany, 5:62
> Hungary, 2:491, 670, 673, 9:614–616
> Netherlands, 2:115–116, 9:*473*
> Poland, 2:164, 663, 5:375, 16:239, 307–308, 310, 311, 312
>> Lodz ghetto, 9:*476, 478*
>> Reichsvereiniung and, 17:202
> Romania, 2:247
> Slovakia, 2:666, 5:357–358, 9:*479*
> *See also* Expulsions
Deportees. *See* Refugees
Deportment. *See* Etiquette
Deposits, of articles or money, 18:373
Depping, Georges-Bernard, 5:**591**
Depression, 14:56–57
Depression, Great. *See* Great Depression
Dépreux, Edouard, 4:10
Deputies of the Jewish people, 5:**591**
The Deputy (Hochhuth), 9:398, 406, 442
The Deputy. See Der Stellvertreter
De-rabbanan. *See* De-oraita vs De-rabbanan
Derash, 3:641, 661–662, 5:**591**, 6:339, 16:8–9, 18:434
Derashah, 3:165
Derashot (Molcho), 14:424
Derashot ha-Ran, 1:636, 5:**591–592**
Derashot ha-Rosh (Shag), 18:361
Derazhnya (Ukraine), 5:**592**
Derbent (Caucasus), 5:**592**
> *See also* Mountain Jews
Derekh Emunah (Abraham ben Shem Tov Bibago), 3:570–571
Derekh erez (behavior of people), 5:**592–593**
Derekh erez (tractate), 5:**593–594**
Derekh ha-Emmunah (Segrè), 18:252
Derekh ha-Kodesh (Hirschensohn-Lichtenstein), 9:136
Derekh ha-Yashar la-Olam ha-Ba (Epstein), 6:474
Derekh Tevunot (Luzzatto), 13:283
Derekh Yesharah (Epstein), 6:473
Deren, Maya, 5:**594**
Derenbourg, Hartwig, 5:594–595
Derenbourg, Joseph Naphtali, 5:594–595
Derenbourg family. *See* Derenburg family
Derenburg, Zevi Hirsch, 5:594
Derenburg family, 5:**594–595**
Derenkowsky, Eleanora. *See* Deren, Maya
Deri, Aryeh, 5:**595**, 18:419
Deri, Machluf. *See* Deri, Aryeh
Dering, Wladyslaw, 8:465
Derishat Ziyyon (Kalischer), 11:737–738

Derjuedisch Gottesdienst in seiner geschichtliehen Entwicklung (Elbogen), 6:291

D'Erlanger. *See* Erlanger family

Dermatology. *See* Medicine

Dernburg, Bernhard, 5:596

Dernburg, Friedrich, 5:596

Dernburg, Heinrich, 5:595–596, 12:551

Dernburg family, 5:**595–596**

Der Nister, 5:**596–598**

De' Rossi, Giovanni Bernardo, 5:**598,** 8:514
   bibliography of, 3:681
   as bibliophile, 3:683

Derrida, Jacques, 3:655, 5:**598–600,** 6:267, 12:716

Dershowitz, Alan M., 5:**600**

Derush. *See* Derash

Déry, Tibor, 5:**600–601**

Derzhavin, Gabriel Romanovich, 5:**601**
   on blood libel, 3:778
   Notkin, Nata, 15:316

Derzhavin, G. R., 15:694

Dés (Romania). *See* Dej (Romania)

De Saulcy. *See* Saulcy, Louis Felicien de Joseph Caignart

Descartes, René
   modern biblical criticism, development of, 3:649
   New Testament critique and, 15:191

Descending and ascending numbers, 15:337

Descent, SeeGenealogy

Descent from the Cross (Rattner), 17:115

Deschenes Commission of Inquiry on War Criminals in Canada, 13:129

Description of the East and some other Countries (Pococke), 16:250

A Descriptive Geography and Brief Historical Sketch of Palestine, 18:191

Desecration, 5:**601–602**

Desertification, 6:452

De-Shalit, Amos, 5:**602**

Desheh, Avraham, 5:**602**

De Shira, Myer. *See* Hart, Myer

Desiderus Erasmus Roterodamus. *See* Erasmus of Rotterdam

Designed as an Easy Guide to the Hebrew Tongue, for Jewish Children and Self-Instruction (Leeser), 6:190

Deskarta (Iraq), 5:**602**

Desmaestre, Jonah, 5:**602–603,** 6:58

Des Moines (IA), 10:7–8

De Sola, Aaron, 18:750

De Sola, Aaron David Meldola, 5:603

De Sola, Abraham, 4:395, 5:603, 18:**750**

De Sola, Benjamin (1818-1882), 18:750

De Sola, Clarence Isaac, 4:400, 401, 5:603

De Sola, David, 18:750

De Sola, David Aaron, 1:509, 18:750–751

De Sola, Isaac, 18:750

De Sola, Juan, 18:750

De Sola, Juan Bartolomé, 5:**604**

De Sola, Raphael Samuel Mendes, 18:750

De Sola family, 5:**603,** 18:**750–751**

Desolation, abomination of. *See* Abomination of desolation

D'Espina, Alfonso. *See* Alfonso de Espina

Desportes, S., 3:778

Dessau, Bernardo, 5:**604**

Dessau, Hermann, 5:**604**

Dessau, Mordecai. *See* Magnus, Marcus

Dessau, Paul, 5:**604**

Dessauer, Friedrich, 5:**604–605**

Dessauer, Jacob, 2:119

Dessauer, Leopold. *See* Dessoir, Ludwig

Dessler, Elijah Eliezer, 5:**605**

Dessoir, Ludwig, 5:**605**

Dessoir, Max, 5:**605–606**

D'Estella, David ben Samuel. *See* Kokhavi, David ben Samuel

Destinee du nationalisme (Sima), 18:590

Destiny (Bursztyn). *See* Goyrl

Destiny's Journey. See Schicksalsreise

The Destiny Waltz (Charles), 4:577

The Destruction of the European Jews (Hilberg), 9:100, 101, 102, 415, 418

De Successionibus (Selden), 18:258

De Synhedriis (Selden), 18:258

Detective Comics, 11:760–761

Detention, 5:**606–608,** 14:360

Detention camps, Cyprus, 5:349

Determinism, 10:825

Detroit (MI), 5:**608–612**
   Fisher, Max M., 7:63–64
   secondhand goods trade, 18:232

Detroit Jewish News, 18:675

Detroit Laundry and Linen Drivers Association, 5:611

Detstvo (Ben-Ammi), 3:316

Detstvo Gor'kogo (Donskoy), 5:752

Dettensee (Germany), 9:315

Deuel, Hans Erwin, 5:**612**

Deuster, Joseph. *See* Anthony, Joseph

Deutch, John M., 5:**612–613**

Deutero-Isaiah
   eschatology in, 6:493
   monotheism, 14:450

Deuteronomy, 3:649, 5:**613–620**
   authorship of, 5:619
   blessing of Moses, 14:545
   book of, 5:613–614
   covenants, 5:249–253
   critical assessment of, 5:613–615
   dates for, 5:615–616
   Decalogue, 5:521–523, 522t
   'eglah 'arufah, 6:220–221
   elders, 6:294–295
   Hosea, Book of and, 9:556–558
   Midrashim, *Mekhilta Deuteronomy,* 13:792–793
   provenance of, 5:616–617
   Shapira fragments, 18:402–403
   Sifrei, 18:562–564
   Tetrateuch, and relation to, 5:617–619
   tithe, 19:738–739
   See also D (Deuteronomy) source of Torah

Deuteronomy Rabbah, 5:**620–621**

Deuterosis. *See* Mishnah

Deutsch, Aladar, 5:**621**

Deutsch, Andre, 5:**621**

Deutsch, Babette, 5:**621**

Deutsch, Benjamin. *See* Nemteanu, Barbu

Deutsch, Bernard Seymour, 5:**621**

Deutsch, Bernát, 8:459

Deutsch, David ben Menahem Mendel, 5:**621–622**

Deutsch, Eliezer Ḥayyim ben Abraham, 5:**622**

Deutsch, Emanuel Oskar, 5:**622**

Deutsch, Ernst, 5:**622**

Deutsch, Felix, 5:**622–623**

Deutsch, Gotthard, 2:47, 5:**623**

Deutsch, Helene, 5:**623**

Deutsch, Ignac, 8:459

Deutsch, Ignaz, 5:**623–624**

Deutsch, Israel, 5:**624**

Deutsch, Jósef, 8:459

Deutsch, Judah Joel, 5:**624**

Deutsch, Leo, 5:**624**

Deutsch, Menahem. *See* Deutsch, Emanuel Oskar

Deutsch, Moritz, 5:**624**

Deutsch, Moses, 5:624

Deutsch, Otto Erich, 5:**625**

Deutsch, Simon, 5:**625**

Deutsch, Tibor. *See* Déry, Tibor

Deutsch de la Meurthe, Émile, 5:**625**

Deutsch de la Meurthe, Henri, 1:429–430, 5:**625**

Deutsche Arbeiterpartei. *See* National Socialism (Nazism)

Der deutsche Charakter in der Geschichte Europas (Kahler), 11:718

Deutsche Konservative Partei. *See* German Conservative Party

Deutscher, Aron. *See* Dotan, Aron

Deutscher, Isaac, 5:**625–626**, 15:326

Deutscher Palaestina-Verein, 5:**626**

Deutsches Evangelisches Institut (Jerusalem), 2:11

Deutsches Reichsstaatsrecht (Laband), 12:407

Deutsch-Israelitischer Germeindebund (DIGB), 5:**626**

Deutschkreutz (Austria), 5:**626–627**

Deutschlaender, Leo, 5:**627**

Deutz (Germany), 5:**627**

Deutz, Emmanuel, 5:627

Deutz, Simon, 5:**627–628**

Devarim. *See* Deuteronomy

Devarim Tovim (Alshekh), 2:10

Devar Moshe (Amarillo), 2:32

Devar she-hayah rules, 9:27

Devar Shemuel (Aboab), 1:268

Devash. *See* Altaras, David ben Solomon

De Vaux, Roland
   Ein Fashkhah, 6:256
   historical criticism of, 3:654
   Jerusalem Bible, 3:617
   sociology of Bible and, 3:658

Devekut, 5:**628–629**, 8:413, 11:104, 661–662
   Dov Baer, 5:767
   Hasidic doctrine, 10:745, 746
   See Also Meditation

Development and Resources Corporation, 13:16

The Development of a Legend (Neusner), 1:461

Development of the Canaanite Dialects (Harris), 8:365

Devenishski, Eisik Meir. *See* Weiter, A.

Dever, 5:573

De Verlatene (Bruggen), 4:222

De Vidas, Elihah, 2:38

Devil. *See* Demons and demonology

The Devil (Molnár), 14:427

The Devil's Arithmetic (Yolen), 18:200

The Devil's General (Zuckmaye), 9:406

Devir. *See* Dvir

De viris illustribus (Jerome), 11:143

De Vita Contemplativa (Philo of Alexandria), 11:589

De vita et moribus Judaeorum, 4:460

Devons, Ely, 5:**629**

Devrei Neḥemiah (Ḥayon), 8:477

De Vries, André, 5:**629**

De Vries, Benjamin, 5:**629**

De Vries, M., 5:**629**, 12:554, 16:349

Dew, 5:**629–630**, 6:73
   prayer for, 5:630

De Wette, Martin, 3:649

De Wette, Wilhelm Martin Lebrecht. *See* Wette, de, Wilhelm Martin Leberecht

Dewey, John, 1:409

Dewey, Thomas E., 4:157

Dhamār (Yemen), 5:**630–631**

Dhamārī, Manṣur Suleiman, 5:**631**

Dhamārī, Saʾid ben David, 5:**631**

Dheka pende imere ana tin Evraikyin Palestinin (Moissis). *See Fifteen Days Across Jewish Palestine* (Moissis)

Dhimma, dhimmi, 5:**631–632**, 15:416–419

Dhimmitude. *See* Dhimma, dhimmi

Dialectic and argumentation. *See* Disputations and polemics

Dialoghi (Sommo), 19:8

Dialoghi d'amore (Abrabanel), 10:791

Dialoghi di Amore (Arabanel), 1:279–280

Dialogi... in quibus judaeorum opiniones... confutanur (Petrus Alfonsi), 16:21

Dialogos sat€ricos (Caceres), 4:330

Dialogue aux Enfers entre Machiavel et Montesquieu, our la politique aux xixe siècle (Joly), 6:297

Dialogue of Solomon and Saturn (poem), 18:761

Dialogues à Byzance (Benda), 3:324

Dialogue with Trypho (Justin Martyr), 11:580

Dialogus inter Philosophum. Judaeum et Christianum (Abelard), 1:246

Diamand, Herman, 5:**632**, 16:347, 18:707

Diamant, Paul Joseph, 5:**632**

Diament, Fred, 2:48

Diamond, David, 5:**632**, 11:413

Diamond, I.A.L., 5:**632–633**

Diamond, Jack (1909-2001), 4:188, 5:**633**

Diamond, Jack (1932-), 5:**633**

Diamond, Jacob, 1:589, 4:360

Diamond, John, 16:342, 18:706

Diamond, John, Baron, 5:**633–634**

Diamond, Leo. *See* Diamond, David

Diamond, Louis Klein, 5:**634**

Diamond, Neil, 5:**634**

Diamond, Sigmund, 5:**634**, 18:732

Diamond, William, 1:589, 6:150

Diamond industry. *See* Gems industry

Diane's Tree. See Arbol de Diana

Diary of a Hunchback. See Zápisky hrbácovy (Leda)

The Diary of Anne Frank. See Diary of a Young Girl (Frank)

Diary of a Seducer. See A Togbikhl fun a Farfirer

Diary of a Shirtwaist Striker (Malkiel), 18:713

Diary of a Young Girl (Frank), 4:630, 6:70, 9:441, 444, 445, 448
   Bloomgarden, Kermit, as producer of play based on, 3:783
   Levin, Meyer, dramatization, 12:712

Diary of Our Own Samuel Pepys (Adams), 1:380

Dias, Luis, 5:**636–637**, 18:320

Diaspora, 5:**637–643**
   aid to Jerusalem, 11:155, 163, 164
   antisemitism, 2:207–209
   apostasy, 2:274–275
   Babylonian, 9:203–204
   Bible reading, 13:658–664
   Borochov, Ber, 4:89–90
   Canada, 4:393–394
   capital punishment in, 4:449–450
   children's literature, 4:625, 626
   creation of centers of hegemony, 6:34–37
   dance, 5:410
   Day of Atonement in, 5:488
   demography and, 5:554–572
   economic history, 6:102–104
   education, 6:172–173
   expulsions, 6:624–626
   extradition to Christian authorities during, 6:627–628
   Graeco-Roman period, Samaritans, 17:722–723
   Iraq, 10:15
   Jewish identity, Philo Judaeus, 16:61
   Jewish identity in, 11:298, 299
   Jewish medicine, 13:724–725, 726, 734–736
   Jewish settlement, 11:163
   Josephus' *Jewish Antiquities* and, 11:439
   laws and legal systems, 14:345
     Berurei Averah/Averot, 3:492

League of Nations, 12:565

Lithuania, 13:117, 120

Persia, 15:785–791

Portuguese Nation in Pesaro (Italy), 16:6–7

Rawidowicz, Simon, on, 17:125

relationship to state of Israel, 16:100, 101, 103

Second Temple period, 9:200–202, 201, *201*

self-government, exilarchs, 6:**600–607**, *601, 602*

Shabbetai Zevi, 18:346–348

sheluḥei erez Israel, 5:721, 18:449–451

ties with Israel, 10:227–228

Torah, reading of, 20:48*t*–49*t*

Zionist socialism and, 18:717–718

See also Galut; *specific nations*

Diaspora, Sephardi. *See* Sephardim

Diaspora Museum (Tel Aviv), 16:127, 128, 130, 18:618

Dibbuk, 5:**643–644**, 7:604, 18:199

Dibbuk ḥaverim, 1:294

Dibon (Israel), 5:**644–645**

Dice games, 7:369, 371

Dichter, Misha, 5:**645**

Dick, Isaac Meir, 15:660

Dickdook Leshon Gnebreet: A Grammar of the Hebrew Tongue, 14:445

Dickens, Charles, 5:**645**, 6:278, 435

Dickenstein, Abraham, 5:**645–646**

Dicker-Brandeis, Frederike, 5:**646**

Dicker-Brandeis, Friedl. *See* Dicker-Brandeis, Frederike

The Dick Gibson Show (Elkin), 6:359

Dickman, Adolfo, 16:349

Dickman, Enrique, 16:349

Dickmann, Max, 11:469

Dickstein, Samuel (1851-1939), 5:**646**

Dickstein, Samuel (1885-1954), 2:53, 5:**646**

Dickstein, Szymon, 5:**646–647**, 18:707

Dictionaries
  Aramaic, 2:353–354
  Bonafos, Menahem ben Abraham, 4:54–55
  Complete Dictionary of Ancient and Modern Hebrew, 3:387–388
  Egyptian, ancient, 6:482
  Galut Yehudah, 14:409
  Hebrew-Arabic, 1:639, 6:47–48, 15:473
  Hebrew-German and German-Hebrew, 3:391
  Hebrew-Persian, 18:772–773
  Hebrew-Russian, 14:519

Milon Olami le-Ivrit Meduberet, 3:389

Thesaurus synonumicus Hebraico-Chaldaico-Rabbinicus, 16:219

Yiddish-English-Hebrew Dictionary, 8:357

Dictionary of All Religions and Religious Denominations (Adams), 1:380

The Dictionary of Cultural Literacy (Hirsch), 9:125

Dictionary of Modern Music and Musicians (Hull), 6:262

Dictionary of National Biography, 9:152

Dictionary of Terms in Photography, 8:670

Dictionnaire général de géographie universelle (Ennery), 6:441

Dictum of Resh Lakish, 21:119

Diderot, Denis, 5:**647**

Didi-Huberman, Georges, 5:**647**

Didumotica (Greece). *See* Didymoteikhon (Greece)

Didymoteikhon (Greece), 5:**647–648**

Dieckhoff, Alain, 11:326

Diego de Barros. *See* Barrassa, Jacob

Diego Roderigo. *See* Zacuto, Abraham ben Samuel

Dien. *See* Razsvet (journal)

Dienchelele, 5:**648–649**

Dienemann, Max, 5:**649**, 11:394

Dienna, Azriel ben Solomon, 5:**649**

Diesendruck, Zevi, 5:**649–650**

Dieses Volk Israel (Baeck), 3:51

Diet. *See* Food

Dietary laws, 5:**650–659**, 652*t*–655*t*, 7:118
  Aaron of Neustadt, 1:219
  abomination, 1:269
  afikoman, 1:434
  amenities, communal, 2:39
  bitterns and herons as unclean birds, 3:729
  blindness and, 3:753
  cholent, 4:664
  Conservative Judaism and, 5:658
  and culture, Jewish, 5:659
  description of permitted foods, 5:650
  explanations for, 5:656–657
  food types
    cheese, 4:587
    eggs, 6:219–220
    fish, 7:59
    honey, 9:517–518
    meat, 5:651

milk regulations, 5:655–656
    parveh, 15:674
    pigs, 16:150–151
  halakhah
    blood, prohibition on consumption of, 3:771–772
    commandments concerning, 5:81*t*–82*t*
    Halakhah le-Moshe mi-Sinai, 8:258
    Ḥazakah of meat, 8:490
    hekhsher, 8:780
    Issur ve-Hetter, 10:773
    Mashgi'ah, 13:601
    nevelah, 5:651, 15:129
    sheḥitah (ritual slaughter), 5:549–550, 18:434–437
    terefah, 5:651
  Hirsch, Samson Raphael, 5:657
  history of, 5:656
  Karaites, 11:799
  niddah, 15:255–256
  Noachian, 6:576
  Passover, 15:678–681
  Reform Judaism and, 5:658
  technology, 19:575
  women and, 5:658–659

Dietrich, Marlene, 14:571

Dietro la porta (Bassani), 3:207

Diez Macho, Alejandro, 5:**659**

Different Trains (Reich), 17:198

Diffesa (Modena), 14:409

Difficult Childhood. See Yaldut Kashah

DiFiglia, Michael Bennett. *See* Bennett, Michael

Di Gara, Giovanni, 5:**659–660**, 15:641

DIGB. *See* Deutsch-Israelitischer Germeindebund

Digestive system, 2:134

Diglat. *See* Tigris

Digne (France), 5:**660**

Dignity. *See* Human dignity and freedom; Human rights

Dihok (Iraq). *See* Dehok (Iraq)

Dijla. *See* Tigris

Dijon (France), 5:**660**

Dik, Ayzik Meir. *See* Dik, Isaac Meir

Dik, Isaac Meir, 5:**660–661**

Dikdukei ha-Te'amim (Ben-Asher), 3:**320,** 13:29–30

The Dikdukei ha-Te'amim of Aaron ben Moses Ben-Asher. See Sefer Dikdukei ha-Te'amim le-Rabbi Aharon ben Moshe ben Asher

Dikdukei Soferim (Rabbinovicz), 17:31

Dikduk Eliyahu (Elijah ben Solomon Zalman), 6:346

Dikdukim (Levita), 13:43
Dikhovsky, Shlomo, 13:682
Dikow (Poland). *See* Tarnobrzeg (Poland)
Diller, Barry, 5:**661**
Dillmann, August, 5:**661–662**
Dillon, Abraham Moses, 5:**662**
Dillon, Mark, 12:553
"Dilly Tante." *See* Kunitz, Stanley Jasspon
DiMaggio, Joe, 14:450, 15:688
Dimanstein, Simon, 5:**662**
Dimat Ashukim (Silberbusch), 18:576
Dimi, 5:**662**
Dimi of Haifa. *See* Avdimi of Haifa
Dimi of Nehardea, 5:**662–663**
Dimitriyevich, Yuli. *See* Engel, Joel
Dimitrov, Emanuil Pop, 4:276
Dimitrovsky, Chaim Zalman, 5:**663**
Dimonah (Israel), 5:**663**
Dimov, Dimitur, 4:276
Dinaburg, Ben Zion. *See* Dinur, Benzion
Dinaburg, Benzion. *See* Dinur, Benzion
Dina de-malkhuta dina, 5:**663–669,** 14:334
　　autonomy, judicial, 2:710–711
　　conflict of laws, 5:151–157
　　Noachide laws and, 15:286
　　public authority, 16:696–710
Dinah, 5:**669,** 8:313, 11:19
Dine, Jim, 5:**669–670**
Dine, Tom, 2:51
Dinei de-Garme (Naḥmanides), 14:742
Dinei kenasot. *See* Obligations, law of
Diner, Hasia R., 5:**670,** 9:153
Diners Club credit organization, 3:784
Dines, Alberto, 4:152, 5:**670–671**
Dineson, Jacob, 5:**671**
Dinin, Samuel, 5:**671**
Dinitz, Simcha H., 5:**671**
Dinitz, Simon, 5:302–303, **671–672**
Diniz, Alavaro. *See* Denis, Albertus
Diniz, Rodrigues. *See* Rodrigues, Dionisius
Dinkins, David N., 15:228–229
Din shamayim, 6:529
Dinstein, Yoram, 11:233
Din Torah, 6:529
Dints, Alvaro. *See* Denis, Albertus
Dinur, Benzion, 5:**672,** 9:160
Dinur, Jehiel. *See* K. Zetnik
Dio Cassius, 5:**672–673,** 11:575
Dio Chrysostom, 5:**673**
Diocletian, Caius Valerianus, 5:**673–674,** 11:478

Diodore of Tarsus, 4:720
Diodorus of Sicily, 5:**674,** 8:749
Diodotus-Tryphon, 5:**674**
Diogenes Laertius, 5:**674**
Diogo Pires. *See* Pyrrhus, Didacus
Dion (Transjordan). *See* Dium (Transjordan)
Dioneo. *See* Shklovski, Isaac Vladimirovich
Dionis, Albert. *See* Denis, Albertus
Dionysius van Ryckel, 5:**674**
Dionysus, cult of, 5:**674–675**
Dio of Prusa. *See* Dio Chrysostom
Dios, 5:**675**
Dioscorides, 2:34
Dioscorides Pedanius, 5:**675**
Diphthongs in Hebrew, 8:570–571
Diplomaticus. *See* Wolf, Lucien
A Diplomat Looks Back (Einstein), 6:264
Diret el-Sunbul. *See* Tadmor (Syria)
Di Rieti. *See* Rieti family
Diringer, David, 5:**675–676**
Diritto Internazionale (Sereni), 18:309
Di Sabato, Elia of Ferma. *See* Elijah ben Shabbetai Be'er
Disabled persons
　　Aaronsohn, Michael, 1:223
　　education of deaf-mutes, 15:759
　　Nazi euthanasia, 6:560–571
Dische, Zacharias, 5:**676**
Discipline, Manual of. *See* Manual of Discipline
Discorso circa il stato degl' Hebrei (Luzzatto), 9:227, 13:287–288
Discours de la servitude volontaire (La Boétie), 12:408
Discourse on the Commerce of the Two Indies (Solis), 18:754
Discourses on the Ecclesiastical and Civil Policy of the Jews (Abendana), 1:250
Discrimination, 5:**679–681**
　　Arab countries, 5:681
　　Canada, 4:397, 409, 422
　　Covenant of Omar, 15:416–419
　　economic history, 6:118–119
　　England, 5:680–681
　　Islam, dhimma, dhimmi, 5:631–632
　　New Christians, 15:133–134
　　numerus clausus, 15:339–343
　　Poland, 16:303
　　U.S., 5:680
　　See also Antisemitism
Discursos Predycaveys (Silva), 18:583
Diseases. *See* Medicine

Disegni, Dario, 5:**681**
Disinterment, 5:**682**
Diskarta (Iraq). *See* Deskarta (Iraq)
Diskin, Chaim, 5:**682**
Diskin, Mordekhai, 5:**682**
Diskin, Moses Joshua Judah Leib, 5:**683**
Disna (Poland), 5:**683–684**
Disney Studios, 15:549
Disney Wars (Stewart), 6:277
Disney World (FL), 15:476
Di sotsyale diferentsiatsye (Shtif), 18:527
Displaced persons (DP), 5:**684–686,** 9:379
　　Beriḥah, 3:433–436
　　Bermuda Conference, 3:466
　　education, Jewish, 6:186
　　Eisenhower, Dwight David, 6:266–267
　　England and, 3:421
　　Germany
　　　　Bergen-Belsen, 3:421–422
　　　　Berlin, 3:451
　　　　Ḥabiru, 8:180–181
　　　　Schmidt, Samuel Myer, aid to, 18:146
　　World Jewish Relief, 4:544–545
Displaced refugees. *See* Displaced persons (DP)
Disputationes adversus Astrologiam Divinatricem (Pico della Miraondola), 16:146–147
Disputation of Barcelona, 3:**145–146,** 4:673, 17:127
Disputation of Paris, 11:103
Disputation of Rimini. *See* Rimini (Italy)
Disputation of Tortosa. *See* Tortosa, Disputation of
Disputations and polemics, 5:**686–699**
　　Amittai ben Shephatiah, 2:81
　　amoraim, 2:93
　　apologetics, 2:263–264
　　Church Fathers, 4:719–721
　　description of, 5:686–687
　　disputations between Jews and Christians (*See also* Tortosa (Spain), disputation of)
　　　　Bibago, Abrahem ben Shem Tov, 3:570
　　　　Brody, 4:199
　　　　Broughton, Hugh, and Loans, Elijah ben Moses, 4:212
　　　　Christiani, Pablo, 4:673
　　　　Odo of Cambrai, 15:383
　　　　Official, Nathan ben Joseph and Joseph, 15:388–389

Oppenheim, Moritz Daniel, paintings of, 15:446

Orobio de Castro, Isaac, 15:481

in Pamplona, 15:609

in Paris, 15:643

in Pavia, 15:698

disputations between Jews and Muslims, 3:669

hebraist, Christian, 8:513

Middle Ages

    Ahimaaz, Chronicle of, 5:691

    Catholic Church, 4:711

    Christian religious drama, 5:691

    Crispin, Gilbert, 5:691

    Duran, Profiat, 5:693

    fifteenth century, 5:693–694

    Gregory of Tours, 5:690

    Ibn Musa, Ḥayyim, 5:693–694

    Islam, 5:692

    Karaites, 5:691, 692–693

    Kimḥi, Joseph, 5:692

    Muelhausen, Yomtov Lipmann, 5:694

    Naḥmanides, 5:693

    Priscus, 5:690

    Sefer Nizzaḥon Yashan, 5:692

    thirteenth century disputations, 5:692–693, 7:153

    twelfth century, 5:691–692

pagan environment, 5:687–690

    Celsus, 5:689–690

    Christianity, 5:687–690

    Justin Martyr, 5:688–689

    Tryphon, 5:688–689

post-fifteenth century

    Buber, Martin, 5:698–699

    Frankist disputations, 5:696

    Lavater, J. C., 5:696

    Mendelssohn, Moses, 5:696

    Orobio de Castro, Isaac, 5:695

    Rosenstock-Heussy, Eugen, 5:696–698

    Rosenzweig, Franz, 5:696–698

    Schmidt, Karl Ludwig, 5:686, 698–699

    Van Limborch, Philipp, 5:695

Reformation, 5:695

    Hizzuk Emunah, 5:695

Renaissance, 5:694–695

    Farissol, Abraham, 5:694–695

See also Polemics and polemical literature

Disputes. *See* Conflict of opinion

Disraeli, Benjamin, 6:414, 12:776, 16:342

    coat of arms, 9:7

    Edelman, Maurice, 6:142–143

    English literature, 6:435–436

Disraeli, Benjamin, Earl of Beaconsfield, 5:**699–702**, 701*t*

D'Israeli, Isaac, 5:**702**, 9:236

Disraeli, Maria, 3:195

Disraeli family, 5:701*t*

Dissection. *See* Autopsies and dissection

Dissection and autopsies, 2:**711–713**

Dissentchik, Aryeh, 5:**702**

Dissolute sisters oracle, 6:639

Distant Journey (Radok), 9:440

Distel, Egon. *See* Goldstein, Moritz

Distenfeld, Henoch. *See* Yalon, Hanoch

District Town. See Okresni město

Dith Pran, 18:106

di Tintori, Abraham ben Ḥayyim, 3:586

Di Trani, Isaiah the Elder. *See* Isaiah ben Mali di Trani

Di Trani, Isaiah the Younger. *See* Isaiah ben Elijah di Trani

Di Trani, Joseph. *See* Trani, Joseph ben Moses

Di Trani, Moses. *See* Trani, Moses ben Joseph

Di Trento. *See* Riva (Italy)

Dittenhoefer, Abram Jesse, 5:**702**

Dium (Transjordan), 5:**702**

Dius. *See* Dios

Divekar, Samaji Hassaji. *See* Divekar, Samuel Ezekiel

Divekar, Samuel Ezekiel, 3:336, 4:51, 5:**702–703**

Divin (Poland), 5:**703**

Divina Commedia (Dante), 5:430–431

Divination, 3:76–81, 5:**703–708**, 16:568

Divine Chariot, 6:299

Divine Comedy (Dante), 10:788, 789

Divine forgiveness, 6:719, 720, 722

The Divine Invasion (Dick), 18:200

Divine judgment, 15:462–463

Divine law. *See* Divine punishment

Divine Presence, 16:**481–484**

Divine providence, 2:460, 461, 13:391

Divine punishment, 5:**708–710**, 7:79

Divine revelation, 11:40

Divine Will. *See* God

Divine wisdom, 11:589

Divorce, 3:72, 4:746–748, 5:**710–721**

    Aaron Simeon ben Jacob Abraham of Copenhagen, 1:221

agency in, 5:715–716

Ash, Abraham, 2:555

Bene Israel, 3:338, 10:298

Bible, 5:710–711

bill of, abbreviations, 1:239

Cleves get, 4:760

consequences of, 5:716–717

    custody of children, 15:635–637

    dowry, 12:94

    ketubbah, 12:93–98

Egypt, statistics, 5:720

Elephantine Papyri, 6:312

Europe, statistics on, 5:719–720

execution of, 5:715

feminism and, 6:753–754

get pitturin, 5:711, 716

grounds for

    bigamy and polygamy, 3:691–694

    head covering, 8:507

    niddah, 15:255

    prostitution, 16:627

ḥaliẓa, 12:726–729

Hillel of Erfurt, 9:115

imprisonment for husband, and refusal of, 9:744, 747

intermarriage, 14:376

Israel, 5:717–719, 10:286, 294, 637

Joseph, Norma Baumel, 11:417

Karaites, 11:795

laws and legal systems, 5:152–153, 154–155, 11:263, 265, 268

    agunah, 1:510–511, 513, 518–519

    apostasy, 2:276

    civil marriage, 4:746–748

    embryo, 6:391

    Maimonides, 5:137

    takkanot, 15:453, 455, 19:452

men's rights, 5:713–714

Morocco, statistics, 5:720

mutual consent and, 5:711–712

niddui vs. ḥerem, 9:14–15

prohibited marriages and, 5:714

Samaritans, 17:732

statistics, 5:720–721, 20:554–559, 554*t*

Talmud, 5:711

tractate *Gittin,* 7:620–621

U.K., statistics on, 5:720

U.S., modern, 6:703

will of parties and, 5:714

women's rights, 5:712–713, 714, 17:7–8

See also Ketubbah

Divorcio nupcial (Eichelbaum), 6:245

Divrei Eliyahu (Chazan), 4:585

Divrei Emet (Adeni), 1:390

Divrei ha-Yamim le-Malkhei Ẓarefat (ha-Kohen), 9:157

Divrei ha-Yamim le-Malkhut Venezia (Capsali), 4:455

Divrei ha-Yamin le-Moseh Rabbenu. See Chronicles of Moses

Divrei Ḥayyim (Halberstam), 8:265

Divrei Ḥiddud (Epstein), 6:467

Divrei Kodesh (Polak), 16:286

Divrei Rivot (Adarbi), 1:383

Divrei Shalom (Adarbi), 1:383

Divrei Shalom ve-Emet (Ḥazzan), 8:506

Divrei Shalom ve-Emet (Wessely), 8:687, 21:19–21

Divrei Yemel Yisrael (Simchoni), 18:590

Divrei Yisrael (Modzhitz), 14:413

The Divulgence of Mysteries and the Appearance of Lights (Aknin). *See Inkishāf al-asrār wa-ṭuhūr al-anwār*

Dīwān (De Piera), 5:590

Dīwān (Eleazar), 6:302

Diwan, Judah ben Amram, 5:**721**

Dixon Group, 11:747

Diyala (Iraq), 5:**721**

Di Yidishe Shtime. *See Yidishe Shtime* (newspaper)

Di Yunge. *See* Yunge, Di

Di-Zahav, Ephraim, 5:**721**

Dizengoff, Meir, 5:**721–722**

Djanet. *See* Zoan (Ancient Egypt)

Djerassi, Carl, 5:**722**

Djerba (Tunisia), 5:**722–723**

Djobar. *See* Jubar

DjubayI. *See* Jubayl (Lebanon)

Dlugosz, Jan, 5:**723**, 15:403

Dluzhnovski, Moyshe. *See* Dluzhnowsky, Moshe

Dluzhnowsky, Moshe, 5:**723**

DMC. *See* Democratic Movement for Change

Dmowski, Roman, 4:109, 5:**723–724**, 6:402

DNA, 4:568, 13:8–9

Dnepropetrovsk (Ukraine), 5:**724–725**

Dnieper Textile Industry Ltd., 6:39

Do'ar ha-Yom (newspaper), 5:**725**

Dobin, Shimon, 5:**725**

Dobin, Shimoni. *See* Dobin, Shimon

Dobkin, Eliyahu, 5:**725**

Dobrath (Israel), 5:**725–726**

Dobrogeanu-Gherea, Constantin, 5:**726**, 12:559

Dobroven, Issay Alexandrovich, 5:**726**

Dobroye utro (Kanovich), 11:766

Dobruschka, Emanuel, 5:**727**

Dobruschka, Franceska, 5:**727**

Dobruschka, Jacob Moses, 4:190, 5:**727**

Dobruschka, Leopoldine, 5:**727**

Dobruschka, Moses, 5:**726–727**, 727

Dobruschka, Solomon, 5:**727**

Dobruschka-Schoenfeld family, 5:**727**

Dobrushin, Yekhezkel, 5:**727–728**

"Dobruska." *See* Frank, Jacob

Dobzhinsky, Abraham ben Raphael. *See* Ciechanow, Abraham ben Raphael Landau of

The Doctor, His Patient, and the Illness (Balint), 3:91

Doctor Addams (Fineman), 7:26

Doctor Falk. *See* Falk, Samuel Jacob Ḥayyim

Doctorow, Edgar Lawrence, 5:**728**, 15:227

Doctorow, E.L. *See* Doctorow, Edgar Lawrence

Doctor Rast (James Oppenheim), 15:445

Doctors. *See* Medicine

Doctors Disagree (Franken), 7:202

Doctors' plot, 5:**728–729**

Doctor Zhivago (Pasternak), 15:684

Doctrine of atoms, 11:730

Doctrine of election, chosenness, 4:669–672, 682–684

Doctrines on Emanation. See Sefer Limmudei Aẓilut (Sarug)

Documentary Hypothesis, 15:752

Document clause, 6:164

Documents
    forgeries, 7:126–127
    interpretation of, 9:821–823
    mistakes, 14:368–369

Dóczy, Lajos, 5:**729**

Dodanim. *See* Rodanim

"Dodecaphony." *See* Twelve tone composition technique

Dod Ḥakhman (Eleazar), 11:735

Dod Mordekhai (Kukizow), 11:792

Doeblin, Alfred, 5:**729–730**

Doeg, 5:**730**

Doenmeh sect, 4:465, 5:**730–733**, 11:295, 18:353, 354, 356

Dogs, 5:**733**

Dohanj, Julije, 5:**733**

Dohm, Christian Wilheim von, 4:550, 5:**733–734**
    Cerfberr and, 2:8
    defense of Jews, 2:268

education, Jewish, 6:178–179

Doing Things with Texts: Essays in Criticism and Critical Theory (Abrams), 1:327

Doiokne. *See* Suftaja

"Do Jews Use Christian Blood for Religious Purposes?" (Alexeyev), 1:636

Dok (Israel), 5:**734**

Dokshitsy (Belarus), 5:**734–735**

Dokszyce (Belarus). *See* Dokshitsy (Belarus)

A doktor úr (Molnár). *See The Lawyer* (Molnár)

Dolgin, Simon Arthur, 5:**735**, 13:200

Dolginovo (Belarus), 5:**735**

Dolgopolsky, Tsipporah. *See* Fleischer, Tsippi

Dolgoposkii, Aaron, 11:322

Dolgorukov (governor of Moscow), 14:517

Dolicocefala bionda (Pitigrilli), 16:188

Dolina (Ukraine), 5:**735**

Doli Siti (Castel-Bloom), 4:512

Dolitzki, Menaḥem Mendel, 5:**735–736**, 8:736

Dollfuss, Engelbert, 5:**736**

Dolls, 1:621–622

Dolly City. See Doli Siti

Dolmatovski, Yevgeni Aronovich, 5:**736**

Dolmens, 5:**736–737**

Dolni Kounice (Czech Republic), 5:**737**

Dolni Kubin (Slovakia), 5:**737–738**

Dolný Kubin (Slovakia). *See* Dolni Kubin (Slovakia)

Dolny Stal (Slovakia). *See* Alistál (Slovakia)

Dołhinów (Belarus). *See* Dolginovo (Belarus)

Domain. *See* Reshut

Domalsky, I., 5:**738**

Dom Antonio, 1:249

Domashevitzky, Isiah. *See* Bershadsky, Isaiah

Dombroveni (Bessarabia), 5:**738**

Domenico Gerosolimitano, 5:**739**

Dome of the Rock, 9:501
    in art, 11:226, 227
    built, 11:154–155
    Even Shetiyyah and, 6:575
    Omar ibn al-Khaṭṭāb, 15:419

Domestic peace, 5:**739**

Domestic violence, 5:**739–741**, 6:704

Domiciles, 5:**741–743**

Domin, Hilde, 5:**743**

Dominic, Alexandru, 5:**743–744**

Domini canes. *See* Dominicans

Dominican Republic, 4:6, 476, 5:*744*, **744–745**

Dominican Republic Settlement Association, 2:60, 5:744

Dominicans, 5:**745–746**
   Berthold of Freiburg, 3:490
   Eckhart, Meister, 6:92
   Hoogstraaten, Jacob, 9:521
   Raymond de Penaforte, 17:126–127

Dominici, Itek. *See* Diamond, I.A L.

Dominion vs. stewardship, 5:164–165

Domitian, 5:**746–747**

Domitilla, 7:69

Domnici, Itek. *See* Diamond, I.A.L.

Domninus of Larissa, 5:**747**

Dom Pedro of Naples, 1:274

Domus Boni Latronis. *See* Latrun (Israel)

Domus Conversorum, 5:**747**

Donalda, Pauline, 5:**747**

Donath, Adolph, 5:**747–748**

Donath, Eduard, 5:**748**

Donath, Ludwig, 5:**748**

Donati, Angelo, 5:**748**, 14:408

Donati, Enrico, 5:**748**

Donati, Lazzaro, 5:**748–749**

Don Bendit. *See* Joseph ben Moses of Troyes

Don Çaq de la Maleha, 16:117

Donchin, Yehudah Leib. *See* Don-Yaḥia, Yehudah Leib

Don Çulema. *See* Ibn Zadok, Solomon

Donen, Stanley, 5:**749**

Donetsk (Ukraine), 5:**749**

Doniach, Deborah, 13:11

Doniger, Wendy, 5:**749–750**

Donin, Hayim Halevy, 5:**750**

Donin, Nicholas, 5:**750**

Don Juan (Simon), 18:617

Dönme sect. *See* Doenmeh sect

Donnolo, Shabbetai, 5:**750–752**, 8:666, 13:725

Don Pacifico affair. *See* Pacifico, David

Don Prophet Tibbon. *See* Jacob ben Makhir

Don Quixote (ballet, Eifman), 6:253

Don Quixote (Cervantes), 4:550

Don Salomon ben Labi. *See* Labi, Solomon

Donskoy, Mark Semenovich, 5:**752**

Don't Worry about the Kids (Neugeboren), 15:119

Don-Yaḥia, Shabbetai, 8:497

Don-Yaḥia, Yehudah Leib, 5:**752**

Donyel, M. *See* Daniel, M.

Door and doorpost, 5:**752–753**

Doppelurkunde, 18:467

Dor (Israel), 2:388, 5:**753–754**

Dor, Moshe, 5:**754–755**

Dor, Z. M., 2:90

Dorati, Antal, 5:**755**

Dor De'ah, 1:346, 11:622

Dor Dor ve-Dorshav (Weiss), 20:733–734

Doré, Paul Gustave, 14:542

Doresh Ẓiyyon (Simḥah ben Joshua), 18:603

Dorff, Elliot N., 5:**755–756**

Dorfman, Joseph (1904-1991), 5:**756**

Dorfman, Joseph (1940-), 5:**756**

Dorfman, Ralph Isadore, 5:**756**

Dori, Ya'akov, 5:**756**

Dorian, Dorel, 5:**757**

Dorian, Emil, 5:**757**

Dorian, Iancovici. *See* Dorian, Dorel

Doris, 5:**757**

Dorls, Fritz, 15:76

Dormido, David Abrabanel, 5:**757–758**

Dormido, Solomon, 5:**757**

Dorohoi (Romania), 5:**758**

Doron, Abraham, 5:**759**

Doron, Haim, 5:**759**

Doros. *See* Dor (Israel)

Dorot (Israel), 5:**759**

Dorot ha-Rishonim (Halevy), 8:270

Dorotheus, 5:**759**

"Dorot Rishonim" (Hazaz), 8:493

Dorozhka, Joseph Ḥayyim, 11:735–736

Dorpat (Estonia). *See* Tartu (Estonia)

Dorph, Sheldon, 5:**759–760**

Dorph, Shelly. *See* Dorph, Sheldon

D'Ortas, Samuel, 4:75

Dortmund (Germany), 5:**760**

Dortn (Segalowitch), 18:249

Dort wo die Zeder (Feld), 6:745

Dosa ben Eleazar, 13:648–649

Dosa ben Harkinas, 5:**760–761**, 6:215

Dosa ben Saadiah, 5:**761**

Dosa the Greek, 4:269

Dosh, Charles. *See* Gardosh, Kariel

Dositheans. *See* Dustan

Dosithean Sect. *See* Dustan

Dositheos. *See* Dustan

Dossetai. *See* Judah ben Dosotheos

Dossin. *See* Malines (Belgium)

Dostai ben Judah, 5:**761**

Dostai ben Yannai, 5:**761–762**

Dostál, Zeno, 5:**762**

Dostrovsky, Aryeh, 5:**762**

Dostrovsky, Israel, 5:**762**

Dostrovsky, Ya'akov. *See* Dori, Ya'akov

Dos Yidishe Morgen Zhurnal. *See* *Jewish Morning Journal* (newspaper)

Dotan, Aron, 5:**762–763**

Dothan (Israel), 5:**763**

Dothan, Moshe, 5:**763–764**

Dothan, Trude, 5:**764**

Double Crown Club, 18:608

Double-decker tenements of New York City, 15:201

The Double Disappointment (Mendes), 6:437

Double dissimilarity, criterion of, 15:192

Double Dying: Reflections on Holocaust Literature (Rosenfeld), 9:414

Double Jeopardy (Chicago), vol. 4: color insert

Double Red Yentl, Split (My Elvis) (Kass), vol. 2: color insert

Doublets, in Torah, 15:734–736, 742, 743

Double V Campaign, 3:735

Doudtchitzky, Dinora, 5:**764**

Douglas, Kirk, 5:**764–765**

Douglas, Melvyn, 5:**765**

Douglas, Michael, 5:**765**

Douwes, Arnold, 5:**765–766**

Dov, Isaac, 3:631

Dov, Issachar. *See* Frenk, Beer

Dov Baer of Lyova, 8:265

Dov Baer of Mezhirech, 1:220, 5:**766–768**

Dov Baer the Maggid of Mezhirech. *See* Dov Baer of Mezhirech

Dov Ber. *See* Schneersohn, Dov Baer

Dov Ber Gdud, 9:496

Dover, John, 15:516

Doves, 5:**768**

Dovid, Pinchas, 4:100

Dovid Bergelson (Dobrushin), 5:727–728

"Dovidl" Karliner. *See* Friedmann, David ben Samuel

Dovrat. *See* Dobrath (Israel)

Doweik ha-Cohen family. *See* Duwayk family

Dow Jones and Company, 11:765–766

Dowries, 5:**768–772**, 12:94, 19:285–286
   conflict of laws, 5:152–153
   Elephantine usage, 6:312
   hakhnasat kallah, 8:247
   head covering, 8:507
   husbands' rights to, 9:639

Dowries, *continued*
  inheritance rights to, 21:157, 161, 166–170, 172, 188
  ketubbah, 12:93–95, 98
  Samaritans, 17:731
  Uzbekistan, 4:264
  See also divorce; marriage
Doyle, Ned, 1:428
Dozy, Reinhart Pieter Anne, 5:**772**
DP's. *See* Displaced persons (DP)
Dr. Seuss, 4:630
Dra (Morocco), 6:**5**
Draa (Morocco). *See* Dra (Morocco)
Drabkin, Abraham, 6:**5**
Drabkin, Moshe. *See* Remez, Moshe David
Drabkin, Moshe David. *See* Remez, Moshe David
Drabkin, Yakov Davidovich. *See* Gusev, Sergei Ivanovich
Drabkina, Elizaveta Yakovlevna, 8:143
Drach, David. *See* Drach, Paul-Louis-Bernard
Drach, Paul-Louis-Bernard, 2:8, 6:**5–6**
Drachman, Bernard, 6:**6**
Drachsler, Julius, 6:**6**
Draguignan (France), 6:**6–7**
Dragunski, David Abramovich, 6:**7**
Draï, Raphaël, 6:**7**
Drama. *See* Plays and playwrights
Drama (Greece), 6:**7–8**
Drancy (France), 6:**8**
Drapkin, Abraham S., 6:**8**
Drapkin, Israel, 6:**8**
Dray, Julien, 6:**8**
Dray Hoyptshtet (Der Nister), 5:597
Dray Shtetlakh (Baal-Makhshoves), 3:8
Dreamers (motion picture), 6:358
Dreamgirls (Bennett), 3:369
The Dream of the Eastern Land (Elkan), 6:357
Dreams, 6:**8–10**
  Daniel, 5:420–421
  divination and, 5:704
  divine revelation, 16:568
  incantations, 2:132
  interpreters of
    Bar Hediya, 3:151–152
    Daniel, 5:419–420
    Jacob and angels, 11:18, 19
    Laban harming Jacob, 11:19
    Nebuchadnezzar, 5:422
  visions
    in Job, 11:351, 352–353
    Joseph's interpretation of, 11:407

  See also Visions
"Dream-Visions." *See* Vision of Seventy Shepherds
Dreben, Sam, 6:**10**
Dregger, Alfred, 3:728
Dreifuss, Ruth, 6:**10**
Dresden (Germany), 3:251, 6:**10–11**
Dresden, Sem, 6:**11**
Dresdner Bank, 11:822
Dresler, Salek, 15:503
Dresner, Samuel Hayim, 6:**11–12**
Dress, 6:**12–17**
  Algeria, 1:647
  Almohads, 1:681
  ancient paintings, 6:54–55
  Bukaran, 4:263–264
  of Bukharan Jews, 4:263–264
  burial customs and, 4:293
  clothing, as dowry, vol. 3: color insert
  crowns, 5:307–309
  Ephod, 6:455–456
  Estori Ha-Parḥi, 6:522
  etiquette, 6:539
  folklore, 7:96, 103, 105, 107, 109
  headdresses, decorative, 5:307–309
  Ḥukkat ha-Goi, 9:580
  infant's circumcision costume, vol. 7: color insert
  Israel Defense Forces, 10:471
  jewelry, 16:479
  marriage, 13:565–566
  mourning, 14:586, 589
  Muslim countries, 5:103
  name-giving ceremony costume, vol. 7: color insert
  Nuremberg, 15:347
  Ottoman empire, 15:527, 528, 529
  priestly vestments, 16:512, 514, 516
  purim, 16:741
  rabbinical, 6:15
  regulations, in Ottoman empire, 15:520, 525–526, 527, 529
  Seljuks, 18:271
  tailoring, 19:435–439
  Tallit, 19:465–466
  Talmid Ḥakham, 19:467
  Tekhelet, 19:586–587
  tombs, 20:34
  Tunisia, 20:178, 180, 183
  See also Clothing and textiles industry; Jewish badges
Dressler, William, 6:**17**
Dressler syndrome, 6:**17**
Dreux (France), 6:**17**

Drexler, "Mickey." *See* Drexler, Millard S.
Drexler, Millard S., 6:**17–18**
Dreyfus, Alfred, 6:**18–19**
Dreyfus, Camille, 6:20
Dreyfus, Françoise. *See* Aimée, Anouk
Dreyfus, Henry, 6:20
Dreyfus, Isaac (1786-1845), 6:18
Dreyfus, Isaac (1849-1909), 6:18
Dreyfus, Jacques, 6:18
Dreyfus, Paul, 6:18
Dreyfus, Samuel, 6:18
Dreyfus, Stanley A., 6:**20**
Dreyfus, Willy, 6:18
Dreyfus Affair, 6:18–19, 7:158, 9:54–55, 11:95
  Barrés, Auguste Maurice, 3:175
  Bloch, Gustave, 3:761
  Bloch, Jean-Richard, 3:763
  Blum, Léon, 4:7
  Canada, 4:396
  Hadamard, Jacques Salomon, 8:185
  Lacretelle, Jacques de, 12:426
  Lazare, Bernard, 12:558
  Levaillant, Isaïe, 12:676
  in Oran, 15:460
  in Paris, 11:724, 15:644
  philosophy, 12:588
Dreyfus-Brodsky, Jules, 6:18
Dreyfus brothers, 6:**20**
Dreyfus family, 6:18
Dreyfus in Kasrilevke (Shalom Aleichem), 18:382–383
Dreyfuss, Barney, 6:**20–21**
Dreyfuss, Richard, 6:**21**
Dreyzl, Leah, 6:**21**
Drezner, Yeḥiel Dov, 6:**21–22**
Dridzo, Solomon Abramovich. *See* Lozovski, Solomon Abramovich
Driesche, Johann Clemens van der. *See* Drusius, Johann Clemens
Drinks Before Dinner (Doctorow), 5:728
Drip irrigation, 6:452
Driver, Godfrey Rolles, 6:22
Driver, S. R., 15:554
Driver, Samuel Rolles, 6:**22**
Driver documents, 2:346
Driving Miss Daisy (Uhry), 2:639
Drob, Max, 6:**22–23**
Drobner, Boleslaw, 6:**23**, 16:347, 18:707
Droga Mlodych, 7:124
Drogobych (Ukraine), 6:**23–24**
Drohobycz (Ukraine). *See* Drogobych (Ukraine)

Drömmen om Österlandet (Elkan). *See The Dream of the Eastern Land* (Elkan)

Dropkin, Celia, 6:**24**

Dropsie, Moses Aaron, 6:**24–25**

Dropsie College, 6:**25–26**
  Adler, Cyrus, 1:395
  establishment, 6:197
  Neuman, Abraham Aaron, 15:120

Drosdoff, Matthew, 6:**26**

Drought. *See* Famine and drought

Dr Phillips, a Maida Vale Idyl (Frankau), 7:196

Drucker, Daniel Charles, 6:**26**

Drudgery Divine: On the Comparison of Early Christianities and the Religions of Late Antiquity (Smith), 18:688

Drug addiction, 12:58–59

Drug use and crime, 5:297

Druja (Belarus). *See* Druya (Belarus)

Drumont, Edouard-Adolphe, 6:**26**
  on blood libel, 3:778
  Dreyfus Affair, 6:18

Drunkenness. *See* Alcohol and drunkenness

Drusilla, 6:**28**, 749

Drusius, Johann Clemens, 6:**28**

Druya (Belarus), 6:**28–29**

Druyanow, Alter, 6:**29**

Druyanow, Asher. *See* Druyanow, Alter

Druyanow, Avraham Abba. *See* Druyanow, Alter

Druze, 10:725, 728
  Bashan, 3:197
  demography, 5:553
  Gadna, 7:332
  Galilee, :332
  Ḥakim bi-Amr Allah, al, 8:249–250
  Hauran, 8:462
  historical survey, 10:182, 224
  holy places in Israel, 9:501–502
  Israel, 10:650–652, 719
    holy places, 9:501, *502*
    Israel Defense Forces, 10:469
  Jethro (father-in-law of Moses), 11:252
  Knesset, 12:237
  Lebanon, 12:578
  Ottoman period, 10:177, 182
  religious court, 10:623
  Shuʿayb, 11:252

Dry bones resurrection, 6:640, 645

Dryden, John, 1:331

Dry Tears (Tec), 4:631

Drzewiecki, Henryk, 6:**29**

D (Deuteronomy) source of Torah, 15:735, 739–740
  identification of, 15:742
  laws in, 15:745–747
  monotheism in, 15:750
  terminology for God, 15:743

Dual Allegiance: An Autobiography (Dunkel), 6:50

Dualism, 6:**29–31**, 7:670, 14:321–322

Duality of Human Existence: an Essay on Psychology and Religion (Bakan), 3:72

Duarte Sanitorium. *See* City of Hope National Medical Center

Du Bartas, Guillaume De Salluste, 6:**31**

Duberman, Martin B., 6:**31**

Dubin, Mordecai, 6:**31–32**, 12:521

Dubinsky, David, 6:**32**, 18:709, 719

Dubin's Lives (Malamud), 20:294

Dubislav, Walter Ernst Otto, 6:**32**

Dublin (Ireland), 6:**32–33**, 10:24–26, 11:73

Dubno (Ukraine), 6:**33–34**

Dubno, Salomon
  Amsterdam, 2:108
  Mendelssohn, Moses, 2:108

Dubno, Solomon ben Joel, 6:**34**, 8:436, 440
  biblical exegesis and study of, 3:646
  as bibliophile, 3:684

Dubno Maggid. *See* Kranz, Jacob

Dubnow, Simon, 6:**34–37**
  Brann, Marcus, 4:129
  Folkspartei, 7:113–114
  on Jewish identity, 11:297
  Jewish Society for History and Ethnography, 11:315
  Sejmists influenced by, 11:314
  Society for the Attainment of Full Civil Rights for the Jewish People in Russia, 18:724

Dubnow, Ze'ev, 6:**37**

Dubnow-Erlich, Sophia, 6:**37–38**, 481

Dubossary (Moldova), 3:779, 6:**38**

Dubrovnik (Croatia), 1:212, 6:**38–39**

Dubrovno (Belarus), 6:**39**

Duchamp, Marcel, 6:255

Duckesz, Eduard, 6:**40**

Duckesz, Yecheskel. *See* Duckesz, Eduard

Duclou, Luigi, 11:568

Duda, Virgil, 6:**40**

Duehring, Karl Eugen, 6:**40**

Duenaburg (Latvia). *See* Daugavpils (Latvia)

Dueñas (Spain), 6:**40–41**

Duenner, Joseph Ẓevi Hirsch, 6:**41,** 15:101
  Amsterdam, 2:111, 114
  Zionism, 2:114

Dueren (Germany), 6:**41**

Dueren, Isaac ben Meir, 2:32, 6:**41–42**

Duerer, Albrecht, 4:70

Duése, Jacques. *See* John XXII

Duesseldorf (Germany), 6:**42**

Dugdale, Blanche Elizabeth Campbell, 6:**42**

Dugi, Menahem ben Solomon ibn. *See* Alroy, David

Duhm, Bernhard, 6:**42–43**

Dühren, Eugen. *See* Bloch, Iwan

Duisburg (Germany), 6:**43**

Dujovne, Leon, 6:**43**

Dukakis, Michael, 4:303

Dukas, Paul, 6:**43**

Duke, David, 15:79

Duke, James B., 6:62

Duke of Sussex Pentateuch, 3:678

Duker, Abraham Gordon, 6:**43–44**

Dukes, Leopold, 6:**44**

Dukhan, 6:**44**

Dukhobors, 11:521

Dulcea of Worms, 6:**44–45**, 7:50

Dulzin, Arye Leib, 6:**45**

Duma, 6:**45–46**, 12:780–781

Dumashevsky, Arnold, 12:553

Dumayet, Pierre, 4:23

"Dumbbell" tenements of New York City. *See* Double-decker tenements of New York City

The Dumb opened their Mouths (Baazov), 3:14

Dummesek. *See* Damascus (Syria)

Dům na předměstí (Poláček), 16:285

Dumuh (Egypt), 6:**46**

Dunajska Streda (Slovakia), 6:**46**

Dunant, Jean Henri, 6:**47**

Dunash ben Labrat, 6:**47–48**, 8:652, 653, 16:265
  biblical exegesis and study, 3:642
  Judah b. Ḥayyuj, biblical exegesis and study, 3:642

Dunash ibn Tamim, 6:**48–49**, 11:532–533, 727

Dunaszerdahely (Slovakia). *See* Dunajska Streda (Slovakia)

Dunayevski, Isaac Osipovich, 6:**49**

Dunayevtsy (Ukraine), 6:**49**

Dunedin (New Zealand), 6:**49–50**

Dunkelman, Benjamin, 6:**50**

Dunkelman, Rose, 6:**50**

Duns Scotus, John, 6:**50–51**

DuPont Company, 18:406
Dupont-Sommer, André, 6:**51**
Du Pré, Jacqueline, 6:**51**
Duque, Simon David, 6:**51**
Dura-Europos (Syria), 6:**51–56**
    anthropomorphism, 2:191
    Aramaic, 2:348
    Catacomb art and, 3:673
    frescoes, 2:494, 6:14
    illuminated manuscript tradition
      and, 3:674
Duran, Aaron, 6:56
Duran, David, 6:56
Duran, Ḥayyim Jonah, 6:56
Duran, Joseph Benjamin, 6:56
Duran, Judah, 6:56
Duran, Moses ben Ẓemaḥ, 6:56
Duran, Profayt. *See* Duran, Profiat
Duran, Profiat, 4:63, 5:693, 6:**56–58**
    apologetics, 2:266
    linguistic literature, 13:34, 42
Duran, Simeon ben Solomon, 6:56, **58**
Duran, Simeon ben Ẓemaḥ, 1:440,
    2:530–531, 6:56, **58–60**, 8:552, 16:89
Duran, Solomon ben Simeon, 6:**61**
Duran, Solomon ben Ẓemaḥ, 6:56
Duran, Ẓemaḥ Astruc, 6:56
Duran, Ẓemaḥ ben Solomon, 6:56, **61**
Duran, Ẓemaḥh ben Benjamin, 6:56
Duran family, 6:**56**
Duran partnership law responsum,
    5:154, 156
Durazzo (Albania), 6:**62**
Durban (Republic of South Africa),
    6:**62**
Durchgangslager. *See* Camps,
    concentration and extermination
Duress
    agunah, 1:518–519
    obligations made by, 15:374
    ones, 15:427–431
    oppression, 15:452–453
    See also Forced conversion
Durham (NC), 6:**62–63**
Durkheim, Émile, 2:185, 3:658, 659,
    6:**63–64**, 18:729–730
    criminology, 5:302
    education, 6:160
    on solidarity, 18:730
Durrës (Albania). *See* Durazzo
    (Albania)
Durrësi (Albania). *See* Durazzo
    (Albania)
Duschak, Mordecai, 6:64
Duschak, Moritz. *See* Duschak,
    Mordecai

Duschinsky, Charles, 6:**64**
Duschinsky, Joseph Ẓevi ben Israel,
    6:**64**
Dushkin, Alexander Mordechai, 6:**64–
    65**
Dushkin, Samuel, 6:**65**
Dushman, Saul, 6:**65**
Dusis ben Fufti, 6:66
Dustan, 6:**65–67**
Dustes ben Pilpeloy, 6:66
Dutch Antilles. *See* Netherlands
    Antilles
Dutch Guiana. *See* Suriname
"Dutch Jerusalem." *See* the
    Netherlands
Dutch literature, 1:287, 6:**67–72**
    Belmonte family, 3:302
    Bible translation, 3:627–628
    biblical influence, 3:671
    Bruggen, Cary van, 4:222
    children's, 4:634
    Costa, Isaäc da, 5:233
    Cunaeus, Petrus, 5:338
    encyclopedias, 6:401
    Hertzveld-Hijmans, Esthella, 9:50
    Herzberg, Abel Jacob, 9:52
    Hond, Meijer de, 9:516–517
    Leeuw, Jacob Ben Ḥayyim, 12:601
    Van Vriesland, Victor Emanuel,
      6:70, 20:475
    Vroman, Leo, 20:588
Dutch National Council of Jewish
    Women (NCJW), 2:118
Dutch West India Company, 4:469,
    471, 472, 15:195
*Duties of the Hearts. See Ḥovot ha
    Levavot*
Duty, 6:**72–73**, 14:372
Duvdevani, Shmuel, 6:**73**
Duveen, Joseph, Lord, 6:**73**
Duveen, Joseph Joel, 6:73
Duveen family, 6:**73**
Duvernois, Henri, 6:**73**
Duwayk, Abraham, 6:73
Duwayk, Jacob Saul, 6:74
Duwayk, Saul, 6:**73–74**
Duwayk family, 6:**73–74**
*Dux neutorum. See Guide of the
    Perplexed*
Dvekut, 18:604
Dvenadtsat stul yev (Ilf), 9:720
Dvinsk (Latvia). *See* Daugavpils
    (Latvia)
Dvir, 6:74, 14:491
Dvoretzky, Aryeh, 6:74
Dvorkin, Elijah, 11:323
Dvorkin, Miriam. *See* Waddington,
    Miriam

Dvorzetsky, Mark Meir, 6:**74**
The Dwarfs (Pinter), 6:440
Dworin, Adela, 5:325
Dworkin, Ronald, 6:**74–75**
Dworkin, Zalman Shimon, 6:**75**
Dyatlovo (Belarus), 6:**75**
Dybbuk. *See* Dibbuk
The Dybbuk (An-Ski), 2:182, 8:179–
    180
    Engel, Joel, 6:408
    Finkel, Shimon, 7:32
    Habimah theater (Moscow),
      14:518
    Justman, Moshe Bunem, 11:581
    Morewski, Abraham, 14:486
    performed by Habimah, 8:179
The Dybbuk (orchestral suite, Engel),
    6:408
Dyche, John Alexander, 6:**75–76**
Dyeing, 3:55, 4:259, 6:**76–77**, 9:68
The Dyeing of Purple in Ancient Israel
    (Herzog), 9:68
Dye plants, 6:77
Dyhernfurth (Poland), 6:**77–78**
Dykman, Shlomo, 6:78
Dykstajn, Szymon. *See* Dickstein,
    Szymon
Dylan, Bob, 4:219, 6:**78–79**, 15:220–
    221
Dymov, Ossip, 6:**79**
Dymshyts, Veniamin E., 6:**79**, 16:348
Dynamic programming, 5:131
The Dynamics of Biblical Parallelism
    (Berlin), 16:257
Dynamics of Prejudice (Bettelheim),
    3:551
Dynow, Ẓevi Elimelech, 6:**79–80**
Dysphemism, 6:**549–551**
Dyte, Charles, 16:339–340
Dywin (Poland). *See* Divin (Poland)
Dzaudzhikau (Soviet Union). *See*
    Ordzhonikidze
Dzerzhinsk (Belarus). *See* Koidanovo
    (Belarus)
Dzhugashvilli. *See* Stalin, Joseph
    Vissarionovich
Dzialoszyce (Poland), 6:**80**
Dzialynski family, 11:17
Dzieckowitz, Eliezer of. *See* Eliezer of
    Dzieckowitz
*Dzieje żydów w Krakowie i na
    Kazimierzu, 1304–1868* (Balaban),
    3:82
Dzigan, Shimon, 6:**80**
Dzikow, Eliezer of. *See* Eliezer of
    Dzieckowitz
Dzisna (Poland). *See* Disna (Poland)

Dzyuba, E.G. *See* Bagritski, Eduard Georgiyevitch

E

E (letter), 6:*81*
Eagle, S.P. *See* Spiegel, Samuel P.
Eagles, 6:**81**
EAJS. *See* European Association for Jewish Studies
The Earliest Chemical Industry (Singer), 18:634
Early Hebrew. *See* Hebrew language
Earth, 6:**82–83,** 7:489
The Earth. See Di Erd
The Earth Is the Lord's (Heschel), 9:71
Earth Pangs. See Erd-Vey
Earthquakes, 6:**83**
    in Amos, 2:97, 98
    relief efforts, 6:321
The Earth's Boundaries. See Gevulot Erez
Easements (servitudes), 18:317, 318
East Berlin (German Democratic Republic), 7:539
East End Jewish Radicals (Fishman), 7:65
Easterners. *See* Kedemites
Eastern Europe
    Agudat Israel, 1:505–506
    American Joint Distribution Committee, 2:59–60, 62
    bankers, moneylenders, 3:116–117
    blood libel in, 3:778
    building and construction, 5:183
    children's literature, 4:621–622
    communal organization, 9:236
    community, nature of, 5:108, 110–111, 9:53
    cooking, traditional Jewish, 7:118
    cultural preservation, 1:323–324
    dress, 6:15–16
    education, Jewish
        eighteenth-early nineteenth century, 6:182–183
        Middle Ages, 6:176
        sixteenth-eighteenth centuries, 6:177–179
        U.S., immigration to, 6:192–195
    emancipation, 6:380–385
    foreign policy and relations with Israel (state), 10:262, 264–265
    glassmaking, 7:631–632
    Hebrew literature, publishing, 16:723
    Holocaust cinema, 9:441–442
    Holocaust studies, 9:423
    ḥukkat ha-goi, 9:580
    immigration
        to Saint Louis (MO), 17:672
        to U.S., 6:192–195
    informers, 9:782
    Jewish artists, 2:507–509
    Jewish identity in, 11:298–299
    Middle Ages
        agriculture, Jewish, 1:495
        education, Jewish, 6:176
    modern period, economic history, 6:135–136
    museums, 14:627–630
    ORT, 15:489, 491
    publishing, 16:714
    relief efforts, 1:324
    shtetl, 18:524–527
    synagogues, shulklapper, 18:531
    Tatar conquest, 5:299–300
    textiles, 19:663
    Yiddish education, 6:188
    Yiddish theater, 19:679, 681–682
    See also specific countries
East Germany. *See* German Democratic Republic (GDR)
East India Company
    Amsterdam, 2:109
    Bushire, 4:306
    Paiva, Jacques, 15:571
East London (Republic of South Africa), 6:**83–84**
East Yiddish language, 11:302
Eating. See Okhlim
Eating etiquette, 6:539
    See also Food
Eaton, Joseph W., 6:**84**
Eban, Abba Solomon, 6:**84–85,** 15:695
Eban, Aubrey Solomon. *See* Eban, Abba Solomon
Eben-Ezer (Israel), 6:**85**
Eber, 2:84, 6:**85**
Ebers. *See* Ephraim family
Ebers, George Moritz, 11:444
Eberst, Isaac ben Judah. *See* Offenbach, Isaac
Ebionites, Jewish identity of, 11:294
Ebla (Syria), 3:656, 657, 6:**85–87,** 223
Eblaite language, 6:85–86
Ebner, Ferdinand, 4:233
Ebner, Meir, 6:**87–88**
Ebner, Meyer. *See* Ebner, Meir
Eboda. *See* Avedat (Negev)
Ebony, 6:**88**
Eborensis, Flavius. *See* Pyrrhus, Didacus
Ebreo, Guglielmo. *See* Guglielmo Da Pesaro
Ebreo, Leone. *See* Abrabanel, Judah ben Isaac
L'ebreo errante in Italia (Morpurgo), 14:509
Ecbatana. *See* Hamadan (Iran)
Ecclesia et synagoga, 6:**88**
Ecclesiastes, Book of, 6:**88–90,** 18:220, 221
    ethical teachings, 6:533
    labor, 12:409
Ecclesiastes Rabbah, 6:**90–91**
Ecclesiasticus. *See* Wisdom of Ben Sira
Écija (Spain), 6:**91**
Écija, Joseph de, 6:**91**
Écija, Yuçaf de. *See* Écija, Joseph de
Eck, Johann, 4:32
Eckardt, Roy A., 6:**91–92**
Eckert, Massimiliano, 14:408
Eckhart, Meister, 6:**92**
Eckman, Julius, 6:**92**
Eckstein, Ze'ev, 11:829
The Eclipse of Both Luminaries, or Two Ẓaddikim Who Harmed One Another. See Likkui Shenei ha-Me'orot, o Shenei Ẓaddikim she-Ḥibbelu Zeh ba-Zeh
Eclipse of God (Buber), 4:233
Ecole Biblique (Jerusalem), 3:617
Ecole de Paris artists, 2:517
Ecole d'Orsay. *See* Ecole Gilbert Bloch (Orsay, France)
Ecole Gilbert Bloch (Orsay, France), 18:210
École Rabbinique. *See* Séminaire Israélite de France
Ecology, 6:**92–95**
    See also Environment
Ecology. *See* Conservation
Economic Development and Cultural Change (Hoselitz), 9:558–559
Economic history, 6:**95–138**
    Babylonian exile, 6:98–99
    economic doctrines, 6:114–117
    Elephantine Papyri, 6:314
    First Temple period, 6:95–98
    French Revolution, 7:254
    Germany, Adler, Georg, 1:397
    Israel (state), 10:489*t*, 490*t*, 491*t*, 492*t*, 493–593, 495*t*, 497*t*, 498*t*, 499*t*, 502*t*, 522*t*, 523*t*, 528*t*, 530*t*, 532*t*, 536*t*, 537*t*, 538*t*, 545*t*, 546*t*, 548*t*, 549*t*, 559*t*, 561*t*, 562*t*, 563*t*, 564*t*, 565*t*, 566*t*, 567*t*, 574*t*, 575*t*
        1954-1959, 10:222
        1983 crisis, 10:241
        1985 stabilization policy, 10:569–573

Economic history, *continued*
  1990s, 10:252–253
  agriculture in Mandate
    period, 10:506–511
  aliyah, and five waves of
    immigration, 10:522–526,
    522*t*, 523*t*
  aliyah and absorption,
    10:343, 348
  Arab boycott, 10:22, 256
  Arabs: demographic growth
    and economic expansion,
    10:493–496, 495*t*, 521–522
  as associate member of
    European Economic
    Community, 10:262–263
  balance of payments, 10:514–
    516, 537*t*, 541–543, 580–
    581
  banking system, 10:586–589,
    586–592, 590–591
  Bank of Israel, 5:54, 10:551–
    557, 581–586
  breakthrough, comparative
    trends and links, 1932-
    1939, 10:500–503, 502*t*
  capital markets, 10:514–516,
    591–592
  centralization, 10:429
  crisis of early twenty-first
    century, 10:463
  crisis of mid-1980s, 10:450
  currency and exchange rate,
    10:546–549
  defense expenditures, 10:561–
    562
  early 1970s, 10:236
  emergence of Jewish
    economy, 1920-31, 10:487–
    493, 489*t*, 490*t*, 491*t*, 492*t*
  employment trends, 10:293,
    533, 535, 539, 545, 557–
    558, 561, 561*t*, 576–577,
    615–617
  Fifth Aliyah, 1932–1939,
    10:496–500, 497*t*, 498*t*,
    499*t*
  fiscal policy, dominant role
    of, 10:543–546, 545*t*, 546*t*
  foreign trade, 10:537*t*, 541–
    542, 550, 563*t*
  government expenditures,
    10:543–545
  growth and restructuring,
    10:573–580, 574*t*, 575*t*
  high-tech, 10:558, 574, 575*t*,
    580, 592–593
  Histadrut and Yishuv,
    10:511–512
  Intifada, 10:725

  "Lost Decade"; war
    expenditures and inflation,
    1974-1985, 10:560–569,
    561*t*, 562*t*, 563*t*, 564*t*, 565*t*,
    566*t*, 567*t*
  Macroeconomic Policy, 1954-
    1973, 10:551–557
  Mandate period, 10:481*t*,
    483*t*, 484*t*, 506–511
  manufacturing, 10:503–505,
    518–520, 557–559, 557–
    560, 559*t*, 570–574, 575*t*,
    592–593
  to mid-1950s, 10:216, 217
  military burden on, 10:234
  monetary and financial
    systems, 10:512–514, 516–
    518, 546–549, 548*t*, 549*t*,
    550, 568–569, 570–573,
    580–586, 581–586
  New Economic Policy, 1952–
    1954, 10:549–551
  Ottoman period, 10:479–485,
    481*t*, 483*t*
  privatization, 10:579–580
  rapid growth, 1948-1973,
    10:534–541, 536*t*, 537*t*,
    538*t*
  resettlement, 10:506–511,
    526–534, 528*t*, 530*t*, 532*t*
  as unique political and
    economic entity, 1918–
    1948, 10:486–487
  urbanization and
    socioeconomic structure,
    10:505–506
  war prosperity, inflation, and
    short-term peace
    reconversion, 10:520–521
  white collar workers, 10:349–
    350
livestock trade, 13:144–145
loans, 13:149–152
mamram, 13:441–442
manufacturing rise, 10:518–520
Middle Ages
  Christianity, 6:108–114
  Islam, 6:104–108
  ma'arufya, 13:307
  mintmasters and moneyers,
    14:298–301
modern period, 6:129–138
  agricultural sector,
    employment in, 6:132–134
  Ashkenazi, 6:118–119
  and community organizaion,
    role of, 6:125–126
  discrimination, 6:118–119
  early, 6:117–127
  Eastern Europe, 6:135–136

  employment patterns, 6:120–
    123
  income, 6:133–134
  incomes, sources of, 6:123–
    124
  industrial employment,
    penetration into, 6:130–131
  migration, Jewish, 6:119–120,
    129–130
  non-Jews, relations with,
    6:124–125
  and Non-Jews, relations with,
    6:124–125
  Palestine (Ottoman), 6:137–
    138
  resource distribution, 6:123–
    124
  Sephardim, 6:118
  service sector, positions in,
    6:131–132
  social stratification, 6:126–
    127
  U.S., 6:136–137
  Western Europe, 6:134–135
  WW II, 6:138
Palestine (Mandate), 10:200–202,
  481*t*, 483*t*, 484*t*, 496–512, 497*t*,
  498*t*, 499*t*, 502*t*
  agriculture and resettlement,
    10:506–511
  balance of payments and
    capital imports, 10:514–516
  breakthrough, comparative
    trends and links, 1932-
    1939, 10:500–503, 502*t*
  historical survay, 10:200–202
  immigration and
    demography, 1932–1939,
    10:496–500, 497*t*, 498*t*,
    499*t*
  immigration and economic
    absorptive capacity, 10:336,
    337–338
  manufacturing, 10:503–505,
    518–520
  monetary and financial
    system, 10:512–514
  money, prices and war
    finance, 10:516–518
  as unique political and
    economic entity, 10:486–
    487
  urbanization and
    socioeconomic structure,
    10:505–506
Palestine (Ottoman), 10:479–485,
  481*t*, 483*t*
Restoration period, 6:98–99
Russia
  1772-1881: First Phase,
    17:535

1881-1917: Second Phase, 17:537, 537t

USSR regime, 17:542, 544, 546, 546t

Second Temple period, 6:99–102

Talmudic period, 6:102–104

transition period, 6:127–129

urban environments, economic doctrines and, 6:115

Yishuv, 10:511–512

Economic History Society, 13:76

The Economic Interpretation of History (Seligman), 18:267

Economics

Aftalion, Albert, 1:441

Akerlof, George A., 1:560

Braverman, Avishay, 4:140

Breitner, Hugo, 4:158

brokers, 4:203–204

Bronfenbrenner, Martin, 4:204–205

Brutzkus, Boris Dov, 4:228

Burns, Arthur Frank, 4:298

Cantoni, Raffaele, 4:437

Colm, Gerhard, 5:58

Council of the Lands, 5:243–244

Czacki, Tadeusz, 5:351

Devons, Ely, 5:629

Dorfman, Joseph (1904-1991), 5:756

Einzig, Paul, 6:264

Fischer, Stanley, 7:55–56

Foerder, Yeshayahu, 7:94

France, 15:759

Frankel, Sally Herbert, 7:199

Frankel, Ya'akov, 7:199–200

game theory, 14:487

Halpern, Georg Gad, 8:284

Heilperin, Michael Angelo, 8:768

Hertzka, Theodor, 9:49–50

Herzenstein, Mikhail Yakovlevitch, 9:53

Hirsch, Julius, 9:126

Hirschman, Albert Otto, 9:140

Horowitz, David, 9:533

Horowitz, Ḥayyim Dov, 9:534

Hoselitz, Berthold Frank, 9:558–559

Jewish identity and, 11:297

Jordan (Hashemite kingdom), 11:404

Landes, David Saul, 12:468

Latin America, 12:509–510

Latvia, 12:520–521

Leiserson, William Morris, 12:629

Lerner, Abba Petachja, 12:656

Levi, Leone, 12:690

Levin, Richard C., 12:712–713

Liberman, Yevsey Grigoryevich, 12:781–782

Lichtenstein, Walter, 12:800

Loria, Achille, 13:192

Lowe, Adolph, 13:234

Lubin, Isador, 13:241–242

Lubin, Simon Julius, 13:242

Luxemburg, Rosa, 13:276–277

Mises, Ludwig Edler von, 14:315

Modigliani, Franco, 14:411

Morgenstern, Oskar, 14:487

Nathan, Robert Roy, 15:12

Neisser, Hans Philipp, 15:66

Pinner, Felix, 16:169–170

Pinto, Issac de, 16:179

Polányi, Karl, 16:326–327

Poznan community brokers, 4:204

Ricardo, David, 17:282

Rivlin, Alice, 17:350

Rostow, Walt Whitman, 17:475–476

Rubinow, Isaac Max, 17:514–515

Rueff, Jacques, 17:526

Ruppin, Arthur, 17:529–530

Sanbar, Moshe, 18:8

Sándor, Pál, 18:17

Schiper, Ignacy, works by, 18:137

Schlesinger, Karl, 18:142

Scholes, Myron S., 18:159–160

Schwartz, Anna Jacobson, 18:182

Seligman, Edwin Robert Anderson, 18:266–267

Sharfman, Isaiah Leo, 18:414

Silberner, Edmund, 18:577

Solow, Robert Merton, 18:780–781

twentieth century, 6:735

U.S., 6:750, 15:778–779

USSR

Dymshyts, Veniamin E., 6:79

Larin, Yuri, 12:493–494

See also Banking and bankers

L'economie politique avant les physiocrates (Einhorn), 6:259

Economy. *See specific countries*

Ecstasy, 6:138–139

Aaron ben Moses ha-Levi of Starosielce and, 1:216

Abraham Joshua Heschel of Apta, 1:313

dance, 5:409

mystical, 11:664–665

Ecstatic Religion (Lewis), 12:765

Ecuador, 6:139–141, 140, 14:460, 21:594

See also New Granada

Ecumenical movement, 4:713, 714–715, 718–719, 12:617–618, 17:521–522

Edah, 6:141–142

Edel, Yiẓḥak, 6:142

Edelman, Gerald Maurice, 6:142

Edelman, Maurice, 6:142–143

Edelman, Raheli, 18:153

Edelmann, Raphael, 6:143

Edelmann, Simḥah Reuben, 6:143

Edelmann, Ẓevi Hirsch, 6:143

Edels, Samuel Eliezer ben Judah ha-Levi, 1:533, 6:143–144, 7:361

Edelstadt, David, 4:108, 6:144–145

Edelstein, Gertrude. *See* Berg, Gertrude

Edelstein, Jacob, 6:145

Eden. *See* Garden of Eden

Eden, Anthony. *See* Eden, Sir Anthony, Earl of Avon

Eden, Bracha, 6:145–146

Eden, Sir Anthony, Earl of Avon, 6:145

Eden-Tamir, 6:145–146

Eder, Montague David, 6:146

Edersheim, Alfred, 16:630

Edessa (Turkey), 6:146–147

Edict of Artaxerxes, 6:659

Edict of Cyrus, 6:658

Edicts of Tolerance. *See* Toleranzpatent

Edinburgh (Scotland), 6:147

Edinger, Ludwig, 6:147

Edinger, Tilly, 6:147–148

Edirne (Turkey), 6:148–150

Edman, Irwin, 6:150

Edmonton (Canada), 1:589–591, 6:150–151

Edneți. *See* Yedintsy (Moldova)

Edom (Transjordan), 6:151–158, 10:127–129, 15:747

Aggadah and, 6:156–157

alphabet, Hebrew, 1:694t, 695

Bible and, 6:152–153

Boẓrah, 4:115

culture, 6:155

Esau, 6:488

identified with Esau, 6:488

inscriptions, 3:658

land, 6:151–152

Moab, 14:399

in Obadiah, 15:366

people, 6:152

political history, 6:153–155

religion, 6:155

Second Temple period, 6:155–156

Edot (origin groups). *See under* Demography
Edrehi, Moses ben Isaac, 6:**158**
Edrei (Galilee), 6:**159**
Edrei (Transjordan), 6:**158–159**
Education, 6:**159–161**
    adult Jewish, 12:621–622, 14:14–15
    American Association for Jewish Education, 2:47–48
    American Gathering of Jewish Holocaust Survivors Summer Seminar Program, 2:49
    American Joint Distribution Committee, 2:63
    ancient schools, 6:170–171
    Asociación Mutual Israelista Argentina, 2:71
    Association for Jewish Studies, 2:613–614
    Australia, Jewish day schools, 14:8, 9
    Austria, Richter, Elise, 17:290–291
    Beth Jacob schools, 3:**533**, 12:455, 18:121
    Bet (ha)-Midrash, 3:537–538
    in Bialystok (Poland), 3:567
    Bible codes, use of, 3:680
    Biram, Arthur, 3:709–710
    Birk, Yehudith, 3:711
    Black, Algernon David, and Ethical Culture, 3:730
    of the blind, 7:86
    Bloom, Benjamin Samuel, 3:780
    Bondy, Max, 4:60
    Brandeis University, 4:124–125
    Brazil, 4:148, 152, 18:32, 33
    Bruna, Jerome Seymour, 4:222–223
    Buechler, Adolf, 4:250–251
    in Bulgaria, 4:270
    Canada, 4:409
        Montreal, 4:405, 14:465–466
        Shapiro, Bernard, 18:404
    Catholic, 4:713, 714
    children studying Torah, vol. 3: color insert
    comparative, 11:760
    Conference on Jewish Social Studies, 5:145
    Confino, Michael, 5:150
    Conservative Judaism, 5:175
    contributions to general, 6:159–161
    crime and, 5:295
    cultural, fraternal orders, 6:712
    Einheitsschule ideas, 11:817
    elementary schools, 6:172–173

    ethics, *Sefer Ḥukkei ha-Torah,* 18:241
    Ethiopia, Hebrew classroom, vol. 3: color insert
    Europe, Jewish Colonization Association, 11:286
    Fez, Morocco, 7:7, 8
    France
        of deaf-mutes, 15:759
        Lévi Alvarès, David, 12:695–696
        Montpellier, 14:463
        Roussillon, 17:499
    Germany
        Engelmann, Susanne Charlotte, 6:410
        Hess, Michael, 9:75
        Jewish, 14:36–37
        Karsen, Fritz, 11:817
        Morgenstern, Lina, 14:487
        theological seminaries, 10:754–755
    in ghettoes and concentration camps, 9:360
    Greece, 18:315
    Hartog, Sir Philip Joseph, 8:378
    Hebrew, Rieger, Eliezer, 17:293
    Hebrew College, 8:553–554
    Holocaust, 6:670–672, 9:447–454
        Meed, Vladka, 13:764
    Hungary, 12:470
        Pest, 4:246
        secondary school system expansion, 11:811
    Iran, 10:11
    Iraq, 10:16–17
        Baghdad, 3:58*t*
        religious, 10:16
        secular, 10:16–17
    Israel
        nineteenth century Jerusalem, 11:173
        twentieth century, 3:386, 389, 15:755–756
    Israel (State), 10:652–674
        Adar, Zvi, 1:383
        aliyah and absorption, 10:343, 344, 526, 657, 658, 668
        Arab, 10:714, 719, 728
        Bar-Ilan University, 3:153–153
        Ben Zvi Institute for the Study of the Jewish Communitities of the East, 3:395–396
        boarding, agricultural and special education schools, 10:667–669

        Christian, 10:642–643, 645
        comprehensive schools, 10:665–666
        compulsory, 10:216
        day care and preschool, 10:661–662
        De-Shalit, Amos, 5:602
        differences among edot, 10:299–300
        Dinur, Benzion, 5:672
        educational system, 10:656–660, 665
        expansion in 1960s, 10:227
        extracurricular education, 10:672–673
        Eẓ Ḥayyim, 6:649–650
        Halperin, Haim, 8:283
        higher education, 10:224, 669–673, 671*t*
        Histadrut and, 10:604
        IDF role, 10:470
        Israel Prize, 10:759–765
        kindergarten, 10:661–664
        labor force level, 10:293
        Lehmann, Siegfried, 12:616
        matriculation examinations and certificates, 10:664–665
        medical research, 10:678–679
        music, 10:689, 749
        post-war of independence to Six-Day War historical survey, 10:227–228
        pre-war of independence period, 10:652–656
        primary schools, 10:661–664
        religious political parties and, 10:429, 431
        religious schools, 10:357, 624–625, 631, 632–633
        secondary schools, 10:661–664
        Shapira, Avraham Elkana Kahana, 18:399
        state system, 10:217
        structure of school system and budget, 10:660–661
        student population, 10:539
        teacher training, 10:672
        television station, 10:708
        vocational technical, 10:612, 666–667
    Istanbul, nineteenth century, 10:781
    Italy, 10:806
        Colombo, Yoseph, 5:64
        Padua, 15:567–568
    Judah (kingdom), 11:112
    Judah Loew ben Bezalel on, 11:507

Juedische Freischule, 11:569

Juedisch Theologisches Seminar, Breslau, 11:572

Justman, Joseph, 11:581

Latin America, 12:512–513

Latvia, 12:522

Levi, Said ben Shalom, 12:692

literacy levels, 10:291–292

Lithuania, 3:462
    Telz, 19:598

Morocco, 13:798–799, 14:500, 502, 505–507
    Corcos, Stella, 5:217

New Zealand, 15:244

Norway, 15:308, 310

Odessa, 15:379, 380

opportunities for women
    nineteenth century, 6:752
    twentieth century, 6:753

Oriental languages, 14:371–372

ORT, 15:490–492

Oxford University, admission of Jews to, 15:554

Ozar Hatorah, 15:556

Palestine (Mandate), 10:623, 653–656
    Arab, 10:712
    Hebrew language, 10:684
    music, 10:689
    religious schools, 10:655

Palestine (Ottoman), 10:652–653
    Hebrew language, 10:683–684
    music, 10:689
    religious schools, 10:621

Palestine Liberation Organization and, 15:592

parental responsibilities in Israeli law, 15:638

Passow, Aaron Harry, 15:683

Persia, 15:786–787, 791

Peru, "León Pinelo" school, 13:21

pluralism, 8:553

Poland, Shapira, Meir, 18:401–402

progressivism, 8:553

Provençal, Abraham ben David, 16:635

Provençal, David ben Abraham, 16:635–636

Provençal, Jacob ben David, 16:636

Rabin, Israel Abraham, 17:33

Rackman, Emanuel, 17:51–52

Radin, Max, 17:54

Rakovsky, Puah, 17:76

Rauch, Eduardo, 17:115

reform, Adler, Mortimer Jerome, 1:403–404

Rivlin, Harry N., 17:350–351

Rivlin, Joseph Joel, 17:351

Rosenbaum, Jonathan, 17:432

Rosin, David, 17:467

Rudavsky, David, 17:519

Ruderman, David B., 17:519–520

Russia, 17:565–566, 568

Russian Federation, 17:583

Russian seizure of Jewish children under Nicholas I, 15:250

Sar, Samuel L., 18:40

scribes, 4:367–368

secular studies, 8:438

Sicily, 18:542–543

Sloss, Israel Wolf, 18:680–681

social work, Perlman, Helen Harris, 15:778

TALI Education Fund, 18:114–115

Talmud, kolel, 12:273

Theresienstadt, 19:703

U.K., 12:458
    Fox, Jacob Samuel, 7:141
    Leitner, Gottlieb Wilhelm, 12:629
    Schonfeld, Victor, 18:160

University in Exile, NYC, 15:219

U.S.
    21th century, 6:203–204
    Baltimore (MD), 3:98–99, 100–101
    Berkson, Isaad Baer, 3:442
    classical, 8:185
    Cremin, Lawrence Arthur, 5:283
    Delougaz, Pierre Pinchas, 5:545
    Deutch, John M., 5:612–613
    Fox, Marvin, 7:141
    Herstein, Lillian, 9:47
    Honor, Leo L., 9:520
    Hurwich, Louis, 9:631
    Hurwitz, Shmarya Leib, 9:633
    Laura and Alvin Siegal College of Judaic Studies, 12:526
    Leipziger, Henry M., 12:628–629
    Levi, Edward H., 12:687
    Levy, Harry Louis, 12:750
    Lieberman, Myron, 12:805
    Los Angeles, 13:207–208
    medical, Perlstein, Meyer A., 15:780
    national organizations, 6:196–197
    non-formal education, 6:195–196

post-WW II 1945-1975, 6:198

public, leaders, 6:747–748

Rice, Joseph Mayer, 17:285

Richman, Julia, 17:288–289

San Diego, 18:13–14

San Francisco, 18:20

San Gabriel-Pomona Valleys, 18:20–21

Sarna, Jonathan Daniel, 18:58–59

Savannah, 18:84

Scharfstein, Zevi, 18:110

Schwab, Joseph J., 18:179–180

Scranton, 18:210

Seattle, 18:229–230

Seman, Philip Louis, 18:274

Shanker, Albert, 18:396

Shapiro, Harold, 18:405

students at Herschel High School (New York City), vol. 20: color insert

Sunday schools, 6:190–191

twentieth century, 6:201–202

of women, 8:438

yeshivas, Polish, 5:468

Yiddish education, 6:187–189

See also Education; Jewish education; Numerus clausus; Yeshivot; Yiddish education; specific countries

Education, Jewish. See Jewish education

Educational Alliance, 2:513, 13:161, 18:320

Educational and Cultural Union, 6:188

Educational Center for the Blind, 13:258

Eduyyot (tractate), 6:214–215, 325

Edward I (King of England), 6:411–413

Edwards, Paul, 6:215

Eerdmans, Bernardus Dirks, 6:215–216

Efeh, 18:695

Efes Damim (Levinsohn), 12:722

Effect, cause and. See Cause and effect, relation between

Efficiency (computer science), 5:129

"Efod." See Duran, Profiat

Efodi, Isaac, 15:655–656

Efraim (Hoffmann), 9:312

Efrat (Israel), 6:216

Efrat, Yaacov, 6:216

Efrat Future Technology Inc., 1:623

Efron, Ilya, 6:216

Efros, Israel Isaac, 3:100, 6:216, 8:736

Egalitatea (periodical), 6:**216–217,** 18:192–193

Eger (Czech Republic). *See* Cheb (Czech Republic)

Eger (Hungary), 6:**217**

Eger, Akiva ben Moses Guens, 6:**217– 218,** 11:425

Eger, Akiva ben Simḥah Bunim, 6:**218**

Eger, Joseph Ginz, 6:219

Eger, Judah Leib of Lublin, 6:**218**

Eger, Moses, 6:219

Eger, Samuel ben Judah Loeb, 6:**218**

Eger, Samuel Genz, 6:219

Eger, Simḥah Bunim ben Moses, 6:**218–219**

Eger, Solomon ben Akiva, 6:217, **219**

Egged, 6:**219**

Eggs, 6:**219–220**

Egidio da Viterbo, 6:**220**

Eglah. *See* Michal

'Eglah 'Arufah, 6:**220–221,** 301

Eglei Tai (Sochaczew), 18:704

Eglon (Canaan), 6:**221–222**

Eglon (King), 6:**222,** 245, 14:401

Az égö csipkebokor (Molnár). *See* The *Emperor's Nurse* (Molnár)

Egozi, David, 6:222

Egozi, Ḥayyim, 6:222

Egozi family, 6:**222**

Egyenlöség (newspaper), 6:**222**

Egy haditudósíto emlekei (Molnár). *See* Memories of a War Correspondent (Molnár)

Egypt, 6:**222–236,** *227*
    Aaronides, 1:219
    Abraham ben Mordecai ha-Levi, 1:304
    Abraham ben Moses ben Maimon, 1:305
    Akhenaton, 1:561
    alabarch, 1:573
    Alashkar, Solomon, 1:577
    alphabet, Hebrew, 1:698, 707
    American Joint Distribution Committee, 2:64
    Anath, 2:131
    ancient and biblical periods, 3:221, 6:222–225
        Aaron, 1:208
        Alexandria, 1:632
        Canaan, 16:120
        ethics, 6:534–535
        Goshen, 8:5
        Hophra, 9:522–523
        influence on Jewish medicine, 13:720, 722
        Jaffa under, 11:60

liberation from, 6:613–616
mythology, rescued infants, 6:613
Neco, 15:52
Old Kingdom capitals, 14:18– 19
oracles against, 6:639–640
pharaoh, 16:27–29
Seti I, 18:319
So, 18:698
    antisemitism, 6:234–235
        Alexandria, 1:632, 634, 635– 636
    Arab period, 6:230
        Alexandria, 1:634
    Arab world 1945-2006, 2:300, 307–308, 309–311, 326–327
    Aramaic, 2:343
    archaeology, Petrie, Sir William Matthew Flinders, 16:18–19
    archives, 2:402
    Armistice Agreement, 10:214
    bar mitzvah, 3:165
    Bible, and literature of, 5:275, 6:225–226
    Bilbeis, 3:697
    Blum Pasha, 4:7
    border skirmishes with, 10:219, 228, 234
    boycotts
        Arab, 4:111–113
        of Israel, 10:218
    Byzantine period, Alexandria, 1:634
    Cairo, 4:342–345
    Cairo genizah, 7:460–483
    Cairo trial, 4:346
    Cambyses, 4:379
    capitulations, 4:452
    Cattaui family, 4:526
    Christian period, 6:229–230
    Cleopatra, 4:754
    Cleopatra III, 2:129
    community organization and structures, 5:104
    Coptic translations of Bible, 3:602
    crocodiles, 5:304
    democracy, 2:326–327, 327, 328
    Diaspora, 5:637–640
    divorce statistics, 5:720
    dress on monuments, 6:12–13
    Egyptian-Israeli peace, 2:311–313
    Elephantine, 15:619
    Eliyahu Hanavi Synagogue, vol. 5: color insert
    embalming, 6:390
    exodus from, 9:166–167

Fatimids and, 6:230–231
Flaccus, Avillius Aulus, 7:66
foreign policy and relations with Israel, 10:257–258, 259, 12:533– 534
    Gaza strip, 7:400–401
    Gaza strip, 1948-1967, 10:303, 717
    geographic location, 6:222
    geonim, 7:386
    government officials, Abu al-Munajjā Solomon ben Shaya, 1:335
    Hasidic movements, 11:599
    Hellenistic period, 6:226–228, *227*
        Alexandria, 1:633–634
    illuminated Hebrew manuscripts from, 3:675–676
    initial immigration of Joseph's brothers to, 11:408–409
    Israel, relations with, 6:236
    Israel-Arab Armistice agreement, 2:475–476
    Jewish quarters, 11:312
    Jewish settlement, 1:434–436
    Judeo-Arabic literature in, 11:530– 531
    Karaite communities, 11:790
    language, 1:329–330, 6:482, 8:622, 624, 18:280
    literature, Ḥabiru, 8:180–181
    literature, She'erit ha-Ḥazzan, 18:431
    Mamluk period, 6:231–232, 13:438–441
        Alexandria, 1:634–635
    Middle Ages, 6:*227*, 16:386
    Miẓrayim, 14:395
    Moses, 14:523–524, 526–527, 532
    mummification, 6:390
    nagid leadership, 14:731–733, 731*t*
    name of country, 6:222
    Niebuhr, Carston, travels of, 15:259
    Onias, Temple of, 15:432–433
    ostraca, 15:508–509
    Ottoman Empire and, 6:231–234, 15:523–524
        Alexandria, 1:634–635
        community leaders, 11:32
        exilarchate of, 6:606
    Palestine Liberation Organization and, 15:592, 594
    papyri, Jewish, 15:619
    Pathros, 15:688
    peace negotiations with Israel, 15:594
    Peace Treaty with, 10:238

Philistines and, 16:53, 54
politics, 16:346
population statistics, 6:234
post-1945 period, 2:300
printing, Hebrew, Alexandria,
  1:635
prominent families, Menasce, de,
  14:28
Ramses, 17:89
responsa literature, 17:232, 233
Roman period, 1:632, 6:228–229
ṣarrāf, 18:61
Second Temple period, 6:229
settlement locations, 6:235
Sinai Campaign and, 10:219–220,
  18:629–632
Six-Day War, 10:229–232, 18:648–
  655
synagogue architecture, 19:375
twentieth century, 6:234–236
Yammit region, 21:278–279
Yom Kippur War, 10:236–237,
  21:383–391, 384, 386, 388, 389
See also specific Egyptian cities
Egypt, Brook of, 6:**236–237**, 286
Egyptian Jewry
  medieval, 5:464–465, 466
    nagidim, 5:467
  sixteenth century, community
    leaders, 5:470–471
      Castro, Abraham, 4:517
      David ben Solomon ibn Abi
        Zimra, 5:470–471
Egyptian Tenses (Polishek), 16:360
Egyptology, 6:391, 482, 13:166, 15:471
Egypto-Semitic Studies (Ember), 6:391
Eḥad Efes le-Tovatenu (Shamir),
  18:392
Eḥad Mi Yode'a (song), 6:**237**
Az éhes város (Molnár). *See The
  Hungry City* (Molnár)
Ehrenberg, Victor Leopold, 6:**237**
Ehrenburg, Ilya Grigoryevich, 6:**237–
  239**
Ehrenfeld, David Ẓevi, 6:239
Ehrenfeld, Isaiah, 6:239
Ehrenfeld, Nathan, 6:**239**
Ehrenfeld, Samuel, 6:239
Ehrenfeld, Samuel ben David Ẓevi,
  6:**239**
Ehrenfeld, Saul, 6:239
Ehrenfeld, Simeon, 6:239
Ehrenfeld, Simḥ Bunim, 6:239
Ehrenfeld family, 6:**239**
Ehrenfest, Paul, 6:**239–240**
Ehrenkranz, Benjamin Wolf Zeeb. *See*
  Ehrenkranz, Benjamin Zeeb

Ehrenkranz, Benjamin Zeeb, 4:194,
  195, 6:**240**
Ehrenkranz, Wolf Zeeb. *See*
  Ehrenkranz, Benjamin Zeeb
Ehrenpreis, Marcus, 4:270, 6:**240**
Ehrenpreis, Mordecai. *See* Ehrenpreis,
  Marcus
Ehrenreich, Bernard Colonius, 6:**240–
  241**
Ehrenreich, Ḥayyim Judah ben
  Kalonymus, 6:**241**
Ehrenreich, Samuel, 18:606
Ehrenstamm, Feith, 6:241
Ehrenstamm, Solomon Jacob, 6:241
Ehrenstamm family, 6:**241**
Ehrenstein, Albert, 6:**241–242**
Ehrentreu, Ernst, 6:242
Ehrentreu, Heinrich, 6:**242**
Ehrlich, Abel, 6:**242**
Ehrlich, Arnold Bogumil, 3:647,
  6:**242–243**
Ehrlich, Eugen, 6:**243**
Ehrlich, Georg, 6:**243–244**
Ehrlich, Henryk. *See* Erlich, Henryk
Ehrlich, Jacob, 6:**244**
Ehrlich, Ludwik, 6:**244**
Ehrlich, Paul, 6:**244–245**, 18:579
Ehrlich, Simḥa, 6:**245**
Ehrlich, Wolf, 3:769
Ehud, 6:**245**
Ehud Banai ve ha-Plittim (Banai),
  3:106
Eibenschitz (Czechoslovakia). *See*
  Ivancice (Czechoslovakia)
Eibeschuetz, Simon Aaron, 6:**245**
Eichelbaum, Samuel, 6:**245**
Eichenbaum, Boris Mikhailovich,
  6:**245–246**
Eichenbaum, Gelber. *See* Eichenbaum,
  Jacob
Eichenbaum, Jacob, 6:**246**
Eichenstein, Isaac Eizik, 21:522
Eichenstein, Ẓevi Hirsch, 21:522
Eichhorn, David Max, 6:**246–247**
Eichhorn, Johann Gottfried, 3:646,
  649, 6:**247**
Eichler, Menahem Max, 6:**247**
Eichmann, Adolf Otto, 6:**247–252**,
  10:226, 12:465
    Blood for Trucks offer, 4:120, 121
    Brunner, Alois, 4:223
    Endre, László, 6:405
Eichmann in Jerusalem (Arendt),
  6:251–252, 9:415
Eichmann in Jerusalem, film, 9:101
Eichmann in Jeruzalem (Herzberg),
  9:52

Eichrodt, Walther, 3:651
Eichthal, Arnold, 6:252
Eichthal, Bernhard, 6:252
Eichthal, Carl, 6:252
Eichthal, David, 6:252
Eichthal, Gustave d', 6:**252**
Eichthal, Louis Aron, 6:252
Eichthal, Simon, 6:252
Eichthal-Seligmann family, 6:**252**
Eicke, Theodor, 4:388
Der Eid eines Judens (Ahlwardt), 1:547
Die Eidesleistung bei den Juden
  (Frankel), 7:201
Eidlitz (Czech Republic). *See* Udlice
  (Czech Republic)
Eidlitz, Abraham Moses. *See* Eidlitz,
  Zerah ben Meir
Eidlitz, Leopold, 6:**252**
Eidlitz, Zerah ben Meir, 6:**252–253**
Eifman, Boris, 5:415–416, 6:**253**
Eig, Alexander, 6:**253**
Eiger, Akiva ben Moses Guens. *See*
  Eger, Akiva ben Moses Guens
Eiger, the Younger. *See* Eger, Akiva
  ben Moses Guens
Eight (number), 15:335
Eighteen Benedictions. *See* Amidah
Eighteen Treatises of the Mishnah (De
  Sola), 18:750
Eighty Years War, 6:67
Eikhah. *See* Lamentations, Book of
Eikhah Zuta, 14:187
Eikhenvald, Aleksandra, 11:323
Eilat (Israel), 6:**253**, 254, vol. 21: color
  insert
    See also Elath (Israel)
Eilberg, Amy, 6:**253–254**, 18:279, 403
"Eili, Eili" (folk song), 18:16
Eilon (Israel), 6:**254**
Eilot (Israel), 6:**254–255**
Eilshemius, Louis M., 6:**255**
Einaeugler, Karol, 6:**255**
Einbeck (Germany), 6:**255**
Eine Geschichte der Juden (Kastein),
  11:827
Einei ha-'Edah (Alemanno), 1:612
Einei Moshe (Alshekh), 2:10
Einei Yisrael (Engelmann), 6:410
Eine Reise nach Freiland (Hertzka),
  9:50
Ein Fashkhah (Israel), 6:**255–256**
Einfeld, Sydney, 6:**256**
Ein Feshkha. *See* Ein Fashkhah (Israel)
*Der Einfluss der Juden auf unsere
  Civilisation* (Endlich), 6:404
Ein Gedi (Israel), vol. 10: color insert
Ein Gev (Israel), 6:**256–257**

Ein ha-Emek (Israel), 6:**257**

Ein ha-Ḥoresh (Israel), 6:**257**

Ein ha-Kore (Jekuthiel ben Judah ha-Kohen), 11:117

Ein ha-Mifraẓ (Israel), 6:**257**

Ein ha-Naziv (Israel), 6:**257**

Ein ha-Sheloshah (Israel), 6:**257**

Ein ha-Shivah. *See* Tabgha (Galilee)

Ein ha-Shofet (Israel), 6:**257**

Ein Hod (Israel), 6:**257–258**

Einhorn, David (1809-1879), 6:**258**
 American Jewish Archives, 2:53
 on Oral Law, 15:457
 on slavery, 3:734

Einhorn, David (1886-1973), 6:**258–259**

Einhorn, Ignaz, 6:**259**

Einhorn, Max, 6:**259**

Einhorn, Moses, 6:**259**

Ein Iron (Israel), 6:**259**

Ein Kapitel aus meinem (Honigmann), 9:518

Ein ke-Elohenu, 6:**259–260**

Ein Kerem (Israel), 6:**260**, 7:173

Einleitung in das Alte Testament (Eissfeldt). *See The Old Testament, an Introduction* (Eissfeldt)

Einleitung in das Alte Testament (Sellin), 18:272

Ein li, plea of, 6:597

Einmal Hunderttausend Taler (Kalisch), 11:736

Ein Peraḥ Sheḥorim (Carmi), 4:484

Einsatzgruppen, 7:564–565, 9:334–336, 13:126

Ein Shemer (Israel), 6:**260**

Ein-Sof, 6:**260–261**, 7:664–665, 11:623–624, 18:351, 356

Einstein, Albert, 6:**261–262**, 8:740, 16:136, 20:751
 Blumenfeld, Kurt Yehudah, 4:11
 Bohm, David, 4:42
 Jewish Palestine Pavilion at the New York World's Fair, 14:462
 Newton-John, Olivia, 15:193
 photographs of, 11:39

Einstein, Alfred, 6:**262–263**

Einstein, Arik, 6:**263**

Einstein, Carl, 6:**263–264**

Einstein, Lewis, 6:**264**

Ein Vered (Israel), 6:**264**

Ein Yahav (Israel), 6:**264**

Ein Zeitim (Israel), 6:**264**

Einzig, Paul, 6:**264**

Ein Zukunftsbild (Eisler), 6:274–275, 21:620

Ein Ẓurim (Israel), 6:**264–265**

Eire. *See* Ireland

Eisen, Arnold, 6:**265**

Eisen, Joel B., 6:452

Eisenbaum, Antoni, 6:**265**

Eisenberg, Aharon Eliyahu, 6:**265–266**

Eisenberg, Denise. *See* Rich, Denise Eisenberg

Eisenberg, Sandy, 18:279

Eisenberg, Shoul, 6:**266**

Eisenberg Companies, 6:266

Eisendrath, Maurice, 1:358

Eisendrath, Maurice Nathan, 6:**266**

Eisenhower, Dwight David, 6:**266–267**, 9:486

Eisenman, Charles, 6:**267**

Eisenman, Peter, 6:**267–268**

Eisenmann, Louis, 6:**268**

Eisenmenger, Johann Andreas, 6:**268**

Eisenstadt (Austria), 6:**268–269**

Eisenstadt (Germany), 6:**271**

Eisenstadt, Abraham Seldin, 6:**269–270**

Eisenstadt, Abraham Ẓevi (1871-1939), 6:**270**

Eisenstadt, Abraham Ẓevi Hirsch ben Jacob (1813-1868), 6:**270**

Eisenstadt, Benjamin, 6:270

Eisenstadt, Benzion, 6:**270**

Eisenstadt, David, 2:18

Eisenstadt, Isaiah, 6:**270–271**

Eisenstadt, Meir, 6:269, **271**

Eisenstadt, Menahem Ẓevi, 6:**271**

Eisenstadt, Mordecai, 18:354

Eisenstadt, Moses Eleazar, 6:**271**

Eisenstadt, Samuel Noah, 6:**271–272**

Eisenstadt, Shmuel Noah, 18:732, 735

Eisenstadt, Yehoshua. *See* Barzilai, Yehoshua

Eisenstadter, Meir ben Judah Leib, 6:**272**

Eisenstadt-Levinson, Lyuba, 6:270

Eisenstaedt, Alfred, 6:**272**, 16:125

Eisenstein, Ferdinand Gotthold, 6:**273**

Eisenstein, Ira, 6:**273**, 274, 17:148

Eisenstein, Judah David, 6:**273**, 400, 8:735

Eisenstein, Judith Kaplan, 6:**273–274**

Eisenstein, Sergei Mikhailovich, 6:**274**, 15:653

Eisinger, Roger. *See* Eydoux, Emmanuel

Eisler, Edmund Menahem, 6:**274–275**

Eisler, Gerhart, 6:**275**, 16:344

Eisler, Hanns, 6:**275**

Eisler, Mátyás, 6:**275**

Eisler, Moritz, 6:**275**

Eisler, Robert, Josephus' *Jewish Antiquities* on Jesus, 11:440

Eisler, Rudolf, 6:**275–276**, 18:731

Eisler, Ruth. *See* Fischer, Ruth

Eismann, Moses, 6:**276**

Eisner, Kurt, 6:**276**, 16:344, 18:705

Eisner, Mark, 2:47, 6:**276**

Eisner, Michael Dammann, 6:**276–277**

Eisner, Pavel, 6:**277**

Eisner, Will, 6:**277–278**

Eiss, Alexander von, 6:**278**

Eissfeldt, Otto, 6:**278**

Eissler, Kurt R., 6:**278**

Eitan, Rafael. *See* Eitan, Raphael

Eitan, Raphael, 6:**279**, 16:357, 358

Eitinger, Leo S., 6:**279**

Eitingon, Max, 6:**279–280**

Eizenberg, Julie, 6:**280**

Eizenstat, Stuart, 6:**280–281**

Eizer, Michael, 11:323

Éjxzakák és hajnalok (Šinko), 18:641

Ekdippa. *See* Achzib (ancient Israel)

Ekonomicheskoye ucheniye Karla Marksa (Slominski), 18:679

Ekron (ancient Israel), 6:**281–282**

Ekron (Israel, state). *See* Mazkeret Batyah (Israel)

Eksati, Boula, 15:541

ʿEl, 7:672–674

Elad (Israel), 6:**282**

Elad, Avraham, 4:346

Elagabalus (Roman emperor), 9:151

Elah, 6:**282**

El Al, 6:**282–283**, 10:233–234

Elam (Khuzistan), 6:**283–284**

Elam (Mesopotamia), 4:587

El-Amarna (Egypt), 6:**284–286,** 8:621–622, 623–624
 archives, 2:402
 Ḥabiru, 8:180–181

El-Amarna letters, 1:414, 2:562, 6:284–285, 12:668
 Amenophis III, 2:41
 Elimelech, 6:348

Elan Vital of the Jewish Woman (Adlerblum), 1:409

El árbol del placer (Steimberg), 19:174–175

El-Arish (Egypt), 6:**286–287**

Elasa (Israel), 6:**287**

Elasah, 6:**287**, 18:398

Elath (Israel), 6:253, **287–288**
 See also Eilat (Israel)

Elath, Eliahu, 6:**288**

Elazar, Daniel, 18:734

Elazar, Daniel J., 6:**288–289**

Elazar, David, 6:**289**

Elazar, Ya'akov, 6:**289–290**

Elazari-Volcani, Yiẓḥak, 6:**290**

Elba ben David. *See* Gaffarel, Jacques

Elbaz, Amram, 6:**290**

Elbaz, Jacob, 6:**290**

Elbaz, Jekuthiel Michael, 1:260

Elbaz, Judah, 6:**290**

Elbaz, Raphael Moses, 6:**290**

Elbaz, Samuel (1790-1844), 6:**290**

Elbaz, Samuel ben Isaac (1698-1749), 6:**290**

Elbaz family, 6:**290**

Elberg, Yehuda, 4:427, 6:**290–291**

'El Berit, 7:674

Elblag (Poland), 6:**291**

Elbogen, Ismar, 6:**291**
   encyclopedias, 6:400
   on Jewish studies, 11:317

Elcan, Marcus, 6:**291–292**

Elchanowicz, Aba. *See* Elḥanani, Aba

Elche (Spain), 6:**292**

Elches, Elkanan, 11:527

Eldad. *See* Shalom Aleichem

Eldad, Israel, 6:**292–293**

Eldad and Medad, 6:**293**

Eldad ha-Dani, 3:706, 6:**293–294**, 7:10–11, 11:727

Eldar, Reuven, 6:**294**

The Elder. *See* Shammai

Elder, Rebellious. *See* Zaken Mamre

Elder, Will, 6:**296–297**

Elderly. *See* Age and the aged

Elders (leaders), 6:**294–296**, 8:253
   See also Batlanim

Elders of Bathyra. *See* Bathyra, sons of

Elders of Zion, Protocols of the Learned, 6:**297**
   American Jewish Committee, 2:55
   Brunschvig, Georges, 4:225
   Endre, László, 6:405
   Estonia, publication, 6:521
   graphic novels, 6:278

El Djudio (newspaper), 6:366

Eldorado (Mosinsohn), 8:720

Elealeh (Trasjordan), 6:**297–298**

Eleasah (Israel). *See* Elasa (Israel)

Eleazar (2nd c. B.C.E.), 6:**298**

Eleazar (son of Aaron), 6:**298**

Eleazar (son of Abinadab), 1:258, 259

Eleazar, Abulfath Abenalazar, 6:**298**

Eleazar, Alaçar, 6:**298**

Eleazar, Alaçar ben Alazrach, 6:**298**

Eleazar, Ezdra, 6:**298**

Eleazar, Judah, 6:**298**

Eleazar, Mosse Aben, 6:**298**

Eleazar, Solomon, 6:**298**

Eleazar ben Ananias, 6:**298–299**

Eleazar ben Arakh, 6:**299**

Eleazar ben Azariah, 6:215, **299–300**
   on excessive biblical study, 3:663
   Moses, 14:534

Eleazar ben Damma, 6:**300–301**

Eleazar ben Dinai, 1:631, 6:**301**

Eleazar ben Ḥalfon ha-Kohen, 6:**301**

Eleazar ben Hananiah ben Hezekiah, 6:**301**

Eleazar ben Ḥarsom, 6:**301–302**

Eleazar ben Jacob ha-Bavli, 6:**302**

Eleazar ben Jair, 6:**302–303**, 18:583

Eleazar ben Judah of Bartota, 6:**303**

Eleazar ben Judah of Worms, 6:44, **303–305**

Eleazar ben Mattathias, 6:**305**, 311

Eleazar ben Matya, 6:**305**

Eleazar ben Moses ha-Darshan of Wuerzburg, 6:**305**

Eleazar ben Parta, 6:**305–306**

Eleazar ben Pedat, 6:**306–307**

Eleazar ben Shammua, 6:**307**

Eleazar ben Simeon (Tanna), 6:**308**
   on extradition, 6:627
   Joshua ben Korḥa, 11:453

Eleazar ben Simeon (Zealot), 6:**307**
   John of Giscala and, 11:383

Eleazar ben Yose ha-Gelili. *See* Eliezer ben Yose ha-Gelili

Eleazar ben Yose I, 6:**308**

Eleazar ben Yose II, 6:**308–309**

Eleazar ben Zadok, 6:**309**

Eleazar family, 6:**298**

Eleazar ha-Kallir. *See* Kallir, Eleazar

Eleazar ha-Kappar (2nd c.), 6:**309**

Eleazar ha-Kappar Beribbi (2nd c.). *See* Eleazar ha-Kappar

Eleazar ha-Kappar Beribbi (3rd c.). *See* Bar Kappara

Eleazar Ḥisma, 6:**309–310**

Eleazar of Bartota. *See* Eleazar ben Judah of Bartota

Eleazar of Modi'in, 6:**310**

Eleazar of Worms. *See* Eleazar ben Judah of Worms

Eleazer ben Arakh, 8:509

The Elected Member (Rubens), 6:438

Election of Israel, Doctrine of. *See* Chosen people

Electrochemistry in Biology and Medicine (Shedlovsky), 18:430

Electrodynamics, quantum, 7:6

Elef ha-magen (Shemariah ben Elijah ben Jacob), 18:457

Elek, Artur, 6:**310**

'El 'Elyon, 7:672

Elements of Financial Analysis (Schwartzman), 18:188

Elephantine (Egypt), 6:**311–314**, 15:619
   Aramaic, 2:345–346
   papyri, 2:345–346, 405, 3:60, 18:467, 469

Elephants, 6:**310–311**

Elfenbein, Israel, 6:**314**

Elfman, Danny, 6:**314–315**

Elfriede Golke, Ruth. *See* Fischer, Ruth

'Elgavish, 16:478

El Hamme. *See* Ḥammat Gader

Elhanan (biblical figure
      son of Dodo), 6:**315**
      son of Jaare-Oregim), 6:**315**

Elhanan, Joseph ben Shabbetai, 17:297

Elhanan ben Ḥushiel, 6:**315**, 11:727

Elhanan ben Isaac of Dampierre, 6:**315–316**

Elhanan ben Shemariah, 6:**316**

Elhanan ben Yakar, 6:**316**, 8:386

Elḥanani, Aba, 6:**316**

Elḥanani, Aryeh, 6:**316**

Elḥanani Prize, 6:**316**

Elhanan of Dampierre. *See* Elhanan ben Isaac of Dampierre

Elhanan of London. *See* Elhanan ben Yakar

El ha-Ẓippor (Bialik), 3:561, 562

Eli, 6:**317**

Elia. *See* Jerusalem (Israel)

Eliab of Norwich. *See* Jurnet of Norwich

Eliachar, Menache, 6:**317**

Elia di Sabato of Fermo. *See* Elijah ben Shabbetai Be'er

Eliakim. *See* Alcimus

Eliakim, Hananiah, 17:296

Eliakim, Marcel, 6:**317–318**

Eliakim Alkimos. *See* Alcimus

Eliakim ben Abraham. *See* Hart, Jacob

Eliakim Goetz ben Meir, 6:**318**

Eliakum Badkhn. *See* Zunser, Eliakum

Elian, Giovanni Battista, 6:**318**

Elias, Eli, 6:**318**

Elias, Josef. *See* Benkow, Jo

Elias, Joseph, 6:**318**

Elias, Ney, 6:**318–319**

Elias, Norbert, 6:**319**, 18:732

Eliasberg, Jonathan, 6:**319**

Eliasberg, Mordecai, 6:**319–320**

Eliashib, 6:**320**

Eliashov, Solomon ben Ḥayyim, 6:**320**

Elias le Eveske, 2:419, 6:**320**

Elias l'Eveske. *See* Elias le Eveske

Elias Sabot. *See* Elijah ben Shabbetai Be'er

Eliassof, Herman, 6:**320**

Elias Sportswear, 6:318

Eliav, Arie Lova, 6:**321**

Eliav, Binyamin, 6:**321–322**

Eli ben Zechariah. *See* Ali ben Zechariah

Eliberis (Spain). *See* Elvira (Spain)

Eli di Sabato of Fermo. *See* Elijah ben Shabbetai Be'er

Eliel, Ernest Ludwig, 6:**322**

Eliezer (biblical figure), 6:**322**
    adoption, 1:415
    Laban and, 12:407
    Moses, 14:524, 526, 535
    on onanism, 15:427
    See also Og (ruler of Bashan)

Eliezer ben David. *See* Bedarida, Guido

Eliezer ben Hyrcanus, 6:**322–325**
    Joshua ben Hananiah, 11:450, 451–452
    Onkelos/Aquila, 15:433
    Orhot Hayyim, 15:469

Eliezer ben Isaac, 6:**325–326**

Eliezer ben Isaac of Krotoszyn, 15:325

Eliezer ben Isaac of Worms, 6:**326**

Eliezer ben Jacob, 6:**326**

Eliezer ben Jacob (1st c.), 6:326

Eliezer ben Jacob (2nd c.), 6:326

Eliezer ben Jacob ha-Levi of Tornogrod, 6:**326**

Eliezer ben Joel ha-Levi of Bonn, 6:**326–327**

Eliezer ben Manasseh ben Baruch, 6:**327**

Eliezer ben Meir ha-Levi of Pinsk, 6:**327**

Eliezer ben Nathan of Mainz, 6:**327–328**

Eliezer ben Samson, 6:**329**

Eliezer ben Samuel ha-Levi, 6:**329**

Eliezer ben Samuel of Metz, 6:**329**, 11:424

Eliezer ben Samuel of Verona, 6:**329**

Eliezer ben Solomon. *See* Eliezer of Touques

Eliezer ben Uri Shraga Phoebus, 8:272

Eliezer ben Yose ha-Gelili, 6:**329–330**

Eliezer Fischel ben Isaac of Strzyzow, 6:**330**

Eliezer ha-Gadol. *See* Eliezer ben Isaac of Worms

Eliezer of Beaugency, 6:**330**
    biblical exegesis and study, 3:642
    exile, meaning of, 7:357–358

Eliezer of Dzieckowitz, 17:420

Eliezer of Dzikow. *See* Eliezer of Dzieckowitz

Eliezer of Dzikow Dzikow. *See* Eliezer of Dzieckowitz

Eliezer of Mainz. *See* Eliezer ben Nathan of Mainz

Eliezer of Metz. *See* Eliezer ben Samuel of Metz

Eliezer of Strzyzow. *See* Eliezer Fischel ben Isaac of Strzyzow

Eliezer of Toul, 6:**330–331**

Eliezer of Touques, 6:**331**

Eliezer of Verona. *See* Eliezer ben Samuel of Verona

Eliezer of Worms. *See* Eliezer ben Isaac of Worms

Eliezer the Great. *See* Eliezer ben Hyrcanus

Elihu, 6:**331**

Elijah (Dupuis), 6:336

Elijah (oratorio, Mendelssohn), 6:337

Elijah (prophet), 6:**331–337**
    Ahab, 1:524
    alchemy, 1:600
    Apocalypse of Elijah, 6:337
    art related to, 6:336–337
    chair of, 6:337–338
    Cherith, 4:594
    cup of, 6:**338**, 15:678, 682
    Elisha, 6:350–351
    folklore of, 6:335
    Jezebel and, 11:334
    John the Baptist and, 11:381
    Kings, Book of, 12:173
    legends about
        journey with Joshua ben Levi, 14:539
        Sabbath and, 14:7
    Messiah, association with, 6:333–334, 496
    Mount Carmel confrontation, 6:332

Elijah, Apocalypse of. See Apocalypse of Elijah

Elijah Bahur ben Asher ha-Levi. *See* Levita, Elijah

Elijah ben Aaron ben Moses, 6:**338**

Elijah ben Abraham, 6:**338**
    Anan ben David, 2:127
    Josiah ben Saul ben Anan, 11:460

Elijah ben Abraham Elmaleh, 6:364

Elijah ben Asher. *See* Levita, Elijah

Elijah ben Baruch the Elder, 6:**338**

Elijah ben Benjamin ha-Levi, 6:**338–339**

Elijah ben Berechiah ha-Kohen. *See* Elias Le Eveske

Elijah ben Eliezer Philosoph ha-Yerushalmi, 6:**339**

Elijah ben Hayyim, 6:**339**

Elijah ben Jacob Elmaleh, 6:364

Elijah ben Joseph ben Isaac Safarty, 18:55

Elijah ben Judah of Paris, 6:**339**

Elijah ben Kalonymus of Lublin, 6:**339**

Elijah ben Loeb of Fulda, 6:**339–340**

Elijah ben Meir Horowitz, 6:**399**

Elijah ben Moses Bashyazi, 3:198, 11:783, 798

Elijah ben Raphael Solomon ha-Levi, 6:**340**

Elijah ben Shabbetai Be'er, 6:**340**, 15:698

Elijah ben Shemaiah, 6:**340**

Elijah ben Solomon Abraham ha-Kohen of Smyrna, 6:**340–341**, 18:352

Elijah ben Solomon ha-Kohen, 6:**341**

Elijah ben Solomon of Vilna. *See* Elijah ben Solomon Zalman

Elijah ben Solomon Zalman, 6:**341–346**, 13:676
    amulets, 2:121–122
    Anim Zemirot, 2:174
    grammarian, 6:345–346
    Hasidism, opposition to, 6:342–343, 14:371
    natural sciences studies, 6:343–344
    publication of papers of, 10:749
    teachings, 6:343–344
    writings, 6:345

Elijah Chelebi ha-Kohen of Anatolia, 6:**346**

Elijah Gaon. *See* Elijah ben Solomon Zalman

Elijah Menahem ben Moses, 6:*346*, **346**

Elijah of Candia. *See* Elijah ben Eliezer Philosoph ha-Yerushalmi

Elijah of Fulda. *See* Elijah ben Loeb of Fulda

Elijah of la Massa, 6:**346–347**

Elijah of Lublin. *See* Elijah ben Kalonymus of Lublin

Elijah of Montalto, 15:644

Elijah of Paris. *See* Elijah ben Judah of Paris

Elijah of Pesaro, 6:**347**

Elijah of Prague, 6:**347**

Elijah of Vilna. *See* Elijah ben Solomon Zalman

Elijah Phineas ben Meir, 6:**347**

Elijah the Elder. *See* Elijah ben Baruch the Elder

Elijahu (Ben Jair), 6:336

Elim (Delmedigo), 5:543–544, 13:675–676

Eli Makower (Orzeszkowa), 15:501

Elimelech, 6:**347–348**, 12:772

Elimelech of Lyzhansk, 6:**348–349**

Elion, Gertrude Bell, 6:**349**

Elionaeus, son of Cantheras, 6:**349**

Eliot, George, 6:**349**, 435, 12:746

Eliphaz, 6:**349–350**

Elisha (biblical figure), 6:**350–351**
    Elijah, 6:332
    Jericho and, 11:139
    Kings, Book of, 12:173

Elisha Ba'al Kenafayim, 6:**351**

Elisha ben Abraham, 6:**351–352**

Elisha ben Abraham ben Benveniste ben Elisha, 3:677

Elisha ben Avuyah, 6:**352–354**

Elisha ben Shemuel, Judeo-Persian poetry of, 11:555

Elishah, 6:**354**

Elisha Ḥayyim ben Jacob Ashkenazi, 6:**354**, 18:347

Elisheba, 1:208, 6:**354**

Elisheva, 6:**354**

Elisofon, Eliot, 6:**354–355**, 16:126

Elison, Abraham Joshua. *See* Belov, A

Elitzur, 6:**355**

Elitzuria games, 6:**355**

Eliyah Margalit (Zemach), 21:503–504

Eliyahu, Mordecai, 18:399

Eliyahu, Mordechai, 6:**355**

Eliyahu, Samuel, 6:355

Eliyahu ha-Navi, 14:7

Eliyahu Hanavi Synagogue (Alexandria, Egypt), vol. 5: color insert

Eliyahu Rabbah (Shapira), 18:400

Eliyahu Zuta (Shapira), 18:400

Eliyia, Joseph, 6:**355–356**

Eliyohu der Novi (Hirschbein), 6:336

Elizabeth (NJ), 20:250

Eli Ẓiyyon ve-Areha, 6:**356**

El-Jish. *See* Giscala (ancient Israel)

El Judío Aarón (Eichelbaum), 6:245

Elk (Poland). *See* Lyck (Poland)

Elkabbach, Jean-Pierre, 6:**356–357**

Elkan, Benno, 6:**357**

Elkan, Sophie, 6:161, **357**

Elkanah, 6:**357**

Elkanah ben Jeroham, 2:24

Elkann, Jean-Paul, 6:**358**

Elkerbout, Ben, 6:**358**

Elkes, Elhanan, 6:**358–359**

Elkin, Adolphus Peter, 6:**359**

Elkin, Stanley, 6:**359**

Elkind, Arkadi Daniilovich, 6:**359**

Elkins Express. *See* Goldberg, Marshall

Elkus, Abram Isaac, 6:**359–360**, 14:445

Elleh Benei ha-Ne'urim (Luzzatto), 8:688, 13:280–281

Elleh Masei Yehudah Halevi (Burla), 4:295

Elleh Toledot Adam (Lisitzky), 13:81

Ellenbogen. *See* Katzenellenbogen family

Ellenbogen, Wilhelm, 6:**360**, 16:340

Ellenbogen, William, 18:705

Ellenson, David Harry, 6:**360**

Ellenstein, Meyer C., 6:**360–361**

Ellinger, Moritz, 6:**361**

Elliot, "Mama" Cass, 6:**361**

Ellis, Vivian, 6:**361**

Ellison, Lawrence J., 6:**361–362**

Ellmann, Richard, 6:**362**

Ellsberg, Daniel, 6:**362**

Ellsberg, Edward, 6:**362–363**

Ellstaetter, Moritz, 6:**363**, 16:344

Ellstein, Abraham, 6:**363**

El Macabeo (Silveyra), 18:589

Elmaleh, Abraham, 6:**364**, 11:735

Elmaleh, Amram, 6:363–364

Elmaleh, Joseph, 6:364

Elmaleh family, 6:**363–364**

El Male Raḥamim, 6:**364–365**

Elman, Mischa, 2:26, 6:**365**

Elman, Ziggy, 6:**365**

El Mansura (Egypt). *See* Mansura (Egypt)

El Melekh Ne'eman, 6:**365**

El Melekh Yoshev, 6:**365**

El-Modari, Judah ha-Kohen ben Eleazar he-Ḥasid. *See* Al-Madari, Judah ha-Kohen ben Eleazar he-Ḥasid

El Mozo. *See* Carvajal y de la Cueva, Luis de

Elnathan ben Achbor, 6:**365–366**

Elnecavé, David, 6:**366**

El Nora Alilah, 6:**366**

'Eloah. *See* 'Elohim

Eloesser, Arthur, 6:**366**

Elohim (Adler), 1:405

'Elohim, 7:674

Elohist source, 3:747

'El 'Olam, 7:673

Elon, Amos, 6:**366–367**

Elon, Binyamin, 6:**367**

Elon, Emuna, 6:367

Elon, Menachem, 6:**367–368**, 13:682, 15:639, 20:467–469
    Englard, Yitzhak, 6:432

on extradition, 6:629–630
mishpat Ivri, 14:358–360, 362
on organ transplantation, 13:749
on patients' rights, 13:742
on physicians' duties, 13:740–741
presumption, legal, 8:490–491
on prolongation of life, 13:743, 745
on role of judge, 13:739
rulings of, 5: 387–389, 12:544–545
on source of basic human rights, 13:739–740

El-Or, Tamar, 18:736

Elousa. *See* Elusa (ancient Israel)

El pan y la sangre (Sneh, Simja), 18:697

El-Paran. *See* Paran (desert, Egypt)

El Paso (TX), 6:**368**

El Paso Jewish Federation, 6:368

'El Ro'i, 7:673–674

Elrov, 1:561–562

El Salvador, 4:475–476, 6:**368–369**

'El Shaddai, 7:673

Elte, Harry, 6:**369**

Eltekeh (ancient Israel), 6:**369–370**

Elton, Geoffrey Rudolph. *See* Elton, Sir Geoffrey Rudolph

Elton, Sir Geoffrey Rudolph, 6:**370**

Elul, 6:**370**

Elusa (ancient Israel), 6:**370–371**

Elvira (Spain), 6:**371**

El-Yam, 6:**371**

Elyan, Isadore Victor. *See* Elyan, Sir Isadore Victor

Elyan, Sir Isadore Victor, 6:**371**

Elyashar, Eliyahu, 6:**372**

Elyashar, Ḥayyim Moshe, 6:372

Elyashar, Isaac, 6:372

Elyashar, Jacob ben Ḥayyim Joseph, 6:**371**

Elyashar, Jacob Saul ben Eliezer Jeroham, 6:**371–372**

Elyashev, Israel Isidor. *See* Baal-Makhshoves

Elyashiv (Israel), 6:**372**

Elyehoenai. *See* Elionaeus, son of Cantheras

Elzas, Barnett Abraham, 6:**372**

Elzet, Yehuda. *See* Avida, Yehuda Leib

Emalia enamelware factory, 18:136

Emanation, 6:**372–374**

Emancipation, 6:**374–386**, 9:231–232
    Allgemeine Zeitung Des Judentums, 1:671
    in Alsace, 2:6, 8
    Amsterdam, 2:109, 110–113, 6:749
    amulets, 2:122

Emancipation, *continued*
    antisemitism, 2:214–223
    apostasy, 2:272
    Board of Deputies of British Jews, 4:20
    in Bohemia, 4:39–40
    Bonald, Louis de, 4:55
    in Bordeaux, 4:83
    Dubnow, Simon, 6:37
    Eastern Europe, 6:380–385
    England, 6:414–415, 422
    Felix Libertate, 2:110, 6:749
    France, 2:216, 4:202, 550, 9:231–232
    Germany, 2:*215*, 215–216, 3:43, 7:528–529, 9:232, 12:778, 17:295
        Luebeck, 13:252
        Mendelssohn, Moses, 14:39–40
    homiletic literature and, 9:513
    humor and, 9:592–594
    Hungarian literature and, 9:605–606
    Hungary, 6:454, 9:609–610
    influence on Jewish philosophy, 16:92
    intermarriage, 14:374–375, 379–381, 381–382
    Italy, 4:437, 525, 10:801–803, 16:7
        Rome, 6:379, 17:414–415
    Jewish identity and, 11:295–296
    Judaism, development of concept of, 11:518–519
    Latin America, 12:508
    medals, 13:715*t*, 716
    medicine and, 13:729–730
    Mirabeau, Honore Gabriel Riqueti, Comte de, 14:305
    mishpat Ivri, 14:340, 351–352
    Moravia, 14:474–475
    Muslim States, 6:385
    opponents, 6:752
    Orthodox Judaism and, 15:493
    in Palatinate, 15:576
    Paris, 15:644
    Poland
        Breslau, 4:164
        Butrymowicz, Mateusz, 4:318
    proposal by Meier Kallir, 11:745
    Protestants and, 16:630
    Prussia, 8:347
    Switzerland, 1:207–208, 6:404, 19:342–343
    theological challenges of, 11:518
    United States, 6:376, 9:231
    Western Europe, 6:375–380
    Westphalia (Germany), 11:54
    See also Civil rights
Emancipation and Counter Emancipation (Duker, Hurin), 6:44
Emancipation of the Jews (Eötvös), 6:454
Emanuel (nominee for gospidar), 6:**386**
Emanuel, George J., 3:713
Emanuel, Isaac, 14:445
Emanuel, Walter Lewis, 6:**386**
Emanu-El Synagogue (San Francisco, CA), 5:40–41, 18:18, 19
Emar (Mesopotamia), 6:**386–390**
Embalming, 6:**390**
Embalming of Jacob, 11:409, 412
The Embassy to Gaius (Philo Judaeus), 16:63
Embden, Gustav, 6:**390–391**
Ember, Aaron, 6:**391**
Embroidery, Parokhet and Kapporet, 15:663–664
Embryo, 6:**391–392**
Embryology
    Auerbach, Leopold, 2:655
    Talmudic, 13:723
Emden (Germany), 6:**392**
Emden, Jacob, 2:24, 6:**392–394**, 18:356
    Abraham ben Isaac ha-Kohen of Zamość, 1:301
    Abraham ben Joseph of Lissa, 1:303
    Abterode, David ben Moses Eliakam, 1:333
    amulets, 2:121
    Anav, Jehiel ben Jekuthiel ben Benjamin Harofe, 2:137
    Anim Zemirot, 2:174
    Baruch ben David Yavan, 3:188
    on extradition, 6:628
    Eybeschuetz, Jonathan, 2:24, 12:459
    on onanism, 15:427
    Saraval, Jacob Raphael ben Simḥah Judah and, 18:52
    Shabbateanism and, 6:633, 7:183
Emden-Eybeschuetz amulet controversy, 2:24, 12:459, 714
Emek Berakhah (Horowitz), 9:532
Emek ha-Bakha (ha-Kohen), 13:109
Emek Ha-Bakha (Joseph ha-Kohen), 7:154, 9:157
Emek ha-Melekh (Bacharach), 3:35
Emek ha-Shaveh (Chorin), 4:667
Emek Yehoshua (Shapira), 18:400
L'Émergence artistique algérienne au XXᵉ siècle (Buzar-Kasbadji), 1:440
Emergency Committee of Atomic Scientists, 6:262
Emerson typeface, 4:12
Emery, Richard Wilder, 6:**394**
Der Emes (newspaper), 14:518
Emesa (Syria), 6:**394**
Emet, me-Erez Yisrael (Aḥ ha-Am), 1:526
Emet ve-Shalom (Sharabi), 18:411
Emigration. *See* Migrations
Êmile, Êmilie: l'ambition feminine au XVIII siècle (Badinter), 3:49
Emin Effendi. *See* Emin Pasha
Emin Pasha, 6:**394**, 18:579
Emiot, Israel, 6:**394–395**
Emissaries of Erez Israel. *See* Sheluḥei Erez Israel
Em la-Mikra (Benamozegh), 3:317
Emma Lazarus Federation of Jewish Women's Clubs, 6:**395**
Emmanuel, Isaac Samuel, 6:**395**
Emmatha. *See* Ḥammat Gader
Emmaus (ancient Israel), 6:**395–396**
Emmendingen (Germany), 3:44
Emmeram of Mainz. *See* Amram of Mainz
Emmeram of Manz, 2:106
Emmerich. *See* Gompertz family
Emmerich, Catherine, 11:384
Emöd, Tamas, 6:**396**
Emori. *See* Amorites
Emotions, 6:**396–397**
Empedocles, 6:**397**
L'Empereur, Constantijn, 6:**397**
The Emperor's Nurse (Molnár), 14:427
Emperor worship, 6:**397**
The Empire of Kalman the Cripple (Elberg), 6:291
Employment
    agriculture, 6:132–133
    Bible, occupational training, 6:165
    business ethics and, 4:311
    discrimination, 4:15
    economic history, 6:120–123
    industrial employment, 6:130–131
    Iran, 10:10–11, 11*t*
    labor law, 12:411–419
    Russia, 1970s, 17:568–569
    service sector, 6:131–132
    See also Labor
"Empty Sky" memorial (NJ), 18:184
Emrāni, 6:**398**
    illuminated manuscripts, 11:556
    Judeo-Persian poetry of, 11:555
Emsheimer, Ernst, 6:**398**
Emuant Ḥakhamim (Basilea), 3:199
Emunah, 6:**398**, 14:391
Emunah, 3:**290–294**

Emunah Omen (Abraham ben Josiah Yerushalmi), 1:303–304

Emunim movement, 6:367

Emunot ve-De'ot (Saadiah Gaon), 6:527

Encounter (Des Pres), 9:408

Encounters Between Judaism and Modern Philosophy: a Preface to Future Jewish Thought (Fackenheim), 6:673, 16:98–99

Encounter with Israel: A Challenge to Conscience (Eckardt), 6:91

Encroachment
 business ethics and, 4:313–314
 land, 18:317

Encyclopaedia Britannica, 1:403, 404, 3:658, 6:401

Encyclopaedia Hebraica (encyclopedia), 6:401

Encyclopaedia Judaica, 6:401
 Baer, Yitzhak, 3:53
 Bayer, Batya, 3:231
 Blumenkranz, Bernhard, 4:11
 Brodie, Israel, 4:196
 Eliav, Binyamin, 6:322
 Hirschberg, Ḥaïm Z'ew, 9:134
 Horodezky, Samuel Abba, 9:527
 Leviant, Curt, 12:696
 Roth, Cecil, 17:479–480
 Simchoni, Jacob Naftali Hertz, 18:590

Encyclopaedia Judaica (Beinart), 3:269

Encyclopaedia Judaica (German encyclopedia), 6:400, 18:753

Encyclopaedia Judaica Castellana (Spanish encyclopedia), 6:400

Encyclopedia of Philosophy (Edwards), 6:215

The Encyclopedia of Russian Jewry, 14:520

Encyclopedia of the Righteous Among the Nations, 17:303

Encyclopedias, 6:399–402
 Greek, 6:355–356
 Holocaust, 9:419
 Philosophy, 6:275–276
 Russian, 14:520
 Swedish language, 6:240

Encyclopedia Talmudica, 14:391

Endecja, 6:402–403, 11:740

Endelman, Halina. *See* Górska, Halina

Endelman, Tom M., 6:**403**

Endingen (Germany), 6:**403–404**

Endingen (Switzerland), 1:207–208, 6:**404**

Endingen Judenspiel (play), 6:403

Endlich, Quirin, 6:**404**

Endocrinology. *See* Medicine

End of Days. *See* Eschatology

The End of Ideology (Bell), 3:298

En-Dor (ancient Israel), 6:**404**

En-Dor (kibbutz), 6:**405**

En-Dor, witch of. *See* Witch of En-Dor

Endowment. *See* Hekdesh

Endre, László, 6:**405**

Enelow, Hyman, 6:**405–406**

Enemy Territory. See Mithḥam Oyev

Engagement with Samuel David Luzzatto. *See Hishtaddelut im Shadal*

En-Gannim (ancient Israel), 6:**406**

En-Gedi (ancient Israel), 6:**406–407**

En-Gedi (Israel), 6:**408**

Engel, Eliot L., 6:**408**

Engel, Joel, 6:**408–409**, 18:725

Engel, Joseph ben Judah, 6:**409**

Engel, József, 6:**409**

Engel, Valerii, 11:323

Engel, Yuli Dimitriyevich. *See* Engel, Joel

Engelberg, Ḥayyim of, 6:**409**

Engelberger, Ferdinand Franz. *See* Engelberg, Ḥayyim of

Engelmann, Gabriel, 6:**409–410**

Engelmann, Susanne Charlotte, 6:**410**

Engelmann, Suzanne Charlotte, 6:160

Der Engel mit der Posaune (Lothar), 13:214–215

Engelsberg, Leon, 6:**410**

Engendering Judaism: An Inclusive Theology and Ethics (Adler), 16:111–112

Engineering
 Austria
  Lieben, Robert von, 12:802
  Schwarz, David, 1:429, 18:189
 Belgium, Lipski, Abraham, 13:75
 bioengineering, 11:772
 construction
  Lipski, Abraham, 13:75
  Rabinovich, Isaak Moseyevich, 17:36
 Czechoslovakia, Gaunse, Joachim, 7:396–397
 England, Blok, Arthur, 3:770
 France
  Carvallo, Jules, 4:502–503
  Citroën, André Gustave, 4:736–737
  Michel-Lévy, Auguste, 14:173
  Weil, R. Adrienne, 20:713
 Germany
  Arco, Georg Wilhelm Alexander Hans, Graf Von, 2:419

Berliner, Emile, 1:430, 3:460–461, 17:149

Hochschild, Mauricio, 9:300

Lilienthal, Otto, 13:17

Marcus, Siegfried, 13:515

Rathenau, Emil Moritz, 17:110

Ruedenberg, Reinhold, 17:525–526

Schlesinger, Georg, 18:140–141

Strauss, Benno, 19:252

Israel
 Frohman, Dov, 7:297
 Harari, Ovadiah, 8:345
 Horev, Amos, 9:525
 Kurrein, Max, 12:393
 Leeuw, Avraham De, 12:601
 Libai, Avinoam, 12:773–774
 Ollendorff, Franz, 15:409
 Ram, Moshe, 17:77
 Reiner, Markus, 17:206
 Schechtman, Dan, 18:430
 Shalon, Raḥel, 18:390
 Singer, Josef, 18:638
 Zarchin, Alexander, 21:458
 Ziv, Jacob, 21:641–642

Italy, Magino, Meir, 13:353

physics, 11:772

Poland, Freudenthal, Alfred Martin, 7:263

Russia
 Goldberg, Emanuel, 7:692, 16:138
 Gurevich, Mikhail Iosifovich, 8:140, 12:630
 Rabinovich, Isaak Moseyevich, 17:36
 Samoilovich, Rudolph Lazarevich, 17:747

U.K.
 Lockspeiser, Ben, 13:153
 Young, Alec David, 21:400

U.S.
 Adler, Charles, 1:395
 Cohen, Morris, 5:28
 Drucker, Daniel Charles, 6:26
 Feld, Jacob, 6:745
 Fondiller, William, 7:114–115
 Goldmark, Peter Carl, 7:717
 Heyman, Moses David, 9:86
 Isaacs, Jacob, 10:55
 Jaffe, Leonard, 11:66–67
 Juda, Walter, 11:474
 Katz, Israel, 12:12
 Kitsee, Isador, 12:207

Engineering, *continued*

Land, Edwin, H., 12:456, 16:125

Langer, Robert S., 12:481

Ledeen, Hyman, 12:596

Lederer, Jerome F., 12:597

Lees, Lester, 12:600

Litman, Samuel, 13:129

Millman, Jacob, 14:257

Nagin, Harry, 14:733

Pinkel, Benjamin, 16:169

Resnick, Judith Arlene, 17:228

Serbin, Hyman, 18:308

Shapiro, Ascher Herman, 18:404

Silverman, Leslie, 18:587

Silverstein, Abe, 18:588

Slepian, Joseph, 18:673

Sporn, Philip, 19:127

Weil, Joseph, 20:712

Wiesner, Jerome Bert, 21:55

Wolman, Abel, 21:152

Zucrow, Maurice Joseph, 21:679

Englaender, Richard. *See* Altenberg, Peter

England, 6:**410–432,** *412*

Anglo-Jewish Historical Exhibition, 14:626

antisemitism, 6:410, 418, 423, 425, 426, 427

badges, Jewish, 3:45

blood libel, 3:775, 4:185, 6:410, 15:301, 312

Canterbury, 4:435–436

caricatures of Jews, 4:477–478

discrimination and, 5:680–681

London, 13:182

cultural and social life

Anglo-Jewish Historical Exhibition, 14:626

architecture, 2:400

archives, 2:408

Ashkenaz, 2:107, 12:747, 13:180–181

assimilation, 2:611

calligraphy, Hebrew, 4:372–373

community organization and structures, 5:108, 110, 119*t*, 9:236

displaced persons (DP) and, 3:421

education, 6:181, 419, 421–422, 429–430, 14:510–511

Freemasons, 7:228

heraldry, Jewish, 9:6–7

Holocaust documentation, resource centers, 9:428

Jewish communities, 11:78, 12:599

journalism, 16:488

medicine, 12:423, 763–764

motion pictures, 14:575

museums, 14:625

philanthropy, 12:746, 16:38, 39–40, 43

resettlement of Jews, 4:331, 5:306, 6:413–414

Sephardim, 13:180, 181

theater, 19:671–672

women in, 21:179

demographics, 6:420–421, 422–426

economic affairs

archa, 2:369–370, 14:442

bankers, moneylenders, 3:116, 12:766

brokers, 4:203

glassmaking, 7:632

moneylending, 12:801, 14:439, 441, 442

occupations, 6:420–421

oil industry development, 16:20

peddling in, 15:710

printing industry, Hebrew, London, 13:184

tailoring, 19:437

tobacco trade, 20:6–7

typographers, 20:213

foreign policy and affairs

Balfour Declaration, 3:85–89

capitulations, 4:453

displaced persons (DP) and, 3:421

Israel, 6:430–432

Jerusalem, 11:167

Libya occupation, 12:792

Mandate for Palestine, 6:419

Ottoman Palestine, 10:183, 184–185

Palestine Liberation Organization, 6:431

Palestinian Authority, 6:431

Sykes-Picot Agreement, 19:350–351, *351*

White Papers, 21:**36–38**

Holocaust

displaced persons (DP) and, 3:421

Irving Holocaust denial, 9:494

rescue efforts, 9:491

immigration, 6:410, 416–417, 418, 419

laws and legal systems, 12:550

capitulations, 4:453

criminology, 5:303

discrimination and, 5:680–681

emancipation, 6:375, 376–377, 9:232

expulsion, 6:411–413

naturalization of Jews, 11:255

prostitution, 16:628

WW II war crimes trials, 20:645–646

Middle Ages, 6:410–413

Jewish affairs department, 6:589–590

London, 13:179–180

military Jewish Brigade Group, 11:271–272

modern period, 6:416–420

motion pictures, 14:575

museums, 14:625

political theories, parties and organizations, 6:414–415, 425–426, 16:339, 342–343

Battle of Cable Street, 3:215

fascism, 3:215

Ha-Shomer ha-Ẓa'ir, 8:385

liberalism, 12:776–777

socialism, 1:504–505

students' movements, 19:265–266

Zionism, 6:417, 418, 423–424, 21:588–589

Zionist socialism, 18:718

population, 6:414–416, 16:387, 392

post-WW II, London, 13:182–183

religious life and scholarship, 6:415, 417–418, 419–420, 421, 422–423, 425, 427–429

Anglo-Orthodox rabbis, 11:51–52

Conservative Judaism, 5:176

ḥazzanim, 8:504

Kabbalah, 6:687–688

Rabbinate, 17:15–16

Reform Judaism rabbis, 11:49–50, 13:697

Sephardim, 13:180, 181

United Synagogue, 20:*404,* 404–405

women, 6:427, 428–429, 19:361

world wars, 6:417, 418–419, 14:510–511

See also Mandate for Palestine; United Kingdom; *specific cities*

Englard, Yitzhak, 6:**432**

Engles, Friedrich, 18:705

English literature, 6:**432–440,** 16:269–270

 Abraham, 1:287

 Abse, Dannie, 1:332

 Adam, 1:375

 Aguilar, Grace, 1:509

 Anglo-Jewish writers, 6:437–440

 Bennett, Salomon Yom Tov, 3:369

 biblical and Hebraic influences, 6:432–434

 biblical influence

  Britain, 3:670

  Canada, 3:672

  United States, 3:672

 Bronowski, Jacob, 4:207

 Brookner, Anita, 4:208

 Browning, Robert, 4:218

 Byron, George Gordon, Lord, 4:324

 Cecil, Henry, 4:535

 Charles, Gerda, 4:577

 Chaucer, Geoffrey, 4:584

 cherub and cherubim, 4:601

 children's, 4:631–634

 Cumberland, Richard, 5:337

 Daleski, Hillel, 5:381–382

 Dickens, Charles, 5:645

 Disraeli, Benjamin, 5:699–702

 D'Israeli, Isaac, 5:702

 encyclopedias, 6:401

 homiletic, 9:514

 Jew, image of, 6:434–436

 Leftwich, Joseph, 12:603

 Levertov, Denise, 12:681–682

 Levy, Amy, 12:747

 Lewis, Leopold Davis, 12:765

 Palestine and Israel, 6:436–437

 Pinter, Harold, 16:177–178

 Pinto, Vivian de Sola, 16:179

 Rodker, John, 17:364–365

 romanticism, Abrams, Meyer H., 1:327

 Rosenberg, Isaac, 17:436–437

 Sinclair, Clive, 18:632

 Sontag, Susan, 19:26

 Spewack, Bella, 19:99–100

 Spiegelman, Art, 4:500–501, 631, 19:107

 Spielvogel, Nathan, 19:109–110

 Steel, Danielle, 19:172

 Stein, Gertrude, 12:661, 19:177–178

 Stein, Joseph, 19:180

 Steiner, George, 19:191

Steinfeld, J.J., 19:192

Stern, Bertha Gladys, 19:204–205

Stern, Steve, 19:217–218

Stine, R.L., 19:228

Stone, Irving, 19:236

Straus, Ralph, 19:251

Strauss, Gustave Louis Maurice, 19:252

Susann, Jacqueline, 19:325–326

Sutro, Alfred, 19:330

Symons, Julian, 19:352

Tarn, Nathaniel, 19:515–516

Taylor, Sydney, 19:560

Tobenkin, Elias, 20:8

Torgov, Morley, 20:54–55

Trillin, Calvin, 20:19

Trilling, Diana, 20:149

Trilling, Lionel, 20:149–150

Turow, Scott, 20:204

Untermeyer, Louis, 8:465, 20:418, 423

Waddington, Miriam, 4:424

Waley, Arthur, 20:608

Wallace, Irving, 20:609

Wallant, Edward Lewis, 20:611

Wasserman, Dale, 20:683–684

Wasserstein, Wendy, 15:227, 20:687

Waten, Judah, 20:688

Weidman, Jerome, 20:698–699

Weinzweig, Helen, 20:729

Weller, Michael, 21:5

Wesker, Arnold, 21:19

West, Nathanael, 21:22

Wolfe, Humbert, 4:116, 21:141

Wolfert, Ira, 21:142

Wouk, Herman, 21:233–234

Yarmolinsky, Avrahm, 21:285

Yezierska, Anzia, 21:328

Zangwill, Israel, 6:437, 14:540, 21:454–456

Zukofsky, Louis, 15:219, 442, 21:681–682

English Standard Version (Bible), 3:621

English translations of Bible, 3:611–627

 Anglo-Saxon and medieval translations, 3:611

 Broughton, Hugh, 4:212

 Catholic versions, 3:625

  early modern, 3:612–613

  World War II, following, 3:614–621

 early modern versions, 3:611–614

 Internet versions, 3:637

 Jewish versions, 3:625

  early modern, 3:614

  World War II, following, 3:621–625

 names for books of Pentateuch, 3:576

 Protestant versions, 3:625

  early modern, 3:611–614

  World War II, following, 3:614–621

 Psalm 23, variations in, 3:625–627

 World War II, following, 3:614–625

  Jewish versions, 3:621–625

  Protestant and Catholic versions, 3:614–621

Engravers. *See* Medalists

Engürüz. *See* Ankara (Turkey)

'En ha-Qore (Jekuthiel ben Judah ha-Kohen), 13:652

En-Harod (Israel), 6:**441,** vol. 11: color insert

En Jodiskfamilies saga. See The Saga of Jewish Family

Enkin, Naum, 2:70

Enlightenment, 9:229

 antisemitism, 2:213–214

 apostasy, 2:271–272

 Assembly of Jewish Notables, 2:599–602, *600*

 deism, 8:436

 integrating religion during, 11:114–115

 Judaism, development of concept of, 11:517–518

 letters and letter writers, 12:673

 literature and humor, 9:592–593

 philosophy during

  influence on Jewish, 16:92

  Jewish contributions to, 16:65–66

  revival of Philo Judaeus, 16:61

 women, 16:109

 See also Haskalah

En-Mishpat (ancient Israel), 11:698

Enneads (Plotinus), 6:373

Ennery, Jonas D', 6:**441**

Enoch (biblical figure), 6:334, **441–442**

Enoch, Ethiopic Book of, 2:257–258, 6:**442–444,** 11:590, 15:290, 18:324

Enoch, Slavonic Book of, 6:**444–445**

Enoch ben Abraham, 6:**445**

Enosh, 6:**445,** 18:319

En-Rimmon (ancient Israel), 6:**445**

Enrique Enriquez de Paz. *See* Enríquez Gómez, Antonio

Enriques, Paolo, 6:**445**

Enriques Miranda, Abraham, 3:695

Enriques Miranda, Joseph, 3:695
Enríquez, Isabel, 6:**446**
Enríquez Basurto, Diego, 6:**446**
Enríquez Gómez, Antonio, 6:**446–447**
En-Rogel (ancient Israel), 6:**447**
Enselberg, Otto. *See* Feraru, Leon
Ensheim, Moses, 6:**447**
Ensisheim (France), 6:**447**
En- Tappuah. *See* Tappuah
Entartung (Nordau), 15:297–298
*Entdecktes Judenthum. See Judaism
   Unmasked* (Eisenmenger)
Entebbe raid, 6:**447–448**
Entelar. *See* Attorneys
Entertainment industry, 6:747
   Benny, Jack, 3:358–359
   Davis, Sammy, Jr., 5:482–483
   Desheh, Avraham, 5:602
   Diller, Barry, 5:661
   Essex County (NJ), 6:513–514
   Hall, Monty, 8:276
   Head, Edith, 8:507–508
   Heckerling, Amy, 8:751
   Jessel, George, 11:244
   Lang, Pearl, 12:479
   Mason, Jackie, 13:603
   Moonves, Les, 14:469
   Morris, William, 14:511
   public relations, 16:711
   Redstone, Sumner Murray, 17:161
   Rose, Billy, 17:425
   Schacht, Alexander, 18:98–99
   Schlamme, Martha Haftel, 18:138–
      139
   Schmidt, Joseph, 18:139–145
   See also Motion pictures;
      Television and radio
Entin, Joel, 6:**448**, 11:327
Entrepreneurship
   Akirov, Alfred, 1:561–562
   Alexander, Kobi, 1:623
   Allen, Paul G., 1:668–669
   Cole, Kenneth, 5:56
   Dell, Michael S., 5:541
   Handler, Ruth Mosco, 8:319–320
   Leviev, Lev, 12:704
   Schlesinger, Isidore William,
      18:141
   Schultz, Howard, 18:174
   Weinberg, Harry, 18:211
Entre Ríos (Argentina), 2:435, 6:**448–
   449**
*Die Entstehung der Psudoisidorischen
   Faelschungen in Le Mans* (Simson),
   18:621
Enuma Elish, 5:274–275

Environment
   afforestation, 6:452
   biodiversity, 5:164
   business ethics and, 4:310
   desertification, 6:452
   destruction of, 5:163
   drip irrigation, 6:452
   global warming, 5:169–170
   grazing, 5:167
   land and people interdependence,
      5:166–168
   nuclear, fossil fuel, solar energy,
      5:169–170
   pollution, 5:166–168
   religions' approach, 5:170–171
   shemittah and yovel, 6:454
   stewardship vs. domination,
      5:164–165
   sustainable development, 6:453–
      454
   See also Conservation;
      Environmental sciences
Environmental law, 6:452–453
Environmental sciences, 6:**449–454**
   atmospheric, 6:449–450
   biological plant protection, 6:452
   desertification, afforestation, 6:452
   environmental law, 6:452–453
   hydrology, 6:451
   oceanography, 6:450–451
   soil microbiology, 6:451
   sustainable development, 6:453–
      454
Envy. *See* Jealousy
Enzikopedyah Le-Ẓiyyonut, 14:426
*Enzyklopaedie der Wissenschaften und
   Kuenste* (Encyclopedia), 6:401
Eötvös, Baron József, 6:454
Eperjes. *See* Presov (Slovakia)
Epernay (France), 6:454
Ephesus (Asia Minor), 6:**454–455**
Ephod, 1:541, 6:**455–456**, 16:512
Ephraim (biblical figure), 1:416, 6:*456,
   456–457,* 11:20
Ephraim, Benjamin, 6:458
Ephraim, David, 6:458
Ephraim, Ḥayyim. *See* Ephraim, Heine
   Ḥayyim
Ephraim, Heine Ḥayyim, 6:457–458
Ephraim, pupil of the Rif. *See*
   Ephraim ibn Avi Alragan
Ephraim, Veitel Heine, 6:457, **458–
   459,** 14:300
Ephraim, Zacharias, 6:458
Ephraim, Zacharias Fraenkel, 6:458
Ephraim ben Gershon ha-Kohen. *See*
   Freudemann, Simḥah

Ephraim ben Isaac, 6:**459**
Ephraim ben Jacob ha-Kohen, 6:**459**
Ephraim ben Jacob of Bonn, 2:87,
   3:770, 6:**460**
Ephraim ben Shemariah, 6:**460**
Ephraim family, 6:**457–458,** 458*t*
Ephraim ibn Avi Alragan, 6:**460**
Ephraimites, 1:218, 6:456–457
Ephraim Moses ben Sender. *See* Cilibi
   Moïse
Ephraim Mountains. *See* Samaria
   (ancient Israel)
Ephraim of Kaleah. *See* Ephraim ibn
   Avi Alragan
Ephraim of Luntshits. *See* Ephraim
   Solomon ben Aaron of Luntshits
Ephraim Solomon ben Aaron of
   Luntshits, 6:**460–461,** 7:361–362,
   9:226, 11:422
Ephraim the Elder. *See* Ephraim ibn
   Avi Alragan
Ephraim the Sephardi. *See* Ephraim
   ibn Avi Alragan
Ephraim the Syrian
   Peshitta and, 3:600
   Peshitta used by, 3:599
Ephrath (Israel), 6:**461**
   See also Bethlehem (Israel)
Ephrati, David Tevele ben Abraham,
   6:**461**
Ephrem the Syrian, 4:720
Ephron (biblical figure), 6:**461–462**
Ephron (mountain, Transjordan),
   6:**461**
Ephron (town, Israel), 6:**461**
Ephron, Nora, 6:**462**
Ephros, Gershon, 6:**462**
Ephrussi, Boris, 6:**462**
The Epic of Russian Literature
   (Slonim), 18:677
Epics, Sumerian literature, 14:101–103
Epictetus, 6:**462–463**
Epicureanism, 6:**463**
Epigraphic materials preservation. *See*
   Archives
Epigraphy. *See* Inscriptions
Epilogue (Bayefsky), 3:232
Epiphanes. *See* Ptolemy V
Epiphanius
   on Judah IV, 11:479
   on Septuagint, 3:596
Epirus (Greece), 6:**463**
Episcopus Judaeorum, 6:**463**
*Episodes from My Life. See Epizoden
   fun Mayn Lebn* (Reisen)
Epistle of Barnabas, 3:664, 4:719
Epistle of Jeremy. *See* Jeremiah, Epistle
   of

The Epistle of the Debate (Falaquera).
  See Iggeret ha-Vikku'ah
*The Epistle of the Mystery of
  Redemption. See Iggeret Sod ha-
  Ge'ullah*
Epistles, Christian, 15:190
  See also New Testament
Epistles of Brethren of Sincerity, 4:**170–
  171**
Epistle to an Apostate (Heller), 8:793
Epistolary conventions, 12:674–675
*Epistola Samuelis Maroccani. See De
  aventu Messiae*
Epitaphs, 6:**464–465**
Epitome on Logic (Averroes), 4:524–
  525
Epizoden fun Mayn Lebn (Reisen),
  17:211
Eppenstein, Simon, 6:**465**
Eppler, Sandor, 6:**465**
Eppstein, Paul, 6:**465–466**
Epshtein, David A., 6:161
Epshtein, Mikhail Semyonovich. *See*
  Golodny, Mikhail
Epstein, Abraham (1841-1918), 6:**466**
Epstein, Abraham (1880-1952), 6:**466**
Epstein, Abraham (1892-1942), 6:**466–
  467**
Epstein, Abraham Meir ben Aryeh
  Leib, 6:**467**
Epstein, Alvin, 6:**467**
Epstein: An Autobiography (Epstein),
  6:**471**
Epstein, Aryeh Leib ben Mordecai,
  6:**467**
Epstein, Baruch ha-Levi, 6:**468**
Epstein, Brian Samuel, 6:**468**
Epstein, Chaim Fischel, 6:**468–469**
Epstein, Charlotte, 6:**469**
Epstein, Claire, 6:**469**
Epstein, Cynthia Fuchs, 18:736
Epstein, Eliyahu. *See* Elath, Eliahu
Epstein, Gilbert, 6:**469–470**
Epstein, Harry H., 6:**470**
Epstein, Helen, 9:383
Epstein, Isaac, 6:183
Epstein, Isaac ben Mordecai, 6:**470**
Epstein, Isidore, 6:**470–471**, 11:332
Epstein, Izhac, 6:**471**
Epstein, Jacob. *See* Epstein, Sir Jacob
Epstein, Jacob (philanthropist), 3:98
Epstein, Jacob Nahum, 6:**472–473**,
  14:325–328, 329–330
Epstein, Jean, 6:**473**
Epstein, Jehiel Michal ben Aaron Isaac
  ha-Levi, 6:**473**
Epstein, Jehiel Michal ben Abraham
  ha-Levi, 6:**473–474**

Epstein, Joseph, 15:668
Epstein, Judith, 6:**474**
Epstein, Julius J. and Philip G., 6:**474**
Epstein, Kalonymus Kalman of
  Cracow, 6:**474–475**
Epstein, Leslie, 6:**475**
Epstein, Louis M., 4:100, 6:**475**
Epstein, Marie, 6:473
Epstein, Meir Harif. *See* Epstein,
  Abraham Meir ben Aryeh Leib
Epstein, Melech, 6:**475**
Epstein, Morris, 6:**475–476**
Epstein, Moses Mordecai, 6:**476**, 18:58,
  674
Epstein, Moshe, 4:180
Epstein, M.S., 6:161
Epstein, Paul Sophus, 6:**476**
Epstein, Seymour, 6:**476**
Epstein, Sir Jacob, 6:**471–472**, 18:223
Epstein, Zalman, 6:**476**
Epstein ha-Levi, Moses Jehiel, 6:**476**
ʾEqdaḥ, 16:478
"Equality" (periodical). *See Egalitatea
  (periodical)*
Equestrian, 19:140
Equidistant Letter Sequences (ELS),
  Bible codes and, 3:679
Equilibrium theory, 2:490
Equus (Shaffer), 18:361
Er, 6:**477**
Er and Onan, 15:426–427
Erasmus of Rotterdam, 6:**477**
  Bible translations by, 3:612
  New Testament of, 15:191
Erastosthenes of Cyrene, 6:**477**, 14:397
Erbil (Iraq). *See* Irbil (Iraq)
Ercole dei Fideli. *See* Sesso, Salamone
  da
Di Erd (Hirschbein), 9:133
Erdély (Romania). *See* Transylvania
  (Romania)
Erder, Y., 11:796
Erd-Vey (Singer), 18:637
Erech (Mesopotamia), 2:402, 3:23,
  6:**477–478**
Erekh Leḥem (Castro), 4:518
Erelei ha-Maḥashavah (Regelson),
  17:187
Erev (Shekhtman), 18:444
Erez ha-Ẓevi (Eliav). *See Land of the
  Hart* (Eliav)
Erez Israel, 6:**478**
Erez Israel (Kann), 11:765
Erez Yisrael (Lurie), 13:269
Erez Yisrael ha-Tovah ve-ha-Yeshanah
  (music album). *See Good Old Israel*
  (music album)

Erfurt (Germany), 6:**478**
Ergas, Joseph ben Emanuel, 6:**478–
  479**, 8:477
Erich, Aron-Hertz. *See* Serbu, Ieronim
Ericson, Walter. *See* Fast, Howard
  Melvin
Erik, Max, 6:**479**
Erik Millin (Rapoport), 17:99
Erikson, Erik Homberger, 6:**479–480**
*Das Erkenntnisproblem in der
  Philosophie und Wissenschaft der
  neuren Zeit* (Cassirer), 4:509
*Erkenntnistheoretisches zur
  Schoepfungsgeschichte der Genesis*
  (Hoenigswald), 9:303
Erlanger, Camille, 6:**480**
Erlanger, Frederic-Emile, 6:480
Erlanger, Joseph, 6:**480**, 13:10
Erlanger, Ludwig, 6:480
Erlanger, Michel, 6:**480–481**
Erlanger, Philippe, 6:**481**
Erlanger, Raphael, 6:480
Erlanger family, 6:**480**, 13:249
Erlau (Hungary). *See* Eger (Hungary)
Erlich, Henryk, 2:18, 6:37, **481**
Erlich, Selma, 12:724
Erlich, Vera Stein, 6:**481**
Erlich, Wolf Hersh. *See* Erlich, Henryk
Erlik, David, 6:**481–482**
Erman, Johann Peter Adolf, 6:**482**
Die Ermordung der Butterblume
  (Doeblin), 5:729–730
Ernakulam (India), 6:**482**
Erotic Poems. See Stihuri venerice
Erpenius, Thomas, 6:**482**
Errera, Carlo, 6:**482**
Errera, Léo, 6:**483**
Errera, Paul Joseph, 6:**483**
Error. *See* Mistakes
er-Routi. *See* Rote family
Er-Routi family. *See* Rote family
Ersekújvár (Slovakia). *See* Nove
  Zamky (Slovakia)
Ertel, Rachel, 11:326
Erter, Isaac, 4:199, 6:**483–484**
Erusin. *See* Betrothal
Eruv, 6:425, 427, **484–485**
Eruv ḥazerot, 6:484, 485
Eruvin (tractate), 6:**485–486**, 18:338
Eruv tavshilin, 6:**484–485**
Eruv ve-Hoẓa'ah (Seigel), 18:253
Erwitt, Elliott, 6:**486**
*Die Erzaehlung des Hexateuch auf ihre
  Quellen untersucht* (Smend), 18:686
L'esaltazione di Salomone (oratorio,
  Porsile), 18:762
Esarhaddon, 3:23, 5:615, 6:**486–487**,
  14:403

Esau, 6:**487–488**
  Adah, 1:370
  birthright, 7:45–46, 11:18
  in commentary, 11:20–22
  Edom, 6:152
  Eliphaz, 6:349
  Eliphaz in Job as son of, 11:351–352
  identified with Edom, 6:488
  identified with Roman Empire, 6:488
  return of Jacob and, 11:19
Esav (Shalev), 18:372
Escalona (Spain), 6:**488**
Escapa, Joseph ben Saul, 6:**489**
Eschatology, 6:**489–504**
  Abrabanel, Isaac ben Judah, 1:279
  Abraham bar Ḥiyya, 1:293
  apocrypha, 6:495–498
  Christian, Jerusalem and, 11:225
  Dead Sea Scrolls, 6:498–500
  in Deutero-Isaiah, 6:493
  Enoch, 6:442–444
  Gehenna, 6:497–498
  Islamic, 6:502–503
  Jewish
      Byzantine empire, 4:326–327
      Jerusalem and, 11:213
  Kabbalistic, 6:500–502
  Levi ben Gershom view, 12:700, 701
  Maimonides, Moses, 13:392–393
  messianism, 6:496–497, 499–500
  Muslim, Jerusalem and, 11:223
  Naḥmanides controversy, 14:747
  paradise, 6:498
  pre-exilic prophets, 6:490–492
  pre-prophetic period, 6:489–490
  Sheol, 6:497
  Talmudic, 6:500
  war, 6:498–499
  Wisdom of Solomon, 18:768
  world to come, 6:497
  Yaḥad, 21:270
  See also Messianism
Eschelbacher, Joseph, 6:**504**
Escrito y sellado (Chocrón), 4:357
Escudero, Lorenzo, 6:**504**
Esdraelon, Plain of. *See* Jezreel (valley, Israel)
Esdras, Book of. *See* Ezra, Greek Book of
IV Esdras, on Bible as closed corpus, 3:579
"Esh Bo'eret" (Hazaz), 8:493
Esh Dat (Epstein), 6:476

Esh Dat (Zamosc), 21:452–453
Eshed, Hagai, 4:346
Eshel, Hanan, 11:525
Eshel, Yitzḥak, 6:**504**
Eshet Ḥayil, 6:**505**
Eshkol. See Sefer ha-Eshkol
Eshkol, Levi, 6:**505–507**, 12:534
  Allon, Yigal, 1:676
  governments of, 10:437–440, 437t, 439t
  Johnson, Lyndon Baines, 11:385
  policies, 10:225
  Six-Day War, 10:229–232
Eshkol, Mamre, and Aner, 2:**145**
Eshkol Anavim (Fischmann), 7:57
Eshkol ha-Kofer (Hadassi), 2:529, 8:188–189
Eshtaol (Israel), 6:**507**
Eshtemoa (ancient Israel), 6:**507**
Eskeles, Bernhard, 6:508
Eskeles, Cecily, 6:508
Eskeles, Gabriel ben Hudah Loew, 6:507
Eskeles, Issachar Berush, 6:507–508
Eskeles, Lea, 6:508
Eskeles family, 6:**507–508**, *508, 508t*
Esom (Transjordan), 1:370
Esotericism. *See* Kabbalah
E (Elohim) source of Torah, 15:735–739
  Aaron and, 15:739
  contradictions and, 15:741–742
  identification of, 15:742
  laws in, 15:745–746
  monotheism in, 15:750
  redactor and, 15:740
  terminology for God, 15:743
España en su historia: Cristianos, Moros y Judíos (Castro Quesada), 4:519
Los Españoles como llegaron a serlo (Castro Quesada), 4:519
Espejo de medicina (Chirino), 4:652
Esperanto, 21:450
Espina, Alfonso de. *See* Alfonso de Espina
Espinelli, Hugo. *See* Saslavsky, Luis Simón
Espinosa, Edouard, 6:508
Espinoza, Enrique, 6:**509**
Espionage
  Aaronsohn family, 1:221–223
  Cairo trial, 4:346
  Lavon Affair, The, 12:533–534
  Pollard Affair, 16:357–359
  Rose, Fred, 17:425–426

  Rosenberg case, 17:440
  Rosenblum, Sigmund Georgievich "Reilly, Ace of Spies," 17:443–444
L'Esprit des lois (Montesquieu), 14:459
Esquisse historique de la musique arabe (Christianowitch), 1:440
Esra, 6:**509**, 18:257
Essais (Montaigne), 14:453
Essai sur l'état actuel des Juifs de Pologne et leur perfectibilité (Calmanson), 4:374
Essaouira (Morocco). *See* Mogador (Morocco)
Essayists and essays
  Berg, Leo, 3:416
  Berger, Lili, 3:425
  Bialoblotzky, Benjamin Jacob, 3:566
  Herschele, 9:44–45
  Holitscher, Arthur, 9:321
  Honigmann, Barbara, 9:518
  Lewisohn, Ludwig, 12:768
  Licht, Michael, 12:796
  Polgar, Alfred, 16:331
  Ravitch, Melech, 17:123
Essay on Man (Cassirer), 4:509
Essay on Rime (Shapiro), 18:406
Essays in the Theory of Economic Fluctuations (Kalecki), 11:732
Essays on Comparative Institutions (Eisenstadt), 6:271
Esseg (Croatia). *See* Osijek (Croatia)
Esselin, Alter, 6:**509**
Essen (Germany), 6:**509–510**
The Essence of Judaism. See Wesen des Judentums
Essenes, 6:**510–512**, 8:390
  Dead Sea sect and, 5:508
  Ein Fashkhah springs, 6:256
  eschatology, 6:498–500
  gnosticism and, 7:651
  Jesus and, 11:248
  John the Baptist and, 11:381
  Jubilees, Book of, 11:474
  Maghāriya and, 18:233
  See also Dead Sea Scrolls; Qumran scrolls
Essex County (NJ), 6:**512–514**
Esslingen (Germany), 6:**514**
Estado da Bahia. *See* Bahia (Brazil)
The Estate (Singer), 18:635
An Estate of Memory (Karmel), 9:408–409, 11:812–813
Estates of deceased, child maintenance, 15:636
Este, João Baptista de, 6:**514**

Estella (Spain), 6:**514–515**

Estella, David ben Samuel. *See* Kokhavi, David ben Samuel

L'Ester (Modena), 14:409

Esterhazy, Ferdinand Walsin, 6:18–19

Esterke, 6:**515**

Estermann, Immanuel, 6:**515**

Estevens, David, 6:**515**

Esther (1880-1943), 6:**518**

Esther (biblical figure), 6:**515–518**, 8:292, 18:215–216
    Esterke, 6:515
    fast of, 6:**519**
    Mordecai, 14:478–479

Esther (Kiera), 12:147–148

Esther, additions to the Book of, 6:**518–519**, 8:294

Esther, Book of, 8:293–294, 18:220, 221
    Ahasuerus, 1:538
    Ahasuerus-Xerxes, 1:538
    Comedia famosa de Aman y Mordochay (Lara), 12:493

Esther Rabbah, 6:**519–520**

Esthersohn, U. *See* Gnessin, Uri Nissan

Estienne, Bible translations by, 3:612

Estonia, 6:**520–522**, *521*
    emancipation, 6:385
    Holocaust
        Tallinn, 19:465
        Tartu, 19:523

Estori Ha-Parḥi, 6:**522**

Estraikh, Gennady, 6:**522–523**

Estrella de Jacob sobre Flores de Lis (Barrios), 3:176

Estrosa, Daniel, 6:**523**, 11:728

Eszék (Croatia). *See* Osijek (Croatia)

Esztendōk (Bródy), 4:201

Esztergom (Hungary), 6:**523**

Etam, 6:**523**

Étampes (France), 6:**523**

. . .*et compagnie* (Bloch), 3:763

E-Temen-an-ki, 3:19

Eten. *See* Manevich, Lev Yefimovich

The Eternal Bride (Orpaz). *See* Ha-Kalah ha-Nitzḥ

Eternal Jew. *See* Wandering Jew

The Eternal Jew. See Der Eybiker Yid

The Eternal Jew documentary, 9:439

Eternal lamp. *See* Ner Tamid

The Eternal Patient and His Beloved (Levin), 12:708

Eternity. *See* Time and eternity

Eternity of universe. *See* Evolution

Ethan, 6:**523–524**

Et ha-Zamir (Be'er), 3:**251**

Ethbaal, 6:**524**

Etheridge, John Wesley, 6:**524**

Ethical culture, 6:**524–525**
    Adler, Felix, 1:407
    Black, Algernon David, 3:730
    Neumann, Henry, 15:122

Ethical idealism. *See* Fichte, Johann Gottlieb

Ethical literature, 6:**525–531**

Ethical wills, 13:106–107, 21:**74–75**
    See also Wills

Ethica Ordine Geometrico Demonstrata (Spinoza), 19:**112**, 113–115, 117

Ethics, 6:**531–537**
    Abraham ben Moses ben Maimon, 1:306–307
    abstinence and asceticism, 8:391
    Al-Nakawa, Israel ben Joseph, 1:686
    animal vs. human life issue, 5:168–169
    Baumgardt, David, 3:221
    in Bible, 6:531–534
    business (*See* Business ethics)
    Calahora, Joseph ben Solomon, 4:349
    Canpanton, Judah ben Solomon, 4:432
    divine transcendence, 6:536–537
    duty and duties, 6:72–73
    economic history, 6:114–116
    Elijah ben Solomon Abraham ha-Kohen of Smyrna, 6:341
    geonic commentaries, 7:493
    Ḥasidei Ashkenaz, 8:388
    Holiness Code, 9:319
    human-assisted evolution, 5:170
    Ibn Bilia, David ben Yom Tov, 9:664–665
    interpersonal relations, 7:129
    Judaism, concept of, 11:512, 514, 12:561–562
    legal and judicial system, taxation, 19:556
    Levinas, Emmanuel, 12:715–716
    literature, 12:671
        Hebrew, 7:13–14, 13:282–283
        homiletic literature and, 9:509
        Jewish, 7:13–14, 13:105–106
    Mivḥar ha-Peninim, 14:372–373
    moderation vs. absolutism, 6:536
    monotheism, 14:449
    Orḥot Ḥayyim, 15:469
    Orḥot Ẓaddikim, 15:469–470
    philosophic analysis of, 16:94, 96, 97, 99

procreation vs. population control, 5:168–169
    Sefer Ḥasidim, 8:392
    Sefer ha-Yashar, 18:240–241
    in Talmud, 6:535–536
    See also Business ethics

Ethics (Spinoza), 16:92–93

Ethics of Judaism. See Ethik des Judentums

Ethics of the Fathers. *See* Avot

Ethik des Judentums (Lazarus), 11:770, 12:561

Ethiopia, 6:**537–539**
    aliyah, 1:661
    American Joint Distribution Committee, 2:62–63
    Bogale, Yona, 4:34
    Boschwitz, Rudolph Eli, 4:95
    boy preparing to pray, vol. 20: color insert
    Enoch, Ethiopic Book of, 6:442–444
    Hebrew classroom, vol. 3: color insert
    immigration to Israel from, 10:241, 243, 263, 353, 453, 631
    Moses, 14:532, 545
    ORT, 15:489–490

Ethiopic translations of Bible, 3:601, 5:661–662

Ethnarch, 6:**539**

Ethnography
    Chorny, Joseph Judah, 4:668
    Israel (land of), 10:107
    Sapir, Edward, 18:37

Ethnomusicology
    Abraham, Otto, 1:290–291
    Brauner, Harry, 4:138–139
    Carp, Paula, 4:493
    Katz, Israel (1930-), 12:**12**
    Lachmann, Robert, 12:423–424

Etienne. *See* Manevich, Lev Yefimovich

Etienne de la Boétie. *See* La Boétie, Etienne de

Etiological legends, Joshua, Book of, 11:447

Etiquette, 6:**539–540**, 18:321

Et Kol ha-Tela'ah asher Meza'atnu (Kara), 11:783

Etlekhe Verter vegn Zhargon Oysleyg (Shalom Aleichem), 18:381

Eto bylo v Leningrade (Chakovski), 4:560

Etrog (fruit), 2:39, 6:**540–541**

Etrog, Sorel, 6:**541**

Etruria. *See* Tuscany (Italy)

Etsi doctoribus gentium, 4:277–278

Etsi Judaeorum, 4:277

Etsi non displiceat, 4:277

Ettelson, Harry William, 6:**541–542**

Ettenberg, Sylvia Cutler, 6:**542**

Ettendorf (France), 6:**542**

Etting, Benjamin, 15:196

Etting, Reuben, 6:542

Etting, Solomon, 6:542

Ettinger, Akiva Jacob, 6:**543**, 15:382

Ettinger, Isaac Aaron, 6:544

Ettinger, Mordecai Ze'ev ben Isaac Aaron Segal, 6:**543–544**

Ettinger, Shmuel, 6:**544–545**

Ettinger, Sholyme. *See* Ettinger, Solomon

Ettinger, Solomon, 6:**545**

Ettinger family, 6:**543**

Etting family, 6:**542–543**

Ettinghausen, Jean-Maurice. *See* Sachs, Maurice

Ettinghausen, Richard, 6:**545**

Ettinghausen, Walter. *See* Eytan, Walter

Ettlingen. *See* Ottolenghi family

Ettlingen (Germany), 6:**545–546**

Ettlinger, Jacob, 6:**546**

Ettlinger, Marion, 6:**546**

"Etudes" (Op. 78, Moscheles), 14:516

Études de grammaire (Polishek), 16:360

Etwas ueber die rabbinische Literatur (Zunz), 21:107, 684, 685–686

Etwas zur Charackteristick der Jude (Bendavid), 3:325

Etyudn un Materyaln tsu der Geshikhte fun der Yidisher Literatur-Bavegung in F.S.R.R. (Abtshuk), 1:333

Etz Hayim (Lieber), 12:803

Etzioni, Amitai Werner, 6:**546–547**

Euboea (Greece). *See* Chalcis (Greece)

Euchel, Isaac Abraham, 6:**547**, 18:722

Eudes of Châteauroux. *See* Odo of Châteauroux

Eudes of Sully. *See* Odo of Sully

Eugenics, 7:393

Eugenio Maria. *See* Zoller, Israel

Eugenius (popes), 6:**547–548**

Eugenius III (pope), 6:547

Eugenius IV (pope), 6:**547–548**, 15:250, 16:374

Euhemerus, 6:**548**

Eulau, Cleo Mishkin, 6:548

Eulau, Heinz, 6:**548**

Eulenburg, Ernst, 6:**548**

Eulenburg, Isaac ben Abraham Moses Israel, 6:**548–549**

Eulenburg, Philipp zu, 9:56, 57, 58, 59, 61

Eulogy. *See* Hesped

Eunuchs, 3:730, 6:**549**

Eupatoria (Ukraine). *See* Yevpatoriya (Ukraine)

Euphemism, 6:**549–551**

Euphrates, 6:51–56, **551–552**

Eupolemus, 6:**552–553**
    chronological concerns of, 3:660
    Moses, 14:531

Eurgetes. *See* Ptolemy III

Eurgetes ll. *See* Ptolemy VII

*Die europaeische Triarchie*i (Hess), 9:75

Europa Plan, 6:**553–554**, 7:75

Europe, 6:**554–560**
    advertising, 1:428
    amulets, 2:122
    anti-Nazi boycott, 4:110, 111
    Antiquity, 6:554
    antisemitism, 2:221–223, 238, 239, 9:244–245
    Anusim, 2:254
    apologetics, 2:267–268
    architecture, 2:399–400
    bar mitzvah, 3:165
    Beriḥah, 3:433–436
    Bet Din in, 3:515
    B'nai Brith activities, 4:16
    business and industries, leather, 12:575
    businesses and industries, diamond trade and industry, 5:636
    capitulations, and Christian states of, 4:452–454
    caricatures of Jews, 4:477–478
    cemeteries, 4:539
    community organization and structures, 5:108–111, 115*t*, 116*t*, 117*t*
    demography, 5:555, 558–559, 562
    department stores and, 5:587–588
    diamond trade and industry, 5:634–635
    divorce statistics, 5:719–720
    education, Jewish, 6:186–187
    eighteenth and nineteenth centuries
        communal organizations, 9:235–236
        religious and cultural differentiation, 9:236
    eighteenth-twentieth century
        hospitals and, 9:562–563
        insurance, 9:809
    emancipation, 6:557–558

French Revolution, and effects on communities, 7:256
    Hasidic movements, 11:599
    and Host, desecration of, 9:565, 565–566
    Jewish intellectual capital, 6:555
    Karaite activities, 11:791
    Leibzoll, 12:624–625
    Middle Ages, 6:555–556
        communal organizations, 9:224
        expulsions from, 6:624–625
        hospitals and, 9:562
    modern, agriculture, Jewish, 1:497–499
    nineteenth century, homiletic literature and, 9:513–514, 514
    peddling in, 15:708–710
    population, 6:557
        1939, 6:558
        1946, 6:559
        2003, 6:560
        twentieth century, 6:559–560
    race theory, 9:244–245
    Renaissance, 6:556–557
    Roman Empire, 6:554–555
    seventeenth-twentieth century, iconography and, 9:705–706
    television and radio, 19:595–596
    See also specific countries and regions

European Association for Jewish Studies (EAJS), 11:318

European Center for Jewish Leadership (LEATID-Europe), American Joint Distribution Committee, 2:64

European Community
    agreements with, 10:265
    Israel as associate member, 10:262–263

The European Community, 6:**560–568**
    development of, 6:560–561
    Jerusalem and, legal aspects of, 11:234
    Mediterrean countries and, 6:562–564
    Palestinians and, 6:564–658

European Council for Nuclear Research (CERN), 13:153

European Council of Jewish Communities, 2:64

European Economic Community. *See* The European Community

European Union, 6:566–568

European Union of Jewish Students, 2:64

Eusebius Pamphili, 2:263, 4:720, 6:**568–569**

Eusebius Sophronius Heironymus. *See* Jerome

Eusebius Sophronius Hieronymus. *See* Jerome

Eustachio, Giovanni Paolo. *See* Nola, Elijah ben Menachem da

Euthanasia, 6:**569–571**, 9:332
  body and soul, concept of, 4:31
  camps, concentration and extermination, 4:384
  historigraphy, 9:419
  Israel Supreme Court decisions, 13:739, 14:360
  Jewish law, 13:743–746
  Kaltenbrunner, Ernst, 11:750

Eutropius, 6:**571**

Evangelical Church of Germany, 16:632

Evans, E.J., 6:62, 15:303

Evans, Eli, 6:**571**

Evans, Jane, 6:**571–572**

Evans, Mary Anne. *See* Eliot, George

Evans, Robert, 6:**572**

Eve (biblical figure), 6:**572–573**
  Adam, 1:371, 372, 373, 375–376, 377–378
  Seth and, 18:319
  symbolism of, 16:106, 107

Eveb ha-To'im, 6:**574**

Eved Ivri. *See* Slavery

Evel. *See* Semaḥot

Even al Pi ha-Be'er (Shaḥam), 18:363

Evenari, Michael, 6:**573–574**

Even Boḥan (Kalonymus ben Kalonymus), 11:749

Even Boḥan (Menahem ben Solomon), 14:23

Even ha-Ezer (Eliezer), 6:270, 328

Even ha-Ezer (Jacob ben Asher), 11:30

Even ha-Shoham (Eliakim Goetz ben Meir), 6:318

Evening Services for Rosh-Hashanah and Yom Kippur (Pinto), 16:178

Even-Or, Mary, 6:**574**

Even Reshef. *See* Firkovich, Abraham

Even Sappir (Saphir), 18:36, 447

Even Shemuel, Judah, 6:**574**, 11:327

Even Shetiyyah, 6:**574–575**

Even Shetiyyah (Abraham ben Judah Leon), 1:304

Even-Shoshan, Avraham, 6:**575**, 8:670

Even-Shoshan, Shelomo, 6:575

Even Tizak (Smilansky), 18:687

Eventov, Yakir, 6:**575**

Even-Yaish. *See* Abenaes, Solomon

Even Yaish, Solomon. *See* Abenaes, Solomon

Even Yehudah (Israel), 6:**575**

Even Yisrael. *See* Steinsaltz, Adin

Even Yiẓḥak (Israel), 6:**575–576**

Evergreen (Plain), 16:214

Ever Hadani, 6:**576**

Ever ha-nahar, 6:551–552

Ever Min ha-Hai, 6:**576**

Everybody's Business (Eisenman), 6:267

Every Friday (newspaper), 18:146

Evian Conference, 2:60, 6:**576–577**, 9:330, 365, 490

Evidence, 6:**577–584**, 12:571–572, 14:353, 360–361
  See also Witnesses

Evidence of Love (Jacobson), 6:438

Evil
  as absence of good, 16:85
  demons and demonology, 5:572–578
  Eichmann trial, 6:250–252
  in Genesis, 7:445–446
  Ḥasidic view of, 8:409
  nature of God and, 11:243
  nature of Nazi, 6:672–674
  problem of, Kabbalah, 11:637–641
  refrain from doing, 6:531
  Satan as personification of, 18:72
  See also Good and evil; Theodicy

Evil eye, 6:**584–585**

Evil inclination. *See* Inclination, good and evil

Evil-Merodach, 6:**585**

Evolution, 5:164, 170, 6:**585–588**, 8:478
  human-assisted, 5:170

Evolutionary Socialism. See Die Voraussetzungen des Sozialismus und die Aufgaben der Sozialdemokratie

The Evolution of Jewish Thought (Agus), 1:522

Evolution of the Horse Brain (Edinger), 6:148

Évora (Portugal), 6:**588**

I Evrai (Schiby), 18:125

Evreul ca simbol (Duda). *See The Jew as a Symbol* (Duda)

Évreux (France), 6:**588**

Evrey i blondinka (Brik), 4:181

Evron (Israel), 6:**588–589**

Evron, Ephraim, 6:**589**

Evron, Gilad, 8:722

Ewald. *See* Friedlaender, Oskar Ewald

Ewald, Heinrich Georg August, 3:649, 6:**589**

Der ewige Jude. *See* Wandering Jew

Exagoge (Ezekiel the Poet), 6:649, 14:539

Examination of witnesses. *See* Witnesses

The Excavation of Tell Beit Mirsim (Albright), 1:596

Excavations, 2:374–377, 5:753–754, 763

Las excelencias y calumnias de los Hebreos (Cardozo), 4:467

Las Excelencias y Calunias de los Hebreos (Cardozo), 18:295

Excerpta Valesiana (historical work), 6:**589**

Exchange, Bill of. *See* Shetar

Exchanges. *See* Stock exchanges

Exchequer of the Jews, 6:**589–590**

Excitable Speech: Politics of the Performative (Butler), 4:317

Excommunication
  Adler, Nathan ben Simeon ha-Kohen, 1:404–405
  Akavyah ben Mahalalel, 1:554
  da Costa, 5:234
  obligations, law of, 15:373
  Schlettstadt, Samuel ben Aaron, 18:142–143
  See also Ḥerem

Execration texts, 6:223–224

Execution (Civil), 6:**590–598**, 9:474

Execution (Judicial). *See* Capital punishment

Exegesis, 13:87–88, 94–95, 107
  biblical (*See* Biblical criticism)
  Eliezer of Beaugency approach, 6:330
  Kimḥi, David, 12:155–156
  La Peyrère, Isaac, 12:488–489
  Midrash Aseret ha-Dibberot, 14:185–186
  Midrash ha-Gadol, 14:186–187
  See also Midrash

Exegetische Terminologie der juedischen Traditonsliteratur (Bacher), 3:**37**

Exempla of the Rabbis (Gaster), 6:**598–599**, 7:12

Exemplar de Penitencia (Castro Sarmento), 4:519

Exemplum, 6:**599–600**

Exeter (England), 6:427, **600**

Ex-Friends (Podhoretz), 16:251

Exhumation. *See* Disinterment

Exilarch, 6:**601**, 602
  Anan ben David, 2:127
  Bustanai ben Ḥaninai, 4:316–317
  establishment, 15:786
  Isaac Iskoi ben Ḥasdai, 18:770
  Jesse ben Hezekaih, 11:244
  Solomon ben Ḥasdai, 18:770

Exilarchs, 6:**600–607**
Exile
city of refuge, 4:743–744
Judah Loew ben Bezalel on,
11:508
Kamenev, Lev, 11:753
See also Galut
The Exile. See Be-Erez Gezerah
Exile, Assyrian. *See* Assyrian exile
Exile, Babylonian. *See* Babylonia, exile
Exiles, Ingathering of the. *See*
Ingathering of the exiles
Existentialism, 6:**611–612**, 672, 16:66,
97–98, 102–103
revelation, 17:258
Soloveitchik, Joseph Baer, 18:779–
780
L'Exode; superflumina Babylonis
(Fondane), 7:114
Exodus (ship), 3:99, 4:10, 9:281, 10:207
The Exodus (Bercovici), 14:541
The Exodus (Ezekiel the Poet). *See*
Exagoge (Ezekiel the Poet)
Exodus (Uris), 8:465, 20:423
Exodus, Book of, 6:**612–623**
Aaron, 1:208–209
Book of the Covenant, 4:67–69
burning bush, 4:297–298
covenants, 5:249–251
Decalogue, 5:520–523, 522t
experience in Numbers, 15:330–
332
historicity, 6:622, 15:747–749
illustration and illumination,
14:541–542
main themes, 6:622–623
Midrashim
Mekhilta of Rabbi Ishmael,
13:793–795
*Mekhilta of Rabbi Simeon ben
Yohai*, 13:795–797
Moses, 14:524–531
Patriarchs in, 15:690
plagues of Egypt, 16:210–214
route, 6:620, *621*
Shovavim Tat, 18:520
strands, 6:619t, 621–622
Wisdom of Solomon, 18:768
Exodus, Rabbah, 6:**624**
Exodus from Egypt, 9:166–167
*Expanding the Palace of Torah:
Orthodoxy and Feminism* (Ross),
16:112
Experanza de Israel (Manasseh Ben
Israel), 18:295
Expiation. *See* Atonement
An Explanation of America (Pinsky),
16:177

Exploration. *See* Travelers and
explorers
Explorers. *See* Travelers and explorers
L'Express (newspaper), 7:616–617
Expressionism
Berlewi, Henryk, 3:443
Bernstein, Theresa, 4:485
Otta, Francisco, 15:516
Expropriation, forfeiture, confiscation,
5:**150–151**
Expulsion of the Jews from Spain
(Beinart), 3:269
Expulsions, 6:**624–626**
Alexandria, 4:326
Argentina, 2:426
Austria, 2:689
Bulgaria, 4:269, 18:745
England, 6:413
France, 2:175, 211, 713, 16:47, 48
Brittany, 7:150
Caen, 4:332
Charles IV, 4:575
Charles VI, 4:576
Draguignan, 6:6–7
Provence, 1:552, 16:638–639
Sens, 18:290
Soissons, 18:745
Germany, 2:212
Duesseldorf, 6:42
medieval, 13:695, 712, 791
Saxony, 18:87
Hungary, 15:708
Bratislava, 4:132
Italy
Bologna, 4:48
Sardinina, 18:53
Lithuania, 4:168
Naples, 1:274
kingdom of, 4:184
under Nicholas I, 15:250
from Nuremberg, 15:347
Pale of Settlement, 15:577–579
Palestinian, Kuwait, 2:316
from Pezinok (Slovakia), 16:24
Poland, 2:423
Portugal, 2:253, 290, 714, 6:413
Russia, 1:621, 9:242
Middle Ages, 9:242
Russian territory, 15:577, 578
Sephardim, 18:293
Sicily, 2:140, 18:543
Spain, 1:276, 311, 2:253, 290, 714,
6:413, 11:14
Albarracín, 1:587
Alfonso de Espina, 1:642
brokers, 4:203

Cádiz, 4:331
Ciudad Rodrigo, 4:745
Dueñas, 6:41
Quincentennial anniversary,
18:304–305
Sargossa, 18:44–45
Seville, 18:328
Sigüenza, 18:571
Ukraine, Sevastopol, 18:324
USSR, 2:221, 235
Western Europe, Middle Ages,
9:216–217, *221*, 221–222
Yemen, 13:694
Extermination camps. *See* Camps,
concentration and extermination
Extirpation. *See* Karet
Extradition, 6:**626–630**
Extrajudicial remedies, 6:630–631
Extralegal remedies, 6:631–632
*The Extraordinary Adventures of Julio
Jurenito* (Ehrenburg), 6:237
Extraordinary remedies, 6:**630–632**
*Extremos y Grandezas de
Constantinopla* (Almosnino), 1:685
Eyal (Israel), 6:**632**
Eybeschuetz, Jonathan, 2:24, 4:194,
6:**632–634**, 684, 8:439, 18:356
Abraham ben Hayyim, 1:300
Abraham ben Isaac ha-Kohen of
Zamość, 1:301
Abraham ben Joseph of Lissa,
1:303
amulets, 2:121
Aryeh Leib ben Mordecai Epstein,
6:467
Baruch ben David Yavan, 3:188
biography, 12:227
Emden, Jacob, 2:24, 6:392, 12:459
Halberstadt, Mordecai, 8:264
Landau, Ezekiel Ben Judah, 12:460
Sheluhei Erez Israel, 18:451
Zerah ben Meir Eidlitz, 6:252
Der Eybiker Yid (Pinski), 16:175
Eydoux, Emmanuel, 6:**634**
Eye banks, 20:107
"Eye writing," 11:667–668
Eylenburg, Issachar Baer ben Israel
Leiser Parnas, 6:**634**
Eynikeyt (periodical), 6:**634**
Eyn Simkhas Touro Lid (Tiktiner),
17:137
Eytan, Rachel, 6:**634–635**
Eytan, Walter, 6:**635**
Ezechias, 9:89
Ezechias (Birck), 9:89
Ezekiel, 6:**635–646**
in art, 6:645–646

Babylonian exile and, 6:611–612
Book of
    altar in, 2:12–13
    on angels, 2:151–152
    fraud, 7:220
    Merkabah Mysticism, 14:66–67
cherub and cherubim, 4:600
Daniel, 5:417
dates, 6:636t
eschatology in, 6:493
Judah, restoration of, 6:493
Noah in, 15:288
style, 6:636–637, 641
tomb, 6:645
withdrawal of, 6:644
Ezekiel, Abraham Ezekiel, 6:**646**
Ezekiel, Apocryphal Books of, 6:**647**
Ezekiel, Ben, 14:454
Ezekiel, Isaac. See Ezekiel, Solomon
Ezekiel, Jacob, 6:**647**
Ezekiel, Mordecai Joseph Brill, 6:**647–648**
Ezekiel, Moses, 6:**648**
Ezekiel, Moses Jacob, 6:**648**
Ezekiel, Nissim, 6:**648**, 15:474
Ezekiel, Solomon, 6:646
Ezekiel ben Reuben Manasseh, 6:**648**
Ezekiel Feivel ben Ze'ev Wolf, 6:**648–649**
Ezekiel ha-Kohen, 17:58
Ezekiel the Poet, 3:660, 6:**649**, 14:532, 539
Eẓel. See Irgun Ẓeva'i Le'ummi
Eżerenai. See Zarasai (Lithuania)
Ezer ha-Dat (Pollegar), 16:3589
Eẓ ha-Da'at (Morpurgo), 14:510
Eẓ ha-Ḥayyim (Vital), 20:547
Eẓ Ḥayyim (Ḥayyim ben Bezalel), 8:481
Eẓ Ḥayyim (Ḥazzan), 1:385
Eẓ Ḥayyim (Aaron ben Elijah), 1:212, 213
Eẓ Ḥayyim (Abrahem ben Shem Tov Bibago), 3:570
Eẓ Ḥayyim (Bacharach), 3:34
Eẓ Ḥayyim (Epstein), 6:474
Eẓ Ḥayyim (educational institution), 6:**649–650**
Eẓ Ḥayyim (Jacob ben Judah of London), 11:34
Eẓ Ḥayyim (Vital), 13:264
Eẓ Ḥayyim yeshivah, 11:716
Ezine (Turkey), 6:**650–651**
Ezion-Geber, 6:**651**
Ezkerah Elohim ve-Ehemayah (Modzhitz), 14:413

Ezobi, Jehoseph ben Hanan ben Nathan, 6:**651–652**
Ezofovich, Abraham Jan, 11:471–472
Ezofovich, Isaac, 11:472
Ezofovich, Michael, 11:472
Ezofovich family. See Józefowicz family
Ez Peri (Finkel), 7:32
Ezra, 3:640, 6:163, **652–654**, 654, 9:187–188
    See also Soferim
Ezra, Apocalypse of, 6:**654–655**
Ezra, Apocryphal. See Ezra, Greek book of
Ezra, Book of, 6:**656–662**
    mishmarot and ma'amadot, 14:317–318
    mishpat Ivri, 14:340
Ezra, David, 6:654
Ezra, Derek, Baron, 6:**655**
Ezra, Elias David ben Joseph, 6:654
Ezra, Greek Book of, 6:**655–656**
Ezra, IV. See Ezra, Apocalypse of
Ezra ben Abraham ben Mazhir, 6:**662**
Ezra ben Ezekiel ha-Bavli, 6:**662**
Ezra ben Joseph Gabbai, 3:57
Ezra ben Nisan, 6:**662–663**
Ezra ben Solomon, 6:**663**
Ezra family, 6:654, **654**
Ezra IV. See Ezra, Apocalypse of
Ezra of Gerona. See Ezra ben Solomon
Ezra of Montcontour, 6:**663**
Ezras Noshim, 2:432
Ezras Torah, 8:807
Ezrat Torah, 3:758, 13:12
Ezrin, Hershell, 6:**663–664**
Eẓyon Bloc, 6:264–265, 20:657

F
F (letter), 6:*665*, 7:5
Faber, Boderianus. See Le Fèvre de la Boderie, Guy
Fabian, Jacob, 15:687
Fabius, Laurent, 6:**665–666**
Fable, 4:619
The Fable of the Ancient (ibn Sahula). See Meshal ha-Kadmoni
Fables, 6:**666–670**
Fables of a Jewish Aesop. See Mishlei Shu'alim
Fabri, Felix, 6:**670**
Fabricant, Solomon, 6:**670**
Fabricius, Guido. See Le Fèvre de la Boderie, Guy
Fabric of My Life (Solomon), 18:764
Fabrikant, V., 18:262

Die Fabrikation der Fiktionen (Einstein), 6:263–264
The Face of God after Auschwitz (Maybaum), 9:397–399
The Face of Joshua: The Small Face (Falk). See Penei Yehoshu'a: Appei Zutrei
Face to Face. See Szemtől szembe
Facing History and Ourselves, 6:**670–672**, 9:451–452
Fackenheim, Emil, 6:**672–674**, 9:393–395, 16:68, 98–99
Factor, Max, 6:**674–675**
Fadenhecht, Yehoshua, 6:**675**
Fadiman, Clifton, 6:**675**
Fadus, Cuspius, 6:**675**
Faenza (Italy), 6:**675**
Făgăraş (Romania). See Fagaras (Romania)
Fagan the Jew (Eisner), 6:278
Fagaras (Hungary). See Fagaras (Romania)
Fagaras (Romania), 6:**675–676**
Fagius, Paulus, 6:**676**
Fahn, Abraham, 6:**676**
Fahn, Reuben, 6:**676–677**
Fain, Sammy, 6:**677**
Fainzilberg, Ilya Arnoldovich. See Ilf, Ilya
Fainzilberg, Ilya Arnoldovieh. See Ilf, Ilya
Fairs. See Market days and fairs
Fairstein, Linda A, 6:**677**
Faith. See Belief
Faith after the Holocaust (Berkovits), 3:439, 9:399–400, 417
Faith and belief, 3:**290–294**
    after the Holocaust, 9:391–401
        Berkovits, Eliezer, 9:399–400
        Cohen, Arthur A., 9:396
        Fackenheim, Emile, 9:393–395
        Funkenstein, Amos, 9:400–401
        Greenberg, Irving, 9:395–396
        Jonas, Hans, 9:396–397
        Levinas, Emmanual, 9:400
        Maybaum, Ignatz, 9:397–399
        Raphael, Melissa, 9:397
        Rubenstein, Richard, 9:392–393
        Wiesel, Elie, 9:401
Faith and Fratricide (Ruether), 4:683–684
Faith and Prejudice (Olson), 16:631
Faith of Judaism (Epstein), 6:471
Faith or Fear: How Jews Can Survive in Christian America (Abrams), 1:327

Faïtlovitch, Jacques, 4:34, 6:**677–678**
  Beta Israel and, 3:504
  Japan and, 11:82
Faitusi, Jacob ben Abraham, 6:**678**
Faivovich Hitzcovich, Angel, 6:**678**,
  16:349
Faiyūm (Egypt), 6:**678–679**
Fajans, Kasimir, 6:**679**
Fajwlowicz, Shlomo Zalman. *See*
  Shragai, Shlomo Zalman
Fakhr al-Dawla Abu al-Fath Is ḥaq.
  See Isaac bar Israel ibn al-Shuwayk
Falaguera family. *See* Falaquera family
Falaise (France), 6:**679**
Falaquera, Nathan ben Joel, 6:**679**
Falaquera, Shem Tov ben Joseph ibn,
  6:399, **679–683**, 8:552, 16:86–87,
  107
Falaquera family, 6:**679**
Falaquero family. *See* Falaquera family
Falcini, Natale, 11:568
Falco, Mario, 6:**683**, 12:552
Falcon, Joseph, 4:82
Falconer, 2:34
Faleshty (Moldova), 6:**683**
Fălești (Moldova). *See* Faleshty
  (Moldova)
Falik, Fernando. *See* Kosice, Gyula
Falk, Aryeh Leib, 6:**685**
Falk, Bernard, 6:**684**
Falk, Issachar Dov, 6:**685**
Falk, Jacob Joshua ben Ẓevi Hirsch,
  6:**684–685**
Falk, Joshua, 6:**685–686**, 8:735
Falk, Joshua ben Alexander ha-Kohen,
  4:779–780, 6:**686**
Falk, Kaufman George, 6:**686**
Falk, Leon, 6:**684**
Falk, Leon, Jr., 6:**684**
Falk, Marcia, 6:**686–687**
Falk, Maurice, 6:**683–684**
Falk, Miksa, 6:**687**
Falk, Peter, 6:**687**
Falk, Samuel, 6:**685**
Falk, Samuel Jacob Ḥayyim, 3:9,
  6:**687–688**
Falk, Sigo, 6:**684**
Falk family, 6:**683–684**
Falkland, Samuel. *See* Heijermans,
  Herman
Falklands War, 2:441
Falkovich, Emanuel, 11:322
Falkowitsch, Joel Baerisch, 6:**688**
Falkowski, Paul G., 6:450
Fall, Leo, 6:**688**
Fallen Angels, 2:155–156
Fallen Angels (Bamberger), 3:102

Fallow year, 6:93
Fall River (MA), 6:**688**
False Papers (Melson), 9:414
False witness. *See* Perjury
Falstein, Max, 16:340
Fălticeni (Romania). *See* Falticeni
  (Romania)
Falticeni (Romania), 6:**688–689**
Faludy, György, 6:**689**
Familial Mediterranean Fever, 6:318
Familiants laws, 4:39, 6:**689–690**,
  13:226, 15:610
Family, 6:**690–695**
  adoption, 1:417–419
  age and the aged, 1:448
  American Jewish, 6:**695–707**
    assimilation, 6:698–700
    contemporary, 6:702–706
    immigration, 6:696–698
  barrenness and fertility, 3:174–175
  biblical, 6:690–693
  commandments concerning, 5:78t
  conduct, 6:539–540
  domestic peace, 5:739
  education, 6:163, 164–165
  importance of, 1:357, 6:693–695
  Talmud, in Jewish education,
    6:170–171
Family. See Mishpaḥ
Family, American Jewish. *See*
  American Jewish family
A Family Album and Other Poems
  (Brody), 4:200
The Family Carnovsky (Singer),
  18:637–638
*Family Diagnosis: An Approach to the
  Preschool Child* (Ackerman), 1:357
Di Familye Tsvi (Pinski), 16:175
Family Institute (NY). *See* The
  Ackerman Institute for Family
  Therapy
*Family in Transition: A study of 300
  Yugoslav villages* (Erlich), 6:481
*The Family Mashber. See Di Mishpokhe
  Mashber*
The Family Moskat (Singer), 18:635
*Family Politics: Love and Power on an
  Intimate Frontier* (Pogrebin), 16:278
*Family Quarrel: The United church and
  the Jews* (Slonim), 18:678
Family Record Book (Modiano), 14:410
Famine and drought, 6:**707–708**
  Earth, 6:82
  Joseph and, 11:20
Fancy's Sketch Book (Moïse), 14:421
Fano (Italy), 6:**708**
Fano, Ezra ben Isaac, 6:708

Fano, Guido Alberto, 6:**708–709**
Fano, Jacob ben Joab Elijah da, 6:708
Fano, Joseph da, 6:708
Fano, Menahem Azariah da, 6:**709**,
  11:392
Fano family, 6:**708**
Fantasia 2000 (periodical), 18:204–205
Fantasy, Jewish. *See* Science fiction
  and fantasy, Jewish
Fantasy on a Hebrew Theme
  (composition, Morawetz), 14:478
Fārābī, Abū Naṣr Muḥammad, al-,
  6:**709–711**
Fārābī, Abū Naṣr Muḥammad al-,
  16:227
Faraj, Murad, 6:**711**, 11:357
Faraj, Samuel ben Nissim al-. *See*
  Mithridates, Flavius
Farāj, Murad, 15:473
Faraj ben Salim. *See* Faraj ben
  Solomon da Agriento
Faraj ben Solomon da Agrigento,
  6:**711–712**
Farband, 6:**712–713**
  Segal, Louis, 18:247
  Yiddesher Kultur Farband, 2:514
Farband fun Zentrales far Yesoimim
  farsorgung in Poylen. *See* Centos
Farber, Marvin, 6:**713**
Farber, Viola, 6:**713**
Farbman, Michael. *See* Abramowitz,
  Grigori
Farbman, W. *See* Abramowitz, Grigori
Farbstein, David Ẓevi, 6:**713–714**
Farbstein, Joshua Heschel, 6:**714**
Fargo (motion picture), 4:782
Farhi, Daniel, 6:**716**
Farhi, Gabriel, 6:**716**
Farhi, Moris, 6:**716**
Farḥi, Ḥayyim, 6:**714**
Farḥi, Joseph Shabbetai, 11:412
Farḥi, Saul, 6:**714**
Farḥi, Shihada. *See* Farḥi, Saul
Farḥi Bible, 3:677
Farḥi family, 6:**714–715**
Farhud, al-, 10:19
Faria, Francisco de, 6:**716**
Farinacci, Roberto, 6:**716–717**
Farissol, Abraham ben Mordecai,
  6:**717**, 12:461
  disputations and polemics, 5:694–
    695
  moneylending, 14:440
Farissol, Jacob ben Ḥayyim, 6:**717**
Farjeon, Benjamin Leopold, 6:49, **717**
Farjeon, Eleanor, 6:717
A farkas (Molnár). *See The Tale of the
  Wolf* (Molnár)

Farkas, Ladislaus, 6:**717–718**, 16:137–138

Farkas, Ruth, 6:**718**

Der Farkishefter Shnayder (Shalom Aleichem), 18:382

Der Farkishefter Shnayder (Shalom Aleichem), 18:382

The Farmer and the Feather. See Ha-Ikkar ver-ha-Noẓah

Farmers' Federation of Israel, 6:**718**

Farmers' Union, 4:317

Farming. *See* Agriculture

Faro (Portugal), 6:**718–719**

Faro (Spain). *See* Haro (Spain)

Faro, Moshe, 15:540

Farragut. *See* Faraj ben Solomon da Agriento

Farrakhan, Louis, 3:736, 20:377

Farrow, Mia, 2:18

Fascism
  Brazil, 18:31, 32
  England, 3:215
  France, 5:438
  Iraq, 10:18–19
  Italy, 6:716–717, 10:793–794, 803–805
  literature opposing, 11:119
  neo-facism, 15:72–73
  Polish literature, 16:336–337

Fashion industry
  Albert, Mildred Elizabeth Levine, 1:589
  Carnegie, Hattie, 4:486
  Delaunay-Terk, Sonia, 5:535
  Drexler, Millard S., 6:17–18
  Karan, Donna, 11:802–803
  Lauren, Ralph, 12:526–527
  Leiber, Judith Maria, 12:618
  Liz Claiborne Inc., 15:492–493
  in New York City, 15:213, 226
  Parnis, Mollie, 15:654
  photography, 16:126
  Scaasi, Arnold, 18:88
  See also Clothing and textiles industry

Faske, Donna. *See* Karan, Donna

Fassūta (Israel State), 6:**719**

Fast, Cheap, and Out of Control (motion picture), 14:510

Fast, Howard Melvin, 6:**719**, 11:511

Fasting and abstinence, 2:546–548, 8:506
  Anan ben David, 2:128
  asceticism, 2:548
  cemetery visiting, 4:538
  fast days, 2:128, 6:719
    Adar, seventh of, 1:382–383

Av, the ninth of, 2:714
Day of Atonement, 5:488, 489, 491
Esther, fast of, 6:519
fast of Tammuz, 19:497–498
fast of the firstborn, 7:46–47
Gedaliah, 7:407
Monday and Thursday, 14:435
Shevat, 18:471
yahrzeit, 21:271
Yom Kippur Katan, 21:382–383

hadran exemption, 8:193
Ḥaliẓah, 12:729
Ḥasidism, 8:415
head covering, 8:506
Karaites, 11:788
laws and customs, 6:720–721
liturgy
  Adonai, Adonai, 1:412
  Akedah, 1:556
  Anenu, 2:75
  Avinu Malkenu, 2:739–740
  haftarah, 8:198, 199
  maftir, 13:335
  seliḥot, 18:268–269
marriage, 13:567
Megillat Ta'anit, 6:301
mishmarot, 14:318
Muslim, 10:90–91
New Moon, 15:151
Nine Days, 15:271
philosophical analysis of, 16:81
prohibited days, 13:769
punishment for assault, 2:596
Purims, special, 16:742
purposes, 6:719, 720, 722
Seliḥot, 18:268, 269
Talmid Ḥakham, 19:467
Talmud, 4:582
Temple, 19:603
Ungar, Joel of Rechnitz, 20:248

Fasting and fast days, 6:**719–723**

Fastlicht, Adolfo, 6:**723**

Fast of Esther, 6:**519**

Fast of Tammuz, 19:**497–498**

Fatah. *See* Al -Fataḥ

Al -Fataḥ
  Arafat, Yasser, 2:333
  Arafat and, 10:279–280
  establishment of, 10:229
  Palestine Liberation Organization and, 15:590, 591, 592, 593
  Palestinian Authority and, 15:597, 599, 600

skirmishes with, 10:233
Syria and, 10:279

Fatal, Moshe. *See* Shahal, Moshe

Fateful Months (Browning), 9:419

Father Justin. *See* Boudin, Jean-François

Father of western misogyny. *See* Philo Judaeus

Fathers
  custody of children, 15:636–637
  maintenance, parental obligation of, 15:635–636
  parables treating God as father, 15:621
  roles, 6:692, 693, 695
    desertion, 6:697
    immigrant, 6:696
    suburbia, 6:701
  See also Children; Parents

Fathers according to Rabbi Nathan. *See* Avot de-Rabbi Nathan

Fathers and Children. See Ha-Avot ve-ha-Banim

Fathers of Zion, 17:111–112

Fath-Nāmeh (Emrāni). *See Book of Victory* (Emrāni)

Fatimids, 6:**723–724**, 11:726–727
  Damascus (Syria) and, 5:392–393
  Egypt and, 6:230–231
  Jerusalem and, 11:157

Fatma Kadin (Kiera), 12:147

Fatmid dynasty, 10:158, 161

Fats. *See* Oils

Fatt, Arthur C., 1:428

Faulhaber, Michael Cardinal von, 4:712

Fauna
  buffaloes, 4:255–256
  camels, 4:380–381
  cats, 4:521
  cattle, 4:526–527
  deer, 5:530–531
  dogs, 5:733
  hyena, 9:647
  hygiene of, 9:648
  hyrax, 9:651
  ibex, 9:656
  koi, 12:267
  mixed species, 14:385, 386, 387
  See also Birds; Reptiles

La fausse industrie (Fourier), 7:139

Fausse route (Badinter), 3:49

Fauvists, 15:648

Fava of Manosque. *See* Hava of Manosque

The Favorite Game (Cohen), 4:423

Favorite Poem Project, 16:176

Fayyūm (Egypt). *See* Faiyūm (Egypt)

Fazallah Tabib al-Hamdani. *See* Rashid al-Din

Fazello, Tommaso, 15:581

Fazlallah Tabib al-Hamdani. *See* Rashid al-Din

Fearing, Kenneth, 6:724–725

Fear of Flying (Jong), 11:399

Fear of God, 6:725–726, 13:230–231

Feast of Fruits. *See* Tu bi-Shevat

The Feast of Pure Reason (Levine), 12:718

Feasts. *See* Festivals

Feather, Leonard, 6:726

Féder, Aizik-Adolphe, 2:517

Feder, Ernesto A. *See* Feder, Ernst

Feder, Ernst, 6:726

Feder, Richard, 6:726–727, 14:476

Feder, Tobias, 6:727

Federacion Agraria Israelita Argentina, 11:775

Federacíon Sefardi Latinoamericana. *See* FESELA (Federación Sefardi Latinoamericana)

Federal Arts Project, 18:617

Federalism, 5:118–120

Federal Republic of Germany. *See* Germany

Federated Department Stores, Inc., 12:560

Federation CJA, 14:464, 466

Federation of Associations for the Care of Jewish Orphans in Poland. *See* Centos

Federation of communities, territorial, 6:727

Federation of Jewish Charities, 18:185

Federation of Jewish Communities (Yugoslavia), 21:416

Federation of Jewish Communities of Romania (FEDROM)
    American Joint Distribution Committee, 2:62
    Filderman, Wilhelm, 7:19

Federation of Jewish Philanthropies (NY), 11:723

Federation of Jewish Welfare Organizations (Los Angeles), 11:816

Federation of Oriental Jews of America, 2:33–34

Federation of Synagogues, 6:415, 419–420

Federation of Zionist Organizations, 4:5

Federation of Zionists of Greater New York and Vicinity, 21:605–606

Federbusch, Simon, 6:727–728

Federjude medals, 13:714

Federman, Max, 6:728

Federn, Paul, 6:728–729

FEDROM. *See* Federation of Jewish Communities of Romania

Fees, for shadkhan, 18:360

Fefer, Itzik, 6:729

Feibelman, Julian Beck, 6:729

Feibusch, Hans, 6:729

Feiczewicz, Louis. *See* Fitch, Louis

Feidman, Giora, 6:729–730, 15:407

Feidman, Levi, 6:730

Feierberg, Mordecai Ze'ev, 6:730–732

Feierstein, Ricardo, 6:732–733

Feiffer, Jules, 6:733

Feigel, Sigi, 6:733

Feigenbaum, Aryeh, 6:733–734

Feigenbaum, Benjamin, 6:734

Feigenbaum, Issac ha-Kohen, 6:734

Feigenberg, Meïr, 6:734

Feigin, Dov, 6:734

Feigin, Samuel Isaac, 6:734

Feiginsohn, Samuel Shraga, 17:418

Feigl, Bedrich, 6:734–735

Feigl, Fredrich. *See* Feigl, Bedrich

Feigl, Fritz, 6:735

Feigl, Herbert, 6:735

Feiler, Arthur, 6:735

Feinberg, Abraham, 6:736

Feinberg, Abraham L., 6:737

Feinberg, Avshalom, 6:736, 15:267–268

Feinberg, David, 6:737

Feinberg, Israel, 6:736

Feinberg, Kai, 15:307, 311

Feinberg, Kenneth, 6:737–738

Feinberg, Leon, 6:738

Feinberg, Lotik. *See* Feinberg, Israel

Feinberg, Louis, 6:738

Feinberg, Nathan, 6:739

Feinberg, Robert, 6:739, 18:707

Feinberg, Samuel Yevgenyevich, 6:739

Feinberg, Yehude-Arye-Leyb. *See* Feinberg, Leon

Feinberg, Yosef, 6:736

Feinberg family, 6:736

Feinbrun-Dothan, Naomi, 6:739

Feiner, Dorothy. *See* Rodgers, Dorothy Feiner

Feiner, Ḥayim. *See* Hefer, Ḥayim

Feiner, Jehiel. *See* K. Zetnik

Feingold, David Sidney, 6:739

Feingold, Russell, 6:739–740

Feinman, Sigmund, 6:740

Feinsilberg, Ilya Arnoldovich. *See* Ilf, Ilya

Feinsinger, Joshua, 6:740

Feinsinger, Shaye. *See* Feinsinger, Joshua

Feinstein, Aryeh Loeb, 6:740

Feinstein, Dianne Goldman, 4:108, 6:740

Feinstein, Elaine, 6:439, 440, 741

Feinstein, Ḥayyim Jacob ha-Hohen, 6:741

Feinstein, Isadore. *See* Stone, I. F.

Feinstein, Meir, 6:741

Feinstein, Moses, 11:255
    abortion, 1:272–273
    Joseph, Norma Baumel, 11:417

Feinstein, Moses (1895-1986), 6:741–742

Feinstein, Moses (1896-1964), 6:742

Feinstone, Morris, 6:743

Feis, Herbert, 6:743

Feischel Buntzl, Mayer. *See* Fischels, Meir ben Ephraim

Feitelson, Menahem Mendel, 6:743, 8:727

Feith, Douglas J., 6:743–744

Feivish, Samuel, 15:437

Feivush, Ḥayyim ben Samuel. *See* Ḥayyim ben Samuel Feivush

Feiwel, Berthold, 6:744

Fejér, Leopold, 6:744

Fejtö, François, 6:744–745

Fekete, Michael, 6:745

Feld, Issac, 6:745

Feld, Jacob, 6:745

Feldbau, Jacques, 2:9

Feldberg, Jacob, 14:454

Feldberg, Leon, 6:745

Felder, Gedalia, 6:745–746

Felder, Jerome Solon. *See* Pomus, Doc

Feldheim, Philipp, 6:746

Der Feldhernnhuegel (Roda Roda), 17:362

Feldman, Abraham Jehiel, 6:746

Feldman, Aharon. *See* Ever Hadani

Feldman, Dora. *See* Shulner, Dora

Feldman, Emanuel, 2:638

Feldman, Herman, 6:746

Feldman, Irving, 6:746

Feldman, Israel. *See* Paldi, Israel

Feldman, József, 6:748

Feldman, Louis H., 6:746–747

Feldman, Martin, 6:747

Feldman, Marty. *See* Feldman, Martin

Feldman, Miroslav, 6:747

Feldman, Morton, 6:747

Feldman, Sandra, 6:747–748

Feldman, Shimshon Simon, 6:748

Feldman, Wilhelm, 6:748

Feldshuh, Tovah, 6:**748–749**

Feldwebel Anton Schmidt (Adler), 1:399

Feleky, Géza, 6:**749**

Felicitations, 5:66

Felicity, two-fold, 3:**239**
See also Beatitude

Feliks, Yehuda, 14:331

Felix, Antonius, 6:28, **749**, 11:396

Felix, Dinah, 17:50

Felix, Eliza Rachel. *See* Rachel (Stage name)

Felix, Raphael, 17:50

Felix, Rebecca, 17:50

Felix, Sarah, 17:50

Felix Libertate, 6:**749–750**

Feller, Abraham Howard, 6:**750**

Feller, Shneyur Zalman, 6:**750**

Fellheim (Germany), 14:17

Fellner, William John, 6:**750**

Felman, Aharon Leib, 6:**750**

Fels, Joseph, 6:**750–751**

Fels, Lazarus, 15:302

Fels, Mary, 6:**751**

Fels, Samuel Simeon, 6:**751**

Felsenthal, Bernhard, 6:**751**
American Jewish Historical Society, 2:58, 59
on Oral Law, 15:457

Fels family, 6:**750–751**

Felsövisó. *See* Viseul-de-Sus (Romania)

Feltre, Bernardino da. *See* Bernardino da Feltre

Felvidek. *See* Slovakia

Felzenbaum, Michael, 6:**751–752**

Felzenbaum, Mikhoel. *See* Felzenbaum, Michael

The Female Face of God in Auschwitz (Raphael), 9:397

Female Hebrew Benevolent Society, 6:190

Females. *See* Women

Feminism, 6:**752–757**, 8:461, 20:347–348, 21:186
ablution, 1:263
Art Movement, Feminist, 2:515
Badinter, Elizabeth, 3:49
Badt-Strauss, Bertha, 3:50
Bernard, Jesse, 3:468
Bible translation and, 3:608
biblical criticism influenced by, 3:655, 658
Boxer, Barbara, 4:108
Broner, Esther M., 4:204
Butler, Judith, 4:317
Canada, 4:406, 409, 417

Chesler, Phyllis, 4:601–602

Cixous, Hélène, 4:749

criticism, 2:87, 8:731–732

German literature
Jelinek, Elfriede, 11:118–119
Lewald, Fanny, 12:757–758

Haggadot, 8:215–216

Hauptman, Judith, 8:461

Jewish philosophy and, 16:105, 110–112

Jewish Theological Seminary, 11:330

Jong, Erica, 11:399–400

Joseph, Norma Baumel, 11:417

Landsberg, Michele, 12:474–475

Mednick, Martha Tamara Schuch, 13:762

Netherlands, suffrage, 11:45

New York City, 15:219, 224

niddah, 15:257–258

Offner, Stacy, 15:389

in Orthodox Judaism, 16:112

Ostriker, Alicia, 15:510

Paley, Grace, 15:600–601

Pappenheim, Bertha, 15:618

Passover observance and, 15:681–682

Pogrebin, Letty Cottin, 16:278–279

Rich, Adrienne, 17:286

Rose, Ernestine Potovksy, 17:425

Schwimmer, Rosika, 18:196

theology, 19:698–699

La Femme de Loth (Bosco), 4:425

Fences, 1:475, 476

Fence to law. *See* Takkanot

Fencing, 19:140

Fenichel, Otto, 6:**757**

Fenichel, Samuel, 6:**757**

Fennel, 6:**757**

Fenton, Paul B., 11:325

Fényes, Adolf, 6:**757**

Fenyö, László, 6:**757**

Fenyö, Miksa, 6:**757–758**

Feodosiya (Ukraine), 6:578, **758**

Ferarius Saladi. *See* Zerahiah ben Isaac ha-Levi

Feraru, Leon, 6:**758**

Ferber, Edna, 6:**758–759**

Ferber, Herbert, 6:**759**, 18:223

Ferber, Zevi Hirsch, 6:**759**

Ferdinand (Holy Roman emperors), 6:**759–760**

Ferdinand, Philip, 6:**760**

Ferdinand and Isabella of Spain, 6:**760–761**
Abrabanel, Isaac ben Judah, 1:276

Alvarez Gato, Juan, 2:27
canonization of Isabella, 11:384
granting of Inquisition in, 18:328
Saragossa Jewish policy, 18:44
Seneor, Abraham, 18:288

Ferdinand I, 6:**759–760**

Ferdinand II, 6:**760**

Ferdinand III, 6:**760**

Ferdman, José Miller, 5:325

Ferenc, François. *See* Fejtö, François

Ferenc Jóska ládájából (Emöd). *See From Ferenc Jóska's Box* (Emöd)

Ferenczi, Sándor, 6:**761**

Ferkauf, Eugene, 6:**761**

Ferme, Moses Cohen. *See* Azevedo, Moses Cohen D'

Fermi, Enrico, 16:137

Fermosa. *See* Jewess of Toledo

Fernandes Villareal, Manoel, 6:**761–762**

Fernandez, Antonio. *See* Carvajal, Abraham Israel

Fernand-Halphen, Alice, 8:285

Fernberger, Samuel, 6:**762**

Fernhof, Isaac, 6:**762**

Ferramonti concentration camp (Italy), 15:581

Ferrara (Italy), 1:303, 6:**762–764**
Anau, Phinehas Hai ben Menahem, 2:136
Lampronti, Isaac, 2:136–137

Ferreira, Abraham Kohen de. *See* Herrera, Abraham Kohen de

Ferrer, Vicente, 3:45, 4:351, 6:**764**, 11:472, 13:192

Ferris, Iris, 6:**764**

Ferris Bueller's Day off (motion picture), 4:195

Ferrizuel, Joseph ha-Nasi, 2:17, 6:**764–765**

Ferrizuel "Cidellus," Joseph. *See* Ferrizuel, Joseph ha-Nasi

Fertile Crescent
1945-2006, 2:300, 301
Aram and Arameans, 2:337

Fertility. *See* Barrenness and fertility

Fertilizers, 1:479–480

FESELA (Federación Sefardi Latinoamericana), 6:**765**

Festival Preludes (Sheriff), 18:462

Festivals, 2:767*t*, 6:**765–771**
altar, 2:12, 15
biblical sources, 6:765–766
calendar, 4:354
cantillation, 13:662
celebrations, 2:766–768
commandments concerning, 5:77*t*

Festivals, *continued*
   dance, 5:409, 410
   dating, according to Meshwi,
     14:80
   diaspora, 6:769–770
   Emar, 6:389–390
   eruvin, 6:484–486
   eschatology, 6:499–500
   exilarch induction, 6:604
   fast days, 6:719
   food, 13:711
   greetings, 8:82, 83
   homilies on readings for, 16:11–12
   intermediate days, 6:769
   Israel, 10:626–628
   Jewish calendar, 4:356–357
   Jubilees, Book of, 11:473–474
   Judaism, development of concept
     of of, 11:514
   Karaites, 11:788, 798
   kibbutz, 7:49, 12:**119–120,** 120*t*
   Lag ba-Omer, 15:420–421
   laws and legal systems, 15:746–747
     Beẓah, 3:556
     burials, 4:293
     domiciles, and observance of,
       5:742–743
     fire, 7:43
     Havdalah, 8:466, 467
     Mishmarot Temple service,
       14:319
     mourning, 14:588
     Mukẓeh, 14:608
     sacrifices, 17:640
     tefillin, 19:579
     Yaknehaz, 21:273–274
   Leviticus, Book of, 12:739
   liturgy
     Amidah, 2:72
     Arvit, 2:537
     azharot, 6:158
     haftarah, 8:198–199
     Hallel, 8:280
     Leipzig Mahzor, 13:365–366
     Mahzor, 13:363–366
     Mahzor Vitry, 13:366–367
     Worms Mahzor, 13:366
   Maghrebi-Ma'aravi, 13:397
   Maiumas, 13:406–407
   meals, eschatological, 6:499–500
   medieval Midrash, 16:12–13
   Mo'ed Katan, 14:413–414
   Passover, 15:677–683
   pilgrim festivals, 10:766, 16:158–
     159
   prayer, 6:770

   religious life and communities,
     Israel, 10:626–628
   Russia, 1970s, 17:566
   Samaritans, 17:729–730
   Second Temple period, 2:768
   Shabbetai Ẓevi, 18:342, 348
   Simḥhat Torah, 18:604–606
   Talmudic literature, 6:768–769
   Temple Scroll, 19:633, 634
   Torah, reading of, 20:46, 49
   Torah ornaments, 20:50–53
   Unleavened Bread, Feast of,
     15:680–681
   women's obligations, 6:770–771
   See specific festivals and holidays
Festschriften, 6:**771–772**
Festus, Porcius, 2:126, 6:**772**
Fetter, Menachem. *See* Elon,
   Menachem
Fettmilch, Vincent, 6:**772,** 7:208
Feuchtwang, David, 6:**772**
Feuchtwanger, Lion, 6:**772–773,**
   11:256, 441, 15:449
Feuer, Henry, 6:**773**
Feuer, Leon Israel, 6:**773–774**
Feuer, Lewis Samuel, 6:**774,** 18:732
Feuerlicht, Morris Marcus, 6:**774**
Feuermann, Emanuel, 6:**774**
Feuerring, Maximilian, 6:**774**
Feuerstein, Aaron, 6:**775**
Feuerstein, Avigdor. *See* Hameiri,
   Avigdor
Feuerstein, Bedřich, 6:**775**
Feuerstein, Henry, 6:**774–775**
Feuerstein, Moses, 6:**775**
Feuerstein, Reuven, 6:**775–776**
Feuerstein, Samuel, 6:197, 775
Feuerstein family, 6:**774–775**
Feuilleton, 4:32, 11:467, 18:578
Feurth, Julius. *See* Firt, Julius
Feygenberg, Rakhel, 7:**5–6**
Feynman, Richard Phillips, 7:**6**
Fez (Morocco), 1:311, 7:**6–8**
Di Fibores (Shalom Aleichem), 18:379
Fichman, David Mironovich. *See*
   Knut, Dovid
Fichman, Jacob, 7:**8–9,** 8:729, 11:217,
   511
Fichmann, Ya'akov. *See* Fichman,
   Jacob
Fichte, Johann Gottlieb, 7:**9–10**
Fiction, Hebrew. *See* Hebrew fiction
Fiction and the Reading Public
   (Leavis), 12:577
Fiddler on the Roof (Harnick and
   Bock), 8:360
Fiddler on the Roof (motion picture),
   18:387

Fiddler on the Roof (musical), 4:26,
   15:220
Fideles. *See* Adelantados
Fiedler, Arthur, 7:**16–17**
Fiedler, Leslie Aaron, 7:**17**
Fiedman, Thomas L., 11:469
Fields, Dorothy, 5:56–57, 7:**17**
Fields, Harvey, 13:204
Fields, Henry, 7:17
Fields, Jackie, 7:**17–18**
Fields, Joseph, 4:658
Fiersohn, Reba. *See* Gluck, Alma
Fieschi, Sinibaldo. *See* Innocent IV
Fifteen Days Across Jewish Palestine
   (Moissis), 14:422
Fifth Aliyah. *See* Aliyah, Fifth
Fifty (number), 15:336, 344
Figdor, Jehiel Michael ben Samuel. *See*
   Kittsee, Jehiel Michael ben Samuel
Figo, Azariah, 7:**18–19**
Figs, 7:**18**
Figure skaters. *See* Ice skating
Filderman, Wilhelm, 7:**19**
Filene, A. Lincoln, 7:**19–20,** 15:205
Filene, Edward Albert, 7:**19–20**
Filene, William, 5:588, 7:19
Filene family, 7:**19–20**
Filipepi, Alessandro di Mariano. *See*
   Botticelli, Sandro
Filipowski, Herschell Philip. *See*
   Filipowski, Ẓevi Hirsch
Filipowski, Ẓevi Hirsch, 7:**20**
Filler, Louis, 7:**20**
Film. *See* Motion pictures
Filosof, Joseph, 18:353
La Filosofia y las teorías científicas
   (Dujovne), 6:43
Filthy pot parable, 6:639
Fima, Efraim, 7:**20–21**
Finale Emilia (Italy), 7:**21,** *21*
Final Solution, 4:385–388, 7:**21–22,**
   9:84–85, 121, 287–289, 305, 325–
   326, 340, 378, 11:828–829
   Bormann, Martin, 4:87
   Eichmann, Adolf Otto, 6:247, 249,
     250, 251
   Frank, Hans Michael, 7:181
   gassing, 7:393
   Germany, 7:536
   Gestapo, 7:564, 565
   Globocnik, Odilo, 7:640
   Goebbels, Paul Josef, 7:680
   Heydrich, Reinhard Tristan, 9:332
   Himmler, Heinrich, 9:121
   Hitler, Adolf, 9:287
   Hoess, Rudolf Franz Ferdinand,
     9:305

Judenrein, 11:529

Kaltenbrunner, Ernst, 11:750

Nazi-Deutsch, 15:42

See also National Socialism (Nazism)

Rauter, Hanns Albin, 17:116

Reichszentrale Fuer Juedische Auswanderung, 17:203

Ribbentrop, Joachim von, 17:280

Schellenberg, Walter, 18:119

SS and SD, 19:155–156

Streicher, Julius, 19:255

Sztójay, Döme, 19:412

Tuka, Vojtech, 20:174

war crimes trials, 20:636, 637, 639

See also Holocaust

The Final Solution (Chabon), 4:555

The Final Solution (Reitlinger), 9:415

Finaly case, 7:**22–23**, 11:776

Finaly family, 11:775–776

Finance. *See* Banking and bankers

Finances, autonomous Jewish, 7:**23–24**, 23t

Financial News (newspaper), 6:264

Financial Times (newspaper), 6:264

Financiers

    Austria, Herz, Leopold Edler von, 9:51–52

    Beit, Sir Alfred, 3:271

    Benedict ben Moses of Lincoln, 3:330

    Belisha family, 3:296

    Belzberg, Samuel, 3:309

    Benveniste, Sheshet ben Isaac ben Joseph, 3:385

    Castiglioni, Camillo, 4:515–516

    Clore, Charles, 4:761

    England

        Isaac of Southwark, 10:53

        Lever, Harold, Baron Lever of Manchester, 12:680

    Hirshhorn, Joseph Herman, 9:143

    Hofmann, Isaac Loew, 9:312–313

    Horowitz, Samuel ben Isaiah Aryeh Leib ha-Levi, 9:541–542

    Icahn, Carl C., 9:702–703

    Lévy, Samuel, 12:755

    Rabinowicz, Oskar K., 17:40

    railroads, 17:69–70

    Rayne, Sir Max, Baron, 17:127

    Riklis, Meshulam, 17:333

    Rohatyn, Felix G., 17:369

    Rosenthal, Leon, 17:454–455

    Rubin, Robert E., 17:513

    Shaw, Benjamin, 18:423–424

    See also Banking and bankers

Das Finanzkapital (Hilferding), 9:106

Finbert, Élian-J., 7:**25**, 15:473–474

Finch, Henry. *See* Finch, Sir Henry

Finch, Sir Henry, 7:**25**

Finci, Eli, 7:**25**

Fine, Diana, 4:440

Fine, H. A., 11:343–344

Fine, Reuben, 7:**25**

Fine, Sidney, 7:**25–26**

Fineberg, Solomon Andhil, 7:**26**

Fineman, Daniel, 7:**26**

Fineman, Hayyim, 7:**26**

Fineman, Irving, 7:**26–27**

Finer, Herman, 7:**27**

Fines, 7:**27–29**, 15:369

    See also Sanctions

Fineshriber, William Howard, 7:**29–30**

Finestein, Israel, 7:**30**

Finestone, Sheila, 7:**30**

A Fine Treatise on Salvation. See Ḥibbur Yafe me-haYeshu'ah

Finf un Tsvantsik Geto Lider (Mlotek, Gottlieb). *See Twenty-Five Ghetto Songs* (Mlotek, Gottlieb)

Fingerman, Gregorio, 7:**30**

Finials, 4:547–548, 20:52

Fininberg, Ezra, 7:**30**

Fink, Janis. *See* Ian, Janis

Fink, Joseph Lionel, 7:**30–31**

Fink, Theodore, 7:**31**, 12:548, 16:340

Finkel, Eliezer Judah, 7:**31**

Finkel, Joshua, 7:**31–32**

Finkel, Nathan Ẓevi Ben Moses, 7:**32**, 18:58

    See also Slobodka Yeshivah

Finkel, Shimon, 7:**32**

Finkelman, Harry. *See* Elman, Ziggy

Finkelstein, Arthur, 7:**33**

Finkelstein, Chaim, 7:**33**

Finkelstein, Heinrich, 7:**33–34**

Finkelstein, Israel, 7:**34**

Finkelstein, Jacob Joel, 7:**34**

Finkelstein, Jacob Yonkel. *See* Fields, Jackie

Finkelstein, Louis, 2:47, 5:173, 7:**34–35**, 17:242

    Jewish Theological Seminary, 11:329–330

    on *Sifra*, 18:560–561

    on *Sifrei*, 18:563, 564

Finkelstein, Nehemiah, 8:476

Finkelstein, Noah, 7:**36**, 8:476

Finkelstein, Norman, 9:495

Finkelstein, Shimon, 7:**36**

Finkelstein, Yonkel. *See* Fields, Jackie

Finkielkraut, Alain, 7:**36–37**

Finklestein, Louis, 2:47

Finland, 7:*37*, **37–39**

    emancipation, 6:385

    libraries, 12:786

    sheḥitah protection, 18:435

Finlay-Freundlich, Erwin, 7:**39**

Finley, Moses. *See* Finley, Sir Moses

Finley, Sir Moses, 7:**39**

Finn, Elizabeth Ann, 7:39

Finn, James, 7:**39**

Finniston, Harold Montague. *See* Finniston, Sir Harold Montague

Finniston, Sir Harold Montague, 7:**39–40**

Finzi, Abraham Raphael, 1:308

Finzi, Aldo, 16:345

Finzi, Gaius, 4:48

Finzi, Gerald, 7:**40**

Finzi, Giuseppe, 7:**40**

Finzi, Gur Aryeh Ha-Levi, 7:**40**

Finzi, Isaac Raphael ben Elisha, 7:**40**, 15:567

Finzi, Joseph, 7:**40**

Finzi, Mario, 4:49, 7:**40**

Finzi, Mordecai ben Abraham, 7:**39–40**, 13:675

Finzi, Samuel, 7:**40**

Finzi, Solomon ben Eliakim, 3:683, 7:**40**

Finẓi, Isaac Raphael ben Elisḥa, 15:567

Finzi family, 7:**40**

Finzi-Norsa Controversy, 7:**40–41**

Fiocchi, Fabiano. *See* Fioghi, Fabiano

Fioghi, Fabiano, 7:**41**

Fiorentino, Salomone, 7:**41**, 10:792

Fiqh, 7:**41–42**

Fir'awn. *See* Pharaoh

Firdaws al-Ḥikma (Ali ibn Sahl ibn Rabbān al-Ṭabar⁻i), 1:660

Fire, 7:**43–44**

Fire and Brimstone; or the Destruction of Sodom (Lesley), 18:739

Firenze (Italy). *See* Florence (Italy)

Firkovich, Abraham, 3:23, 7:**44–45**, 8:356, 11:548, 558, 793–794

Firkovitch Collections, 13:493–494

Firoz Koh (Afghanistan), 1:432

First Aliyah. *See* Aliyah, First

First Amendment (U.S. Constitution)

    Abrams, Floyd M., 1:327

    Adams, Arlin Marvin, 1:379–380

    American Jewish Congress, 2:58

    Brandeis, Louis Dembitz, 4:124

    Jewish settlement in America and, 2:42

First American Jewish Families: 600 Genealogies, 1654–1988 (Stern), 2:54

The First Book of Michael Singermann (Brinig), 4:184
Firstborn, 7:**45–48**
  Commandments, the 613, 5:75, 80
  embryo, 6:391
  Exodus, Book of, 6:612, 614
  first fruits, 7:48
  inheritance rights, 19:288
  levirate marriage, 12:726
  lots, casting of, 13:219
  Passover, 15:680
  Plagues of Egypt, 16:29
  priest and redemption of, 16:525
The Firstborn (Fry), 14:540
First Cincinnati Haggadah. *See* Cincinnati Haggadah
First Esdras. *See* Ezra, Greek book of
The First Forty Years (Morris), 14:510
First fruits, 7:**48–49**
  Agrippa I, 1:503
  Bikkurim, 3:697
  ḥerem, 9:12
  incense offering, 9:754
  leap year, 12:567
  offerings, Bikkurim, 3:697
  pilgrimage, 16:154
  See also Shavuot
First Generation (Altauzen). *See* *Pervoye pokoleniye* (Altauzen)
"First Generations." *See* "Dorot Rishonim"
First International Anti-Jewish Congress, 15:434
First International Conference on Children of Holocaust Survivors, 9:383
First Joshua Ibn Gaon Bible, 3:677
The First Kantakion on the Nativity (Romanos Melodos), 17:405
First Kennicott Bible, 3:677
First Person (television show), 14:510
First Vatican Council. *See* Vatican Council I
Firt, Julius, 7:**49–50**
Firuz, Al-Shams Al-Karim, 7:50
Firuz, Daniel ben Moses, 7:50
Firuz, Moses ben Isaiah, 7:50
Fīrūz family, 7:**50**
Firzogerin, 7:**50–51**
Fisch, Aharon Harel. *See* Fisch, Harold
Fisch, Harold, 3:622, 7:**51**
Fischel, Arnold, 7:**51**
Fischel, Harry, 7:**51–52**, 15:205
Fischel, Walter Joseph, 7:**52**
Fischel family. *See* Fishel family
Fischels, Meir. *See* Fischels, Meir Ben Ephraim; Fischels, Meir ben Ephraim

Fischels, Meir ben Ephraim, 7:**52**
Fischer, Annie, 7:**53**
Fischer, Bernard, 7:**53**
Fischer, Bobby. *See* Fischer, Robert
Fischer, Carolus, 7:**53**
Fischer, David Hackett, 4:125
Fischer, Edmond, 7:**53**, 13:10
Fischer, Emil. *See* Makai, Emil
Fischer, Eugene, 4:681
Fischer, Gyula, 7:**53–54**
Fischer, Jean, 7:**54**
Fischer, Josef, 7:**54**, 55
Fischer, Julius. *See* Fischer, Gyula
Fischer, Karl. *See* Fischer, Carolus
Fischer, Leo, 7:**54**
Fischer, Louis, 7:**54**
Fischer, Maier. *See* Fischer, Marcus
Fischer, Marcus, 7:52
Fischer, Maurice, 7:53–54
Fischer, Meir. *See* Fischer, Marcus
Fischer, Moritz von, 7:**54**
Fischer, Moses, 7:52
Fischer, Otokar, 7:**54–55**
Fischer, Robert, 4:604, 605
Fischer, Ruth, 7:**55**, 16:344
Fischer, Samuel, 7:**55**
Fischer, Stanley, 7:**55–56**
Fischer family, 7:**52**
Fischhof, Meshullam Zalman, 2: 650
Fischhof, Meshullam Zalman II, 2: 650
Fischhoff, Adolf, 7:**56**, 16:340
Fischhoff, Joseph, 7:**56–57**
Fischl, Viktor. *See* Dagan, Avigdor
Fischler, Abraham, 4:213
Fischler, Stan, 7:**57**
Fischman, William, 15:205
Fischmann, Naḥman Isaac, 7:**57**
Fiscus Judaicus, 7:**57**, 11:294, 18:448
Fish, gefilte, 7:118
Fish, Harel, 7:**57–58**
Fish, Harold. *See* Fish, Harel
Fish, Morris, 14:464
Fish, Stanley, 7:**58**
Fish and fishing, 2:553, 7:**58–59**
Fishbane, Michael, 4:125, 7:**59–60**
Fishbein, Morris, 7:**60**
Fishberg, Maurice, 7:**60**
Fishblate, Solomon, 15:303
Fishcl, Otto, 18:665
Fishel, Efrayim, 1:221
Fishel, Ephraim, 7:61
Fishel, Ephraim (d. 1475), 7:61
Fishel, Ephraim (late 15th-early 16th century), 7:61
Fishel, Moses (d. 1504), 7:61

Fishel, Moses (d. 1542), 7:61
Fishel, Rachel, 7:61
Fishel, Stephan, 7:61
Fishel family, 7:**60–61**
Fishels, Roizl of Cracow, 7:**61–62**
Fisher, Carrie Frances, 7:**62**
Fisher, Donald, 7:**62**
Fisher, Dudu, 7:**62–63**
Fisher, Eddie, 7:**63**
Fisher, Edwin Jack. *See* Fisher, Eddie
Fisher, Lee, 15:393
Fisher, Max M., 5:611, 7:**63–64**
Fisher, Samuel, Baron Fisher of Camden, 7:**64**
Fisher, Sir Woolf, 7:**64**
Fisher, Woolf. *See* Fisher, Sir Woolf
Fish industry, Israeli, 2:553
Fishke der Krumer (Abramovitsh), 1:321
Fishke the Lame. See Fishke der Krumer
Fishko, Asher David. *See* Dagon, Barukh
Fishman, Ada. *See* Maimon, Ada
Fishman, Jacob, 7:**64**, 11:307
Fishman, Joshua Aaron, 7:**64–65**
Fishman, Judah Leib. *See* Maimon, Judah Leib
Fishman, Sylvia Barack, 18:736, 20:367
Fishman, William, 7:**65**
Fishman, William Harold, 7:**65**
Fiszel. *See* Fishel family
Fitch, Louis, 7:**65**
Fitelberg, Gregor. *See* Fitelberg, Grzegorz
Fitelberg, Grzegorz, 7:**65**
Fitelberg, Jerzy, 7:65
Fiterman, Charles, 7:**66**
Fiterman, Jacobo, 16:350
Fitzenhagen, W., 2:26
Fiume. *See* Rijeka; Rijeka (Croatia)
Five (number), 15:335
Five Books of Moses. *See* Pentateuch
The Five Books of Moses (Robert Alter), 3:624
Five Communities. *See* Mattersdorf (Austria)
Five Finger Exercise (Shaffer), 18:361
The Five Scrolls, 13:768, 18:**220–222**, 222t
Five species, 7:**66**
"The Fixer." *See* Rothstein, Arnold
Fiziki i liriki (Slutski), 18:685
Flaccus (Philo Judaeus), 16:63
Flaccus, Avillius Aulus, 7:**66**
Flaccus, Valerius, 6:100, 7:**66–67**
"Flagellation." *See* Makkot

Flagellum Calumniantium seu Apologia in qua Anonymi cujusdam calumniae refutantur (de Castro), 4:518

Flags, 7:**67–69**, *68*, 18:605
  See also Banners

Flam, Gila, 13:12

Flam, Herb, 7:**69**

Flanagan, Bud, 7:**69**

Flaut, Hezekiah Feivel. *See* Plaut, Hezekiah Feivel

Flavia Ioppe. *See* Jaffa (Israel)

Flavia Neapolis. *See* Nablus (Israel)

Flavius, Clemens, 7:**69**

Flavius Arrianus. *See* Arrian

Flavius Claudius Julianus. *See* Julian the Apostate

Flavius Eborensis. *See* Pyrrhus, Didacus

Flavius Josephus. *See* Josephus Flavius

Flavius Petrus Sabbatius Justinianus. *See* Justinian I (Cyzantine emperor)

Flavius Theodosius Junior. *See* Theodosius II

Flax, 7:**69–70**, vol. 16: color insert
  See also Sha'atnez

Fleas, 7:**70**

Flechtheim, Alfred, 7:**70–71**

Fleck, Bela, 7:**71**

Fleckeles, Eleazar ben David, 7:**71**, 12:460–461

Fleg, Edmond, 7:**71–72**, 12:661, 18:761

Flegenheimer, Arthur Simon. *See* Schultz, Dutch

Flegenheimer, Edmond. *See* Fleg, Edmond

I fleghomeni vatos (Schiby), 18:125

Fleischer, Charles, 7:**72**

Fleischer, E., 6:669

Fleischer, Ernö. *See* Emöd, Tamas

Fleischer, Ezra, 7:73, 8:729

Fleischer, Judah Loeb, 7:**72–73**

Fleischer, Leopold. *See* Fleischer, Judah Loeb

Fleischer, Lipot. *See* Fleischer, Judah Loeb

Fleischer, Max, 7:**73**

Fleischer, Michael, 7:**73**

Fleischer, Nat. *See* Fleischer, Nathaniel Stanley

Fleischer, Nathaniel Stanley, 7:**74**

Fleischer, Richard, 7:73

Fleischer, Tsippi, 7:**74**

Fleischman, Miksa. *See* Fenyö, Miksa

Fleischmann, Gisi, 7:**74–75**

Fleischmann, Julius, 7:75

Fleischmann, Karel, 2:519

Fleisher, Alfred, 7:75–76

Fleisher, Benjamin Wilfred, 7:75

Fleisher, Benjamin Wolf, 7:75

Fleisher, Charles, 4:100

Fleisher, Edwin Adler, 7:75

Fleisher, Hannah Tuchnor, 7:75

Fleisher, Larry, 7:**76**

Fleisher, Leon, 7:**76**

Fleisher, Moyer, 7:75

Fleisher, Samuel Stuart, 7:75

Fleisher, Simon B., 7:75

Fleisher family, 7:**75–76**

Fleming, Alexander, 4:558

Flersheim, L. H., 4:255

Flesch, Abraham, 7:76

Flesch, Adolph, 7:76

Flesch, Carl, 7:**77**

Flesch, Gumpel. *See* Flesch, Mordecai

Flesch, Heinrich, 7:76

Flesch, Joseph (1781-1841), 7:76

Flesch, Joseph (d. 194?), 7:76–77

Flesch, Mordecai, 7:76

Flesch, Philip, 7:76

Flesch, Solomon. *See* Flesch, Philip

Flesch-Birnbaum. *See* Flesch family

Flesch family, 7:**76–77**

Flesh, 7:**77**

The Fleuron, 18:608

Flexer, A. L. *See* Volynski, Akim Levovich

Flexner, Abraham, 2:53, 6:161, 7:**78**

Flexner, Bernard, 4:123, 7:77, 15:588

Flexner, James Thomas, 7:77

Flexner, Jennie Maas, 7:77

Flexner, Simon, 7:77

Flexner, Washington, 7:77

Flexner family, 7:**77–78**

Fleyta Marsiya (Livshits), 13:146

Flieg, Helmut. *See* Heym, Stefan

Floating charge, 12:817

Floggings, 7:**78–80**

Flohr, Salo, 7:**80**

Flohr, Solomon Mikhailovitch. *See* Flohr, Salo

The Flood, 7:**80–83**

Flora
  box, 4:108
  broom, 4:210
  burning bush, 4:297–298
  calamus, sweet, 4:350–351
  caper, 4:442–443
  carob, 4:492
  castor-oil plant, 4:516
  cedar, 4:535
  flowers, 7:89–91
  frankincense, 7:213

  hyssop, 9:654
  Israel, 10:141–142
  ivy, 10:822
  mallow, 13:435
  mandrake, 13:466
  medicinal, mastic, 13:669
  mixed species, 14:385–387

Die Flora der Juden (Loew), 13:163

Flor de Apolo (Barrios), 3:176

Florence (Italy), 5:475, 7:**83–86**

Florentin, Mevorah, 7:**86**

Flores, Giorgio. *See* Momigliano, Attilio

Floreta Ca Noga, 7:**86**

Florey, Howard, 4:558

Florida, 7:**86–89**, *88*
  Boca Raton, 15:605
  Broward County, 4:212–213
  Disney World, 15:476
  Lee and Charlotte counties, 12:598–599
  Levy, Moses Elias, 12:754
  Orlando, 15:475–476
  Palm Beach County, 15:604–606

Florina. *See* Phlorina

Florio, John, 6:437

Florus of Lyons, 7:**89**

Floryanowa. *See* Narol (Poland)

Floss (Germany), 7:**89**

Flossenburg concentration camp, 13:129

Flower, Constance Rothschild, 17:490

Flowers, 7:**89–91**
  See also Flora

Le Fluor et ses composés (Moissan), 14:422

Flusser, David, 7:**91**, 11:462, 15:192

Flute music, 14:647

The Flute of Marsyas. See Fleyta Marsiya (Livshits)

Fly and flies, 7:**91–92**

Foa, Carlo, 7:92

Foa, Cesare, 7:92

Foa, Edouard, 7:92

Foa, Elia Emanuel, 7:92

Foa, Eliezer, 7:92

Foa, Eliezer Nahman, 7:92

Foa, Esther Eugénie Rebecca, 7:**92**

Foa, Isaac ben Gad, 7:92

Foa, Mordecai, 7:92

Foa, Moses Benjamin, 4:78, 7:92

Foa, Raimondo, 7:**92–93**

Foa, Salvatore, 7:92

Foa family, 7:**92**

Foà family. *See* Foa family

Focşani (Romania). *See* Focsani (Romania)

Focsani (Romania), 7:**93**

Focus (Miller), 14:251

Fodder, 7:**93–94**

Fodor, Andor, 7:**94**

Foe from the North, 11:131–132

    See also Nebuchadnezzar

Foerder, Herbert. *See* Foerder, Yeshayahu

Foerder, Yeshayahu, 7:**94**

Foester, Johann. *See* Forster, Johann

Fogaras (Romania). *See* Fagaras (Romania)

Fogelberg, Dan, 7:**94**

Fogelman, Eva, 9:382–383, 386

The Fog of War (motion picture), 14:510

Fohrer, Georg, 11:354

Foi. *See* Foa family

Foighel, Isi, 7:**94**

Foix (France), 7:**94**

Földes, Jolán, 7:**94–95**

Foley, Francis, 7:**95**

Foligno, Hananel, 7:**95**

Foligno, Hananel Da. *See* Foligno, Hananel

Folk customs and superstitions

    about night, 5:487

    Anatoli, Jacob ben Abba Mari ben Samson, 2:132

    Eisenstadt (Germany), 6:269

    Institute of Folklore (Romania), 4:138

    Kabbalah and, 11:670–671

    life cycle, 7:109–110

    niddah, 15:256

    Noy, Dov, 15:326–327

Folk dance, 5:409–410, 413, 10:693–694

    of Bukharan Jews, 4:264

    Horah, 9:523–524

    Kadman, 11:700

    Oved, Margalit, 15:548–549

    See also Folklore

Folk dances. *See* Dance

Folkistishe Heftn, 7:113

Folkist Party. *See* Folkspartei

Folklore, 7:**95–113**

    abbreviations, 1:239

    Absalom, 1:331

    Adam Ba'al Shem, 1:378

    Aden, 1:389

    Afghanistan, 1:433

    aggadah, 1:455–456

    Ahikar, Book of, 1:542–543

    'Alef, 1:607–608

    amulets, 2:122

Angel of Death, 2:148, 149

    apostasy, 2:277

    astrology, 2:620

    audio-oral transmission literature, 7:96–103

        dramas, 7:102–103

        narratives, folk, 7:97–100

        proverbs, 7:102

        riddles, 7:102

        songs and lyrics, 7:100–102

    circumcision, 4:734

    classifications for, 7:96

    cogitative, 7:106–111

        deception, 7:108–110

        sacrifice and compromise, 7:108

        spirits and demons, 7:106–108

    defined, 7:96

    Dibbuk, 5:643–644

    Elijah, 6:335

    evil eye, 6:584–585

    folk medicine, 7:110–111

    Grunwald, Max, 8:114

    Herschele, 9:44–45

    humor and, 9:592

    Israel Folklore Society, 18:724

    lamed vav zaddikim, 12:446

    lions, 13:62–63

    Lipson, Mordekhai, 13:76

    paradise in Eden narrative, 15:626–627

    Poland, Chelm, 4:588–589

    Rapoport, Samuel, 17:98

    Russia, 1970s, 17:566

    studies, 11:49

    visual, 7:103–105

    Yiddish, 4:628–629

        Bernstein, Ignatz, 3:479

        Bialoblotzky, Benjamin Jacob, 3:566

        Cahan, Judah Loeb, 4:336

        Landau, Alfred, 12:458

        Mayse-Bukh, 13:702–703

        Peretz, Issac Leib, 15:767–768

Folkman, Judah, 7:**113**

Folk music

    Beregovski, Moshe, 3:408

    Broder, Berl, 4:194, 195

    Broder singers, 4:194, 195

    of Bukharan Jews, 4:264

    Carlebach, Shlomo, 4:481–482

    Carp, Paula, 4:493

    Dylan, Bob, 6:78–79

    Ehad mi Yode'a, 6:237

    Elliot, "Mama" Cass, 6:361

    Engel, Joel, 6:408–409

    Europe, 13:694

    Hirsh, Nurit, 9:141–142

    India, 9:773

    Jerusalem in, 11:229

    Mlotek, Chana, 14:396

    Morocco, 1:438–439

    Moses in, 14:543

    Noy, Meir, 15:327

    Ochs, Philip David, 15:376

    recordings, 17:150–151

    Rubin, Ruth, 17:513

    Society for Jewish Folk Music, 18:725

    studies, Emsheimer, Ernst, 6:398

Folksbiene Yiddish theater, 21:**372–373**

Folk Song in Israel (Smoira-Cohn), 18:690

Folksongs. *See* Folk music

Folkspartei (Poland), 7:**113**

Folkspartei (Russia), 7:**113–114**, 14:288–289

Folks-shtime (newspaper), 18:690

Folk tales. *See* Folklore

Fomin, Yefim Moiseyevich, 7:**114**

Fondane, Benjamin, 7:**114**

Fondiller, William, 7:**114–115**

Fondo Communal of Clara (Argentina), 11:775

Fonds Social Juif Unifié. *See* FSJU

Foner, Sarah Feiga Meinkin, 8:443

Fonseca, Alvaro da, 7:**115**

Fonseca, Daniel de, 7:**115**, 15:541

Fonseca, Isaac Aboab da, 4:144

Fonseca, Moses, 15:197

Fontainebleau (France), 7:**115**

Fontenoid. *See* Kiriath-Jearim (ancient city)

Food, 7:**115–121**

    Ashkenazi traditional style, 7:118

    Atonement, Day of, 7:120

    Av, 7:120

    consumption

        prohibitions, 13:711

        ritual handwashing after, 13:701

    cookbooks, 5:200–203

    dairy products, 7:117

    dietary laws, 7:118

    forbidden food, 7:116

    Hanukkah, 7:120–121

    hygiene, 9:648

    Jewish style cookery, 7:117–118

    leek, 12:600

    legumes, 12:610–611

lentils, 12:641
meals, 7:116
Morris, Nelson, 14:511
oil, 7:117
Passover, 7:119
produce, 7:116, 12:675
Purim, 7:121
religious quality of meals, 18:321
Rosh Ha-Shanah, 7:120
Sabbath, 7:118–119, 14:6–7
Sephardi traditional style, 7:118
se'udah, 18:321–322
Shavout, 7:119–120
spices, 7:116–117
Sukkot, 7:120
Tu bi-Shevat, 7:121
wine, 7:117
See also Dietary laws; *specific food*
Food and Agricultural Organization, 20:271
Food laws. *See* Dietary laws
Food products. *See* Dairy products; Vegetables
Food Supplies in the Aftermath of World War II (Hirsch), 9:126
A Fool There Was, 3:124
Foot, hand washing, 1:262–263
Football (American, Canadian), 5:479, 19:140–142
Levy, Marv, 12:753
Luckman, Sidney, 13:249
Mix, Ronald Jack, 14:373
Modell, Arthur B., 14:407
Rosenbloom, Carrol, 17:442
Sherman, Alexander, 18:463–464
The Forbidden Zone (motion picture), 6:314
Forcalquiers (France), 7:**121–122**
Forced baptism, 3:**121–122**, 6:50
Forced conversion, 2:211, 251–252, 253, 274–275, 470, 3:121–122
in Bari, 3:152
Basil I, 3:198
Bibago brothers, 3:570, 571
Boudin, Jean-François, 4:105
in Brindisi, 4:184
Byzantine empire, 4:326, 327
Byzantine Greece, 8:45–47
Cabessa family, 4:329–330
cantonists, 4:437–439
Draguignan, 6:6
Duns Scotus, John, 6:50
Duran, Profiat, 6:50
Isaac ben Sheshet Perfet, 10:49
to Islam, 11:58
in Bukhara, 4:259

in Iran, 3:15
in Persia, 15:788, 789
Julius III's fines for, 11:574
Mortara, Edgardo, 4:19
Nicholas III forbidding, 15:249
Oppenheim, 15:442
Oppenheimer, Joseph ben Issachar Suesskind, 15:449
Otranto, 15:516
Ottoman empire, 15:522
by Pastoureaux, 15:685
penal law and, 15:721–722
Portugal, 4:469
See also Finaly Case
Forced labor, 7:**122–124**
Chelmno concentration camp, 9:485
corvée, 5:226
Germany, 9:122
Holocaust
France, 7:161
Germany, 18:75
Force majeure. *See* Ones
Ford, Alexander, 7:**124–125**
Ford, Harrison, 7:**125**
Ford, Henry
American Jewish Committee, 2:55
antisemitism of, 18:39
The Ford of the Jabbok. See Ma'avar Yabbok (Halkin)
Foreigners. *See* Strangers and gentiles
Foreign Volunteers. *See* Maḥal
Foreiro, Francisco, 7:**125**
Foreman, Carl, 7:**125**
Foreman, Milton J., 7:**125**
Forensic medicine
Helpern, Milton, 8:802
Karplus, Heinrich, 11:816–817
Forerio, Francisco. *See* Foreiro, Francisco
Forerius, Francisco. *See* Foreiro, Francisco
Forewords and Introductions. *See* Haskamah
Forfeiture, expropriation, confiscation, 5:**150–151**
Forgeries, 7:**125–126**, 18:402–403
Forgery, 5:54, 7:**126–127**
Forgiveness, 7:**127–129**
Day of Atonement and, 5:488, 491
fasting, 6:719
Kipper, 12:182–183
Forlì (Italy), 7:**129–130**
Forma Kleshnyov (Slonimsky), 18:679
Der Formalismus in der Ethik und die materiale Wertethik (Scheler), 18:119

Formal method (literary criticism), 6:246
Forman, Milos, 7:**130**
Forman, Phillip, 7:**130**
Form and matter, 7:**130–131**, 324–326
Formation of the Soviet Union (Pipes), 16:182
Form criticism, 3:646, 650–651, 653, 15:191, 315
Formentera (Spain). *See* Ibiza and Formentera (Spain)
Former Soviet Union
Estonia, 6:521–622
Latvia, 12:520–524
See also Kazakhstan; Union of Soviet Socialist Republics (USSR)
Formiggini, Angelo Fortunato, 7:**131**
Form letters, 12:672–673
Form of the Earth and Figure of the Celestial Spheres. See Ẓurat ha-Areẓ ve-Tavnit Kaddurei ha Raki'a
Forms of Prayer (Marks), 16:465
Forms of Prayer According to the Custom of the Spanish and Portuguese Jews (De Sola), 18:750
Formstecher, Solomon, 7:**131–132**, 665, 15:35, 16:94
The Forsaken Woman (Bruggen). *See De Verlatene*
Forst, Siegmund, 4:371
Forster, Johann, 7:**132**
Forsthemius, Johann. *See* Forster, Johann
Fortalitium fidei contra Judeos, Saracenos et alios Christianae fidei inimicos (Espina), 1:642
Fortas, Abe, 7:**132–133**, 12:556
Fortes, Meyer, 2:186, 7:**133**
For the Parents' Sins. See Be-Ovoyn Oves
Forti, Baruch Uzziel ben Baruch, 3:706, 7:**133**
Forti, Jacob Raphael Hezekiah ben Abraham Israel, 7:**133**
Fortis, Abraham Isaac, 7:**134**
Fort Meyers (FL), 12:598–599
Fort Michilimackinac (MI), 18:764
Fortresses
Agrippina, 1:504
Herodium, 9:39
Sarkil, 18:57
Sarṭaba, 18:63
Fort St. George. *See* Madras (India)
Fortunatus. *See* Szerencsés, Imre
Fortunoff, Max and Clara, 15:226
Fortunoff Video Archive for Holocaust Testimony, 7:**134**

Forty (number), 15:336

Forty-seven Identifications of the British Nation with the Lost Ten Tribes of Israel (Hine), 4:188

Forum on the Air (radio show), 6:266

Forverts (newspaper). *See Jewish Daily Forward* (newspaper)

Forward (newspaper). *See Jewish Daily Forward* (newspaper)

Foss, Lukas, 7:**134–135**

Fossanno (Italy), 7:**135**

Fossil Brains (Edinger), 6:148

Fossil fuel energy, 5:169–170

Fossoli (Italy), 7:**135**

Fostat. *See* Cairo (Egypt)

Fould, Achille, 7:135–136, 16:343

Fould, Achille Charles, 16:343

Fould, Benoît, 7:135, 15:443

Fould, Ber Leon, 7:135

Fould, Edourard Mathurin, 7:136, 16:343

Fould, Ernest Adolphe, 7:136, 16:343

Fould, Gustave Eugène, 7:136, 16:343

Fould family, 7:**135–136**

The Foundation of the World (Israeli). *See Yesod Olam* (Israeli)

Foundations, 7:**136–138**

Foundations of Law Act of 1980, 14:358

Foundations of Set Theory (Bar-Hillel), 3:152

Foundations of the Torah (Luzzatto). *See Yesodei ha-Torah* (Luzzatto)

Foundations of Understanding and Tower of Faith. See Yesodei ha-Tevunah u-Migdal ha-Emunah

Foundation Stone. See Even Shetiyyah

The Fountainhead (Rand), 17:90

Fouquet, Jean, 14:542

Four (number), 15:334–335

Four Aspects (Ephraim ben Isaac), 6:459

Fourcade, Simón. *See* Saslavsky, Luis Simón

The four captives, 7:**138–139**, 18:457

Four Columns. See Even Shetiyyah

Four Cups. *See* Arba kosot

Le Four Electrique (Moissan), 14:422

Fourier, Charles, 18:704

Fourier, François Marie Charles, 7:**139**

Four Lands, Council of. *See* Council of Four Lands

Fournier, Jacques, 15:608

Four questions of Passover. *See* Mah Nishtannah

Four Seasons Hotel Inc., 18:418

Four species, 7:**139–140**

Fourth Aliyah. *See* Aliyah, Fourth

Fourth Crusade, 4:327

Fourth Lateran Council. *See* Lateran Councils III, IV

The Fourth of July War (Topol), 18:200

Four Worlds. *See* Worlds, The Four

Fowl. *See* Chicken

Fox, Bernard Joshua, 7:**140**

Fox, Chaim-Leib, 7:**140**

Fox, Charles, 7:**140**

Fox, Emanuel Philips, 7:**140**

Fox, Everett, 3:623, 625

Fox, Eytan, 7:**140**

Fox, Gerson, 2:652

Fox, Isaac Solomon, 7:**141**

Fox, Jacob Samuel, 7:**141**

Fox, John Jacob. *See* Fox, Sir John Jacob

Fox, Marvin, 4:125, 7:**141**

Fox, Moses, 2:652

Fox, Samuel I., 18:14

Fox, Sidney, 13:11

Fox, Sir John Jacob, 7:**141**

Fox, William, 7:**141–142**, 14:570, 571

Foxes, 6:667, 7:**140**, 15:622

Fox Fables. See Mishlei Shu'alim

Foxman, Abraham, 2:195, 7:**142**

Foy. *See* Foa family

Fraenckel, Jonas, 7:143

Fraenckel, Liepmann, 7:**142**

Fraenckel family. *See* Fraenkel family

Fraenkel, Abraham, 7:143

Fraenkel, Abraham Adolf, 7:**143**

Fraenkel, Baermann, 7:143

Fraenkel, David ben Moses, 7:143

Fraenkel, David ben Naphtali Hirsch, 7:**143**

Fraenkel, David Isaac, 7:142

Fraenkel, Elkan, 7:**144**, 14:407

Fraenkel, Enoch, 7:142

Fraenkel, Faiwel, 7:**144**

Fraenkel, Gabriel, 7:143

Fraenkel, Isaac Seckel, 4:167, 7:**144**

Fraenkel, Israel, 7:142

Fraenkel, Jonah, 1:461, 462, 463

Fraenkel, Jonas, 7:**144**, 11:572

Fraenkel, Koppel Ha-Levi, 7:142

Fraenkel, Levi ben Saul, 7:**144–145**

Fraenkel, Levi Schaulsohn. *See* Fraenkel, Levi ben Saul

Fraenkel, Louis, 7:**145**

Fraenkel, Moses, 7:143

Fraenkel, Osmond K., 7:**145**

Fraenkel, Sándor. *See* Ferenczi, Sándor

Fraenkel, Zacharias, 7:143

Fraenkel, Ẓevi Hirsch, 7:144

Fraenkel family, 7:**142–143**

Fraenkel-Teomim, Baruch ben Joshua Ezekiel Feiwel, 7:**145**

Fraga (Spain), 7:**146**

Fragile (music album), 6:263

Fragmenta Commentarii ad Pentateuchum Samaritano-arabicum (Drabkin), 6:5

Fragmente și romanțe (Aderca), 1:390

Fragments and Romances. See Fragmente și romanțe

Fraihait Gezang Ferain. *See* Paterson Jewish Folk Chorus

"Frailach in Swing" (Elman), 6:365

Fram, David, 7:**146**

Franc, G. Venetus. *See* Giorgio, Francesco

France, 7:**146–170,** *148*

    antisemitism, 2:217, 220

        Action Française, 1:369–370

        Agde, 1:446

        Agen, 1:449

        Aix-en-Provence, 1:552

        Albi, 1:591–592

        Alphonse of Poitiers, 1:730

        Amulo, 2:124

        Arles, 2:470

        badges, Jewish, 2:6, 81, 3:45–46, 47

        Bergheim, 3:427

        Béziers, 3:559

        Blois, 1:609

        blood libel, 4:105, 106, 12:754

        Bordeaux, 4:82

        Cadenet, 4:331

        Caen, 4:332, 460–461, 515

        Carcassone, 4:460

        Carcassonne, 4:460–461

        Carpentras, 4:493–494

        Castelsarrasin, 4:515

        Châlons-sur-Marne, 4:563

        Chalon-sur-Saône, 4:563

        Chambéry, 4:564

        Champagne, 4:565

        Charles II, 1:310

        Charles IV, 4:575

        Charles VI, 4:576

        Chateaubriand, François René, 4:582–583

        Chinon, 4:651

        Clermont-Ferrand, 4:755

        Cluny, 4:763

        Crusaders, 5:313

        Draguignan, 6:6–7

        Dreyfus Affair, 6:18–19, 7:158

Drumont, Edouard-Adolphe, 6:26
Enlightenment, 2:213–214
Ensisheim, 6:447
French Revolution, 7:252–255
Lyons, 1:469
Middle Ages, 4:460, 563
Morhange, 14:491
Pastoureaux, 15:685
post-revolution, 7:158
Proudhon, Pierre Joseph, 16:633
Provence, 1:592, 16:638
Savoy, 18:86
Third Republic, 7:158
twentieth century, 2:233, 234, 238, 3:378, 5:438, 441, 7:167–168, 13:692
assimilation, 2:611, 7:156
Assembly of Jewish Notables (1806), 2:599–602, *600*
Crypto-Jews, 4:82
linguistic, 8:436, 437
Marranos, 4:189, 16:24
oath, Jewish, 7:156
Ribeauville community, 11:576
Sanhedrin assembly (1807), 18:24
social status, 7:157, 160, 163
cultural and social life, 7:159–160, 164, 165
architecture, 2:400
archives, 2:408–409
art and artists, 2:505, 509, 510–511, 517, 3:673, 16:144–145, 186–187
Bibliothèque Nationale, 3:685
cantatas and choral works, Hebrew, 4:434–435
classical scholars, 4:750
community organization, 7:163–164, 165–167
film, 9:442, 443, 12:487, 634
journalism, 5:305, 11:467, 803, 12:559, 563, 16:490
Judeo-French language, 11:545
liberalism, 12:777
motion pictures, 14:575–576
museums, 14:625
philanthropy, 12:678–679, 16:39
printing, 16:537
publishing, 12:589, 16:717
seals, use of, 18:226–227
social welfare, 7:156

theater, 19:672
typography, 20:217
yeshivot, 21:316
demography, 16:387–388, 391–392
changes in, 7:159
distribution of communities, 7:162–163, 164–165
population statistics, 7:159, 164
settlements, locations of, 7:*148*
seventeenth-eighteenth centuries, 7:154
early civilization to Middle Ages, 7:147, 149, 150–152
economic life, 7:149
economic affairs, 7:157, 159–160, 163, 168
bankers and banking, 3:116, 14:441
Colbert, Jean Baptiste, 5:56
French Revolution, 7:254
leather industry and trade, 12:575
Lévy, Samuel, 12:755
moneylending, 7:152, 14:441
oil industry development, 16:20
pre-French Revolution, 7:254
pre-Middle Ages, 7:149
education
Jewish, 6:174–175, 180, 7:156–157, 165, 12:615
Lévi Alvarès, David, 12:695–696
Montpellier, 14:463
Roussillon, 17:499
emancipation, 2:218, 4:202, 6:375–376, 377–378, 9:231–232
expulsion of Jews from
Arles, 2:470
Languedoc, 12:484
Orange, 15:460
Paris, 15:643, 644
Provence, 7:153–154
foreign policy and affairs with Israel, 7:168–170, 10:266
1990s, 10:265
armaments, 10:219, 235
arms purchases, 10:470–471
borders guarantees, 10:217
Sinai Campaign, 10:220
Six-Day War, 10:230
French Revolution to 1930
post-Revolution period, 7:155–156, 158
Second Empire period, 7:157

WW I, 7:159
Holocaust, 4:83, 7:160–162, 9:339
Aix-en-Provence, 1:552
Alsace-Lorraine, 2:9
Bayonne, 3:232
Belfort, 3:280
Besançon, 3:494
Bordeaux, 4:83
Centre de Documentation Juive Contemporaine, 4:547
Chambon-sur-Lignon, 4:564–565
cinema, 9:442, 443
Colmar, 5:58–59
deportations, 7:161
Dijon, 5:660
documentation, resource centers, 9:428
Drancy, 6:8
Fontainebleau, 7:115
forced labor, 7:161
Lyons, 3:141, 13:297
Marseilles, 13:578–579
memorials, 9:430–431
Metz, 14:136
Montpellier, 14:463
Mulhouse, 14:610
Nancy, 14:772–773
Nantes, 14:773
Nice, 15:249
Paris, 7:160
resistance, 7:162
Rosheim, 17:467
Sarreguemines, 18:62
Saverne, 18:84
Sélestat, 18:260
Strasbourg, 19:245
Thionville, 19:704
Toulouse, 20:74
Tours, 20:77
Troyes, 20:158
Jewish movements and organizations
Assembly of Jewish Notables (1806), 2:599–602, *600*
Centre de Documentation Juive Contemporaine, 4:547
Comité des Delegations Juives, 5:72–73
Consistory, 5:178–180, *578*, 7:155
Etudiantes Juifs de France, 19:266
Jewish scout movement, 18:209–210

France, *continued*
  Les Colloques des
      Intellectuels Juifs De
      Langue Française, 12:661–
      662
  opposition to Nazism, 7:161–
      162
  ORT, 15:489, 490
  tosafists, 17:340–341
  Union Générale des Israélites
      de France, 12:443, 20:250–
      251
  Zionism, 12:489, 21:586–587
late twentieth to twenty first
    century, 7:164–170
laws and legal systems, 12:550–551
  blood libel, 4:105, 106, 12:754
  civil rights, 4:755, 7:157, 158,
      254–255
  Finaly case, 7:22–23
  Neuwirth Law, 18:615
Middle Ages to French
    Revolution, 7:152–153
  agriculture, Jewish, 1:495
  Carolingian dynasty, 7:147–
      149
  Crusaders, 5:313
  Jewish communities, 4:493–
      494, 6:588, 11:44
  kings, 13:219–222, 16:47–48
  Ottoman empire, German
      Jews settling in, 15:522
  pre-revolutionary period,
      7:252–253
  return of Jews to Paris,
      15:643, 644
  revolutionary period, 7:253–
      254
  scholars, 5:468
  scholarship, centers of, 7:153
  sephardim, 7:253–254
  settlements, locations of,
      7:148
migrations, 5:295–296, 11:724
  to North America, 2:62
  Ottoman empire, German
      Jews settling in, 15:522
  Portuguese people, 4:82–83
  post-WW II, 7:162
  return of Jews to Paris,
      15:643, 644
political theories, parties and
    organizations
  Action Française, 1:369–370
  capitulations, 4:452–453
  government officials, 6:665–
      666, 12:676
  Jerusalem and, 11:165–166,
      167, 169, 171, 221–222

kings, 13:219–222, 16:47–48
liberalism, 12:777
military, 5:439, 12:442, 479,
    746, 14:244
Neo-Nazism, 15:81
Ottoman Palestine and,
    10:182–183, 184–185, 405
political participation, 16:338,
    343
Sanhedrin assembly (1807),
    18:24
separation of church and
    state, 7:158–159
socialism, 6:8, 18:704, 706
Sykes-Picot Agreement,
    19:350–351, *351*
Vichy government, 4:7,
    14:501–502
politicians
  Blum, Léon, 4:7–8
  Daudet, 5:441
  Ennery, Jonas D', 6:441
  Lang, Jack, 12:479
  Laval, Pierre, 12:530–531
  Mayer, Daniel, 13:698
  Mayer, René, 13:699
  Mendès-France, 14:43–44
  Mitterand, François, 7:168
  Napoleon Bonaparte, 7:155
  Schrameck, Abraham, 18:167
  Schumann, Maurice, 18:175–
      176
  Schwartzenberg, Roger-
      Gerard, 18:187
post-WW II, 7:162–164, 165
  Besançon, 3:494
  Fontainebleau, 7:115
  immigration to France, 7:162
  Lyons, 13:297
  Mitterand, François, 7:168
  Neo-Nazism, 15:81
pre-WW II, 7:159
religious life and scholarship
  Albigensis Christian sect,
      1:592
  apologetics, 2:265–266
  Ashkenazim, 7:253
  Bible translated into French
      and Provençal, 3:628–629
  biblical translations, 3:628–
      629
  chief rabbi, 11:724
  Conservative Judaism, 5:176
  Haggadot, 8:212
  Hasidei Ashkenaz, 11:599–
      602
  illuminated manuscripts,
      Hebrew, 9:730–731

Jewish studies in, 11:324–326
la'az and, 12:405–406
missionaries, 4:99
Orthodox Judaism, 7:157–158
Rabbinical training, 17:23
Reform Judaism, 7:157–158
Séminaire Israélite de France,
    12:615, 18:279–280
tosafists, 17:340–341
yeshivot, 21:316
WW II, 7:160–162
  Besançon, 3:494
  partisans, 15:668
  Resistance to German
      occupation, 3:141, 18:209–
      210
  Vichy government, 4:7,
      14:501–502
  See also Algeria; Alliance Israélite
      Universelle; French literature;
      French Revolution; specific
      French cities
France, Gourdi. *See* Giroud, Françoise
La France juive (Drumont), 6:26
Frances, Immanuel ben David, 7:**170–
    171**
Frances, Immanuel Bocarro. *See*
    Rosales, Jacob Hebraeus
Frances, Isaac, 7:**171**
Frances, Jacob ben David, 7:**171–172**,
    18:347
Francesco, Giorgio, 17:95
Francesco della Rovere. *See* Sixtus IV
    (pope)
Franche-Comté (France), 7:**172**
Franchetti, Raimondo, 7:**172**
The Franchiser (Elkin), 6:359
Francia, Francis, 7:**172**
Franciscan order, 3:469, 490, 6:260,
    7:**173–175**
Franciscus de Sant Jordi. *See* Rimoch,
    Astruc
Franciscus Georgius Venetus. *See*
    Giorgio, Francesco
Francis Elizabeth, Countess
    Waldegrave, 4:117
Francis I, 7:**172–173**, 12:625
Francis Joseph I of Hapsburg, 7:**175**,
    14:475
Franck, Adolphe, 7:**175–176**
Franck, Henri, 7:**176**
Franck, Jacob. *See* Franck, Adolphe
Franck, James, 7:**176**
Franckenstein, C., 11:444
Franco. *See* Francos
Franco, Avraham, 7:**176–177**
Franco, Gad, 7:**177**
Franco, Hizkiya, 7:**177**

Franco, Jacob de Moses, 7:176
Franco, Moses, 2:33, 7:**177**
Franco, Rahamim, 7:177
Franco, Ralph, 7:176
Franco, Raphael, 7:176
Franco, Solomon, 4:99, 7:176
Franco family, 7:**176**, 9:6
Franco-Mendes, David, 6:399, 7:**177–178**
Francos, 1:614–615, 4:452, 6:298, 7:**178**
Francos of Aleppo, 4:451
Franc Tireurs et Partisans Français (FTP), 15:668
Franji. *See* Francos
Frank, A., 11:363
Frank, Adolf, 4:492
Frank, Albert Rudolph, 7:**178**
Frank, Anne, 4:630, 6:70, 7:**178–179**, 12:457, 14:478
Frank, Barney, 7:**179–180**
Frank, Bruno, 7:**180**
Frank, David, 4:190
Frank, Eli, 7:**180**
Frank, Eva, 7:**180–181**, 191, 15:386
Frank, Hans, 4:251
Frank, Hans Michael, 7:**181**
Frank, Henry I., 14:454
Frank, Ilya Mikhailovich, 7:**181**
Frank, Irvin, 15:398
Frank, Jacob, 3:712, 7:**182–192**, 8:439, 15:386, 538, 18:357–358
    arrest of, 7:188
    Breunn (Moravia), and community of, 7:189
    Frankist disputations and polemics, 5:696
    incarceration in Czestochowa (Poland), 7:188–189
    and Iwanie (Ukraine), revelations in, 7:184–185
    Lvov (Ukraine), 13:289
    Offenbach (Germany), and community of, 7:189
    personality of, 7:191
    Podolia (Poland), 7:182–183
    Shabbateanism, 7:182, 18:357–358
    See also Frankist movement
Frank, Jerome New, 7:**192**, 12:556
Frank, Jocob, 4:199
Frank, John, 16:341
Frank, Josef, 7:**192**
Frank, Karl Hermann, 7:**192**
Frank, Leo Max, 7:**192–193**
Frank, Menahem Mendel, 7:**193**
Frank, Paul. *See* Elad, Avraham
Frank, Philipp, 7:**193**

Frank, Ray, 7:**193–194**
Frank, Robert, 7:**194**, 16:125
Frank, Semyon Lyudvigovich, 7:**194–195**
Frank, Waldo David, 7:**195**
Frank, Ẓevi Pesaḥ, 7:**195–196**
Frankau, Gilbert, 7:196
Frankau, Julia, 7:196
Frankau, Pamela, 7:196
Frankau family, 7:**196**
Frankel, Benjamin, 7:**196**, 9:112
Frankel, Heinrich Walter, 7:196
Frankel, Hiram D., 7:**196–197**
Frankel, Lee Kaufer, 7:**197**
Frankel, Leo, 7:**197**, 16:343
Frankel, Léo, 18:705
Frankel, Marvin Earl, 7:**197–198**
Frankel, Max, 7:**198**, 12:636
Frankel, Naomi, 7:**198–199**
Frankel, Sally Herbert, 7:**199**
Frankel, Samuel Benjamin, 7:**199**
Frankel, William, 7:**199**
Frankel, Ya'akov, 7:**199–200**
Frankel, Zacharias, 5:171, 7:143, **200–201**, 15:494
    in Dresden, 6:11
    Jewish Theological Seminary, 6:182
    Juedisch Theologisches Seminar, Breslau, 11:572
    Monatsschrift (periodical), 14:433
    on Oral Law, 15:457
    on Septuagint, 3:597
Frankel family. *See* Fraenkel family
Franken, Rose Dorothy Lewin, 7:**201–202**
Frankenberg, Joyce Penelope Wilhelmina. *See* Seymour, Jane
Frankenburger, Paul. *See* Ben-Haim, Paul
Frankenburger, Wolf, 7:**202**, 16:344
Frankenheimer, John Michael, 2:104, 7:**202–203**
Frankenstein, Carl, 7:**203**
Frankenthal, Käte, 7:**203**
Frankenthaler, George, 7:**203**
Frankenthaler, Helen, 7:**203–204**
Frankford Woolen Mills, 18:74
Frankfort, Henri, 3:651, 7:**204**
Frankfort, Henriette Groenwegen, 7:204
Frankfort, Jacob, 13:195
Frankfurt (Germany). *See* Frankfurt on the Main (Germany)
Frankfurt, Henri, 2:371
Frankfurt, Moses ben Mendel. *See* Mendelsohn, Frankfurt Moses

Frankfurt, R. Moses ben Simon, 2:108
Frankfurter, David, 7:**204**
Frankfurter, Felix, 3:685, 4:123, 7:**204–207**, 11:817–818, 12:555, 20:751
Frankfurter, Moses, 2:38, 7:**207**
Frankfurter, Solomon Friedrich, 7:**207**
Frankfurter Zeitung (newspaper), 14:487
Frankfurt on the Main (Germany), 7:**207–212**, 11:697, 16:534–535
    15th to 17th centuries, 7:208
    18th century, 7:208–209
    Abraham Abusch ben Ẓevi Hirsch, 1:291–292
    Adler, Nathan ben Simeon ha-Kohen, 1:404–405
    book fairs, 4:77–78
    Hebrew printing, 7:211
    liturgical music, 7:211
    Middle Ages, 7:207–208
    Mizrachi, 14:390
    Orthodox Judaism, 7:209–210
    post-WW II, 7:210
    Reform Judaism, 7:209
Frankfurt on the Oder (Germany), 7:**212**
Frankincense, 7:**212–213**
Frankist movement, 7:**182–192**
    Birkenthal, Dov Ber, 3:712
    Brody, resistance to, 4:199
    conversions to Christianity, 7:189–190
    disputation in Lvov, 7:185–187
    disputations with the Church, 7:183–187
    Dobruschka, Moses, 5:726–727
    economic activities, 7:189
    Frank, Eva, 7:180–181
    Frank, Jacob, 7:182–183
    Landau, Ezekiel Ben Judah, 12:460
    Landau, Samuel, 12:461
    literature, 7:190
    Offenbach (Germany), and community of, 7:180–181, 189
    Prague (Bohemia), 7:190–191
    religious beliefs, 7:184–185
    social activities, 7:189
    social structure, 7:187–188, 190
    See also Shabbateanism
Frankl, Adolf, 7:**213**
Frankl, Lothar, 7:**213**
Frankl, Ludwig August, 2:408, 7:**213–214**, 12:435
Frankl, Oscar Benjamin, 7:**214**
Frankl, Pinhas Fritz. *See* Frankl, Pinkus Fritz
Frankl, Pinkus Fritz, 7:**214**

Frankl, Viktor Emil, 7:**214**

Frankl family. *See* Fraenkel family

Frankl-Gruen, Adolf Abraham, 7:**214**

Frankl-Hochwart, Ludwig August, Ritter von. *See* Frankl, Ludwig August

Franklin, Abraham, 7:214

Franklin, Arthur Ellis, 7:215

Franklin, Beatrice, 7:215

Franklin, Benjamin, 7:214

Franklin, Benjamin Wolf, 7:214

Franklin, Ellis, 7:215

Franklin, Ellis Abraham, 7:215

Franklin, Jacob, 7:214

Franklin, Leo Morris, 7:**215**

Franklin, Lumley, 7:216

Franklin, Rosalind Elsie, 7:**215–216**, 13:8

Franklin, Selim, 7:**216**

Franklin, Sidney, 7:**216**

Franklin family, 7:**214–215**

Franks, 4:761

Franks (Germanic people), 1:313, 4:615

Franks, Aaron, 7:217

Franks, Abigail, 12:674, 15:197, 20:307–308

Franks, Abraham, 7:216–217

Franks, Benjamin, 4:51, *7:216*

Franks, Bilhah Abigail Levy, 7:**217**

Franks, David, 7:**217–218**, 15:196, 197

Franks, David Salisbury, 7:**218**

Franks, Fila, 15:197

Franks, Henry, 15:199

Franks, Jacob (1688-1769), 7:**218**, 15:196, 197, 563

Franks, Jacob (c.1766-c.1823), 7:**218**

Franks family, 7:**216–217**, 217t

   American Jewish Archives, 2:53

Frantseyzishe Poezye: Ibersetsungen un Komentarn (Litvine), 13:140–141

Franzblau, Abraham Norman, 7:**218**

Franzblau, Rose Nadler, 7:**218**

Franz Joseph. *See* Francis Joseph I of Hapsburg

Franz Kafka and Prague (Eisner), 6:277

Franzos, Karl Emil, 7:**219**

Fraser, Clara Goodman, 18:713–714

Fra synagogen til Løvebakken (Benkow), 3;365

Fraternal societies, 7:**219**

   B'nai B'rith's origins in, 4:13

   Brith Abraham, 4:186

   Farband, 6:712–713

Fraternidad Agraria, 2:432, 433

Fraud, 5:292–293, 7:**219–220**, 14:367–369

   See also Marriage; Practice and procedure

Frauenstaedt, Christian Martin. *See* Frauenstaedt, Julius

Frauenstaedt, Julius, 7:**220**

Fraye Arbeter Shtime (periodical), 6:144

Frayheyt trial, 19:175

Frederick Augustus II (King of Saxony), 18:87

Frederick Augustus III (King of Saxony), 18:87

Frederick I (Grand Duke of Baden), 7:**220–221**

Frederick I (Holy Roman Emperor), 11:420, 421

Frederick II (King of Prussia), 3:446, 7:**221**, 14:300

Frederick II (King of Sicily). *See* Frederick II of Hohenstaufen (Holy Roman Emperor)

Frederick III (Duke of Austria). *See* Frederick III of Hapsburg (Holy Roman Emperor)

Frederick III (King of Germany). *See* Frederick III of Hapsburg (Holy Roman Emperor)

Frederick III of Hapsburg (Holy Roman Emperor), 7:**222**

Frederick II of Babenberg (Duke of Austria), 7:**221**

Frederick II of Hohenstaufen (Holy Roman Emperor), 3:776, 7:**221–222**

Frederick Schwartz Architects, 18:184

Frederick the Belligerent. *See* Frederick II of Babenberg

Frederick the Great. *See* Frederick II (King of Prussia)

Frederick the Great (King of Prussia). *See* Frederick II (King of Prussia)

Frederick William III (King of Prussia), 6:458, 7:222–223, **222–223**

Frederick William IV (King of Prussia), 7:223, **223**

Fredriksson, Marianne, 18:91–92

Freed, Alan, 7:**223**

Freed, Arthur, 7:**223–224**

Freed, Isadore, 7:**224**

Freed, James Ingo, 7:**224**

Freedman, Barnett, 7:**224**

Freedman, David Noel

   Anchor Bible, 3:616

   on Hebrew poetry, 3:655

Freedman, Harry, 7:**224–225**

Freedman, James O., 7:**225**

Freedman, Marcia, 15:682

Freedman, Martin, 7:222

Freedman, Ronald, 18:732, 733

Freedman, Samuel, 7:**225**

Freedom, 7:**225–227**

   moral perfection and, Mendelssohn, Moses, 14:34

natural vs. abstract, 16:94–95

   of speech, 17:314–316

   See also Human dignity and freedom

Freedom Flight (Balin), 3:91

Freedom of the City of Jerusalem (award), 11:706

Freedom of the press. *See* First Amendment (U.S. Constitution)

Freedom Tower, 18:589

Freehling, Allen, 13:205

Freehof, Solomon Bennett, 7:**227–228**, 15:457

Freeland: A Social Anticipation. See Freiland, ein sociales Zukunftsbild

Freeland League, 19:650

Freeman, Arthur. *See* Liebermann, Aaron Samuel

Freeman, Joseph, 7:**228**

Freemasons, 3:324, 5:437, 7:**228–230**, 9:136–137, 14:426

   See also Fraternal societies

Free Sons of Israel, 7:**230**

Free speech. *See* Freedom, of speech

Free to Be You and Me (Pogrebin), 16:278

Free verse, 11:721

The Freewheelin' Bob Dylan (Dylan), 6:78

Free will, 7:**230–234**

   Aaron ben Elijah, 1:213

   absence of, 16:93

   criminal responsibility and, 15:720–721

   Duns Scotus, John, 6:50–51

   Ibn Daud, Abraham ben David Halevi, 9:664

   nature of, 16:87

   Pharisaic concept, 16:31

Freha bat Avraham, 7:**234**

Freiberg, Albert Henry, 7:**234**

Freiberg, Joseph A., 7:**234**

Freiberg, Julius, 7:**234**

Freiberg, Julius Walter, 7:**234**

Freiberg, Maurice J., 7:**234**

Freiberg, Stella, 7:**234**

Freiberger, Miroslav/Šalom, 7:**234–235**

Freiberg family, 7:**234**

Freiburg (Switzerland). *See* Fribourg (Switzerland)

Freiburg im Breisgau (Germany), 3:43, 7:**235**

Freidenreich, Harriet, 9:152

Freidlaender, Salomo. *See* Mynona

Freidlina, Rakhil Khatskelevna, 7:**235–236**

Freidman, Gino, 14:408

Freidus, Abraham Solomon, 7:**236**

Freier, Recha, 7:**236**

Freifeld, Abraham, 7:**236**

Freiheit. *See Morning Freiheit* (newspaper)

Freiland: Ein Sociales Zukunftbild (Hertzka), 18:202

Freiland, ein sociales Zukunftsbild (Hertzka), 9:49

Freilich, Max Melech, 7:**236**

Freiman, Archibald Jacob Freiman, 3:727, 7:**236–237**, 15:516, 517

Freiman, Lawrence, 7:237, 15:517

Freiman, Lillian, 4:404, 406, 7:236, 15:517

Freiman, Moses Bilsky, 7:236

Freiman family, 7:**236–237**

Freimann, Abraham Ḥayyim, 7:**237**

Freimann, Alfred. *See* Freimann, Abraham Ḥayyim

Freimann, Aron, 2:47, 7:**237–238**

Freimann, Isaac, 7:**237**

Freimann, Israel Meir, 7:**237**

Freimann, Jacob, 7:**238**

Freimann family, 7:**237**

Freimuetige Kaffeegespreache zweier juedischer Zuschauerinnen ueber Juden Pinkus (Herz), 9:52

Freire, Leonara, 15:346

Freistadt. *See* Hlohovek

Freistadt, Abraham Leib, 4:66

Freleng, "I.J.". *See* Freleng, Isadore "Friz"

Freleng, Isadore "Friz", 7:**238**

French Enlightenment and the Jews (Hertzberg), 9:49

French Jewish Representative Council, 11:721

French literature, 7:**238–252**

    Abraham, 1:287

    antisemitism, 5:441, 7:241–242

    in Arabic world, 15:473–474

    Benda, Julien, 3:324–325

    Berl, Emmanuel, 3:442

    biblical influence, 3:670, 7:238–240, 240

    Canada, 4:425

    Chateaubriand, François René, 4:582–583

    cherub and cherubim, 4:601

    children's, 4:634

    Classical period, 7:239–240

    Créhange, Alexandre, 5:280

    Daniel, 5:425–426

    Daniel-Rops, 5:429

    Daudet, 5:441

    David in, 5:456

    Dreyfus affair, effect of, 7:241–242

    Du Bartas, Guillaume De Salluste, 6:31

    eighteenth century, philosophy, 7:241

    Fleg, Edmond, 7:71–72

    Halévy, Elie Halfon, 8:270

    Harry, Myriam, 8:366–367

    Holocaust, 7:245–251

    homiletic, 9:514

    Hourwitz, Zalkind, 9:569

    images of Jews, 7:240–241

    Ionesco, Eugène, 10:6

    Kaplan, Jacob, 11:775–776

    La Boétie, Etienne de, 12:408

    Lacretelle, Jacques de, 12:426

    Lambert, Mayer, 12:442

    Langfus, Anna, 12:482

    Lattes, Judah, 12:519

    Lazare, Bernard, 12:558

    Lévy, Alfred, 12:747

    Levy, Bernard-Henri, 12:748

    Middle Ages, 7:238–239, 243

    Mikhaël, Ephraïm, 14:221

    National Socialism (Nazism), 7:242

    Némirovsky, Irène, 15:69

    nineteenth century, 5:435, 7:243–245

    Old French modification of Hebrew, 7:243

    orientalist, 12:724–725

    poetry, 7:251–252

        Claudel, Paul, 4:751

        Fondane, Benjamin, 7:114

        Hertz, Henri, 9:48

        Le Fèvre De La Boderie, Guy, 12:601

        medieval, 11:33–34, 16:269

        Morhange, Pierre, 14:491

        nineteenth century, 14:43

        twentieth century, 11:6

    pro-Jewish, Péguy, Charles-Pierre, 15:712

    Proust, Marcel, 16:634–635

    Renaissance period, 7:239

    Romantic period, 7:240

    Sarraute, Nathalie, 18:62

    Schwarz-Bart, André, 18:191

    Schwob, Marcel, 18:197

    Sephardi authors, 7:249–251

    twentieth century, 6:634, 7:243–245

        Chalier, Catherine, 4:562–563

        Duvernois, Henri, 6:73

        Jacob, Max, 11:28

        Maurois, André, 13:691

        Memmi, Albert, 14:16–17

        Perec, Georges, 15:758

        Pierre-Bloch, Jean, 16:148

    WW I, 7:242

    WW II, 7:242

French Poetry: Translations and Comments. See Frantseyzishe Poezye: Ibersetsungen un Komentarn (Litvine)

French Revolution, 7:155, 165, **252–257**

    emancipation, 6:375, 377–378, 9:231–232

    Grégoire, Henri Baptiste, 8:84

    Mirabeau, Honore Gabriel Riqueti, Comte de, 14:305

    in Paris, 15:644

    Switzerland, 6:404

French Sanhedrin, 18:24

The French States of the Pope (Lunel), 13:259

Frenel. *See* Frenkel, Itzḥak

Frenel, Itzḥak. *See* Frenkel, Itzḥak

Frenk, Azriel Nathan. *See* Frenk, Ezriel Nathan

Frenk, Beer, 7:257

Frenk, Ezriel Nathan, 7:257

Frenkel, Itzḥak, 7:**257**, 15:650

Frenkel, Izḥak Yedidiah, 7:**257**

Frenkel, Jacob Ilich, 7:**257–258**

Frenkel, Vera, 7:258

Frensdorff, Ferdinand, 7:258

Frensdorff, Solomon, 7:**258**

Fresco, David, 7:258

Freud, Anna, 7:**258–259**

Freud, Jonathan, 18:93

Freud, Lucian, 7:**259**

Freud, Sigmund, 1:290, 4:181–182, 5:302, 7:**259–262**, 14:538

Freudemann, Simḥah, 7:**262–263**, 11:398

Freudenthal, Alfred Martin, 7:**263**

Freudenthal, Gad, 11:325

Freudenthal, Jacob, 7:**263**

Freudenthal, Max, 7:**263**

Freund, Ernst, 7:**263**

Freund, Gisèle, 7:**263–264**

Freund, Martin, 7:**264**

Freund, Paul Abraham, 7:**264**, 12:556

Freund, Samuel ben Issachar Baer, 7:**264**

Freund, Vilmos, 7:**264**

Freundlich, Otto, 7:**264–265**

Freund-Rosenthal, Miriam Kottler, 7:**265**

Frey, Jean Baptiste, 6:464, 7:**265**

Frey, William, 2:88

Frey Ruiz Tagle, Eduardo, 4:643

Fribourg (Switzerland), 7:265–266

Frida, Emil. *See* Vrchlický, Jaroslav

Fridényi bankja (Acsády), 1:369

Fridenyi's Bank. See Fridényi bankja

Fridland, Mikhail Yefimovich. *See* Kol'tsov, Mikhail

Fridman, Gal, 7:266

Fridman, Isaac, 4:42–43

Fridman, Shoyl. *See* Rashkin, Leyb

Fried, Aaron, 7:266

Fried, Alfred Hermann, 7:266–267

Fried, Erich, 7:267

Fried, Heidi, 18:94

Fried, Lazar, 7:267

Fried, Miriam, 7:267

Fried, Morton Herbert, 7:267–268

Fried, Norbert. *See* Frýd, Norbert

Friedan, Betty, 7:268, 15:219, 18:733

Friedberg (Germany), 7:268–269

Friedberg, Abraham Shalom, 7:269, 8:300

Friedberg, Bernard, 3:682, 7:269

Friedberg Genizah Project, 7:478–479

Fried-Bliss, Miriam. *See* Fried, Miriam

Friede, Shalom, 7:270

Friedell, Egon, 7:270

Friedemann, Adolf, 4:28, 7:270

Friedemann, Ulrich, 7:270

Friedenberg, Albert Marx, 7:270

Friedenberg, Samuel, 7:270–271

Friedenthal, Karl Rudolf, 16:344

Friedenwald, Harry, 3:99, 7:271

Friedenwald, Jonas, 7:271

Friedenwald family, 3:98, 7:271

Frieder, Armin, 7:271

Friederman, Zalman Jacob, 7:271–272

Friedjung, Heinrich, 7:272

Friedkin, William, 7:272, 12:485

Friedlaender, Bernhardt, 4:70

Friedlaender, David, 4:70, 78, 620, 7:272–273, 8:436, 437, 440, 11:569, 16:344

Friedlaender, Elfriede. *See* Fischer, Ruth

Friedlaender, Henri, 4:369

Friedlaender, Israel, 7:273–274, 15:209

Friedlaender, Johnny, 7:274

Friedlaender, Max, 7:274

Friedlaender, Michael, 3:614–617, 622, 7:274

Friedlaender, Moritz, 7:274–275

Friedlaender, Oskar Ewald, 7:275

Friedlaender, Ruth. *See* Fischer, Ruth

Friedlaender, Saul, 7:275–276

Friedlaender, Solomon Judah, 7:276

Friedland, Abraham Hyman, 7:276–277

Friedland, Ḥayyim Abraham. *See* Friedland, Abraham Hyman

Friedland, Judah Aryeh. *See* Friedlaender, Solomon Judah

Friedland, Natan, 7:277

Friedland, Raḥel. *See* Shalon, Raḥel

Friedland, Samuel, 4:213

Friedland, Solomon Judah. *See* Friedlaender, Solomon Judah

Friedland collection, 13:491–493

Friedlander, Isaac, 7:277

Friedlander, Israel, 4:439

Friedlander, Kate, 7:277

Friedlander, Lee, 7:277–278

Friedlander, Walter, 7:278

Friedland family, 7:276

Friedman, Benjamin, 7:278–279

Friedman, Benny. *See* Friedman, Benjamin

Friedman, Bruce Jay, 7:279

Friedman, Deborah Lynn, 7:279

Friedman, Dénes, 7:279

Friedman, Herbert A., 7:280, 9:381

Friedman, Isaac, 4:256–257

Friedman, Jacob (1910-1972), 7:280

Friedman, Jacob K. (1856-1905), 15:355

Friedman, Jerome Isaac, 7:280

Friedman, Kinky, 7:280–281

Friedman, Lee Max, 2:58, 59, 7:281

Friedman, Michel, 16:344

Friedman, Milton, 7:281–282

Friedman, Moshal, 11:378

Friedman, Naphtali, 7:282, 15:579, 611

Friedman, Nathan. *See* Yellin-Mor, Nathan

Friedman, Pauline Esther, 11:469

Friedman, Philip, 7:282–283

Friedman, Richard Elliott, 3:624

Friedman, Richard F. *See* Friedman, Kinky

Friedman, Rosemary, 6:439–440

Friedman, Shamma, 1:462–463, 7:283–284

amoraim, 2:90

on Judah ha-Nasi, 11:505

Friedman, Szajko. *See* Szajkowski, Zosa

Friedman, Theodore, 7:284

Friedman, Thomas L., 7:284–285

Friedmann, Abraham, 7:285

Friedmann, Aron, 7:285

Friedmann, Daniel, 7:285

Friedmann, David Aryeh, 7:285

Friedmann, David ben Samuel, 7:285–286

Friedmann, Desider, 7:286

Friedmann, Egon. *See* Friedell, Egon

Friedmann, Georges, 7:286, 18:730

Friedmann, Israel. *See* Ruzhin, Israel

Friedmann, Jane, 7:286

Friedmann, Kornel. *See* Capa, Cornell

Friedmann, Meir, 3:647, 7:287

Friedmann, Moritz, 7:287

Friedmann, Paul, 7:287–288

Friedmann, Simon, 15:438

Friedrich Nietzsche, sein Leben und sein Werk (Richter), 17:291

Friedrichsfeld, David, 7:288

Friedrichstadt (Latvia). *See* Jaunijelgava (Latvia)

Friedrich Wilhelm III. *See* Frederick William III

Friedrich Wilhelm IV. *See* Frederick William IV

Friedsam, Michael, 2:21, 7:288

Friend, Charlotte, 7:288, 13:9

Friend, Fred, 15:677

Friend, Hugo Morris, 7:288

Friendly, Edwin S., 11:468

Friendly, Fred W., 7:289

Friendly, Fred Wachenheimer. *See* Friendly, Fred W.

Friendly, Henry Jacob, 7:289

Friendly Fire (Kanin), 11:763

Friends (de Vries), 6:72

Friends (television show), 18:196

Friendship, 7:289–290

Friendship leagues with Israel, 7:290

Fries, Jakob Friedrich, 7:290–291

Frigeis, Lazaro de, 7:291

Friling 1942 (Shayevitsh), 18:424

Frisch, Daniel, 7:291

Frisch, Efraim, 7:291

Frisch, Ephraim, 7:291–292

Frisch, Otto Robert, 7:292, 16:137

Frischmann, David, 7:292–295, 8:181, 456, 476, 726, 12:424, 18:370

Fritsch, Theodor, 7:295

Fritta, 7:295–296

Fritz the Cat (Bakshi), 3:74

Friuli-Venezia Giulia (Italy), 7:296

Frizzi, Benedetto, 7:296

Froehlich, Alfred, 7:296–297

Froehlich, Joachim. *See* Gay, Peter Jack

Froelich, Joachim. *See* Gay, Peter Jack

Frogs, 7:297

Frohlich, Herbert, 7:297

Frohman, Charles, 7:297

Frohman, Daniel, 7:297, 14:570

Frohman, Dov, 7:**297**

Frohman family, 7:**297**

Frolik, Josef, 11:403

Frolkis, Vladimir Veniaminovich, 7:**297–298**

Froman, Ian, 7:**298**

From an American Legation (Morris), 14:511

From Ararat to Suburbia: A History of the Jewish Community of Buffalo (Adler), 1:408

Frome, Anthony. *See* Feinberg, Abraham L.

From Ferenc Jóska's Box (Emöd), 6:396

From Generation to Generation: Age Groups and Social Structure (Eisenstadt), 6:271

From Here and There (Brenner). *See Mi-Kan u-mi-Kan*

From Inside and Outside. See Mi-Bayit u-mi-Ḥuẓ

Fromm, Erich, 2:187, 7:**298**

Fromm, Herbert, 7:**298–299**

From Magic to Science (Singer), 18:634

Fromm-Reichmann, Frieda, 7:**299**

From Near and Far (Epstein), 6:466

From Shelomo ha-Elkoshi's Book of Reminiscences (Epstein), 6:476

From the City, from the Plough (Baron), 3:171

From the Diary of Anne Frank (composition, Morawetz), 14:478

From the Life of Poetry. See Iz zhizni piezii

From the Stone Age to Christianity (Albright), 1:596

From the Synagogue to Lion Hill. See Fra synagogen til Løvebakken

From Wandering Afar. See Mi-Shut ba-Merhakim

From Within the Walls. See Mi-Bein ha-Homot

Fronto, Marcus Cornelius, 7:**299**

Frost, Martin, 7:**299–300**

Zur Fruehgeschichte des Machzor (Edelmann), 6:143

Frug, Shimon, 4:635

Frug, Shimon Shmuel, 7:**300**

Das Früheste Vorkommen der Juden in Deutschland; Juden in romischen Trier (Altmann), 2:23

Fruit of the goodly tree. *See* Etrog

Fruits and fruit trees

    apples, 2:287

    Bible, 7:116

    peaches, 15:704

    pears, 15:705

    prohibition on felling, 6:93

    tree cutting, 5:166–167

Frum, Barbara Rosenberg, 7:300

Frum, David, 7:300

Frum, Linda, 7:300

Frum, Murray, 7:300

Frum family, 7:300

Frumkin, Aleksandr Naumovich, 7:**300–301**

Frumkin, Aryeh Leib, 7:**301**

Frumkin, Boris Markovich, 7:**301**

Frumkin, Gad, 8:466, 12:557

Frumkin, Israel Dov, 3:71, 7:**301–302**, 8:466, 13:257–258

Frumkin, Malkah. *See* Esther (1880-1943)

Frumkin, Michael Levi. *See* Rodkinson, Michael Levi

Frumkin, Sidney. *See* Franklin, Sidney

Fry, Christopher, 14:540

Fry, Varian, 7:**302**, 9:490

Frýd, Nora F. *See* Frýd, Norbert

Frýd, Norbert, 7:**302–303**

Frydman, Sjaiko. *See* Szajkowski, Zosa

Frymer-Kensky, Tikva, 7:**303**

FSJU (Fonds Social Juif Unifié), 2:62

FTP. *See* Franc Tireurs et Partisans Français

Fubini, Guido, 7:**303**

Fubini, Mario, 7:**303–304**

Fuchs, Abraham Moshe, 7:**304**

Fuchs, Alfred, 7:**304**

Fuchs, Bina. *See* Abramowitz, Bina

Fuchs, Chaim-Leib. *See* Fox, Chaim-Leib

Fuchs, Daniel, 7:**304**

Fuchs, Jacob Samuel. *See* Fox, Jacob Samuel

Fuchs, Lillian, 7:**304–305**

Fuchs, Lukas. *See* Foss, Lukas

Fuchs, Moses Ẓevi, 7:**305**

Fuchs, William. *See* Fox, William

Fuchsberg, Jacob D., 7:**305**

Fuenfkirchen (Hungary). *See* Pecs (Hungary)

Fuenn, Samuel Joseph, 7:**305–306**, 8:725

Fuerst, Julius, 3:682, 7:**306**

Fuerst, Milán. *See* Fust, Milán

Fuerstenberg, Carl, 7:**306**

Fuerstenberg, Pontus, 11:433

Fuerst Lazar (Kapper), 11:782

Fuerth (Germany), 7:**306–307**

Fuerth, Henriette, 7:**307**

Fugitive Pieces (Michaels), 14:170

Fugtazki, Malka, 9:496

Fuhrmann, Israel. *See* Furman, Yisroel

Fuks, Abraham Moshe. *See* Fuchs, Abraham Moshe

Fuks, Alexander, 7:**307–308**

Fuks, Chaim-Leib. *See* Fox, Chaim-Leib

Fuks, Lajb, 7:**308**

Fulani, Lenora, 15:224

Fulbert of Chartres, 7:**308**

Fulbright, William J., 2:51

Fuld, Aaron ben Moses, 7:**308**

Fuld, Felix, 6:513

Fuld, Stanley Howells, 7:**308–309**, 12:556

Fulda (Germany), 3:776, 7:**309**

Fulda, Ludwig, 7:**309–310**

Fuller, Samuel Michael, 7:**310**

Fulvia, 7:**310**

The Functions of Social Conflict (Coser), 5:228

Fundam, Isaac, 4:78

Fundamental Principles of the Sociology of Law (Ehrlich), 6:243

Fundamentals of Belief. *See* Articles of faith

Fundamenta punctationis linguae sacrae (Alting), 2:21

Fund for Jewish Documentary Filmmaking, 15:23

Fundoianu, Barbu. *See* Fondane, Benjamin

Fund-raising. *See* Philanthropy

Funem Yarid (Shalom Aleichem), 18:379, 388

Funerals

    depicted on Burial Society glass (18th c.), vol. 7: color insert

    Elmaleh Raḥamim, 6:364–365

    epitaphs, 6:464–465

    flute playing, 14:647

    hakkafot, 8:250

    head covering, 8:506

    hesped, 9:74

    ḥever ir, 8:470

    ḥevra kaddisha, 9:81–82

    post-Biblical traditions, 4:292–293

    in Prague (painting), vol. 7: color insert

    prayers, 6:364–365

    Sephardim, 4:293–294

    tohora, 20:15

    tombs and tombstones, 20:32–33

    women, role of, 4:293

    Ẓidduk ha-Din, 21:528

    See also Burial customs

Funerary art, 2:497

Funerary inscriptions. *See* Epitaphs

Funerary rites. *See* Burial customs
Funes (Spain), 7:**310**
Fun Finften Yor (Der Nister), 5:596
Fun Ineveynik (Smolar), 18:690
Funk, Casimir, 7:**310**
Funk, Solomon, 7:**310–311**
Funken im Abgrund (Morgenstern),
    14:487–488
Funkenstein, Amos, 7:**311**, 9:400–401
Fun Mayn Velt (Segal), 18:247
Fun Minsker Geto (Smolar), 18:690
*A Funny Thing Happened on the Way
    to the Forum* (Shevelove), 18:472
Funt, Alan, 7:**311**
Furaydis, al- (Israel), 7:**311**
Furchgott, Robert F., 7:**311**, 13:10
Furie, Sidney J., 7:**312**
Furman, Yisroel, 7:**312**
Furst, Moritz, 7:**312**
Furstenberg, Hillel, 7:**312**
Furtado, Abraham, 4:83, 7:**312–313**
Fur trade and industry, 7:**313–314,**
    12:627
Furtună, Enric, 7:**314**
Fust, Milán, 7:**315**
Fustat. *See* Cairo (Egypt)
Futoransky, Luisa, 7:**315**
The Future (periodical). *See Die
    Zukunft*
"The Future of Jewish Art" (Raskin),
    17:107

G

G (letter), 7:*317*, 8:5
Gaal, 7:**317**
Ga'aton (Israel), 7:**317**
Gabanyi, Ewa, 2:518
Gabara (Israel). *See* Araba (Israel)
Gabata. *See* Gevat (Israel)
Gabbai, 7:**318–319**
Gabbai, Aaron, 7:318
Gabbai, Ezekiel, 7:318, 15:525, 542
Gabbai, Ezekiel ben Joseph Nissim
    Menahem, 7:318
Gabbai, Ezekiel ben Joshua, 7:318
Gabbai, Ezekiel ben Ṣāliḥ, 7:318
Gabbai, Isaac ben David ben
    Yeshu'ah, 7:317–318
Gabbai, Meir ben Ezekiel ibn, 7:**319**
Gabbai, Moses ben Shem-Tov, 7:**319**
Gabbai Ereẓ Yisrael, 18:450
Gabbai family (Iraq), 7:**317–318**
Gabbai family (Italy), 7:**317**
Gabbai Izidro, Abraham, 7:**319**
Gabba'im. *See* Tax gatherers
Gabbay, Abraham ben Jedidiah,
    10:828

Gabe, Dora, 4:276
Gabel, Heinrich, 15:652, 16:340
Gabel, Max, 7:**319**
Gabès (Tunisia), 7:**319–320**
Gabin (Poland), 7:**320**
Gabiniana. *See* Kenath (ancient city)
Gabinius, Aulus, 1:629–630, 7:**320**
Gabirol, Solomon ben Judah, ibn,
    4:170, 7:**321–327**, 16:80–81, 91
    Amina, 2:77–78
    angels, 2:160–161
    beatitude, 3:237–238
    biblical study, influence of, 3:662
    emanation, 6:373
    form and matter, 7:130–131
    God, attributes of, 7:666–667
    Judeo-Arabic literature and,
        11:534
    Neoplatonism, 15:85
    philosophy, 7:323–326
        microcosm, 14:179
    piyyut, language of, 8:659
    poetry, 7:320–323, 16:265
    soul, immortality of, 19:36
    space and place, 19:66–67
Gabler, Johann, modern biblical
    exegesis by, 3:649
Gabler, Milton, 7:**327**
Gablonz an der Neisse. *See* Jablonec
    Nad Nisou (Czechoslovakia)
Gabo, Naum. *See* Pevsner, Naum
    Nehemia
Gábor, Andor, 7:**327**
Gabor, Dennis, 7:**327**
Gabor, Eva, 7:**327–328**
Gábor, Ignác, 7:**327**
Gabor, Jolie, 7:**327–328**
Gabor, Magda, 7:**327–328**
Gabor, Zsa Zsa, 7:**327–328**
Gabriel (angel), 2:152, 153, 5:421,
    14:**167–169**
Gabriel, Dan. *See* Gordon, Judah Leib
Gabriel, Gilbert W., 7:**328**
Gabrielovitch, Osip Solomonovitch,
    7:**328**
Gabriel Solmar (Lorm), 13:193
Gad (deity), 7:**328–329**
Gad (seer), 7:**330**
Gad (tribe), 7:*329,* 329–330
Gad, Devorah, 7:**330**
Gadara (ancient Israel), 7:**331,** *331*
Gad ben Isaac Foa, 7:92
Gad ben Samuel Foa, 7:92
Gad-Bernard, Esther, 18:579
Gadna, 3:256, 7:**332**
Gadol, Moise S., 7:**332–333**

Gadres. *See* Gaza (Israel)
Gadyach (Ukraine), 7:**333**
Gaelic, Bible translated into Gaelic,
    3:636
Gaer, Felice D., 7:**333**
Gaeta (Italy), 7:**333–334**
Gafeniyyah. *See* Gofnah (ancient
    Israel)
Gaffarel, Jacques, 7:**334**
Gagin, Ḥayyim, 7:**334**
Gagin, Ḥayyim ben Abraham ben
    Moses, 7:**334**
Gagin, Shalom Moses ben Ḥayyim
    Abraham, 7:**334–335**
Gagin, Shalom Moshe Hai, 1:516
Gaḥal, 3:261, 6:245, 7:**335**
Gaines, William M., 7:**335**
Gai Oni (Lapid), 12:490
Gaisin, (Ukraine), 7:**335**
Gaitskell, Dora, 16:343
Gál, Fedor, 7:**336**
Galaction, Gala, 3:633, 7:**336**
Galai, Binyamin, 7:**336**
Galant, Eliahu Vladimirovich, 7:**336**
Galanta (Slovakia), 7:**336–337**
Galant Commission, 7:336
Galanté, Abraham, 7:**338**
Galante, Abraham ben Mordecai,
    7:**338**
Galante, Jedidiah ben Moses, 7:**338**
Galante, Mordecai, 7:337
Galante, Moses, 1:516, 4:102, 7:**337–
    338**
Galante, Moses ben Jonathan, 7:**338–
    339**
Galante, Moses ben Mordecai, 7:**339**
Galante family, 7:**337–338**
Galantia (Asia Minor), 7:**339–340**
Galati (Romania), 7:**339**
Galatinus, Pietro Columna, 7:**340**
Galatz. *See* Galati
Galba (Roman emperor), Josephus'
    prophecy on Vespasian and,
    11:435–436
Galbanum, 7:**340**
Gal-ed. *See* Gilead (ancient Israel)
Galen, Claudius, 4:31, 7:**340–341**
Galerie Louise Leiris, 11:726
Galerie Simon, 11:725–726
Galgameš. *See* Carchemish (Syria)
Galgóc. *See* Hlohovek
Galgolah, Jeshua ben, 3:160
Gal Ḥadash ba-Sifrut ha-Ivrit
    (Shaked), 18:367
Gal Ḥadash ba-Sipporet ha-Ivrit
    (Shaked), 18:367
Galich. *See* Halicz

Galich, Alexander Arkadyevich, 7:**341**

Galicia (Eastern Europe), 7:**341–345,**
345t

  agriculture, Jewish, 1:498–499

  Aguddat Aḥim, 1:508

  annexation of, 2:690

  antisemitism, Lvov, 4:724

  candle tax, 4:430

  education, Jewish, 6:182, 12:529

  emancipation, 6:383

  Hasidism, founders, 11:39–41

  Haskalah, 15:773–774

  Holocaust, 16:312

  Kerem Ḥemed, 12:81

  Mizrachi Movement, 6:675

  oil development, 16:19–20

  politicians, Einaeugler, Karol,
6:255

  rabbis, 5:468–469

  Zionist movement, Braude,
Markus, 4:135

  Zionist socialism in, 18:718

Galicja. *See* Galicia (Eastern Europe)

Galil, Uzia, 7:**345**

Galilean Aramaic, 2:349

"Galilean" Mona Lisa (3rd c.), vol. 14:
color insert

Galilean Targum, 3:590, 591

Galilee (Israel), 7:**345–348**, 10:119

  Aharoni, Yoḥanan, 1:531–532

  Kedesh, 11:698–699

Galilee, Sea of. *See* Kinneret (Lake)

Galileo, Giovanni Battista. *See* Jona,
Giovanni Battista

Galili, Israel, 7:**348–349**

Galinski, Heinz, 7:**349**

Galipapa, Elijah Mevorakh, 7:**349**

Galipapa, Ḥayyim ben Abraham,
7:**349**, 15:609

Galipapa, Maimon, 7:**349–350**

Galitsiya. *See* Galicia

Galizien. *See* Galicia

Galizyah Kol Titten (Kallir), 11:745

Gall, Rose. *See* Jacobs, Rose Gell

Gallego, Joseph Shalom, 7:**350**

Gallei Razayya, 11:617

Gallican Psalter, 3:598

Gallichi family. *See* Gallico family

Gallico, Elisha ben Gabriel, 7:**350**

Gallico family, 7:**350**

Galling, Kurt, 7:**350**

Gallipoli (Turkey), 7:**350–351**

Gallipoli Campaign, 11:303, 15:694

Gallus, Cestius. *See* Cestius Gallus

Gallus, revolt against, 10:154–155

Galmudah, 15:255

Galon (Israel), 7:**351–352**

Galop (Fininberg), 7:30

Galpern, Bella, 9:496

Galský, Desider, 7:**352**

Galsworthy, John, 6:436

Galt, Alexander, 4:395

Galut, 7:**352–363**

  Middle Ages, 7:355–362

  Mishnaic period, 7:353–355

  modern, 7:362–363

  Muslim world, 7:356–357, 358–
359

  Second Temple period, 7:353

  sources of, 7:352–353

*Galut: Modern Jewish Reflection on
Homelessness and Homecoming*
(Eisen), 6:265

Galut mawza', 13:694

Galut Yehudah (Modena), 14:409

Galveston Plan, 7:**363–364**

Gama, Gaspar da, 4:142, 7:**364**

Gamala (ancient Israel), 4:568, 7:**364**

Gamaliel, Rabban, 7:**364–366**

Gamaliel, Rabban ha-Zaken, 3:589,
592, 7:364

Gamaliel, Rabban II, 7:365, 10:145–
147, 12:410

  Amidah, 2:73

  Birkat ha-Minim, 3:711

  Dosa ben Harkinas, 5:760–761

  Eleazar ben Azariah, 6:300

  Eliezer ben Hyrcanus, 6:324

  Joshua ben Hananiah, 11:450–451

  Onkelos/Aquila, 15:433–434

  targumim, dating of, 3:589

  See also Simeon ben Gamaliel II

Gamaliel, Rabban III, 7:366

Gamaliel, Rabban IV, 7:366

Gamaliel, Rabban V, 7:366

Gamaliel, Rabban VI, 7:366

Gamaliel ben Pedahzur, 7:**366**

Gamaliel be-Rabbi, Rabban. *See*
Gamaliel, Rabban III

Gamaliel of Jabneh, Rabban. *See*
Gamaliel, Rabban II

Gamarnik, Yan Borisovich, 7:366

Gambling, 7:**366–370**

Games, 7:**370–373**

  cards and cardplaying, 4:467–468

  chess, 4:602–605

Games, Abram, 4:368, 7:**373**

Gamoran, Emanuel, 7:**373**

Gamoran, Mamie Goldsmith, 7:**373**

Gamus Gallegos, Paulina, 7:**373–374**

Gamzon, Robert, 7:**374**, 18:209, 210

Gamzu, Ḥayyim, 7:**374**

Gancheshty (Moldova). *See*
Kotovskoye (Moldova)

Ganchoff, Moses, 7:**374–375**

Gand. *See* Ghent (Belgium)

Gandelsonas, Mario, 1:471, 7:**375**

Gandhi, Mohandas Karamchand,
4:107, 7:**375–376**, 11:743

Gandhi's Truth (Erikson), 6:480

Gandz, Solomon, 7:**376**

Gan Eden. *See* Garden of Eden

Gan Eden (Aaron ben Elijah), 1:212,
213

Ganelin, Sholom Izrailovich, 6:161

Ganganelli, Giovanni Vincenzo
Antonio. *See* Clement XIV (pope)

Ganganelli, Lorenzo (cardinal). *See*
Clement XIV (pope)

Gan ha-Meshalim ve-ha-Ḥidot
(Abulafia), 1:344

Gan Ḥayyim, 7:**376**

Gani, Meir, 10:6

Ganj-Nāmeh (Emrāni). *See Book of
Treasure* (Emrāni)

Gannei Tikvah, 7:**376**

Gannei Yehudah, 7:**376**

Gans, Bird Stein, 7:**376–377**

Gans, David ben Solomon, 4:39,
7:**377**, 13:675

  Esterke, 6:515

    Joseph ben Mordecai Gershon ha-
Kohen of Cracow, 11:424

Gans, Eduard, 7:**377–378**, 12:551

Gans, Mozes Heiman, 7:**378**

Gan she-Ḥarav (Raab, Esther), 17:5

Gan Shelomo (Israel), 7:**378**

Gan Shemu'el (Israel), 7:**378**

Gan Shomron (Israel), 7:**379**

Ganso, Joseph, 7:**379**

Gantman, Judah Leib, 7:**379**

Gan Yavneh (Israel), 7:**379**

Ganz, Joachim, North Carolina,
15:302

Ganzfried, Solomon ben Joseph,
7:**379–380**

Gaon. *See* Geonim

Gaon, Moses David, 7:**386**

Gaon, Nissim David, 7:**387**, 21:223

Gaon, Saadiah, 11:730, 13:29–30, 32

Gaon, Solomon, 7:**387**

Gaon, Yehoram, 7:**387**

Gaon, Yehudai, 8:262

Gaon of Vilna. *See* Elijah ben
Solomon Zalman

Ga'on va-Shever (Smolenskin), 18:692

Ga'on Ẓevi (Horowitz), 9:545

Gap, Inc., 6:17–18, 7:62

Gaponov, Boris, 7:**387**, 11:322

Gaponov, Dov. *See* Gaponov, Boris

Gara, Giovanni di. *See* Di Gara, Giovanni

The Garbage, the City, and the Death (Fassbinder), 4:237

Garbell, Alexander, 15:649

Garbuz, Yair, 7:**388**

Garcia, Alvar, 15:563

García de la Huerta, Vicente, 11:256

Garcia de Orta. *See* Orta, Garcia de

Garcia de Santa Maria, Gonzalo, 15:563

Garcian, Lobell, 4:299

Garcian, Vidal, 4:299

Garden of Eden, 7:**388–389**, 15:628–629

    Adam, 1:371, 372, 373, 374

    biblical narrative of paradise in, 15:623–627

    location of, 15:624

Garden of Eden (Aaron ben Elijah). *See Gan Eden* (Aaron ben Elijah)

Garden of God. *See* Garden of Eden

Garden of the Finzi-Contini (Bassani), 3:207

The Garden of the Finzi-Contini (motion picture), 9:442

Garden of Wisdow. See Firdaws al-Ḥikma

Gardosh, Kariel, 7:**389**

Garfield, John, 3:783, 7:**389**

Garfinkle, Julius. *See* Garfield, John

Garfunkel, Art, 7:**389–390**, 15:221, 18:614

Garganin. *See* Georgia (Transcaucasia)

Garih, Üzeyir, 7:**390**

Garlic, 7:**390**, vol. 16: color insert

Garlock, John Henry, 7:**390**

Garme and gerama, 7:**502–505**

Garment, Leonard, 7:**390–391**

Garment industry. *See* Clothing and textiles industry; Fashion industry

Garments

    rending of (*See* Keri'ah)

    See Dress

Garmison, Samuel, 7:**391**

    Amigo, Abraham, 2:77

    Mishpetei Zedek, 2:130

Garmon family. *See* Darmon family

Garmu, Bet. *See* Bet Garmu family

Garstang, John, 7:**391**, 8:499

Gartner, Lloyd P., 7:**391**

Gary (IN), 6:195, 7:**391**

Gary, Romain, 7:247, **391–392**

Gary Plan, 6:195

Gas chambers, 2:664–665, 3:309–311, 9:305–306, *484*

    See also Holocaust

Gascony (France), 7:**392**

Gaskell, Sonja, 7:**392**

Gaspar d'Almeida. *See* Gama, Gaspar Da

Gaspar de Leão. *See* Leão, Gaspar de

Gass, Adolfo, 16:350

Gasser, Herbert Spencer, 7:**392**

Gassing, 7:**393**

Gassner, John, 7:**393**

Gaster, Moses, 2:123, 6:598, 7:**394**, 12:463

Gaster, T. H., form criticism of, 3:651

Gaston-Marin, Gheorghe, 7:**394**

Gastroenterology. *See* Medicine

Gasur (Iraq). *See* Nuzi

Gas vans, 9:340

Gat (Israel), 7:**394**

The Gate. See Vrata

Gate of the Gates. *See* Bāb al-Abwāb (Caucasus)

Gates, Bill, 1:668

Gateshead on Tyne (England), 7:**395**

Gates of Heaven (motion picture), 14:510

Gates of Hope. *See* Sha'arei Tikvah

The Gates of Prayer, 17:171

Gates of Prayer for Shabbat and Weekdays, 4:546

"Gateway of the Golan" (Israel). *See* Sha'ar ha-Golan (Israel)

"Gateway of the Valleys" (Israel). *See* Sha'ar ha-Amakim (Israel)

"Gateway to Hefer". *See* Sha'ar Ḥefer-beit Yizḥak (Israel)

"Gateway to Hefer Plain". *See* Sha'ar Ḥefer-beit Yizḥak (Israel)

Gateway to Jewish Song (Eisenstein), 6:274

Gath (ancient Israel), 1:355, 7:**395**

Gath-Hepher (ancient Israel), 7:**396**

Gath-Rimmon (ancient Israel), 7:**396**

Gatigno, Eliakim ben Isaac, 7:**396**

Gatigno, En Solomon Astruc, 7:**396**

Gatigno, Ḥayyim Abraham Benveniste, 2:31, 7:**396**

Gatigno family, 7:**396**

Gato, Juan. *See* Álvarez Gato, Juan

Gaul. *See* France

Gaunse, Joachim, 7:**396–397**

Gaup, Peter, on Nuremberg laws, 15:350

Gavison, Ruth, 7:**397**

Gavison family, 7:**397**

Gavronsky, Helen. *See* Suzman, Helen

Gawler, George, 7:**397–398**

Gawler, John Cox, 7:**398**

Gay, Peter Jack, 7:**398**

Gaya (Czech Republic). *See* Kyjov (Czech Republic)

Gayane (ballet, Eifman), 6:253

Ga'ya system (Hebrew grammar), 11:117, 13:635–637

Gaylord, Mitchell, 7:**398**

Gay rights, 18:19

Gaysin. *See* Gaisin

Gaza (Israel), 7:**398–400**

Gaza Strip (Israel), 2:333, 7:*400,* **400–403**

    American Joint Distribution Committee, 2:64

    Arab population

        after Six-Day war, 10:717–718

        Egyptian control, 10:303, 717

    Arab population, 1948–67, 10:303, 717

    Egyptian rule, 7:400–401

    feminist organizations, 6:754

    Gush Katif, 8:147–148

    Israeli rule, 7:400–401, 403

    Palestinan nationalism, 7:401–402

    security lockout, 10:726

    Sharon unilateral withdrawal policy, 10:463, 464

    See also Intifada; West Bank

Gazelle, 7:**403**

Gazeta de Amsterdam (newspaper), 16:487, 492

A Gazetteer of Hebrew Printing (Freimann), 7:237

Gazit (Israel), 7:**403–404**

Gazov-Ginzberg, Anatolii, 11:321

Gdansk (Poland), 7:**404–405**

GDR (German Democratic Republic). *See* German Democratic Republic (GDR)

Geba (Erez Israel), 7:**405**

Gebal-Byblos. *See* Jubayl

Gebiha of Be-Katil, 7:**406**

Gebini, 7:**406**

Gebirtig, Mordechai, 7:**406**

Gebrente Trit (Segalowitch), 18:249

Gebrueder Simon, 18:611–612

Gecas, Antony, 6:424, 426

Gecko, 7:**406**

Gedakht (Der Nister), 5:596

Gedalecia, Joseph, 2:33

Gedalge, Andre, 7:**406–407**

Gedali (Babel), 3:**18**

Gedaliah, 3:8, 7:**407**, 9:182

    ha-Levi, 7:**407–408**

Gedaliah, Don Judah. *See* Gedaliah, Judah

Gedaliah, Judah, 3:587, 7:**407**

Gedaliah, Judah ben Moses, 7:**407**

Gedaliah Ibn Yaḥia, 11:419

Gedaliah of Siemiatycze, 7:**408**

Gedanken un Motivn–Lider in Proze (Der Nister), 5:596, 597

Geddes, Alexander, 7:**408**

Geder. *See* Gedor (ancient Israel)

Gederah (Israel), 7:**408**

Gederah, Gederoth (ancient Israel), 7:**408–409**

Gediliah, Abraham ben Samuel, 7:**409**

Gedola. *See* Masorah Magna

Gedolei Saloniki le-Dorotam (Emmanuel), 6:395

Gedor (ancient Israel), 7:**409**

Gedud ha-Avodah (Palestine Mandate), 6:441, 7:**409**

Ge'ez language, 18:283

Geffen, Aviv, 7:**409–410**

Geffen, David, 7:**410**

Geffen, Joel, 7:**410–411**

Geffen, Tobias, 7:**411**

Gehazi, 7:**411–412**

Geheime Staats Polizei. *See* Gestapo

Gehenna (Israel). *See* Gehinnom (Israel)

Gehinnom (Israel), 6:497–498, 7:**412**, 15:111–112, 627–629
    Abaddon and, 1:224
    Kabbalistic, 6:501

Gehlin, Jan, 18:93

Gehrig, Lou, 1:668

Gehry, Frank Owen, 7:**412**

Gehsperre Aktion, 13:159

Geidels family. *See* Jeiteles family

Geiger, Abraham, 3:448, 4:164, 165, 7:**412–415**
    aggadah, 1:463
    Hochschule fuer die Wissenschaft des Judentums, 6:182
    on Jewish culture and Islam, 11:539
    on Jewish studies, 11:316
    Juedisch Theologisches Seminar, Breslau, 11:572
    on Oral Law, 15:456–457
    progressive revelation, 15:494

Geiger, Bernard, 7:**415**

Geiger, Ludwig, 7:**415–416**

Geiger, Moritz, 7:**416**

Geiger, Solomon Zalman, 7:**416**

Gei Ḥizzayon (Jagel), 3:706, 7:15, 11:70–71

Gei Oni. *See* Rosh Pinnah (Israel)

Geiringer, Karl, 7:**416**

Geis, Gilbert, 5:302

Geisel, Theodore, 4:630

Geist der Utopie (Bloch), 3:760

Gekht, Semen Grigorevitch, 7:**416–417**

Geklibene Verk fun I.M. Dik (Dik), 5:660–661

Gelasius I, 7:**417**

Gelb, Arthur, 7:**417**

Gelb, Ignace Jay, 7:**417–418**

Gelb, Max, 7:**418**

Gelb, Saadia, 20:337

Gelber, Arthur E., 7:419

Gelber, Jack, 7:**419**

Gelber, Jacob. *See* Eichenbaum, Jacob

Gelber, Louis, 7:418

Gelber, Moses, 7:418

Gelber, Nathan Michael, 7:**419**

Gelber, Rose Ann. *See* Chasman, Rose Ann

Gelber, Sholome Michael, 7:419

Gelber family, 7:**418–419**

Gelbhaus, Sigmund, 7:**419**

Gelbrun, Artur, 7:**419**

Geldern, Joseph Jacob, 7:**420**

Geldern, Simon von, 7:**419–420**

Geldern, Van, family, 6:42, 7:**420**

Geldman, Mordecai, 7:**420**, 8:706

Gelfand, Izrail Moisevitch, 7:**420**

Gelfond, Aleksandr Osipovitch, 7:**420**

Gelfond, Alexander Lazarvevitch, 7:**420–421**

Gelil ha-Goyim. *See* Galilee (Israel)

Gelil Yam (Israel), 7:**421**

Geller, Laura, 13:204, 17:179

Gelléri, Andor Endre, 7:**421**

Gellért, Oszkár, 7:**421**

Gellman, Leon, 7:**421**, 14:391

Gell-Man, Murray, 7:**421–422**

Gellner, František, 7:**422**

Gelman, Juan, 7:**422–423**

Gelman, Manuel, 7:**423**

Gelnhausen (Germany), 7:**423**

Gelsenkirchen (Germany), 7:**423**

Gemara, 7:**423**
    Ahilot, 15:394
    Bible
        order of books in, 3:581
        religious impact of, 3:662
    Mo'ed Katan, 14:414
    See also Talmud

Gemariah, 7:**423**, 18:398

Gematria, 7:**424–427**, 11:597–598

Gemen (Germany), 7:**427**

Gemilut Ḥasadim, 7:**427–428**

Geminder, Bedřich, 18:665

A Gemini. See Blíženci

Gems industry, 5:**634–636**
    Barnato, Barney, 3:167–168

Biet, Sir Alfred, 3:271
Israel, 6:566
Leibler, Isi Joseph, 12:619–620
in New York City, 15:196, 226
Oppenheimer, Sir Ernest, 15:447
Paiva, Jacques, 15:571
See also Precious stones and jewelry

Gemul ha-Yesharim (Smolenskin), 18:692

Genazzano, Elijah of, 8:479

Gender and the Politics of History (Scott), 9:152

Gender equality, Shekhinah and, 18:444

Gender-neutral language in Bible translation, 3:608

Gender Trouble: Feminism and the Subversion of Identity (Butler), 4:317

Genealogical scroll. *See Megillat Yuḥasin*

Genealogy, 7:**428–438**, 429*t*
    Benjamin (tribe), 3:354–355
    biblical, 7:428–430
    biblical literature, 8:290
    Bischhoffsheim family, 3:725*t*
    Elijah Menahem ben Moses, 6:346
    Herod I, 9:33*t*
    Kaifeng community, 11:726
    Latin America, 7:437
    Megillat Yuḥasin, 13:769–770
    priesthood, 1:217–219
    research and methodology, 7:432–437
    Sassoon family, 18:69*t*
    Second Temple Period, 7:430–432
    Yad Vashem, 7:432–433
    See also names of specific families

Génébrard, Gilbert, 7:**438–439**

General Council of Women Workers of Israel. *See* Mo'eẓet ha-Po'alot

General Dutch Diamond Workers Union, 16:286–287

General Dynamics Corporation, 5:307

General Electric Co., 6:65

General Enumeration of the Jews Tolerated in the Province of Alsace, 1784, 2:6

General Federation of Jewish Labor. *See* Histadrut

General Federation of Jewish Workers in Palestine. *See* Histadrut

General Federation of Labor in Israel. *See* Histadrut

General Jewish Workers' Union. *See* Bund

General Journal of Judaism. See Allgemeine Zeitung Des Judentums (periodical)

The General Line (motion picture), 6:274

General Motors Building in Detroit, 11:718

Generalprovediteur. *See* Court Jews

General Zionist party (Argentina), 2:435

General Zionists, 4:317, 7:**439–440**
   Ha-Boker, 8:182
   Poland, 16:304–305

The Generations of Noah Edon. See Dos Hoyz fun Joyakh Edon

Genesis (sculpture, Epstein), 6:471

Genesis, Book of, 7:**440–447**, 441*t*, 443*t*, 447*t*
   Abimelech, 1:257
   Abraham, 1:281–282
   composition and author, 7:440–442, 443*t*
   covenants, 5:249–251
   Creation, 5:273–280
   distinct character of, 7:442–443
   Edom, 6:153
   Gilgamesh Epic compared with flood account, 7:82–83
   historicity of, 15:747
   paradise in Eden narrative, 15:623–627
   patriarchs, 12:444
   Patriarchs in, 15:690
   themes, 7:445–446
      age of, 7:444–445
   two creation accounts, 7:441–442

Genesis Rabbah, 7:**448–449**

Genesis Rabbati, 7:**449–450**

Genetic ancestry, Jewish, 7:**450–458**
   and alcoholism, 6:27–28
   Buerger's disease, 4:254
   Lemba, 7:455
   maternal mitochondrial DNA, 7:456, 457
   paternal ancestry and, 7:452–456, 457
   philogenetics application, 7:451–452

Genetic diseases in Jews, 7:**458**

Genetics
   blindness, 3:755–756
   Brenner, Sydney, 4:161–162
   Brown, Michael Stuart, 4:215–216
   Cedar, Chaim, 4:435, 13:9
   Cohen, Stanley N., 5:36
   Ephrussi, Boris, 6:462
   Jacob and, 13:*8*
   Lederberg, Joshua, 12:596, 13:9
   molecular basis, 13:8–9
   Sachs, Leo, 13:10, 17:635

Geneva (Switzerland), 7:**458–460**

Geneva Bible, 3:613, 628

Genghis Khan, 14:443–444

Genital organs. *See* Reproductive system

Genius of Judaism (D'Israeli), 5:702

Geniva, 6:603

Genizah, 7:**460**

Genizah, Cairo, 7:**460–483,** 9:160
   Abraham ben Moses ben Maimon, 1:304, 305
   Adler, Elkan Nathan, 1:396
   Ali, 1:658
   Amalfi, 2:31
   Amidah, 2:73, 75
   Amram Gaon, 2:104, 105
   apologetics, 2:264
   Arabic and Judeo-Arabic translations of Bible, 3:603, 604, 605
   bibliography and cataloguing, 7:479–481
   bibliography in, 3:681
   bibliophiles and, 3:683
   Bilbeis, 3:697
   Biriyyah, 3:710
   Birkat ha-Minim, 3:711
   Bodleian Library, 4:29
   book trade in, 4:77
   Bornstein, Ḥayyim Jehiel, 4:88
   Cambridge records, 7:477–478
   Cambridge Yiddish Codex, 4:379
   collections, 7:461–462
   discoveries, history of, 7:462–465
   Eleazar ben Ḥalfon ha-Kohen, 6:301
   Elhanan ben Shemariah, 6:316
   Galilean Aramaic, 2:349
   historical discoveries, 7:466–470, 475
   illuminated fragments, 7:469
   Jubayl, 11:473
   Judeo-Arabic culture and, 11:541
   Judeo-Persian in, 11:551, 552
   Kahle, Paul Ernst, 11:717
   Katsh, Abraham Isaac, 12:6
   Khayabar (ancient city), 12:108
   liturgy and poetry, 7:465–466, 474, 18:598
   location, 4:342
   Nissi ben Berechiah al-Nahrawani and, 15:278
   Obadiah the Norman proselyte in, 15:367
   poetry, 7:474–475
   treatment of books, 4:73
   Yannai's works, 21:281

Gennanzo, Elijah Ḥayyim ben Benjamin of, 7:**483**

Gennesar, Water of. *See* Kinneret, Lake

Genoa (Italy), 7:**483–484,** 16:391

Genocide
   eight stages of, 9:390
   historiography, 9:418–419, 419
   impact from Holocaust, 9:402
   See also Holocaust

Genocide Convention, 7:**484–485**

Gens, Jacob, 20:532–533
   Judenrat institution, 11:526
   Oshmyany, 15:503

Gent. *See* Ghent (Belgium)

Gentiles, 7:**485–487**
   cheesemakers and, 4:587
   courts, 14:342–343, 18:468
   medieval Jewish view of, 13:787
   purity and impurity, ritual, 16:753–754
   Second Temple, 19:622

Gentili, Gershom ben Moses, 7:488

Gentili, Moses ben Gershom, 7:487

Gentili, Moses Hefetz, 3:663, 13:676

Gentili family, 7:**487–488**

Gentleman's Agreement (Hobson), 9:299

Genua und die Maechte am Mittelmeer 1257-1311 (Caro), 4:487

La génuflexion d'Alénou (Schulsinger), 18:173

Geografyah Mezuyyeret shel Erez Yisrael (Kamenetzky), 11:753

Geographica (Eratosthenes of Cyrene), 6:477

Geographica (Strabo), 6:477, 19:239–240

Géographie de la Palestine (Abel), 1:246

Geography, 7:**488–492**
   biblical, Smith, Sir George Adam, 18:687–688
   Braslavi, Joseph, 4:131
   Brawer, Abraham Jacob, 4:140
   Brawer, Moshe, 4:140–141
   earthquakes, 6:83
   Israel
      area total, 10:374
      Carmel, Mount, 4:483–484
      Coastal Plain, 10:375
      dew, 5:630
      historical boundaries, 9:105, 10:186–192, 188, 189
      Negev, 10:384–386
      post-Six-Day War boundaries, 10:232–233

Rift Valley, 10:383–384
topography, 3:386
urban geography, 18:360
Italy
Almagià, Roberto, 1:677–678
Errera, Carlo, 6:482
Farissol, Abraham ben
Mordecai, 6:717
Jordan (Hashemite kingdom),
11:404
Jordan (river), 11:*400*, 400–403
Middle Ages, 7:490–491
Mnaseas of Patara, 14:397
modern, 7:491–492
Palestine
Horowitz, Israel Ze'ev, 9:537
Sapir, Eliyahu, 18:38
Raisz, Erwin J., 17:75
settlement and, 10:373–374
Talmudic, 7:488–490
Geology
Austria, Suess, Eduard, 19:291
Denmark, Cohen, Emil Wilhelm,
5:14
Germany
Bentor, Jacob, 3:380
Berendt, Gottlieb Michael,
3:410
Blanckenhorn, Max, 3:738
Goldschmidt, Victor, 7:721
Oppenheim, Paul Leo, 15:446
Rosenbuch, Karl Harry
Ferdinand, 17:444
Salomon-Calvi, Wilhelm,
17:698
Holland, Vroman, Akiva, 20:588
Israel
Ben-Abraham, Zvi, 3:313
Picard, Leo Yehuda, 16:144
Shiftan, Ze'ev, 18:475–476
Italy, Ancona, Cesare D', 2:142
Norway, Goldschmidt, Victor
Moritz, 7:721
Russia, Loewinson-Lessing, Frank
Yulevich, 13:170–171
U.S., Benioff, Hugo, 3:353
Geometry. *See* Mathematics
Geonic literature, 1:639–641, 7:**492–
495**, 12:759
Geonic period
liturgy, 13:132–133
moneylending, 14:438
mysticism during, 11:596–599
response, 17:229–230
Takkanot, 19:446–447
Geonim, 7:**380–386**
Babylonia
Aaron ben Joseph ha-Kohen
Sargado, 1:214

Abba, 1:225
Abraham ben Nathan ha-
Baghdadi, 1:309
Aha of Shabha, 1:529–531
Al-Bazak, Mazli'ah ben Elijah
ibn, 1:587
Ali ben Zechariah, 1:659
Amram ben Sheshna, 2:104–
105
Azariah ben Solomon, 2:762–
763
Daniel ben Eleazar ben
Nethanel Hibbat Allah,
5:427
David ben Judah, 5:467
David ben Zakkai, 5:472
Dosa ben Saadiah, 5:761
Hai Bar Rav David Gaon,
8:232
Hai ben Nahshon, 8:232
Hai ben Sherira, 8:232–233
Hananel ben Hushi'el, 8:314–
315
Hanina ben Kahana ben
Huna, 8:323
Hefez ben Yazli'ah, 8:753
Hezekiah ben David, 9:91
Isaac, 10:35
Israel ben Samuel ha-Kohen,
10:748
Jacob ha-Kohen bar
Mordecai, 11:37
Joseph bar Abba, 11:418–419
Joseph bar Hiyya, 11:419
Joseph ben Jacob bar Satia,
11:422
Kohen-Zedek bar Ivomai,
12:260
Kohen Zedek of Pumbedita,
12:260
Moses Kahana ben Jacob,
14:558
Mubashshir ben Nissi ha-
Levi, 14:594
Mubashshir ben Rav Kimoi
ha-Kohen, 14:594
Nahshon bar Zadok, 14:757
Natronai ben Nehemiah,
15:33
Nehemiah bar Kohen Zedek,
15:62
Nissi ben Berechiah al-
Nahrawani, 15:278
Paltoi Bar Abbaye, 15:607–
608
Pirkoi ben Baboi, 16:183
Rabbah, 17:7–8
Saadiah Gaon, 17:606–614

Samuel ben Hophni, 17:770–
771
Sar Shalom ben Boaz, 18:62–
63
Sherira ben Hanina Gaon,
18:463
Simona, 18:617
Yehudai ben Nahman, 21:297
Zadok bar Mar Yishi, 21:442
Zemah ben Hayyim, 21:505
Zemah ben Paltoi, 21:505
Zemah Zedek ben Isaac,
21:505
Baghdad, 7:384, 384*t*
Ben 'Alān, Joshua, 3:315
biblical exegesis and study, 3:641,
662
Egypt
Elhanan ben Shemariah,
6:316
Nethanel ben Moses ha-Levi,
15:93
Sar Shalom ben Moses ha-
Levi, 18:63
Shemariah ben Elhanan,
18:457
Egypt and Damascus, 7:386
Erez Israel, 7:384–385, 385*t*, 386
Germany, Simeon bar Isaac,
18:592–593
gezerta imprecation, 7:569–571
Israel
Nathan ben Abraham I, 15:12
Nathan ben Abraham II,
15:12–13
mishpat Ivri, 14:340
North Africa
Dunash ibn Tamim, 6:48–49
Hushi'el ben Elhanan, 9:640–
641
Jacob ben Dunash ben Akiva,
11:31
Judah ben Joseph of
Kairouan, 11:488
Nissim ben Jacob ben Nissim
ibn Shahin, 15:279–280
Palestine
Abiathar ben Elijah ha-
Kohen, 1:255, 18:770
Abraham ben Nathan, 1:308
Abraham Gaon, 1:311
Daniel ben Azariah, 5:427
David ben Daniel, 4:466
Elijah ben Solomon ha-
Kohen, 6:341
Ephraim ben Shemariah,
6:460
Josiah ben Aaron he-Haver,
11:460

Geonim, *continued*

Solomon ben Judah, 18:770–771

Persia

Albaradani, Joseph, 1:586

Samuel ben Ali, 17:768

Samuel ben Daniel Abu Rabīʿa ha-Kohen, 17:769

Spain, Ibn Abitur, Joseph ben Isaac, 9:658

Sura and Pumbedita, 7:380–384, 383*t*, 384*t*

Tunisia, Elhanan ben Ḥushiel, 6:315

Geʾon Yaʾakov (Kahana), 11:711

Geophysics

Haurwitz, Bernard, 8:462

Kaplan, Joseph, 11:776

George, Manfred, 7:**495**

George, Stefan, 4:81

George, Walte Lionel, 7:**495**

Georgia (Transcaucasia), 7:**495–501**, *496*

communist era, 7:498–500

eighteenth, nineteenth centuries, 7:497–498

Georgian Jews in Israel, 10:296

Middle Ages, 7:496–497

Republic, 7:500

See also Judeo-Georgian language

Georgia (U.S.), 1:261, 7:*501*, **501–502**

Georgiopolis. *See* Lydda (Israel)

Georgius Florentius. *See* Gregory of Tours

Gephrous. *See* Ephron (town, Israel)

Ger (Poland). *See* Gora Kalwaria (Poland)

Geradike. *See* Gerar (ancient Israel)

Gerama and garme. *See* Garme and gerama

Gerar (ancient Israel), 7:**505**, 14:316

Gerasa (Jordan), 3:150, 7:**505–506**

Gerber, Maynard, 7:**506**

Gerchunoff, Alberto, 7:**506**, 11:469

Gercke, Achim, 15:349

Ger de Cordova, Abraham. *See* Escudero, Lorenzo

Die gerettete Zunge (Canetti), 4:430

Gerez, Josef Habib, 7:**506**, 15:474

Gerhardt, Charles Frederic, 7:**506–507**

Geri, Jacob, 7:**507**

Geriatrics. *See* Age and the aged

Gerizem, Mount (ancient Israel). *See* Mount Gerizim (ancient Israel)

Gerizim, Mount (Israel). *See* Mount Gerizim (Israel)

German, D.A. *See* Granin, Daniel Aleksandrovich

German, Daniel Aleksandrovich. *See* Granin, Daniel Aleksandrovich

German Botanical Society, 13:7

German Christian Social Party. *See* Christian Social Party (Germany)

German Conservative Party, 5:**177**

German Democratic Liberal Party, 11:704

German Democratic Republic (GDR), 6:275, 7:539

German Education and Reeducation (Engelmann), 6:410

Germania Judaica, 4:129

Germanicus. *See* Wechsler, Max

German Jewish Emancipation, Auerbach, Berthold, 2:653

German literature, 7:**509–518**

Adler, Hermann, 1:398–399

Adler, Paul, 1:405

Aichinger, Ilse, 1:549

apologetics, 2:267

Ben-Chorin, Schalom, 3:324

Ben-Gavriel, Moshe Yaʾakov, 3:342

Berg, Leo, 3:416

biblical and Hebraic influences, 3:671, 7:509–510

biblical influence, 3:671

Braun, Felix, 4:137–138

Broch, Hermann, 4:191–192

Brociner, Marco, 4:192

Brod, Max, 4:192–193

Bruckner, Ferdinand, 4:220

children's, 4:620–621, 634

criticism, Mendelssohn, Moses, 14:35

Daniel in, 5:418

David in, 5:456

Doeblin, Alfred, 5:729

Domin, Hilde, 5:743

Donath, Adolph, 5:747–748

Ehrentreu, Heinrich, 6:242

Eloesser, Arthur, 6:366

encyclopedias, 6:400, 401

feminist, Jelinek, Elfriede, 11:118–119

Frank, Bruno, 7:180

Goethe, 7:681–682

Hartmann, Moritz, 8:377

Heine, Heinrich, 8:770–773

Hermlin, Stephan, 9:30

Herzberg, Wilhelm, 9:52

Hessel, Franz, 9:78

Heyse, Paul, 9:87

Hildesheimer, Wolfgang, 9:105

Hilsenrath, Edgar, 9:119

Hitzig, Julius Eduard, 9:294

Holocaust, post-holocaust, 7:517–518

Honigmann, Barbara, 9:518

Hundt-Radowsky, Joachim Hartwig, 9:602

Jewish contribution, 7:513–517, 535

Jewish image in, 7:511–513

Landauer, Meyer Heinrich Hirsch, 12:467–468

Landsberger, Arthur, 12:475

Lazarus, Nahida Ruth, 12:562

Leonhard, Rudolf, 12:647

Lessing, Theodor, 12:665–666

Lewald, Fanny, 12:757–758

Lewin, Kurt Zadek, 12:760–761

Lewysohn, Yehudi Leib Ludwig, 12:772

Mosenthal, Salomon Hermann, 14:521–522

Neumann, Alfred, 15:120–121

Neumann, Robert, 15:122

novels

Hermann, Georg, 9:24

Heym, Stefan, 9:85

Hirschfeld, Georg, 9:137

Holitscher, Arthur, 9:321

Landsberger, Arthur, 12:475

Pistorius, Johannes, 16:187

poetry

Bab, Julius, 3:14

Beck, Karl Isidor, 3:243

Beer, Michael, 3:253

Calé, Walter, 4:353

Celan, Paul, 4:536

Ehrenstein, Albert, 6:241–242

Heymann, Walther, 9:86–87

Hiller, Kurt, 9:116

Kaleko, Mascha, 11:733

Kara, Avigdor ben Isaac, 11:783

Lasker-Schueler, Else, 12:498

medieval, 16:269

Mombert, Alfred, 14:430

Picard, Jacob, 16:144

Rubiner, Ludwig, 17:514

Rodenberg, Julius, 17:363

Roessler, Carl, 17:367

Roth, Joseph, 17:482–483

Rubiner, Ludwig, 17:514

Schiller, Friedrich von, 18:133–134

Schwiefert, Peter, 18:195–196

Seghers, Anna, 18:249

Sternheim, Carl, 19:222

Strich, Fritz, 19:257–258

studies, 11:53

Sturmann, Manfred, 19:276

Suesskind von Trimberg, 19:291

Susman, Margarete, 19:327–328

Tabori, Georg, 19:427–428

Toller, Ernst, 20:29–30

Torberg, Friedrich, 20:53–54

Trebitsch, Siegfried, 20:124

Tucholsky, Kurt, 20:168–169

twentieth century
    Ehrenstein, Albert, 6:241–242
    Einstein, Carl, 6:263–264
    Jacob, Heinrich Eduard, 11:28
    Mehring, Walter, 13:772–773

Ury, Else, 20:428

Van Hoddis, Jakob, 20:473

Viertel, Berthold, 20:524–525

Walden, Herwarth, 20:601

Waldinger, Ernst, 20:604–605

Wassermann, Jakob, 20:685–686

Weiss, Ernst, 20:732–733

Weiss, Peter, 20:736

Wengeroff, Pauline Epstein, 21:10–11

Werfel, Franz, 21:12–13

Wihl, Ludwig, 21:57

Winder, Ludwig, 21:80

Wolf, Friedrich, 21:136

Wolfenstein, Alfred, 21:142

Wolfskehl, Karl, 21:148

Wolfsohn-Halle, Aaron, 21:148

Yiddish and Hebrew influences, 7:510–511

Zuckermann, Hugo, 21:678

Zuckmayer, Carl, 21:678–679

Zweig, Arnold, 21:694

Zweig, Stefan, 21:694–695

German Literature on Czechoslovak Soil (Eisner), 6:277

German Orthodoxy. *See* Neo-Orthodoxy

German Press Association of Pennsylvania, 14:514

German reparations, 10:216–217, 430–431, 550, 553–554, 17:**220–221,** 239–240

American Jewish Committee, 2:55

American Joint Distribution Committee, 2:62

Conference on Jewish Material Claims Against Germany, 2:49, 62, 5:143–145, 6:186, 7:124

Eizenstat, Stuart, 6:280–281, 20:381

Goldman, Ya'akov ben Asher, 7:715

Memorial Foundation for Jewish culture, 14:18

"Policy of Fulfillment," 4:64

successor organizations, 11:327

United Restitution Organization, 20:274–275

World Jewish Restitution Organization, 2:49

German Social Democratic Party (Czechoslovakia), 5:352

German Social Democratic Party (Germany), 16:344

German Templars, 8:235

Germany, 7:**518–545,** *521*

antisemitism, 2:215–216, 7:532–535, 534*t*, 19:255
    Agrarian League, 1:470
    Ahlwardt, Hermann, 1:547
    Baden-Baden, 9:*466*
    badges, 3:46–48
    Berlin, 3:445, 447, 448–451
    blood libel, 3:31, 775, 776, 778, 7:309, 17:334–335
    Boycott Sabbath, 5:61
    Calwer, Richard, 4:378
    Carben, Victor von, 4:460
    censorship, 4:540
    Central-Verein Deutscher Staatsbuerger Juedischen Glaubens, 4:546
    Charles IV, 4:575
    Chemnitz, 4:593–594
    Cleves, 4:759
    Coburg, 4:764
    Cochem, 4:765
    Delitzsch, Friedrich, 5:540–541
    Einbeck, 6:255
    Emden, 6:392
    Erfurt, 6:478
    Essen, 6:509
    Esslingen, 6:514
    film propaganda, 5:54
    Frankfurt on the Main, 7:208–209
    Freiburg im Breisgau, 7:235
    Fulda, 7:309
    Hamburg, 8:296
    Hanover, 8:330
    Heidingsfeld, 8:764
    Hep!Hep!, 8:811–812
    Host, desecration of, 3:445
    Kristallnacht, 3:449, 4:64, 9:*463*, 12:362–363
    League of Nations censure, 5:73
    Middle Ages, 5:436
    minority rights, 5:73
    Mommsen, Theodor, 14:431
    Mosbach, 14:515
    Neo-Nazism, 2:238, 15:80–81
    Nuremberg laws, 15:348–350
    political parties and organizations, 2:216–219, *217,* 4:695, 5:177
    post-WW I, 9:243–244
    publications, 19:275
    Reichstag members, 2:*215,* 19:232
    Saxony, 18:88
    Unified Germany, 7:543
    Verein zur Abwehr des Antisemitismus, 20:509–510

building and construction, 5:183
    architecture, 2:400, 14:29–30
    synagogue architecture, 19:376–377, 379, 381

cultural and social life
    archives, 2:407–408
    assimilation, 3:446
    censorship, 4:540
    Center for Jewish History, 4:542–543
    cinema, 9:442
    community organization, 5:108–110, 7:307
    cooperatives, 5:206
    film propaganda, 5:54
    Freemasons, 7:228–229
    Gesellschaft der Freunde, 7:560–561
    integration of Jews, 14:39–40
    Jewish artists, 2:505–506, 507
    Jewish communities in German Democratic Republic, 7:539
    Juedischer Kulturbund, 3:14, 11:570
    language, 8:436, 668–669, 12:482–483
    letters and letter writers, 12:673
    libraries, 12:784, 786
    linguistic assimilation, 8:436
    motion pictures, 14:576
    museums, 14:627–628
    social history, 4:487
    theater, 19:672–674

economic affairs
    banking, 3:115–116
    coinage, 14:299
    moneylending, 7:519–520, 14:441, 442
    Ottoman Palestine, 10:183–184
    stock exchanges, 19:230

Germany, *continued*

    trade and commerce, 15:709, 19:664, 20:85

    education, 8:437–438

        Jewish during Middle Ages, 6:174–176

        Jewish during nineteenth and early twentieth centuries, 6:181–182

        Jewish during sixteenth to eighteenth centuries, 6:177–179

    foreign policy and affairs

        Bitburg Controversy, 3:727–728

        emigration, 1930's, 5:61, 7:534, 534t

        international aid to Jews, 16:40, 43

        with Israel (state), 10:228

        Israel, relations with, 7:543–544

        Ottoman Palestine, 10:183–184

    Holocaust

        Andernach, 7:143

        Ansbach, 7:180

        Germany, 19:101

        Jebenhausen, 11:99

        Juelich, 11:572

        Katowice, 12:6

        Kempen, 12:73

        Kiel, 12:146

        Kissingen, 12:202

        Kitzingen, 12:209

        Koblenz, 12:243

        Krefeld, 12:347–348

        Kreuznach, 12:355

        Meiningen, 13:776

        Memmingen, 14:17

        Mergentheim, 14:64

        Merseburg, 14:71

        Minden, 14:265

        Muehlhausen, 14:594

        Muenster, 14:599

        Munich, 14:613

        Nauheim, 15:36–37

        Pforzheim, 16:27

        Spandau, 19:83

        Speyer, 19:101

        Stendal, 19:201

        Straubing, 19:248

        Stuttgart, 19:277

        Sulzbach, 19:306

        Tauberbischofsheim, 19:528

        Thuringia, 19:711

        Trier, 20:144

        Tuebingen, 20:173

        Ulm, 20:243

        Villingen, 20:528

        Warendorf, 20:650

        Weinheim, 20:721

        Westphalia, 21:29

        Wiesbaden, 21:52

        Wolfenbuettel, 21:141–142

        Worms, 21:227

        Wuerttemberg, 21:247

        Wuerzburg, 21:248

        Wuppertal, 21:250

        Xanten, 21:257

        Zerbst, 21:515

        Zwickau, 21:265, 695

    Holocaust and WW II, 7:535–536

        Ahlem, 1:547

        Austrian annexation, 2:693

        Baden, 3:43

        Bayreuth, 3:232

        Bremen, 4:158

        Chemnitz, 4:593–594

        Coburg, 4:764

        Cochem, 4:765

        Darmstadt, 5:436

        Department of Jewish Matters and Deportation, 6:248–251

        displaced persons, 3:451, 20:430–431

        documentation, resource centers, 9:425

        Dresden, 6:11

        Dueren, 6:41

        Duesseldorf, 6:42

        Duisburg, 6:43

        Eichmann, Adolf Otto, 6:248–252

        Einbeck, 6:255

        einsatzgruppen, 7:564–565

        Eisenstadt, 6:269

        Elblag, 6:291

        Emden, 6:392

        Erfurt, 6:478

        Essen, 6:510

        Esslingen, 6:514

        eugenics, 7:393

        expansion of the Reich, 9:330–331

        film propaganda, 9:439, 440

        Frankfurt on the Main, 7:210

        Freiburg im Breisgau, 7:235

        Gestapo, 7:564–565

        ghettos, 7:575–577

        guilt, 15:344–345

        Halberstadt, 8:263

        Halle, 8:279

        Hamburg, 8:297

        Hitler, Adolf, 9:286–290

        Jewish participation in military service, 14:243–244

        Kindertransport, 8:282

        Landau, 12:457

        Leipzig, 12:628

        Lithuania, occupation of, 13:125–127

        Mainz, 13:405

        memorials, 9:431

        Mosbach, 14:515

        Nuremberg, 15:347–348

        Ohdruf concentration camp photograph, 9:*486*

        pre-war rescue, 9:490–492

        Ravensburg, 17:121

        refugees, 17:183–185, 186t

        Regensburg, 17:188–189

        Schweinfurt, 18:195

        Sephardim, 18:301

        St. Louis, voyage of the, 19:228–229

        study of, 9:421–422, 457–458

        Theresienstadt, 6:465–466

        Wannsee Conference, 20:617–619

        Wobbelin camp photographs, 9:*489*

Jewish movements and organizations

    Akademie Fuer Die Wissenschaft Des Judentums, 1:554

    Blau-Weiss, 3:746–747

    Central-Verein Deutscher Staatsbuerger Juedischen Glaubens, 4:546–547, 9:245

    Deutscher Palaestina-Verein, 5:626

    Deutsch-Israelitischer Germeindebund (DIGB), 5:626

    ESRA, 6:509, 18:257

    Gesellschaft zur Foerderung der Wissenschaft des Judentums, 7:561, 18:722–723

    Hasidic movement, 11:600

    Haskalah, 3:446

    He-Ḥalutz, 8:760

    Hilfsverein der Deutschen Juden, 3:105, 9:106–107, 12:482

    ḥud Habonim, 9:717t

    Juedische Freischule, 3:446–447, 11:569

Juedische Kultusvereinigung, 17:202

Juedischer Frauenbund, 11:570

Juedischer Kulturbund, 3:14, 11:570

Juedische Volkspartei, 11:571, 20–574

Juedisch-Literarische Gesellschaft, 11:571–572, 18:723

Kartell-Convent der Verbindungen Deutscher Studenten Juedischen Glaubens (KC), 11:818

Kartell Jeudischer Verbindungen (KJV), 11:818–819

Landjudenschaft, 12:471–472

Reichsbund Juedischer Frontsoldaten, 17:201

Soncino Gesellschaft der Freunde des Juedischen Buches, 19:11

Verband der Deutschen Juden, 20:506

Verband der Vereine Fuer Juedische Geschichte und Literatur, 20:506

Verband Nationaldeutscher Juden, 20:507

Verein Fuer Kultur und Wissenschaft des Judentums, 20:509

Vereinigung Fuer das Liberale Judentum in Deutschland, 20:509

Verein zur Abwehr des Antisemitismus, 20:509–510

Zentralrat der Juden in Deutschland, 21:510

Zentralwohlfahrtstelle der Deutschen Juden, 21:511

Zionism, 3:448, 7:534–535, 9:55–51, 12:466, 800, 21:587–588

laws and legal systems, 12:551

anti-sheḥitah movements, 18:435

civil rights, 4:546, 7:209

crime, 5:291, 292, 293

emancipation, 2:215–216, 3:43, 6:379–380, 9:232, 12:778, 13:712, 17:295

farmers' settlement law, 18:311

intermarriage, 21:180

Nuremberg laws, 15:348–350

Oppenheimer, Fritz E., 15:448

prostitution, 16:628

statute of limitations on Nazi crimes, 2:234

Middle Ages, 7:518–524, 521

antisemitism, 5:436

Black Death, 3:445, 4:125, 126, 167, 7:309

Crusades, 7:519–520

expulsions, 13:695, 712, 791

fur trade, 7:313, 314

Jewish education, 6:174–176

Mainz, 13:403–404

moneylending, 7:519–520

Ottoman empire settlement, 15:522

persecutions, 7:522–525, 529

seals, use of, 18:226, 227

settlement, 6:556

social life, 7:520–521

Swabian League, 19:334–335

music, 12:688

choral singing, 4:659–661, 12:758

ethnomusicology, 12:423–424

folks songs, 6:237

liturgical music, 7:211

political theories, parties and organizations, 2:216–218, 217, 218–219

Agudat Israel, 1:505

anarchism, 18:710

Christian Socialist Workingmen's Union, 16:630–631

Christian Social Party, 4:695

denazification, 5:578–579

German Conservative Party, 5:177

Gestapo, 14:597–598

Heimwehr, 8:770

liberalism, 12:497, 777–778

Marxism, 12:476

participation, 16:339, 343–344, 354

Reichsvereinigung, 17:202–203

Reichszentrale Fuer Juedische Auswanderung, 17:203

socialism, 12:691, 18:705–706

SS and SD, 19:154–156

students' fraternities, 19:264–265

Weimar Republic, 11:52

politicians, 6:726, 12:475

Adenauer, Konrad, 1:390

Bernstein, Aron David, 3:476–477

Brandt, Willy, 4:128

Humboldt, Wilhelm von, 9:588–589

Lasker, Eduard, 12:497

Lassalle, Ferdinand, 12:501–502

Levi, Paul, 12:691

Rathenau, Walther, 17:110–111

Schaeffer, Hans, 18:103

Scholem, Werner, 18:159

Simson, Martin Eduard von, 18:621

population, 7:307, 9:326, 16:388, 391, 395

post-WW II, 7:537–539, 537t, 9:401–402

denazification, 5:578–579

displaced persons, 3:451

Frankfurt on the Main, 7:210–211

guilt, 15:344–345

Oppenheimer, Fritz E., 15:448

printing and publishing, 5:61, 16:534–536, 537, 715–716

Berlin, 3:452

Frankfurt on the Main, 7:211

Frankfurt on the Oder, 7:212

Freiburg im Breisgau, 7:235

Fuerth, 7:307

Juedischer Verlag, 11:571

Schocken Press, 18:153

Soncino Gesellschaft der Freunde des Juedischen Buches, 19:11

typography, 20:216–217

Reformation to WW I, 7:524–529

assimilation, 7:527

court Jews, 7:526

emancipation, 7:538–539

French revolution, influence of, 7:526–527

Jewish education, 6:177–179, 181–182

settlement, 6:557, 8:296

social life, 7:525–526, 527–528, 528t

women in, 6:752

religious life and scholarship

Chief Rabbinate, 4:613

Christian-Jewish relations, 12:642–643, 16:632

Haggadot, 8:212, 213

Ḥasidei Ashkenaz, 11:599–602

Hochschule Fuer die Wissenschaft des Judentums, 2:570, 6:182, 9:300, 12:561

Germany, *continued*

Institutum Judaicum
Delitzschianum, 9:809

Juedisch-Literarische
Gesellschaft, 11:571–572,
18:723

Juedisch Theologisches
Seminar (Breslau), 11:572

Neo-Orthodoxy, 6:546,
15:82–83

Orthodox Judaism, 1:384,
3:448, 7:209–210, 12:616,
15:493–495

Protestant Church response
to Holocaust, 9:375–376,
12:797

rabbis, 17:16–17

Reform Judaism, 3:448, 7:209

responsa literature, 17:231,
232–233, 234

secular studies, 8:438

tosafists, 17:340–341

yeshivot, 21:316

Weimar Republic, 7:529–532, *530,*
11:52

women, 6:752, 21:180

Juedischer Frauenbund,
11:570

prostitution, 16:628

See also Holocaust; National
Socialism (Nazism); Prussia;
specific German cities and
individual people

Germany Is Our Problem
(Morgenthau), 14:489

Gernsback, Hugo, 18:197

Gernsheim, Friederich, 7:**546**

Gerö, Ernö, 7:**546**

Gerona (Spain), 7:**546–548,** 11:605–
606

Gerondi, Abraham ben Isaac. *See*
Abraham ben Isaac

Gerondi, Isaac ben Judah, 7:**548**

Gerondi, Jacob ben Sheshet, 7:**548–
549**

Gerondi, Johan ben Abraham. *See*
Jonah ben Abraham Gerondi

Gerondi, Moses ben Solomon ben
d'Escola, 7:**549**

Gerondi, Nissim ben Reuben. *See*
Nissim ben Reuben Gerondi

Gerondi, Samuel ben Meshullam,
7:**549**

Gerondi, Solomon ben Isaac, 7:**549**

Gerondi, Zerahiah ben Isaac ha-Levi,
7:**549–550**

Geronimo de Santa Fe. *See* Lorki,
Joshua

Gerousia. *See* Gerusia

Gerovich, Eliezer Mordecai ben Isaac,
7:**550**

Gershenzon, Mikhail Osipovich, 7:**551**

Gershman, Joe, 7:**551**

Gershom, 7:**551,** 14:526, 535

Gershom, Hillel. *See* Enelow, Hyman

Gershom, Levi ben, 5:278, 16:133,
18:658

Gershom ben Judah Me'or ha-Golah,
7:**551–552,** 8:489

apostasy, 2:274

ban of, 17:324–325

on bigamy and polygamy, 3:692

herem bet din, 9:16

taxes, 7:23

Gershom ben Solomon, 6:399, 7:**552–
553**

Gershon, Gershonites, 7:**553**

Gershon, Isaac, 7:**553–554**

Gershon, Karen, 6:438, 7:**553**

Gershon, Pinchas, 7:**554**

Gershon ben Solomon of Arles,
7:**554–555,** 8:663

Gershon Ephros Cantorial Anthology
Foundation, 6:462

Gershon Ḥayyot Manasse of
Hotzenplotz, 15:505

Gershoni, Ẓevi Hirsch. *See* Gersoni,
Henry

Gershon of Kitov. *See* Abraham
Gershon of Kutow

Gershovitz, Samuel, 7:**555**

Gershoy, Leo, 7:**555**

Gershuni, Grigori, 18:707

Gershuni, Grigori Andreyevitch, 7:**555,**
16:348

Gershuni, Moshe, 7:**555–556**

Gershwin, George, 7:**556**

Gersoni, Henry, 7:**556–557**

Gersonides. *See* Levi ben Gershom

Gerson-Kiwi, Edith, 7:**557**

Gerstein, Kurt, 3:**311,** 7:**557**

Gersten, Berta, 7:**557**

Gerstle, Lewis, 7:**557–558**

Gertler, Mark, 7:**558**

Gertner, Levi, 6:207, 7:**558**

Gertner, Meir, 7:**558**

Gertsa (Ukraine), 7:**558–559**

Gertz, Elmer, 7:**559**

Gerunda (Spain). *See* Gerona (Spain)

Gerupina. *See* Agrippina (ancient
Israel)

Gerusia, 7:**559–560**

Geruzyah. *See* Georgia (Transcaucasia)

Gery, 7:**560**

Gesammelte Schriften (Eisner), 6:276

Gesammelte Schriften (Liebermann),
12:808

Gesamtarchiv der deutschen Juden,
2:407–408

Gesang, Nathan-Nachman, 7:**560**

Geschichte der Augenheilkunde
(Hirschberg), 9:134

*Geschichte der israelitischen und
jüdischen Religion* (Hoelscher), 9:302

Geschichte der jeudischen Reformation
(Ritter), 17:346

Geschichte der Juden am Bodensee
(Loewenstein), 13:169

Geschichte der Juden in Rom (Rieger),
17:293–294

*Geschichte der Juden in Stadt and Land
Salzburg* (Altmann), 2:22–23

Geschichte der juedischen Literatur
(Karpeles), 11:816

Geschichte der Stadt Danzig (Simson),
18:621

*Geschichte des juedischen Volkes und
seiner Literatur...* (Baeck), 3:52

Gesellschaft der Freunde, 7:**560–561**

Gesellschaft der Jungen Hebraeer,
7:**561**

Gesellschaft zur Foerderung der
Wissenschaft des Judentums, 7:**561–
562,** 18:722–723

Gesenius, Heinrich Friedrich Wilhelm,
7:**562,** 13:57–58, 15:753

Geshem, Gashmu, 7:**562**

Gesher (Israel), 7:**562–563**

Gesher Benot Ya'akov (Israel), 7:**563**

Gesher ha-Ziv (Israel), 7:**563**

Geshikhte fun der Literatur bay Yidn
(Zinberg), 21:536–537

Geshuri, Meir Shimon, 7:**563**

Gesiv. *See* Achzib (ancient Israel)

Gessius Florus, 7:**563–564**

La Gesta del Marrano (Aguinis), 1:510

Gestaendnisse (Heine). *See Confessions*
(Heine)

Gestalt psychology, 21:17

Gestapo, 7:**564–565,** 14:597–598

Barbie, Nikolaus, 3:140

Eichmann, Adolf Otto, 6:247–252

Heydrich, Reinhard Tristan, 9:84

Himmler, Heinrich, 9:121

Gestetner, David, 7:**565**

The Gests of Alexander of Macedonia
(Kazis), 7:13

Gesundheit, Jacob ben Isaac, 7:**565–
566**

Get. *See* Divorce

Get mekushar, 18:467

Get mi-humrah, 4:746–747

Geto Fabrik 76 (Bryks), 4:229

Getz, Stan, 7:**566**

Ge'ulei Teiman (Israel), 7:**566**

Ge'ulim (Israel), 7:**566**
Ge'ullah, 7:**566–567**
Geva (Israel), 7:**567**
Gevarim (Israel), 7:**567**
Gevat (Israel), 7:**567**
Gévaudan (France), 7:**567**
Gevim (Israel), 7:**567**
Gevirtz, Stanley, 7:**567**
Gevulot (Israel), 7:**567–568**
Gevulot Erez (Abraham ben Elijah of Vilna), 1:299
Gewitsch (Czech Republic). *See* Jevicko (Czech Republic)
Der Geyer (Boraisha), 4:80
Gezamlte Lider (Ludwig), 13:251
Gezamlte Shiftn (Entin). *See Collected Works* (Entin)
Gezang un Gebet (Der Nister), 5:596
Der Gezeichnete (Picard), 16:144
Gezer (ancient Israel), 7:**568–569**, 18:601
Gezer (Israel), 2:377, 7:**569**
Gezerah. *See* Takkanot
Gezerah shalvah rule, 9:26
Gezerat ha-Sheniyyot. *See* Familiants Laws
Gezer calendar, 6:167, 7:**569**
Gezerta, 7:**569–571**
Gezerta imprecation, 7:**569–571**
Gharadaia (Algeria), 14:712
Ghazālī, abu Ḥamid Muḥammad ibn Muḥammad al-Tūsī al-, 7:**571–573**
Ghazni (Afghanistan), 1:432
Ghelerter, Ludwig Litman, 7:**574**
Ghent (Belgium), 7:**574**
Gheron, Yakkir Mordecai ben Eliakim, 7:**574**
Ghetto (Sobol), 8:722, 18:702
Ghetto Fighters' House (Israel), 7:**578**, 9:426–427
 See also Loḥamei ha-Getta'ot (Israel)
"The Ghetto Fighters" kibbutz. *See* Loḥamei ha-Getta'ot (Israel)
The Ghetto Inside Them. See Ghetto v nich
Ghettos, 7:**574–578**
 art and artists, 2:515, 516–521
 Belorussia (Russia), 16:313–314
 Bialystok, 3:568
 Bialystok (Poland), 16:313
 Bologna, 4:48
 in Boskovice, 4:97
 Chicago, 4:608
 Christian, 11:310–311
 Cracow (Poland), 5:262–263, 16:311

 education in, 9:360
 establishment and leadership, 9:333–334
 Galicia (Eastern Europe), 16:312
 historigraphy, 9:419
 Hungary, 9:614–615, 614t
 Italy, 10:800–801, 802
  Padua, 15:566
 Lithuania, 16:313–314
 Lublin (Poland), 16:310–311
 Muslim, 11:312
 Palencia (Spain), 15:577
 Paul IV and *Cum nimis absurdum,* 15:695
 Piotrkow, 16:181
 Plock (Poland), 16:239
 Poland, 16:315–316
  Sokolka, 18:746
 Radom (Poland), 16:311–312
 Rome, 17:413–415
 Ukraine, Sokal, 18:746
 Volhynia (Ukraine), 16:314
 Warsaw (Poland), 16:309–310
 See also Jewish quarters; specific ghettos and concentration camps
Ghetto v nich (Hostovský), 9:568
Ghez, David, 7:**578**
Ghez, Mathilda, 7:**578**
Ghez family, 7:**578**
Ghillany, Friedrich Wilhelm, 7:**578**
Ghiron, Isaiah, 7:**579**
Ghiron, Johanan, 7:**579**
Ghiron, Judah Ḥayyim, 7:**579**
Ghirondi, Mordecai Samuel ben Benzion Aryeh, 7:**579**
Ghiron family, 7:**578–579**
Ghirshman, Roman, 2:371, 7:**579**
Ghitter, Ron, 4:360
Ghivelder, Zevi, 11:469
Ghosts of the Past: Anti-Semitism at Elite Colleges (Freedman), 7:225
Ghrenassia, Gaston. *See* Macias, Enrico
Giacomo Marchi. *See* Bassani, Giorgio
Giacomo Savelli. *See* Honorius IV
Giants, Nephilim, 15:86–87
Gibbethon (ancient Israel), 7:**579**
Gibbethon (Israel), 7:**580**
Gibbor, Judah ben Elijah, 7:**580**
Gibbs, Terry, 7:**580**
Gibeah, Geba (ancient Israel), 7:**580–582**
Gibeon (ancient Israel), 1:414, 7:**582–583**
Gibeonites and Nethinim, 7:**583–585**

Gibiletto. *See* Jubayl (Lebanon)
Gibli, Binyamin, 4:346
Gibraltar, 7:**585**
Gibson, Mel, 7:142, 13:202
Gibstein, Ya'akov, 1:445
Gidal, Nahum T. *See* Gidal, Tim
Gidal, Tim, 7:**585–586**, 16:128
Gidalewitsch, Ignaz Nachum. *See* Gidal, Tim
Giddal, 7:**586**
Giddulei Terumah (Figo), 7:18
Gide, André, 9:246–247
Gideon, 7:**586–588**, 587, 9:170
 Abimelech and, 1:258
 Jotham son of Gideon, survival of, 11:465
 Judges, Book of, 11:564
 Midianites, 6:404
Gideon (Chayefsky), 4:585
Gideon, Miriam, 7:**588–589**
Gideon, Samson, 7:**589**
Gidonim, 1:222
Giehse, Threse, 7:**589**
Giessen (Germany), 7:**589**
Gifter, Mordecai, 7:**592**
Gift law, 5:138–139
Gifts, 7:**590–592**
 betrothal and, 3:539
 ones in, 15:428
Gikatilla, Isaac ibn, 7:**592–593**
Gikatilla, Joseph ben Abraham, 6:668, 7:**593–594**
Gikatilla, Moses ben Samuel ha-Kohen, 3:642, 7:**594–595**, 11:533
Gikow, Ruth, 7:**595**
Gilāan (Iran), 7:**596**
Giladi, Alex, 7:**595**
Giladi, Israel, 7:**595–596**, 11:731
Gilbert, Brad, 7:**596–597**
Gilbert, Felix, 7:**597**
Gilbert, Ina, 7:**597**
Gilbert, Martin. *See* Gilbert, Sir Martin
Gilbert, Melissa Ellen, 7:**597–598**
Gilbert, Milton, 7:**598**
Gilbert, Shlomo, 7:**598**
Gilbert, Sir Martin, 7:**597**
Gilbert, Walter, 4:593, 7:**598**, 13:9
Gilbert Crispin. *See* Crispin, Gilbert
Gilboa (Israel), 7:**598–599**
Gilboa, Amir, 7:**599**, 8:703, 705
Gilboa, Jacob, 7:**599**
Gilead (ancient Israel), 7:**600–601**, 10:129–130
 adoption, 1:416
 Elijah, 6:331

Gilead (ancient Israel), *continued*
  Jacob and Laban, 11:19
  regions, 11:6
Gilead, Dorothea. *See* Krook,
  Dorothea
Gilead, Zerubavel, 7:**601**
Gilels, Emil Grigoryevich, 7:**601**
Gilgal (ancient Israel), 7:**601–602**
Gilgamesh Epic, biblical flood and,
  7:81–83, 14:539
Gilgul, 7:**602–604**, 11:597
  Abraham bar Ḥiyya, 19:37
  Balbo, Michael ben Shabbetai
    Cohen, 3:84–85
  Bikayam, Meir ben Ḥalifa, 3:695
  dibbuk, 7:604
  Garden of Eden, 15:628–629
  Gehinnom, 6:501, 15:628–629
  Ibbur, 7:604
  Kabbalah, 11:655
  neoplatonism, 15:84
  punishment, 7:603
Giliyonot (Leibowitz), 12:**621–622**
Gilligan, Carol Friedman, 7:**604–605**
Gillman, Alfred, 13:10
Gillman, Neil, 7:**605**
Gillman, Sid, 7:**605**
Gillui arayot. *See* Sexual offenses
Gilman, Alfred G., 7:**605–606**, 13:10
Giluni. *See* Golan (ancient Israel)
Gilyonei ha-Shas (Joseph ben Judah
  Engel), 6:409
Gilyonot (Monthly), 7:**606**, 12:621–
  622
Gimbel, Adam, 7:606
Gimbel, Bruce A., 7:606
Gimbel, Isaac, 7:606
Gimbel family, 5:588, 7:**606**
Gimmel, 7:**606**
Ginaea. *See* En-Gannim (ancient
  Israel)
Gingold, Hermione, 7:**606–607**
Gingold, Pinchas M., 7:**607**
Giniewski, Paul, 7:**607**
Ginjalek. *See* Cranganore (India)
Ginnabris. *See* Sennabris (Galilee)
Ginnat Egoz (Gikatilla), 7:593
Ginnegar (Israel), 7:**607**
Ginnosar (Israel), 7:**607**
Ginnosar, plain of (Israel), 7:**607**
Ginnosar, Rosa, 7:**607–608**
Ginott, Haim G., 7:**608**
Ginsberg. *See* Guenzburg (East
  European family name)
Ginsberg, Allen, 7:**608–609**, 15:687
Ginsberg, Asher Hirsch. *See* Aḥad
  ha-Am

Ginsberg, Edward, 7:**609**
Ginsberg, Harold Lewis, 7:**609–610**
  English translations of Bible,
    3:621, 622
  Job, Book of, 11:343, 344, 346,
    351, 352, 353, 355
  Ugaritic language and biblical
    exegesis, 3:652
Ginsberg, Louis, 15:687
Ginsberg, Mitchell I., 7:**610**
Ginsberg, Morris, 5:302, 7:**610**, 18:731
Ginsburg, Christian David, 3:588,
  7:**610–611**
Ginsburg, David, 7:**611**
Ginsburg, Evgenia Semionova, 7:**611**
Ginsburg, Jacob Cohen, 4:25
Ginsburg, Jekuthiel, 7:**611**
Ginsburg, Norton Sidney, 7:**611**
Ginsburg, Ruth Joan Bader, 7:**611–
  612**, 12:556–557, 15:225
Ginsburg, Saul, 7:**612**
Ginsburg, Shimon. *See* Ginzburg,
  Simon
Ginsburger. *See* Guenzburg (East
  European family name)
Ginsburger, Ernest, 7:**612**
Ginzay, Amnon. *See* Gazov-Ginzberg,
  Anatolii
Ginzberg. *See* Guenzburg (East
  European family name)
Ginzberg, Eli, 7:**612–613**
Ginzberg, Louis, 2:47, 7:**613–614**
  aggadah, 1:460
  on Oral Law, 15:458
Ginzburg. *See* Guenzburg (East
  European family name)
Ginzburg, Ilya Yakovlevich. *See*
  Guenzburg, Ilya Yakovlevich
Ginzburg, Iser, 7:**614–615**
Ginzburg, Natalia, 7:**615**, 10:794
Ginzburg, Pesah, 7:**615**
Ginzburg, Simon, 7:**615**
Ginzburg, Vitaly Lazarevitch, 7:**615–
  616**
Ginzburg court appointment, 20:374–
  375
Ginzburger. *See* Guenzburg (East
  European family name)
Ginzei Qedem (periodical), 7:480
Ginzei Ẓiyyon vi-Yrushalayim (Badhav),
  3:49
Ginzell, F. K., 4:88
Giorgio, Francesco, 7:**616**, 12:601
Giovanni, Maria, 7:**616**
Giovanni Ambrogio. *See* Guglielmo
  Da Pesaro
Giovanni Maria Ciocchi del Monte.
  See Julius III

Gipstein, Yaacov. *See* Agam, Yaacov
Girgan. *See* Georgia (Transcaucasia)
Girgashites, 7:**616**
Girgasite, Land of. *See* Georgia
  (Transcaucasia)
Girgenti. *See* Agrigento
Girona (Spain). *See* Gerona (Spain)
Giroud, Françoise, 7:**616–617**
Giscala (ancient Israel), 7:**617**
Giselle (ballet, Eifman), 6:253
Giser, Moses David, 7:**617**
Gislebertus. *See* Crispin, Gilbert
Giso, Pino, 4:184
Gissin, Avshalom, 7:**617–618**
Giszkalay, János, 7:**618**
Gitai, Amos, 7:**618**
Giterman, Isaac, American Joint
  Distribution Committee, 2:61
Gitin, Seymour, 7:**618–619**
Gitlin, Jacob, 7:**619**
Gitlow, Benjamin, 7:**619**
Gittaim (ancient Israel), 7:**619–620**
Gittelsohn, Roland Bertram, 7:**620**
Gittin (tractate), 7:**620–621**
Gittleman, Len, 16:126
Giuliani, Rudolph, 3:782, 15:225
Giustiniani, Agostino, 7:**621–622**
Giustiniani, Marco Antonio, 7:**622**
Givat Ada (Israel), 7:**622**
Givatayim (Israel), 7:**622**
Givat Brenner (Israel), 7:**622**, 18:309
Givat ha-Sheloshah, 7:**622–623**
Givat Ḥavivah (Israel), 14:485
Givat Ḥayyim (Israel), 7:**623**
Givat Ḥen (Israel), 7:**623**
Givat Shemuel (Israel), 7:**623**
Givat Ze'ev (Israel), 7:**623**
"Givers of Smooth Interpretations".
  See Seekers after smooth things
Givet, Jacques, 7:**624**
Givins, Philip, 7:**623–624**, 16:341
Givton. *See* Gibbethon (ancient Israel)
Glaber, Raoul. *See* Raoul Glaber
Glaber, Rodulphus. *See* Raoul Glaber
Gladiator, 7:**624**
Gladstein, Moses, 6:62
Gladstone, Jacob. *See* Glatstein, Jacob
Glagau, Otto, 7:**624**
Glan, A. *See* Osherowitch, Mendl
Glanc, Levi Hirsch, 4:30
Glantz, Jacobo, 7:**624**
Glantz, Margo, 7:**624–625**
Glantz, Ya'akov. *See* Glantz, Jacobo
Glanville, Brian Lester, 6:438, 7:**625**
Glanz, A. *See* Glanz-Leyeles, Aaron

Glanz, Leib, 7:**625**
Glanz-Leyeles, Aaron, 4:6, 7:**625–626**
Glaphyra, 2:398, 7:**626**
Glasberg, Abraham, 4:199
Glaser, Daniel, 5:302
Glaser, Donald Arthur, 7:**626**
Glaser, Eduard, 7:**626**
Glaser, Joseph, 7:**626–627**
Glaser, Joshua. *See* Glaser, Julius
    Anton
Glaser, Julius Anton, 7:**627**, 12:549
Glasgow (Scotland), 7:**627–628**
Glasgow Hebrew College, 14:510
Glashow, Sheldon Lee, 7:**628**
Glasman, Baruch, 7:**628**
Glasner, Moses Samuel, 7:**628**
Glass, 7:**628–632**
    gold glass, 7:629–630
    Hellenistic and Roman, 7:629–630
    medieval to modern, 7:631–632
    third century to Arab conquest,
      7:630–631
Glass, Louis, 3:713
Glass, Montague Marsden, 7:**632**
Glass, Philip, 7:**632–633**
Glass Hat (Semel), 9:386
Glass manufacturing, 11:49
Glatstein, Jacob, 4:6, 7:**633–634**
Glatzer, Nahum Norbert, 4:125,
    7:**634–635**
Die Glaubens schwere Wege (Barasch),
    3:135
Glauber, Roy J., 7:**635**
Glazer, Nathan, 7:**635**, 18:733
Glazer, Simon, 7:**635–636**
Glaziers. *See* Glass
Glazman, B. *See* Glasman, Baruch
Glazman, Josef, 15:667
The Gleaner (periodical), 6:92
Gleb. *See* Mutnik, Abraham
Glebokie. *See* Glubokoye (Poland)
Glebovitch, M. *See* Osherowitch,
    Mendl
Glebovskoye podvorye inn (Moscow),
    14:517
Gleiwitz. *See* Gliwice
Gleizer, Jenny, 4:149
Glicenstein, Enrico, 7:**636**
Glicenstein, Henoch. *See* Glicenstein,
    Enrico
Glick, David, 7:**636**
Glick, Hirsch, 7:**637**
Glick, Irving Srul, 7:**637**
Glickman, Daniel Robert, 7:**637–638**
Glickman, Martin Irving, 7:**638**
Glickson, Moshe. *See* Gluecksohn,
    Moshe

Glid, Nandor, 7:**638**
*Gli ebreia Firenze nell' età del
    rinascimento* (Cassuto), 4:511
Glière, Reinhold Moritzevitch, 7:**638–
    639**
Gli Indifferenti (Moravia). *See The
    Time of Indifference* (Moravia)
Glikin, Moshe, 7:**639**
Gliksberg, Haim, Nikel, Lea, 15:265
Glinyani (Ukraine), 7:**639**
Gli occhiali d'oro (Bassani), 3:207
Gliwice (Poland), 7:**639–640**
Global warming, 5:169–170
Globes (newspaper), 7:**640**
Globke, Hans, Nuremberg laws,
    15:350
Globocnik, Odilo, 3:569, 7:**640**
Globus, Yoram, 7:**640–641**
Glock, Charles Y., 7:**641**
Glogau (Poland), 7:**641**, 18:578
Glogau, Jehiel Michael ben Asher
    Lemmel ha-Levi, 7:**641–642**
Glogau, Moses, 7:**642**
Glogauer, Israel. *See* Lovy, Israel
Glogó. *See* Glogau (Poland)
The Glory of Gershwin (Adler), 1:402
Glosk, Abraham Abba. *See* Glusk,
    Abraham Abba
Glossaries, biblical, 3:605–606, 628,
    12:406
Glosses
    Berlin, Isaiah ben Judah Loeb,
      3:457
    Blondheim, David Simon, 3:771,
      12:405
Glotz, Gustave, 7:**642**
Gloucester (England), 7:**642**
Glubokoye (Poland), 7:**642–643**
Gluck, Alma, 7:**643**
Gluck, Hannah, 7:**643**
Gluck, Louise, 7:**643**
Gluckman, Henry, 7:**643–644**, 16:349
Gluckman, Max, 2:186, 7:**644**
Glucksman, Harry L., 7:**644**
Gluckstein, Isidore, 7:**644**
Gluckstein, Samuel George. *See*
    Joseph, Samuel George
Gluckstein family, 7:**644**
Glueck, Abraham Isaac, 7:**644**
Glueck, Nelson, 2:371, 7:**644–645**,
    17:171
    biblical archaeology of, 3:650, 654
    Edom, 6:152, 153
Glueck, Sheldon, 5:301–302, 7:**645**
Glueckberg, Alexander Mikhailovich.
    See Cherny, Sasha
Glueckel of Hameln, 3:707, 708,
    7:**645–646**, 13:110–111

Gluecks, Richard, 7:**646**
Gluecksohn, Moshe, 7:**646**
Glueckstadt (Germany), 7:**646**
Glueckstadt, Isaac Hartvig, 7:**646–647**
Glueck-Touroff, Eleanor, 5:301–302,
    7:**645**
Der Gluehende (Mombert), 14:430
Glusberg, Samuel. *See* Espinoza,
    Enrique
Glusk, Abraham Abba, 7:**647**
Gluska, Zekharyah, 7:**647**
Gluskin, Ze'ev, 7:**647**
Gluskina, Gita, 11:323
Glussk (Russia), 7:**647**
Gnaeus Pompeius Magnus. *See*
    Pompey
Gnats, 7:**647–648**
Gnesen (Poland). *See* Gniezno
    (Poland)
Gnesin, Mikhail Fabianovitch, 7:**648**
Gnessin, Menahem, 7:**648**
Gnessin, Uri Nissan, 4:159, 6:24,
    7:**648–650**, 8:696
Gniezno (Poland), 7:**650**
Gnostic Christianity. *See* Gnosticism
Gnosticism, 7:**650–651**
    body and soul, concept of, 4:31
    dualism, 6:30
    Epistle of Barnabas on, 3:664
    Jonas, Hans, 11:393
    Joseph and Asenath, 11:418
    Kabbalah and, 11:590–591
    Nag Hammadi Codices, 14:728–
      729
Goa (India), 7:**651**, 9:796
Goats, 5:488, 492–493, 7:**651–652**
Gobineau, Joseph Arthur, Comte de,
    7:**652**
God, 7:**652–672**
    Abba, 1:224–225
    abbreviations for, 1:238
    Abraham, 1:284–285
    Academy on High, 1:353
    Adam, 1:371, 372
    Adam Kadmon, 1:378–379
    Adonai, Adonai, El Raḥum
      veḤannun, 1:412
    adoption, 1:417
    amulets, 2:121
    anthropomorphism regarding,
      11:516
    anthropomorphized, 15:738,
      16:83–84
    attributes of, 7:662–663, 666–669,
      11:578, 16:82–83, 85, 88, 92
    as basic principle of religion, 16:89
    biblical culture, 7:652–658
      creator, 7:653–654

God, *continued*

Genesis, 7:445–447

and history, 7:447–448

in history, 7:654–655

human relationship, 7:657–658, 663–664

lawgiver, 7:655–656

personality of, 7:657

self-limitation of, 7:656–657

suffering, 7:656

biblical literature, 3:290

cause and effect, 4:528–529

characteristics of, 11:514

conception of, 2:102–103, 5:274, 287

development of relationship with, 15:732–733

devotion to, 11:104

divine forgiveness, 7:128–129

divine presence, 16:481–484

divine providence of, 16:85, 89

dualism, 6:30–31

euphemisms for, 7:660

evil and nature of God, 11:243

existence of

Aaron ben Elijah, 1:213

Crescas, Ḥasdai, 16:89

Halevi, Judah, 16:83

Ibn Daud, Abraham, 16:84

Karaite, 16:79–80

Maimonides, 16:85

Mendelssohn, Moses, 14:34–35

Neoplatonic, 16:77, 81

Philo Judaeus, 16:75–76

Saadiah Gaon, 16:78–79

as father, 15:621

free will and, 10:824–825, 16:87, 89

as giver of freedom, 16:94–95

Godliness, Schulweis, Harold on, 18:174

Hellenistic culture, 7:658–660

Philo, 7:659–660

host of heaven, 2:150–151

as husband, 15:621–622

images of, Shi'ur Komah, 18:491

jealousy shown by, 11:98

justice and mercy of, 7:669, 11:578

Kabbalistic literature, 7:664–665

as king, 15:621–622

labor of, 12:408–409

Levi ben Gershom view, 12:699–700

location of worship of, 11:127

love of, 3:66–67

medieval Jewish philosophy, 7:661–664, 678

metaphoric marriage to, 11:126

modern Jewish Philosophy, 7:665–666, 668–669

monotheism, 14:448–450

Mukammis conception of, 14:608

names of, 2:139–140, 7:672–678

ba'al shem, 3:9

in Jonah (biblical book), 11:388

Kabbalah, 6:260–261

Moses, 14:524, 527

in Patriarch narratives, 15:691

Shekhinah, 18:440–444

nature of, Saadiah Gaon, 17:610

oneness of, Ḥasidic idea of, 8:408

parables about, 15:621–622

Pharisaic concept, 16:30–31

place of judgment of, 11:112

protocols of messengers of, 11:131

providence, Divine, 7:663–664

Rabbinical literature, 3:291–293

relationship with humans, 16:98, 104

self-limitation, 16:95

Talmudic literature, 7:660–661

terminology in Torah for, 15:735, 742, 743

theistic conceptions of, 7:669–672

theosophy, 11:587

trancendentalist philosophy of, 16:62–63

unity of, declaring, 18:453–456

wealth and closeness to, 11:42

God, Chariot of. *See* Throne of God

God, Man and History (Berkovits), 3:438–439

God, Throne of. *See* Throne of God

Godal, Eric, 7:**678**

Goddard, Paulette, 7:**678–679**

The Goddess Anath. See Ha-Elah Anat

Godefroi, Michael Henry, 2:112, 7:**679,** 12:552, 16:345

Goder Pereẓ (Norzi), 15:313

Godfather. *See* Sandak

God fearers, 11:293, 520

Godik, Giora, 7:**679**

Godiner, Samuel Nissan, 7:**679**

Godínez, Felipe, 7:**679–770,** 11:568

God in Search of Man (Heschel), 9:71

"Go Down Moses" (folk song), 14:543

Godowsky, Leopold, 7:**680,** 16:125

God rozhdeniya (Aliger), 1:659

Gods and goddesses. *See* Myths and mythology

God's Presence in History (Fackenheim), 9:393–395

Goebbels, Paul Josef, 7:**680**

Goeding (Czech Republic). *See* Hodonin (Czech Republic)

Goering, Hermann Wilhelm, 2:665, 7:**680–681**

Goeritz, Mathias, 7:**681**

Goerlitz (Germany), 7:**681**

Goetel, Ferdynand, 9:354–355

Goeth, Amon, 16:226

Goethe, Johann Wolfgang von, 7:**681–682**

Goethe Medal, Blumenthal, Werner Michael, 4:13

Goetschel, Jules, 7:**682**

Goettingen (Germany), 7:**682**

Goetze, A., 8:621, 622

Goffman, Erving Manual, 7:**682–683,** 18:732

Gofnah (ancient Israel), 7:**683**

Gog, J.L. *See* Ginsburg, Jekuthiel

Gog and Magog, 6:640, 7:**683–684**

Goi. *See* Gentiles

Goido, Isaac. *See* Gorin, Bernard

Goiim, 7:**684**

Goitein, Baruch Benedict, 7:**684**

Goitein, Fritz. *See* Goitein, Shlomo Dov

Goitein, Shlomo Dov, 7:**685–686,** 9:160

Golah. *See* Galut

Golan (ancient Israel), 7:**686,** 10:130

Golan, Menahem, 7:**686–687**

Golan Heights. *See* Ramat ha-Golan (Israel)

Golani Brigade, Amit, Meir, 2:80

Golant, Yevgeni Y., 6:161

Golavski, Ḥayyim, 6:22

Golb, Norman, 7:**687**

Golcuv Jenikov (Czech Republic), 7:**687**

Gold, 1:596, 14:124–125, 127, 15:439

Gold, Benjamin, 7:**687–688**

Gold, Henry Raphael, 7:**688**

Gold, Herbert, 7:**688**

Gold, Hugo, 7:**688**

Gold, Michael, 7:**688–689**

Gold, Philip, 7:**689**

Gold, Wolf, 7:**689,** 18:211

Gold, Ze'ev. *See* Gold, Wolf

Goldbeck, Edward, 1:224

Goldbeck, Eva, 1:224

Goldberg, Aaron, 16:124

Goldberg, Abraham, 7:**689–690**

Goldberg, Alexander, 7:**690**

Goldberg, Arthur Joseph, 4:174, 7:**690,** 12:556

Goldberg, Baer ben Alexander, 7:**690–691**

Goldberg, Ben Zion, 7:**691**

Goldberg, Bertrand, 7:**691**

Goldberg, Boris, 7:**691–692**

Goldberg, Dov ben Alexander. *See* Goldberg, Baer ben Alexander

Goldberg, Emanuel, 7:**692**, 16:138

Goldberg, Gumpertz, 14:454

Goldberg, Harvey E., 7:**692**

Goldberg, Helena, 14:454

Goldberg, Isaac, 7:**692**, 8:740

Goldberg, Isaac Leib, 7:**692–693**

Goldberg, Isaiah-Nissan Hakohen. *See* Yaknehaz

Goldberg, J. B., 7:**693**

Goldberg, Jeanette Miriam, 7:**693**

Goldberg, Lea, 7:**693–695**, 8:698, 721

Goldberg, Manehem. *See* Boraisha, Menahem

Goldberg, Marshall, 7:**695**

Goldberg, Menahem. *See* Boraisha, Menahem

Goldberg, Milton M. *See* Gordon, Milton M.

Goldberg, N., parodies of, 15:659

Goldberg, Oscar, 7:**695–696**

Goldberg, Rube, 7:**696**

Goldberg, Sylvie Anne, 11:325–326

Goldberg, Szymon, 7:**696**

Goldberger, Izidor, 7:**696–697**

Goldberger, Joseph, 7:**697**

Goldblatt, David, 6:399

Goldbloom, Alton, 7:**697**

Goldbloom, Jacob Koppel, 7:**697**

Goldbloom, Michael, 11:470

Goldbloom, Richard, 7:**697**

Goldbloom, Victor Charles, 7:**697**

Goldbloom family, 7:**697**

Goldblum, Israel Isser, 7:**697**

Goldblum, Jeff, 7:**697–698**

Goldblum, Michael. *See* Ben-Zvi, Shlomo

Goldblum, Natan, 7:**698**

Goldbogen, Avrom Hirsch. *See* Todd, Mike

Goldemberg, Isaac, 7:**698**

Golden, Harry Lewis, 4:579, 7:**698**, 11:468, 15:303

Golden, John, 7:**698–699**

Goldenberg, Baerish, 7:**699**

Goldenberg, Charles Robert, 7:**699**

Goldenberg, David, 6:25

Goldenberg, Emanuel. *See* Robinson, Edward G.

Goldenberg, Lazar, 18:704

Goldenberg, Leo. *See* Hamon, Leo

Goldenberg, Samuel, 7:**699–700**

Goldenberg, Samuel Leib, 7:**699**

Goldenberg-Getroitman, Lazar, 7:**699**

Golden Calf, 6:618, 622, 7:**700–701**

    Aaron and, 1:209, 210

    Aaronides and, 1:218

    Jeroboam I and, 11:140–141

    Moses, 14:525, 527, 528, 530, 535–536

Goldene Keyt, Di (Quarterly), 7:**701–702**

Golden Haggadah, 8:213

Goldenson, Samuel Harry, 7:**702**

Goldenthal, Jacob, 4:199, 7:**702**

Goldenweiser, Alexander Alexandrovich, 2:186, 7:**702**, 12:554

Goldenweiser, Emanuel Alexandrovich, 7:**702–703**

Goldfaden, Abraham, 4:194, 195, 7:**703–704**

Goldfaden era, the, 19:678–679

Goldfarb, Israel, 7:**704–705**

Goldfeder, Fishel, 7:**705**

Goldfish, Samuel. *See* Goldwyn, Samuel

Goldflam, Arnošt, 7:**705**

Goldfodem, Avrom. *See* Goldfaden, Abraham

Goldfogle, Henry M., 15:211

Gold glass, 7:**629–630**

Goldhagen, Daniel Jonah, 4:217

Goldhammer-Sahawi, Leo, 7:**705–706**

Goldhar, Pinchas, 7:**706**

Goldhurst, Herschel. *See* Golden, Harry Lewis

Goldin, Daniel Saul, 7:**706–707**

Goldin, Ezra, 7:**707**

Goldin, Harrison J., 15:224

Goldin, Hyman Elias, 7:**707**

Goldin, Jay. *See* Goldin, Harrison J.

Goldin, Judah, 7:**707**

Goldin, Nan, 7:**707–708**

Golding, Louis, 7:**708**

Goldkorn, George, 15:650

Goldman, Aharon HaLevi, 7:**709**

Goldman, Anita, 18:94

Goldman, Bernard, 7:**709**, 16:347

Goldman, Charles, 6:450

Goldman, Edwin Franco, 7:**709**

Goldman, Eliezer, 7:**709–711**, 8:375

Goldman, Emma, 7:**711**, 18:710

Goldman, Eric Frederick, 7:**711–712**

Goldman, Frank, 4:16

Goldman, Hetty, 2:370, 7:**712**

Goldman, Israel, 7:**712**

Goldman, Joel, 6:450

Goldman, Marcus, 7:**708**

Goldman, Martin Jacob, 7:**712**

Goldman, Max. *See* Reinhardt, Max

Goldman, Mayer Clarence, 7:**713**

Goldman, Michael. *See* Liber, Marc

Goldman, Moises, 7:**713**

Goldman, Mordecai. *See* Goldman, Martin Jacob

Goldman, Moses ha-Kohen, 7:**713**

Goldman, Paul L., 7:**713**

Goldman, Peirre, 7:248

Goldman, Ralph J., American Joint Distribution Committee, 2:62

Goldman, Solomon, 7:**713–714**, 11:330

Goldman, William, 7:**714**

Goldman, Ya'akov ben Asher, 7:**714**

Goldman family, 7:**708–709**

Goldmann, Isaac, 6:399

Goldmann, Lucien, 7:**714**

Goldmann, Max. *See* Reinhardt, Max

Goldmann, Nahum, 6:400, 7:**714–716**

Goldmann, Sidney, 7:**716**

Goldmark, Joseph, 7:**716**, 16:340

Goldmark, Karl, 7:**717**, 18:762

Goldmark, Pauline, 7:**716**

Goldmark, Peter Carl, 7:**717**

Goldmark, Rubin, 7:**716–717**

Goldmark family, 7:**716–717**

The Gold-Rimmed Spectacles. See Gli occhiali d'oro

Goldring/Woldenberg Institute Southern Jewish Life. *See* Institute of Southern Jewish Life, Goldring/Woldenberg

Gold Rush of 1849

    Jewish immigration to California, 13:195

    Jewish immigration to U.S., 2:43

Goldscheid, Rudolf, 7:**717**, 18:731

Goldschmidt, Adolf, 2:525

Goldschmidt, D., 13:133

Goldschmidt, Ernst Daniel, 7:**717**

Goldschmidt, Guido, 7:**717**

Goldschmidt, Hans, 7:**718**

Goldschmidt, Heinrich Jacob, 7:**718**

Goldschmidt, Henriette, 7:**718**

Goldschmidt, Hermann, 7:**718**

Goldschmidt, Hugo, 7:**718**

Goldschmidt, Jakob, 7:**718–719**

Goldschmidt, Johanna Schwabe, 7:**719**

Goldschmidt, Lazarus, 7:**719**

    forgeries, 7:126

    German translation of Bible by, 3:631

Goldschmidt, Levin, 12:551

Goldschmidt, Meir Aron, 7:**719–720**

Goldschmidt, Neal Edward, 7:**720**

Goldschmidt, Richard Benedict, 7:**720**

Goldschmidt, Richard Hellmuth, 7:**720–721**

Goldschmidt, Victor, 7:**721**

Goldschmidt, Victor Moritz, 7:**721**

Goldschmidt family, 3:724–725, 9:77

Goldschneider, Calvin, 18:732

Goldsmid, Aaron, 7:**721**

Goldsmid, Abraham, 4:117, 7:**721**

Goldsmid, Albert Edward Williamson, 7:**723**

Goldsmid, Benjamin, 7:**721**

Goldsmid, Henry d'Avigdor, 16:342

Goldsmid, Isaac Lyon, 7:**721**

Goldsmid, Julian, 16:342

Goldsmid, Sir Francis, 16:342

Goldsmid, Sir Frederick, 16:342

Goldsmid family, 4:181, 7:**721–723**, 722t

Goldsmid-Stern-Salomons, David Lionel. *See* Goldsmid-Stern-Salomons, Sir David Lionel

Goldsmid-Stern-Salomons, Sir David Lionel, 7:**723**

Goldsmith, Horace Ward, 7:**723**

Goldsmith, Jacob, 15:464

Goldsmith, Lewis, 7:**723–724**, 11:467

Goldsmith, Raymond William, 7:**724**

Goldsmith, Samuel Abraham, 7:**724**

Goldsmith, Dayyan E., 15:639

Goldsmith Memorial Library (Kansas), 11:767

Goldsmiths and silversmiths, 7:**724–727**

Gold standard, 5:52

Goldstein, Abraham Samuel, 7:**727**

Goldstein, Alexander, 7:**727**

Goldstein, Angelo, 7:**727**

Goldstein, Baruch, 10:245

Goldstein, Elyse, 7:**727–728**

Goldstein, Ephraim. *See* Di-Zahav, Ephraim

Goldstein, Eugen, 7:**728**

Goldstein, Fanny, 7:**728**

Goldstein, Herbert S., 7:**728–729**

Goldstein, Isaac, 18:746

Goldstein, Isidore. *See* Isou, Isidore

Goldstein, Israel, 7:**729**

Goldstein, Jennie, 7:**729**

Goldstein, Josef, 7:**729**

Goldstein, Joseph, 14:446

Goldstein, Joseph Leonard, 4:215–216, 7:**729–730**, 13:10

Goldstein, Judah Jamison, 7:**730**

Goldstein, Julius, 7:**730**

Goldstein, Kurt, 7:**730–731**

Goldstein, Leopold. *See* Baltazar, Camil

Goldstein, Mateo, 12:555

Goldstein, Moritz, 7:**731**

Goldstein, Raymond, 7:**731**

Goldstein, Rebecca, 7:**731**

Goldstein, Richard Frank, 7:**731–732**

Goldstein, Richard Joseph, 7:**732–733**

Goldstein, Robert J., 6:452–453

Goldstein, Ruby, 7:**732**

Goldstein, Salwian, 7:**732**

Goldstein, Sholem. *See* Goldenberg, Samuel

Goldstein, Sidney, 7:**732**, 18:732

Goldstein, Sidney Emanuel, 7:**732**

Goldstein, W., 11:378

Goldsteucker, Eduard, 7:**733**

Goldstick, Hyman, 6:150

Goldszmidt, Henryk. *See* Korczak, Janusz

Goldszmit, Henryk. *See* Korczak, Janusz

Goldwasser, I. *See* Emiot, Israel

Goldwasser, Israel Edwin, 7:**733**

Goldwater, Barry M., 7:**734**

Goldwater, John L., 7:**734**

Goldwater, Joseph, 7:**733–734**

Goldwater, Michael, 7:**733–734**

Goldwater, Sigmund Schulz, 7:**734**

Goldwater family, 7:**733–734**

Goldwyn, Samuel, 7:**734–735**, 14:571

Goldziher, Ignaz, 7:**735**, 11:539, 542

Goldziher, Isaac Judah. *See* Goldziher, Ignaz

Golem, 1:287–288, 2:579, 7:**735–738**, 18:199, 200–201

Golem, 12:630

Golf, 1:605, 19:142

Goliath, 6:226, 315, 7:**738–739**

Goliger, Silviu. *See* Silviu, George

Golinkin, David, 7:**739**

Golinkin, Mordecai, 7:**739–740**

Golinkin, Mordecai Ya'akov, 7:**740**

Golinkin, Noah, 5:175, 7:**740–741**

Golitsyn, A., on blood libel, 3:779

Golitsyn, Count Nikolai Nikolayevich, 7:**741**

Golke, Elfriede. *See* Fischer, Ruth

Goll, Claire, 7:**741–742**

Goll, Yvan, 7:**742**

Gollancz, Hermann. *See* Gollancz, Sir Hermann

Gollancz, Israel. *See* Gollancz, Sir Israel

Gollancz, Sir Hermann, 7:**742**

Gollancz, Sir Israel, 7:**743**

Gollancz, Sir Victor, 7:**743**

Gollancz, Victor. *See* Gollancz, Sir Victor

Goller, Izak, 7:**743**

Golluf, Eleazar, 7:**743–744**

Goloboff, Gerardo Mario, 7:**744**

Golodny, Mikhail, 7:**744**

Golomb, Abraham, 7:**744**

Golomb, Eliyahu, 7:**744–745**

Golombek, Harry, 7:**745**

Golovanevsk (Ukraine), 7:**745**, 18:263

Golphon, Joseph ben Mako, early printed editions of Hebrew Bible, 3:587

Golschmann, Vladimir, 7:**745–746**

Goltsch-Jenikau. *See* Golcuv Jenikov

Golub, Leon, 7:**746**

Goluchowski, Agenor Sen., Count, 7:**746**

Goluchowski, Agenor von, Count, 9:65–66

Gomberg, Moses, 7:**746**

Gombin. *See* Gabin

Gombiner, Abraham Abele ben Ḥayyim ha-Levi, 7:**746–747**

Gombrich, Ernst Hans. *See* Gombrich, Sir Ernst Hans

Gombrich, Sir Ernst Hans, 7:**747**

Gomel (Russia), 7:**747–748**

Gomel blessing, 7:**748**

Gomelsky, Alexander Yankelovich, 7:**748**

Gomer (biblical figure), 7:**748**

Gomer (biblical nation), 7:**748**

Gomer (daughter of Diblaim). *See* Hosea

Gomez, Benjamin, 15:199

Gomez, Daniel, 15:196

Gomez, Lewis Moses, 7:**748–749**

Gomez, Louis Moses, 5:329–330

Gómez, Mari, 4:645

Gomez, Mordecai, 15:196

Gómez de Sossa, Isaac, 7:**749**

Gomez family, 7:**748–749**

Gomez Mill House (Newburgh, NY), 5:329–330

Gomorrah. *See* Sodom and Gomorrah (ancient cities)

Gompel, Solomon ben Mordecai, 7:**750**

Gompers, Samuel, 7:**749–750**, 12:411, 18:708

Gomperts. *See* Gomperz family

Gompertz, Benjamin, 7:**750**

Gompertz, Ephraim, 7:**750**

Gompertz, Isaac, 7:**750**

Gompertz, Joseph, 7:**750**

Gompertz, Lewis, 7:750

Gompertz family, 7:**750**

Gomperz, Benedict Reuben. *See* Wesel, Baruch Bendet ben Reuben

Gomperz, Julius von, 14:475

Gomperz, Moses Levi, 7:750–751

Gomperz, Reuben Elias, 7:750

Gomperz, Salomon Emmerich, 7:751

Gomperz, Theodor, 7:**752**

Gomperz family, 7:**750–751**, 751*t*

Gone: The Last Days of the New Yorker (Adler), 1:406

Gonen, Shmuel, 8:722

Gonzague, Hyacinthe de. *See* Deutz, Simon

Goodall, Charles, 15:398

Good and evil, 7:**752–754**

   Aaron ben Elijah on, 1:213

   demons and demonology, 5:572–578

   dualism, 6:29–31

   Edwards, Paul, 6:215

   Ḥasidei Ashkenaz, 8:388

   See also Evil

Goodblat, Morris, 7:**754–755**

Goodbye, Children, 9:443

Goodbye, My Fancy (Kanin), 11:763

The Goodbye Girl, 6:21

Goodenough, Erwin Ramsdell, 7:**755**, 11:589

Good Faith principle, 5:196–197

Goodfriend, Isaac, 2:637

Goodhart, Arthur Lehman, 7:**755–756**

Good Jew of Gostynin. *See* Jehiel Meir of Gostynin

Goodman, Abraham Vossen, American Jewish Historical Society, 2:59

Goodman, Allegra, 7:**756**

Goodman, Andrew, 7:**756**, 15:215

Goodman, Arnold Abraham, Lord, 7:**756–757**

Goodman, Benny, 7:**757**, 15:220

Goodman, Martin David, 7:**757**

Goodman, Nelson, 7:**757**

Goodman, Paul, 18:709

Goodman, Paul (Author), 7:**758**

Goodman, Paul (Zionist), 7:**757–758**

Goodman, Percival, 7:**758**

Goodman, Theodosia. *See* Bara, Theda

Goodman, Tobias, 7:**758–759**

Good Old Israel (music album), 6:263

Goodrich, Frances, 7:**759**

Good Samaritan Law of 1998, 14:360

The Good Soldier Schweik (Hašek), 4:193

Google, 4:183

Goor, Yehudah, 7:**759**

Goose, 7:**759**

Gophna. *See* Gofnah (ancient Israel)

Gophna, Ram, 7:**760**

Gora Kalwaria (Poland), 7:**760–761**

Goral. *See* Lots

Gorban, Motta. *See* Gur, Mordecai

Gorcey, Bernard, 7:**761–762**

Gorcey, Leo, 7:**761–762**

Gordimer, Nadine, 7:**762**

Gordin, Abba, 7:**762**

Gordin, Jacob (1853-1909), 1:393, 3:739, 7:**763–764**, 18:370, 19:679–680

Gordin, Jacob (1897-1947), 7:**764**

Gordis, Robert, 7:**764**, 11:343, 353

Gordon, Abraham, 7:**764–765**

Gordon, Aharon David, 4:279, 7:**765–766**, 9:247, 15:35

Gordon, Albert I., 7:**766–767**

Gordon, Cyrus Herzl, 7:**767**

Gordon, David, 7:**767**, 8:293

Gordon, Eliezer, 7:**767–768**, 11:715

Gordon, George. *See* Byron, George Gordon, Lord

Gordon, George Lord, 7:**768**

Gordon, Harold, 7:**768**

Gordon, Jacob (1877-1934), 7:**768–769**

Gordon, Jacob (1902-1943), 7:**769**

Gordon, Jekuthiel ben Leib, 7:**769**

Gordon, Judah Leib, 4:119, 6:669, 7:**769–772**, 8:442, 690, 726

   Jerusalem in writings, 11:216

   in Panevezys, 15:611

   parodies, 15:659

   Shalom Aleichem and, 18:381

Gordon, Max, 7:**772–773**

Gordon, Michael, 7:**773**

Gordon, Mikhl, 7:**773**

Gordon, Milton, 18:733

Gordon, Milton M., 7:**773**

Gordon, Nathan, 7:**773–774**

Gordon, Phil, 16:124

Gordon, Samuel, 7:**774**

Gordon, Samuel Leib, 6:183, 7:**774**

Gordon, Shmuel, 7:**774**

Gordon, Sid, 7:**774–775**

Gordon, Willy, 7:**775**

Gordonia, 7:**775–776**

Gore, Al, 12:805

Gorelik, Shemarya, 7:**776**

Goren, Charles Henry, 4:467, 7:**776–777**

Goren, Natan, 7:**777**

Goren, Shlomo, 7:**777–778**

Gorgias, 7:**778**

Gorin, Bernard, 7:**778**

Gorizia (Italy), 7:**778–779**

Gorki (Russia), 7:**779**

Gorki, Maxim, 7:**779–780**

   antisemitism, 5:93

   on Bellis blood libel case, 3:779

Gorky, Maxim. *See* Gorki, Maxim

Gorky's Childhood. See Detstvo Gor'kogo

Gorlice (Poland), 7:**780**

Gorlin, Alexander, 7:**780–781**

Gorme, Eydie, 12:**545–546**

Gorni, 7:**781**

Gornick, Vivian, 7:**781**

Goro, Fritz, 16:126

Gorochov, Yedidyah. *See* Admon, Yedidyah

Gorodenka (Ukraine), 7:**781–782**

Gorodok (Molodechno district, Belarus), 7:**783**

Gorodok (Ukraine), 7:**782**

Gorodok (Vitebsk district, Belarus), 7:**783**

Gorodok dynasty Hasidism, 5:473

Gorokhovskaya, Maria, 7:**783**

Goron, Land of. *See* Georgia (Transcaucasia)

Gorshman, Shira, 7:**783**

Górska, Halina, 7:**783**

Gorzow Wielkopolski (Poland), 7:**783–784**

Goshen (Ancient Egypt), 8:5, 9:166

Goshen-Gottstein, Moshe, 8:5

Goslar (Germany), 8:**5–6**

Goslar, Hans, 8:6

Goslar, Naphtali Hirsch ben Jacob, 8:6

Göslöw. *See* Yevpatoriya (Ukraine)

Gospel of John, logos, 13:175

Gospels, 15:190, 191

   Jesus in, 11:246–249

   Sanhedrin in, 18:22

   See also New Testament

Gossip, slander, 17:324–325

Gostynin (Poland), 8:**6–7**

Gota, Moses Zerahiah ben Shneur, 8:7

Gotbaum, Victor, 15:224

Göteborg (Sweden), 8:7

Got Fun Nekome (Asch), 12:660–661

Gotha (Germany), 8:7

Gotlieb, Allan, 8:**7–8**

Gots, Abram Rafailovich, 8:8

Gots, Mikhail Rafailovich, 8:8, 16:348

Gots family, 8:8

Gotsfeld, Bessie, 2:80, 8:**8–9**

Gotsiridze, Manana, 11:322

Der Gott der Vaeter (Alt), 2:11

Die Gottesdienstlichen Vortraege der Juden (Zunz), 1:460, 462
Gottesfeld, Chone, 8:**9**
Gottesman, Benjamin, 8:9
Gottesman, David Samuel, 8:9
Gottesman, Mendel, 8:9
Gottesman family, 8:**9**
Gottheil, Gustav, 6:242–243, 8:**9**
Gottheil, Richard James Horatio, 8:**9–10**
Gotti, John, 5:345
Gottlieb, Adolph, 8:**10**
Gottlieb, Allan. *See* Gotlieb, Allan
Gottlieb, Bernhard, 8:**10**
Gottlieb, Edward, 8:**10–11**
Gottlieb, Ephraim, 8:**11**
Gottlieb, František, 8:**11–12**
Gottlieb, Heinrich, 8:**12**
Gottlieb, Hinko, 8:**12**
Gottlieb, Hirsch Leib, 8:**12**
Gottlieb, Jacob, 8:**12**
Gottlieb, Jedidiah ben Israel, 8:**12–13**
Gottlieb, Leopold, 15:649
Gottlieb, Malke, 14:396
Gottlieb, Maurycy, 8:**13**, 15:649
Gottlieb, Yankev. *See* Gottlieb, Jacob
Gottlieb, Yehoshua, 8:**13**
Gottlober, Abraham Baer, 1:319, 8:**13–14**, 416
Gottlober, Avraham-Ber. *See* Gottlober, Abraham Baer
Gottschalk, Alfred, 8:**14–15**
Gottschalk, Louis Moreau, 8:**15**
Gottschalk, Louis Reichenthal, 8:**15–16**
Gottschalk, Marius, 15:397
Gottschalk, Max, 8:**16**
Gottschalk of Bacharach, 3:31–32
Gottschall, Morton, 8:**16**
Gottstein, Jacob, 1:577
Gottwald, Norman, sociology of Bible and, 3:659
Goudchaux, Michel, 8:**16**, 16:343
Goudeket, Maurits, 2:117, 8:**16–17**
Goudsmit, Joel Emanuel, 8:**17**, 12:552
Gougenot Des Mousseaux, Henri, 8:**17**
Gould, Barbara, Ayrton, 16:342
Gould, Elliott, 8:**17**
Gould, Milton S., 8:**17–18**
Gould, Morton, 8:**18**
Gould, Samuel Brookner, 8:**18**
Gould, Stephen Jay, 8:**18–19**
Göndör, Ferenc, 7:**752**
Gourary, Moishe. *See* Gray, Morris Abraham
Gourd, 8:**19**, vol. 16: color insert
Gouri, Haim, 8:**19–20**, 703, 704

The Governance of England (Low), 13:232
Government, prayer for the, 8:**20–21**
The Governor of Jericho. See Moshel Yeriho
Goy. *See* Gentiles
Goyim. *See* Goiim
Goyrl (Bursztyn), 4:203
Gozan (ancient city), 8:21
Gozhansky, Samuel, 8:**21**, 18:714
Gozlan, Elie, 8:**21–22**
Grabski, Stanislaw, 8:22
Grabski, Wladyslaw, 8:22
Grace. *See* Love
Grace after meals, 8:**22–23**
   five species, 7:66
   Shir ha-Ma'alot, 18:489
Grace and law, 4:683
Grace before meals, 8:24
Gracian, Shealtiel ben Soloman, 8:24
Grade, Chaim, 8:**24–25**
Grade, Lew, Baron, 8:**25**
Graded numbers, 15:337
Gradenwitz, Peter Emanuel, 8:**25**
Gradis, David, 4:82, 83
Gradis family, 8:**25–26**
Gradner, Yisroel, 4:195
The Graduate, 9:307
Grady, T., 15:586
Graebe, Hermann Friedrich, 8:**26**, 9:335
Graeber, Schealtiel Eisik, 8:**26**
Graeco-Roman period
   Diaspora, 17:722–723
   laws, antichresis, 2:193
   See also Greece; Roman Empire
Graes, Ortwln Van De, 8:**26**
Graetz. *See* Grodzisk Wielkopolski (Poland)
Graetz, Heinrich, 8:**26–29**
   Judaism, essential principles of, 11:512
   modern biblical exegesis by, 3:646
   on Oral Law, 15:457
   piyyut, language of, 8:652
   Silesia, 18:579
Graetz, Hirsch. *See* Graetz, Heinrich
Graetz Theory of Diacriticals, 13:622–623
Graf, Herbert, 8:**29**
Graf, Karl Heinrich, 8:**29**, 16:630
Graf, Moses ben Menahem. *See* Moses ben Menahem Graf
Graffman, Gary, 8:**29**
Grafman, Milton, 3:713
Grafstein, Jerahmiel S., 8:**29**

Grafstein, Jerry. *See* Grafstein, Jerahmiel S.
Graham, Bill, 8:**30**
Graham, Martha, 3:214, 5:414, 12:479, 695
Grain. *See* Five species
Le grain de sable (Bacri), 3:42
Grajewo (Poland), 8:**30**
Grajewski, Aryeh Leib, 8:**30–31**
Grajewski, Eliezer Zalman, 8:**31**
Grajewsky, Pinchas, 8:**31**
Grajonca, Wolfgang. *See* Graham, Bill
Grajonca, Wulf Woloodia. *See* Graham, Bill
Grammar, 4:664
   Rashi, 17:103–104
   Reicherson, Moses, 17:199
Grammar, Hebrew. *See* Hebrew grammar
Grammarians
   Balmes, Abraham ben Meir de, 3:94
   Benevento, Immanuel ben Jekuthiel, 3:341
   Benveniste, Emile, 3:382
   Benveniste, Joshua Raphael Ben Israel, 3:384
   Ben Ze'ev, Judah Leib, 3:390
   Berechiah Berakh ben Eliakim Getzel, 3:406–407
   Censorinus, 4:539
   Duran, Profiat, 6:56–57
   Hanau, Solomon Zalman ben Judah Loeb ha-Kohen, 8:318
   Hayyuj, Judah ben David, 8:484
   Heidenheim, Wolf, 8:763
   Ibn Altabban, Levi ben Jacob, 9:659–660
   Ibn Bal'am, Judah ben Samuel, 9:658–659, 660
   Ibn Danan, Saadiah ben Maimun, 9:662
   Ibn Habib, Moses ben Shem Tov, 9:678–679
   Ibn Janāh, Jonah, 9:680–683
   Ibn Kapron, Isaac, 9:684–685
   Ibn Mar Saul, Isaac ben Levi, 9:685–686
   Ibn Quraysh, Judah, 9:688
   Ibn Shoshan family, 9:693
   Ibn Yahya, David ben Joseph, 9:697
   Ibn Yahya, David ben Solomon, 9:697
   Ibn Yashush, Isaac Abu Ibrahim, 9:699
   Kimhi, Moses, 12:158
   Shapiro, Aryeh Leib ben Isaac, 18:404

Grammar of Mishnaic Hebrew (Segal), 14:330

A Grammar of Politics (Laski), 12:499

Grammatik der aethiopischen Sprache (Dillmann), 5:661–662

Gran. *See* Esztergom (Hungary)

Grana. *See* Gorni

Granach, Alexander, 8:**31**

Granada (Spain), 8:**32**
    Abraham ben Isaac of, 1:301–302
    Arabic officials, 11:111

Granada, Gabriel De, 8:**32–33**

Granat, Joseph. *See* Rimon, Joseph Ẓevi

Granat, Joseph Ẓevi. *See* Rimon, Joseph Ẓevi

Grande, Benzion Moiseevich, 8:**33**

Grand Hotel. See Menschen im Hotel

Granditsky, Palle, 8:**33**

Grand Jury: An Institution on Trial (Frankel), 7:197

Grandma Sultana's Salty Biscuits (Seri). *See Ugiyot ha-Melah shel Savta Sultana* (Seri)

Grandparents' roles, 6:703–704

Grand to Be an Orphan (Slonim), 18:678

Grandval, Gilbert Yves Edmond, 8:**33**

Granice nauki (Chwistek), 4:724

Granich, Irwin. *See* Gold, Michael

Granin, Daniel Aleksandrovich, 8:**33**

Granott, Abraham, 8:**33**

Granovsky, Abraham. *See* Granott, Abraham

Granovsky, Alexander, 8:**33–34**

Grant, Baron Albert, 8:**34**

Grant, Lee, 8:**34**

Grant, Robert, 6:377

Grant, Ulysses Simpson, 8:**34–35**
    Board of Delegates of American Israelites, 4:19
    Browne, Edward B. M., 4:216

Granz, Norman, 8:**35**

Grapefruit, 4:737

Grapes. *See* Vines

Grapes of Wrath operation, 10:247–248

Grapheus, Benvenutus, 13:727

Graphic novels. *See* Cartoonists and cartoons

Graphic Storytelling (Eisner), 6:278

Grasovski, Yehudah. *See* Goor, Yehudah

Grass, Alex, 8:366

Grasshopper, 8:**35–36**

Gratian, 8:**36**

Gratianus, Franciscus. *See* Gratian

Gratius, Ortwln Van De. *See* Graes, Ortwln Van De

Grattenauer, Karl Wilhelm Friedrich, 8:**36**

Gratuity. *See* Ha'anakah

Gratz, Hyman, 8:37

Gratz, Jacob, 8:37

Gratz, Rebecca, 6:190, 191, 8:**37–38**, 21:183

Gratz College (U.S.), 2:104, 6:193, 8:**38–39**

Gratz family, 2:53, 8:**36–37**, 37t

Graubard, Moritz, 15:211

Graubart, Judah Leib. *See* Graubart, Y.L.

Graubart, Y.L., 8:**39**

Graumann, Harry. *See* Graumann, Sir Harry

Graumann, Sir Harry, 8:**39**, 11:377

Graur, Alexandru, 8:**39–40**

Graur, Constantin, 8:40

Gravenhage. *See* Hague, The

Graves, Philip, 6:297

Gravity (Serra), 18:314

Gray, Herb. *See* Gray, Herbert Eser

Gray, Herbert Eser, 8:**40**, 16:341

Gray, Martin, 8:**40–41**

Gray, Morris Abraham, 8:**41**

Gray, Naomi Ellington. *See* Jacob, Naomi Ellington

Grayzel, Solomon, 8:**41**

Graz (Austria), 8:**41–42**

Grazer, Brian, 8:**42**

Graziadio, 4:77

Graziani, Yitzhak, 8:**42**

Graziano, Abraham Joseph Solomon ben Mordecai, 8:**42–43**

Grazing rights, 5:167

Great Academy. *See* Sanhedrin (judicial body)

Great arenda. *See* Arenda

Great Assembly. *See* Synagogue, The Great

The Great Baba. *See* Baba Rabbah

The Great Betrayal. See La trahison des cle

Great Books of the Western World (Adler), 1:403

Great Britain. *See* United Kingdom

Great Debate. *See* Vikkuḥa Rabbah

Great Depression
    art and artists, 2:514
    New York City and, 15:214, 216, 221

Great Fire of 1871, 4:608

Great Greek Encyclopaedia (encyclopedia), 6:355–356

Great Hallel, 8:280

Great Poland (historical entity), 8:**43–44**

Great Sanhedrin. *See* Sanhedrin

The Great Seder Olam. See Seder Olam

"Great Society" programs, 11:385

Great Synagogue (London), 18:129

Great Synagogue (Moscow), 18:143

Great Synagogue, men of, 8:254

Grebniov, Leonid. *See* Feinberg, Leon

Greco-Roman period. *See* Graeco-Roman period

Greece, 8:**44–57**, 46
    ancient
        dramatists, 6:649
        European settlement by Jews, 6:554
    antisemitism, Chalcis, 4:561
    artisans, 5:266
    boule, 4:105
    Byzantine period, 8:45–48
        Salonika, 17:699–700
    community, nature of, 5:110–111
    contemporary Jewish life, 8:53–57
    contemporary period, 8:52–56
    Cuomotini, 5:339–340
    Diaspora, 5:638
    Don Pacifico affair, 15:564
    Egypt, 6:226–228
    eighteenth-nineteenth centuries, Salonika, 17:702
    emancipation, 6:381
    forced conversions, 8:45–47
    Hebrew publishing, Salonika, 17:706
    Holocaust, 8:50–52, 9:339, 340
        Athens, 7:631–632
        Chalcis, 4:561
        Kavalla, 12:38–39
        Kos, 12:317
        Salonika, 17:703–705
        Sephardim, 18:301
        Serrai, 18:316
        Trikkala, 20:148–149
        Veroia, 20:512–513
        Volos, 20:574–575, 575
    immigration to, Byzantine period, 8:48
    Independence, 8:50
    Jewish Archives, 2:409
    Jewish music, 8:55–56
    Jewish participation in military service, 14:245–246
    Larissa, 12:494
    late nineteenth-early twentieth centuries, Salonika, 17:702–703

Greece, *continued*
  letters and letter writers, 12:669
  Middle Ages, agriculture, Jewish, 1:495
  modern, Jewish communities, 13:684
  museums, 14:627
  Naupaktos, 15:38
  Nehama, Joseph, 15:59
  Ottoman period, 8:48–50
  partisans, 8:50–52
  Patras, 15:688–689
  post-WW II, Salonika, 17:705–706
  relations with Israel, 8:55
  Second Temple period, 8:44–45
  Sephardi immigration to, Salonika, 17:700–701
  seventeenth century, Salonika, 17:701–702
  Turkish period, Salonika, 17:700–701
  See also Orientalists
Greed, envy, 5:254
Greek Apocalypse of Baruch, 3:**186**
Greek Bible
  Aquila's translation, 15:433–434
  Coptic translations based on, 3:602
  Ethiopic translations based on, 3:601
  Hellenistic canon, 3:579, 579*t*
  Judeo-Greek translations, 3:636
  Judith, Book of, 11:567
  modern translations, 3:636
  Old Greek (OG) or Hexaplaric versions, 3:597, 598, 601, 602, 666
  order of books in, 3:579*t*
  Septuagint or LXX, 3:595–598, 652, 660, 666
  See also Hexapla
Greek calendars, 4:705
Greek language, 8:647–648
  Bible passages originally containing, 3:578
  Dead Sea scrolls influence, 8:638–639
  Hellenism, 8:785–786
  as Jewish language, 11:301
  linguistics, 8:58
  in Mishnaic Hebrew, 8:647–648
  of New Testament, 15:190
  in Qumran texts, 3:596
  rabbincal knowledge of, 8:57–59
  Scroll of Esther translation, 18:218
  of Septuagint, 3:596
  See also Judeo-Greek language

Greek literature (ancient), 8:**59–62**
  Belleli, Lazarus Menahem, 3:299
  biblical influence, 3:671
  Caecilius of Calacte, 4:331–332
  Choerilos of Samos, 4:658
  Demetrius, 5:549
  Eliyia, Joseph, 6:355
  Hadas, Moses, 8:185
  Plutarch, 16:242–243
  Testament of Solomon, 18:768
Greek literature (modern), 8:**62–65**
  Caïmis, Julius, 4:339
  Moissis, Asher, 14:422
Greek mythology. *See* Myths and mythology
Greek Orthodox Church
  Israel, 10:638–639, 641, 644
  Jewish relations with, 11:278
Green, Abel, 8:**65**
Green, Adolph, 5:71, 8:**65**
Green, Arthur, 4:125, 8:**65–66**
Green, David Ezra, 8:**66**
Green, Gerald, 8:**66**
Green, Monroe, 1:428
Green, Philip, 8:**66**
Green, Shawn David, 8:**66–67**
Green, William Scott, 2:90
Greenacre, Phyllis, 8:**67**
Greenbaum, Edward Samuel, 8:**67**
Greenbaum, Elias, 8:78
Greenbaum, Henry, 8:78
Greenbaum, Henry Everett, 8:78
Greenbaum, Michael, 8:78
Greenbaum family, 8:78
Greenberg, Blu, 20:367–368
Greenberg, Clement, 8:**67–68**
Greenberg, David Morris, 8:**68**
Greenberg, Eliezer, 8:**68**
Greenberg, Hank, 15:222
Greenberg, Hayim, 8:**68**
Greenberg, Ḥayyim, 20:340–341
Greenberg, Henry Benjamin, 8:**69–70**
Greenberg, Irving, 8:**70**, 9:383, 395–396, 473
Greenberg, Joanne, 8:**70**
Greenberg, Joseph, 8:**70–71**
Greenberg, Leopold, 8:**71**, 9:63–64, 65, 12:554
Greenberg, Leopold Jacob, 8:**71**
Greenberg, Lorry, 15:517
Greenberg, Louis, 8:**71**
Greenberg, Maurice R., 8:**72**
Greenberg, Moshe, 8:**72–73**
Greenberg, Noah, 8:**73**
Greenberg, Samuel Bernard, 8:**73**

Greenberg, Sidney, 8:**73**
Greenberg, Simon, 8:**73–74**
Greenberg, Susanne, 11:463
Greenberg, Uri Ẓevi, 8:**74–76**, 698
  Amir, Anda, 2:78
  Jerusalem in writings, 11:216
Greenberg, Yitz. *See* Greenberg, Irving
Greenberg family, 15:225
Greenberg,Samuel Bernard, 8:**73**
Greenblatt, Aliza Waitzman, 8:**76**
Greenblatt, Eliyahu, 8:**76**
Greene, Harold H., 8:**76–77**
Greene, Lorne, 8:**77**
Greene, Shecky, 8:**77**
Greenebaum, Gary, 13:204–205
Greenfield, Albert Monroe, 8:**78**
Greenfield, Howard, 18:234
Greenfield, Jonas Carl, 8:**79**
Greengard, Paul, 8:**79**, 13:10
Greenglass, David, 15:215
Green Lantern (comic strip), 11:761
Green Line settlements, 10:361–366, 369–370, 440, 441, 630
Green Onion (music group), 6:263
Greenshpan. *See* Aviv, Haim
Greenspan, Alan, 8:**79–80**
Greenspan, Bud, 8:**80–81**
Greenspan, Jay, 4:372
Greenspon, Edward, 11:470
Greenstein, E. L., Job, Book of, 11:348, 352, 353
Greenstein, Harry, 8:**81**
Greenstein, Jesse Philip, 8:**81**
Greenstein, Julius Hillel, 8:**81**
Greenwald, Jekuthiel Judah, 8:**81**
Greenwald, Leopold. *See* Greenwald, Jekuthiel Judah
Greenwald, Yekutiel. *See* Greenwald, Jekuthiel Judah
Greetings and congratulations, 8:**81–84**, 82*t*–84*t*
Grego, Isaac, 16:345
Grégoire, Abbé. *See* Grégoire, Henri Baptiste
Grégoire, Henri Baptiste, 2:8, 3:703, 8:**84**
Gregorius. *See* Bar Hebraeus, Johanan
Gregorius Bar Hebraeus. *See* Bar Hebraeus, Johanan
Gregorovius, F., 18:231
Gregory (popes), 8:**84–86**
Gregory, Sir Theodore, 8:**86**
Gregory, Theodore. *See* Gregory, Sir Theodore
Gregory I (pope), 4:277, 721, 8:**84–85**, 9:207, 15:580, 16:372
Gregory VII (pope), 16:372

Gregory IX (pope), 4:277, 7:150, 8:85, 16:373

Gregory X (pope), 8:85

Gregory XI (pope), 18:690

Gregory XIII (pope), 4:278, 8:85–86, 16:375, 18:313

Gregory XVI (pope), 16:376

Gregory Bar Hebraeus. *See* Bar Hebraeus, Johanan

Gregory of Nyssa, 4:720

Gregory of Tours, 5:690, 8:**86**

Gregory the Great (pope). *See* Gregory I (pope)

Gregos. *See* Romaniots

Greidling. *See* Gorodok

Greiner, Andor. *See* Gábor, Andor

Grenoble (France), 8:**86–87**

An den Grenzen des Geistes (Améry), 2:65

Gresh, Alain, 8:**87**

Gressman, Hugo, 8:**87**

Grey, Joel, 8:**87**

Grey Advertising, 1:428

Greyshirt movement, resistance to, 13:232

Griberg, Abraham. *See* Grunberg, Abraham

Die griechischen Inschriften der Palaestina Tertia westlich der Aruba (Alt), 2:11

Die Griechische Plastik (Loewy), 13:172

Grigorevna, Shirke. *See* Gorshman, Shira

Grigoryevich, Lev. *See* Deutsch, Leo

Griliches, Avenir, 8:**88**

Grillparzer, Franz, 11:256

Grinberg, Aleksander Abramovich, 8:**88**

Grine Felder (Hirschbein), 9:133

Grininke Beymelekh (periodical), 8:767

Grinker, Roy Richard Sr., 8:**88**

Grinspun, Bernardo, 8:**88**, 16:350

Grishaber, Isaac, 8:**88**

Grishin. *See* Kopelson, Ẓemaḥ

Gritse (Poland). *See* Grojec (Poland)

Grobart, Fabio, 8:**89**

Grobman, Michael, 2:500

Grock, 8:**89**

Gródek Jagiellónski. *See* Gorodok (Ukraine)

Grodek Wilenski. *See* Gorodok

Grodno (Lithuanian), 8:**89–91**, 11:715

Grodzinski, Ḥayyim Ozer, 2:77, 8:**91–92**

Grodzinski, Zvi Hirsch, 8:**92**

Grodzisk Mazowiecki (Poland), 8:**92**

Grodzisk Wielkopolski (Poland), 8:**92–93**

Die groessere Hoffnung (Aichinger), 1:549

Grof, Andros. *See* Grove, Andrew Stephen

Grojec (Poland), 8:**93**

Gronach, Isaiah. *See* Granach, Alexander

Gronemann, Sammy. *See* Gronemann, Samuel

Gronemann, Samuel, 8:**93**, 18:761

Groner, Dovid Yitzchok, 8:**93–94**

Groper, Jacob, 8:**94**

Gropius, 4:172

Gropper, William, 8:**94**, 13:239

Grosman, Ladislav, 8:**94**

Gross, Adolf, 8:**94–95**

Gross, Chaim, 4:9, 8:**95**, 15:221

Gross, Charles, 8:**95**

Gross, David J., 8:**95**

Gross, Elly, 4:370–371

Gross, Heinrich, 8:**96**, 11:324

Gross, Henri. *See* Gross, Heinrich

Gross, John Jacob, 8:**96**

Gross, Michael, 8:**96**

Gross, Moshe. *See* Gross-Zimmerman, Moshe

Gross, Naphtali, 8:**96–97**

Gross, Nathan, 8:**97**

Grossberg, Menasseh, 8:**97**

Grosser, Bronislaw, 8:**97**

Das grosse Synhedrion in Jerusalem und, das grosse Beth-din in der Quaderkammer des jerusalemischen Tempels (Buechler), 4:250

Grosseteste, Robert, bishop of Lincoln, *Testaments of the Twelve Patriarchs*, 15:692

Grossfeld, Abie. *See* Grossfeld, Abraham Israel

Grossfeld, Abraham Israel, 8:**97–98**

Grossinger, Jennie, 8:**98**

Grossman, Allan (1910-1991), 8:**98–99**, 15:436

Grossman, Allen (1932-), 8:**99**

Grossman, Allen (U.S. poet), 20:298

Grossman, Arthur. *See* Freed, Arthur

Grossman, Avraham, 8:**98**

Grossman, David, 8:**99–100**, 708

Grossman, Gheorghe. *See* Gaston-Marin, Gheorghe

Grossman, Larry, 8:**98–99**

Grossman, Leonid Petrovich, 8:**100**

Grossman, Mary Belle, 15:393

Grossman, Meir, 8:**100–101**

Jewish legion and, 11:303

Jewish State Party, 11:315–316

Grossman, Mendel, 9:362

Grossman, Morton Irvin, 8:**101**

Grossman, Reuven. *See* Avinoam, Reuven

Grossman, Steven, 8:**101–102**

Grossman, Vasili Semyonovich, 8:**102**

Grossman, Yiẓak-David, 8:**102**

Grossmanites. *See* Jewish State Party

Grossmann, Kurt Richard, 8:**102–103**

Grossmichel. *See* Michalovce (Slovakia)

Grosswardein (Romania). *See* Oradea

Gross-Zimmerman, Moshe, 8:**103**

Grosz, Bandi, 4:120

Groteska (Kaleve), 18:205

Grotius, Hugo, 8:**103**

on blood libel, 3:776

on Jews, 9:227, 17:164

modern biblical criticism, development of, 3:649

Group for the Ordination of Women (GROW), 6:254

The Group of five, 3:703

Group Psychotherapy with Children (Ginott), 7:**608**

Group Theater, 1:408, 4:763

Grove, Andrew Stephen, 8:**103–104**

Groves, sacred, 8:**104**

See also Asherah

GROW (Group for the Ordination of Women), 6:254

The Growth of Reform Judaism (Plaut), 16:228

Growth of the Law (Cardozo), 4:466

Dos Groyse Gevins (Shalom Aleichem), 18:385

Grozny (Chechen Republic), 8:**104**

Gruber, Mayer I., 11:348, 352

Gruber, Ruth, 8:**104–105**

Gruberger, Philip. *See* Berg, Philip

Gruby, David, 8:**105**

Grueber, Heinrich, 8:**105**

Gruen, Adolf, 8:**105**

Gruen, David. *See* Ben-Gurion, David

Gruen, J. M., 11:340

Gruenbaum, Henry, 8:**105–106**

Gruenbaum, Max, 8:**106**

Gruenbaum, Yitzhak, 16:347

Gruenbaum, Yiẓhak, 8:**106–107**

Gruenberg, Abraham. *See* Grunberg, Abraham

Gruenberg, Karl, 8:**107**

Gruenberg, Louis, 8:**107**

Gruenberg, Mendel. *See* Milian, Maximin

Gruenberg, Samuel, 8:**107**

Gruenberg, Sidonie Matsner, 8:**107**

Gruenblatt, Natan. *See* Goren, Natan

Gruenblatt, Nathan. *See* Goren, Natan

Gruenebaum, Elias, 15:576

Gruenewald, Max, 8:**107–108**

Gruenfeld, Judah, 8:**108**

Gruenhut, David ben Nathan, 8:**108**

Gruenhut, Eleazar, 8:**108**

Gruenhut, Lazar. *See* Gruenhut, Eleazar

Gruenhut, Max, 8:**108–109**

Gruening, Ernest Henry, 8:**109**

Gruensfeld (Germany), 3:43

Gruenspan, Herschel. *See* Grynszpan, Herschel

Gruenstein, Nathan, 8:**109**

Gruenthal, Josef. *See* Tal, Josef

Gruenvald, Philipp. *See* Grünvald, Philip

Gruenwald, Judah. *See* Grünwald, Judah

Gruenwald, Malkiel, 10:224

Gruenwald, Moritz, 8:**109**

Grulëv, Mikhail Vladimirovich, 8:**109**

Grumbach, Antoine, 8:**109–110**

Grumbach, Salomon, 8:**110**, 16:343

Grumberg, Jean-Claude, 7:246–247, 8:**110**

Grünbaum, Adolf, 8:**110**

Grunberg, Abraham, 8:**111**, 15:382

Grunberg, Arnon, 6:71–72

Grünberg, Carlos Moisés, 8:**111**

Grundig, Hans, 8:**111**

Grundig, Lea, 8:**111**

Die Grundlagen der allgemeinen Relativitaetstheorie (Einstein). *See Relativity, the Special and the General Theory, a Popular Exposition* (Einstein)

Die Grundlagen des 19. Jahrhunderts (Chamberlain), 4:563

Grundlegung der Soziologie des Rechts (Ehrlich). *See Fundamental Principles of the Sociology of Law* (Ehrlich)

Grundman, Zwi, 8:**111–112**

Gruner, Dov, 6:22, 8:**112**

Grunfeld, Ernie, 8:**112**

Grunfeld, Isidor, 8:**112**

Gruntal, Robert. *See* Nathan, Robert

Grünvald, Fülöp. *See* Grünvald, Philip

Grünvald, Philip, 8:**112–113**

Grünwald, Amram, 8:**113**

Grunwald, Henry Anatole, 8:**113**

Grünwald, Judah, 8:**113**

Grunwald, Max, 8:**114**

Grünwald, Moses, 8:**113**

Grunwald, Yekusiel Yehudah. *See* Greenwald, Jekuthiel Judah

Grusenberg, Oscar Osipovich, 3:770, 8:**114–115**

Gruzenberg, Michael Markovitsch. *See* Borodin, Michael Markovitsch

Gruzenerg, Michael. *See* Borodin, Michael Markovitsch

Gruziya (Transcaucasia). *See* Georgia (Transcaucasia)

Grydzewski, Mieczyslaw, 8:**115**

Gryn, Hugo, 8:**115**

Grynberg, Anne, 11:326

Grynberg, Berl, 8:**115**

Grynberg, Henryk, 8:**115**

Grynszpan, Herschel, 8:**115**

Grynszpan, Jechiel, 15:632

Grytzhendler, Mieczyslaw. *See* Grydzewski, Mieczyslaw

Guadalajara (Spain), 8:**115–116**

Guadalupe (Spain), 8:**116**

Guadeloupe (French Antilles), 4:473

Un guapo del 900 (Eichelbaum), 6:245

Guarantee. *See* Suretyship

Guardian. *See* Apotropos

"Guardian of Israel." *See* Shomer Israel

Guard of the House. See Mishmeret ha-Bayit

The Guardsman (Molnár), 14:427

Guastalla, Enrico, 8:**116–117**

Guatemala, 8:*117*, **117–118**, 9:798

Guayaquil (Ecuador), 6:139–140

Gubelman. *See* Yaroslavsky, Yemelyan

Gubenko, Julius. *See* Gibbs, Terry

Guber, Howard. *See* Guber, Peter

Guber, Peter, 8:**119**

Guber, Rivka, 8:**119**

Guccio, Gionnino, 11:379

Guebwiller (France), 8:**119**

Guedalla, Haim, 8:**119**

Guedalla, Philip, 8:**119–120**

Guedemann, Moritz, 8:**120**

Guelman, Jacobo, 16:349

Guens (Hungary). *See* Köszeg (Hungary)

Guens, Akiva Eger. *See* Eger, Akiva ben Moses Guens

Guens, Simḥah Bunim ben Moses. *See* Eger, Simḥah Bunim ben Moses

Guenzburg (East European family name), 8:**120–121**

Guenzburg, Baron David, 3:684, 8:122

Guenzburg, Baron Horace, 8:121–122, 12:678

Guenzburg, Baron Joseph Yozel, 8:121, 18:726

Guenzburg, David. *See* Guenzburg, Baron David

Guenzburg, Horace. *See* Guenzburg, Baron Horace

Guenzburg, Ilya Yakovlevich, 8:**122–123**

Guenzburg, Joseph Yozel. *See* Guenzburg, Baron Joseph Yozel

Guenzburg, Mordecai Aaron, 8:**123**, 441

Guenzburg, Naphtali Herz. *See* Guenzburg, Baron Horace

Guenzburg, Shimon. *See* Ginzburg, Simon

Guenzburg family (Russian bankers), 8:**121–122**

Guenzburg Library, 13:491

Guenzig, Ezriel, 8:**123**

Guenzler, Abraham, 8:**123–124**

Guer de Cordova, Abraham. *See* Escudero, Lorenzo

Guérin, Victor, 8:**124**

Guernsey. *See* Channel Islands (U.K.)

Gueron, Yakir, 15:527, 530, 537, 574

Guerrilla warfare, Palestine Liberation Organization and, 15:590–591

A Guest for the Night (Agnon), 11:216

Gufnah. *See* Gofnah (ancient Israel)

Gufnin. *See* Gofnah

Guf Rishon Rabbim (Shaḥam), 18:363

Guggenheim, Camille, 8:**125**

Guggenheim, Charles, 8:**126**

Guggenheim, Daniel, 8:124

Guggenheim, Harry Frank, 1:430, 8:124

Guggenheim, Isaac, 8:124

Guggenheim, Meyer, 8:124

Guggenheim, Paul, 8:**126**

Guggenheim, Simon, 8:124

Guggenheim, Solomon Robert, 8:124, 15:221

Guggenheim, Willy. *See* Varlin

Guggenheim family, 8:**124–125**, 125*t*

Guggenheim-Gruenberg, Florence, 8:**126**

Guggenheim Museum (NYC), 15:221

Guglielmo Da Pesaro, 8:**126–127**

Guglielmo Ebreo. *See* Guglielmo Da Pesaro

Guglielmo Raimondo de Moncada. *See* Mithridates, Flavius

Guglielmus Siculus. *See* Mithridates, Flavius

Guiana, 8:**127**

The Guianas, Caribbean, Spanish-Portuguese Nation of the: La Nacion, 4:470–471

Guibert of Nogent. *See* Vibert of Nogent

Guidacerio, Agacio, 8:**127–128**

Guidacerius, Agathius. *See* Guidacerio, Agacio

Guide of the Perplexed (Maimonides), 1:212, 230, 338, 2:548, 7:232, 667–668, 8:242, 11:730, 13:103–104, 384–385, 388–393, 16:84–86
  Alexander of Hales, 1:629
  commentaries, 6:681–682
    Latif, Isaac B. Abraham ibn, 12:506
  free will, 7:232
  mathematics in, 13:674
  Moses, 14:536–537
  naturalistic prophecy, 16:583
  platonism, 16:227
  Solomon ben Abraham of Montpelier, 18:770
  translations, 8:513, 19:712
    Al-Ḥarizi, Judah ben Solomon, 1:657
    Levin, Menahem Mendel, 12:712

The Guide of the Reader. See Hidāyat al-Qāri

A Guide to Jewish Religious Practice (Klein), 12:**222**

The Guide to the Guide (Falaquera), 6:681–682

Guilbert of Nogent. *See* Vibert of Nogent

Guilds, 5:268–269, 8:**128–129**
  ancient Israel, 6:97
  employment, 6:121–122
  Middle Ages, 6:110–111
  See also Freemasons

Guilt, inheriting, 21:498

Guinsburg, Jacó, 4:152

Guinzberg, Harold Kleinert, 8:**129**

Gukovsky, Grigory Aleksandrovich, 8:**129–130**

Gulak, Asher, 8:130

Guldenfenning. *See* Opferpfennig

Guldenpfennig, 15:438

Gulf and Western Industries (G&W), 4:6

Gulf War (1991), 8:**130–135**, 10:243, 453, 473–474
  Arab boycott and, 4:113
  U.S.-Israel relationship and, 4:304

Gull, 8:**135**

Gumpert. *See* Gomperz family

Gumpert, Martin, 8:**135–136**

Gumpertz. *See* Gomperz family

Gumplowicz, Ludwig, 8:**136**, 18:729–730

Gumprecht ben Abraham, 2:20

Gundbert. *See* Gomperz family

Gundelfinger, Friedrich. *See* Gundolf, Friedrich

Gundolf, Friedrich, 8:**136–137**

Gunkel, Hermann, 3:650–651, 8:**137**

Gunsberg, Isidor, 8:**137**

Gunzberg, Aryeh Leib ben Asher, 8:**137–138**, 768

Gunzberg, Niko, 8:**138**

Gunzburg, Aileen Mindel Bronfman de, 4:205–206

Gunzenhauser, Azriel, 8:138

Gunzenhauser, Joseph ben Jacob, 8:**138**

Gunzhausen, Leah, 1:221

Gur (Poland). *See* Gora Kalwaria (Poland)

Gur, Batya, 8:**138**

Gur, Mordecai, 6:279, 8:**138–139**

Gura-Humorului (Romania), 8:**139**

Guralnik, David B., 8:**139–140**

Gurama, 18:572

Gurarie, Morris. *See* Gray, Morris Abraham

Gur Aryeh. *See* Judah ben Isaac (1166-1224)

Guraryeh, Moishe, 8:41

Gur dynasty, 7:760–761, 8:424

Gurevich, Mikhail Iosifovich, 8:**140**, 12:630

Gurevich, Moshe, 8:**140**

Gurevicz. *See* Horowitz family

Gurevitch, Michael, 8:722

Gurfein, Rivka, 8:**140–141**

Gurfinckel, Sorana. *See* Gurian, Sorana

Gurian, Sorana, 8:**141**

Gurji, Joseph, 3:57

Gurland, Ḥayyim Jonah, 8:**141**

Gurs concentration camp, 3:44, 8:**141**, 11:728

Gurshtein, Aaron, 8:**141–142**

Gurvich, Alexander Gavrilovich. *See* Gurwitsch, Alexander Gavrilovich

Gurvich, Fyodor Ilyich. *See* Dan, Fyodor Ilyich

Gurvitch, Georges, 8:**142**, 18:730

Gurwicz. *See* Horowitz family

Gurwitsch, Aaron, 8:**142**

Gurwitsch, Alexander Gavrilovich, 8:**142**

Gusev, Sergei Ivanovich, 8:**142–143**

Gush Emunim, 8:**143–145**, 10:362–363, 364, 365–366, 630

Gush Etzyon (Israel), 6:216, 8:**145–147**, *146*, 12:59

Gush Halav (ancient Israel). *See* Giscala (ancient Israel)

Gush Halav, János. *See* Giszkalay, János

Gush Katif (Israel), 8:*147*, **147–148**, 12:58–59, 524

Gusikow, Joseph Michael, 8:**148**

Gusinsky, Vladimir Alexandrovich, 8:**148–149**

Gustav, Freidrich. *See* Henle, Elkan

Gustman, Ze'ev, 15:668

Guston, Philip, 8:**149**

Guta bat Nathan, 7:50

Gutenberg, Beno, 8:**149**

Guterman, Jacob Aryeh ben Solomon, of Radzymin, 17:61

Guterman, Solomon, 17:61

Gutfreund, Otto, 8:**149–150**

Gutgeld, Mordekhai. *See* Bentov, Mordekhai

Guth, Katjy, 6:18

Guthe, Hermann, 8:**150**

Gutheim, James Koppel, 8:**150–151**, 13:224

Guthrie, Arlo David, 8:**151**

Gutman, Alexander B., 8:**151**

Gutman, Chaim, 8:**151**

Gutman, Israel, 8:**151–152**

Gutman, Nahum, 8:**152–153**

Gutman, Simhah Alter, 3:**392–393**

Gutman, Tobais. *See* Feder, Tobias

Gutman, Tobias. *See* Feder, Tobias

Gutmann, Amy, 8:**153**

Gutmann, David, 8:**154–155**, 14:475

Gutmann, David Meir, 8:**153–154**

Gutmann, Eugen, 8:**154**

Gutmann, Jacob. *See* Guttmann, Jacob

Gutmann, Jean. *See* Babilée, Jean

Gutmann, Joseph, 8:**154**

Gutmann, Joshua, 8:**154**

Gutmann, Wilhelm Ritter Von, 8:**154–155**, 14:475

Gutnick family, 8:**155**

Gutt, Camille, 8:**155**

Guttapershah (Hoffmann), 9:312

Guttmacher, Alan F., 8:**155**

Guttmacher, Elijah, 8:**155–156**

Guttmacher, Manfred, 8:**156**

Guttman, Eliahu. *See* Guttman, Louis

Guttman, Jacob, 18:223

Guttman, Louis, 8:**156**, 18:735

Guttman, Ludwig. *See* Guttmann, Sir Ludwig

Guttmann, Alexander, 8:**156**

Guttmann, Jacob, 8:**156–157**

Guttmann, Julius, 8:**157–158**, 16:69–70, 71

Guttmann, Michael, 8:**159**

Guttmann, Robert, 8:**159**

Guttmann, Sir Ludwig, 8:**158–159**

Guttmann, Yitzhak. *See* Guttmann, Julius

Guttural letters, Hebrew, 8:558
Gutzkow, Karl Ferdinand, 4:32, 8:**159–160**
Guy, Philip Langstaffe Ord, 8:**160**
Guzik, David, 2:61
Guzik, Hanna, 8:**160**
Guzik, Jacob, 8:**160**
Guzman de Alfarache (Alemán), 1:611
Gvati, Chaim, 8:**160**
Gyges, 13:295
Gymnasium, 8:**160–161**
Gymnastics, 19:142
    Grossfeld, Abraham Israel, 8:97–98
    Keleti, Agnes, 12:68
Gyongyos (Hungary), 8:**161**
Györ (Hungary), 8:**161**
Gypsy Princess (Kalman), 11:745
Gyulafehérvár (Transylvania). *See* Alba Iulia (Transylvania)

H

H (letter), 8:*163*, 9:5
Ha-Abir. *See* Rosanes, Abraham ben Israel
Ha-Aderet veha Emunah (Levin), 12:710
Den Haag. *See* Hague, The
Ha-Ai (ancient Israel). *See* Ai (ancient Israel)
Ha-Akarah (Shami), 18:391
Ha-Am (newspaper), 14:518
Ha-Am, Aḥ. *See* Aḥad ha-Am
Ha-Am ve-Ruḥo (Bergmann), 3:430
Haan, Carryvan Bruggen de, 2:114
Haan, Jacob Israël De, 6:70, 8:**163–164**
Haan, Meijer De, 8:**164–165**
Ha'anakah, 8:**165–168**
Ha-Arakhim ha-Ḥinnukhiyyim shel ha-Tanakh (Adar), 1:383
Haarburger, Ivan, 3:769
Haaretz (newspaper), 8:**168**, 10:705, 706, 707, 12:458, 18:153–154
Haas, Fritz, 8:**168–169**
Haas, Georg, 8:**169**
Haas, Hugo, 8:**169**
Haas, Leo, 8:**169**
Haas, Ludwig, 3:43, 8:**169**
Haas, Robert D., 18:659–660
Haas, Solomon ben Jekuthiel Kaufmann, 8:**169–170**
Haas, Willy, 8:**170**
Haase, Hugo, 8:**170**, 16:344
Ha-Ashuri. *See* Ḥefeẓ ben Yaẓli'ah
Ha-asif (annual), 8:**170–171**
Haavara, 8:**171**
Ha-Avot ve-ha-Banim (Abromovitsh), 1:319

Habakkuk (book and prophet), 8:**171–173**
Habakkuk, Prophecy of (Apocrypha), 8:**173**
Habakkuk commentary, 8:636, 12:208, 16:10
Habas, Bracha, 4:624, 8:**173**
ha-Bavli, David. *See* Mukammiṣ, ibn Marwān al-Rāqi al-Shirazi al-
Ḥabban (Yemen), 8:**173–174**
Ḥabbarei, 8:**174**
Habe, Hans, 8:**174**
Haber, Fritz, 8:**174–175**, 18:579
Haber, Moritz, 8:**174**
Haber, Samuel L., 8:**175**
Haber, Shamai, 8:**175**
Haber, Solomon, 8:**174**
Haber, William, 8:**175–176**
Ha-Berekhah (Bialik), 3:563
Haber family, 8:**174**
Haberlandt, Gottlieb, 8:**176**
Haberman, Joshua O., 8:**176**
Habermann, Abraham Meir, 8:**176–177**
Habet (painting, Solomon), 18:767
Habib, Philip, 12:582, 583
Ḥabib, Ḥayyim ben Moses ben Shem Tov, 8:**177**
Ḥabib, Moses ben Solomon Ibn, 8:**177**
Ḥabiba, Joseph, 8:**177–178**
Habibi, Emil, 8:**178**, 10:737
Ḥabil (Yemen), 8:**178**
Habillo, David, 8:**178**, 18:342
Habillo, Elijah ben Joseph, 8:**178**
Habillo, Elisha, 8:**179**
Habimah, 8:**179–180**, 10:686, 11:753, 12:796, 14:518
Ha-Boker, 8:**181–182**
Ha-Boneh (Modena), 14:409
Ha-Bonim (Israel), 8:**182**
Habor (Mesopotamia), 8:**182**
Habraeus, Leo. *See* Abrabanel, Judah ben Isaac
Das Habsburgerlied (Frankl), 7:213
Habsburg monarchy. *See* Hapsburg monarchy
Ḥabshush, Shalom ben Yaḥya, 8:**182**
Ḥaçen, Jahuda Aben, 8:454
Hackenburg, William Bower, 8:**182**
Hacker, Leonard. *See* Hackett, Buddy
Hackett, Albert, 7:**759**
Hackett, Buddy, 8:**183**
Hacohen, David, 8:**183**
Hacohen, Mordecai, 8:**183**
Hacohen, Mordecai ben Hillel, 8:**183–184**
Hacohen, Raphael Ḥayyim, 8:**184**

Hacohen, Rosa. *See* Ginnosar, Rosa
Hadad, 8:**184–185**
Hadad (King of Edom), 6:154
Hadad son of Bedad (King of Edom), 6:153–154
Hadamard, Jacques Salomon, 8:**185**
Ḥadareh (Smilansky), 18:687
Hadar ha-Karmel (Lerner), 12:658
Ḥadarim, 6:183–185, 189, 204–205
    See also Jewish education
Ḥadar Morim (Shabtai), 18:359
Ha Darom, 17:237
Hadas, Moses, 8:**185**
Hadas-Lebel, Mireille, 11:326
Hadassah (Smilansky), 18:687
Hadassah, the Women's Zionist Organization of America, 8:**185–188**
    American Joint Distribution Committee, 2:60
    Canada, 4:401, 406, 6:50
    Dunkelman, Rose, 6:50
    Epstein, Judith, 6:474
    Hadassah Choral Union, 3:703
    Hadassah Medical Organization, 2:60, 8:186, 187, 188
    Halprin, Rose Luria, 8:286
    Hospital and Medical School, 8:187, 13:737
    in Jerusalem, 8:186, 11:177, 179–180, 188
    Kansas City, MO., 11:768
    leaders, 11:50–51
    Palestine (Mandate), 10:674
    Seligsberg, Allice Lillie, 18:268
    Youth Aliyah, 10:338, 11:51, 257, 258, 261
Hadassi, ha-Avel ben Elijah. *See* Hadassi, Judah ben Elijah
Hadassi, Judah ben Elijah, 8:**188–189**
    angels, 2:159
    articles of faith, 2:529
    Eldad ha-Dani, 6:294
    Josiah ben Saul ben Anan, 11:460
Ha-Dat ve-ha-Ḥayyim (Braudes), 4:136
Hadayah, Ovadiah, 8:**189**
Haddad, Ezra, 8:**189**
Haddad, Sarit, 8:**189**
Ḥaddad, Ezra, 15:473
Ḥaderah (Israel), 8:**189–190**
Ha-Derashah (Hazaz), 8:493
Ha-Deror (journal), 12:696
Ha-Devorah (Mohr), 14:420
Ḥad Gadya, 8:**190**
Ha-Di'alektikah shel ha-Sevel (Weltsh), 9
Hadid (ancient Israel), 8:**190–191**

Hadith, 8:**191–192,** 11:729

Hadoar, 9:151

Ha-Dod Peretz Mamri (Shabtai), 18:359

Hadoram. *See* Adoniram

Hadrach (Syria), 8:**192**

Hadran, 8:**193**

Hadrian, Publius Aelius (Roman emperor), 3:158, 8:**193–194,** 9:202, 18:275
    Aquila and, 15:433
    Leghorn, 12:610

Hadrian I (pope), 8:**193**

Ḥaḍramawt (Yemen), 8:**192–193**

Haduta ben Abraham, 8:**194**

Ha-Efrati, Joseph, 8:**195,** 18:369

"Ha-Egel" (Feierberg), 6:731

Ha-Elah Anat (Cassuto), 4:511

Ha-Elim Aẓelim (Shaḥam), 18:363

Ha-Emet (periodical), 8:**195,** 12:709

Ha-Emunah ha-Ramah (Ibn Daud), 7:231, 12:408

Haendel, Ida, 8:**195**

Ha-Enẓiklopedyah ha-Ivrit (encyclopedia). *See Encyclopaedia Hebraica* (encyclopedia)

Ha-Eshkol (Goldmann), 6:399

Haezraḥi, Yehuda, 8:**195–196**

Ḥafeẓ Ḥayyim. *See* Israel Meir ha-Kohen

Ḥafeẓ Ḥayyim (Israel), 8:**196**

Haffkine, Waldemar Mordecai, 8:**196**

Hafka'at She'arim, 5:185, 8:**196–198**

Ḥafor perot, 14:424

Hafsids, 8:**198**

Haftarah, 8:**198–200**

The Haftarah Commentary (Plaut), 16:228

Ha-Gadol, Aaron, 6:327

Hagai, Baruch, 8:**200**

Haganah, 8:**200–205,** 10:465–467
    Amit, Meir, 2:80
    Arazi, Yehuda, 2:361, 362
    archives, 2:417
    Ben-Gurion, David, 3:346
    Ben-Zvi, Izhak, 3:394
    Beriḥah, 3:435
    British measures against, 10:205, 207
    development of, 9:250–251, 10:201, 204
    Dunkelman, Benjamin, 6:50
    early Mandate years, 8:201–203
    Jabotinsky, Vladimir, 11:11–12, 13
    Laskov, Ḥayyim, 12:500
    leaders, Dayan, 5:485
    Palmaḥ, 15:603–604

Ratner, Yohanan, 17:113
    responsibilities after UN partition, 10:208
    War of Independence, 8:204–205
    WW II, 8:203–204

Hagar, 1:287, 8:**205–206,** 18:46, 47

Ha-Gashash ha-Ḥiver, 8:**206–207**

Hagbaha, gelilah, 8:**207**

Hagbahah, 1:360–361

Hagège, Daniel. *See* Hajjāj, Daniel

Ha-Gelilit (Israel). *See* Bet Leḥem (Israel)

Ha-Gemul (Smolenskin), 18:691

Hagen (Germany), 8:**207**

Hagenbach (Germany), 8:**207**

Hager, Baruch, 20:564

Hager, Israel, 20:564

Hager, Menahem Mendel ben Ḥayyim, 20:564

Hager dynasty. *See* Vizhnitz dynasty

Ha-Gevul (Shamir), 18:392

Ḥagga. *See* Haggai

Haggadah. *See* Aggadah or Haggadah

Haggadah, Passover, 8:**207–217,** 15:681–682
    Abraham bar Jacob, 1:294
    commentaries and ritual, 8:208–210
    components, 8:208–209
    Eḥad mi Yode'a, 6:237
    Ehrenfeld, Samuel ben David ẒEvi, 6:239
    feminist haggadot, 8:215–216
    Ha laḥma anya, 8:251
    illustration and illumination, 4:76, 8:210–215, 14:541–542
    manuscripts and editions, 8:210–215
    music and singing, 8:215–216

Haggadah Shelemah (Kasher), 11:821

Haggahot, 8:**217–221**

Haggahot literature, 8:219–220

Haggahot Maimuniyyot, 8:**221–222**

Haggahot Mordekhai (Schlettstadt), 14:480–481

Haggai (Amora), 8:**223**

Haggai (prophet), 6:493, 8:**222–223**

Haggai of Sepphoris, 8:**223**

Ḥagigah, 8:**223–224**
    Elisha ben Avuyah, 6:352

Ha-Ginnah (journal), 8:283

Hagin of Lincoln, 2:419

Hagiography, 8:**224–226**
    angels, 2:151
    biography and autobiography influenced by, 3:705–706
    Kabbalah, 7:14

mishpat Ivri, 14:337

Hagiz, Jacob, 15:524

Hagiz, Moses, 18:298, 299

Ḥagiz, Abraham, 8:226

Ḥagiz, Jacob, 8:226
    Amigo, Abraham, 2:77

Ḥagiz, Jacob (Scholar), 8:**226–227**

Ḥagiz, Moses, 8:**227,** 477, 478

Ḥagiz, Samuel, 8:226

Ḥagiz family, 8:226

Ḥagorat Mazzalot (Hazaz), 8:494

Ha-Gosherim (Israel), 8:**227**

Hagozer, Gershom, 8:**227–228**

Hagozer, Jacob, 8:**227–228**

Ha-GRA. *See* Elijah ben Solomon Zalman

Hagramah, 18:434

Hagronia (Mesopotamia), 8:**228**

Hague, The, 8:**228–229**

Hague Convention, domicile of minors, 5:742

Hague Convention on the Civil Aspects of International Child Abduction (1980), 1:242–243

Haguenau (France), 8:**229–230**

Ha-Ḥalutz, 8:757

Ha-Ḥaverot Hakhi Tovot (Mazia), 8:723

Ha-Hed (periodical), 14:426

Ha-Hekkesh ha-Yashar (Gershom), 13:173

Ha-Ḥerev ha-Mithappekhet (Bedersi), 3:248

Ha-Hesder (motion picture), 4:535–536

Ha-Ḥeshbon ve-ha-Nefesh (Bartov), 3:181

Ha-Ḥevrah le-Ḥakirat Ereẓ Israel ve-Attikoteha. *See* Israel Exploration Society

HaḤibbur ha-Gadol (Zacuto), 21:434

Ha-Ḥinnukh, 2:38, 3:15, 8:**230**

Ha-Histadrut ha-Kelalit shel ha-Ovedim be-Ereẓ Israel. *See* Histadrut

Ha-Histadrut ha-Kelalit shel ha-Ovedim ha-Ivriyyim be-Ereẓ Israel. *See* Histadrut

Hahn, Albert L., 8:**230–231**

Hahn, Joseph ben Moses, 8:**231**

Hahn, Joseph Yuspa ben Phinehas Seligmann, 6:178, 8:**231**

Hahn, Kurt, 6:160, 8:**231**

Hahn, Michael, 8:**231**

Hahn, Reynaldo, 8:**231–232**

Ha-Ḥozeh Ḥezyonot be-Arba'ah Olamot (Sobel), 18:699

Ha-Ḥozeh mi-Lublin. *See* Jacob Isaac ha-Ḥozeh mi-Lublin

Ḥai, amulets, 2:122
Hai Bar Rav David Gaon, 8:232
Hai ben Nahshon, 8:232
Hai ben Sherira, 8:232–233, 18:463
    amulets, 2:121
    Judeo-Arabic literature and,
        11:531
Haidamacks, 3:96, 4:37, 6:49, 8:233–
234
Haifa (Israel), 8:234–238
    aerial view
        1920s, vol. 11: color insert
        1990s, vol. 11: color insert
    Crusades, 8:234–235
    growth during Mandate, 10:506
    Jewish settlement, 8:236–237
    Levi, Shabbetai, 12:693
    Ottoman rule, 8:235–236
    plain, 10:118
    population, 10:289, 292, 481t
    Wadi Salib neighborhood riots,
        10:535–536
Haifa, University of. See University of
    Haifa
Haifa Bay Plain (Israel), 10:111
Haifa Municipal Theater, 8:238
Haifa Symphony Orchestra, 10:688–
689
Haifa Technion
    Blok, Arthur, 3:770
    Kaplansky, Shelomo, 11:780–781
Hai Gaon, 1:439, 587
Haigerloch (Germany), 9:315
Ḥaikin, Simon Menahem, 8:747
Ha-Ikkar ver-ha-Noẓah (Dolitzki),
    5:735–736
Hailperin, Herman, 8:238–239
Haimovici, Bercu. See Bonciu, H.
Haimovici, Mendel, 8:239
Haimowitz, Morris Jonah, 8:239
Ḥa'im Yesh Mekhubad ba-Ulam?
    (Rosenblum), 18:206
Haindorf, Alexander, 8:239
Hainovitz, Asher, 8:239
Hair and beard care, 5:230
Ha-Irgun ha-Ẓeva'i ha-Leummi (IZL),
    11:13
Ha-Ishah ha-Gedolah min ha-Ḥalomot
    (Kenaz), 12:75
Ha-Ish mi-Sham (Ben-Ner), 3:367
Haiti (Caribbean), 4:473, 8:239–240
Hajdu, André, 8:240
Hajdu, Miklós, 8:240–241
Hajdu, Vavro, 18:665
Hajek, Markus, 8:241
Hajim, Jisrael, 8:241

Hajjāj, Daniel, 8:241
Hajnal, Anna, 8:241
Hajós, Alfréd, 8:241, 15:413
Ha-Kalah ha-Nitzḥ (Orpaz), 15:483
"Ha-Kame'a" (Feierberg), 6:731
Ha-Karmel (periodical), 8:242
Ha-Katuv(im), 3:574
Hakdamah, 8:242–243
Ha-Ketav ve-ha-Kabbalah
    (Meklenburg), 13:797–798
Ḥaketía, 8:243–244
Ḥakham, 8:245
Ḥakham, Simon, 8:245
    Judeo-Persian literature, 11:557
Ḥakham bashi, 8:245–247, 15:536–
    537, 17:14–15
    am ha-areẓ, 2:67, 68
Ḥakhamim ba-Layla (Banai), 3:106
Ḥakham Lev (Judah Leib ben Hillel of
    Schwersenz), 11:506
Hakhasat Kallah (Agnon), 1:466
Hakhel, 8:247
Ḥakhirah, 12:572–573
Hakhnasat kallah, 8:247–248
Hakhsharah farms, 8:760–761
Ha-Kibbutz ha-Artzi ha-Shomer
    Ha-ẓair, 8:248, 12:124
Ha-Kibbutz ha-Dati, 8:248, 12:125–
    126
Ha-Kibbutz ha-Me'uḥad, 2:416, 8:248,
    12:124–125
Ḥākim, al-, 6:724
Ḥakim, Eliahu, 8:248–249
Ḥakim, Samuel ben Moses ha-Levi
    ibn, 8:249
Ḥakim bi-Amr Allah, al, 8:249–250
Hakkafot, 8:250
Hakkarat Panim le-Rabbi Yishma'el,
    4:653
Ha-Kohen (13th c.). See Daniel ben
    Samuel ibn Abī Rabi'
Ha-Kohen, Abraham Issachar, 17:58
Ha-Kohen, Ezekiel, 17:58
Ha-Kohen, Issac, 17:92
Ha-Kohen, Samuel, 15:523
Ha-Kohen, Solomon ben Naḥman,
    17:97
Ha-Kohen, Solomon Enoch, 17:58
Ha-Kongres (Oren), 18:206
Ha-Kumkum, 8:299
Ḥalab (Syria). See Aleppo (Syria)
Ḥaladah, 18:434
Ḥalaf ibn Sargado. See Aaron ben
    Joseph ha-Kohen Sargado
Ḥalafta, 8:250
Ḥalafta ben Saul, 8:250–251
Ha laḥma Anya, 8:251

Halakhah, 8:251–258, vol. 17: color
insert
    613 commandments, 5:73, 74t–
        84t, 85
    Aaron ben Jacob ha-Kohen of
        Lunel and, 1:213–214
    academies, 1:348, 349, 351
    admission, 1:410–411
    agency, 1:449–454
    agriculture
        demai, 5:547–548
        five species of seed, 7:66
        jubilee, 17:626–628
        sabbatical year, 17:626–628
    Agudat Israel, 1:505–508
    agunah, 1:509–520, 510–520
    Aḥad ha-Am, 1:528–529
    Aḥai ben Josiah, 1:529
    Aḥaronim, 1:532–537
    Aḥ ha-Am, 1:528–529
    Akiva, 1:562–563
    Alexander Suslin ha-Kohen of
        Frankfurt, 1:630
    Alfandari, Jacob, 1:638
    Alfasi, Isaac ben Jacob, 1:639–641
    Algazi, Israel Jacob ben Yom Tov,
        1:644
    algorithms, 5:130
    Allon, Gedalya, 1:675
    Almosnino, Joseph ben Isaac,
        1:685
    altars in, 2:14–16
    Ammonites in, 2:86–87
    amoraim, 2:89, 94
        Adda Bar Ahavah, 1:384
        Eleazar ben Pedat, 6:306–307
        Eleazar ben Yose II, 6:308–
            309
        Johanan ben Nappaḥa,
            11:371–372
        Rabbah bar bar Ḥana, 17:8
        Rabbah bar Naḥamani, 17:9
        Rashi, 17:102–103, 104, 105
        Rava, 17:118–119
        Saadiah Gaon, 17:608–609
    antinomianism, 2:200–201
    arba ammot, 2:362
    Ashkenazim, 6:41
    asmakhta, 2:590–592
    assault, 2:595–598
    attorneys, 2:648
    authority on halakhah, 5:649,
        11:805–806
    Baschko, Ẓevi Hirsch ben
        Benjamin, 3:195
    Bat Kol, 3:213
    bat kol, 17:507

Bava Batra, 3:223–224
Bava Kamma, 3:224–226
Bava Metzia, 3:226–227
in *Beit ha-Beḥirah,* 13:786
Bene Israel and, 10:298
Benjamin Ze'ev Ben Mattathias of
    Arta, 3:364
Berab, Jacob, 3:397–398
Berlin, Noah Ḥayyim Ẓevi Hirsch,
    3:458
Bet Hillel and Bet Shammai,
    3:530–533
Bible, interpretation of, 9:815–816,
    816, 818
blood in, 3:772
Buber, Martin, 4:234
business ethics, 4:308–309
cards and cardplaying, 4:467
Caro, Joseph ben Ephraim, 4:489–
    491
Case, Joseph ben Abraham, 4:505
Cases family, 4:505
Castro, Jacob ben Abraham, 4:518
Christianity, 4:679
codification, 4:765–780, 11:30
coins, 5:52
competition, restriction of, 8:450–
    451
Conservative Judaism, 8:257,
    11:518–519
conversion, 16:587–589
    Anusim, 2:251
    maranos, 15:134
customary law, 8:254
    aggadah vs., 1:454
    ha'takah, 20:11–12
    minhag, 10:49
David ben Shalom Mizraḥi, 14:393
day-and-night cycle, 5:487–488
Day of Atonement, 5:488
deaf-mute people and, 5:509–510
debt
    Apoteke, 12:815–816
    cancellation of claims, debts,
        rights, 13:770–771
    debt assignment, 2:603–605
    debt recovery in, 6:591
    liens and debts, 12:812–817
    suretyship, 19:317–322
    usury, 20:438–443
definition of Jew, 11:254–255
detention, 5:607
development of, 8:254–257
dina de-malkhuta dina, 5:664–665
disinterment, 5:682
Diskin, Moses Joshua Judah Leib,
    5:683

Dosa ben Saadiah, 5:761
Dostai ben Judah, 5:761
economic history, 6:117
Eduyyot, 6:214–215
Eldad ha-Dani, 6:294
Eleazar ben Arakh, 6:299
Eleazar ben Azariah, 6:299–300
Eleazar ben Judah of Worms,
    6:303–304
Eleazar ben Yose I, 6:308
Eliezer ben Hyrcanus, 6:322–325,
    323–324
Eliezer ben Jacob (1st century),
    6:326
Eliezer ben Jacob (2nd century),
    6:326
Eliezer ben Joel ha-Levi of Bonn,
    6:326–327
Eliezer ben Samuel of Metz, 6:329
Elijah ben Ḥayyim, 6:339
Elijah ben Judah of Paris, 6:339
Ellenson, David Harry, 6:360
Emden, Jacob, 6:392–393
encyclopedias, 13:760
Ephraim ibn Avi Alragan, 6:460
evolution in, 6:586, 587
family law
    adoption, 1:417–418
    adultery, 1:425–427
    annulment, 1:514–517
    child marriage, 4:616–617
    civil marriage, 4:746–748
    Cleves get, 4:760
    ḥaliẓa, 12:726–729
    ḥaliẓah, 12:725–729
    paternity, 21:423–426
feminist, 6:755, 756
fish and fishing, 7:59
five species of seed, 7:66
gematria, 7:425
geonic, 7:492–493
geonim, 7:380–385
God's will at variance with,
    10:824–825
Goldman, Eliezer, 7:710–711
Halakhah le-Moshe mi-Sinai,
    8:258
Hananiah, 8:315
Ḥanina, 8:321
Ḥasidei Ashkenaz, 8:388
Ḥasidism, 8:391
Haskalah, 8:436, 439
ḥerem, 9:10–16
Herschorn, Joshua Halevy, 9:44
Hillel (the Elder), 9:109
historical school (Germany),
    11:518–519

Horovitz, Marcus, 9:529
Ḥukkat ha-goi, 9:580
human rights issues, 17:330–332
Ḥumra, 9:600
Ibn Danan, Saadiah ben Maimun,
    9:662
Ibn Gaon, Shem Tov ben
    Abraham, 9:676
Ibn Ghayyat family, 9:676–677
Ibn Sahl, Joseph ben Jacob, 9:688–
    689
insanity, 15:722
insults, 9:807–808
insurance, 9:808–809
interpretation of, 9:821
Isaac ben Meir Dueren, 6:41
Ishmael ben Elisha, 10:83
Islam, 10:98, 11:270
Islamic law and, 11:**262–270**
Israeli politics, 10:434
Israeli rabbinical courts, 13:682
Jabneh (ancient Israel), 11:10
Jerusalem in, 11:210–211
Jewish identity and, 11:292, 295,
    298, 299
Job in, 11:356
Joseph ben Emanuel Ergas, 6:478–
    479
Joseph ben Judah Engel, 6:409
Josephus' *Jewish Antiquities* and,
    11:438
Jubilees, Book of, 11:473
Judaism, development of concept
    of, 11:518–519
Judeo-Persian, 11:551
Kabbalah, 11:588, 589, 591, 601,
    606, 611, 613, 619, 668–669,
    680–681, 685
Karaite, 10:50
Karelitz, Abraham, 11:805–806
karet, 11:806–807
kelal Israel, 12:68
kingship, 12:196
Krochmal, Nachman, 12:368
law and morality, 12:538–544
Lawat, Abraham David Ben Judah
    Leib, 12:541
legal and judicial system
    of Israel, 10:403
        vs. religious, 14:333–334
        Takkanot legislation, 19:441–
            444, 448–449
        taxation, 19:557–558
Leibowitz, Yeshayahu, 12:623–624
Levi, Isaac Ben Solomon, 12:688–
    689
Levi, Jacob Ben Israel, 12:689

Halakhah, *continued*

Levites, 12:733

literature

issur ve-hetter, 10:773

prayer books, 16:462

responsa, 17:228–239

Samaritans, 17:736–737

liturgical, 13:133

ma'aseh, 13:308–313

ma'aser sheni, 13:314

majority rule, 13:414–417, 416–417

maritime law, 13:546–547

mathematics and, 13:671–673, 677

medical, 13:738–757

artificial insemination, 13:751–753

euthanasia, 13:743–746

organ transplantation, 13:746–751

patients' rights, 13:739–743

physicians' duties, 13:739–741

in vitro fertilization, 13:755–756

Megillat Setarim, 13:768

minority opinions, 13:416–417

Mishnah, 14:321–322

mishpat Ivri, 14:337, 345

mixed species, 14:386–387

Mizrahi, Elijah, 14:394

modern Judaism, 8:251, 253, 257

Monzon, Abraham, 14:467

Mordacai ben Hillel ha-Kohen, 14:481

Mordecai Joseph Leiner of Izbica, 10:824–825

mukzeh objects, 14:608

mushrooms, 14:636

Nahmanides novellae, 14:741–743

niddah, 15:253, 255, 21:162

Niddui vs. herem, 9:13–15

Noachide laws, 15:286–287

Not in Heaven (Berkovits), 3:439

oral and written, 8:252–253

ordination, 17:14

Orthodox Judaism, contemporary responsa, 6:742, 745–746

ownership and possession, 8:486–491

Pharisees, 8:254–255

Philo Judaeus, 16:61

philosophical analysis of, 16:103–104

piety and, 16:149

pigs, 16:150–151

pilpul, 16:162

Pittsburgh Platform, 16:191

posekim, 16:415

pre-Middle Ages, 13:88–91

Priestly Blessing, 16:510–511

proselytes, 16:588, 591, 593, 594

Provençal, 11:35, 16:639

proverbs, 16:646–647

psychology, 16:687

punishment, 4:447–448

de-oraita vs de-rabbanan, 8:253–254

herem, 9:10–16

karet, 11:806–807

Niddui vs. herem, 9:13–15

purity

impurity laws, 12:737–738

mikvah, 14:225, 226, 229–230

ritual purity and impurity, 16:750–755

rabbinical authority, 2:703–705

rabbinical literature, 17:22

rabbis

Aaron ben Joseph ha-Levi and, 1:215

Aaron of Neustadt and, 1:219

Abraham ben Moses ben Maimon, 1:306

Abraham Zevi Hirsch ben Jacob Eisenstadt, 6:270

Adarbi, Isaac ben Samuel, 1:383

Ehrenfeld, Samuel ben David Zevi, 6:239

Elijah ben Solomon Zalman, 6:343

Greek rabbis, 5:466

Halevi, Hayyim David, 8:268

Halevi, Joseph Zevi ben Abraham, 8:268

Heller, Yom Tov Lipmann ben Nathan Ha-Levi, 8:797

Hirsch, Samson Raphael, 9:130–131

Horowitz, Phinehas ben Zevi Hirsch ha-Levi, 9:540–541

Israel Meir ha-Kohen, 10:756

Judah Loew ben Bezalel, 11:507

Landau, Ezekiel Ben Judah, 12:459–461

Laniado, Raphael Solomon Ben Samuel, 12:484

Maimonides, Moses, 13:385–388, 395

Nahmanides, 8:252

Sasson, Aaron ben Joseph, 18:62–63

Shammai, 18:394

Soloveitchik, Joseph Baer, 18:777, 778–779

Rapoport, Abraham ben Israel Jehiel ha-Kohen, 17:98

Rashi, 17:105

Rav, 17:116–117

Reform Judaism, 8:257

religious impact of Bible and, 3:661

reshut, 17:227

responsa, 12:671, 15:771–772

rishonim, 17:339–343

ru'ah ha-kodesh, 17:507

Saadiah Gaon, 17:608–609

Sadducees, 18:254–255

sages, authority of, 5:64–65, 8:253–254

Samuel ben Meir, 17:772–773

Sanhedrin, 18:22

Saraval, Samuel Ben Isaac, 18:52

Sardi, Samuel Ben Issac and, 18:52–53

Schwarzschild, Steven Samuel, 18:194

Second Temple, Temple Mount, 19:627

Sefer ha-Ma'asim Li-venei Erez Yisrael, 18:240

Sefer ha-Neyar, 18:240

Sephardim, 18:296, 298, 299–300

sevarah, 18:322–323, 323

Shulhan Arukh, 18:529–530

Sikarikon, 18:573–574

Soferim (tractate), 18:744

sources of, 8:251–254

succession and inheritance, 19:284–289

synagogues, 19:356, 362–363, 368, 384

takkanot ha-kahal, 10:753, 19:453–460

Tannaitic, Amoraic periods, 8:255–256

technology and, 19:572–573

Temple Scroll, 19:633, 634

tenancy rights, 8:449–450

transplants, 20:106–108

trespassing, 8:449, 450–451

Turei Zahav (David ben Samuel ha-Levi), 5:469–470

weights and measures, 20:708–709

widows, 21:42–44

witness, 21:115–125

woman Torah study, 21:199–200

writing of Bible, 13:606–607

yuhasin, 21:423–426

See also Bet Hillel; Bet Shammai; Laws and legal systems; Mishpat Ivri

Halakhah le-Moshe (Amarillo), 2:32

Halakah le-Moshe mi-Sinai, 8:**258**

Halakhic Man (Soloveitchik), 18:778–779

Halakhic Mind (Soloveitchik), 18:779

Halakhic periodicals, 8:**258–259**

Halakhot Gedolot, 1:640, 8:**259–261**, 753, 9:104

Halakhot Ketannot (Schlettstadt), 14:481

Halakhot Pesukot (Abba), 1:225, 8:653

Halakhot Rabbati. See Sefer ha-Halakhot

Ḥalakim Enoshiyim (Castel-Bloom), 4:512

Halakot Keẓuvot, 4:769

Halakot Pesukot, 4:769, 8:260–261, **262–263**

Ḥalap, Jacob Moses ben Zebulun, 8:**358**

Ha-Lašon we-Sifrutah (Aḥad Ha-Am), 8:675

Ha-Layla la-Ish (Shamir), 18:392

Halberstadt (Germany), 8:**263**, 12:614

Halberstadt, Abraham ben Menahem Menke, 8:**263–264**

Halberstadt, Meir, 4:132

Halberstadt, Menahem Mendel, 8:264

Halberstadt, Mordecai, 8:**264**

Halberstaedter, Ludwig, 8:**264**

Halberstam, Aaron, 8:265

Halberstam, Baruch, 8:265

Halberstam, Ben Zion, 4:23, 8:265

Halberstam, David, 8:**265–266**

Halberstam, Ezekiel Shraga of Sieniawa, 8:265

Halberstam, Ḥayyim ben Leibush, 8:264

Halberstam, Hayyim of Zanz, 8:452

Halberstam, Isaac ben Ḥayyim, 8:**266**

Halberstam, Jacob Samson, 8:265

Halberstam, Jekuthiel Judah, 8:265

Halberstam, Naftali, 4:24, 8:265

Halberstam, Shlomo, 15:230–231

Halberstam, Solomon Ḥayyim, 4:23–24, 8:**266**

    as bibliophile, 3:684

    in Bielsko, 3:690

Halberstam, Zalman Ḥayyim. *See* Halberstam, Solomon Ḥayyim

Halberstam dynasty, 8:**264–265,** 424

Halberszdadt, Solomon, 4:200

Halbwachs, Maurice, 8:**266–267,** 18:730

Haleva, Isak, 8:**267**

Haleva, Naphtali, 8:267

Ha-Levanon (newspaper), 4:182, 8:**267,** 466

Ha-Levi, Abraham, 15:536

ha-Levi, Bet family. *See* Levi family (Salonika, Greece)

Ha-Levi, David Ẓadok, 8:474

Ha-Levi, Eliezer. *See* Loewe, Louis

Halevi, Ezekiel Ezra ben Joshua, 8:**267**

Halevi, Ḥayyim David, 8:**267–268**

Ha-Levi, Israel b. Moses, of Zamosc, 4:199

Halevi, Joseph Ẓevi ben Abraham, 8:**268**

Halevi, Judah. *See* Judah Halevi

Ha-Levi, Sasson ben Elijah ben Moses, 8:**268**

Halevi, Saul, 4:21

Ha-Levi, Zerahiah, 8:454

Ḥalevi, Solomon. *See* Pablo de Santa Maria

Halevy, Abraham H., 8:**269**

Halévy, Daniel, 8:269

Halevy, David of Ostrog, 8:507

Halévy, Élie, 8:**269–270**

Halévy, Elie Halfon, 8:270

Halévy, François Fromental Élie. *See* Halévy, Jacques Fromental Élie

Halevy, Isaac, 8:270

Halévy, Jacques Fromental Élie, 8:**270–271**

Halévy, Joseph, 8:**271**

Halévy, Léon, 8:268–269, 18:704

Halévy, Ludovic, 8:269

Halevy, Meyer Abraham, 8:**271–272**

Halevy, Moshe, 8:**272**

Halevy, Yosef, 8:272

Halévy family, 8:**268–269**

Halfan, Elijah Menahem, 8:**272,** 14:424

Halfan family. *See* Halfanus family

Halfanus, Abba Mari, 8:272

Halfanus, Elias, 8:272

Halfanus family, 8:**272**

Half-Jews. *See* Partial Jews

Ḥalfon, Abraham, 8:**273**

Ḥalfon, ben Nethanel ha-Levi abu Sai-ʿd, 8:**273**

Halhul (ancient Israel), 8:**273**

Halicz (Poland), 8:**273–274**

Halicz, Asher, 8:274

Halicz, Elyakim, 8:274

Halicz, Samuel, 8:274

Halicz family, 8:**274**

Halifax (Nova Scotia), 2:639, 640

Ḥalifin, 1:361, 363

    onaʾah, not subject to, 15:425

Halikhot Olam (Jeshua ben Joseph ha-Levi), 11:242

Halikhot Sheva (Almoli), 1:682

Halikhot Teiman (Kafah), 11:703–704

Halivni, David Weiss, 2:47, 8:**274–275**

Halivni, Weiss, 11:331

Ḥaliẓah, 12:**725–729,** 14:448, 21:323

Halkin, Abraham Solomon, 8:**275**

Halkin, Shmuel, 8:**275–276**

Halkin, Simon, 8:**276,** 736–737

Hall, Monty, 8:**276–277**

Hall, Owen, 8:**277**

Ḥallah (bread), 7:118

Ḥallah (precept), 8:**277–278**

Ḥallah (tractate), 8:**278**

Halle (Germany), 8:**278–279**

Halle, Morris, 8:**279**

Hallegua, Ḥayyim Joseph, 8:279

Hallegua, Joseph, 8:279

Hallegua, Moses, 8:279

Hallegua family, 8:**279**

Hallel, 6:770, 8:**279–280**

    Four species, 7:139

    New Moon, 15:151

    See also Midrash Hallel

Hallel ha-Gadol, 8:280

Hallel Miẓri, 8:280

Hallelujah, 8:**280–281**

Haller's Army, 8:**281**

Hallgarten, Charles, 8:281

Hallgarten, Julius, 8:281

Hallgarten, Lazarus, 8:281

Hallgarten family, 8:**281–282**

Hallo, Rudolf, 8:**282**

Hallo, William, 8:**282**

Halmi, Robert, 8:**282–283**

Halmi, Robert, Jr., 8:**283**

Halokh va-Shov (Shaham), 18:363

Ḥalomot be-Aspazia (periodical), 18:206

Ḥalom shel Tammuz (Shaḥar), 18:364

Halper, Albert, 8:**283**

Halper, Benzion, 8:**283**

Halperin, Haim, 8:**283**

Halperin, Israel. *See* Halpern, Israel

Halperin, Jacob, 12:553

Halpérin, Jean, 2:28

Halperin, Maurice. *See* Hall, Monty

Halperin, Mikhl. *See* Helpern, Michael

Halperin, Uriel. *See* Ratosh, Yonathan

Halperin, Yeḥiel, 8:**283**

Halperin, Zeʾev, 13:798

Halpern, Abraham, 16:340

Halpern, Benjamin, 4:125, 8:**284,** 18:734

Halpern, Georg Gad, 8:**284**

Halpern, Harry, 8:**284**

Halpern, Israel, 8:**284–285**

Halpern, Jack, 8:**285**

Halpern, Leyvik. *See* Leivik, H.

Halpern, Lipman, 8:**285**

Halpern, Moyshe-Leyb, 8:**285**

Halphen, Achille-Edmond, 8:**285**

Halphen, Fernand, 8:**285**

Halphen, Georges-Henri, 8:**285**

Halphen, Louis, 8:**285–286**

Halphen family, 8:**285**

Halprin, Ann, 8:**286**

Halprin, Rose Luria, 8:**286**

Halsman, Philippe, 8:**286**, 16:126

Halter, Marek, 8:**286–287**, 15:650

Halt in the Wilderness (Brodsky). *See Ostanovka v pustyne*

Ḥalukkah, 3:387, 8:**287–290**

Ḥalutzei ha-Sifrut ha-Ivrit ba-Amerikah (Kabakoff), 11:584

Ḥalutz plays, 8:**718–719**

Ham, 4:391

Ham (son of Noah), 8:**290–291**

Ham (Transjordan), 8:**290**

Ḥama (amora), 8:**291**

Ha-Ma'abarah (Ballas), 3:92

ha-Ma'aravi. *See* Samuel ben Moses al-Maghribī

Ḥama Bar Bisa, 8:**291**, 15:501

Ḥama Bar Ḥanina, 8:**291**

Ha-Mabbit (periodical), 18:692

Hamadan (Iran), 8:**292–293**

Ḥamadyah (Israel), 8:**293**

Hamafdal. *See* National Religious Party

Ha-Mafte'aḥ (Shatzkes), 18:421

Ha-Maggid (newspaper), 6:240, 8:**293**

Ha-Maḥazeh ha-Ivri ha-Histori bi-Tekufat ha-Teḥiyyah (Shaked), 18:368

Ha-Malakh. *See* Abraham ben Dov of Mezhirech

Hama massacre, 2:541

Ha-Mamon (Horowitz), 9:534

Haman, 2:31, 6:334, 8:**294–295**, 14:478, 18:215, 217
    Scroll of Esther, 18:215

"*Haman and his Demise*" (Dubnow-Erlich), 6:37

Haman the Agagite. *See* Haman

Ḥama of Nehardea, 8:**291**

Ha-Ma'or (Gerondi), 7:549–550

Ha-Ma'pil (Israel), 8:**294**

"Ha-Ma'pil" (Kabak), 11:584

Hamas, 8:**294–295**, 10:725
    Palestine Liberation Organization and, 15:594, 595
    Palestinian Authority and, 15:597, 600

theft and robberies, 19:680

Hamashbir Hamerkazi, 8:**295**

Ha-Mashbir ha-Merkazi, 9:148

Ha-Mashbir he-Ḥadash (Schoenhack), 18:157

Ha-Maspik le-Ovedei ha-Shem. See Kifayat al-abidin

Ha-Matmid (Bialik), 3:563

Ha-Mavdil, 8:**295**

Hambro, Carl Joachim, 8:**295**

Hambro, Joseph, 8:**295**

Hamburg (Germany), 8:**295–297**
    Altona, 2:23–24
    banishment, 3:111

Hamburg, Abraham Benjamin, 8:**297–298**

Hamburg City Theater, 16:360

Hamburger, Jacob, 6:400, 8:**298**

Hamburger, Michael, 8:**298**

Hamburger, Mordechai. *See* Moses, Marcus

Hamburger, Sidney. *See* Hamburger, Sir Sidney

Hamburger, Sir Sidney, 8:**298**

Hamdī, Levi ben Yeshu'ah, 8:**298**

ham Dov MikhailishkerAbra. *See* Lebensohn, Abraham Dov

Ha-Me'assef (Franco-Mendes), 7:177

Hame'assef (journal), 8:**298–299**, 437, 440

Hameiri, Avigdor, 8:**299–300**

Ha-Meiri, Menahem, 8:667

Hameiri, Moshe, 8:**300**, 14:390

Hamel, Jacob, 4:77

Ha-Meliẓ (newspaper), 6:476, 8:**300**, 476, 12:744, 18:684–685

Hameln (Germany), 8:**300–301**

Hamenaḥem, Ezra, 8:**301**

Ha-Me'orer (monthly), 8:**301**

Der Hamer (newspaper), 6:475

Hamerow, Theodore Stephen, 8:**301**

Ḥameẓ, 8:**301–303**
    sale of, 8:**303**

Ha-Mikra be-Rambam (Kafah), 17:341–342

Hamilton (Canada), 8:**303–305**

Hamilton, Ian, Zion Mule Corps, 11:303

Ha-Minah Lizah (Castel-Bloom), 4:512

Ḥamishah Kinyanim (Lonzano), 13:187

Ḥamisha Perakim bi-Ysodot ha-Shirah (Goldberg), 7:694

Ha-Mishpat ha-Ivri (Elon), 6:367

Ha-Mishpat ha-Ivri Society, 14:352

Ḥamiẓ, Joseph ben Judah, 8:**305**

Hamizpeh (newspaper), 8:**305**

Hamlet (Slonimsky), 18:680

Hamlet: oder Die lange Nacht nimmt ein Ende (Doeblin), 5:729–730

Hamlisch, Marvin, 8:**305–306**

Hamlyn, Paul, Baron, 8:**306**

Ḥammat Gader (ancient Israel), 8:**306**

Hammath (ancient Israel), 8:**306–307**

Hammel, Shimon, 18:201

Hammer, Armand, 8:**307–308**

Hammer, Reuven, 8:**308**

Hammer, Robert A. *See* Hammer, Reuven

Hammer, Zevulun, 8:**308–309**

"Hammerin' Hank." *See* Greenberg, Henry Benjamin

Hammerstein, Arthur, 8:**309**

Hammerstein, Oscar, 8:**309**

Hammerstein, Oscar II, 8:**309**

Hammerstein, William, 8:**309**

Hammerstein family, 8:**309**

Ḥammuda, Yaḥya, 10:280

Hammurapi, 3:23, 8:**309–310**
    Amraphel, 2:106

Hammurapi, Code of, 5:133–134, 8:**310**
    Book of the Covenant's similarity to, 4:67

Hamnuna, 8:**310**

Hamnuna amoraim, 8:**310**

Hamnuna Saba, 8:**310**

Hamnuna Zuta, 8:**310**

Ha-Moda'i. *See* Eleazar of Mod'in

Ha-modi'a (newspaper), 8:**310–311**

Hamon, Aaron ben Isaac, 8:**312**

Hamon, Abraham Yesha, 8:312

Hamon, Av, 8:312

Hamon, Isaac, 8:311, 312

Hamon, Joseph, 8:312

Hamon, Joseph the Elder, 8:311

Hamon, Judah, 8:312

Hamon, Leo, 8:**312–313**, 16:343

Hamon, Moses, 2:33, 8:**311–312**

Hamon family, 8:**311–312**, 15:541

Hamor, 8:**313**

Ha-Mora (Shemariah ben Elijah ben Jacob), 18:457

Ha-Moreh. *See* Gozhansky, Samuel; Nahum, Aaron Sassoon ben Eliahu

Ḥamsa, amulets, 2:122, 123

Hamta. *See* Ammatha (ancient city)

Ha-Musikah (Smoira-Cohn), 18:690

Ḥana Bar Ḥanilai, 8:**313**

Ḥana ben Bizna, 8:**313**

Hanafi Muslim terrorist attack on B'nai B'rith headquarters, 4:16

Hanamel, 8:**314**

Hananel ben Ḥushi'el, 2:529, 6:315, 8:**314–315**

Hananel ben Samuel, 8:**315**

Hanani, Ḥaim, 8:**315**

Hananiah (2nd c.), 8:**315**

Hananiah (3rd-4th c.). *See* Ḥanina (3rd-4th c.)

Hananiah (Book of Daniel), 5:418, 419

Hananiah ben Ḥakhinai, 8:**315–316**

Hananiah ben Teradyon, 6:305, 8:**316**

Hananiah of Sephoris, 8:**316**

Hananiah son of Azzur, 8:**316–317**

Hanan the Egyptian, 8:**314**

Hana of Manosque. *See* Hava of Manosque

Hanau (Germany), 8:**317–318**

Hanau, Solomon Zalman ben Judah Loeb ha-Kohen, 8:**318**

Hanbury, Lily, 8:**318**

Hânceşti (Moldova). *See* Kotovskoye (Moldova)

Hand, foot washing, 1:262–263

Handali, Esther, 8:**318**, 15:541

Handali, Joshua ben Joseph, 8:**318–319**

Hand an sich legen. Diskurs ueber den Freitod (Améry), 2:65

Handatlas der Hautkrankheiten (Kaposi), 11:781

Handball, 9:45–46, 19:142–143

Handbuch der alttestamentlichen Theologie (Dillmann), 5:661–662

Handbuch der historisch-geographischen Pathologie (Hirsch), 9:123

Handbuch der Schulhygiene (Baginsky), 3:59

Handbuch des medizinischen Klinik (Cannstadt), 4:431

Handel, George Friderich, 18:762

Handel, Georg Friedrich, 14:542

Handelsgeschichte der Juden des Altertums (Herzfeld), 9:53

Handelsman, Marceli, 8:**319**

Handicrafts. *See* Crafts

Handler, Evelyn, 4:124

Handler, Milton, 8:**319**

Handler, Miriam, 8:319

Handler, Philip, 8:**319**

Handler, Ruth Mosko, 8:**319–320**

Handler, Simon. *See* Hevesi, Simon

Handlin, Oscar, 8:**320**

Hands, symbolism of, 18:570

Handshakes. *See* Teki'ata

The Hand that Signed the Paper (Demidenko), 18:202

Ha-Ne'ehovim ve-ha-Ne'imim oder der Shvartse Yungermantshik (Dineson), 5:671

Ha-Ner Lo Kavah (Shalom), 18:377

Ha-Nesikhah ha-Amerikait (Aloni), 1:687, 8:723

ha-Neẓiv. *See* Berlin, Naphtali Ẓevi Judah

Hanfmann, G. M., 2:370

Hanfmann, George Maxim Anossov, 8:**320**

Hangchow (China), 8:**320–321**

Hanging (execution method). *See* Capital punishment

Hanhagot ha-Rosh (Asher ben Jehiel), 2:564

Hanhagot literature, 6:526

Ḥanīf, 8:**321**

Hanina. *See* Hananiah

Ḥanina (3rd-4th c.), 8:**321**

Ḥanina bar Ḥama, 8:**321–322**

Ḥanina ben Abbahu, 8:**322**

Ḥanina ben Antigonus, 8:**322**

Ḥanina ben Dosa, 8:**323**, 390

Ḥanina ben Gamaliel, 8:**323**

Hanina ben Ḥakhinai. *See* Hananiah ben Ḥakhinai

Ḥanina ben Kahana ben Huna, 8:**323**

Ḥanina of Brat Hauran. *See* Ḥunya of Beth-Horon

Ḥanina Segan ha-Kohanim, 5:760–761, 6:215, 8:**323–324**

Ḥanitah (Israel), 8:**324**

Hankin, Yehoshua, 8:**324**

Hannah (wife of Elkanah), 2:201, 6:317, 8:**324–325**

Peninnash and, 15:726

Hanna Senesh (Megged), 8:720

Hannathon (ancient Israel), 8:**326**

Ḥanneles, Judah Leib ben Meir, 8:**326**

Hannemann, Pablo, 8:**326**

Hannover, Adolph, 8:**326**

Hannover, Nathan Nata, 8:**326–327**, 11:670

Hannover, Raphael Levi, 8:**327**, 13:676

Ha-No'ar ha-Ivri-Akiba, 8:**327**

Ha-No'ar ha-Oved Ve-ha-Lomed, 8:**327–328**

Hanokh, Shalom, 8:**328**

Ḥanokh ben Moses, 8:**328–329**

Ḥanokh of Aleksandrow, 8:**329**

Ḥanokh Zundel ben Joseph, 8:**329**

Hanover (Germany), 8:**329–330**

Hanray, Lawrence, 8:**330–331**

Hanseatic League, 13:252

Hanson, Norman Leonard, 8:**331**

Hantke, Arthur, 8:**331**

Hantke, Menahem. *See* Hantke, Arthur

Ḥanukkah, 8:**331–333**
  altar dedication during, 2:15
  Amidah, 2:75
  celebration in Israel, vol. 6: color insert
  celebration in New York City, vol. 20: color insert
  celebration in Yemen, vol. 6: color insert
  clown in dreidel costume, vol. 17: color insert
  folklore, 7:104
  food, 7:120–121
  games, 7:371–372
  Hallel, 8:279
  lighting the candles, vol. 17: color insert
  Ma'oz Ẓur, 13:496–497
  meals, 7:120–121
  parodies of, 15:657
  Scroll of Antiochus, 18:214
  woman rabbi celebrating, Italy, vol. 5: color insert
  See Also Hasmoneans

Ḥanukkah lamp, 6:357, 8:**333–335**
  amulets, 2:122, 123
  bas relief (3rd c.), vol. 14: color insert
  catacombs, 4:522
  image of, 11:224–225

Hanun, 2:84

Ha-Ogen (Israel), 8:**335–336**

Haolam (Weekly), 8:**336**

Ha-Olam ha-Zeh (periodical), 2:742

Ha-Olam ha-Zeh-Ko'ah Hadash, 2:742

Ha-On (Israel), 8:**336**

Ha-Onah ha-Bo'eret (Megged), 8:722

Ha-Or, 3:387

Ha-Oved ha-Ẓiyyoni, 8:**336–337**

Ha-Pardes (periodical), 15:633

Ha-Parḥi, Estori, 15:343

Ha-Parnas, Sefer (Parnas), 8:**337**

Ha-Patriyot (Levin), 8:721

Hapax Legomena, 8:**337**

Ha-Penini. *See* Jedaiah ben Abraham Bedersi

Hapharaim (ancient Israel), 8:**337**

Ha-Pisgah (periodical), 8:735, 18:176

Hapoel, 8:**338**

Ha-Po'el ha-Mizrachi, 4:18, 6:355, 8:**338–340**, 10:607–608, 14:390–392

Ha-Po'el ha-Za'ir (newspaper), 1:537, 8:**340**, 14:420

Ha-Po'el ha-Za'ir (political party), 1:537, 540, 3:138, 8:**340–342**, 9:247, 286–287

Happiness, eternal. *See* Beatitude
Hapsburg monarchy, 8:**342–343**
    antisemitism, 2:219
    Francis Joseph I of Hapsburg,
        7:175
    Jews in, 2:688–689, 11:115
Haqqoni, 4:264
Ha-Rabbah. *See* Rabbah (ha-Rabbah)
HaRAH. *See* Aaron ben Joseph ha-
    Levi
Ha-Ramah. *See* Ramah (ancient Israel)
Ha-Ramathaim-Zophim. *See* Ramah
    (ancient Israel)
Ha-Ramkol (Shamir), 18:392
Haran (Babylon), 8:**343–344**
Haran, Menahem, 3:653, 8:**344**
Harare (Zimbabwe). *See* Salisbury
    (Rhodesia)
Harari, Ḥayyim (1883-1940), 8:**344**
Harari, Ḥayyim (1940-), 8:**344–345**
Harari, Ḥayyim Solomon, 8:**344**
Harari, Isaac ben Moses, 8:**344**
Harari, Izhar, 8:**344**
Harari, Moses ben Isaac, 8:**344**
Harari, Nissim ben Isaiah, 8:**344**
Harari, Ovadiah, 8:**345**
Harari, Shalom, 8:**344**
Harari, Sir Victor Raphael, 8:**345**
Harari, Victor Raphael. *See* Harari, Sir
    Victor Raphael
Harari, Yehudit, 8:**344**
Harari family, 8:**344**
Haratin, 6:5
Ha-Rav Aharon ha-Levi. *See* Aaron
    ben Joseph ha-Levi
Harbin (China), 8:**345–346**
Harburg, E. Y., 8:**346**
Harby, Isaac, 8:**346**, 9:161
Harby, Levi Myers, 8:**346**
Harden, Maximillian, 8:**346–347**,
    21:682–683
Hardenberg, Karl August von, 8:**347**
Hardman, Jacob Benjamin, 8:**347**
Hardy, Nell. *See* Carter, Nell
Hardy, René, 3:141
Hare, 8:**347–348**
Ḥaredi. *See* Orthodox Judaism
Ḥaredim, 8:311, **348–352**
Harei Besamim (Horowitz), 9:532–533
Harel (Israel), 8:**352**
Harel, David, 8:**352**
Harel, Menashe, 8:**352**
Harel, Yisrael, 8:**352–353**
Harendorf, Samuel Jacob, 8:**353**
Ha-Reubeni, Ephraim, 8:**353**
Ha-Reubeni, Hannah, 8:353

Hareven, Gail, 8:**353**
Hareven, Shulamith, 8:**353–354**
Hareven, Tamara, 9:152
Harf, Hanns, 8:**354**
Harf, Suse Hallenstein, 8:**354**
Har ha-Keramim (Hillels), 9:115
Har ha-Melekh (ancient Israel), 8:**354**
Ḥarif, Ḥayyim ben Joseph, 8:**355**
Ḥarif, Israel, 8:**354**
Ḥarif, Jacob Isaac, 8:**355**
Ḥarif, Joseph, 8:**355**
Ḥarif, Joseph Segal, 8:**355**
Ḥarif, Judah Leib, 8:**354**
Ḥarif, Moses Ḥayyim, 8:**354–355**
Ḥarif, Moses Ḥayyim ben Eleazar,
    8:**354–355**
Ḥarif, Moses ha-Zaken ben Israel,
    8:**354**
Ḥarif, Moses Phineas, 8:354
Ḥarif, Solomon ben Isaac Abraham,
    8:**355**
Ḥarif, Ẓevi Hirsch, 8:**354**
Ḥarif family, 8:**354–355**
Ḥarif Ha-Levi family, 8:**355**
Ḥariri, Abraham ben Phineas, 8:355
Ḥariri, Ḥayyim, 8:355
Ḥariri, Isaac, 8:355
Ḥariri, Isaac ben Moses, 8:355
Ḥariri, Isaac ha-Levi, 8:355
Ḥariri, Moses, 8:355
Ḥariri, Phineas, 8:355
Ḥariri, Solomon ben Isaac Abraham,
    8:355
Ḥariri family, 8:**355**
Ḥarizi, Abu Isaac Abraham, 8:**355**
Harkavi, Abraham Elijah. *See* Harkavy,
    Albert
Harkavi, Isaac. *See* Harkavi, Yitzhak
Harkavi, Yitzhak, 8:**355–356**
Harkavy, Albert, 8:**356–357**
Harkavy, Alexander, 8:**357**
Harkavy, Minna B., 8:**357–358**
Harlau (Moldavia), 8:**358–359**
Harlem Globetrotters, 18:34
Harlow, Julius, 8:**359**
Harman, Avraham, 8:**359**
Harman, Herman. *See* Harman,
    Avraham
Harman, Jane, 8:**360**
Harmatz, William, 8:**360**
Harmonica, 1:401–402
Harmony, numerical, 15:337
Harnick, Sheldon, 4:26, 8:**360–361**
Haro (Spain), 8:**361**
The Harod Valley (Israel), 10:118
*Ha-Ro'eh u-Mevakker Sifrei Meḥaberei
    Zemannenu* (Mohr), 14:420

Harofe ha-Ivri (periodical), 6:259
Ḥaroset, 8:**361**
Ha-Rosh. *See* Shalom, Abraham
Harosheth-Goiim (ancient Israel),
    8:**361**
Harran, Don, 8:**361–362**
The Harrassment (Duda), 6:40
Harris, Barbara, 8:**362**
Harris, Cyril Kitchener, 8:**362**, 11:378
Harris, David. *See* Harris, Sir David
Harris, Jed, 8:**362**
Harris, Louis, 8:**362–363**
Harris, Mark, 8:**363**
Harris, Marvin, 8:**363**
Harris, Maurice, 8:**363–364**
Harris, Milton, 8:**364**
Harris, Percy Alfred. *See* Harris, Sir
    Percy Alfred
Harris, Sam Henry, 8:**364**
Harris, Sir David, 8:**362**, 16:349
Harris, Sir Percy Alfred, 8:**364**
Harris, Sol, 3:769
Harris, Sydney, 8:**364–365**
Harris, Zellig Sabbetai, 8:**365**, 13:60
Harrisburg (PA), 8:**365–366**
Harrison, Earl G., 20:430–431
Harrison, Leon, 8:**366**
Harrison, Lester, 8:**366**
Ḥarrison, Rex, 15:606
Harrisse, Henry, 8:**366**
Harry, Myriam, 8:**366–367**
Harry Fischel Institute for Research in
    Talmud and Jewish Law, 18:724
Harshav, Benjamin, 8:**367**
Hart, Aaron, 4:394, 8:**367**, 16:341
    Judah family (Canada), 11:479
Hart, Abraham, 8:**368**
Hart, Benjamin, 8:**368**
Hart, Bernard, 8:**368–369**, 15:200
Hart, Cecil M., 8:**369**
Hart, Daniel, 8:**369**
Hart, Eli, 15:199
Hart, Emanuel Bernard, 8:**369**, 15:198,
    200
Hart, Ephraim, 8:**369**, 15:197
Hart, Ernest Abraham, 8:**369–370**
Hart, Ezekiel, 8:**370**, 16:341
Hart, Henry, 4:19
Hart, Herbert Lionel Adolphus, 8:**370**
Hart, Isaac, 8:**370**
Hart, Jacob, 8:**370**
Hart, Joel, 8:**370–371**
Hart, Kitty Carlisle, 8:**371**
Hart, Levy, 14:445
Hart, Lorenz, 8:**371–372**
Hart, Moses, 8:367

Hart, Moss, 8:**372**

Hart, Myer, 8:**372**

Hart, Samuel, 8:**372**

Hart, Solomon Alexander, 8:**372**

Hart family, 4:394–395

Hart family (England), 8:**367**

Hart family (United States), 8:368*t*

Hartford (CT), 5:162, 8:**372–374**

Hartglas, Maximilian Meir Apolinary, 8:**374**

Hartman, David, 8:**374–376,** 16:103–104

Hartman, Geoffrey, 8:**376–377**

Hartman, Harriet, 18:736

Hartman, Hella, 4:369

Hartman, Moritz, 11:782

Hartmann, Hansi, 4:120

Hartmann, Heinz, 8:**377**

Hartmann, Ludo Moritz, 8:377

Hartmann, Moritz, 8:**377–378**

Hartog, Levie de, 8:**378**

Hartog, Numa Edward, 8:378

Hartog, Philip Joseph. *See* Hartog, Sir Philip Joseph

Hartog, Sir Philip Joseph, 6:161, 8:**378**

Hartogensis, Benjamin Henry, 8:**378**

Hartogh, Abraham, 16:345

Hartt, Maurice, 16:341

Hartt, Stanley, 14:464

Hărtuiala (Duda). *See The Harrassment* (Duda)

Harun al-Yahudi. *See* Aaron ben Batash

Hārūn a-Yehūdī. *See* Aaron ben Batash

Harvard University
    Frankfuter, Felix, 7:205
    law school, 12:555–556
    numerus clausus at, 15:343

Harvest of Hate. See Bréviaire de la haine

Harvey, Laurence, 8:**378**

Hary, B., 3:605

Harẓaʿot al ha-Islam (Plessner), 16:237

Har Ẓevi (Frank), 7:196

Harzfeld, Avraham, 8:**378–379**

Ha-Safarty, Raphael Menahem, 18:55

Hasambah (Mossinsohn), 4:626

Ḥasan
    abu Ali Jepheth ibn Bundār, 8:**379**
    ben Mashi'ah, 8:**379**

Hasan, Japeth al-. *See* Barqamani, Japeth al-

Hasan, King of Morocco, 1:580

Hasan-Rokem, Galit, 1:461

Ha-Sarfaty, Isaac, 18:55

Ha-Sarfaty, Vidal, 18:55

Ha-sar mi-Coucy. *See* Samson ben Samson of Coucy

Ha-Sar mi-Evreux. *See* Samuel of Evreux

Ḥasdai ben Baradoi, 8:379

Ḥasdai ben Bustanai, 8:379

Ḥasdai ben David ben Hezekiah, 8:379

Ḥasdai ben Natronai, 8:379

Ḥasdai Benvenist. *See* Benvenist, Adzay

Ḥasdai Crescas
    articles of faith, 2:530
    Duns Scotus, John, 6:51
    Duran, Profiat, 6:56–57
    miracles, 14:308–309
    physics and, 16:133
    prophets and prophecy, 16:584–585

Ḥasdai family, 8:379

Ḥasdai ibn Shaprut. *See* Ḥisdai ibn Shaprut

Ha-Sefarim, 3:574

Hasefer, 8:**379–380**

Hašek, Jaroslav, 4:193

Haselkorn, Abraham, 9:380

Hasenclever, Walter, 8:380

Ha-Shaḥar (journal), 8:**380–381,** 442–443, 18:691–692

"Ha-Shalom" (Halévy), 8:270

Ha-Shavui (Yizhar), 21:378

Ha-Shelah ha-Kodosh. *See* Horowitz, Isaiah ben Abraham ha-Levi

ha-Shelavim ha-Aḥaronim be-Ḥakamat ha-Medinah (Sherf), 18:462

Hashemite Kingdom, 1:243

Ha-Shilo'aḥ (journal), 1:526, 6:240, 8:**381,** 12:762

Ha-Shirim asher li-Shelomo (Rossi), 14:409

Hashkavah prayer, 2:567

Hashkivenu, 8:**381–382**

Ḥashmal, 14:128

Ha-Shomer (military group), 8:201, 10:464–465

Ha-Shomer ha-Ẓa'ir, 8:382, **382–385,** 13:146
    Anielewicz, Mordecai, 2:164
    archives, 2:416
    Ben-Zvi, Izhak, 3:394
    bi-nationalism promoted by, 3:702, 703
    Canada, 4:407
    development as Marxist movement, 18:721
    founding of, 18:720

Ha-Kibbutz ha-Arzi ha-Shomer ha-Ẓa'ir, 12:124

Horowitz, David, 9:533

Ha-Shunra ve-ha-Schmetterling (Hoffmann), 9:312

Ḥasidei Ashkenaz, 8:**386–389,** 11:599–602
    gematria, 7:425–426
    Ḥasidim, sefer, 8:392

Ḥasidei Ummot ha-Olam, 8:**389–390,** 17:303–307

Ḥasidic literature, 8:414, 417–419
    autobiographical elements in, 3:706
    fiction, 7:16
    parables in, 15:623

Ḥasidim, 8:**390–392**
    abstinence and asceticism, 8:391
    Iowa, 10:8
    Israel, early settlement, 10:625
    Judah ben Samuel he-Ḥasid, 11:490–491

Ḥasidim, Sefer. See Sefer Ḥasidim

Ḥasidim, sefer, 6:529, 600

Ḥasidism, 8:**393–434,** 394, 400*t*–407*t,* 9:237
    Aaron ben Moses ha-Levi of Starosielce and, 1:216–217
    Aaron Samuel ben Naphtali Herz ha-Kohen, 1:220
    Abraham ben Alexander Katz of Kalisk, 1:294
    Abraham ben Dov of Mazhirech, 1:298
    Abraham Dov Baer of Ovruch, 1:311
    Abraham Gerson of Kutow, 1:311–312
    Abraham Ḥayyim ben Gedaliah, 1:312
    Abraham Joshua Heschel of Apta, 1:312–313
    Abramovitsh, Sholem Yankev, 1:319
    Adam Ba'al Shem, 1:378
    Adel, 1:385
    Adler, Nathan ben Simeon ha-Kohen, 1:404–405
    Admor, 1:412
    Agnon, Shmuel Yosef, 1:465
    aliyah of, 8:395, 10:332
    Aminshov dynasty, 20:651
    angels, 2:161
    Argentina, 2:447
    Ashkenaz, 6:44
        Eleazar ben Judah of Worms, 6:303–305
        Eleazar ben Moses ha-Darshan of Wuerzburg, 6:305

Ḥasidism, *continued*

Elhanan ben Yakar, 6:316

ba'al shem, 3:9

basic ideas of

Creator and the universe, 8:408

hitlahavut and joy, 8:409

kavannah and Ẓakkism, 8:409–410

Belarus, 16:171

Belz dynasty, 3:308–309

Bick, Jacob Samuel, 3:685

in Bistrita, 3:727

Bobover, 4:23–24

Bodrogkeresztúr, 4:30

Bratslav (Ukraine), 14:751–753

Bratslaver, 14:751–753, 19:222

Breslov Ḥasidism, 11:773

Buber and, 4:231, 234, 8:416–417

centers of, Medzibezh (Ukraine), 13:763

Chabad, 4:553–555, 18:503–505

Chernobyl dynasty, 5:474–475

Ciechanow, Abraham ben Raphael Landau of, 4:726

contemporary Judaism and, 11:519

dance, 5:410–411

dance niggunim, 8:428, 429, *431, 433*

devekut, 8:413

devotion to God, 11:104, 14:24

Dov Baer of Mezhirech, 5:766–768, 8:394–395, 411–412

dynastic geneology, 8:400t–407t

dynastic musical styles, 8:427–428

dynasties, Izbica Radzyn, 10:824–825

dynasties and descendants, 8:419–425

Eliezer ben Jacob ha-Levi of Tarnogrod, 6:326

Elijah ben Solomon Zalman, 6:342–343

Elimelech of Lyzhansk, 6:348–349

emotions, 6:397

Epstein, Kalonymus Kalman of Cracow, 6:474–475

founder, 10:743–745

founders, Jacob Isaac, 11:39–41

Galicia, 7:343

Gorodok dynasty, 5:473

Gur dynasty, 7:760–761

hagiography, 8:226

Halberstam dynasty, 8:264–265

ḥamez, 8:302

Ḥanokh of Aleksandrow, 8:329

Ḥaredim, 8:348–352

ḥasidim ha-rishonim period, 8:390

Haskalah and, 8:416

Ḥavazzelet, 8:466

Ḥayyim ben Solomon Tyrer of Czernowitz, 8:482

Ḥayyim Ḥaykl ben Samuel of Amdur, 8:482

history

Bunin, Ḥayyim Isaac, 4:284

first three generations, 8:393–395

modern period, 8:396–397, 398

Horowitz, Pinchas David ha-Levi, 9:541

Hungary and, 9:610

influence on Jewish philosophy, 16:104–105

Israel ben Eliezer Ba'al Shem Tov, 8:393–394, 395

joy, concept of, 11:471

Judaism, development of concept of, 11:517

Kabbalah, 11:622

Kabbalistic writings, 8:414

Kahana, Abraham, 11:710

King, parable of, 8:408

Lachowicze, 12:425

leaders

Menahem Mendel of Vitebsk, 14:25–26

Menahem Mendel Peremyshlany, 14:24

Levi Isaac ben Meir of Berdichev, 12:704–706

literature, 6:600, 7:16, 8:414, 417–419

ethical, 6:529–530

Zava'at Ribash, 21:462–463

Lithuania, 11:809, 12:425

Lublin, Poland, 13:243

meditation and, 13:762

Meir Jehiel ha-Levi of Ostrowiec, 13:788

Mitnaggedim, 14:371

mitzvot performance, 8:413

modern developments, 8:417–419

music traditions, 8:425–430, *431–434,* 14:676

Naḥman of Bratslav, 14:748–751

narratives, 8:415

in New York City

Boro Park, 15:230–231

Williamsburg, 15:237

niggun, 14:676

opposition, 8:395–396, 415–416, 11:41

David of Makow, 5:474

Ornstein, Jacob Meshullam ben Mordecai Ze'ev, 15:480

Ostrow Mazowiecka, dispute between Hasidim and Mitnaggedim in, 15:514

in Pabianice, 15:561

in Pale of Settlement, 15:579

Palestine (Ottoman), support of, 10:748

parodies of, 15:658–660

Peremyshlyany (Ukraine) and, 15:762–763

Piekarz, Mendel, 11:684

piety, 16:150

Poland, 1:610

polemical opposition to, 16:329–330

Polonnoye, 16:360

prayer, 16:460

prayer books, 16:464

principles of, 21:463

psychology, 16:688

publications, 8:419

Tanya, 18:504–505

repentance, 7:128–129, 17:223

Romania, 5:433

Jassy, 11:92

satires, Erter, Isaac, 6:483–484

Savran dynasty, 18:86

Shabbatean influence on, 11:42–43

sheḥitah, 18:435–436

spread of

eighteenth century, 11:52, 104

twentieth century, 11:677

teachings, 10:745–746

ethical values, 8:412

worship through physical acts, 8:410–412

Twersky dynasty, 20:208–209

United States, 8:397, 15:495

Vizhnitz dynasty, 20:564

Warka dynasty, 20:650–651

way of life

dynastic geneology, 8:400t–407t

leadership, 8:398–399

prayer and customs, 8:399, 408

women and, 8:397–398, 21:177–178, 185

World Wars influence, 8:397

Yiddish literature, 21:345, 357–358

Ẓaddik, 11:40, 41–42

descent of, 6:348–349

doctrine of, 6:348

Zanz and Sadagora controversy, 8:264–265

Zhidachov dynasty, 21:522

Ḥasidut (Abraham ben Eliezer ha-Levi Berukhim), 1:299

Ḥasifat Gernuzim mi-Teiman (Nahum), 17:342

Ha-Sifrut ha-Ivrit ha-Ḥadashah li-Zrameha (Shaanan), 18:335

Ha-Sifrut ha-Yehudit ha-Hellinistit (Gutmann), 8:154

Haskalah, 8:**434–444**, *435, 9:237*
  Bally, Davicon, 3:94
  Barit Jacob, 3:154–155
  Berdichev, 3:402–403
  Bialystok (Poland), 3:567
  Bick, Jacob Samuel, 3:685
  Brody, diffsuion by Jews of, 4:199
  children's literature, 4:620–621
  community, 5:109
  Czechoslovakia, 4:39
  David in literature, 5:455
  Dik, Isaac, 5:660–661
  drama, 8:714, 19:678
  education, 6:159, 8:437–439
  education curricula, 4:620–621
  Elijah ben Solomon Zalman, 6:344
  Galicia, 7:342–343
    Mieses, Judah Leib, 14:206
  Galician, 8:688–689
  Germany, 8:434–436
    Frederick the Great, 3:446
  Gordon's poetry, 7:770–771
  Hame'assef, 8:298–299, 437, 440
  Ha-Meliẓ, 8:300
  Ha-Shahar, 8:442–443
  Ha-ShaḤar, 8:380–381
  Ḥasidism, 8:416
  Hebrew
    development of, 8:437
    influence on, 8:671
  Hebrew newspapers, 15:155
  Hebrew poetry, 16:598
    Franco-Mendes, David, 7:177
  history, 8:434–436
  Hochschule Fuer die Wissenschaft des Judentums, 9:300
  Homberg, Naphtali Herz, 9:504–505
  ideology, 8:439–440, 442–443
  Juedische-theologisches Seminar, 21:108–109
  Kerem Ḥemed, 12:81–82
  labor, 12:411
  leaders
    German Euchel, 6:547
    Krochmal, Nachman, 16:95
    Meisel, Moses ben Mordecai, 13:789

Mendelsohn, Frankfurt Moses, 14:30
Mendelssohn, Moses, 14:33–40
Peretz, Abraham, 15:764
Perl, Joseph, 15:773–774
Schorr, Joshua Heschel, 18:163–164
Lebensohn, Abraham Dov, 12:589–590
Lebensohn, Micah Joseph, 12:590–591
Leopold Zunz, 21:684–688
linguistic assimilation, 8:436–437
literature, 6:727, 8:686–691
  Bikkurei ha-Ittim, 3:696–697, 8:688
  biography and autobiography, 3:707
  Bloch, Samson ha-Levi, 3:767–768
  Franzos, Karl Emil, 7:219
  Jerusalem, 11:215–217
  Levin, Menahem Mendel, 12:710–711
  Levinsohn, Isaac Baer, 12:720–722
  Mendelssohn, Moses, 8:687
  Russia, 8:441, 443
  types of, 8:687–688
  Wessely, Naphtali Hartwig, 8:687
Lithuania, 13:120
  Raseiniai, 17:101
mathematics and, 13:677–678
mediators with Orthodox Judaism, 11:121
Menahem Mendel Levin, 12:**710–711**
Netherlands, 8:436–437
opponents, 13:790
Ornstein, Jacob Meshullam ben Mordecai Ze'ev, 15:480
parody, Hebrew, 15:658–660
Poland, Breslau, 4:164
Prague, leaders, 11:115
Rapoport, Solomon Leib, 17:99
Romania, 3:135
Russia, 8:440–443, 12:707–708, 17:535
Russian, 8:688–691
satires, Erter, Isaac, 6:483–484
Schick, Baruch ben Jacob, 18:125–126
Smolenskin, Perez, 18:693
Society for the Promotion of Culture Among the Jews of Russia, 18:725–728

Toleranzpaten, 4:39
Ukraine, 11:755
Wessely's poetry, 21:20
Wissenschaft des Judentums, 21:**105–114**
women, 8:435, 438, 443, 21:178–179, 181–182
women's writing, 8:699–700
Yiddish, 8:436–437
  view of, 8:686–687
Yiddish literature used to propagate, 15:773
Haskamah, 8:**444–445**
Haskell, Arnold Lionel, 8:**445**
Haskil, Clara, 8:**445**
Hasmonean bet din, 8:**445**
Hasmonean coinage, 5:48–49
Hasmoneans, 2:631, 8:*446*, **446–448**, 447t, 13:299
  Antigonus, 2:197–198
  Antigonus II, 2:197–198
  Antioch, 2:201
  Assumption of Moses, 14:544–555
  Eleazar ben Mattathias, 6:305
  European cultural influences, 6:554
  fall of, 2:457
  historiography, 9:154
  Jaffa under, 11:60
  Jerusalem under, 11:148–149
  Josephus Flavius, 11:439
  Josippon on, 11:461
  Judah Maccabee, 11:509–511
  Judea, 9:194–197
  Mattathias, 13:685
  revolt, 9:193–194, 11:90
Ha-Solelim (Israel), 8:**448**
Ha-Sozyalism ha-Ma'aravi u-She'elat ha-Yehudim (Silberner), 18:577
Hassagot, 1:297, 8:**453–454**
Hassan. See Chao Ch'eng
Hassan, David, 8:454
Hassan, Jahuda aben Haçen, 8:454
Hassan, Joshua. See Hassan, Sir Joshua
Hassan, Raphael, 8:454
Hassan, Salvador, 8:454
Hassan, Shemayyah, 8:454
Hassan, Sir Joshua, 8:**454**
Hassan family, 8:**454**
Ḥassān ibn Ḥassān, 8:**454**
Hassan II (king of Morocco), 14:503–504
Hasse, Hugo, 18:705
Hassegat gevul, 8:**448–453**
  copyright law, 8:450–451, 453
  intellectual property rights, 8:451, 453

Hassegat gevul, *continued*
    monopoly infringement, 8:452–453
    tenancy rights, 8:449–450
    trespassing, 8:449–451
Hassenfeld, Sylvia Kay, 8:**454–455**
Hassid, William Zev, 8:**455**
Hassideans, 8:**455**
Hast, Marcus, 8:**455**
Ḥatam Sofer. *See* Sofer, Moses
Ḥatan Damim (Hazaz), 8:492
Hatan Sofer (Hungarian rabbi). *See* Ehrenfeld, Samuel ben David ẒEvi
Ḥatan Sofer (Ehrenfeld), 6:239
Hatchwell, Sol, 8:**455–456**
Ha-Tefillah. *See* Amidah
Hatefutsoth, Beth, 16:130
Ha-Tekufa (Elisheva), 6:354
Ha-Tekufah (periodical), 8:**456**, 12:424
Ha-Tekufah ha-Gedolah (Kasher), 11:821
Ha-Telai ha-Shaḥor (Avnery), 18:206
Ha-Telem ha-Rishon (Raab, Judah), 17:6
Ha-Tenu'ah ha-Demokratit Le-Shinu'i. *See* Democratic Movement for Change
Ha-Tenu'ah le-Ma'an Ereẓ Israel ha-Shelemah, 8:456, **456–457**
Ha-Tikvah, 8:**457–458**
Ha-Tikvah, 11:229
Ha-To'eh be-Darkhei ha-Hayyim (Smolenskin), 18:692
Ha-To'eh be-Darkhei ha-Ḥayyim (Smolenskin), 18:691
Hatokai, Aldin, 8:**458**
Ha-Tor (newspaper), 8:123–124
Ha Torah ve ha-Medinah, 17:237
Ha-Toren (periodical), 8:735
Hatra, Aramaic, 2:348
Hatred, ill-will, 8:**458–459**
Hatry, Clarence Charles, 8:**459**
Hats, medieval Jewish, 15:*561*
Hattarat hora'ah, semikhah, 18:276–278
Ḥaṭṭ'at, on altars, 2:12–13
Ḥaṭṭe'ot Ne'urim (Lilienblum), 13:15
Ḥatti, 9:290–292
Hattusas (Turkey)
    archives, 2:403
    library, 2:404
Hattušili I, 9:292
Hatvany, Bertalan, 8:459–460
Hatvany, Ferenc, 8:459
Hatvany-Deutsch, Antonia, 8:459
Hatvany-Deutsch, József, 8:459
Hatvany-Deutsch, Lajos, 8:459

Hatvany-Deutsch, Sándor, 8:459
Hatvany-Deutsch family, 8:**459–460**
Haubenstock-Ramati, Roman, 8:**460**
Haunch, Paunch, and Jowl (Ornitz), 15:479
Haupt, Paul, 8:**460**, 470
Hauptman, Herbert Aaron, 8:**460–461**
Hauptman, Judith, 8:**461**
Hauran (Syria), 8:**461–462**, 10:131
Haurowitz, Feliz, 13:11
Haurwitz, Bernard, 8:**462**
Hausdorf, Azriel Zelig, 8:**462**
Hausdorff, Felix, 8:**463**
Hauseman, John. *See* Houseman, John
Hauser, Emil, 8:**463**
Hauser, Henri, 8:**463**
Hauser, Philip Morris, 8:**463**, 18:731
Hauser, Rita Eleanor, 8:**463–464**
Hauser, Robert, 18:732
Hauser Foundation, 8:464
Hauser's Memory (Siodmak), 18:199
Hausman, Theo, 4:371
Hausman, Tzvi. *See* Hausman, Theo
Hausner, Bernard, 8:**464**
Hausner, Gideon, 6:250, 8:**464**
Hautval, Adelaïde, 8:**464–465**
Ḥavalim (Be'er), 3:**251–252**
Havana (Cuba), 5:318, 8:**465**
Havaner Lebn (periodical), 11:780
Hava of Manosque, 8:**466**
Havas, Géza, 8:**466**
Ḥavaẓẓelet (newspaper), 8:267, **466**
Ḥavaẓ Ẓ elet ha-Sharon (Alshekh), 2:10
Ḥavaẓẓelet ha-Sharon (Babad), 3.14
Havdalah, 8:**466–468**
    Amidah, 2:75
    candles, 4:429
    fire, 7:44
    Ha-Mavdil, 8:295
    Provençal, Moses, 16:636
Ḥaver, Ḥaverim, 8:**468–470**
Ḥaver, Ḥayyim, 8:468
Ḥaver, Isaac, 8:468
Ḥaver family, 8:468
Ḥaverim, am ha-areẓ, 2:67, 68
Ḥaver ir, 8:**470**
Havilah (ancient Israel), 8:470, **470–471**
Havinenu, 2:72, 76
Ḥaviv, Avshalom, 8:**471**
Ḥaviv-Lubman, Avraham Dov, 8:**471**
Havre, Le (France), 8:**471**
Havurah, 5:175, 6:705, 8:**471–472**
    congregations, Amsterdam, 2:117–118

New York City, 15:233–234
Ḥavurah kaddisha. *See* Ḥevra kaddisha
Havurat Ẓedakah, 12:605–606
Havvah. *See* Eve
Ḥavvat Da'at (Lorbeerbaum), 13:191
Ḥavvat Yair (Bacharach), 3:34
Havvoth-Jair (ancient Israel), 8:**472**
Hawaii (HI), 8:**472–473**, *473*
Hawaja Mussa. *See* Smilansky, Moshe
Hawatmeh, Nayef, 10:281
Hawerim (de Vries). *See* Friends (de Vries)
Hawk, 8:**473**
Hawn, Goldie, 8:**473–474**
Háy, Gyulah, 8:**474**
Hay, John Milton, 8:**474**
Háy, Julius. *See* Háy, Gyulah
Ha-Yad ha-Ḥazakah (Kalischer), 11:736–737
al-Ḥayat al-Jadida (newspaper), 15:596
Hayatizadé, Mustapha, 18:349
Ḥaycraft, W., 15:582
Ḥaycraft Commission of Inquiry (1921), 15:582–583
Ḥaydān (Yemen), 8:**474**
Hayden, Henri, 8:**474–475**
Hayden, Melissa, 8:**475**
Hayden, Tom, 15:141
Ha-Yehudi ha-Aḥaron (Kaniuk), 11:763–764
Ha-Yehudi ha-Aḥaron (Weinshall), 18:206
Ha-Yehudi ha-Kadosh. *See* Przysucha, Jacob Isaac ben Asher
Ha-Yerushah (Smolenskin), 18:692–693
Hayes, Isaac Israel, 8:**475**
Hayes, Saul, 4:422, 8:**475–476**
Hayesod, Keren, 4:242, 12:714
Ha-Yevani. *See* Joab the Greek
Haynt (newspaper), 7:35–36, 36, 8:**476**
Hayntike Kinder (Shalom Aleichem), 18:385
Ha-Yom (newspaper), 8:**476**, 11:771
Ḥayon, Nehemiah Ḥiyya ben Moses, 1:213, 637, 4:181, 8:**476–478**, 15:444, 538, 769, 18:355–356
    Sheluḥei Ereẓ Israel, 18:451
Ha-Yored le-Ma'alah (Kaniuk), 11:763–764
Ha-Yoresh (Shamir), 18:392
Ha-Yoshevet ba-Ganim (Hazaz), 8:493
Hays, Arthur Garfield, 8:**478**, 12:547
Hays, Baruch, 4:70
Hays, Benjamin, 8:478
Hays, Daniel Peixotto, 8:**478–479**

Hays, David, 8:478

Hays, Isaac, 8:**479**

Hays, Jacob, 8:478

Hays, Judah, 8:478

Hays, Michael, 8:478

Hays, Michael Solomon, 15:196

Hays, Moses Michael, 4:99

Hays, Solomon, 8:478

Hays family, 8:**478**

   in New York State, 15:239

Ḥayyai Im Ishma'el (Shamir), 18:393

Ḥayyat, Reuven. *See* Trebitsch, Abraham

Ḥayyat, Judah ben Jacob, 8:**479**

Ḥayyat Kaneh (Molcho), 14:424

Ḥayyei Adam (Danzig), 5:432

Ḥayyei Ahava (Shalev), 18:373

Ḥayyei Amram (Elbaz), 6:290

Ḥayyei Avraham (Ḥalfon), 8:273

Ḥayyei Olam (Lerner), 12:658

Ḥayyei Yehonatan (Klemperer), 12:227

Ḥayyei Yehudah (Modena), 3:706, 7:15, 14:409

Ḥayyim, Samuel, 15:536

Ḥayyim Abraham Raphael ben Asher, 8:**479**

Ḥayyim ben Abraham ha-Kohen, 8:**479–480**

Ḥayyim ben Bezalel, 4:778, 8:**480**

Ḥayyim ben David, 2:32

Ḥayyim ben Hananel ha-Kohen, 8:**481**

Ḥayyim ben Isaac, 8:**481–482**

Ḥayyim ben Jehiel Ḥafeẓ Zahav, 8:**482**

Ḥayyim ben Mas'ud Raphael Alfasi, 1:638

Ḥayyim ben Samuel ben David of Tudela, 8:**482**

Ḥayyim ben Samuel Feivush, 6:686

Ḥayyim ben Shabbetai, 8:**483–484**

Ḥayyim ben Solomon Tyrer of Czernowitz, 8:**482**

Ḥayyim Ḥaykl ben Samuel of Amdur, 8:**482–483**

Ḥayyim Judah ben Ḥayyim, 8:**483**

Ḥayyim le-Olam (Modai), 14:405

Ḥayyim Mordecai of Nadwozna, 8:419

Ḥayyim Paltiel ben Jacob, 8:**483**

Ḥayyon, Nehemiah, 3:571

Ḥayyot, Menahem Manish ben Isaac, 8:**484**

Ḥayyuj, Judah ben David, 8:**484**

   Judeo-Arabic literature of, 11:533

   weak and geminative verbs, 13:39–40

Ḥayyun, Abraham ben Nissim, 8:**485**

Ḥayyun, Joseph ben Abraham, 8:**485**

Haza, Ofra, 8:**485**

Hazael, 6:350, 8:**485–486**, 18:375–376

Hazai, Samu, 8:**486**

Ḥazak, 8:**486**

Hazak, Abraham Isaac. *See* Fortis, Abraham Isaac

Hazak, Jacob Raphael Hezekiah ben Abraham Israel. *See* Forti, Jacob Raphael Hezekiah ben Abraham Israel

Ḥazakah, 1:361, 8:**486–491**, 15:551–552

Ha-Zaken. *See* Abraham ben Eliezer ha-Levi; Jacob ben Yakar; Shammai

Ḥazal (Urbach), 1:462

Ḥazan, Ya'akov, 8:**491**

Ḥazani, Mikha'el Ya'akov, 8:**491**

Hazards Prevention Law, 5:167

Ha-Ẓarefati, Joseph, 3:677

Ḥazas. *See* Slonimski, Ḥayyim Selig

Hazaz, Ḥayyim, 8:**491–495**, 716–717

Ha-Ẓedakah be-Yisrael (Bergmann), 3:430

Ha-Ẓefirah (newspaper), 8:476, **495**, 12:759, 18:679, 747–748747–748

Ha-Ẓe'irim (music group), 6:263

"Ha-Zelalim" (Feierberg), 6:731

Ha-Zeman (periodical), 12:9

Ḥaẓerim (ancient Israel), 8:**495**

Ḥaẓerim (Israel), 8:**495–496**

Hazeroth (ancient Israel), 8:**496**

Ḥaẓevah (Israel), 8:**496**

Ha-Zevi (periodical), 3:**387–388**

Ha-Ẓevi (newspaper), 10:704, 705, 12:526

Ḥazit Dor Benei Midbar, 13:159

Ḥazit ha-Moledet, 6:292

Ha-Ẓiyyonut mi-Nekuddat Hashkafat ha-Dat (Don-Yaḥia), 5:752

Hazkarat neshamot, 8:**496–497**

Hazketto. *See* Forti, Baruch Uzziei ben Baruch

Ḥazkuni, Abraham, 8:**497**

Ha-Ẓ Naḥash (Ergas), 6:479

Ha-Ẓofeh (newspaper), 8:**497–498**, 12:759, 14:391

Ha-Ẓofeh ba-Areẓha-Ḥadashah (periodical), 8:735

Ha-Ẓofeh le-Veit Yisrael (Erter), 6:483–484

Hazomir Choral Society, 4:662

Ḥazon Ish, 11:805–806

Ḥazon Yeḥezkel (Abramsky), 1:328

Hazor (Canaan), 2:371, 378, 11:7–8

Ḥazor (ancient Israel), 8:**498–500**

Ḥazor (Israel), 8:**500–501**

Ḥazor Ashdod (Israel), 8:**500–501**

Ha-Zore'a (Israel), 8:**501**

Ḥazut Kashah (Arama), 13:230

Ḥazzan. *See* Ḥazzanim

Ḥazzan, David, 2:31, 8:501

Ḥazzan, Elijah ben Abraham, 8:502

Ḥazzan, Elijah Rachamim, 8:502

Ḥazzan, Ḥayyim, 8:501

Ḥazzan, Ḥayyim David, 8:502

Ḥazzan, Israel Moses ben Eliezer, 8:**506**

Ḥazzan, Jacob, 1:385, 8:501

Ḥazzan, Joseph Raphael ben Ḥayyim, 8:501–502

Ḥazzan, Solomon, 8:502

Ḥazzan family, 8:**501–502**

Ḥazzanim, 8:**502–505**

   Al-Gharīd al-Yahūdī, 1:652

   Amsterdam, 2:119

   Bacon, Hirsch Leib, 3:40

   Bacon, Israel, 3:40

   Bacon, Shlomo Reuven, 3:41

   Bacon, Yidel, 3:41

   Baer, Abraham, 3:52

   Bagely, David, 3:59–60

   Beer, Aaron, 3:250–251

   Belorussia, Beimel, Jacob, 3:268

   ben Elijah, 8:501

   Bouzaglo, David, 4:107

   Braun, Arie, 4:137

   Brod, Dovidi, 4:192

   Burla, Jacob Hai ben Judah, 4:295

   Danto, 5:431

   Deutsch, Mortiz, 5:624

   Duque, Simon David, 6:51

   Ephros, Gershon, 6:462

   Eshel, Yitzḥak, 6:504

   Fisher, Dudu, 7:62–63

   Hast, Marcus, 8:455

   Heilmann, Yitzhak, 8:767

   Henle, Moritz, 8:808

   Herschman, Mordechai, 9:43

   Hershovits, Bela, 9:46

   Herstik, Naftali, 9:47

   Israel

      Ben-Haim, Yigal, 3:351

      Lerer, Joshua, 12:653

      Lerer, Shmuel, 12:653–654

   Jacob ben Moses Moellin, 14:414

   Karmon, Israel, 11:814

   Katz, Shalom, 12:16

   Kirschner, Emanuel, 12:189

   Lefkowitz, David, 12:601–602

   Leoni, Myer, 12:647–648

   Lerer, Joshua, 12:653

   Lerer, Shmuel, 12:653–654

   Mendelson, Jacob ben-Zion, 14:30

Ḥazzanim, *continued*
 Mendelson, Solomon, 14:30–31
 Miller, Ben-Zion, 14:252
 Minkowski, Pinchas, 14:282–283
 Mizrahi, Asher, 14:393
 Morgowski, Jacob Samuel, 14:507–508
 musical style, 14:*651*, 651–653, *652, 653*
 Naumbourg, Samuel, 15:37
 Ne'eman, Yehoshua Leib, 15:**54**
 Netherlands, Brandon, Oheb Isaa, 4:127
 Ostfeld, Barbara Jean, 15:507
 Pinchik, Pierre, 16:164–165
 Polachek, Sender, 16:285
 Poland, Berggrün, Heinrich, 3:426
 recordings, 17:150, 151
 Russia, Bernstein, Abraham Moshe, 3:476
 Schorr, Baruch, 18:162–163
 Schulhof, Moshe, 18:171
 Sharlin, William, 18:414–415
 Shestapol, Wolf, 18:466
 Singer, Josef, 18:638
 Sirota, Gershon, 18:644
 Sobol, Mordechai, 18:702
 Sola, Abraham De, 18:750
 U.K., Bueno de Mesquito, David, 4:252
 U.S.
  Brown, Saul Pardo, 4:216
  Lefkowitz, David, 12:601–602
  Morais, Sabato, 14:471
Ḥazzanut
 Ashkenazi styles, 14:663, *664, 665,* 671–676, 681–685, *682–683, 684, 688*
 Sephardi styles, 14:*662,* 664–665, *665*
Hd. *See* Hadad
He, 8:**506**
He, She and It (Piercy), 18:200
Head, covering of, 8:**506–507,** 18:752
Head, Edith, 8:**507–508**
Headdresses, decorative, 5:**307–309**
Head of the French yeshivot. *See* Perez ben Elijah of Corbeil
Head shaving, women, 8:507
Health. *See* Medicine
Heaps, Abraham Albert, 8:**508,** 16:341
Hear, Ye Sons (Fineman), 7:26
Hearst, William Randolph, 15:211
Heart, 2:134, 8:**508–510**
Heartburn (Ephron), 6:462
Heartfield, John, 8:**510,** 16:125

Heart of the Comet (Benford, Brin), 18:200
Hearts of Gold (Sinclair), 18:632
Heart transplants, 20:107
Heaven. *See* Paradise
Heavenly host, 2:150–151
Heavenly voice. *See* Bat Kol
Heavy Traffic (Bakshi), 3:74
Hebelt, J., 2:26
Heber, 8:**510**
Heber koltok antologiaja, 11:805
Die hebraeischen Handschriften der k. und k. Hofbibliothek in Wien (Schwarz), 18:189
Die hebraeischen Handschriften in Oesterreich (Schwarz), 18:189
Die hebraeischen Uebersetzungen des Mittelalters und die Juden als Dolmetscher (Steinschneider), 19:198
Hebraeorum gens, 4:278
Hebraeorum supremus. *See* Praefectus Judaeorum
Hebraists
 Baranowicz, David Eliezer, 3:134
 Bar-Asher, Moshe, 3:137
 Burstein, Israel, 4:301
 Christian
  Bacon, Roger, 3:40
  Bartolocci, Giulio, 3:180–181
  Bate, Julius, 3:210
  Beck, Michael, 3:243
  Bialoblotzky, Christian Heinrich Friedrich, 3:566
  Danz, Johann Andreas, 5:431–432
  Imbonati, Carlo Giuseppe, 9:737
  Plantavit de la Pause, Jean, 16:219
 Drusius, Johann Clemens, 6:28
 Ferdinand, Philip, 6:760
 Filipowski, Zevi Hirsch, 7:20
 Fischer, Carolus, 7:53
 German, Pellicanus, Conrad, 15:718–719
 Halper, Benzion, 8:283
 Le Fèvre de la Boderie, Guy, 12:601
 Lemans, Moses, 12:636
 Lowth, Robert, 13:237
 Pococke, Edward, 16:250
 U.S., 15:792
Hebraists, Christian, 8:**510–551,** 518*t*–551*t*
 Broughton, Hugh, 4:212
 Budde, Karl Ferdinand Reinhard, 4:249

Budny, Szymon, 4:249–250
Buxtorf, Johannes
 the Elder, 4:321
 the Younger, 4:321–322
 correlated listing of, 8:518*t*–551*t*
Danby, Herbert, 5:408
De' Rossi, Giovanni Bernardo, 5:598
Domincans, 8:512
Forster, Johann, 7:132
Franciscans, 8:512
Kabbalah study, 8:513–514
Mendicant orders, 8:512–513
nineteenth century, 8:515–516
Rashi influence on, 8:511
Reformation, 8:514–515
Ricius, Paulus, 17:292
Hebrew alphabet, 1:**689–728,** 8:554, 559*t*
 10th c. primer, vol. 3: color insert
 'Alef, 1:607
 bet, 3:499
 in Bible, 13:607–608
 Braille, 1:726–727, 3:*754*
 cursive script, 1:697–706, *698, 700–705,* 12:445
  Ashkenzic type, 1:*705,* 706
  Babylon type, 1:698–699, *701,* 706
  Egypt type, 1:698, *700, 701*
  Italkian type, 1:699–700, *704,* 706
  Jewish cursive hand, 1:697
  Karaitic types, 1:706, 718
  Maaravic type, 1:699, *702, 703*
  Palestine-Syria type, 1:698
  Palestine type, 1:*698, 700*
  Parsic type, 1:699, *702*
  Sephardic type, 1:699, *703*
  Temanic type, 1:699, *702*
  Yevanic type, 1:699, *703t, 704, 705*
  Yevano-Karaitic type, 1:*705,* 706
  Zarphatic type, 1:*704,* 706
 epistolary conventions, 12:674–675
 ḥet, 9:79
 in Kabbalah, 1:728–730
 letters used as numbers, 1:726, *726*
 manual or finger spelling for the deaf, 1:727
 mashait script, 1:718–721, *721–726*
 mathematics, 13:671
 mem, 14:16
 in Midrash, 1:728–730

North-West Semitic, 1:689–697,
690t, 691t, 692, 694t, 696t
Aramaic script, 1:694t, 695–
697
Hebrew script, 1:692, 693,
694t
Jewish script, 1:696t, 697
Moabite, Edomite, and
Ammonite scripts, 1:694t,
695
Paleo-Hebrew script, 1:694t,
695
Phoenician script, 1:691,
691t, 692, 694t
proto-Canaanite and
Cuneiform Canaanite,
1:689, 690t, 691, 691t
Samaritan script, 1:692, 695
printing, 5:478
pronunciation, 8:560–573, 561t,
563t
punctuation, 8:560, 560t
shorthand, 1:728
square script, 1:706–718, 709–717
appearance and basic types,
1:706–707
Aramaic type, 1:706, 709
Ashkenazic type, 1:716, 717,
718
Babylon type, 1:707, 712
Egypt type, 1:707, 711
Italkian type, 1:708, 715, 716
Jewish square script, 1:706,
709, 710
Maaravic type, 1:708, 713,
714
Parsic type, 1:707–708, 712
Sephardic type, 1:708, 714
Temanic type, 1:708, 713
Yevanic type, 1:715
Ẓarphatic type, 1:708, 716,
718
in Talmud, 1:728–730
vowel signs, origins, 13:623, 624,
627–628, 630–632, 633–634
See also specific letters
A Hebrew and English Lexicon of the
Old Testament (Brown, Driver,
Briggs), 6:22
Hebrew Benevolent Society Anshe
Sholom, 8:304
Hebrew Bible. See Pentateuch
Hebrew Bible illumination, 2:495
Hebrew Bible in Art (Leveen), 12:678
Hebrew bibliography, 3:681–683
Hebrew book titles, 8:551–553
Hebrew cantatas and choral works,
4:433–435

Hebrew College, 8:553–554
Hebrew Committee for National
Liberation, 21:606–607
Hebrew Deeds of Catalan Jews (Klein),
18:471
Hebrew Enoch. See Sefer Heikhalot
Hebrew fiction, 7:10–16
aggadah, 1:455
allegory, 1:666, 667
animal tales, 2:174
Ashkenazi literature, 7:14
based on Second Temple period,
7:11–12
bible stories, 7:11
children's literature, 4:619–620
Chronicles of Moses, 14:545–546
collections, 7:12
ethical literature, 7:13–14
exemplum, 6:599
fables, 6:669
hagiography, 8:224
Hassidic literature, 7:14, 16
Hazaz, Ḥayyim, 8:491–494
historiography, 7:12
Italian Renaissance, 7:15
Jesus' life, 7:13
Kabbalah, 7:14–16
Laor, Yitzhak, 12:488
Lapid, Shulamit, 12:490
Midrashic themes, 7:10
novel, 11:584, 18:691–694
romance, 6:13
Talmudic and Midrashic narrative,
7:10
visions, 20:544, 545
wisdom literature, 21:96
Yiddish literature, 17:553
See also specific authors and works
Hebrew Free Trade School, 3:695
Hebrew grammar, 8:554–620, 11:31,
116–117
Abraham ha-Bavli, 1:312
Almoli, Solomon ben Jacob, 1:681
alphabet, 8:559, 559t
Aramaic influence, 8:573
beginnings, 13:612–614, 648–653
Ben-Asher approach, 3:320, 321
biblical patterns, 8:554–558
Buchner, Ze'ev Wolf ben David
ha-Kohen, 4:243
Buttenweiser, Moses, 4:319
Calimani, Simḥah ben Abraham,
4:363
consonants, 8:560–565, 561t
early, 15:718
Eblaite language, 6:87

Elijah ben Solomon Zalman,
6:345–346
Emden approach to, 6:393
genizah records, 7:476
Ḥayyuj writings, 8:484
Heidenheim, Wolf, 8:763
Ibn Balʿam, Judah ben Samuel,
9:660–661
Ibn Barun, Abu Ibrahim Isaac ben
Joseph ibn Benveniste, 9:661
Ibn Ḥabib, Moses ben Shem Tov,
9:678–679
Ibn Janāḥ, Jonah, 9:680–681
Ibn Quraysh, Judah, 9:688
Ibn Yashush, Isaac Abu Ibrahim,
9:699
Lerner, Ḥayyim Ẓevi Ben Todros,
12:657
Levita, Elijah, 12:730–732
Lonzano, Abraham, 13:187
Mishnaic, 14:330–331
modern, 8:678–680
Mordell, Phinehas, 14:482–483
morphology
basic elements, 8:575–576
formatives, morphemes,
8:576–577
parts of speech, 8:577, 598
roots, stems, 8:574–575
Natonek, Joseph, 15:32
noun formation, 3:134, 8:577–587
adverbs, 8:585–586
conjugations, 8:587–859
declension, 8:582–584
numerals, 8:586–587
particles, 8:585–586
patterns, pattern formations,
8:577–580
prefixes, compounds, 8:581–
582
prepositions, 8:585
pronouns, 8:584–585, 584t
suffixes, 8:580–581
pronunciation, 8:554–557, 558–
559, 559
accentuation, 8:569–570
community variations, 8:562,
563t
consonants, 8:560–565, 561t
dipthongs, 8:570–571
ḥatef, 8:568–569
šewa, 8:568–569
vowel elison and exchanges,
8:571–573
vowels, 8:565–569, 570–571
punctuation, 8:560, 560t
Rabbinowicz, Israel Michel, 17:31–
32

Hebrew grammar, *continued*
  Rashi's language, 17:103–104
  spelling, writing, 8:559–560, 559*t*–560*t*
  syllables, 8:567–568
  syntax, 8:596–618
    adjuncts, 8:603–607, *605*
    adverbial sentences, 8:609–611
    concords, 8:612–614
    copula, 8:602
    dependency, 8:611–615
    foreign influence, 8:597
    fragmentary sentences, 8:615–616
    objects, 8:607–609
    obligatoriness, 8:6i4–615
    part order, 8:615
    parts of speech, 8:577, 598
    prepositional phrases, 8:605–606, *606*
    pronouns, personal and demonstrative, 8:615
    relative clauses, 8:606–607
    sentence connection, 8:617
    sentences, 8:598–611
    sentence subordination, 8:617–618
    subjects, predicates, 8:598–603
    transitive, intransitive verbs, 8:608
  verb formation, 3:124, 8:484, 557–558, 587–596
    assimilated forms, 8:592–594, 593*t*
    defective verbs, 8:592–594
    inflection, 8:589–592, 590*t*
    mute forms, 8:594–596, 594*t*, 595*t*, 596*t*
  vowels, 8:554–555
Hebrew Hillbilly. *See* Goldberg, Marshall
"Hebrew Humanism" of Martin Buber, 4:231, 234
Hebrew Immigrant Society, 8:**620,** 9:245, 14:503–504
Hebrew journalism
  Rabinowitz, Ya'akov, 17:42
  Rosenberg, Abraham Ḥayyim, 17:434
  Rosenfeld, Samuel, 17:447
Hebrew language, 8:**620–683,** 10:684
  abbreviations, 1:237–240
  Abrech, 1:329–330
  Academy of the Hebrew Language, 1:351–353
  Alting, Jacobus, 2:20–21

Amchai, Yehuda, 2:71–72
Amelander, Menahem Mann ben Solomon Ha-Levi, 2:38
Amen, 2:38–39
Amorites, 2:96
Aramaic influences, 2:357
astronomy texts, 2:132
authorized translation of Mandatory statues, 10:415
autonomous
  Ben-Gurion, David, 3:344
  Ben-Yehuda, Eliezer, 3:387–388
Ben Ḥayyim, Ze'ev, 3:351–352
Ben Yehuda, Netiva, 3:389
biblical, 3:216, 581–582, 8:626–634
  adjectives, 8:633–634
  Ancient evidence, 8:626
  Aramaic, 2:345*t*, 346–347
  clause formation, 8:634
  conjugation of verbs, 2:*345*
  consonants, 8:628
  Masoretic text, 8:627–628
  numerals, 8:634
  pronouns, 8:629–630
  verbs, tenses, 8:630–633
  vowels, 8:628–629
Blau, Joshua, 3:743–744
Brit Ivrit Olamit, 4:189
Canada, 4:419
Dead Sea scrolls, 5:499–500, 8:634–639
dictionaries
  Alcalay, Reuven, 1:598
  Alfasi, David ben Abraham, 1:639
  Maḥberet, 14:22
Dontan, Aron, 5:762–763
Driver, Samuel Rolles, 6:22
early treatises on *Even Boḥan* (Menahem ben Solomon), 14:23
Eblaite language, 6:87
Ecclesiastes, 6:88–89
Edelmann, Simḥah Reuben, 6:143
education
  Chomsky, William, 4:665–666
  England, 6:422
epitaphs, 6:464–465
Erasmus of Rotterdam, 6:477
Erez Israel, 6:478
euphemisms, Bible, 13:616
evolution, 9:252
Foreiro, Francisco, 7:125
glosses, 3:771, 11:546, 547, 12:405–406
Goshen-Gottstein, Moshe, 8:5

grammar
  Abu al-Faraj Harun ibn al-Faraj, 1:334
  Campen, Johannes van, 4:383
  Isaac benSamuel ha-Levi, 10:46–47
  Monis, Judah, 14:444–445
  Scneider, Mordecai Bazalel, 18:150–151
Guidacerio, Agacio, 8:127
guttural letters, 8:558
Histadrut Ivrit of America, 9:151
Hungarian literature, influences of, 9:602–604
IDF instruction in, 10:470
influence of Greek language, 8:58
Israel (state)
  cultural life, 10:683–684
  mishpat Ivri, 14:353–354
  revival, 10:683–684
Italian pronunciation, 10:815
Jabotinsky, Vladimir and, 11:13
Jewish language, 11:301, 302
Jewish studies in Soviet Union and, 11:321–322
joy, concept of, 11:470–471
Judah Halevi on, 11:499
Judah ha-Nasi on, 11:503
Judeo-Persian grammars, 11:551, 554
Kipper, 12:181–183
Language war, 12:482–483
Lara, David ben Isaac Cohen De, 12:492–493
law, 14:353–354
Leaf, Hayim, 12:563
linguistic development, newspapers, 15:157
logic texts, 2:132
Masoretic text, 8:627–628
medicine and, 13:601, 724
Mendelssohn view of, 8:437
Middle Ages, 8:650–671
  Arabic influence, 8:655, 658–665
  Aramaic influence, 8:669–670
  Ashkenazaic, 8:667–670
  France, 8:667
  German influence, 8:667–669
  Haskalah influence, 8:671
  Italian, 8:666
  Karaitic, 8:666
  piyyut, 8:651–653
  pure Hebrew concept, 8:654
  Saadia Gaon's influence, 8:653–655
  Samaritan, 8:666

Spanish Hebrew poetry,
8:655–660, 16:263
Yiddish influence, 8:667–669
miracles, 14:305
Mishnaic, 2:356, 8:639–650,
14:330–331
Aramaic influence, 8:648
Ashkenazaic and, 8:669
Dead Sea scrolls, 8:638
dialects, 8:649
foreign loan words, 8:647–
648
morphology, 8:642–650, 642t,
643t, 644t
nouns, 8:645–646
Palestinian, Babylonian,
8:649–650
phonetics, 8:642
problems and issues, 8:640–
642
syntax, 8:646, 648
tanna and amora, 8:639
types of, 8:639
verbs and tenses, 8:644–645,
648
vocabulary, 8:646–648
mnemonic devices, Bible, 13:619
modern, 8:67, 671–680
foreign words, 8:676
grammar, 8:678–680
pronunciation, 8:672–673
revival period, 8:671–672
spelling, 8:673–675
verbal innovations, 8:677–678
vocabulary, 8:675
names, 1:333
nineteenth century, homiletic
literature and, 9:514
origin of, 18:285
Oxford University, study at,
15:554
Palestine (Mandate), 10:198
Palestine (Ottoman)
journalism, 10:704–705
schools, 10:652, 653
Parḥon, Salomon ben Abraham
Ibn, 15:641–642
philology
Morag, Shlomo, 14:470
poetry and, 16:264
philosophy translated into, 16:86
pre-biblical, 8:620–626
morphology, 8:624–626
phonology, 8:622–624
pronounciation, Bible, 13:609,
612, 624–648
relation to other Semitic
languages, 18:284–285

revival in Israel, 10:291
Rosén, Haiim B., 17:428
Russia
1970s, 17:564–565
USSR regime, 17:543
in science books, 18:157
Second Aliyah, 10:196
semitic language influences,
8:621–625
sheluḥei ereẓ Israel, 18:452
sin, 18:621–622
spelling, 8:556, 557, 559–560
stress structure of ancient, 13:637–
639
summer camps, 11:272
teaching, 6:471, 14:520
tenses, 8:557–558
theory, 6:589
Tibbonian, 8:659
Tiberian vocalization, 8:628–629
Torah and
dating of, 15:742
terminology in, 15:734–736
translation, Tibbonian, 8:659
United Kingdom, education, 6:207
Yiddish codevelopment, 9:252
See also Alphabet; Pronunciations
of Hebrew; specific names of
letters of alphabet
The Hebrew Leader (periodical), 4:58
Hebrew linguistic literature, 13:29–61,
37t
authors and works, 13:45–54
nineteenth–twentieth
centuries, 13:57–60
sixteenth–eighteenth
centuries, 13:53–57
tenth–eleventh centuries,
13:45–49
twelfth–fifteenth centuries,
13:49–53
bases, joint, 13:31
beginnings, 13:29–30
Biblical Hebrew, 13:35
description and definition, 13:29–
30
development of, 13:31–43
Aramaic and Arabic
comparisons, 13:35–36
dictionaries, 13:36–38, 37t
four periods, 13:31–34
grammatical works, 13:36,
38–43
languages, 13:35
motivations for writings,
13:34–35
dictionaries, 13:36–38, 37t

four periods of development,
13:31–34
creative period, 13:32–33
criteria of division, 13:31
dissemination period, 13:33
first attempts, 13:31–32
standstill, 13:33–34
Gesenius, Heinrich Friedrich
Wilhelm, 13:57–58
history of, 13:29–31
language, 13:35
lexicography, 13:36–38
modern trends, 13:58–60
monographs, 13:45
motivations for writing, 13:34–35
phonetics, 13:60
post-Biblical Hebrew, 13:35
publication of the works, 13:43–44
reconstruction, 13:57–58
study of, 13:43–45
Christian Hebrew studies,
13:54–57
classical historical method,
13:57–58
See also Hebrew literature
Hebrew linguistics. See Hebrew
language
Hebrew literature, 10:684–685, 18:582
Aaron ben Elijah, 1:212
abbreviations, 1:237–240
Aboab da Fonseca, Isaac, 1:269
Abraham, 1:286–287
Abraham, Apocalypse of, 1:288–
289
Abraham bar Ḥiyya, 1:293
Abramovitsh, Sholem Yankev,
1:318–322
Aden, 1:387
Aescoly, Aaron Ze'ev, 1:430–431
Agmon, Nathan, 1:465
Agnon, Shmuel Yosef, 1:465–468
Aḥ ha-Am, 1:525–529
Akavya, Avraham Aryeh Leib,
1:554
Akedah, 1:558–559
Alexandria, 1:635
Alfes, Benzion, 1:641
Almanzi, Joseph, 1:679
Almog, Ruth, 1:680
awards, Israel Prize, 10:762–763
Band, Arnold, 3:107
Barash, Asher, 3:135–136
Behak, Judah, 3:262
Beilinson, Moses Eliezer, 3:267
Ben-Amitai, Levi, 3:316
Ben Eliezer, Moshe, 3:340

Hebrew literature, *continued*
  Ben-Yehuda, Eliezer, 3:386–388
  Ben-Yehuda, Ḥemdah, 3:388
  Ben-Zion, S., 3:392–393
  Berdyczewski, Micha Josef, 3:404–406
  Berkowitz, Yitzḥak Dov, 3:440–441
  Bloch, Samson ha-Levi, 3:768
  book titles, 8:551–553
  Brandstaedter, Mordecai David, 4:127
  Braudes, Reuben Asher, 4:136
  Braunstein, Menahem Mendel, 4:139
  Brenner, Joseph Ḥayyim, 4:159–161
  Bresselau, Meyer Israel, 4:167
  Brill, Joseph, 4:183
  Burla, Yehuda, 4:295–296
  Cantarini, Isaac Vita ha-Kohen, 4:433
  Carmoly, Eliakim, 4:485
  Caro, David, 4:487
  Castel-Bloom, Orly, 4:512
  censorship, 4:540–541, 5:739
  children's, 4:619–628, 11:779
  Churgin, Ya'akov Yehoshua, 4:723–724
  collections, 6:598–599
  Comtino, Mordecai ben Eliezer, 5:132–133
  criticism, 6:743, 8:723–733
    Ahad ha-Am and Berdiczewski controversey, 8:726–727
    Eisenstadt, Benzion, 6:270
    encomiastic, 8:725
    Epstein, Zalman, 6:476
    Jaffe, Abraham B., 11:64
    Lachower, Yeruḥam Fishel, 12:424–425
    Miron, Dan, 14:313
    modern era, 8:727–733
    nineteenth century, 8:724–727
    Shapira, Hayyim Nachman, 18:400
    utilitarian-sociological, 8:725–726
  Dagon, Barukh, 5:378–379
  Dahan family, 5:379
  Day of Atonement in, 5:491
  Deinard, Ephraim, 5:532
  Dolitzki, Menaḥem Mendel, 5:735–736
  Dor, Moshe, 5:754–755

  drama, 8:713–723
    early beginnings, 8:713–714
    expressionist-historical, 8:716–717
    ḥalutz play, 8:718–719
    Haskalah, 8:714
    historical melodrama, 8:714–715
    holocaust dramaturgy, 8:720–721, 722–723
    Israel, 8:719–723
    national renaissance period, 8:714–719
    poetic, 8:715–716
    Zionist melodrama, 8:717
  dualism in, 13:668–669
  Edelmann, Ẓevi Hirsch, 6:143
  Ehrenpreis, Marcus, 6:240
  eighteenth century, 11:35
  L'Empereur, Constantijn, 6:397
  encyclopedias, 6:399, 400–401, 401–402
  in England, 6:143
  essayists, 6:688
  ethical, 6:525–526
  European cultural hegemony, 6:556, 730–732
  European period
    Berdyczewski influence, 8:694
    Bialik influence, 8:694–696
    Galician Haskalah, 8:688–689
    Haskalah literature, 8:686–691
    Russia and Poland, 8:691–696
    Seforim influence, 8:693
  fables, 6:669
  father of American, 6:685–686
  folklore, Schwadron, Abraham, 18:181–182
  Frankel, Naomi, 7:198–199
  Freha bat Avraham, 7:234
  Gnessin's writings, 7:649
  Grossman, David, 8:99–100
  Guenzburg, Mordecai Aaron, 8:123
  Ha-asif, 8:170–171
  Habas, Bracha, 8:173
  Hapax Legomena, 8:337
  Harshav, Benjamin, 8:367
  Ha-Tekufah, 8:456
  Hendel, Yehudit, 8:806
  Herschberg, Abraham Samuel, 9:42–43
  Hillels, Shelomo, 9:115
  Histadrut Ivrit of America, 9:151
  Horowitz, Aaron Judah Loeb, 9:531

  Horowitz, Ya'akov, 9:544
  Hurwitz, Judah ben Mordecai ha-Levi, 9:632
  Hurwitz, Phinehas Elijah, 9:632
  Hurwitz, Samuel Justin, 9:632–633
  Ibn Zabara, Joseph ben Meir, 9:699
  imaginative language in, 18:197–198, 203
  Israel period, 8:702–712
    1970's, 8:704–705
    1980's onward, 8:706–712
    drama, 8:719–723
    Holocaust, 8:709
    new wave, 8:705–706
    poetry, 8:703, 711–712
    prose, 8:704
    women writers, 8:710–711
  Katzir, Judith, 12:23
  Kenaani, David, 12:**74**
  Kenan, Amos, 12:**74–75**
  Kenaz, Yehoshua, 12:75–76
  Keret, Etgar, 12:**84**
  Kipnis, Levin, 12:179
  Kishon, Ephraim, 12:200
  Kleinmann, Moshe, 12:227
  Landau, Judah Loeb, 12:463
  Laor, Yitzhak, 12:488
  Lapid, Shulamit, 12:**490**
  legal sources, 14:336–337
  Leon, Messer Judah Ben Jehiel, 12:646
  Lerner, Joseph Judah, 12:658
  Letteris, Meir, 12:667–668
  Levin, Shmarya, 12:713–714
  Levner, Israel Benjamin, 12:744
  Levontin, Jehiel Joseph, 12:744
  Lewinsky, Elhanan Leib, 12:762
  Lewinsky, Yom-Tov, 12:762–763
  Libowitz, Samuel Nehemiah, 12:783
  Lichtenbaum, Joseph, 12:796–797
  Lichtenfeld, Gabriel Judah, 12:797
  Liebman, Charles, 12:810
  Liebrecht, Savyon, 12:811–812
  Luzzatto, Moses Ḥayyim, 13:282–283
  masculine bias, 6:754–755
  Mezaḥ, Joshua ha-Levi, 14:155
  Michael, Sami, 14:166–167
  Middle Ages, 2:261, 264–268
    Alexander the Great, 1:627
    Ashkenazai-Hasidic, 6:529–530
    Brody, Heinrich, 4:200
    Davidson, Israel, 5:475–476

exempla, 6:599–600

Nevu'at Ha-Yeled, 15:130

philosophical-ethical, 6:527–528, 680–683

publication of scholarly, 13:797

rabbinic-ethical, 6:528

Schirmann, Jefin, 18:137–138

Mirsky, Aaron, 14:314–315

Mishnah, 14:320–321

modern, 8:**684–738**

   Afro-American influence, 8:736

   anthologies, 8:734

   beginning of, 8:685–686

   British Mandate period, 8:700–702

modern Israel

   Matalon, Ronit, 13:670

   Megged, Aharon, 13:765–766

Mohr, Meir, 14:420–421

nineteenth century, Peretz, Issac Leib, 15:765–768

novels, 3:489, 8:19–20, 9:312

Ottoman period, 8:696, 700–702

Palestine (Mandate), 10:684–685

patrons, 13:689, 16:263

Pineles, Hirsch Mendel ben Solomon, 16:166

Pines, Noah, 16:167

Plungian, 16:242

poetry, 8:697–698

   Rodin, Elisha, 17:364

   Schwartz, Abraham Samuel, 18:182

Polak, Gabriel Isaac, 16:286

post-WW II, Russia, 17:563

printing, 1:300, 301, 6:708, 11:64, 169

prose, 8:698–699

prose, Maqāma, 13:508–509

publishing, 16:721–724

Rabbinowitz, Saul Phinehas, 17:32

Rabinovitz, Alexander Siskind, 17:38–39

Rabinowitz, Eliahu Wolf, 17:40

Rabinowitz, Ya'akov, 17:42

Rabinowitz, Zina, 17:43

Raisin, Jacob Zalman, 17:74

Raisin, Max, 17:74–75

Rakovsky, Puah, 17:76

Ravikovitch, Dalia, 17:122

Ravina, Menashe, 17:123

Rawidowicz, Simon, 17:125–126

Rawnitzki, Yehoshua Ḥana, 17:126

Reich, Asher, 17:196

Reifmann, Jacob, 17:203–204

Rimon, Jacob, 17:344

Rodkinson, Michael Levi, 17:365

Rosenberg, Yehuda Yudel, 17:439

Rosenfeld, Aharon, 17:445

Rossi, Azariah ben Moses dei, 17:471–473

Rubin, Solomon, 17:514

Satanow, Isaac, 18:73–74

satires, Erter, Isaac, 6:483–484

Schaechter, Joseph, 18:101–102

Schapira, Noah, 18:108

Schatz, Ẓevi, 18:111

Schiller, Friedrich von, influence on, 18:133–134

Schulman, Kalman, 18:172

Sefer ha-Yashar, 1:286–287

Selikovitch, George, 18:269–270

Seri, Dan Benaya, 18:310–311

Shaanan, Avraham, 18:334–335

Shaḥam, Nathan, 18:363

Shaḥar, David, 18:363–364

Shakespeare, William, 18:369–370

Shalev, Meir, 18:372–373

Shami, Yitzḥak, 18:391

Shamir, Moshe, 18:392–393

Shatzkes, Moses Aaron, 18:420–421

Shenhar, Yitzhak, 18:459–460

short stories, 6:730–732

Slonimski, Ḥayyim Selig, 18:678

Slucki, Abraham Jacob, 18:685

Smilansky, Meir, 18:687

Smilansky, Moshe, 18:687

Smolenskin, Peretz, 18:691–694

Smoli, Eliezer, 18:694

Sobel, Jacob Ẓevi, 18:699

Sokolow, Nahum, 18:747–749

Someck, Ronny, 19:6

translations, 8:733–734

   from Arabic, 11:31

   Germany, 6:744

   into Italian, 18:52

   Perski, Joel Dov Baer, 15:792

   into Russian literature, 17:591

   science fiction, 18:204

   U.S., 6:686–687

translations of Shakespeare, 18:369–370

United States, 8:734–737, 11:584, 12:563

visions, 20:544

women's, 8:699–702

women writers, 8:443

Writers' Association in Israel, 21:234–235

See also Hebrew linguistic literature; Hebrew parody; Hebrew prosody

"Hebrew Liturgical Poetry and Christian Hymnology (Schirmann)," 18:138

Hebrew manuscripts, 13:**488–495**

   500 B.C.E.-1970, 13:488–489

   Almanzi, Joseph, 1:679

   Ben-Asher, Aaron ben Moses, 3:320

   Bodleian Library, 4:29

   Buchanan, Claudius, 4:238–239

   Cambridge University, 4:378

   Canada, Library and Archives of, 15:517

   collections of, 13:489–490

   illuminated Hebrew Bibles, 3:675–679

   Oesterreichische Nationalbibliothek, 15:384

   owners of, 13:489

   Palatina Library, Parma, 15:653

   Russia, 13:490–495

Hebrew newspapers, 15:**154–189**

   duration, 15:156

   Europe

      daily newspapers, 15:157–158

      decline, 15:158–159

      early newspapers, 15:157

      yearbooks and periodicals, 15:156–157

   first Hebrew daily newspaper, 11:770

   Ha-Boker, 8:181–182

   Ha-Levanon, 8:267, 466

   Ha-Maggid, 8:293

   Ha-Meliz, 8:300, 476

   Ha-Me'orer, 8:301

   Hamizpeh, 8:305

   Ha-modi'a, 8:310–311

   Ha-Shahar, 8:442–443

   Haskalah, 15:155

   Ḥavazzelet, 8:267, 466

   Ha-Yom, 8:476

   Ḥa-Zefirah, 8:495

   Ḥa-Ẓefrah, 8:476

   Ḥa-Ẓofeh, 8:497–498

   Hebrew linguistic development, 15:157

   ideology, 15:155

   Israel, labor, 5:443

   Kantor, Judah Leib, 11:770

   Latin America, 12:513–515

   list of newspapers and periodicals, 15:160t–188t

   North America, 15:159

Hebrew newspapers, *continued*
   Russia, 8:442
   stages of development, 15:155–156
   Yated Ne'eman, 8:311
   See also Press
Hebrew Observer (periodical), 3:353,
   6:92
Hebrew parody, 15:**654–663**
   in Bible, rabbinic, and early
      Hebrew literature, 15:654–655
   defined, 15:654
   in medieval and early modern
      periods, 15:655–660
   in modern times, 15:660–663
Hebrew poetry. *See* Hebrew prosody
Hebrew printing, 16:**529–540,** *541*
   Amsterdam, 16:533–534
      Benveniste, Immanuel, 3:383
      Castro Tartas, David de,
         4:520
      Foa family, 7:92
   Baghdad, 3:59
   Berdichev, 3:403
   Bible
      early Hebrew editions, 3:586–
         588, 8:514–515
   Buxtorf dynasty, 8:515
   Czechoslovakia, 4:190
      Eliezer ben Isaac, 6:325–326
   Egypt, 4:345
      Alexandria, 1:635
      Cairo, 4:345
   England, London, 13:184
   Fez, Morocco, 7:6
   France, Plantin, Christophe,
      16:219
   Frankfuter, Moses, 7:207
   Geneva, 7:459
   genizah records, 7:477
   Germany, 16:534–536
      Berlin, 3:452
      Frankfurt on the Main, 7:211
      Frankfurt on the Oder, 7:212
      Freiburg im Breisgau, 7:235
      Fuerth, 7:307
      Hanau, 8:317
      Hena, Hans Jacob, 8:317
      Homburg, 9:505
      Leipzig, 12:628
   Halberstadt, 8:263
   Hamburg, 8:297
   India, 4:353
   Israel, 16:538–539, 539*t*
   Italy, 16:532–533, 536
      Bologna, 4:48
      Brescia, 4:163

      Cremona, 5:283–284
      Florence, 7:86
      Foa family, 7:92
      Naples, 14:776–777
   Jerusalem, 16:538
   Metz, 14:136
   modern period, 16:536–540
   Naḥmias, ibn, brothers, 14:754
   Naples, 14:776–777
   Poland, 7:404
      Breslau, 4:165
      Cracow, 5:262
      Krotoszyn, 12:374
      Lublin, 13:243–244
   Polonnoye, 16:360
   Portugal, Lisbon, 13:80
   pre-modern period, 16:529–531
   Romania, Bacau, 3:30
   seventeenth–eighteenth centuries,
      16:533–536
   sixteenth century, 16:531–533
   Slovakia, Bratislava, 4:133
   Strasbourg, 19:245
   Sulzbach, 19:306–307
   Ukraine
      Bratslav, 4:134
      Lvov, 13:291
   U.S., 16:538
   Venice, 5:659–660, 20:502–503
   Vienna, 20:523
   women printers, 16:539–540
   See also Incunabula; Printing
Hebrew pronunciations. *See*
   Pronunciations of Hebrew
Hebrew prosody, 16:**595–623**
   Abdallah, Yusef, 1:240
   Abraham ben Daniel, 1:295
   Abraham ben Ḥalfon, 1:299
   Abraham of Sarteano, 1:313–314
   Abulafia, Todros ben Judah ha-
      Levi, 1:344–345
   Alamani, Aaron he-Ḥaver ben
      Yeshu'ah, 1:575
   Alashkar, Joseph ben Moses, 1:576
   Alḥadib, Isaac ben Solomon ben
      Ẓaddik, 1:654
   Al-Ḥarizi, Judah ben Solomon,
      1:655–657
   Almanzi, Joseph, 1:679
   Baghdad, seventeenth–eighteenth
      centuries, 6:662
   Bat-Miriam, Yokheved, 3:213–214
   Bavli, Hillel, 3:230
   Bedersi, Abraham ben Isaac, 3:248
   Bejerano, Maya, 3:273
   Ben Yiẓḥak, Avraham, 3:389

   Bergel, Joseph, 3:418
   Bergstein, Fania, 3:433
   Bialik, Ḥayyim Naḥman, 3:561–
      565
   biblical principles of, 16:598–600
   Broides, Abraham, 4:202–203
   Broido, Ephraim, 4:203
   Bukarat, Abraham ben Solomon
      ha-Levi, 4:257
   Cahan, Yaakov, 4:336–337
   Calimani, Simḥah ben Abraham,
      4:363
   "Canaanites," 4:393
   Carmi, Isaiah Ḥ ben Joseph, 4:484
   Carmi, T., 4:484
   Caspi, Saul, 4:506
   Castello, Abraham Isaac, 4:514
   Chomsky, Dov, 4:664
   composition, forms of, 16:601–
      603, 621, 622*t*
   contemporary, 14:15, 15:726
   De Piera, Solomon ben
      Meshullam, 5:590
   Dunash ben Labrat, 6:47–48
   Efros, Israel Isaac, 6:216
   Ehrenkranz, Benjamin Zeeb, 6:240
   Eichenbaum, Jacob, 6:246
   Eleazar ben Ḥalfon ha-Kohen,
      6:301
   Eleazar ben Jacob ha-Bavli, 6:302
   Elijah ben Eliezer Philosoph ha-
      Yerushalmi, 6:339
   Elisheva, 6:354
   Fichman, Jacob, 7:8–9
   Fischmann, Naḥman Isaac, 7:57
   Fleischer, Ezra, 7:73
   Frances, Immanuel ben David,
      7:170–171
   Frances, Jacob ben David, 7:171–
      172
   Franco-Mended, David, 7:177
   girdle poems, 16:609
   Gottlober, Abraham Baer, 8:13–14
   Gouri, Haim, 8:19–20
   Greenberg, Uri Ẓevi, 8:74–75
   Habermann, Abraham Meir,
      8:176–177
   Halévy, Elie Halfon, 8:270
   Halkin, Simon, 8:276
   Hameiri, Avigdor, 8:299
   Hamon, Aaron ben Isaac, 8:312
   Ḥarizi, Abu Isaac Abraham, 8:355
   Haskalah revival, 16:613–615
   Ḥisdai ibn Ḥisdai, Abu al-Faḍl,
      9:145
   history, 16:596–597
   Ibn al-Taqana, Moses, 9:660

Ibn Ezra, Isaac, 9:672–673

Ibn Ezra, Moses ben Jacob, 9:673–675

Ibn Ḥabib, Moses ben Shem Tov, 9:678–679

Ibn Ḥasdai, Abraham ben Samuel ha-Levi, 9:679

Ibn Kapron, Isaac, 9:684

Ibn Khalfun, Isaac, 9:685

Ibn Mar Saul, Isaac ben Levi, 9:685–686

Ibn Paquda, David ben Eleazar, 9:687

Ibn Shuwayk, Isaac ben Israel, 9:694

Ibn Zakbel, Solomon, 9:700

Italy, 16:611–613

Karni, Yehuda, 11:814–815

Keshet, Yeshurun, 12:89–90

Kinderfreund, Aryeh Leib, 12:160

Lebensohn, Abraham Dov, 12:589–590

Lebensohn, Micah Joseph, 12:590–591

Lenski, Ḥayyim, 12:640–641

Letteris, Meir, 12:667–668

Levi, Joshua Joseph Ben David, 12:689–690

Levi-Perotti, Giustina, 12:724

Lisitzky, Ephraim, 13:81

medieval, 5:428, 10:38–39, 767, 11:33–34, 100–101, 111

medieval, Merecina of Gerona, 14:63

meter, 6:606t, 607t, 608t, 16:606–609, 613–614, 616, 617–618

Mishol, Agi, 14:331

modern, 6:742, 16:615–621

Morpurgo, Rachel Luzzatto, 14:509

parallelism, 16:598–599

Peretz, Issac Leib, 15:765–768

periods of, 16:597–598

Phinehas ben Joseph ha-Levi, 16:117

Pincas, Israel, 16:164

piyyut, 8:651–653

    classical, 16:599–603

prose, rhymed, 16:609–610

Provençal, 6:717

Psalms of Solomon, 18:766–777

Raab, Esther, 17:6

rhyme, 16:603–605, 609–611, 618–621, 622–623

rhythm and sound, 16:598–599, 604, 605, 608–609

Rimon, Jacob, 17:334

Rimon, Joseph Ẓevi, 17:334

Rokeaḥ, David, 17:372

Romanelli, Samuel Aaron, 17:374

Rosen, Abraham, 17:427

Rossena, Daniel ben Samuel of, 17:471

Ruebner, Tuvia, 17:525

Shabazi, Shalem, 18:337

Shalev, Yitzḥak, 18:373

Shalom, Shin, 18:377–378

Shapiro, Abba Constantin, 18:403

Silberschlag, Eisig, 18:578

Silkiners, Benjamin Nahum, 18:581

Sivan, Aryeh, 18:647

Solodar, Abraham, 18:754

Someck, Ronny, 19:6

Spanish, 8:655–660

    medieval, 16:605–610

terminal rhyme, 16:610–611

twentieth century, 12:443–444, 463, 13:792

versification, syllabic system of, 16:614–615

See also Piyyut; Poetry

Hebrew publishing

Austria, Schmid, Anton von, 18:145

Bologna, 8:392

China, Shanghai, 18:396

Ereẓ Israel, 4:622–628

Europe, 4:620–622

Greece, Salonika, 17:706

Ḥasidim, sefer, 8:392

Histadrut Ivrit of America, 9:151

Palestine (Mandate), 10:684

Palestine (Ottoman), 4:182–183

Parma, 8:392

Safed (Galilee), 17:661

Turkey, Izmir, 10:828

See also Hebrew printing; Publishing

"Hebrewpunk" literature, 18:206

Hebrew Reader (Solodar), 18:754

The Hebrew Sabbath School Visitor (periodical), 6:192

Hebrew script

development, 1:693, 694t, 695

French written in, 11:545

Jewish languages and, 11:303

Judeo-Provençal written in, 11:560

Lachish, 12:421–422

Nun, 15:344

Pe, 15:700

writing implements for, 4:73

Hebrew Seminar movement, 6:207

Hebrew Sheltering and Immigrant Aid Society (HIAS), 2:444, 15:208

Hebrew Socialist Union. *See* Agudat ha-Soẓyalistim ha-Ivrim

Hebrew Sunday School Society, 6:190

Hebrew Teachers' Association, 8:673

Hebrew Technical Institute, 13:161

Hebrew theater

Cameri, 4:381

Habimah, 8:179–180

Israel dramatic literature, 8:719–723

Hebrew Theological College, **8:738–739,** 13:12, 17:29, 18:576

Hebrew Union College-Jewish Institute of Religion, 6:197, **8:739–740,** 13:207, 17:26–27

Adler, Elkan Nathan, 1:396

American Jewish Archives, 2:53

Binder, Abraham Wolf, 3:703

Central Conference of American Rabbis, 4:545

Cincinnati, 4:727, 728

Ellenson, David Harry, 6:360

establishment, 6:192

Morgenstern, Julian, 14:486–487

West Coast branch, 6:198

See also Gottschalk, Alfred; Hebrew Union College-Jewish Institute of Religion

Hebrew University of Jerusalem, **8:740–744**

Albert Einstein Archives, 6:268

American Joint Distribution Committee, 2:60, 62

Birk, Yehudith, 3:711

Center of Criminology, 2:79

Department of Education, 6:65

Dvoretzky, Aryeh, 6:74

Institute of Jewish Studies, 14:470–471

Institute of Mathematics, 2:79

library, 12:788

physics, study of, 16:137–138

The Hebrew Worker (sculpture), 6:316

Hebron (Israel), **8:744–749**

Anak, Anakim son of Arba, 2:125, 126

biblical period, 8:744

oak of Abraham, 15:357

post-biblical period, 8:744–745

Hebron Agreement, 15:598

Hebron Mountains (Israel), 10:114–115

Hebron Stores (Shami), 18:391

Hecateus of Abdera, **8:749**

Judea as term, use of, 11:523

Moses, 14:531

Hechal Shlomo, **8:749–750**

Hechingen (Germany), 9:315
Hechinger, Fred M., 6:161
Hechler, William Henry, 8:**750**, 9:56
Hecht, Ben, 8:**750–751**
Hecht, Reuben, 8:**751**
Hecht, Selig, 8:**751**, 13:10
Hechter, Josef. *See* Sebastian, Mihail
Heckerling, Amy, 8:**751**
Heckscher, Eli Filip, 8:**751–752**
Heckscher, Ephraim, 2:24
Hedegård, Oscar David Leonard, 8:**752**
Ḥeder, 6:182, 8:752
    New York (NY), 6:192, 194
    Russia, 6:187
    See also Jewish education
Hedvata. *See* Haduta ben Abraham
Heeger, Alan J., 8:**752**
Hefer, Ḥayim, 4:96, 8:**752**
Hefer Plain (Israel), 8:**752–753**, *753*
Ḥefeẓ ben Yaẓli'aḥ, 8:**753**
    Judeo-Arabic literature and,
        11:531
Ḥefeẓ family. *See* Gentili family
Hefker, 8:**753–755**
Hefter, Alfred, 8:**755**
Hefter, Hidalgo. *See* Hefter, Alfred
Ḥefẓi Bah (Israel), 8:**755**
Hegedüs, Armin, 8:**755**
Hegel, Georg William Friedrich,
    8:**755–756**, 12:503
Hegenheim (France), 8:**756**
Hegesippus, 11:461
Hegner, Jacob, 1:405
Hegyon ha-Hefesh ha-Aẓuvah
    (Abraham bar Ḥiyya), 1:293
He-Ḥalutz, 8:**756–761**, 9:490, 18:425
    Ben-Gurion, David, 3:344–345
    Central Europe, 8:760
    established, 10:335
    immigration to Palestine, 8:759
    Iran, 1:224
    Lithuania, 8:759
    North America, 8:759–760
    origins, 8:756–757, 13:277–278
    Poland, 8:758–759
    Romania, 8:760
    Russia, 8:757–758, 18:606
    Trumpeldor, Joseph, 8:757
He-Ḥalutz (periodical), 8:**761**
He-Ḥalutz ha-Ẓa'ir, 8:759
He-Ḥaver, 8:**761**
Heichelheim, Fritz Moritz, 8:**761–762**
Heidegger, Martin
    Arendt relationship, 2:424
    Jonas, Hans, 11:393

Levinas, Emmanuel, 12:715
Heidelberg (Germany), 8:**762**, 15:575
Heidelberger, Michael, 8:**762–763**,
    13:11
Heidenberg, Johann, of Tritheim. *See*
    Trithemius, Johannes
Heidenhain, Rudolf, 8:**763**
Heidenheim, Benjamin Ze'ev. *See*
    Heidenheim, Wolf
Heidenheim, Wolf, 2:158, 4:157,
    8:**763**, 13:653
Heidentum, Christentum, Judentum
    (Brod), 4:192
Heidingsfeld (Germany), 8:**763–764**
Heifers. *See* Red heifers
Heifer's neck, ceremony of breaking
    of, 11:374
Heifetz, Jascha, 8:**764**
Ḥei ha-Olamim (Alemanno), 1:612
Heijermans, Herman, 6:70, 8:**764–765**
Heikhal ha-Kelim ha-Shevurim
    (Shaḥar), 18:363
Heikhal ha-Shem (Luria), 13:267
Heikhal Kodesh (Albaz), 1:587, 6:290
Heikhalot, 11:592–595
Heikhalot (Zohar), 21:648
Heilborn, Ernst, 8:**765**
Heilbron, Dame Rose, 8:**765**
Heilbron, Ian Morris. *See* Heilbron,
    Sir Ian Morris
Heilbron, Sir Ian Morris, 8:**765**
Heilbronn (Germany), 8:**765–766**
Heilbronn, Jacob ben Elhanan, 8:**766**
Heilbronn, Joseph ben David of
    Eschwege, 8:**766**
Heilbrun, Carolyn, 18:736
Heilbrun, Carolyn G., 8:**766–767**
Heilbut, Eleazar Lazi ben Joseph ben
    Lazi, 8:**767**
Das heilige Experiment (Hochwaelder),
    9:301
Die heilige Geschichte der Menschheit
    (Hess), 9:75
Heiligkeitsgesetz. See Holiness Code
Heilmann, Yitzhak, 8:**767**
Heilperin, Falk, 8:**767–768**
Heilperin, Michael Angelo, 8:**768**
Heilpern, Yom Tov Lipman ben Israel,
    8:**768**
Heilprin, Angelo, 8:**768**
Heilprin, Jehiel (20th c.), 6:183
Heilprin, Jehiel Ben Solomon (1660-
    1746), 3:681, 8:**768–769**
Heilprin, Louis, 8:768
Heilprin, Michael, 8:768, 15:200
Heilprin, Phinehas Menahem, 8:**769**
Heilprin, Samuel Helmann ben Israel,
    8:**769**

Heilprin family, 8:**768**
Heilprun, Eliezer Leizer ben Mordecai,
    8:**769**
Heiman, Eugenio, 4:49
Heimann, Moritz, 8:**769–770**
Heimeinkaufsvertraege, 17:202
Heimern, R. *See* Auernheimer, Raoul
Heimkehr der Fronttruppen (Doeblin),
    5:729–730
Heimwehr, 8:**770**
Heine, Harry. *See* Heine, Heinrich
Heine, Ḥayyim. *See* Heine, Heinrich
Heine, Heinrich, 5:365, 7:514, 8:**770–
    773**
    Bieber, Hugo, on, 3:687
    Boerne, Ludwig, 4:32
    Heine, Solomon, 15:305
    Judah Halevi in poetry of, 11:500
    Lassalle, Ferdinand, 12:501
    Moser, Moses, 14:522
    Moses, 14:540
    Solomon, 18:761
Heine, Solomon, 8:**773**, 15:305
Heine, Thomas Theodor, 8:**773**
Heine-Heimowitz, Morris, 8:**773**
Heinemann, Fritz, 8:**773–774**
Heinemann, Isaac. *See* Heinemann,
    Yiẓak
Heinemann, Jeremiah, 8:**774**
Heinemann, Wolf, 15:243
Heinemann, Yiẓak, 1:461, 462, 8:**774**
Heinrich, Friedberg von, 16:344
Heinrich Feuchtwanger Collection,
    18:227–228
Heir to the Glimmering World (Ozick),
    20:295
Heisinovitch, Abba Shaul. *See*
    Aḥimeir, Abba
Hejaz (Saudi Arabia), 8:**775**
Hejaz period, Arabian Jewish
    communities, 2:294–295
Hekdesh, 2:40, 8:**775–780**, 9:562–563,
    12:605
Hekher fun der Erd (Der Nister), 5:596
Hekhsher, 8:**780**
Helam (Gilead). *See* Alamah (Gilead)
Ḥelbo, 8:**780**
Ḥelbo, Menahem, 11:783–784
Held, Adolph, 8:**780–781**
Held, Anna, 8:**781**
Held, Moshe, 8:**781**
Der Held der Erde (Mombert), 14:430
Heldman, Gladys Medalie, 8:**781**
Helena (MT), 14:454
Helena (Queen of Adiabene), 1:391,
    8:**781–782**, 14:447
Helena Augusta, 8:**782**

Ḥelez (Israel), 8:**782–783**

Helfand, Ḥayyim Yankel. *See* Litwak, A.

Helfman, Elḥanan, 8:**783**

Helfman, Hessia Meyerovna, 8:**783**

Helicz family. *See* Halicz family

Heliodorus, 8:**783**, 18:261

Heliopolis (Ancient Egypt), 8:**783**

Ḥelkat Meḥokkek (Alshekh), 2:10

Helkias and Ananias, 2:**129**

Hell

    in apocalyptic literature, 15:628

    in medieval literature, 15:628–629

    in modern period, 15:629

    in post-biblical Jewish thought, 15:627–628

    in rabbinic literature, 15:628

Helladius on Antinoupolis, 8:**783**

Hellenism, 2:388–390, 8:**784–791**

    anthropomorphism, 2:189–190

    apologetics, 2:262–263

    architecture, 2:399

    art, 2:493

    blood libel in, 3:775

    Canon, 3:579, 579t

    coinage, 5:48

    Diaspora, 5:637–639, 642–643

    Eichthal, Gustave D', 6:252

    Greek language, 8:785–786

    Gutmann, Joshua, 8:154

    and illuminated manuscripts, Hebrew, 9:726–727

    influence on Jews, 8:786–790

    Jerusalem, 11:147–148

    Jewish identity, 11:293

        Philo Judaeus, 16:60–61

    Josephus' *Jewish Antiquities* as product of, 11:438

    Judaism

        allegorical interpretation of scripture and, 3:644, 660

        development of concept, 11:515

        religious impact of Bible on, 3:659–660

    Kabbalah and, 11:589

    literature, 13:86–87

        belief, faith, 3:291

        commandments, reasons for, 5:86

        God, 7:658–660

        logos, 13:174

        Wisdom of Solomon, 18:768–769

    Moses, 14:531–533

    Phoenicia, 16:119–120

    political history, boule, 4:105–106

    political power, 8:784–785

    pottery, 16:425

    scholars of, 6:747, 7:755

    Second Temple, 19:610–611

    spiritual resistance, Jewish, 8:790–791

    Tadmor (Syria), 19:430–431

Hellenistic Jewish literature, 8:**791–792**

Heller, Anna. *See* Rosenthal, Anna

Heller, Aryeh Leib ben Joseph Ha-Kohen of Stry, 8:**792–793**

Heller, Bernard, 8:**793**

Heller, Bernát, 8:**793–794**

Heller, Bunim, 8:**794**

Heller, Ḥayyim, 4:193, 8:**794**

Heller, Hermann, 8:**794–795**

Heller, James Gutheim, 8:792

Heller, Jehiel ben Aaron, 8:**795**

Heller, Joseph, 8:**795**

Heller, Joseph Elijah, 8:**795**

Heller, Joshua ben Aaron, 8:**795**

Heller, Judah, 8:**795–796**

Heller, Maximilian, 8:792

Heller, Meshullam Feivush of Zbarazh, 14:79

Heller, Michael, 20:299–300

Heller, Samuel, 13:186

Heller, Stephen, 8:**796**

Heller, Theodor, 6:160, 8:**796**

Heller, Yom Tov Lipmann ben Nathan Ha-Levi, 1:390, 4:779, 8:**796–798**, 11:422, 455, 14:329

Heller family, 8:**792**

Hellerstein, Alvin K., 8:**798–799**

Hellinger, Mark, 8:**799**

Hell in Islamic literature, 6:503

Hellman, Clarisse Doris, 8:**799**

Hellman, Herman Wolf, 8:**800**

Hellman, Isaias Wolf, 8:**799–800**

Hellman, Jacob, 8:**800**

Hellman, Lillian Florence, 3:783, 8:**800–801**

Hellman, Meyer, 15:415

Hellman's Scrapbook (Majzels), 4:424

Hello, Dolly! (Herman), 9:24

Helmanowitch, Nat. *See* Holman, Nathan

Helmsley, Harry, 18:150

Helmsley, Leona, 8:**801**, 18:150

Helmsley-Spear, 18:150

Helpern, Michael, 8:**801–802**

Helpern, Milton, 8:**802**

Helpern, Yermiyahu, 8:802

Helsingfors Program, 7:37, 8:**802–803**

Heltai, Jenö, 8:**803**

Ḥemah, 16:283

Heman, 8:**803**

Hemar, Marian, 8:**803–804**

Hematology. *See* Medicine

Ḥemdat Shelomo (Lipschitz), 13:71–72

Ḥemdat Yamim, 8:**804**, 18:357

Ḥemdat Yisrael (Plotzki), 16:241

Hemerobaptists, 18:233

Hemlock, 8:**805**, vol. 16: color insert

Hemp, 8:**805**

Hemsi, Alberto, 8:**805**

Hena, Hans Jacob, 8:317

Hendel, Neḥama, 8:**805–806**

Hendel, Yehudit, 8:**806**

Hendeles et al. v. Kupat Am Bank Ltd., 13:214, 14:358

Henderson the Rain King (Bellow), 3:301

Hendricks, Harmon, 8:806, 15:197, 198

Hendricks, Henry Harmon, 8:807

Hendricks, Henry S., 8:807

Hendricks, Uriah, 8:806, 15:197

Hendricks family, 8:**806–807**

Hengstenberg, Ernst Wilhelm, 8:**807**

Ḥenikh of Olesko, 3:308

Henkin, Joseph Elijah, 8:**807**

Henle, Elkan, 8:**807**

Henle, Jacob, 2:135, 8:**807–808**, 13:7

Henle, Moritz, 8:**808**

Henna, 8:**808**

Henochsberg, Edgar Samuel, 8:**808**

Henriette Jacoby (Hermann), 9:24

Henriques, Basil Lucas Quixano. *See* Henriques, Sir Basil Lucas Quixano

Henriques, Cyril Quixano, 8:**809**

Henriques, Isabel. *See* Enríquez, Isabel

Henriques, Jacob Cohen, 15:195

Henriques, Robert David Quixano, 8:**809**

Henriques, Sir Basil Lucas Quixano, 8:**809**

Henriques de Castro, David, 4:517

Henriques family, 8:**808–809**

Henriquez, Basurto Diego. *See* Enríquez Basurto, Diego

Henríquez, Gómez Antonio. *See* Enríquez Gómez, Antonio

Henry, Buck, 8:**810**

Henry, Emma, 8:**810**

Henry, H.J., 6:18–19

Henry, Jacob, 8:**810**, 15:302

Henry, Jules, 8:**810**

Henry, Michael, 8:**810**

Henry, Richard. *See* Sellers, Peter

Henry III (King of England), 6:411, 413

Henry IV (German emperor), 8:**809**

Henry IV of Spain, 2:27

Henry VII (King of Bavaria), 15:346

Henry M. Jackson School of International Studies (Seattle, WA), 18:230

Henry of Cossey, 8:512

Henry of Winchester, 8:**810**

Henschel, George. *See* Henschel, Sir George

Henschel, Isidor Georg. *See* Henschel, Sir George

Henschel, Sir George, 8:**810**

Henschel brothers, 8:**811**

Hensel, Kurt, 8:811

Henshel, Harry D., 8:811

Hentoff, Nat, 8:811

Ḥen Tov (Badiḥi), 3:49

Hep! Hep!, 8:**811–812**, *812*

Hepher (ancient city), 8:**812–813**

Heppner, Aron, 8:**813**

Heptaplomeres (Bodin), 9:227

Heptaplus (Pico della Miraondola), 16:146–147

Heracles, 9:**5**

Heraclitus, 9:**5**

Heraclius, 4:326, 9:**5–6**

Heraldry, 9:**6–7**

Herat (Afghanistan), 9:**7**

Herberg, Will, 9:**7–8**

Herbert de Bosham. *See* Bosham, Herbert de

Herbert of Bosham. *See* Bosham, Herbert de

Herblock. *See* Block, Herbert Lawrence

Herbs, medicinal, 9:**8–7**

Herbst, Josif, 4:276

Herbst, Karl, 9:**7**

Herbstein, Joseph, 9:**7**

Hercules. *See* Heracles

Herdan, Kurt Lucian, 9:**7**

Herder, Johann Gottfried, 9:**7–10**, 13:57

    modern biblical exegesis by, 3:646

Herder, Moses, 2:87

Hereafter. *See* Afterlife

Here and Now (Layton), 12:557

Hereford (England), 9:**10**

Ḥerem, 9:**10–16**, 21

    Amalekites, 2:28, 29

    categories, 9:10–11

    Deuteronomy's reinterpretation, 9:12–13

    etymology, 9:11–12

    mishpat Ivri, 14:342

    Niddui vs. ḥerem, 9:13–15

    procedure, 9:15–16

Ḥerem bet din, 9:**16–17**

Ḥerem ha-Ikkul, 9:**17**

Ḥerem ha-Yishuv, 9:**17–18**

Ḥerem setam, 9:**18–20**

Herennius Philo. *See* Philo of Byblos

Heresy, 9:**20–22**

    Judaism viewed as, 11:579

Ḥeret Enosh (Mohr), 14:420

Ḥerev le-Et (Israel), 9:**22**

Ḥerev Nokemet Nekam-Berit (Bresselau), 4:167

Here We Are: Songs of the Holocaust (Mlotek), 14:396

Herford, Robert Travers, 9:**22**, 16:630

Heritage (periodical), 2:59

A Heritage Affirmed (Lurie), 13:269

Herlands, William Bernard, 9:**22–23**

Herlingen, Aaron Wolff of Gewitsch, 4:367, 9:**23**

Herlitz, Esther, 9:23

Herlitz, Georg, 6:400, 9:**23**

Herman, Abraham. *See* Harman, Avraham

Herman, David, 9:**23**

Herman, Jerry, 9:**23–24**

Herman, Josef, 9:**24**

Herman, Max. *See* Gluckman, Max

Herman, Mildred. *See* Hayden, Melissa

Herman, Nathan-David. *See* Herman, David

Herman, Oskar, 9:**24**

Hermann, Georg, 9:**24**

Hermann, Hugo, 9:**41–42**, 42

Hermann, Leo, 9:**24–25**

Hermann, Oscar. *See* Herman, Oskar

Hermann Mestetz (Czech Republic). *See* Hermanuv Mestec (Czech Republic)

Hermannstadt (Romania). *See* Sibiu (Romania)

Herman of Scheda. *See* Hermanus Quondam Judaeus

Hermanus Quondam Judaeus, 9:**25**

Hermanuv Mestec (Czech Republic), 9:**25**

Hermaphrodite. *See* Androgynos

Hermaphroditism, 11:418

Hermeneutics, 9:**25–29**

    Baraita of 32 Rules, 3:129, 6:329

    Bible, interpretation of, 9:818–819

    Karaite doctrine, 11:797–800

    See also Bible; Midrash

Hermer, Manfred, 9:**29**

Hermes. *See* Mercury

Hermes Trimegistos, 9:29

Hermetic writings, 9:**29**

Hermippus of Smyrna, 9:**29–30**

Hermlin, Stephan, 9:**30**

Hermogenes, 9:**30**

Hermon (stream), 3:109, 11:401

Hermon (Bader), 3:45

Hermon, Mount. *See* Mount Hermon

Hero (Rosenberg), 18:200

Herod, 2:458, 9:**31**, 197–198

Herod I, 9:**31–38**

    Agrippa, Marcus Vipsanius, 1:504

    Alexander, 1:618–619

    Alexandra, 1:631

    Alexas, 1:636

    Archelaus, 4:455

    in the arts, 9:37–38

    Assumption of Moses, 14:544

    Bathyra, 3:212

    Caesar, Sextus Julius, 4:332

    Cleopatra of Jerusalem, 4:754

    Cleopatra VII, 4:754

    coinage, 5:48–49

    Cypros and, 5:347

    Doris, 5:757

    dynastic murders, 9:34–35

    Edom, 6:157

    emperor worship, 6:397

    Erez Israel under, 9:35–36

    genealogy, 9:33*t*

    Herod's day, 15:792

    Jerusalem and, 11:149–150

    Joseph (brother), 11:414

    Josephus' *Jewish Antiquities,* 11:439–440

    Joshua ben Phabi, ousting of, 11:454–455

    in music, 9:38

    Nicholas of Damascus and, 15:251, 252

    Obedas II, 15:367

    relationship with Jewish subjects, 9:36

    Second Temple, reconstruction, 19:612–613

    Simeon ben Boethus, 4:33

Herod II, 9:**38**

Herod Agrippa, 11:150

Herod Agrippa II. *See* Agrippa II

Herod Antipas. *See* Antipas, Herod

Herod Antipater, 15:252

Herodians, 9:**38–39**

Herodias, 9:**39**

    John the Baptist and, 11:381

Herodium, 9:**39**

Herodotus, 9:**39**

    Jewish identity in Hellenistic period and, 11:293

jujube and lotus eaters of, 11:572
on Palestine, 15:581
Herod Philip, 2:398
Herod Philip I, 9:**39–40**
Herod's Children (Aichinger), 9:412
Herod the Great. *See* Herod I
Heroes Go into Battle. See Hrdinové táhnou do boje
Heroic tales, myths. *See* Hagiography
Herold, Jacques, 15:648
The Heron. See L'airone
Herons, 3:729
Herrera, Abraham Kohen de, 9:**40–41**
Herrera, Alonso Nunez de. *See* Herrera, Abraham Kohen de
Herrera de Pisuegra (Spain), 9:**41**
Herrmann, Bernard, 9:**41**
Hersch, Jeanne, 9:**42**
Hersch, Pesach Liebman, 9:**42**
Hersch, Seymour, 9:**44**
Herschberg, Abraham Samuel, 9:**42–43**
Herschel, Solomon. *See* Hirschel, Solomon
Herschele, 9:**44–45**
Herscher, Uri David, 9:**43**, 18:659
Herschman, Mordechai, 9:**43**
Herschorn, Joshua Halevy, 9:**44**
Herschorn, Sheea Halevy. *See* Herschorn, Joshua Halevy
Hersh, Wolf. *See* Erlich, Henryk
Hershele Ostropoler. *See* Ostropoler, Hershele
Hershey, Barbara, 9:**45**
Hershfield, Harry, 4:499
Hershko, Avram, 4:593, 9:**45**, 13:10
Hershkowitz, Victor, 9:**45–46**
Hershl Shamay (Abtshuk), 1:333
Hershman, Abraham M., 9:**46**
Herskovits, Bela, 9:**46**
Herskovits, Melville Jean, 9:**46**
Herskovitz, Marshall, 9:**46–47**
Herskovitz, Melville J., 2:186
Herstein, Lillian, 9:**47**
Herstik, Naphtali, 9:**47**
Herta. *See* Gertsa
Hertz, Benedykt, 9:**47**
Hertz, Emanuel, 9:**47**
Hertz, Gustav, 9:**47–48**
Hertz, Henri, 9:**48**, 11:358
Hertz, Henrik, 9:**48**
Hertz, Ilse. *See* Roberg, Ilse
Hertz, Joseph Herman, 3:614, 9:**48–49**, 11:328, 378
Hertzberg, Arthur, 9:**49**
Hertzberg-Fraenkel, Leo. *See* Herzberg-Fraenkel, Leo

Hertzka, Emil, 9:**49**
Hertzka, Theodor, 9:**49–50**
Hertzveld-Hijmans, Esthella, 9:**50**
Ḥerut (Israel), 9:**50**
Ḥeruti. *See* Smilansky, Moshe
Ḥerut movement, 9:**50–51**, 17:262–267
    Begin, Menaḥem, 3:261
    Shamir, Yitzhak, 18:393
Herxheimer, Salomon, 2:163, 9:**51**
Herz, Henri, 9:**51**
Herz, Henriette, 9:**51**
Herz, Leopold Edler von, 9:**51–52**
Herz, Marcus, 9:**52**
Herz, Michael, 4:86
Herzberg, Abel Jacob, 6:70, 9:**52**
Herzberg, Judith, 6:71
Herzberg, Wilhelm, 9:**52**
Herzberg-Fraenkel, Leo, 4:199, 9:**53**
Herzberg-Fraenkel, Sigmund, 4:199
Herzenstein, Mikhail Yakovlevich, 9:**53**
Herzfeld, Ernst Emil, 2:371, 9:**53**
Herzfeld, Helmut. *See* Heartfield, John
Herzfeld, Levi, 4:226, 9:**53–54**
Herzheimer, Solomon, 3:631
Herzl (Elon), 6:366
Herzl, Binyamin Ze'ev. *See* Herzl, Theodor
Herzl, Jenö. *See* Heltai, Jenö
Herzl, Theodor, 9:**54–66**, 54*t*, 247, 605, 12:779
    Abdul-Hamid II and, 15:542
    Aḥ ha-Am, 1:526
    antisemitism, 9:55
    Bliokh, Ivan Stanislavovich, 3:756
    Bloch, Ernst, criticism by, 3:760
    Bloch, Joseph Samuel, 3:764
    Bodenheimer, Max Isidor, 4:27
    Buber, Martin, 4:235
    Chamberlain, Joseph, 4:564
    Dreyfus Affair, 6:19
    El-Arish, 6:286
    flag of Israel, 7:68
    Frederick I (Grand Duke of Baden), 7:221
    German relationship, 9:55–60
    Ḥibbat Zion, 9:94
    Landau, Saul Raphael, 12:465
    Levontin, Zalman David, 12:745
    Nobel, Nehemiah Anton, 15:291
    Nordau, Max, 15:298
    Nussenblath, Tulo, 15:354
    Odessa Committee, 15:382
    protestrabbiner and, 16:633
    Schachtel, Hugo-Hillel, 18:99
    Schalit, Isidor, 18:104, 105

Schnirer, Moritz Tobias, 18:151
Turkish relationship, 9:61–63
Uganda controversy, 9:63–66
on utopian vision of Israel, 18:202–203
vision at First Zionist congress, vol. 21: color insert
Zionist financial institutions, 11:285
See also Newlinski, Philipp Michael
Herzliah Hebrew Teachers' Institute, 9:**66–67**
Herzlia High School (Israel), 14:522
Herzliyyah (Israel), 9:**67**, vol. 11: color insert
Herzl Museum, 2:414
Herzog (Bellow), 3:300, 301
Herzog, Chaim, 9:**67–68**
Herzog, David, 9:**68**
Herzog, Emile. *See* Maurois, André
Herzog, George, 9:**68**
Herzog, Isaac, 6:33, 9:**68–70**
Herzog, Jacob, 9:70
Herzog, Reginald Oliver, 9:**70**
Herzog, Sarah, 9:69
Herzog, Shira, 9:**70**
Herzog, Z., 2:330
Herzstein, Barbara. *See* Hershey, Barbara
Heschel, Abraham Joshua, 3:736, 9:**70–72**, 11:330, 16:104
    Dresner, Samuel Hayim, 6:11
    Existentialism, 6:612
    free will, 7:233–234
    good and evil, 7:754
    miracles, 14:309–310
    National Conference on Soviet Jewry, 15:20
    redemption, 17:154
    revelation, 17:258
Heschel, Abraham Joshua ben Jacob, 9:**72–73**
Heschel, Abraham Joshua of Apta. *See* Abraham Joshua Heschel of Apta
Hescheles, Marian. *See* Hemar, Marian
Ḥesed le-Avraham (Weinberg), 18:677
Heshbon (ancient Israel), 6:297, 9:**73**
Ḥeshbon Mahalekhot ha-Kokhavim (Abraham bar Ḥiyya), 1:293
Ḥeshek Shelomo (Alemanno), 1:611–612
Ḥeshek Shelomo (Solomon ben Judah of Lunel), 18:772
Heshel, Abraham Joshua, of Machnovka, 8:420
Heshin, Schneur Zalman, 9:**73–74**

Ḥeshvan. *See* Marḥeshvan

Heskes, Irene, 9:**74**

Hesped, 6:526, 9:**74**, 11:494–495
   See also Kinah

Hesperides. *See* Benghazi (Libya)

Hess, Dame Myra, 9:**76**

Hess, Mendel, 9:**74**

Hess, Michael, 9:**75**

Hess, Moses, 9:**75–76**, 12:439, 13:255,
   18:577, 705, 21:541–542
      Duenner, Joseph Ẓ Hirsch, 6:41

Hess, Rudolph, 4:87

Hesse (Germany), 9:**77–78**

Hesse-Darmstadt (Germany), 9:77

Hesse-Homburg. *See* Homburg
   (Germany)

Hesse-Kassel (Germany), 9:77

Hessel, Franz, 9:**78**

Hessen, Joseph Vladimiovich, 9:**78**

Hessen, Julius Isidorovich, 9:**78–79**,
   18:724

Hester Street (motion picture), 18:585

Hestrin, Shlomo, 9:**79**

Hestrin-Lerner, Sarah, 9:**79**

Ḥet, 9:**79**

Het dendende hart van de barak
   (Hiller), 9:116

Hetter iskah. *See* Shetar

Het verstoorde leen (Hiller), 9:116

Ḥevel Sedom (Almog), 1:680

Ḥevel Yam ha-Melaḥ (Almog), 1:680

Ḥever, Ḥanan, 8:731

Ḥever ha-Yehudim, 9:**79**

Ḥever ir, 8:**470**

Hevesi, Alan, 15:224

Hevesi, András, 9:79

Hevesi, Lajos, 9:**79**

Hevesi, Ludwig. *See* Hevesi, Lajos

Hevesi, Sandor, 9:**79**

Hevesi, Simon, 9:**80**, 13:254

Hevesy, George Charles de, 9:**80**

Ḥevrah, ḥavurah, 4:572, 9:**80–81**

Ḥevra kaddisha, 4:548, 572, 9:**81–82**
      Altschul, Emil, 2:25
      taxes, 7:24

Ḥevrat ha-Ovedim, 9:**82–83**, 147

Ḥevrat Ḥayyim, 3:742

*He Walked in the Fields. See Hu
   Halakh ba-Sadot*

He Will Light the Way. See Ya'ir Nativ

Hewitt, Don, 9:**83**

Hexagram, 2:122, 123

Hexapla, 7:463

Hexapla (Origen), 3:597, 598, 601,
   666, 15:474

Hexateuch, 6:278, 11:444

Hexter, Jack H., 9:**83–84**

Heyd, Uriel, 9:**84**

Heydemann, Heinrich, 2:370

Heydenfeldt, Solomon, 9:**84**

Heydius, Thomas. *See* Hyde, Thomas

Heydrich, Reinhard Tristan, 9:**84–85**,
   332, 336, 11:526, 527

Heyermans, Herman. *See* Heijermans,
   Herman

Heykhan Ani Nimzet (Castel-Bloom),
   4:512

Heym, Stefan, 9:**85–86**

Heyman, Henrik. *See* Hertz, Henrik

Heyman, Moses David, 9:**86**

Heyman, Seymor C., 15:397

Heymann, Fritz, 9:**86**

Heymann, Lewis, 15:316

Heymann, Walther, 9:**86–87**

Heymans, Gerardus F., 9:**87**

Heyse, Paul, 9:**87**

Hezekiah (amora), 9:**90**

Hezekiah (freedom fighter), 9:**90**,
   18:290

Hezekiah (King of Judah), 1:539,
   9:**87–90**, 180–181, 18:582
      Kings, Book of, 12:173–174
      Nehushtan, 15:64
      priestly source of Torah and,
         15:738, 739

Hezekiah, the High Priest, 9:**90–91**

Hezekiah ben David, 9:**91**

Hezekiah ben David da Silva, 9:**91–92**

Hezekiah ben Jacob, 9:**92**

Hezekiah ben Manoah, 9:**92**

Hezekiah of Ventura, 4:48

Ḥezi, 18:440

Hezir, 9:**92**

Hezir family tomb, vol. 10: color
   insert

HIAS. *See* Hebrew Sheltering and
   Immigrant Aid Society

Ḥibat Allah
      abu al-Barakāt ben All
         al-Baghdādi, 9:**92–93**, 16:84
      ibn Jumay' ibn Zayn, 9:93

Ḥibat Allah ibn al-Ḥasan ben
   Ephraim, 11:536

Hibbath Zion (Sokolow), 18:749

Ḥibbat Zion (Israel), 9:**94**

Ḥibbat Zion (movement), 3:140,
   8:443, 9:**94**, 11:68, 724, 755, 756,
   16:44
      Aḥ ha-Am, 1:525, 526
      Bambus, Willy, 3:105
      Barishansky, Raphael, 3:154
      Barzilai, Yehoshua, 3:194
      Benei Moshe, 3:334–335

Berliand, Shlomo Meir, 3:444
      Bermann, Vasili, 3:466
      in Bialystok (Poland), 3:567
      Eliasberg, Mordecai, 6:319
      Fez, Morocco, 7:7
      First Aliyah and, 10:333–334
      Grunberg, Abraham, 8:111
      Guttmacher, Elijah, 8:155–156
      ḥalukkah, 8:289
      Ha-ShaḤar, 8:381
      Helpern, Michael, 8:801
      Kattowitz Conference, 12:7–8
      Landau, Adolph, 12:457
      Lapidot, Alexander Moses, 12:490
      Levin, Judah Leib, 12:709–710
      Levontin, Zalman David, 12:744–
         745
      Lilienblum, Moses Leib, 13:15
      Lippe, Karpel, 13:69
      Meerovitch, Menaché, 13:765
      Mohilewer, Samuel, 14:418–419
      Schapira, Hermann, 18:107–108
      Smolenskin, Peretz, 8:381
      See also Zionism

Ḥibbat Ẕiyyon (Dinur), 5:672

Ḥibbur ha-Meshiḥah ve-ha-Tishboret
   (Abraham bar Ḥiyya), 1:293, 13:673

Ḥibbur Yafeh Min ha-Yeshu'a
   (Nissim). *See Sefer ha-Maasiyyot*

Ḥibbur Yafe me-haYeshu'ah (Nissim),
   10:97–98, 14:539, 15:280

Ḥibbut ha-Kever, 9:**94**

Hibshūsh, Ḥayyim, 9:**94–95**

HICEM, 4:639

Hickl, Max, 9:**95**

Hida, 2:774–775

Ḥidah parables, 15:620

Hidalgo, Alfred. *See* Hefter, Alfred

Hidāyat al-Qāri, 1:334, 13:650, 651

*Hidden Holocaust? Gay and Lesbian
   Persecution in Germany* (Grau),
   9:419

*The Hidden Puddle. See Shelulit
   Genuzah*

Hidden Songs (Elisheva), 6:354

Ḥiddushei Aggadot (Edels), 6:144

Ḥiddushei Halakhot (Edels), 6:143–144

Ḥiddushei ha-Ritba (Yom Tov),
   21:391–392

Ḥiddushei Maharḥa (Alfasi), 1:638

Ḥiddushim, 1:422–423, 9:**95–97**,
   14:337

Hidekel. *See* Tigris

The Hiding Place, 9:444

Ḥidka, 9:**97**

Hiel, 9:**97**

Hier, Marvin, 9:**97**, 13:200–201, 18:618–620

Hierapolic (Syria), 9:**97–98**

Hieroglyphic writing, Hittite, 9:293

Hieronymus de Sancta Fide. *See* Lorki, Joshua

Hierosolymitanische Stiftung, 9:**98**

Higgayon (Reines), 17:207

Higger, Michael, 9:**98**

High Commissioner for Palestine, 9:**98–99**

Higher Criticism, 11:25

Higher Freedom (Polish), 16:334

Higher School for Jewish Science (Berlin). *See* Hochschule Fuer die Wissenschaft des Judentums

Higher Than the Earth. See Hekher fun der Erd

High Holiday Prayer Book (Silverman), 18:587

High Holidays
Book of Life, 4:69
folklore, 7:104

High Holy Days: A Commentary on the Prayerbook of Rosh Hashanah and Yom Kippor (Kieval), 12:153

High places. *See* Cult Places, Israelite

High priests, 9:**99–100**
Aaron, 1:209, 210–211
Aaronide, 1:217–219
breastpiece precious stones, 16:475–479, 476t
Caiaphas, Joseph, 4:339
Jaddua, 11:57–58
Jason, 11:90
Jeshua, 11:241–242
red heifer, 17:156–158
Second Temple, 19:618–619
selection, 16:117
Simeon ben Boethus, 18:594
Simeon the Just, 18:602

Highway 61 Revisited (Dylan), 6:78

Hija, David de, 4:257

Hijackings, plane, 6:447–448

Hijar (Spain), 9:**100**

Ḥikrei Halakhah u-She'elot u-Teshuvot (Mohilewer), 14:419

Hilberg, Raul, 4:217, 9:**100–102**

Hildebert of Lavardin, 9:**102**

Hildesheim (Germany), 9:**102–103**

Hildesheimer, Azriel, 6:269, 8:260–261, 9:**103–104**, 12:616, 17:19
Juedische Presse, 11:569

Hildesheimer, Hirsch, 9:**104–105**
Juedische Presse, 11:569

Hildesheimer, Meir, 9:**105**

Hildesheimer, Wolfgang, 9:**105**

Hilduin, 9:**106**

Hilewitz, Alter, 9:**106**

Hilf, Alois, 15:509

Hilf: a Zaml-Bukh fir Literatur un Kunst (Shalom Aleichem), 18:383

Hilfai. *See* Ilfa

Hilferding, Rudolf, 9:**106**, 16:344, 18:729

Hilfsverein der deutschen Juden, 3:105, 9:**106–107**, 12:482
Levin, Shmarya, 12:713

Hilkhot Bekhorot (Naḥmanides), 14:743

Hilkhot Ḥallah (Naḥmanides), 14:742

Hilkhot niddah. *See* Niddah

Hilkhot Niddah (Naḥmanides), 14:743

Hilkhot Re'u. See Halakot Pesukot

Hilkhot Sheḥitah u-Vedikah (Weil), 20:**711–712**

Hilkhot Yom Tov (Algazi), 1:645

Hilkiah, 9:**107**

Ḥilla (Iraq), 9:**107–108**

Hillel (3rd century C.E.), 9:**110**

Hillel (330–365 C.E.), 9:**110**

Hillel (organization), 6:196, 9:**111–112**, 15:132, 20:371–372
Canada, 4:17
founding, 4:14
Joel, Richard M., 11:364–365
Jospe, Alfred, 11:462–463
Pekarsky, Maurice Bernard, 15:715

Hillel (the Elder), 3:530–533, 641, 8:391, 9:**108–110**
academies, 1:348
calendar, 4:357
creation, 5:275–276
halakhah, approach to, 6:486, 8:255
Ḥanukkah lamp, 8:333
Johanan ben Zakhai and, 11:373
on marriage, 8:255, 21:324
on New Year, 15:193
on non-Jewish women and niddah, 15:256–257
on praising the bride, 8:247–248
resurrection, 17:242

Hillel, David d'Beth, 2:28

Hillel, Shelomo, 9:**112–113**

Hillel II, 4:357, 9:**110–111**

Hillel ben Eliakim, 9:**113**

Hillel ben Jacob of Bonn, 3:770

Hillel ben Naphtali Ẓevi, 2:24, 9:**113**

Hillel ben Samuel, 3:239, 7:129, 9:**113–115**, 16:87

Hillel Ben Shakhar. *See* Landau, Judah Loeb

Hillel of Erfurt, 9:**115**

Hillel of Greece. *See* Hillel ben Eliakim

Hillels, Shelomo, 9:**115**

Hillel the Elder. *See* Hillel of Erfurt

Hillel und Schamai (Adler), 1:402

Hiller, Arthur, 9:**115**

Hiller, Ferdinand, 9:**115**

Hiller, Kurt, 9:**116**

Hillesum, Etty, 9:**116**

Hillesum, Jeremias, 9:**116–117**

Hillman, Bessie Abramowitz, 18:713

Hillman, Bessie "Bas Sheva" Abramowitz, 9:**117**

Hillman, David, 9:**117**

Hillman, Samuel Isaac, 9:**117**

Hillman, Sidney, 9:117, **118**

Hillquit, Morris, 9:**118–119**, 15:212, 18:708

Ḥilluk ha-Kara'im ve-ha-Rabbanim (Elijah ben Abraham). *See The Controversy between the Karaites and the Rabbanites* (Elijah ben Abraham)

Hillula, 1:439, 9:**119**

Hillula dance, 5:411, vol. 5: color insert

Hillula de-Rabbi Shimon bar Yoḥai, the Festivity, 9:**119**

Ḥillul ha-Shem. *See* Kiddush ha-Shem and Ḥillul ha-Shem

Hilsenrath, Edgar, 9:**119**

Hilsner, Leopold. *See* Hilsner Case

Hilsner Case, 9:**119–120**, 15:352

Him, George, 4:368, 12:769

Himmelfarb, Gertrude, 9:**120–121**, 152

Himmelstein, Lena, 9:**121**

Himmelweit, Hildegarde, 9:**121**

Himmler, Heinrich, 9:**121–122**
Blood for Trucks offer, 4:120
camps, concentration and extermination, 4:384
as commander of Auschwitz, 2:662, 667
Hoess, Rudolf, 9:304–306
Ravensbrueck concentration camp, 17:121
Schellenberg, Walter, 18:119

Ḥimyar, 4:326, 9:**122**

Hinatuna. *See* Hannathon (ancient Israel)

Hindakah. *See* Ḥidka

Hindemith, Paul, 2:31

Hindenberg. *See* Zabrze (Poland)

Hindenburg. *See* Zabrze (Poland)

Hindus, Maurice Gerschon, 9:**123**

Hine, Edward, 4:188

Hīneni he-ani mi-ma'as, 9:**123**

Hinkel, Hans (Staatskommissar), 11:570
Hinnom, valley of, 6:503
Ḥinnukh Beit Yehudah (Judah Leib ben Enoch Zundel), 11:506
Hinrichsen, Henri, 9:123
Hinrichsen, Max, 9:123
Hinrichsen, Max Abraham, 9:123
Hinrichsen, Michael, 13:712
Hinrichsen, Walter, 9:123
Hinrichsen family, 9:**123**
Hippo (Algeria). *See* Bone (Algeria)
Hippolytus of Rome, 4:720
Hippopotamus, 3:**263**
Hippo Regius. *See* Bone
Hippo Regius (Algeria). *See* Bone (Algeria)
Ḥīra (Persia), 9:**123**
Hiram, 9:**123–124**, 18:757
Hiram (craftsman), 9:124
Hiram (King of Tyre), 9:123–124
Hiram (King of the Zidonians), 9:124
Hirchmann, Ira A., 9:490
Hire. *See* Lease and hire
Hirsch, Aron Siegmund, 9:**124**
Hirsch, August, 9:**124**
Hirsch, Baron Maurice de, 1:500, 501, 3:173, 9:**127–128**
    Jewish settlement in America, 2:46
    railroads, 17:70
Hirsch, Clara, 9:128
Hirsch, Don. *See* Harran, Don
Hirsch, Edith, 9:126
Hirsch, Emil Gustave, 9:**124–125**
Hirsch, Eric Donald, Jr., 9:**125**
Hirsch, John Stephen, 9:**125–126**
Hirsch, Joseph, 9:**126**
Hirsch, Judd, 9:**126**
Hirsch, Julius, 9:**126–127**
Hirsch, Markus, 9:**127**
Hirsch, Max, 16:344
Hirsch, Mendel, 9:**128**
Hirsch, Moritz Freiherr von. *See* Hirsch, Baron Maurice de
Hirsch, Otto, 9:**128**
Hirsch, Paul, 16:344
Hirsch, Rachel, 9:**128**
Hirsch, Richard, 9:**129**
Hirsch, Robert Paul, 9:**129**
Hirsch, Robert von, 2:524
Hirsch, Samson Raphael, 9:**129–132**
    Breuer, Isaac, 4:171
    Breuer, Joseph, 4:171–172
    Breuer, Mordecai, 4:172–173
    Breuer, Solomon, 4:173
    on dietary laws, 5:657

education, 6:181–182, 9:130
Frankel, Zacharias, 7:200–201
Hirsch Pentateuch, 3:614, 623, 631
Moses, 14:537
Orthodox Judaism, development of, 15:493–494, 496
See also Neo-Orthodoxy
Hirsch, Samuel, 7:665, 9:**132–133**, 16:94–95
    miracles, 14:309
    nature, 15:35
Hirsch, Solomon, 9:**133**
Hirsch, Ẓevi. *See* Bruck, Grigori
Hirschbein, Esther. *See* Shumiatcher-Hirschbein, Esther
Hirschbein, Peretz, 9:**133–134**, 19:680
Hirschberg, Ḥaïm Z'ew, 9:**134**
Hirschberg, Julius, 9:**134**
Hirschel, Levie, 9:**134–135**
Hirschel, Meyer. *See* Hirshel, Meyer
Hirschel, Saul. *See* Berlin, Saul ben Ẓevi Hirsch Levin
Hirschel, Solomon, 1:621, 9:**135**
Hirschensohn, Ḥayyim, 9:135
Hirschensohn, Isaac, 9:135
Hirschensohn, Jacob Mordecai, 9:135
Hirschensohn family, 9:**135–136**
Hirschensohn-Lichtenstein, Jehiel Ẓevi Hermann, 9:**136**
Hirschfeld, Al, 9:**136**
Hirschfeld, Ephraim Joseph, 9:**136–137**, 14:426
Hirschfeld, Georg, 9:**137**
Hirschfeld, Gustav, 9:**137**
Hirschfeld, Hartwig, 9:**137–138**
Hirschfeld, Heinrich Otto, 9:**138**
Hirschfeld, Isador, 9:**138**
Hirschfeld, Magnus, 9:**138–139**
Hirschfeld, Otto, 2:370
Hirschfeld-Mack, Ludwig, 9:**139**
Hirschfield, Siegfried, 14:446
Hirschhorn, Samuel, 9:**139**
Hirschkahn, Ẓvi, 9:**139**
Hirschler, Ignác, 9:**140**
Hirschler, Pál, 9:**140**
Hirschler, René, 2:9, 9:**140**
Hirschman, Albert Otto, 9:**140**
Hirschmann, Ira Arthur, 9:**140–141**
Hirsch-Ollendorf, Gilbert Yves Edmond. *See* Grandval, Gilbert Yves Edmond
Hirschprung, Pinhas, 9:**141**
Hirsh, Nurit, 9:**141–142**
Hirshberg, Jehoash, 9:**142**
Hirshberg, Yehoash. *See* Hirshberg, Jehoash

Hirshberg, Yehudah, 9:**142**
Hirshel, Meyer, 9:**142**
Hirshenberg, Samuel, 9:**142**
Hirshenson, Hayim, 9:**142–143**
Hirshfield, Morris, 9:**143**
Hirshhorn, Joseph Herman, 9:**143**
Hirst, L. F., 3:731
Hirszfeld, Ludwik, 9:**143**
Hirszowicz, Abraham, 9:**143–144**
Hirz, Naphtali ben Judah Selke. *See* Hirshel, Meyer
Hisab al-Gubar (Dunash ibn Tamim), 6:47–48
al-Ḥisād al-Awwal (Shaul), 18:421
Ḥisda, 9:**144**, 17:8–9, 9
Ḥisdai. *See* Ḥasdai
Ḥisdai ibn Ḥisdai, Abu al-Faḍl, 9:**145**
Ḥisdai ibn Shaprut, 9:**145–146**, 11:414
    Khazar Correspondence, 12:112–113
    letters of, 12:*670*
    Pamplona, 15:609
Hishtaddelut im Shadal (Bachrach), 3:39
Ḥisin, Ḥayyim, 9:**146**
Hista'arut Melekh ha-Negev im Melekh ha-Ẓafon (London), 13:185
Histadrut, 3:345, 9:**146–150**
    Aḥdut ha-Avodah-Po'alei Zion, 1:540, 541
    Ben-Gurion, David, 3:345
    Ben-Zvi, Izhak, 3:394
    economic affairs, 10:511–512
    Ha-Oved ha-Ẓiyyoni, 8:336–337
    Ha-Poel ha-Mizrachi relations, 8:339
    Institute for Social Research, 11:762
    Israel (state), 10:600–605, 618
        newspaper, 10:705
    Israel Arab integration, 10:727–728
    Israel Labor Party and, 10:755
    Katznelson, Berl, 12:25
    Kessar, Israel, 12:90
    Lavon, Pinḥas, 12:532–533
    Mo'eẓet ha-Po'alot, 14:415
    Palestine (Mandate), 10:201, 511–512, 594–600
    Shem-Tov, Victor, 18:458
    Solel Boneh, 18:752–753
Histadrut ha-No'ar ha-Amamit ha-Halutzit Gordonia. *See* Gordonia
Histadrut ha-Ovedim ha-Le'ummit, 3:428, 9:**150–151**
Histadrut ha-Rabbanim. *See* Rabbinical Council of America

Histadrut Harabinim. *See* Rabbinical Council of America

Histadrut ha-Ẓofim be-Israel, 18:201

Histadrut Ivrit b'America, Birnbaum, Philip, 3:716

Histadrut Ivrit of America, 9:**151**, 13:240

Histoire de la Palestine (Abel), 1:246

Histoire de la Russie (Milyukov), 6:267

Histoire de l'Espagne musulmane (Lévi-Provençal), 12:725

Histoire des Juifs de France (Berman), 13:20

Histoire des Musulmans d'Espagne, jusqu'a la conquête de l'Andalousie par les Almoravides 711-1110 (Dozy), 5:772

Histoire du peuple anglais au XIXe siècle (Halevi), 8:269

L'Histoire et la Religion des Juifs depuis Jésus Christ jusqu'à Présent (Basnage), 16:629

Historia Augusta, 9:**151**

Historia Judaica. See Revue des etudes juives

Historians, 9:**151–153**
- ancient
  - Herodotus, 9:39
  - Jason of Cyrene, 11:90
  - Philo Judaeus, 16:63
  - Philo of Byblos, 16:64
- Australia, Levi, John Simon, 12:689
- Austria, Buedinger, Max, 4:251
- authors of Torah, 15:731, 750
- Babai ben Farhad, 3:15
- Babai ben Luṭ, 3:15
- Belgium, Hyman, Paul, 9:651
- biographers, Melville, Lewis, 14:16
- Bohemian Jewry, Lieben, Salomon Hugo, 12:803
- Canada, Rome, David, 17:417
- Chinese history, Levenson, Joseph Richmond, 12:680
- classical literature, 12:644
- Dalven, Rachel, 5:384
- Danish Jewry, Fischer, Josef, 7:54
- economy, Beer, George Louis, 3:251
- Egypt, Chaeremon, 4:555–556
- England
  - architecture, 16:23
  - Finestein, Israel, 7:29, 30
  - Fishman, William, 7:65
  - Hyamson, Albert Montefiore, 9:646
  - Israel, Jonathan, 10:741
  - Judaica, 11:49

Momigliano, Arnaldo Dante, 14:430–431
  - twentieth century, 11:16
- English history, Victorian England, 9:120–121
- Europe
  - Pinson, Koppel S., 16:177
  - politics, 17:204–205
- European history, Hurwitz, Samuel Justin, 9:632
- Fine, Sidney, 7:25–26
- Finley, Sir Moses, 7:39
- France
  - Adler, Alexandre, 1:394
  - Depping, Georges-Bernard, 5:591
  - Hauser, Henri, 8:463
  - Isaac, Jules Marx, 10:36
  - Kaspi, Andre, 11:823
  - Lévy, Arthur, 12:747
  - Lévy, Paul, 12:754
  - Liber, Maurice, 12:775
- Germany
  - Bresslau, Harry, 4:167–168
  - Isaacsohn, Siegfried, 10:56–57
  - Mayer, Gustav, 13:698
  - Mommsen, Theodor, 14:431
  - Perlbach, Max, 15:775
  - Rieger, Paul, 17:293–294
  - Riess, Ludwig, 17:294
  - Simson, Bernhard von, 18:621
  - Simson, Paul, 18:621
  - Synder, Louis Leo, 18:698
- Graetz, Heinrich, 8:26–29
- Greco-Jewish, 6:552–553
- Greece
  - Agatharchides of Cnidus, 1:445–446
  - Emmanuel, Isaac Samuel, 6:395
- Guttman, Jacob, 8:156–157
- Guttman, Julius, 8:157–158
- Halevy, Isaac, 8:270
- Halpern, Israel, 8:284–285
- Halphen, Louis, 8:285–286
- Heichelheim, Fritz Moritz, 8:761–762
- Heilprin, Jehiel Ben Solomon, 3:681, 8:768–769
- Hellenism, Cleodemus Malchus, 4:753
- Holocaust
  - Bauer, Yehuda, 3:218–219
  - Bensoussan, Georges, 3:378
  - Braham, Randolph Louis, 4:118

  - Browning, Christopher R., 4:217
  - Poliakov, Léon, 16:331
  - Reitlinger, Gerald, 17:213
- Hungary
  - Acsády, Ignác, 1:369
  - Buechler, Alexander, 4:251
  - Dukes, Leopold, 6:44
  - Kardos, Albert, 11:804–805
  - Lánczy, Gyula, 12:456
- international relations, Beloff, Max, Baron, 3:302–303
- of Islamic art, 6:545
- Islamic studies, Lewis, Bernard, 12:764
- Israel
  - Brawer, Abraham Jacob, 4:140
  - Ettinger, 6:544
  - Mazar, Benjamin, 13:705–706
  - Schalit, Abraham Chaim, 18:104
  - Sermoneta, Joseph Baruch, 18:312
- Italy
  - Coen, Achille, 4:781
  - Mondolfo, Rodolfo, 14:435
  - Romanin, Samuele, 17:402
  - Segrè, Arturo, 18:251
  - Soave, Moise, 18:699
- Jewish history, 1:431, 11:97, 13:791
  - Allon, Gedalya, 1:675
  - Baron, Salo Wittmayer, 3:172–173
  - Bédarride, Israél, 3:247
  - Bégin, Emile Auguste, 3:261
  - Ben-Sasson, Haim Hillel, 3:373
  - Berger, David, 3:424
  - Berlin, Israel, 3:457
  - Bernstein, Béla, 3:477
  - Bershadski, Sergey Alexandrovich, 3:488–489
  - Bevan, Edwyn Robert, 3:555–556
  - Biale, David, 3:560
  - Brilling Bernhard, 4:183
  - Cantera Burgos, Francisco, 4:435
  - Capsali, Elijah, 4:455–456
  - Carlebach, Elisheva, 4:480
  - Carmilly-Weinberger, Moshe, 4:485
  - Caro, Georg Martin, 4:487
  - Cassel, Paulus Stephanus, 4:508

Historians, *continued*

    Cassuto, Umberto, 4:510–511

    Cazès, David, 4:533

    Cesarani, David, 4:551

    Chazan, Robert, 4:585

    Churgin, Pinkhos, 4:723

    Dessau, Hermann, 5:604

    Deutsch, Gotthard, 5:623

    Diamant, Paul Joseph, 5:632

    Dimitrovsky, Chaim Zalman, 5:663

    Diner, Hasia R., 5:670

    Dinur, Benzion, 5:672

    Dohm, Christian Wilhelm von, 5:733–734

    Hellenistic and Roman, 17:75

    Herzfeld, Levi, 9:53–54

    Herzog, David, 9:68

    Hessen, Julius Isidorovich, 9:78–79

    Hildesheimer, Hirsch, 9:104–105

    Hirschberg, Ḥaïm Z'ew, 9:134

    Hock, Simon, 9:301

    Horodezky, Samuel Abba, 9:527

    Horovitz, Marcus, 9:529

    Hungarian Jewry, 17:196

    Hyman, Paula E., 9:650–651

    Ibn Daud, Abraham ben David Halevi, 9:662–665

    Levin, Nora, 12:712

    Lévy, Alfred, 12:747

    Lewin, Adolf, 12:759

    Lewin, Louis, 12:761

    Menes, Abram, 14:46–47

    Pines, Shlomo, 16:167

    Rabbinowitz, Saul Phinehas, 17:32

    Rabin, Israel Abraham, 17:33

    Rabinowicz, Oskar K., 17:40

    Raphael, Chaim, 17:94

    Reinharz, Jehuda, 17:209

    Riviln, Eliezer, 17:350

    Rivkin, Ellis, 17:349

    Romain, Jonathan A., 17:373

    Rome, David, 17:417

    Rosanes, Solomon Abraham, 17:422

    Roth, Cecil, 17:479–480

    Rubens, Alfred, 17:510

    Rubinstein, William D., 17:518

    Ruderman, David B., 17:519–520

    Spanish Jewry, 3:268–269

Josephus, 11:437, 439, 441

Karaites, Lelewel, Joachim, 12:634

Katz, David S., 12:**10**

Katz, Jacob, 12:12–13

Katz, Solomon, 12:16

Kayserling, Meyer, 12:42–43

Kehimkhar, Ḥayim Samuel, 12:67

Kisch, Guido, 12:197

Klausner, Joseph Gedaliah, 12:215–217

Klein, Samuel, 12:225–226

Klemperer, Gutmann, 12:227

labor history, Hobsbawm, Eric John, 9:298–299

Lea, Henry Charles, 12:563

legal, Radin, Max, 17:54

legal history, Hyman, Harold Melvin, 9:650

literary history, 7:144

    Bab, Julius, 3:14

    Beider, Chaim, 3:265

    Benichou, Paul, 3:352–353

    Berendsohn, Walter A., 3:409–410

    Bernays, Michael, 3:470

    Calin, Vera, 4:363–364

    Iodifescu, Silvian, 10:7

    Karpeles, Gustav, 11:816

    Rejzen, Kalman, 17:213–214

Marxism, Deutscher, Isaac, 5:625–626

medical, Leibowitz, Joshua O., 12:620–621

Mesopotamian culture, Lehmann-Haupt, Carl Friedrich, 12:616

Meyer, Michael A., 14:148–149

Middle Ages

    Cantor, Norman Frank, 4:440–441

    Davidsohn, 5:475

    Europe, Jewish life, 13:785

    Levison, Wilhelm, 12:729–730

    Liebermann, Felix, 12:808

Milano, Attilio, 14:232

Moravia

    Bretholz, Berthold, 4:170

    D'Elvert, Christian Ritter von, 5:547

of Moravian Jewry

    Flesch, Heinrich, 7:76

    Frankl-Gruen, Adolf Abraham, 7:214

musical history

    Botstein, Leon, 4:104

    Heskes, Irene, 9:74

    Rosenthal, Harold, 17:453

Nazi Germany, Kempner, Robert Max Wasilii, 12:**74**

Netherlands, Meijer, Jacob, 13:774–775

Neuman, Abraham Aaron, 15:120

Phoenicia

    Claudius Iolaus, 4:752

    Dios, 5:675

Poland

    Balaban, Meir, 3:82

    Brann, Marcus, 4:129

    Czacki, Tadeusz, 5:351

    Dembitzer, Ḥayyim Nathan, 5:548

    Handelsman, Marceli, 8:319

    Ringelbaum, Emanuel, 17:335–336

    Shatzky, Jacob, 18:421

of prehistory, 15:782

religious history

    Baudissin, Wolf Wilhelm, Graf von, 3:216

    Bauer, Bruon, 3:216

    Doniger, Wendy, 5:749–750

    Heyd, Uriel, 9:84

    Lévy, Isidore, 12:750

    Reinach, Solomon, 17:205

Roman history

    Hirschfeld, Heinrich Otto, 9:138

    Pliny the Elder, 16:237–238

Romania, 12:531–532

Rosenberg, Arthur, 17:435

Russia

    Agursky, Mikhail, 1:520

    Braudo, Alexander Isayevich, 4:137

    Dubnow, Simon, 6:34–37

    Pipes, Richard Edgar, 16:182

    Schwarz, Solomon, 18:190–191

Russian and Slavic law, Leontovich, Fedor, 12:649

Shahar, Shulamit, of Middle Ages, 18:364

Simonsohn, Shlomo, 18:618

Singer, Charles Joseph, 18:634

Slavic history, Eisenmann, Louis, 6:268

Slouschz, Nahum, 18:681

Smith, Morton, 18:688–689

Snyder, Louis Leo, 18:698

socialism, Beer, Max, 3:252

Spanish Jewry

    Castro Quesada, Americo, 4:519

    Millás Vallicrosa, José Mariá, 14:251

    Vendrell, Francisca, 14:251

Sweden
   Heckscher, Eli Filip, 8:751–752
   Lamm, Martin, 12:452–453
U.K.
   Adler, Michael, 1:403
   Alderman, Geoffrey, 1:606
   Schama, Simon, 18:105
U.S.
   Adelson, Howard Laurence, 1:386
   Adler, Selig, 1:408
   Bailyn, Bernard, 3:68–69
   Bernstein, Harry, 3:479
   Davis, David Brion, 5:479–480
   Davis, Natalie Zemon, 5:482
   Dawidowicz, 5:483
   diplomatic history, 17:99
   Duberman, Martin B., 6:31
   economic history, 17:113
   Eisenstadt, Abraham Seldin, 6:269–270
   Emery, Richard Wilder, 6:394
   Endelman, Todd M., 6:403
   Evans, Eli, 6:571
   Feis, Herbert, 6:743
   Filler, Louis, 7:20
   Handlin, Oscar, 8:320
   Hartogensis, Benjamin Henry, 8:378
   Hertz, Emanuel, 9:47
   Hexter, Jack H., 9:83–84
   Hofstadter, Richard, 9:313
   Janowsky, Oscar Isaiah, 11:80
   Lea, Henry Charles, 12:563
   Levy, Leonard Williams, 12:752
   Mayer, Arno Joseph, 13:698
   Morris, Richard Brandon, 14:511
   Rischin, Moses, 17:339
   Schapiro, Jacob Salwyn, 18:109
   Schappes, Morris U., 18:110
   Semmel, Bernard, 18:286
Warsaw ghetto, Ringelbaum, Emanuel, 17:335–336
women's history, Lerner, Gerda Kronstein, 12:657
See also Pentateuch
Historiarum adversum paganos libri septem (Orosius), 15:482
Historia Sacra Real (Acosta), 1:359
Historia Universal Judia (Shaki), 18:371
An Historical Account of the Ten Tribes Settled Beyond the River Sambatyon in the East (Edrehi), 6:158

Historical critical method, 3:650–654
Historical Geography of the Holy Land (Smith), 18:687
Historical Judaism. See Conservative Judaism
Historical Society of Israel, 18:724
Histories of Lot and Abraham, 18:739
Historiography, 9:**153–163**
   Baer, Yitzhak, 3:54
   Bible, 9:153–154
   Harrisse, Henry, 8:366
   Holocaust, 9:415–421
   Israel, 9:161
   local Jewish history, 9:160–161
   Middle Ages, 7:12–13, 9:155–156
   Poland, 3:82
   Second Temple, 9:154–155
   Spain and Portugal, 9:156–157, 695
   systematic, 9:158–163
   twentieth century, 9:159–163
   United States, 9:161–163
   Wissenschaft period, 9:158–159
   women's studies, 9:163
   See also Jewish studies
History, 9:**163–285**, 254t–280t, 12:121
   Abrabanel, Isaac ben Judah, 1:278
   Bar Kokhba revolt, 9:202
   David and Solomon, 9:172–174
   diaspora, Babylonian, 9:203–204
   diaspora, Second Temple period, 9:200–202, 201
   early Christianity, 9:205–207
   Eastern Europe, 9:232–233
   economic (See Economic history)
   eighteenth and nineteenth centuries, 9:228–241, 267t–274t
      communal organization, 9:234–236
      emancipation era, 9:231–232
      enlightenment, 9:229
      Ḥasidism, 9:237
      Haskalah movement, 9:237
      mercantilist states, 9:229–230
      migration, 9:234, 240
      Moses Mendelssohn, 9:230–231
      Polish partitions, 9:232–233
      Russia, 9:233, 235
      Zionism, nationalism, 9:238–239
   European settlement, 9:207–208
   Ezra, 9:187–188
   fourth to seventh centuries, 9:204–208, 258t
   French revolution and emancipation, 9:231–232

   God and, 7:447–448, 654–655
   Haskalah view of, 8:440
   Hasmonean rule, 9:194–198
   Hellenistic rule, 9:191–193
   Herod's rule, 9:197–198
   Islam, appearance of, 9:207
   Israel, kingdom of, 9:177–179
   Jerusalem rebuilt, 9:188–189
   Judah, kingdom of, 9:175–177, 179–182
   judges, 9:169–170
   kingdoms divide, 9:174–175
   Middle Ages
      Black Death and expulsions, 9:215–216
      Christian attitudes, 9:209–210, 213–214, 221, 227–228, 230
      Eastern Europe, 9:220, 227
      expulsions and Black Death, 9:215–216
      Germany, 9:220
      under Islam, 9:208–209, 212
      Jewish leadership, 9:210–213, 217–218
      Karaism, 9:211
      Khazar kingdom, 9:212
      Maimonides, 9:219
      seventh to eleventh centuries, 9:208–213, 258t–259t
      Spain, 9:214–215, 216–217
      twelfth century, 9:218
      Western Europe, 9:215, 217–220
   Nehemiah, 9:188–191
   Patriarchs to Exodus, 9:165–167, 254t
   philosophy of, Krochmal, Nachman, 12:367–368
   Ptolemaic rule, 9:191–193
   revolts against Rome, 9:199–202
   Roman rule, 9:198–204
   Samuel and Saul, 9:170–172
   Second Temple destruction, 9:200
   Selucid rule, 9:193
   Sinai to Canaanite settlement, 9:165–169
   sixteenth to seventeenth centuries, 9:222–228, 264t–267t
   social stucture, 9:182–185
      classes, 9:182–184
         slaves and laborers, 9:184–185
         tribes to urbanization, 9:182–184
   statistics, 19:167–170
   Temple destruction to exile, 9:180, 180, 186–188

History, *continued*
  Temple rededication, post exile, 9:189–190
  tribes to urbanization, 9:182–184
  twentieth and twenty-first centuries, 9:241–253, 274t–280t
    German Jewry, 9:243–245
    Hebrew and Yiddish, 9:252
    Holocaust and World War II, 9:252–253
    Israel establishment, 9:281–282
    migrations, 9:251, *251*
    Nazism, National Socialism, 9:244–245, 252–253
    pogroms and migration, 9:243
    population, 9:241–242, 242t
    racism and antisemitism, 9:244–245
    Russian Jewry, 9:242–243, 245
    Soviet Russia, 9:245, 246
    World War I, effect of, 9:248–249
    Yishuv in Palestine, 9:249–252
    Zionism, 9:245–246, 247–249
History and Destiny of the Jews. See Eine Geschichte der Juden (Kastein)
History and Legend Concerning the Wailing Wall (Moissis), 14:422
History of Hungarian Serfhood. See A magyar jobbágyság története
A History of Jewish Education (Simon), 18:609
History of Matzah (Rivers), 17:347
A History of Messianic Speculation in Israel (Silver), 18:584
History of Modern Hebrew Literature. See Toledot ha-Sifrut ha-Ivrit ha-Hadashah
"The History of My Dovecote" (Babel), 3:17
History of One Family (Kabak). *See Toledot Mishpahah Ahat*
History of Our Families. See Korot Bateinu
History of Religions (Moore), 14:469
History of Rome (Mommsen), 14:431
History of the Assyrian Script, Vowels and Accents. *See Sefer ha-yah li-Khetav Ashuri ve-Toledot ha-Nekuddot ve-ha-Te'amim*
History of the Holocaust (Bauer), 9:418
History of the Hugarian Empire. See A magyar birodalom története
A History of the Inquisition of Spain (Lea), 12:563

A History of the Inquisition of the Middle Ages (Lea), 12:563
A History of the Jewish People in the Time of Jesus Christ (Schuerer), 18:170
History of the Jews (Graetz), 8:27–28, 17:32
History of the Jews from the Destruction of Jerusalem to the Present Time (Adams), 1:380
History of the Jews in Christian Spain (Baer), 3:54, 9:160–161
History of the Jews in Palestine in the Period of the Mishnah and the Talmud. See Toledot ha-Yehudim be-Erez Yisrael be-Tekufat ha-Mishnah ve-ha-Talmud
History of the Jews in Russia and Poland (Dubnow), 6:34
History of the Jews in the United States (Levinger), 12:720
A History of the Jews of Krakow. See Dzieje żydów w Krakowie i na Kazimierzu, 1304–1868
History of the United Synagogue of America (Karp), 11:815
History of Tithes (Selden), 18:258
History of Yiddish Literature: From the Beginning to the Haskalah Period (Erik), 6:479
History of Zionism, 1600-1918 (Sokolow), 18:**748**
Hit (Mesopotamia), 9:**285**
Hitahadut, 9:**285–286**
Hitahadut ha-Ikarim be-Yisrael. *See* Farmers' Federation of Israel
Hitbonenut. *See* Meditation
Hitchcock, Alfred, 12:748
A hitehagyott (Molnár). *See The Apostate* (Molnár)
Hitganvut Yehidim (Kenaz), 12:76
Hitlahavut and joy, 8:409
Hitler, Adolf, 9:**286–290**
  Nuremberg laws, 15:348–350
  The Producers, 15:228
  rise to power, 9:327–328
  Seyss-Inquart, Arthur and, 18:333
  See also National Socialism (Nazism); Neo-Nazism
Hitler: Diagnosis of a Destructive Prophet (Redlich), 17:159
Hitler's Willing Executioners (Goldhagen), 9:335, 419, 20:381
"Hitler Victorious" alternate history, 18:201
Hitman, Uzi, 9:**290**
Hitschmann, Edward, 9:**290**
Hittites, 9:**290–293**, *291*
  archives, 2:403

  Ephron, 6:461
  Kadesh, 11:699
  Mesopotamia, 14:85–86
  treaties and covenants, 5:250–252
Hitzig, Ferdinand, 9:**293–294**
Hitzig, Julius Eduard, 9:**294**
HIV. *See* AIDS/HIV
Hivites, 9:**294**, 14:388
Hiwi al-Balkhi, 6:176, 9:**295**
Hiyya, 9:**295–296**, 14:437–438, 18:597
Hiyya bar Abba, 6:306, 9:**297**, 18:448
Hiyya bar Avin, 9:**297**
Hiyya Bar Ba. *See* Hiyya bar Abba
Hiyya Bar Va. *See* Hiyya bar Abba
Hiyya ben Joseph Dayyan, 5:495, 18:451
Hiyya Rofe, 9:**297**
Hizbolla, 9:**297–298**
Hizb ut-Tahrir, 6:426
Hizzuk Emunah (Troki), 5:695
Hizzuk Emunah (Troki), 11:792, 14:404, 20:155–156
Hkam al family, 8:**241–242**
Hladik, Abraham, 9:**298**
Hladni krematorijum (Debrecenji), 5:520
Hlasy (Fischer), 7:54–55
Hlohovek (Slovakia), 9:**298**
Hlusk. *See* Glussk
HMO (Hadassah Medical Organization), 2:60, 8:186, 187, 188
The Hoax of the Twentieth Century (Butz), 9:416, 493
Hobab. *See* Jethro (father-in-law of Moses)
Hobsbawm, Eric John, 9:**298–299**
Hobson, Laura Z., 9:**299**
Hochberg, Isidore. *See* Harburg, E. Y.
Hocheimer, Henry, 9:**299**
Hocheimer, Lewis, 9:299
Hocheimer's Criminal Law (Hocheimer), 9:299
Hochhuth, Rolf, 9:**299**
Hochman, Julius, 9:**299–300**
Hochschild, Mauricio, 4:47, 9:**300**
Hochschule Fuer die Wissenschaft des Judentums, 6:182, 9:**300**, 12:561
Hochwaelder, Fritz, 9:**301**
Hock, Simon, 9:**301**
Hoda'ah. *See* Admission
Hodayah ben Jesse ha-Nasi, 11:460
Hodayot. *See* Thanksgiving Psalms
Hoddu. *See* India
Hodel. *See* Adel
Hodess, Jacob, 9:**301**
Hod ha-Sharon (Israel), 9:**301**

Hodl (Shalom Aleichem), 18:385–386

Hodmezovasarhely (Hungary), 9:**302**

Hódmezövásárhely (Hungary). *See* Hodmezovasarhely (Hungary)

Hodonin (Czech Republic), 9:**302**

Hoechheimer, Moses ben Ḥayyim Cohen, 9:**302**

Hoeflich, Eugen. *See* Ben-Gavriel, Moshe Ya'akov

Hoellriegel, Arnold. *See* Bermann, Richard Arnold

Hoelscher, Gustav, 9:**302**, 11:442

Hoenig, Aaron Moses, 9:303

Hoenig, Adam Albert, 9:303

Hoenig, Enoch, 9:303

Hoenig, Israel, 9:303

Hoenig, Leopold, 9:303

Hoenig, Loebel, 9:303

Hoenig, Marianne, 9:303

Hoenig, Maximillian, 9:303

Hoenigsberg, Soliman von, 9:303

Hoenigsberg family, 9:**303**, 13:129

Hoenigswald, Richard, 6:160, 9:303

Hoenlein, Malcolm, 9:**304**

Hoeschel, Joshua. *See* Hoeschel ben Saul

Hoeschel, Rebbi Reb. *See* Joshua Hoeschel ben Jacob

Hoeschel ben Saul, 9:**304**

Hoess, Rudolf Franz Ferdinand, 2:662, 9:**304–306**

Hofagent. *See* Court Jews

Ho Feng-Shan, 9:**306**

Hofer, Andreas, 9:**306–307**

Hoff, Hans, 9:**307**

Hoffaktor. *See* Court Jews

Hoffer, Willi, 9:**307**

Hoffer, Yeḥiel, 9:**307**

Hoffman, Chaim. *See* Yahil, Chaim

Hoffman, Charles Isaiah, 9:**307**

Hoffman, Dustin, 4:219, 9:**307–308**

Hoffman, Eduard. *See* Reményi, Eduard

Hoffman, Isidore B., 9:307

Hoffman, Jacob, 9:**308**

Hoffman, Jeffrey, 9:**308**

Hoffman, Julius Jennings, 9:**308–309**

Hoffman, Lawrence A., 9:**309**

Hoffman, Philip E., 9:**309–310**

Hoffman, Sandor. *See* Hevesi, Sandor

Hoffmann, Camill, 9:**310**

Hoffmann, David Ẓevi, 9:**310–311**

Hoffmann, Eduard. *See* Reményi, Eduard

Hoffmann, Jacob, 9:**311**

Hoffmann, Roald, 9:**311–312**

Hoffmann, Sandor. *See* Hevesi, Sandor

Hoffmann, Yoel, 8:708–709, 9:**312**

Hofjude. *See* Court Jews

Hofjude diplomacy, 2:54

Hofman, Lonek, 4:86

Hofmann, Isaac Loew, 9:**312–313**

Hofmannsthal, Hugo von, 4:81, 138, 9:**313**, 11:412

Hofshi-Mendes, David. *See* Franco-Mendes, David

Hofstadter, Richard, 9:**313**

Hofstadter, Robert, 9:**313**

Hofstaetter, Osias, 2:518

Hofstein, David, 9:**313–314**

Hoga, Stanislav, 9:**314**

Hogei ha (Bergman), 3:428

Ḥoglah (Israel), 9:**314**

Hohenau (Austria), 9:**314**

Hohenems (Austria), 9:**314–315**

Hohensalza (Poland). *See* Inowroclaw (Poland)

Hohenzollern (Germany), 9:**315**

Der Hohe Rabbi Loew. *See* Judah Loew ben Bezalel

Ho'il Moshe (Alfalas), 1:636

Ho'il Moshe (Benjamin), 3:358

Ḥokher, 12:572

Ḥokhmat Adam (Danzig), 5:432

Ḥokhmat ha-Ḥizzayon (Abraham bar Ḥiyya), 1:293

Ḥokhmat ha-Misken (Shaḥam), 18:363

Ḥokhmat ha-Ẓeruf (Abulafia), 13:761–762

Ḥokhmat Shelomo (Luria), 13:269

Ḥokhmat Yisrael (collection), 18:686

Ḥokhmat Yisrael (Slutzki), 18:686

Hol. *See* Phoenix (bird)

Holbach, Paul Henri Dietrich, Baron D', 9:**315–316**

Holbein, Hans (the younger), 14:542

Holbert, Ludvig, 18:89

Holbrooke, Richard, 9:**316**

Holdheim, Samuel, 9:**316–317**

    Einhorn, David (Reform rabbi), 6:258

    on Oral Law, 15:457

Holdheim, Theodore, 9:**317**

Holesov (Czech Republic), 9:**317–318**

ḥol ha-mo'ed, 14:413

Holidays. *See* Festivals; *specific holidays*

Holiness. *See* Kedushah (holiness)

Holiness and Humanity: Ritual in the Making of a Religious LIfe (Rappaport), 17:100

Holiness code, 9:**318–321**, 12:738–740

Holitscher, Arthur, 9:**321**

Hollaender, Felix, 9:321

Hollaender, Friedrich, 9:321

Hollaender, Gustav, 9:321

Hollaender, Ludwig, 9:**321–322**

Hollaender, Victor, 9:321

Hollaender family, 9:**321**

Holland. *See* The Netherlands

Hollandaerski, Leon, 16:346–347

Hollander, Felix C., 6:62

Hollander, Franklin, 9:**322**

Hollander, Isaiah ben Aaron, 9:**322**

Hollander, John, 9:**322**, 20:299

Hollandersky, Abraham, 9:**322**

Holleschau (Czech Republic). *See* Holesov (Czech Republic)

Holliday, Judy, 9:**322–323**

Hollósy, Simon, 15:353

Hollzer, Harry Aaron, 9:**323**

Holman, Nathan, 9:**323–324**, 15:222

Holman Christian Standard Bible, 3:621

Holmes-Einstein Letters: Correspondence of Mr. Justice Holmes and Lewis Einstein (Holmes, Einstein), 6:264

Holocaust, 9:252–253, **324–489**

    aftermath and impact, 9:401–402

    aliyah and absorption, 10:215

    alternative history literature, 18:201, 206

    American Israel Public Affairs Committee, 2:50

    American Jewish press, 9:367–368

    American Judaism, 4:93

    anti-zionism, 2:243–244

    Association of Holocaust Children (Poland), 2:64

    Association of Holocaust Organizations (AHO), 2:614–615

    Bitburg Controversy, 3:727–728

    chess players, 4:604

    children of survivors, 9:382–387

    Conference on Jewish Material Claims Against Germany, 5:143–145

    demography, 5:556–558, 557t, 568–570, 569t

    denial, 2:234–235, 240, 9:493–495, 10:30–32, 20:380

    displaced persons, 9:379

    economic impact, 6:138

    faith, post Holocaust, 9:391–401

    Halakha, 9:362–363

    legislation in Israel, 10:414

Holocaust, *continued*

meaning, search for, 9:387–388

Neo-Nazism, 9:416, 15:75

New York Times coverage of, 15:222

philosophical response to, 6:673, 16:99

postwar trials, 9:381, 10:226

rabbinic, 9:362–363

relief and rehabilitation, 18:40

restitution from banks, 6:280–281, 18:637

uniqueness of, 9:388–391

United Restitution Organization, 20:274–275

U.S., 9:364–368, 379–381

victims, 9:352–355

world, 9:364–377

yishuv, 9:377–379

Zionism, 21:554–556, 571–573

Albania, 1:584

Algeria, 1:649

archives, memorials and museums

American Jewish Archives, 2:53

archives, 2:407, 410–413, 9:362

Belgium, 3:286–287

Berlin Memorial to the Murdered Jews of Europe (Germany), 6:267

Center for Advanced Holocaust Studies, 20:277

Fortunoff Video Archive for Holocaust Testimony, 7:134

Ghetto Fighter's House, 7:578

historiography, 9:415–421

The Holocaust Martyrs' and Heroes' Rememberance Authority, 21:266–268

Holocaust Survivors Film Project, 8:376

Latvia, 12:523–524

Los Angeles Holocaust Museum, 13:201

memorials and monuments, 9:429–432, 21:401

Museum of Jewish Heritage: A Living Memorial to the Holocaust, 14:623–624

museums, 9:432–438, 438*t*–439*t*, 14:635–636

New York's Museum of Jewish Heritage, 11:734

remembrances, 6:716

Simon Wiesenthal Center, 18:618–620

Survivors of the Shoah Visual History Foundation, 19:324–325

United States Holocaust Memorial Museum, 20:275–277

Wiener Library, 9:428, 21:50–51

Yad la-Yeled, 7:578

Yad Vashem, 11:818, 17:303, 21:266–268

art and literature, 2:502–503, 507, 6:729, 9:402–415, 13:684

alternative history, 18:201

art of ghettos and camps, 2:515, 516–519, 3:41

children of survivors, 9:384

children's, 4:625–627, 630–631, 633, 9:414, 15:477

drama, 8:720–723, 9:405–406

encyclopedias, 9:419

fiction, 4:265

films and cinema, 7:134, 9:439–446, 12:487

French, 7:245–251

historiography, 9:415–421

Holocaust studies, 3:408–409, 9:421–424

Hungarian, 9:604–605, 606, 607

influence on literature, 18:90, 95–96

Israeli, 8:709

Italian, 10:790, 793–795

journalism, 12:666

journals and diaries, 7:178–179, 9:403–405, 412–413

music, 14:697–699

Neo-nazi, 9:416

Paris school of artists, 15:649

photography, 9:460–489, 16:129–130

poetry, 1:398–399, 9:407–408, 410, 21:327

Polish, 9:416

Romanian, 17:401–402

scholar of, 12:480–481

Shoah (motion picture), 12:487

survivor testimonies, 9:446–447

Yiddish, 21:351, 358–361

Austria, 2:693–695

Ehrlich, Jacob, 6:244

Judenburg, 11:525

Klagenfurt, 12:210

Krems, 12:354

Kristallnacht, pogroms, 9:330–331

Mattersdorf, 13:686

Styria, 19:279

Tyrol, 20:220

Vienna, 20:521–522

Wiener Neustadt, 21:51

Belarus

Baranovichi, 3:134

Bereza, 3:413–414

Braslav, 4:130–131

Bykhov, 4:324

David-Godorok, 5:473–474

Dolginovo, 5:735

Druya, 6:28–29

Dubrovno, 6:39

Dyatlovo, 6:75

Ilya, 9:736

Ivanovo, 10:821

Ivye, 10:822

Kobrin, 12:244

Koidanovo, 12:267

Krichev, 12:356

Lachva, 12:426

Lida, 12:802

Lyakhovichi, 13:293

Minsk, 14:295

Mir, 14:304–305

Mogilev, 14:417

Molodechno, 14:429

Mozyr, 14:592–593

Mstislavl, 14:593

Novogrudok, 15:321

Novy Dvor, 15:324

Oshmyany, 15:502–503

Ostryna, 15:515

Pinsk, 16:172

Polotsk, 16:361

Pruzhany, 16:657

Radoshkovichi, 17:59

Radun, 17:59

Rechitsa, 17:144

Rogachev, 17:367–368

Ruzhany, 17:597–598

Shchedrin, 18:426

Slonim, 18:676–677

Stolbsty, 19:234

Stolin, 19:234

Svisloch, 19:334

Vitebsk, 20:560

Volkovysk, 20:573–574

Volpa, 20:578

Vysokoye, 20:590

Zelva, 21:502

Belgium, 3:282–283, 9:339
    Antwerp, 2:250
    Brussels, 4:227
Belorussia (Russia), 16:313–314
    Ozery, 15:557
Bessarabia
    Dombroveni, 5:738
    Kaushany, 12:37
    Khotin, 12:117–118
    Kiliya, 12:154
    Kishinev, 12:199
    Sekiryany, 18:256–257
    Vad Raskov, 20:457
    Valea-Lui-Vlad, 20:459
    Yedintsy, 21:292–293
Bohemia, Kosová Hora, 12:321
Bohemia-Moravia, 5:358–359
Bolivia, 4:46
Bosnia-Herzegovina
    Sarajevo, 18:49
    Travnik, 20:122
Bulgaria, 9:339, 19:172
    deportation policy, 4:271–273
    Law to Protect the Nation, 19:172
    Ruse, 17:530–531
    survivors, 4:275
Canada, 4:18, 408, 419, 423, 9:370
children
    art and literature, 4:625–627, 630–631, 633, 9:414, 15:477
    Association of Holocaust Children (Poland), 2:64
    Auschwitz survivors, 9:369
    Finaly case, 7:22–23
    Frank, Anne, 7:178–179
    hidden Jewish children, 9:374
    Kindertransport, 9:369, 12:160–161
    literature, 4:625, 626, 627, 630–631, 633, 15:477
    pictures of, 9:468–470, 473, 476–477
    rescue of, 16:318, 17:305
    of survivors, 9:382–387
    victims, 6:755, 16:318
Chile, 4:639–640
Christian response
    Catholic Church, 9:370–375, 453–454
    Catholic guilt, 11:280
    Christian antisemitism, 4:685
    John Paul II, 11:383, 384
    John XXIII, 11:379–380
    Lichtenberg, anti-nazi priest, 12:797

Orthodox Churches, 9:377
Pope Pius XII, 9:371–372, 402, 17:415–416
Protestant Churches, 9:375–377
chronology, 9:344–452t
    1932-1935, 9:344t
    1936-1938, 9:344–346t
    1938-1940, 9:346–347t
    1941-1942, 9:347–349t
    1943-1945, 9:349–351t
    1946-2000, 9:351–352t
Croatia, 9:340
    Dubrovnik, 6:39
    Osijek, 15:504
    Rijeka, 17:332–333
    Split, 19:126
    Zagreb, 21:444
Czechoslovakia, 5:357–359, 9:340
    Tachov, 19:429
Czech Republic
    Brno, 4:190
    Cheb, 4:586
    Chodova Plana, 4:658
    Chomutov, 4:666
    Jablonec Nad Nisou, 11:8
    Jemnice, 11:121
    Jevicko, 11:253
    Jihlava, 11:337
    Jindrichuv Hradec, 11:337
    Klatovy, 12:212
    Kojetin, 12:269
    Kolin, 12:273
    Kromeriz, 12:369
    Kyjov, 12:402
    Mikulov, 14:223
    Miroslav, 14:314
    Mlada Boleslav, 14:395
    Moravia, 14:476
    Moravske Budejovice, 14:477
    Moravske Krumlov, 14:477
    Nachod, 14:721
    Ostrava, 15:509
    Pilsen, 16:163
    Pobezovice na Sumave, 16:249
    Pohorelice, 16:282
    Polna, 16:360
    Prague, 16:453–454
    Prostejov, 16:625
    Roudnice nad Labem, 17:497
    Tabor, 19:426
    Theresienstadt, 6:145
    Trebic, 20:124
    Trest, 20:134

    Turnov, 20:203–204
    Udlice, 20:224
    Uherske Hradiste, 20:231
    Uhersky Brod, 20:231
    Usov, 20:433
    Usti nad Labem, 20:437
    Votice, 20:585
    Zatec, 21:462
    Znojmo, 21:646
Denmark, 5:582–583, 9:341–342
    influence on literature, 18:90
education, 6:670–672, 9:100–102, 423
    American Gathering of Jewish Holocaust Survivors Summer Seminar Program, 2:49
    American Youth and the Holocaust, 9:449
    Berenbaum, Michael, 3:408–409
    Center for Advanced Holocaust Studies, 20:277
    Facing History and Ourselves Program, 9:451–452
    Germany, 9:457–458
    Hilberg, Saul, 9:100–102
    Holocaust literature, 3:408–409, 9:421–424
    Israel, 9:455–457
    Italy, 10:810
    Jewish, 6:185–186
    Langer, Lawrence L., 12:480–481
    Meed, Vladka, 13:764
    Moreshet, 14:484–486
    National Catholic Center for Holocaust Education, 9:453–454
    Sweden, 9:458–459
    Task Force for International Cooperation on Holocaust Education, Remembrance, and Research, 9:457, 459
    U.S., 9:422–423, 447–454
    Yad Vashem International Institute for Holocaust Research, 9:426
Estonia, 6:521
    Tallinn, 19:465
    Tartu, 19:523
faith
    Buber, Martin, 4:233
    destruction of synagogues, 16:306, 19:356–357
    post Holocaust, 9:391–401
    spiritual resistance, 9:360–363
Finland, 7:38

Holocaust, *continued*
France, 4:83, 7:160–162, 9:339
Aix-en-Provence, 1:552
Alsace-Lorraine, 2:9
Bayonne, 3:232
Belfort, 3:280
Besançon, 3:494
Bordeaux, 4:83
Centre de Documentation
Juive Contemporaine,
4:547
Chambon-sur-Lignon, 4:564–
565
Colmar, 5:58–59
Dijon, 5:660
Drancy, 6:8
Fontainebleau, 7:115
Lyons, 3:141, 13:297
Marseilles, 13:578–579
Metz, 14:136
Montpellier, 14:463
Mulhouse, 14:610
Nancy, 14:772–773
Nantes, 14:773
Nice, 15:249
Paris, 7:160, 15:645
Paris school of artists affected
by, 15:649
Rosheim, 17:467
Sarreguemines, 18:62
Saverne, 18:84
Sèlestat, 18:260
Strasbourg, 19:245
Thionville, 19:704
Toulouse, 20:74
Tours, 20:77
Troyes, 20:158
Galicia (Eastern Europe), 16:312
genocide and euthanasia
Baranovich aktion, 3:134
death camps, 9:355–356
disabled victims, 6:569–570
Einsatzgruppen massacres,
6:251, 7:564–565, 9:334–
336
euthanasia program, 9:332
Final Solution, 4:385–388,
7:21–22, 9:84–85, 121,
287–280, 305, 325–326,
340, 378, 11:828–829
gas chambers, 7:393
gas vans, 9:340
genocide, eight stages of,
9:390
Genocide Convention, 7:484–
485
Golovanevsk massacre, 7:745

impact from Holocaust, 7:162
Lida massacre, 12:802
mass shootings, 9:334–336
Ponary massacres, 16:369
racist ideology, 9:327
Germany
Ahlem, 1:547
Andernach, 7:143
Ansbach, 7:180
Baden, 3:44
Bayreuth, 3:232
Bielefeld, 3:688
Bremen, 4:158
Chemnitz, 4:593–594
Coburg, 4:764
Cochem, 4:765
Darmstadt, 5:436
Dresden, 6:11
Dueren, 6:41
Duesseldorf, 6:42
Duisburg, 6:43
Einbeck, 6:255
Eisenstadt, 6:269
Elblag, 6:291
Emden, 6:392
Erfurt, 6:478
Essen, 6:510
Esslingen, 6:514
Frankfurt on the Main, 7:210
Halberstadt, 8:263
Halle, 8:279
Hamburg, 8:297
Jebenhausen, 11:99
Juelich, 11:572
Katowice, 12:6
Kempen, 12:73
Kiel, 12:146
Kissingen, 12:202
Kitzingen, 12:209
Koblenz, 12:243
Krefeld, 12:347–348
Kreuznach, 12:355
Kristallnacht, pogroms,
9:330–331
Landau, 12:457
Leipzig, 12:628
Mainz, 13:405
Meiningen, 13:776
Memmingen, 14:17
Mergentheim, 14:64
Merseburg, 14:71
Minden, 14:265
Mosbach, 14:515
Muehlhausen, 14:594
Muenster, 14:599

Munich, 14:613
Nauheim, 15:36–37
Nuremberg, 15:347–348
Pforzheim, 16:27
Ravensburg, 17:121
Regensburg, 17:188–189
Saxony, 18:88
Schweinfurt, 18:195
Sephardim, 18:301
Spandau, 19:83
Speyer, 19:101
Stendal, 19:201
Straubing, 19:248
Stuttgart, 19:277
Sulzbach, 19:306
Tauberbischofsheim, 19:528
Theresienstadt, 5:54, 6:465–
466
Thuringia, 19:711
Trier, 20:144
Tuebingen, 20:173
Ulm, 20:243
Villingen, 20:528
Wannsee Conference, 9:336,
20:617–619
Warendorf, 20:650
Weinheim, 20:721
Westphalia, 21:29
Wiesbaden, 21:52
Wolfenbuettel, 21:141–142
Worms, 21:227
Wuerttemberg, 21:247
Wuerzburg, 21:248
Wuppertal, 21:250
Xanten, 21:257
Zerbst, 21:515
Zwickau, 21:265, 695
ghetto life, 7:575–578, 9:333–334,
16:308, 309–313
Aeltestenrat, 6:358–359
collaborators, 9:359
cultural life, 9:361
currency, 5:53, 54
humor, 9:360–361
Jewish councils, 2:599, 9:356–
357, 11:526–529, 15:104–
105
Jewish police, 9:356–357
Judenrein concept, 11:529
Nazi film propaganda, 5:54,
9:439, 440
uprisings, 9:338, 13:764,
21:125, 676
yellow badges, 3:47–48
Greece, 8:50–52, 9:339, 340
Athens, 2:631–632

Chalcis, 4:561
Drama, 6:7–8
Kavalla, 12:38–39
Kos, 12:317
Patras, 15:689
Salonika, 17:703–705
Serrai, 18:316
Trikkala, 20:148–149
Veroia, 20:512–513
Volos, 20:574–575
historians
Bauer, Yehuda, 3:218–219
Braham, Randolph Louis,
4:118
Browning, Christopher R.,
4:217
Dawidowicz, Lucy, 5:483
Friedlaender, Saul, 7:275–276
Gutman, Israel, 8:151–152
Novitch, Miriam, 15:320–321
Poliakov, Léon, 16:331
Hungary, 4:18, 9:341, 612–616,
614t
Baia-Mare, 3:67
Baja, 3:70
Bak, 3:70
Blood for Trucks offer, 4:120
Bonyhád, 4:66
Budapest, 4:246–248
Eger, 6:217
Endre, László, 6:405
Hungarian Arrow Cross
Party, 2:491
Kaposvar, 11:781
Kasztner, Rezsö Rudolf,
11:828–829
Kecskemet, 12:48
Kistarcsa, 12:205
Kisvarda, 12:205
Köszeg, 12:322
Miskolc, 14:364
Nagykanizsa, 14:734
Nyiregyhaza, 15:355–356
Pestszenterzsebet, 16:14
population statistics, 18:606
refugees, 6:465
Satoraljaujhely, 18:75
Senta, 18:291
Simleul-Silvaniel, 18:606
Sopron, 19:27
Szeged, 19:404
Szekesfehervar, 19:405
Szolnok, 19:405, 411
Szombathely, 19:412
Vac, 20:457
Veszprem, 20:515

Italy, 9:339, 10:803–805, 808, 810
Alessandria, 1:618
Bologna, 4:49
Bolzano, 4:51
Cueno, 5:338–339
Delegazione Assistenza
Emigrati Ebrei, 7:484
Ferrara, 6:763
Florence, 7:86
Genoa, 7:483–484
Gorizia, 7:779
Leghorn, 12:609
Lugo, 13:253–254
Milan, 14:231
Modena, 14:408
Pisa, 16:184
Reggio Emilia, 17:190
Rome, 17:415–416
Rovigo, 17:500
Trieste, 20:145–146
Turin, 20:194
Venice, 20:503–504
Vercelli, 20:508
Verona, 20:514
Latvia, 12:522–523
Daugavpils, 5:442
Jaunijelgava, 11:95
Jekabpils, 11:116
Jelgava, 11:118
Kraslava, 12:337
Krustpils, 12:375
Liepaja, 12:818
Ludza, 13:252
Riga, 6:35, 17:300
Tukums, 20:174
Ventspils, 20:505
Libya, 12:791–792
Tripoli, 20:151–152
Lithuania, 4:170, 13:125–127, 126t,
16:313–314
Birzai, 3:724
Jonava, 11:399
Jurbarkas, 11:577
Kaunas, 12:36
Kedainiai, 12:49
Kelme, 12:71
Kretinga, 12:355
Kupiskis, 12:388
Kybartai, 12:401
Memel, 14:16
Ninth Fort, 15:273
Plunge, 16:242
Rokiskis, 17:372
Seduba, 18:237
Taurage, 19:529

Telsiai, 19:598
Troki, 20:155
Ukmerge, 20:234
Utena, 20:444
Vilkaviškis, 20:526–527
Vilkaviškis, 20:526–527
Vilna, 20:532–533
Virbalis, 20:539
Zagare, 21:443
Zarasai, 21:458
Luxembourg, 9:339, 13:276
Macedonia
Monastir, 14:432
Phlorina, 16:118
Skoplje, 18:662
medical experiments, 2:669–670,
5:376, 15:42–43
Mengele, Josef, 4:387–388,
14:47
sterilization experiments,
8:464–465
Moldova, 4:178
Dubossary, 6:38
Falticeni, 6:688–689
Kaushany, 12:37
Khotin, 12:117–118
Kiliya, 12:154
Kishinev, 12:199
Kotovskoye, 12:324
Leovo, 12:650
Lipkany, 13:64
Novoselitsa, 15:322
Orgeyev, 15:468–469
Soroki, 19:30
Teleneshty, 19:594
Tiraspol, 19:729
Vad Rashkov, 20:457
Vad Raskov, 20:457
Valea-Lui-Vlad, 20:459
Yedintsy, 21:292–293
Zguritsa, 21:521
Moravia
Trebic, 20:124
Trest, 20:134
Uhersky Brod, 20:231
Nazi officials and organizations
Barbie, Klaus, 13:297
Bormann, Martin, 4:87
Brunner, Alois, 4:223
Buehler, Josef, 4:251–252
Demjanjuk, John, 5:551–552,
18:462
Eichmann, Adolf Otto,
6:248–252
Frank, Hans Michael, 7:181
Frank, Karl Hermann, 7:192

Holocaust, *continued*

Gestapo, 7:564–565

Globocnik, Odilo, 7:640

Gluecks, Richard, 7:646

Goebbels, Paul Josef, 7:680

Goering, Hermann Wilhelm, 2:665, 7:680–681

Heydrich, Reinhard Tristan, 9:84–85, 336

Himmler, Heinrich, 9:121–122

Hitler, Adolf, 9:286–290

Hoess, Rudolf Franz Ferdinand, 9:304–306

Kaltenbrunner, Ernst, 11:750

Katzmann, Friedrich, 12:23

Lecca, Radú, 12:593–594

Mengele, Josef, 4:387–388, 14:47

Mueller, Heinrich, 14:597–598

Nazi war criminals, 9:373–374

Pohl, Oswald, 16:282

Rademacher, Franz, 17:53–54

Rauter, Hanns Albin, 17:116

Ribbentrop, Joachim von, 17:280

Rosenberg, Alfred, 17:434–435

RSHA, 17:506

Sauckel, Fritz, 18:76–77

Schellenberg, Walter, 18:119

Seyss-Inquart, Arthur, 18:333

sonderkommando, 19:11–13

SS and SD, 19:154–155

Streicher, Julius, 4:478–479, 15:349, 19:255

Stroop, Juergen, 19:261

Tiso, Josef, 19:734–735

Treuhandstelle, 16:453

Tuka, Vojtech, 20:174

Vašek, Anton, 20:478

Wirth, Christian, 21:93

Wisliceny, Dieter, 21:104–105

Netherlands, 9:339, 359

Amsterdam, 2:115–116, 5:105, 8:11

Calmeyer, Hans-Georg, 4:374–375

Dutch literature, 6:70–71

Mauthausen, 13:693

Sephardim, 18:301

Westerbork, 9:116, 21:24

Norway, 9:341, 15:306, 309, 310–311

influence on literature, 18:95–96

refugees, 6:279

Poland, 4:323, 16:306–318

Aleksandrow Lodzki, 1:611

Association of Holocaust Children (Poland), 2:64

Augustow, 7:659

Auschwitz, 2:661–675, 9:304–306, 337–338

Bedzin, 3:249–250

Belchatow, 3:279

Belzyce, 3:312

Biała Podlaska, 3:560

Bialystok, 3:568–569, 16:312–313

Bielsko, 3:690

Bielsk Podlaski, 3:690

Bilgoraj, 3:698

Bochnia, 4:26

Breslau, 4:165

Brzeg, 4:230

Brzesk Kujawksi, 4:230

Brzeziny, 4:231

Buchach, 4:238

Bydgoszcz, 4:323, 16:308

Chelmno, 4:589–590

Chiciny, 4:586, 588

Chmielnik, 4:657

Chorzów, 4:669

Chryzanow, 4:707

Ciechanow, 4:726, 16:308–309

Cracow, 5:262–263, 16:311

Czestochowa, 5:373

Dabrowa Gornicza, 5:375

Danzig, 16:308

David-Gorodok, 5:473–474

Disna, 5:683–684

Dzialoszyce, 6:80

Endecja party, 6:402–403

Glubokoye, 7:642–643

Gniezno, 7:650

Gorlice, 7:780

Hrubieszow, 9:574

Inowroclaw, 9:790, 16:307–308

Izbica Lubelska, 10:824

Janow Lubelski, 11:79–80

Janowska Road camp, 13:291

Jaroslaw, 11:89

Jaslo, 11:90

Jedrzejow, 11:102

Kalisz, 11:738–740

Kielce, 12:147

Kielce pogram, 3:435

Kletsk, 12:230

Klodawa, 12:232

Kock, 12:250

Kolo, 12:278

Konin, 12:287

Konskie, 12:288

Konskowola, 12:288

Kosov, 12:320–321

Kozienice, 12:331

Kozle, 12:332

Krasnik, 12:338–339

Krasnystaw, 12:339

Kristallnacht, pogroms, 9:330–331

Krosno, 12:372–373

Krotoszyn, 12:374

Krynki, 12:376

Krzepice, 12:377

Kutno, 12:399

Lachva, 12:426

Lancut, 12:455–456

Lask, 12:496

Leczyca, 12:595

Leszno, 12:667

Lezajsk, 12:772

Lida, 12:802

Lipno, 13:68–69

Lodz, 5:53, 13:158–160, 16:307–308

Lomza, 13:179

Lowicz, 13:236

Lubaczow, 13:239

Lubartow, 13:240

Lublin, 13:244, 16:310–311

Lukow, 13:255–256

Lutomiersk, 13:272–273

Makow Mazowiecki, 13:420

Miedzyrzec Podlask, 14:204–205

Mielec, 14:205

Minsk Mazowiecki, 14:298

Mlawa, 14:396

Narol, 14:782

Nasielsk, 14:787

Nowy Dwor Mazowiecki, 15:325

Nowy Sacz, 15:326

Olkusz, 15:408–409

Opatow, 15:437–438

Opoczno, 15:441

Opole Lubelskie, 15:441

Ostroleka, 15:512

Ostrowiec, 15:513–514

Ostrow Mazowiecka, 15:514

Otwock, 15:546

Ozorkow, 15:559

Pabianice, 15:561–562

Parczew, 15:632

Peremyshlyany (Ukraine), 15:762
Piaseczno, 16:142
Pinczow, 16:165
Piotrkow, 16:181
Plock, 16:239
Plonsk, 16:241
Pogrebishchenski, 16:259
Poznan, 16:307–308, 432
Przedborz, 16:659
Przemysl, 16:660
Przeworsk, 16:660
Przysucha, 16:660–661, 661
Przytyk, 16:662
Pulawy, 16:731
Pultusk, 16:732
Radom, 16:311–312, 17:56–57
Radomsko, 17:57–58
Radzymin, 17:61
Radzyn, 17:61
Ropczyce, 17:420
Rozwadow, 17:505
Rymanow, 17:602
Rypin, 17:602–603
Rzeszow, 17:604
Sandomierz, 18:17
Sanok, 18:26
Siedlce, 18:553
Siemiatycze, 18:557–558
Sieradz, 18:558–559
Sierpc, 18:559
Skalat, 18:656
Skarzysko-Kamienna, 18:657
Skierniewice, 18:658–659
Sochaczew, 18:703
Sokolka, 18:746
Sokolow Podlaski, 18:750
Sosnowiec, 19:32
Srem, 19:154
Staszow, 19:167
Stettin, 19:223–224
Stopnica, 19:237–238
Strykow, 19:263, 264
Suwalki, 19:332
Swidnica, 19:340
Szczebrzeszyn, 19:403
Szczercow, 19:403–404
Szydlowiec, 19:413
Tarnobrzeg, 19:516
Tarnogrod, 19:516
Tarnow, 19:520
Tomaszow Lubelski, 20:31–32
Tomaszow Mazowiecki, 19:32, 20:32
Torun, 16:308, 20:67

Trzcianka, 20:162
Tykocin, 20:211
Tyszowce, 20:221
Warsaw, 16:309–310, 20:670–674, 671
Wegrow, 20:696–697
Wieliczka, 21:45
Wielun, 21:45–46
Wislica, 21:104
Wloclawek, 21:130
Wlodawa, 21:130–131
Wodzislaw, 21:131
Wolbrom, 21:133
Wolomin, 21:153
Wronki, 21:246
Wyszkow, 21:254
Wyszogrod, 21:255
Yavorov, 21:291
Zabludow, 21:432
Zabrze, 21:432
Zambrow, 21:450
Zamosc, 21:452
Zawiercie, 21:464
Zdunska Wola, 21:466–467
Zelechow, 21:500
Zelow, 21:502
Zgierz, 21:520–521
Zmigrod Nowy, 21:645
Zwolen, 21:696
Zychlin, 21:696
Zyrardow, 21:697
Portugal, 2:117, 16:412
    Mendes, Aristides de Sousa, 14:42–43
Prussia, Pomerania, 16:365
refugees and survivors, 6:465, 9:495–496
    aliyah and absorption, 10:215, 216
    American Gathering of Jewish Holocaust Survivors, 2:48–49
    American Joint Distribution Committee, 2:62
    Association of Holocaust Children (Poland), 2:64
    Australia, 14:8, 9
    Benjamin and Vladka Meed Registry of Jewish Holocaust Survivors, 2:59
    Bulgaria, 4:275
    children from Auschwitz, 9:369
    First International Conference on Children of Holocaust Survivors, 9:383
    Fortunoff Video Archive for Holocaust Testimony, 7:134

    Ḥasidism, 8:397
    Holocaust Survivors Film Project, 8:376
    Japan, 11:81
    Lantos, Tom, 12:486–487
    Lerman, Miles, 12:655–656
    New York City, 15:223
    psychological trauma, 6:279
    testimonies, 9:446–447
    U.K., 9:368–369
    U.S. Army chaplains, 9:379–381
    U.S. leaders, 13:764
    post war, 9:141
    World Gathering of Jewish Holocaust Survivors, 2:48
resistance and rescue, 9:342, 357–359, 490–492, 495–496, 20:740
    Aliav, Ruth, 1:658
    armed, 3:511, 9:338–339
    Beriḥah, 3:433–436
    Blood for Trucks offer, 4:120
    B'nai Brith, 4:16
    defiance, 9:359–363
    Denmark, 5:582–583
    Dzialosyce, 6:80
    Europa Plan, 6:553–554
    Fareynigte Partizaner Organizatsye, 20:532–533
    Fleischmann, Gisi, 7:74–75
    France, 7:162
    funding, 13:700
    ghetto uprisings, 9:333, 338, 13:764, 20:532–533, 21:125, 676
    Japan, 11:84
    Kasztner, Rezsö Rudolf, 11:828–829
    liberation, death camps, 9:342–343
    Lichtenberg, anti-Nazi priest, 12:797
    Mendes, Aristides de Sousa, 14:42–43
    Netherlands, 15:105–106
    Nèvejean, Yvonne, 15:129
    Operation Texas, 15:323
    Palestine, 9:281, 492
    Poland, 2:643, 16:314–317
    Righteous Among the Nations, 17:303–307
    Romania, 17:388–391
    spiritual resistance, 9:360–363
    Stefan, Metropolitan, 19:172–173
    Sugihara, Japanese diplomat, 19:294–295

Holocaust, *continued*
uprisings in camps, 15:707
USSR, 17:548–550
Wallenberg, Rauol, 20:611–612
War Refugee Board, 20:665
Yugoslavia, 21:415
Zakynthos, 21:456–457
Romania, 4:240–241, 5:433–434, 9:339, 11:92–93, 12:593–594, 17:385–391
Bacau, 3:31
Beltsy, 3:307
Bendery, 3:327
Braila, 4:118
Bucharest, 4:240–241
Bukovina, 4:266
Cluj, 4:762–763
Darabani, 5:433–434
Dorohoi, 5:758
Focsani, 7:93
Galati, 7:339
Jassy, 11:92
Mihaileni, 14:220
Nasaud, 14:783
Nasna, 14:787–788
Piatra-Neamt, 16:143
Ploesti, 16:240
Radauti, 17:53
Reghin, 17:190
Roman, 17:373–374
Salonta, 17:708
Seini, 18:254
Sighet, 18:568
Stefanesti, 19:173
Suceava, 19:290
Sulita, 19:305
Targu-Mures, 19:515
Timisoara, 19:726–727
Tirgu-Frumos, 19:730
Tirgu Neamt, 19:731
Transylvania, 20:110
Turda, 20:192
Vaslui, 20:479
Vatra Dornei, 20:486
Viseul-de-Sus, 20:543
Russia
Birobidzhan, 3:719
commemorations, 17:566
Klintsy, 12:232
Koenigsberg, 12:252
Krasnodar, 12:339
Kursk, 12:393
ORT, 15:489–490
Pochep, 16:250

rescue efforts, 9:491–492
Rostov, 17:475
Smolesk, 18:691
Starodub, 19:166
Taganrog, 19:432
Velizh, 20:493
Voronezh, 20:582
Yalta, 21:277
Scandinavia, Thanks to Scandinavia Scholarship Fund, 4:84–85
Serbia, 9:339–340
Belgrade, 3:288–289
Niš, 15:275
Novi Sad, 15:320
Subotica, 19:283
Zrenjanin, 21:671–672, 672
Silesia (region), 16:309
Teschen, 19:654
Slovakia, 5:357–358, 9:340–341
Banska, Bystrica, 3:120
Bratislava, 4:132–133
deportations, 9:479
Dunajska Streda, 6:39
Kosice, 12:318
Michalovce, 14:173
Pezinok, 16:25
Piestany, 16:149
Presov, 16:486
Topolcany, 20:38–39
Trencin, 20:131
Trnava, 20:154
Zilina, 21:531
Spain, 19:81
statistics
death in camps, 4:390
mortality estimates, 16:397–398
numbers of the dead, 9:343
population, prewar, 9:326–327
Subcarpathian Ruthenia, 19:282
Sweden, 9:342, 19:337–338
influence on literature, 18:92–93
Switzerland, 12:528, 19:344–345
asylum policy, 6:10, 12:528
Transylvania, 20:110
Tunisia, 20:188–189
Tunis, 20:188–189
Turkey, Sephardim, 18:301
U.K., 9:368–370
Channel Islands, 4:566
Ukraine, 4:86, 178, 238, 316
Aleksandriya, 1:610
Babi Yar, 3:22–23

Bar, 3:123
Belgorod-Dnestrovski, 3:288
Berestechko, 3:413
Berezhany, 3:414
Berezino, 3:414
Berezovka (Ukraine), 3:414
Birzula, 3:724
Bolekhov, 4:45
Borislav, 4:86
Bratslav, 4:134
Brody, 4:199–200
Busk, 4:316
Cherkassy, 4:595
Chernigov, 4:596
Chernobyl, 4:597
Chernovtsy, 4:598
Chortkov, 4:668–669
Drogobych, 6:24
Dubno, 6:33–34
Dunayevtsy, 6:49
Glinyany, 7:639
Gorodenka, 7:782
Gorodok, 7:782
Izyaslav, 10:830
Kalush, 11:750–751
Kazatin, 12:44
Kerch, 12:81
Kharkov, 12:105–106
Kherson, 12:114
Khmelnik, 12:115
Khorol, 12:117
Khust, 12:119
Kiev, 12:151–152
Kirovograd, 12:187–188
Kolomyya, 12:280
Komarno, 12:282
Konotop, 12:288
Korets, 12:307–308
Korosten, 12:316
Korsun-Shevchenkovski, 12:316
Kosov, 12:320–321
Kovel, 12:328
Kovno, 6:358–359
Krasnoye, 12:339
Kremenchug, 12:351
Kremenets, 12:352
Krivoi-Rog, 12:365
Krivoye Ozero, 12:365
Kuty, 12:399–400
Leshnev, 12:662
Lutsk, 13:274
Lvov, 13:291–292
Lyuboml, 13:301
Medzibezh, 13:763

Melitopol, 14:13
Mezhirech, 14:156
Mogilev-Podolski, 14:418
Monastyriska, 14:433
Mostiska, 14:568
Mukachevo, 14:607
Nadvornaya, 14:727
Odessa, 15:381
Olesko, 15:402
Olyka, 15:412
Ostrog, 15:511–512
Piryatin, 16:184
Podgaitsy, 16:250–251
Podkamen, 16:252
Podolia, 16:253
Podvolochisk, 16:254
Polonnoye, 16:361
Poltava, 16:363
Priluki, 16:527
Proskurov, 16:595
Radomyshl, 17:58
Radziwillow, 17:60
Rogatin, 17:368
Romny, 17:418
Rovno, 17:502
Rozdol, 17:503
Sadagora, 17:651
Sambor, 17:744–745
Sarny, 18:60
Sasov, 18:66
Satanov, 18:73
Sekiryany, 18:256–257
Sevastopol, 18:324
Shargorod, 18:414
Shepetovka, 18:460
Skalat, 18:656–657
Smela, 18:686
Snyatyn, 18:697
Sokal, 18:746
Stanislav, 19:163
Staro-Konstantinov, 19:166
Storozhinets, 19:239
Stry, 19:263
Talnoye, 19:491
Tarnopol, 19:518
Tarutino, 19:524
Tlumach, 19:749–750
Tolstoye, 20:30
Tomashpol, 20:31
Torchin, 20:54
Transnistria, 20:102–106, *103*
Tuchin, 20:167–168
Tulchin, 20:174
Turka, 20:195
Tysmenitsa, 20:221

Uman, 20:245
Uzhgorod, 20:448
Vasilkov, 20:479
Vinnitsa, 9:*475*, 20:538
Vishnevets, 20:543
Vizhnitsa, 20:564
Vladimir Volynski, 20:565
Volhynia, 16:314, 20:573
Voznesensk, 20:586
Yavorov, 21:291
Yefingar, 21:293–294
Yevpatoriya, 21:325
Zabolotov, 21:432
Zaleshchiki, 21:448
Zaporozhe, 21:457
Zastavna, 21:462
Zbarazh, 21:465
Zbarzh, 21:465
Zborov, 21:466
Zhdanov, 21:521
Zhidachov, 21:521
Zhitomir, 21:524
Zhmerinka, 21:525
Zholkva, 21:526
Zhuravno, 21:526
Zlatopol, 21:643
Zolochev, 21:667
Zolotonosha, 21:667
Zvenigorodka, 21:693
U.S.
   Army, 20:429–431
   Catholic Church, 4:714
women, 6:755
Wuerttemberg, Talheim, 19:463
Yom ha-Shoah, 9:455–456
Yugoslavia, 9:339, 18:49, 21:412–415
   Monastir, 14:432
   Sarajevo, 18:49
   Sephardim, 18:301
   Sombor, 19:6
   Zemun, 21:508
See also Camps, concentration and extermination; German reparations; National Socialism (Nazism)
The Holocaust (Green), 9:442–443, **493**
The Holocaust (Segal), 18:246
The Holocaust: A History of the Jews during the Second World War (Gilbert), 9:418
The Holocaust (U.S. monument), 9:431
Holocaust: A History (Dwork & van Pelt), 9:418
Holocaust and Genocide Studies, 9:424

Holocaust and Jewish Resistance Teachers Program, 2:49
Holocaust and Return to Zion (Spero), 19:98
The Holocaust and the Literary Imagination (Langer), 9:414, 12:481
Holocaust denial, 2:234–235, 240, 9:**493–495**, 10:30–32, 15:75, 20:380
Holocaust Documentation and Education Center (Hollywood, FL), 4:213
Holocaust Education Center and Memorial Museum (Houston, TX), 9:572
Holocaust in Historical Perspective (Bauer), 9:416
Holocaust in It's Historical Context (Katz), 9:389–390
The Holocaust in Romania: The Destruction of the Jews and Gypsies under the Antonescu Regime, 1940–1944 (Ioanid), 9:419
The Holocaust Kingdom (Donat), 9:404
The Holocaust Martyr's and Heroes' Rememberance Authority, 21:266–268
Holocaust Martyrs' and Heroes' Rememberance Day. *See* Yom ha-Shoah
Holocaust mini series, 9:442–443
Holocaust Organizations, Association of. *See* Association of Holocaust Organizations
Holocaust Project: From Darkness Into Light (Chicago, IL), 4:612
Holocaust Rememberance Day, 9:**495**, 13:138
Holocaust rescuers, Jewish. *See* Jewish Holocaust rescuers
Holocaust scholars
   Bauer, Yehudah, 3:218–219
   Berenbaum, Michael, 3:408–409
   Braham, Randolph Louis, 4:118
   Browning, Christopher R., 4:217
   Dawidowicz, Lucy, 5:483, 9:152
   Dvorzetsky, Mark Meir, 6:74
   Friedlaender, Saul, 7:275–276
   Gutman, Israel, 8:151–152
   Hilberg, Raul, 4:217, 9:100–102
   Langer, Lawrence L., 12:480–481
   Lanzmann, Claude, 12:487
   Novitch, Miriam, 15:320–321
   Young, James E., 21:401
Holocaust Survivors Film Project, 2:412, 8:376
Holocaust Testimonies: The Ruins of Memory (Langer), 9:413
Holofcener, Larry, 4:26
Holofernes, 9:**496–497**
   Judith, Book of, 11:566–569

Holon (ancient Israel), 9:**497**
Ḥolo shel mo'ed, 6:769
Holtzman, Elizabeth J., 9:**497–498**
Holtzman, Kenneth Dale, 9:**498**
Holtzman, Kenny. See Holtzman, Kenneth Dale
Holtzmann, Fanny E., 2:53
Holy, concept of, Otto, Rudolph, 15:518
Holy Ark. See Ark
Holy Blossom Temple (Toronto, ON), 6:737, 11:51–52
Holy Child of La Guardia (Spain), 3:775
Holy Congregation in Jerusalem, 9:**498–499**
Holy Cross Day (Browning), 4:218
Holy days
    Holiness Code, 9:319–320
    shofar, 18:507
The Holy Inquisition. See Svyataya Inkvizitsiya (Lozinski)
Holy Land. See Israel (land of)
The Holy Land (Zubrin), 18:200
Holy places, 9:**499–503**, 502
Holy Roman Empire
    bankers, moneylending, 3:114, 7:221, 14:442
    civil rights of Jews, 7:221
    Ferdinand I-III, 6:759–760, 12:650
    Francis I, 7:172–173
    Landjudenschaft, 12:471–472
    Leopold I, 12:650
    population, medieval, 16:388
    Schutzjuden, 18:179
Holy See. See Vatican
Holy Spirit. See Ru'aḥ ha-Kodesh
"Holy Spirit, The." See Ru'aḥ ha-Kodesh
Holzberg, Simchah, 9:**503**
Holzman, "Red." See Holzman, William
Holzman, William, 9:**503–504**
Holzstock-Holzstick, Meir Jehiel. See Meir Jehiel ha-Levi of Ostrowiec
Ḥoma, 9:**504**
Ḥomat Anakh (Azulai), 1:390
Homberg, Naphtali Herz, 6:179, 182, 8:436, 439, 9:**504–505**, 12:455
    Francis I, 7:173
    Galician Haskalah, 8:688
Homburg (Germany), 9:**505**
"Home buying agreements." See Heimeinkaufsvertraege
The Homecoming (Pinter), 16:177
Home Depot, 3:739
Homel. See Gomel

Homeland. See Vaderland
Homely and Religious Topics (Baar), 3:13
Homem, Antonio, 9:**505–506**
Homer, 9:**506**
    allegorical interpretation of, 3:660
    Cartesian method applied to works of, 15:191
    number of books in Bible and, 3:580
Homicide, 9:**506–507**
    accidental, bloodguilt for, 3:774
    animals
        in Book of the Covenant, 4:68
        homicidal, bloodguilt of, 3:774
        unauthorized slaughter of, 3:774
    Babi Yar, 3:22–23
    blood-avengers, 3:772–773
    bloodguilt, 3:773–774
    dynastic, Herod 1, 9:34–35
    'eglah 'arufah, 6:220–221
    heifer's neck, ceremony of breaking of, 11:374
    Lithuania, civilians, 9:474
    ritual, 9:579
    Vinnitsa, Jews, 9:474
Homiletic literature, 6:526, 9:73, **507–516**, 16:469–470
    Alba, Jacob di, 1:581
    allegories, 1:665–666
    Benjamin ben Aaron of Zalozce, 3:360
    Bernard of Clairvaux, 3:469
    biblical commentary, 3:641, 660–662
    Derashot ha-Ran and, 5:591–592
    Deuteronomy Rabbah and, 5:620
    Ḥemdat Yamim, 8:804
    Middle Ages and, 9:508–512
    nineteenth century, 9:508–512
    See also Aggadah or Haggadah; Derashot ha-Ran; Midrash; Preaching
Homilies. See Homiletic literature
Homiyyah. See Gomel
Homolka, Oscar, 9:**516**
Homonna (Slovakia). See Humenne (Slovakia)
Homosexuality, 5:175, 9:**516**, 17:179–180
    Amsterdam, 2:118–119
    Benjaminites of Gibeah in Judges, 11:565
    Brinig, Myron, 4:184

    Busch, Charles, 4:303
    Butler, Judith, 4:317
    feminist scholarship, 6:756
    Hirschfeld, Magnus, 9:138–139
    Jonathan and David, love between, 11:396
    Mithridates, Flavius, 14:370
    Reform Judaism, 6:20
    San Francisco activism, 18:19
    scholarship, 6:31
    as sexual offense, 18:329
    United States, 20:368
    See also Lesbianism
Homs. See Emesa
Homunculus. See Golem
Hond, Meijer de, 9:**516–517**
Honduras, 4:475, 476, 9:**517**
Honein (ancient city), 9:**517**
Honesty. See Truth
Honey, 3:250, 9:**517–518**
    figs, 7:18
Hong Kong (China), 9:**518**
Honigmann, Barbara, 9:**518**
Honigsmann, Peter, 2:407
Ḥoni ha-Me'aggel, 9:**518–519**
Honor, 9:**519–520**
    oil as symbol of, 15:395
Honor, Leo L., 9:**520**
Honoratus de Bonafide. See Duran, Profiat
Honoring parents. See Parents, honoring
Honorius (popes), 9:**520–521**
Honorius I (pope), 9:520
Honorius III (pope), 4:277, 9:**520–521**, 16:373
Honorius IV (pope), 9:521
Honorius Flavius (Roman emperor), 9:**521**
Hoofien, Eliezer Sigfried, 9:**521**
Hoogstraaten, Jacob, 9:**521**
Hook, Sidney, 9:**521–522**, 18:708
Hoopoes, 9:**522**
Hope is the Last to Die (Birenbaum), 9:404
Hope-Simpson, John, and Hope-Simpson Report, 15:583
Hophni, Samuel, 11:730
Hophni and Phinehas, 6:317, 9:**522**
Hophra, 9:**522–523**
Hopkins, Harry, 15:266
Hor (Israel), 9:**523**
Hora'ah, 2:565
Horace, Quintus Horatius Flaccus, 9:**523**, 11:582
Horah, 9:**523–524**

Horayat ha-Qore, 13:650

Horayot (tractate), 9:**524**

Hore-Belisha, Leslie, 16:342

Hore-Belisha, Leslie, Lord, 9:**524**

Horeb – Essays on Israel's "Duties" in the Diaspora. See Choreb, oder Versuche ueber Jissroels Pflichten in der Zerstreung

Ḥoref Aḥaron (Ballas), 3:92

Horenstein, Jascha, 9:**525**

Horesh, Raya. *See* Jaglom, Raya

Ḥorev, 6:184

Ḥorev, Amos, 9:**525**

Ḥorev Commission, 9:**525**

Horites, 6:151, 152

Horkheimer, Max, 9:**525–526**, 18:739

Hormah (ancient city), 9:**526**

Hormuz (Iran), 9:**526**

Horn, Eduard. *See* Einhorn, Ignaz

Hornbostel, E.M. von. *See* Hornbostel, Erich Moritz von

Hornbostel, Erich Moritz von, 1:290, 291, 9:**526**

Horner, Henry, 9:**526–527**

Hornets, 9:**527**

Horns, altar, 2:12, 14, 15

Horodenka. *See* Gorodenka

Horodezky, Samuel Abba, 9:**527**

Horodisch, Abraham, 9:**527–528**

Horodischtsch, Leon, 9:**528**

Horodno. *See* Grodno (Lithuanian)

Horologium Hebraeum (Schickard), 18:128

Horonaim (Israel), 9:**528**

Horontchik, Simon, 9:**528**

Horovitz, Eliezer. *See* Eliezer ben Jacob Ha-Levi of Tornogrod

Horovitz, Israel, 9:**528**

Horovitz, Jacob, 9:**528–529**

Horovitz, Jacob Isaac, 18:604

Horovitz, Josef, 9:**529**

Horovitz, Leopold, 9:**529**

Horovitz, Marcus, 9:**529–530**

Horovitz, Saul, 9:**530**, 18:565, 567

Horowitz, Aaron Judah Loeb, 9:**531**

Horowitz, Aaron Meshullam Zalman, 9:530

Horowitz, Abraham, 9:530

Horowitz, Abraham ben Isaiah, 9:**531**

Horowitz, Abraham ben Shabbetai Sheftel, 9:**532**, 16:295–296

Horowitz, Aron, 9:531

Horowitz, Aryeh Leib ben Eleazar ha-Levi, 9:**532**

Horowitz, Aryeh Leib ben Isaac, 9:**532–533**

Horowitz, Ber, 9:**533**

Horowitz, Danny, 8:722

Horowitz, David, 9:**533**

Horowitz, David ben Eleazar, 9:**539**

Horowitz, David Joshua Hoeschel ben Zevi Hirsch ha-Levi, 9:**533–534**

Horowitz, Edler von. *See* Horowitz, Samuel ben Isaiah Aryeh Leib ha-Levi

Horowitz, Eleazar, 9:**539**

Horowitz, Eleazar ben David Joshua Hoeschel. *See* Horowitz, Lazar ben David Joshua Hoeschel

Horowitz, Ḥayyim Aryeh, 9:**539**

Horowitz, Ḥayyim Dov, 6:399, 9:**534**

Horowitz, Isaac, 9:**539**

Horowitz, Isaac ha-Levi ben Jacob Jokel, 9:**534**

Horowitz, Isaiah ben Abraham ha-Levi, 6:33, 8:552, 670, 746, 9:530, 531, **534–537,** 15:524

Horowitz, Isaiah ben Jacob ha-Levi, 9:**537**

Horowitz, Isaiah ben Moses ha-Levi, 9:530

Horowitz, Isaiah ben Shabbetai Sheftel, 9:**537**

Horowitz, Israel Albert, 9:**537**

Horowitz, Israel Ze'ev, 9:**537**

Horowitz, Jacob. *See* Harris, Jed

Horowitz, Jacob ben Abraham, 9:**537–538**

Horowitz, Jacob Jokel ben Meir ha-Levi, 9:**538**

Horowitz, Jakob Yokel, 9:**539**

Horowitz, Joseph, 9:**539**

Horowitz, Lazar ben David Joshua Hoeschel, 9:**538**

Horowitz, Leon. *See* Horowitz, Aaron Judah Loeb

Horowitz, Levi Yitzchok, 4:100, 9:**541**

Horowitz, Louis J., 9:**538**

Horowitz, Meir Jacob, 9:**541**

Horowitz, Meshullam Issachar ben Aryah Leib ha-Levi, 9:**538–539**

Horowitz, Moses ben Judah, 9:**539**

Horowitz, Moshe, 9:**541**

Horowitz, Phinehas ben Israel ha-Levi, 9:**539–540**

Horowitz, Phinehas ben Zevi Hirsch ha-Levi, 4:165, 7:209, 9:**540–541**

Horowitz, Pinchas David ha-Levi, 9:**541**

Horowitz, Pinhas ben Zevi Hirsch ha-Levi. *See* Horowitz, Phinehas ben Zevi Hirsch ha-Levi

Horowitz, Samuel, 9:**539–540**

Horowitz, Samuel ben Isaiah Aryeh Leib ha-Levi, 9:**541–542**

Horowitz, Samuel Edler von ben Isaiah Aryeh Leib ha-Levi. *See* Horowitz, Samuel ben Isaiah Aryeh Leib ha-Levi

Horowitz, Samuel Shmelke of Nikolsburg, 9:**542**

Horowitz, Sarah Rebecca Rachel Leah, 9:**542–543**

Horowitz, Saul Ḥayyim ben Abraham ha-Levi, 9:**543**

Horowitz, Shabbetai Sheftel ben Akiva, 9:**543**

Horowitz, Shabbetai Sheftl, 9:530

Horowitz, Shraga Feivel ha-Levi, 9:**543–544**

Horowitz, Vladimir, 9:**544**

Horowitz, Winona. *See* Ryder, Winona

Horowitz, Ya'akov, 9:**544**

Horowitz, Zevi Hirsch, 9:**541**

Horowitz, Zevi Hirsch ben Ḥayyim Aryeh Leibush ha-Levi, 9:**544–545**

Horowitz, Zevi Hirsch ben Joshua Moses Aaron ha-Levi, 9:**545**

Horowitz, Zevi Hirsch ben Phinehas ha-Levi, 9:**545**

Horowitz, Zevi Joshua ben Samuel Shmelke, 9:**545**

Horowitz family, 9:**530–531**
    Joseph ben Gershon of Rosheim, 11:421

Horowitz family (Canada), 9:**531**

Horror, Cave of, 11:524

Horse racing, 19:143–144
    Harmatz, William, 8:360
    trainers, 11:47

Horses, 9:**545–546**

Horst, August, 17:121

Hort, Abraham, Jr., 15:242

Hort, Abraham, Sr., 9:**546**, 15:242

Horthy, Miklos, 13:274

Horthy, Regent, 12:205

Horthy Offer, 13:275

Horvitz, Sam, 4:212

Horwitz, Aaron ben Moses ha-Levi of Starosielce. *See* Aaron ben Moses ha-Levi of Starosielce

Horwitz, Aaron ben Moses ha-Levy of Starosielce. *See* Aaron ben Moses ha-Levi of Starosielce

Horwitz, H. Robert, 9:**546**, 13:9

Horwitz, Jerome. *See* Howard, Moe, Shemp, and Curly

Horwitz, Moses. *See* Howard, Moe, Shemp, and Curly

Horwitz, Phineas Jonathan, 9:**547**

Horwitz, Samuel. *See* Howard, Moe, Shemp, and Curly

Hos, Dov, 9:**547**

Hosannah. *See* Hoshanot

Hoschander, Jacob, 9:**547**

Hosea, Book of, 9:**547–558**
    Aggadah and, 9:558

Hosea, Book of, *continued*
　　Deuteronomy and, 9:556–558
　　eschatology in, 6:490–491
　　Hosea A, 9:548–552
　　Hosea B, 9:552–556
　　Jacob story, 11:20
　　Jeremiah and, 11:126
　　text summary, 9:547–548
Hosea ben Nun. *See* Joshua (biblical figure)
Hoselitz, Berthold Frank, 9:**558–559**
Hoshaiah, Rav, 9:**559**
Hoshaiah Rabbah. *See* Oshaiah Rabbah
Hoshana Rabba, 7:120, 9:**559–560**, 19:301
Hoshanot, 9:**560**
Hoshaya of Tiriah. *See* Abba Oshaya of Tiriah
Hoshea (King of Israel), 9:180, **560–561**, 18:376
Hoshea ben Elah. *See* Hoshea
Ḥoshen Mishpat. See Shulḥan Arukh
Ḥoshen mishpat (breastplate), 4:156
Hospitality, 9:**561–562**
Hospitals, 4:573, 741–742, 9:**562–565**
Host, desecration of, 9:214, 565, 565–**566**
　　Berlin (Germany), 3:445
　　Boniface VIII, 4:63
　　Brandenburg, 4:125, 126
　　Breslau, 4:164
　　Brunswick, 4:226
　　Brussels, 4:226
　　Sochaczew, 18:703
Hostages. *See* Captives, ransoming of
Host libels
　　in Paris, 15:643
　　in Passau, 15:677
Host of Heaven, 2:150–151, 9:**566–567**
Hostovský, Egon, 9:**567–568**
Ḥotam Toknit (Firkovich), 7:44
Hotel du Lac (Brookner), 4:208
Hotel Gellért, 8:755
Hoter ben Solomon. *See* Dhamārī, Manṣur Suleiman
Hottinger, Johann Heinrich, 2:21, 9:**568**
Hotzenplatz (Czech Republic). *See* Osoblaha
Hotzenplotz. *See* Osoblaha (Czech Republic)
Houbigant, C. F. H., 3:646
Houdini, Harry, 9:**568**
Hourvitz, Ya'ir, 9:**568–569**
Hourwitz, Zalkind, 8:436, 439, 9:**569**
Household gods, possession of, 15:355

Households, legal heads of, 3:7, 6:692
A House Is Not a Home (Adler), 1:406
Houseman, John, 9:**569**
House of Castile, 18:589
House of Elder Artists. *See* THEA
House of Este, 13:253
House of Israel community, 9:**569–570**
House of Ivory plaques, 2:493
House of Omri. *See* Israel, Kingdom of
House of the Forest of Lebanon, 9:**570**
The House on the Outskirts. See Dům na předměstí
Houses
　　door and doorpost, 5:752–753
　　lease and hire, 12:568–574
Housing, 1:326
Housing and Construction Holding Company Ltd., 18:753
Housman, Clarence, 14:446
Houston (TX), 3:170, 9:**570–572**
Ḥovah, 9:**572**
Hovevei Zion. *See* Ḥibbat Zion (movement)
Hovevi Zion. *See* Ḥibbat Zion
Ḥovot ha-Levavot (Ibn Paquda), 3:66–67, 6:527–528, 7:14, 8:660
　　free will, 7:231
Howard, Curly. *See* Howard, Moe, Shemp, and Curly
Howard, Leslie, 9:**572**
Howard, Melvin. *See* Torme, Mel
Howard, Michael, 6:425, 426, 9:**572**, 16:343
Howard, Moe, Shemp, and Curly, 9:**572–573**
Howard, Shemp. *See* Howard, Moe, Shemp, and Curly
Howard *v.* Miarah, 5:196
Howe, Geoffrey, 6:431
Howe, Irving, 9:**573**, 15:227, 18:709
How goodly. See Mah tovu
Howl and other Poems (Ginsberg), 7:608
How to Organize Learning (Moravchik), 6:177
Dos Hoyz fun Joyakh Edon (Pinski), 16:175–176
Hoẓa'ah Ivrit, 11:571
Hoẓin, Ẓedakah ben Saadiah, 9:**573**
Hrabanus Maurus, 9:**573**
Hranice (Czech Republic), 9:**574**
Hrdinové táhnou do boje (Poláček), 16:285
Hrobonovo (Slovakia). *See* Alistál (Slovakia)
Hroznětín (Czech Republic). *See* Hroznetin (Czech Republic)

Hroznetin (Czech Republic), 9:**574**
Hrubieszow (Poland), 9:**574–575**
Hrushkovski, Benjamin. *See* Harshav, Benjamin
Huarte de San Juan, Juan, 9:**575**
Huarte of Navarra, Juan de Dios. *See* Huarte de San Juan, Juan
Huberman, Bronislaw, 9:**575**, 10:758
Hubeş, Rozet, 9:**575**
Hubmann, Franz, 16:127
Ḥabiru, 8:**180–181**, 12:668
H.U.C. *See* Hebrew Union College-Jewish Institute of Religion
Huche. *See* Archa
Húd, 9:**575–576**
Hudal, Alois, 9:373
Hudson, Stephen, 9:**576**
Hudson County (NJ), 9:**576**
Huebsch, Adolph, 9:**576–577**
Huehner, Leon, 2:59
Huepte (Spain). *See* Huete (Spain)
Huesca (Spain), 9:**577–579**
　　Bibago brothers, conversion activities of, 3:570, 571
　　Juan de Ciudad, conversion of, 11:472
Huessy, Margrit. *See* Rosenstock-Huessy, Margrit
Huete (Spain), 9:**579**
Hughes, Sarah Elizabeth, 9:**579**
Hugh of Lincoln, 3:775, 6:411, 434, 9:**579**
Hugh of St. Victor, 8:512
Hugó, Károly, 9:**579**
Hugo, Victor, 14:540
Hu Halakh ba-Sadot (Shamir), 4:381, 18:392
Huig de Groot. *See* Grotius, Hugo
Ḥukkat ha-Goi, 9:**580**
Ḥukkei Ha-Elohim (Polak), 16:286
Ḥukkei ha-Torah, 6:175, 177
Hukok (Israel), 9:**580**
Ḥulatah (Israel), 9:**580**
Huldah, 9:**580–581**
Huldah (Israel), 9:**581**
Ḥuleh (Israel), 9:**581–582**
Ḥuleh Basin (Israel), 10:125–126
Ḥuleh Valley (Israel), 9:**582–583**, 583, 15:620
Hull (England), 9:**584**
Hull House (Chicago, IL), 18:320
Ḥullin (tractate), 9:**584–585**
Human (Ukraine). *See* Uman (Ukraine)
Human dignity and freedom, 9:**585–588**
　　human rights and, 17:309–332
　　　body search, 17:326–327

privacy, 17:323
Jewish law, 6:583–584
sanctity of human life, 13:722
source of, 13:739–740
Torah and, 15:750
Humane slaughter, 18:434–435
The Human Factor in Changing Actor (Herskovits), 9:46
Humanism
Buber, Martin, 4:231, 234
Buhler, Charlotte, 4:256
Erasmus of Rotterdam, 6:477
ethical culture, 6:524–525
Hadas, Moses, 8:185
La Boétie, Etienne de, 12:408
Leibowitz, Yeshayahu, 12:623
Montaigne, Michel de, 14:453
Montesquieu, Charles Louis de Secondat, 14:459
physics and, 16:132–133
Humanistic Values in the Bible. See Ha-Arakhim ha-Ḥinnukhiyyim shel ha-Tanakh
Die Humanistische Front (Berendsohn), 3:409
The Humanitarian Hour, 7:30
Humanitarian Principles. See Principiile umanitariste (Relgis)
Humanity Uprooted (Hindus), 9:123
Human life vs. animal life ethics, 5:168–169
See also Life and death
Human nature. *See* Man, nature of
Human Parts. See Ḥalakim Enoshiyim
Human race. *See* Son of Man
Human rights, 17:**309–332**
assembly, demonstration, 17:318
balancing of, 17:322
body search, 17:326–327
Cotler, Irwin, 5:237
creditor's, 17:325
definitions, 17:311
embryos, 6:391–392
entrapment, 17:327
Fichte, Johann Gottlieb, 7:9–10
freedom of expression, 17:314–316
halakhic pluralism, 17:330–332
Israeli courts, 17:316, 317, 320, 322, 327–330
to life, 17:313
marital relations privacy, 17:325–326
movement, 17:318–320
Muslim residents, 17:329
non-Jews, converts, 17:328–330
occupation, 17:320–321

privacy, 17:323–328
property, 17:321–322
rights and obligations, 17:310–311
source of, 17:312–313
vote and be elected, 17:316–317
The Human Stain (Roth), 20:297
Human trafficking, abduction, 1:242–243
Human Traits and Their Social Significance (Edman), 6:150
Humboldt, Wilhelm von, 9:**588–589**
Humboldt's Gift (Bellow), 3:300
Humenne (Slovakia), 9:589
Humenné (Slovakia). *See* Humenne (Slovakia)
Humielnik. *See* Khmelnik (Ukraine)
Humility, 9:**589–590**
Humility for the sake of Heaven, 8:388
Ḥummash, 9:**590**
ḥummash. *See also* Pentateuch
Humor, 9:**590–599**
American literature and, 9:595–596
Bible and, 9:590
emancipation period and, 9:592–594
folklore and, 6:29, 9:592
Israel and, 9:597–598
psychology and, 9:599
Talmud and, 9:591
U.S. and, 9:594–595
Yiddish theatre and, 9:594
See also Comedians
Humphrey, Hubert H., 2:51, 9:**599–600**, 11:757
Ḥumra, 9:**600**
Huna (amora), 8:450, 9:600–601
obligations, law of, 15:370
Huna (name), 9:**600–601**
Huna, Rav. *See* Rav Huna Resh Galuta
Huna ben Avin ha-Kohen, 9:**601**
Huna ben Bereih de-Rav Joshua. *See* Huna ben Joshua
Huna ben Joshua, 8:450, 9:**601**, 15:614
Huna ben Nathan, 2:37, 9:**601–602**
Ḥuna name. *See* Huna (name)
Huna of Sepphoris, 9:**602**
Huna Resh Galuta, 9:600
Huncovce (Slovakia), 9:**602**
Hundakas. *See* Ḥidka
Hundt-Radowsky, Joachim Hartwig, 9:**602**
Hunfalu (Slovakia). *See* Huncovce (Slovakia)
"Hungarian Jewish Review" (periodical). *See Magyar Zsidó Szemle* (periodical)

Hungarian-Jewish Society for Literature. *See* Izraelita Magyar Irodalmi Társulat
Hungarian literature, 6:749, 9:**602–608,** 12:441
Adler, Shalom ben Menaheim, 1:408
Ágai, Adolf, 1:445
Benjámin, Lázló, 3:358
biblical influence, 3:671
Bródy, László, 4:201
Bródy, Lili, 4:201
Bródy, Sándor, 4:201
children's, 4:635
Csergö, Hugo, 5:315
Csermely, Gyula, 5:315
Déry, Tibor, 5:600–601
Deutsch, David ben Menahem Mendel, 5:621–622
Dóczy, Lajos, 5:729
encyclopedias, 6:402
Földes, Joan, 7:94–95
Illés, Béla, 9:724
Karacsony, Beno, 11:785
Kiss, József, 12:201–202
Lederer, Abraham, 12:596
Lengyel, József, 12:638
Lengyel, Menyhért, 12:638–639
Lenkei, Henrik, 12:640
Mohácsi, Jenö, 14:418
Molnár, Ákos, 14:427
Molnár, Ferenc, 14:427
poetry, 6:689
Skamander group, 11:94
Somlyó, Zoltan, 19:7
Spiro, György, 19:120
Szabó, Imre, 19:400
Szabolcsi, Lajos, 19:401
Szántó, György, 19:402
Szenes, Béla, 19:406
Szenes, Erzsi, 19:406
Szép, Ernö, 19:406–407
Szerb, Antal, 19:407
Szilágyi, Géza, 19:408
Szomory, Dezsö, 19:412
Turóczi-Trostler, József, 20:204
Ujvári, Péter, 20:232
Vándor, Lajos, 20:473
Várnai, Zseni, 20:477
Vas, István, 20:478
Vészi, Endre, 20:515
Zelk, Zoltan, 21:501
Zsigmond, Ede, 21:673
Zsoldos, Jenö, 21:673
Zsolt, Béla, 21:673
Hungary, 9:**608–620,** 612
antisemitism, 2:217, 219–220, 9:244–245, 612, 618–619, 19:401–402
Alberti-Irsa, 1:591

Hungary, *continued*
  Arrow Cross party, 2:491
  censorship, 4:540
  Ónody, Géza, and antisemitic
    party, 15:434
  cultural and social life
    architecture, 2:400, 12:440
    art, 5:373
    assimilation and, 9:611, 618
    communal life, 6:272
    communities, 5:110, 9:610–
      611, 618, 619
    education, Jewish, 6:186,
      9:619
    Jewish history, preservation
      of, 18:117
    Jewish settlements, 1:270,
      9:611
    journalism, 6:222, 687,
      11:467–468, 12:676, 16:493
    Judaizers in, 11:520
    language, biblical translations,
      3:632
    linguistic assimilation, 8:437
    migration of Bulgarian Jews,
      4:269
    museums, 14:629
    music, 11:745, 785
    secondary school system
      expansion, 11:811
  economic affairs
    banking, 12:456
    coinage, 14:299
    publishing, 16:717–718
  eighteenth to mid-nineteenth
    century, 9:609
  foreign policy and affairs
    Bulgarian Jews migrating to,
      4:269
    Israel, 9:619–620
  Holocaust, 4:18, 246–248, 9:341,
    612–616, 614t, 11:828–829,
    12:486
    Baia-Mare, 3:67
    Baja, 3:70
    Bak, 3:70
    Blood for Trucks offer, 4:120,
      9:122
    Bonyhád, 4:66
    Bratislava, 4:132
    Budapest, 4:246–248
    deportation and, 9:614–616
    Eger, 6:217
    Endre, László, 6:405
    ghettoization, 9:614–615, 614t
    Kaposvar, 11:781
    Kasztner, Rezsö Rudolf,
      11:828–820

Kecskemet, 12:48
Kistarcsa, 12:205
Kisvarda, 12:205
Köszeg, 12:322
Miskolc, 14:364
Nagykanizsa, 14:734
Nyiregyhaza, 15:355–356
Pestszenterzsebet, 16:14
population statistics, 18:606
refugees, 6:465
Satoraljaujhely, 18:75
Senta, 18:291
Simleul-Silvaniei, 18:606
Sopron, 19:27
Szeged, 19:404
Szekesfehervar, 19:405
Szolnok, 19:405, 411
Szombathely, 19:412
Vac, 20:457
Veszprem, 20:515
laws and legal systems, 12:551–552
  (*See also* Slovakia)
  dayyanim, 11:711
  emancipation, 6:380, 9:609–
    610, 18:683
  neology, 15:73–74
  numerus clausus in, 15:342–
    343
  politicians, 6:687
  population statistics during
    Holocaust, 9:616
  population statistics in
    twentieth century, 9:618
  post-Communist period,
    9:618–619
  post-WW II, 9:616–618
  Rabbinical training, 17:23
  resistance during WW II and,
    9:616
  seals, use of, 18:227
  siege of Buda (1686), 18:171
  Simleul-Silvaniei, 18:**606–607**
  textiles, 19:663
  transportations, 3:67, 84
Middle Ages, 9:608
Ottoman Empire, 9:608–609,
  15:524
political theories, parties and
  organizations
  Communist regime and,
    9:611–612
  Hungarian Arrow Cross
    Party, 2:491
  Ónody, Géza, and antisemitic
    party, 15:434
religious life and scholarship
  education, Jewish, 6:186,
    9:619

  Hasidism and, 9:610, 11:745
  ḥazzanim, 11:815
  Judaizers in, 11:520
  language, biblical translations,
    3:632
  Orthodoxy, development of,
    15:493–495
  Rabbinical seminaries, 12:470
WW II
  refugees, 20:740
  war crimes trials, 20:643
See also Austria-Hungary;
  Czechoslovakia
The Hungry City (Molnár), 14:427
Hunsdorf (Slovakia). *See* Huncovce
  (Slovakia)
Hunt Foods Inc., 18:614
Hunting, 5:166, 9:**621–622**
Hunya ben Avin ha-Kohen. *See* Huna
  ben Avin ha-Kohen
Ḥunya of Beth-Horon, 9:622
Hupfeld, Hermann Christian Karl,
  9:**622**
Ḥuppah Sheḥorah (Ratosh), 17:114
Ḥuppah ve-Tabba'at (Hazaz), 8:494
Ḥuppat Eliyahu. *See* Aggadat Bereshit
Ḥuppat Ne'urim, 18:573
Hur, 9:**622–623**
Hur (grandfather of Bezalel of tribe of
  Judah), 9:622–623
Hur (King), 9:623
Hur (son of Caleb and Miriam), 9:623
*Ḥurban: Responses to Catastrophe in
  Hebrew Literature* (Mintz), 9:415
Ḥurfaysh (Israel), 9:**623**
Hurok, Sol. *See* Hurok, Solomon
Hurok, Solomon, 9:**623**
Hurrian, 9:**623–630**
  Amarna tablets, 9:623–624
  culture, religion and mythology,
    9:629–630
  Hivites, 9:294
  Hurrian language, 9:623, 625–626,
    628–629
  Mespotamia, 14:86–87
  and Mittanni, land of, 9:626–628
  Ñanigalbat, land of, 9:628
  Ñurri, land of, 9:624, 625–626
  Subarian language, 9:626
  and Subartu, land of, 9:626
Hurricane Katrina, 13:224
Hurst, Fannie, 9:**630**
Hurvitz, Eli, 9:**630–631**
Hurvitz, Joseph Yozel, 9:**631**
Hurwich, Louis, 9:**631**
Hurwitz, Adolf, 9:**631**
Hurwitz, Chaim, 8:441, 9:**631–632**

Hurwitz, Haykl. *See* Hurwitz, Chaim

Hurwitz, Henry, 9:**632**

Hurwitz, Hirsch, 8:441

Hurwitz, Hyman, 6:204

Hurwitz, Israel Zalman. *See* Libin, Z.

Hurwitz, Judah ben Mordecai ha-Levi, 9:**632**

Hurwitz, Phinehas Elijah, 8:439, 9:**632**

Hurwitz, Phyllis. *See* Lewis, Shari

Hurwitz, Samuel Justin, 9:**632**

Hurwitz, Saul Israel, 9:**632–633**

Hurwitz, Shmarya Leib, 9:**633**

Hurwitz, Shmuel. *See* Litvin, A.

Hurwitz, Stephan, 9:**633**

Hurwitz, Yigael, 9:**633–634**

Hurwitz, Zalkind. *See* Hourwitz, Zalkind

Husband and wife, 9:**634–640**
    abortion, 1:273
    adultery, 1:424–427
    agunah, 1:510–520
    domestic peace, 5:739
    domestic violence, 5:739–741
    dowries, 5:768–772
    imprisonment of husband, 9:744, 747
    laws and legal systems, maintenance, 13:399–403

Hushai the Archite, 9:**640**

Ḥushi'el ben Elhanan, 9:**640–641**

Hu-și (Romania). *See* Husi (Romania)

Husi (Romania), 9:**641**

Husid, Mordkhe, 4:426–427

Husik, Isaac, 9:**641–642**

Huss, John, and Hussites, 4:38

Ḥussayn bin Ṭalāl. *See* Hussein

Hussein (King of Jordan), 9:**642**, 10:246, 11:404–405
    Palestine Liberation Organization and, 15:589, 590, 593, 594
    Palestinian Authority and, 15:596

Hussein, Saddam, 2:326–328
    See also Gulf War (1991)

Husseini, Ḥājj Amīn al-, 9:**642–643**, 10:275–276

Husseini, Ḥājj Muhammad Amīn al-. *See* Husseini, Ḥājj Amīn al-

Husseini, Mūsā Kāẓim al-, 10:274, 275

Husserl, Edmund Gustav Albrecht, 9:**643–644**

Hussites, 9:**644–645**
    Hungarian translations of Bible and, 3:632
    Jihlava, Jews of, 11:337

Husté. *See* Khust (Ukraine)

Huszt. *See* Khust (Ukraine)

Ḥuṭ ha-Meshullash (Diwan), 5:721

Ḥut ha-Shani (Bacharach), 3:34

Le Hutin. *See* Louis (Kings of France)

Hutner, Isaac, 9:**645**

Hutterites, 6:84

Ḥutz, Solomon Bekhor, 3:59

Hutzman. *See* Ruediger

Hutzmann. *See* Ruediger

Ḥuẓal (ancient city), 9:**645**

Ḥuẓal of Benjamin (ancient city). *See* Ḥuẓal (ancient city)

Ḥuẓpit ha-Meturgeman, 9:**646**

Hyacinthe de Gonzague. *See* Deutz, Simon

Hyamson, Albert Montefiore, 9:**646**

Hyamson, Moses, 9:**646**

Hyamson, Nathan, 9:**646**

Hybrid. *See* Mixed species

Hyde, Ida Henrietta, 9:**646–647**

Hyde, Thomas, 9:**647**

Hydius, Thomas. *See* Hyde, Thomas

Hydraulis. *See* Organs

Hydrology, 6:451, 17:77

Hyenas, 9:**647**

Hyères (France), 9:**647**

Hygiene, 9:**647–648**
    rules of, 13:721, 724

The Hygiene of Healthy Souls and the Therapy of Ailing Souls (Aknin). *See* Ṭibb al-Nufūs al-Salīma wa-Muʿālajat al-Nufūs al-Alīma

Hyksos, 6:224, 9:166, **648–649**

Hylaea, 13:146

Hyman, Aaron, 9:**649–650**

Hyman, Arthur, 2:47, 16:70

Hyman, Harold Melvin, 9:**650**

Hyman, Henry, 15:198

Hyman, Jeffrey. *See* Ramone, Joey

Hyman, Joseph C., 9:**650**

Hyman, Libbie Henrietta, 9:**650**

Hyman, Marcus, 9:649

Hyman, Paula E., 2:47, 9:152, **650–651**

Hyman, William, 16:341

Hymans, Paul, 9:**651**

Hymn of Hate (Lissauer), 13:82

"Hymn of Unity." *See* Shir ha-Yiḥud

Hymns
    Adon Olom, 1:414–415
    Aḥot Ketannah, 1:547–548
    Ein ke-Elohenu, 6:259–260
    El Nora Alilah, 6:366
    Ha-Mavdil, 8:295
    Hamdī, Levi ben Yeshu'ah, 8:298
    Kargau, Menaham Mendel, 11:808
    Lekhah Dodi, 12:632–634
    Luria, Isaac, 13:265

Hymns, Liturgical. *See* Liturgy

Hymns, Table. *See* Zemirot

Hyndman, H.M, 18:704

Hypermoderne Schachpartie (Tartakover), 4:604

Hyporcoristica, 14:766

Hypsicrates of Amisus, 9:**651**

Hypsistarians, 18:232–233

Hyraxes, 9:**651**

Hyrcania (Israel), 9:**651–652**

Hyrcanian exile, 2:522–523

Hyrcanus, 3:26

Hyrcanus, Johanan. *See* Hyrcanus, John

Hyrcanus, John, 6:157, 9:**653–654**

Hyrcanus, John II. *See* Hyrcanus II

Hyrcanus II, 1:629–630, 6:539, 8:446, 9:196, **652–653**, 11:574–575, 12:487

Hyssop, 9:**655**

I

I (letter), 9:*655*, 10:5

I. Schocken Soehne, 18:153

Iacobescu, D., 9:*655*

Iacobson, Armand. *See* Iacobescu, D.

Ia-'-kin. *See* Jehoiachin (King of Judah)

Ialo. *See* Aijalon (ancient Israel)

Iamnia. *See* Jabneh (ancient Israel)

Ian, Janis, 9:**655–656**

Iancovici, Dorel. *See* Dorian, Dorel

Iancu-Agou, Danièle, 11:324, 325

I and Thou (Buber). *See* Ich und Du (Buber)

IA-Sha-R. *See* Reggio, Isacco Samuel

Iasi (Romania). *See* Jassy (Romania)

Ibāḍīs, 9:**656**

Ibbei ha-Naḥal (Shapira), 18:401

Ibbur, 7:604

Ibbur ha-shanah. *See* Calendars

Ibbur Shanim (Susan), 19:325

Iber di Khurves fun Ployne (Bursztyn), 4:302

Iberian peninsula
    See Portugal; Spain

Ibex, 9:**656**

Ibillin. *See* Avelim (Israel)

Ibiza and Formentera (Spain), 9:**656–657**

Ibleam (Israel), 9:**657**

Ibn Abbas, Judah. *See* Abbas, Judah ben Samuel ibn

Ibn Abbas, Judah ben Samuel II, 6:173–174, 9:**657**

Ibn Abbasi, Jacob. *See* Abbasi, Jacob ben Moses ibn

Ibn ʾAbd al-ʾAzīz, Umayya. *See* Ibn Abī al-ṣalt

Ibn Abī al-Bayān Suleimān al-Isrāʾīlī, Abū al-Fadl Dāʿūd. *See* David ben Solomon

Ibn Abī al-Ṣalt, 9:**657–658**

Ibn Abitur, Joseph ben Isaac, 8:328–329, 9:**658**

Ibn Abi Zimra, David. *See* David ben Solomon ibn Abi Zimra

Ibn Adiya, Samuel. *See* Samuel ibn ʾĀdiyā

Ibn Adonijah, Jacob ben Ḥayyim. *See* Jacob ben Ḥayyim ben Isaac ibn Adonijah

Ibn Adret, Moses. *See* Adret, Moses ibn

Ibn Adret, Solomon ben Abraham. *See* Adret, Solomon ben Abraham

Ibn Aknin, Joseph. *See* Aknin, Joseph ben Judah ben Jacob ibn

Ibn al-Amshata, Daniel. *See* Daniel ben Saadiah ha-Bavli

Ibn al-Athīr, 15:419

Ibn al-Barqūlī, Ezra, 9:658

Ibn al-Barqūlī, Joseph, 9:658

Ibn al-Barqūlī, Mevorakh, 9:658

Ibn al-Barqūlī, Samuel, 9:658

Ibn al-Barqūlī family, 9:**658–659**

Ibn Alfakhar, Abraham Abu Isḥak, 9:659

Ibn Alfakhar, Ezra, 9:659

Ibn Alfakhar, Joseph, 9:659

Ibn Alfakhar, Judah, 9:659

Ibn Alfakhar, Solomon, 9:659

Ibn Alfakhar family, 9:**659**

Ibn al-Ḥītī, David ben Seʾadel, 9:**659**, 11:425

Ibn al-ʾIbri, Johanan. *See* Bar Hebraeus, Johanan

Ibn al-Muʾallim. *See* Dhamārī, Manṣur Suleiman

Ibn al-Rabīb, Abraham, 9:**659**

Ibn al-Saigh. *See* Avempace

Ibn al-Ṣāʾigh. *See* Avempace

Ibn al-Sawdā. *See* Abdallah ibn Sabāʾ

Ibn Altabban, Levi ben Jacob, 9:**659–660**

Ibn al-Taqana, Moses, 9:**660**

Ibn Ardut, Ḥayyim Joseph ben Azriel ha-Kohen, 9:**660**

Ibn Arundi. Isaac. *See* Arundi, Isaac

Ibn Asad, Joshua ben Judah Abu-l-Faraj Furqān, 11:532

Ibn Atar family. *See* Atar family

Ibn Avi Zimra, David ben Solomon. *See* David ben Solomon ibn Abi Zimra

Ibn Bakoda, David. *See* Ibn Paquda, David ben Eleazar

Ibn Bakoda, David ben Eleazar. *See* Ibn Paquda, David ben Eleazar

Ibn Balʿam, Judah ben Samuel, 9:**660–661**

biblcal exegesis and study, 3:642

Judeo-Arabic literature of, 11:533

Ibn Barun, Abu Ibrahim Isaac ben Joseph ibn Benveniste, 9:**661**

Ibn Barzel, Joseph, 9:**661**

Ibn Biklārish, Jonah ben Isaac. *See* Ibn Biklārish, Junas ben Isaac

Ibn Biklārish, Junas ben Isaac, 9:**661**

Ibn Bilia, David ben Yom Tov, 2:530, 9:**662**

Ibn Crispin Cohen, Moses, 11:536

Ibn Danan, Saadiah ben Maimun, 9:**662**

Ibn Danan family. *See* Abendanan family

Ibn Dannan, Saadiah ben Maimun. *See* Ibn Danan, Saadiah ben Maimun

Ibn Dannān family. *See* Abendanan family

Ibn Daud, Abraham ben David Halevi, 2:17, 127, 461, 462, 8:260, 9:**662–665**, 13:247, 16:84

Abraham ben Solomon of Torrutiel, 1:310

allegorical interpretation and, 3:644

angels, 2:160

biographical material of, 3:705

chronology, 4:707

commandments, reasons for, 5:87

The Four Captives, 7:138–139

free will, 7:231–232

good and evil, 7:753

Ha-Emunah ha-Ramah, 12:408

Judeo-Arabic literature and, 11:535

Ohev ben Meir ha-Nasi, 15:392

Sefer ha-Kabbalah, 7:12–13

soul, immortality of, 19:37

space and place, 19:67

Ibn Ezra, Abraham, 15:655

Ibn Ezra, Abraham ben Meir, 2:618, 9:**665–672**, 670t, 13:673, 16:82–83, 267

allegorical interpretation of scripture, 3:644

angels, 2:160

astrology, and theories of, 9:670–671

Bible, and exegetes of, 9:666–669

Bonfils, Joseph ben Eliezer, 4:62

commandments, reasons for, 5:87

in Dreux, 6:17

Fleischer, Judah Loeb, 7:73

good and evil, 7:753

grammatical works, 13:41

hakdamah, 8:242–243

Italian Jewish scholarship, 6:174

Joshua ben Elijah ha-Levi, 11:450

Judah Halevi's friendship with, 11:493

on Judah ha-Parsi, 11:505

language of, 8:659

modern biblical criticism, as precursor of, 3:648

Moses, 14:537

Neoplatonic philosophy of, 9:669–671

Neo-Pythagorean philosophy of, 9:670, 670t

piyyut language, 8:651–652, 652, 660

poetry and, 9:665–666

on Saadiah Gaon's Bible translations, 3:603–604

synthetic approach to biblical exegesis, 3:642–643

Torah, 20:40

Ibn Ezra, Isaac, 9:**672–673**

Ibn Ezra, Joseph ben Isaac, 9:**673**

Ibn Ezra, Moses ben Jacob, 4:170, 8:283, 652, 9:**673–675**, 16:82

biblical exegesis and study, 3:642, 662

Joseph ben Tanḥum Yerushalmi, 11:426, 427

Judeo-Arabic literature of, 11:534, 535

literary criticism, 8:723–724

poetic Hebrew, 8:657, 658

Ibn Ezra, Solomon ben Moses, 9:**675**

Ibn Fadanj, Ibrahim, 9:675

Ibn Fadanj, Jacob, 9:675

Ibn Fadanj family, 9:**675–676**

Ibn Fadanq family. *See* Ibn Fadanj family

Ibn Falaquera, Shem Tov ben Joseph. *See* Falaquera, Shem Tov ben Joseph ibn

Ibn Gabbai, Meir ben Ezekiel. *See* Gabbai, Meir ben Ezekiel ibn

Ibn Gabirol, Solomon ben Judah. *See* Gabirol, Solomon ben Judah, ibn

Ibn Gaon, Shem Tov ben Abraham, 9:**676**

Ibn Ghayyat, Judah, 9:677

Ibn Ghayyat, Solomon, 9:677

Ibn Ghayyat family, 9:**676–677**

Ibn Ghiyyat family. *See* Ibn Ghayyat family

Ibn Gikatilla, Moses ben Samuel ha-Kohen. *See* Gikatilla, Moses ben Samuel ha-Kohen

Ibn Ḥabib, Isaac ben Menahem, 2:32

Ibn Ḥabib, Jacob ben Solomon, 3:571, 9:**677–678**

Ibn Ḥabib, Moses ben Shem Tov, 9:**678–679**

Ibn Hajjar,David, 5:**474**

Ibn Ḥasan, Jekuthiel ben Isaac, 9:**679**

Ibn Ḥasdai. *See* Joseph ben Aḥmad Ibn Ḥasdai

Ibn Ḥasdai, Abraham ben Samuel ha-Levi, 9:**679**

Ibn Ḥassin, David ben Aaron. *See* David ben Aaron ibn Ḥassin

Ibn Hawkal, 15:580

Ibn Ḥayyim, Aaron, I, 9:**679**

Ibn Ḥayyim, Aaron, II, 9:**679–680**

Ibn Ḥayyim, Abraham ben Judah, 9:**680**

Ibn Ḥayyim, Joseph, 3:677, 9:**680**

Ibn Ḥazm, Aḥmad, 1:422

Ibn Hussein, David ben Aaron. *See* David ben Aaron ibn Ḥassin

Ibn Isḥak, Ḥunain, 1:657

Ibn Jamil, Isaac Nissim, 9:**680**

Ibn Janāḥ, Jonah, 8:454, 653, 9:**680–683**

  biblical exegesis and study, 3:642
  Judeo-Arabic literature of, 11:533

Ibn Jau, Jacob, 8:328–329, 9:**683–684**

Ibn Kammūna, Sa'd ibn Manṣūr, 9:**684**

  Judeo-Arabic literature and, 11:537

  Mongols, 14:444
  as Orientalist, 15:471

Ibn Kapron, Isaac, 9:**684–685**

Ibn Kaspi, Joseph. *See* Kaspi, Joseph ben Abba Mari ibn

Ibn Kastar, Abu Ibrahim. *See* Ibn Yashush, Isaac Abu Ibrahim

Ibn Khalfun, Isaac, 9:**685**

Ibn Killis, Abu al-Faraj Ya'qūb ibn Yūsuf, 9:**685**

Ibn Latif, Isaac B. Abraham. *See* Latif, Isaac B. Abraham ibn

Ibn Latimi, Joseph. *See* Joseph ben Sheshet Ibn Latimi

Ibn Lev, Joseph. *See* Lev, Joseph ben David ibn

Ibn Malca. *See* Malca family

Ibn Malik, Menahem ben Abraham, 3:676

Ibn Malkah family. *See* Malca family

Ibn Mar Saul, Isaac ben Levi, 9:**685–686**

Ibn Matkah. *See* Matkah, Judah ben Solomon ha-Kohen

Ibn Matkah, Judah. *See* Matkah, Judah ben Solomon ha-Kohen

Ibn Matud, Samuel. *See* Ibn Motot, Samuel ben Saadiah

Ibn Matud, Samuel ben Saadiah. *See* Ibn Motot, Samuel ben Saadiah

Ibn Matut, Samuel ben Saadiah. *See* Ibn Motot, Samuel ben Saadiah

Ibn Migash, Joseph ben Meir ha-Levi, 9:**686**

Ibn Motot, Samuel ben Saadiah, 9:**686–687**

Ibn Muhāajir, Abraham ben Meir, 9:**687**

Ibn Muhajir, Abu Sulayman. *See* David ibn Hajjar

Ibn Mukammis. *See* Mukammiṣ, ibn Marwān al-Rāqi al-Shirazi al-

Ibn Munabbih, Wahb, 3:669

Ibn Mūsā, Ḥayyim ben Judah, 5:693–694, 9:**687**

Ibn Pakuda, Baḥya. *See* Baḥya ben Joseph Ibn Paquda

Ibn Pakuda, David ben Eleazar. *See* Ibn Paquda, David ben Eleazar

Ibn Paquda, Baḥya. *See* Baḥya ben Joseph Ibn Paquda

Ibn Paquda, David ben Eleazar, 2:177, 9:**687**

Ibn Plat, Joseph, 9:**687–688**

Ibn Pollegar, Isaac. *See* Pollegar, Isaac ben Joseph ibn

Ibn Quraysh, Judah, 9:**688**, 11:533

Ibn Roshd. *See* Averroes

Ibn Rushd, Abu al-Walid Muhammad. *See* Averroes

Ibn Sahl, Abu-Amr. *See* Ibn Sahl, Joseph ben Jacob

Ibn Sahl, Abu Isḥāq Ibrāhīm, 9:**688**

Ibn Sahl, Joseph ben Jacob, 9:**688–689**

Ibn Sahl, Solomon. *See* Ibn Zakbel, Solomon

Ibn Sahula, Isaac. *See* Sahula, Isaac ben Solomon Abi

Ibn Sahula, Isaac ben Solomon. *See* Sahula, Isaac ben Solomon Abi

Ibn Sahula, Meir. *See* Sahula, Meir ben Solomon Abi

Ibn Sa'īd, Isaac, 9:**689**

Ibn Sakatar, Abu Ibrahim. *See* Ibn Yashush, Isaac Abu Ibrahim

Ibn Sakuyah. *See* Ibn Sāqawayh

Ibn Sāqawayh, 9:**689**

Ibn Saquya. *See* Ibn Sāqawayh

Ibn Saquyah. *See* Ibn Sāqawayh

Ibn Saruq, Menahem. *See* Menahem ben Jacob ibn Saruq

Ibn Sasson, Samuel ben Joseph, 9:**689–690**

Ibn Saud (King of Saudi Arabia), 18:77

Ibn Shabbat, Joseph B. Ephraim Ha-Levi. *See* Écija, Joseph de

Ibn Shahin, Jacob. *See* Jacob ben Nissim ibn Shahin

Ibn Shaprut, Hisdai. *See* Ḥisdai ibn Shaprut

Ibn Shatanash. *See* Ibn Abitur, Joseph ben Isaac

Ibn Shem Tov, Isaac ben Shem Tov, 9:**690**

Ibn Shem Tov, Joseph ben Shem Tov, 3:645, 9:**690–691**

Ibn Shem Tov, Shem Tov, 9:**691–692**

Ibn Shem Tov, Shem Tov ben Joseph ben Shem Tov, 9:**692**

Ibn Shortmeqas. *See* Ohev ben Meir ha-Nasi

Ibn Shoshan (Morocco). *See* Bensusan

Ibn Shoshan, Abraham, 9:**693**

Ibn Shoshan, Abu Omar Joseph, 9:**693**

Ibn Shoshan, David, 9:**693**

Ibn Shoshan, Jacob ben Joseph, 9:**693**

Ibn Shoshan, Meir, 9:**693**

Ibn Shoshan, Samuel ben Zadok, 9:**693**

Ibn Shoshan family (Spain), 9:**692–693**

Ibn Shuaib, Joel, 9:**693–694**

Ibn Shuaib, Joshua, 3:645, 9:**694**

Ibn Shuwayk, Isaac ben Israel, 9:**694**

Ibn Sid, Isaac. *See* Ibn Sa'īd, Isaac

Ibn Sid, Samuel, 12:644

Ibn Sighmar family, 11:727

Ibn Sūsā. *See* Bensusan

Ibn Sūsā, Issachar ben Mordecai. *See* Susan, Issachar ben Mordecai

Ibn Tamim, Dunash. *See* Dunash ibn Tamim

Ibn Tibbon, Judah ben Saul, 19:712

  Arabic language, 6:173, 14:372
  as bibliophile, 3:683

  Hebrew linguistic purity, 8:659, 660, 663

Ibn Tibbon, Moses ben Samuel ben Judah, 8:660, 19:712

Ibn Tibbon, Samuel ben Judah, 2:132, 3:239, 8:659–660, 661, 12:698, 16:86, 19:712

Ibn Tibbon family, 19:**712–714**

  Arabic language, 6:173
  as Orientalists, 15:471

Ibn Tūmart, 1:681

Ibn Verga, Joseph, 9:**694–695**

Ibn Verga, Solomon, 4:25, 9:225, **695–696**

  exile, meaning of, 7:360
  Shevet Yehuda, 7:15

Ibn Waqar, Abraham, 9:**696**

Ibn Waqar, Isaac, 9:696

Ibn Waqar, Joseph, 9:696

Ibn Waqar, Joseph ben Abraham, 9:**696–697**, 11:536

Ibn Waqar, Joseph ben Isaac ben Moses, 9:696

Ibn Waqar, Judah, 9:696

Ibn Waqar, Samuel, 9:696, 11:536

Ibn Waqar family, 9:**696**

Ibn Yaḥya, David ben Joseph, 9:**697**

Ibn Yaḥya, David ben Solomon, 9:**697**

Ibn Yaḥya, Gedaliah ben David, 9:**698**

Ibn Yaḥya, Gedaliah ben Joseph, 7:13, 9:**698**

 bibliography of, 3:681
 biographical material of, 3:705
 Shalshelet ha-Kabbalah, 7:13

Ibn Yaḥya, Gedaliah ben Tam, 9:**698**

Ibn Yaḥya, Joseph ben David, 9:**698–699**

Ibn Yaḥya family, 13:80

Ibn Yaʾish, Solomon, 15:541

Ibn Yashush, Isaac Abu Ibrahim, 9:**699**

Ibn Yihyah, Gedaliah ben Joseph. *See* Ibn Yaḥya, Gedaliah ben Joseph

Ibn Zabara, Joseph ben Meir, 6:667, 9:**699**, 15:655

Ibn Zabara, Judah. *See* Ibn Zabarra, Judah

Ibn Zabara, Moses Jacob, 3:677

Ibn Zabarra, Joseph ben Meir. *See* Ibn Zabara, Joseph ben Meir

Ibn Zabarra, Judah, 9:**700**

Ibn Ẓaddik, Joseph. *See* Ẓaddik, Joseph ben Jacob ibn

Ibn Zadok, Abbās Rabīʾa Solomon. *See* Ibn Zadok, Solomon

Ibn Zadok, Solomon, 9:**700**

Ibn Zakbel, Solomon, 9:**700**

Ibn Zarzal, Abraham. *See* Zarzal, Abraham ibn

Ibn Ẓur, Jacob ben Reuben, 9:**700–701**

Ibo, 9:**701**

Ibrāhīm. *See* Abraham

Ibrāhīm, Ibrāhīm Mūsā, 15:473

Ibrāhīm ibn Sahl, 15:472

Ibrahim ibn Sahl al-Andalusī al-Israʾili, 9:**701**

Ibrahim ibn Yaʾqūb of Tortosa, 9:**701–702**

Ibrahim Pasha (?-1536), 15:525

Ibrāhīm Pasha (1789-1848), 9:**702**

Ibraila (Romania). *See* Braila (Romania)

Ibzon, 11:565

ICA. *See* Jewish Colonization Association (ICA)

Icahn, Carl C., 9:**702–703**, 15:225

Icarus (Slonimsky), 18:680

Ice hockey, 18:150, 19:144
 Fischler, Stan, 7:57
 Hart, Cecil M., 8:369

Icel. *See* Mersin (Turkey)

Iceland, Reubin, 9:**703**

Icelandic language, 3:632–633

Ice skating, 19:144
 Hughes, Sarah Elizabeth, 9:579
 Rubenstein, Louis, 17:510–511
 Slutskaya, Irina, 18:685

Ichabod, 9:**703**

Ich und Du (Buber), 4:231, 232–233, 234, 7:233

ICJW. *See* International Council of Jewish Women (ICJW)

Iconoclastic period
 Jewish life in Byzantine empire affected by, 4:327
 manuscript illumination and, 3:674

Iconography, 1:561, 9:**703–706**, *704*, 15:736–737

Icor (American Association for Jewish Colonization in the Soviet Union), 3:718

Idaho, 1:624, 9:**706–707**, *707*

Iddiyyot. *See* Eduyyot (tractate)

Idealism, critical, 2:643

Idealism and Liberal Education (Freedman), 7:225

The Idea of Biblical Poetry: Parallelism and Its History (Kugel), 16:256

The Idea of Self: East and West: A Comparison between Buddhist Philosophy and the Philosophy of David Hume (Hoffmann), 9:312

The Idea of the Jewish State (Halpern), 8:283

Ideas Face Reality, Jewish Law & Life in Poland, 1550-1655 (Fran), 18:471

L'Idea Sionnista (periodical), 14:408

Ideen zu einer kuenftigen Dynamik der Geschichte (Molitor), 14:426

Idel, Moshe, 9:**707–708**

Idelovitch, David, 9:**708**

Idelsohn, Abraham, 9:**709**

Idelsohn, Abraham Zvi, 8:426, 457, 503, 9:**708–709**

Idelsohn, Beba, 9:**709–710**

Idelsohn, Benjamin, 9:**710**

Idelson, Abraham, 8:336

Idelson, Israel. *See* Bar-Yehudah, Israel

Identification imagery, 2:503

Identité juive, identité humaine (Draï), 6:7

Identity, Jewish. *See* Jewish identity

IDF. *See* Israel Defense Forces (IDF)

Idi, 9:**710**

Idi bar Avin, 9:**710**

Idiglat. *See* Tigris

Idigna. *See* Tigris

The Idiot (ballet, Eifman), 6:253

Idishe gas (periodical). *See* Jewish Street (periodical)

Idolatry, 8:376, 9:**710–715**
 Aaron and, 1:209
 Abba Gulish, 1:227
 adultery, 1:425
 Ahab, 1:524
 akkum, 1:569
 commandments concerning, 5:77t, 78t–79t
 dysphemisms, 6:550, 551
 Jeremiah, Epistle of, 11:134
 Nazism as form of, 16:99
 Noachide laws on, 15:284
 Wisdom of Solomon, 18:768–769

IDP. *See* International Development Program

Idra de-Vei Mashkena (Zohar), 21:648

Idra Rabba (Zohar), 21:648

Idrīs. *See* Enoch

al-Idrisi, 2:81

Idumea (Palestine, Roman)
 Edom, 6:156–157
 leaders, 11:36

Idunum. *See* Judenburg (Austria)

I Enoch. *See* Enoch, Ethiopic Book of

IES. *See* Israel Exploration Society

Ieṣṣau. *See* Wechsler, Max

Iewes in America, or Probabilities that the Americans Are of that Race (Thorowgood), 14:460

Iezer. *See* Abiezer

Ifrane (Morocco). *See* Ofran

Ifranji. *See* Francos

If This Be a Man (Levi), 4:631, 9:355–356, 405, 447, 12:692

If You Can Believe Your Eyes and Ears (album), 6:361

Ig'eret Rav Sherira Ga'on (Sherira), 18:463

Iggeret (Pirkoi ben Baboi), 16:183

Iggeret Ba'alei Ḥayyim (Kalonymus ben Kalonymus), 6:668

Iggeret el Ro'ei Seh Pezurah Yisrael (Homberg), 9:504–505

Iggeret ha-Ḥalomi (Falaquera), 6:681

Iggeret ha-Hitnaẓẓelut (Jedaiah ben Abraham Bedersi), 11:101

Iggeret ha-Kodesh, 9:**715**, 14:470

Iggeret ha-Kohanim (Bali), 3:90

Iggeret Ḥamudot (Genazzano), 8:479

Iggeret ha-Musar (Alami), 1:575

Iggeret ha-Musar (Lipkin), 13:65

Iggeret ha-Purim (Almoli), 1:682

Iggeret ha-Vikku'ah (Falaquera), 6:680

Iggeret Issur Ner Shabbat (Bali), 3:90

Iggeret kelalit, 18:447

Iggeret li-nedivim, 18:447

Iggeret Magen Avraham (Cardozo),
  4:464

Iggeret Nidḥei Yisrael (Pigit), 16:151

Iggeret Orḥot Olam (Farissol), 6:717

Iggeret Sod ha-Ge'ullah (Abraham ben
  Eliezer ha-Levi), 1:298

Iggeret Tokheḥah (Judah ben Asher),
  11:483

Iggerot Moshe (Feinstein), 6:742,
  11:255

Iggud ha-Rabbonim. *See* Rabbinical
  Alliance of America

"I give thanks." *See Modeh Ani*

Iglau. *See* Jihlava

Iglesia Israelita, 11:521

Ignace, Edouard, 16:343

Ignatius of Loyola, 11:245

Ignatoff, David, 9:**715**

Ignatow, David, 9:**715–716**

Ignatyev, Count Nikolai Pavlovich,
  9:**716**

Ignatyev, Nikolai Pavlovich. *See*
  Ignatyev, Count Nikolai Pavlovich

Ignotus, Hugó, 9:**716**

Ignotus, Pál, 9:716

Igra, Meshullam ben Samson, 9:**716–
  717**

Igra, Moses ben Samson. *See* Igra,
  Meshullam ben Samson

I Haven't Got a Hat, 7:238

"I Have Set a Memorial to God's
  Miracles" (Aboab). *See* "Zekher
  Asiti le-Nifle'ot El"

Iḥud, bi-nationalism promoted by,
  3:703

Iḥud Habonim, 9:**717–719**, 717t

Iḥud ha-Kevuẓot ve-ha-kibbutzim,
  9:**719**, 12:123–124

Iḥyā 'Ulūm al Din (al-Ghazālii, 7:571

II Enoch. *See* Enoch, Slavonic Book of

I.IẒ.L. *See* Irgun IẒeva'i Le'ummi

IJA. *See* Institute of Jewish Affairs
  (IJA)

Ijon (Israel), 9:**719**

Ikkarim. See Sefer ha-Ikkarim

Ikkur, 18:434

Ikkuv ha-keri'ah. *See* Bittul ha-Tamid

Ikonicoff, Moisés, 16:350

Ikor, Roger, 9:**719**

Ikriti. *See* Shemariah ben Elijah Ben
  Jacob

Ilai (3rd–4th c.), 9:**720**

Ilai (c. 3rd c.). *See* Tanḥum ben
  Ḥanilai

Ilai (c. 100 C.E.), 9:**719–720**

Ilan, Ornit, 2:330

Ilaniyyah (Israel), 9:**720**

Il Caso Pinedus (Levi), 12:691

Ilf, Ilya, 9:**720–721**

Ilfa, 9:**721**

Ilgen, Karl David, 9:**721**

ILGWU. *See* International Ladies
  Garment Workers Union

Iliad (Homer), 3:580

Ilin, M., 9:**721–722**

Ilintsky, Gedaliah ben Issac of. *See*
  Lunietz, Gedaliah ben Issac of

Ilintsy (Ukraine), 9:**722**

Ilja (Belarus). *See* Ilya (Belarus)

Illafsky family. *See* Illowy family

Illai. *See* Mamzer

Illawy family. *See* Illowy family

Illegal contracts, 5:193–194, 196

Illegal immigration, 4:9–10, 9:250,
  281, **722–724**, 10:204

  Ben-Gurion, David, 3:346

  Patria, 15:689

  post World War II, 10:10:206–207

  See also Aliyah and absorption;
    Beriḥah; Migrations

Illereichen-Altenstadt. *See* Altenstadt
  (Germany)

Illés, Béla, 9:**724**

Illescas (Spain), 9:**724**

Illiberis. *See* Elvira

Illinois, 9:526–527, *725*

Illinois (U.S.), 9:**724–725**

Illness. *See* Sicknesses

Illovy family. *See* Illowy family

Illoway family. *See* Illowy family

Illowy, Bernard, 9:**725–726**

Illowy, Jacob, 9:725

Illowy, Jacob Loeb, 9:725

Illowy, Phineas, 9:725

Illowy, Samuel, 9:725

Illowy, Solomon, 9:725

Illowy family, 9:**725**

Los Illuminados (Aguinis), 1:510

Illuminated amulets, 2:122–123

Illuminated Kettubot, 12:97–98

Illuminated manuscripts, 1:375, 2:495–
  496, 497–498, 11:226

  aggadah, 1:463

  Avicenna's medical treatise (15th
    c.), vol. 8: color insert

  Bible with masoretic notes (13th
    c.), vol. 8: color insert

biblical influence, 3:674–679

  David in, 5:456–457

  Hebrew Bibles, 3:675–679

  Ibn Ḥayyim, Abraham ben Judah,
    9:680

  Ibn Ḥayyim, Joseph, 9:680

  Islamic, 3:674

  Joel ben Simeon, 11:366

  Jonah portrayed in, 11:391

  Joseph ha-Ẓarefati, 11:430

  Joseph portrayed in, 11:412–413

  Josephus depicted in, 11:441–442

  Joshua depicted in, 11:444

  Judah Maccabee portrayed in,
    11:511

  Judeo Persian, 11:556, vol. 8: color
    insert

  Kosher preparation of meat (14th
    c.), vol. 8: color insert

  man with covered Torah (15th c.),
    vol. 8: color insert

  Moses receiving Tablets of the
    Law (14th c.), vol. 8: color
    insert

  Noah's ark (13th c.), vol. 8: color
    insert

  Passover, men reading the
    Haggadah (15th c.), vol. 8:
    color insert

  sacrifice of Isaac (13th c.), vol. 8:
    color insert

  Second Temple, implements,
    19:626

  Tisha Be-Av prayer (15th c.), vol.
    8: color insert

  Tower of Babel, 3:21

Illuminated manuscripts, Hebrew,
  9:**726–735**

  Adam and Eve, 1:375

  characteristics of, 9:727–728

  French school of, 9:730–731

  German school of, 9:731–732

  Hellenistic period and, 9:726–727

  Italian school of, 9:732–733

  materials and techniques for,
    9:728

  Oriental styles of, 9:728–729

  seventeenth-eighteenth century,
    9:733–734

  Spanish school of, 9:729–730

Illuminating the Eyes of the Wise. See
  Me'ir Einei Ḥakhanim (Lublin)

Illustrated books, 4:75–76

Illustrated Monthly for the Jewish
  Home (periodical). *See* Menorah
  (journal)

Illustrerad svensk litteraturhistoria
  (Schück, Warburg), 18:169

Ilna'e, Eliezer Isaac, 9:**735**

Ilovy, Rudolf, 9:725

Ilu Rak (Almagor), 18:206

Ilya (Belarus), 9:**735–736**

Ilya Ehrenburg: Writing, Politics and the Art of Survival (Goldberg), 6:238

Ilyās (prophet). *See* Elijah (prophet)

Image of God. *See* God

Imagination, 9:**736**

Imagined. See Gedakht

Imagining Religion: From Babylon to Jonestown (Smith), 18:688

Imagining Robert: My Brother, Madness, and Survival (Neugeboren), 15:119

I Married a Communist (Roth), 20:296–297

Imatatio Dei. See Imitation of God

Im australischen Busch (Semon), 18:286

Imber, Naphtali Herz, 8:457, 736, 9:**736–737**

Imber, Samuel Jacob, 9:**737**

Imber, Shmuel-Yankev. *See* Imber, Samuel Jacob

Imbonati, Carlo Guiseppe, 3:681, 8:514, 9:**737**

Imbonatus, Carlo Guiseppe. *See* Imbonati, Carlo Guiseppe

Im Eruw (Placzek), 16:210

Im Eshkaḥekh, 18:450

Imit. *See* Izraelita Magyar Irodalmi Társulat

Imitatio Deí. *See* Imitation of God

Imitation of God, 9:**737–738**

The Immanence of God in Rabbinical Literature (Abelson), 1:249

Immanuel, 9:**738–740**

Immanuel ben Solomon of Rome. *See* Immanuel of Rome

Immanuel Bin-Gorion, 3:406

Immanuel of Rome, 4:75, 5:430–431, 8:724, 9:**740–741**, 10:791, 16:612

    Anatoli, Jacob ben Abba Mari ben Samson, 2:132

    Anav, Zedekiah ben Abraham, 2:139

    Ancona, 2:140

"Immanuel the Jew" of Rome. *See* Immanuel of Rome

Imma Shalom, 9:**741–742**

Immersion. *See* Ablution; Ritual immersion

Immigration. *See* Aliyah and absorption; Illegal immigration; Migrations

Immigration to Israel. *See* Aliyah and absorption in Israel

Immortal Adventure (Lindheim), 13:28

Immortality of soul. *See* Soul, immortality of

Immortality of the soul. *See* Soul, immortality of

Immovable property. *See* Property

Immunology. *See* Medicine

Imola (Italy), 9:**742**

Impalement, 9:**742**

Im Paradies (Heyse), 9:87

Imperfect Justice: Looted Assets, Slave Labor, and the Unfinished Business of World War II (Eizenstat), 6:281

Imperio de Dios en la harmonía del mundo (Barrios), 3:176

Importancia por contacto (Aguinis), 1:510

Impossibility theorem, 2:490

Impotence. *See* Barrenness and fertility

Imprecation. *See* Blessing and cursing

Impressionism

    Brauner, Isaac, 4:139

    Fichman, Jacob, 7:8

    Oppenheimer, Joseph, 15:448–449

    Pissarro, Camille, 16:186–187

    in poetry, 4:138

    post-impressionism, Ballin, Moegens, 3:93

Imprisonment, 9:**742–747**

    for debt, 9:**747–752**

    See also Detention

Impurity, ritual. *See* Purity and impurity, ritual

Imrāni. *See* Emrāni

Imrei Binah (Birkenthal), 3:712

Imrei Binah (Rossi), 17:472

Imrei Higyonai Ashir ve-Azamer la-Adonai (Kapuzato), 11:782–783

Imrei Regesh (Schmelkes), 18:144

Imrei Shefer (Wessely), 21:20

Imri, Rakhel. *See* Feygenberg, Rakhel

Im Tishtaḥ Ei Pa'am (Shaked), 18:367

In a Different Voice (Gilligan), 18:736

In a Forest Settlement. See Be-Yishuv shel Ya'ar

Inbal, Eliahu, 9:**752**

Inbal Dance Theater, 9:**752**

    Levi-Tannai, Sara, 12:732–733

    Oved, Margalit, 15:548–549

Inber, Vera Mikhailovna, 9:**752–753**

In Canada. See In Kanade

Incantations, 2:132

Incense and perfumes, 9:**753–755**, 16:191

    cult sacrifices and, 5:333

    frankincense, 7:212–213

    incense altars, 2:14

    onycha used in making of, 15:436

Incest, 9:**755–756**

    Aaron ben Judah Kusdini on, 1:216

    commandments, 5:84t

    as sexual offense, 18:329

    Talmud, 4:582

Incident at Vichy (Miller), 14:252

Incidents of Travel and Adventure in the Far West (Carvalho), 4:502

Inclination, good and evil, 9:**756–757**

The Incoherence of the Philosophers. See Tahāfut al-Falāsifa

In Commendam transactions, 15:671

Incunabula, 9:**757–769**

    collections, 9:759

    history and dates, 9:757–758

    Italy, 6:708

    list of, 9:762–768

    Portugal, 6:718

    printing of, 9:758–762

    scholarship, 9:759

    statistics on, 9:758

In Darkness Striding (Burla). *See Naftulei Adam*

In Days of Cain (Dunn), 18:200

Indebtedness bonds, 5:154–155

Indelman, Moshe. *See* Yinnon, Moshe

Indemnification, restitution, 17:**239–240**

Independence Day (Israel), 9:**769–770**

Independent Jewish Workers Party, 9:**770–771**

Independent Liberal Party, 9:**771**

Independent Order of True Sisters, 4:220

In der Medinas Yisroel in Yor 2000 (Zeitlin), 18:202, 21:620–621

Index Dioscorides (Lusitanus), 2:34

India, 9:**771–776**, 772

    Abraham, Samuel, 1:291

    Abrahams, Lionel, 1:316

    Abrahão, Coje, 1:317

    Bene Israel, 3:335–338

    Bene Menashe, 3:340

    Black Jews, 6:741

    Bombay, 4:51–52

    botanists, 6:648

    foreign policy and relations with Israel, 10:265

    Israel, communities of Indian Jews in, 10:298

    Jewish dress, 6:15

    literature, 15:474

        Barnett, Lionel David, 3:169

        Kalila and Dimna, 11:735

        twentieth century, 5:463

military, 11:28

museums, 14:635

newspapers, 16:493–494

ORT, 15:489–490

Orta, Garcia de, 15:492

philanthropists, 6:648

poets, 6:648

prominent families, 6:654

sabbath service (New Delhi), vol. 5: color insert

theater, 5:463

trade, 7:468

See also Kehimkhar, Ḥayim Samuel

India-Book, 11:821

Indiana (U.S.), 9:**776–777**, *777*, *777t*

Indianapolis (IN), 9:**778**

Indians, American. *See* American Indians

The Indian Wants the Bronx (Horovitz), 9:528

The Indifferent Ones (Moravia). *See The Time of Indifference* (Moravia)

Indigo, 3:55

Individual

business ethics, 4:308

Duns Scotus, John, 6:50–51

ideal, 6:531–532

The Individual and His Society (Kardiner), 11:804

Indonesia, 9:**778–779**

Indre-et-Loire. *See* Touraine (France)

Industrial Air Sampling and Analysis (Silverman), 18:587

Industrialists

Australia, Blaustein family, 3:745–746

Austria, Bunzi family, 4:285

Canada

Bronfman, Edgar Miles, 4:206

Davis, Mortimer B., 5:481

Lastman, Melvin Douglas, 12:503–504

Citroën, André Gustave, 4:736–737

England

Bagrit, Sir Leon, 3:60

Bejerano family, 3:272

France, Deutsch de la Meurthe, Henri, 5:625

Germany

Hirsch, Aron Siegmund, 9:124

Hirsch, Baron Maurice de, 9:127

Rathenau, Emil Moritz, 17:110

Rathenau, Walther, 17:110–111

Rosenthal, Philipp, 17:457

Israel

Hecht, Reuben, 8:751

Hurvitz, Eli, 9:630

Lautman, Dov, 12:530

Shenkar, Arie, 18:460

Italy, Blayer, Pietro, 3:747

Japanese, Eisenberg, Shoul, 6:266

Netherlands, Bergh, Van Den family, 3:426–427

Russia, Baron, Bernhard, 3:171

U.K.

Bagrit, Sir Leon, 3:60

Burton, Montague, 4:302

Cazalet, Edward, 4:533

Davis, Sir Edmund, 5:480

Levinstein, Herbert, 12:723

Schon, Frank, 18:160

U.S.

Bamberger, Simon, 3:105

Brown, David Abraham, 4:214

Davidson, William, 5:477

Hammer, Armand, 8:307–308

Lauterbach, Edward H., 12:529

Lewisohn family, 12:767–768

Shapero, Nate S., 18:398

Shapiro, Irving Saul, 18:406

Shapp, Milton Jerrold, 18:408–409

Simon, Norton, 18:614

Industrial Removal movement, 9:**779**

Indyk, Martin, 9:**779**

Inebahti. *See* Naupaktos (Greece)

Inés, the Maiden of Herrera, 4:645, 9:41, 15:474

I Never Saw Another Butterfly (art collection), 5:646

Infamous decree of March 17, 1808, 2:8, 15:576

Infant baptism, 3:121

Infeld, Leopold, 9:**779–780**

Infertility. *See* Barrenness and fertility

Infinite. *See* Ein-Sof

Infinity, concept of, 15:333

Infinity Broadcasting, 11:812

Informaciones para los Immigrantes Israelitas (periodical), 6:140, 141

Information technology (IT), 15:491

Information technology, Internet

Bible translation on, 3:637

Brin, Sergey, 4:183

The Informed Heart (Bettelheim), 3:551, 9:415

Informers, 9:**780–786**

Ingathering of the exiles, 9:282, **786–787**

aliyah and absorption, 10:339–340

Ben-Gurion, David, 3:346

post-war of independence to Six-Day War historical survey, 10:215–216

Ingber, Lou. *See* Stillman, Louis

In generali concilio, 4:277

Ingolstadt (Germany), 9:**787**

Ingwiller (France), 9:**787**

Inheritance. *See* Succession

The Inheritance of the Fathers (Meir ben Elijah). *See Naḥalat Avot* (Meir ben Elijah)

In Heysn Vint. See In the Hot Wind (Dropkin)

Initials. *See* Abbreviations

In Kanade (Shtern), 4:426

Inkeles, Alex, 9:**787**

Inkishāf al-asrār wa-ṭuhūr al-anwār (Aknin), 1:570

Ink making, 18:241–242

Inlander, Heinz. *See* Inlander, Henry

Inlander, Henry, 9:**787**

In Likht fun Doyres (Lee), 12:598

In Memory of May 4, 1970: Kent State - Abraham and Isaac (Segal), 18:246

In Memory of the Czech Transport to the Gas Chambers (Bacon), 3:41

In Mr. Lublin's Shop. See Ba-Ḥanuto shel Mar Lublin

In My Father's Pastures (Morgenstern), 14:487

Innocence Project, 18:116

Innocent, 9:**788–789**

Innocent II (pope), 9:788

Innocent III (pope), 9:788

Innocent IV (pope), 9:788–789

Innocent Vlll (pope), 9:788–789

Innocent IV, 16:373

Innocent X (pope), 16:376

Innocent III, 16:373

Innocent III (pope), 4:277, 9:215

Innocent IV (pope), 4:277, 15:383

L'Innominato (Momigliano), 14:431

Innsbruck (Austria), 9:**789–790**

Inowroclaw (Poland), 9:**790**, 16:307–308

In Polish Woods (Opatoshu). *See In Poylishe Velder*

In Potiphar's House (Kugel), 1:461

Inquisition, 9:**790–804**

Abenatar Melo, David, 1:250

Alfonso de Espina, 1:642

America, 2:41

Inquisition, *continued*
  Bahia, 3:61
  Bibago brothers, conversion
    activities of, 3:570, 571
  Brazil, 4:142, 143
  Canary Islands, 4:428
  Carcassonne (France), 4:461
  Caribbean, Spanish-Portuguese
    Nation of the: La Nacion,
    4:468–469
  Cartagena (Colombia), 5:62
  censorship, 5:739
  Chile, 4:636–637
  Dias, Luis, 5:636–637
  Dominicans, 5:745
  Enríquez Gomez, Antonio, 6:446
  Europe, 9:799–800
  Goa, 7:651
  history of, 9:790–791
  Hoogstraaten, Jacob, 9:521
  Italy, 10:798
    Palermo, 15:580, 581
  late eighteenth century, 9:795
  laws and legal systems of, 9:800–
    803
  Orobio de Castro, Isaac, 15:481
  Portugal, 4:469, 520–521, 9:793–
    794, 796, 12:567, 13:79–80,
    16:411
    John III, 11:379
    John XXII on jurisdiction
      over Jews, 11:379
    Lisbon, 13:80
    Oporto, 15:441
    possessions, 9:796–797
  records, 9:796
  Sánchez, Gabriel, 18:9
  scholarship approach to, 9:792–
    793
  Spain, 4:290, 9:791–792, 794–796,
    18:44–45
    Andalusia, 11:58
    Barcelona, 3:144
    Biel, 3:688
    Cavalleria, Alfonso de la,
      4:532
    Chirino family, 4:652
    Ciudad Real, 4:745
    colonies, 9:797–799
    Cuenca, 5:327–328
    Escalona, 6:488
    Seville, 18:328
  statistics, 9:795–796
  See also New Christians
The Inquisition and Judaism
  (Mocatta), 14:404
Inquit. *See* Goldstein, Moritz

Insanity, Jewish law, 15:722
Inscriptions, 21:241–244
  Bonsphorus, kingdom of, 4:98
  Hebrew, 1:693
  Phoenician, 16:124
Insdorf, Annette, 9:**804**
*In Search of Lost Time. See A la
  Recherche du temps perdu*
Insects
  centipedes, 4:543
  fleas, 7:70
  hornets, 9:527
  lice, 13:226–227
Insemination, artificial, 2:**532–533**
Insight and Responsibility (Erikson),
  6:479
Insolvency, oaths of, 15:363
Institute for Historical Research, 9:493
Institute for Jewish Policy Analysis,
  11:318
Institute for Judaism and
  Contemporary Society. *See* Fisch,
  Harold
Institute for Microfilmed Hebrew
  Manuscripts, 13:133
Institute for Research in Jewish Law,
  18:724
Institute for Science and Halakhah,
  19:574–576
Institute for Social Research, 11:762
Institute for the Research of Medieval
  Hebrew Poetry, 9:**804–805**
Institute of Folklore (Romania), 4:138
Institute of Geophysics, University of
  California, Los Angeles, 11:776
Institute of Jewish Affairs (IJA), 2:411,
  9:**805**
Institute of Jewish Studies (England),
  2:23
Institute of Musical Art, 13:160
Institute of Psychological Research,
  13:192
Institute of Science and Halakhah,
  13:233–234
Institute of Social and Religious
  Studies, 13:129
Institute of Southern Jewish Life,
  Goldring/Woldenberg, 9:**805–806**
The Institute of Traditional Judaism
  (ITJ), 9:**806–807,** 17:26
Institute on Human Relations, 18:586
Institutions for the Care of
  Handicapped Immigrants. *See*
  Malben
Instituto Convitto Rabbinico, 17:23
Institutum Judaicum Delitzschianum,
  9:**807**
Institut zur Foerderung der
  Israelitischen Literatur, 18:723

Instruction of Amenemope
  (instructional text), 6:226
Insults, 9:**807–808**
Insurance, 1:397, 9:**808–809**
Integral Judaism, 15:563
Intel Corporation. *See* Grove, Andrew
  Stephen
Intellect, 9:**809–810**
  Alexander of Aphrodisias, 1:628
  Duns Scotus, John, 6:50–51
Intellectual property, 8:451, 453
Intelligence operations. *See* Espionage
Intention. *See* Kavvanah
Inter-American Development Bank,
  2:71
Intercalation. *See* Calendars
Intercollegiate Menorah Association,
  6:196
Interdizioni israelitiche (Cattaneo),
  4:525
Interest. *See* Usury
Interfaith relations
  Brasch, Rudolph, 4:130
  Brazil, 4:151–152
  Brickner, Balfour, 4:179
  Bronstein, Herbert, 4:207
  conference, 13:67
  Protestants, 16:632–633
  Schiffman, Larence H., 18:132
  See also specific faiths
Intermarriage. *See* Mixed marriages
Intermarriage in New York City
  (Drachsler), 6:6
Inter multiplicis (papal bull, Leo X),
  14:461
International Anti-Jewish Congress,
  4:109
International Association of Jewish
  Genealogical Societies, 9:**810–811**
International Catholic-Jewish Liaison
  Committee (ILC), 11:279–280
International Chess Federation, 11:807
International Commission on
  Holocaust Era Insurance Claims
  (ICHEIC), 18:462
International Committee of Museums
  and Sites (Israel) of UNESCO,
  3:710
International Conference of Jewish
  Communal Service, 9:**811–812**
International Conference of Jewish
  Social Work, 11:816
International Council of Christians
  and Jews (ICCJ), 11:281–282
International Council of Jewish
  Women (ICJW), 2:118, 9:**812**
International Court of Justice, 4:254
International Development Program
  (IDP), 2:64

International Emergency Conference of Jews and Christians (1947), 16:631

International Executive Service Corps (IESC), 13:61

International Forum on the Holocaust, 2:412

International Jewish Colonization Society, 19:650

International Jewish Committee on Interreligious Consultations (IJCIC), 9:49, 11:276, 277–278, 280

International Jewish Labor Bund, 4:283

International Jewish Newspaper (newspaper), 14:520

International Labor Organization, 14:512–513, 20:271

International Ladies Garment Workers Union (ILGWU), 9:**812–813,** 12:411, 18:151
  Chaikin, Sol C., 4:557–558
  Dubinsky, David, 13:708–709
  Dyche, John Alexander, 6:75–76
  Mazur, Jay, 13:708–709
  Pesotta, Rose, 16:13
  Schlesinger, Benjamin, 18:140
  Shavelson, Clara Lemlich, 18:421–422
  Sigman, Morris, 18:568

International Military Tribunal, 20:634–635

International Museum of War and Peace (Switzerland), 3:756

International Network of Children of Jewish Holocaust Survivors, 9:383

International Order (left-wing organization), 6:189

International Refugee Organization, 17:186

International Society of Musicology, 1:398

International Tracing Service, 2:411, 9:**813–814**

International Union of Crystallography, 11:809

International Working Men's Association, 18:705

Internet. *See* Information technology (IT)

Internment camps. *See* Camps, concentration and extermination

Interpretation, 9:**814–827**
  contracts, 5:197–198, 9:823–824
  definition of terms, 9:814
  documents, 9:821–823
  Halakhah, 9:821
  Takkanot ha-Kahal, 9:824–826
  See also Bible scholars

Interpretation of Dreams. See Mefasher Ḥelmin

An Interrupted Life. See Het verstoorde leen

Interruption of prayers. *See* Bittul ha-Tamid

Intertextuality and the Reading of Midrash (Boyarin), 1:461

In the Almost Promised Land: American Jews and Blacks, 1915-1935 (Diner), 9:153

In the Australian Bush (Semon). *See Im australischen Busch (Semon)*

In the Depths of the Forest (Byadulya-Yasakar). *See V dremuchikh lesakh*

In the Hot Wind (Dropkin), 6:24

In the Light of Generations. See In Likht fun Doyres (Lee)

In the Middle of It All. See Be-Emẓa ha-Roman

In the Steps of Pope Paul (Slonim), 18:678

Intifada, 7:402, 403, 9:**827–837,** 10:241–242, 720–725
  1987, 15:594
  Arabic literature, 10:747
  Arab Israelis, 9:837, 10:720–721
  causes of, 9:827–830
  characteristics of uprising, 9:830–834
  economic developments and, 9:836
  England, 6:431
  IDF response, 10:473, 474–475
  Israeli responses to, 9:829, 835–836, 836–837
  political ramifications of, 9:834–835, 837
  second, 10:251–252, 732–733
  social upheavals in territories and, 9:836–837

Intifada (2000). *See* Al-Aqsa Intifada

Intoarcerea poetului la uneltele sale (Baltazar), 3:96

Intorno a Gramsci e alla filosofia della prassi (Mondolfo), 14:435

Into That Darkness: From Mercy Killing to Mass Murder (Sereny), 9:415

Introductions and forewords. *See* Hakdamah

Introduction to Group Therapy (Slavson), 18:672

An Introduction to the Literature of the Old Testament (Driver), 6:22

Introduction to the Philosophy of Dialectical Materialism. See Vvedeniye v filosofiyu dialekticheskogo materializma

Introduction to the Talmud (Mielziner), 14:206

Introduction to the Text of the Mishnah (Epstein), 14:327

Introductory Study of the Civil Laws of the Jewish Family in Greece (Moissis), 14:422

Introspective movement, 4:6

Invalidation of transactions, 15:425

Inventors. *See* Engineering

Invertebrates, 2:172

The Investigation (Weiss), 9:405–406

The Invisible Sun (Pinto), 16:179

Inyanei ha-Yehudim: She'elat ha-Yeẓi'ah (Eismann). *See Concerning Jewish Affairs: the Emigration Question* (Eismann)

In-Zikh, 10:**5,** 13:251

Ioannina (Greece), 10:**5–6**

Ionesco, Eugène, 10:**6–7**

Ioppe (Israel, Ancient). *See* Jaffa (Israel)

Iosifescu, Silvian, 10:7

I.O.U. *See* Shetar

Iowa (U.S.), 10:**7–8,** *8, 8t*

IPF. *See* Israel Policy Forum

Ippolito, Joseph. *See* Fano, Joseph da

Ipswich (England), 10:9

Iqbal, Muhammad, 10:94

Iquitos (Peru), 10:9, 15:794–795

"Ira." *See* Slutskaya, Irina

Iran, 10:**9–14,** *10, 10t, 11t*
  Abbasids and, 1:233
  American Embassy hostages, 15:571
  antisemitism, Hamadan, 8:292–293
  Aramaic, 2:343
  immigration to Israel (state), 10:340
  Iran-Iraq war, 2:313
  Islamic Revolution, 15:571
  Israel, relationship with, 15:571
  Judeo-Iranian dialect, 11:548, 550
  Judeo-Tat language, 11:560–561
  Kashan, 11:820
  Kerman, 12:86–87
  Kermanshah, 12:87
  Kurdistan, 12:389, 391–392
  Lar, 12:492
  Meshed, 14:76–77
  Nehavand, 15:60
  Omar, Covenant of, 15:418
  ORT, 15:489–490
  Pahlavi, Mohammad Reza Shah, 15:569–570
  Pahlavi, Reza Shah, 15:570–571

Iran, *continued*

See also Persia; *specific cities*

Iran stele, 3:657

Iraq, 2:327, 10:**14–24,** 16*t*, 12:187

Abadan (Iran), 1:224

American Joint Distribution Committee, 2:62

Amsterdam immigrants, 2:117

antisemitism, 3:206, 5:681, 10:18–19, 20–21

Arabic literature written by Jews of, 15:473

Arab world (1945-2006), 2:301

Aramaic, 2:343

Birs Nimrud, 4:94

Communism, 10:19

communities of Jews, Israel (state), 10:295–296

demography, 10:15–16, 16*t*

Diaspora, 10:15

education and literature, 10:16–17

emmigration from, 10:20

foreign policy and relations with Israel, 10:21–22

Six-Day War, 10:230–232

Gulf War (1991), 8:130–135

Iran-Iraq war, 2:313

Islamic period, 10:14–15

Jews in, 1:224

Khanaqin, 12:**101**

Kurdistan, 12:389–390

literature

Shashu, Salim, 18:420

Shaul, Anwar, 18:421

Someck, Ronny, 19:6

Mandate period, 10:17–18

Middle Ages

exilarchs, 5:427, 466–467, 469, 472

gaons, 5:427, 429

modern

Jewish community leaders, 5:426

literature, 5:438

rabbis, 5:417

Mongolian period, 10:15

music, 10:22–24

Niebuhr, Carston, travels of, 15:259

Nissim, Abraham Ḥayyim, 15:278

Nuzi, 15:355

occupation and British Mandate period, 10:17–18

Ottoman period, 10:15–16, 15:525

Palestine (Ottoman), 10:295–296

politics, 16:346

ṣarrāf, 18:61

Sassoon, Sir Ezekiel, 18:71

Zionism, 10:19

See also Babylonia; Mesopotamia; *specific cities*

Irāqī, Eleazar ben Aaron ha-Kohen, 4:353, 10:**24**

Irāqī, Shalom ha-Kohen, 10:**24**

Irāqī, Shalom Joseph, 10:**24**

Irbil (Iraq), 10:**24–25**

Ir Dammesek Eliezer (Eliezer), 6:327

Ir David (Lara), 12:492

Ireland, 10:25, **25–27**

Bible translated into Gaelic, 3:636

Briscoe, Robert, 4:185

Dublin, 6:32–33

foreign policy and relations with Israel, 10:27

industrialists, 11:68

museums, 14:626

political participation, 16:343

rabbis, chief, 11:73

sheḥitah protection, 18:435

Irgun. *See* Irgun Ẓeva'i Le'ummi

Irgun Sanitari Ivri. *See* OZE (Russian Jewish Health Organization)

Irgun Vitkin, 8:753

Irgun Ẓeva'i Le'ummi, 10:**27–28,** 208, 210, 211, 15:402, 17:264–265

Begin, Menaḥem, 3:261

Ben-Gurion, David, 3:346

Beriḥah, 3:435

Briscoe, Robert, 4:185

operations of, 10:207, 17:129

during World War II, 10:206

Ir ha-Gefanim. *See* Avignon (France)

Ir ha-Niddaḥat, 10:**28–29**

Irira, Abraham. *See* Herrera, Abraham Kohen de

Irira, Alonzo Nunez de. *See* Herrera, Abraham Kohen de

Irish Free State. *See* Ireland

Irkutsk (Russia), 10:**29**

Ir Lavan. *See* Belgorod-Dnestrovski (Ukraine)

Ir Miklat (Ben-Ner), 3:368

Irmiyā ben Ḥilfiyā, 14:539

Ir-Nahash (Judah), 10:**29**

Iron (ancient Israel), 10:**29**

Iron and Iron Age, 14:125–126, 127–128

archaeology, 2:125, 387–388, 12:420–421

architecture, 2:399

Early Iron Age, 14:89

Finkelstein, Israel, 7:33–34

Late Iron Age, 14:89–92

Tell Arad, 2:329–330

The Iron Council (Miéville), 18:200

Iron Guard, 4:781, 10:**29–30,** 18:590

Ironic Tales. See Ironishe Mayselekh

Ironishe Mayselekh (Baal-Makhshoves), 3:8

Irrigation, Ereẓ Israel, 1:481–482

Irsa (Hungary). *See* Alberti-Irsa (Hungary)

IRSO. *See* Jewish successor organizations

Ir u-Melo'ah (Agnon), 1:467

Irving, Amy, 4:115, 10:**30**

Irving, David, 6:425, 9:494–495, 10:**30–32,** 15:245

antisemitism, 2:243

Browning, Christopher R., 4:217

Irving, Jules, 3:742, 10:**30**

Irving *v.* Lipstadt, 10:**30–32**

Ir Yamim Rabbim (Hareven), 8:353

Ir Yizre'el. *See* Afulah (Israel)

Isaac (7th c.), 10:**35**

Isaac (8th c.), 10:**35**

Isaac (biblical figure), 10:**32–35**

Abimelech and, 1:257, 258

Abraham, 1:282

Abraham's bosom, 1:316

Akedah, 1:555–560

ancient portrayals, 6:52–53

Esau, 6:487

Jacob and, 11:18

as Patriarch, 15:689–691

sacrifice of, vol. 8: color insert

Sarah and, 18:47

Isaac (c.12th-13th c.), 10:**35–36**

Isaac (mid-2nd c.), 10:**35**

Isaac, Aaron, 10:**36**

Isaac, Beer Loeb, 11:765

Isaac, Jules Marx, 10:**36,** 11:380

Isaac, Sacrifice of. *See* Akedah

Isaac, Saul, 16:342

Isaac, Testament of, 10:**36**

Isaac Arondi of Huesca, 4:54

Isaac Baer Ashers. *See* Issachar Baer ben Solomon Zalman

Isaac bar Dorbelo, 10:**37**

Isaac bar Israel ibn al-Shuwayk, 10:**37**

Isaac bar Joseph, 10:**37**

Isaac bar Rav Judah, 10:**37**

Isaac ben Abba Mari of Marseilles, 4:103, 10:**37–38,** 11:559, 12:405

Isaac ben Abraham, 10:**38**

Isaac ben Abraham di Molina, 10:**38**

Isaac ben Abraham ha-Gorni, 6:6, 10:**38–39**

Isaac ben Abraham of Narbonne, 10:**39**

Isaac ben Abraham of Posen, 10:**39**

Isaac ben Abraham Troki. *See* Troki, Isaac ben Abraham

Isaac ben Asher ha-Levi, 10:**39–40**

Isaac ben Avdimi, 10:**40**

Isaac ben Bezalel of Vladimir, 10:**40**

Isaac ben Eleazar, 10:**40–41**

Isaac ben Eliakim of Posen, 10:**41**

Isaac ben Eliezer, 10:**41**

Isaac ben Ezekiel of Russia. *See* Isaac of Chernigov

Isaac ben Ḥayyim ben Abraham, 10:**41**

Isaac ben Ḥayyim Moses. *See* Bardach, Israel

Isaac ben Israel Ibn Shuwaykh. *See* Isaac bar Israel ibn al-Shuwayk

Isaac ben Jacob ha-Kohen, 10:**41–42**, 14:463

Isaac ben Jacob ha-Lavan of Prague, 10:**42**

Isaac ben Jacob Min ha-Leviyyim, 10:**42**

Isaac Benjamin Wolf ben Eliezer Lipman, 10:**42–43**

Isaac ben Joseph ibn Pollegar. *See* Pollegar, Isaac ben Joseph ibn

Isaac ben Joseph Israeli. *See* Israeli, Isaac ben Joseph

Isaac ben Joseph of Corbeil, 10:**43**

Isaac ben Judah, 10:**43**

Isaac ben Judah ha-Kohen. *See* Rappaport, Isaac ben Judah ha-Kohen

Isaac ben Judah ha-Seniri, 10:**43–44**

Isaac ben Judah of Mainz, 10:**44**

Isaac ben Meir, 10:**44**

Isaac ben Meir Dueren. *See* Dueren, Isaac ben Meir

Isaac ben Meir of Dueren. *See* Dueren, Isaac ben Meir

Isaac ben Melchizedek of Siponto, 10:**44**

Isaac ben Menahem the Great, 10:**44–45**

Isaac ben Merwan ha-Levi, 10:**45**

Isaac ben Mordecai, 10:**45**

Isaac ben Mordecai Gershon Treves. *See* Gershon, Isaac

Isaac ben Moses ha-Levi. *See* Duran, Profiat

Isaac ben Moses of Beja, 4:270

Isaac ben Moses of Vienna, 2:87, 10:**45–46**, 12:627, 18:603

Isaac ben Noah Kohen Shapira, 10:**46**

Isaac ben Perez of Northampton, 15:301

Isaac ben Samson ha-Kohen, 10:**46**
Yiddish translations of Bible, 3:611

Isaac ben Samuel ha-Levi, 10:**46–47**

Isaac ben Samuel of Acre, 10:**47–48**

Isaac ben Samuel of Dampierre, 10:**48**
Judah ben Isaac (Sir Leon of Paris), 11:487

Isaac ben Sheshet Perfet, 1:515, 6:58, 10:**49**

Isaac ben Solomon, 10:**49–50**

Isaac ben Todros, 10:**50**

Isaac ben Todros of Barcelona, 10:**50**

Isaac ben Yakar, 10:**50–51**

Isaac da Fonseca Aboab. *See* Aboab da Fonseca, Isaac

Isaac from Ourville, 10:**52**

Isaac Hezekiah ben Samuel Lampronti. *See* Lampronti, Isaac Hezekiah ben Samuel

Isaac Ḥilo of Larissa, 8:746

Isaac ibn Ezra. *See* Ibn Ezra, Isaac

Isaac Judaeus. *See* Israeli, Isaac ben Solomon

Isaac Katznelson Ghetto Fighter's Museum, 2:411

Isaacks, Jacob. *See* Isaacs, Jacob (c.1730-1798)

Isaac Laquedem. *See* Wandering Jew

Isaac Luria of Safed, 6:599

Isaac Nappaḥa, 10:**52–53**

Isaac of Bohemia. *See* Isaac ben Jacob ha-Lavan of Prague

Isaac of Chernigov, 10:**53**

Isaac of Corbeil, 15:769

Isaac of Evreux, 10:**53**

Isaac of Norwich, 11:577

Isaac of Regensburg. *See* Isaac ben Jacob ha-Lavan of Prague

Isaac of Southwark, 10:**53**

Isaac Or Zaru'a. *See* Isaac ben Moses of Vienna

Isaac Or Zaru'a. *See* Isaac ben Moses of Vienna

Isaacs, Abraham, 15:196

Isaacs, Abram Samuel, 2:58, 10:**53–54**

Isaacs, Barnett. *See* Barnato, Barney

Isaacs, Edith Juliet, 10:**54**

Isaacs, Edith Juliet Rich. *See* Isaacs, Edith Juliet

Isaacs, Eva Violet (Marchioness of Reading), 17:134

Isaacs, Gerald Rufus (2nd Marquess of Reading), 17:134

Isaacs, Henry, 15:243

Isaacs, Isaac Alfred, 10:**54–55**, 12:548, 16:340

Isaacs, Isaiah, 10:**55**

Isaacs, Jacob (1896–1973), 10:**55**

Isaacs, Jacob (c.1730-1798), 10:**55**

Isaacs, Jeremy. *See* Isaacs, Sir Jeremy

Isaacs, Jorge, 10:**55–56**

Isaacs, Joseph, 10:**56**

Isaacs, Lewis Montefiore, 10:54

Isaacs, Myer Samuel, 3:173, 10:53, 11:306, 15:200

Isaacs, Nathan, 10:**56**

Isaacs, Nathaniel, 10:**56**, 16:349

Isaacs, Rufus Daniel (1st Marquess of Reading), 16:342, 17:133–134

Isaacs, Sampson, 15:198

Isaacs, Samuel Myer, 4:19, 10:53, 11:306, 15:198–199, 200

Isaacs, Sir Jeremy, 10:**55**

Isaacs, Solomon J., 15:198

Isaacs, Stanley Myer, 10:54, 15:214

Isaacs, Susan, 6:161, 10:**56**

Isaac Sagi Nahor. *See* Isaac the Blind

Isaacs family, 10:**53–54**

Isaacsohn, Siegfried, 10:**56–57**

Isaacson, Jose, 10:**57**

Isaac Tauroci. *See* Isaac ben Todros

Isaac Tauroci ben Todros. *See* Isaac ben Todros

Isaac the Blind, 1:300, 2:563, 10:**51–52**, 11:603–604

Isaac the Great. *See* Isaac ben Abraham of Posen

Isabella (Queen of Spain). *See* Ferdinand and Isabella of Spain

Isabella of Castile. *See* Ferdinand and Isabella of Spain

Isaghoyi is to Oikoyeniakon Dhikyeon ton en Elldi Israiliton (Moissis). *See Introductory Study of the Civil Laws of the Jewish Family in Greece* (Moissis)

Isaiah (biblical figure)
eschatology in, 6:491–492
Judah, king of, 6:491–492
Kings, Book of, 12:173–174
prophecies, 5:424

Isaiah, Ascension of. See Ascension of Isaiah

Isaiah, Book of, 10:**57–75**
Aggadah, 10:73
apocalypse, 6:494
arts, 10:74–75
authorship, 10:57–58
The Book of Pronouncements, 10:64–66
Christianity, 10:73
Deutero-Isaiah, 6:493, 10:68–73
eschatology in, 6:493
First Isaiah
chapters 1-12, 10:60–64
chapters 13-33, 10:64–67
chapters 34-35, 10:68

Isaiah, Book of, *continued*
  chapters 36-39, 10:67–68
  introduction to, 10:57–60
  Isaiah's rebuke, 18:428–429
  Isaiah-Trito, 6:494
  Islam, 10:73–74
  themes, 10:59
  Trito-Isaiah, 6:494
  Zion vision in, 10:61–62
Isaiah, Martyrdom of. See Martyrdom of Isaiah
Isaiah, Second. *See* Isaiah, Book of, Deutero-Isaiah
Isaiah ben Abraham, 10:**76–77**
Isaiah ben Elijah di Trani, 10:**77**
Isaiah ben Elijah di Trani the Younger. *See* Isaiah ben Elijah di Trani
Isaiah ben Israel Hezekiah, 3:208
Isaiah ben Mali di Trani, 4:113, 6:62, 10:**77**
Isaiah ben Mali di Trani the Elder. *See* Isaiah ben Mali di Trani
Isaiah ben Uzziah ha-Kohen, 10:**77–78**
Isaiah Ḥasid from Zbarazh, 10:**78**, 18:355
Isaiah Menahem ben Isaac, 10:**78**
Isaiah's Vision of Eternal Peace, tryptych (Ardon), 2:421
Isaiah Trani the Elder. *See* Isaiah ben Mali di Trani
Isak, Aron. *See* Isaac, Aaron
Isbakh, Alexander Abramovich, 10:**78**
Iscah, 18:46
Iscandari, Abba, 6:233, 15:523
Iscandari, Abraham, 15:523
Iscandari, Abraham ben Eleazar, 10:79
Iscandari family, 10:**78–79**
Isenstein, Kurt Harald, 10:**79**
Iser, Josif, 10:**79**
Isfahan (Iran), 2:253, 3:15, 10:**79–80**, 15:789
Isfahanians. *See* Isunians
Ish, Ishah ve-Ish (Liebrecht), 12:811
Ishak. *See* Isaac (c.12th-13th c.)
Ishbaal, David and, 5:447
Ishbibenob, 1:260
Ishbili, Yom Tov ben Abraham. *See* Yom Tov ben Abraham Ishbili
Ish-Bosheth, 8:744, 10:**80–81**, 15:606, 17:142–143
Ishei Yisrael (Modzhitz), 14:413
Ish Emunim (Elyashar), 6:371, 372
Ish Ger. *See* Graziano, Abraham Joseph Solomon ben Mordecai
Ish ha-Halakhah (Soloveitchik). *See* *Halakhic Man* (Soloveitchik)

Ish ha-Halakhah ve-ha-Ma'aseh (Silver), 18:585
Ish ha-Kazav. *See* Lies, Man of
Ish-Horowitz, Samuel Joseph, 8:417
Ish-Kishor, Ephraim, 10:**81**
Ishmael (son of Abraham), 1:282, 286, 10:**81–82**
Ishmael (son of Nethaniah son of Elishama), 10:**82**
Ishmael ben Abraham Isaac ha-Kohen, 10:**82–83**, 14:441
Ishmael ben Elisha, 10:**83–84**
  Bible text treated as binding authority by, 3:585
  biblical exegesis and study, 3:641
  Josiah and, 11:459
  Levi Ben Gershom, 12:698
Ishmael ben Johanan ben Beroka, 10:**84**
Ishmael ben Phabi II. *See* Ishmael ben Phiabi II
Ishmael ben Phiabi II, 2:129, 10:**84**
Ishmael ben Yose ben Ḥalafta, 6:333, 10:**84–85**
Ishmaelites, 10:**85–86**
Ishmael of Barcelona. *See* Izmel of Barcelona
Ishmael of 'Ukbara, 10:**86**, 11:788
Ishon, Moshe, 8:497
Ishrū Maqālāt (Mukammis), 14:608
Ish-Shalom. *See* Friedmann, Meir
Ish Shalom, Meir. *See* Friedmann, Meir
Ishto ha-Senu'ah (Burla), 4:295
Ish Vilna be-Kherson. *See* Behak, Judah
Ish Yehudi. *See* Rabinovich, Yehudah Leib
Isidor, Lazare, 10:**86**
Isidore of Seville, 4:721, 8:511, 10:**86–87**
Isidoros. *See* Lampon and Isidoros
Isidorus Hispalensis. *See* Isidore of Seville
Isis, 10:**87**
Iska, 15:671
Iskah. *See* Shetar
Iskandari, Eliezer, 15:542
Iskat ha-Shokold (Gouri), 8:20
Iskenderun (Turkey), 10:**87**
Iskorasten. *See* Korosten (Ukraine)
Iskorost (Ukraine). *See* Korosten (Ukraine)
Iskowitch, Isidor. *See* Cantor, Eddie
Iskowitz, Gershon, 10:**87**
Islam, 10:**87–98**
  Abdallah ibn Salāam, 1:241

Adam, 1:374–375
Ahl al-Kitāab, 1:546
Almohads, 1:681
Almoravids, 1:684
Amen, 2:38
amenities, 2:40
American Jewish Committee, 2:55
American Joint Distribution Committee, 2:64
Amran, 2:106
Amsterdam, 2:119
antisemitism
  dhimma, dhimmi, 5:631–632
  in early Islamic period, 2:210
apologetics, 2:265
apostasy, 2:270, 275
archaeology, 2:391–392
  Abbasids, 1:233–234
  Aghlabids, 1:464–465
  Iraq, 10:14–15
  Jews during, 1:234
  pre-Islamic, 10:88
Aristotelianism in, 3:644, 648
art, 2:495
  Jerusalem in, 11:228
  scholars of, 13:698
badges, Jewish, 3:45
Balaam, 3:80
banking, 1:211–212, 3:111–112
brokers, 4:203
Brunschvig, Robert, 4:225
Cain, 4:341
caliph, 4:364
Canaan (son of Ham), 4:390–391
characteristics of, 10:91–93
Christianity and, 3:668
community organization and structures, 5:103–105, 118t
conversion to, 11:223
Daniel in, 5:418
David in, 5:454–455, 18:760
democracy, 2:326
discrimination, 5:631–632
divorce, 5:720
Doenmeh, 5:730–733
economic history, 6:104–108
Elijah, 6:335–336
Elisha, 6:351
emancipation, 6:385
Enoch, 6:442
Eve in, 6:9
Even Shetiyyah in, 6:574–575
exilarchs and, 6:604–605
expansion of, 10:91
Ezekiel in, 6:645

Ezra in, 6:653
fiqh, 7:41–42
forced conversions, 11:58
Ḥanīf, 8:321
historians, 12:764
holy places in Israel, 9:501, *502*
influence on Jewish philosophy,
  16:77, 78–79, 78–80, 84, 87–88
Isaac in, 10:34
Isaiah, Book of, 10:73–74
Ishmael (son of Abraham), 10:82
Israel (state)
  religious courts, 10:419–422,
    420
  religious life and
    communities, 10:646–650
Jacob in, 11:22
Jeremiah in, 11:133–134
Jerusalem and, 11:154, 159–160,
  222–224
Jethro in, 11:252
Jewish access to holy sites, 11:312–
  313
Jewish culture under, 11:538–543
Jewish languages and, 11:302
Jewish quarters in Muslim
  communities, 1:436, 11:311–313
Jewish relations, 9:208–209
  Abd al-Ḥaqq al-Islāmī, 1:240
  Morocco, 14:504, 505
jihād, 11:336–337
Jihad, 15:597
Job in, 11:357
Jonah, Book of, 11:390
Joseph in, 11:412
Joshua and, 11:443
Josippon, 11:462
Judaism and, 10:96–98, 11:519,
  538–542
Kāam, 11:729–731
kehalim, 2:40
Korah, 12:299
Koran, 12:301–304
Marrano diaspora, 13:560
messianism and appearance of,
  4:326
Middle Ages
  disputations and polemics,
    5:692
  domestic violence, 5:740
Miriam, 14:312
Moses, 14:538–539, 16:29
music Maqām, 13:507
naming of, 10:87–88
Nebuchadnezzar, 15:50–51
Nimrod in, 15:269–270

as Noachide religion, 15:284
Noah in, 15:288–289
Omar, Covenant of, 15:416–419
Omar ibn al-Khaṭṭāb, 15:416, 419
Orientalists and Orientalism,
  15:471
Oriental literature, 15:471–474
Palermo, 15:580
Palestine (Mandate) governance
  and, 10:406–407, 408, 646
Palestine (Ottoman) governance
  and, 10:404, 646
Pharaoh in, 16:29–30
philosophy
  acceptance regardless of
    source, 16:69
  Averroes, 2:723–726
  Avicenna, 2:727–729
"The Pillars of Islam," 10:88–91
polemic against Judaism and
  Christianity, 3:669, 10:95–96
pre-Islamic period, 10:88
Queen of Sheba, 16:765
racism, 2:119
Samaritans, 17:738
Samuel, 17:756
Saragossa (Spain), 18:41
Saul, 18:81
scholars of, Perlmann, Moshe,
  15:779
Seth, 18:319
Seville (Spain), 18:326
Shi'a, rulers, 6:723–724
Solomon, 18:760–761
Terah, 19:646
Torah and, 11:263
Umayyad dynasty, 20:245–247
view of Isaiah, Book of, 10:73–74
See also Conversion to Islam;
  Koran; Ottoman empire
Islamic law, 10:97
  development of, 10:92–93
  dhimma, dhimmi, 5:631–632
  fiqh, 7:41–42
  Jewish law and, 11:**262–270**
  Kharaj and Jizya, 12:101–104
  sources, 11:267
  See also Fiqh
Islamic literature
  Aaron, 1:211
  Abraham, 1:286
  Adam, 1:374–375
  aggadah, 1:463
  Balaam, 3:80
  Benjamin, tribe of, 3:356
  biblical influence, 3:672

Elijah, 6:335–336
Elisha, 6:351
Enoch, 6:442
eschatology, 6:502–503
Goliath, 7:738–739
Hadith, 8:191–192
Haman, 8:294–295
Ḥanīf, 8:321
hell, 6:503
Hinnom, valley of, 6:503
Israelite, 10:754
judgment day, 6:502–503
Potiphar, 16:419–420
resurrection, 6:502–503
retribution, 6:502
Islamic Republic of Iran (IRI). *See*
  Iran
Islamic Resistance Movement. *See*
  Hamas
Islamic States. *See* Muslim States
Isle-sur-la-Sorgue, L' (France), 10:**98**
Isma'il. *See* Ishmael (son of Abraham)
Ismail (Alawid sharif), 1:580, 14:497–
  498
Ismail (Romania). *See* Izmail
  (Romania)
Ismā'īl al-'Ukbarī. *See* Ishmael of
  'Ukbara
Ismail ibn Nagrel'a. *See* Samuel ha-
  Nagid
Ismā'īliyya movement, 4:170
Isnimit (Turkey). *See* Izmit (Turkey)
Isolationist Impulse (Adler), 1:408
Isou, Isidore, 10:**98**
Ispoved. See Confession
Israel (ancient). *See* Israel (land of)
Israel (Jewish people), 10:99–100,
  11:253
Israel (land of), 10:**99, 100–179,** *157,*
  163, 166, 169
  antisemitism, 2:206–207
  Arab period, 10:*157,* 157–161
  archaeology
    agricultural land-management
      methods and implements
      in, 1:471–486
    architecture, 2:401–402
    Baal-Berith, 3:5–6
    cities, 4:739, 741
    El-Amarna letters, 6:285
    fortresses, 11:698
    Hyksos, 9:649
    later idealization, 3:654
    origins of, 2:379–380
    ostraca, use of, 15:508
    "spice route" and, 9:753
  boundaries, 10:*101,* 101–108, *102,*
    103, 104, 105

Israel (land of), *continued*
    Byzantine period, 10:156
    climate, 10:131–136
        cloudiness, 10:132
        humidity, 10:134–135
        precipitation, 10:132–133
        research, 10:135–136
        temperature, 10:133–134
        UV radiation, 10:132
        winds, 10:135
    Crusader period, 5:312, 10:161–
        165, *163*
    cultural and social life
        academies in, 1:347–351, *350*
        age and the aged, 1:447
        amulets, 2:121
        archives, 2:405
        Armenian community, 2:474
        census, 4:541–542
        dance, 5:409
        education, 6:163–169
        elders, 6:295
        ethnography, 10:107
        European influence, 6:554
        Freemasons, 7:228, 229–230
        Galilean Aramaic, 2:349
        headdresses, 5:307–309
        hospitality and, 9:561
        humor, 9:597
        nomadism, 15:294–295
        sculpture, 18:222, 223
        social structure, 9:182–186
        travelers and travels to,
            20:116–121
    economic affairs
        coins and currency, 5:47–48,
            52
        history, 6:95–102
        "spice route" and, 9:753
    flora and fauna, 1:347, 7:18, 89,
        10:140–143, 17:5
        agriculture, 1:486–490, 12:762
        cattle, 6:93
    foreign policy and affairs
        Amalekites and, 2:28–30
        amphictyonic hypothesis,
            3:658–659
        capitulations, 4:453–454
        illegal immigration, 9:281
        Judah (Kingdom) and,
            11:111–112, 141
        Moab (Jordan), 14:401–402
        Philistines and, 16:53–55
        Phoenicia and, 16:121–122
        Sheluḥei Ereẓ Israel, 18:446–
            452
    geography, 18:191
        illustrated, 11:753
        names, 10:100–101
    geology, 10:136–140, 16:144
        stratigraphic evolution,
            10:136–139
        structural pattern, 10:139–140
    Hellenistic-Roman period, 9:191–
        200
        crucifixion, 5:309
        Diaspora, 5:643
        First Roman War, 9:199–200
        Hasmonean revolt, 9:193–194
        Hasmonean rule, 9:194–196
        Herod's rule, 9:197–198
        independent Judea, 9:194
        procurators, 9:198–199
        Ptolemaic period, 9:191–193
        Selucid Empire, 9:193
    laws and legal systems, 12:557,
        728, 14:341, 354
        capitulations, 4:453–454
        census, 4:541–542
        dietary laws, 5:656
        elders, 6:295
        hospitality and, 9:561
        illegal immigration, 9:281
        labor in, 12:411
    Mamluk period, 10:165–168, *166*
    maps of
        Abraham Bar Jacob (17th c.),
            vol. 13: color insert
        Adrichom, Christian van
            (16th c.), vol. 13: color
            insert
        anonymous (20th c.), vol. 13:
            color insert
        Blau, Willem Janszoon (16th
            c.), vol. 13: color insert
        Bunting, Heinrich (16th c.),
            vol. 13: color insert
        Crusader's map (11th c.), vol.
            13: color insert
        Hogenberg, Franz (16th c.),
            vol. 13: color insert
        Jode, Gerard de (16th c.),
            vol. 13: color insert
        ornamental plaque (20th c.),
            vol. 13: color insert
        Plancius, Petrus (16th c.),
            vol. 13: color insert
    nineteenth century to WW I,
        1:505, 506–508, *507t*, 10:175–
        179
    Ottoman period, 10:168–172, *169*
    Persian period, 10:156
    physiography, 10:108–131
        coastal plains, 10:109–111
        Galilee mountains, 10:119–
            121
        introduction, 10:108–109
        Rift Valley, 10:121–126
        Transjordan, 10:126–131
        valley sequence, 10:118
        Western mountain zone,
            10:111–118
    political leaders
        Abulafia, Isaac, 1:340
        Ahab, 1:522–524
        Ahaziah, 1:539
        Boule, 4:105–106
        Solomon, 18:755–759, *18:756*
    political theories, parties and
        organizations
        Agudat Israel, 6:505–508
        Esra settlement organization,
            6:509
        Mizrachi, 14:390
    post-Second Temple until Arab
        conquest, 10:143–156
        anarchy, revolts and stability,
            10:147–151, 153–155
        Jerusalem Talmud, 10:155–
            156
        leadership, 10:144–147, 151–
            153, 155–156
        political history, 10:144–145,
            154
        post-Roman rule, 10:155–156
        resettlement and economic
            recovery, 10:147
        wars, 10:143–144, 147
    religious life and scholarship
        amulets, 2:121
        Anath, 2:131
        birth of, 6:622
        Day of Atonement in, 5:488,
            489
        dietary laws, 5:656
        Franciscans, 7:173–174
        Geonim, 7:384–385, *385t*, *386*
        Jeshurun, 11:**243**
        J (YHWH) source of Torah
            and, 15:736–737
        Kadesh-Barnea, 11:698–699
        Levi Ben Gershom view,
            12:700–701
        oaths, 15:359–360
        pilgrimages to, 16:154–156
        Sephardim, 18:303
        Torah, reading of, 20:48t–49t
    settlement, 9:239, 247, 249–250
    seventeenth and eighteenth
        centuries, 10:173–175
    See also Palestine (Ottoman)

Israel (Mandate). *See* Mandate for Palestine

Israel (name), 10:**98–99**

Israel (Pedersen), 15:711–712

Israel (patriarch). *See* Jacob

Israel (poet), 2:17

Israel (State), 9:279*t*–280*t*, 281–282, 10:**179–740,** 715*t*

  agriculture

    Arab, 10:713

    citrus culture, 4:737–738, 6:750

    climate, 2:557

    dew, 5:630

    exports, 6:562, 563–564, 565–566

    Farmers' Federation of Israel, 6:718

    flowers, 7:89–91

    land reclamation projects, Ḥuleh Valley, 9:582–583, *583*

    Mandate period, 10:506–511

    olive cultivation in, 15:407

    pigs, 16:151

    rain, 17:72–73

  aliyah and absorption, 1:443, 661, 5:685, 10:329–373, 334*t*, 342*t*, 344*t*, 349*t*, 358*t*, 526, 658, 668

    1880–1948, 10:333–339, 334*t*

    1948-1967, 10:339–345, 339–354, 341*t*, 355–357, 360–361

    1967-1982, 10:345–350

    1982-1992, 10:344*t*, 345–350, 345*t*, 347*t*, 349*t*, 350–353, 351*t*, 352–353, 361–365

    1993-2002, 10:345*t*, 347*t*, 351*t*, 353–354

    absorption methods, 10:340–345

    Afghan migrations, 1:433

    Asia, 10:341*t*

    difficulties, 10:330

    displaced persons, 6:186, 9:281

    education and, 10:343, 344, 526, 657

    Ethopia, 10:352*t*

    health services, 10:675

    housing, 2:76–77, 10:354–355, 355, 357–359, 358*t*, 365–366

    ingathering of exiles, 10:339–340

    land ownership, 10:371–372, 527

    land reclamation, 10:372–373

Landsmannschaften, 12:477–478

Law of Return, 12:541–545

Libyan immigration, 12:792

motives for aliyah, 10:329–330

regional and settlement planning, 10:370–371

rural development, 10:366–370

Russia, 17:558, 569–571, 570*t*, 571*t*, 572, 573

Second Temple period to Ḥibbat Zion, 10:330–333

urbanization, 10:366–370

USSR, 10:345–349, 349*t*

Yemenite immigration, 21:307

  antisemitism

    caricatures, 4:479

    Waldheim Affair, 20:602–604

  Arab population, 10:485–486, 521–522, 679, 712–715, 712–739, 712*t*, 714, 719, 728

    1948–1967, 10:712–715

    1970s, 10:719–721

    1980s - mid-1990s, 10:721–728

    1995 - 2005, 10:728–733

    in administered territories, 10:239, 241–242

    Arab refugees, 10:256, 267–271

    arts and popular culture, 10:733–734

    Bedouin, 10:737–739

    demography, 10:485–486, 521–522

    farming and urbanization, 10:485–486

    Gaza Strip, 1948–67, 10:303, 717

    health services, 10:679

    Jordanian Rule, 1948–67, 10:715–717

    Knesset representation, 10:424

    literature, 10:734–737

    Military Administration and, 10:436–437

    post-Six-Day War, 10:231, 232, 717–719

    property abandoned by, 10:270

    refugees, 10:256, 267–271, 278

    Six-Day War and, 10:231, 232

    standard of living, 10:224–225

voting by, 10:250–251

  archaeology

    Israel Antiquities Authority, 2:378–379

    Israel Exploration Society, 10:750

    synagogue architecture, 19:381–382

  cultural and social life, 10:682–683, 682–710

    age and the aged, 1:448–449

    Akedah, 1:558–559

    alcohol consumption, 6:28

    American Joint Distribution Committee, 2:63

    architecture, 10:701–704, 702–704, 17:144–145

    archives, 2:414–417

    art, 2:509–513, 10:695–701, 12:532, 678

    Ashkenaz tensions with other edot, 10:298–299, 300

    assimilation, 2:613

    bar mitzvah, 3:166

    blindness in, 3:755

    calligraphy, Hebrew, 4:369–371

    "Canaanites," 4:393

    choral singing, 4:662

    commemorative medals and coins, 13:716

    cookbooks, 5:202

    cooperatives, 5:207–210

    dance, 3:214–215, 254, 5:412–413, 12:695

    displaced persons, 6:186, 9:281

    edot, 10:294–298

    encyclopedias, 6:400–402

    festivals and holidays, 10:626–627

    film industry, 10:709–710

    folk dances, 10:693–695

    Freemasons, 7:229

    galleries and museums, 10:697–698, 704, 757–758

    gender equality, myth of, 6:754

    Habimah, 8:179–180

    health services, 10:674–679

    Hebrew language, 10:683–684

    humor and, 9:597–598

    Independence Day, 17:566

    influence on self-hate, 18:264–265

    intercommunal problems, 10:298–300

    Jewish identity and, 11:297–298

Israel (State), *continued*

Jewish National Fund and, 11:308–309

journalism and press, 10:704–707

Karaites and Karitism, 11:794–795

kibbutz movement, 1:378, 5:209–210

libraries, 10:685–686, 12:783, 784–785, 786–787, 788

ma'barah, 13:315

Maccabiah, 13:320

Maccabi World Union, 13:321

medical research, 10:678–679

Moshavim, 5:209–210

museums, 14:631

music, 5:433, 10:688–693, 749, 14:639–640, 695–697

orphans and orphanages, 15:485–486

parody, Hebrew, 15:662

philanthropy, 16:42–43, 45–46

philosophy, 16:99–103

photographs, 16:130

Project Renewal, 16:544–547

public transportation, 6:219

refugees, 17:186

revisionism, influence of, 17:262–267

revival of Hebrew language, 10:291

sculpture, 18:222

social welfare, 10:679–682

songs, 10:691–693

Soviet immigrant influence, 14:697

sports, 19:129–133

stamps, 19:161

television and radio, 10:707–709

theater, 8:179–180, 719–723, 10:686–688, 21:312–313

Yom ha-Zikkaron, 21:382

defense forces, 4:464–479

espionage and sabotage activities, 4:346

General Security Service (Shabak), 15:771

Haganah, 10:466–467

IDF formation and focus, 10:467–474

Naḥal, 14:735

space program, 10:478

terrorist attacks against, 12:584–586

war against terrorism, 10:474–479

demography, 5:554, 560, 562

birth rates, 10:525–526

crime rates after Six Day War, 5:297–298

Druze population, standard of living, 10:224–225

emigration, 10:524

fertility patterns, 10:286–288

growth and demographic change, 10:524–526

Habitation in Israel and the Administered Territories, 10:306–329t

health statistics, 10:675

household statistics, 10:293–294

human resources, 10:293–298

immigration, 10:523t

monogamy, 10:288

mortality, 10:288

student population, 10:539

white-collar worker excess, 10:349–350

economic affairs, 10:479–593

1960-1966, 10:225, 227–228

1985 stabilization policy, 10:569–573

advertising, 1:428–429

air travel, 6:282–283

aliyah and absorption, 10:343, 348, 522–526, 522t, 523t

Arabs: demographic growth and economic expansion, 10:495t, 521–522

Arabs' demographic growth and economic expansion, 10:493–496

artisans, 5:270, 271

as associate member of European Economic Community, 10:262–263

balance of payments, 10:514–516, 537t, 541–543, 580–581

banking system, 10:586–589, 586–592, 590–591

bank notes, 5:55

Bank of Israel, 5:54, 10:551–557, 581–586

boycott, Arab, 4:111–113

breakthrough, comparative trends and links, 1932-1939, 10:500–503, 502t

business ethics, 4:315

capital markets, 10:514–516, 591–592

centralization of, 10:429

chemical industry, 4:591–592

coins and currency, 5:54–55

construction, 18:752–753

crisis of 1980s, 10:241, 450

crisis of early twenty-first century, 10:463

currency and exchange rate, 10:546–549

defense expenditures, 10:561–562

department stores and, 5:588

diamond trade and industry, 5:636

early 1970s, 10:236

economic development, 6:137–138, 12:704

emergence of Jewish economy, 1920-31, 10:487–493, 489t, 490t, 491t, 492t

employment trends, 10:293, 533, 535, 539, 545, 557–558, 561, 561t, 576–577, 615–617, 618t

European Economic Community, 6:561–566

expansion, 10:495t

Fifth Aliyah, 1932–1939, 10:496–500, 497t, 498t, 499t

fiscal policy, 10:543–546, 545t, 546t

fishing industry, 2:553

foreign trade, 10:537t, 541–542, 550, 563t

glass industry, 7:632

government expenditures, 10:543–545

growth and restructuring, 10:573–580, 574t, 575t

high-tech industries, 10:558, 574, 575t, 580, 592–593, 19:576

Histadrut and Yishuv, 10:511–512

housing, 10:529

leather industry and trade, 12:577

"Lost Decade"; war expenditures and inflation, 1974-1985, 10:560–569, 561t, 562t, 563t, 564t, 565t, 566t, 567t

Macroeconomic Policy, 1954-1973, 10:551–557

Mandate period, 10:481t, 483t, 484t, 506–511

manufacturing, 10:503–505, 518–520, 557–559, 557–560, 559t, 570–574, 575t, 592–593

monetary and financial
systems, 10:502*t*, 512–514,
516–518, 546–549, 548*t*,
549*t*, 550–553, 568–569,
570–573, 580–586, 581–586
New Economic Policy (NEP),
1952–1954, 10:549–551
political history, 10:521
printing and publishing,
16:538–539, 725–726,
20:218, 539*t*
privatization, 10:579–580
rapid growth, 1948-1973,
10:534–541, 536*t*, 537*t*,
538*t*
reparations, 10:550, 553–554,
17:220–221
resettlement, 10:506–511,
526–534, 528*t*, 530*t*, 532*t*
State of Israel Bonds, 4:58–
59, *59*
sugar industry and trade,
19:294
sustainable development,
6:453–454
tailoring, 19:438
taxation, 19:558–559
textiles, 19:664–665
tobacco trade, 20:7
tourism, 6:367
urbanization and
socioeconomic structure,
10:505–506
war prosperity, inflation, and
short-term peace
reconversion, 10:520–521
wine and liquor trade, 21:85–
86
education, 10:652–674, 12:616
Academy of the Hebrew
Language, 1:351–353
boarding, agricultural and
special education schools,
10:667–669
comprehensive schools,
10:665–666
day care and preschool,
10:661–662
educational system, 3:263,
10:656–660, 665
extracurricular education,
10:672–673
higher education, 10:669–673,
671*t*
kindergarten, primary and
secondary schools, 10:661–
664
matriculation examinations
and certificates, 10:664–665
scholarly societies, 18:724

structure of school system
and budget, 10:660–661
students' movements, 19:268
teacher training, 10:672
ulpan, 20:243–244
vocational-technological
education, 10:666–667
flag of, 7:70–71
foreign policy and relations,
10:254–267
Abdullah ibn Hussein, 1:244
Africa, 1:437, 10:257–258,
260, 262, 264, 265
aims, 10:254
airlifts of refugees, 10:263
Albania, 1:584
Algeria, 1:651
American Judaism, impact of
establishment of Israel on,
4:93
Arab countries, 10:264
Arab nations' boycott of,
10:22, 256, 453
Arab refugees, 10:256
Argentina, 2:448–450
armistice agreements, 2:475–
476
Asia, 10:265
Australia, 2:687
Belguim, 3:287
Beta Israel, 3:508–509
Bolivia, 4:48
borders, 10:186–192, *188,
189*, 217–218, 232–233,
254–255, *255*
Brazil, 4:153–154
Bulgaria, 4:275
Burma, 4:297
Camp David Accords, 10:260,
20:398
Canada, 4:415–416, 419, 420–
421
Capucci affair, 20:483
Ceylon, 4:553
Chile, 4:643–645
China, 4:647–651
Churchill, Winston, 4:723
Conference of Presidents of
Major American Jewish
Organizations, 5:140–143
Costa Rica, 5:236
Cuba, 5:325–326
Cyprus, 5:349
Czechoslovakia, 5:361–362
Denmark, 5:585
Eastern Europe, 10:262, 264–
265

Egypt, 10:257–258, 259
Egyptian, 14:593
El Salvador, 3:369
England, 6:419, 430–432
Entebbe raid, 6:447–448
Ethiopia, 6:538–539
European Union, 6:566–568
Extradition Law, 6:629–630
Finland, 7:38
France, 7:168–170, 10:266
Gaza strip, 7:401–403
Germany, 1:390
Holy See, 10:266
Hungary, 9:619–620
incarcerated prisoners' rights,
4:743–744
India, 9:775–776, 10:265
international aid and
cooperation, 10:267
Intifada, 7:402, 403
Iran, 10:12, 15:571
Iraq, 10:21–22
Ireland, 10:27
Italy, 10:813–814
Japan, 11:83–84
Jerusalem, status of, 10:255–
256
Latin America, 10:260, 263,
266, 12:515–516
Libya, 12:794–795
Luxembourg, 13:276
Madagascar, 13:330
Madrid Peace Conference,
10:262, 263–264
Malta, 13:436
Middle East, 10:256–257, 265
Morocco, 14:503–504, 505
New Zealand, 15:244, 245–
246
Nicaragua, 15:248
Norway, 15:311
Oslo Accords, 2:316–320
Pakistan, 15:572
Palestinian Authority, 2:318,
319
Palestinian Liberation
Organization (PLO),
10:258
Palestinians, 10:258–259,
17:35
Panama, 15:610
Paraguay, 15:630
Partition Resolution of 1947,
20:259–260
peace negotiations with
Egypt, 15:594
Philippine, 16:49

Israel (State), *continued*

Poland, 16:323–325

Portugal, 16:412–413

reparations, 10:430–431, 550, 553–554, 17:220–221

Romania, 17:394, 395

Russia, 17:558–560, 563–564

Russian Federation, 14:519, 520, 17:580

Saudi Arabia, 18:77, 78

Scandanavia, 10:266

South Africa, 19:53–54

Soviet Jewry, 17:563–564

Soviet Union, 10:263

Spain, 19:82

Sweden, 19:339–340

Switzerland, 19:346

Syria, 19:394–395

technical assistance and, 10:266–267

terrorist activities, 10:259

Turkey, 20:200–201

Uruguay, 20:427–428

USSR, 5:96, 10:262, 264

Uzbekistan, 4:263

Vatican, 11:277, 280

Venezuela, 20:498

war in Lebanon, 1980s, 10:260–262

Western Europe, 10:260, 263, 265–266

White Paper of 1939, 4:722

world communities, influence on, 5:121

Yugoslavia, 21:418–419

foreign policy and relations with UN, 10:254–255, 258, 266

anti-Israel campaign, 20:273–274

internationalization of Jerusalem, 10:214–215

Israel admitted, 10:214

Jerusalem status, 10:255

partition of Mandate Palestine, 10:207

Sinai Campaign, 10:220

Six-Day War, 10:229–232

U.N. Partition Resolution of 1947, 20:259–260

foreign policy and relations with U.S., 10:258–260, 262, 263, 266–267, 434, 16:357–359, 20:394–400, 751

1970s-1980s, 10:259–260

armaments, 10:235

Bush, George H. W., 4:303–304

Bush, George W., 4:304–305

economic aid, 10:550, 578

Eisenhower Doctrine, 10:221

first Gulf War, effects of, 4:304

peace proposals, 10:235

private aid, 6:736

Reagan, Ronald, 17:135–136

recognition, 11:53, 18:19

governance, 10:387–403

alternative models, 10:729–730

central government, 10:398–400, *400*, 424

Chief Rabbinate and councils, 10:634–636

civil service, 10:400–401

comptroller, state, 10:397–398, 422–423

constitution and basic laws, 10:394, 397–398, 410–412, 429, 434, 453

Declaration of Independence, 10:409–410

electoral system, 10:394–395

Ha-Tikvah, 8:457–458

Kahan Commission, 11:713–714

Knesset, 10:394–395, 396–397, 403, 413–414, 424

local government, 10:401–402

Ministry of Health, 10:675

police, 10:423

policy research centers, 11:239

political parties, 10:395–397, 424–428, 427*t*, 755

president, 10:397

prime minister role, 10:398

reform of civil law, 10:415–416

reform of criminal law, 10:416

religion and, 10:403

Religious Affairs Ministry, 10:634

separation of powers, 10:402–403

state comptroller, 10:397–398, 422–423

state of emergency, 10:417–418

translation of Mandatory statutes to Hebrew, 10:415

historical survey, 10:179–282

1954 to 1959, 10:222

1990s, 10:252–253

Arab National Movement, 10:271–278

Arab refugees, 10:267–271

economic history, 10:252–253

to mid-1950s, 10:216, 217

military burden on, 10:234

Oslo process, 10:245–246

Palestinian Arabs post-1948, 10:278–281

post-Oslo, 10:246–254

pre-Oslo, 10:242–245

Six-Day War and aftermath, 10:229–235

terrorist warfare, 10:251–252

Yom Kippur War to first Intifada, 10:235–242

Holocaust

documentation, resource centers, 9:425–426, 426–428

Eichmann trial, 10:226

reparations, German, 10:216, 217, 430–431

studies, 9:422

WW II war crimes trials, 20:644

Yom ha-Shoah, 9:495

human geography, 10:373–387

Acre Plain, 10:379

Carmel Coast region, 10:378

Coastal Plain, 10:373, 375–383, 376–377

distribution of population, 10:374–375

Haifa Bay area, 10:378–379

Hills region, 10:379, 380

introduction, 10:373–374

Judean Plain, 10:377–378

Mount Hermon, 10:386

Negev, 10:384–386

Rift Valley, 10:383–384

Sharon region, 10:378

Southern Plain, 10:377

independence to Six-Day War, 10:208–229

Arab states, 10:209–210

battles, 10:210–211, 212, *213*

borders, war on, 10:217–219

economic history, 10:216–217, 222–223, 226–227

education, 10:227–228

elections, 10:212–213

ingathering of exiles, 10:215–216

international relations, 10:228–229

political history, 10:208–209, 210, 211–212, 214–215, 225–226

religious history, 10:226
Sinai campaign and
   aftermath, 10:219–220
social history, 10:216–217,
   223–224
Jewish population, 10:282–293,
   284t, 287t, 289t, 290t, 291t,
   292t, 304, 304t, 305, 305t, 306–
   329t
   Administered Territories,
      10:303–304, 306–329t
   aliyah, growth by, 10:282–283
   composition by place of
      birth, 10:284–285, 284t
   distribution by sex, 10:285
   geographic distribution,
      10:289–290, 289t, 290t
   growth of, 10:283–284
   Israel Place List (2004) –
      Places of Jewish Habitation
      in Israel and the
      Administered Territories,
      10:306–329t
   languages and literacy,
      10:291–292, 291t, 292t
   marriages, births, deaths and
      natural increases, 10:285–
      289, 287t
   regional distribution, 10:292
   statistics, 10:290–291, 291t,
      304, 304t, 305, 305t
labor, 10:594–600, 594–619, 600–
   605, 618t
   1980s and after, 10:618–619,
      618t
   Almogi, Yosef Aharon, 1:681
   developments, 1970-1980,
      10:615–618
   employment, 10:614–615
   employment trends, 10:293,
      533, 535, 539, 545, 557–
      558, 561, 561t, 576–577,
      601, 615–617, 618t
   Ha-Oved ha-Ziyyoni, 8:336–
      337
   Histadrut, 9:146–150, 10:600–
      605
   Histadrut and, 10:604
   Histadrut ha-Ovedim ha-
      Leumit, 9:150–151
   ideology, 10:605–607
   juveniles, 10:611–612
   labor relations, 10:607–614
   laws, 12:415–419
   legislation, 10:608–609, 617–
      618
   pensions, 10:614
   standard work day and
      vacation, 10:610–611

strikes and lockouts, 10:612–
   613
unemployment, 10:613–614
unemployment insurance,
   10:681
vocational, 10:612
wages and deductions,
   10:609–610, 616–617
women, 10:611
laws and legal systems, 10:403–
   423, 418–420, 418–422, 634–
   636, 637, 14:354–362, 16:701–
   703
   abandoned property, 8:754–
      755
   abortion, 1:273
   acquisition, 1:362, 363
   adoption, 1:418–419
   agency, 1:453–454
   agunah, 1:513, 517–520
   application of Jewish criminal
      law, 15:725
   artificial insemination,
      13:753–755
   assault, 2:596–598
   attorney general, 10:422
   bar, 10:422
   bigamy and polygamy, 3:693–
      694
   bribery, 4:176–177
   capital punishment, 4:448–
      449, 448–451, 450–451
   child marriage, 4:617
   citizenship, 10:636–637
   civil rights, 15:138–139
   coffins, 4:783
   commercial, 5:188–189
   commission of offense to
      avoid harm, 15:722
   compounding offenses, 5:124
   compromise, 5:126–128
   comptroller, state, 10:397–
      398, 422–423
   concubines, 5:135–136
   conditions, 5:138–139
   confessions, 5:147–148
   conflict between democracy
      and Judaism, 13:739
   "Constitutional Revolution,"
      10:243–244
   Constitution and Bill of
      Rights, 10:213, 394, 410–
      412, 434, 623–624
   consumer protection, 5:188–
      189
   contracts, 5:195–198
   copyright, 8:453
   Covenant and, 5:249–253

crime, 5:291–292, 293–298,
   293t, 294t
crime rates immigrants,
   5:295–296
crime rates juvenile
   delinquency, 5:296
crime rates women, 5:297
criminology, 5:303–304, 6:8
damages, 5:389, 7:504
debt, 6:597–598, 9:751–752
Declaration of Independence,
   5:528–529, 10:409–410
definition of Jew, 10:415
detention, 5:608
dina de-malkhuta dina,
   5:667–669
divine punishment, 5:710
divorce, 5:717–719
domestic violence, 5:740–741
domiciles and jurisdiction,
   5:742
dowries, 5:771–772
duress, 15:431, 453
effect of English legal
   precedents, 10:415–416
Eichmann trial, 10:226
election law, 10:411
embryos, 6:392
euthanasia, 13:743–746, 745–
   746
forgery, 7:127
fraud, 7:220
Freedom of Occupation,
   20:466–469
gambling, 7:368–369, 370
garme and gerama, 7:503–504
gifts, 5:138–139
ḥaliẓa, 12:728–729
ḥazakah, 8:490–491
Hazards Prevention Law,
   5:167
hefker, 8:754–755
human rights, 9:585–586,
   587, 17:309–310, 316, 317,
   320, 322, 327–330, 20:466–
   469
human trafficking, abduction,
   1:242–243
imprisonment, 5:303, 608,
   9:745–747, 751–752,
   16:739–740
incest and, 9:756
interpretation of Declaration
   of Independence, 10:409–
   410
Islam and, 10:647, 649
Jerusalem, legal status of,
   11:234–235

Israel (State), *continued*

judges, 10:420–422

labor, 12:415–419

land ownership, 10:719, 730–731

law of evidence, 6:581, 582, 583

law of maẓranut, 13:708

Law of Return, 10:414–415, 12:541–545, 19:170

legislation, 10:410, 413–418, 657

liens, 12:816, 817

limitation of actions, 13:24–25

lost property, 13:213–215, 214–215

maintenance, 13:401–403

mamzer, 13:445, 21:425

marriage and divorce, 3:74, 4:617, 748, 9:638–639, 12:728–729, 13:573, 576, 14:376

maternity, establishing, 21:426

matrimonial property, 13:680–683

mediation, 13:720

mishpat Ivri, 14:354–358, 358

mistakes, 14:369

moral rights, 8:453

Muslim residents rights, 17:329

national health insurance, 10:676

natural rights, 10:412

obligations, 15:372

official position of Jewish law, 14:354–356

organ transplantation, 13:749

parental rights and obligations, 15:638–640

partnerships in, 15:672–673

paternity laws, 21:423–426

performers right, 8:453

pigs, 16:151

planning and construction, 16:218–219

pledges, 16:236

police, 10:423

position of Jewish law, 12:540–541, 14:354–358

profiteering, 8:198

property, 16:565

prostitution, 16:628

rabbinical courts, 13:681–683, 14:352–353, 362, 16:440–446, 701

rape, 17:93

sales, 17:687

separation of powers, 18:292

servitudes, 18:318

sexual offenses, 18:330–332, 331

shomerim, 18:515–518

slander, 18:663–665

state of emergency, 10:417–418

status of Basic Laws, 10:411, 412

status of Jewish law, 14:358–362

succession and inheritance, 19:288–289

Supreme Court, 3:130–131, 10:418, 16:701

suretyship, 19:320–322

Takkanot, 19:451

Takkanot ha Kahal, 19:459–460

torts, 20:66–67

translation of Mandatory statues to Hebrew, 10:415

values of, as Jewish state, 13:739

widows, 21:40–42

wills, 1:363, 21:72, 73–74

women's status, 21:194–207

WW II war crimes trials, 20:644

yuḥasin, 21:424–426

non-Jewish population, 10:300–305, *301, 302t, 303, 303t, 304t, 305, 713t*

Bedouin, 10:737–739

Christian, 10:643–644

Druze, 10:469

political history, 10:423–464

early, 6:292

First Knesset, 1949-1951, 10:428–430, 428t, 429t, 430t

Fourth Knesset, 1959-1961, 10:434–436, 434t, 435t

Fifth Knesset, 1961-1965, 10:436–438, 436t, 437t

Eighth Knesset, 1973-77, 10:442–444, 442t, 443t

Eleventh Knesset, 1984-1988, 6:279, 10:448–451, 448t, 449t, 450t

Einstein, Albert, 6:262

Fourteenth Knesset, 1996-99, 10:456–458, 456t, 457t

Fifteenth Knesset, 1999-2003, 10:458–462, 458t, 459t, 460t–461t

Independence Day, 9:769–770

Likud, 13:13–14

Mandate period, 10:481t, 483t, 484t, 506–511

Mapai, 13:497–498

Mapam, 13:498–499

Ninth Knesset, 1977-81, 10:444–446, 444t, 445t

Ottoman period, 10:479–485, 481t, 483t

political parties, 10:395–397, 424–428, 427t

Second Knesset, 1951-1955, 10:430–432, 430t, 431t, 432t

Seventh Knesset, 1969-73, 10:440–442, 440t, 441t

Sixteenth Knesset, 2003-2006, 10:461–464, 462t, 463t

Sixth Knesset, 1965-1969, 10:438–440, 438t, 439t

Tenth Knesset, 1981-1984, 10:446–448, 446t, 447t

Third Knesset, 1955-1959, 10:432–434, 433t, 434t

Thirteenth Knesset, 1992-96, 10:453–456, 453t, 454t, 456t

Twelfth Knesset, 1988-92, 6:279, 10:451–453, 451t, 452t

as unique political and economic entity, 1918–1948, 10:486–487

political theories, parties and organizations, 10:394–395

Aḥdut ha-Avodah (political party), 1:540

ba'alei tesuvah, 3:7

Bene Israel, 3:338–339

Beta Israel, 3:507

B'nai Brith activities, 4:16

communism, 5:99–100

Council of Settlements of Judea, Samaria, and Gaza, 8:353

friendship leagues, 7:290

Ha-Poel ha-Mizrachi, 8:339–340

Ha-Po'el ha-Ẓa'ir, 8:340–342

Ha-Shomer ha-Ẓa'ir, 8:384–385

Ḥerut, 17:262–267

Ḥerut Movement, 9:50–51

Histadrut, 3:345

Iḥud Olami, 21:222

Independent Liberal Party, 9:771

Islamic Movement and, 10:727, 731

Israel Labor Party, 1:676, 681,
4:483, 6:321, 10:755–756,
18:362, 432
Israel Women's Network,
21:193, 194
Jewish Agency for Israel,
20:257–258
Kach, 11:693
Knesset, 12:235–239, 235t,
236t, 237t
La'am, 8:456–457
labor, 21:222–223
Land of Israel Movement,
8:457–458
Loḥamei Ḥerut Israel,
13:175–176
Maki communist party, 5:100
Mandate era politics, 3:345–
346
Mapam, 8:491
Masorti movement, 5:175–
176
National Religious Party,
8:308–309
ORT, 15:490
Po'alei Agudat Israel, 16:243–
244
Po'alei Zion, 16:249
Rafi, 17:64
recognition of Palestine
Liberation Organization,
10:455
religious, 10:429, 431
revisionism, influence of,
17:262–267
scouting, 18:210
Shas (political party), 18:419–
420
Shinui, 18:484–485
student's movements, 19:268
theocracy, 19:692
Tnu'at ha-Teḥiyah, 8:457
Tsomet, 20:165
Values of a Jewish and
Democratic State, 20:466–
469
Youth Aliyah, 21:403–406
politicians, 5:485–486
Allon, Yigal, 1:675
Almogi, Yosef Aharon, 1:681
Barak, Ehud, 3:131–132
Baram, Moshe, 3:132
Baram, Uzi, 3:133
Bar-Yehudah, Israel, 3:192
Begin, Menaḥem, 3:261–262
Begin, Ze'ev Binyamin,
3:261–262
Beilin, Yossi, 3:266–267

Ben-Eliezer, Binyamin, 3:339–
340
Ben-Gurion, David, 3:344348
Ben-Natan, Asher, 3:367
Ben-Porat, Miriam, 3:371–
372
Ben-Porat, Mordekhai, 3:372
Bentov, Mordekhai, 3:380–
381
Bernstein, Perez, 3:483
Chaim Weitzman, first
President, 20:751
Chouraqui, André, 4:672–673
Dapkin, Abraham S., 6:8
Dizengoff, Meir, 5:721–722
Dulzin, Arye Leib, 6:45
Eban, Abba Solomon, 6:84
Ehrlich, Simha, 6:245
Elath, Eliahu, 6:288
Eliav, Arie Lova, 6:321
Elon, Binyamin, 6:367
Eshkol, Levi, 6:505–506
Hammer, Reuven, 8:308
Harman, Avraham, 8:359
Hillel, Shelomo, 9:112–113
Hurwitz, Yigael, 9:633–634
Lahat, Shlomo, 12:439
Leibowitz, Yeshayahu, 12:624
Levi, Shabbetai, 12:693
Levy, David, 12:749
Libai, David, 12:774
Meir, Golda, 13:777–779
Modai, Yitzhak, 14:406
Netanyahu, Binyamin, 15:91–
92
Peres, Shimon, 15:763–764
Peretz, Amir, 15:764–765
Sapir, Pinḥas, 18:38–39
Shahal, Moshe, 18:362
Shalom, Silvan, 18:378
Shamir, Yitzhak, 18:393–394
Shapira, Ḥayyim Moshe,
18:400
Shapiro, Ya'akov Shimshon,
18:408
Sharansky, Natan, 18:411–412
Sharett, Moshe, 18:412
Sharon, Ariel, 18:415–417
Shazar, Shneur Zalman,
18:425–426
Sheetrit, Meir, 18:431–432
Shem-Tov, Victor, 18:458–
459
Sherf, Ze'ev, 18:462
population, 10:282–329, 302t, 303,
303t, 304t, 305, 306–329t, 522t
increases, 10:287t

War of Independence effect,
10:521–522
pre-war of independence period,
10:652–656
religious life and scholarship,
10:619–652
1960s, 10:226
1970s to early 1990's, 10:628–
632
1990s and after, 10:632–638
aggadah, 1:460–463
apostasy, 2:276–277
Bahā'ī, 10:650
bar mitzvah, 3:166
Chief Rabbi, 7:777–778
Chief Rabbinate, 4:613
Christian, 10:642–643, 645
Christian attitude, 4:685–686
Christianity, 10:638–646
Christians, 10:638–646
Christian sects and, 11:283
controversy about, 10:224
Druze, 10:650–652
as framework for struggle for
Torah, 16:100
Franciscan presence, 10:640
Ḥanukkah, 8:333
Ḥaredim, 8:350–352
ḥazzanim, 8:503–504
holy places, 9:499–503, 502
ingathering of the exiles,
9:787
interfaith dialogue, 10:643,
645–646
Islam, 10:646–650, 647–650
John Paul II's visit to, 11:384
kehillot or community
councils, 10:622–623
military hesder, yeshivot,
21:320
non-Orthodox Jewish
congregations, 10:628–630
Orthodoxy, 15:494
Ottoman to post-war of
independence period,
10:619–626
Protestants, 16:633–634
rabbis, 17:18–19
Reform Judaism, 17:181–182
religious schools, 10:624–625,
631, 632–633
Sabbath and holiday
observances, 10:626–628
scholarly societies, 18:724
Sephardim, 18:303–304
synagogues, 19:357–358
Torah, approach to, 20:44

Israel (State), *continued*

war of independence-Six Day War, 10:623–626

as world Jewry center, 10:227–228

yeshivot, 21:320–321

terrorist attacks against, 10:233–234, 245, 247, 258

Hamas, 8:294–295

Hizbolla, 9:297–298

Intifada (second) and, 10:252

wars

Lebanese War, 10:239–241, 260, 447–448, 472–473, 12:580, 581–584

Lebanon invasion, 1982, 17:135–136

Sinai Campaign, 18:629–632, 20:265–266

Six-Day War, 12:691, 18:648–655, 20:267–268

War of Independence, 3:346, 5:485, 7:347, 11:177–178, 20:260–261

Yom Kippur War, 21:383–391, *384, 386, 388, 389*

water supply, 10:531–532, 13:799

Arab diversion of Jordan River, 10:228–229

border skirmishes with Syria, 10:218

rural planning, 10:10:368

See also Erez Israel; Israel (land of); Jerusalem (Israel); Mandate for Palestine; specific locations

Israel, Abner R., 18:55

Israel, Abraham ben Moses, 10:740

Israel, Edward, 10:**740**

Israel, Edward Leopold, 10:**740**

Israel, Jonathan, 10:**741**

Israel, Jossif, 4:276

Israel, Jules. *See* Irving, Jules

Israel, Kingdom of, 10:**741**

Israel, Melvin. *See* Allen, Mel

Israel, Michael Boaz. *See* Cresson, Warder

Israel, Moses, 10:740

Israel, New. *See* New Israel

Israel, People of. *See* Congregations

Israel, Richard J., 10:**741–742**

Israel, Steve, 10:**742**

Israel, Wilfrid, 10:**742**

Israel, Yom Tov ben Elijah, 10:**742–743**

Israel Academy of Sciences and Humanities, 10:**743**

Israel Agricultural Bank, 8:283

Israel Among the Nations (Ehrenreich), 6:241

Israel and the Diaspora (Dinur), 5:672

"Israel and the Diaspora" (Scholem), 16:100

Israel Antiquities Authority, 2:378–379

Israel-Arab armistice agreements, 2:**475–476**

Israel Archives Association, 18:724

Israel Ba'al Shem Tov. *See* Israel ben Eliezer Ba'al Shem Tov

Israel bar Samuel bar Hophni. *See* Israel ben Samuel ha-Kohen

Israel ben Benjamin of Belzec, 10:**743**

Israel ben Eliezer Ba'al Shem Tov, 1:311, 378, 385, 3:9, 4:94, 309–310, 5:410, 8:393–394, 10:**743–748,** *744*

Israel Benjamin. *See* Benjamin, Israel

Israel ben Joel, 10:**748**

Israel ben Jonathan from Leczyca, 10:**748**

Israel ben Moses Najara. *See* Najara, Israel ben Moses

Israel ben Perez of Polotsk, 10:**748**

Israel ben Samuel ha-Dayyan ha-Ma'aravi. *See* Israel ha-Dayyan ha-Ma'aravi

Israel ben Samuel ha-Kohen, 10:**748–749**

Israel ben Samuel of Shklov, 10:**749**

Israel Chamber Ensemble. *See* Israel Chamber Orchestra

Israel Chamber Orchestra, 10:**749–750**

Israel Communist Party, 18:696

Israel Corporation, 6:266

Israel Declaration of Independence. *See* Declaration of Independence, Israel

Israel Defense Forces (IDF), 10:467–474

Amit, Meir, 2:80

archives, 2:417

in art, 11:77–78

Ben-Gurion, David, 3:346

campaigns, 10:471–474

Dayan, 5:485–486

festivals and holidays observance in, 10:627

Grapes of Wrath operation in Lebanon, 10:247–248

integration of varied Jewish communities and, 10:467–468

Intifada and, 10:242

Intifada (second) and, 10:252

leaders, Eitan, Raphael, 6:279

Lebanese War, 10:239–241, 260

Lebanon withdrawal, 10:250

Mofaz, Shaul, 14:415

organization of, 10:468–470

radio station, 10:708

war against terrorism, 10:474–479

War of Independence, 10:209–212

Israele disperso e ricostruito (Bachi), 3:38

Israel Eliakim. *See* Benjamin, Israel

Israel Exploration Society, 3:710, 10:**750,** 18:724

Israel family, 10:**740**

Israel Federation of Ha-Shomer ha-Za'ir, 8:384

Israel Film Art Archives, 2:416

Israel Folklore Society, 18:724

Israel Geographic Society, 2:79

Israel Gymnastic Club. *See* Maccabi World Union

Israel ha-Dayyan ha-Ma'aravi, 10:**750,** 11:537

Israel Haraf of Satanov, 10:**750–751**

Israel ha-Zifroni. *See* Zifroni, Israel ben Daniel

Israel-Holy *See* Basic Agreement, 10:265

Israeli, Benzion, 10:**751**

Israeli, Isaac ben Joseph, 10:**751**

Israeli, Isaac ben Solomon, 3:238, 10:**751–753,** 16:80

angels, 2:160

Judeo-Arabic literature and, 11:531

Kairouan, 11:727

Neoplatonism, 15:85

soul, immortality of, 19:36

Israeli, Isaac d'. *See* D'Israeli, Isaac

Israeli, Israel, 10:**753**

Israeli, Isserl ben Isaac Segal, 10:**753**

Israeli, Shaul, 10:**754**

Israeli literature, 10:684–685

Adelman, Uri, 1:386

Agmon, Nathan, 1:465

Aloni, Nissim, 1:687

Be'er, Haim, 3:251–252

Ben-Amotz, Dahn, 3:317

Ben-Natan, Asher, 3:367

for children, 4:622–628, 633

Even-Shoshan, 6:575

Danker, 5:430

David in, 5:455–456

dramatic, 8:719–723

encyclopedias, 6:400–401, 400–402, 402

Ever Hadani, 6:576

fiction, Eytan, 6:634–635

Hareven, Shulamith, 8:353

historiography, 9:161

Levin, Hanoch, 12:708

novels

Bartov, Hanoch, 1:181

Gur, Batya, 8:138

Gurfein, Rivka, 8:140–141

poetry, 17:5

Canaanites, 4:393

Hourvitz, Ya'ir, 9:568–569

Ragen, Naomi, 17:64–65

science fiction and fantasy, Jewish, 18:202–203, 206–207

Seneed, Alexander, 18:288

Shabtai, Ahron, 18:359

Shabtai, Yaakov, 18:359–360

Sobol, Yehoshua, 18:702

Israel in Egypt (oratorio, Handel), 14:542

Israel Institute of Technology. *See* Technion, Israel Institute of Technology

The Israelis: Founders and Sons (Elon), 6:366

Der Israelit (periodical), 10:**754**, 12:616

Israelita, Paulus. See Ricius, Paulus

Israelite, The. See American Israelite (periodical)

Die Israeliten in der Wueste (oratorio, C.P.E. Bach), 14:542

De Israëliten te Mekka van Davids tijd tot in de vijfde eeuw onzer tijdrekening (Dozy), 5:772

Israelites, 3:668–669, 10:**754**

British, biblical influence, 3:670

liberation from enslavement, 6:613–616

monarchal concept, 1:258

Second Temple, 19:617–618

Israelitisches Familienblatt (periodical), 10:**754**

Israelitisches Gebetbuch (Seligmann), 18:267

Israelitisch-Theologische Lehranstalt, 10:**754–755**

Israelitul Roman, 3:135

Israeli viper, 18:695

Israel Labor Party, 1:676, 681, 6:321, 10:**755–756**

Carmel, Moshe, 4:483

Shahal, Moshe, 18:362

Sheetrit, Meir, 18:432

Israel Meir ha-Kohen, 10:**756–757**

Israel Meir Kagan. *See* Israel Meir ha-Kohen

Israel Moses ben Aryeh Loeb, 10:**757**

Israel Movement for Progressive Judaism, 17:181–182

Israel Museum (Jerusalem), 2:47, 10:697, 699–700, 704, **757–758**

Israel National Opera Company, 5:589

Israel of Bamberg, 10:**758**

Israel of Belzec. *See* Israel ben Benjamin of Belzec

Israel of Krems, 10:**758**

Israel of Leczyca. *See* Israel ben Jonathan from Leczyca

Israel of Modzhitz, 14:413

Israel of Polotsk. *See* Israel ben Perez of Polotsk

Israel of Ruzhin. *See* Ruzhin, Israel

Israel of Shklov. *See* Israel ben Samuel of Shklov

Israel of Zamosc, 8:415

Israel Philharmonic Orchestra, 10:688, **758–759,** 11:757, 14:693–694

Israel Policy Forum (IPF), 10:**759**

Israel Prize, 10:**759–765,** 11:695, 700, 704

Israëls, Isaac, 10:765

Israëls, Jozef, 10:765

Israel Samuel ben Solomon Calahorra. *See* Calahorra, Israel Samuel ben Solomon

Israel Sifroni. *See* Zifroni, Israel ben Daniel

Israel Society for Biblical Research, 18:724

Israelsohn, Jacob Izrailevich, 10:**765–766**

Israels Propheten (Duhm), 6:42–43

Israel State Archives, 9:427

Israel Tuito, Chairman of Mikol Halev, Kikar Halehem, The Association for Reducing Social Disparities in Israel, et al. *v.* Municipality of Jerusalem, 16:218

Israel und Aegypten (Alt), 2:11

Israel United Nations Association, 2:678

Israel Women's Network, 6:754, 21:193, 194

Israel Zifroni. *See* Zifroni, Israel ben Danie

Isrā'īl. See Jacob

Isrā'īliyyāt. See Israelite

Isra'iliyyät. See Israelite

Isru Ḥag, 10:**766**

Issac ben Aaron of Karlin, 11:29

Issachar, 10:*766,* **766–767**

Issachar, Simḥah, 10:767

Issachar Baer ben Solomon Zalman, 10:**767**

Issachar Baer ben Tanḥum, 10:**767–768**

Issachar Baer of Radoszyce. *See* Radoshitser, Issachar Baer

Issachar Berman ben Naphtali ha-Kohen, 10:**768**

Issachar Ber Rosenbaum of Strezhnitz, 8:419

Issachar Dov Baer ben Aryeh Leib of Zloczow, 10:**768**

Issachar Dov of Belz, 3:308

Issakov, Simcho, 4:276

Issar Judah ben Nehemiah of Brisk, 10:**768**

Isserlein, Israel ben Pethahiah, 1:219, 3:705, 10:**768–770,** 15:442

apostasy, 2:274

descendants, 14:508

Jacob ben Moses Moellin, 14:414

Joseph ben Moses (talmudist and author), 11:424

Mordacai ben Hillel ha-Kohen, 14:481

Isserlein, Redel, 10:769

Isserlein, Schoendlein, 10:769

Isserlein family, 10:769

Isserles, John. *See* Isserles, Steven

Isserles, Moses ben Israel, 1:532, 10:**770–772,** 13:268

Arab-influenced Hebrew, 8:670

Bragadini, 4:117

competition, 8:451

divination, 5:706

Elijah ben Solomon Zalman, 6:344

halakhic codification, 4:777–780

Ḥayyim ben Bezalel, 8:480

Joseph ben Mordecai Gershon ha-Kohen of Cracow, 11:423

Luria, Solomon ben Jehiel, 16:295–296

Meir ben Baruch of Rothenburg and, 13:782

Shulḥan Arukh, 18:529–530

Isserles, Moshe, 6:628

Isserlin, Israel Issar ben Mordecai, 4:193

Isserlis, John. *See* Isserlis, Steven

Isserlis, Steven, 10:**772**

Isserman, Ferdinand M., 10:**772–773**

Issi. *See* Assi

Issi ben Akavyah. *See* Yose ben Akavyah

Issur Giyyora, 10:**773**

Issur "the Proselyte." *See* Issur Giyyora

Issur ve-Hetter, 6:41, 10:**773**

Istanbul (Turkey), 10:**773–786,** *774*

1923 to present, 10:782–784

eighteenth-early twentieth centuries, 10:779–783

fifteenth, sixteenth and seventeenth centuries, 10:773–779, *774*

Hebrew publishing, 10:784–785

Jewish quarters, 11:312

transfer of Jews to, 15:521–522

See also Constantinople (Turkey)

Istituto Convitto Rabbinico. *See* Collegio Rabbinico Italiano

Istóczy, Gyözö, 10:**786**, 11:781

Istomin, Eugene, 10:**786**

Istomin, George. *See* Istomin, Eugene

Istoria kye Thrili yiro apo to Tikhos ton Dhakrion (Moissis). *See History and Legend Concerning the Wailing Wall* (Moissis)

Istoriya yevreyskogo naroda, 4:137

Istria (northern Adriatic), 10:**787**

Istrumsa, Daniel. *See* Estrosa, Daniel

Istrumsa, Ḥayyim Abraham, 10:**787**

Isunians, 1:337

IT. *See* Information technology (IT)

Itabyrion. *See* Mount Tabor

"Itala Fragments," 3:674

Italia, Shalom, 10:**787**

L'Italia Economica, 3:37

The Italian Conception of International Law (Sereni), 18:309

Italian literature, 10:**787–795**
  Abraham, 1:287
  Bible, 10:787–788
  biblical influence, 3:670–671
  Cantoni, Alberto, 4:436–437
  Castelnuovo, Enrico, 4:514
  children's, 4:634
  conflict, literature of, 10:793
  criticism, 12:687–688
  De Benedetti, Aldo, 5:516
  Holocaust and aftermath, 10:793–795
  image of Jews in, 10:788–790
  Levi, Benedetto, 12:686
  Levi, Carlo, 12:686
  Levi, David, 12:686–687
  Levi, Joshua Joseph Ben David, 12:689–690
  Levi, Paolo, 12:691
  Levi, Primo, 12:691–692
  medieval, 16:268–269, 270–271
  Middle Ages-twentieth century, 10:790–793
  modern, 5:444
  Momigliano, Attilio, 14:431
  Moravia, Alberto, 14:476–477
  Morpurgo, Giuseppe, 14:509
  Pitigrilli, 16:188
  poetry, 5:544
  responsa, 17:232, 233
  Rieti, Moses ben Isaac da, 17:297–298
  Roman period, 17:403–404
  Svevo, Italo, 19:333–334
  translations, 16:270–271
  Vivante Chartres, Annie, 20:563
  See also Judeo-Italian literature

The Italian Madrigal (Einstein), 6:262

Italiener, Bruno, 10:**795**

Italkian. *See* Judeo-Italian language

Italy, 10:**795–816**, *796, 804,* 804*t*
  antisemitism, 2:233, 3:469, 4:382, 445, 10:799–801, 803–805, 810–811
    Acqui, 1:359
    Agrigento, 1:502
    Alessandria, 1:618
    badges, Jewish, 2:137, 140, 292, 3:46, 47, 12:506, 608
    Bergamo, 3:418
    blood libel, 3:469, 4:163, 7:414, 10:798, 15:566
    Bologna, 4:49
    Brescia, 4:163
    Calabria, 4:348
    Capistrano, John of, 4:445
    Capua, 4:457
    carnival celebrations, 4:486
    Casale Monferrato, 4:504
    Catania, 4:523
    Catanzaro, 4:523
    censorship, 4:541
    Chieri, 4:615
    Crusader period, 3:469
    Fascist regime, 6:716–717
    Franciscan order, 3:469
    Palermo, 15:581
    Rome, 4:523–524
  catacombs, 4:521–522
  cultural and social life (*See also* Renaissance, Italy; *specific Italian cities*)
    architecture, 2:400
    archives, 2:409
    art, biblical influence, 3:673
    artisans, 5:266–267
    artists, 2:505, 5:748–749
    bar mitzvah, 3:165
    cantatas and choral works, Hebrew, 4:433–434
    community organization, 10:806, 809
    education, Jewish, 6:174, 179–180, 181, 16:635–636
    ḥazakah, 8:490
    illuminated Hebrew Bibles, 3:678–679
    illuminated manuscripts, Hebrew, 9:732–733
    immigration to Israel, 10:295
    Jewish heritage, 10:807, 809–810
    journalism, 11:467, 12:519, 16:494

    language, biblical translations, 3:633
    letters and letter writers, 12:673
    libraries, 12:787
    Marranos, 2:140
    medicine, 12:688
    museums, 14:626
    music, 10:814–815, 12:690, 14:668–669
    synagogue architecture, 19:375–376, *376*
    theater, 19:674
  demography and population statistics, 2:*290,* 10:*796, 804,* 804*t,* 805–806, 807, 16:389
  economic affairs
    bankers, moneylending, 3:115, 14:441, 442–443, 461
    Hebrew printing, 3:586, 587, 4:163, 7:86
    leather industry and trade, 12:575
    printing and publishing, 9:760–761, 10:806, 16:532–533, 536, 537–538, 716–717
    silk trade, Bozzolo, 4:116
    typography, 20:216
    yeshivot, 21:316–317
    Yiddish literature, 21:343–344
    Zionism, 10:806–807, 12:703, 21:592–593
  foreign policy and affairs
    Ethiopia, 3:504–505
    Israel, 10:814
    Libya occupation, 12:791
  French Revolution, and effects on communities, 7:256
  historians, Bonfil, Robert, 4:61–62
  Holocaust, 9:339, 10:803–805, 810
    Alessandria, 1:618
    camps, internment and detention, 7:135
    cinema, 9:442, 445–446
    Florence, 7:86
    Genoa, 7:483–484
    Gorizia, 7:779
    Leghorn, 12:609
    literature, 10:793–795
    Lugo, 13:253–254
    Milan, 14:231
    Modena, 14:408
    Pisa, 16:184
    Reggio Emilia, 17:190
    Rome, 17:415–416
    Rovigo, 17:500

studies, 10:810
Trieste, 20:145–146
Turin, 20:194
Venice, 20:503–504
Vercelli, 20:508
Verona, 20:514
Jewish participation in military
service, 14:243
laws and legal systems, 10:809,
12:552
anti-sheḥitah movements,
18:435
emancipation, 6:378–379,
12:779
freedom and equality, 1815-
1838, 10:801–803
ḥazakah, 8:490
Middle Ages, 10:796, 797–799
agriculture, Jewish, 1:495
political theories, parties and
organizations, 10:807–809,
16:345
liberalism, 12:779
neo-fascism, 15:72
post-WW II to 1995, 10:805–812
religious life and scholarship
anti-sheḥitah movements,
18:435
baptism, forced, 3:122
bar mitzvah, 3:165
Catholic-Jewish relations,
10:797, 798, 811
conferences, 5:145–146
Haggadot, 8:212, 213–214
Inquisition, 9:799
Kabbalists, 11:618
language, biblical translations,
3:633
liturgy, 13:135
Marranos, 2:140
missionarie, 4:94
Rabbinical training, 17:22–23
Risorgimento, 4:49
Shabbateanism center,
18:353–354
tosafists, 17:342
Roman period, 10:795–796
San Nicandro community, 11:520
WW II
Beriḥah, 3:434
partisans in, 15:667–668
Itchele. See Justman, Moshe Bunem
Itelson, Gregor, 10:816–817
Ithai. See Ittai
Ithamar, 10:817
It Happened in Leningrad. See Eto bylo
v Leningrade

Ithiel (biblical figure). See Solomon
(biblical figure)
Itil (Turkey). See Atil (Turkey)
Itineraries of Ereẓ Israel, 10:817–818
Itinerarium Antonini, 10:818
Itinerarium Burdigalense. See
Itinerarium Hierosolymitanum
Itinerarium Hierosolymitanum, 10:818
ITO (International Trade
Organization), 19:649
I Trionfi (Alatrini), 1:579
I.T.S. See International Tracing Service
It's Garry Shandling's Show (television
show), 18:396
Ittai (of Gath), 10:818
Ittai (son of Ribai of Gibeah), 10:818
Ittim. See Sefer ha-Ittim
Ittinga, Mordecai Ze'ev ben Isaac
Aaron Segal. See Ettinger, Mordecai
Ze'ev ben Isaac Aaron Segal
'Ittur soferim, 13:609
Itzele Ponovezher. See Rabinovich,
Isaac Jacob; Rabinovih, Issaac Jacob
Itzelle Peterburger. See Blaser, Isaac
Itzhak Bakhrakh. See Isbakh,
Alexander Abramovich
Itzhak Katzenelson Ghetto Fighters'
House. See Ghetto Fighters' House
(Israel)
Itzig, Daniel, 10:818–819, 819t
Itzig, Isaac Daniel, 10:819, 11:569
Itzig, Julius Eduard. See Hitzig, Julius
Eduard
Itzig family, 3:446, 9:294, 10:819, 819
Itzik, Dalia, 10:819–820
Iudex Judaeorum, 10:820
Iunu. See Heliopolis (Ancient Egypt)
Ivah le-Moshav (Duckesz), 6:39
Ivan III (Czar of Russia), 11:521
Ivan Alexander (Czar of Bulgaria),
18:47
Ivanćice (Czechoslovakia). See Ivancice
(Czechoslovakia)
Ivancice (Czechoslovakia), 10:820
Ivanhoe (Scott), 6:435, 18:208
Ivanitchev Yar, 13:253
Ivanji, Ivan, 10:820
Ivanov Frankovsk (Ukraine). See
Stanislav (Ukraine)
Ivanovo (Belarus), 10:820–821
Ivan the Terrible. See Demjanjuk, Jan
Ivan the Terrible (film trilogy), 6:274
Ivan the Terrible (Slonimsky), 18:680
Ivanyi-Grunwald, Bela, 10:821
I vegetariani dell'amore (Pitigrilli),
16:188
Ivgy, Moshe, 10:821

Ivo of Chartres, 10:821
Ivory, 6:310–311, 10:821–822
Ivrīm. See Eber
Ivrit be-Ivrit, 6:194, 205, 471
Ivy, 10:822
Ivye (Belarus), 10:822
Iwanie (Ukraine), 7:184–185
Iwje (Belarus). See Ivye (Belarus)
Ixar. See Hijar (Spain)
Iyov of Minsk. See Brill, Joseph
Iyyar, 10:823
the 14th of (See Passover, Second)
the 18th of (See Lag ba-Omer)
Izates II (King of Adiabene), 1:391,
2:129, 10:823, 14:447
Izban, Shmuel, 10:823–824
Izbica Ḥasidim, 11:40–41
Izbica Lubelska (Poland), 10:824
Izbica Radzyn family, 10:824–825
Izbitski, Joseph. See Mikhalevich,
Beinish
Izenberg, Jerry, 10:825
Izis, 10:825–826
Izl, 8:202, 203, 204
Izmail (Romania), 10:826
Izmel of Barcelona, 3:382
Izmir (Turkey), 1:339, 10:826–828,
20:202
Izmit (Turkey), 10:828–829
Izniknid (Turkey). See Izmit (Turkey)
Izraelita (periodical), 10:829
Izraelita Magyar Irodalmi Társulat,
3:120, 10:829
Izvestiya o Khazarakh (Chwolson),
4:724
Izyaslav (Ukraine), 3:779, 10:829–830
Iz zhizni piezii (Dolmatovski), 5:736

J

J (letter), 11:5
J. Lyons and Company, 13:298
J. & W. Seligman & Company, 18:266
Jaakobs Traum (Beer), 3:255
Jaazaniah, 6:287, 11:5, 18:398
Jaazaniahu. See Jaazaniah
Jabal, 11:5–6
Jabal az-Zevedani. See Amana
Jabali language, 11:301
Jabbok, 11:6
Jabbok (river), 2:83, 11:401
Jabès, Edmond, 7:244–245, 11:6,
15:474, 546
Jabesh-Gilead (ancient Israel), 11:6–7
Jabez, Joseph ben Ḥayyim, 2:531,
6:149, 11:7
Jabez, Solomon, 6:149, 11:7

Jabez family, 10:784, 11:**7**

Jabin (King of Hazor), 8:497, 11:**7–8**

Jablonec Nad Nisou (Czechoslovakia), 11:**8**

Jablonna (detention camp), 11:**8–9**

Jablonski, Daniel Ernst, 3:587

Jabneel (ancient Israel), 11:**9**

Jabneel (Israel, State), 11:**9**

Jabneh (ancient Israel), 6:309, 11:**9–10**
  Eleazar ben Azariah, 6:299–300
  Eleazar ben Matya, 6:305
  Eleazar ben Yose I, 6:308
  Eliezer ben Hyrcanus, 6:323
  Johanan ben Zakhai at, 11:376
  sages of, 10:145–146, 147–148

Jabotinsky, Eric, 11:14

Jabotinsky, Vladimir, 11:**10–14**
  Amery, Leopold Charles Maurice Stennet, 2:66
  Ben-Gurion, David, 3:345
  Jewish Legion, 9:249, 10:465, 11:303, 304, 306
  Jewish State Party, 11:315–316
  Nordau, Max, 15:298, 299
  pogrom self-defense, 18:262
  Society for the Attainment of Full Civil Rights for the Jewish People in Russia, 18:724

Jabotinsky, Ze'ev. See Jabotinsky, Vladimir

Jabotinsky Institute, 2:415

Jaca (Spain), 11:**14–15**

Jachia, Samuel. See Denis, Albertus

Jachin and Boaz (sanctuary pillars), 11:**15–16**

Jacie, Henry. See Jessey, Henry

Jackal, 11:**16**

Jackan, Samuel Jacob, 8:476

Jack Solomons Tells All (Solomons), 18:773

Jackson, Andrew, 14:422, 15:198, 291

Jackson, Bernard S., 11:**16**

Jackson, Daniel, 15:198, 199

Jackson, Harry, 11:**16**

Jackson, Henry, 2:51

Jackson, Jesse, 2:51, 3:736, 15:228, 20:378

Jackson, Solomon Henry, 11:**16**, 15:199

Jacksonville (FL), 11:**16–17**

Jacob (3rd/4th c. amora), 11:**25**

Jacob (biblical figure), 11:**17–25**
  abduction, 1:243
  Abraham's bosom, 1:316
  adoption, 1:415–416
  Bilhah, 3:698
  birthright, 7:45–46

blessing of, 11:**26–27**
  commentary, 11:20–22
  Dinah and, 5:669
  embalming of, 11:409, 412
  Ephraim, 6:456, 457
  Esau, 6:487–488
  Jabbok river and, 11:6
  Joseph and, 11:406, 408, 410
  Laban and, 12:406–407, 13:8
  Midrash Va-Yissa'u, 14:192
  Midrash va-Yisse'u, 7:11
  as Patriarch, 15:689–691

Jacob (Hekim Yakub), 10:776

Jacob, Benno, 11:**25**

Jacob, Berthold, 11:**25–26**

Jacob, Edmund, 3:651

Jacob, François, 11:**27–28**, 13:9

Jacob, Gyula. See Major, Julius

Jacob, Heinrich Eduard, 11:**28**

Jacob, Jack Frederick Raphael, 11:**28**

Jacob, Max, 11:**28**, 15:648

Jacob, Naomi Ellington, 11:**28**

Jacob, Testament of, 11:**29**

Jacob, Walter, 11:**29**

Jacob Anatoli. See Anatoli, Jacob ben Abba Mari ben Samson

Jacob and the Angel (sculpture, Epstein), 6:471

Jacob Ashkenazi. See Temerls, Jacob ben Eliezer

Jacob bar Samson. See Jacob ben Samson

Jacob ben Aaron of Karlin, 11:**29**

Jacob ben Abba Mari Anatoli. See Anatoli, Jacob ben Abba Mari ben Samson

Jacob ben Abraham Solomon, 11:**29–30**

Jacob ben Aḥa, 11:**30**

Jacob ben Asher, 3:712, 4:489, 774–775, 11:**30–31**, 422, 12:462
  business ethics, 4:307
  metaphorical titles, 8:552

Jacob ben Benjamin Ze'ev, 11:**31**

Jacob ben Dunash ben Akiva, 11:**31**

Jacob ben Eleazar, 11:**31**

Jacob ben Ephraim Naphtali Hirsch of Lublin, 11:**31–32**

Jacob ben Hananel Sikili. See Sikili, Jacob ben Hananel

Jacob ben Ḥayyim ben Isaac ibn Adonijah, 4:52, 11:**32**, 13:620–621, 652
  early printed editions of Hebrew Bible, 3:587

Jacob ben Ḥayyim Talmid, 11:**32**, 312

Jacob ben Idi, 11:**32–33**

Jacob ben Isaac, 11:536

Jacob ben Isaac ha-Levi of Roethelsee, 3:611

Jacob ben Isaac Roman. See Roman, Jacob ben Isaac

Jacob ben Jacob ha-Kohen, 11:**33**

Jacob ben Jakar. See Jacob ben Yakar

Jacob ben Joseph, 1:613

Jacob ben Judah, 11:**33–34**

Jacob ben Judah de Lotra. See Jacob ben Judah

Jacob ben Judah of London, 11:**34**

Jacob ben Korshai, 11:**34**

Jacob ben Machir ibn Tibbon, 14:463

Jacob ben Makhir, 19:712

Jacob ben Meir Tam. See Tam, Jacob ben Meir

Jacob ben Mordecai of Schwerin, 11:**34–35**, 12:558

Jacob ben Moses of Bagnols, 11:**35**

Jacob ben Naphtali, 11:**35**

Jacob ben Nethanel ben (Al-)Fayyūmī, 11:**35**

Jacob ben Nissim ibn Shahin, 11:**35**

Jacob ben Reuben, 11:**35–36**
  allegorical interpretation of scripture, 3:645
  apologetics, 2:265–266

Jacob ben Samson, 11:**36**

Jacob ben Saul of Lunel. See Jacob Nazir

Jacob ben Simeon, 11:**36**

Jacob ben Sosas, 11:**36**

Jacob ben Yakar, 11:**36**

Jacob ben Ẓemaḥ ben Nissim, 11:**36–37**

Jacob Blaustein Institute for Desert Research, 3:**349**

Jacob David ben Israel Issar, 11:**37**

Jacob de Lunel. See Lunel, Jacob de

Jacob de Sequeira. See Rodrigues, Bartholomew

Jacob ha-Bachri. See Bachrach, Jacob Ben Moses

Jacob ha-Katan, 11:**37**

Jacob ha-Kohen. See Mazeh, Jacob

Jacob ha-Kohen bar Mordecai, 11:**37**

Jacob ha-Levi of Marv, 11:460

Jacobi, Abraham, 11:**37**

Jacobi, Erwin Reuben, 11:**37–38**

Jacobi, Frederick, 11:**38**

Jacobi, Georg, 11:**38**

Jacobi, Hanoch, 11:**38**

Jacobi, Heinrich. See Jacobi, Hanoch

Jacobi, Johanna Alexandra. See Jacobi, Lotte

Jacobi, Karl Gustav Jacob, 11:**38**, 16:135

Jacobi, Lotte, 11:**38–39**

Jacobi, Moritz Hermann, 11:**39**

Jacob ibn Ḥabib, 15:537

Jacob ibn Jau. *See* Ibn Jau, Jacob

Jacobins. *See* Dominicans

Jacob Isaac ben Shalom, 11:**39**

Jacob Isaac ha-Ḥozeh mi-Lublin, 8:395, 11:**39–41**, 12:455

Jacob Isaac of Przysucha, 11:40

Jacob Israel ben Benjamin of Belzec. *See* Israel ben Benjamin of Belzec

Jacob Joseph ben Ẓevi ha-Kohen Katz of Polonnoye, 11:**41–42**

Jacob Joseph of Ostrog, 11:**42**

Jacob Koppel ben Aaron Sasslower, 11:**42**

Jacob Koppel ben Moses of Mezhirech, 11:**42–43**

Jacob Meir. *See* Meir, Jacob

Jacob Nazir, 11:**43**

Jacob of Belzyce, 11:**43**

Jacob of Corbeil, 11:**43–44**

Jacob of Dubno. *See* Kranz, Jacob ben Wolf

Jacob of Edessa, 3:599

Jacob of Eger. *See* Jacob of Vienna

Jacob of Fulda. *See* Jacob ben Mordecai of Schwerin

Jacob of Kefar Sakhnayya, 11:**44**

Jacob of Lissa. *See* Lorbeerbaum, Jacob ben Jacob Moses of Lissa

Jacob of Malitsch, 17:420

Jacob of Marvège, 11:**44**

Jacob of Orleans, 11:**44**

Jacob of Oxford, 15:554

Jacob of Pont-Sainte-Maxence, 11:**44**

Jacob of Serugh, 4:720

Jacob of Vienna, 11:**44–45**

Jacobowski, Ludwig, 11:**45**

Jacob Qerido. *See* Querido, Jacob

Jacob Rader Marcus Center of the American Jewish Archives, 2:410

Jacobs, Aletta Henriëtte, 11:**45**, 16:345

Jacobs, Arthur, 11:**45–46**

Jacobs, Bernard B., 11:**46**

Jacobs, Cecil Isidore, 4:267

Jacobs, David. *See* Jacobs, Arthur

Jacobs, Ferdinande, 4:394

Jacobs, Frances Wisebart, 11:**46–47**

   See also National Jewish Center for Immunology and Respiratory Medicine

Jacobs, George, 11:**47**

Jacobs, Henry, 14:454

Jacobs, Hirsch, 4:8, 11:**47**

Jacobs, Irwin M., 11:**47–48**

Jacobs, James Leslie, 11:**48**

Jacobs, Jim. *See* Jacobs, James Leslie

Jacobs, Jimmy. *See* Jacobs, James Leslie

Jacobs, Joe, 11:**48–49**

Jacobs, Joseph, 2:49, 11:**49**

Jacobs, Lazarus, 4:185, 11:**49**

Jacobs, Louis, 6:420, 11:**49–50**

Jacobs, Manis, 13:223

Jacobs, Michael Strauss, 11:**50**

Jacobs, Rose Gell, 11:**50–51**

Jacobs, Sam, 4:404, 11:**300**

Jacobs, Samuel William, 11:**51**, 16:341

Jacobs, Simeon, 11:**51**, 12:554, 16:348–349

Jacobs, Solomon (civic leader), 11:**51**

Jacobs, Solomon (rabbi), 11:**51–52**

Jacobs, Wolf. *See* Jacobs, Samuel William

Jacobs, Yosef. *See* Jacobs, Joe

Jacob Samson of Shepetovka, 11:**52**

Jacobsen, Arne Emil, 11:**52**

Jacobsen, David, 2:505

Jacob's Ladder (Levertov), 12:682

Jacobsohn, Jacob, 2:407

Jacobsohn, Siegfried, 11:**52–53**

Jacobson, Anna, 11:**53**

Jacobson, Avigdor. *See* Jacobson, Victor

Jacobson, Dan, 11:**53**

Jacobson, Edward, 4:16, 11:**53**

Jacobson, Harry. *See* Jackson, Harry

Jacobson, Howard, 6:439, 11:**53–54**

Jacobson, Israel, 4:226, 6:160, 11:**54–55**

Jacobson, Kurt, 11:**55**

Jacobson, Ludvig Levin, 11:**55**

Jacobson, Nathan, 11:**55**

Jacobson, Paul Henrich, 11:**55**

Jacobson, Sydney Baron, 11:**55–56**

Jacobson, Victor, 11:**56**

Jacob's staff, 13:674

Jacobsthal, Gustav, 11:**56**

Jacobs *v.* Karotz, 5:196

Jacob the Liar (Becker), 3:246

Jacob the Small. *See* Jacob ha-Katan

Jacobus Apella Vicedominus, 4:37, 11:**56**

Jacoby, Johann, 11:**56–57**, 12:778, 16:344

Jacoby, Lee. *See* Cobb, Lee J.

Jacoby, Oswald, 11:**57**

Jacques, M. E. *See* Zhernensky, Moshe Eliyahu

Jadassohn, Josef, 11:**57**

Jadassohn, Salomon, 11:**57**

Jaddua (high priest), 1:625, 11:**57–58**, 18:602

Jadid al-Islam, 2:253–254

Jadīd al-Islām, 11:**58**

Jadlowker, Hermann, 11:**58**

Jaecklin, Jud, 11:**58**

Jael, 11:**58–59**, 562, 563

Jaén (Spain), 11:**59**

Jaffa (Israel), 11:**59–64**

   economic center of Arab sector, 10:486

   growth of, 10:485, 486

   population, 1882-1944, 10:481*t*

   See also Tel Aviv (Israel); Tel Aviv-Jaffa (Israel)

Jaffa, Henry N., 11:**64**

Jaffa, Nathan, 11:**64**

Jaffa brothers, 11:**64**

Jaffe, Abraham B., 11:**64**

Jaffe, Bezalel, 11:**64–65**

Jaffe, Daniel. *See* Itzig, Daniel

Jaffe, Eli, 11:**65**

Jaffe, Israel ben Aaron, 11:**65**

Jaffe, Leib, 11:**65–66**

Jaffe, Leonard, 11:**66–67**

Jaffe, Maurice Abraham, 11:**67**

Jaffe, Meir of Ulm, 4:74, 11:**67**

Jaffe, Mordecai ben Abraham, 1:532, 2:174, 4:778–779, 8:552, 11:**67–68**

Jaffe, Mordecai-Gimpel (1820-1891), 11:**68**

Jaffe, Otto. *See* Jaffe, Sir Otto

Jaffe, Rona, 11:**68–69**

Jaffe, Sam, 11:**69**

Jaffe, Samuel ben Isaac Ashkenazi, 11:**69**

Jaffe, Sir Otto, 11:**68**

Jaffee, Irving W., 11:**69–70**

Jaffe family, 11:**64**, 66*t*

Jaffe-Margoliot, Israel David, 11:**70**

JAFI (Jewish Agency for Israel). *See* Jewish Agency

Jagel, Abraham, 3:706, 7:15, 11:**70–71**

Jagel, Abraham ben Ḥananiah dei Galicchi, 11:**71**

Jaglom, Henry, 11:**71**

Jaglom, Raya, 11:**71–72**

Jagt, Marek van der. *See* Grunberg, Arnon

Jahaz (Moab), 11:**72**

Jahaza (Moab). *See* Jahaz (Moab)

Jāhiliyya, 10:95

Jahoda, Marie, 11:**72–73**, 18:735

Jahrbuecher des fraenkischen Reichs unter Ludwig dem Frommen (Simson), 18:621

Jahrzeit. *See* Yahrzeit

Jahzah. *See* Jahaz (Moab)

Jai Alai, 19:144

Jails. *See* Prisons

Jair, 11:**73**, 564

Jair family, 11:73

Jair of Gilead, 11:73

Jakab, Dezsö, 11:**73**

Jakeh (biblical figure). *See* Solomon (biblical figure)

Jakim. *See* Alcimus

Jakob der Lugner (Becker), 3:**246**

Jakób of Belzyce. *See* Jacob of Belzyce

Jakobovits, Lord Immanuel, 6:33, 427, 11:**73**

Jakobovits, Tobias, 11:**73–74**

Die Jakobsleiter (Schoenberg), 11:24

Jakobson, Roman, 11:**74**

Jakobstadt (Latvia). *See* Jekabpils (Latvia)

Jakubovish, Isaac. *See* Jekeles, Isaac ben Jacob

Jakubowski, Jackie, 11:**74**

Jama, Samuel ibn, 11:**74**

Jamaica, 4:473–474, 11:**74–75**
　　government officials, 13:670
　　Jewish settlement in, 2:41

Jamal Sulaymān, 11:**75–76**

Jámbor, Ferenc-Iosef, 11:**76**

Jambres (Egyptian sorcerer), 11:78

James (brother of Jesus), 11:449

James, David, 11:**76**

James, Harry, 11:**76**

James, Protoevangelium of. See Protoevangelium of James

James, Sidney, 11:**76**

James I, King of Aragon, 1:253, 17:127, 18:42, 572

James Joyce (Ellmann), 6:362

James Joyce: A Critical Introduction (Levin), 12:709

Jāmiʿ al-Tvaārīkh (Rashid al-Din), 14:444, 17:106

Jammer, Max, 11:**76–77**

Jammer, Moshe, 11:**77**

Jamnia. *See* Jabneh (ancient Israel)

Jamnitz (Czechoslovakia). *See* Jemnice (Czechoslovakia)

Jampel, Sigmund, 11:**77**

Janáček, Leoš, 4:193

Janah (ancient Israel). *See* Janoah (ancient Israel)

Janco, Marcel, 6:257, 11:**77–78**, 14:470, 15:648

Janīn (Palestinina Authority). *See* Jenin (Palestinian Authority)

Janina (Greece). *See* Ioannina (Greece)

Janissaries, Jewish relationship with, 15:526–527

Jankélévitch, Vladimir, 11:**78**

Jannaeus, Alexander. *See* Yannai, Alexander

Janner, Barnett, 11:**78**, 16:342

Janner, Greville Ewan, 11:78

Jannes (Egyptian sorcerer), 11:**78**

Janoah (ancient Israel), 11:**78–79**

Janovi al-Yad Pinsk (Belarus). *See* Ivanovo (Belarus)

Janovo. *See* Jonava (Lithuania)

Janovsky, Saul Joseph, 11:**79**, 18:710

Janowitz, Henry D., 11:**79**

Janowitz, Morris, 11:**79**, 18:733

Janow Lubelski (Poland), 11:**79–80**

Janów Lubelski (Poland). *See* Janow Lubelski (Poland)

Janów Poleski (Belarus). *See* Ivanovo (Belarus)

Janów Polski. *See* Ivanovo (Belarus)

Janowska Road camp, 13:291

Janowski, David Markelovich, 11:**80**

Janowski, Max, 11:**80**

Janowsky, Oscar Isaiah, 11:**80**

Jansenists, 15:674–675

Januarius, 11:**80**

January, Pepper. *See* Rivers, Joan

Jaoui, Agnes, 3:42

Japan, 11:**81–85**
　　antisemitism in, 2:240–242, 11:81, 85
　　conversion to Judaism in, 11:82
　　Judaizers in, 11:521
　　Makuya, 13:420–421
　　relations with Israel and, 10:265
　　trade with Israel, 11:83

Japanese language, 3:637

Japhet, Israel Meyer, 11:**85**

Japheth (son of Noah), 11:**86**

Japheth al-Barqamani, 11:**86**

Japheth ben David ibn Ṣaghīr, 11:**86**

Japheth ben Eli ha-Levi, 2:128, 3:604–605, 11:**86–87**, 532

Japhia (ancient Israel), 11:**87**

Jarash. *See* Gerasa

Jarblum, Marc, 4:10, 11:**87–88**

Jaré family, 11:**88**

Jargon. *See* Yiddish language

Jarkon. *See* Yarkon river

Jarman, 3:**16**

Jarmona family. *See* Darmon family

Jarmon family. *See* Darmon family

Jarmuth (Canaan), 11:**88**

Jaroczynski school, 13:157

Jaroslavsky, César, 16:350

Jaroslavsky, Naum, 16:349

Jaroslaw (Poland), 11:**88–89**

Jasenovac concentration camp, 9:340

Jashar, Book of. *See* Book of Jashar

Jasieński, Bruno, 11:**89**

Jasinowski, Israel Isidore, 11:**89**

Jaslo (Poland), 11:**89–90**

Jasny, Naum, 11:**90**

Jason (high priest), 9:193, 11:**90**, 147–148

Jason of Cyrene, 9:154, 11:**90**

Jassinowsky, Pinchas, 11:**91**

Jassy (Romania), 11:**91–93**, 13:257

Jastrow, Joseph, 11:**94**

Jastrow, Marcus Mordecai, 2:104, 11:93

Jastrow, Morris, 11:93

Jastrow family, 11:**93–94**

Jastrun, Mieczyslaw, 11:**94**

Jászi, Oszkár, 11:**94**

Játiva (Spain), 11:**94–95**

Jattir (Judea), 11:**95**

Jau, Jacob Ibn. *See* Ibn Jau, Jacob

Jaunijelgava (Latvia), 11:**95**

Jaurès, Jean Léon, 11:**95**

Javal, Emile, 11:**96**

Javal, Leopold, 11:**95–96**

Javal family, 11:**95–96**

Javan (grandson of Noah), 11:**96**

Javetz, Barzillai ben Baruch, 11:**96**

Javid Bey, Mehmed, 11:**96**

Javitch, David, 8:365

Javitch, Lee, 8:365

Javits, Jacob, 2:51

Javits, Jacob Koppel, 11:**97**

Javorov. *See* Yavorov (Ukraine)

Jawitz, Ze'ev, 11:**97–98**, 14:389

Jawnieli, Shemuel. *See* Yavne'eli, Shemuel

Jaworów (Ukraine). *See* Yavorov (Ukraine)

Jaws, 6:21

Jaww, Jacob Ibn. *See* Ibn Jau, Jacob

Jay, Allan Louis Neville, 11:**98**

Jazaniah. *See* Jaazaniah

Jazaniahu. *See* Jaazaniah

Jazer (ancient Israel), 11:**98**

Jazirat ibn ʿUmar (Iraq), 11:**98**

The Jazz Singer (motion picture), 14:571, 20:336

JBC. *See* Joint Boycott Council

JCCs. *See* Jewish Community Centers

J.C.R. *See* Jewish Cultural Reconstruction, Inc. (JCR)

JDC. *See* American Jewish Joint Distribution Committee (JDC)

JDL. *See* Jewish Defense League

Jealousy, 5:254, 11:**98–99**, 15:462–463

Jean de Saint-Rémy, 15:314

Jeanette and Harry Weinberg Foundation, 18:211

Jebel. *See* Dok (Israel); Seir, Mount (ancient Israel)

Jebel Abu Ḥasan (Eqypt), 3:13

Jebenhausen (Germany), 11:**99**

Jebus, 11:**99–100**

   See also Jerusalem (Israel)

Jebusites, 11:**99–100**

   See also Jerusalem (Israel)

Jechoniah. *See* Jehoiachin (King of Judah)

Jeconiah. *See* Jehoiachin (King of Judah)

Jedaiah (priestly ancestral house), 11:**100**

Jedaiah ben Abraham Bedersi, 11:**100–101**

Jedermann (Hofmannsthal), 9:313

Jedidiah (biblical figure). *See* Solomon (biblical figure)

Jedidiah ben Moses of Recanati, 11:**101–102**

Jedidiah ben Moses of Rimini. *See* Jedidiah ben Moses of Recanati

Jedidiah Solomon Raphael ben Abraham, 13:652–653

Jedrzejow (Poland), 11:**102**

Jeduthun (biblical harpist), 11:**102**

Jefferson, Thomas, 11:**102–103**

Jefferson Airplane, 3:90, 91

Jeffries, Leonard, 3:736

Jehiel ben Abraham, 2:136

Jehiel ben Gershom. *See* Bauer Jacob

Jehiel ben Joseph of Paris, 11:**103**

Jehiel Lifschits of Gostynin. *See* Jehiel Meir of Gostynin

Jehiel Meir of Gostynin, 11:**103**

Jehiel Michael ben Abraham Meir of Cifer, 11:**103**

Jehiel Michael ben Eliezer, 11:**103–104**

Jehiel Michael ben Judah Leib he-Ḥasid, 11:**104**

Jehiel Michael of Zloczow, 11:**104**

Jehiel Michel ben Abraham Meir of Cifer. *See* Jehiel Michael ben Abraham Meir of Cifer

Jehiel Michel ben Eliezer. *See* Jehiel Michael ben Eliezer

Jehiel Michel ben Judah Leib he-Ḥasid. *See* Jehiel Michael ben Judah Leib he-Ḥasid

Jehiel Michel of Zloczow. *See* Jehiel Michael of Zloczow

Jehiel of Paris. *See* Jehiel ben Joseph of Paris

Jehoahaz (King of Israel), 11:**105**

Jehoahaz (King of Judah), 9:179, 11:**105–106**

Jehoash (King of Israel), 9:178, 11:**106**

Jehoiachin (King of Judah, 6th c. B.C.E.), 11:**106–107**

Jehoiada (chief priest), 11:**107–108**

Jehoiakim (King of Judah, 609-598 B.C.E.), 2:86, 6:365–366, 9:181–182, 11:**108–109**

Jehoiarib (priestly division), 11:**109**

Jehoram (King of Israel), 1:539–540, 11:**110–111**

Jehoram (King of Judah), 6:332, 350, 9:177, 11:**109–110**

Jehoseph ha-Nagid, 11:**111**

Jehoshabath, 11:107

Jehoshaphat (King of Judah), 9:176–177, 11:**111–112**

   Edom, 6:155

   Elisha, 6:350

   judicial system, 6:166

   Ophir, 15:439

Jehoshaphat, Valley of (ancient Israel), 11:**112**

Jehosheba, 11:107

Jehosiphiah the Proselyte. *See* Josiphiah the Proselyte

Jéhouda, Josué, 11:**112–113**

Jehovah's Witnesses, 4:383–384

Jehu (Evron), 8:722

Jehu (King of Israel), 6:332, 9:177–178, 11:**113–114**

Jehu (prophet), 3:13, 11:**113**

Jeiteles, Andreas Ludwig Joseph Heinrich, 11:115

Jeiteles, Berthold, 11:115–116

Jeiteles family, 11:**114–116**, 114*t*, 12:460

Jeitteles family. *See* Jeiteles family

Jekabpils (Latvia), 11:**116**

Jekeles, Eisik Reb. *See* Jekeles, Isaac ben Jacob

Jekeles, Isaac ben Jacob, 11:116

Jekeles, Moses ben Isaac, 11:116

Jekeles, Moses ben Jacob, 11:116

Jekeles family, 11:**116**

Jekel of Eiger. *See* Jacob of Vienna

Jekuthiel ben Isaac ha-Nakdan, 13:635, 637

Jekuthiel ben Judah ha-Kohen, 11:**116–117**, 13:652

Jekuthiel ben Judah ha-Kohen ha-Naqden. *See* Jekuthiel ben Judah ha-Kohen

Jelenski, Jan, 11:**117–118**

Jelgava (Latvia), 11:**118**

Jelinek, Elfriede, 11:**118–119**

Jellin, Aryeh Loeb ben Shalom Shakhna, 11:**119**

Jellinek, Aaron. *See* Jellinek, Adolf

Jellinek, Adolf, 3:764, 11:**119–120**

   journey of Elijah and Joshua ben Levi, 14:539

Jellinek, Georg, 12:547, 551

Jellinek, Hermann, 11:**120–121**

Jellinek, Karl, 11:**121**

Jellinik, Adolf, 2:269

Jemdat Nasr archives, 2:402

Jemnice (Czechoslovakia), 11:**121**

Jener, Abraham Naphtali Hirsch ben Mordecai, 11:**121**

Jenin (Palestinian Authority), 11:**121–122**

Jenin, Jenin (Bakri), 3:73

Jenkinson, Hilary. *See* Jenkinson, Sir Hilary

Jenkinson, Sir Charles. *See* Jenkinson, Sir Hilary

Jenkinson, Sir Hilary, 11:**122**

Jennikau, Aaron. *See* Kornfeld, Aaron ben Mordecai Baer

Jennis, Dennis. *See* Aboab, Isaac de Mattathias

Jenufa (Janáček), 4:193

Jędrzejów (Poland). *See* Jedrezjow (Poland)

Jephtah's Daughter (Seter), 18:319

Jephthah (biblical figure), 1:416, 11:**122–124**, 564–565, 14:388

Jerahmeel ben Solomon, 11:**124**

Jerba (Tunisia). *See* Djerba (Tunisia)

Jeremiah, 11:**124–135**

   Ahab, 1:525

   Babylonian exile and, 6:611, 612

   Baruch, 3:181–182

   eschatology in, 6:492

   foe from the North and, 11:131–132

   historicity of, 11:125

   Hosea and, 11:126

   Lamentations, Book of, 12:449

   Temple sermon, 11:126–127

   versions of Book of, 11:128–129

Jeremiah (priest), 2:132

Jeremiah, Chronicles of. *See* Baruch, Rest of the Words of

Jeremiah, Epistle of, 3:185–186, 11:**135**

Jeremiah ben Abba, 11:**135–136**

Jeremiah ben Isaac, 11:**136**

Jeremiah und seine Zeit (Cornill), 5:224

Jeremias, Alfred, 3:651, 11:**136**

Jerez de la Frontera (Spain), 11:**137**

Jeriboam (biblical figure), 12:172

Jericho (Palestine), 11:**137–140**

   Jordan (river) and, 11:402

   Joshua and, 11:442, 443, 446

Jeroboam (King of Israel), 1:257, 3:13,
9:174–175, 11:**140–141**
Ahijah the Shilonite, 1:542
golden calves, 6:622, 14:525
Solomon, 18:758
Jeroboam II (King of Israel), 2:85,
9:178–179, 11:**141–142**
Jeroham ben Meshullam, 4:773, 6:41,
11:**142**
Jerome, 11:**142–143**
Church Fathers, 4:720
Latin translation of Bible by,
3:598, 666
oak of Abraham in Hebron,
15:357
Jerome, William Travers, 15:211
Jerrold Electronics Corporation,
18:408
Jersey Homesteads, 14:446
Jersey Rain (Pinsky), 16:176
Jerubaal. *See* Gideon
Jerusalem (Chateaubriand), 4:583
Jerusalem (Israel), 11:**143–232**
Abba Sakkara and, 1:234
Abraham ha-Levi, 1:312
Absalom, monument of, 1:332
Acra, the, 1:363–364
Adoni-Zedek, 1:413–414
Aelia Capitolina, 1:429, *429*
agoranomos, 1:469–470
Aleppo Jewish community in,
10:296
Alexandrians in, 1:632–633
aliyah to, 10:332
alternate names, 2:453
Arabs, 11:153–157
after Six-Day war, 10:718
population of, 10:486, 494
Aramaic, 2:348
archaeology, 10:631, 11:200–205
architecture, 10:703
archives, 2:405
Ariel, 2:453
arts, 11:224–229
Ashkenazi community, renewal of,
14:24–25
British rule, 11:173–178
as capital of Israel, 10:213, 214,
239, 259
centricity of, 7:489
Christianity, 10:638, 11:152, 164–
165, 218–222, 224–226
Crusades and, 10:161, 162, 163,
165, 11:157–159, 221
Ethiopian church, 6:537–538
fortification of, 9:188
governance, during Mandate,
10:390

government, 10:211
Hadassah hospital, 8:187
Hajj Muhammad Amīn al-
Husseini as, 10:275
Ha-modi'a, 8:310–311
Hasmonean Tunnel at western
Wall, 10:247–248
history of, 11:144–196, 212–213
Arab rule, 11:153–157
British rule, 11:173–178
Crusades, 11:157–159, 221
as divided city, 11:178–182
Mamluk rule, 11:159–161
Ottoman period, 8:245–247,
267, 10:170–171, 172–173,
683, 704–705, 11:161–173
pre-Roman, 11:144–150
Roman rule, 11:36, 150–153,
219–220
united, 11:182–196, 199
housing construction, 10:354
as hub of universe, 11:212, 215,
222
Isaiah, Book of, 10:59
Islam and, 10:89, 11:222–224
Israel Museum, 10:757–758
Jebusites and, 11:99–100
Jewish settlement
Arab attacks, 11:175–176,
177–178, 186
prohibition of, 11:152, 153,
154, 158
revival of, 11:162–164, 167–
168, 169, 170, 171, 172,
173, 174–175
Josiah, expansion under, 11:457
in Judaism, 11:208–218
as Judeo-Persian literary center,
11:557
kabbalists, 11:621
Karaites, 10:161, 298
ketubbah depiction of, vol. 12:
color insert
Knesset in, 10:428–429
kolelim, 8:289
Kurds (Targum Jews) in, 10:297–
298
labor organization, 10:605
legal aspects, 11:210, 211, **232–239**
Mamluk period, 10:168, 11:159–
161
municipal government, 11:181–
182
necropolises, 11:202, 203–204, 210
Old City, aerial view, vol. 10:
color insert
Ophel, 15:438
oracle of unclean, 6:639

Orthodox Jews and, 6:64
Ottoman period, 10:170–171, 172–
173, 11:161–173
Ḥakham Bashi, 8:245–247
Hebrew language, 10:683
journalism, 10:704–705
newspapers, 8:267
Palestine
Exploration Fund survey of,
15:589
Mandate, anti-Jewish riots,
10:197, 200
Ottoman, 10:683, 704–705
Persian Jews, 10:297
pilgrimages, 16:155–156
planning and construction,
16:217–218
population, 10:292
1882-1944, 10:481t
Arab, 10:486, 494
Jewish, 10:506
printing and publishing, 16:538
rebuilding of, Nehemiah and,
6:660–661
Rehavia neighborhood, 14:425
Roman rule, 11:36, 150–153, 219–
220, 436
Schick, Conrad, study by, 18:126
schools, 6:649–650
security fence, 11:195–196
Sha'alu Shelom Yerushalayim,
7:408
Shalem (ancient Israel), 18:371
Six Day War, 10:230, 231, 255,
18:651–652
status of, 10:255–256
symbols of, 11:225
temple dedication, 9:189–191
Titus, Flavius Vespasianus,
19:743–744
United Nations, 20:261–262
internationalization and,
10:214–215
Jerusalem status, 20:261–262
partition of, 10:208
status and, 10:255–256
urban planning, 10:368
Urfalis in, 10:298
War of Independence, 10:209,
20:658, 662
water supply, 11:169–170, 174,
177, 179, 182, 194, 205–207,
13:799
Western Wall, 9:188, 21:24–27
Jerusalem (Mendelssohn), 14:34, 37–
39, 16:93–94
Jerusalem, Karl Wilheim, 11:**232**

Jerusalem, Little. *See* Béziers (France)

Jerusalem: The Topography, Economics, and History from the Earliest Times to A.D. 70 (Smith), 18:688

Jerusalem, Wilhelm, 11:**239**, 18:731

Jerusalem ancienne et nouvelle (Abel), 1:246

Jerusalem Bible, 3:617

Jerusalem Chamber of Commerce, 6:317

Jerusalem City of Peace (Karavan), 11:804

Jerusalem College of Technology, 13:234

Jerusalem Did Not Fall (Elon), 6:366

Jerusalem Foundation. *See* Hierosolymitanische Stiftung

Jerusalem Institute for Israel Studies (JIIS), 11:**239**

"Jerusalem Itinerary." *See* Itinerarium Hierosolymitanum

Jerusalem Koren Edition (Bible), 3:617

Jerusalem Mountains (Israel), 10:114–117, 115

Jerusalem of Lithuania (Ran), 16:127

The Jerusalem Post (newspaper), 1:504, 11:**240**

The Jerusalem Publishing House, 11:**240**

Jerusalem Report (periodical), 11:**241**

Jerusalem Syndrome (Sobol), 18:702

Jerusalem Talmud, 19:**483–487**
  amoraim, 2:93, 95, 13:90–91
  Bava Kamma differences, 3:225–226
  Beit ha-Beḥirah and, 13:786
  biblical orthography, 13:612
  cheese, 4:587
  commentators
    on aggadot, 11:69
      Ratner, Dov Baer, 17:112
      Sirillo, Solomon ben Joseph, 18:643–644
  detention, 5:607
  Elijah ben Loeb of Fulda, 6:339
  Elijah ben Solomon Zalman, 6:342
  Elisha ben Avuyah, 6:352
  Eruvin (tractate), 6:485–486
  finalized, 10:155
  Galilean Aramaic, 2:349
  Johanan ben Nappaḥa, 11:370–372
  on Judean boundaries, 11:523
  Megillah (tractate), 13:768
  mishpat Ivri, 14:337, 346
  Orlah, 15:475
  patients' rights, 13:742
  redaction, 9:206
  savora, 18:85
  Torah divisions, 13:607, 609–610
  tractates, 13:667

Jerusalimski, Moses Naḥum ben Benjamin, 11:**241**

Jeschurun (periodicals), 9:133, 11:**241**

Jeshua (high priest), 11:**241–242**

Jeshua ben Elijah ha-Levi. *See* Joshua ben Elijah ha-Levi

Jeshua ben Joseph ha-Levi, 11:**242**

Jeshua ben Judah, 2:17, 3:605, 11:**242–243**

Jeshurun, 11:**243**

Jesi, Samuel, 11:**243**

JESNA (Jewish Education Service of North America), 2:48, 6:201, 11:**290–291**

Jesse (father of David), 5:446, 459, 11:**243–244**

Jesse ben Hezekiah, 11:**244**

Jessel, George. *See* Jessel, Sir George

Jessel, George Albert, 11:**244**

Jessel, Sir George, 11:**244**, 12:550, 16:342

Jesselson, Ludwig, 11:**244–245**

Jessey, Henry, 11:**245**, 15:252

Jessner, Leopold, 11:**245**

Jessurun, Isaac ben Abraham Ḥayyim. *See* Jesurun, Isaac ben Abraham Ḥayyim

Jessurun family. *See* Jesurun family

Jesters, court. *See* Court jesters

Jesuits, 11:**245**

Jesurun, Isaac ben Abraham Ḥayyim, 11:**246**

Jesurun, Reuel, 11:**246**

Jesurun family, 11:**246**

Jesus, 11:**246–251**
  Aaron and, 1:210–211
  Adam, 1:374, 375
  Ben Stada, 3:378–379
  Bethphage (Israel), 3:536
  David and, 5:454, 455, 460
  James, brother of Jesus, 11:449
  John the Baptist and, 11:380, 381
  Joseph as type of, 11:412
  Josephus' *Jewish Antiquities* on, 11:439–440
  Joshua as type of, 11:443, 444
  Josippon on, 11:462
  Judeo-Christian disciples, 11:44
  jujube thorns and, 11:572
  Moses, 14:538
  Noah as type of, 15:289
  Toledot Yeshu, 7:13
  See also Christianity; Nazareth (Israel)

Jesus (son of Sapphas). *See* Joshua

Jesus (son of Seth). *See* Joshua

Jesus the Jew (Barth), 4:681, 687

Jether. *See* Jethro

Jethira (Judea). *See* Jattir (Judea)

Jethro (father-in-law of Moses), 6:614–615, 11:**251–253**, 14:524, 526, 545

Jettchen Gebert (Hermann), 9:24

Jeuschsohn, B. *See* Justman, Moshe Bunem

Jevicko (Czech Republic), 11:**253**

Jevičko (Czech Republic). *See* Jevicko (Czech Republic)

Jew, 11:**253–255**

"A Jew." *See* "Adam mi-Yisrael"

The Jew (Cumberland), 5:337

The Jew and the Blonde. See Evrey i blondinka

The Jew as a Symbol (Duda), 6:40

Jew Bill Controversy (England), 11:**255**

Jew Castle. *See* Chufut-Kale (Crimea)

The Jew-Eater. See Endlich, Quirin

Jewelry. *See* Precious stones and jewelry

"The Jewess" (Babel), 3:18

Jewess of Toledo, 11:**255–256**

The Jew in American Literature (Liptzin), 13:78

Jewish Advocate, 9:368

Jewish Agency, 11:**256–262**, 20:257–258
  Adler-Rudel, Salomon, 1:409
  Amidar, 2:76
  Amir, Eli, 2:78
  Argentina, 2:444
  Asociación Mutual Israelita Argentina, 2:71
  Ben-Gurion, David, 3:345–346
  Beriḥah, 3:434
  Dulzin, Arye Leib, 6:45
  education, Jewish, 6:186
  Filderman, Wilhelm, 7:19
  Horev Commission and, 9:525
  Morocco, 14:506
  Neumann, Emanuel, 15:121
  Project Renewal, 16:544–547
  rescue from Holocaust, 9:490
  Sokolow, Nahum, 18:749

Jewish Agency for Israel (JAFI). *See* Jewish Agency

Jewish Agency for Palestine. *See* Jewish Agency

Jewish Agricultural (and Industrial Aid) Society, 11:**262**, 14:446

Jewish American Poetry: Poems, Commentary, and Reflections, 20:301

Jewish Anti-Fascist Committee, 2:**196–197**, 5:301, 14:518

Jewish Antiquities (Josephus), 9:155, 11:438–440, 18:762

Jewish Archives and Historical Society of Edmonton and Northern Alberta, 6:151

Jewish Art Theater (NYC), 18:186

Jewish Autonomous Region. *See* Birobidzhan (Russia)

Jewish badges, 3:**45–48**, 9:*460, 464*
> Austria, 2:689
> Belgium, 2:250
> Boniface IX, 4:63
> France, 2:6, 81, 3:45–46, 47
> Germany, 3:46–47, 450
> Italy, 2:137, 140, 292, 3:46, 47, 12:506, 608
> Netherlands, 2:115
> Spain, 6:91, 12:643
> *See also* Dress

Jewish Blind Society, 6:428

The Jewish Book Council, 11:**270–271**, 13:78

Jewish Braille Institute, 1:223

Jewish Brigade Group, 11:**271–272**, 17:120, 18:610
> Benjamin, Ernest Frank, 3:357
> Beriḥah, 3:434–435
> in Italy, 12:500, 13:253–254, 16:8

Jewish camping, 6:196, 199–200, 11:**272–275**
> B'nai B'rith, 4:15
> Camp Kawaga (WI), 6:241

Jewish Cantillation and Song in the Isle of Djerba (Lachmann), 12:424

Jewish Care, 6:428

Jewish catechism. *See* Articles of faith

Jewish Centers Association, 13:197

Jewish Central Information Office. *See* Wiener Library

Jewish Chautauqua Society, 6:192, 7:693

Jewish-Christian relations, 4:93, 11:**275–284**, 775–776, 16:632–633

Jewish Chronicle (newspaper), 6:415, 7:199, 8:71, 11:**284–285**

Jewish Civilization: The Jewish Historical Experience in a Comparative Perspective (Eisenstadt), 18:735

Jewish Colonial Trust, 11:**285**

Jewish Colonization Association (ICA), 11:**285–288**
> American Joint Distribution Committee, 2:60
> Anglo-Jewish Association, 2:162
> Ansell, David Abraham, 2:181
> Argentina, 6:448
>> Alpersohn, Marcos, 1:688
>> Birobidzhan, 3:718
>> Bliokh, Ivan Stanislavovich, 3:756
>> Brandt, Boris, 4:128
>> Brazil, 4:145–146
>> Canada, 4:399
>> Dubrovno, 6:39
>> Hirsch, Baron Maurice de, 9:127
>> Latvia, 12:521

The Jewish Communal Association of North America, 11:**288**

The Jewish Communal Register (statistics), 6:697

Jewish Community Center of Dallas, 5:383

Jewish Community Centers (JCCs), 3:99, 6:195, 200, 13:209–210

Jewish Community Council of Montreal, 14:465

Jewish Community for Cuba (JCC), 5:317–318

Jewish Congregation Anshe Sholom (Ontario), 8:304

Jewish Consciousness program, 10:224

Jewish Contemporary Documentation Center. *See* Centre de Documentation Juive Contemporaine

Jewish Continuity (organization), 6:428–429

Jewish Continuity Act, 6:428

Jewish Continuity and Change (Goldscheider), 18:736

Jewish cookbooks, 5:**200–203**, 14:456

Jewish Correspondence Bureau. *See* Jewish Telegraphic Agency (JTA)

Jewish Council on Public Affairs (JCSA), 2:52, 11:**288–289**

Jewish Court. *See* Bet din and judges

Jewish Cultural Association. *See* Juedischer Kulturbund

Jewish Cultural Reconstruction, Inc. (JCR), 11:**289**

Jewish Daily Forward (newspaper), 4:335–336, 6:696–697, 11:**289–290**, 719, 14:396, 15:210, 21:356
> Cahan, Abraham, 16:503–504, 20:325–326
> Held, Adolph, 8:780–781
> influence of, 18:708
> *Morning Freiheit* (newspaper), 14:493

Jewish Day (newspaper), 11:**290**

Jewish Defense League, 11:715, 18:264
> Kach party, 11:693
> in New York City, 15:215

Jewish Democratic Committee, Comitetul Democrat Evreiesc. *See* C.D.E.

Jewish Demography and Statistics (Schmelz), 18:145

Jewish Drama Studio Shalom, 14:520

Jewish education, 6:**162–214**
> academies
>> in Babylonia, 1:347–351
>> in Erez Israel, 1:347–351, 14:522
>>> Hebrew language, 1:351–353
>> on High, 1:353
> Agudat Israel, 1:506, 507
> Agus, Irving Abraham, 1:521
> Alliance Israelite Universelle, 1:672–675, 673*t*
> Argentina, 4:587, 6:211–212
> art, 5:626, 646
> Australia, 6:207–208
> Bei-Rav, 3:269
> Bible, 6:162–169
>> curriculum, 6:167–168
>> diplomats and government officials, 6:166
>> educational institutions, 6:164–169
>> priests and prophets, 6:168
>> religious education, 6:163–164, 165, 166–167
>> royalty, 6:165–166
>> scribal education, 6:167
>> sources, 6:162–163
>> survey, historical, 6:163
>> women, 6:168–169
> Brazil, 6:212
> Canada, 4:402, 405, 419–420, 6:208–210, 209*t*, 14:465–466
> Chile, 4:641
> Cuba, 5:321, 324–325
> Czechoslovakia, 5:355
> Dan, Joseph, 5:407–408
> Della Torre, Lelio, 5:541–542
> dukhan platform for teachers and, 6:44
> eighteenth-early nineteenth century, 6:181–186
> England, 6:419, 421–22, 429–430, 14:510–511
> Europe
>> Middle Ages, 9:220–221
>> sixteenth and seventeenth centuries, 9:224
>> WW II, 6:186–187
> Germany, 1:547, 8:437–438
>> Akademie fuer die Wissenschaft des Judentums, 1:554
>> Hirsch, Mendel, 9:128
>> Hochschule Fuer die Wissenschaft des Judentums, 9:300

government intervention, 8:438–439

Harari, Ḥayyim, 8:344

Haskalah and, 8:437–439

Hebrew, 4:621, 623

ḥeder, 8:752

Hirsch views, 9:130

homiletic literature and, 9:515

Hungary, 9:619

Hurwitz, Henry, 9:632

intermarriage, 14:375, 382

Iran, 6:214

Jewish Education Service of North America, 2:48, 11:290–291

Kaplan, Aryeh, 11:773–774

Kaplan, Chaim Aron, 11:774–775

Mexico, 3:425, 6:213

Middle Ages, 6:172–177, 9:517–518

Mizrachi, 14:390–391

modern, 6:742

Mo'ezet ha-Po'alot, 14:415

Morocco, 14:500, 502, 505–507

North Africa, 6:213–214

parental role, 4:618

Pines, Noah, 16:167

pre-World War II, 6:184–185

Russia, 8:442

Schweid, Eliezer on, 18:194

sixteenth-eighteenth centuries, 6:177–180

South Africa, 6:210–211

summer camps and, 11:271–272

Syria, 5:396

Talmud, 6:169–172

teacher training, 8:438

U.K., 6:204–207

Uruguay, 6:212–213

U.S., 4:713, 6:189–204, 705, 706, 12:469, 16:34, 35

   Adler, Joseph, 1:401

   Alper, Michael, 1:688

   Alperstein, Avraham Eliezer ben Yeshaya, 1:688

   Belkin, Samuel, 3:296

   Benderly, Samson, 3:327–328

   Ben-Horin, Meir, 3:352

   CAJE, 4:763–764

   Chanover, Hyman, 4:566

   Chipkin, Israel, 4:652

   Chomsky, William, 4:665–666

   Churgin, Pinkhos, 4:723

   Cincinnati, 4:727–728

   colonial and national period, 6:189–190

   congregational education 1960's and 1970's, 6:199

   day schools, growth of, 5:68, 6:198–199

   Dinin, Samuel, 5:671

   Dorph, Sheldon, 5:759–760

   Eastern Europe immigration 1881-1910, 6:192–195

   Essex County (NJ), 6:513

   German-Jewish immigration 1840-1880, 6:191–192

   Hebrew College, 8:553–554

   Herzliah Hebrew Teachers' Institute, 9:66–67

   higher learning, 6:196–197

   Hirshenberg, Samuel, 9:142–143

   innovations in settings for, 6:199–201

   institutional development 1910-1945, 6:195

   Lamm, Norman, 12:453

   Maximon, Shalom Dov Ber, 13:695

   Mendlowitz, Shraga Feivel, 14:44

   Monmouth County (NJ), 14:447

   Mordecai, Jacob, 14:480

   Pekarsky, Maurice Bernard, 15:715

   Perlberg, Abraham Nathan, 15:775

   Pilch, Judah, 16:153

   Progressivism, 8:553

   women leaders, 6:542

   See also specific academies and organizations

Jewish Educational Society (San Francisco), 11:722

Jewish Education Service of North America (JESNA), 2:48, 6:201, **11:290–291**

Jewish Educators Assembly, 6:199

Jewish emancipation. *See* Emancipation

Jewish Emancipation under Attack (Duker, Weinryb), 6:44

The Jewish Emergence from Powerlessness (Bauer), 9:416

Jewish Encyclopedia, 6:400, 11:724, 18:636

Jewish Examiner (periodical), 2:49

Jewish Family Album (Hubmann), 16:127

Jewish Family Bible, 3:617, 622

Jewish Family Papers. See Juedische Familienpapiere

Jewish Family Service (JFS), 5:383

Jewish Federation Council, 13:208–209

Jewish Federation of Greater Dallas, 5:382–383

Jewish Federation of Monmouth County, 14:447

Jewish Fighters' Organizations, 15:667

Jewish Fighting Organization (ZOB), 13:240

The Jewish Foundation for the Righteous, 18:174

Jewish Freemasons. *See* Freemasons

Jewish Free School. *See* Juedische Freischule

Jewish Funders Network, 7:137

The Jewish Gauchos of the Pampas (Gerchunoff), 7:506

Jewish hat, 3:45, 46

Jewish-Hellenistic literature, 2:262–263

The Jewish Herald (newspaper), 4:216

Jewish Historical Institute (Warsaw, Poland), 2:408, 411, 11:**291**, 18:723

Jewish Historical Society of England, 1:315, 2:408, 6:417, 7:29, 9:160, 11:**292**, 13:67, 18:723

Jewish History (Graetz), 6:35

Jewish Holocaust rescuers, 9:**495–496**

Jewish-Hungarian Literary Society. *See* Izraelita Magyar Irodalmi Társulat

Jewish identity, 11:**292–299**

   biblical period, 11:292–293

   Bolshevik theory of communism and, 5:92–93

   Christian period, 11:293–294

   Comintern and, 5:97

   Conference of Presidents of Major American Jewish Organizations and, 5:142

   demography and, 5:557–558

   Hellenistic period, 11:293

   Hungarian literature and, 9:605–606

   intermarriage, 6:379–381, 379–384

   Israel, 14:355

   Judah Halevi, 11:498–499

   Judah Loew ben Bezalel, 11:508

   Judaism, development of concept of, 11:514–515

   in literature, 6:730–732

   medieval and early modern period, 11:294–295

   modern period, 11:295–299

   Netherlands, 15:108–109

   photography and, 16:126–128

   Sarachek, Bernard, 18:40–41

Jewish Images and Traditions (Silvain), 16:128

Jewish Immigrant Aid Services of Canada (JIAS), 11:**299–300**

Jewish Immigrant Aid Society of Canada, 11:707

Jewish Institute of Religion. *See* Hebrew Union College-Jewish Institute of Religion

Jewish International Cigar Makers Union, 18:708

Jewish Journal, 13:209

The Jewish Journal of Sociology (journal), 18:734

Jewish Labor Committee, 2:49, 11:**300–301**

Jewish Labor Committee (JLC), 4:110–111

Jewish Labour Committee (Canada), 11:780

Jewish Lads' Brigade, 18:209

Jewish languages, 3:609–611, 11:**301–303**

See also specific languages

Jewish law. *See* Halakhah

Jewish Law: History, Sources, Principles (Elon), 18:471

Jewish Law and Modern Ideology (Dorff), 5:755

Jewish Legion, 9:249, 10:465, 11:**303–306**

Amery, Leopold Charles Maurice Stennet, 2:66

Ben-Gurion, David, 3:344

Canada, 4:400

Nordau, Max, 15:298

Patterson, John Henry, 15:694

World War I, 11:11

Jewish Life (periodical), 18:110

Jewish Literary Society, 10:17–18

Jewish literature, 13:**84–117**

abbreviations, 1:239

Dead Sea scrolls, 5:505

encyclopedias, 6:399–402, 18:636

Esther, representation of, 6:516–518

Greece, 5:643

Heine, Heinrich, 8:770–773

Jewish condition in, 6:730–732

Judah Halevi in, 11:500

Levinas, Emmanuel, 12:716

methodologies, 13:102–117

didactic literature, 13:111

ethical wills, 13:106–107

ethics, 13:105–106

Ladino literature, 13:116–117

mystical literature, 13:107–108

philosophical exegesis, 13:107

philosophy and theology, 13:102–105

polemical and apologetic literature, 13:112–113

prose literature, 13:108–111

Yiddish literature, 13:113–116

Middle Ages, 7:10–13, 13:93–117

Bible exegesis, 13:94–95

grammar and lexicography, 13:93–94

Judeo-Arabic writings, 9:68

poetry, 13:95–96

rabbinic literature, 13:96–102

Norway, 18:96

Pinsker, Simḥah, 16:174–175

pre-Middle Ages, 13:84–93

Aggadah, 13:88–89, 91–93

Apocalyptic literature, 13:86

Apocryphal literature, 13:85–86

Bible, 13:84–85, 87–88

Halakhah, 13:88–91

Hellenistic literature, 13:86–87

history and philosophy, 13:88

publishing, 16:721–724

Russia, 1881-1917: Second Phase, 17:538, 540

Singer, Howard, 18:634

Singer, Isaac Bashevis, 18:634–636

Singer, Isidore, 18:636

Sodom and Gomorrah, 18:739–741

Sola, Abraham de, 5:603

Solomon, 18:761

Sweden, 18:93–94

See also Hebrew fiction

On Jewish Liturgy (Goldschmidt), 13:133

The Jewish Manual (Montefiore), 14:456

The Jewish Marriage Contract (Epstein), 6:475

Jewish Meditation (Kaplan), 11:773

The Jewish Messenger (periodical), 11:**306**

Jewish Morning Journal (newspaper), 11:**306–307**, 15:210

Jewish Museum (NYC), 11:**307–308**, 15:228

Jewish Mysticism (Abelson), 1:249

Jewish National and University Library, 4:580, 581, 12:**788**, 13:133

Jewish National Council. *See* Nationalrat

Jewish National Fund (JNF), 9:246, 11:**308–309**, 16:45

afforestation, 6:452

Bischoffsheim, Amalia, 3:725

Bodenheimer, Max Isidor, 4:27, 28

Boehm, Adolf, 4:31

donor's certificate, vol. 21: color insert

Schachtel, Hugo-Hillel, 18:99

Schloessinger, Max, 18:144

Jewish National Library, 8:740

Jewish National Party (Austria). *See* Juedische Volkspartei (Austria)

Jewish National Workers Alliance. *See* Farband

Jewish New Year. *See* Rosh Ha-Shanah

Jewish oath. *See* Oath More Judaico

Jewish Organization for Resistance and Mutual Aid, 15:668

Jewish Palestine Exploration Society. *See* Israel Exploration Society

Jewish Passages (Goldberg), 7:692

Jewish People's Party (Russia), 6:36

Jewish philosophy, 16:**67–114**

Aaron ben Elijah, 1:212–213

Abraham, 1:284–285

Abraham bar Ḥiyya, 1:292–293

Adlerblum, Nima, 1:409

Agus, Jacob B., 1:521–522

Albalag, Isaac, 1:582–583

Albo, Joseph, 1:593–595

Aldabi, Meir ben Isaac, 1:605

Alexander, Samuel, 1:624–625

Alexander of Aphrodisias, 1:628

angels, 2:159–161

anthropomorphism, 2:190

antisemitism on, 16:92

Aquinas, Thomas, 2:292

Arama, Isaac ben Moses, 2:340–341

Aristotelianism, 16:78, 83, 84, 88, 106–107

Ibn Daud, Abraham ben David Halevi, 9:663–665

imagination and, 9:736

Ashʿarite Kalām, 16:77

Averroes, 2:723

Avicenna, 2:727–728

Bar-Hillel, Yehoshua, 3:152

Bibago, Abraham ben Shem Tov, 3:570–571

Brinker, Menachem, 4:184–185

Buber, Martin, 4:232–233

Canpanton, Judah ben Solomon, 4:432

Christian influence on, 5:686–687, 16:91

classification of commandments, Saadiah Gaon, 17:610

contextual approach, 16:71

creation

analysis of, 16:72–73, 75, 82, 85, 88

Maimonides, Moses, 13:390

Saadiah Gaon, 17:609–610

Decalogue in, 5:526

defined, 16:**68–71**

Delmedigo, Elijah ben Moses Abba, 5:542
Delmedigo, Joseph Solomon, 5:543–544
divine providence, 13:391
Duran, Profiat, 6:56–58
Duran, Simeon ben Ẓemaḥ, 6:58–60
Eisler, Moritz, 6:275
emanation, 6:372–374
emotions, 6:396–397
end of days, 13:448
Enlightenment period, 14:33–40
essentialism, 16:69–70, 71
exegesis, 13:107
favors Christianity over Judaism, 16:98–99
feminism in, 16:105, 110–112
Finkielkraut, Alain, 7:36–37
Frankel, Zecharias, 7:200–201
freedom, 7:226
free will, 13:447, 16:93
goal of modern education, 11:742
God
    anthropomorphized, 16:83–84
    attributes of, 16:82–83, 85, 88, 92
    divine providence of, 16:85, 89
    free will and, 16:87, 89
    as giver of freedom, 16:94–95
    imitation of, 9:737–738
    proof of existence of, 16:75–76, 77, 78–79, 79–80, 81, 83, 84, 85, 89
    relationship with humans, 16:98, 104
    self-limitation, 16:95
Greek influence on, 5:674, 16:73–74, 76–77, 77–78, 80–81
halakhah, 16:103–104
Hasidic influence on, 16:104–105
Heinemann, Yiẓak, 8:774
Hellenistic period, 16:59–64, 62–63, 74–76
Horovitz, Saul, 9:530
Husik, Isaac, 9:641–642
Ibn Ḥabib, Moses ben Shem Tov, 9:678–679
Ibn Kammūna, Saʿd ibn Manṣūr, 9:684
Ibn Shem Tov, 9:691
immortality, nature of, 16:88
imperative of resistance to Nazi purpose, 6:673
influence on Christian thought, 16:91

Israeli, 16:99–103
Israeli, Isaac ben Solomon, 10:751–752
I-Thou and I-It relations, 16:98, 109–110
Joseph ben Shem Tov, 9:691
Judeo-Arabic, 11:534–536
Judeo-Persian, 11:553–554
justice, Jewish concept of, 11:578–579
Kalām, influence of, 11:730–731
Kaplan, Abraham, 11:773
Kaplan, Mordecai Menahem on Judaism, 11:777–778
Kaufmann, Walter, 12:33
Krochmal, Nachman, 12:366–367
Landauer, Meyer Heinrich Hirsch, 12:467–468
Law of Moses, 13:392
Maimon, Solomon, 13:370–371
Maimonides, 2:292, 9:736
Maimonides, Moses, 13:388–393, 14:536–537
Middle Ages, 6:680–683, 11:101
    categories, 4:524
    cause and effect, 4:529
    chosen people doctrine, 4:671
    Denburg, Chaim, 5:579
    ethical literature, 7:14
    Judah ben Joseph Moscato, 14:515–516
    Matkah, Judah ben Solomon ha-Kohen, 13:679
    miracles, 14:307
    nature, 15:34
    redemption, 17:152–153
    repentance, 17:222
moral virtue, 13:392
Moses, 13:392, 14:536–538
Muslim influence on, 16:77, 78–79, 78–80, 84, 87–88
Muʿtazilite Kalām, 16:77, 79–80
names of man, 13:446
nature of God, 17:610
nature of man
    Maimonides, Moses, 13:392
    Saadiah Gaon, 17:610–611
Neher, André, 15:62–63
neoplatonism, 15:84–86, 84–87, 16:77, 80–81, 82–83, 106
    Ibn Ezra, Abraham ben Meir, 9:669–671
    Ibn Ezra, Moses ben Jacob, 9:675
neo-Pythagorean, 9:670, 670t
opposition to, 5:471, 11:7
Pines, Shlomo, 16:167

Ravitzky, Aviezer, 17:124
Rawidowicz, Simon, 17:125–126
Reconstructionist school of thought, 11:777–779
redemption, 17:151–155
Reichenbach, Hans, 17:199
Reines, Alvin Jay, 17:207
religious thought, Akedah, 1:556–558
Renan, Ernest, 17:218
repentance, 17:222
response to Holocaust, 16:99
Ruʿaḥ ha-Kodesh, 17:507–509
Saadiah Gaon, 17:609–612
Sabbath, 17:619
Saint-Simonism, 17:678
Salonika, 1:433
Scheler, Max Ferdinand, 18:118–119
schools of, 16:67–68
Schopenhauer, Arthur, 2:560
Schweid, Eliezer, 18:194
Shalom, Abraham ben Isaac ben Judah ben Samuel, 18:376–377
Shekhinah, 18:441, 442
Shemariah ben Elijah ben Jacob, 18:457
Shestov, Lev, 18:466–467
sin, 18:621–625
Slonimsky, Henry, 18:679–680
social, 12:291
Solomon ben Judah of Lunel, 18:679–680, 772
soul, nature of, 16:76, 81, 83, 87, 106, 108
theory of knowledge, 17:609
truth
    acceptance regardless of source, 16:68–69
    historical experience as source, 16:83
    revelation as source, 16:96
    types of, 16:87
    See also Business ethics; Haskalah movement; Metaphysics
Jewish police, 9:357–358
Jewish Publication Society, 11:**309–310**, 12:601, 18:722
    Adler, Cyrus, 1:395
    Amram, David Werner, 2:104
    education, Jewish, 6:192–193
    English translations of Bible, 3:614, 621–622
Jewish Quarterly Review (periodical), 1:395, 6:25, 11:**313**, 14:455
Jewish quarters, 11:**310–313**
    Bratislava, 4:132

Jewish quarters, *continued*
Brno, 4:190
Bursa, 4:300, 301
Cologne (Germany), 5:60
Constantinople, 4:327
Dra valley, 6:5
Fez, Morocco, 7:7
Ottoman empire, 15:529
Pamplona, 15:609
Paris, 15:642, 643
Provence, France, 16:638
Senlis (France), 18:289
Spain
Buitrago, 4:257
Majorca, 13:413–414
Segovia, 18:250–251
Seville, 18:326
Ukraine, 6:23–24
See also Ghettoes
Jewish Reconstructionist Foundation, 11:777
Jewish Reform Action Center (Washington, D.C.), 18:34
Jewish Relief Committee for War Victims. *See* YEKOPO
Jewish Religious Education Board, 6:205
See also Association for the Diffusion of Religious Knowledge
Jewish Religious Union (Great Britain), 14:452, 455
Jewish Renewal movement, 16:36, 18:100–101
Jewish Resistance, 10:206, 207
Belarus
Braslav, 4:131
Minsk, 14:296
Novogrudok, 15:321
Oshmyany, 15:503
Bielski brothers, 3:688–689
Bloch, Marc, 3:765
Brest-Litovsk (Lithuania), 4:170
Ereẓ Israel, 1:658
France, 5:748, 9:358
Ha-Shomer ha-Ẓa'ir, 8:384
Paris (France), 15:645
partisans, 15:664–668, 665
Poland, 5:373, 16:314–317
Bialystok, 3:569–570
Cracow, 5:263
Parczew Forest, 15:632
Romania, 17:388–391
Slovakia, 5:358
Summer Seminar Program on Holocaust and Jewish Resistance, 2:49

Ukraine
Bolekhov, 4:44–45
Brody, 4:200
Buchach, 4:238
USSR, 17:548–550
Jewish Restitution Successor Organization (JRSO), 11:327
Jewish Rifles. See Judenflinten
Jewish School of Paris, 15:647–648
Jewish Science (Moses), 4:694
Jewish science fiction and fantasy, 18:**197–207**
antisemitism, 18:201–202
counterfacts and historical events, 18:201
history of, 18:197–198
Israeli literature, 18:202–203, 206–207
myths, 18:198–199, 200–201
themes, 18:199–200
Yiddish literature, 18:199
Zionism, 18:204–206
Jewish Scientific Institute. *See* YIVO Institute for Jewish Research
Jewish Scout Movement, 18:209
Jewish Self-Government in the Middle Ages (Finkelstein, L.), 7:23, 35
Jewish self-hatred, 4:116–117, 18:**264–265**
Jewish Social Democratic Party (ZhPSD), 4:211, 6:255, 11:**313–314**
Jewish socialism, 18:**714–721**
beginnings of the movement, 18:714–715
Bund, 18:715–716
Europe, 18:718
Morning Freiheit (newspaper), 14:492–493
relations with Communist Party, 18:719–720
U.S., 18:718–719
youth movements, 18:720–721
zionist socialism, 18:717–718
Jewish Socialist Federation, 18:709
Jewish Socialists. *See* Jewish Socialist Workers' Party
Jewish Socialist Verband, 11:**314**
Jewish Socialist Workers' Party, 11:**314–315**, 12:524
Jewish Social Studies (journal), 18:734
Jewish Social Welfare Foundation (JMW), 2:118
Jewish Society for History and Ethnography, 11:**315**
Jewish Sociology and Social Research (journal), 18:734
Jewish Souls. See Yidishe Neshomes (Litvin)

The Jewish South (newspaper), 4:216
The Jewish State. See Der Judenstaat
Jewish State Party, 11:**315–316**
Jewish Street (periodical), 14:520
Jewish Student Movement, 21:610–615
Jewish studies, 11:**316–327**
Aaron ben Jacob ha-Kohen of Lunel, 1:213–214
Aaron ben Joseph ha-Kohen Sargado, 1:214
abbreviations, 1:240
Abraham ben Azriel, 1:295
Abraham ben David of Posquières, 1:296–298
Abramowicz, Dina, 1:323–324
Abramson, Shraga, 1:329
Blumenkranz, Bernhard, 4:11
Bonfil, Robert, 4:61–62
Borovoy, Saul, 4:92
Breuer, Mordecai, 4:173
Canada, 4:427, 11:316–320
Center for Jewish History, 4:542–543
Chile, 4:642
Chotzner, Joseph, 4:672
CLAL, 4:749–750
defined, 11:316
Dropsie College (Philadelphia, PA), 6:25–26
France, 11:324–326
Harf, Suse Hallenstein, 8:354
historical development of, 11:316–317
Jost, Isaac Marcus, 11:464
Judenrat institution, historiography of, 11:527–529
Juedisch-Literarische Gesellschaft, 11:571–572
Kabbalah, 11:673–674, 681–686
Latin America, 12:440
Neusner, Jacob, 15:124–125
at Oxford University, 15:554
Rabba ben Matnah, 17:7
Schalit, Abraham Chaim, 18:104
Soviet Union, 11:319–324
U.S., 11:316–320, 12:526
Jewish successor organizations, 11:**327**
Jewish Supernumerary Police (Palestine, Mandate), 10:466
Jewish Supplementary Schooling: An Educational System in Need of Change (report), 6:201
"Jewish Survival" (Ben Gurion), 10:217
Jewish Symbols in the Greco-Roman Period (Goodenough), 7:755, 11:589
Jewish Synagogue Association. *See* Juedische Kultusvereinigung

Jewish Tax. *See* Fiscus Judaicus

Jewish Teachers' Seminary and People's University, 11:**327–328**

Jewish Telegraphic Agency (JTA), 11:**328**, 12:462–463, 603

Jewish Territorialist Organization. *See* ITO

Jewish Theocracy (Weiler). *See Teokratiah Yehudit* (Weiler)

Jewish Theological Seminary (JTS), 5:172–173, 11:**328–331**, 17:25–26

　Amateau, Albert Jean, 2:34

　Americana Judaica collection, 11:815

　American Jewish Historical Society, 2:58

　benefactors, Adler, Elkan Nathan, 1:396

　Blumenthal, Joseph, 4:12

　diaries of Mordecai Kaplan, 11:778

　Eichler, Menahem Max, 6:247

　Eilberg, Amy, 6:254

　establishment, 6:182, 193

　Finkelstein, Louis, 7:34–35

　Halpern, Harry, 8:284

　Morais, Sabato, 14:471

　Schechter, Solomon, 2:113–114

　Schneeberger, Henry William, 18:147

　West Coast branch, 6:198

The Jewish Times, 5:26

Jewish Travellers (Adler), 6:347

Jewish Travellers (Volterra), 20:579

Jewish Trust Corporation (JTC), 11:327

Jewish United Federation of Teachers, 6:161

Jewish Volunteer Corps (JVC), 20:369–370

Jewish War (1st c.)

　caves in Judean Desert used during, 11:524

　Joseph of Gamala, 11:431

　Joshua son of Sapphas, 11:449

　Juster, Jean, on, 11:578

　Justus of Tiberias and, 11:440, 581–582

　leaders, 11:36

　overview of, 10:143–144

　See also Josephus Flavius; *Josippon*

The Jewish War (Josephus), 9:155, 11:436–437, 461

Jewish War Veterans of the U.S.A. (JWV), 11:**331**, 12:222

Jewish Way of Life (Karp), 11:815

The Jewish Wedding (Oppenheim), vol. 3: color insert

Jewish Welfare Board, 6:195, 428, 11:814, 12:742

　See also Jewish Community Centers

Jewish Welfare Federation of Detroit, 18:700

Jewish Western Bulletin (newspaper), 4:187

The Jewish Wife (Lazarus), 12:562

The Jewish Woman (periodical), 11:**331–332**

Jewish Women: A Comprehensive Encyclopedia, 9:163

Jewish Women in America: An Historical Encyclopedia, 9:163

Jewish Women's Archive, 2:410

Jewish Women's Congress, 2:53

Jewish World (newspaper), 11:**332**

Jewish yearbooks, 4:305

Jewish Y movement, 11:271–272

Jewnin, Abraham Jonah, 11:**332**

Jews: Their History, Culture, and Religion (Finkelstein), 7:35

The Jews: A Study of Race and Environment (Fishberg), 7:60

The Jews and the Inquisition (Mocatta), 14:404

"Jews-by-choice." *See* Proselytes

Jews' College (U.K.), 6:204–205, 206, 415, 429, 11:**332–333**

Jew Seuss documentary, 9:439

Jews in America, or Probabilities that those Indians are Judaical, Made More Probable by Some Additionals to the Former Conjectures (Thorowgood), 14:460

The Jews in Russia. See Yevrei v Rossii (Leskov)

"The Jews in the 19th Century or Considerations of their Civil and Political Status in Europe" (Bail), 3:68

Jews of China (Finn), 7:39

The Jews of Georgian England, 1714-1830: Tradition and Change in a Liberal Society (Endelman), 6:403

The Jews of Germany (Lowenthal), 13:235

The Jews of Languedoc Provence (Lunel), 13:259

The Jews of Lvov at the Turn of the 17th Century. See Zydzi lwówscy na przełomie XVI–XVII wieku

The Jews of Perpignan in the Thirteenth Century: An Economic Study Based on Notarial Records (Emery), 6:394

Jews of South Carolina: From Earliest Times to the Present Day (Elzas), 6:372

The Jews of Warsaw (Gutman), 8:151–152

Jews' Pennies. *See* Judenpfennige

Jews' Temporary Shelter (London, England), 11:**333**

Jew Suess. *See* Oppenheimer, Joseph ben Issachar Suesskind

The Jew Within: Self, Family, and Community in America (Eisen, Cohen), 6:265

Jezebel, 1:524, 6:331–332, 335–336, 11:**333–334**

Jeziory (Belarus). *See* Ozery

Jezreel (city, Israel), 11:**334–335**

Jezreel (valley, Israel), 2:80, 10:118, 11:**335**

Jhabvala, Ruth Prawer, 11:**336**

JIAS. *See* Jewish Immigrant Aid Services of Canada

Jidah ben David. *See* Bondavin, Bonjudas

Jidyó. *See* Ladino

Jihād, 11:**336–337**

Jihlava (Czech Republic), 11:**337**

Jilovsky family. *See* Illowy family

Jilovy family. *See* Illowy family

Jimenes. *See* Ximenes

Jimenes de Cisneros, Francisco. *See* Ximenes de Cisneros, Francisco

Jindrichuv Hradec (Czech Republic), 11:**337**

J.I.R. *See* Hebrew Union College-Jewish Institute of Religion

Jirku, Anton, 11:**337–338**

Jischuw (Badt-Strauss), 3:50

Jitta, Daniel Josephus, 11:**338**

Jizfān, Judah ben Joseph, 11:**338**

JLC. *See* Jewish Labor Committee

JMW (Jewish Social Welfare Foundation), 2:118

JNF. *See* Jewish National Fund

Joab, 11:**338–339**

　Abner, 1:264

　Amasa, 2:32–33

　Solomon, 18:755

Joab ben Jeremiah, 11:**339–340**

Joab the Greek, 11:**340**

Joachim, Al. *See* Ritz, Al

Joachim, Harry. *See* Ritz, Harry

Joachim, Jimmy. *See* Ritz, Jimmy

Joachim, Joseph, 11:**340**

Joachimsen, Philip J., 11:**340**

João II, King of Portugal, 1:313

João Rodrigues de Castelo Branco. *See* Amatus Lusitanus

Joash (King of Judah), 2:35–36, 11:107, 108, **341**

Joazar. *See* Joezer, son of Boethus

Job (biblical figure), 2:456

　in art, 11:358

Job (biblical figure), *continued*
 in halakhah, 11:356
 Islam and, 11:357
 Job the Impatient (JIP)
  framework, 11:344–351
 Job the Patient (JP) framework,
  11:342–344
 Kedemites, 11:352
 Kettuvim, position within, 11:341–
  342
 in literature, 11:357–358
 in liturgy, 11:356
 meaning and message of, 11:353–
  355
 in music, 11:358–359
 one-book datum theory of,
  11:343–344
 origins and literary evolution of,
  11:350–351
 targum to, 3:593
 two-book theory (JP and JIP) of,
  11:342, 343–344, 350
Job (Schwartz), 18:182
Job, Book of, 2:456, 11:**341–359**
 in aggadah, 11:356–357
 anthropodicy vs. theodicy of,
  11:355–356
 in art, 11:358
 Christianity and, 11:342, 357, 358,
  360
 critical analysis of, 11:342–350
  complaint of Job, 11:346
  Elihu, 11:347–348
  Epilogue, 11:342–343
  failure of friends to comfort
   Job, 11:346–347, 351–352
  God and Job, 11:348–350
  Prologue, 11:342
  three friends cycles, 11:344–
   346
 dream visions in, 11:351, 352–353
 Elihu, 6:331
 Eliphaz, 6:349
  name, significance of,
   11:351–352
  three friends cycles, 11:344–
   346
 ethical teachings, 6:533
 in halakhah, 11:356
 Hapax Legomena, 8:337
 holistic interpretation, 11:353
 in literature, 11:357–358
 in liturgy, 11:356
Job, Testament of. See Testament of Job
Jobab. *See* Job (biblical figure)
Jobards, Jason, Jr., 3:30
Jochanan Hakkadosh (Browning),
 4:218

Jochebed, 11:**360–361,** 14:523, 526,
 17:101–102, *102,* 105–106
Jochelson, Vladimir, 11:**361**
Jochelson, Waldemar. *See* Jochelson,
 Vladimir
Jochsberger, Tzipora, 11:**361**
Jocul de-a vacantaţa (Sebastian),
 18:231
Joel, Asher. *See* Joel, Sir Asher
Joel, Billy, 11:**362–363**
Joel, Book of, 11:**361–362**
 dreams, 6:9
 eschatology in, 6:494
 locust plague, 6:494
Joel, Carl. *See* Joel, Raphael
Joel, David Heymann, 11:**363**
Joel, Karl, 11:**363**
Joel, Manuel, 11:**363–364**
Joel, Otto J., 11:**364**
Joel, Raphael, 11:**364,** 12:547
Joel, Richard M., 6:142, 9:112, 11:**364–
365**
Joel, Sir Asher, 11:**362,** 16:340
Joel, Solomon Barnato "Solly," 11:**365,**
 377
Joel ben Isaac ha-Levi, 11:**365**
Joel ben Moses Gad, 11:**365–366**
Joel ben Simeon, 11:**366**
Joelish Teitelbaum of Satmar. *See* Joel
 Teitelbaum of Satmar
Joel of Bonn. *See* Joel ben Isaac ha-
 Levi
Joelson, Charles S., 15:687
Joezer, son of Boethus, 11:**366–367**
Joezer ben Boethus, 2:128
Joffe, Abraham Feodorovich, 11:**367**
Joffe, Abram Moiseyevich. *See*
 Deborin, Abram Moiseyevich
Joffe, Adolph Abramovich, 11:**367**
Joffe, Eliezer Lipa, 11:**367–368**
Joffe, Hillel, 11:**368**
Joffe, Judah Achilles, 11:**368**
Joffe, Maria, 11:**367**
Joffe, Shalom Elhanan, 8:735
Joffen, Abraham, 11:**368**
Joffe-Raykin, Ruth, 17:126
Jogiches, Leon, 11:**368–369**
Johanan (son of Kareah), 11:**369**
Johanan ben Beroka, 11:**369**
Johanan ben Gudgada, 11:**369**
Johanan ben ha-Horanit, 6:309,
 11:**369**
Johanan ben ha-Horoni. *See* Johanan
 ben ha-Horanit
Johanan ben ha-Huranit. *See* Johanan
 ben ha-Horanit
Johanan ben ha-Hurni. *See* Johanan
 ben ha-Horanit

Johanan ben Jehoiada, 11:**369**
Johanan ben Joshua ha-Kohen,
 11:**369–370**
Johanan ben Levi. *See* John of Giscala
Johanan ben Levi of Giscala. *See* John
 of Giscala
Johanan ben Nappaha, 11:**370–372,**
 397
Johanan ben Nuri, 11:**372–373**
 Eleazar Hisma, 6:309–310
 five species, 7:66
 Joshua ben Korha, 11:452
Johanan ben Torta, 11:**373**
Johanan ben Zakkai, 1:234, 6:725,
 10:146–147, 11:**373–377**
 on altars, 2:16
 am ha-arez, 2:66
 Elazar ben Zadok, 6:309
 Eleazar ben Arakh, 6:299
 Eliezer ben Hyrcanus, 6:323
 on heart and ethics, 8:509
 Jabneh and, 11:10
 Josephus' prophecy on Vespasian
  and, 11:435
 Joshua ben Hananiah, 11:450, 451,
  452
 on Judean boundaries, 11:523
 Kahana, 11:708–709
 Moses, 14:534
 Simeon ben Nethanel, 18:599
Johanan ha-Sandelar, 11:**377**
Johanan the Hasmonean, 11:**377**
Johanan Hyrcanus. *See* Hyrcanus,
 John
Johanan the Essene. *See* John the
 Essene
Johan Maurits van Nassau, 4:144
Johannan the Essene. *See* John the
 Essene
Johannesburg (South Africa), 11:**377–
378**
Johannes de Capua. *See* John of
 Capua
Johannes Faustus (opera), 6:275
Johannes Hispalenis. *See* Avendauth
Johison, Josef, 3:631
John (King of England), 6:411
John I (King of Aragon), 15:562
John II (King of France), 11:**379**
John II (King of Portugal), 11:**378–
379**
John II (King of Spain), 4:551
John III (King of Portugal), 11:**379**
John XXII (pope), 11:**379,** 16:374
John XXIII (pope), 3:725, 9:374,
 11:**379–380,** 16:377
John ben Levi. *See* John of Giscala

John Chrysostom, 4:326, 720, 11:**382**

John Hall (Elkan), 6:357

John Hyrcanus
olam ha-ba, 15:399
Scroll of Esther, 18:216

John Monash: A Biography (Serle), 14:432

John of Bristol, 8:512

John of Capistrano
in Nuremberg, 15:347
Oleśnicki, Zbigniew, 15:403
Pope Nicholas V and, 15:250

John of Capua, 11:**382–383,** 735

John of Giscala, 2:127, 3:150–151, 6:307, 11:**383**

John Paul II (pope), 11:**383–385,** 16:377–378
antisemitism, 2:243
Bethlehem, visit to, 15:599
Jewish community and, 9:375, 11:280

John Skelton's Poetry (Fish), 7:58

Johnson, Eyvind, 18:92

Johnson, Lyndon Baines, 11:**385,** 13:235, 15:323
Fortas, Abe, 7:132–133
Lewin, Nathan, 12:761

Johnson, Mary Lea. *See* Richards, Mary Lea Johnson

Johnson, Meyer Albert "Jonny," 11:470

Johnson-Reed Act of 1924, 20:335

Johnston plan, 11:403

John the Baptist, 2:547, 6:260, 11:247, **380–381**
Elijah, 6:336
as Hemerobaptist, 18:233

John the Essene, 11:**382,** 15:263

Joiachin. *See* Jehoiachin (King of Judah)

Joigny (France), 11:**385**

Joint. *See* American Joint Distribution Committee

The Joint. *See* American Jewish Joint Distribution Committee

Joint Authority of Jewish-Zionist Education, 13:147

Joint Boycott Council
American Jewish Congress, 2:57
boycotts, anti-Nazi, 4:111

Joint Distribution Committee. *See* American Jewish Joint Distribution Committee

Joint Foreign Committee. *See* Anglo-Jewish Association (AJA)

Joint ownership in Jewish law, 15:671–672

Jokneam (Israel), 11:**385**

Joktan, 11:**385–386**

Jolles, Jacob Ẓevi ben Naphtali, 11:**386**

Jolles, Zechariah Isaiah, 11:**386,** 13:677

Jolles, Zvi Enrico, 11:**386**

Jolowicz, Herbert Felix, 11:**386**

Jolson, Al, 11:**386–387,** 14:571

Jolson, Julius. *See* Stahl, Friedrich Julius

Joly, Maurice, 6:297

Jona, Giovanni Battista, 11:**387**

Jonadab son of Rechad, 17:143

Jonah, 7:59

Jonah (amora), 11:**387–388**

Jonah, Book of, 11:**388–392**

Jonah, Moses, 11:**392,** 13:263

Jonah ben Abraham Gerondi, 6:525, 11:**392–393,** 14:463
repentence, 6:528
Solomon ben Abraham of Montpelier, 18:770

Jona Quadrilinguis (Pragensis), 6:315

Jonas, Abraham, 11:**393–394,** 13:27

Jonas, Benjamin Franklin, 11:394, 13:223–224

Jonas, Emile, 11:**393**

Jonas, Hans, 9:396–397, 11:**393**

Jonas, Joseph, 11:**393–394,** 15:392

Jonas, Nathan S., 11:**394**

Jonas, Regina, 11:**394,** 13:139, 17:17

Jonathan (biblical name), 11:**394–395**

Jonathan (father of priest Zechariah in Nehemiah), 11:395

Jonathan (high priest). *See* Aristobulus III (high priest)

Jonathan (levite in reign of Jehoshaphat), 11:395

Jonathan (one of David's valiant men), 11:**394**

Jonathan (scribe in Jeremiah), 11:395

Jonathan (son of Abiathar), 11:394–395

Jonathan (son of Absolom), 11:**398–399**

Jonathan (son of Gershom), 11:394

Jonathan (son of Jerahmeel), 11:395

Jonathan (son of Joiada), 11:395

Jonathan (son of Kareah), 11:395

Jonathan (son of Mattathias), 18:213–214

Jonathan (son of Saul), 11:**395–396,** 18:79, 82

Jonathan (son of Shimea), 11:394

Jonathan (son of Uzziah), 11:394

Jonathan (tanna), 11:**396**

Jonathan (uncle of David), 11:394

Jonathan, Targum of. *See* Targum

Jonathan Apphus, 8:446

Jonathan ben Abraham Isaac, 11:**396**

Jonathan ben Amram, 11:**396**

Jonathan ben Anan, 11:**396–397**

Jonathan ben David ha-Kohen of Lunel, 11:**397,** 14:329

Jonathan ben Eleazar, 11:**397**

Jonathan ben Jacob, 6:34, 11:**397–398**

Jonathan ben Joseph of Ruzhany, 11:**398**

Jonathan ben Moses Jacob of Wielowicz, 15:325

Jonathan ben Nathan Nata. *See* Eybeschuetz, Jonathan

Jonathan ben Uzziel, 11:**398**
Targum Jonathan, 3:592
Targum Yerushalmi I, 3:591

Jonathan ha-Kohen. *See* Jonathan ben David ha-Kohen of Lunel

Jonathan the Hasmonean, 5:674, 11:**398–399**

Jonathan Logan Dress Co., 18:183

Jonathan Logan Inc., 18:183

Jonathan of Lunel. *See* Jonathan ben David ha-Kohen of Lunel

Jonathan of Ruzhany. *See* Jonathan ben Joseph of Ruzhany

Jonathan the Hasmonean, 2:201, 9:194

Jonathan the Weaver, 12:789–790

Jonava (Lithuania), 11:**399**

Jonavici v. Minister of the Interior, 12:542

Jones, Arthur, 15:79

Jones, Henry, 4:13

Jones, Jacqueline, 4:125

Jong, Erica, 11:**399–400**

Jong, Loe De. *See* Jong, Louis De

Jong, Louis De, 11:**400**

Het Joodsche Lied (de Haan), 6:70

Joppa (Israel). *See* Jaffa (Israel)

Joppah. *See* Jaffa (Israel)

Jordan (river), 6:83, 10:125–126, 11:*400,* **400–403**

Jordan (valley), 10:123–124

Jordan, Charles Harold, 11:**403**

Jordan, Hashemite kingdom of, 11:**404–405**
Abdullah ibn Hussein, 1:243–244
Akaba, 1:553
Allon, Yigal, 1:676
Arabah, 2:293
Arab refugees in, 10:278
attacks from, 10:218
borders post War of Independence, 10:214, 12:517–518
change of name to, 15:582
diplomatic representation, 10:265

Jordan, Hashemite kingdom of, *continued*
 Al-Fataḥ in, 10:280
 Hashemite Kingdom, 2:301, 305
 holy sites, 11:236
 Intifada and, 10:723–724
 Israel, Arab population under Jordanian Rule, 1948–67, 10:715–717
 Jerusalem and, 10:256, 11:178–179, 181
 Palestine Liberation Organization and, 15:592, 593
 Six-Day War, 10:230–232
 Washington Declaration, 10:246
Jortner, Joshua, 11:**405**
Josaphat, Israel Beer. *See* Reuter, Paul Julius, Freiherr von
Josce of York, 11:**405–406**
Josefowicz. *See* Jozefowicz family
Josel ben Gershon of Rosheim. *See* Joseph ben Gershon of Rosheim
Josel ben Ze'ev Wolf ha-Levi. *See* Joseph ben Ze'ev Wolf ha-Levi
Joselein ben Moses. *See* Joseph ben Moses (1423-1490?)
Joselewicz, Berek, 11:**406**, 16:346
Joselewicz, Berko, 15:321
Joselit, Jenna Weissman, 9:153
Joselman ben Gershon of Rosheim. *See* Joseph ben Gershon of Rosheim
Joselmann of Rosheim. *See* Joseph ben Gershon of Rosheim
Joseph (biblical figure), 11:**406–413**
 adoption, 1:415, 416
 in aggadah, 11:411–412
 agrarian measures of, 11:409, 410
 in art, 11:412–413
 Bible
  in Genesis, 11:406–410
  outside of Genesis, 11:410–411
 brothers
  immigration to Egypt, 11:408–409
  reconciliation with, 11:408
  sale into bondage by, 11:406, 411–412
 death of, 11:410
 dreams, interpretation of, 9:*704*, 11:407
 Ephraim, 6:456, 457
 incarceration of, 11:407
 in Islam, 11:412
 Jacob and, 11:20, 22, 27, 406, 408, 410
 in literature, 11:411–412
 in music, 11:413

 name, meaning of, 11:411
 nature and meaning of, 11:410
 Pharaoh and, 11:407–408, 16:28
 Potiphar and Potiphar's wife, 6:225, 11:407, 411, 413
 The Tribe of Joseph (Chagall), vol. 4: color insert
Joseph (King of the Khazars), 11:**414**
Joseph (son of Antipater and Cypros), 11:**414**
Joseph, Abraham, 11:**415**
Joseph, Annette Pinto, 11:**415**
Joseph, Bernard. *See* Joseph, Dov
Joseph, Dov, 11:**416**
Joseph, Henry (1785-1832), 11:**415**
Joseph, Henry (1838-1913), 2:70, 11:**416**
Joseph, Jacob, 10:747, 11:**416–417**
Joseph, Jacob Henry, 11:**415**
Joseph, Jesse Joseph, 11:**415**
Joseph, Keith, 11:**415–416**, 16:342
Joseph, Lazarus, 11:**416–417**, 15:215
Joseph, Morris, 11:**417**, 15:703
Joseph, Norma Baumel, 11:**417**
Joseph, R., 1:235
Joseph, Raphael, 18:343
Joseph, Samuel, 11:**417**, 18:731
Joseph, Samuel George, 7:644, 11:**415**
Joseph, Saul Abdallah, 11:**417**
Joseph II (King of Germany), 4:39–40, 11:**414**, 14:474, 475
Joseph al-Baradani, 11:**419**
Joseph and Asenath, 11:**418**
Joseph and His Brethren (Wells), 6:433
Joseph bar Abba, 11:**418–419**
Joseph bar Ḥiyya, 11:**419**
Joseph bar Jacob. *See* Joseph ben Jacob bar Satia
Joseph bar Nissan, 11:**419**
Joseph Bekhor Shor. *See* Bekhor Shor, Joseph ben Isaac
Joseph ben Aaron ben Benjamin. *See* Joseph (King of the Khazars)
Joseph ben Aaron Elmaleh, 6:364
Joseph ben Abitur. *See* Ibn Abitur, Joseph ben Isaac
Joseph ben Abraham ben Seth, 11:**423**
Joseph ben Abraham ha-Kohen Haro'eh al-Baṣir. *See* Baṣir, Joseph ben Abraham ha-Kohen Haro'eh al-
Joseph ben Aḥmad Ibn Ḥasdai, 11:**419**
Joseph ben Amran, 18:572
Joseph ben Asher of Chartres, 11:**419**
Joseph ben Ashkenazi. *See* Joseph ben Moses (Darshan of Przemyslany)
Joseph ben Ayyush Elmaleh, 6:363
Joseph ben Baruch of Clisson, 11:**419**

Joseph ben David. *See* Joseph David
Joseph ben David ha-Yevani, 11:**419–420**
Joseph ben Elem, 11:**420**
Joseph ben Eliezer Tov Elem of Jerusalem, 2:103
Joseph ben Elijah of Zaslaw, 11:**420**
Joseph ben Ezra ben Joseph Khlef, 6:654
Joseph ben Gershon of Rosheim, 2:6, 81, 4:377, 451, 576, 11:**420–421**
Joseph ben Gorion, 11:461–462
Joseph ben Ḥama, 3:594
Joseph ben Ḥiyya, 11:**421–422**
Joseph ben Isaac Bekhor Shor. *See* Bekhor Shor, Joseph ben Isaac
Joseph ben Isaac ha-Levi, 11:**422**
Joseph ben Isaac ha-Sefardi. *See* Ibn Abitur, Joseph ben Isaac
Joseph ben Israel, 11:**422**
Joseph ben Issachar Baer of Prague, 11:**422**
Joseph ben Jacob (liturgical poet), 11:**422**
Joseph ben Jacob bar Satia, 11:**422**
Joseph ben Joshua Moses of Frankfurt, 11:**423**
Joseph ben Justu of Jaén, 11:**423**
Joseph ben Kalonymus Ha-Nakdan I, 11:**423**
Joseph ben Kalonymus Ha-Nakdan II, 11:**423**
Joseph Ben Mattathias. *See* Josephus Flavius
Joseph ben Mordecai Gershon ha-Kohen (of Cracow), 11:**423–424**
Joseph ben Mordecai Gershon ha-Kohen (of Jerusalem), 11:**424**
Joseph ben Moses (1423-1490?), 11:**424**, 15:368
Joseph ben Moses, Darshan of Przemyslany, 11:**424**
Joseph ben Moses Babad. *See* Babad, Joseph ben Moses
Joseph ben Moses of Kremenets, 11:**424**
Joseph ben Moses of Troyes, 11:**424**
Joseph ben Moses Phinehas, 11:**425**
Joseph ben Moses Trani. *See* Trani, Joseph ben Moses
Joseph ben Nathan of Etampes, 11:**419**
Joseph ben Nathan Official. *See* Official, Joseph ben Nathan
Joseph ben Noah, 11:**425**
Joseph ben Phinehas, 11:**425**
Joseph ben Plat. *See* Ibn Plat, Joseph
Joseph ben Samuel ben Isaac ha-Mashbir, 11:**425**

Joseph ben Samuel ha-Nagid. *See* Jehoseph ha-Nagid

Joseph ben Shalom Ashkenazi, 11:**425–426**

Joseph ben Shemtov. *See* Ibn Shem Tov, Joseph ben Shem Tov

Joseph ben Sheshet Ibn Latimi, 11:**426**

Joseph ben Solomon of Carcassonne, 11:**426**

Joseph ben Tanḥum Yerushalmi, 11:**426–427**, 537

Joseph ben Uzziel, 11:**427**

Joseph ben Ẓaddik, 2:17, 11:**427**

Joseph ben Zechariah, 11:**418**

Joseph ben Ze'ev Wolf ha-Levi, 11:**427–428**

Joseph Darshan. *See* Calahora, Joseph ben Solomon

Joseph David, 11:**428**

Joseph della Raina, 11:**428–429**

Joseph family (British), 11:**415–416**

Joseph family (Canadian), 11:**415**

Joseph of Gamala, 11:**431**

Joseph the Greek. *See* Joseph ben David ha-Yevani

Joseph ha-Arokh. *See* Joseph ben Shalom Ashkenazi

Joseph ha-Kohen, 9:157, 225, 11:**429**

Joseph ha-Ma'aravi. *See* Joseph Maman al-Maghribi

Joseph ha-Mekanne. *See* Official, Joseph ben Nathan

Joseph ha-Nagid. *See* Jehoseph ha-Nagid

Joseph Ḥayyim ben Elijah al-Ḥakam, 11:**429**

Joseph Ḥayyim of Baghdad, 2:122

Joseph ha-Ẓarefati, 11:**430**

Joseph Ḥazzan ben Judah of Troyes, 11:**430**

Joseph ibn Abitur. *See* Ibn Abitur, Joseph ben Isaac

Joseph ibn Lev. *See* Lev, Joseph ben David ibn

Joseph ibn Migash. *See* Ibn Migash, Joseph ben Meir ha-Levi

Joseph Ibn Shraga, 11:**430**

Joseph Ibn Ṭabūl, 11:**430**

Joseph Issachar Baer ben Elhanan, 11:**430–431**

Joseph Joske ben Judah Judel of Lublin, 11:**430–431**

Joseph Maman al-Maghribi, 11:**431**

Joseph Meir Weiss of Spinka. *See* Spinka, Joseph Meir Weiss of

Joseph Moses ben Jekuthiel Zalman, 11:**431**

Joseph Moses of Salositz, 11:**431**

Joseph of Arimathea, 4:188

Joseph of Carcassone. *See* Joseph ben Solomon of Carcassonne

Joseph of Chartres. *See* Joseph ben Asher of Chartres

Joseph of Clisson. *See* Joseph ben Baruch of Clisson

Joseph of Israel. *See* Joseph ben Baruch of Clisson

Joseph of Jaén. *See* Joseph ben Justu of Jaén

Joseph of Kremenets. *See* Joseph ben Moses of Kremenets

Joseph of Lublin. *See* Joseph Joske ben Judah Judel of Lublin

Joseph of Prague. *See* Joseph ben Issachar Baer of Prague

Joseph of Rosheim. *See* Joseph ben Gershon of Rosheim

Joseph of Salositz. *See* Joseph Moses of Salositz

Joseph of Spinka. *See* Spinka, Joseph Meir Weiss of

Joseph of Tiberias, 18:448–449

Joseph of Troyes. *See* Joseph ben Moses of Troyes

Joseph of Zaslaw. *See* Joseph ben Elijah of Zaslaw

Joseph Porat. *See* Joseph ben Moses of Troyes

Joseph the Righteous. *See* Joseph ben Moses Phinehas

Joseph Rosh ha-Seder, 11:**432**

Joseph Samuel ben Ẓevi of Cracow, 11:**432**

Joseph Solomon Rofe of Candia. *See* Delmedigo, Joseph Solomon

Joseph Solomon Zalman ben Meir, 11:**432**

Josephson, Brian David, 11:**434**

Josephson, Erland, 11:**433**

Josephson, Ernst Abraham, 11:**433**

Josephson, Gunnar, 11:**433**

Josephson, Jacob Axel, 11:**432–433**

Josephson, Ludwig Oscar, 11:**433**

Josephson, Lyon, 15:239

Josephson, Manuel, 11:**434**, 15:239

Josephson, Matthew, 11:**434**

Josephson, Ragnar, 11:**433**

Josephson effect, 11:**434**

Josephson family, 11:**432–433**

Josephsthal, George. *See* Josephtal, Giora

Josephsthal, Israel Beer. *See* Reuter, Paul Julius, Freiherr von

Joseph Strauss Rabbinical Seminary. *See* Ohr Torah Stone

Josephtal, Louis Maurice, 11:**434**

Josephthal, Giora, 11:**434**

Josephthal, Senta, 11:**434**

Joseph the Zealot. *See* Official, Nathan ben Joseph

Josephus Flavius, 2:405, 11:**435–442**

  Abraham, 1:284

  agriculture, 1:490–491

  apologetics, 2:263

  Areios (King of Sparta), 15:431

  in art, 11:441–442

  autobiography of, 3:705

  Bible

    as closed and inviolate corpus, 3:579, 584

    names for, 3:574

    tripartite canon of, 3:576

  biography, 11:435–436

  Butnah, 4:318

  Christianity and Jesus, 11:439–440, 441

  chronological concerns of, 3:660

  on Eleazar ben Jair, 6:302–303

  Essenes, 6:510–511

  as historian, 11:437, 439, 441

  historiography, 9:154–155

  Izates, 14:447

  as Jew, 11:440–441

  Jewish distaste for, 11:436

  Jewish War

    as commander of Galilee in, 11:435

    as historian of, 11:436–437

    as Roman prisoner/collaborator, 11:436–437

  on John the Baptist, 11:380

  on John the Essene, 11:382

  on John of Giscala, 11:383

  Jonathan ben Anan, 11:397

  Jonathan the Hasmonean, 11:399

  Joseph ben Elem, 11:420

  on Joshua ben Gamla, 11:450

  Joshua ben Phabi, 11:454

  Josippon and, 11:461

  on Jotapata, 11:464

  on Judean boundaries, 11:523

  on Julius Archelaus, 11:574

  Justus of Tiberias and, 11:440, 581–582

  in literature, 11:441

  Moses, 14:531, 533

  Nicanor's gate, location of, 15:248

  Nicholas of Damascus quoted by, 15:252

  Numenius, son of Antiochus, 15:339

  oak of Abraham in Hebron, 15:357

Josephus Flavius, *continued*
on Obedas II, 15:367
olam ha-ba, 15:399
Onias, Temple of, 15:432
Onias IV, 15:432
Pamphylia, 15:608
papyri confirming or correcting, 15:619
Philo Judaeus and, 16:63
on Philo the Elder, 3:660
on Sanhedrin, 18:21
on Second Temple menorah, 14:51
with Titus in Jerusalem, 11:435–436
Vespasian, prophecy regarding, 11:435–436
works of, 11:436–440
as writer, 11:437, 441
Jose Solomon Rofe of Candia. *See* Delmedigo, Joseph Solomon
Joshua (biblical figure), 11:**442–445**
Eldad and Medad, 6:293
Hazor conquest by, 8:497, 11:8
Jericho conquest by, 11:138
Moses, 14:525–526, 528
Joshua (liturgical poet), 11:**445**
Joshua (son of Sapphas), 11:**449**
Joshua (son of Seth), 11:**449**
Joshua (tanna), 11:**445**
Joshua, Book of, 11:444*t*, **445–449**
Alt School or Alt-Noth trend, 2:11
Book of Jashar, 4:69
Joshua ben Abraham Maimuni, 11:**449**
Joshua ben Damnai, 11:**449**
Joshua ben Elijah ha-Levi, 11:**450**
Joshua ben Gamla, 6:171, 11:**450**
Joshua ben Hananiah, 11:**450–452**
Hadrian, Publius Aelius, 8:194
on Johanan ben Nuri, 11:373
Joshua ben Hyrcanus, 11:**452**
Joshua ben Jehozadak. *See* Jeshua (high priest)
Joshua ben Joseph. *See* Joshua Hoeschel ben Joseph of Cracow
Joshua ben Joseph ha-Levi. *See* Jeshua ben Joseph ha-Levi
Joshua ben Judah. *See* Jeshua ben Judah
Joshua ben Korḥa, 2:69, 6:627, 11:**452–453**
Joshua ben Levi, 6:333–334, 11:**453–454**, 14:539, 18:599
Joshua ben Mordecai Falk ha-Kohen, 11:**454**
Joshua ben Peraḥyah, 11:**454**, 15:282
Joshua ben Phabi, 11:**454–455**

Joshua ben Saul. *See* Hoeschel ben Saul
Joshua Boaz ben Simon Baruch, 11:**455**
Joshua ha-Garsi, 11:**455**
Joshua Heschel ben Isaac Babad, 3:14
Joshua Hoeschel ben Jacob ("the Rebbi Reb Hoeschel"), 11:**455–456**
Joshua Hoeschel ben Joseph of Cracow, 11:**456**
Joshua Ibn Nun, 6:67, 11:**456–457**
Joshua Joseph ben David Levi. *See* Levi, Joshua Joseph ben David
Joshua Lorki. *See* Lorki, Joshua
Joshua of Belz, 3:308
Joshua of Kurnik. *See* Joshua ben Mordecai Falk ha-Kohen
Joshua of Lorca. *See* Lorki, Joshua
Joshua son of Jehozadak. *See* Jeshua (high priest)
Joshua Then and Now (Richler), 17:288
Josiah (amora), 11:**460**
Josiah (biblical figure), 12:174
Josiah (King of Judah), 9:181, 11:**457–459**
Deuteronomy and, 15:740
rated by God, 15:743
Josiah (tanna), 11:**460**
Josiah ben Aaron he-Ḥaver, 11:**460**
Josiah ben Jesse, 11:**460**
Josiah ben Saul ben Anan, 11:**460**
Josiah the Great. *See* Josiah (tanna)
Josiah of Usha, 11:**460**
Josiphiah the Proselyte, 11:**460**
Josipovici, Gabriel, 6:439, 11:**461**
Josippon, 8:325, 11:**461–462**
Amelander, Menahen Mann ven Solomon Ha-Levi, 2:38
Byzantine empire, 4:327
illustration of, 4:76
Otranto, 15:516
printing of, 2:108
Josko, 11:**462**
Jospe, Alfred, 11:317, 319, **462–463**
Jospe, Eva Scheyer, 11:462, 463
Jospe, Raphael, 11:463
Josse bar Nissan. *See* Joseph bar Nissan
Jossel ben Joshua Moses of Frankfurt. *See* Joseph ben Joshua Moses of Frankfurt
Jossko. *See* Josko
Jost, Isaac Marcus, 2:163, 9:158–159, 11:**463–464**
Jotabah (Gulf of Elath), 11:**464**
Jotapata (Israel), 11:**464–465**

Jotbath (Sinai Desert), 11:**465**
Jotham (King of Judah), 11:**465–466**
Ammonites, 2:85
training, 6:166
Jotham (son of Gideon the Judge), 11:**465**
Jothbatah. *See* Jotbath
Journalism, 11:**466–470**
Aḥimeir, Abba, 1:544
Allouche, Felix Nissim S'Aidou, 1:677
Austria
Baumgarten, Emanuel Mendel, 3:221–222
Beda, 3:246–247
Benedikt, Moritz, 3:333
Bermann, Richard Arnold, 3:465
Bettauer, Hugo, 3:550–551
Braunthal, Julius, 4:140
Brunner, Sebastian, 4:224
Beider, Chaim, 3:265
Brazil, Dines, Alberto, 5:670–671
Brick, Daniel, 4:178
Bulgaria, 4:270–271
Canada
Landsberg, Michele, 12:474–475
Littman, Sol, 13:129
Rosenfeld, Fanny, 17:445
Schlesinger, Joe, 18:141
caricatures, 4:478–479
Chakovski, Alexander Borisovich, 4:560–561
Chile, 4:641–642
Chamudes Reitich, Marcos, 4:565
Levy, Robert, 12:755
Elnecavé, David, 6:366
Finland, 11:74
France, 5:425
Cahen, Isidore, 4:337
Chalom, Marcel, 4:563
Elkabbach, Jean-Pierre, 6:356–357
Hourwitz, Zalkind, 9:569
Lazareff, Pierre, 12:559
Lazurick, Robert, 12:563
Lecache, Bernard, 12:593
Levy, Sam Saadi, 12:755
Raphael, John, 17:95
Reinach, Joseph, 17:204–205
Schiller, Armand, 18:133
Schumann, Maurice, 18:175–176
Germany, 6:726
Becker, Julius, 3:245

Ben-Chorin, Schalom, 3:324
Bernhard, Georg, 3:472–473
Heymann, Fritz, 9:86
Hock, Simon, 9:301
Hundt-Radowsky, Joachim
    Hartwig, 9:602
Pinner, Felix, 16:169–170
Reich-Ranicki, Marcel, 17:201
Schwab, Hermann, 18:179
Simon, Heinrich, 18:611
Greece
    Bensanchi, Mentesh, 3:373
    Caimis, Moisis, 4:339–340
    Molho, Isaac Raphael,
        14:425–426
    Recanati, Abraham Samuel,
        17:141
    Schiby, Baruch, 18:125
Hebrew
    Carlebach, Ezriel, 4:480
    Chicago, 4:612
    Eimann, Moses, 6:276
    Ludvipol, Abraham, 13:251
    Rabbi Binyamin, 17:19
    Rabinovich, Yehudah Leib,
        17:38
    Rabinowitz, Ya'akov, 17:42
    Ratosh, Yonathan, 17:113–
        114
    Rawnitzki, Yehoshua Ḥana,
        17:126
Hermann, Leo, 9:24–25
Hungary, 6:687, 11:76
    Bródy, Lili, 4:201
    Bródy, Zsigmond, 4:202
    Havas, Géza, 8:466
    Hevesi, Lajos, 9:79
    Ignotus, Hugó, 9:716
    Lévai, Jenö, 12:676
    Radó, Antal, 17:56
Israel, 10:704–707
    Agron, Gershon, 1:504
    Bar-Ilan, David, 3:153
    Barnea, Nahum, 3:168
    Beilin, Asher, 3:266
    Ben-Avi Ithmar, 3:322
    Broido, Ephraim, 4:203
    Danker, 5:430
    Dissentchik, Aryeh, 5:702
    Eliav, Binyamin, 6:321
    Elon, Amos, 6:366–367
    Harel, David, 8:352
    Hodess, Jacob, 9:301
    Landa, David, 12:458
    Laquer, Walter Ze'ev, 12:492
    Lurie, Ted, 13:270

Nimrodi family, 15:270
Pearlstein, Moshe, 15:705–
    706
Ragen, Naomi, 17:64–65
Rager, Itzhak, 17:65
Riviln, Eliezer, 17:350
Rosenblum, Herzl, 17:443
Rosenfeld, Shalom, 17:447
Sarid, Yossi, 18:56
Schnitzer, Shmuel, 18:152
Sokolow, Nahum, 18:747–748
Kaplan, Sender Meyer, 11:780
Landau, Jacob, 12:462–463
Latin America, 12:513–515
Lattes, Dante, 12:519
Levin, Poul Theodor, 12:712
Levy, Louis, 12:752
Lithuania, Schachnowitz, Selig,
    18:98
Ottoman Empire, 15:540
Palestine, Di-Zahav, Ephraim,
    5:721
Pitigrilli, 16:188
Poland
    Erlich, Henryk, 6:481
    Hirschhorn, Samuel, 9:139
    Izraelita, 10:829
    Kaplan, Pesaḥ, 11:779
    Rochman, Leib, 17:359
Roest, Meijer Marcus, 17:367
Romania
    Călugăru, Ion, 4:376
    Carp, Horia, 4:493
    Dan, Sergiu, 5:408
    Hefter, Alfred, 8:755
    Lazareanu, Barbu, 12:559
    Relgis, Eugen, 17:214
    Semilian, Savin Solomon,
        18:279
Rosenberg, Moishe, 17:438
Rotem, Cvi, 17:477
Rouleau, Eric, 17:498
Russia
    Ben-Ammi, Mordecai, 3:316–
        317
    Bernstein, Simon, 3:484
    Dan, Fyodor Ilyich, 5:407
    Landau, Adolph, 12:457–458
    Landau, Gregory Adolfovich,
        12:461
    Latzky-Bertholdi, Jacob Ze'ev
        Wolf, 12:524
    Leviné, Eugene, 12:717–718
    Pines, Meyer Isser, 16:167
    Schmidt, Samuel Myer,
        18:145–146

Sandler, Boris, 18:15–16
Selig, Phineas, 18:265
Simone, Andre, 18:617
South Africa, 6:745
    De Lima, Joseph Suasso,
        5:539
    Levinson, Olga, 12:723
Sweden, 11:74
Turkey, 14:28–29
    Benroya, Avraham, 3:319
    Leyon, Avram, 12:772
U.K., 11:55–56, 12:457, 546–547,
    707
    Beer, Rachel, 3:253
    Bermant, Chaim Icyk, 3:466
    Lewis, Hyman, 12:764–765
U.S.
    Adams, Franklin Pierce, 1:380
    Adler, Julius Ochs, 1:401
    Adler, Renata, 1:406
    Berger, Meyer, 3:425
    Berger, Victor, 3:426
    Bernstein, Carl, 3:477–479
    Bernstein, Herman, 3:479
    Bourke-White, Margaret,
        4:106–107
    Brainin, Joseph, 4:119
    Brill, Isaac Lipa, 4:182
    Broder, David Salzer, 4:194–
        195
    Brody, Jane E., 4:200–201
    Bublick, Gedaliah, 4:237
    Buchwald, Art, 4:243
    De Hass, Jacob, 5:532
    Fischer, Louis, 7:54
    Frankel, Max, 7:198
    Freeman, Joseph, 7:228
    Gruber, Ruth, 8:104–105
    Hersch, Seymour, 9:44
    Hewitt, Don, 9:83
    Laurence, William L., 12:527
    Lawrence, David, 12:545
    Lederer, Esther Pauline,
        12:596
    Leeser, Isaac, 12:600–601
    Lelyveld, Joseph, 12:636
    Lerner, Max, 12:658
    Levy, Albert J., 12:746
    Lewis, Anthony, 12:763
    Liebling, A. J., 12:809
    Lippmann, Walter, 13:70
    Los Angeles, 13:209
    Lyons, Eugene, 13:297
    Minsky, Louis, 14:298
    Morning Freiheit (newspaper),
        14:492–493

Journalism, *continued*

    Morwitz, Edward, 14:514

    Newman, Peter Charles, 15:148

    Ochs, Adolph Simon, 15:375–376

    Opper, Frederick Burr, 15:451

    Pearl, Daniel, 15:705

    Pearlstine, Norman, 15:**706–707**

    Remnick, David, 17:217–218

    Richards, Bernard Gerson, 17:287

    Rogoff, Harry, 17:369

    Rosenthal, A. M., 17:451–452

    Rosewater, Edward, 17:463

    Rukeyser, Merryle Stanley, 17:528

    Schanberg, Sydney H., 18:106

    Schlesinger, Benjamin, 18:140

    Schorr, Daniel, 18:163

    Schur, Zev Wolf, 18:176

    Seldes, George, 18:259

    Seltzer, Louis Benson, 18:272

    Silverman, Sime, 18:587–588

    Singer, Isaac Bashevis, 18:634–635

    Singer, Israel Joshua, 18:637

    Slomovitz, Philip, 18:675

  Yiddish

    Argentina, 4:253

    Cahan, Abraham, 4:335–336

    Chicago, 4:611–612

    Elberg, Yehuda, 6:290–291

    Held, Adolph, 8:780–781

    Litvin, A., 13:140

    Der Moment (newspaper), 14:430

    Resnick, Solomon, 17:227–228

    Ressler, Benjamin, 17:239

    Rogoff, Harry, 17:369

  Yugoslavia, 12:489

  See also Photojournalism; *specific journalists and publications*

Journal of General Physiology, 13:160

Journal of the American Medical Association, 7:60

Journal of the History of Philosophy, 7:141

Journals of Sexual Science (Hirschfeld), 9:138

"The Journey" (Mandel). *See Le périple* (Mandel)

Journey, prayer for. *See* Travel, prayer for

A Journey Through A Haunted Land (Elon), 6:366

Joy, 11:**470–471**

Joyce, James, 6:436

Joyce at 34 (motion picture), 4:666

Jozefowicz, Michael, 4:168

Józefowicz family, 4:168, 11:**471–472**

The JPS Guide to Jewish Women: 600 B.C.E.-1900 C.E., 9:163

JRSO. *See* Jewish Restitution Successor Organization

J (YHWH) source of Torah, 15:735–739

  Aaron and, 15:739

  contradictions and, 15:741–742

  identification of, 15:742

  monotheism in, 15:750

  redactor, 15:740

  terminology for God, 15:743

JTA. *See* Jewish Telegraphic Agency

JTC. *See* Jewish Trust Corporation

JTS. *See* Jewish Theological Seminary

Juan de Ciudad, 11:**472**

Juan de Dios Huarte of Navarra. *See* Huarte de San Juan, Juan

Juan de España, 11:**472**

Juan de Valladolid, 11:**472**, 14:462

Juan el Viejo. *See* Juan de España

Juan Espera en Dios. *See* Wandering Jew

Juan Poeta. *See* Juan de Valladolid

Juarez, Pedro, 15:563

Jubail. *See* Jubayl

Jubal, 11:**472**

Jubar (Syria), 11:**473**

Jubayl (Lebanon), 11:**473**, 16:120

Jubilees, Book of, 5:166, 11:**473–474**

  devil in, 13:668–669

  Fallen Angels, 2:155

  Noah, Books of, 15:290

Jubilee Year. *See* Sabbatical Year and Jubilee

Jubilus, 8:281

Jud, Michel, 4:125

Juda, Leo, 3:681

Juda, Walter, 11:**474**

Judaesaptan (Austria), 11:**474–475**

Judah (biblical figure and tribe), 9:174–179, 11:**475–478**, *476*

  Ahab, 1:522

  Ahaz, 1:539

  Ahaziah, 1:539–540

  borders, 6:236

  David and, 5:446, 448–451

  eschatology, 6:493

  Mizpeh, 14:388

  Tamar and, 19:493–494

Judah (King of Judea). *See* Aristobulus I (King of Judea)

Judah (kingdom), 4:698–699, 10:*103, 104*

  decline, 11:109–110

  Edom, 6:155–156

  E (Elohim) source of Torah and, 15:736–737

  exile to Babylonia, 6:608–610

  Israel (kingdom) and, 11:111–112, 141

  restoration of, 6:493

  Solomon, 18:758

Judah (Nesiah, 3rd c.), 11:**478**

Judah (son of Zipporai), 11:**480**

Judah, Baruch, 11:479

Judah, Baruch H., 11:479

Judah, Benjamin S., 4:70, 11:479, 15:198

Judah, Bernard, 11:479

Judah, Daniel. *See* Oliver Y Fullana, Nicolás de

Judah, Emanuel, 11:479

Judah, Hillel, 11:479

Judah, Manuel, 11:479

Judah, Michael, 11:479–480, 15:304

Judah, Naphtali, 11:479, 15:198

Judah, Samuel, 11:479, 15:197

Judah, Samuel Benjamin Helbert, 11:444, 479, **480,** 14:540

Judah, Uriah, 11:479

Judah, Walter, 15:197

Judah, Walter Jonas, 8:735, 11:479

Judah III (Judah Nesiah II, 3rd-4th c.), 11:**478–479**

Judah IV (4th-5th c.), 11:**479**

Judah Areyeh mi-Modena. *See* Modena, Leon

Judah Aristobulus. *See* Aristobulus I (King of Judea)

Judah Aryeh Leib ben David, 11:**480**

Judah bar Ezekiel, 11:**480–481**

Judah bar Ilai, 2:14, 11:**481–482**

Judah bar Pazzi. *See* Judah bar Simeon

Judah bar Shalom, 11:**482**

Judah bar Simeon, 11:**482**

Judah ben Asher, 11:**483**

Judah ben Barzillai al-Bargeloni, 11:**483–484,** 20:40

  Abraham bar Ḥiyya, 1:292, 293

  Abraham ben Isaac of Narbonne, 1:302

  on functions of rabbinate, 18:275–276

Judah ben Bathyra, 3:27, 11:**484**

Judah ben Bava, 11:**484–485,** 18:593

Judah ben David. *See* Hermanus Quondam Judaeus

Judah ben Dosotheos, 11:**485**

Judah ben Eleazar, 11:**485–486,** 553

Judah ben Eli, 11:**486**

Judah ben Eliezer, 11:460, **486**

Judah ben Farḥon, 18:572

Judah ben Gerim, 11:**486**, 18:593

Judah ben Ḥiyya, 3:642, 11:**486–487**

Judah ben Ilai, 3:589

Judah ben Isaac (14th or 15th c.), 11:**487**

Judah ben Isaac (1166-1224), 11:**487**

　Joseph ben Baruch of Clisson, 11:419

　Joseph ben Moses of Troyes, 11:424

　in Paris, 15:643

Judah ben Isaac Ibn Shabbetai, 11:**487–488**, 15:655–656

Judah ben Jacob. *See* Prossnitz, Judah Leib ben Jacob Holleschau

Judah ben Jacob ha-Kohen, 11:**488**

Judah ben Jacob Hayyat, 6:625

Judah ben Joseph of Kairouan, 11:**488**

Judah ben Judah. *See* Jaecklin, Jud

Judah ben Kalonymus ben Meir, 11:**488–489**

Judah ben Kalonymus ben Moses of Mainz, 11:**489**

Judah ben Menahem of Rome, 11:**489**

Judah ben Mordecai Elmaleh, 6:364

Judah ben Moses. *See* Leonte ben Moses

Judah ben Moses ha-Darshan, 11:**489**

Judah ben Moses of Lublin, 11:**489–490**

Judah ben Naḥamani, 2:88, 89, 11:**490**, 18:598

Judah ben Nathan, 11:**490**

Judah ben Nissan, 11:**490**

Judah ben Pedaya, 11:**490**

Judah ben Samuel ben Abbas, 2:77

Judah ben Samuel he-Ḥasid, 6:175–176, 8:389, 11:**490–491**

Judah ben Shammua, 11:**491**

Judah ben Sheshet. *See* Yehudi ben Sheshet

Judah ben Simeon ben Pazzi. *See* Judah bar Simeon

Judah ben Solomon Al-Ḥarizi. *See* Al-Ḥarizi, Judah ben Solomon

Judah ben Solomon ibn Matka, 6:399

Judah ben Tabbai, 11:**491**, 18:600

Judah ben Tema, 11:**491–492**

Judah ben Yakar, 11:**492**

Judah families, 11:**479–480**

Judah the Galilean, 11:**492**

Judah Hadassi. *See* Hadassi, Judah ben Elijah

Judah Halevi, 2:618, 8:273, 11:**492–501,** 16:83–84

　Abraham, 1:285

　Adam, 1:373

　Alamani, Aaron he-Ḥaver ben Yeshu'ah, 1:575

　apologetics, 2:265

　beatitude, 3:238

　biblical study, influence of, 3:662

　biography of, 11:493–494

　Brody, Heinrich, 4:200

　cause and effect, 4:529

　chosen people doctrine, 4:671

　commandments, reasons for, 5:87

　Divine attributes, 19:284

　evolution and, 6:586

　free will, 7:231

　Ibn Ezra, Abraham, friendship with, 11:493

　Jerusalem and, 11:214–215, 216

　Jewish philosophy, 1:409

　Joshua ben Elijah ha-Levi and, 11:450

　Judeo-Arabic literature and, 11:535

　Kuzari, commentary on, 6:717

　miracles, 14:307–308

　Moses, 14:536

　philosophy of, 11:497–500

　poetry of, 11:494–497, 16:266

　prophets and prophecy, 16:582

　revelation, 17:257

　Ru'aḥ ha-Kodesh, 17:508–509

　on Shekhinah, 18:442

　skeptics and skepticism, 18:658

　soul, immortality of, 19:37

　Torah, 20:40

　Zionism of

　　immigration to Ereẓ Israel, 11:493–494

　　philosophical position, 11:499

　　"Poems of Zion" or Zionides, 11:495–497

Judah ha-Levi bei-Rabbi Hillel, 11:**492–501**

Judah ha-Nasi, 3:212, 4:767–768, 9:203, 10:151–153, 11:**501–505**

　altar of Temple, 2:15

　am ha-areẓ, 2:70

　amoraim, 2:89, 90

　amora of, 2:88

　Bet She'arim (Israel) (Besara), 3:547

　Eleazar ben Shammua, 6:307

havdallah, 8:467

Ḥiyya, 9:295

Joshua ben Korḥa, 11:453

labor, 12:409–410

Mishnah, 14:319–320

Oshaiah Rabbah, 15:501

Sefrei Numbers, 18:565–566

Sikarikon, 18:573–574

Simeon ben Gamaliel, 18:595

Simeon ben Ḥalafta, 18:597

Simeon ben Judah ha-Nasi, 18:597

Simeon ben Menasya, 18:598

Judah ha-Nasi al-Bargeloni. *See* Judah ben Barzillai al-Bargeloni

Judah ha-Nasi II

　Ammi bar Nathan, 2:82

　Diocletian, Caius Valerianus and, 5:673–674

Judah ha-Parsi, 11:**505**

Judah Ḥasid, ha-Levi, 11:**505–506,** 18:354

Judah he-Hasid

　Anim Zemirot, 2:174

　piety and, 16:150

Judah ibn Abbas. *See* Abbas, Judah ben Samuel ibn

Judah ibn Quraysh. *See* Ibn Quraysh, Judah

Judah Ibn Sūsā, 3:379

Judah Jonah of Safed. *See* Jona, Giovanni Battista

Judah L. Magnes Museum (California), 13:**354–355,** 15:358

Judah Leib ben Baruch, 11:**506**

Judah Leib ben Enoch Zundel, 11:**506**

Judah Leib ben Hillel of Schwersenz, 11:**506**

Judah Liwa ben Bezalel. *See* Judah Loew ben Bezalel

Judah Loeb ben Bezalel. *See* Judah Loew ben Bezalel

Judah Loebush ben Isaac, 11:456

Judah Loew ben Bezalel, 2:174, 4:778, 779, 6:178, 9:225–226, 11:**506–509**

　exile, meaning of, 7:360–361

　Moses, 14:537

Judah Maccabee, 8:446, 11:**509–511,** 13:316

　Alcimus, 1:603

　Bacchides, 3:31

　Elasa, 6:287

　Hasmonean revolt, 9:194

　Mizpeh, 14:388

　Nicanor, 15:247

　Scroll of Antiochus, 18:213–214

Judah Messer Leon, 2:141

Judah Nesiah. *See* Judah (Nesiah, 3rd c.)

Judah Nesiah II. *See* Judah III

Judah of Dueren, 6:41

Judah of Fez. *See* Abbas, Judah ben Samuel ibn

Judah of Kairouan. *See* Judah ben Joseph of Kairouan

Judah of Lublin. *See* Judah ben Moses of Lublin

Judah of Mainz. *See* Judah ben Kalonymus ben Moses of Mainz

Judah of Prague. *See* Judah Loew ben Bezalel

Judah of Rome. *See* Judah ben Menahem of Rome

Judah of Schwersenz. *See* Judah Leib ben Hillel of Schwersenz

Judah Sir Leon of Paris. *See* Judah ben Isaac

Judah the Tiberian. *See* Judah ben Eli

Judaica. *See* Wissenschaft des Judentums

Judaic studies. *See* Jewish studies

Judaism, 11:**511–520**

    Aish HaTorah, 1:551

    Bible, religious education, 6:165

    body and soul, concept of, 4:30–31

    Buber on, 4:234

    contemporary, 11:519

    development of, 11:514–519

    essential principles of, 11:511–513

    historical perspectives of, 6:36–37

    influence of, 11:519–520

    integral, 15:563

    Islam and, 1:546, 11:538–542

    Maimonides, Moses, 13:393

    mysticism in, 5:407–408, 11:589–590

    New Testament's relationship to, 15:191–192

    normative Judaism, concept of, 11:513

    of Paul, 15:192

    postmodern, 4:93

    Protestant study of, 16:629

    tenets, 6:59

    Torah and, 11:511–512, 516

Judaism (Epstein), 6:471

Judaism (Hertzberg), 9:49

Judaism (journal), 18:734

Judaism (periodical), 2:58

Judaism, Conservative. *See* Conservative Judaism

Judaism, conversion to. *See* Proselytes

Judaism, Liberal. *See* Reform Judaism

Judaism, Positive Historical. *See* Conservative Judaism

Judaism, Reconstructionist. *See* Reconstructionism

Judaism: The Evidence of the Mishnah (Neusner), 15:124

Judaism and Hebrew Prayer (Reif), 13:133

Judaism and Modern Man: An Interpretation of Jewish Religion (Herberg), 9:8

Judaism and the Scientific Spirit (Plaut), 16:228

Judaism and the Solitary Jew (Schweid), 16:102

Judaism - A Quarterly Journal (periodical), 18:193

Judaism as a Civilization (Kaplan), 11:779

Judaism in German Christian Theology (Stendhal), 4:687

Judaism in Islam (Katsh), 12:6

Judaism in Palestine (Smith), 18:688

Judaism in the First Centuries of the Christian Era: The Age of the Tannaim (Moore), 14:469, 17:241–242

Judaism in Theory and Practice (Lookstein), 13:189

Judaism Unmasked (Eisenmenger), 6:268

Judaistica. *See* Wissenschaft des Judentums

Judaizers, 11:**520–523**

    Bible translations by, 3:635

    in Bohemia, 4:38

    Juvenal on, 11:582

    See also God fearers

Judas (Christian writer), 11:**523**

Judas Iscariot. See Yehudah Ish-Keriyyot

Der Jude (periodical), 4:231, 11:**523**

Judea (Roman province), 9:196–197, 10:*105*, 11:**523**

    Agrippa I, 1:502–503

    Caligula, Caius Caesar Augustus, 4:363

    Edom, 6:157

    government, 6:675

    procurators, 6:749

    See also Intifada

Judea Capta coinage, 5:51

Judean coins and currency, 5:48

Judean Desert (Israel), 10:115

Judean Desert caves, 11:**523–525**

Judean Mountains (Israel), 10:114–117

Judean Plain (Israel), 10:110

Judean Scrolls (Driver), 6:22

The Judean Scrolls and Karaism (Wieder), 11:796

Judea Reform Congregation (Durham, NC), 6:62

Judel ben Moses of Lublin. *See* Judah ben Moses of Lublin

Judenburg (Austria), 11:**525**

Judenflinten (Ahlwardt), 1:547

Zur Judenfrage in Ungarn (Einhorn), 6:259

Judenfrei. *See* Judenrein

Judenfresser. *See* Endlich, Quirin

Judengasse. *See* Jewish quarters

Judengeleit. *See* Leibzoll

Judenpfennige, 11:**525**

Judenrat, 9:332, 11:**526–529**

    behavior, 9:356–357

    Bialystok, 3:137, 568, 569

    in Borislav, 4:86

    Kovno, 6:358

    Lachva (Poland), 12:426

    Oshmyany, 15:503

    Warsaw (Poland), 5:371

Judenrat: The Jewish Councils in Eastern Europe Under Nazi Occupation (Trunk), 9:416, 20:161

Judenrein, 11:**529**

Der Judenstaat (Herzl), 9:54–56

Der Judenstaat Altneuland (Herzl), 21:620

Die Judenstadt von Lublin (Balaban), 3:82

Judenstern. *See* Badge, Jewish

Judentums, Wissenschaft Des, 15:458

Das Judentum und das Wesen des Christentums (Eschelbacher), 6:504

Das Judentum und seine Geschichte (Geiger), 7:414

Die Juden von Barnow (Franzos), 7:219

Judenzoll. *See* Leibzoll

Judeo-Alsatian language, 2:7

Judeo-Arabic Biblical Exegesis Project, 7:480

Judeo-Arabic culture, 11:538–543

Judeo-Arabic Halakhic Literature Project, 7:480

Judeo-Arabic language, 3:743–744, 8:243, 11:302, **529–530**

Judeo-Arabic literature, 11:**530–545**

    Abu al-Faraj Harun ibn al-Faraj, 1:334

    Abu al-Fat, 1:334

    after thirteenth century, 11:536–538

    Al-Avani, Isaac, 1:579

    in Babylonia, Palestine, and Egypt, 11:530–531

    culture of, 11:538–543

    Hirschfeld, Hartwig, 9:137–138

Joseph story, use of, 11:412

Karaites, 11:530, 531–532

in North Africa and Spain, 11:532–534

religious philosophy and theology, 11:534–536

Judeo-Aramaic language, 11:301

Judeo-Berber language, 11:530

Judeo-Christian dialogue

Anselm of Canterbury, 2:181

Disputation of Barcelona, 3:145–146

Judeo-Christians of early Christian period, 11:293–294, 453, 520

Judeo-French language, 11:**545**

Judeo-Georgian language, 11:302

Judeo-German. *See* Yiddish language

Judeo-Greek language, 3:636, 11:**545–546**

Judeo-Iranian dialect, 11:548, 550

Judeo-Italian language, 11:**546–548**

Judeo-Italian literature, 11:547–548

Carmi, Joseph Jedidiah, 4:484

Judith, Book of, 11:568

Judéo-Niçois dialect, 15:249

Judeo-Persian language, 11:302, **548–559**

Bible translated into, 3:609, 8:245

characteristics of, 11:548–550

dialectical characteristics of, 11:548–549

Judeo-Iranian dialect, 11:548, 550

manuscripts and research history, 11:558

modern, 11:557–558

See also Judeo-Persian literature; Judeo-Tat language

Judeo-Persian literature, 11:550–558

Aklar Mordecai ben Raphael, 1:569

Bacher, Wilhelm studies of, 3:37

biblical influence, 3:670

of Bukharan Jewry, 4:262–263

early period, 11:550–552

Emrāni, 6:398

manuscripts and research history, 11:558

medieval to early modern, 11:550–556

modern period, 11:556–558

Judeo-Provençal language, 11:**559–560,** *560*

Judeo-Roman. *See* Judeo-Italian language

Judeo-Romance languages and literature, 11:301, 546

Bible's influence, 3:670

Bible translated into, 3:609–610

Blondheim, David Simon, 3:771

See also specific languages

Judeo-Spanish language. *See* Ladino

Judeo-Tajik dialect, 11:556–557

Judeo-Tatar language, 3:609

Judeo-Tat language, 11:302, 550, **560–561**

Judezmo. *See* Ladino

Judge. *See* Bet din and judges

Judge Jerry. *See* Sheindlin, Gerald

Judge Judy. *See* Sheindlin, Judith

Judgement at Nuremberg, 9:441

"Judge of the Jews." *See* Iudex Judaeorum

Judges, Book of, 1:258, 9:153, 11:*561,* **561–566**

Judges and judiciary

Admon ben Gaddai, 1:412

Agranat, Shimon, 1:470

Albalia, Baruch ben Isaac, 1:583

appointment of, 3:514–515

Battat, Reuben, 3:215

Botein, Bernard, 4:101–102

Brandeis, Louis Dembitz, 4:121–124

Bregstein, Marcel Henri, 4:157

Breitel, Charles, 4:157–158

Breyer, Stephen Gerand, 4:174–175

Butzel, Henry M., 4:320

Canada, 12:549

Cardozo, Benjamin Nathan, 4:466

Colorni, Vittore, 5:68–69

Cowen, Zelman, 5:255–256

Daube, 5:441

dina de-malkhuta dina, 5:666

drunkenness, 6:27

duties of, 13:739, 741

Ehrlich, Eugen, 6:243

elders, 6:295

Elon, Menachem, 6:367–368

Errera, Paul Joseph, 6:483

Feller, Shneyur Zalman, 6:750

Forman, Philip, 7:130

Fortas, Abe, 7:132

Fox, Bernard Joshua, 7:140

France

Bédarride, Israél, 3:247

Cassin, René Samuel, 4:508–509

Frank, Eli, 7:180

Frank, Jerome New, 7:192

Frankel, Marvin Earl, 7:197–198

Frankfurter, Felix, 7:204–206

Freimann, Abraham Ḥayyim, 7:237

general courts, 14:355, 356, 361

gentile courts, 14:342–343

Germany

Behrend, Jacob Friedrich, 3:264

Riesser, Jacob, 17:296

Greene, Harold H., 8:76–77

Hellerstein, Alvin K., 8:798–799

Hoffman, Julius Jennings, 9:308–309

International Court of Justice, 4:254

Israel, 9:73–74

Barak, Aharon, 3:130–131

Beinisch, Dorit, 3:269

Ben-Porat, Miriam, 3:371–372

separation of powers, 18:292

Smoira, Moshe, 18:689

Italy

Cammeo, Federico, 4:381–382

Cattaneo, Carlo, 4:525

Mortara, Lodovico, 14:513

Polacco, Vittorio, 16:285

Segrè, Gino, 18:252

Jessel, Sir George, 11:244

Kantorowicz, Hermann, 11:772

Karminski, Seymour, 11:814

Kaufman, Irving R., 12:29

Kaye, Judith S., 12:41

Kelsen, Hans, 12:**71–72**

Landau, Moshe, 12:465

Lapidot, Ruth, 12:490

Laserson, Max, 12:494–495

Laskin, Bora, 12:499–500

Lauterpacht, Sir Hersch, 12:530

Lauterpacht, Sir Hersh, 12:530

lay tribunals, 14:343–344

Levin Smith, Sir Archibald, 12:720

Libedinsky Tschorne, Marcos, 12:775

Meijer, Eduard Maurits, 13:775

Meyer, Jonas Daniel, 14:147

mishpat Ivri, 14:341–362

Moses, 14:525, 527

Newman, Jon O., 15:146

Pinanski, Abraham, 16:164

Piperno Beer, Sergio, 16:181–182

principles of judicial conduct, 3:515

punishment, 16:737

qualifications of judges, 3:515

rabbinical courts, 14:352–355, 356, 362

Reinhardt, Stephen R., 17:208–209

Judges and judiciary, *continued*
Robinson, Jacob, 17:355–356
Rode, Walther, 17:362
Rosenberg, Abraham Ḥayyim, 17:433–434
Russian
Belkowsky, Ẓevi Hirsch, 3:297–298
Pobedonostsev, Konstantin Petrovich, 16:249
Sliozberg, Henry, 18:673–674
Sand, Leonard B., 18:9–10
Sanhedrin, 18:21–23
Satanowski, Marcos, 18:74
Schnitzer, Adolf, 18:152
semikhah, 18:274–275, 276
Sereni, Angela Piero, 18:309
Shamgar, Meir, 18:391
Sheftel, Mikhail, 18:433–434
Sheindlin, Gerald, 18:437
Sheindlin, Judith, 18:437
Sicily, 18:542
Silberg, Moshe, 18:577
Sloss, Marcus Cauffman, 18:680
Smoira, Moshe, 18:689
Soboloff, Simon Ernest, 18:700
Sodom and Gomorrah, 18:738
Sofaer, Abraham, 18:741
Solomon, 18:759
South Africa
Chaskalson, Arthur, 4:581
Herbstein, Joseph, 9:9
Talmudic duties, 13:741
U.S., 12:556–557
Bazelon, David L., 3:233–234
Becker, Edward Roy, 3:244
Calabresi, Guido, 4:347–348
Choper, Jesse H., 4:666
Herlands, William Bernard, 9:22–23
Heydenfeldt, Solomon, 9:84
Hollzer, Harry Aaron, 9:323
Lehman, Irving, 12:614
Leibowitz, Samuel Simon, 12:622
Levin, Theodore, 12:714
Levy, Moses, 12:555, 753–754
Licht, Frank, 12:796
Redlich, Norman, 17:159
Rifkind, Simon Hirsch, 17:298–299
Rosenman, Samuel Irving, 17:448–449
Rothenberg, Morris, 17:485
Judgment. *See* Practice and procedure
Judgment, Day of. *See* Day of the Lord

Judgment, Divine. *See* Day of the Lord
Judi ben Sheshet. *See* Yehudi ben Sheshet
Judicial autonomy, 2:**710–711**, 14:341–344, 351–352
Judicial Review and the National Political Process: A Functional Reconsideration of the Role of the Supreme Court (Choper), 4:666
Judin, Samuel, 11:**566**
Judisk Kronika (newspaper), 4:178
Judisk Tidskrift (periodical), 6:240
Judith (Du Bartas), 6:31
Judith (Seter), 18:319
Judith (wife of Rabbi Ḥiyya), 11:**566**
Judith, Book of, 11:**566–569**
dance, 5:409
as example of alternative history, 18:201
Judith Epstein Memorial Award, 6:474
Judith Lady Montefiore College, 6:206
Judo, 19:144
Jud Seuss (Feuchtwanger), 6:772
Jud (Jew) Suess. *See* Oppenheimer, Joseph ben Issachar Suesskind
Jud Suess (L. Feuchtwanger), 15:449
Die Juedin von Toledo (Grillparzer), 11:256
Juedische Apologetik im neutestamentlichen Zeitalte (Bergmann), 3:429–430
Juedische Colonial Bank. *See* Jewish Colonial Trust
Juedische Familienpapiere (Herzberg), 9:52
Juedische Freischule, 3:**325**
Juedische Freischule (school), 3:446, 447, 11:**569**
Juedische Gemeinschaft Holstein, 13:252
Juedische Hochschule. *See* Hochschule Fuer die Wissenschaft des Judentums
Juedische Jugendblaetter, 3:156
Juedische Klaenge (Loewenstein), 13:168
Juedische Kultusvereinigung, 17:202
Juedische Merkwuerdigkeiten (Schudt), 18:169
Juedische Presse (periodical), 11:**569–570**
Juedischer Central-Verein. *See* Central-Verein Deutscher Staatsbuerger Juedischen Glaubens
Juedischer Frauenbund, 11:**570**
Juedischer Frauenbund (Kaplan), 9:152
Juedischer Kulturbund, 3:14, 11:**570**
Juedischer Parlamentsklub, 15:**652**

Juedische Rundschau (periodical), 11:**570–571**
Juedischer Verlag, 11:**571**
Der juedische Selbsthass (Lessing), 12:665
Juedisches Lexicon (Herlitz, Kirschner), 6:400
Juedisches Nachrichtenblatt (Bulletin), 17:202
Juedische-theologisches Seminar, 21:108–109
Juedische Volkspartei (Austria), 20:**574**
Juedische Volkspartei (Germany), 11:**571**
Juedische Volkszeitung (newspaper), 18:684
Das juedische Weib (Lazarus), 12:562
Juedische Zeitung, 1:247
Juedisch-Literarische Gesellschaft, 11:**571–572**, 18:723
Juedisch Theologisches Seminar (Breslau), 11:**572**
Juelich (Germany), 11:**572**
Die juengsten Urteile ueber das Judenthum (Schreiner), 18:167
The Juggler (Schwartz), 18:186
The Jug of Tears (Pann), 15:612
Le Juif imaginaire (Finkielkraut), 7:36
Le Juif Polonais (opera, Erlanger), 6:480
Juifs de Chine (Dehergne and Leslie), 11:726
Les Juifs russes: extermination ou émancipation (Errera), 6:483
Juilliard Musical Foundation, 13:160
Juiverie. *See* Jewish quarters
Jujube, 11:**573**
Julia Neapolis. *See* Nablus (Israel)
Julian the Apostate, 9:205, 10:155, 11:**573–574**, 12:670
aftermath of reign, 4:325
Ambrose of Milan on, 2:37
rebuilding of Temple, attempt at, 2:82
Julianus. *See* Pappus and Julianus
Julianus, Flavius Claudius. *See* Julian the Apostate
Julius II (pope), 16:374
Julius III (pope), 11:**574**, 16:375
Amatus Lusitanus, 2:34
Marranos, 2:140
Julius Archelaus, 11:**574**
Julius Caesar (Roman emperor), 6:228, 9:196–197, 11:**574–575**
Julius Firmicus Maternus, 4:720
Julius Florus, 11:**575**
Julius Severus, 11:**575**
Jun-Broda, Ina, 11:**575**

Jung, Guido, 16:345

Jung, Julius, 11:575

Jung, Leo, 11:**575–576**

Jung, Moses, 11:575

Jungbunzlau (Czech Republic). *See* Mlada Boleslav (Czech Republic)

Der junge David (Beer), 3:**255**

Jungholz (France), 11:**576**

Jungman, Moshe. *See* Yungman, Moshe

Jungreis, Abraham ha-Levi, 11:576

Jungreis, Asher Anshel, 11:**576**

Jungreis, Moses Nathan Nata ha-Levi, 11:576

Jungreis, Samuel Ze'ev ha-Levi, 11:576

Jungreisz. *See* entries at Jungreis

Junior congregation. *See* Children's services

Juniper, 11:**576**

Junosza, Klemens, 11:**577**

Jurados. *See* Adelantados

Juramentum Judaeorum, 15:362. *See* Oath More Judaico

Jurbarkas (Lithuania), 11:**577**

Jurburg. *See* Jurbarkas

Jurnet of Norwich, 11:**577**, 15:312

Jurors. *See* Judges and judiciary

Juster, George, 11:**577**

Juster, Jean, 9:159, 11:**577–578**

Justice, 11:**578–579**
   commandments concerning, 5:83*t*–84*t*
   Ecclesiastes, 6:89–90

Justice and Judaism: The Work of Social Action (Lipman), 13:67

Justice and mercy of God. *See* God

Justin, 4:719, 11:**579**

Justinian I (Byzantine emperor), 9:207, 11:**579–580**

Justinian I (Cyzantine emperor), 4:326

Justinianus, Augustus. *See* Giustiniani, Agostino

Justin Martyr, 5:688–689, 11:**580**

Justinus, Marcus Junianius. *See* Justin

Justitz, Alfred, 11:**581**

Just Like Beauty (Lerner), 18:200

Justman, Joseph, 11:**581**

Justman, Moshe Bunem, 11:**581**

Justus of Tiberias, 11:**581–582**
   chronological concerns of, 3:660
   Josephus and, 9:154, 11:440, 581–582

Jutrzenka (newspaper), 15:**117–118**

Juvenal, 11:**582**

Juvenile delinquency, 5:296, 7:645

A Juvenile Enthusiast (Altauzen). *See* *Bezusy entuziast* (Altauzen)

JVC. *See* Jewish Volunteer Corps

JWB. *See* National Jewish Welfare Board

JWV. *See* Jewish War Veterans of the U.S.A.

K

K (letter), 11:*583*, 12:5

K. Zetnik, 6:251, 12:**402–403**

Kaaba, 1:286

Kaaden. *See* Kadan (Czech Republic)

"Ka'arat ha-Kesef " (Ezobi), 6:651

Ka'at, 15:550

Kaatz, Saul, 11:**583**

Kabachnik, Martin Izrailovich, 11:**583**

Kabak, Aaron Abraham, 11:**583–584**

Kabakoff, Jacob, 11:**584**

Ka'b al-Aḥbār, Omar ibn al-Khaṭṭāb, 15:419

Ka'b al-Aḥbār, 11:**584–585**

Ka'b al-Ashraf, 11:**585**

Kabars. *See* Khazars

Kabbala Denudata (Knorr von Rosenroth), 11:673

Kabbalah ("tradition"), 11:585, 14:338

Kabbalah (mysticism), 11:**585–692**
   abbreviations, 1:239
   Abraham, 1:287
   Abraham Abulafia, 11:607–608
   Abraham ben Dov of Mazhirech, 1:298
   Abraham ben Eliezer ha-Levi, 1:298–299
   Abraham ben Eliezer ha-Levi Berukhim, 1:299
   Abraham ben Isaac of Granada, 1:301
   Abraham ben Moses ben Maimon, 1:308
   Abulafia, Abraham ben Samuel, 1:337–339, 338
   Abulafia, Todros ben Joseph ha-Levi, 1:343–344
   Academy on High, 1:353
   Adler, Nathan ben Simeon ha-Kohen, 1:404–405
   Adret, Solomon ben Abraham, 1:423
   aggadah, 11:589, 591, 593, 602, 603, 605
   Ahijah the Shilonite, 1:542
   allegories, 1:666–667, 3:643, 645
   alphabet, Hebrew, 1:729–730
   angels and angelology
      Gabriel, 14:169
      Metatron, 14:133–134
      Michael, 14:169
      Raziel, 17:128–129
      sacred names, angels, 11:597
      Sandalfon, 18:10
      Uriel, 20:421–422
   Anna be-Khoh, 2:177
   anthropology, 11:651–657
   anti-philosophical elements, 11:612–613
   astrology, 2:619–620
   astronomy, 2:624
   ba'al shem, 3:9
   Bacharach, Naphtali ben Jacob Elhanan, 3:35
   Baruch, 3:182–183
   Baruch (ben Abraham) of Kosov, 3:190–191
   Bashiri, Yaḥya, 3:197
   basic ideas, 11:622–668
   Benevento, Immanuel ben Jekuthiel, 3:341
   Bet El, 11:621
   bibliography, 11:686–692
   Bikayam, Meir ben Ḥalifa, 3:695
   Blake, William, 3:737
   Bloom, Harold, 3:781
   Bonfrère, Jacques, 4:62–63
   Botarel, Moses ben Isaac, 4:101
   Brandwein, Yehuda Ẓevi, 4:128–129
   Burgos (Spain), 4:290
   Buzaglo, Shalom ben Moses, 4:322
   Cardozo, Abraham Miguel, 4:465, 466
   Caro, Joseph ben Ephraim, 4:491
   Chabad, 4:554
   chosen people, 4:671
   Christian Kabbalah, 11:671–673, 17:292
   circumcision, 4:733
   Commandments, 11:602, 608, 610, 611
   David, 5:454
   David b. Abraham ha-Lavan, 11:612
   David ben Solomon ibn Abi Zimra, 5:471
   demons, demonology, 5:575–577
      Asmodeus, 2:593
      female demons, 5:576
      Samael, 17:715
   devekut, 5:628–629, 11:661–662
   development of, 11:43
   dissemination of kabbalistic doctrines, 11:678
   Dor De'ah opposition, 11:622
   Duran, Profiat, 6:57
   Dynow, Ẓevi Elimelech, 6:79–80

Kabbalah (mysticism), *continued*
    ecstasy, 11:664–665
    Eleazar of Worms, 11:602
    Eliezer Fischel ben Isaac of
        Strzyzow, 6:330
    Elijah ben Solomon Zalman,
        6:341–345
    Eliyahu, Mordecai, 6:355
    Emden, Jacob, 6:392–393
    England, 6:687–688
    Enoch, Book of, 11:590
    esoteric nature, 11:587
    ethical literature
        kabbalistic-ethical, 6:530
        rabbinical-ethical, 6:528
    evil, 11:638–641
        kelippot, 11:639
        sitra aḥra, 11:638–639
    exile, 11:657–659, 17:153–154
    Ezra ben Solomon, 6:663
    fear of God, 6:726
    folk customs, influence on,
        11:670–671
    The Four Worlds, 21:224–225
    Gan Eden, 15:629
    gematria, 11:597–598
    Germany, 11:622
    Gerona, 11:605–606
    God and creation, 11:623–626
        Adam Kadmon, 1:378–379
        beḥinot, 11:634–635
        breaking of the vessels,
            11:644–646
        channels, 11:635
        creation, Lurianic, 11:641–
            648
        din, 11:631, 635, 638, 642–
            644, 646, 670
        earlier worlds, 11:635–636
        Ein-Sof, 11:623–626
        emanation, 6:374
        light, 11:624, 626, 629, 630,
            634, 635–636, 640, 641–
            646
        lower worlds, 11:635–637
        Lurianic Kabbalah, 11:617–
            619, 641–648
        nothingness, 11:626
        parẓufim, 11:646–648
        primal will, 11:625
        reshimu, 11:642–644
        sefirot, 5:220–221, 11:596,
            627–630, 630–635, 18:244
        thought, 11:625–626
        three lights, 11:626–627
        tikkun, 11:646–648
        ẓinẓum, 11:641–644, 17:283

Habillo, David, 8:178
halakhah, 8:250
Hart, Jacob, 8:370
Ḥasidic schools, 11:677
havurot, 18th century, 8:393
Ḥayyim Vital, 20:546–549
Hellenism and, 11:589
historical development, 11:589–
    622
        after expulsion from Spain,
            11:614–619
        apocalyptic esotericism,
            11:589–591
        apocalyptic movement, post-
            expulsion, 11:615–616
        creative period, 11:681–682
        critical period, 11:684–685
        early beginnings, 11:589–590
        fourteenth-fifteenth century
            Spain, 11:610–614
        Geonic period, 11:596–597
        nineteenth century, 11:37
        post-expulsion to Safed,
            11:613–619
        pre-Safedian, 11:759
        reproductive period, 11:682–
            684
        Safed during Ottoman
            period, 10:170
        seventeenth-nineteenth
            centuries, 11:620–622
        twentieth century, 11:677–681
Horowitz, Samuel ben Isaiah
    Aryeh Leib ha-Levi, 9:541–542
influence
        Ashkenazi, 11:615–616
        Bible, 3:661, 662–663
        Christianity, 11:671–673
        Judaism, 11:668–671
        messianism, 11:614
        Philo of Alexandria, 11:589
        Shabbateanism, 11:42–43
interpretations
        nationalistic, 11:678
        psychological, 11:679
Isaac ben Jacob ha-Kohen, 10:41–
    42
Isaac ben Samuel of Acre, 10:47–
    48
Isaac Luria Ashkenazi, 11:617–618
Isaac the Blind, 10:51–52, 11:603–
    604
Italy, 5:440–441, 6:709, 11:618
Jerusalem, 11:215, 621
Joel, David Heymann, 11:363
Jonah, Moses, 11:392
Joseph ben Emanuel Ergas, 6:478–
    479

Joseph ben Judah Engel, 6:409
Joseph Ibn Shraga, 11:430
Joseph Ibn Ṭabūl, 11:430
Joseph Moses ben Jekuthiel
    Zalman, 11:431
Judah ben Joseph Moscato, 14:515
kabbalists
    Aaron Berechiah ben Moses
        of Modena, 1:217, 14:407
    Aaron Selig ben Moses of
        Zolkiew, 1:220–221
    Abi-Ḥasira family, 1:256
    Abraham ben Alexander of
        Cologne, 1:294
    Abraham ben Israel of Brody,
        1:303
    Abraham ben Jehiel Michal
        ha-Kohen, 1:303
    Abraham ben Simeon of
        Worms, 1:310
    Abulafia, Abraham ben
        Samuel, 1:337–339
    Abulafia, Todros ben Joseph
        ha-Levi, 1:343–344
    Adadi, Abraham Ḥayyim ben
        masoud Ḥai, 1:370
    Adam Kadmon, 1:378–379
    Adani, Mizraḥi Shalom, 1:381
    Akiva Baer ben Joseph, 1:563
    Albaz, Moses ben Maimon,
        1:587, 6:290
    Albotini, Judah ben Moses,
        1:595–596
    Alcastiel, Joseph, 1:599
    Aldabi, Meir ben Isaac, 1:605,
        6:399
    Alemanno, Johanan ben
        Isaac, 1:611–613
    Alexander Susskind ben
        Moses of Grodno, 1:630–
        631
    Alfandari, Ḥayyim ben Isaac
        Raphael, 1:637–638
    Algazi, Israel Jacob ben Yom
        Tov, 1:644
    Algazi, Yom Tov ben Israel
        Jacob, 1:645
    Alkabeẓ, Solomon ben Moses
        ha-Levi, 1:662–663, 662t
    Almosnino, Joseph ben Isaac,
        1:685
    Amarillo, Aaron ben
        Solomon, 2:31–32
    Angel, Baruch, 2:147
    Ankawa, Abraham ben
        Mordecai, 2:176, 13:24
    Arḥa, Eliezer ben Isaac, 2:451
    Arzin, Joseph ben Jacob,
        2:539–540

Asher ben David, 2:563

Ashkenazi, Malkiel, 2:576

Ashlag, Yehudah, 2:579–580

Attar, Ḥayyim ben Moses, 2:645–646

Attia, Shem Tov, 2:647

Ayllon, Solomon ben Jacob, 2:760–761

Azikri, Eleazar ben Moses, 2:768–769

Azriel of Gerona, 2:771–772

Azulai (Castilian family), 2:773, 773

Azulai, Abraham ben Israel, 2:774

Azulai, Abraham ben Israel, 2:774, 2:773, 773

Azulai, Abraham ben Mordecai, 2:774

Azulai, Ḥayyim Joseph David, 2:77, 7:16, 774–775

Azulai, Masʿud, 2:775

Barazani, Samuel ben Nethaniel Ha-Levi, 3:138–139

Basilea, Solomon Aviad Sar-Shalom, 3:199

Bavli, Menahem ben Moses, 3:230

Benamozegh, Elijah ben Abraham, 3:317

Benjamin, Israel, 3:208, 357

Benjamin, Moses, 3:358

Benjamin ben Eliezer ha-Kohen Vitale of Reggio, 3:360–361, 18:354

Busal, Ḥayyim ben Jacob Obadiah de, 4:302–303

Byron, George Gordon, Lord, 4:324

Cuenque, Abraham Ben Levi, 5:328

Dato, Mordecai ben Judah, 5:440–441, 11:547

Daʾud, Sultana, 1:440

Delacrut, Mattathias ben Solomon, 5:535

Eliashov, Solomon ben Ḥayyim, 6:320

Elijah ben Raphael Solomon ha-Levi, 6:340

Elijah Phinehas ben Meir, 6:347

Epstein, Aryeh Leib ben Mordecai, 6:467

Ergas, Joseph ben Emanuel, 6:478–479

Eybeschuetz, Jonathan, 2:24, 4:194, 6:632–634, 8:439, 18:356, 684

Falk, Samuel Jacob Ḥayyim, 3:9, 6:687–688, 18:356

Fano, Menahem Azariah da, 6:709

Forti, Jacob Raphael Hezekiah ben Abraham Israel, 7:133

Frank, Jacob, 3:712, 7:182–192, 8:439, 15:386, 18:357–358, 538

Gabbai, Meir ben Ezekiel ibn, 7:319

Galante, Abraham ben Mordecai, 7:338

Galante, Moses ben Mordecai, 7:339

Galatinus, Pietro Columna, 7:340

Gallico Elisha ben Gabriel, 7:350

Gedaliah, ha-Levi, 7:407

Gerondi, Jacob ben Sheshet, 7:548–549

Gikatilla, Joseph, 11:610

Gikatilla, Joseph ben Abraham, 6:668, 7:593–594

Giorgio, Francesco, 7:616, 12:601

Gordon, Jekuthiel ben Leib, 7:769

Gruenhut, David ben Nathan, 8:108

Hagiz, Moses, 18:298, 299

Halfan, Elijah Menahem, 8:272

Ḥamiẓ, Joshua ben Judah, 8:305

Hannover, Nathan Nata, 8:326–327, 11:670

Ḥariri family, 8:355

Ḥayon, Nehemiah Ḥiyya ben Moses, 1:213, 4:181, 8:476–478, 15:444, 18:355–356, 538, 637, 769

Ḥayyat, Judah ben Jacob, 8:479

Ḥayyim Abraham Raphael ben Asher, 8:479

Ḥayyim ben Abraham ha-Kohen, 8:479–480

Ḥazkuni, Abraham, 8:497

Herrera, Abraham Kohen de, 9:40–41

Horowitz, Isaiah ben Abraham ha-Levi, 9:534–537

Horowitz, Jacob ben Abraham, 9:537–538

Horowitz, Shabbetai Sheftel ben Akiva, 9:543

Horowitz, Ẓevi Hirsch ben Joshua Moses Aaron ha-Levi, 9:545

Horowitz of Nikolsburg, Samuel Shmelke, 9:542

Ibn Gaon, Shem Tov ben Abraham, 9:676

Ibn Motot, Samuel ben Saadiah, 9:686–685

Ibn Shem Tov, Shem Tov, 9:691–690

Ibn Waqar, Joseph ben Abrahm, 9:696–695

Idel, Moshe, 9:707–706

Isaiah ben Abraham, 10:76–77

Israel ben Jonathan from Leczyca, 10:748

Israel Haraf of Satanov, 10:750–751

Jacob ben Jacob ha-Kohen, 11:33

Jacob David ben Israel Issar, 11:37

Jacob Koppel ben Moses of Mezhirech, 11:42–43

Jacob Nazir, 11:43

Jaffe, Israel ben Aaron, 11:65

Jaffe, Mordecai ben Abraham, 8:552, 11:67–68

Jamal Sulaymān, 11:75–76

Jehiel Michael ben Eliezer, 11:103–104

Jolles, Jacob Ẓevi ben Naphtali, 11:386

Joseph ben Shalom Ashkenazi, 11:425–426

Joseph della Raina, 11:428–429

Joseph Issachar Baer ben Elhanan, 11:430–431

Joseph Joske ben Judah Judel of Lublin, 11:430–431

Joshua Ibn Nun, 6:67, 11:456–457

Judah ben Yakar, 11:492

Judah Leib ben Baruch, 11:506

Knorr von Rosenroth, Christian, 11:673, 12:240–241

Koraḥ, Ḥayyim ben Joseph, 12:300

Koraḥ, Yiḥye ben Shalom, 12:300

Labi, Simeon, 12:408

Latif, Isaac B. Abraham ibn, 11:607, 12:506–507

Leon, Isaac de, 12:644–645, 15:375

Kabbalah (mysticism), *continued*

Lipschutz, Shabbetai ben Jacob Isaac, 13:74

Loanz, Elijah ben Moses, 13:152–153

Lonzano, Abraham ben Raphael de, 13:187

Lonzano, Menahem ben Judah de, 13:187–188

Luria, Isaac ben Solomon, 13:262–267

Luria, Jehiel ben Israel Ashkenazi, 13:267

Luzzatto, Moses Ḥayyim, 6:180, 13:281–286, 18:357, 530

Mahalalel ben Shabbetai Hallelyah, 13:358

Marcus, Aaron, 1:301, 13:512

Menahem Ẓiyyoni, 14:27

Meyuḥas, Abraham ben Samuel, 14:154

Molcho, Solomon, 11:584, 14:423–424, 18:315

Molitor, Franz Joseph, 14:426

Moses ben Menahem Graf, 14:554

Moses ben Shem Tov de Leon, 14:554–555

Moses ben Solomon ben Simeon of Burgos, 14:555–556

Mueller, Ernst, 14:597

Naḥmanides, 2:548, 14:739–747

Naḥman of Kosov, 14:753–754

Navon, Benjamin Mordecai ben Ephraim, 15:39

Nehemiah Ha-Kohen, 15:62, 18:348–349

Nethanel ben Meshullam Ha-Levi, 15:93

Ornstein, Mordecai Ze'ev, 15:480, 481

Ostropoler, Samson ben Pesaḥ, 15:513

Ottolengo, Samuel David ben Jehiel, 15:518, 519

Pinto, Josiah ben Joseph, 16:179

Poppers, Meir ben Judah Loeb ha-Kohen, 16:381

Reuben Hoeshke ben Hoeshke Katz, 17:247

Reuchlin, Johannes, 16:26, 17:247–249

Ricchi, Raphael Immanuel ben Abraham Ḥai, 17:283

Ricci, Raphael Immanuel ben Abraham Ḥai, 17:283

Ricius, Paulus, 17:292

Rovigo, Abraham ben Michael, 3:360–361, 17:500–501

Runkel, Solomon Zalman, 17:529

Saba, Abraham ben Jacob, 17:614–615

Sahula, Meir ben Solomon Abi, 17:668

Samuel ben Eliezer of Kalwaria, 17:770

Scholem, Gershom Gerhard, 3:62–63, 16:100–103, 18:158–159, 359

Sharabi, Shalom, 18:410–411

Shephatiah ben Amittai, 18:460–461

Spira, Nathan Nata ben Solomon, 19:119

Taitaẓak, Joseph, 2:10, 4:302, 15:537, 19:439–440

Tayyib, Isaac ben Benjamin, 19:562

Temerls, Jacob ben Eliezer, 19:599–600

Tishby, Isaiah, 11:682–683, 19:733

Uceda, Samuel ben Isaac, 20:223

Valle, Moses David ben Samuel, 20:465

Vidas, Elijah ben Moses de, 20:517–518

Vigenère, Blaise de, 20:525

Vital, Ḥayyim ben Joseph, 1:254, 2:10, 20:546–549

Vital, Samuel ben Ḥayyim, 20:549–550

Vital family, 20:546

Wanneh, Isaac ben Abraham, 20:617

Wormser, Seckel, 21:229

Yakhini, Abraham ben Elijah, 18:345, 21:273, 352

Yiẓḥaki, Abraham ben David, 21:377

Zacuto, Moses ben Mordecai, 1:287, 12:690, 18:347, 21:435–437

Ẓayyaḥ, Joseph ben Abraham ibn, 21:464–465

Ẓemaḥ, Jacob ben Ḥayyim, 21:505

kapparot, 11:782

Kara, Avigdor ben Isaac, 11:783

Katz, Naphtali ben Isaac, 12:15

Khalaẓ, Judah ben Abraham, 12:100

Lamed vav ẓaddikim, 12:445–446

Landauer, Meyer Heinrich Hirsch, 12:467–468

Lara, Ḥiyya Kohen de, 12:493

in legal disputation, 5:471

León, Luis de, 12:645

Leon, Messer David Ben Judah, 12:645–646

Levi, Isaac Ben Solomon, 12:688–689

literature, English, 6:434

Lithuania, 11:621–622

Lurianic, 13:264–266, 14:666, 17:283

maggid and maggidim, 13:340–341

Maimonides, 5:465

man, 11:651–657

measure of the body, 11:592–593

Merkabah mysticism, 11:590, 591, 593–595

Metatron mysteries, 11:33

Modena, 14:407–408

Modena, Leon, 14:409–410

Molcho, Solomon, 14:423–424

Mopsik, Charles, 14:470

Morocco, 11:620–621, 14:496–497

Moses, 14:537

Moses b. Jacob Cordovero, 5:220–221, 11:616

Moses Botarel, 11:613

Moses de Leon, 11:609–610

movements

Ḥasidei Ashkenaz, 11:599–602

Ḥasidism, 11:622

New Age, 11:680

Safed, 14:666–667

Shabbateanism, 11:619–620

Zhidachov Ḥasidism, 11:622

music, 14:660–661, 663, 666–667

mysteries of the Throne, 11:590

Naḥmanides concepts, 14:743–747

Naḥmanides' use of, 3:643

name of God, 6:260–261

non-Ḥasidic ultra-orthodox world, 11:677

non-Jewish Kabbalah, 11:678

notarikon, 15:314–315

Omer, 15:420, 421

opposition to, 11:619, 16:329–330

Oriental Jewish world, 11:677

original sin, 11:652

Ostropoler, Samson ben Pesaḥ, 15:513

Ottoman Empire, 15:538

paradise, 15:629

philosophy and theology
  anthropomorphism, 2:191, 10:771
  antinomianism, 2:200, 201
  dualism, 6:30
  eschatology, 6:500–502
  gnosticism, 11:590–591, 595–596, 608–609
  pantheism, 11:648–651
piety, 16:150
Poland, 11:619, 621–622
practical, 11:665–668
  alchemy, 1:600–601, 11:667
  amulets, 2:121, 122, 123
  chiromancy, 4:653
  dibbuk, 5:643–644
  golem, 7:736, 737
  levitating tables, 11:668
  magic, 1:310, 11:665–668
  occult phenomena, 11:668
prayer and meditation
  Anna be-Khoh, 2:177
  kavvanah, 11:662–664
  meditation, 11:612, 662–664, 13:761–762
  prayer, 11:662–664, 16:459
Provence (France), 11:602–605
providence, 16:651–652
psychology of, 11:651–657
Raza Rabba, Sefer Raza Rabba, 17:128
Recanati, Menahem ben Benjamin, 17:142
redemption, 11:657–659, 17:153–154
Reformation, 17:163
Reggio, Abraham ben Ezriel, 17:189
repentance, 17:223
righteousness, 17:309
Rovigo, Abraham ben Michael, 17:500–501
Sabbath, 17:620–621
sacred persons, 11:679–680
sacred space, 11:679–680
sacrifices, 17:649
Safed, 11:614–619
Sandzer, Ḥayyim ben Menahem, 18:18
Sarug, Israel, 18:63
scholarship and, 11:673–674
secrecy of, 11:587–588
Sefer Yeẓirah, 11:595–596
Shabbetai Ẓevi, 18:351–352
Sharabi, Shalom, 18:410–411
Sheḥitah, 18:435

Shekhinah, 11:597, 18:442–443
shemittot, 11:637–638
Solomon ben Ḥayyim Eliashov, 6:320
soul, 11:651–657
  Adam's soul, 11:656–657
  curtain of souls, 11:654–655
  ḥayyah, 11:654
  immortality of, 19:38–39
  nefesh, 11:652–653
  neshamah, 11:652–653
  ru'ah, 11:652–653
  transmigration of, 11:597, 655
  ẓelem, 11:654
Spain, 5:467, 11:605–614
sparks, uplifting of, 8:410
stories, 7:14–16
studies, 11:680–686
symbols and symbolism, 11:588, 589, 596, 602, 606–607, 609–610, 622–623, 628, 630
  light, 11:624–625, 626
  menorah, 14:52–53
  sefirot, 11:630–635
  ushpizin, 19:301
Tagin, 19:433
Talmud interpretations, 11:585
tefillin, 19:577–580
terminology, 11:588
Torah, 11:659–661
women in, 11:681, 21:176–177
Yom Kippur Katan, 21:382
ẓaddik, 6:79–80, 17:309
Ẓemaḥ ben Solomon Duran, 6:61
Zohar, 11:609–610, 639, 640
See also Kabbalistic literature
The Kabbalah; or the Religious Philosophy of the Hebrews (Franck), 7:175
The Kabbalah Centre, 3:417–418
Kabbalah certificates, for sheḥitah, 18:434
Kabbalah me-Inyan ha-Tefillah le-Rabbi Avraham (Abraham ben Isaac), 1:300
Kabbalat Shabbat, 11:**692**
Kabbalistic literature
  abbreviations, 1:239
  Abraham ben Alexander of Cologne, 1:294
  Abraham ben David of Posquières, 1:298
  Abraham ben Eliezer ha-Levi, 1:298–299
  Abraham ben Isaac, 1:300
  Abraham ben Isaac of Granada, 1:301–302

Abraham ben Israel of Brody, 1:303
Abraham ben Jehiel Michal ha-Kohen, 1:303
Abulafia, Todros ben Joseph ha-Levi, 1:343–344
Academy on High, 1:353
Adam Ba'al Shem, 1:378
Adani, Mizraḥi Shalom, 1:381
afterlife, 1:442
Agrat bat Mahalath, 1:470–471
Akiva Baer ben Joseph, 1:563
Albaz, Moses ben Maimon, 1:587
Albotini, Judah ben Moses, 1:595–596
Alcastiel, Joseph, 1:599
Aldabi, Meir ben Isaac, 1:605
Alemanno, Johann ben Isaac, 1:611
Alexander Susskind ben Moses of Grodno, 1:630
Algazi, Israel Jacob ben Yom Tov, 1:644
Algazi, Yom Tov ben Israel Jacob, 1:645
Alkabeẓ, Solomon ben Moses ha-Levi, 1:662–663
alphabets or kolmosin, 11:667
autobiographical elements in, 3:706
azilut, 6:374
Bahir, Sefer Ha, 3:62–63
chiromancy, 4:653
Chotsh, Ẓevi Hirsh ben Jerahmeel, 4:672
commandments, reasons for, 5:89–90
Cordovero, Moses ben Jacob, 5:220–221, 13:262
creation, Gerondi formulation, 7:549
Cuenque, Abraham ben Levi, 5:328
Delacrut, Mattathias ben Solomon, 5:535
Delmedigo, Joseph Solomon, 5:544
dibbuk and, 5:643
Ein-Sof, 6:260–261, 7:664–665
Elijah, 6:334
Elijah ben Solomon Zalman, 6:342–345, 344
emanation and creation, 6:374
Emden critique of, 6:393
eschatology, 6:500–502
"eye writing," 11:667–668
fiction, Hebrew, 7:14–15, 16
forgeries, 7:126

Kabbalistic literature, *continued*
    Forti, Jacob Rephael Hezekiah ben Abraham Israel, 7:133
    Gallei Razayya, 11:617
    Gehinnom, 6:501
    gematria, 7:424, 425–427
    genizah records, 7:477
    Gikatilla writings, 7:593–594
    gilgul, 7:602–604
    God, 7:664–665
        names of, 7:677–678
    Golem, 7:736–737
    hagiography, 8:225
    Ḥasidei Ashkenaz, 8:386–387, 11:599–602
    Ḥasidic, 8:414
    Ḥayon writings, 8:476–478
    Heikahalot books, 11:591
    Heikhalot Rabbati, 11:592, 593
    Ḥemdat Yamim, 8:804
    ibbur, 7:604
    Jewish Gnosis, 11:595–596
    Kanah and Peliyah, books of, 11:759
    Labi, Simeon, 12:408
    life after death, 6:500–501
    Luzzatto, Moses Ḥayyim, 13:283
    Mafte'ah ha-Kabbalah (Baruch), 3:182–183
    Masoret ha-Berit, 11:612
    Merkabah, 11:593–595
    Merkabah Shelemah, 11:593
    messiah and redemption, 6:501–502
    messianic literature, 7:15
    Midrash Avkir, 11:597
    The Mystery of the Names, Letters, and Vowels, and the Power of the Magical Operations, according to the Sages of Lunel, 11:610
    nitẓoẓot ha-neshamot, 7:603
    Pardes, 11:593
    punishment and gilgul, 7:603
    Raphael, 17:94
    Raza Rabba, 11:597, 602, 17:128
    Raziel, Book of, 17:129
    Recanati, Menahem ben Benjamin, 17:142
    resurrection, 6:502
    Sefer ha-Bahir, 11:597
    Sefer ha-Peli'ah, 11:613
    Sefer ha-Razim, 17:129–130
    Sefer Yeẓirah, 11:595–596, 21:328–331
    sefirot, 7:664–665
    soul, 1:442

    Tohorot, 20:15–16
    Toledot ha-Ari, 20:28
    visions, 20:545
    Zohar, 11:609–610, 639, 21:647–664
Ka'b ben Asad, 11:692
Kabinettfakrtr. *See* Court Jews
Kabīr, Abraham Ṣāliḥ al-, 11:692
Kabīr, Joseph, 11:692–693
Kabri (Israel), 11:693
Kabritha (ancient Israel), 11:693
Kabul (Afghanistan), 1:432
Kacew, Romain. *See* Gary, Romain
Kach, 11:693, 715, 18:264
Kacyzne, Alter, 11:693–694, 16:131
Kaczér, Illés, 11:694
Kaczerginsky, Symerke, 11:694
Kadan (Czech Republic), 11:694
Kádár, Ján, 11:695
Kadari, Shraga, 11:695
Kaddari, Menachem Zevi, 11:695
Kaddish, 11:695–698, vol. 3: color insert
Kaddish de-Rabbanan. *See* Kaddish
Kaddosh (Gitali), 1:244–245
Kadduri. *See* Kadoorie school
Kadelburg, Gustav, 4:13
Kadelburg, Lavoslav, 11:698, **698**
Kadesh (ancient Israel), 11:698–699
Kadesh, Operation. *See* Sinai Campaign
Kadesh-Barnea (ancient Israel). *See* Kadesh (ancient Israel)
Kadimah (Israel), 11:699
    Bialystok (Poland), Jewish resistance in, 3:570
    Bierer, Rubin, involvement of, 3:691
Kadimah (student association), 11:699–700, 18:151
Kadimah-Zoran, 11:699
Kadishman, Menashe, 10:696–697, 699, 11:**700**
Kadison, Luba, 4:278
Kadman, Gurit, 11:**700**
Kadmut ha-Tanḥuma (Epstein), 6:466
Kadoorie, Eliezer, 3:57
Kadoorie, Horace, 11:701
Kadoorie, Lawrence, Baron, 11:**701**
Kadoorie, Sasson, 11:**701**
Kadoorie Agricultural Aid Loan Fund, 11:701
Kadoorie family, 11:**701**
Kadoorie school, 11:**701**
Kadushin, Max, 11:**701–702**
Kael, Pauline, 1:406, 11:**702**

Kaempf, Saul Isaac, 11:**702–703**
Kaernten (Austria). *See* Carinthia (Austria)
Kaf, 11:**703**
Kafaḥ, Yiḥye ben Solomon, 11:**703**
Kafaḥ, Yosef, 11:**703–704**
Kaffa. *See* Feodosiya (Ukraine)
Kafka, Bruno Alexander, 11:**704**
Kafka, František, 11:**704**
Kafka, Franz, 6:612, 11:**704–705,** 12:480
    Brod, Max, 4:193
Kafra, Phinehas ben Jacob ha-Kohen. *See* Phinehas ben Jacob ha-Kohen
Kafr Bir'am. *See* Kefar Baram (Galilee)
Kafr Kamā (Israel), 11:**705–706**
Kafr Kanna. *See* Kefar Kanna (Israel)
Kafr Qāsim (Israel), 11:**706**
Kagan, Elie, 11:**706**
Kagan, Ḥafeẓ Ḥayyim. *See* Israel Meir ha-Kohen
Kagan, Helena, 11:**706**
Kagan, Israel Meir. *See* Israel Meir ha-Kohen
Kagan, Joseph, Baron, 11:**706**
Kagan, Koppel. *See* Kahana, Koppel
Kagan, Solomon Robert, 11:**706**
Kagan, Yaakov, Novogrudok, Jewish Resistance in, 15:321
Kaganovich, Lazar Moiseyevich, 11:**706–707,** 16:348
Kaganowski, Efraim, 11:**707**
Kage, Joseph, 11:300, **707**
Kahal. *See* Community
Kahan, Abraham Isaac, 17:479
Kahan, Baruch Mordecai, 11:**707–708**
Kahan, Louis, 11:**708**
Kahan, Salomon, 11:**708**
Kahan, Samuel. *See* Kursky, Franz
Kahana, 11:**708–710**
Kahana, Abraham, 9:160, 11:**710**
    biblical exegesis and study, 3:647
Kahana, Abraham Aryeh Leib ben Shalom Shakhna, 11:**710**
Kahana, Aharon, 11:**710**
Kahana, David, 11:**710–711**
Kahana, Ḥayyim Aryeh, 11:**711**
Kahana, Hermann. *See* Kahana, Aharon
Kahana, Hillel, 4:103
Kahana, Jacob ben Abraham, 11:**711**
Kahana, Jehiel Ẓevi ben Joseph Mordecai, 11:**711**
Kahana, Joseph Mordechai, 11:711
Kahana, Kalman, 11:**711**
Kahana, Koppel, 11:**711–712**
Kahana, Loeb Scheines. *See* Kahana, Abraham Aryeh Leib ben Shalom Shakhna

Kahana, Naḥman, 11:**712**

Kahana, Samuel. *See* ha-Kohen, Samuel

Kahana, Solomon David, 11:**712**

Kahana-Carmon, Amalia, 8:706, 11:**712–713**

Kahan Commission, 6:279, 11:**713–714**

Kahane, Arthur, 11:**714–715**

Kahane, Isaak, 11:**715**

Kahane, Meir, 11:**715**
　　Kach party, 11:693, 18:264
　　in New York City, 11:715, 15:215

Kahaneman, Joseph, 11:**715–716**

Kahanov, Moses Nehemiah, 11:**716**

Kahanovich, Israel Isaac, 11:**716–717**

Kahanovich, Pinkhes. *See* Der Nister

Kahanovitsch, Pinkhes. *See* Der Nister

Kahanstam, A. *See* Kahnshtam, Aharon

Kāhina, 11:717, **717**

Kahle, Paul Ernst, 3:588, 8:626, 11:**717**

Kahler, Erich, 11:**717–718**

Kahler, Eugen von, 15:648

Kahn, Albert (Architect), 11:**718–719**

Kahn, Albert (Philanthropist), 11:**718**

Kahn, Alexander, 11:**719**

Kahn, Alfred Joseph, 11:**719**

Kahn, Bernard, 11:**719**

Kahn, Dorothy C., 11:**719–720**

Kahn, Ely Jacques, 11:**720**

Kahn, Erich Itor, 11:**720**

Kahn, Florence Prag, 11:**720**

Kahn, Franz, 11:**721**

Kahn, Gustave, 11:**721**

Kahn, Jean, 11:**721**

Kahn, Julius, 11:**721–722**

Kahn, Léon, 11:**722**

Kahn, Louis, 11:**722**

Kahn, Louis I., 11:**722**

Kahn, Madeline, 11:**722–723**

Kahn, Max, 15:303

Kahn, Otto Hermann, 11:**723**, 15:220

Kahn, Richard Ferdinand, Lord, 11:**723**

Kahn, Robert I., 11:**723–724**

Kahn, Roger, 11:**724**

Kahn, Sam, 16:349

Kahn, Zadoc, 11:**724**, 18:721
　　French Bible translation by, 3:629

Kahneman, Daniel, 11:**724–725**

Kahnshtam, Aharon, 11:**725**

Kahnweiler, Daniel-Henry, 11:**725–726**

Kâhya, 15:534

Kaidan. *See* Kedainiai (Lithuania)

Kaidanover, Aaron Samuel ben Israel. *See* Koidonover, Aaron Samuel ben Israel

Kaidanover, Ẓevi Hirsch. *See* Koidonover, Ẓevi Hirsch

Kaidanovo (Belarus). *See* Koidanovo (Belarus)

Kaifeng (China), 11:**726**, 15:474

Kaireng (China). *See* P'ien-liang (China)

Kairouan (Tunisia), 1:464–465, 6:315, 11:**726–727**, 14:730–731

Kaiser, Alois, 11:**728**

Kaiser Friedrich der Zweite (Kantorowicz), 11:772

Kaiserlautern (Germany), 11:**728**

Der Kaizer in Geto (Bryks), 4:230

Kākhya, 11:**728**, **728**

Kakungulu, Semei, 11:521

Kaladei (Czech Republic). *See* Kolodeje nad Luzici (Czech Republic)

Kalahora family. *See* Calahora family

Kalai, Joseph B. Jacob, 11:**728**

Kalai, Mordecai ben Solomon, 4:102, 11:**728–729**

Kalai, Samuel ben Joseph, 11:**729**

Kalai, Samuel ben Moses, 11:**729**

Kala-i Sultaniye (Turkey). *See* Canakkale (Turkey)

Kalakaua, David (King of Hawaii), 8:473

Kalām, 11:**729–731**
　　allegorical interpretation of scripture and, 3:644
　　God, attributes of, 7:666
　　Judah Halevi, 11:498

Kalām cosmology, 5:231

Kalarash (Moldova), 11:**731**

Kalb, Bernard, 11:**731–732**

Kalb, Marvin, 11:**732**

Kalckar, N. S., 11:412

Kaldor, Nicholas, Baron, 11:**732**

Kalecki, Michal, 11:**732**

Kalef, Yehoshua, 11:**733**

Kaléko, Golda Malka. *See* Kaléko, Mascha

Kaléko, Mascha, 11:**733**

Kales (Turkey). *See* Koila (Turkey)

Kalfa, Isaac ben Joseph, 11:**733**

Kali, Mordecai. *See* Kalai, Mordecai ben Solomon

Kal'i, Samuel ben Moses. *See* Kalai, Samuel ben Moses

Kalib, Sholom, 11:**733**

Kalich, Bertha, 11:**734**

Kalichstein, Joseph, 11:**734**

Kalik, Mikhail, 11:**734**

Kalikow, Peter S., 11:**734–735**, 15:225

Kalila and Dimna, 6:667, 11:**735**, **735**

Kalinin, Mikhail, 3:718

Kalinindorf (Ukraine), 4:24, 11:**735**

Kaliningrad (Russia). *See* Koenigsberg (Russia)

Kalininskoye. *See* Kalinindorf (Ukraine)

Kalinkovichi (Belarus), 11:**735–736**

Kalir, Avraham, 11:**736**

Kalisch. *See* Kalisz (Poland)

Kalisch, David, 11:**736**

Kalisch, Markus Moritz, 11:**736**

Kalischer, Judah Leib ben Moses, 11:**736–737**

Kalischer, Ẓevi Hirsch, 11:**737–738**, 21:541

Kalish. *See* Kalisz (Poland)

Kalish, Isaac, of Warka, 20:650–651

Kalish, Leib. *See* Judah Aryeh Leib ben David

Kalish, Sophie. *See* Tucker, Sophie

Kalisli. *See* Warka dynasty

Kalisz (Poland), 11:**738–740**

Kalisz, Statute of, 4:45

Kalladay (Czech Republic). *See* Kolodeje nad Luzici (Czech Republic)

Kallah, 11:**741**
　　months of, 11:**741–742**

Kallah Rabbati, 11:**741**

Kallen, Horace Meyer, 11:**742–743**, 18:660

Kallenbach, Hermann, 11:**743**

Kallier, Meier. *See* Kallir, Meier

Kallir, Eleazar, 11:369, **743–745**

Kallir, Eleazar ben Eleazar, 11:**745**

Kallir, Meier, 11:**745**

Kallirian rhyme, 11:**743–744**, 16:603–605

Kallo, Yizḥak Isaac, 11:**745**

Kalm, Peter, 15:197

Kálmán, Emmerich, 11:**745**

Kalman, Maira, 11:**745–746**

Kalman, Tibor, 11:**746**

Kalman Kalikes Imperye (Elberg). *See* The Empire of Kalman the Cripple (Elberg)

Kalman of Worms, 11:**746**

Kalmanovitch, Zelig, 11:**746–747**

Kalmanowitz, Abraham, 11:**747**

Kalmin, Richard
　　aggadah, 1:461
　　amoraim, 2:90

Kalms, Harold Stanley. *See* Kalms, Sir Harold Stanley

Kalms, Sir Harold Stanley, 11:**747**

Kalnitsky, George, 11:**747**

Kalonymus, Eleazar ben Judah, 11:**748**

Kalonymus ben David, 4:52

Kalonymus ben Kalonymus, 6:668, 11:**749–750,** 15:656–657

Kalonymus ben Meshullam, 2:87

Kalonymus ben Mordecai Jaffe, 11:64

Kalonymus family, 1:219, 11:600–601, **747–749,** 13:247

Kalov dynasty, 8:421

Kaltenbrunner, Ernst, 11:**750**

Kalush (Ukraine), 11:**750–751**

Kaluszyn (Poland), 11:**751**

Kal va-ḥomer, 9:25–26

Kalvarier Beth Hamidrash, 2:556

Kalvarija (Lithuania), 11:**751**

Kambujiya. *See* Cambyses

Kam-bu-zi. *See* Cambyses

Kam-bu-zi-ia. *See* Cambyses

Kamelhar, Jekuthiel Aryeh ben Gershon, 11:**751–752**

Kamenetsky, Nathan, 11:**752**

Kamenetsky, Yaakov, 11:**752**

Kamenets-Podolski (Ukraine), 11:**752–753**

Kamenetzky, Abraham Shalom, 11:**753**

Kamenev, Lev, 11:**753–754**

Kamenka, Ẓevi Hirsch of, 11:**754**

Kamenka-Bugskaya (Ukraine), 11:**754**

Kamenszain, Tobias, 11:**754**

Kamhi, Jak V., 11:**755**

Kamhi, Leon, 11:**755**

Kami'a. *See* Amulets

Kamienna. *See* Skarzysko-Kamienna (Poland)

Kaminer, Isaac, 11:**755**

Kaminetsky, Jean-Paul, 11:**755–756**

Kaminetsky, Joseph, 11:**755**

Kaminka, Armand, 11:**756–757**

Kaminker, Simone. *See* Signoret, Simone

Kaminska, Esther Rachel, 11:757

Kaminska, Ida, 11:757

Kaminska family, 11:**757**

Kaminski, Abraham Isaac, 11:757

Kaminski, Joseph, 11:757

Kaminski family, 11:**757**

Kaminsky, David Daniel. *See* Kaye, Danny

Kaminsky, Melvin. *See* Brooks, Mel

Kamionka Strumilowa (Ukraine). *See* Kamenka-Bugskaya (Ukraine)

Kamish, 6:86

Kammerknechtschaft, 18:317

Kammi i travy (Aliger), 1:659

Kammon. *See* Cumin

Kammona. *See* Jokneam (Israel)

Kamniel, Abu Al-Hasan Meir Ibn, 11:**757**

Kampelman, Max M., 11:**757–758**

Kampf (Lasker), 4:603

Der Kampf um den Lebenssinn unter den Vorlaeufern der modernen Ethik (Baumgardt), 3:221

Kamson, Ya'akov David, 11:**758**

Kamẓa and Bar Kamẓa, 11:**758**

Kanada: A Zamelbuch (Rosenberg), 4:402

Kanah (ancient Israel), 11:**759**

Kanah and Peliyah, books of, 11:**759**

Kanatha. *See* Kenath (ancient city)

Kanbuzi. *See* Cambyses

Kandel, Eric Richard, 11:**759–760,** 13:10

Kandel, Isaac Leon, 11:**760**

Kandlein family, 11:760

Kandlein of Regensburg, 11:**760**

Kane, Bob, 11:**760–761**

Kane, Carol, 11:**761**

Kane, Gil, 11:**761**

Kane, Irving, 11:**761**

Kanee, Sol, 11:**761–762**

Kanee family, 11:761–762

Kaneh. *See* Calamus, sweet

Kanengeiser, Henrietta. *See* Carnegie, Hattie

Kaneti, Selim, 11:**762**

Kanev (Ukraine), 11:**762**

Kanev, Isaac, 11:**762**

Kanfer, Moses, *Nowy Dziennik,* 15:326

Kanievsky, Jacob Israel, 11:**762–763**

Kanin, Fay Mitchell, 11:**763**

Kanin, Garson, 3:783, 11:**763**

Kanitz (Czech Republic). *See* Dolni Kounice (Czech Republic)

Kaniuk, Yoram, 8:706, 11:**763–764**

Kann, Beer Loeb Isaac, 11:765

Kann, Jacobus Henricus, 11:**765**

Kann, Moses, 11:765

Kann, Peter R., 11:**765–766**

Kanna'im. *See* Zealots

Kannegiser, Leonid Akimovich, 11:**766**

Kanner, Abraham Otto, 15:475, 476

Kanner, Leo, 11:**766**

Kanof, Abram, 2:59

Kanovich, Grigory, 11:**766**

Kanovitz, Howard, 11:**767**

Kansas (U.S.), 11:*767,* 767, 767t

Kansas City (MO), 11:**767–769**

Kant, Immanuel, 11:**769–770,** 16:65–66

  autonomy and duty, 6:72, 12:562

  Leibowitz, Yeshayahu, 12:623

  modern biblical criticism, development of, 3:649

Kanter, Rosabeth Moss, 18:736

Kantian ethics, 3:**221**

Kantor, Jacob, 11:322–323

Kantor, Jacob Robert, 11:**770**

Kantor, Joel, 16:130, 131

Kantor, Judah Leib, 8:476, 11:**770–771**

Kantor, Michael, 11:**771**

Kantor, "Mickey ". *See* Kantor, Michael

Kantorberg, Friedrich. *See* Torberg, Friedrich

Kantorovich, Leonid, 11:**771**

Kantorowich, Roy, 11:**771–772**

Kantorowicz, Ernst Hartwig, 11:**772**

Kantorowicz, Hermann, 11:**772,** 12:551, 18:731

Kantorowiez, Yasha, Novogrudok, Jewish Resistance in, 15:321

Kantrowitz, Adrian, 11:**772**

Kantrowitz, Arthur, 11:**772**

Kant und der Marxismus (Adler), 1:402

Kaparot. *See* Kapparot custom

Kaparot ceremony, vol. 6: color insert

Kaplan, Abraham, 11:**773**

Kaplan, Abraham Elijah, 15:495

Kaplan, Alexander Sender ben Zerah ha-Kohen, 11:**773**

Kaplan, Anatoli Lvovich, 11:**773**

Kaplan, Aryeh, 11:**773–774**

  English translations of Torah, 3:623, 625

Kaplan, Bob. *See* Kaplan, Robert P.

Kaplan, Chaim Aron, 11:**774–775**

Kaplan, Eliezer, 11:**775**

Kaplan, Enrique, 16:350

Kaplan, Isaac, 11:**775**

Kaplan, Jacob, 11:**775–776**

Kaplan, Johanna, 11:**776**

Kaplan, Joseph, 11:**776**

Kaplan, Louis Lionel, 11:**776**

Kaplan, Marion, 18:736

Kaplan, Mordecai Menahem, 5:172–173, 7:666, 11:**776–779,** 15:208, 209, 218, 20:411–412

  Eisenstein, Ira, 6:273

  Eisenstein, Judith Kaplan, 6:274

  free will, 7:234

  good and evil, 7:754

  Jewish Theological Seminary, 6:193, 11:328, 329

  Reconstuctionist Judaism, 17:146–149

  redemption, 17:155

Kaplan, Pavel, Am Olam, 2:88

Kaplan, Pesaḥ, 11:**779**

Kaplan, Robert P., 11:**779–780**

Kaplan, Sender Meyer, 11:**780**

Kaplansky, Kalmen, 11:**780**

Kaplansky, Shelomo, 11:**780–781**
  Ben-Gurion, David, 3:345

Kaplinski, Hirsch, 15:667

Kapos, 11:**781**

Kaposi, Moritz, 11:**781**

Kaposvar (Hungary), 11:**781**

Kaposvár (Hungary). *See* Kaposvar (Hungary)

Kapp. *See* Hoenigsberg family

Kapparot custom, 11:**781–782**

Kappel, Alexander. *See* Mukdoni, A.

Kapper, Siegfried, 11:**782**

Kappler, Herbert, 10:808

Kapporet, 2:466, 467. *See* Parokhet and Kapporet

Kapuzato, Moses ha-Yevani, 11:**782–783**

Kara. *See* Menahem ben Ḥelbo

Kara, Avigdor ben Isaac, 11:**783**

Kara, Joseph, 11:**783–784**
  biblical exegesis and study, 3:642

Kara, Menahem ben Jacob, 11:783, **784–785**

Karácsony, Benö, 11:**785**

Karaczewski, Ḥanina, 11:**785**

Karaferia. *See* Veroia

Karaghiozi ou la comédie grecque dans l'ame de théatre d'ombres (Caïmis), 4:339

Kara'im. *See* Karaites

The Karaite Mourners of Zion and the Qumran Scrolls (Erder), 11:796

Karaites, 8:188–189, 9:211, 11:**785–802,** *786*
  Aaron ben Elijah, 1: 212, 213
  Aaron ben Judah Kusdini, 1: 216
  Abner of Burgos, 1:264
  Abraham ben Josiah Troki, 1:303
  Abraham ben Josiah Yerushalmi, 1:303–304
  Abraham ben Judah ben Abraham, 1:304
  Abu ʿImrān al-Tiflīsī, 1:336
  Aden, 1:387
  Afendopolo, Caleb ben Elijah, 1:431
  Aga family, 1:443
  Ali ibn Suleiman, 1:660
  aliyah and, 10:329, 330–331
  alphabet, Hebrew, 1:705*t*, 706
  Al-Tarā;s, Sīdī ibn, 2:17
  angels, 2:159
  anti-Rabbanite groups, 11:788
  apologetics, 2:264
  areas of settlement, 11:*786*

articles of faith, 11:797

Babovich, Simḥah ben Solomon ben Nahamu, 3:23

Bakhchisarai, 3:72

Beim Solomon ben Abraham, 3:268

Belarus, Braslav, 4:130

beliefs, 3:200, 11:785, 14:737

Benjamin ben Elijah Duwan, 3:361

Bible, 11:785–786

Bible translations, 3:604–605

biblical commentary, 5:428, 11:35–36

biblical exegesis and study stimulated by rise of, 3:641

biography of Anan, 3:706

"burden of inheritance," 11:786

in Byzantine empire, 4:327

Cairo (Egypt), 4:342, 343, 344

calendar, 11:798

characteristic of the sect, 11:785–786

Chufut-Kale, 4:709

commandments, reasons for, 5:86, 11:798

communities in Israel, 10:298, 13:707

consolidation, 11:789–790

Constantinople, 5:182–183

contemporary life, 11:794–795

creed, 11:797–800

Crimea, 5:299–300

Damascus Document, 11:787

Daniel ben Moses al-Qumisì, 5:428

Dead Sea Scrolls, 11:786–787, 796

dietary laws, 11:799

distinguished from Rabbanites, 11:785–802

doctrine, 11:785, 797–800

Elijah ben Aaron ben Moses, 6:338

Elijah ben Abraham, 6:338

Elijah ben Baruch, 6:338

exilarchate and, 6:603

Firkovich, Abraham, 7:44

Firuz family, 7:49–50

genizah, 7:462

Halicz, 8:273

Ḥasan, ben Mashi'ah, 8:379

Hebrew of, medieval, 8:666

historical development, 11:785–786, 787–795

history, 8:356

holidays, 11:798

Ibn al-Hītī, David ben Se'adel, 9:659

Istanbul (Ottoman period), 10:775, 782

Jerusalem, 10:161, 11:155, 156, 163

Jewish identity and, 11:294

Josippon, 11:462

Jubar, 11:473

Judah Halevi on, 11:500

Judah ha-Parsi as, 11:505

Judaizers, Russian, 11:522

Judeo-Arabic literature of, 11:530, 531–532

Kazaz, Elijah ben Elijah, 12:44

Kirkisani, Jacob Al-, 12:186

Kukizow dynasty, 12:382–383

Labanos family, 12:407–408

languages used by, 11:302

leadership, 5:467, 11:793

Lelewel, Joachim, 12:634

Leonovich family, 12:648

literature, 8:188–189, 11:789–790, 16:151

liturgy, 11:799

mamzer, 13:443–444

map, 11:*786*

marriage laws, 11:242, 799, 14:448

Middle Ages, disputations and polemics, 5:691, 692–693

Mizraḥi, Elijah, 14:394

Mordecai ben Nisan, 14:482

music, 11:800–802

ninth-twelfth century, 11:787–790

opinions towards, Kimḥi, Solomon ben Nissim Joseph David, 12:159

Oraḥ Ẓaddikim, 11:792

Oral Law, 15:456

in Panevezys, 15:611

Passover, 13:689

philosophy, 16:79–80

physicians, 5:470, 6:662–663

poets, 5:434, 6:711

population statistics, 11:794

prayer services, 11:799

previous name, 11:787

printing industry, 11:800

rikkuv theory, 11:799

rise of, 15:786

ritual purity, 11:799

Romania, 17:375

Russian rule, 11:793–794

Saporta, Ḥanokh, 18:39

Saul ben Anan, 18:83

scholars, 5:465–466, 467, 11:86–87, 242
  Isaac ben Solomon, 10:49–50

Karaites, *continued*

  Isaiah ben Uzziah ha-Kohen, 10:77–78

  Israel ha-Dayyan ha Ma'aravi, 10:750

  Levi ben Japheth, 12:702

  Luzki, Abraham ben Joseph Solomon, 13:278

  Luzki, Joseph Solomon ben Moses, 13:278

  Luzki, Simḥah Isaac ben Moses, 13:278–279

  Menahem ben Michael ben Joseph, 14:22–23

  Poki, Judah ben Eliezer Chelebi, 16:284–285

 scholarship, 11:795–797

  Kalam, influence of, 11:730

 sevel ha-yerushah (tradition), 11:786

 seventeenth-eighteenth century, 11:792

 Shapshal Seraya ben Mordechai, 18:409

 Solomon ben Aaron, 18:769

 Solomon ben Judah, 18:771

 study of, 6:676–677

 tefillin, 11:799

 theologians, 6:711

 Tobias ben Moses ha-Avel, 20:11–12

 translators of literature of, 11:36

 Troki (Lithuania), 20:154–155

 Turkey, 3:198, 6:148

 twelfth-sixteenth centuries, 11:790–792

 ẓiẓit, 11:799

The Karaite tradition of Hebrew Grammatical Thought in Its Classical Form: A Critical Edition and English Translation of al-Kitāb al-kāfi fī al-luga al-'Ibrāniyya by Abu al-Faraj Hārūn ibn al-Faraj. See Al-Kitāb al-Kāfi

Karan, Donna, 11:**802–803**

Karasik et al. v. the State of Israel, 16:218

Karasu, Albert, 11:**803**

Karasubazar (Ukraine), 11:**803**, 12:634

Karate, 19:144

Karavan, Dani, 10:697, 11:**803–804**

Karben, Victor von. *See* Carben, Victor von

Kar-Ben/Lerner, 11:**804**

Kar-Ben Publishing. *See* Kar-Ben/Lerner

Kardiner, Abram, 2:187, 11:**804**

Kardos, Albert, 11:**804–805**

Kardos, László, 11:**805**

Kar-duniash. *See* Babylonia

Kareh, Soleiman. *See* Kareh, Solomon

Kareh, Solomon, 11:**805**

Karel, Rudolph, 11:**805**

Karelitz, Avraham Yeshayahu, 11:762, **805–806**

Karen tribe of Burma, supposed Jewish origins of, 4:296–297

Karet, 7:79, 11:**806–807**

Karff, Mona May, 11:**807**

Karfunkel, Aaron ben Judah Leib ha-Kohen, 11:**807**

Kargau, Menaḥem Mendel ben Naphtali Hirsch, 11:**808**

Karigal, Raphael Ḥayyim Isaac. *See* Carigal, Raphael Ḥayyim Isaac

Karinthy, Ferenc, 11:**808**

Kariv, Avraham Yiẓḥak, 8:729, 11:**808**

Kariyah, al-, 11:**808**

Kariyah, Qar'iyya, al-. *See* Kariyah, al-

Karkamiš. *See* Carchemish (Syria)

Karka'ot. *See* Property

Karkar (Syria), 11:**808–809**

Karkar, battle of, 1:523, *523*, 11:808

Karle, Jerome, 8:460, 11:**809**

Karliner, Baruch, 11:**810**

Karliner, "Dovidel." *See* Friedmann, David ben Samuel

Karlin family, 11:**809–810**

Karlin Ḥasidim, 8:421, 429

Karl Marx School (Berlin-Neukoelln), 11:817

Karl-Marx-Stadt (Germany). *See* Chemnitz (Germany)

Karlovy Vary (Czech Republic). *See* Carlsbad (Czech Republic)

Karlsbad (Czech Republic). *See* Carlsbad (Czech Republic)

Karlsburg (Transylvania). *See* Alba Iulia (Transylvania)

Karlsruhe (Germany), 3:44, 11:**810–811**

Karl und Rosa (Doeblin), 5:729–730

Kármán, Mór, 11:**811**

Kármán, Theodore von, 11:**811–812**

Karmazin, Mel, 11:**812**

Karmel. *See Ha-Karmel* (periodical)

Karmel, Ilona, 11:**812–813**

Karmi, Dov, 11:**813**

Karmi'el (Israel), 11:**813**

Karmi family, 11:**813**

Karminski, Hannah, 11:**813–814**

 Juedischer Frauenbund, 11:570

Karminski, Seymour Edward, 11:**814**

Karmiyyah (Israel), 11:**814**

Karmon, Israel, 11:**814**

Karnaim (biblical city), 2:**581**, 11:**814**

Karnei Shomron (Samaria), 11:**814**

Karni, Yehuda, 11:217, **814–815**

Karnik, Moses ben Akiva. *See* Kronik, Moses ben Akiva

Karniol, Alter Yehiel, 11:**815**

Karp, Abraham J., 11:**815**

Karp, Max and Sophie, 11:**815–816**

Karp, Sophie. *See* Karp, Max and Sophie

Karpel, Herman, 11:**816**

Karpeles, Gershon. *See* Karpeles, Gustav

Karpeles, Gustav, 11:**816**

Karpeles, Jiří. *See* Kars, Jiří

Karpf, Fay, 18:735

Karpf, Maurice Joseph, 11:**816**

Karpinovitsh, Avrom, 11:**816**

Karplus, Heinrich, 11:**816–817**

Karregal, Ḥayyim Moses ben Abraham. *See* Caregal, Ḥayyim Moses ben Abraham

Kars, George, 15:648

Kars, Jiří, 11:**817**

Karsen, Fritz, 11:**817**

Karski, Jan, 11:**817–818**

Kartell-Convent der Verbindungen Deutscher Studenten Juedischen Glaubens (KC), 11:**818**

Kartell Jeudischer Verbindungen (KJV), 11:**818–819**

Kartir (high priest), 3:29

Kartusskaya Bereza (Belarus). *See* Bereza (Ukraine)

Karu, Baruch, 11:**819**

Kasabi, Joseph ben Nissim, 11:**819**

Kaschau (Slovakia). *See* Kosice (Slovakia)

Kasdan, Lawrence Edward, 11:**819**

Kasejovice (Czech Republic), 11:**819–820**

Kashan (Iran), 3:15, 11:**820**

Kashani, Eliezer, 6:22, 11:**820**

Kashdan, Isaac, 11:**820–821**

Kasher, 11:**821**

 cooking, 5:200–201

 dietary laws, 5:651, 13:601

 Mishnah, 14:327

 mishpat Ivri, 14:355–356

 porging, 18:437

 preparation of meat (14th c.), vol. 8: color insert

 winery (France), vol. 20: color insert

Kasher, Israel. M., 3:682

Kasher, Menahem, 11:**821**, 15:498

Kasher, Shimon, 11:821

Kashisha. *See* Abbaye Kashisha

Kashmir region, 11:**821–822**

Kashrut
anatomy, 2:133
chicken controversy, 2:579
Coca-Cola formula hekhsher, 7:411
enforcement, 6:23
hekhsher, 8:780
milk, 14:249
reform Judaism, 17:173
ritual slaughter, 10:620

Kasimerz. *See* Cracow

Kaskel, Karl, 11:822

Kaskele family. *See* Kaskel family

Kaskel family, 11:**822**

Kasovsky, Chayim Yehoshua, 11:**822–823**

Kaspare Cohn Hospital, 13:196

Kasparov, Gary, 4:104, 605, 11:**823**

Kaspi, André, 11:**823**

Kaspi, Joseph ben Abba Mari ibn, 11:**823–825**, 16:87

Kaspi, Nethanel ben Nehemiah, 11:**825**

Kasr ibn Hubayrah. *See* Qaṣr ibn Hubayrah

Kasrilevke series (Shalom Aleichem), 18:382–383

Kasrils, Ronnie, 11:**825–826**, 16:349

Kass, Deborah, 2:516

Kassa (Slovakia). *See* Kosice (Slovakia)

Kassel (Germany), 11:**826–827**

Kassel, David, 11:**827**

Kasselowitz (Czech Republic). *See* Kasejovice (Czech Republic)

Kassil, Lev Abramovich, 4:635, 11:**827**

Kassites, 2:106

Kassovitz (Czech Republic). *See* Kasejovice (Czech Republic)

Kastein, Josef, 11:**827**

Kastoria (Greece), 11:**827–828**

Kaszab, Judy. *See* Cassab, Judy

Kasztner (Lerner), 8:722–723

Kasztner, Israel, 10:224. *See* Kasztner, Rezsö Rudolf

Kasztner, Rezsö Rudolf, 11:**828–829**

Kataf. *See* Balsam

Katav, Shalom, 15:473

Katchalski, Aharon. *See* Katzir, Aharon

Katchalski, Ephraim. *See* Katzir, Ephraim

Katchen, Julius, 12:**5**

Kathleen Mavourneen, 3:124

Katholische Dogmatik (Schmaus), 4:682

Katkov, Mikhail Nikiforovich, 12:**5–6**

Katowice (Germany), 12:**6–7**

Katschen and the Book of Joseph. See Sefer Yosef

Katsh, Abraham Isaac, 12:**6**

Kattan, Naïm, 4:425, 12:**7**

Kattina, Jacob, 12:**7**

Kattowitz Conference, 12:**7–8**

Kattowiz. *See* Katowice

Katuv Shum (Abraham ben David of Posquières), 1:297

Katz, Abraham Isaac. *See* Katsh, Abraham Isaac

Katz, Albert, 12:**8**

Katz, Aleph, 12:**8**

Katz, Alex, 12:**8–9**

Katz, Avigdor, 18:604

Katz, Benzion (1875-1958), 12:**9**

Katz, Benzion (1907-1968), 12:**9**

Katz, Bernard, 13:10. *See* Katz, Sir Bernard

Katz, Daniel, 12:**10**

Katz, David, 12:**10**

Katz, David S., 12:**10**

Katz, Dovid, 12:**10–11**

Katz, Elihu, 12:**11–12**, 18:735

Katz, Emanuel. *See* Mané-Katz

Katz, Hanns Ludwig, 12:**11**

Katz, Illés. *See* Kaczér, Illés

Katz, Israel (1917-2003), 12:**12**

Katz, Israel (1927-), 12:**12**

Katz, Israel (1930-), 12:**12**

Katz, Jacob, 9:161, 12:**12–13**, 18:735

Katz, Jake, 15:397

Katz, Joel. *See* Grey, Joel

Katz, Joseph. *See* Katz, Israel (1930-)

Katz, Joseph ben Elijah, 12:**13**

Katz, Label A., 12:**13**

Katz, Mack, 4:212

Katz, Menahem, 12:**13**

Katz, Menke, 12:**13–14**

Katz, Mickey, 12:**14**

Katz, Mindru, 12:**14**

Katz, Moe, 4:212

Katz, Morris Abraham. *See* Katz, Aleph

Katz, Moses, 12:**14–15**

Katz, Moshe, 15:265

Katz, Naphtali ben Isaac, 12:**15**

Katz, Nina. *See* Cassian, Nina

Katz, Otto. *See* Simone, André

Katz, Reuben Hoeshke ben. *See* Reuben Hoeshke ben Katz

Katz, Reuven, 12:**15**

Katz, Ruth, 12:**15–16**

Katz, Sam, 3:81, 16:341

Katz, Shmuel, 12:**16**

Katz, Sholom, 12:**16**

Katz, Sir Bernard, 12:**9–10**

Katz, Solomon (1855-1920). *See* Dobrogeanu-Gherea, Constantin

Katz, Solomon (1909-1990), 12:**16**

Katz, Steven T., 9:389–390, 12:**16–17**

Katzav, Moshe, 12:**17–18**

Katzburg, David Ẓevi, 12:**18**

Katzenberg, Jeffrey, 12:**18**

Katzenelenbogen, Uriah, 12:**19**

Katzenellenbogen, David Tevel, 12:**19**

Katzenellenbogen, Meir ben Issac, 4:117, 8:451, 11:423, 12:**19–20**

Katzenellenbogen, Saul, 4:199, 13:261

Katzenellenbogen, Ẓevi Hirsh, 12:**20**

Katzenellenbogen family, 12:**19**

Katzenelson, Baruch, 12:**20**

Katzenelson, Itzhak, 12:**20–21**

Katzenelson, Judah Leib Benjamin, 8:476, 12:**21**

Katzenelson, Nissan, 12:**21–22**

Katzenelson, Yosef, 12:**22**

Katzenstein, Julius. *See* Kastein, Jodeph

A Katz in Geto (Bryks), 4:230

Katzir, Aharon, 12:**22**

Katzir, Ephraim, 12:**22–23**, 13:10

Katzir, Judith, 12:**23**

Katzman, Sam, 12:**23**

Katzmann, Friedrich, 12:**23**

Katznelson, Avraham. *See* Nissan, Avraham

Katznelson, Beeri. *See* Katznelson, Berl

Katznelson, Berl, 12:**23–26**

Katznelson, I., 8:715–716

Katznelson, Jacob Benjamin, 11:511

Katznelson, Raḥel, 12:**26**

Katznelson, Reuben, 12:**26**

Katznelson, Shmuel. *See* Tamir, Shmuel

Katznelson, Shulamit, 12:**26–27**

Katz-Suchy, Juliusz, 12:**27**, 16:347

Kauder, Samuel Judah ben David, 12:**27**

Kauders, Shmuel Loeb. *See* Kauder, Samuel Judah ben David

Kauen. *See* Kaunas (Lithuania)

Kauffman, Stuart, 13:11

Kauffmann, Felix, 12:**27**

Kauffmann, Isaac, 12:**27**

Kaufman, Andy, 12:**27–28**

Kaufman, Avraham Yosifovich, 12:**28**

Kaufman, Bel, 12:**28**

Kaufman, Boris, 12:**28**

Kaufman, Debra Renée, 18:736

Kaufman, Denis. *See* Vertov, Dziga

Kaufman, Donald, 4:191

Kaufman, George Simon, 12:**28–29**

Kaufman, Gerald. *See* Kaufman, Sir Gerald

Kaufman, Gurit. *See* Kadman, Gurit

Kaufman, Irving R., 12:**29**, 15:215

Kaufman, Jan, 18:403

Kaufman, Joyce Jacobson, 12:**29–30**

Kaufman, Judah. *See* Even Shemuel, Judah

Kaufman, Louis, 14:454

Kaufman, Philip, 12:**30**

Kaufman, Sir Gerald, 12:**29**

Kaufman, Yoram J., 6:450

Kaufman Haggadah, 8:213

Kaufmann, David, 12:**30–31**
    as bibliophile, 3:684
        Brann, Marcus, 4:129

Kaufmann, Felix, 12:**31**

Kaufmann, Fritz, 12:**31**

Kaufmann, Fritz Mordecai, 12:**31–32**

Kaufmann, Hanne, 12:**32**

Kaufmann, Ignatz, 12:27

Kaufmann, Isidor, 12:**32**

Kaufmann, Judah. *See* Even Shemuel, Judah

Kaufmann, Oskar, 12:**32**

Kaufmann, Pierre, 15:546

Kaufmann, Richard, 12:**32–33**

Kaufmann, Rosa, 15:684

Kaufmann, Walter, 12:**33**

Kaufmann, Yeḥezkel, 12:**33–35**
    biblical exegesis and study, 3:648, 650
    Job, Book of, 11:347
    Joel, Book of, 11:362
    Jonah, Book of, 11:388
    Joshua and book of Joshua, 11:442, 449

Kaulla family, 12:**35**

Kaunas (Lithuania), 6:358–359, 12:**35–37**

Kaunas University, 13:124

Kausalitaet und Teleologie im Streite um die Wissenschaft (Adler), 1:402

Kaushanski, Baruch. *See* Agadati, Baruch

Kaushany (Moldova), 12:**37**

Kautsky, Karl, 4:137

Kautzsch, Emil Friedrich, 12:**37**

Kauvar, Charles Eliezer Hillel, 12:**37–38**

Kavalla (Greece), 12:**38–39**

Kavar Erez Noshevet (Sened), 18:288

Kaverin, Benjamin Aleksandrovich, 12:**39**

Kav ha-Yashar (Koidonover), 13:106

Kavner, Julie, 12:**39**

Kavod, 8:387

Kavod le-Ish (Elyashar), 6:372

Kavod-ve-Ometz school, 5:217

Kavvanah, 12:**39–40**
    See Also Meditation

Kav ve-Naki (Elisha ben Abraham), 6:351

Kawamorita Eiji, 11:84–85

Kawkabān (Yemen), 12:**40**

Kay, Barry, 12:**40**

Kaye, Danny, 12:**40–41**

Kaye, Emmanuel. *See* Kaye, Sir Emmanuel

Kaye, Judith S., 12:**41**

Kaye, Nora, 12:**41–42**

Kaye, Sir Emmanuel, 12:**41**

Kayfetz, Ben, 12:**42**

Kayser, Rudolf, 12:**42**

Kayserling, Meyer, 3:682, 12:**42–43**

Kayserling, Moritz. *See* Kayserling, Meyer

Kayyara, Simeon, 8:260

Kazakevich, Emmanuil Genrikhovich, 12:**43**

Kazakhstan, 12:**43**

Kazan (Tatarstan autonomous republic), 12:**43**

Kazan, Elia, 2:104

Kazan, Lanie, 12:**43–44**

Kazarnovski, Isaac Abramovich, 12:**44**

Kazatin (Ukraine), 12:**44**

Kazaz, Elijah ben Elijah, 12:**44**

Kazaz, Mordekhai. *See* Ben-Porat, Mordekhai

Kazdan, Ḥayyim Solomon, 12:**44–45**

Kazimierz (Poland), 5:257–259

Kazimierz dynasty, 12:**45**

Kazimierz Wielke. *See* Casimir III

Kazin, Alfred, 12:**45**

Kazin, Judah ben Yom Tov, 12:**45**

Kazin, Raphael ben Elijah, 3:57, 12:**45–46**

Kazir Ḥarish (Israel), 12:**46**

Kazis, I.J., 7:13

Kaznelson, Siegmund, 11:571, 12:**46**

Kazrin (Israel), 12:**46**

Kazvin (Iran), 12:**46–47**

Kazyonny ravvin, 8:442, 12:**47–48**, 713

KBC Band, 3:90

Kecskemet (Hungary), 12:**48**

Kecskeméti, Ármin, 12:**48**

Kecskeméti, György, 12:**48**

Kecskeméti, Lipót, 12:**48–49**

Kedainiai (Lithuania), 12:**49**

Kedar, 12:**49–50**

Kedem, Ora, 12:**50**

Kedemites, 12:**50**
    Job, Book of, 11:352

Kedemoth (desert and ancient city), 12:**50**

Kedesh, Galilee (Israel), 11:698–699

Kedmah Mizrahah, bi-nationalism promoted by, 3:702–703

Kedushah (blessing), 12:**56–57**

Kedushah (holiness), 12:**50–56**
    idea of, Kook, Abraham Isaac, 12:291–292

Kedushah, Amidah, 2:74

Kedushta'ot, 18:598

Keegstra, James, 1:590

Kefar Akko (ancient village), 12:**57**

Kefar Azar (Israel), 12:**57**

Kefar Baram (Galilee), 12:**57–58**

Kefar Barukh (Israel), 12:**58**

Kefar Bialik (Israel), 12:**58**

Kefar Blum (Israel), 12:**58**

Kefar Darom (Philistia), 12:**58–59**

Kefar Ezyon (Israel), 12:**59**

Kefar Gamala (Israel), 12:**59**

Kefar Gideon (Israel), 12:**59**

Kefar Giladi (Israel), 12:**59**

Kefar Glickson (Israel), 12:**60**

Kefar Ḥabad (Israel), 12:**60**

Kefar ha-Ḥoresh (Israel), 12:**60**

Kefar ha-Maccabi (Israel), 12:**60**

Kefar Ḥananyah (ancient village, Israel), 12:**60**

Kefar ha-Nasi (Israel), 12:**60**

Kefar ha-Ro'eh (Israel), 4:18, 12:**61**

Kefar Ḥasidim (Israel), 12:**61**

Kefar Ḥattin (ancient village), 12:**61**

Kefar Ḥayyim (Israel), 12:**61**

Kefar Hess (Israel), 12:**61**

Kefar Ḥittim (Israel), 12:**61**

Kefar Jawitz (Israel), 12:**61**

Kefar Kanna (Israel), 12:**62**

Kefar Kisch (Israel), 12:**62**

Kefar Malal (Israel), 12:**62**

Kefar Mandi (Israel), 12:**62**

Kefar Masaryk (Israel), 12:**62**

Kefar Menaḥem (Israel), 12:**62–63**

Kefar Monash (Israel), 12:**63**

Kefar Mordekhai (Israel), 12:**63**

Kefar Neburaya (Israel), 12:**63**

Kefar Netter (Israel), 12:**63**

Kefar Otnay (ancient city), 12:**63**

Kefar Pines (Israel), 11:695, 12:**63**

Kefar Rosh ha-Nikrah (Israel), 12:**63**

Kefar Ruppin (Israel), 12:**64**

Kefar Sava (Israel), 12:**64**

Kefar Shemaryahu (Israel), 12:**64**

Kefar Shiḥlayim (ancient village), 12:**64**
Kefar shittufi, Jokneam, 11:385
Kefar Silver (Israel), 18:584
Kefar Syrkin (Israel), 12:**64–65**
Kefar Szold (Israel), 12:**65**
Kefar Tavor (Israel), 12:**65**
Kefar Truman (Israel), 12:**65**
Kefar Uriyyah (Israel), 12:**65**
Kefar Veradim (Israel), 12:**65**
Kefar Vitkin (Israel), 12:**65**
Kefar Warburg (Israel), 12:**65**
Kefar Yasif (Upper Galilee), 12:**66**
Kefar Yeḥezkel (Israel), 12:**66**
Kefar Yehoshu'a (Israel), 12:**66**
Kefar Yonah (Israel), 12:**66–67**
Kehillah (New York, NY), 6:64, 193–194, 11:777, 12:411, 15:209, 217
Kehilla Kaddisha de-vi-Yrushalayim. *See* Holy Congregation in Jerusalem
Kehillat Hadar (NY), 8:472
Kehillath Anshe Ma'arav (Chicago), 4:607
Kehimkhar, Ḥayim Samuel, 12:**67**
Kehunnat Avraham (Abraham ben Shabbetai ha-Kohen), 1:310
Keil, Karl Friedrich, 12:**67**
Keilah (ancient city), 12:**67**
Keilin, David, 13:10
Keiras, 8:318
Keitel, Harvey, 12:**67**
Keiẓad Seder Mishnah (Moravchik). *See How to Organize Learning* (Moravchik)
Kelaḥ Pitḥei Ḥokhman (Luzzatto), 13:283–284
Kelal, Talmudic, 12:603–604
Kelalei ha-Dikduk (Altaras), 2:16
Kelal Kaẓer mi-Kol ha-rashum bi-Khetav (Bulat), 6:399
Kelal u-ferat rules, 9:27
Kelal Yisrael, 12:**67–68**
Kelen, Emerich. *See* Kelen, Imre
Kelen, Emery. *See* Kelen, Imre
Kelen, Imre, 12:**68**
Keleti, Agnes, 12:**68**
Keli Ḥemdah (Plotzki), 16:241
Kelim (tractate), 12:**69**
Kelimat ha-Goyim (Duran), 6:56, 57, 13:112
Kelin, Samuel ben Nathan ha-Levi. *See* Kolin, Samuel ben Nathan ha-Levi
Kelitah. *See* Aliyah and absorption
Keli Yakar (Ephraim Solomon ben Aaron of Luntshits), 6:461
Keli Yakar (Laniado), 12:484, 485
Kellendonk, Frans, 6:69

Keller, Morton, 12:**69**
Kellerman, Faye, 12:**69–70**
Kellerman, Jonathan, 12:**70**
Kellermann, Benzion, 12:**70**
Kellner, Leon, 12:**70**
Kelm. *See* Kelme (Lithuania)
Kelman, Wolfe, 12:**71**
Kelme (Lithuania), 12:**71**
Kelmer, Samuel, 17:66
Kelmer Maggid. *See* Moses Isaac
Kelmy. *See* Kelme (Lithuania)
Kelsen, Hans, 12:**71–72**, 548, 549, 551
Kemal Mustafa, 12:**72**
Kemelman, Harry, 12:**72**
Kemény, Ferenc, 6:160
Kemény, Simon, 12:**72**
Kemer. *See* Parium
Kemi. *See* Egypt
Kempen (Germany), 12:**72–73**
Kempf, Franz Moshe, 12:**73**
Kempinsky, Aharon, 12:**73**
Kempner, Aviva, 12:**73–74**
Kempner, Harris, 12:**74**
Kempner, Robert Max Wasilii, 12:**74**
Kenaani, David, 12:**74**
Kenaf Renanim (Carmi), 4:484
Kenan, Amos, 12:**74–75**, 18:205
Kenan-Ofri, Esti, 15:407
Kenasot, 15:369
Kenath (ancient city), 12:**75**
Kenaz, 1:356
Kenaz, Yehoshua, 8:708–709, 12:**75–76**
Der Keneder Adler (newspaper), 4:425–426, 18:247, 21:152
Keneder Odler (newspaper). *See Der Keneder Adler* (newspaper)
Kenen, I. L., 2:50, 51
Keneset ha-Gedolah (Benveniste), 1:637, 3:383
Keneset Yisrael, 12:**76**
    See also Kelal Yisrael
Kenig Artis Houf. See Vidvilt
Kenite, 2:30, 12:**76–77**
Kenna. *See* Kefar Kanna (Israel)
Kennedy, Edward M., 4:174
Kennedy, John Fitzgerald, 2:83, 12:**77**, 761
Kennedy Center Honors, 15:253
Kenneth Cole Productions, 5:56
Kent, Allegra, 12:**77**
Kent, Roman R., 2:48, 49, 12:**77–78**
Kentner, Louis, 12:**78**
Kentridge, Morris, 12:**78**, 16:349
Kentridge, Sir Sydney, 12:**78–79**
Kentridge, Sydney. *See* Kentridge, Sir Sydney

Kentucky (U.S.), 12:**79–80**
Kenya, 12:**80**
Kenyon, Dame Kathleen Mary, 11:201, 12:**80–81**, 15:589
Kerak (ancient city), 12:**81**
Keranot. *See* Horns, altar
Kerber, Linda, 9:152
Kerch (Ukraine), 12:**81**
Kerem Ḥemed (periodical), 12:**81–82**, 465
Kerem Shelomo (Amarillo), 2:32
Kerem Shelomo (Plungian), 16:242
Keren Hayesod, 1:247, 9:24, 246, 12:**82–84**
Keresztúr (Austria). *See* Deutschkreutz (Austria)
Keret, Etgar, 12:**84**
Keri'ah, 12:**84–85**
Keri and ketiv. *See* Qere and ketiv
Keriat *Shema. See* Shema, reading of
Keri'at Shema al ha-Mittah. See Night Prayer
Kerith. *See* Cherith
Keritot (tractate), 12:**85**
Kerler, Dov-Ber, 12:**85–86**
Kerler, Yoysef, 12:**86**
Kerman (Iran), 12:**86–87**
Kermanshah (Iran), 12:**87**
Kern, Jerome, 7:17, 12:**87**
Kerovah, 2:75, 12:**88**, 16:193
Kerr, Alfred, 12:**88**
Kersh, Gerald, 12:**88–89**
Kersten, Felix, 17:121
Kertesz, Andre, 12:**89**
Kertész, Imre, 12:**89**
Kertesz, Istavan, 12:**89**
Kesef Mezukkak (Pinto), 16:179
Kesef Mishneh (Caro, Joseph ben Ephraim), 4:490
Kesef Nimas (Pinto), 16:179
Kesef Nivḥar (Pinto), 5:394, 16:179
Kesef Ẓaruf (Pinto), 16:179
Kesef Ẓaruf (Ṣefirah), 18:243–244
Keshet (periodical), 2:78
Keshet, Yeshurun, 12:**89–90**
Kessar, Israel, 12:**90**
Kessel, Barney, 12:**90**
Kessel, Joseph, 12:**90–91**
Kessler, David, 12:**91**
Kessler, Leopold, 12:**91**
Kessler-Harris, Alice, 9:152
Kestelman, Morris. *See* Kestleman, Morris
Kesten, Hermann, 12:**91**
Kestenberg, Leo, 12:**91–92**
Kestleman, Morris, 12:**92**

Keszi, Imre, 12:**92**

Ketāb-e sargozasht-e Kāshān (Babai ben Farhad), 3:**15**

Ketā-e Anusi (Babai ben Luṭf, 3:15

Ketavim le Toledot Ḥibbat Ẓiyyonve-Yishuv Erez Yisrael (Druyanow). *See Writings on the History of Hibbat Zion and the Settlement of Palestine*

Ketav yad, 18:468

Ketef Hinnom (Israel), 3:657

Ketem Paz (Labi), 12:408

Keter Kehunnah (Lara), 12:492

Keter Malkhut (Ibn Gabirol), 7:325–326

Keter Publishing House, 12:**92–93**

Keter Shem Tov (Abraham ben Alexander of Cologne), 1:294

Keter Torah (Aaron ben Elijah), 1:212, 213

Keti'a Bar Shalom, 12:**93**

Ketiv and qere, 13:609, 615–617, 15:751–752

Ketoret ha-Mizbe'aḥ (Mordecai ben Naphtali Hirsch of Kremsier), 14:482

Ketoret ha-Sammim (Mordecai ben Naphtali Hirsch of Kremsier), 14:482

Ketubbah, 12:**93–98**, 21:44
    animal motif, Morocco (19th c.), vol. 12: color insert
    Bible scenes motif, Italy (18th c.), vol. 12: color insert
    bond of indebtedness, 5:154–155
    calligraphy, modern Hebrew, 4:366–367
    concubines and, 5:134–135
    flower and leaf motif, Yemen (18th c.), vol. 12: color insert
    flower motif
        Georgia (19th c.), vol. 12: color insert
        Iran (19th c.), vol. 12: color insert
        Italy (17th c.), vol. 12: color insert
        Tunis (19th c.), vol. 12: color insert
    gate motif, Netherlands (17th c.), vol. 12: color insert
    genizah records of, 7:471–472
    Holy City motif, Italy (18th c.), vol. 12: color insert
    illuminated, 10:787
    illuminated kettubot, 12:97–98
    leaf motif, Singapore (19th c.), vol. 12: color insert
    legal aspects, 12:93–95

lien, 12:812–813
    marriage and divorce law, 5:152–153, 712–713, 716, 769, 771
    payment of, 18:600
    shown during wedding ceremony, Israel, vol. 3: color insert
    status in modern times, 12:95–97
    widow's claim, 13:22–23
    See also Divorce; Get; Marriage

Ketubbot (Aaron ben Joseph ha-Levi), 1:215

Ketubbot (tractate), 12:**98–99**

Ketubot, illuminated, 2:498

Keturah, 12:**99**

Ketuvim, 3:576
    books of, 3:577t
    canonization of, 3:578–579
    Judeo-Persian translations of, 11:553
    order of books in, 3:582, 582t
    poetry, 16:255–256
    targumim to, 3:593–594

Ketuvim (periodical), 8:697

Ketuvim Aḥaronim (Fraenkel), 7:144

Kevallim (motion picture). *See Cables* (motion picture)

Kever Avot, 12:**99–100**

Kevi. *See* Koi

Kevod Ḥakhamim (Abraham ben Shabbetai ha-Kohen), 1:310

Kevod Ḥkhamim (Meshullam Phoebus ben Israel Samuel), 14:79–80

Kevurat Ḥamor (Smolenskin), 18:692

Kevuẓat Kesef (Shapiro), 18:404

Kevuẓot Kesef (Pinto), 16:179

Kewall, Benjamin, 11:444

Keyfitz, Nathan, 18:732

Keyserling, Leon H., 12:**100**

Di Keytn fun Meshiekh (Leivik), 12:630

Keẓaẓah, 12:**100**

Keẓi'ah. *See* Cinnamon

Keẓot ha-Ḥoshen (Heller), 8:792, 795–796

Kfar Darom (Israel), 20:657

Khalaẓ, Judah ben Abraham, 12:**100**

Khalfon, Abraham. *See* Ḥalfon, Abraham

Khalid ben Jasikhi, 1:602

Khallenberg, Pinḥas, 8:504

Khalyastre (journal), 12:**100–101**

Khanaqin (Iraq), 12:**101**

Khanikin. *See* Khanaqin (Iraq)

Khaniqin. *See* Khanaqin (Iraq)

Khān Yūnis (Gaza Strip), 12:**101**

Kharāj and Jizya, 12:**101–104**

Kharasch, Morris Selig, 12:**104**

Kharik, Izi, 4:141, 12:**104–105**

Kharik, Yitskhok. *See* Kharik, Izi

Kharkov (Ukraine), 12:**105–106**

Kharkov Conference, 12:**106**

Khave (Shalom Aleichem), 18:386

Khavkin, M., 3:719

Khaybar (ancient city), 12:**106–108**

Khayml. *See* Siemiatycki, Chaim

Khazarian Hebrew Documents of the Tenth Century (Golb & Printsak), 7:472

Khazars, 9:145, 212, 11:414, 12:**108–114**, *110*, 16:83
    Būlān, 4:266–267
    conversion to Judaism, 12:111–112
    Eldad ha-Dani, 6:294
    Jewish community, 7:472
    Jews after Khazar kingdom, 12:113–114
    Khazar Correspondence, 12:112–113
    kingdom and political rule, 2:130, 12:109–111, 112
    Nitra, 15:281
    origin, 12:108–109
    Sarkil fortress, 18:57

Kherson (Ukraine), 12:**114–115**

Khirbat al-Muqanna', 6:281

Khirbat al-Rabba. *See* Rabbath-Moab (ancient Israel)

Khirbat Mird (West Bank), 5:505

Khirbat Miyămăs (Israel), 13:407

Khirbat Sīmūniyya (Canaan). *See* Shimron (Canaan)

Khirbet El-Qom (Israel), 3:656

Khirbet Faḥil. *See* Pella (Canaan)

Khmelnik (Ukraine), 12:**115**

Khmelnitski, Bogdan. *See* Chmielnicki, Bogdan

Khnum (Egyptian god), 6:311, 312

Khnumhotep II (pharaoh), 6:223

Khodasevich, Vladislav Felitsianovich, 12:**115**

Khodorkovsky, Mikhail Borisovich, 12:**115–116**

Khomeini, Ayatollah, 12:**116**, 15:569, 570

Khorasan. *See* Khurasan (Persia)

Khorazin (Galilee). *See* Chorazin (Galilee)

Khorezm (Uzbekistan), 12:**116–117**

Khorol (Ukraine), 12:**117**

Khorsabad archives, 2:404

Khotin (Moldova), 12:**117–118**

Khouri, Makram, 12:**118**

Khoushi, Abba, 12:**118**

Khrushchev, Nikita S., 3:720, 18:163

Khurasan (Persia), 12:**118–119**
  See also Afghanistan
Khurbn & Other Poems (Rothenberg), 20:298–299
Khust (Ukraine), 12:**119**
Khuzestani Jews of Bushire, 4:306
Khuzistan (Persia), 11:548, 549
Khvolson, Daniel Avaraamovich. *See* Chwolson, Daniel
Khwarizm. *See* Khorezm (Uzbekistan)
Kibarty (Lithuania). *See* Kybartai (Lithuania)
Kibbuta movement, Adamit, 1:378
Kibbutz Arẓi Ha-Shomer ha-Ẓa'ir, 8:383–384, 14:484–485
Kibbutz Buchenwald, 15:246
Kibbutz festivals, 7:49, 12:**119–120**, 120*t*
Kibbutzim
    Ḥanitah, 8:324
    Ha-Ogen, 8:335–336
    Ha-On, 8:336
Kibbutz movement, 5:209–210, 12:**121–138**
    absorption of immigrants by, 10:342, 359, 527–529, 528*t*
    Afikim, 1:433
    age and the aged, 1:448–449
    Al ha-Mishmar, 1:655
    Allonim, 1:677
    American, 8:385
    Ben-Gurion, David, 3:344, 346, 348
    beyond Green Line, 10:361–362, 364–365
    Biranit, 3:710
    Biriyyah, 3:711
    Busel, Joseph, 4:303
    Carol, Aryeh, 4:492–493
    choral singing, 4:662
    economics, 10:618, 12:129–131, 136–137
    education, 12:122–123, 132–133
    Eilon, 6:254
    Eilot, 6:254–255
    Ein Gev, 6:256–257
    Ein ha-Emek, 6:257
    Ein ha-Mifraẓ, 6:257
    Ein ha-Naziv, 6:257
    Ein ha-Sheloshah, 6:257
    Ein ha-Shofet, 6:257
    Ein Shemer, 6:260
    Ein Ẓurim, 6:264–265
    En-Dor, 6:405
    En-Gedi, 6:408
    English, 8:385
    En-Harod, 6:441, vol. 11: color insert

family roles, 12:128–129
festivals and holidays observance in, 10:627
folklore and customs, 7:110
Gedud ha-Avodah, 7:409
governing responsibilities, 10:393
Ha-Kibbutz ha -Arzi ha-Shomer ha-Za'ir, 12:124
Ha-Kibbutz ha-Dati, 12:125–126
Ḥamadyah (Israel), 8:293
Ha-Ma'pil, 8:294
Harel, 8:352
Ha-Solelim, 8:448
Ḥaẓor Ashdod, 8:501
Ha-Zore'a, 8:501
Ḥefẓi Bah, 8:755
Histadrut and, 10:595–596, 601
Japan support, 11:83
kibbutz federations, 12:135–136
Lahavot ha-Bashan, 12:439
Lavi, 12:531
during Mandate
    growth, 10:492
    mixed farming strategy, 10:510–511
Misgav Am, 14:315–316
Mishmar ha-Emek, 14:316
Mishmar ha-Negev, 14:316
Mishmar ha-Sharon, 14:317
Mishmar ha-Yarden, 14:317
Mishmarot, 14:317
Mizra, 14:388
Neẓer Sereni, 15:246
Nir Am, 15:273
Nir David, 15:273, vol. 11: color insert
Nirim, 15:274
Niẓẓanim, 15:284
northern Israel, 13:666
Or Ha-Ner, 15:**469**
political representation of, 10:432
political structure, 12:131–132
population, 10:289, 292, 375
population change, 12:126–128
post-Holocaust aliyah and, 10:215
relations with Israeli society, 12:133–135
Sarid, 18:56
Sasa, 18:64
Sedeh Boker, 18:234
Sedeh Eliyahu, 18:234
Sedeh Naḥum, 18:235
Sedeh Neḥemyah, 18:235
Sedot Yam, 18:237
Shaalbim, 18:334
Sha'ar ha-Golan, 18:335, 336

Shamir, 18:391
Shefayim, 18:432
Sheluḥot, 18:452–453
Third Aliyah and, 10:510
women participation, 21:192, 194
Yodefat, 11:464
See also Agriculture
Kibel, Wolf, 12:**138**
Ki-Bukh (fable collection), 12:**138**
Kidd, Captain, 4:51
Kidd, Michael, 12:**138**
Kiddah. *See* Cinnamon
Kiddush, 6:505, 12:**138–139**
Kiddush ha-Ḥayyim, 12:**139**
Kiddush ha-Shem and Ḥillul ha-Shem, 12:**139–145**
    Barukh shem kavod malkhuto le-olam va-ed, 3:192
    biblical literature, 12:140
    ethical conduct, 12:141–142
    Ḥasidei Ashkenaz, 8:388
    historical aspects, 12:142–145
    jihād and, 11:337
    love of God, 13:230–231
    martyrdom, 12:140–142
    prayer, 12:142
    Rabbinic literature, 12:140–142
Kiddushin (tractate), 4:616–617, 746–748, 12:**145–146**, 15:428
Kiddush Levanah (prayer). *See Sanctification of the Moon* (prayer)
Kidnapping. *See* Abduction
Kidney transplants, 20:107
Kidron, 12:**146**
Kidron (biblical place), 6:464
Ki Eirom Attah (Shamir), 18:392
Kiel (Germany), 12:**146**
Kiel, Yehuda, 12:**146**
Kielce (Poland), 12:**146–147**
Kielce pogrom, 3:435, 9:374
Kiera, 12:**147–148**
Kiera, Esther, 16:345–346
Kieras, 8:318
Kierkegaard, Søren, 1:285, 557, 4:126, 16:105
Kiesler, Frederick John, 12:**148**
Kiesler, Hedwig Eva Maria. *See* Lamarr, Hedy
Kiev (Ukraine), 12:**148–153**
    1793-1941, 12:149–151
    Babi Yar, 3:22–23
    Holocaust period, 12:151–152
    pogram self-defense, 18:262
    pre-1667, 12:148–149
    post World War II, 12:152–153
    Yidishe Kultur Lige, 13:267

Kiev (Ukraine), *continued*
    See also Beilis blood libel trial
Kieval, Hayyim, 12:**153**
Kieval, Herman. *See* Kieval, Hayyim
Kifayat al-abidin (Ben Maimon),
    1:306, 307
Kikayon. *See* Castor-oil plant
Kik-oil, 15:396
Kikoine, Michel, 12:**153**
Kilayim (tractate), 12:**154**
Kiliya (Moldova), 12:**154**
Killing centers. *See* Camps,
    concentration and extermination
The Killing Fields (motion picture),
    18:106
Kiln People (Brin), 18:200
Kilye (Turkey). *See* Koila (Turkey)
Kimberley (South Africa), 12:**154–155**
Kimche, Jon, 12:**155**
Kimha de-Avishuna (Treves), 20:135
Kimhi, David, 12:**155–156**
    on Amos, 2:97
    Bible editions containing
        commentaries of, 3:586, 610,
        677
    Joshua, Book of, 11:444
    Landau, Jacob, 12:462
    linguistic literature, 13:33–54
    modern biblical criticism, as
        precursor of, 3:648
    moneylending, 14:439
    NJV influenced by commentaries
        of, 3:621
    on peace, 15:702
    synthetic approach to biblical
        exegesis and study, 3:642, 643
Kimhi, Dov, 12:**156–157**
Kimhi, Jacob ben Samuel, 12:**157**
Kimhi, Joseph, 2:158, 8:566, 12:**157–**
158
    disputations and polemics, 5:692
    synthetic approach to biblical
        exegesis and study, 3:643
Kimhi, Mordecai, 12:**158**
Kimhi, Moses, 12:**158**, 13:41
Kimhi, Solomon ben Nissim Joseph
    David, 12:**159**
Kimhi, Raphael Israel ben Joseph,
    12:**158–159**
Kimhit family, 12:**159**
Kimmel, Sidney, 12:**159–160**
Kimpetbriv paper-cuts, 15:615–616
Kimpulung (Romania). *See*
    Campulung Moldovenesc
    (Romania)
Kimshonim (Raab, Esther), 17:5, 6
Kinah
    See also Av, Ninth of; Hesped

Kinah (poem), 12:**160**
"Kinah Shemor" (Modena), 14:409
Kinases enzymes, 5:31
Kinder der Welt (Heyse), 9:87
Kinderfreund, Aryeh Leib, 12:**160**
Kindergartens, 6:159–160
    Theresienstadt ghetto, 9:*473*
Kindertransport, 8:282, 9:369, 12:**160–**
161
Kindī, Abu Yūsuf YaʿQūb ibn Ishaq
    Al-, 12:**161–162**
Kineset Yisrael, 1:507
The King (Elkan), 6:357
King, Alan, 12:**162–163**
King, Carole, 12:**163**
King, Colin, 15:243
King, H. C., 15:582
King, Larry, 12:**170**
King, Martin Luther, Jr., 3:736
    Borowitz, Eugene B., 4:93
    Braude, William Gordon, 4:135
King, William Lyon Mackenzie, 4:404
The King and the Cobbler
    (Gronemann), 18:761
King-Crane Palestine Inquiry
    Commission (1919), 15:582
King David Hotel, 10:207
The King David Report (Heym), 9:86
Kingdom Come (Brant), 4:130
Kingdom of Bosphorus, 4:**98**
Kingdom of God (Buber). *See*
    Koenigtum Gottes
The Kingdom of Love (Brod). *See Das*
    Zauberreich der Liebe
Kingdom of Samaria. *See* Israel,
    Kingdom of
The King in Exile (Elkan), 6:357
The King Is Cruelest of All. See Akhzar
    mi-Kol ha-Melekh
King James Bible, 2:144, 3:611–614
The King of Lampedusa (Harendorf),
    8:353
"The King of Swing." *See* Sampras,
    Pete
The King of the Jews (Epstein), 6:475
King parables, 15:621–622
Kings, Book of, 4:76–77, 12:**170–175**
Kings and kingship, 1:279, 12:**163–170**
    Adoni-Zedek, 1:413–414
    adoption, 1:416–417
    ancient Israeli view, 5:445, 9:184
    Biblical literature, 12:167–168
    commandments concerning, 5:84*t*
    concept of monarchy, 12:168–169
    coronation, 12:165–166
    education, 6:165–166
    law, 14:349

    oils, anointing with, 15:396
    origins in Judaism, 12:164
    Phoenicia, 16:120
    Polemon II, 16:330
    Rabbinic literature, 12:169
    separation of powers, 18:291
    Sisebut, 18:644–645
    Solomon, 18:755–763
    succession, 12:166–167
The King's Archives (Ibn Latif), 12:506
The King's Delicacies (Mizrahi), 14:393
The King's Law, Noachide laws and,
    15:286–287
Kingsley, Charles, 6:435
The King's New Clothes. See Bigdei ha-
    Melekh ha-Hadashim
King Solomon and Asmodeus (Raban),
    vol. 2: color insert
"King Solomon's Mines". *See* Timna
    (Israel)
King's seer. *See* Jeduthun (Biblical
    harpist)
Kingston (Jamaica), Anglo-Orthodox,
    rabbis, 11:51
The King's Valley. See Emek ha-Melekh
Kinnamon. *See* Cinnamon
Kinneret (kibbutz, Israel), 4:303,
    12:**176**
Kinneret (Lake), 10:124–126
    Jordan (river) and, 10:125–126
Kinneret (Moshav, Israel), 12:**176**
Kinneret, Lake, 11:401, 12:**176–178**
Kinneret Kinneret (Alterman), 8:720
Kinnim (tractate), 12:**178**
Kinnor, 14:641
Kinross, Albert, 12:**178**
Kinship and Marriage in Early Arabia
    (Smith, William Robertson), 18:689
Kinsky, Georg Ludwig, 12:**178**
Kinyan. *See* Acquisition
Kinyan Avraham (Lonzano), 13:187
Kiov. *See* Kiev (Ukraine)
Kipen, Aleksander Abramovich,
    12:**178–179**
Kipen, Grigoriy Abromovich, 12:179
Kipnis, Alexander, 12:**179**
Kipnis, Itzik, 12:**179**
Kipnis, Levin, 12:**179**
Kipnis, Menahem, 12:**179–180**
    Justman, Moshe Bunem, 11:581
Kipper, 12:**180–183**
Kippod, 15:550–551
Kippoz, 15:550
Kira. *See* Kiera
Kirby, Jack, 12:**183–184**, 598
Kirchheim, Raphael, 12:**184**

Kirchheimer, Otto, 12:**184**

Kirchner, Leon, 12:**184**

Kirghizia. *See* Kyrgyzstan

Kir-Hareseth (ancient city), 12:**184–185**

Kiriath-Arba. *See* Hebron

Kiriath-Jearim (ancient city), 12:**185**

Kirimi, Abraham, 12:**185**

Kirjath Sepher (quarterly), 12:**185–186**, 16:146

al-Kirkisani, Jacob, 8:292
    apologetics, 2:265

al-Kirkisānī, Jacob, 12:**186**

Kirkpatrick, Alexander Francis, 12:**186–187**

Kirkuk (Iraq), 12:**187**

Kirovograd (Ukraine), 12:**187–188**

Kirsanov, Semyon Isaakovich, 12:**188**

Kirschbaum, Eliezer Sinai, 12:**188**

Kirschbraun, Elijah, 12:**188**

Kirschenbaum, Mordecai, 12:**188–189**

Kirschner, Bruno, 6:400

Kirschner, Emanuel, 12:**189**

Kirschner, Marc, 13:**10**

Kirschstein, Moritz, 12:**189**

Kirschstein, Salli, 12:**189**

Kirshblum, Mordecai, 12:**189–190**

Kirshon, Vladimir Mikhailovich, 12:**190**

Kirstein, Lincoln, 12:**190**, 15:220

Kirstein, Louis Edward, 4:100, 12:**190**

Kirszenbaum, Jesekiel David, 12:**190**

Kirszenstein-Szewinska, Irena, 12:**190–191**

Kiryas Joel (NY), 12:**191–192**

Kiryat Anavim (Israel), 12:**192**

Kiryat Ata (Israel), 12:**192**

Kiryat Bialik (Israel), 12:**192**

Kiryat Ekron (Israel), 12:**192**

Kiryat Gat (Israel), 12:**192–193**

Kiryat Ḥaroshet (Israel), 12:**193**

Kiryat Malakhi (Israel), 12:**193**

Kiryat Motzkin (Israel), 12:**193**

Kiryat Ono (Israel), 12:**193**

Kiryat Ponevezh, 11:715

Kiryat Sefer (Lattes), 12:519

Kiryat Sefer (Meiri), 13:787

Kiryat Shemonah (Israel), 12:**193–194**

Kiryat Tivon (Israel), 12:**194**

Kiryat Yam (Israel), 12:**194**

Kirzhnitz, Abraham, 12:**194**

Kiš, Danilo, 12:**194–195**

Kisch, Abraham, 11:364, 12:195

Kisch, Alexander, 12:**195–196**

Kisch, Bruno Zecharias, 12:**196**

Kisch, Cecil. *See* Kisch, Sir Cecil

Kisch, Daniel Montagu, 12:195

Kisch, Egon Erwin, 12:**196**

Kisch, Frederick Hermann, 12:**196–197**

Kisch, Guido, 12:**197**

Kisch, Hermann Michael, 12:195

Kisch, Sir Cecil, 12:195

Kisch family (Prague), 12:195

Kisch family (U.K.), 12:195

Kisel, Dovid. *See* Kassel, David

Kish (biblical figure), 12:**197**

Kishinev (Moldova), 12:**197–200**, 18:261
    pogroms
        Bialik, Ḥayyim Naḥman, 3:563
        Blumenfeld, Felix Mikhaylovich, 4:11
        B'nai B'rith, 4:14
        Pann, Abel, 15:612

Kishon (river), 12:**200**

Kishon, Ephraim, 12:**200**
    Ofir, Shaike, 15:390
    Ohel, 15:392

Kislev, 12:**200–201**

Kisling, Moise, 12:**201**, 15:648

Kismarton. *See* Eisenstadt

Kisos. *See* Ivy

Kiss, Gershon, parodies of, 15:661

Kiss, József, 12:**201–202**

Kiss and kissing, 12:**202**

Kisse Kavod (Abbas), 1:232

Kisse Ve-Ippodromin Shel Shelomo Ha-Melekh, 14:188

Kissin, Baron Harry, 12:**202**

Kissingen (Germany), 12:**202**

Kissinger (Kalb), 11:732

Kissinger, Henry Alfred, 3:728, 10:257, 258, 12:**202–204**, 20:354

Kissinger, The Price of Power: Kissinger in the Nixon White House (Hersch), 9:44

Kiss of death, 5:**513**

The Kiss of God: Mythical and Spiritual Death in Judaism (Fishbane), 7:60

Kissufim (Israel), 12:**204–205**

Kistarcsa (Hungary), 12:**205**

Kister, Meir J., 12:**205**

Kisvarda (Hungary), 12:**205**

Kitāab al-Aghānī (Al-Gharīḍ al-Yahūdī), 1:652

Kitāb al-Anwār wa-al-Marāqib (al-Kirkisānī). *See Book of Lights and Watch Towers* (al-Kirkisānī)

Kitāb al-Din wa al-Dawla (Ali ibn Sahl ibn Rabbān al-Ṭabar⁻i), 1:660

Kitab al-Hadaiq (Batalyawsi), 3:210

Kitāb al-Hidāya ilā Faraā'iḍ al-Qulū (Baḥya), 3:66

Kitāb al-Ḥujja wa al-Dalīl fi Naṣr al-Dhalī (Halevi), 16:83–84

Kitāb al-Ḥulaf alladī al-Muʿallimayn ben Asher wa-ben Naftali (Mishael ben Uzziel), 13:650

Kitāb-al-Kullīyāt fī al-Ṭibb (Averroes), 2:725

Kitab al-Luma (ibn Janah), 13:40–41

Kitab al-Masalik (Ibn Khurdadhbah). *See The Book of Routes* (Ibn Khurdadhbah)

Kitab al-Muḥadara wal-Mudhakara (Ibn Ezra), 8:283

Kitāb al-Muḥāḍ ara wa al-Mudhākara (Ibn Ezra), 9:674

Kitāb al-Muʾtābar (Ḥibat Allah), 9:93

Kitāb al-Muʿtabar (Abu al-Barakā), 9:93

Kitāb al-Nuqat (Ḥayyuj), 8:484

Kitāb al-Nutaf (Ḥayyuj), 8:484

Kitāb al-Tabbākh (Abu al-Hasan of Tyre), 1:335

Kitāb al-Tanqīṭ (Ḥayyuj), 8:484

Kitāb al-Tarīkh (Abu al-Fat), 1:334

Kitāb al-Tashwīr (Ibn Janāah, Jonah), 9:681–682

Kitāb Maʿānī al-Nafs (author unknown), 16:81

Kitaj, R. B., 12:**205–206**

Kitchener, H. H. H., Palestine Exploration Fund, 15:589

Kite, 12:**206**

Ki-Tekoʾa Shofar (Lisitzky), 13:81

Kitel, 12:**206**

Kitev (Ukraine). *See* Kuty (Ukraine)

Kitniyot, 12:610–611

Kitrón, Moshe, 12:**206–207**

Kitsee, Isador, 12:**207**

Kitser Masoes Binyomen Hashlishi (Abramovitsh), 1:320

Kittel, Rudolf, 12:**207**

Kittim, 12:**207–208**, 16:9–10

Kittsee, Ḥayyim ben Isaac, 12:**208–209**

Kittsee, Jehiel Michael ben Samuel, 12:**209**

Kitvei ha- Geʾonim (Horowitz), 9:544

Kitvei ha-Kodesh (*Kitve ha-Qodesh*; "Holy Writings"), 3:574

Kitvei R. Avraham Epstein (Epstein), 6:466

Kitz, Leonard, 16:341

Kitzingen (Germany), 12:**209**

Kivrot ha-Taʾavah (Loebel), 13:161

Kivsat ha-Rash (Shamir), 18:392

Kiẓẓur Aggadah (Sultansky), 19:306

Kiẓẓur Mordekhai (Schlettstadt), 18:143

Kizzur Or Zaru'a (Ḥayyim ben Isaac), 8:481

Kizzur Piskei ha-Mordekhai (Ottolengo), 14:481

Kizzur Shelah (Epstein), 6:473–474, 474

Kizzur Shulkḥan Arukh (Ganzfried), 7:379

Kizzur Talmud Yerushalmi ve-Talmud Bavli (Pinner), 16:169

KKK. *See* Ku Klux Klan (KKK)

Klabin family, 12:**209**, 436

Klaczko, Julian, 4:128, 12:**209–210**

Kladderadatsch (periodical), 11:736

Klaermann, Bernát. *See* Karácsony, Benö

Die Klagegedichte des Jeremia... (Baumgartner), 3:222

Klagenfurt (Austria), 12:**210**

Klaipėda (Lithuania). *See* Memel (Lithuania)

Klalei Leshon Ever (Calimani), 4:363

Klang, Heinrich, 12:**210**, 549

Klapper, Paul, 12:**210**

Klar, Benjamin Menaḥem, 12:**210–211**

Klarman, Yosef, 12:**211**

Klarsfeld, Beate Auguste, 12:**211**

Klarsfeld, Serge, 12:**211–212**

Klarwein, Joseph, 12:**212**

Klasky, Arlene, 5:315–316

Klasky Csupo, Inc., 5:315–316

Klatovy (Czech Republic), 12:**212**

Klatzkin, Elijah ben Naphtali Hertz, 12:**212–213**

Klatzkin, Jacob, 6:400, 12:**213–214**, 17:155

Klatzko, Mordecai ben Asher, 12:**214**

Klauber, Abraham, 18:14

Klausenburg (Romania). *See* Cluj (Romania)

Klausner, Abraham, 8:483, 12:**214–215**

Klausner, Israel, 12:**215**

Klausner, Joseph Gedaliah, 8:686, 727, 12:**215–217**

Klausner, M. A., 3:631

Klausner, Zevi Hirsch, 12:**218**

Klavan, Israel, 12:**218**

Klee, Alfred, 12:**218**

Kleerekoper, Asser Benjamin, 12:**218**, 16:345

Klein, Abraham Moses, 4:423, 424, 12:**218–219**

Klein, Agnes. *See* Keleti, Agnes

Klein, Alberto, 12:**219–220**

Klein, Anne, 12:**219–220**

Klein, Calvin, 12:**220**, 526

Klein, Edward E., 12:**220**

Klein, Franz, 16:340

Klein, George, 12:**220–221**

Klein, Gerda Weissman, 4:631, 12:**221**

Klein, Gottlieb, 12:**221–222**

Klein, Henry. *See* Avidov, Zvi

Klein, Hyman, 12:**222**

Klein, Isaac, 12:**222**

Klein, Julius, 12:**222–223**

Klein, Julius Leopold, 12:**223**

Klein, Kurt, 12:**221**

Klein, Lawrence Robert, 12:**223**

Klein, Mannie, 12:**223**

Klein, Melanie Reizes, 12:**224**

Klein, Moritz, 12:**224**

Klein, Morton, 12:**224**

Klein, Morton Richard. *See* Richards, Martin

Klein, Philip (1849-1926), 12:**225**

Klein, Philip (1890-?), 12:**225**

Klein, Philip Hillel, 4:5

Klein, Ralph, 12:**225**

Klein, Salomon Wolf, 2:8, 12:**225**

Klein, Samuel, 12:**225–226**

Klein, Samuel Shmelka, 12:**226**

Klein, Samy, 2:9

Klein, Theodore, 12:**226**

Klein, Viola, 18:736

Klein, Wilhelm, 12:**226**

Klein, Yves, 12:**226–227**

Kleinbaum, Moshe. *See* Sneh, Moshe

Kleinman, Mór. *See* Kármán, Mór

Kleinmann, Moshe, 12:**227**

Klemperer, Gutmann, 12:**227**

Klemperer, Otto, 12:**227**

Klemperer, Paul, 12:**227–228**

Klemperer, Victor, 12:**228**

Klenbart, Hanan J. *See* Ayalti, Hanan J.

Klenicki, Leon, 12:**228–229**

Klepfish, Samuel Zanvil, 12:**229**

Klepfisz, Irena, 12:**229**

Kletsk (Poland), 12:**229–230**

Kletzki, Paul, 12:**230**

Kley, Eduard, 12:**230–231**

Dos Kleyne Mentshele (Abramovitsh), 1:319–320

Klezmer music, 14:674–675, *675*
    Feidman, 6:729–730

Kl Herzogenbusch. *See* Vught concentration camp

Kligler, Israel Jacob, 12:**231**

Klíma, Ivan, 12:**231**

Kline, Franz, 12:**231**

Kline, Nathan S., 12:**232**

The Klinger Quartet (painting, Mopp), 14:470

Klintsy (Russian Federation), 12:**232**

Klober, Isaac, 13:268

Klodawa (Poland), 12:**232**

Klopstock, Friedrich Gottlieb, 18:761

Klosterneuburg (Austria), 12:**232–233**

Klotz, Louis-Lucien, 12:**233**, 16:343

Klug, Aaron, 4:593, 12:**233**, 13:9

Kluger, Ruth. *See* Aliav, Ruth

Kluger, Solomon ben Judah Aaron, 4:199, 12:**233**

Klugman, Jack, 12:**233–234**

Klumel, Meir, 12:**234**

Klutznick, Philip Morris, 4:497, 498, 12:**234–235**

Klutznick National Jewish Museum, 4:15

Di Klyatshe; Oder Tsar Baley Khayim (Abramovitsh), 1:320

Di Klyatshe (Sforim), 21:346

Klytemnestra (Beer), 3:253

Knefler, Frederick, 12:**235**

Kneset Yisrael
    Constitution and, 10:213–214
    first election, 10:213

Knesset, 12:**235–239**, 235t, 236t, 237t
    Agudat Israel, 1:507t
    Amit, Meir, 2:80
    Burg, Avraham, 4:286–287
    Burg, Yosef, 4:287–288
    Eban, Abba Solomon, 6:84
    Eitan, Raphael, 6:279
    Kach, 11:693
    Lapid, Joseph, 12:489
    mishpat Ivri, 14:356

Knesset Assembly Hall (Jerusalem), 11:804

Knesset Foreign Affairs and Defense Committee, 16:358

Knesset main gate (Jerusalem), vol 2: color insert

Kniberg, Irwin Alan. *See* King, Alan

Knieža, Emil, 12:**239**

Kniga moey zhizni (Dubnow), 6:36

Knihy a osudy (Firt), 7:50

Knives, for sheḥitah, 18:434

Knohl, Israel, Job, Book of, 11:348

Knopf, Abraham. *See* Knopf, Alfred A.

Knopf, Alfred A., 12:**239–240**

Knopf, Blanche Wolf, 12:**240**

Knopfler, Mark, 12:**240**

Knorr von Rosenroth, Christian, 11:673, 12:**240–241**

Knowing God (Dorff), 5:755

Knowledge, Tree of, paradise in Eden narrative, 15:624–626

Knox, John, 3:613

Knox, Ronald Arbuthnott, and *Knox Bible*, 3:598, 614–615

Knoytn (Esselin). *See Candlewicks* (Esselin)

Knut, Dovid, 12:**241**

Kobayashi, Masayuki, 12:**242**

Kobe (Japan), 11:82–83, 12:**242**

Kober, Adolf, 12:**242**

Kober, Arthur, 12:**242**

Kobielski, Franciszek Antoni, 12:**242**

Koblenz (Germany), 12:**242–243**

Kobler, Franz, 12:**243**

Kóbor, Tamás, 12:**243–244**

Kobrin (Belarus), 12:**244**

Kobrin, Leon, 12:**244–245**

Kobrin, Moses ben Israel Polier of, 12:**244–245**

Kobrin, Solomon, 12:**245–246**

Kobrin Ḥasidism, 12:**425**

Kobryń (Belarus). *See* Kobrin (Belarus)

Koc, Adam, 15:558

Koch, Adelheid Lucy, 12:**246**

Koch, Edward Irving, 3:736, 12:**246**, 15:224

Koch, Johannes. *See* Cocceius, Johannes

Koch, Kenneth, 12:**246–247**

Kochan, Lionel, 12:**247**

Kochav. *See* Mazeh, Jacob

Kochi (India), 8:279, 12:**247–250**, 15:759, 17:67

    Bene Israel, 3:335–336

    Bombay, 4:51

Kochubiyevski, Boris, 12:153

Kock (Poland), 12:**250**

Kodashim, 12:**250–251**

    commentary on, 3:188

    Me'ilah, 13:**775**

    Menaḥot, 14:27–28

Koder, Samuel Shabdai, 12:**251**

Koder, Shabdai Samuel, 12:**251**

Kodesh Hillulim (Aaron Samuel ben Naphtali Herz ha-Kohen), 1:220

Koebner, Richard, 12:**251**

Koenig, Ghisha, 12:**251**

Koenig, Leo, 12:**251–252**

Koenig, Samuel S., 15:214

Die Koenigin von Saba (opera, Goldmark), 18:762

Koenigsberg (Russia), 12:**252**

Koenigsberg, David, 12:**252–253**

Koenigsberg, Moses, 11:468, 12:**253**

Koenigsberger, Bernhard, 12:**253**

Koenigswarter, Moritz von, 16:340

Koenigswarter family, 12:**253–254**

Koenigtum Gottes (Buber), 4:231

Koenig v. Cohen, 14:359

Koeningsberg, Benjamin, 15:205

Koepfel, Wolfgang Fabricius. *See* Capito, Wolfgang Fabricius

Koerner, Moses ben Eliezer Phoebus, 12:**254**

Koestler, Arthur, 12:**254**

Kof, 12:**254–255**

Kofer. *See* Ransom

Koffka, Kurt, 12:**255**

Koffler, Camilla, 16:126

Koffler, Murray, 12:**255**

Kogan, Abraham, 12:**255**

Kogan, Chaim. *See* Kahana, David

Kogan, David. *See* Kahana, David

Kogan, Koppel. *See* Kahana, Koppel

Kogan, Leonid Borissovich, 12:**256**

Kogan, Moyse, 12:**256**, 15:649

Kogen, David, 12:**256**

Kohath and Kohathites, 12:**256–257**

Koheleth (biblical figure). *See* Solomon (biblical figure)

Koheleth America (Deinard), 5:532

Koheleth Mussar (periodical), 8:437, 12:**257**, 14:36

Kohelet Moshe (Wiener), 21:50

Kohelet publishing house, 4:623

Kohelet Shelomo (London), 13:186

Kohelet Zuta, 14:187

Kohen, Albert, 12:**258**

Kohen, Benjamin, 18:354

Kohen, Benzion Raphael. *See* Frizzi, Benedetto

Kohen, Eleazar ben Ze'ev Wolf, 12:**258**

Kohen, Gershon and Gronen, 4:76

Kohen, Moiz. *See* Tekinalp, Munis

Kohen, Raphael ben Jekuthiel Suesskind, 12:**258–259**

Kohen, Sami, 12:**259**

Kohen family, 12:**257–258**

Kohen-Solal. *See* Solal family

Kohen-Solal, Abraham, 18:751

Kohen-Solal, David, 18:751

Kohen-Solal, Ḥayyim, 18:751

Kohen-Solal, Moses ben Isaac, 18:751

Kohen-Solal, Nathan, 18:751

Kohen-Solal, Nathan ben Saadiah, 18:751

Kohen-Solal, Nissim, 18:751

Kohen- Zedek, Joseph, 12:**259–260**

Kohen-Ẓedek bar Ikhumai. *See* Kohen-Ẓedek bar Ivomai

Kohen-Ẓedek bar Ivomai, 12:**260**

Kohen Ẓedek of Pumbedita, 12:**260**

Kohl, Helmut, 3:727–728

Kohl, Herbert, 12:**260**

Kohlbach, Bertalan, 12:**260–261**

Kohler, Kaufmann, 6:197, 12:**261**

    Einhorn, David (Rabbi), 6:258

    on Oral Law, 15:457

    Ru'aḥ ha-Kodesh, 17:509

Kohler, Max, 9:161

Kohler, Max James, 2:59, 12:**261–262**

Kohn, Abraham, 12:**262**, 15:710

Kohn, Eugene, 12:**262**

Kohn, Feibel, 13:254

Kohn, Hans, 12:**262–263**

Kohn, Jacob, 12:**263**

Kohn, Jindřich, 12:**263**

Kohn, Leo, 12:**263**

Kohn, Maier, 12:**263–264**

Kohn, Moritz. *See* Kaposi, Moritz

Kohn, Ottó. *See* Komoly, Ottó

Kohn, Phinehas. *See* Kohn, Pinchas

Kohn, Pinchas, 2:180, 12:**264**

Kohn, Salomon, 12:**264**, 616

Kohn, Samuel, 12:**264**

Kohn, Theodor, 12:**264**

Kohn, Walter, 4:593, 12:**264–265**

Kohn, Zsigmond. *See* Kunfi, Zsigmond

Kohr, Howard, 2:52

Kohs, Samuel Calmin, 12:**265**

Kohut, Adolf, 12:**266**

Kohut, Alexander, 12:**265–267**

Kohut, George Alexander, 12:**266**

    American Jewish Historical Society, 2:59

Kohut, Rebecca, 12:**266**

Kohut family, 12:**265–267**

Koi, 12:**267**

Koidanov dynasty, 12:**267**

Koidanovo (Belarus), 12:**267–268**

Koidanovo dynasty. *See* Koidanov dynasty

Koidonover, Aaron Samuel ben Israel, 12:**268**

Koidonover, Ẓevi Hirsch, 12:**268**

Koigen, David, 12:**268–269**, 18:731

Koil (Poland). *See* Kolo (Poland)

Koila (Turkey), 12:**269**

Kojetein (Czech Republic). *See* Kojetin (Czech Republic)

Kojetin (Czech Republic), 12:**269**

Kojetín (Czech Republic). *See* Kojetin (Czech Republic)

Kojève, Alexandre, 12:**269**

Kokand (Uzbekistan), 12:**269**

Kokesch, Ozer, 12:**269–270**

Kokhavei Yitzhak (periodical), 14:509

Kokhavi, David ben Samuel, 2:530, 12:**270**

Kokhav Yair (Israel), 12:**270**

Kokhevei Boker (Shazar), 18:426

Kokhva de-Shavit (Slonimski), 18:679

Kokovtsov, Paul Konstantinovich, 12:**270**

Kokovtsov, Pavel, 11:321

Kol, Moshe, 12:**270–271**

Kol Aggadot Yisrael (Levner), 12:744

Kolarovgrad (Bulgaria), 12:**271**

Kol Aryeh (Schwartz), 18:182

Kolatch, Alfred Jacob, 12:**271**

Kolb, Leon, 12:**271–272**

Kolberg (Poland), 12:**272**

Kol Bo, 1:214, 12:**272**

Koldewey, R., 3:24, **24**

Kol Dodi Dofek (Soloveitchik), 18:779

Koldychevo Camp, 12:**272–273**

Koldyczewo camp. *See* Koldychevo camp

Kolel, 12:**273**
> Amsterdam, 2:118
> U.S., 6:199, 202

Kolelim of Palestine, 8:288–289

Kolel Shomerei ha-Ḥomot, 8:288

Kolender, William, 18:15

Kol ha-Am (newspaper), 11:733

Kol ha-Osher ha-Mufraz ha-Zeh (Almog), 1:680

Kolin (Czech Republic), 12:**273–274**

Kolin, Samuel ben Nathan ha-Levi, 12:**274**

Kolin, Solomon Jacob. *See* Ehrenstamm, Solomon Jacob

Kolisch, Ignaz von, 12:**274**

Kolisch, Rudolf, 12:**274**

Kolischer, Heinrich, 12:**274**

Kol Israel, 10:707–708

Kolkata (India). *See* Calcutta (India)

Kol Kitvei (Greeberg), 8:75

Kollek, Teddy, 11:189–190, 12:**274–275**

Kollek, Theodore. *See* Kollek, Teddy

Kollen, Horace M., American Jewish Archives, 2:53

Koller, Carl, 12:**275**

Kollonitsch, Leopold, 12:**275**

Kol Maḥazike Hadas (newspaper), 8:124

Kolman, Arnošt, 12:**275–276**

Kolmar, Gertrud, 12:**276**

Kol Mevaser tsu der Yidisher Folksbibliotek (Shalom Aleichem), 18:381–382

Kol Mevasser (periodical), 7:8, 12:**276**, 13:11, 15

Koln. *See* Cologne

Kol Nevu'ah (Cohen), 5:13

Kolnick, Arthur, 15:650

Kol Nidrei, 12:**276–278**
> Amidah, 2:76
> Anim Zemirot, 2:174
> text, 13:785

Kolnik, Arthur, 12:**278**

Kolo (Poland), 12:**278**

Kolodeje nad Luzici (Czech Republic), 12:**278–279**

Kolodin, Irving, 12:**279**

Kolodny, Moshe. *See* Kol, Moshe

Kolomea (Ukraine). *See* Kolomyya (Ukraine)

Kol Omerim Hodu (Segrè), 18:252

Kol Omer Kera (Caro), 4:492

Kolomyya (Ukraine), 12:**279–280**

Kolonymus ben Kalonymus, 4:170

Kolozsvár (Romania). *See* Cluj (Romania)

Kol Shavat Bat Yehudah (Nevakhovich), 8:441

Kol Simḥah o Nizu'ah ha-Hokhmah (Calimani), 4:363

Koło (Poland). *See* Kolo (Poland)

Kołobrzeg (Poland). *See* Kolberg (Poland)

Kołomyya (Ukraine). *See* Kolomyya (Ukraine)

Koltanowski, George, 12:**280**

Kolthoff, Izaak Maurits, 12:**280–281**

Kol'tsov, Mikhail, 12:**280–281**

Kol u-Vat Kol (Kariv), 11:808

Kolvirt Emes (daily), 11:735

Kol Yehudah (Moscato), 14:515

Kol Zimrah (Eichenbaum), 6:246

Koma, Herz. *See* Coma, Herz

Komarno (Slovakia), 12:**281–282**

Komarno (Ukraine), 12:**282**

Komárno (Slovakia). *See* Komarno (Slovakia)

Komárom (Slovakia). *See* Komarno (Slovakia)

Komáromi Csipkés, György, 12:**282–283**

Komarovsky, Mirra, 12:**283**, 18:736

Komemiyut (Abram), 18:202

Komlós, Aladár, 12:**283**

Komoly, Ottó, 12:**283–284**

Komor, Andras, 12:**284**

Komor, Marcell, 11:73

Komorn (Slovakia). *See* Komarno (Slovakia)

Komotau. *See* Chomutov

Kompert, Leopold, 12:**284–285**, 15:126, 384

Komroff, Manuel, 12:**285**

Komzet, 12:**285**

Kon, Feliks, 12:**286,** 16:347

Konarmiya. See Red Cavalry

Der Kondor (Hiller), 9:116

Konfino, Ẓak, 12:**286**

Konig, Lea, 12:**286**

Konigsberg, Allen Stewart. *See* Allen, Woody

Konin (Poland), 12:**286–287**

Koning, Hendrick, 6:280

Koning Eizenberg Architects Inc., 6:280

Konir, Mordecai (Marcus, Marx) ben Samuel. *See* Meisel, Mordecai ben Samuel

Konitz (Poland), 12:**287**

Konitz, Lee, 12:**287**

Konner, Josef, 14:512

Konner, Lena, 14:512

Konotop (Ukraine), 12:**287–288**

Konrád, György, 12:**288**

Konrad of Megenberg, 3:733

Konsk (Poland). *See* Konskie (Poland)

Końskawola (Poland). *See* Konskowola (Poland)

Końskie (Poland). *See* Konskie (Poland)

Konskie (Poland), 12:**288**

Konskowola (Poland), 12:**288**

Konstantinov, Konstantin, 4:276

Konstanz (Germany). *See* Constance (Germany)

Konvitz, Joseph, 12:**288–289**

Konvitz, Milton Ridvas, 12:**289**

Konzentrationslager KZ. *See* Camps, concentration and extermination

Kook, Abraham Isaac, 8:358, 10:620, 12:**289–293**, 18:297
> Chief Rabbinate, 14:352
> Kabbalah, 11:678
> Mizrachi, 14:390
> nature, 15:35
> Orthodox Judaism and, 15:498, 499
> Ouziel, Ben Zion Meir Ḥai, 15:547
> on peace, 15:703
> redemption, 17:155
> repentance, 17:223
> shemittah decision, 10:621
> soul, immortality of, 19:38

Kook, Hillel, 12:**293**

Kook, Rav, 5:165

Kook, Saul Ḥone ben Solomon Zalman, 12:**293**

Kook, Ẓevi Judah ben Abraham Isaac ha-Kohen, 12:**293**

Kook family, 11:66t

Kopeliovitch, Leonard. *See* Koppett, Leonard

Kopeliovitz, Almog. *See* Almog, Yehuda

Kopeliovitz, Yehuda. *See* Almog, Yehuda

Kopelman, Arie Leonard, 12:**293–294**

Kopelowitz, Lionel, 12:**294**

Kopelson, Zemaḥ, 12:**294**

Kopf, Maxim, 12:**294**

Kopit, Arthur, 12:**294–295**

Koplewitz, Jacob. *See* Keshet, Yeshurun

Koplik, Henry, 12:**295**

Koppel, Heinz, 12:**295**

Koppel, Jacob. *See* Duschinsky, Charles

Koppel, Ross, 18:733

Koppel, Ted, 12:**295–296**

Koppelman, Jacob ben Samuel Bunim, 12:**296**

Koppett, Leonard, 12:**296**

Kopple, Barbara, 12:**296**

Kopplemann, Herman Paul, 12:**296–297**

Köprülü, Ahmed, in Turkey, 18:345–346

Kops, Bernard, 12:**297**

Kopytman, Mark Ruvimovich, 12:**297–298**, 600

Korah, 12:**298–299**, 14:525, 528

Koraḥ, Amram ben Yiḥye, 12:**299–300**

Koraḥ, Ḥayyim ben Joseph, 12:**300**

Koraḥ, Ḥayyim ben Yiḥye, 12:**300**

Koraḥ, Shalom ben Yiḥye, 12:**300**

Koraḥ, Yiḥye ben Shalom, 12:**300**

Koran, 12:**301–304**

    Aaron in, 1:211

    Adam legend, 1:374–375

    Ahl al-Kitāab, 1:546

    Arabic language, 2:297

    Bible and, 3:667–669

    democracy, 2:326

    eschatology, 6:502–503

    Haman, 8:294

    Ḥanīf, 8:321

    Húd, 9:575–576

    Jerusalem holiness, 11:222–223

    Jethro, 11:252

    Kalām, 11:730

    kiss of death, 5:513

    language, 16:263

    Moses, 14:538–539

    New Testament's influence on, 3:668

    Pharaoh, 16:29–30

    poetry, 16:263–264

    Queen of Sheba, 16:765

    Seth in, 18:319

    Solomon, 18:760

    Yahūd, 21:271

    See also Islam

Korban Aharon (Abiob), 1:259

Korban Todah (Ḥarshush), 8:182

Korbon ha-Edah (Fraenkel), 7:143

Korchnoy, Viktor, 12:**305**

Korczak (Wadja), 9:444

Korczak, Janusz, 9:444, 12:**305–306**

Korczak-Marla, Rozka, 12:**306**

Korda, Alexander. *See* Korda, Sir Alexander

Korda, Sir Alexander, 3:717, 12:**306**

Koreff, David Ferdinand, 12:**306–307**

Kore ha-Dorot (Conforte), 5:158

Kore me-Rosh (Aaron Samuel ben Naphtali Herz ha-Kohen), 1:220

Korène, Vera, 12:**307**

Korets (Ukraine), 12:**307–308**

Korets, Phinehas ben Abraham Abba Shapiro of, 12:**308**

Koret School of Veterinary Medicine, 8:743

Koretz, Zvi, 12:**308–309**

Koriat, Asher, 12:**309**

Korine, Ezra, 12:**309**

Koritzinsky, Harry M., Norway, 15:307

Korkis, Abraham Adolf, 12:**309**

Korman, Edward R., 12:**309–310**

Körmendi, Ferenc, 12:**310**

Kormis, Fred, 12:**310**

Korn, Arthur, 12:**310**

Korn, Bertram Wallace, 2:59, 12:**310–311**

Korn, Rachel Häring, 4:426, 12:**311**

Korn, Rochl. *See* Korn, Rachel Häring

Kornberg, Arthur, 12:**311**, 13:9

Kornberg, Hans Leo. *See* Kornberg, Sir Hans Leo

Kornberg, Sir Hans Leo, 12:**311–312**

Korneuburg (Austria), 12:**312**

Kornfeld, Aaron ben Mordecai Baer, 12:**312**

Kornfeld, Joseph Saul, 12:**312–313**

Kornfeld, Paul, 12:**313**

Kornfeld, Zsigmond, 12:**313**

Korngold, Erich Wolfgang, 12:**313**

Kornheiser, Tony, 12:**313–314**

Kornienko, Yurii, 11:322

Kornik (Poland), 12:**314**

Kórnik (Poland). *See* Kornik (Poland)

Kornik, Meir ben Moses, 12:**314**

Kornik, Moses ben Akiva. *See* Kronik, Moses ben Akiva

Kornitzer, Leon, 12:**314**

Korn Jude medals, 13:714

Korobka, 7:23–24, 12:**314–315**

Korolenko, Vladimir Galaktionovich, 3:779, 11:441, 12:**315–316**

Korone (Greece), 12:**316**

Korosten (Ukraine), 12:**316**

Korot Bateinu (Agnon), 1:467–468

Korot ha-ittim li-Yshurun be-Erez Yisrael (Baum), 3:219

Korot Yemei Kedem (Fischer), 7:52

Korsun-Shevchenkovski (Ukraine), 12:**316**

Kortner, Fritz, 12:**316**

Korzec (Ukraine). *See* Korets (Ukraine)

Kos (Greece), 12:**316–317**

Kos (owl, biblical), 15:550

Kosciuszko, Thaddeus, 11:406

Kosciuszko rising, 11:406, 18:703

Kosel (Poland). *See* Kozle (Poland)

Koshar (god), 3:11

Kosher. *See* Kasher

"Kosher Knockout." *See* Salita, Dmitriy

Koshetz, Nina, 12:**317**

Košice (Slovakia). *See* Kosice (Slovakia)

Kosice (Slovakia), 12:**317–319**

Kosice, Gyula, 12:**319**

Kosinski, Jerzy, 12:**319**

København (Denmark). *See* Copenhagen (Denmark)

Koslov (Ukraine). *See* Yevpatoriya (Ukraine)

Koslowsky, Pinhas. *See* Sapir, Pinhas

Kosmin, Barry, 12:**319**

Kosner, Edward A., 12:**319–320**

Kosov (Ukraine), 12:**320–321**

Kosová Hora (Bohemia), 12:**321**

Kosów (Ukraine). *See* Kosov (Ukraine)

Kosow, Sophia. *See* Sidney, Sylvia

Kosściuszko, Tadeusz, 12:**317**

Kossoff, David, 6:438, 12:**321**

Kossoff, Leon, 12:**321**

Kossovski, Vladimir, 12:**321**

Kossowsky, Isaac, 11:378

Kossowsky, Michel, 11:378

Kossuth, Lajos, 12:**321–322**

Kostelanetz, André, 12:**322**

Kosterlitz, Hans, 13:10

Kostomarov, Nikolai Ivanovich, 12:**322**

Köszeg (Hungary), 12:**322–323**

Kotarbińska, Janina, 12:**323**

Kothar. *See* Koshar

Kotik, Ezekiel. *See* Kotik, Yekheskl

Kotik, Yekheskl, 12:**323**

Kotler, Aaron, 1:508, 12:**323**, 441

Kotler, Oded, 8:721

Kotlier, Abraham, parodies of, 15:661

Kotovskoye (Moldova), 12:**324**

Kotovskoye (Russia), 12:**323**

Kotoynti (Shalom Aleichem), 18:385

Kotsk, Menahem Mendel Morgenstern of. *See* Kotsk, Menahem Mendel of

Kotsk, Menahem Mendel of, 12:**324–325**

Kotsker Ḥasidim, 8:424

Kotsuji, Abraham. *See* Kotsuji, Setsuzo

Kotsuji, Setsuzo, 12:**325**

Kottek, Samuel, 11:325

Kottler, Moses, 12:**325**

The Kotzker, 16:104–105

Kouchner, Bernard, 12:**325**

Koufax, Sandy, 12:**325–326**, 15:222

Koufax, Sanford Braun. *See* Koufax, Sandy

Koussevitzky, Moshe, 12:**326**

Koussevitzky, Serge, 12:**326–327**, 13:226

Kovachev, Yordan, 4:276

Kovad I, 3:29–30

Kovadloff, Santiago, 12:**327**

Kovel (Ukraine), 12:**327–328**

Kovner, Abba, 3:434, 8:703, 12:**328–329**, 14:484, 15:667

Kovner, Abraham Uri, 8:300, 725, 12:**329–330**, 15:616

Kovner, B. *See* Adler, Jacob

Kovno (Lithuania). *See* Kaunas (Lithuania)

Kowalski, Max, 12:**330**

Kowalsky, Judah Leib, 12:**330**

Kowno. *See* Kaunas (Lithuania)

Kozakov, Mikhail Emmanuilovich, 12:**330**

Kozenitsy (Poland). *See* Kozienice (Poland)

Kozer, José, 12:**330**

Kozienice (Poland), 12:**330–331**

Kozienice, Israel ben Shabbetai Hapstein, 12:**331**

Kozinski, Alex, 12:**331–332**

Kozle (Poland), 12:**332**

K.P. Pobedonostsev i yeo korrespondenty(Pobedonostsev), 16:249

Kracauer, Isidor, 12:**332**

Kracauer, Siegfried, 12:**332–333**, 18:731

Kraft, Louis, 12:**333**

Kraft, Robert K., 12:**333**

Kraft, Werner, 12:**333–334**

Krakauer, Leopold, 12:**334**

Kraken, Blau, Herbert, 3:742

Krakover, Isaac, 4:199

Kraków (Poland). *See* Cracow (Poland)

Kramer (television character/New Yorker), 15:228

Kramer, Imre. *See* Keszi, Imre

Kramer, Jacob, 12:**334**

Kramer, Larry, 12:**334**, 15:227–228

Kramer, Moses ben David, of Vilna, 12:**334–335**

Kramer, Samuel Noah, 2:371, 12:**335**

Kramer, Stanley E., 12:**335–336**

Kramer, Theodor, 12:**336**

Kramm, Joseph, 12:**336**

Krantz, Judith, 12:**336**

Krantz, Philip, 12:**336–337**

Kranz, Jacob ben Wolf, 6:33, 669, 12:**337**, 461

Kraslava (Latvia), 12:**337**

Krasna, Norman, 12:**337–338**

Krasner, Lee, 12:**338**

Krasnik (Poland), 12:**338–339**

Krasnodar (Russia), 12:**339**

Krasnostav (Poland). *See* Krasnystaw (Poland)

Krasnoye (Ukraine), 12:**339**

Krasnystaw (Poland), 12:**339**

Krasucki, Henri, 12:**339–340**

Kraus, Adolf, 12:**340**

Kraus, Eliyahu, 12:**343**

Kraus, František R., 12:**340**

Kraus, Gertrud, 12:**340**

Kraus, Ivan, 12:**340–341**

Kraus, Karl, 12:**341**

Kraus, Lili, 12:**341**

Kraus, Michael, 12:**342**

Kraus, Moshe, 12:**342**

Kraus, Oskar, 12:**342**

Kraus, Ota B., 12:**342**

Kraus, Paul Eliezer, 12:**342–343**

Krauskopf, Friedrich Salamo, 12:**343–344**

Krauskopf, Joseph, 12:**343**

Krauss, Judah ha-Kohen, 12:**344**

Krauss, Samuel, 12:**344–345**, 14:331
Joseph, Saul Abdallah, 11:417

Krausz, Zsigmond, 12:**345**

Kravis, Henry R., 12:**345–346**, 15:225

Kravitch, Phyllis, 12:**346**

Krayn, Hugo, 12:**346**

Krayzelburg, Lenny, 12:**346–347**

Krebs, Hans Adolf. *See* Krebs, Sir Hans Adolf

Krebs, Sir Hans Adolf, 12:**347**, 13:10

Krefeld (Germany), 12:**347–348**

Krein, Alexander Abramovich, 12:**348**

Kreinin, Meir, 12:**348**

Kreisel, Henry, 4:424, 12:**348**

Kreiser, Jacob Grigoryevich, 12:**348–349**

Kreisky, Bruno, 12:**349–350**, 16:341, 18:706

Kreisler, Fritz, 12:**350**

Kreitman, Benjamin Zvi, 12:**350–351**

Krelenboim, Yosef Aharon. *See* Almogi, Yosef Aharon

Krémègne, Pinchas, 12:**351**

Kremenchug (Ukraine), 12:**351–352**

Kremenets (Ukraine), 12:**352**

Kremenetzki, Eliezer Naruch Ashkenazi. *See* Meyer, Paulus

Kremenetzky, Johann, 12:**352–353**

Kremer, Aaron. *See* Kremer, Arkadi

Kremer, "Alexander." *See* Kremer, Arkadi

Kremer, Arkadi, 4:279, 280, 12:**353**, 18:714

Kremer, Isa, 12:**353**

Kremer, Jonathan, 4:372

Kremnička (Slovakia), 3:120

Kremnitzer, Johanan ben Meir, 12:**353–354**

Krems (Austria), 12:**354**

Krengel, Menahem Mendel, 12:**354**

Kreslavka (Latvia). *See* Kraslava (Latvia)

Krespin, Joshua Abraham. *See* Krispin, Joshua Abraham

Kressel, Getzel, 12:**354**

Kressyn, Miriam, 12:**354–355**

Krestin, Lazar, 12:**355**

Kretchnif family, 8:420

Kretinga (Lithuana), 12:**355**

Kreuzburg (Latvia). *See* Krustpils (Latvia)

Kreuznach (Germany), 12:**355**

Kreymborg, Alfred, 12:**355**

Krichev (Belarus), 12:**355–356**

Kriegel, Annie, 12:**356**

Kriegel, Maurice, 11:326

Kriegel-Valrimont, Maurice, 12:**356**

Krieger, Leonard, 12:**356**

Kriegsgefangenlager. *See* Camps, concentration and extermination

Krim, Mathilde, 12:**356–357**

Krimchak language, 12:**357**

Krimchaks, 12:**357–360**
communities of Jews, Israel (state), 10:297
Krimchak language, 12:357

Simferopol (Ukraine), 18:602
Krinitzi, Avraham, 12:**360–361**
Krinki (Poland). *See* Krynki (Poland)
Krinsky, Henry. *See* Crown, Henry
Kripke, Dorothy, 15:416
Kripke, Myer, 15:416
Kripke, Saul Aaron, 12:**361**
Krips, Josef, 12:**361**
Kris, Ernst, 12:**361–362**
Die Krise der heutigen Maedchenerziehung (Engelmann), 6:410
Krispin, Joshua Abraham, 12:**362**
Kriss, Grigori, 12:**362**
Kristallnacht, 3:449, 9:84, 330–331, *463*, 11:811, 12:**362–363**, 797
   Berlin, 3:449
   Bonn, 4:64
   Brandt, Willy, 4:128
   Dueren, 6:41
   Duesseldorf, 6:42
   Duisburg, 6:43
   Kassel, 11:826
   Leipzig, 12:628
   Schnaittach, 18:147
Kristeller, Paul Oskar, 12:**363**
Kristeller, Samuel, 12:**363**
Kristianpoller family, 12:**363–364**
Kristol, Irving, 12:**364**
Kristol, William, 12:**364–365**
Krivoi-Rog (Ukraine), 12:**365**
Krivoye Ozero (Ukraine), 12:**365**
Di Krizis fun der Yidisher Kolonizatsie in Argentine (Chasanowich), 4:581
Kroch, Jacob Leib ben Shemaiah, 12:**365–366**
Krochmal, Abraham, 12:**366**
Krochmal, Menahem Mendel ben Abraham, 12:**366,** 14:474
Krochmal, Nachman, 4:199, 7:665, 12:**366–368**, 16:95
   Letteris, Meir, 12:667
   miracles, 14:309
   nature, 15:35
   on Shekhinah, 18:442
   Torah, 20:43
Krock, Arthur, 12:**368**
Krojanker, Gustav, 12:**369**
Krol, Abram, 15:650
Kromeriz (Czech Republic), 12:**369**
Kroměříž (Czech Republic). *See* Kromeriz (Czech Republic)
Kronecker, Hugo, 12:**369–370**
Kronecker, Leopold, 12:**370**
Kronenberg, Samuel Leizer, 12:370
Kronenberger, Louis, 12:**370–371**

Kronenberg family, 12:**370**
Kroner, Richard, 12:**371**
Kroner, Theodor, 12:**371**
Kroniek der Jodenvervolging (Herzberg), 9:52
Kronik, Moses ben Akiva, 12:**371**
Kronish, Leon, 12:**371–372**
Kronstadt (Romania). *See* Brașov (Romania)
Krook, Dorothea, 12:**372**
Kroshner, Mikhail Yefimovich, 12:**372**
Krosno (Poland), 12:**372–373**
Kross, Ann, 2:53, 12:**373**
Kroto, Harold Walter. *See* Kroto, Sir Harold Walter
Kroto, Sir Harold Walter, 12:**373**
Krotonsky polden (Livshits), 13:146
Krotoschin (Poland). *See* Krotoszyn (Poland)
Krotoschin, Benjamin, 3:9
Krotoszyn (Poland), 12:**373–374**
Krottingen (Lithuana). *See* Kretinga (Lithuana)
Krouch, Max and Julius, 15:397
Kruger, Barbara, 12:**374–375**
Kruger, Haim, 14:42
Kruger, Paul, 11:378
Krulewitch, Melvin Levin, 12:**375**
Krupnik, Baruch. *See* Karu, Baruch
Krupnik, Igor, 11:323, 324
Krushevan, Pavolaki, 12:**375**
Krustpils (Latvia), 12:**375**
Kruta leta (Kafka), 11:704
Krygier, Rivon, 12:**375–376**
Krymov, Yuri, 12:**376**
Krynki (Poland), 12:**376**
Krystal, Henry, 9:385
Krzemieniec (Ukraine). *See* Kremenets (Ukraine)
Krzepice (Poland), 12:**376–377**
Księg przysłów, przypowieści i wyrażeń przysłówiowych polskich (Adalberg), 1:371
Kuba (Azerbaijan), 3:75, 12:**377**
Kubelsky, Benny. *See* Benny, Jack
Kubie, Lawrence, 12:**377**
Kublin, Hyman, 12:**377**
Kubovy, Aryeh Leon, 12:**378**
Kubowitzki, Aryeh Leon. *See* Kubovy, Aryeh Leon
Kubrick, Stanley, 12:**378**
Kucinsky, Meir, 4:152
Kudrow, Lisa, 12:**378**
Kuenen, Abraham, 12:**378–379**
Kufa (Iraq), 12:**379**
Kugel, Ḥayyim, 12:**379**

Kugel, James L., 1:461, 12:**379–380**
Kuh, Anton, 12:**380**
Kuh, David, 12:**380**
Kuh, Ephraim Moses, 12:**380–381,** 18:579
Kuḥayl, Shukr ben Sālim, 12:**381**
The Kuhbuch (fables), 6:668–669
Kūhīn, Raḥamīm, 15:473
Kūhīn, Salīm Zakī, 15:473
Kuhn, Abraham, 12:381–382
Kuhn, Loeb and Co. *See* Kuhn-Loeb
Kuhn, Thomas, 18:732
Kuhn, Thomas S., 12:**381**
Kuhn-Loeb, 12:**381–382**, 18:130
Kuibyshev (Russian Federation), 12:**382**
Kuk, Abraham Isaac. *See* Kook, Abraham Isaac
Kukizow, David ben Mordecai, 12:**382–383**
Kukizow, Mordecai ben Nisan, 12:382
   Joseph ben Samuel ben Isaac ha-Mashbir, 11:425
   treatises on Karaism, 11:792
Kukizow dynasty, 12:**382–383**
Ku Klux Klan (KKK)
   antisemitism, 2:233
   in Birmingham, 3:713
   in New York City, 15:215
Kulbak, Moyshe, 12:**383**
Kulisher, Joseph, 12:**384**
Kulisher, Michael, 12:**384**
Kulisher, Reuben, 12:**383–384**
Kulisher family, 12:**383–384**
Kulka, Erich, 12:**384**
Kulmhof. *See* Chelmno
Kultur-Lige, 12:**384**
Kulturverein. *See* Verein Fuer Kultur und Wiessenschaft des Judentums
Kultusverein, 12:**385**
Kun, Béla, 12:**385,** 638, 18:705
Kuneitra (Ramat ha-Golan). *See* Qunayṭira, al- (Ramat ha-Golan)
Kunfi, Zsigmond, 12:**385**
Kung Salomo och Morolf (Levertin), 18:761
Kunin, Madelein May, 12:**385–386**
Kunitz, Stanley Jasspon, 12:**386**
Kunschak, Leopold, 4:694
Kunstadt, Isaac ben Eliezer Lipman, 12:**386**
Die Kunst des 20. Jahrhunderts (Einstein), 6:263
Kunstler, William, 12:**386–387**
Kunteres, 12:**387**
Kunteres Beit Avraham (Weinberg), 18:677

Kunteres ha-Semikhah (Ibn Ḥabib), 18:275

Kunteres ha-Teshuvot (Cohen), 5:11

Kunteres Kitvei Kodesh (Weinberg), 18:677

Kunteres Yefalles Nativ (Baranowicz), 3:134

Kuntillet 'Ajrud (Israel), 3:656–657

Kuntres ha-Hitbonenut (Schneersohn), 1:216

Kuntres ha-Hitpa'alut (Schneersohn), 1:216

Kuntres ha-sefekot (Heller), 8:795–796

Kunungen (Elkan). *See The King* (Elkan)

Kunungen i landsflykt (Elkan). *See The King in Exile* (Elkan)

Kunya, 1:333

Kunz, Josef Laurenz, 12:**387**

Kuper, Emil Albertovich. *See* Cooper, Emil Albertovoch

Kuper, G. *See* Singer, Israel Joshua

Kuper, Jack, 12:**387**

Kuper, Simon Meyer, 12:**388**

Kuperman, Diane, 11:470

Kupernik, Abraham, 12:**388**

Kuperstock, Daryl, 4:372

Kupferman, Moshe, 10:696, 698–699, 12:**388**

Kupishki (Lithuania). *See* Kupiskis (Lithuania)

Kupishok (Lithuania). *See* Kupiskis (Lithuania)

Kupiškiai (Lithuania). *See* Kupiskis (Lithuania)

Kupiškis (Lithuania). *See* Kupiskis (Lithuania)

Kupiskis (Lithuania), 12:**388**

Kupleten Komishe un Humoristishe (Mogulesko), 14:418

Kupovetskii, Mark, 11:323, 324

Kuppah, 2:39

Kuppat Ḥolim, 11:762

Kuppat Ḥolim ha-Kelalit, 10:674, 675–676, 677, 679

Kuppot Ereẓ Yisrael, 18:450

Kura (Eblaite deity), 6:86

Kuranda, Ignaz, 12:**389**, 16:340

Kurdistan, 12:**389–393**
    Alroy, David, 2:5–6, 27
    'Amadiya, 2:27–28
    American Joint Distribution Committee, 2:62
    dance, 5:410, 411
    Niego, Joseph, 15:260
    Sheluḥei Ereẓ Israel, 18:452

Kurdistan Jewish community, 3:**138**

Kurds, communities of Jews, Israel (state), 10:297–298

Kurg, Wilhelm Traugott, 12:**374**

Kurland. *See* Courland

Kurnik (Poland). *See* Kornik (Poland)

Kurnik, Meir ben Moses. *See* Kornik, Meir ben Moses

Kurrein, Max, 12:**393**

Kursheedt, Gershom, 13:223

Kursheedt, Isaac B., 15:198

Kursheedt, Israel Baer, 12:**393**

Kursk (Russian Federation), 12:**393**

Kursky, Franz, 12:**393**

Kurth, Ernst, 12:**393**

Kurtz, Aaron, 12:**393–394**

Kurtz, Vernon H., 12:**394**

Kurtzer, Daniel Charles, 12:**394–395**

Kurtzman, Harvey, 6:296, 12:**395**

Kurz, Selma, 12:**395**

Kurzweil, Baruch, 8:686, 729, 12:**395–396**

Kurzweil, Benedict. *See* Kurzweil, Baruch

Kusel, R., 3:43

Kusevitsky, Moshe. *See* Koussevitzky, Moshe

Kush. *See* Cush (Africa); Cush (son of Ham)

Kush (Africa). *See* Cush (Africa)

Kushner, Aleksander Semenovich, 12:**396**

Kushner, Harold S., 11:349, 12:**396–397**

Kushner, Lawrence, 12:**397**

Kushner, Tony (1956-), 12:**397–398**, 15:227

Kushner, Tony (1960-), 12:**398**

Kushnirov, Aaron, 12:**398**

Kussû. *See* Thrones

Kutais (Russia), blood libel in, 3:779

Kutno (Poland), 12:**398–399**

Kutscher, Edward Yechezkel, 8:649, 12:**399**

Kuttenplan (Bohemia). *See* Chodova Plana (Bohemia)

Kutub al-Lugha (Gaon), 13:29–30, 32, 38–39

Kutur-ogly (Ukraine). *See* Berdyansk (Ukraine)

Kuty (Ukraine), 12:**399–400**

Kuwait, Gulf War (1991), 8:130–135

Kuweiti, Salah, 12:**400**

Kuzari (Judah Halevi), 1:251, 7:358, 11:497–500
    commentary on, 6:717
        Solomon ben Judah of Lunel, 18:772

Kuzhmir. *See* Kazimierez dynasty

Kuzkovski, Joseph, 12:**400**

Kuznets, Simon, 12:**400–401**

Kuznetsov, Anatoly, 9:354, 405

Kuznetsov, Eduard, 4:65

Kvaternik, Eugen, 15:698

Kvitko, Leib, 12:**401**

Kwartin, Zavel, 12:**401**

Kwartin, Zevulun. *See* Kwartin, Zavel

Kwasniacy (Drzewiecki), 6:29

Kwasnik, Oscar. *See* Rabinowicz, Oskar K.

Kwasnik, Oskar K. *See* Rabinowicz, Oskar K.

Kybartai (Lithuania), 12:**401**

Kyjov (Czech Republic), 12:**401–402**

Kyra. *See* Kiera

Kyrgyzstan, 12:**402**

Kyustendil (Bulgaria), 12:**402**

L

L (letter), 12:*405*, 13:5

La'am, 8:456–457

La'az, 12:**405–406**

Lab, Joseph ben David ibn. *See* Lev, Joseph ben David ibn

Laban, 11:18–19, 22, 12:**406–407**
    abduction, 1:243
    adoption, 1:415–416

Laban, Rudolf von, 10:694

Laband, Paul, 12:**407**, 547, 551

Labanos, Abraham ben Samuel, 12:407

Labanos, Abraham ben Samuel II, 12:407–408

Labanos family, 12:**407–408**

Labanowski family. *See* Labanos family

Labi, Salomon. *See* Labi, Solomon

Labi, Simeon, 12:**408**

Labi, Solomon, 12:**408**

La Boétie, Etienne de, 12:**408**

Labor, 12:**408–411**
    Austria, Adler, Friedrich, 1:397
    Canada, 4:401–402, 405, 406–407
        Caiserman, Hanane Meier, 4:346
        Heaps, Abraham Albert, 8:508
        women, 4:400
    compulsory, 6:591–592
    corvée, 5:226
    economic doctrines and, 6:116, 12:629
    Ereẓ Israel, *Aḥdut ha-Avodah*, 1:540
    forced, 1:413, 5:226
    Germany, Adler, Georg, 1:397
    Israel (state), 9:547, 10:594–619, 618t
        1980s and after, 10:618–619, 618t

developments, 1970-1980, 10:615–618
employment, 10:614–615
employment trends, 10:293, 533, 535, 539, 545, 557–558, 561, 561t, 576–577, 601, 614–615, 618t
Histadrut, 9:146–150, 10:600–605, 12:532–533
Histadrut ha-Ovedim ha-Le'ummit, 9:150–151
ideology, 10:605–607
juveniles, 10:611–612
labor organizations, 10:594–600, 600–605
labor organizations, 1948-1970s, 10:600–605
labor organizations in pre-war of independence period, 10:594–600
labor relations, 10:607–614, 12:410–411
legislation, 10:608–609, 617–618
newspaper, 10:705
pensions, 10:614
standard work day and vacation, 10:610–611, 627
strikes and lockouts, 10:612–613
unemployment, 10:613–614
unemployment insurance, 10:681
wages and deductions, 10:609–610, 616–617
women, 10:611
Palestine (Mandate)
Aharonovitch, Yosef, 1:537–538
Aḥdut ha-Avodah, 1:540
employment trends, 10:491t, 494, 495t, 500, 520
Histadrut, 10:594–600
legislation and voluntary agreements, 10:607–608
Palestine (Ottoman), Teachers' Association, 10:653
political parties, Israel Labor Party, 10:755
U.S., Chaikin, Sol C., 4:557–558
Labor activism, Harzfeld, Avraham, 8:378–379
Labor Archives and Museum, 2:417
Laboratory Experiments in Direct and Alternating Currents (Litman), 13:129
Labor camps. See Camps, concentration and extermination
Labor laws, 5:153–154, 12:411–419
Bible, 12:411–412

conflict of laws, 5:151, 153
contracts, 12:412–414
economic history, 6:116
employees, 12:412, 413, 415
employers, 12:412–415
Filene, Edward, 7:20
ha'anakah and severance pay, 8:166
Israel (state), 12:415–419
oaths, 15:361
public authority, 16:697, 699
Sabbath, 17:616, 619–620
Labor movement
Austria, 12:625
Ben-Aroya, Avraham, 3:318–319
Ben-Zvi, Izhak, 3:393–394
Ben-Zvi, Raḥel Yanait, 3:395
in Bialystok (Poland), 3:567
Bienenstock, Max, 3:690
Bookbinder, Hyman H., 4:66–67
Borochov, Ber, 4:88–90
Breslaw, Joseph, 4:166–167
cooperatives, 5:208
in Detroit (MI), 5:611
Hardman, Jacob Benjamin, 8:347
Jewish Labor Committee, 11:300–301
Jewish Socialist Verband, 11:314
Landau, Saul Raphael, 12:465
Newman, Pauline, 15:147–148
in New York City, 15:202–206, 209–210, 214
Padway, Joseph Arthur, 15:568
Pat, Jacob, 15:685
Polak, Henri, 16:286–287
Russia, 1:324
Samuel Gompers, 7:749–750
Selekman, Benjamin Morris, 18:260
Shavelson, Clara Lemlich, 18:421–422
Sheinkman, Jacob, 18:438
Sigman, Morris, 18:568
Soviet Union, 5:96–97
See also Bund; Guilds
Labor relations. See Labor movement; Trade unions
Labor unions. See Trade unions
Labor Zionism
body and soul, concept of, 4:31
Canada, 4:406–407
Chasanowich, Leon, 4:581
fraternal orders, 6:712–713
Katznelson, Berl, 12:23–26
Landau, Saul Raphael, 12:465
Shazar, Shneur Zalman, 18:425

Labor Zionist Alliance, 12:419–420
Labour Committees for Human Rights (Canada), 11:780
Labut' (Dostál), 5:762
Lace industry, Kalisz, 11:738–740
La Chaux-de-Fonds (Switzerland), 12:420
Lachish (ancient city), 12:420–421
Lachish ostraca, 12:421–422
Lachish region (Israel), 12:422, 422–423
Lachmann, Peter Julius. See Lachmann, Sir Peter Julius
Lachmann, Robert, 1:439, 12:423–424
Lachmann, Sir Peter Julius, 12:423
Lachower, Yeruḥam Fishel, 12:424–425
Lachowicze, Mordecai ben Noah of, 12:425
Lachrymabilem Judaeorum, 4:277
Lachs, Manfred, 12:425
Lachva (Belarus), 12:425–426
Lachwz (Belarus). See Lachva (Belarus)
Lackritz, Steven. See Lacy, Steve
Lacombe Lucien (Modiano), 14:410
La Comunidad Israelita de El Salvador, 6:369
La Coruña. See Corunna
Lacretelle, Jacques de, 12:426
Lacrosse, 19:144–145
Lacy, Steve, 12:426–427
Ladder of saintliness, 16:116
Ladder of Tyre, 18:601, 20:219
Ladejinsky, Wolf Isaac, 12:427
Ladenburg, Albert, 12:427
Ladenburg family, 12:427
Ladino, 11:302, 12:427–435
Bible translated into, 3:610, 633
biblical commentaries, Me-Am Lo'ez, 13:710–711
Culi, Jacob, 5:328
dialects, 12:431
Greek Jews using, 11:546
history of, 12:427–428
literature, 12:432–433, 13:116–117, 18:295
biblical influence, 3:670
children's, 4:629–630
Joseph story, use of, 11:411
in Ottoman empire, 15:539–540
poetry, 12:432–433
music, 12:434
newspapers, 16:494–496
nineteenth-twentieth centuries, 12:433–434

Ladino, *continued*
Sephiha Haim Vidal, study of, 18:306
topography of, 12:428–431
writing system, 12:431–432
Ladmir (Ukraine). *See* Vladimir Volynski (Ukraine)
Lady of the Manor. See Ba'alat ha-Armon
Laemel, Simon von, 12:**435–436,** 781
Laemmel, Simon von. *See* Laemel, Simon von
Laemmle, Carl, 12:**436,** 14:570, 571
Laetus, 12:**436**
Lafer, Celso, 16:350
Lafer, Horacio, 12:**436,** 16:349, 350
Lagarde, Paul de, 11:558, 12:**436**
Lagash archives, 2:402
Lag ba-Omer, 12:**436–437,** 15:420–421, 18:594, vol. 17: color insert
Lagos (Portugal), 12:**437**
La Guardia, Fiorello Henry, 12:**437–438,** 15:214–215, 216
La Guardia, holy child of, 12:**438**
Laguna, Daniel Israel Lopez, 12:**438–439**
Laharanne, Ernest, 12:**439**
Lahat, Shlomo, 12:**439**
Lahavot ha-Bashan (Israel), 12:**439**
Lahr, Bert, 12:**439–440**
Lahrheim, Irving. *See* Lahr, Bert
Laibach (Slovenia). *See* Ljubljana (Slovenia)
L'airone (Bassani), 3:207
La'itos. *See* Laetus
LAJSA, 12:**440**
Lajta, Béla, 12:**440**
Lakatos, Imre, 12:**440**
Lakatos, László, 12:**441**
Lake Kinneret. *See* Kinneret (Lake)
Lakewood (NJ), 12:**441**
Lakner, Yehoshua, 12:**441–442**
Lamarr, Hedy, 12:**442**
Lamb, Charles, 6:435
Lambert, Aimé, 12:**442**
Lambert, Mayer, 12:**442**
Lambert, Phyllis, 12:**442–443**
Lambert, Raymond Raoul, 12:**443**
Lamdan, Yiẓhak, 12:**443–444**
Lame and blind man parable, 6:647
Lamech, 1:370–371, 12:**444–445**
Lamech, Book of, 12:**445**
Lamed, 12:**445**
Lamed-vav Shirim al Lezer Tsipres (Shamri), 18:395
Lamed vav ẓaddikim, 12:**445–446**

Lamego family, 12:**446**
Lamentations, 14:586–587
of Judah Halevi, 11:494–495
mourning, 14:585–586
Lamentations, Book of, 12:**446–451,** 447, 18:220, 221–222
in the arts, 12:450
authorship and date, 12:449–450
contents and ideology, 12:446–448
in music, 12:450–451
relation to Mesopotamian lamentations, 12:450
style, 12:448–449
Lamentations: Four Folk-Plays of the American Jew (Brody), 4:200
Lamentations Rabbah, 12:**451–452,** 452
La Migresse, Sarah, 13:727
Lamm, Martin, 12:**452–453**
Lamm, Norman, 12:**453**
Lamm, Pavel Aleksandrovich, 12:**453**
Lammlin, Asher. *See* Lemlein, Asher
L'amour en plus (Badinter), 3:49
L'Amour et son Amour (Babilée), 3:21
Lampon and Isidoros, 1:635–636, 12:**453–454**
Lamport, Nathan, 15:205
Lampronti, Isaac Hezekiah ben Samuel, 4:181, 12:**454**
encyclopedias, 6:399
Ferrara, 2:136–137
Lancaster (PA), 12:**454–455**
Lańcut (Poland). *See* Lancut (Poland)
Lancut (Poland), 12:**455–456**
Lánczy, Gyula, 12:**456**
Lánczy, Leó, 12:**456**
Land, Edwin H., 12:**456,** 16:125
Landa, Abram, 12:**456–457,** 16:340
Landa, Liva, 14:301
Landa, Myer Jack, 12:**457**
Land and people interdependence, 5:166–168
Landau (Germany), 12:**457**
Landau, Adolph, 12:**457–458**
Landau, Alfred, 12:**458**
Landau, Annie, 12:**458**
Landau, David, 12:**458**
Landau, Edmund, 12:**458–459**
Landau, Elazar. *See* Rokeaḥ, Elazar ben Shmelke
Landau, Elazar ben Shmelke. *See* Rokeaḥ, Elazar ben Shmelke
Landau, Eleazar ben Eugen, 12:**459**
Landau, Eleazar ben Israel, 12:**459**
Landau, Eliezer ben Samuel, 4:193
Landau, Ezekiel ben Judah, 8:444, 12:**459–461,** 13:5, 15:493
Joseph ben Moses Phinehas, 11:425

retirement age, 12:417
secular education, 8:438
Zerah ben Meir Eidlitz, 6:252
Landau, Gregory Adolfovich, 12:**461**
Landau, Herman, 11:333
Landau, Isaac Elijah ben Samuel, 12:**461–462**
Landau, Israel, 12:**461**
Landau, Israel Jonah ben Joseph ha-Levi, 12:**462**
Landau, Jacob (15th c.), 8:444, 12:**462**
Landau, Jacob (1745/1750–1822), 12:460–461
Landau, Jacob (1892–1952), 11:328, 12:460, **462–463**
Landau, Jacobke. *See* Landau, Jacob
Landau, Jacob M., 12:**463**
Landau, Judah Loeb, 11:378, 12:**463–464**
Landau, Leib, 12:**464,** 553
Landau, Leibush Mendel, 12:**464**
Landau, Leo. *See* Landau, Judah Loeb
Landau, Leopold, 12:**464**
Landau, Lev Davidovich, 12:**464**
Landau, Mark Aleksandrovich. *See* Aldanov, Mark
Landau, Martin, 12:**464–465**
Landau, Moses, 3:631, 12:**465**
Landau, Moshe, 6:250–251, 12:**465,** 14:359
Landau, Nathan, 12:**465**
Landau, Samuel, 12:460–461
Landau, Saul Raphael, 12:**465**
Landau, Shemuel Ḥayyim, 12:**465–466**
Landau, Zishe, 12:**466**
Landauer, Georg, 12:**466**
Landauer, Gustav, 12:**466–467**
Landauer, Meyer Heinrich Hirsch, 12:**467–468**
Landauer, Samuel, 12:**468**
Landers, Ann. *See* Lederer, Esther Pauline
Landes, David Saul, 12:**468**
Landes, Ruth, 2:186, 12:**468–469**
Landesjudenschaft, Boehmische, 12:**469**
Lichtenstadt, Abraham Aaron, 12:797–798
Moravia, 14:474
Landesjudenschaften
Ansbach, 2:180
taxes, 7:24
Landesman, Alter, 12:**469**
Landesman, Rocco, 12:**470**
Landesmann, Heinrich. *See* Lorm, Hieronymus

Landesrabbinerschule (Hungary),
12:**470,** 14:474–475, 16:210

Landflucht movement, in Bohemia,
4:40

Landis, John, 12:**470–471**

The Land is Already Inhabited (Sened).
See Kavar Erez Noshevet (Sened)

Landjudenschaft, 12:**471–472**

Land Law of 1969, 14:362

Land lottery (1909, Jaffa, Israel), vol.
21: color insert

Landman, Isaac, 12:**472–473**
The American Hebrew, 2:49

Land management, Erez Israel, 1:**472–
486**

Landmarks, 1:474–476, 8:448–449,
9:523, 12:**473**

Land of Israel Movement. *See* Ha-
Tenu'ah le-Ma'an Erez Israel ha-
Shelemah

Land of the Hart (Eliav), 6:321

Landon, Michael, 12:**473**

Land ownership
Israel (ancient), 9:184–185
legal aspects, 11:265–266
Middle ages, 6:109–110

Landowska, Wanda, 12:**473–474**

Landrabbiner, 4:63, 12:**474**

Land reclamation projects, Israel
(state), Huleh Valley, 9:582–583,
583, *583*

Land robbery. *See* Hassegat gevul

Landsberg, Michele, 12:**474–475**

Landsberg, Otto, 12:**475,** 551, 16:344,
18:705

Landsberg, Yitzhak. *See* Sadeh, Yitzhak

Landsberg an der Warthe. *See* Gorzow
Wielkopolski

Landsberger, Arthur, 12:**475**

Landsberger, Benno, 12:**475–476**

Landshut (Germany), 12:**476**

Landshut, Siegfried, 12:**476**

Landshuth, Eliezer, 12:**476–477**

Landsleit congregations, 15:207–208

Landsmannschaften, 4:399, 12:**477–
478,** 627, 15:208, 20:327
See also Fraternal societies

Landsofer, Jonah ben Elijah, 6:144,
12:**478**

Landsteiner, Karl, 12:**478**

Land tenancy law, 5:154

Land Without Shade (Sened). *See
Adamah le-Lo Zel* (Sened)

Laney, Joseph, North Carolina, 15:302

Lang, Fritz, 12:**478–479**

Lang, Heinrich, 3:745

Lang, Jack, 12:**479**

Lang, Pearl, 12:**479**

Langallerie, Philippe Gentil de, 12:**479**

Langdon, David, 12:**479**

Lange, Hope, 15:572

Langer, František, 12:**479–480**

Langer, Jiří Mordechai, 12:**480**

Langer, Lawrence L., 12:**480–481**

Langer, Robert S., 12:**481**

Langermann, Max, 12:**481**

Langfus, Anna, 12:**482**

Language and Information (Bar-Hillel),
3:152

Language and languages
Akkadian, 6:284–285
Ammonites, 2:84
Amorites, 2:96
Canaan, 16:119
dialects vs., 11:302
Elamite, 6:284
European, Aramaic influences,
2:356
gender-neutral language in Bible
translation, 3:608
Halakhah, technology, 19:573
Judeo-Alsatian, 2:7
Ladino, 12:427–435
Moabites, 14:400–401
Nazi-Deutsch, 15:42
Neo-Aramaic, 15:70–72
Phoenician, 16:123–124
Samaritans, 17:735
Tower of Babel, 3:19–21
*See also specific languages and
subheading "language" under
country names*

Language and Responsibility
(Chomsky), 4:665

Language Loyalty in the United States
(Fishman), 7:64

Language War, 10:653, 684, 12:**482–
483**

Languedoc (France), 12:**483–484**

Laniado, Abraham ben Isaac, 12:**484**

Laniado, Raphael Solomon ben
Samuel, 12:**484**

Laniado, Samuel ben Abraham, 12:**485**

Laniado, Solomon ben Abraham,
12:**485**

La nokhri tashikh, 14:437

Lansberger, Franz, 2:526

Lansdorfer, Jonah ben Elijah, 12:**478**

Lansing, Sherry Lee, 12:**485**

Lansky, Meyer, 12:**485–486**

Lantos, Robert, 12:**486**

Lantos, Tom, 12:**486–487**

Lanzmann, Claude, 12:**487**

Laodicea (ancient city), 12:**487–488**

Laor, Yitzhak, 12:**488**

Lapapa, Aaron ben Isaac, 12:**488,**
18:345

La Peyrère, Isaac, 3:649, 12:**488–489**

Lapid, Joseph, 12:**489**

Lapid, Shulamit, 8:723, 12:**490**

Lapidot, Alexander Moses, 12:**490**

Lapidot, Ruth, 12:**490**

Lapidus, Morris, 12:**491**

Lapidus, Sidney, 2:59

Lapin, Berl, 12:**491**

Lapin, Bezalel, 12:**491**

Lapin, Daniel, 13:202

Lapin, Israel Moses Fischel, 12:**491**

Lapseki (Turkey), 12:**491–492**

Lapson, Dvora, 12:**492**

Lapwings. *See* Hoopoes

La Québécoite (Robin), 17:354

Laqueur, Walter Ze'ev, 12:**492**

Lar (Iran), 12:**492**

Lara, David ben Isaac Cohen de,
12:**492–493**

Lara, Hiyya Kohen de, 12:**493**

Lara, Isaac Cohen de, 12:**493**

Larin, Mikhail, 3:718

Larin, Yuri, 12:**493–494**

La-Rishonah (Shurer), 8:718

Larissa (Greece), 12:**494**

La Rochelle (France), 17:**357**

L'Arrabiata (Heyse), 9:87

The Larry Sanders Show (television
show), 18:396

Larsa archives, 2:402

Larsen, Terje, 15:598

Larsfeld, Paul F., 18:731

Larsson, Zenia, 18:93

La Ruche, 15:649

Lasansky, Mauricio, 12:**494**

The Lasansky Method, 12:**494**

Lasar Segall Museum (Brazil), 18:33

Lasdun, Denys. *See* Lasdun, Sir Denys

Lasdun, Sir Denys, 12:**494**

Laser, Simon Menahem, 8:305

Laserson, Max, 12:**494–495**

Lashkowitz, Herschel, 15:304

Lashon, 11:530

Lashon ha-Ra, 12:**495**

Lask (Poland), 12:**495–496**

Lask, Emil, 12:**496**

Lasker, Albert David, 1:428, 12:**496–
497**

Lasker, Eduard, 3:726, 12:**497,** 16:344

Lasker, Emanuel, 4:603, 604, 605,
12:**497**

Lasker, Florina, 12:**497**

Lasker, Loula Davis, 12:**497**

Lasker, Morris, 12:496
Lasker family, 12:**496–497**
Lasker-Schueler, Else, 12:**498,** 18:590
Laski, Esther Pearl, 12:499
Laski, Harold, 18:706
Laski, Harold Joseph, 12:**499,** 16:342
Laski, Nathan, 12:498
Laski, Neville Jonas, 12:498
Laski family, 12:**498–499**
Laskin, Bora, 12:**499–500,** 16:341–342
Laskov, Ḥayyim, 12:**500,** 534
Lasky, Jesse Jr., 12:500
Lasky, Jesse L., 12:**500–501,** 660, 14:570
Lassalle, Ferdinand, 12:**501–502,** 16:344, 18:705
Lassar, Oscar, 12:**502**
Lassar-Cohn. *See* Cohn, Lassar
Lassaw, Ibram, 12:**502–503**
Lasser, Louise, 12:**503**
Lasson, Adolf, 12:**503**
Last Day in Vietnam (Eisner), 6:278
The Last Jew. See Di Familye Tsvi; Ha-Yehudi ha-Aḥaron
Lastman, Melvin Douglas, 12:**503–504,** 16:341
The Last of the Just (Schwarz-Bart), 9:410–411, 18:191
The Last Reckoning. See Dos Letste Sakhakl
The Last Stand of the Aryan Peoples against Judaism. See Der Verzweiflungskampf der arischen Voelker mit dem Judentum
The Last Stop, 9:440
The Last Way (painting; Kuzkovski), 12:400
Last Winter. See Ḥoref Aḥaron
The Last Worker (Sobol), 18:702
Las Vegas (NV), 12:**504–505,** 15:127–128
Laszczower, Joshua, 4:199
Laszlo, Philip Alexius de Lombos, 12:**505**
Late California Notes. See Tarziu: insemnari californiene
Lateran Councils III, IV, 4:716–717, 12:**505–506**
    Jewish badges, 3:45, 46, 7:152
    sumptuary laws, 6:14
Lathyrus. *See* Ptolemy VIII
Latif, Isaac B. Abraham ibn, 11:607, 12:**506–507,** 20:40
Latin, Howard, 6:453
Latin America, 12:**507–517,** 512*t*
    agriculture, Jewish, 1:500–501
    American Jewish Committee, 2:55

antisemitism, 2:235, 238, 12:511
B'nai B'rith activities, 4:16
Caribbean, 12:508
children's literature, 4:635
colonial period, 12:507–508
communal organizations, 12:510–512
community organization and structures, 5:113–114, 115*t*, 116*t*, 120*t*
Conservative Judaism, 5:176
Crypto-Jews, 12:507–508
demography, 12:512
education, 12:512–513
emancipation, 12:508
foreign policy and relations with Israel, 10:260, 263, 266, 12:515–516
immigration to, 2:41, 45–46, 12:477, 508–509
journalism, 11:469–470, 16:496–497
    Jewish, 12:513–515
laws and legal systems, 12:554–555
museums, 14:634
ORT, 15:489, 491
politics, 16:349–350
publishing, 16:718
socialism, 18:709
socioeconomic status, Jewish, 12:509–510
Yiddish education, 6:189
Yiddish theater, 19:681
youth movements, 9:717*t*, 718–719
Zionism, 12:512, 21:593–595
Latin American Jewish Studies Association. *See* LAJSA
Latin America Training and Research Center for the Development of Jewish Communal Leadership (LEATID), 2:64
Latin language, 8:647–648
    grammarians, 14:753
    Jewish languages and, 11:301
    linguistics, 8:58
    in Mishnaic Hebrew, 8:647–648
    rabbincal knowledge of, 8:57–59
    Spinoza's works of Hebrew grammar, 13:56
    translations of Bible
        Council of Trent on authenticity of, 3:612
        Old Latin Bible (OL), 3:598, 609
        Vulgate, 3:598, 666
Latin literature
    Claudian, 4:751–752

Josippon and, 11:461
Latino. *See* Judeo-Italian language; Ladino
Latino literature, Ottoman empire, 10:780
Latrun (Israel), 12:**517–518**
Latteiner, Joseph, 12:**518**
Lattes, Abraham ben Isaac, 12:**518**
Lattes, Adolfo, 14:408
Lattes, Bonet, 12:**518–519**
Lattes, Dante, 12:**519,** 15:564
Lattes, Isaac ben Jacob, 12:**519**
Lattes, Isaac Joshua, 12:**519**
Lattes, Judah, 12:**519–520**
Lattes family, 12:**518**
Latvia, 12:**520–524,** 520*t*, *521*
    Braun, Abraham, 4:137
    courts, Laserson, Max, 12:494–495
    emancipation, 6:385
    He-Ḥalutz, 8:759–760
    Holocaust, 12:522–523, 13:252
        Daugavpils, 5:442
        Jaunijelgava, 11:95
        Jekabpils, 11:116
        Jelgava, 11:118
        Kraslava, 12:337
        Krustpils, 12:375
        Liepaja, 12:818
        Ludza, 13:252
        Riga, 17:300
        Tukums, 20:174
        Ventspils, 20:505
    minority rights, 12:521, 522, 14:290
    politicians
        Dubin, Mordecai, 6:31–32, 12:521
        Meisel, Noah, 12:521, 13:789–790
        Mintz, Paul, 12:521
        Nurock, Mordechai, 12:521
Latzky-Bertholdi, Jacob Ze'ev Wolf, 12:**524**
Lau, Israel Meir, 12:**524–525**
Laub, Gabriel, 12:**525**
Lauda (Germany), 3:43
The Lauda and the Origins of the Italian Melodic Style. See La Lauda e i primordi della melodia italiana
La Lauda e i primordi della melodia italiana (Liuzzi), 13:143
Laudanum, 12:**525**
Lauder, Estée Mentzer, 12:**525,** 15:226
Lauder, Leonard, 12:525
Lauder, Robert, 15:224
Lauder, Ronald, 12:**525–526**

Lauer, Chaim, 3:688

Laufbahn, Yitshak, 12:**526**

Lauingen (Germany), 12:**526**

Laun (Czech Republic). *See* Louny (Czech Republic)

Laura and Alvin Siegal College of Judaic Studies, 12:**526**

Lauren, Ralph, 12:**526–527**

Lauren Bacall by Myself (Bacall), 3:30

Laurence, William L., 12:**527**

Laurents, Arthur, 12:**527–528**

Lausanne (Switzerland), 12:**528**

Lautenberg, Frank R., 12:**528–529**, 15:141, 687

Lauterbach, Asher Zelig, 12:**529**

Lauterbach, Edward H., 12:**529**, 15:211

Lauterbach, Jacob Zallel, 2:47, 12:**529**

Lauterpacht, Elihu, 11:233

Lauterpacht, Hersch. *See* Lauterpacht, Sir Hersch

Lauterpacht, Sir Hersch, 12:**530**, 548, 550, 15:326

Lautman, Dov, 12:**530**

Laval, Pierre, 12:**530–531**

Lavater, Johann Caspar, 5:696, 14:35, 16:93

Laver, 2:492–493

L'Aveu-Dans l'engrenage du proces de Prague (London), 13:184

Lavi (Israel), 12:**531**

Lavi, Shelomo, 12:**531**

Lavi, Theodor, 12:**531–532**

Lavi, Yoḥanan. *See* Loewenson, Jean

Lavie, Raffi, 10:696, 12:**532**

Lavin, Linda, 12:**532**

Lavon, Pinḥas, 4:346, 10:225, 12:**532–533**

   Ben-Gurion, David, 3:347

   Eshkol, Levi, 6:506

The Lavon Affair, 6:506, 10:431–432, 435–436, 437, 12:**533–534**

Lavrovy (Slonimsky), 18:679

Lavry, Marc, 12:**534–535**

Law, Islamic. *See* Islamic law

Law, Liberty and Psychiatry (Szasz), 19:402–403

Law and grace, 4:683

Law and Literature (Cardozo), 4:466

Law and morality, 12:**535–541**

   biblical literature, 12:535

   morality as source of law, 12:535–536

   morality as source of liability, 12:536–537

   moral sanctions, 12:537–539

   role of *Bet Din*, 12:539–540

Lawāni, Da'ud, 12:**541**

Lawat, Abraham David ben Judah Leib, 12:**541**

Lawn bowling, 19:145

Law of Obligations. *See* Obligations, law of

Law of Return, 10:215, 340, 414–415, 626, 632, 636–637, 12:**541–545**, 14:212, 19:170

   demography and, 5:558

   mishpat Ivri, 14:355

Law of the House. See Torat ha-Bayit

Lawrence, David, 12:**545**

Lawrence, Gerald, 12:**545**

Lawrence, M. Larry, 18:15

Lawrence, Steve, 12:**545–546**

Lawrence, Thomas Edward, 12:**546**

Laws and legal systems, 13:212–215

   613 commandments, 5:74t–84t, 85

   Abrabanel, Isaac ben Judah, 1:278–279

   acquisition, 1:359–363

   administration, 14:347

   admission, 1:410–411

   adultery, 1:425–427

   advertising, misrepresentation, 5:188

   agency, 1:449–454

   agunah, 1:509–520

   agunot, 5:173

   antisemitic, Aargau, 1:208

   Apoteke, 12:815–816

   Austria, Middle Ages, 10:820

   Babylonian Talmud, divine punishment, 5:709

   benei ha-Ir, 12:605

   Bet Hillel, 3:530–533

   Bet Shammai, 3:530–533

   Bible, 12:535

      shomerim, 18:513–514

   bonds of indebtedness, 5:154–155

   breach and compensation, 5:195

   bribery, 4:175–177

   Cairo trial, 4:346

   Canada, 12:499–500

   capital punishment, 4:445–451, 9:507

   captives, ransoming of, 4:456–457

   civil laws

      conflicts, 5:154

      divine punishment, 5:709–710

      domiciles and communal enactments, 5:742

      in Jewish law, 18:52

      theft and robberies, 19:686–687

   classification, 14:347–348

Codification of Law, 4:765–781

commandments, reasons for, 5:85–90

Committee on Jewish Law and Standards, 5:173, 174

compounding offenses, 5:123–124

concubine, 5:133–136

conditions, 5:136–139

confessions, 5:147–148

confiscation, expropriation, forfeiture, 5:150–151

conflict of laws, 5:151–157

consideration, 5:190–191

constitutional law, 12:407

construction and planning, 16:215–219

consumer protection, 5:184–189

contempt of court, 5:189

   imprisonment and, 9:744

copyright, 8:450–451, 453

corporation, 12:604–608

crime, 5:291–298, 14:347

crimes, imprisonment and, 9:744–745

criminal law, theft and robberies, 16:332, 19:687–688

customs, influence of, 5:192–193

damage, evidentiary, 7:504

death and, 5:512–513

debt, 12:812–817

dietary, 5:81t–82t

dina de-malkhuta dina, 5:663–669

divine punishment, 5:708–710

divorce, 7:620–621

documents, shetar, 18:467–471

dowries, 5:769–772

Duran law responsum, 5:154, 156

Dustan version, 6:66

Eichmann trial, 6:250–251

Elon approach, 6:367–368

embryo rights, 6:391–392

English case law, 14:356, 358

environmental, 5:166–168, 6:452–453

Epstein approach to study, 6:476

Familiants Laws, 4:39

family law, Takkanot, 19:449–450

floating charge, 12:817

foreign law, 14:349–351

gambling, 7:368–370

gentile courts, shetar, 18:468

gentile status, 7:486

gerama and garme, 7:502–504

gifts, 5:138–139, 7:590–592

Gittin, 7:620–621

Good Faith principle, 5:196–197

Laws and legal systems, *continued*
Hafka'at She'arim, 8:196–198
Halakhic literature, ḥumra, 9:600
ḥaliẓa, 12:726–729
Hammurapi, Code of, 8:310
Hapsburg empire, Raphael Joel as first Jewish advocate in, 11:364
Hasmonean bet din, 8:445
hassegat gevul, 8:448–453
Havurat Zedakah, 12:605–606
ḥazakah, 8:486–491
hazards prevention, 5:167
hekdesh, 12:605
ḥerem, 9:10–16, 21
ḥerem bet din, 9:16
Ḥerem ha-Ikkul, 9:17
ḥerem ha-Yishuv, 9:17–18
ḥerem setam, 9:18–19
homicide, 9:506–507
husbands and wives, maintenance, 13:399–403
illegal contracts, 5:193–194
impurity, 12:737–738
incest and, 9:755–756
informers, 9:783–785
Inquisition, 9:800–803
intellectual property rights, 8:451, 453
international, 6:739, 12:425, 637–638
Israel
    divine punishment, 5:710
    dowries, 5:771–772
Israel (Mandate), mishpat Ivri, 14:354
Israel (Ottoman), Berurei Averah/ Averot, 3:492
Israel (state), 10:403–423
    attorney general, 10:422
    bar, the, 10:422
    Chief Rabbinate and councils, 10:634–636
    comptroller, state, 10:397–398, 422–423
    constitution and basic laws, 10:394, 397–398, 429, 434, 453, 623–624
    Constitution and Bill of Rights, 10:410–412
    courts, 10:418–420, 634–636, 637
    and debt, imprisonment for, 9:751–752
    Declaration of Independence, 10:409–410
    human dignity and freedom laws, 9:585–586, 587

imprisonment and, 9:745–747
incest and, 9:756
Islam and, 10:647, 649
judges, 10:420–422
labor, 12:415–419
Lapidot, Ruth, 12:490
Law of Return, 10:215, 340, 414–415, 626, 632, 636–637
legislation, 10:410, 413–418, 657
limitation of actions, 13:24–25
maintenance, 13:401–403
mamzer, 13:445
marriage, prohibited, 13:576
and marriages, rights in, 9:638–639
mishpat Ivri, 14:354–358
mistakes, 14:369
national health insurance, 10:676
official position of Jewish law, 14:354–356
police, 10:423
position of Jewish law, 14:354–358
rabbinical courts, 14:352–353, 362
reform of civil law, 10:415–416
reform of criminal law, 10:416
Religious Affairs Ministry, 10:634
religious courts, 10:419–422
sales, 17:687
shomerim, 18:515–518
status of Jewish law, 14:358–362
theft and robbery, 19:688
translation of Mandatory statues to Hebrew, 10:415
Italy, 10:809
Judaism, development of concept of, 11:517
Judeo-Arabic culture and, 11:541–542
kelal, 12:603–604
"King's law," punishments, 16:737
labor law, 5:153–154, 12:411–419
land robbery, 8:449
land tenancy, 5:154
Law of Moses, 13:392
lease and hire, 12:568–574
legal analysis, Shi'buda de-Rabbi Nathan, 18:474–475
legal maxims, 12:603–604

legal person, 12:604–608
leket, shikhḥah, and pe'ah, 12:631–632
leprosy laws, 12:650–653
liability, 12:536–537, 773
liens and debts, 12:812–817
loans, 13:149–152
    interest-bearing, 5:185
lost property, 13:212–215
lotteries, 7:369–370
love of neighbor, 13:231
ma'aseh, 13:308–313
Magdeburg law, 13:336
majority rule, 13:414–417
mamzer, 13:442–445
mandatory commandments, 5:74t–78t
maritime law, 13:546–547
marriages, 13:569–574
    marriage, prohibited, 13:575–576
    monogamy, 14:447–448
matrilineal descent, 5:174–175
medicine and, 13:738–757
Middle Ages, Magdeburg law, 13:336
Miller case, 5:156
minority opinions, 13:416–417
mistaken transactions, 5:186–188
mistakes, 14:366–369
monopoly infringement, 8:452–453
Moses, 14:528–529
    Maimonides, Moses, 13:392
natural vs. divine, 16:90
negligence and liability, 20:62–64, 65, 66
Niddui vs. ḥerem, 9:13–15
Noachide laws, 15:284–287
novellae of Justinian I concerning Jews, 11:579–580
obligations, 5:190, 191–192, 192–193
oral, 8:252–253
overreaching, 5:186
ownership, 16:564–565
ownership and possession, 8:486–491
Palestine (Mandate), 10:405–409, 412–413
    Jewish courts, 10:621–622
Palestine (Ottoman), 10:403–405, 412
    Jewish courts, 10:620
partnership, 5:154
Passover, 12:605, 16:5–6
penalties, theft and robbery, 19:689

performance, 5:194–195

personal status, 14:354

pleas, 16:228–231

pledges, 16:231–236

Poland, 12:425

police offenses, 16:331–332

pollution, 5:166–168

post-Talmudic period, limitation of actions, 13:23–24

pre-Sinaitic laws, 15:286

presumptions, 8:489, 490–491

price-fixing, 8:196

profiteering, 5:185, 8:196–198

prohibitions, 5:78t–84t

property, 12:536, 16:563–565

property and obligations, public authority, 16:697–698

prosbul, 16:586–587

punishment, 16:736–737

rabbinical courts
    Morocco, 14:504
    theft and robbery, 19:689

rape, 6:677

reasonable standard, 5:167–168

reshut, 17:227

rights, 6:74–75
    proprietary, 16:564–565

rites and rituals, mishpat Ivri, 14:333–334

Roman period, limitation of actions, 13:23

Rosh Ha-Shanah, 17:465–466

Russia
    attorneys, 12:553–554
    deputies of the Jewish people, 5:591
    historians, 12:649
    May laws, 12:508–509, 13:701–702, 15:579
    restricting Jewish settlement and businesses, 13:701–702

Sabbath, 12:761, 17:619–620

Sabbatical Year and Jubilee, 17:629–630
    ancient Near East, 17:625–626

sales, 17:683–684

separation of powers, 18:291–292

Sephardi, ma'amad, 13:305

servitudes, 9:216, 18:317–318

sevarah, 18:322–323

sexual relations, illicit, 12:739

Sha'arei Shevu'ot, 18:335

shalish, 18:373–374

Shema, reading of, 18:455

shomerim, 18:513–518

Sicily, Dienchelele, 5:648–649

Sikarikon, 18:573–574

Spain, Berurei Averah/Averot, 3:492

states, theft and robbery, 19:689–690

stipulation, 5:193, 194

stolen property, 5:77t–78t

substantive law, Shi'buda de-Rabbi Nathan, 18:474

succession and inheritance, 19:284–289

Supreme Court, mamzer, 13:445

suretyship, 19:317–322

Talmud, limitation of actions, 13:22–23

talmudic literature, ḥumra, 9:600

taxation, 19:534–558
    adjudication and evidence, 19:552–553
    Bible, 19:534
    date of accrual of liability, 19:543–545
    ethics of tax payments, 19:556
    Halakhah, 19:557–558
    Israel, 19:558–559
    post-Talmudic period, 19:536–539
    principles of interpretation, 19:554–555
    property, 19:540–543
    Talmud, 19:534–536
    tax appeals, 19:551–552
    tax assessment, 19:539–540, 548–551
    tax collection procedures, 19:555–556
    tax relief and immunity, 19:545–548

teaching, 6:164

tenancy rights, 8:449–450

tort, 7:502–504

torts, 5:78t, 12:773, 20:63–67

trespassing, 8:449–450, 450–451

unjust enrichment, 20:413–414

usury, 20:437–443

widows, 21:**40–45**

wills, 5:156, 21:**65–74**

witnesses, 21:**115–125**

written, 8:252

ye'ush, 21:322–323

yuḥasin, 21:**423–426**

See also Halakhah; Laws and legal systems; Mishpat Ivri; Natural law; Practice and procedure; Rites and rituals; *specific laws and classes of laws; specific legal cases*

Laws and Regulations for all the Ashkenazi Synagogues in the British Empire (Adler), 1:405

Law's Empire (Dworkin), 6:74

Laws of Edward the Confessor, 18:317

Lawson, John Howard, 12:**547**

Lawson family, 12:**546–547**

Lawton, Samuel T., 12:**547**

The Lawyer (Molnár), 14:427

Lawyers, 12:**547–557**
    Adams, Arlin Marvin, 1:379
    Australia, 12:456–457, 548
    Austria, 12:548–549
    Canada, 12:549
    England, 12:550, 764
    France, 12:550–551
    Germany, 12:551
    Hamon, Leo, 8:312–313
    Handler, Milton, 8:319
    Harman, Jane, 8:360
    Harris, Sydney, 8:364–365
    Hart, Daniel, 8:369
    Hauser, Rita Eleanor, 8:463–464
    Hausner, Gideon, 8:464
    Hays, Arthur Garfield, 8:478
    Hays, Daniel Peixotto, 8:478–479
    Hungary, 12:551–552
    Israel, 12:557, 774
    Italy, 12:552
    Jewish lawyers in history, 12:547–548
    Levi, Paul, 12:691
    Levin, Lewis Charles, 12:710
    Levinson, Salmon Oliver, 12:723
    Netherlands, 12:552–553
        Hartog, Levie de, 8:378
    Neumeyer, Karl, 15:124
    Poland, 12:553, 804
    Rankin, Harry, 17:91
    Ratner, Marc Borisovich, 17:113
    Rauh, Jospeh L., Jr., 17:115–116
    Rayner, Isidor, 17:127
    Redlisch, Joseph, 17:159
    Rice, Isaac Leopold, 17:285
    Riegelman, Harold, 17:293
    Rifkind, Simon Hirsch, 17:298–299
    Robinson, Nehemiah, 17:356
    Rosenberg, James Naumburg, 17:437
    Rosenblatt, Bernard Abraham, 17:440
    Rosenblatt, Sol Arieh, 17:442
    Rosendale, Simom Wolfe, 17:444
    Rostow, Eugene Victor Debs, 17:475

Lawyers, *continued*
  Rubenstein, Harold Frederick, 17:516–517
  Rubinstein, Hilary Michael, 17:516–517
  Rubinstein, Michael, 17:516
  Russia, 12:553–554
  Silkin, Lewis, First Baron, 18:**581**
  South Africa, 12:554–555
    Alexander, Bernard, 1:622
  South America, 12:554–555
  U.S., 5:548, 12:555–557, 614, 622
  USSR, 12:553–554
  See also Attorneys
La-Yesharim Tehillah (Play), 8:714
Laylah be-Mai (Yehoshua), 8:721
Layton, Irving, 4:423, 12:**557–558**
Laza of Frankfurt, 12:**558**
Lazar, David, *Nowy Dziennik*, 15:326
Lazar, Hirsch. *See* Teller, Zevi Lazar
Lazar, Samson, 12:**558**
Lazar ben Pedat. *See* Eleazar ben Pedat
Lazard, Alexandre, 12:558
Lazard, Elie, 12:558
Lazard, Gilbert, Judeo-Persian literature, 11:558
Lazard, Simon, 12:558
Lazard family, 12:**558**
Lazare, Bernard, 6:18, 12:**558**, 18:710
Lăzăreanu, Barbu, 12:**559**
Lazareff, Pierre, 12:**559**
Lazaron, Morris Samuel, 12:**559**
Lazarsfeld, Paul F., 12:**559–560**
Lazarus, Aaron, 15:302
Lazarus, Emma, 6:395, 12:**560–561**, 13:298, 15:202
Lazarus, Fred, 12:560
Lazarus, Fred, Jr. (1884-1973), 12:560
Lazarus, Jeffrey, 12:560
Lazarus, Mel, 12:**561**
Lazarus, Moritz, 12:**561–562**, 16:96
  duty, 6:72
  Kantian ethical imperative and, 11:770
  soul, immortality of, 19:38
Lazarus, Moses, 15:200
Lazarus, Nahida Ruth, 12:**562**
Lazarus, Ralph, 12:560
Lazarus, Simon, 12:560
Lazarus family, 12:**560**
Lazerowitz, Morris, 12:**562**
Lazne Kynzvart (Czech Republic), 12:**562–563**
Lazurick, Robert, 12:**563**
Lea, Henry Charles, 12:**563**
Leachman, Cloris, 12:**563**

Lead, 14:126, 128
Leadership Conference on Civil Rights, 3:736
Leaf, Hayim, 12:**563**
League for Human Rights (Canada), 4:18
League for Israel, The American Jewish. *See* The American Jewish League for Israel
League for Jewish-Arab Rapprochement and Cooperation, 3:703
League of Czech Jews. *See* Svaz čechů-Židů
League of Nathans (Sherman), 18:465
League of Nations, 12:**564–566**
  Bernheim Petition, 3:475
  Dugdale, Blanche Elizabeth Campbell, 6:42
  holy places in Israel and, 9:503
  numerus clausus, 15:342
Leah (biblical figure), 12:**566–567**
  adoption, 1:415
  Dinah and, 5:669
  Jacob and, 11:17, 19, 22, 12:406–407
  as Matriarch, 15:691
  See Also Matriarchs
Leah, the Forsaken (Mosenthal), 14:521
Le'an? (Feierberg), 6:730, 732
Leander, Pontus, 13:58
Leão, Gaspar de, 12:**567**
Leap year, 12:**567**
Lear, Evelyn, 12:**567–568**
Lear, Norman, 12:**568**
Learned societies, 18:**722–724**
Learn to Do Well. See Limdu Heitev
Lease and hire, 12:**568–574**
  acquisition and rent of property, 12:568
  contract and obligations, 12:569–570, 572
  contract termination, 12:571
  exemption and liability, 12:570–571
  lease in Jewish law, 12:573
Leather industry and trade, 12:**574–577**
LEATID. *See* Latin America Training and Research Center for the Development of Jewish Communal Leadership
Leaven. *See* Hamez
Leavetaking as Exile (Weiss), 20:736
Leavis, Queenie Dorothy, 12:**577**
Leavitt, Moses A., 12:**577**
Leb, Joseph ben David ibn. *See* Lev, Joseph ben David ibn
Lebanon, 2:301, 313, 314, 12:**577–581**, 578
  Arafat, Yasser, 2:333–334

  borders post War of Independence, 10:214, 12:579
  cedar, 4:535
  IDF withdrawal, 10:250
  invasion of, European Economic Community and, 6:565
  Jubayl, 11:473
  Palestine Liberation Organization and, 12:581, 15:592, 593, 594
  terrorist attacks from, 10:247–248, 12:584–586
  war with Israel, 10:239–241, 260, 447–448, 472–473, 12:580, 581–584
Lebanon War, 10:239–241, 260, 447–448, 472–473, 12:**581–589**
  aftermath, 12:589
  ceasefire, 12:582–584
  Eitan, Raphael, 6:279
  Occupied Territories and, 10:722
  operations and warfare, 12:584–588
  political origins, 12:581–582
  Sharon, Ariel, 18:416–417
  terrorist attacks by PLO, 12:582–584
  U.S. and, 17:135–136
  See also Hizbolla
Le Bé, Guillaume, 12:**589**, 15:641
Lebeau, Samuel S. *See* Leibowitz, Samuel Simon
Lebedeff, Aaron, 12:**589**
Der lebendige Heine im Germanischen Norden (Berendsohn), 3:409
Lebensboym, Rosa. *See* Margolin, Anna
Lebensohn, Abraham Dov, 12:**589–590**, 15:618
Lebensohn, Adam ha-Kohen. *See* Lebensohn, Abraham Dov
Lebensohn, Micah Jospeh, 12:**590–591**, 15:618
Lebert, Sigmund, 12:**591**
Lebhar, Jacob, 5:542
Lebhar family. *See* Delmar family
Lebo-Hamath, 11:699, 12:**591–592**
Lebork (Poland), 12:**592**
Lebović, Djordje, 12:**592**
Lebow, Fred, 12:**592–593**
Lebrecht, Fuerchtegott, 12:**593**
Lebrowitz, Barney. *See* Levinsky, Battling
Lec, Stainslaw Jerzy, 12:**593**
Lecache, Bernard, 12:**593**, 15:629
Lecca, Radú, 12:**593–594**
Lecce (Italy), 12:**594**
Leçons d'Hygiène (Albu), 1:596
Lectures on Jewish Philosophy in the Middle Ages (Eisler), 6:275

Lectures on Sacred Poetry of the Jews (Lowth), 16:256

Lectures on Structural Poetics. See Lektsii po struktural'nou poetike (Lotman)

Lectures on the Religion of the Semites (Smith), 18:689

Leczna (Poland), 12:**594**

Leczyca (Poland), 12:**594–595**

Leda, Eduard, 12:**595–596**

Ledeen, Hyman, 12:**596**

Leder, Phil, 13:11

Leder, Rudolph. *See* Hermlin, Stephan

Lederberg, Joshua, 12:**596**, 13:9

Lederer, Abraham, 12:**596**

Lederer, Anna Marie. *See* Rosenberg, Anna Marie Lederer

Lederer, Eduard, Jindrichuv Hradec, 11:337

Lederer, Esther Pauline, 11:469, 12:**596–597**

Lederer, Francis, 12:**597**

Lederer, Ignác. *See* Gábor, Ignác

Lederer, Jerome F., 12:**597**

Lederer, Reuven. *See* Eldar, Reuven

Lederman, Leon Max, 12:**597**

Le-doresh ha-ḥokhmot (Dunash ben Labrat), 6:47

Lee, David, 12:**597**

Lee, Elizabeth, 12:598

Lee, Malke, 12:**597–598**

Lee, Sidney. *See* Lee, Sir Sidney

Lee, Sir Sidney, 9:151, 12:**598**

Lee, Stan, 12:**598**

Leeches, 12:**599**

Lee County (FL), 12:**598–599**

Leeds (U.K.), 12:**599–600**

Leef, Yinam, 12:**600**

Leeks, 12:**600**, vol. 16: color insert

Lees, Lester, 12:**600**

Leeser, Isaac, 2:635–636, 11:393, 12:**600–601**, 16:433
    education, Jewish, 6:190–191, 192
    English translations of Bible, 3:614

Le-Et Attah (Baron), 3:171

Leeuw, Avraham de, 12:**601**

Leeuw, Jacob ben Ḥayyim de, 12:**601**

Lefanim Le'aḥor (Landau), 8:717

Lefeu oder der Abbruch (Améry), 2:65

Le Fèvre de la Boderie, Guy, 12:**601**

Lefin, Menahem Mendel. *See* Levin, Menahem Mendel

Lefkowitz, David, 12:**601–602**

Lefkowitz, Louis, 12:**602**, 15:224

Lefkowitz, Robert, 13:10

Lefrak, Samuel J., 12:**602**

Lefshetz, Solomon, 12:**603**

Left and right. *See* Right and left

Left Behind series (Jenkins, LaHaye), 18:199

Leftwich, Joseph, 12:**603**

Legacy Senior Communities, Inc., 5:383

Legal documents. *See* Shetar

Legal Documents of the Talmud, in Light of Greek Papryi and Greek and Roman Law (Gulak), 18:470

Legal maxims, 12:**603–604**

Legal person, 12:**604–608**, 15:672

Legal profession. *See* Attorneys; Lawyers

Legal systems. *See* Laws and legal systems

Legboymer (Shalom Aleichem), 18:380

Legendary autobiography, 3:706

Legenden der Juden (Bergmann), 3:430

Legender och visor (Levertin), 12:681

Legend of Four Glasses (Pappenheim). *See* Aggadat Arba Kosot

The Legend of the Ten Martyrs. See Aggadat Aseret Harugei Malkhut

Legends and Songs. See Legender och visor (Levertin)

The Legends of Genesis (Gunkel), 8:137

Legends of the Jews (Ginzberg), 1:460

Legends of the Prophets. See Qiṣaṣ Al-Anbiya'

Leghorn (Italy), 12:**608–609**, 790, 16:390

Legio (ancient Israel), 12:**609–610**

La législation civile du Thalmud (Rabbinowicz), 17:32

La législation criminelle du Thalmud (Rabbinowicz), 17:32

Legnica (Poland), 12:**610**

Legrel, Florin. *See* Mugur, Florin

Legumes, 12:**610–611**

Lehavim (Israel), 12:**611**

Lehem ha-Panim (Aboab), 1:267

Lehem Shamayim (Emden), 6:392

Lehem Todah (Badiḥi), 3:49

Lehem Yehudah (Zarco), 21:458–459

Leḥi. *See* Loḥamei Ḥerut Israel

Lehigh Valley (PA), 12:**611–612**

Leḥishat Saraf (Ḥagiz), 8:478

Lehman, Allan S., 12:612

Lehman, Arthur, 12:612

Lehman, Emanuel, 12:612

Lehman, Ernest, 12:**613**

Lehman, Henry (1821-1855), 12:612, 15:203

Lehman, Herbert Henry, 4:101, 12:612, **613–614**, 15:214, 215, 241

Lehman, Irving, 12:556, 612, **614**

Lehman, Mayer, 12:612

Lehman, Philip, 12:612

Lehman, Robert, 12:612

Lehman, William, 12:**614**

Lehman family, 12:612

Lehmann, Arthur, 20:588

Lehmann, Behrend, 7:212, 8:263, 11:765, 12:**614–615**

Lehmann, Emil, 12:**615**

Lehmann, Fritz, 13:10

Lehmann, Joseph, 12:**615**

Lehmann, Karl, 2:370, 12:**615**

Lehmann, Léonce, 12:**615**

Lehmann, Marcus, 12:**616**

Lehmann, R. P., bibliography of, 3:682

Lehmann, Sigfried, 12:**616**

Lehmann-Haupt, Carl Friedrich, 12:**616**

Lehrbuch der alttestamentlichen Religionsgeschichte (Smend), 18:686

Lehrbuch der Kinderheilkunde (Baginsky), 3:59

Lehren, Akiva, 12:**617**

Lehren, Hirschel, 12:**616–617**

Lehren, Jacob Meir, 12:**617**

Lehren, Moses, 12:**616**

Lehren family, 12:**616–617**
    Amsterdam, 2:112

Lehrer, Liebush, 12:**617**

Die Lehre von den Geistigen und vom Volk (Brunner), 4:224

Lehrhaus Judaica (Oakland), 15:358

Lehrman, Daniel S., 12:**617**

Lehrman, Irving, 12:**617–618**

Lehrman, Max, 4:212

Leib, Moshe, 18:604

Leiber, Jerry, 12:**618–619**

Leiber, Judith Maria, 12:**618**

Leiber and Stoller, 12:**618–619**

Leibl, Daniel, 12:**619**

Leibler, Isi Joseph, 12:**619–620**

Leibmauth. *See* Liebzoll

Leibniz' System in seinen wissenschaftlichen Grundlagen (Cassirer), 4:509

Leibovici, Aurel. *See* Baranga, Aurel

Leibovici, Rubin. *See* Duda, Virgil

Leibovitz, Annie, 12:**620**

Leibowitz, Baruch Ber, 12:**620**

Leibowitz, Joshua O., 12:**620–621**

Leibowitz, Keren, 12:**621**

Leibowitz, Neḥama, 3:625, 12:**621–622**

Leibowitz, René, 12:**622**

Leibowitz, Samuel Simon, 12:**622**

Leibowitz, Yeshayahu, 1:285, 8:375, 12:**622–624**, 16:99–100, 101, 102, 103, 20:44

Leibzoll, 2:6, 157
Leicester (England), 12:**625**
Leichtentritt, Hugo, 12:**625**
Leichter, Kaethe Pick, 12:**625–626**
Leidesdorf, Aaron, 12:626
Leidesdorf, Babetta, 12:626
Leidesdorf, Markus, 12:626
Leidesdorf, Menahem Mendel, 12:626
Leidesdorf, Samuel David, 12:**626**
Leidesdorfer, Isaac, 12:626
Leidesdorfer, Joachim, 12:626
Leidesdorfer, Moses, 12:626
Leidesdorfer, Samuel, 12:626
Leidesdorfer family, 12:**626**
Leigh, Adèle, 12:**626**
"Leil Aviv" (Feierberg), 6:731
Leimdoerfer, David, 12:**626–627**
Leiner, Benjamin. See Leonard, Benny
Leiner, G., *Oholot*, 15:394
Leiner, Gershon Ḥanokh ben Jacob, 12:**627**
Leininger, Harald. See Munk, Kaj
Leinsdorf, Erich, 12:**627**
Leipnik (Czech Republic). See Lipnik nad Becvou (Czech Republic)
Leipzig (Germany), 12:**627–628**
Leipziger, Emil William, 12:**628**
Leipziger, Henry M., 12:**628–629**
Leipzig Mahzor, 13:365–366
Leiria (Portugal), 12:629, **629**
Leiserson, William Morris, 12:**629**
Leitmeritz (Czech Republic). See Litomerice (Czech Republic)
Leitner, Elisabeth, 2:66
Leitner, Gottlieb Wilhelm, 12:**629**
Leivik, H., 11:357–358, 12:**629–631**
Lekaḥ Tov (Jagel Abraham ben Ḥananiah dei Galicchi), 11:71
Lekert, Hirsch, 4:280, 12:**631**
Leket, shikhḥah, and pe'ah, 12:**631–632**
Leket Peraḥim (Bader), 3:45
Lekhah Dodi, 1:662, 11:500, 12:**632–634**, *633*
Lekh-Lekho (Shalom Aleichem), 18:386
Lekh-Lekho (Shayevitsh), 18:424
Lekhno, David, 12:**634**
Lekket Shikḥah (Solomon ibn Mekekh), 1:251
Le-Korot ha-Kehillot be-Polanyah (Horowitz), 9:544–545
Leksikon fun der Yidisher Literatur, Prese, un Filologye (Rejzen), 17:213–214
Lektsii po struktural'nou poetike (Lotman), 13:217
Lelewel, Joachim, 12:**634**

Lel Ikd ill Yas, 4:734
Lelouch, Claude, 12:**634**
Lelov (Poland), 12:**635**
Lelov dynasty, 8:421–422, 12:**635**
Lelyveld, Arthur Joseph, 12:**635–636**, 15:393
Lelyveld, Joseph, 12:**636**
Lemaire, André, 11:326
Lemans, Moses, 12:**636**
Lemansky, P. See Hersch, Pesach Liebman
Lemba, 7:455, 12:**636–637**
Lemberg (Ukraine). See Lvov (Ukraine)
Lemberger, Moses ben Aaron, 12:**637**, 14:474
Le-Mizmor Todah (Modzhitz), 14:413
Lemkin, Raphael, 6:62, 12:**637–638**
Lemlein, Asher, 12:**638**
Lemon, H. de H., 16:345
Lemuel, 12:**638**
Lemuel (alias of Solomon). See Solomon (biblical figure)
Lender, Marvin, 15:137
Lending. See Obligations, law of
Lengnau (Switzerland), 1:207–208, 6:**404**
Lengyel, Emil, 12:**638**
Lengyel, József, 12:**638**
Lengyel, Menyhért, 12:**638–639**
Lenin, Vladimir Ilyich, 5:92–94, 12:**639–640**
      See also Communism
Leningrad (Russia). See Saint Petersburg (Russia)
Lenkei, Henrik, 12:**640**
Lenkinski, Louis, 12:**640**
Lenski, Ḥayyim, 12:**640–641**
Lentils, 12:**641**, vol. 16: color insert
Leo (popes), 12:**641–642**
Leo III (Byzantine emperor), 12:**642**
Leo VI (Byzantine emperor), 4:327, 12:**642**
Leo VII (pope), 12:641
Leo X (pope), 3:587, 12:641, 14:461, 16:375
Leo XII (pope), 16:376
Leo XIII (pope), 3:784, 12:642, 16:377
A Leo and a Scorpio. See Lev a Štír
Leo Baeck Institute, 4:542, 9:425, 12:**642–643**, 18:723
Leo Hebraeus. See Abrabanel, Judah
Le-Olam Al Tomar Ilu (Sivan), 18:206
León (Spain), 12:**643–644**
Leon, Abraham de, 12:644
Leon, Abraham Judah, 12:644
Léon, Adrien, 4:83

Leon, Anthony James, 12:**644,** 16:349
Leon, David ben Judah, 17:13
Leon, Elijah de, 12:644
Leon, Harry Joshua, 12:**644**
Leon, Henry Cecil. See Cecil, Henry
Leon, Isaac ben Eliezer, 12:644
Leon, Isaac de, 12:**644–645,** 15:375
Leon, Jacob de, 12:644
Leon, Jacob Rodriguez de, 12:644
Leon, Joseph de, 12:644
Leon, Judah Ḥayyim, 12:644
León, Luis de, 12:645
Leon, Manuel de, 12:644
Leon, Meir de, 12:644
Leon, Messer David ben Judah, 12:**645–646**
Leon, Messer Judah ben Jehiel, 12:**646**
Leon, Moses, 12:644
Leon, Moses P. de, 12:644
Leon, Pedro de, 12:644
Léon, Robert, 4:8
Leon, Samuel de, 12:644
Léon, Xavier, 12:**646–647**
Leonard, Benny, 12:**647**
Leone, Leon di, 12:**647**
Leone de Ser Danial. See Romano, Judah ben Moses ben Daniel
Leone Ebreo. See Abrabanel, Judah
Leon family, 12:**644**
Leonhard, Rudolf, 12:**647**
Leoni, Myer, 4:117, 12:**647–648**
Leonidov, Leonid Mironovich, 12:**647–648**
Leon of Paris. See Judah ben Isaac
Leonovich, Abraham, 8:273
Leonovich, Abraham ben Levi, 12:648
Leonovich, Joseph, 12:648
Leonovich, Zara ben Samuel, 12:648
Leonovich family, 8:273, 12:**648**
León Pinelo family, 13:21
Leon Pinelo School, 13:21
Leonte ben Moses, 12:**648**
Leontopolis (Egypt), 12:**648–649**
Leontovich, Eugenie, 12:**649**
Leontovich, Fedor, 12:**649**
Leopard, 12:**649**
Leopold, Isaiah Edwin. See Wynn, Ed
Leopold, Lipot. See Fleischer, Judah Loeb
Leopold I, 12:**650**
Leopold II, 11:364
Leopold Morse Home for Infirm Hebrews and Orphanage, 14:513
Leo the Great (pope), 4:721
Leo the Isaurian. See Leo III (Byzantine emperor)

Leo the Wise. *See* Leo VI (Byzantine emperor)

Leovo (Moldova), 12:**650**

Lepanto. *See* Naupaktos (Greece)

Lepel (Belarus), 12:**650**

Le Prestre, Jacob, 2:419

Leprosy, 12:**650–653**
    Gehazi, 7:411–412
    motif, 16:28
    oil used in ritual purification of those recovered from, 15:395

Le Puy (France), 16:**757**

Lerer, Joshua, 12:**653**

Lerer, Shmuel, 12:**653–654**

Lerer, Yehiel, 12:**654**

Lérida (Spain), 12:**654–655**, 14:466–467

Lerma, Judah ben Samuel, 12:**655**

Lerman, Miles, 12:**655–656**

Lermontov (Eichenbaum), 6:246

Lerner, Abba Petachja, 12:**656**

Lerner, Alan Jay, 12:**656–657**, 13:164

Lerner, Alec, 2:161

Lerner, Gerda, 18:736

Lerner, Gerda Kronstein, 9:152, 12:**657**

Lerner, Ḥayyim Ẓevi ben Todros, 12:**657**

Lerner, Jaime, 12:**657–658**

Lerner, Joseph Judah, 12:**658**

Lerner, Max, 12:**658**

Lerner, Mayer ben Mordecai of Altona, 12:**658–659**

Lerner, Michael, 12:**659**

Lerner, Moti, 8:722–723

Lerner, Ralph, 12:**659**

Lerner, Reuben, 11:322

Lerner, Tillie. *See* Olsen, Tillie

Lerner Publishing Group. *See* Kar-Ben/Lerner

Le Roith, Harold Hirsch, 12:**659**

Le Roy, Mervyn, 12:**660**

Lert, Ernst, 12:**660**

Leśman, Jan Wiktor. *See* Brzechwa, Jan

Leśmian, Bolesław, 12:**664**

Lesbianism, 12:**660–661**
    Amsterdam, 2:118, 119
    feminist scholarship, 6:756
    Rich, Adrienne, 17:286
    See also Homosexuality

Lesebuch fuer jeudische Kinder, 4:620

Leshnev (Ukraine), 12:**662**

Leshonenu (journal), 8:673, 18:724

Leshon ha-Zahav (Alḥadib, Isaac ben Solomon ben Ẓaddik), 1:654

Lesko (Poland), 12:**662**

Leskov, Nikolay Semyonovich, 12:**662–663**

Leslau, Wolf, 12:**663**

Leslie, Robert L., 12:**663**

Les Miserables (play), 7:63

Less, Emil, 12:**664**

Lesser, Isaac, 6:25

Lesser Poland (Poland), 12:**664**

Lessing, Gotthold Ephraim, 8:436, 9:230, 12:**664–665**, 14:33, 35, 39
    Il Decamerone (Boccaccio), influence of, 4:25
    modern biblical criticism, development of, 3:649

Lessing, Theodor, 4:81, 12:**665–666**

Lessman, Boleslaw. *See* Leśmian, Boleslaw

Lessons for Life (Kahn), 11:723

Lester, Richard, 12:**666**

L'Estrange, Hamon, 14:460

Lestschinsky, Jacob, 12:**666**, 15:204

Lestschinsky, Joseph, 12:**666**

Leszno (Poland), 12:**667**

Letichev (Ukraine), 12:**667**

Let's Call Him Leon (Sened). *See Nikra Lo Leon* (Sened)

Dos Letste Sakhakl (Pinski), 16:175

Letter Concerning Toleration (Locke), 9:228

Letteris, Max, 15:384

Letteris, Meir, 12:**667–668**

Letter of Aristeas, 2:**456–457**, 4:73
    allegorical interpretation of scripture, 3:644
    Bible, names for, 3:574
    Septuagint, 3:595–596

Letters, Cave of, 11:524

Letters and letter writers, 12:**668–675**, 669
    agronim, 12:672–673
    biblical period, 12:668–669
    formulas and style, 12:674–675
    Franks, Bilhah Abigail Levy, 7:217
    Lachish, 12:421–422
    Middle Ages, 12:670–673
    modern period, 12:673–674
    Sheluḥei Ereẓ Israel, 18:447
    Talmudic literature, 12:670
    women letter writers, 12:673–674

Letters of protection. *See* Schutzbrief

Letters of the Jews Through the Ages (Crescas), 5:284

Letter to My Mother (Meijer), 6:71

Let There Be Sculpture (Epstein), 6:471

Lettre au Président Bouteflika sur le retour des Pieds-Noirs en Algérie (Draï), 6:7

Lettres Persanes (Montesquieu), 14:459, 460

Lettuce, 12:**675**

Das letzte Passahmahl Christi und der Tag seines Todes (Chwolson), 4:725

Leusden, Johann, 12:**675**

Leuvielle, Gabriel-Maxmillien. *See* Linder, Max

Lev, Abraham, 12:**675–676**

Lev, Joseph ben David ibn, 12:**676**, 15:534, 537

Lev, Levav, 8:508–510

Lev, William Ze'ev. *See* Low, William Ze'ev

Levaddah (Kabak), 11:584

Lévai, Jenö, 12:**676**

Levaillant, Isaïe, 12:**676**

Levanda, Lev Osipovich, 12:457, **676–677**

Levanda, Vitali Osipovich, 12:**677–678**

Levanon, Mordecai, 12:**678**

Levant, Oscar, 12:**678**

Lev Aryeh (Modena), 14:409

Lev a Štír (Dostál), 5:762

Leveen, Jacob, 12:**678**

Leven, Narcisse, 12:615, **678–679**

Levene, Peter, Baron Levene of Portsoken. *See* Levene, Sir Peter, Baron Levene of Portsoken

Levene, Phoebus Aaron Theodor, 12:**679**

Levene, Sam, 12:**679**

Levene, Sir Peter, Baron Levene of Portsoken, 12:**679**

Levenson, Jon D., 12:**679–680**

Levenson, Joseph Richmond, 12:**680**

Levenson, Sam, 12:**680**

Leventman, Seymour, 18:733

Lever, Harold, 18:706

Lever, Harold, Baron Lever of Manchester, 12:**680**, 16:342

Lever, Norman. *See* Lever, Harold, Baron Lever of Manchester

Leverson, Ada, 12:**680–681**

Levertin, Oscar Ivar, 12:**681**, 18:761

Levertoff, Paul Philip, 12:**681**

Levertov, Denise, 12:**681–682**

Levey, Barnett, 12:**682**

Levi (Amora), 12:**684–685**

Levi (biblical figure, tribe), 12:**682–684**
    in Abel-Maul, 1:248
    ablution, 1:263
    day of penance and prayer of, 6:659–660
    firstborn and priestly service, 7:46
    in the Halakhah, 12:733
    mishmarot and ma'amadot, 14:317–319

Levi (biblical figure, tribe), *continued*
   Moses, 14:526
   Second Temple, 19:617
   Shechem, 11:19
   See also Cities, of the Levites
Levi (Dustan priest), 6:66
Levi, Aaron. *See* Montezinos, Anatonio de
Levi, Abraham ben Joseph, 12:**685**
Levi, Alexander, 10:7
Levi, Behrend, 12:**685**
Levi, Benedetto, 12:**686**
Levi, Benjamin, 4:70
Levi, Carlo, 10:794, 12:**686**
Levi, David (1742-1801), 3:614, 4:211, 12:**686**
Levi, David (1816-1898), 12:**686–687**
Levi, Doro, 2:370, 12:**687**
Levi, Edward H., 12:**687**
Levi, Ernst Josef Maria. *See* Lert, Ernst
Levi, Eugenio, 12:**687–688**
Levi, Giorgio Renato, 12:**688**
Levi, Giulio Augusto, 12:**688**
Levi, Giuseppe, 12:**688**
Levi, Graziadio David, 10:792
Levi, Harry, 4:100
Levi, Hermann, 12:**688**
Levi, Isaac, 3:614
Levi, Isaac ben Solomon, 12:**685**, **688–689**
Levi, Isaac I, 12:**685**
Levi, Isaac II ben Solomon II. *See* Levi, Isaac ben Solomon
Lévi, Israel, 12:**689**, 18:721
Levi, Jacob, 12:**685**
Levi, Jacob ben Israel, 12:**688–689**
Levi, James, 4:78
Levi, John Simon, 12:**689**
Levi, Joseph (18th c.), 15:526
Levi, Joseph I, 12:**685**
Levi, Joseph II, 12:**685**
Levi, Joshua Joseph ben David, 12:**689–690**
Levi, Judah, 12:**685**
Levi, Leo, 2:58, 12:**690**
Levi, Leone, 12:**690**
Levi, Mario, 12:**690**
Levi, Mario Giacomo, 12:**690**
Levi, Moritz, 12:**690–691**
Levi, Moshe, 12:**691**
Levi, Nathaniel, 16:339–340
Levi, Paolo, 12:**691**
Levi, Paul, 12:**691**, 16:344
Levi, Primo, 4:631, 10:794, 12:**691–692**
Levi, Raphael. *See* Hannover, Raphael Levi

Levi, Rino, 12:**692**
Levi, Said ben Shalom, 12:**692**
Levi, Samuel Gershon, 12:**692–693**
Levi, Shabbetai, 12:**693**
Levi, Solomon ben Isaac (1532-1600), 12:**693–694**
Levi, Solomon ben Isaac (1581-1634), 12:**694**
Levi, Solomon I, 12:**685**
Lévi, Sylvain, 12:**694**
Levi, Testament of, 12:**694–695**
Levi, Yoel, 12:**695**
Levi-Agron, Hassia, 12:**695**
Lévi Alvarès, David, 12:**695–696**
Lévi Alvarès, Eugène, 12:696
Lévi Alvarès, Theodore, 12:696
Leviant, Curt, 12:**696**
Levias, Caspar, 12:**696**
Leviathan, 12:**696–697**
Leviathan artistic group, 15:385
Levi ben Abraham ben Ḥayyim, 12:**697–698**
   antinomianism, 2:200
Levi ben Abraham of Villefranche, allegorical interpretation of scripture, 3:645
Levi ben Gershom, 2:461–462, 462, 624–625, 724, 12:**698–701**, 13:674, 16:88
   allegorical interpretation of scripture, 3:645
   beatitude, 3:239
   Duns Scotus, John, 6:51
   emanation, 6:374
   free will, 7:232
   God, attributes of, 7:667
   moneylending, 14:440
   nature, 15:34–35
   prophets and prophecy, 16:583–584
   Solomon ben Judah of Lunel, 18:772
Levi ben Ḥabib, 12:**702**, 15:537
Levi ben Japheth, 12:**702**
   Judeo-Arabic literature and, 11:532
Levi ben Sisi, 12:**702–703**
Levi-Bianchini, Angelo, 12:**703**
Levi-Civita, Tullio, 12:**703**
Levi della Vida, Giorgio, 12:**703–704**
Levie, Werner, Juedischer Kulturbund, 11:570
Levien, J.F., 16:339–340
Levien, Sonya, 12:**704**
Leviev, Lev, 12:**704**
Leviev, Manos, 4:264
Levi family (Salonika, Greece), 1:208, 209, 217–219, 12:*685*, **685**

Levi family (San Diego, CA), 18:14
Levi Isaac ben Meir of Berdichev, 8:396, 12:**704–706**
Levi-Montalcini, Rita, 12:**706**, 13:10
Levin, A. Leo, 12:**706**
Levin, Alter Isaac, 12:**706**
Levin, Aryeh, 12:**706–707**
Levin, Bernard, 12:**707**
Levin, Carl, 12:**707**
Levin, Eliezer, 4:152
Levin, Emanuel (1820-1913), 4:199, 12:**707–708**
Levin, Hanoch, 8:721, 722, 723, 12:**708–709**
Levin, Harry, 12:**709**
Levin, Hirschel, 12:477
Levin, Ira, 12:**709**
Levin, Judah Leib (1844-1925), 12:**709–710**
Levin, Judah Leib (1863-1926), 12:**710**, 14:518–519
Levin, Lewis Charles, 12:**710**
Levin, Ludwig. *See* Robert, Ludwig
Levin, Maksim Grigoryevich, 12:**710**
Levin, Menahem Mendel (1749-1826), 3:611, 4:199, 12:**710–711**
Levin, Menahem Mendel (1820-1913). *See* Levin, Emmanuel (1820-1913)
Levin, Mendel, 9:593
Levin, Meyer, 12:**711–712**
Levin, Michael, 3:737
Levin, Mona, 18:96
Levin, Nathaniel William, 12:**712**
Levin, Nora, 9:152, 12:**712**
Levin, Poul Theodor, 12:**712**
Levin, Richard C., 12:**712–713**
Levin, Robert, Norway, 15:310
Levin, Sander, 12:**713**
Levin, Shmarya, 6:74, 12:**713–714**
   Language war, 12:482–483
Levin, Theodore, 12:**714**
Levin, Y., Birobidzhan, 3:719
Levin, Yehudah Leib, 8:310–311
Levin, Yiẓḥak Meir, 12:**714**
Levin, Ẓevi Hirsch ben Aryeh Loeb, 12:**714–715**
Levinas, Emmanuel, 9:400, 12:**715–717**, 15:546, 16:99, 109, 110–111
   Blanchot, Maurice, 3:738
   Lévy, Benny, 12:748
   Torah, approach to, 20:44
The Levinas Reader (Levinas), 9:400
Levine, Baruch, 12:**717**
Levine, Charles A., 1:430
Leviné, Eugene, 12:**717–718**
Levine, Hillel, 21:613

Levine, Jack, 12:**718**

Levine, James, 12:**718**

Levine, Joseph E., 12:**718–719**

Levine, Lee, 18:114

Levine, Leon, North Carolina, 15:303

Levine, Les, 12:**719**

Levine, Norman, 4:424, 12:**719**

Levine, Philip, 12:478, **719**

Levine, Raphael, 12:**719–720**

Levinger, Lee Joseph, 12:**720**

Levin-Shatzkes, Yiẓhak, 12:**720**

Levinsky, Battling, 12:**720**

Levin-Smith, Archibald. *See* Levin Smith, Sir Archibald

Levin Smith, Sir Archibald, 12:**720**

Levinsohn, Isaac Baer, 12:**720–722**
  apologetics, 2:269
  on blood libel, 3:779
  education, Jewish, 6:182

Levinsohn, Nahum Mendel. *See* Kossovski, Vladimir

Levinsoḥn, Isaac Dov, parodies, 15:659

Levinson, Abraham, 12:**722**

Levinson, Albert, 15:589

Levinson, Andre, 12:**722–723**

Levinson, Barry, 12:**723**

Levinson, Joshua, 1:461

Levinson, Norman David. *See* Norell, Norman

Levinson, N.P., 3:43

Levinson, Olga, 12:**723**

Levinson, Salomon Oliver, 12:**723**

Levinson, Wilhelm, 12:**729–730**

Levinstein, Herbert, 12:**723**

Levinthal, Bernard Lewis, 12:723–724

Levinthal, Bernard Louis, 12:723

Levinthal, Helen Hadassah, 12:724, 18:278

Levinthal, Herbert, 12:724

Levinthal, Israel Herbert, 12:724

Levinthal, Lewis Edward, 12:724

Levinthal, Louis Edward, 12:724

Levinthal family, 12:**723–724**

Levi-Perotti, Giustina, 12:**724**

Lévi-Provençal, Evariste, 12:**725–726**

Levirate marriage and Ḥaliẓah, 12:**725–729**, 14:448, 21:323

Leviseur, Moritz, 3:769, 16:349

Leviseur, Sophie, 3:769

Levisohn, Solomon, 18:369

Levisohn, V., on blood libel, 3:779

Levison, Wilhelm, 12:**729–730**

Levi-Strauss, Claude, 2:186, 12:**730**

Levita, Elijah, 4:23, 52, 8:444, 12:**730–732**, 13:652, 15:651, 16:612, 21:343–344
  Bachrach, Jacob ben Moses, 3:39

Bible editions and translations, 3:587, 588, 610

Bove-Bukh, 4:107–108, 15:651

Egidio Da Viterbo, 6:220

grammatical works, 13:43, 55

Italian biblical study and exegesis, 3:663

Osiander, Andreas, 15:503

Levita, Joseph ben Naphtali Hirz. *See* Hirshel, Meyer

Levita, Joseph Naphtali Hirz. *See* Hirshel, Meyer

La levita gris: cuentos judíos de ambiente porteño (Espinoza), 6:509

Levitan, Isaac Ilitch, 12:**732**

Levitan, Solomon, 12:**732**

Levi-Tannai, Sara, 12:**732–733**

Levites in the Halakhah, 12:**733**
  See also Levi (biblical figure, tribe)

Levitical cities (ancient Israel), 12:**733–734,** *734*

Leviticus, Book of, 12:**734–740,** 735*t*
  Holiness code, 12:**738–740**
  impurity laws, 12:651, 737–738
  sacrificial system, 12:735–737
  Sifra, 18:560–564

Leviticus Rabbah, 12:452, **740–742**

Levitsky, Jacob, 12:**742**

Levitsky, Louis Moses, 12:**742**

Levitsky, Mischa, 12:**742**

Levitsky, Sara. *See* Adler, Sara

Levitt, Abraham, 12:742

Levitt, Alfred S., 12:**743**

Levitt, Andrew, 12:743

Levitt, Arthur, Jr., 15:224

Levitt, Arthur, Sr., 12:**743,** 15:224

Levitt, Esther, 12:**743**

Levitt, Helen, 12:**743–744**

Levitt, John, 12:743

Levitt, William Jaird, 12:742–743

Levitt family, 12:**742–743**

Levitzki, Alexander, 12:**744**

Levner, Israel Benjamin, 12:**744**

Levontin, Jehiel Joseph, 12:**744**

Levontin, Zalman David, 12:**744–745**

Lev Same'ah (Alegre), 1:608

Lev Tolstoy (Eichenbaum), 6:246

Lev Tov (Isaac ben Eliakim of Posen), 10:41

Levush Malkhut (Jaffe), 4:779, 11:67–68

Levush Mordekhai (Epstein), 6:476

Levy, Aaron (1742-1815), 12:**746**

Levy, Aaron (1771-1852), 12:**746,** 15:239

Levy, Aaron J., 15:205, 211

Lévy, Abraham Eugène, 12:**746**

Levy, Albert. *See* Levy, Sir Albert

Levy, Albert J., 12:**746**

Lévy, Alfred, 12:**747**

Levy, Amy, 12:**747**

Levy, Arthur (1878-1946). *See* Liebert, Arthur

Lévy, Arthur (1847-1931), 12:**747**

Levy, Asser, 12:555, **747,** 15:195, 239

Levy, Benjamin, 12:**747, 747,** 15:242

Levy, Benn Wolff, 12:**747–748**

Lévy, Benny, 12:**748**

Levy, Bernard-Henri, 12:**748**

Lévy, Calmann, 12:**746**

Levy, Chapman, 12:**748**

Levy, Clifton Harby, 12:**748**

Levy, Daniel. *See* Levy, Sir Daniel

Levy, David, 12:**749**

Levy, Elias, 12:**747**

Levy, Felix Alexander, 12:**749–750**

Levy, Harry Louis, 12:**750**

Levy, Hayman, 12:**750,** 15:197, 199, 239

Levy, Henry. *See* Russell, Henry

Levy, Hyman, 12:**750**

Levy, Isaac, 12:**745**

Levy, Isaac (d. after 1555), 12:**745**

Lévy, Isaac (1835-1912), 12:**750**

Lévy, Isidore, 12:**750**

Levy, Jacob, 12:**751**

Lévy, Jean-Pierre, 15:668

Levy, Jefferson Monroe, 12:**751**

Levy, Jonas Phillips, 12:**751**

Levy, Joseph, 12:**745**

Levy, Joseph Langley, 12:**751**

Levy, Joseph Leonard, 12:**751**

Levy, Joseph Moses, 12:**546**

Levy, Judah, 12:**745**

Levy, Judah ben Menahem, 12:**751–752**

Levy, Julius. *See* Rodenberg, Julius

Lévy, Lazare, 12:**752**

Levy, Leonard Williams, 12:**752**

Lévy, Léopold, 15:648

Lévy, Lexandre Nathan, 12:**746**

Levy, Louis, 12:**752**

Levy, Louis Edward, 12:**752**

Levy, Lucien, 12:**752**

Levy, Marion Joseph, Jr., 12:**752–753**

Levy, Marv, 12:**753**

Levy, Marvin David, 12:**753**

Levy, Michael Abraham, Baron Levy of Mill Hill, 12:**753**

Lévy, Michel, 12:**746**

Levy, Moses (1757-1826), 12:555, **753–754**

Levy, Moses (c.1665-1728), 12:**753**

Levy, Moses (d. after 1620), 12:**745**

Levy, Moses Elias, 7:87, 12:**754**

Levy, Nathan, 12:**754**

Lévy, Paul, 12:**754**

Levy, Pauline Marion. *See* Goddard, Paulette

Lévy, Raphael (1898-1972). *See* Ryvel

Lévy, Raphaël (c.1612-1670), 4:105, 12:**754**

Levy, Reuben, 12:**754–755**

Levy, Robert, 11:469, 12:**755**

Levy, Roland Alexis Manuel. *See* Roland-Manuel

Levy, Rudolf, 12:**755**, 15:648

Levy, Sam Saadi, 12:**755**

Lévy, Samuel, 12:**755**

Levy, Sion, 12:**755–756**

Levy, Sir Albert, 12:**746**

Levy, Sir Daniel, 12:548, **749**, 16:340

Levy, Solomon, 15:242

Levy, Uriah Phillips, 12:**756**

Levy, William, 14:446

Levy-Alvares, Eugène. *See* Lévy, Abraham Eugene

Levy-Bacrat, Abraham ben Solomon, 12:**756**

Lévy-Bensusan, Joshua, 3:380

Lévy-Bruhl, Henri, 12:**756–757**, 18:730

Lévy-Bruhl, Lucien, 2:185, 12:**756–757**, 18:730

Lévy-Dhurmer, Lucien, 12:**757**

Levy family (Morocco), 12:**745**

Lévy family (French musicians), 12:**745**

Lévy family (French publishers), 12:**746**

Levy-Lawson, Edward, 12:546

Levy-Lawson, Harry Lawson Webster. *See* Levy-Lawson, Sir Harry Lawson Webster

Levy-Lawson, Sir Harry Lawson Webster, 12:547

Levy-Yuly. *See* Yuly family

Lew, Jacob, 12:**757**

Lewald, Fanny, 12:**757–758**

Lewandowski, Louis, 4:660, 661, 8:504, 12:**758**

Lewek, Jordanis. *See* Lewko, Jordanis

Lewenthal, Raymond, 12:**758**

Lewi, Maurice J., 12:**758**

Lewin, Aaron ben Nathan of Rzeszow, 12:**758–759**

Lewin, Adolf, 12:**759**

Lewin, Benjamin Manesseh, 2:76, 12:**759**

Lewin, George. *See* Walden, Herwarth

Lewin, Gershon, 12:**759**

Lewin, Joshua Heshel ben Elijah Ze'ev ha-Levi, 12:**759–760**

Lewin, Judah Leib, 12:**760**

Lewin, Kurt Zadek, 2:610, 12:**760–761**, 18:264, 265

Lewin, Louis, 12:**761**

Lewin, Nathan, 12:**761–762**

Lewin-Epstein, Eliahu Ze'ev, 12:**762**

Lewinsky, Elhanan Leib, 12:**762**

Lewinsky, Yom-Tov, 12:**762–763**

Lewinstein, Joseph ben Abraham Abush, 12:**763**

Lewis, Anthony, 12:**763**

Lewis, Aubrey Julian. *See* Lewis, Sir Aubrey Julian

Lewis, Bernard, 6:25–26, 12:**764**

Lewis, David, 12:**764**, 16:341, 18:706

Lewis, George. *See* Lewis, Sir George

Lewis, Hyman, 12:**764–765**

Lewis, I. M., 12:**765**

Lewis, Jerry, 12:**765**

Lewis, Leopold Davis, 12:**765**

Lewis, Oscar, 2:187, 12:**766**, 18:733

Lewis, Peter B., 12:**766**

Lewis, Ruth. *See* Farkas, Ruth

Lewis, Samuel, 12:**766**

Lewis, Samuel Alexander, 12:**766**

Lewis, Shari, 12:**766–767**

Lewis, Sir Aubrey Julian, 12:**763–764**

Lewis, Sir George, 12:**764**

Lewis, Stephen, 12:**767**

Lewis, Ted, 12:**767**

Lewisohn, Adolph, 12:**767**, 15:211
  The American Hebrew, 2:49

Lewisohn, Frederick, 12:**768**

Lewisohn, Julius, 12:**767**

Lewisohn, Leonard, 12:**767–768**, 14:487–488

Lewisohn, Ludwig, 12:**768**

Lewisohn, Sam Adolph, 12:**768**

Lewisohn, Solomon, 8:724

Lewisohn family, 12:**767–768**

Lewit, Tonya, 18:777

Lewite, Leon, 12:**768–769**

Le Witt, Jan, 4:368, 12:**769**

Lewitt, Sol, 12:**769–770**

Lewitzky, Bella, 12:**770**

Lewko, Jordanis, 12:**770**

Lewkowitsch, Julius, 12:**770–771**

Lewkowitz, Albert, 12:**771**

Lewy, Israel, 12:**771**

Lewy, Julius, 12:**771**

Lewy, Yoḥanan, 12:**771–772**

Lewysohn, Abraham, 12:**772**

Lewysohn, Yehudi Leib Ludwig, 12:**772**

Lewin, Gershon, 12:759

A Lexicon of Musical Invective (Slonimsky), 18:680

Lexicography
  Alcalay, Reuven, 1:598
  Barth, Jacob, 3:179–180
  Ben-Yehuda, Eliezer, 3:386–388
  Ben Ze'ev, Judah Leib, 3:390
  Castell, Edmund, 4:513
  Guralnik, David B., 8:139–140
  Ibn Barun, Abu Ibrahim Isaac ben Joseph ibn Benveniste, 9:661
  Ibn Janāḥ, Jonah, 9:680–683
  Ibn Quraysh, Judah, 9:688
  Lara, David Ben Isaac Cohen De, 12:492–493
  Levita, Elijah, 12:730–732
  Lifshits, Shiye-Mordkhe, 13:11
  Loew, Immanuel, 13:163
  Nathan ben Jehiel of Rome, 15:13–14
  Parḥon, Salomon ben Abraham Ibn, 15:641–642
  Schoenhack, Joseph, 18:157

Lexicon linguae aethiopicae cum indice latino (Dillmann), 5:661–662

Lexicon of Yiddish Literature, Press, and Philology. See Leksikon fun der Yidisher Literatur, Prese, un Filologi

Lex talionis, blindness and, 3:753

Leycester, John, 1:412

Leyeles, A., Judah Halevi in poetry of, 11:500

Leyl ha-Esrim (Sobol), 8:721

Leyl ha-Esserim (Sobol), 18:702

Leyon, Avram, 12:**772**

Lezajsk (Poland), 12:**772–773**

Lhevinne, Josef, 12:**773**

Liability, 12:536–537, **773**
  labor law, 12:414–415
  negligence and, 20:62–64, 65, 66
  Noachide laws, violations of, 15:286
  of a shalish, 18:374

Liacho, Lázaro, 12:**773**

Liachovitzky, Jacobo Simon, 12:**773**

Libai, Avinoam, 12:**773–774**

Libai, David, 12:**774**

Libations and cult sacrifices, 5:333

Libau. *See* Liepaja

Libava. *See* Liepaja

Libedinski, Yuri Nikolayevitch, 12:**774–775**

Libedinsky Tschorne, Marco, 12:**775**

Libel, 1:406
  antisemitic (*See* Blood libel)

Liber, Marc, 12:**775**

Liber, Maurice, 12:**775**

Liberalism, 12:**775–781**
    Austro-Hungary, 12:778–779
    Canada, 4:414
    children's services, 4:636
    England, 12:776–777
    France, 12:777
    Germany, 12:777–778
    Italy, 12:779
    Russia, 12:780–781
    United States, 12:779–780
Liberal Judaism
    England
        Mattuck, Israel I., 13:688
        Montagu, Lily, 14:452
        Montefiore, Claude Joseph Goldsmid, 14:455
        Kant, Immanuel and, 11:769–770
        Seligmann, Caesar, 18:267
        See also Reform Judaism
Liber Antiquitatum Biblicarum (Philo), 14:533, 16:**58–59**
Libération (organization), 15:668
Liberation movements, Passover and Seder as framework of expression for, 15:681–682
Liberation theology, 11:282–283
Liberberg, Joseph, 3:719
Liber de Trinitate et Incarnatione adversus Judaeos et Sarracenos (Ramon), 17:85–86
Liberec (Czech Republic), 12:781
Liberman, Serge, 12:781
Liberman, Yevsey Grigoryevich, 12:**781–782**
Liber Profetiae Moysis. See Assumption of Moses
Liberty Union Party (U.S.), 18:11–12
Libeshey (Lithuania). *See* Lyubeshov (Lithuania)
Libeskind, Daniel, 12:782
    Nussbaum, Felix, 15:352
    World Trade Center site, design for, 15:225
Libin, Z., 12:**782–783**
Libman, Isaac. *See* Lipman, Levi
Libnah (Canaan), 12:**783**
Libowitz, Samuel Nehemiah, 12:**783**
Libraries, 12:**783–788**
    Aden, 1:387–388
    Ashurbanipal, 2:404
    Assur, 2:404
    Bibliothèque Nationale, 3:685
    Bodleian Library, 4:29
    Canada, Library and Archives of, 15:517
    Edelmann, Raphael, 6:143
    Hattusas, 2:404

Jewish National Library, 8:740
Leveen, Jacob, 12:678
Library of Congress for the Jewish People, 2:410
Maimonides Library, 4:14
Mocatta, 2:408
modern, 12:783–784
national and public, 12:784–785
Oesterreichische Nationalbibliothek, 15:384
Oppenheim, David ben Abraham, 15:444
twenty first century collections, 12:785–786
virtual and digitized, 12:786
Library (Ullman), 20:241
Library, Jewish National, 8:740
Library, Jewish National and University. *See* Jewish National and University Library
Library of Congress for the Jewish People, 2:410
Libre del gentilo e los savis (Ramon), 17:85
Le Libre de Mondell (Schwob), 18:197
La Libre Parole (periodical), 6:26, 7:158
Libre Predicationis Contra Judaeos (Ramon), 17:85–86
Libro del Alborayque, 1:595
Libschitz, Baruch Mordecai ben Jacob, 12:**788–789**
Libschitz, Jacob Zalman, 12:789
Libschitz, Meir Ezekiel, 12:788–789
Libya, 12:*789*, **789–795**
    antisemitism, discrimination, 5:681
    early history, 12:789–791
    Holocaust, Tripoli, 20:151–152
    Holocaust period, 12:791–792
    Israeli relations, 12:794–795
    modern period, 12:792–793
    Zionism, 12:792, 793–794
Lice, 13:**226–227**
Lichine, David, 12:**795–796**
Licht, Alexander, 12:796
Licht, Frank, 12:796
Licht, Michael, 12:796
Lichtenbaum, Joseph, 12:**796–797**
Lichtenberg, Bernhard, 12:**797**
Lichtenfeld, Gabriel Judah, 12:**797**
Lichtenstadt (Czech Republic). *See* Hroznetin (Czech Republic)
Lichtenstadt, Abraham Aaron, 12:**797–798**
Lichtenstein, Aaron, 12:**798**, 15:703
Lichtenstein, Aharon, 18:780

Lichtenstein, David. *See* Lichine, David
Lichtenstein, Hillel ben Baruch, 12:**798–799**
Lichtenstein, Morris, 4:694
Lichtenstein, Roy, 12:**799**
Lichtenstein, Tehillah, 4:694, 12:**799–800**
Lichtenstein, Walter, 12:**800**
Lichtheim, George, 12:**800**
Lichtheim, Richard, 12:**800**
Lichtknecht, Wilhelm, 4:137
Lichtstein, Abraham ben Eliezer Lipman, 12:**800**
Lichtstein, Abraham Jekuthiel Zalman ben Moses Joseph, 12:**800–801**
Licoricia of Winchester, 12:**801**
Lida (Belarus), 12:**801–802**
Lida, David ben Aryeh Leib, 2:107, 8:480
Lider (Adler), 1:400
Lider (Emiot). *See* Songs (Emiot)
Lider fun a Midbernik (Esselin). *See Poems of a Hermit* (Esselin)
Lidzbarski, Abraham Mordechai, 12:**802**
Lidzbarski, Mark, 12:**802**
Lieben, Robert von, 12:**802–803**
Lieben, Salomon, 12:**803**
Lieben, Salomon Hugo, 12:**803**
Lieber, David, 12:**803–804**, 20:412
Lieberman, A. S., 18:704
Lieberman, Chaim, 12:**804**
Lieberman, Elias, 12:**804**
Lieberman, Herman, 12:**804**, 16:347
Lieberman, Joseph, 3:129, 12:**804–805**, 15:137
Lieberman, Judith, 12:**807**
Lieberman, Myron, 12:**805**
Lieberman, Nancy Elizabeth, 12:**805–806**
Lieberman, Saul, 2:47, 8:274, 12:**806–807**, 16:73
Liebermann, Aaron Samuel, 1:504, 4:279, 12:709, **807**, 18:714–715
Liebermann, Carl Theodor, 12:**808**
Liebermann, Felix, 12:**808**
Liebermann, Herman, 18:707
Liebermann, Max, 12:**808**
Liebermann, Rolf, 12:**808–809**
Liebermann, Solomon, Joseph ben Mordecai Gershon ha-Kohen of Cracow, 11:423
Lieberson, Goddard, 12:**809**
Lieberson, Stanley, 18:733
Liebert, Arthur, 12:**809**
Lieb Kalish. *See* Judah Aryeh Leib ben David

Liebknecht, Karl, Jogiches, Leon, 11:369

Liebliche Tefillah (Aaron ben Samuel of Hergerhausen), 1:217

Liebling, A.J., 12:**809**

Liebling, Estelle, 12:**809–810**, 18:581

Liebling, Roman. *See* Polanski, Roman

Liebman, Charles, 12:**810**, 17:24–25

Liebman, Joshua Loth, 12:**810**

Liebman, Max, 4:332

Liebman, P. *See* Hersch, Pesach Liebman

Liebmann, Esther Schuloff Aaron, 12:**810–811**

Liebmann, Jost, 1:213, 12:**810–811**

Liebmann, Max, 2:49

Liebmann, Otto, 12:**811**

Liebmann-Beer, Jacob. *See* Meyerbeer, Giacomo

Liebrecht, Savyon, 12:**811–812**

Liebschuetz family. *See* Lipschuetz family

Liebson, Sarah Gertrude. *See* Millin, Sarah Gertrude

Liebstein, Jacov. *See* Lovestone, Jay

Liebzoll, 12:**624–625**

Lieder vom armen Mann (Beck), 3:**243**

Liége (Belgium), 12:**812**

Liens and debts, 12:**812–817**
    admission, 1:410–411
    agency status, 1:451–452
    Apoteke, 12:815–816
    assignment of, 2:**603–605**
    chattels, 12:814–815
    collection, 6:590–598
        from impoverished, 6:590, 594–597
        Israel (State), 6:597–598
        penalties for debtors, 6:591–592
    communities, 13:152
    creation of, 12:813–814
    indebtedness bonds, 5:154–155
    inherited, 19:287–288
    obligation, security, 12:816–817
    obligations, 5:191–192
    pledges, 16:231–232
    prosbul, 16:586–587
    shetar, 18:468, 469
    taking pledges, 16:232–233
    waiver of, 7:79, 13:770–771
    See also Loans; Obligations, law of; Usury

Liepaja (Latvia), 12:**817–818**

Liepman, Eliezer. *See* Prins, Liepman Philip

Lies, Man of, 12:**818–819**

Lies, Prophet of, 12:**819**

Liessin, Abraham, 12:**819**

Lietuva. *See* Lithuania

Lifchitz, Alexander, 5:415

Life (Béjart), 3:21

Life (periodical), 6:272, 355, 16:125

The Life (Josephus), 11:440

Life, A User's Manual (Perec). *See La Vie mode d'emploi* (Perec)

Life, Book of. *See* Book of Life

Life: The Unfinished Experiment (Luria), 13:268

Life, Tree of. *See* Tree of Life

Life after death
    Judaism, development of concept of, 11:516
    kabbalistic, 6:500–501

Life and death, 13:**5–6**
    Kever Avot, 12:99–100
    sanctity of human, 13:5–6, 722
        conversion or threat of death and, 15:721–722

Life cycle events
    bar Mitzvah, 3:164–166
    dance, 5:409–410, 411–412
    See also Greetings and congratulations

Life Is Beautiful. See La vita è bella

Life Is with People (Zborowski and Herzog), 7:50

Life of Adam and Eve. See Book of the Life of Adam and Eve

The Life of David (Pinsky), 16:176–177

The Life of Jesus. See Toledot Yeshu

The Life of Moïse Cilibi the Famous. See Viaţa lui Cilibi Moïse Vestitul

The Life of the Dead (Levin), 12:708

A Life on the Stage. See Die Varheit

Life Plus 99 Years (Leopold), 13:162

Life sciences, 13:**6–11**, *8*

Lifnei Arba Me'ot Shanah (Shalkovich), 18:375

Lifnim min ha-Ḥomah (Agnon), 1:467

Lifschitz, Malkah. *See* Esther (1880-1943)

Lifschitz, Uri, 13:**11**

Lifschitz family. *See* Lipschuetz family

Lifshits, Shiye-Mordkhe, 13:**11–12**

Lifshitz, David, 13:**12**

Lifshitz, Nehamah, 13:**12**

Lifshyts family. *See* Lipschuetz family

Lifson, Shneior, 13:**12**

Ligeti, György, 13:**12–13**

"The Light". *See* Lumina

Light, creation of, 5:276

Lightfoot, John, 13:**13**, 59

Light of the Lord (Crescas), 16:584

Light of the Wise. See Sirāj al-'Uqūl

Ligue de la Patrie Française, 6:19

Ligue des Droits de l'Homme, 6:19

Likkui Shenei ha-Me'orot, o Shenei Ẓaddikim she-Ḥibbelu Zeh ba-Zeh (Dolitzki), 5:735–736

Likkut Aẓamot, 13:**13**

Likkutei Amarim (Abraham ben Israel of Brody), 1:303

Likkutei Amarim (Shneur Zalman of Lyady). *See Tanya*

Likkutei Ḥaver Ben Ḥayyim (Plaut), 16:227

Likkutei Kadmoniyyot (Pinsker), 16:174–175

Likkutei Moharan (Naḥman of Bratslav), 8:427

Likkutei Shikhḥah u'Fe'ah (Elmalik), 6:363

Likkutim (Alemanno), 1:612

Likkutim mi-Sefer Mekor Ḥayyim (Falaquera), 6:682

Likud, 13:**13–14**
    American Israel Public Affairs Committee, 2:51
    peace process, 2:312, 315–316, 318–319
    See also Netanyahu, Binyamin

Likud party, 3:**261**
    formed, 10:451

Lilien, Ephraim Moses, 4:70, 13:**14**

Lilienblum, Moses Leib, 8:436, 13:**14–16**

Lilienthal, David Eli, 13:**16**

Lilienthal, Max, 6:182, 8:442, 13:**16–17**, 15:198

Lilienthal, Menahem. *See* Lilienthal, Max

Lilienthal, Otto, 13:**17**

Liliom (Molnár), 14:427

Lilith, 5:573, 7:107–108, 13:**17–20**
    Agrat bat Mahalath, 1:470
    Alphabet of ben Sira, 2:122
    amulets, 2:122
    in feminist science fiction, 18:199
    Joseph della Raina legend, 11:428
    relationship to night, 5:487

Lilith (periodical), 13:**20**

Lilith Fair, 13:19

Liliuokalani (Queen of Hawaii), 8:473

Lille (France), 13:**20**

Lillienblum, M. L., 8:726

Lillienthal, Max, Jolles, Zechariah Isaiah, 11:386

Lillit, 15:551

Lily (flower), 7:70, vol. 16: color insert

Lily Montagu: Sermons, Addresses, Letters, and Prayers (Montagu), 14:452

Lima (Peru), 13:**20–21**

Lima, Moses ben Isaac Judah, 13:**21–22**

Liman, Arthur L., 13:**22**

Limborch, Philip van, Orobio de Castro, Isaac, 15:481

Limburg, Joseph, 13:**22**, 16:345

Limdu Heitev (Abramovitsh), 1:319

Limerick (Ireland), 13:**22**

Limitation of actions, 13:**22–25**

Limitations to Psychotherapy of Schizophrenics (Eissler), 6:278

The Limits of Love (Raphael), 17:94

The Limits of Science. See Granice nauki

Limmudei Dat u-Musar (Halévy), 8:270

Limoges (France), 13:**25**

Limoux (France), 13:**25**

Limpieza de sangre, 11:294, 13:**25–26**

Lincoln (England), 3:775, 13:**26**

Lincoln, Abraham, 4:162, 13:**26–27**

Lincoln, Trebitsch, 13:**27**

Lincoln Square Synagogue (NYC), 15:234

Lindau (Germany), 13:**27**

Linder, Jakub, 4:200

Linder, Max, 13:**27–28**

Lindheim, Irma Levy, 13:**28**

Lindmann (Raphael), 17:94

Lindo, Joshua, 15:610

Lindo family, 13:**28**

Lindsay, John V., 15:215, 216

Lindzen, Richard Siegmund, 6:450

Linets (Ukraine). *See* Ilintsy (Ukraine)

Linetzky, Isaac Joel, 13:**28**

Lingle, Linda, 8:473, 13:**28–29**

Linguistic literature, Hebrew. *See* Hebrew linguistic literature

Linguistics
    Ballagi, Mór, 3:91
    Barth, Jacob, 3:179–180
    Benveniste, Emile, 3:382
    Bloomfield, Leonard, 3:783
    Bréal, Michel, 4:155
    Buchner, Abraham, 4:243
    Chomsky, Noah Avram, 4:664–665
    Fishman, Joshua Aaron, 7:64–65
    Halle, Morris, 8:279
    Harris, Zellig Sabbetai, 8:365
    Jakobson, 11:74
    Lévy, Paul, 12:754
    PIamenta, Moshe, 16:142
    Radin, Paul, 17:54–55
    Reicherson, Moses, 17:199

    Rosén, Haiim B., 17:428
    Sapir, Edward, 18:37
    Sarfatti, Gad B., 18:55
    Schaechter, Mordkhe, 18:102
    semitic languages, 3:**216**
    Sephiha, Haim Vidal, 18:306
    Sievers, Eduard, 18:560
    See also Hebrew language

Linitz-Rabinowitz Ḥasidim, 8:421

Linkabit Inc., 11:47

Linnas, Karl, 15:388, 18:461–462

Linowitz, Sol Myron, 13:**61**

Linz (Austria), 13:**61**

Linz program, 18:157

Lion, 18:570

Lion, Leon M., 13:**63**

Lion of wrath, 13:**63**

Lions, 13:**61–63**

Liozno (Belarus), 13:**63**

Lipcani (Moldova). *See* Lipkany (Moldova)

Lipchitz, Chaim Jacob. *See* Lipchitz, Jacques

Lipchitz, Jacques, 13:**63–64**

Lipiner, Siegfried, 13:**64**

Lipitz, Dov, 4:188

Lipkany (Moldova), 13:**64**

Lipkin, Israel ben Ze'ev Wolf, 3:741, 4:202, 13:**64–65**

Lipkin, Yom Tov Lipman, 13:**66**

Lipkin-Shahak, Amnon, 13:**66**

Lipman, Eugene, 9:380–381

Lipman, Eugene Jay, 13:**66–67**

Lipman, Jacob Goodale, 13:**67**

Lipman, Levi, 13:**67**

Lipman, Vivian David, 13:**67–68**

Lipmann, Fritz Albert, 13:**68**

Lipmann, Otto, 13:**68**

Lipmann, Yom Tov. *See* Zunz, Leopold

Lipnik nad Becvou (Czech Republic), 13:**68**

Lipnik nad Bečvou (Czech Republic). *See* Lipnik nad Becvou (Czech Republic)

Lipno (Poland), 13:**68–69**

Lipovets (Ukraine), 13:**69**

Lippe (Germany), 13:**69**

Lippe, Ḥayyim David, bibliography of, 3:682

Lippe, Karpel, 13:**69**

Lippe-Detmold (Germany). *See* Lippe (Germany)

Lippmann, Edmund Oskar von, 13:**70**

Lippmann, Eduard, 13:**70**

Lippmann, Gabriel, 13:**70**

Lippmann, Walter, 13:**70**

Lippmann, Zev, 4:370

Lippold, 4:125, 13:**70–71**, 14:300

"Lippy". *See* Lipshitz, Israel

Lipschitz, Jacob ha-Levi, 13:**71**

Lipschitz, Jacques, 18:223

Lipschitz, Rudolf Otto Sigismund, 13:**71**

Lipschitz, Solomon ben Moses, 13:**71**

Lipschitz, Solomon Zalman, 13:**71–72**

Lipschuetz, Baruch Isaac ben Israel, 13:**72**

Lipschuetz, Eliezer Meir, 13:**72**

Lipschuetz, Gedaliah, 13:**73**

Lipschuetz, Gedaliah ben Solomon Zalman, 13:**73**

Lipschuetz, Hillel Aryeh Leib ben Ze'ev Dov, 13:**73**

Lipschuetz, Israel ben Eliezer, 4:760, 13:**73**, 14:329

Lipschuetz, Solomon ben Moses. *See* Lipschitz, Solomon ben Moses

Lipschuetz family, 13:**72**

Lipschutz, Aryeh Leib, 13:**73**

Lipschutz, Eliezer ben Solomon, 13:**73–74**

Lipschutz, Enrique, 11:469

Lipschutz, Israel ben Gedaliah, 13:**74**, 14:537

Lipschutz, Shabbetai ben Jacob Isaac, 13:**74**

Lipschutz, Solomon ben Mordecai, 13:**74–75**

Lipschutz family. *See* Lipschuetz family

Lipset, Seymour Martin, 13:**75**

Lipshitz, Israel, 13:**75**

Lipski, Abraham, 13:**75**

Lipski, Louis, 13:**75–76**

Lipson, Edna. *See* Charles, Gerda

Lipson, Ephraim, 13:**76**

Lipson, Mordekhai, 8:497, 13:**76**

Lipstadt, Deborah, 4:217, 9:494–495, 10:30, 31

Lipsyte, Robert Michael, 13:**76–77**

Lipszyc family. *See* Lipschuetz family

Lipton, Seymour, 13:**77**, 18:223

Liptószentmiklós (Czech Republic). *See* Liptovsky Mikulas (Czech Republic)

Liptovsky Mikulas (Czech Republic), 13:**77–78**

Liptovsky Mikulás (Czech Republic). *See* Liptovsky Mikulas (Czech Republic)

Liptzin, Sol, 13:**78**

Lipzin, Keni, 13:**78**

Lis, Joseph de. *See* Castro Tartas, Isaac de

Lisbon (Portugal), 13:**78–81**

Lishansky, Batya, 13:**81**, 18:223

Lishansky, Yosef, 8:382, 13:**81**, 15:267–268

Li-She'elat ha-Agunah (Epstein), 6:475

Lishem, David (b. Lichtenstein), 5:416

Lisitzky, Ephraim E., 13:**81**

Lismann, Hermann, 13:**81**

Lispector, Clarice, 4:152, 13:**81–82**

L'Israélite Français (journal), 8:270

Lissa, Zofia, 13:**82**

Lissak, Moshe, 13:**82**, 18:735

Lissauer, Ernst, 13:**82**

Lisser, Joshua Falk, 13:**82**

Lissitzky, El, 13:**82–83**

Lissitzky, Lazar. *See* Lissitzky, El

List, Emanuel, 13:**83**

List, George Harold, 13:**83**

Listening to the Growing Grass (Brauner). *See Să auzi iarba cum crește*

Listopad, František, 13:**83**

Liszt, Franz, Joachim, Joseph, 11:340

Lit, Samuel, 13:**83–84**

Lita. *See* Lithuania

Litauer, Jan Jakub, 13:**84**

Lite. *See* Lithuania

Das Literarische Quartette (television show), 17:201

Literary criticism
  Abraham ben Azriel, 1:295
  Abrams, Meyer H., 1:327
  Admoni, Vladimir Grigoryevich, 1:412
  Aḥad ha-Am, 8:726–727
  Aikhenvald Yuli Isayevich, 1:550
  American, 8:737
  anthologies, 8:732
  Auerbach, Erich, 2:654
  Baal-Makhshoves, 3:8
  Bab, Julius, 3:14
  Belinkov, Arkhadii Viktorovich, 3:295–296
  Benichou, Paul, 3:352–353
  Benjamin, Walter, 3:359–360
  Bercovitch, Sacvan, 3:401–402
  Berdiczewski, Micha Josef, 8:726–727
  Berendsohn, Walter A., 3:409–410
  Bernays, Michael, 3:470
  Bialik, Ḥayyim Naḥman, 8:725, 727–728
  Brainin, Reuben, 8:726
  Brenner, Joseph Ḥayyim, 8:728
  Brill, Joel, 8:724
  Caecilius of Calacte, 4:331–332

Camerini, Eugenio Salomone, 4:381

Campen, Michael Herman van, 4:383

Coèn, Graziadio Vita Anania, 4:781

Crohmǎlniceanu, Ovid S., 5:305

Czechoslovakia, 5:367

Dahlberg, Edward, 5:379

Daiches, David, 5:381

Debenedetti, Giacomo, 5:516–517

Delaunay-Terk, Sonia, 5:535

Derrida, Jacques, 5:598

Dobrogeanu-Gherea, Constantin, 5:726

Dobrushin, Yekhezkel, 5:727–728

Fadiman, Clifton, 6:675

Feitelson, Menaham Mendel, 8:727

feminist, 8:731–732

Fichman, Jacob, 7:8–9

Fichmann, Jacob, 8:729

Fiedler, Leslie Aaron, 7:17

Fish, Harel, 7:58

Fish, Stanley, 7:58

Fleischer, Ezra, 8:729

Frischmann, David, 8:726

Fuenn, Samuel Joseph, 8:725

Gordon, Judah Leib, 8:726

Hartman, Geoffrey, 8:376–377

Hebrew, 8:723–733

Ḥever, Ḥanan, 8:731

Hirsch, Eric Donald, Jr., 9:125

Hollander, John, 9:322

Howe, Irving, 9:573

Ibn Ezra, Moses, 8:723–724

Immanuel of Rome, 8:724

Josipovici, Gabriel, 11:461

journals
  academic and popular, 8:730–731
  children's literature, 8:731–732

journals, American, 8:737

Kariv, Avraham Yitzḥak, 8:729

Klausner, J., 8:727

Klausner, Joseph Gedaliah, 12:215–217

Kovner, A. U., 8:725

Kurzweil, Baruch, 8:729

Lachower, Yeruḥam Fishel, 12:424–425

Levertin, Oscar Ivar, 12:681

Levi, Eugenio, 12:687–688

Levin, Harry, 12:709

Lewisohn, Solomon, 8:724

Lillienblum, M. L., 8:726

Lubetzski, I. E., 8:727

Luz, Zvi, 8:732

Miron, Dan, 8:732

Paperna, A. J., 8:725

Pinsky, Robert, 16:176

poetry, 8:731, 732

Polgar, Alfred, 16:331

Rabinowicz, Oskar K., 17:40

Rahv, Philip, 17:69

Rapoport, Judah, 8:725

reading, ways of, 8:731

Reichard, Piroska, 17:199

Reich-Ranicki, Marcel, 17:201

Rivkin, Boruch, 17:348–349

Rosenfeld, Isaac, 17:445–446

Sadan, Dov, 8:729

Sanielevici, Henric, 18:24

Saphir, Moritz Gottlieb, 18:36–37

Satanow, Isaac ha-Levi, 8:724

Shaked, Gershon, 18:366–368

Sinclair, Clive, 18:632

Singer, Isaac Bashevis, 18:634

Smolenskin, Perez, 8:726

Sokolow, Nahum, 8:726

Solotaroff, Theodore H., 18:773

Steinberg, J., 8:727–728

Wessely, Naphtali Herz, 8:724

Literatura, Teoriya, Kritika, Polemika (Eichenbaum), 6:246

Literature
  Abraham, 1:287
  Abraham, Apocalypse of, 1:288–289
  Abraham, Testament of, 1:291
  Absalom, 1:331
  acrostics, 1:368–369
  Adam, 1:375, 377–378
  Akedah, 1:556
  alchemy, 1:602–603
  allegories
    Middle Ages, 1:665–666
    modern, 1:667
  Anglo-Saxon, Daniel in, 5:418
  apocalypse, 2:256–258
  Apocalyptic, 5:418, 421
    Daniel, 5:423–424
    Ezra, 6:654–655
    Vision of Daniel (thirteenth century), 5:426
  apologetic, 2:262–269, 16:114
  Argentina, 6:732–733
  assimilationist, Feldman, Wilhelm, 6:748
  autobiographies, 3:705–709
  Bible's impact on, 3:669–672

Bikkurei ha-Ittim, 3:696–697
biographies, 3:705–709
Bloom, Harold, and Western canon, 3:781
Brazil, 4:152
of Bukharan Jewry, 4:262–263
Cain, 4:341
courtier tales, 5:424
history of, Fraenkel, Jonas, 7:144
Iraq, 10:16–17
Israel, 10:684–685
    Akedah, 1:558–559
    Spanish language, 15:707
Jacob in, 11:23
Jephthah in, 11:123
Jeremiah in, 11:134
Jerusalem in, 11:215–217, 224
Jewish image in
    Danish literature, 18:89–90
    French literature, 7:240–241
    Norwegian literature, 18:94–96
    Swedish literature, 18:92–93
Job in, 11:357–358
Jonah, Book of, 11:390–391
Joseph in, 11:411–412
Josephus and, 11:441
Joshua in, 11:443–444
Judah Maccabee in, 11:510–511
Judith, Book of, 11:567–568
Ladino, 12:432–433
Lamentations, Book of, 12:450
medieval Hebrew, 2:261, 264–268
Moses in, 14:539–541
naturalist school, 4:118, 126
New York City and, 15:210–211, 219, 221, 227
Noah in, 15:289
Odessa as center for, 15:380
paradise in Eden narrative, 15:626–627
parodied, 15:662–663
Portuguese, 2:109, 12:438–439
psalms, *Psalms, Book of,* 16:677–678
psychology approach to, 4:159
Saint Louis (MO), 17:673
Salome, 17:694
Solomon, 18:761
Tower of Babel in, 3:21
U.K., 6:684, 741
U.S., twentieth century, 6:733
See also nams of authors and specific types of literature; Talmudic literature
Literature, Czechoslovak. *See* Czechoslovak literature

Literature, Jewish. *See* Jewish literature
Literature of Destruction: Jewish Responses to Catastrophe (Roskies), 9:415
Literaturgeschichte der synagogalen Poesie (Zunz), 21:686
Lit family, 13:**83–84**
Lithography
    Bien, Julius, 3:690
    Kaplan, Anatoli Lvovich, 11:773
    Sima, Miron, 18:590
Lithuania, 5:432, 13:**117–128,** *118,* 118t–119t, 122t, 126t
    Agudat Israel, 1:505
    antisemitism
        Aleksander Jagiellonczyk, 1:610
        Brest-Litovsk, 4:168–170
    arenda, 2:422
    artisans, 5:268, 12:631
    banishment from community, 3:111
    birth of Jewish socialism in, 18:714
    Birzai, 3:724
    Bloch, Joseph Leib, 3:763
    blood libel in, 3:778
    brokers, 4:204
    communal organization, 9:236
    community, nature of, 5:108, 110
    contemporary period, 20:533
    cooperatives, 5:206
    Council of the Lands, 5:239–244, *241*
    education, 13:123–124, 19:598
    emancipation, 6:385
    emigration, 13:122
    exiles from, 13:121
    expulsions, 4:168
    Fareynigte Partizaner Organizatsye, 20:532–533
    Gaon, 11:712
    Germany, occupation by, 13:125–127
    Grodno, 8:89–91
    Hasidism, 11:809, 12:425
    Haskalah, 13:120
    He-Ḥalutz, 8:759
    He-Ḥalutz (movement), 8:759
    Ḥibbat Zion, 13:120
    history of, 13:117, *118,* 118t–119t, 121–124
    Holocaust, 4:170, 13:125–127, 126t, 16:313–314
        Dvorzetsky, Mark Meir, 6:74
        Jonava, 11:399
        Jurbarkas, 11:577

        Kaunas, 12:36
        Kedainiai, 12:49
        Kelme, 12:71
        Kretinga, 12:355
        Kupiskis, 12:388
        Kybartai, 12:401
        Memel, 14:16
        Plunge, 16:242
        Rokiskis, 17:372
        Seduba, 18:237
        Taurage, 19:529
        Telsiai, 19:598
        Troki, 20:155
        Ukmerge, 20:234
        Utena, 20:444
        Vilkaviškis, 20:526–527
        Vilkaviškis, 20:526–527
        Vilna, 20:532–533
        Virbalis, 20:539
        Wehrmact murders, 9:*474*
        Zagare, 21:443
        Zarasai, 21:458
    independence period, 13:121–124, 122t
    Jewish autonomy, 13:122–123
    Jewish dress, 6:16, 17
    Johannesburg, Jewish immgrants to, 11:377
    Jonava, 11:399
    Jurbarkas, 11:577
    Kabbalists, 11:619, 621–622
    Karaites, 11:792
    Kaunas, 12:35–37
    Kedainai, 12:49
    Labanos family, 12:407–408
    language, 13:117
        translations of Bible, 3:636
    leather industry and trade, 12:577
    liberation of, 13:127
    Lyubeshov dynasty, 13:300
    map, 13:118t
    Middle Ages, agriculture, Jewish, 1:495
    minority rights, 14:290
    Musar movement, 13:119
    nineteenth century scholarship, 6:740
    Ninth Fort, 15:273
    Orthodox Judaism, 11:519
    Palanga, 15:575
    parliamentary elections, 13:124
    peddling in, 15:709
    poetry, Kamson, Ya'akov, 11:758
    Poland and, 16:291–293, 295–296, 299–300
    population, 13:122t

Lithuania, *continued*
post-WW II, 13:127–128
preaching, 16:471–472
responsa, 17:231, 234
scholars
Edelmann, Simḥah Reuben, 6:143
Landau, Isaac Elijah Ben Samuel, 12:461–462
Skuodas, 18:662
Socialist movement, 13:121
spiritual trends and leaders, 13:119–120
USSR rule, 13:124–125
war crimes trials, 13:127
yeshivot, 21:318–319
Leibowitz, Baruch Ber, 12:620
Lewin, Joshua Heshel Ben Elijah Ze'ev Ha-Levi, 12:759–760
YIVO headquarters, WW II, 21:376
Zionism, 13:120
Lithuanian Council, 3:111
Litin (Ukraine), 13:**128–129**
Litinski, Genrikh Ilyich, 13:**129**
Litman, Samuel, 13:**129**
Litomerice (Czech Republic), 13:**129**
Litoměřice (Czech Republic). *See* Litomerice (Czech Republic)
Littauer, Lucius Nathan, 13:**129–130**
Little Annie Fannie (comic strip), 6:296
"The Little Champ." *See* Attell, Abraham Washington
Little Golden Books, 18:177
The Little Golden Calf. See Zolotoy Telenok
"The Little Hebrew." *See* Attell, Abraham Washington
Little Sister. See Ahot Ketannah
Little Tales in Verse. See Mayselekh in Ferzn
Littman, Joseph Aaron, 13:**130**
Littman, Sol, 13:**130**
Littman Library of Jewish Civilization, 13:129
Liturgy, 13:**131–139**, 16:276
acrostics, 1:368–369
Addir bi-Melukhah, 1:384–385
Addir hu, 1:385
Adonai, Adonai El Raḥum ve-Ḥannun, 1:412
Adon Olam, 1:*414*, 414–415
Akedah, 1:556
alphabet, Hebrew, 1:729
Amen, 2:38–39

Amidah, 2:72–76
Amsterdam, 2:111
angelic song, 19:14
angels and, 2:158
antisemitism, *Kol Nidrei*, 12:277
Arvit, ma'aravot, 13:305
Ashkenazi
Mi-Sinai Niggunim, 14:363–364
shtayger, 18:522–523
Ashkenazi rites, 13:134
Babylonian, 13:602
Baer, Seligman Isaac, 3:53
Bakkashah, 3:72–73
Barekhu, 3:149
benedictions, 13:131–132
Bible's impact on, 3:661–662
biblical period, 13:131
Bittul ha-Timid as interruption of daily prayers over injustice, 3:729–730
Bridegrooms of the Law, 4:179–180
Bronstein, Herbert, 4:207–208
Canaanite rites, 13:134
Christian, 4:676–677
David, 5:453–454
Decalogue in, 5:525–526
eighteenth century, 5:463
Elbogen, Ismar, 6:291
feasts and festivals
Leipzig Mahzor, 13:365–366
Mahzor, 13:363–366
Mahzor Vitry, 13:366–367
Worms Mahzor, 13:366
French rites, 13:134
geonic period, 13:132–133
ge'ullah, 7:566–567
gomel blessing, 7:748
Great Hallel, 8:280
Hallel, 8:279–280
Ha-Mavdil, 8:295
hashkivenu, 8:381–382
Ḥasidic, 8:414
havdalah, 8:466–468
hazkarat neshamot, 8:496–497
Heidenheim, Wolf, 8:763
hīneni he-ani mi-ma'as, 9:123
hymns to Creation, 15:760
ingathering of the exiles, 9:786
Iran, 10:13
Iraq, 10:22–23
Italy, 10:814–816
Jerusalem in, 11:213–215
Job in, 11:356
Justinian I's interference with, 11:579

Kaddish, 11:695–698
Karaites, 11:799
Kieval, Hayyim, 12:153
Kol Nidrei, 12:276–278
Lekhah Dodi, 12:632–634, *633*
Mah tovu, 13:362–363
Maḥzor for Rosh Hashanah and Yom Kippur, 8:359
memorial liturgies, 13:134
mornings, Monday and Thursday, 14:435
mourning, 14:588–589
musaf, 14:620–621
Musaf, Malkhuyyot, 13:433–434
music, Maqām, 13:507–508
Passover, Berah Dodi, 3:398
piyyut, 13:132, 14:650–653, *651, 652, 653*, 16:192–209
poetry, 4:243
Alashkar, Moses ben Isaac, 1:576–577
Benjamin ben Azriel, 3:360
Benjamin ben Ḥiyya, 3:361
Benjamin ben Solomon Ha-levi, 3:361
Benjamin Ben Zerah, 3:362
Buchner, Ze'ev Wolf ben David ha-Kohen, 4:243
Byzantine empire, 4:326
Elijah ben Raphael Solomon ha-Levi, 6:340
Elijah ben Shemaiah, 6:340
Elijah Chelebi ha-Kohen of Anatolia, 6:346
Ephraim ben Jacob of Bonn, 6:460
Leonte Ben Moses, 12:648
Meir ben Judah Leib Eisenstadter, 6:272
Silano, 18:575
Simeon ben Megas ha-Konen, 18:598
Solomon Suliman ben Amar, 18:773
Polish rites, 13:134
prayer chant, 14:646–647, 650–653
prayer schedules, 13:131–139
Priestly Blessing, 16:510–511
Provencal rites, 13:135–136
psalms, 13:132
Psalms, Book of, 16:676–677
rain, prayer for, 17:73
Reform Judaism, 4:545–546
reforms of the liturgy, 13:137
Rhineland rites, 13:134
rites, post-geonic, 13:133–136
ritual and
Nine Days, 15:271

Parokhet and Kapporet,
15:663–664
Passover, 15:677–682
Romanian (Greek) rites, 13:135
Roman (Italian) rites, 13:135
Saadiah Gaon, 17:613
Sabbath, maftir, 13:335
Samaritans, 17:736
Satan, 18:73
scholarship
Abudarham, David ben
Joseph, 1:336
Landshuth, Eliezer, 12:476–
477
Sea, Song of the, 18:224, *224*
Seder, Passover, Mah Nishtannah,
13:362
Selihot, 18:268–269
Sephardic, Sola, David Aaron de,
18:751
Sephardi (Spanish) rites, 13:135–
136
seventeenth-twentieth century,
13:136–139
Shaharit, 18:364
Shalom Aleikhem, 18:389–390
Sheikh, Abraham ben Shalom ha-
Levi al-, innovations by, 18:437
Shema, reading of, 18:453–456
Shemoneh Esreh, 18:458
Siddur Sim Shalom, 8:359
Song of the Sea, 18:224
sun, blessing of, 19:314
Talmudic period, 13:131–132
Targumim in, 3:589
tkhines, 13:136–137
U-Netaneh Tokef, 20:247–248
Women involved in, 4:204
worship and
Arabic literature, 15:473
organs used in, 15:466–468
Ya'aleh ve-Yavo, 21:262
Yaknehaz, 21:273–274
Yekum Purkan, 21:299–300
Yemenite rites, 13:136
Yeziv pitgam, 21:331–332
Yiddish, 21:341
Yigdal, 21:373–374
Yishtabbah, 21:375
Yom Kippur, 14:488
yozerot, 21:406–407
Zidduk ha-Din, 21:528
Zikhronot, 21:529
zur mi-Shello, 21:690
See also Azharot, Azharah;
Hazzanim; Liturgical music;
Masoretic Accents, Musical;
Prayer; Prayers; Torah service

Litva. *See* Lithuania
Litvak, Anatole, 13:**139**
Litvak, Michael. *See* Litvak, Anatole
Litvakov, Moses, 13:**139–140**
Litvakov, Moyshe. *See* Litvakov, Moses
Litvin, A., 13:**140**
Litvine, M., 13:**140–141**
Litvinoff, Emanuel, 13:**141**
Litvinov, Maxim Maximovich, 13:**141,**
16:348
Litvinovsky, Pinchas, 13:**141–142**
Litwa. *See* Lithuania
Litwack, Harry, 13:**142**
Litwak, A., 13:**142**
Litzmanstadt (Poland). *See* Lodz
(Poland)
Liuzzi, Fernando, 13:**143**
Liuzzi, Giorgio, 13:142–143
Liuzzi family, 13:**142–143**
Liveright, Horace Brisbin, 13:**143**
Liverpool (England), 13:**143–144**
Liverpool Memorandum Book, 13:143
Lives of the Philosophers (Diogenes
Laertius), 5:674
Livestock, 1:493–494
trade in, 13:**144–145**
Living Bible, 3:619, 621
The Living End (Elkin), 6:359
Living Root (Heller), 20:299
Livingston, Leon, 15:654
*The Living Torah: A New Translation
Based on Traditional Jewish Sources*
(Aryeh Kaplan), 3:623
A Living Tree (Dorff), 5:755
Livnat, Limor, 13:**145–146**
Livni, Hillel, 13:**146**
Livni, Tzipi, 13:**146**
Livorno. *See* Leghorn
Le livre des questions (Jabès), 11:6
Livret de famille (Modiano). *See
Family Record Book* (Modiano)
Livshits, Benedikt Konstantinovich,
13:**146–147**
Livy, 13:**147**
Livyat Hen (Levi), 12:697–698
Liwerant Szclar, Daniel, 13:**147**
Lizards, 13:**147**
Liz Claiborne Inc., 15:492–493
Lizkor ve-Lishko'ah (Ben-Amotz),
3:317
Ljubljana (Slovenia), 13:**147–148**
Lleida. *See* Lérida
Llerda. *See* Lérida
Llerena (Spain), 13:**148**
Lloyd George, David, 3:85–88, 13:**148–
149**

Lloyd-George, Earl. *See* Lloyd George,
David
Loan Bank Ltd., Palestine Economic
Corporation and, 15:588
Loans, 13:149–152, **149–152**
antichresis, 2:193
banks, 2:554
interest-bearing, 5:185
interest on, 12:606
U.S. loan guarantees to Israel,
4:304
See also Obligations, law of; Usury
Loans, Elijah ben Moses, 4:212, 11:421
Loans, Jacob Jehiel, 11:420
Loans and business, commandments
concerning, 5:82t–83t
Loans family, 11:420
Loanz, Elijah ben Moses, 13:**152–153**
Lobato family, 13:**153**
Lobbying, American Israel Public
Affairs Committee, 2:50–52
Locke, John, 9:228
on Bible, 3:664
Orobio de Castro, Isaac, 15:481
Locker, Berl, 13:**153**
Locker, Malke, 13:**153**
Lockspeiser, Ben. *See* Lockspeiser, Sir
Ben
Lockspeiser, Edward, 13:**154**
Lockspeiser, Sir Ben, 13:**153**
Locusts, 6:494, 11:361, 362, 13:**154**
Lod (Israel). *See* Lydda (Israel)
Lo-Debar (Israel), 13:**154–155**
The Lodestone. See Magnet
Lodève (France), 13:**155**
Lodge, Thomas, 11:441
Lodi (Italy), 13:**155**
Lodmer. *See* Vladimir Volynsk
(Ukraine)
Lodmir (Ukraine). *See* Vladimir
Volynski (Ukraine)
Lods, Adolphe, 3:658, 13:**155**
Lodskh (Poland). *See* Lodz (Poland)
Lodz (Poland), 13:**155–160,** 155t,
16:301t, 307–308
coins and currency, 5:53
ghetto, 7:576, 9:467, 469, 470–471,
476–478, 13:158–160, 16:308
Jewish residents, 9:462
Loeb, Aaron. *See* Jeiteles, Andreas
Ludwig Joseph Heinrich
Loeb, Aryeh. *See* Mandelstamm, Leon
Loeb, Baruch, 11:114–115
Loeb, Benedict. *See* Loeb, Baruch
Loeb, Ignaz, 11:115
Loeb, Isaac. *See* Loeb, Ignaz
Loeb, Isaac. *See* Wormser, Sekel

Loeb, Isidore, 13:**160,** 18:721
Loeb, Jacques, 13:7, **160**
Loeb, James, 13:**160–161**
Loeb, Jonas, 11:114
Loeb, Judah, 11:115. *See* Dukes, Leopold
Loeb, Leo, 13:**161**
Loeb, Mishel, 11:114
Loeb, Morris, 13:**161**
Loeb, Solomon, 12:381–382
Loebel, Hirsch. *See* Levin, Ẓevi Hirsch ben Aryeh Loeb
Loebel, Israel, 8:415, 13:**161–162**
Loebl, Eugen, 13:**162**
Loebl, Evžen, 18:665
Loeb-Leopold case, 13:**162**
Loehner, Fritz. *See* Beda
Loerrach (Germany), 3:44
Loesener, Bernhard, Nuremberg laws, 15:348, 349, 350
Loesser, Frank, 13:**162**
Die Loesung der Judenfrage (Schrenzel), 18:168
Loetscher, Hugo, Noah in writings of, 15:289
Loevenstein, Fedor, 13:**162**
Loew, Asher, 15:385
Loew, Eleazar, 13:**162–163**
Loew, Immanuel, 13:**163**
Loew, Judah ben Bezalel, 7:360–361
Loew, Leopold, 13:**163–164**
Loew, Lipót. *See* Loew, Leopold
Loew, Marcus, 13:**164**
Loew, Moritz, 13:**164**
Loew-Beer family, 13:**164**
Loewe, Bril. *See* Loewe, Joel
Loewe, Eliakim. *See* Loewe, Heinrich
Loewe, Frederick, 13:**164–165**
Loewe, Fritz Philipp, 13:**165**
Loewe, Heinrich, 11:570, 13:**165**
Loewe, Herbert Martin James, 13:**165–166,** 15:554
Loewe, Isidor. *See* Loewe, Ludwig and Isidor
Loewe, Joel, 13:**166**
Loewe, Louis, 13:**166–167**
Loewe, Ludwig and Isidor, 13:**167,** 16:344
Loewe, Maximilian, 13:232
Loewe, Victor, 13:**167**
Loewe family. *See* Low family
Loewenson, Hans. *See* Loewenson, Jean
Loewenson, Jean, 13:**167**
Loewenstamm, Aryeh Loeb ben Saul, 2:107, 13:167
Loewenstamm, Saul, 2:107, 13:167–168

Loewenstamm family, 2:108, 13:**167–168**
Loewenstein, Bernhard, 13:**168**
Loewenstein, Captain Leo, 17:201
Loewenstein, Hilde. *See* Domin, Hilde
Loewenstein, Karl, 13:**168**
Loewenstein, Kurt, 13:**168**
Loewenstein, Leopold, 13:**169**
Loewenstein, Nathan, 13:**169**
Loewenstein, Rudolph Maurice, 13:**169**
Loewenstein-Strashunsky, Joel David, 13:**169–170**
Loewenstein von Opoka, Nathan. *See* Loewenstein, Nathan
Loewenthal, Eduard, 13:**170**
Loewenthal, Johann Jakob, 13:**170**
Loewenthal, Zdenko, 13:**170**
Loewi, Otto, 13:10, **170**
Loewinger, David Samuel, 13:**170**
Loewinson-Lessing, Franz Yulyevich, 13:**170–171**
Loewisohn, Solomon, 8:440, 687, 13:**171**
Loewith, Karl, 13:**171–172**
Loewy, Emanuel, 13:**172**
Loewy, Fritz. *See* Beda
Loewy, Isaac, 13:**172**
Loewy, Jacob Ezekiel ben Joseph, 13:**172**
Loewy, Maurice, 13:**172**
Loggem, Manuel van, 13:**172–173**
Logic, 13:**173–174**
　Anatoli, Jacob ben Abba Mari ben Samson, 2:132
　literature, Luzzatto, Moses Ḥayyim, 13:283
　Maimonides, Moses, 13:173
　sevarah, 18:322–323
　Sheffer, Henry M., 18:432–433
Logic (Reines). *See* *Higgayon* (Reines)
Logical empiricism. *See* Logical positivism
Logical positivism, 6:735
The Logical Structure of Linguistic Theory (Chomsky), 4:665
Logical Terms (Maimonides), 4:524
The Logic of Moral Discourse (Edwards), 6:215
Logic of the Heart, Logic of the Mind (Soloveichik), 18:775
Logos, 2:159, 13:**174–175**
Loḥamei ha-Getta'ot (Israel), 13:**175**
　See also Ghetto Fighters' House (Israel)
Loḥamei Ḥerut Israel, 1:211–212, 3:435, 6:292, 10:206, 207, 208, 13:**175–176**
　Amir, Aharon, 2:78

Olei ha-Gardom, 15:402
　Shamir, Yitzhak, 18:393
Lohr, I., Joshua, Book of, 11:448
Loisy, Alfred Firmin, 13:**176**
Lollard Bible, 3:611
Lolli, Eude, 13:**176–177**
Lom, Herbert, 13:**177**
Lo Matimim le-Ḥalom ha-Ẓiyyoni (Yemini), 18:206
Lombard, Peter, 4:96
Lombardy (Italy), 13:**177–178**
Lombroso, Cesare, 5:301–302, 13:**178**
Lomdim, 6:212
Lomza (Poland), 13:**178–179**
Lomzer, Ḥayyim. *See* Wasserzug, Ḥayyim
Lomzha (Poland). *See* Lomza (Poland)
Lomzhe (Poland). *See* Lomza (Poland)
London (England), 13:**179–184,** *183*
　diamond trade and industry, 5:635
　Elias Le Eveske, 6:320
　map, 13:183*t*
　Medieval period, 13:179–180
　Middle period, 13:180
　Orthodox Judaism, 1:328
　postwar period, 13:182–183
　Resettlement period, 12:747, 13:180–182
　secondhand goods trade, 18:231–232
　synagogue archives, 2:408
　twentieth century developments, 13:183–184
　United Synagogue, 20:*404,* 404–405
　See also England
London, Artur, 13:**184,** 18:665
London, Fritz, 13:**184–185**
London, George, 13:**185**
London, Jacob ben Moses Judah, 13:**185**
London, Mayer, 18:708
London, Meyer, 13:**185–186,** 15:205, 211
London, Solomon Zalman ben Moses Raphael, 13:**186**
London Board of Jewish Religious Education, 6:206
London Conference. *See* Saint James's Conference
London Jews' Society, New Testament in Hebrew published by, 3:681
A London Plane Tree (Levy), 12:747
London Polyglot (Walton), 13:56
London Pride (Lyons), 13:297
London Talmud Torah Council, 6:205
The Lonely Crowd: A Study of the Changing American Character (Riesman), 17:294

Lonely Man of Faith (Soloveitchik), 1:285, 18:778

The Lonely Years (Babel), 3:19

Long Beach (CA), 13:**186–187**

Long Night's Journey into Day: A Revised Retrospective on the Holocaust (Eckardt), 6:91

Longo, Saadiah, 4:302, 13:**187**

The Long Voyage (Semprun), 9:411

Lons-le-Saunier (France), 13:**187**

Lonzano, Abraham ben Raphael de, 13:**187**

Lonzano, Menaham ben Judah de, 3:587, 588, 13:**187–188**

Looking Ahead (Mendes), 18:202, 21:620

Looking for Fred Schmidt (Epstein), 6:476

Lookstein, Haskel, 13:**188**

Lookstein, Joseph Hyman, 3:153, 11:575, 13:**188–189**, 15:495

Loon Lake (Doctorow), 5:728

Lopès-Dubec, Camille, 4:83

Lopès-Dubec, S., 4:83

Lopes family, 9:6, 13:**189**

Lopez, Aaron, 13:**189**
   American Jewish Archives, 2:53
   North Carolina, 15:302

López, Alexis, 4:643

Lopez, Isaac, 4:99

Lopez, Robert Sabatino, 13:**189–190**

Lopez, Roderigo, 2:66, 13:**190,** 18:369

Lopez, Sabatino, 13:**190**

Lopez Rosa family, 13:**190**

Lopian, Elijah, 13:**190–191**

Lopoliansky, Uri, 13:**191**

Lo raḥok mi-Merkaz ha-Ir (Castel-Bloom), 4:512

Lorbeerbaum, Jacob ben Jacob Moses of Lissa, 13:**191–192**

Lorber, Judith, 18:736

Lord George Bentinck (Disraeli), 6:436

Lord Horror (Britton), 18:202

Lord of the Covenant. *See* Baal-Berith

Lord's Day Alliance, 4:396

The Lord's Fight. See Malḥamot ha-Shem

Lorentz, Einhart, 18:96

Lorenzo the Magnificent, 7:84

Lorge, Irving, 13:**192**

The Lorge-Thorndike Intelligence Tests (Lorge), 13:192

Loria, Achille, 13:**192**

Loria family. *See* Luria family

Loritz, Alfred, 15:76

Lorje, Chaim, 13:**192**

Lorki, Joshua, 6:61, 13:**192–193**
   Geronimo de Santa Fé, 11:472

Pablo de Santa Maria, 15:562

Lorm, Hieronymus, 13:**193**

l'Oronaise, Reinette. *See* Da'ud, Sultana

Loronha, Fernão de. *See* Noronha, Fernão de

Lorraine (France), 7:154, 13:**193–194**

Lorre, Peter, 13:**194–195**

Lortel, Lucille, 13:**195**

Los Angeles (CA), 13:**195–211**
   1970-2005, 13:198–200
   community organization, 13:196–197
   demographic revolution of the 1980s, 13:198
   early beginnings, 13:195–196
   education, 13:205–207, 207–208
   history of, 13:195–196
   Jewish Federation Council, 13:208–209
   Jewish population of the 1980s, 13:198–199
   journalism, 13:209
   population growth, 13:196–198
   religious developments, 13:197–200
   religious organization, 13:197–198, 200–207
      rabbi-community builders, 13:203–204
      rabbi-educators, 13:205–207
      rabbi-institution builders, 13:200–203
      rabbi-social activists, 13:204–205
   Sinai Temple, 12:804
   Skirball Cultural Center, 18:**659–660**
   welfare organizations, 13:210–211

Los Angeles Conservation Corps, 11:771

Loschitz (Czech Republic). *See* Lostice (Czech Republic)

Loshits (Poland). *See* Losice (Poland)

Losice (Poland), 13:**211**

Lositsy (Poland). *See* Losice (Poland)

Los Nuestros (Bendelac), 8:244

Losonc (Slovakia). *See* Lucenec (Slovakia)

L'Osservatore Romano, 9:371

Lost and Found (Adelman), 1:386

The Lost Childhood (Nir), 9:414

Lostice (Czech Republic), 13:**211–212,** 15:117

Loštice (Czech Republic). *See* Lostice (Czech Republic)

Lost property, 13:**212–215,** 14:358
   basis of the Law, 13:212

commandments concerning, 5:77t–78t, 13:213–215
   Hendeles judgment, 13:214
   loss of ownership, 13:213
   mitzvah, 13:212
   resignation, concept of, 13:213
   restoration, 13:212
   retention of ownership, 13:212

The Lost Shore (Langfus), 9:408, 12:482

Lot, 13:**215–216,** 18:738
   Abraham, 1:281
   Ammonites, 2:83, 86
   in the arts, 18:739–740
   Moab, 14:399
   See also Sodom and Gomorrah (ancient cities)

Lotan, Giora, 13:**216**

Loterai, 11:550

Lothaire. *See* Clotaire II

Lothar. *See* Clotaire II

Lothar, Ernst, 13:**216–217**

Lothar, Rudolf, 13:**217**

Lothar of Segni. *See* Innocent

Lotman, Yuri Mikhailovich, 13:**217**

Lots, 7:369–370, 13:**217–219**
   Biblical data, 13:217–218
   post-Talmudic times, 13:219
   Qumran, 13:218–219
   Second Temple period, 13:218–219
   "throwing" lots, 13:218

Lot's wife, 18:739–740

Lotteries, 7:369–370

Lotus jujube, 11:572

Louchheim, Stuart F., 7:76

Louis (kings of France), 1:313, 13:**219–222**

Louis, Joe, 11:50

Louis, Morris, 13:**222**

Louis VII (King of France), 15:643

Louis-Dreyfus, Julia, 13:**222,** 15:228

Louisiana (U.S.), 13:**222–224,** *223,* 223t

Louis IV (Emperor of Germany), 15:438

Louis IX (King of France), 4:673, 7:150, 15:643

Louis Napoleon. *See* Napoleon III

Louis the Pious. *See* Louis (kings of France)

Louisville (KY), 13:**224–226**
   See also Kentucky (U.S.)

Louny (Czech Republic), 13:**226**

Lourie, Arthur (1892-1966), 13:**226**

Lourie, Arthur (1903-1978), 13:**226**

Lourie, Norman Victor, 13:**226**

Lourie, Vincent. *See* Lourie, Arthur (1892-1966)

Lourie family. *See* Luria family

Louse. *See* Lice

Louvish, Simon, 6:440

Love, 13:**227–232**

   and fear of God, 13:230–231

   Ḥasidic, 8:408

   Hebrew words for love, 13:227

   intermarriage, 14:373–374

   Jonathan and David, love between, 11:396

   justice and, 11:578

   neighbor, 13:231

   of neighbor, 13:231

   poetry, of Judah Halevi, 11:494

   post-Biblical, 13:229–230

   reciprocal love of God and people, 13:227–229

   Song of Songs, 13:229

   songs, taboos, 2:132

   spontaneous relationship, as, 13:227

   in the Bible, 13:227

Love. *See* Szerelem

A Love in Germany (Hochhuth), 9:299

Lovell, Leopold, 13:**232**, 16:349

The Love of Aaron. *See* Aronova ljubav

Love of God, 3:**240**, 6:725

The Love of King David and Fair Bethsabe (Peele), 1:331

The Lover (Pinter), 16:177

Lovers (Eisner), 6:277

Lovestone, Jay, 13:**232**

Love Story (Segal), 18:245

The Love Story of Aliette Brunton (Frankau), 7:196

Love Your Neighbor and Yourself (Dorff), 5:755

Lovy, Israel, 13:**232**

Low, Maurice, 13:233

Low, Minnie, 13:**233**

Low, Seth, 15:211

Low, Sidney James Mark, 13:232–233

Low, William Ze'ev, 13:**233–234**

Lowdermilk, Walter Clay, 13:**234**

Lowe, Adolph, 13:**234**

Lowe, Elias Avery, 13:**234**

Lowenstein, Allard Kenneth, 13:**235**

Lowenstein, Laszlo. *See* Lorre, Peter

Lowenstein, Solomon, 13:**235**

Lowenthal, Kathe. *See* Gershon, Karen

Lowenthal, Marvin, 13:**235**

Lowenthal, Wilhelm, 2:429

Lower, Arthur, 4:404

Lower East Side (New York City), 5:414

Lowey, Nita Melnikoff, 13:**235–236**

Low family, 13:232, **232–233**

Lowicz (Poland), 13:**236**

Lowie, Robert Harry, 2:186, 13:**236–237**

Lowinsky, Edward Elias, 13:**237**

Lown, Philip W., 2:47, 13:**237**

Lown Institute for Advanced Judaic Studies (Brandeis University), 2:23

Lowry, Israel, 4:660

Lowth, Robert, 3:737, 13:**237**

Lowy, Frank, 13:**237–238**

Lowy, Israel. *See* Lovy, Israel

Lowy, Israel Glogauer. *See* Lovy, Israel

de Loya family. *See* Delouya family

Loyalties (Galsworthy), 6:436

Loyeva, Olga, 18:379–380

Loyter, Efraim Barukhovich, 13:**238**

Loytsker, Khaim, 11:322

Lozano, Menahem di, 14:667

Lo Zeh ha-Derekh (Aḥ ha-Am), 1:525–526, 527

Lozinski, Samuel, 13:**238**

Lozinsky, Kadish. *See* Luz, Kadish

Lozniany (Belarus). *See* Liozno (Belarus)

Lozovski, Solomon Abramovich, 13:**238–239**

Lozowick, Louis, 13:**239**

Łachowicze (Belarus). *See* Lyakhovichi (Belarus)

Łomża (Poland). *See* Lomza (Poland)

Łosice (Poland). *See* Losice (Poland)

Łowicz (Poland). *See* Lowicz (Poland)

Łubaczów (Poland). *See* Lubaczow (Poland)

Łuck (Ukraine). *See* Lutsk (Ukraine)

Lubaczow (Poland), 13:**239**

Lubarsky, Abraham Elijah, 13:**239–240**

Lubartow (Poland), 13:**240**

Lubartów (Poland). *See* Lubartow (Poland)

Lubavich (Russia), 13:**240**

Lubavitch Ḥasidim, 8:421

Lubavitch movement

   Dworkin, Zalman Shimon, 6:75

   education, Jewish, 6:197, 214

   in Johannesburg, 11:378

Lubetkin, Zivia, 13:**240–241**

Lubetzky, Judah, 13:**241**

Lubetzski, I. E., 8:727

Lubianiker, Pinḥas, 12:532–533

Lubicz-Milosz, Oscar Vencelas de. *See* Milosz, Oscar

Lubieszów (Lithuania). *See* Lyubeshov (Lithuania)

Lubin, Abraham, 13:**241**

Lubin, Isador, 13:**241–242**

Lubin, Simon Julius, 13:**242**

Lubinski, Georg. *See* Lotan, Giora

Lubitch, Joseph, 15:649

Lubitsch, Ernst, 13:**242**, 14:571

Lublin (Poland), 1:300, 13:**242–245**

   arenda, 2:423

   blood libel in, 3:776

   Holocaust, 16:310–311

Lublin, Lilly Applebaum, 9:337–338

Lublin, Meir ben Gedaliah, 1:532, 4:779, 13:**245**

Lubliner, Stanislaus Hernisz Ludwig, 16:346–347

Lublin Hasidism, 11:39–41

Lublinski, Samuel, 13:**245–246**

Lubny (Ukraine), 13:**246**

Luboshitzki, Aaron, 13:**246**

Luboshutz family, 13:**246**

Lubotzky, Binyamin. *See* Eliav, Binyamin

Lubraniec (Poland), 13:**246–247**

Lubrentsk (Poland). *See* Lubraniec (Poland)

Luca, B., 13:**247**

Lucan, 13:**247**

Lucca (Italy), 13:**247**

Lucca, Pauline, 13:**247**

Lucena (Spain), 13:**247–248**

Lucena, Abraham de, 15:195

Lučenec (Slovakia). *See* Lucenec (Slovakia)

Lucenec (Slovakia), 13:**248**

Lucent Technologies, 12:713

Lucerna family. *See* Ma'or Katan family

Lucerne (Switzerland), 13:**249**

Lucian of Samosata, 6:483, 13:**249**

Lucille Lortel Theater, 13:195

Lucius Annaeus Seneca. *See* Seneca the Younger

Luck (Czech Republic). *See* Luka (Czech Republic)

Lucki, Aben Yashar. *See* Luzki, Abraham ben Joseph Solomon

Lucki, Simḥah Isaac ben Moses. *See* Luzki, Simḥah Isaac ben Moses

Lucki, Yashar. *See* Luzki, Joseph solomon ben Moses

Luckman, Sid. *See* Luckman, Sidney

Luckman, Sidney, 13:**249**

Luckner, Gertrud, 4:712

Lucretius. *See* Widmanstetter, Johann Albrecht

Lucuas, 13:**249–250**

Ludmir. *See* Vladimir Volynski

Ludo, Isac Iacovitz, 1:376–377, 13:**250**
Ludomir, Maid of, 8:398, 13:**250,** 21:177–178
Ludvík, Frejka, 18:665
Ludvipol, Abraham, 8:497, 13:**251**
Ludwig, Emil, 11:412, 13:**251**
Ludwig, Jack, 4:424
Ludwig, Reuben, 13:**251**
Ludwig Kossuth (Einhorn), 6:259
Ludwig of Bavaria, 2:476–477
Ludza (Latvia), 13:**251–252**
Luebeck (Germany), 13:**252**
Lueger, Karl, 13:**252–253**
Lueneberg (Germany), 13:**253**
Luettich (Belgium). *See* Liége (Belgium)
Luftspring, Sammy, 13:**253**
Lugansk (Ukraine), 13:**253**
Luge, 19:145
Lugo (Italy), 13:**253–254**
Lugoj (Romania), 13:**254**
Lugos (Romania). *See* Lugoj (Romania)
Luḥot Edut (Emden), 6:393
Luidor, Joseph, 13:**254**
Luik (Belgium). *See* Liége (Belgium)
Luiz, Thomás. *See* Castro Tartas, Isaac de
Luka (Czech Republic), 13:**254**
Lukács, Georg, 13:**254–255,** 18:729
Lukács, György. *See* Lukács, Georg
Lukas, Paul, 13:**255**
Luke, H. C., 15:582
Lukhes (Bader), 3:45
Lukov (Poland). *See* Lukow (Poland)
Lukow (Poland), 13:**255–256**
Luków (Poland). *See* Lukow (Poland)
Lul (television show), 6:263
Lulav, 8:332, 13:**256**
Lulianus. *See* Pappus and Julianus
Lumbroso, Abraham ben Isaac, 13:**256**
Lumbroso, Alberto Emmanuele, 13:**256**
Lumbroso, Giacomo, 13:**256**
Lumbroso, Isaac ben Jacob, 13:**256**
Lumbroso family, 13:**256**
Lumen ad Revelationem Gentium (Alfonso de Oropesa), 1:643
Lumen Gentium (Sforno), 18:334
Lumet, Sidney, 13:**256–257**
Lumina, 13:**257**
Luna: Gan Eden Geneti (Moav), 18:205
Lunacharsky, A., 4:90
Lunah (Burla), 4:295
Lunar calendar, 2:128, 4:354–359, 14:468

Luncz, Abraham Moses, 13:**257–258**
Lundenburg (Czech Republic). *See* Breclav
Lunel (France), 13:**258–259**
Lunel, Armand, 13:**259**
Lunel, Jacob de, 13:**259**
    Judeo-Provençal literature, 11:560
Lunéville (France), 13:**259**
Lunge, Georg, 13:**259**
Lunietz, Gedaliah ben Issac of, 13:**259**
Lunts, Lev Natanovich, 13:**259–260**
L'Uomo delinquente (Lombroso), 13:178
Lupin, Henry, 14:454
Luria, Aaron, 13:**260**
Luria, Abraham, 8:735
Luria, Alexander Romanovich, 6:161, 13:**261**
Luria, David ben Jacob Aaron, 13:**261**
Luria, David ben Judah, 13:**261–262**
Luria, Gabriel, 4:77
Luria, Isaac, 2:10, 4:128, 13:134
    Abraham ben Eliezer ha-Levi Berukhim, 1:299
    Adam Kadmon, 1:379
    angels, 2:158
    Jonah, Moses, 11:392
    Joseph ben Shalom Ashkenazi, 11:426
    Joseph della Raina legend, 11:428
    Joseph Ibn Shraga, 11:430
    Joshua ben Nun, 11:456
    literature, 7:15, 16
    Sarug, Israel, 18:63
    on Shekhinah, 18:444
Luria, Isaac ben Solomon, 13:**262–267**
    Berurei Averah/Averot and, 3:492
Luria, Jehiel ben Israel Ashkenazi, 13:**267**
Luria, Johanan, 2:6, 13:260
Luria, Noah, 13:**267**
Luria, Salvador Edward, 13:9, **267–268**
Luria, Solomon ben Jehiel, 1:532, 4:778, 11:423, 13:**268–269,** 18:675
    on competition, 8:451
    Ḥayyim ben Bezalel, 8:480
    Isserles, Moses ben Israel, 16:295–296
Luria family, 13:**260–261**
Lurianic mysticism. *See* Kabbalah
Lurie, Esther, 2:517
Lurie, Harry Lawrence, 13:**269**
Lurie, Joseph, 6:399, 13:**269**
Lurie, Ranan Raymond, 13:**270**
Lurie, S., Amusin, Joseph, 2:124
Lurie, Ted, 13:**270**

Lurie, Zvi, 13:**270**
Lurja family. *See* Luria family
Lurje family. *See* Luria family
Lurye, Noyekh. *See* Luria, Noah
Luschan, Felix von, 13:**270**
Luser Segermacher (Moses), 14:544
Lusitanus. *See* Amatus Lusitanus
Lusitanus, Amatus, 13:727
Lust (Jelinek), 11:119
Lustig, Arnost, 13:**270–271**
Lustig, Moses, 13:**271**
Die lustigen Weiber von Windsor (libretto, Mosenthal). *See The Merry Wives of Windsor* (libretto, Mosenthal)
Lustiger, Jean-Marie Aron, 13:**271**
Luther, Martin, 13:**271–272**
    Abraham, 1:285
    antisemitism of, 13:272, 17:163–164
    Bible translations by, 3:612, 630–631
        Danish translations influenced by, 3:627
        Dutch translations influenced by, 3:627
        French translations influenced by, 3:628
        Icelandic translations influenced by, 3:632
    on issues of, 3:607
    biblical canon for, 3:666
    Joseph ben Gershon of Rosheim, 11:421, 13:272
    on Judith (biblical book) as dramatic theme, 11:567
    Osiander, Andreas, 15:503
    Rashi's influence on, 3:648
Lutheran Church
    in Germany, Jewish relations, 11:281
    Holocaust, response to, 9:376
    Israel (state), 10:640–641
Lutomiersk (Poland), 13:**272–273**
Lutostanski, Hippolyte, 3:779, 13:**273**
Lutsk (Ukraine), 13:**273–274**
Lutz, Carl, 13:**274–275**
Lutz, Charles. *See* Lutz, Carl
Lutzerner family. *See* Ma'or Katan family
Lutziner, Itzele, 13:251–252
Lutzki, Yashar. *See* Luzki, Joseph Solomon ben Moses
Lutzky, A., 13:**275**
Lux, Lilian, 4:301
Lux, Stefan, 13:**275**
Luxembourg, 13:**275–276**
    Holocaust, 9:339

Luxembourg, *continued*
    relations with Israel, 13:276
Luxemburg. *See* Luxembourg
Luxemburg, Rosa, 11:368–369,
    13:**276–277**, 16:344, 347, 18:705,
    713
    on capitalism, 18:729
    women in revolution, 18:736
Luz (Israel), 13:**277**, 279
    See also Bet-El (Israel)
La Luz (newspaper), 6:366
Luz, Kadish, 13:**277–278**
Luz, Zvi, 8:732
Luzern (Switzerland). *See* Lucerne
    (Switzerland)
Luzerner family. *See* Ma'or Katan
    family
Luzki, Abraham ben Joseph Solomon,
    13:**278**
Luzki, Joseph Solomon ben Moses,
    11:793, 13:**278**
Luzki, Simḥah Isaac ben Moses,
    11:792, 13:**278–279**
Luz of the spine, 13:**279**
Luzzati family. *See* Luzzatto family
Luzzato, Simhah
    apologetics, 2:267
    exile, meaning of, 7:362
Luzzato, Simone. *See* Luzzato, Simhah
Luzzatti, Luigi, 13:**279–280**, 16:345
Luzzatto, Angelo. *See* Luzzatto,
    Ephraim
Luzzatto, Ephraim, 8:688, 13:**280–281**
Luzzatto, Gino, 13:**281**
Luzzatto, Isaac, 13:**281**, 18:10
Luzzatto, Isacco. *See* Luzzatto, Isaac
Luzzatto, Jacob ben Isaac, 13:**281**
Luzzatto, Moses Ḥayyim, 6:180, 530,
    13:**281–286**, 16:345, 18:357
    autobiographical elements of
        writings, 3:706, 13:281–286
    categories, propositions, and
        syllogisms, 13:283
    ethical works, 13:284–285
    kabbalistic writings, 13:283–284
    Lachower, Yeruḥam Fishel, 12:424
    Lampronti, Isaac Hezekiah Ben
        Samuel and, 12:454
    letters, 13:285
    literary criticism, 8:724
    Maggid, divine voice of, 13:282
    Mesillat Yesharim, 13:284
    messianic doctrine, 13:282
    order or gradation, 13:283
    plays, 13:285
    poetry, 13:285
    reasoning's three modes, 13:283

Sheluḥei Erez Israel, 18:451
    treatises on logic, 13:283
    ẓimẓum, 13:284
Luzzatto, Samuel David, 10:802–803,
    12:519, 13:**286–287**, 16:96, 21:107–
    108
    biblical exegesis and study, 3:646
    on derivation of term masorah,
        13:614–615
    education, Jewish, 6:181
    Italian translation of Bible by,
        3:633
    miracles, 14:309
    Morpurgo, Rachel Luzzatto,
        14:509
    Padua, 15:567
    piyyut, language of, 8:652
Luzzatto, Simone ben Isaac Simḥah,
    13:**287–288**
Luzzatto family, 13:**280**
Lvov (Ukraine), 11:735, 13:**288–292**
    from 1684 to 1772, 13:289
    from 1772 to 1914, 13:289–290
    from 1914 to 1939, 13:290–291
    assimilationist intelligentsia
        groups, 13:290
    early settlements, 13:288
    Frankist movement, 7:185–187
    Ḥasidism, 13:290
    Hebrew printing, 13:291
    Janowska Road camp, 13:291
    refugees' arrival, 13:290
    trades and craftsmen, 13:288–289
    trends within the community,
        13:290
    two communities, 13:288–289
    Zionist influences, 13:290
Lvovich, David, 13:**292–293**
Lvovich, Marc. *See* Slonim, Marc
Lwoff, André Michel, 13:9, **293**
Lwów (Ukraine). *See* Lvov (Ukraine)
Lyady (Russia), 13:**293**
Lyakhovichi (Belarus), 13:**293**
Lyakhovichi, Mordecai ben Mordecai
    ben Noah of. *See* Lachowicze,
    Mordecai ben Mordecai ben Noah
    of
Lybartov (Poland). *See* Lubartow
    (Poland)
Lybavichi (Russia). *See* Lubavich
    (Russia)
Lychnidos. *See* Ochrida
Lyck (Poland), 13:**293–294**
Lydda (Israel), 13:**294–295**
Lydda, Council of, Judaism, essential
    principles of, 11:512
Lydia and Lydians, 13:**295–296**

Lykeus. *See* Popper, Jozef
Lykke-Per (Pontoppidan), 18:90
Lynen, Feodor, Bloch, Konrad, 3:765
Lyon, Emma. *See* Henry, Emma
Lyon, George Lewis, *Jewish World*,
    11:332
Lyon, Hart. *See* Levin, Ẓevi Hirsch
    ben Aryeh Loeb
Lyon, Morton Sahl. *See* Sahl, Mort
Lyon-Caen, Charles Léon, 12:550,
    13:**296**
Lyons (France), 13:**296–297**
    early Jewish population, 13:296
    Holocaust, 13:297
    postwar period, 13:297
    Sephardi community, 13:297
Lyons, Albert Michael Neil, 13:**297**
Lyons, Eugene, 13:**297**
Lyons, Israel, 13:**297–298**
Lyons, Jacques Judah, 13:**298**, 15:198
    American Jewish Historical
        Society, 2:59
Lyons, Joseph. *See* Lyons, Sir Joseph
Lyons, Leonard, 13:**298**
Lyons, Robert, 15:199
Lyons, Sir Joseph, 13:**298**
Lyotard, Jean-François, 13:**298–299**
Lyriske Forsøg (Siesby), 18:560
Lysanias, 13:**299**
Lysias, 9:194, 13:**299–300**
    Nicanor, 15:247
    Silas, 18:575
Lysimachus of Alexandria, 13:**300**,
    14:531
Lyubeshov (Lithuania), 13:**300**
Lyuboml (Ukraine), 13:**300–301**
Lyuboml (Ukraine). *See* Lyuboml
    (Ukraine)
Lyubranets (Poland). *See* Lubraniec
    (Poland)
Lyudi, gody, zhizn (Ehrenburg). *See*
    Memoirs (Ehrenburg); *People and
    Life 1891-1921, 1962* (Ehrenburg)
Lyutsin (Latvia). *See* Ludza (Latvia)
Lyzhansk Ḥasidim, 8:421

M

M (letter), 13:*303*, 14:5
M. Cocceius Nerva. *See* Nerva
M. Valerius Martialis. *See* Martial
Maacah, 13:**303–304**
*Ma'adanei Melekh. See The King's
    Delicacies* (Mizrahi)
Ma'agan Mikha'el (Israel), 13:**304**
Ma'aleh Adumim (Israel), 13:**304**
Ma'aleh Akrabbim (Israel), 13:**304**
Ma'aleh ha-Ḥamishah (Israel), 13:**304**

Ma'alot ha-Torah (Ragoler), 17:65

Ma'alot-Tarshīḥā, 13:**304–305**

Ma'amad, 13:**305**

Ma'amadot. *See* Mishmarot and Ma'amadot

Ma'amad Sheloshtan, 2:604

Ma'amar be-Kabbalah Nevu'it. See Keter Shem Tov

Ma'amarei Ḥokhmah (newspaper), 18:679

Ma'amar ha-AḥdutI (Jabez), 2:531

Ma'amar ha-Ishut al Tekhunat ha-Rabbanim ve-ha- Kara'im (Holdheim), 9:317

Ma'amar Ḥayyei Olam (Pisa), 16:185

Ma'amar Mordekhai (Halberstadt), 8:264

Ma'amarot, the ten. See Sefirot

Ma'amar Peloni Almoni. See Keter Shem Tov

Ma'amar Perek Ḥelek (Abraham ben Eliezer ha-Levi), 1:298

Ma'amar Yikkavu ha-Mayim (Ibn Tibbon), 3:239, 19:712

Ma'aneh Lashon (Jacob ben Abraham Solomon), 11:29, 30

Ma'anit (Israel), 13:**305**

Ma'aravot, 13:**305**

Ma'arekhet (Ḥayyat), 8:479

Ma'arekhet ha-Elohut, 13:**305–306**

Ma'ariv. *See* Arvit

Maariv (newspaper), 10:706, 707, 13:**306–307**, 18:152

Ma'arivim. *See* Ma'aravot

Maarsen, Isaac, 13:**307**

Maarsen, Moses, 2:24

Ma'arufya, 13:**307**

Ma'as (Israel), 13:**307–308**

Ma'aseh, 13:**308–313**, 14:338

Ma'aseh Adonai (Ashkenazi), 2:573

Ma'aseh Alfes (Alfes), 1:641–642

Ma'aseh Efod (Duran), 6:57, 13:34, 42

Ma'aseh Ḥoshev (Levi ben Gershom), 13:674

Ma'aseh Merkavah. *See* Merkabah mysticism

Ma'aseh Nissim (Aaron ben David Cohen of Ragusa), 1:212

Ma'aseh Nissim (Edrehi). *See An Historical Account of the Ten Tribes Settled Beyond the River Sambatyon in the East* (Edrehi)

Ma'aseh Rav (Benjamin), 3:358

Ma'aseh Rav (Elijah ben Solomon Zalman), 6:345

Ma'aseh Roke'aẓ (Masud Ḥai Roke'aḥ), 8:482

Ma'aseh Torah. *See* Midrash Sheloshah Ve' Arba'ah

Ma'aseh Tuviyyah (Cohn), 5:45, 6:399

Ma'aseh Yerushalmi (Zlotnik, J.L.), 7:13

Ma'aser. *See* Terumot and Ma'aserot; Tithes

Ma'aserot (offerings), 19:**652–654**

Ma'aserot (tractate), 13:**313–314**

Ma'aser sheni, 13:**314**

Ma'avar Yabbok (Aaron Berechiah ben Moses of Modena), 1:217

Ma'avar Yabbok (Halkin), 8:276

Maayani, Ami, 13:**314–315**

Maaz. *See* Ahimaaz

Maazel, Lorin, 13:**315**

Maazel, Lorin Varencove. *See* Maazel, Lorin

Ma'barot (Israel), 13:**315**

Ma'barot (transitional camps), 10:341–342, 343, 13:**315**

MaBaSh. *See* Chajes, Gerson ben Abraham

Mabkḥsh, Evariste. *See* Lévi-Provençal, Evariste

Der Mabl (Shalom Aleichem), 18:384

Mabovitch, Golda. *See* Meir, Golda

Macalister, Robert Alexander Stewart, 2:377, 13:**315**, 15:589

Macaulay, Lord. *See* Macaulay, Thomas Babington

Macaulay, Thomas Babington, 13:**315–316**

Maccabea (Budapest Zionist youth society), 18:157

The Maccabean (periodical), 2:104

Maccabean martyrs, 8:447, 448

Maccabean revolt, 3:**31**, 13:316, 20:627
   Hassideans, 8:455
   Hebron, 8:744
   Jabneel, 11:9
   Modi'in, 14:411–412

Maccabeans. *See* Hasmoneans

Maccabeans, Order of Ancient. *See* Order of Ancient Maccabeans

Maccabee (name), 13:**316**
   See also Hasmoneans; Judah Maccabee

The Maccabee. See El Macabeo (Silveyra)

Maccabee, Judah. *See* Judah Maccabee

Maccabees, book of, 8:325, 331

Maccabees, Second Book of, 9:154, 13:**317–318**
   abomination of desolation, 1:270
   Judah Maccabee, 11:510
   tripartite canon referred to in, 3:576

Maccabees, First Book of, 9:154, 13:**316–317**
   Judah Maccabee, 11:509–510

olam ha-ba, 15:399

Maccabees, Third Book of, 13:**318–319**

Maccabees, Fourth Book of, 13:**319–320**

Maccabiah, 13:**320**

Maccabiah games, 19:130

Maccabi World Union, 13:**320–321**

Maccabi Youth Games, 20:372

Maccobi, Ḥayyim Zundel. *See* Maccoby, Ḥayyim Zundel

Maccoby, Ḥayyim Zundel, 13:**321–322**

Maccoby, Hyam, 13:**322**

MacDonald, Ramsay, Shaw Commission, 15:583

Macedonia, 13:**322**
   Egptian Jews, 6:228
   Holocaust
      Monastir, 14:432
      Phlorina, 16:118
      Skoplje, 18:662
   Ochrida, 15:375
   Phlorina, 16:117–118
   Skoplje, 18:661–662
   Yugoslavia, 21:411, 415
   See also Bulgaria; Byzantine Empire; Yugoslavia

Macedonian calendar, 4:705

Macedonian Jewry, 11:755

Machabey, Armand, 13:**323**

Machado family, 13:**323**

Machaerus (Jordan), 13:**323**

Machaut, Denis de, 13:**323–324**, 15:643–644

Machir, 1:416, 13:**324**

Machir ben Judah, 13:**324**

Machlup, Fritz, 13:**324–325**

Machon Schechter l'Mada'ey Hayahadut. *See* Schechter Institute of Jewish Studies, The

Machpelah, Cave of, 9:499, 13:**325–327**, *326*

Macht, David I., 13:**327**

Die Macht der Verhaeltnisse (Robert), 17:354

Macias, Enrico, 13:**327**

Mack, Julian W., 4:123

Mack, Julian William, 12:556, 13:**327–328**
   American Jewish Committee, 2:55

MacKenzie, D. N., 11:558

Macklowe, Harry, 13:**328**

Mack Raymond, 18:733

Macnin, Meir, 16:346

Macnin, Meyer, 14:499

Macnin family, 13:**328**

Mâcon (France), 13:**328–329**

Macready, Sir, 11:305

Macrobius, Ambrosius, 13:**329**

Macy's (department store), 5:588

Madaba, 13:**329–330,** 14:401

Madách, Imre, 14:418, 540

Madagascar, 13:**330**

Madagascar Plan, 13:**330–331**

Madame Alexander Doll Company, 1:621, 622

Madame Rosa, 9:442

Madi group, founded by Blazko, Martin, 3:747

Madīna (Saudi Arabia). *See* Medina (Saudi Arabia)

Madison (WI), 13:**331**

Madison, James, 13:**331–332,** 15:290

Madison Square Garden (New York City), 11:50

Madjanek concentration camp, 9:*484*

Mad Magazine, 4:500, 6:296, 7:335

Mad Marshal. *See* Goldberg, Marshall

Madmūn ben Japheth ben Bundār, 1:387, 13:**332**

Madon (Israel), 13:**332**

Madras (India), 13:**332–333**

Madrid (Spain), 13:**333–334**

Madrid Conference for Peace in the Middle East (1991), 4:304, 10:243, 262, 263, 453, 11:235–236

Maduro, Eric Shalom Delvalle, 15:610

Maduro, Ricardo, 13:**334**

Madzovitch, Yitzhak. *See* Modai, Yitzhak

Maehren (Czech Republic). *See* Moravia (Czech Republic)

Maehrisch-Budwitz (Czech Republic). *See* Moravske Budejovice (Czech Republic)

Maehrisch-Kromau (Czech Republic). *See* Moravsky Krumlov (Czech Republic)

Maehrisch-Ostrau (Czech Republic). *See* Ostrava (Czech Republic)

Maehrisch-Weisskirchen (Czech Republic). *See* Hranice (Czech Republic)

Maerchen des Lebens (Altenberg), 2:17

Maerich-Aussee. *See* Usov

Maes, Andreas, 13:**334**

Maestre Bonjua. *See* Bondavin, Bonjudas (Bonjusas, or Judah ben David)

Maestre Leo de Bagnols. *See* Levi ben Gershom

Maestre Vidal Bellsom. *See* Moses ben Joshua of Narbonne

Maestro, Jacko. *See* Maestro, Yaakov

Maestro, Yaakov, 13:**334–335**

Maestro Gaio, Isaac ben Mordecai, 15:250

Maestro Juan of Paris, 4:101

Maestro Manoel, Xabillo. *See* Habillo, Elijah ben Joseph

Mafia, 12:485–486

Mafte'ah ha-Kabbalah (Baruch), 3:182–183

Mafte'ah ha-Talmud (Guttman), 8:159

Maftir, 13:**335**

  See also Haftarah

Magadan (Israel). *See* Magdala (Israel)

Ma'gal Tov ha-Shalem (Azulai), 18:447

Magāsidal-Falāsifa (al-Ghazālī), 1:582, 583

Magdala (Israel), 13:**335**

Magdeburg (Germany), 13:**335–336,** 18:690

Magdeburg Law, 13:**336**

  in Ozery, 15:557

Magdi'el (Israel). *See* Hod ha-Sharon (Israel)

Magen Avot (Duran), 1:440, 2:530–531, 6:60

Magen Avraham (Farissol), 6:717

Magen Avraham (Laniado), 12:484

Magen David, 3:53, 9:*460, 464,* 13:**336–339**

  amulets, 2:122

  flags, 7:68

  Morocco, 14:506

Magen David Adom, 13:**339,** 16:45

Magen ha-Hokhmah (Mohr), 14:420

Magen va-Herev (Modena), 14:409

Magen ve-Zinnah (Modena), 14:409

Magerit (Spain). *See* Madrid (Spain)

Maggid, 4:491, 13:**339–341**

Maggid, David, 13:**341–342**

Maggid of Brody. *See* Kluger, Solomon ben Judah Aaron

Maggid of Deretschin, 6:648–649

Maggid of Dubno. *See* Kranz, Jacob ben Wolf

Maggid of Kamenets. *See* Maccoby, Hayyim Zundel

Maggid-Steinschneider, Hillel Noah, 13:**342**

Maggishei Minhah (Amelander), 2:38

Maghar, al- (Israel), 13:**342**

Maghāriya, 18:233

al-Maghārrīya sect, 2:159

Maghreb, 2:300, 320–324, 4:344, 5:106

  communities of Jews, Israel (state), 10:295

  Omar, Covenant of, 15:418

  Palestine (Ottoman), 10:295

Maghrebi-Ma'aravi, 13:**342,** 397

Maghribim. *See* Maghreb

Magic, 13:**342–352**

  Abracadabra, 1:280

angels, 2:153

Apochrypha, literature, 13:343–344

biblical curses, power of, 3:752

Copperfield, David, 5:213

divination and, 5:703

Egyptian, 11:78

evil eye, 6:584–585

history of, 13:342–345

Houdini, Harry, 9:568

Judeo-Persian literature on, 11:552, 553–554

Kabbalah, 1:310, 11:665–668

Middle Ages, literature, 13:345–351

Moses, 14:533

rabbinic literature, 13:345

sorcery, 13:344–345

Magician among the Spirits (Houdini), 9:568

The Magician of Lublin (Singer), 18:635

Magidor, Menachem, 13:**352**

Magidov, Jacob, 13:**352–353**

Magidson, Beverly, 18:403

Magino, Meir, 13:**353**

Magister Benjamin of Cambridge. *See* Benjamin of Cambridge

Magister Leo Hebraeus. *See* Levi ben Gershom

Magna Carta, 6:411

Magnes, Judah Leon, 4:5, 13:**353–354**

  bi-nationalism promoted by, 3:703

  Dushkin, Alexander Mordecai, 6:64

  New York City and, 15:205, 209, 217

Magnes Museum, Judah L. *See* Judah L. Magnes Museum (California)

Magnet (Banus), 3:121

Magnin, Edgar Fogel, 13:197, **355**

Magnin, Mary Ann Cohen, 13:**355–356**

Magnum Photos, 18:332

Magnus, Eduard, 13:**356**

Magnus, Heinrich Gustav, 13:**356–357**

Magnus, Katie, 6:193, 13:**356**

Magnus, Laurie, 13:**356**

Magnus, Marcus, 1:213, 13:**357**

Magnus, Paul Wilhelm, 13:**357**

Magnus, Philip, 13:**356**

Magnus, Philip Montefiore, 13:**356**

Magnus, Rudolph, 13:**357**

Magnus, Solomon Wolff, 13:**357**

Magnus-Allcroft, Philip. *See* Magnus, Philip Montefiore

Magnus family, 13:**356**

Magreb (North Africa), nagid
leadership, 14:733

Magyar language, 13:248

Magyar Zsidó Szemle (periodical),
3:36, 13:**357–358**, 18:613

Mahadurah, 2:565–566

Maḥal, 13:**358**

Mahalakh Sheviler ha-Daʿat (Kimḥi),
13:41–42

Mahalalel. *See* Gottlober, Abraham
Baer

Mahalalel ben Shabbetai Hallelyah,
13:**358**

Mahalla al-Kubra (Egypt), 13:**358–359**

Mahallal ben Shalom ben Jacob. *See*
Adani, Mahalal

Mahamad. *See* Maʾamad

Mahanaim (Jordan), 13:**359**

Maḥanayim (Israel), 13:**359–360**

Maḥaneh Levi (Horowitz), 9:545

Maḥaneh Sheli political party, 6:321

MaHaRaf. *See* Perez ben Elijah of
Corbeil

Maharal. *See* Judah Loew ben Bezalel

MaHaRaL mi-Prag. *See* Judah Loew
ben Bezalel

Maharal of Prague. *See* Judah Loew
ben Bezalel

MaHaRaM. *See* Lublin, Meir ben
Gedaliah; Schiff, Meir ben Jacob ha-
Kohen

MaHaRaM ESH. *See* Eisenstadt, Meir

Maharam of Lublin. *See* Lublin, Meir
ben Gedaliah

Maharam of Padua. *See*
Katzenellenbogen, Meir ben Issac

Maharam Schick. *See* Schick, Moses
ben Joseph

Maharanaḥ. *See* Elijah ben Ḥayyim

Maharashdam. *See* Medina, Samuel
ben Moses de

MaHaRDaKh. *See* David ben Hayyim
of Corfu

Maharhash. *See* Ḥayyim ben Shabbetai

Maharik. *See* Colon, Joseph ben
Solomon

Maharikas, Jacob ben Abraham. *See*
Castro, Jacob ben Abraham

Maharil musical minhag, 14:662–663

Maharit. *See* Trani, Joseph ben Moses

Mahariv. *See* Wanneh, Isaac ben
Abraham

MaHaRiVaL. *See* Lev, Joseph ben
David ibn

Maharlah. *See* Ḥanneles, Judah Leib
ben Meir

MaHaRShA. *See* Edels, Samuel Eliezer
ben Juday ha-Levi

Maharsha. *See* Alfandari, Solomon
Eliezer ben Jacob

Maharsha, exile, 7:361

Maharshak. *See* Koidonover, Aaron
Samuel ben Israel

Maharshal. *See* Luria, Solomon ben
Jehiel

Maḥashovot u-Maʾasim (Lewinsky),
12:762

Maḥazeh Ragil (Matmor), 8:720

Mahazike Hadas (newspaper), 8:124

Mahazikei ha-Dat. *See* Maḥzike Hadas

Maḥazikei Torah institutions, 20:198

Maḥbarot Itiʾel, 1:656

Maḥberet (Menahem ben Jacob ibn
Saruq), 6:47, 14:22

Maḥberet ha-Tene (Ahitub ben Isaac),
1:546

Maḥberet ha-Tijān, 13:651

Maḥ beret ḥe-Arukh (Parḥon), 15:642

Maḥberot Immanuʾel (Immanuel of
Rome), 8:724

Maher Shalal Hash Baz, 13:**360**

Maḥ ha-Shir (Shalom), 18:378

MAHJ. *See* Musée d'Art d'Histoire du
Judaïsme

Mahler, Arthur, 13:**360**, 15:652, 16:340

Mahler, Eduard, 13:**360**

Mahler, Gustav, 13:**360–361**
Jihlava, Jews of, 11:337

Mahler, Margaret, 13:**361**

Mahler, Raphael, 9:161, 13:**361**

Mahler-Kalkstein, Menahem. *See*
Avidom, Menahem

Mahlon and Chilion, 13:**361–362**

Mah Nishtannah, 13:**362**, 15:678–679

*Mahnruf an seine Stammesgenossen von
einem russischen Juden* (Pinsker),
16:173

Maḥoza (Iraq), 13:**362**

Mah tovu, 13:**362–363**

Maḥzike Hadas, 13:**363**

Maḥzor, 8:763, 13:**363–366**
See also Kieval, Hayyim

*Maḥzor for Rosh Hashanah and Yom
Kippur* (Harlow), 8:359, 14:488

Maḥzor Romania, 6:325, 11:728,
13:135

Maḥzor Vitry, 6:175, 16:462

Maḥzor Vitry (Simḥah), 13:**366–367**

Maidanek. *See* Majdanek

Maiden. *See* Virgin, virginity

The Maidens' Land. See Tara fetelor

The Maid of Midian (Judah), 14:540

Maier, Chaim. *See* Améry, Jean

Maier, Hans. *See* Améry, Jean

Maier, Joseph, 13:**367**

Maierzuk, Hanna. *See* Meron, Hanna

Mailer, Norman, 4:218, 13:**367–368**,
15:221, 18:709

Mailman, Abraham, 4:213

Maimaran, Abraham, 16:346

Maimi, Simon, 13:**368**

Maimon, Ada, 13:**368**

Maimon, J., 1:728

Maimon, Judah Leib, 13:**368–369**,
14:390

Maimon, Solomon, 7:10, 8:688,
13:**369–371**

Maimon, Yaʾacov, 13:**371**

Maimon ben Joseph, 13:**371**

Maimonidean controversy, 3:**239**,
8:434, 13:**371–381**
aftermath of, 13:380–381
defined, 13:371–372
first clash, 13:372–373
first stage in Europe, 13:373–374
fourth climax, 13:378–380
second climax in Europe, 13:374–
377
Solomon ben Abraham of
Montpelier, 18:770
third climax in Europe, 13:377–
378

Maimonides, 16:84
Aaron ben Elijah, 1:212, 213
Aaron ben Meshullam of Lunel,
1:216
Abba Mari ben Moses ben Joseph
Astruc of Lunel, 1:230
Abbasi, Jacob ben Moses ibn,
1:232–233
Aboab, Isaac I, 1:266
Abraham, 1:284–285
Abraham ben Azriel, 1:295
Abraham ben David of
Posquières, 1:296, 297–298
Abraham ben Hillel of Fostat,
1:300
Abraham ben Isaac of
Montpellier, 1:302
Abraham ben Moses ben Maimon,
1:304–306, 307, 308
Abulafia, Meir, 1:342
Adam, 1:373–374
Adani, David ben Yesha ha-Levi,
1:381
Adret, Solomon ben Abraham,
1:421–422, 423
advertising, misrepresentation,
5:188
Ahitub ben Isaac, 1:546
Albertus Magnus, 1:591
Albotini, Judah ben Moses, 1:595–
596
Alegre, Abraham ben Solomon,
1:608
Alexander of Aphrodisias, 1:628

Maimonides, *continued*

Alexander of Hales, 1:629

Alfasi, Isaac ben Jacob, 1:640

Al-Ḥarizi, Judah ben Solomon, 1:657

Amatus Lusitanus, 2:35

amulets, 2:121

Anatoli ben Joseph, 2:133

anatomy, 2:134

angels, 2:160, 13:390

Ani Maamin, 2:165

anthropomorphism, 2:190

apologetics, 2:265

Aristotelianism, miracles, 14:308

arms-bearer supporters, 4:772–773

Articles of Faith, 2:165, 529–530

asceticism, 2:548

asmakhta, 2:590, 591

astrology, 2:619

atomism, 2:644

belief, faith, 3:293–294

Bible, interpretation of, 9:818

biographical material of, 3:706

on bloodletting, 3:774

Bonafed, Solomon ben Reuben, 4:54

business ethics, 4:307, 312

capital punishment, 4:449, 451

Caro, Joseph ben Ephraim, 4:489–490

categories, 4:524–525

on categories of beings, 4:524

cause and effect, 4:529

on chastity, 4:582

circumcision, 4:732

codification of law, 4:770–773, 774–775, 776, 777, 778

commandments, 16:150
reasons for, 5:87–88

commentaries on, 6:681–682, 16:86, 87, 88
Mendelssohn, Moses, 14:36
Persian, 14:6

commentary, Adani, Saadiah ben David, 1:381

compromise, 5:127

conditions, 5:137

confession of sins, 5:149

creation, 5:278

Crescas critique, 5:285, 287

criticisms of, 5:429, 11:30, 16:86, 88, 89

on dietary laws, 5:657

divination, 5:706–707

Divine attributes, 19:284

dreams and, 6:9–10

Duns Scotus, John, 6:50–51

Duran, Profiat, 6:57–58

Duran, Simeon ben Ẓemaḥ, 6:58, 59

Eckhart, Meister, 6:92

economic doctrines and, 6:114, 115

economic issues, 6:114–115

election, 9:219

emanation and creation, 6:373–374

ethical middle way, 6:536

ethics vs. philosophy, 6:528

evolution and, 6:586

exile, meaning of, 7:358–359

on extradition, 6:628

faith and reason, 2:461

fallow year and, 6:93

fear of God, 6:725–726

fines, 7:29

forgiveness of sin, 7:128

form and matter, 7:131

free will, 7:232

gendered Torah interpretation, 16:107

genizah discoveries, 7:474

gentiles, 7:487

Ghazālī influence, 7:572

God
attributes of, 7:667–668
nature of, 7:662, 663

good and evil, 7:753–754

hakdamah, 8:242

halakhah, 8:252, 257

Ḥasidei Ummot ha-Olam, 8:389

Hebrew of, 8:665–666

illegal contracts, 5:194

imagination and, 9:736

immortality of the soul, 1:442, 3:238–239

inclination, good and evil, 9:757

influence on
al-Fārābī, 6:709, 710–711
Christian thought, 16:91
Kafaḥ, Yosef, 11:704
modern Israeli philosophers, 16:99

informers, penal laws for, 9:784

Islamic influence on, 10:97, 11:266–267

Jonah ben Abraham Gerondi, 11:392

Jonathan ben David ha-Kohen of Lunel, 11:397

Judaism, 13 essential principles of, 11:512–513

Judeo-Arabic literature and, 11:531, 533–534, 535, 536, 537

kabbalists and, 5:465

kitniyot, 12:610

Latif, Isaac B. Abraham ibn, 12:506

law of evidence and, 6:577–578, 579, 580–581, 582, 583

legal practice and procedure, 16:436

letters' influence, 12:671–672

mathematics and, 13:673–674

medical works, 13:726

medicinal herbs, 9:8

Meiri and, 13:787

mikveh and purity, 14:225

Mishnah, 14:328–329

Mishneh Torah, 4:770–771

monotheism, 14:450

Morocco, 14:494–495

mukẓeh objects, 14:608

music, 14:658–659

nature, 15:34

New Christians, 15:133

Noachide laws, 15:285–286

numismatics, interest in, 15:343

olam ha-ba, 15:400

opposition to, 11:7
Solomon ben Abraham of Montpellier, 18:770

oppression, 15:453

Oral Law, 15:456

orphans and orphanages, 15:483

ownership and possession, 8:489

peace, 15:702

philosophy, Jewish, 2:292

platonism, 16:227

polemical opposition, 16:329

prayer, 16:459

prophets and prophecy, 16:582–583

proselytism, 16:590–592

punishment, 16:735

Rabbinate, 17:13

Ravitzky, Aviezer, 17:124

redemption, 17:153

repentance, 17:222

resurrection, 3:292–293, 17:243

revelation, 17:257

righteousness, 17:309

right of self-redress in civil cases, 6:631

rishonim, 17:341–343

Ru'aḥ ha-Kodesh, 17:509

Second Temple, floor plan, 19:*617*

shofar, 18:508

skepticism, 18:658

soul, immortality of, 19:37

space and place, 19:67
substance and accident, 19:283
Thirteen Principles of Faith,
2:529–530
Toledo opposition, 20:25
Torah, 20:40, 42, 45
Torah authorship, 15:734, 751
Ukẓin, 20:239
veneration of, 2:158
witness competency, 21:115–117
Yad, 21:264
See also Guide of the Perplexed
Maimonides, Moses, 13:**381–397**
in Abendanan family, 1:251
allegorical interpretation and,
3:644–645
astronomy, 13:395
beatitude, 3:238–239
biography of, 13:381–384
Creation, 13:390
divine providence, 13:391
eschatology, 13:392–393
God, 13:389–390
Guide of the Perplexed, 13:384–
385, 388–393
Halakhah, 13:385–388, 395
influence of, 13:384–385, 393
Judeo-Persian translation of Bible,
attestation to, 3:609
Law of Moses, 13:392, 14:536–537
logic, 13:173
Mishneh Torah, 13:387–388
moral virtue, 13:392
Moses, 13:392, 14:536–537
nature of man, 13:392
philosophy, 13:388–393
physician and medicine, 13:393–
395
priniciples of Judaism, 13:393
prophecies, 13:391
responsa literature, 13:386
secularization and Sephardim,
18:299
Sefer ha-Mitzvot, 12:461, 13:386–
387
Shalom, Abraham ben Isaac ben
Judah ben Samuel on, 18:376–
377
on Shekhinah, 18:442
translations, 13:395
*Maimonides: Torah and Philosophic
Quest* (Hartman), 16:103–104
Maimonides College (Boston, MA),
6:197, 18:777
Maimonides College (Philadelphia,
PA), 6:25, 192
Maimonides College (Vienna), 11:756

Maimonides Library (New York City,
NY), 4:14
Maimonides of Polish Jewry. *See*
Isserles, Moses ben Israel
Maimonides the Man (Elfenbein),
6:314
Maimoran family. *See* Maymeran
family
Maimuna, 1:439, 13:**397**, vol. 6: color
insert
Maine, 13:**397–399**, 398t
Mainstreet (motion picture), 9:441–
442
Maintenance, 13:**399–403**
parental obligation of
in Israeli law, 15:638–639
in Jewish law, 15:635–636,
637
widow's claim, 13:23
Mainz (Germany), 13:**403–405**
Crusader massacre, 5:311–312
Eliezer ben Nathan of Mainz,
6:327
Shum, 18:532–533
Mainz, Ernest, 11:558
Maiorescu, George Toma, 13:**405**
Mairovich, Zvi, 13:**406**
Maisel, Elijah Ḥayyim, 13:**406**
Maisels, Israel Aaron, 13:**406**
Maisels, Maxine. *See* Amishai-Maisels,
Ziva
Maisels, Misha. *See* Maisels, Moses
Ḥayyim
Maisels, Moses Ḥayyim, 13:**406**
Maisel-Shoḥat, Hannah, 13:**406**
Maisler, Benjamin. *See* Mazar,
Benjamin
Maiumas (festival), 13:**406–407**
Maiumas (Gaza), 13:407
Majdal (Egypt), 2:568
Majdal al-Shams (Israel), 13:**407**
Majd al-Karūm (Israel), 13:**407**
Majdanek (Poland), 13:**407–408**
Majdanek concentration camp, 9:342,
484, 13:244, 17:121
Majjani family, 11:727
Major, Ervin, 13:**408–409**
Major, John, 6:431
Major, Julius, 13:**409**
Majorca (Spain), 4:708–709, 6:58–59,
13:**409–414**
Majority rule, 13:**414–417**
Major Trends in Jewish Mysticism
(Scholem), 11:681–682, 18:158
Majzels, Robert, 4:424
Makai, Emil, 13:**417**
Makarov (Ukraine), 13:**417**

*Makbilot bein ha-Besorot le-Sifrut ha-
Tanna'im* (Smith), 18:688
Makers of Hebrew Books in Italy
(Amram), 2:104
Makhon Yerushalayim, 17:237–238
Makhshirin (tractate), 13:**418**
Maki communist party, 5:100
Making Americans (Razovsky), 17:131
Making It (Podhoretz), 16:251
Making Movies (Lumet), 13:257
The Making of a Gadol (Kamenetsky),
11:752
*The Making of a Public Man, A
Memoir* (Linowitz), 13:61
The Making of Nazis (Kandel), 11:760
The Making of the Jewish Middle Class
(Kaplan), 9:152
Makkabim-Re'ut, 13:**418**, 14:412
Makkedah (Israel), 13:**418**
Makkel No'am (Ehrenkranz), 6:240
Makkot, 7:79
Makkot (tractate), 13:**418–419**
Makleff, Aryeh Leib, 13:419
Makleff, Mordechai, 13:419
Makleff family, 13:**419**
Mako (Hungary), 13:**419–420**
Makom. *See* Space and place
Makom Tov la-Laylah (Liebrecht),
12:811
Makov (Poland). *See* Makow
Mazowiecki (Poland)
Makow Mazowiecki (Poland), 13:**420**
Makuya, 11:85, 13:**420–421**
Malabaila, Damiano. *See* Levi, Primo
Malach, Leib, 13:**421**
Malachi, Book of, 6:494, 13:**421–423**
Malachi, Eliezer Raphael, 13:**423–424**
Malachi ben Jacob ha-Kohen, 13:**424**
Málaga (Spain), 13:**424**
Malakh, Ḥayyim ben Solomon,
13:**424–425**, 18:354, 355
Malakh ha-Mavet. *See* Angel of Death
Malakhim Ba'im (Ben-Ner), 3:367
Malakhovka (Russia), 14:519
Malamat, Abraham, 13:**425–426**
Malamud, Bernard, 13:**426**, 15:227
Blitzstein, Marc, operas of, 3:757
Malamud, Samuel, 4:152
Malaria, 11:368
Malavsky, Samuel, 13:**426–427**
Malaysia, 13:**427**
Malben, 13:**427**
American Joint Distribution
Committee, 2:62
Jordan, Charles Harold, 11:403
Malbim, Meir Loeb ben Jehiel Michael
Weisser, 13:**427–429**
biblical exegesis and study, 3:643,
646

Malca family, 13:**429–430**

Malchi, Esperanza, 12:148, 13:**430,** 15:541

Malcolm MacDonald White Paper, 21:38

Maldonado de Silva, Francisco, 4:637, 13:**430**

Malediction. *See* Blessing and cursing

Malerei, Fotographie, Film (Moholy-Nagy). *See Painting, Photography, and Film* (Moholy-Nagy)

Males. *See* Men

Malesherbes, Chretien Guillaume de la-Moignon de, 13:**431**

Malesherbes Commission, 4:82

Malev, William S., 13:**431**

Malik al-Ramlī, 13:**431**

Malines (Belgium), 13:**431–432**

Malino, Jerome, 13:**432**

Malinowski, Joseph ben Mordecai, 11:792, 13:**432**

Malitsch, Jacob of. *See* Jacob of Malitsch

Malkah, Judah ben Nissim ibn, 11:536, 13:**432–433**

Malkat Ester (Alterman), 8:720

Malkhi, Ezra ben Raphael Mordecai, 13:**433**

Malkhi, Moses, 13:**433**

Malkhi, Moses ben Raphael Mordecai, 13:**433**

Malkhuyyot, 2:75, 13:**433–434**

Malki, Ezra. *See* Malkhi, Ezra ben Raphael Mordecai

Malkī, Sa'd Litto, 15:473

Malkiel, Theresa Serber, 13:**434**

Malkiel, Theresaz, 18:713

Malkiel, Yakov, 13:**434**

Malkiyyah (Israel), 20:660

Maller, Julius Bernard, 13:**434–435**

Mall of America, 18:608

Mallorca (Spain). *See* Majorca (Spain)

Mallow, 13:**435,** vol. 16: color insert

Malmö (Sweden), 13:**435**

Málnai, Béla, 13:**435**

Malovany, Joseph, 13:**435,** 15:308

Malshinim. *See* Informers

Malsin, Lane Bryant, 13:**435–436.** *See* Himmelstein, Lena

Malta, 13:**436**

    Bible translated into Maltese, 3:636

    Inquisition, 9:799

Malter, Henry, 2:47, 13:**436–437**

Maltin, Leonard, 13:**437**

Maltz, Albert, 13:**437**

Malvano, Giacomo, 13:**437**

Malzberg, Benjamin, 13:**437–438**

The Mamas and the Papas (music group), 6:361

Mamelukes. *See* Mamluks

Mamet, David, 13:**438**

Mamistabolob, Abraham, 13:**438**

Mamluks, 13:**438–441**

    Egypt, 1:634–635, 6:231–232

    Israel, land of, 10:165–168, *166*

    Jerusalem, 11:159–161

    Omar, Covenant of, 15:418

    Ottoman conquest of, 15:523

    sheluḥei Erez Israel, 18:447, 449

Mammals, 2:167–171

Mamon, 14:334

Mamon, obligations, law of, 15:369

Mampsis (Israel), 13:**441**

Mamram, 13:**441–442**

Mamran. *See* Mamram

Mamre (Israel), 13:**442**

Mamre, Aner, and Eshkol, 2:**145**

Mamroth, L., 11:739

Mamshit (ancient city), vol. 10: color insert

Mamshit (Israel). *See* Mampsis (Israel)

Mamurra. *See* Vitruvius, Pollo

Mamuzio, Aldus. *See* Aldo Manuzio

Mamzer, 1:272, 13:**442–445**

Mamzerut, 21:425

Man

    bigamy and polygamy, 3:691

    birth of male children, 3:721–723

    divine justice, 17:610–611

    divorce, and rights of, 5:713–714

    Levi Ben Gershom view, 12:700

    nature of, 13:392, **446–450,** 17:610–611

Man, Mendl. *See* Mann, Mendel

Mana ben Jonah. *See* Mani

Mana II. *See* Mani

Manākhah (Yemen), 13:**450**

Manarah (Israel), 13:**450**

Manasse (Roman-Ronetti), 17:399

Manasseh (King), 1:416, 2:88, 9:181, 13:**452–453**

    Ephraim, 6:456, 457

    Esarhaddon, 6:486

Manasseh (son of Joseph), 18:592

    birthright, 11:20

Manasseh (tribe), 13:**450–452,** *451*

    Abiezer, 1:255

    En-Dor, 6:404

Manasseh, Ezekiel ben Reuben, 3:57

Manasseh, Japheth, 8:746

Manasseh, Prayer of. See Prayer of Manasseh

Manasseh B, Athaṅ. *See* Māshā'Allah ben Athaṅ

Manasseh ben Israel, 4:78, 13:**454–455**

    An Apology for the Honourable Nation of the Jews, and all the Sons of Israel (Nicholas), 15:252

    bibliography of, 3:681, 682

    as bibliophile, 3:683

    Cromwell, Oliver and, 5:306

    English Jews, 6:413

    exile, meaning of, 7:362

    lost tribes of Israel, 14:460

    moneylending, 14:441

    Palache family, 15:573

Manasseh ben Joseph of Ilya, 8:440, 13:**455–456**

Manasseh ben Porat. *See* Manasseh ben Joseph of Ilya

Man at the Crossroads (Rivera), 18:365

Manchester (England), 13:**456–457**

Manchuria, 11:81, 13:**457**

    Jewish community, 4:646, 647

    Kaufman, Avraham Yosifovich, 12:28

The Manchurian Candidate (motion picture), 2:104

Mancroft family, 13:**457**

Mandate for Palestine, 15:582

    agriculture, 6:543

        Irgun Vitkin, 8:753

        irrigation, 10:509–510

        leaders, 11:9

    aliyah and absorption, 1:660–661, 10:201, 204, 206–207, *301,* 354, 358t, 359–360, 371

        housing and settlements, 10:354, 358t, 359–360

        "Illegal" immigration and, 9:722–723, 724

        Jewish Colonization Association, 11:287

        land ownership, 10:371

        non-Jewish population, 10:*301,* 301–302

    borders, 10:185–187, 197–198, 479–480

    Comintern and, 5:97

    cultural and social life

        architecture, 10:701–702

        art, 10:695

        Bedouin, 10:737

        community organization, 10:391–393, 392t

        displaced persons and, 5:685

        health services, 10:674–675

        Hebrew publishing, 10:684

        humor, 9:597–598

Jewish folk dance, 10:693–694
journalism and press, 10:705
museums, 14:631
music, 10:688, 691
Palestine Orchestra, 14:693–694
scouting, 18:210
sculpture, 18:222
Sephardim, 18:303
sports, 19:129–130
stamps, 19:161
theater, 10:686
defense, 10:464–467, 465–467
    Arab attacks against Jews,
      10:200, 202, 203, 207–208,
      277
    Arab Revolt, 10:277
    Arab riots, 10:465, 466
    Haganah, 10:201, 204, 205,
      207, 208
    stockade and watchtower,
      19:230
economic affairs, 10:481t, 483t,
    484t, 496–512, 497t, 498t, 499t,
    502t
    advertising, 1:428
    agriculture and resettlement,
      10:506–511
    Arab-Jewish economic links,
      10:493–494, 501
    balance of payments and
      capital imports, 10:514–516
    banking system, 10:586–587
    comparative trends and links,
      1932–1939, 10:500–503,
      502t
    employment, 10:491t, 494,
      495t, 500, 520
    historical survey, 10:200–202
    immigration and
      demography, 1932–1939,
      10:496–500, 497t, 498t,
      499t
    land purchases by Jews,
      10:488
    manufacturing, 10:503–505,
      518–520
    monetary and financial
      system, 10:512–514
    money, prices and war
      finance, 10:516–518
    as unique political and
      economic entity, 10:486–
      487
    urbanization and
      socioeconomic structure,
      10:494, 505–506
education, 10:623, 653–656
    Arab, 10:712

Hebrew University, 8:740–741
    music, 10:689
foreign policy and affairs
    Abdullah ibn Hussein, 1:243–
      244
    England, 6:419
    Holocaust rescue efforts,
      9:281, 492
    League of Nations, 12:564–
      565
    Sykes-Picot Agreement,
      19:350–351, 351
    White Paper of 1939, 3:345–
      346, 4:722
governance, 10:388, 389–391, 393,
    406–407, 486
historical survey, 10:197–208
    Arab national movement and
      revolts, 10:202–203
    economic history, 10:200–202
    partition, 10:203, 207
    resistance and Haganah,
      10:203–204, 206–207
    Third, Fourth and Fifth
      Aliyah, 10:199–200, 201
    war of independence, 10:207–
      208
    WW II, 10:204–206
immigration to, 10:198
    Arab, 10:712
    economic absorptive capacity
      and, 10:336, 337–338
    illegal, 10:499–500
    quotas, 10:198, 336, 497
    restrictions, 10:338–339
    total number, 10:339
labor
    Aharonovitch, Yosef, 1:537–
      538
    Histadrut, 10:594–600
    legislation and voluntary
      agreements, 10:607–608
laws and legal systems, 10:405–
    409, 412–413, 14:352–353, 354
partition, 10:187, 189, 190, 203,
    207, 273–274, 427
political theories, parties and
    organizations, 3:345–346
    Agudat Israel, 1:507
    Aḥdut ha-Avodah, 1:540
    Aḥdut ha-Avodah-Po'alei
      Zion, 1:541
    Arab nationalism, 9:642–643,
      10:196
    Beriḥah, 3:435–436
    Berit ha-Biryonim
      organization, 3:436
    Berit Shalom, 3:436–437

    Betar, 3:510–511
    Irgun Ẓeva'i Le'ummi,
      10:206, 207, 208
    Jewish Agency, 11:256–258
    Loḥamei Ḥerut Israel, 10:206,
      207, 208
    National Socialism (Nazism),
      19:632
    political parties of yishuv,
      10:425–428
population, 10:282, 283, 285
    Arab, 10:481t, 710–712, 712t
    Ashkenaz dominance, 10:298
    Bukharan Jews, 10:297
    Christian, 10:638
    Coastal Plain, 10:376
    emigration from, 10:497
    Hills region, 10:379–380
    Jewish, 10:481t, 487
    non-Jewish, 10:301–302
    Persian Jews, 10:297
    by religion, 10:711, 712t
    statistics, 10:392t
religious life and scholarship,
    Islam, 10:646–647
See also Israel (land of); Palestine
    (Ottoman); Palestine Inquiry
    Commissions
Mandatory commandments, 5:74t–78t
Mandel, Arnold, 13:458
Mandel, Eli, 4:424, 13:458–459
Mandel, Georges, 13:459, 16:343
Mandel, Marvin, 13:459
Mandel, Mordekhai. See Avi-Shaul,
    Mordekhai
Mandel, Shelomoh, 13:459
Mandel, Stephen, 6:151, 16:341
Mandelbaum, Allen, 20:300–301
Mandelbaum, Bernard, 13:459–460
Mandelbaum, David Goodman,
    13:460
Mandelbaum, Dov, 3:682
Mandelberg, Avigdor, 13:460
Mandelberg, Victor. See Mandelberg,
    Avigdor
Mandelbrot, Benoit, 13:460–461
Mandel Foundation, 6:203
Mandelker, Dan, 6:453
Mandelkern, Solomon, 13:461
Mandel-Mantello, George, 6:369
Mandelshtam, Leonid Isaakovich,
    13:461–462
Mandelshtam, Nadezhda Yakovlevna,
    13:462
Mandelshtam, Osip Emilyevich,
    13:462–464
Mandelson, Peter, 13:464

Mandelstamm, Aryeh Loeb. *See* Mandelstamm, Leon

Mandelstamm, Benjamin, 13:**464**

Mandelstamm, Leon, 3:635, 13:**465**

Mandelstamm, Max Emmanuel, 3:137, 13:**465**

Mandeville, John, 6:436

Mandiac Aramaic, 2:353

Mandl, Ignaz, 13:252

Mandl, Jacob Koppel. *See* Theben, Jacob Koppel

Mandl, Saadia, 13:**465–466**

Mandrake, 9:8, 13:**466,** vol. 16: color insert

Manduzio, Danato, 18:25

Manehem. *See* Boraisha, Menahem

Mané-Katz, 13:**466**

Manescu, Corneliu, 4:34

Manessier de Vesoul, 13:**466–467**

Manetho, 13:**467**
  antisemitism of, 11:293
  Josephus, as source for, 11:438, 440
  Judea as term, use of, 11:523
  Moses, 14:531

Manetti, Giannozzo, 8:514, 13:**467**

Manevich, Lev Izrailovich. *See* Manevich, Lev Yefimovich

Manevich, Lev Yefimovich, 13:**467–468**

The Man from There. See Ha-Ish mi-Sham

Manger, Itsik. *See* Manger, Itzik

Manger, Itzik, 13:**468**, 21:350

Manhanaim (Canaan), 11:19

Manhattan Project, 11:809, 16:137

Manheim, Bilhah, 13:**468–469**

Manhig Olam. See Sefer ha-Manhig

Mani, 13:**469**

Mani, Abraham, 13:469

Mani, Elijah ben Suleiman, 8:747, 13:469

Mani, Elijah Moses, 13:469

Mani, Ezra, 13:**469–470**

Mani, Isaac Malchiel, 13:469

Mani, Israel, 13:469

Mani, Suleiman Menahem, 13:469

Manichaeism, 13:**470**

Mani family, 13:**469**

Mani Leib, 13:**470**

Manilow, Barry, 13:**470–471**

Manin, Daniele, 13:**471**

Manischewitz, Hirsch, 13:**471**

Manischewitz Company, 15:393

Man Is Not Alone (Heschel), 9:71

Manissa (Turkey), 13:**471–472**

Manitoba (Canada), 4:615, 13:**472–473**
  Freedman, Samuel, 7:225

Maniyevich, Frederic Rand. *See* Mann, Frederic Rand

Mankiewicz, Herman Jacob, 13:**473–474**

Mankiewicz, Joseph Leo, 13:**474**

Mankowitz, Wolf, 13:**474**

Mann, Abby, 13:**474**

Mann, Abraham Aaron of Posnan, 13:**474–475**

Mann, Daniel, 13:**475**

Mann, Delbert, 13:**475**

Mann, Erika, 13:**477–478**

Mann, Frederic R., 2:46

Mann, Frederic Rand, 13:**475**

Mann, Herbie, 13:**475–476**

Mann, Jacob, 7:466, 9:160, 13:**476**

Mann, Mendel, 13:**476**

Mann, Theodore R., 13:**476–477**

Mann, Thomas, 2:65, 3:410, 13:**477–478**

Manna, 6:614, 13:**478–479**, 14:525

Mannaseh Ben Israel, 9:227

Manne, Mordecai Ẓevi, 13:**479**

Manne, Sheldon. *See* Manne, Shelly

Manne, Shelly, 13:**479–480**

Manners and Customs of New Zealanders (Polack), 16:286

Mannes, Leopold, 13:**480**, 16:125

Mannes family, 13:**480**

Mannheim (Germany), 3:44, 13:**480**

Mannheim, Hermann, 5:302, 303, 13:**480–481**

Mannheim, Karl, 6:161, 13:**481**, 18:729

Mannheim, Lucie, 13:**481–482**

Mannheimer, Isaac Noah, 3:687, 12:779, 13:**482**, 16:340

Mannheimer, Theodor, 13:**482–483**

Manoah of Narbonne, 13:**483**

Manoello Giudeo. *See* Immanuel of Rome

Man of Lies, 12:**818–819**

Manof *v.* Saleima, 5:128

The Manor (Singer), 18:635

Manor, Ehud, 13:**483**

Manosque (France), 13:**483**

Manov, Emil, 4:276

Le Mans (France), 13:**483–484**

Mansfeld, Alfred, 13:**484**

Manslaughter. *See* Homicide

Manso, Leo, 13:**484**

Man's Quest for God (Heschel), 9:71

Man's Search for Meaning (Frankl), 7:214

Manssier de Vezou. *See* Manessier de Vesoul

A Man Stands Behind a Sitting Woman (Levin), 12:708

Mansteling. *See* Abduction

Manṣūr, 13:**484–485**
  al- (*See* Manṣūr)

Mansura (Egypt), 13:**485**

Mansurah, Saadiah ben Judah, 13:**485**

Mansurah, Shalom ben Judah, 13:**485**

Man the Measure (Kahler), 11:718

Mantinga, Hector. *See* Mok, Maurits

Mantino, Jacob ben Samuel, 8:272, 13:**485–486**, 14:424

Mantua (Italy), 13:**486–487**, 16:635–636

Mantua edition Haggadah, 8:214

Manual of Discipline, 5:**676–679**, 6:443

Manual on School Hygiene. See Handbuch der Schulhygiene (Baginsky)

Manuel, Frank Edward, 13:**488**

Manuel I, 4:469, 13:**487–488**

Manuel I Comnenus, 13:**488**

Manufacturing
  Freilich, Max Melech, 7:236
  Rabinowitz, Louis Mayer, 17:41
  Rée, Hartvig Philip, 17:16

Manufacturing Consent (Chomsky), 4:665

Manuscripts, colophons, 5:65–67

Manuscripts, Hebrew. *See* Hebrew manuscripts

Manutius, Aldus. *See* Aldo Manuzio

The Man Who Never Was (Montagu), 14:451

Maon. *See* Ma'on

Ma'on (Israel), 13:**495–496**

Ma'onites, 13:495

Maor, Galia, 13:**496**

Ma'or Katan family, 13:**496**

Maor program, 17:30

Ma'ot Erez Yisrael, 18:450

Ma'ot ḥittim. *See* Me'ot ḥittim

Ma'oz Ḥayyim (Israel), 13:**496**

Ma'oz Ẓur, 13:**496–497**

Mapai, 1:540, 9:287, 11:762, 12:531, 13:**497–498**

Mapam, 1:655, 8:491, 13:270, **498–499**

Map Is Not Territory: Studies in the History of Religions (Smith), 18:688

Map makers, 1:677–678, 5:288, 13:**499–500**, 14:397, 17:75

Mapolska. *See* Lesser Poland (Poland)

Mappah (Isserles), 4:777–778

Maps (Israel). *See* Mampsis (Israel)

Maps of Erez Israel, 13:**500–505**
  Abraham Bar Jacob (17th c.), vol. 13: color insert

Adrichom, Christian van (16th c.), vol. 13: color insert

anonymous (20th c.), vol. 13: color insert

Blau, Willem Janszoon (16th c.), vol. 13: color insert

Bunting, Heinrich (16th c.), vol. 13: color insert

Crusader's map (11th c.), vol. 13: color insert

Hogenberg, Franz (16th c.), vol. 13: color insert

Jode, Gerard de (16th c.), vol. 13: color insert

ornamental plaque (20th c.), vol. 13: color insert

Plancius, Petrus (16th c.), vol. 13: color insert

Mapu, Abraham, 4:119, 159, 8:690–691, 13:505–507

Maqām, 13:507–508

Maqāma, 1:656, 666, 13:508–509, 16:266

Maqāmāt, 13:685–686

Maqam Nawa, 12:633

Maqueda (Spain), 13:509

Mar (Samuel). *See* Samuel (2nd-3rd c.)

Mar (term of respect), 13:509–510

Mar, Jehiel. *See* Mohar, Jehiel

Mara de-atra rabbi, 17:12–13

MaRaF. *See* Perez ben Elijah of Corbeil

Máramarossziget (Romania). *See* Sighet (Romania)

Marathi literature, 15:474

Mar Bar Rav Ashi, 13:510

Mar Bar Ravina, 13:510

Marbeh Eẓah (Shapira), 18:401

Marbeh Tevunah (Shapira), 18:401

Mar Berei de-Ravina. *See* Mar Bar Ravina

Marbiz-Torah, 17:14

Marburg (Germany), 13:510–511. *See* Maribor (Germany)

Marburg system, 5:18–19

Marceau, Marcel, 13:511

Marcellus II, 16:375

The March (Doctorow), 5:728

Marche (Italy). *See* Ancona (Italy)

Marchon Products, 18:160

Marck, Siegfried, 13:511

Marckwald, Willy, 13:511

Marcoff, Cella. *See* Serghi, Cella

Marcos, Fedinand, 18:752

Marcos, Imelda, 18:752

Marcosson, Isaac, 13:511

Marcous, Louis. *See* Marcoussis, Louis

Marcoussis, Louis, 13:511–512

Marculeşti (Bessarabia), 13:512

Marcus, Aaron, 1:301, 13:512

Marcus, Bernard, 13:512–513

   Blank, Arthur M., 3:739

Marcus, David Daniel, 13:513

Marcus, Eduard. *See* Voronca, Ilarie

Marcus, Ernst, 13:513

Marcus, Frank, 13:513

Marcus, Gill, 16:349

Marcus, Jacob Rader, 2:53, 54, 59, 410, 9:160, 162, 13:513–514

Marcus, Joseph, 13:514

Marcus, Mickey. *See* Marcus, David Daniel

Marcus, Ralph, 13:514–515

Marcus, Rudolph Arthur, 4:593, 13:515

Marcus, Ruth Barcan, 13:515

Marcus, Siegfried, 13:515

Marcus, Stanley, 13:515–516

Marcus Annaeus Lucanus. *See* Lucan

Marcus Aurelius Antoninus, 2:82, 13:516

Marcus ben Binah. *See* Hirsch, Aron Siegmund

Marcus ben Yeuzel Donath of Nitra. *See* Mordecai ben Yeuzel Donath of Nitra

Marcuse, Herbert, 13:516–517, 18:709, 739

Marcuse, Ludwig, 13:517

Marcuse, Moses, 13:517

Marcus Fabius Quintilianus. *See* Quintilian

Marcus Julius. *See* Agrippa II

Marcus Junian(i)us Justinus. *See* Justin

Marczali, Henrik, 13:517

Mardin (Turkey), 13:518

Marduk, 3:23, 24, 13:518–519

Marduk-apla-iddina. *See* Merodach-Baladan

Marek, Pesach, 13:519

Marek, Piotr. *See* Marek, Pesach

Mareshah (Israel), 13:519–521, *520*

Maresius, Samuel, 2:21

De Le Mar family. *See* Delmar family

De Le Mar family. *See* Delmar family

Margaliot, Mordecai, 13:521

Margaliot, Reuben, 13:521

Margalit, Dan, 13:521–522

Margalit, Meir, 13:522, 15:392

Margalita, Anton. *See* Margarita, Anton

Margalita, Moses. *See* Margoliouth, Moses

Margareten, Regina, 13:522

Margaretten (Romania). *See* Marghita (Romania)

Margarita, Anton, 11:420–421, 13:522

Marget, Arthur W., 13:522

Marghita (Romania), 13:522–523

"Marginal man" concept, 18:733–734

Margita (Romania). *See* Marghita (Romania)

Margitta (Romania). *See* Marghita (Romania)

Margo, Boris, 13:523

Margolies, Isaac ben Elijah, 13:523–524

Margolies, Morris S., 4:100

Margolies, Moses Zevulun, 13:524

Margolies family. *See* Margolioth family

Margolies-Schlesinger-Jaffe, Israel David ben Mordecai. *See* Jaffe-Margoliot, Israel David

Margolin, Anna, 13:524–525

Margolin, Arnold, 13:525

Margolin, Eliezer, 11:304, 306, 13:525

Margolin, Julij, 13:525–526

Margolin, Moses, 13:526

Margolin, Sarah. *See* Rabinowich, Sarah

Margoliot, Moses ben Simeon, 13:526

Margolioth, Ephraim Zalman ben Menahem Mannes, 13:527

Margolioth, Ḥayyim Mordecai, 6:34

Margolioth, Jacob, 13:527

   Nuremberg, 15:347

Margolioth, Judah Loeb, 13:527–528

Margolioth family, 13:526–527

Margoliouth, David Samuel, 13:528

Margoliouth, Meir of Ostraha, 13:528

Margoliouth, Moses, 13:528

Margoliouth family. *See* Margolioth family

Margoliouth of Ostrog, Meir. *See* Margoliouth of Ostraha, Meir

Margolis, Asher, 11:322

Margolis, Berl. *See* Broder, Berl

Margolis, Gabriel. *See* Margolis, Gavriel Zev

Margolis, Gavriel Zev, 4:100, 13:528–529

Margolis, Laura, 2:61

Margolis, Max Leopold, 3:614, 13:529–530

Margolis, Selig, 14:672–673

Margolis-Kalvaryski, Haim, 3:703, 13:530

Margolius, Rudolf, 18:665

Margoshes, Samuel, 13:530

Margoulies, Berta, 13:530–531

Margowitz, Dan. *See* Daniel, Dan
Margueron, Jean-Claude, 6:386–387
Margules, Max, 13:**531**
Margulies, Emil, 13:129, **531**
Margulies, Ephraim Zalman. *See* Margolioth, Ephraim Zalman ben Menahem Mannes
Margulies, Mordecai. *See* Margaliot, Mordecai
Margulies, Mordecai. *See* Schlesinger, Marx
Margulies, Samuel Hirsch, 6:181, 13:**531–532**, 15:563
Margulies family. *See* Margolioth family
Margulois, David. *See* Merrick, David
Margul-Sperber, Alfred, 13:**532**
Marḥab al-Yahūdī ibn al-Ḥārith, 13:**532–533**, 15:472
Marḥeshvan, 13:**533**
Mari (Mesopotamia), 13:**533–542**, *534*, *536t*
    Anath, 2:131
    Bible, 13:537–541
    excavations, 13:533–535
    Patriarchial period, 13:537, 538–540
    prophecies, 13:540–541
    royal archives, 2:403
    West Semitic rule, 13:535–538, 539
Mari (son of Samuel's daughter). *See* Maari ben Issur
Maria (Babel), 3:17
Maria, Eugenio. *See* Zoller, Israel
Maria Hebraea. *See* Mary the Jewess
Mariamme. *See* Mariamne
Mariamne (daughter of Agrippa I), 11:574
Mariamne (c. 60-29 B.C.E.), 1:631, 5:347, 13:542–543, **542–543**
Mariamne II (d. c. 20 B.C.E.), 11:455, 13:543
Mariampol (Lithuania). *See* Marijampole (Lithuania)
Marianos, 3:509, 13:**543**
Mariánské Lázně (Czech Republic). *See* Marienbad (Czech Republic)
Maria Prophetissa, Moysis Soror. *See* Mary the Jewess
Maria Stuart (Slonimsky), 18:680
Maria Theresa, 2:690, 13:**543–544**
    Judith, as type of, 11:568
    Moravia, 14:474
Mari ben Issur, 13:**544**
Mari ben Rachel. *See* Mari ben Issur
Maribor (Germany), 13:**544**
Marienau School (Germany), 4:60

Marienbad (Czech Republic), 12:563, 13:**544**
Marienbad (Shalom Aleichem), 18:387
Marijampole (Lithuania), 11:751, 13:**545**
Maril, Herman, 13:**545**
Marini, Shabbethai Ḥayyim, 6:180, 13:**545–546**
Marini, Vita. *See* Marini, Shabbethai Ḥayyim
Marinoff, Jacob, 13:**546**
Marissa (Israel). *See* Mareshah (Israel)
Maritain, Jacques, 3:784, 13:**546**
Maritain, Raïsa, 3:784
Maritain, Raïssa, 13:**546**
Marital rape, 18:331
Maritime law, 13:**546–547**
Mariupol (Ukraine). *See* Zhdanov (Ukraine)
Marix, Adolph, 13:**547**
Mark, Berl. *See* Mark, Bernard
Mark, Bernard, 13:**547**
Mark, Julius, 13:**547–548**
Mark, Mary Ellen, 13:**548**
Mark, Yudel, 11:368, 13:**548**
Markabah mysticism, 17:128
Markah, 13:**548–549**
Markel, Lester, 13:**549**
Markel-Mosessohn, Miriam, 8:443, 699, 13:**549**
Market days and fairs, 13:**550–552**
    Butnah, 4:318
    economic history, 6:111
"The Market for 'Lemons': Quality Uncertainty and the Market Mechanism" (Akerlof), 1:560
Marketing, 4:315
Market overt, oaths in, 15:362–363
Markish, Peretz, 13:**552**
The Mark of Cain (Ram Oren). *See Or Kain*
Markon, Isaac Dov Ber, 13:**552–553**
Markova, Alicia, 5:416, 13:**553**
Markovits, Jakabs. *See* Markovits, Rodion
Markovits, Rodion, 13:**553**
Markowitz, Harry M., 13:**553**
Markowitz, Sandra. *See* Harris, Barbara
Marks, Alice Lilian. *See* Markova, Alicia
Marks, Barnett E., 16:124
Marks, Harry Hananel, 13:**553**
Marks, Hayman, 13:**553–554**
Marks, Hertha. *See* Ayrton, Hertha
Marks, Lewis, 15:198
Marks, Marcus M., 13:**554**

Marks, Samuel, 11:377, 13:**554**, 16:349
Marks, Simon, 5:588, 13:**554–555**
Markson, Aaron David, 13:**555**
Markus, Ludwig, 13:**555**
Markus, Samuell, 15:541
Markuse, Moses, 8:441
Markus-Studien (Chajes), 4:559
Marlé, Arnold, 13:**555**
Marli, Raphael ben Maẓli'aḥ. *See* Marli, Samuel ben Maẓli'aḥ
Marli, Samuel ben Maẓli'aḥ, 13:**555**
Marlowe, Christopher, 13:**555–556**
Marmor, Kalman, 13:**556**
Marmor, Ẓevi. *See* Marmor, Kalman
Marmorek, Alexander, 13:**556–557**
Marmori, Hanokh, 13:**557**
Marmorosh, Jacob, 3:739
Marmorstein, Arthur, 13:**557**
Marmur, Dow, 13:**557–558**
Maron, Hanna. *See* Meron, Hanna
Maronite Christian community, 3:599, 7:617
Maror, 13:**558**
Marosvásárhely (Romania). *See* Targu-Mures (Romania)
Mar'ot Elohim (Al-Constantini), 1:604
Marot ha-Ẓove'ot (Alshekh), 2:10
Marquis d'Argens. *See* Argens, Jean Baptiste de Boyer
Marr, Wilhelm, 13:**558**
Marrakesh (Morocco), 11:757, 13:**558–559**
Marranism, 10:9
Marrano diaspora, 13:**560–563**
Marranos, 3:121, 122, 13:**559**
    Abenaes, Solomon, 1:249–250
    Abenatar Melo, David, 1:250
    Abendana, Isaac, 1:250
    Abendana family, 1:250
    Aboab, Immanuel, 1:265–266
    Aboab, Isaac de Mattathias, 1:268
    Acosta, Christobal, 1:358–359
    adventurers, 6:716
    Aguilar, Diego D', 1:508–509
    Alemán, Mateo, 1:611
    Alvares family, 2:27
    America, 2:41
    Ames family, 2:66
    Amsterdam, 2:109
    Amsterdam (Netherlands), 2:108, 109, 119
    Antuñes family, 2:249
    anusim, 2:251
    apologetics, 2:267
    apostasy, 2:271
    Arias, Joseph Semah, 2:451–452

Assumpção, Diogo da, 2:615
Azevedo, Moses Cohen D', 2:768
Bargas, Abraham de, 3:150
Barrassa, Jacob, 3:174
Barros, Basto, Arturo Carlos De, 3:177–178
Belgium, 3:281–282
Belmonte family, 3:302
Bernal family, 3:467
Brazil, Recife, 17:145–146
Brudo, Manuel, 4:220–221
Brussels, 4:226
Bueno family, 4:252
Caceres, Francisco de, 4:330–331
Caceres, Simon de, 4:331
Cardoso family, 4:463
Cardozo, Abraham Miguel, 1:637, 4:464–466, 12:791, 15:538
Cardozo, Isaac, 4:466–467
Carvajal, Abraham Israel, 4:502
Castelo Branco, 4:515
Castro, de, family, 4:518
Castro, Pedro de, 4:518
Castro family, 4:517
Castro Sarmento, Jacob de, 4:519–520, 13:728
Castro Tartas, Isaac de, 4:520–521
Catholic Church, 4:711
Chaves family, 4:584
Chirino family, 4:652
Chuetas, 4:708–709
Coronel Chacon, Sir Augustin, 5:225
Coutinho family, 5:248–249
Curiel family, 5:341
Desecration of the Host, 9:566
Dias, Luis, 5:636–637, 18:320
England, 6:414–415
     Bristol, 4:185
Enríquez Basurto, Diego, 6:446
Faria, Francisco de, 6:716
Fonseca, Daniel de, 7:115
France, 4:82, 189, 16:24
     Badajoz, 3:42
     Bayonne, 3:231–232
     Biarritz, 3:570
     Bordeaux, 4:82
     Languedoc, 12:484
Gómez de Sossa, Isaac, 7:749
Granada, Gabriel De, 8:32–33
halakhah, 15:134
heraldry, 9:6
Herrera, Abraham Kohen de, 9:40–41
Homem, Antonio, 9:505–506
Inés of Herrera, 9:41

Italy, 2:140, 4:50
     Ancona, 15:695
     Ferrara, 6:763
Jesurun, Reuel, 11:246
Jesurun family, 11:246
Jewish identity and, 11:294–295, 12:428
John III of Portugal, 11:379
Juan de España, 11:472
Juan de Valladolid, 11:472, 14:462
Julius III, 2:140
Laguna, Daniel Israel Lopez, 12:438–439
Lamego family, 12:446
literature of, 15:730
Lobato family, 13:153
Lopez, Roderigo, 2:66, 13:190
Lopez Rosa family, 13:190
Machado family, 13:323
Maldonado de Silva, Francisco, 4:637, 13:430
in medicine, 13:727–728
Mendes, Diogo, 14:43
Mesquita family, 14:110
Mexico, 14:137–138
Mocatta family, 14:404
Montezinos Antonio de, 14:460
Morocco, 14:496
Nasi, Gracia, 14:785
Nasi, Joseph, 1:249, 2:34, 10:777, 14:786–787, 15:524, 532, 541, 16:345–346
Nuñez, Hector, 15:345, 346
Nuñez family, 15:345–346
Oliver Y Fullana, Nicolás de, 15:408
Orta, Garcia de, 13:728, 15:492
Paz, Duarte de, 15:699–700
Penso de la Vega, Joseph, 2:125, 15:730, 18:299–300
Philippines, 16:49
philosophy, 16:65
Pina, Jacob, 16:164
Pineda, Juan de, 16:166
Pinto Delgado, João, 16:179–180
Portugal, 2:140, 5:47
     Chaves family, 4:584
     Oporto, 15:441
Prado, Juan de, 16:446–447, 18:298
Pyrrhus, Didacus, 16:757–758
rescue of, 14:43
Rio de Janeiro, 17:337
Robles, Antonio Rodrigues, 17:356
Rojas, Fernando de, 17:370–371
Sanchez, Antonio Nuñes Ribeiro, 18:9

Senior, Solomon, 18:289
ships and sailing, 18:488
Silva, Rodrigo Mendez Da, 18:583
Silva, Samuel Da, 18:583
Silverya, Miguel De, 18:589
Solis family, 18:753–754
Spain, 19:76–78, 77
     Toledo, 20:26
     Valencia, 20:461
Spanish and Portuguese literature, 19:85–86, 87–88
sugar industry and trade, 19:293–294
Teixeira, Pedro, 19:585
Teixeira de Sampaio, Abraham Senior, 19:585–586
Teixeira Pinto, Bento, 19:586
Torre, Alfonso de la, 20:59
trade and commerce, 20:83–85
Treviño de Sobremonte, Tomás, 20:136
Treviño de Sorbemonte, 20:136
Usque, Abraham, 3:636, 20:433
Usque, Samuel, 9:225, 11:429, 20:433–434
Usque, Solomon, 20:434
Vitoria, Francisco de, 20:561
Zacutus Lusitanus, 21:437
See also Conversos; Curiel; New Christians
Marre, Alan. See Marre, Sir Alan
Marre, Sir Alan, 13:**563**
Marriage, 13:**563–574**
     adultery, 1:424–427, 4:582
     agunah, 1:510–520
          Epstein, Louis M., 6:475
          Takkanot, 19:452
     annulment, 1:514–517
     apostasy, 2:276
     arrangements, 6:693
     Asia and African statistics, 20:555–556, 555t
     badhan, 3:48
     barrenness and fertility, 3:174–175
     betrothals and, 3:541–542
     Bible, 13:563–564, 565
     bigamy and polygamy, 3:691–694
     celibacy vs., 4:537
     ceremony, 13:565–569
     child, 4:616–617
     civil, 4:746–748
     common law, 13:683
     concept of marriage, 13:563–565
     contemporary U.S., 6:702
     contracts and, 9:638
     divorces, Samaritans, 17:732

Marriage, *continued*

dowries, 4:264, 5:768–772

Elephantine Papyri, 6:312

feminism and, 6:753–754

forbidden, 2:128, 5:466, 6:691–692

Aaron ben Judah Kusdini, 1:216

Germany, Bergen-Belsen, 3:421

ḥuppah, 13:568

husband and wife, rights and obligations of, 9:634–640

immigration strains on, 6:696

importance of, 6:694–695

interfaith

children of, 11:268

definition of Jew and, 11:254

intermarriage, 20:554–555, 555t

contemporary U.S., 6:703

Ezra and, 6:652, 659

Nehemiah and, 6:661, 662

Samaritans, 17:731–732

Israel (state), 9:638–639, 13:573

endogamous, 10:286, 289

Ethiopian, 10:631

imprisonment, and marital relations, 9:746–747

Muslim, 10:649

rate, 10:293–294

religious status and, 10:637

sexual offenses, 18:331

Italy, interfaith, 10:806, 807

Jewish identity and, 11:292, 298

Karaite permissible, 11:242

Kiddushin, 13:569–573

laws and legal systems, 5:152–153, 154–155, 6:689–690, 691–692, 11:263, 265, 13:569–574

Bakshi-Doron, Eliahu, 3:74

Karaites, 11:799

Maimonides, 5:137

Mendes claim dispute, 5:153

prohibited, 13:575–576

lesbian, 12:660

Levirate marriage and ḥalizah, 12:**725–729**

mamzer, 13:442–445

metaphorically to God, 11:126

Middle Ages, 13:564–565

mixed, 2:114, 9:187–188 (*See* Mixed marriages, intermarriages)

monogamy, 14:447–448

niddah, 15:253, 255

Nissu'in, 13:570–571

North America, 13:573–574

Nuremberg laws, 15:348–350

ones in, 15:428

in Ottoman empire, 15:539

parables based on, 15:621–622

post-Talmudic period, 12:727, 13:566–568

prohibited, 5:83t–84t, 714, 13:**574–576**

property relations, 13:680–683

rabbinic literature, 13:564

rebellious husbands' rights and, 9:639

remarriage, 6:329

restrictive clauses, 11:19

ring, 13:568

rites and rituals, 13:568–569

Samaritans, 17:731–732

shadkhan, 18:360–361

statistics, 20:554–556, 554t, 555t, 558–559

Talmud, 12:727, 13:565–566

trial marriage advocated by Léon Blum, 4:7

wife's earnings, 9:639–640

wife's property rights, 9:639

Zelophehad's daughters, 15:332

See also Ketubbah; *Kiddushin* (tractate); Mikvah; Mixed marriages, intermarriages

Marriage and the Family in Australia (Elkin), 6:359

Marriage Laws in the Bible and Talmud (Epstein), 6:475

Marron, Hanna. *See* Meron, Hanna

Marrus, Michael R., 13:**576**

Marsala (Italy), 13:**576–577**

Marschak, Jacob, 13:**577**

Marseilles (France), 13:**577–579**

Marshak, Ilya Yakovlevich. *See* Ilin, M.

Marshak, Samuel Yakovlevich, 13:**579–580**

Marshall, Bob, 14:454

Marshall, David Saul, 13:**580**

Marshall, Louis, 11:256–257, 12:547, 13:**580–581**

American Jewish Archives, 2:53

American Jewish Committee, 2:54, 55, 56

Billikopf, Jacob, 3:699

Jewish Theological Seminary, 11:329

New York City and, 15:205, 210, 217

parochial schools, 6:161

Marshall, Mel, 15:549

Marshrut v bessmertiye (Eichenbaum). *See A Route to Immortality* (Eichenbaum)

Marsus, C. Vibius, 13:**581**

Martha, 11:450, 13:**581**

Marti, Karl, 13:**581–582**

Martial, 13:**582**

Martin (popes), 13:**582**

Martin, Alvin Morris. *See* Martin, Tony

Martin, Benno, 15:348

Martin, Bernard, 13:**582–583**

Martin, David, 13:**583**

Martin, Tony, 13:**583**

Martin IV (pope), 13:582

Martin V (pope), 3:122, 4:48, 13:582

Martín Buber (Dujovne), 6:43

Martinez, Ferrant, 13:**583–584**, 18:327

Martínez de Oviedo, Gonzalo, 13:**584**

Martinez Dormido, Manuel. *See* Dormido, David Abrabanel

Martin I, King of Aragon, 1:250

Martini, Raymond, 3:146, 7:126, 8:513, 13:**584–585**

Martinique (French Antilles), 4:473

Marton, Ernö Jechezkel, 13:**585**

Martov, Julius, 1:325, 4:279, 13:**585–586**, 16:348, 18:705, 714

Märturia unei generatii (Aderca), 1:391

Marty (Chayefsky), 4:585

Marty Balin's Greatest Hits (Balin), 3:91

Martyrdom

Aaron of Neustadt, 1:220

Amnon of Mainz, 2:87

Babi Yar, 3:22–23

Black Death, as result of, 3:733–734

Blois, 3:770

Bonn, 4:63

Boppard, 4:79

Brandenburg, 4:126

Bratislava, 4:131

Breslau, 4:164

Brzesk Kujawksi, 4:230

Cantor, Bernard, 4:439

Carvajal family, 4:501

Castro Tartas, Isaac de, 4:521

Eleazar (martyr), 6:298

in fiction, 7:10

Hananiah ben Teradyon, 8:316

Hatchwell, Sol, 8:455–456

Homem, Antonio, 9:505–506

Josce of York, 11:405–406

Joseph ben Gershon of Rosheim, 11:420, 421

Kiddush ha-Shem, 12:140–142

lists of, *Memorbuch*, 14:17–18

Maccabean, 8:447, 448

Morrocco, 8:455–456

Nordhausen, 15:299

Nuñes family, 15:345

Obernai, 15:368

Ofran, 15:391

Oppenheim, 15:442

Oppenheimer, Joseph ben Issachar Suesskind, 15:449

Selucid rule, ancient Israel, 9:193

Suleika, 8:455–456

Martyrdom of Isaiah, 10:**76**

Martyrologic hagiography, 8:225

Martyrs, Acts of Alexandrian. *See* Alexandrian Martyrs, Acts of

Martyrs' and Heroes' Remembrance Authority. *See* Yad Vashem

Martyrs Memorial Museum, 13:201

Martyrs' suicide, 5:313–314

Marum, L., 3:43

Marvel Comics, 11:761, 12:598

Marwick, Lawrence, 13:**586**

Marx, Adolf Bernhard, 12:758, 13:**586**

Marx, Alexander, 11:329, 13:**586–587**

Marx, David, 2:637

Marx, Frank, 14:446

Marx, G. A. *See* Dalman, Gustaf Hermann

Marx, Karl, 13:**587**

Marx, Karl Heinrich, 13:**587–590**
    antisemitism, 9:232
    biblical criticism and, 3:655, 659
    criminology, 5:302
    First International, 18:705
    on Jewish identity, 11:297
    Landshut, Siegfried, 12:476
    Lassalle, Ferdinand, 12:501
    sociology and, 18:728–729

Marx-Aveling, Eleanor, 18:704

Marx Brothers, 13:**590–591**

Marxism
    Adler, Max, 1:402
    biblical criticism and, 3:655, 659
    Borochov, Ber, 4:88–90
    Deborin, Abram Moiseyevich, 5:519–520
    Dickstein, Szymon, 5:646–647
    influence on sociology, 18:729
    Landshut, Siegfried, 12:476
    Schaff, Adam, 18:103
    See also Marx, Karl Heinrich; New Left

Mary (mother of Jesus)
    Aaron and, 1:211
    as new Eve, 6:573

Maryam (biblical figure). *See* Miriam (biblical figure)

Maryan, 13:**591**, 15:650

Maryland, 13:**591–592**, *592,* 592*t*

Mary the Jewess, 1:602

Mar Zadok. *See* Zadok, bar Mar Yishi

Marzeahs, 6:27

Il Marzocco (periodical), 15:500

Marzouk, Moshe, 4:346, 13:**592**

Mar Zutra ben Mari, 21:693

Mar Zutra ben R. Naḥman, 21:693

Masa be-Merḥav ha-Zeman (Pal), 18:206

Masada (Israel), 6:302–303, 13:**593–599**
    aerial view, vol. 14: color insert
    Eleazar ben Jair, 6:302–303
    lots, 13:219
    Silva, Flavius, 18:583
    Yadin, Yigal, 2:161, 371

The Masada Plan (Harris), 18:200

Masa le-Erez Yisrael bi-Shenat Tat be-Elef ha-Shishi (Lewinsky), 18:202

Māsarjawayh of Basra, 3:205
    Judeo-Arabic literature and, 11:531

Masaryk, Jan Garrigue, 3:435, 5:443, 13:**599**

Masaryk, Thomas Garrigue, 13:**600**

Masat Binyamin (Slonik), 18:675

Masat Moshe (Alshekh), 2:10

Masci, Girolamo. *See* Nicholas IV

Māshā'Allah ben Athaň, 13:**600**

Mashad. *See* Meshed (Iran)

Mashā'Irī, al- family, 13:**600–601**

Mashal. *See* Allegories; Parables; Proverbs

Mashal, 15:620–623

Mashalim. *See* Fables

Mashallah of Egypt, 11:531

Mashash, Shlomo, 13:**601**

Ma Shelomekh, Dolores? (Hoffmann), 9:312

Mashgi'ah, 13:**601**

Mashina, 3:106

Mashiv ha-Ru'ah, 13:**601**

Mashkin. *See* Mo'ed Katan

Mashkon. *See* Pledges

Mashkoni, Judah Leon ben Moses. *See* Moskoni, Judah Leon ben Moses

Mashreh Kitrin (Abraham ben Eliezer ha-Levi), 1:298

Masie, Aaron Meir, 13:**601**

Masius, Andreas. *See* Maes, Andreas

Maskil. *See* Haskalah

Maskileison, Abraham ben Judah Leib, 13:**601–602**

Maskilim
    Akiva ben Moses Guens Eger, 6:217

Chelm, Solomon ben Moses, 4:589

Elijah Phinehas ben Meir, 6:347

Kantor, Judah Leib, 11:771

Mohr, Abraham Menahem Mendel, 14:420

Nevakovich, Judah Leib, 15:128

Ornstein, Jacob Meshullam ben Mordecai Ze'ev, 15:480

parody, Hebrew, 15:658–660

Romania, 17:379

of Slonim, 17:428–429

Maskil le-Eitan, Abraham ben Judah Leib. *See* Maskileison, Abraham ben Judah Leib

The Masks (Duda), 6:40

Maṣli'aḥ Ṣāliḥ, 13:**602**

Masliansky, Zvi Hirsch, 13:**602**, 15:207

Maslow, Abraham H., 4:256, 13:**602**

Maslow, Sophie, 13:**602–603**

Masnut, Samuel ben Nissim, 13:**603**

Mason, Jackie, 13:**603**

Masora, 13:**603–656**
    accuracy, 15:751–752
    Babylonian system, 13:630–633
        contamination of, 13:618
        notations, 13:619–620
        terminology, 13:617–618
        tonal meanings in, 13:624
        Torah divisions, 13:607, 609–610
        written symbols, 13:616
    editing, 13:620–621
    masoretes, 13:648–651
        Ben-Asher, Aaron ben Moses, 3:319–320
        Ben-Asher, Moses, 3:**320**
        Ben-Naphtali, Moses Ben David, 3:367
    Masoretic Notes, 13:617
    Palestinian system, 13:618
        notations, 13:620
        pronounciation, 13:624–629
        Tiberian influence on, 13:644
    Samaritan Pentateuch, 15:753–754
    Tiberian system, 13:633–642
        accentuation, 13:637–642
        contamination of, 13:618
        influence of, 13:631–632, 644
        non-conventional system, 13:642–646
        pronounciation, 13:625–626, 628, 629
    vowel signs, 13:623
    vowel signs, origins, 13:624, 627–628, 630–632, 633–634
    written, 13:614–622

Masorah, comparative tables in illuminated Spanish Hebrew Bibles, 3:677

Masorah Magna, 13:618–621

Masorah Parva, 13:615–618, 620

Masorah vocalization, 7:475–476

  Ben-Asher, Aaron ben Moses,
    3:320

  Ben-Asher, Moses, 3:320

Masoret. *See* Masorah; Tradition

Masoret ha Berit (David ben Abraham
  ha-Lavan), 5:463

Masoret ha-Berit (Ha-Lavan), 11:612

Masoret ha-Gedolah. *See Okhlah ve-
Okhlah*

Masoret ha-Masoret (Levita), 12:731,
  13:652

Masoretic accents, musical, 13:**656–
664**, *657*

  notation, 13:*657, 658, 659, 660,
    661, 662, 663*

  styles, 13:661–664

Masoretic Cantillation. *See*
  Cantillation; Music

Masoretic scholars

  Baer, Seligman Isaac, 3:53

  Heidenheim, Wolf, 8:763

  Heilbronn, Joseph be David of
    Eschwege, 8:766

  Kahle, Paul Ernst, 11:717

Masoretic text, 3:583, 8:627–628,
  13:652

  al tikrei, 2:20

  authorities, 11:42

  exegesis and, 3:641

  hegemony of, 3:585

  mene, mene, tekel, u-farsin, 14:46

  micrography in illuminated
    Hebrew manuscripts, 3:676, 678

  Okhlah ve-Okhlah, 15:397

  printed editions of Hebrew Bible,
    3:588

Masoret Seyag la-Torah (Abulafia),
  1:341–342, 13:652

Masorti Judaism, 6:428, 8:308. *See*
  Conservative Judaism

Masorti Olami, 5:176–177

Masorti Peace Corps, 18:588

Massa ba-Arav (Romanelli), 17:374

Massachusetts (U.S.), 13:**664–666**, *665*

Massacre of the Innocents, 9:37

Massacres

  Armleder, 2:6, *477*

  Bury St. Edmunds, 4:302

  Haidamaks, 3:96

  Of Heraclius, 4:326

  Rindfleisch, 2:36

Massadah (Israel), 13:**666**

Massad Camps, 11:272

Massa ha-Am (Abraham ben Josiah
  Troki), 1:303

Massah and Meribah. *See* Rephidim

Massa le-Erez Yisrael bi-Shenat Tat
  (Leib), 21:620

Massarani, Tullo, 13:**666–667**

Massarano, Isacchino. *See* Massarano,
  Jacchino

Massarano, Jacchino, 13:**667**

Massarik, Friederike. *See* Massary,
  Fritzi

Massary, Fritzi, 13:**667**, 15:602

Massekhet, 13:**667**

Massekhet Ḥanukkah, 15:657

Massekhet Purim (Kalonymus ben
  Kalonymus), 7:121, 11:749, 15:656–
  657

Massell, Sam, Jr., 13:**667–668**

Massenpsychologie (Broch), 4:191

Massepha (ancient Israel), 14:388

Masserman, Jules Homan, 13:**668**

Masse und Macht (Canetti), 4:431

Massias, Enrico, 1:440

Mass murder. *See* Camps,
  concentration and extermination;
  Genocide Convention; Holocaust

Massorah. *See* Masorah

The Massorah (Ginsburg), 7:610

Massuah Institute for the Study of the
  Holocaust, 9:427

Massu'ot Yiẓḥak, 13:**668**

Mastbaum, Joel, 13:**668**

Mastema, 13:**668–669**

Master, Arthur M., 13:**669**

Master Aaron. *See* Aaron of Baghdad

The Master and Margarita
  (Slonimsky), 18:680

Master of the Divine Name. *See* Ba'al
  Shem

*Masters of Death: The SS-
Einsatzgruppen and the Invention of
the Holocaust* (Rhodes), 9:419

Mastic (plant), 13:**669**

Măstile (Duda). *See The Masks* (Duda)

Masturbation, 15:427

Masud Ḥai Roke'aḥ, 8:482

Masur, Norbert, 17:121

Mat, Moses, 13:**669–670**, 18:675

Matalon, Eli, 13:**670**

Matalon, Ronit, 13:**670**

Mata Meḥasya (Babylon), 13:**670**

Matas, David, 13:**670–671**

Matatron. *See* Metatron

Matchmakers. *See* Shadkhan

Materia medica (Castro Sarmento),
  4:519

De Materia Medica (Dioscorides
  Pedanius), 5:675

La Maternelle (motion picture), 6:473

Maternity, establishing, 21:426

Mathematics, 13:**671–679**

  Abraham bar Ḥiyya, 1:293

  ancient education, 6:167

  biblical, 15:333

  Brodetsky, Selig, 4:196

  Bronowski, Jacob, 4:207

  computation, 5:129–131

  Creizenach, Michael, 5:280–281

  England

    Mordell, Louis Joel, 14:482

    Roth, Klaus Friedrich, 17;483

  Ensheim, Moses, 6:447

  Filipowski, Ẓevi Hisrch, 7:20

  Fraenkel, Abraham Adolf, 7:143

  France

    Levi Ben Gershom, 12:698–
      702

    Levy, Lucien, 12:752

  geometry, Mishnat ha-Middot,
    14:331

  Germany

    Bendavid, Lazarus, 3:325

    Bernays, Paul Isaac, 3:470

    Cantor, Moritz Benedict,
      4:440

    Courant, Richard, 5:245

    Eisenstein, Ferdinand
      Gotthold, 6:273

    Hausdorff, Felix, 8:463

    Hurwitz, Adolf, 9:631

    Jacobi, Karl Gustav Jacob,
      11:38

    Lipschitz, Rudolf Otto
      Sigismund, 13:71

  Germany Landau, Edmund,
    12:458–459

  Hadamard, Jacques Salomon,
    8:185

  Hanani, Ḥaim, 8:315

  Hannover, Raphael Levi, 8:327

  Hungary, Fejér, 6:744

  Israel

    Agmon, Shmuel, 1:465

    Bernstein, Joseph, 3:480

    Dvoretzky, Aryeh, 6:74

    Fekete, Michael, 6:745

    Levitsky, Jacob, 12:742

    Pekeris, Chaim Leib, 15:716

    Shelah, Saharon, 18:445

  Italy

    Levi-Civita, Tullio, 12:703

    Segrè, Beniamino, 18:251

    Segrè, Corrado, 18:251

  Lefschetz, Solomon, 12:603

  Mishnat ha-Middot, 14:331

Netherlands, Lemans, Moses, 12:636

Neugebauer, Otto, 15:119

Neumann, Johann Ludwig von, 15:122

Perelman, Chaim, 15:760–761

physics and, 16:135, 136

Poland

Dickstein, Samuel (1853-1939), 5:646

Lichtenfeld, Gabriel Joseph, 12:797

Rabin, Michael Oser, 17:33

Rosenhead, Louis, 17:447–448

Russia, Besicovitch, Abram Samoilovitch, 3:494–495

Schur, Issai, 18:176

Schwartz, Laurent, 18:185–186

Syria, Domninus of Larissa, 5:747

U.K., Levy, Hyman, 12:750

U.S.

Hauptman, Herbert Aaron, 8:460–461

Simons, James H., 18:618

Matif ha-Kazav. *See* Prophet of Lies

Matisyahu, vol. 20: color insert

Matkah, Judah ben Solomon ha-Kohen, 11:536, 13:**679**

Matlin, Marlee, 13:**679–680**

Matlin, Moshe Meir, 13:**680**

Matmor, Yoram, 8:720

Matriarchs, 13:**680**, 15:691

Matrilineal descent, 5:174–175

Matrimonial property, 13:**680–683**

Matrimony. *See* Marriage

La matriz del infierno (Aguinis), 1:510

Matsas, Joseph, 13:**684**

Matsas, Nestoras, 13:**684**

Matt, C. David, 13:**684–685**

Matta'ei Mosheh (Aaronsohn), 1:223

Mattan Torah. *See* Revelation

Mattathias (Hasmonean), 9:193–194, 13:**685**, 18:601

Mattathias (poet), 13:**685–686**

Mattathias ben Ḥeresh. *See* Mattiah ben Ḥeresh

Mattathias ben Simeon, 13:**686**

Mattathias ha-Yiẓhari, 13:**686**

Matteh Aharon (Bacharach), 3:4

Matteh Dan (Nieto), 18:295

Matteh Moshe (Benjamin), 3:358

Mattel, 8:320

Mattenot Kehunnah (Issachar Berman ben Naphtali ha-Kohen), 10:768

Matter and form. *See* Form and matter

A Matter of Principle (Dworkin), 6:74

A Matter of Taste: How Names, Fashions, and Culture Change (Lieberson), 18:733

Mattersburg (Austria). *See* Mattersdorf (Austria)

Mattersdorf (Austria), 13:**686–687**

Mattersdorf, Jeremiah ben Isaac, 13:**687**

Matters of Life and Death (Dorff), 5:755

Matthau, Walter, 13:**687**

Matthew of Paris, 14:444

Matthias ben Theophilus (high priests), 13:**687–688**

Matthias ben Theophilus I, 13:687, **688**

Matthias ben Theophilus II, 13:687

Matthioli, 2:34

Mattiah ben Ḥeresh, 13:**688**

Mattityah ben Moshe. *See* Mattathias (poet)

Mattityahu. *See* Mattiah ben Ḥeresh

Mattityahu ben Ḥeresh. *See* Mattiah ben Ḥeresh

Mattnah, 13:**688**

Mattuck, Israel I., 13:**688**

Ma'tuk, Sulayman ben David, 13:**688–689**

Maturity

age of (*See* Puberty)

religious and legal (*See* Bar Mitzvah, Bat Mitzvah)

Matz, Israel, 13:**689**

Matzah, 7:119, 13:**689–690**, 15:678, 680–681

Matzah of Zion (Tlass), 3:780

Matzenauer, Margarete, 13:**690**

Matzliah, Nissim, 15:544

Matzo. *See* Matzah

Matẓot and matẓah meal. *See* Matzah

Mauiel, Mordecai ben Samuel. *See* Meisel Mordecai ben Samuel

Mauriac, François, 7:23

Maurier, George du, 6:436

Mauritius, 13:**690–691**

Maurogonato, Isaac, 16:345

Maurois, André, 3:763, 13:**691**

Maurras, Charles, 1:369–370, 13:**691–692**

Maus (periodical), 4:500–501

Maus (Spiegelman), 4:631, 9:414, vol. 2: color insert

Mauşel Marcus ben Samuel. *See* Meisel Mordecai ben Samuel

Mauşel Marx ben Samuel. *See* Meisel Mordecai ben Samuel

Mauşel Mordecai ben Samuel. *See* Meisel Mordecai ben Samuel

Mauss, Marcel, 2:185, 13:**692**, 18:730

Mauthausen concentration camp, 13:**692–693**

Mauthner, Fritz, 12:467, 13:**693–694**

Mautner, Konrad, 13:**694**

Mavet (god), 5:573

Mavet ba-Geshem (Almog), 1:680

Mavo Histori (Smoira-Cohn), 18:690

Mavo le-nusaḥ ha-Mishnah (Epstein), 6:472

Ma-Wara-n-Nahr. *See* Transoxiana

Mawza' (Yemen), 13:**694**

Max Factor & Company, 6:674–675

Maxie, Slapsie. *See* Rosenbloom, Max Everitt

Maximalists, 3:655

Maximianupolis (ancient Israel). *See* Legio (ancient Israel)

Maximilian I (Holy Roman emperor), 13:**694–695**

Maximilian II (Holy Roman emperor), 13:695

Maximon, Shalom Dov Ber, 13:**695**

Maximoswki, Shalom Dov Ber. *See* Maximon, Shalom Dov Ber

Maxims, legal. *See* Legal maxims

Maximus (Emperor), 2:37

Maximus, Magnus Clemens, 13:**695–696**

Maximus of Turin, 4:721

Maximus the Usurper. *See* Maximus, Magnus Clemens

Max Weber: An Intellectual Portrait (Bendix), 3:328

Maxwell, Robert, 6:425, 13:**696**

Maxwell Street market, 4:608

Maxwell Street Settlement House, 13:233

Maxy, Max Herman, 13:**696**

May, Elaine, 13:**696–697**

May, Lewis, 15:200, 464

Maya ben Heresh, 3:754

Mayakovsky, V., 4:181

Ma'yan Barukh (Israel), 13:**697**

Ma'yan Gannim (Judah ben Yakar), 11:492

Ma'yan Ẓevi (Israel), 13:**697**

Maybaum, Ignaz, 9:397–399, 13:**697**

Maybaum, Sigmund, 13:**697–698**

Maydanski, Moses, 11:322

Mayence (Germany). *See* Mainz (Germany)

Ma'yenei ha-Yeshu'ah (Abrabanel), 7:133

Mayer, Arno Joseph, 13:**698**

Mayer, Astorre, 13:700

Mayer, Daniel, 13:**698**, 16:343, 18:706

Mayer, George Toma. *See* Maiorescu, George Toma

Mayer, Gustav, 13:**698**

Mayer, Lehrer. *See* Mayer, Leopold

Mayer, Leo Ary, 2:371, 13:**698**

Mayer, Leopold, 13:**698–699**

Mayer, Levy, 13:**699**

Mayer, Louis Burt, 12:442, 13:**699**, 14:571

Mayer, Morris. *See* Myer, Morris

Mayer, René, 13:**699**, 16:343

Mayer, Robert. *See* Mayer, Sir Robert

Mayer, Sally, 13:**700**

Mayer, Saly, 13:**700**

   American Joint Distribution Committee, 2:61

Mayer, Sir Robert, 13:**699–700**

Mayerchik, Hanna. *See* Chapbooks; Meron, Hanna

Mayerowitz, Berachya, 2:636

Mayers, Baruch, 4:133–134

Mayim, Aḥaronim, 13:**701**

Maykapar, Samuil Moyseyevich, 13:**701**

May laws (Russia, 1882), 12:508–509, 13:**701–702**, 15:579

Maymeran, Joseph, 14:497

Maymeran family, 13:**702**, 14:497

Maynard, Fredelle Bruser, 13:**702**

Mayne Lider (Einhorn). *See* *My Poems* (Einhorn)

Mayn Leksikon (Ravitch), 17:123

Mayse-Bukh, 13:**702–703**, 21:342

Dos Mayse-bukh fun Mayn Lebn (Ravitch), 4:426

Mayselekh in Ferzn (Der Nister), 5:596

Maysles, Albert, 13:**703–704**

Maysles, David Paul, 13:**703–704**

Mayzel, Maurycy, 13:**704**

Mayzel, Nachman, 13:**704**

Mazaca. *See* Caesarea (Cappadocia)

Mazaga. *See* Caesarea (Cappadocia)

Māzandarān (Iran), 13:**704–705**

Mazar, Amihai, 13:**705**

Mazar, Benjamin, 2:371, 9:159, 13:**705–706**

   Bet She'arim (Israel), 3:547

Mazarinades, 4:106

Mazdaism. *See* Zoroastrianism

Maze, Ida, 4:426, 13:**706**

Mazeh, Jacob, 6:47, 13:**706**, 14:517–518

Mazer, Abraham, 13:707

Mazer, William, 2:46

Mazer family, 13:**707**

Mazhdunarodnaya evreiskaya gazeta (newspaper). *See* *International Jewish Newspaper* (newspaper)

Mazia, Edna, 8:723

Mazie, Aharon. *See* Masie, Aaron Meir

Mazkeret Batyah (Israel), 8:300, 13:**707**

Mazkeret Ḥakhmei Italyah (Mortara), 14:513

Mazkir. *See* Hazkarat neshamot

Maẓli'aḥ (Israel), 13:**707**

Maẓli'aḥ ben Solomon ha-Kohen, 1:387, 13:**707**

Mazon, 13:210, 18:175

Mazowiecki (Poland). *See* Grodzisk Mazowiecki (Poland)

Maẓranut, 13:**707–708**

Maẓref ha-Avodah (Bachrach), 3:38–39

Mazur, Eliyahu, 13:**708**

Mazur, Jay, 13:**708–709**

Mazursky, Paul, 13:**709**

Mazuz, Meni, 13:**709**

Maẓẓah. *See* Matzah

Mazzot Festival, 6:614

Maẓẓuvah (Israel), 13:**709–710**

McCarthy, Eugene, 13:235

McCarthy, Joseph R., 3:769

McCarthyism

   Block, Herbert Lawrence, 3:769

   Bohm, David, 4:41

   Oppen, George, 15:442

   Oppenheimer, J. Robert, 15:450

McDonald, James Grover, 9:490, 13:**322**

McGill University, 4:397, 6:209

McHugh, Jimmy, 7:17

McKinley, William, 15:304

McKinney, Cynthia, 2:52

McKinsey Is Coming (Hochhuth), 9:299

McLeod, Norman, 11:84

M&Co, 11:746

McWilliams, Joseph E., 15:215

Me, Shimon and Little Moise. See Ani ve-Shimon u-Moise ha-Kattan

Mě, Heřmanů, (Bohemia). *See* Hermanuv Mestec (Bohemia)

Me-Aggot Lod (Shamir), 18:392

Meal. *See* Se'udah

Meals, Grace after. *See* Grace after meals

Me-Am Lo'ez (Culi), 5:328–329, 12:432, 13:**710–711**, 18:295

The Meaning of Jewish Existence (Altmann), 2:23

Mears, Otto, 13:**711**

Me'assef le-Khol ha-Maḥanot (Almoli), 1:682, 6:399

The Measure of Righteousness. See Kav ha-Yashar (Koidonover)

Measures. *See* Weights and measures

Meat, 13:**711**

   eating, 5:165–166, 9:319

   preparation of, 5:651

     hygiene, 9:648

     kasher, 11:821

     sheḥitah, 18:434–437

     shoḥet, 18:434

   regulations about, 5:651, 652t–655t, 655

Meat tax. *See* Korobka

Me-Az u-mi-Kedem (Shenhar), 18:459

Mecca (Saudi Arabia), 14:602

Mechelen (Belgium). *See* Malines (Belgium)

Mechnikov, Ilya, 13:11

Mechoulam, Raphael, 13:**711–712**

Mecklenburg (Germany), 13:**712–713**

Medad (1859-1944). *See* Rawnitzki, Yehoshua Ḥana

Medad (prophet), 6:293

Medalie, George Zerdin, 13:**713**

Medalists, 1:328, 13:**713**

   Bendix, Benedict Heinrich, 3:327

   Bennett, Salomon Yom Tov, 3:369

   Brenner, Victor, 4:162

   Doudtchitzky, Dinora, 5:764

   Picart, Bernard, 16:144–145

   Simon, Jean Henri, 18:612

   Soldi, Emile-Arthur, 18:752

Medallion Fund, 18:618

Medals, 13:**713–717**, *714*, 715t –716t

   Judin, Samuel, 11:566

Medeba. *See* Madaba

Medem, Vladimir, 13:142, **717**

Medes and Media, 13:**717–718**

Media. *See* Medes and Media

Mediation, 13:**718–720**

Medical Education in the United States and Canada (Flexner), 7:78

Medici, Cosimo de', 1:274, 7:84

Medici, Giovanni de'. *See* Leo X (pope)

Medici, Lorenzo de', 7:84

Medici family, 7:84, 12:608

Medicine, 13:**720–738**

   abortion, Morgentaler, Henry, 14:488

   amoraim, 2:94

   anatomy, 2:133–135

     Bbodian, David, 4:28

     biblical knowledge, 13:721–722

     Frigeis, Lazaro de, 7:291

     Henle, Jacob, 8:807–808, 13:7

     Jacobson, Ludvig Levin, 11:55

Levi, Giuseppe, 12:688
Tandler, Julius, 19:499–500
Tobias, Phillip Vallentine, 20:10–11
Zuckerkandl, Emil, 21:675
Zuckerman, Solly, Lord, 21:677
anointing, 2:179
anthropology, Fishberg, Maurice, 7:61
anthropometrism, 6:359
antibiotics, Chain, Ernest Boris, 4:558
apothecaries, Calahora family, 4:348–349
artificial insemination, 2:532–533
autopsies, 2:711–713
Padua, 15:567
bacteriology, 16:227–228
Friedemann, Adolf, 4:28, 7:270
Kligler, Israel Jacob, 12:231
Olitzki, Aryeh Leo, 15:405
Plaut, Hezekiah Feivel, 16:227
Salomonsen, Carl Julius, 17:699
Van der Hoeden, Jacob, 20:473
Wassermann, August von, 20:685
blindness, 3:753–756, 754, 7:86
bloodletting, 3:774
blood libel and, 3:776
blood research
Landsteiner, Karl, 12:478
Ramot, Bracha, 17:87–88
botanical, 9:8–9
Acosta, Christobal, 1:358–359
balsam, 3:95–96
flora, 7:90
cancer, 3:768–769
Bloch, Richard, 3:768–769
Blumberg, Baruch Samuel, 4:9, 13:9
Folkman, Judah, 7:113
Gold, Michael, 7:689
Gutman, Alexander B., 8:151
Klein, George, 12:220–221
MIT Center for Cancer Research, 13:268
Pressman, David, 16:506
cardiology, 13:733
Bamberger, Heinrich Von, 3:103
Dressler, William, 6:17
Kantrowitz, Adrian, 11:772
Kisch, Bruno Zecharias, 12:**196**

Master, Arthur M., 13:669
Mirowski, Michel, 14:314
Neufeld, Henry, 15:118
Schrire, Velva, 18:168
Stein, Yehezkiel, 19:182
cholera
Ballin, Samuel Jacob, 3:93
Cannstadt, Karl Friedrich, 4:431
Scialom, David Dario, 18:197
Civil War (U.S.) hospitals, 15:719–720
communal amenities, 2:40
copper staff, 5:213–214
dentistry
Gottlieb, Bernhard, 8:10
Seldin, Harry M., 18:259–260
dermatology, 13:730, 733
Dostrovsky, Aryeh, 5:762
Jadassohn, Josef, 11:57
Kaposi, Moritz, 11:781
Lassar, Oscar, 12:502
Unna, Paul Gerson, 20:416–417
Diaspora
contributions of, 13:734–736
restrictions on, 13:724–725, 726
duties of, in Jewish law, 13:739–741
education, 13:725–727, 728, 729
Eliakim, Marcel, 6:317–318
Lewi, Maurice J., 12:758
in Padua, 15:567
Prywes, Moshe, 16:658–659
Rosenheim, Max, 17:448
Sheba, Chaim, 18:427–428
twentieth century, 15:780
emancipation period and, 13:729–730
endocrinology
Reichstein, Tadeus, 17:201–202
Schally, Andrew Victor, 18:105
epidemiology, Mer, Gideon, 14:61
ethics, 2:35, 3:748
experimentation, 2:669–670
concentration camp, 5:376, 14:47
fertility, Winston, Robert, Baron, 21:90
folklore, 7:110–111
forensic
Helpern, Milton, 8:802
Karplus, Heinrich, 11:816–817

gastroenterology, 13:733
Crohn, Burrill Bernard, 5:305
Einhorn, Max, 6:259
Einhorn, Moses, 6:259
Grossman, Morton Irvin, 8:101
Janowitz, Henry D., 11:79
general
Abraham ben Solomon of Saint Maximin, 1:310
Abrahams, Isaac, 1:315
Abramowitz, Emil, 1:324
Ackord, Elias, 1:358
Alguades, Meir, 1:654
Ali ibn Sahl ibn Rabbān al-Ṭabarī, 1:659–660
Ardut family, 2:421
Asaph ha-rofe, 2:543–544
Astruc, Saul ha-Kohen, 2:627, 4:56
Benchetrit, Aaron, 3:323
Benveniste, Isaac ben Joseph, 3:383
Benveniste, Joshua Raphael Ben Israel, 3:384
Benveniste, Moses, 3:384
Benveniste, Samuel, 3:385
Benveniste, Sheshet ben Isaac ben Joseph, 3:385
Bergel, Joseph, 3:418
Bernard, Ḥayyim David, 3:468
Berr, Jacob, 3:487
Bessels, Emil, 3:498
Bibago, Isaac, 3:571
Brecher, Gideon, 4:156
Brudo, Manuel, 4:220–221
Bueno, Joseph, 4:252
Castro, Pedro de, 4:518
Castro family, de, 4:518
Castro Sarmento, Jacob de, 4:519–520
Cohen, Henry, Baron, 5:18
David ben Solomon, 5:470
Duran, Profiat, 6:56
Falaquera, Nathan ben Joel, 6:679
Faraj (Moses) ben Solomon da Agriento, 6:711–712
Fortis, Abraham Isaac, 7:134
Garcian, Lobell, 4:299
Garcian, Vidal, 4:299
Ḥalfan, Elijah Menahem, 8:272
Hart, Joel, 8:370–371
Herz, Marcus, 9:52
Ḥibat Allah, abu al-Barakāt ben All al-Baghdādi, 9:92–93

Medicine, *continued*

Ḥibat Allah, ibn Jumay' ibn Zayn, 9:93

Hillel ben Samuel, 9:113–114

Hirsch, Rachel, 9:128

Huarte de San Juan, Juan, 9:575

Hurwitz, Judah ben Mordecai ha-Levi, 9:632

Ibn Barzel, Joseph, 9:661

Ibn Biklārish, Junas ben Isaac, 9:661

Ibn Daud, Abraham ben David Halevi, 9:662–665

Isaac ben Todros, 10:50

Israeli, Isaac ben Solomon, 10:752–753

Jacob of Belzyce, 11:43

Lampronti, Isaac Hezekiah ben Samuel, 12:454

Lattes, Bonet, 12:518–519

Lattes, Isaac ben Jacob, 12:519

Loeb family, 11:114–115

Luzzatto, Ephraim, 13:280

Maimonides, Moses, 13:393–395, 726

Ma'or Katan family, 13:496

Masie, Aaron Meir, 13:601

Morwitz, Edward, 14:514

Nassy, David de Isaac Cohen, 14:789

Nifoci, Isaac, 15:262

Nostradamus, 15:314

Orta, Garcia de, 15:492

Padeḥ, Baruch, 15:564–565

Peixotto, Daniel, 15:713

Pick, Alois, 16:145–146

Polak, Jacob Eduard, 16:287

Rieti, Moses ben Isaac da, 17:297–298

Rimoch, Astruc, 17:334

Rosenthal, Pavel, 17:456–457

Rufus of Samaria, 17:527–528

Samson ben Joshua Moses Morpurgo, 14:509–510

Schnirer, Moritz Tobias, 18:151

Sequeyra, John de, 18:307–308

Sheba, Chaim, 18:427–428

Tarnopolsky, Samuel, 19:518–519

Wallach, Moshe, 20:610

Watters, Leo Laizer, 20:688–689

Weidner, Paulus, 20:699

Worms, Asher Anshel, 21:228

Zacutus Lusitanus, 21:437

Zondek family, 21:668–669

genetics, 12:596

Brenner, Sydney, 4:161–162

Brown, Michael Stuart, 4:215–216

Cedar, Chaim, 4:535

Cohen, Stanley N., 5:36

Ephrussi, Boris, 6:462

Goldstein, Joseph Leonard, 4:215–216, 7:729–730, 13:10

Lederberg, Joshua, 12:596, 13:9

Muller, Benjamin, 14:610–611

Sachs, Leo, 13:10, 17:635

Greek, 13:722, 724

gynecology, Landau, Leopold, 12:464

health activism, 18:746

hematology

Dameshek, William, 5:402

Diamond, Louis Klein, 5:634

Rachmilewitz, Moshe, 17:50

Wintrobe, Maxwell Myer, 21:92

herbs, 9:8–7

homeopathy, Altschul, Emil, 2:25

hygiene, 9:647–648, 13:721, 724

immunology

Benacerraf, Baruj, 3:313–314, 13:11

Besredka, Alexander, 3:495

Ehrlich, Paul, 6:244

Heidelberger, Michael, 8:762–763

Hirszfeld, Ludwik, 9:143

Lachmann, Peter Julius, 12:423

Levine, Philip, 12:719

Milstein, Cesar, 14:260

Nossal, Sir Gustav, 15:313–314

Rahbar, Samuel, 17:68

research, 6:142, 12:423

Wiener, Alexander S., 21:46

influences on early, 13:720, 722

instruments of God, 13:720–722

internal medicine, Senator, Hermann, 18:287

Islamic Spain, 13:726

Israel, 13:736–738

Arab population, 10:679

medical research, 10:678–679

Istanbul (Ottoman period), court physicians, 10:776–777, 779, 781

Italy, 13:728–729

Jewish law and, 13:**738–757**

artificial insemination, 13:751–753

euthanasia, 13:743–746

organ transplantation, 13:746–751

patients' rights, 13:739–743

physicians' duties, 13:739–741

in vitro fertilization, 13:755–756

knowledge of Hebrew, 13:601, 724

leeches, 12:599

literature

Fishbein, Morris, 7:60

Israeli, Isaac ben Solomon, 10:753

Judeo-Arabic, 11:531, 536–537

Judeo-Persian, 11:552, 553–554

Marranos, 13:727–728

Amatus Lusitanus, 2:34–35, 135

Mendes, Fernando Moses, 14:41

Petrus Aldonsi, 16:21

Rodrigues, Dionisius, 17:366

Sanchez, Antonio Nuñes Ribeiro, 18:9

medical ethics, 19:184–185

medical history

Davisohn, Robert, 5:475

Leibowitz, Joshua O., 12:620–621

Neuberger, Max, 15:116–117

Preuss, Julius, 16:508

mesmerism, Koreff, David Ferdinand, 12:306–307

microscopy, 13:730

Hannover, Adolph, 8:326

modern clinical, 13:731–734

nephrology

de Vries, André, 5:629

Rosenheim, Max, Baron, 17:448

neurology

Axel, Richard, 2:755–756, 13:10–11

Bender, Morris Boris, 3:326

Benedikt, Moritz, 3:333

Benzer, Seymour, 3:391

Bernheim, Hippolyte, 3:474

Edinger, Ludwig, 6:147

Eldar, Reuven, 6:294

Gasser, Herbert Spencer, 7:392

Greengard, Paul, 8:79, 13:10

Grinker, Roy Richard Sr., 8:88

Halpern, Lipman, 8:285

Kisch, Bruno Zecharias, 12:196

Oppenheim, Hermann, 15:445

Prusiner, Stanley S., 13:9–10, 16:652–653

Remak family, 17:215

Romberg, Moritz Heinrich, 17:406

Sachs, Bernard, 6:439, 17:634

Wechsler, Israel, 20:694

Weisenburg, Theodore H., 20:730

Wolf, Abner, 21:134

Zimmerman, Harry M., 21:535

neurophysiology, Breuer, Joseph, 4:171

neuropsychology, Luria, Alexander Romanovich, 13:261

nutrition, Yudkin, John, 21:408–409

obstetrics
De Lee, Joseph B., 5:537

De Leon, Dabid Camden, 5:537

Guttmacher, Alan F., 8:155

Kristeller, Samuel, 12:363

Simon, Pierre, 18:615

ophthalmology
Benevenutus Grapheus Heirosolymitanus, 3:341, 13:727

Feigenbaum, Aryeh, 6:733–734

Friedenwald family, 3:98, 7:271

Hart, Ernest Abraham, 8:369–370

Hays, Isaac, 8:479

Hirschberg, Julius, 9:134

Hirschler, Ignác, 9:140

Koller, Carl, 12:275

Meyerhof, Max, 14:150–151

Michaelson, Isaac Chesar, 14:171

Stein, Richard, 19:182

oral surgery
Hirschfeld, Isador, 9:138

Seldin, Harry M., 18:259–260

otolaryngology
Hajek, Markus, 8:241

Korine, Ezra, 12:309

Semon, Sir Felix, 18:286

Steinberg, Martin R., 19:188

otology
Bárány, Robert, 3:134

Politzer, Adam, 16:354

Rosen, Samuel, 17:430

papal physicians, Elijah ben Shabbetai Be'er, 6:340

parasitology
Adler, Saul Aaron, 1:407

Gruby, David, 8:105

Sandground, Jack Henry, 18:12

pathology
Angrist, Alfred Alvin, 2:163

Berenblum, Isaac, 3:409

Bueno, Ephraim Hezekiah, 4:252

Cohnheim, Julius, 5:45

Davidsohn, Israel, 5:475

Hirsch, August, 9:124

Karplus, Heinrich, 11:816–817

Klemperer, Paul, 12:227–228

Loeb, Leo, 13:161

Rappaport, Henry, 17:99–100

Salaman, Redcliffe Nathan, 17:681

Traube, Ludwig, 20:112

Weigert, Carl, 20:700

Widal, Fernand, 21:39

pediatrics, 13:733
Abt, Isaac Arthur, 1:333

Baginsky, Adolf Aron, 3:59

Finkelstein, Heinrich, 7:33–34

Jacobi, Abraham, 11:37

Koplik, Henry, 12:295

Levinson, Abraham, 12:722

Perlstein, Meyer A., 15:780

Rice, Joseph Mayer, 17:285

Rosen, Fred Saul, 17:428

Schick, Bela, 18:126

pharmacology, 13:734
Dioscorides Pedanius, 5:675

Donnolo, Shabbetai, 5:751

Elion, Gertrude Bell, 6:349

Froehlich, Alfred, 7:296–297

Furchgott, Robert F., 7:311, 13:10

Gilman, Alfred G., 7:605–606, 13:10

Ibn Birklārish, Junas ben Isaac, 9:661

Loewi, Otto, 13:10, 170

Macht, David I., 13:327

Pick, Ernst Peter, 16:146

Starkenstein, Emil, 19:165

Vane, Sir John R., 13:10, 20:473

physiology
Bakst, Nicolai Ignatyetvich, 3:74–75

Bernstein, Julius, 3:480

Bernstein, Nathan Osipovitch, 3:482–483

Cyon, Elie de, 5:346

Erlanger, Joseph, 6:480

Frolkis, Vladimir Veniaminovich, 7:297–298

Heidenhain, Rudolf, 8:763

Hestrin-Lerner, Sarah, 9:79

Hollander, Franklin, 9:322

Hyde, Ida Henrietta, 9:646–647

Kandel, Erich Richard, 11:759–760, 13:10

Katz, Sir Bernard, 12:9–10

Kronecker, Hugo, 12:369–370

Loewi, Otto, 13:170

Magnus, Rudolph, 13:357

Munk, Hermann, 14:614–615

Oppenheimer, Hillel Reinhard, 15:448

Rahamimoff, Rami, 17:67

Stern, Lina Solomonovna, 19:213–214

Valentin, Gabriel Gustav, 20:463

physiotherapy, Brandes, Ludwig Israel, 4:126

plastic surgery, Penn, Jack, 15:727

prohibition, 2:128

Provence, France, 16:637–638

psychology
Rapaport, David, 17:92

Stern, Erich, 19:207–208

public health and hygiene, 13:721, 724, 734
Albu, Isidor, 1:596

Doron, Haim, 5:759

Goldberger, Joseph, 7:697

Hart, Ernest Abraham, 8:369–370

Lieben, Salomon, 12:803

Marcuse, Moses, 13:517

Orenstein, Alexander Jeremiah, 15:465–466

OZE, 15:556

Saliternik, Zvi, 17:691

Sarphati, Samuel, 18:60–61

Stern, Arthur C., 19:204

radiology
Bucky, Gustav, 4:244

Halberstaedter, Ludwig, 8:264

Rigler, Leo George, 17:332

rheumatology, Ziff, Morris, 21:528–529

Medicine, *continued*
  Roman, Celsus, Aulus Cornelius,
    4:538
  sexuality, Hirschfeld, Magnus,
    9:138–139
  spinal injuries, Guttman, Sir
    Ludwig, 8:158–159
  status in Talmud of, 13:722
  surgery
    Adam, Lajos, 1:377
    Barnett, Sir Lewis Edward,
      3:170
    Cohen, Harry, 5:17
    Davidoff, Leo Max, 5:474
    Erlik, David, 6:481
    Garlock, John Henry, 7:390
    Hava of Manosque, 8:466
    Horwitz, Phineas Jonathan,
      9:547
    Papo, Iẓidor Joseph, 15:617
    Pirogov, Nikolai, 16:183
    Steg, Adolphe, 19:173
    Stilling, Benedict, 2:135,
      19:227
    Teller, Issachar Baer, 19:597
    Voronoff, Serge, 20:583
  Tay-Sachs disease, 19:561–562
  texts
    al-Qānū fī al-Ṭibb
      (Avicenna), 2:728–729, vol.
      8: color insert
    Kitāb-al-Kullīyāt fī al-Ṭibb,
      2:725
    Sefer Asaph ha-Rofe, 2:543–
      544
  translators, 11:37, 13:724, 726, 727
  transplants, 20:106–108
  urology
    Buerger, Leo, 4:254
    Tenenbaum, Joseph L.,
      19:638
  venereal diseases, Gumpert,
    Martin, 8:135–136
  virology, 13:9–10
    Baltimore, David, 3:100
    Goldblum, Natan, 7:698
    Nathans, Daniel, 13:9, 15:17–
      18
    Revel, Michel, 17:253
    Sabin, Albert Bruce, 13:11,
      17:631–632
    Salk, Jonas, 13:11, 17:691
    Temin, Howard Martin, 13:9,
      19:600
  women
    Cohen, Elizabeth D. A.
      Magnus, 5:14
    Cori, Gerty Theresa, 5:223,
      13:10

    Floreta Ca Noga, 7:86
    Frankenthal, Käte, 7:203
    Freud, Anna, 7:258–259
    Friedlander, Kate, 7:277
    Friend, Charlotte, 7:288, 13:9
    Fromm-Reichmann, Frieda,
      7:299
    Greenacre, Phyllis, 8:67
    Hava of Manosque, 8:466
    Hestrin-Lerner, Sarah, 9:79
    Hyde, Ida Henrietta, 9:646–
      647
    Jacobs, Aletta Henriëtte,
      11:45, 16:345
    Kagan, Helena, 11:706
    Klein, Melanie Reizes, 12:224
    Koch, Adelheid Lucy, 12:246
    Krim, Mathilde, 12:356–357
    La Migresse, Sarah, 13:727
    Levi-Montalcini, Rita, 12:706,
      13:10
    Mahler, Margaret, 13:361
    Straus, Rahel Goitein,
      19:250–251
    Wolff, Charlotte, 21:143–144
    Yalow, Rosalyn Sussman,
      21:277
    Zaiẓov, Rina, 21:445–446
  See also Psychiatry; Psychology
Medicine and law, 13:738–757
Medieval Hebrew. *See* Hebrew
  language
*Medieval History: the Life and Death of
  a Civilization* (Cantor), 4:440–441
Medieval Jewish Chronicles
  (Neubauer), 9:160
Medieval period. *See* Middle Ages
*Medieval Trade in the Mediterranean
  World* (Lopez), 13:189–190
Medina (Saudi Arabia), 13:**757**, 14:602
Medina, Avihu, 13:**758**
Medina, Moses ben Samuel de, 13:759
Medina, Samuel ben Moses de, 1:259,
  383, 13:**758–759**, 15:537
Medina, Sir Solomon de, 13:**759**
Medina, Solomon de. *See* Medina, Sir
  Solomon de
Medinaceli (Spain), 13:**759**
Medina del Campo (Spain), 13:**759–
760**
Medina de Pomar (Spain), 13:**760**
Medinah, 13:**760**
*Medinah Mizraḥit Ketanah le-Lo
  Taskbikh* (Bartal), 18:206
Medinat Zamet (Lithuania). *See*
  Samogitia (Lithuania)
Medini, Ḥayyim Hezekiah ben
  Raphael Elijah, 8:747, 13:**760**

Meditation, 13:**761–762**, 16:14
Meditation and the Bible (Kaplan),
  11:773
*Meditation of the Sad Soul. See Hegyon
  ha-Hefesh ha-Aẓuvah*
Mediterranean countries
  insurance, 9:808–809
  travels in, 3:362–364, *363*
  See also Western Mediterranean
A Mediterranean Society (Goitein),
  7:468, 470, 471, 685–686, 18:470–
  471
Mednick, Martha Tamara Schuch,
  13:**762**
Medres, Israel Jonah, 13:**763**
Medurot Do'akhot (Lisitzky), 13:81
Medved, Michael, 13:202, **763**
Medvedev, Mikhail, 13:**763**
Medzhibozh (Ukraine). *See* Medzibezh
  (Ukraine)
Medzibezh (Ukraine), 13:**763**
Meed, Benjamin, 2:48, 49, 13:**764**
Meed, Vladka, 2:49, 13:**764**
Meek, Theophile, 3:622
Me-Emesh (Baron), 3:171
Me-Ereẓ el Ereẓ (Shenhar), 18:459
Meerovitch, Menaché, 13:**764–765**
Me-Ever la-Gevulin (Brenner), 4:160
Me-Ever Nehar ha-Lethe (Lenski),
  12:640
Mefarshim. *See* Posekim
Mefasher Ḥelmin (Almoli), 1:682
Mefiẓei Haskalah. *See* Society for the
  Diffusion of Englightenment
Megaddef. *See* Lorki, Joshua
Megallah Amukkot (Spira), 7:425–426
Megallah Temirin (Perl), 15:774
Megapolensis, Johannes, 15:195
Megasthenes, 13:**765**
Meged Geresh Yeraḥim (periodical),
  15:384
Megged, Aharon, 8:704, 720–721, 722,
  13:**765–766**
Megged, Eyal, 13:**766**
Megged, Matityahu. *See* Megged,
  Matti
Megged, Matti, 13:**766**
Megiddo (ancient Israel), 13:**766–767**,
  767
Megillah (biblical scroll), 13:**768**
  See also specific scrolls
Megillah (tractate), 13:**768**
  See Also Purim; Scroll of Esther
*Megillat Aḥima'aẓ. See Megillat
  Yuḥasin*
Megillat Eifah (Shabbetai ben Meir
  Ha-Kohen), 18:338

Megillat Eivah (Heller), 8:796, 798

Megillat Ester. See Scroll of Esther

Megillat ha-Esh (Bialik), 3:564

Megillat ha-Megalleh (Abraham bar Ḥiyya), 1:293

Megillat Ofen (Schulhof), 18:171

"Megillat Paras" (Elyashar), 6:371

Megillat Purei a-Ketayim (Altschul), 2:24

Megillat Sefer (Emden), 6:393

Megillat Setarim, 13:**768–769**

Megillat Setarim (Naḥman), 14:749

Megillat Setarim (Nissim ben Jacob ben Nissim Ibn Shahin), 15:279–280

Megillat Setarim (Sherira), 18:463

Megillat Ta'anit (Eleazar ben Hananiah ben Hezekiah), 6:301

Megillat Yuḥasin, 8:653, 13:**769–770,** 21:374

    See also specific "Megillat" titles

Megillat Yuḥasin (Ahimaaz ben Paltiel), 1:219, 543–544, 7:12, 9:155, 15:470, 18:448

    Amalfi, 2:31

    Amittai, 2:81

    Byzantine empire, 4:327

Megillat Zuta (Abraham ben Hillel of Fostat), 1:300

Megillot

    17th-18th c., 18:*219*

    and calligraphy, modern Hebrew, 4:367

    engravings and etchings, 10:787

    illuminated, 2:497–498

    order of, after the Pentateuch, 18:222*t*

    order of books in, 3:582, 582*t*

    Scroll of Esther, 18:218, 220

    targum to, 3:593–594

    See also Scrolls, The Five

Meginnei Zahav (Joel ben Moses Gad), 11:365

Megszabaditottál a haláltól (Pap), 15:613–614

Mehagerim (Shaked), 18:368

Me-ha-Ibbur u-Minyan ha-Shanim (Bachrach), 3:39

Meḥayyeh ha-metim, 13:6

Meheimanuta de-Khulah (Ḥayon), 8:477

Mehemet Ali. *See* Muhammad Ali

Meḥikat Afassim (Modai), 14:406

Meḥilah, 13:**770–771**

Meḥizah, 13:**771–772**

Meḥkerei Areẓ (Loewisohn), 13:171

Mehlsack, Eliakim ben Judah ha-Milzahgi, 13:**772**

Mehmed IV, 18:349

Mehring, Walter, 13:**772–773**

Mehta, Zubin, 13:**773**

Mei Ammi (Israel), 13:**773**

Meidner, Ludwig, 13:**773–774**

Meier, Julius, 13:**774**

Meier, Richard, 12:782, 13:**774**

Meijer, Ischa, 6:71

Meijer, Israel Chaim. *See* Meijer, Ischa

Meijer, Jaap. *See* Meijer, Jacob

Meijer, Jacob, 13:**774–775**

Meijers, Eduard Maurits, 13:**775**

Me'ilah (tractate*)*, 13:**775**

Me'il Katon (Almog), 1:680

Me'il Shemu'el (Kalai), 11:729

Me'il Ẓedakah (Elijah ben Solomon Abraham ha-Kohen of Smyrna), 6:341

Meimad, 15:703

Mei Marom (Ḥalap), 8:358

Meinertzhagen, Richard Henry, 13:**775**

Meinhardt, Gustav. *See* Herzberg, Wilhelm

Meinhold, Johannes Friedrich, 13:**775–776**

Meiningen (German), 4:695

Meiningen (Germany), 13:**776**

Mein Kampf (Hitler), 9:286–287, 327

Meinkin, Sarah Feiga Foner, 8:700

Mein Leben (Reich-Ranicki), 17:201

Mein System (Nimzovitch), 4:604

Mein Weg zu Marx (Lukacs), 13:255

Mein Werden und mein Wirken (Erman), 6:482

Meir (fabulist), 6:667

Meir (rabbi), 8:640

    Aḥerim, 1:541

    Bible text treated as binding authority by, 3:585

Meir (tanna), 13:**776–777,** 779

    Oenomaus of Gadara, 15:383

Meir, Golda, 13:**777–779**

    governments of, 10:440–443, 440*t*, 441*t*, 443*t*

    Moscow visit, 14:518

    Shem-Tov, Victor, 18:458

Meir, Jacob, 13:**779**

Meir, Ofra, 1:461

Meir, Samuel ben, 2:175

Meir, Ya'akov. *See* Meir, Jacob

Me'ira Dakhya (Carvalho), 4:502

Me'irat Einayim (Eliakim Goetz ben Meir), 6:318

Me'irat Einayim (Isaac ben Samuel of Acre), 10:47

Me'irat Einayyim (Luzki), 13:279

Meir Ba'al ha-Nes Tomb, 13:**779**

Meir ben Aaron Leib. *See* Peremyshlyany, Meir ben Aaron Leib of

Meir ben Baruch ha-Levi, 13:**779–780**

Meir ben Baruch of Rothenburg, 11:419, 13:**780–783**, 15:442, 443

    Isaac ben Meir Dueren, 6:41

    Nicholas IV's plea for release of, 15:250

    Nuremberg, as rabbi of, 15:347

    Perez ben Elijah of Corbeil and, 15:769

Meir ben Elijah, 13:**783**

Meir ben Elijah of Norwich, 13:**783,** 15:312

Meir ben Ephraim of Padua, 13:**783**

Meir ben Gedaliah of Lublin. *See* Lublin, Meir ben Gedaliah

Meir ben Ḥiyya Rofe, 13:**783–784**

Meir ben Isaac Nehorai. *See* Meir ben Isaac Sheli'aḥ Ẓibbur

Meir ben Isaac of Trinquetaille, 13:**784**

Meir ben Isaac Sheli'aḥ Ẓibbur, 1:555, 13:**784**

Meir ben Judah Loeb. *See* Leoni, Myer

Meir ben Samuel of Ramerupt, 13:**784–785**

Meir ben Samuel of Shcherbreshin, 13:**785**

Meir ben Simeon ha-Me'ili, 13:**785**

Meir ben Simeon of Narbonne

    apologetics, 2:266

    moneylending, 14:439, 440

Meir Dan of Ostrova Plotzki. *See* Plotzki, Meir Dan of Ostrova

Meire, Menahem ben Solomon ha-, 13:652

Me'ir Einei Ḥakhanim (Lublin), 13:245

Meir Eshel. *See* Absalon

Meir Ezofowicz (Orzeszkowa), 15:501

Meir ha-Kohen, 8:221

Meiri, Menahem ben Solomon, 7:487, 13:**785–788**, 14:438

Meir Jehiel ha-Levi of Ostrowiec, 13:**788**

Meir Loeb ben Jehiel Michael Weisser. *See* Malbim, Meir Loeb ben Jehiel Michael Weisser

Meir of England. *See* Meir ben Elijah of Norwich

Meirov, Shaul. *See* Avigur, Shaul

Meirovitch, Menashe. *See* Meerovitch, Menaché

Me'ir Shefeyah, 13:**788**

Meir Simḥah ha-Kohen of Dvinsk, 13:**788–789**, 18:262

Meisel, Hugo, 19:133

Meisel, Mordecai ben Samuel, 4:39, 13:**789**

Meisel, Moses ben Mordecai, 13:**789**

Meisel, Noah, 12:521, 13:**789–790**

Meisel, Willy, 19:133

Meisels, David Dov, 13:**790**, 16:347

Meisels, Dov Berush, 13:**790**, 16:340

Meisels, Saul, 13:**791**

Meisels, Uzziel ben Zevi Hirsch, 13:**791**

Meisl, Joseph, 13:**791**

Meisl, Marcus ben Samuel. *See* Meisel, Mordecai ben Samuel

Meisl, Marx ben Samuel. *See* Meisel, Mordecai ben Samuel

Meisl, Mordecai ben Samuel. *See* Meisel, Mordecai ben Samuel

Meissen (Germany), 13:**791**

Der Meister (Brod), 4:192

Meister Eckhart. *See* Eckhart, Meister

Meister Joseph, 4:48

Meitar (Israel), 13:**791**

Meitner, Lise, 13:**792**, 16:137

Meitus, Eliahu, 13:**792**

Mekabbel, 12:572

Mekhilta (Elijah ben Solomon Zalman), 6:345

Mekhilta (Rabin), 17:33

Mekhilta de-Arayot, 18:561–562

Mekhilta de-Milu'im, 18:561

Mekhilta de-Sanya. See Mekhilta of Rabbi Simeon ben Yoḥai

Mekhilta Deuteronomy, 13:**792–793**

Mekhilta of Rabbi Ishmael, 12:529, 13:**793–795**

Mekhilta of Rabbi Simeon ben Yoḥai, 13:**795–797**

Mekhilta ve-Elleh Shemot. See Mekhilta of Rabbi Ishmael

Mekhiltin de-Rabbi Akiva. See Mekhilta of Rabbi Simeon ben Yoḥai

Mekhirat Ḥamez. *See* Ḥamez, sale of

Mekhirot Shetarot, 2:604

Mekhlis, Lev Zakharovich, 13:**797**

Mekize Nirdamim, 7:238, 8:266, 13:**797**

Meklenburg, Jacob Zevi, 13:**797–798**

Mekler, Eliezer. *See* Wolf, Lucien

Meknès (Morocco), 13:**798–799**

Mekor Barukh, 11:728–729

Mekor Chaim Judaic Studies educational center (Moscow), 2:63

Mekor Ḥayyim (Ḥayyim ben Abraham ha-Kohen), 8:480

Mekor Ḥayyim (Halevi), 17:236–237

Mekor Ḥayyim (Ibn Gabirol), 7:323–326

Mekor Ḥayyim (ibn Gabirol), 7:130–131, 15:85–86

Mekorot Water Company, 13:**799**

Melafefon. *See* Cucumber

Melamed, Ezra Zion, 14:**5–6**

Melamed, Hirsch, 11:412

Melamed, Jak, 4:276

Melamed, Meir, 14:**6**

Melamed, Raḥamim Reuven, 14:**6**

Melamed, Siman Tov, 14:**6**

Melammed le-Ho'il (Hoffmann), 9:310

Melanchthon, Philipp, 11:421, 14:**6**

The Melanesians of British New Guinea (Seligman), 18:266

Mélanges inédits (Montesquieu), 14:460

Melavveh, Malkah, 14:**6–7**

Melbourne (Australia), 14:**7–10**, 634

Melchett family. *See* Mond family

Melchior, Carl, 14:**10**

Melchior, Carl Henriques, 14:10

Melchior, Marcus, 14:**10–11**

Melchior, Michael, 14:**11**, 15:307–308, 504, 703

Melchior, Moritz Gerson, 14:10

Melchior family, 14:**10**

Melchizedek, 6:444, 14:**11–12**

Meldola, Raphael (1754-1828), 14:**12**

Meldola, Raphael (1849-1915), 14:**12**

Meldola family, 14:**12**

Meleager of Gadara, 14:**12**

Melekh Basar va-Dam (Shamir), 18:392

Melekhet Maḥashevet (Eidlitz), 6:253

Melekhet Shelomo (Adeni), 1:390, 14:329

Meleze-Modrzejewski, Joseph, 11:326

Méline, F.J., 6:19

Melito of Sardis, 14:**12–13**

Melitopol (Ukraine), 14:**13**

Melizat Yeshurun (Lewisohn), 8:724

Melizat Yeshurun (Loewisohn), 13:171

Melkman, Joseph, 6:71

Mellah. *See* Jewish quarters

Meller, Berish. *See* Kimḥi, Dov

Mello, Antonio Rodriguez. *See* Abenatar Melo, David

Melnikoff, Avraham, 14:**13**, 18:223

Melodics of Verse (Eichenbaum), 6:246

Melodika stikha (Eichenbaum). *See Melodics of Verse* (Eichenbaum)

Melokhim-Bukh, 14:**13–14**

Melons, 14:**14**

Melton, Florence, 14:**14–15**

Melton, Samuel Mendel, 14:14, **15**

Meltzer, Isser Zalman, 14:**15**, 18:674

Meltzer, Shimshon, 14:**15**

Melun (France), 14:**16**

Melville, Lewis, 14:**16**

Melvin Simon & Associates, 18:608

Melzer, Marcos, 16:349

Melzer, Mordecai ben Asher. *See* Klatzko, Mordecai ben Asher

Melzer, Shimshon. *See* Meltzer, Shimshon

Mem, 14:**16**

Memel (Lithuania), 3:778, 8:759, 14:**16**

Memmi, Albert, 14:**16–17**, 15:473

Memmingen (Germany), 14:**17**

Memoiren einer Grossmutter. Bilder aus der Kulturgeschichte der Juden Russlands in 19. Jahrhundert (Wengeroff), 21:10–11

Mémoires d'outre-tombe (Chateaubriand), 4:583

Mémoires Inédits (Solis), 18:754

Memoirs (Ehrenburg), 6:238

The Memoirs of Elias Canetti. See Die gerettete Zunge

Memoirs of Mischa Elman's Father (Elman), 6:365

Memoirs of the Peace Conference (Lloyd George), 13:148

Memorable Encounters (Kaminetsky), 11:756

Memoram. *See* Mamram

Memora technica. *See* Mnemonics or memora technica

Memorbuch, 14:**17–18**

Memorial. *See* Yad

Memorial Day. *See* Yom ha-Zikkaron

Mémorial des Martyrs de la Déportation, 9:430

Memorial Foundation for Jewish Culture, 14:**18**

Memorial light, 14:**18**

Memorial of Six Pillars, 13:201

Memorial prayer. *See* Hazkarat neshamot

Memories of a War Correspondent (Molnár), 14:427

Memories of My Home. See Zikhroynes fun Mayn Haym

Memphis (Egypt), 6:46, 14:**18–19**

Memphis (TN), 14:**19–20**

Men. *See* Man

Menachem Munish ben Joshua Heschel Babad, 3:14

Menahem. *See* Alroy, David

Menahem (King of Israel), 9:179, 14:**20**

Menahem ben Aaron ibn Zeraḥ, 14:**20–21**, 15:655

Menahem ben Aaron of Volterra, 3:683

Menahem ben Ḥelbo, 14:**21**
    biblical exegesis and study, 3:642
    Judah ben Moses ha-Darshan,
        11:489
Menahem ben Jacob, 14:**21–22**
Menahem ben Jacob ibn Saruq, 14:**22**
    biblical exegesis and study, 3:642
    Dunash ben Labrat, 6:47
Menahem ben Jacob Kara. *See* Kara,
    Menaham ben Jacob
Menahem ben Joseph Bashyazi, 3:198
Menahem ben Judah de Lonzano. *See*
    Lonzano, Menahem ben Judah de
Menahem ben Judah the Galilean. *See*
    Menahem son of Judah
Menahem ben Michael ben Joseph,
    14:**22–23**
Menahem ben Moses Egozi, 6:222
Menahem ben Moses ha-Bavli, 14:**23**
Menahem ben Perez of Joigny, 11:385
Menahem ben Solomon, 14:**23**
Menahem ben Solomon ha-Me'iri. *See*
    Meiri, Menahem ben Solomon
Menahem ben Solomon ibn Duji. *See*
    Alroy, David
Menaḥem ha-Sofer (Shalkovich),
    18:374
Menahem ibn Dugi. *See* Alroy, David
Menahem ibn Saruq. *See* Menahem
    ben Jacob ibn Saruq
Menahem Isaiah ben Isaac. *See* Isaiah
    Menahem ben Isaac
Menahemites, 2:6
Menaḥemiyyah (Israel, state), 14:**24**
Menahem-Mendel Avigdors. *See* Isaiah
    Menahem ben Isaac
Menaḥem Mendel be-Ereẓ Yisrael
    (Berkowitz), 3:441
Menahem Mendel ben Isaac, 14:**24**
*Menaḥem Mendel in Ereẓ Israel. See
    Menaḥem Mendel be-Ereẓ Yisrael*
Menaḥem Mendel Morgenstern,
    10:824
Menahem Mendel of Kotsk. *See* Kotsk,
    Menahem Mendel of
Menahem Mendel of Lubavich, 8:408
Menahem Mendel of Peremyshlany,
    14:**24**
Menahem Mendel of Rymanow. *See*
    Rymanower, Menahem Mendel
Menahem Mendel of Shklov, 14:**24–25**
Menahem Mendel of Vitebsk, 8:395,
    14:**25–26**
Menahem Mendl of Kotzk, 16:104–
    105
Menahem of Merseburg, 14:**26**
Menahem of Worms, Rabbi. *See*
    Menaham ben Jacob

Menahem son of Judah, 14:**26–27**
    Ananias ben Nedebeus, 2:129
Menahem the Essene, 14:**23**
Menahem Ẓiyyoni, 14:**27**
Menahen ben Judah di Lonzano,
    13:652
Menaḥot (tractate*)*, 14:**27–28**
Menaker, Abraham. *See* Morewski,
    Abraham
Menakhem-Mendl (Aleichem), 21:347
Menakhem-Mendl (fictional
    character), 18:385
Menakhem-Mendl letters (Shalom
    Aleichem), 18:385
Menander of Ephesus, 14:**28**
Menander of Laodicea, 14:**28**
Menasce, Alfred de, 14:**28**
Menasce, de, family, 14:**28**
Menasce, Felix de, 14:**28**
Menasce, Jacob David de, 14:**28**
Menashe ben al-Farrar. *See* Qazzāz,
    Manasseh ben Abraham ibn
Menasseh ben Israel. *See* Manasseh
    ben Israel
Menda, Eliezer, 14:**28–29**
Mendel, Arthur, 14:**29**
Mendel, David. *See* Neander, August
Mendel, Hermann, 14:**29**
Mendel, Lafayette Benedict, 14:**29**
Mendel, Menahem, 6:218
Mendel Avigdors. *See* Isaiah Menahem
    ben Isaac
Mendele Moykher Sforim. *See*
    Abramovitsh, Sholem Yankev
Mendele the Book Peddler. *See*
    Abramovitsh, Sholem Yankev
Mendel family, 14:**29**
Mendel Menahem Avigdors. *See* Isaiah
    Menahem ben Isaac
Mendeloff, Gershon. *See* Lewis, Ted
Mendel of Novy Bydzov, 15:323
Mendel of Satanov. *See* Levin,
    Emanuel
Mendels, Maurits, 14:**29**
Mendels, Moses. *See* Bachrach, Jacob
    ben Moses
Mendelsohn, Eric, 14:**29–30**
Mendelsohn, Frankfurt Moses, 14:**30**
Mendelsohn, Shelomo, 14:**30**
Mendelson, Jacob ben-Zion, 14:**30**
Mendelson, José, 14:**30**
Mendelson, Solomon, 14:**30–31**
Mendelson, Yoysef. *See* Mendelson,
    José
Mendelssohn, Abraham, 14:**31**
Mendelssohn, Arnold, 14:**32**
Mendelssohn, Brendel. *See*
    Mendelssohn-Veit-Schlegel,
    Dorothea

Mendelssohn, Fanny Caecile, 14:**33**
    See also Mendelssohn Hensel,
        Fanny Caecile
Mendelssohn, Felix, 11:340, 14:**32–33**
Mendelssohn, Heinrich, 14:**33**
Mendelssohn, Henriette, 14:**31–32**
Mendelssohn, Jakob Ludwig Felix. *See*
    Mendelssohn, Felix
Mendelssohn, Kurt Alfred Georg,
    14:**33**
Mendelssohn, Maria. *See*
    Mendelssohn, Henriette
Mendelssohn, Moses, 8:437, 687,
    14:**33–40**, 16:65, 93–94
    Anhalt, 2:163
    Bamberger, Fritz, 3:102
    biblical exegesis and study of,
        3:645–646, 649, 663
    Bloch, Marcus Eliezer, 3:765
    chosen people doctrine, 4:671
    commandments, reasons for, 5:88
    concept of hell rejected by, 15:629
    disputations and polemics, 5:696
    Dubno, Salomon, 2:108, 6:34
    Emden, Jacob, 6:393
    German translation of Bible by,
        3:631, 12:460
    on God, 7:665, 668, 671
    Haskalah, 8:434–435, 436
    Haskalah literature, 8:687
    Hebrew, 8:437
    human perfectability, 8:440
    initiation of learned societies,
        18:722
    Judaism, development of concept
        of, 11:517–518
    Juedische Freischule, 11:569
    Lessing, Gotthold Ephraim, 12:665
    Levin, Ẓevi Hirsch ben Aryeh
        Loeb, 12:714
    Mirabeau, Honore Gabriel
        Riqueti, Comte de, 14:305
    miracles, 14:309
    Orthodx attitudes towards
        Pentateuch translation of,
        15:493
    Phaedon, 2:108
    principles of faith, 2:532
    soul, immortality of, 19:38
    Torah, 20:43
Mendelssohn, Zipporah. *See*
    Mendelssohn, Fanny Caecile;
    Mendelssohn Hensel, Fanny Caecile
Mendelssohn family, 14:**31–32**, 31*t*
Mendelssohn Hensel, Fanny Caecile
    See also Mendelssohn, Fanny
        Caecile
Mendelssohn Hensel, Fanny Caecilie,
    14:**40–41**

Mendelssohn-Veit-Schlegel, Dorothea, 14:**41**

Mendelvich, Nathan. *See* Bogoraz, Vladimir Germanovich

Mendes, Alvaro. *See* Abenaes, Solomon; Ibn Yaʾish, Solomon

Mendes, Aristides de Sousa, 14:**42–43**

Mendes, Catherine. *See* Costa, Catherine da

Mendès, Catulle, 14:**43**

Mendes, David Franco, 11:569

Mendes, Diogo, 14:**43**

Mendes, Fernando Moses, 14:41

Mendes, Frederic de Sol, 14:42

Mendes, Gracia, 10:777, 15:524, 532, 537, 541, 19:303

Mendes, Hannah Garcia, 5:153

Mendes, Isaac, 4:70

Mendes, Moses, 6:437, 14:41

Mendes, Rachel. *See* Costa, Catherine da

Mendes, Rui, 19:104

Mendes, Sam, 14:**43**

Mendes da Costa family. *See* Costa family

Mendes family (England), 14:**41–42**

Mendes family (Istanbul), 10:777

Mendes family (Morocco and Algeria), 14:**41**

Mendes family (United States), 14:**42**

Mendes-France, Pierre, 18:706

Mendès-France, Pierre, 14:**43–44**, 16:343

Mendes legal dispute, 5:153

Mendez, Alvaro. *See* Abenaes, Solomon

Mendez, Jael Henrietta. *See* Pye, Jael Henrietta

Mendez family. *See* Mendes family (England)

Mendicancy. *See* Begging and beggars

Mendicants, 3:**258–260**

Mendiz family. *See* Mendes family (Morocco and Algeria)

Mendlowitz, Shraga Feivel, 6:197, 14:**44**

Mendoza (Argentina), 14:**44–45**

Mendoza, Daniel, 14:**45**

Mene, mene, tekel, u-farsin, 14:**45–46**

Meneket Rivkah (Tiktiner), 17:136–137

Menelaus (high priest), 9:193, 14:**46**

Menem, Carlos Saúl, 2:442–443, 449, 450

Menes (Egyptian king), 6:223

Menes, Abram, 14:**46–47**

Mengele, Josef, 2:669–670, 4:387–388, 14:**47–48**, 15:43, 630

Mengenlehre (Hausdorff), 8:463

Menhuhin, Yehudi. *See* Menhuhin, Sir Yehudi

Meninsky, Bernard, 14:**48**

Menken, Adah Isaacs, 14:**48**

Menken, Alan, 14:**48–49**

Menken family, 14:**48**

Menkes, Hershadovid. *See* Katz, Dovid

Menkes, Zygmunt, 14:**49**

Menkin, Moshe Ẓevi. *See* Neriah, Moshe Ẓevi

Menma ʿrē-Sety. *See* Seti I

Menois (Gaza), 13:495

Menorah. *See* Ḥanukkah lamp

Menorah (journal), 14:**55**

Menorah (periodical), 11:721

Menorah Association, 6:196, 14:**55**

Menorah Journal, 6:196. *See* Menorah Association and Menorah Journal

Menorah Medical Center (Missouri), 11:768

Menorah Monthly (periodical), 6:361

Menorah paper-cuts, 15:616

Menorahs, 14:**49–55**

Menorah Society. *See* Menorah Association and Menorah Journal

Menorat ha-Maʾor (Aboab), 1:266–267, 686, 13:106

Menorat ha-Maʾor (Al-Nakawa), 1:266, 686, 6:406

El menor daño de medicina (Chirino), 4:652

Menschen im Hotel (Baum), 3:220

Der Menschensohn (Ludwig), 13:251

Menschen und Affen (Ehrenstein), 6:242

Menssier de Vesoul. *See* Manessier de Vesoul

Menstrual blood, 3:772, 776

Menstruation. *See* Niddah

Mental Health Law Project (MHLP), 3:234

Mental illness, 3:9, 14:**55–59**, 15:119

Di Mentshn fun Godlbozhits (Rashkin), 17:107

Menuhin, Hephzibah, 14:**60**

Menuhin, Sir Yehudi, 14:**60**

Menzel, Wolfgang, 4:32

Meʾon Arayot (Shapiro), 18:404

Meʿor Einayim (Pinto), 16:179

Meʾor Einayim (Rossi), 9:157, 17:471–473

Meʾorerei Yeshenim, 7:20

Meʾot ḥittim, 14:**60**

Mephibosheth, 14:**60–61**

Mer, Gideon, 14:**61**

Merab, 1:423, 14:**61**

Merano (Italy), 14:**61**

Méray, Tibor, 14:**61**

Mercado. *See* Alfandari, Solomon Eliezer ben Jacob; Habillo, Elisha

Mercado. *See* Alfandari, Solomon Eliezer ben Jacob

Mercantile economy, 15:449

Mercerus, Joannes. *See* Mercier, Jean

Merchant, Larry, 14:**61–62**

Merchant bankers, 3:115–116

Merchant of Venice (Shakespeare), 4:25, 6:435, 18:368–369

Bouwmeester, Louis Frederik Johannes, 4:107

film adapation by Steve Suissa, 18:371

Yiddish translation by Bovshover, Joseph, 4:108

Merchants. *See* Brokers; Crafts; Economic history; Guilds; Trade and commerce

Mercier, Jean, 14:**62**

Mercurius. *See* Mercury

Mercury, 14:**62**

Mercy, 14:**62–63**

justice and, 11:579

Mercy killing. *See* Euthanasia

Merecina of Gerona, 14:**63**

Meremar, 14:**63**

Merenids. *See* Merinids

Mererah, 16:283–284

Meretz, 14:**63–64**

Mergentheim (Germany), 14:**64**

Merḥav, 8:327

Merḥavyah (Israel), 14:**64**

Meri. *See* Buffaloes

Meribah. *See* Rephidim

Meribah, waters of (ancient Israel). *See* Kadesh-Barnea (ancient Israel)

Mérida (Spain), 14:**65**

Meridi. *See* Ibn Abitur, Joseph ben Isaac

Meridor, Dan, 14:**65**

Merin, Moshe, 11:526

Merinid dynasty, 14:**66**

Merinids, 14:495

Merism, 17:302

Merit, inheriting, 21:497–498

Merit of the Fathers. *See* Zekhut avot

Merkabah mysticism, 11:591, 593–595, 14:**66–67**

anthropomorphism, 2:191

chiromancy, 4:653

dualism, 6:30

Johanan ben Nappaḥa, 11:370–371

Joseph ben Ḥiyya, 11:421

Kabbalah and, 13:761

literature, 11:591–595

Metatron, 14:133

Raza Rabba, 17:128

Razeil, Book of, 17:129

See also Kabbalah

Merkaz ha-Rav Yeshivah, 18:399

Merkin, Zalmen. *See* Erik, Max

Merkulis. *See* Mercury

Mermelstein, Mel, 15:462

Merneptah, 14:67

Merodach, 14:68

Merodach-Baladan, 3:23, 14:68

Merom (Israel). *See* Meron (Israel)

Meron (Israel), 14:68–69

Meron, Hanna, 14:69

Merovingian kingdom, 4:761

Meroz (ancient city), 14:70

Merrick, David, 14:70

Merrick, Leonard, 14:70

Merrill, Robert, 14:70

Merritt, Ruth Newlander, 4:372

The Merry Wives of Windsor (libretto, Mosenthal), 14:521

Merseburg (Germany), 14:71

Mersin (Turkey), 14:71

Merton, Robert C., 14:72, 18:159–160

Merton, Robert K., 18:731

Merton, Robert King, 14:72–73

Merton family, 14:71

Merv (ancient city), 14:73

Merzbacher, Abraham, 14:73

Merzbacher, Eugen, 14:73

Merzbacher, Gottfried, 14:73

Merzbacher, Leo, 14:73–74, 15:198

Merzbacher family, 14:73

Merzer, Arieh, 14:74

Meselson, Matthew, 13:9, 14:74

Mesene (ancient geographic location), 14:74–75

Dos Meserl (Shalom Aleichem), 18:380

Mesha (King of Moab), 14:75, 400, 401

  Baal-Meon, 3:8

  as noqed, 2:97

Meshach. *See* Shadrach, Meshach, Abed-Nego

Meshal ha-Kadmoni (ibn Sahula), 6:668

Meshalim (Fleischer), 6:669

Mesharshia Kahana ben Mar. Rav Ashi. *See* Moses Kahana ben Jacob

Mesha Stele, 14:75–76, 400

  Chemosh, name of, 4:594

Meshcherskii, Nikita, 11:321

Meshech (ancient nation), 14:76

Meshed (Iran), 1:432, 14:76–77

Meshel, Yeruham, 14:77

Meshikhah, 1:360–361

Meshiv Devarim Nekhoḥim (Gerondi), 7:548–549

Meshullaḥim, 16:44

Meshullam, Asher Levi. *See* Del Banco, Anselmo

Meshullam, Vita, 15:566

Meshullam ben Jacob of Lunel, 1:296, 13:258, 14:77

Meshullam ben Kalonymus, 14:77–78

Meshullam ben Moses, 14:78

Meshullam ben Nathan of Melun, 2:105, 14:78–79

Meshullam da Volterra, 3:697

Meshullam de Piera, 16:267

Meshullam Feivush Heller of Zbarazh, 8:411–412, 14:79

Meshullam of Volterra, 8:744

Meshullam Phoebus ben Israel Samuel, 14:79–80

Meshullam Sofer. *See* Zimel Sofer

Meshullam Zalman ha-Kohen, 14:80

Meshullam Zusya of Hanipoli. *See* Zusya of Hanipoli

Meshwi al-ʿUkbarī, 14:80

Mesillat Yesharim (Luzzatto), 11:671, 13:284

Mesillat Zion (Israel), 14:80

Mesillot (Israel), 14:80

Mesirah, 1:361

Mesirow, Milton. *See* Mezzrow, Milton

Meskin, Aharon, 14:80–81

Mesolelot, tribadism, 12:660

Mesopotamia, 14:81, 81–109, 82, 83

  Amorite period, 14:81–84

  archeological excavations, 14:92–93

  archives, 2:402–405

  astronomy, 14:90

  biblical religion, influences on, 6:386–390

  borders, 6:551

  chronological history, 14:93

  Dark Age, 14:85–86

  dress on monuments, 6:12–13

  Early Iron Age, 14:89

  Elam, 6:283

  ethics, 6:535

  exile in, 6:607–608

  Feudal Era, 14:86–87

  flood epics, 7:80–82

  Hammurapi, Code of, 8:310

  Hammurapi, Era of, 14:84–85

  Hurrians, 14:85–86

  Late Iron Age, 14:89–92

  legal practice, 14:93–97

  literature, 14:97–98

    creation, 5:274–275

    lamentations, 12:450

    Sumerian, 14:99–105

  myth, Noah story and, 15:287

  Patriarchs associated with, 15:690

  Sencherib, 14:90–91

  Shinar, 18:484

  Shu-Sin, 14:83

  Ur, 14:83–84

  See also Babylonia; Iraq

Mesorah Publications, 2:534–535

Mesorot. *See* Masorah

Mesquita, Benjamin Bueno de, 14:110

Mesquita, Joseph Bueno de, 14:110

Mesquita family, 14:110

The Message (English translation of Bible), 3:621

Messalamus. *See* Andronicus son of Meshullam

Messel, Alfred, 14:110

Messel family, 14:110

Messerer, Asaf Mikhailovich, 5:415, 14:110

Messerer, Sulamith, 14:110

Messer Leon, David ben Judah. *See* Leon, Messer David ben Judah

Messiah, 14:110–115

  Adam Kadmon, 1:379

  aliyah and, 10:330

  birth pangs of, 6:496

  Christianity, and sermons on, 7:308

  Elijah, 6:334

  Elijah's association with, 6:333–334

  Enoch, Ethiopic Book of, 6:443

  eschatology, 6:499–500, 501–502

  Jesus as, 11:249

  Luzzatto, Moses Ḥayyim, 13:282–283

  pseudo-messiah, 18:325

    Jonathan the Weaver, 12:789–790

    Lemlein, Asher, 12:638

    Molcho, Solomon, 14:423–424

  redemption, kabbalistic, 6:501–502

  Schneersohn, Menachem Mendel, 18:149

  son of man, 6:496–497

  See also Shabbateanism

The Messiah of Stockholm (Ozick), 15:557

Messianic Days. See Yemot ha-Mashiʾaḥ

Messianic movements, 14:115–122

Messianism, 6:496–497
  Abdallah, Yusef, 1:240
  Abdallah ibn Sabā, 1:240–241
  Abraham ben Eliezer ha-Levi, 1:298, 299
  Abu 'Īā, Isaac ben Jacob al-Iṣfahīnī, 1:337
  Abulafia, Abraham ben Samuel, 1:338
  Aescoly, Aaron Ze'ev, 1:431
  Agmon, Nathan, 1:465
  Alroy, David, 2:5–6
  Arabanel, Isaac ben Judah, 1:279
  Birkenthal, Dov Ber, 3:712
  Botarel, Moses ben Isaac, 4:101
  Cahan, Yaakov, 4:337
  Christian, 6:496–497
  Davidic dynasty, 5:453, 460, 462
  eschatology, 6:496–497
  Essene, 6:499–500
  Ḥasidei Ashkenaz, 8:387
  Haskalah and, 8:439
  illuminated Spanish Hebrew manuscripts expressing, 3:677
  impact of Emancipation, 16:92
  Islam, appearance of, 4:326
  Jerusalem, 1:312
  Judaism, development of concept, 9:223, 11:514
  Judeo-Arabic culture and, 11:540, 541
  literature, 7:15
  Luzzatto, Moses Ḥayyim, 13:282–283
  Maimonides view of, 16:86
  in Netherlands, 4:252
  Obadiah the Norman proselyte, 15:367
  Pablo de Santa Maria, 15:562
  parody, Hebrew, 15:657–658
  Shabbatean movement, 13:265, 14:480
  world to come, 6:497
  See also Eschatology
Messibbot ha-Po'al (Baranowicz), 3:134
Messibbot ha-Shem (Baranowicz), 3:134
Messina (Italy), 14:**122**
Messing, Shep, 14:**122**
Messinger, Ruth Wyler, 14:**122–123**, 15:224
Mestechko. *See* Shtetl
Mestel, Jacob, 14:**123**
Metaethical thought, 6:536–537
Metals and mining, 14:**124–131**
  antimony, 14:128
  biblical literature, 14:123–126

copper, 14:125, 127
  gold, 14:123–124, 127
  iron, 14:125–126
  lead, 14:126
  metalworkers, 14:128–131
  metalworking, 5:264
  Rabbinic literature, 14:126–128
  silver, 14:124–125
  symbolism, 5:424, 14:128
  tin, 14:126, 128
Metamorfozele mastilor comice (Calin), 4:364
The Metamorphosis of Comic Masques. See Metamorfozele mastilor comice
Metaphor
  adoption as, 1:416–417
  adultery, 1:425
  blindness as, 3:753–754
Metaphoric Judaism, 5:599
Metaphysics, 1:280, 624–625, 9:93, 14:**131–132**, 18:779
Metatron, 11:593–594, 14:**132–134**
  alphabet, 11:667
  dualism, 6:30
Metatron mysteries, 11:33
Metchnikoff, Elie, 14:**134**
Meteg system (Hebrew grammar), 11:117
Metei Midbar (Bialik), 3:563
Metek Sefatayim (Frances), 7:171
Metempsychosis. *See* Gilgul
Metempsychosis (Moore), 14:469
Meteor Farm (Brant), 4:130
Meteorology
  Asbel, Dov, 2:556–557
  Berson, Arthur Joseph Stanislav, 3:489–490
  Conrad, Victor, 5:162–163
  Less, Emil, 12:664
  Loewe, Fritz Philipp, 13:165
  Pepper, Joseph, 15:757
  Rubenson, Robert, 17:510
  Rubin, Morton Joseph, 17:512
Die Methegsetzung (Baer), 3:53
Method acting, 1:408–409
La méthode (Morin), 14:492
Methodik des deutschen Unterrichts (Engelmann), 6:410
Methone (Greece). *See* Modon (Greece)
Methuselah, 14:**134**
Metivta. *See* The Institute of Traditional Judaism (ITJ)
Metivta de-Raki'a. *See* Academy on High
Metman-Cohen, Yehudah Leib, 14:**134**

Metro-Goldwyn-Mayer, 13:164
Metro-Goldwyn-Mayer (MGM), 14:571
Metrologische Voruntersuchungen zu einer Geschichte des. . . altjuedischen Handels (Herzfeld), 9:53
Metrology. *See* Weights and measures
Metternich, Prince Klemens Wenzel von, 4:224, 14:**134–135**
Metulah. *See* Metullah (Israel)
Metullah (Israel), 14:**135**
Meturgeman, 3:589
  See also Amora
Metz (France), 7:156, 12:754, 13:194, 14:**135–136**
Metz, Moses. *See* Ensheim, Moses
Metzenbaum, Howard M., 15:393
Metzger, Arnold, 14:**136**
Metzger, Ottilie, 14:**136**
Metzger, Tom, 15:79
Metzger-Latterman, Ottilie. *See* Metzger, Ottilie
Metzlein-Auerbach family. *See* Auerbach family
Me'un, 4:616–617
Meunites, 14:**137**
Mevakker. *See* Gordon, Judah Leib
Mevakshei Derekh (Israel), 5:22–23
Mevasseret Zion (Israel), 14:**137**
Mevasser ha-Levi, 11:531
Mevo Ḥammat (Israel), 8:306
Mevo ha-Talmud (Aknin), 1:570
Mevo ha-Yerushalmi (Frankel), 7:201
Mevo le-Massekhot ve-Avot de Rabbi Natan (Finkelstein), 17:242
Mevo'ot le-Sifrut ha-Amora'im (Epstein), 6:472
Mevo'ot le-Sifrut ha-Tanna'im (Epstein), 6:472
Mevorah, Valeri, 4:276
Mevorakh, Valeri. *See* Petrov, Valeri
Mevorakh ben Saadiah, 6:231, 14:**137**
Mevorakh ha-Bavli, 14:**137**
Mevorakh ibn al-Barqūlī. *See* Ibn al-Barqūlī
Mexico, 14:**137–146**, *138*
  antisemitism, 14:141–142
  Ashkenaz, 6:748
  Blis, David, 3:756
  Colonial period, 14:137–139
  communal organizations, 14:140–141, 142–143
  demography, 14:144
  economic status, 14:141
  education, Jewish, 6:213
  education and culture, 14:142, 144–145
  immigration, 14:140

Indians as Judaizers, 11:520, 521
Inquisition, 9:797
journalism, 12:514–515, 17:438
literature, Seligson, Esther, 18:268
nineteenth century, 14:139–140
religious life, 14:145
socioeconomic status, 14:143–144
Zionism, 6:723, 21:594–595
Me-Yarkon. *See* Yarkon river
Meyer, Annie Nathan, 14:**146**
Meyer, Baron de Hirsch, 14:**146**
Meyer, E., on Joshua, 11:442
Meyer, Eduard, 9:159, 14:**146**
Meyer, Ernst Hermann, 14:**146–147**
Meyer, Eugene, 11:468, 14:**147**
Meyer, Hans Johannes Leopold,
14:**147**
Meyer, Hirshel. *See* Hirshel, Meyer
Meyer, Jonas Daniel, 2:112, 12:552,
14:**147**, 16:345
Meyer, Julius, 15:**48**, 415
Meyer, Leon, 14:**147**
Meyer, Ludwig Beatus, 14:**148**
Meyer, Marshall T., 14:**148**
Meyer, Martin Abraham, 14:**148**
Meyer, Michael A., 14:**148–149**
Meyer, Paulus, 3:764, 14:**149**
Meyer, Richard Emil, 14:150
Meyer, Richard Joseph, 14:**149**
Meyer, Richard Moritz, 14:**149**
Meyer, Seligmann, 14:**149–150**
Meyer, Torben Louis, 14:**150**
Meyer, Victor, 14:**150**
Meyerbeer, Giacomo, 13:247, 14:**150**
Meyer Ḥayyim (Ibn Gabirol), 16:80–81
Meyerhof, Max, 14:**150–151**
Meyerhof, Otto, 13:10, 14:**151**
Meyerhoff, Hans, 14:**151**
Meyerhoff, Harvey, 14:**151–152**
Meyerhoff, Joseph, 3:99, 14:**152**
Meyerhoff, Lyn, 14:**151–152**
Meyerhoff, Joseph, 15:589
Meyer-Lévy, Claude, 14:**152**
Meyerovich, Mark. *See* Daniel, M.
Meyerovich, Mordecai. *See* Daniel, M.
Meyerowitz, Herbert Vladimir, 14:**152**
Meyerowitz, Joel, 14:**152–153**
Meyers, Eric, 18:307
Meyers, Nancy Jane, 14:**153**
Meyerson, Emile, 14:**153**
Meyerson, Golda. *See* Meir, Golda
Meyerstein, Edward Harry WIlliam,
14:**153–154**
Meyerstein, Edward William, 14:**154**
Meynes Rivko. See Meneket Rivkah

Meysl, Marcus ben Samuel. *See*
Meisel, Mordecai ben Samuel
Meysl, Marx ben Samuel. *See* Meisel,
Mordecai ben Samuel
Meysl, Mordecai ben Samuel. *See*
Meisel, Mordecai ben Samuel
Meyuḥas, Abraham ben Samuel,
14:**154**
Meyuḥas, Moses Joseph Mordecai ben
Raphael Meyuḥas, 14:**154**
Meyuḥas, Raphael Meyuḥas ben
Samuel, 14:**154**
Meyuḥas, Yosef Baran, 14:**154–155**
Meyuḥas, Yosef Baran ben Rahamim
Natha. *See* Meyuḥas, Yosef Baran
Mezaḥ, Joshua ha-Levi, 14:**155**
Mézan, Saul, 4:270
Mezei, Mór, 14:**155**
Mezey, Ferenc, 14:**155**
Mezhibezh (Ukraine). *See* Medzibezh
(Ukraine)
Mezhirech (Poland). *See* Miedzyrzec
Podlask (Poland)
Mezhirech (Ukraine), 14:**155–156**
Mezhirichi. *See* Mezhirech (Ukraine)
Meẓiẓah, 4:734
Meẓiẓim. See Peeping Toms (motion
picture)
Mezo, Ferenc, 15:413
Mezöfi, Vilmos, 14:**156**
Mezonot. *See* maintenance
Mezrich (Poland). *See* Miedzyrzec
Podlask (Poland)
Mezrits Gadol (Ukraine). *See*
Mezhirech (Ukraine)
Mezuzah, 14:**156–157**
amulets, 2:121
cases, vol. 15: color insert
Mezz. *See* Mezzrow, Milton
Mezzrow, Milton, 14:**157**
MGM (Metro-Goldwyn-Mayer),
14:571
MGWJ. *See Monatsschrift fuer
Geschichte und Wissenschaft des
Judentums*
Mi al Har Ḥorev ha-Amidi (Obadiah),
14:543
Miami-Dade County (FL), 7:88,
14:**158–161**
Miasteczko. *See* Shtetl
Mibashan. *See* Braunstein, Menahem
Mendel
Mi-Bayit u-mi-Ḥuẓ (Dolitzki), 5:735–
736
Mi-Bein ha-Homot (Carmel), 4:483
Mi-Birkenshtadt. *See* Chajes, Gerson
ben Abraham
Mica, 14:**161**

Micah (book), 6:492, 14:**162–164**
Micaiah (Ephraimite), 14:**164**
Micaiah (son of Imlah), 14:**164–165**
Micaiah (son of Shaphan), 18:398
Mice, 14:**589–590**
Michael (angel), 2:152, 14:**167–169**,
533, 18:768
Michael, Heimann Joseph Ḥayyim,
3:684, 4:29, 14:**165**
Michael, Jakob, 14:**165**
Michael, Moses, 14:**166**
Michael, Sami, 14:**166–167**
Michael, Simon, 4:132
Michael II, 14:**165**
Michaelis, Archie. *See* Michaelis, Sir
Archie
Michaelis, J. H., 3:587
Michaelis, J. H., early printed editions
of Hebrew Bible, 3:588
Michaelis, Johann David, 8:515,
14:**169**
Michaelis, Leonor, 14:**169–170**
Michaelis, Max. *See* Michaelis, Sir Max
Michaelis, Sir Archie, 14:**169**, 16:340
Michaelis, Sir Max, 14:**170**
Michaels, Alan Richard, 14:**170**
Michaels, Anne, 14:**170**
Michaels, Lorne, 14:**171**
Michaels, Moses. *See* Michael, Moses
Michaelson, Ezekiel Ẓevi ben
Abraham Ḥayyim, 14:**171**
Michaelson, Isaac Chesar, 14:**171**
Michael VIII Palaeologus, 14:**165**
Michaes, Moses. *See* Michael, Moses
Michal, 14:**171–172**, 15:607
Michali, Binyamin Yiẓḥak, 14:**172**
Michall, Moses. *See* Michael, Moses
Michalovce (Slovakia), 14:**172–173**
Michel, Ernest, 2:48
Michel, Jud, 14:**173**
Michelangelo
biblical influence, 3:673
Moses, 14:541
Michel Berr de Turique. *See* Berr,
Michel
Michel de Nostre-Dame. *See*
Nostradamus
Michelet Shazar, 6:212
Michel Ḥasid. *See* Jehiel Michael ben
Judah Leib he-Ḥasid
Michel-Lévy, Auguste, 14:**173**
Michelson, Albert Abraham, 14:**173–
174**
Michelson, Charles, 14:**174**
Michelstaedter, Carlo, 14:**174–175**
Michigan (U.S.), 14:*175*, **175–177**
Fine, Sidney, 7:25–26

Michigan (U.S.), *continued*
    Holocaust Memorial Center
      (Farmington Hills), vol. 9: color
      insert
    Levin, Theodore, 12:714
    Solomon, Ezekiel, 18:764–765
Michlelet Shazar, 2:448
Michmas (ancient city). *See* Michmash
    (ancient city)
Michmash (ancient city), 14:**177–178**
Michonze, Grégoire, 15:648
Michrovsky, Issachar. *See* Miron,
    Issachar
Michzyński, Sebastian, 14:**179–180**
Mickiewicz, Adam, 4:128, 136, 14:**178,**
    16:302
Microbiology
    Chet, Ilan, 4:605–606
    Hirszfeld, Ludwik, 9:143
    Rager, Bracha, 17:65
    soil, 6:451
Micrococcus prodigiosus, 9:565
Microcosm, 14:**178–179**
Microcosm (Ẓaddik), 21:438
Micrography, 3:676, 678, 4:367
Micropolyphony, 13:12
Microsoft, 1:668, 3:93–94
Miczyński, Sebastian, on brokers,
    4:204
Midbar Yehudah (Modena), 14:409
Middle Ages
    agriculture, 1:494–497
    amulets, 2:121
    anatomy, 2:135
    anthropomorphism, 2:190
    antisemitism, 2:211–212, 6:555–
      556
        badges, 3:45–47
        caricatures of Jews, 4:477
        France, 4:460, 563
        Germany, 5:436
        Hugh of Lincoln, 9:579
        Spain, 5:437
        stereotypes, 7:511
    Anusim, 2:251–252
    arts
        choral singing, 4:659–660
        Creation, 5:279–280
        dance, 5:410
        ḥazzanim, 8:502
        music, 14:653–656, *654, 656*
        Sabbath, 17:621
        sculpture, 18:222
        synagogue architecture,
          19:*368,* 368–376, *370, 372,*
          373, 374

Ashkenaz, domestic violence,
    5:740
astrology, 2:617–618, 618–619
astronomy, 2:622–625
    Bet Din and, 3:514–515
    Bohemia, 4:37–38
captives, ransoming of, 4:457
Carinthia (Austria), 4:480
charity, 4:571–573
chosen people doctrine, 4:670–671
coffins, 4:783
concubine, 5:134
conferences, 5:145–146
Court Jews, 5:246–248
Crimea, 5:298–300
cultural and social life
    age and the aged, 1:447–448
    archives, 2:405–406
    bathing, 3:210–211
    community organization,
      5:102–108, 6:176–177
    dietary laws, 5:656
    dress, 6:14–15
    gambling, 7:367
    head covering, 8:506
    Hebrew language, 8:650–671
    humor and, 9:591
    hygiene, 9:648
    market days and fairs,
      13:550–552
    marriages, 13:564–565
    shaving and beards, 3:235–
      236
    sports, 19:128–129
    women, dress, 6:14–15
divination, 5:707–708
dreams, 6:9–10
economics
    banking, 2:554, 3:111–115
    begging and beggars, 3:259,
      260
    Christianity, 6:108–114
    Lopez, Robert Sabatino,
      13:189–190
    ma'arufya, 13:307
    mintmasters and moneyers,
      14:298–301
    moneylending, 2:554
education, Jewish
    Asia, 6:176
    Babylonian period, 6:172–173
    community organization,
      6:176–177
    Eastern Europe, 6:176
    France, 6:174–176
    Geonic period, 6:172–173

    Germany, 6:174–176
    pre-Geonic period, 6:172–173
    universities, 20:406–407
    Western Mediterranean,
      6:173–174
    yeshivot, 21:316–317
Egypt, 6:*227*
England
    Canterbury, 4:*435,* 435–436
    Liebermann, Felix, 12:808
    London, 13:179–180
Europe
    hospitality and, 9:562
    hospitals, 9:562
exile, 7:355–362
expulsions, 3:110–111, 9:215–216,
    221, 221–222, 13:695, 791
federations of communities, 6:727
France
    Carpentras, 4:493–494
    education, Jewish, 6:174–176
    Jewish communities, 5:442
galut, 7:355–362
gentiles, 7:486–487
geography, 7:490–491
Germany, 7:518–524, *521*
    Berlin, 3:444–445
    education, Jewish, 6:174–176
    Mainz, 13:403–404
ḥazakah, 8:490
ḥerem ha-Yishuv, 9:17–18
ḥerem setam, 9:18–19
history
    Christian attitudes, 9:209–210
    historiography, 9:155–156
    under Islam, 9:208–209
Hungary, 9:608
imprisonment, 9:743, 748–749
India, 9:773
informers, 9:780, 783–785
Islam
    domestic violence, 5:740
    economic history, 6:104–108
Italy, 10:790–791, *796,* 797–799
Khazar kingdom, 9:212
Levison, Wilhelm, 12:729–730
Lisbon (Portugal), 13:78–79
literature
    Alexander the Great, 1:627
    animal tales, 2:173
    Apocrypha and
      Pseudepigrapha, 2:261
    children's, 4:619
    Creation, 5:279–280
    Dutch, 6:68

ethical, 6:527–531, 535–536
homiletic, 9:508–512
Italy, 10:790–791
Jewish, 13:93–117
letters, 12:670–673
magic, 13:345–351
poetry, 5:428, 468, 6:651,
    13:95–96, 16:262–270
polemic, 16:328–329
rabbinical, 17:22
scholarly Hebrew, 13:797
Magdeburg law, 13:336
maps of Erez Israel, 13:501–502
Moses, 14:536–537
names, 14:768–769
Palestine (Ottoman), 4:286
philosophy
    Adam, 1:373–374
    afterlife, 1:442
    belief, faith, 3:293–294
    disputations and polemics,
        5:690–694
    emotions and, 6:396–397
    ethical thought, 6:527–530
    God, 7:661–664
    good and evil, 7:753–754
    miracles, 14:307, 309
    redemption, 17:152–153
    repentance, 17:222
    resurection, 17:243–244
    reward and punishment,
        17:270–271
    righteousness, 17:309
    Ru'ah ha-Kodesh, 17:508–509
    soul, 19:33–35, 36–38
    stoicism, 19:233
physicians, 6:711–712
property transfer, 5:137
psychiatry, 16:684–685
psychology, 16:688
publishing
    book titles, 8:551–552
    book trade, 4:77–78
religious life and scholarship
    baptism, forced, 3:121–122
    biblical exegesis, 13:94–95
    Catholic Church, 4:710–711
    Christianity, 6:88, 108–114
    commandments, reasons for,
        5:86–88
    cosmology, 5:231–232
    Crusades, 5:310–315, 9:210,
        213–214
    Day of Atonement, 5:489–
        490, 491
    elders, 6:296

hagiography, 8:224–226
Hallelujahs, long, 8:281
Hanukkah, 8:333
Hanukkah lamp, 8:333
Hebraists, Christian, 8:511–
    514
Hebrew manuscripts, 13:489
iconography and, 9:703–705
prayer, 16:459, 460
preaching, 5:438, 16:470–472
principles of faith, 2:530–531
proselytism, 16:590–592
providence, 16:649–651
rabbis, 17:11–12
synagogues, 18:531, 19:352–
    355
theology, 19:695–696
Saragossa (Spain), 18:41–43
semikhah, 18:275–276
Spain
    Carrion de Los Condes, 4:496
    Seville, 18:326–327
titles, 19:740–741
trade and commerce
    crafts, 5:265–269
    dyeing, 6:76–77
    goldsmiths and silversmiths,
        7:725–726
    hunting and, 9:621–622
    leather industry and trade,
        12:574–575
    Mediterannean trade, 3:143
    textiles, 19:662
    wine and liquor trade, 21:82–
        83
Tyre, 20:219
visions, 20:544–545
See also Black Death
Middle Aramaic. See Aramaic, middle
Middle East
    antisemitism, 2:225–226, 236
    coinage, 14:300
    foreign policy and relations with
        Israel (state), 10:256–257, 265,
        12:546
    Ozar Hatorah in, 15:556
    post-WW II, Russian policies,
        17:559
    rites and rituals, liturgy, 13:136
    See also Arab countries; Near East;
        Western Mediterranean; specific
        countries
Middle Kingdom (Egypt), 6:223–224
Middlesex County (NJ), 14:**180**
Middot (tractate), 14:**180–181**
Mi-Devarav (Lurie), 13:270
Midian, Midianites, 2:29, 6:404,
    14:**181–182**, 523–524, 526, 16:114–
    115

Midler, Bette, 14:**182**
Midnight Vigil (Seter), 18:319
Midrash, 14:**182–185**, 184t
    Abraham ben Elijah of Vilna,
        1:299
    aggadah, 13:91–92
    Aggadat Bereshit, 1:464
    Akedah, 1:556, 560
    alchemy, 1:603
    allegorical interpretation of
        scripture in, 3:643–644
    alphabet, Hebrew, 1:728–730
    amoraim, 2:89
    angels, 2:156–158
    animal tales, 2:173
    apologetics, 2:263
    astrology, 2:617
    astronomy, 2:621, 624
    Belkin, Samuel, 3:296
    Bereshit-Nāmeh (Shāhin), 18:365
    on birth, 3:721
    circuses and theater, 4:735, 19:670
    commentary
        Braude, William Gordon,
            4:135
        Buber, Solomon, 4:236
        Hanokh Zundel ben Joseph,
            8:329
        Rashi, 17:102–103
        Schick, Abraham ben Aryeh
            Loeb, 18:126
    Dead Sea sect, 5:506–508, 14:182–
        183
    death, 5:511–512
    demons, demonology, 5:574–575,
        577
    dress, 6:13
    drunkenness, 6:27
    Dura-Europos (Syria), 6:51–56
    Ecclesiastes, 6:89
    Ecclesiastes Rabbah, 6:90–91
    Eleazar ben Damma, 6:300–301
    Eleazar ben Parma, 6:305–306
    Eliezer ben Nathan of Mainz,
        6:328
    Eliezer ben Yose ha-Gelili, 6:329–
        330
    Ephraim, 6:457
    eschatology, 6:500
    Eshet Hayil, 6:505
    euphemisms, 6:550–551
    Exodus
        Mekhilta of Rabbi Ishmael,
            13:793–795
        Mekhilta of Rabbi Simeon ben
            Yohai, 13:795–797
    Exodus Rabbah, 6:624

Midrash, *continued*

fables, 6:667

fiction, 7:10

flags, *7:67*

folklore, 7:95–113

Galilean Aramaic, 2:349

Haman, 8:294

heart references, 8:510

Hellenistic Jewish literature, 8:791–792

iconography, 9:703–704, *704*

influence
apocalypse, 2:258
Philo Judaeus, 16:64
stoicism, 19:232

interpretation
Adam, 1:373–375, 379
allegorical, 3:643–644
biblical exegesis and study, 3:640–641, 9:815, 816
Ḥemdat Yamim, 8:804, 18:357
homiletic literature, 9:507–516
illuminated manuscripts, 1:375, 463, 2:495–496, 3:674–679, 11:226–227
legal maxims, 12:603–604

Jesus in, 11:250–251

Jewish literature, 13:84–117

Jubilees, Book of, 11:474

Judeo-Persian, 11:551, 553

Leviticus Rabbah, 12:740–742

Lilith, 13:17–20

mediation in, 13:719

Mekhilta Deuteronomy, 13:792–793

metals and mining, 14:127–128, 131

mishpat Ivri, 14:338

Nations, The Seventy, 15:31–32

Numbers Rabbah, 15:337–338

olive trees and olives in, 15:406–407

Omar ibn al-Khaṭṭāb, 15:419

parables, 15:621–623

parody in, 15:654

Pesikta de-Rav Kahana, 16:11–12

plagues of Egypt, 16:214

proselytes, 16:589–590

Provence (France), 16:639

proverbs, Talmudic, 16:646–648

Psalms, Book of, 16:675–676

rabbinical literature, 3:291–293

rain, 17:71

Rashi, 17:102–103

religious impact of Bible and, 3:661–662

Renaissance commentaries, 11:69

resistance literature, 3:283, 9:361

Revelation, 17:254–256

Satan in, 18:72–73

Shāhin, 18:365

Shekhinah, 18:441

spiritual resistance, 8:790–791, 9:360–363

Tanḥuma, 8:291

tannaitic
Abba Kolon, 1:229
Mattiah ben Ḥeresh, 13:688

in vernacular, *Mayse-Bukh,* 13:702–703

Wisdom of Solomon, 18:768–769

Yannai (poet), 21:281

See also Aggadah or Haggadah

Midrash Aggadah, 14:189
Esther Rabbah, 6:519–520
Lamentations Rabbah, 12:451–452

Midrash Agur, 14:187

Midrashah (Argentina), 6:211

Midrash Ahasuerus. See Esther Rabbah

Midrash Alẓi'ani (Abraham ben Solomon), 1:310

Midrash and Mishnah (Lauterbach), 12:529

Midrash and Theory (Stern), 1:461

Midrash Aseret ha-Dibberot, 7:12, 14:**185–186**

Midrashat Sedeh Boker. *See* Midreshet Sedeh Boker

Midrash Avkir, 11:597, 14:188

Midrash David (Shapiro), 18:404

Midrash Elleh Ezkerah. See Aggadat Aseret Harugei Malkhut

Midrash Eser Galuyyot, 14:188

Midrash Esfah, 14:188

Midrash Ezraḥim, 13:261

Midrash ha-Gadol, 13:792–793, 795, 14:**186–187**

Midrash ha-Ḥokhmah (Matkah), 6:399, 13:679

Midrash ha-Ittamari (Elijah ben Solomon Abraham ha-Kohen of Smyrna), 6:341

Midrash Hallel, 14:187–188

Midrash ha-Ne'lam (Zohar), 21:649

Midrash ha-'ur (Dhamārī), 5:631

Midrash ha-Zohar. See Zohar

Midrash Ḥ Vi-Yterot, 14:188

Midrashic literature
Dhamārī, Manṣur Suleiman, 5:631
Dhamārī, Sa'id ben David, 5:631
Genesis Rabbah, 7:448–449
Genesis Rabbati, 7:449–450
rabbinical literature, 17:22

rain, 17:71

reeds, 17:161

Midrashim. *See* Midrash

Midrashim, Smaller, 14:**187–190**

Midrash Kinot. See Lamentations Rabbah

Midrash Kohelet. See Ecclesiastes Rabbah

Midrash Konen, 1:224, 14:189

Midrash la-Perushim (Eliezer Fischel ben Isaac of Strzyzow), 6:330

Midrash Lekaḥ Tov (Tobias ben Eliezer), 14:**190**

Midrash Mah Rabbu, 14:189

Midrash Megillat Esther. See Esther Rabbah

Midrash of 32 Hermeneutic Rules, 6:406

Midrash Panim Aḥherim Le-Esther, Hosaḥ Alef, 14:187

Midrash Pinkhas (Altman), 2:21

Midrash Proverbs, 14:**190–191**

Midrash Rabbi David ha-Nagid (David ben Abraham Maimuni), 5:465

Midrash Samuel, 14:**191**

Midrash Sheloshah Ve' Arba'ah, 14:188

Midrash Sheloshim u-Shetayim Middot. See Midrash Agur

Midrash Shir ha-Shirim, 14:187

Midrash Tadshe, 14:188

Midrash Talpiyyot (Elijah ben Solomon Abraham ha-Kohen of Smyrna), 6:341

Midrash Tanḥuma (Amelander), 2:38

Midrash Tehillim, 14:**191–192**

Midrash Temurah, 14:189

Midrash Va-yekhulu (Rabbati), 14:189

Midrash Va-Yissa'u, 8:224, 14:**192**

Midrash ve-Aggadah (Fraenkel), 1:461, 462

Midrash Yehi Or. *See* Zohar

Midrash Yelammedenu. See Tanḥuma Yelammedenu

Midrash Yonah, 14:187

Midreshei Halakhah, 14:**193–204, 193t**

Aggadic material, 14:199–200
characteristics of, 14:193–197
editing and codification, 14:202–203
relation to other works, 14:200–202
schools of thought, 14:197–199
sources of early halakhah, 14:200

Midreshei Ḥanukkah, 14:189

Midreshet Sedeh Boker, 18:234

Midreshet Yerushalayim, 18:115

Midstream (periodical), 14:**204**, 18:734

Midwest Council of the Society for the Advancement of Judaism, 11:701–702

Miedzyborz (Ukraine). *See* Medzibezh (Ukraine)

Miedzyrzec Korecki. *See* Mezhirech (Ukraine)

Miedzyrzec Podlask (Poland), 14:**204–205**

Mielec (Poland), 14:**205**

Mielziner, Moses, 14:**205–206**

Mieses, Fabius, 14:**206**

Mieses, Jacob. *See* Mieses, Jacques

Mieses, Jacques, 14:**206**

Mieses, Matthias, 14:**206**

Miesis, Judah Leib, 14:**206**

Mifalot Elohim, 3:9

Miflagah Datit Le'ummit. *See* Ha-Poel ha-Mizrachi

Mifleget ha-Avodah ha-Yisra'elit. *See* Israel Labor Party

Mifleget ha-Po'alim ha-Me'uḥedet. *See* Mapam

Mifleget Po'alei Erez Yisrael. *See* Mapai

Migdal (Israel), 14:**207**. *See* Magdala (Israel)

Migdal-Ashkelon (Israel). *See* Ashkelon (Israel)

Migdal David (Ephrati), 6:461

Migdal David (Kokhavi), 2:530

Migdal David (Lida), 8:480

Migdal ha-Emek (Israel), 14:**207**

Migdal Nunaiya (Israel). *See* Magdala (Israel)

Migdal Senaah. *See* Senaah

Migdol (ancient city), 14:**207**

Migrations, 14:**207–219**
    1881-1914, 14:207–208, 208*t*
    1915-1948, 9:*251,* 14:209–212, 210*t*
    1948-1965, 14:213*t*
    during Abbasid dynasty, 1:234
    from Afghanistan, 1:433
    to Afghanistan, 1:432
    from Africa, 1:437
    to Africa, 1:436
    to Alberta, 1:590
    from Algeria, 1:650
    Alliance Israelite Universelle, 1:672
    in art, 11:77–78
    from Bohemia-Moravia, 5:358–359
    to Brazil, 18:30, 31, 32
    to Cairo, 4:344
    to Canada, 1:500, 4:395, 398, 404–405, 408, 410, 411, 414, 421–422
    to Caracus (Venezuela), 4:459–460
    children's literature, 4:625
    to Chile, 4:638, 639–640
    to China, 4:646–647
    to Colombia, 5:63
    from Czechoslovakia, 5:356–357
    demography and, 5:554–572
    to Denmark, 5:584
    economic history, 6:119–120, 129–130
    to Ecuador, 6:139–141
    effect on philanthropy, 16:38
    eighteenth-early nineteenth century
        Europe, 9:233–234
        intercontinental, 9:*240*
    to England, 1:398, 6:413–415, 416–417
    Fez, Morocco, 7:7–8
    intermarriage, 14:374–375
    international migrations, 1969-2002, 14:214*t*
    to Israel, 1:442–443, 14:215–219
        1915-1948, 14:211*t*
        1947-2004, 5:685, 14:216*t,* 217*t*
        1948-1967, 14:215*t,* 16:321, 324–325
        Jabotinsky, Vladimir and, 11:13
        Jewish Agency, 1:409, 11:257, 259, 260, 278
        Law of Return, 12:541–545, 14:212
        ma'barah, 13:315
        sociological aspects, 14:215–218
    Israeli emigration, 14:218–219, 219*t*
    Jewish Colonization Association, 11:285–288
    Landsmannschaften, 12:476–477
    to Latin America, 2:41, 45–46, 12:477, 508–509
    from Latvia, 12:523
    Morocco
        Casablanca, 4:503–504
        from Europe, 14:493–496
        to Israel, 14:503–505
    Nazi Germany
        Reichsvereinigung and, 17:202
        Reichszentrale Fuer Juedische Auswanderung and, 17:203
    to New World, 4:469, 470
    Palestinan emigration, 14:215, 215*t*
    to Palestine, 1:507, 3:433–436
    philanthropy in England, 16:43
    philanthropy in U.S., 16:41
    from Poland, 16:319–320
    population estimates, 1900-2005, 14:214*t*
    from Syria, 1:616, 4:495–496, 5:396
    to U.K., 1:659
    to U.S., 1:499–500, 4:537, 14:209*t*
        1915-1948, 14:211*t*
        artisans, 5:269–270
        Colorado, 5:67–68
        Columbus (OH), 5:69
        Dallas (TX), 5:382
        Denver (CO), 5:586
        Detroit (MI), 5:609–610
        economic aspects, 6:136–137
        education, Jewish, 6:191–195
        family units, 6:696–698
        New York, 11:828
        Pittsburgh (PA), 16:188–189
        quotas, 6:697
        San Antonio (TX), 18:7
        San Diego (CA), 18:15
        San Francisco (CA), 18:18, 19
        Schenectady (NY), 18:120
        Scranton (PA), 18:210
        settlement as farmers, 11:262
    See also Aliyah; Illegal immigration; *specific countries*

Mihael, Albert, 4:276

Mihaileni (Romania), 14:**219–220**

Mihaly, Eugene, 14:**220**

Mihṭileni. *See* Mihaileni (Romania)

Mi'ilya (Israel), 14:**220**

Mi-Kadmoniyyot ha-Yehudim (Epstein), 6:466

Mi-Kan u-mi-Kan (Brenner), 4:159

Mikardo, Ian, 14:**220,** 16:342

Mi-Karov u-me-Raḥok (Epstein). *See From Near and Far* (Epstein)

Mikdash Me'at (Rieti), 17:297

Mikes, George, 14:**220**

Mikhaël, Ephraïm, 14:**221**

Mīkhā'īl, Murad, 14:**221**

Mikhailishker, Abraham Dov. *See* Lebensohn, Abraham Dov

Mikhailovitch, Solomon. *See* Flohr, Salo

Mikhal. *See* Lebensohn, Micah Jospeh

Mikhalevich, Beinish, 14:**221–222**

Mikhlelet Yehudah ve-Shomron, 2:453

Mikhlol (Kimḥi), 13:42

Mikhlol Yofi (Solomon ibn Mekekh), 1:251

Mikhmoret (Israel), 14:**222**

Mikhoels, Solomon, 4:141, 14:**222,** 518, 18:370

Mikhtav al Devar ha-Moreh (Falaquera), 6:682

Mikhtavim el Aḥ (Silman), 18:582

Mi-Kitov ad Yerushalayim (Locker), 13:153

Mikneh Avram (Balmes), 3:94, 13:34, 42–43

Mikra. *See* Ḥummash

Mikra (*Miqra'*; "reading"), 3:574

Mikra ki-Feshuto (Ehrlich), 6:243

Mikulov (Czech Republic), 14:**223– 224**

Mikva, Abner J., 14:**224**

Mikva'ot (tractate), 14:**224**

Mikveh Israel, 2:40, 14:**225–230, 230,** 15:254, vol. 21: color insert
        See also Ablution

Mikveh Israel Agricultural School, 15:114

Mikveh Israel Congregation (Philadelphia, PA), 16:33, 34

Mikvot
        feminism and, 6:752–753
        in Offenburg, 15:387, 388
        in Ostia, 15:508

Mila 18 (Uris), 9:406–407

Milan (Italy), 14:**231–232**

Milan, Gabriel, 4:474

Milano, Attilio, 14:**232**

Milbauer, Joseph, 14:**232**

Milchig. *See* Milk

Milcom, 2:84, 85

Milenky (Eisner). *See Lovers* (Eisner)

Miletus (ancient city), 14:**232**

Milevsky, Aharón, 14:**232**

Mi-Lev va-Nof (Mohar), 14:420

Mileykowsky, Nathan, 14:**232–233**

Mileykowsky, Netanyahu. *See* Mileykowsky, Nathan

Milgram, Stanley, 14:**233,** 18:732

"Milgram experiments," 18:732

Milgrom, Jacob, 14:**233**

Milḥamot Adonai (Hart), 8:370

Milḥamot ha-Shem (Ben Maimon), 1:305, 306–307

Milḥamot ha-Shem (Solomon ben Yerucham), 16:328

Milhaud, Darius, 13:259, 14:**234**

Milḥemet Benei-Or (Shamir), 18:392

Milḥemet ha-Minim (Damron), 18:205–206

Milḥemet ḥovah, 11:337

Milḥemet Mitzvah (Duran), 6:61

Milḥemet Mitzvah (Meir ben Simeon). *See Obligatory War* (Meir ben Simeon)

Milian, Maximin, 14:**234**

Miliband, David, 14:234

Miliband, Ralph, 14:**234**

Milich, Adolphe, 14:**234**

Military contracting, 5:198–200

Military law, 14:**235–238**

Military service, 14:**238–249**
        Australia, Monash, Sir John, 14:432
        Austria, Pick, Alois, 16:145–146
        Austria-Hungary
                Eiss, Alexander von, 6:278
                Singer, Joseph, 18:638
        Bible, 5:159–160
                military training, 6:165
        Bulgaria, 14:245
        Canada, 4:407–408, 422, 6:50
                Cass, Samuel, 4:507
        cantonists, 4:437–439
        chaplaincy, 14:247–248
        conscription, 4:437–439
        Czarist Russia, 14:240
        Egypt (ancient), Elephantine garrison, 6:311–312, 313–314
        France, 14:244
                Moch, Jules, 14:404
                Moch, Jules Salvador, 14:404–405
                nineteenth century, 12:442
                Sée, Léopold, 18:237–238
                twentieth century, 5:439
        Germany, 14:243–244
        Greece, 14:245–246
        Israel
                Ben-Eliezer, Binyamin, 3:339–340
                Ben Yehuda, Netiva, 3:388–389
                Carmel, Moshe, 4:483
                Dori, Ya'kov, 5:756
                Elazar, David, 6:289
                Herzog, Chaim, 9:67–68
                Laskov, Ḥayyim, 12:500
                Shaltiel, David, 18:390
                Sharon, Ariel, 18:415–417
        Italy, 14:243
                Capon, Augusto, 4:454
                Levi-Bianchini, Angelo, 12:703
                Modena, Angelo, 14:408
                Segrè, Roberto, 18:252
                Sesso, Salmone da, 18:318
        Jewish participation in WW I, 9:248–249, 14:239t
        Jews in
                Brandão, Ambrósio Fernandes, 4:121
                Brociner, Mauriciu, 4:192
                Burg, Meno, 4:287
                Bush, Solomon, 4:305
                Harby, Levi Myers, 8:346
                Jewish Legion, 11:303–306
                Jewish War Veterans of the U.S.A., 11:331
                Ottoman Empire, Molcho, David Effendi Isaac Pasha, 14:423
        Poland, 14:244–245
                Czarniecki, Stefan, 5:351
                Mond, Bernhard Stanislaw, 14:435
        Roman Empire, Cassius Longinus, 4:510
        Romania, 14:245
        Russia
                compulsory military service for Jews, 15:250
                Mordvinov, Nicolai Semionovich, 14:483
        Slovakia, Magyar Revolution, 18:683
        Spain, Enríquez Gomez, Antonio, 6:446
        Switzerland, 14:46
        U.K., 14:240–241
                Divekar, Samuel Ezekiel, 5:702–703
                Seligman, Herbert Spencer, 18:267
        U.S., 14:238
                Davis, Abel, 5:478–479
                Ellsberg, Edward, 6:362–363
                Frankel, Samuel Benjamin, 7:199
                Levy, Aaron, 12:746
                Mordecai, Alfred (1804-1887), 14:479
                Mordecai, Alfred (1840-1920), 14:479
                Moreel, Ben, 14:483
                Morris, Nelson, 14:511
                Morse, David Abner, 14:512
                twentieth century, 7:125
        USSR, 14:242, 242t
                Diskin, Chaim, 5:682
        women's participation, 14:246

Milk, 7:117, 14:**249**

Milken, Michael, 4:33

Milken, Michael R., 14:**249–250**

Milken Family Foundation, 13:211

Milkovsky, Roni. *See* Milo, Roni

Milkweed, 14:**250**

Mill, John. *See* Mill, Joseph Solomon

Mill, Joseph Solomon, 4:279, 280, 14:**250**

Millais, John, 14:542

Millás Vallicrosa, José Mariá, 14:**251**

Millbank, Joseph Duveen. *See* Duveen, Joseph

Mille'el, 13:622–624

Millenarianism, Christian, 3:737

Miller, Arthur, 14:**251–252**
- Bloomgarden, Kermit, 3:783
- Monroe, Marilyn, 14:450–451
- New York City and, 15:215, 220, 227

Miller, Ben-Zion, 14:**252**

Miller, Betty, 14:253

Miller, Emanuel, 14:**252–253**

Miller, Irving, 14:**253**

Miller, Israel, 14:**253**

Miller, Jonathan, 14:253

Miller, Louis, 14:**253–254**

Miller, Louis E., 14:**254**

Miller, Martin Rudolf, 14:**254**

Miller, Marvin Julian, 14:**254**

Miller, Mitch, 14:**255**

Miller, Shaye, 14:**255**

Miller, Stanley, 13:11

Millera', 13:622–624

Miller v. Miller, 5:156

Millet (grain), 14:255, vol. 16: color insert

Millet (Ottoman Empire), 14:**255–256**

Millet (sorghum), vol. 16: color insert

Millett, Peter, Baron. *See* Millett, Sir Peter, Baron

Millett, Sir Peter, Baron, 14:**256**

Millgram, Abraham Ezra, 14:**256**

Millin, Philip, 12:554, 14:**256**

Millin, Sarah Gertrude, 14:**257**

Millman, Irving, 4:9

Millman, Jacob, 14:**257**

Millo, Josef, 4:381, 14:**257**

Millon Olami le-Ivrit Meduberet (Ben Yehuda), 3:389

Millstones, 14:**257**

Milner, Moses Michael, 14:**257–258**

Milnsky, Joan Alexandra. *See* Rivers, Joan

Milo, Roni, 14:**258–259**

Milosz, Oscar, 14:**259**

Milstein, Cesar, 14:**260**

Milstein, Nathan, 14:**260**

Milstein, Paul, 14:259

Milstein, Seymour, 14:259
- and brothers, 15:226–227

Milstein family, 14:**259–260**

Milton, Ernest, 14:**260**

Milton, John, 6:435, 14:**260–261**

Milwaukee (WI), 14:**261–263**

Milyukhin, 11:522

Mi Ma'amikim (Feinstein), 17:236

Mimesis (Auerbach), 2:654

Miminalists, 3:655

Mi-Mizraḥ u-mi-Ma'arav (periodical), 4:119

Mimmation, 8:622

Mimouna festival, vol. 21: color insert

Mimram, 18:470. *See* Mamram

Mimrane. *See* Mimram

Mimran family. *See* Maymeran family

Min, 14:**263–264**

The Mina Lisa. See Ha-Minah Lizah

Mi Natan Ha-Hora'ah (Eshed), 4:346

Minc, Hilary, 14:**264**, 16:347

Minco, Marga, 6:71, 14:**264**

Minda, Albert Greenberg, 14:**264**

Minden (Germany), 14:**265**

Mind Evolution: An East-West Synthesis (Razran), 17:131

Mindlin, Henrique, 14:**265**

Mindlin, Sam, 14:512

The Mind of Paul (Edman), 6:150

Mines and mining, Drogobych (Ukraine), 6:23

Mingahim, rabbinical literature, 17:22

Minhag, 10:49, 14:**265–278**, 18:605
- halakhah and, 8:254, 10:773
- mistakes, 14:369
- as a source of law, 14:266–269, 338

Minhagei Maharil (Moellin), 14:414

Minhag Elzos, 2:6

Minhagim books, 4:76, 14:**278–280**

Minḥah, 14:**280–281**
- Amidah, 2:72, 74, 75

Minḥ Aharon (Aaron ben Meir Brisker), 1:216

Minḥah Belulah (Porto), 16:406, 407

Min ha-Masorah el Reshit ha-Milona'ut ha-Ivrit (Dotan), 5:763

Minḥat Avraham (Shapira), 18:399

Minḥat Eliyahu (Elijah ben Solomon Abraham ha-Kohen of Smyrna), 6:341

Minḥat ha-Omer, 1:260

Minḥat Ḥinnukh (Babad), 3:**15**

Minḥat Kena'ot (Pisa), 16:185

Minḥat Kena'ot (Abba Mari), 1:230, 2:530

Minḥat Shai (Jedidiah Solomon Raphael ben Abraham), 13:652–653

Minḥat Shai (Norzi), 15:313

Minḥat Yehudah (Ḥayyat), 8:479

Minḥat Yehudah (Alkalai), 1:663–664

Minḥat Yehudah (Schreiber), 8:735

Min ha-Zekenim. *See* Del Vecchio

Min ha-Zekenim, Shabbetai el-Hanan ben Elisha. *See* Del Vecchio, Shabbetai el-Hanan ben Elisha

Minhelet ha-Am, 11:775

Minim ve-Ugav (Zweifel), 21:693

Minis, Abraham, 14:281

Minis, Philip, 14:281

Minis family, 14:**281**

Minkin, Jacob Samuel, 14:**281**

Minkoff, Nahum Baruch, 4:6, 14:**281–282**

Minkowski, Eugène, 14:**282**

Minkowski, Hermann, 12:458, 13:678, 14:**282**

Minkowski, Pinchas, 14:**282–283**

Minkowski, Pinie. *See* Minkowski, Pinchas

Minneapolis-St. Paul (MN), 14:**283–285**

Minnesota (U.S.), 7:196–197, 14:**285–286**

Minnesota Center for Philosophy of Science, 6:735

Minnith, 14:**286**

Minor, Joseph. *See* Minor, Osip S.

Minor, Osip S., 14:**286**, 518

Minor, Solomon Zalman, 14:**286**, 517

Minor, Zalkind. *See* Minor, Solomon Zalman

Minorca, 14: **286–287**

Minority. *See* Majority rule

Minority Bloc, 14:**287–288**

Minority rights, 5:72–73, 14:**288–291**

Minor Prophets, 14:**291–292**

Minors, puberty, 16:695–696
- *See also* Child marriages

Minor tractates, 4:292–293, 14:**292–293**

Minow, Newton Norman, 14:**293**

Minram family. *See* Maymeran family

Minsk (Belarus), 14:**293–297**
- community archives, 2:408
- hanging of Jewish partisans, 9:474
- partisans, 15:667

Minsk Conference, 14:**297**

Minsker, Sender. *See* Polachek, Sender

Minski, Nikolai Maximovich, 14:**297**

Mińsk Mazowiecki (Poland). *See* Minsk Mazowiecki (Poland)

Minsk Mazowiecki (Poland), 14:**297–298**

Minsky, Louis, 14:**298**

Minstrelsy, 14:657–658, *658*

Mint, vol. 16: color insert

Mintchine, Abraham, 14:**298**

Mintmasters and moneyers, 14:**298–301**
- Court Jews, 5:246–247

Mintmasters and moneyers, *continued*
  Denis, Albertus, 5:580
  Levi, Gerd, 12:627
  Poland, 16:288–289
  See also Banking; Coins and
    currency; Court Jews; Medalists;
    Moneylending; Numismatics
Mintz, Alan, 18:207
Mintz, Moses ben Isaac, 12:462,
  14:**301**
Mintz, Paul, 12:521, 14:**301–302**
Mintz, Shlomo, 14:**302**
Minutes (Elisheva), 6:354
Minuty (Elisheva). *See Minutes*
  (Elisheva)
Minyan, 14:**302**
Minyan (Shapiro), 18:407
Minyat Zifta (Egypt), 14:**302–303**
Minz, Abraham ben Judah ha-Levi,
  14:**303**
    Abraham ben Moses ha-Kohen
      ha-Sephardi, 1:308
Minz, Benjamin, 14:**303**
Minz, Judah ben Eliezer ha-Levi,
  14:**303**
Minz, Moses ben Isaac ha-Levi. *See*
  Muenz, Moses ben Isaac ha-Levi
Miqdash. *See* Tabernacle
Miqra' soferim, 13:609
Mir (Belarus), 14:**304–305**
Mirabeau, Honore Gabriel Riqueti,
  2:8, 213
Mirabeau, Honore Gabriel Riqueti,
  Comte de, 14:**305**
Miracle Mongers and Their Methods
  (Houdini), 9:568
Miracles, 14:**305–310**
  Elijah, 6:333
  Elisha, 6:350–351
  Elisha Ba'al Kenafayim, 6:351
  Ḥoni ha-Me'aggel, 9:518–519
  Mordecai of Neskhiz, 14:482
  Moses, 14:524, 527, 530
  See also Signs and symbols
Miracle working. *See* Hagiography
Miranda, Salomon Rodrigues de,
  14:**310**, 16:345, 18:705
Miranda de Ebro (Spain), 14:**310**
Mirandola, Giovanni Pico della. *See*
  Pico della Mirandola, Giovanni
Miransky, Peretz, 14:**310–311**
Mirele Efros (Gordin), 18:370
Mirelman, David, 14:311
Mirelman, Jose, 14:311
Mirelman, Leon, 14:311
Mirelman, Roberto, 14:311
Mirelman, Simon, 14:311

Mirelman, Victor, 14:311
Mirelman family, 14:**311**
Miriam (biblical figure), 14:**311–312**
  Aaron and, 1:208, 209, 210
  Abraham's bosom, 1:316–317
  dance, 5:409
  Moses, 14:523–531
  Passover observance and, 15:681,
    682
Miriam (Daughter of Rashi), 17:102,
  102*t*, 105–106
Miriam (mother of Jesus). *See* Mary
  (mother of Jesus)
Miriam bat Benayah, 14:**312**
Miriamne II, 4:33
Mirisch, Harold. *See* Mirisch brothers
Mirisch, Marvin. *See* Mirisch brothers
Mirisch, Walter. *See* Mirisch brothers
Mirisch brothers, 14:**312–313**
Mirisch Co., 14:312
Mirkevet ha-Mishneh (Chelm), 4:589
Mirkin, Moshe Aryeh, 14:471
Mirkin, Shlomo. *See* Morag, Shlomo
Mirles, David. *See* Fraenkel, David ben
  Naphtali Hirsch
Miron, Dan, 8:732, 14:**313**, 331
Miron, Issachar, 14:**313–314**
Mironov, P.G., 3:770
Miroslav (Czech Republic), 14:**314**
Mirovská, Inna. *See* Rottová, Inna
Mirowski, Michel, 14:**314**
*The Mirror and the Lamp: Romantic
  Theory and the Critical Tradition*
  (Abrams), 1:327
The Mirror Has Two-Faces, 3:30
Mirsky, Aaron, 14:**314–315**
Mirsky, Jacob, 15:516
Mirsky, Samuel Kalman, 14:**315**
Mirtala (Orzeszkowa), 15:501
Mir Trogn A Gesang (Mlotek). *See* The
  New Book of Yiddish Songs
  (Mlotek)
Mirvish, David, 14:315
Mirvish, Edwin, 14:315
Mirvish family, 14:**315**
*Mir Zaynen Do: Lider fun di getos un
  lagern* (Mlotek). *See Here We Are:
  Songs of the Holocaust* (Mlotek)
Mi-Saviv la-Nekuddah (Brenner),
  4:160
Mischlinge. *See* Partial Jews
*Mi-Sefer ha-Zikhronot shel Shelomo
  ha-Elkoshi* (Epstein). *See From
  Shelomo ha-Elkoshi's Book of
  Reminiscences* (Epstein)
Mises, Ludwig Edler von, 14:**315**
The Misfits (motion picture), 14:450–
  451

Misgav Am (Israel), 14:**315–316**
Misgeret, 14:503
Mishael. *See* Shadrach, Mishach,
  Abed-Nego
Mishael (Book of Daniel), 5:418, 419
Mishael (Seri), 18:310
Mishale ben Uzziel, 13:650
Mishawayh. *See* Meshwi Al-Ukbari
Mishcon, Victor, Baron, 14:**316**
Mishcon de Reya (law firm), 14:316
Mi she-Berakh, 14:**316**
Mishḥa de-Ravevata (Alfasi), 1:638
Mishkan. *See* Tabernacle
Mishkan Tefillah, 13:138
Mishkan T'filah, 4:546
Mishkovsky, Zelda. *See* Zelda
Mishle. *See* Proverbs, Book of
Mishlei. *See* Proverbs, Book of
Mishlei Irasto (Uziel), 6:668
Mishlei Sendabar, 6:668, 7:13, 18:632
Mishlei Shu'alim (Berechiah), 3:406–
  407
Mishlei Shu'alim (Berechiah ben
  Natronai ha-Nakdan), 6:437, 667–
  668
Mishlei Sindbad. See Mishlei Sendabar
Mishmar ha-Emek (Israel), 14:**316**
Mishmar ha-Emek, battle for, Amit,
  Meir, 2:80
Mishmar ha-Negev (Israel), 14:**316**
Mishmar ha-Sharon (Israel), 14:**317**
Mishmar ha-Yarden (Israel), 14:**317**,
  20:661
Mishmarot (Israel), 14:**317**
Mishmarot and Ma'amadot, 14:**317–
  319**
Mishmeret ha-Bayit (Adret), 1:215, 423
Mishmerot Kehunnah (Lara), 12:493
Mishna, dyeing, 6:77
Mishnah, 14:**319–331**, 19:472*t*, 473*t*
  Abendana, Jacob ben Joseph,
    1:251
  Abraham ben David of
    Posquières, 1:297
  Aggadah, 14:322–323
  am ha-arez, 2:66–67
  amoraic period, 14:327–328
  amoraim, 2:89
  Amorites, 2:97
  androgyny, 2:145
  animals, 2:167, 172
  apes, 2:254
  Arakhin, 2:336
  Aramaic influences, 2:356
  Avot, 6:525
  baraita, 3:124–127

Bar Kappara, 3:155
Bava Batra, 3:223–224
Bava Kamma, 3:224–226
Bava Metzia, 3:226–227
Bekhorot, 3:275–276
Bikkurim, 3:697
blasphemy in, 3:741
blemishes in, 3:750
Book of Life, 4:69
burial customs, 4:292–293
codification of law, 4:767–768
commentary
    Adeni, Solomon bar Joshua,
        1:390
    Bertinoro, Obadiah ben
        Abraham Yare, 3:491–492
concordances, 11:822
defined, 14:319–320
demai, 5:547
desecration, 5:601–602
development of, 13:776
division of Torah into verses,
    13:610
dyeing, 6:76
ecology and, 6:95
editions, translations, and aids,
    14:330–331
Eduyyot, 6:214–215
'eglah 'arufah, 6:220–221
Eleazar ben Pedat, 6:306
Eleazar ben Shammua, 6:307
Eliezer ben Hyrcanus, 6:325
Eliezer ben Jacob (1st century),
    6:326
Elijah ben Solomon Zalman,
    6:344–345
environmental responsibility,
    6:449
Epstein, Jacob Nahum, 6:472
Eruvin (tractate), 6:485–486
famine in, 6:707–708
final redaction, 10:152–153
format and style, 4:768
hakhel, 8:247
Halakhah, 13:89–90, 14:321–322
Ḥallah, 8:278
Hallel ha-Gadol, 8:280
Hebrew manuscripts, 13:489–490
Italian commentary on, first, 10:44
Jacob in, 11:34
Judah ha-Nasi, 11:504
Kasovsky, Chaym Yehoshua,
    11:822
Kelim, 12:69
Keritot, 12:85
Ketubbot, 12:98–99

Kiddushin, 12:145–146
Kilayim, 12:154
Kinnim, 12:178
legal maxims, 12:603–604
as literature, 14:320–321
Maimonides, Moses, 13:385–386
mathematics in, 13:671–673
mediation in, 13:719
Megillah, 13:768
Me'ilah, 13:**775**
Menaḥ, 14:**27–28**
Middot (tractate), 14:180–181
Mikva'ot, 14:**224**
minor tractates, 14:292–293
mishpat Ivri, 14:346
mixed species, 14:386–387
modern interpretation, 14:329–330
Mo'ed, 14:413
Mo'ed Katan, 14:413–414
moneylending, 14:437–438
monogamy, 14:448
Moses, 14:533–534
Nashim, 14:783, 15:52–54
Nazir, 15:44–45
Nezikin, 15:246–247
Niddah, 15:258–259
oaths, 15:361
Oholot, 15:394
Omer, 15:420
Orlah, 15:475
Parah, 15:630
peaches in, 15:704
as philosophy and not theology,
    16:73–74
Rabbah bar Naḥamani, 17:9
redaction of, 14:326–327
religious impact of Bible and,
    3:662
Rieger, Paul, 17:293–294
Sanhedrin, 18:23–24
Seder, 15:678–679
Shas, 18:235, 419–420
Shema reading, 18:454
Shevi'it, 18:472
Shevu'ot, 18:472–473
Sikarikon, 18:573–574
Simeon ben Lakish, 14:413
sources of, 14:324–326
summaries, 13:786
Tannaitic Halakhah, 14:323–324
Tohorot, 15:55
tractates, 13:667, 15:704–705
traditional interpretation, 14:328–
    329
See also Simeon ben Gamaliel II of
    Jabneh

Mishnah de-Rabbi Akiva (Egar), 6:218
Mishnaic literature
    advertising, misrepresentation,
        5:188
    air pollution, 5:167
    commentary, 8:797–798
    cotton, 5:238
    crowns and wreaths, 5:308–309
    figs, 7:18
    Gemilut Ḥasadim, 7:427
    genealogy, 7:431
    geonic commentaries, 7:492
    Gittin, 7:620–621
    Gnostic speculation probition,
        11:590
    grazing rights, 5:167
    ḥaver ir, 8:470
    Kallah, 11:741
    plants and products of plants,
        16:220t–225t
    Sukkah, 19:298–299
    Ukẓin, 20:239
    usury, 20:442
    virgin, virginity, 20:539–540
    vocalization, 7:465
    wages for services, 5:185
    Yadayim, 21:264
    Yevamot, 21:323–325
    Yoma, 21:381–382
    Zavim, 21:463–464
    Zera'im, 21:515
    Zevahim, 21:518
*Mishnat Eliezer. See Midrash of 32
    Hermeneutic Rules*
Mishnat ha-Gra (Elijah ben Solomon
    Zalman), 6:345
Mishnat ha-Middot, 13:672, 14:**331**
*Mishnat Melekhet ha-Mishkan. See
    Baraita de-Melekhet ha-Mishkan*
Mishneh Torah (Maimonides), 4:770–
    773, 776, 777, 778, 13:5, 387–388,
    17:243, 19:37
    Alfasi family, 1:638
    business ethics, 4:307
    copyright of, 8:451
    Rosanes, Judah ben Samuel,
        disquisitions on, 17:422
    Solomon ben Abraham of
        Montpelier, 18:770
Mishnet Torah. See Deuteronomy
Mishol, Agi, 14:**331**
Mishpacha, 8:472
Mishpaḥ ha-Adamah (Smilansky),
    18:687
Mishpat ha-Shalom ha-Ivri, 14:352
Mishpat Ivri, 14:**331–363**
    Aaron ben Elijah, 1:212

Mishpat Ivri, *continued*

Aaron ben Jacob ha-Kohen of Lunel, 1:213–214

Aaron ben Joseph ha-Levi, 1: 214–215

Aaron ben Judah Kusdini, 1:216

Abbas, Moses Judah ben Meir and, 1:232

Abbasi, Jacob ben Moses ibn and, 1:233

abduction, 1:241–243

ablution, 1:261–263

abortion, 1:270–273

acquisition, 1:359–363

admission, 1:410–411

adoption, 1:417–418

adultery, 1:425–427

agency, 1:449–454

apostasy, 2:275–277

apotropos, 2:278–279, 281–283

appeals, 2:283

artificial insemination, 2:532–533

assignment of debt, 2:603–605

attorneys, 2:648

bigamy and polygamy, 3:691–694

Birkat ha-Torah, 3:712

birth control, 3:723

blindness in, 3:754–755

blood-avengers, 3:772–773

branches of law, 14:346–348

cancellation of claims, debts, rights, 13:770–771

capital punishment, 4:446–451

Caro, Joseph ben Ephraim, 4:489–490

castration, 4:516–517

codification, 4:766–767, 11:30

contradictions in, 6:644

criminal responsibility, 15:720–723

damages, 2:751–753, 5:385–389

Damascus, Book of the Covenant of, 5:398–399

definintion and terminology, 14:332–333

de-oraita and de-rabbanan, 14:335–336

Deuteronomy, Book of and, 5:617

dina de-malkhuta dina and, 5:663–669

divine origin, 6:616–617

divorce, 5:711–719

dowry, 5:769

duress, 15:721–722

emancipation period, 14:351–352

Englard, Yitzhak, 6:432

evidence, 6:**577–584**

evolution of laws, 14:344–346

exceptions to penalties, 15:722–723

extrajudicial redress, 6:630–631

family, 6:691

fines, 7:27–29

fire, 7:43

firstborn, 7:45–48

first fruits, 7:49

forced conversion, 15:721–722

foreign law, 14:349–351

forgery, 7:126–127

government, legitimacy of, 13:782

historical periods, 14:339–341

human rights, 17:309–332

ignorance of, 15:723, 724

intermarriage, 14:376–377

Israel (state)

Hebrew language, 14:353–354

position of Jewish law, 14:354–358

rabbinical courts, 14:352–353, 362

status of law, 14:358–362

Jerusalem as special case, 11:210, 211

joint ownership in, 15:671–672

labor, 12:415–419

laws of life and practice, 14:341–344

leadership in development of law, 14:348–349

legal persons, 15:672

lien, 12:812–816

literature, 14:345–346

marriage, civil, 4:746–748

matrimonial, 13:**680–683**

mediation, 13:718–720

medical, 13:738–757

artificial insemination, 13:751–753

euthanasia, 13:743–746

organ transplantation, 13:746–751

patients' rights, 13:739–743

physicians' duties, 13:739–741

in vitro fertilization, 13:755–756

medieval English, 11:34

morals and laws, 14:334–335

nationalism, 14:352–354

Noachide laws in, 15:285–287

norm of, 14:338–339

nuisance, 15:327–329

on oaths, 15:362–364

Ona'ah, 15:423–426

onanism, 15:426–427

ones, 15:427–431

oppression, 15:452–453

Oral Law, 11:269

ordeal, 15:462–463

orphans and orphanages, 15:483–484

ownership, 15:551–552

parent and child in, 15:635–638

partnerships in, 15:669–673

Paul's attitude towards, 15:697

perjury, 15:**772–773**

Phinehas, 16:115

privacy rights, 6:583–584

property, 8:753–755

punishment in, 15:723–724

real estate, 13:707–708

ritual and civil law, 14:333–334

Sanhedrin (tractate) on, 18:23

severence pay, 8:166–168

similarity of Torah to treaties of ancient era, 15:744–745, 751

slander, 18:663–665

Slavery, 18:667–670

sources, 11:267, 268

sources of law, 14:336–339

Supreme Court case law, 2:281–283, 597–598

transmission context, 15:733

war, 15:739

women in, 6:755

Zionism, 14:352–354

See also Appeals; Arbitration; Gulak, Asher; Halakhah; Law, Jewish; Obligations, law of; Oral Law; Talmudic law

Mishpat Kohen (Kook), 17:235

Mishpat Pythagoras (Alterman), 8:720

Mishpat Shalom (Abramovitsh), 1:319

Mishpeh Soferim (Albeck), 1:587

Mishpetei ha-Ḥerem (Naḥmanides), 14:743

Mishpetei Ketubbah (Eliezer ben Joel ha-Levi of Bonn), 6:327

Mishpetei Shemu'el (Kalai), 11:729

Di Mishpokhe Mashber (Der Nister), 5:596, 597

Mi-Shut ba-Merḥakim (Bialik), 3:562

Mi-Sinai Niggunim, 14:*363*, **363–364**

Miška, Marcus ben Samuel. *See* Meisel, Mordecai ben Samuel

Miška, Marx ben Samuel. *See* Meisel, Mordecai ben Samuel

Miška, Mordecai ben Samuel. *See* Meisel, Mordecai ben Samuel

Miskolc (Hungary), 14:**364**

Misogynism, 1:313–314, 11:487–488, 16:63–64

Miṣr. *See* Egypt

Misraki. *See* Mizraḥi

Misrephoth-Maim, 14:**364**

Missile Crisis (Abel), 1:245

Missionaries

    Alexander, Michael Solomon, 1:623–624

    Anselm of Canterbury, 2:181

    Bossuet, Jacques Benigne, 4:99

    Christianity, 4:238–239

    Fioghi, Fabiano, 7:41

    Hirschensohn-Lichtenstein, Jehiel Ẓevi Hermann, 9:136

    Italy, 4:94

    Protestants, 4:366, 16:629–630, 632

    Schick, Conrad, 18:126

    See also Apostasy

Missionary sermons, 15:580

Mississippi (U.S.), 14:**364–366**, *365*, 365*t*

Misslitz (Czech Republic). *See* Miroslav (Czech Republic)

Missouri (U.S.), 14:*366*, **366**, 366*t*

Mistakes, 14:**366–369**

Mistra. *See* Sparta

Mitah yafah. *See* Euthanasia

Mitau (Latvia). *See* Jelgava (Latvia)

Mitava (Latvia). *See* Jelgava (Latvia)

Mitchell, Alice. *See* Rivlin, Alice

Mitchell, Yvonne, 14:**369**

Mitelberg, Louis. *See* Tim

Mithḥam Oyev (Ben-Ner), 3:368

Mithradates. *See* Mithredath

Mithredath, 14:**370**

Mithridates, Flavius, 1:502, 2:130, 14:**370–371**

Mitin, Mark Borisovich, 14:**371**

Mitnaddevei Ḥuẓ la-Areẓ. *See* Maḥal

Mitnaggedim, 8:410, 14:**371**, 621

    in Brest-Litovsk, 4:169

    David of Makow, 5:474

    Ostrow Mazowiecka, dispute between Hasidim and Mitnaggedim in, 15:514

Mitpaḥat Sefarim (Emden), 6:393

Mitpaḥat Soferim (Duschinsky), 6:64

Mitpaḥot, 4:73

Mittanni, land of, 9:626–628

Mitteilhungen des Gesamtarchivs der Deutschen Juden, 2:407

Mittelman, Judah, 1:223, 2:556

Mittwoch, Eugen, 14:**371–372**

Mitz, Phoebe, 18:763

Mitzvah, 14:**372**

    Amsterdam, 2:116

dance, 5:411

duty and duties, 6:72–73

    Kavvanah, 12:40

    loans, 13:149

    sick, visiting the, 18:543–544

    See also Commandments

Mi'ut and ribbui rules, 9:28

Mivḥar ha-Peninim (Gabirol), 13:111, 14:**372–373**

Mivḥar ha-Shirah ha-Ivrit ha-Ḥadashah (Barash), 3:136–137

Mivḥar ve-Ḥadashim (Mishol). *See* Selection and New Poems (Mishol)

Mivrak (periodical), 2:78

Mivtaḥyah (bride), 6:312

Mix, Ron. *See* Mix, Ronald Jack

Mix, Ronald Jack, 14:**373**

Mixed marriages, 14:**373–385**

    Amsterdam, 2:114

    Canada, 4:417

    in colonial-period New York City, 15:197

    Conservative Judaism, 14:376–377

    Drachsler, Julius, 6:6

    Israel (state), 14:376

    Jewish identity and, 11:292, 298

    Joseph and Asenath, 11:418

    by Judaizers, 11:522

    legal aspects, 14:376

    Nuremberg laws, 15:348–350

    prevention, 14:376

    Reform Judaism, 14:376–377

    size of community, 14:374–376

    social factors, 14:373–374

    statistics, 14:373, 374*t*, 20:555*t*

    world-wide, 14:382–385

    See also Marriages

Mixed species, 14:**385–387**

Mi-Zimrat Kedem (Siroussi, ed.), 8:504

Mizmor le-David, 14:**387**

Mizmor Shir le-Yom ha-Shabbat, 14:**387**

Mizpah (ancient Israel). *See* Mizpeh or Mizpah (ancient Israel)

Mizpah (Israel), 14:**387–388**

Mizpeh of Moab (ancient Israel), 14:**388**

Mizpeh or Mizpah (ancient Israel), 14:**388**

Mizpeh Ramon (Israel), 14:**388**

Mizra (Israel), 14:**388**

Mizrachi, 14:**389–392**

    Abramowitz, Dov Baer, 1:324

    Amiel, Moshe Avigdor, 2:77

    Bettelheim, Samuel, 3:552

    Bloch, Chaim Isaac, 3:758

Churgin, Pinkhos, 4:723

Dolgin, Simon Arthur, 5:735

Don-Yaḥia, Yehudah Leib, 5:752

Duenner, Joseph Ẓevi Hirsch, 6:41

Galicia, 6:675, 727–728

Ha-Poel ha-Mizrachi, 8:338–340

Juedische Presse as official organ in Germany, 11:570

Landau, Leibush Mendel, 12:464

Landau, Shemuel Ḥayyim, 12:466

Minsk Conference, 14:297

Mizrachi Women's Organization of America, 2:80

Orthodox Judaism, development of, 15:494

Pick, Ḥayyim Hermann, 16:146

Pinkas, David Ẓvi, 16:169

Poland, 6:714, 16:305

Rabin, Israel Abraham, 17:33

Rubinstein, Isaac, 17:517

Shapira, Ḥayyim Moshe, 18:400

Shapira, Yeshayahu, 18:402

Slucki, Abraham Jacob, 18:685

Soloveitchik, Joseph Baer, 18:778

    See also Zionism

Mizrachi, Shimon, 14:**392**

Mizrachi Organization of America, 4:6

Mizrachi Teachers' Seminary, 13:72

Mizrachi Women's Organization of America (AMIT), 2:**80**

Mizraḥ, 14:**392–393**

Mizrahi, Asher, 1:440, 14:**393**

Mizrahi, Haninah, 14:**395**

Mizraḥi, Abraham, 6:22

Mizraḥi, David ben Shalom, 14:**393**

Mizraḥi, Elijah, 13:675, 14:**393–395**, 15:534, 537, 19:315

Mizraḥi, Elijah ben Abraham. *See* Mizraḥi, Elijah

Mizraḥi, Gershon, 14:**394**

Mizraḥi, Israel, 14:**394**

Mizraḥi, Reuben, 14:**394**

Mizraḥ paper-cuts, 15:615

Mizrayim, 14:**395**

Mizvot he-Areẓ (Kahana), 11:711

MJH: ALMTTH. *See* Museum of Jewish Heritage: A Living Memorial to the Holocaust

Mlada Boleslav (Czech Republic), 14:**395**

Mlava (Poland). *See* Mlawa (Poland)

Mlawa (Poland), 14:**395–396**

Mlot, Jan. *See* Dickstein, Szymon

Mlotek, Chana, 14:**396–397**

Mlotek, Joseph, 14:**396**

MLP (Mental Health Law Project), 3:234

Mława (Poland). *See* Mlawa (Poland)

Mnaseas of Patara, 14:**397**

Die Mneme (Semon), 18:286

The Mneme (Semon). *See* Die Mneme (Semon)

Mnemonics or memora technica, 14:**397–398**

Mnouchkine, Alexandre, 14:**398–399**

Mnouchkine, Ariane, 14:399

Mo. *See* Rene, Roy

Moab (Jordan), 14:*401*
 alphabet, Hebrew, 1:694*t,* 695
 Amalekites, 2:29
 Chemosh, god of Moabites, 4:594
 Ehud, 6:245
 Israelite encampment on plains of, 15:331–332
 Kir-Hareseth, 12:184–185
 Mesha, 14:75
 Mesha Stele, 14:75–76
 Moses, 14:528, 529
 See also Rabbath-Moab (ancient Israel)

Moab (Transjordan), 14:**399–404**

Moab-Ammon (Transjordan), 10:129

Moabite language, 18:284, 285

Moabite Stone. *See* Mesha Stele

Moartea unei republici roşii (Aderca), 1:391

Moati, Serge, 14:**404**

Mobsters, 5:479, 12:485–486, 504

Mocatta, Abraham, 14:404

Mocatta, Alan Abraham, 14:404

Mocatta, David, 2:400, 14:404

Mocatta, Edgar, 14:404

Mocatta, Frederick David, 14:404

Mocatta, Isaac Lindo, 14:404

Mocatta, Moses (diamond broker), 14:404

Mocatta, Moses (scholar), 14:404

Mocatta, Rebecca, 14:404

Mocatta family, 14:**404**

Mocatta library, 2:408

Moch, Jules, 14:**404**, 16:343, 18:705

Moch, Jules Salvador, 14:**404–405**

Mocha (Yemen), 14:**405**

Moda'ah, 15:428–429, 430–431

Modai, Ḥayyim, 14:**405–406**

Modai, Yitzhak, 14:**406**

Modal music, synagogue, 14:663–664, *664*

Modeh Ani, 14:**406**

Model, Marx, 14:**406–407**

Model Homes Company, 18:289

Modell, Art. *See* Modell, Arthur B.

Modell, Arthur B., 14:**407**

A Model World, and Other Stories (Chabon), 4:555

Modena (Italy), 14:**407–408**
 See also Finale Emilia

Modena, Aaron Berakhiah. *See* Aaron Berechiah ben Moses of Modena

Modena, Angelo, 14:**408**

Modena, Avtalyon, 14:**408**

Modena, bat Sheva. *See* Modena, Fioretta

Modena, Fioretta, 14:**408**

Modena, Leon, 13:287, 14:**408–410**
 alchemy, 1:602–603
 apologetics, 2:267
 autobiography, 13:110–111
 bibliography of, 3:681
 cantatas and choral works, Hebrew, 4:433
 cardplaying, 4:467
 Ḥayyei Yehudah, 3:706, 7:15, 14:410
 Italian translation of Bible by, 3:633

Modena, Samuel. *See* Medina, Samuel ben Moses de

Modena, Solomon, 14:408

Moderation
 in etiquette, 6:539
 in sex, 18:329

Modern, Judah, 14:**410**

Modern British Jewry (Alderman), 1:606

Modern dance, 5:414–415

Modern German Literature (Eloesser), 6:366

Modern Hebrew calligraphy, 4:366–373, **366–373**
 education, 4:367–368
 England, 4:372–373
 history, 4:366–367
 Israel, 4:369–371
 U.S., 4:371–372

Modernity and the Holocaust (Bauman), 3:220, 9:418

Modern Language Bible (MLB), 3:616

Modern Library, 13:143

Modern Orthodox Judaism, 15:497–499
 halakhlic responsa, 6:742
 Kaddish recitation by women, 11:698
 Kamenetsky, Yaakov, 11:752

Modern Philosophies of Judaism (Agus), 1:521

Modern Research as Illustrating the Bible (Driver), 6:22

Modern Russian Art (Lozowick), 13:239

Modern Russian Literature from Chekov to the Present (Slonim), 18:677

Modesty. *See* Humility

Modiano, Patrick, 14:**410–411**

Modigliani, Amedeo, 14:**411**, 15:478, 648, 18:223

Modigliani, Enrico, 16:345

Modigliani, Franco, 14:**411**

Modigliani, Guiseppe, 16:345

Modigliani, Vittorio Emanuele, 14:411

Modi'im (Israel). *See* Modi'in (Israel)

Modi'in (Israel), 14:**411–412**

Modim de-Rabbanan, 2:74

Modon (Greece), 14:**412–413**

Modzhitz, Saul Jedidiah Eleazar, 14:413

Modzhitz dynasty, 14:**413**

Mo'ed, 13:768, 14:**413**, 18:401

Mo'ed Katan (tractate), 14:**413–414**

Mo'ed Mo'adim (Filipowski), 7:20

Das Moeglichkeitsproblem der Kritik der reinen Vernunft, der modernen Phaenomenologie und der Gegenstandstheorie (Baumgardt), 3:221

Moellin, Jacob ben Moses, 7:211, 12:462, 14:**414–415**, 18:390

Mo'ezet Gedolei ha-Torah, 1:506

Mo'ezet ha-Po'alot, 14:**415**

Mofaz, Shaul, 14:**415**

Mogador (Morocco), 1:444, 14:**415–416**

Moghrabi, 5:470

Mogilev (Belarus), 14:**416–418**

Mogilev-Podolski (Ukraine), 14:**418**

Mogul, The. *See* Gottlieb, Edward

Mogulesko, Sigmund, 14:**418**

Mogulesko, Zelig. *See* Mogulesko, Sigmund

Mohácsi, Jenö, 14:**418**

Mohamed VI, King of Morocco, 1:580

Mohammad. *See* Muhammad

Mohammed. *See* Muhammad

Mohar. *See* Dowry

Mohar, Jehiel, 14:**420**

Mohar, Meir. *See* Mohr, Meir

Mohar betulot. *See* Dowry

Mohel. *See* Circumcision

Mohilever, Samuel. *See* Mohilewer, Samuel

Mohilewer, Josef, 14:**419**

Mohilewer, Samuel, 14:**418–419**, 15:277

Moholy-Nagy, László, 14:**419–420**

Mohr, Abraham Menahem Mendel, 4:27, 14:**420**

Mohr, Meir, 14:**420–421**

Moineşti (Romania). *See* Moinesti (Romania)

Moinesti (Romania), 14:**421**

Moïse (de Vigny), 14:540

Moïse (Montesquiou-Fézensac), 14:540

Moïse (opera, Rossini), 14:542

Moïse, Abraham, 14:**421**

Moïse, Penina, 14:**421**

Moïse, Theodore Sydney, 14:**421–422**

Moiseiwitsch, Benno, 14:**422**

Moiseiwitsch, Tanya, 14:**422**

Moisesville Teachers Seminary, 6:211

Moissan, Henri, 14:**422**

Moissis, Asher, 14:**422**

Moi universitety (Donskoy), 5:752

Mojecki, Przeclaw, 14:**423**

Mok, Maurits, 6:71

Mokady, Moshe, 14:**423**

Mokhi'aḥ ben Ḥayyim of Eisenstadt. *See* Mordecai ben Ḥayyim of Eisenstadt

Moladah (Israel), 14:**423**

Molcho, David Effendi Isaac Pasha, 14:**423**

Molcho, Solomon, 11:584, 14:**423–424**, 18:315

Ancona, 2:140

Moldavia. *See* Moldova

Moldova, 14:**424–425**

Brichany, 4:178

Holocaust, 4:178

Dubossary, 6:38

Kaushany, 12:37

Khotin, 12:117–118

Kiliya, 12:154

Kishinev, 12:199

Kotovskoye, 12:324

Leovo, 12:650

Lipkany, 13:64

Soroki, 19:30

Teleneshty, 19:594

Tiraspol, 19:729

Vad Rashkov, 20:457

Valea-Lui-Vlad, 20:459

Yedintsy, 21:292–293

Zguritsa, 21:521

Kaushany, 12:37

Kiliya, 12:154

Kishinev, 12:196–199

Novoselitsa, 15:322

Orgeyev, 15:468–469

Romanian history of, 117:375–377

Moledet (Israel), 14:**425**

Moles, 14:**425**

Molho, Isaac Raphael, 14:**425–426**

Molhov, Iako, 4:276

Molitor, Franz Joseph, 11:673, 14:**426**

Moller, Erich, 14:**426–427**. *See* Moller, Hans and Erich

Moller, Hans, 14:**426–427**

Molnár, Ákos, 14:**427**

Molnár, Ferenc, 14:**427**

Moloch, cult of, 2:84, 14:**427–429**

Molodechno (Belarus), 14:**429**

Molodowsky, Kadia, 14:**429–430**

Molodoy Tolstoy (Eichenbaum). *See Young Tolstoy* (Eichenbaum)

Moloka'i Free Press (newspaper), 13:29

Molokan sect, 11:521

Mombach, Israel, 4:660

Mombert, Alfred, 14:**430**

Der Moment (Yiddish newspaper), 8:476

Der Moment (newspaper), 14:**430**

Moment (Polish newspaper). *See Chwila*

Momigliano, Arnaldo Dante, 14:**430–431**

Momigliano, Attilio, 14:**431**

Momigliano, Felice, 14:**431**

Mommsen, Theodor, 11:578, 14:**431**

Monājāt-Nāmeh (Babai ben Luṭf, 3:15

Monarchy. *See* Kings and kingship

Monash, John. *See* Monash, Sir John

Monash, Sir John, 14:**432**

Monasterzyska (Ukraine). *See* Monastyriska (Ukraine)

Monastir (F.Y.R. of Macedonia), 14:**432–433**, 16:118

Monastyriska (Ukraine), 14:**433**

Monatsschrift Fuer Geschichte Und Wissenschaft Des Judentums (periodical), 4:129

Monatsschrift Fuer Geschichte und Wissenschaft Des Judentums (periodical), 14:**433–434**

Moncada, Guglielmo Raimondo. *See* Mithridates, Flavius

Moncada, Salvador, 13:10

I Moncalvo (Castelnuovo), 4:514

Moncalvo (Italy), 14:**434**

The Moncalvos. See I Moncalvo

Moncorvo (Portugal), 14:**434**

Mond, Alfred Moritz, 4:123, 14:**434–435**

Mond, Bernhard Stanislaw, 14:**435**

Mond, Henry, 14:**434–435**

Mond, Julian Edward Alfred, 14:**435**

Mond, Ludwig, 14:**434**

Monda, Virgiliu, 14:**435**

Monday and Thursday, 14:**435**

Mond family, 14:**434–435**

Mond Nickel Co., 14:434

Mondolfo, Rodolfo, 14:**435**

Mondzain, Simon, 14:**435**

Monefiore, Hugh, apostasy, 2:273, 274

Money, 20:441

See also Numismatics

The Money. See Ha-Mamon

Money changers, 3:112–113, 14:**435–436**

Arabs, Ṣarrāf, 18:61–62

Moneyers. *See* Mintmasters and moneyers

Moneylending, 3:112–119, 4:710, 745, 14:**436–443**

Bible, 14:436–437

development of, 6:555–556

economic doctrines, and interest for, 6:116–117

ethics, 6:116–117

formulas for, 10:78

France, 7:152, 14:462

geonic period, 14:438

Germany, 7:519–520

history of, 6:103, 106–107, 112–113, 14:441–443

illuminators of manuscripts supported by, 3:679

monti di pietà, 14:461

otherhood and brotherhood, 14:441

Poland, 16:293

Provence, France, 16:637

rabbinic period, 14:438–441

secondhand goods trade and, 18:231

stock exchanges, 19:230–231

Talmud, 14:437–438

U.K., 12:766, 801

See Also Banking and bankers; Economic history; Obligations, law of; Usury

Mongolia, 10:15, 14:**443**

Mongols, 1:234, 4:258, 14:**443–444**

Monis, Judah, 4:99, 8:735, 14:**444–445**

Monitors (animal), 14:**445**

"Monkey" (drypoint print, Moreh), 14:483

Monmouth County (NJ), 14:**445–447**

Monobaz I and II, 1:391, 392, 14:**447**

Monogamy, 14:**447–448**

See also Bigamy and polygamy

Monomachia sive certamen medicum (de Castro), 4:518

Monopoli, Marchisio da, 4:184

Monoszon, Elye I., 6:161

Monotheism, 7:669–670, 14:**448–450**, 15:750

Abraham, 1:283, 284, 286

Monotheism, *continued*
  Deuteronomy, Book of and, 5:618
  disputations, 5:687
  Judaism during biblical period, development of, 11:514
  Julian the Apostate and, 11:573
  Koran, 12:301
  Moses, 14:538
  See also Islam
Monroe, Marilyn, 4:112, 14:**450–451**
Monsanto, Isaac Rodriguez, 13:223
Monsey (NY), 17:360–361
Monsky, Harry, 4:16
Monsky, Henry, 14:**451**, 15:416
Monsky, Ẓevi. *See* Monsky, Henry
Monson (Spain). *See* Monzón (Spain)
Monsterus. *See* Muenster, Sebastian
Montagu, Edwin Samuel, 14:**451–452**, 16:342
Montagu, Ewen Edward, 14:451
Montagu, Lily, 14:**452**
Montagu, Louis Samuel, 14:451
Montagu, Montague Francis Ashley, 2:188, 14:**452–453**
Montagu, Samuel, 14:451
Montagu, Venetia Stanley, 14:452
Montagu family, 14:**451–452**
Montaigne, Michel de, 14:**453**
Montalcino, Cornelio de, 11:574
Montalto, Philotheus Eliajus, 13:729
Montana (U.S.), 14:**453–454**, *454,* 454t
Montano, Benito Arias, 12:601. *See* Arias Montano, Benito
Montclus (Spain), 14:**455**
Monte, Andrea del. *See* Sarfati, Joseph
Monte di Pietá
  in Bologna, 4:48
  in Orvieto, 15:500
  Padua, 15:566
Montefiore, Abraham, 14:457
Montefiore, Claude Joseph Goldsmid, 14:452, **455–456**
  Anglo-Jewish Association, 2:162
  Balfour Declaration, 2:162
  English translations of Bible, 3:614
  Jewish Quarterly Review, 11:313
Montefiore, Eliezer Levi, 1:385
Montefiore, Francis Abraham, 14:459
Montefiore, Hugh William, 14:459
Montefiore, Jacob, 14:457, 16:339–340
Montefiore, J.B. *See* Montefiore, Joseph Barrow
Montefiore, Joseph, 14:457
Montefiore, Joseph Barrow, 1:385, 14:**456**, 15:241–242
Montefiore, Joseph Elias, 14:457

Montefiore, Joseph Mayer, 14:457, 459
Montefiore, Joshua, 14:**456**
Montefiore, Judith, 14:**456**
Montefiore, Moses, 6:415, 8:747, 9:6–7, 15:529–530
  Board of Deputies of British Jews, 4:20
  bookplate of, 4:70
  Jerusalem and, 11:169, 170
  Moroccan Jews and, 14:499
  Mortara case, 14:513
  Persian Jews and, 15:790
  See Montefiore, Sir Moses
Montefiore, Moses Vita, 14:457
Montefiore, Nathaniel, 14:457
Montefiore, Sebag-Montefiore family, 2:682, 14:**457–459**, 458t
Montefiore, Sir Moses, 14:**457**
Montefiore College. *See* Judith Lady Montefiore College
Montélimar (France), 14:**459**
Montereau (France), 14:**459**
Montereau-Faut-Yonne (France). *See* Montereau (France)
Montes Pietatis. *See* Monti di Pietá
Montesquieu, Charles Louis de Secondat, Baron de la Brede et de, 14:**459–460**
Montesquiou-Fézensac, Ambroise Anatole de, 14:540
Monteux, Pierre, 14:**460**
Montevideo (Uruguay), 14:**460**
Montezinos, Antonio de, 14:**460**
Montezinos, David, 14:**460**
  as bibliophile, 3:684
Months. *See* Calendar; Year
Monti di Pietá, 14:**461**
Montiel (Spain), 14:**461**
Montini, Giovanni Battista. *See* Paul VI
Montisson (Spain). *See* Monzón (Spain)
Montor, Henry, 14:**461–462**
  State of Israel Bonds, 4:58
Móntoro, Antón de, 14:**462**
Montparnasse school of art, 15:647, 648, 649
Montpellier (France), 14:**462–463**
Montreal (Canada), 14:**463–466**
Montreal (QC), 2:41, 4:394–395
  education, 4:405, 6:210
  Finestone, Sheila, 7:30
  Jewish community leaders, 11:51
  Jewish history, 4:395–396
  kashrut supervision, 5:21
  literature, 4:423, 424
  philanthrophy, 5:481

Monument against Facism, 9:431
Monuments, 1:332, 12:473
  Holocaust, 9:429–432
Monument (Denkmal) to the Murdered Jews of Europe, 9:431
Monzón (Spain), 14:**466–467**
Monzon, Abraham, 14:**467**
Monzon, Abraham (18th c.), 14:467
Monzon, Abraham (d. after 1603), 14:467
Moon, 4:354–359, 14:**467–468**
  blessing of the, 14:**468**
Moonman, Eric, 14:**468–469**
Moonves, Les, 14:**469**
Moore, Deborah Dash, 9:152–153
Moore, George Foot, 14:**469**, 16:630, 17:241–242
Moorish Spanish art. *See* Spain, Moorish art and design
Mopp, 14:**469–470**, 15:443
Mopsik, Charles, 11:325, 14:**470**
La morada en el tiempo (Seligson), 18:268
Morag, Shlomo, 14:**470–471**
Morais, Sabato, 6:193, 11:328–329, 14:**471**
Moral behavior, religious observance vs., 10:59
Moral blemishes, 3:750
The Moral Conquest of Germany (Ludwig), 13:251
Morality
  Berkovits, Eliezer, 3:439
  dietary laws and, 5:656–657
  dualism, 6:29–30
  duty and duties, 6:72, 12:535–537
  Leibowitz, Yeshayahu, 12:624
  Misphat Ivri, 14:334–335
  moral virtue, 13:392
  perfection, 6:528
  standards of conduct, 5:592–593
  tales about, 6:599–600
  Trees of Life and of Knowledge in Eden narrative, 15:624–625
The Moral Life of the Hebrews (Smith, John Merlin Powis), 18:688
Moral Reproofs (Ezra ben Ezekiel ha-Bavli). *See* Tokhehot Musar
Moral rights, 8:453
Morava (Czech Republic). *See* Moravia (Czech Republic)
Moravchik, Moses, 6:177
Moravia (Czech Republic), 14:**471–476**, *473,* 473t, 475t, 18:682–683
  blood libel in, 3:776
  Chajes, Gershon ben Abraham, 4:558

Duschak, Mordecai, 6:64
historians, Flesch, Heinrich, 7:76
Holocaust, 14:476
Holocaust Period, 5:358–359
laws controlling Jewish
   population, 6:689–690
leather industry and trade,
   12:575–576
peddling in, 15:709
textiles, 19:663–664
Moravia, Alberto, 10:794, 14:**476–477**
Moravia, Holocaust
   Trebic, 20:124
   Trest, 20:134
   Uhersky Brod, 20:231
Moravska Ostrava (Czech Republic).
   See Ostrava
Moravske Budejovice (Czech
   Republic), 14:**477**
Moravské Budějovice (Czech
   Republic). *See* Moravske Budejovice
   (Czech Republic)
Moravský Krumlov (Czech Republic).
   See Moravsky Krumlov (Czech
   Republic)
Moravsky Krumlov (Czech Republic),
   14:**477**
Morawetz, Oskar, 14:**477–478**
Morawitz, Karl Ritter von, 14:**478**
Mordecai (5th c. B.C.E.), 8:292,
   14:**478–479**, 18:215–216, 217
Mordecai (biblical figure, Zerubbabel
   period), 14:478
Mordecai, Alfred (1804-1887), 14:**479–
   480**
Mordecai, Alfred (1840-1920), 14:**479–
   480**
Mordecai, George Washington, 15:302
Mordecai, Ḥayyim, 4:48
Mordecai, Jacob, 14:**480**, 15:302
Mordecai ben Eliezer Comtino. *See*
   Comtino, Mordecai ben Eliezer
Mordecai ben Ḥayyim of Eisenstadt,
   14:**480**
Mordecai ben Hillel ha-Kohen,
   14:**480–481**, 15:346, 347
Mordecai ben Judah ha-Levi, 14:**481–
   482**
Mordecai ben Manlin Dessau. *See*
   Magnus, Marcus
Mordecai ben Naphtali Hirsch of
   Kremsier, 14:**482**
Mordecai ben Nathan Nata Broda,
   4:193
Mordecai ben Nisan, 14:**482**
Mordecai ben Noah of. *See*
   Lachowicze, Mordecai ben Noah of
Mordecai ben Yeuzel Donath of Nitra,
   4:367

Mordecai family, 15:302
Mordecai Joseph Leiner of Izbica,
   10:824–825
Mordecai of Duesseldorf. *See*
   Halberstadt, Mordecai; Halberstadt,
   Mordechai
Mordecai of Izbica. *See* Mordecai
   Joseph Leiner of Izbica
Mordecai of Kremsier. *See* Mordecai
   ben Naphtali Hirsch of Kremsier
Mordecai of Lachowicze. *See*
   Lachowicze, Mordecai ben Noah of
Mordecai of Neskhiz, 14:**482**
Mordecai of Nesukhoyshe. *See*
   Mordecai of Neskhiz
Mordekai ha-Gadol (Mordecai ben
   Hillel ha-Kohen). *See Sefer
   Mordekhai* (Mordecai ben Hillel ha-
   Kohen)
The *Mordekhai* (Mordecai ben Hillel
   ha-Kohen). *See Sefer Mordekhai*
   (Mordecai ben Hillel ha-Kohen)
Mordekhai ha-Katan (Schlettstadt),
   14:**480–481**
Mordell, Louis Joel, 14:**482**
Mordell, Phinehas, 14:**482–483**
Mordkowski, Shmuel, 13:293
Mordovtsev, Daniil Lukich, 14:**483**
Mordvinov, Nicolai Semionovich,
   14:**483**
More, Hannah, 14:540
More, Mulla Elijahu Chayin, 11:558
Moreel, Ben, 14:**483**
Moreh, Mordecai, 14:**483–484**
Moreh, Shmuel, 14:**484**
Moreh ha-Lashon (Lerner), 12:657
Moreh ha-Moreh (Falaquera), 6:681–
   682, 8:552
Moreh Nevukhei ha-Zeman
   (Krochmal), 21:108
Moreh ẓedek. *See* Teacher of
   Righteousness
Moreinu ha-Rav Shelomo Eliezer. *See*
   Alfandari, Solomon Eliezer ben
   Jacob
Morell, S., 8:261
More Nevuké ha-Lašon (Shapiro),
   8:678
Moreno, Jacob L., 14:**484**
Morenu ha-Rav ibn Ḥayyim. *See*
   Elijah ben Ḥayyim
Morenu Ha-Rav Meir. *See* Lublin,
   Meir ben Gedaliah
Morenu Ha-Rav Meir Schiff. *See*
   Schiff, Meir ben Jacob ha-Kohen
Morenu ha-Rav Perez. *See* Perez ben
   Elijah of Corbeil
Morenu ha-Rav Shelomo Luria. *See*
   Luria, Solomon ben Jehiel

Morenu Ha-Rav Shemu'el Adels. *See*
   Edels, Samuel Eliezer ben Judah ha-
   Levi
Morenu Ha-Rav Shemu'el Kaidanover.
   See Koidonover, Aaron Samuel ben
   Israel
Morenzi, Isaiah, 4:270
Moreshet, 8:650, 14:**484–486**
Moresheth-Gath (ancient city), 14:**486**
Moreshet Publishing House, 14:484
More Wandering Stars (anthology),
   18:199
Morewski, Abraham, 14:**486**
Morgen Journal (daily newspaper). *See
   Jewish Morning Journal* (daily
   newspaper)
Morgenstern, Julian, 3:651, 14:**486–
   487**
Morgenstern, Lina, 14:**487**
Morgenstern, Oskar, 14:**487**
Morgenstern, Salomo. *See*
   Morgenstern, Soma
Morgenstern, Soma, 14:**487–488**
Morgentaler, Henry, 14:**488**
Morgenthau, Hans Joachim, 14:**489–
   490**
Morgenthau, Henry, Jr., 14:**489**,
   15:224
   State of Israel Bonds, 4:58
Morgenthau, Henry, Sr., 14:**488–489**
Morgenthau, Henry S.
   American Joint Distribution
      Committee, 2:59
   in Ottoman empire, 15:543
Morgenthau, Robert, 14:489, 15:224
Morgenthau Commission, 14:489, **490**
Morgenthau family, 14:**488–489**
Morgen-Zhurnal (daily newspaper).
   See Jewish Morning Journal (daily
   newspaper)
Morgn-Frayhayt (newspaper). *See
   Morning Freiheit* (newspaper)
Morgulis, Manasseh, 14:**490–491**
Morgulis, Mikhail. *See* Morgulis,
   Manasseh
Morhange (France), 14:**491**
Morhange, Charles Henri-Valentin.
   See Alkan, Charles Henri-Valentin
Morhange, Pierre, 14:**491**
Moriah (publishing house), 4:621,
   6:74, 14:**491**, 17:126
Moriah (unknown biblical location),
   14:**491**
Moriah, Angel of the Lord, 2:151
Móricz, Zsigmond, 15:614
Morin, Edgar, 14:**491–492**
Möring, Marcel, 6:71
Morning benedictions, 14:435, **492**
   See also Shaḥarit

"Morning Freedom" (newspaper). *See Morning Freiheit* (newspaper)

Morning Freiheit (newspaper), 6:475, 14:**492–493**

Morning Journal (daily newspaper). *See Jewish Morning Journal* (daily newspaper)

Morning of Fools. See Boker shel Shotim

Morning service. *See Shaḥarit*

Morocco, 2:306, 314, 320–322, 326, 327, 14:**493–507**, *494*
  Aaron ben Batash, 1:212
  Abendanan family, 1:251–252
  Abitbol family, 1:260
  Agadir, 1:444
  Alawid dynasty, 1:579–580
  aliyah, 2:646
  Alliance Israélite Universelle, 14:500, 502–503, 504, 505–507
  Amsterdam immigrants, 2:117
  amulets, 2:123
  antisemitism, 14:499, 501, 502–503
  bakkashot, 3:73
  Bibas family, 3:571–572
  Cabessa family, 4:329–330
  capitulations, 4:453
  Chriqui family, 4:673
  community, nature of, 5:112, 118
  community organization and structures, 5:108, 118t
    118t, 5:110
  demographics, 14:501, 504, 505
  divorce statistics in, 5:720
  Dra region, 6:5
  early history, 14:493–496, 497–500
  education, 14:500, 502, 505–507
  emigration to Israel, 11:288, 14:503–504
  emigration to Palestine from, 5:296, 470
  Fez, 7:6–8
  French Morocco, 14:500, 501, 502
  immigration to Israel from, 10:523
  important Jewish communities, 13:798–799
  Jewish music, 1:438–439
  Jewish quarters, 11:312
  Kabbalists, 11:620–621
  leading families, 13:702
  Mogador, 14:415–416
  museums, 14:627
  musical traditions, 1:438–439
  Muslim-Jewish relations, 14:504, 505
  mysticism, 14:496–497
  Ofran, 15:390–391
  photography of Jewish life, 16:129
  politics, 14:500–501, 502, 16:346
  population, medieval, 16:386
  population statistics, 14:499, 504, 505
  professions, 14:496, 498
  Rabbin délégué, 17:15
  rabbinical courts, 14:504
  relations with Israel, 14:505
  scholars, Moses ben Isaac Edrehi, 6:158
  Sijilmassa, 18:572–573
  social welfare, 14:502
  Spanish Morocco, 14:500, 501–502
  succession and inheritance laws, 19:289
  Tangier zone, 14:500, 502
  WW II, 14:501–502
  Zionism, 4:502, 14:501
  See also Azemmour

Morogowski, Jacob Samuel, 14:**507–508**

Morosini, Giulio, 14:**508**

Morphology in Hebrew, 8:574–577

Morpungo, Elijah, 14:508

Morpungo, Giuseppe Lazzaro, 14:508

Morpungo, Mosé, 14:508

Morpurgo, Abraham Vita, 14:508

Morpurgo, Benedetto, 14:508

Morpurgo, Edgardo (architect), 14:508

Morpurgo, Edgardo (historian), 14:508

Morpurgo, Elio, 14:508

Morpurgo, Emilio, 14:508

Morpurgo, Gino, 14:508

Morpurgo, Giulio, 14:508

Morpurgo, Giuseppe, 14:**509**

Morpurgo, Jacob, 14:509

Morpurgo, Luciano, 14:508

Morpurgo, Marco, 14:508

Morpurgo, Rachel Luzzatto, 14:508, **509**, 21:178–179

Morpurgo, Salomone, 14:508, **509**

Morpurgo, Samson ben Joshua Moses, 2:141, 14:508, **509–510**

Morpurgo, Vittorio, 14:508

Morpurgo family, 2:141, 14:**508–509**

Morris, Alvin. *See* Martin, Tony

Morris, Errol M., 14:**510**

Morris, Henry, 15:302

Morris, Henry Harris, 14:**510**

Morris, Ira Nelson, 14:511

Morris, Nathan, 14:**510–511**

Morris, Nelson, 14:**511**

Morris, R. H., 15:583

Morris, Richard Brandon, 14:**511**

Morris, William, 14:**511**

Morris and Sussex Counties (NJ), 14:**511–512**

Morrison, Herbert, 15:586

Morrison-Grady scheme for partition of Palestine, 15:586–588

Morse, David Abner, 14:**512–513**

Morse, Leopold, 14:**513**

Mortality and Morbidity after Excessive Stress (Eitinger), 6:279

Mortara, Edgardo
  abduction, 14:513
  Board of Delegates of American Israelites, 4:19
  Bologna, 4:49

Mortara, Lodovico, 12:552, 14:**513**

Mortara, Marco, 14:**513**

Mortara case, 3:122, 14:**513**, 15:199

Morteira, Saul Levi, 14:**514**
  Amsterdam Talmud Torah school, 2:109
  Andrade, Velosino Jacob de, 2:144

Mortensen, Norma Jean. *See* Monroe, Marilyn

Mortgage. *See* Pledge; Property

Mortifcation of the body, 8:388

Mortiz, Ricardo, 11:568

Morton, Louis C., 14:**514**

Mor u-Keẓi'ah (Emden), 6:392

Morvedre. *See* Murviedro

Morwitz, Edward, 14:**514**

Mosad Le-Aliyah Bet, 1:658

Mosaics
  Jacob in, 11:23
  Tower of Babel, 3:21

Mosbach (Germany), 14:**514–515**

Mosbacher, Emil, Jr, 14:**515**

Moscati, Sabatino, 14:**515**

Moscato, Judah ben Joseph, 14:**515–516**

Moscheles, Ignaz, 14:**516**

Mosconi, Judah Leon, 15:375

Moscovich, Cíntia, 4:152

Moscovici, A. *See* Toma, A.

Moscovici, Virgiliu. *See* Monda, Virgiliu

Moscovitch, Maurice, 14:**516**

Moscow (Russian Federation), 14:**516–521**

Moscow Cantorial Academy, 2:63

Moscow Chamber Orchestra, 3:178

Moscowitz, Ann. *See* Kross, Ann

Moscowitz family, 8:420

Moscow Jewish Theater, 2:22

Moscow Yiddish Theater, 8:275

Mosè (Orvieto), 14:541

Mosedei Ḥokhmah (Slonimski), 18:679

Mosedot le-Tippul be-Olim Neḥshalim. *See* Malben

Mosé e il cavalier Levi (Pitigrilli), 16:188

Mosé in Egitto (opera, Rossini), 14:542

Mosenthal, Adolph, 14:521

Mosenthal, Harry, 14:521

Mosenthal, Joseph, 14:521

Mosenthal, Julius, 14:521

Mosenthal, Salomon Hermann, 14:**521–522**

Mosenthal, William, 14:521

Mosenthal family, 14:**521**

Moser, Claude. *See* Moser, Sir Claude, Baron

Moser, Jacob, 4:115, 14:**522**

Moser, Moses, 14:**522**

Moser, Sir Claude, Baron, 14:**522**

Moserim. *See* Informers

Moses, 14:**522–543**, 15:733–734

    Aaron and, 1:208–211

    Aaronides and, 1:218, 219

    Abraham, Testament of, 1:291

    Adar, 1:382–383

    Aggadah, 14:534–536

    ancient paintings, 6:53, 54

    arts, 14:539–540, 541–542

    Bible, 14:523

    biography, 14:523–527

    Bithiah, 3:729

    blessing of, 14:**545**

    Christianity, 14:538

    critical assessment of, 14:526–531

    Decalogue and, 5:520–521

    Eldad and Medad, 6:293

    Elijah, 6:334

    Hellenistic period, 14:531–533

    historicity of, 15:748

    interpretations, Philo Judaeus, 16:62

    Islam, 14:538–539

    Joshua and, 11:442, 443

    journey, 14:539

    justice, as model of, 11:579

    Kadesh-Barnea, 11:698

    in Koran, 16:29

    Middle Ages, 14:536–537

    Miriam, 14:311–312

    mishmarot and ma'amadot, 14:319

    modern interpretations, 14:537–538

    Mount Sinai, 18:627

    music, 14:542–543

    name, 14:526

    ordination of elders, 18:274

    Pharaoh and, 16:29

    rabbinic period, 14:533–536

    receiving Tablets of the Law, 9:*704*, vol. 8: color insert

    revolt against, 5:440

    rod of, 17:365–366

    twentieth century literature, 14:540–541

    See also Exodus, Book of

Moses (Asch), 14:541

Moses (Buber), 14:538

Moses (Rosenberg), 14:540

Moses, Abraham, 15:302

Moses, Adolph, 13:225, 14:**543–544**

Moses, Alfred, 4:694

Moses, Assumption of. See Assumption of Moses

Moses, Banin, 1:388–389

Moses, Chin-Shih. *See* Chao Ying-Ch'eng

Moses, Chronicles of. See Chronicles of Moses

Moses, Eliezer Adolph. *See* Moses, Adolph

Moses, Five Books of. *See* Bible; Pentateuch

Moses, Isaac and Mrs. Isaac, 15:198

Moses, Isaac S, 14:**546**

Moses, Judah, 20:316

Moses, Marcus, 14:**546**

Moses, Menahem, 1:388

Moses, Myer, 14:**546**

Moses, Raphael J., 2:53, 14:**546**

Moses, Robert, 14:**546–547**, 15:216

Moses, Selim, 1:389

Moses, Song of. *See* Sea, Song of the

Moses and Jesus (Zangwill), 14:540

Moses and Monotheism (Freud), 14:538

Moses ben Aaron of Shirvan, 11:554

Moses ben Abraham of Pontoise, 14:**547–548**

Moses ben Abraham of Przemysl. *See* Mat, Moses

Moses ben Asher, 5:66

Moses ben Attar, 14:497

Moses ben Daniel of Rohatyn, 14:**548**

Moses ben David Ben-Naphtali, 13:644, 650

Moses ben Don David Elmaleh, 6:363

Moses ben Elias Pobian, 3:636

Moses ben Elijah ha-Levi, 14:**548**

Moses ben Elijah Pasha, 14:**548**

Moses ben ha-Nesi'ah, 14:**548**

Moses ben Ḥanokh, 14:**548–549**

Moses ben Isaac. *See* Ibn al-Taqana, Moses

Moses ben Isaiah Katz, 14:**549**

Moses ben Israel Polier of Kobrin. *See* Kobrin, Moses ben Israel Polier of

Moses ben Jacob ibn Ezra. *See* Ibn Ezra, Moses ben Jacob

Moses ben Jacob of Coucy, 14:**549–550**

Moses ben Jacob of Kiev, 14:**550–551**

Moses ben Joab, 14:**551**

Moses ben Joseph ben Merwan Levi, 14:**551**

Moses ben Joseph ha-Levi, 14:**551–552**

Moses ben Joseph Trani. *See* Trani, Moses ben Joseph

Moses ben Joshua of Narbonne, 2:461, 14:**552**, 16:87–88

Moses ben Judah, Noga, 14:**552–553**

Moses ben Kefa, 3:599

Moses ben Levi, 14:**553–554**

Moses ben Maimon. *See* Maimonides, Moses

Moses ben Menahem. *See* Mendelssohn, Moses

Moses ben Menahem Graf, 14:**554**

Moses ben Mendel Frankfurt. *See* Mendelsohn, Frankfurt Moses

Moses ben Mevorakh, 14:**554**

Moses ben Mordecai of Brescia, 3:610

Moses ben Mordecai of Mantua, 3:610

Moses ben Naḥman. *See* Naḥmanides

Moses ben Raphael Mordecai. *See* Malkhi, Moses

Moses ben Samuel of Damascus, 14:**554**

Moses ben Schne'or. *See* Moses of Evereux

Moses ben Shem Tov de Leon, 14:**554–555**

Moses ben Shem Tov de León, 12:643

Moses ben Shem-Tov Gabbai. *See* Gabbai, Moses ben Shem-Tov

Moses ben Shem Tov ibn Ḥabib. *See* Ibn Ḥabib, Moses ben Shem Tov

Moses ben Solomon ben Simeon of Burgos, 14:**555–556**

Moses ben Solomon of Salerno, 2:132

Moses ben Yom-Tov, 14:**556**

Moses de Leon, 1:344, 11:609–610, 12:643, 14:746–747

Moses de Toledo. *See* Toledo, Moses de

Moses de Vushal, 17:278

Moses di Trani. *See* Trani, Moses ben Joseph

Moses Esrim ve-Arba, 14:**556**

Moses game, 7:372

Moses Germanus. *See* Späth, Johann
Peter

Moses Gerondi. *See* Naḥmanides

Moses Gikatilla. *See* Gikatilla, Moses
ben Samuel ha-Kohen

Moses ha-Darshan, 14:**556–557**

Moses ha-Goleh. *See* Moses ben Jacob
of Kiev

Moses ha-Kohen of Tordesillas, 14:**557**

Moses Ḥayyim Ephraim of Sudylkow,
14:**557–558**

Moses ibn Crispin. *See* Ibn Crispin
Cohen, Moses

Moses ibn Ezra, 16:265–266

Moses ibn Ḥabib. *See* Ibn Ḥabib,
Moses ben Shem Tov

Moses in the Bulrushes (More), 14:540

Moses Isaac, 14:**558**

Moses Kahana ben Jacob, 14:**558**

Moses Leib of Sasov, 14:**558–559**

Moses Meir. *See* Meir ben Ephraim of
Padua

Moses Meir ben Ephraim of Padua.
See Meir ben Ephraim of Padua

Moses Mendels. *See* Bachrach, Moses
ben Isaiah Menachem; Bachrach,
Moses ben Isaiah Menahem

Moses Mendessohn Academy
(Halberstadt, Germany), 8:263

Moses Moḥeh, 13:649

Moses Montefiore Library, 13:257

Moses Nathan, 14:**559**

Moses of Chorene, 2:472, 473

Moses of Coucy, 7:487

Moses of Dessau. *See* Mendelssohn,
Moses

Moses of Evreux, 14:**559**

Moses of Kiev, 14:**559**

Moses of Kiev II. *See* Moses ben Jacob
of Kiev

Moses of Mantua. *See* Moses ben
Mordecai of Mantua

Moses of Narboni. *See* Moses ben
Joshua of Narbonne

Moses of Narbonne. *See* Moses ben
Joshua of Narbonne

Moses of Padua. *See* Meir ben
Ephraim of Padua

Moses of Palermo, 14:**559–560**, 15:581

Moses of Pavia, 14:**560**

Moses of Salerno. *See* Moses ben
Solomon of Salerno

Moses of Trani. *See* Trani, Moses ben
Joseph

"Moses on Nebo" (Nathan), 14:541

Moses Shoham ben Dan of Dolina,
14:**560**

Moses und Aaron (cantata,
Schoenberg), 14:543

Moses und Jesus (Buchholtz), 18:89–90

Moses Ze'ev ben Eliezer of Grodno,
14:**560**

Moshav, Moshav Ovedim, 14:**560–562**

Moshavim, 5:209–210, 14:561

absorption of immigrants by,
10:342, 359, 360, 527–529, 528*t*

Allonei Abba, 1:676–677

Almagor, 1:678

Almah, 1:678

Amazyah, 2:36

Amirim, 2:79

Amminadav, 2:83

Arbel, 2:363

Bat Shelomo, 3:214

Be'er Toviyyha, 3:258

beyond Green Line, 10:364–365

Binyaminah, 3:705

Biriyyah, 3:711

Bitan Aharon, 3:727

Bizzaron, 3:730

Bozrah, 4:115

Christian, 10:643

coastal plain, 13:668

Ein Iron, 6:259

Ein Vered, 6:264

Ein Yahav, 6:264

Elyashiv, 6:372

Eshtaol, 6:507

governing responsibilities, 10:393

Ha-Bonim, 8:182

Ha-Poel ha-Mizrachi, 8:339

Ḥazevah, 8:496

Ha-Zore'im, 8:501

Histadrut and, 10:601

Joffe, Eliezer Lipa, 11:367–368

Jokneam, 11:385

Kadimah, 11:699

during Mandate
growth, 10:492
mixed farming strategy,
10:510–511

Mazkeret Batyah, 13:**707**

Mazli'ah, 13:**707**

Menaḥemiyyah (Israel, state),
14:**24**

Mizpah, 14:387–388

Moledet, 14:425

Nir Ezyon, 15:274

Orot, 15:**482**

Petaḥ Tikvah, 16:14–15

population, 10:289, 292, 375

Sedeh Warburg, 18:235

Sedeh Ya'akov, 18:235

Sha'ar Ḥefer-beit Yiẓḥak, 18:336

Shadmot Devorah, 18:361

Sharonah, 18:418

Shavei Zion, 18:421

She'ar Yashuv, 18:427

Third Aliyah and, 10:510

See also Agriculture; Moshav

Moshav Shittufi, 14:**562**

Moshe bar Jehiel. *See* Michael, Moses

Moshel ba-Elyonim Attah Yadat
(Bachrach), 3:39

Moshel Yeriḥo (Mundy), 8:721

Moshe Rabbenu. *See* Moses

Moshinsky, Elijah, 14:**563**

Mosinsohn, Y., 8:720

Moskoni, Judah Leon ben Moses,
14:**563**

Josippon, 11:462

Moskovitz, Shalom, 14:**563**

Moskowitz, Belle Linder Israels,
14:**563–564**

Moskowitz, Henry, 14:**563–564,** 15:205

Moskva (Russian Federation). *See*
Moscow (Russian Federation)

Moslems. *See* Islam

Mosler, Henry, 14:**564**

Mosley, Oswald, 3:215

Mosque of Omar. *See* Dome of the
Rock

Moss, Celia, 14:**564**

Moss, David, 4:371

Moss, John, 14:**565**

Moss, Marion, 14:**564**

Moss, Matthew, 16:340

Mossad, 11:714

Amit, Meir, 2:80

Morocco, 14:503

Mossadeq, 15:569, 570

Mosse, Albert, 14:565

Mossé, B., 3:629

Mosse, George L., 14:**566**

Mosse, Markus, 14:565

Mosse, Rudolf, 14:565

Mosse family, 14:**565–566**

Mosseri, Albert, 14:566

Mosseri, Mathilda. *See* Mosseri, Mazal

Mosseri, Mazal, 13:469

Mosseri family, 14:566

Mossinsohn, Yigal, 4:626, 14:**566–567**

Mossinson, Benzion, 14:**567**

Mossner, Walther von, 14:**567**

Most (Czechoslovakia), 14:**567**

Mostel, Samuel Joseph. *See* Mostel,
Zero

Mostel, Zero, 4:26, 14:**567–568**

Mostiska (Ukraine), 14:**568**

Mosul (Iraq), 3:138, 139, 14:**568–569**
exilarchs, 5:472
Moszkowicz, Daniel, 3:569
Moszkowicz, Daniel, Bialystok
(Poland), Jewish resistance in, 3:570
Moszkowski, Moritz, 14:**569**
Mot, 3:11
Mota, Nehemia, 14:**569**
Motal, Abraham ben Jacob, 14:**569**
Motanul incălţat (Silviu), 18:590
Mother of Charities (Denver). *See*
Jacobs, Francis Wisebart
The mother of Yiddish writers. *See*
Maze, Ida
Mothers
custody of children, 15:636–637
maintenance, parental obligation
of, 15:635
role
biblical, 6:692
contemporary U.S., 6:701,
704
immigrant, 6:696
See also Children; Parents
Moths, 14:**569–570**
*Motif Index of Talmudic-Midrashic
Literature* (Noy), 1:461
Motion Picture Patents Co., 14:570
Motion pictures, 14:**570–578**
Bloom, Claire, 3:780–781
Canada, 12:486
critics, 13:763
directors
Aldrich, Robert, 1:606–607
Allen, Woody, 1:669–670
Bakri, Mohammed, 3:73
Bakshi, Ralph, 3:73
Benjamin, Richard, 3:358
Bergman, Andrew, 3:427–428
Bogdanovich, Peter, 4:34–35
Brooks, Albert, 4:209
Brooks, James L., 4:209
Brooks, Mel, 4:209–210
Brooks, Richard, 4:210
Cedar, Joseph, 4:535–536
Chetwynd, Lionel, 4:606
Corwin, Norman Lewis,
5:226–227
Cukor, George, 5:328
Curtiz, Michael, 5:343
Dassin, Jules, 5:440
Donen, Stanely, 5:749
Donskoy, Mark Semenovich,
5:752
Dostál, Zeno, 5:762
Eisenstein, Sergei
Mikhailovich, 6:274

Elkerbout, Ben, 6:358
Forman, Milos, 7:130
Hershkovitz, Marshall, 9:46–
47
Jhabvala, Ruth Prawer,
11:336
Kanin, Garson, 11:763
Kasdan, Lawrence, 11:819
Lang, Fritz, 12:478–479
Lanzmann, Claude, 12:487
Lelouch, Claude, 12:634
Le Roy, Mervyn, 12:660
Lester, Richard, 12:666
Levinson, Barry, 12:723
Litvak, Anatole, 13:139
Lubitsch, Ernst, 13:242
Lumet, Sidney, 13:256–257
Maysles, Albert, 13:703–704
Mazursky, Paul, 13:709
Mendes, Sam, 14:43
Morris, Errol M., 14:510
Paul, David, 13:703–704
Penn, Arthur, 15:726–727
Perry, Frank, 15:782
Polanski, Roman, 16:326
Rasky, Harry, 17:108
Reiner, Carl, 17:205–206
Reiner, Rob, 17:206–207
Reisz, Karel, 17:213
Ritt, Martin, 17:345
Ross, Herbert, 17:469
Rossen, Robert, 17:471
Rubens, bernice, 17:510
Saslavsky, Luis Simón, 18:66
Saville, Victor, 18:84
Schlesinger, John, 18:141–143
Singer, Bryan, 18:633–634
U.S., 5:440, 13:703–704, 709,
14:43, 15:726, 782
Zwick, Edward, 9:46–47
documentaries, Rasky, Harry,
17:108
executives
Balaban, Barney, 3:81
Eisner, Michael Dammann,
6:276–277
Lansing, Sherry Lee, 12:485
Loew, Marcus, 13:164
Mayer, Louis Burt, 13:699
Fields, Dorothy, 7:17
Fox, Eytan, 7:140
French, 14:575–576
German, 14:576
Hackett, Buddy, 8:183
Holocaust, 9:439–446
Israel, 10:709–710
Dayan, Assaf, 5:484

Jolson, Al, 11:386–387
Los Angeles movie industry,
13:197–198
Nazi propaganda, 5:54, 9:439, 440
nickelodeon era, 14:570
Ovitz, Michael, 15:549
Pakula, Alan Jay, 15:572
Pasternak, Joseph, 15:684
Poland, 14:576–577
producers
Balcon, Sir Michael, 3:85
Belasco, David, 3:278
Bergman, Andrew, 3:427–428
Berman, Pandro S., 3:464
Bruckheimer, Jerry, 4:219–
220
Chopra, Joyce, 4:666
Coen, Ethan, 4:781–782
Coen, Joel, 4:781–782
Cronenberg, David, 5:306
DeMille, Cecil B., 5:551
Deren, Maya, 5:594
Douglas, Michael, 5:765
Evans, Robert, 6:572
Ford, Alexander, 7:124
Foreman, Carl, 7:125
Fox, William, 7:141–142
Freed, Arthur, 7:223–224
Hershkovitz, Marshall, 9:46–
47
Kasdan, Lawrence, 11:819
Laemmle, Carl, 12:436
Lasky, Jesse L., 12:500
Lehman, Ernest, 12:613
Le Roy, Mervyn, 12:660
Levine, Joseph E., 12:718–719
Levinson, Barry, 12:723
Mnouchkine, Alexandre,
14:398
Pasternak, Joseph, 15:684
Penn, Arthur, 15:726–727
Rafelson, Robert, 17:63
Rasky, Harry, 17:108
Richards, Martin, 17:287–288
Ritt, Martin, 17:345
Rossen, Robert, 17:471
Rudin, Scott, 17:522–523
U.S., 6:572, 12:436, 15:726
Zwick, Edward, 9:46–47
Rasky, Harry, 17:108
Richter, Hans, 17:291
Sandler, Adam Richard, 18:15
screenwriters
Bergman, Andrew, 3:427–428
Biró, Lajos, 3:717
Brooks, James L., 4:209

Motion pictures, *continued*
 Brooks, Richard, 4:210
 Diamond, I.A.L., 5:632–633
 Hershkovitz, Marshall, 9:46–47
 Horovitz, Israel, 9:528
 Kasdan, Lawrence, 11:819
 Lehman, Ernest, 12:613
 Levien, Sonya, 12:704
 Levinson, Barry, 12:723
 Levy, Benn Wolfe, 12:748
 Rafelson, Robert, 17:63
 Raphael, Frederic, 17:94
 Raphaelson, Samson, 17:96
 Rossen, Robert, 17:471
 Rubens, bernice, 17:510
 Schary, Dore, 18:110
 Zwick, Edward, 9:46–47
 U.K., 14:575
 U.S., 14:570–575
 USSR, 14:577
 Yiddish films, 14:575
Motives and Symphonies. See Motive și simfonii
Motive și simfonii (Aderca), 1:390
Motke Ḥabad, 14:**578**
Motl Peyse dem Khazns (Shalom Aleichem), 18:379, 385
Motorboat racing, 19:145
Motorcycling, 19:145
Motot, Samuel ibn. *See* Ibn Motot, Samuel ben Saadiah
Mottelson, Ben R., 14:**578**
Motti, Felix Josef, 14:**578**
Motzi. *See* Grace before meals
Motzkin, Leo, 14:**578–579**
Moulay al-Ḥasan (Morocco). *See* Al-Ḥasan (Mulay of Morocco)
Moulay al-Rashid (Morocco). *See* Al-Rashid (Mulay of Morocco)
Moulay al-Yazid (Morocco). *See* Al-Yazid (Mulay of Morocco)
Moulay Ismail (Morocco). *See* Ismail (Alawid sharif)
Moulay Muhammad ben Abdallah (Morroco). *See* Muhammad ben Abdallah (Mulay of Morocco)
Moulay Muhammad ben ʿAbd al-raḥman (Morroco). *See* Muhammad ben ʿAbd al-raḥman (Mulay of Morocco)
Moulay Suleiman (Morocco). *See* Suleiman (Mulay of Morocco)
Moulin, Jean, 3:141
Mountain Jews, 14:**579–584**
 early history, 14:579–580
 literature, 14:584

Russian rule, 14:580–582
 social structure, 14:581
 Soviet rule, 14:582–583
 See also Azerbaijan
Mount Carmel (Israel), 4:**483–484**, 6:332, 10:116–118
Mount Gerizim (ancient Israel), 9:501
Mount Gerizim (Israel), 7:**507–508**
Mount Gilboa (Israel), 10:116
Mount Hermon, 3:7, 9:**30–31**, 10:131
Mount Horeb. *See* Sinai, Mount
Mount Meron (Israel). *See* Meron (Israel)
Mount of Olives, 9:499, 14:**584–585**
Mount of Olives cemetery (Israel), vol. 10: color insert
Mount of Vineyards. See Har ha-Keramim
Mount Perazim. *See* Baal-Perazim
Mount Seir. *See* Edom (Transjordan)
Mount Sinai, 2:76, 6:616, 14:523, 527, 535, 18:**627–629**
Mount Sinai, Melodies from. *See* Mi-Sinai Niggunim
Mount Sinai Hospital (New York), 11:720
Mount Tabor, 19:**426–427**
Mount Zion
 Franciscan order, 7:173
 tomb of David, 5:453
Mourners of Zion. *See* Avelei Zion
Mourning, 12:84–85, 14:**585–589**
 abstinence and, 2:547–548, 13:711
 aninut, 2:174, 14:587–588
 apostasy, 2:276
 Biblical, 14:585–586
 Day of Atonement, 5:490–491
 head covering, 8:506
 Kever Avot, 12:99–100
 lamentations, 14:586–587
 modern practice, 14:588
 Nine Days, 15:271
 Omer's association with, 15:420–422
 prayers and liturgy, 14:588–589
 Samaritans, 17:732
 sheloshim, 18:446
 talmudic period, 14:587–588
 texts, *Semaḥot*, 18:273–274
 See also Kinah
Mouse. *See* Mice
Moussorgsky, Modest, 11:444
Mousy. *See* Blum, Walter
Movement for Revival. *See* Tnu'at ha-Teḥiyah
Movie palaces, 3:81

Movies. *See* Motion pictures
Movietone News, 7:141
Mowinckel, Sigmund, 3:651
Mowinckel, Sigmund Olaf Plytt, 14:**590**
Mowshowitz, Israel, 14:**590**
Moyal, Abdallah Nadīm, 15:473
Moyal, Avraham. *See* Muyal, Avraham
Moyal, Esther, 14:**590**
Moynihan, Daniel Patrick, 15:225
Moyse, Edouard, 2:505
Moyshe (Asch). *See* Moses (Asch)
Moysheles Kinderyorn (Kassel), 11:827
Moy vremennik (Eichenbaum). *See My Chronicle* (Eichenbaum)
Moyẓeszowa, Raszka. *See* Fishel, Rachel
Moẓa (ancient Israel), 14:**590–591**
Moẓa (Israel), 14:**591**
Mózes (Madách), 14:540
Mózes (Pap), 14:541
Mozes, Noah, 14:591–592
Mozes family, 14:**591–592**
Mozley, Charles, 13:144
Moznayim (journal), 14:**592**
Mozyr (Belarus), 14:**592–593**
Mr. Sammler's Planet (Bellow), 3:300, 9:407, 20:293–294
Mr. Wildcatter. *See* Davis, Marvin H.
Mrgillat Ta'anit, 13:**769**
Mrs. Woods (Bavli), 8:736
Mstislavl (Belarus), 14:**593**
Muʿāwiya (Umayyad caliph), 11:154
Mubarak, Ḥusni, 15:594
Mubarak, Muhammed Husni Sa'id, 14:**593–594**
Mubashshir ben Nassi ha-Levi, 14:**594**
Mubashshir ben Rav Kimoi ha-Kohen, 14:**594**
Mucianus, Caius Licinius, 14:**594**
Muehlhausen (Germany), 14:**594–595**
Muehsam, Erich, 14:**595**
Muelhausen (France). *See* Mulhouse (France)
Muelhausen, Yom Tov Lipmann, 14:**595–597**
 apologetics, 2:267
 disputations and polemics, 5:694
 movements opposing veneration of, 2:158
Mueller, Anton von. *See* Bienenfeld, Franz Rudolf
Mueller, David Heinrich, 14:**597**
Mueller, Ernst, 14:**597**
Mueller, Ernst Lothar. *See* Lothar, Ernst
Mueller, Heinrich, 14:**597–598**

Mueller, Joel, 14:**598**

Mueller-Cohen, Anita, 14:**598**

Muenchener Juedische Nachrichten, 13:271

Muenster (Germany), 14:**598–599**

Muenster, Sebastian, 8:515, 14:**599–600**

Muensterberg, Hugo, 14:**600**

Muenz, Eleazar ben Aryeh Leib, 14:**600**

Muenz, Moses ben Isaac ha-Levi, 3:705, 14:**600–601**
   in Bingen, 3:705

Muenzer, Thomas, 3:760

Muessner, Franz, 4:683

Die Muetter (Hirschfeld), 9:137

Mugur, Florin, 14:**601**

Muhajir, Abu Sulayman ibn. *See* David ibn Hajjar

Muhammad
   Aaron and, 1:211
   Abdallah ibn Salām and, 1:241
   Abraham, 1:286
   Ahl al-Kitāab, 1:546
   Bible and, 3:667–669
   eschatology, 6:502–503
   Jerusalem and, 11:222–223
   Jews of Medina and, 13:757
   as messiah, 1:240
   Moses, 14:538–539
   See also Islam

Muhammad Ali, 10:182, 14:**605–606**

Muhammad ben Abdallah (Mulay of Morroco), 14:497

Muhammad ben ʾAbd al-Raḥman (Mulay of Morroco), 14:499

Muhammad V (king of Morocco), 14:503

Muhammad VI (king of Morocco), 14:505

Muhammed, 14:**601–605**
   Jewish tribes, relations with, 14:602–605
   Mecca and Medina, 14:602

Muhlstock, Louis, 14:**606**, 15:252

Muhr, Abraham, 14:**606–607**

Mukachevo (Ukraine), 14:**607**

Mukachevo family. *See* Shapira family

al-Mukammis, David, 2:265

Mukammiṣ, ibn Marwān al-Rāqi al-Shirazi al-, 14:**607–608**
   Judah ben Barzillai al-Bargeloni, 11:483
   Judeo-Arabic literature and, 11:531, 534

Mukdoni, A., 14:**608**

Mukẕeh, 14:**608**

Mulay al-Ḥasan (Morroco). *See* Al-Ḥasan (Mulay of Morroco)

Mulay al-Rashid (Morroco). *See* Al-Rashid (Mulay of Morroco)

Mulay al-Yazid (Morroco). *See* Al-Yazid (Mulay of Morroco)

Mulay Ismail (Morocco). *See* Ismail (Alawid sharif)

Mulay Muhammad ben Abdallah (Morroco). *See* Muhammad ben Abdallah (Mulay of Morroco)

Mulay Muhammad ben ʾAbd al-Raḥman (Morroco). *See* Muhammad ben ʾAbd al-raḥman (Mulay of Morroco)

Mulay Suleiman (Morroco). *See* Suleiman (Mulay of Morroco)

Mulberries, 14:**609**, vol. 16: color insert

Mulder, Samuel Israel, 2:113, 14:**609**

Mule, 14:**609–610**

Mule Corps. *See* Zion Mule Corps

Mulhouse (France), 14:**610**

Mulisch, Harry, 14:**610**

Mulisch, Harry, 6:71

Mullā Murād. *See* Aklar Mordecai ben Raphael

Muller, Benjamin, 14:**610–611**

Muller, Herman Joseph, 14:**611**

Muller, Hermann, 13:8

Muller, Robert, 14:**611**

Mul Ohel Timmorah (Silkiner), 8:736

Mul Ohel Timmurah (Silkiner), 18:581

Mult És Jövö (journal), 14:**611**

The Multilanguage Bibliography of Jewish Law, 18:471

Multiplier theory, 11:723

Mulūk al-Ṭwaā'if, 14:**611–612**

Mumar, 9:20

Mumbai (India). *See* Bombay (India)

Mummification, 6:390. *See* Embalming

Mum ve-Ḥalom (Carmi), 4:484

Munchik, Eliahu, 8:757

Mundy, Yosef, 8:721

Muni, Paul, 14:**612**

Munich (Germany), 14:**612–614**
   blood libel in, 3:775

Municipal regulations for Jews
   Bialystok (Poland), 3:567
   Joseph II, 11:414
   in Noerdlingen, 15:293
   in Osnabrueck, 15:505

Muñiz-Huberman, Angelina, 14:**614**

Munk, Elias, 14:614

Munk, Elie, 14:614

Munk, Hermann, 14:**614–615**

Munk, Kaj, 14:615

Munk, Leo, 14:614

Munk, S., 15:529

Munk, Solomon, 14:**615**

Munkács (Ukraine). *See* Mukachevo (Ukraine)

Munkacs family. *See* Shapira family

Munkácsi, Bernát, 14:**615–616**

Munkácsi, Ernö, 14:**616**

Munk family, 14:**614**

Muntner, Alexander Suessman, 14:**616**

Munweis, Paula. *See* Ben-Gurion, Paula

Muqaddim, 14:**616**

Muquddāmin. *See* Adelantados

Murabbaʿat Caves, 11:524

Murabbaʿat scrolls, 14:**616–617**

Murashu's sons, 14:**617–618**

Murcia (Spain), 14:**618**

Murder. *See* Homicide

Murderers Among Us (Staudte), 9:440

Murder Incorporated, 18:173, 174

Murmelstein, Benjamin, 14:**618–619**

Murphy, Franklin D., 18:659

Murray, Arthur, 14:**619**

Murviedro (Spain), 14:**619–620**

Mūsā. *See* Moses

Musaf, 14:**620–621**
   Amidah, 2:72, 74, 75
   Rosh Ha-Shannah, 13:433–434
   U-Netanneh Tokef, 2:87

Musar Haskel, 14:**621**

Musar literature. *See* Ethical literature

Musar movement, 3:741, 14:**621–623**
   Broida, Simḥah, 4:202
   Dessler, Elijah Eliezer, 5:605
   dualism, 6:29
   duty, 6:72
   Finkel, Nathan Ẓevi ben Moses, 7:32
   Hurvitz, Joseph Yozel, 9:631
   Joffen, Abraham, 11:368
   Kabbalah, 11:679
   Kamenetsky, Yaakov, 11:752
   Lipkin, Israel ben Ze'ev Wolf, 13:64–65
   Lithuania, 13:119
   Moses Isaac, 14:558
   Phinehas ben Jair, 16:116
   repentance, 17:223
   righteousness, 17:309
   See also Finkel, Nathan Ẓevi Ben Moses; Heller, Joshua ben Aaron; Kelme (Lithuania)

Musée d'Art d'Histoire du Judaïsme (MAHJ), 14:**623**

Muselevitsh, Iser. *See* Tolush

Muselmann, 9:355–356, 14:**623**

Muserei ha-Filosofim (Al-Ḥarizi, Judah ben Solomon), 1:657

Museum of Istanbul, 18:582

Museum of Jewish Heritage: A Living Memorial to the Holocaust (MJH: ALMTTH), 9:436, 14:**623–624**

Museum of the Southern Jewish Experience, 14:633

Museum of Tolerance, 9:436, 13:201, 18:619

Museums, 14:**624–636**

  Anglo-Jewish Historical Exhibition, 14:626

  Australia, 14:634

  Berlin, 14:628

  Berlin (Germany) Jewish Museum, 4:13

  B'nai B'rith Klutznick National Jewish Museum, 4:15

  Brazil, 18:33

  Canada (North America), 14:634

  Caribbean, 14:634

  China, 14:635

  curators, Sandberg, Willem Jacob, 18:11

  Eastern Europe, 14:627–630

  ghetto, 14:629–630

  Holocaust, 9:432–438, 438t, 439t, 14:635–636

  India, 14:635

  International Committee of Museums and Sites (Israel) of UNESCO, 3:710

  International Museum of War and Peace, 3:756

  Israel, 14:631

  Israel Museum, Billy Rose Sculpture Garden, 2:47

  Labor Archives and Museum, 2:417

  Latin America, 14:634

  Los Angeles Holocaust Museum, 13:201

  Musée d'Art d'Histoire du Judaïsme, 14:623

  Museum of Jewish Heritage: A Living Memorial to the Holocaust, 14:623–624

  National Museum of American Jewish History, 15:25–26

  South Africa, 14:634–635

  Strauss collection, 14:625

  U.S., 14:631–634

  Western Europe, 14:625–627

  See also United States Holocaust Memorial Museum

Musher, Sidney, 14:**636**

Mushrooms, 14:**636**

Music, 14:**636–701**

  Abraham, 1:288

  accentuation, reading symbols, 14:649–650, *650*

  Adam, 1:376

  Aḥot Ketannah, 1:547–548

  Akdamut Millin (prayer), 1:555

  Akedah, 1:560

  Alarizi, Judah ben Solomon, 1:657

  Aleinu le-Shabbe'aḥ (prayer), 1:608t, 609–610

  Aleppo (Syria), 1:616–617

  Amen, 2:39

  American Society for Jewish Music, 2:65

  Amidah, 2:76

  Amsterdam, 2:119, 120

  Andalusian nūba, Bouzaglo, David, 4:107

  Arabic, 1:679, 6:711

  art music, 14:668–669, 676–677, *677*, 687–689, *690*, *691*

  Ashkenazi, shtayger, 18:522–523

  Ashkenazi styles, 14:671–676, *672*, *673*, *674*, *675*

  Babylonian opposition, 14:647

  Bible reading by chant, 14:645–646, 649–650

  Bible's impact on, 3:672–673

  Broadway theater, 15:220, 228

  Bukharan Jews, 4:264

  Cain, 4:431–432

  cantatas and choral works, Hebrew, 4:433–435, 14:363–364

  cantillation, 4:436, 10:815

  choirs, 4:658–663, 14:679–681

  collections, archives, 14:639–640

  criticism

    David, Ernest, 5:463

    Jacobs, Arthur, 11:45–46

    Mendel, Arthur, 14:29

    Rosenfeld, Paul, 17:447

  Daniel in, 5:419

  David and, 5:457–458

  dirges, *Eli Ẓiyyon ve-Areha*, 6:356

  Elijah, 6:336–337

  ethnomusicology, 1:290–291, 12:423–424

  Ezekiel in, 6:646

  female voice prohibition, 14:649

  flute playing, 14:647

  folk, 14:689–692, 17:150–151

  funeral, 6:365

  Hallel, 8:281

  hallelujah-singing, 8:281

  Ḥanukkah, *Ma'oz Ẓur,* 13:496–497

  harmonica, Adler, Larry, 1:401

  Hasidic, Kazimierz dynasty, 12:45

  Ḥasidic niggun, 14:676

  Ha-Tikvah, 8:457–458

  hazzanut, Danto, 5:431

  history

    12th to14th centuries, 14:658–661

    16th to 18th centuries, 14:666–676

    19th century, 14:676–685, *679*, *680*

    20th century, 14:685, 685–689, *688*, *689*

    Biblical period, 14:640–642

    Middle Ages, 14:653–656, *654*, *656*

    Reform movement, 14:677–681

    Second Temple, 14:642–643

    sources, 14:637–640

  Holocaust, 14:697–699

  humanistic approach, 14:667–668

  Hungary, Kallo, Yiẓhak Isaac, 11:745

  India, 9:776, 12:249–250

  Iran, 10:13

  Iranian Jewish, 10:13

  Iraq, 10:22–24

  Isaac in, 10:34–35

  Isaiah in, 10:74–75

  Islam, Maqām, 13:507

  Israel, 3:123, 5:433, 10:688–691

    art music, 14:692–697

    Haifa Symphony Orchestra, 10:688–689

    Israel Chamber Orchestra, 10:749–750

    Israel Philharmonic Orchestra, 10:758–759

    song, 10:692–693

  Israel Arab, 10:734

  Italian, librettists, 5:433

  Italy, 10:814–815

  Jacob in, 11:24–25

  jazz, 6:726

  Jephthah in, 11:123–124

  Jeremiah in, 11:134

  Jerusalem in, 11:228–229

  Jewish

    preservation of, 10:689–690

    Sodom and Gomorrah, 18:741

    Solomon, 18:762–763

    spiritual objectives, 6:57

  Job in, 11:358–359

Joel, Book of, 11:362

Jonah, Book of, 11:391

Joshua, story of, 11:444

Judah ben Isaac's Hebrew treatise on, 11:487

Judah Maccabee story used as theme in, 11:511

Judeo-Arabic culture and, 11:542

Judith, Book of, 11:568–569

Kaddish, 11:697

Karaites and Karitism, 11:800–802

Kol Nidrei, 12:277–278

Kurdistan, 12:392

Ladino, 12:434

Lamentations, Book of, 12:450–451

liturgy
   Addir bi-Melukhah, 1:385
   Addir Hu, 1:385
   Maqām, 13:507–508
   Seliḥot, 18:268–269, *269*

Maccabees themes, 8:448

Maharil minhag, 14:662–663

managers, Epstein, Brian, 6:468

Mandate period art music, 14:692–695

masoretic accents, 13:656–664

metrical poetry, 14:656–657

minstrelsy, 14:657–658, *658*

modal scale, 14:663–664, *664*

Moscow Chamber Orchestra, 3:178

Moses, 14:542–543

musicology, Rosen, Charles, 17:428

mystical approaches, 14:660–661, 663, 666–667

National Sound Archives, 14:639–640

New York City, 15:220–221

Noah in, 15:290

North Africa, 1:437–440

Nusaḥ, 15:351

Obadiah the Norman proselyte, 15:367

organs, 15:466–468

oriental sephardi style, 14:669–671, *670, 671*

Palestine (Mandate), 10:688, 691

Palestine (Ottoman), 10:691

philanthropists, Mayer, Sir Robert, 13:699–700

phonetic punctuation, 4:84

pizmon, 16:210

popular and social, 14:657–658, *658*

prayer chant, 14:646–647, 650–653

producers, Chess, Leonard, 4:605

promoters, Bernstein, Sid, 3:484

psalmody, 14:644–645, *645*

psalms, 16:678–682

publishers
   Eulenburg family, 6:548
   Hertzka, Emil, 9:49
   Hinrichsen family, 9:123

rabbinic attitude, 14:658–659

Rachel (biblical figure), 17:49

recordings, 17:149–151

regional styles, 14:662, 662–665, *664, 665*

religious, Absalom, 1:331

Renaissance, 13:237

Russia, nineteenth century, 5:483

Safed mystical movement, 14:666–667

Salome, 17:694

Samaritans, 17:738–739

Saul, 18:82–83

scientific approach, 14:653–655

script, 14:649–650

Scrolls, The Five, 18:221

Second Temple, 19:621

Sephardic, 10:814

songs, Israel (state), 10:691–693

spatial music, 4:130

studies, 11:37–38, 56
   Emsheimer, Ernst, 6:398
   Mendel, Hermann, 14:29

synagogue, 14:663–664, *664*, 669

synagogue song and chant, 14:643–649, *644, 645, 646, 648*

Talmud, 19:487–488, *487t*

Tehillot le El-Elyon (Kirschner), 12:189

theater, musical, 1600 to 20th century, 19:675–676

theory
   Schachter, Carl, 18:99
   Schenker, Heinrich, 18:122
   Schillinger, Joseph, 18:134–135

Tiberian system of accentuation, 14:650

Tower of Babel, 3:21

Tunisia, 14:393

Turkey, Edirne, 6:148–150

Wisdom of Ben Sira, 3:377–378

women's folk, 14:689–692

Yemenite, 21:309–311

Yemenite instruments, 21:311

Yiddish
   Broder, Berl, 4:194, 195
   Broder Singers, 4:194, 195, 19:678

Noy, Meir, 15:327

U.S., 13:791

See also Composers; Liturgical music; Musicians and dancers; *specific musicians*

Musical instruments, Temple, 14:641–643

Musical theater, Yiddish, 19:680

Musical Tradition of the Eastern European Synagogue (opus), 11:733

Musicians and dancers
   Abeliovich, Lev Moysseyevich, 1:247
   Aber, Adolf, 1:253
   Abileah, Arie, 1:257
   Abraham, Gerald, 1:289–290
   Abraham, Otto, 1:290–291
   Abrass, Osias, 1:329
   Abravanel, Maurice de, 1:329
   Achron, Joseph, 1:355–356
   Ackerman, Shabtai, 1:358
   Adaskin, Murray, 1:384
   Adler, Guido, 1:397–398
   Adler, Hugo Chaim, 1:399
   Adler, Israel, 1:399
   Adler, Larry, 1:401–402
   Adler, Richard, 1:406–407
   Admon, Yedidyah, 1:411
   Agadati, Baruch, 1:443–444
   Aguilar, Emanuel Abraham, 1:509
   Aharon, Ezra, 1:531
   Aldema, Gil, 1:606
   Alexander, Haim, 1:622–623
   Algazi, Leon, 1:644–645
   Al-Gharīḍ al-Yahūdī, 1:652
   Al-Ḥarizi, Judah ben Solomon, 1:655–657
   Alkan, Charles Henri-Valentin, 1:665
   Alman, Samuel, 1:678–679
   Al-Manṣūr al-Yahūdī, 1:679
   Alpert, Herb, 1:688–689
   Alshvang, Arnold Aleksandrovich, 2:11
   Alter, Israel, 2:18
   Altschul, Joseph, 2:25
   Altschuler, Modest, 2:26
   Amar, Licco, 2:31
   Amiran, Emanuel, 2:79
   Amram, David, 2:104
   Ančerl, Karel, 2:139
   Ancona, Mario, 2:142
   Anhalt, István, 2:163–164
   Apel, Willi, 2:254
   Applebaum, Louis, 2:288
   Arbatova, Mia, 2:362–363

Musicians and dancers, *continued*

Argov, Alexander, 2:451
Argov, Zohar, 2:451
Arie, Rafael, 2:453
Arlen, Harold, 2:469–470
Arom, Simha, 2:484
Aroni, Tsvi, 2:485
Aronovich, Yuri Mikhaylovich, 2:486
Arpa, Abramo Dall', 2:489
Artzi, Shlomo, 2:535
Ashkenazy, Vladimir Davidovich, 2:579
Atzmon, Moshe, 2:648–649
Auer, Leopold, 2:649–650
Austria, pianists, 9:51
Avenary, Hanoch, 2:722
Avidom, Menahem, 2:730
Avni, Tzevi, 2:743–744
Avshalomov, Aaron, 2:754
Avshalomov, Jacob, 2:754
Ax, Emmanuel, 2:755
Babbitt, Milton, 3:16–17
Babilée, Jean, 3:21
Babin, Victor, 3:21–22
Bacharach, Burt, 3:32
Bachauer, Gina, 3:35
Bachmann, Jacob, 3:38
Bacon, Hirsch Leib, 3:40
Bacon, Israel, 3:40
Bacon, Shlomo Reuven, 3:41
Bacon, Yidel, 3:41
Baer, Abraham, 3:52
Bagley, David, 3:59–60
Bar, Shlomo, 3:123
Bardanashvili, Yosef, 3:147
Barenboim, Daniel, 3:149–150
Bar-Ilan, David, 3:153
Barmas, Issay, 3:163–164
Barnea, Ezra, 3:168
Barnett, John, 3:169
Barnett, John Francis, 3:169
Barshai, Rudolf, 3:178
Bart, Lionel, 3:179
Bauer, Jacob, 3:217
Bauer, Marion Eugenie, 3:217
Bayer, Batya, 3:231
Beda, 3:246–247
Beer, Aaron, 3:250–251
Be'er Rami, 3:254
Beimel, Jacob, 3:268
Bekker, Paul, 3:277
Bell, Joshua, 3:299
Bellison, Simeon, 3:299–300
Bely, Viktor Arkadyevich, 3:307–308

Benatzky, Ralph, 3:312
Bendix, Otto, 3:327
Bendix, Victor Emanuel, 3:328
Benedict, Sir Julius, 3:330
Ben-Haim, Paul, 3:350–351
Ben-Haim, Yigal, 3:351
Benn, 3:366
Ben-Shabetai, Ari, 3:373–374
Beregovski, Moshe, 3:408
Bergel, Bernd, 3:418
Berger, Arthur Victor, 3:423–424
Berggrün, Heinrich, 3:426
Bergman, Alan and Marilyn, 3:427
Bergson, Michael, 3:433
Berk, Fred, 3:437
Berlijn, Anton, 3:444
Berlin, Irving, 3:455–456
Berlinski, Herman, 3:461
Bernstein, Abraham Moshe, 3:476
Bernstein, Elmer, 3:478
Bernstein, Leonard, 3:480–481
Bertini, Gary, 3:490–491
Bertonoff, Deborah, 3:492
Bie, Oscar, 3:687
Binder, Abraham Wolf, 3:703
Birnbaum, Abraham Baer, 3:714
Birnbaum, Eduard, 3:714
Blanes, Jacob, 3:738
Blanter, Matvey Isaakovich, 3:740–741
Blaustein, Abraham, 3:746
Blech, Leo, 3:747
Blindman, Yeruham, 3:753
Blitzstein, Marc, 3:757
Bloch, André, 3:758
Bloch, Charles (hazzan), 3:759
Bloch, Ernest, 3:759–760
Bloch, Rosine, 3:767
Bloomfield-Zeisler, Fanny, 3:783
Blum, René, 4:8
Blumenfeld, Felix Mikhaylovich, 4:10
Blumenthal, Nissan, 4:12–13
Bodanzky, Arthur, 4:27
Bodky, Erwin, 4:29
Boehm, Yohanan, 4:31–32
Boghen, Felice, 4:36
Bolaffi, Michele, 4:44
Bolm, Adolph Rudolphovich, 4:48
Borge, Victor, 4:84–85
Boris, Ruthanna, 4:85
Borovsky, Alexander, 4:92
Boscovitch, Alexander Uriyah, 4:96
Botstein, Leon, 4:104

Bouzaglo, David, 4:107
Braham, John, 4:117
Brailowsky, Alexander, 4:119
Brandon, Oheb Isaac, 4:127
Brant, Henry Dreyfus, 4:129–130
Braudo, Yevgeni, Maximovich, 4:137
Braun, Arie, 4:137
Braun, Yehezkiel, 4:138
Brauner, Harry, 4:138–139
Brecher, Gustav, 4:156
Brecker Brothers, 4:156
Brecker brothers, 4:156
Bréval, Lucienne, 4:174
British, cellists, Du Pré, Jacqueline, 6:51
Brod, Dovidl, 4:192
Brod, Max, 4:192–193
Broder Singers, 4:195
Brodsky, Adolf, 4:197–198
Bronfman, Yefim, 4:206–207
Brook, Barry Shelley, 4:208
Browning, John, 4:217–218
Bruell, Ignaz, 4:221
Brussilovsky, Yevgeni Grigoryevich, 4:227–228
Buchwald, Theo, 4:244
Bukofzer, Manfred, 4:265
Burle Marx, Walter, 4:296
Caceres, Abraham, 4:330
Cahn, Sammy, 4:338
Caregal, Hayyim Moses ben Abraham, 4:468
Carlebach, Shlomo, 4:481–482
Carp, Paula, 4:493
Caspi, Matti, 4:506
Castelnuovo-Tedesco, Mario, 4:515
Cervetto, Jacob Basevi, 4:551
Chagrin, Francis, 4:557
Chagy, Berele, 4:557
Chasins, Abraham, 4:581
Cherkassky, Shura, 4:594
Cherney, Brian, 4:595
Cherniavsky family, 4:595
Chujoy, Anatole, 4:709
Churgin, Bathia, 4:723
Civita, Davit, 4:749
Cohen, Harriet, 5:17
Cohen, Jacob Raphael, 5:23
Cohen, Leonard, 5:25–26
Cohen, Selma Jeanne, 5:34
Cohen, Yardena, 5:38
Cohen Melamed, Nissan, 5:39
Coleman, Cy, 5:56–57
Colonne, Jules Edouard, 5:65

INDEX

Comissiona, Sergiu, 5:72
composers
    Aguilar, Emanuel Abraham,
      1:509
    Aharon, Ezra, 1:531
    Bardanashvili, Josef, 3?147
Conried, Heinrich, 5:163
Consolo, Federico, 5:180
Cooper, Emil Albertovich, 5:205
Copland, Aaron, 5:212
Costa, Sir Michael, 5:234
Cowen, Sir Frederic Hymen, 5:255
Cranko, John, 5:273
Damari, Shoshana, 5:390
Damrosch family, 5:403–404
Danto, Louis, 5:431
Da-Oz, Ram, 5:433
Da Ponte, Lorenzo, 5:433
Daus, Avraham, 5:443
Davičo, Lujo, 5:444
David, Ernest, 5:463
David, Ferdinand, 5:463
David, Samuel, 5:464
Davydod, Karl Yulyevich, 5:483
Denmark
    Bendix, Otto, 3:327
    Bendix, Victor Emanuel,
      3:328
De Philippe, Edis, 5:589
Dessau, Paul, 5:604
Deutsch, Moritz, 5:624
Deutsch, Otto Erich, 5:625
Diamond, David, 5:632
Diamond, Neil, 5:634
Dichter, Misha, 5:632
Di-Zahav, Ephraim, 5:721
Dobroven, Issay Alexandrovich,
    5:726
Donalda, Pauline, 5:747
Dorati, Antal, 5:755
Dorfman, Joseph, 5:756
Dresden, Sem, 6:11
Dukas, Paul, 6:43
Dunayevski, Isaac Osipovich, 6:49
Du Pré, Jacqueline, 6:51
Duque, Simon David, 6:51
Dushkin, Samuel, 6:65
Edel, Yizḥak, 6:142
Eden-Tamir, 6:145–146
Ehrlich, Abel, 6:242
Eifman, Boris, 6:253
Einstein, Alfred, 6:262–263
Einstein, Arik, 6:263
Eisenstein, Judith Kaplan, 6:273–
    274
Eisler, Hanns, 6:275

Ellstein, Abraham, 6:363
Elman, Mischa, 2:26, 6:365
Elman, Ziggy, 6:365
Emsheimer, Ernst, 6:398
Engel, Joel, 6:408–409
Ephros, Gershon, 6:462
Erlanger, Camille, 6:480
Eshel, Yitzḥak, 6:504
Espinosa, Edouard, 6:508
Eulenburg, Ernst, 6:548
Even-Or, Mary, 6:574
Fain, 6:677
Fall, Leo, 6:688
Fano, Guido Alberto, 6:708–709
Farber, Viola, 6:713
Feidman, Giora, 6:729–730, 15:407
Feinberg, Samuel Yevgenyevich,
    6:739
Feinsinger, Joshua, 6:740
Feldman, Morton, 6:747
Feuermann, Emanuel, 6:774
Fiedler, Arthur, 7:16–17
Fields, Dorothy, 7:17
Fischer, Annie, 7:53
Fisher, Dudu, 7:62–63
Fitelberg, Grzegorz, 7:65
Fleischer, Tsippi, 7:74
Fleisher, Leon, 7:76
Flesch, Carl, 7:77
Fogelberg, Dan, 7:94
Foss, Lukas, 7:134–135
Frankel, Benjamin, 7:196, 9:112
Freed, Isadore, 7:224
Freedman, Harry, 7:224–225
Fried, Miriam, 7:267
Friede, Shalom, 7:270
Friedlaender, Max, 7:274
Friedman, Deborah Lynn, 7:279
Friedman, Kinky, 7:280–281
Friedmann, Aron, 7:285
Friedmann, Moritz, 7:287
Fromm, Herbert, 7:298–299
Fuchs, Lillian, 7:304–305
Gabrielovitch, Osip
    Solomonovitch, 7:328
Ganchoff, Moses, 7:374–375
Gantman, Judah Leib, 7:379
Gebirtig, Mordechai, 7:406
Gedalge, Andre, 7:406–407
Geiringer, Karl, 7:416
Gelbrun, Artur, 7:419
Gerber, Maynard, 7:506
Gernsheim, Friederich, 7:546
Gerovich, Eliezer Mordecai ben
    Isaac, 7:550

Gerson-Kiwi, Edith, 7:557
Geshuri, Meir Shimon, 7:563
Getz, Stan, 7:566
Gibbs, Terry, 7:580
Gideon, Miriam, 7:588–589
Gilboa, Jacob, 7:599
Gilels, Emil Grigoryevich, 7:601
Giovanni, Maria, 7:616
Glanz, Leib, 7:625
Glass, Philip, 7:632–633
Glick, Irving Srul, 7:637
Glière, Reinhold Moritzevitch,
    7:638–639
Gluck, Alma, 7:643
Gnesin, Mikhail Fabianovitch,
    7:648
Godowsky, Leopold, 7:680, 16:125
Goldberg, Szymon, 7:696
Goldfarb, Israel, 7:704–705
Goldman, Edwin Franco, 7:709
Goldmark, Karl, 7:717, 18:762
Goldschmidt, Hugo, 7:718
Goldstein, Josef, 7:729
Goldstein, Raymond, 7:731
Golinkin, Mordecai, 7:739–740
Golschmann, Vladimir, 7:745–746
Goodman, Benny, 7:757, 15:220
Gottschalk, Louis Moreau, 8:15
Gould, Morton, 8:18
Gradenwitz, Peter Emanuel, 8:25
Graf, Herbert, 8:29
Graffman, Gary, 8:29
Graziani, Yitzhak, 8:42
Greenberg, Noah, 8:73
Greenblatt, Eliyahu, 8:76
Gruenberg, Louis, 8:107
Guglielmo Da Pesaro, 8:126–127
Gusikow, Joseph Michael, 8:148
Haendel, Ida, 8:195
Hahn, Reynaldo, 8:231–232
Hainovitz, Asher, 8:239
Hajdu, André, 8:240
Halévy, Jacques Fromental Élie,
    8:270–271
Halprin, Ann, 8:286
Hamdī, Levi ben Yeshu'ah, 8:298
Hammerstein family, 8:309
Hanokh, Shalom, 8:328
Harburg, E. Y., 8:346
Harran, Don, 8:361–362
Haskell, Arnold Lionel, 8:445
Haskil, Clara, 8:445
Hast, Marcus, 8:455
Haubenstock-Ramati, Roman,
    8:460
Hauser, Emil, 8:463

ENCYCLOPAEDIA JUDAICA, *Second Edition, Volume 22*

691

Musicians and dancers, *continued*

Hayden, Melissa, 8:475
Hebrew, Noy, Meir, 15:327
Heifetz, Jascha, 8:764
Heilmann, Yitzhak, 8:767
Heller, Samuel, 13:186
Hemsi, Alberto, 8:805
Henle, Moritz, 8:808
Henschel, Sir George, 8:810
Herrmann, Bernard, 9:41
Herschman, Mordechai, 9:43
Herskovits, Bela, 9:46
Herstik, Naphtali, 9:47
Hertzka, Emil, 9:49
Herz, Henri, 9:51
Herzog, George, 9:68
Heskes, Irene, 9:74
Hess, Dame Myra, 9:76
Hiller, Ferdinand, 9:115
Hinrichsen family, 9:123
Hirsh, Nurit, 9:141–142
Hirshberg, Jehoash, 9:142
Hitman, Uzi, 9:290
Holdheim, Theodore, 9:317
Hollaender family, 9:321
Horenstein, Jascha, 9:525
Hornbostel, Erich Moritz von,
    1:290, 9:526, 291
Horowitz, Vladimir, 9:544
Huberman, Bronislaw, 9:575,
    10:758
Hungary, pianists, 18:129
Hurok, Solomon, 9:623
Ian, Janis, 9:655–656
Ibn Abī al-Ṣalt, 9:657–658
Idelsohn, Abraham Zvi, 8:426,
    9:708–707, 503
Inbal, Eliahu, 9:752
Isserlis, Steven, 10:772
Istomin, Eugene, 10:786
Jacobi, Abraham, 11:37
Jacobi, Frederick, 11:38
Jacobi, Georg, 11:38
Jacobi, Hanoch, 11:38
Jacobs, Arthur, 11:45–46
Jacobsthal, Gustav, 11:56
Jadassohn, Salomon, 11:57
Jadlowker, Hermann, 11:58
Jaffe, Eli, 11:65
Janowski, Max, 11:80
Japhet, Israel Meyer, 11:85
Jassinowsky, Pinchas, 11:91
Joachim, Joseph, 11:340
Jochsberger, Tzipora, 11:361
Jonas, Emile, 11:393

Judah ben Isaac (14th or 15th c.),
    11:487
Kadman, Gurit, 11:700
Kahn, Erich Itor, 11:720
Kaiser, Alois, 11:728
Kalib, Sholom, 11:733
Kalichstein, Joseph, 11:734
Karaczewski, Ḥanina, 11:785
Karel, Rudolph, 11:805
Karliner, Baruch, 11:810
Karmon, Israel, 11:814
Karniol, Alter Yehiel, 11:815
Katchen, Julius, 12:5
Katz, Israel (1930–), 12:12
Katz, Mindru, 12:14
Katz, Ruth, 12:15–16
Katz, Sholom, 12:16
Kaye, Nora, 12:41–42
Kent, Allegra, 12:77
Kentner, Louis, 12:78
Kern, Jerome, 7:17, 12:87
Kertesz, Istavan, 12:89
Kestenberg, Leo, 12:91–92
Kidd, Michael, 12:138
Kinsky, Georg Ludwig, 12:178
Kipnis, Alexander, 12:179
Kirchner, Leon, 12:184
Kirschner, Emanuel, 12:189
Kirstein, Lincoln, 12:190, 15:220
Klemperer, Otto, 12:227
Kletzki, Paul, 12:230
Klezmer, Feidman, 2:119, 6:729–
    730, 14:674–675, 675
Kogan, Abraham, 12:255
Kohn, Maier, 12:263–264
Kolisch, Rudolf, 12:274
Kolodin, Irving, 12:279
Kopytman, Mark Ruvimovich,
    12:297–298, 600
Korngold, Erich Wolfgang, 12:313
Kornitzer, Leon, 12:314
Koshetz, Nina, 12:317
Kostelanetz, André, 12:322
Koussevitzky, Serge, 12:326–327,
    13:226
Kowalski, Max, 12:330
Kraus, Gertrud, 12:340
Kraus, Lili, 12:341
Kraus, Moshe, 12:342
Krein, Alexander Abramovich,
    12:348
Kreisler, Fritz, 12:350
Kremer, Isa, 12:353
Krips, Josef, 12:361
Kroshner, Mikhail Yefimovich,
    12:372

Kurth, Ernst, 12:393
Kurz, Selma, 12:395
Kuweiti, Salah, 12:400
Kwartin, Zavel, 12:401
Lachmann, Robert, 1:439, 12:423–
    424
Lakner, Yehoshua, 12:441–442
Lamm, Pavel Aleksandrovich,
    12:453
Landowska, Wanda, 12:473–474
Lang, Pearl, 12:479
Lapson, Dvora, 12:492
Lavry, Marc, 12:534–535
Lear, Evelyn, 12:567–568, 567–568
Lebert, Sigmund, 12:591
Leef, Yinam, 12:600
Lefkowitz, David, 12:601–602,
    601–602
Leiber and Stoller, 12:618–619
Leibowitz, René, 12:622
Leichtentritt, Hugo, 12:625
Leigh, Adèle, 12:626
Leinsdorf, Erich, 12:627
Leoni, Myer, 4:117, 12:647–648
Lerer, Joshua, 12:653
Lerer, Shmuel, 12:653–654
Lert, Ernst, 12:660
Levant, Oscar, 12:678
Levi, Hermann, 12:688
Levi, Leo, 2:58, 12:690
Levi, Yoel, 12:695
Levi-Agron, Hassia, 12:695
Levine, James, 12:718
Levinson, Andre, 12:722–723
Levi-Tannai, Sara, 12:732–733
Levitsky, Mischa, 12:742
Lévy, Lazare, 12:752
Levy, Marvin David, 12:753
Lévy family, 12:745
Lévy family (French musicians),
    12:745
Lewandowski, Louis, 4:660, 8:504,
    12:758, 661
Lewenthal, Raymond, 12:758
Lewitzky, Bella, 12:770
Lhevinne, Josef, 12:773
Lichine, David, 12:795–796
Liebermann, Rolf, 12:808–809
Liebling, Estelle, 12:809–810
Mendelson, Jacob ben-Zion, 14:30
Mendelson, Solomon, 14:30–31
Mintz, Shlomo, 14:302
Moiseiwitsch, Benno, 14:422
Moscheles, Ignaz, 14:516
Piatigorsky, Gregor, 16:142
Poland, pianists, 3:433, 12:473–
    474

Rabinovicz, Pinchas, 17:38
Radzynski, Jan, 17:61–62
Raisa, Rosa, 17:74
Rambert, Dame Marie, 5:416, 17:84
Ramone, Joey, 17:87, 18:87
The Ramones, 17:87
Ran, Shulamit, 17:89
Rappaport, Jacob, 17:100
Raskin, Judith, 17:107
Rathaus, Karol, 17:109
Ravina, Menashe, 17:123
Ravitz, Shelomo, 17:124
Razumni, Ephraim Zalman, 17:133
Redlich, Hans Ferdinand, 17:159
Reed, Lou, 17:162
Reich, Steve, 17:198
Reiner, Fritz, 17:206
Reisenberg, Nadia, 17:211–212, 211–212
Reizenstein, Franz, 17:213
Reményi, Eduard, 17:216–217, 216–217
Resnik, Regina, 17:228
Réti, Rudolf, 17:244
Ricardo, David (1904-1982), 17:282–283
Rice, Elmer Leopold, 17:284–285
Rich, Buddy, 17:286
Rich, Denise Eisenberg, 17:287
Rieti, Vittorio, 17:297, 298
Ringer, Alexander L., 17:336
Rivlin, Shelomo Zalman, 17:351
Robbins, Jerome, 5:414–415, 17:353–354
Rochberg, George, 12:600, 17:357
Rodan, Mendi, 17:361–362
Rodgers, Mary, 17:363–364
Rodgers, Richard, 17:364
Rodney, Red, 17:364–365
Rodzinsky, Artur, 17:366
Rogers, Bernard, 17:368
Roitman, David, 17:370
Roland-Manuel, 17:372
Roll, Michael, 17:372–373, 372–373
Romanos Melodos, 4:326, 17:405
Romberg, Sigmund, 17:406
Ronly-Riklis, Shalom, 17:419
Rosé, Arnold Josef, 17:424
Rosé, Edward, 17:424
Rose, Leonard, 17:426
Rosen, Charles, 17:428
Rosenblatt, Josef, 17:441
Rosenfeld, Abraham Isaac Jacob, 17:445

Rosenstock, Joseph, 17:450
Rosenthal, Harold, 17:453
Rosenthal, Manuel, 12:451, 17:455
Rosenthal, Moriz, 17:456
Rosowsky, Solomon, 17:468, 18:725
Ross, Herbert, 17:469
Rossi, Madama Europa de', 17:473
Rossi, Salamone de', 17:473–474
Roth, David Lee, 17:480–481
Rothmueller, Aaron Marko, 17:487
Rózsavölgyi, Márk, 17:505
Rubin, Ruth, 17:513
Rubinstein, Anton Grigoryevich, 13:193, 17:516
Rubinstein, Artur, 17:516
Rubinstein, Ida, 17:517
Rudel, Julius, 17:519, 18:581
Rudinow, Moshe, 17:523
Rudolf, Max, 17:524
Russell, Henry, 17:531
Sacerdote, David, 17:632
Sachs, Curt, 17:634
Sadai, Yitzhak, 17:651
Sadie, Stanley, 17:657
Saint-Léon, Arthur Michel, 17:670
Salaman family, 17:680–681
Salmon, Karel, 17:692–693
Salzman, Pnina, 17:713–714
Samburphy, Daniel, 17:745
Saminsky, Lazare, 17:746–747, 18:725
Samuel, Harold, (1879-1937), 17:764
Sanderling, Kurt, 18:11
Sandler, Jacob Koppel, 18:16
Schachter, Carl, 18:99
Schaechter-Gottesman, Bella, 18:102
Schalit, Heinrich, 18:104
Schenker, Heinrich, 18:122
Schidlowsky, Leon, 18:128
Schiff, András, 18:129
Schifrin, Lalo, 18:132
Schillinger, Joseph, 18:134–135
Schindler, Kurt, 18:136
Schlamme, Martha Haftel, 18:138–139
Schlesinger family (Germany), 18:139
Schmidt, Joseph, 8:504, 18:145
Schnabel, Artur, 18:146–147
Schneider, Alexander, 18:150
Schoenberg, Arnold, 18:155–156
Schoene, Lotte, 18:156

Schorr, Baruch, 18:162–163
Schorr, Friedrich, 18:163
Schreker, Franz, 18:167
Schubert, Lia, 18:168–169
Schulhof, Moshe, 18:171
Schulhoff, Julius, 18:171–172
Schuller, Gunther, 18:172
Schuman, William Howard, 18:175
Schwartz, Stephen, 18:187
Schwarz, Rudolf, 18:190
Secunda, Sholom, 18:233–234
Segal, Uri, 18:248
Seiber, Mátyás György, 18:253
Sendrey, Alfred, 18:287
Serkin, Peter Adolf, 18:311
Serkin, Rudolf, 18:311
Seter, Mordechai, 18:318–319
Sevitzky, Fabien, 18:329
Shaham, Gil, 18:362–363
Shallon, David, 18:375
Shapero, Harold, 18:397–398
Sharett, Yehudah, 18:413
Sharlin, William, 18:414–415
Shaw, Artie, 18:423
Shelem, Mattityahu, 18:445–446
Shemer, Naomi, 18:457–458
Sheriff, Noam, 18:462–463
Shestapol, Wolf, 18:466
Shiloah, Amnon, 18:476–477
Shlonsky, Verdina, 18:496–497
Shmueli, Herzl, 18:498
Shulsinger, Bezalel, 18:532
Siegmeister, Elie, 18:556–557
Silbermann, Alphons, 18:577
Sills, Beverly, 18:581–582
Simon, Carly Elisabeth, 18:610
Singer, George, 18:634
Singer, Josef, 18:638
Singer, Kurt, 18:638–639
Sinigaglia, Leone, 18:641
Siprutini, Emanuel, 18:642
Sirota, Gershon, 18:644
Slatkin, Leonard, 18:666
Slonimski, Nicolas, 18:680
Slonimsky, Sergei Mikhailovich, 18:680
Smoira-Cohn, Michal, 18:689–690
Sobol, Mordechai, 18:702
Sokolow, Anna, 18:747
Solomon, 18:764
Solomon (British pianist), 14:516
Solti, Sir Georg, 18:781
Sondheim, Stephen, 19:13–14
Spector, Johanna, 19:93

Musicians and dancers, *continued*

Spivacke, Harold, 19:124
Spivak, Nissan, 19:125
Spivakovsky, Tossy, 19:125
Starer, Robert, 19:164
Stark, Edward, 19:165
Stein, Erwin, 19:177
Steinberg, Maximilian Ossejevich, 19:188
Steinberg, William, 19:190
Stenn, Rebecca, 19:201
Stern, Isaac, 19:210–211
Stern, Julius, 19:212
Stern, Moshe, 19:215–216
Sternberg, Erich-Walter, 19:219
Steuermann, Edward, 19:224
Stolyarski, Peter Solomonovich, 19:235
Strakosch, Maurice, 19:240
Stransky, Josef, 19:243
Straus, Oscar Solomon, 19:250
Strauss, Johann, Jr., 19:252–253
Stutschewsky, Joachim, 19:276
Styne, Jule, 19:278–279
Suliţeanu, Ghisela, 19:305
Sulzer, Solomon, 19:308–309
Susskind, Walter, 19:328
Szabolcsi, Bence, 19:400–401
Szell, George, 19:405
Szerman, Pinchas, 19:408
Szeryng, Henryk, 19:408
Szigeti, Joseph, 19:408
Tal, Josef, 19:461
Talmon, Zvi, 19:469
Tamiris, Helen, 19:496
Tansman, Alexander, 19:508–509
Taruskin, Richard, 19:523–524
Taube, Michael, 19:527
Taube, Moshe, 19:527
Taube, Samuel Baruch, 19:527
Tauber, Richard, 19:528
Tausig, Karl, 19:529–530
Temianka, Henri, 19:600
Tertis, Lionel, 19:650
Thalberg, Sigismund, 19:666
Thomas, Michael Tilson, 19:705–706
Tischler, Hans, 19:733
Toch, Ernst, 20:14
Tourel, Jennie, 20:75
Tsfassman, Alexander Naumovich, 20:165
Tucker, Richard, 20:169
Tugal, Pierre, 20:173
Tureck, Rosalyn, 20:192
Ullman, Viktor, 20:241

Ungar, Benjamin, 20:248
Unger, Max, 20:248–249
Valabrega, Cesare, 20:458
Vardi, Arie, 20:476
Veinberg, Moissey Samiulovich, 20:490
Veprik, Alexander Moiseyevitch, 20:505–506
Vicol, Adrian, 20:516
Vigoda, Samuel, 20:525–526
Vinaver, Chemjo, 20:534
Vogel, Wladimir, 20:567
Volpe, Arnold, 20:578
Waghalter, Ignatz, 20:594
Wagner, Richard, 20:594–595
Waldman, Leibele, 20:605
Waldteufel, Emil, 20:606
Wallenstein, Alfred, 20:612
Walter, Bruno, 20:613
Wasserzug, Ḥayyim, 20:687
Weill, Kurt, 20:714
Weinberg, Jacob, 20:717
Weinberger, Jaromir, 20:719
Weiner, Lazar, 20:720
Weiner, Leo, 20:720
Weinstock, Herbert, 20:728–729
Weintraub, Solomon, 20:729
Weinzweig, John, 20:729–730
Weisball, Hugo, 20:731
Weisgal, Abba Joseph, 20:731
Weissberg, Julia Lazarevna, 20:737
Weissenberg, Alexis, 20:737
Weisser, Albert, 20:738
Weisser, Joshua, 20:738
Weissmann, Adolf, 20:740
Wellesz, Egon Joseph, 21:5–6
Werner, Eric, 21:13–14
Wertheim, Rosalie Marie, 21:15–16
Wiener, Jean, 21:47
Wienlawski, Henri, 21:51
Wilensky, Moshe, 21:61
Williams, Charles, 21:64
Winternitz, Emanuel, 21:91–92
Wittgenstein, Paul, 21:127
Wohlberg, Moshe, 21:131–132
Wolff, Albert Louis, 21:143
Wolff, Hermann, 21:144
Wolfsohn, Juliusz, 21:148
Wolfsthal, Chune, 21:151
Wolpe, Stefan, 21:155
Wormser, André, 21:229
Yampolsky, Berta, 21:279
Yasser, Joseph, 21:288
Yellin-Bentwich, Thelma, 21:448

Zaludkowski, Elijah, 21:448
Zefira, Brachah, 21:493
Zehavi, David, 21:493
Zeira, Mordecai, 21:494
Zemach, Benjamin, 21:503
Zhitomirski, Alexander Matveyevich, 21:525
Zilberts, Zavel, 21:530
Zimbalist, Efrem, 21:534
Zukerman, Pinchas, 21:681
Zukofsky, Paul, 21:682
Zur, Menachem, 21:688
Music of Latin America (Slonimsky), 18:680
Musicologists
Adler, Guido, 1:397–398
Adler, Israel, 1:399
Bayer, Batya, 3::231
Bely, Viktor Arkadyevich, 3:307–308
Beregovski, Moshe, 3:408
Braudo, Yevgeni Maximovich, 4:137
Brook, Barry Shelley, 4:208
Bukofzer, Manfred, 4:265
Churgin, Bathia, 4:723
Deutsch, Otto Erich, 5:625
Einstein, Alfred, 6:262
Eisenstein, Judith Kaplan, 6:273–274
Harran, Don, 8:361–362
Herzog, George, 9:68
Hirshberg, Jehoash, 9:142
Hornbostel, Erich Moritz von, 9:526
Idelsohn, Abraham Zvi, 9:708–709
Katz, Ruth, 12:15
Leichtentritt, Hugo, 12:625
Levi, Leo, 12:690
Pincherle, Marc, 16:164–165
Pisk, Paul Amadeus, 16:186
Plamenac, Dragan, 16:214
Redlich, Hans Ferdinand, 17:159
Ringer, Alexander L., 17:336
Rosowsky, Solomon, 17:468
Silbermann, Alphons, 18:**577**
Singer, Kurt, 18:638–639
Slonimski, Nicolas, 18:680
Slonimsky, Sergei Mikhailovich, 18:680
Smoira-Cohn, Michal, 18:689–690
See also Music
Músicos y relojeros (Steinberg), 19:174
Music Since 1900 (Slonimsky), 18:680
Music Teachers Training College (Tel Aviv), 2:79

Musiklexicon (Riemann), 6:262
Musil, Alois, 14:**701**
Musil, Robert, 2:65
Muskmelon, 14:14
Muslim Caliphate communities, 5:103–104
Muslims. *See* Islam
Muslims, new. *See* Jadid al-Islam
Musolino, Benedetto, 14:**701–702**
Mussaf he-Arukh (Mussafia), 14:702
Mussafia, Abraham Ḥai, 14:702
Mussafia, Adolfo, 14:702
Mussafia, Benjamin ben Immanuel, 3:609, 14:**702**
Mussafia, Ḥayyim Isaac, 14:702
Musselmen. *See* Muselmann
Mussert, Anton Adriaan, 14:**702–703**
Mussili I, 9:292
Mussili II, 9:292
Mussolini, Benito, 4:9, 9:287–288, 14:**703–704**
Mustafa, son of Suleiman the Magnificent, 2:33
Mustaʿrab, Mustaʿrabs, 4:344, 10:298, 14:**704**
Mustard, 14:**704**, vol. 16: color insert
Muṣuri (king of Moab), 14:403
Muszkat, Marion, 14:**704**
Mutakallimūn, 11:729–730
Muʿtazila, 11:729–730
Muʿtazilite Kalām, 16:77, 79–80
Muʾtazilite philosophy, 1: 212, 213
Muter, Mela, 14:**704–705**
Mutnik, Abraham, 14:**705**
Mutnikovich, Abraham. *See* Mutnik, Abraham
Mutual aid societies. *See* Fraternal societies
Muwashshaḥāt, 1:616
Muwatalli, 9:292
Muyal, Avraham, 14:**705**
Myanamar. *See* Burma
My Chronicle (Eichenbaum), 6:246
Mydans, Carl, 4:107
Myer, Morris, 14:**705**
Myer, Sidney Baevski, 14:**705–706**
Myerhoff, Barbara, 2:187
Myerhoff, Barbara Gay Siegel, 14:**706**
Myers, Abraham C., 12:598
Myers, Arthur, 15:243
Myers, Asher Isaac, 14:**706**
Myers, Charles Samuel, 14:**707**
Myers, Gustavus, 14:**707**
Myers, Lawrence E., 14:**707**
Myers, Michael, 15:243
Myers, Mordecai, 4:255, 14:**708**, 15:198

Myers, Moses, 14:**708**, 15:299
Myers, Myer, 14:**708**, 15:196
Myers, Samuel, 14:**708–709**
Myers, Sir Arthur Melziner, 14:**706**
Myers, Sir Michael, 14:**707–708**
Myerson, Bess, 14:**709**
Myerson, Golda. *See* Meir, Golda
My Father Is My Help (Eliezer ben Joel ha-Levi of Bonn), 6:327
My Jerusalem (ballet, Eifman), 6:253
My Lai 4: A Report on the Massacre and Its Aftermath (Hersch), 9:44
My Life (Adler), 1:394
My Life As A Rebel (Balabanoff), 3:82–83
My Models Were Jews (Reiss), 17:212
Mynona, 14:**709**
My People's Prayer Book (Hoffman), 9:309
My Poems (Einhorn), 6:258
Myrrh, 14:**709–710**, vol. 16: color insert
Myrtle, 14:**710**
Mysh, Michael, 14:**710**
Myslitel (Aldanov), 1:606
My Spring Will Come. See Pridet vesna moya
The Mysteries of Pittsburgh (Chabon), 4:555
Mysterium Novum (Elhanan), 6:315
The Mystery of the Names, Letters, and Vowels, and the Power of the Magical Operations, according to the Sages of Lunel, 11:610
Mystery plays, 3:669
Mystici Corpus Christi (Piux XII), 9:371
Mysticism, 11:585, 587–588, 589–590
    Aaron of Baghdad, 1:219
    Abelson, Joshua, 1:249
    Aberlin, Rachel, 1:254
    Abraham ben Alexander Katz of Kalisk, 1:294
    Abraham ben Alexander of Cologne, 1:294
    alphabet, Hebrew, 1:728–730
    angels, 2:158–159
    anthropomorphism, 2:190, 191
    antinomianism, 2:199, 200–201
    asceticsm, 2:549
    Botarel, Moses ben Isaac, 4:101
    of Buber, 4:234
    commandments, reasons for, 5:89–90
    contemplation and, 13:761
    dietary laws and, 5:657
    Dionysius van Ryckel, 5:674

    dualism, 6:30
    Elijah, 6:334
    emotions, role of, 6:397
    Geonic period, 11:596–599
    God, 11:623, 659–660
    Ḥasidei Ashkenaz, 8:386–389
    Ḥasidism, 11:599–602
    Horodezky, Samuel Abba, 9:527
    Johanan ben Zakhai, 11:375
    Joseph and Asenath, 11:418
    Joseph ben Ḥiyya, 11:421
    kavod, 8:387
    Kook, Abraham Isaac, 12:290–291
    literature, English, 6:434
    Maimonidean controversy, 13:374–375, 380
    Morocco, 14:496–497
    music, 14:649, 650, 651, 660–661, 660–663, 666–667, 675, 676, 678
    Muslim, Jerusalem and, 11:223–224
    mystical literature, 7:15, 13:107–108
    mystic way, 11:661–665
    neoplatonism, 15:84, 85
    Ramon, Lull, 17:85–86
    Raza Rabba, 17:128
    Raziel, Book of, 17:129–130
    Safed as center, 10:170
    Satanow, Isaac, 18:73–74
    Scholem, Gershom Gerhard, 18:158–159
    Sefer Raza Rabba, 17:128
    Torah, 11:659–660
    See also Kabbalah (mysticism); Merkabah mysticism; Neoplatonism; Sufism
Mystiek Lichaam (Kellendonk), 6:69
The Myth of the Negro Past (Herskovits), 9:46
Myths and mythology, 14:**710–711**
    Akedah, 1:558, 559
    Anath, 2:131
    Ares, 2:425
    Baal, 3:9–12, 8:184, 11:113
    Balaam, 3:76–81
    Barnacle goose, 3:167
    Dagon, 5:378, 6:387
    Egyptian, 6:613
    golem, 18:199, 200–201
    Hadad, 8:184–185
    Heracles, 9:5
    Hurrian, 9:629–630
    leviathan, 12:696–697
    paradise in Eden narrative, 15:626

Myths and mythology, *continued*
science fiction and fantasy, Jewish, 18:198–199, 200–201
Sumerian literature, 14:99–101
Titans, 19:735
Tower of Babel, 3:19–21
Ugaritic, 3:10, 11, 12, 6:22
See also Hagiography
Mytilene, Duke of. *See* Abenaes, Solomon
My Universities. See Moi universitety
M'zab (Algeria), 14:**711–712**

N
N (letter), 14:*713*, 15:5
Naamah, 14:**713**
Naaman, 11:520, 14:**713–714**
Na'amat. *See* Pioneer Women
Na'an (Israel), 14:**714**
Naar, David, 14:**714**
Naarah (ancient Israel), 14:**714**, *715*
Na'ari, Moses ben Judah. *See* Nagari, Moses ben Judah
Nabal, 1:255, 14:**714–716**
Nabateans, 14:**716–718**, *717t*
Aramaic inscriptions, 2:348
Elusa, 6:370–371
Glueck, Nelson, 2:371
Nabi Samuil (Israel), 14:**388**
Nablus (Israel), 14:**718–719**
Nabonidus, 14:**719**
Naboth, 1:524, 14:**719–720**
Naboth's Vineyard (Dane), 6:336
Naçan, Moses. *See* Açan, Moses de Tarrega
Nachéz, Tivadar, 14:**720**
Nachgelassene Schriften (Calé), 4:353
Nach Jerusalem (Frankl), 7:213
Nachlas, Wolf. *See* Alexeyev, Alexander
Nachmanides, 7:359
Nachmann, Werner, 14:**720**
Nachmanovich, Isaac, 14:**721**
Nachmanovich, Isaac ben Naḥman, 14:**720**
Nachmanovich, Mordecai ben Isaac, 14:**720**
Nachmanovich, Naḥman Isaakovitch, 14:**720**
Nachmanovich family, 14:**720–721**
Nachod (Czech Republic), 14:**721**
Nachod, Jacob, 14:**721**
Nachod, Oskar, 14:**721**
Nachsommer (Lorm), 13:193
Nacht (Hilsenrath), 9:119
Die Nacht des Dr. Herzfeld (Hermann), 9:24

Die Nachtmuetze... (opera, Kreutzer), 6:337
La Nacion. *See* The Spanish-Portuguese Nation of the Caribbean: La Nacion
Nadab (King), 4:13
Nadab (King of Israel), 1:256–257, 542, 543, 14:**722**
Nadab (son of Aaron), 14:**721–722**
Nadan. *See* Nadab (King of Israel)
Nadav, Ẓevi, 14:**722**
Naddaf, Abraham Ḥayyim, 14:**722–723**
Nadel, Arno, 14:**723**
Nadel, Siegfried Ferdinand Stephan, 14:**723**
Nadel, Yizḥak. *See* Oren, Yizḥak
Nadelman, Elie, 14:**723–724**
Nāder, Shah, 14:**724**
Nadich, Judah, 14:**724–725**
Nadie la conoció nunca (Eichelbaum), 6:245
Nadir, Moyshe, 14:**725–726**
Nadjus, Leo. *See* Naidus, Leib
Nadler, Jerrold Lewis, 14:**726**
Nadler, Marcus, 14:**726**
Nadler, Serge. *See* Natra, Sergiu
Nadn. *See* Dowry
Nad Ned (Bartal), 18:206
Nad Ned (Ben-Tovim), 18:206
Nadson, Semyon Yakovlevich, 14:**726–727**
Naḍīr Banū I-, 14:**725**
Nadvornaya (Ukraine), 14:**727**
Nadwórna (Ukraine). *See* Nadwornaya (Ukraine)
Naeh, Barukh ben Menahem, 14:**727**
Naemlich (Adler), 1:405
Naftali, Peretz, 14:**727**
Naftulei Adam (Burla), 4:295
Nafusi, Isaac. *See* Nifoci, Isaac
The Nag; or, Cruelty to Animals. See Di Klyatshe; Oder Tsar Baley Khayim
Nagara (Spain). *See* Nájera (Spain)
Nagari, Moses ben Judah, 14:**727**
Nagasaki (Japan), 11:81, 82, 14:**728**
Nagel, Ernst, 14:**728**
Nag Hammadi Codices, 14:**728–729**
Nagid, 14:**729–733**
Nagids. *See* Negidim
Nagin, Harry S., 14:**733**
Nagler, Isadore, 14:**734**
Nagy, Endre, 14:**734**
Nagybaczoni-Nagy, Vilmos, 14:**734**
Nagybánya (Romania). *See* Baia-Mare (Romania)

Nagybecskerek (Serbia). *See* Zrenjanin (Serbia)
Nagykanizsa (Hungary), 14:**734–735**
Nagykàroly (Romania). *See* Carei (Romania)
Nagymarton (Austria). *See* Mattersdorf (Austria)
Nagymihá`ly. *See* Michalovce (Slovakia)
Nagyszalonta (Romania). *See* Salonta (Romania)
Nagyszeben (Romania). *See* Sibiu (Romania)
Nagytapolcsány. *See* Topolcany (Slovakia)
Nagyvárad (Romania). *See* Oradea
Naḥal, 14:**735**
Naḥal (IDF), 10:469
Naḥalah le-Yisrael (Ḥazzan), 8:506
Nahalal (ancient Israel), 14:**735**
Nahalal (Israel), 14:**735**
Naḥalat Ari'el (Shapiro), 18:404
Naḥalat Avot (Meir ben Elijah), 13:783
Naḥalat Binyamin (Isaac Benjamin Wolf ben Eliezer Lipman), 10:42
Naḥalat Shivah (Bacharach), 3:34
Naḥalat Ya'akov (Jacob Koppel ben Aaron Sasslower), 11:42
Naḥalat Ya'akov (Naumberg), 18:273
Naḥalat Yehoshu'a (Shapira), 18:400–401
Naḥalat Yehudah (Israel), 14:**736**
Naḥalat Yosef (Adani), 1:382
Naḥal Miẓrayim. *See* Egypt, Brook of
Naḥal Oz (Israel), 14:**736**
Naham of Bratzlav, 5:410
Naham of Bratzlav, dance, 5:411
Naharin, Ohad, 3:214, 14:**736**
Nahariyyah (Israel), 14:**736–737**
Nahash, 2:84, 14:**737**
Nahavand (Iran). *See* Nehavand (Iran)
Nah'āwendī, Benjamin ben Moses al-, 14:**737–738**
biblical exegesis of, 3:641
Judeo-Arabic literature and, 11:532
Karaites, 11:789
Naḥman Bar Rav Huna, 14:**738**
Naḥman ben Isaac, 14:**738**
Naḥman ben Jacob, 14:**738–739**
Naḥmanides, 2:548, 14:**739–748**
Abraham, 1:285
Abraham ben David of Posquières, 1:297
Abraham ben Isaac, 1:300
Abulafia, Meir, 1:341
Adret, Solomon ben Abraham, 1:421, 423

amulets, 2:121

biblical commentary, 6:271

Christiani, Pablo, 4:673

commentators, 14:745–746

Disputation of Barcelona, 3:145–146

disputations and polemics, 5:693

eschatology, 6:500–502

eschatology controversy, 14:747

halakhah, 8:252

Halakhist, 14:741–743

ḥiddushim, 9:96

Judah ben Yakar as teacher of, 11:492

Kabbalist, 14:743–747

Maimonides controversy, 14:739

miracles, 14:308

mishpat Ivri, 14:335

Moses, 14:537

Moses de Leon controversy, 14:746–747

Peshitta, use of, 3:599

on physicians, 13:740, 741

religious influence in Spain, 11:605

ressurection, 17:243

Sefer ha-Mitzvot, 8:259

space and place, 19:67

synthetic approach to biblical exegesis and study, 3:642, 643

Naḥman of Bratslav, 8:427, 14:**748–753**

forgiveness of sin, 7:128–129

ḥasidic narrative, 7:16

Naḥman of Horodenka, 14:**753**

Naḥman of Kosov, 14:**753–754**

Nahmias, Samuel ben David. *See* Morosini, Giulio

Naḥmias, ibn, family, 14:**754**

Naḥmias, Joseph ben Joseph, 14:**754**

Naḥmias, R. Eliezer Raphael, 2:31

Nahmias family. *See* Abendana family

Naḥmias family, 10:784

Naḥmijas, Danilo, 14:**754**

Naḥmuli, Joseph, 2:31

Nahon, Gerard, 14:**754–755**

Nahon, Gérard, 11:325

Nahon, Isaac, 14:754

Nahon, Isaac ben Joseph, 14:754

Nahon, Moses, 14:754

Nahon family, 14:**754**

Nahor, 14:**755–756**

Naḥote, 2:93

Nahoum, Ḥaim, 14:**756,** 16:346

Nahoum, Ḥayyim, 15:537, 543, 544

Nahr Abu Futrus. *See* Yarkon river

Nahrai ben Nissim, 2:405, 4:77, 14:**756**

Nahrawān (Iraq), 14:**756–757**

Nahr Barada (Syria). *See* Amanah (Syria)

Nahshon, 14:**757**

Nahshon Bar Zadok, 14:**757**

Nahum, Aaron Sasson ben Elijah, 14:**759**

Nahum, Aaron Sassoon ben Eliahu, 10:17–18

Nahum, Book of, 6:492, 14:**757–759**

Nahum, Eliezer ben Jacob, 14:**759**

Nahum of Gimzo, 14:**759**

Bible text treated as binding authority by, 3:584

Nahum the Mede, 14:**759**

Nahum the Scrivener, 18:602

Naian (ancient Israel). *See* Ai (ancient Israel)

Naiditsch, Isaac Asher, 14:**760**

Naidus, Leib, 14:**760**

Naiera (Spain). *See* Nájera (Spain)

Naim, Aziz ben Jonah, 11:557, 558

Naimovich, Isak, 4:276

Naimovich, Maxim, 4:276

Nain (ancient Israel), 14:**760**

Naissus (Serbia). *See* Niš

Najar, Judah ben Jacob, 14:760

Najar, Maimon, 14:760

Najara (Spain). *See* Nájera (Spain)

Najara, Israel, 2:17, 11:556, 13:188, 14:667, *671*

Najara, Israel ben Moses, 14:**761**

Najara, Moses, 14:760–761

Najara family, 14:**760–761**

Najar family, 14:**760**

Najāt al-Ghāriqīn (Adani), 1:381

Najdorf, Miguel, 14:**761–762**

Nájera (Spain), 14:**762**

Najīb al-Dawla, 14:**762**

Najjar, Nathan, 6:61

Najman, Julija, 14:**762**

Najnudel, León David, 14:**762**

Najrān (Yemen), 14:**762–763**

Nakam (Frankfurter), 7:204

Nakar, Meir, 14:**763**

Nakba, 10:730

Nakdimon ben Guryon, 14:**763**

The Nakedness of the Fathers: Biblical Visions and Revisions (Ostriker), 20:299

Name, change of, 14:**763–764**

Naményi, Ernest, 14:**764**

Namer Ḥavarburot (Shabtai), 8:722

Names, 14:**764–770**

abbreviation of, 1:238

Abu, 1:333

Biblical, 14:**764–766**

clothing for name-giving ceremony, vol. 7: color insert

folklore, 7:108

of God, 3:608–609

of God, Bible translations, rendering in, 3:631

for Jewish communities, 11:545

Middle Ages, 14:768–769

modern times, 14:769–770

Patriarchs, 15:690

surnames, establishment of, 14:768

Talmudic, 14:767–768

Namias, Jerome, 14:**770**

Namibia. *See* South West Africa

Namier, Sir Lewis, 14:**770–771**

Naming ceremonies, 3:721–722

Namir, Mordechai, 14:**771–772**

Namir, Ora, 14:**772**

Nancy (France), 14:**772–773**

Goudchaux, Michel, 8:16

Ñanigalbat, land of, 9:628

Nanotime (Kosko), 18:200

Nansen Office, 17:184

Nantes (France), 14:**773**

Naomi, 1:416, 6:347–348, 14:**773**

Naon, Avram. *See* Nom, Ibrahim

Naphtali, 14:**773–775,** *774*

Bilhah, 3:698

Naphtali, Testament of. See Testament of Naphtali

Naphtali ben Isaac ha-Kohen. *See* Katz, Naphtali ben Isaac

Naples (Italy), 14:**775–777**

Naples, kingdom of

Abrabanel family, 1:274, 275–276

Amalfi, 2:31

Brindisi, 4:184

expulsions, 2:140, 4:184

Naples and Collier County (FL), 14:**777**

Napoleon Bonaparte, 10:173–174, 175, 182, 11:54, 14:**777–778**

in Alsace, 2:8

Ancona, 2:141

Assembly of Jewish Notables, 2:599–602

emancipation, 4:202, 6:378, 7:155, 9:231–232

Florentine Jews under, 7:85

Frankfurt on the Main (Germany), 7:209

Infamous Decree, 2:8, 15:576

Paduan Jews under, 15:567

Palatinate Jews under, 15:576

Napoleon III, 2:110–111

Napoléon intime (Lévy), 12:747

Nappaha, Isaac, 2:16

Naquet, Alfred Joseph, 14:**778–779**

NARA, 14:**779**

Naram-Sin, 1:564

Narbata (ancient city), 14:**779**

Narboni. *See* Moses ben Joshua of Narbonne

Narboni, Alla ben Sidun ben Joshua, 14:**779**

Narboni, André, 14:779

Narboni family, 14:**779**

Narbonne (France), 1:213, 14:**779–781**

Narcissus (flower), 7:91

Nard. *See* Spikenard

Nardi, Nahum, 14:**781**

Naresh (Babylonia), 14:**781**

Narkis, Zvi, 4:370

Narkiss, Bezalel, 14:**781–782**

Narkiss, Mordechai, 14:**782**

Narmer (pharaoh). *See* Menes (Egyptian king)

Narodietsky, Nahum. *See* Nardi, Nahum

Narodnaya Volya, 18:707

Narodnaya Volya movement, Osipovich, Nahum, 15:504

Narodniki, 18:707

Narodowa Demokracja. *See* Endecja

Narodowa Demokracja (Poland). *See* Endecja

Narol (Poland), 14:**782**

Narot, Joseph, 14:**782**

Narrowe, Morton, 14:**782–783**

The Narrows (Irvine), 18:200

Narseh, 3:29

NASA. *See* National Aeronautics and Space Administration (NASA)

Nasatir, Abraham Phineas, 14:**783**

Nasaud (Romania), 14:**783**

Naschitz, Theodor. *See* Nachéz, Tivadar

Nashāshībī, Rāghib Bey al-, 10:274, 275

Nashim, 14:**783**

Nashim (Almog), 1:680

Nashim (Shapira), 18:401

Nash papyrus, 14:**783–784**

Nashville (TN), 14:**784**

Nasi, 4:614, 10:155–156, 14:**784–785**, 15:525

Nasi, Dona Gracia
Abrabanel, Benvenida, 1:276
Ancona, 2:140
Lev, Joseph Ben David Ibn, 12:676

Nasi, Gracia, 14:**785–786**

Nasi, Joseph, 2:34, 10:777, 14:**786–787**, 15:524, 532, 541, 16:345–346
Abenaes, Solomon and, 1:249

Nasielsk (Poland), 14:**787**

Nasi family, 10:777

Nasim
of Holy Land, 6:543–544
of Isfahan, 15:789
Johanan ben Zakhai, 11:376

Nasi Rabban Gamaliel, 10:146–147

Nasna (Romania), 14:**787–788**

Nasrallah, Sheik Hassan, 9:298

Nassau (Germany), 14:**788**

Nassauer, Rudolf, 14:**788**

Nasser, Gamal Abdul, 6:234, 12:795, 14:**788–789**
Ben-Gurion, David, 3:347
Palestine Liberation Organization, 15:589–590
Six Day War, 18:648–655

Nass family. *See* Leidesdorfer family

Nassy, David de Isaac Cohen, 14:**789**

Nasz Przegląd (newspaper), 14:**789–790**

Nataf. *See* Balsam

Natal, founding, 10:56

Natanson, Ludwik, 15:**5**

Natanson, Marc, 18:707

Natanson, Mark, 15:**5–6**

Nathan (prophet), 15:**6**

Nathan, Abraham, 15:**8**

Nathan, Annie. *See* Meyer, Annie Nathan

Nathan, Benjamin, 15:200

Nathan, David, 15:**8**, 242

Nathan, Emile, 16:349

Nathan, Ernesto, 15:**8**, 16:345

Nathan, Frederic Lewis, 15:6

Nathan, George Jean, 15:**8**

Nathan, Harry, 18:706

Nathan, Harry Louis, Baron, 15:**9**, 16:342

Nathan, Henry, 4:186, 187, 15:**9**, 16:341

Nathan, Ibrahim, 4:51

Nathan, Isaac, 4:117, 15:**9**

Nathan, Joseph Edward, 15:**9–10**, 243

Nathan, Louis Edward, 4:673

Nathan, Manfred, 12:554, 15:**10**

Nathan, Matthew, 15:6

Nathan, Maud, 15:**10**

Nathan, Mordecai, 15:**10–11**

Nathan, Moses. *See* Açan, Moses de Tarrega

Nathan, Mulla Ibrahim, 15:**11**

Nathan, Nathaniel, 15:6

Nathan, Paul, 12:482, 15:**11**

Nathan, Philip, 4:226

Nathan, Robert, 14:541, 15:6–7, 289

Nathan, Robert Roy, 15:**11–12**

Nathan, Simon, 15:7–8

Nathan, Venguessone, 15:**12**

Nathan ben Abraham I, 15:**12**

Nathan ben Abraham II, 15:**12–13**

Nathan ben Isaac Ha-Kohen Ha-Bavli, 15:**13**

Nathan ben Jehiel of Rome, 12:465, 15:**13–14**
Judeo-Greek glosses of, 11:546
Judeo-Italian glosses of, 11:547
le'azim and, 12:405

Nathan ben Samuel, 3:586

Nathan der Weise, 9:230

Nathan der Weise (Lessing), 8:436, 12:665

Nathan de-Ẓuẓita Resh Galuta, 15:**14**

Nathanel ben Jehiel Foa, 7:92

Nathan family (U.K.), 15:**6–7**

Nathan family (U.S.), 15:**7–8**, 7t

Nathan Ha-Bavli, 15:**15**, 278
See also Avot de-Rabbi Nathan

Nathaniel of Chinon. *See* Nethanel of Chinon

Nathan Note of Shklov. *See* Notkin, Nata

Nathan of Churt. *See* Nathan, Harry Louis, Baron

Nathan of Gaza, 1:339, 11:43, 15:**15–17**, 538
Amigo, Abraham, 2:77
beginning of Shabbatean movement, 18:342, 343
Elisha Ḥayyim ben Jacob Ashkenazi, 6:354
influence on Shabbatean movement, 18:346, 353
Shabbetai Ẓevi's apostasy, 18:349–350, 351
Shabbetai Ẓevi's imprisonment, 18:348
Sheluḥei Ereẓ Israel, 18:451

Nathan of Trinquetaille, 13:784

Nathans, Daniel, 13:9, 15:**17–18**

Nathansen, Henri, 15:**18**

Nathan Shklover. *See* Notkin, Nata

Nathanson, Bernhard, 15:**18**

Nathanson, Dov Baer. *See* Nathanson, Bernhard

Nathanson, Joseph Saul, 6:543–544, 8:452, 15:**18–19**

Nathanson, Mendel Levin, 15:**19**

Nathan Sternhartz of Nemirov. *See* Naḥman of Bratslav

Nathan Sternherz of Nemirov. *See* Naḥman of Bratslav

National Academy for Adult Jewish Studies, 6:200

National Advisory Committee on Aeronautics, 18:588

National Aeronautics and Space Administration (NASA), 1:430, 18:588

National Association for the Advancement of People of Color (NAACP), 3:734, 735, 736

National Association of Jewish Chaplains, 9:564

National Association of Social Workers, 18:585

National Association of Temple Educators, 6:199

National Basketball Association
    Auerbach, Red, 2:656–657
    Fleisher, Larry, 7:76
    Podoloff, Maurice, 16:253

National Catholic Center for Holocaust Education, 9:453–454

National Center for Jewish Healing, 6:254

National Committee for Rescue from Nazi Terror, 17:109–110

The National Community Relations Advisory Council (NCRAC). *See* Jewish Council on Public Affairs

National Conference of Christians and Jews, 6:199

National Conference of Jewish Charities
    Bijur, Nathan, 3:695
    Low, Minnie, 13:233

National Conference of Jewish Communal Service, 18:585

National Conference of Jewish Communal Services, 18:723

National Conference of Jewish Welfare, 11:816

National Conference of Synagogue Youth (NCSY), 3:6

National Conference on Soviet Jewry, 15:**20–21**

National Council of Jewish Education (U.S.), 4:652, 6:196, 11:776

National Council of Jewish Federations and Welfare Funds. *See* Council of Jewish Federations and Welfare Funds

National Council of Jewish Women (NCJW), 15:**21–22**, 16:46, 18:610
    American, Sadie, 2:47
    American Jewess, 2:53
    Brenner, Rose, 4:161
    Dutch, 2:118

Solomon, Hannah Greenbaum, 13:233, 18:765

National Council of Young Israel, 21:**401–402**

National Democracy (Poland). *See* Endecja

The National Diffusion Network: Two Unique Holocaust Education Programs, 9:451–452

National Federation of Slovak Jews, 18:684

National Federation of Temple Sisterhoods, 15:**22**, 18:610
    See also Simon, Carrie Obendorfer

National Foundation for Jewish Culture, 15:**22–23**, 18:584

National Front (England), 6:423

National Havurah Committee, 15:**23–24**

National Heart Savers Association, 18:746

Nationalism
    Borochov, Ber, 4:90
    Cuba, 5:319
    Cuza, Alexander C., 5:345
    Jewish, 5:92–95
        Birnbaum, Nathan, 3:714–716
        Judaism, development of concept of, 11:518
        Po'alei Zion, 16:244
        relationship to religion, 6:36–37
        Smolenskin, Perez, 18:693
    Kook, Abraham Isaac, 12:292
    Lenin, Vladimir Ilyich, 5:92–94
    Poland, 16:347
    race, theory of, 17:46
    roots of, 16:102
    Stalin, Joseph, 5:94
    See also Zionism

Die Nationalitaetenfrage und die Sozialdemokratie (Bauer), 3:217

Die Nationalitaetenfrage und die Sozialdemonkratie (Bauer), 18:705

National Jewish Center for Immunology and Respiratory Medicine, 15:24

National Jewish Center for Learning and Leadership (CLAL), 4:**749–750**

National Jewish Coalition. *See* Republican Jewish Coalition

The National Jewish Community Relations Advisory Council. *See* Jewish Council on Public Affairs

National Jewish Democratic Council, 15:**25**

National Jewish Hospital for Consumptives, 16:185–186

National Jewish Outreach Program, 3:**7**

National Jewish Population Study, 18:736

National Jewish Welfare Board, 6:247

Nationaljudentum (Guedemann), 8:120

National Labor Federation. *See* Histadrut ha-Ovedim ha-Leumit

National Military Organization. *See* Irgun IẒeva'i Le'ummi

National Museum of American Jewish History, 15:**25–26**

National Parks in Israel, 15:**26–27**

Nationalrat, 15:**27**

National Religious Party, 8:308–309, 14:390, 391
    Shapira, Ḥayyim Moshe, 18:400

National Religious Party (political party), 15:**27–28**

National Scholarship Service and Fund for Negro Students, 18:183

National Socialism (Nazism), 1:292, 9:244–245, 252–253, 327–328, 15:**28–29**
    Adolf Hitler, 9:286–289
    Adorno, Theodor W., 1:420
    Alsace under, 2:9
    American Jewish Committee, 2:55
    American Joint Distribution Committee, 2:60–61
    Amsterdam, 2:114–115
    Ancona, 2:141
    Anti-Fascist Committee, Jewish, 2:196–197
    antisemitism
        course of, 9:244–245
        source of, 9:417
    Bitburg Controversy, 3:727–728
    Black-Jewish relations in U.S. and, 3:735
    blood libel used by, 3:778
    Bormann, Martin, 4:87
    boycott, anti-Nazi, 4:110–111
    boycotts, anti-Jewish, 4:110, 9:461
    Brunner, Alois, 4:223
    Buehler, Josef, 4:251
    Calmeyer, Hans-Georg, 4:374–375
    camps, concentration and extermination, 4:383–390, 9:253
    caricatures of Jews, 4:478–479
    Catholic Church, 4:712
    Czech Republic, 4:534–535
    denazification and, 5:578–579
    development, 6:560
    Dollfuss, Engelbert, 5:736
    Eichmann, Adolf Otto, 6:247–252
    England, 6:418
    euthanasia, 6:560–570

National Socialism (Nazism), *continued*
Final Solution, 7:21–22
forced labor, 7:122–124
as form of idolatry, 16:99
Frank, Hans Michael, 7:181
Frank, Karl Hermann, 7:192
Haavara, 8:171
Himmler, Heinrich, 9:121–122
Jewish settlement in America, 2:46
Judenraete, 11:526–529
Judenrein concept, 11:529
Juedischer Kulturbund, 11:570
Kristallnacht, 9:330–331
Madagascar Plan, 13:330–331
neo-Nazism, 2:233, 238
Nietzsche, Friedrich Wilhelm, 15:262
in Nuremberg, 15:347–348
Nuremberg laws, 15:348–350
Office of Special Investigations (OSI), U.S., 15:388, 18:461–462
opponents, Russian, 6:237–239
Palestine (Mandate), 19:632
Pavelić, Ante, 15:698
physics and, 16:136–137
Pohl, Oswald, 16:282
Protocols of the Learned Elders of Zion, 6:297
Schacht Plan, 18:101
Seyss-Inquart, Arthur, 18:333
SS and SD, humiliation of Polish Jews, 9:465
Statute of Limitations on Nazi crimes, 2:234
See also Fascism; Germany; Holocaust; Nazi-Deutsch; Neo-Nazism
National Society for Hebrew Day Schools. *See* Torah Umesorah
National Sound Archives, 14:639–640
National Theater of Israel, 8:719–723
National Women's League of the United Synagogue of America. *See* Women's League for Conservative Judaism
National Yiddish Book Center, 15:**29**–**30**
A Nation Dedicated to Religious Liberty (Adams), 1:380
Nationhood
Berkovits, Eliezer, 3:439
biblical development of, 15:733–734, 743
historicity of Exodus, 15:747–749
Nation of Islam, 3:736
Nations. *See* Goiim

Nations, The Seventy, 15:**30**–**32**, *31*
Native American Party, 15:291
Native Americans
Angel, Marc D., 2:147
Bunzel, Ruth Leah, 4:285
as Israelites, 4:121
as Judaizers, 11:520, 521
languages, biblical translations, 3:637
Natonek, Joseph, 15:**32**
Natorei Karta. *See* Neturei Karta
Natra, Sergiu, 15:**32**
Natronai bar Nehemiah, 15:**33**
Natronai ben Ḥavivai, 11:726–727, 15:**33**
Natronai ben Hilai, 2:104, 105, 15:**32**–**33**
Natronai Gaom, 2:127
Natufian period architecture, 2:399
The Natural and Supernatural Jew (Cohen), 5:10
Naturalis Historia (Pliny the Elder), 16:237–238
Naturalism
of Nissim ben Moses of Marseilles, 15:280
school of literature, 4:118, 126
Naturalization
Romania, 17:381–382
United Kingdom, 16:630
Naturalization Act of 1740, 20:305–306
Natural law, 11:508, 15:284–287
Natural Supernaturalism: Tradition and Revolution in Romantic Literature (Abrams), 1:327
Nature, 15:**33**–**35**
parables from, 15:622–623
in poetry, 7:9
See Also Ecology
Nature of man. *See* Man, nature of
Nature of the Judicial Process (Cardozo), 4:466
Nature Reserves Authority (Israel), 15:36
Nature reserves in Israel, 15:**35**–**36**
Natzweiler-Struthof (France), 15:36
Nauheim (Germany), 15:**36**–**37**
Nauman, Fred, 15:216
Naumann, Max, 20:507
Naumbourg, Samuel, 4:660, 15:37
Naumburg, Elkan, 15:37
Naumburg, Elsie Margaret Binger, 15:37
Naumburg, George Washington, 15:37
Naumburg, Margaret, 15:38
Naumburg, Robert Elkan, 15:37

Naumburg, Walter Wehle, 15:37
Naumburg family, 15:37
Naupaktos (Greece), 15:38
Navarro, Abraham, 15:**38**–**39**
Navarro, Moses (d. 1370), 15:38
Navarro, Moses (d. 1410), 15:38
Navarro, Solomon, 11:428
Navarro family, 15:38
Naveh (ancient city), 15:39
Navon, Benjamin Mordecai ben Ephraim, 15:39
Navon, David, 15:39
Navon, Ephraim ben Aaron, 15:39
Navon, Isaac Eliyahu, 15:39
Navon, Jonah ben Hanun, 15:**39**–**40**
Navon, Jonah Moses ben Benjamin, 15:**40**
Navon, Joseph, 15:40
Navon, Yitzhak, 15:**40**–**41**
Nawi, Reuben ben David, 15:41
Nawi family, 15:41
Naxos, Duke of. *See* Nasi, Joseph
Naysants (Poland). *See* Nowy Sacz
Nazarenes, 2:74
Nazarenus (Toland), 16:629
Nazareth (Israel), 15:**41**–**42**, 20:661
Nazarites
commandments concerning, 5:82t
John the Baptist and, 11:381
The Nazi and the Barber (Hilsenrath), 9:119
Nazi Concentration Camps (motion picture), 9:440
Nazi-Deutsch, 9:253, 15:42
See also National Socialism (Nazism)
Nazi Germany and the Jews (Friedlander), 9:418
Nazi hunters
Klarsfeld, Beate Auguste, 12:211
Klarsfeld, Serge, 12:211–212
Simon Wiesenthal Center, 18:618–620
Nazi medical experiments, 15:**43**–**44**
Dachau concentration camp, 5:376
Nazimova, Alla, 15:44
Nazi party. *See* National Socialism (Nazism)
The Nazi Persecution of the Gypsies (Lewy), 9:419
Nazir (tractate), 15:**44**–**45**
Nazir, Joseph ha-Levi, 15:45
Nazir, Moses ha-Levi, 15:45
Nazirite, 15:**45**–**47**
alcohol, 6:26
Samson, 11:565

Nazism. *See* National Socialism (Nazism)

NCJW (National Council of Jewish Women). *See* National Council of Jewish Women

NCSY. *See* National Conference of Synagogue Youth (NCSY)

Neander, August, 15:**47**, 16:630

Near East
ancient
demons, demonology, 5:572
ethics, 6:532–533, 534–535
Congress of Berlin, 3:453–454
dyeing, 6:77
idolatry, and religions of, 9:712–713
See also Middle East

Near East Report (periodical), 2:50

Nebaioth, 15:**47**

Nebezhal, Itzhak Ernst, 15:**47**

Nebmare Amunhotpe. *See* Amenophis III

Nebo (ancient location), 15:**47–48**

Nebraska (U.S.), 15:**48**, 48

Nebuchadnezzar, 3:24, 15:**48–51**
Ahab, 1:525
Ahasuerus, 1:538
Ammonites, 2:85–86
in arts, 5:418–419
Babylonian exile and, 6:611
conquests, 6:225, 641–642
Daniel and, 5:418, 419–420, 422
Jehoiachin and, 11:106
Jehoiakim and, 11:109
Jeremiah and, 11:127–128
Moab, 14:403
Philistines and, 16:54
Shadrach, Mishach, Abed-Nego, 18:361
Zedekiah, 9:182

Nebuchadnezzar II, 3:24, 14:91

Nebuzaradan, 15:**52**

Nechayanno (Sobol), 18:701

Necho, 11:458–459

The Necklace. See Sefer ha-Anak

Neco, 9:181, 15:**52**

Necoh. *See* Neco

Necromancy. *See* Divination; Magic

Nedarim (tractate), 15:**52–54**

Neder, Vows and vowing

Nedunyah. *See* Dowries

Needleman, Joseph, 15:303

Ne'eman, Yehoshua Leib, 15:**54**

Ne'eman, Yuval, 15:**54–55**, 16:139–140

Nefesh ha-Ḥayyim (Volozhiner), 8:415–416

Nefesh Yehudah (Frankfurter), 7:207

Nefesh Yehudi (Sobol), 8:721–722, 18:702

Nefilat appayim. See Taḥanun

Nefuẓot Yehudah, (Moscato, Judah ben Joseph), 14:515, 516

Nega'im (tractate), 15:**55**

Negative Dialectics (Adorno), 1:420

Negbah (Israel), 15:**55–56**

Negerplastik (Einstein), 6:263

Negev (Israel), 3:**349**, 15:56, **56–59**
the Arabah, 2:293
highlands, 10:112–114

Negidim, 6:231–232, 233, 724

Negligence and liability, 20:62–64, 65, 66

Negre, Astruc de Sen. *See* Abba Mari ben Eligdor

Negri, Giuditta. *See* Pasta, Giuditta

Negropont (Greece). *See* Chalcis (Greece)

Neḥalim (Israel), 15:**59**

Nehama, Joseph, 15:**59**

Nehamah, Judah, 15:540

Nehamias, Baruch. *See* Castro, Bendito de

Nehardea (Babylonia), 1:350, 2:37, 15:**59–60**

Nehar Pekod (ancient city), 15:**60**

Nehar Shalom (Sharabi), 18:411

Nehāvand (Iran), 15:**60**

Nehemiah (2nd c.), 15:**61–62**

Nehemiah (5th c. B.C.E.), 9:188–191, 15:**60–61**
Ezra and, 6:652
rebuilding of Jerusalem, 6:660–661
Samaritans, 17:720
Sanballat I and, 6:652
Tosefta attribution, 20:71

Nehemiah, Book of, 6:**656–662**
as autobiography, 3:705
economic aspects, 6:99
mishmarot and ma'amadot, 14:317–318
mishpat Ivri, 14:340

Nehemiah bar Kohen Ẓedek, 15:**62**

Nehemiah Ha-Kohen, 15:**62**, 18:348–349

Neher, André, 2:28, 15:**62–63**, 16:102–103

Neher-Bernheim, Renée, 15:**63**

Neḥmad ve-Na'im (Gans), 13:675

Nehorah (Israel), 15:**63**

Nehorai (2nd c.), 15:**63**

Nehorai (11th c.). *See* Meir ben Isaac Sheli'aḥ Ẓibbur

Nehrungsbilder (Heymann), 9:86

Nehunya ben Avin ha-Kohen. *See* Huna ben Avin ha-Kohen

Neḥunya ben ha-Kahah, 15:**64**

Neḥunya of Brat Hauran. *See* Ḥunya of Beth-Horon

Nehushtan, 15:**64–65**

Neḥutei, 15:**65**

Neighbor, love of. *See* Love, of neighbor

Neighborhood Playhouse (New York City, NY), 5:414

Neighbors: The Destruction of the Jewish Community in Jedwabne, Poland (Gross), 9:419

Ne'ilah, 2:72, 76, 15:**65–66**

Neilson, Julia, 15:**66**

Neiman, Yehudah, 15:**66**

Neipris, Joseph, 15:**66**

Neisser, Hans Philipp, 15:**66**

Neizvestny, Ernst, 15:**66–67**

Nekamah, 15:667

Neklyudov, Nicoloai Adrianovich, 15:**67**

Nekudah (journal), 8:353

Nekuddot (vocalization), 4:101

Nelson, Benjamin, 15:**67**, 18:732

Nelson, Harry, 4:180

Nelson, Lemrick, Jr., 15:228

Nelson, Leonhard, 15:**67**

Nelson, Louis, 15:**67–68**

Nemalim (Orpaz Averbuch), 1:667

Ne'manin. *See* Adelantados

Nemerov, Howard, 15:**68**

Németh, Andor, 15:**68**

Németkeresztír (Austria). *See* Deutschkreutz (Austria)

Nemetz, Nathan, 4:188

Nemetz, Nathan Theodore, 15:**68**

Nemirov (Ukraine), 15:**68–69**

Némirovsky, Irène, 15:**69**

Nemirovsky, Mordechai. *See* Namir, Mordechai

Nemon, Oscar, 15:**69**

Nemoy, Leon, 15:**69–70**

Nemoy, Maury, 4:372

Nemţeanu, Barbu, 15:**70**

Neo-Aramaic, 15:**70–72**, 71t

Neobychaynye pokhozhdeniya Khulio Khurenito (Ehrenburg). *See The Extraordinary Adventures of Julio Jurenito* (Ehrenburg)

Neoconservatism, 1:326

Neo-Facism, 15:**72–73**

Neofiti, 3:122

Neolithic period, architecture, 2:399

Neologism. *See* Neology

Neology, 15:**73–74**, 342

Neo-Nazism, 15:**74–82**
  caricatures of Jews, 4:479
  France, 15:81
  Germany, 15:80–81
  growth of movements, 15:74–75
  Holocaust denial, 15:75
  political participation, 15:75
    1945-1960, 15:76–77
    1970-2006, 15:76–78
  Russia, 15:82
  Scandinavia, 15:82
  United Kingdom, 15:81–82
  U.S., 15:78–80
Neo-Orthodoxy, 15:**82–83**
  Agudat Israel, 1:505
  development in Germany, 6:546
  Germany, 1:384
  Jewish identity and, 11:296
Neo-plasticism, 4:50
Neoplatonism, 3:237, 15:**84–86,** 16:77,
  80–81, 82–83, 106
  allegorical interpretation of
    scripture and, 3:644
  beatitude, 3:237–240
  cosmology, 5:231
  creation, 5:277–278, 10:752
  Damascius, 5:390
  Domninus of Larissa, 5:747
  dualism, 6:29
  emanation, 6:372–374
  Empedocles, 6:397
  God, attributes of, 7:666–667
  Ibn Gabirol's, 7:324–325
  Latif, Isaac B. Abraham Ibn,
    12:506–507
  matter and form, 7:324–325
  miracles, 14:307
  nature, 15:34
  revelation, 17:256–257
  Torah, 20:40
Neoromanticism, 15:648
Ne'ot Mordekhai (Israel), 15:**86**
NEPA Law and Litigation
  (Mandelker), 6:453
Nephilim, 2:126, 15:**86–87**
Neppi, Grazziadio. *See* Neppi, Hananel
Neppi, Hananel, 15:**87**
Nergal-Sharezer, 15:**87**
Neriah, Moshe Zevi, 15:**87**
Neriglissar. *See* Nergal-Sharezer
Nerium oleander. See Oleander
Ner Ma'aravi (periodical), 8:735
Ner neshamah. *See* Memorial light
Nero (Roman emperor), 11:435–436,
  15:**87–88**
Neronias. *See* Banias (ancient Israel)

Ner Tamid, 15:**88**
Nerva (Roman emperor), 11:294,
  15:**88**
Nervi, Pier Luigi, 4:172
Nervous system, 13:10–11
Nes. *See* Banners
Neshamah Yeterah, 15:**88**
Nesher (Israel), 15:**88–89**
Nesher, Zevi. *See* Adler, Hermann
Neshkiz dynasty, 8:421
Nesib (Turkey). *See* Nisibis
Neşibin (Turkey). *See* Nisibis
Nesi'im. *See* Nasi
Nes Lo Karah lanu (Shamir), 18:393
Nessana (Israel). *See* Nizzanah
Nessiat kappayim. *See* Priestly Blessing
Nesvizh (Belarus), 15:**89**
Nes Ziyyonah (Israel), 15:**89–90**
Nes Ziyyonah (organization), 15:**90**
Neta'im (Israel), 15:**90**
Netanya (Israel), 3:316, 15:**90–91**
Netanyahu, Benjamin. *See* Netanyahu,
  Binyamin
Netanyahu, Benzion, 15:**91**
Netanyahu, Bibi. *See* Netanyahu,
  Binyamin
Netanyahu, Binyamin, 9:159, 10:248–
  250, 15:**91–92**
  American Israel Public Affairs
    Committee, 2:51
  government of, 10:457–458, 457t,
    12:749
  Palestinian Authority and, 15:598
  Shamir, Yitzhak and, 18:394
  Sharon, Ariel and, 18:417
  Sheetrit, Meir and, 18:432
Netanyahu, Johnathan, 6:448
Nethanel (3rd c.), 3:16
Nethanel al-Fayyūmī, 16:84
Nethanel ben Al-Fayyumi, 15:**92–93**
Nethanel ben Isaiah, 15:**93**
Nethanel ben Meshullam ha-Levi,
  15:**93**
Nethanel ben Moses ha-Levi, 15:**93**
Nethanel ben Yesha, 11:538
Nethanel ibn al-Fayyūmī, 11:537
Nethanel of Chinon, 15:**93**
The Netherlands, 15:**93–110,** *94*
  1870-1940
    cultural life, 15:103
    demography, 15:100–101
    education, 15:102–103
    political participation,
      15:101–102
    religious practices, 15:101
    social structure, 15:100

Abraham, Samuel, 1:291
Amsterdam Haggadot, 8:215
architecture, 2:400, 5:534–535,
  6:369
art of, biblical influence, 3:673
Ashkenazim, 15:97
bankers, moneylending, 3:114, 117
Bible, Dutch translations of,
  3:627–628
Brazil as Dutch colony, 4:144
brokers, 4:203
cantatas and choral works,
  Hebrew, 4:435
children's literature, 4:634
Christian-Jewish relations, 16:632
Church response to Holocaust,
  9:373
colonization, 4:469–473
communal organization, 15:98
crime, 5:292–293
diplomats, 3:302
Dutch Labour Party, 14:310
Dutch literature, 6:67–72
early settlement, 15:93–95
economic expansion, 15:96
Education Act of 1857, 2:114
emancipation, 6:378, 749, 15:97–
  98
French Revolution, and effects on
  communities, 7:255–256
German refugees, 15:103
Grotius, Hugo, 8:103
Halakhah responsa, 15:771–772
Haskalah, 8:436–437
Hebraists, 12:636
Holocaust, 9:339, 359
  anti-Jewish laws, 15:104
  Calmeyer, Hans-Georg,
    4:374–375
  deportation, 15:105
  Jewish badges, 3:47
  Jewish Council, 15:104–105
  Mauthausen, 13:693
  Nazi occupation, 15:103
  resistance, 15:105–106
  Sephardim, 18:301
  Westerbork transit camp,
    9:116, 21:24
India, 12:248
Jewish archives, 2:409
Jewish identity, 15:108–109
Jewish scholarship, 15:97
journalism, 11:467, 12:462–463,
  16:492–493
laws and legal systems, 12:552–553
libraries, 12:787

linguistic assimilation, 8:436–437
Marranos, 15:95
messianism in, 4:252
museums, 14:627
music, 6:11
nationalization, 1815-1870, 15:98–100
    communal organinzation, 15:99
    economic conditions, 15:99
    emancipation, 15:99–100
    religious practices, 15:100
New York City, Dutch colonial period in, 15:195
Orthodox Judaism in, 15:494
Palache family, 15:573
philanthropists, Eibeschuetz, Simon Aaron, 6:245
plague, 15:94–95
political participation, 16:344–345
politicians, Mendel Maurits, 14:29
population, 16:391
Portuguese community, 15:96–97
postwar period
    communal organizations, 15:107–108
    demography, 15:106–107
    integration, 15:107
    restoration, 15:106
publishing, 16:714
Reform movement, 15:101, 108
relations with Israel, 15:109–110
religious liberties, 15:95
scholars, Biblical, Eerdmans, Bernardus Dirks, 6:215–216
sculpture, 5:377
socialism, 15:102
synagogues, 15:107i
theater, 19:674
tobacco trade, 20:6
trade and commerce, 20:85
Vught transit camp, 20:588–589
WW II war crimes trials, 20:643
Yiddish language, 15:99
Zionism, 15:101, 102, 108, 21:589–590
Zionist Organization, 11:765
See also Amsterdam; Dutch literature
Netherlands, Holocaust, Amsterdam, 2:115–116, 5:105, 18:11
Netherlands Antilles, 4:471–472
Netherworld, 15:**110–112**, 400
    eschatology, 6:497
Nethinim and Gibeonites. *See* Gibeonites and Nethinim
Netilat yadayim, 15:**112–113**
    See also Ablution

Netimah la-Ger (Adler), 1:405
Netira, 14:441, 15:**113**
Netiv ha-Lamed-He (Israel), 15:**113**
Netivot (Israel), 15:**113**
Netivot ha-Mishpat (Lorbeerbaum), 8:792
Netivot Shalom, 15:703
Netivot Ziyyon vi-Yrushalayim (Luncz), 13:257–258
Netophah (ancient city), 15:**113**
Netter, Charles, 11:738, 15:**114**
Netter, Richard, 4:84
Netter, Yizhak. *See* Netter, Charles
Nettl, Paul, 15:**114**
Nettles, vol. 16: color insert
Neturei Karta, 15:**114–115**
    Blau, Amram, 3:742
Network, 21:613
Netzer, Amnon, 11:558
Netzler, Iosef. *See* Trivale, Ion
Neuaegyptische Grammatik (Erman), 6:482
Neubauer, Abraham. *See* Neubauer, Adolf
Neubauer, Adolf, 4:250, 15:**115**
Neubauer, Jacob, 15:**115–116**
Neubauer, Jekuthiel. *See* Neubauer, Jacob
Neuberg, Gustav Embden Carl, 15:**116**
Neuberger, Albert, 15:**116**
Neuberger, H. Maurine, 15:**116**
Neuberger, Joseph, 16:344
Neuberger, Richard Lewis, 15:**116**
Neubitschow. *See* Novy Bydzov
Neuburger, Max, 15:**116–117**
Neuchâtel (Switzerland), 12:420, 15:**117**
Neuda, Abraham, 15:**117**
Neuda, Fanny, 15:**117**
Das Neue Denken (Rosenzweig), 6:612
Neue Freie Presse, 3:36, 333, 13:217
Neue Juedische Presse (periodical). *See* *Israelitisches Familienblatt* (periodical)
Das neue Musiklexicon (Einstein), 6:262
Neufeld, Daniel, 15:**117–118**
Neufeld, Henry, 15:**118**
Neugarten, Bernice, 15:**118–119**
Neugebauer, Otto, 15:**119**
Neugeboren, Jay, 15:**119–120**
Neugeboren, Michael. *See* Neugeboren, Jay
Neugroeschel, Mendel, 15:**120**
Neuhaeusel. *See* Nove Zamky
Neuhaus, Solomon. *See* Newhouse, Samuel Irving

Neukollin (Czech Republic). *See* Kolin (Czech Republic)
Neulander, Arthur H., 15:**120**
Neuman, A. A., 11:313
Neuman, Abraham Aaron, 15:**120**
Neumann, Alfred, 15:**120–121**
Neumann, Emanuel, 15:**121**
Neumann, Erich, 15:**121**
Neumann, Ferenc. *See* Molnár, Ferenc
Neumann, Franz Joseph, 4:190
Neumann, Henry, 15:**122**
Neumann, Johann Ludwig von, 15:**122**
Neumann, Jonny. *See* Neumann, Johann Ludwig von
Neumann, Robert, 15:**122**
Neumann, Yeheskel Moshe, 15:**123**
Neumark, Celia. *See* Rosenbloom, Celia Neumark
Neumark, David, 15:**123**
Neumark, Ephraim, 8:292, 15:**123**
Neumark, Martha, 18:278
Neumarkt (Romania). *See* Targu-Mures (Romania)
Neumeyer, Alfred, 15:**123**
Neumeyer, Karl, 15:**123–124**
Neunzehn Briefe ueber Judentum (Hirsch), 9:129–130
Neuoderberg. *See* Novy Bohumin
Neuroses, 14:58
Neu Sandec (Poland). *See* Nowy Sacz
Neusatz. *See* Novi Sad
Neu-Sedlitz. *See* Austerlitz (Czech Republic)
Neusner, Jacob, 15:**124–125**, 16:73–74
    aggadah, 1:461, 462–463
    amoraim, 2:90
    on Judah ha-Nasi, 11:504–505
    Mishnah, 14:330
Neusohl (Slovakia). *See* Banska, Bystrica (Slovakia)
Neustadt, David. *See* Ayalon, David
Neustadt, Israel. *See* Isserlein, Israel ben Pethahiah
Neustadt, Leib, 2:61
Neustaedter, Helmut. *See* Newton, Helmut
Neustein, Joshua, 10:697
Neutitschein (Czech Republic). *See* Novy Jicin (Czech Republic)
Neutra. *See* Nitra
Neutra, Richard Joseph, 15:**125**
Neuwert, Adolf. *See* Nowaczynski, Adolf
Neuwirth, Bebe, 15:**125–126**
Neuwirth Law, 18:615
Die Neuzeit. See *Neuzeit, Die* (periodical)

Neuzeit, Die (periodical), 15:**126–127**

Nevada (U.S.), 15:*127*, **127–128**

Nevakhovich, Judah Leib, 8:688, 15:**128**

Nevatim (Israel), 15:**128**

Neveh Eitan (Israel), 15:**128**

Neveh Oved (Israel). *See* Poriyyah (Israel)

Neveh Shalom (Shalom), 18:376

Neveh Shalom synagogue (Istanbul), 20:198

Neveh Ya'ir (Israel). *See* Ein ha-Sheloshah (Israel)

Neveh Yam (Israel), 15:**128–129**

Nèvejean, Yvonne, 15:**129**

Nevel, 14:642

Nevelah, 15:**129**

Nevelson, Louise, 15:**129–130**, 18:223

Nevers (France), 15:**130**

Nevi'im, 3:576

books of, 3:577*t*

canonization of, 3:577–578

Jonathan ben Uzziel, 11:398

Judeo-Persian translations of, 11:553

order of books in, 3:580*t*

targumim, 3:592–593

Nevins, Sheila, 15:**130**

Nevis (British West Indies), 4:474

Nevu'at Ha-Yeled, 15:**130**

Nevzelin, Leonid Borisovich, 15:**131**

New Age movement, 11:680

New American Bible (NAB), 3:617–618

New American Standard Bible (NASB), 3:619

New Amsterdam, 15:195

See also New York City

New and Collected Poems (Pinsky), 16:176

A New Approach to the Teaching of the Torah (Kaplan), 11:776

Newark (NJ), 6:360–361, 512–514

See also Essex County

New Bedford (MA), 13:665, 15:**131**

New Brunswick (NJ), 2:639, 640, 15:**131–133**

Newcastle-Upon-Tyne (England), 15:**133**

New Century Bible, 3:621

New Christians, 15:**133–134**

Barros, Basto, Arturo Carlos De, 3:177–178

Bayonne, 3:231–232

Bonafed, Solomon ben Reuben, 4:53, 54

Brandão, Ambrósio Fernandes, 4:121, 143

Brazil, 4:142–144, 18:30

Caribbean, Spanish-Portuguese Nation of the: La Nacion, 4:469, 476

Carvajal family, 4:501

Cervantes Saavedra, Miguel de, 4:550

Italy, 4:523

limpieza de sangre, 13:25–26

Noronha, Fernão de, 15:301

Portuguese, 3:60–61, 16:410–411, 18:30

Recife, 17:145–146

Rio de Janeiro, 17:337

Spain, 4:467, 18:57–58

See also Conversos; Inquisition; Marranos

New Colophon, 1:396

The New Colossus (Lazarus), 15:202

the New Daily (periodical). *See Nowy Dziennik*

New Deal, New York City and, 15:214

New Dictionary (Even-Shoshan), 8:670

New England Holocaust Memorial (Boston, MA), vol. 9: color insert

New English Bible (NEB), 3:618–619

New English Translation (NET) (Bible), 3:637

Newfield, Morris, 3:713, 15:**134–135**

New France (French colony). *See* Quebec (Canada)

New Granada, 9:798

New Haggadah (Eisenstein, ed.), 6:273

New Hampshire (U.S.), 15:*135*, **135–136**

New Haven (CT), 5:161, 15:**136–137**

The New History and the Old: Critical Essays and Reappraisals (Himmelfarb), 9:120

The New History and the Old (Himmelfarb), 9:152

Newhouse, Samuel Irving, 15:**137–138**

New Idealism, 11:363

New International Version (NIV) (Bible), 3:620–621

New Israel, 15:**138**

The New Israel Fund, 15:**138–139**

New Jersey (U.S.), 12:441, 15:**139–141**

Middlesex County, 14:180

Passaic-Clifton, 15:676–677

Paterson, 15:686–688

New Jersey Jewish News (periodical), 15:132–133

New Jerusalem, 11:219

New Jerusalem Bible, 3:617

New Jewish Version (NJV) (Bible), 3:614, 617, 621–622

New Kingdom (Egypt), 6:224

New Leader (periodical), 11:719

New Left, 12:659, 15:**141–143**, 18:709

New Light from the Phrophets (Finkelstein), 7:35

A New Light on Zion. See Or Ḥadash al Ziyyon (Reines)

Newlinski, Philipp Michael, 15:**143–144**

New Living Translation (Bible), 3:621

New London (CT), 15:**144–145**

Newman, Abe, 4:212

Newman, Alfred, 15:**145**

Jewish Historical Society of England, 11:292

Newman, Arnold, 15:**145**, 16:126

Newman, Aubrey, 15:**145**

Newman, Barnett, 2:514, 15:**145–146**

Newman, Isidore, 15:**146**

Newman, Jon O., 15:**146**

Newman, Louis Israel, 15:**146**

Newman, Paul, 15:**147**

Newman, Pauline, 12:661, 15:**147–148**, 18:713

Newman, Peter Charles, 15:**148**

Newman, Randy, 15:**148**

Newmark, Harris, 15:148

Newmark, Joseph, 13:195, 15:**148**

Newmark, Marco Ross, 15:**148–149**

Newmark family, 15:**148–149**

New Methods of Geostatistical Analysis and Graphical Presentation: Distribution of Populations over Territories (Bachi), 3:38

New Mexico (U.S.), 15:*149*, **149–150**

New Moons, 15:**150–151**

Amidah, 2:74, 75

announcement of, 15:**151–152**

New Muslims. *See* Jadid al-Islam

Newmyer, Arthur Grover, 15:**152**

New Odessa (OR), 2:88

New Orleans (LA), 3:264, 8:150–151, 13:222–224, 15:**152–153**

Newport (RI), 2:41, 15:**153–154**

New Revised Standard Version (NRSV) (Bible), 3:615–616

News from the American Diaspora (Neugeboren), 15:119

Newsom, Carol, 11:349

Newsom, Carol, Job, Book of, 11:353

New South Wales (Australia). *See* Australia

Newspapers. *See* Hebrew newspapers; Press

A New Spirit. See Ru'aḥ Ḥadashah

New Square (NY), 15:**189**

See also Skvira (Ukraine)

New Testament, 15:**189–192**

Abaddon, 1:224

Abraham, 1:285

Abraham's bosom, 1:316

adoption, 1:417

apocrypha, 15:191

Aramaic, 2:348

canonicity of, 15:190–191

Christianity, 4:674

contents, 15:190

Dead Sea scrolls and, 15:192

demons, demonology, 5:574

Gehenna, 15:628

Jewish sensitivities regarding translation of, 3:608

Jews, versions intended for, 3:681

Jezebel in, 11:334

Job in, 11:342

Judaism, relationship with, 15:191–192

Koran, influence on, 3:668

language and style, 15:190, 192

letters and letter writers, 12:669–670

Moses, 14:538

Muhammad, 1:546

Noah in, 15:288

paradise, 15:628

Passover in, 15:681

Patriarchs in, 15:689

Sadducees, 17:655

Salome, 17:693

Satan, 18:72

scholarship of, 15:191

as term, 3:574

tripartite canon referred to in, 3:577

view of Pharisees, 16:31

The New Thinking (Rosenzweig), 6:612

Newton, Francis. *See* Hobsbawm, Eric John

Newton, Helmut, 15:**192–193**

Newton-John, Olivia, 15:**193**

The New Vision: From Material to Architecture (Moholy-Nagy), 14:420

New Wave movement (literature), 18:366, 368, 374

   Kahana-Carmon, Amalia, 11:712

   Oz, Amos, 15:555

New Wave movement (photography), 16:127

New World Translation (NWT) (Bible), 3:616

New Year, 15:**193–194**

   sacrifices, 17:647

   Samaritans, 17:730

   See also Rosh Ha-Shanah

New Year for Trees. *See* Tu Bi-Shevat

New Year's cards, 15:**194**

New Year's Day. *See* Rosh Ha-Shanah

New York (state, U.S.), 15:**239–241**, *240*

   Levitt, Arthur, Sr., 12:743

   Levy, Hayman, 12:750

   Levy, Moses, 12:753

New York City (NY), 15:**194–239**

   1870-1920, 15:200–212

      communal life, 15:202, 206–210

      cultural life, 15:210–211

      demographics, 15:200–203, 201*t*

      economy, 15:202–203, 203–206, 204*t*

      political life and civic affairs, 15:211–212

   1920-1970, 15:212–222

      communal life, 15:216–219

      cultural life, 15:219–222

      demographics, 15:212–213

      economy, 15:213–214

      political life and civic affairs, 12:437–438, 15:214–216

   1970-2006, 15:222–238

      cultural life, 15:227–228

      demographics, 15:222–223

      economy, 15:225–227

      neighborhoods, Jewish, 15:223, 231–238

      political life and civic affairs, 15:223–225

      race relations, 15:228–229

      Russian Jewish immigrants, 15:229–231

   Aaronsohn, Moses in, 1:223

   Abrams, Robert, 1:327–328

   Am Olam immigrants in, 2:88

   antisemitism and civil rights of Jews

      1920-1970, 15:214, 215

      1970-2006, 15:228–229

      colonial period, 15:195, 196

      post-Revolutionary period, 15:197, 199

      real estate and housing in modern cities, 15:227

   Black-Jewish relations

      1920-1970, 15:215, 216, 219, 220

      1970-2006, 15:228–229

      Crown Heights incident, 1991, 15:228–229

   Bloomberg, Michael, 3:782

   Brooklyn Orthodox community, vol. 5: color insert

   building and construction trade, 5:184

   Civil War, 15:200

   closing prayer at a seder, vol. 5: color insert

   clothing industry, 6:318

   colonial period, 15:194–197

   communal life

      1870-1920, 15:202, 206–210

      1920-1970, 15:216–219

      Kehillah, 15:209, 217

      post-Revolutionary period, 15:198–199

      UJA-Federation/Federation for the Support of Jewish Philanthropies, 15:209, 217, 229

   crime amongst Jews of, 15:209

   cultural life

      1870-1920, 15:210–211

      1920-1970, 15:219–222

      1970-2006, 15:227–228

   demographics

      1870-1920, 15:200–203, 201*t*

      1920-1970, 15:212–213

      1970-2006, 15:222–223

      colonial period, 15:196–197

      post-Revolutionary period, 15:197, 198

      present-day, 15:194

      Russian Jewish immigrants, modern, 15:229–231

   double-decker tenements, 15:201

   as Dutch colony, 3:179, 15:195

   economy of

      1870-1920, 15:202–203, 203–206, 204*t*

      1920-1970, 15:213–214

      1970-2006, 15:225–227

      colonial period, 15:195–196

      post-Revolutionary period, 15:199–200

      Stock Exchange, 15:197, 224, 225–226

   education in

      1870-1920, 15:202, 207, 208

      1920-1970, 15:214, 215–216, 218–219

      city colleges, 15:218–219

      colonial period, 15:197

      education, Jewish, 6:188–195, 197

      post-Revolutionary period, 15:199

      Russian Jewish immigrants, modern, 15:231

      Yonkers desegregation lawsuit, 18:9–10

New York City (NY), *continued*
  Ḥanukkah celebration by
    congregation Beth Simchat
    Torah, vol. 20: color insert
  Helmsley-Spear managed real
    estate, 18:150
  Holocaust survivors in, 15:223
  hospitals
      1870-1920, 15:200, 206–207,
        208
      1920-1970, 15:217
      in Civil War, 15:200
      post-Revolutionary period,
        15:199
  housing, 1:326
  Jewish neighborhoods, 6:697
  journalism in
      1870-1920, 15:210, 211
      1920-1970, 15:221–222
      post-revolutionary period,
        15:199
  Judah family, 11:479
  lawyers in
      1870-1920, 15:205
      1920-1970, 15:214
      colonial period, 15:196
      post-Revolutionary period,
        15:197
  Marathon, 12:592–593
  Metropolitan Opera, 11:723
  mobsters, 12:485–486
  museums, 14:632–633
  neighborhoods, Jewish
      1870-1920, 15:200–202, 203
      1920-1970, 15:212–213
      1970-2006, 15:223, 231–238
      Boro Park, 15:203, 213, 217,
        223, 231–232
      Brighton Beach, 15:230, 231
      colonial period, 15:196–197
      post-Revolutionary period,
        15:198
      Upper West Side, 15:201,
        223, 232–234
      Washington Heights, 15:202,
        203, 230, 234–236
      Williamsburg, 15:202–203,
        207, 212–213, 217, 224,
        231, 234–238
  New School for Social Research,
    11:742
  political life and civic affairs
      1870-1920, 15:211–212
      1920-1970, 15:214–216
      1970-2006, 15:223–225
      Beame, Abraham David,
        3:234–235

    colonial period, 15:196
    Eisner, Mark, 6:276
    feminism in, 15:219, 224
    Morgenthau, Robert Morris,
      14:489
    post-Revolutionary period,
      15:197–198
    Tammany Hall, Jewish
      involvement in, 15:198,
      205, 211, 214, 290
  post-Revolutionary period and
    early nineteenth century,
    15:197–200
  real estate development, 11:734
  real estate interests in, 15:226–227
  Revolutionary period, 15:197–198
  school strikes (1968), 18:396–397
  September 11, 2001 terrorist
    attacks, 15:225
  settlement of Jews in, 2:45
      1870-1920, 15:200–203, 201t
      colonial period, 15:195, 197
      post-Revolutionary period,
        15:197
      Russian Jewish immigrants,
        modern, 15:229–231
  societies and associations
      1870-1920, 15:202, 206–210
      1920-1970, 12:799, 15:217
      post-Revolutionary period,
        15:198–199
      UJA-Federation/Federation
        for the Support of Jewish
        Philanthropies, 15:209,
        217, 229
  students at Herschel High School,
    vol. 20: color insert
  synagogues
      1870-1920, 15:201–202, 203,
        206, 207–208
      1920-1970, 15:217–218
      Civil War, 15:200
      colonial period, 15:195, 197,
        198
      post-Revolutionary period,
        15:197
      of Upper West Side, 15:233–
        234
      of Washington Heights,
        15:235
  Yiddish theater, 19:680–681
The New York Daily News, 11:469–470
New Yorker, 1:406, 11:746, 12:809
New York Federation of Jewish
  Philanthropies, 2:25
New York Places and Pleasures
  (Simon), 18:613
New York Post (newspaper), 11:469–
  470, 734, 12:545, 15:222

New York's Museum of Jewish
  Heritage, 11:734
New York Times, 1:327, 401, 4:484,
  7:417, 12:763, 809, 15:221–222
  Frankel, Max, 7:198
New Zealand, 2:649, 15:**241–246**, *242*
  assimilation, 2:611
  Australia and New Zealand Army
    Corps, 14:432
  businessmen, 5:480–481, 12:712
  Jewish community founder, 9:546
  libraries, 12:787
  newspapers, 16:487
  politicians, 3:299
  Zionism, 21:580–581
New Zealand (Polack), 16:286
New Zionist Organization. *See*
  Revisionist movement; Zionists
The Next War (Hayek), 18:205
Neyhus, David K. *See* Mordecai of
  Neskhiz; Niles, David K.
Neyrac, Pierre, 8:477, 15:**246**
Neẓaḥ, 8:385
Neẓaḥ Yisrael (Schur), 18:176
Nezed ha-Dema' (Zamosc), 21:453
Neẓer Sereni (Israel), 15:**246**
Nezhdanov, Andrey. *See* Sobol,
  Andrey Mikhailovich
Nezhin (Ukraine), 15:**246**
Nezibiin (Turkey). *See* Nisibis
Nezikin (tractate), 11:741, 15:**246–247**,
  18:401, 744–745
Nicanor (Syrian commander), 9:194,
  15:**247**
Nicanor of Alexandria, 15:248
Nicanor's gate (Jerusalem), 15:**247–
248**
Nicaragua, 15:**248**
Nicarchus, 14:532, 15:**248–249**
Nicator. *See* Demetrius II
Nice (France), 15:**249**
Nicholas, Edward, 15:**252**
Nicholas I (czar), 9:235, 15:**250**,
  16:372, 17:533–534
  Judaizers under, 11:522
  Levanda, Lev Osipovich, 12:677
  Pale of Settlement under, 15:578
Nicholas II (czar), 15:**250**
  Octobrists, 15:376
  *Protocols of the Learned Elders of
    Zion*, 6:297
Nicholas III (pope), 4:277, 15:**249–
250**, 16:373
Nicholas IV (pope), 15:**250**
Nicholas V (pope), 15:**250**, 16:374
Nicholas of Damascus, 15:**251–252**
Nicholas de Lyre, 8:512, 15:**251**
  Luther influenced by Rashi via,
    3:648

modern biblical criticism, as precursor of, 3:648
Pablo de Santa Maria, 15:562
Nicholas of Cusa, 5:**343**
Nicholas of Damascus, 9:154, 11:439
Nicholas of Hereford, 3:611
Nicholas of Lyre. *See* Nicholas de Lyre
Nicholas soldiers, residence rights of, 15:579
Nichols, Jack, 15:**252–253**
Nichols, Mike, 15:**253**
Nickelodeons, 14:570
Nicolai, Friedrich, 14:35
Nicomedia (Turkey). *See* Izmit (Turkey)
Nicopolis (Bulgaria). *See* Nikopol
Niddah (menstruating woman), 1:262, 263, 2:133, 135, 3:128–129, 15:**253–258**, 21:162
    sexual intercourse with, 18:330
Niddah (tractate), 15:**258–259**
Niddui vs. ḥerem, 9:13–15
Niebuhr, Carston, 15:259
Niebuhr, Reinhold, 15:259
Niederstetten (Germany), 15:**259–260**
Niego, Joseph, 15:**260**
Niemirów. *See* Nemirov (Ukraine)
Niemirower, Jacob Isaac, 15:**260**
Nierman, Leonardo, 15:**260–261**
Nierop, Ahasverus Salomon Van, 15:261
Nierop, Frederik Salomon Van, 15:261
Nierop, Hendrik Abraham Van, 15:261
Nierop, Van, family, 15:**261**
Nieswiez. *See* Nesvizh (Belarus)
Nieszawa statutes, 15:403
Nieto, David, 6:515, 15:**261**
Nieto, Isaac, 15:**261–262**
Nietzsche, Friedrich Wilhelm, 15:**262**
    antisemitism, 7:512
    Brandes, Georg, 4:126
    Richter, Raoul, 17:291
Nieuwe Bijbelvertaling (Bible), 6:67
Nifoci, Isaac, 15:**262**
Niger, Peter. *See* Nigri, Petrus
Niger, Petrus. *See* Nigri, Petrus
Niger, Shmuel, 15:**262–263**
Niger of Perea, 11:449, 15:**263**
Niggun, Ḥasidism, 14:676
Niggunim (Seter), 18:318
Niggunim, Ḥasidic, 8:426–429
Niggunim Mi-Sinai. *See* Mi-Sinai Niggunim
Night (Wiesel), 4:630–631, 9:401, 409
Night and day. *See* Day and night

Night and Fog (Renais), 9:440
Night and Hope (Lustig), 13:270
Nightingale (Byadulya-Yasakar). *See* Salavey
Nightingales, 15:**263–264**
A Night in May. See Laylah be-Mai
The Night in Meron (Gidal), 16:128
Nightmare Before Christmas (motion picture), 6:315
Night of the Broken Glass. *See* Kristallnacht
The Night of the Twentieth. See Leyl ha-Esrim
Night Prayer, 15:**264**
Night Round (Modiano), 14:410
Nights and Dawns. See Éjxzakák és hajnalok
Nigri, Petrus, 15:**264–265**
Nikel, Lea, 15:**265**
Nikitin, Victor, 15:**265**
Nikmat ha-Avot (Shami), 18:391
Nikodem, Theophil. *See* Beer, Peter
Nikolayev (Ukraine), 15:**265–266**
Nikolsburg. *See* Mikulov (Czech Republic)
Nikopol (Bulgaria), 15:**266**
Nikova, Rina, 5:412, 15:**266**
Nikra Lo Leon (Sened), 18:288
Nile (river), 15:**266**
Niles, David K., 15:**266–267**
Nili, 1:221–223, 13:81, 15:**267–268**
Nîmes (France), 15:**268–269**
Nimmukei ha-Grib (Bachrach), 3:39
Nimoy, Leonard, 15:**269**
Nimrod, 15:**269–270**
Nimrod (Danziger), 5:432, 18:223, vol. 2: color insert
Nimrod, Nomi, 15:682
Nimrodi, Ofer, 15:270
Nimrodi, Yaacov, 15:270
Nimrodi family, 15:**270**
Nimzovitch, Aaron, 4:603, 604, 605, 15:**270**
Nine (number), 15:335
Nine Days, 15:**271**
Nineteen Letters of Ben Uziel (Hirsch), 6:6
Nineteen Letters on Judaism. See Neunzehn Briefe ueber Judentum
Nineveh (Assyria), 15:**271–272**
Nineveh archives, 2:403–404
Niñez Coronel, Fernando. *See* Seneor, Abraham
Niñez da Costa family. *See* Curiel
Ningpo (China), 15:**272**
Ningsia (China), 15:**272**
Nini, Achinoam, 15:**272–273**

Ninth Fort (Lithuania), 15:**273**
Ninth of Av. *See* Av, the ninth of
The Ninth of Av (Horovitz), 9:529
Nipur archives, 2:404
Nir, Yeshayahu, 16:127
Nir Am (Israel), 15:**273**
Nir David (Israel), 15:**273**, vol. 11: color insert
Nirenberg, Harry and Minerva, 15:476
Nirenberg, Marshall Warren, 13:9, 15:**273–274**, 476
Nir Ezyon (Israel), 15:**274**
Nirim (Israel), 15:**274**
Nir-Rafalkes, Nahum, 15:**274**
Niš (Serbia), 15:**274–275**
Nisan, 15:**275**
Nishapur (Persia), 15:**275**
Nishmat Adam (Aaron Samuel ben Moses Shalom of Kremenets), 1:220
Nishmat Kol Ḥai, 15:**275–276**
Nisibis (Turkey), 15:**276**
Niskier, Arnaldo, 11:470
Nissan, Avraham, 15:**276–277**
Nisselovich, Eliezer. *See* Nisselovich, Leopold
Nisselovich, Leopold, 6:45, 15:**277**, 579
Nissenbaum, Isaac, 15:**277**
Nissenson, Aaron, 15:**277–278**
Nissenson, Hugh, 15:**278**
Nissi ben Berechiah al-Nahrawani, 15:**278**
Nissi ben Noah, 15:**278**
Nissim, Abraham Ḥayyim, 15:**278**
Nissim, Isaac, 15:**278–279**
Nissim, Jacob, 11:727
Nissim, Moshe, 15:**279**
Nissim ben Berechiah al-Nahrawani. *See* Nissi ben Berechiah al-Nahrawani
Nissim ben Ḥayyim Egozi, 6:222
Nissim ben Jacob ben Nissim ibn Shahin, 6:527, 667, 15:**279–280**
    Islamic influence on, 10:97–98
    journey of Elijah and Joshua ben Levi, 14:539
    Judeo-Arabic literature of, 11:533
    Sefer ha-Maasiyyot, 7:12
    Sherira ben Ḥanina Gaon, 18:463
Nissim ben Moses of Marseilles, 15:**280**
Nissim ben Noah. *See* Nissi ben Noah
Nissim ben Reuben Gerondi, 15:**280–281**
Nissim Gaon. *See* Nissim ben Jacob ben Nissim ibn Shahin
Nissim-Oglu, Ilya Sherbatovich. *See* Anisimov, Ilya Sherbatovich

Nitra (Slovakia), 15:**281–282**
Nittai of Arbela, 15:**282**
    Joshua ben Peraḥyah, 11:454
Nitẓoẓot ha-neshamot, 7:603
Nivḥar mi-Kesef (Pinto), 16:179
Nixon, Richard Milhous, 15:**282–283,**
    18:163
    Bitburg Controversy, 3:728
    Block, Herbert Lawrence, 3:769
    Watergate, 11:468
Nizer, Louis, 15:**283**
Nizhni Novgorod. *See* Gorki
Niẓoẓei Or (Plotzki), 16:241
Niẓẓaḥon (Kabak), 11:584
Niẓẓanah (Israel), 15:**283–284**
Niẓẓanim (Israel), 15:**284**
NJOP. *See* National Jewish Outreach
    Program
No (Egypt). *See* Thebes (Egypt)
Noa. *See* Nini, Achinoam
Noachide, laws of the sons of. *See*
    Noachide laws
Noachide laws, 15:**284–287**
    cruelty to animals, 2:166
    dietary, 6:576
    Pallière, Aimé, 15:602
Noah (biblical figure), 8:290, 12:444–
    445, 15:**287–290**
    Canaan, curse of, 4:391
    the Flood, 7:80
    Japeth and, 11:86, 18:453
    Shem and, 18:453
    wine, 6:27
Noah (purported books of), 12:445,
    15:**290**
Noah, laws of the sons of. *See*
    Noachide laws
Noah, Mordecai Manuel, 9:161,
    11:468, 15:**290–291**
    in Buffalo, NY, 4:255
    on Jewish studies, 11:317
    Judah, Samuel Benjamin Helbert,
        11:480
    New York City and, 15:198, 199,
        200
    Sarna, Jonathan Daniel on, 18:58
Noahian, laws of the sons of. *See*
    Noachide laws
Noah's Ark, 2:469
No'am (Kasher), 11:821, 17:237
No'am ha-Middot (Amram), 2:104
No'am Meggadim (Eliezer ben Jacob
    ha-Levi of Tarnogrod), 6:326
No-Amon (Egypt). *See* Thebes (Egypt)
No'am Yerushalmi (Shapira), 18:401
No'ar Ḥaluẓi Loḥem (IDF), 10:469
Nob (Israel), 1:544, 15:**291**

Nobel, Joseph, 15:**291**
Nobel, Nehemiah Anton, 15:**291**
Nobel Prizes, 15:**291–292,** 292*t*
*The Noble Faith. See Ha-Emunah ha-
    Ramah*
Noda bi-Yehudah (Landau), 12:460
Nodus Salomonis (choral canon,
    Valentini), 18:762
Noeldeke, Theodor, 15:**292–293**
Noerdlingen (Germany), 15:**293,** 384
Noether, Amalie. *See* Noether, Emmy
Noether, Emmy, 15:**293**
Noether, Fritz, 15:**293**
Noether, Max, 15:**293**
Noether family, 15:**293–294**
Nofekh, 16:477
Noise pollution, 5:168, 6:94–95
Nokh Alemen (Bergelson), 3:419
Nokhn Got fun Midber (Molodowsky).
    See Toward the God of the Desert
    (Molodowsky)
Nola, Elijah ben Menachem da, 15:**294**
Nom, Ibrahim, 15:**294,** 474
Nomadism, 15:**294–296**
    Ishmaelites, 10:85–86
    Kenite, 12:76–77
Nomberg, Hersh David, 8:497,
    15:**296–297**
Nomologia o Discursos legales (Aboab),
    1:265–266
None Is Too Many (Abella and
    Troper), 4:415
None Is Too Many (Sherman), 18:464–
    465
Nones, Benjamin, 15:**297,** 20:312
Nones, Joseph B., 15:297
None Shall Escape, 9:439
Nonius, Petrus. *See* Nuñez, Pedro
The Non-Jewish Jew and Other Essays
    (Deutscher), 5:625–626
Non-Jewish Kabbalah, 11:678
Non-Jews
    modern period, 6:124–125
    National Socialism (Nazism),
        9:331
    sacrifices from, 17:647
    sexual intercourse with, 18:330
    women, niddah, 15:256–257
Noqed, 2:97
Norcia, de, family. *See* Norzi family
Norcia, Manuele de, 15:312
Nordau, Max, 1:526, 9:64, 15:**297–299,**
    299, 18:749
Norden, Benjamin, 15:299, 16:348
Norden, Joshua Davis, 15:299
Norden, Samuel, 15:299
Norden family, 15:**299**

Nordhausen (Germany), 15:**299–300**
Nordlingen, Joseph Yuspa ben
    Phinehas Seligmann. *See* Hahn,
    Joseph Yuspa ben Phinehas
    Seligmann
Nord-Vest. *See* Minski, Nikolai
    Maximovich
Norell, Norman, 15:**300**
Norfolk (VA), 15:**300–301**
Norman, Edward Albert, 2:46, 15:**301**
Norman, Norman K., 1:428
Norman Conquest of 1066, 6:410
Norman Fund. *See* America-Israel
    Cultural Foundation
Normative Judaism, concept of,
    11:513
Norodnia Volia, 11:361
Noronha, Fernão de, 15:**301**
Norsa, Abramo Immanuel. *See* Norzi,
    Immanuel di
Norsa, da. *See* Norzi family
Norsa, Hannah, 15:**301**
Norsa, Immanuel. *See* Norzi,
    Immanuel di
Norsa, Isaac ben Moses, 15:313
Norsa, Paolo, 15:313
Norsa, Umberto, 15:313
Norsa or de Norsa family. *See* Norzi
    family
North Africa
    Berbers, 3:400–401
    capitulations, 4:452–453
    communities, 5:104–105
    demography, 5:558
    education, Jewish, 6:180, 213–214
    Jewish immigration to France,
        2:62
    Jewish settlements, 1:436–437,
        10:223–224
    Judaizers in, 11:520
    Judeo-Arabic language used in,
        11:529–530
    Judeo-Arabic literature in, 11:532–
        534
    Kairouan, 11:726–727
    leather industry and trade, 12:575
    literature, 5:435–436, 12:433
    Maghrebi-Ma'aravi, 13:342
    medieval, 11:35
    music, 1:437–440
    musical traditions, 1:437–440
    ORT, 15:489–490
    Ottoman attempts to expand into,
        15:524–525
    Oẓar Hatorah in, 15:556
    Phoenician colonization of,
        16:122–123

synagogue architecture, 19:375
North America. *See* Canada; United States
North American Federation of Temple Youth, 5:200, 17:172, 175–176
Northampton (U.K.), 15:*301*
North-Arabic. *See* Arabic language
North Carolina (U.S.), 6:62–63, 15:*302*, **302–304**
North Dakota (U.S.), 15:*304*, **304**
Northern Ireland, 10:27
Northern Kingdom. *See* Israel, Kingdom of
Northern Negev Highlands (Israel), 10:113–114
Northern Rhodesia. *See* Zambia (Africa)
Northern Territory Times (newspaper), 18:763
North Ossetian Autonomous Republic, 15:**463**
Norton, John Lewis, 6:83
Norton, Joshua Davis, 15:299
The Norton Anthology of Modern Poetry, 6:362
Norton Simon Inc., 18:614
Norwalk (CT), 15:**304–305**
Norway, 15:*305*, **305–312**
    anti-sheḥitah movements, 18:435
    Constitution Day, 21:13
    emancipation, 6:377
    Holocaust, 9:341
        influence on literature, 18:95–96
        refugees, 6:279
    language, biblical translations, 3:633
    Oslo, 15:504–505
    Oslo chief rabbi, 14:11
    politicians, Benkow, Jo, 3:365
    restitution by, 15:504
Norwegian literature, 15:310–311, 18:94–96
Norwich (England), 15:**312**
    blood libel in, 3:775
Norzi, Benjamin ben Immanuel, 15:312
Norzi, Eliezer ben David, 15:312
Norzi, Ḥayyim ben Jehiel, 15:313
Norzi, Immanuel di, 1:308, 7:40–41
Norzi, Isaac ben Daniel, 15:312
Norzi, Jedediah Solomon Raphael ben Abraham, 3:587, 588, 15:**313**
Norzi, Jehiel Vidal ben Jedediah Solomon, 15:313
Norzi, Moses ben Jedediah Solomon, 15:313
Norzi, Nathan, 15:312

Norzi, Raphael ben Gabriel, 15:312
Norzi family, 15:**312–313**
Nosaḥ. *See* Nusaḥ
Nossal, Gustav. *See* Nossal, Sir Gustav
Nossal, Sir Gustav, 15:**313–314**
Nossig, Alfred, 15:314
Nostalgia and Nightmare (Band), 1:468
Nostra Aetate, 9:374, 402, 11:380, 15:695
Nostradamus, 15:314
Notarikon, 3:129, 15:**314–315**
Notation, musical. *See* Cantillation; Music
Note, Nathan, of Shklov. *See* Notkin, Nata
Notes from a Private Journal (Montefiore), 14:456
Notes of a Journey from Cornhill to Grand Cairo (Thackeray), 6:435
Notes on the Hebrew Text and the Topography of the Books of Samuel (Driver), 6:22
Not Far from the Center of Town. See Lo raḥok mi-Merkaz ha-Ir
Not for Glory (Rosenberg), 18:200
Noth, Albrecht, 15:416
Noth, Martin, 2:11, 3:651, 658, 11:446, 447, 449, 15:315
Notification. *See* Moda‘ah
Not in Heaven (Berkovits), 3:439
Notkin, Nata, 15:**315–316**
Notovich, Osip Konstantinovich, 15:**316**
Nottingham (U.K.), 15:**316**
Notzot (Be'er), 3:**251**
Nouă Suliţa (Moldova). *See* Novoselitsa
Nouns, Hebrew. *See under* Hebrew grammar
Novak, David, 15:**316**
Novak, Robert, 15:**316–317**
Novakhovich, Benzion. *See* Vinchevsky, Morris
Novakhovichi, Benzion. *See* Vinchevsky, Morris
Novakovsky, Alexander. *See* Nove, Alec
Novaredok. *See* Novogrudok
Nova Scotia, 2:639, 640
Novatian, 4:720
Novation. *See* Assignment of debt
Nova Trajana Bostra (Israel). *See* Bozrah (Israel)
Nova Trajana Bostra (Roman Palestine), 4:114–115, *115*
Novaya Aleksandriya (Poland). *See* Pulawy (Poland)
Novaya Ushitsa (Ukraine), 15:**317**

Nove, Alec, 15:**317**
Noveck, Simon, 15:**318**
A Novel about a Horse Thief (Opatoshu). *See Roman fun a Ferd Ganev*
Novellae. *See* Ḥiddushim
Novellae of Justinian I concerning Jews, 9:5, 11:579–580
Noveln (Shapiro), 18:407
Novelot Ḥokhmah (Bacharach), 3:35
Novels and novelists. *See entries under national literature terms*
November 1918 (Doeblin), 5:729–730
November pograms. *See* Kristallnacht
Nove Mesto Nad Vahom (Slovakia), 15:**318–319**
Nové Sedlice. *See* Austerlitz (Czech Republic)
Nove Zamky (Slovakia), 15:**319**
Novgorod-Seversk (Ukraine), 15:**319–320**
Novi Sad (Serbia), 15:**320**
Novitch, Miriam, 15:**320–321**
Novoaleksandrovsk (Lithuania). *See* Zarasai (Lithuania)
Novogrudok (Belarus), 15:**321–322**
Novogrudok school of Musar, 11:368
Novomeysky, Moshe, 15:**322**
Novomisky, Moses Joseph. *See* Olgin, Moshe J.
Novo-Nogaisk (Ukraine). *See* Berdyansk (Ukraine)
Novoselitsa (Moldova), 15:**322**
Novosiltsev, Nicolai Nikolayevich, 15:**322**
Novozybkov (Russia), 15:**323**
Novy, J., 11:385
Novy, Jim, 15:**323**
Novy Bohumin (Czech Republic), 15:**323**
Nový BydŇov-Israelites. *See* Abrahamites
Novy Bydzov (Czech Republic), 15:**323**
Novy Dvor (Belarus), 15:**323–324**
Novy Izrail. *See* New Israel
Novy Jicin (Czech Republic), 15:**324**
Novy Oleksiniec (Ukraine), 15:**324**
Now (Bacall), 3:30
Nowack, Wilhelm Gustav Hermann, 15:**324**
Nowaczynski, Adolf, 15:**324–325**
Nowakowski, David, 4:660, 15:**325**
Nowogródek. *See* Novogrudok
Nowy Dwor Mazowiecki (Poland), 15:**325–326**
Nowy Dziennik (periodical), 15:**326**
Nowy Sacz (Poland), 15:**326**

Noy, Dov, 1:461, 15:**326–327**
Noy, Meir, 15:**327**
Nuclear energy, 5:169–170, 6:261–262
Nuclear physics
    Bethe, Hans Albrecht, 3:529
    Italy, 16:137
    Oppenheimer, J. Robert, 15:450
    Segrè, Emilio Gino, 18:251–252
Nuclear Weapons and Foreign Policy
  (Kissinger), 12:203
Nudel Ida, 15:**327**
Nudelman, Santiago Israel, 15:**327,**
  16:349
Nuernberg (Germany). *See* Nuremberg
  (Germany)
Nueva carta esperanzada a un General
  (Aguinis), 1:510
Nūḥ. See Noah (biblical figure)
Nuisance law, 15:**327–329**
Nulman, Macy, 15:**329–330**
Nuʿmān ibn abi al-Riḍāāʿ, 11:536
Number Our Days (Myerhoff), 14:706
Numbers, Book of, 15:**330–333**
Numbers, typical and important,
  15:**333–337**, 513
    See also specific numbers
Numbers in Hebrew, 8:586–587
Numbers Rabbah, 15:**337–338**
Numenius, son of Antiochus, 15:**339**
Numenius of Apamea, 14:531, 15:**339**
Numerus clausus, 15:**339–343**
Numhauser, Jacobo Schaulson, 16:349
Numinous, sense of, 15:518
Numismatics, 13:716, 15:**343–344**
    Reifenberg, Adolf, 17:203
Numquam dubitavimus, 4:278
Nun, 15:**344**
Nunberg, Herman, 15:**344–345**
Nuñes, Isaac Israel. *See* Alvares, Isaac
Nuñes family. *See* Nuñez family
Nunes Vais, Abraham Joseph, 15:345
Nunes Vais, Isaac Joseph, 15:345
Nunes-Vais, Italo, 15:345
Nunes Vais family, 15:**345**
Nuñez, Beatrice, 15:345
Nuñez, Clara, 15:345
Nuñez, Daniel, 15:346
Nuñez, Hector, 15:345, **346**
Nuñez, Helen, 15:345
Nuñez, Henrique, 15:345
Nuñez, Joseph Israel. *See* Alvarez,
  Antonio
Nuñez, Maria, 15:345
Nuñez, Moses, 15:346
Nuñez, Pedro, 15:345
Nuñez, Robert, 15:346

Nuñez, Samuel Ribeiro, 15:345–346
Nuñez, Violante, 15:345
Nuñez, Zipporah, 15:346
Nuñez Alvarez, Isabel, 15:345
Nuñez family, 15:**345–346**
Nuñez-Torres, David, 15:345
Nunez-Vaez family. *See* Nunes Vais
  family
Nur Banu, 8:318
Nuremberg (Germany), 15:**346–348**
Nuremberg laws, 2:693, 9:244–245,
  287–289, 330, 15:**348–350**
Nuremberg trials, 4:128, 9:381,
  11:828–829, 12:553, 20:637–638
Nurock, Mordecai, 12:521, 15:**350–351**
Nurock, Mordechai, 12:521
Ñurri, land of, 9:624, 625–626
*The Nursemaid of Rebecca. See
  Meneket Rivkah*
Nursia, Daniel de, 15:312
Nursia, de, family. *See* Norzi family
Nursia, Leone de, 15:312
Nusaḥ, 15:**351**
Nusaḥ ha-Ari (Luria), 13:134
Nusaḥ Yagur (Sharett), 14:543
Nusinov, Isaac, 15:**351–352**
Nusinov, Yitzhak. *See* Nusinov, Isaac
Nussaḥ. *See* Nusaḥ
Nussbaum, Arthur, 15:**352**
Nussbaum, Felix, 2:507, 15:**352**
Nussbaum, Hilary, 15:**352**
Nussbaum, Hillel. *See* Nussbaum,
  Hilary
Nussbaum, Jakob, 15:**353**
Nussbaum, Max, 15:**353**
Nussbaum, Perry, 15:**353–354**
Nussenbaum, Yitzḥak. *See* Ben-
  Aharon, Yitzḥak
Nussenblath, Tulo, 15:**354**
Nuts, 15:**354**
Nuzi (Iraq), 15:**355**
  archives, 2:404, 6:322
  historic documents, 9:165
Nyilaskeresztes Párt-Hungarista
  Mozgalom. *See* Arrow Cross Party
Nyiregyhaza (Hungary), 15:**355–356**
Nyitra. *See* Nitra
Nyons (France), 15:**356**
Nyu-yorkish (Shapiro), 18:407

O

O (letter), 15:*357*
Oʾah. *See* Owls
Oʿaḥ, 15:550
Oak, 15:**357–358**, vol. 16: color insert
Oakes, John B., 15:376

Oakland (CA), 15:**358**
Oak of Abraham (Hebron), 15:357
Oaorio family. *See* Abendana family
Oates, Joyce Carol, 4:666
Oath More Judaico, 15:**364–365**
*The Oath of a Jew. See Der Eid eines
  Judens*
Oaths, 15:**358–364**
  in Bible, 15:358–360
  curses, relationship to, 15:358, 462
  hired service, 12:412
  more Judaico or juramentum
    Judaeorum, 15:362
  obligations, law of, 15:373
  ordeal and, 15:462
  ordeal of jealousy, 15:462–463
  in post-Talmudic law, 15:362–364
  sanctions for, 15:360, 362
  Shevuʿot, 18:472–473
  in Talmudic law, 15:360–362
Oaths (tractate). *See Shevuʿot* (tractate)
Oaths and gezerta, 7:570–571
Oats. *See* Five species
Obadia, Meyer, 16:346
Obadiah (King of the Khazars), 15:**365**
Obadiah (Norman proselyte), 14:543,
  15:**366–367**
Obadiah, Book of, 15:**365–366**
Obadiah ben Abraham, 11:537
Obadiah ben Pethahiah. *See* Perl,
  Joseph
Obadiah of Bertinoro, 8:744
Obadiah Scroll, 15:367
Obadya, Abraham, 15:**367**
Obed (biblical figure), 15:**367**
Obedas I (Arabian king), 15:**367**
Obedas II (Arabian king), 15:**367**
Obed-Edom (biblical figures), 15:**368**
Oberehnheim. *See* Obernai
Oberhoffaktor. *See* Court Jews
Obermann, Julian Joël, 15:**368**
Obermayer, Leon J., 2:59
Obermeyer, Jacob, 11:429, 15:**368**
Obermilizfaktor. *See* Court Jews
Obernai (France), 15:**368**
Obernik, Judah, 15:**368**
Obey, André, 15:289
*Objective Criteria of Recovery from
  Neuropsychiatric Disorders* (Eissler),
  6:278
Objectivists, 15:442
Oblations. *See* Sacrifice
Obligations, law of, 5:189–193,
  14:346–347, 15:**368–375**
  bypass routes, 12:537–540, 15:373
  coercion, 15:374

contents of obligations, 15:373
contracts, arising from, 15:369, 372, 373–374
creation of obligation, 15:369
custom, 15:373
execution of obligations, 15:372
extinction of obligations, 15:372
imperfect or unenforceable obligations, 15:369–370
inherited obligations, 15:374
labor, 12:412–415
lease and hire, 12:569
liabilities and fines, 15:369
Mishnah, 14:321
mishpat Ivri, 14:334
obligees, benefits derived by, 15:372–373
ones and, 15:430
oral vs. written, 15:371
parties to obligations, 15:369, 371
personal nature of, 15:368, 370
proprietary aspects of, 15:368, 370
public acts, 15:373–374
in state of Israel, 15:372
third party, recovery via encumbered and alienated assets in hands of, 15:370–371
torts, arising from, 15:369, 372
undertaking, obligation as, 15:372
Obligatory War (Meir ben Simeon), 14:439
Oboda (Negev). *See* Avedat (Negev)
Obóz Zjednoczenia Narodowego (OZON). *See* OZON
Obrecht Shul (Amsterdam, Netherlands), 6:369
Obrist, Hermann, 1:397
Obrister der Juedischkeit. *See* Praefectus Judaeorum
Obscenity. *See* Profanity
Observances. *See* Mitzvah
Obshestvo Remeslenofo zemledelcheskofo Truda. *See* ORT
Obsidio Szigetiana (Zriny), 9:603
Obuda (Hungary), 4:245
Óbuda (Hungary). *See* Obuda (Hungary)
Ocaña (Spain), 15:375
The Occident (newspaper), 12:600
Occult sciences, 11:668
Nostradamus, 15:314
Occupational training. *See* Vocational training
An Occupation of Angels (Tidhar), 18:206
Occupations. *See specific occupations and disciplines*

Occupied territories
administered territories, 10:239
administration, 10:231
Arab population, 10:241–242, 279, 720–721, 722–725
attacks on Israelis in, 10:249
Dayan and, 5:485
European Economic Community and, 6:565, 566, 567–568
feminist organizations, 6:754
Gaza Strip, 10:464
government, 10:247
Intifada, 10:241–242
Jewish settlements, 10:253
Oslo Accords and, 10:246
population, 10:303–305, 380–383
UN and refugees in, 10:270–271
Wye Plantation Agreement, 10:249
See also Gaza Strip; Green Line settlements; West Bank
Oceanography, 6:450–451
Ochberg, Isaac, 15:375
Ochrida (Macedonia), 15:375
Ochs, Adolph Simon, 1:398, 11:468, 15:375–376
Ochs, George Washington, 15:376
Ochs, Julius, 15:375
Ochs, Milton B., 15:376
Ochs, Phil. *See* Ochs, Philip David
Ochs, Philip David, 15:376
Ochs, Siegfried, 15:376
Ochs-Cakes, George. *See* Ochs, George Washington
Ochs family, 15:375–376
O ciclo das águas (Moacyr), 18:207
Octavianus, Caius Julius Caesar. *See* Augustus
October (motion picture), 6:274
October Revolution (1917), 15:378
Octobrists (political party), 15:376–377
Odem, 16:476
Odenathus and Zenobia, 15:377
Odenathus Septimus, 15:377
Odenburg (Hungary). *See* Sopron (Hungary)
Odes of Solomon, 18:765–766
Odessa (Ukraine), 3:562, 563, 15:377–382, 18:261, 262
Odessa Committee, 15:382
Odessa Tales (Babel), 3:17, 18
Odesser, Bezalel. *See* Shulsinger, Bezalel
Odessus. *See* Varna
Odets, Clifford, 15:289, 290, **382–383**
Odo of Cambrai, 15:383
Odo of Châteauroux, 15:383

Odo of Sully, 15:383
Odors, air pollution, 5:167–168
Odyssey (Homer), 3:580
The Odyssey of a Faith (Heller), 8:793
Oea (Libya). *See* Tripoli (Libya)
Oedenberg. *See* Sopron (Hungary)
Oels (Poland). *See* Olesnica
Oenomaus of Gadara, 15:383
Oesterley, William Oscar Emil, 15:**383–384**
Oesterreicher, John, 4:712
Oesterreicher, Tobias Von, 15:**384**
Oesterreicher, Vojěch. *See* Rakous, Vojtěch
Oesterreichische Geschichte bis zum Ausgange des 13. Jahrhunderts (Buedinger), 4:251
Oesterreichische-Israelitische Union, 20:**249**
Oesterreichische Nationalbibliothek (Austria), 15:**384**
Oesterreichisches Central-Organ Fuer Glaubensfreiheit, Cultur, Geschichte und Literatur der Juden (periodical), 15:**384**
Oettingen (Germany), 15:**384–385**
Oeuvre de Secours aux Enfants. *See* OSE
Oeuvre de Secours aux Enfants (OSE), 2:62, 9:496
Ofakim (Israel), 15:**385**
Ofek, Avraham, 15:**385–386**
Ofek, Uriel, 15:**386**
Ofen (Hungary). *See* Budapest (Hungary)
Ofen community. *See* Buda community
Ofer, Avraham, 15:**386**
Oferet. *See* Lead
Offenbach (Germany), 15:**386–387**
Frank, Eva, 7:180–181
Frank, Jacob, 7:189
Offenbach, Isaac, 15:**387**
Offenbach, Jacques, 15:**387**
Offenburg (Germany), 3:43, 15:**387–388**
Offerings
frankincense, 7:212–213
incense, 9:754–755
pascal, 9:108
See also Cults; Sacrifices
Office, public. *See* Public authority
Office of Special Investigations (OSI), 15:**388**
Official, Joseph, 14:439, 15:**388–389**
Official, Nathan ben Joseph, 2:162, 11:419, 14:439, 15:**388–389**
Official Aramaic. *See* Aramaic, official

Offner, Stacy, 15:**389**

Of Horrible and Woeful Destruction of Sodome and Gomorra (anonymous), 18:739

Ofir, Arie, 15:**389**

Ofir, Shaike, 15:**389–390**

Ofir, Yeshayahu. *See* Ofir, Shaike

O'Flaherty, Wendy. *See* Doniger, Wendy

Ofner, Francis-Amir, 15:**390**

Ofner, Julius, 12:547, 15:**390**

Ofran (Morocco), 15:**390–391**

Og (ruler of Bashan), 6:158, 322, 14:528, 15:**391–392**
    See also Eliezer (biblical figure)

O'Hare, Berta. *See* Margoulies, Berta

Ohavei Torah, 6:409

Oh Canada! Oh Quebec: Requiem for a Divided Country (Richler), 17:288

Ohel, 8:272, 15:**392**

Ohel Abraham (Shag), 18:361

Ohel Moed. *See* Makuya

Ohel Mo'ed (Gerondi), 7:549

Ohel Moshe vi-Yhudit. *See* Judith Lady Montefiore College

Ohev ben Meir ha-Nasi, 15:**392**

Ohev Mishpat (Duran), 2:530–531

Oh God, What Next? (Montefiore), 14:459

Ohio (U.S.), 11:393, 15:**392–393**, *393*

Ohio State University, 5:69–70

Ohio Steel Foundry Company Building, 11:718

Oholah, 6:639

Oholei Shem, 4:139

Oholei Ya'akov (Castro), 4:518

Oholiab (tractate), 15:**393–394**

Oholibah, 6:639

Oholot (tractate), 15:**394**

Ohrbach, Jerome Kane, 15:394

Ohrbach, Nathan M., 15:394

Ohrbach family, 15:**394**

Ohrbach's department store chain, 15:394

Ohrenstein, Jiří. *See* Orten, Jiří

Ohrenstein, O. *See* Ornest, Ota

Ohr Torah Stone, 17:29–30, 345

Ohud, 11:562–563

Oif Kiddush Ha-Shem (Bryks), 4:229–230

Oil and petroleum products, 16:**19–20**

Oil Imperialism (Fischer), 7:54

Oil of Life, 15:**394**

Oils, 7:117, 15:**395–396**

Oingo Boingo (music group), 6:314–315

L'Oiseau n'a plus d'ailes (Schwiefert), 18:196

Oistrakh, David Fedorovich, 15:**397**

Oistrakh, Igor, 15:397

Okhlah ve-Okhlah, 13:621, 622–623, 15:**397**

Okhlim (Shabtai), 8:722

Oklahoma (U.S.), 15:**397–398**, *398*, 18:178

Oko, Adolph S., 15:398

Okresni město (Poláček), 16:285

Olah, George A., 4:593, 15:**399**

Olah Ḥadashah (Sanguinetti), 18:21

Olam ha-ba, 15:**399–400**
    fourth, 6:497–498
    Orthodox Judaism and, 15:497
    See also Beatitude; Hell

Olam katan. *See* Microcosm

Olam Va'ed (Eliezer Fischel ben Isaac of Strzyzow), 6:330

Olan, Levi Arthur, 15:**400–401**

Olat Hodesh (Fleckeles, Eleazar ben David), 7:71

Olat Ish (Elyashar), 6:372

Olat Tamid (Albelda), 1:588

Olat Yiẓḥak (Lutẓiner), 13:251–252

Olat Ẓibbur (Fleckeles), 7:71

Olbracht, Ivan, 15:**401**

Old and Young (Braudes). *See* Zekenim im Ne'arim

Old Arabic. *See* Arabic language

Old clothes. *See* Secondhand goods and old clothes, trade in

The Old Country (Shulman), 16:127

Oldenburg (Germany), 15:**401–402**

Old French. *See* Judeo-French language

Old Greek (OG) or Hexaplaric versions of Bible, 3:597, 598, 601, 602

The Old Huntsman (Sassoon), 18:71

Old Kingdom (Egypt), 6:223

Old Konstantin (Ukraine). *See* Staro-Konstantinov (Ukraine)

Old Latin Bible (OL), 3:598, 609

The Old Man of the Mountains (Nicholson), 6:336

Old Testament, 3:574, 15:190, 191

The Old Testament, an Introduction (Eissfeldt), 6:278

Oleander, 15:**402**

Olei ha-Gardom, 15:**402**

Oleśnicki, Zbigniew, 15:**403**

Olesko (Ukraine), 15:**402**

Olesnica (Poland), 15:**402–403**

Olevski, Buzi, 15:**403**

Olgin, Moshe J., 15:**403**

Olgopol (Ukraine), 15:**403–404**

Olim, 1:660–661

Oliphant, Laurence, 15:**404**

Olitski, Jules, 15:**404–405**

Olitzki, Aryeh Leo, 15:**405**

Olitzky, Baruch, 15:405

Olitzky, Kerry M., 15:**405–406**

Olitzky, Leib, 15:405

Olitzky, Mattes, 15:405

Olitzky family, 15:**405**

Olive, 15:**406–407**, vol. 16: color insert
    oils made from, 15:395–396
    Tree of Life viewed as, 15:394

Olivero, Betty, 15:**407–408**

Oliver Twist (Dickens), 5:645, 6:278, 435

Oliver Y Fullana, Nicolás de, 15:**408**

Olivétan, Pierre Rovert, 3:628–629

Olivetti, Adriano, 15:408

Olivetti, Camillo, 15:408

Olivetti family, 15:**408**

Oliveyra, Solomon ben David de, 15:**408**

Olkusz (Poland), 15:**408–409**

Ollendorff, Franz, 15:**409**

Ollendorff, Friedrich, 15:**409**

Olmedo (Spain), 15:**409–410**

Olmert, Ehud, 13:191, 15:**410**

Olmo, Jacob Daniel, 2:136

Olmo, Jacob Daniel ben Abraham, 15:**410–411**

Olmuetz (Czech Republic). *See* Olomouc

Olofernes. *See* Holofernes

Olomouc (Czech Republic), 15:**411**

Olschwanger, Isaac Wolf, 15:**411**

Olsen, Tillie, 15:**411–412**

Olshan, Isaac, 15:**412**

Olshausen, Justus, 13:58, 15:**412**

Olson, B.E., 16:631

Olsvanger, Immanuel, 15:**412**

Olszowy-Schlanger, Judith, 11:326

Olyka (Ukraine), 15:**412**

Olympic Games, 1:314–315, 15:**413–415**, *413t–415t*, 19:145
    1936, 9:329–330
        athletes, Jewish, 7:638
        Copeland, Lillian, 5:211
        Fields, Jackie, 7:17

Omaha (NE), 14:451, 15:**415–416**

Omaha Blues (Lelyveld), 12:636

Omanut, 4:624

Omar (caliph), 3:45, 11:153–154

Omar, covenant of. *See* Covenant of Omar

Omar, Mosque of. *See* Dome of the Rock

Omar, Ẓāhir al-, 10:173, 174

Omar ibn al-Khaṭṭāb, 15:416, **419**

Omen. *See* Divination

Omer, 4:359

Omer (Israel), 15:**419**

Omer (offering and time period), 15:**419–422**

Omer, Hillel, 15:**422**

Omer ba-Sadeh (Luria), 13:261

Omnam Ken, 15:**422**

Omri (King of Israel), 9:175–176, 15:**422–423**

Omride dynasty, 9:177–179

Omsk (Russia), 15:**423**

O My America! (Kaplan), 11:776

On (Ancient Egypt). *See* Heliopolis (Ancient Egypt)

Ona'ah, 5:186, 15:**423–426**

Onagers, 15:**426**

On Aging ((Améry)). *See Ueber das Altern* (Améry)

Onan, 3:723, 15:**426**

Onanism, 15:**426–427**

On Being a Christian Jew (Montefiore), 14:459

On Chestnuts, Peacocks and Tokens from Heaven (Sened). *See Armonium, Tavasim, u-Petakim mi-Shamayim* (Sened)

On Contemporary Jewish Existence (Rotenstreich), 16:101

Onderwijzer, Abraham ben Samson ha-Kohen, 15:**427**

One (number), 15:334

The One-and-a-Half-Eyed Archer. See Polutoraglazy strelets (Livshits)

On Eastern and Western Foundations in the Music of Israel (Smoira-Cohn), 18:690

Oneg Shabbat archives, 2:410

Oneg Yom Tov (Heilpern), 8:768

O nekotoryh srednevekovykh obvineniyakh protiv Yevreyev (Chwolson), 4:724

Onen. *See* Aninut

Ones, 15:**427–431**

One thousand (number), 15:336–337

Onex Corporation, 18:184

On Foreign Ground. See Oyf Fremder Erd

Oni. *See* Rosh Pinnah (Israel)

Onias, Temple of, 12:649, 15:**432–433**

Onias I, 15:**431**

Onias II, 15:**431**

Onias III, 15:**431–432**

Onias IV, 12:649, 15:**432**

Onions, 15:**433**, vol. 16: color insert

On Jerusalem (Philo, the Elder), 16:**58**

Onkelos, 15:**433–434**
    anthropomorphism, 2:189

God fearers as ancestors of, 11:293

Only Yesterday. See Temol Shilshom

On Meanings in Music (Smoira-Cohn), 18:690

Ono (Judea), 15:**434, 500**

Ónody, Géza, 15:**434**

Onolzbach (Germany). *See* Ansbach (Germany)

Onomasticon (Eusebius), 6:568–569

Onomastics. *See* Names

On Our Young Poetry. See Shiratenu ha-Ze'irah

On Ployne's Ruins (Bursztyn). *See Iber di Khurves fun Ployne*

On Several Medieval Accusations Against the Jews. See O nekotoryh srednevekovykh obvineniyakh protiv Yevreyev

On Suicide (Améry). *See Hand an sich legen. Diskurs ueber den Freitod* (Améry)

Ontario (Canada), 15:**434–436**

On the Brink of Crisis. See Ad Mashber

On the Death of Hitler's Assassin (Yarden), 18:206

On the Dnieper. See Baym Dnieper

On the Essence of the Soul (Baḥya), 3:65

On the Improvement of the Jews as Citizens. See Ueber die buergerliche Verbesserung der Juden

On the Jews (Aristeas), 2:456

On the Jews (Artapanus), 2:521

On the Kings of Judah (Eupolemus), 6:552–553

On the Old Yiddish Novel: 14th-16th Centuries (Erik), 6:479

On the Soul (Alexander of Aphrodisias), 1:628

On the Threshold of the House of Study. See Al Saf Beit ha-Midrash

Onycha, 15:**436**

Opatoshu, David, 15:437

Opatoshu, Joseph, 15:**436–437**

Opatovsky, Joseph. *See* Opatoshu, Joseph

Opatow (Poland), 15:**437–438**

Opava (Czech Republic), 15:**438**

The Open Society and Its Enemies (Popper), 16:380

Open the Gate (Molodowsky), 14:430

Opera
    Amsterdam, 2:108, 119
    Bréval, Lucienne, 4:174
    De Phillippe, Edis, 5:589
    Halévy, Jacques Fromental Élie, 8:270–271
    Israel National Opera Company, 5:589, 11:814

    Lear, Evelyn, 12:567–568
    Leigh, Adèle, 12:626
    Lert, Ernst, 12:660
    librettists, Beda, 3:246
    Liebermann, Rolf, 12:808–809
    Liebling, Estelle, 12:809–810
    London, George, 13:185
    Lucca, Pauline, 13:247
    New York Metropolitan Opera, 11:723
    Pasta, Giuditta, 15:683–684
    Pauly, Rosa, 15:697–698
    Peerce, Jan, 15:712
    Peters, Roberta, 16:16
    Pollini, Bernhard, 16:360
    Raisa, Rosa, 17:74
    Raskin, Judith, 17:107
    Resnik, Regina, 17:228
    Schoene, Lotte, 18:156
    Schorr, Friedrich, 18:163
    Sills, Beverly, 18:581–582
    tenors, 11:58, 13:763
    women, 13:690

"Operation Barbarosa," 9:334

"Operation Blot Out," 9:335–336

Operation Defensive Shield, 10:252, 477–479, 18:417

Operation Ezra, 9:112, 10:20, 340

Operation Joshua, 4:304

Operation Kadesh. *See* Sinai Campaign

Operation Magic Carpet, 10:340

Operation Moses, 10:353

Operation Nehemiah, 9:112, 10:20, 340

Operations, War of Independence. *See* War of Independence

Operation Solomon, 4:95, 304, 10:353, 453

Operation T4, 6:570–571

Operation Texas, 15:323

Operativo Siesta (Aguinis), 1:510

Operetta, 11:745

Opferpfennig, 15:**438**

Ophel (Jerusalem), 15:**438**

Ophir, 15:**439, 439**

Ophir, Noah, 4:370

Ophrah (ancient Israel), 15:**439**

Ophuels, Max, 15:**439–440**

L'Opinion Nationale (newspaper), 4:503

The Opinions of the Philosophers (Falaquera). *See De'ot ha-Philosofim*

Opler, Marvin Kaufmann, 15:**440**

Opler, Morris Edward, 15:**440**

Opoczno (Poland), 15:**440–441**

Opole Lubelskie (Poland), 15:**441**

Oporto (Portugal), 15:**441**

Oppé, Adolph Paul, 15:**441**

Oppen, George, 15:**441–442**

Oppenheim (Germany), 15:**442–443**

Oppenheim, Abraham, 15:**443**

Oppenheim, Beer ben Isaac, 15:**443**

Oppenheim, Dagobert, 15:**443**

Oppenheim, David, 4:29, 78, 11:398, 15:**443–444**

Oppenheim, David ben Abraham, 15:**444–445**
　bibliography of, 3:681
　as bibliophile, 3:683, 684

Oppenheim, Friedrich Carl, 15:**443**

Oppenheim, Ḥayyim (Hebrew scholar), 15:**445**

Oppenheim, Ḥayyim (Rabbi). *See* Oppenheim, Joachim

Oppenheim, Helene, 15:**443**

Oppenheim, Hermann, 15:**445**

Oppenheim, Jacques, 12:553, 15:**445**

Oppenheim, James, 15:**445**

Oppenheim, Joachim, 15:**445**

Oppenheim, Joel, 15:**443**

Oppenheim, Lassa Francis Lawrence, 15:**445–446**

Oppenheim, Martha, 11:393

Oppenheim, Max. *See* Mopp

Oppenheim, Meir, 15:**443**

Oppenheim, Meret, 15:648

Oppenheim, Moritz Daniel, 15:**446**

Oppenheim, Paul Leo, 15:**446**

Oppenheim, Sally, 15:**446**

Oppenheim, Sally, Baroness Oppenheim-Barnes, 16:342–343

Oppenheim, Samuel, 2:59

Oppenheim, Seligmann, 3:704–705

Oppenheim, Seligmann, in Bingen, 14:301

Oppenheim, Simon, 15:**443**

Oppenheim, Solomon, Jr., 15:**443**

Oppenheim, Waldemar, 15:**443**

Oppenheimer, Carl, 15:**447**

Oppenheimer, David, 4:187

Oppenheimer, David ben Abraham. *See* Oppenheim, David ben Abraham

Oppenheimer, Emanuel, 15:**451**

Oppenheimer, Ernest. *See* Oppenheimer, Sir Ernest

Oppenheimer, Franz, 4:28, 15:**447–448**, 18:730

Oppenheimer, Fritz E., 15:**448**

Oppenheimer, Harry Frederick (H.F.O.), 15:**447**

Oppenheimer, Heinz Reinhard. *See* Oppenheimer, Hillel Reinhard

Oppenheimer, Hillel Reinhard, 15:**448**

Oppenheimer, J. Robert, 15:**450**

Oppenheimer, Joseph, 15:**448–449**

Oppenheimer, Joseph ben Issachar Suesskind, 15:**449–450**

Oppenheimer, Karl, 15:**450**

Oppenheimer, Max. *See* Mopp

Oppenheimer, Samuel, 4:132, 15:**444**, **450–451**

Oppenheimer, Sir Ernest, 15:**447**

Oppenheimer family (from Oppenheim). *See* Oppenheim family

Oppenheim family (from Frankfurt and Bonn), 15:**443**

Oppenheim family (from Oppenheim), 15:**443**

Oppenhejm, Ralph Gerson, 15:**451**

Opper, Adolf. *See* Blowitz, Henri Georges Stephane Adolphe Opper de

Opper, Frederick Burr, 4:499, 15:**451**

Oppert, Gustav Salomon, 15:**451–452**

Oppert, Jules Julius, 15:**452**

The Opponents, 11:433

Opposite the Tent of Timmorah. See Mul Ohel Timmorah

Oppression, 15:**452–453**

Optimisti (Sinko), 18:641

Opus Dei, 15:317

Orabuena, Ishmael, 15:453

Orabuena, Joseph, 15:562

Orabuena, Joseph I, 15:453

Orabuena, Joseph II, 15:453

Orabuena family, 15:**453**

Orach, 15:**453**

Oracle. *See* Divination; Ephod; Prophets and prophecy

Oracle Corp., 6:361–362

Oracles. *See* Prophets and prophecy; Sibyl and Sibylline Oracles

Oradea (Romania), 15:**453–454**

Oradea Mare (Romania). *See* Oradea

Or Adonai (Crescas), 2:530, 5:285–288, 16:89

Oraḥ Ḥayyim (Abraham Ḥayyim ben Gedaliah), 1:312

Oraḥ Ḥayyim (Ehrenfeld), 6:239

Oraḥ Ḥayyim (Jacob ben Asher), 11:30

Oraḥ Ḥayyim (Kahana), 11:712

Oraḥ Ḥayyim (Shapira), 18:400

Oraḥ Selulah le-Dikduk Sefat Ever (Baranowicz), 3:134

Oraḥ Ẓaddikim (Luzki), 11:792, 13:279

Or Akiva (Israel), 15:**454**

Orality, 2:93

Oral Law, 8:252–253, 15:**454–459**
　Bet Hillel and Bet Shammai, 3:530–533

Bloch, Hermann, 3:762

in Conservative Judaism, 15:457–458

Duran, Simeon ben Ẓemaḥ, 6:59

Eleazar ben Pedat, 6:306–307

Elijah ben Solomon Zalman, 6:343

instruction, 6:171

Luria, David ben Judah, 13:261

mishpat Ivri, 14:339

Moses, 14:534

in Reform Judaism, 15:456–457

Written Law, relationship to, 15:454–456

See also Soferim

Oral obligations, 5:192–193, 15:**371**

Oral tradition
　children's literature, 2:619
　kabbalah and, 11:585–586
　rise of concept, 11:515

Oram ben Ner, 4:276

Or Ammim (Sforno), 18:334

Oran (Algeria), 15:**459–460**

Orange (France), 15:**460**

Orange County (CA), 15:**460–462**

Oranges, 4:737–738

Oranit (Samaria), 15:**462**

Orașul Stalin (Romania). *See* Brașov (Romania)

Orașuo Stalin (Romania). *See* Brașov (Romania)

Oration on the Dignity of Man (Pico della Miraondola), 16:146–147

Orations, Balaam, 3:77–80

Orbister der Judischlait. *See* Praefectus Judaeorum

Ordeal, 15:**462**
　trial by, 15:462

Ordeal of jealousy, 15:**462–463**

Order of Ancient Maccabeans, 13:**316**

The Order of the World. See Seder Olam

Ordinance. *See* Takkanot

Ordinary Men: Reserve Police Battalion 101 and the Final Solution in Poland (Browning), 4:217, 9:336, 419

Ordination, 17:13–14, 643, 18:274–279

L'Ordination (Benda), 3:324

Ordman, Jeanette, 15:**463**

Ordo Fratrum Praedicatorum. *See* Dominicans

Az ördög (Molnár). *See The Devil* (Molnár)

Ordzhonikidze (Russia), 15:**463**

Ore'aḥ Natah Lalun (Agnon), 1:467, 11:216

Oreb (Midianite prince), 15:**463–464**

Oregon (U.S.), 9:133, 13:774, 15:**464**, **464**

Orel (Russia), 15:**464–465**

Oren, Ram, 15:**465**

Oren, Yiẓhak, 15:**465**

Orense (Spain), 15:**465**

Orenstein, Alexander Jeremiah, 15:**465–466**

Orenstein, Arbie, 15:**466**

Orenstein, Ẓevi Hirsch ben Mordecai, 4:169

L'or et la cendre (Abécassis), 1:244

Orgad, Ben Zion, 11:444, 15:**466**

Organ donation, 3:755

Organic chemistry
  Bergmann, Ernst David, 3:429
  Bergmann, Felix Eliezier, 3:429
  Herzog, Reginald Oliver, 9:70
  Lewkowitsch, Julius, 12:770–771
  Liebermann, Carl Theodor, 12:808
  Pinner, Adolf, 16:169
  Raphael, Ralph Alexander, 17:95
  Reichstein, Tadeus, 17:201–202
  See also Chemistry

The Organism as a Whole (Loeb), 13:160

Organization, Jewish. *See* Community

Organization and Pathology of Thought (Rapaport), 17:92

Organization of Greek Concentration Camp Survivors, 17:131

Organización Pasi Cefi, 4:641

Organized crime, 18:173–174
  See also Mobsters

Organize? With 1,250,000 Workers Backing Us, Of Course We Will Organize (Shahn), vol. 4: color insert

Organs, 15:**466–468**

Orgel, Leslie, 13:11

Orgelbrand, Hipolit, 15:468

Orgelbrand, Maurycy, 15:468

Orgelbrand, Mieczyslaw, 15:468

Orgelbrand, Samuel, 15:**468**

Orgeyev (Moldova), 15:**468–469**

Or Hadash (Hammer), 8:308

Or Ḥadash (Kallir), 11:745

Or Ḥadash al Ẓiyyon (Reines), 17:208

Orhai (Mesopotamia). *See* Osroene

Or ha-Levannah (Solomon), 11:793

Or ha-Me'ir (Shapira), 18:402

Or ha-Mizraḥ, 17:237

Or Ha-Ner (Israel), 15:**469**

Or ha-Yashar (Aaron Simeon ben Jacob Abraham of Copenhagen), 1:221

Or ha-Yashar (Copenhagen), 4:760

Or ha-Ẓafun (Finkel), 7:32

Orhei (Moldova). *See* Orgeyev

Orḥot Ḥayyim (Aaron ben Jacob ha-Kohen), 1:213–214, 12:405

Orḥot Ḥayyim (Eliezer ben Hyrcanus), 15:**469**

Orḥot Ḥayyim (Eliezer ben Isaac of Worms), 6:326

Orḥot Ḥayyim (Kahana), 11:712

Orḥot Ẓaddikim, 15:**469–470**

Oria (Italy), 2:81, 15:**470–471**

Orient, Middle Ages, dress, 6:14–15

Oriental illuminated Hebrew Bibles, 3:675–676

Oriental Institute at Bonn, 11:717

Orientalists, 15:**471**
  Barnett, Lionel David, 3:169
  Baumgartner, Walter, 3:222
  Beck(ius) Matthias Friedrich, 3:250
  Beek, Martinus Adrianus, 3:250
  Benzinger, Immanuel, 3:391–392
  Bernard, Edward, 3:467–468
  Brunschvig, Robert, 4:225
  Burchardt, Hermann, 4:285–286
  Burckhardt, Johann Ludwig, 4:286
  Chwolson, Daniel, 4:724–725
  Clermont-Ganneau, Charles, 4:755
  Crowfoot, John Winter, 5:307
  Delitzsch, Friedrich, 5:540–541
  Derenbourg, Hartwig, 5:594–595
  Derenbourg, Joseph Naphtali, 5:594–595
  Deutsch, Emanuel Oskar, 5:622
  Dillmann, August, 5:661–662
  Diringer, David, 5:675–676
  Erpenius, Thomas, 6:482
  Finkel, Joshua, 7:31–32
  Fischel, Walter Joseph, 7:52
  Halévy, Joseph, 8:271
  Halkin, Abraham Solomon, 8:275
  Harkavi, Albert, 8:356–357
  Haupt, Paul, 8:460
  Herzfeld, Ernst Emil, 9:53–54
  Huebsch, Adolph, 9:576–577
  Hyde, Thomas, 9:647
  and illuminated manuscripts, Hebrew, 9:728–729
  Landauer, Samuel, 12:468
  Leitner, Gottlieb Wilhelm, 12:629
  Lévi, Sylvain, 12:694
  Levias, Caspar, 12:696
  Lévi-Provençal, Evariste, 12:724–725
  Levy, Reuben, 12:754–755
  PIamenta, Moshe, 16:142
  Plessner, Martin, 16:237
  Pococke, Edward, 16:250

Reckendorf, Herman Solomon, 17:146

Reland, Adrian, 17:214

Renan, Ernest, 17:218

Robinson, Edward, 17:355

Rosenmueller, Ernst Friedrich Karl, 17:449

Rosenthal, Erwin, 17:453

Rosenthal, Franz, 17:453

Schultens, Albert, 18:173

Oriental Jewish Community of New York, 2:34

Oriental Jews
  alcoholism and, 6:28
  aliyah and absorption of, 10:215, 223–224, 226, 235–236
  Caribbean, 4:477
  dance, 5:410
  descriptions, nineteenth century, 5:472–473
  Israel (state), music, 10:693
  resurgence in twentieth century, 11:677

Oriental literature, 15:**471–474**

Origen, 1:290, 4:720, 15:**474**
  Bible's importance to, 3:665, 666
  Greek Bible texts collected by, 3:597, 598, 601

Original sin, 1:374

Origin and Growth of Religion as Illustrated by the Religion of the Ancient Hebrews (Montefiore), 14:455

The Origin of Language (Herder), 13:57

The Origin of the Egyptian Language (Loewe), 13:166

Origins of life, 13:**11**

The Origins of Nazi Genocide from Euthanasia to the Final Solution (Friedlander), 9:419

Origins of the Fifth Amendment (Levy), 12:752

The Origins of the Final Solution: The Evolution of Nazi Jewish Policy September 1939–March 1942 (Browning & Mathaus), 9:419

Origins of the Kabbalah (Scholem), 18:158

Orihuela (Spain), 15:**474**

Or Ishim (Shazar), 18:426

Or Israel (Israel ben Jonathan from Leczyca), 10:748

Or Kain (Ram Oren), 15:465

Orlah (tractate), 15:**475**

Orland, Herschl, 15:**475**

Orland, Yaakov, 15:**475**

Orlando (FL), 15:**475–476**

Or la-Yesharim (Eidlitz), 6:252–253
Or la-Yesharim (Epstein), 6:473
Orléans (France), 15:**476–477**
Orlev, Uri, 15:**477**
Orlik, Emil, 15:**477–478**
Orlikow, David, 15:**478**, 18:706
Orlinsky, Harry Meyer, 2:47, 3:614, 621, 622, 15:**478**
Orloff, Chana, 15:**478**
Ormandy, Eugene, 15:**479**
Or Mayer: Catalogue of the Old Hebrew Manuscripts and Printed Books of the Library of the Hon. Mayer Sulzberger of Philadelphia (Deinard), 5:532
Ormian, Ḥayyim, 15:**479**
Ormódy, Bertalan, 15:**479**
Ormuz (Iran). *See* Hormuz (Iran)
Ornea, Zigu, 8:380
Ornest, Ota, 15:**479**
Ornias (demon), 18:768
Ornitz, Samuel Badisch, 15:**479**
Ornstein, Abraham Frederick, 15:**479**
Ornstein, Jacob Meshullam ben Mordecai Ze'ev, 15:**479–480**
Ornstein, Leo, 15:**480–481**
Ornstein, Leonard Salomon, 15:**481**
Ornstein, Mordecai Ze'ev, 15:480, 481
Ornstein, Mordecai Ze'ev ben Moses, 15:**481**
Ornstein, O. *See* Ornest, Ota
Ornstein, Ẓevi Hirsch, 15:480
Ornstien, Abraham Frederick. *See* Ornstein, Abraham Frederick
Orobio de Castro, Balthazar. *See* Orobio de Castro, Isaac
Orobio de Castro, Isaac, 15:**481–482**
    disputations and polemics, 5:695
Orofernes. *See* Holofernes
Oropesa, Alfonso de. *See* Alfonso de Oropesa
Orosius, Paulus, 15:**482**
Orot (Israel), 15:**482**
Orpah, 15:**482**
Orpaz Averbuch, Yitzhak, 1:667, 8:706, 15:**482–483**
The Orphan Colony of the Jews of China (Finn), 7:39
Orphans and orphanages, 15:**483–487**
    American Joint Distribution Committee, 2:59–60, 62
    B'nai B'rith, 4:13–14
    Canada, 4:404
    Centos, 4:544
Orpheus: histoire generale des religions (Reinach), 17:205
Orrhoene (Mesopotamia). *See* Osroene (Mesopotamia)

Or Rishon be-Ḥokhmat ha-Lashon (Dotan), 5:763
Orsha (Belarus), 15:**487**
Orshanski, Elijah. *See* Orshanski, Ilya Grigoryevich
Orshanski, Ilya Grigoryevich, 12:457, 15:**487–488**
Orsini, Giovanni Gaetano, 15:249–250
Orsova (Romania), 15:**488**
ORT (Obshestvo Remeslenofo zemledelcheskofo Truda), 3:75, 15:**488–492**
    American Joint Distribution Committee, 2:60, 62
    Lvovich, David, 13:292
    Panken, Jacob, 15:612
    Shabad, Ẓemaḥ, 18:337
    trade schools, 6:185
Orta, Garcia de, 4:51, 13:728, 15:**492**
Orten, Jiří, 4:64, 15:479, **492**
Ortenberg, Arthur, 15:**492–493**
Ort-Farband, 3:718
Orthodox Churches
    Holocaust, response to, 9:377
    Jewish relations with, 4:678, 11:278, 282
Orthodox day schools, 11:756
Orthodox Islam, 18:270–271
Orthodox Judaism, 15:**493–500**, 20:349, 350, 366
    Abécassis, Eliette, 1:244–245
    ablution, 1:263
    Adams, Theodore L., 1:380–381
    Adar, 1:383
    Agudat Israel, 1:505–508
    alcoholism among members, 6:28
    in America, 2:45
    The American Hebrew, 2:49
    angels, 2:161
    Argentina, 2:430, 433, 439, 447
    Austria, Deutsch, Ignaz, 5:623–624
    ba'alei tesuvah, 3:6–7
    bar mitzvah, 3:166
    Bergen County (NJ), 3:423
    Bismark, Otto von, on, 3:726
    Breuer, Solomon, 4:173
    Canada, 4:410, 416, 417, 419
        Montreal, 14:465
        rabbis, 6:745–746
    Caribbean, 4:476
    children's literature, 4:627, 633
    choral singing, 4:661
    coffins, 4:783
    defined, 15:493
    dress, 6:17
    education, Jewish, 6:198

English-language literature, 6:746
feminism in, 6:753, 12:661, 16:112
Germany
    Adass Jeshurun, 1:384
    Adass Jisroel, 1:384
    Berlin, 3:448
    Deutsch, Israel, 5:624
    Hildesheimer, Azriel, 9:103
    Hirsch, Samson Raphael, 9:129–132
    Lehmann, Marcus, 12:616
    periodicals, 10:754
halakhah and development of concept of Judaism, 11:518–519
Ḥaredim, 8:348–352
Hungary, Sofer, Ḥayyim ben Mordecai Ephraim Fischel, 18:742–743
intermarriage, 6:381
Israel
    Elad, 6:282
    women, 6:754
Jerusalem, 6:64
Juedisch-Literarische Gesellschaft, 11:571–572
Jung, Leo, 11:575–576
Lithuanian pattern, 11:519
mediators with Haskalah, 11:121
Mizrachi, 15:494
modern Orthodoxy, trends and developments in, 15:495–499
Mo'ezet Gedolei ha-Torah, 1:506
Monatsschrift (periodical), 14:433
Monmouth County (NJ), 14:446
National Council of Young Israel, 21:**401–402**
neo-Orthodoxy, 11:519
Netherlands, Schuster, Aaron, 18:177
in New York City, 15:207, 208, 217–218
non-Orthodox Jews, attitude towards, 15:494, 498–499
origins and development, 15:493–494
periodicals, 11:241
rabbincal conferences, 17:20–21
Rabbinical Alliance of America, 17:20
Rabbinical Council of America, 17:21
rabbinical training, 17:28–30
    Rabbiner-Seminar Fuer das Orthodoxe Judentum, 17:19–20
resurrection, 1:442
Rosenheim, Jacob, 17:448

separation of women in
synagogues, 13:**771**
separatism, 15:**493–494**
Breuer, Isaac, 4:**171**
spread of, 15:**494–495**
television and, 10:**708**
Torah authorship, 15:**751–752**
Torah Umesorah, 11:**755–756**
U.K.
Abramsky, Yeḥezkel, 1:**328**
Adler, Nathan Marcus, 1:**405**
ultra-orthodox
Edah, 6:**141**
in Jerusalem, 11:**189, 190,
192, 195**
Union of Orthodox Jewish
Congregations of America,
20:**253**
Union of Orthodox Rabbis of the
United States and Canada,
20:**253**
U.S.
Adler, Joseph, 1:**401**
birth rate, 6:**703**
Borough Park, Brooklyn, vol.
5: color insert
children of immigrants, 6:**698**
contemporary families,
6:**705–706**
Donin, Hayim Halevy, 5:**750**
Drachman, Bernard, 6:**6**
Edah, 6:**141–142**
education, 14:**44**
immigrants, 6:**696**
rabbis, 6:**6, 741–742, 14:42**
Saint Louis, 17:**671–672**
Schachter, Jacob J., 18:**100**
Scheinfeld, Solomon Isaac,
18:**118**
Schwab, Shimon, 18:**180–181**
Scranton, 18:**211**
Seattle, 18:**229**
Soloveichik, Aaron, 18:**774–
775**
Soloveichik, Moshe, 18:**776–
777**
Soloveitchik, Joseph Baer,
18:**777–780**
summer camps, 11:**272–274**
Young Israel movement, 4:**284**
See also Modern Orthodox
Judaism; Neo-Orthodoxy
Orthodoxy. See Orthodox Judaism
Orthodoxy, German. See Neo-
Orthodoxy
Or Torah (Menahen ben Judah di
Lonzano), 13:**652**

Orvieto (Italy), 15:**500**
Orvieto, Angiolo, 10:**793**, 14:**540–541**,
15:**500**
Or Yehudah (Israel), 15:**500–501**
Or Yisrael (Jaffe), 11:**65**
Or Yisrael (Lipschuetz), 4:**760**, 13:**73**
Or Zaru'a (Isaac ben Moses of
Vienna), 10:**45–46**
Orzeszko, Eliza. See Orzeszkowa, Eliza
Orzeszkowa, Eliza, 15:**501**
Oświęcim (Germany). See Auschwitz
concentration camp
Osborn, Max, 15:**501**
Osca (Spain). See Huesca (Spain)
Oscar Wilde (Ellmann), 6:**362**
Oschinsky, Lawrence, 15:**501**
OSE (Oeuvre de Secours aux Enfants),
2:**62**, 9:**496**
OSE (Russian Jewish Health
Organization). See OZE (Russian
Jewish Health Organization)
Oseh Pele (Farḥi), 6:**335**
Oshaiah, 8:**291**
Oshaiah, Rav. See Hoshaiah, Rav
Oshaiah Rabbah, 15:**501–502**
Oshek. See Oppression
Osheroff, Douglas Dean, 15:**502**
Osherowitch, Mendl, 15:**502**
Oshmyany (Belarus), 15:**502–503**
Oshry, Ephraim, 15:**503**
Oshyanski, Abel-Aaron Itskovich. See
Ashanski, Abel-Aaron Itskovich
OSI. See Office of Special
Investigations
Osiander, Andreas, 15:**503**
Osijek (Croatia), 15:**503–504**
Osinsky, Moishe. See Burton, Sir
Montague
Osipenko (Ukraine). See Berdyansk
(Ukraine)
Osipovich, Nahum, 15:**504**
Osiris, Daniel Illffa, 15:**504**
Oslo (Norway), 15:**504–505**
Oslo Accords (1993), 2:**316–320**,
8:**747**, 10:**245–246, 455**
American Israel Public Affairs
Committee, 2:**51**
Elon, Binyamin, 6:**367**
England, 6:**431–432**
Jerusalem and, 11:**236**
Palestine Liberation Organization
and, 15:**594**
Palestinian Authority and, 15:**597,
598, 599**
Osnabrueck (Germany), 15:**505**
Osoblaha (Czech Republic), 15:**505–
506**

Osobyi archive, 2:**413**
Osofsky, Simḥa. See Assaf, Simḥa
O sprawe Steigera (Loewenstein),
13:**169**
Osrhoene (Mesopotamia). See Osroene
Osroene (Mesopotamia), 15:**506**
Ossowetzky, O. Yehoshua, 15:**506**
Ossuaries, 15:**506–507**
Ostanovka v pustyne (Brodsky), 4:**198**
Osten, Michael. See Goldstein, Moritz
Österlind, 11:**433**
Ostermann, Helmut. See Avnery, Uri
Ostfeld, Barbara Jean, 15:**507**
Ostia (Italy), 15:**507–508**
Ostra Brama, Legende aus der Zeit des
grossen Untergangs (Adler), 1:**398–
399**
Ostraca, 1:**692, 693**, 15:**508–509, 619**
Ostraca collections, 2:**405**
Ostrava (Czech Republic), 15:**509–510**
Ostriches, 15:**510**
Ostrich farming, 15:**547**
Ostriker, Alicia, 15:**510**, 20:**299**
Ostriker, Jeremiah P., 15:**510**
Ostrog (Ukraine), 15:**510–512**
Ostrog Ḥasidim, 8:**421**
Ostrogorski, Moses, 15:**512**
Ostroleka (Poland), 15:**512**
Ostrolenk, Bernhard, 15:**512**
Ostrolenka (Poland). See Ostroleka
Ostropoler, Hershele, 9:**592**, 15:**512–
513**
Ostropoler, Samson ben Pesaḥ, 15:**513**
Ostrov Lomzinsky (Poland). See
Ostrow Mazowiecka
Ostrovsky, Moshe. See Hameiri,
Moshe
Ostrower, Fayga, 15:**513**
Ostrowiec (Poland), 15:**513–514**
Ostrowiec Swietokrzyski (Poland). See
Ostrowiec
Ostrow Mazowiecka (Poland), 15:**514**
Ostryna (Belarus), 15:**514–515**
Osvát, Ernö, 15:**515**
Oswiecim (Poland), 12:**465**, 15:**515**
See also Auschwitz
Oszmiana (Belarus). See Oshmyany
Otaci (Moldavia). See Ataki
(Moldavia)
The Other Kingdom (Rousset), 9:**404–
405**
Othmar, R. See Auernheimer, Raoul
Othniel, 1:**356**, 9:**170**, 11:**562**, 15:**515**
Otiyyoy De-R. Akiva, 14:**188**
Otranto (Italy), 15:**516**
Otros son los sueños (Seligson), 18:**268**

Otta, Francisco, 15:**516**

Ottawa (Canada), 15:**516–517**

Ottensosser, David, 15:**517–518**

Ottepel (Ehrenburg). *See The Thaw* (Ehrenburg)

Ottinger, Albert, 15:**518**

Otto, Rudolph, 15:**518**

Ottolenghi, Abraham Azariah, 15:518

Ottolenghi, Adolfo, 15:518

Ottolenghi, Bonaiuto. *See* Ottolenghi, Abraham Azariah

Ottolenghi, Donato, 15:518
    See also Ottolenghi, Nathan

Ottolenghi, Eleazar, 15:518

Ottolenghi, Emilio, 15:518

Ottolenghi, Giuseppe, 15:518, **519**, 16:345

Ottolenghi, Joseph ben Nathan, 14:481, 15:518, **519**

Ottolenghi, Joshua, 15:518

Ottolenghi, Lazzaro. *See* Ottolenghi, Eleazar

Ottolenghi, Mario, 15:518–519

Ottolenghi, Michael, 15:519

Ottolenghi, Moses Jacob, 15:518, **519**

Ottolenghi, Nathan, 15:518

Ottolenghi, Raffaele, 15:518

Ottolenghi, Salvatore. *See* Ottolenghi, Joshua

Ottolenghi family, 15:**518–519**

Ottolengo, Samuel David ben Jehiel, 15:518, **519**

Ottolengo family. *See* Ottolenghi family

Ottoman Empire, 15:**519–546**, *521*, *522*
    Abdul Mejid I, 1:244
    Alliance Israélite Universelle, 15:530, 542
    Antebi, Albert, 2:184
    Arab alleigance during, 10:272
    archaeology, 2:392–393
    Bashan region, 3:197
    Bayazid II, 3:230
    blood libels in, 15:529–531
    Bulgaria under, 4:269
    capitulations, 4:452–454
    Chief Rabbinate, 4:613
    Christian-Jewish tensions in, 15:530
    clothing regulations for Jews, 15:520, 525–526, 527, 529
    community organization and structures, 5:106–108
    Constantinople, conquest of and transfer of Jews to, 15:521–522
    conversion of Jews to Islam and Christianity in, 15:531
    Covenant of Omar, 8:246
    disputes within Jewish community, settlement of, 15:535–536
    economic life of Jews in, 15:531–534
    Egypt, Alexandria, 1:634–635
    Egypt and, 6:231–234
    emancipation, 6:381, 385
    expansion of, *15:521*
        initial growth to conquest of Constantinople, 15:520–521
        in Middle East, Eastern Europe, and North Africa, 15:523–525
    Four Communities, concept of, 15:526
    Ḥakham Bashi, 8:**245–247**, 15:536–537, 17:14–15
    Hamon family, 8:311–312
    Herzl, relations with, 9:61–63
    holy places in Israel and, 9:501
    Hungary, 9:608–609
    Iraq, 10:15–16
    Janissaries, Jewish relationship with, 15:526–527
    Jerusalem under, 11:161–173
        European interest in, 11:164–166, 168–169
        Jewish activity in, 11:162–164, 166
    Jewish quarters, 11:312, 15:529
    judicial autonomy, 14:351–352
    Kawkabān, 12:40
    keiras, 8:318
    Kiera, 12:147–148
    Ladino literature development, 10:780
    Ladino literature in, 12:433, 15:539–540
    leather industry and trade, 12:575
    Mediterranean countries, insurance, 9:808–809
    Millet, 14:255–256
    Mizraḥi, Elijah, 14:393–394
    music, 14:670
    Nasi under, 15:525
    officials, 11:96
    Omar, Covenant of, 15:418
    organization of Jewish communities in, 15:534–537
    political power exercised by Jews in, 15:541–542
    refugee Jews settling in
        from Germany and France, 15:522
        from Spain and Portugal, 15:522–523
    Rose Law or Rescript of the Rose Chamber, 15:526
    Sarajevo, 18:48
    ṣarrāf, 18:61
    Selim I, 18:270
    Selim II, 18:270
    Sephardim in, 18:300–301
    sheluḥei erez Israel, 18:449
    slaves and slavery, 15:529
    social and family life of Jews in, 15:538–539
    sources of information regarding, 15:520
    spiritual life of Jews in, 15:537–538
    stagnation and decline
        nineteenth century, status of Jews in, 15:526–528
        reign of Abdul-Hamid II and last days of empire, 15:542–543
        sixteenth-eighteenth centuries, 15:525–526
    Suleiman the Magnificent, 19:302–304
    Sykes-Picot Agreement, 19:350–351, *351*
    synagogues, restrictions on, 15:528–529
    taxation of Jews by, 15:520, 525, 528, 533
    textiles, 19:662
    tobacco trade, 20:7
    Tunisia, 20:181–185
    Turkey, 2:147, 6:148, 149
    World War I, 15:543
    Young Turk revolution, Jewish participation in, 15:542–543, 544
    Zionist movement in, 15:542, 543–545
    See also Palestine (Ottoman); Turkey

Otwock (Poland), 15:**546**

OU (Union of Orthodox Jewish Congregations of America). *See* Union of Orthodox Jewish Congregations of America

Ouaknin, Jacques, 15:546

Ouaknin, Marc-Alain, 15:**546–547**

Oudtshoorn (South Africa), 15:**547**

Oulif, Charles Narcisse, 15:**547**

Our Hitler: A Film from Germany, 9:443

Our Religion and Our Neighbors (Schwartzman), 18:188

Our Review (newspaper). *See Nasz Przegląd* (newspaper)

Our Stake in World Trade (Lubin), 13:241–242

Oury, Gerard, 15:**547**

An Outline of Jewish History
(Dubnow), 6:34

Outlines of Jewish History (Magnus),
6:193

Out-marriage. *See* Mixed marriages

Outrageous Fortune (Franken), 7:202

*The Outside Chance of Maximilian
Glick* (Torgov), 20:54

Outside the Law. See Vne zakona
(Lunts)

Ouziel, Ben Zion Meir Ḥai, 14:390,
15:**547–548**

Ovadia, David, 4:276

Ovadia, Nissim J., 15:**548**

Ovchinski, Levi, 15:**548**

Ovdat (Negev). *See* Avedat (Negev)

Ovdei kokhavim u-mazalot. See
Akkum

Oved, Margalit, 15:**548–549**

Oved avodah zarah. *See* Akkum

Ovelim (Israel), 2:**721**

Oven Cave (Israel), vol. 10: color
insert

Overcoming Anti-Semitism (Fineberg),
7:26

Overreaching, law of. *See* Ona'ah

Overture to a Fairy Tale (composition,
Morawetz), 14:478

Ovid, 15:**549**

Ovitz, Michael, 15:**549**

Ovodovski, M. *See* Osherowitch,
Mendl

Ovruch (Ukraine), 15:**549–550**

Ovsay, Joshua, 15:**550**

Owen, Robert, 18:704

Owls, 15:**550–551**

Owner of Orchard (periodical). *See
Bustenai* (periodical)

Ownership, 1:474–476, 15:**551–552**
ḥazakah, 8:486–491
See also Hefker

Ownership rights, 1:359–363, 16:564–
565

Owning Up: the Art Modell Story
(Modell), 14:407

Oxford (England), 15:**552–554**, *553*

Oxford Center for Hebrew and Jewish
Studies, 15:554

Oxford University (England)
admission of Jews to, 15:554
Bodleian Library, 4:29

Oyabe Zen'ichiro, 11:84

Oybervisha. *See* Viseul-de-Sus
(Romania)

Oyf der Letster (Smolar), 18:690

Oyf Fremder Erd (Singer), 18:637

Oyfn Sheydveg (Shekhtman), 18:444

Oyf Vos Badarfn Yidn a Land (Shalom
Aleichem), 18:382

Oyf Yishev Erts-Yisroel: Zelik Mekhanik
(Shalom Aleichem), 18:382

Oysgetreyselt (Shalom Aleichem),
18:383

Oysher, Moishe, 15:**554**

Der Oysvorf: oder Shmuel Pasternak
(Shalom Aleichem), 18:383–384

Der Oytser (Pinski), 16:175

O yunost moya! (Selvinski), 18:272–
273

Oyved, Moyshe, 15:**554**

Oz, Amos, 8:705–706, 15:**554–556**

Oẓar Beduyei ha-Shem (Chajes),
4:559–560

Oẓar ha-Beraitot (Higger), 9:98

Oẓar ha-Ge'onim (Lewin), 12:759

Oẓar ha-Hayyim (Ẓahalon), 6:399

Oẓar ha-Ḥokhmah (Barasch), 6:399

Oẓar ha-Kavod (Abulafia), 1:343–344

Oẓar ha-Mishpat (Rakover), 18:471

Oẓar ha-Shemot (Rosenberg), 17:434

Oẓar ha-Shorashim (Ben Ze'ev), 3:391

Oẓar Hatorah, 6:214, 15:**556**
American Joint Distribution
Committee, 2:62
Morocco, 14:507

Oẓar Ḥayyim (Isaac ben Samuel of
Acre), 10:47

Oẓar Leshon ha-Mishnah (Kasovsky),
11:822

Ozarow dynasty, 2:539

Oẓar Razei (Bar Hebraeus), 3:151

Oẓar Yisrael (Eisenstein), 6:273, 400

OZE (Russian Jewish Health
Organization), 2:59, 15:**556–557**,
18:337

Ozery (Belorussia), 15:**557**

Ozhor (Belorussia). *See* Ozery
(Belorussia)

Ozick, Cynthia, 15:**557–558**

Oz le-Elohim (Ḥayon), 8:477, 18:356

OZON (Obóz Zjednoczenia
Narodowego), 15:**558**

Ozorkow (Poland), 15:**558–559**

Oẓ ve-Shalom, 15:703

P

P (letter), 15:*561*, 16:5

P. Virgily. *See* Kahan, Baruch
Mordecai

PA. *See* Palestinian Authority;
Palestinian Authority (PA)

Pa'amei ha-Heikhal (Talmon), 8:504

Pa'amon, 14:642

Pa'amon be-Kijong-dzu (Shaḥam),
18:363

Pabianice (Poland), 15:**561–562**

Pablo Christiani. *See* Christiani, Pablo

Pablo de Santa Maria, 4:290, 15:**562–
563**

Pabyanits. *See* Pabianice (Poland)

Pabyanitse. *See* Pabianice (Poland)

De Pace fidei (Cusa), 5:343

Pacelli, Eugenio Maria Giuseppe
Giovanni. *See* Pius XII

*Las paces de los reyes ye judía de
Toledo* (Vega), 11:256

Pacheco, Rodrigo Benjamin Mendes,
15:196, **563**

Pacht, Isaac, 15:**563**

Pachter, Charles, 15:**563**

Pacifici, Alfonso, 15:**563–564**

Pacifici, Riccardo, 15:**564**

Pacific Jewish Center, 13:202

Pacifico, David, 15:**564**

Pacifism, 3:756

Pacino, Al, 18:371

Packman, James Joseph, 15:**564**

PACT. *See* Parents and Children
Together

Paddan-Aram (Mesopotamia), 12:406,
15:**564**

Padeh, Baruch, 15:**564–565**

Padeia Institute, 19:232

Paderborn (Germany), 15:**565–566**

Paderewski, Ignace, 14:490

Padico. *See* Palestinian Development
and Investment Company

Padova (Italy). *See* Padua (Italy)

Padovan, Giuseppe. *See* Luzzatto,
Gino

Padua (Italy), 15:**566–568**
Heilbronn, Jacob ben Elhanan,
8:766

Padway, Joseph Arthur, 15:**568**

Paganism, 16:94–95, 96
disputations and polemics, 5:687–
690
Jacob story symbolism, 11:20–21
Julian the Apostate and, 11:572–
574
monotheism, 14:449–450

Pagan Martyrs, Acts of. *See*
Alexandrian Martyrs, Acts of

The Pagan Rabbi, and Other Stories
(Ozick), 15:557

Page, Larry, 4:183

Pagel, Julius Leopold, 15:**568**

Pagel, Walter, 15:**568**

Pagis, Dan, 15:**569**

Pagnini, Santes, 8:514, 15:**569**

Paḥad Yiẓhak (Lompronti), 6:399

Paḥad Yiẓḥak (Cantarini), 4:433

Paḥal (Canaan). *See* Pella (Canaan)

Pahlavi, Mohammad Reza Shah (shah of Iran), 15:**569–570**

Pahlavi, Reza Shah (shah of Iran), 15:**570–571**

P.A.I. *See* Po'alei Agudat Israel

Paicovitch, Yigal. *See* Allon, Yigal

Pa'il, Meir, 15:**571**

Pailes, Isaac, 15:**571**

The Painted Bird (Kosinski), 9:411–412

Painted in Words: A Memoir (Bak), 3:71

Painters and painting

    Australia

        Cassab, Judy, 4:507

        Feuerring, Maximilian, 6:774

        Fox, Emanuel Philips, 7:140

        Kahan, Louis, 11:708

        Kempf, Franz Moshe, 12:73

    Austria

        Birnbaum, Uriel, 3:716–717

        Dicker-Brandeis, Frederike, 5:646

        Herlingen, Aaron Wolf, 9:23

        Inlander, Henry, 9:787

        Kopf, Maxim, 12:294

        Krestin, Lazar, 12:355

        Kupferman, Moshe, 10:698–699

        Mopp, 14:469–470

    Belorussia, Chagall, Marc, 4:556–557

    Brazil, Segall, Lasar, 4:152, 18:248–249

    Bulgaria, Pascin, Jules, 15:648, 675

    Canada

        Gilbert, Ina, 7:597

        Iskowitz, Gershon, 10:87

        Muhlstock, Louis, 14:606

        Nichols, Jack, 15:252–253

        Pachter, Charles, 15:563

        Raphael, William, 17:95–96

    Chile

        Herdan, Kurt Lucian, 9:7

        Otta, Francisco, 15:516

    China, Fima, Efraim, 7:20–21

    Czechoslavakia

        Feigl, Bedrich, 6:734–735

        Fritta, 7:295–296

        Guttman, Robert, 8:159

        Haas, Leo, 8:169

        Justitz, Alfred, 11:581

        Kars, Jiri, 11:817

Steiner-Prag, Hugo, 19:192

        Ticho, Anna, 19:717–718

    Denmark

        Ballin, Moegens, 3:93

        Estevens, David, 6:515

    England

        Cooper, Alexander, 5:204

        Costa, Catherine da, 5:233

        Ezekiel, Abraham Ezekiel, 6:646

        Feibusch, Hans, 6:729

        Freud, Lucian, 7:259

        Gertler, Mark, 7:558

        Hart, Solomon Alexander, 8:372

        Kestleman, Morris, 12:92

        Kossoff, Leon, 12:321

        Meninsky, Bernard, 14:48

        Rogers, Claude Maurice, 17:368

        Salaman, Charles, 17:680–681

        Solomon, Simeon, 18:767

        Solomon, Solomon Joseph, 18:767–768

        Sutton, Philip, 19:330

        Towne, Charles, 20:78

        Uhlman, Fred, 20:232

        Ziegler, Archibald, 21:528

    France

        Caro-Delvaille, Henri, 4:492

        Delaunay-Terk, Sonia, 5:535

        Friedlaender, Johnny, 7:274

        Kikoine, Michel, 12:153

        Kisling, Moise, 12:201

        Klein, Yves, 12:226–227

        Kolnik, Arthur, 12:278

        Lévy-Dhurmer, Lucien, 12:757

        Loevenstein, Fedor, 13:162

        Mané-Katz, 13:466

        Marcoussis, Louis, 13:511–512

        Milich, Adolphe, 14:234

        Mondzain, Simon, 14:435

        Muter, Mela, 14:704–705

        Pailes, Isaac, 15:571

        Picart, Bernard, 16:144–145

        Pissarro, Camille, 16:186–187

        Pressmane, Joseph, 16:507

        Soutine, Chaim, 3:781, 19:63–64

        Zak, Eugen, 21:446

    Germany

        Fraenckel, Liepmann, 7:142

        Freundlich, Otto, 7:264–265

        Henschel brothers, 8:811

Hirschfeld-Mack, Ludwig, 9:139

        Katz, Hanns Ludwig, 12:11

        Kaufmann, Isidor, 12:32

        Kirschstein, Salli, 12:189

        Koppel, Heinz, 12:295

        Krayn, Hugo, 12:346

        Levy, Rudolf, 12:755

        Liebermann, Max, 12:808

        Lismann, Hermann, 13:81

        Magnus, Eduard, 13:356

        Meidner, Ludwig, 13:773–774

        Nussbaum, Felix, 2:507, 15:352

        Nussbaum, Jakob, 15:353

        Oppenheim, Moritz Daniel, 15:446

        Oppenheimer, Joseph, 15:448–449

        Orlik, Emil, 15:477–478

        Salomon, Charlotte, 17:696

        Segal, Arthur, 18:244

        Steinhardt, Jakob, 19:192–193

        Struck, Hermann, 4:70, 249, 19:261–262

        Ury, Lesser, 20:428–429

        Wolf, Gustav, 21:137

        Wollheim, Gert H., 21:151–152

    Hungary

        Czobel, Béla, 5:373

        Fényes, Adolf, 6:757

        Horovitz, Leopold, 9:529

        Ivanyi-Grunwald, Bela, 10:821

        Laszlo, Philip Alexius de Lombos, 12:505

        Lavie, Raffi, 10:696, 12:532

        Moholy-Nagy, László, 14:419–420

        Perlmutter, Izsák, 15:780

    Israel

        Castel, Moshe Elazar, 4:511–512

        Cohen Gan, Pinhas, 5:38–39

        David, 5:463

        Engelsberg, Leon, 6:410

        Frenkel, Itzhak, 7:257

        Garbuz, Yair, 7:388

        Gershuni, Moshe, 7:555–556

        Gross, Michael, 8:96

        Grundig, Hans, 8:111

        Grundig, Lea, 8:111

        Grundman, Zwi, 8:111–112

        Gutman, Nahum, 8:152–153

        Halevy, Yosef, 8:272

        Kadishman, Menashe, 10:696–697, 699, 11:700

Kahana, Aharon, 11:710
Karavan, Dani, 11:803–804
Kupferman, Moshe, 10:696
Levanon, Mordecai, 12:678
Lifschitz, Uri, 13:11
Litvinovsky, Pinchas, 13:141–142
Mairovich, Zvi, 13:406
Mokady, Moshe, 14:423
Neiman, Yehudah, 15:66
Nikel, Lea, 15:265
Paldi, Israel, 15:576
Pann, Abel, 15:612–613
Rubin, Reuven, 17:512–513
Sebba, Shalom, 18:231
Shemi, Menahem, 18:458
Sima, Miron, 18:590
Stematsky, Avigdor, 15:265, 19:200
Tagger, Sionah, 19:432–433
Weill, Shraga, 20:715
Zaritsky, Yossef, 13:11, 21:460

Italy
Castellazzo, Moses da, 4:513
Coen, Giuseppe, 4:781
Donati, Enrico, 5:748
Donati, Lazzaro, 5:748–749
Modigliani, Amedeo, 14:411
Tivoli, Serafino da, 19:745–746

Lebanon, Safdie, Sylvia, 17:658

Lithuania
Rosenberg, Lazar, 4:402, 17:437–438
Schatz, Boris, 2:501, 10:695, 696, 13:14, 18:110–111, 223
Streichman, Yehezkel, 19:225–256

Mexico, Nierman, Leonardo, 15:260–261

Netherlands
Citroen, Roelof Paul, 4:737
De Chaves, Aaron, 5:528
Haan, Meijer De, 8:164–165
Israëls, Jozef, 10:765
Rembrandt van Rijn, 3:673, 17:215–216

Poland
Centerszwer, Stanisława, 4:543
Feuerring, Maximilian, 6:774
Gottlieb, Maurycy, 8:13
Halter, Marek, 8:286–287
Hayden, Henri, 8:474–475
Herman, Josef, 9:24
Hirshenberg, Samuel, 9:142

Kirszenbaum, Jesekiel David, 12:190
Maryan, 13:591
Pilichowski, Leopold, 16:159
Rosenthal, Max, 17:455–456
Szalit-Marcus, Rachel, 19:402
Szyk, Arthur, 4:76, 19:413
Topolski, Feliks, 20:39

Romania
Gluck, Hannah, 7:643
Iser, Josif, 10:79
Janco, Marcel, 11:77–78
Juster, George, 11:577
Maxy, Max Herman, 13:696
Probst-Kraid, Riza, 16:542

Russia
Chapiro, Jacques, 4:568
Kuzkovski, Joseph, 12:400
Levitan, Isaac Ilitch, 12:732
Lissitzky, El, 13:82–83
Pasternak, Leonid Osipovich, 15:684–685
Rabin, Oscar, 17:33–34
Raskin, Saul, 17:107–108
Ryback, Issachar, 17:601
Serov, Valentin, 18:314
Soutine, Chaim, 19:63–64
Tatlin, Vladimir E., 19:526
Zhitnitski, Mark, 21:524

Slovakia, Szobel, Géza, 19:409

South Africa
Kibel, Wolf, 12:138
Stern, Irma, 19:210
Ullmann, Ernest, 20:242

Sweden
Salomon, Geskel, 17:697
Varlin, 20:477

U.K.
Cohen, Bernard, 5:11
Cohen, Harold, 5:17
Daniels, Alfred, 5:429
David, Jean, 5:463
Freedman, Barnett, 7:224
Hillman, David, 9:117
Kramer, Jacob, 12:334
Rothenstein, Sir William, 17:486–487
Solomon, Simeon, 14:542, 18:767
Wilson, "Scottie," 21:78
Wolmark, Alfred, 21:152

U.S.
Carvalho, Solomon Nunes, 4:502, 16:125
Chicago, Judy, 4:612
Dine, Jim, 5:669–670

Eilshemius, Louis, 6:255
Frankenthaler, Helen, 7:203–204
Gikow, Ruth, 7:595
Golub, Leon, 7:746
Gottlieb, Adolph, 8:10
Guston, Philip, 8:149
Hirsch, Joseph, 9:126
Hirshfield, Morris, 9:143
Kanovitz, Howard, 11:767
Katz, Alex, 12:8–9
Kitaj, R. B., 12:205–206
Kline, Franz, 12:231
Krasner, Lee, 12:338
Levine, Jack, 12:718
Lichtenstein, Roy, 12:799
Louis, Morris, 13:222
Lozowick, Louis, 13:239
Manso, Leo, 13:484
Margo, Boris, 13:523
Maril, Herman, 13:545
Menkes, Zygmunt, 14:49
Moïse, Theodore Sydney, 14:421–422
Mosler, Henry, 14:564
Newman, Barnett, 2:514, 15:145–146
Olitski, Jules, 15:404–405
Pearlstein, Philip, 15:706
Rattner, Abraham, 17:114–115
Ray, Man, 14:419, 17:126
Reder, Bernard, 17:155–156
Reiss, Lionel, 17:212–213
Rivers, Larry, 17:347
Rose, Herman, 17:426
Rosenthal, Maz, 17:455–456
Rothko, Mark, 4:50, 17:487
Schames, Samson, 18:106
Schanker, Louis, 18:106–107
Schor, Ilya, 18:162
Schwartz, Manfred, 18:186
Seligmann, Kurt, 15:648, 18:267–268
Shahn, Ben, 4:76, 16:125–126, 18:365–366
Simon, Sidney, 18:617
Soyer, Raphael, 4:9, 19:65–66
Spero, Nancy, 19:97–98
Spiro, Eugen, 19:120
Sterne, Hedda, 19:220–221
Sterne, Maurice, 19:221
Tworkov, Jack, 20:210
Walkowitz, Abraham, 20:609
Weber, Max, 20:692–693
Wilson, Sol, 21:78

Painters and painting, *continued*
  Zucker, Jacques, 21:674
  Yugoslavia, Herman, Oskar, 9:24
Painting, Photography, and Film
  (Moholy-Nagy), 14:420
Pairs (sages). *See* Zugot
Pais, Aaron, 16:345
Paiva, Jacques, 15:**571**
The Pajama Game (musical), 1:406
Pak family. *See* Bak family
Pakistan, 15:**571–572**
Pakku'at sadeh. *See* Cucumber
Pakku'ot. *See* Cucumber
Pakn Treger (periodical), 15:30
Paks (Hungary), 15:**572**
Pakula, Alan Jay, 15:**572**
"Palace of Shushan" (Iran). *See*
  Shushan (Iran)
Palache, Abraham (Netherlands),
  15:573
Palache, Abraham (of Izmir), 15:573,
  574
Palache, David, 15:573
Palache, Ḥayyim, 15:**573–574**
Palache, Isaac ("the lame"), 15:573
Palache, Isaac (rabbi), 15:573
Palache, Isaac (son of Samuel
  Palache), 15:573
Palache, Jacob Carlos, 15:573
Palache, Joseph, 15:573
Palache, Judah Lion, 15:573, **574**
Palache, Moses, 15:573
Palache, Samuel, 14:497, 15:573
Palache family, 14:497, 15:**572–573**
Palacio family. *See* Palache family
*Palaestina ex monumentis veteribus
  illustrata* (Reland), 17:214
Palaggi, Ḥayyim. *See* Palache, Ḥayyim
Palaggi family. *See* Palache family
Palagi, Ḥayyim, 15:537
Palágyi, Lajos, 15:**574–575**
Palágyi, Melchior. *See* Palágyi,
  Menyhért
Palágyi, Menyhért, 15:**575**
Palanga (Lithuania), 15:**575**
Palatina Library (Parma), 15:653
Palatinate (Germany), 12:457, 15:**575–
  576**
Palatnik, Rosa, 4:152
Paldi, Israel, 15:**576**
Palecke, Samuel, 16:344–345
Palencia (Spain), 15:**576–577**
Pale of Settlement (Russia), 9:233,
  234, 15:**577–580**, *578*, 18:602
  birth of Jewish socialism in,
    18:714
  blood libel cases in, 3:779

cantonists from, 9:235
contraction of, 13:701–702
Duma, 6:45
emancipation, 6:383, 384
Haskalah, 8:442
Mogilev, 14:417
occupations in, 12:411
Octobrists on, 15:377
peddling in, 15:709–710
Paleography, Hebrew, 7:**477**
Paleography, Latin, 13:234
Palermo (Italy), 15:**580–581**
Palestine, 15:**581–582**, 18:38
Palestine (Byzantine)
  agriculture, 1:492
  Aḥa, 1:522
  Aḥa bar Ḥanina, 1:525
  amoraim, 2:89, 89–95, *92*
  Caesarea, 4:333
  hexagonal glass bottles, 7:631
Palestine (Crusader)
  Caesarea, 4:333
  massacres, 5:311–312
Palestine (Mamluk)
  Caesarea, 4:333
  Mamluks, 13:438–441
Palestine (Ottoman), 4:286, 15:523–
  524, 581
  agriculture, 1:492–493
    land reclamation, 10:372
  aliyah and absorption, 1:660,
    10:180–181, 193–196, 300–302
    Ḥibbat Zion period, 1880s,
      10:330–333
    non-Jewish population,
      10:300–301
  cultural and social life
    architecture, 10:701
    Ashkenazim, 8:288–289
    Bedouin, 10:737
    communities, 9:239
    ḥalukkah, 8:287–288
    Hebrew publishing, 4:182–
      183
    Hebrew revival, 8:671–672
    journalism and press, 10:704–
      705
    Judaizers, Russian, 11:522
    Moroccan aliyah, 2:646
    museums, 14:630–631
    music, 10:691, 693
    orphans and orphanages,
      15:485–486
    parody, Hebrew, 15:661
    Perushim, 8:288
    philanthropy, 16:44

  press, 4:182–183
    women, 21:190–192
  defense forces, 10:464–465, 464–
    467
  economic affairs, 10:479–485,
    481t, 483t
    agricultural sector, 10:486
    banking system, 10:586
    boycott, Arab, 4:111–113
    community tokens,
      currencies, 5:121–122
    currency, 5:53
    funds for Istanbul and,
      10:779–780
    ḥalukkah, 8:287–288
    World War I, 10:517–518
  education, 10:652–653
    Hebrew language, 10:683–684
    music, 10:689
    religious schools, 10:621
  foreign policy and affairs
    capitulations, 4:453–454
    Congress of Berlin, 3:454
    international affairs, 10:181–
      186
    Nili, 15:267–268
    Sykes-Picot Agreement,
      19:350–351, *351*
    travels, 6:670
  governance, 10:387, 387–388, 390,
    391
  historical survey, 10:181–186, 192–
    197
  Israel, land of, 10:168–179, *169*
    eighteenth century, 10:173–
      175
    nineteenth - early twentieth
      century, 10:175–179
    sixteenth–seventeenth
      centuries, 10:168–172, *169*,
      172–173
  Jewish movements and
    organizations
    Bilu, 3:701
    Jewish Legion, enlistment in,
      11:304
    kolelim, 8:288–289
    Po'alei Zion, 16:246
    political parties of yishuv,
      10:424–425
    Va'ad ha-Pekidim ve-ha-
      Amarkalim, 20:455
    Va'ad Pekidei Erez Israel be-
      Kushta, 20:456–457
    Zionist aliyot, 9:247–248
  labor
    legislation, 10:607
    Teachers' Association, 10:653

trade unions, 10:594
laws and legal systems, 10:403–405, 412
    autonomy of Jews, 10:178
    land ownership, 10:371
    religious courts, 10:620
Middle Ages, 4:286
Napoleonic invasion, 10:173–174, 175, 182
political theories, parties and organizations
    Bar-Giora society, 8:382
    Board of Delegates of American Israelites, 4:20
    exilarchate of, 6:606
    Ha-Shomer, 8:382
    political parties of yishuv, 10:424–425
population, 10:174, 175, 192, 282, 392*t*
    Arab, 10:481*t*, 485–486
    Ashkenazim, 10:294, 619–621
    Christian, 10:638
    Coastal Plain, 10:375–376
    Georgian Jews, 10:296
    Hills region, 10:379
    Iraqi Jews, 10:295–296
    Jewish, 10:481*t*
    Maghrebs, 10:295
    non-Jewish, 10:300–301
    Persian Jews, 10:297
    Sephardim, 10:295, 619–621
    Yemenite Jews, 10:296
religious life and scholarship, 10:619–621, 646
    chief rabbi position instituted, 11:168
    gaons, 5:427
    Islam, 10:646
    Jewish leadership, 10:178–179
    missionaries, 10:176–177
    religious courts, 10:620
    support of Hasidism, 10:748
Sykes-Picot Agreement, 19:350–351, *351*
See also Ottoman Empire
Palestine (Roman)
    agriculture, 1:490–492
    Bar Kokhba revolt, 10:148–151
    Boule, 4:105–106
    Caesarea, 4:333
    Christianity as offical religion and, 10:154, 155
    destruction of Second Temple, 10:144
    economy, 10:148
    geography, 11:143

governors, 16:32
Hananiah ben Teradyon martyrdom, 8:316
Herod's kingdom, 9:*32*
Jabneel, 11:9–10
Jaffa, 11:60–61
Jewish leadership during, 10:145–147
Jewish War (66-70 C.E.)
    changes as result, 10:144–145
    overview of, 10:143–144
judges and judicial courts, Sanhedrin, 18:21–23
Nablus, 14:718
pilgrims, Melito of Sardis, 14:12–13
political history, Sanhedrin, 18:21–23
procurator, 16:542–543
during Severan dynasty, 10:151–153
synagogue architecture, 19:*374*, 374–375
Palestine, Mandate for. *See* Mandate for Palestine
Palestine and Roumania, a Description of the Holy Land, and the Past and Present State of Roumania and the Roumanian Jews (Sneersohn), 18:696
Palestine Archaeological Musem. *See* Rockefeller Museum
Palestine Conservatoire, 14:694
Palestine Cooperative Co., Inc., 15:588
Palestine Economic Corporation, 4:123, 7:77, 15:**588–589**, 18:613
Palestine Electric Company, 15:589
Palestine Entity, 10:278–279
Palestine Exploration Fund, 2:161, 15:**589**
Palestine Foundation Fund. *See* Keren Hayesod
Palestine Historical and Ethnographical Society, 18:724
Palestine Inquiry Commissions, 15:**582–585**
Palestine Jewish Colonization Association (PICA), 2:26, 16:**143**
Palestine Labor Party. *See* Mapai
Palestine—Land of Promise (Lowdermilk), 13:234
Palestine Liberation Front (PLF), 15:594
Palestine Liberation Organization (PLO), 15:**589–595**
    Arab world (1964-1970), 2:304–305
    Arafat, Yasser, 2:309, 332, 334
    Charter, 15:591, 595

    England, relations with, 6:431
    establishment of, 15:589–590
    Al-Fataḥ and, 10:280
    foreign policy and relations with, Israel (state), 10:258
    funding, 15:593
    Germany, position on, 7:544
    guerilla groups, 15:590–591
    ideology of, 15:591
    Intifada and, 10:241–242
    Israeli recognition of, 10:455
    Lebanese War and, 10:240, 12:581–584
    Lebanon, 2:313
    Oslo Accords, 10:246
    Palestinian Authority and, 15:594–595
    peace talks, participation in, 15:593–594
    recognition by Israel and U.S. as legal representative of Palestinians, 15:594
    recognition of Israel by, 10:455
    relationship with Arab states, 15:589–590, 592–593
    shift toward acceptance of Palestinian state in West Bank and Gaza Strip only, 15:593
    social and political institutions, 15:591–592
    terrorism, association with, 15:591, 593
    terrorist attacks by, 10:258
    See also Hamas; Intifada
Palestine Mortgage and Credit Bank Ltd., 15:588
Palestine Office, 15:**595**
Palestine Orchestra. *See* Israel Philharmonic Orchestra
Palestine partition and partition plans, 15:584–585, **585–588**, *586, 587*
Palestine Partition Commission (1938), 11:175, 15:584, 586, *587*
The Palestine Post. See The Jerusalem Post (newspaper)
Palestine Potash Ltd., 15:589, 18:739
Palestine Royal Commission (1937). *See* Peel Commission
Palestine Symphony Orchestra. *See* Israel Philharmonic Orchestra
Palestine viper, 18:695
Palestine Water Company Ltd., 15:588–589
Palestinian Authority (PA), 2:302–303, 15:**596–600**
    antisemitism, 2:328
    Arab world (1945-2006), 2:300, 301, 318, 320, 326

Palestinian Authority (PA), *continued*
demography, 2:328
England, relations with, 6:431
Gaza strip, 7:401–403
Hamas, 8:295
Intifada, 7:402, 403
Israel, 2:318, 319, 320
Japan and, 11:83
Palestine Liberation Organization
and, 15:594–595
See also Gaza Strip; Intifada; Sinai;
West Bank
Palestinian Christian Aramaic, 2:351–
352
Palestinian city coins and currency,
5:51
Palestinian Development and
Investment Company (Padico),
15:598
The Palestinian Girl (Sobol), 18:702
Palestinian Masorah system, 13:618
notations, 13:620
pronounciation, 13:624–629
Tiberian influence on, 13:644
Palestinian National Authority. *See*
Palestinian Authority
Palestinian National Council, 15:592
Palestinian Pentateuch Targumim,
3:591–592
Palestinians
See also Arab population
Palestinians, foreign policy and
relations with Israel, 10:258–259
Palestinian Talmud. *See* Talmud
*Palet: een boek gewijd aan de
hedendaagsche Nederlandsche
schilderkunst* (Citroen), 4:737
Paley, Grace, 15:**600–601**
Paley, William Samuel, 15:**601**
Palgrave, Francis Turner, 9:151,
15:**601–602**
Palgrave, Reginald Francis Douce,
15:602
Palgrave, Robert Harry Inglis, 15:602
Palgrave, William Gifford, 15:602
Palgrave family, 15:**601–602**
Pallache family. *See* Palache family
Palladius, 11:382
Pallas family. *See* Palache family
Pallenberg, Max, 15:**602**
Pallière, Aimé, 15:**602**
La Palma (Spain), 15:**603**
Palmaḥ, 8:203
Palmaḥ, 15:**603–604**
Chizbatron, 15:389
Palmaḥ generation, 11:712, 18:203
Palm Beach County (FL), 7:88,
15:**604–606**

Palmer, Edward Henry, 15:**606**
Palmer, Lilli, 15:**606**
Palmerston, Lord, 15:564
Palmistry. *See* Chiromancy
Palms, 15:**602–603**
Palm Springs and Desert Area (CA),
15:**606**
Palmtree of Deborah (Cordovero),
5:221
Palmyra (Syria). *See* Tadmor (Syria)
Palmyrene inscriptions, 2:348
Palombo, David, 15:**606–607**
Palontritti, Melchior, 13:288
Palquera, Shem Tov ben Joseph ibn.
See Falaquera, Shem Tov ben
Joseph ibn
Palquera family. *See* Falaquera family
Palti, 15:**607**
Paltiel, 15:**607**
Paltoi bar Abbaye, 15:**607–608**
Paltrow, Bruce, 15:608
Paltrow, Gwyneth, 15:**608**
A Pál utcai fiúk (Molnár). *See The
Paul Street Boys* (Molnár)
Palyäj family. *See* Palache family
Pam, Hugo, 15:**608**
Pamiers (France), 15:**608**
Pampeluna (Spain). *See* Pamplona
Pamphilius. *See* Rode, Walther
Pamphylia (Asia Minor), 15:**608**
Pamplona (Spain), 15:**609**
Pan, Y., 4:141
Panǎ, Saşa, 15:**609**
Panama, 12:**755–756**, 15:**610**
Caribbean, Spanish-Portuguese
Nation of the: La Nacion, 4:475
Levy, Sion, 12:755–756
Pancosmosophia (Ambron), 2:36
Paneas. *See* Banias (ancient Israel)
Paneriai (Lithuania). *See* Ponary
(Lithuania)
Panet, Ezekiel ben Joseph, 15:**610–611**
Panet, Menaḥem Mendel, 15:611
Panet family. *See* Banet family
Paneth, Ezekiel ben Jacob. *See* Baneth,
Ezekiel ben Jacob
Paneth, Friedrich Adolf, 15:**611**
Panevezhis (Lithuania). *See* Panevezys
(Lithuania)
Panevezys (Lithuania), 15:**611**
Pan Graba (Orzeszkowa), 15:501
Panias. *See* Banias (ancient Israel)
Panigel, Eliyahu Moshe, 15:**612**
Panigel, Raphael Meir ben Judah,
15:**612**
Panim el Panim (Shalom), 18:377
Panim Me'irot (Eisenstadt), 6:271

Panken, Jacob, 15:212, **612**
Pann, Abel, 15:**612–613**
Panofsky, Erwin, 2:370, 15:**613**
Panov, Valery, 5:415, 15:**613**
Panteleone, Agostino. *See* Giustiniani,
Agostino
Pantheism, 7:670–671
Pantheism and Kabbalah, 11:648–651
Panther, Peter. *See* Tucholsky, Kurt
Panticapaecum (kingdom of
Bosphorus), 4:98
Pao-Pao (Selvinski), 18:272
Pap, Arthur, 15:**613**
Pap, Károly, 14:541, 15:**613–614**
Papa (amora), 15:370, **614**
Papa (Hungary), 15:**614–615**
Papacy. *See* Catholic Church; Popes
Papageorgios, 11:546
Papal bulls, 4:**277–278**
Benedict XIII, 3:330
Calixtus II, 4:365
Catholic Church, 4:277–278, 711
Clement III, 4:752
Clement IV, 4:752
Clement VI, 4:752–753
Gregory IX, 8:85
Gregory XIII, 8:85
Paul IV, 15:696
Perugian Jews banished, 15:798
Papal States
emancipation, 6:379
Jewish dress, 6:15
restriction on Jews in, 6:547–548,
16:7
Papareschi, Gregorio. *See* Innocent
Paper, H. H., 11:558
Paper-cuts, 15:**615–616**
Papermaster, Benjamin, 15:304
Paperna, Abraham Baruch, 15:**616**
Paperna, Abraham Jacob, 8:725,
15:**616–617**
Paperna, I., 6:669
Papi, 15:**617**
Di Papierne Kroyn (Bryks), 4:230
Papiernikov, Joseph, 15:**617**
Papi I, 15:617
Papi II, 15:617
Papir Brigade, 11:694
Papirofsky, Joseph. *See* Papp, Joseph
Papo, Izidor Josef, 15:**617**
Papo, Samuel Shemiah, 15:**617–618**
Papp, Joseph, 15:220, **618**
Pappa. *See* Papa (Amora)
Pappenheim, Bertha, 11:570, 15:**618**
Pappenheim, Solomon, 8:687, 15:**618**
Pappus and Julianus, 15:**618–619**

Pappus ben Judah, 15:**619**
Papyri (documents), 15:**619–620**
Papyrus (plant), 15:**620**, 21:237–238
Parables, 15:**620–623**
    allegories vs., 1:665
    animals, 2:173
Parables in Midrash (Stern), 1:461
Parables of Erasto, 18:632–633
Parables of Sindbad. See Mishlei Sendabar
Paracelsus (Browning), 4:218
Paradise, 15:**623–629**
    in apocalyptic literature, 15:628
    in Eden narrative, 15:623–627
    eschatological, 6:498
    forfeiture of place in, 11:109
    Gan Eden, 15:628–629
    in medieval literature, 15:628–629
    in modern period, 15:629
    in post-biblical Jewish thought, 15:627–628
    in rabbinic literature, 15:628
Paradise Lost (Milton), 14:260
Il Paradiso (Moravia), 14:477
Paradoxes of Legal Science (Cardozo), 4:466
Paraf, Pierre, 15:**629**
Paraguay, 15:**629–630**, 21:594
Parah (ancient Israel), 15:**631**
Parah (tractate), 15:**630–631**, 17:157
Parah adumah. *See* Red heifers
Parallelism in poetry, 13:237, 16:256–258, 598–599
Parallel Quest (Lindheim), 13:28
Paralympic Games, 12:621
Paramagnetic Resonance in Solids (Low), 13:233
Paramount Pictures, 3:81, 14:570–571
Paran (desert, Egypt), 15:**631**
Paran (tribe), 15:631
Paranoia, 14:57–58
Paran Plateau (Israel), 10:113
Parapets, 15:**631**
Al Parashat Derakhim (Aḥad Ha-Am), 14:456
Parashat Ki-Tavo, 3:677
Parashiyyot of Bible, 13:607
Parchment, use of, 4:71, 72–73
Parchment making, 18:241
Parczew (Poland), 15:**631–632**
Pardes, 11:593, 15:**632**
Pardes, Eliyahu, 15:**633**
Pardes, Shmuel Aaron, 15:**633**
Pardes ha-Binah (Aaronsohn), 1:223
Pardes ha-Ḥokhmah (Aaronsohn), 1:223

Pardes Ḥannah-Karkur (Israel), 15:**632**
Pardesiyyah (Israel), 15:**633**
Pardez, 3:641
Pardo, Abraham, 15:**634**
Pardo, David, 15:633, 634
Pardo, David Samuel ben Jacob, 15:**633–634**
Pardo, Isaac, 15:634
Pardo, Jacob, 6:39, 15:634
Pardo, Joseph, 2:109
Pardo, Joseph I, 15:**634**
Pardo, Joseph II, 15:634
Pardo, Moses ben Raphael, 15:**634**
Pardo, Saul. *See* Brown, Saul Pardo
Pardo family, 15:**633**
Pardon. *See* Forgiveness
Pardon wird nicht gegeben (Doeblin), 5:729–730
Parents
    honoring, 4:618
    honor of, 15:**641**
Parents and children, 4:617–618, 15:**635–640**
    adoption, 1:417–419
    "best interest of the child" concept, 15:639–640
    child marriage, 4:616
    corporal punishment of children, 15:640
    embryos, 6:391–392
    Israeli law, 15:638–640
    Jewish law, 15:635–638
    one parent not Jewish, 15:637–638
    parables treating God as father, 15:621
    See also Custody of children; Maintenance, parental obligation of
Parents and Children Together (PACT), 2:63
Parentucelli, Tommaso. *See* Nicholas V
Parenzo, Asher, 15:641
Parenzo, Gershon ben Moses, 15:641
Parenzo, Jacob, 15:641
Parenzo, Meir, 15:641
Parenzo family, 15:**641**
Parḥon, Salomon ben Abraham Ibn, 15:**641–642**
Parḥon, Samuel ben Abraham Ibn, 6:174
Der Paria (Beer), 3:253
Pariente, Abraham, 15:642
Pariente, Barbara, 15:605
Pariente, Jacob I, 15:642
Pariente, Jacob II, 15:642
Pariente, Joseph, 15:642

Pariente, Judaḥ ben Abraham, 15:642
Pariente, Samuel, 15:642
Pariente, Solomon, 15:642
Pariente family, 15:**642**
Parion. *See* Parium
Paris (France), 15:**642–647**, 19:482
Paris, Hailu, 15:647
Paris, Matthew, 3:775
Parish-Alvars, Eli, 2:27
Paris Jewish School, 6:5
Paris-Midi (newspaper), 12:559
Paris Peace Conference
    Bigarte, Jacques, and, 3:694
    Sokolow, Nahum and, 18:748
Paris school of art, 15:**647–651**
Paris-Soir (newspaper), 12:559
Parium (Asia Minor), 15:**651**
Der Parizer Haynt, 7:35–36
Pariz un Viene (Levita), 15:**651**
Park, Robert E., 18:733–734
Parker, Dorothy, 15:**651**
Parker, John, 15:**651**
Parker, Sarah Jessica, 15:**652**
Parkes, James William, 4:679–680, 683, 9:159, 15:**652**
Park Synagogue (NY), 8:505
Parlamentsklub, Juedischer. *See* Juedischer Parlamentsklub
Les parlers judéo-romans et la Vetus Latina (Blondheim), 3:771
Parma (Italy), 15:**652–653**
Parnakh, Valentin Yakovlevich, 15:**653**
Parnas, 15:**653–654**
Parnas, Ḥayyim Naḥman, 15:**654**
Parnas, Joseph, 11:527
Parnas, Yakub Karol, 15:**654**
Parnasim, 1:386
Parnis, Mollie, 15:**654**
Parody. *See* Hebrew parody
Paroisse Universitaire (France), 13:271
Parokhet and Kapporet, 4:548, 15:**663–664**
Parosh. *See* Fleas
Parrot, André, 15:**664**
Parsci. *See* Judeo-Persian language
Parshiyyot (Baron), 3:171
Parsley, 20:488
Parthian Empire, 6:600–601
Parthians, 3:26
Partial Jews, Nuremberg laws, 15:349–350
Particles in Hebrew, 8:585–586
Particularism, 11:514–515
Parti Québécois, 14:464, 466
Partisan Review (periodical), 16:58
Partisans, 9:357–359, 15:**664–668**, *665*
    hangings, 9:*474*

Partisans, *continued*
in Oshmyany, 15:503
Poland, 16:316–317
Russia, 17:548, 549–550
Le Parti Socialiste et la politique financière (Moch), 14:405
Partition plans for Palestine. *See* Palestine partition and partition plans
Partnership 2000, 6:202
The Partnership for Excellence in Jewish Education, 7:137
Partnership law, 5:154
Partnerships, 15:**669–673**
lease and hire, 12:570
ona'ah and, 15:425
Partos, Oedoen, 15:**673**
Part Real Part Dream (Seter), 18:319
Partridges, 15:**673**
Parturition. *See* Birth
Parvaim (Arabia), 15:**673–674**
Parveh, 15:**674**
Parzel. *See* Iron
Parzela. *See* Iron
Parzen, Herbert, 15:**674**
Parẓufim, 11:646–647
Pascal, Blaise, 15:**674–675**
Pascani (Romania), 15:**675**
Pascheles, Wolf, 15:**675**
Pascheles, Ze'ev. *See* Pascheles, Wolf
Pascin, Jules, 15:648, **675**
Pasha, Djemal, 1:221
Pasha, Jacob, 15:541
Pashanel. *See* Desheh, Avraham
Pashhur, 15:**675–676**
Pashman, Morris, 15:**677**
Pasmanik, Daniel, 15:**676**
Pasovsky, Josef. *See* Millo, Josef
Passaic-Clifton (NJ), 15:**676–677**
Passau (Germany), 15:**677**
Passfield White Paper, 13:148, 21:37
Passi, David, 15:541, **677–678**
Passigi. *See* Albigenses
Passing Ceremony (Weinzweig), 20:729
Passing for Touchdowns (Luckman), 13:249
Passion. *See* Love
The Passion of Joseph D. (Chayefsky), 4:585
The Passion of the Christ (motion picture), 7:142, 13:202
Les passions intellectuelles (Badinter), 3:49
Passover, 15:**678–683**
Addir bi-Melukhah, 1:384–385
Addir hu, 1:385

afikoman, 1:434
altar ceremonies, 2:16
Amsterdam, 2:116
arba kosot, 2:362
bedikat ḥameẓ, 3:249
blood libel associated with, 3:775–776, 778
burning levened food to prepare for, vol. 6: color insert
Coca-Cola heksher, 7:411
Cup of Elijah, 6:335, 338
Eḥad mi Yode'a, 6:237
Elephantine Papyri, 6:313
fasting, 6:723
food, 7:119
freedom, 7:226
games, 7:372
Ḥad Gadya, 8:190
Haggadah, 8:**207–217**
Dayyeinu, 5:496
Jerusalem in, 11:226
Ha laḥma Anya, 8:251
Hallel, 8:279–280
ḥameẓ, 8:301–303
sale of, 8:303
Ḥaroset, 8:361
Holocaust, 2:116
hymns, 1:385
Jesus and, 11:247
kitniyot, 12:610
Lag ba-Omer, 12:436
laws concerning, 12:605, 16:5–6
matzah, 7:119, 13:689–690
men reading the Haggadah, vol. 8: color insert
origin, 6:614
pascal offerings, 9:108
pilgrim festivals and, 16:158–159
plagues of Egypt, 16:210–214, 211t
Samaritans, 17:729
Seder
Mah Nishtannah, 13:362
maror, 13:558
Seder plates, 16:24
Ya'aleh ve-Yavo, 21:262
Passover, Alexander, 12:553
Passover, Second. *See* Second Passover
Passover Haggadah (Silverman), 18:587
Passow, Aaron Harry, 15:**683**
Pasta, Giuditta, 15:**683–684**
Pasternak, Boris Leonidovich, 2:272–273, 15:**684**
Pasternak, Joseph, 15:**684**
Pasternak, Leonid Osipovich, 15:**684–685**
Pasteur (motion picture), 6:473

Pasteur Institute, 13:293
Pastoral nomadism. *See* Nomadism
Pastoureaux, 15:**685**
John XXII and, 11:379
massacres, 14:455
persecutions in France, 4:515
Pas Yed'a (Abraham ben Josiah Troki), 1:303
Pat, Jacob, 15:**685**
Patai, Edith, 15:686
Patai, József, 15:**685–686**
Patai, Raphael, 2:188, 15:**686**
Paternity laws, 6:391–392, 21:423–426
Paternity testing, 2:598
Paterson (NJ), 15:**686–688**
Paterson Jewish Folk Chorus, 4:663
The Path of the Upright. See Mesillat Yesharim (Luzzatto)
Pathologie und Therapie der Hautkrankheiten (Kaposi), 11:781
Pathology
Karplus, Heinrich, 11:816–817
Rappaport, Henry, 17:99–100
Pathros (Egypt), 15:**688**
Paths of Faith. See Shevilei Emunah
Paths of Zion and Jerusalem. See Netivot Ẓiyyon vi-Yrushalayim (Luncz)
The Path to Cubism (Kahnweiler), 11:725
Patinkin, Dan. *See* Patinkin, Don
Patinkin, Don, 15:**688**
Patinkin, Mandy, 15:**688**
Patkin, Max, 15:**688**
Patoureaux persecutions, 3:732
Patras (Greece), 15:**688–689**
Pătrășcanu's trial, 4:138
Patraselka, Jacob, 3:762
Patria (vessel), 15:**689**
Patriarchal merit termination, 21:498
Patriarchs
Abraham, 1:282, 283
Abraham's bosom, 1:316
education in period, 6:163
eschatology, 6:489–490
history, 9:165–166
interpretations, 16:61, 62
Machpelah, Cave of, 13:325–327, 326
Mari (Mesopotamia), 13:537, 538–540
overview, 15:732
Philistines and, 16:55
See also Abraham; Jacob
The Patriarchs, 15:**689–691**
Patriarchs, Testaments of the Twelve. See Testaments of the Twelve Patriarchs

Patriarchy, 6:690–691, 754–756

Patricof, Alan, 15:**693**

The Patriot. See Ha-Patriyot

Patt, Gideon, 15:**693**

Patterson, David, 15:554, **693–694**

Patterson, John Henry, 11:303, 304, 305, 15:**694**

Patterson Jewish Folk Chorus, 4:662

Pauker, Ana, 15:**694**

Pauker, Marcel, 15:**694**

Paul (biblical figure), 4:682
  on Bible, 3:665
  in Corinth (Greece), 5:223–224
  Ephesus, 6:454–455
  epistle, 1:417
  Judaism of, 15:192

Paul, Gabe. *See* Paul, Gabriel Howard

Paul, Gabriel Howard, 15:**695**

Paul, Gus, 15:397

Paul I (emperor of Russia), 15:**694–695**

Paul III (pope), 16:375

Paul IV (pope), 3:46, 4:48, 278, 15:531–532, **695,** 16:375
  antisemitism, 2:140
  ghettoes and Jewish quarters, 11:311

Paul VI (pope), 11:384, 15:**695,** 16:377
  Bisgyer, Maurice, 3:725
  Israel and, 11:277
  Jewish-Catholic relations, 11:276
  Nissim, Isaac, 15:279

Paul Baerwald School of Social Work (Hebrew University of Jerusalem), 2:62

Paul Baerwald School of Social Work (Paris), 2:62

Pauli, Johannes, 15:**695–696**

Pauli, Wolfgang, 15:**696**

Paulker, Fred, 4:370

Paulli, Holger, 18:89

Paulo de Pina. *See* Jesurun, Reuel; Pablo de Santa Maria

Paul of Tarsus, 15:691, 692, **696–697**

Paul of Tella, 3:601

The Paul Street Boys (Molnár), 14:427

Paulus Israelita. *See* Ricius, Paulus

Paulus of Sancta Maria. *See* Pablo de Santa Maria

Pauly, Rosa, 15:**697–698**

Pausanius, 15:**698**

Pavel, Ota, 15:**698**

Pavelić, Ante, 15:**698**

Pavia (Italy), 13:177, 15:**698–699**

Pavlograd (Ukraine), 15:**699**

Pavlova, Galina, 15:613

Pavoloch (Ukraine), 15:**699**

Pawlikowski, Józef, 15:**699**

Pawlikowski, Konstantin Cholewa de, 3:778

Pawly. *See* Meyer, Paulus

The Pawnbroker (Lewis), 9:441

The Pawnbroker (motion picture), 9:407

Payis. *See* Lots

Paz, Duarte de, 15:**699–700**

Paz, Enrique Enriquez de. *See* Enríquez Gómez, Antonio

Paziza. *See* Aricha, Yosef

Pe, 15:**700**

Peace, 15:**700–703**
  Aaron and, 1:210
  agunah, 1:518
  Broner, Esther M., 4:204
  sacrifices, 17:643
  See Also Mediation

Peace movements, religious, 15:**703–704**

Peace Now, 15:555, **704**

Peace of Mind (Liebman), 12:810

Peaches, 15:**704**

Peacocks, 15:**704**

Pe'ah. *See* Leket, shikhḥah, and pe'ah

Pe'ah (tractate), 15:**704–705**

Pearl, Daniel, 11:469, 15:**705**

Pearlman, Moshe, 15:**705–706**

Pearls and Other Stories. See Perl un Andere Dertseylungen

Pearls of Yiddish Poetry (Mlotek), 14:396

Pearlstein, Leah, 18:746

Pearlstein, Philip, 15:**706**

Pearlstine, Norman, 15:**706–707**

Pears, 15:**705**

Peas. *See* Legumes

Pe'at ha-Shulḥan (Elijah ben Solomon Zalman), 6:344

PEC. *See* Palestine Economic Corporation

Pecar, Samuel, 15:**707**

Pecci, Vincenzo Gioacchino. *See* Leo XIII (pope)

Pechersky, Alexander, 15:**707**

Péchi, Simon, 15:**707–708**

Pechina (Spain), 15:**708**

PEC Israel Economic Corporation. *See* Palestine Economic Corporation

Peckelman, Henry. *See* Furtună, Enric

Pecs (Hungary), 15:**708**

Pécs (Hungary). *See* Pecs (Hungary)

Pedaayets. *See* Podgaitsy

Pedagogy. *See* Education

Peddlers, 15:302

Peddler storage cooperatives, 5:206

Peddling, 4:396, 398–399, 568, 608, 15:**708–711**

Pedersen, Johannes, 3:651, 658, 659, 15:**711–712**

Pediatrics. *See* Medicine

Pediatrics (Abt), 1:333

Pedro de Cartagena, 15:563

Pedro de Luna. *See* Benedict XIII (antipope)

Pedro I, King of Castile and Leon, 1:343

Pedro the Cruel. *See* Pedro I, King of Castile and Leon

Peel, Earl, 15:584

Peel Commission, 15:583–584, 585–586, *586,* **712**

Peele, George, 1:331

Peeping Tom (Jacobson), 6:439, 11:54

Peeping Tom (motion picture), 6:263

Peerce, Jan, 15:**712**

Pee Wee's Big Adventure (motion picture), 6:314–315

Pegai river. *See* Yarkon river

Péguy, Charles-Pierre, 8:269, 12:558, 15:**712**

Peierls, Rudolf Ernst. *See* Peierls, Sir Rudolf Ernst

Peierls, Sir Rudolf Ernst, 15:**712–713**

P'ein-Liang. *See* Kaifeng

Peiper, Tadeusz, 15:**713**

Peixotto, Benjamin Franklin, 4:19, 15:**713**

Peixotto, Daniel Levi Maduro, 8:735, 15:392, 713

Peixotto, George da Maduro, 15:**713–714**

Peixotto, Jessica Blanche, 15:**714**

Peixotto, Judith Salzedo, 15:**714**

Peixotto family, 15:**713–714**

Pekah (King of Israel), 9:179, 15:**714–715**

Pekahiah (King of Israel), 9:179, 15:**715**

Pekarsky, Maurice Bernard, 15:**715**

Pekelis, Alexander H., 2:57

Pekelis, Alexander Haim, 15:**715–716**

Pekeris, Chaim Leib, 15:**716**

Pekerman, José Nestor, 15:**716**

Pekid Ereẓ Yisrael, 18:450

Peki'in (Israel), 15:**716–717**

Peking (China), 15:**717**

Pekod (Aramean tribe), 15:**717**

Pelethites, 16:54–55

Peli. *See* Heilprin, Phinehas Menahem

Pelicans, 15:**717–718**

Pella (Canaan), 15:**718**

Pelleg, Frank, 15:**718**

Pellicanus, Conrad, 15:**718–719**
   Pauli, Johannes, 15:696

Pellicanus, Kuerschner. *See* Pellicanus, Conrad

Pellicanus, Kuersner. *See* Pellicanus, Conrad

Pellicanus, Kursiner. *See* Pellicanus, Conrad

Pellicanus Rubeaquensis. *See* Pellicanus, Conrad

Pellikan, Conrad. *See* Pellicanus, Conrad

Pellikan, Kuerschner. *See* Pellicanus, Conrad

Pellikan, Kuersner. *See* Pellicanus, Conrad

Pellikan, Kursiner. *See* Pellicanus, Conrad

Pelte, Feyge. *See* Meed, Vladka

Peltin, Samuel Hirsch, 15:**719**

Peltz, Isac, 15:**719**

Pelugta. *See* Conflict of opinion

Pember, Phoebe Yates, 15:**719–720**

Penal law, 5:57, 15:**720–723**, **720–726**, 723
   See also Laws and legal systems

Penalty. *See* Fines; Punishment

Penei Aharon (Amarillo), 2:31–32

Penei Shelomo (Amarillo), 2:32

Penei Yehoshu'a: Appei Zutrei (Falk), 6:684

Penei Yizḥak (Abulafia), 1:340

Penguin Books, 4:217, 10:30

Peniel (ancient Israel). *See* Penuel

Peninnah (wife of Elkanah), 15:**726**

Penitence. *See* Repentance

Penitence, Ten Days of. *See* Ten Days of Penitence

Penitential Prayers. *See* Seliḥot

Penker, Joseph David. *See* David, Joseph

Penn, Alexander, 15:**726**

Penn, Arthur, 15:**726–727**

Penn, Irving, 15:**727**, 16:126

Penn, Jack, 15:**727**

Penn, Sean, 15:**727–728**

Pennsylvania, 12:454–455, 611–612, 15:**728–730**

Pensacola (FL), 7:87

Pensées sur la religion (Pascal), 15:674

Penso, Joseph. *See* Penso de la Vega, Joseph

Penso de la Vega, Joseph, 15:**730**, 18:299–300
   Amzalak, Moses Bensabat, 2:125
   Confusion de Confusiones, 2:109

Pentacle, amulets, 2:122

Pentagon Papers, 6:362

Pentateuch, 15:**730–753**
   Aaron ben Elijah, 1:212
   Abraham ben Shabbetai ha-Kohen, 1:310
   Adani, David ben Amram, 1:381
   Akedah, 1:555–560
   Aristobulus' interpretation, 2:459
   authors, 15:734–744, 743, 745–747, 749, 750, 751–752
   commentaries, 7:492, 9:662, 11:30–31, 15:499–500
      Caro, Isaac ben Joseph, 4:488
      Gabirol, Solomon ben Judah, ibn, 7:321–327
      Ha-Ketav ve-ha-Kabbalah, 13:797–798
      Ibn Bal'am, Judah ben Samuel, 9:660–661
      Ibn Ezra, Abraham ben Meir, 9:666–670, 19:315–316
      Ibn Tibbon, Moses ben Samuel ben Judah, 8:660, 19:712
      Mekor Ḥayyim (Ibn Gabirol), 7:130–131, 7:323–326
      Mizraḥi, Elijah, 15:534, 537, 19:315
      Naḥmanides, 2:548, 14:739–747, 19:315–316
      Rashi, 1:301, 17:101–106, 102*t*, 19:315–316
      Sorotzkin, Zalman ben Ben-Zion, 19:30–31
      Spinka, Joseph Meir Weiss of, 19:111
      Spira, Nathan Nata ben Solomon, 19:119
      Steinhardt, Joseph ben Menahem, 19:193
      Supercommentaries on the Pentateuch, 19:315–316
      Tanḥum ben Eliezer, 19:504
      Toledano, Jacob, 20:19–21
      Vivante, David Abraham, 20:563
   contradictions in, 15:741–742
   Dead Sea scrolls and, 5:504
   Decalogue and, 5:521
   Deuteronomy, Book of and, 5:613–614
   development of scholarship of, 15:744
   elders, 6:295
   historicity of, 9:153, 15:747–750
   vs. kabbalah, 11:585
   literature, Samaritans, 17:737–738

mishpat Ivri, 14:335, 337
moneylending, 14:436
Moore, George Foot, 14:469
Moses, 14:523–531
Nazirite, 15:45–47
Oral Law and, 15:455
poetical sections, 15:621
reading, 15:734, 740, 20:46, 47*t*–49*t*
   accents, 13:*659, 660*
   cantillation, 13:*657, 658*, 661, *661*
   triennial cycle, 20:46
revelation, 17:253–259
Sefer Torah, 4:547, 18:241–243
Segal, Moses Hirsch on, 18:248
Sforno, Obadiah ben Jacob on, 18:334
Sidrah, 18:552
Spinoza, Baruch de, 16:65, 92–93, 19:111–119
supercommentaries. *See* Supercommentaries on the Pentateuch
Tanakh, 19:499
Tanḥuma bar Abba, 19:502–503
Tanḥuma Yelammedenu, 19:503–504
tannaim, 19:505–507
teki'ata, 19:587
tithe, 19:737–738
Tokheḥah, 20:18
Tractatus Theologico-Politicus (Spinoza), 19:116–118
translations
   Aramaic, 2:347
   Galilean Aramaic, 2:349
   German, 14:36
   Judeo-Persian, 11:552, 19:531
   Mandarin Chinese, 18:122–123
   Onkelos, 15:433–434
   Russian, 19:187
   Septuagint, 11:717, 18:307
Wellhausen, Julius, 15:743–745, 749, 21:6–7
See also Torah

Pentateuch, Samaritan. *See* Samaritan Pentateuch

Pentateuchal oaths, 15:361

The Pentateuch and Book of Joshua Critically Examined (Colenso), 5:57

Pentecost. *See* Shavuot

Penuel (ancient Israel), 15:**755**

Penueli, Shemuel Yeshayahu, 15:**755–756**

Penzance (U.K.), 15:**756**

Penzance archives, 2:408

Penzias, Arno Allan, 15:**756**

The People, Food for Kings (Laor), 12:488

People and Life 1891-1921, 1962 (Ehrenburg), 6:238

People and Polity: The Organizational Dynamics of World Jewry (Elazar), 6:289

The People of Godlbozhits. See Di Mentshn fun Godlbozhits (Rashkin)

People of the land. *See* Am ha-areẓ

People's Administration. *See* Minhelet ha-Am

People's Art Guild, 2:513

The People's Choice (Lazarsfeld), 12:560

People's Front for the Liberation of Palestine, 6:282–283

Pe'ot, 15:**756**

Pepper, 15:**756**–757

Pepper, Joseph, 15:**757**

Perahia, Murray, 15:**757**

Peraḥyah, Aaron ben Ḥayyim Abraham ha-Kohen, 15:**757**

Peraḥyah, Aaron ha-Cohen, 2:32

Peraḥyah, Ḥasdai ben Samuel ha-Kohen, 15:**757**

Peraḥyah ben Nissim, 15:**757**–758

Perath, 15:**631**

Perath (Israel). *See* Parah

Per Atum (Egypt). *See* Pithom (Egypt)

Perchersky, Alexander, 18:701

Percival. *See* Raphael, John

Percy, Charles, 2:52

Perec, Georges, 4:23, 15:**758**

Pereferkovich, Nehemiah, 15:**758–759**

Peregrine. *See* Deutscher, Isaac

Peregrino, Abraham Israel. *See* Escudero, Lorenzo

Pereira, Abraham, 8:747, 18:299, 348

Pereira, Francisco Nuñez. *See* Leão, Gaspar de

Pereira, Francisco Nuñez. *See* Abendana, David

Pereira, Jacob Rodrigues. *See* Péreire, Jacob Rodrigues

Pereira, Moses Lopez. *See* Aguilar, Diego D'

Pereira de Paiva, Moses, 15:**759**

Péreire, Émile, 15:**759**, 17:69–70, 18:704

Péreire, Isaac, 6:26, 15:**759**, 18:704

Péreire, Jacob Rodrigues, 13:728, 15:**759**

Perek Shirah, 5:164, 15:**760**

Perel, Martin Lewis, 15:**774–775**

Perelman, Chaim, 15:**760–761**

Perelman, Joseph. *See* Dymov, Ossip

Perelman, Ronald Owen, 15:**761**

Perelman, Sidney Joseph, 15:**761**

Perelmann, Jerohman Judah Leib ben Solomon Zalman, 15:**762**

Perelmuth, Jacob Pincus. *See* Peerce, Jan

Peremyshlany family, 8:419–420

Peremyshlyany (Ukraine), 15:**762**

Peremyshlyany, Meir ben Aaron Leib of, 15:**762–763**

Peres, Shimon, 10:247–248, 12:534, 15:**763–764**, 18:362

American Israel Public Affairs Committee, 2:51

Ben-Gurion, David, 3:347

governments of, 10:449–450, 449*t*, 455–456, 455*t*

Modai, Yitzhak, 14:406

Palestinian issue, 10:261

Shamir, Yitzhak and, 18:393–394

Perets, Y.L. *See* Peretz, Isaac Leib

Peretz, Abraham, 15:**764**

Peretz, Amir, 15:**764–765**

Peretz, Gregory, 15:**764**

Peretz, Isaac Leib, 8:694, 718, 15:**765–768**, 21:347–348

Nomberg, Hersch David, 15:296, 297

Shalom Aleichem and, 18:381

Yiddish translations of Bible, 3:611

Peretz, Yitskhok Leybush. *See* Peretz, Isaac Leib

Peretz, Yitzhak Ḥayyim, 18:419

Peretz, Y.L. *See* Peretz, Isaac Leib

Pereyslav (Ukraine). *See* Pereyslav-Khmelnitski (Ukraine)

Pereyslav-Khmelnitski (Ukraine), 15:**768–769**

Pereyv (Sobol), 18:701

Perez (son of Judah), 15:**769**, 19:493, 21:512–513

Perez, João, 1:313

Perez, Juan. *See* Senior, Solomon

Perez, Judah ben Joseph, 15:**769**

Perez, Jung, 17:130–131

Perez Bayer, Francisco, 15:**769**

Perez ben Elijah of Corbeil, 15:**769–770**

Perez ben Moses of Brody, 15:**770**

Perfect de Pratis. *See* Benveniste, Sheshet ben Isaac ben Joseph

Perfection

biblical, 6:531–532

Mendelssohn, Moses, 14:34

The Perfection of Actions (Falaquera). *See Shelemut ha-Ma'asim*

Perfet, Isaac ben Sheshet. *See* Isaac ben Sheshet Perfet

Performance arts, 6:517–518

Perfumes, 3:95, 5:230, 9:753–754

Pergament, Moses, 15:**770**

Pergament, Osip Yakovlevich, 15:**770**

Pergamum (ancient city and kingdom), 15:**770–771**

Pergola, Raphael Della, 15:**771**

Peri, Eẓ-Ḥayyim (periodical), 12:493, 601, 15:**771–772**

Peri, Hiram, 15:**771**

Peri, Ya'akov, 15:**771**

Peri'ah, 4:731, 734

Peri Hadash (Amigo), 2:77

Peri Hadash (Hezekiah), 9:91

Periodicals. *See* Press

Peripatos. *See* Aristotle

Perizzites, 15:**772**

Perjury, 15:**772–773**

Perl, Joseph, 8:689, 9:593, 15:658, 762, **773–774**

Perl, Néstor, 16:350

Perl, William, 9:496

Perla, Jeroham Fischel ben Aryeh Ẓevi, 15:**775**

Perlbach, Max, 15:**775**

Perlberg, Abraham Nathan, 15:**775**

Perle, Joshua, 15:**775–776**

Perle, Richard Norman, 15:**776**

Perle, Yehoshua. *See* Perle, Joshua

Perles, Felix, 15:**776**, 777

Perles, Isaac Moses, 15:**777**

Perles, Joseph, 3:600, 15:**776**

Perles, Moses Meir ben Eleazar, 15:**777**

Perles, Rosalie, 15:**776–777**

Perles family, 15:**776–777**

Perl fun der Yidisher poezye (Mlotek). *See Pearls of Yiddish Poetry* (Mlotek)

Perlhefter, Issachar Behr ben Judah Moses, 15:**777**

Perlin, Ḥayyim Lipmann. *See* Sonnenfels, Aloys von

Perlman, Alfred Edward, 15:**777–778**

Perlman, Helen Harris, 15:**778**

Perlman, Itzhak, 15:**778**

Perlman, Jacob, 15:**778–779**

Perlman, Samuel, 15:**779**

Perlman, Selig, 15:**779**

Perlmann, Moshe, 15:**779**

Perlmutter, Abraham Ẓevi, 15:**779**

Perlmutter, Izsák, 15:**780**

Perlmutter, Yehiel. *See* Yeshurun, Avot

Perlov, Aaron. *See* Aaron the Second

Perlov, Aaron ben Jacob, 11:809

Perlov, Asher, 11:809–810

Perlov, Asher (d. 1873), 11:810

Perlov, Yitskhok, 15:**780**

Perlov family. *See* Karlin family

Perlow, Issac. *See* Perlov, Yitskhok

Perls, Isaac Moses. *See* Perles, Isaac Moses

Perlstein, Meyer A., 15:**780**

Perl un Andere Dertseylungen (Singer), 18:637

Perlzweig, Maurice L., 15:**780**

Perlzweig, William Alexandre, 15:**780**

Pernambuco (Brazil). *See* Recife (Brazil)

Pernerstorfer, Engelbert, 15:**780–781**

Peròn, Isabel, 2:441

Peròn, Juan, 2:440–441, 449

Perpignan (France), 3:**248**, 6:394, 15:**781–782**

Perpignan archives, 2:406

Perrault, Emile. *See* Harry, Myriam

Perreau, Pietro, 15:782

Perrot, Jean, 15:782

Perry, Frank, 15:782

Persecutions. *See* Antisemitism

Persecutions of 1391, 3:144, 18:327

La Persévérance du mal (Chalier), 4:562

Persia, 2:766, 15:**782–792**

    Ahasuerus, 1:538

    Ahasuerus-Xerxes, 1:538

    Angaria, 2:146

    Anusim, 2:253–254

    Aramaic, 2:348

    archaeology, 2:388

    Cambyses, 4:379

    community leaders, Melamed, Siman Tov, 14:6

    crypto-Jews, 11:58

    dress, 6:14

    education, Jewish, 6:176

    Israel (ancient), 10:156

    Jewish communities in, 15:*783*, 786, 787

        Israel (state), 10:297

        Lar, 12:492

    Jewish quarters in, 11:312

    Josephus' *Jewish Antiquities* and, 11:438–439

    Judaism, development of concept of, 11:515

    letters and letter writers, 12:669

    Niebuhr, Carston, travels of, 15:259

    Nishapur, 15:275

    Ottoman conquest of, 15:525

    pottery, 16:422

pre-Islamic, 15:782–785

Scroll of Esther, depiction of, 18:217

sects, Isunians, 1:337

Talmud, Middle Persian culture, 19:488–491

See also Iran

Persian apples. *See* Peaches

Persian Empire

    Phoenicia, 16:122

    political history, satrap, 18:75

Persian Gulf Crisis

    Argentina support, 2:450

    El Al airline, 6:283

    England, 6:431

Persian language, 8:647

    in Mishnaic Hebrew, 8:647

    Sefer ha-Meliẓah (Solomon ben Samuel), 18:772–773

    Solomon ben Samuel, 18:772

    See also Judeo-Persian language

Persian literature

    Daniel, influence on, 6:495

    Sarmad, Muhammad Sa'id, 18:57

    Shāhin, 18:365

    See also Judeo-Persian literature

Persitz, Alexandre, 15:**792**

Persitz, Shoshanah, 15:**792**

Persius, 15:**792**

Perski, Joel Dov Baer, 15:**792**

Persky, Daniel, 8:737, 15:**792**

Persky, Shimon. *See* Peres, Shimon

Persoff, Nehemiah, 15:**793**

A Personal Repertoire (Smoira-Cohn), 18:690

Persov, Shmuel, 15:**793**

A Perspective of Jewish Life Through Its Festivals (Adlerblum), 1:409

Perth (Australia), 15:**793**

Peru, 15:**793–797**

    Inquisition, 9:798

    Judaizers in, 11:520, 521

    León Pinelo school, 13:21

    Zionism, 21:594

Perugia (Italy), 15:**798**

Perush (Falaquera), 6:681

Perush al Ḥamishah Perakim min ha-Haysharah le-Abu Nasr (Bali), 3:90

Perushim, 8:287–288, 288, 14:337, 18:35

Perush Inyan Sheḥitah (Bali), 3:90

Perush Rabbi Yehudah ben Binyamin Anav (Mirsky), 14:315

Perush Rabbi Yonatan ha-Kohen mi-Lunel al-Megillah u-Mo'ed Katan (Mirsky), 14:315

Perutah, 18:439–440

Perutz, Leo, 15:**798**

Perutz, Max Ferdinand, 15:**798**

Pervomaisk (Ukraine), 15:**798**

Pervoye pokoleniye (Altauzen), 2:17

Pervye gody (Slonimsky), 18:679

Pesah. *See* Passover

Pesaḥ. *See* Passover

Pesaḥ, Sheni. *See* Passover, Second

Pesaḥim, 16:**5–6**

Pesaḥson, Isaac Mordecai, 16:6

Pesante, Moses ben Ḥayyim ben Shem Tov, 16:6

Pesaro (Italy), 16:**6–8**

Pesaro, Abramo, 16:**8**

Peschkowsky, Michael Igor. *See* Nichols, Mike

Pesharah and biẓẓa, 5:124

Peshat, 3:641, 661, 16:**8–9**

    biblical commentaries, 11:783–784

Pesher, 16:**9–11**

Pesher Habakkuk. *See* Habakkuk Commentary

Peshev, Dimiter, 4:271–272

Peshitta (Syriac Bible), 3:599–600

Peshkov, Aleksey Maksimovich. *See* Gorki, Maxim

Peshkova, Ekaterina, 7:779

Pesikta de-Rav Kahana, 12:452, 741, 16:**11–12**

Pesikta Ḥta, 14:189

Pesikta Rabbati, 16:**12–13**

Pesikta Zutarta, 16:12

Peskin, Benjamin, 14:446

Pesnya o Dnepre (Dolmatovski), 5:736

Pesnya o schast'e (Donskoy), 5:752

Pesotta, Rachelle. *See* Pesotta, Rose

Pesotta, Rose, 16:**13**

Pest (Hungary), 4:245–246

Pestszenterzsebet (Hungary), 16:**13–14**

Pestszenterzsébet (Hungary). *See* Pestszenterzsebet (Hungary)

Pesukei de-Zimra, 3:191–192, 16:**14**

Petach Tikva Local Planning and Construction Committee and others *v.* M. Zitman and Sons Ltd., 16:218

Petaḥ Tikvah (Israel), 16:**14–15**, 17:5–6

Petegorsky, David W., 16:**15**

Peten, 18:696

Peter de Luna. *See* Benedict XIII (antipope)

Peter I, Czar of Russia, 1:359

Peter IV of Aragon (Holy Roman Emperor), 3:733

Peter Niger. *See* Nigri, Petrus

Peter of Blois, 16:**15**

Peter of Cluny, 11:454, 16:**15–16**

Peters, Roberta, 16:**16**

Peterson, Eugene, 3:621

Peter the Hermit, 5:311

Peter the Venerable. *See* Peter of Cluny

Pethahiah of Regensburg, 2:89, 16:**16**

Petiḥah, 16:**16–17**

Petiot, Jean Charles Henri. *See* Daniel-Rops, Henri

Petit, David, 4:82

Petit, Jean Charles Henri. *See* Daniel-Rops, Henri

"Petite métaphysique du meurtre" (Abécassis), 1:244

Petlyura, Simon, 11:753, 16:**17**, 18:191

Petlyura gangs, 4:119

Petra (Jordan), 14:716, 16:**17–18**

Petrarch, 12:724

Petrie, Sir William Matthew Flinders, 15:589, 16:**18–19**

Petrie, William Matthew Flinders. *See* Petrie, Sir William Matthew Flinders

Petrikau (Poland). *See* Piotrkow (Poland)

Petrograd (Russia). *See* Saint Petersburg (Russia)

Petrograd Conference, 16:**19**

Petrokow (Poland). *See* Piotrkow (Poland)

Petroleum and oil products, 6:23, 16:**19–20**

Petronius, Publius, 16:**20–21**

Petronius Arbiter, Gaius, 16:**21**

Petrov, Valeri, 4:276, 16:**21**

Petrus Abaelardus. *See* Abelard, Peter

Petrus Aldefonsi. *See* Petrus Alfonsi

Petrus Alfonsi, 16:**21**

Petrus Damiani. *See* Damian, Peter

Petrus Venerabilis. *See* Peter of Cluny

Petschek family, 16:**22**

Petter ben Joseph, 16:**22**

Petuchowski, Jakob Josef, 16:**22–23**

Petuḥot of Bible, 13:607

Pevsner, Anton, 16:**23**

Pevsner, Naum Nehemia, 16:**23**

Pevsner, Nikolaus. *See* Pevsner, Sir Nikolaus

Pevsner, Sir Nikolaus, 16:**23**

Pevzner, Samuel Joseph, 16:**23**

Pewter plates, 16:**23–24**

Peyrehorade (France), 16:**24**

Peyrère, Isaac, La. *See* La Peyrère, Isaac

Pezinok (Slovakia), 16:**24–25**

Pezurai (Kaplan), 11:774

Pfalz (Germany). *See* Palatinate

Pfeffer, Leo, 16:**25**
    American Jewish Congress, 2:58

Pfefferkorn, Johannes, 16:**25–26**

Pfefferkorn, Joseph. *See* Pfefferkorn, Johannes

Pfefferman, Abba. *See* Pann, Abel

Pfeiffer, Robert Henry, 16:**26–27**

Pflaum, Heinz. *See* Peri, Hiram

Pforzheim (Germany), 3:44, 16:**27**

Pforzheimer, Carl Howard, 16:**27**

Pfundtner, Hans, 15:348

Phainon (Edom). *See* Punon (Edom)

Phalange, Christian, 11:713–714

Phalsbourg (France), 16:**27**

Phanagoria (kingdom of Bosphorus), 4:98

Pharaoh, 1:561, 16:**27–30**, 212–213
    Moses, 14:523–535
    Solomon, 18:757, 760

Pharaonic laws. *See* Familiants laws

Pharisaic Judaism, 3:27

Pharisees, 4:680–681, 16:**30–32**
    ablution, 1:261–262
    Amidah, 2:73
    Ananias son of Zadok, 2:130
    angels, 2:153
    Finkelstein, Louis, 7:35
    House of David and, 5:453
    Jesus and, 11:248
    Jubilees, Book of, 11:474
    polemics, 16:327–328

Pharmacology. *See* Medicine

Pharos (Egypt), 16:**32**

Phasael, 16:**32**

Phasaelis (Jordan Valley), 16:**32**

Pheasants, 16:**32–33**

Pheibush family. *See* Phillips family

Phenomenology, 3:79, 6:611, 713

Pheroras, 16:**33**

PḤḤ (Partisans, Soldiers, Pioneers), 15:668

Philadelphia (PA), 16:**33–38**
    Dropsie College, 6:25–26
    education, Jewish, 6:190, 12:723
    philanthropy, 5:437–438, 6:24–25, 16:34–35, 37
    See also Gratz, Rebecca; Gratz family

Philadelphia, Jacob, 16:**38**

Philadelphia Zionist Council, 2:104

Philadelphus. *See* Ptolemy II

Philanthropy, 4:728, 16:**38–47**
    Blaustein family, 3:746
    Bloomingdale family, 3:784
    Broad, Eli, 4:191
    Bronfman family, 4:205–206

Canada, 4:418
    Bennett, Avie J., 3:368
    Dan, Leslie L., 5:408
coordination of communal efforts, 16:39–40, 41–42, 43
Cullman family, 5:329–330
Day of Atonement customs, 5:489–490
effect of emigration, 16:38, 40
England, 16:38, 39–40
    twentieth century, 13:699–700
First Aliyah, 10:334, 357–358
Fischel, Harry, 7:51
foundations, 7:136–138
France, 16:39
    Deutsch de la Meurthe, Henri, 5:625
    Lehmann, Léonce, 12:615
    Leven, Narcisse, 12:678–679
Germany
    Hirsch, Baron Maurice de, 9:127–128
    Simon, James, 18:611–612
ḥalukkah, 8:287–290
Hassenfeld, Sylvia Kay, 8:454–455
Hauser Foundation, 8:464
Holy Roman Empire, Meisel Mordecai ben Samuel, 13:789
Ibn Ḥasan, Jekuthiel ben Isaac, 9:679
India, 6:648, 654
Iraq, 11:36–37
Israel (state)
    early years, 10:216
    late 1960s, 10:234
    post-Six-Day War, 10:231–232
Jewish Colonization Association, 11:285–288
Jewish Communal Association of North America, 11:288
Jewish communities in Palestine (Ottoman) and, 10:619
to Jews in Mandate Palestine, 10:200
to Jews in Ottoman Palestine, 10:178, 192–193
Kadoorie family, 11:701
Kimmel, Sidney, 12:159–160
Netherlands
    Eibeschuetz, Simon Aaron, 6:245
    Lehren family, 12:616–617
for Palestine (Ottoman), Istanbul and, 10:779–780
Palestine (Ottoman) schools, 10:652–653

Philanthropy, *continued*

Pollin, Abe, 16:360

Rabinowitz, Louis Mayer, 17:41

Reese, Michael, 17:162

Reichmann, Samuel, 17:200

Reichmann, Saul, 17:200

Reisman, Heather, 17:212

Rosenberg, James Naumburg, 17:437

Rosenbloom, Solomon, 17:442–443

Rosenthal, Leon, 17:454–455

Rothschild, Baron Edond James de, 17:491–492

Rothschild, James Armand de, 17:493–494

Rothschild, Kurt, 17:494

Rubin, Samuel, 17:513–514

Russia, Baron, Bernhard, 3:171

Saint Louis (MO), 17:671–672

Schneider, Irving, 18:150

Swiss, Dunant, Jean Henri, 6:47

Syria, 6:714–715

U.K.

Braude, Jacob, 4:135

Burton, Sir Montague, 4:302

Clore, Charles, 4:761

Sassoon, Vidal, 18:71–72

U.S., 16:40–42, 46–47

Adler, Max, 1:402

Baltimore (MD), 3:98–99

Barnert, Nathan, 3:168

Bernheim, Isaac Wolfe, 3:474

Bernstein, Zalman Chaim, 3:485

Boyar, Louis H., 4:108–109

Carter, Victor M., 4:498–499

Crown, Henry, 5:307

Davidson, William, 5:477–478

Eisenman, Charles, 6:267

Evans, Eli, 6:571

Falk family, 6:683–684

Fels, 6:750–751

Hackenburg, William Bower, 8:182

Jacobs, Francis Wisebart, 11:46–47

Jesselson, Ludwig, 11:244–245

Kahn, Otto Herman, 11:723

Lefrak, Samuel J., 12:602–603

Levitt family, 12:742–743

Levy, Sir Albert, 12:746

Lewis, Peter B., 12:766

Lewis, Samuel Alexander, 12:766

Lewisohn family, 12:767–768

Matz, Israel, 13:689

Mazer family, 13:707

Melton, Florence, 14:14–15

Memphis, 14:19–20

Philadelphia, 5:437–438, 16:34–35, 37

Philips, Rebecca Machado, 16:57

San Diego, 18:13

San Francisco, 18:20

Sapirstein-Stone-Weiss family, 18:39

Schiff, Jacob Henry, 18:130–131

Schusterman, Charles and Lynn, 18:177–179

Schwartz, Gerald, 18:184

Shalom, Isaac I., 18:377

Sharp, Isadore Nataniel, 18:418

Sherman, Archie, 18:464

voluntary societies vs. obligatory contributions, 16:38–39

See also specifc organizations

Philately. *See* Stamps

Philharmonic Orchestra. *See* Israel Philharmonic Orchestra

Philhellene. *See* Aristobulus I

Philip (kings of France), 16:**47–48**

Philip (ruler of Judea). *See* Herod Philip I

Philip, Harvey. *See* Spector, Phil

Philip, Herschell. *See* Filipowski, Zevi Hirsch

Philip Augustus (King of France), 7:150, 15:643, 16:47

Philip II (King of France), 16:47

Philip III, the Bold (King of France), 16:47–48

Philip IV, the Fair (King of France), 7:150–151, 13:25, 16:48

Philip Morris Tobbaco, 5:329–330

Philip of Bathyra, 16:**48–49**

Philipopolis (Bulgaria). *See* Plovdiv (Bulgaria)

Philippines, 16:**49**

Inquisition, 9:797–798

overthrow of Marcos, 18:752

Philippson, Alfred, 16:51

Philippson, Franz Moses, 16:50

Philippson, Johanna, 16:51

Philippson, Ludwig, 16:50

Anhalt, 2:163

German translation of Bible by, 3:631

Philippson, Martin Emanuel, 16:50

Philippson, Moses, 16:49–50

Philippson, Paul, 16:50–51

Philippson, Phoebus Moritz, 16:50

Philippson, Robert, 16:51

Philippson family, 16:**49–51**

Philips, Jacob, 3:769

Philips, Philip A., 15:243

Philipson, David, 16:**51–52**

American Jewish Archives, 2:53

Philip V, the Tall (King of France), 16:48

Philip W. Lown School of Near Eastern and Judaic Studies, 13:237

Philistia, 16:52

Philistine ostraca, 3:657

Philistines, 7:619, 16:**52–55**

Ashekelon, 2:567

David and, 5:445, 447, 448, 18:79

Ekron, 6:281–282

Judah, tribe of, 11:475–476

Samson and, 6:626

Saul and, 18:80

Shamgar and, 18:390–391

Phillippson, Ludwig, 11:500

Phillips, Coleman, 15:243

Phillips, Edis. *See* De Philippe, Edis

Phillips, Jacob, 16:55–56

Phillips, Jonas, 15:197

Phillips, Lazarus, 16:56

Phillips, Lionel. *See* Phillips, Sir Lionel

Phillips, Marion, 16:**56**, 342

Phillips, N. Taylor, 2:59

Phillips, Naphtali, 15:198, 199, 290, 16:56

Phillips, Nathan, 16:**56–57**, 341

Phillips, Philip, 12:555, 15:475, 16:57

Phillips, Rebecca Machado, 16:**57–58**

Phillips, Sir Lionel, 16:**56**, 349

Phillips, William, 16:58

Phillips Company, 20:588–589

Phillips family, 16:**55–56**

Phillips Manufacturing Company, 18:746

Phillipson, Irving Joseph, 16:58

Philo, Solomon, 4:187

Philo (1st c.), *Liber Antiquitatum Biblicarum,* 14:533, 16:**58–59**

Philo (the Elder), 16:**58**

Philo and the Oral Law (Belkin), 3:**296**

Philodemus, 16:**59**

Philo Judaeus, 4:732, 16:**59–64**, 75–76, 106

Abraham, 1:284

Adam, 1:372, 373

afterlife, 1:441

Akedah, 1:556

allegorical interpretation of scripture, 3:643, 644

angels, 2:159

apologetics, 2:263

Bible, names for, 3:574

Bible's importance to, 3:665

on Bithynia, 3:729

circumcision, 4:732

Clement of Alexandria, 4:753

commandments, reasons for, 5:86

creation, 5:277

Day of Atonement, 5:491

De Vita Contemplativa, 11:589

dualism, 6:29

economic policies of Flaccus, 6:104

ecstasy, 6:138

Essenes, 6:510–511

free will, 7:230–231

God, 7:659–660

    attributes of, 7:666

ḥallah, 8:277

historical work, 9:154

Jewish identity in Hellenistic period and, 11:293

logos, 13:174–175

moneylending, 14:437

Moses, 14:531, 532–533

nature, 15:34

platonism, 16:226

revelation, 17:256

Ru'aḥ ha-Kodesh, 17:507–508

on Septuagint, 3:596

soul, immortality of, 19:36

space and place, 19:66

Torah, 20:44

Wisdom of Solomon, 18:768

Philological commentary on Bible, 3:642, 648

Philology

    Benardete, Mair José, 3:318

    Benfey, Theodor, 3:342

    Dunash ben Labrat, 6:47–48

    Frankfurter, Solomon Friedrich, 7:207

    Frankl, Oscar Benjamin, 7:214

    Humboldt, Wilhelm von, 9:588–589

    Ibn Janāaḥ, Jonah, 9:683

    Ilgen, Karl David, 9:721

    Lara, David Ben Isaac Cohen De, 12:492–493

    Leslau, Wolf, 12:663

    Levita, Elijah, 12:730–732

    Lewy, Julius, 12:771

    Morpurgo, Salomone, 14:509

    Reinach, Solomon, 17:205

    Scaliger, Joseph Jsutus, 18:88–89

Schwabe, Moshe, 18:181

Philometor, Ptolemy Vl

Philo of Alexandria. *See* Philo Judaeus

Philo of Alexandria

    Palestine, 15:581

    Pamphylia, 15:608

    papyri confirming or correcting, 15:619

Philo of Byblos, 16:**64**

Philopator. *See* Ptolemy IV

Philo-Semitism

    Finch, Sir Henry, 7:25

    Finn, James, 7:39

    Soloviev, Vladimir, 18:780

Philosoph, Jacob. *See* Querido, Jacob

Philosopher's Holiday (Edman), 6:150

The Philosophers of Our Time. See Hogei ha

Philosopher's Quest (Edman), 6:150

Philosophia libera (Cardozo), 4:467

Philosophical commentary on Bible, 3:643

Philosophical determinism, 8:370

Die Philosophic der Tat (Hess), 18:705

Philosophie der Geschichte oder ueber die Tradition (Molitor), 11:673, 14:426

Philosophie der symbolischen Formen (Cassirer), 4:509

Philosophie des Geldes (Simmel), 18:607

Philosophie sociale, dediée au peuple français (Dobruschka), 5:727

Philosophies of Judaism (Guttmann), 16:69–70, 71

Philosophy, 16:64–67, **64–67**

    14th-17th centuries, 16:65

    18th-19th centuries, 16:65–66

    20th century, 16:66–67

    afterlife, 13:447–448

    Arab, Kindī, Abu Yūsuf Ya'Qūb ibn Ishaq Al-, 12:161–162

    British

        Hart, Herbert Lionel Adolphus, 8:370

        Lakatos, Imre, 12:440

    Czechoslovakia, Bergman, Samuel Hugo, 3:428–429

    destiny of man, 13:449

    determinability, law of, 13:370

    determinism, 8:370, 11:232

    dualism, 6:29–31

    Edwards, Paul, 6:215

    England

        Berlin, Sir Isaiah, 3:456

        Bevan, Edwyn Robert, 3:555–556

Polanyi, Michael, 16:327

existentialism, 6:611–612, 672, 16:97–98, 102–103

France, 17:115

    Basch, Victor Guillaume, 3:194–195

    Bergson, Henri Louis, 3:432–433

    Bernheim, Gilles, 3:474

    Brunschvicg, Leon, 4:224–225

    Derrida, Jacques, 5:598

    Fourier, François Marie Charles, 7:139

    Franck, Adolphe, 7:175–176

    Holbach, Paul Henri Dietrich, Baron D', 9:315–316

    Léon, Xavier, 12:646–647

    Levi Ben Abraham Ben Ḥayyim, 12:697–698

    Levinas, Emmanuel, 12:715–716

    Lévy, Benny, 12:748

    Levy, Bernard-Henri, 12:748

    Lyotard, Jean-Francois, 13:298

    Raul, Fréd, 17:115

    Schuhl, Pierre-Maxime, 18:170–171

Frank, Philip, 7:193

Frank, Semyon Lyudvigovich, 7:194–195

Frank, Waldo David, 7:195

Frauenstaedt, Julius, 7:220

Germany

    Adorno, Theodor W., 1:420

    Albertus Magnus, 1:591

    Baumgardt, David, 3:221

    Ben-Chorin, Schalom, 3:324

    Bendavid, Lazarus, 3:325

    Benjamin, Walter, 3:359–360

    Brunner, Constantin, 4:224

    Brunswig, Alfred, 4:226

    Buber, Martin, 4:232–233

    Cassirer, Ernst, 4:509–510

    Dessoir, Max, 5:605–606

    Dubislav, Walter Ernst Otto, 6:32

    Fichte, Johann Gottlieb, 7:9–10

    Hegel, Georg William Friedrich, 8:755–756

    Heinemann, Fritz, 8:773–774

    Herder, Johann Gottfried, 9:9–10

    Herz, Marcus, 9:52

    Hirsch, Samuel, 9:132–133

Philosophy, *continued*
  Hoenigswald, Richard, 9:303
  Husserl, Edmund Gustav Albrecht, 9:643–644
  Idealism, 8:755–756
  Landauer, Gustav, 12:466–467
  Lask, Emil, 12:496
  Lasson, Adolf, 12:503
  Lazarus, Moritz, 12:561–562
  Lessing, Gotthold Ephraim, 12:664–665
  Lessing, Theodor, 12:665–666
  Lewkowitz, Albert, 12:771
  Liebert, Arthur, 12:809
  Liebmann, Otto, 12:811
  Mauthner, Fritz, 13:693
  Mendelssohn, Moses, 14:33–40
  Nelson, Leonard, 15:67
  Regelson, Abraham, 17:187
  Reinahc, Adolf, 17:205
  Richter, Raoul, 17:291
  Rosenstock-Huessy, Eugen, 17:450–451
  Rosenzweig, Franz, 17:458–462
  Schelling, Friedrich Wilhelm Joseph, 18:119–120
  Simmel, Georg, 18:607
God, image of, 13:447
Greek, ancient
  Aelian, 1:429
  Celsus, 4:537–538
  Clearchus of Soli, 4:752
  Empedocles, 6:397
  Epicurean, 16:58
  Islamic interpretation, 6:709–710
  logos, 13:174
  Plato, 1:279, 280
Gutmann, Amy, 8:153
Ḥibat Allah, abu al-Barakāt ben All al-Baghdādi, 9:93
Hungary
  Horovitz, Saul, 9:530
  Lukacs, Georg, 13:254–255
intellect, 9:809–810
  elite vs. masses, 13:388–389
  infinite, 13:370
Israel
  Leibowitz, Yeshayahu, 12:622–623
  Rotenstreich, Nathan, 17:478–479
Italy
  Leon, Messer David Ben Judah, 12:645–646

Lerma, Judah Ben Samuel, 12:655
Luzzatto, Samuel David, 13:286–287
Michelstaedter, Carlo, 14:174
Momigliano, Felice, 14:431
Romano, Judah ben Moses ben Daniel, 17:404
Kaufmann, Felix, 12:31
law, Cahn, Edmond Nathaniel, 4:337–338
letters and letter writers, 12:671–672
literature
  English, 6:434, 16:110–112
  philosophy and theology, 13:102–105
logical positivism, 6:735
man, origins of, 13:449
mathematical logic, Perelman, Chaim, 15:760–761
metaphysics of time, 11:78
  Meyerhoff, Hans, 14:151
microcosm, 14:178–179
nature, 15:35
Netherlands, Polak, Leonard, 16:287
new idealism, 11:363
phenomenology, 6:713
Pinto, Isaac de, 16:179
Poland
  Chwistek, Leon, 4:724
  Schaff, Adam, 18:103
providence, 16:648–652
Ramon, Lull, 17:85–86
Rand, Ayn, 17:89–90
reason vs. faith, 4:562
Renaissance Italy, 11:71
Romania, Cilibi Moïse, 4:726
Roth, Leon, 17:483
Rousseau, Jean Jacques, 17:498
Russia, Soloviev, Vladimir, 18:780
Schrecker, Paul, 18:167
science and, 16:131–132
  Meyerson, Emile, 14:153
Seneca the Younger, 18:288
Singer, Peter, 18:640
skepticism, 18:657–658
Spain
  Ibn Daud, Abraham ben David Halevi, 9:662–665
  Ibn Kapron, Isaac, 9:684
  Ibn Shem Tov, Joseph ben Shem Tov, 9:692
  Ibn Waqar, Joseph ben Abrahm, 9:696–697
Swiss, Hersch, Jeanne, 9:42

Turkey, Banrubi, Isaac, 3:372–373
U.K., Bronowski, Jacob, 4:207
U.S.
  Adler, Felix, 1:396–397
  Adler, Mortimer Jerome, 1:403–404
  Aiken, Henry David, 1:550
  Berkson, Isaac Baer, 3:442
  Butler, Judith, 4:317
  Cherniss, Harold Fredrik, 4:596–597
  Edman, Irwin, 6:150
  Heschel, Abraham Joshua, 9:70
  Hook, Sidney, 9:521–522
  Katz, Steven T., 12:16–17
  Lazerowitz, Morris, 12:562
  Scheffler, Israel, 18:116–117
women
  gender in, 16:105–111
  origins of, 13:449
The Philosophy of Space and Time. See Axiomatik der relativistischen Raum-Zeit-Lehre (Reichenbach)
The Philosophy of Spinoza (Wolfson), 21:149–150
Philostratus, 16:**114**
Philo the Elder, 3:660
Philo the Epicist, 3:660
Philo Verlag, 16:**114**
Philoxenian version of Bible, 3:600–601
Phinehas. *See* Hophni and Phinehas
Phinehas (biblical figures), 16:**114–115**
Phinehas (son of Eleazar), 11:99
Phinehas (son of Eli). *See* Hophni and Phinehas
Phinehas (Temple official), 16:**116**
Phinehas ben Ḥama, 11:479
Phinehas ben Ḥama ha-Kohen, 16:**116**
Phinehas ben Jacob ha-Kohen, 16:**116**
Phinehas ben Jair, 8:391, 16:**116–117**
Phinehas ben Joseph ha-Levi, 16:**117**
Phinehas ben Samuel, 11:383, 16:**117**
Phinehas Shapira, 1:220
Phlorina (Macedonia), 16:**117–118**
Phocas (Byzantine emperor), 4:326
Phoebus, Ḥayyim (Abraham) ben Samuel. *See* Ḥayyim ben Samuel Feivush
Phoebus, Uri Shraga, 8:272
Phoebus ben Aaron ha-Levi. *See* Uri ben Aaron ha-Levi
Phoenicia, Phoenicians, 16:**118–124**
  alphabet, Hebrew, 1:691, 691t, 692t, 694t, 12:445
  colonization, 16:122–123

Daniel, 5:417
history, 16:119–122
kings, 6:524
names, 16:118–119
people and language, 16:119, 123–124, 18:281, 284, 285
shekel weights, 18:439
Phoenix (AZ), 16:**124–125**
Phoenix (bird), 16:**125**
Phologombos, Terentius. *See* Judah, Samuel Benjamin Helbert
Phonetic punctuation, 4:84
Phonograph records. *See* Records, phonograph
Phorcensis. *See* Reuchlin, Johannes
Photis (ancient Israel), 16:**125**
Photius, 15:377
Photography, 16:**125–131**
Bar-am, Micha, 3:132
Ben Dov, Yaakov, 3:328
Bing, Ilse, 3:704
Bourke-White, Margaret, 4:106–107
Brenner, Frédéric, 4:158–159
Capa, Cornell, 4:441
Capa, Robert, 4:441–442
celebrations and customs, 16:128
Coen, Giuseppe, 4:781
Elisofon, Eliot, 6:354–355
faces, 16:127–128
France, 10:825–826
Frank, Robert, 7:194
Germany/U.S., 11:38–39
Halsman, Phillippe, 8:286
Heartfield, John, 8:510
Holocaust, 9:362, 16:129–130, 130
Israel (state), 10:701
Judaica, 16:126–131
Kagan, Elie, 11:706
Land, Edwin H., 12:456
Meyerowitz, Joel, 14:152–153
Moholy-Nagy, László, 14:419–420
Newman, Arnold, 15:145
Newton, Helmut, 15:192–193
in New York City, 15:221
nostagia, 16:128–129
Plachy, Sylvia, 16:210
Ray, Man, 17:126
Ringl+Pit, 17:336–337
Seymour, David, 18:332
Siskind, Aaron, 18:645–646
synagogues, 16:129–130
themes and motifs, 16:127–128
U.S.
Carvalho, Solomon Nunes, 4:502

Eisenstaedt, Alfred, 6:272
Erwitt, Elliott, 6:486
Ettlinger, 6:546
Leibovitz, Annie, 12:620
Levitt, Helen, 12:743–744
Penn, Irving, 15:727
Rubin, Gail, 17:512
Photojournalism, 16:125–126, 17:514
Photo-Realism (Kanovitz), 11:767
Phylacteries. *See* Tefillin; Ẓiẓit
Phyrgia (Asia Minor), 16:**131**
Physical chemistry
Bauer, Simon Harvey, 3:218
Bernstein, Harold Joseph, 3:478–479
Hirshberg, Yehudah, 9:142
Polanyi, Michael, 16:327
Reichinstein, David, 17:200
See also Chemistry
Physical education, 1:687–688, 2:541
Physicians. *See* Medicine
Physics, 16:**131–141**
11th to sixteenth centuries, 16:133–134
Aharonov, Yakir, 1:537
Alferov, Zhores I., 1:641
atomic
Meitner, Lise, 13:792
Peierls, Sir Rudolf Ernst, 15:712–713
Perl, Martin Lewis, 15:774
Bacher, Simon, 3:36
Bernal, John Desmond, 3:467
Brown, Harold, 4:214
Charpak, Georges, 4:580
Cooper, Leon N., 5:205
cryogenics, Mendelssohn, Kurt Alfred Georg, 14:33
Dember, Harry L., 5:548
De-Shalit, Amos, 5:602
Dessau, Bernardo, 5:604
Dessauer, Friedrich, 5:604–605
doctrine of atoms, 11:730
Dostrovsky, Israel, 5:762
Ehrenfest, Paul, 6:239–240
eighteenth-nineteenth centuries, 16:134
Einstein, Albert, 6:261–262, 16:136–137
Epstein, Paul Sophus, 6:476
Feynman, Richard Phillips, 7:6
Frank, Ilya Mikhailovich, 7:181
Frank, Philip, 7:193
Gross, David J., 8:95
Harari, Ḥayyim, 8:344–345
Haskalah, 16:134

Hecht, Selig, 8:751
Heeger, Alan J., 8:752
Hertz, Gustav, 9:47–48
Ḥibat Allah, abu al-Barakāt ben Alī al-Baghdādī, 9:93
Infeld, Leopold, 9:779–780
Israel, 11:76–77, 16:137–141
London, Fritz, 13:184–185
Low, William Ze'ev, 13:233–234
Michelson, Albert Abraham, 14:173–174
Nazi Germany, 16:136–137
Ne'eman, Yuval, 15:54–55
nineteenth–twentieth centuries, 16:134–136
Rabi, Isidor Isaac, 17:33
Rabinovich, Yehudah Leib, 17:38
Racah, Giulio, 17:44–45
radio astronomy, Penzias, Arno Allan, 15:756
Reines, Frederick, 17:207
Richter, Burton, 17:290
Rosen, Moshe, 17:429
Rotbla, Sir Joseph, 17:476
Rotenberg, Mattie Levi, 17:477–478
Saxon, David, 18:86–87
Schawlow, Arthur L., 18:112
Schwinger, Julian Seymour, 18:196–197
Schwartz, Melvin, 18:187
Simon, Sir Francis Eugene, 18:611
sixteenth–seventeenth centuries, 16:134
U.S.
Estermann, Immanuel, 6:515
Franck, James, 7:176
Hofstadter, Robert, 9:313
Karle, Jerome, 11:809
Lee, David, 12:597
vacuum, Dushman, Saul, 6:65
women, 16:136–137
Physiology. *See* Medicine
Piacenza (Italy), 16:**142**
Piamenta, Moshe, 16:**142**
The Pianist (Polanski), 9:446, 16:210
Piaseczno (Poland), 16:**142**
Piatigorsky, Gregor, 16:**142**
Piatra-Neamt (Romania), 16:**142–143**
Piattelli, Phinehas Hai ben Menahem. *See* Anau, Phinehas Ḥai ben Menahem
Piattoli, Scipione, 16:**143**
PICA (Palestine Jewish Colonization Association), 2:26, 16:**143**
Picard, Edmond, 16:**144**
Picard, Jacob, 16:**144**

Picard, Leo Yehuda, 16:**144**

Picart, Bernard, 16:**144–145**

Picciotto, Elijah, 16:145

Picciotto, Ḥai Moses, 16:145

Picciotto, Hillel, 16:145

Picciotto, Hillel Ḥayyim, 16:145

Picciotto, James, 16:145

Picciotto, Joseph, 16:145, 346

Picciotto, Moses ben Ezra, 16:145

Picciotto, Moses Haim, 16:145

Picciotto, Raphael, 16:145

Picciotto family, 16:**145**, 346

Picho, Azariah. See Figo, Azariah

Picho, Joseph, 16:**145**

Pick, Alois, 16:**145–146**

Pick, Ernst Peter, 16:**146**

Pick, Ḥayyim Hermann, 16:**146**

Pick, Isaiah. See Berlin, Isaiah ben Judah Loeb

Pick, Jiří Robert, 16:**146**

Pico della Mirandola, Giovanni, 1:279, 11:671–672, 16:133–134, **146–147**

Picon, Molly, 16:**147**

Picquart, Georges, 6:18–19

Picquigny, Baron of. See Calmer, Moses Eliezer Liefmann

Pidyon ha-ben, 7:46–47

Pidyon shevuyim. See Captives, ransoming of

A Piece of the Pie: Blacks and White Immigrants since 1880 (Liberson), 18:733

Piedmont (Italy), 16:**147–148**

Piekarz, Mendel, 11:684

Piera, Solomon da. See Da Piera, Solomon ben Meshullam

Da Piera, Meshullam ben Solomon. See De Piera, Meshullam ben Solomon

Pierce, William, 15:79

Pierleone, Peter. See Anacletus II

Pierleoni, Baruch, 16:148

Pierleoni, Leo, 16:148

Pierleoni, Pietro di Leone, 16:148

Pierleoni family, 16:**148**

Pierre-Bloch, Jean, 16:**148**

Pierre de Nostra-Donna, 15:314

Piésni Salomona (Ujejski), 18:761

Piestany (Slovakia), 16:**148–149**

Piety and the pious, 12:537, 16:83, **149–150**

   Abraham ben Moses ben Maimon, 1:308

   display of, 2:132

   Eleazar ben Judah of Worms, 6:304–305

   Ḥasidei Ashkenaz, 8:389

   Ḥasidim, 8:390–391

Pigeons. See Doves

Piggul. See Abomination

Pigit, Samuel ben Shemaria, 16:**151**

Pigs, 16:**150–151**

Pi-Hahiroth (Egypt), 16:**151–152**

Piḥas, Yehudah. See Kohn, Leo

Pijade, Mośa, 15:667, 16:**152**

Pike, Lipman Emanuel, 16:**152**

Pikku'aḥ nefesh, 16:**152–153**

Pilate, Pontius. See Pontius Pilate

Pilch, Judah, 2:47, 9:368, 16:**153**

Pilchik, Ely Emanuel, 16:**153–154**

Pilderwasser, Joshua. See Weisser, Joshua

Pilev (Poland). See Pulawy (Poland)

Pilevsky, Meir. See Pa'il, Meir

Pilgrimages, 16:**154–158**

   archaeology, 2:391

   Christian, 16:156–157

   Christian to Jerusalem, 11:220–221, 222

   Elkanah, 6:357

   Erez Israel, 10:817–818

   Muslim, 10:90

   pilgrim accounts, 16:157–158

   pilgrim festivals, 16:158–159

   post-Temple period, 16:155–156

   Second Temple period, 16:154–155

Pilgrim festivals, 16:**158–159**

   mourning during, 18:446

   sacrifices, 17:646–647

   Second Temple, 19:621

   Shavuot, 18:422–423

   Shir ha-Ma'alot, 18:489

   See also Festivals

Pilichowski, Leopold, 16:**159**

Pillar of cloud and pillar of fire, 16:**161**

The Pillar of Fire. See Ammud ha-Esh

Pillars, 16:**159–161**

Pillory punishment, 9:745

Pilpul, 1:532, 2:658–659, 12:493, 16:**161–163**

Pilsen (Czech Republic), 16:**163**

Pilsudski, Józef, 4:110, 14:490, 16:**163–164**

Piltene (Latvia), 5:245

Pina, Jacob, 16:**164**

Pinanski, Abraham, 16:**164**

Pincas, Israel, 16:**164**

Pinchasoff, Solomon Babajan, 11:557

Pincherle, Alberto. See Moravia, Alberto

Pincherle, Leone, 16:345

Pincherle, Marc, 16:**164**

Pinchik, Pierre, 16:**165**

Pinck, Bernard D., 15:677

Pincus, Barry Alan. See Manilow, Barry

Pincus, Gregory Goodwin, 16:**165**

Pincus, Jules. See Pascin, Jules

Pincus, Louis Arieh, 16:**165**

Pinczow (Poland), 16:**165**

Pine, 16:**165–166**, vol. 16: color insert

Pineda, Juan de, 16:**166**

Pinel, Duarte. See Usque, Abraham

Pineles, Hirsch Mendel ben Solomon, 16:**166**

Pineles, Samuel, 16:**166–167**

Pineles, Shemuel Yeshayahu. See Penueli, Shemuel Yeshayahu

Pinelo family, 12:554, 13:21

Pines, Jehiel Michael. See Pines, Yehiel Michael

Pines, Meyer Isser, 16:**167**

Pines, Noah, 16:**167**

Pines, Shlomo, 16:**167**

Pines, Yehiel Michael, 16:**167–168**

Pinheiro, Moses, 16:**168–169**

Pinhel, Duarte. See Usque, Abraham

Pinkas, 2:406, 4:71, 72, 16:**169**

Pinkas, David Zvi, 16:**169**

Pinkas ha-sheilhut, 18:447

Pinkel, Benjamin, 16:**169**

Pinkerfeld, Anda. See Amir, Anda

Pinkowitz, Morris. See Halle, Morris

Pinner, Adolf, 16:**169**

Pinner, Ephraim Moses ben Alexander Susskind, 16:**169**

Pinner, Felix, 16:**169–170**

Pinner, Moritz, 16:**170**

Pinochet, Augusto, 4:642, 644

Pins, Jacob, 16:**170**

Pinsk (Belarus), 16:**170–172**

Pinsker, J.L., 11:700

Pinsker, Leon, 9:247, 16:**173–174**

   Levanda, Lev Osipovich, 12:677

   Odessa Committee, 15:382

Pinsker, M.L., 12:8

Pinsker, Simḥah, 16:**174–175**

Pinski, David, 1:399, 16:**175–176**, 19:680

Pinsky, Robert, 16:**176–177**

Pinson, Koppel S., 16:**177**

Pinter, Harold, 6:438, 439, 440, 16:**177–178**

Pinto, Aaron Adolf de, 12:552, 16:178

Pinto, Abraham ben Reuben, 16:178

Pinto, Abraham de, 16:**178**

Pinto, de, family (Netherlands), 16:**178**

Pinto, Isaac (1720-1791), 16:**178**

Pinto, Isaac de (1717-1787), 2:109, 4:70, 16:**179**

Pinto, Josiah ben Joseph, 2:130, 16:**179**

Pinto, R. Abraham, 16:178

Pinto, R. Ḥayyim, 16:178

Pinto, R. Jacob, 16:178

Pinto, Vivian de Sola, 16:179

Pinto Delgado, João, 16:**179–180**

Pinto families (Morocco), 16:**178**

Pinto family (U.S.), 5:161

Pioneers

    Calof, Rachel Bella Kahn, 4:375–376

    De Cordova, Jacob, 5:529–530

    Hankin, Yehoshua, 8:324

    Levy, Moses Elias, 12:754

    Sapir, Eliyahu, 18:37–38

Pioneers of Liberty, 18:710

Pioneer Women, 4:406–407, 16:**180**

Piotrkow (Poland), 16:**180–181**

"The Pious". *See* Louis (Kings of France)

Piove di Sacco (Italy), 16:**181**

Pipano, David, 4:270

Piperno Beer, Sergio, 16:**181–182**

Pipes, Richard Edgar, 16:**182**

Piratin, Phil, 16:342

Pirḥei Ẓafon (Lebensohn), 8:725

Pirkeh Avot, 6:525

    Jacob ben Korshai, 11:34

Pirkei de Rabbi Eliezer, 6:323, 7:11, 16:**182–183**

Pirkei Eliyahu (Levita), 12:731

Pirkei Rabbenu ha-Kadosh. See Aggadat Bereshit

Pirkei Rudorfer (Barash), 3:135

Pirkheimer, Willibald, 4:70

Pirkoi ben Baboi, 8:262, 16:**183**

Pirogov, Nikolai, 16:**183**

Piryatin (Ukraine), 16:**183–184**

Pisa (Italy), 16:**184**

Pisa, Abram da, 16:185

Pisa, da, family, 16:**184–185**

Pisa, Daniel da, 16:185

Pisa, Emanuele da, 16:185

Pisa, Franco, 16:185

Pisa, Giuseppe da, 16:185

Pisa, Giusta da, 16:184–185

Pisa, Isaac da, 16:185

Pisa, Isaac di Manuele da Rimini da, 16:184–185

Pisa, Jehiel Vitale da, 16:185

Pisa, Luigi della Torre da, 16:185

Pisa, Luigi Israel da, 16:185

Pisa, Matassia di Sabato da, 16:184

Pisa, Moses-Aron, 16:185

Pisa, Salomon da, 16:185

Pisa, Samuel da, 7:40–41

Pisa, Simone Samuel da, 16:185

Pisa, Ugo da, 16:185

Pisa, Vitale Jehiel da, 16:184

Pisa, Vitale Jehiel Nissim da, 16:185

Piscator Bible, 3:630, 631

A Pisces. See Ryby

Pisco, Seraphine Eppstein, 16:**185–186**

Pisetzky, Naomi, 11:463

Pisgah (ancient Israel), 16:**186**

Pi Shenayim (Asher ben Jehiel), 6:352

Pisk, Paul Amadeus, 16:**186**

Piskei ha-Rosh (Asher ben Jehiel), 2:564, 4:773

Pissarro, Camille, 16:**186–187**

Pissarro, Lucien, 16:187

Pistachios, 16:**187**, vol. 16: color insert

Pister, Hermann, 4:241, 242

"Pistol Pete." *See* Sampras, Pete

Pistorius, Johannes, 16:**187**

Pistrak, Moses M., 6:161

Pistyan. *See* Piestany

Pita, Jan, 1:312

Piṭah, 16:476

Pitch Dark (Adler), 1:406

Pithei Teshuvah (Eisenstadt), 6:270

Pithom (Egypt), 16:**187–188**

Pithu et ha-Sha'ar (Molodowsky). *See Open the Gate* (Molodowsky)

Pitigrilli, 16:**188**

Pitron Ḥalomot. See Mefasher Ḥelmin

Pitshe Odesser. *See* Abrass, Osias

Pittsburgh (PA), 16:**188–190**

Pittsburgh Pirates, 6:20–21

Pittsburgh Platform (1885), 6:193, 258, 14:471, 544, 16:**190–191**

Pittsburgh Platform (1999), 6:203

Pittum ha-Ketoret, 16:**191**

Pity. *See* Charity; Compassion; Mercy

Pius IV, 16:375

Pius V, 4:48–49, 16:375

Pius VI, 16:376

Pius VII, 16:376

Pius VIII, 16:376

Pius IX, 14:513, 16:376–377

Pius X, 16:191, 377

Pius XI, 11:384, 16:**191–192**, 376, 377

Pius XII, 9:371–372, 11:379, 384, 15:695, 16:**192**, 377

    Holocaust, response to, 9:371–372, 402, 17:415–416

Pius XII and the Third Reich (Friedlaender), 9:417

Piyyut, 9:212, 14:650–653, *651, 652, 653*, 16:**192–209**

    Adonim ben Nisan ha-Levi, 1:413

    collections, 16:195

    Day of Atonement, 5:489

    for Day of Atonement, 5:489

    Eleazar ben Ḥalfon ha-Kohen, 6:301

    Eleazar ben Jacob ha-Bavli, 6:302

    Eleazar ben Judah of Worms, 6:304

    Eleazar Kallir, 11:743–744

    Elijah ben Shemaiah, 6:340

    England, 13:783

    history of, 16:192–193

    Jacob ben Ḥayyim Joseph Elyashar, 6:371

    Jerusalem in, 11:214–215

    of Judah Halevi, 11:495

    Judeo-Persian, 11:554

    Kallir, Eleazar, 11:743–744

    Kara, Joseph, 11:783–784

    kerovot, 18:598

    language of, 8:651–653

    liturgy, 13:132

    Menahem ben Jacob, 14:21–22

    Moses, 14:543

    North African music, 1:438, 439

    Omnam Ken, 15:422

    paytanim, poets, 16:196*t*–202*t*

    Phinehas ben Jacob ha-Kohen, 16:116

    pizmon and, 16:210

    Provençal, 10:43

    rhyme and meter, 16:193–194

    Saadiah Gaon, 17:613

    for Shavuot, 13:784

    Simeon bar Isaac, 18:592–593

    Solomon ben Judah, 18:770–771

    Solomon ben Judah ha-Bavli, 18:771

    Solomon Suliman ben Amar, 18:773

    transmission of, 13:627–628

    types of, 16:193–194

    Yannai, 21:280–282

    Yose ben Yose, 21:398

    yoẓerot, 21:406–407

    See also Hebrew prosody; Poetry

Pizarnik, Alejandra, 16:**209–210**

Pizei Bagrut (Bartov), 3:181

Pizmon, 16:**210**

Pizzighettone, David, 4:52

Place. *See* Space and Place

La Place de L'Etoile (Modiano), 14:410

Places of Remembrance, 9:431

Plachy, Sylvia, 16:**210**

Placzek, Abraham, 16:**210**

Placzek, Baruch Jacob, 16:210

Plague of locusts, 13:154
Plagues of Egypt, 6:614, 16:**210–214**, 211*t*
 Aaron and, 1:208, 209
 of firstborn, 16:29
 louse, 13:226–227
 Moses, 14:524, 527
"Plagues of Egypt" (poem), 14:540
Plain, Belva, 16:**214**
Plaisir de la Musique (Roland-Manuel). *See* Roland-Manuel
Plamenac, Dragan, 16:**214**
Plamondon, Joseph Edward, 4:397
Plane hijackings, 6:447–448
Planet of the Jews (Gaubart), 18:200
Plane trees, 16:**215**, vol. 16: color insert
A Planned Economy or Free Enterprise: The Lessons of History (Lipson), 13:76
Planning and construction, 16:**215–219**
 laws of
  biblical, 16:215–216
  Israel, 16:218–219
  Jerusalem, 16:217–218
  talmudic, 16:216–218
 synagogues, 16:216
Plantavit de la Pause, Jean, 16:**219**
Plantavitius. *See* Plantavit de la Pause, Jean
Plantin, Christophe, 6:67, 12:601, 16:**219**
Plants, Biblical and Mishnaic, 6:77, 16:**219–225**, 220, 220*t*–225*t*
 acorns, vol. 16: color insert
 almonds, vol. 16: color insert
 almond tree, vol. 16: color insert
 anise, vol. 16: color insert
 apple blossoms, vol. 16: color insert
 balm, vol. 16: color insert
 barley, vol. 16: color insert
 briar, vol. 16: color insert
 broad bean blossoms, vol. 16: color insert
 carob pods, vol. 16: color insert
 cattails, vol. 16: color insert
 cedar, vol. 16: color insert
 citron, vol. 16: color insert
 coriander, vol. 16: color insert
 cumin, vol. 16: color insert
 dates and date palms, vol. 16: color insert
 flax, vol. 16: color insert
 garlic, vol. 16: color insert
 gourds, vol. 16: color insert

hemlock (gall), vol. 16: color insert
leeks, vol. 16: color insert
lentils, vol. 16: color insert
lilies, vol. 16: color insert
mallow, vol. 16: color insert
mandrakes, vol. 16: color insert
millet (grain), vol. 16: color insert
millet (sorghum), vol. 16: color insert
mint, vol. 16: color insert
mulberrries, vol. 16: color insert
mustard, vol. 16: color insert
myrrh, vol. 16: color insert
nettles, vol. 16: color insert
oak tree, vol. 16: color insert
olive tree, vol. 16: color insert
onions, vol. 16: color insert
pine tree, vol. 16: color insert
pistachios, vol. 16: color insert
plane tree, vol. 16: color insert
reeds, vol. 16: color insert
rue, vol. 16: color insert
saffron, vol. 16: color insert
tamarisk, vol. 16: color insert
thistles, vol. 16: color insert
thorns, vol. 16: color insert
weeds, vol. 16: color insert
white poplars, vol. 16: color insert
willow, vol. 16: color insert
 See also Botany
The Plants and Animals of the Mishnah (Feliks), 14:331
Plaques, House of Ivory, 2:493
Plasencia (Spain), 16:**225**
Plaskow, Judith, 16:111
Plaszow, 16:**225–226**
Platanus orientalis. See Plane trees
Platek, Felka, 15:352
Plates for Passover and Seder use, 15:682
Platkes, Elijah. *See* Rivlin, Elijah
Plato and Platonism, 16:**226–227**
 Arabanel, Isaac ben Judah, 1:279, 280
 Cartesian method applied to works of, 15:191
 Crescas critique, 5:287
 dualism, 6:29
 interpretations, Philo Judaeus, 16:62
 Islamic interpretation, 6:710
Plato of Tivoli, 1:293
Platt, Polly, 4:34
Plaut, Hezekiah Feivel, 16:**227**
Plaut, Hugo Carl, 16:**227–228**

Plaut, W. Gunther, 3:625, 16:**228**, 17:174
Plavnik, Samuil Yefimovich. *See* Byadulya-Yasakar, Zmitrok
Plays and playwrights
 Aloni, Nissim, 8:723
 Alterman, Nathan, 8:720
 Austria, Hofmannsthal, Hugo von, 9:313
 Avi-Shaul, Mordekhai, 8:719
 Baazov, Herzl, 3:14
 Bacri, Jean-Pierres, 3:41
 Baranga, Aurel, 3:133
 Barrios, Daniel Levi De, 3:176–177
 Bar-Yosef, Y., 8:720
 Beer, Michael, 3:253
 Behrman, Samuel Nathaniel, 3:264–265
 Bernard, Tristan, 3:468
 Bernstein, Henri-Leon, 3:479
 Bible's impact on, 3:669
 Bruckner, Ferdinand, 4:220
 Busch, Charles, 4:303
 Chayefsky, Paddy, 4:584–585
 Chilton, Nola, 8:721
 Chocrón, Isaac, 4:657
 Chodorov, Edward, 4:657–658
 Chodorov, Jerome, 4:658
 Claudel, Paul, 4:751
 Eichelbaum, Samuel, 6:245
 Evron, Gilad, 8:722
 Franken, Rose Dorothy Lewin, 7:201–202
 Germany
  Hirschfeld, Georg, 9:137
  Hochhuth, Rolf, 9:299
  Hochwaelder, Fritz, 9:301
 Goldberg, Leah, 8:721
 Gurevitch, Michael, 8:722
 Hall, Owen, 8:277
 Hart, Moss, 8:372
 Háy, Gyulah, 8:474
 Hecht, Ben, 8:750
 Heijermans, Herman, 8:764–765
 Hellman, Lillian Florence, 8:800–801
 Hertz, Henrik, 9:48
 Horovizt, Israel, 9:528
 Horowitz, Danny, 8:722
 Hugó, Károly, 9:579
 Hungary, 11:808
 Israel (state), 10:687
 Jephthah in, 11:123
 Jerusalem in, 11:216–217
 Kalisch, David, 11:736
 Kanin, Garson, 11:763

Karinthy, Ferenc, 11:808
Kotler, Oded, 8:721
Landau, Judah Loeb, 12:463
Langer, Frantisek, 12:479–480
Lapid, Shulamit, 8:723
Laurents, Arthur, 12:527–528
Lawson, John Howard, 12:547
Lerner, Moti, 8:722–723
Levi, Paolo, 12:691
Levin, Hanoch, 8:721, 722, 723
Levy, Benn Wolfe, 12:747–748
Lewis, Leopold Davis, 12:765
Matmor, Yoram, 8:720
Megged, Aharon, 8:720–721, 722
Miller, Arthur, 14:251–252
Mosinsohn, Y., 8:720
Mundy, Yosef, 8:721
Pinski, David, 16:175
Pinter, Harold, 16:177–178
Purim-shpil, 16:745
Rabinovich, José, 17:37
Raboy, Isaac, 17:44
Racine, Jean, 17:50–51
Ragen, Naomi, 17:64–65
Raphael, John, 17:95
Raphaelson, Samson, 17:96
Refisch, Hans Jose, 17:191
Rice, Elmer Leopold, 17:284–285
Robert, Ludwig, 17:354
Roessler, Carl, 17:367
Rosenvof, Mauricio, 17:444
Rovinsky, Samuel, 17:501
Różewicz, Tadeusz, 17:503–504
Rozenmacher, Germán, 17:503
Rubens, Paul Alfred, 17:510
Rubenstein, Harold Frederick,
    17:516–517
Saul, portrayals of, 18:81, 82
Schisgal, Murray, 18:138
Schnitzler, Arthur, 18:152
Shabtai, Yaakov, 8:722
Silva, Antonio Jose Da, 18:582–
    583
Simon, Neil, 18:614
Singer, Israel Joshua, 18:637
Sobol, Yehoshua, 8:721, 722,
    18:703
Sommo, Judah Leone ben Isaac,
    19:8
Song of Songs, 19:20
Yerushalmi, Rina, 8:722
See also names of specific plays;
    Theater
Pleas, 16:228–231
Pleasure. See Joy
Pledges, 16:231–236
    antichresis, 2:193

debt related, 16:231–234
    mortgaged property, 16:234–236
Plehve, Vyacheslav Konstantinovich
    von, 9:64, 65, 16:236–237
Plessner, Martin, 16:237
Pletten, 16:237
Pleven (Bulgaria), 16:237
PLF. See Palestine Liberation Front
Pliny the Elder, 6:510–511, 16:237–
    238, 18:753
Pliny the Younger, 3:729
Plisetskaya, Maya, 16:238
PLO. See Palestine Liberation
    Organization
PLO (Palestine Liberation
    Organization). See Palestine
    Liberation Organization (PLO)
Plock (Poland), 16:238–239
Ploesti (Romania), 16:239–240
Plonsk (Poland), 16:240–241
The Plot: The Secret Story of the
    Protocols of the Elders of Zion
    (Eisner), 6:278
The Plot against America (Roth), 9:413
Plotinus, 6:373
    form and matter, 7:130
    platonism, 16:226–227
Plotnicka, Frumka, 16:241
Plotsk (Poland). See Plock (Poland)
Plotzki, Meir Dan of Ostrova, 16:241
Plough, Abe, 14:20
Plovdiv (Bulgaria), 16:241–242
Plowing, Erez Israel, 1:483–484
Plummer, Beatrice, 16:343
Plums, 16:242
Plunge (Lithuania), 16:242
Plungian, Mordecai, 16:242
Plungiansky, Mordecai. See Plungian,
    Mordecai
Plungyany (Lithuania). See Plunge
    (Lithuania)
Pluralism, 5:118–120, 17:314–316
    educational, 8:553
    halakhic, 17:330–332
Plutarch, 4:331–332, 16:242–243
Plutocracy and Politics in New York
    City (Almond), 1:683
Plymouth (England), 16:243
Plyushchevka. See Yefingar (Ukraine)
Plywood Minnesota (company), 4:95
Plzeń (Czech Republic). See Pilsen
    (Czech Republic)
Plzen (Czech Republic). See Pilsen
    (Czech Republic)
Pnueli, Amir, 16:243
Po'alei Agudat Israel, 1:507–508,
    11:711, 14:303, 16:243–244

Po'alei Tzion Party (Argentina), 2:435
Po'alei Zion, 4:320, 6:188–189, 712–
    713, 9:286–287, 11:87, 16:244–249,
    18:717
    Austria, 11:780–781, 13:153
    Austro-Hungaria, 16:245
    Borochov, Ber, 4:88–90
    Buxbaum, Nathan, 4:320
    Canada, 4:406
    Fineman, Hayyim, 7:26
    Jewish Legion and, 11:305
    Jewish Social Democratic Party
        and, 11:313, 314
    Palestine (Ottoman), 16:246
    pogram self-defense, 18:262
    post-WW I, 16:247–249
    Russia, 16:244–245
    Schussheim, Aaron Leib, 18:176
    Sejmists and, 11:314, 315
    Shazar, Shneur Zalman, 18:425
    socialism, 18:711
    split of (1920), 18:720
    U.S., 12:419, 16:245–246
    World Socialist Union, 16:246–248
    See also Labor Zionist Alliance
Po'alei Zion Oyf der Shvel (periodical),
    18:425
Pobedonostsev, Konstantin Petrovich,
    15:250, 16:249
Pobezovice na Sumave (Czech
    Republic), 16:249
Pochep (Russia), 16:250
Pocket Books, Inc., 18:177
Pococke, Edward, 2:20, 15:554, 16:250,
    250
Pococke, Richard, 16:250
Pococke, Thomas, 16:250
Podagra (Lucian of Samosata), 13:249
Podgaitsy (Ukraine), 16:250–251
Podhajce. See Podgaitsy
Podhoretz, Norman, 15:225, 16:251
Podkamen (Ukraine), 16:251–252
Podolia (Ukraine), 16:252–253
    Shabbateanism, 7:182–183
Podoloff, Maurice, 16:253
Podolyer, Menakhem. See
    Osherowitch, Mendl
Podvolochisk (Ukraine), 16:253–254
Podzemní město (Poláček), 16:285
Poel, Jacob, 4:63
Poema de la Reyna Ester,
    Lamentaciones del Propheta Jeremias
    y Historia de Rut y varias poesías
    (Pinto), 16:179–180
Poems. See Lider
Poems de la Reyna Esther (Barrios),
    18:295

Poems of a Hermit (Esselin), 6:509
Poems of a Jew (Shapiro), 18:406
Poésie lyrique hébraïque contemporaine (Slouschz), 18:681
Poésies hébraïques de Don Jehouda Abrabanel (Slouschz), 18:681
Poesing (Slovakia). *See* Pezinok (Slovakia)
The Poet and the World (Pinsky), 16:177
Poeta of Valladolid, Juan. *See* Juan de Valladolid
Poetry, 16:**254–278**
  Aaron Ḥakiman, 1:217
  Abbas, Moses Judah ben Meir, 1:232
  Abi Zimra, Isaac Mandil ben Abraham, 1:260
  Abraham ben Daniel, 1:295
  Abraham ben Hillel of Fostat, 1:300
  Ali, 1:658
  Arabanel, Isaac ben Judah, 1:279
  Arabic, 15:473
    post 1948, 10:735–736
    medieval, 5:428
  Austria, Lipiner, Siegfried, 13:64
  Austrian
    Beer-Hofmann, Richard, 3:254
    Frankl, Ludwig August, 7:213
  Babylonian, 13:602
  biblical, 3:76–81, 16:254–262
    Psalms, 5:453
  Book of Jashar, 4:69
  Bulgarian, 16:21
  Canadian, 4:423–424, 424
    Layton, Irving, 12:557–558
  children's, 4:627
  Chile, Rosenmann-Taub, David, 17:449
  Christian, *Odes of Solomon*, 18:766
  Czechoslovakia, Hoffmann, Camill, 9:310
  Denmark, Hertz, Henrik, 9:48
  Dutch
    Correa, Isabel de, 5:225
    Hertzveld-Hijmans, Esthella, 9:50
  English
    Abse, Dannie, 1:332
    Hamburger, Michael, 8:298
    Levy, Amy, 12:747
    Rosenberg, Isaac, 17:436–437
  ethical, 6:526
  Favorite Poem Project, 16:176
  France
    Bekhor Shor, Joseph ben Isaac, 3:276–277

Hertz, Henri, 9:48
French
  Franck, Henri, 7:176
  Le Fèvre de la Boderie, Guy, 12:601
  medieval, 11:33–34
  nineteenth century, 14:43
  twentieth century, 11:6
German
  Bassan, Abraham Hezekiah ben Jacob, 3:206–208
  Feld, Isaac, 6:745
  Hasenclever, Walter, 8:380
  Hiller, Kurt, 9:116
  Jacobowski, 11:45
  Kaleko, Mascha, 11:733
  Kara, Avigdor ben Isaac, 11:783
  Lasker-Schueler, Else, 12:498
  medieval, 5:468
  Rubiner, Ludwig, 17:514
Greek
  Eliyia, Joseph, 6:355–356
  Homer, 9:506
Hellenistic Judaism and, 3:660
Hungarian
  Emöd, Tamas, 6:396
  Kiss, József, 12:201–202
  Somly Zoltan, 19:7
imagery and metaphor, 16:259–261
impressionist, 4:138
introspective movement, 4:6
Iranian Jewish, 10:13
Israel
  Bernstein, Ori, 3:483
  Hefer, Ḥayim, 8:752
Israel Arab, 10:733
Italian, 10:790–792
  Concio, Joseph ben Gerson, 5:133
  da Ponte, 5:433
  Fiorentino, Salomone, 7:41
  Levi-Perotti, Giustina, 12:724
  Rieti, Moses ben Isaac da, 17:297–298
Jacob in, 11:23
Jerusalem in, 11:214–215, 217, 224
of Judah Halevi, 11:494–497
Judeo-Persian, 11:551, 554–556
kabbalistic, 12:408
Kalai, Joseph b. Jacob, 11:728
Kaleko, Mascha, 11:733
Kallir, Eleazar, 11:743–744
Kaminer, Isaac, 11:755
Kaminka, 11:756

Kamson, Ya'akov David, 11:758
Karaite, medieval, 5:428
Ladino, 12:432–433
Lazarus, Emma, 12:560–561
Lithuanian, Kamson, Ya'akov, 11:758
liturgical, 11:743–744
  Abun, 1:346
  Buchner, Ze'ev Wolf ben David ha-Kohen, 4:243
  Byzantine empire, 4:326
  tenth century, 11:31
liturgy, 4:243
Ludwig, Reuben, 13:251
Luria, Isaac, 13:265
Luzzatto, Moses Ḥayyim, 13:282–283, 285
medieval, 13:95–96, 16:262–270
  Al-Andalus, 16:262–266
  England, 16:269–270
  France and Germany, 16:269
  Italian, 16:268–269
  maqāma, 16:266
  neo-Hebrew poetry of, 3:662
  Spain and Provence, 16:266–268, 270
meter and rhythm, 16:258–259
metrical, 14:656–657
modern biblical criticism and, 3:655
paradigmatic, syntagmatic, 16:257–258
parallelism, 16:256–258
Persian
  Albaradani, Joseph, 1:586
  liturgical, Al-Bargeloni, Isaac ben Reuben, 1:586
  Turkish, Alceh, Matilde, 1:599
Polish, 11:89
  Karmel, Ilona, 11:812–813
  Lec, Stanislaw Jerzy, 12:593
  Luboshitzki, Aaron, 13:246
  Peiper, Tadeusz, 15:713
  Różewicz, Tadeusz, 17:503–504
proverbs, 16:640
Rabinovich, José, 17:37
Rabon, Israel, 17:44
Raboy, Isaac, 17:44
Radnóti, Miklos, 17:55–56
Raḥel, 17:68
Raisin, Jacob Zalman, 17:74
Ratosh, Yonathan, 17:113–114
Ravikovitch, Dalia, 17:121–122
Ravitch, Melech, 17:123

Regelson, Abraham, 17:187

Reich, Asher, 17:196

Reichard, Piroska, 17:199

Reisen, Abraham, 17:211

Remos, Moses ben Isaac, 17:218

repetition and pattern, 16:261–262

Rodin, Elisha, 17:364

Rodker, John, 17:364–365

Rokeaḥ, David, 17:372

Rolnick, Joseph, 17:373

Romanelli, Samuel Aaron, 17:374

Romanian, 17:400–401

    Iacobescu, D., 9:655

    Rudich, Mayer, 17:520–521

Romano, Samuel, 17:405

Rosenblatt, H., 17:440–441

Rosenfeld, Morris, 17:446–447

Rossena, Daniel ben Samuel of, 17:471

Rubin, Hadassah, 17:512

Rubinstein, Joseph, 17:517–518

Russian

    Kannegiser, Leonid Akimovich, 11:766

    Kanovich, Grigory, 11:766

Samuel ibn ʿAdiyā, 17:778

Santob de Carrión, 18:29–30

scholarship, modern, 16:270–277

Shimoni, David, 18:482–483

Shlonsky, Abraham, 18:494–496

Spain

    Barrios, Daniel Levi De, 3:176–177

    Benveniste, Sheshet ben Isaac ben Joseph, 3:385

    Ibn Ezra, Abraham ben Meir, 9:665–666

    Ibn Ezra, Moses ben Jacob, 9:674–675

    Isaacson, Jose, 10:57

    León, Luis de, 12:645

    medieval, 13:685–686

Spanish-Hebrew, 10:35–36, 41

sweatshop, 19:335–336

Teixeira, Bento, 17:45

terseness, 16:258–259

Turkey, Benveniste, Joshua Raphael Ben Israel, 3:384

Ukrainian

    Kaminer, Isaac, 11:755

    Kariv, Avraham, 11:808

U.S.

    Hollander, John, 9:322

    Moïse, Penina, 14:421

    Nemerov, Howard, 15:68

    Rich, Adrienne, 17:285–286

Rukeyser, Muriel, 17:528

twentieth century, 6:724–725, 746

Yugoslavian, twentieth century, 5:444, 6:747

See also Hebrew prosody; Piyyut; Psalms; Yiddish poetry

The Poet's Return to his Tools. See Intoarcerea poetului la uneltele sale

Poety Izrailya (collection), 18:686

Pogranichniki (Bill-Belotserkovski), 3:699

Pogrebin, Letty Cottin, 16:278–279

Pogrebishchenski (Poland), 16:279

Pogroms, 16:279–282

    1880s, 16:279–280

    1903-1906, 16:280–281

    1917-1921, 16:281–282

    accounts of, 13:785

    Aden, 1:389

    Belarus, 11:735–736, 14:417

    Bialystok (Poland), 3:567

    Birzula, 3:724

    Brailov, 4:119

    Bratslav, 4:134

    Bryansk, 4:229

    "cold pogrom," anti-Jewish boycotts regarded as, 4:110

    Egypt, Roman era, 16:28

    Endecja party in Kalisz, 11:740

    Hep!Hep!, 8:811–812

    Iraq, 10:19

    Kamenets-Podolski, 11:753

    migration and, 9:243

    Nezhin, 15:246

    Nikolayev, 15:265

    Nuremberg, 15:348

    Ochberg, Isaac, 15:375

    Odessa, 15:379–380

    Orsha, 15:487

    Romania, 5:433

    Russia, 6:558

        Alexander, 1:620

        by Cossacks, 13:763

        Ukraine, 14:13

    Russia/Romania, 10:826

    Second Aliyah and, 10:334

    self-defense, 18:261–263

    Sheftel, Mikhail, investigations by, 18:433

    Ukraine, 1:610, 16:17, 279–281, 18:686

        Chernigov, 4:596

        Chernobyl, 4:597

        Mogilev-Podolski, 14:418

Pohl, Baruch. See Pollini, Bernhard

Pohl, Oswald, 16:282

Pohorbishch. See Pogrebishchenski

Pohorelice (Czech Republic), 16:282

Pohrlitz. See Pohorelice

Pointers, Torah, 20:52–53

Poison, 16:283–284

Poitiers (France), 16:284

Poitou (France), 1:730, 2:175, 16:284

Der Pojaz (Franzos), 7:219

Poki, Judah ben Eliezer Chelebi, 16:284–285

Pol. See Beans

Poláček, Karel, 16:285

Polacco, Vittorio, 16:285

Polachek, Sender, 16:285

Polachek, Solomon, 16:285–286

Polachek, Victor Henry, 16:286

Polack, Joel Samuel, 16:286

Polack family. See Polak family

Polak, Carel, 16:345

Polak, Gabriel Isaac, 2:113, 16:286

Polak, Henri, 16:286–287, 345

Polak, Jacob Eduard, 16:287

Polak, Leonard, 16:287

Polak, Moritz, 12:553

Polak and Sons, 3:75

Polakevich, Mattityahu Moshe. See Shoham, Mattityahu Moshe

Polak family, 4:70

Poland, 16:287–326, 290, 292, 294

    antisemitism, 1:508, 2:217, 220, 229, 4:445, 11:102, 12:594–595, 16:317–318

        Aleksander Jagiellonczyk, 1:610

        anti-Jewish laws, 15:403

        Bialystok, 3:567, 6:45

        blood libel, 3:778

        boycotts, anti-Jewish, 4:109–110

        Breslau, 18:319

        Capistrano, John of, 4:445

        censorship, 4:540

        Checiny, 4:586

        Chelm, 4:588

        Chmielnicki, Bogdan, 4:654–656

        Chmielnik, 4:656, 657

        Chryzanow, 4:707

        Ciechanow, 4:725

        Cracow, 5:261–262

        Dmowski, Roman, 5:723–724

        Endecja party, 6:402–403, 11:740

        Haller's Army, 8:281

        Jedrzejow, 11:102

Poland, *continued*

Kalisz, 11:740

late twentieth century, 16:322–323

Legnica, 12:610

Leszno, 12:667

literature, 16:335–338

Mlawa, 14:395–396

Nara, 14:779

OZON, 15:558

Pilsudski, Józef, 16:163–164

Plock, 9:*465*

post-WW II, 16:319–320, 321

Reformation to WW I, 11:117–118, 16:300–305

Rozwój, 17:505–506

Samuel Commission, 17:775

Skarga, Piotr, 18:657

cultural and social life, 16:293–296, 298–299, 299*t*, 310*t*

archives, 2:408

artisans, 5:268, 269, 269*t*

assimilation, 4:318, 5:351–352, 6:265, 16:302

censorship, 4:540

community, nature of, 5:108, 110, 9:222

cooperatives, 5:206, 207

education, Jewish, 5:261, 6:182–183, 186

emancipation, 4:164, 6:382–383

ḥazakah, 8:490

intercommunal institutions, 11:88

Jewish dress, 6:15–16, 17

Jewish Historical Institute, 2:408, 411, 11:291, 18:723

Jewish identity in, 11:298–299

journalism, 11:467, 779, 16:497–498

language, biblical translation, 3:634, 16:334–335

Lithuanian Jewry, 13:121

motion pictures, 14:576–577

museums, 14:630

synagogue architecture, 19:373, *373*

tobacco trade, 20:6

yeshiva education method, 5:468

Yiddish education, 6:188

Yiddish theater in interwar period, 19:682

early settlement, 4:45, 11:738–740

economic affairs, 16:293, 298, 302, 304

arenda, 2:423

bankers, moneylenders, 3:117, 12:770, 14:443

brokers, 4:204

chemical industry, 4:591

coinage, 14:299, 300

fur trade, 7:313

Israeli relations, 16:323–325

leather industry and trade, 12:577

peddling, 15:709, 710

wine and liquor trade, 21:83–85

Holocaust, 4:323, 21:182

Aambrow, 21:450

Aleksandrow Lodzki, 1:611

Bedzin, 3:249–250

Belchatow, 3:279

Belzyce, 3:312

Biała Podlaska, 3:560

Bialystok, 3:567–570, 567*t*, *568*

Bialystok district, 16:312–313

Bielsko, 3:689–690

Bilgoraj, 3:698

Bochnia, 4:26

Breslau, 4:165

Brzeg, 4:230

Brzesk Kujawksi, 4:230

Brzeziny, 4:231

Buchach, 4:238

Bydgoszcz, 4:323, 16:308

Chelm, 4:588–589

Chiciny, 4:586, 588

Chmielnicki massacres, 4:654–656

Chmielnik, 4:657

Chorzów, 4:669

Chryzanow, 4:707

Ciechanow, 4:726, 16:308–309

cinema, 9:444

Cracow district, 5:262–263, 16:311

Dabrowa Gornicza, 5:375

David-Gorodok, 5:473–474

Disna, 5:683–684

Divin, 5:703

documentation, resource centers, 9:428

Dvorzetsky, Mark Meir, 6:74

Dzialosyce, 6:80

educational visits, 14:485–486

Elblag, 6:291

Endecja party, 6:402–403

Gabin, 7:320

Galicia district, 16:311–312

Gdansk, 7:405

general government, 16:309–314

ghettos, 16:308, 309–313

Gliwice, 7:640

Glogau, 7:641, 18:578

Glubokoye, 7:642–648

Gniezno, 7:650

Gora, Kalwaria, 7:760

Gorlice, 7:780

Gorzow Wielkopolski, 7:784

Gostynin, 8:6–7

Grajewo, 8:30

Grodzisk Mazowiecki, 8:92

Grodzisk Wielkopolski, 8:93

Grojec, 7:760

Halicz, 8:273

historiography, 9:416

Hrubieszow, 9:574

Inowroclaw, 9:790, 16:307–308

Israeli Holocaust study tours, 9:456

Izbica Lubelska, 10:824

Janow Lubelski, 11:79–80

Jaroslaw, 11:89

Jaslo, 11:90

Jedrzejow, 11:102

Jewish participation in military service, 14:244–245

Kalisz, 11:738–740

Kaluszyn, 11:751

Kielce, 3:435, 9:374, 12:147

Kletsk, 12:230

Klock, 12:250

Klodawa, 12:232

Kock, 12:250

Kolberg, 12:272

Kolo, 12:278

Konin, 12:287

Konskie, 12:288

Konskowola, 12:288

Kornik, 12:314

Kosov, 12:320–321

Kozienice, 12:331

Kozle, 12:332

Krasnik, 12:338–339

Krasnystaw, 12:333, 339

Krosno, 12:372–373

Krotoszyn, 12:374

Krynki, 12:376

Krzepice, 12:377

Kutno, 12:399

Lachva, 12:425–426

Lancut, 12:455–456

Lask, 12:496

Lebork, 12:592

Leczna, 12:594

Leczyca, 12:595

Legnica, 12:610

Leszno, 12:667

Lezajsk, 12:772

Lipno, 13:68–69

Lithuania, Belorus districts, 16:313–314

Lodz, 5:53, 7:575, 9:467, 469, 470–471, 476–478, 13:158–160, 16:307–308

Lomza, 13:179

Losice, 13:211

Lowicz, 13:236

Lubaczow, 13:239

Lubartow, 13:240

Lublin, 13:244, 16:310–311

Lubraniec, 13:246

Lukow, 13:255–256

Lutomiersk, 13:272–273

Lyck, 13:294

Makow Mazowiecki, 13:420

memorials, 9:430

Miedzyrzec Podlask, 14:204–205

Mielec, 14:205

Minsk Mazowiecki, 14:298

Mlawa, 14:396

Narol, 14:782

Nasielsk, 14:787

Nowy Dwor Mazowiecki, 15:325

Nowy Sacz, 15:326

occupation districts, 16:306–309

Olesnica, 15:403

Olkusz, 15:408–409

Opatow, 15:437–438

Opoczno, 15:440–441

Opole Lubelskie, 15:441

Ostroleka, 15:512

Ostrowiec, 15:513–514

Oswiecim, 12:465, 15:515

Otwock, 15:546

Ozorkow, 15:558–559

Pabianice, 15:561–562

Pale of Settlement, 15:577

Parczew, 15:631–632

partisans, 15:666–667, 16:316–317

Piaseczno, 16:142

Pinczow, 16:165

Piotrkow, 16:181

Plock, 16:239

Plonsk, 16:241

Pogrebishchenski, 16:259, 279

Polish-Jewish relations, 16:317–318

Poznan, 16:307–308, 432

Przedborz, 16:659

Przemysl, 16:660

Przeworsk, 16:660

Przysucha, 16:660–661, 661

Przytyk, 16:662

Pulawy, 16:731, 732

Pultusk, 16:732

Radom, 16:311–312, 17:56–57

Radomsko, 17:57–58

Radymno, 17:60

Radzymin, 17:61

Radzyn, 17:61

Rawicz, 17:125

religions, 16:303t

Ropczyce, 17:420

Rozwadow, 17:505

Rymanow, 17:602

Rypin, 17:602–603

Rzeszow, 17:604

Sandomierz, 18:17

Sanok, 18:26

Siedlce, 18:553

Siemiatycze, 18:557–558

Sieradz, 18:558–559

Sierpc, 18:559

Skalat, 18:656

Skarzysko-Kamienna, 18:657

Skierniewice, 18:658–659

Skloe, 18:661

Smolar, Hersh, 18:690

Sochaczew, 18:703

Sokolka, 18:746

Sokolow Podlaski, 18:749–750, 750

Sosnowiec, 19:32

Srem, 19:154

Staszow, 19:154, 167

Stettin, 19:223–224

Stopnica, 19:237–238

Strykow, 19:263, 264

Suwalki, 19:332

Swidnica, 19:340

Szczebrzeszyn, 19:403

Szczercow, 19:403–404

Szydlowiec, 19:413, 414

Tarnobrzeg, 19:516

Tarnogrod, 19:516

Tarnow, 19:520

Tomaszow Lubelski, 20:31–32

Tomaszow Mazowiecki, 19:32, 20:32

Torun, 16:308, 20:67

Trzcianka, 20:162

Tykocin, 20:211

Tyszowce, 20:221

Warsaw district, 16:309–310, 670–674, 20:670–674, 671

Wegrow, 20:696–697

Wieliczka, 21:45

Wielun, 21:45–46

Wislica, 21:104

Wloclawek, 21:130

Wlodawa, 21:130–131

Wodzislaw, 21:131

Wolbrom, 21:133

Wolomin, 21:153

Wronki, 21:246

Wyszkow, 21:254

Wyszogrod, 21:255

Yavarov, 21:291

Zabludow, 21:255, 432

Zabrze, 21:432

Zambrow, 21:450

Zamosc, 21:452

Zawiercie, 21:464

Zdunska Wola, 21:466–467

Zelechow, 21:500

Zelow, 21:502, 520–521

Zgierz, 21:520–521

Zmigrod Nowy, 21:645

Zwolen, 21:696

Zyardow, 21:697

Zychlin, 21:696

Zyrardow, 21:697

Jewish movements and organizations

  Beriḥah, 3:434–435

  Folkspartei, 7:113

  Gordonia, 7:775–776

  Ha-No'ar ha-Ivri-Akiba, 8:327

  Haskalah movement, 4:164

  He-Ḥalutz (movement), 8:758–759

  Jewish Social Democratic Party, 11:313–314

  Kabbalists, 11:619, 621–622

  Maḥzike Hadas, 13:363

  Mizrachi Movement, 6:714

  ORT, 15:489

  Shomer Israel, 18:518

  TOZ, 15:556, 20:78

  United Jewish Socialist Worker's Party, 20:259

  Zionism, 12:466, 768–769, 21:597–599

late twentieth century

  American Joint Distribution Committee, 2:64

Poland, *continued*

    Israeli relations, 16:323–325

  laws and legal systems

    anti-Jewish, 15:403

    anti-sheḥitah movements, 18:435

    arenda, 2:423

    crime, 5:292

    emancipation, 6:382–383

    ḥazakah, 8:490

    legal status, 16:289–293, 300

    minority rights, 14:290

    numerus clausus in, 15:341

    ugoda, 20:230

    war crimes trials, 20:643

  Middle Ages

    agriculture, Jewish, 1:495

    anti-Jewish laws, 15:403

    center of Ashenaz, 6:556

    early settlement, 16:288–289

    seals, use of, 18:227

    trade and commerce, Jewish, 1:496–497

  political theories, parties and organizations

    Agudat Israel, 1:507, 12:714

    Bund, 2:18, 4:282–283

    Casimir III, 4:505

    communism, 3:462, 5:97–98

    Endecja party, 6:402–403

    Folkspartei, 7:113

    Jewish Social Democratic Party, 11:313–314

    Jewish socialism in, 18:720

    Maḥzike Hadas, 13:363

    Minority Bloc, 14:287

    Nara, 14:779

    OZON, 15:**558**

    PPS socialist party, 16:433–434

    Rozwój, 17:505–506

    Sejm, 18:256

    socialism, 6:23, 12:804, 18:707–708

    United Jewish Socialist Worker's Party, 20:259

  politicians, 16:302, 304–305, 346–347

    Chajn, Leon, 4:560

    Dmowski, Roman, 5:723–724

    Einaeugler, Karol, 6:255

    Pilsudski, Józef, 16:163–164

    Slawoj-Skladkowski, Felicjan, 18:673

  post-WW II, 16:318–323

    American Joint Distribution Committee, 2:62

    antisemitism, 16:319–320, 321

    children's rescue, 16:318

    emigration, liquidation, 16:320–321, 324–325

    renewal of Jewish life, 16:318–320

  post-WW I – WW II, 16:302–306

    agriculture, Jewish, 1:498–499

    American Joint Distribution Committee, 2:59

    boycotts, anti-Nazi, 4:110

    Fourth Aliyah and, 10:199, 200, 337

    Morgenthau Commission, 14:489, 490

  printing and publishing, 16:533, 536, 537, 718

    Breslau, 4:165

    Hebrew, 12:374, 13:243–244

  Reformation to WW I, 16:299–300

    Amsterdam immigrants, 2:107

    antisemitism, 11:117–118, 16:300–305

    independence movement proponents, 13:790

    partition era, 9:232–233, 288, 16:300–302

    Ukraine, colonization of, 16:296–298, 296*t*

    Uprising of 1830, 6:382

  religious life and scholarship

    apologetics, 2:267–268

    biblical exegesis and study in, 3:643

    Catholic-Jewish relations, 11:282

    Chief Rabbinate, 4:613

    church opposition, 16:291

    Hasidism, 11:39–41

    historiography, 3:82

    Jewish Historical Institute, 2:408, 411, 11:291, 18:723

    Kabbalists, 11:619, 621–622

    language, biblical translation, 3:634, 16:334–335

    preaching, 16:471–472

    Rabbinical training, 17:23

    religions, 16:303*t*

    responsa literature, 17:231, 232, 234

    Schorr, Moses, 18:164

  WW II

    American Joint Distribution Committee, 2:61

    invasion, 9:331–332

    Jewish participation in military service, 14:244–245

    partisans, 15:666–667

    resistance, 5:263, 9:574–575, 16:314–317

    underground organizations, 3:434–435, 16:315–316, 18:287

    See also Camps, concentration and extermination; Council of the Lands; *specific Polish cities and locations*

Poland/1931 (Rothenberg), 20:298

Polangen (Lithuania). *See* Palanga

Polanski, Roman, 16:**326**

Polanyi, John C., 16:**326**

Polányi, Karl, 16:**326–327**

Polanyi, Michael, 16:**327**

Polaroid cameras, 12:456

Polemics and polemical literature, 16:**327–330**

  Abraham ben Moses ben Maimon, 1:305

  biography as element in, 3:706

  Christian

    Abner of Burgos, 1:264–265

    Barruel, Augustin, 3:178

    Chiarini, Luigi, 4:607

    John Chrysostom, 11:382

    Justin Martyr, 11:580

    Loisy, Alfred Firmin, 13:176

    Nigri, Petrus, 15:264

    Orosius, 15:482

    in Orvieto, 15:500

  Islamic, 3:669

  Jewish

    Briel, Judah ben Eliezer, 4:181

    Brociner, Joseph, 4:192

    Brudo, Manuel, 4:221

    Celsus, 4:537–538

    Ḥerev Nokemet Nekam-Berit (Bresselau), 4:167

    Job and, 11:357

    Jonathan ben Eleazar, 11:397

    Judah ben Barzillai al-Bargeloni, 11:483

    Judah ben Eleazar, 11:485–486

    of Judah Halevi, 11:499–500

    Levi, David, 12:686

    Official, Nathan ben Joseph and Joseph, 15:388–389

    parodic forms of, 15:656, 657–658

  Kalonymus ben Kalonymus, 11:749–750

  letters and letter writers, 12:671

  See also Disputations and polemics

Polemon II, 16:**330**

Polemon of Ilium, 16:**331**

Polgar, Alfred, 16:**331**

Poli, Umberto. *See* Saba, Umberto

Poliakov, Israel, 8:206–207

Poliakov, Léon, 11:324, 16:**331**

Policar, Isaac ben Joseph ibn. *See* Pollegar, Isaac ben Joseph ibn

Police offenses, 9:357–358, 16:**331–332**

"Policy of fulfillment," 4:64

Polier, Justine Wise, 21:102–103

Polier, Shad, 16:**332–333**

Polier of Kobrin, Moses ben Israel. *See* Kobrin, Moses ben Israel Polier of

Poliker, Yehudah, 16:**333**

Polio vaccines, 4:28

Polish, David, 16:**333–334**

The Polish Boy. See Dos Poylishe Yingle

Polish Communist party, 5:97–98

Polish literature, 16:**334–338**

  Adalberg, Samuel, 1:371

  apologetics, 2:267–268

  assimilationist, 6:748

  biblical influence, 3:672

  Biegeleisen, Henryk, writings of, 3:688

  Brandstaetter, Roman, 4:127–128

  Brandys, Kazimierz, 4:129

  children's, 4:629, 635

  Drzewiecki, Henryk, 6:29

  Hertz, Benedykt, 9:47

  Lewin, Aaron Ben Nathan of Rzeszow, 12:758–759

  Lewinstein, Joseph Ben Abraham Abush, 12:763

  Lewy, Israel, 12:771

  Lewysohn, Abraham, 12:772

  Libschitz, Baruch Mordecai Ben Jacob, 12:788–789

  nineteenth century, Peltin, Samuel Hirsh, 15:719

  poetry, 13:246

    Behr, Issachar Falkensohn, 3:263

    Braun, Mieczyslaw, 4:138

    Brzechwa, Jan, 4:230

    Karmel, Ilona, 11:812–813

    Lec, Stanislaw Jerzy, 12:593

    Lesmian, Boleslaw, 12:664

    Mickiewicz, Adam, 14:178

    Różewicz, Tadeusz, 17:503–504

    Slonimski, Antoni, 18:678

  Rudnicki, Adolf, 17:523–524

  Schultz, Bruno, 18:175

    Stande, Stanislaw Ryszard, 19:162

    Stern, Anatol, 19:203–204

    Stryjkowski, Juljan, 19:263–264

    Szenwald, Lucjan, 19:406

    Tuwim, Julian, 20:207–208

    Wat, Alexander, 20:687–688

    Ważyk, Adam, 20:691

    Winawer, Bruno, 21:79

    Wittlin, Jozef, 21:128

    Wittlin, Józef, 21:128

    Woroszylski, Wiktor, 21:229–230

    Wygodzki, Stanisllaw, 21:251

  Yiddish, 21:350–351, 353

Political history

  Canada, 4:401–402, 405–406, 413–415, 420–421

  France, Algeria, 1:648–649

  Hellenistic period, 4:105–106

  holy places in Israel and, 9:501, 503

  Iran, 10:12

  Israel (ancient), 4:105–106

  Israel (state), 10:423–464, 427t, 428t, 429t, 430t, 431t, 432t, 433t, 434t, 435t, 436t, 437t, 438t, 439t, 440t, 441t, 442t, 443t, 444t, 445t, 446t, 447t, 448t, 449t, 450t, 451t, 452t, 453t, 454t, 456t, 457t, 458t, 459t, 460t–461t, 462t, 463t, 521

    Eighth Knesset, 1973-77, 10:442–444, 442t, 443t

    Eleventh Knesset, 1984-88, 10:448–451, 448t, 449t, 450t

    Fifteenth Knesset, 1999-2003, 10:458–462, 458t, 459t, 460t–461t

    Fifth Knesset, 1961-1965, 10:436–438, 436t, 437t

    First Knesset, 1949-1951, 10:428–430, 428t, 429t, 430t

    Fourteenth Knesset, 1996-99, 10:456–458, 456t, 457t

    Fourth Knesset, 1959-1961, 10:434–436, 434t, 435t

    Independent Liberal Party, 9:771

    introduction, 10:423–424

    Knesset, 12:235–239, 235t, 236t, 237t

    Likud, 13:13–14

    Mapai, 13:497–498

    Mapam, 13:498–499

    Ninth Knesset, 1977-81, 10:444–446, 444t, 445t

    political parties, 10:395–397, 424–428, 427t

    post-war of independence to Six-Day War, 10:208–209, 210, 211–212, 214–215, 225–226

    Second Knesset, 1951-1955, 10:430–432, 430t, 431t, 432t

    Seventh Knesset, 1969-73, 10:440–442, 440t, 441t

    Shas (political party), 18:419–420

    Shinui, 18:484–485

    Sixteenth Knesset, 2003-2006, 10:461–464, 462t, 463t

    Sixth Knesset, 1965-1969, 10:438–440, 438t, 439t

    Tenth Knesset, 1981-1984, 10:446–448, 446t, 447t

    Third Knesset, 1955-1959, 10:432–434, 433t, 434t

    Thirteenth Knesset, 1992-96, 10:453–456, 453t, 454t, 456t

    Twelfth Knesset, 1988-92, 10:451–453, 451t, 452t

  Italy, 10:807–809

  Morocco, 14:500–501

  Palestine (Roman), 18:21–23

  Persian Empire, 18:75

  Poland

    Rozwój, 17:505–506

    Sejm, 18:256

  public relations, 16:711–712

  shtadlan, 18:521–522

  Turkey, 16:762

  U.S., 4:497–498

Political participation. *See* Politics

Political parties

  antisemitic, 2:*217*

  Austria, Christian Social Party, 4:694

  Germany, Christian Social Party, 4:694

  Israel

    Agudat Israel, 1:507–508

    National Religious Parties, 15:27–28

  Meretz, 14:63–64

  See also National Jewish Democratic Council; *specific parties*

Political science

  Almond, Gabriel Abraham, 1:683

  behaviorism, 6:548

  Beilin, Yossi, 3:266–267

  Berger-Barzilai, Joseph, 3:426

  Berlin, Sir Isaiah, 3:456

  Finer, Herman, 7:26–27

Political science, *continued*
  Landau, Jacob M., 12:463
  Laqueur, Walter Ze'ev, 12:492
  Laski, Harold Joseph, 12:499
  Morgenthau, Hans Joachim, 14:489–490
  Robson, William Alexander, 17:356–357
  Rowe, Leo Stanton, 17:502
  Schapiro, Leonard, 18:109
  Simon, Herbert Alexander, 18:611
The Political Systems of Empires (Eisenstadt), 6:271
Political Zionism. *See* Zionism
Politics, 16:**338–354**
  Abrabanel, Isaac ben Judah, 1:278–279
  Argentina, 16:350
  Australia, 12:456–457, 749, 16:339–340
  Austria, 4:323–324, 12:625, 778–779, 16:338, 340–341
  Bosnia-Herzegovina, 18:49
  Canada, 16:341–342
    Croll, David Arnold, 5:305–306
    Lewis, Stephen, 12:767
  censorship, 4:540
  Colombia, 5:63–64
  Egypt, 16:346
  England, 12:776–777, 16:339, 342–343
    Cromwell, Oliver, 5:306
    Rifkind, Sir Malcom, 17:298
    Rothschild, James Armand de, 17:493–494
  France, 5:45, 627, 12:479, 530–531, 775–781, 16:338, 343
  Germany, 4:236–237, 12:475, 497, 501–502, 777–778, 16:339, 343–344, 354
  Iraq, 16:346
  Israel, 12:489, 624, 749
    Rosen, Pinḥas, 17:430
    Rosen, Shelomo, 17:430–431
    Rubinstein, Amnon, 17:515–516
  Italy, 12:779, 16:345
  Jewish political tradition, 6:288–289
  Latin America, 16:349–350
  Latvia, 12:521
  liberalism, 12:775–781
  Morocco, 16:346
  muslim states, 16:345–346
  Netherlands, 16:344–345
  Panama, 5:546

  Poland, 16:346–347, 17:468
  radical, 16:338–339
  Romanin Jacur, Leone, 17:402
  Russia, 12:780–781, 16:236–237, 347–348
  South Africa, 12:644, 16:348–349
  Soviet Union, 16:348
  Tunisia, 16:346
  Turkey, 16:345–346
  U.S., 12:437–438, 486–487, 602, 613–614, 659, 779–780, 16:338, 339, 350–354
    Rickover, Hyman George, 17:292–293
    Rosenthal, Benjamin Stanley, 17:452
    Rosewater, Edward, 17:463
    Ross, Dennis, 17:469
    Rudman, Warren, 17:523
    Ruef, Abraham, 17:526
Politics among Nations (Morgenthau), 14:490
Politics in the Twentieth Century (Morgenthau), 14:490
The Politics of Genocide: The Holocaust in Hungary (Braham), 9:419–420
The Politics of Meaning (Lerner), 12:659
Politische Gemeinde, 16:**354**
Politsche oder soziale Demokratie (Adler), 1:403
Politzer, Adam, 16:**354**
Politzer, H. David, 16:**354–355**
Pollack, Egon, 16:**355**
Pollack, Israel, 16:**355**
Pollack, Jacob, 15:347
Pollack, Jacob ben Joseph, 6:178, 16:**355**
Pollack, Michael Solomon. *See* Alexander, Michael Solomon
Pollack, Milton, 16:**356**
Pollack, Sydney, 16:**356**
Pollack, Walter Heilprin, 12:556
Pollak, Frank. *See* Pelleg, Frank
Pollak, Ḥayyim Joseph, 6:44
Pollak, Miksa, 16:**356**
Pollak, Moses ha-Levi, 16:**356**
Pollak, Rose. *See* Pauly, Rosa
Pollak, Walter Heilprin, 16:**356**
Pollak, Zalman, 16:**356–357**
Pollard, Jonathan Jay, 16:357–359
  Blitzer, Wolf, 3:757
Pollard, Sidney, 16:**357**
Pollard Affair, 10:450, 16:**357–359**
Pollegar, Isaac ben Joseph ibn, 1:264, 265, 16:87, **359**
  apologetics, 2:266

Pollin, Abe, 16:**359–360**
Pollini, Bernhard, 16:**360**
Pollio, Gaius Asinius. *See* Asinius Pollio, Gaius
Poll taxes. *See* Taxation
Pollution, 5:166–168, 167–168, 6:93–95
Polna (Czech Republic), 3:779, 15:352, 16:**360**
Polo, 19:145
  water (*See* Water polo)
Polonnoye (Ukraine), 16:**360–361**
Polotsk (Belarus), 16:**361**
Polotsky, Hans Jacob, 16:**361–362**
Polshek, James, 16:**362**
Polska Partia Socjalityczna. *See* PPS
Poltava (Ukraine), 16:**362–363**
Polutoraglazy strelets (Livshits), 13:146
Polyakevich. *See* Kopelson, Ẓemaḥ
Polyakov, Eliezer, 14:517, 16:364
Polyakov, Samuel, 16:363–364, 17:70
Polyakov family, 16:**363–364**
Polybius of Megalopolis, 16:**364**
Polycarp, Philoxenian version of Bible, 3:600
Polygamy. *See* Bigamy and polygamy
Polyglotta. See Biblia Polyglotta
Polyglot texts of Bible, 3:588, 613, 636, 13:56
Polygyny. *See* Bigamy and polygamy; Monogamy
Polykoff, Shirley, 16:**364**
Polytheism, 7:670
Pomaria (Algeria). *See* Tlemcen (Algeria)
Pomegranates, 16:**364–365**
Pomer, Hector, 4:70
Pomerania, 16:**365**
Pomerantz, Berl, 16:**365–366**
Pomerantz, Fred P., 16:**366**
Pomerantz, Sydney Irving, 16:**366**
Pomeranus. *See* Bugenhagen, Johann
Pomi, David de', 16:366–367
  Italian translation of Bible by, 3:633
  moneylending, 14:440
Pomi, de', family, 16:**366–367**
Pomi, Elijah de', 16:366
Pomis, David de'. *See* Pomi, David de'
Pommer, Erlich, 16:**367**
Pompeii (Italy), 16:**367**
Pompeius. *See* Pompey
Pompeius Trogus, 14:532, 16:**367–368**
Pompey, 2:82, 457, 16:**368**
  Julius Caesar and, 11:574–575
  Julius Florus on, 11:575

Pomplona (Spain). *See* Pamplona

Pomponius Mela, 16:**368**

Pomus, Doc, 16:**368**

Ponary (Lithuania), 16:**369**

Poner, Meir, 8:715

Ponevezh (Lithuania). *See* Panevezys

Ponevezher Rav. *See* Kahaneman, Joseph

Ponholzer, Bartholomaeus, 11:568

Ponidi family. *See* Bondi family

Ponte, Lorenzo da. *See* Da Ponte, Lorenzo

Pontecorvo, Bruno, 16:**369**

Pontius Pilate, 9:198, 16:**369–370**

Pontoise (France), 16:**370**

Pontrémoli, Emmanuel, 16:**370**

The Pool. See Ha-Berekhah

Pool, Cave of, 11:524

Pool, David de Sola, 16:**370–371**

    American Jewish Historical Society, 2:59

Poona (India), 16:**371**

Poor, provision for, 15:704–705, 16:**371–372**

Pope Pius XII and the Holocaust (Wills), 9:374

Popes, 16:**372–378**

    antisemitism, 1:619, 4:710–711, 711

    blood libel, opposition to, 3:776, 778

    bulls, papal, 4:277–278

    forced baptism, 3:121–122

    Paz, Duarte de, 15:699–700

    physicians, 6:340

    See also Catholic Church; *specific names of popes*

Popgueorguiev, Stoyan. *See* Stefan, Metropolitan

Popjak, George, 3:765

Poplars, 16:**378**

Poppaea, Sabina, 16:**378**

Popper, David, 16:**379**

Popper, Hayyim, 16:**378**

Popper, Joachim, 4:175

Popper, Josef, 1:429, 16:**379**

Popper, Julius, 16:**379**

Popper, Karl. *See* Popper, Sir Karl

Popper, Siegfried, 16:**380**

Popper, Sir Karl, 16:**380**

Popper, William, 16:**380**

Popper, Wolf, 4:175

Popper Bozian, Wolf, 16:**380–381**

Popper family, 16:**378–379**

Poppers, Jacob ben Benjamin ha-Kohen, 16:**381**

Poppers, Meir ben Judah Loeb ha-Kohen, 16:**381**

Popular Front for the Liberation of Palestine (PFLP), 6:447–448, 10:233–234, 281

Population, 16:**381–400**

    1900-2005, 14:214*t*

    Ashkenazi, morbidity, 18:546

    Babylonia, 16:386

    Belarus, 12:650

    Black death and, 16:388

    Boston, 4:99

    Brazil, 4:142, 146*t*, 154

    Bucharest, 4:239*t*, 241

    Buenas Aires, 4:253

    Bulgaria, 4:*268*, 271*t*

    Byzantine Empire, 16:386

    Caribbean, 16:392

    Chicago, 4:609–610

    control, vs. procreation ethics, 5:169

    conversions and mixed marriages, 16:395

    during Crusader period, 10:161

    Czechoslovakia, 12:781, 16:393

    Egypt, medieval, 16:386

    England, 12:625, 16:392

    Europe, 16:387–389, 389*t*, 393–394, 396*t*

        1880, 6:*557*

        1939, 6:*558*

        1946, 6:*559*

        2003, 6:*560*

        laws controlling Jewish, 6:689–690

        pre-WW II, 9:326–327

    France, 16:391–392

    Germany, 16:391, 395

        Fuerth, 7:307

        Leipzig, 12:627

    growth and distribution, 9:241–243, 242*t*

    Holocaust

        estimates, 16:397–398

        Hungary, 9:616

    Iberia, medieval, 16:386

    Israel (ancient), 16:382–385, 384*t*

    Israel (Byzantine period), 10:159–160

    Israel (Crusader period), 10:163–165

    Israel (Mamluk period), 10:167–168

    Israel (state), 10:282–329, 302*t*, *303*, 303*t*, 304*t*, *305*, 306–329*t*

        1958, 10:223

        Administered Territories, 10:303–304, 306–329*t*

        aliyah, growth by, 10:282–283

        composition by place of birth, 10:284–285, 284*t*

        distribution by sex, 10:285

        distribution of population, 10:374–375

        geographic distribution, 10:289–290, 289*t*, 290*t*

        growth of, 10:283–284

        household statistics, 10:293–294

        human resources, 10:293–298

        intercommunal problems, 10:298–300

        Israel Place List (2004) – Places of Jewish Habitation in Israel and the Administered Territories, 10:306–329*t*

        Jewish population, 10:282–293, 284*t*, 287*t*, 289*t*, 290*t*, 291*t*, 292*t*, 304, 304*t*, *305*, 305*t*, 306–329*t*

        languages and literacy, 10:291–292, 291*t*, 292*t*

        marriages, births, deaths and natural increases, 10:285–289, 287*t*

        non-Jewish, 10:300–305, *301*, 302*t*, *303*, 303*t*, 304*t*, *305*, 713*t*

        regional distribution, 10:292

        statistics, 10:290–291, 291*t*, *304*, 304*t*, *305*, 305*t*

    Italy, 16:390–391

    Jerusalem

        after reunification, 11:183, 186, 190, 191–192, 196

        during British rule, 11:174, 176

        as divided city, 11:178, 181

        medieval, 16:385

        during Ottoman rule, 11:163, 164, 169, 171, 172

    Latin America, 16:392

    Latvia, 12:520, 817–818

    lifetime longevity, 18:545

    Middle Ages, 16:385–389

    Moldova, 12:650

    morbidity, 18:546–548, 548*t*

    Netherlands, 16:391

    nineteenth century to WW II, 16:392–395, 396*t*–397*t*

    Palestine (Mandate), 10:282, 283, 285

    Palestine (Ottoman), 10:282

    Pest (Hungary), 4:246*t*

    Poland, 12:635

    Provence, France, 16:637

    Russia, 16:394

Population, *continued*

sixteenth to eighteenth centuries, 16:389–392

sources, 16:382

Soviet Union, 16:399

twentieth century, Hungary, 9:618

U.S., 16:392–394, 395, 397*t*, 399

WW II to 1971, 16:397–399

See also Demography; *specific cities and countries*

Porat, Joseph. *See* Joseph ben Moses of Troyes

Porat, Orna, 16:**400**

Porath, Israel, 16:**400–401**

Porchetus Salvagus, 16:**401**

Porges, Heinrich, 16:**401**

Porges, Moses ben Israel Naphtali, 16:**401**

Porges, Nathan, 16:**401**

Porging, 18:437

Poriyyah (Israel), 16:**401–402**

Pornind dela clasici (Calin), 4:364

Porodica u transformaciji (Erlich). *See Family in Transition: A study of 300 Yugoslav villages* (Erlich)

Porphyry, 5:421–422, 16:**402**

Portaleone, Abraham, 16:403

Portaleone, Abraham ben David II, 16:**403–404**

Portaleone, Benjamin, 16:402–403

Portaleone, Eleazar, 16:403

Portaleone, Elhanan ben Menahem, 16:402

Portaleone, Leone de' Sommi. *See* Sommo, Judah Leone ben Isaac

Portaleone family, 16:**402–403**

Portals, 16:**402**

Port Elizabeth (South Africa), 16:**404**

Portella, de, family, 16:**404**

Portella, Ishmael de, 16:404

Portella, Muça de, 16:404

Portents. *See* Signs and symbols

Porter, Dame Shirley, 16:404

Porter, John, 4:413

Porter, Leslie. *See* Porter, Sir Leslie

Porter, Sarah Ricardo, 17:282

Porter, Sir Leslie, 16:**404**

Portland (OR), 16:**404–405**

Port Natal (South Africa). *See* Durban (Republic of South Africa)

Portnoy, Alicia, 18:714

Portnoy, Antonio, 11:469

Portnoy, Jekuthiel, 16:**405**

Porto, Abraham de. *See* Alvarez, Fernando

Porto, Abraham Menahem ben Jacob ha-Kohen, 16:**406**

Porto, Menahem Zion, 13:675

Porto Allegre (Brazil), 16:**406–407**

Porto family, 16:**405–406**

Porto-Rafa, Abraham Menahem, 16:407

Porto-Rafa, Moses ben Jehiel ha-Kohen, 16:**407–408**

Porto-Riche, Georges de, 16:**408**

Portrait medals, commissioning of, 18:222

Portrait of Jeanne Hebuteren, Seated (Modigliani), vol. 4: color insert

Portrait of Max (Behrman), 3:264

Portrait photography, 16:126

Portraits

as book illustrations, 4:76

Brodskii, Isaac, 4:197

Portraits of Jews, 16:**408**

Port Said (Egypt), 16:**408–409**

Portsmouth (England), 16:**409**

Portugal, 16:**409–414**, *410*

Abenaes, Solomon, 1:249

Aboab, Isaac II, 1:267–268

Abrabanel, Isaac ben Judah, 1:276

Affonso, 1:431–432

Agadir, 1:444

antisemitism, 13:79–80

Bordeaux, Portuguese merchants of, 4:82–83

Braganza, 4:117

Brazil as colony of, 4:142–144

Chief Rabbinate, 4:613

Crypto-Jews, 3:178, 4:117

early printed editions of Hebrew Bible in, 3:586–587

expulsion of Jews from

fifteenth century, 13:79

Ottoman empire, Portuguese Jews settling in, 15:522–523

forced conversion, 3:122, 4:469

historiography, 9:156–157

Holocaust, 2:117, 14:42–43, 16:412

Inquisition, 4:520–521, 9:793–794, 796, 13:80, 16:411

Israeli relations, 16:412–413

Jewish communities, 6:588

Jewish immigration

to Amsterdam, 2:108, 109, 117

to France, 4:82–83

to Norway, 15:305

to U.S., 2:42–45

John II of Portugal, 11:378–379

John III of Portugal, 11:379

language and literature, 2:109, 117, 3:633

Benarus, Adolfo, 3:319

biblical influence, 3:671

Pina, Jacob, 16:164

Silva, Antônio José Da, 18:582–583

Leão, Gaspar de, 12:567

limpieza de sangre, 13:25–26

marranos, conversos, 2:140, 249, 4:584, 5:47

Middle Ages, 2:489–490

Lagos, 12:437

Lisbon, 13:78–79

modern period, 16:412, 413

Morocco, 14:496

New Christians, Marranos, 16:410–412

Oporto, 15:441

Paz, Duarte de, 15:699–700

printing

Hebrew, 13:80

incunabula, 9:761–762

Talmud, 6:718

scholarship, 13:80

Portugalov, Benjamin Osipovich, 16:**414**

Portugies, Michael. *See* Hinrichsen, Michael

Portuguese communities, Caribbean, 4:468–470, 476–477

Portuguese literature. *See* Spanish and Portuguese literature

Porumbacu, Veronica, 16:**414**

Porush, Israel, 16:**414**

Porush, Menachem, 16:**414–415**

Porzecanski, Teresa, 16:**415**

Posekim, 8:256–257, 16:**415–416**

Lev, Joseph Ben David Ibn, 12:676

Mordecai ben Judah ha-Levi, 14:481

Nathanson, Joseph Saul, 15:18–19

Posen (Poland). *See* Poznan (Poland)

Posen, Isaac ben Abraham of. *See* Isaac ben Abraham of Posen

Posener, Edith Claire. *See* Head, Edith

Posener, Georges Henri, 16:**416**

Posener, Solomon, 16:**416**

A Posheter Zelner (Smolar), 18:690

Posidonius, 14:531, 532, 16:**416**

Posidonius of Apamea. *See* Posidonius

Posnanski, Adolf, 16:416

Posnanski, Samuel Abraham, 16:416–417

Posnanski family, 16:**416–417**

Posner, Akiva Barukh, 16:**417**

Posner, David ben Naphtali, 16:**417**

Posner, Richard Allen, 16:**417–418**

Posner, Sam, 12:599

Posner, Solomon Zalman. *See* Lipschitz, Solomon Zalman

Posner, Solomon Zalman ben Joseph, 16:**418**

Posquières (France), 16:**418**

Poss. *See* Ashkenazi, Gershon

Possession. *See* Ḥazakah; Ownership

Possessor of the Name. *See* Ba'al Shem

Post. *See* Pillar

Postal systems, 2:146

Postan, Michael Moissey, 16:**418**

Post-biblical period
love, 13:229–230
psychology, 16:687–688
Sabbatical Year and Jubilee, 17:626, 628–629
Satan, 18:72–73
seal, seals, 18:226–228
ships and sailing, 18:487
theater, 19:670–671

Postel, Guillaume, 11:672, 12:601, 16:**418–419**

Postemus. *See* Apostomos

Post-geonic period, 19:447–448

Post-geonic period, Takkanot, 19:449–450

Postillae Perpetuae (Nicholas de Lyre), 15:251

Post-impressionism, 3:93

Postman, Neil, 18:732

Post Miserabile, 4:277

Postmodernism
Derrida, Jacques, 5:599
Josipovici, Gabriel, 11:461

Post-mortem. *See* Autopsies and dissection

Post Mortem (Kaniuk), 11:764

Postolsky, Shalom, 16:**419**

Postrelko, Avraham. *See* Harzfeld, Avraham

Post-structuralism, 3:655

Post-Talmudic period
Bible, interpretation of, 9:818, 821
laws and legal systems, 13:23–24, 19:536–539
lots, 13:219
ma'aseh, 13:310
maritime law, 13:546–547
marriages, 12:727, 13:566–568
Pumbedita academy, 16:733–734
sea of the Talmud, 18:228
See also Rabbinic period

Post-Temple period, 18:446–447

Post-Temple period, sheluḥei erez Israel, 18:448–449

Postville (IA), 10:8

Post-World War I
education, Jewish, 6:184–185

Hungarian literature and, 9:606
"Illegal" immigration and, 9:722–723
self-defense, 18:263–264
Sephardim, 18:301

Post-World War II
denazification, 5:578–579
England, London, 13:182–183
Europe, education, Jewish, 6:186–187
France, Lyons, 13:297
Greece, Salonika, 17:705–706
Hungary, 9:616–618
"Illegal" immigration and, 9:723–724
Italy, 10:805–812
Lithuania, 13:127–128
Sephardim, 18:301–302
U.S., education, Jewish, 6:198

Potash and Perlmutter (Glass), 7:632

Potash works, Dead Sea, 3:767

Potiphar, 6:225, 11:407, 411, 413, 16:28, **419–420**

Poti-Phera, 16:**420**

Potocki, Valentine, 16:**420**

Potofsky, Jacob Samuel, 16:**420–421**

Potok, Chaim, 16:**421**

Potomok Chingis Khana (Brik), 4:181

Potovsky, Ernestine Potovsky. *See* Rose, Ernestine Potovsky

Pottery, 16:**421–426**
Bronze age, 16:422–424
Byzantine, 16:426
Hellenistic and Roman, 16:425–426
Iron age, 16:424–425
Neolithic period, 16:422
Philistine, 16:52

Pougatchov, Emanuel. *See* Amiran, Emanuel

Pöstyén. *See* Piestany

Pound, Ezra Loomis, 15:442, 16:**426–427**

Poupko, Bernard, 16:**427**

Poupko, Israel Meir. *See* Israel Meir ha-Kohen

Pourquoi je suis Juif (Fleg), 7:72

Poussin, Nicolas, 14:541

Poverty, 16:**427–428**

Povich, Shirley Lewis, 16:**428–429**

Powdermaker, Hortense, 2:186, 16:**429**

Powecki, Piotr. *See* Skarga, Piotr

Powell, Bruce, 13:207

In Poylishe Velder (Opatoshu), 15:437

Dos Poylishe Yingle (Linetzky), 13:28

Pozitsye mit der Letster Hofenung (Smolar), 18:690

Poznan (Poland), 16:307–308, **429–432**
artisans, 5:269
community, 4:204

Poznanski, Gustavus, 16:**433**

Poznanski, Menaḥem, 16:**433**

Poznański, Edward, 16:**432–433**

Pozner, Solomon. *See* Posener, Solomon

Pozsony (Slovakia). *See* Bratislava (Slovakia)

PPS, 16:**433–434**

Praag, Siegfried Emanuel van, 16:**434**

Practical Contributions to Pediatrics. See Praktische Beitraege zur Kinderheilkunde

Practice and procedure, 16:**434–446**
civil, 16:434–438
penal, 16:438–440
Rabbinical court rules, Israel, 16:440–446

The Practice of Arithmetic (Levi ben Gershom). *See* Ma'aseh Ḥoshev (Levi ben Gershom)

Prado, Dan. *See* Prado, Juan de

Prado, Juan de, 16:**446–447**, 18:298

Praefectus Judaeorum, 16:**447**

Praeger, Moses. *See* Moses ben Menaham Graf

Pragensis, Paulus. *See* Elhanan (biblical figure)

Prager, Dennis, 16:**447–448**

Prager, Richard, 16:**448**

Prager Presse (Eisner), 6:277

Prag Kahn, Florence. *See* Kahn, Florence Prag

Prague (Czech Republic), 5:363, 16:**448–456**, *449*
Afike Jehuda, 1:433
Altschul family, 2:24–25
Burial Society glass, vol. 7: color insert
cemetery, vol. 7: color insert
early settlement, 16:448–449
Elijah of Prague, 6:347
fifteenth-eighteenth centuries, 16:450–451
funeral (painting), vol. 7: color insert
Holocaust period, 16:453–454
influential families, Jeiteles, 11:114–115
Jewish archives, 2:408
Landesjudenschaft, Boehmische, 12:469
modern period, 16:454–455
museums, 14:628–629
nineteenth century to WW II, 16:*451,* 451–453

Prague (Czech Republic), *continued*
  printing, publishing, 12:465,
    16:536
  rabbis, Ehrenfeld, Nathan, 6:239
  scholars, 12:478
  seals, use of, 18:227
Prague Circle, 4:192
Prague edition Haggadah, 8:214, 215
Praha. *See* Prague
Prais, Simon, 4:373
*Praktische Beitraege zur
  Kinderheilkunde* (Baginsky), 3:59
Pranaitis, J., 3:779
Pratensis, Felix, 4:52
  early printed editions of Hebrew
    Bible, 3:587
Prathet Thai. *See* Thailand
Prato, David, 16:**456**
Pratt, Richard, 16:**456**
Pravda (newspaper), 11:753
Prawer, Joshua, 16:**456**
Prawer, Siegbert, 16:**456**
Prayer, 16:**456–461**
  Abraham Gerson of Kutow, 1:312
  Adonai, Adonai, El Raḥum
    veḤannun, 1:412
  Ahavah Rabbah, 1:538–539
  Ahavat Olam, 1:538–539
  Aleinu le-Shabbe'aḥ, 1:608–610
  Al ha-Nissim, 1:655
  alphabet, Hebrew, 1:729
  Amidah, 2:72–76, 13:601
  Amram Gaon, 2:105
  apocryphal literature, 16:458
  benedictions, 3:330–333
  biblical, 16:456–458
  Birkat ha-Minim, 3:711–712
  Birkat ha-Torah, 3:712
  Bittul ha-Timid as interruption of,
    3:729–730
  chant, 14:646–647, 650–653
  Conservative Judaism, morning
    benedictions, 14:492
  contemporary events, 16:467
  Day of Atonement, 5:489
  devotion to God and, 14:24
  dew, prayer for, 5:**630**
  Dov Baer, 5:767
  dreams, 6:9
  El Male Raḥamim, 6:364–365
  El Melekh Yoshev, 6:365
  fasts, 6:720
  government, prayer for the, 8:20
  grace before and after meals, 8:22–
    23, 24
  Ḥasidei Ashkenaz, 8:387–388

  hasidic, 16:460
  Ḥasidic, 8:399, 408, 412–413
  Hazkarat neshamot, 8:496–497
  Jerusalem, 11:213–214
  Judeo-Persian, 11:554
  Kaddish, 11:695–698
  Karaites, 11:799
  Kavvanah, 12:39–40
  Kiddush ha-Shem, 12:**139–145**
  medieval thought, 16:459
  meditation and, 13:761
  Mi she-Berakh, 14:316
  mizraḥ, 14:392–393
  Modeh Ani, 14:406
  Moon, blessing of the, 14:468
  morning benedictions, 14:406, 492
  Muslim, 10:88–90
  Ne'ilah, 15:65–66
  New Moon, announcement of,
    15:151–152
  Night Prayer, 15:264
  of Nine Days, 15:271
  Nishmat Kol Ḥai, 15:275–276
  opening Ark, 16:16–17
  piyyut, 16:192–209
  Rabbinic thought, 16:458–459
  for rain, 13:601
  recitation, 11:41
  role in Hasidism, 10:746
  seder, 18:235
  sick, prayer for the, 18:543
  for travel, 20:**112–113**
  women, firzogerin, 7:50
  women and, 16:460–461
  Yiddish, 1:217
  See also Kaddish
Prayer books, 16:**461–467**
  Baer, Seligman Isaac, 3:53
  Central Europe, *Memorbuch,*
    14:17–18
  children's, 4:636
  early siddurim, 16:462–463
  German translation, *Siddur li-
    Venei Yisrael* (Heidenheim),
    8:763
  Middle Ages, 16:462
  modern, 16:464
  printed, 16:463
  reform, 16:464–466
  Reform Judaism, 4:545–546
  Schliefer, Solomon, 18:143
  Sephardic, Sola, Abraham De,
    18:750
  Silverman, Morris, 18:**587**
  textual editions, 16:463–464
  veneration of, 2:158

"Prayer for the State of Israel"
  (Herzog), 9:70
Prayer of Azariah. *See* Song of Three
  Children and the Prayer of Azariah
Prayer of Manasseh, 13:**453–454**
*Prayers for Sabbath, Rosh-Hashanah
  and Yom Kippur, with the Amidah
  and Musaph of the Moadim* (Pinto),
  16:178
Prayer shawl. *See* Tallit
Prayers of Consolation (Silverman),
  18:587
*Pray Tell: A Hadassah Guide to
  Prayer*(Harlow), 8:359
Preacher of Morals. See Kohelet Musasr
Preaching, 16:**467–475**
  Aḥa of Shabḥa, 1:529–530
  Alfalas, Moses, 1:636
  Eliezer ben Manasseh ben Baruch,
    6:327
  Elijah ben Kalonymus of Lublin,
    6:339
  Elijah ben Solomon Abraham ha-
    Kohen of Smyrna, 6:340–341
  Ephraim Solomon ben Aaron of
    Luntshits, 6:460–461
  forms, 16:468–469, 471
  homiletic, 16:469–470
  homiletic literature and, 9:509–
    511, 513–514
  Judah ben Joseph Moscato,
    14:515–516
  maggid and maggidim, 13:339–
    340
  medieval, 5:438
  medieval period, 16:470–472
  modern times, 16:472–475
  nineteenth century, 14:6
  Olah Ḥadashah, 18:21
  Rabba, Menahem, 17:7
  role, 11:41
  seventeenth century, 15:770
  Talmudic period, 16:467–470
  twentieth century, U.S., 13:602
  *Witness from the Pulpit: Topical
    Sermons 1933-1980,* 18:35
Pre-biblical Hebrew. *See* Hebrew
  language
*Precarious Life: The Power of Mourning
  and Violence* (Butler), 4:317
Precedent, legal. *See* Ma'aseh
Precepts. *See* Commandments, the 613
Precious stones and jewelry, 16:**475–
  479,** 476t
  of Bukharan Jews, 4:264
  wedding rings (17th c.), vol. 3:
    color insert
Predah (Frankel), 7:199

Predestination, 16:88

Prediction and clairvoyance, 16:571
   divination and, 5:707
   famine, 6:707

Prefixes in Hebrew, 8:581–582

Pre-Geonic period, 6:172–173

Preger, Jacob, 16:**479**

Pregnancy, 2:122
   artificial insemination, 13:750–755
   embryos, 6:391–392
   Talmudic embryology, 13:723
   in vitro fertilization, 13:755–756
   See also Abortion; Barrenness and
     fertility

Prehistoric period, 2:381–383

Preil, Elazar Meir, 16:**479–480**

Preil, Gabriel Joshua, 16:**480**

Preis, Eli, 4:371

Preiskel, Abram, 15:677

Prejudice
   against Catholics, 4:713
   sociological studies, 11:79
   See also Antisemitism

Pre-marital sex, Talmud, 4:582

Preminger, Otto Ludwig, 16:**480**

Přemysl Ottokar II, 14:472, 16:**480–481**

Prés, Josquin de, 18:762

Presbyter Judaeorum, 16:**481**

Presbyter of the Jews, 2:**419**

Prescription, extinctive. *See* Limitation
   of actions

Presence, Divine. *See* Divine Presence

*The Presentation of Self in Everyday
   Life* (Goffman), 7:683, 18:732

The Present Danger (Podhoretz),
   16:251

The Present State of the Jews
   (Addison), 6:180

Present Tense (periodical), 2:56

President of Israel, 16:**484–485**

President's Commission on the
   Holocaust, 6:280

Presidents' Conference. *See*
   Conference of Presidents of Major
   American Jewish Organizations

President's Residence gates (Israel),
   vol. 4: color insert

Pre-Sinaitic laws, Noachide laws and,
   15:286

Presley, Elvis, 12:619

Presov (Slovakia), 16:**485–486**

Prešporek (Slovakia). *See* Bratislava
   (Slovakia)

Press, 16:**486–505**
   Australia, New Zealand, 16:487
   Austria, 16:491–492

Balkans, 16:495

Bécsi Magyar Ujság, 8:282

Belgium, 16:487

Brazil, 4:148, 16:496

Bulgaria, 16:495

Canada, 16:487–488

Czechoslovakia, 16:488

Damascus Affair and, 5:400–401

Egypt, 1:635, 6:234

England, 16:488–489

France, 16:490

Germany, 16:490–491

Harby, Isaac, 8:346

Harden, Maximillian, 8:346–347

Hungary, 16:493

India, 16:493–494

Italy, 16:494

Ladino, 12:433, 16:494–496

Latin America, 16:496–497

Middle East, North Africa, 16:497

Netherlands, 16:492–493

Palestine (Ottoman), 4:182–183

Poland, 3:396–397, 16:497–498

Romania, 16:498

Russia, 16:498–501

Scandinavia, 16:501–502

South Africa, 16:502

Switzerland, 16:502–503

Turkey, 12:772, 16:497

U.K., 12:546–547

U.S., 9:367–369, 12:596, 600–601,
   16:495–496, 503–505

Yiddish, 3:485–486, 16:487, 488,
   489, 492, 496, 499, 500, 501,
   503–504

   See also Hebrew newspapers

Press, Frank, 16:**505–506**

Press, Yeshayahu, 16:**506**

Pressburg (Slovakia). *See* Bratislava
   (Slovakia)

Presser, Harriet, 18:732–733

Presser, Jacob, 6:70, 9:409, 16:**506**

Pressler, Menahem, 16:**506**

Pressman, David, 16:**506**

Pressman, Jacob, 13:203, 16:**506–507**

Pressman, Lee, 16:**507**

Pressmane, Joseph, 16:**507**

The Press of the Widow and Romm
   Brothers. *See* Defus ha-Almanah
   ve-ha-Aḥim Romm

Prestes, Luis Carlos, 4:149

Pretoria (South Africa), 16:**507–508**

Preuss, Hugo, 12:551, 16:344, **508,**
   18:705

Preuss, Julius, 16:**508**

Preussen (Germany). *See* Prussia
   (Germany)

Previn, André, 16:**508**

Pre-World War II, 6:184–185

Preziosi, Giovanni, 16:**508–509**

Pribram, Alfred Francis, 16:**509**

Pribram, Karl, 16:**509**

Price, Abraham A., 16:**509**

Price cutting, 4:314–315

Price fixing, 5:185, 8:196–198

Pride. *See* Ethics; Humility

Pridet vesna moya (Domalsky), 5:738

Prières d'un coeur israélite (Ennery),
   6:441

Priesand, Sally Jane, 13:139, 15:234,
   393, 16:**509–510**, 17:178, 18:279

Priest, High. *See* High Priest

Priestly blessing, 16:510–511, **510–511**
   ablution, 1:263
   amen, 2:38, 39
   amulets, 2:121
   Birkat ha-Minim, 3:711–712
   blessing of children, 3:752
   covering of head, 8:507
   dukhan and, 6:44
   folklore, 7:105
   liturgy, 13:131
   minyan, 14:302
   mourning, 14:589
   peace, 15:701
   stress on words, 2:137
   Ta'anit, 19:416
   tallit, 19:465
   temple, 19:619, 624

Priestly Code, menorah, 14:50

Priestly source, 3:649, 652

Priestly vestments, 16:**511–513**

Priests and priesthood, 16:**513–526**
   Aaron, 1:217–218
   Aaronides, 1:217–219, 218*t*
   Abihu, 1:256–257
   ablution, 1:261, 263
   Abraham, 1:283
   Ahijah, 1:541
   Ahitub, 1:545
   Alcimus, 1:603
   anatomy, 2:133
   ancestral house, 11:100
   ark, carrying, 16:518
   blemishes, 3:749–750
   chief priests, Jehoida, 11:107–108
   commandments concerning, 5:81*t*
   descent, 6:694, 10:84
   Diez Macho, Alejandro, 5:659
   divisions, 11:109, 15:738–740
   dynasties, 16:515
   education, 6:168

Priests and priesthood, *continued*
Eli, 6:317
functions of
cultic, 16:517–518
judging and instructing,
16:519–521
mantic, 16:518–519
purification, 12:651, 16:519
halakhic role, 16:524–525
ḥallah, 8:277
Hanamel, 8:314
history of
Hellenistic era to Second
Temple, 16:523–524
Patriarchal period to
Babylonian return, 16:521–
523
holiness and purity of, 16:520–521
Holiness Code, 9:319, 320
investiture, 6:617
levels of, 16:516–517
medicine and, 13:720
Melchizedek, 14:11
mishmarot and ma'amadot,
14:317–319
modern times, 16:525–526
Moses, 14:529
Phinehas, 16:114–115
power of, 15:743, 744
Psalms, Book of, 16:670–671
right to, 16:513–516
sacrifical system, 21:231
Second Temple, 19:616–617
vestments, 16:511–513
Wicked Priest, 21:**38–39**
Zadok, 21:439–441
See also High priests; Nazirite
Prigogine, Ilya, 4:593, 16:**526**
Prijs, Joseph, 16:**526–527**
Priluker, Jacob, 15:138
Priluki (Ukraine), 16:**527**
*Prime Linee di Storia della Tradizione
Maccabaica* (Momigliano), 14:431
Primera Sociedad Agricola Israelita,
2:429
Primitive Religion (Lowie), 13:236
Primitive Society (Lowie), 13:236
Primo, Samuel, 6:148, 16:**527–528,**
18:348
Primogeniture, 7:47, 19:285
Jacob and Esau, 11:18, 21
Manasseh and Ephraim, 11:20
Primordial Man. *See* Adam Kadmon
Primrose, Albert. *See* Primrose, Harry
Mayer Archibald
Primrose, Hannah Rothschild, 17:491

Primrose, Harry Mayer Archibald,
17:491
Prince, Harold, 16:**528**
The Prince and the Hermit (fable). *See
Ben ha-Melekh Ve-ha-Nazir*
Prince des Juif. *See* Praefectus
Judaeorum
Prince of Egypt (motion picture), 8:485
Princeton University, 1:396
Principiile umanitariste (Relgis), 17:214
Principles of faith, 2:529–532
*Principles of Grammar. See Kelalei ha-
Dikduk*
Principles of Neural Science (Kandel),
11:759–760
Principles of Psychology (Kantor),
11:770
Pringle, Mia, 16:**528**
Pringsheim, Hans, 16:**528**
Pringsheim, Nathanael, 13:7
Prinicipi di scienza economica (Bachi),
3:38
Prin lentile negre (Aderca), 1:390–391
Prins, Liepman Philip, 16:**528–529**
Printcipen un Oyfgaben, 8:757
Printer's marks, 16:**529**
Prostitz, Isaac ben Aaron, 16:629
Printing, 16:*541*
Aldo Manuzio, 1:606
Alexander family, 1:621
Alkan, Alphonse, 1:664
Alnakar, Abraham ben Joseph,
1:685–686
Altaras family, 2:16–17
Altona, 2:24
Amsterdam, 2:108, 109, 122
Anhalt, 2:163
Appiryon Shlomo catalogue, 2:108
art, 2:497–498
ArtScroll/Mesorah series, 21:644–
645
Bak family, 3:70–71
Bekache, Shalom, 3:273
Belforte, Solomon, 3:280
Blumenthal, Joseph, 4:12
Bomberg, Daniel, 4:52
Bragadini family, 4:117
colophon, 5:67
Conat, Abraham ben Solomon,
5:133
Concio, Joseph ben Gerson, 5:133
copyright, 8:450–451, 453
Cracow, 5:262, 6:629
Cremona, 5:283–284
decorative borders, 4:75
Dubno, 6:34
Dutch, 4:520

European cultural hegemony,
6:556
Ferrara, 6:763–764
Fez, Morocco, 7:8
Fishels, Roizl of Cracow, 7:61–62
Germany, 4:305
Gunzenhauser, Joseph ben Jacob,
8:138
hakdamah, 8:242–243
Halicz family, 8:274
haskamah, 8:444–445
Hebrew alphabet, 5:478
Hebrew Bible, 3:586–588
Hebrew grammars, 15:718
Hebrew literature, 1:300, 301,
6:708, 7:16, 11:7, 64, 13:783
illustrated books, 4:75–76
illustrations of Jerusalem, 11:226–
227
India, 10:24
Istanbul, 10:784–785
Italy, 16:532–533
Adelkind, Israel Cornelius,
1:386
incunabula, 9:760–761
Leghorn, 12:609
in Jerusalem, 11:169
Karaites and Karitism, 11:800
Landau, Moses, 12:465
Lasansky, Mauricio, 12:494
Le Bé, Guillaume, 12:589
Leipzig, 12:628
Levy, Louis Edward, 12:752
Lévy family, 12:746
Lichtenstein, Roy, 12:799
in Nowy Dwor Mazowiecki,
15:325
in Nuremberg, 15:347
in Offenbach, 15:386
in Olesnica, 15:402
otiyyot Amsterdam, 2:108
in Ozery, 15:557
in Padua, 15:568
Parenzo family, 15:641
in Paris, 15:645
Pins, Jacob, 16:170
Poland, Dyhernfurth, 6:77–78
Polonnoye, 16:360
Portugal, incunabula, 9:761–762
Prague, 16:455, 533
prayer books, 16:463
printer's marks, 16:529
printmakers, Moreh, Mordecai,
14:483–484
in Romania, 11:92
Romania, Seini, 18:254

Rome, 17:415
Sefer Yeẓiran, 2:*121*
Shaḥor family, 18:366
sidurim, 2:108
Slavuta, 18:672–673
Spain, 2:633
    incunabula, 9:761–762
Syria, Aleppo, 1:615–616
Talmud, 6:718, 16:629
    in U.S., 6:746
title pages, engraved, 4:75
Turkey, 10:828
    Constantinople, 9:762
    incunabula, 9:762
typographers, 20:212–213
typography, 20:213–218
U.S., 11:16
Venice, 16:532–533
Verona, 20:513
Vienna, 20:523
Vilna, 20:530–531
Warsaw, 20:670
Zhitomir, 21:524–525
Zholkva, 21:526
Zurich, 21:690
See also Hebrew printing;
    Publishing; *specific printers*
Printing, Hebrew. *See* Hebrew printing
Prinz, Joachim, 3:736, 16:**540–541,**
    20:352
Prinz, Zalman ben Moses, 2:38
Das Prinzip des Mosaismus (Einhorn),
    6:258
Das Prinzip Hoffnung (Bloch), 3:760
Prior, Matthew, 18:761
The Prioress' Tale (Chaucer), 3:775–
    776, 4:584
Prior of Crato. *See* Antonio
Případ profesora Körnera (Hostovský),
    9:568
The Pripet Marshes (Feldman), 9:407
Prisco, Moses, 15:536
Priscus, 4:615, 15:642, 16:**541**
    disputations and polemics, 5:690
Prisoner-of-war camps. *See* Camps,
    concentration and extermination
Prison reform, 4:550, 5:303
Prisons
    Israel, 5:303
    treatment of prisoners, 9:745
    See also Jails
Pritzker, Jay, 16:541
Pritzker, Nicholas, 16:541
Pritzker family, 16:**541–542**
Privacy rights, 17:17:323–328
    Jewish law, 6:583–584

Private International Law, 5:151–157
The Prizefighter and the Lady, 3:53
*Probleme der Bevoelkerungs-Bewegung
    bei den Juden* (Lestschinsky), 12:666
Probleme des modernen Judentums
    (Klatzkin), 12:213
*The Problem from Hell: America in the
    Age of Genocide* (Parker), 9:390–391
*Problems of Human Pleasure and
    Behavior* (Balint), 3:91
Problems of the Hebrew Verbal System
    (Driver), 6:22
Probst, Menaham Mendel, 16:**542**
Probst-Kraid, Riza, 16:**542**
*Procession on Simḥat Torah in the
    Synagogue of Copenhagen* (Ballin),
    3:93
Procopius, 11:464
Procreation vs. population control,
    5:169
Procurators, 9:198–199, 16:**542–543**
The Producers (musical), 4:209, 210,
    15:228
Production cooperatives, 5:210
Proem type preaching, 16:469
Profanity, 16:**543–544**
Profatius Judaeus. *See* Jacob ben
    Makhir
Professional societies, 18:723
The Professional Soldier (Janowitz,
    Morris), 11:79
Professor Bernhardi (Schnitzler), 18:152
Profiat Duran. *See* Duran, Profiat
Profil107 (Fink, Koren), 18:206
Profiteering, 5:185, 8:196–198
Pro Flacco (Cicero), 4:725
Progressive Jewish Alliance, 16:**544**
Progressive Judaism. *See* Reform
    Judaism
Progressive movement, 19:46
Progressive revelation, 15:494
Progressive Women's Councils, 18:422
Progressivism, educational, 8:553
Prohibited practices, 2:97
Prohibition era, U.S., 15:661
Prohibitions
    on clothing, 18:336
    commandments concerning,
        5:78t–84t
Prohovnik, Abraham, 16:**544**
Pro-Israel (newspaper), 14:425
Project Renewal, 12:749, 16:**544–547**
*Prolegomena to Every Future
    Metaphysic* (Kant), 11:769
Prometheus (Bruggen), 4:222
Promiscuity. *See* Sex; Sexual offenses
Promissory note. *See* Mamram

Pronouns in Hebrew, 8:584–585, 584t
Pronunciations of Hebrew, 16:**547–
    562,** 556t–557t
    Ashkenazi, 16:551–553, *552*
    classifications of, 16:553, 553t,
        554t
    consonants, 16:553–555, 556t–
        557t, 558–559
    Sephardi, 16:550–551
    specimen texts, 16:561–562
    vowels, 16:556t–557t, 559–561
    Yemenite, 16:549–550, *550*
    See also Hebrew grammar
Proops, Abraham, 15:386, 16:563
Proops, Marjorie, 16:563
Proops, Samuel, 2:108
Proops, Solomon ben Joseph, 16:562–
    563
Proops family, 16:**562–563**
Propaganda
    Anti-Defamation League, 2:194
    Anti-Fascist Committee, Jewish,
        2:196
    communism, 5:92
    historiography, 9:416
    Nazi Germany, 4:478–479, 5:54
    for Sheluḥei Ereẓ Israel, 18:450
Pro-Palestine Association. *See* Pro
    Palesztina Szovetsseg
Pro Palesztina Szovetsseg, 3:124
Property, 16:**563–565**
    acquisitiion by agency, 1:452
    acquisition, 1:359–363
    communal, 5:60
    demarcation, 1:474–476
    lost or stolen, commandments
        concerning, 5:77t–78t
    pledges, 16:234
    real, ona'ah, not subject to, 15:424
    shalish, 18:374
    ye'ush, 21:322–323
    See also Sikarikon
Property development
    Levy, Aaron, 12:746
    Ratner, Bruce C., 17:112
    Ratner, Leonard, 17:112–113
    Reichmann, Samuel, 17:200
    Reichmann, Saul, 17:200
    Ross, Stephen, 17:470
    Rudin family, 17:521
    Silverstein, Larry, 18:589
Property law
    antichresis, 2:193
    conditions, 5:137
    hefker, 8:753–755
    lease and hire, 12:568–573

Property law, *continued*
  matrimonial, 13:680–683
  obligations, law of, 15:368, 370
  ona'ah, 15:423–426
  ones in, 15:428
  oppression, 15:452–453
  ownership, 8:486–491, 15:551–552
  servitudes, 18:317–318
  sevarah, 18:323
Property ownership. *See* Ḥazakah
Prophacius Judaeus. *See* Jacob ben
  Makhir
Prophecy. *See* Prophets and prophecy
Prophecy (Krasner), vol. 2: color insert
Prophetic literature
  covenant, 5:252–253
  dietary laws, 5:656
  dualism, 6:30–31
  humility and, 9:590
  sacrifices, 17:644
Die Prophetie (Heschel), 9:71
"Prophet of a Nameless God" (Hart),
  6:336
Prophet of Avila, 2:**736**
Prophet of lies, 12:**819**
Prophets, lives of the, 16:**565–566**
Prophets and prophecy, 3:239, 5:422,
  16:**566–586**
  Abrabanel, Isaac ben Judah, 1:278
  Abraham, 1:282, 283, 284–285
  Ahijah the Shilonite, 1:542
  alchemy, 1:599–600
  in Amos, 2:100–103
  on angels, 2:151–152
  angels and, 2:151
  of Avila, 2:736
  books of
    Abrabanel, Isaac ben Judah,
      1:277–278
    Aramaic, 2:347
  classical, 16:574–578
    pre-classical comparison,
      16:571–574
  classification, 16:566–567
  Columbus, Christopher interest in,
    5:70
  Conversos, 4:645
  Daniel, 5:418, 421
  Dead Sea scrolls, 5:504
  Dias, Luis, 5:636–637
  divination, 5:703–704
  dreams and divination, 16:568
  ecstasy and, 6:138–139
  education, 6:168
  Elijah, 6:331–337
  Elisha, 6:350–351

end of days and, 16:9, 10
  eschatology, 6:490–495
  false, 1:525, 16:576–577
  function of, 16:567
  group prophecy, 16:569–570
  Hananiah son of Azzur, 8:316–317
  Ibn Daud, Abraham ben David
    Halevi, 9:664
  intercessor role, 16:577–578
  Isaiah, 5:424
  Islam, 10:92
  Jacob, 11:17–18
  Jeremiah, 11:126, 127, 130, 132,
    133
  kabbalistic literature and, 5:628–
    629
  Koran, 12:301–302
  Maimonides, Moses, 13:391
  mantics, 5:703
  Mari (Mesopotamia), 13:540–541
  Michah, 14:162–164
  mishpat Ivri, 14:337
  morality, supremacy of, 16:578–
    579
  Moses, 14:530, 536–537
  Nathan, 15:**6**
  nature of, 16:567–568
  philosophers' views of, 16:581–586
    Baruch Spinoza, 16:585
    Ḥasdai Crescas, 16:584–585
    Judah Halevi, 16:582
    Maimonides, 16:582–583
    medieval, 16:585–586
    modern, 16:585–586
    Saadia Gaon, 16:581–582
  philosophical analysis of, 16:76,
    83, 85, 88
  politics of, 16:570–571
  pre-classical, 16:568–571
  reluctance of, 16:575–576
  repentance, 16:579–580
  separation of powers, 18:291
  Shemaiah (era of Rehoboam),
    18:456
  symbolic acts of, 18:569
  Talmud's view of, 16:580–581
  visions, 16:573–574
  wonder working, 16:571
  See also Eschatology; *names of*
    specific prophets
Propper, Dan, 16:**586**
Proprietary rights, 16:**564–565**
Prosbul, 16:**586–587**
Prose, Francine, 16:**587**
Proselytes, 5:200, 16:**587–594**
  ablution, 1:262

adoption, 1:418, 419
  Agrippa II, 6:394
  Aquila, 15:433–434
  Bodo, 4:30
  Catechumens, house of, 4:523–524
  conversion, laws of, 16:587–589
  Domus Conversorum, 5:747
  Du Pré, Jacqueline, 6:51
  Ehrlich, Arnold Bogumil, 6:242–
    243
  embryos, 6:391–392
  Escudero, Lorenzo, 6:504
  evangelical Christian sects, 11:283
  Halakhic definition of Jew and,
    11:254–255
  in Hellenistic and early Christian
    periods, 11:293
  in Japan, 11:82
  Joseph and Asenath, 11:418
  by Judaizers, 11:520
  Khazars, 16:83
  Maimonides views of, 16:591
  medieval, 16:590–592
  mixed marriages, Jewish identity
    of children of, 11:298
  modern times, 16:592–594
  non-orthodox views, 16:594
  in Norway, 15:307
  Obadiah the Norman proselyte,
    15:366–367
  Onkelos, 15:433–434
  Oshaiah Rabbah, 15:501–502
  Pallière, Aimé, 15:602
  post-Talmudic views of, 16:590–
    592
  Russia, Judaizing sects of, 11:521
  Talmudic view of, 16:589–590
  U.S., 16:593–594
  See also Apostasy
Proselytizing
  in Israel by Christian churches,
    11:279
  in Japan, 11:82
Proskauer, Joseph Meyer, 16:**594**
Proskurov (Ukraine), 16:**594–595**
Prosody, Hebrew. *See* Hebrew prosody
Prosopopéia (Teixeira), 17:45
Prospero, Joseph M., 6:450
Prossnitz (Czech Republic). *See*
  Prostejov (Czech Republic)
Prossnitz, Daniel. *See* Prosstitz, Daniel
Prossnitz, Judah Leib ben Jacob
  Holleschau, 15:444, 16:**623–624**,
  18:355
Prossnitz, Menahem. *See* Katz,
  Menahem
Prosstitz, Daniel, 16:**624**

Prostejov (Czech Republic), 16:**624–625**

Prostitution, 16:**625–629**
  Adler, Polly, 1:405–406
  banishment, 3:111
  Canada, 4:400
  concubine, 5:134
  ethics, 6:533, 535
  imprisonment, 9:744
  modern period, 16:627–628
  perfumes, 9:754
  post-Talmudic views of, 16:626–627
  priestly restrictions, 16:521
  punishment of, 18:330
  Rahab, 17:66–67
  sexual offenses, 18:330
  Talmudic, Halakhahic views of, 16:626
  Tzvi Migdal traffic network, Brazil, 4:147–148
  white slave trade, 16:627–628

Prostitz, Isaac ben Aaron, 16:**629**

Prostration prayer. See Taḥanun

Protectorate of Bohemia-Moravia. See Moravia

Protestant Bibles
  canon of, 3:666
  English translations, 3:625
    early modern, 3:611–614
    World War II, following, 3:614–621
  German, 3:630
  translation spurrred by Reformation period, 3:606

Protestant Churches, 10:640–641, 642

Protestantism, Bible, meaning of, 3:664

Protestants, 4:683, 684–685, 690–693, 16:**629–634**
  antisemitism, 2:231, 16:631
  Benzinger, Immanuel, 3:391–392
  biblical drama, 7:509–510
  Canada, 4:397
  Holocaust, response to, 9:375–377
  Marrano diaspora, 13:560–561
  Reformation, 17:163–165
  Réveil movement, 6:70
  scholars of Judaism, 6:589, 16:630
  theologians
    Callenberg, Johann Heinrich, 4:366
    Calvin, John, 4:376–377
    Hottinger, Johann Heinrich, 9:568
  See also World Council of Churches

Protestrabbiner, 16:**634**

"Protest Rabbis." See Protestrabbiner

Protests, Bittul ha-Timid, 3:729–730

Protocol of 110, 13:185

Protocols of the Learned. See Elders of Zion, Protocols of the Learned

Protoevangelium of James, 11:380

Das Protokollbuch der Landjudenschaft des Herzogtums Kleve (Baer), 3:54

Proto-Semitic language, 18:283–284, 283t

Proto-Yiddish, 11:301–302

Protsentnaya norma. See Numerus clausus

Proudhon, Pierre Joseph, 16:**634,** 18:705

Proust, Marcel, 16:**634–635**

Provençal, Abraham ben David, 16:**635**

Provençal, David ben Abraham, 16:**635–636**

Provençal, Jacob ben David, 16:**636**

Provençal, Moses ben Abraham, 13:674, 16:**636**

Provençal language, biblical translations, 3:629

Provence (France), 16:**636–639,** 637
  expulsion from, 7:153–154
  Hebrew language of, 8:667
  Jewish communities, 9:219
    Draguignan, 6:6
    leaders of, 13:785
  Kabbalah, establishment of, 11:602–605
  poetry, medieval, 16:266–268, 270
  See also Judeo-Provençal language

Proverbios morales (Santob de Carrión), 18:29, 295

Proverbs, 16:**639–642**
  ancient education, 6:168
  Halakhah, 16:646–647
  Hillel (the Elder), 9:109–110
  mnemonics or memora technica, 14:398
  Talmudic, 16:646–648

Proverbs (Egyptian), 6:534

Proverbs, Book of, 16:**642–646**
  Agur, 1:521
  calligraphy, vol. 2: color insert
  commentaries, 6:526
  commentary, Meiri, Menahem ben Solomon, 13:787
  Eshet Ḥayil, 6:505
  ethical teachings, 6:533
  Lemuel, 12:638
  Midrash Proverbs, 14:190–191
  targum to, 3:593

Proviantliefirant. See Court Jews

Providence, 16:**648–652**
  anthropocentrism, 2:188
  emanation, 6:373
  free will, 7:230, 232
  God in history, 7:656
  miracles, 14:307, 309
  stoicism, 19:232
  views on
    Aaron ben Elijah, 1:212
    Aboab, Isaac I, 1:267
    Abrabanel, Isaac ben Judah, 1:278
    Crescas, Ḥasdai ben Judah, 5:266
    ḥasidic thought, 8:408
    Jewish philosophy, 16:83, 85
    Levi ben Gershom, 12:699, 700
    Maimonides, 13:388, 391
    Moses ben Joseph ha-Levi, 14:551

Providence, Divine, 8:408

Provins (France), 16:**652**

Proxies, attorneys, 2:648

Prudence of Troyes, 4:81

Pruewer, Julius, 16:**652**

Prunk, Michael. See Dorian, Emil

Prusa (Anatolia). See Bursa (Anatolia)

Prusiner, Stanley S., 13:9–10, 16:**652–653**

Prussia (Germany), 16:**653–656,** 654
  antisemitism, 4:374
  Bialystok, 3:567, 568
  coinage, 14:300
  emancipation, 8:347
  Freemasons, 7:229
  politicians, 11:56, 12:778
  See also specific rulers

Prussia, Holocaust, Pomerania, 16:365

Pruzana (Belarus). See Pruzhany (Belarus)

Pruzhany (Belarus), 16:**656–657**

Prylucki, Noah, 7:113, 16:**657–658**

Prylucki, Zevi Hirsch, 8:476, 14:430, 16:**658**

Prynne, William, 16:**658**

Prystor, Janina, 16:**658**

Prywes, Moshe, 16:**658–659**

Przedborz (Poland), 16:**659**

Przedbórz (Poland). See Przedborz (Poland)

Przedborz family, 16:**659**

Przemyśl (Poland). See Przemysl (Poland)

Przemysl (Poland), 16:**659–660**

Przemyslany. *See* Peremyshlyany (Ukraine)

Przeworsk (Poland), 16:**660**

Przybyslawa, Isaac. *See* Eulenburg, Isaac ben Abraham Moses Israel

Przysucha (Poland), 16:**660–661**

Przysucha, Jacob Isaac ben Asher, 16:**661–662**

Przytyk (Poland), 16:**662**

A Psalm, a Song for the Sabbath Day. *See* Mizmor Shir le-Yom ha-Shabbat

Die Psalmen (Baethgen), 3:55

Psalmody. *See* Music

Psalms, 14:644–645
  apocryphal, 16:**662–663**
  Book of Life, 4:69
  Talmudic period, 13:132
  Thanksgiving, 5:507, 19:**667–669**

Psalms, Book of, 5:457, 16:**663–683**
  Abenatar Melo, David, 1:250
  Aboab, Isaac I, 1:266
  Abraham ben Shabbetai ha-Kohen, 1:310
  arts, 16:678
  commentary, Meiri, Menahem ben Solomon, 13:787
  composition, 16:666–667
  dates, 16:667–668
  David, 16:668–669
  education, 6:164
  Egyptian literature, 6:226
  English translations Psalm 23, variations in, 3:625–627
  Jerusalem in, 11:209
  liturature, 16:677–678
  liturgy, 3:661, 16:676–677
  Midrash Tehillim, 14:191
  Mizmor le-David, 14:387
  Mizmor Shir le-Yom ha-Shabbat, 14:387
  modern biblical criticism and, 3:655
  music, 12:632–634, 16:678–682
  number of psalms and verse division, 16:664–666
  paraphrase, 12:438–439
  place in canon, 16:664
  priestly cult, 16:670–671
  Psalms of Solomon, 18:766–767
  superscription and technical terminology, 16:671–675
  Talmud and Midrash, 16:675–676
  targum to, 3:593
  text, 16:671
  title, 16:663–664
  types of, 16:669–670

Psalms of Solomon, 18:**766–767**

A Psalm to David. See Mizmor le-David

Psalter. *See* Psalms, Book of

Psantir, Jacob, 16:**683**

Pseudepigrapha, 2:**258–261**, 6:495–498
  See also specific works

Pseudocerastes fieldi, 18:695–696

Pseudo-Clement, 15:394

Pseudo-Eupolemus, 3:660, 6:553

Pseudo-Hecateus. *See* Hecateus of Abdera

Pseudo-Longinus, 16:**683**

Pseudo-Philo. *See* Philo (1st c.), *Liber Antiquitatum Biblicarum*

Pseudo-Phocylides, 16:**683–684**

Pseudo-Scylax, 16:**684**

Pshishkha, Jacob Isaac ben Asher. *See* Przysucha, Jacob Isaac ben Asher

P (Priestly) source of Torah, 15:735–736
  contradictions and, 15:741–742
  dating of, 15:738, 739, 743–744
  identification of, 15:742
  laws in, 15:745–747
  monotheism in, 15:750
  redactor and, 15:740
  Tabernacle, 15:749

Psychiatric Examination among Refugees in Norway (Eitinger), 6:279

Psychiatry, 16:**684–687**
  Abraham, Karl, 1:290
  Adler, Alfred, 1:394–395, 5:302, 6:160–161
  Balint, Michael, 3:91
  Baruk, Henri, 3:191
  biodynamics, Masserman, Jules Homan, 13:668
  criminology and, 5:302
  Deutsch, Felix, 5:622–623
  Eissler, Kurt R., 6:278
  Eitenger, Leo S., 6:279
  Eitingon, Max, 6:279–280
  Erikson, Erik Homberger, 6:479–480
  Federn, Paul, 6:728–729
  Fenichel, Otto, 6:757
  Ferenczi, Sándor, 6:761
  Frankl, Viktor Emil, 7:214
  Franzblau, Abraham Norman, 7:218
  Freud, Sigmund, 1:290, 4:181–182, 5:302, 7:259–262, 14:538
  Fromm, Erich, 2:187, 7:298
  Gold, Henry Raphael, 7:688
  Hartmann, Heinz, 8:377
  Hautval, Adelaïde, 8:464–465
  Hitschmann, Edward, 9:290

Hoff, Hans, 9:307
Hoffer, Willi, 9:307
Kanner, Leo, 11:766
Kardiner, Abram, 2:187, 11:804
Kline, Nathan S., 12:232
Kubie, Lawrence, 12:377
law and, 3:234
Lewis, Sir Aubrey Julian, 12:763–764
Loewenstein, Rudolph Maurice, 13:169
Malzberg, Benjamin, 13:437–438
Masserman, Jules Homan, 13:668
Miller, Emanuel, 14:252–253
Miller, Louis, 14:253–254
Minkowski, Eugène, 14:282
Nunberg, Herman, 15:344–345
Rado, Sandor, 17:56
Rank, Otto, 17:91
Redlich, Frederick C., 17:158–159
Reik, Theodore, 17:204
Roth, Sir Martin, 17:484
Rothschild, Friedrich Salomon, 17:493
Sakel, Manfred Joshua, 17:679
Schilder, Paul Ferdinand, 18:133
Spitz, Rene A., 19:121–122
Stekel, Wilhelm, 19:200
Stengel, Erwin, 19:201
Szasz, Thomas Stephen, 19:402–403
Tausk, Viktor, 19:530
Tramer, Moritz, 20:90–91
Winnik, Henry Zvi, 21:88
Wolberg, Lewis Robert, 21:132–133
Woolf, Moshe, 21:212
Zilboorg, Gregory, 5:302, 21:530–531

The Psychic Life of Power (Butler), 4:317

Psychoanalysis
  Abraham, Karl, 1:290
  Alexander, Franz, 1:622
  Balint, Michael, 3:91
  Bendek, Therese F., 3:329
  Bernfeld, Siegfried, 3:472
  Breuer, Joseph, 4:171
  Brill, Abraham Arden, 4:181–182
  criminology and, 5:302
  Eissler, Kurt R., 6:278
  Eitingon, Max, 6:279–280
  Erikson, Erik Homberger, 6:479–480
  Fenichel, Otto, 6:757
  Ferenczi, Sándor, 6:761

Fine, Reuben, 7:25

Hartmann, Heinz, 8:377

Kardiner, Abram, 11:804

Klein, Melanie Reizes, 12:**224**

Loewenstein, Rudolph Maurice, 13:169

Rado, Sandor, 17:56

Rank, Otto, 17:91

Redlich, Frederick C., 17:158–159

Reich, Wilhelm, 17:198–199

Reik, Theodor, 17:204

Róheim, Géza, 17:369–370

Slavson, Samuel Richard, 18:672

The Psychoanalytical Theory of Neurosis (Fenichel), 6:757

Psychology, 16:**687–693**

    Alexander of Aphrodisias, 1:628

    Bakan, David, 3:72

    Beit-Hallahmi, Benjamin, 3:271–272

    Ben-Shakhar, Gershon, 3:374

    Bettelheim, Bruno, 3:551–552

    biodynamics, Masserman, Jules Homan, 13:668

    Brodsky, Stanley L., 4:198

    Brothers, Joyce, 4:211

    Bruna, Jerome Seymour, 4:222–223

    Buhler, Charlotte, 4:256

    Chein, Isidor, 4:587–588

    cognitive, 4:222

    criminology and, 5:302

    Denmark, Florence Levin, 5:586

    Dessoir, Max, 5:605–606

    early, 6:681

    empirical research in, 11:72

    Feurstein, Reuven, 6:775–776

    Fingerman, Gergorio, 7:30

    Fishman, Joshua Aaron, 7:64–65

    Fox, Charles, 7:140

    Frankenstein, Carl, 7:203

    Franzblau, Abraham Norman, 7:218

    Freudian, 6:728

    Gurwitsch, Aaron, 8:142

    Heller, Theodor, 8:796

    Ḥibat Allah, abu al-Barakāt ben Ali al-Baghdādi, 9:93

    Himmelweit, Hildegard, 9:121

    humor and, 9:599

    individual, 1:394

    Jungian, Oz, Amos, 15:555

    kabbalah and, 11:679

    Kahneman, Daniel, 11:724–725

    Kantor, Jacob Robert, 11:770

    Karpf, Maurice Joseph, 11:816

Katz, Daniel, 12:**10**

Lehrman, Daniel S., 12:617

Lévy-Bruhl, Lucien, 12:756

Lewin, Kurt Zadek, 12:760–761

Lipmann, Otto, 13:68

literature, psychology approach to, 4:159

Luria, Alexander Romanovich, 13:261

Milgram, Stanley, 14:233

Neugarten, Bernice, 15:118

Neumann, Erich, 15:**121**

personality theory, Maslow, 13:602

psychotraumatology, Eitinger, Leo S., 6:279

Rapaport, David, 17:92

Razran, Gregory, 17:131

Redl, Fritz, 17:158

Roback, Abraham Aaron, 17:352

Rodin, Judith, 17:364

Rubin, Edgar, 17:511–512

Rubinstein, Sergey Leonidovich, 17:518

self-hatred, Jewish, 18:264–265

Selz, Otto, 18:273

of women, Mednick, Martha Tamara Schuch, 13:762

The Psychology of Gang Formation and the Treatment of Juvenile Delinquents (Redl), 17:158

Psychotechnics, 18:141

Psychotherapeutic Techniques in Medicine (Balint), 3:91

Psychotherapy

    Balint method, 3:91

    family, 1:357

Ptashne, Mark Stephen, 13:9, 16:**693**

Ptolemaeus, Claudius. *See* Ptolemy the Geographer

Ptolemaic cosmology, 5:231

Ptolemaic period

    Egypt, 6:226–227

    Ereẓ Israel, 9:191–193

    Josephus' *Jewish Antiquities* on, 11:439

Ptolemais (Israel). *See* Acre (Israel)

Ptolemy (c. 85-40 B.C.E.), 1:631, 16:**695**

Ptolemy (c. 135 B.C.E.), 16:**694–695**

Ptolemy (Macedonian Dynasty monarchs), 16:**693–694**

Ptolemy I, 6:227, 9:191, 16:**693–694**

Ptolemy II, 3:595, 660, 4:71, 73, 6:227, 16:694

Ptolemy III, 6:227, 16:694

Ptolemy IV, 6:227, 16:694

Ptolemy V, 16:694

Ptolemy VI, 1:625, 16:694

Ptolemy VII, 16:694

Ptolemy VIII, 16:694

Ptolemy X. *See* Ptolemy VIII

Ptolemy Macron, 16:**695**

Ptolemy of Chennos, 16:**695**

Ptolemy of Mende, 16:**695**

Ptolemy Philadelphus. *See* Ptolemy II

Ptolemy the Biographer, 16:**695**

Ptolemy the Geographer, 16:**695**

Puah. *See* Shiphrah and Puah

Puberty, 16:**695–696**

Public Access (Singer), 18:633

Publications. *See specific publications*

Publications (periodical), 2:59

Public authority, 16:**696–710**

    communal leaders, 16:696–697

    elected officials

        elections, 16:699–701

        rights and obligations, 16:703–709

    elections of public officeholders, 16:699–701

    employees, 16:703–709

    employers, 16:698–699

    exercise of discretion, 16:698

    Israel (state)

        court rulings, 16:701–703

        rabbincal courts, 16:701

        Supreme Court, 16:701

    laws on property and obligations, 16:697–698

    Responsa Index, 16:709–710

    takkanot ha-kahal, 16:709–710

Public health. *See* Medicine

Publicists

    Berr, Jacob, 3:487

    Lewald, Fanny, 12:757–758

    Lewin, Gershon, 12:759

Public offic. *See* Public authority

Public relations, 3:470–471, 16:**710–713**

Publishing, 2:534–535, 16:**713–728**

    Adler, Emanuel Philip, 1:396

    Adler, Harry Clay, 1:398

    Beilinson, Moses Eliezer, 3:267

    Bemporad, Enrico, 3:312–313

    Bisliches, Mordecai Lieb, 3:726

    Bloch family, 3:758

    Block, Paul, 3:769

    Blogg, Solomon ben Ephraim, 3:770

    Bobruisk, 4:25

    Chile, 4:641–642

    Conat, Abraham ben Solomon, 5:133

Publishing, *continued*
Concio, Joseph ben Gerson, 5:133
Deutsch, Andre, 5:621
Dvir publishing house, 6:74
Efron, Ilya, 6:216
England, Cass, Frank, 4:506
Filipowski, Zevi Hirsch, 7:20
Fink, Theodore, 7:31
Firt, Julius, 7:49
Fischer, Samuel, 7:55
France
    Alcan family, 1:599
    Lévy family, 12:746
general, 16:714–721
    Austria, 16:715–716
    Brazil, 18:33
    Czechoslovakia, 16:717
    Europe, Eastern, 16:714
    France, 16:717
    Germany, 16:715–716
    Hungary, 16:717–718
    Italy, 16:716–717
    Latin America, 16:718
    Netherlands, the, 16:714
    Poland, 16:718
    publishers, 16:727–728
    Romania, 16:717
    Russia, 16:718
    Scandinavia, 16:716
    Spain, 16:718
    U.K., 16:718–719
    U.S., 16:719–721, 723–724
    Yugoslavia, 16:717
Germany
    Hessel, Franz, 9:78
    Hitzig, Julius Eduard, 9:294
    Philo Verlag, 16:114
    Schocken Press, 18:153
Hamlyn, Paul, Baron, 8:306
Hart, Abraham, 8:368
Hebraica and Judaica, 16:721–724
    Europe, Central and Western, 16:721–722
    Europe, Eastern, 16:723
    U.K., 16:722–723
Hoza'ah Ivrit, 11:571
international, Maxwell, Robert, 13:696
Israel
    The Jerusalem Publishing House, 11:240
    Laufbahn, Yitshak, 12:526
    Moreshet Publishing House, 14:484
    Perlman, Samuel, 15:779
    Persitz, Shoshanah, 15:792

Israel (state), 16:725–726
    1950s, 10:224
    religious works, 10:628
Italy, 10:806, 813–814
    Sabbioneta, 17:630–631
The Jewish Publication Society, 11:309–310
Joshua Boaz ben Simon Baruch, 11:455
Juedischer Verlag, 11:571
Keter Publishing House, 12:**92–93**
Landau, Moses, 12:465
Leaf, Hayim, 12:563
Newhouse, Samuel Irving, 15:137–138
in New York City, 15:198, 199, 221
in Nowy Dwor Mazowiecki, 15:325
in Nuremberg, 15:347
Orgelbrand, Samuel, 15:468
Poland, Dyhernfurth, 6:77–78
publishers, 16:727–728
Rawnitzki, Yehoshua Hana, 17:126
Rodker, John, 17:364–365
Russia, Moriah publishing house, 14:491
of scholarly medieval Hebrew literature, 13:797
of scholarly works, 18:722–723
sheluhei Erez Israel, 18:452
sixteenth century Italy, 16:8
Slutzki, David, 18:686
by Society for the Promotion of Culture Among the Jews of Russia, 18:726–727
travel guides to Erez Israel, 10:817–818
U.K., Schonfield, Hugh Joseph, 18:161
U.S.
    Cerf, Bennett Alfred, 4:549
    Cowen Philip, 5:255
    Kar-Ben/Lerner, 11:804
    Polachek, Victor Henry, 16:286
    Schiff, Dorothy, 18:129–130
    Schuster, Max Lincoln, 18:177
    Schwarzberg, Samuel Benjamin, 18:192
Yiddish publishing
    Russia, 17:543, 553, 581–583
    Sarasohn, Kasriel Hersch, 18:50
See also Hebrew publishing; Printing
Puchowitzer, Judah Leib. *See* Pukhovitser, Judah Leib

Puduil, King of Ammon. *See* Buduilu, king of Ammon
Puerta del cielo (Herrera), 9:41
Puerto del Cielo (Gershon). *See* Sha'ar ha-Shamayim (Gershon)
Puerto Rico, 16:**728–729**
Pugio Fidei (Martini), 3:146, 8:513
Pugliese, Emanuele, 16:**729**
Pugliese, Umberto, 16:**730**
Pukh. *See* Antimony
Pukhachewsky, Michael Zalman, 16:**730**
Pukhovitser, Judah Leib, 16:**730**
Pul. *See* Tiglath-Pileser III
Pulawy (Poland), 16:**730–731**
Pulcelina of Blois, 16:**731**
Pulgar, Isaac ben Joseph ibn. *See* Pollegar, Isaac ben Joseph ibn
Pulitzer, Joseph, 11:468, 16:**731–732**
Pulitzer Prize
    Block, Herbert Lawrence, 3:769
    Lewis, Anthony, 12:763
Pulkau (Austria), 16:**732**
Pull My Daisy (motion picture), 2:104
Pułtusk (Poland). *See* Pultusk (Poland)
Pultusk (Poland), 16:**732**
Pulu. *See* Tiglath-Pileser III
Pulvermacher, Oscar, 16:**732–733**
Pulzer, Peter G. J., 16:**733**
Pumbedita (Babylonia), 15:62, 16:**733–734**
Pumbedita Academy, 1:350, 659, 6:603, 604, 7:380–384, 10:15, 11:25, 14:340, 16:8, 17:7, 9
Punctuator of Prague. *See* Jekuthiel ben Judah ha-Kohen
Pundak ha-Ruhot (Alterman), 8:720
Punishing sword oracle, 6:639
Punishment, 16:**734–740**
    Aaron ben Elijah on, 1:213
    adultery, 1:424–427
    blindness as, 3:753, 754
    bloodguilt, 3:773–774
    divine, 5:708–710, 7:79
    flogging, 7:78–80
    fraud, 7:220
    gilgul, 7:603
    impalement, 9:742
    judicial, 14:342
        commandments concerning, 5:78t
    karet, 11:806–807
    Mishnah, 14:321
    Noachide laws, violations of, 15:286, 287
    pillory, 9:745

purification for sinning, 19:292

See also Capital punishment; Netherworld; Reward and punishment

Punishment and gilgul, 7:603

Punishment Without Crime (Fineberg), 7:26

Punon (Edom), 16:**740**

Purification. *See* Ablution

Purification for sinning, 19:292

Purim, 16:**740–741**

    Adloyada, 1:410

    Adloyada festival, Tel Aviv, vol. 6: color insert

    Al ha-Nissim, 1:655

    Altschul family, 2:24

    Amidah, 2:75

    Amsterdam, 2:108

    Anim Zemirot, 2:174

    clown performing in Hebron, vol. 20: color insert

    drunkenness, 6:27

    Esther and Mordecai tombs, 8:292

    food, 7:121

    games, 7:371, 372

    gift offerings, 16:24

    haircutting custom, vol. 17: color insert

    Haman, 8:294–295

    parody, Hebrew, 15:656–657

    Purim Katan, 16:**741**

    Purim Meshullash, 16:**741**

    Purims, special, 16:**742–744,** 742*t*–744*t*

    Purimshpil, 2:108, 16:**744–746,** 19:684

    Scroll of Esther, 18:215–220, *219*

Purim d'Amchislav, 14:593

Puritans, 6:433

Purity and impurity, ritual, 16:**746–756**

    ablution, 1:261–263

    Baraita de-Niddah, 3:128–129

    Bible, 16:746–750

    commandments concerning, 5:75*t–76t*

    leprosy, 12:651–652

    Mishnah, 14:321–322

    Samaritans, 17:730

    Shevu'ot, 18:472–473

Purity laws

    Abraham ben Hillel of Fostat, 1:300

    Baraita de-Niddah, 3:128–129

    birth, 3:721, 722

    blemishes, 3:749–750

    blood prohibitions, 3:771–772

    canonical books of the Bible, 3:575

    Karaites, 11:799

    menstrual blood, 3:772

    niddah, 15:253–258

    in Numbers, 15:330

Purity of blood. *See* Limpieza de sangre

Purple worm. *See* Crimson worm

Pusey, E. B., 15:554

Puss-in-Boots. See Motanul incălțat (Silviu)

Put (son of Ham), 16:**756**

Putiel, 16:**756**

Putnam, Hilary, 16:**756–757**

Putterman, David, 16:**757**

The Puttermesser Papers (Ozick), 15:558

Puy, le (France). *See* Le Puy (France)

Puy-en-Velay, le (France). *See* Le Puy (France)

Puzi (music album), 6:263

Puzzles, acrostics, 7:372

Pyckoon, Maragret. *See* Picon, Molly

Pye, Jael Henrietta, 16:**757**

Pyl (Sobol), 18:701

Pynson Printers, 1:396

Pyrrhus, Didacus, 16:**757–758**

Pyrrhus Lusitanus. *See* Pyrrhus, Didacus

Pythagoras, 9:29–30, 16:**758**

Q

Q (letter), 16:*759*

Q (Quelle text of New Testament), 15:191

Qāʿ al-Yahūd, 18:6

Qabbalah. *See* Kabbalah

Qaddoumi, Farouq, 15:595, 597, 598

Qal'a-e-Shush (Iran). *See* Shushan (Iran)

Qal'at Ḥammād (Algeria), 16:**759**

Qar'iyya, al-. *See* Kariyah, al-

Qaryat al-'Inab. *See* Abu Ghosh

Qaṣīda

    Judah Halevi's use of, 11:494

    Morocco, 1:439

Qaṣr ibn Hubayrah (Babylonia), 16:**759–760**

Qātāya. *See* Sambari, Joseph ben Isaac

Qaynuqāʾ, Banū, 16:**760**

Qazzāz, Manasseh ben Abraham ibn, 16:**760**

    al- (*See* Qazzāz, Manasseh ben Abraham ibn)

Qen (ancient city). *See* Kenath (ancient city)

Qeranot. *See* Horns, altar

Qere and ketiv, 13:609, 615–617, 15:751–752

Qesse-ye Haft Barādarān (Emrāni). *See* Story of the Seven Brothers (Emrāni)

Qetanna. *See* Masorah Parva

Qinot. *See* Lamentations, Book of

Qirmisin. *See* Kermanshah (Iran)

Qirqer (Crimea). *See* Chufut-Kale (Crimea)

Qirqisani, Jacob al-. *See* Kirkisani, Jacob

Qirqyer (Crimea). *See* Chufut-Kale (Crimea)

Qiṣ aṣ al-Anbiyaʿ, 1:463, 3:669, 674

Qiṣaṣ min al-Gharb (Shaul), 18:421

Qittner, Zsigmond, 16:**760–761**

Qof. *See* Kof

Qohelet. *See* Ecclesiastes

Qos (god of Edom), 6:156

Quadratus, Ummidius Caius, 11:396, 16:**761**

Quails, 16:**761**

Qualcomm Inc., 11:47–48

Quality of goods, Jewish law regarding, 5:187–188

Quamvis perfidiam, 4:277

Quantum crystallography, 11:809

Quantum electrodynamics, 7:6

Quantum Mechanics of Molecular Rate Processes (Levine), 12:719

Quaresmius, Franciscus, 16:**761**

"The Quarreler". *See* Louis (kings of France)

Quastel, Judah Hirsch, 16:**761–762**

Qubbah, 2:468

al-Quds (newspaper), 15:596

Que (Turkey), 16:**762**

Quebec (Canada), 4:397, 403–404, 405, 408–409, 14:466, 16:**762–765**

La Québécoite (Robin), 4:425

Queen Elizabeth (motion picture), 14:570

Queen mothers, 6:692

Queen of Sheba, 13:18, 16:**765,** 18:757, 759, 762

Queensland (Australia). *See* Australia

Queen Theodora of Bulgaria. *See* Sarah of Turnovo

Queer theory, 4:317

Queler, Eve, 16:**765–766**

Querido, Israël, 2:114, 6:70, 16:**766**

Querido, Jacob, 16:**766,** 18:353

Queries and replies. *See* Responsa

Questions and Answers on Genesis and Exodus (Philo Judaeus), 16:60

Quetsch, Solomon, 16:**766**

Quf. *See* Kof

Quiet Chants (Einhorn), 6:258

Quietus, Lusius, 16:**766–767**

Quilmes, 2:438

Quilon inscription (Southern India), 11:548

Quince, 16:**767**

Quincentennial Foundation of Istanbul, 11:755, 18:305

Quintilian, 16:**767**

Quintilius Varus, 16:**767**

Quintus Septimus Florins Tertullianus. *See* Tertullian

Quirinius, P. Sulpicius, 11:367, 16:**767–768**

Quisling, Vidkun Abraham Lauritz Jonssøn, 15:309, 505, 16:**768**

Quito (Ecuador), 6:140

Quixano Henriques family. *See* Henriques family

Qumran (Abécassis), 1:244

Qumran (Israel), 12:818–819, 16:**768–775**, *769, 772t, 773*
    Amusin, Joseph Davidovich, 2:124
    caves, 16:771–775, *773*
        Copper scroll, 5:213–214
        Dead Sea scrolls, 5:500–501
    cylindrical jars, 16:773–774
    Damascus, Book of the Covenant of, 5:397–399
    Enoch, Ethiopic Book of, 6:443
    eschatology, 6:496, 498–500
    Essenes, 6:510–511
    Judean Desert caves used by, 11:524
    Khirbet Qumran, 16:768–771, *769, 772t*
    libraries of, 16:774–775
    pottery in caves, 16:773
    Russian language, 2:124
    See also Dead Sea scrolls

Qumran community. *See* Dead Sea sect

Qumran sect. *See* Dead Sea sect

Qumran scrolls
    Melchizedek and, 14:11
    pesher, 16:9, 10
    raz, 16:9
    Samaritan Pentateuch and, 15:753–754
    See also Dead Sea scrolls

Qunaytira, al- (Ramat ha-Golan), 16:**776**

Quodvultdeus, 4:721

Quorum. *See* Minyan

Quotas. *See* Numerus clausus

Quotas and affirmative action, 3:737

Qura (Eblaite deity). *See* Kura (Eblaite deity)

Qurayẓa, Banū, 16:**776**

R

R (letter), 17:5

R. A. Bloch Cancer Support Center, 3:768

RA. *See* Rabbinical Assembly

Raab, Esther, 17:**5**, 6

Raab, Judah, 17:**5–6**

Ra'ah. *See* Buzzards

Raamses. *See* Ramses (Egyptian rulers)

Ra'anannah (Israel), 17:6

Ra'aya Meheimna (Zohar), 21:650

Raba, 1:235

Rabad. *See* Abraham ben David of Posquières

Rabad I. *See* Ibn Daud, Abraham ben David Halevi

RaBaN. *See* Eliezer ben Nathan of Mainz

Raban, Avner, 17:6

Rabanus Maurus. *See* Hrabanus Maurus

Rabat (Morocco). *See* Salé-Rabat (Morocco)

Rabb, Maxwell Milton, 17:**6–7**

Rabb, Theodore K., 17:40

Rabba, Menahem, 17:7

Rabba ben Matnah, 17:7

Rabbah. *See* Ḥiyya

Rabbah (8th century). *See* Abba

Rabbah (ha-Rabba), 17:7

Rabbah (Mar-Rava), 17:**7–8**

Rabbah bar bar Ḥana, 17:8

Rabbah bar Ḥana, 17:8

Rabbah bar Huna, 17:**8–9**

Rabbah bar Naḥamani, 1:235, 17:**9**

Rabbah ben Avuha, 17:**9–10**

Rabbah ben Shilah, 17:**10**

Rabbah Tosfa'ah, 17:**10**

Rabbana. *See* Ashi

Rabbana Simeon. *See* Simeon bar Isaac

Rabbanei Minsk va-Ḥakhameha (Eisenstadt), 6:270

Rabbanites, 10:297, 17:**10**
    Al-Tarā;s, Sīdī ibn, 2:17
    Anan ben David, 2:127
    Cairo, 4:344
    distinguished from Karaites, 11:785–802
    Hadassi, Judah ben Elijah, 8:188–189
    Mizraḥi, Elijah, 14:394

Saporta, Ḥanokh, 18:39

Rabbath-Ammon (ancient Israel), 2:83, 84, 86, 17:**7**, **10–11**

Rabbath-Moab (ancient Israel), 2:425, 17:7

Rabbathmoba. *See* Rabbath-Moab (ancient Israel)

Rab Battalion, 15:667

Rabbenu. *See* Tam, Jacob ben Meir

Rabbenu Asaph. *See* Asaph ha-Rofe

Rabbenu Ephraim. *See* Ephraim ibn Avi Alragan

Rabbenu Gershom. *See* Gershom ben Judah Me'or ha-Golah

Rabbenu ha-Kadosh. *See* Judah ha-Nasi

Rabbenu Moses Gerondi. *See* Naḥmanides

"Rabbi." *See* Judah ha-Nasi

Rabbi, Rabbinate. *See* Rabbis

Rabbi Abraham Ben David. *See* Abraham ben David of Posquières

Rabbi Ben Ezra (Browning), 4:218

Rabbi Binyamin, 8:497, 17:19
    bi-nationalism promoted by, 3:703

Rabbi Emanuel Rackman Program for Practical Rabbinics, 17:30

Rabbi Esriel Hildesheimer and the Creation of a Modern Jewish Orthodoxy (Ellenson), 6:360

Rabbi Isaac. *See* Isaac ben Samuel of Dampierre

Rabbi Isaac ben Sheshet Perfet and his Times (Hershman), 9:46

Rabbi Isaac Elhanan Theological Seminary, 2:486, 6:193, 197, 17:28–29, 18:774, 776–777

Rabbi Joseph B. Soloveitchik Institute (Boston, MA), 18:100

Rabbi Judah Leib Zlotnik Seminary, 6:210

Rabbi Meir of Rothenburg (Agus), 1:521

Rabbi Mór. *See* Arraby Moor

Rabbi Moses ben Maimon. *See* Maimonides, Moses

Rabbinate. *See* Rabbis

The Rabbinate of the Great Synagogue, London, from 1756-1842 (Duschinsky), 6:64

"Rabbi Nathan's Lien". *See* Shi'buda de-Rabbi Nathan

Rabbin délégué, 17:15

Rabbiner, Ẓemaḥ, 4:270

Rabbiner-Seminar fuer das Orthodoxe Judentum, 17:**19–20**

Rabbinic academies. *See* Rabbinical seminaries

Rabbinical Alliance of America, 17:**20**

Rabbinical Assembly (RA), 17:**20**
  admission of women members,
    18:403
  Eichler, Menahem Max, 6:247
  Eilberg, Amy, 6:253–254
  Finkelstein, Louis, 7:34–35
  Kelman, Wolfe, 12:71
  Segal, Bernard, 18:244
  Shapiro, Alexander M., 18:403
  Silverstein, Alan, 18:588
Rabbinical authority, 2:**703–705**
Rabbinical Conferences, 17:**20–21**
Rabbinical Council of America (RCA),
  17:**21**
Rabbinical Council of the Israeli Chief
  Rabbinate, 11:704
Rabbinical courts
  Chief Rabbinate, Takkanot,
    19:450–451
  Israel, 12:607–608, 14:352–353,
    352–355, 356, 362, 16:440–446
  legal and judicial systems
    Levirate marriage and
      Ḥaliẓah, 12:728–729
    theft and robbery, 19:689
  limitation of actions, 13:24
  Morocco, 14:504
  shammash, 18:395
  Takkanot, 19:451–452
Rabbinical disputes. See Conflict of
  opinion
Rabbinical education. See Rabbinical
  training
Rabbinical High Court, 11:704
Rabbinical literature, 13:96–102, 17:**22**
  Abelson, Joshua, 1:249
  Adret, Moses ibn, 1:421
  Akedah, 1:556
  Alashkar, Joseph ben Moses, 1:576
  ants, 2:184
  apes, 2:254
  apikoros, 2:255–256
  articles of faith, 2:529
  atmospheric pollution, 5:167
  atonement, 2:644
  authors, Aḥa of Shabḥa, 1:529–
    531
  belief, faith, 3:291–293
  Bible
    exegesis and study, 3:641–
      643, 660–662
    history of text, 3:583–584
    Septuagint, 3:597
  Bokser, Baruch M., 4:43–44
  bread, 4:155
  Buber, Solomon, 4:236
  burial customs, 4:292–293

cabbage, 4:329
Chajes, Ẓevi Hirsch, 4:560
charity, 4:569–570
chosen people doctrine, 4:670–671
circumcision, 4:732
codes, 13:97–98, 100–101
commentaries, 13:96–97, 99–100
confession of sins, 5:149
creation, 5:275–277
creation hierarchy, 5:165
crimson worm dye, 5:304
Decalogue, 5:525
detention, 5:606–607
Dorff, Elliot N., 5:755
dualism, 6:30
Duran, Simeon ben Ẓemaḥ, 6:58–
  60
Duran, Solomon ben Simeon, 6:61
Duschak, Mordecai, 6:64
dyeing, 6:77
environment and beauty, 5:168
female voices prohibition, 14:649
foreign law applicability, 5:155–
  156
forgiveness, 7:129
fruit trees, 5:166–167
Hadayah, Ovadiah, 8:189
hagiography, 8:225–226
Hannah and her seven sons, 8:325
hassagot, 8:453–454
heresy, 9:20–22
hospitality and, 9:561–562
host of heaven and, 9:567
hunting, 9:621, 622
hygiene, 9:648
imprisonment, 5:607–608
and inclination, good and evil,
  9:757
indebtedness, 5:154–155
Jabneh and, 11:10
joy, concept of, 11:471
Kings, Kingship, 12:169
la'az, 12:405
labor, 12:410–411
le'azim, 12:405
Lightfoot, John, 13:13
magic, 13:345
mamzer, 13:444–445
marriage and divorce law, 5:152–
  153, 154–155
marriages, 13:564
Mishnah, 19:319–331
music, 14:649, 658–659
nature, 15:33–34
nature of man, 13:448–450
noise pollution, 5:168

olam ha-ba, 15:399–400
olive trees and olives in, 15:406–
  407
onions in, 15:433
paradise in, 15:628
parody in, 15:654–655
profiteering, 5:185
Ranschburg, Bezalel ben Joel,
  17:91
Rath, Meshullam, 17:109
Reifmann, Jacob, 17:203–204
Reischer, Jacob ben Joseph,
  17:210–211
responsa, 13:98–99, 101–102
righteousness, 17:308–309
rishonim, 17:339–343
Risikoff, Menahem Hakohen,
  17:344–345
Rosenbaum, Moses Ḥayyim Lits,
  17:433
Rosenberg, Yehuda Yudel, 17:439
Rosenblatt, Samuel, 17:441
Rosenthal, Ludwiga, 17:455
Rosh Ha-Shanah, 17:464
Roth, Joel, 17:482
Ru'aḥ ha-Kodesh, 17:506–507
Rubio, Mordecai, 17:518
Sabbath, 17:618–619
Samael, 17:714–715
sha'atnez, 18:336–337
shippon, 21:34–35
sin, 18:624–625
Sukkot, 19:300–301
synaptic study of, 8:461
Talmud, Babylonian, 19:475–477
town planning, 5:168
Ẓemaḥ ben Solomon Duran, 6:61
Rabbinical Ordination/Leadership
  Program, 17:30
Rabbinical School at Hebrew College
  in Greater Boston, 17:27–28
Rabbinical seminaries, 12:784, 17:**22–
  27**
  Babylonian, 3:27
  Hebrew Theological College,
    8:738–739
  Hebrew Union College Jewish
    Institute of Religion, 8:739–740
  See also specific institutions
Rabbinical Seminary for Orthodox
  Judaism. See Rabbiner-Seminar Fuer
  das Orthodoxe Judentum
Rabbinical Seminary of America,
  Chofetz Chaim Yeshiva, 17:30
Rabbinical training
  American, 17:**23–31**
    Conservative, 17:25–26

Rabbinical training, *continued*
  orthodox, 17:28–30
  Reconstuctionist, 17:27
  Reform, 17:26–27
  transdenominational, 17:27–28
  ultra-orthodox, 17:30
  Jewish Theological Seminary of America, 5:172–173
  Orthodox, Rabbiner-Seminar Fuer das Orthodoxe Judentum, 17:19–20
  Reconstructionist Judaism, 17:148–149
  Schechter Institute of Jewish Studies, 5:176
  seminaries, 17:22–27
  University of Judaism, 5:173
  See also specific institutions
A Rabbinic Anthology (Loewe, Montefiore, eds.), 13:165–166, 14:455
Rabbinic education. *See* Rabbinical training
Rabbinic Judaism
  New Testament's relationship to, 15:191–192
  orphans and orphanages, 15:483
  piety and, 16:149–150
Rabbinic literature. *See* Rabbinical literature
Rabbinic period
  dress, 6:14
  Judaism, development of concept of, 11:515–516
  moneylending, 14:438–441
  Moses, 14:533–536
  proverbs, 16:647–648
  purity and impurity, ritual, 16:750–754
  theology, 19:695
  usury, 12:606, 20:440–441
Rabbinic seminaries. *See* Rabbinical seminaries
Rabbinic training. *See* Rabbinical training
Rabbinism. *See* Rabbanites
Rabbinovicz, Raphael Nathan Nata, 17:**31**
Rabbinowicz, Israel Michel, 17:**31–32**
Rabbinowicz, Joseph Samuel, 17:31
Rabbinowitz, Saul Phinehas, 4:183, 17:**32**
Rabbi of Apta. *See* Abraham Joshua Heschel of Apta
Rabbis, 17:**11–19**
  ablution, 1:262–263
  Ashkenazi, dress, 6:15

of Buda, 4:245
Bulgaria, 4:270
Canadian, 12:692–693
Central Conference of American Rabbis, 4:545–546
emolument, pay, 17:12
England, 17:15–16
Epicureanism, 6:463
female ordination, 17:16, 17, 18
of Fez, Morocco, 7:7
Germany, 17:16–17
Holy Roman Empire, 12:472
Hungary, 12:470
Iraqi, Dangoor, 5:417
Israel, 17:18–19
Landrabbiner, 12:474
Middle Ages, 5:102–103, 17:11–12
modern period, 17:15–16
Muslim countries, 17:13–15
ordination, 17:16, 18, 18:274–275, 278–279
  Sephardic, 17:13–14
  women, 17:17
Reform Judaism, 17:13
restriction of title, 18:276
Sephardim, dress, 6:15
Spain, 17:13
U.S., 17:17–18
  Danglow, Jacob, 5:417
women, Eilberg, Amy, 6:253–254
Yugoslavia, 12:693–694
See also Chief rabbi and rabbinate; *names of specific rabbis*
Rabbi Shelomo ben Shimon. *See* Duran, Solomon ben Simeon
Rabbi Shimon ben Shelomo Ha-Sheni. *See* Duran, Simeon ben Solomon
Rabbi Shimon ben Ẓemaḥ. *See* Duran, Simeon ben Ẓemaḥ
The Rabbi's Melody. See Dem Reben Nign
A Rabbi Talks with Jesus (Neusner), 15:125
Der Rabbi von Bacherach (Heine), 3:31
Rabbi Ya'akov Elyashar (Benayahu), 6:371
Rabchik, Joseph, 11:471
Rab de la Corte, 17:**32**
Rabi, Isidor Isaac, 17:**33**
Rabi Abad. *See* Abraham ben Isaac of Narbonne
Rabī' ibn Abi al-Ḥuqayq, 17:**33**
Rabin. *See* Avin
Rabin, Israel Abraham, 17:33
Rabin, Michael Oser, 17:33
Rabin, Oscar, 17:**33–34**
Rabin, Sam, 17:**34**

Rabin, Yitzhak, 12:439, 17:**34–36**
  agreements signed with Arafat, 10:245, 246
  agreements signed with Jordan, 10:246
  Allon, Yigal, 1:676
  American Israel Public Affairs Committee, 2:51
  assassination of, 10:246–247, 455
  government of, 10:454–455, 454t
  governments of, 10:443–444, 443t
  Palestine Liberation Organization and, 15:594, 595
  as prime minister
    1973 government, 10:237, 238
    1992 government, 10:244–245
  Shamir, Yitzhak and, 18:394
  Sharon, Ariel and, 18:416
  Shas (political party) and, 18:419
Rabin family, 17:**33**
Rabinkovich family. *See* Józefowicz family
Rabinoff, George W., 17:**36**
Rabinovich, Benzion. *See* Benn
Rabinovich, Isaac Jacob, 17:**36**
Rabinovich, Isaak Moseyevich, 17:**36**
Rabinovich, Isaiah, 8:737
Rabinovich, Itamar, 17:**36–37**
Rabinovich, José, 17:**37**
Rabinovich, Joseph, 17:**37**
Rabinovich, Osip Aronovich, 17:**37–38**
Rabinovich, Yehudah Leib, 17:**38**
Rabinovicz, Haim ben Zion, 17:**38**
Rabinovicz, Pinchas, 17:**38**
Rabinovitch, Osip, 12:553
Rabinovitz, Alexander Siskind, 17:**38–39**
Rabinovitz, Raphael Natahan Nata. *See* Rabbinovicz, Raphael Nathan Nata
Rabinovitz, Sholem. *See* Shalom Aleichem
Rabinowich, Eliyahu Akiva, 17:**39**
Rabinowich, Sarah, 17:**39**
Rabinowich, Solomon ha-Kohen. *See* Rabinowich, Solomon ha-Kohen of Radomsko
Rabinowich, Solomon ha-Kohen of Radomsko, 17:**58**
Rabinowicz, Mordecai. *See* Ben-Ammi, Mordecai
Rabinowicz, Oskar K., 17:**40**
Rabinowitch, Eugene, 17:**40**
Rabinowitsch, Eliyahu Akiva. *See* Rabinowich, Eliyahu Akiva
Rabinowitz, Aharon. *See* Yariv, Aharon
Rabinowitz, Cilla Cypora. *See* Cohn, Cilla Cypora

Rabinowitz, Eliyahu Wolf, 17:**40**

Rabinowitz, Isaac. *See* Halevy, Isaac

Rabinowitz, Jacob. *See* Rabinowitz, Ya'akov

Rabinowitz, Jerome. *See* Robbins, Jerome

Rabinowitz, Joel, 17:**40–41**

Rabinowitz, Louis Isaac, 11:378, 17:**41**

Rabinowitz, Louis Mayer, 17:**41**

Rabinowitz, Menashe. *See* Ravina, Menashe

Rabinowitz, Moritz, 15:311

Rabinowitz, Raphael. *See* Rabbinovicz, Raphael Nathan Nata

Rabinowitz, Ruth, 16:349

Rabinowitz, Samuel Jacob, 17:**41**

Rabinowitz, Stanley, 17:**41–42**

Rabinowitz, Ya'akov, 17:**42**

Rabinowitz, Yehoshua, 17:**42–43**

Rabinowitz, Ẓevi ha-Cohen, 17:**43**

Rabinowitz, Ẓevi Judah, 17:**43**

Rabinowitz, Zina, 17:**43**

Rabinowitz family, 8:420

Rabinowitz-Teomim, Elijah David ben Benjamin, 17:**43**

Rabin-Pelossof, Dalia, 17:35

Rabinsohn, Ana. *See* Pauker, Ana

Rabnovitsh, Sholem. *See* Shalom Aleichem

Rabon, Israel, 17:**44**

Rab-Saris, Rab-Mag, 6:549, 17:**44**

Rab-Shakeh, 17:**44**

Raby, Naphtali Eliahu. *See* Rahabi, Naphtali Eliyahu

Racah, Giulio, 17:**44–45**

Raccah, Mas'ūd ben Aaron, 17:**45**

Racconti romani (Moravia). *See Roman Tales* (Moravia)

Race, theory of, 9:244–245, 327, 17:**45–47**

    Boas, Franz, 4:21–22

    Jewish identity and, 11:297

    See also Antisemitism

Race against Death: Peter Bergson, America, and the Holocaust (Wyman & Medoff), 9:420

Rachel (biblical figure), 17:**47–49**

    adoption, 1:415, 416

    Bilhah and, 3:698

    Jacob and, 11:17, 19, 22, 12:406–407

    as Matriarch, 15:691

    See Also Matriarchs

Rachel (daughter of Rashi), 17:102, *102*, 105–106

Rachel (stage name), 17:**50**

Rachel (wife of Akiva), 17:**49–50**

Rachel, Tomb of. *See* Rachel (biblical figure)

Rachel Calof's Story: Jewish Homesteader on the Northern Plains (Calof), 4:375–376

Rachlis, Arnold, 15:461

Rachman, Peter, 17:**50**

Rachmilewitz, Moshe, 17:**50**

Racial persecution. *See* Race, theory of

Racial theory. *See* Race, theory of

Racine, Jean, 17:**50–51**

Racism. *See* Antisemitism

Racker, Efraim, 17:**51**

Rackman, Emanuel, 17:**51–52**

Racquetball, 19:146

Rad, Gerhard von, 17:**52**

Radak. *See* Kimḥi, David

Radanites. *See* Radaniya

Radaniya, 1:234, 6:106, 7:313, 17:**52**

Radauti (Romania), 17:**52–53**

Radautz. *See* Radauti

RaDBaZ. *See* David ben Solomon ibn Abi Zimra

Radek, Karl, 17:**53**

Rademacher, Franz, 17:**53–54**

Radhanites. *See* Radaniya

Radical idealism, Hungarian literature and, 9:605

Radical insecurity doctrine, 6:537

Radical Zionist Alliance, 21:614–615

Radimin (Poland). *See* Radzymin (Poland)

Radin (Poland). *See* Radzyn (Poland)

Radin, Adolph Moses, 17:**54**

Radin, Max, 12:556, 17:**54**

Radin, Paul, 17:**54–55**

Radio. *See* Television and radio

Radio Corporation of America (RCA), 18:59

Radishes, 17:**55**

Radler-Feldmann, Yehoshua. *See* Rabbi Binyamin

Radner, Gilda, 17:**55**

Radnitz, Gerty Theresa. *See* Cori, Gerty Theresa

Radnōtl, Miklos, 17:**55–56**

Radó, Antal, 17:**56**

Rado, Sandor, 17:**56**

Radom (Poland), 16:311–312, 17:**56–57**

Radomsk. *See* Radomsko (Poland)

Radomsko (Poland), 17:**57–58**

Radomsko, Solomon ha-Kohen Rabinowich of. *See* Rabinowich, Solomon ha-Kohen of Radomsko

Radomyshl (Ukraine), 17:**58**

Radomyslski, Grigory Yevseyevich. *See* Zinoviev, Grigori Yevseyevich

Radoshitser, Issachar Baer, 17:**58**

Radoshkovichi (Belarus), 17:**59**

Radoszkowice. *See* Radoshkovichi (Belarus)

Radszyche, Issachar Baer. *See* Radoshitser, Issachar Baer

Radu, Vasile, Romanian translation of Bible by, 3:633

Raduń. *See* Radun (Belarus)

Radun (Belarus), 17:**59**

Radvanyi, Netty. *See* Seghers, Anna

Radymno (Poland), 17:**59–60**

Radzinowicz, Leon. *See* Radzinowicz, Sir Leon

Radzinowicz, Sir Leon, 17:**60**

Radziwillow (Ukraine), 17:**60**

Radzkowitz, Saul Benjamin ha-Kohen, 6:650

Radzymin (Poland), 17:**61**

Radzymin dynasty, 17:**61**

Radzyn (Poland), 17:**61**

Radzyń-Podlaski. *See* Radzyn (Poland)

Radzynski, Jan, 17:**61–62**

Die Raeuber (Schiller), 18:134

RaF. *See* Perez ben Elijah of Corbeil

Rafa. *See* Porto, Menahem Zion

Rafa (Gaza), 17:**62**

Rafaeli, Samuel, 17:**64**

Rafah (Gaza). *See* Rafa (Gaza)

Rafailovich, M. *See* Gots, Mikhail Rafailovich

Rafalin, David Shlomó, 17:**62–63**

Rafa-Rapaport, Abraham Menahem. *See* Porto, Abraham Menahem ben Jacob ha-Kohen

Rafelson, Robert, 17:**63**

Rafes, Moses, 17:**63**

Raffa, Jonah ḥa-Kohen, 15:658

Raffalovich, Arthur Germanovich, 17:**63–64**

Raffalovich, Isaiah, 4:145, 17:**64**

Rafi, 3:347, 17:**64**

Rafi'ah (Gaza). *See* Rafa (Gaza)

Rafoul, Elie. *See* Rouleau, Eric

Ragen, Naomi, 17:**64–65**

Rager, Bracha, 17:**65**

Rager, Ijo. *See* Rager, Itzhack

Rager, Itzhack, 17:**65**

Rāghib. *See* Elisha ben Shemuel

Ragoler, Abraham ben Solomon, 17:**65**

Ragoler, Elijah ben Jacob, 17:**65–66**

Ragtime (Doctorow), 5:728, 15:227

Rag trade. *See* Secondhand goods and old clothes, trade in

Ragusa (Croatia). *See* Dubrovnik (Croatia)

Rahab, 17:**66–67**

Rahabi, Ezekiel, 17:**67**

Rahabi, Naphtali Eliyahu, 17:**67**

Raḥamei ha-Av (Kattina), 12:7

Raḥamim ben Reuben, 3:59

Raḥamim ha-Kohen, 1:340

Rahamimoff, Rami, 17:**67**

Raḥbah, al- (Mesopotamia), 17:**67–68**

Rahbar, Samuel, 17:**68**

Raḥel, 17:**68**

Rahel Morpurgo and the Contemporary Hebrew Poets in Italy (Morpurgo), 14:509

Rahv, Philip, 17:**69**

Raicu, Lucian, 6:40

Railroads, 1:395, 12:611, 17:**69–70**

    Los Angeles population, increase in, 13:19

    Rice, Isaac Leopold, 17:285

Raimundus Lullus. *See* Ramon, Lull

Rain, 17:**70–73**, *71*

    Baal worship, 3:12

    Israel (state), 10:132–133

    prayer for, 6:574, 13:601, 17:**73**

Rainbow, 17:**73–74**

Rainbow Haggadah, 4:42

Rainer, Luise, 17:**74**

Rain from Heaven (Behrman), 3:264

Raisa, Rosa, 17:**74**

Raisin, Jacob Zalman, 17:**74**

Raisin, Max, 17:**74–75**

Raising Arizona (motion picture), 4:782

Raisman, Abraham. *See* Raisman, Sir Jeremy

Raisman, Jeremy. *See* Raisman, Sir Jeremy

Raisman, Sir Jeremy, 17:**75**

Raisz, Erwin J., 17:**75**

Rajak, Tessa, 17:**75**

Rajpurkar, Joseph Ezekiel, 17:**75**

Rakadeti, Amadeti (Shalev), 18:373

Rakaḥ communist party, 5:100

Rakh va-Tov (Solomon ben Aaron), 12:407

Rakishik. *See* Rokiskis

Rákosi, Mátyás, 17:**75–76**

Rakous, Vojtĕch, 17:**76**

Rakovsky, Puah, 17:**76**

RaLBaG. *See* Levi ben Gershom

Ralberg. *See* Levi ben Gershom

Rall, Yisrael, 17:**77**

Ram, Moshe, 17:**77**

Rāma, al- (Israel), 17:**77**

Ramadan, Jewish culture and, 11:540

Ramah (ancient Israel), 17:**77**

Ramah camps, 6:542, 18:616

Rām Allāh. *See* Ramallah (Palestine)

Ramallah (Palestine), 17:**77–78**

Ramatayim (Israel). *See* Hod ha-Sharon (Israel)

Ramat David (Israel), 17:**78**

Ramat Gan (Israel), 17:**78**

    Kahana, Aharon, 11:710

    museum of ceramic art, 11:710

Ramat Hadar (Israel). *See* Hod ha-Sharon (Israel)

Ramat ha-Golan (Israel), 17:**78–80**, 18:653–654

Ramat ha-Kovesh (Israel), 17:**81**

Ramat ha-Sharon (Israel), 17:**81**

Ramat ha-Shofet (Israel), 17:**81**

Ramat Raḥel (Israel), 17:**81–83**

Ramat Raziel (Israel), 17:**83**

Ramat Yishai (Israel), 17:**83**

Ramat Yoḥanan (Israel), 17:**83–84**

Ramat Ẓevi (Israel), 14:451, 17:**84**

Ramaz School (New York, NY), 6:197, 13:188

"Rambam." *See* Maimonides, Moses

Rambam, Cyvia. *See* Rambert, Dame Marie

Rambam hospital, 6:482

Rambam Lehrhaus (Berlin), 2:23

RaMBan. *See* Naḥmanides

RaMBeMaN. *See* Mendelssohn, Moses

Rambert, Dame Marie, 5:416, 17:**84**

Ramerupt (France), 17:**84**

Rames (Israel). *See* Ramleh (Israel)

Rameses. *See* Ramses (Egyptian rulers)

RaMHaL. *See* Luzzatto, Moses Ḥayyim

Ramlah. *See* Ramleh (Israel)

Ramleh (Israel), 17:**84–85**

Ramon, Haim, 9:149, 17:**86–87**

Ramon, Ilan, 17:**87**

Ramon, Lull, 17:**85–86**

Ramone, Joey, 17:**87**

The Ramones (musical group), 17:**87**

Ra'mot, 16:478

Ramot, Bracha, 17:**87–88**

Ramoth (ancient Israel), 17:**88**

Ramot ha-Shavim (Israel), 17:**88**

Ramoth-Gilead (ancient Israel), 14:388, 17:**88**

Ramot Menasheh (Israel), 17:**88**

Ramot Naftali (Israel), 17:**88**

Rams. *See* Sheep

Ramses (Egypt), 17:**88–89**

Ramses (Egyptian rulers), 17:**89**

Ramses I (Pharaoh), 17:**89**

Ramses II (Pharaoh), 17:**89**

Ramses III (Pharaoh), 17:**89**

Ram's horn. *See* Shofar

Ramukh family. *See* Benremokh family

The RaN. *See* Nissim ben Reuben Gerondi

Ran, Leyzer, 16:127

Ran, Shulamit, 17:**89**

Ranch, H.J., 18:761

Rand, Ayn, 17:**89–90**

Rand, Ya'akov, 17:**90**

Randall, Tony, 17:**90–91**

Randglossen zur hebraeischen Bibel (Ehrlich), 6:243

Randolph, A. Philip, Black-Jewish relations in U.S., 3:734

Rank, Otto, 17:**91**

Ranke, Hans, Nuremberg laws, 15:350

Rankin, Harry, 17:**91**

Ranschburg, Bezalel ben Joel, 17:**91**

Ransom, 9:20, 17:**91–92**

Ransoming of captives, 4:**456–457**

Raoul Glaber, 17:**92**

Rapa, Abraham Menaham ben Jaco ha-Kohen, 17:**97**

Rapa family. *See* Rapoport family

Rapaport, David, 17:**92**

Rapaport, David ha-Kohen, 2:77, 17:**92**, 97

Rapaport, Jacob, 17:92

Rapaport, Moses. *See* Porto-Rafa, Moses ben Jehiel ha-Kohen

Rapaport, Nathan, 17:**92–93**

Rapaport, Robert, 15:605, 606

Rapaport, Simon, 17:**97–98**

Rapaport family. *See* Rapoport family

Rape, 11:565, 17:**93**, 18:330

    See also Marital rape; Sexual offenses

Rape ending in consent, 18:331–332

Raphael (angel), 17:**93–94**

Raphael, Alexander, 17:**94**

Raphael, Benjamin I., 4:70

Raphael, Chaim, 17:**94**

Raphael, Frederic, 17:**94**

Raphael, Gideon, 17:**94–95**

Raphael, John, 17:**95**

Raphael, Marco. *See* Raphael, Mark

Raphael, Mark, 17:**95**

Raphael, Melissa, 9:397

Raphael, Nathaniel. *See* Raphael, John

Raphael, Percival. *See* Raphael, John

Raphael, Ralph Alexander, 17:**95**

Raphael, William, 17:**95–96**

Raphael, Yitzhak, 17:**96**

Raphael, Yom Tov Lipman ben Israel. *See* Heilpern, Yom Tov Lipman ben Israel

Raphael ben Joseph, 15:523

Raphael Kohen. *See* Kohen, Raphael ben Jekuthiel Suesskind

Raphael Levi of Hanover. *See* Hannover, Raphael Levi

Raphael of Bershad, 17:**96**

Raphaels. *See* Kellner, Leon

Raphaelson, Samson, 17:**96**

Raphall, Morris Jacob, 3:713, 734, 15:198, 199, 200, 17:**97**

Rapkine, Louis, 17:**97**

Rapoport, Abraham ben Israel Jehiel ha-Kohen, 17:**98**

Rapoport, Alexander, 17:98

Rapoport, Benjamin ben Simḥah ha-Kohen, 17:**97**

Rapoport, Benjamin Ze'ev Wolf ha-Kohen ben Isaac, 17:**97**, **98**

Rapoport, Charles, 17:98

Rapoport, Ḥayyim ben Simḥah ha-Kohen, 17:**97**

Rapoport, Jitzhak, 15:308

Rapoport, Samuel, 17:**98**

Rapoport, Solomon Judah Leib, 8:725, 12:465, 17:97, 99

   Bikkurei ha-Ittim, 3:696

   biographical writings of, 3:707

Rapoport, Solomon Zainwil. *See* An-Ski, S.

Rapoport family, 17:**97–98**

Rapp, James, 2:48

Rappaport, Armin H., 17:**99**

Rappaport, Henry, 17:**99–100**

Rappaport, Isaac ben Judah ha-Kohen, 17:**97**, **100**

Rappaport, Isaac ha-Kohen, 3:695

Rappaport, Jacob, 17:**100**

Rappaport, Reuben Kohen, 3:15

Rappaport, Roy, 17:**100**

Rappaport, Samuel. *See* Rapoport, Samuel

Rappaport, Solomon Judah Leib. *See* Rapoport, Solomon Judah Leib

Rappaport family. *See* Rapoport family

Rappeduni be-Tappuhim (Eliakim Goetz ben Meir), 6:318

Rappoltsweiler. *See* Ribeauvillé

Rappoport, Charles, 17:**100–101**, 18:707

Rappoport, Shloyme-Zanvl. *See* An-Ski, S.

Rappoport family. *See* Rapoport family

Raqqa (Mesopotamia), 17:**101**

La Raquel (García de la Huerta), 11:256

Raquel, the Jewess of Toledo (Feuchtwanger). *See Spanische Ballade* (Feuchtwanger)

Râşcani (Moldova). *See* Ryshkany (Moldova)

Raschkow, Suesskind, 11:412

Raseiniai (Lithuania), 17:**101**

Rashal. *See* Luria, Solomon ben Jehiel

RaShBa. *See* Adret, Solomon ben Abraham

Rashbad. *See* Samuel ben David

Rashbam. *See* Samuel ben Meir

RaSHBaSh (1400-1467). *See* Duran, Solomon ben Simeon

RaSHBaSh (1438-after 1510). *See* Duran, Simeon ben Solomon

RashbaẒ. *See* Duran, Simeon ben ZemaḤ

Rashei Besamim (Mizraḥi), 14:393

Rashei tevot. *See* Abbreviations

Rashgolski, Hillel. *See* Bavli, Hillel

Rashi, 17:**101–106**, 102*t*

   Abulrabi, Aaron, 1:345–346

   Amram Hasida, 2:105

   amulets, 2:123

   apologetics, 2:266

   art, 2:495

   biblical exegist, 3:641, 17:102–103

   on biblical study, 3:662

   commentaries, 5:435, 17:104–105

   daughters of, 17:105–106

   early editions of Bible containing commentaries of, 3:586, 610

   on excessive biblical study, 3:663

   exile, meaning of, 7:357

   glosses, 12:405–406

   grammarian, 17:103–104

   halakhist, 17:105

   Hebraists, influence on, 8:511

   Herbert de Bosham, 4:96

   on informers, 9:780

   Isaac ben Meir and, 10:44

   Isaac ben Menaham the Great and, 10:44–45

   Joseph ben Issachar Baer of Prague, supercommentary of, 11:422

   Joseph ben Solomon of Carcassonne, 11:426

   Joshua, Book of, 11:444

   Judah ben Nathan, 11:490

   literal commentary style founded by, 3:642

   Luria family, 13:260

   Luther influenced by, 3:648

   Menahem ben Ḥelbo and, 14:21

   Mizraḥi, Elijah, 14:394

   modern biblical criticism, as precursor of, 3:648

   Pappus and Julianus, 15:619

   Pentateuch commentary, 1:301

   peshat, 3:661

   Shemaiah of Troyes, 18:456–457

   on Tabernacle story, 6:617–618

   targum readings, substitution of commentaries for, 3:662

   teachers of, 11:36

Rashid. *See* Rosetta (Egypt)

Rashid (Egypt). *See* Rosetta (Egypt)

Rashīd, Moulay, 7:7

Rashid al-Din, 14:444, 17:**106–107**

Rashid Effendi. *See* Vambery, Arminius

Rashkin, Leyb, 17:**107**

Rashkov (Moldova). *See* Vad Rashkov (Moldova)

Rasht (Iran), 7:596

Ras Kasrun, 3:13

Raskin, Judith, 17:**107**

Raskin, Leib. *See* Rashkin, Leyb

Raskin, Saul, 17:**107–108**

Rasky, Harry, 17:**108**

Raslovleff, Michael, 6:297

Rasminsky, Louis, 16:341–342, 17:**108**

Rasofsky, "Beryl". *See* Ross, Barney

Rasofsky, David. *See* Ross, Barney

Rasofsky, David "Beryl." *See* Ross, Barney

La Rassegna Mensile di Israel (journal), 12:519, 17:**108–109**

Ras Shamra (Ugarit, Syria), 18:103

Rasskazy v pis'makh (Sobol), 18:701

Rath, Meshullam, 17:**109**

Rathaus, Karol, 17:**109**

Rathbone, Eleanor, 17:**109–110**

Rathenau, Emil Moritz, 12:459, 17:**110**

Rathenau, Walther, 12:459, 16:344, 17:**110–111**

Rationalism, 6:682–683

   Abba Mari ben Moses ben Joseph Astruc of Lunel, 1:230

   Abbas, Judah ben Samuel ibn, 1:231

   Abelard, Peter, 1:246

   Abrabanel, Isaac ben Judah, 1:277

   Abraham, 1:284–285

   Cloots, Jean Baptiste du Val-de-Grâce, 4:761

   Deists, 5:533–534

   metaphysics, 14:34–35

   opposition to, 11:7

Ratisbon. *See* Regensburg (Germany)

Ratisbonne, Alphonse, 17:**111–112**

Ratisbonne, Marie Alphonse. *See* Ratisbonne, Alphonse

Ratisbonne, Théodore, 17:**111–112**

Ratisbonne brothers, 17:**111–112**

Ratisbonne family, 2:8

Ratmistrovka family, 8:420

Ratner, Bruce C., 17:**112**

Ratner, Dov Baer, 17:**112**

Ratner, Leonard, 17:**112–113**

Ratner, Marc Borisovich, 17:**113**

Ratner, Sarah, 13:10

Ratner, Sidney, 17:**113**

Ratner, Yohanan, 17:**113**

Ratosh, Yonathan, 2:78, 4:393, 17:**113–114**

Rat Pack, 3:726

Rats, 17:**109**

Ratshesky, Abraham Captain, 17:**114**

Ratti, Angelo, 11:379

Rattner, Abraham, 15:649, 17:**114–115**

Rau, Heinz, 17:**115**

Raubach. *See* Magnus, Marcus

Rauch, Eduardo, 17:**115**

Raudnitz an der Elbe (Czech Republic). *See* Roudnice nad Labem (Czech Republic)

Rauh, Frédéric, 17:**115**

Rauh, Joseph L., Jr., 17:**115–116**

Rauter, Hanns Albin, 17:**116**

Rav, 17:**116–118**
  amoraim, 2:90, 93, 94, 11:708
  Amram I, 2:103
  Johanan ben Nappaḥa, 11:371
  Moses, 14:534
  Shela, 18:444–445

Rava, 17:**118–119**
  Adda bar Ahavah, 1:384–385
  Aḥ ben Jacob, 1:525
  Ameimar, 2:37
  am ha-arez, 2:69
  Ammi bar Nathan, 2:82
  amoraim, 2:94, 95

Rava, Maurizio, 17:**119**

Rava Abba. *See* Rava

Rava Abba ben Joseph ben Ḥama. *See* Rava

Ravad. *See* Av Bet Din

Rav Adda. *See* Avila, Eliezer ben Samuel ben Moses De

Ravalia. *See* Ravaya family

Rav Assi. *See* Assi, Rav

Rav Avina. *See* Ravina

Ravaya, Astrug, 17:119

Ravaya, Joseph, 17:119

Ravaya, Moses, 17:119

Ravaya family, 17:**119**

Ravaylla. *See* Ravaya family

Ravelstein (Bellow), 3:300

Ravenna (Italy), 17:**120**

Ravens, 17:**119**

Ravensbrueck concentration camp, 17:**120–121**

Ravensburg (Germany), 17:**121**

Rav Huna
  Ammi ben Nathan, 2:82
  amoraim, 2:89, 94, 95
  Anan, 2:126

Rav Huna Resh Galuta, 9:**600**

Ravikovich, Dalia, 17:**121–122**

Ravin. *See* Avin

Ravina, 17:**122–123**

Ravina, Menashe, 17:**123**

Ravina I, 17:122

Ravina II, 17:122–123

Ravintzky, Yehoshua. *See* Rawnitzki, Yehoshua Ḥana

Ravitch, Melech, 4:426, 12:675, 17:**123**

Ravitch, Richard, 15:224

Ravitz, Shelomo, 17:**124**

Ravitzky, Aviezer, 15:703, 16:71, 17:**124**

Rav Metivta (Zohar), 21:649

Rav Pe'alim (Abraham ben Elijah of Vilna), 1:299

Rav Peninim (Alshekh), 2:10

Rav Shalom (Adler), 1:408

Rav Shalom (Fischhof II), 2:650

Rav Shisha. *See* Abitbol, Saul Jeshua ben Isaac

Rav Shlomo ben Abraham. *See* Adret, Solomon ben Abraham

Ravyah (Eliezer), 6:327

Rav Yenuka. *See* Natronai bar Nehemiah

Rav Yosef (Kasabi), 11:819

Rav Za'ir. *See* Tchernowitz, Chaim

Rawanduz (Iraq). *See* Ruwandiz (Iraq)

Rawet, Samuel, 4:152, 17:**124**

Rawicz (Poland), 17:**125**

Rawidowicz, Simon, 4:188, 17:**125–126**

Rawitz, Solomon, 18:702

Rawnitzki, Yehoshua Ḥana, 1:460, 4:621, 6:74, 14:491, 17:**126**

Ray, Man, 14:419, 17:**126**

Raykin, Arkadi Isaakovich, 17:**126**

Raykin, Konstantin, 17:126

Raykin, Yekaterina, 17:126

Raymond de Penaforte, 17:**126–127**

Raymond Martini. *See* Martini, Raymond

Raymond VI, Count of Toulouse, 1:592

Raynal, David, 16:343, 17:**127**

Rayne, Max, Baron. *See* Rayne, Sir Max, Baron

Rayne, Sir Max, Baron, 17:**127**

Rayner, Isadore, 17:**127**

Raynor, Bruce, 17:**127–128**

Rayss, Tscharna, 17:**128**

Raz, 16:9

Raza de-Meheimanuta (Shabbetai Ẓevi), 8:477

Raza de-Razin (Cardozo), 4:466

Raza de-Razin (Zohar), 21:648

Raza de-Yihuda (Ḥayon), 8:477

Raza di-Meheimanuta (Shabbetai Ẓevi), 18:351

RaZaH. *See* Zechariah ben Solomon-Rofe

Raza Rabba, Sefer, 17:**128**

Războuiul amintirilor (Duda). *See The War of Remembrances* (Duda)

Razgon, Aleksandr, 11:324

Raziel (angel), 2:159, 17:**128–129**, 130

Raziel (Pseudonym). *See* Abulafia, Abraham ben Samuel

Raziel, Book of, 2:121, 17:**129**

Raziel, David, 17:**129**

Razim, Sefer ha-. See Sefer ha-Razim

Razin, Aharon, 17:**130**

Razofsky, Cecilia, 17:**131**

Razon, Jacko, 17:**130–131**

Razran, Gregory, 17:**131**

Razsvet (journal), 17:**131–133**

Razumni, Ephraim Zalman, 17:**133**

Razumni, Solomon. *See* Razumni, Ephraim Zalman

Razumny, Mark, 17:**133**

Razzia, in Novi Sad, 15:320

RCA. *See* Rabbinical Council of America

RCA (Radio Corporation of America), 18:59

Reader. *See* Sheli'aḥ ẓibbur

Reading, Eva Violet, 14:434–435

Reading, Fanny, 17:**134–135**

Reading family, 17:**133–134**

Reading Hebron (Sherman), 18:465

Reading of the law. *See* Torah, reading of

Reading the Hands by an Indian Sage. See Re'iyyat ha-Yadayim le-Eḥad me-Ḥakhmei Hodu

Reagan, Ronald Wilson, 17:**135–136**
  American Gathering of Jewish Holocaust Survivors, 2:48, 49
  Bitburg Controversy, 3:727–728
  Bloomingdale, Alfred S., 3:784

Reagan Plan, 15:593, 17:**136**

Re'aḥ ha-Sadeh (Eliezer ben Meir ha-Levi of Pinsky), 6:327

Reale, Miguel, 4:149

Real-Encyklopaedie des Judentums (Hamburger), 6:400, 8:298

Real-Encyklopaedie fuer Bibel und Talmud (Hamburger), 8:298

Real estate. *See* Property

Real estate development. *See* Property development

The Real Messiah (Kaplan), 11:773

Real property. *See* Property

Reason, 3:65
  belief and, 3:293–294, 6:682–683

Reasonable standard, 5:167–168

Reasons for Naturalizing the Jews in Great Britain and Ireland, On the same footwith all other Nations, Containing also, A Defence of the Jews against All Vulgar Prejudices in all Countries (Toland), 9:230

The Reawakening (Levi), 12:692

Rebbenu Ephraim. *See* Ephraim ibn Avi Alragan

Rebbetzin, 17:**136**

"The Rebbi Reb Hoeschel." *See* Joshua Hoeschel ben Jacob

Rebecca bat Meir Tiktiner, 17:**136–137**

Rebekah (biblical figure), 15:691, 17:**137–138**
  Abimelech and, 1:257, 258
  children of, 11:17–18
  Esau, 6:487
  See Also Matriarchs

Rebellious son, 17:**138–139**

Dem Reben Nign (Bader), 3:45

Rebenstein, A. *See* Bernstein, Aron David

Rebi, Joseph. *See* Rabchik, Joseph

Rebichkovich family. *See* Józefowicz family

Rebreanu (Romania), 17:**139**

Rebuke and reproof, 17:**139–140**

Recanati (Italy), 17:**140**

Recanati, Abraham Samuel, 17:**141**

Recanati, Amadeo, 11:547, 17:140

Recanati, Daniel, 17:141

Recanati, Emanuele, 17:140

Recanati, Harry Rafael, 17:141

Recanati, Jacob Ḥayyim ben Isaac Samuel, 17:140

Recanati, Jedidiah. *See* Recanati, Amadeo

Recanati, Judah Ḥayyim, 17:140

Recanati, Leon, 17:140, **141–142**

Recanati, Menaham. *See* Recanati, Emanuele

Recanati, Menaham ben Benjamin, 17:140, **142**
  on Targum Yerushalmi I, 3:591

Recanati, Shabbetai Elhanan (17th c.), 17:140

Recanati, Shabbetai Elhanan (18th c.), 17:140

Recanati, Yehuda. *See* Recanati, Leon

Recanati, Yehudah Leib. *See* Recanati, Leon

Recanati family, 17:**140–141**

Reccared, 4:716, 17:**142**

Rechab and Baanah, 17:**142–143**

Rechabites, 17:**143–144**
  seminomadism of, 15:295

Recherches Bibliques (Halévy), 8:271

Recherches sur les calcul différentiels et intégrals (Ensheim), 6:447

Rechitsa (Belarus), 17:**144**

Rechter, Ya'akov, 17:144–145

Rechter, Ze'ev, 17:144

Rechter family, 17:**144–145**

Recife (Brazil), 1:269, 4:142, 144, 17:**145–146**
  archives, 2:406–407
  Caribbean, Spanish-Portuguese Nation of the: La Nacion, 4:469

Recitation, amoraim, 2:93

Reckendorf, Ḥayyim ẓevi. *See* Reckendorf, Hermann (1825-1875)

Reckendorf, Hermann (1825-1875), 17:146

Reckendorf, Hermann Solomon (1863-1923), 17:**146**

Reckless, Walter, C., 5:302–303

Reckless Disregard: Westmoreland v. CBS et al.; Sharon v. Time (Adler), 1:406

Recklinghausen (Germany), 17:**146**

The Reckoning and the Soul. See Ha-Ḥeshbon ve-ha-Nefesh

Reclamation projects, land. *See* Land reclamation projects

Reconstruction Foundation, 11:719

Reconstructionism, 17:**146–149**

Reconstructionist Judaism, 6:273, 11:146–149, 20:366
  Alper, Michael, 1:688
  bar mitzvah, 3:166
  Becker, Lavy M., 3:246
  Canada, 4:416
  Cohen, Jack Joseph, 5:22–23
  Eisenberg, Sandy, 18:279
  Eisenstein, Ira, 6:273
  gender equality, 6:753
  havurot, 8:471–472
  ḥazzanim, 8:505
  Kaddish recitation by women, 11:698
  Kaplan, Mordecai Menaham, 11:776–779
  Kohn, Eugene, 12:262
  lesbianism, 12:661
  Mevakshei Derekh, Israel, 5:22–23
  niddah, 15:257

prayer, women's role in, 16:461
  Reconstructionist Rabbinical College, 17:27, 147, 148, 149, 18:586
  Sasso, Sandy Eisenberg, 18:67
  Shapiro, Rami, 18:407
  siddur, publications, 11:148–149
  Strassfeld, Michael, 19:247
  Teutsch, David, 19:656–657
  theology, 11:147–148
  Vorspan, Max, 20:583

Reconstructionist Rabbinical College (RRC), 17:27, 147, 148, **149**, 18:586

Reconstruction of Religious Thought in Islam (Iqbal), 10:94

Recorders. *See* Scribes

Records, phonograph, 17:**149–151**

Records of the Trials of the Spanish Inquisition in Ciudad Real (Beinart), 3:269

The Recruit. See Rekrut

Redaction criticism, 15:191

Redactor (R) of Torah, 15:737–738, 740–741

Red Cavalry (Babel), 3:17, 19

Red coral, 5:215

The Red Cross and the Holocaust (Favez), 9:420

"Red Danny." *See* Cohn-Bendit, Daniel

Redeemer. *See* Messiah

The Redeemers (Schwarz), 18:189

Redem (Poland). *See* Radymno (Poland)

Redemption, 16:98, 17:**151–155**
  biblical views, 17:151–152
  Judah Loew ben Bezalel on, 11:508
  kabbalistic, 6:501–502, 17:153–154
  Kalischer's ideas and teachings, 11:737–738
  medieval views, 17:152–153
  modern thought, 17:154–155
  stages of, 11:737–738
  talmudic views, 17:152

Redemption of the Firstborn, 7:46–47

Reden an die deutsche Nation (Fichte), 7:9

Reder, Bernard, 17:**155–156**

Reder, Rudolph, 3:**308, 309–310**

Rede unter dem Galgen (Aichinger), 1:549

Red Friday, Bialystok (Poland), 3:568

Red heifers, 1:262, 15:630, 17:**156–158**

Redl, Fritz, 17:**158**

Redler-Feldman, Yehoshua, 8:497, 17:19

Redlich, Frederick C., 17:**158–159**

Redlich, Hans Ferdinand, 17:**159**

Redlich, Joseph, 16:340, 17:**159**

Redlich, Norman, 17:**159**

Red Light (Plachy), 16:210

The Red Magician (Goldstein), 18:200

Redmans road Talmud Torah, 6:205

Red Russia arenda, 2:422

Red Sea, 17:**159–161**

 Moses, 14:524, 527, 532

 Song of the Sea, 18:224

"Red Shield of David." *See* Magen David Adom

Redstone, Ostrovsky. *See* Redstone, Sumner Murray

Redstone, Sumner Murray, 17:**161**

Rée, Hartvig Philip, 17:**161**

Reed, 17:**161–162**, vol. 16: color insert

Reed, Lewis Allen. *See* Reed, Lou

Reed, Lou, 17:**162**

Re'em. *See* Antelope

Reese, Jimmie, 17:**162**

Reese, Michael, 17:**162**

Reeve, Ada, 17:**162**

Refaeli, S. *See* Refaeli, Samuel

Refaeli, Samuel, 17:**64**

Reflections of a Russian Statesman (Pobedonostsev), 16:249

Reflections on Language (Chomsky), 4:665

Reformation, 17:**163–165**

 antisemitism, 2:212–213

 Anti-Trinitarians, 4:249–250

 apostasy, 2:271

 Bible and literature during, 3:669

 Bible's significance and, 3:664

 Bible translation in, 3:606, 611–614

 disputations and polemics, 5:695

 effect on European Jewry, 9:222–223

 Hungarian literature and, 9:602–604

 Judaizers, 11:520

 modern biblical criticism and, 3:648–649

Reformed Church of the Netherlands, 16:632

Reform Jews (Ben-Sion), 15:138

Reform Judaism, 17:**165–183**

 ablution, 1:262

 adult education committment, 17:176–177

 alcoholism among members, 6:28

 Aleinu le-Shabbe'ah, 1:609

 America, 2:45

 angels, 2:161

 Argentina

  history, 2:439

  Klenicki, Leon, 12:228–229

  presence, 2:447

 Australia, Brasch, Rudolph, 4:130

 Austria

  Kohn, Abraham, 12:262

  Mannheimer, Isaac Noah, 13:482

 Bauer critique, 3:216

 Beth Adam decision, 17:174–175

 bimah, location of, 3:701

 Birkat ha-Minim, 3:712

 Bismark, Otto von, on, 3:726

 burial customs, 4:293

 Canada

  growth, 4:410

  Montreal, 14:465

  Scheuer, Edmund, 18:123–124

 cantors, women, 8:505

 Caribbean, 4:476

 CCAR, 4:545–546

 Central Conference of American Rabbis, 4:545–546

 classic period, 17:168–169

 contemporary, 11:519

 converts, 16:594

 Curaçao, Goudeket, Maurits, 8:16–17

 Declaration of Principles, 17:168–169

 dietary laws and, 5:658

 education, Jewish, 6:198

 feminism, 6:753, 754, 17:177–180

 France

  Bebe, Pauline, 3:241–242

  Farhi, Daniel, 6:716

  Farhi, Gabriel, 6:716

  history, 7:157–158

 Germany

  Adler, Lazarus Levi, 1:402

  Aub, Joseph, 2:649

  Auerbach, Isaac Levin, 2:655

  Berlin, 3:448

  Berlin, Saul ben Zevi Hirsch Levin, 3:459–460

  Bloch, Philipp, 3:767

  Bresselau, Meyer Israel, 4:167

  Dienemann, Max, 5:649

  Einhorn, David, 6:258

  Eppenstein, Simon, 6:465

  Formstecher, Solomon, 16:94

  Frankl, Pinkus Fritz, 7:214

  Geiger, Abraham, 7:412–415

  Herxheimer, Salomon, 9:51

  Hess, Mendel, 9:74

  Hirsch, Samuel, 9:132–133, 16:94–95

  Holdheim, Samuel, 9:316–317

  Jonas, Regina, 6:753

  Jost, Isaac Marcus, 11:463–464

  Kley, Eduard, 12:230–231

  Kober, Adolf, 12:242

  Lehmann, Emil, 12:615

  Leimdoerfer, David, 12:626–627

  Maybaum, Ignaz, 13:697

  pioneers, 11:54–55

  reaction to development in, 6:546

  reestablishment after World War II, 11:29

  Rieger, Paul, 17:293–294

  Ritter, Immanuel Heinrich, 17:346

  Schottlaender, Benedet, 18:165

 halakha, approach to, 17:173–174

 halakhah and development of concept of Judaism, 11:518–519

 hazzanim, 8:505

 Hebrew Union College-Jewish Institute of Religion, 8:739–740 26-27, 17:26–27

 Hirsch, Samson Raphael on, 9:130–131

 Hoffman, Lawrence A., 9:309

 homiletic literature and, 9:513, 515

 homosexuality, 17:179–180

 Hungary

  Chorin, Aaron, 4:667–668

  Einhorn, Ignaz, 6:259

  Fischer, Gyula, 7:53–54

  Kohlbach, Bertalan, 12:260–261

  Leimdoerfer, David, 12:626–627

  Loew, Immanuel, 13:163

  Loew, Leopold, 13:163–164

  Schick, Moses ben Joseph, opposition to, 18:127

  Zipser, Majer, 21:639

 identity, approaches to, 17:177–178

 intermarriage, 19:211

 Israel (state), 10:629–630, 636, 17:181–182

 Italy

  growth, 10:812–813

  Sheluhei Erez Israel, 18:451–452

Kaddish recitation by women, 11:698
kashrut, 17:173
ketubbot, 12:97
lesbianism, 12:661
Levend Joods Gellof, 2:117
Liebliche Tefillah, 1:217
liturgy, 4:545–546
mixed marriage, intermarriage, 14:376–377, 381
Modena, Leon as precursor, 14:410
Monatsschrift (periodical), 14:433
Netherlands
 Amsterdam, 2:114, 117
 Goudeket, Maurits, 8:16
niddah, 15:257
nineteenth century, 17:165–169
North American Federation of Temple Youth, 17:172, 175–176
opponents, early, 11:70
Oral Law, 15:456–457
ordination, 17:178
organs, use of, 15:467
Orthodox Judaism vs., 15:493
Palestine, Wilhelm, Kurt, 21:62
Pittsburgh Platform, 6:193, 203, 258, 14:471, 16:190–191
Poland
 Joel, Manuel, 11:364
 Loewenstein, Bernhard, 13:168
 Peltin, Samuel Hirsh, 15:719
 Rosenthal, Ferdinand, 17:453
post-WW II, 17:170–171
prayer books, 4:545–546, 7:227–228, 16:464–467
prayers
 Hazkarat neshamot, 8:497
 women's role in, 16:461
preaching, 16:475
rabbi, rabbinate, 17:13
rabbinical conferences, 17:20–21
Rabbinic training, 17:26–27
Religious Action Center, 9:129
resurrection, 1:442
re-traditionalization, 17:172, 175
ritual prayers for opening Ark, 16:16–17
Russia, Lilienthal, Max, 13:16–17
Schindler period, 17:171–172
separation of women in synagogues, 13:771
siddur, 17:171
Sweden
 Klein, Gottlieb, 12:221–222

Wilhelm, Kurt, 21:62
theological boundaries, 17:174–175
twentieth century, 17:169–172
twenty-first century, 17:180–182
U.K.
 Gryn, Hugo, 8:115
 Joseph, Morris, 11:417
 Maybaum, Ignaz, 13:697
 Perlzweig, Maurice L., 15:780
Union of Reform Judaism, 20:254–255
U.S.
 Aaron, Israel, 1:211
 Aaronsohn, Michael, 1:223
 Adler, Liebman, 1:402
 Adler, Samuel, 1:407
 Asher, Joseph, 2:561
 Backman, Jules, 3:40
 Bamberger, Bernard Jacob, 3:102
 Barnston, Henry, 3:170
 Baron, Joseph Louis, 3:172
 Beerman, Leonard, 3:255–256
 Benjamin, Raphael, 3:358
 Bergen County (NJ), 3:423
 Berger, Elmer, 3:424
 Berkowitz, Henry, 3:440
 Berman, Morton Mayer, 3:463–464
 Bernstein, Philip Sidney, 4:483–484
 Bettan, Israel, 3:550
 Blank, Sheldon Haas, 3:740
 Bloch, Joshua, 3:764
 Braude, William Gordon, 4:135–136
 Brickner, Balfour, 4:178–179
 Brickner, Barnett Robert, 4:179
 Bronstein, Herbert, 4:207–208
 Browne, Edward B.M., 4:216–217
 Browne, Lewis, 4:217
 Calisch, Edward Nathan, 4:364
 Coffee, Rudolph Isaac, 4:482
 Cohen, Henry, 5:17–18
 Cohen, Jacob Xenab, 5:23
 Cohn, Elkan, 5:40–41
 Cohon, Samuel Solomon, 5:46–47
 Cook, Samuel, 5:200
 Cronbach, Abraham, 5:306
 Currick, Max Cohen, 5:341–342
 Davidson, David, 5:475

Dreyfus, Stanley A., 6:20
Ehrenreich, Bernard Colonius, 6:240–241
Eichhorn, David Max, 6:246–247
Einhorn, David, 6:258
Eisendrath, Maurice Nathan, 6:266
Eliassof, Herman, 6:320
Ellenson, David Harry, 6:360
Ellinger, Moritz, 6:361
Elzas, Barnett Abraham, 6:372
Enelow, Hyman, 6:405–406
Ettelson, Harry William, 6:541–542
Feibelman, Julian Beck, 6:729
Feinberg, Abraham L., 6:737
Feldman, Abraham Jehiel, 6:746
Felsenthal, Bernhard, 6:751
Feuer, Leon Israel, 6:773–774
Feuerlicht, Morris Marcus, 6:774
Fineberg, Solomon Andhil, 7:26
Fineshriber, William Howard, 7:29
Fink, Joseph Lionel, 7:30–31
Franklin, Leo Morris, 7:215
Freehof, Solomon Bennett, 7:227–228
Freudenthal, Max, 7:263
Frieder, Armin, 7:271
Frisch, Ephraim, 7:291–292
Glaser, Joseph, 7:626–627
Goldenson, Samuel Harry, 7:702
Goldstein, Elyse, 7:727–728
Goldstein, Sidney Emanuel, 7:732
Gordon, Nathan, 7:773
Gottheil, Gustav, 8:9
Gottschalk, Alfred, 8:14–15
Gutheim, James Koppel, 8:150–151
Harby, Isaac, 8:346
Harris, Maurice, 8:363–364
Harrison, Leon, 8:366
Heller family, 8:792
Hirsch, Emil Gustave, 9:124–125
Hirsch, Richard, 9:129
Hirsch, Samuel, 9:132–133
Hocheimer, Henry, 9:299
Israel, Edward Leopold, 10:740

Reform Judaism, *continued*

Isserman, Ferdinand M., 10:772–773

Jacob, Walter, 11:29

Kahn, Robert I., 11:723–724

Klein, Edward E., 12:220

Kohler, Kaufmann, 12:261

Korn, Bertram Wallace, 12:310–311

Krauskopf, Joseph, 12:343

Kronish, Leon, 12:371–372

Kushner, Lawrence, 12:397

Landman, Isaac, 12:472–473

Lauterbach, Jacob Zallel, 12:529

Lazaron, Morris Samuel, 12:559

Leipziger, Emil William, 12:628

Lelyveld, Arthur Joseph, 12:635–636

Lerner, Michael, 12:659

Levinger, Lee Joseph, 12:720

Levy, Clifton Harby, 12:748

Levy, Felix Alexander, 12:749–750

Levy, Joseph Leonard, 12:751

Liebman, Joshua Loth, 12:810

Lilienthal, Max, 13:16–17

Lipman, Eugene Jay, 13:66–67

Lookstein, Haskel, 13:188

Magnin, Edgar Fogel, 13:355

Malino, Jerome, 13:432

Marcus, Jacob Rader, 13:513–514

Mark, Julius, 13:547–548

Martin, Bernard, 13:582–583

Mayer, Leopold, 13:699

Mendes, Frederic de Sola, 14:42

Merzbacher, Leo, 14:73–74

Meyer, Martin Abraham, 14:148

Mielziner, Moses, 14:205–206

Mihaly, Eugene, 14:220

Minda, Albert Greenberg, 14:264

Morgenstern, Julian, 14:486–487

Moses, Adolph, 14:543–544

Moses, Isaac S., 14:546

Narot, Joseph, 14:782

Neumark, David, 15:123

Newfield, Morris, 15:134–135

Newman, Louis Israel, 15:146

New York City (NY), 15:217–218

Nussbaum, Max, 15:353

Nussbaum, Perry, 15:353–354

Offner, Stacy, 15:389

Olan, Levi Arthur, 15:400–401

Olitzky, Kerry M., 15:405–406

opponents, 11:93

Petuchowski, Jakob Josef, 16:22–23

Philipson, David, 16:51–52

Pilchik, Ely Emanuel, 16:153–154

Plaut, W. Gunther, 16:228

Polish, David, 16:333–334

Poznanski, Gustavus, 16:433

Priesand, Sally Jane, 16:509–510

Raisin, Jacob Zalman, 17:74

Raisin, Max, 17:74–75

Regner, Sidney L., 17:191

Rosenau, William, 17:431

Rothschild, Jacob M., 17:493

Ruderman, David B., 17:519–520

Rudin, A. James, 17:521–522

Rudin, Jacob Philip, 17:522

Saint Louis (MO), 17:671–672

Samfield, Max, 17:746

Saperstein, David N., 18:34–35

Saperstein, Harold I., 18:35

Schaalman, Herman E., 18:96–97

Schanfarber, Tobias, 18:106

Schartzman, Sylvan David, 18:188

Schindler, Alexander M., 18:135–136

Schindler, Solomon, 18:137

Schulman, Samuel, 18:171–173

Schwartzman, Sylvan David, 18:188

Seattle (WA), 18:229

Shankman, Jacob K., 18:397

Shulman, Charles E., 18:531

Silver, Abba Hillel, 18:583–584

Silver, Daniel Jeremy, 18:584

Silverman, Joseph, 18:586–587

Simon, Abram, 18:608–609

Sobel, Ronald, 18:699–700

Sonderling, Jacob, 19:13

statistics, 20:365

Steinbach, Alexander Alan, 19:183

Steinberg, Paul, 19:189

Stern, Chaim, 19:205–206

Stern, Jack, 19:211

Stern, Malcolm Henry, 19:214–215

Stolz, Joseph, 19:235

summer camps, 11:272–273

Trachtenberg, Joshua, 20:79

Voorsanger, Jacob, 20:581

Washofsky, Mark E., 20:682

Wechsler, Judah, 20:694

Weinstein, Jacob, 20:727–728

Wiener, Max, 21:48

Wise, Isaac Mayer, 21:99–100

Wise, Jonah Bondi, 21:100

Wolf, Alfred, 21:134–135

Wolf, Arnold Jacob, 21:135

Wolsey, Louis, 21:156

women, ordination of, 18:278–279

Yoffie, Eric H., 17:172, 21:380

Zeldin, Isaiah, 21:499–500

Zimmerman, Sheldon, 21:535

Zlotowitz, Bernard M., 21:644

Zola, Gary Phillip, 21:665

Vereinigung Fuer das Liberale Judentum in Deutschland, 20:509

women, 17:172, 177–180, 21:179

ordination of, 20:349–350

as rabbis, 17:178–179

status, nineteenth century, 6:752

youth education programs, 17:172, 175–176

Zionism of, 17:170

See also Liberal Judaism

Reform movement

Columbus platform, 18:583

Hamburg, 8:296

Haskalah and, 8:439–440

Hungary, neology, 15:73–74

of Josiah, 11:457–458

music, 14:677–681

Netherlands, 15:101

philosophers, 15:123

Pittsburgh platform, 18:583

Simon, Abram, 18:608–609

See also Neo-Orthodoxy

Refuge, cities of. *See* Cities, of refuge

Refugees, 17:**183–187,** 186t

in 16th century Sarajevo, 18:47–48

American Joint Distribution Committee, 2:60–62

Arab, 20:262–264
in Austria, 2:692
Berihah, 3:433–436
Bosnian War (1992-1994), 18:49
Central British Fund, 4:544–545
Chambon-sur-Lignon, 4:564–565
China, 4:646–647
displaced persons and, 5:683–686
ORT, 15:489
Levy family, 12:745
Schmolka, Marie, aid to, 18:146
See also Displaced persons (DP)
Refugiados (Aguinis), 1:510
Refuseniks, 3:6–7, 11:299, 17:**187**
1970s, 17:564, 571
1980s, 17:573–576, 574
Nudel Ida, 15:327
Refutation of the Christian Principles
(Crescas), 5:285
Regavim (Israel), 17:**187**
Regbah (Israel), 17:**187**
Regelson, Abraham, 17:**187**
Regem-Melech, 17:**187**
Regensburg (Germany), 3:**229,**
17:**188–189**
Kandlein family, 11:760
Reggio, Abraham ben Ezriel, 17:**189**
Reggio, Isacco Samuel, 15:384, 17:**189**
Reggio di Calabria (Italy), 17:**189**
Reggio Emilia (Italy), 17:**189–190**
Reghin (Romania), 17:**190**
Regina (Saskatchewan), 18:65
Regius (Algeria). See Bone (Algeria)
Les régles de la méthode sociologique
(Durkheim), 6:64
Regner, Sidney L., 17:**191**
Regulations, legal. See Takkanot
Rehayim Shevurim (Hazaz), 8:492
Rehfisch, Hans Jose, 17:**191**
Rehine, Zalma, 17:**191**
Rehinul Săsesc. See Reghin (Romania)
Rehob (ancient Israel), 17:**191–192**
Rehob, Tel. See Tel Rehov
Rehoboam, 9:174–175, 17:**192**
Ammonites, 2:85
Rehoboh ha-Nahar. See Rehoboth
(ancient Israel)
Rehoboh-in-the-Negev. See Rehoboth
(ancient Israel)
Rehoboth (ancient Israel), 17:**193**
Rehov ha-Maderegot (Hendel), 8:806
Rehovot (Israel), 6:265, 17:**195**
Rehovot (Smilansky), 18:687
Rehovot ha-Nahar, 2:10
Rehovot ha-Nahar (Sharabi), 18:411
Rehum, 17:**196**

Rehumei, 17:**196**
Rehumei I, 17:196
Rehumei II, 17:196
Rehumei III, 17:196
Reibcheid, Samuel, 4:152
Reich, Asher, 17:**196**
Reich, Ignác, 17:**196**
Reich, Koppel, 17:**196–197**
Reich, Leon, 17:**197**
Reich, Marc David. See Rich, Marc
Reich, Robert Bernard, 4:125, 17:**197–
198**
Reich, Steve, 17:**198**
Reich, Wilhelm, 17:**198–199**, 19:173–
174
Reichard, Piroska, 17:**199**
Reich Association of the Jews in
Germany. See Reichsvereinigung
Reichenbach, Hans, 17:**199**
Reichenberg. See Liberec
Reicher, Emanuel, 17:**199**
Reicherson, Moses, 17:**199**
Reichert, Israel, 17:**199–200**
Reichinstein, David, 17:**200**
Das Reich Judaea im Jahre 6000
(Austerberg-Verakoff), 18:602,
21:620
Reichman, Albert, 17:200
Reichman, Avram Adolf. See Dominic,
Alexandru
Reichman, Hananiah, 6:669
Reichmann, Edward, 17:200
Reichmann, Eva, 17:200
Reichmann, Louis, 17:200
Reichmann, Paul, 17:200
Reichmann, Renée, 17:200
Reichmann, Samuel, 17:200–201
Reichmann family, 17:**200–201**
Reich-Ranicki, Marcel, 17:**201**
Reich-Ranicki — Solo, 17:201
Reich Representation of German Jews.
See Reichsvereinigung
Reich Representation of the Jews in
Germany. See Reichsvereinigung
Reichsbund Juedischer Frontsoldaten,
17:**201**
Reich Security Main Office. See RSHA
Reichslandbund, 1:470
Reichssicherheitshauptamt. See RSHA
Reichstein, Tadeus, 17:**201–202**
Reichsvereinigung, 9:128, 17:**202–203**
Reichsvereinigung der Juden in
Deutschland. See Reichsvereinigung
Reichsvertretung der Juden in
Deutschland. See Reichsvereinigung
Reichszentrale fuer juedische
Auswanderung, 17:**203**

Reicin, Bedřich, 18:665
Reif, S., 13:133
Reifenberg, Adolf, 17:**203**
Reifmann, Jacob, 17:**203–204**
Reik, Emma. See Reik, Havivah
Reik, Havivah, 17:**204**
Reik, Theodor, 2:187
Reik, Theodore, 17:**204**
Reiling, Anna. See Seghers, Anna
Reiling, Netty. See Seghers, Anna
"Reilly, Ace of Spies". See Rosenblum,
Sigmund Georgievich
Reilly, Sidney. See Rosenblum,
Sigmund Georgievich
Reimarus, Hermann Samuel, 16:629
Rein, Raphael. See Abramowitz,
Raphael
Reina, Joseph Della, 7:15
Reinach, Adolf, 17:**205**
Reinach, Joseph, 17:204–205
Reinach, Solomon, 2:370, 17:205
Reinach, Theodore, 2:370, 11:324,
17:205
Reinach family, 17:**204–205**
Reincarnation. See Gilgul
Das reine Denken und die
Seinskonstituierung bei Hermann
Cohen (Soloveitchik), 18:777
Reineman, Solomon, 4:296
Reiner, Carl, 17:**205–206**
Reiner, Fritz, 17:**206**
Reiner, Markus, 17:**206**
Reiner, Rob, 4:209, 17:**206–207**
Reines, Alvin Jay, 17:**207**
Reines, Frederick, 17:**207**
Reines, Isaac Jacob, 14:389, 17:**207–
208**, 18:576
Reinhardt, Max, 4:118, 15:602, 17:**208**
Reinhardt, Stephen R., 17:**208–209**
Reinharz, Jehuda, 4:124–125, 17:**209**
Reinharz, Shulamit, 18:736
Reinmann, Salomon, 17:**209–210**
Reinsdorf, Jerry, 17:**210**
Reis. See Auerbach, Isaac Eisig ben
Isaiah
Reis, Isaac. See Nadir, Moyshe
Reischer, Jacob ben Joseph, 17:**210–
211**
Reise durch das juedische Palaestina
(Holitscher), 9:321
Reisen, Abraham, 11:827, 17:**211**
Reisen, Zalman. See Rejzen, Zalman
Reisenberg, Nadia, 17:**211–212**
Reiser, Paul, 17:**212**
Reisler, Jerzy. See Sawicki, Jerzy
Reisman, David, 18:731
Reisman, Heather, 17:**212**

Reisman, Sammy, 3:726

Reiss, Abraham Joseph. *See* Rice, Abraham Joseph

Reiss, Herz, 15:386

Reiss, Lionel, 17:**212–213**

Reiss, Naḥ. *See* Avigad, Naḥman

Reiss, Seligmann, 15:386

Reisz, Karel, 17:**213**

Reitlinger, Gerald, 17:**213**

Re'iyyat ha-Yadayim le-Eḥad me-Ḥakhmei Hodu, 4:653

Reizeles, Ḥayyim. *See* Reizes, Ḥayyim ben Isaac ha-Levi

Reizeles, Ḥayyim ben Isaac ha-Levi. *See* Reizes, Ḥayyim ben Isaac ha-Levi

Reizenstein, Elmer Leopold. *See* Rice, Elmer Leopold

Reizenstein, Franz, 17:**213**

Reizes, Ḥayyim ben Isaac ha-Levi, 17:**213**

Reizes, Joshua, 17:**213**

Rejzen, Zalman, 17:**213–214**

Rekev Eliyahu (Katz, Joseph ben Elijah), 12:13

Rekhasim (Israel), 17:**214**

Rekhev Eliyahu (Joseph ben Elijah of Zaslaw), 11:420

Rekhush Natush (Lapid), 8:723

Rekrut (Dostál), 5:762

Reland, Adrian, 17:**214**

Reland, Hadrian. *See* Reland, Adrian

Relating Religion: Essays in the Study of Religion (Smith), 18:688

Relationships, forbidden. *See* Marriage, prohibited

Relativity (physics), 6:261–262

Relativity, the Special and the General Theory, a Popular Exposition (Einstein), 6:261

Relgis, Eugen, 17:**214**

Relief Organization of German Jews. *See* Hilfsverein der deutschen Juden

Religion Behind the Iron Curtain (Fineberg), 7:26

Religion der Vernunft aus den Quellen des Judentums (Cohen), 5:19–20

Die Religion des Geistes (Formstecher), 7:131–132

Religion of Reason Out of Sources of Judaism (Cohen). *See Religion der Vernunft aus den Quellen des Judentums*

Religions

    Buber on, 4:233–234

    Cohen approach, 5:19–20

    German Christian reformers, 14:6

    idolatry, and Near Eastern, 9:712–713

Palestine (Mandate) governance and, 10:406–407, 408

Phoenician, 16:123

Poland, 16:303*t*

religious courts

    Israel (state), 10:419–422

    Palestine (Mandate), 10:621–622

    Palestine (Ottoman), 10:620

social psychology, 3:271–272

See also Scholars and scholarship; *specific religions and topics*

Die Religionsphilosophie der Juden (Hirsch), 9:132

Religious Action Center, UAHC, 9:129

Religious ecstasy. *See* Ecstasy

Religious freedom and coercion

    Chile, 4:638

    England

        Caceres, Simon de, 4:331

        Carvajal, Abraham Israel, 4:502

    Orthodox views on, 15:499

    U.S.

        Adams, Arlin Marvin, 1:379–380

        Adams, John, 1:380

        early advocates, 11:102–103

    See also Forced conversion

Religious Freedom Restoration Act, 18:752

Religious News Service, 14:298

Religious peace movements. *See* Peace movements, religious

The Religious Right: the Assault on Tolerance and Pluralism in America (Foxman), 7:142, 20:378

The Rema. *See* Isserles, Moses ben Israel

"Remaining land," Joshua, Book of, 11:447

Remak. *See* Kimḥi, Moses

Remak, Ernst Julius, 17:215

Remak, Robert, 13:7, 17:215

Remak family, 17:**215**

Rembrandt (Bródy), 4:201

Rembrandt van Rijn, 3:673, 14:542, 17:**215–216**

Remedies. *See* Medicine

Remembrance of Things Past. See A la Recherche du temps perdu

Remenik, Hersh, 11:322

Reményi, Eduard, 17:**216–217**

Remeth (ancient Israel). *See* Ramoth (ancient Israel)

Remez, 3:641

Remez, Aharon, 17:217

Remez, Moshe David, 17:**217**

Reminiscences of an Amnesiac. See Zikhronot shel Ḥoleh Shikheḥah (Reich)

Remire (French Guyana), 4:532–533

Remnant of Israel, 17:**217**

Remnants (A Fable) (Sherman), 18:465

Remnick, David, 17:**217–218**

Remoch family. *See* Benremokh family

Remos, Moses, 15:581

Remos, Moses ben Isaac, 17:**218**

La Renaissanca (newspaper), 14:425

Renaissance

    Apocrypha, 2:261

    astronomers, 2:625–626

    Catholic Church, 4:711

    cultural life, 6:556

    dance, 5:410

    disputations and polemics, 5:694–695

    Italy

        cultural life, 6:556

        Hebrew fiction, 7:15

        Judah ben Joseph Moscato, 14:515–516

        Kabbalah, 5:440–441, 6:709

        literature, 7:15, 10:791–792

        Pico della Mirandola, Giovanni, 16:146–147

    music, 13:237

    pseudepigrapha, 2:261

Renaissance de la littérature hébraïque (Slouschz), 18:681

The Renaissance of Judaism (Silverman), 18:586

Renaissance Technologies, 18:618

ReNaK. *See* Krochmal, Nachman

Renan, Ernest, 6:36, 17:**218**

Renassia, Yossef, 17:**218–219**

Rendell, Edward Gene, 17:**219**

Rending of garments. *See* Keri'ah

René (King of France), 16:638

Rene, Roy, 17:**219–220**

René of Anjou, 1:310

Rent. *See* Lease and hire

Repair of the House. See Bedek ha-Bayit

Reparations

    Austria, 2:697

    Bienenfeld, Franz Rudolf, on, 3:690

Reparations, German. *See* German reparations

Repentance, 3:6–7, 17:**221–224**

    fasting, 6:719, 720, 722

    Rabba, Menahem, 17:7

    Shabbateanism and, 18:347

Repetition of the Law. See Mishneh Torah

Repetitorium der organischen, beziehungsweise anorganischen Chemie (Pinner), 16:169

Rephaim, 17:**224–225**

Rephidim (ancient Israel), 2:28, 29, 17:**225**

Replicación (Chirino), 4:652

Replies and queries. *See* Responsa

Le Reporter engage: trente ans d'instantanes (Kagan), 11:706

Report of the Commission for the Study of Jewish Education in the United States (report), 6:199

A Report on Kurdistan and the Kurds (Driver), 6:22

"Report to the Secretary on the Acquiescence of this Government in the Murder of the Jews" (U.S. Treasury), 9:365

Representational art, 2:492, 493–494, 495, 496, 497

The Representative. See Der Stellvertreter

The Reproduction of Mothering (Chodorow), 18:736

Reproductive system, 2:135

Reproof. *See* Rebuke and reproof

Reptiles, 2:172
    chameleon, 4:565
    lizards, 13:147
    monitor, 14:444

De Republica Hebraeorum libri tres (Cunaeus), 5:338

Republican Jewish Coalition, 17:**225**

Republic of Georgia. *See* Georgia (Transcaucasia)

Republic of Ireland. *See* Ireland

La République Universelle (Cloots), 4:761

La repudiée (Abécassis), 1:245

Repulsion (Polanski), 16:326

Requisition. *See* Confiscation, expropriation, forfeiture

Rereading the Rabbis: A Woman's Voice (Hauptman), 8:461

Rescue from Holocaust, 9:342, **490–492,** 495–496
    Aliav, Ruth, 1:658
    Fleischmann, Gisi, 7:74–75
    funding, 13:700
    Japan, 11:84
    Mendes, Aristides de Sousa, 14:42–43
    Nèvejean, Yvonne, 15:129

Rescue of Jews in World War II. *See* Refugees

Research Institute for Medieval Hebrew Poetry (Jerusalem), 18:155

Resen (Mesopotamia), 17:**225–226**

Resettlement period, London, England, 13:180–181

Resh, 17:**226**

Reshef, Even. *See* Firkovich, Abraham

Resheph, 5:573, 17:**226**

Reshevsky, Samuel Herman, 17:**226–227**

Resh Galuta. *See* Exilarch

Reshimat Poalei Israel. *See* Rafi

Reshit Bikkurim (Enoch ben Abraham), 6:445

Reshit Bikkurim (Judah Leib ben Enoch Zundel), 11:506

Reshit Da'at (Albelda), 1:588

Reshit Ḥokhmah (Amelander), 2:38

Reshit Ḥokhmah (Vidas), 20:517

Resh kallah, 11:726–727, 17:**227**

Resh Lakish. *See* Simeon ben Lakish

Reshumot (periodical), 6:29

Reshut, 17:**227**

Reshut (possession), 15:551–552

Residences. *See* Domiciles

Residency, laws controlling, 6:690

Resident aliens. *See* Strangers and gentiles

Resilience and Courage: Women, Men and the Holocaust (Tec), 9:420

Resistance, Jewish. *See* Jewish resistance

Resistance during World War II, 9:358, 15:664–668, 665
    Austria-Hungary, 14:241–242, 18:263
    Belarus, 9:358, *474,* 15:645, 667, 668, 16:148, 20:209–210
        Braslav, 4:131
        Minsk, 14:296
        Novogrudok, 15:321
        Oshmyany, 15:503
    Belgium, 3:282–283
    Belgrade, 3:283–284
    Bielski brothers, 3:688–689
    Bloch, Marc, 3:765
    Bulgaria, 15:668
    Denmark, 5:582–583
    Erez Israel, 1:658
    France, 3:141, 5:748
    Greece, 8:50–52
    Ha-Shomer ha-Ẓa'ir, 8:384
    Hungary, 9:616
    Italy, 15:667–668
    Lithuania, 4:170, 15:666–667, 17:548–550, 21:125
    Netherlands, 15:105–106
    Poland, 5:373, 15:566–667, 16:314–317
        Bialystok, 3:569–570

        Cracow, 5:263
        Hrubieszow, 9:574–575
        Parczew Forest, 15:632
        Sobibor, 15:707
        Warsaw, 9:253, 338, 13:240–241, 20:672, 673–674, 21:676
    Romania, 17:388–391
    Russia, 17:548–550
    Slovakia, 5:358, 15:668
    Summer Seminar Program on Holocaust and Jewish Resistance, 2:49
    Ukraine
        Bolekhov, 4:44–45
        Brody, 4:200
        Buchach, 4:238
    USSR, 15:666–667, 17:548–550

Resnais, Alain, 3:41

Resnick, Hirsch Yosef Hakohen. *See* Resnick, Zvi Yosef Hakohen

Resnick, Salomon, 17:**227–228**

Resnick, Zvi Yosef Hakohen, 17:**228**

Resnik, Judith Arlene, 17:**228**

Resnik, Regina, 17:**228**

Respiratory system, 2:134

Responsa, 17:**228–239**
    Adret, Solomon ben Abraham, 1:421–423
    archives, 2:405
    Caro, Joseph ben Ephraim, 4:490–491
    David ben Solomon ibn Abi Zimra, 5:471
    Fraenkel-Teomim, Baruch ben Joshua Ezekiel Feiwel, 7:145
    geonic, 7:494
    geonic period, 9:210–211, 17:229–230
    geonim, 7:380, 384
    Halakhic, 12:671, 15:771–772, 17:228–239
        Holocaust, 9:362–363
    Hoffmann, David Ẓevi, 9:310–311
    Jacob ben Moses Moellin, 14:414
    Judah ben Eliezer ha-Levi Minz, 14:303
    Judeo-Arabic culture and, 11:541–542
    Landau, Ezekiel Ben Judah, 12:459–460
    Lapapa, Aaron Ben Isaac, 12:488
    Lauterbach, Jacob Zallel, 12:529
    ma'aseh, 13:310
    Maimonides, Moses, 13:386
    Meir ben Baruch of Rothenburg, 13:780–783

Responsa, *continued*
mishpat Ivri, 14:337–338
Mizraḥi, Elijah, 14:394
Moses ben Isaac Mintz, 14:301
nineteenth century, 17:233–234
psychology, 16:688
publishing, 17:237–239
rabbinic office, 13:98–99, 101–102
Responsa Index, public authority,
16:709–710
rishonim, 17:230–231
Sar Shalom ben Boaz, 18:62
Schick, Moses ben Joseph,
opposition to, 18:127–128
Schlettstadt, Samuel ben Aaron,
18:143
separation of powers, 18:291–292
Shalem, Samuel, 18:371–372
Shalom ben Yiẓhak of Neustadt,
18:390
Shapiro, Saul ben Dov, 18:408
significance of, 17:231
sixteenth to eighteenth centuries,
17:231–233
Slonik, Benjamin Aaron ben
Abraham, 18:676
Slonim, Reuben, 18:678
twentieth century, 11:29, 17:234–
236
U.S., 17:236–237
See also Halakhah
Responsa Project, Bar-Ilan, 5:131–132
Response to Modernity (Meyer), 14:149
Responsorial psalmody. *See* Music
Ressler, Benjamin, 17:**239**
Ressner, Franz. *See* Roessler, Carl
Restitution and indemnification,
17:**239–240**
in Bulgaria, 4:273
by Germany
American Jewish Committee,
2:55
American Joint Distribution
Committee, 2:62
successor organizations,
11:327
World Jewish Restitution
Organization, 2:49
legal claims of, ona'ah and, 15:425
by Norway, 15:309, 310, 504
by Swiss banks, 5:401–402, 18:637
Restitution of Jewish Cultural
Reconstruction, 8:793
Rest of the Words of Baruch, 3:187–188
Restoration of Jews (Hechler), 8:750
Restraint. *See* Rebuke and reproof
Resurrection, 3:239, 292, 13:6, 17:**240–
244**
afterlife, 1:441–442

Boethusians, 2:198
Daniel prophecy, 6:495, 497
Essenes, 6:511
Karaites, 11:798
legend
luz of the spine, 13:279
Mount of Olives, 14:585
literature
Apocalypse of Isaiah, 6:494,
495
Bible, 3:644, 645, 673, 13:448
medieval philosophy, 17:243–244
Pharisaic concept, 16:30, 31
theology
Abulafia concept, 1:342
article of faith, 3:291, 292
body and soul, 4:30
intertestamental eschatology,
6:493–495, 497–499
Islamic, 6:502–503
kabbalistic, 6:502
man's nature, 13:392, 448,
17:612
olam ha-ba, 15:399–400
Orthodox Judaism and,
15:497
soul's immortality, 3:239,
19:35–39
Talmudic, 17:241–243
word to come, 15:399–400
views on
Aaron ben Elijah, 1:213
Abraham bar Ḥiyya, 1:292
Albo, Joseph, 1:594, 618–619,
16:90
Levi ben Gershom, 12:701
Maimonides, 3:239, 13:372,
373, 374
modern, 17:244
Muhammad, 6:502–503
Saadiah Gaon, 17:612
Retail stores, 4:729, 5:69–70, 9:121,
18:608
Reth, Alfred, 15:648
*Rethinking Modern Judaism: Ritual,
Commandment, Community* (Eisen),
6:265
Rethymnon (Greece), 17:**244**
Réti, Richard, 17:**244**
Réti, Rudolf, 17:**244**
Retirement, 12:417
Le retour de Silbermann (Lacretelle),
12:426
Retribution, 6:497
divine (*See* Reward and
punishment)
Essene, 6:499

Islamic, 6:502
Reuben, 17:**244–246,** *245*
Bilhah, 3:698
Reuben, Abraham, 15:571
Reuben ben Ḥayyim, 17:**246**
Reuben ben Strobilius, 17:**246–247**
Reuben Hoeshke ben Hoeshke Katz,
17:**247**
Reubeni, David. *See* Reuveni, David
Reuchlin, Johannes, 16:26, 17:**247–249**
Bible translations by, 3:612
biography of, 7:415
education, 6:159
Kabbalah, 11:672
Luther influenced by Rashi via,
3:648
Melanchthon, Philipp, 14:6
Pfefferkorn, Johannes, 16:26
Pforzheim Jews, 16:27
Talmud defense, 19:482
Reuel. *See* Jethro (father-in-law of
Moses)
Reuss, Eduard, 17:**249**
Reuter, Paul Julius, Freiherr von,
17:**249–250**
Reuti, ar-. *See* Rote family
Reutlingen (Germany), 17:**250**
Reuveni, Aharon, 17:**250–251**
Reuveni, David, 3:42, 706, 9:264*t,*
17:**251–252,** 18:315
Azemmour community, 2:765
Badajoz, 3:42
Beirut, 3:270
Castro, Abraham, 4:523
Charles V, 4:576
Clement VII, 4:753
Glanz-Leyeles, Aaron, drama,
7:625
ḥiddushim, 8:465
Joseph ben Gershon of Rosheim,
11:421
Kabbalah, 11:616
Llerena, 13:148
Messianism, 6:497
Molcho, Solomon, 14:424
Ten Lost Tribes, 3:706, 7:99,
19:639–640
travel book, 9:133, 11:710
Reuytenberg, Efraim. *See* Fima, Efraim
Revadim (Israel), 17:**252**
Révah, Israel Salvator, 17:**252**
Reval (Estonia). *See* Tallinn (Estonia)
Revealer of Secrets (Eliezer ben Nathan
of Mainz), 6:328
Revel (Estonia). *See* Tallinn (Estonia)
Revel, Bernard, 6:193, 17:**252–253**

Revel, Bernard Dov, 15:398, 495, 498
Revel, Michel, 17:**253**
Revelation, 17:**253–259**
    biblical literature, 17:253–254
    continuous, 15:494
    dreams, 6:8–10
    in Orthodox Judaism, 15:497–498
    progressive, 15:494
    Steinheim view, 19:195
    Talmudic literature, 17:254–256
Revere, Giuseppe Prospero, 17:**259**
Reverence of God, 6:725
Reverii sculptate (Aderca), 1:390
Révész, Béla, 17:**259**
Revesz, Geza, 17:**259**
Revi'a, 18:440
Reviczky, Imre, 3:67, 17:**259–260**
Revid ha-Zahav (Mizrahi), 14:393
The Review (periodical), 2:686
Revi'iyat Rosendorf (Shaham), 18:363
Revised Standard Version (RSV)
    (Bible), 3:615–616
Revisionist movement
    Bodenheimer, Max Isidor, 4:28
    Briscoe, Robert, 4:185
    Hecht, Ben, 8:750
    Hoffmann, Jacob, 9:311
    on Jewish legion, 11:306
    Jewish State Party, 11:315–316
    Zionist, 1:544, 3:345, 4:495,
        17:**260–267**, 18:705
Revista Cultului Mozaic (journal),
    17:**267**
Revival of the Religious Sciences
    (al-Ghazālī), 7:571
Revivim (Israel), 17:**267–268**
Revolte (Aderca), 1:391
Revolutionary movements
    Abbasid, 1:233
    American Revolution, 2:43–44
    Bar Kokhba, 3:158–161
    Clermont-Tonnerre, Stanislas de,
        4:755
    Deutsch, Leo, 5:624
    Deutsch, Simon, 5:625
    Dimanstein, Simon, 5:662
    Hofer, Andreas, 9:306
    Jewish identity and, 9:238, 11:296–
        297
    Leviné, Eugene, 12:717–718
    Pijade, Moša, 16:152
    See also American Revolution;
        French Revolution
Revolution of 1848
    emancipation, 6:379
    Meisels, Dov Berush, 13:790

proponents, 11:120–121
*The Revolving Sword. See Ha-Ḥerev
    ha-Mithappekhet*
Revson, Charles Haskell, 17:**268**
Revson Foundation, 6:571
Revue de métaphysique et de morale
    (journal), 12:646
Revue des études juives (periodical),
    11:724, 17:**268**, 18:722
Revue européenne des études hébraiques
    (periodical), 4:189
Revusky, Abraham, 17:**268–269**
Reward and punishment, 17:**269–272**
    medieval philosophy, 17:270–271
    modern thought, 17:271–272
    naturalism, supernaturalism,
        17:270–271
Rexingen (Germany), 17:**272**
Reyakh fun Erd (Horowitz), 9:533
Reyzn, Avrom. *See* Reisen, Abraham
Reyzn, Zalman. *See* Rejzen, Zalman
Rezchik. *See* Gordon, Abraham
Rezekne (Latvia), 17:**272**
Rezhitsa. *See* Rezekne
Rezin, 17:**272–273**
Rezina (Moldova), 17:**273**
Reznik, David, 17:**273**
Reznik, Lipe, 17:**273**
Reznikoff, Charles, 15:442, 17:**273–274**
Rhatyn. *See* Rogatin (Ukraine)
Rheims (France), 17:**274**
Rhetorical criticism, 3:653
Rhineland Jews
    judenpfennige, 11:525
    Judeo-French language used by,
        11:545
Rhineland Protestant Synod, 4:685
Rhinewine, Abraham, 17:**274–275**
Rhode Island (U.S.), 17:**275–277**, *276*
Rhodes (Greece), 7:177, 17:**277–279**
Rhodesia, community organization
    and structures, 5:108, 110, 119*t*
Ri. *See* Isaac ben Samuel of Dampierre
"Riaz." *See* Isaiah ben Elijah di Trani
Riba. *See* Isaac ben Asher ha-Levi;
    Judah ben Eleazar
Rib-Adda of Byblos, 6:285
Riba II, 10:40
Ribal. *See* Levinsohn, Isaac Baer
Ribalow, Menachem, 17:**279–280**
Ribam (12th c.). *See* Isaac ben Meir
Ribash. *See* Isaac ben Sheshet Perfet
Riba the Younger, 10:40
Ribbentrop, Joachim von, 17:**280**
Ribbentrop-Molotov Pact, 9:331
Ribbui and mi'ut rules, 9:28

Ribeauvillé (France), 11:576, 17:**280**
Ribeiro, Bernardim, 17:**280**
Ribeiro dos Santos, Antonio, 17:**280–
    281**
Ribeiro Sanchez, Antonio, 13:728,
    17:**281**
Ribes de Majorca, Jaime. *See* Cresques,
    Judah
Ribicoff, Abraham A., 17:**281–282**
Riblah (Ancient Syria), 17:**282**
Ricardo, David (1772-1823), 17:**282**
Ricardo, David (1904-1982), 17:**282–
    283**
Ricardo, Halsey Ralph, 17:**282**
Ricardo, Harry Ralph, 17:**282**
Ricardo, John Lewis, 17:**282**
Ricchi, Raphael Immanuel ben
    Abraham Ḥai, 17:**283**
Ricci, Matteo, 1:552, 11:726
Ricci, Paulus. *See* Ricius, Paulus
Rice, 17:**283–284**
Rice, Abraham Joseph, 17:**284**
Rice, Elmer Leopold, 17:**284–285**
Rice, Isaac Leopold, 17:**285**
Rice, James P., 17:**285**
Rice, Joseph Mayer, 17:**285**
Ricercar (Seter), 18:319
*Ricerche sull' organizzazione della
    Giudea sotte il dominio romano*
    (Momigliano), 14:431
Rich, Adrienne, 17:**285–286**, 18:736
Rich, Bernard. *See* Rich, Buddy
Rich, Buddy, 17:**286**
Rich, Daniel, 17:**285**
Rich, Denise Eisenberg, 17:**287**
Rich, Emanuel, 17:**285**
Rich, Marc, 17:**286–287**
Rich, Morris, 17:**285**
Rich, Walter Henry, 17:**285**
Richard I (King of England), 6:410–
    411
Richards, Anne, 4:125
Richards, Bernard Gerson, 17:**287**
Richards, Martin, 17:**287–288**
Richards, Mary Lea Johnson, 17:**287–
    288**
Richards Medical Research Building,
    11:722
Richenza of Nürenberg, 7:50
Rich family, 17:**285**
Richietti, Joseph Shallit ben Eliezer,
    17:**288**
Richler, Mordecai, 4:423–424, 6:439,
    12:486, 17:**288**
The Rich Man (Kreisel), 4:424
Richman, Julia, 17:**288–289**
Richmond (VA), 6:291–292, 17:**289–
    290**

Richter, Burton, 17:**290**

Richter, Elise, 17:**290–291**

Richter, Hans, 17:**291**

Richter, Raoul, 17:**291**

Richtmann, Mozés, 17:**291–292**

Rici, Paulus. *See* Ricius, Paulus

Ricinus plant, 11:388

Ricius, Paulus, 17:**292**

Rickles, Don, 17:**292**

Rickover, Hyman George, 6:161, 17:**292–293**

Riddles

hidah parables, 15:620

parodic, 15:655

Rie, Dame Lucie, 17:**293**

Riegelman, Harold, 17:**293**

Rieger, Eliezer, 17:**293**

Rieger, Paul, 17:**293–294**

Riegner, Gerhart, 17:**294**

R.I.E.I.T.S. *See* Rieti, Moses ben Isaac da

Riesman, David, 17:**294**

Riess, Ludwig, 17:**294**

Riesser, Gabriel, 6:379, 12:547, 16:344, 17:**295–296**

Der Jude, 11:523

Riesser, Jacob, 17:**296**

Riesser, Lazarus Jacob, 17:296

da Rieti. *See* Rieti family

Rieti, Angelo da, 17:296

Rieti, Arturo, 17:297

Rieti, Asael Raphael, 17:296

Rieti, C., Italian translation of Bible by, 3:633

Rieti, David Naphtali, 17:296–297

Rieti, Elhanan ben Isaac Eliakim da, 17:296

Rieti, Eliezer ben Isaac, 17:297

Rieti, Elijah Isaac, 17:296

Rieti, Fabio, 17:297

Rieti, Hezekiah ben Gabriel, 17:297

Rieti, Isaac, 17:296

Rieti, Laudadio Ishmael da, 17:296

Rieti, Maestro Gaio da. *See* Rieti, Moses ben Isaac da

Rieti, Malka, 17:296–297

Rieti, Michael ben Juda da, 17:296

Rieti, Mordecai ben Isaac da, 17:297

Rieti, Moses ben Elchana da, 17:296

Rieti, Moses ben Isaac da, 11:460, 547, 17:**297–298**

Rieti, Moses da, 17:296

Rieti, Serena, 17:297

Rieti, Simone da, 17:297

Rieti, Solomone da, 17:296

Rieti, Solomon Moses da, 17:296

Rieti, Vittorio, 17:297, **298**

Rieti family, 17:**296–297**

Rieto, Nicky, 17:297

Rietti. *See* Rieti family

Rietti family. *See* Rieti family

Rif. *See* Alfasi, Isaac ben Jacob

Rifkind, Malcolm. *See* Rifkind, Sir Malcolm

Rifkind, Simon Hirsch, 3:435, 17:**298–299**

Rifkind, Sir Malcolm, 6:425–426, 17:**298**

Riga (Latvia), 6:35, 12:520, 17:**299–301**

Right and left, 17:**301–302**

Righteous Among the Nations, 17:**303–307**

Benoit, Pierre-Marie, 3:370–371

Douwes, Arnold, 5:765–766

Eichmann trial, 6:252

Foley, Francis, 7:95

Hasidei Ummot ha-Olam, 8:389

Hautval, Adelaïde, 8:464–465

Ho Feng-Shan, 9:306

Johan Westerweel, 21:27

Karski, Jan, 11:818

Sandberg, Willem Jacob, 18:11

Schindler, Oskar, 18:136

Sendler, Irena, 18:287

Zakynthos, 21:456–457

Righteous gentiles

Mendes, Aristides de Sousa, 14:42–43

Nèvejean, Yvonne, 15:129

Righteous men. *See* Zaddikim

Righteousness, 17:**307–309**

Maimonides' views, 17:309

medieval thought, 17:309

of Noah, 15:288

zaddik, 17:308–309

Rights

human (*See* Human rights)

proprietary (*See* Proprietary rights)

Rights of the Kingdom (Brothers), 4:188

Rights organizations. *See specific organizations*

Rigler, Leo George, 17:**332**

Rīhāniyyah, al- (Israel), 17:**332**

Riijksinstituut voor Oollogsdocumentatie, 2:411

Riis, Jacob, 15:204

Rijeka (Croatia), 17:**332–333**

Rikam. *See* Kimhi, Joseph

Riklis, Meshulam, 17:**333**

Rimini (Italy), 17:**333**

Rimmon, 17:**333–334**, 18:594

Rimmonim. *See* Finials

Rimmon-Perez (ancient Israel), 17:**334**

Rimoc family. *See* Benremokh family

Rimoch, Astruc, 4:54, 17:**334**

Rimokh family. *See* Benremokh family

Rimon, Jacob, 17:**334**

Rimon, Joseph Zevi, 17:**334**

Rimonim (art periodical), 2:527

Rinat ha-Heikhal (Talmon), 8:504

Rindfleisch, 2:36, 17:**334–335**

Bamberg, 3:101

Bohemia, 4:38

Niederstetten, 14:480, 15:259

Noerdlingen, 15:293

Oettingen, 15:384

The Ring, 7:74

Ringel, Michael, 17:**335**

Ringelblum, Emanuel, 9:333, 362, 17:**335–336**

American Joint Distribution Committee, 2:61

Judenrat institution, 11:527

Ringelblum, Menahem. *See* Ringelblum, Emanuel

Ringer, Alexander L., 17:**336**

Ringl+Pit, 17:**336–337**

Rio de Janeiro (Brazil), 17:**337–339**

Ri of Dampierre. *See* Isaac ben Samuel of Dampierre

Riots, anti-Jewish. *See* Pogroms

Riproduzione nei protozoi (Enriques), 6:445

Rips, Eliyahu, 3:679

Risālat al-ibānah fi usūl al-diyānah (Aknin), 1:569

Risālat al-Tanbīh (Ibn Janāh), 9:681

Risani, 18:573

Rischin, Moses, 17:**339**

The Rise of Anthropological Theory (Harris), 8:363

The Rise of David Levinsky (Cahan), 4:336, 20:281

The Rise of Reform Judaism (Plaut), 16:228

Risha (Poland). *See* Rzeszow (Poland)

Rishonim, 1:532, 14:340, 17:**339–343**

Austria

Aaron of Neustadt, 1:219–220

Jacob of Vienna, 11:44–45

Petter ben Joseph, 16:22

Tyrnau, Isaac, 20:219–220

Avigdor ben Elijah ha-Kohen, 2:732

Babylonia

Daniel ben Saadiah ha-Bavli, 5:429

Daniel ben Samuel ibn Abī
Rabī', 5:429

David ben Hezekiah, 5:466–467

Natronai bar Hilai, 15:32–33

Ben Meir, Aaron, 3:366

Bulgaria, Moskoni, Judah Leon
ben Moses, 14:563

Crimea, Kirimi, Abraham, 12:185

Czechoslovakia

Isaac ben Jacob ha-Lavan of
Prague, 10:42

Muelhausen, Yom Tov
Lipmann, 14:595–597

Taku, Moses ben Ḥisdai,
19:460–461

David ben Zakkai II, 5:472

Egypt

Abraham ben David
Maimuni, 1:296

Alamani, Aaron he-Ḥaver
ben Yeshu'ah, 1:575

Ali ben Amram, 1:659

Anatoli ben Joseph, 2:133

David ben Abraham
Maimuni, 5:464–465

David ben Daniel, 5:466

David ben Joshua Maimuni,
5:467

Hananel ben Samuel, 8:315

Joseph Rosh ha-Seder, 11:432

Joshua ben Abraham
Maimuni, 11:449

Maẓli'ah ben Solomon ha-
Kohen, 13:707

Peraḥyah ben Nissim,
15:757–758

Tanḥum ben Joseph
Yerushalmi, 19:504–505

England

Elhanan ben Yakar, 6:316

Elijah Menahem ben Moses,
6:346

Moses ben Yom Tov, 14:556

France

Aaron ben Jacob ha-Kohen
of Lunel, 1:213–214

Aaron ben Meshullam of
Lunel, 1:216

Abba Mari ben Eligdor, 1:229

Abraham ben David of
Posquières, 1:296–298

Abraham ben Isaac of
Montpellier, 1:302

Abraham ben Isaac of
Narbonne, 1:302–303

Abraham ben Nathan ha-
Yarhi, 1:309

Abraham ben Samuel of
Dreux, 1:310

Asher ben Meshullam ha-
Kohen of Lunel, 2:564–565

Asher ben Saul, 2:565

Bekhor Shor, Joseph ben
Isaac, 2:276–277

Benjamin ben Samuel ha-
Levi, 3:361

Bondavin, Bonjudas, 4:56–57

Bonfils, Joseph ben Samuel,
4:62

Crescas, Asher ben Abraham,
5:284

David ben Levi of Narbonne,
5:468

David ben Saul, 5:470

Elhanan ben Isaac of
Dampierre, 6:315–316

Eliezer ben Samuel of Metz,
6:329

Eliezer of Beaugency, 6:330

Eliezer of Toul, 6:330–331

Eliezer of Touques, 6:331

Elijah ben Judah of Paris,
6:339

Ezra of Montcontour, 6:663

Gershom ben Solomon,
7:552–553

Gershon ben Solomon of
Arles, 7:554–555

Ḥayyim ben Hananel ha-
Kohen, 8:481

Hezekiah ben Manoah, 9:92

Isaac ben Abba Mari of
Marseilles, 10:37–38

Isaac ben Abraham, 10:38

Isaac ben Abraham of
Narbonne, 10:39

Isaac ben Joseph of Corbeil,
10:43

Isaac ben Menahem the
Great, 10:44–45

Isaac ben Merwan ha-Levi,
10:45

Isaac ben Samuel of
Dampierre, 10:48

Isaac from Ourville, 10:52

Isaac of Evreux, 10:53

Jacob ben Moses of Bagnols,
11:35

Jacob ben Samson, 11:36

Jacob of Corbeil, 11:43–44

Jacob of Marvège, 11:44

Jacob of Orleans, 11:44

Jacob of Pont-Sainte-
Maxence, 11:44

Jehiel ben Joseph of Paris,
11:103

Jonathan ben David ha-
Kohen of Lunel, 11:397

Joseph ben Baruch of
Clisson, 11:419

Joseph ben Moses of Troyes,
11:424

Joseph Ḥazzan ben Judah of
Troyes, 11:430

Judah ben Isaac, 11:487

Judah ben Moses ha-
Darshan, 11:489

Judah ben Nathan, 11:490

Kimḥi, David, 12:155–156

Kimḥi, Joseph, 12:157

Kimḥi, Mordecai, 12:158

Kimḥi, Moses, 12:158

Kokhavi, David ben Samuel,
12:270

Lattes, Isaac ben Jacob,
12:519

Lattes, Judah, 12:519

Levi ben Gershom, 12:698–
701

Machir ben Judah, 12:324

Manoah of Narbonne, 13:483

Meir ben Isaac of
Trinquetaille, 13:784

Meir ben Samuel of
Remerupt, 13:784–785

Meir ben Simeon ha-Me'ili,
13:785

Meiri, Menahem ben
Solomon, 13:785–788

Menahem ben Ḥelbo, 14:21

Meshullam ben Jacob of
Lunel, 14:77

Meshullam ben Moses, 14:78

Meshullam ben Nathan of
Melun, 14:78–79

Moses ben Abraham of
Pontoise, 14:547–548

Moses ben Jacob of Coucy,
14:549–550

Moses ben Joseph ben
Merwan Levi, 14:551

Moses ha-Darshan, 14:556–
557

Moses of Evreux, 14:559

Nethanel of Chinon, 15:93

Official, Joseph, 15:388–389

Official, Nathan ben Joseph,
15:388–389

Perez ben Elijah of Corbeil,
15:769–770

Rashi, 17:101–106

Reuben ben Ḥayyim, 17:246

Samson ben Abraham of
Sens, 17:752–753

Rishonim, *continued*

Samson ben Isaac of Chinon, 17:753

Samson ben Joseph of Falaise, 17:753–754

Samson ben Samson of Coucy, 17:754

Samuel ben David, 17:769

Samuel ben Meir, 17:771–773

Samuel Ben Solomon of Falaise, 17:774

Samuel of Evreux, 17:778

Schlettstadt, Samuel ben Aaron, 18:142–143

Shemaiah of Troyes, 18:456–457

Simeon ben Samuel of Joinville, 18:600

Solomon ben Abraham of Montpellier, 18:770

Solomon ben Judah of Dreux, 18:772

Solomon ben Meir, 18:772

Tam, Jacob ben Meir, 19:491–492

Treves, Johanan ben Mattathias, 20:135–136

Germany

Abraham ben Azriel, 1:295

Abraham ben Samuel he-Ḥasid, 1:309

Alexander Suslin ha-Kohen of Frankfurt, 1:630

Amram of Mainz, 2:106

Asher ben Jehiel, 2:563–564

Ashkenazi, Dan, 2:573

Bamberg, Samuel ben Baruch, 3:101–102

Baruch ben Isaac of Regensburg, 3:188

Baruch ben Isaac of Worms, 3:189

Baruch ben Samuel of Mainz, 3:190

Bruna, Israel ben Ḥayyim, 4:222

Dueren, Isaac ben Meir, 6:41–42

Eleazar ben Judah of Worms, 6:303–305

Eleazar ben Moses ha-Darshan of Wuerzburg, 6:305

Eliezer ben Isaac of Worms, 6:326

Eliezer ben Joel ha-Levi of Bonn, 6:326–327

Ephraim ben Isaac of Regensburg, 6:459

Ephraim ben Jacob of Bonn, 6:460

Ḥayyim ben Isaac, 8:481–482

Ḥayyim ben Jehiel Ḥafeẓ Zahav, 8:482

Ḥayyim Paltiel ben Jacob, 8:483

Hezekiah ben Jacob, 9:92

Hillel of Erfurt, 9:115

Isaac bar Dorbelo, 10:37

Isaac ben Asher ha-Levi, 10:39–40

Isaac ben Eliezer, 10:41

Isaac ben Judah of Mainz, 10:44

Isaac ben Meir, 10:44

Isaac ben Mordecai, 10:45

Isaac ben Moses of Vienna, 10:45–46

Israel ben Joel, 10:748

Israel of Bamberg, 10:758

Israel of Krems, 10:758

Isserlein, Israel ben Pethahiah, 10:768–769

Jacob ben Yakar, 11:36

Joel ben Isaac ha-Levi, 11:365

Judah ben Kalonymus ben Meir, 11:488–489

Judah ben Kalonymus ben Moses of Mainz, 11:489

Judah ben Samuel he-Ḥasid, 1:490–491

Kalonymus family, 11:747–749

Meir ben Baruch ha-Levi, 13:779–780

Meir ben Baruch of Rothenburg, 13:780–783

Meir ben Isaac Sheli'aḥ Ẓibbur, 13:784

Menahem ben Jacob, 14:21–22

Menahem of Merseburg, 14:26

Mordecai ben Hillel ha-Kohen, 14:480–481

Samson ben Eliezer, 17:753

Samuel ben Kalonymus he-Ḥasid of Speyer, 17:771

Samuel ben Natronai, 17:774

Shalom ben Yizḥak of Neustadt, 18:390

Solomon ben Samson, 18:772

Weil, Jacob ben Judah, 20:711–712

Gershom ben Judah Me'or ha-Golah, 7:551–552

Hillel ben Eliakim, 9:113

Isaac of Chernigov, 10:53

Italy

Abenafia, Joseph, 1:250

Ahitub ben Isaac, 1:546

Anan ben Marinus ha-Kohen, 2:128

Anatoli, Jacob ben Abba Mari ben Samson, 2:132–133

Anau family, 2:136

Anav, Benjamin ben Abraham, 2:137

Anav, Jehiel ben Jekuthiel ben Benjamin ha-Rofe, 2:137–138

Anav, Zedekiah ben Abraham, 2:138–139

Anav Judah ben Benjamin ha-Rofe, 2:138

Bonavoglia, Moses de' Medici, 4:56

Daniel ben Jehiel of Rome, 5:428

Eliezer ben Samuel of Verona, 6:329

Elijah of la Massa, 6:346–347

Isaac ben Melchizedek of Siponto, 10:44

Isaiah ben Elijah di Trani, 10:77

Isaiah ben Mali de Trani, 10:77

Meshullam ben Kalonymus, 14:77–78

Moses of Pavia, 14:560

Nathan ben Jehiel of Rome, 15:13–14

Menahem ben Solomon, 14:23

Morocco

Adonim ben Nisan ha-Levi, 1:413

Aghmati, Zechariah ben Judah, 1:465

Alfasi, Isaac ben Jacob, 1:639–641

Gagin, Ḥayyim, 7:334

Najar family, 14:760

North Africa

Duran, Solomon ben Simeon, 6:61

Duran, Zemaḥ ben Solomon, 6:61

Ephraim ibn Avi Alragan, 6:460

Ibn Plat, Joseph, 6:685–686

Jama, Samuel ibn, 11:74

Persia

David ben Samuel, 5:469

Isaac bar Israel ibn al-Shuwayk, 10:37

Zechariah ben Barachel, 21:486

responsa, 17:230

Russia

Eliezer ben Nathan of Mainz, 6:327

Moses of Kiev, 14:559

Solomon ben Samuel, 18:772–773

Spain

Aaron ben Joseph ha-Levi, 1:214–215

Abbas, Moses ben Samuel, 1:231–232

Aboab, Isaac I, 1:266–267

Aboab, Isaac II, 1:267–268

Abudarham, David ben Joseph, 1:336

Abudarham family, 1:335

Abulafia, Meir, 1:341–342

Abzardiel, Moses, 1:346

Adret, Solomon ben Abraham, 1:421–423

Albalia, Baruch ben Isaac, 1:583

Albalia, Isaac ben Baruch, 1:583–584

Al-Bargeloni, Isaac ben Reuben, 1:586

Aldubi, Abraham ben Moses ben Ismail, 1:607

Alguades, Meir, 1:654

Al-Nakawa, Israel ben Joseph, 1:686

Astruc ha-Levi, 2:627

Baḥya ben Asher ben Ḥlava, 3:65–66

Bonafed, David ben Reuben, 4:53

Canpanton, Isaac ben Jacob, 4:431–432

Canpanton, Judah ben Solomon, 4:432

David ben Saadiah, 5:469

David ibn Haijar, 5:474

Duran, Simeon ben Ẓemaḥ, 6:58–60

Gabbai Moses ben Shem-Tov, 7:319

Galipapa, Ḥayyim ben Abraham, 7:349

Gatigno family, 7:396

Gerondi, Moses ben Solomon d'Escola, 7:549

Gerondi, Samuel ben Meshullam, 7:549

Gerondi, Zerahiah ben Isaac ha-Levi, 7:549

Gracian, Shealtiel ben Solomon, 8:24

Ḥabiba, Joseph, 8:177

Ḥanokh ben Moses, 8:328–329

Ḥayyim ben Samuel ben David of Tudela, 8:482

Ibn Balʿam, Judah ben Samuel, 9:660–661

Ibn Ezra, Abraham ben Meir, 9:663–671

Ibn Gaon, Shem Tov ben Abraham, 9:676

Ibn Ghayyat family, 9:676–677

Ibn Migash, Joseph ben Meir ha-Levi, 9:686

Ibn Shuaib, Joshu, 9:694

Isaac ben Sheshet Perfet, 10:49

Isaac ben Todros of Barcelona, 10:50

Israeli, Israel, 10:753

Jacob ben Asher, 11:30–31

Jeroham ben Meshullam, 11:142

Jonah ben Abraham Gerondi, 11:392–393

Joseph ben Justi of Jaén, 11:423

Judah ben Asher, 11:483

Judah ben Barzillai al-Bargeloni, 11:483–484

Maimon ben Joseph, 13:371

Maimonides, Moses, 13:381–395

Mattathias ha-Yiẓhari, 13:686

Menahem ben Aaron ibn Zeraḥ, 14:20–21

Moses ha-Kohen of Tordesillas, 14:557

Naḥmanides, 14:739–747

Naḥmias, Joseph ben Joseph, 14:754

Nissim ben Reuben Gerondi, 15:280–281

Sardi, Samuel ben Isaac, 18:52

Sikili, Jacob ben Hananel, 18:574

Tamakh, Abraham ben Isaac ha-Levi, 19:492–493

Vidal, Crescas, 20:516

Vidal Yom Tov of Tolosa, 20:517

Yom Tov ben Abraham Ishbili, 21:391–392

Zerahiah ben Isaac ha-Levi, 21:515

Syria

Abraham ben Mazhir, 1:304

Al-Madari, Judah ha-Kohen ben Eleazar he-Ḥasid, 1:677

Baruch ben Isaac of Aleppo, 3:188

Baruch ben Samuel of Aleppo, 3:190

Ezra ben Abraham ben Mazhir, 6:662

Jesse ben Hezekiah, 11:244

Shim'on, Joseph ben Judah ibn, 18:480–481

Solomon ben Elijah ha-Kohen, 18:770

Yemen

Abraham ben Solomon, 1:310

Adani, David ben Amram, 1:381

Adani, David ben Yesha ha-Levi, 1:381

Adani, Saadiah ben David, 1:381

Dhamārī, Manṣur Suleiman, 5:631

Dhamārī, Sa'id ben David, 5:631

Jacob ben Nethanel ben (Al-) Fayyūmī, 11:35

Nethanel ben al-Fayyumi, 15:92

Nethanel ben Isaiah, 15:93

Zechariah ben Solomon-Rofe, 21:486–487

Rishon le-Zion, 6:289, 17:**344**

Rishon le-Zion (Israel), 12:745, 17:**344**

Rishpon (Israel), 17:**344**

Risikoff, Menahem Hakohen, 17:**344–345**

Risikoff, Mendel Hakohen. See Risikoff, Menahem Hakohen

Riskin, Shlomo, 6:216, 17:**345**

Ritba. See Yom Tov ben Abraham Ishbili

Rites and rituals

ablution, 1:261–263

betrothal, 3:541

births, Sholem Zokhor, 18:512–513

candles, 4:429–430

cemeteries, 4:538–539

Christian, 4:676–677

circumcision, 4:730–734

circumcisions, sandak, 18:10

dance, 5:409, 8:286

deaths, shofar, 18:507

festivals, Temple Scroll, 19:633

First Temple, 19:606–608

Holiness Code, 9:319

Rites and rituals, *continued*
Holy days, shofar, 18:507
homicides, 'eglah 'arufah, 6:220–221
iconography and, 9:704
kapparot custom, 11:781–782
Keri'ah, 12:84–85
laws and legal systems, mishpat Ivri, 14:333–334
laws pertaining to, 15:746
liturgy, 13:133–136, 265
minyan, 14:302
mishmarot and ma'amadot, 14:318–319
mourning, sheloshim, 18:446
Netilat Yadayim, 15:112–113
objects used in, Kasher, 11:821
perfumes and, 9:754
photographs of, 16:128
pilgrimages, 16:154–155
Rosh Ha-Shanah, 17:465–466
Tashlikh, 19:524–525
Russia, 1970s, 17:568
Samaritans, 17:727–732, 730–732
Second Temple, 19:616–621
Shavuot, 18:423
Shema, reading of, 18:454–455
Simḥat Torah, 18:604–605
Sukkot, lulav, 13:256
Women involved in, 4:204
See also Purity and impurity, ritual; *specific rites and rituals*
Ri the Elder. *See* Isaac ben Samuel of Dampierre
Ritratto di provincia in rosso (Levi), 12:691
Ritt, Martin, 17:**345**
Rittenberg, David, 3:765, 13:10, 17:**345–346**
Ritter, Immanuel Heinrich, 17:**346**
Ritterman, Ignatius, 15:198
Rittner, Edward, 12:553
Ritual art, 2:496–497
Ritual bath. *See* Mikveh
Ritual immersion, 3:**210–211**, 5:490
See also Ablution
Ritual impurity. *See* Purity and impurity, ritual
Ritual murder. *See* Blood libel
Ritual purity. *See* Purity and impurity, ritual
Rituals. *See* Rites and rituals
Ritual slaughter (sheḥitah). *See under* Dietary laws
Ritual uncleaness. *See* Purity and impurity, ritual
Der Ritus des synagogalen Gottesdienstes (Zunz), 21:686

Ritz, Al, 17:346
Ritz, Harry, 17:346
Ritz, Jimmy, 17:346
Ritz brothers, 17:**346**
Riva (Italy), 17:**346**
Riva di Trento. *See* Riva (Italy)
Rivan. *See* Judah ben Nathan
Riveles, Benjamin. *See* Rivlin, Benjamin
Riveles, Elijah. *See* Rivlin, Elijah
Riveles family. *See* Rivlin family
Rivera, Diego, 18:365
Rivera, Jacob Rodriguez, 17:**346**
River Cave (Israel), vol. 10: color insert
Rivers, Joan, 17:**347**
Rivers, Larry, 17:**347**
Rivers, Melissa, 17:347
Rivevot Efrayim (Ephraim Solomon ben Aaron of Luntshits), 6:461
Riviera Girl. See Gypsy Princess
Rivista Israelitica (periodical), 17:**348**
Rivkes, Moses ben Naphtali Hirsch, 17:**348**
Rivkin, Boruch, 17:**348–349**
Rivkin, Ellis, 17:**349**
Rivkind, Isaac, 17:**349**
Rivlin, Alice, 17:**350**
Rivlin, Benjamin, 17:349–350
Rivlin, Eliezer, 17:**350**
Rivlin, Elijah, 17:349
Rivlin, Harry N., 17:**350–351**
Rivlin, Hillel, 17:350
Rivlin, Isaac Eisik, 17:**350**
Rivlin, Joseph Joel, 17:**351**
Rivlin, Moses, 17:350
Rivlin, Shelomo Zalman, 17:**351**
Rivlin, Yosef Yitzḥak, 17:**351–352**
Rivlin, Zalman, 13:241
Rivlin family, 17:**349–350**
Rizaieh (Iran), 17:**352**
Riẓba. *See* Isaac ben Abraham
Rizhinashvili, Itzko, 3:14
Rizius, Paulus. *See* Ricius, Paulus
Rizpah, 17:**352**
Rizzi, Paulus. *See* Ricius, Paulus
RJF. *See* Reichsbund Juedischer Frontsoldaten
R'-ms-sw. *See* Ramses (Egyptian rulers)
Roach, Hal, 14:572
Roads, 1:476
The Road to Ein Harod (Kenan), 12:74
The Road to H: Narcotics, Delinquency, and Social Policy (Chein), 4:587
Road to Reaction (Finer), 7:26

Roback, Abraham Aaron, 17:**352**
Roback, Lea, 17:**352–353**
The Robber Barons (Josephson), 11:434
Robberies. *See* Theft and robberies
Robbins, Archie, 4:212
Robbins, Harold, 17:**353**
Robbins, Jerome, 5:414–415, 15:220, 17:**353–354**
Roberg, Ilse, 4:372
Robert, Ludwig, 17:**354**
Robert of Reading, 17:**354**
Roberts, Tony, 17:**354**
Robespierre, 2:8
Robin, Régine, 4:425, 17:**354–355**
Robinson (Siesby), 18:560
Robinson, Albert, 6:62
Robinson, Charles Phineas, 6:62, 16:349
Robinson, Dove-Myer, 15:243
Robinson, Edward, 17:**355**
Robinson, Edward G., 17:**355**
Robinson, Jacob, 17:**355–356**
Robinson, Nehemiah, 17:**356**
Robison, Sophia, 17:**356**, 18:733
Robles, Antonio Rodrigues, 17:**356**
Robock, Alan, 6:450
Robson, William Alexander, 17:**356–357**
Robusti, Jacob. *See* Tintoretto
Roby, Naphtali Eliyahu. *See* Rahabi, Naphtali Eliyahu
Rocamora, Isaac de, 17:**357**
Rocamora, Solomon de, 17:357
Rocamora, Vincente de. *See* Rocamora, Isaac de
Rocca, Moses Della. *See* Basola, Moses
Rochberg, George, 12:600, 17:**357**
Rochelle, La (France). *See* La Rochelle (France)
Rochester (England), 17:**359**
Rochester (NY), 17:**357–359**
Rochman, Leib, 17:**359**
Rock and Roll Hall of Fame, 18:614
Rock Drill (sculpture, Epstein), 6:471
Rockefeller Museum, 17:**359**
Rocker, Henry A., 17:360
Rocker, Rudolf, 17:**360**, 18:710
Rocker, Samuel, 17:360
Rocker family, 17:**360**
Rocket (plant), 17:**360**
The Rocking Chair (Klein), 4:423
Rock Justice (Balin), 3:90
Rockland County (NY), 17:**360–361**
Rockler, Walter, 15:388
Rock of Ages. See Ma'oz Ẓur
Rodan, Mendi, 17:**361–362**

Rodanim, 17:**362**

Roda Roda, Alexander, 17:**362**

Rodbell, Martin, 13:10, 17:**362**

Rode, Walther, 17:**362**

Rodell, Fred M., 17:262–263, **362–363**

Rodenberg, Julius, 17:**363**

Rodensky, Shemuel, 17:**363**

Rodericus, Joannus. *See* Amatus
    Lusitanus

Rodgers, Adam, 17:**363**

Rodgers, Dorothy Feiner, 17:363–364

Rodgers, Mary, 17:**363–364**

Rodgers, Richard, 17:**364**

Rodin, Elisha, 17:**364**

Rodin, Judith, 17:**364**

Rodker, John, 17:**364–365**

Rodkinson, Michael Levi, 17:**365**

Rodney, Red, 17:**365**

Rodnik (periodical), 17:182

Rod of Aaron, 17:**365**

Rod of Moses, 17:**365–366**

Rodrigues, Abraham, 4:83

Rodrigues, Bartholomew, 17:**365–366**

Rodrigues, Dionisius, 17:**366**

Rodrigues, Isaac, 4:83

Rodrigues, Joseph, 4:83

Rodrigues, Joseph Jessurun. *See*
    Salvador, Joseph (1716-1786)

Rodriguez, Dionisius. *See* Rodrigues,
    Dionisius

Rodulphus, Glaber. *See* Raoul Glaber

Rodzinsky, Artur, 17:**366**

Roedelheim (Germany), 17:**366–367**

Roedelsheim, Eliezer Zussman, 2:38

Roederer, Count Pierre Louis, 17:**367**

Roederer, Pierre Louis. *See* Roederer,
    Count Pierre Louis

Roehricht, Reinhold, 17:**367**

Roeper, Annemarie Bondy, 4:60

Roeper School (Michigan), 4:60

Roessler, Carl, 17:**367**

Roest, Meijer Marcus, 17:**367**

Roest, Rust. *See* Elkan, Sophie

Rofe, Johanan Levi, 4:78

Rofe, Joseph Solomon. *See* Delmedigo,
    Joseph Solomon

Rogachev (Belarus), 17:**367–368**

Rogachover, The. *See* Rozin, Joseph

Rogatin (Ukraine), 17:**368**

Roger II of Sicily, 8:342

Rogers, Bernard, 17:**368**

Rogers, Claude Maurice, 17:**368**

Rogers, Ernesto, 17:**368**

Rogers, Richard, 8:371

Rogers plan, 15:283

Roginski, Simon Zalmanovich, 17:**369**

Rogoff, Harry, 17:**369**

Rogoff, Hillel. *See* Rogoff, Harry

Rogoznizki, Gedalya. *See* Allon,
    Gedalya

Rohaleh (Smilansky), 8:718–719

Rohatyn (Ukraine). *See* Rogatin
    (Ukraine)

Rohatyn, Felix G, 17:**369**

Rohatyn, Felix G., 15:224, 225

Róheim, Géza, 2:187, 17:**369–370**

Rohling, August, 3:764, 778, 4:711–
    712, 17:**370**

Rohrlich, Oscar. *See* Cosașu, Radu

Roitman, Arie, 15:385

Roitman, David, 17:**370**

Roitt, Ivan, 13:11

Rojas, Fernando de, 17:**370–371**

Rokach, Eleazar, 17:**371**

Rokach, Israel, 17:371

Rokach, Shimon, 17:**371**

Rokach dynasty, 8:423

Rokaḥ, Elazar. *See* Rokeaḥ, Elazar ben
    Shmelke

Roke'ah (Eleazar), 6:304

Roke'ah, Aaron, 3:308–309

Rokeaḥ, David, 17:**372**

Rokeaḥ, Elazar ben Shmelke, 4:199,
    17:**372**

Roke'aḥ, Eleazar. *See* Rokach, Eleazar

Roke'aḥ, Eleazar ben Judah. *See*
    Eleazar ben Judah of Worms

Roke'aḥ, Issachar Dov, 3:308

Roke'aḥ, Shalom, 3:308

Rokiskis (Lithuania), 17:**372**

Rol, P. *See* Rosenthal, Pavel

Roland-Manuel, 17:**372**

*The Role of the Jews in the Russian
    Revolutionary Movement. See Rol
    yevreyev v russkom revolyutsionnom
    dvizhenii*

Roll, Michael, 17:**372–373**

Roller Skating, 19:145

Rolling Stone (periodical), 12:620

Rolnick, Joseph, 17:**373**

*Rol yevreyev v russkom revolyutsionnom
    dvizhenii* (Deutsch), 5:624

Rom, Yosef, 17:**373**

Romain, Jonathan A., 17:**373**

Roman (Romania), 17:**373–374**

Roman, Jacob ben Isaac, 17:**374**

Roman calendar, 4:705

Roman Catholicism. *See* Catholic
    Church

Romance languages
    Blondheim, David Simon, 3:771
    la'az and, 12:405–406
    Ladino and, 12:427–435

Romanelli, Samuel Aaron, 1:438,
    10:792, 17:**374**

Roman Emperors, 17:**374–375**

Roman Empire
    Aelia Capitolina, 1:429
    Agrippa, Caius Julius, 1:503
    Agrippa, Marcus Vipsanius, 1:504
    Agrippa I, 1:502–503
    Agrippa II, 1:503
    alabarch, 1:573
    Albinus, Lucceius, 1:593
    antisemitism, 4:486, 12:453–454
    apocalypse, 2:257
    archaeology, 2:390–391
    architecture, 2:399
    art, 2:494–495
    Caesar, Sextus Julius, 4:332
    Caligula, Caius Caesar Augustus,
        4:363
    Caracalla, Marcus Aurelius
        Antoninus, 4:458–459
    carnival, 4:486
    Catholic Church, 4:709–710
    Cestius Gallus, 4:552–553
    Chalcis, 4:561
    Cicero, Marcus Tullius, 4:725
    Claudius, 4:752
    coins and currency, 5:51
    Diaspora, 5:637–643
    economic history, 6:101–104
    Edom, 6:156–158
    Egypt, 1:632, 635–636, 6:228–229
    emperor worship, 6:397
    epitaphs, 6:464
    Esau, 6:488
    exilarchs and, 6:601
    expulsions from, 6:624
    extradition of criminals to
        authorities, 6:627
    Festus, Porcius, 6:**772**
    Fiscus Judaicus, 7:57
    Herod 1, 9:32, 34
    identified with Esau, 6:488
    Italy, 10:795–796
    Jacob story symbolism, 11:20–21
    Jewish settlements, 6:554–555
        Africa, 1:435–436
    Jewish war against, overview of,
        10:143–144
    Jonah (amora), 11:387
    Judah ha-Nasi and, 11:501–502
    Judea as province of, 11:523
    law, biblical interpretation of,
        9:816
    laws and legal systems, limitation
        of actions, 13:23

Roman Empire, *continued*
   Masada (Israel), 13:594–599
   Numenius, son of Antiochus, 15:339
   pottery, 16:425–426
   Samaritans, 17:723–724
   Second Temple, 19:611
   Severus, Alexander, 18:325
   Severus, Septimius, 18:325
   Tadmor (Syria), 19:430–431
   taxation, 2:481
   Trajanic revolt, 5:641
   See also Graeco-Roman period; Josephus Flavius; Palestine (Roman)
A Roman fun a Ferd Ganev (Opatoshu), 15:436
Romania, 17:**375–397**, **380**, *386*
   agriculture, Jewish, 1:499, 4:177–178
   American Jewish Joint Distribution Committee, 7:19
   American Joint Distribution Committee, 2:62
   antisemitism, 2:*217*, 220–221, 5:433–434, 8:474, 11:91, 92, 17:382, *17:383*, 17:396
      Campulung Moldovenesc, 4:390
      Cluj, 4:762
      Codreanu, Corneliu Zelea, 4:781
      Iron Guard, 10:29–30
   Bistrita, 3:727
   Blank, Maurice, 3:739
   Board of Delegates of American Israelites, 4:19–20
   Bogdan, Corneliu, 4:34
   Borsa, 4:94
   Botosani, 4:103
   boycotts, anti-Jewish, 4:109
   Braila, 4:118
   Brașov, 4:131
   Brociner, Joseph, 4:192
   Cajal, Nicolae, 4:347
   C.D.E., 4:533–534
   children's literature, 4:634–635
   Communism, 4:241
   communist period, 17:391–394
   communities
      life in, 17:384–385, 393–395
      nature of, 5:111
      organizations, 17:379–381
   Congress of Berlin, 3:454
   emancipation, 6:381–382, 15:713
   Filderman, Wilhelm, 7:19
   Gura-Humorului, 8:139

   Hasidim, 17:379
   He-Ḥalutz (movement), 8:760
   history, 12:531–532, 17:375–379
   Holocaust, 4:240–241, 5:433–434, 9:339, 11:828–829, 12:593–594, 17:385–391
      Bacau, 3:31
      Beltsy, 3:307
      Bendery, 3:327
      Braila, 4:118
      Bucharest, 4:240–241
      Cluj, 4:762–763
      Darabani, 5:433–434
      Dorohoi, 5:758
      Focsani, 7:93
      Galati, 7:339
      Jassy, 11:92
      Lecca, Radú, 12:592–593
      Mihaileni, 14:220
      Nasaud, 14:783
      Nasna, 14:787–788
      Piatra-Neamt, 16:143
      Ploesti, 16:240
      Radauti, 17:53
      Reghin, 17:190
      Roman, 17:373–374
      Salonta, 17:708
      Seini, 18:254
      Sephardim, 18:301
      Sighet, 18:568
      Stefanesti, 19:173
      Suceava, 19:290
      Sulita, 19:305
      Targu-Mures, 19:515
      Timisoara, 19:726–727
      Tirgu-Frumos, 19:730
      Tirgu Neamt, 19:731
      Transylvania, 20:110
      Turda, 20:192
      Vaslui, 20:479
      Vatra Dornei, 20:486
      Viseul-de-Sus, 20:543
   Institute of Folklore, 4:138
   Iron Guard, 18:590
   Israel relations, 17:394, 395
   Jewish participation in military service, 14:245
   journalism, 16:498
      Dan, Sergiu, 5:408
      Lazareanu, Barbu, 12:559
   jurists, 6:750
   language, biblical translations, 3:633
   liturgy, 13:135
   maskilim, 17:379
   Mihaileni, 14:219–220

   naturalization, 17:381–382
   numerus clausus in, 15:341–342
   Oradea, 15:453–454
   Orsova, 15:488
   Pascani, 15:675
   Pauker, Ana, 15:694
   peasant revolt of 1907, in Botosani, 4:103
   periodicals, 1:376–377, 6:216–217
   political life, 17:379–384, *383*, 392–393
   political organizations, 17:392–393
   politicians, Ebner, Meir, 6:87–88
   post-communist period, 17:394–397
   publishing, general, 16:717
   resistance, 17:388–391
   Siret, 18:643
   socialism, 18:707–708
   sports, Adelstein-Rozeanu, Angelica, 1:386–387
   Transylvania, 20:108–110
   Union of the Communities, 17:389–390
   Zionism, 21:599–601
      Kasztner, Rezso Rudolf, 11:828–829
      Lavi, Theodor, 12:531–532
   Zionist movement
      Braunstein, Menahem Mendel, 4:139
      Brociner, Joseph, 4:192
Romanian literature, 17:**397–402**
   Aderca, Felix, 1:390–391
   Benador, Ury, 3:314
   biblical, 17:397–398
   biblical influence, 3:671
   Blecher, Marcel, 3:747
   Breslasu, Marcel, 4:163–164
   Călugăru, Ion, 4:376
   Cassian, Nina, 4:508
   children's, 4:634–635
   Dan, Sergiu, 5:408
   Dominic, Alexandru, 5:743–744
   Dorian, Dorel, 5:757
   Dorian, Emil, 5:757
   Duda, Virgil, 6:40
   Fondane, Benjamin, 7:114
   Holocaust, 17:401–402
   Iacobescu, D., 9:655
   image of a Jew, 17:398–400
   Lazar, Samson, 12:558
   Lazareanu, Barbu, 12:559
   Luca, B., 13:247
   Ludo, Isac Iacovitz, 13:250
   Monda, Virgiliu, 14:435

Peltz, Isac, 15:719

poets, playwrights, 17:400–401

Roman-Ronetti, Moïse, 17:405–406

Rudich, Mayer, 17:520–521

Sebastian, Mihail, 18:230–232

Serbu Ieronim, 18:308

Serghi, Cella, 18:310

Sever, Alexandru, 18:325

Soare, Iulia, 18:698–699

Steuerman, Adolf Rodion, 19:224

Tertulian, Nicolae, 19:650–651

Toma, A., 20:31

Trivale, Ion, 20:153

Verea, Adrian, 20:508

Voronca, Ilarie, 20:582

Weiss, Aureliu, 20:732

Romanin, Samuele, 9:151, 17:**402**

Romanin Jacur, Leone, 17:**402**

Romaniots, 15:520, 534, 535, 17:**402–403**

Bulgaria, 18:745

Istanbul (Ottoman period), 10:774, 775, 777–778

Romanish languages, Bible translated into, 3:633

Roman literature, 5:672–673, 9:523, 17:**403–404**

Romano, Judah ben Moses ben Daniel, 11:547–548, 17:**404**

Romano, Marco, 17:**405**

Romano, Samuel, 17:**405**

Romano, Solomon. See Elian, Giovanni Battista

Romanos Melodos, 4:326, 17:**405**

Roman Pomaria (Algeria). See Tlemcen (Algeria)

Roman-Ronetti, Moïse, 17:**405–406**

Roman Rusi (Shalev), 18:372

Romans. See Roman Empire

Roman Tales (Moravia), 14:477

Romantiker (Locker), 13:153

Romanus I Lecapenus, 15:516, 17:**406**

Roman von einem Kinde (Honigmann), 9:518

Romberg, Moritz Heinrich, 17:**406**

Romberg, Oswaldo, 10:699

Romberg, Sigmund, 17:**406**

Rombro, Jacob. See Krantz, Philip

Rombro, Jacob Barukhovitsh. See Krantz, Philip

Rome (Italy), 16:390, 17:**406–417**, 414t

Abba Kolon and, 1:229

Alatri, Samuel, 1:578–579

Bar Kochba rebellion, 3:158–161, 158, 159

Brunetti, Angelo, 4:223

catacombs, 4:521–522

Christian empire, 17:411

classical period, 17:406–407

Counter-Reformation, 17:413

Diaspora, 5:638, 640

early empire, 17:407–408

emancipation, 6:379, 17:414–415

ghetto period, 17:413–414

Holocaust period, 17:415–416

Jewish archives, 2:409

Jewish rebellions, 3:150–151

Jewish War, influence of, 17:407

late empire, 17:408–409

literary activities, 17:411–412

modern period, 17:416

Papal legislation, 17:412

printing, 17:415

rebellions, 20:628

Samaritans, 7:508

Renaissance, 17:412–413

scholarshaip, 17:411–412

Talmud, burning of, 19:482–483

Talmudic literature, 17:409–411

See also Bar Kokhba revolt; Vatican

Rome, David, 17:**417**

Rome and Jerusalem (Hess), 9:75–76

Romemot El (Alshekh), 2:11

Romes, Adam. See Costa, Uriel da

Romm, Baruch ben Joseph, 17:**417**

Romm, David, 17:**418**

Romm, Deborah, 17:**418**

Romm, Joseph Reuben, 17:**418**

Romm, Menahem Mannes, 17:**417–418**

Romm family, 17:**417–418**

Romny (Ukraine), 17:**418**

Rómpase en case de incendio (Chocrón), 4:657

Rona, Peter, 17:**418**

Rónai, János, 17:**418–419**

Ronald, Landon, 17:531

Ronald Dworkin and Contemporary Jurisprudence (Cohen), 6:75

Roncalli, Angelo Giuseppe. See John XXIII

La ronde de nuit (Modiano). See *Night Round* (Modiano)

Ronly-Riklis, Shalom, 17:**419**

Ronsburg, Bezalel, 2:25

Ronsperg. See Pobezovice na Sumave

Roobot (ancient Israel). See Rehoboth (ancient Israel)

Roosevelt, Anna Eleanor, 17:**419**

Roosevelt, Eleanor. See Roosevelt, Anna Eleanor

Roosevelt, Franklin Delano, 17:**419–420**

Evian Conference, 6:576

liberalism, 12:779–780

meeting with Jan Karski, 11:817–818

Morgenthau, Henry, Jr., 14:489

New York City and, 15:214, 215

Niles, David K., 15:266

Roosevelt, Theodore, 15:211, 17:**420**

B'nai B'rith, 4:14

Brenner, Victor, 4:162

Roots (periodical), 6:395

The Roots of Crime (Alexander), 1:622

Roots of Light. See Shorshei Avir

Ropczyce (Poland), 17:**420**

Ropczyce, Naphtali Zevi. See Ropshitser, Naphtali Zevi

Ropshits (Poland). See Ropczyce (Poland)

Ropshitser, Naphtali Zevi, 17:**420**

Ropshitz dynasty, 8:422

Rosa, Moses da. See Provencal, Moses ben Abraham

Rosales, Immanuel Bocarro Frances. See Rosales, Jacob Hebraeus

Rosales, Jacob, 17:**420–421**

Rosales, Jacob Hebraeus, 17:**421**

Rosales family. See Rosanes family

Rosanes, Abraham Abele, 17:**421**

Rosanes, Abraham ben Hayyim, 17:**421**

Rosanes, Abraham ben Israel, 17:**421–422**

Rosanes, Abraham ben Joseph, 17:**421**

Rosanes, Abraham ben Meir, 17:**421**

Rosanes, Ha-Rav Abraham ben Isaac. See Rosanes, Abraham ben Israel

Rosanes, Isaac ben David, 17:**421**

Rosanes, Isaac ben Hayyim, 17:**421**

Rosanes, Jacob, 17:**421**

Rosanes, Judah ben Samuel, 17:**421, 422**

Rosanes, Judith, 17:**423**

Rosanes, Mordecai, 17:**422**

Rosanes, Solomon Abraham, 4:270, 17:**422**

Rosanes, Zevi Hirsch ben Issachar Berish, 17:**421, 422–423**

Rosanes family, 17:**421–422**

Rosario (Argentina), 17:**423**

Rose, Alex, 17:**424**

Rosé, Arnold Josef (1863-1946), 17:**424**

Rose, Arnold Marshall (1918-1968), 17:**424–425**, 18:731

Rose, Billy, 4:177, 17:**425**

Rose, Ernestine Potovsky, 17:**425**

Rose, Ernie. *See* Rose, Irwin

Rose, Fred, 4:406, 16:341, 17:**425–426**

Rose, Herman, 17:**426**

Rose, Irwin, 17:**426**

Rose, Leonard, 17:**426**

Rose, Mauri. *See* Rose, Maurice (1906-1981)

Rose, Maurice (1899-1945), 17:**426**

Rose, Maurice (1906-1981), 17:**426–427**

Rose, Max, 15:547

Rose, Noel, 13:11

Roseanne (television show), 3:174

Rose family (South Africa), 15:547

Rose Law or Rescript of the Rose Chamber, 15:526

Rosemary's Baby (Levin), 12:709

Rosen, Abraham, 17:**427**

Rosen, Al. *See* Rosen, Albert Leonard

Rosen, Albert Leonard, 17:**427**

Rosen, Andrew, 17:427

Rosen, Carl, 17:**427**

Rosen, Charles, 17:**428**

Rosen, Felix. *See* Rosen, Pinḥas

Rosen, "Flip". *See* Rosen, Albert Leonard

Rosen, Fred Saul, 17:**428**

Rosén, Haiim B., 17:**428**

Rosen, Jack, 12:599

Rosen, Joseph A., 17:**428**

Rosen, Joseph ben Isaac, 17:**428–429**

Rosen, Kopul, 6:206

Rosen, Leonard, 12:599

Rosen, Mathias, 17:**429**

Rosen, Moses, 17:**429**

Rosen, Moshe, 17:**429**

Rosen, Nathan, 16:138–139

Rosen, Norma, 17:**429–430**

Rosen, Pinḥas, 12:534, 17:**430**

Rosen, Samuel, 17:**430**

Rosen, Shelomo, 17:**430–431**

Rosen, Yehoshua, 17:**431**

Rosenak, Leopold, 17:**431**

Rosenau, William, 11:317, 17:**431**

Rosenbach, Abraham Simon Wolf, 17:**431–432**

   American Jewish Historical Society, 2:58–59

   American Joint Distribution Committee, 2:60

Rosenbach, Helene. *See* Deutsch, Helene

Rosenbach, Philip, 17:432

Rosenbaum, Alissa Zinovievna. *See* Rand, Ayn

Rosenbaum, Borge. *See* Borge, Victor

Rosenbaum, Daniel. *See* Ranschburg, Bezalel ben Joel

Rosenbaum, Dov. *See* Drezner, Yeḥlel Dov

Rosenbaum, Eli M., 15:388

Rosenbaum, Hercel. *See* Drzewiecki, Henryk

Rosenbaum, Jeremiah ben Isaac. *See* Mattersdorf, Jeremiah ben Isaac

Rosenbaum, Jonathan, 17:**432**

Rosenbaum, Morris, 17:**432**

Rosenbaum, Moses Ḥayyim Lits, 17:**433**

Rosenbaum, Samuel, 17:**433**

Rosenbaum, Semyon, 17:**433–434**

Rosenbaum, Shimshon. *See* Rosenbaum, Semyon

Rosenbaum, Yankel, 15:228

Rosenberg, Abraham, 17:**434**

Rosenberg, Abraham Ḥayyim, 17:**434**

Rosenberg, Alfred, 17:**434–435**

Rosenberg, Anna Marie Lederer, 17:**435**

Rosenberg, Arthur, 17:**435**

Rosenberg, Benjamin. *See* Benn, Ben

Rosenberg, Ellen. *See* Auerbach, Ellen Rosenberg

Rosenberg, Ethel, 7:26, 15:215, 17:440

Rosenberg, Eugene, 17:**435–436**

Rosenberg, Fred. *See* Rose, Fred

Rosenberg, Harold, 17:**436**

Rosenberg, Hilding, 11:413

Rosenberg, Isaac, 6:437, 14:540, 17:**436–437**

Rosenberg, Israel, 17:**437**

Rosenberg, James Naumburg, 17:**437**

Rosenberg, Julius, 7:26, 15:215, 17:440

   See also Kaufman, Irving R.

Rosenberg, Lazar, 4:402, 17:**437–438**

Rosenberg, Leonard. *See* Randall, Tony

Rosenberg, Lev Samuilovich. *See* Bakst, Leon

Rosenberg, Louis, 17:**438**

Rosenberg, Ludwig, 17:**438**, 18:706

Rosenberg, M. J., 21:612–613

Rosenberg, Moishe, 17:**438**

Rosenberg, Stuart E., 17:**438–439**

Rosenberg, Walter, 14:446

Rosenberg, William Samuel. *See* Rose, Billy

Rosenberg, Yehuda Yudel, 17:**439**

Rosenberg, Yoav, 3:679

Rosenberg case, 17:**440**

Rosenblatt, Bernard Abraham, 17:**440**

Rosenblatt, H., 17:**440–441**

Rosenblatt, John, 15:415

Rosenblatt, Josef, 17:**441**

Rosenblatt, Leo, 8:504

Rosenblatt, Mordecai ben Menahem, 17:**441**

Rosenblatt, Samuel, 17:**441**

Rosenblatt, Sol Arieh, 17:**442**

Rosenblatt, Yossele. *See* Rosenblatt, Josef

Rosenbloom, Carroll, 17:**442**

Rosenbloom, Celia Neumark, 17:443

Rosenbloom, Charles, 17:443

Rosenbloom, Max Everitt, 17:**442**

Rosenbloom, "Slapsie Maxie". *See* Rosenbloom, Max Everitt

Rosenbloom, Solomon, 17:**442–443**

Rosenblueth, Felix. *See* Rosen, Pinḥas

Rosenblueth, Ḥayyim. *See* Rosenblatt, H.

Rosenblueth, Pinḥas. *See* Rosen, Pinḥas

Rosenblum, Arnold Josef. *See* Rosé, Arnold Josef

Rosenblum, Arnold Joseph. *See* Rosé, Arnold Josef

Rosenblum, Frank, 17:**443**

Rosenblum, Herzl, 17:**443**

Rosenblum, Sigmund Georgievich, 17:**443–444**

Rosenbourg, Isaac, 4:13

Rosenbusch, Karl Harry Ferdinand, 17:**444**

Rosencof, Mauricio, 17:**444**

Rosendale, Simon Wolfe, 17:**444**

Rosenfarb, Chava, 4:427, 17:**444–445**

Rosenfeld, Abraham Isaac Jacob, 17:**445**

Rosenfeld, Aharon, 17:**445**

Rosenfeld, Fanny, 17:**445**

Rosenfeld, Isaac, 17:**445–446**

Rosenfeld, Jonah, 17:**446**

Rosenfeld, Lev Borisovich. *See* Kamenev, Lev

Rosenfeld, Morris, 4:108, 12:466, 16:125, 17:**446–447**

   Bloy, Léon, 3:784

Rosenfeld, Otto. *See* Rank, Otto

Rosenfeld, Paul, 17:**447**

Rosenfeld, Samuel, 17:**447**

Rosenfeld, Sándor Friedrich. *See* Roda Roda, Alexander

Rosenfeld, Shalom, 17:**447**

Rosenhead, Louis, 17:**447–448**

Rosenheim, Arthur, 17:**448**

Rosenheim, Jacob, 17:**448**

Rosenheim, Leonard. *See* Rosenheim, Max

Rosenheim, Max, 17:**448**

Rosenheim, Otto, 17:**448**

Rosenman, Samuel Irving, 17:**448–449**

Rosenmann-Taub, David, 17:**449**

Rosenmueller, Ernst Friedrich Karl, 17:**449**

Rosenroth, C. Knorr von. *See* Knorr von Rosenroth, Christian

Rosensaft, Josef, 17:**449–450**

Rosensaft, Menachem Z., 3:727, 728, 9:383–384, 386, 17:450

Rosensohn, Etta Lasker, 12:497, 17:**450**

Rosenstein, Neil, 13:261

Rosenstein, Sami. *See* Tzara, Tristan

Rosenstock, Joseph, 17:**450**

Rosenstock, Julius, 6:139

Rosenstock-Huessy, Eugen, 5:696–698, 17:**450–451**, 18:731

    Rosenzweig, Franz, 17:450–451, 458, 461

Rosenstock-Huessy, Gritli. *See* Rosenstock-Huessy, Margrit

Rosenstock-Huessy, Margrit, 17:450–451, 460–461

Rosenthal, A. M., 17:**451–452**

Rosenthal, Aaron, 15:516

Rosenthal, Abraham Michael. *See* Rosenthal, A. M.

Rosenthal, Anna, 17:457

Rosenthal, Benjamin Stanley, 2:51, 17:**452**

Rosenthal, David. *See* Rosenthal, Harold

Rosenthal, Eliezer. *See* Rosenthal, Leser

Rosenthal, Elijah, 17:456

Rosenthal, Emmanuel. *See* Rosenthal, Manuel

Rosenthal, Erich, 17:**452–453**, 18:734

Rosenthal, Erwin, 17:**453**

Rosenthal, Ferdinand, 17:**453**

Rosenthal, Franz, 17:**453**

Rosenthal, Fritz. *See* Ben-Chorin, Schalom

Rosenthal, Harold, 17:**453**

Rosenthal, Herman, 17:**453–454**

    Am Olam, 2:88

Rosenthal, Ida, 17:**454**

Rosenthal, Isaac Jacob. *See* Rosenthal, Erwin

Rosenthal, Joe, 16:125

Rosenthal, Judah, 17:**454**

Rosenthal, Judah Leib. *See* Rosenthal, Leon

Rosenthal, Leiser, as bibliophile, 3:684

Rosenthal, Leon, 17:**454–455**, 18:725

Rosenthal, Leser, 17:**455**

Rosenthal, Ludwig A., 17:**455**

Rosenthal, Lyova, 8:34

Rosenthal, Manuel, 12:451, 17:**455**

Rosenthal, Mark Mordecai. *See* Rózsavölgyi, Márk

Rosenthal, Maurycy. *See* Rosenthal, Moriz

Rosenthal, Max, 17:**455–456**

Rosenthal, Moriz, 17:**456**

Rosenthal, Naphtali, 17:**456**

Rosenthal, Pavel, 17:**456–457**

Rosenthal, Philipp, 17:**457**

Rosenthal, Pinhas. *See* Rosenthal, Pavel

Rosenthal, Samuel, 15:517

Rosenthal, William, 17:**457**

Rosenwald, Julius, 5:588, 17:**457–458**

Rosenwald, Lessing Julius, 17:**458**

Rosenwald, William, 17:**458**

Rosenwald family, 17:**457–458**

Rosenweiler (France). *See* Rosenwiller (France)

Rosenwiller (France), 17:**458**

Rosenzweig, A. *See* Ágai, Adolf

Rosenzweig, Abraham. *See* Rosen, Abraham

Rosenzweig, Adolf. *See* Ágai, Adolf

Rosenzweig, Franz, 4:93, 6:612, 8:282, 16:97–98, 109, 110, 17:**458–462**, 18:609

    Adler, Hugo Chaim, 1:399

    Buber, Martin, 4:231, 233, 235

    disputations and polemics, 5:696–698

    duty, 6:73

    German translation of Bible by, 3:631

    miracles, 14:309

    redemption, 17:154–155

    repentance, 17:223

    revelation, 17:258

    Rosenstock-Huessy, Eugen, 17:450–451, 458, 461

    on Shekhinah, 18:442

    Torah, 20:41, 43–44

Rosenzweig, Gerson, 15:661, 17:**462**

Rosenzweig, Walther. *See* Rode, Walther

The Rose of Tibet (Davidson), 18:204

Rose oil, 15:396

Roses, 17:**424**

Roses (flower), 7:90

Rosetta (Egypt), 17:**462–463**

Rosewater, Edward, 15:48, 415, 17:**463**

Rosewater, Victor, 17:463

Rosh Amanah (Abrabanel), 2:531

Rosheim (France), 17:**467**

Rosh ha-Ayin (al-Ayn), 2:205

Rosh ha-Ayin (Israel), 17:**463**

Rosh ha-Keneset. *See* Archisynagogos

Rosh Ha-Nikrah (Israel). *See* Kefar Rosh Ha-Nikrah (Israel)

Rosh Ha-Shanah, 15:193–194, 17:**463–466**

    Adonai, Adonai El Rahum ve-Hannun, 1:412

    Ahot Ketennah, 1:547–548

    Aleinu le-Shabbe'ah, 1:608, 609

    Amidah, 2:72, 75

    Amidah, 18:508

    calendar, 4:354–355

    food, 7:120

    mourning during, 18:446

    Musaf, 13:433–434

    Tashlikh, 19:524–525

    Yamim Nora'im, 21:277–278

    Zikhronot, 21:529

Rosh Ha-Shanah (Lazarus), 13:298

Rosh Ha-Shanah (tractate), 17:**466**

Rosh Keneset. *See* Archisynagogos

Rosh Pinnah (Israel), 17:**466–467**

Roshwald, Mordecai, 18:204

Rosh yeshivah, 1:349–350, 351

    Leibowitz, Baruch Ber, 12:620

    Lichtenstein, Aaron, 12:798

    Sarna, Ezekiel, 18:58

Rosi, Abraham. *See* Ben-Adir

Rosin, David, 17:**467**

Rosin, Heinrich, 17:467

Rositten. *See* Rezekne

Roskies, David G., 17:**467–468**

Rosmarin, Trude. *See* Weiss-Rosmarin, Trude

Rosmaryn, Henryk, 17:**468**

Rosmersholm (Brecher), 4:156

Rosofsky, Barnet David. *See* Ross, Barney

Rosowsky, Solomon, 17:**468**, 18:725

Ross, Barney, 17:**468–469**

Ross, Calvin. *See* Abrams, Cal

Ross, Dennis, 17:**469**

Ross, Herbert, 17:**469**

Ross, Jerry, 1:406

Ross, Leonard Q. *See* Rosten, Leo Calvin

Ross, Lillian, 17:**470**

Ross, Stephen, 17:**470**

Ross, Tamar, 16:112

Rosselli, Carlo, 17:**470**

Rosselli, Nello, 17:470

Rosselli family, 17:**470–471**

Rossen, Robert, 17:**471**

Rossena, Daniel ben Samuel of, 17:**471**

Rossi, Azariah ben Moses dei, 9:157, 17:**471–473**
  Amatus Lusitanus, 2:35
  biographical material of, 3:706
  Italian biblical study and exegesis, 3:663
Rossi, Azariah Bonaiuto. *See* Rossi, Azariah ben Moses dei
Rossi, Boniauto. *See* Rossi, Azariah ben Moses dei
Rossi, Giovanni Bernardo de'. *See* De' Rossi, Giovanni Bernardo
Rossi, Madama Europa de', 17:**473**
Rossi, Salamone de', 1:415, 4:433, 660, 17:**473–474**
Rossieni. *See* Raseiniai
Rossienie. *See* Raseiniai (Lithuania)
Rossiiskaya evreiskaya entsiklopedia (encyclopedia). *See The Encyclopedia of Russian Jewry*
Rossin, Samuel, 17:**474**
Rossini, Gioacchino, 14:542
Rosskam, Edwin, 16:126
Rossman, I. *See* Dan, Sergiu
Rossow, William, 6:450
Rosten, Leo Calvin, 17:**474**
Rostov (Russia), 17:**474–475**
Rostow, Eugene Victor Debs, 17:**475**
Rostow, Walt Whitman, 17:**475–476**
Rotbaum, Jacob, 17:**476**
Rotblat, Sir Joseph, 17:**476**
Rote, Abraham (d. after 1525), 17:**476**
Rote, Abraham (d. after 1603), 17:**477**
Rote, Abraham (d. after 1730), 17:**477**
Rote, Isaac ben Jacob, 17:**477**
Rote, Jacob (16th c.), 17:**476–477**
Rote, Jacob (d. after 1622), 17:**477**
Rote, Jacob (d. after 1730), 17:**477**
Rote, Moses, 17:**477**
Rote family, 17:**476–477**
Rotem, Cvi, 17:**477**
Rotem, Simcha, 13:240–241
Rotem, Zvi. *See* Rotem, Cvi
Rotenberg, Mattie Levi, 17:**477–478**
Rotenburg, Joseph, 17:**478**
Rotenburg, Naphtali, 17:**478**
Rotenburg, Simon Samson, 17:**478**
Rotenburg family, 17:**478**
Rotenstreich, Fischel, 17:**478**
Rotenstreich, Nathan, 16:101–102, 103, 17:**478–479**
Roth, Aaron, 17:**479**
Roth, Abraham Ḥayyim, 17:479
Roth, Bezalel. *See* Roth, Cecil
Roth, Cecil, 15:554, 17:**479–480**
Roth, David Lee, 17:**480–481**

Roth, Ḥayyim Judah. *See* Roth, Leon
Roth, Henry, 17:**481–482**
Roth, Joel, 17:**482**
Roth, Joseph, 11:357, 17:**482–483**
Roth, Klaus Friedrich, 17:**483**
Roth, Leon, 17:**483**
Roth, Mark, 17:**483–484**
Roth, Philip Milton, 3:781, 15:140, 17:**484–485**
Roth, Sir Martin, 17:**484**
Rothberg, Samuel, 17:**485**
Rothberg School for Overseas Students, 8:743
Rothburg, Sam, 4:58
Rothchild, Jeroboam. *See* Mandel, Georges
Rothchild, Louis (1885-1944). *See* Mandel, Georges
Rothenberg, Jerome, 20:298
Rothenberg, Morris, 17:**485**
Rothenberg, Robert C., 2:53
Rothenberg ob der Tauber (Germany), 17:**485–486**
Rothenstein, Michael, 17:**486**
Rothenstein, Sir William (1872-1945), 4:116, 17:**486–487**
Rothenstein, William (1908-1993). *See* Rothenstein, Michael
Rothko, Mark, 4:50, 17:**487**
Rothman, Daryl. *See* Kuperstock, Daryl
Rothman, James, 13:10
Rothmueller, Aaron Marko, 17:**487**
Rothmüller, Erich. *See* Rotem, Cvi
Rothschild, Adolf Carl, 17:**489**
Rothschild, Alain, 17:**490**
Rothschild, Alfred, 17:**490**
Rothschild, Alphonse, 15:530, 17:**490**
Rothschild, Alphonse Mayer, 17:**489**
Rothschild, Amschel Mayer, 17:**489**
Rothschild, Amschel Moses, 17:**487**
Rothschild, Annie. *See* Yorke, Annie Rothschild
Rothschild, Anselm Salomon, 17:**489**
Rothschild, Anselm von, 16:340
Rothschild, Anthony, 17:**490**
Rothschild, Anthony Gistav, 17:**491**
Rothschild, Baron Edmond James de, 4:334, 10:334, 17:**490, 491–492**
  Aḥ ha-Am, 1:526
  First Aliyah and, 10:357–358
  immigration to Israel, 11:287, 14:418–419
  Mazkeret Batyah and, 13:707
  Odessa Committee, 15:382
  Ossowetzky, O. Yehoshua, 15:506
  Petaḥ Tikvah and, 16:14

Rothschild, Bethsabée, 17:**490**
Rothschild, Binyamin de, 3:705
Rothschild, Carl Mayer, 17:**489**, 490
Rothschild, Charlotte, 17:**490**
Rothschild, Constance. *See* Flower, Constance Rothschild
Rothschild, Edmond (1926-1997), 17:**490**
Rothschild, Edmond James de. *See* Rothschild, Baron Edmond James de
Rothschild, Edmund Leopold, 17:**491**
Rothschild, Edouard, 17:**490**
Rothschild, Evelina, 17:**490**
Rothschild, Ferdinand James, 17:**490**
Rothschild, Friedrich Salomon, 17:**493**
Rothschild, Gustave, 17:**490**
Rothschild, Guy, 17:**490**
Rothschild, Hannah. *See* Primrose, Hannah Rothschild
Rothschild, Isaac Elhanan, 17:**487**
Rothschild, Jacob M., 17:**493**
Rothschild, James Armand de, 4:123, 17:**69**, 491, **493–494**
Rothschild, James Jacob, 17:**489–490**
Rothschild, Kurt, 17:**494**
Rothschild, Leopold, 17:**490**
Rothschild, Lionel Nathan (1808-1879), 6:414, 16:342, 17:**490**
Rothschild, Lionel Nathan (1882-1942), 17:**491**
Rothschild, Lionel Walter, 17:**490**
Rothschild, Mayer Amschel, 17:**487**, 489
Rothschild, Mayer Carl, 17:**489**
Rothschild, Nathaniel Charles Jacob, Fourth Baron Rothschild, 17:**494**
Rothschild, Nathaniel Mayer (1840-1915), 17:**490**
Rothschild, Nathaniel Mayer Victor, Lord (1910-1990), 17:**491, 494**
Rothschild, Nathan Mayer (1777-1836), 6:414, 417, 17:**69**, 489
Rothschild, Natty. *See* Rothschild, Nathaniel Mayer
Rothschild, Robert Philippe, 17:**490**
Rothschild, Robert Phineas, 17:**494–495**
Rothschild, Sally. *See* Rothschild, Friedrich Salomon
Rothschild, Salomon, railroads, 17:69
Rothschild, Salomon Albert, 17:**489**
Rothschild, Salomon Mayer, 17:**489**
Rothschild, Uri, 17:**487**
Rothschild, Walter N., 17:**495, 495**
Rothschild, Wilhem Karl, 17:**489**
Rothschild Bank, oil industry development, 16:20

Rothschild family, 3:75, 17:**487–491**, 488*t*
  heraldry, 9:7
  Oppenheim, Moritz Daniel, 15:446
The Rothschilds (musical), 4:26
Roth-Shachamorov, Esther, 17:**495**
Rothstein, "A. R.". *See* Rothstein, Arnold
Rothstein, Arnold, 17:**495–496**, 18:173
Rothstein, Arthur, 16:126
Rothstein, Irma, 17:**496**
Rothstein, Theodor, 18:704
Roth *v.* Yeshufeh, 5:196–197
Roti. *See* Rote family
Roti family. *See* Rote family
Rotkin, Charles, 16:126
Rotnemer, Dory, 15:547
Rottembourg, Henri, 17:**496**
Rottová, Inna, 17:**496**
Rottweil-Villingen (Germany), 3:44
Roudnice nad Labem (Czech Republic), 17:**496–497**
Rouen (France), 17:**497–498**
Rouffach (France), 17:**498**
Rouleau, Elie Rafoul. *See* Rouleau, Eric
Rouleau, Eric, 17:**498**
Rousseau, Jean Jacques, 17:**498**
Roussillon (France), 17:**498–499**
Rousso, Henry, 11:324
Rousso, Isaac Beḥor Moses, 11:828
A Route to Immortality (Eichenbaum), 6:246
Routi, er-. *See* Rote family
Routtenberg, Max Jonah, 17:**499**
Rove, Karl, Novak, Robert, 15:317
Rovere, Francesco della. *See* Sixtus IV (pope)
Rovigo (Italy), 17:**499–500**
Rovigo, Abraham ben Michael, 3:360–361, 17:**500–501**
Rovigo *mikveh* dispute, 18:52
Rovina, Hanna, 17:**501**, 18:590
Rovinsky, Samuel, 17:**501**
Rovner, Sejdel. *See* Morogowski, Jacob Samuel
Rovner, Zaydel. *See* Morogowski, Jacob Samuel
Rovno (Ukraine), 17:**501–502**
Rowanduz (Iraq). *See* Ruwandiz (Iraq)
Rowe, Leo Stanton, 17:**502**
Rowing (sport), 19:145–146
Rowley, Harold Henry, 17:**502–503**
Równe (Ukraine). *See* Rovno (Ukraine)
Royal Canadian Mounted Police, 11:779

Royal Commission on Palestine. *See* Peel Commission
Royal Fusiliers, Jewish legion and, 11:303–306
Royals, Cincinnati, 8:366
Royal Stoa, 3:199
Royalty, prayer for. *See* Government, prayer for the
Royselekh paper-cuts, 15:615
Royz, Olesh. *See* Rose, Alex
Royzenblit, Ḥayyim. *See* Rosenblatt, H.
Różana (Belorus). *See* Ruzhany (Belorus)
Rozanes, Judah ben Samuel. *See* Rosanes, Judah ben Samuel
Rozdol (Ukraine), 17:**503**
Rozdół (Ukraine). *See* Rozdol (Ukraine)
Rozenberg, Zvi Hirsh, 4:170
Rozenblit, Marsha, 9:152
Rozenblum, Schlomo ben Hirsh. *See* Rosenblum, Sigmund Georgievich
Rozenmacher, Germán, 17:**503**
Rozenzweig, Franz, 7:666
Różewicz, Tadeusz, 17:**503–504**
Rozhanoy (Belorus). *See* Ruzhany (Belorus)
Rozhany (Belorus). *See* Ruzhany (Belorus)
Rozhinoy (Belorus). *See* Ruzhany (Belorus)
Rozin, Joseph, 11:821, 17:**504**
Rozovski, Pinḥas, 17:**504–505**
Rozprawa o Żydach i Karaitach (Czacki), 5:351
Rózsavölgyi, Márk, 17:**505**
Rozwadow (Poland), 17:**505**
Rozwój, 17:**505–506**
RRC. *See* Reconstructionist Rabbinical College (RRC)
R.S.F.S.R. (Russian Soviet Federative Socialist Republic). *See* Russia
RSHA, 17:202, **506**
Ru'aḥ Ḥadashah (Coèn), 4:781
Ru'aḥ ha-kodesh, 17:**506–509**
Ru'aḥ ha-Zeman (periodical). *See* Ha-Zeman (periodical)
Ru'aḥ Ḥen (Solomon ben Judah of Lunel), 18:772
Ruaḥ Ḥen (Zamosc), 21:453
Rubashov (Poland). *See* Hrubieszow (Poland)
Rubashov, Shneur Zalman. *See* Shazar, Shneur Zalman
Rubenovitz, Herman H., 4:100, 17:**509–510**
Rubenovitz, Mignon, 17:510

Rubens, Alfred, 17:**510**
Rubens, Bernice, 6:438, 17:**510**
Rubens, Paul Alfred, 17:**510**
Rubens, Peter Paul, 14:542
Rubenson, Robert, 17:**510**
Rubenstein, Jacob. *See* Ruby, Jack
Rubenstein, Jeffrey L.
  aggadah, 1:461
  amoraim, 2:90
Rubenstein, Louis, 17:**510–511**
Rubenstein, Moses M., 6:161
Rubenstein, Richard, 9:392–393
Rubenstein, Richard Lowell, 17:271–272, **511**
Rubin, David, 6:428
Rubin, Edgar, 17:**511–512**
Rubin, Gail, 17:**512**
Rubin, Hadassah, 17:**512**
Rubin, Harry, 13:9
Rubin, Israel. *See* Rabon, Israel
Rubin, Morton Joseph, 17:**512**
Rubin, Reuven, 17:**512–513**
Rubin, Robert E., 15:225, 17:**513**
Rubin, Ruth, 17:**513**
Rubin, Samuel, 2:46, 17:**513–514**
Rubin, Solomon, 17:**514**
Rubin dynasty, 8:422
Rubiner, Ludwig, 17:**514**
Rubinger, David, 17:**514**
Rubinow, Isaac Max, 15:205, 17:**514–515**
Rubinowitz, Ephraim. *See* Ha-Reubeni, Ephraim
Rubinstein, Akiva, 4:605, 17:**515**
Rubinstein, Amnon, 17:**515–516**
Rubinstein, Anton Grigoryevich, 13:193, 17:**516**
Rubinstein, Artur, 17:**516**
Rubinstein, Harold Frederick, 17:**516–517**
Rubinstein, Helena, 15:213, 17:**517**
Rubinstein, Hilary Michael, 17:516–517
Rubinstein, Ida, 17:**517**
Rubinstein, Isaac, 17:**517**
Rubinstein, Joseph, 17:**517–518**
Rubinstein, Michael, 17:516
Rubinstein, Sergey Leonidovich, 6:161, 17:**518**
Rubinstein, William D., 17:**518**
Rubio, Mordecai, 8:747, 17:**518**
Ruboy, Isaac, 17:44
Ruby, Jack, 17:**518–519**
Rudavsky, David, 17:**519**
Rudel, Julius, 17:**519**, 18:581
Ruderman, David B., 2:47, 17:**519–520**

Ruderman, Jacob Isaac, 17:**520**
Rudich, Mayer, 17:**520–521**
Rudin, A. James, 17:**521–522**
Rudin, Jack, 17:521
Rudin, Jacob Philip, 17:**522**
Rudin, Lewis, 15:226, 17:521
Rudin, Sam. *See* Rudin, Samuel
Rudin, Samuel, 17:521
Rudin, Scott, 17:**522–523**
Rudin, William, 17:521
Rudin family, 17:521
Rudinow, Moshe, 17:**523**
Rudinsky, Louis, 17:521
Rudman, Warren, 17:**523**
Rudner, Rita, 17:**523**
Rudnicki, Adolf, 17:**523–524**
Rudolf, Max, 17:**524**
Rudolf I of Hapsburg, 13:782, 17:**524**
Rudolf II of Hapsburg, 11:507, 17:**524**
Rudolph (monk), 17:**525**
Rudolph, Arthur, 11:446, 447, 15:388, 18:461
Rudolph, Jack, 15:304
Rudolph, Marvin, 17:**525**
Rudolph, Mendy. *See* Rudolph, Marvin
Rudolph I (emperor of Germany). *See* Rudolf I of Hapsburg
Rudolph II (Holy Roman Emperor). *See* Rudolf II of Hapsburg
Rudorfer's Episodes, 1920-27. See Pirkei Rudorfer
Rudorfer's Stories, 1936-44. See Sippurei Rudorfer
Rue, vol. 16: color insert
Ruebner, Tuvia, 17:**525**
Ruedenberg, Reinhold, 17:**525–526**
Rue des boutiques obscures (Modiano). *See Dark Shops Street* (Modiano)
Ruediger, 17:**526**
Ruef, Abraham, 17:**526**
Rueff, Jacques, 17:**526**
Ruehs, Christian Friedrich, 17:**526**
Ruelf, Isaac, 17:**526–527**
Ruether, Rosemary, 4:683, 685, 687
Rueti, al-. *See* Rote family
Rueti, Jacob ben Samuel al-, 17:476
Rufach (France). *See* Rouffach (France)
Rufeisen, Joseph, 17:**527**
Rufeisen, Oswald, 2:273, 274
Rufeisen v. Minister of the Interior, 12:542
Rufus of Samaria, 17:**527–528**
Rufus Tinneius. *See* Tinneius Rufus
Rugby, 19:146

Ruḥamah (Israel), 17:**528**
Rujm al-Mushayrifa, 14:388
Rujm malfūf, Ammonites, 2:83
Rukeyser, Merryle Stanley, 17:**528**
Rukeyser, Muriel, 17:**528**
The Rule of the Community. See Manual of Discipline
Rules of Evidence Amendment Law (Cautioning of Witnesses and Annulment of Oath) of 1980, 14:360–361
Rules of the Hebrew Language. See Klalei Leshon Ever
Rules of the Noun. See Messibbot ha-Shem
Rules of the Verb. See Messibbot ha-Po'al
Ruma (Canaan), 17:**528**
Ruma (Galilee), 17:**528**
Rumanyah va-Amerikah (Horowitz), 9:531
Rumkowski, Chaim Mordechai, 3:782, 4:230, 17:**528–529**
Rumpler, Eduard, 17:**529**
Runitsch, Ossip, 17:**529**
Runkel, Solomon Zalman, 17:**529**
Ruppin, Arthur, 15:595, 17:**529–530**, 18:731
Ruppin Agricultural College (Israel), 8:283
Ruse (Bulgaria), 17:**530–531**
Rusish-yidisher verter-bikh (Lifshits), 13:11
Ruslander, Sylvan, 15:393
Russe (Bulgaria). *See* Ruse (Bulgaria)
Russell, Henry, 17:**531**
Russell, Landon Ronald. *See* Ronald, Landon
Russell, William Clark, 17:531
Russia, 17:**531–587**, 532t, 537t, 539, 545t, 546t, 554t, 555t, 557
  pre-1772, 17:531–532
  1772-1881: First Phase, 9:233–234, 17:532–535, 532t
    Alexander II, 17:534
    economic history, 17:535
    Haskalah, 17:535
    the "Jewish Problem," 17:533
    Nicholas 1, 17:533–534
    population statistics, 17:535
  1881-1917: Second Phase, 17:535–542, 537t
    Civil War, 17:541–542
    demography, 17:537t, 539
    economic history, 17:537, 537t
    February Revolution (1917), 17:540–541

    Jewish literature, 17:538, 540
    population statistics, 17:535, 537, 537t, 539
    socio-political ideologies, 17:537–538
    WW I, 17:540
    Yiddish language, 17:538, 540
  1970s, 17:564–571
    antisemitism, 17:569
    arts, 17:566
    assimilation, 17:564–566
    demography, 17:569
    education, 17:565–566, 568
    emmigration from Russia, 17:569–571, 570t
    employment, 17:568–569
    festivals, 17:566
    folklore, 17:566
    Hebrew language, 17:564–565
    Holocaust commemorations, 17:566
    immigration to Israel, 17:569–571, 570t
    Israeli Independence Day, 17:566
    population statistics, 17:569
    "refuseniks", 17:564, 571
    rites and rituals, 17:568
    symposium on Jewish culture, 17:567–568
    synagogues, 17:568
    Yiddish language, 17:564, 568
    Yiddish literature, 17:568
  1980s, 17:571–579
    aliyah and absorption in Israel, 17:571t, 572, 573, 579
    antisemitism, 17:572–573
    community organization, 17:574, 577–579
    demography, 17:571–572, 571t
    emmigration from Russia, 17:571t, 572, 573, 579
    perestroika and glasnost, 17:576–579
    population statistics, 17:571–572
    "refuseniks", 17:573–576, 574
    Western support, 17:575–576
Abkhaziya, 1:261
actors
  Leonidov, Leonid Mironovich, 12:648
  Leontovich, Eugenie, 12:649
agriculture, Jewish, 1:498–499, 4:177–178
American Jewish Committee, 2:54–56

Am Olam, 2:87–88

Amusin, Joseph, 2:124

Anapa, 2:130

anarchism, 18:710

An-Ski collections, 2:182–183

antisemitism, 1:620–621, 2:*217*, 221–222, 4:525, 5:92–94

    Beilis blood libel, 3:266–267

apostasy, 2:272

architecture, 2:400

archives, 2:408

assimilation, 2:611–613

bankers, moneylenders, 3:116–117

    Horodischtsch, Leon, 9:528

Bet Din in, 3:515

Bialystok (Belostok), 3:567

Bilu, 3:700–701

blood libel in, 3:778–780

boycotts, anti-Jewish, 4:109–110

building and construction, 5:183

Bukhara, conquest of, 4:259–261

candle tax, 4:430

cantonists, 4:437–439

Catherine II, 4:525

Caucasus, 4:527–528

censorship, 4:540

children's literature, 4:635

choreographers, Eifman, Boris, 6:253

communism, 5:91–96

community, nature of, 5:108, 109, 110

community leaders, 6:737

composers

    Dunayevski, Isaac Osipovich, 6:49

    Litinski, Genrikh Ilyich, 13:129

compulsory military service, Jewish children seized for, 15:250, 265

Congress of Berlin, 3:453–454

cooperatives, 5:205–206

crime, 5:291, 292, 293

Crimean conquest, 5:300

Czarist, Kazyonny Ravvin, 12:47–48

dance, 5:415

Duma, 12:780–781

Duma and, 6:45–46

education, Jewish, 6:176, 182–183, 187–188

emancipation, 6:383–385

emigration, 6:558, 559

exclusion of Jews from, 15:577

film directors, 11:734

Folkspartei, 7:113–114

forced baptism, 3:122

fur trade, 7:313, 314

Ha-Shomer ha-Ẓa'ir, 8:385

Haskalah movement, 8:440–443, 12:707–708, 720–722

ḥazakah, 8:490

Hebrew manuscripts, 13:490–495

He-Ḥaver, 8:761

Holocaust

    extermination activities, 17:547–548, 551–553

    Klintsy, 12:232

    Koenigsberg, 12:252

    Krasnodar, 12:339

    Kursk, 12:393

    Pochep, 16:250

    Rostov, 17:475

    Smolesk, 18:691

    Starodub, 19:166

    Taganrog, 19:432

    Velizh, 20:493

    Voronezh, 20:582

    Yalta, 21:277

informers, 9:782–783

Jerusalem and, 11:167

Jewish dress, 6:16

Jewish labor, 12:411

Jewish participation in military service, 14:241

Jewish political parties, 6:383–384

Jewish Socialist Workers' Party, 11:314–315

Jewish Society for History and Ethnography, 11:315

Jews prohibited in, 6:625

journalism, 5:407, 11:467, 12:457–458, 461, 524, 717–718

Judaizers in, 11:520, 521–522

Klintsy, 12:232

labor movement, Abramowitz, Emil, 1:324

language

    Bible translated into, 3:634–635

    Qumran, 2:124

laws and legal systems

    attorneys, 12:553–554

    deputies of the Jewish people, 5:591

    historians, 12:649

    May laws, 12:508–509, 13:701–702, 15:579

    restricting Jewish settlement and businesses, 13:701–702

leather industry and trade, 12:577

liberalism, 12:780–781

libraries, 12:787

military contracting, 5:198–200

musicians, 12:453, 773

Neo-Nazism, 15:82

newspapers, 16:498–501

New York City, modern Russian Jewish immigrants to, 15:229–231

nineteenth century, Decembrists, 5:528

Novozybkov, 15:323

numerus clausus in, 15:339–340

occupational restrictions on Jews in, 15:577, 579

Octobrists, 15:376–377

oil industry development, 16:20

Omsk, 15:**423**

Ordzhonikidze, 15:463

Orel, 15:464–465

orphans and orphanages, 15:486

Orshanski on Jews of, 15:487–488

ORT, 15:488, 491

Orthodox Judaism, ba'alei tesuvah, 3:6

OZE, 15:556

Pale of Settlement, 15:577–580, *578*

philanthropy, 16:40

poetic cinema, 11:734

pogroms, 16:279–282

    by Cossacks, 13:763

political participation, 16:339, 347–348

population, 16:394, 395

population statistics, 16:396t, 17:572

post-WW II, 17:553–558, 555t, 557t

    aliyah and absorption in Israel, 17:558

    antisemitism, 17:553–554, 556, 558

    demography, 17:554–556, 554t, 555t, 557

    Hebrew literature, 17:563

    Israel (state) assistance, 17:563–564

    Middle East policies, 17:559

    population statistics, 17:554–556, 554t, 555t, 557, 557t

printing, publishing, 16:537

publishing

    Efron, Ilya, 6:216

    general, 16:718

rabbis, government-appointed, 8:442

relations with Israel (state), 17:558–560

Russia, *continued*
> Russian Federation, 17:579–586
>> antisemitism, 14:517–518, 520–521, 17:583–586
>> community organization, 14:520, 17:580–581
>> education, 17:583
>> population statistics, 14:518, 519–520, 521, 17:580
>> relations with, Israel (state), 14:519, 520, 17:580
>> synagogues, Moscow, 14:518–519
>> Yiddish publishing, 17:581–583
> Social Democrats, Schwarz, Solomon, 18:190–191
> twentieth century, Lewin, Judah Leib, 12:760
> Uzbekistan, 4:259–261
> Voronezh, 20:582
> Zionist movement, Brandt, Boris, 4:128
> Zionist Socialism, 18:717

Russian Federation. *See* Russia; Union of Soviet Socialist Republics (USSR)

Russian Hamlet (ballet, Eifman), 6:253

Russian Jewish Encyclopedia. See Yevreyskaya Entsiklopediya

Russian Jewish Health Organization. *See* OZE

Russian Jewish Historical Ethnographic Society, 18:723

Russian Jewish Scientific Society, 13:165

Russian literature, 12:774–775, 17:**587–591**, 589–591
> Aizman, David Yakolevich, 1:553
> Aldanov, Mark, 1:605–606
> biblical influence, 3:672
> Brik, Osip Maksimovich, 4:181
> children's, 4:635
> Ehrenburg, Ilya Grigoryevich, 6:237
> encyclopedias, 6:400, 402
> Ilf, Ilya, 9:720–721
> image of Jews in, 17:588–591
> Jabotinsky, Vladimir, 11:13–14
> Leskov, Nikolay Semyonovich, 12:662–663
> Levanda, Lev Osipovich, 12:676–678
> Levin, Emanuel, 12:707–708
> Levinsohn, Isaac Baer, 12:720–722
> Libedinski, Yuri Nikolayevich, 12:774–775
> Mordovtsev, Danil Lukich, 14:483
> Morgulis, Manasseh, 14:490–491

Pines, Yehiel Michael, 16:167–168
poetry
> Aliger, Margarita Yosifovna, 1:659
> Broadsky, Joseph, 4:198
> Cherny, Sasha, 4:599
> Derzhavin, Gabriel Romanovich, 5:601
> Dolmatovski, Yevgeni Aronovich, 5:736
> Domalsky, I., 5:738
> Dubnow-Erlich, Sophia, 6:37
> Eichenbaum, Jacob, 6:246
> Inber, Vera Mikhailovna, 9:752–753
> Kannegiser, Leonid Akimovich, 11:766
> Kanovich, Grigory, 11:766
> Selvinski, Ilya Lvovich, 18:272–273
> Slutski, Boris Abramovich, 18:685–686
Rabinovich, Ospi Aronovich, 17:37–38
scholars
> Eichenbaum, Boris Mikhailovich, 6:245–246
> Slonim, Marc, 18:677
science fiction, 18:206
Shalkovich, Abraham Leib, 18:374–375
Sobol,. Andrey Mikhailovich, 18:701–702
Svirski, Alexey Ivanovich, 19:334
Tur brothers, 20:192
twentieth century
> Belinkov, Arkhadii Viktorovich, 3:295–296
> Belov, A, 3:305–306
> Chakovski, Alexander Borisovich, 4:560–561
> Ehrenburg, Ilya Grigoryevich, 6:237–239
> Isbakh, Alexander Abramovich, 10:78
> Perefertkovich, Nehemiah, 15:758–759
> Slonimsky, Mikhail Leonidovich, 18:679
Tynyanov, Yuri Nikolayevich, 20:212
Utkin, Joseph Pavlovich, 20:445
Wengeroff, Semyon Afanasyevich, 21:11
Yevtushenko, Yegeni Alexandrovich, 3:22, 21:327
Yushkevich, Semyon Solomonovich, 21:428

Russian Mendelssohn, the. *See* Levinsohn, Isaac Baer

Russian Orthodox Church, Israel (state), 10:639, 641

Russian Palestine Society, 11:321

Russian Revolution
> Bolshevik theory of communism, 5:92–94
> Bund and, 4:281–282
> Lenin, Vladimir Ilyich, 12:639–640
> in Ovruch, 15:549

Russian Social Democratic Party, 5:92–93

Russian Socialist Revolutionary Party, 18:707

Russian Soviet Federative Socialist Republic (R.S.F.S.R.). *See* Russia

Russo, Baruchiah, 18:353

Russo, Nissim, 15:544

Rustchuk (Bulgaria). *See* Ruse (Bulgaria)

Rustic Sunset. See Sheki'ah Kaf

Rute. *See* Rote family

Rute family. *See* Rote family

Rutenberg, Pinḥas, 4:104, 17:**591–592**
> Jewish legion and, 11:303

Rutenberg, Piotr. *See* Rutenberg, Pinḥas

Rutgers University, 15:132

Ruth
> adoption, 1:416
> Davidic dynasty, 5:459

Ruth, Book of, 17:**592–596**, 18:22, 220–221
> Elimelech, 6:348
> *Ruth Rabbah,* 17:596

Ruthenia. *See* Subcarpathian Ruthenia

Rutherston, Albert, 4:116

Ruth Rabbah, 17:**596**

Ruth y Noemí (Espinoza), 6:509

Ruth Zuta, 14:187

Ruti family. *See* Rote family

Rutilius Namatianus, 17:**596**

Rutland, Suzanne, 17:**597**

Rutty family. *See* Rote family

Ruwandiz (Iraq), 17:**597**

Ruzhany (Belorus), 17:**597–598**

Ruzhin, Israel, 17:**598–601**, 599*t*

Ryan, Allan A., Jr., 15:388

Ryback, Issachar, 17:**601**

Rybczykowicz, Michael, 4:168

Ryby (Dostál), 5:762

Rydberg, Abraham Viktor, 18:91

Ryder, Winona, 17:**601**

Rye. *See* Five species

Rymanow (Poland), 17:**601–602**

Rymanow, Menahem Mendel of. *See* Rymanower, Menahem Mendel

Rymanower, Menahem Mendel, 17:**602**

Rymanower, Ẓevi Hirsh, 17:**602**

Rypin (Poland), 17:**602–603**

Ryshkanovca (Moldova). *See* Ryshkany (Moldova)

Ryshkany (Moldova), 17:**603**

Ryssel, Victor, 17:**603**

Ryvel, 15:473, 17:**603**

Ryzhey, Peter Lvovich. *See* Tur brothers

Ryzhyn, Israel. *See* Ruzhin, Israel

Rzeszow (Poland), 17:**603–604**

S

S (letter), 17:*605*, 18:5, 19:5

Sa'ad (Israel), 17:**605**

Saada, Jacques, 16:341

Ṣa'adī, Judah ben Solomon, 17:**605**

Saadiah (16th c. poet), 17:**605–606**

Saadiah al-Fayyumi. *See* Saadiah Gaon

Saadiah bar Joseph. *See* Saadiah Gaon

Saadiah ben Joseph Gaon. *See* Saadiah Gaon

Saadiah ben Joseph ha-Levi, 17:**606**

Saadiah Gaon (882-942), 5:472, 6:527, 604, 16:78–79, 17:**606–614**

    Aaron ben Joseph ha-Kohen Sargado, 1:214

    Abraham, 1:285

    allegorical interpretation and, 3:644

    Amidah, 2:73, 75

    angels, 2:159–160

    anthropomorphism, 2:190

    apologetics, 2:265

    Bible translations of, 3:603–604, 605, 17:612–613

    biblical exegesis of, 3:641–642, 644, 648, 662

    biography, 3:705, 17:606–608

    calendar dispute, 7:385

    commandments, reasons for, 5:86

    commentaries, 7:492

    creation, 5:277

    Divine attributes, 19:283

    divine immanence, 8:387

    exile, meaning of, 7:356–357

    faith, 3:293

    free will, 7:231

    God, 7:661, 662, 678

    good and evil, 7:753

    as grammarian, 17:612

    hakdamah, 8:242

    Halakhah, 17:608–609

    and Ḥasidei Ashkenaz, 8:386–387

    Hebrew Language, 8:653–655

    ḥerem setam, 9:18–19

    infinity of God, 6:261

    Judeo-Arabic literature and, 11:531

    kavod, 8:387

    liturgy, 17:613

    miracles, 14:307

    music, 14:654–655

    nature, 15:34

    philosophy

        classification of commandments, 17:610

        Creation, 17:609–610

        nature of God, 17:610

        nature of man and divine justice, 17:610–611

        theory of knowledge, 17:609

    piyyut, language of, 8:651, 653–655

    piyyutim, 17:613

    prophets and prophecy, 16:581–582

    redemption, 17:152–153

    repentance, 17:222

    resurrection, 17:243

    revelation, 17:256

    Ru'aḥ ha-Kodesh, 17:508

    Sargado, conflict with, 1:214

    Siddur Saadia Gaon, 16:462

    soul, immortality of, 19:36

    space and place, 19:66

    substance and accident, 19:283

    Torah, 20:40, 42, 44–45

Saalschuetz, Joseph Lewin, 17:**614**

Saarbruecken (Germany), 17:**614**

Ša'ar ha-Šamayim (Gershon ben Solomon), 8:663

Saatchi, Charles, 17:**614**

Saatchi & Saatchi, 1:428

Să auzi iarba cum creşte (Brauner), 4:138

Saaz. *See* Zatec (Czech Republic)

Saba, Abraham ben Jacob, 17:**614–615**

Saba, Umberto, 17:**615**

Saba'ai (Saudi Arabia). *See* Sabea (Saudi Arabia)

Saban, Haim, 17:**615–616**

Sabath, Adolf Joachim, 17:**616**

Sabba of Kelme. *See* Broida, Simḥah Zissel ben Israel

Sabbatarian sect, 15:**707–708**

Sabbateanism. *See* Shabbetai Ẓevi

Sabbath, 17:**616–622**

    Aaron of Neustadt, 1:219

    Amidah, 2:72, 73, 74–76

    bread, 4:155

    calendar reform, 4:359–360

    Canada, 4:396

    candles, 4:429–430, vol. 17: color insert

    children practicing candle lighting, vol. 6: color insert

    communal, 11:42

    contract obligations, 5:194

    dress, 6:13, 14, 16–17

    end of, meal and festivities at, 14:6–7

    eruvin, 6:484–486

    fasting, 6:723

    fire prohibition, 2:128, 7:43

    first after Sukkot, 18:338

    food, 13:711

        fish, 7:59

        traditional foods, 7:118–119

    homilies on readings for special, 16:11–12

    Israel (state), legal and judicial systems, 19:576

    Jubilees, Book of, 11:473

    laws pertaining to, 12:761, 15:746

    liturgy, maftir, 13:335

    Mizrachi, 14:391

    Nehemiah's interpretation of regulations, 6:661, 662

    Neshamah Yeterah, 15:88

    Phlorina, 16:118

    poems, 2:128

    preceding Passover, 18:338

    religious life and communities, Israel (state), 10:626–628

    rites and rituals, Samaritans, 17:729

    Sabbaths, special, 17:**622–623**

    sacrifices, 17:646

    sanctity of life and, 13:744

    Second Temple, 19:621

    service in India, vol. 5: color insert

    se'udah shelishit, 18:322

    Shabbat Bereshit, 18:338

    Shabbat ha-Gadol, 18:338

    Torah, reading of, 20:47*t*

The Sabbath (Heschel), 9:71

Sabbath and Festival Prayer Book (Silverman), 18:587

Sabbath Cantata (Seter), 18:318

Sabbatical year and Jubilee, 5:166, 17:**623–630**

    ancient Near East, 17:625–626

    Bible, 17:623–625

    commandments concerning, 5:76*t*

Sabbatical year and Jubilee, *continued*
famine, 6:707, 708
laws and customs, 17:629–630
obligations, extinction of, 15:372
post-biblical period, 17:626, 628–629
Second Temple period, 17:626–628

Sabbati Sevi, the Mystical Messiah (Scholem), 18:158

Sabbatyon (river). *See* Sambatyon (river)

Sabbioneta (Italy), 17:**630–631**

Sabea (Saudi Arabia), 1:546, 17:**631**

Sabin, Albert Bruce, 13:11, 17:**631–632**

Sabina Poppaea. *See* Poppaea, Sabina

Sabinus, 17:**632**

Sabot, Elias. *See* Elijah ben Shabbetai Be'er

Sabotage activities, Cairo trial, 4:346

Sabra refugee camp, 10:240–241, 251

Sabri, Sheikh hamza]Ikrameh, 15:596

Sabsovich, H. L., 17:**632**

Sabsovich, Hirsch Loeb. *See* Sabsovich, H. L.

Sabu (Saudi Arabia). *See* Sabea (Saudi Arabia)

Sabum (Saudi Arabia). *See* Sabea (Saudi Arabia)

Sabzanov, Yahiel, 4:264

Sacchetti, Franco, 10:789

Sacerdote, David, 17:**632**

Sacerdoti, Angelo-Raphael Chaim, 17:**632–633**

Sacerdoti, Eugenio Cohen, 15:568

Sachar, Abram, 9:111

Sachar, Abram Leon, 4:124, 17:**633**

Sachar, Harry, 3:86, 87, 89

Sachar, Howard Morley, 17:633

Sachar, Kreine Sonia. *See* Lipzin, Keni

Sachenhausen currency, 5:54

Sacher, Harry, 17:**633**

Sachnowitz, Herman, 15:309

Sachs, Andrew, 17:**634**

Sachs, Bernard, 6:439, 17:**634**

Sachs, Curt, 17:**634**

Sachs, Hanns, 17:**634–635**

Sachs, Julius (1832-1897), 17:**635**

Sachs, Julius (1849-1934), 17:**635**

Sachs, Leo, 13:10, 17:**635**

Sachs, Leonard, 17:**635**

Sachs, Leonie. *See* Sachs, Nelly

Sachs, Maurice, 17:**635–636**

Sachs, Michael, 3:631, 17:**636**

Sachs, Nelly, 9:410, 17:**636–637**, 18:94

Sachs, Senior, 17:**637**

Sachse, Heinrich. *See* Loewe, Heinrich

Sachsen (Germany). *See* Saxony (Germany)

Sachsenhausen Holocaust memorial (Germany), vol. 9: color insert

Sachsenhausen-Oranienburg (Germany), 5:54, 17:**637**

Sachs family, 17:634

Sack, Benjamin G., 17:**637–638**

Sackler, Harry, 8:736, 17:**638**

Sacks, Jonathan Henry, 6:427–429, 17:**638–639**

Sackur, Otto, 17:**639**

Sacramento (CA), 17:**639**

Sacred property, misuse of. *See* Me'ilah (tractate)

Sacred Dramas (More), 14:540

Sacred music. *See* Music

Sacred places. *See* Holy places

Sacred Service (Bloch), 4:661–662

Sacrifical system, 21:231

The Sacrifice (Wiseman), 4:424, 21:103

Sacrifice of Isaac, 11:700

Sacrifices, 17:**639–649**
Akedah, 1:555–556, 10:32
altars for, 2:11–16
ancient paintings, 6:52–53
animal, 7:46
Elephantine Temple, 6:312, 313
Parah, 15:630
Bible, 17:639–643
biblical traditions and history, 17:643–644
blemishes, 3:749–750
blood, role of, 3:771–772
children, 14:427–429
commandments concerning, 5:74t–75t, 80t–81t
Day of Atonement, 5:492–493
grain offerings, 7:48
Holiness Code, 9:319
human, Jephthah's daughter, 11:122
interpretations, 17:647–649
meal-offerings, 14:27–28
frankincense, 7:212–213
Moloch, cult of, 14:427–429
oils, use of, 15:395
Omer, 15:419–422
Passover, 15:677, 679
red heifer, 17:156–158
revolt against Rome, 66-70 C.E., 6:298–299
Second Temple period, 17:644–647
semikhah, 18:274

slaughter, place of, 2:11, 15
See also Cults; First Fruits; Priests and priesthood

Sacrificial system, 12:735–737

Sacrilege, 17:**649–650**

Śatāru. *See* Shetar

Śitzer, Juraj, 19:**122–123**

Sacy, Antoine Isaac Silverstre de, 17:**650**

Sadagora (Ukraine), 17:**650–651**

Sadagura (Ukraine). *See* Sadagora (Ukraine)

Ṣa'dah (Yemen), 17:**651**

Sadai, Yitzhak, 17:**651**

Sa'd al-Dawla al-Ṣafī ibn Hibbatallah, 3:56, 14:444, 17:**651–652**

Sadan, Dov, 8:684, 729, 17:**652–653**, 21:365–366

Sadat, Muhammad Anwar al-, 11:235, 15:591, 594, 17:**653–654**

Sa'd ben Manṣūr. *See* Ibn Kammūna, Sa'd ibn Manṣūr

Sadducees, 17:**654–655**
Anan ben David, 2:128
angels, 2:153
calendar, 4:358
doctrine of world to come, 2:198
Oral Law, 15:455, 456
polemics, 16:327–328

Ṣade, 17:**655**

Sadeh, Pinhas, 17:**655–656**

Sadeh, Yitzhak, 17:**656–657**

Sadeh, Yizhak, 15:603, 604

Sadie, John. *See* Sadie, Stanley

Sadie, Stanley, 17:**657**

Sa'dis family, 17:**657**

Sadler, John, 4:188

Sadness and Happiness (Pinsky), 16:176

Sadosky, Manuel, 16:350

Sadowsky, Reuben, 15:204

Sad Villa (Modiano), 14:410

Saechsisch. *See* Reghin

Saechsisch-Regen. *See* Reghin

Saeki Yoshiro, 11:84

Saertels, Moses, 3:610

Safah Berurah (Hannover), 8:327

Safarty, Israel Jacob, 18:55

Safdie, Moshe, 17:**657–658**

Safdie, Sylvia, 17:**658**

Safed, 14:666–667

Safed (Israel), 1:311, 17:**658–661**
Abraham ben Eliezer ha-Levi Berukhim, 1:299
Absaban, Solomon, 1:330
Adadi, Abraham Ḥayyim ben Masoud Hai, 1:370

aliyah to, 10:331
amulets, 2:121
Baum, Menaḥem ben Aaron of Kamenetz, 3:219
Berab, Jacob, 3:397–398
Caro, Joseph ben Ephraim, 4:488
earthquakes, 6:83
Hebrew used, 8:670
Kabbalistic literature, 7:15
Ottoman empire, 10:171, 172, 177–178, 749, 15:524
printing, publishing, 16:538
Safed Landscape (Shemi), vol. 2: color insert
Saferty, Abner Israel, 18:55
Saferty, Zemah, 18:55
Safety. *See* Peace
Saffron, 17:**661**, vol. 16: color insert
Safi (Morocco), 12:745, 17:**661**
Safire, William, 17:**661–662**
Ṣafiyya, 1:211
Safra (4th c. C.E.), 17:**662**
Safra, Edmond, 17:**663**
Safra, Jacob, 17:**662–663**
Safra, Joseph, 17:**663**
Safra Benayah ben Sa'adiah. *See* Benayah family
Safra family, 17:**662–663**
Safrai, Shmuel, 15:192, 17:**663**
Safran, Alexander, 17:**663**
Safran, Bezalel Ze'ev, 17:**663**
Safran, Joseph, 17:**663–664**
Safriel, Uriel, 6:452
Safrin, Isaac Judah Jehiel, 17:**664**
Sagalowitz, Benjamin, 17:**664**
Sagan, Carl Edward, 17:**664–665**
The Saga of Jewish Family (Cohn), 5:40
The Sage in Jewish Society of Late Antiquity (Kalmin), 1:461
Sages, halakhic authority, 8:253–254
See also specific sages
The Sages: Their Concepts and Beliefs. See Ḥazal
Sagi Nahor. *See* Isaac the Blind
Sagis, Joseph, 17:**665**
Sagis family, 17:**665**
Sagunto. *See* Murviedro
Sahagún (Spain), 17:**665**
Sahl, Mort, 17:**665–666**
Sahlān ben Abraham, 17:**666**
Sahl ben Maẓli'aḥ ha-Kohen Abu al-Surrī, 17:**666**
Sahl ibn Faḍl, 17:**666–667**
Sahlins, Marshall, 17:**667**
Sahula, Isaac ben Solomon Abi, 6:668, 17:**667–668**

Sahula, Meir ben Solomon Abi, 17:**668**
Sa'id. *See* Saadiah (c. 16th c. poet)
Sa'īd ben Shelomo, 17:**657**
Sa'id ibn Hasan, 17:**668**
Sai'id ibn Daud. *See* Adani, Saadiah ben David
Sailing. *See* Ships and Sailing
Sailor with Guitar (Lipchitz), vol. 4: color insert
Ṣaineanu, Lazar, 17:**668–669**
Saint-Denis (France), 17:**669**
Saintes (France), 17:**669**
Saint Gall (Switzerland), 17:**669**
Saint-Giles (France), 17:**670**
Saint James's Conference, 3:345, 17:**670**
Saint-Jean-de-Luz (France), 17:**670**
Saint-Léon, Arthur Michel, 17:**670**
Saint Louis (MO), 17:**671–674**
Saint Louis voyage. *See St. Louis,* voyage of the
Saint-Paul-Trois-Châteaux (France), 17:**674**
Saint Petersburg (FL), 17:**674–675**
Saint Petersburg (Russia), 17:**675–677**
Saint-Rémy-de-Provence (France), 17:**677–678**
Saints, 1:228, 12:445–446
Saint-Simon, Henry Claude de Rouvroy de, 18:704
Saint-Simonism, 6:252, 17:**678**
Saint-Symphorien-D'Ozon (France), 17:**678**
Sa'ir, 15:551
Saitowitz, Stanley, 17:**678–679**
Sajaroff, Miguel, 17:**679**
Sajet, Ben, 16:345
Sakel, Manfred Joshua, 17:**679**
Sakharov, Andrei, 4:65
Saki (Lithuania). *See* Sakiai (Lithuania)
Sakiai (Lithuania), 17:**679**
Sakic, Dinko, 4:16
Sakis Adassi (Greece). *See* Chios (Greece)
Sakler, Harry, 8:715
Sakmér (Romania). *See* Satu-Mare (Romania)
Sakowitz, Bernard, 17:**679–680**
Sakrī, Isaac ben Moses ibn, 3:56
Saks, Gene, 17:**680**
Salāam, Abdallah ibn. *See* Abdallah ibn Salāam
Saladin, 10:162, 17:**680**
Salafiyya Jihadiyya, 14:505
Salah, Ra'id, 10:731
Ṣālaḥ, Sheikh Sassoon B., 18:68

Salah al-Dīn. *See* Saladin
Salāma ben Mevorakh, 11:536
Salaman, Charles, 17:**680–681**
Salaman, Redcliffe Nathan, 17:**681**
Salamanca (Spain), 17:**681–682**
Der Salamander (Heyse), 9:87
Salaman family, 17:**680–681**
Salami Netofah family, 21:210
Salamon, Erno, 17:**682**
Salamone de' Rossi. *See* Rossi, Salamone de'
Salampsio. *See* Salome Alexandra
Salant, Joseph Sundel ben Benjamin Benish, 17:**682–683**
Salant, Samuel, 17:**683**
Salanter, Israel ben Ze'ev Wolf. *See* Lipkin, Israel ben Ze'ev Wolf
Salavey (Byadulya-Yasakar), 4:323
Salchah (Bashan), 17:**683**
Saldae (Algeria). *See* Bougie; Bougie (Algeria)
Salelli, Cencio. *See* Honorius III
Salem. *See* Jerusalem (Israel)
Salem, Emmanuel Raphael, 17:**687**
Sale of human beings. *See* Slavery; Slave trade
Sale of property, 15:428
Sale of stolen animals. *See* Theft and robberies
Salé-Rabat (Morocco), 17:**687–688**
Salerno (Italy), 17:**688–689**
Sales, 14:367–368, 17:**683–687**
Salesky, Charles, 15:304
Salfeld, Siegmund, 15:346, 17:**689**
Salgado, Plínio, 4:149
Sālih, Yaḥya ben Joseph, 13:652–653
Ṣāliḥ, Abraham, 17:**689**
Ṣāliḥ, Yaḥya ben Joseph, 17:**689**
Ṣāliḥ, Yihye Maharis. *See* Ṣāliḥ, Yaḥya ben Joseph
Ṣāliḥ ibn Yaḥya ibn Joseph, 17:**689–690**
Ṣāliḥ ibn Yihye ibn Joseph. *See* Ṣāliḥ ibn Yaḥya ibn Joseph
Sālim (ancient Israel). *See* Shalem Rabta (ancient Israel)
Salina. *See* Salome Alexandra
Salinger, Jerome David, 17:**690**
Salisbury (Rhodesia), 17:**690**
Salit, Norman, 17:**690–691**
Salita, Dmitriy, 17:**691**
Saliternik, Zvi, 17:**691**
Saljūq. *See* Seljuks
Salk, Jonas, 13:11, 17:**691**
Salkind, Jacob Meir, 17:**691**
Salkinson, Eliezer. *See* Salkinson, Isaac Edward

Salkinson, Isaac Edward, 17:**691–692**, 18:369

Sallah Shabati (motion picture), 6:263

Salmon, Alexander, 17:**692**

Salmon, Barnett, 17:692

Salmon, Cyril Barnet, 17:**692**

Salmon, Karel, 17:**692–693**

Salmon ben Jeroham, 17:**693**
Judeo-Arabic literature and, 11:532

Salmon family, 17:**692**

Salome, 17:**693–695**
Alexas, 1:636
John the Baptist and, 11:381
Obedas II, 15:367

Salome Alexandra, 8:446, 17:**695**, 18:600

Salomo (Heine), 18:761

Salomo (Klopstock), 18:761

Salomon. *See* Mulder, Samuel Israel

Salomon (Fleg), 18:761

Salomon, Albert, 17:**695**

Salomon, Alice, 17:**695–696**

Salomon, Berthold. *See* Jacob, Berthold

Salomon, Charlotte, 17:**696**

Salomon, Erich, 16:125, 17:**696–697**

Salomon, Gavriel, 17:**697**

Salomon, Geskel, 17:**697**

Salomon, Gottfried, 17:**697**

Salomon, Gotthold, 17:**697**

Salomon, Haym, 15:197, 17:**697–698**, 20:309

Salomon, Henry. *See* Sloman, Henry

Salomon, Irving, 18:15

Salomon, Joel Moses, 17:**698**

Salomon, Julius, 17:**698**

Salomon, Karl. *See* Salmon, Karel

Salomon, Moses, 4:182

Salomon Brothers, 3:782

Salomon-Calvi, Wilhelm, 17:**698**

Salomon de la Tour. *See* Salomon, Gottfried

Salomons, David, 6:377, 16:342, 17:**699**

Salomons, Julian Emanuel, 12:548, 16:340, 17:**699**

Salomonsen, Carl Julius, 17:**699**

Salonika (Greece), 17:**699–707**
Byzantine-Turkish period, 17:699–701
community, nature of, 5:107
community leaders
Adarbi, Isaac ben Samuel, 1:383
Almosnino, Moses ben Baruch, 1:685

Levi, Abraham Ben Joseph, 12:685
Medina, Samuel ben Moses de, 13:758
Hebrew publishing, 17:706
Holocaust, 9:340, 17:703–705
labor movement, 3:318–319
in Ottoman empire, 15:520, 526, 543–544
philosophers, Afia, Aaron, 1:433
post-WW II, 17:705–706
Renaissance Jews, 5:428
responsa, 17:233
Sephardi immigration to, 17:700–701
Sephardim contributions to, 18:300–301
seventeenth century-early twentieth centuries, 17:701–703
Shabbateanism center, 18:353
yeshivah, 12:494
Zionist movement in, 15:543–544

Salonikan Federation, 2:420

Salon Jewesses, 8:435, 9:51

Salons, 17:**707**

Salonta (Romania), 17:**707–708**

Salsberg, Joseph B., 4:406, 5:99, 17:**708**

Salt, 7:116, 17:**708–709**
Drogobych (Ukraine), 6:23
salt trade and industry, 11:750, 17:709–710

Salten, Felix, 17:**709**

Saltpeter, Mechel. *See* Gordon, Max

Salt trade and industry, 17:**709–710**

Saltzman, Harry, 17:**710**

Saltzman, Maurice, 17:**710**

Salus, Hugo, 17:**711**

Salusque Lusitano. *See* Usque, Solomon

Salutsky, Jacob Benjamin. *See* Hardman, Jacob Benjamin

Saluzzo (Italy), 17:**711**

Salvador, Francis, 17:711–712

Salvador, Joseph (1716-1786), 17:711

Salvador, Joseph (1796-1873), 17:**712**

Salvador family, 17:**711–712**

Salvaged Pages (Zapruder), 4:631

Salvation. *See* Redemption

The Salvation of the Drowning. See Najāt al-Ghāriqīn

Salvendi, Adolf, 17:**712**

Salvo de Cassetta, 15:580

Salz, Abraham Adolph, 17:**712**

Salzberg (Poland). *See* Bochnia (Poland)

Salzburg (Austria), 17:**712–713**

Salzman, Leib. *See* Malach, Leib

Salzman, Pnina, 17:**713–714**

Salzman, William, 17:**714**

Salzmann, Laurence, 16:130

Salzmann, Samuel Ezekiel, 13:156

Salzmann, Siegmund. *See* Salten, Felix

Samael, 17:**714–715**

Samama, Nessim, 16:346, 17:**716**

Samandar (Khazaria), 17:**716**

Samara (Russian Federation). *See* Kuibyshev (Russian Federation)

Samaria (ancient Israel), 1:522–524, 17:**716–718**, *717*

Samarian Mountains (Israel), 10:116

Samaritan Aramaic, 2:352

Samaritan community, 3:**16**, 8:666

Samaritan Masorah system, 13:646–648

Samaritan Pentateuch, 15:**753–755**

Samaritans, 17:**718–740**, 734t
Āl-Asāṭīr, 1:576
Alexander the Great, 1:625, 626
Alexander the Zealot, 1:631
calendar, 4:358
chronology, 17:732–735
Dustan sect, 6:65–67
history of, 17:719–727
demography, 17:726–727
Graeco-Roman Diaspora, 17:722–723
late Roman to Crusader period, 17:723–724
Mt. Gerizim excavations, 17:723
Nehemiah, time of, 17:720
origins, 17:719–720
population statistics, 17:726–727
post-Crusader period, 17:724–726
Second Temple period, 17:720–722
holy places in Israel, 9:501, *502*
in Islam, 17:738
Jewish identity and, 11:292–293
Josephus' *Jewish Antiquities*, possible Samaritan source for, 11:438–439
Josippon, 11:462
languages, 3:351–352, 17:735
literature, 17:735–738
Abu al-Fat, 1:334
Abu al-Hasan of Tyre, 1:335
Mount Gerizim, 7:507–508
music, 17:738–739
Passover, 15:678
polemics, 16:327–328
religion and customs, 17:727–732

Roman rebellion, 7:508

Samaritan translation of Bible, 3:599, 652

Samarkand (Uzbekistan), 17:**740–741**

Samau'al ben Judah ibn 'Abbās al-Maghribī, 1:643, 17:**741–742**

Sambari, 15:534

Sambari, Joseph ben Isaac, 17:**742–743**

Sambatyon. *See* Eldad, Israel

Sambatyon (river), 6:293, 17:**743–744**

Samberg, Aizik. *See* Samberg, Isaac

Samberg, Isaac, 17:**744**

Sambor (Ukraine), 17:**744–745**

Samburcky, Daniel, 17:**745**

Samburcky, Samuel, 17:**745**

Samegah, Joseph ben Benjamin, 17:**745–746**

Samekh, 17:**746**

Samfield, Max, 17:**746**

Samiel. *See* Samael

Saminsky, Lazare, 17:**746–747**, 18:725

Samiro, S. *See* Tzara, Tristan

Samizdat, 11:323

Samkalden, Ivo, 16:345

Sammlung juedischer Geschichten in der Schweiz (Ulrich), 9:158

Sammuel. *See* Samael

Samogitia (Lithuania), 17:**747**

Samoilovich, Reuben Lazarevich. *See* Samoilovich, Rudolph Lazarevich

Samoilovich, Rudolph Lazarevich, 17:**747**

Samokov (Bulgaria), 17:**748**

Samokovlija, Isak, 17:**748**

Sampras, Pete, 17:**748**

The Sampson Option (Hersch), 9:44

Sampter, Jessie Ethel, 17:**748–749**

Samra, David, 17:**749**

Samson, 9:170, 17:**749–752**

Delilah and, 5:539

extradition of, 6:626

Judges, Book of, 11:565

Samson (Brandys), 4:129

Samson, Benjamin Abraham, 17:**752**

Samson Agonistes (Milton), 6:435

Samson ben Abraham of Sens, 17:**752–753**

Samson ben Eliezer, 17:**753**

Samson ben Isaac of Chinon, 17:**753**

Samson ben Joseph of Falaise, 17:**753–754**

Samson ben Pesaḥ of Ostropol, 11:456

Samson ben Samson of Coucy, 17:**754**

Samson ha-Nakdan, 17:**754**

Samson Resources Company, 18:178

Samson the Nazarite (Jabotinsky), 11:14

Samter, Ernst, 17:**754**

Samuda, Joseph d'Aguilar, 17:**754**

Samuel (2nd-3rd c.), 3:28–29, 9:204, 14:534, 17:**757–758**

Amidah, 2:76

Johanan ben Nappaḥa, 11:371

Judah bar Ezekiel, 11:480

Rav, 17:116–117

Samuel (biblical figure), 9:170–171, 17:**754–757,** 18:78–80, 81

Agag, 1:445

Samuel (Mar). *See* Samuel (2nd-3rd c.)

Samuel, Alexander, 15:554

Samuel, Book of, 17:**758–763**

Book of Jashar, 4:69

Elkanah, 6:357

historiography, 9:153, 154

labor, 12:409

Midrash, Samuel, 14:191

sin, concept of, 18:622

Samuel, Edwin, 17:**764**

Samuel, Emanuel, 11:467

Samuel, Harold (1912-1982), 17:**764**

Samuel, Harold, (1879-1937), 17:**764**

Samuel, Herbert Louis, 3:86–87, 10:198, 388, 15:582, 16:342, 17:**764–765**

Samuel, Howard, 17:**766**

Samuel, Marcus, Viscount Bearstead, 16:20

Samuel, Maurice, 17:**766**

Samuel, Morris, 2:53

Samuel, Ralph E., 17:**766**

Samuel, Raphael, 17:**766–767**

Samuel, Saul, 16:339–340, 17:**767**

Samuel, Sigmund, 4:398, 17:**767**

Samuel, Sydney Montagu, 17:**767**

Samuel, Wilfred Sampson, 17:**767–768**

Samuel ben Abraham, 11:790

Samuel ben Abraham de Ortas, 12:629

Samuel ben Abraham Safarty, 18:55

Samuel ben Ali, 17:**768**, 18:275

Samuel ben Avigdor, 17:**768–769**

Samuel ben Azariah, 17:**769**

Samuel ben Baruch Levy Aben-Yuly, 21:427

Samuel ben Daniel Abu Rabī'a ha-Kohen, 17:**769**

Samuel ben David (12th c.), 17:**769**

Samuel ben David (d. 1673), 17:**769**

Samuel ben David Moses ha-Levi, 17:**769–770**

Samuel ben Eliezer of Kalwaria, 17:**770**

Samuel ben Hananiah, 17:**770**

Samuel ben Hophni, 17:**770–771**

biblical exegesis and study, 3:662

Judeo-Arabic literature and, 11:531

Samuel ben Isaac ha-Sardi. *See* Sardi, Samuel ben Isaac

Samuel ben Jacob of Kelmy, 17:**771**

Samuel ben Kalonymus he-Ḥasid of Speyer, 17:**771**

Samuel ben Kalonymus "the Pious" of Speyer. *See* Samuel ben Kalonymus ha-Ḥasid of Speyer

Samuel ben Maẓli'aḥ Marli. *See* Marli, Samuel ben Maẓli'aḥ

Samuel ben Meir, 17:**771–773**

biblical exegesis and study, 3:642

Joseph ben Moses of Troyes, 11:424

Samuel ben Moses al-Maghribī, 11:537, 17:**773**

Samuel ben Moses ha-Ma'aravi. *See* Samuel ben Moses al-Maghribī

Samuel ben Naḥman, 17:**773–774**

Samuel ben Naḥmani. *See* Samuel ben Naḥman

Samuel ben Natronai, 17:**774**

Samuel ben Samson, 17:**774**

Samuel ben Shilat, 17:**774**

Samuel ben Solomon of Falaise, 17:**774**

Samuel ben Uri Shraga Phoebus, 17:**774–775**

Samuel Benveniste. *See* Benveniste, Samuel

Samuel Commission, 17:**775**

Samuel de Medina, 2:40

Samuel ha-Katan, 17:**775–776**

Samuel ha-Levi ben al-Dastur. *See* Samuel ben Ali

Samuel ha-Nagid, 3:669, 16:265, 17:**776–777**

as bibliophile, 3:683

Nissim ben Jacob ben Nissim Ibn Shahin and, 15:279

Samuel ha-Shelishi ben Hoshana, 17:**777**

Samuel ibn 'Ādiyā, 11:530, 17:**778**

Samuel ibn Adiyā, 15:472

Samuel ibn Sid. *See* Sid, Samuel ibn

Samuel Jachia. *See* Denis, Albertus

Samuel Montagu and Co., 14:451

Samuel of Derenburg. *See* Smol

Samuel of Evreux, 17:**778**

Samuel of Lublin, 2:650

Samuel of Primo, 18:451

Samuel of Wych Cross. *See* Samuel, Harold (1912-1982)

Samuel Sir Morel. *See* Samuel ben Solomon of Falaise

Samuelson, Bernhard, 17:**778**

Samuelson, Paul Anthony, 17:**778–779**

Samuel Yarhina'ah. *See* Samuel (2nd-3rd c.)

Samuilov, Victor, 4:277

Ṣanʿā (Yemen). *See* Sanʾa (Yemen)

Sanʾa (Yemen), 18:**5–6**

Sanandaj (Iranian Kurdistan), 18:**6**

San Antonio (TX), 18:**7**

Sanatoria, 5:68

Sanatorium pod klepsydrąá (Schulz), 18:175

Sanballat, 18:**7–8**

Sanballat I, 18:**7–8**

Sanballat II, 18:**8**

Sanballat III, 18:**8**

Sanbar, Moshe, 18:**8**

Sanbatyon (river). *See* Sambatyon (river)

Sanches, Francisco, 18:**8–9**

Sanchez, Antonio Nuñes Ribeiro, 18:**9**

Sánchez, Gabriel, 18:**9**

Sanchez, Juan (de Sevilla). *See* Abrabanel, Samuel (of Seville)

Sanchez de Cartagena, Alvar, 15:563

Sancho IV (King of Castile), 1:311

Sancta, 11:777–779

Sancta mater ecclesia (papal bull), 4:278, 18:313

Sanctification. *See* Kedushah

Sanctification of the Moon (prayer), 14:468

Sanctions

agunah, 1:519–520

for oaths, 15:360, 362

obligations, law of, 12:537–540, 15:369

See also Fines

Sanctuary. *See* Tabernacle; Temples

Sand, Leonard B., 18:**9–10**

Sandak, 18:**10**

Sandalfon, 18:**10**

San Daniele del Friuli (Italy), 18:**10–11**

Sandberg, Moshe. *See* Sanbar, Moshe

Sandberg, Willem Jacob, 18:**11**

Sandek. *See* Sandak

Sanderling, Kurt, 18:**11**

Sanders, Bernard, 18:**11–12**

Sanders, James, 3:653

Sanders, Leo, 15:205

Sandground, Jack Henry, 18:**12**

San Diego (CA), 18:**12–15**

Sandler, Adam Richard, 18:**15**

Sandler, Boris, 18:**15–16**

Sandler, Jacob Koppel, 18:**16**

Sandmel, Samuel, 18:**16**

Sandomierz (Poland), 18:**16–17**

Sandomir (Poland). *See* Sandomierz (Poland)

Sándor, Pál, 18:**17**

Sandrow, Edward T., 18:**17–18**

Sandstrom, Emil, 15:585

Sandz dynasty. *See* Halberstam dynasty

Sandzer, Ḥayyim ben Menahem, 18:**18**

San Francisco Bay Area (CA), 18:**18–20**

Eckman, Julius, 6:92

San Gabriel-Pomona Valleys (CA), 18:**20–21**

Sanger, Adolph L., 15:211

Sanguinetti, Azariah Ḥayyim, 18:**21**

Sanhedrin (Abulafia), 1:341

Sanhedrin (judicial body), 18:**21–23**

of 1807, 2:8

as academy, 1:348, 349

Berab, Jacob, 3:397–398

France, 7:155–156, 9:231, 18:24

Herod I, 9:31–32

at Jabneel, 11:10

Pharisees, 16:30

re-establishment after Bar Kokhba revolt, 10:150–151

separated from office of nasi, 10:153

Simeon ben Gamaliel II, 18:595

temple genealogical archives, 2:405

Sanhedrin (tractate), 18:**23–24**

Sanhedrin, French. *See* French Sanhedrin

Sanhedrin, Tombs of. *See* Sanhedrin (judicial body)

Sanīʿ al Dawla. *See* Abu al-Munajjā Solomon ben Shaya

Sanielevici, Henric, 18:**24**

Sanim (ancient Israel). *See* Shalem Rabta (ancient Israel)

Sanipu of Ammon, 2:85

San Jose (CA), 18:**25**

San Marino, 18:**25**

San Nicandro (Italy), 18:**25**

San Nicandro community (Italy), 11:520

Sanok (Poland), 12:662, 18:**25–26**

San Quentin prison, 3:742

San Remo Conference, 18:**26**

San Remo Drive: A Novel from Memory (Epstein), 6:475

Santa Coloma de Queralt (Spain), 18:**26–27**

Santa Cruz (CA), 18:**27**

Santa Fe (Argentina), 18:**27–28**

Santa Fé, Gerónimo de, 20:62

Santangel, Luis de, 18:**28**

Santarém (Portugal), 18:**28–29**

Santiago Jewish community, 4:640–641

Sant Jordi, Franciscus de. *See* Rimoch, Astruc

Santob de Carrión, 12:432, 18:**29–30**

Sants (Poland). *See* Nowy Sacz (Poland)

Sanū', James. *See* Sanū', Yaʾqub

Ṣanū', Yaʾqūb, 15:472, 18:**30**

Sanuel of Norwich, 11:577

Sanwel, Perez. *See* Eger, Samuel

Sanz dynasty. *See* Halberstam dynasty

São Paulo (Brazil), 12:209, 18:**30–34**

Ṣapā, Mount, 3:10, 11

Sapci Basi. *See* Carmona, Bekhor Isaac David

Saperstein, Abe. *See* Saperstein, Abraham M.

Saperstein, Abraham M., 18:**34**

Saperstein, David N., 18:**34–35**

Saperstein, Harold I., 18:**35**

Saphet (Israel). *See* Safed (Israel)

Saphir, Jacob, 6:49, 18:**35–36**

Saphir, Moritz Gottlieb, 18:**36–37**

Saphir, Moses Gottlieb. *See* Saphir, Moritz Gottlieb

Saphir, Naomi. *See* Shemer, Naomi

Saphire, Saul, 11:412, 444, 18:**37**

Sapientia Salomonis (Birck), 18:761

Sapir, Edward, 2:186, 13:60, 18:**37**, 731

Sapir, Eliyahu, 18:**37–38**

Sapir, Joseph, 15:693, 18:**38**

Sapir, Pinḥas, 18:**38–39**

Sapiro, Aaron, 18:**39**

Sapirstein-Stone-Weiss family, 18:**39**

Saporta, Ḥanokh, 18:**39–40**

Saporta family, 13:727

Sappho and Socrates (Hirschfeld), 9:138–139

Sappir, 16:477

Sar, Samuel L., 18:**40**

Sar, Shmuel Leib. *See* Sar, Samuel L.

Sārā al-Qurayẓiyya, 15:472

Sarachek, Bernard, 18:**40–41**

Sarachek, Joseph, 18:**41**

Sarachek, "Red". *See* Sarachek, Bernard

Saraga, Lascar. *See* Lazar, Samson

Saragossa (Spain), 1:215, 18:**41–46**

Abbas, Moses ben Samuel and, 1:231

Sarah, 18:**46–47**

Abimelech and, 1:257

Abraham, 1:281, 282, 285

adoption, 1:415

interpretations, Philo Judaeus, 16:62, 64

as Matriarch, 15:691

See Also Matriarchs

Sarah (wife of Shabbetai Ẓevi), 18:342

Sarah of Turnovo, 4:269, 276, 18:47

Sarai. *See* Sarah

Sarajevo (Bosnia-Herzegovina), 12:690–691, 14:629, 18:47–49

rabbis, 8:179, 12:690–691

Sarajevo Haggadah, 8:213–214

Sarasohn, Kasriel Hersch, 18:50

Sarasota (Florida), 18:50–51

Saratov (Russia), 18:51

blood libel in, 3:779

Saraval, Jacob Raphael ben Simḥah Judah, 18:52

Saraval, Judah Leib, 18:52

Saraval family, 18:51–52

Sarcophagi, 15:506–507

Sarcophagus, Ahiram. *See* Hiram

Sardi, Samuel ben Isaac, 4:773, 18:52–53

Sardinia (Italy), 1:652, 4:335, 18:53

Sardis (Lydia), 13:295–296, 18:53–54, 54, 292

Sardis synagogue, 13:296, 18:54

Sarei ha-Elef (Kasher), 11:821

Sarezer. *See* Sharezer

Sarfati, 18:54–55

Sarfati, Giosifante. *See* Sarfati, Joseph

Sarfati, Isaac, 15:522

Sarfati, Jacob Ben Solomon, 18:54–55

Sarfati, Joseph, 18:54

Julian III as godfather, 11:574

Sarfati, Josiphon. *See* Sarfati, Joseph

Sarfati, Samuel, 18:54

Sarfatti. *See* Sarfati

Sarfatti, Gad B., 18:55

Sarfaty, Isaac, 18:55

Sarfaty family, 18:55

Sargado, Aaron, 11:422

Sargenes. *See* Kitel

Sargon II (King of Assyria), 2:126, 404, 3:23, 6:607, 9:180, 18:56

Sargon of Agade, 2:469

Sargon of Akkad, 6:85

Sarha, Adulammi. *See* Edelmann, Simḥah Reuben

Sar Ha-Adulammi. *See* Edelmann, Simḥah Reuben

"Sar ha-Birah." *See* Jonathan ben Eleazar

Sar ha-Panim. *See* Metatron

Sarid (Israel), 18:56

Sarid (Zebulun), 18:56

Sarid, Yossi, 18:56–57

Sarique family. *See* Chriqui family

Saris. *See* Eunuchs

Sārīs, 6:549

Sarkil (Khazaria), 18:57

Sarmad, Muhammad Saʿid, 15:474, 18:57

Sarmad the Jew. *See* Sarmad, Muhammad Saʿid

Sarmento, Jacob de Castro. *See* Castro Sarmento, Jacob de

Sarmiento, Pedro, 18:57–58

Sarna, Ezekiel, 18:58

Sarna, Jonathan Daniel, 4:125, 18:58–59

Sarna, Nahum M., 4:125, 18:59

Sarnoff, David, 18:59–60

Sarnoff, Robert, 18:60

Sarny (Ukraine), 18:60

Sarphati, Samuel, 16:345, 18:60–61

Ṣarrāf, 18:61–62

Sarraute, Nathalie, 18:62

Sarreguemines (France), 18:62

Sar Shalom ben Boaz, 3:590–591, 18:62–63

Sar Shalom ben Moses ha-Levi, 18:63

Sarsur. *See* Agency

Sarṭaba (Jordan Valley), 18:63

Sarto, Giuseppe Melchiorre. *See* Pius X

Sartre, Jean-Paul, 2:65

Sarug, Israel, 13:264–265, 18:63–64

Sarūj (Turkey), 18:64

Saruk, Israel. *See* Sarug, Israel

Sārūm, Abraham, 18:64

Saruq, Menahem ben Jacob ibn, *See.* *See* Menahem ben Jacob ibn Saruq

Sasa (Israel), 18:64

Sasanid dynasty, 3:28–29

Saskatchewan (Canada), 18:64–65

Saskatoon (SK), 18:65

Saslavsky, Luis Simón, 18:66

Sason. *See* Solomon ben Samson

Sasov (Ukraine), 18:66

Sasów (Ukraine). *See* Sasov (Ukraine)

Sasporta, Ḥanokhanokh. *See* Saporta, Ḥanokh

Sasportas, Jacob, 4:252, 18:66–67, 346

Sassanids, 6:602

Sasso, Dennis, 18:67

Sasso, Sandy Eisenberg, 18:67

Sasson, Aaron ben Joseph, 18:67–68

Sasson, Eliyahu, 18:68

Sassoon, Aaron, 18:70

Sassoon, Abdulla, 18:70

Sassoon, Albert. *See* Sassoon, Abdulla

Sassoon, Arthur, 18:70

Sassoon, David Solomon, 3:684, 4:51, 18:68

Sassoon, Edward Albert, 18:70

Sassoon, Elias David, 18:70

Sassoon, Ezekiel. *See* Sassoon, Sir Ezekiel

Sassoon, Flora, 18:70

Sassoon, Jacob Elias, 18:70

Sassoon, Philip, 18:70–71

Sassoon, Rachel, 18:70

Sassoon, Reuben D., 18:70

Sassoon, Sassoon David, 18:70

Sassoon, Siegfried Lorraine, 18:71

Sassoon, Sir Ezekiel, 16:346, 18:71

Sassoon, Solomon, 18:70

Sassoon, Solomon David (1880-1942), 18:70

Sassoon, Solomon David (1915-1985), 18:70

Sassoon, Victor, 18:71

Sassoon, Vidal, 18:71–72

Sassoon ben Ẓalaḥ, 3:57

Sassoon family, 9:7, 18:68–71, 69t

Satan, 18:72–73

Adam, 1:372, 373, 374

Adam Kadmon, 1:379

Akedah, 10:33

Moses, 14:533, 535–536

Samael, 17:714–715

shofar, 18:508

See also Belial; Mastema

Satan in Goray. See Sotn in Goray

Satanov (Ukraine), 18:73

Satanow, Isaac, 8:724, 18:73–74

Satanowski, Marcos, 12:555, 18:74

Satinsky, Sol, 18:74

Satire

Beda, 3:246–247

Bonafed, Solomon ben Reuben, 4:53, 54

Christianity, 6:56–57

Horace, Quintus Horatius Flaccus, 9:523

humor and, 9:593–594

Laub, Gabriel, 12:524

Saphir, Moritz Gottlieb, 18:36–37

Schorr, Joshua Heschel, 18:164

Slominski, Antoni, 18:678

Satire (Juvenal), 11:582

Satires (Horace), 9:523

Satmar Hassidim, 12:191–192

Satoraljaujhely (Hungary), 18:74–75

Satorra family. *See* Stora family

Satrap, 18:75

Satu-Mare (Romania), 18:**75–76**

Satz, Ludwig, 18:**76**

Satz, Mario, 18:**76**

Sauckel, Ernst Friedrich Christoph. *See* Sauckel, Fritz

Sauckel, Fritz, 18:**76–77**

Saudi Arabia, 2:296, 301, 18:**77–78**
    Aden, 1:387–389
    aircraft to, 2:52
    Arab-Israeli conflict, 2:311
    armistice agreements, 2:475
    democracy in Iraq and, 2:327
    Egypt and, 2:304
    Hejaz, 8:775
    inter-Arab disputes, 2:310
    peace plans, 18:78
    See also Arabia

Saul, 9:170–172, 18:**78–83,** *79*
    Abishai and, 1:260
    Abner, 1:263–264
    Adriel, 1:423
    Agag, 1:444–445
    Ahimelech, 1:544, 545
    dance, 5:409
    David and, 5:445, 447–448, 18:80–81
    death of, 13:743
    Doeg and, 5:730
    ecstasy, 6:139
    in literature, 18:81–82
    in music, 18:82–83
    Witch of En-Dor, 6:404, 405

Saul (Alfieri), 10:788

Saul ben Anan, 18:**83**

Saul ben Nafusi of Palermo, 15:581

Saulcy, Louis Felicien de Joseph Caignart, 18:**83**

Saul D. ibn Danān, 14:504

Saul Judycz. *See* Wahl, Saul ben Judah

Saul of Tarsus. *See* Paul of Tarsus

Saul Silber Memorial Library, 8:738

Saute Barbara (Langfus), 12:482

Sava de-Mishpatim (Zohar), 21:649

SAVAK, 15:569, 570

Savanization, 6:452

Savannah (GA), 7:501–502, 18:**83–84**
    Minnis family, 14:281

Savannah Jewish Archives (GA), 18:84

Savelli, Giacomo. *See* Honorius IV

Saverne (France), 18:**84**

Saville, Victor, 12:545, 18:**84**

Savior. *See* Messiah

Savir. *See* Sevirin

Savitt, Dick. *See* Savitt, Richard

Savitt, Richard, 18:**85**

Savoie (France). *See* Savoy (France)

Savoir (France). *See* Savoy (France)

Savora, savoraim, 1:529, 14:340, 18:**85,** 617

Savoraim. *See* Savora, savoraim

Savoy (France), 18:**85–86**

Savoy Big Five. *See* Harlem Globetrotters

Savran, Bella, 9:382

Savran dynasty, 18:**86**

Savyon (Israel), 18:**86**

Sawdust Caesar (Seldes), 18:259

Sawicki, Jerzy, 18:**86**

Sax, Ruben. *See* Brooks, Richard

Saxon, David Stephen, 18:**86–87**

Saxony (Germany), 18:**87–88**

Say, Is This the U.S.A.? (Bourke-White and Caldwell), 4:107

Scaasi, Arnold, 18:**88**

Scales. *See* Balance; Weights and measures

Scalfaro, Oscar Luigi, 16:345

Scaliger, Joseph Justus, 8:515, 18:**88–89**

Scallions, 15:433

Scandals, 12:533–534

Scandarani family. *See* Iscandari family

Scandari, Eleazar ben Abraham Scandari, 10:79

Scandari family. *See* Iscandari family

Scandinavia
    bankers, moneylenders, 3:117
    education, Jewish, 6:181
    emancipation, 6:377
    Neo-Nazism, 15:82
    newspapers, 16:501–502
    publishing, 16:716
    relations with Israel, 10:266
    Thanks to Scandinavia Scholarship Fund, 4:84–85

Scandinavian literature, 18:**89–96**
    Danish literature, 18:89–90
    Norweigian literature, 18:94–96
    Schück, Johan Henrik Emil, 12:453, 18:169
    Swedish literature, 18:90–94
    Warburg, Karl Johan, 12:453, 20:632
    Warrens, Rosa, 20:666
    Wergeland, Henrik Arnold, 15:305, 21:13

Scantrel, Félix André Yves. *See* Suarès, André

Scapegoat. *See* Azazel

The Scapegoat (Caine), 6:436

Scaraboid seals, 18:225

Scarab seals, 18:225

Scarlet Thread. See Ḥut ha-Shani

Scaurus, 2:457

Scepter, 18:**96**

Schaalman, Herman E., 18:**96–97**

Schaap, Dick. *See* Schaap, Richard J.

Schaap, Richard J., 18:**97–98**

Schach, Fabius, 18:**98**

Schach, Leonard Lazarus, 18:**98**

Schach, Miriam, 18:98

Schachnowitz, Selig, 18:**98**

Schacht, Al. *See* Schacht, Alexander

Schacht, Alexander, 15:688, 18:**98–99**

Schacht, Hjalmar, 18:101

Schachtel, Hugo-Hillel, 18:**99**

Schachter, Carl, 18:**99**

Schachter, Herschel, 9:380, 18:**99–100**

Schachter, Jacob J., 18:**100**

Schachter, Raphael, 4:79

Schachter-Shalomi, Zalman, 18:**100–101**

Schacht Plan, 18:**101**

Schaechter, Joseph, 18:**101–102**

Schaechter, Mordkhe, 18:**102**

Schaechter-Gottesman, Bella, 18:**102**

Schaeffer, Claude F.A., 18:**102–103**

Schaeffer, Hans, 18:**103**

Schaeffle, Albert, 18:733

Schafer, Stephen, 18:**103**

Schaff, Adam, 18:**103**

Schaffhausen (Switzerland), 18:**103–104**

Schaken (Lithuania). *See* Sakiai (Lithuania)

Schakowsky, "Jan". *See* Schakowsky, Janice D.

Schakowsky, Janice D., 18:**104**

Schalek, Malva, 2:517, 518

Schalit, Abraham Chaim, 9:161, 18:**104**

Schalit, Heinrich, 18:**104**

Schalit, Isidor, 18:**104–105**

Schally, Andrew Victor, 18:**105**

Schama, Simon, 18:**105**

Schames, Samson, 18:**106**

Schanberg, Sydney H., 18:**106**

Schanfarber, Tobias, 18:**106**

Schanker, Louis, 18:**106–107**

Schanzer, Carlo, 18:**107**

Schapera, Isaac, 18:**107**

Schapira, David, 16:349, 18:**107**

Schapira, Hermann, 8:740, 18:**107–108**

Schapira, Noah, 18:**108**

Schapira, Ẓevi Hirsch. *See* Schapira, Hermann

Schapiro, Israel, 18:**108–109**

Schapiro, Jacob Salwyn, 18:**109**

Schapiro, Leonard, 18:**109**

Schapiro, Meyer, 18:**109–110**

Schapiro, Miriam, 4:612

Schappes, Morris U., 18:**110**

Scharfstein, Ẓevi, 18:**110**

Schary, Dore, 18:**110**

Schary, Isidore. *See* Schary, Dore

Schatz, Bezalel, 18:**111**

Schatz, Boris, 2:501, 10:695, 696, 13:14, 18:**110–111**, 223

Schatz, Louise, 18:**111**

Schatz, Zahara, 18:**111**

Schatz, Ẓevi, 18:**111**

Schatz-Anin, Max, 18:**111**

Schaulen (Lithuania). *See* Siauliai (Lithuania)

Schaulsohn. *See* Fraenkel, Levi ben Saul

Schaulson Brodsky, Jorge, 18:**111–112**

Schaulson Numhauser, Jacobo, 18:**112**

Schau-Platz der Eitelkeit... (play), 18:761

Schawlow, Arthur L., 18:**112**

Schayes, Adolph, 18:**112**

Schayes, "Dolph". *See* Schayes, Adolph

Schechter, Abraham Israel, 18:**112–113**

Schechter, Mathilde Roth, 18:**113**

Schechter, Shneur Zalman. *See* Schechter, Solomon

Schechter, Solomon, 2:750–751, 5:172, 11:777, 18:**113–114**, 115

    Jewish Quarterly Review, 11:313

    Jewish Theological Seminary, 1:395, 6:193, 11:329

Schechter, Yerachmiel, 4:369–370

Schechter Institute of Jewish Studies (Jerusalem), 5:176, 18:**114–115**

Schechtman, Joseph B., 18:**115–116**

Scheck, Barry, 18:**116**

Scheckter, Jody, 18:**116**

Scheer, Eva, 15:310

Scheffler, Israel, 18:**116–117**

Schefftel, Rosalie. *See* Perles, Rosalie

Scheftelowitz, Isidor, 18:**117**

Scheib, Israel. *See* Eldad, Israel

Scheiber, Alexander, 18:**117**

Scheid, Elie, 18:**117–118**

Schein, Lazar. *See* Ṣaineanu, Lazar

Scheindlin, Raymond P., 18:**118**

Scheinerman, Arik. *See* Sharon, Ariel

Scheinert, David, 18:**118**

Scheines, Loeb. *See* Kahana, Abraham Aryeh Leib ben Shalom Shakhna

Scheinfeld, Solomon Isaac, 18:**118**

Scheinman, Arieh, 4:170

Schekman, Randy, 13:10

Scheler, Max Ferdinand, 18:**118–119**, 729

Schellenberg, Walter, 18:**119**

Schelling, Friedrich Wilhelm Joseph, 18:**119–120**

Schelomo, Rhapsodie Hébraïque (symphony, Bloch), 18:762

Schenectady (NY), 18:**120–121**

Schenirer, Sarah, 18:**121–122**

Schenk, Faye L., 18:**122**

Schenker, Heinrich, 18:**122**

Schenker, Joel W., 18:**122**

Scherer, Moshe, 17:30

Schereschewsky, Samuel Isaac Joseph, 18:**122–123**

Scherlag, Mark, 18:**123**

Scherman, Nosson, 18:**123**

Schermeister, Ḥayyim Ze'ev. *See* Bar-Daroma, Ḥayyim Ze'ev

Scheuer, Edmund, 18:**123–124**

Scheuer, James H., 18:**124–125**

Scheyer, Eva. *See* Jospe, Eva Scheyer

Schiber, Chaim. *See* Sheba, Chaim

Schiby, Baruch, 18:**125**

Schichardus, Guillielmus. *See* Schickard, Wilhelm

Schick, Abraham ben Aryeh Loeb, 18:**125**

Schick, Baruch ben Jacob, 8:440, 18:**125–126**

Schick, Bela, 18:**126**

Schick, Conrad, 18:**126–127**

Schick, Moses ben Joseph, 18:**127–128**

Schickard, Wilhelm, 18:**128**

Schickardus, Guillielmus. *See* Schickard, Wilhelm

Schickart, Wilhelm. *See* Schickard, Wilhelm

Schickhard, Wilhelm. *See* Schickard, Wilhelm

Schicksalsreise (Doeblin), 5:729–730

Schidlowsky, Leon, 18:**128**

Schieber, Chaim. *See* Sheba, Chaim

Schiff, Adam, 18:**128–129**

Schiff, András, 18:**129**

Schiff, David Tevele, 18:**129**

Schiff, Dorothy, 3:40, 11:468, 15:222, 18:**129–130**

Schiff, Ernst, 11:333

Schiff, Frieda. *See* Warburg, Frieda

Schiff, Hugo, 18:**130**

Schiff, Jacob Henry, 18:**130–131**

    The American Hebrew, 2:49

    American Jewish Archives, 2:53

    American Jewish Committee, 2:54

    Jewish Theological Seminary, 11:329

    New York City and, 15:203, 205, 207, 208, 211, 217

    railroads, 17:70

Schiff, Meir ben Jacob ha-Kohen, 18:**131**

Schiff, Morenu Ha-Rav Meir. *See* Schiff, Meir ben Jacob ha-Kohen

Schiff, Otto M., 11:333

Schiff, Sydney. *See* Hudson, Stephen

Schiff, Sydney Alfred. *See* Hudson, Stephen

Schiff bases, 18:130

Die Schiffbruechigen (Améry), 2:65

Schiffman, Lawrence H., 18:**131–132**

Schifrin, Boris. *See* Schifrin, Lalo

Schifrin, Lalo, 18:**132**

Schild, Edwin, 18:**132–133**

Schilder, Paul Ferdinand, 18:**133**

Schildkraut, Joseph, 18:133

Schildkraut, Rudolph, 18:**133**

Schiller, Armand, 18:**133**

Schiller, Friedrich von, 14:540, 18:**133–134**

Schiller, Solomon, 18:**134**

Schiller Dramatic Society, 11:815

Schiller-Szinessy, Solomon Mayer, 18:**134**

Schilling, Berthe. *See* Bréval, Lucienne

Schillinger, Joseph, 18:**134–135**

Schimpf und Ernst (Pauli), 15:696

Schindler, Alexander M., 17:171–172, 179–180, 18:**135–136**, 20:254–255

    Bitburg Controversy, 3:728

Schindler, Emilie, 18:136

Schindler, Kurt, 18:**136**

Schindler, Oskar, 16:226, 18:**136**

Schindler, Rudolph M., 18:**137**

Schindler, Solomon, 4:100, 18:**137**

Schindler's List (motion picture), 9:444–445, 18:136, 20:380

Schiper, Ignacy, 18:**137**

Schiper, Yiẓḥak. *See* Schiper, Ignacy

Schirmann, Ḥyyim. *See* Schirmann, Jefim

Schirmann, Jefim, 18:**137–138**

Schisgal, Murray, 18:**138**

Schizophrenia, 6:278, 14:57

Schkolnick, Meyer. *See* Merton, Robert King

Die Schlafmuetze des Propheten Elias (opera, Kreutzer). *See Die Nachtmuetze...* (opera, Kreutzer)

Die Schlafwandler (Broch), 4:191

Schlamme, Martha Haftel, 18:**138–139**

Schleiermacher, Friedrich, 18:**139**

    form criticism influenced by, 3:650

Schlesien. *See* Silesia (region)

Schlesinger, Abraham von, 7:76

Schlesinger, Adolf Martin, 18:139

Schlesinger, Akiva Joseph, 18:**139–140**

Schlesinger, Béla. *See* Szenes, Béla

Schlesinger, Benjamin, 6:32, 18:**140**

Schlesinger, Benjamin Wolf, 18:139

Schlesinger, Bruno Walter. *See* Walter, Bruno

Schlesinger, Frank, 18:**140**

Schlesinger, Georg, 18:**140–141**

Schlesinger, Guillermo, 18:**141**

Schlesinger, Ḥayyim ben Isaac. *See* KittSee, Ḥayyim ben Isaac

Schlesinger, Heinrich, 18:139

Schlesinger, Isidore William, 18:**141**

Schlesinger, Israel, 18:139

Schlesinger, Joe, 18:**141**

Schlesinger, John, 18:**141–142**

Schlesinger, Karl, 18:**142**

Schlesinger, Markus. *See* Schlesinger, Marx

Schlesinger, Marx (d. 1683), 18:139

Schlesinger, Marx (d. 1754), 18:139

Schlesinger, Mortiz Adolf, 18:139

Schlesinger, Simḥah Bunim ben Moses. *See* Eger, Simḥah Bunim ben Moses

Schlesinger family (Austria), 18:**139**

Schlesinger family (Germany), 18:**139**

Schleswig-Holstein (Germany), 13:252, 18:**142**

Schlettstadt (France). *See* Sèlestat (France)

Schlettstadt, Samuel ben Aaron, 14:480–481, 18:**142–143**

Schliefer, Solomon, 12:760, 14:518–519, 18:**143–144**

Die schlimme Botschaft (Einstein), 6:263

Schloessinger, Max, 18:**144**

Schloss, Arthur David. *See* Waley, Arthur

Schloss, Moses, 15:200

Schlossberg, Joseph, 18:**144**

Schluesselburg fortress, 13:261

Schmeling, Max, 11:48–49

Schmelkes, Gedaliah ben Mordecai, 18:**144**

Schmelkes, Isaac Judah, 8:452, 18:**144**

Schmelling-Baer boxing match, 3:52

Schmelt, Albrecht, 2:665

Schmelz, Usiel Oscar, 18:**145**

Schmerling, Louis, 18:**145**

Schmid, Anton von, 8:688–689, 13:171, 18:**145**

Schmidt, David. *See* Ephraim, David

Schmidt, Joseph, 8:504, 18:**145**

Schmidt, Karl Ludwig, 5:686, 698–699

Schmidt, Menaham. *See* Shemi, Menahem

Schmidt, Samuel Myer, 18:**145–146**

Schmidt, Simon. *See* Benador, Ury

Schmiedl, Adolf Abraham, 18:**146**

Schmitz, Ettore. *See* Svevo, Italo

Schmolka, Marie, 18:**146**

Schnabel, Artur, 18:**146–147**

Schnaittach (Germany), 18:**147**

Schnapper, Ber, 18:**147**

Schnee (Hermann), 9:24

Schneeberger, Henry William, 18:**147**

Schneersohn, Dov Baer, 18:501–502

Schneersohn, Isaac, 11:324, 18:**147–148**

Schneersohn, Joseph Isaac, 6:31, 8:397, 18:502

Schneersohn, Menachem Mendel (1902-1994), 3:6, 6:75, 15:228, 498, 18:**148–149**, 502

Schneersohn, Menaḥem Mendel (1789-1866), 18:502

Schneersohn family, 18:**147**, 148*t*

Schneesohn family, 18:501–502

Schneider, Abram Leopoldovich. *See* Schneider, Alan

Schneider, Alan, 18:**149–150**

Schneider, Alexander, 18:**150**

Schneider, Irving, 18:**150**

Schneider, Leonard Alfred. *See* Bruce, Lenny

Schneider, Mathieu, 18:**150**

Schneider, Mordecai Bezalel, 18:**150–151**

Schneider, Yossi. *See* Sarid, Yossi

Schneiderman, Harry, 18:**151**

Schneiderman, Rose, 18:**151**, 713

Schneller, Abba. *See* Khoushi, Abba

Schneurson, Zelda. *See* Zelda

Schnirer, Moritz Tobias, 11:699–700, 18:**151**

Schnittke, Alfred, 18:**151–152**

Schnitzer, Adolf, 18:**152**

Schnitzer, Eduard. *See* Emin Pasha

Schnitzer, Shmuel, 18:**152**

Schnitzler, Arthur, 18:**152**

Schocken, Amos, 18:154

Schocken, Gershon, 18:153–154

Schocken, Gustav. *See* Schocken, Gershon

Schocken, Salman, 18:153, **154–155**

as bibliophile, 3:684

Shenhar, Yitzhak, 18:459

Schocken, Theodore, 18:153

Schocken Bible, 3:623, 678

Schocken family, 18:**153–154**

Schocken Institute, 18:**155**

Schocken Library (Jerusalem), 18:155

Schocken Press, 18:153

Schoeffer, Nicolas, 18:**155**, 223

Schoem, Ira, 15:677

Schoen, Jacob, 4:186

Schoenbaum, Eliezer Isaac. *See* Ilna'e, Eliezer Isaac

Schoenberg, Alexander Julius Wilhelm, 18:**155**

Schoenberg, Arnold, 18:**155–156**

Die Jakobsleiter, 11:24

Moses, 14:543

Schoenberg, Isaac, 2:517

Schoenberger, Margaret. *See* Mahler, Margaret

Schoene, Lotte, 18:**156**

Schoenerer, Georg von, 13:252, 18:**156–157**

Schoenerer nationalism, 15:438

Die schoene Wienerin (Lorm), 13:193

Schoenfeld, Joseph, 18:**157**

Schoenfeld family. *See* Dobruschka-Schoenfeld family

Schoenhack, Joseph, 18:**157**

Schoenheimer, R., 3:765

Schoenheimer, Rudolf, 18:**157–158**

Schoenlanke (Poland). *See* Trzcianka (Poland)

Die Schoepfung (Mombert), 14:430

Schoeps, Hans Joachim, 18:**158**

Schoffmann, G., 4:159

Schoffmann, Gershon. *See* Shofman, Gershon

Scholars and scholarship

   Aggadah (Haggadah), 1:460–463

   Bohemia, 9:298

   Bulgaria, 4:270

   classical scholarship, 4:750–751, 8:185, 12:771–772

   England, 6:415–416

   Fez, Morocco, 7:7

   France, 4:750, 5:468, 7:153

   Germany, 4:750, 751, 12:615

      of Jewish culture, 16:630

   Hellenism, 6:747, 7:755

   Holocaust scholars

      Bauer, Yehudah, 3:218–219

      Berenbaum, Michael, 3:408–409

      Braham, Randolph Louis, 4:118

      Browning, Christopher R., 4:217

      Dawidowicz, Lucy, 5:483, 9:152

Dvorzetsky, Mark Meir, 6:74
Friedlaender, Saul, 7:275–276
Gutman, Israel, 8:151–152
Hilberg, Raul, 4:217, 9:100–102
Langer, Lawrence L., 12:480–481
Lanzmann, Claude, 12:487
Moreshet, 14:484–486
Novitch, Miriam, 15:320–321
Young, James E., 21:401
Israel (State), 1:460–463, 18:724
Italy, 4:750, 17:411–412
Kabbalah (mysticism), 11:673–674
Karaites, 5:465–466, 467, 11:86–87, 242, 730, 795–797
   Isaac ben Solomon, 10:49–50
   Isaiah ben Uzziah ha-Kohen, 10:77–78
   Israel ha-Dayyan ha Ma'aravi, 10:750
   Levi ben Japheth, 12:702
   Luzki, Abraham ben Joseph Solomon, 13:278
   Luzki, Joseph Solomon ben Moses, 13:278
   Luzki, Simḥah Isaac ben Moses, 13:278–279
   Menahem ben Michael ben Joseph, 14:22–23
   Poki, Judah ben Eliezer Chelebi, 16:284–285
languages and literature
   Abraham ha-Bavli, 1:312
   Alcalay, Reuven, 1:598
   Almoli, Solomon ben Jacob, 1:682, 6:399
   Auerbach, Isaac Eisig ben Isaiah, 2:654–655
   Avé-Lallemant, Friedrich Christian B., 2:720
   Avineri, Yitzhak, 2:738
   Avrunin, Abraham, 2:753–754
   Baer, Seligman Isaac, 3:53, 587–588, 631, 13:653
   Baranowicz, David Eliezer, 3:134
   Bar-Asher, Moshe, 3:137
   Barth, Jacob, 3:179
   Ben-Asher, Aaron ben Moses, 3:319–320
   Ben-Asher, Moses, 3:312, 320
   Ben Ḥayyim, Ze'ev, 3:351–352, 13:615
   Ben-Naphtali, Moses Ben David, 3:367
   Ben-Yehuda, Eliezer, 3:386–388, 8:671–673, 675, 10:683, 704–705

   Ben Ze'ev, Judah Leib, 3:391
   Blau, Joshua, 3:743–744
   Buchner, Ze'ev Wolf ben David ha-Kohen, 4:243
   Burstein, Israel, 4:301
   Campen, Johannes van, 4:383
   Castell, Edmund, 4:513
   Dotan, Aron, 5:762–763
   Even-Shoshan, Avraham, 6:575, 8:670
   Goshen-Gottstein, Moshe, 8:5
   Harkavy, Alexander, 8:357
   Ḥayyuj, Judah ben David, 8:484, 11:533, 13:39–40
   Ibn Barun, Abu Ibrahim Isaac ben Joseph, 9:661
   Ibn Janāḥ, Jonah, 8:454, 653, 9:680–683
   Ibn Quraysh, Judah, 9:688, 11:533
   Ibn Yashush, Isaac Abu Ibrahim, 9:699
   Jacob ben Ḥayyim ben Issac, 4:52, 11:32, 13:620–621
   Jacob Koppel ben Aaron Sassflower, 11:42
   Jekuthiel ben Judah ha-Kohen, 11:116–117, 13:652
   Joseph ben David ha-Yevani, 11:419–420
   Kaddari, Menahem Zevi, 11:695
   Kutscher, Edward Yechezkel, 8:649, 12:399
   Lara, David ben Isaac Cohen de, 12:492–493
   Lerner, Ḥayyim Ẓevi ben, 12:657
   Levita, Elijah, 12:730–732
   Lifshits, Shiye-Mordkhe, 13:11–12
   Mani, Ezra, 13:469–470
   Menahem ben Jacob ibn Saruq, 3:642, 6:47, 14:22
   Morag, Shlomo, 14:470–471
   Mordell, Phinehas, 14:482–483
   Moses ben ha-Nesi'ah, 14:548
   Plantavit de la Pause, Jean, 16:219
   Polotsky, Hans Jacob, 16:361–362
   Samson ha-Nakdan, 17:754
   Sarfatti, Gad B., 18:55
   Schaechter, Mordkhe, 18:102
   Schneider, Mordecai Bezalel, 18:150–151
   Schulmann, Eliezer, 18:173

   Steinberg, Joshua, 3:635, 19:187
   Warshawsky, Isaac, 20:676
   Weinreich, Uriel, 20:724
   Wizen, Moshe Aharon, 21:128
   Yalon, Hanoch, 8:640–641, 653, 21:276–277
   Yeivin, Israel, 21:298
   Zamenhof, Ludwig Lazar, 21:450–451
   Zand, Michael, 11:322, 21:454
legal, 3:353, 5:464, 17:362–363
Lisbon (Portugal), 13:80
Lithuania, 6:143
Masoretic scholars, 3:53, 8:763, 766, 11:717
medieval and modern period
   Ayalon, David, 2:759
   Baer, Gabriel, 3:52
   Billig, Levi, 3:699
   Brunschvig, Robert, 4:225
   Burckhardt, Johann Ludwig, 4:286
   Cazès, David, 4:533
   Goitein, Shlomo Dov, 7:685–686, 9:160
   Goldenthal, Jacob, 4:199, 7:702
   Goldziher, Ignaz, 7:735, 11:539, 542
   Heyd, Uriel, 9:84
   Hirschfeld, Hartwig, 9:137–138
   Horovitz, Joseph, 9:529
   Kister, Meir J., 12:205
   Landau, Jacob M., 12:463
   Levi della Vida, Giorgio, 12:703–704
   Lewis, Bernard, 6:25–26, 12:764
   Mann, Jacob, 7:466, 9:160, 13:476
   Mayer, Leo Ary, 2:371, 13:698
   Moreh, Shmuel, 14:484
   Mueller, David Heinrich, 14:597
   Piamenta, Moshe, 16:142
   Roman, Jacob ben Isaac, 17:374
   Rosenthal, Franz, 17:453
   Somekh, Sasson, 15:473, 19:7
   Stern, Samuel Miklós, 19:217
   Stillman, Norman Arthur, 19:227–228
   Weil, Gotthold, 20:711
   Weil, Gustav, 20:711
Protestants, 16:629–630

Scholars and scholarship, *continued*
　Provence (France), 16:639
　South Africa, 12:463–464
　Spain, 5:469
　Torah, 19:269–275, 20:41
　　historical aspects, 19:272–273
　　scope of, 19:271–272
　　women and, 19:273–275
　U.S., 18:723
　See also Bible scholars; Education;
　　Talmudic scholars
Scholars' Festival. *See* Lag ba-Omer
Scholars of Evreux, 10:53
Scholem, Emmy Wiechelt, 18:159
Scholem, Gershom Gerhard, 3:62–63,
　359, 9:159, 16:100–101, 102, 103,
　18:**158–159**
　forgeries, 7:126
　Kabbalah studies, 11:681–684
Scholem, Werner, 18:**159**
Scholes, Myron S., 18:**159–160**
Schomberg, Isaac, 18:160
Schomberg, Meyer Loew, 18:160
Schomberg, Ralph. *See* Schomberg,
　Raphael
Schomberg, Raphael, 18:160
Schomberg family, 18:**160**
Schon, Frank, Baron, 18:**160**
Schonberg, Al. *See* Shean, Al
Schonfeld, Andrew. *See* Shonfield, Sir
　Andrew
Schonfeld, Avigdor. *See* Schonfeld,
　Victor
Schönfeld, P. *See* Tigrid, Pavel
Schonfeld, Solomon, 18:160–161
Schonfeld, Victor, 6:205, 15:495,
　18:**160–161**
Schonfield, Hugh Joseph, 18:161
Schonwald, Dave, 15:397
Schoolman, Albert, 11:273, 18:161
Schoolman, Bertha S., 18:**161**
School of Montparnasse. *See* Paris
　school of art
School of Salerno, 13:725–726
Schools. *See* Education; Universities
Schopenhauer, Arthur, 2:560
*Schopfung und Chaos in Urzeit and
　Endzeit* (Gunkel), 8:137
Schor, Alexander Sender ben Ephraim
　Zalman, 18:**161–162**
Schor, Ephraim Solomon ben
　Naphtali Hirsch, 18:**162**
Schor, Ephraim Solomon the Elder
　ben Naphtali Hirsch. *See* Schor,
　Ephraim Solomon ben Naphtali
　Hirsch
Schor, Ilya, 18:**162**

Schor, Jacob, 18:162
Schor, Meir, 4:196–197
Schor family. *See* Wolowski family
Schorr, Abraham Ḥayyim ben
　Naphtali Ẓevi Hirsch, 18:**162**
Schorr, Baruch, 18:**162–163**
Schorr, Daniel, 18:**163**
Schorr, Friedrich, 18:**163**
Schorr, Israel, 18:163
Schorr, Joshua Heschel, 4:199, 8:761,
　18:**163–164**
　See also He-Ḥalutz (periodical)
Schorr, Mojżesz. *See* Schorr, Moses
Schorr, Moses, 18:**164**
Schorr, Naphtali Mendel, 18:**164–165**
Schorr, Osias. *See* Schorr, Joshua
　Heschel
Schorsch, Gustav, 18:**165**
Schorsch, Ismar, 6:202, 8:461, 505,
　11:331, 18:**165**
Schossberger, Eliezer, 4:182
Schott, Benedict. *See* Schottlaender,
　Bendet
Schottlaender, Bendet, 18:**165**
Schottland, Charles Irwin, 4:124,
　18:**165–166**
Schottlander, Bernard, 18:**166**
Schotz, Benno, 18:**166**
Schrader, Abe, 18:**166–167**
Schrag, Daniel P., 6:450
Schrameck, Abraham, 16:343, 18:**167**
Schramm, Hanna, 2:518
Schrecker, Paul, 18:**167**
Schreiber, Geri. *See* Spina, Geri
Schreiber, Moses Aaron, 8:735
Schreiber, Simon, 6:217
Schreiber family. *See* Sofer family
Schreiner, Abraham, 16:19–20
Schreiner, Martin, 18:**167**
Schreiner, Mordechai. *See* Schreiner,
　Martin
Schreker, Franz, 18:**167**
Schrenzel, Abraham. *See* Rapoport,
　Abraham ben Israel Jehiel ha-Kohen
Schrenzel, Moses, 18:**168**
Schrift, Shirley. *See* Winters, Shelley
Die Schrift und ihre Verdeutschung
　(Buber and Rosenzweig), 4:231
"Schrijver." *See* Mulder, Samuel Israel
Schrimm (Poland). *See* Srem (Poland)
Schrire, Velva, 18:**168**
Schroeder, Rudolf Alexander, 4:81
Schub, Moshe David, 18:**168**
Schubert, Kurt, 18:**168**
Schubert, Lia, 18:**168–169**
Schubert theaters, 11:46

Schück, Johan Henrik Emil, 12:453,
　18:**169**
Schudt, Johann Jakob, 18:**169**
Schueck, Jenö, 18:**169–170**
Schuerer, Emil, 4:250, 18:**170**
Schuhl, Pierre-Maxime, 18:**170–171**
Schulberg, Budd Wilson, 18:**171**
Die Schuldlosen (Broch), 4:191
Die Schule der Werdenden Gesellschaft
　(Karsen), 11:817
Schulhof, Isaac, 18:**171**
Schulhof, Moshe, 18:**171**
Schulhoff, Erwin, 18:171–172
Schulhoff, Julius, 18:**171–172**
Schuller, Alexander. *See* Schuller,
　Gunther
Schuller, Gunther, 18:**172**
Schulman, Kalman, 18:**172**
Schulman, Salomon, 18:94
Schulman, Samuel, 18:**172–173**
Schulmann, Eliezer, 18:**173**
Schulner, Dora. *See* Shulner, Dora
Schulsinger, Joseph, 18:**173**
Schulstein, Moses, 11:511
Schultens, Albert, 8:515, 13:57, 18:**173**
Schultz, Dutch, 18:**173–174**
Schultz, Howard, 18:**174**
Schulweis, Harold Maurice, 13:203,
　18:**174–175**
Schulz, Bruno, 18:**175**
Schulzstaffeln. *See* SS and SD
Schumacher, Gottlieb, 18:**175**
Schuman, Howard, 18:732
Schuman, William Howard, 18:**175**
Schumann, Horst, 15:**43**
Schumann, Maurice, 16:343, 18:**175–
　176**
Schumer, Charles, 15:224, 241, 18:752
Schur, Isaiah. *See* Schur, Issai
Schur, Issai, 13:678–679, 18:**176**
Schur, William. *See* Schur, Zev Wolf
Schur, Zev Wolf, 18:**176**
"Schur's lemma," 18:**176**
Schussheim, Aaron Leib, 18:**176**
Schuster, Aaron, 18:**177**
Schuster, Arthur. *See* Schuster, Sir
　Arthur
Schuster, Claude, 18:**177**
Schuster, Ernest Joseph, 18:**176**
Schuster, Felix, 18:**176–177**
Schuster, Francis Joseph, 18:**176**
Schuster, George Ernest, 18:**177**
Schuster, Henry, 18:**176**
Schuster, Joseph Samuel, 18:**176**
Schuster, Judel Joseph, 18:**176**
Schuster, Leo, 18:**176**

Schuster, Max Lincoln, 18:**177**
Schuster, Samuel, 18:176
Schuster, Samuel Judah, 18:176
Schuster, Sir Arthur, 18:**177**
Schuster, Son and Co., 18:176
Schuster family, 18:**176–177**
Schusterman, Charles, 15:398, 18:**177–179**
Schusterman, Lynn, 15:398, 18:**177–179**
Schutz, Alfred, 18:732
Schutzbrief, 5:60, 18:179
Schutzbund, Republikanischer, 18:179
Schutzer, Paul, 16:126
Schutzjuden, 7:221, 13:253, 18:87, **179**
Schutzstaffein. See SS and SD
Schutzstaffel. See SS
Schwab, Hermann, 18:179
Schwab, Joseph J., 18:**179–180**
Schwab, Löw, 18:**180**
Schwab, Moïse, 18:**180**
Schwab, Shimon, 18:**180–181**
Schwabacher, Henri Simon. See Duvernois, Henri
Schwabacher, Simeon Aryeh, 18:181
Schwabe, Max. See Schwabe, Moshe
Schwabe, Moshe, 18:181
Schwadron, Abraham, 18:**181–182**
Schwanda the Bagpiper (Weinberger), 4:193
Schwartz, Abraham Judah ha-Kohen, 18:182
Schwartz, Abraham Samuel, 18:182
Schwartz, Anna Jacobson, 18:182
Schwartz, Bernard. See Curtis, Tony
Schwartz, David, 18:183
Schwartz, Delmore, 18:183
Schwartz, Eddy, 4:277
Schwartz, Felice Nierenberg, 18:**183–184**
Schwartz, Frederic, 18:**184**
Schwartz, Gerald, 18:**184**
Schwartz, Israel Jacob, 18:**185**
Schwartz, Joseph ha-Kohen, 18:**185**
Schwartz, Joseph J., 2:61, 62, 63, 12:577, 18:**185**
Schwartz, Laurent, 18:**185–186**
Schwartz, Manfred, 18:**186**
Schwartz, Maurice, 4:278, 12:782, 18:**186–187**, 370–371, 19:680–681
Schwartz, Melvin, 18:**187**
Schwartz, Morris, 4:125
Schwartz, Phinehas Selig ha-Kohen, 18:**187**
Schwartz, Pinḥas Sigmund. See Schwartz, Phinehas Selig ha-Kohen
Schwartz, Richard J., 18:183

Schwartz, Sigmund. See Schwartz, Phinehas Selig ha-Kohen
Schwartz, Stephen, 18:**187**
Schwartz, William, 18:183
Schwartzenberg, Roger-Gerard, 18:**187**
Schwartz family. See Shaḥor family
Schwartzman, Sylvan David, 18:**188**
Schwarz, Adolf, 18:**188–189**
Schwarz, Arthur Zechariah, 18:188–189
Schwarz, Aryeh. See Schwarz, Adolf
Schwarz, Benjamin, 18:189
Schwarz, David, 1:429, 18:**189**
Schwarz, Harry Heinz, 16:349, 18:**189**
Schwarz, Ḥayyim, 4:76, 15:402
Schwarz, Leo Walder, 9:160, 18:**189–190**
Schwarz, Peter. See Nigri, Petrus
Schwarz, Rudolf, 18:**190**
Schwarz, Samuel, 18:**190**
Schwarz, Solomon, 18:**190–191**
Schwarz, Tamar, 18:189
Schwarz, Walter. See Evenari, Michael
Schwarz, Yehoseph, 18:**191**
Schwarzbard, Samuel. See Schwarzbard, Sholem
Schwarzbard, Sholem, 18:**191**
Schwarz-Bart, André, 18:**191–192**
Schwarzbart, Isaac Ignacy, 13:241, 16:347, 18:**192**
Schwarz-Bart, Simone, 18:191
Schwarzberg, Samuel Benjamin, 18:**192**
Schwarzerd, Philipp. See Melanchthon, Philipp
Schwarzfeld, Benjamin, 18:192
Schwarzfeld, Elias, 6:216–217, 18:192
Schwarzfeld, Moisi. See Schwarzfeld, Moses
Schwarzfeld, Moses, 6:216–217, 18:**192–193**
Schwarzfeld, Wilhelm, 18:193
Schwarzfeld family, 18:**192–193**
Schwarzfuchs, Simon, 11:325
Schwarzman, Asher, 18:**193**
Schwarzmann, Lev Issakovich. See Shestov, Lev
Schwarzschild, Karl, 18:193
Schwarzschild, Martin, 18:193
Schwarzschild, Steven Samuel, 18:**193–194**
Schwefelberg, Veronica. See Porumbacu, Veronica
Schweid, Eliezer, 16:102, 103, 18:**194–195**
Schweidnitz. See Swidnica (Poland)
Schweinfurt (Germany), 18:**195**

Schweinfurt, Jacob, 11:392
Schweitzer, Albert, 4:167
Schweitzer, Daniel, 16:349
Schweitzer, Eduard von, 18:**195**
Schweitzer, Helena. See Bresslau, Helena
Schweitzer, Miguel, 16:349
Schweitzer, Recha. See Freier, Recha
Schwerin-Goetz, Eliakim ha-Kohen, 18:**195**
Schwerner, Armand, 20:301
Schwerner, Michael, 15:215
Schwesig, Karl, 2:518
Schwiefert, Peter, 18:**195–196**
Schwimmer, David, 18:**196**
Schwimmer, Rosika, 18:**196**
Schwinger, Julian Seymour, 4:94, 18:**196–197**
Schwob, Marcel, 18:**197**
Sciaki, Joseph, 18:**197**
Sciaki, Pepo. See Sciaki, Joseph
Scialom, David Dario, 18:**197**
Science
    awards, Israel Prize, 10:760, 764
    Elijah ben Solomon Zalman, 6:343–345
    Israel Academy of Sciences and Humanity, 10:743
    Judaism, influence of, 11:519–520
    Judeo-Persian, 11:553–554
    Kook, Abraham Isaac, 12:292
    Leibowitz, Yeshayahu, 12:622–623
    Rabbinical attitude towards, 2:564
    Slonimski Ḥayyim Selig, 18:678–679
    See also specific disciplines
Science fiction and fantasy, Jewish. See Jewish science fiction and fantasy
The Science of Behavior and the Image of Man (Chein), 4:587
Science of Judaism. See Wissenschaft des Judentums
Scientific Liason Unit, 16:357, 358
Scientific Man vs. Power Politics (Morgenthau), 14:490
Scliar, Moacyr, 4:152, 18:**207**
Scopes monkey trial, 8:478
Scorpions, 18:**207**
Scotland, 18:**207–208**
    Gaelic translations of Bible, 3:636
Scott, C. P. See Scott, Charles Prestwich
Scott, Charles Prestwich, 18:**208**
Scott, Joan Wallach, 9:152
Scott, Sir Walter, 6:435, 18:**208**
Scott, Walter. See Scott, Sir Walter
Scotus, John Duns. See Duns Scotus, John

Scouting, 18:**208–210**
Scranton (PA), 18:**210–211**
Scranton, William, 15:283
Scriabin, 2:26
Scribes, 13:606, 609, 18:**212–213,** 212t
  Benayah family, 3:322
  biblical exegesis and study, 3:640
  calligraphy, Hebrew, 4:366–367
  education, 4:367–368, 6:167–168, 187
  halakhic sayings, 8:253
  history of, 4:366
  Meir ben Ephraim of Padua, 13:783
  Miriam bat Benayah, 14:312
  mishpat Ivri, 14:340
  See also Sefer Torah
Script, Ammonites, 2:84
Script, Hebrew. *See* Hebrew script
Scriptura Beneventana (Lowe), 13:234
Scripture. *See* Bible
Scroll of Antiochus, 9:155, 18:**213–215**
Scroll of Esther, 10:787, 18:**215–220,** *219,* vol. 15: color insert
The Scroll of Genealogies. See Megillat Aḥima'aẓ
Scroll of the Hasmoneans. See Scroll of Antiochus
Scroll of the Law. *See Sefer Torah*
Scroll of the Revealer. See Megillat ha-Megalleh
Scrolls. *See specific scrolls*
Scrolls, The Five. *See The Five Scrolls*
Scrutinium Scripturarum (Pablo de Santa Maria), 15:562
Sculpture, 18:**222–224**
  Argentina
    Blazko, Martin, 3:747
    Hannemann, Pablo, 8:326
    Kosice, Gyula, 12:319
  Austria, Ehrlich, Georg, 6:243–244
  Canada
    Etrog, Sorel, 6:541
    Frenkel, Vera, 7:258
    Levine, Les, 12:719
    Singer, Yvonne, 18:640
  Chile, Freifeld, Abraham, 7:236
  Czechoslovakia
    Beer, Samuel Friedrich, 3:254
    Gutfreund, Otto, 8:149–150
    Vogel, Karel, 20:567
  David in, 5:457
  Denmark
    Isenstein, Kurt Harald, 10:79
    Wagner, Siegfried, 20:595
  France
    Aronson, Naum, 2:488

Astruc, Zacharie, 2:627
    Bernstein-Sinaieff, Leopold, 3:486
    Bloc, André, 3:757–758
    Elkan, Benno, 6:357
    Gordon, Willy, 7:775
    Kogan, Moyse, 12:256
    Krémègne, Pinchas, 12:351
    Orloff, Chana, 15:478
    Schoeffer, Nicolas, 18:155
    Zadkine, Ossip, 21:439
  Germany
    Elkan, Benno, 6:357
    Glicenstein, Enrico, 7:636
    Kogan, Moyse, 12:256
    Kormis, Fred, 12:310
    Nossig, Alfred, 15:314
    Ullman, Micha, 20:240–241
    Zadikow, Arnold, 21:439
  Hungary
    Bokros-Birman, Dezsö, 4:43
    Engel, József, 6:409
    Schoeffer, Nicolas, 18:155
  Israel, 6:541, 734, 10:696, 697, 698–699, 18:222
    Absalon, 1:332
    Agam, Yaacov, 1:445
    Ben-Zvi, Zeev, 3:395
    Danziger, Itzhak, 5:432
    Etrog, Sorel, 6:541
    Feigin, Dov, 6:734
    Haber, Shamai, 8:175
    Kadishman, Menashe, 11:700
    Karavan, Dani, 11:803–804
    Lishansky, Batya, 13:81
    Melnikoff, Avraham, 14:13
    Palombo, David, 15:606–607
    Rapaport, Nathan, 17:92–93
    Shemi, Yehi'el, 18:458
    Sternschuss, Moshe, 19:223
    Tevet, Nahum, 19:657
    Tumarkin, Igael, 20:175
    Ullman, Micha, 20:240–241
  Italy, Glicenstein, Enrico, 7:636
  Jacob in, 11:24
  Neolithic, 11:138
  Netherlands, Da Costa, Joseph Mendes, 5:377
  Poland, Nossig, Alfred, 15:314
  Russia
    Antokolski, Mark, 2:246–247
    Aronson, Naum, 2:488
    Guenzburg, Ilya Yakovlevich, 8:122–123
    Neizvestny, Ernst, 15:66–67
    Pevsner, Anton, 16:23

Pevsner, Naum Nehemia, 16:23
    twentieth century, 16:23
  South Africa
    Kottler, Moses, 12:325
    Lipshitz, Israel, 13:75
    Meyerowitz, Herbert Vladimir, 14:152
    Wald, Herman, 20:600
  Sweden, Gordon, Willy, 7:775
  United Kingdom
    Caro, Anthony, 4:487
    Ehrlich, Georg, 6:243–244
    Elkan, Benno, 6:357
    Epstein, Jacob, 6:471–472
    Koenig, Ghisha, 12:251
    Kormis, Fred, 12:310
    Nemon, Oscar, 15:69
    Schottlander, Bernard, 18:166
    Schotz, Benno, 18:166
    Vogel, Karel, 20:567
    Werner, Michael, 21:14
    Zvia, 21:693
  U.S.
    Baizerman, Saul, 3:69
    Baskin, Leonard, 3:201
    Borofsky, Jonathan, 4:91
    Davidson, Jo, 5:476
    Etrog, Sorel, 6:541
    Ezekiel, Moses Jacob, 6:648
    Ferber, Herbert, 6:759
    Glicenstein, Enrico, 7:636
    Gross, Chaim, 8:95
    Harkavy, Minna B., 8:357–358
    Lassaw, Ibram, 12:502–503
    Lewitt, Sol, 12:769–770
    Lichtenstein, Roy, 12:799
    Lipchitz, Jacques, 13:63–64
    Lipton, Seymour, 13:77
    Margoulies, Berta, 13:530–531
    Nevelson, Louise, 15:129–130
    Rattner, Abraham, 17:114–115
    Rothstein, Irma, 17:496
    Segal, George, 18:246
    Serra, Richard, 18:314
    Simon, Sidney, 18:617
    Tewi, Thea, 19:659
    Zadkine, Ossip, 21:439
    Zorach, William, 21:669
  U.S., Nadelman, Elie, 14:723–724
  Yugoslavia, Glid, Nandor, 7:638
Sculptured Reveries. See Reverii sculptate

SD. *See* SS and SD

Sea, Song of the. See Song of the Sea

Seabees, 14:483

Seagram's, 4:205–206

Seal of Solomon. *See* Magen David

Seals, 3:656–657, 14:388, 18:**225–228**

Seamail (Herzberg), 6:71

Sea of Galilee. *See* Kinneret (Lake)

Sea of Reeds. *See* Red Sea

Sea of the Talmud, 18:**228**

Sea Peoples, 16:52

Searchlights on Delinquency (Eissler), 6:278

Seasongood, Alfred, 18:228

Seasongood, Lewis, 18:228

Seasongood, Murray, 18:228

Seasongood family, 18:**228**

Seattle (WA), 18:**229–230**

Sebag (North African surname), 18:**230**

Sebag, Hananiah, 18:230

Sebag, Isaac ben Abraham, 18:230

Sebag, Joseph, 14:459, 18:230

Sebag, Judah ben Mas'ud, 18:230

Sebag, Robert, 14:459

Sebag, Sarah Montefiore, 14:459

Sebag, Solomon, 18:230

Sebag, Solomon ben Mas'ud ben Abraham, 18:230

Sebag, Solomon ben Shalom, 18:230

Sebag-Montefiore, Harold, 14:459

Sebag-Montefiore, Oliver, 14:459

Sebag-Montefiore, T.H., 14:459

Sebag-Montefiore family. *See* Montefiore, Sebag-Montefiore family

Sebaste (ancient Israel). *See* Samaria (ancient Israel)

Sebastian, Mihail, 18:**230–231**

Sebba, Shalom, 18:**231**

Sebestyén, Artur, 8:755

Sebta (Morocco). *See* Ceuta (Morocco)

Secco, M. *See* Smilansky, Meir

Second Aliyah, 1:660, 9:247–248, 10:180–181, 194–196, 282, 334–335, 358–359, 482–485, 523, 606

    Katznelson, Berl, 12:23–26

    Luidor, Joseph, 13:254

Second City (improvisational theater company), 15:253

La Seconde Semaine (Du Bartas), 6:31

Secondhand goods and old clothes, trade in, 18:**231–232**

Second Passover, 15:679, **683**

The Second Scroll (Klein), 4:423, 12:**219**

Second Sejm (Poland), 18:256

Second Temple period

    aliyah and absorption, 10:330–333

    am ha-arez, 2:66–67

    Amidah, 2:73

    Bible, history of, 3:583–584

    destruction, 11:758

    economic history, 6:99–102

    Edom (Transjordan), 6:155–156

    education, 6:171

    Egypt, 6:229

    fruit offerings, 7:49

    Greek language, 8:57–59

    hasidim ha-rishonim, 8:390–391

    historiography, 9:154–155

    hunting and, 9:621

    leprosy, 12:652–653

    lots, 13:218–219

    money changers, 14:435–436

    Phinehas, 16:116

    Sabbatical Year and Jubilee, 17:626–628

    sacrifices, 17:644–647

    Sadducees, 17:654–655

    Samaritans, 17:720–722

    Simeon of Mizpah, 18:602

    tithe, 19:739

    See also Soferim

Second Vatican Council. *See* Vatican Council II

Second War with Rome. *See* Bar Kokhba revolt

Second Wave feminist movement, 6:753–754

Secrets of Secrets (Eleazar ben Judah of Worms), 6:304

Secret State Police. *See* Gestapo

The Sectarian Document. See Manual of Discipline

Sections, Jewish. *See* Yevsektsiya

Sects, minor, 1:312, 336, 337, 592, 4:674–675, 18:**232–233**

Secular and Religious Works (Moïse), 14:421

Secularism, 16:102

    economic impact, 6:127–129

    Humanist Jews, in Orange County, 15:461

    mishpat Ivri, 14:357

    Schechter, Joseph on, 18:102

Secularization. *See* Haskalah

Secunda, Sholom, 18:**233–234**

Secureni (Ukraine). *See* Sekiryany (Ukraine)

Securing Religious Liberty: Principles for Judicial Interpretation of the Religion Clauses (Choper), 4:666

Security for loans. *See* Suretyship

Sedaca, 4:82

Sedaka, Neil, 12:545, 18:**234**

Sedarim. *See* Mishnah

Sedarim of Bible, 13:607

Sedeh Boker (Israel), 3:346–347, 18:**234**

Sedeh Bokhim (Calahora), 4:349

Sedeh Eliyahu (Israel), 18:**234**

Sedeh Nahum (Israel), 18:**235**

Sedeh Nehemyah (Israel), 18:**235**

Sedeh Warburg (Israel), 18:**235**

Sedeh Ya'akov (Israel), 18:**235**

Seder, 15:678–679, 681–682, 18:**235**

    afikoman, 1:434

    Cup of Elijah, 6:335, 338

    Ehad mi Yode'a, 6:237

    Miriam's cup, vol. 17: color insert

    translation and commentary, 18:123

    See also Passover

Seder (Gaon), 2:105

Seder Avodah bi-Kezarah (Aldubi), 1:607

Seder de-Eliyahu (Elijah ben Raphael Solomon ha-Levi), 6:340

Seder Eliyah. See Tanna de-Vei Eliyahu

Seder Eliyahu. See Tanna de-Vei Eliyahu

Seder Eliyahu Rabbah. See Aggadat Bereshit

Seder Eliyahu Zuta (Capsali), 4:455

Seder Gittin va-Halizah (Minz), 14:303

Seder ha-Dorot (Heilprin), 3:681, 8:768–769, 9:158

Seder Halizah (Slonik), 18:675

Seder ha-Tefillot - Forms of Prayer, 16:465, 466

Seder Leil Pesa]hudot] (Shemaiah of Troyes), 18:456

Seder Mitzvot Nashim (Slonik), 18:675

Seder Olam, 4:706–707, 9:155, 18:**235–236**, 603

Seder Olam Zuta, 5:462, 18:235, 236

Sederot (Israel), 18:**236–237**

Seder plates, 16:24

Sedom. *See* Sodom and Gomorrah (ancient cities)

Sedom (Israel), 18:739

Sedot Yam (Israel), 18:**237**

Sedran, Barney, 18:**237**

Sedransky, Barney. *See* Sedran, Barney

Sedud (Israel). *See* Sarid (Israel)

Seduva (Lithuania), 18:**237**

Sée, Camille, 16:343, 18:237

Sée, Edmond, 18:**237**

Sée, Germain, 18:237

Sée, Henri, 18:237

Sée, Léopold, 18:**237–238**

See Aggadah or Haggadah
  See also Haggadah, Passover

Seeds, 14:386–387

Sée family, 18:**237**

Seekers after smooth things, 18:**238**

Die Seele und die Formen (Lukacs), 13:255

Seeligmann, Arieh. *See* Seeligmann, Isac Leo

Seeligmann, Isac Leo, 18:**238–239**

Seeligmann, Sigmund, 18:**239**

Seer of Lublin. *See* Jacob Isaac ha-Ḥozeh mi-Lublin

See-*See* partridges, 15:673

Seesen (Germany), 18:**239**

Seetzen, Ulrich Jasper, 18:**239**

Sefaradim. *See* Sephardim

Sefardi, Moisés. *See* Petrus Alfonsi

Sefardi, Mosé. *See* Petrus Alfonsi

Sefat Emet (Heidenheim), 8:763

Sefat Emet (Kirimi), 12:185

Sefat Emet u-Leshon Zehorit (Emden), 6:393

Sefat ha-Naḥal (Shapira), 18:401

Sefei Ḥemed (Medini), 13:760

Sefer Abudarham (Abudarham), 1:336

Sefer Alfa Beta (Muelhausen), 14:596–597

Sefer Asaph ha-Rofe (Asaph ha-Rofe), 2:543–544

Sefer Asheri. See Piskei ha-Rosh

Sefer Beḥinat Olam (Jedaiah ben Abraham Bedersi), 11:100

Sefer Bikkurim (Bassani), 3:207

Sefer Dikdukei ha-Teʿamim le-Rabbi Aharon ben Moshe ben Asher (Dotan), 5:762–763

Sefer Dinaburg (Dinur), 5:672

Sefer EzḤayyim (Vital), 20:547

Sefer ha-Aggadah (Bialik and Rawnitzki), 1:460, 14:491

Sefer ha-Anak (Al-Ḥarizi, Judah ben Solomon), 1:656

Sefer ha-Bahir, 3:**62–63**, 7:602–603, 11:597

Sefer ha-Baḥur (Levita), 8:444

Sefer ha-Bedihah ve-ha-Ḥiddud (Druyanow). *See The Book of Jokes and Witticisms*

Sefer ha-Beri'ah, 11:828

Sefer ha-Berit, 3:574

Sefer ha-Berit (Elijah), 6:347, 399

Sefer ha-Dema'ot (Bernfeld), 9:160

Sefer ha-Dikduk. See Kitāb al-Tashwīr (Ibn Janāaḥ, Jonah)

Sefer ha-Ebronot (Slonik), 18:675

Sefer ha-Eshkol (Abraham ben Isaac), 1:302

Sefer ha-Eshkol (Abraham ben Isaac of Narbonne), 1:302

Sefer Hafla'ah (Horowitz), 9:540–541

Sefer ha-Gallui (Saadiah), 18:213

Sefer ha-Gematriyyot (Eleazar ben Moses ha-Darshan of Wuerzburg), 6:305

Sefer ha-Gittin (Badhav), 3:49

Sefer ha-Halakhot (Alfasi), 1:639–640, 4:770

Sefer ha-Hashlamah (Meshullam ben Moses), 14:78

Sefer ha-Hassagah (Ibn Janaḥ), 8:454

Sefer ha-Ḥayyim (Ḥayyim), 8:480–481

Sefer ha-Ḥayyim (Ashkenaz), 8:386, 18:**239–240**

Sefer ha-Ḥeshbon ve-ha-Middot (Comtino), 13:674–675

Sefer ha-Ḥezyonot (Vital), 1:254, 7:15

Sefer ha-Higgayon (Luzzatto), 13:283

Sefer ha-ḥinnukh. See Ha-Ḥinnukh

Sefer ha-Ḥizzayon (Satanow), 8:724

Sefer ha-Hokhmah (Baruch), 3:190

Sefer ha-Hokhmah (Eleazar ben Judah of Worms), 6:304

Sefer ha-Huzari (Halevi), 16:83–84

Sefer ha-Ibbur (Abraham bar Ḥiyya), 1:293

Sefer ha-Ikkarim (Albo), 1:593–595, 2:531, 11:7, 14:439–440, 16:89–90

Sefer Ḥai Ro'i (Shalom), 18:377

Sefer ha-Ittim (Judah ben Barzillai al-Bargeloni), 1:302, 11:483, 484

Sefer ha-Ittur (Isaac ben Abba Mari of Marseilles), 10:37–38

Sefer ha-Kabbalah (Ibn Daud), 1:310, 2:127, 4:707, 7:12–13, 138, 8:260, 9:156, 662, 17:13

Sefer ha-Koḥah (Ḥayyuj), 8:484

Sefer ha-Ma'alot (Falaquera), 6:680–681

Sefer ha-Ma'asim Li-venei Erez Yisrael, 18:**240**

Sefer ha-Maasiyyot (Nissim), 6:527, 667, 7:12

Sefer ha-Manhig (Abraham ben Nathan ha-Yarhi), 1:309

Sefer ha-Massa le-Erez Yisrael (Bachrach), 3:39

Sefer ha-Massa'ot (Chorny), 4:668

Sefer ha-Mefo'ar (Molcho), 14:424

Sefer ha-Melizah (Solomon ben Samuel), 18:772–773

Sefer ha-Meshalim (Gikatilla), 6:668

Sefer ha-Mevakesh (Falaquera), 6:681, 16:107

Sefer Ha-Middot. See Orḥot Ẓaddikim

Sefer ha-Minhagim (Ḥayyim), 8:483

Sefer ha-Minhagim (Klausner), 12:214

Sefer ha-Minhagot (Asher ben Saul), 2:565, 4:653

Sefer ha-Mispar (Levi), 12:698

Sefer ha-Mispar (Mirzraḥi), 13:675, 14:394

Sefer ha-Mitzvot (ben Yazli'ah), 8:283, 753, 13:386–387

Sefer ha-Mitzvot (Naḥmanides), 8:259

Sefer ha-Mo'adim. See Book of Festivals

Sefer ha-Musar (Aknin), 1:570

Sefer ha-Musar (Kaspi), 13:107

Sefer ha-Navon, 8:386

Sefer ha-Nefesh (Falaquera), 6:681

Sefer ha-Ner (Aghmati), 1:465

Sefer ha-Neyar, 18:**240**

Sefer ha-Nezirim (Fraenkel), 7:144

Sefer ha-Niẓẓaḥon (Muelhausen), 13:112, 14:595–596

Sefer ha-Olam ha-Katan (Ẓaddik), 16:82, 21:438

Sefer ha-Orah (Jacob ben Jacob ha-Kohen), 11:33

Sefer ha-Osher (Jacob ben Reuben), 11:35–36

Sefer ha-Otiyyot (Agnon), 1:468

Sefer ha-Pardes, 6:326

Sefer ha-Peles. See Eshkol ha-Kofer

Sefer ha-Peli'ah (Botarel), 11:613

Sefer ha-Pitronot mi-Leipzig, 12:406

Sefer ha-Raban (Eliezer), 6:328

Sefer ha-Razim, 17:**129–130**

Sefer ha-Roke'aḥ (Eleazar ben Judah of Worms). *See Book of Wisdom* (Eleazar ben Judah of Worms)

Sefer ha-She'illot (Aḥa), 4:769

Sefer ha-She'iltot. *See She'iltot* (Aḥa of Shabḥa)

Sefer ha-Shirim (Hameiri), 8:299

Sefer ha-Shoham (Moses), 14:548

Sefer ha-Shorashim (Abraham ha-Bavli), 1:312

Sefer Ḥasidim, 7:487

Sefer Ḥasidim (Judah ben Samuel he-Ḥasid), 7:14, 8:386, 388, **392–393**, 668–670, 11:491
  captives, ransoming of, 4:457

Sefer Ḥasidim (Margalioth), 7:129

Sefer ha-Sod (Kaspi), 11:824

Sefer ha-Temunah, 11:759

Sefer ha-Temunah. See Temunah, The Book of

Sefer ha-Terumot (Sardi), 4:773

Sefer ha-Vikku'aḥ (Loebel), 8:415

Sefer ha-Yaḥas (Sikili), 18:574

Sefer ha-yah li-Khetav Ashuri ve-Toledot ha-Nekuddot ve-ha-Te'amim (Bachrach), 3:39

Sefer ha-Yakar (Donnolo), 13:725

Sefer ha-Yalkut (Abraham ben Daniel), 1:295

Sefer ha-Yare'ah (Abba Mari ben Moses ben Joseph Astruc of Lunel), 1:230

Sefer ha-Yashar, 1:286–287, 6:6, 7:11, 12:433, 14:188–189, 18:**240–241**

Sefer ha-Yashar (Abraham ben Daniel), 1:295

Sefer ha-Yeḥud (Asher ben David), 2:563

Sefer ha-Yuḥasin (Zacuto), 21:434

Sefer Ḥayyat al-Rukh (Melamed), 14:6

Sefer ha-Ẓara (Elijah ben Solomon Zalman), 6:345

Sefer ha-Zekhut (Naḥmanides), 14:742

Sefer ha-Zikhronot, 14:345–346

Sefer ha-Zohar (de Leon), 1:344

Sefer ha-Ẓoref (Ẓoref), 18:354

Sefer ha-Ẓoref (Zoref), 1:378

Sefer Ḥefeẓ (ben Yazli'ah), 8:753

Sefer Heikhalot, 11:592

Sefer Higgayon al Derekh She'elot u-Teshuvot (Elijah ben Eliezer Philosoph ha-Yerushalmi), 6:339

Sefer Hitabbekut (Emden), 6:393

Sefer Ḥukkei ha-Torah, 18:**241**

Sefer Ḥukkim u-Mishpatim (Aknin), 1:569

Sefer Josippon. See Josippon

Sefer Kerovot (Heidenheim), 8:763

Sefer Leshem Shevo ve-Aḥlamah (Eliashov), 6:320

Sefer Limmudei Aẓilut (Sarug), 13:264

Sefer Ma'aseh Ḥoshev (Levi), 12:698

Sefer Mafte''aḥ Manulei ha-Talmud (Nissim ben Jacob ben Nissim Ibn Shahin), 15:279

Sefer Maḥazikei ha-Dat (Lipschitz), 13:71

Sefer Mareh Einayim (Bahlul), 3:64

Sefer Massa' Teiman. See Even Sappir

Sefer Me'irat Einayim (Falk), 6:686

Sefer Mesharim (Jeroham ben Meshullam), 11:142

Sefer Mikhlol (Kimḥi), 13:33–34

Sefer Milhamot Adonai (Reuben), 2:265

Sefer Milḥamot Adonai (Levi ben Gershom), 12:698, 701, 16:88

Sefer Milḥamot ha-Shem (Kafah), 11:703

Sefer Mitzvot Gadol (Moses of Coucy), 4:773, 9:73, 14:394, 549–550, 19:179–180

Sefer Mitzvot Katan (Isaac ben Joseph of Corbeil), 10:43

Sefer Mitzvot Katan (Perez ben Elijah of Corbeil), 15:769–770

Sefer Mordekhai (Mordecai ben Hillel ha-Kohen), 14:480–481

Sefer Netivot ha-Shalom (Mendelssohn), 14:34

Sefer Niẓẓaḥon Yashan, 5:692

Sefer Olam Barur (Eliezer Fischel ben Isaac of Strzyzow), 6:330

Sefer Olam Eḥad (Eliezer Fischel ben Isaac of Strzyzow), 6:330

Sefer Olam Hafukh (Eliezer Fischel ben Isaac of Strzyzow), 6:330

Sefer Olam ha-Gadol (Eliezer Fischel ben Isaac of Strzyzow), 6:330

Sefer Peratei Peratin (Abulafia), 1:341

Sefer Raza Rabba, 17:**128**

Sefer Razi'el. See Raziel, Book of

Sefer Refu'ot (Abraham ben Josiah Troki), 1:303

Sefer Refu'ot (Markuse), 8:441

Sefer Sha'arei Ẓedek (Gikatilla), 7:593–594

Sefer Sha'ashu'im (Ibn Zabara), 6:667

Sefer Shemuel. See Shmuel-Bukh

Sefer Shimmush (Emden), 6:393

Sefer Taḥkemoni (Al-Ḥarizi), 1:656, 8:660

Sefer Toledot ha-Teva (Abramovitsh), 1:320

Sefer Toledot Yeshu. See Toledot Yeshu

Sefer Torah, 4:547, 18:**241–243**, 744, 20:50

  breastplate, 4:156
  correction, emendation, 8:216–220
  hagbaha, gelilah, 8:207
  haggahot, 8:217–218

Sefer va-Yedabber, 18:565

Sefer Vikku'aḥ (Loebel), 13:161

Sefer Yehoshu'a (Babad), 3.14

Sefer Yemin Moshe (Caregal), 4:468

Sefer Yere'im (Eliezer ben Samuel of Metz), 6:329

Sefer Yeẓirah, 1:287, 11:595–596, 13:671, 21:**328–331**

  amulets, 2:121
  Dunash Ibn Tamim, 6:48, 49
  Elhanan ben Yakar, 6:316
  Judah ben Barzillai al-Bargeloni, 11:483, 484
  Latif, Isaac B. Abraham ibn, 12:507
  Mordell, Phinehas, 14:482–483

Sefer Yosef (Hoffmann), 9:312

Sefer Yuḥasin, 13:109, 770

Sefer Ẓaḥot (Ibn Ezra), 13:41

Sefer Ẓaḥot (Saadia Gaon), 8:652, 653

Sefer Zekhirah. See Book of Remembrance

Sefer Zeraḥ (Bali), 3:90

Sefer Zerubbavel, 7:10

Sefer Zikkaron (Kimḥi), 13:41

Sefer Zot, 18:565

Sefirah. *See* Omer

Ṣefirah, Saadiah ben Joseph, 18:**243–244**

Sefire, treaty of, 5:251

Sefirot, 7:664–665, 11:627–635, 12:437, 18:**244**

  contemplation of, 5:220–221, 12:645, 13:761, 762
  development of, Shabbatean influence on, 11:43
  menorah as symbol of, 14:52–53
  Shekhinah and, 18:442

Seforim, Mendele Mokher. *See* Abramovitsh, Sholem Yankev

Sefwi Sui and Sefwi Wiawso, 9:569–570

Segal, Arthur, 18:**244**

Segal, Bernard, 18:**244–245**

Segal, Bernard Gerard, 12:556, 18:**245**

Segal, D. *See* Singer, Isaac Bashevis

Segal, Erich, 18:**245**

Segal, Esther, 18:**245**

Segal, Gedaliah ben Eliezer, 18:**246**

Segal, George (1924-2000), 18:223, **246**

Segal, George (1934–), 18:**246**

Segal, H. C., 2:50

Segal, Hugh, 18:**246–247**

Segal, Isaac, 8:355

Segal, J. J., 4:426

Segal, Jacob Isaac, 18:**247**

Segal, Jekuthiel Zalman, 8:355

Segal, Joseph, 8:355

Segal, Judah Ḥasid. *See* Judah Ḥasid, ha-Levi

Segal, Louis, 18:**247**

Segal, M. H., 3:650, 8:640–641

Segal, M. Z., 3:647, 8:574

Segal, Marc. *See* Chagall, Marc

Segal, Moses, 8:355

Segal, Moses Hirsch, 13:59, 14:330, 18:**247–248**

Segal, Pinchas. *See* Pinchik, Pierre

Segal, Robin David. *See* Benson, Robby

Segal, Samuel, Baron, 18:**248**

Segal, Simon, 15:650

Segal, Uri, 18:**248**

Segal, Zevi. *See* Segal, Moses Hirsch

Segall, Lasar, 18:**248–249**

Segall, Lazar, 4:152

Segalowitch, Zusman, 18:**249**

Segan ha-Kohanim. *See* Ḥanina Segan ha-Kohanim

Segan Leviyyah. *See* Isaac ben Eliezer

Seghers, Anna, 18:**249**

Segni, Lothair of. *See* Innocent III

Segorbe (Spain), 18:**249–250**

Segovia (Spain), 18:**250–251**

Segre, Abraham ben Judah (17th-18th c.), 18:251

Segre, Abraham ben Judah (d. 1772), 18:251

Segre, Abraham ben Zerah, 18:251

Segrè, Arturo, 18:**251**

Segrè, Beniamino, 18:**251**

Segrè, Corrado, 18:**251**

Segre, Dino. *See* Pitigrilli

Segre, Don. *See* Pitigrilli

Segre, Elisha, 18:251

Segrè, Emilio Gino, 18:**251–252**

Segrè, Gino, 18:**252**

Segre, Ḥayyim, 18:251

Segre, Jacob ben Isaac, 18:251

Segre, Joshua Benzion (1729-1809). *See* Segre, Salvatore (1729-1809)

Segrè, Joshua Benzion (c. 1705-c. 1797), 18:252

Segre, Judah, 18:251

Segre, Nethanel, 18:251

Segre, Nethanel ben Aaron Jacob, 18:251

Segrè, Roberto, 18:**252**

Segrè, Salvador (c.1705-c.1797). *See* Segrè, Joshua Benzion (c.1705-c.1797)

Segre, Salvatore (1729-1809), 18:**252–253**

Segre family, 18:251

Segrè family. *See* Segre family

Segullat Melakhim (Abraham ben Simeon of Worms), 1:310

Seiber, Mátyás György, 18:**253**

Seid, Ruth, 18:**253**

Seiffert, Ernst. *See* Tauber, Richard

Seigel, Joshua, 18:**253–254**

Seinfeld (television show), 5:463–464, 13:222, 15:228, 18:254

Seinfeld, Jerry, 13:222, 15:228, 18:**254**

Seini (Romania), 18:**254**

Seipel, Ignaz, 18:**254–255**

Seir. *See* Esau

Seir, Land of. *See* Edom (Transjordan)

Seir, Mount (ancient Israel), 18:**255**

Seitlin, Rose, 4:212

Seixas, Abraham Mendes (broker), 18:255

Seixas, Abraham Mendes (revolutionary war officer), 18:255

Seixas, Benjamin Mendes, 15:197, 18:255

Seixas, David G., 18:256

Seixas, Gershom Mendes, 6:189–190, 9:156, 15:197, 198, 18:255

Seixas, Hayman, 15:198

Seixas, Isaac Mendes, 18:255

Seixas, Moses Mendes, 4:15, 18:255–256

Seixas, Rachel, 11:393

Seixas family, 18:**255–256**

Seize the Day (Bellow), 3:301

Sejera (Israel). *See* Ilaniyyah (Israel)

Sejm, 4:89, 18:**256**

    Jewish Socialist Workers' Party, 11:314–315

    Minority Bloc, 14:287

Sekhel. *See* Reason

Sekhel Tov (Menahem ben Solomon), 14:23

Sekiryany (Ukraine), 18:**256–257**

Sela, Michael, 13:11, 18:**257**

Sela ha-Yehudim (Crimea). *See* Chufut-Kale (Crimea)

Selbstbewusstsein und Persoenlichkeitsbewusstein (Schilder), 18:133

Selbstemanzipation (newspaper), 18:**257–258**

Selbstwehr (newspaper), 18:**258**

Selden, John, 8:515, 18:**258–259**

Seldes, George, 18:**259**

Seldes, Marian, 18:**259**

Seldin, Harry M., 18:**259–260**

Selected Poems and Fables: An English/Yiddish Collection (Miransky), 14:311

Selected Works (Lipsky), 13:75–76

Selection and New Poems (Mishol), 14:331

Selekman, Benjamin Morris, 18:**260**

Sélestat (France), 18:**260**

Seleucia, 18:**260**

Seleucia (Iraq), 3:24, 26, 18:260

Seleucia (Transjordan), 18:260

Seleucid Acra. *See* Acra

Seleucid dynasty, 5:423, 424

Seleucid Empire, 5:549–550, 18:601

    Osroene, 15:506

Seleucid Era, 18:**260**

Seleucus IV Philopator, 18:**260–261**

Self-consuming Artifacts (Fish), 7:58

Self-control, in sex, 18:329

Self-defense, 18:**261–264**

    Ananyev, 2:130

Lancut, 12:455

legal ruling, 2:596–597

Slonim, 18:676

Self-Defense (newspaper). *See* *Selbstwehr* (newspaper)

Self-hatred, Jewish. *See* Jewish self-hatred

Self-incrimination, 5:147–148

    See also Confessions

Self Portrait (Ray), 17:126

Self-Portrait (Soutine), vol. 2: color insert

Self Portrait with Cows Going Home (Plachy), 16:210

Selig, Allan H., 18:**265**

Selig, Bud. *See* Selig, Allan H.

Selig, Gottfried, 11:523

Selig, Phineas, 18:**265**

Seligman, Brenda Zara, 18:266

Seligman, Charles Gabriel, 18:**266, 267**

Seligman, Edwin Robert Anderson, 18:**266–267**

Seligman, Herbert Spencer, 18:**267**

Seligman, Isaac Newton, 2:49, 4:19, 15:211, 18:266

Seligman, Jesse, 18:266

Seligman, Joseph, 15:200, 211, 18:266

Seligman, Margaret, 12:768

Seligman family, 18:**266**

Seligmann, Aron (elder), 6:252

Seligmann, Aron (younger), 6:252

Seligmann, Aron Elias, 6:252

Seligmann, Caesar, 18:**267**

Seligmann, Elias, 6:252

Seligmann, Kurt, 15:648, 18:**267–268**

Seligmann, Lemle, 6:252

Seligmann, Liebmann, 6:252

Seligmann, Mayer, 6:252

Seligsberg, Alice Lillie, 18:**268**

Seligson, Esther, 18:**268**

Seliḥot

    in Alsace, 2:6

    Elijah ben Shemaiah, 6:340

    piyyut and, 16:194

    See also Forgiveness

Seliḥot, 18:**268–269**, *269*

Selikman, Benjamin M., 20:337

Selikovitch, George, 18:**269–270**

Selim I, 15:523, 18:**270**

Selim II, 18:**270**

Seljuks, 10:159, 18:**270–271**

Selke, Naphtali Hirz ben Judah. *See* Hirshel, Meyer

Sella, Aviem, 16:357, 358

Sellers, Peter, 18:**271–272**

Sellin, Ernst, 18:**272**

Seltzer, Louis Benson, 18:**272**

Selucid Empire, 3:25–26, 9:193

Selvinski, Ilya Lvovich, 18:**272–273**

Selz, Otto, 18:**273**

Selznick, David Oliver, 18:273

Selznick, Lewis B., 18:273

Selznick, Myron, 18:273

Selznick family, 18:**273**

Semag. See Sefer Mitzvot Gadol

Semah, David, 15:473

Semahes, Solomon ben Jacob, 4:189

Semaḥot, 18:**273–274**

La Semaine (Du Bartas), 6:31

Semak. See Isaac ben Joseph of Corbeil

Se-Ma-K. See Sefer Mitzvot Katan

SeMaK (Perez ben Elijah of Corbeil). *See Sefer Mitzvot Katan* (Perez ben Elijah of Corbeil)

Seman, Philip Louis, 18:**274**

Semenovich, Yakov. *See* Kanovich, Grigory

Semikhah, 3:**397–398**, 12:702, 16:330, 18:**274–279**

Semilian, Savin Solomon, 18:**279**

Séminaire Israélite de France, 12:615, 18:**279–280**

Seminaries, rabbinical. *See* Rabbinical seminaries

Seminario Docente para Escuelas Israelitas. *See* Midrashah (Argentina)

Seminary of Judaic Studies. *See* Schechter Institute of Jewish Studies

Seminomadism, 15:294, 295–296

Semites, 16:119, 18:**280**

Semitic, Aryan races, 17:46–47

Semitic Action, 4:393

Semitic languages, 18:**280–286**, 283*t*

   Akkadian language, 1:564–569

   Ammonites, 2:84

   Amorites, 2:96

   Anath, 2:131

   Asherah, 2:131

   Barth, Jacob, 3:179–180

   Bergstraesser, Gotthelf, 3:433

   Caquot, Andre, 4:458

   Ebla (Syria), 6:85–86

   Eblaite, archaeological site in northern Syria, 6:85–87

   Finkel, Joshua, 7:31–32

   Leslau, Wolf, 12:663

   Lidzbarski, Mark, 12:802

   linguistics, 3:216

   Moscati, Sabatino, 14:515

   West Semitic, 16:119

Semitic Writing (Driver), 6:22

Semler, Johann, 3:649

Semlin (Yugoslavia). *See* Zemun (Yugoslavia)

Semmel, Bernard, 18:**286**

Semon, Felix. *See* Semon, Sir Felix

Semon, Richard Wolfgang, 18:**286**

Semon, Sir Felix, 18:**286**

Semyatitski, Chaim. *See* Siemiatycki, Chaim

Senaah, 18:**286–287**

Sen Astruc de Noves. *See* Abba Mari ben Eligdor

Senator, David Werner, 18:**287**

Senator, Hermann, 18:**287**

Senators

   Boxer, Barbara, 4:108

   Feinstein, Diane, 4:108

   Lautenberg, Frank R., 12:528–529

   Levin, Carl, 12:707

   Lieberman, Joseph, 12:804–805

   Neuberger, Richard Lewis, 15:116

Sender, Anne, 15:308

Sender, Ruth Minsky, 4:631

Sender Blank un Zayn Gezindl (Shalom Aleichem), 18:380

Senderey, Israel. *See* Drapkin, Israel

Sender Minsker. *See* Polachek, Sender

Sendler, Irena, 18:**287**

Sendrey, Alfred, 18:**287**

Die Sendung Mosis (Schiller), 14:540

Seneca the Elder, 18:**287–288**

Seneca the Younger, 13:247, 18:**288**

Sened, Alexander, 18:**288**

Sened, Yonat, 18:288

Seneh. *See* Burning bush

Seneor, Abraham, 12:438, 18:250, **288–289**

Senigallia (Italy), 18:**289**

Senior, Abraham. *See* Seneor, Abraham

Senior, Max, 18:**289**

Senior, Solomon, 18:**289**

Senior services, 4:15

Senir (stream), 11:401, 402

Seniri, Isaac ben Judah ha-. *See* Isaac ben Judah ha-Seniri

Senko, Yasue, 18:**289**

Senlis (France), 18:**289**

Sennabris (Galilee), 18:**289–290**

Sennacherib, 1:421, 6:281, 369, 14:90–91, 18:**290**

Señorita (Eichelbaum), 6:245

Sens (France), 18:**290–291**

Sense of Injustice (Cahn), 4:338

Senta (Hungary), 18:**291**

Sentences, Hebrew. *See under* Hebrew grammar

Separation of powers, 18:**291–292**

Separatist Orthodoxy, 4:171, 15:493–494

Sepharad (Lydia), 18:**292**

Sepharadim. *See* Sephardim

Sephardic Brotherhood of America, 2:34

Sephardic Home for the Aged, 18:303

Sephardic House, 2:64

Sephardi Diaspora (20th c.), 18:302

Sephardi language. *See* Ladino

Sephardim, 2:571, 18:**292–305**, *293*

   alphabet, Hebrew, 1:699, 703*t*, 708, 714*t*

   Amsterdam, 2:108–110, 110, 111, 114, *116*, 117

   amulets, 2:122

   Argentina, 2:427, 430, 433, 437, 445, 447

   arts, Sabbath, 17:621

   betrothals and, 3:541–542

   Bible cantillation, 13:658, 664

   birth customs and folklore, 3:722

   burial customs, 4:293–294

   Canada, Montreal, 14:464

   Caribbean, Spanish-Portuguese Nation of the: La Nacion, 4:476

   Chile, 4:638–639, 640, 641, 643

   China, 18:396

   communities of Jews, Israel (state), 10:294–295

   Cuba, 5:317

   demography, 5:571

   Dutch literature and, 6:69

   eclipse of, 18:300–301

   England, 6:414–415

      London, 13:180, 181

   Erez Israel

      Chelouche family, 4:590

      Elmaleh, Abraham, 6:364

   Europe, 9:222

   expulsions, 18:*293*

   Fesela, 6:765

   France, pre-French Revolution, 7:253–254

   Greece, 10:5–6

      Larissa, 12:494

      Salonika, 17:700–701

   ḥalukkah, 8:288, 289–290

   Hamburg community, 8:295–296

   ḥameẓ, 8:302

   Ḥisdai ibn Shaprut, 9:145

   history of, 18:292–294

   Holocaust, 18:301

   Israel (Mandate), 18:303

   Israel (Ottoman), 18:303

Sephardim, *continued*
Israel (state), 18:303–304
Eliyahu, Mordecai, 6:355
religious schools, 10:633
Shas (political party), 18:419–420
Istanbul (Ottoman period), 10:774, 775, 777–778
Jacob Saul ben Eliezer Jeroham Elyashar, 6:371–372
in Jerusalem, 11:172–173
chief rabbis, 13:601
Elazar, Ya'akov, 6:289–290
Franco, Raphael, 7:176–177
Kaddish, 11:697
Ladino literature, 4:629–630
language, 12:427–435, 18:294
Latin America, 12:510–511
laws and legal systems
Berurei Averah/Averot, 3:492
ma'amad, 13:305
literature, 3:176, 12:493, 18:294–295
modern period, early, economic history, 6:118
Monmouth County (NJ), 14:447
music, 10:814
New York, 2:147
Palestine (Ottoman), 10:295, 619–621
post-WW I, 18:301
post-WW II, 18:301–302
prominent families, Meldola, 14:12
rabbis, dress, 6:15
religious practices, 18:295–296
reorganization, 9:223
rites and rituals, liturgy, 13:135–136
secularization of laws, 18:296–300
Spain
emigration from, 18:*293*
language, 12:427–435
Quincentennial anniversary of expulsion, 18:304–305
Syria, Aleppo, 1:614
traditional cookery style, 7:118
U.S., 18:302–303
Seattle, 18:229
Venezuela, 4:459
Caracas, 4:459–460
Yugoslavia, Alcalay, Isaac, 1:598
Sephardi prosody, 11:13
Sephardi Report (periodical), 2:64
Sephardi Torah Guardians. *See* Shas (political party)
Sepharvaim (ancient Israel), 2:126, 18:**305**

Sephiha, Haim Vidal, 18:**306**
Sepphoris (Galilee), 11:370, 371, 18:**306–307**
September 11, 2001 terrorist attacks
American Israel Public Affairs Committee, 2:52
Bush, George W., 4:304
New York City, 15:225
September 11, 2001 terrorist attacks, Victim Compensation Fund, 6:737–738
Septimius Severus. *See* Severus, Septimius
Septuagint, 3:595–598, 652, 660, 666, 11:717, 18:**307**
Josephus' *Jewish Antiquities* and, 11:438
Letter of Aristeas, 2:456
Pharos translation, 16:32
Samaritan Pentateuch and, 15:754
The Septuagint version of Issiah (Seeligmann), 18:238
Sepulchers. *See* Tombs and tombstones
Sepúlveda (Spain), 18:**307**
Sequeira, Jacob de. *See* Rodrigues, Bartholomew
Sequeyra, John de, 18:**307–308**
Seradz (Poland). *See* Sieradz (Poland)
Serafimovicz, Simeon, 6:426–427
Seraiah, 18:**308**
Seraiah (captain of Judean forces), 18:308
Seraiah (chief priest), 18:308
Seraiah (officer of King Jehoiakim), 18:308
Seraiah (son of Neriah), 18:308
Serajevo (Bosnia-Herzegovina). *See* Sarajevo (Bosnia-Herzegovina)
Seraph, 18:**308**
Seraph (semidivine being), 18:308
Seraph (serpent), 18:308
Seraphim, 2:150
Serapion Brothers, 13:260
Serbia
Albala, David, 1:582
emancipation, 6:381
Holocaust, 9:339–340
Belgrade, 3:288–289
Subotica, 19:283
Zrenjanin, 21:671–672, 672
language, biblical translation, 3:635
literature, 5:444
museums, 14:629
Niš, 15:274–275
Novi Sad, 15:320

Serbo-Croatian children's literature, 4:635
Zionism, 1:663
Serbin, Hyman, 18:**308**
Serbo-Croatian language. *See* Croatia, language; Serbia, language
Serbu, Ieronim, 18:**308**
Ser Daniel, Leone de. *See* Romano, Judah ben Moses ben Daniel
Sered, Susan Starr, 18:736
Serekh, 18:**308–309**
Sereni, Ada, 18:309
Sereni, Angelo Piero, 18:**309**
Sereni, Enzo Ḥayyim, 18:**309**
Serenus. *See* Severus
Serero, David, 2:31
Serero, Emanuel ben Menahem, 18:309, 310
Serero, Ḥayyim David (1750-1826), 18:310
Serero, Ḥayyim David (d. 1968), 18:310
Serero, Jacob, 18:310
Serero, Jonathan ben Ḥayyim David, 18:310
Serero, Joseph ben Raphael Joshua Zion, 18:310
Serero, Joshua (1670-1740), 18:**309–310**
Serero, Joshua (1748-1819), 18:310
Serero, Judah, 18:310
Serero, Mattathias (1806-1891), 18:310
Serero, Mattathias (d. 1935), 18:310
Serero, Mattathias ben Menahem, 18:310
Serero, Menahem, 18:310
Serero, Menahem ben David, 18:309
Serero, Naḥman, 18:310
Serero, Saul, 18:**310**
Serero, Saul ben David, 18:309
Serero family, 18:**309–310**
Sereth. *See* Siret (Romania)
Serf, Monique. *See* Barbara
Serfaty, Benazar, 16:349
Serghi, Cella, 18:**310**
Sergius IV, 16:372
Serhatlya, Suljo. *See* Krauskopf, Friedrich Salamo
Seri, Dan Benaya, 18:**310–311**
Seridei Esh (Weinberg), 20:717
Sering, Max, 18:**311**
Serkin, Jeanette, 15:605
Serkin, Max, 15:605
Serkin, Peter Adolf, 18:**311**
Serkin, Rudolf, 18:**311**
Serl bas Jacob ben Wolf Kranz, 18:**311–312**

Serling, Rod, 18:**312**

Serman. *See* Homiletic literature

The Sermon. See Ha-Derashah

Sermoneta, Joseph Baruch, 18:**312**

Sermons. *See* Homiletic literature; Preaching

Sermons to Jews, 18:**312–313**

    See also Preaching

Seror, Joseph (d. 1625), 18:313

Seror, Joseph (d. 1755), 18:313

Seror, Raphael Jedidiah Solomon ben Joshua ben Solomon, 18:313

Seror, Solomon, 18:313

Seror, Solomon ben Tobias, 18:313

Seror, Tobias, 18:313

Seror family, 18:**313**

Serota, Beatrice, 16:343

Seroussi, Elías, 18:**313–314**

Seroussi, Raphael, 18:313–314

Serov, Valentin, 18:314

SERP. *See* Jewish Socialist Workers' Party

Serpec (Poland). *See* Sierpc (Poland)

Serpent, copper. *See* Copper serpent

Serpents. *See* Snakes

Serpent's Walk (Caverhall), 18:202

Serra, Richard, 18:314

Serrai (Greece), 18:**314–316**

Serrarius, Peter, 18:346

Serravalle (Italy). *See* Vittorio Veneto (Italy)

Serres (France), 18:**316**

Serres (Greece). *See* Serrai (Greece)

Serubabel (periodical), 12:8

Serusi, Abraham, I, 18:316

Serusi, Abraham, II, 18:316

Serusi, Ḥai, 18:316

Serusi family, 18:**316**

Seruya, Isaac, 18:316

Seruya, Jacob, 18:316

Seruya, Solomon, 18:316

Seruya, Solomon (1926–), 18:316

Seruya family, 18:**316**

Servant of the Lord, 18:**316**

Servant of the Lord image, 10:71–72

Servants, 12:412–415

Servants of Solomon. *See* Solomon, Servants of

Servants of the Royal Chamber. *See* Servi Camerae Regis

Serverus, Marcus Aurelius Alexander. *See* Severus, Alexander

Servetus, Michael, 4:376

Servetus, Miguel. *See* Servetus, Michael

Servi, Ephraim. *See* Servi, Flaminio

Servi, Ferruccio, 18:317

Servi, Flaminio, 18:**316–317**

Servi Camerae Nostrae. *See* Servi Camerae Regis

Servi Camerae Regis, 16:289–293, 18:**317**

Service cooperatives, 5:210

Services. *See* Daily services; Liturgy

Servitudes, 18:**317–318**

Sessa, Karl Borromaeus Alexander, 18:**318**

Sesso, Salamone da, 18:**318**

Seter, Mordechai, 11:569, 18:**318–319**

Seth, 15:394, 18:**319**

Sethos I. *See* Seti I

Seti I, 18:**319–320**

The "Settlement" Cookbook (Kander), 5:201

Settlement houses, 18:**320**

Settlement movements (Israel). *See* Gush Emunim; Gush Etzyon

The Settlement of the Jews in North America (Daly & Kohler), 9:161

Setubal (Portugal), 18:**320–321**

Setubal, "Messiah" of. *See* Dias, Luis

Setumot of Bible, 13:607

Setzer, Aaron. *See* Aaron ben Elijah ha-Kohen

Se'udah, 18:**321–322**

Se'udah shelishit, 18:**322**

Se'udat livyatan, 18:**322**

Sevaʿ (Saudi Arabia). *See* Sabea (Saudi Arabia)

Sevarah, 14:338, 18:**322–323**

Sevastopol (Ukraine), 18:**324**

Seven (number), 15:335

Seven Arts Feature Syndicate, 4:119

Seven Books of Histories Against the Pagans (Orosius). *See Historiarum adversum paganos libri septem*

Seven Communities. *See* Mattersdorf (Austria)

Seven-fold Pillars. See Ammudei Sheva

Seven Noachide laws. *See* Noachide laws

Seven species, 3:163, 7:18, 116

Seventh Day Adventists, 11:520

Seventh of Adar, 1:**382–383**

Seventh Palestinian Conference, 10:275

Seventh Year (tractate). *See Shevi'it* (tractate)

Seventy (number), 15:336

Seventy Shepherds, Vision of. *See* Vision of Seventy Shepherds

Seven Wicks. See Sheva Petilot

Seven Year Itch (motion picture), 14:450

"Seven Zamero sons." *See* Benzamero

Sever, Alexandru, 18:**325**

Severan Dynasty, 10:151–153

Severence pay, 8:166–168, 12:413–414, 415

Severus, 18:**325**

Severus, Alexander, 18:**325**

Severus, Lucius Septimius. *See* Severus, Septimius

Severus, Septimius, 4:458, 11:502, 18:**325**

Severus, Sextus Julius. *See* Julius Severus

Sevilla (Spain). *See* Seville (Spain)

Seville (Spain), 18:**325–329**

Sevirin, 13:618

Sevitzky, Fabien, 18:**329**

Šewa, 13:633–634, 636–637, 651–652

Sewage and human waste, 6:93–94

Sex, 18:**329**

    See also Sexual offenses

sex, lies and videotape (motion picture), 18:737

Sexagesimal system, 15:333

Sexism. *See* Feminism

Sex Laws and Customs in Judaism (Epstein), 6:475

Sex of the Soul (Mopsik), 14:470

Sextus Empiricus, 18:**329**

Sextus Julius Severus. *See* Julius Severus

Sexual behavior. *See* Sex

Sexual degradation, 18:333

Sexual ethics

    in Bible, 6:532–533

    forbidden relationships, 6:691–692, 9:516

Sexual imagery, 18:442–443

Sexuality

    Boteach, Shmuel, 4:101

    Brandeau, Esther, living disguised as boy, 4:121

    Hirschfeld, Magnus, 9:138–139

    Jonathan and David, love between, 11:396

    Joseph and Potiphar's wife, 11:407, 411, 413

    niddah, 15:253, 254, 255, 257

    Nuremberg laws, 15:348, 349

    onanism, 15:426–427

    Trees of Life and of Knowledge in Eden narrative, 15:625

Sexual offenses, 18:**329–332**

    Phinehas, 16:114–115

Sexual relations

    abstinence, 4:582

    commandments concerning, 5:83t–84t

Sexual relations, *continued*
Holiness Code, 9:319
illicit, 12:739
Seymour, Chim. *See* Seymour, David
Seymour, David, 16:126, 18:**332**
Seymour, Jane, 18:**332–333**
Seyss-Inquart, Arthur, 18:**333**
Sezer, Robert, 15:474
Sfaira der Alte (Mombert), 14:430
Sfard (Lydia). *See* Sardis (Lydia)
Sfard, David, 18:**333**
Sforno, Hananel, 18:334
Sforno, Obadiah, 4:48
Italian biblical study and exegesis, 3:663
Sforno, Obadiah ben Israel, 18:334
Sforno, Obadiah ben Jacob, 18:**333–334**
Sforno, Shemaiah ben Nissim, 18:334
Sha'agat Aryeh (Gunzberg), 8:137–138
Sha'agat Aryeh (Modena), 14:409
Shaalabbin. *See* Shaalbim
Shaalbim, 18:**334**
Sha'al ha-Ish (Elyashar), 6:372
Sha'alu Shelom Yerushalayim (Plotzki), 16:241
Sha'alu Shelom Yerushalayim (Gedalliah), 7:408
Sha'alu Shelom Yerushalayim (Kahanov), 11:716
Shaanan, Avraham, 18:**334–335**
Sha'ar Efraim (Ha -Kohen), 2:538
Sha'ar Efrayim (Ephraim ben Jacob ha-Kohen), 6:459
Sha'arei Dimah (Albelda), 1:588
Sha'arei Dura (Dueren), 6:41–42
Sha'arei ha-Avodah (Aaron ben Moses ha-Levi of Starosielce), 1:216
Sha'arei ha-Yiḥud ve-ha-Emunah (Aaron ben Moses ha-Levi of Starosielce), 1:216
Sha'arei Ḥokhmah (Edels), 6:144
Sha'arei Musar Haskel. See Musar Haskel
Sha'arei Ne'imah (Dubno), 6:34
Sha'arei Orah (Gikatilla), 7:593
Sha'arei Shevu'ot, 18:**335**
Shaarei Tefila, Gates of Prayer, 4:545
Sha'arei Tevunah (Kanievsky), 11:762–763
Sha'arei Tikvah (London), 6:204
Sha'arei Tikvah (Samaria), 18:**335**
Sha'arei Torah (Hanau), 8:318
Sha'arei Ẓedek, 14:405
Sha'arei Ẓiyyon (Hannover), 8:327, 11:670
Sha'ar ha-Amakim (Israel), 18:**335**

Sha'ar ha-Golan (Israel), 18:**335–336**
Sha'ar ha-Harkavah ve-ha-Shimmush (Balmes), 3:94
Sha'ar ha-Razim (Abulafia), 1:343
Sha'ar ha-Shamayim (Gershon), 6:399, 7:554–555
Sha'ar ha-Shamayim (Horowitz), 9:535
Sha'ar ha-Shem he-Ḥadash (Almoli), 1:682
Sha'ar ha-Yesod (Almoli), 1:682
Sha'ar Ḥefer-beit Yizḥak (Israel), 18:**336**
Sha'ar Shimon (Bacher), 3:36
Sha'ar Yehudah (Poki), 16:284–285
Sha'ar Zekenim (Hamburg), 8:297–298
Sha'atnez, 18:**336–337**
Shabad, Ẓemaḥ, 18:**337**
Shabak, 15:771
Shabazi, Shalem, 18:**337**
Shabbat
Havdalah, 8:466–468
Kabbalat Shabbat, 11:692
Kiddush, 12:138–139
mukẓeh objects, 14:608
pikkua'ah nefesh, 16:153
Safed mystical movement, 14:666–667
Torah reading, 20:45–50
See also Sabbath
Shabbat (tractate), 18:**337–338**
Shabbateanism, 6:530, 11:619–620, 16:527, 21:435
1680-1700, 18:352–355
Aboab, Samuel ben Abraham, 1:268
Abraham ben Ḥayyim, 1:300
Abraham ben Isaac ha-Kohen of Zamość, 1:301
Adam Ba'al Shem, 1:378
Adam Kadmon, 1:379
aliyah and, 10:332
Amsterdam, 2:109
beginning of, 18:342–343
Bikayam, Meir ben Ḥalifa, as crypto-Shabbatean, 3:695
Bloch, Mattathias ben Benjamin Ze'ev Ashkenazi, 3:766
Bonafoux, Daniel ben Israel, 4:55
Brudo, Abraham ben Elijah, 4:220
Busk as center of, 4:316
Cardozo, Abraham Miguel, 4:464–466
controversy about, 6:633, 684
eighteenth century, 18:355–358
Elijah ben Solomon Abraham ha-Kohen of Smyrna, 6:340–341

Emden opposition to, 6:392–393
evil, 11:640
expulsion from Yemen, 13:694
Frank, Eva, 7:180–181
Frank, Jacob, 7:182–183, 18:357–358
gematria, 7:426
Hamburg, 8:296
Ḥayon, Nehemiah Ḥiyya ben Moses, 8:476–478
Hebron, 8:747
history of, 18:340–341
influence of, 11:42–43
Jerusalem and, 11:163, 164
Joseph della Raina legend, 11:428
Judah Ḥasid, ha-Levi, 11:505–506
Landau, Ezekiel Ben Judah, 12:460
Laniado, Solomon Ben Abraham, 12:485
leaders
Isaiah Ḥasid from Zbarazh, 10:78
Jamal Sulaymān, 11:76
Meir ben Ḥiyya Rofe, 13:783
literature, 7:16
Ḥayon writings, 8:476–478
Ẓevi Muddaḥ, 7:171
Nehemiah Ha-Kohen, 15:62
opposition, 11:104
Frances, Jacob ben David, 7:171–172
Landsofer, Jonah ben Elijah, 12:478
in Ottoman empire, 15:538
Pinheiro, Moses, 16:168–169
polemical opposition, 16:330
Possnitz, prophet of, 16:623–624
Rovigo, Abraham ben Michael, 17:500–501
Sasportas, Jacob, opposition to, 18:66
Sheluḥei Ereẓ Israel, 18:451
sheluḥei ereẓ israel, 18:451
women, 21:177
Zoref, Joshua Heshel ben Joseph, 21:670–671
See also Frankist movement; Nathan of Gaza; Shabbetai Ẓevi
Shabbatean propaganda
18th century, 18:358
education of propagandists, 18:357
Eybeschuetz, Jonathan and, 18:356
polarization of, 18:355
Serrarius, Peter, 18:346
in Turkey, 18:345
Shabbat ha-Olam (Shalom), 18:**377**
Shabbat lights, Ba-Meh Madlikin, 3:105

A Shabbat Manual (Plaut), 17:174
Shabbaton movement, 3:**33**
Shabbetai, Ḥayyim, 2:32
Shabbetai ben Meir ha-Kohen, 14:472, 18:**338–339**
Shabbetai ben Yom Tov ibn Boded. *See* Ehrlich, Arnold Bogumil
Shabbetai ben Ẓevi Hirsch of Raszkow, 3:33, 18:**339–340**
Shabbetai movement, 5:730–733
Shabbetai Ẓevi, 2:77, 6:148, 10:778, 15:538, 18:**340–359**, *341*
   Algazi, Solomon ben Abraham, 1:645
   apostasy, 18:348–349
   arrest and imprisonment in Turkey, 18:344–346, 348
   Cardozo, Abraham Miguel, 4:464
   Diaspora, 18:346–348
   Doenmeh and, 5:730–733
   early years and personality, 18:341–342
   in Gaza and Jerusalem, 18:341–342
   Joseph ben Saul Escapa, 6:488
   journeys of, 18:*341*
   Kabbalah, 18:351–352
   Lapapa, Aaron Ben Isaac, 12:488
   map, 18:*341*
   opposition, Lapapa, Aaron ben Isaac, 12:488
   post-apostasy, 18:349–351
   Shabbateanism
      1680-1700, 18:352–355
      beginning of, 18:342–343
      eighteenth century, 18:355–358
      Frank, Jacob, 18:357–358
      history of, 18:340–341
      Laniado, Solomon Ben Abraham, 12:485
      Mordecai ben Ḥayyim of Eisenstadt, 14:480
      Morocco, 14:497
   Sheluḥei Ereẓ Israel, 18:451
   in Smyrna and Constantinople, 18:343–346
Shabbetai Ẓevi (Agmon), 1:465
Shabbetai Zvi
   Amsterdam, 2:109
   amulets, 2:121
   See also Ayllon, Solomon ben Jacob
Shabbezi, Shalem. *See* Shabazi, Shalem
Shablul (motion picture). *See Snail* (motion picture)
Shabtai, Aharon, 18:**359**

Shabtai, Yaakov, 8:722, 18:**359–360**
Shach, Eliezer Menaḥem, 18:419
Shachar, Arie, 18:**360**
SHaDaL. *See* Luzzatto, Samuel David
Shaddai. *See* God
Shadkhan, 18:**360–361**
Shadmot Devorah (Israel), 18:**361**
Shadov (Lithuania). *See* Seduva (Lithuania)
Shadovsky, Israel Ḥayyim. *See* Shulman, Victor
Shadows on the Hudson (Singer), 18:635
Shadrach, Meshach, Abed-Nego, 5:419, 420, 18:**361**
Shaffer, Anthony, 18:361
Shaffer, Peter. *See* Shaffer, Sir Peter
Shaffer, Sir Peter, 18:**361**
Shag, Abraham, 18:**361–362**
Shahal, Moshe, 18:**362**
Shaham, Gil, 18:**362–363**
Shaham, Nathan, 18:**363**
Shahar, Shulamit, 18:**364**
Shaḥar, David, 18:**363–364**
Shaḥarit
   Amidah, 2:72, 74
   Barukh she-Amar, 3:191–192
Shaḥarit, 18:**364**
Shāhin, 18:**365**
Shāhīn, Mawlānā
   illuminated manuscripts, 11:556
   Judeo-Persian poetry of, 11:554–555
Shahn, Ben, 4:76, 16:125–126, 18:**365–366**
Shaḥor, Ḥayyim, 18:366
Shaḥor, Isaac, 18:366
Shaḥor family, 18:**366**
Shahpuhr. *See* Shapur
Shaikevich, Nahum Meyer. *See* Shomer
Shaked, Gershon, 18:**366–368**
Shakespeare, William, 4:25, 6:435, 18:**368–371**
Shakespeare a mai szinpadon (Bánóczi), 3:120
Shakespeare on the Contemporary Stage. See Shakespeare a mai szinpadon
Shakhna, Shalom. *See* Shalom Shakhna ben Joseph
Shaki (Lithuania). *See* Sakiai (Lithuania)
Shaki, Isaac, 18:**371**
Shakvay (Lithuania). *See* Sakiai (Lithuania)
Shakyai (Lithuania). *See* Sakiai (Lithuania)

Shakyay (Lithuania). *See* Sakiai (Lithuania)
Shalag. *See* Gordon, Samuel Leib
Shalakh, 15:550
Shalekhet - Fallen Leaves (Kadishman), 11:700
Shalem (ancient Israel), 18:**371**
Shalem, Samuel, 18:**371–372**
Shalem, Solomon, 4:270
Shalem Rabta (ancient Israel), 18:371
Shalev, Avner, 18:**372**
Shalev, Meir, 8:708, 18:**372–373**
Shalev, Yitzḥak, 18:**373**
Shalev, Zeruya, 18:**373**
Shali'aḥ. *See* Agency
Shalish, 18:**373–374**
Shalit, Leon, 2:161
Shalit case, 11:298, 12:542
Shaliyah ibn Ṭīrūn ibn Nīn, 6:66
Shalkovich, Abraham Leib, 4:622, 18:**374–375**
Shallon, David, 18:**375**
Shallots, 15:433
Shallum, 18:**375**
Shalmaneser III, 1:523, 18:**375–376**
Shalmaneser V, 2:126, 3:23, 18:**376**
Shalmei Nedarim (Kaplan), 11:773
Shalom. *See* Peace
Shalom, Abraham, 18:**376**
Shalom, Abraham ben Isaac ben Judah ben Samuel, 18:**376–377**
Shalom, Gershom Gerhard. *See* Scholem, Gershom Gerhard
Shalom, Isaac I, 15:556
Shalom, Isaac I., 18:**377**
Shalom, Shin, 11:441, 18:**377–378**
Shalom, Silvan, 18:**378**
Shalom Akhshav. *See* Peace Now
Shalom Aleichem, 15:207, 18:**378–389**, 21:346–347
   Altman, Nathan, 2:22
   autobiography, 18:384, 388
   biographies, 18:389
   biography of, 18:378, 379–380, 382, 385, 388
   early writings, 18:379
   English translations, 18:389
   Hebrew literature, 18:387–388
   humor and, 9:593–594
   lecture tours, 18:383–384, 388
   stock exchange, 18:380, 382
   Tevye der Milkhiker cycle, 18:385–387
   works and correspondence, 18:388–389
   writings as sole income, 18:382–383

Shalom Aleichem, *continued*
  Yiddish literature, 18:378–379, 380–382
  Yiddish theater, 18:383–384
Shalom Aleichem Folk Institute, 6:189
Shalom Aleikhem, 18:**389–390**
Shalom al Yisrael (Zweifel), 21:693
Shalom ben Abraham, 3:610
Shalom ben Obadiah ha-Cohen, 4:352
Shalom ben Yiẓḥak of Neustadt, 18:**390**
Shalom Hartman Institute, 8:375
Shalom of Safed. *See* Moskovitz, Shalom
Shalom Shakhna ben Joseph, 18:**390**
Shalom Zakhar. *See* Sholem Zokhor
Shalon, Raḥel, 18:**390**
Shalosh. *See* Pineles, Hirsch Mendel ben Solomon
Shalosh Ḥidot (Ensheim), 6:447
Shalosh se'udah. *See* Se'udah shelishit
Shalshelet ha-Kabbalah (Ibn Yaḥya), 7:13, 9:156
Shaltiel, David, 18:**390**
Shalvi, Alice, 18:115
Shamah, Joseph, 15:556
Shamdon. *See* Ben Temalyon
Shamerim. *See* Samaritans
Shamgar, 18:**390–391**
  Judges, Book of, 11:563
Shamgar, Meir, 18:**391**
Shamgar son of Anath, 2:131
Shami, Yitzḥak, 18:**391**
Shamir (Israel), 18:**391**
Shamir, Moshe, 4:381, 8:704, 705, 18:**392–393**
Shamir, Yitzhak, 18:**393–394**
  American Israel Public Affairs Committee, 2:51
    Bush, George H. W., 4:304
  governments of, 10:242, 448, 448*t*, 450–453, 450*t*, 452*t*
  Modai, Yitzhak, 14:406
  Sharon, Ariel and, 18:417
Shammah, 18:**394**
Shammah (Edomite chief), 18:394
Shammah (son of Agee), 18:394
Shammah (son of Jesse), 18:394
Shammai, 3:530–533, 6:486, 18:**394**
  creation, 5:275–276
  Eduyyot, 6:214–215
  halakhah, approach to, 6:486, 8:255
  Ḥanukkah lamp, 8:333
  on marriage, 8:255, 21:324
  on New Year, 15:193

on non-Jewish women and niddah, 15:256–257
on praising the bride, 8:247–248
resurrection, 17:242
Shammash, 8:334, 18:**395**
Shamosh, Yitzḥak, 18:**395**
Shamouti, 4:737
Shamri, Arie, 18:**395**
Shamsky, Art. *See* Shamsky, Arthur Louis
Shamsky, Arthur Louis, 18:**395**
Shanah Rishonah (Zemach), 21:504
Shandling, Garry, 18:**395–396**
Shanghai (China), 18:**396**
  American Joint Distribution Committee, 2:61
  museums, 14:635
  refugees, 4:646, 647
Shanker, Albert, 6:161, 18:**396–397**
Shankman, Jacob K., 18:**397**
Shanks, Hershel, 18:**397**
Shaool, Anwar. *See* Shaul, Anwar
Sha'ot Metot (Adelman), 1:386
Shapera, Robert. *See* Evans, Robert
Shapero, Harold, 18:**397–398**
Shapero, Nate S., 18:**398**
Shapero, Samuel. *See* Shapero, Harold
Shaphan, 6:287, 18:**398**
Shapira, Abraham, 18:**399**
Shapira, Avraham Elkana Kahana, 18:**399**
Shapira, Elijah ben Benjamin Wolf, 18:**400**
Shapira, Ḥayyim Eleazar, 18:398–399
Shapira, Ḥayyim Moshe, 14:391, 18:**400**
Shapira, Ḥayyim Nachman, 18:**400**
Shapira, Isaac ben Noah Kohen. *See* Isaac ben Noah Kohen Shapira
Shapira, Joshua Isaac ben Jehiel, 18:**400–401**
Shapira, Kalonymous Kalman, 18:**401**
Shapira, Meir, 18:**401–402**
Shapira, Moses William, 18:402–403
Shapira, Myriam. *See* Harry, Myriam
Shapira, Shalom Joseph. *See* Shalom, Shin
Shapira, Yeshayahu, 18:**402**
Shapira, Ẓevi Hirsch, 18:398
Shapira family, 18:**398–399**
Shapira fragments, 18:**402–403**
Shapiro, A. Y., 8:678
Shapiro, Abba Constantin, 18:**403**
Shapiro, Alexander M., 18:**403–404**
Shapiro, Aryeh Leib ben Isaac, 18:**404**
Shapiro, Ascher Herman, 18:**404**

Shapiro, Benjamin, 18:**404**
Shapiro, Bernard, 18:**404**
Shapiro, David S., 18:**404**
Shapiro, Esther June, 18:**404–405**
Shapiro, Ezra Z., 18:**405**
Shapiro, Feliks, 11:322
Shapiro, Harold, 18:**405**
Shapiro, Harry Lionel, 2:187, 18:**405–406**
Shapiro, Harvey, 20:301
Shapiro, Irving Saul, 18:**406**
Shapiro, Jonathan, 1:540
Shapiro, Joseph ben Abraham. *See* Case, Joseph ben Abraham
Shapiro, Karl Jay, 18:**406–407**
Shapiro, Lamed, 18:**407**
Shapiro, Leah, 11:322
Shapiro, Levi Joshua. *See* Shapiro, Lamed
Shapiro, Milton Jerrold. *See* Shapp, Milton Jerrold
Shapiro, Moses, 11:322
Shapiro, Moshe. *See* Shapira, Ḥayyim Moshe
Shapiro, Phinehas. *See* Korets, Phinehas ben Abraham Abba Shapiro of
Shapiro, Rami, 18:**407**
Shapiro, Robert, 18:**407–408**
Shapiro, Samuel Harvey, 18:**408**
Shapiro, Saul ben Dov, 18:**408**
Shapiro, Ya'akov Shimshon, 18:**408**
Shapka, Shalom Joseph. *See* Shalom, Shin
Shapp, Milton Jerrold, 18:**408–409**
Shapshal Seraya ben Mordechai, 18:**409**
Shapshilevich, Moise ben Haim. *See* Schappes, Morris U.
Shapur, 18:**409–410**
Shapur I, 3:28, 18:410
Shapur II, 18:410
Shar'ab (Yemen), 18:**410**
Sharabi, Shalom, 18:**410–411**
Sharansky, Natan, 4:125, 14:520, 18:**411–412**
Sharett, Moshe, 3:345–346, 12:533–534, 18:**412–413**
  Blood for Trucks offer, 4:120, 121
  governments of, 10:431–432, 432*t*
Sharett, Yehudah, 14:543, 18:**413**
Sharezer, 18:**413–414**
Sharfman, Isaiah Leo, 18:**414**
Shargorod (Ukraine), 18:**414**
Sharh, 3:605
Sharḥ al-Alfāẓ (Abu al-Faraj), 1:334
Sharḥ-i Torah (Shāhin), 18:365

Sharigrad (Ukraine). *See* Shargorod (Ukraine)

Sharlin, William, 18:**414–415**

Sharm el-Sheikh (Sinai Peninsula), 6:287–288, 18:**415**

Sharon, Abraham. *See* Schwadron, Abraham

Sharon, Ariel, 1:406, 10:250–251, 252, 253, 18:**415–417**
  governments of, 10:460–464, 460t– 461t, 462t–463t
  Lebanese War and, 10:240
  Novak, Robert, 15:317
  Sharansky, Natan and, 18:412
  Sheetrit, Meir and, 18:432
  unilateral withdrawal from Gaza and, 10:463, 464

Sharon, Aryeh, 18:**417–418**

Sharon, Nathan, 18:**418**

Sharon, Omri, 18:417

Sharon, Ariel, 15:599

Sharonah (Israel), 18:**418**

Sharon Plain (Israel), 10:110–111

Sharp, Isadore Nataniel, 18:**418**

Sharp, Issy. *See* Sharp, Isadore Nataniel

Sharuhen (territory of Simeon), 18:**418–419**

Shas (Mishnah), 18:**419**

Shas (political party), 5:595, 18:**419–420**

Shasha. *See* Sholem Zokhor

Shashu, Salim, 18:**420**

Shasu, 2:30

Shatilla refugee camp, 10:240–241, 251

Shatkin, Aaron, 13:9

Shatner, William, 18:**420**

Shatt el-Nil. *See* Chebar

Shatzkes, Moses, 18:**420**

Shatzkes, Moses Aaron, 18:**420–421**

Shatzky, Jacob, 18:**421**

Shaul, Anwar, 15:473, 18:**421**

Sha'ul – Der Letster Meylekh fun Yisroel (Hofstein), 9:314

Shaul – the Last King of Israel. See Sha'ul – Der Letster Meylekh fun Yisroe

Sha'ul ve-Yohannah (Frankel), 7:199

Shaulyai (Lithuania). *See* Siauliai (Lithuania)

Shavei Zion (Israel), 18:**421**

Shavelson, Clara Lemlich, 18:**421–422**, 713

Shaving and beards, 3:**235–236**

Shavir (music album). *See Fragile* (music album)

Shavl (Lithuania). *See* Siauliai (Lithuania)

Shavli (Lithuania). *See* Siauliai (Lithuania)

Shavuot, 12:436, 18:**422–423**
  flowers, 7:91
  food, 7:119–120
  games, 7:372
  Hallel, 8:280
  offering of first fruits, vol. 6: color insert
  pilgrim festivals and, 16:158–159
  Samaritans, 17:729–730
  Sheloshet Yemei Hagbalah, 18:446
  Sunday festival day, 2:128
  Yeziv pitgam, 21:331–332

Shaw, Artie, 18:**423**

Shaw, Benjamin, 18:**423–424**

Shaw, Irwin, 18:**424**

Shaw, Walter, 15:583

Shaw Commission (1929), 15:583

The Shawl (Ozick), 15:558

Shawn, Dick, 18:**424**

Shawn, Karen, 4:630

Shayele, Reb. *See* Steiner, Shaye

Shayevitsh, Simkha-Bunim, 18:**424–425**

Shazar, Rahhel. *See* Katznelson, Rahel

Shazar, Shneur Zalman, 18:**425–426**

Shazar, Zalman, 4:189
  Johnson, Lyndon Baines, 11:385

ShaZHah. *See* Halberstam, Solomon Hayyim

Shcharansky, Anatoly. *See* Sharansky, Natan

Shchebreshin (Poland). *See* Szczebrzeszyn (Poland)

Shchedrin (Belarus), 18:426

A Sheaf of Leaves (Solomon), 18:764

Shealtiel, 18:**426–427**

Shean, Al, 18:**427**

Shear, Murray Jacob, 18:**427**

Shearer, Norma, 18:**427**

Shearith Israel (NY), 6:189–190, 8:735

She'ar Yashuv (Israel), 18:**427**

Sheba, Chaim, 18:**427–428**

Sheba, Queen of. *See* Queen of Sheba

Sheba ben Bichri, 18:**428**

Shebnah, 18:**428–429**

Shebreshin (Poland). *See* Szczebrzeszyn (Poland)

Shechem (ancient Canaan and Israel), 8:313, 18:*429*, **429–430**
  Abimelech, 1:258
  Baal-Berith, 3:5–6
  Covenant of, 11:449
  rape of Dinah, 11:19

Shechem temple, 3:**5–6**

Shechtman, Dan, 18:**430**

Shechtman, Eli. *See* Shekhtman, Elye

SHeDal. *See* Luzzatto, Samuel David

Shedlovsky, Theodore, 18:**430**

Sheduva (Lithuania). *See* Seduva (Lithuania)

She'elat Yavez (Emden), 6:392

She'elot u'Teshuvot. *See* Responsa

Sheep, 13:8, 18:**431**

She'eris Yisroel, 21:343

She'erit ha-Hazzan, 18:**431**

She'erit Yisrael (Amelander), 2:38

Sheetrit, Meir, 18:**431–432**

Shefaram (Galilee), 18:**432**

Shefa tal (Horowitz), 9:543

Shefayim (Israel), 18:**432**

Shefeyah. *See* Me'ir Shefeyah

Sheffer, Henry M., 18:**432–433**

Shefferstroke function, 18:433

Sheffield (England), 18:**433**

Sheftall, Benjamin, 18:433

Sheftall, Levi, 18:433

Sheftall, Mordecai, 18:433

Sheftall, Moses, 18:433

Sheftall, Sheftall, 18:433

Sheftall family, 18:433

Sheftel, Mikhail, 18:**433–434**

Shehelet, 15:436

Shehitah, 18:**434–437**

Shehiyyah, 18:434

Shehsel. *See* Shabbetai Zevi

Sheikh, Abraham ben Shalom ha-Levi al-, 18:**437**

Sheikh Ishaq Pasha. *See* Gabbai, Isaac ben David ben Yeshu'ah

She'iltot (Aha of Shabha), 1:529–531, 14:315

Sheiltot Avyah (Karfunkel), 11:807

Sheindlin, Gerald, 18:437

Sheindlin, Judith, 18:437

Sheinkin, Menahem, 18:**437–438**

Sheinkman, Jacob, 18:**438**

Shekalim (tractate), 18:**438–439**

Shekanzib (Babylonia), 18:**439**

Shekel, 18:**439–440**

Shekels and talents, 20:703–705, 703t, 704t

Shekhinah, 11:597, 18:**440–444**
  Abelson, Joshua, 1:249
  angels and, 2:159
  kabbalistic influence, 11:670–671

Shekhol ve-Khishalon (Brenner), 4:159, 160

Shekhtman, Elye, 18:**444**

Shekhunat Borokhov (Israel). *See* Givatayim (Israel)

Sheki'ah Kaf (Ben-Ner), 3:367

Shela, 18:**444–445**

Shelag bi-Yrushalayim (Carmi), 4:484

Shelah. See Shenei Luhot ha-Berit

Shelah, pool of. *See* Shiloah, Siloam (ancient Israel)

Shelah, Saharon, 18:**445**

Shelah, Uriel. *See* Ratosh, Yonathan

Sheldon, Sidney, 18:**445**

Shelem, Mattityahu, 18:**445–446**

Shelemut ha-Ma'asim (Falaquera), 6:681

Shelhim. *See* Sheluhei Erez Israel

Sheli'ah Zibbur, 18:**446**

Shelihim le-azmam, 18:448

Shel Mi Attah Yeled? (Bartov), 3:181

Shelomi (Israel), 18:**446**

Shelomo ha-Elkoshi. *See* Epstein, Zalman

Shelomo Min-ha-Adummim. *See* Rossi, Salamone de'

Shelomo Molkho (Kabak), 11:584

Shelomo ve-Kohelet (Lebensohn), 12:591

Shelomo Yitzhaki. *See* Rashi

Shelom Yerushalayim (Alkalai), 1:663

Sheloshah Kadmonei Mefareshei ha-Moreh (Moses), 14:552

Sheloshah Yamim, 12-14.5.48 (Sherf), 18:462

Sheloshet Yemei Hagbalah, 18:**446**

Sheloshim, 14:588, 18:**446**

Sheluhei Erez Israel, 18:**446–452**

Sheluhot (Israel), 18:**452–453**

Shelulit Genuzah (Hazaz), 8:492–493

Shem, 4:391, 18:**453**, 19:493

Shema, reading of, 1:538–539, 3:399, 6:365, 18:**453–456**
    hashkivenu, 8:381–382

Shema eli Kol Bekhi ve-Kinah (Mordecai ben Naphtali Hirsch of Kremsier), 14:482

Shemaiah
    Baasha, 3:13
    biblical exegesis and study, 3:641
    God fearers as ancestors of, 11:293

Shemaiah (1st c. B.C.E.), 18:**456**

Shemaiah (era of Rehoboam), 18:**456**

Shemaiah of Troyes, 18:**456–457**

Shemama, Nessim. *See* Samama, Nessim

"Shem and Jepeth on the Train." *See* "*Shem ve-Yefet ba-Aggalah*"

Shemariah ben Elhanan, 18:**457**

Shemariah ben Elijah ben Jacob, 18:**457**

Shemen. *See* Oils

Shemenah Lahmo (Anshel), 2:562

Shemen ha-Mor (Abiob), 1:259

Shemen ha-Tov (Solomon Ohev), 1:212

Shemen Roke'ah (Loew), 13:162–163

Shemer, Naomi, 3:106, 18:**457–458**

Shemesh Zedakah (Morpurgo), 14:510

Shem ha-Gedolim ha-Kelali (Badhav), 3:49

Shem ha-Gedolim me-Erez Hagar (Schwartz), 18:187

Shemi, Menahem, 18:**458**

Shemi, Yehi'el, 10:697, 18:**458**

Shemini Azeret, 18:**604–605**, 19:301
    hakkafot, 8:250
    Samaritans, 17:730

Shemittah, 6:454
    hefker, 8:754–755
    Palestine (Ottoman), 10:621

Shem mi-Shmu'el (Sochaczew, Samuel), 18:704

Shemoneh esreh. *See* Amidah

Shemoneh Esreh, 18:**458**

Shemot Devarim (Levita), 6:28, 12:732

Shem Tov, Isaac ibn. *See* Ibn Shem Tov, Isaac ben Shem Tov

Shem Tov, Joseph ben Shem Tov. *See* Ibn Shem Tov, Joseph ben Shem Tov

Shem-Tov, Victor, 18:**458–459**

Shem Tov ben Abraham Ibn Gaon. *See* Ibn Gaon, Shem Tov ben Abraham

Shem Tov ben Isaac Ardutiel. *See* Santob de Carrión

Shem Tov ben Isaac Shaprut, 15:609

Shem Tov ben Joseph iben Shem Tov. *See* Ibn Shem Tov, Shem Tov ben Joseph ben Shem Tov

Shem Tov Bible, 3:677

Shem Tov family, 16:90

Shem Tov Ibn Shem Tov. *See* Ibn Shem Tov, Shem Tov

Shem Tov Katan, 3:9

Shem Tov Katan (Krotoschin), 3:9

Shemu'el Ben-Natan. *See* Pevzner, Samuel Joseph

Shemuel Bukh, 3:610, 611

"Shemu'el Frankfurte" (Hazaz), 8:492

"*Shem ve-Yefet ba-Aggalah*" (Abramovitsh), 1:321

Shenabazzar. *See* Sheshbazzar

Shenaton ha-Mishpat ha-Ivri (Sasson), 18:470

Shenazzar. *See* Sheshbazzar

Shenberg, Yitzhak. *See* Shenhar, Yitzhak

Shenei Dimyonot (Fernhof), 18:202, 21:620

Shenei ha-Me'orot, 11:754

Shenei Luhot ha-Berit (Horowitz), 8:552, 670, 9:535

Shenhab. *See* Ivory

Shenhar, Yitzhak, 8:718, 18:**459–460**

Sheni va-Hamishi. *See* Monday and Thursday

Shenkar, Arie, 18:**460**

Shenut (India). *See* Chennamangalam (India)

Sheol. *See* Netherworld

Shepetovka, (Ukraine), 18:**460**

Shepham Hariblah. *See* Riblah (Ancient Syria)

Shephatiah ben Amittai, 2:81, 15:470, 18:**460–461**

Shephatiah ben Amittai of Oria. *See* Shephatiah ben Amittai

Shephelah (ancient Israel), 10:116, 18:**461**

SHePHeR. *See* Rabbinowitz, Saul Phinehas

Shepherd, Cybill, 4:34–35

"Shepherds." *See* Pastoureaux

Sheps (Poland). *See* Sierpc (Poland)

Sher, Anthony. *See* Sher, Sir Anthony

Sher, Neal M., 15:388, 18:**461–462**

Sher, Sir Anthony, 18:**461**

Sher'ab (Yemen). *See* Shar'ab (Yemen)

Shereshevsky, Simon, bi-nationalism promoted by, 3:703

Sherf, Ze'ev, 18:**462**

Sheriff, Noam, 18:**462–463**

Sherira ben Hanina Gaon, 1:214, 2:405, 11:418, 18:**463**
    Amram Gaon, 2:104
    amulets, 2:121
    biographical material of, 3:705–706
    Elhanan ben Shemariah, 6:316
    on functions of rabbinate, 18:275

Sherira Gaon. *See* Sherira ben Hanina Gaon

Sherith Synagogue (San Francisco, CA), 18:18–19

Sherman, Alexander, 18:**463–464**

Sherman, Allan, 18:**464**

Sherman, Allie. *See* Sherman, Alexander

Sherman, Archie, 18:**464**

Sherman, Avraham, 13:682–683

Sherman, Jason, 18:**464–465**

Sherry, Larry. *See* Sherry, Lawrence and Norman Burt

Sherry, Lawrence and Norman Burt, 18:**465**

Sherry, Norm. *See* Sherry, Lawrence and Norman Burt

Sherry, Norman Burt. *See* Sherry, Lawrence and Norman Burt

Shertok, Moshe. *See* Sharett, Moshe

Shertok, Yehudah. *See* Sharett, Yehudah

Shesh, 16:478

Sheshai, 1:**544**

Sheshbazzar, 18:**465–466**

Sheshet, 2:103, 546, 3:142, 8:313, 18:**466**

Shesh-Kenafayim, 4:62, 14:414

Sheshonq. *See* Shishak

Shestapol, Wolf, 18:**466**

Shestov, Lev, 18:**466–467**

Shestoy strelkovy (Slonimsky), 18:679

Shetar, 14:338, 18:**467–471**

Shetar Hov, 18:469

Shetar Iska, 18:469–470

Shetar ko'ah harsha'ah mishpati, 18:447

Shetar marriage, 4:747

Shetar pitturin, 18:447

Shetar tena'ei ha-shelihut, 18:447

Shetei ha-Kezavot (Braudes), 4:136

Shetei Yadot (Lonzano), 13:187–188

Shetikah (Sobol), 18:702

Shetilei Zeitim (Mizrahi), 14:393

Shetzer, Simon, 18:**471**

Sheva' (Saudi Arabia). *See* Sabea (Saudi Arabia)

Sheva Petilot (Aboab), 1:266

Shevat, 18:**471**

Shevelei David (Silberstein), 18:578

Shevelove, Burt, 18:**471–472**

Shever Beit Ahav (Kaminka), 11:756

Shevet Musar (Elijah), 6:340–341

Shevet Yehudah (Ibn Verga), 7:15, 9:156–157, 225

Shevi'it (tractate), 18:**472**

Shevilei Emunah (Aldabi), 1:605, 6:399

Shevilei Olam (Bloch), 3:768

Shevil ha-Zahav (Eliasberg), 6:319

Shevo, 16:477

Shev Shemateta (Heller), 8:792–793

Shevu'a haben, 4:734

Shevuoslekh paper-cuts, 15:615

Shevu'ot (tractate), 18:**472–473**

Shewbread or showbread, 18:**473–474**

Shi'a Islam
    Abdallah ibn Saba, 1:240
    rulers, 6:723–724

Shibaam (Yemen), 18:**474**

Shi'buda de-Rabbi Nathan, 18:**474–475**

Shi'budim. *See* Servitudes

Shiddukhim, 3:540

Shield of David. *See* Magen David

Shieren, Jacob. *See* Ben-Ami, Jacob

Shifat Revivim (Habillo), 8:179

Shifman, Elijah, 11:321

Shifrah of Brody, 18:**475**

Shiftan, Ludwig. *See* Shiftan, Ze'ev

Shiftan, Ze'ev, 18:**475–476**

Shihin (Galilee), 18:**476**

Shihor, Shihor-Libnath, 18:**476**

Shihor-Libnath. *See* Shihor, Shihor-Libnath

Shikhhah. *See* Leket, shikhhah, and pe'ah

Shikkun, 9:148

Shikkun Vatikim (Shaham), 18:363

Shikun u-Fitu'ah (case), 12:607

Shila of Kefar Tamarta, 18:**476**

Shill, Louis, 16:349, 18:**476**

Shills, Edward, 18:732

Shiloah, Amnon, 18:**476–477**

Shiloah, Siloam (ancient Israel), 18:**477–478**

Shiloah, Reuben, 18:**477**

Shiloah Inscription. *See* Siloam Inscription

Shiloh (ancient Israel), 6:317, 18:**478–479**

Shiloh, Yigal, 18:**479**

Shils, Edward Albert, 18:**479–480**

Shimei, 18:**480**, 755

Shimmush, 6:168

Shim'on, Joseph ben Judah ibn, 18:**480–481**

Shimon ben Shelomo "the Second". *See* Duran, Simeon ben Solomon

Shimon ben Zemah. *See* Duran, Simeon ben Zemah

Shimoni, David, 18:**481–483**

Shimoni, Youval, 18:**483**

Shimonovitz, David. *See* Shimoni, David

Shimron (Canaan), 18:**483**

Shimshelevich, Izhak. *See* Ben-Zvi, Izhak

Shin, 18:**483–484**

Shinah, Selman, 18:**484**

Shinan, Avigdor, 1:461

Shinar, 18:**484**

Shindookh, Moses ben Mordechai, 18:**484**

Shinov, Chavdar, 4:277

Shinui, 18:**484–485**

Shinui party, 12:489

Shinwell, Emanuel, Baron, 16:342, 18:**485–486**, 705

Shion (territory of Issachar), 18:**486**

Shiphrah and Puah, 14:523, 18:**486**

Shiplacoff, Abraham Isaac, 18:**486**

Ship of the Hunted (Elberg), 6:291

Shippon, 21:34–35

Ships and sailing, 3:476, 18:**486–489**

Shipwrecks, archaeological study of, 17:6

Shir. *See* Rapoport, Solomon Judah Leib

Shira. See Shirah

Shirah (Agnon), 1:467, 11:216

Shiratenu ha-Ze'irah (Bialik), 8:727–728

Shirat Yisrael (Halper), 8:283

Shiraz (Iran), 18:**489**

Shirei Korban (Fraenkel), 7:143

Shirei Makkot Mizrayim (Alterman), 2:19

Shirei Musar Haskel. See Musar Haskel

Shirei Sefat Kodesh (Lebensohn), 12:590

Shirei Tehillah (Buchner), 4:243

Shirei Tiferet (Wessely), 8:687, 14:540, 21:20

Shirei Yerushalayim (Karni), 11:815

Shir ha-Ma'alot, 18:**489**

Shir-Hamales paper-cuts, 15:615–616

Shir ha-Yihud, 8:387, 18:**490**

Shir ha-Yihud la-Matbe'a (Kaminer), 11:755

Shirim (Silkiner), 18:581

Shirim (Solodar), 18:754

Shirim Nivharim (Shapiro), 18:403

Shirtwaist Strike (1909), 18:713

Shir u-Mizmor (hymn)(Kargau), 11:808

Shir Zahav li-Kveod Yisrael ha-Zaken (Sobel), 18:699

Shishah Sedarim. *See* Shas (Mishnah)

Shishak (King of Egypt), 2:85, 6:224, 11:140, 18:**490**

Shitah Mekubbetzet (Ashkenazi), 2:572

Shita Sidra. *See* Shas (Mishnah)

Shith. *See* Seth

Shitrit, Behor Shalom, 18:**490**

Shittah. *See* Acacia

Shittim. *See* Abel Shittim

Shittim (ancient Israel). *See* Abel Shittim (ancient Israel)

Shitz (Levin), 8:722

Shi'urei Maran ha-Gaon Rav Avraham Shapira (Shapira), 18:399

Shi'ur Komah, 18:**491**

Shivah, 14:587

Shivat Am-mudei ha-Tanakh (Kariv), 11:808

Shivat Ziyyon (Slucki), 18:685

Shivhei ha-Besht, 1:378

Shivhei Yerushayim (Basola), 3:204

Shivrei Luḥot (Longo), 13:187

Shivtah (Negev), 18:**491–492**

Shivtei Yeshurun Lekha be-Shir No'amim (She'erit ha-Ḥazzan), 18:431

Shivviti, 18:**492**

Shivviti paper-cuts, 15:615

Shklov (Belarus), 18:**492–493**

Shklover, Baruch. *See* Schick, Baruch ben Jacob

Shklover, Nathan. *See* Notkin, Nata

Shklovski, Isaac Vladimirovich, 18:**493**

Shkolnik, Levi. *See* Eshkol, Levi

Shkop, Simeon Judah, 13:12, 18:**493**

Shliḥei ẓibbur, 2:118

Shlof, Mayn Kind (Shalom Aleichem), 18:382

Shlom the Mintmaster, 18:**493–494**

Shlomzion party, 18:416

Shlonsky, Abraham, 18:**494–496**
    influence on Fichman, Jacob, 7:9

Shlonsky, Verdina, 18:**496–497**

Shloyme, Reb Khayims (Abramovitsh), 1:321, 322

Shmeruk, Chone, 18:**497**

Shmeterlingen (Altman), 2:21

Shmeykhl, Tvye. *See* Gottesfeld, Chone

Shmittah year, 16:586–587

Shmuel-Bukh, 18:**497–498**

Shmueli, Ephraim, 18:**498**

Shmueli, Herzl, 18:**498**

Shmuel Yosef Agnon, Yiddish Work (Agnon), 1:467

Shmushkevich, Yaacov, 18:**498–499**

Shneour, Zalman, 18:**499–501**

Shneur, Zalkind. *See* Shneour, Zalman

Shneur Zalman of Liozna-Lyady. *See* Shneur Zalman of Lyady

Shneur Zalman of Lyady, 1:216, 8:396, 414, 18:**501–505**
    Abraham ben Alexander Katz of Kalisk, 1:294
    Chabad, 4:554
    Judah Leib ben Baruch, 11:506

Shoah. *See* Holocaust

Shoah (Lanzmann), 9:443–444, 12:487

Shoah (motion picture), 9:386

Shoah Foundation Institute for Visual History and Education. *See* The Survivors of the Shoah Visual History Foundation

Shoah Visual History Foundation. *See* The Survivors of the Shoah Visual History Foundation

Shobi, 2:84

Shochat, Israel, 10:464–465, 18:**505–506**

Shochat, Mania Wilbushewitch, 18:**506**

Sho'el ka-Inyan (Joffe), 8:735

Shofar, 14:642, 18:**506–508**
    Amidah, 2:75
    laws on reading, 2:128
    Rosh Ha-Shanah, 17:464–465
    Yemenite Jew at the Western Wall, vol. 17: color insert

Shofarot, 18:508

Shofman, Gershon, 18:**508–509**

Shohal, Isaac ha-Kohen, 15:523

Shoham (Israel), 18:**509**

Shoham (stone), 16:478

Shoham, Mattityahu Moshe, 8:716, 11:216, 18:**509–511**

Shoham, Shlomo-Giora, 18:**511**

Shohat, Avraham Beiga, 18:**511**

Shoḥat, Eliezer, 18:**511–512**

Shoḥet, 2:39, 18:**434, 435**

Shohetman, Baruch, 18:**512**

Sholal. *See* Solal family

Sholal, Isaac, 18:**512**

Sholal, Isaac ben Abraham ha-Kohen, 18:751

Sholal, Jonathan ha-Kohen. *See* Sholal, Nathan ha-Kohen

Sholal, Nathan ha-Kohen, 18:**512**

Sholem Aleykhem. *See* Shalom Aleichem

Sholem Zokhor, 4:734, 18:**512–513**

Sholtz, David, 7:87

Shomer, 18:**513**
    See also Mashgi'ah

Shomer Emunim (Ergas), 6:479

Shomerim, 18:399, **513–518**

Shomer Israel, 18:**518**

Shomers Mishpet (Shalom Aleichem), 18:380

Shomrat (Israel), 18:**518**

Shomron (ancient Israel). *See* Samaria (ancient Israel)

Shomron, Dan, 18:**518–519**

Shonfield, Andrew. *See* Shonfield, Sir Andrew

Shonfield, Sir Andrew, 18:**519**

Shoop, Simon, 18:211

Shooting, 19:146
    Vinnitsa (Ukraine), 9:475

The Shop Around the Corner (motion picture), 4:26

The Shop on Main Street (Grossman), 9:407, 441–442, 11:695

Shore, Dinah, 18:**519**

Shore, Francis Rose. *See* Shore, Dinah

Shoresh (Israel), 18:**519**

Shorshei Avir (Almog), 1:680

Shorshei Halakhah (Loewy), 13:172

Short, Renee, 16:342–343, 18:**519**

Shoshan, Ilan. *See* Ranschburg, Bezalel ben Joel

Shoshanat Yeriḥo (Kenan), 12:**75**

Shoshannat ha-Amakim (Alshekh), 2:10

Shoshannat ha-Melekh (Ḥarshush), 8:182

Shoshannat Ya'akov (Leeuw), 12:601

Shostak, Eliezer, 18:**519**

Should the Baby Live? The Problem of Handicapped Infants (Singer), 18:640

Shoval (Israel), 18:**519–520**

Shovavim Tat, 18:**520**

Showbread. *See* Shewbread or showbread

Showbread (Aboab). *See* Lehem ha-Panim

Shpiglblat, Aleksander, 18:**520**

Afn Shpits fun a Mast (Elberg). *See* Ship of the Hunted (Elberg)

Shpola (Ukraine), 18:**520**

Shprintse (Shalom Aleichem), 18:386

Shragai, Shlomo Zalman, 18:**520–521**

Der Shrayber Geyt in Keyder (Shapiro), 18:407

Shraybman, Yekhiel, 18:**521**

Shreier, Feiwel, 18:**521**

Shrek! (Steig), 19:173, 174

Shriki family. *See* Chriqui family

Shroder, William J., 18:**521**

A Shroud of Stories. See Takhrikh shel Sippurim

Shtadlan, 11:751, 18:**521–522**

Shtaplen (Sfard), 18:333

Shtayger, 18:**522–523**

Shtaynbarg, Eliezer. *See* Steinbarg, Eliezer

Shtentsl, Avrom-Nokhem. *See* Stencl, Abraham Nahum

Shterenberg, David, 2:21

Shtern, Israel, 18:**523–524**

Shtern, Israel Hirsch, 18:523

Shtern, Sholem, 4:426, 18:523

Shtern family, 18:523

Shtetl, 1:322, 18:**524–527**
    Eastern European, 9:234
    photographs of, 16:128–129

Shtetlakh. *See* Shtetl

Shtiblekh, 8:399

Shtif, Nokhem, 18:**527**

Shtile Gezangen (Einhorn). *See* Quiet Chants (Einhorn)

Shtile Troymen (Segalowitch), 18:249

Shtol un Ayzn (Singer), 18:637

Shtoptsi. *See* Stolbsty (Belarus)

A Shtot Mit Yidn (Bickel), 3:686

Shtoybits (Belarus). *See* Stolbtsy (Belarus)

Shua, Ana María, 18:**527**

Shuadit. *See* Chuadit

Shuau, Joab. *See* Joab the Greek

Shu'ayb, 11:252

Shub, David, 18:**527–528**

Shub, Katriel. *See* Chasanowich, Leon

Shubert, Jacob J., 18:**528**

Shubert, Lee, 18:528

Shubert, Sam, 18:528

Shubert family, 18:**528**

Shubitu (Negev). *See* Shivtah (Negev)

Shubow, Joseph Shalom, 18:**528–529**

Shuchat, Wilfred G., 18:**529**

Shulal. *See* Solal family

The Shulammite, 18:**529**

Shulent. *See* Cholent

Shulḥan Arukh, Jacob ben Asher, 11:30

Shulḥan Arukh (Caro, Joseph), 1:532–537, 4:490, 776–780, 6:473, 18:**529–530**

Abraham Ẓevi Hirsch ben Jacob Eisenstadt, 6:270

business ethics, 4:307

commentaries in, 6:686

David ben Shalom Mizraḥi, 14:393

Falk, Joshua ben Alexander ha-Kohen, 6:686

Job, Book of, 11:356

Judah Leib ben Baruch, 11:506

Meir ben Baruch of Rothenburg and, 13:782

organs, use of, 15:467

Shulḥan Arukh, parodies of, 15:659

Shulḥani, 14:435–436

Shulim, Joseph Isidore, 18:**530–531**

Shulklapper, 18:**531**

Shulman, Abraham, 16:127

Shulman, Charles E., 18:**531**

Shulman, Harry, 18:**531**

Shulman, Max, 18:**531**

Shulman, Milton, 18:**531**

Shulman, Victor, 18:**531–532**

Shulman, Valery Matyevich. *See* Panov, Valery

Shulmānu-asharid. *See* Shalmaneser III

Shulner, Dora, 18:**532**

Shulsinger, Bezalel, 18:**532**

Shultz, Samuel, 18:**532**

Shul un Kultur Farband. *See* Educational and Cultural Union

Shulvass, Moses Avigdor, 18:**532**

Shum, 18:**532–533**

Shuman, Mort, 16:368

Shumen (Bulgaria). *See* Kolarovgrad (Bulgaria)

Shumiatcher-Hirschbein, Esther, 18:**534**

Shumlin, Herman, 3:783

Shummai, 1:348

Shunami, S., 3:682, 683

Shunary, Jonathan, 1:727

Shunem (Jezreel Valley), 18:**534**

Shunning. *See* Ḥerem

Shuqba Cave, 20:593

al-Shuqeiri, Aḥmad, 15:589, 590, 591

Shura Greizel, 6:187

Shurat ha-Mitnadvim, 18:618

Shurer, Haim, 18:**534**

Shurūṭ al-Dhabaḥāt (Elijah ben Aaron ben Moses), 6:338

Shushan (Iran), 18:**534–535**

Shushtar (Iran), 18:**535**

Shuster, Frank, 20:691

Shuster, Joe, 18:**536**

Shuval, Judith, 18:**536**

Shvadron, Shalom Mordecai ben Moses, 18:**536–537**

Shvambraniya (Kassil), 11:827

Shwed, Gil, 18:**537**

Shylock (fictional character), 14:486, 516, 18:369, 371

Shylock and Shakespeare (Morewski), 14:486

Si'aḥ ha-Sadeh (Eliezer ben Meir ha-Levi of Pinsky), 6:327

Si'aḥ ha-Se'udah (Heilprun), 8:769

Siauliai (Lithuania), 18:**537**

Siawek. *See* Grosser, Bronislaw

Siberia (Russian Federation), 12:710, 18:**537–539**

Sibir (Russian Federation). *See* Siberia (Russian Federation)

Sibirya (Gordin), 7:763, 19:680

Sibiu (Romania), 18:**539**

Siboni family, 18:**539**

Sibraim (ancient Israel). *See* Sepharvaim (ancient Israel)

Sibyl and Sibylline Oracles, 3:290, 18:**539–541**

Sibylline Oracles. *See* Sibyl and Sibylline Oracles

Sicarii, 18:**541**, 21:**467–480**

Ananias ben Nedebeus, 2:129

Athronges, 21:476

Eleazar ben Jair, 6:302–303

Felix and, 6:749

fourth philosophy, 21:467–471

Jerusalem zealots, 21:471–474

John of Giscala, 21:476–478

Jonathan ben Anan, 11:397

Judah the Galilean, 11:492

late scholarship, 21:478–479

Simeon bar Giora, 21:474–476

suicide, 21:470

See also Sikarikon; Zealots

Sichar (Samaria), 18:**541**

Sichel, Meir, 5:167–168

Sicher, Benjamin Ze'ev. *See* Sicher, Gustav

Sicher, Gustav, 18:**541**

Sicherheitsdienst des Reichsfuehrers. *See* SS and SD

Sichrovsky, Heinrich von, 18:**541–542**

Sicily (Italy), 18:**542–543**

expulsion, 2:140

laws and legal systems, Dienchelele, 5:648–649

Palermo, 15:580–581

rights of Jews, 7:222

Sick fund. *See* Kuppat Ḥolim

Sicknesses, 18:**545–548**, 548*t*

sick

prayer for the, 18:543

visiting the, 18:543–544

sick care, communal, 18:544–545

See also Medicine

Sicut Judaeis, 1:619, 4:277

Sid, Samuel ibn, 18:**549**

Siddur (Amram Gaon). *See* Seder

Siddur (prayerbook), 4:546

Siddur (Shabbetai ben Ẓevi Hirsch), 18:339

Siddur Beit ya'akov (Emden), 6:393

Siddur ha-Rav (Shneur Zalman of Lyady), 8:414

Siddur ha-Shalom, 14:519

Siddurim

Reconstuctionist, 17:148–149

Reform, 17:171

Siddur Rashi, 16:462

Siddur Rav Amram Gaon, 16:462

Siddur Saadia Gaon, 16:462

Siddur Sim Shalom (Harlow), 8:359

Sidelocks. *See* Pe'ot

Sidi, Samuel ibn. *See* Sid, Samuel ibn

Sidi Muhammed Ben-Abdallah, 14:498

Sidjelmessa. *See* Sijilmassa (Morocco)

Sidney, Sylvia, 18:**549**

Sidon (Lebanon), 16:121–122, 18:**549–551**

Sidon, Karol Efraim, 18:**551–552**

Sidon, Simeon, 18:**552**

Sidrah, 18:**552**

Siebenbuergen. *See* Transylvania

Siebert, Muriel, 18:**552**

Siedlce (Poland), 18:**552–553**

Siedlungsgesetz, 18:311

Sieff, Israel Moses, Baron, 5:588, 18:**553**

Sieff, Rebecca, 18:**554**

Sieff Research Institute. *See* Weizmann Institute of Science

Siegel, Benjamin "Bugsy," 18:**554**

Siegel, "Bugsy." *See* Siegel, Benjamin "Bugsy"

Siegel, Ida Lewis, 18:**554–555**

Siegel, Jerry, 18:**555**

Siegel, Mark, 4:498, 18:**555**

Siegel, Morton K., 18:**556**

Siegel, Seymour, 18:**556**

Der Siegelring des Salomo (Bueschenthal), 18:761

Siege of Buda (Hungary) (1686), 18:171

Siegmeister, Elie, 18:**556–557**

Siemiatycki, Chaim, 18:**557**

Siemiatycze (Poland), 18:**557–558**

Siena (Italy), 18:**558**

Sieradz (Poland), 18:**558–559**

Sierpc (Poland), 18:**559**

Sierra, Sergio Joseph, 18:**559–560**

Siesby, Gottlieb Isaschar, 18:**560**

Los siete dias de la semana (Caceres), 4:330

Sievers, Eduard, 18:**560**

Sifra, 6:345, 12:660, 18:**560–562**

Sifrei, 6:345, 9:113, 18:**562–564**

Sifrei ha-Kodesh or *Sifre ha-Qodesh*, 3:574

Sifrei ha-Minim, 18:**564–565**

Sifrei Numbers, 18:**565–566**

Sifrei Torah. *See* Sefer Torah

Sifrenu books, 4:624

Sifre Zuta Deuteronomy, 18:**566**

Sifre Zuta Numbers, 18:**566–567**

Sifrut Az, Ka'an ve-Akhshav (Shaked), 18:367

Sifrut ha-Historyah ha-Yisre'elit (Kahana), 9:160

Siftei Kohen (Shabbetai ben Meir Ha-Kohen), 14:472, 18:338

Sighet (Romania), 18:**568**

Sighmar family, ibn. *See* Ibn Sighmar family

Sigismund I, King of Poland, 1:313

Sigler, Eugen. *See* Relgis, Eugen

El siglo pitagórico y vida de don Gregorio Guadaña (Enríquez Gomez), 6:446

Sigman, Morris, 18:**568**

Sigmund Freud and the Jewish Mystical Tradition (Bakan), 3:72

Signature. *See* Autographs

Signatures, on shetar, 18:468

Signoret, Simone, 18:**568**

Signs and symbols, 18:**568–570**
  divination and, 5:706
  iconography and, 9:704
  Moses, 14:524, 527, 530
  sacrifices, 17:647–648
  women, Shekhinah, 18:442–443
  See also Masora; Miracles

Signs & Relics (Plachy), 16:210

Sigüenza (Spain), 18:**570–571**

Sihah be-Erezha-Hayyim (Wolfsohn-Halle), 8:688

Sihon, 14:528, 15:391–392, 18:**571**

Sihot ha-Sabba mi-Slobadka (Kaplan), 7:32

Sijill, 18:**571**

Sijilmassa (Morocco), 18:**572–573**

Sikarikon, 18:**573–574**

Sikhnin (Israel), 18:**574**

Sikili, Jacob ben Hananel, 18:**574–575**

Sikkumim ba-She'elah ha-Le'ummit: Le-Or ha Marksizm-Leninizm (Sneh, Moshe), 18:696

Sikkuth and Chiun, 18:**575**

Silano, 18:**575**

Silas, 18:**575–576**

Silas the Babylonian, 15:263

Silber, Abraham Hillel. *See* Silber, Abba Hillel

Silber, Saul, 18:**576**

Silberberg, Mendel, 18:**576**

Silberbusch, David Isaiah, 4:103, 18:**576**

Silberfarb, Moses, 18:**576–577**

Silberg, Moshe, 18:**577**

Silberman, Jerry. *See* Wilder, Gene

Silbermann (Lacretelle), 12:426

Silbermann, Abraham Moritz, 18:**577**

Silbermann, Alphons, 18:**577**

Silbermann, Eliezer Lipmann, 8:293

Silberner, Edmund, 18:**577**

Silberschlag, Eisig, 18:**578**
  Judah Halevi in poetry of, 11:500

Silbersky, Leif, 18:94

Silberstein, Abe. *See* Silverstein, Abe

Silberstein, David Judah Leib, 18:**578**

Silberstein, Isaiah, 18:578

Silberstein, Solomon Joseph, 18:**578**

Silberstein-Ötvös, Adolf, 18:**578**

Silence (Sobol), 18:703

Silent Wigwams. *See* Vigvammim Shotekim

Silesia (region), 16:309, 18:**578–580**
  anti-Jewish legislation, 6:689–690, 11:589

Holocaust, Teschen, 19:654

Silius Italicus, Tiberius Catius Asconius, 18:**580**

Silk, 18:**580**
  Lugoj (Romania), 13:254
  trade, 3:27, 4:116
  weaving, 15:580, 687

Silk City (NJ). *See* Paterson (NJ)

Silkin, John, 18:706

Silkin, Jon, 16:342, 18:**580–581**

Silkin, Lewis, First Baron, 16:342, 18:**581**, 706

Silkiner, Benjamin Nahum, 8:736, 18:**581**

Silk or Wool in the High Priest's Ephod (Ainsworth), 1:550

Sill. *See* Door and doorpost

Sillein (Slovakia). *See* Zilina (Slovakia)

Sills, Beverly, 18:**581–582**

Silman, Kadish Yehuda Leib, 15:661, 18:**582**

Siloam (ancient Israel). *See* Shiloah, Siloam (ancient Israel)

Siloam Inscription, 18:**582**

Silva, Antônio José Da, 18:**582–583**

Silva, Duarte da, 18:753

Silva, Flavius, 18:**583**

Silva, Hezekiah da. *See* Hezekiah ben David da Silva

Silva, Joshua Da, 18:**583**

Silva, Judith da, 18:754

Silva, Myer da, 18:754

Silva, Rodrigo Mendez Da, 18:**583**

Silva, Samuel Da, 18:**583**

Silvain, Gerard, 16:127, 128, 129

Silver, 14:124–125

Silver, Abba Hillel, 15:393, 18:**583–584**, 20:341

Silver, Daniel Jeremy, 18:**584**

Silver, Edward S., 18:**584**

Silver, Eliezer, 18:**585**

Silver, Harold M., 18:**585**

Silver, Joan Micklin, 18:**585**

Silver, Ron, 18:**585–586**

Silver, Sheldon, 15:224

Silverblatt, Howard. *See* Da Silva, Howard

Silverman, Alexander, 18:**586**

Silverman, Belle. *See* Sills, Beverly

Silverman, Ira, 18:**586**

Silverman, Joseph, 18:**586–587**

Silverman, Joy, 2:18

Silverman, Leslie, 18:**587**

Silverman, Morris, 18:**587**

Silverman, Samuel. *See* Silverman, Sidney

Silverman, Sidney, 16:342, 18:**587**, 706

Silverman, Sime, 18:**587–588**

"The Silver Plate" (Ezobi). *See* "Ka'arat ha-Kesef " (Ezobi)

Silvers, Herbert. *See* Ferber, Herbert

Silvers, Phil, 18:**588**

Silversmith, Philip. *See* Silvers, Phil

Silverstein, Abe, 18:**588**

Silverstein, Alan, 18:**588**

Silverstein, Larry, 15:225, 18:**589**

Silverstone, Gedalyah, 18:**589**

Silveyra, Miguel de, 18:**589**

Silviu, George, 18:**590**

Silviu, Goliger. *See* Silviu, George

Sima, Horia, 18:**590**

Sima, Miron, 18:**590**

Simanei Kizzur Or Zaru'a (Hayyim ben Isaac), 8:481

Simanim, 13:619, 14:398

Siman Tov Melammed, 11:555

Simchoni, Jacob Naftali Hertz, 18:**590–591**

Simchovich, Abraham. *See* Grobart, Fabio

Simchowitz, Jacob Naftali Hertz. *See* Simchoni, Jacob Naftali Hertz

Simeon, 11:19

Simeon (biblical figure), 18:**591–592**

Simeon (son of Boethus), 11:454

Simeon, Elijah, 2:27

Simeon, Testaments of. See Testaments of the Twelve Patriarchs

Simeon Akiva Baer. *See* Akiva Baer ben Joseph

Simeon Bar Giora. *See* Bar Giora, Simeon

Simeon bar Isaac, 18:**592–593**

Simeon bar Kokhba. *See* Bar Kokhba

Simeon bar Kosevah. *See* Bar Kokhba

Simeon bar Yohai, 18:**593–594**

Simeon ben Abba, 18:**594**

Simeon ben Boethus, 4:33, 18:**594**

Simeon ben Eleazar, 12:410, 18:**594–595**

Simeon ben Gamaliel I, 18:**595**

Simeon ben Gamaliel II, 10:151, 11:453, 18:**595–596**

See also Gamaliel, Rabban II

Simeon ben Giora, 11:435, 436

Simeon ben Halafta, 2:184

Simeon ben Halafta, 18:**596–597**

Simeon ben Jehozadak, 18:**597**

Simeon ben Jeshua ben Sira. *See* Ben Sira, Simeon ben Jesus

Simeon ben Jesus ben Sira. *See* Ben Sira, Simeon ben Jesus

Simeon ben Johanan. *See* Simeon the Just

Simeon ben Judah ha-Nasi, 18:**597**

Simeon ben Lakish, 5:169, 18:**597–598**
   Amittai ben Shephatiah, 2:81
   amoraim, 2:95
   amora of, 2:88
   Johanan ben Nappaha, 11:372
   Judah and, 11:478
   Judah ben Nahamani, 11:490
   Mo'ed, 14:413
   Nezikin, 15:246
   Torah, 20:40

Simeon ben Megas ha-Kohen, 18:**598**

Simeon ben Menasya, 18:**598–599**

Simeon ben Nanas, 18:**599**

Simeon ben Nethaniel, 2:66, 18:**599**

Simeon ben Pazzi, 18:**599–600**

Simeon ben Samuel Duwayk, 6:73

Simeon ben Samuel of Joinville, 18:**600**

Simeon ben Shetah, 18:**600–601**
   Judah ben Tabbai, 11:491
   public education, 6:163, 171

Simeon ben Yohai, 12:437
   Eleazar ben Yose I, 6:308
   Elijah, 6:333
   Judah ben Gerim, 11:486
   Labi, Simeon, on, 12:408
   on labor, 12:410
   Moses, 14:537
   See Also Mekhilta of Rabbi Simeon ben Yohai

Simeon ha-Gadol. *See* Simeon bar Isaac

Simeon ha-Pakuli, 18:**601**

Simeon ha-Timni, 18:**601–602**

Simeon Kayyara. *See* Kayyara, Simeon

Simeon of Mizpah, 18:**602**

Simeon Son of Onias I, 18:**602**

Simeon the Great. *See* Simeon bar Isaac

Simeon the Hasmonean, 9:194, 11:399, 14:412, 18:**601**

Simeon the Just, 18:**602**
   See also Soferim

Simferopol (Ukraine), 18:**602–603**

Simfonii Prokofieva (Slonimsky), 18:680

Simhah. *See* Joy

Simhah ben Joshua of Zalozhtsy, 18:**603**

Simhah ben Samuel of Speyer, 18:**603–604**

Simhah ben Samuel of Vitry, 13:366

Simhah Bunem of Przysucha (Pshiskha), 18:**604**

Simhah Bunim ben Moses Guens. *See* Eger, Simhah Bunim ben Moses

Simhah Bunim ben Moses Schlesinger. *See* Eger, Simhah Bunim ben Moses

Simhat Aniyyim (Alterman), 2:19

Simhat Bat, 3:722

Simhat Hanef (Smolenskin), 18:692

Simhat Hanef (Smolenskin), 18:691

Simhat Torah, 18:604–605, **604–606,** 19:301–302
   Bridegrooms of the Law, 4:179–180
   celebration in Tel Aviv, vol. 6: color insert
   women, 4:180

Simhoni, Assaf, 18:**606**

Simhoni, Yehudit, 18:606

Simiente (Seligson), 18:268

Simin, Moshe, 2:71

Simlai, 18:**606**

Simla'i, R. *See* Mohr, Meir

Simlat Binyamin (Hamburg), 8:298

Simleul-Silvaniei (Hungary), 18:**606–607**

Simmel, Georg, 11:363, 18:**607,** 730, 733

Simmons, Gene, 18:**607–608**

Simon, Abram, 18:**608–609**

Simon, Akiba Ernst, 18:**609–610**

Simon, Aron. *See* Hirsch, August

Simon, Aryeh, 18:**610**

Simon, Carly Elisabeth, 18:**610**

Simon, Carrie Obendorfer, 18:609, **610–611**

Simon, David, 18:608

Simon, Ernst, 6:161, 18:**611**

Simon, Francis Eugene. *See* Simon, Sir Francis Eugene

Simon, Heinrich, 18:**611**

Simon, Herbert, 18:608

Simon, Herbert Alexander, 18:**611**

Simon, James, 18:**611–612**

Simon, Jean Henri, 18:**612**

Simon, John. *See* Simon, Sir John

Simon, Joseph (Hungary), 18:**612–613**

Simon, Joseph (U.S.), 12:454, 18:**612**

Simon, Julius, 18:**613**

Simon, Kate, 18:**613**

Simon, Leon. *See* Simon, Sir Leon

Simon, Maurice, 18:**614**

Simon, Melvin, 18:608

Simon, Moses, 6:291, 15:676

Simon, Neil, 15:220, 18:**614**

Simon, Norton, 18:**614–615**

Simon, Oliver, 18:608

Simon, Paul Frederic, 15:221, 18:**615**

Simon, Pierre, 18:**615–616**

Simon, Ralph, 18:**616**

Simon, Richard, 3:649, 18:177, **616**

Simon, Shlome, 11:736, 18:**616–617**

Simon, Sidney, 18:**617**

Simon, Sir Francis Eugene, 18:**611**

Simon, Sir John, 16:342, 18:**612**

Simon, Sir Leon, 18:**613–614**

Simon, Tamás, 18:**617**

Simon, Uriel, 15:703

Simona, 18:**617**

Simon and Schuster, 18:177, 610

Simon ben Joachim. *See* Simon, Richard

Simone, André, 18:**617–618**, 665

Simon family (U.K.), 18:**608**

Simon family (U.S.), 18:**608**

Simon of Trent, 3:776, 4:163

Simon Property Group, 18:608

Simons, James H., 18:**618**

Simons, Solomon, 15:302

Simonsen, David Jacob, 18:**618**

Simonsohn, Shlomo, 18:**618**

Simon Wiesenthal Center, 9:97, 18:**618–620**

Simpson, O. J., 18:408

Simpson, Sampson, 15:196, 197.198, 199

Simpson, Solomon, 15:197

The Simpsons (television show), 4:209

Simson, Bernhard von, 18:**621**

Simson, Martin Eduard von, 16:344, 18:**621**

Simson, Nathan, 15:196

Simson, Paul, 18:**621**

Simson, Sampson, 18:620

Simson, Samson, 18:620

Simson, Solomon, 18:620

Simson family, 18:**620–621**

Simultanschules, 6:160

Sin, 12:448, 18:**621–625**

    Al Ḥet, 1:658

    forgiveness, 7:127–128

    Satan responsible for, 18:73

    Solomon, 18:760

Sin, Original. *See* Original sin

Sin, Wilderness of, 18:**625**

Sin-ab-usur. *See* Sheshbazzar

Sin-aḥḥê-eriba. *See* Sennacherib

Sinai, 18:**625–627**, *626*

    Abu Aweigila, 1:335

    Moses, 14:528, 18:627

    in Numbers, 15:330

    wanderings in, 9:166–167

Sinai, Mount. *See* Mount Sinai

Sinai Campaign, 6:145, 11:706, 18:606, **629–632**, *630*

    Amit, Meir, 2:80

    Ben-Gurion, David, 3:346–347

    Egyptian antisemitism, 6:235

    Eisenhower, Dwight David, 6:267

    El-Arish, 6:286

    Sharm el-Sheikh, 18:415

    Sharon, Ariel, 18:416

Sinai Covenant, significance of, 8:375–376

Sinatra, Frank, 3:726, 4:338

Sinbad. *See* Sindabar

Since Last Night. See Me-Emesh

Sincere Brethren, 4:170–171

Sinclair, Clive, 6:439, 440, 18:**632**

Sinclair, Jo. *See* Seid, Ruth

Sindabar, 18:**632–633**

Sindabot. *See* Sindabar

Sinfonietta (Seter), 18:319

Singapore, 18:**633**

Singer, Abraham, 18:**633**

Singer, André, 4:153

Singer, Bryan, 18:**633–634**

Singer, Charles Joseph, 18:**634**

Singer, Dorothea Waley, 18:634

Singer, E. F., 15:436

Singer, George, 18:**634**

Singer, Howard, 18:634

Singer, Isaac Bashevis, 15:217, 227, 234, 18:**634–636**

Singer, Isidore, 6:400, 18:**636**

Singer, Israel, 18:**636–637**

Singer, Israel Joshua, 18:**637–638**

Singer, Josef (1841-1911), 18:**638**

Singer, Josef (1923-), 18:**638**

Singer, Joseph, 18:**638**

Singer, Kurt, 18:**638–639**

    Juedischer Kulturbund, 11:570

Singer, Leo, 18:633

Singer, Ludvik, 18:**639**

Singer, Milton B., 18:**639**

Singer, Paul, 18:**639**

Singer, Pesaḥ, 18:**639–640**

Singer, Peter, 18:**640**

Singer, Simeon, 18:**640**

Singer, Yvonne, 18:**640**

Singerman, Berta, 18:**640–641**

Singerman, Paulina, 18:641

Singermann (Brinig), 4:184

Singer of Zion. *See* Judah Halevi

"Singer of Zion." *See* Judah Halevi

Singers. *See* Cantors; Music

Singer's Prayer Book (Singer), 18:640

Single tax movement, 6:750–751

Sinigaglia, Abraham Vita (fl. 18th century), 18:641

Sinigaglia, Abraham Vita (fl. 19th century), 18:641

Sinigaglia, Jacob Samson Shabbetai, 2:141, 18:641

Sinigaglia, Leone, 18:641, **641**

Sinigaglia, Moses Elijah, 18:641

Sinigaglia, Solomon (fl. 18th century), 18:641

Sinigaglia, Solomon Jedidiah (fl. 1639), 18:641

Sinigaglia family, 18:**641**

Sinim (Lebanon). *See* Tripoli (Lebanon)

Šinko, Ervin, 18:**641**

Sinneh (Iranian Kurdistan). *See* Sanandaj (Iranian Kurdistan)

Sinning and purification, 19:292

Sin rumbo (Sneh, Simja, 18:**697**

Sins, Confession of. *See* Confession of sins

Sinscheimer, Aaron, 4:13

Sinsheim (Germany), 3:43

Sint Maarten (Netherlands Antilles), 4:472

Sin-uballiṭ. *See* Sanballat

Sinuhe, 6:225–226

Sinyavsky, Andrei, 5:427

Sinzheim, David, in Bischheim, 3:724

Sinzheim, Joseph David, 1:333

Sinzheim, Joseph David ben Isaac, 18:**641–642**

Sion, Yael. *See* Dayan, Yael

Sionistsko-Sotsialisticheskaya Rabochaya Partiya. *See* Zionist Socialist Workers' Party

Siponto (Italy), 18:**642**

Sippar (ancient Israel). *See* Sepharvaim (ancient Israel)

Sippurei Ereẓ ha-Galil (Simḥah ben Joshua), 18:603

Sippurei ha-Besht (Agnon), 1:468

Sippurei Ma'asiyot (Naḥman), 14:749

Sippurei Rudorfer (Barash), 3:135

Sippurei Sindabar. See Mishlei Sendabar

Sippur ha-Aggadah—Aḥdut shel Tokhen ve-Ẓurah (Fraenkel), 1:462

Sippurim (Luidor), 13:254

Sippurim (Pascheles), 15:675

Siprutini, Emanuel, 18:**642**

Sirāj al-'Uqūl (Dhamārī), 5:631

Sirat, Colette, 16:70, 71–72

Sirat, Rene Samuel, 18:**642–643**

Sire, Henry, 14:512

Sire, Rosena, 14:512

Siret (Romania), 18:**643**

Sirillo, Solomon ben Joseph, 18:**643–644**

Sirilyo, Samuel ibn. *See* Sid, Samuel ibn

Sirion. *See* Mount Hermon

Sirius Satellite Radio, 11:812

Sirizli. *See* Israel, Yom Tov ben Elijah

Sirizli, Yom Tov ben Elijah. *See* Israel, Yom Tov ben Elijah

Sirkes, Joel, 4:780, 6:144, 13:255, 18:**644**

    on extradition, 6:628

    organs, use of, 15:467

Sir Leon of Paris. *See* Judah ben Isaac

Sir Morel. *See* Samuel ben Solomon of Falaise

Sirota, Gershon, 8:503, 18:**644**

Sirotsky, Naum, 11:470

Sis. *See* Swifts

Sisebut, 18:**644–645**

Sisera, 8:361, 18:**645**

    Judges, book of, 11:563

    slaying of, 11:58–59

Siskind, Aaron, 16:126, 18:**645–646**

Siso, Astruc Jacob, 4:299

Sisteron (France), 18:**646**

The Sisters (Brinig), 4:184

Sisters of Zion, 17:111–112

Sistine Chapel (Vatican City), 14:542

Sitbon, Abraham, 18:**646**

Sitbon, Joseph, 18:**646**

Sitbon, Judah, 18:**646**

Sitbon, Samuel, 18:**646**

Sitbon family, 18:**646**

Sitrei Torah (Zohar), 21:649

Sitruk, Joseph, 18:**646**

Sitteon Dabbah, Shaul David, 18:**646–647**

La situazione giuridica di Gerusalemme (Sereni), 18:309

Sitz im Leben, 14:436

Sivan, 18:**647**

Sivan, Aryeh, 18:**647**

Si vera sunt, 4:277

Silversmiths and goldsmiths. *See* Goldsmiths and silversmiths

Sivitz, Moshe, 18:**647–648**

Six (number), 15:335

Six Day War, 10:229–232, 255, 18:**648–655**, *649*, 18:*653*

    aliyah and, 10:345–346

    American Israel Public Affairs Committee, 2:50

    antisemitism in Egypt, 6:235

    background, 18:648–650

    cease-fire lines, 10:191–192

    diplomacy, 6:84

    El-Arish, 6:286

    Elath, 6:288

    England, 6:431

Eshkol, Levi, 6:506

Eshtaol, 6:507

European Economic Community, 6:562

    Golan Heights and Syrian front, 18:*653*, 653–654

    Iraq, 10:22

    Jerusalem and Jordanian front, 11:182, 404, 18:*651*, 651–652

    Levi, Moshe, 12:691

    music and, 10:692, 693

    New Left, 15:142

    Old City, 18:652–653

    Protestants and, 16:633

    Russia, 14:519–520

    Sharon, Ariel, 18:416

    southern front, 18:650–651

    Suez Canal, 18:653

    territorial occupation policy, 5:485

Sixteen Years in Siberia (Deutsch), 5:624

Sixtus IV (pope), 4:278, 16:374, 18:**655–656**

Sixtus V (pope), 4:49, 278, 16:375

Sixtus of Siena, 18:**656**

Sixty (number), 15:336

Siyyum, 18:**656**

Siyyum ha-Shas, 13:202

S. K. *See* Kohn, Salomon

Skalat (Ukraine), 18:**656–657**

Skarbowe Niggunim. *See* Mi-Sinai Niggunim

Skarga, Piotr, 18:**657**

Skarzysko-Kamienna (Poland), 18:**657**

Skeleton, 2:134

Skeptics and skepticism, 18:9, **657–658**

Sketches from the Brewery. See Temunot mi-Beit Mivshal ha-Shekhar

Skidel (Belarus), 18:**658**

Skierniewice (Poland), 18:**658–659**

Skin. *See* Nevel

Skin creams, 5:229

Skin diseases

    blemishes, 3:749–750

    Bloch, Iwan, 3:762–763

Skink, 18:**659**

Skirball, Jack, 18:**659**

Skirball Cultural Center, 9:43, 18:**659–660**

Sklare, Marshall, 4:125, 18:**660**, 734

Sklarew, Myra, 18:**660–661**

Sklat (Ukraine). *See* Skalat (Ukraine)

Sklepy cynamonowe (Schulz), 18:175

Skole (Ukraine), 18:**661**

Skoplje (Macedonia), 18:**661–662**

Skoss, Solomon Leon, 18:**662**

Skoss, Zalman Leib. *See* Skoss, Solomon Leon

Skotnicki, Alexander, 15:632

Skowhegan School of Painting and Sculpture, 18:617

Skulnik, Menasha, 18:**662**

Skulsky, Shlomo, 11:444

Skuodas (Luthuania), 18:**662**

Skver (Ukraine). *See* Skvira (Ukraine)

Skver dynasty. *See* Twersky dynasty

Skverer Ḥasidim, 15:230

Skvira (Ukraine), 18:**662–663**

    See also New Square (NY)

Skvoz literaturu (Eichenbaum). *See Through Literature* (Eichenbaum)

Slander, 12:495, 17:324, 18:**663–665**

Slanderers. *See* Informers

Slánský, Rudolf, 18:665

Slánský Trial, 18:**665–666**

The Slanting Light (Charles), 4:577

Slapsie Maxie. *See* Rosenbloom, Max Everitt

Slar, Kathyrn Kish, 9:152

Slask. *See* Silesia (region)

Slater, Oscar, 18:**666**

Slatkin, Leonard, 18:**666**

Slatkine, Menahem Mendel, 18:**666–667**

Slaughter, ritual. *See* Sheḥitah

Slaughtering, commandments concerning, 5:76*t*–77*t*

Slaughter of stolen animals. *See* Theft and robberies

The Slave (Singer), 18:635

Slave labor. *See* Forced labor

Slavery, 18:**667–670**

    Bondi, August, 4:57

    in Book of Covenant, 6:616

    in Byzantine empire, 11:579

    commandments concerning, 5:78*t*, 82*t*–83*t*

    for debt, 6:590

    economic history, 6:97–98, 102, 103

    Emin Pasha, 6:394

    extradition of slaves, 6:626

    Germany, payment of taxes and, 13:782

    imposed by Egyptians, 16:28

    Israel (ancient), 9:186

    liberation of Israelites from, 6:613–616, 623

    New York City, views of Jews in, 15:200

    obligations, law of, 12:773, 15:370

    ona'ah, not subject to, 15:424

Slavery, *continued*

    in Ottoman empire, 15:529

    Palermo slave market, 15:581

    Passover and Seder, significance of, 15:681–682

    Patras Jews sold as slaves, 15:689

    Pinner, Moritz, 16:170

    Raphall, Morris Jacob, on, 17:97

    study of, 5:480

    U.S. Jews and slave trade, 3:734

    See also Ha'anakah; Slave trade

Slave trade, 16:627–628, 18:**670–672**

Slaveykov, Petko Rachev, 4:275

Slavin, Ezra, 11:776

Slavische Melodien (Kapper), 11:782

Slavkov u Brna. *See* Austerlitz (Czech Republic)

Slavonic languages, biblical translations, 3:634–636

Slavson, Samuel Richard, 18:**672**

Slavuta (Ukraine), 18:**672–673**

Slawoj-Skladkowski, Felicjan, 18:**673**

Slawson, John, 2:56, 18:**673**

Slaying (execution method). *See* Capital punishment

The Sleepwalkers. See Die Schlafwandler

Slepian, Joseph, 18:**673**

Slezko. *See* Silesia (region)

Sling, Otto, 18:**665**

Sliozberg, Henry, 16:348, 18:**673–674**

Slobodka Yeshivah, 7:32, 18:**674**

Sloman, Henry, 18:**675**

Slomon, Solomon. *See* Sloman, Henry

Slomovitz, Philip, 18:**675**

Slonik, Benjamin Aaron ben Abraham, 18:**675–676**

Slonim (Belarus), 18:**676–677**

Slonim, Marc, 18:**677**

Slonim, Reuben, 18:**677–678**

Slonim dynasty, 18:676, **677**

Slonimer, Yoshke. *See* Altschul, Joseph

Slonim Ḥasidim, 8:424

Slonimski, Alexander, 18:679

Slonimski, Antoni, 18:**678**

Slonimski, Ḥayyim Selig, 8:495, 18:**678–679**

Slonimski, Henry, 18:**679–680**

Slonimski, Leonid Zinovyevich, 18:**679**

Slonimski, Nicolas, 18:**680**

Slonimsky, Mikhail Leonidovich, 18:**679**

Slonimsky, Sergei Mikhailovich, 18:**680**

Sloss, Marcus Cauffman, 18:**680**

Slotki, Israel Wolff, 18:**680–681**

Slotki, Judah Jacob, 18:681

Slouschz, Nahum, 18:**681**

Slovakia, 5:**369–370**, 18:**681–684**

    Bratislava, 4:131–134

    change in Jewish political status, 18:683–684

    Holocaust, 9:340–341

        attempted purchase of Jews, 6:553

        Banska, Bystrica, 3:120

        Bratislava, 4:132–133

        deportations, 9:479

        Dunajska Streda, 6:39

        Kosice, 12:318

        Michalovce, 14:173

        Pezinok, 16:25

        Piestany, 16:149

        Presov, 16:486

        Topolcany, 20:38–39

        Trencin, 20:131

        Trnava, 20:154

        Zilina, 21:531

    Jewry, 5:363–364

    language, Bible translated into, 3:634

    literature, 5:363–364

    museums, 14:629

    Nitra, 15:281–282

    Nove Mesto Nad Vahom, 15:318–319

    Nove Zamky, 15:319

    partisans, 15:668

    printing industry, Hebrew, 4:133

    Slovak People's party, 18:684

    transport to Auschwitz, 2:666

    See also Czechoslovakia; Czech Republic

Slovensko. *See* Slovakia

Slovo, Joe, 16:349, 18:**684**

Slovo–The Unfinished Autobiography (Slovo), 18:684

Slowakei. *See* Slovakia

Slucki, Abraham Jacob, 18:**684–685**

Slute. *See* Slutskaya, Irina

Sluter, Claus, 14:541

Slutsk (Belarus), 18:**685**

Slutskaya, Irina, 18:**685**

Slutski, Boris Abramovich, 18:**685–686**

Slutzki, David, 18:**686**

Slutzky, Abraham, 14:389

Slutzky, Meir. *See* Amit, Meir

Sma. *See* Falk, Joshua ben Alexander ha-Kohen

The Small Seder Olam. See Seder Olam Zuta

Smart Alecks. See Ḥakhamim ba-Layla

Smela (Ukraine), 18:**686**

Smell, air pollution, 5:167–168

Smell of Earth. See Reyakh fun Erd

Smelser, Neil Joseph, 18:**686**, 731

Smend, Rudolph, 6:278, 18:239, **686–687**

Smiela. *See* Smela (Ukraine)

Smilansky, Meir, 18:**687**

Smilansky, Moshe, 11:304, 18:**687**

Smilansky, Yizhar. *See* Yizhar, S.

Smith, Alfred E., 15:214

Smith, George Adam. *See* Smith, Sir George Adam

Smith, Goldwin, 4:396

Smith, John Merlin Powis, 18:**688**

Smith, Jonathan Z., 18:**688**

Smith, Morton, 18:**688–689**

Smith, Sir George Adam, 18:**687–688**

Smith, William Robertson, 18:**689**

    sociology of Bible and, 3:658

Smith's Gazelle (Davidson), 6:438

Smoira, Moshe, 18:**689**

Smoira-Cohn, Michal, 18:**689–690**

Smoke pollution, 5:167–168, 6:94

Smoking, cigarette, 5:329

Smol, 18:**690**

Smolar, Hersh, 18:**690**

Smolensk (Russia), 18:**690–691**

Smolenskin, Perez, 4:119, 8:442–443, 726, 18:**691–694**

    Am Olam, 2:87

    Ha-ShaḤar, 8:380–381

    Kadimah, 11:699

Smolenskin, Pereẓ, 18:369

Smoler, Eliezer. *See* Smoli, Eliezer

Smoli, Eliezer, 18:**694**

Smollett, Tobias, 6:435

Smorgon (Belarus), 18:**694**

Smorgon, Gershon, 18:**694**

Smorgon, Victor, 18:**694**

Smorgon dynasty, 18:**694–695**

Smorgonie. *See* Smorgon (Belarus)

Smuts, Jan Christiaan, 18:**695**

Smyrna (Turkey). *See* Izmir (Turkey)

Snail (motion picture), 6:263

Snakes, 18:**695–696**

    in Eden narrative, 1:371, 372, 373, 374

    Eve and, 6:572, 573

    paradise in Eden narrative, 15:626

Sneersohn, Ḥayyim Ẓevi, 18:**696**

Sneh, Ephraim, 18:**697**

Sneh, Moshe, 18:**696–697**

Sneh, Simja, 18:**697**

Snell, Ḥarry, 15:583

Sniatýn. *See* Snyatyn (Ukraine)

Snow Crash (Stephenson), 18:200

Snyatyn (Ukraine), 18:**697–698**

Snyder, Louis Leo, 18:**698**

So, 18:**698**

Soap, 4:591, 18:**698**

Soare, Iulia, 18:**698–699**

Soave, Moise, 18:**699**

Sobata (Negev). *See* Shivtah (Negev)

Sobedruhy (Czech Republic), 18:**699**

Sobel, Bernard, 18:**699**

Sobel, Henry I., 18:33

Sobel, Jacob Ẓevi, 18:**699**

Sobel, Ronald, 18:**699–700**

Sobeloff, Isidor, 18:**700**

Sobeloff, Simon Ernest, 12:556, 18:**700**

Sobelsohn, Karl. *See* Radek, Karl

Sobelson, Karl. *See* Radek, Karl

Sobibor (Poland), 9:336, 18:*700*, **700–701**

Sobibor, uprising, Pechersky, 15:707

Sobieski, Jan III (King of Lithuania), 12:407

Soble, James H. *See* Sobel, Jacob Ẓevi

Sobol, Andrey Mikhailovich, 18:**701–702**

Sobol, Mordechai, 8:503, 18:**702**

Sobol, Yehoshua, 8:721, 722, 10:687, 18:**702–703**

Soborten. *See* Sobedruhy (Czech Republic)

Sobotka, Harry Herman, 18:**703**

Sobremonte, Tomás Treviño de. *See* Treviño de Sobremonte, Tomás

Soccer, 2:118

Sochaczew (Poland), 18:**703**

Sochaczew, Abraham ben Ze'ev Nahum Bornstein of, 18:**703–704**

Sochaczew, Samuel, 18:704

Sochaczew dynasty, 8:423

Sochaczewer, Amos. *See* Horev, Amos

Social and Religious History of the Jews (Baron), 3:173, 9:159

Social Class and Mental Illness (Redlich), 17:158–159

Social customs, 13:509–510

Social demand, theory of, 4:181

Social Democratic Party (Austria), 1:409, 6:360, 18:179

Social Democratic Party (Germany), 4:378

Social Democratic Party (Poland), 13:277

Social Democratic Party (Russia), 1:324, 18:190–191

Social ethics, 6:531–532

Social Gospel, 16:633

Social history

　　Discursos Predycaveys (Silva), 18:583

Germany, 4:487

homosexuality and, 9:516

Jews in London, 18:583

Socialism, 18:**704–714**, 706–707

　Aḥdut ha-Avodah-Po'alei Zion, 1:540–541

　Amsterdam, 2:113

　anarchism, 18:709–710

　Asia and Africa, 18:709

　attitudes towards Jews, 18:710–712

　Austria, 16:341

　　Adler, Friedrich, 1:397

　　Adler, Max, 1:402–403

　　Adler, Victor, 1:409

　　Bauer, Otto, 3:217

　　Braunthal, Julius, 4:140

　Belgium, 16:144

　Bloch, Joseph, 3:763

　Borochov, Ber, 4:88–90

　Breitner, Hugo, 4:158

　of Buber, 4:231, 235

　Canada, 4:400, 401–402, 406, 12:764

　England, Agudat ha-Soẓyalistim ha-Ivrim, 1:504–505

　France, 6:8, 14:404–405, 16:148, 633, 18:704

　Germany, 16:344, 18:705

　　1914-1939, 18:705–706

　　Adler, Georg, 1:397

　　Beer, Max, 3:252

　　Bernstein, Eduard, 3:478

　　Braun, Adolph and Heinrich, 4:137

　　Calwer, Richard, 4:378

　　Eisner, Kurt, 6:276

　　Hess, Moses, 9:75–76

　　Lassalle, Ferdinand, 12:501–502

　　Levi, Paul, 12:691

　　Singer, Paul, 18:639

　Hilferding, Rudolph, 9:106

　Hungary, Frankel, Leo, 7:197

　International Working Men's Association, 18:705

　introduction, 18:704

　Italy, Modigliani, Vittorio Emanuele, 14:411

　Jewish contribution to, 18:712–713

　Jewish identity and, 11:297, 12:807

　Jewish Social Democratic Party, 11:313–314

　Jewish Socialist Verband, 11:314

　Jewish Socialist Workers' Party, 11:314–315

　Lasalle, Ferdinand, 12:501–502

　Latin America, 18:709

　Latvia, Shatz-Anin, Max, 18:111

　Lithuania, 13:121

　Netherlands, 15:102, 16:286–287

　New York City, 15:209–210, 211–212

　Palestine, Aḥdut ha-Avodah, 1:540

　Panken, Jacob, 15:612

　parody, Hebrew, 15:660

　Po'alei Zion, 16:244

　Poland, 5:632, 646–647, 6:23, 12:804, 16:347, 18:707–708

　post-WW II, 16:339, 18:706

　Romania, 18:707–708

　Russia, 18:706–707

　　Abramowitz, Emil, 1:324

　　Abramowitz, Raphael, 1:325

　　Dan, Fyodor Ilyich, 5:407

　　Eisenstadt, Isaiah, 6:270

　　Latzky-Bertholdi, Jacob Ze'ev Wolf, 12:524

　　Lestschinsky, Joseph, 12:666

　　Leviné, Eugene, 12:717–718

　　Narodnaya Volya, 18:707

　　Russian Socialist Revolutionary Party, 5:92–93, 18:707

　　Zemla i Volya, 18:707

　U.K., 12:499, 18:704

　U.S., 4:336, 5:538, 7:619, 687–688, 9:118, 18:708–709, 21:214–215

　　Levin-Shatzkes, Yiẓhak, 12:720

　women, 18:713–714

　Zionist movement and, 4:88–90, 12:709–710

　See also Bund; Jewish socialism

Socialism, Jewish. *See* Jewish socialism

Socialist Party of America, 9:118

Socialist Trade and Labor Alliance, 18:568

Socialist Workers' Party. *See* Jewish Socialist Workers' Party

Socialist Zionism, 4:89

Social justice

　business ethics and, 4:310–312

　Judaism, influence of, 11:519–520

　labor and, 12:410–411

Social Science and the Distrust of Reason (Bendix), 3:328

Social services

　Brazil, 18:33

　Kahn, Alfred Joseph, 11:719

　Low, Minnie, 13:233

　state taxation for, 16:38

Social solidarity, 6:63, 16:322–323

Social standards of conduct, 5:592–593

Social status

　concubines, 5:135–136

Social status, *continued*
    Cuba, 5:318–319
    Latin America, 12:509–510
    modern period, early, 6:126–127
    pre-French Revolution, 7:252–253
Social theory
    humor and, 9:598–599
    self-hatred, Jewish, 18:264–265
Social welfare
    Caspary, Eugen, 4:505–506
    charity, 4:573–575
    Council of Jewish Federations and
        Welfare Funds, 5:238–239
    Council of the Lands, 5:244
    Hadassah, the Women's Zionist
        Organization of America,
        8:185–188
    loans, 13:149
    Morocco, 14:502
    Schottland, Charles Irwin, 18:165–
        166
    settlement houses, 18:320
    sick
        communal care of, 18:544–
            545
        visiting the, 18:543–544
    Solomons, Adolphus Simeon,
        18:773
Social work
    Adler-Rudel, Salomon, 1:409–410
    Barrett, David, 3:175–176
    Bressler, David Maurice, 4:168
    Doron, Abraham, 5:759
    education, Perlman, Helen Harris,
        15:778
    Germany, Karminski, Hannah,
        11:813–814
    Hirschler, René, 9:140
    Klein, Philip, 12:225
    Lourie, Norman Victor, 13:226
    Lowenstein, Solomon, 13:235
    Newfield, Morris, 15:134–135
    Razovsky, Cecilia, 17:131
    Rosen, Joseph A., 17:428
    Rubinow, Isaac Max, 17:514–515
    Silver, Harold M., 18:585
    Slawson, John, 18:673
    Sobeloff, Isidor, 18:700
    U.S.
        Beckelman, Moses W., 3:244
        Bernheimer, Charles
            Seligman, 3:475
        Bernstein, Ludwig Behr,
            3:482
        Frankel, Lee Kaufer, 7:197
        Karpf, Maurice Joseph,
            11:816

Lurie, Harry Lawrence,
    13:269
    Silver, Harold, 18:585
Sociedad Hebraica Argentina, 2:71,
    12:511
Société des Études Juives, 11:724,
    14:625, 18:**721–722**
Societies, learned. *See* Learned
    societies
Societies and associations. *See*
    Fraternal societies; Freemasons;
    specific society or association
Society. *See* Ḥevrah, ḥavurah
Society for Ethical Culture, 1:396
Society for Handicrafts and
    Agricultural Work. *See* ORT
Society for Jewish Folk Music, 18:**725**
Society for Jewish Science, 4:694,
    12:799
Society for Jewish Writers and
    Journalists (Warsaw), 11:774–775
Society for the Advancement of
    Judaism, 11:777
Society for the Attainment of Full
    Civil Rights for the Jewish People in
    Russia, 6:384, 18:724–725, **724–725**
Society for the Culture and Science of
    Judaism. *See* Verein Fuer Kultur
    und Wissenschaft des Judentums
Society for the Diffusion of Culture,
    11:725
Society for the Diffusion of
    Englightenment, 6:187–188
Society for the Enlightenment of the
    Jews in Russia, 3:635
Society for the Full and Equal Rights
    of the Jewish People in Russia, 6:36
Society for the Promotion of Culture
    among the Jews of Russia, 3:137,
    4:116, 6:36, 182–183, 18:722, **725–
    728**
"The Society for the Restoration of
    Things to Their Former Glory" or
    "The Community of Hebraists"
    (Schlesinger), 18:139–140
Society for the Safeguarding of the
    Health of the Jewish Population. *See*
    TOZ
Society for the Support of Jewish
    Farmers and Artisans in Syria and
    Palestine. *See* Odessa Committee
Society for the Welfare of the Jewish
    Deaf, 2:34
Society of Jesus. *See* Jesuits
Sociology, 3:**298**, 14:72–73, 18:**728–
737**
    Adorno, Theodor W., 1:420
    Bauman, Zygmunt, 3:220
    Bell, Daniel, 3:298
    Ben-David, Joseph, 3:325

    Bendix, Reinhard, 3:327–328
    Cahnman, Werner J., 4:338–339
    Coser, Lewis A., 5:228
    Coser, Rose Laub, 5:228–229
    criminology and, 5:302–303
    demographers, 18:732–733
    Diamond, Sigmund, 5:634
    Dinitz, Simon, 5:671–672
    Drachsler, Julius, 6:6
    Durkheim, Émile, 6:63–64
    early development
        Europe, 18:739–741
        U.K., 18:731
        U.S., 6:6, 18:731–732
    Eaton, Joseph W., 6:84
    Eisenstadt, Samuel Noah, 6:271–
        272
    Elias, Norbert, 6:319
    Endelman, Todd M., 6:403
    Eppstein, Paul, 6:465
    Epstein, Abraham, 6:466–467
    Gumplowicz, Ludwig, 8:136
    Gurvitch, Georges, 8:142
    Guttman, Louis, 8:156
    Halbwachs, Maurice, 8:266–267
    Halpern, Benjamin, 8:283
    Hauser, Philip Morris, 8:463
    Horkheimer, Max, 9:525–526
    Inlander, Henry, 9:787
    intercultural relations, 18:733
    intermarriage, 14:373–385
    Jewish alcohol consumption, 6:27–
        28
    Jewish topics, 18:733–734
    Lazarsfeld, Paul F., 12:559–560
    Levy, Marion Joseph, Jr., 12:752–
        753
    Marxian sociology, 18:729
    Moreno, Jacob L., 14:484
    Morin, Edgar, 14:491–492
    Moser, Claude, 14:522
    Nelson, Benjamin, 15:67
    Oppenheimer, Franz, 15:447–448
    Riesman, David, 17:294
    Robinson, Sophia, 17:356
    Rose, Arnold Marshall, 17:424–
        425
    Rosenthal, Erich, 17:452–453
    Rosenthal, William, 17:457
    Ruppin, Arthur, 17:529–530
    Schafer, Stephen, 18:103
    Scheler, Max Ferdinand, 18:118–
        119
    Simmel, Georg, 18:607
    Sklare, Marshall, 18:660
    Smelser, Nell Joseph, 18:686

sociology of religion, 18:735

theory and empiricism, 18:732

women in sociology, 18:735–737

Sociology and History (Cahnman), 4:338–339

Sociology of the Bible, 3:658–659

Soco (ancient city), 18:**737**

Socoh (ancient city), 18:**737**

Sod (mystical or allegorical meaning), 3:641

Sod Adonai li-Yre'av (Cardozo), 4:466

Sodei Razayya (Eleazar ben Judah of Worms). *See Secrets of Secrets* (Eleazar ben Judah of Worms)

Soderbergh, Steven, 18:**737**

Sod ha-Ibbur. See Sefer ha-Ibbur

Sod ha-Sodot (Elhanan), 6:316

Sodom (Israel). *See* Sedom (Israel)

Sodom and Gomorrah (ancient cities), 18:**737–740**

    Abraham, 1:281, 282

Sodome et Gomorrhe (Giraudoux), 18:739

Sodom Region. See Hevel Sedom

Sodomy, 18:329

Sod Yesharim (Modena), 14:409

Soest (Germany), 18:**740**

Sofaer, Abraham (1896-1988), 18:**740**

Sofaer, Abraham (1939-), 18:**741**

Sof Davar (Shabtai), 18:360

Sofer. *See* Scribes; Soferim

Sofer, Abraham (1897-), 18:**742**

Sofer, Abraham Samuel Benjamin Wolf, 18:618, 741, 743

Sofer, Akiva, 18:**742**

Sofer, Hatam (1762-1839). *See* Sofer, Moses

Sofer, Hayyim ben Mordecai Ephraim Fischel (1821-1886), 18:**742**

Sofer, Moses, 4:132, 133, 18:**742–743**

    Adler, Nathan ben Simeon ha-Kohen, 1:404

    Bloch, Issachar Baer ben Samson, correspondence with, 3:762

    Dukes, Leopold, 6:44

    Duschak, Mordecai, 6:64

    Ehrenfeld, Samuel ben David Zevi, 6:239

    hassegat gevul, 8:451

    Lehren, Hirschel, 12:617

    Orthodox Judaism and, 15:494

Sofer, Simeon (1820-1883), 18:**741**

Sofer, Simeon (1850-1944), 18:**742**

Sofer, Simhah Bunem, 18:**741–742**

Sofer, Solomon, 18:**742**

Sofer family, 18:**741–742,** 741t

Soferim, 13:606, 609, 615, 18:**743–744**

Soferim (Epstein). *See Writers* (Epstein)

Soferim (tractate), 8:506, 18:**744–745**

Sof ha-Olam (Shamir), 18:392

Sofia (Bulgaria), 18:**745**

Sogane (Israel). *See* Sikhnin (Israel)

Soharet, 16:478

Der Sohn des verlorenen Sohnes (Morgenstern). *See The Son of the Lost Son* (Morgenstern)

A Soho Address (Lewis), 12:765

Soil chemistry, 17:203

Soil conservation, 13:234

Soil Microbiology, 6:26, 451

Soissons (France), 18:**745**

Sokal (Ukraine), 18:**745–746**

Sokhachev. *See* Sochaczew (Poland)

Sokhko. *See* Socoh (ancient city)

Sokolka (Poland), 18:**746**

Sokolof, Phil, 18:**746**

Sokolow, Anna, 18:**747**

Sokolow, Nahum, 8:495, 726, 14:297, 18:**747–749**

Sokolow Podlaski (Poland), 18:**749–750**

Sola, Aaron de. *See* De Sola, Aaron

Sola, Abraham de. *See* De Sola, Abraham

Sola, Clarence Isaac de. *See* De Sola, Clarence Isaac

Sola, David Aaron de. *See* De Sola, David Aaron

Sola, de, family. *See* De Sola family

Solal, Maimon, 18:751

Solal, Saadiah, 18:751

Solal family, 18:**751**

Solar day, 5:487

Solar energy, 5:169–170

Solarz, Stephen, 18:**752**

Soldaat van Oranje. See Soldier of Orange

Şoldăneşti (Romania). *See* Falticeni (Romania)

Sol de la vida (Barrios), 3:176

Soldi, Emile-Arthur, 18:**752**

Soldi-Colbert, Emile-Arthur. *See* Soldi, Emile-Arthur

Soldier of Orange (Roelfzema), 6:69

Soldiers, Necrology on Geneva (Hochhuth), 9:299

Sold Out. See Vyprodáno

Soldyck, Emile-Arthur. *See* Soldi, Emile-Arthur

Solel Boneh, 9:147–148, 10:201, 511, 512, 595, 597, 601, 18:**752–753**

Solidarite, 9:496

Solieli, Max. *See* Solieli, Mordecai

Solieli, Mordecai, 18:**753**

Solinus, Caius Julius, 18:**753**

Solis, Benjamin de, 18:**754**

Solis, Diego da, 18:**754**

Solis, Duarte Gomes de, 18:**753–754**

Solis, Duarte Gomez, 2:125

Solis, Eleazar. *See* Solis, Henrique

Solis, Francisco, 18:**753**

Solis, Gomes da, 18:**754**

Solis, Henrique, 18:**753**

Solis, Isaac Diogo da Silva, 18:**753**

Solis, Isaac Fernando da Silva, 18:**753**

Solis, Jacob da Silva, 18:**754**

Solis, Joseph de, 18:**754**

Solis, Simão Pires, 18:**753**

Solis, Solomon da Silva, 18:**754**

Solis-Cohen, David da Silva, 18:**754**

Solis-Cohen, Emily da Silva Jr., 18:**754**

Solis-Cohen, Jacob da Silva (1838-1927), 18:**754**

Solis-Cohen, Jacob da Silva (1890-1968), 18:**754**

Solis-Cohen, Leon da Silva, 18:**754**

Solis-Cohen, Solomon da Silva, 18:**754**

Solis-Cohen family, 18:**754,** 754t

Solis family, 18:**753–754**

"Solly." *See* Solomon, Harold

Solnik, Benjamin Aaron ben Abraham. *See* Slonik, Benjamin Aaron ben Abraham

Solo (Ballas), 3:92

Solo (Sobol), 18:702

Solodar, Abraham, 18:**754–755**

Solodukho, Judah, 11:321

Solomon (biblical figure), 5:451, 18:**755–763**

    Abishag the Shunammite and, 1:259

    Adonijah, 1:413

    Adoniram, 1:413

    Aggadah, 18:759–760

    Ahijah the Shilonite, 1:542

    alchemy, 1:600

    Chronicles, Book of, 4:699–701

    Ecclesiastes, 6:88, 89

    economy and society, 18:757–758

    Edom, 6:154

    Jerusalem and, 11:146

    Joab, death of, 11:339

    kingdom, 9:173–174, 18:755–757, 756

    Kings, Book of, 12:170–172

    lineage, 18:755

    representation in Islam, 18:760–761

    wisdom and kingship, 18:758–759

Solomon (biblical figure), *continued*
 See also Temple; Timna (Israel)
Solomon (oratorio, Handel), 18:762
Solomon (pianist), 18:**764**
Solomon, Benjamin (Australian censor), 18:763
Solomon, Benjamin (South African court usher), 18:763
Solomon, Bertha, 16:349, 18:**764**
Solomon, Edward, 18:764
Solomon, Edward Philip, 18:764
Solomon, Elias Louis, 18:**764**
Solomon, Emmanuel, 1:385, 18:763
Solomon, Ezekiel, 18:**764–765**
Solomon, Hannah Greenbaum, 13:233, 18:**765**
Solomon, Harold, 18:**765**
Solomon, Haym. *See* Salomon, Haym
Solomon, Ḥayyim's Son. See Shloyme, Reb Khayims
Solomon, Herbert. *See* Mann, Herbie
Solomon, Isaac b., 11:793
Solomon, James Hymie. *See* Reese, Jimmie
Solomon, Jonas, 14:445
Solomon, Judah Moss, 1:385, 16:340, 18:763
Solomon, Moses, 14:454
Solomon, Nathaniel, 18:763
Solomon, Odes of. See Odes of Solomon
Solomon, Psalms of. See Psalms of Solomon
Solomon, reign of, 4:698
Solomon, Richard, 18:764
Solomon, Saul I, 16:348–349, 18:763
Solomon, Saul II, 18:763–764
Solomon, Saul III, 18:764
Solomon, Servants of, 18:**767**
Solomon, Simeon, 14:542, 18:**767**
Solomon, Solomon Joseph, 18:**767–768**
Solomon, Testament of. See Testament of Solomon
Solomon, Vabian Louis, 1:385, 16:340, 18:763
Solomon, William Ewart Gladstone, 18:764
Solomon, William Henry, 18:764
Solomon, Wisdom of. See Wisdom of Solomon
Solomon Adeni. *See* Adeni, Solomon bar Joshua
Solomon Almoli. *See* Almoli, Solomon ben Jacob
Solomon ben Aaron, 12:407, 18:**769**
Solomon ben Abraham Adret. *See* Adret, Solomon ben Abraham

Solomon ben Abraham of Montpellier, 14:463, 18:**770**
Solomon ben David, 1:216
Solomon ben Elijah ha-Kohen, 18:**770**
Solomon ben Ḥasdai, 18:**770**
Solomon ben Isaac. *See* Rashi
Solomon ben Isaac Abraham of Przmysl, 8:355
Solomon ben Jacob Almoli. *See* Almoli, Solomon ben Jacob
Solomon ben Jesse, 11:460
Solomon ben Judah, 6:341, 18:**770–771**
Solomon ben Judah ha-Bavli, 18:**771**
Solomon ben Judah "of Dreux," 18:772
Solomon ben Judah of Lunel, 18:**772**
Solomon ben Kohen-Ẓedek, 11:557
Solomon ben Masʿud Raphael Alfasi, 1:638
Solomon ben Meir, 18:**772**
Solomon ben Meir ha-Levi of Karlin, 11:810
Solomon ben Meshullam de Piera, 4:53
Solomon ben Meyer Nathan Halberstam, 8:265
Solomon ben Samson, 18:**772**
Solomon ben Samuel, 18:**772–773**
Solomon ben Shaya. *See* Abu al-Munajjā Solomon ben Shaya
Solomon Enich ha-Kohen, 17:58
Solomon family (Australia), 18:763
Solomon family (England), 18:**763–764**
Solomon Gursky Was Here (Richler), 4:423, 17:288
Solomon ha-Levi. *See* Pablo de Santa Maria
Solomon Ḥayyim of Koidanov, 12:267
Solomon Ḥayyim Perlow of Koidanov. *See* Solomon Ḥayyim of Koidanov
Solomon ibn Adret. *See* Adret, Solomon ben Abraham
Solomon ibn Gabirol, 6:50, 527
Solomon ibn Yaish, 15:524
Solomon Jacob of Kolin. *See* Ehrenstamm, Solomon Jacob
Solomon Oef. *See* Solomon Ohev
Solomon Ohev, 1:212
Solomon on the Vanity of the World (Prior), 18:761
Solomonovich, Joseph. *See* Grossman, Vasili Semyonovich
Solomons, Adolphus Simeon, 18:**773**
Solomons, Jack, 18:**773**
Solomons, Jacob. *See* Parker, John
Solomon Salmatic ben Maimon, 3:586

Solomon Schechter Day School Association, 6:198
Solomon Seneor ben Ephraim. *See* Szerencsés, Imre
Solomon Suliman ben Amar, 18:**773**
Solomon Vidal ben Pourtaya, 15:608
Solomon Yedidya. *See* Solomon ben Aaron
Solotaroff, Theodore H., 18:**773**
Soloveichik, Aaron, 18:**774–775**
Soloveichik, Abraham, 18:773
Soloveichik, Ḥayyim (1853-1918), 2:77, 18:773, **775**
Soloveichik, Ḥayyim Simḥah (d. 1921), 18:773
Soloveichik, Isaac, 18:773
Soloveichik, Isaac Ze'ev, 18:773
Soloveichik, Isaac Ze'ev Ha-Levi, 18:773, **775–776**
Soloveichik, Joseph, 18:773
Soloveichik, Joseph Baer, 6:197, 17:155, 18:774
 of Volozhin, 18:**776**
Soloveichik, Joseph Dov, 18:773, 774
Soloveichik, Joseph ha-Levi (1700s), 18:773
Soloveichik, Max. *See* Solieli, Mordecai
Soloveichik, Mordecai. *See* Solieli, Mordecai
Soloveichik, Moses, 6:197, 18:773
Soloveichik, Moshe, 18:**776–777**
Soloveichik, Samuel, 18:774
Soloveichik, Simḥah ha-Levi, 18:773
Soloveichik, Zalman, 18:773
Soloveichik family, 18:**773–774**, 774*t*
Soloveitchik, Haym, 18:780
Soloveitchik, Joseph Baer, 1:285, 4:100, 18:**777–780**
 existentialism, 6:612
 modern Orthodoxy and, 15:495, 497, 498, 499
Soloviev, Vladimir, 18:**780**
Solow, Robert Merton, 18:**780–781**
Solti, Georg. *See* Solti, Sir Georg
Solti, Sir Georg, 18:**781**
Solvay, Ernest, 14:434
Solvo o zavtrashnem dne (Dolmatovski), 5:736
Solyma (ancient Israel). *See* Shalem (ancient Israel)
Somalia, 15:439
Somary, Felix, 19:5
Sombart, Werner, 18:733, 19:**5–6**
 on Jewish identity, 11:297
Sombor (Yugoslavia), 19:**6**
Someck, Ronny, 19:**6**
Somekh, Abdallah ben Abraham, 19:**6–7**

Somekh, Sasson, 15:473, 19:**7**

Somen, Israel, 19:**7**

Somi, Leone Ebreo de. *See* Sommo, Judah Leone ben Isaac

Somi, Leone Ebreo di. *See* Sommo, Judah Leone ben Isaac

Somlyó, Zoltan, 19:**7**

Sommelsdyk, Aerssen van, 4:70

Sommer, Emil, 19:**7**

Sommerhausen, Zevi Hirsch, parodies of, 15:658

Sommerstein, Emil, 19:**7–8**

Sommi Portaleone, Leone de. *See* Sommo, Judah Leone ben Isaac

Sommo, Judah Leone ben Isaac, 10:791, 19:**8–9**

Sommo, Yehuda. *See* Sommo, Judah Leone ben Isaac

Somogyi, Béla, 19:**9**

Somrei Sabat, 11:520

Ṣomrei Sabat, 19:**9**

Son, rebellious. *See* Rebellious son

Sonata Tragica (composition, Morawetz), 14:478

Soncino, Eliezer Gershon, 15:540

Soncino, Gershom ben Eliezer, 4:345

Soncino, Gershom ben Moses, 4:77, 163, 6:708, 19:10

Soncino, Joshua, 19:**10–11**

Soncino, Joshua Solomon, 19:10

Soncino, Menzlein. *See* Soncino, Gershom ben Moses

Soncino brothers, early printed editions of Hebrew Bible by, 3:586, 587

Soncino family, 4:75, 9:760, 18:699, 19:**10**, 10t

Soncino Gesellschaft der Freunde des Juedischen Buches, 19:**11**

Soncinus, Hieronymus. *See* Soncino, Gershom ben Moses

Sonderkommando, Jewish, 9:355, 19:**11–13**

Sonderling, Jacob, 19:**13**

Sondheim, Stephen, 19:**13–14**

Sondheimer, Franz, 19:**14**

"*Sone ha-Nashim*" (Abraham of Sarteano), 1:313–314

Song, angelic, 19:**14**

Song and Prayer. See Gezang un Gebet

Song Behind the Wire. See Spiew za Drutami (Karmel)

"Song of Ascent". *See* Shir ha-Ma'alot

Song of Deborah, 5:518, 18:390, 391

Song of Happiness. See Pesnya o schast'e

Song of Songs, 18:220, 221, 19:**14–20**

Abishag the Shunammite, 1:259

Aknin, Joseph ben Judah ben Jacob ibn, 1:570

allegorical nature of, 19:16–17

in the arts, 19:18–19

authorship, date, and origin, 19:18

balsam, 3:95

character of, 19:15–16

flowers, 7:90

interpretation of, 19:16, 17–18

love, 13:229

Song of Songs Rabbah, 19:**20**

Song of the Dnieper. See Pesnya o Dnepre

Song of the Sea, 6:614

Song of the Sea, 18:224, **224–225**

Song of Three Children and the Prayer of Azariah, 19:**20**

Songs. *See* Music

Songs (Emiot), 6:394–395

Songs of Israel. See Zemirot Yisrael

Songs of the Land. See Zemirot ha-Arez

Sonik (Poland). *See* Sanok (Poland)

Sonnabend, Yolanda, 19:**20**

Sonne, Avraham. *See* Ben Yizhak, Avraham

Sonne, Isaiah, 19:**21**

Sonneborn, Rudolf Goldschmidt, 19:**21**

Der Sonne-Geist (Mombert), 14:430

Sonnemann, Leopold, 16:344, 19:**21**

Sonnenborn, Rudolph G., State of Israel Bonds, 4:58

Sonnenfeld, Barry, 19:**21–22**

Sonnenfeld, Iulia, 18:**698–699**

Sonnenfeld, Joseph Ḥayyim ben Abraham Solomon, 19:**22**

Sonnenfeld, Sigismund, 19:**22–23**

Sonnenfeldt, Helmut, 19:**23**

Sonnenfels, Aloys von, 19:**23**

Sonnenfels, Joseph von, 11:414

Sonnenschein, Rosa, 19:**24**

Sonnenthal, Adolf Ritter von, 19:**24**

Sonnenwendhof (Mosenthal), 14:521

Sonneschein, Rosa, 2:53

Sonnino, Sidney, 19:23

Sonntag, Joseph, 19:**25**

Son of a Smaller Hero (Richler), 17:288

Son of Man, 6:496–497, 11:249, 19:**25**

Son of Mennaeus. *See* Ptolemy (85-40 B.C.E.)

The Son of the Lost Son (Morgenstern), 14:487

Sons of Bava. *See* Benei Binyamin

Sons of Darkness. *See* Sons of Light

Sons of Israel (Providence), 17:275

Sons of Light, 19:**25–26**

Sons of Singermann (Brinig), 4:184

Sons of the Fathers (Halper), 8:283

Sons of Zadok. *See* Zadokites

Sontag, Susan, 19:**26**

Sophia Church (Japan), 11:82

Sophie's Choice (motion picture), 9:443, 15:572

Sophie's Choice (Styron), 9:413

Soprano singers

Donalda, Pauline, 5:747

Leigh, Adèle, 12:626

Sopron (Hungary), 19:**26–27**

Sopronkeresztúr (Austria). *See* Deutschkreutz (Austria)

Sorauer, Paul Karl Moritz, 19:**27**

The Sorcerer's Apprentice (Dukas), 6:43

Sorcery, 19:**27–28**

magic, 13:344–345

Witch of En-Dor, 18:80, 81

witch of En-Dor, 6:404, 405

Sorek, valley of (ancient Israel), 19:**28**

Sores (Greece). *See* Serrai (Greece)

Sorgum, 19:**28**

Soria (Spain), 19:**28–29**

Sorkin, Aaron, 19:**29**

Sorkin, Michael, 19:**29–30**

Soroca. *See* Soroki (Moldova)

Soroki (Moldova), 19:**30**

Soros, George, 12:766, 15:225–226, 19:**30**

Sorotzkin, Zalman ben Ben-Zion, 6:75, 19:**30–31**

The Sorrow and the Pity (Ophuls), 9:442

The Sorrows of Job. See Yissurei Iyov

Sorstalanság (Kertész), 9:413

Sosis, Israel, 11:322–323, 19:**31**

Sosius, Gaius, 19:**31**

Soskice, Frank, baron Stow Hill. *See* Soskice, Sir Frank, baron Stow Hill

Soskice, Sir Frank, baron Stow Hill, 19:**31–32**

Soskin, Selig Eugen, 19:**32**

Søby, Espen, 18:96

Sosnovets. *See* Sosnowiec

Sosnowiec (Poland), 19:**32**

Sotah, 19:**32–33**, 21:161–162

See also Ordeal of jealousy

Soter. *See* Ptolemy I

Soter II. *See* Ptolemy VIII

Sotn in Goray (Singer), 18:635

Sotsialisticheskaya Yevreyskaya Rabochaya Partiya. *See* Jewish Socialist Workers' Party

Souirah (Morocco). *See* Mogador (Morocco)

Soul, 19:**33–35**

Adam and Eve as parts of, 16:106

Soul, *continued*

afflicting during Day of
Atonement, 5:488

afterlife, 1:441–442

On the Essence of the Soul, 3:65

immortality of, 3:238–240, 19:**35–
39**

Biblical literature, 19:35

body and soul, concept of,
4:31

Kabbalah, 19:38–39

Maimonides' interpretation,
2:462, 13:6

medieval philosophy, 1:442,
19:36–38

Mendelssohn, Moses, 14:34

modern philosophy, 19:38

nature of, 16:88

Talmudic literature, 19:35–36

nature of, 9:114, 663–664, 16:76,
81, 83, 87, 108

Paquda's concept, 3:66

resurrection of, 17:240–244

transmigration (*See* Gilgul)

See also Body and soul; Gilgul

The Soul of a Jew. See Nefesh Yehudi

Soul of Wood (Lind), 9:411

Souls on Fire (Wiesel), 9:410

Soultz (Germany), 19:**39**

Sourasky family, 19:**39**

Source criticism, 3:646, 649, 652–653

*Les sources et les courants de la
philosophie contemporaine en France*
(Banrubi), 3:373

Sources of Courage (Lookstein), 13:189

Sous (Morocco), 19:**40**

Sous le règne de la Licorne et du Lion
(Finbert), 7:24

South Africa, 19:**40–53,** *41, 43t*

antisemitism, 2:238

architects and architecture, Le
Roith, Harold Hirsch, 12:659

assimilation, 2:611

Bloemfontein, 3:769–770

businesses and industries

agricultural exports, 14:521

diamond trade and industry,
5:636

mining, 3:167–168, 12:481

communty organization, 19:44–48

department stores, 5:588

economic, social structure, 19:51–
52

education, 19:47–48

education, Jewish, 6:210–211

immigration, 19:42–43, *43t*

Israel relations, 19:53–54

Jewish settlement, 1:437

Johannesburg, 11:377–378

journalism, 6:745, 12:723

journalism in, 11:470

law, 9:9, 11:51, 12:554

legal, social status, 19:43–44

libraries, 12:787

museums, 14:634–635

newspapers, 16:502

Ochberg, Isaac, 15:375

Oudtshoorn, 15:547

political particpation, 19:50–51

politicians

Leon, Anthony James, 12:644

Schwarz, Harry Heinz, 18:189

Slovo, Joe, 18:684

politics, 16:348–349

religious institutions, 19:45–46

resistance leaders, Kasrils, Ronnie,
11:825–826

scholars, 12:463–464

settlement, 19:41–42

shehitah protection, 18:435

Smuths, Jan Christiaan, 18:695

social, cultural life, 19:48–50,
52–53

Solomon family, 18:763–764

wedding, vol. 5: color insert

youth movements, Iḥud Habonim,
9:717t, 719

Zionism, 19:49–50, 21:604–605

South African Board of Jewish
Education, 6:210–211

South African Institute of Town
Planners, 11:772

South African literature

biography, memoirs, 19:56–57

De Lima, Joseph Suasso, 5:539

English, 6:439

English writers, 19:54–55

Jacobson, Dan, 11:53

Jewish image, 19:54

Levinson, Olga, 12:723

Millin, Sarah Gertrude, 14:257

poetry, drama, 19:55–56

Yiddish writers, 19:59–60

See Also Dutch literature

South African War. *See* Boer War

South America. *See* Latin America

South Arabia. *See* Arabia

South Carolina (SC), 19:*61,* **61–62**

South Dakota (SD), 19:**62–63,** *63*

Southern Rhodesia. *See* Zimbabwe

A Southern Woman's Story (Pember),
15:719–720

Southhampton (England), 19:**60–61**

South West Africa, 19:**63**

Southwood, Julius Salter Elias, First
Viscount, 19:**63**

Soutine, Chaim, 3:781, 19:**63–64**

Souvenirs, 7:94

Sovern, Michael Ira, 19:**64**

Sovetish Heymland (journal), 14:519,
19:**64–65**

Soviano, Henry, 16:346

Soviet Jewry, 9:282–283, 20:269–270

Soviet Literature (Slonim), 18:677

The Soviets in World Affairs (Fischer),
7:54

Soviet Union. *See* Union of Soviet
Socialist Republics (USSR)

Soyer, Moses, 4:9, 19:**65**

Soyer, Raphael, 19:**65–66**

Soyer brothers, 15:221

Sozanda, 4:264

Sozialistiche Monatshefte (newspaper),
18:705

*Sozial- und Wirtschaftsgeschichte der
Juden im Mittelalter und der Neuzeit*
(Caro), 4:487

*Das Soziologische in Kants Erkenntnis-
Kritik* (Adler), 1:402

Sozusa (Israel). *See* Apollonia (Israel)

Sozvezdiye (Dolmatovski), 5:736

Space and place, 19:**66–67**

Spain, 19:**67–83**

antisemitism, 2:213, 4:519

Alba de Tormes, 1:581

Albarracín, 1:587

autos-da-fé, 18:45

badges, Jewish, 3:46

Barcelona, 17:126–127

blood libel, 3:775, 12:438

Cádiz, 4:331

Calahorra, 4:350

Calatayud, 4:351–352

Carmona, 4:485

Carrion de los Condes, 4:496

Cartagena, 4:496–497, 497

Castellón de la Plana, 4:514

Castile, 1:643

Castrojeriz, 4:518–519

Cea, 4:534

Chillón, 4:645

Ciudad Real, 4:745

Ciudad Rodrigo, 4:745

Coca, 4:764–765

Dueñas, 6:40–41

Middle Ages, 5:437

persecutions of 1391, 3:144,
20:461

Anusim, 2:252–253

civil war, Abraham Lincoln
Brigade, 15:218
conversos, 9:209, 19:76–78, *77*
Alboraycos, 1:595
Madrid, 13:333
Majorca, 13:413
Saragossa, 18:43–44, 45
Seville, 18:328
Toldeo, 18:57–58
cultural and social life, 1:386,
4:435, 9:214–215, 18:292, 19:79–
80
archives, 2:406
art, 2:496
Caribbean, Spanish-
Portuguese Nation of the:
La Nacion, 4:468–470,
476–477
communal life, 9:217
community, nature of, 5:105,
108
community organization,
13:411, 18:41, 326
deterioration of, 9:216–217
dress, 6:15
education, Jewish, 6:173–174
golden age, 19:71–73
Hebrew language used, 8:670
intellectual life in Islamic,
6:555
Jewish identity, 11:294–295
Ladino, 12:427–428, 427–435
language, biblical translations,
3:636
letters and letter writers,
12:673
limpieza de sangre, 13:25–26
medicine, 13:726
Moorish, 2:464, 495, 14:611–
612, 729–733
museums, 14:626
music, 12:434
population, 16:386, 388–389
seals, use of, 18:227
synagogue architecture,
19:373–374, *376*
economic affairs
artisans, 5:267
coinage, 14:299
contractors, 5:198
leather industry and trade,
12:575
moneylending, banking,
3:113, 14:439
printing and publishing,
9:761–762, 16:718
taxes, 7:23
typography, 20:213, 216

wine and liquor trade, 21:83
expulsions, 3:707, 7:15, 18:44–45,
19:78–79
Middle Ages, 6:556, 625, 626
Ottoman empire, 15:522–523
Palencia, 15:577
Palermo, Sicily, 15:581
Pamplona, 15:609
Quincentennial anniversary,
18:304–305
foreign policy and affairs
Israel, 19:82
Jewish immigrants to
America, 2:41
Holocaust, 19:81
Inquisition, 4:485, 9:791–792,
794–796, 18:44–45, 20:58–59
Badajoz, 3:42
Beinart, Haim, 3:269
laws and legal systems
banishment, 3:110
Berurei Averah/Averot, 3:492
Bet Din in, 3:515
capital punishment, 4:449–
450
informers, 9:780–781
Jewish immigrants to
America, 2:41
Middle Ages, 6:582, 18:41–42
Middle Ages
agriculture, Jewish, 1:494–495
antisemitism, 5:437
conversions, 6:528
expulsions, 6:556, 625, 626
intellectual life in Islamic,
6:555
Jewish law in, 6:582
Jewish privileges, 18:41–42
kabbalists, 5:467
officials, 9:145, 14:6
physicians, 6:679
population, 16:388–389
scholars, 5:469
modern period, 19:80–81
Muslim rule, 18:326, 19:68– 71, *70*
political theories, parties and
organizations
Calatrava Order, 4:352
Chief Rabbinate, 4:613
conferences, 5:145
post-WW II, 19:81–82
religious life and scholarship,
3:142–145
Bet Din, 3:515
biblical exegesis in, 3:642, 662
Christian reaction, 19:73–75

conferences, 5:145
early printed editions, 3:586–
587
Haggadah, 8:212, 213
illuminated Bibles, 3:676–678,
9:729–730
Kabbalistic mysticism,
11:605–606
language, biblical translations,
3:636
limpieza de sangre, 13:25–26
Middle Ages, 5:467
piyyut, 16:194, 195
preaching, 16:471–472
rabbis, 12:644–645, 17:13
Rab de la Corte, 17:32
talmudic school, 1:341–342
tosafists, 17:341
transporting a medieval
Torah scroll, vol. 5: color
insert
yeshivot, 21:316
Umayyad dynasty, 20:246–247
Visigoth rule, 19:67–68
See also Ferdinand and Isabella;
Iberian peninsula; *specific
Spanish towns and cities*
Spalato. *See* Split (Croatia)
Spandau (Germany), 19:**83**
Spanel, Abram Nathaniel, 19:**83**
Spanier, Arthur, 19:**83–84**
Spanier, Israel. *See* Wechsler, Israel
Spaniolish. *See* Ladino
Spanische Ballade (Feuchtwanger),
11:256
Spanish and Portuguese literature,
19:**84–91**
Aboab da Fonseca, Isaac, 1:269
Alemán, Mateo, 1:611
biblical influence, 3:671
Biblical influences, 19:84–85
Cervantes Saavedra, Miguel de,
4:550
Christian polemics, 1:265
conversos, marranos, 19:85–86,
87–88
Crescas, Ḥasdai ben Abraham,
5:285–286
encyclopedias, 6:400, 402
Enríquez Gomez, Antonio, 6:446
Jew, image of, 19:85, 86
Jewish contribution, 19:86–87,
88–89
Latin America, Isaacs, Jorge, 10:55
modern writers, 19:86, 87
poetry
Abbas, Moses Judah ben
Meir and, 1:232

Spanish and Portuguese literature, *continued*

Abun, 1:346

Açan, Moses de Tarrega, 1:354

Cota de Maguaque, Rodrigo de, 5:237

Enríquez, Isabel, 6:446

Enríquez Basurto, Diego, 6:446

Ibn Sasson, Samuel ben Joseph, 9:689–690

León, Luis de, 12:645

Móntoro, Antón de, 14:462

Rabinovich, José, 17:37

Rojas, Fernando de, 17:370–371

Schindlin, Raymond P., 18:118

Steimberg, Alicia, 19:174–175

Sverdlik, Oded, 19:333

Tarnopolsky, Samuel, 19:518–519

Tiempo, César, 19:718

Toker, Eliahu, 20:17–18

Verbitsky, Bernardo, 11:469, 20:1507

Wechsler, Elina, 20:693

The Spanish-Portuguese Nation of the Caribbean: La Nacion, 4:**468–477**

British West Indies, 4:473–474

Central America, 4:475–476

Colombia, 4:475

Dutch West India Company, 4:469

French Antilles, 4:473

The Guianas, 4:470–471

Inquisition, 4:468–469

Netherlands Antilles, 4:471–472

New Christians, 4:469

Panama, 4:475

Portuguese Jewish communities, 4:468–470

Recife, 4:469

Sephardim, 4:476

Spanish Jewish communities, 4:468–470, 476–477

Surinam, 4:471

Tobago, 4:472–473

Venezuela, 4:474–475

Virgin Islands, 4:474

See also Cayenne (French Guyana)

Sparrow, 19:**91**

Sparta (Ancient Greece), 19:**91–92**

Numenius, son of Antiochus, 15:339

Spartakusbund, 13:277

Spartakusgruppe, 13:277

Sparzenstein, Baron von. *See* Ricius, Paulus

Spassovich, D. V., 3:770

Späth, Johann Peter, 19:**92**

Spatial music, 4:130

"Spatiodynamism," 18:155

Species, the four. *See* Four species

Spectator. *See* Feder, Ernst

Specter, Arlen, 19:**92–93**

Spector, Johanna, 19:**93**

Spector, Mordecai, 19:**93–94**

Spector, Morris, 3:726

Spector, Norman, 14:464, 19:**94**

Spector, Phil, 19:**94**

Spectroscopy, 18:177

Speculation and Revelation (Shestov), 18:467

Speculative Kabbalah. *See* Kabbalah

Speech

etiquette, 6:539

free, 17:314–316

parts of, in Hebrew grammar, 8:577, 598

Speeches on Zionism (Balfour), 3:8

Speedboat (Adler), 1:406

Speiser, Ephraim Avigdor, 9:159, 294, 19:**94–95**

Spektor, Isaac Elḥanan, 19:**95–96**

Spelling, Aaron, 19:**96**

Spellman, Frank, 19:**96**

Spells. *See* Blessing and cursing; Magic

Spencer, John, 19:**96–97**

Spengler, Oswald, 7:512

Sperber, Alexander, 13:59

Sperber, Dan (scientist), 19:**97**

Sperber, Daniel (historian), 19:**97**

Sperber, Manès, 19:**97**

Spero, George, 16:342

Spero, Nancy, 19:**97–98**

Spero, Shubert, 19:**98**

Spertus Institute of Jewish Studies, 19:**98–99**

Spewack, Bella, 19:**99–100**

Speyer (Germany), 19:**100–102**

Crusader massacre, 5:311

Shum, 18:532–533

Speyer, Benjamin, 19:**102**

Speyer, Edgar. *See* Speyer, Sir Edgar

Speyer, Edward Beit, 19:102

Speyer, Philipp, 19:102

Speyer, Sir Edgar, 19:**102**

Speyer family, 19:**102**

Spice box, Havdallah, 8:467–468

Spice Garden. See Arugat ha-Bosem

Spicehandler, Ezra, 11:558

Spices, 19:**102–104**

calamus, sweet, 4:350–351

cinnamon, 4:730

Laudanum, 12:524

Spice trade, 19:**104–105**

Spiders, 19:**105**

Spiegel, Dora, 19:**105**

Spiegel, Isaiah, 19:**105–106**

Spiegel, Ludwig, 19:**106**

Spiegel, Marcus, 20:317–318

Spiegel, Nathan, 19:**106**

Spiegel, Paul, 19:**106**

Spiegel, Samuel P., 19:**106**

Spiegel, Shalom, 11:355, 19:**106–107**

Spiegel, Sidney, 13:11

Spiegel-Adolf, Mona, 19:**107**

Spiegelberg, Herbert, 19:**107**

Spiegelblatt, Aleksander. *See* Shpiglblat, Aleksander

Spiegelgeschichte (Aichinger), 1:549

Spiegelman, Art, 4:500–501, 631, 19:**107**

Spiegelman, Sol, 13:9, 19:**107–108**

Spielberg, Steven, 8:485, 11:819, 13:206, 19:**108**

Spielman, Emily, 19:109

Spielman, Isidore, 19:108

Spielman, Marion Harry Alexander, 19:108–109

Spielman, Meyer Adam, 6:161, 19:109

Spielman family, 19:**108–109**

Spielmann, Rudolf, 19:109

Spielmann family. *See* Spielman family

Spielvogel, Carl, 19:109

Spielvogel, Nathan, 19:**109–110**

Spier, Leslie, 2:186, 19:**110**

Spies, Reilly, Ace of. *See* Rosenblum, Sigmund Georgievich

Spiew za Drutami (Karmel), 11:812

Spikenard, 19:**110**

Das Spil von Kunig Salomon mit den zewyen Frawen (mystery), 18:761

Spina, Alonso de. *See* Alfonso de Espina

Spina, Geri, 19:**110**

Spingarn, Joel and Arthur, 3:734

Spinka, Joseph Meir Weiss of, 19:**111**

Spinka dynasty, 8:425

Spinoza, Baruch de, 16:65, 92–93, 19:**111–119**

Bible scholar, 19:118–119

commandments, reasons for, 5:88

dogmas of universal faith, 2:531–532

influence of, 19:117–118

Latin works of Hebrew grammar, 13:56

life and works, 19:111–112

metaphysics, 19:113–114

modern biblical criticism, development of, 3:649

New Testament critique and, 15:191

Nieto, David, 15:261

Oko, Adolph S., 15:398

Orobio de Castro, Isaac, 15:481, 482

philosophy, 19:112–118

prophets and prophecy, 16:585

psychology, ethics, 19:114–115

religion, critique of, 19:115–117

revelation, 17:257

secularization and Sephardi, 18:298–299

Torah, 20:43, 45

translations by Auerbach, Berthold, 2:652

Spinoza, Benedictus. *See* Spinoza, Baruch de

Spinoza, Bento. *See* Spinoza, Baruch de

"Spinoza of chess." *See* Rubinstein, Akiva

The Spinoza of Market Street (Singer), 18:635–636

Spira, Nathan Nata ben Solomon, 19:**119**

Spira family. *See* Shapira family

Spiral Press, 4:12

Spire. *See* Speyer

Spire (Germany). *See* Speyer (Germany)

Spire, André, 19:**119–120**

Spires (Germany). *See* Speyer (Germany)

Spirit. *See* Soul

The Spirit (comic strip), 6:277–278

The Spirit of Hebrew Poetry. See Vom Geiste der hebraeischen Poesie

The Spirit of Judaism: In Defense of Her Faith and Its Professors (Aguilar), 1:509

Spiritual movements, 18:451
See also specific movements

Spiro, Eugen, 19:**120**

Spiro, György, 19:**120**

Spiro, Karl, 19:**120**

Spiro, Melford Elliot, 19:**120–121**

Spiro, Nathan. *See* Spira, Nathan Nata ben Solomon

Spiro, Nathan Nata ben Solomon. *See* Spira, Nathan Nata ben Solomon

Spitz, Hirsch, 15:386

Spitz, Joseph, 15:677

Spitz, Mark Andrew, 19:**121**

Spitz, Rene A., 19:**121–122**

Spitzer, Benjamin Solomon Zalman. *See* Spitzer, Solomon

Spitzer, Eliot, 15:224, 19:**122**

Spitzer, Frederic, 19:**122**

Spitzer, Hugo, 19:**122**

Spitzer, Karl Heinrich, 19:**123**

Spitzer, Leo, 19:**123**

Spitzer, Moshe, 19:**123–124**

Spitzer, Rudolf. *See* Lothar, Rudolf

Spitzer, Samuel, 19:**124**

Spitzer, Solomon, 19:**124**

Spitzer, Zalman. *See* Spitzer, Solomon

Spivacke, Harold, 19:**124**

Spivak, Elijah, 11:320

Spivak, Elye, 19:**124–125**

Spivak, Nissan, 19:**125**

Spivakovsky, Tossy, 19:**125**

Splendor in the Grass (motion picture), 2:104

Spliet. *See* Split (Croatia)

Split (Croatia), 19:**125–126**

Spoehr, Alexander, 19:**126**

Spoleto (Italy), 19:**127**

Sponheim, Abbot of. *See* Trithemius, Johannes

Sporkin, Stanley, 19:**127**

Sporn, Philip, 19:**127**

Sports, 19:**127–150**

Albert, Marv, 1:588–589

Allen, Mel, 1:667–668

Alouf, Yehoshua, 1:687–688

arenas, 16:359–360

Cosell, Howard, 5:227–228

fencing, 11:98

Formula One racing, 18:116

handball, 11:48

Hapoel, 8:338–340

historical opposition to, 19:127–128

horse racing, 19:143–144

ice hockey, 3:552, 7:57, 18:150, 19:144

Israel, 19:130–133

Elitzur, 6:355

Maccabiah, 13:320

Maccabi Tel Aviv basketball team, 14:392

Jewish athletes, 19:133–150

Maccabiah games, 19:130

Middle Ages, 19:128–129

in New York City, 12:592–593, 15:222

pre-1948 Israel, 19:129–130

public relations, 16:711

Rosenfeld, Fanny, 17:445

Roth-Shachamorov, Esther, 17:495

Rubenstein, Louis, 17:510–511

skating

ice, 19:144

speed, 11:69–70

soccer, 15:716, 19:133–134

swimming, 19:146–147

Epstein, Charlotte, 6:469

Leibowitz, Keren, 12:621

table tennis, Adelstein-Rozeanu, Angelica, 1:386–387

team owners

Cuban, Mark, 5:326

Davidson, William, 5:477

Dreyfus, Barney, 6:20–21

Mizrachi, Shimon, 14:392

Modell, Art, 14:407

Pollin, Abe, 16:359–360

track and field, 1:328–329, 5:211, 19:148–149

writers

Abramson, Jesse, 1:328–329

Daniel, Dan, 5:425

Fischler, Stan, 7:57

Izenberg, Jerry, 10:825

Kahn, Roger, 11:724

Schaap, Richard J., 18:97–98

See also specific sports

Sports education, 2:541

The Spotted Tiger. See Namer Havarburot

Spouses (Property Relations) Law (Israel, 1973), 13:681, 682

Sprachman, Abraham, 19:**150–151**

Sprachman, Mandel, 19:**150–151**

Springarn, Arthur Barnett, 19:110

Springarn, Joel Elias, 19:110

Springarn brothers, 19:110

Der Springbrunnen (Heymann), 9:86

Springer, Axel Caesar, 19:**151**

Springer, Béla. *See* Dénes, Béla

Springfield (MA), 19:**151–152**

Springs (water)

Ein Fashkhah, 6:255–256

En-Gedi, 6:408

En-Haron, 6:441

En-Rogel, 6:447

Springs, Alice, 15:192

Springtime in Budapest. See Budapesti tavasz (Karinthy)

Sprinzak, Joseph, 19:**152–153**

Spying. *See* Espionage

Squadron, Howard Maurice, 19:**153**

Squash, 19:146, 147–148

Squill, 19:**153**

Sraffa, Piero, 19:**153**

Srem (Poland), 19:**153–154**

Sri Lanka. *See* Ceylon

Srole, Leo, 18:733

SS and SD, 19:**154–156**

Auschwitz trials, 2:676

SS and SD, *continued*
Bergen-Belsen concentration camp, burial of prisoners, 9:*487*
Eichmann, Adolf Otto, 6:248–251
Himmler, Heinrich, 9:121–122
Hoess, Rudolf, 9:304–306
humiliation of Polish Jews, 9:*465*
St. Croix. *See* Virgin Islands
St. Eustatius (Netherlands Antilles), 4:472
St. Jean d'Acre (Israel). *See* Acre (Israel)
St. Louis, voyage of the, 2:60, 4:213, 5:320, 9:366, 19:**228–229**
St. Martin (Netherlands Antilles). *See* Sint Maarten (Netherlands Antilles)
St. Paul (MN). *See* Minneapolis-St. Paul (MN)
St. Thomas. *See* Virgin Islands
St. Urbain's Horseman (Richler), 4:423–424, 6:439, 17:288
Die Staatenbildung der Israeliten in Palaestina (Alt), 2:11
Stachel, Jacob, 19:**156**
Stacked Steel Slabs (Serra), 18:314
Stade, Bernard, 13:58
Stadthagen, Joseph, 19:**156**
Staff of Aaron. *See* Rod of Aaron
Staff of Moses. *See* Rod of Moses
Stage design, 1:553, 2:487
Stahl, Friedrich Julius, 12:551, 16:344, 19:**156–157**
Stahl, Heinrich, 19:**157**
Stalin (Bulgaria). *See* Varna (Bulgaria)
Stalin, Joseph Vissarionovich, 19:**157–158**
American Joint Distribution Committee, 2:60
antisemitism, doctors' plot, 5:728–729
Block, Herbert Lawrence, 3:769
nationalism, 5:94
See also Communism
Stalino (Ukraine). *See* Donetsk (Ukraine)
Stalin vedyot nas k pobede komunizma (Kaganovich), 11:707
Stamford (CT), 19:**158–159**
Stamford (England), 19:**158**
Stampfer, Jehoshua, 19:**159**
Stampfer, Joshua, 19:**160**
Stamps, 19:**160–162**
Stand, Adolf, 15:652, 16:340, 19:**162**
Standard (symbol). *See* Banners
Stande, Stanislaw Ryszard, 19:**162**
Stangl, Franz, 18:700
Stanislav (Ukraine), 19:**162–163**

Stanislavsky, Konstantin, 1:408, 409
Stanislavsky, Simon Judah, 19:**163**
Stanislawow. *See* Stanislav (Ukraine)
Stantsye Baranovitsh (Shalom Aleichem), 18:384
Star, Darren, 19:**164**
Stara Zagora (Bulgaria), 19:**164**
Starbucks, 18:174
Starer, Robert, 19:**164**
Stark, Abe, 15:215
Stark, Albert, 19:**164–165**
Stark, Edward, 19:**165**
Stark, Louis, 19:**165**
Stark, Pesach. *See* Stryjkowski, Juljan
Starkenstein, Emil, 19:**165**
Starkey, John Llewelyn, 19:**165**
Starkova, Klavdiia, 11:321
Starobinski, Jean, 19:**165**
Starodub (Russia), 19:**166**
Star of David. *See* Magen David
"Star of David" (boxer). *See* Salita, Dmitriy
Star of Redemption (Rosenzweig), 16:110, 17:450, 460–461
Star of Solomon amulets, 2:122
Staro-Konstantinov (Ukraine), 19:**166**
Starominsky, Marc. *See* Seter, Mordechai
Starominsky, Mordechai. *See* Seter, Mordechai
Starr, Joshua, 19:**166**
Starting from the Classics. See Pornind dela clasici
Star Trek (television show), 18:440
Stary Bykhov (Belarus). *See* Bykhov (Belarus)
Stashev. *See* Staszow (Poland)
Stasov, Vladimir, 2:508
Staszow (Poland), 19:**166–167**
The State in Theory and Practice (Laski), 12:499
Statement on Race (UNESCO report), 14:453
Statenbijbel (Bible), 6:67, 68
State of Israel. *See* Israel
State of Israel Bonds, 4:58–59, *59*
State of Nationalities (social concept), 6:34
Statistics, 19:**167–171**
population (*See* Demography)
See also Vital statistics
Statius, Publius Papinius, 19:**171**
Statue of Liberty (New York City, NY), 15:202
Status quo ante, 19:**171**
Statute of Kalisz, 4:45
Statutes of the Kings, Temple Scroll, 19:633, 634–635

Staub, Hermann, 19:**171**
Stavi, Moses, 19:**171–172**
Stawsky, Moses. *See* Stavi, Moses
Stealing. *See* Theft and robberies
Steaua fără nume (Sebastian), 18:231
Steel, Danielle, 19:**172**
Steel and Iron. See Shtol un Ayzn
Stefan, Metropolitan, 19:**172–173**
Ştefăneşti. *See* Stefanesti (Romania)
Stefanesti (Romania), 19:**173**
Stefen, Oskar, 3:569
Steg, Adolphe, 19:**173**
Steiermark (Austria). *See* Styria (Austria)
Steig, William, 19:**173–174**
Steiger trial, 19:**174**
Steiman, Beynush, 19:**174**
Steimberg, Alicia, 19:**174–175**
Steimer, Molly, 19:**175**
Stein, Arthur, 19:**175**
Stein, August, 19:**175–176**
Stein, Aurel. *See* Stein, Sir Aurel
Stein, Baron Karl vom und Zum, 19:**181**
Stein, Benno, 6:481
Stein, Edith, 11:384, 19:**176**
Stein, Edmund Menahem, 19:**176–177**
Stein, Eliezer Lipman, 19:**177**
Stein, Erwin, 19:**177**
Stein, Gertrude, 12:661, 19:**177–178**
Stein, Henri, 19:**178**
Stein, Herbert, 19:**178–179**
Stein, Herman D., 19:**179**
Stein, Isaac, 19:**179–180**
Stein, Israel, 4:180
Stein, Janice Gross, 19:**180**
Stein, Joseph, 19:**180**
Stein, Jules Caesar, 19:**180–181**
Stein, Leonard, 19:**181**
Stein, Leonard J., 2:162
Stein, Ludwig, 18:731, 19:**181–182**
Stein, Richard, 19:**182**
Stein, Sir Aurel, 2:371, 19:**176**
Stein, William Howard, 13:10, 19:**182**
Stein, Yehezkiel, 19:**182**
Steinach, Eugen, 19:**182–183**
Steinamanger. *See* Szombathely
Steinbach, Alexander Alan, 19:**183**
Steinbach, Emil, 12:547, 19:**183**
Steinbach, John, 14:446
Steinbarg, Eliezer, 19:**183,** 21:350–351
Steinberg, Aaron, 19:**184**
Steinberg, Arnold, 19:**184**
Steinberg, Avraham, 19:**184–185**
Steinberg, Isaac Nahman, 19:**185**

Steinberg, Jacob, 8:727–728, 19:**185–187**

Steinberg, Joshua, 19:**187**
   Russian translation of Bible by, 3:635

Steinberg, Judah, 19:**187–188**

Steinberg, Martin R., 19:**188**

Steinberg, Maximilian Ossejevich, 19:**188**

Steinberg, Milton, 19:**188–189**

Steinberg, Moses, 4:199

Steinberg, Paul, 19:**189**

Steinberg, Sam, 14:464, 19:184

Steinberg, Saul, 15:225, 19:**189–190**

Steinberg, William, 19:**190**

Steinberger, Jack, 19:**190**

Steinberg family, 19:**183–184**

Steinbruch, Aarão, 16:349, 350, 19:**190**

Steinem, Gloria, 15:219, 19:**190–191**

Steinem, Pauline, 15:393

Steiner, Clarence, 14:446

Steiner, Drago. *See* Eventov, Yakir

Steiner, George, 19:**191**

Steiner, Hannah, 19:**191**

Steiner, Jean Fançois, 5:21

Steiner, Leslie. *See* Howard, Leslie

Steiner, Shaye, 4:30

Steiner-Prag, Hugo, 19:**192**

Steinfeld, J.J., 19:**192**

Steingut, Irwin, 19:192

Steingut, Stanley, 19:192

Steingut family, 19:192

Steinhardt, Frank, 5:318

Steinhardt, Jakob, 4:70, 15:648, 19:**192–193**

Steinhardt, Joseph ben Menahem, 19:**193**

Steinhardt, Laurence Adolf, 19:**193–194**

Steinhardt, Menahem Mendel ben Simeon, 19:**194**

Steinhardt, Michael H., 15:226, 19:**194**

Steinhaus, Hugo Dyonizy, 19:**194–195**

Steinheim, Salomon Ludwig, 16:96, 17:258, 19:**195**

Steinherz, Natan, 4:134

Steinherz, Samuel, 19:**195–196**

Steinitz, Wilhelm, 4:603, 604–605, 12:497, 19:**196**

Steinman, Eliezer, 19:**196–197**

Steinsaltz, Adin, 19:**197**

Steinschneider, Daniel. *See* Prosstitz, Daniel

Steinschneider, Moritz, 19:**197–199**, 21:108
   bibliography of, 3:682
   on Jewish studies, 11:316–317

Orientalism, 15:471

Steinthal, Hermann Heymann, 2:163, 15:468, 19:**199–200**

"The Steipler." *See* Kanievsky, Jacob Israel

Stekel, Wilhelm, 19:**200**

Stekelis, Moshe, 2:187, 19:**200**

Stella (Spain). *See* Estella (Spain)

Der Stellvertreter (Hochhuth), 9:299

Stematsky, Avigdor, 15:265, 19:**200**

Stempenyu (Shalom Aleichem), 18:378, 381, 383–384

Stencl, Abraham Nahum, 19:**200**

Stendal (Germany), 19:**200–201**

Stendal, Moses, 3:611

Stengel, Erwin, 19:**201**

Stenheim, Solomon Ludwig, 7:665

Stenn, Rebecca, 19:**201**

Stent, Gunther Siegmund, 13:9, 19:**202**

Stephen III, 16:372

Stephen S. Wise Temple, 21:499

Sterility. *See* Barrenness and fertility

Sterilization experiments, 8:464–465

Sterk, Izidor, 8:755

Sterling, Jeffrey, Baron Sterling of Plaisow. *See* Sterling, Sir Jeffrey, Baron Sterling of Plaisow

Sterling, Sir Jeffrey, Baron Sterling of Plaisow, 19:**202**

Stern, Abraham Jacob, 19:**202–203**

Stern, Adolphe, 19:**203**

Stern, Alfred, 19:**203**

Stern, Anatol, 19:**203–204**

Stern, Arthur C., 19:**204**

Stern, Avraham, 19:**204**

Stern, Bernhard Joseph, 19:**204**

Stern, Bertha Gladys, 19:**204–205**

Stern, Bezalel, 19:**205**

Stern, Bill, 19:**205**

Stern, Chaim, 3:625, 19:**205–206**

Stern, Clara Josephy, 6:160, 19:218

Stern, David, 1:461, 11:468, 19:**206**

Stern, David de, 19:202

Stern, Elizabeth Gertrude Levin, 19:**207**

Stern, Emma, 15:650

Stern, Ephraim, 19:**207**

Stern, Erich, 19:**207–208**

Stern, Ernest, 19:**208**

Stern, Frederick Claude. *See* Stern, Sir Frederick Claude

Stern, Fritz Richard, 19:**208**

Stern, Gershon, 19:**208–209**

Stern, Grete, 17:336–337

Stern, Grigori, 19:**209**

Stern, Guenther. *See* Anders, Guenther

Stern, Hans, 19:**209**

Stern, Harry Joshua, 19:**209**

Stern, Horace, 12:556, 19:**209–210**

Stern, Howard, 11:812, 19:**210**

Stern, Irma, 19:**210**

Stern, Isaac, 2:46, 19:**210–211**
   Bronfman, Yefim, 4:206

Stern, Jack, 19:**211–212**

Stern, Jacques, 19:**212**

Stern, Joseph, 19:**212**

Stern, Joseph Zechariah, 19:**212**

Stern, Julius, 19:**212**

Stern, Julius David, 19:**212–213**

Stern, Kurt Gunter, 19:**213**

Stern, Leonard, 19:**213**

Stern, Lina Solomonovna, 19:**213–214**

Stern, Louis, 19:**214**

Stern, Malcolm Henry, 2:54, 3:697, 19:**214–215**

Stern, Max, 19:**215**

Stern, Max Emanuel, 19:**215**

Stern, Menahem (Historian), 19:**215**

Stern, Menahem (Rabbi), 19:**215**

Stern, Moritz, 9:159, 19:**215**

Stern, Moshe, 19:**215–216**

Stern, Noah, 19:**216**

Stern, Otto, 19:**216**

Stern, Philip Cohen, 19:**216**

Stern, Robert A.M., 19:**216–217**

Stern, Samuel Miklós, 19:**217**

Stern, Sigismund, 19:17, **217**

Stern, Sir Frederick Claude, 19:**208**

Stern, Steve, 19:**217–218**

Stern, Vera, 2:46

Stern, William, 19:**218–219**

Sternberg, Erich-Walter, 11:413, 19:**219**

Sternberg, Jacob, 19:**219**

Sternberg, Josef von, 14:571, 19:**219**

Sternberg, Kurt, 19:**219**

Sternberg, Lev Yakovlevich, 11:361, 19:**219–220**

Sternberg, Sarah Frankel, 8:397, 19:**220**

Sternberg, Sigmund. *See* Sternberg, Sir Sigmund

Sternberg, Sir Sigmund, 19:**220**

Sternberger, Estelle, 11:331

Sternberger, Leon, 15:198

Stern der Erloesung. See The Star of Redemption

Sterne, Hedda, 19:**220–221**

Sterne, Maurice, 19:**221**

Sterne, Simon, 15:211, 19:**221–222**

Stern family, 19:**202**

Stern Gang. *See* Loḥamei Ḥerut Israel

"Stern Group." *See* Loḥamei Ḥerut Israel

Sternharz, Nathan, 19:**222**

Sternheim, Carl, 19:**222**

Stern, Jenö. *See* Zsoldos, Jenö

Sternschuss, Moshe, 19:**223**

Stern's Department Store, 15:226

Sternstein, Joseph Philip, 19:**223**

Stern-Taeubler, Selma, 19:**223**

Stetit autem Salomon (motet, de Prés), 18:762

Stettin (Poland), 12:592, 19:**223–224**

Steuerman, Adolf Rodion, 19:**224**

Steuermann, Edward, 19:**224**

Steuernagel, Carl, 19:**224**

Steuss, David, 19:**224–225**

Stewardship vs. dominion, 5:164–165

Stibium. *See* Antimony

Stieglitz, Alexander, 19:**225**

Stieglitz, Alfred, 19:**225**

Stieglitz, Julius Oscar, 19:**225–226**

Stieglitz family, 19:**225**

Stiglitz, Joseph E., 19:**226**

Stihuri venerice (Aderca), 1:391

Stiles, Ezra, 4:479, 19:**226**

Stiller, Ben, 19:**227**

Stiller, Mauritz, 14:577–578

Stilling, Benedict, 19:**227**
    anatomy, 2:135

Stillman, Louis, 19:**227**

Stillman, Norman Arthur, 19:**227–228**

Stine, R.L., 19:**228**

Stipulation in contract law, 5:193, 194

Stirring Times (Finn), 7:39

Stobbe, Otto, 19:**229–230**

Stock, Dov. *See* Sadan, Dov

Stockade and watchtower, 19:**230**

Stock exchanges, 2:109, 15:730, 19:**230–231**

Stockholm (Sweden), 19:**231–232**

Stoecker, Adolf, 3:726, 4:695, 11:811, 19:**232**

Stoicism, 6:462–463, 19:**232–233**

Stokes, Rose Pastor, 19:**233**

Stolbsty (Belarus), 19:**233–234**

Stolen property
    commandments concerning, 5:77t–78t
    economic history, 6:111–112

Stolin (Belarus), 19:**234**

Stoller, Ezra, 16:126

Stoller, Mike, 12:618–619

Stoller, Samuel, 19:**234–235**

Stolpce. *See* Stolbsty (Belarus)

Stolyarski, Peter Solomonovich, 19:**235**

Stolypin, Peter, 4:36–37

Stolz, Blanche A., 19:**235**

Stolz, Joseph, 19:**235**

Stone, Dewey D., 19:**235**

Stone, I. F., 18:709, 19:**235–236**

Stone, Irving, 19:**236**

Stone, Julius, 12:548, 19:**236**

Stone, Mickey. *See* Marcus, David Daniel

Stone, Oliver, 19:**236**

Stone, Peter, 19:**236–237**

Stone, Richard Bernard, 19:**237**

Stone, Steven Michael, 19:**237**

Stone family. *See* Sapirstein-Stone-Weiss family

Stonequist, Everett, 18:733

Stoner, J.B., 15:79

Stones and Herbs. See Kammi i travy

Stoning. *See* Capital punishment

Stopnica (Poland), 19:**237–238**

Stora, Abraham, 19:238

Stora family, 19:**238**

Storax, 19:**238**

Storia degli Ebrei in Italia (Milano), 14:232

Storia della letteratura italiana (Momigliano), 14:431

Storie di poveri amanti (Bassani), 3:207

Stories, animal, 2:173–174

Stories of an Imaginary Childhood (Bukiet), 4:265

Stork, 19:**238**

The Stormy Life of Lazik Roitschwantz (Ehrenburg), 6:238

Storojinet. *See* Storozhinets

Storozhinets (Ukraine), 19:**238–239**

Storrs, Ronald. *See* Storrs, Sir Ronald

Storrs, Sir Ronald, 19:**239**

Story of a Secret State (Karski), 11:818

"The Story of Hannah," 8:448

"The Story of the Jerusalemite." *See* Ma'aseh Yerushalmi

The Story of the Jews. See History of Matzah (Rivers)

Story of the Seven Brothers (Emrāni), 6:398

Strabo, 6:477, 19:**239–240**

Strack, Hermann Leberecht, 19:**240**

Strakosch, Maurice, 19:**240**

Strand, Paul, 19:**240–241**

Strange, James, 18:307

The Strange Nation of Raphael Mendes (Moacyr), 18:207

"Stranger" concept and Jewish identity, 11:292, 18:730, 733

Strangers and gentiles, 19:**241–242**

Strangers within Our Gates (Woodsworth), 4:396

Strangling (execution method). *See* Capital punishment

Stránský, Jaroslav, 19:**242–243**

Stransky, Josef, 19:**243**

Strasberg, Lee, 1:408–409, 14:450, 15:220, 19:**243**

Strasbourg (France), 19:**243–245**

Strasburger, Eduard, 13:7, 19:**245–246**

Strashimirov, Anton, 4:276

Strashun, Mathias, 19:**246–247**

Strashun, Samuel ben Joseph, 19:**247**

Strashunsky, Joel David. *See* Loewenstein-Strashunsky, Joel David

Strassburg. *See* Strasbourg

Die Strasse meiner Jugend (Eloesser), 6:366

Strassfeld, Michael, 15:233, 19:**247**

Strassfeld, Sharon, 19:**247–248**

Straton's Tower. *See* Caesarea (Israel)

Straton's Tower (Israel). *See* Caesarea (Israel)

Stratten, Dorothy, 4:35

Straubing (Germany), 19:**248**

Straucher, Benno, 15:652, 16:340

Straus, Isidore, 15:203, 207, 211, 19:**248–249**

Straus, Jesse Isidore, 19:**249**

Straus, Lazarus, 15:203

Straus, Nathan, 15:203, 211, 19:**249**

Straus, Nathan, Jr., 15:214, 19:**249–250**

Straus, Oscar (1850-1926), 15:211, 19:**249**
    The American Hebrew, 2:49
    American Jewish Committee, 2:54
    American Jewish Historical Society, 2:59

Straus, Oscar Solomon (1870-1954), 19:**250**

Straus, R. Peter, 19:**250**

Straus, Rahel Goitein, 19:**250–251**

Straus, Ralph, 19:**251**

Straus, Roger, Jr., 19:**251**

Straus, Roger Williams, 19:**250**

Strausberg, Baruch Hirsch. *See* Strousberg, Bethel Henry

Straus family, 5:588, 19:**248–250**

Strauss, Aryeh Ludwig, 19:**252**

Strauss, Benno, 19:**252**

Strauss, Berthold, 3:684

Strauss, Claude. *See* Vigée, Claude

Strauss, David Friedrich, 15:191

Strauss, Eduard, 19:**252**

Strauss, Eliyahu. *See* Ashtor, Eliyahu

Strauss, George Russell, Baron, 16:342, 18:706, 19:**252**

Strauss, Gustave Louis Maurice, 19:**252**

Strauss, Herbert D., 1:428
Strauss, Johann, Jr., 19:**252–253**
Strauss, Leo, 19:**253**
Strauss, Levi, 5:588, 19:**253**
Strauss, Lewis Lichtenstein, 15:450, 19:**254**
Strauss, Meyer. *See* Strouse, Myer
Strauss, Oscar, 15:203
Strauss, Peter E., 19:253
Strauss, Robert Schwarz, 19:**254–255**
Strauss-Kahn, Dominique, 19:**255**
Strazzaria, 18:231
Streckfuss, Adolf Friedrich Karl, 19:**255**
The Street of Crocodiles (Schulz), 18:175
Streicher, Julius, 4:478–479, 19:**255**
  Nuremberg laws, 15:349
Streichman, Yehezkel, 19:**255–256**
  Nikel, Lea, 15:265
Streisand, Barbra, 19:**256**
Streit, Shalom, 19:**257**
Strelisk, Uri ben Phinehas of, 19:**257**
Strelisker, David. *See* Brod, Dovidl
Strelisker, Marcus, 19:**257**
Stretyn, Judah Zevi Hirsch, 19:**257**
Strich, Fritz, 19:**257–258**
Strick, Joseph, 19:**258**
Stricker, Robert, 1:247, 15:390, 16:341, 19:**258**
Strigler, Mordecai, 19:**258**
The Strike (motion picture), 6:274
Strikes, labor, 12:411
Strim (Poland). *See* Srem (Poland)
Strindberg, August, 18:91, 92
  Josephson, Ernst Abraham, 11:433
  Josephson, Ludwig Oscar, 11:433
String Quartet No. 1 (composition, Morawetz), 14:478
Stripes. *See* Floggings
Strisower, Leo, 19:**258–259**
Strnad, Oskar, 19:**259**
Strochlitz, Sigmund, 19:**259**
Stroheim, Erich von, 14:571, 19:**259**
Strominger, Jack, 13:11, 19:**260**
The Strong Are Lonely. See Das heilige Experiment
Strongila, Fatima, 15:541
Stronilah, 19:303
Stroock, Allan, 19:261
Stroock, Hilda, 19:260
Stroock, Joseph, 19:260
Stroock, Marcus, 19:260
Stroock, Moses J., 19:260
Stroock, Solomon Marcuse, 19:260
Stroock family, 19:**260–261**

Stroop, Juergen, 19:**261**
Strousberg, Bethel Henry, 17:70, 19:**261**
Strouse, Myer, 19:**261**
Struck, Hermann, 4:70, 249, 19:**261–262**
Structuralism, 3:653, 655
Structure of Society (Levy), 12:752
Structure of Spanish History. See España en su historia: Cristianos, Moros y Judíos
Structurists, 4:88
Strug, Kerri, 19:**262**
Struggle. See Kampf
Strunsky, Simeon, 19:**262**
Stry (Ukraine), 19:**262–263**
Stryj. *See* Stry (Ukraine)
Stryjkowski, Juljan, 19:**263–264**
Strykow (Poland), 19:**264**
Stubbs, J. N., 15:582
Stubrin, Marcelo, 16:350
Stuckart, Wilhelm, 15:348, 349, 350
Students' fraternities, German, 19:**264–265**
Students' movements, Jewish, 19:**265–269**
  England, 19:265–266
  France, 19:266
  Hillel, 9:111–112
  Israel, 19:268
  U.S., 19:266–268
  World Union of Jewish Students, 19:269
Student Struggle for Soviet Jewry, 19:269
Student Zionist Organization, 19:266
Studer, Claire. *See* Goll, Claire
Studia Instrumentorum Musicae Popularis (study series), 6:398
Studies and Materials for the History of the Yiddish Literature Movement in Soviet Russia. See Etyudn un Materyaln tsu der Geshikhte fun der Yidisher Literatur-Bavegung in F.S.R.R.
Studies in Aramaic Legal Papyri from Elephantine (Muffs), 18:470
Studies in Contemporary Jewish Thought (Rotenstreich), 16:101
Studies in Economic Dynamics (Kalecki), 11:732
Studies in Historiography (Momigliano), 14:431
Studies in Prejudice and Other Sociological Studies (AJC), 2:56
"Studies of Jewish Intermarriage in the United States" (Rosenthal), 14:377
Studium Biblicum Franciscanum, 7:174

Study, 19:**269–275**
  Angel of Death, 2:148
  David, 5:452
  Ezra, 6:652
  fasting, 2:772
  halakhah, 8:251
  Hasidism, 8:396–397, 398, 409, 411, 413, 416
  impurity, 16:755
  Kaddish, 11:696
  Kotsk, Menahem Mendel of, 12:324
  Ma'aseh Efod (Duran), 6:57
  manna, 13:479
  marriage, 13:564
  Meir (tanna), 13:777
  Midrash, 14:182
  mourning, 14:587
  niddui and herem, 9:13
  Pentateuch, 15:752
  pilpul, 16:161–163
  prayer, 16:458
  Rava, 17:118–119
  siyyum, 18:656
  swaying, 16:460
  talmid hakham, 19:466–468
  Tohorot ha-Kodesh, 20:17
  women, 19:273–275, 21:199–200
A Study of Gersonides in His Proper Perspective (Adlerblum), 1:409
Study of Japanese Hebrew Songs (Kawamorita Eiji), 11:85
study of Jews in, methods developed, 6:544
Der Stuermer (periodical), 4:478–479, 19:**275**
Stuhlweissenberg. *See* Szekesfehervar
Stulberg, Louis, 19:**275**
Stunning, prior to shehitah, 18:435
Sturman, Hayyim, 19:**275–276**
Sturmann, Manfred, 19:**276**
Sturmhoefel, Nahida. *See* Lazarus, Nahida Ruth
Stutschewsky, Joachim, 19:**276**
Stuttgart (Germany), 19:**276–277**
Stuttgart Psalter, 3:675
Stutthof (concentration camp), 19:**277–278**
Stuyvesant, Peter, 15:195
Stybel, Abraham Joseph, 8:456, 19:**278**
Styne, Jule, 19:**278–279**
Styria (Austria), 19:**279**
Suarès, André, 19:**279**
Suarez family, 19:**279–280**
Suasso, Abraham Israel, 19:280
Suasso, Antonio, 19:280

Suasso, Antonio Lopez, 19:280

Suasso, Francisco, 19:280

Suasso, Isaac Lopez. *See* Suasso, Antonio Lopez

Suasso family, 19:**280**

Suba (Israel), 11:381

Subarian language, 9:626

Subartu, land of, 9:626

Subbotin, Andrey Pavlovich, 19:**280**

Sub camuflaj (Banus), 3:121

Subcarpathian Ruthenia, 19:**280–282**
    Holocaust, 19:282

Subotica (Serbia), 19:**282–283**

Subpoena. *See* Ḥerem bet din

Subriana Lobo, Ricardo. *See* Wolf, Richard Riegel

Substance and accident, 19:**283–284**

Substanzbegriff und Funktionsbegriff (Cassirer), 4:509

Suburban experience, family structure, 6:699–700, 701

Succession, 19:**284–290**
    adoption, 1:415, 417–418
    apostasy, 2:276
    cancellation of rights of, 13:770
    criminology and, 5:301–302
    daughters' rights, 15:332, 19:286–287, 21:501–502
    Elephantine Papyri, 6:312
    embryos, 6:391–392
    firstborn, 7:45
    household gods, possession of, 15:355
    husbands' rights, 19:285–286
    Israel, 19:288–289
    legal aspects, 11:263–264
    obligations, law of, 15:374
    order of, 19:284
    primogeniture, 19:285
    renunciation, 19:287
    wives' rights, 19:286

Successor organizations, 11:**327**

Succoth (ancient Israel), 14:710, 19:**290**

Succoth-Benoth, 19:**290**

Suceava (Romania), 19:**290**

Suchowo, Yeḥezkelsky. *See* Danin, Yeḥezkel

Suczawa. *See* Suceava

Sudan, 2:300–301

Sude. *See* Se'udah

Sudomir (Poland). *See* Sandomierz (Poland)

Suedfeld, Gabriel, 19:**291**

Suedfeld, Simon Maximilian. *See* Nordau, Max

Suess, Eduard, 19:**291**

Suess, Joseph. *See* Oppenheimer, Joseph ben Issachar Suesskind

Suesskind von Trimberg, 19:**291**

Suetonius, 19:**291**

Suez Canal, 10:219, 220
    Arab boycott and, 4:112

Suffering, 3:**292**, 7:656, 19:**291–292**
    biblical literature, 7:656
    Talmudic literature, 7:752–753

Suffixes in Hebrew, 8:580–581

Sufism, 1:307, 10:93, 19:**292–293**
    Abraham ben Moses ben Maimon, 1:307–308
    Judeo-Arabic culture and, 11:542–543

Suftaja, 18:470

Sugar, Alan. *See* Sugar, Sir Alan

Sugar, Sir Alan, 19:**293**

Sugar industry and trade, 19:**293–294**

Sugerman, Bernard. *See* Sugerman, Sir Bernard

Sugerman, Sir Bernard, 19:**294**

Sugihara, Chiune-Sempo, 11:84, 19:**294–295**

Suicide, 14:59, 19:**295–297**
    body and soul, concept of, 4:31
    Jewish prisoner, 9:*488*
    of Judenrat leaders, 11:526–527

Le suicide: étude de sociologie (Durkheim), 6:64

Sukenik, Eliezer Lipa, 2:371, 378, 19:**297**
    Bet Alfa (Israel), 3:509
    numismatics, 15:344

Sukenik, Yigal. *See* Yadin, Yigael

Sukkah (Aaron ben Joseph ha-Levi), 1:215

Sukkah (booth), 19:**297–298**
    on a boat (Venice, Italy), vol. 20: color insert
    Germany (19th c.), vol. 6: color insert
    Marrakesh (Morocco), vol. 20: color insert

Sukkah (tractate), 19:**298–299**

Sukkat Shalom (Adani), 1:381

Sukkot, 2:15–16, 5:675, 19:**299–302**
    in Art, 19:302
    Biblical literature, 19:299–300
    blessing at the Western Wall, vol. 17: color insert
    dance, 5:409
    etrog, 6:540
    food, 7:120
    four species, 7:139–140
    Hallel, 8:279–280
    Hoshana Rabba and, 9:559–560

hoshanot and, 9:560

ivy and, 10:822

laws, customs, 19:301

pilgrim festivals and, 16:158–159

Rabbinic literature, 19:300–301

rites and rituals, lulav, 13:256

Samaritans, 17:730

Shemini Atzeret, 19:301

Simḥat Torah, 19:301–302

sukkah, 19:297–298

See also Simḥat Torah

Sukkot (Ryback), vol. 4: color insert

Sukkoth
    Ushpizin, 20:432
    willow, 21:65

Sulal, Isaac. *See* Sholal, Isaac

Sulam (periodical), 6:292

Sulamith (periodical), 19:**302**

Sulam Ya'akov program, 17:182

Sulaymān (Islamic figure). *See* Solomon (biblical figure)

Sulaym ibn Ruhaym. *See* Salmon ben Jeroham

Suleiman (Mulay of Morroco), 14:499

Suleiman I, 15:523–524, 19:**302–304**
    Jerusalem and, 11:161–162, 165

Suleiman ibn Ya'qūb (Solomon Jacob), 4:51

Suleimaniya (Iraq), 19:**304**

Suleiman the Magnificent. *See* Suleiman I

Suliṭa (Moldova). *See* Novoselitsa

Sulita (Romania), 19:**304–305**

Suliṭeanu, Ghisela, 19:**305**

Sullam, Sara Coppio, 12:674, 19:**305–306**

Sulle orme di Marx (Mondolfo), 14:435

Sullivan, Ed, 12:680

Sullivan, Louis, 1:395–396

Sulpicius Severus, 4:106, 19:**306**

Sultansky, Mordecai ben Joseph, 12:407, 19:**306**

Sulum. *See* Marduk

Sulz. *See* Soultz (Germany)

Sulzbach (Germany), 19:**306–307**

Sulzbach, Abraham, 19:**307**

Sulzbach, Walter, 18:731, 19:**307**

Sulzberger, Arthur, Jr., 11:468

Sulzberger, Arthur Hays, 11:468, 15:221–222, 19:**307–308**

Sulzberger, Arthur Ochs, 11:468

Sulzberger, Cyrus L., 2:49

Sulzberger, Mayer, 19:**308**
    American Jewish Committee, 2:54
    as bibliophile, 3:684

Jewish Museum collection and, 11:307

Jewish Theological Seminary, 11:329

Sulzer, Solomon, 3:714, 4:660–661, 8:504, 505, 19:**308–309**

Sumac, 19:**309**

Sumbal, Joseph Ḥayyim, 16:346

Sumbal, Samuel, 16:346, 19:**309**

Sumer, Sumerians, 19:**309–312**, *310*
  ethics, 6:535
  Halévi, Joseph, 8:271
  history, 19:309–311
  mythology, 6:572–573
  temple archives, 2:403

Sumerian literature, 14:98–106
  Eblaite texts, 6:85–86
  flood epics, 7:81–82
  Myths, 14:88–101

Summa doctrinae de foedere et testamento Dei (Cocceius), 4:765

Summa universae theologiae (Alexander of Hales), 1:628–629

Summer camps. *See* Jewish Camping

Summerfield, Myer, 6:62

Summerland (Chabon), 4:555

The Summer of Aviya (Almagor), 1:678

Summers, Lawrence H., 19:**312–313**

Summer School for Modeling Systems, 13:217

Summi Polificatus (Piux XII), 9:371

Sumptuary laws, 6:14–16, 19:**313**

Sun, 4:354–359, 19:**313–314**
  blessing of the, 19:**314**

Sunbal, Samuel, 14:498

Sunbat (Egypt), 19:**314–315**

The Sun Chemist (Davidson), 18:204

Sunday Commons, 7:72

Sunday Jews (Calisher), 4:365

Sunderland, 19:**315**

Sundials, 19:**315**

Sundukov, 11:521

The Sunflower (Wiesenthal), 4:631

Sunnism. *See* Orthodox Islam

Sunset, 5:486

The Sunset (Babel), 3:17

Sun Yatsen, 4:647–648

Sun Yat-Sen, 4:91

Suomi. *See* Finland

Super, Arthur Saul, 11:378

Supercommentaries on the Pentateuch, 19:**315–316**

Supernaturalism, 17:270

Superstitions. *See* Folk customs and superstitions

Šuppiluliuma I, 9:292

Šuppiluliuma II, 9:292

Supplemento alle opere volgari a stampa dei secoli XIII e XIV, indicate e descritte da F. Zambrini (Morpurgo), 14:509

Support of Faith. See Ezer ha-Dat

Suprasky, Yehoshua, 19:**316**

Supreme Court
  Israel, 3:130–131, 10:418, 18:292
    Agranat, Shimon, 1:470
    Berenson Zvi, 3:412
    bribery decisions, 4:176–177
    definition of Jew, 10:415
    effect of English legal precedents, 10:415–416
    election law and, 10:411
    Heshin, Schneur Zalman, 9:73–74
    human dignity and freedom laws, 9:587–588
    imprisonment and, 9:745–747
    imprisonment for debt and, 9:751
    interpretation of Declaration of Independence, 10:409–410
    lost property, 13:214–215
    natural rights, 10:412
    on sexual offenses, 18:332
    Silberg, Moshe, 18:577
    status of Basic Laws, 10:411, 412
  mamzer, 13:445
  marriages, 9:639–640
  New York State, 3:13
  U.S.
    Brandeis, Louis Dembitz, 4:121–124, 12:556
    Breyer, Stephen Gerand, 4:174–175, 12:556–557
    Frankfurter, Felix, 7:204–206
    Ginsburg, Ruth Joan Bader, 12:556–557

Sura (Babylonia), 19:**316–317**

Sura Academy, 1:350, 6:603, 604, 7:380–384, 10:15, 748
  mishpat Ivri, 14:340
  Rav, founded by, 17:116–117
  Rava and, 17:118

Surat (India), 19:**317**

Sure, Barnett, 19:**317**

Surely the People Is Grass. See Akhen Ḥaz-Am

Surenhuis, Wilhelm, 19:**317**

Surenhuysen, Gulielmus Surenhusius. *See* Surenhuis, Wilhelm

Surenhuysen, Wilhelm. *See* Surenhuis, Wilhelm

Suretyship, 19:**317–323**
  arev and arev kabbelan, 19:318–319
  debtor, right of recourse, 19:320
  Israel, 19:320–322
  scope of, 19:319–320
  srevut and asmakhta, 19:320

Surfing, 19:146

The Surgeon's Daughter (Scott), 18:208

Surgun, Isaac, 19:**323**

Sürgüns, 10:774

Surinam. *See* Suriname

Suriname, 19:**323–324**
  America, Jewish immigration to, 2:41
  Ashkenaz, 2:107
  Caribbean, Spanish-Portuguese Nation of the: La Nacion, 4:471
  Dutch literature, 6:69

Sur me-Ra (Modena), 4:467

Sur Moses Mendelssohn, sur la réforme politique des Juifs (Mirabeau), 14:305

Surnames, 14:768

Surowiecki, Wawrzyniec, 19:**324**

Surprised by Sin: The Reader in "Paradise Lost" (Fish), 7:58

Surrealism, 15:648
  Blecher, Marcel, 3:747
  Brauner, Victor, 4:139

Suruc (Turkey). *See* Sarūj (Turkey)

Survey of American Jewish Public Opinion (AJC), 2:56

Survival in Auschwittz. See If This Be a Man

The Survivor: An Anatomy of Life in the Death Camps (Des Pres), 9:414–415

Survivor from a Dead Age (Lozowick), 13:239

The Survivors (Feinstein), 6:440

The Survivors of the Shoah Visual History Foundation, 2:412, 9:425, 446, 13:201, 19:**324–325**

Suryah ha-Deromit asher le-Ḥofo shel ha-Yam ha-Tikhon (Bar-Navi), 18:206

Susa (Iran). *See* Shushan (Iran)

Susan, Issachar ben Mordecai, 3:379, 19:**325**

Susann, Jacqueline, 19:**325–326**

Susanna and the Elders, 19:**326–327**

Susita or Hippos (ancient Israel), 19:**327**

Susman, Margarete, 19:**327–328**

Sussex County (NJ). *See* Morris and Sussex Counties (NJ)

Susskind, David, 19:**328**

Susskind, Walter, 19:**328**

Susslin. *See* Israel ben Joel

Susslin, Israel ben Joel. *See* Israel ben Joel

Sussman, Abraham, 19:**328–329**
　　Odessa Committee, 15:382

Sussman, Berthold, 14:446

Sussman, Ezra, 19:**329**

Sussman, Yoel, 19:**329**

Sustainable development, 6:453–454

Sustar (Iran). *See* Shushtar (Iran)

Sutro, Abraham, 19:**329**

Sutro, Adolph Heinrich Joseph, 19:**329–330**

Sutro, Alfred, 19:**330**

Sutton, Philip, 19:**330**

Sutzkever, Abraham, 19:**330–331**

Suvalk. *See* Suwalki (Poland)

Suwalki (Poland), 19:**331–332**

Suwalski, Isaac, 19:**332**

Suzin, Solomon Moses, 19:**332**

Suzman, Helen, 16:349, 19:**332**

Suzman, Janet, 19:**332–333**

Svaz čechů-Židů, 4:**534–535**

Svechi na vetru (Kanovich), 11:766

Svengali (fictional character), 6:436

Svenska Dagbladet (newspaper), 12:681

Sverdlik, Oded, 19:**333**

Sverdlov, Yakov Mikhailovich, 19:**333**

Svetlov, Mikhail, 19:**333**

Svevo, Italo, 19:**333–334**

Svirski, Alexey Ivanovich, 19:**334**

Svisloch (Belarus), 19:**334**

Svive (periodical), 14:429–430

Svyataya Inkvizitsiya (Lozinski), 13:238

Swabian League, 19:**334–335**

Swadesh, Morris, 19:**335**

The Swan. See Labut'

Swans. *See* Tinshemet

Swansea (Wales), 19:**335**

Swarsensky, Hardi, 19:**335**

Swaythling, First Baron. *See* Montagu, Samuel

Swaziland, 6:371
　　See also South Africa

Sweatshop poetry, 19:**335–336**

Sweatshops
　　Canada, 4:396
　　Chicago, 4:608–609
　　in New York City, 15:202, 204

Sweden, 19:**336–340**, *337*
　　anti-sheḥitah movements, 18:435
　　Denmark, relations with, 5:583
　　emancipation, 6:377
　　founding of Jewish community in, 10:36

government officials, 3:466–467

Holocaust, 9:342, 19:**337–338**
　　influence on literature, 18:92–93

Holocaust education, 9:458–459

Israel, relations with, 19:**339–340**

Josephson family, 11:432–433

Lamm, Martin, 12:452–453

language, biblical translations, 3:636

libraries, 12:787

literature, 18:90–94
　　Elkan, Sophie, 6:357
　　Levertin, Oscar Ivar, 12:681

museums, 14:627

newspapers, 16:501–502

publishing, 6:240

Sweet calamus. *See* Calamus, sweet

Swet, Gershon, 19:**340**

Swidnica (Poland), 19:**340**

Swifts, 19:**340–341**

Swig, Benjamin Harrison, 19:**341**

Swig, Richard, 19:**341**

Swill literature. *See* French literature; German literature

The Swimmers (Mishol), 14:331

Swimming, 19:146–147
　　Epstein, Charlotte, 6:469
　　Leibowitz, Keren, 12:621

Swines. *See* Pigs

Swingtime, 7:17

Swisłocz. *See* Svisloch (Belarus)

Swiss Federation of Jewish Communities
　　Bloch, Rolf, 3:767
　　jubilee, 6:454

Switzerland, 19:**341–347**, *343*
　　American Joint Distribution Committee, 2:61
　　antisemitism, 19:345
　　　Berne, 3:471
　　anti-sheḥitah movements, 18:435
　　architecture, 2:400
　　Berne, 3:688
　　Biel, 3:688
　　Black Death, Berne, 3:471
　　blood libel, Berne, 3:471
　　community, nature of, 5:109
　　community leaders, 6:733
　　emancipation, 1:207–208, 6:380–381, 404, 19:342–343
　　French Revolution, and effects on communities, 7:256
　　Holocaust, restitution, 6:280–281
　　Holocaust period, 12:528, 19:344–345

Israel relations, 19:346

Jewish life, 19:345–346

Jewish participation in military service, 14:246

La Chaux-de-Fonds, 12:420

Lausanne, 12:528

medieval period, 19:341–342

museums, 14:627

Neuchâtel, 15:**117**

newspapers, 16:502–503

Orthodox Judaism in, 15:494

politicians, 6:713–714
　　Dreifuss, Ruth, 6:10

reparations, Eizenstat, Stuart, 6:280–281, 20:381

synagogues, Berne, 3:472

Swope, Gerard, 19:**347**

Swope, Herbert Bayard, 19:**347**

The Sword Extended in Refutation of the Rabbis of the Jews (Abd al-Ḥaqq al-Islāmī), 1:240

Sybil (Disraeli), 5:700

Sycamina (Israel). *See* Haifa (Israel)

Sycamore, 18:461, 19:**347–348**

Sydney (Australia), 19:**348–349**

Sykes, Mark. *See* Sykes, Sir Mark

Sykes, Sir Mark, 19:**349–350**

Sykes-Picot Agreement (1916), 10:184–185, *10:188*, 19:**350–351**, *351*

Syllables in Hebrew, 8:567–568

Syllaeus, Obedas II, 15:367

Sylvester, James Joseph, 15:554, 19:**351**

Sylvia, Sarah, 11:377, 19:**351**

Sylvia Plachy's Unguided Tour (Plachy), 16:210

Symbolic interactionism, 18:732

Symbols and symbolism
　　catacombs, 4:522
　　dreams, 6:8–10
　　food, 7:120
　　four species, 7:138–139
　　Kabbalah and, 11:588
　　See also Signs and symbols

Symbolum Apostolicum (Pragensis), 6:315

Symmachus, 3:585, 597, 601

Symmachus ben Joseph, 19:**351–352**

Symonds, Saul, 19:**352**

Symons, Julian, 19:**352**

Symphonic Bashrav (Ehrlich), 6:242

Symphonic Poem on Ukrainian Folk Themes (Alshvang), 2:11

Symphony (Alshvang,), 2:11

The Symphony (painting, Mopp), 14:470

Die synagogale Poesie des Mittelalters (Zunz), 21:686

Die Synagoge (periodical), 1:402

Synagogue, The Great, 19:**383–385**

The Synagogue Council of America, 13:188, 18:609, 19:**385**

Synagogues, 19:**352–383**

    Altneushul (Prague), vol. 19: color insert

    Amran, 2:106

    Amsterdam, 2:106, 107, 109, 111, 114, 117–118

    Ancona, 2:140, 141

    Anhalt, 2:163

    Ansbach, 2:180

    archisynagogos, 2:398

    architecture, 11:722, 16:160–161, 19:364

        5th century, 19:367, *367*

        18th,19th centuries, 19:376–378

        20th, 19:376–383

        Brunner, Arnold, 4:224

        early, 19:*365*, *366*

        Europe, 19:381–383

        Germany, 19:376–377, 379, 381

        Israel, 19:381–382

        Italy, 10:815

        Middle Ages to emancipation, 19:*368*, 368–376, *370*, *372*, *373*, *374*

        Netherlands, 6:369

        Palestine, 19:*374*, 374–375

        Poland, 4:588

        Polish wooden, 19:*373*, *373*

        Spain, 19:373–374, *376*

        United States, 19:379–381

    Ark design, 2:463–464

    art in, Jerusalem in, 11:227

    Beth Sholom (Elkins Park, PA), vol. 19: color insert

    bimah, 3:701–702

    Brazil, 18:33

    of Buda, 4:245

    Callinicum, 2:37

    Canada, Edmonton, 6:150–151

    candles, 4:429

    cantatas and choral works, Hebrew, 4:433–435

    cantillation, 4:436, 10:815

    Capernaum, vol. 19: color insert

    ceremonial objects, 4:547–549

    Chodorow (Ukraine), vol. 19: color insert

    choirs, 14:679–681

    construction and building, 5:183

    Croatia, Dubrovnik, 6:39

    design and location, 19:362–363

    Druya, 6:28

    dukhan and, 6:44

    Eastern Europe

        shtetl, 18:524–526

        shulklapper, 18:531

    ecclesia et synagoga, 6:88

    education, Jewish, 6:198–199

    Egypt

        ancient, 6:228

        Dumuh, 6:46

        modern, 6:236

    El Ghriba (Djerba, Tunisia), vol. 19: color insert

    El Salvador, 6:369

    England, 6:422

        London, 6:414

    family affilation, in U.S., 6:700–701

    in France, 4:494–495, 530

    France, Béziers, 3:559

    Galilean Aramaic, 2:349

    Galilee, Chorazin, 4:666–667, *667*

    gambling, 7:367–368

    Germany

        Dresden, 6:10, 11

        Duesseldorf, 6:42

        Duisburg, 6:43

        Erfurt, 6:478

        Frankfurt, 9:*463*

    glass vessels, 7:630

    Hallel, 8:280

    Ḥazzan, 14:*651*, 651–653, *652*, *653*

    Holocaust destruction of, 16:306, 19:356–357

    Hungary, 3:222, 4:246

        Pest, 4:245

    India, 4:352

        Ernakulam, 6:482

    Isfahan (Iran), vol. 19: color insert

    Israel, 4:443, *443*, 19:357–358

        Bet Alfa, 3:509

        Bet Yeraḥ, 3:*553*, 553–554

        En-Gedi, 6:407

        Eshtaol, 6:507

    Johanan ben Zakkai (Jerusalem), vol. 19: color insert

    London Great Synagogue, 2:107

    Magen Aboth (Alibag, India), vol. 19: color insert

    Middle Ages, 19:352–355

        shulklapper, 18:531

    mizraḥ, 14:392–393

    modal music, 14:663–664, *664*

    modern period, 19:355–356

    music, U.S., 11:38, 80

    Ner Tamid, 15:88

    in New York City, 15:195

    New Zealand, Dunedin, 6:49–50

    organizations of, 19:359–360

    origins, early history, 19:352–355

    Ostia, 15:507–508

    Ostin (Italy), vol. 19: color insert

    Ottoman empire's restrictions on, 15:528–529

    Ozery, 15:557

    Pabianice, 15:561

    Padua, 15:567

    Parokhet and Kapporet, 15:663–664

    of Pest, 4:246

    Pharisees fostered, 16:31

    photographs of, 16:129–130

    planning and construction, laws of, 16:216

    proscribed uses of, 19:363–364

    public services, minyan, 14:302

    Puerto Rico, 16:729

    Russia, 1970s, 17:568

    Russian Federation, Moscow, 14:518–519, 520

    Sardis, 18:53–54, *54*

    Scotland, Edinburgh, 6:147

    separation of men and women, 13:771–772

    shammash, 18:395

    sheli'aḥ ẓibbur, 18:446

    shulklapper, 18:531

    Slovakia, Dunajska Streda, 6:46

    song and chant, 14:643–649, *644*, *645*, *646*, *648*

    South Africa, East London, 6:83

    Soviet Bloc, 19:358–359

    Spain, Seville, 6:91

    Switzerland

        Berne, 3:472

        Engingen and Lengnau, 6:404

    Syria, Dura-Europos, 6:52–55

    Temple imitation, 2:128

    Toledo, 20:23

    Trencin (Slovakia), vol. 19: color insert

    Turkish musical traditions, 20:201–202

    Ukraine, 4:598

    U.S., 19:357, 360–361

        Baron Hirsch Congregation, 14:19

        Essex County (NJ), 6:512–513

        Mississippi, 14:365

        Monmouth County (NJ), 14:445–447

        Morris County (NJ), 14:511–512

Synagogues, *continued*
    Saint Louis, 17:671
    San Francisco, 18:18–19
    Savannah, 18:84
    Schenectady, 18:120
    Schulweis, Harold,
        innovations introduced by,
        18:174
    Scranton, 18:211
    Sussex County (NJ), 14:511–
        512
    Veroia (Greece), vol. 19: color
        insert
    Warsaw ghetto, young worshipper,
        9:468
    women in, 6:753
    women's integration into, 19:360–
        362
    Yemen, 2:106, 18:6
    Yiddish language, 2:111
    See also Liturgy; New York City
Synaptic study, 8:461
Synek, Jiří. *See* Listopad, František
Syngalowski, Aron, 19:**385**
Synods, 17:20–21, 19:**385–386**
Synoptic gospels, 14:455, 15:190, 191
The Synoptic Gospels (Montefiore),
    14:455, 456
*Die syntaktischen Vehaeltnesse des
    Arabischen* (Reckendorf), 17:146
Syntax
    in Hebrew, 8:596–618
    Reckendorf, Hermann Soloman,
        17:146
    See also Hebrew grammar
Syntaxe Amharique et syntaxe Turque
    (Polotsky), 16:362
"Synthetic Zionism." *See* Helsingfors
    Program
Syphilis, 6:244
Syracuse (Italy), 19:**386–387**
Syracuse (NY), 19:**387–388**
Syria, 2:302–303, 306, 19:**388–397**, *389*
    antisemitism, 4:495–496
        Aleppo, 1:614, 615, 616,
            4:587
        discrimination, 5:681
    Arab conquest, 19:388–393
    Aramaic, 2:343
    art, *5:394*
    Biblical, Second Temple period,
        19:388
    blood libel in, 3:780
    border skirmishes with, 10:229
    borders post War of
        Independence, 10:214
        demilitarized, 10:218

cities, 4:739, 741
city states, 2:489
community organization and
    structures, 5:108, 110, 118*t*
contemporary period, 19:393–397
Damascus, 5:390–397
Diaspora, 5:638
Al-Fataḥ and, 10:279
financiers, 6:714–715
important families, 5:495, 6:714–
    715
Israel relations, 19:394–395
Jubar, 11:473
language, 13:623, 631
Laniado, Samuel Ben Abraham,
    12:485
Lebanese War and, 10:241,
    12:581–584, 586–587
literature, Shamosh, Yitzḥak,
    18:395
Mamluks, 13:438–441
medieval leaders, Masnut, 13:603
modern, 2:541–542
Niebuhr, Carston, travels of,
    15:259
Ottoman empire, 19:391–393
Ottoman empire's conquest of,
    15:523–524
Palestine (mandate) as part of,
    10:273–274
Palestine Liberation Organization
    and, 15:590, 592
philanthropy, 6:714–715
Quirinius, 2:128
Semetic languages, 18:282
Six Day War, 10:229–232, 18:648–
    655, *18:653*
synagogues, Dura-Europos, 6:52–
    55
Yom Kippur War, 10:236–237,
    21:383–391, *384, 386, 388, 389*
Syriac Aramaic, 2:352–353, 353*t*
Syriac Bible, 3:599–601
    Philoxenian version, 3:600–601
Syrian Orthodox Church
    Israel (state), 10:639
    Peshitta used by, 3:599, 600
Syrkin, Joshua, 19:**397–398**
Syrkin, Marie, 19:**398**
Syrkin, Moses Nahum Solomonovich,
    19:**398**
Syrkin, Nachman, 12:524, 18:717,
    19:**398–400**
Syrkin, Yakov Kovovich, 19:**400**
Syro-Hexapla, 3:601
Systemalpatent, 6:690
*System and History of Nature. See
    System und Geschichte des
    Naturalismus* (Loewenthal)

*System und Geschichte des
    Naturalismus* (Loewenthal), 13:170
Szabad, Ẓemaḥ. *See* Shabad, Ẓemaḥ
Szabó, Imre, 19:**400**
Szabolcsi, Bence, 19:**400–401**
Szabolcsi, Lajos, 11:441, 19:**401**
Szabolcsi, Miksa, 6:222, 19:**401**
Szadów (Lithuania). *See* Seduva
    (Lithuania)
Szajkowski, Zosa, 19:**401**
Szaki (Lithuania). *See* Sakiai
    (Lithuania)
Szálasi, Ferenc, 19:**401–402**
Szalit-Marcus, Rachel, 19:**402**
Szaniawski, Klemens. *See* Junosza,
    Klemens
Szántó, György, 19:**402**
Szántó, Simon, 15:126, 384, 19:**402**
Szapszał Seraya ben Mordecai. *See*
    Shapshal Seraya ben Mordechai
Szarogród (Ukraine). *See* Shargorod
    (Ukraine)
Szasz, Thomas Stephen, 19:**402–403**
Szászrégen. *See* Reghin
Szatmár (Romania). *See* Satu-Mare
    (Romania)
Szatmárnémeti (Romania). *See* Satu-
    Mare (Romania)
Szbadka. *See* Subotica
Szczebrzeszyn (Poland), 19:**403**
Szczecin (Poland). *See* Stettin (Poland)
Szczercow (Poland), 19:**403–404**
Szᴅ. *See* Sifre Zuta Deuteronomy
Szeged (Hungary), 19:**404**
Szekely, Eva, 19:**404–405**
Szekesfehervar (Hungary), 19:**405**
Szell, George, 19:**405**
Szemtől szembe (Déry), 5:600–601
Szende, Pál, 19:**405**
Szende, Stefan, 4:128, 19:**405–406**
Szendrei, Aladar. *See* Sendrey, Alfred
Szenes, Béla, 19:**406**
Szenes, Erzsi, 19:**406**
Szenes, Hannah, 19:**406**
Szentesi, Rudolf. *See* Kiss, József
Szenwald, Lucjan, 19:**406**
Szép, Ernö, 19:**406–407**
Szer, Seweryn, 19:**407**
Szerb, Antal, 19:**407**
Szerelem (Déry), 5:600–601
Szerencsés, Imre, 14:427, 19:**407**
Szereszewski, Moses David, 19:**407–
    408**
Szereszewski family, 19:407–408
Szerman, Pinchas, 19:**408**
Szeryng, Henryk, 19:**408**

Szigeti, Imre, 19:**408**

Szigeti, Joseph, 19:**408**

Szilágyi, Géza, 19:**408**

Szilágysomlyó. *See* Simleül-Silvaniei (Hungary)

Szilard, Leo, 19:**408–409**

Szinérváralja (Romania). *See* Seini (Romania)

Szklów (Belarus). *See* Shklov (Belarus)

Szlovákia. *See* Slovakia

Szn. See Sifre Zuta Numbers

Sznajder, Edward, 16:347

SZO. *See* Student Zionist Organization

Szobel, Géza, 19:**409**

Szold, Benjamin, 19:**409**
  biblical exegesis and study, 3:647

Szold, Henrietta, 15:209, 19:**409–411**
  Jewish Publication Society, 11:310
  Woman of Valor (Fineman), 7:26

Szold, Robert, 4:123, 19:**411**

Szold, Robert, 15:588, 589

Szolnok (Hungary), 19:**411**

Szombathely (Hungary), 19:**411–412**

Szomory, Dezsö, 19:**412**

Szrem. *See* Srem

Sztejnbarg, Dina. *See* Kotarbińska, Janina

Sztejnbarg, Janina. *See* Kotarbińska, Janina

Sztójay, Döme, 19:**412**

Sztybel, A. J. *See* Stybel, Abraham Joseph

Szulwas, Moses Avigdor. *See* Shulvass, Moses Avigdor

Szwarc, Michael, 19:**412**

Szydlowiec (Poland), 19:**412–413**

Szyk, Arthur, 4:76, 19:**413**

Szyr, Eugeniusz, 16:347, 19:**413**

T

T (letter), 19:*415*, 20:*5*

T. Carmi. *See* Carmi, T.

T4, 6:570–571, 9:332

Ta'alumot Ḥokhmah (Bacharach), 3:35

Ta'amei ha-Mikra. *See* Cantillation

Ta'amei ha-Mitzvot (Brudo), 4:221

Ta'amei ha-Mitzvot (Recanati), 17:142

Ta'amei Torah (Bardach), 3:147

Taanach (Canaan), 8:621, 622, 12:668, 19:**415–416**

Ta'anit Esther. See Esther, fast of

Ta'anit Megillat (Eleazar ben Hananiah ben Hezekiah). *See Megillat Ta'anit* (Eleazar ben Hananiah ben Hezekiah)

Ta(scedil)awwuf. *See* Sufism

Taba Agreement (1995), 10:455

Tabachnik, Abraham ber, 19:**417**

Tabachnik, Shelomo. *See* Ben-Yosef, Shelomo

Tabak, Solomon Leib, 19:**417**

Ṭabarī, 15:419

Tabeel, The Son of, 19:**417**

Tabenkin, Yiẓḥak, 3:345, 19:**417–418**

Tabernacle, 19:**418–424**
  Aaron and, 1:209
  acacia, 1:347
  Baraita de-Melekhet ha-Mishkan, 3:128
  building, 6:617, 618
  historicity of, 15:744, 749–750
  incense alters, 2:14
  menorah, 14:49–50
  Moses, 14:525
  sacrificial altars, 2:12
  See also Sukkot

Tabernacle of Peace. See Sukkat Shalom

Tabernacles, Feast of. *See* Sukkot

Tabgha (Galilee), 19:**424**

Tabi, 19:**424–425**

Tabib, Avraham, 19:**425**, 425–426

Tabib, Mordekhai, 19:**425**

Tabick, Jacqueline, 17:16

Table hymns. *See* Zemirot

Table Talk (Selden), 18:258

Table tennis, 1:386–387, 3:430, 19:147

The Tablets (Schwerner), 20:301

Tablets of the Law, 19:**425**

Tabor (Czech Republic), 19:**426**

Tábor (Czech Republic). *See* Tabor (Czech Republic)

Tabor, David, 19:**426**

Tabor, Harry Zvi, 19:**426**

Tabor, Mount. *See* Mount Tabor

Tabor, Paul, 19:**427**

Tabori, Georg, 19:**427–428**

Tábori, Paul. *See* Tabor, Paul

Taborites, 4:38

Tabor oak, 15:357

Tabriz (Iran), 19:**428**

Tabrizi, Mahomet Abu-bekr-at-ben Mahomet, 19:**428**

Tachau (Czechoslovakia). *See* Tachov (Czechoslovakia)

Tachov (Czechoslovakia), 19:**428–429**

Tacitus, 19:**429**

Tadef (Syria), 19:**429–430**

Tadjer, Salis, 4:276

Tadmor (Syria), 15:377, 19:**430–431**

Tadmor, Hayim, 19:**431**

Tadzhikistan (CIS), 19:**432**

Taenzer, Aaron. *See* Taenzer, Arnold

Taenzer, Arnold, 19:**432**

Taeubler, Eugen, 2:407, 19:**432**

Tafilalet. *See* Sijilmassa (Morocco)

Tafsir Megillat Ester (Shāhin), 18:365

Taganrog (Russia), 19:**432**

Tageblat (newspaper), 15:210

Tagger, Sionah, 19:**432–433**

Tagger, Theodor. *See* Bruckner, Ferdinand

Tagin, 19:**433**

Taglicht, David Israel, 19:**433**

Tagmulei ha-Nefesh (Hillel ben Samuel), 7:129, 9:114

Tâgru-Neamt (Romania). *See* Tirgu Neamt (Romania)

Tag und Nacht (Mombert), 14:430

Der Tag X (Heym), 9:85

Tahāfut al-Falāsifa (al-Ghazālī), 11:730

Tahal, 19:**433–434**

Taḥanun, 12:437, 19:**434–435**

Taharah. *See* Tohorah

Taharat ha-Mishpaḥah, 1:263, 19:**435**

Taḥash, 19:**435**

Ta Ḥazei (Zohar), 21:649–650

Taḥkemoni. See Sefer Taḥkemoni

Tailoring, 19:**435–439**

"Tailor of Cordoba." *See* Móntoro, Antón de

Taima (Arabia). *See* Tayma (Arabia)

Taine, Hippolyte-Adolphe, 6:36

Tainye Pesni (Elisheva). *See Hidden Songs* (Elisheva)

Taitaẓak, Joseph, 2:10, 4:302, 15:537, 19:**439–440**

Takala be-Ḥalal (Argaman), 18:206

Takhrikh shel Sippurim (Agnon), 1:468

Taking Rights Seriously (Dworkin), 6:74

Takkanot, 2:422–423, 19:**440–453**
  Agunah, 19:452
  amoraic period, 19:446
  annulment of, 19:445
  Chief Rabbinate in Mandate to post-war of independence period, 19:450–451
  definition and substance, 19:440–441
  divorce law, 17:7–8
  domestic life, 18:600
  education, 18:600
  exiles of Castile, 14:495
  family law, 19:449–450
  geonic period, 19:446–447
  Halakhah, 19:441–444, 448–449
  Halakhic through Tannaitic period, 19:445–446
  ḥerem bet din, 9:16

Takkanot, *continued*

Herzog, Isaac, 9:69

legislation, 19:441–444, 444–445, 448–449, 451

mishpat Ivri, 14:338, 353

post-geonic period, 19:447–448, 449–450

public welfare, Knesset legislation for, 19:451

rabbinical courts, 19:451–452

Rappaport, Issac ben Judah ha-Konen, 17:100

of Toledo, 10:753

Troyes (France), 6:328

women's rights, 19:451–452

Takkanot ha-Kahal, 19:**453–460**

history of, 19:457–459

imprisonment for debt and, 9:749–751

interpretation of, 9:824–826

legal and judicial systems, 19:459–460

legal aspects of, 19:453–457

mishpat Ivri, 14:349

public authority, 16:709–710

research, 19:459

Der Takkif (Placzek), 16:210

Di Takse (Abramovitsh), 1:320

Taku, Moses ben Ḥisdai, 19:**460–461**

Tal, Josef, 18:762–763, 19:**461**

Tal, Mikhai., 19:**461–462**

Talavera de la Reina (Spain), 19:**462**

Tale of Sinuhe (tale), 6:225–226

The Tale of the Allergist's Wife (Busch), 4:303

"Tale of the Centaur" (play), 18:761

The Tale of the Wolf (Molnár), 14:427

Tale of Two Brothers (tale), 6:225

Tales. *See* Tallit

Tales, animal, 2:**173–174**

Tales from the Talmud (Bayefsky), 3:231–232

Tales of a Long Night. See Hamlet: oder Die lange Nacht nimmt ein Ende

Tales of Galilee. See Sippurei Erez ha-Galil (Simḥah ben Joshua)

Tales of Irasto (Uziel). *See Mishlei Irasto*

Tales of Sendabar. See Mishlei Sendabar

Tales of the Ba'al Shem Tov. See Sippurei ha-Besht

Talev, Dimitur, 4:276

Talheim (Wuerttemberg), 19:**462–463**

TALI Education Fund, 18:114–115

Talion, 19:**463**

Talismans. *See* Amulets

Talker, Bahais Joseph, 15:474

Talker, Ezekiel Samuel, 19:**463–464**

Talker, Moses Daniel, 15:474

Tallahassee (FL), 19:**464–465**

Tallinn (Estonia), 19:**465**

Tallit, 6:13, 18:364, 19:**465–466,** vol. 18: color insert

Tallit katan, 19:**466**

Talmaciu (Romania), 19:**466**

Tálmaciu (Romania). *See* Talmaciu (Romania)

Talmai, 1:**544**

Talmi, Igal, 19:**466**

Talmid, Jacob ben Ḥayyim. *See* Jacob ben Ḥayyim Talmid

Talmid family, 11:32

Talmid Ḥakham, 19:**466–468**

Talmon, Jacob Leib, 19:**468–469**

Talmon, Shemaryahu, 19:**469**

Talmon, Yonina, 18:735

Talmon, Zvi, 8:504, 19:**469**

Talmud, 19:**469–470,** 472t, 473t

32 rules, 3:129

Aaron of Pesaro, 1:220

Abaddon, 1:224

Abba (scholar), 1:225

Abba Bar Aḥa, 1:225

abbreviations, 1:237–240

abomination, 1:269–270

abortion, 1:271–272

Abraham Abele ben Abraham Solomon, 1:291

Abraham's bosom, 1:317

Academy on High, 1:353

Admon ben Gaddai, 1:412

age and the aged, 1:447

agriculture

crossbreeding animals, 7:403

demai, 5:547

flax, 7:70

Kilayim, 12:154

leather production, 12:574

leket, 12:631–632

ma'aserot, 19:652–653

pe'ah, 12:631–632

rain, 17:70–71

shikhḥah, 12:631–632

Terumot, 19:651–652

yoke, 21:381

allegories, 1:665–666

alphabet, Hebrew, 1:728–730

Amen, 2:39

am ha-arez, 2:67–70

amoraim, 2:89, 11:708

Amorites, 2:97

Amram Hasida, 2:105

amulets, 2:121

Anan ben David, 2:127–128, 128

Anan family, 2:129

anatomy, 2:133, 134

angels, 2:156–158

Angel of Death, 2:148–149

cherub and cherubim, 4:600

Gabriel, 14:167–169

Michael, 14:167–169

Raphael, 17:93

Raziel, 17:128–129

Uriel, 20:421–422

animals, 2:167, 12:696–697

birds, 2:171–172

camels, 4:381

fish, 2:172

koi, 12:267

mammals, 2:167–171

mules, 14:609–610

reptiles, 2:172

tales of, 2:173

anointing, 2:179–180

anthropomorphism, 2:190

antichresis, 2:193

Antoninus Pius, 2:248–249

apikoros, kofer, mumar, 9:20

apocalypse, 2:257–258

Apocalypse of Baruch, 3:184–185

apologetics, 2:263

Apostomos, 2:278

astrology, 2:617

astronomy, 2:621–622

atonement, 2:644

attitudes toward

Haskalah, 8:436

kabbalah, 11:585

baraita, 3:124–128

bar mitzvah, 3:165

Bei-Rav, 3:269

belief, 3:292–293

benedictions, 3:331, 332

biblical exegesis and study, 3:640–641, 660–663

bibliography and, 3:681

birth, 3:721

blasphemy in, 3:741–742

blemishes in, 3:750

blessing and cursing in, 3:751–752

blindness in, 3:754–755

body and soul, concept of, 4:31

bribery, 4:175

bribery in, 4:175

burning of, 7:150, 184, 15:383, 19:**481–483**

business ethics and, 4:312–315

captives, ransoming of, 4:456

cards and cardplaying, 4:467

censorship, 4:540

charity, 4:569

choral singing, 4:658–659

Chronicles, Book of, 4:696, 703

chronology, 4:706–707

circumcision, 4:732

circuses, 4:735

city of refuge, 4:742–744

civil law

    acquisition, 1:359–363

    avot nezikin, 2:751–753

    Bava Batra (tractate), 3:223–224

    Bava Kamma (tractate), 3:224–226

    Bava Metzia (civil law), 3:226–227

    breach of contract, 5:195

    competition, restriction of, 8:450–451

    compromise, 5:124–126

    conditions, 5:137–138

    confiscation, expropriation, forfeiture, 5:150–151

    contractual obligations, 5:190, 191–192

    contractual ties, 5:190

    embryo rights, 6:391–392

    Hafka'at She'arim, 8:196–198

    hassegat gevul, 8:449

    human rights, 17:309–332

    illegal contracts, 5:194

    mistaken transactions, 5:186–188

    moneylending, 14:437–438

    monopoly, right of, 8:450

    ownership and possession, 8:486–491, 15:551–552

    performance, contractual, 5:194–195

    planning and construction, laws of, 16:216–218

    pleas, 16:228–231

    pledges, 16:231–236

    possession and ownership, 15:551–552

    profiteering, 5:185

    property, 20:414–416

    suretyship, 19:317–318

    unjust enrichment, 20:413–416

    usury, 20:438–440

cloth and clothing

    cotton, 5:238

    crowns, 5:308

dyeing, 6:76, 77

    ephod, 6:456

    head covering, 8:506–507

    veil, 20:489

    women, 6:13

    zizit, 21:642–643

codification of law, 4:768–770

coins and currency, 5:51–52, 51*t*, 52*t*

commentary

    Abner of Burgos, 1:264

    Abraham ben David of Posquières, 1:296–298

    Abraham ben Elijah of Vilna, 1:299

    Abramsky, Yeḥezkel, 1:328

    Abulafia, Meir, 1:341–342

    Adani, Saadiah ben David, 1:381

    Adret, Moses ibn, 1:421

    Adret, Solomon ben Abraham, 1:422–423

    Aghmati, Zechariah ben Judah, 1:465

    Aḥaronim, 1:532–537

    Aḥ bar Rav, 1:525

    Akiva Baer ben Joseph, 1:563

    Akrish, Isaac ben Abraham, 1:571

    Alashkar, Moses ben Isaac, 1:576–577

    Albalia, Isaac ben Baruch, 1:583–584

    Al-Bargeloni, Isaac ben Reuben, 1:586

    Albeck family, 1:587–588

    Aldubi, Abraham ben Moses ben Ismail, 1:607

    Alexander Suslin ha-Kohen of Frankfurt, 1:630

    Alfasi, Isaac ben Jacob, 1:639–641

    Al-Madari, Judah ha-Kohen ben Eleazar he-Ḥasid, 1:677

    Baruch ben Samuel of Alleppo, 3:190

    Boton, Abraham ben Judah di, 4:102

    Boton, Abraham ben Moses de, 4:102

    Boyarin, Daniel, 4:109

    Breslau, Aryeh Loeb ben Ḥayyim, 4:165–166

    Breslau, Joseph Mozes ben David, 4:166

    Breuer, Mordecai, 4:172–173

    Bruell, Jacob, 4:221–222

Buchner, Abraham, 4:243

Bukarat, Abraham ben Solomon ha-Levi, 4:257

Bulat, Judah ben Joseph, 4:267

Busal, Ḥayyim ben Jacob Obadiah de, 4:302–303

Calahorra, Israel Samuel ben Solomon, 4:350

Canpanton, Isaac ben Jacob, 4:431–432

Carmoly, Issachar Baer ben Judah Lima, 4:485

Caro, Joseph ben Ephraim, 4:489–490

Carvalho, Mordecai Baruch, 4:502

Casès, Benjamin ben David, 4:505

Castro, Jacob ben Abraham, 4:518

Chajes, Ẓevi Hirsch, 4:560

Chavel, Charles Ber, 4:584

Chazan, Eliyahu Simcha, 4:585

Ciechanow, Abraham ben Raphael Landau of, 4:726

Deutsch, Eliezer Ḥayyim ben Abraham, 5:622

Dimitrovsky, Chaim Zalman, 5:663

Edels, Samuel Eliezer ben Judah Ha-Levi, 6:143–144

Ehrentreu, Heinrich, 6:242

Falk, Jacob Joshua ben Ẓevi Hirsch, 6:684

Fano, 6:709

Fischels, Meir ben Ephraim, 7:52

Fraenkel, David ben Naphtali Hirsch, 7:143

Frankel, Zecharias, 7:201

Ḥagigah (tractate), 8:223–224

Hananel ben Ḥushi'el, 8:314

Italian Renaissance, 6:709

Jellin, Aryeh Loeb ben Shalom Shakhna, 11:119

Landau, Jacob, 12:462

Levi ben Gershom, 12:698

Leviticus Rabbah, 12:740–742

Lewin, Joshua Heshel Ben Elijah Ze'ev Ha-Levi, 12:759–760

Meiri, Menahem ben Solomon, 13:786

Meir Simḥah ha-Kohen of Dvinsk, 13:788–789

Melamed, Ezra Zion, 14:5–6

Pesikta de Rav Kahana, 12:741

Talmud, *continued*

    Pinner, Ephraim Moses ben Alesander Susskind, 16:169

    Pinto, Josiah ben Joseph, 16:179

    Rabbinovicz, Raphael Nathan Nata, 17:31

    Ragoler, Elijah ben Jacob, 17:65–66

    Ranschburg, Bezalel ben Joel, 17:91

    Rapoport, Abraham ben Israel Jehiel ha-Kohen, 17:98

    Rapoport, Solomon Leib, 17:99

    Rashi, 17:101–106

    Rath, Meshullam, 17:109

    Ratner, Dov Baer, 17:112

    Reifmann, Jacob, 17:203–204

    Rivkes, Moses ben Naphtali Hirsch, 17:348

    Rosenblatt, Mordecai ben Menahem, 17:441

    Rozin, Joseph, 17:504

    Samuel ben Judah Loeb Eger, 6:218

    Simḥah Bunim ben Moses Eger, 6:218–219

    Song of Songs Rabbah, 19:20

    tosafot, 20:67–70

compassion, 5:123

computation, 5:129–130

concordance, 11:822–823

coral, 5:215

cosmetics, 5:229–230

cosmology, 5:231

courts of law

    admission, 1:410–411

    attorneys, 2:648

    bet din, 3:514

    contempt of court, 5:189

    dictum of Resh Lakish, 21:119

    Jewish vs. non-Jewish lawsuits, 5:155

    jurists' duties, 13:741

    law of evidence, 6:577–580, 582–583, 584

    legal practice and procedure, 16:434–446

    limitation of actions, 13:22–23

    witnesses, 21:115–124

crime and criminal law

    compounding offenses, 5:123

    confessions, 5:147–149

    homicide, 6:221, 9:507

    human trafficking, abduction, 1:242

    rape, 17:93

    trespassing, 8:449–451

Dama, son of Netina, 5:384–385

Damascus (Syria), 5:392

deaf-mute people, 5:508–509

death, 5:511–512

    afterlife, 1:441–442

    burial customs, 4:292–293

    coffins, 4:782–783

    cremation, 5:281

    suicide, 19:296

the deep, 5:530

Dembitzer, Ḥayyim Nathan, 5:548

demons, demonology, 5:574–575

    Agrat bat Mahalath, 1:470–471

    Samael, 17:715

    Satan, 18:72

Derekh erez, 5:593–594

dietary laws, 5:655–656, 657

    cheese, 4:587

    eggs, 6:219–220

    fish and fishing, 7:59

    ḥamez, sale of, 8:303

dina de-malkhuta dina, 5:663–664, 666

disputations, 5:687

divination, 5:705–707

domiciles, 5:741

dreams, 6:9

drunkenness, 6:27

dukhan and, 6:44

dysphemisms, 6:551

earth in, 6:82–83

ecology, 6:93, 95

education, 6:159, 169–172, 12:273

elders, 6:296

emotions, 6:396

environment, 6:449

Eruvin (tractate), 6:485–486

eschatology, 6:500

ethics, 6:535–536

euphemisms, 6:550–551

even ha-to'im, 6:574

evil eye, 6:585

extradition of slaves, 6:626, 627

Eybeschuetz controversey, 8:264

fables, 6:667

family law

    abortion, 1:271

    adultery, 4:582

    barrenness and fertility, 3:174–175

    child marriage, 4:616

    civil marriage, 4:746–748

    divorce, 5:711

    dowries, 5:769

    Gittin, 7:620–621

    Ketubbot, 12:98–99

    Kiddushin, 12:145–146

    levirate marriage and Ḥalizah, 12:725–729

    marriages, 12:725–726, 13:565–566

    orphans and orphanages, 15:483–484

    rebellious son, 17:138–139

    Sotah (tractate), 19:33

    Usha, takkanot of, 20:432

    widows, 21:40–45

    Yevamot, 21:323–325

fiction, 7:10

figs, 7:18

fire, 7:43

flax, 7:70

flies, 7:91

forgiveness, 7:128–129

freedom, 7:226

free will, 7:232–233

friendship, 7:290

gambling, 7:366, 368–369

Garden of Eden, 7:388–389

gematria, 7:424–425

Gemilut Ḥasadim, 7:427

genealogy, 7:431

Genesis Rabbah, 7:448–449

genizah discoveries, 7:473–474

gentiles, 7:485–487

geographic references, 7:488–490

Geonic responsa, 7:384

Gittin, 7:620–621

God, 7:660–661

    names of, 7:677

Gog and Magog, 7:684

good and evil, 7:752–753

grace after meals, 8:22–23

Greek language, 8:57–58

haggahot, 8:217–220

Ḥagigah, 8:223–224

hagiography, 8:224–226

halakhah, 8:251–258

    crucifixion, 5:309–310

    Halakhah le-Moshe mi-Sinai, 8:258

    Halakot Gedolot, 8:259–261

    Halakot Kezuvot, 8:261

    Halakot Pesukot, 8:260–261, 262–263

Halberstam, Isaac ben Ḥayyim, 8:265

Halivni, David Weiss, 8:274–275
Hallel, 8:280
Hamburg, Abraham Benjamin, 8:297–298
Hananiah, 8:315
Ḥanina bar Ḥama, 8:321–322
Ḥanina ben Dosa, 8:323
Ḥanukkah, 8:332
hatred, 8:458
heart, 8:509–510
ḥerem, 9:13–14, 13–19
heresy, 9:20–22
honey, 9:517
honor, 9:519–520
humor, 9:591
ḥumra, 9:600
idolatry, 9:713–714
informers, 9:780, 783
ingathering of the exiles, 9:786
insults, 9:807
insurance, 9:808, 809
Jashar, Book of, 4:69
jealousy in, 11:99
Jerusalem Talmud, 10:155–156, 19:472t, 473t
Jesus in, 11:249–250
joy, concept of, 11:470–471
Judaism, essential principles of, 11:512
Julian III's commission on, 11:574
Kavvanah, 12:39–40
ketubbah bond, 5:154–155
labor, 12:409–410, 417
lamed vav ẓaddikim, 12:445
landmarks, 8:449–450
land robbery, 8:449–450
legal person, 12:605
leprosy laws, 12:652–653
letters and letter writers, 12:670
Leviathan, 12:696–697
Levirate marriage and ḥaliẓah, 12:725–727
lexicography, 5:435, 11:93
maritime law, 13:546
mathematics in, 13:671–673
medicine, 13:722, 723, 724
    bloodletting, 3:774
    leprosy, 12:652–653
    medicinal herbs, 9:8–9
    physicians' duties, 13:739
Megillah (tractate), 13:768
Middle Ages, 13:780–782, 17:256–257
miracles, 14:306–307
mishmarot and ma'amadot, 14:318

mitzvah, 14:372
modern philosophy, 17:257–258
morality and law, 12:535–537
Mordacai ben Hillel ha-Kohen, 14:481
mukẓeh objects, 14:608
mushrooms, 14:636
musical rendition, 19:**487–488,** 487t
oaths in, 15:44–45, 360–362
oils in, 15:396
Onias, Temple of, 15:433
Onkelos, 15:433–434
Palestinian, language validity, 8:641
parables, 15:621–623
parody in, 15:654
Patriarchal merit termination, 21:498
peace, concept of, 15:701–702
pikkua'ah nefesh, 16:152–153
pilpul, 16:161–163
polemical, 16:327–329
police offenses, 16:332
pomegranates, 16:364–365
poverty, 16:427–428
prayer, 16:458–459
precious stones and jewelry, 16:478–479
printing of, 1:386, 6:746, 11:7
profanity, 16:543–544
proofreaders, 8:218–219
prophets and prophecy, 16:580–581
proselytes, view of, 16:589–590
proverbs, 16:646–648
providence, 16:649
Psalms, Book of, 16:675–676
psychiatry, 16:684
psychology, 16:687–688
punishments, 16:735
    banishment, 3:110
    capital punishment, 4:446–448
    crucifixion, 5:309–310
    fines, 7:27–29
    flogging, 7:78–79
    imprisonment, 5:606–607, 9:743, 748
rabbinical literature, 17:22
rabbis, 17:11, 15
rain, 17:71
Rashi commentary, 17:104–105
rebuke and reproof, 17:139–140
redaction, 9:206–207
redemption, 17:152

red heifer, 17:157–158
repentance, 17:221–222
reshut, 17:227
responsa, 17:228–239
Responsa Project, 5:131–132
resurrection, 17:241–243
revelation, 17:254–256
reward and punishment, 17:269–270
rice, 17:283–284
right and left, 17:302
righteousness, 17:308–309
    Ḥasidei Ummot ha-Olam, 8:389
    ẓaddik, 21:437
rishonim, 17:339–343
ritual purity
    hand washing, 13:701
    hygiene, 9:648
    niddah in, 15:254–256
Rome (Italy), 17:409–411, 19:482–483
Rosenblatt, Mordecai ben Menahem, 17:441
Rosenzweig, Gerson, 17:463
Rossi, Azariah ben Moses dei, 17:**471–473**
saints, 1:228
sanctity of life, 13:744
Scroll of Esther, 18:218
serekh, 18:308–309
se'udah, 18:321–322
sexual relations
    abstinence, 4:582
    celibacy, 4:537
    chastity, 4:582
    homosexuality, 9:516
    incest, 4:582
    lesbianism, 12:660
    onanism, 15:426–427
    pre-marital sex, 4:582
    prostitution, 16:626
    virginity, 20:540–541
shaving and beards, 3:235–236
Shekhinah, 18:441
Sicarii, 21:469
sorcery, 19:27–28
soul, immortality of, 19:35–39
spices, 19:102
stipulation, 5:193, 194
structure
    book titles, 8:551–553
    minor tractates, 14:292–293
    Mishnah, 14:327–329
study and methodology
    cantillation, 4:436

Talmud, *continued*

contoversy, rules of, 5:157–158

halakhic decision and exegesis, 13:90–91, 92

intonation of Bible, 13:656–657

legal maxims, 12:604

mnemonics or *memora technica,* 14:397–398

peshat, 16:89

pilpul, 16:162

principles of legality, 15:720

Telz style of Talmudic study, 3:759

suffering, 7:752–753

summaries, *Beit ha-Beḥirah,* 13:786

taxation, 19:534–536

textiles, 19:661–662

thunder and lightning, 19:710

titles, 19:740–741

Tosefta, 20:70–72

translations

Aquila, 15:433–434

Hebrew manuscripts, 13:490

Onkelos, 15:433–434

Rabbinowicz, Israel Michel, 17:31–32

Schwab, Moïse, 18:180

Tu Bi-Shevat, 20:167

twilight, 20:209–210

vengeance, 20:499

in vernacular, *Mayse-Bukh,* 13:702–703

vows and vowing, 20:586

wages for services, 5:185–186

weights and measures, 20:706–709, 707t, 708t

wine, 21:80–81

Zaken Mamre, 21:446

zeal in, 11:99

zekhut avot, 21:497–498

Zevahim, 21:518–519

Zugot, 21:680

See also Babylonian Talmud; Haggadah, Passover; Jerusalem Talmud; Obligations, law of

Talmud, David L., 19:**483**

Talmud, Jerusalem. *See* Jerusalem Talmud

Talmud and Middle Persian culture, 19:**488–491**

Talmud de-Erez Yisrael. *See* Talmud

The Talmud for Every Jew (Simon), 18:616

Talmudic academies. *See* Academies in Babylonia and Erez Israel

Talmudic period

archives, 2:405

bathing, 3:210–211

Bet Din, 3:514

liturgy, 13:131–132

scripture, 12:535–537

sculpture, 18:222

Talmudic scholars

Abba, 1:224–225

Abba bar Aḥa, 1:225

Abba bar Avina, 1:225–226

Abba bar Kahana, 1:226

Abba bar Marta, 1:226

Abba bar Zavda, 1:226–227

Abba bar Zemina, 1:227

Abba ben Abba ha-Kohen, 1:227

Abba Benjamin, 1:227

Abba Guryon of Sidon, 1:227–228

Abba Ḥilkiah, 1:228

Abbahu, 1:228–229, 18:594

Abba Kohen Bardela, 1:229

Abba of Akko, 1:230

Abba Oshaya of Tiriah, 1:230–231

Abba Saul, 1:232

Abba Saul ben Batnit, 1:232

Abbaye, 1:235–236

Abbaye Kashisha, 1:236

Abba Yose ben Dostai, 1:236

Abba Yose ben Ḥanin, 1:236

Abraham ben David of Posquères, 1:296–298

Abraham ben Elijah of Vilna, 1:299

Abraham ben Isaac of Montpellier, 1:302

Abraham ben Isaac of Narbonne, 1:302

Adda bar Ahavah, 1:384–385

Aḥa bar Ḥanina, 1:525

Aḥa bar Rav, 1:525

Aḥa ben Jacob, 1:525

Aḥai, 1:529

Aḥai ben Josiah, 1:529

Aibu, 1:549

Akavyah ben Mahalalel, 1:554, 5:760–761, 6:215

Akiva, 1:562–563

Alexandri, 1:631–632

Ameimar, 2:37–38

Ammi bar Nathan, 2:82

Amram, 2:103

Amram Ḥasida, 2:105

Anan, 2:126, 3:641, 706

Ashi, 2:565–566

Assi, 2:82, 103, 603, 11:478

Assi, Rav, 2:603, 18:598

Avdan, 2:717

Avdimi of Haifa, 2:717

Avia, 2:726

Avimi, 2:737

Avimi ben Abbahu, 2:737

Avin, 2:737

Avina, 2:737–738

Avira, 2:740

Avtalyon, 2:754–755, 3:641, 11:293, 18:456

Azariah, 2:762

Bacharach, Jair Ḥayyim ben Moses Samson, 3:33–34

Bachrach, Moses ben Isaiah Menahem, 3:39

Baneth family, 3:107

Barazani, Asenath, 3:138

Bar Hediya, 3:151–152

Bar Kappara, 3:155–156, 11:504, 18:597–598

Baruch ben Isaac of Regensburg, 3:188

Bebai, 3:241

Bebai Bar Abbaye, 3:241

Bena'ah, 3:313

Ben Azzai, Simeon, 3:322–323, 8:391, 18:601

Ben Bag Bag, 3:323

Ben He He, 3:352

Benjamin ben Japheth, 3:361

Ben Kalba Savu'a, 3:365

Ben Petura, 3:371

Ben Stada, 3:378

Ben Zoma, Simeon, 3:393, 18:601

Berechiah, 3:406

Berlin, Naphtali Ẓevi Judah (ha-Neẓiv), 3:457–458

Bialoblocki, Samuel Sheraga, 3:566

Bischhoff, Erich, 3:724

Coronel, Naḥman Nathan, 5:225

Daniel Ḥayyata, 5:429

de Vries, Benjamin, 5:629

Dimi, 5:662

Dimi of Nehardea, 5:662–663

Dosa ben Harkinas, 5:760–761, 6:215

Dostai ben Judah, 5:761

Dostai ben Yannai, 5:761–762

Duenner, Joseph Ẓevi Hirsch, 6:41

Eleazar ben Arakh, 6:299

Eleazar ben Azariah, 3:663, 6:215, 299–300, 14:534

Eleazar ben Damma, 6:300–301

Eleazar ben Hananiah ben Hezekiah, 6:301

Eleazar ben Judah of Bartota, 6:303

Eleazar ben Matya, 6:305

Eleazar ben Parta, 6:305–306

Eleazar ben Pedat, 6:306–307

Eleazar ben Shammua, 6:307

Eleazar ben Simeon, 6:308, 627,
11:453

Eleazar ben Yose I, 6:308

Eleazar ben Yose II, 6:308–309

Eleazar (Eliezer) ben Zadik, 6:309

Eleazar (Eliezer) ha-Kappar, 6:309

Eleazar Ḥisma, 6:309–310

Eleazar of Mod'in, 6:310

Elfenbein, Israel, 6:314

Eliezer ben Hyrcanus, 6:322–325,
11:450, 451–452, 15:433, 469

Eliezer ben Isaac of Worms, 6:326

Eliezer ben Jacob, 6:326

Eliezer ben Yose ha-Gelili, 6:329–
330

Elijah ben Judah of Paris, 6:339

Elisha ben Avuyah, 6:352–353

Epstein, Jacob Nahum, 6:472

Eybeschuetz, 6:633

Gamaliel, Rabban ha-Zaken,
3:589, 592, 7:364

Gebiha of Be-Katil, 7:406

Haggai, 6:493, 8:222–223

Haggai of Sepphoris, 8:223

Ḥalafta, 8:250

Ḥalafta ben Saul, 8:250–251

Ḥama Bar Bisa, 8:291

Ḥama of Nehardea, 8:291

Hamnuna, 8:310

Ḥana Bar Ḥanilai, 8:313

Ḥana ben Bizna, 8:313

Hananel ben Ḥushi'el, 8:314

Hananel ben Samuel, 8:315

Hananiah, 8:315

Hananiah ben Ḥakhinai, 8:315–
316

Hananiah ben Teradyon, 6:305,
8:316

Hananiah of Sephoris, 8:316

Hanan the Egyptian, 8:314

Ḥanina, 8:321

Ḥanina bar Ḥama, 8:321–322

Ḥanina Bar Papa, 8:322

Ḥanina ben Abbahu, 8:322

Ḥanina ben Antigonus, 8:322

Ḥanina ben Dosa, 8:323, 390

Ḥanina ben Gamliel, 8:323

Ḥanina Segan ha-Kohanim,
5:760–761, 6:215, 8:323–324

Ḥanokh ben Moses, 8:328–329

Ḥayyim ben Bezalel, 8:480

Ḥayyim ben Jehiel Ḥafeẓ Zahav,
8:482

Ḥayyim ben Samuel ben David of
Tudela, 8:482

Ḥayyim Judah ben Ḥayyim, 8:483

Ḥayyim Paltiel ben Jacob, 8:483

Hazkarat neshamot, 8:496–497

Ḥefeẓ ben Yaẓli'aḥ, 8:753

Helbo, Menahem, 11:783–784

Heschel, Abraham Joshua, 9:70–72

Hezekiah, 9:90

Ḥidka, 9:97

Higger, Michael, 9:98

Hilewitz, Alter, 9:105

Hillel (330-365 C.E.), 9:110

Hillel (the Elder), 9:108–109

Hillel II, 9:110

Hillel ben Eliakim, 9:113

Hillel ben Samuel, 9:113–114

Hillel of Erfurt, 9:115

Hirschprung, Pinhas, 9:141

Ḥisda, 9:144, 17:8–9

Ḥiyya, 9:295–297, 14:437–438,
18:597

Ḥiyya bar Abba, 6:306, 9:297,
18:448

Ḥiyya bar Avin, 9:297

Hoffmann, David Ẓevi, 9:310–311

Horovitz, Saul, 9:530

Horowitz, Abraham ben Shabbetai
Sheftel, 9:532

Horowitz, Jacob ben Abraham,
9:537–538

Horowitz, Phinehas ben Israel ha-
Levi, 9:539–540

Horowitz, Ẓevi Hirsch ben
Ḥayyim Aryeh Leibush ha-Levi,
9:544–545

Hoshaiah, Rav, 9:559

Ḥozin, Ẓedakah ben Saadiah,
9:573

Huna, 8:450, 9:600–601, 15:370

Huna ben Avin ha-Kohen, 9:601

Huna ben Joshua, 8:450, 9:601

Huna ben Nathan, 2:37, 9:601–
602

Huna of Sepphoris, 9:602

Ḥunya of Beth-Horon, 9:622

Ḥushi'el ben Elhanan, 9:640–641

Ḥuzpit ha-Meturgeman, 9:646

Ibn Abitur, Joseph ben Isaac,
9:658

Ibn Migash, Joseph ben Meir ha-
Levi, 9:684

Ibn Shoshan, David, 9:692

Idi, 9:710

Idi bar Avin, 9:710

Ilai (c. 100 C.E.), 9:719–720

Ilai (end of 3rd-4th c. C.E.), 9:720

Ilfa, 9:721

Isaac, 10:35

Isaac bar Joseph, 10:37

Isaac bar Rav Judah, 10:37

Isaac ben Avdimi, 10:40

Isaac ben Eleazar, 10:40–41

Isaac Nappaḥa, 10:52–53

Ishmael ben Elisha, 10:83–84

Ishmael ben Johanan ben Beroka,
10:84

Ishmael ben Yose ben Ḥalafta,
6:333, 10:84–85

Jacob, 11:25

Jacob ben Aḥa, 11:30

Jacob ben Idi, 11:32–33

Jacob ben Korshai, 11:34

Jacob ben Moses Moellin, 14:414

Jeremiah ben Abba, 11:135–136

Johanan ben Beroka, 11:369

Johanan ben Gudgada, 11:369

Johanan ben ha-Ḥoranit, 6:309,
11:369

Johanan ben Nappaḥa, 11:370–
372, 397

Johanan ben Nuri, 6:309–310,
7:66, 11:372–373, 452

Johanan ben Torta, 11:373

Johanan ben Zakkai, 11:373–377

Johanan ha-Sandelar, 11:377

Jonah, 11:387–388

Jonathan, 11:396

Jonathan ben Amram, 11:396

Jonathan ben Eleazar, 11:397

Joseph ben Ḥiyya, 11:421–422

Joshua, 11:444

Joshua ben Hananiah, 8:194,
11:373, 450–452

Joshua ben Hyrcanus, 11:452

Joshua ben Korha, 2:69, 6:627,
11:452–453

Joshua ben Levi, 6:333–334,
11:453–454, 14:539, 18:599

Joshua ben Peraḥyah, 11:454

Joshua ha-Garsi, 11:455

Josiah (amora), 11:460

Josiah (tanna), 11:459

Judah bar Ezekiel, 11:480–481

Judah bar Ilai, 2:14, 11:481–482

Judah bar Shalom, 11:482

Judah bar Simeon, 11:482

Judah ben Bathyra, 3:27, 11:484

Judah ben Bava, 11:484–485,
18:593

Judah ben Dosotheos, 11:485

Judah ben Gerim, 11:486, 18:593

Judah ben Ḥiyya, 11:486–487

Talmudic scholars, *continued*
Judah ben Pedaya, 11:490
Judah ben Shammua, 11:491
Judah ben Tabbai, 11:491, 18:600
Judah ben Tema, 11:491–492
Judah ha-Nasi, 3:212, 11:501–505
Kahana, 11:708–710
Kalman of Worms, 11:746
Kalonymus family, 11:748
Karelitz, Avraham Yeshayahu,
    11:805–806
Kimhi, Jacob ben Samuel, 12:157
Kimhi, Solomon ben Nissim
    Joseph David, 12:159
Klein, Hyman, 12:222
Landau, Eleazar Ben Israel, 12:459
Lauterbach, Jacob Zallel, 6:239,
    12:529
Levi, 12:684
Levi ben Sisi, 12:702–703
Lieberman, Saul, 12:806–807
Mani, 13:469
Mar Bar Rav Ashi, 13:510
Mar Bar Ravina, 13:510
Mari ben Issur, 13:544
Mattiah ben Heresh, 13:688
Mattnah, 13:688
Meir, 1:541, 3:585, 8:640, 13:776–
    777, 779, 15:383
Meremar, 14:63
Mordecai ben Naphtali Hirsch,
    14:482
Nahman Bar Rav Huna, 14:738
Nahman ben Isaac, 14:738
Nahman ben Jacob, 14:738–739
Nahum of Gimzo, 3:584, 14:759
Nahum the Mede, 14:759
Nakdimon ben Guryon, 14:763
Nathan Ha-Bavli, 15:15, 278
Nehemiah (2nd c. C.E.), 15:61–62
Nehorai, 15:63
Nehunya ben Ha-Kahan, 15:64
Nittai of Arbela, 11:454, 15:282
Oshaiah Rabbah, 15:501–502
Papa, 15:614
Papi, 15:617
Pappus ben Judah, 15:619
Phinehas ben Hama ha-Kohen,
    16:116
Phinehas ben Jair, 8:391, 16:116–
    117
Pirkoi ben Baboi, 16:183
Plaut, Hezekiah Feivel, 16:227
Polachek, Solomon, 16:285–286
Rabba ben Matnah, 17:7
Rabbah bar bar Hana, 17:8

Rabbah bar Huna, 17:8–9
Rabbah bar Nahamani, 17:9
Rabbah ben Avuha, 17:9–10
Rabbah ben Shilah, 17:10
Rabbah Tosfa'ah, 17:10
Rabbinovicz, Raphael Nathan
    Nata, 17:31
Rav, 17:116–118
Rava, 17:118–119
Ravina, 17:122–123
Rehumei, 17:196
Reuben ben Strobilius, 17:246–247
Safra, 17:662
Samuel, 17:757–758
Samuel ben Nahman, 17:773–774
Samuel ben Shilat, 17:774
Samuel ha-Katan, 17:775–776
Schiff, Meir ben Jacob ha-Kohen,
    18:131
Schmelkes, Gedalliah ben
    Mordecai, 18:144
Schmelkes, Isaac Judah, 18:144
Schwarz, Adolf, 18:188
Shammai, 3:530–533, 18:394
Shela, 18:444–445
Shemaiah, 3:13, 641, 11:293,
    18:456
Sheshet, 2:103, 546, 3:142, 8:313,
    18:466
Shila of Kefar Tamarta, 18:476
Simeon bar Yohai, 18:593–594
Simeon ben Abba, 18:594
Simeon ben Eleazar, 12:410,
    18:594–595
Simeon ben Gamaliel I, 18:595
Simeon ben Gamaliel II, 10:151,
    11:453, 18:595–596
Simeon ben Halafta, 2:184,
    18:596–597
Simeon ben Jehozadak, 18:597
Simeon ben Judah ha-Nasi, 18:597
Simeon ben Lakish, 11:478, 490,
    14:413, 15:246, 18:597–598,
    20:40
Simeon ben Menasya, 18:598–599
Simeon ben Nanas, 18:599
Simeon ben Nethanel, 2:66, 18:599
Simeon ben Pazzi, 18:599–600
Simeon ben Shetah, 6:163, 171,
    11:491, 18:600–601
Simeon ha-Pakuli, 18:601
Simeon ha-Timni, 18:601–602
Simeon of Mizpah, 18:602
Simlai, 18:606
Singer, Pesah, 18:639–640
Sirkes, Joel, 18:644
Solomon ben Abraham of
    Montpellier, 18:770

Soloveichik, Joseph Baer, of
    Volozhin, 18:776
Symmachus ben Joseph, 19:351–
    352
Tanhuma bar Abba, 19:502–503
Tanhum ben Hanilai, 19:504
Tanhum ben Hiyya, 19:504
Tarfon, 6:627, 11:580, 19:512–513
Ukba, Mar, 20:232–233
Ulla I, 20:240
Yannai, 11:487, 21:280
Yeshevav the Scribe, 21:313–314
Yose, 11:387
Yose bar Hanina, 21:394–395
Yose ben Akavyah, 21:395
Yose ben Avin, 21:395
Yose ben Dormaskos, 21:395
Yose ben Halafta, 21:396
Yose ben Joezer of Zeredah,
    21:396–397
Yose ben Johanan ha-Tanna of
    Jerusalem, 21:397
Yose ben Judah, 21:397
Yose ben Kippar, 21:397
Yose ben Kisma, 21:397
Yose ben Meshullam, 21:397–398
Yose ben Zimra, 21:398–399
Yose ha-Gelili, 3:129, 21:399–400
Yose ha-Kohen, 21:400
Yudan, 21:407–408
Zadok, 21:441
Zechariah ben Avkilus, 21:486
Ze'eira, 21:490–491
Ze'iri, 21:495
See also Amoraim; Tannaim
Talmudic Stories: Narrative Art,
Composition and Culture
(Rubenstein), 1:461
The Talmud in its Emptiness. See
Talmud in seiner Nichtigkeit
Der Talmud in seiner Nichtigkeit
(Buchner), 8:436
Talmudische Archäologie (Krauss),
14:331
Talmud Katan (Alfasi). *See Sefer ha-*
Halakhot (Alfasi)
Talmud Lashon Ivri (work), 3:**391**
Talmud of the West, The. *See* Talmud
The Talmud Student. See Ha-Matmid
Talmud Torah. *See* Study
Talmud Torah (Sikili), 18:574
Talmud Torah schools
    Algeria, 6:214
    Conservative Judaism, 6:196
    Constantinople, 6:180
    Lodz, 11:725
    Morocco, 14:505, 506

New York (NY), 6:190, 191–195
Russia, 6:187
U.K., 6:204–205
Talmud Torah Society, 6:180
Talnoye (Ukraine), 19:**491**
Talnoye family, 8:420
Talpiot, 17:236–237
Talpir, Gabriel Joseph, 19:**491**
Tal Shaḥar, 19:**491**
Talut. *See* Saul
Ṭālūt. *See* Saul
Tam, Jacob ben Meir, 3:770, 19:**491–492**
  agunah, 1:518
  Amram Gaon, 2:105
  Ephraim ben Isaac, 6:459
  Joseph ben Moses of Troyes, 11:424
  moneylending, 14:438
  taxes, 7:23
Tam, Rabbenu
  Anjou, 2:175
  fines and damages, 7:28
  medieval education, 6:176–177
Tamakh, Abraham ben Isaac ha-Levi, 19:**492–493**
Tamar (daughter of Absalom), 19:**494**
Tamar (daughter of David), 19:**494**
Tamar (daughter of Sarah of Turnovo), 18:47
Tamar (Judah), 19:**493**
Tamar (wife of Er and Onan), 2:87, 6:477, 19:**493–494**
  Zerah and, 21:512
Tamares, Aaron Samuel, 19:**494**
Tamarisk, 19:**494–495**, vol. 16: color insert
Tamaroff, Mordecai. *See* Tenenbaum, Mordecai
Tamḥui, 2:39
Tam ibn Yaḥya, Jacob ben David, 19:**495**
Tamid (tractate), 18:602, 19:**495**
Tamid Anaḥnu (Shaham), 18:363
Tamir, Alexander, 6:145–146
Tamir, Shmuel, 19:**495–496**
Tamiris, Helen, 19:**496**
Tamm, Igor Yevgenyevich, 19:**496**
Tammany Hall, Jewish involvement in, 15:198, 205, 211, 214, 290
Tammuz (fourth month of the Jewish year), 19:**497**
Tammuz (Sumerian-Babylonian fertility god), 19:**496–497**
Tammuz, Benjamin, 4:393, 19:**497**
Tammuz, Fast of. *See* Fast of Tammuz
Tampa (FL), 19:**498–499**

Tamrah (Israel). *See* Ramat Ẓevi (Israel)
Tamuda (Morocco). *See* Tetuán (Morocco)
Tamut (bride), 6:312
Tan, N. A. *See* Bogoraz, Vladimir Germanovich
Tan, V. G. *See* Bogoraz, Vladimir Germanovich
Tanais (kingdom of Bosphorus), 4:98
Tanakh, 19:**499**
  See also Bible
Tancred (Disraeli), 5:700, 6:435–436, 12:710
Tandler, Julius, 19:**499–500**
Tanenbaum, Joey, 19:**500**
Tanenbaum, Larry, 19:**500**
Tanenbaum, Max, 19:**500**
Tanenbaum, "Sid." *See* Tanenbaum, Sidney Harold
Tanenbaum, Sidney Harold, 19:**500–501**
Tanenbaum family, 19:**500**
Tang, Abraham ben Naphtali. *See* Abrahams, Abraham
Tang-i Azao inscriptions (Central Afghanistan), 11:548
Tangier (Morocco), 14:500, 501, 19:**501–502**
Tangiers (Morocco). *See* Tangier (Morocco)
Tanḥuma bar Abba, 19:**502–503**
Tanḥuma Yelammedenu, 19:**503–504**
Tanḥum ben Eliezer, 19:**504**
Tanḥum ben Ḥanilai, 19:**504**
Tanḥum ben Ḥiyya, 19:**504**
Tanḥum ben Joseph ha-Yerushalmi. *See* Tanḥum ben Joseph Yerushalmi
Tanḥum ben Joseph Yerushalmi, 11:537, 19:**504–505**
Tanḥum mi-Kefar Yano'ah (Zemach), 21:504
Tanḥum of Kefar Acco. *See* Tanḥum ben Ḥiyya
Ta'anit (tractate), 19:**416**
Tanja (Morocco). *See* Tangier (Morocco)
Tanna de-Vei Eliyahu, 6:333, 338–339, 19:**508**
  See also Aggadat Bereshit
Tannaim, 1:350, 2:89, 19:**505–507**, *507*
  Aḥerim, 1:541
  Akiva, 1:562–563
  baraita, 3:124–128
  biblical exegesis and study, 3:640
  Dosa ben Harkinas, 5:760–761
  Dostai ben Judah, 5:761
  Dostai ben Yannai, 5:761–762

Eleazar ben Arakh, 6:299
Eleazar ben Azariah, 6:299–300
Eleazar ben Damma, 6:300–301
Eleazar ben Hananiah ben Hezekiah, 6:301
Eleazar ben Judah of Bartota, 6:303
Eleazar ben Matya, 6:305
Eleazar ben Parta, 6:305–306
Eleazar ben Shammua, 6:307
Eleazar ben Simeon, 6:308
Eleazar ben Yose I, 6:308
Eleazar ben Zadok, 6:309
Eleazar ha-Kappar, 6:309
Eleazar Ḥisma, 6:309–310
Eleazar of Modi'in, 6:310
Eliezer ben Hyrcanus, 6:322–325
Eliezer ben Jacob (1st century), 6:326
Eliezer ben Jacob (2nd century), 6:326
Eliezer ben Yose ha-Gelili, 6:329–330
Elisha ben Avuyah, 6:352–354
Hananiah, 8:315
Hananiah of Sephoris, 8:316
Hanan the Egyptian, 8:314
Ḥanina ben Antigonus, 8:322
Ḥanina ben Dosa, 8:323
Ḥanina ben Gamaliel, 8:323
Ḥanina Segan ha-Kohanim, 8:323–324
Hillel (the Elder), 9:108–110
Ḥiyya, 9:295–297
Judah, 8:487
legal maxims, 12:603
Mattiah ben Ḥeresh, 13:688
Meir, 13:776–777
Mishnah, 14:320–321
mishpat Ivri, 14:337, 340
Nehorai, 15:63
Neḥunya ben ha-Kahah, 15:64
Simeon ben Eleazar, 18:594–595
Simeon ben Ḥalafta, 18:596–597
Simeon ben Menasya, 18:598–599
Simeon ben Nanas, 18:599
Simeon ben Nathaniel, 18:599
Simeon Ha-Timni, 18:601–602
Simeon of Mizpah, 18:602
Tannenbaum, Frank, 19:**508**
Tannenbaum, Jacob. *See* Tennenbaum, Jacob
Tannenbaum, Judith. *See* Shuval, Judith
Tanner, Celia, 12:598
Tannim, 15:550

Tansman, Alexander, 19:**508–509**

Tansman, Alexandre. *See* Tansman, Alexander

Tanta (Egypt), 19:**509**

Tanuji, Ishmael ha-Kohen, 19:**509**

Tanuji, Joseph ben Shalom ha-Kohen, 19:**509–510**

Tanuji family, 19:**509**

Tanya (Shneur Zalman of Lyady), 4:554, 18:504–505

Tanzhaus, 19:**510**

Tapestry of the Three Coronations (tapestry), 18:762

Tappuah, 19:**510**

    Tappuah (territory of Ephraim), 19:510

    Tappuah (territory of Judah), 19:510

Tappuḥei Zahav (Alshekh), 2:10

Tappuḥim min ha-Midbar (Liebrecht), 12:811–812

Tara fetelor (Banus), 3:120

Taragan, Ben-Zion, 19:**510**

Taranto (Italy), 19:**510–511**

Tarascon (France), 19:**511**

Tarazona (Spain), 19:**511–512**

Tarbiz (periodical), 19:**512**

Tarbut, 4:622, 6:185, 11:725, 12:455, 801, 14:518, 19:**512**

Tares, 19:**512**

Tarfon (Rabbi), 6:627

Tarfon (tanna), 11:580, 19:**512–513**

Târgu-Frumos (Romania). *See* Tirgu-Frumos (Romania)

Targum, 10:297–298, 19:**513**

    anthropomorphism, 2:189

    Aramaic translations of Bible, ancient, 3:588–594

    dating, 3:589

    defined, 3:588

    Erez Israel, 3:591

    Galilean Aramaic, 2:349

    genizah records, 7:476–477

    Jonathan, 3:592

    Jonathan ben Uzziel, 11:398

    Joseph ben Ḥiyya, 11:421

    Ketuvim, 3:593–594

    liturgical role of, 3:589

    Nevi'im, 3:592–593

    Onkelos, 3:589–591, 13:621, 630

    origins and purpose, 3:589

    Peshitta and, 3:600

    Shekhinah, 18:441

    Toraic, 3:589–592

    use of, 3:589

Targum Sheni, 19:**513–515**

Targu-Mures (Romania), 19:**515**

Targum Yerushalmi I (Pseudo-Jonathan), 3:591

Targum Yerushalmi II (Fragmentary Targum), 3:591–592

Targum Yerushalmi to the Prophets, 3:593

Tarif, Amin, 19:**515**

The Tarikh-i-Rashidi (Elias), 6:319

Tarkinus. *See* Trajan, Marcus Ulpius

Tarlov, Malcolm, 15:304

Tarn, Nathaniel, 19:**515–516**

Tarnegol Kaparot (Amir), 2:78

Tarnobrzeg (Poland), 19:**516**

Tarnograd (Poland). *See* Tarnogrod (Poland)

Tarnogrod (Poland), 19:**516**

Tarnopol (Ukraine), 19:**516–518**

Tarnopol, Joachim Ḥayyim, 19:**518**

Tarnopolsky, Samuel, 19:**518–519**

Tarnow (Poland), 19:**519–520**

Taronji y Cortés, José, 19:**520**

Tarragona (Spain), 19:**520–521**

Tarrasch, Siegbert, 4:605, 12:497, 19:**521–522**

Tárrega (Spain), 19:**522**

Tarshish, 4:485, 16:477–478, 19:**522**

    Tarshis (port of unknown Biblical location), 19:522

    Tarshis (son of Bilhan), 19:522

Tarski, Alfred, 19:**522**

Tartakover, David, 10:699

Tartakover, Savielly Grigoryevich, 4:603, 604, 605, 19:**522–523**

Tartakower, Arieh, 4:189, 18:735, 19:**523**

Tartakower, Aryeh. *See* Tartakower, Arieh

Tartan, 19:**523**

Tartu (Estonia), 19:**523**

Taruskin, Richard, 19:**523–524**

Tarutino (Ukraine), 19:**524**

Taryag mitzvot. *See* Commandments, the 613

Tarziu: insemnari californiene (Calin), 4:364

Tashbez. See Teshuvot Shimon ben Zemah

Tash dynasty, 8:425

Tashkent (Uzbekistan), 19:**524**

Tashlikh, 19:**524–525**, vol. 17: color insert

Ta-Shma, Israel Moses, 19:**525**

Tashrak, 19:**525–526**

Task Force for International Cooperation on Holocaust Education, Remembrance, and Research, 9:457, 459

Taslitt, Israel Isaac, 11:444

Tasmania, 19:**526**

Tatar conquest, 5:299–300

Tatarjaras (operetta), 11:745

Tatlin, Vladimir E., 19:**526**

Tats. *See* Mountain Jews

Tattenai, 19:**526**

Tattoo, 19:**526–527**, 21:240

TAU. *See* Tel Aviv University

Tau, Max, 19:**527**

Taub, Ezekiel ben Zevi-Hirsch of Kazimierz, 12:45

Taub, Henry, 15:687

Taub, Isaac, 15:610

Taub, Joe, 15:687

Taube, Michael, 19:**527**

Taube, Moshe, 19:**527**

Taube, Samuel Baruch, 19:**527**

Taubenschlag, Raphael, 19:**527–528**

Tauber, Richard, 19:**528**

Tauberbischofsheim (Germany), 3:43, 19:**528**

Taubes, Aaron Moses ben Jacob, 19:**528**

Taubes, Ḥayyim Zevi, 19:**528**

Taubes, Loebel, 19:**528–529**

Taubman, A. Alfred, 19:**529**

Tauf Aleph (Gotlieb), 18:200

Taurage (Lithuania), 19:**529**

Tauroci, Isaac. *See* Isaac ben Todros

Tauroggen (Lithuania). *See* Taurage (Lithuania)

A Taurus, an Aries and a Libra. See Býk, Beran a Váhy

Tausig, Karl, 19:**529–530**

Tausk, Viktor, 19:**530**

Taussig, Frank William, 19:**530**

Taussig, Friedrich. *See* Fritta

Taussig family, 19:**530**

Tauste (Spain), 19:**530**

Tav, 19:**530**

Tavern-keepers. *See* Wine and liquor trade

Tavrig (Lithuania). *See* Taurage (Lithuania)

Tavus, Jacob ben Joseph, 19:**531**

    Judeo-Persian translation of Bible by, 3:609

    Judeo-Persian translations of Bible, 11:552

Taw. *See* Tav

Tawiow, Israel Ḥayyim, 19:**531**

Tawrizi, Judah Meir ben Abraham, 19:**531**

The Tax. See Di Takse

Tax, Sol, 2:187, 19:**531–532**

Taxation, 19:**532–558**

    amoraic tax exemption, 2:95

Aurum Coronarium, 2:661
in Bukhara, 4:259
Burgundy, 4:290
candle tax, 4:430
Courland (Latvia), 5:245–246
Covenant of Omar, 15:416–419
dina de-malkhuta dina, 5:665
easing burden of, 18:448
Eleazar family (Aragon), 6:298
fiscus Judaicus, 18:448
half-shekel tax, 18:438–439
history of, 6:104–108, 19:532–534
imprisonment for debt and,
9:748–749
Kallah months, 11:741–742
korobka, 12:314–315
legal and judicial system, 19:534–
558
adjudication and evidence,
19:552–553
Bible, 19:534
date of accrual of liability,
19:543–545
ethics of tax payments,
19:556
Halakhah, 19:557–558
Israel, 19:558–559
post-Talmudic period,
19:536–539
principles of interpretation,
19:554–555
property, 19:540–543
Talmud, 19:534–536
tax appeals, 19:551–552
tax assessment, 19:539–540,
548–551
tax collection procedures,
19:555–556
tax relief and immunity,
19:545–548
Leibzoll, 2:6, 157, 12:624–625
medieval education, 6:176–177
medieval Spain, 3:42, 18:42–43,
327
Noerdlingen, 15:293
Olyka, 15:412
opferpfennig, 15:438
Oppenheim, 15:442
Orense, 15:465
Orléans, 15:477
Ottoman empire, 15:520, 525, 528,
533
Oxford, 15:552
Ozery, 15:557
Palatinate, 15:575, 576
Palencia, 15:576
Palermo, 15:580

philanthropic foundations, 7:136
Provence (France), 16:638–639
Russia, 4:525
sheḥitah tax, 18:436
Turkey, 6:148–149
See also Finances, autonomous
Jewish
Tax farming, 2:422–423
Dueñas, 6:40
Écija, Joseph, 6:91
Middle Ages, 6:113–114
Montiel (Spain), 14:461
Tax gatherers, 9:142, 19:558–559
Tayeb, Isaac. See Tayyib, Isaac ben
Benjamin
Taylor, Elizabeth, 19:559
Taylor, Kenneth, 3:619
Taylor, Peter Murray. See Taylor, Sir
Peter Murray
Taylor, Richard, 3:680
Taylor, Sir Peter Murray, 19:559–560
Taylor, Sydney, 19:560
Taylor-Schechter Genizah Research
Unit, 7:478, 480
Tayma (Arabia), 19:560–561
Taymor, Julia, 19:561
Tay-Sachs disease, 3:755–756, 19:561–
562
Tayyib, Isaac ben Benjamin, 19:562
Ṭayyiba, al-, 19:562
Taz. See David ben Samuel ha-Levi
Tbilisi (Georgia). See Tiflis (Georgia)
Tchaikovsky (ballet, Eifman), 6:253
Tcherikover, Avigdor. See Tcherikover,
Victor
Tcherikover, Victor, 9:159, 19:562
Tcherikower, Elias, 19:563
Tchernichovsky, Saul. See
Tchernichowsky, Saul
Tchernichowsky, Saul, 4:119, 11:444,
19:563–567
Tchernowitz, Chaim, 19:567
Tchernowitz, Jacob. See Tsur, Jacob
Tchernowitz, Samuel, 19:567–568
Tchernowitz-Avidar, Yemimah, 19:568
Teacher of Righteousness, 5:508,
12:818, 16:9, 10, 19:568–570
Teachers' Association in Israel,
19:570–571
Tebi. See Tabi
Tebriz (Iran). See Tabriz (Iran)
Tec, Nechama, 4:631, 19:571
Tecanus. See Teka
Techanus. See Teka
Technion, Israel Institute of
Technology, 2:254, 19:571–572
Technology and Halakhah, 19:572–576

Teddy the Jewboy. See Davis, Edward
Tedeschi, Isaac Refael, 19:577
Tedeschi, Moses Isaac ben Samuel,
19:577
Tedeschi family, 19:576–577
Tedesci, Solomon. See Ashkenazi,
Solomon
Tedesco, Moses Isaac ben Samuel. See
Tedeschi, Moses Isaac ben Samuel
Tedesco family. See Tedeschi family
Te'enah. See Figs
Tefillah. See Amidah
Tefillat Geshem. See Rain, prayer for
Tefillat ha-Derekh. See Travel, prayer
for
Tefillat laḥash. See Amidah
Tefillin, 19:577–580
amulets, 2:121
Karaites, 11:799
obligation, 3:164
worn during morning services,
18:364
Teheran (Iran), 19:580–581
education, Jewish, 6:214
Judeo-Persian literature and
language in, 11:557–558
Tehilimzeiger, Moshe. See Ben-Amotz,
Dahn
Tehillot le-El Elyon (Kirschner), 12:189
Teḥinnah, 19:581
Teḥiyyat ha-metim, 13:6
Teḥiyyat Israel, 3:387
Tehom. See The deep
Tehomi, Avraham, 19:581–582
Teichman, Moses. See Murray, Arthur
Teicholz, Bruce B., 19:582
Teif, Moshe, 19:582
Teima (Arabia). See Tayma (Arabia)
Teitel, Jacob, 12:553, 19:582
Teitelbaum, Aaron, 19:583–584
Teitelbaum, Abraham, 19:584
Teitelbaum, Benjamin. See Demblin,
Benjamin
Teitelbaum, David, 11:522
Teitelbaum family, 8:422–423, 19:582–
583
Teitelboim Volosky, Volodia, 16:349,
19:584
Teitler, Samuel, 19:584
Teitsh, Moyshe, 19:584
Teitz, Mordecai Pinchas. See Teitz,
Pinchas
Teitz, Pinchas, 19:584–585
Teixeira, Pedro, 19:585
Teixeira de Sampaio, Abraham Senior,
19:585–586
Teixeira de Sampaio, Diego. See
Teixeira de Sampaio, Abraham
Senior

Teixeira Pinto, Bento, 4:121, 143, 17:145, 19:**586**

Teka, 19:**586**

Tekhelet, 19:**586–587**

Tekhelet Lavan. *See* Blau-Weiss

Teki'ata, 1:362, 19:**587**

Tekinalp, Munis, 19:**587–588**

Teki'to. *See* Teki'ata

Tekoa (territory of Judah), 19:**588**

Tekoah, Yosef, 19:**588**

Tekufah de-Rav Adda. See Baraita de-Rav Adda

Tekumah (Israel), 19:**589**

Tel Adashim (Israel), 19:**589**

Tela Ignea Satanae (Wagenseil), 9:228

Tel al-Rimah stele, 3:657

Telamyon. *See* Ben Temalyon

Tel Aviv-Jaffa (Israel), 3:444, 19:**589–593**

    aerial view, vol. 21: color insert

    architecture and architects, 11:813

    journalism center, Palestine (Mandate), 10:705

    during Mandate

        governance, 10:390

        growth, 10:492, 505–506

        population, 10:487

    population, 10:289, 292

    printing, publishing, 16:538–539

    public sculpture, 10:698

Tel Aviv Municipality *v.* the Estate of the Deceased Leterhaus, 16:218

Tel Aviv Museum of Art, 10:695, 697, 700

Tel Aviv University, 12:557, 19:**593–594**

Tel-Dan, 3:657, 5:459

Teleneshty (Moldova), 19:**594**

Teleneşti (Moldova). *See* Teleneshty (Moldova)

Television and radio, 19:**594–596**

    Brazil, 4:152

    Brice, Fanny, 4:177

    Brooks, James L., 4:209

    Brothers, Joyce, 4:211

    Bruckheimer, Jerry, 4:220

    Burns, George, 4:298–299

    Burrows, Abe, 4:299

    Burrows, James, 4:299

    Buttons, Red, 4:319–320

    comedy, 5:463–464

    Corwin, Norman Lewis, 5:226–227

    Cosell, Howard, 5:227–228

    directors

        Benson, Robby, 3:378

        Hiller, Arthur, 9:115

Lumet, Sidney, 13:256–257

        Rafelson, Robert, 17:63

        Singer, Bryan, 18:633–634

    Di-Zahav, Ephraim, 5:721

    football, 14:407

    Freed, Alan, 7:223

    Hackett, Buddy, 8:183

    Halmi, Robert, 8:282–283

    Hart, Kitty Carlisle, 8:371

    Israel (state), 10:707–709

    Lasser, Louise, 12:503

    Latin America, 12:515

    Lear, Norman, 12:568

    Lewis, Shari, 12:766–767

    Moati, Serge, 14:404

    Moonves, Les, 14:469

    New York City Jewish cultural life and, 15:221, 228

    producers

        Bernstein, Sidney Lewis, 3:484

        England, 10:55

        Rafelson, Robert, 17:63

        Shapiro, Esther June, 18:404–405

        U.S., 3:177

    Reiner, Carl, 17:205–206

    Rotenberg, Mattie Levi, 17:477–478

    San Diego (CA), 18:15

    Serling, Rod, 18:312

    Sherman, Allan, 18:464

    See also specific programs

Television and the Child (Himmelweit), 9:121

Telgener, 3:770

Tel Ḥai (Israel), 19:**596**

Tel Hazor (Israel) archaeological site, vol. 10: color insert

Tel Kazir (Israel), 19:**596**

Tell al-Balāṭa, 18:*429*

Tell al-Khalayfa, 6:651

Tell al-Qīdāh, 8:498–499

Teller, Edward, 19:**596–597**

    Oppenheimer, J. Robert, 15:450

Teller, Hirsh Lazar. *See* Teller, Ẓevi Lazar

Teller, Israel, 4:103, 19:**597**

Teller, Issachar Baer, 19:**597**

Teller, Ẓevi Lazar, 4:103, 19:**597**

Tell eş-Şarem. *See* Tel Reḥov

Tell Mardikh (Syria). *See* Ebla (Syria)

Tell Me Another Morning (Berger), 9:408

Tell Qadis, 11:699

Tel Miqne (Israel), 6:281

Tel Mond (Israel), 19:**597**

Tel Reḥov, 17:**193–195**

Telschen (Lithuania). *See* Telsiai (Lithuania)

Tel Shalem. *See* Legio

Telshi (Lithuania). *See* Telsiai (Lithuania)

Telsiai (Lithuania), 3:779, 19:**597–598**

Tel Talpiot (periodical), 12:18

Telushkin, Nissan, 19:**598**

Tel Yitzḥak (Israel), 19:**598–599**

Tel Yosef (Israel), 19:**599**

Telz (Lithuania). *See* Telsiai (Lithuania)

Telz style of Talmudic study, 3:759

Tema (Arabia), 19:**599**

    See also Tayma (Arabia)

Teman, 19:**599**

Temerls, Jacob ben Eliezer, 19:**599–600**

Temesvár (Romania). *See* Timisoara (Romania)

Temianka, Henri, 19:**600**

Temidi. *See* Aharonovitch, Yosef

Temin, Howard Martin, 13:9, 19:**600**

Temkin, Asher, 19:**600**

Temkin, Mordecai, 19:600

Temkin, Moshe, 19:600

Temkin family, 19:**600**

Temol Shilshom (Agnon), 1:467, 11:216

Tempelgesellschaft. *See* Templers

Temperance Advocate (journal), 12:710

"Le Temple" (Hugo), 14:540

Temple Beth Zion (Buffalo, NY), 1:211

Temple Mount, 9:501, 19:**627–631**, *628–629*

Templers, 8:235–236, 19:**631–633**

Temples, 19:**601–627**, *612, 617*

    Abba Yose ben Ḥanin and, 1:236

    Acra, 1:363, 364

    altars, 2:12, 13, 14

    Alypius of Antioch, 2:82

    Amidah, 2:72

    Amos on worship at, 2:100, 102

    architecture, 16:160

    Bible manuscripts as substitute for, 3:677

    breastpiece precious stones, 16:475–479, *476t*

    cherub and cherubim, 4:600

    commandments concerning, 5:74t, *76t, 80t*

    crimson worm dye, 5:304

    destruction of, Passover offering, 15:678

donations to, commandments concerning, 5:76t

Elephantine, 6:311–312, 313

Ephod, 6:455–456

Eupolemus account, 6:552

fasting, 6:720–721, 723

First Temple, 19:601–608

    Aggadah, 11:212

    altar, 2:12, 14, 13

    building materials and ornamentation, 19:606

    centralization of cult at, 11:458

    centralization of worship, 15:740

    cult of, 11:126–127

    furniture, 19:605–606

    history, 19:601–603

    Jachin and Boaz (pillars), 11:15–16

    Jerusalem during, 11:145–147

    Josiah, reforms of, 11:457–458

    menorahs, 14:50

    plans, 19:603–605, 606

    rituals, 19:606–608

    significance for people, 19:608

    site and orientation, 19:606

    Solomon's building of, 18:760

    sources and purpose for, 19:603

    Temple Mount, 19:631

genealogical archives, 2:405

genealogy, 7:430–432

great laver, 2:492–493

Hekdesh, 8:775–780

High Priest, 9:99–100

Holy of Holies, 6:574

implements, illuminated Spanish Hebrew manuscripts illustrating, 3:676–677

Julian the Apostate's attempt at rebuilding, 2:82

liturgy, musical intonation, 13:656

meal-offerings, 14:27–28

mishmarot and ma'amadot, 14:318–319

mizraḥ, 16:421–426

music, musical instruments, 14:641–643

Onias, Temple of, 15:432–433

priestly blessing, 16:510–511

priests, 5:81t

purification, 5:492–493

rebuilding, 6:610, 611, 658

sacrifical system, 21:231

Second Temple, 19:608–626, 612, 617

    Aggadah, 11:212

    altar, 2:14–16

    arts, 19:625–626

    courts, 19:614–616

    Day of Atonement rituals, 5:488, 492–493

    destruction, 10:144–145, 11:373, 375–376, 19:743–744

    first building, 19:611–612, 612

    functionaries and participants, 19:616–619

    gentiles, 19:622

    Hellenistic period, 19:610–611

    high priests, 11:57–58

    Jerusalem during, 11:147–151

    Johanan ben Zakhai and, 11:373, 374

    menorahs, 14:50–51

    music, 19:621

    Nicanor's gate, 15:247–248

    organs used in, 15:466, 467

    Petronius, Publius, 16:20

    Pilgrim Festivals, 19:621

    priests, power of, 15:743, 744

    provisions, 19:624

    reconstruction, 11:152, 19:612–613

    Roman period until destruction, 19:611

    Sabbath, 19:621

    significance for people, 19:624–625

    Temple Mount, 19:613–614, **627–631**, 628–629

    Temple Square, 19:614

    Titus, Flavius Vespasianus, 19:743–744

    treasury, 19:622–624

    Zerubbabel period, 19:608–610

shewbread or showbread, 18:473–474

tax, opferpfennig and, 15:438

Temple Scroll, 19:634

Third Temple, Julian the Apostate's promise to raise, 11:573–574

Trajan's permission to rebuild, 15:619

treasure, 5:214

unlawful use of hekdesh, 13:775

Western Wall, 21:**24–27**

wood offerings, 21:210

See also specific temple names and locations

Temple Scroll, 6:499, 19:**633–635**

Temple sermon of Jeremiah, 11:126–127

Temple worship, 21:231–233

Templo, Jacob Judah Aryeh Leon. See Templo, Jacob Judah Leon

Templo, Jacob Judah Leon, 19:**635**

Templum Solomonis. See Dome of the Rock

Die Tempora im Semitischen (Bauer), 3:216

Temporary Laws of 1881 (Russia). See May Laws (Russia, 1882)

Temunah, The Book of, 19:**635–636**

Temunot mi-Beit Mivshal ha-Shekhar (Barash), 3:136

Temurah (tractate), 19:**636–637**

Ten (number), 15:335–336

    Patriarchs and, 15:287

The Ten (artists' group), 4:50

Tenancy rights, 8:449–450

Tenants Protection Law of 1972, 14:361–362

Ten Commandments. See Decalogue

The Ten Commandments (Carl), vol. 4: color insert

Ten Days of Penitence, 19:**637**

    Amidah, 2:75

    Book of Life, 4:69

    Elul, 6:370

Tendler, Aron, 13:202

Tendler, Moshe, 19:**637**

Tene, Benjamin, 19:**638**

Tenements of New York City, 15:201

Tenenbaum, Helen. See Weinzweig, Helen

Tenenbaum, Joseph L., 4:111, 19:**638**

Tenenbaum, Joshua, 19:**638**

Tenenbaum, Mordecai, 3:137, 569, 570, 19:**638–639**

Tenenbaum, Shelly, 18:736

Tenenbaum, Shia. See Tenenbaum, Joshua

Tenets of faith. See Articles of faith

Ten Lost Tribes, 19:**639–640**

    Brazilian Indians, 4:121

    British Israelites, 4:188

    in Burma, 4:296–297

    Ecuador, 14:460

    Eldad ha-Dani, 11:727

    fictional accounts, 7:10–11

    Japanese as, 11:84–85

The Ten Martyrs, 12:452, 18:595, 19:**640–641**

The Ten Martyrs of the Kingdom (Emrāni), 6:398

Ten Men of Leisure. *See* Batlanim

Tennenbaum, Jacob, 19:**641**

Tennesee Valley Authority (TVA), 13:16

Tennessee (U.S.), 19:**641–642**, *642*, *642t*

Tennis, 19:147–148
Buxton, Angela, 4:320–321
Flam, Herb, 7:69
France, 5:436
Savitt, Richard, 18:85
Solomon, Harold, 18:765

Tennuat Ha'am political party, 6:321

Ten plagues. *See* Plagues of Egypt

"Ten Points of Seelisberg," 16:631

Tenses, Hebrew. *See* Hebrew language

The Tenth Man (Chayefsky), 4:585

Tent of meeting. *See* Tabernacle

Tenu'ah le-Magga (Gouri), 8:20

Tenuval. *See* Tnuva

Teokratiah Yehudit (Weiler), 16:104

Teologia dogmatica e apologetica (Benamozegh), 3:317

Teomim, Aaron ben Moses, 19:**642–643**

Teomim, Aryeh Leib, 4:199, 12:459, 19:**643**

Teomim, Aryeh Loeb. *See* Teomim, Aryeh Leib

Teomim, Joseph ben Meir, 19:**643–644**

La teoria cellulare (Enriques), 6:445

Teoría de los valores y filosofía de la historia (Dujovne), 6:43

Te'oriyah u-Vikoret: Bamah Yisrelit (journal), 8:730

Teplice (Czech Republic), 19:**644**

Teplice-Šanov (Czech Republic). *See* Teplice (Czech Republic)

Teplitz (Czech Republic). *See* Teplice (Czech Republic)

Teplitz, Saul I., 19:**644–645**

Teplitz-Schoenau (Czech Republic). *See* Teplice (Czech Republic)

Tepper, Kolya, 19:**645**

Tepper, Morris, 19:**645**

Terah, 19:**645–646**

Terahides, 8:343

Teraphim, 19:**646**

Terebinth, 19:**646–647**

Terefah, 18:597, 19:**647**

Terentius Phologombos. *See* Judah, Samuel Benjamin Helbert

Terezín (Czech Republic). *See* Theresienstadt (Czech Republic)

Terezin Requiem (Bor), 9:405

Terkel, Louis. *See* Terkel, Studs

Terkel, Studs, 19:**647–648**

Terminally Ill Persons Act of 2005, 14:360

Terni, Daniel ben Moses David, 4:44, 19:**648**

Ternopol (Ukraine). *See* Tarnopol (Ukraine)

Terracing, 1:472–473, 474, 482

Terracini, Benvenuto Aron, 19:**648**

Terracini, Umberto Elia, 16:345, 19:**648**

The Terrible Secret: The Suppression of Information Regarding the Final Solution (Laquer), 9:378

Territorial federations of communities. *See* Federation of communities, territorial

Territorialism, 16:167, 19:**648–650**

Territories. *See* Gaza strip; Judea; Samaria

Terrorism
al-Qaeda, 18:77–78
in Brazil, 4:153
in Buenos Aires, 4:253–254
Entebbe Raid, 6:447–448
Hamas, 8:294–295
Hanafi Muslim terrorist attack on B'nai B'rith headquarters, 4:16
Lebanon, 12:584–586
Palestine Liberation Organization associated with, 15:591, 593
West Berlin, 15:143

Tertis, Lionel, 19:**650**

Tertulian, Nicolae, 19:**650–651**

Tertullian, 4:719–720
on blood libel, 3:775

Tertz, Abram, 5:427

Teruel (Spain), 19:**651**

Terumat ha-Deshen (Isserlin), 10:769, 14:481

Terumat Yad (Eliasberg), 6:319

Terumot (tractate), 19:**651–652**

Terumot and ma'aserot (offerings), 19:**652–654**

Teschen (Silesia), 19:**654**

Teshuvah, 1:663, 3:572, 11:773

Teshuvah Shelemah (Epstein), 6:469

Teshuvot. *See* Responsa

Teshuvot 'al Rav Sa'adyah Ga'on (Dunash ben Labrat), 6:48

Teshuvot Ba'alei ha-Tosafot (Agus), 1:521

Teshuvot be-Anshei Aven (Heilprin), 8:769

Teshuvot ha-Ranah (Elijah ben Hayyim), 6:339

Teshuvot Rashi (Elfenbein), 6:314

Teshuvot Shimon ben Zemah (Simeon ben Zemah), 8:552

Testament, New. *See* New Testament

Testament, Old. *See* Bible

Testament of Abraham, 1:**291**

Testament of Job, 11:**359–360**

The Testament of Moses. See Assumption of Moses

Testament of Naphtali, 14:**775**

Testament of Solomon, 18:**768**

The Testament of the Lost Son (Morgenstern), 14:487

Testaments. *See* Wills

Testaments of the Twelve Patriarchs, 15:**691–693**

Testamentum Moses. See Assumption of Moses

Testimonies. *See* Evidence; Witnesses

Testimony of a Generation. See Märturia unei generatii

A testör (Molnár). *See The Guardsman* (Molnár)

Tet, 19:**654–655**

Tetrarch, 19:**655**

Tetuán (Morocco), 19:**655–656**

Teubal, Ezra, 15:556, 19:**656**

Teucer of Cyzicus, 15:651, 19:**656**

Te'udah be-Yisrael (Levinsohn), 12:721

Te'udat Shelomo (Lipschitz), 13:71

Teutsch, David, 17;149, 19:**656–657**

Teuv'ot ha-Arez (Schwarz), 18:191

Teva, Musar u-Mediniyyut (Weltsh), 9

Tevah, 3:701

Tevele ben Nathan of Lissa. *See* David ben Nathan of Lissa

Teveryah (Jordan Valley). *See* Tiberias (Jordan Valley)

Tevet, 19:**657**

Tevet, Nahum, 19:**657–658**

Tevet, Shabbetai, 19:**658**

Tevul Yom, 19:**658**

Tevunah (journal), 8:795

Tevu'ot Shor (A. Shor), 18:161

Tevu'ot Shor (E. Shor), 18:162

Tevye der Milkhiker: A Familyen-Bild in Fir Aktn (Shalom Aleichem), 18:387

Tevye der Milkhiker cycle (Shalom Aleichem), 18:385–386

Tevye Fort keyn Erts-Yisroel (Shalom Aleichem), 18:386

Tevye the dairyman (fictional character), 18:382, 385–387

Teweles, Judah, 1:433, 19:**658–659**

Tewi, Thea, 19:**659**

Texas (U.S.), 12:496–497, 19:**66t**, **659–661**, *660*

The Texas-Israeli War (Waldrop), 18:199–200

Texeda, Fernando de, 4:496

Texeira, Myer Hart. *See* Hart, Myer

Text and Texture: Studies in Biblical Literature (Fishbane), 7:60

Textbook of Aramaic Documents from Ancient Egypt (Porton, Yardeni), 18:470

A Text-book of North Semitic Inscriptions (Cooke), 5:201

Textbook of Pediatrics. See Lehrbuch der Kinderheilkunde

Textes d'auteurs grec et romain relatifs au Judaisme (Reinach), 17:205

Textiles, 15:663–664, 19:**661–665**

    See also Clothing and textiles industry; Fashion industry

T'filat Shalom (Adaskin), 1:384

Thackeray, William Makepeace, 6:435

Thadamora (Syria). *See* Tadmor (Syria)

Thailand, 19:**665–666**

Thalberg, Irving Grant, 18:427, 19:**666**

Thalberg, Sigismund, 19:**666**

Thallus, 19:**667**

Thamna, 13:294

Thanksgiving Psalms, 5:507, 19:**667–669**

Thanks to Scandinavia Scholarship Fund, 4:84–85

Tharaud, Jean. *See* Tharaud, Jérôme and Jean

Tharaud, Jérôme and Jean, 19:**669**

Thassis. *See* Simeon the Hasmonean

Thatcher, Margaret, Baroness, 4:189, 11:416, 16:343, 19:**669**

The Thaw (Ehrenburg), 6:238

THEA, 7:781

Theater, 4:**735**, 19:**669–685**

    1600 to 20th century, 19:671–677, 674

        England, 19:671–672

        entertainers, 19:676–677

        France, 19:672

        Germany, 19:672–674

        Holland, 19:674

        Italy, 19:674

        musicals, 19:675–676

        Russia, 19:674

        U.S., 19:674–675

    Amsterdam, 2:108, 119

    Arabic, 15:472–473

    Blau, Herbert, 3:742–743

    Bloom, Claire, 3:780–781

    Bloomgarden, Kermit, 3:783

    of Bukharan Jews, 4:264

    Canada, Hirsch, John Stephen, 9:125–126

    critics

        Bab, Julius, 3:14

        Brahm, Otto, 4:118

        Brustein, Robert Sanford, 4:228

        Buchwald, Nathaniel, 4:243

    Denmark, 6:734

    England

        nineteenth century, 11:16

        twentieth century, 3:438, 5:538

    France, 17:50

        Ionesco, Eugène, 10:6

        Theatre du Soleil, 14:399

    Germany, 5:484

        Barnowsky, Viktor, 3:170

        Bruckner, Ferdinand, 4:220

        Jessner, Leopold, 11:245

    Halevy, Moshe, 8:272

    Harris, Sam Henry, 8:364

    Hart, Lorenz, 8:871

    Harvey, Laurence, 8:378

    Hebrew, 8:179–180, 719–723

    Hungary, Hevesi, Sandor, 9:79

    India, 5:463

    Israel (state), 10:686–688

        1950s, 10:224

        Schach, Leonard Lazarus, 18:98

    Israel, Arab, 10:734

    Jacob as subject of plays, 11:23

    Loyter, Efraim Barukhovich, 13:238

    Maccabees theme, 8:447

    Moscow Jewish Theater, 2:22

    Moses in, 14:539–541

    New York City, 15:210, 219–220, 227–228

        Comden, Betty, 5:71–72

        Schubert, 11:46

    Odets, Clifford, 15:382

    origins, 19:669–670

    Palestine (Mandate), 10:686

    post-Biblical period, 19:670–671

    producers

        Houseman, John, 9:569

        Richards, Martin, 17:287–288

        Rotbaum, Jacob, 17:476

        Rudin, Scott, 17:522–523

        Schenker, Joel W., 18:122

    Reinhardt, Max, 17:208

    revolutionary period, 8:179

    Russia

        Hirschbein, Peretz, 9:133–134

        Raykin, Arkadi Isaakovich, 17:126

        Sanū', Ya'qub, 18:30

    Shevelove, Burt, 18:471–472

    South Africa, Schach, Leonard Lazarus, 18:98

    U.K., Brook, Peter Stephen Paul, 4:208

    U.S.

        actors, 6:748–749

        Adler, Stella, 1:408–409

        Bennett, Michael, 3:369

        Bernstein, Aline, 3:476

        Burrows, Abe, 4:299

        Busch, Charles, 4:303

        Clurman, Harold, 4:763

        Fiddler on the Roof, 8:360

        Harris, Jed, 8:362

        Herman, Jerry, 9:23–24

        Landesman, Rocco, 12:470

        Lortel, Lucille, 13:195

        May, Elaine, 13:696–697

        Mendes, Sam, 14:43

        Schildkraut, Joseph, 18:133

        Schildkraut, Rudolph, 18:133

        Schneider, Alan, 18:149–150

        Sobel, Bernard, 18:699

    Warsaw ghetto, 9:472

    See also Yiddish theater

The Theater of Revolt; An Approach to the Modern Drama (Brustein), 4:228

Theater of the Absurd, 11:705

Theatro comico portuguez (Silva), 18:582–583

Theben Jacob Koppel, 19:**685**

Thebes (Egypt), 19:**685**

Thebes (Greece), 19:**685**

Thebez (near Shechem), 19:**685–686**

Theft and robberies, 16:332, 19:**686–691**

    business ethics and, 4:308–309

    employee, 12:416

    Ḥabiru and, 8:180–181

Their Brothers' Keepers (Friedman), 9:415

Theism. *See* God

Thémanlys, Pascal, 19:**691**

Themistius, 19:**691**

Theocracy, 19:**691–692**

Theodicy

    Buber, Martin, 4:233, 7:754

    Job as anthropodicy vs., 11:355–356

    Jonas, Hans, 11:393

    justice and, 11:578–579

Theodor, Julius, 4:43, 19:**692**

Theodora of Bulgaria, Queen. *See* Sarah of Turnovo

Theodore (son of Zeno), 2:81

Theodore, Adah Isaacs. *See* Menken, Adah Isaacs

Theodore Herzl, A Memorial (Hechler), 8:150

Theodore of Mopsuestia, 19:**692**
  importance of Bible to, 3:666
  modern biblical study, as precursor of, 3:648
  Peshitta used by, 3:599

Theodosia (Ukraine). *See* Feodosiya (Ukraine)

Theodosius (Samaritan spokesperson), 19:**692**

Theodosius I, 2:37, 19:**692–693**

Theodosius II, 4:326, 9:206, 19:**693**

Theodosius of Rome, 19:**693**

Theodotion, 3:585, 597, 601

Theodotus, 3:660, 19:**693–694**

Theological Interpretation of the Holocaust (Funkenstein), 9:400–401

Theological Seminary (Budapest), 6:186

Theologico-Political Treatise (Spinoza), 16:93

Die Theologie der Propheten (Duhm), 6:42–43

Theology, 19:**694–699**
  belief, faith, 3:290–294
  Benzinger, Immanuel, 3:391–392
  body and soul, concept of, 4:30–31
  Borowitz, distinctively American theology of, 4:93
  Buber, Martin, 4:233–234
  Budny, Szymon, 4:249–250
  Buechler, Adolf, 4:250–251
  cosmology, 5:231–232
  Cusa, Nicholas of, 5:343
  Dalman, Gustaf Hermann, 5:383–384
  Damian, Peter, 5:402
  Delitzsch, Franz, 5:539–540
  Deutsch, Gotthard, 5:623
  Dionysius van Ryckel, 5:674
  divine immanence, 8:387, 18:440–444
  Donnolo, Shabbetai, 5:751–752
  Emancipation period, theological challenges of, 11:518
  L'Empereur, Constantijn, 6:397
  feminist, 6:755
  Fioghi, Fabiano, 7:41
  Forster, Johann, 7:132
  God, Man and History (Berkovits), 3:438–439
  Green, Arthur, 8:65–66

Hartman, David, 8:374–376

Hedegård, Oscar David Leonard, 8:752

Herberg, Will, 9:7–8

Herder, Johann Gottfried, 9:9–10

Herford, Robert Travers, 9:22

Hitzig, Ferdinand, 9:293–294

Hottinger, Johann Heinrich, 9:568

Judeo-Arabic, 11:534–536

Juedisch Theologisches Seminar, Breslau, 11:572

Rosenstock-Huessy, Eugen, 17:450–451

Rosenzweig, Franz, 17:458–462

Rowley, Harold Henry, 17:502–503

Rubenstein, Richard Lowell, 17:511

Ruth, Book of, 17:593

Schleiermacher, Friedrich, 18:139

Schulweis, Harold Maurice, 18:174

Smith, William Robertson, 18:689

Soloviev, Vladimir, 18:780

Tabernacle, 19:423
  of wealth, 4:307

Theophany, 6:616

Theophilus (Greek author), 19:**699**

Theophilus (son of Hanan son of Seth), 19:**699**

Theophrastus of Eresos, 19:**699**

Theoredet, 15:377

Théorie du Judaïsme (Chiarini), 4:607

Die Theorien uber Wesen und Ursprung der Tosephra (Duenner), 6:41

Theory and Practice of Modern Government (Finer), 7:26

A Theory of Evolving Tonality (Yasser), 21:288

Theory of Games and Economic Behavior (Morgenstern, Neumann), 14:487

The Theory of the Names. See Nomologia o Discursos legales

Theosophy, 11:587

Therapeutae, 2:547, 18:233, 19:**699–701**

Theresienstadt (Czech Republic), 19:**701–703**

Theresienstadt ghetto and concentration camp, 6:145, 249–250, 9:341, 11:765, 19:*702*
  bank notes, 5:54
  Bor, Josef, novels of, 4:79
  education in, 9:360
  Eppstein, Paul, 6:465–466
  "home buying agreements," 17:202
  kindergarten, 9:473

There Will Be A Time (Tidhar), 18:206

Thermuthis, 14:533

Thesaurus of Scales and Melodic Patterns (Slonimsky), 18:680

Thesaurus synonumicus Hebraico-Chaldaico-Rabbinicus (Plantavit de la Pause), 16:219

These Are the Children of My Youth. See Elleh Benei ha-Ne'urim (Luzzatto)

Thessaloniki (Greece). *See* Salonika (Greece)

Theudas, 19:**703–704**

Thiasoi, 4:98

Thieberger, Friedrich, 19:**704**

Thieme, Karl Otto, 19:**704**

Thier, Samuel O., 4:124

Thijn, Ed van, 16:345

The Thin Blue Line (motion picture), 14:510

The Thinker. See Myslitel

Thinking About the Holocaust: After Half a Century (Rosenfeld), 9:414

The Thinking Heart of the Camp. See Het dendende hart van de barak

Thionville (France), 19:**704**

Third Aliyah, Israel (state), 1:660–661, 680, 8:338, 10:199, 335, 489, 510, 523

Third Book of Enoch. See Sefer Heikhalot

Third Esdras. *See* Ezra, Greek book of

Third Great Cycle in Jewish History (Greenberg), 9:396

Third Lateran Council. *See* Lateran Councils III, IV

The Third Man. See Elad, Avraham

"Third Stream" (jazz), 18:172

Third Way, 10:245

Thirteen, the. *See* Minhelet ha-Am

Thirteen Attributes of God, 1:412

Thirteen Principles of Faith, 2:529–530

Thirteen rules of R. Ishmael, 9:25–28

Thirty Years' War
  in Bohemia, 4:39
  Levi, Behrend, 12:685

This Is My England (Pinto), 16:179

This Is My Life (motion picture), 6:462

This Man Is My Brother (Brinig), 4:184

This People Israel. See Dieses Volk Israel

Thistles. See Kimshonim

Thistles and thorns, 19:**704–705**, vol. 16: color insert

This Way to the Gas, Ladies and Gentlemen (Borowksi), 9:412

Thomalla, Richard, 18:700

Thomar (Portugal). *See* Tomar (Portugal)

Thomas, Michael Tilson, 19:**705–706**

Thomashefsky, Bessie, 19:**706**

Thomashefsky, Boris, 19:**706–707**

Thomas Muenzer als Theologe der Revolution (Bloch), 3:760

Thomas of Heraclea, 3:600–601

Thomsen, Peter, 19:**707**

Thon, Albert, 19:**707**

Thon, Jehoshua. *See* Thon, Osias

Thon, Osias, 19:**707–708**
  Nowy Dziennik, 15:326

Thon, Ya'akov Yoḥanan, 19:**708**

Thorenberg (Romania). *See* Turda (Romania)

Die Thorheiten des weisen Koenigs (Bodmer), 18:761

Thorman, Simson, 15:392

Thorn (Poland). *See* Torun (Poland)

Thorn, Jules. *See* Thorn, Sir Jules

Thorn, Sir Jules, 19:**708**

Thorns. *See* Thistles and thorns

Thorowgood, Thomas, 14:460

"Those Who Advocate the Unity of Allah." *See* Almohads

Thought, freedom of, 7:226–227

Thoughts and Motifs–Poems and Prose. See Gedanken un Motivn–Lider in Proze

Thou Hast Delivered Me from Death. See Megszabaditottál a haláltól

A Thousand (number), 15:336–337

Thrasyllus of Mendes, 19:**708**

Three (number), 15:334

Three Bathers (painting, Eilshemius), 6:255

The Three Branches (Moses ben Isaac Mintz), 14:301

Three Capitals. See Dray Hoyptshtet

Three Essays of...al-Jahiz (Finkel), 7:31–32

Three Stooges. *See* Howard, Moe, Shemp and Curly

Three Towers. See Dray Shtetlakh

Three weeks, 19:**708–709**

Throne of God, 19:**709–710**

Thrones, 11:590, 18:760, 19:**709**

Through Black Lenses. See Prin lentile negre

Through Literature (Eichenbaum), 6:246

Through the Binding Ropes (Ben Yehuda), 3:389

Through the Sound of Many Voices (Plaut), 16:228

Thunder and lightning, 19:**710**

Thunder Over Mexico (motion picture), 6:274

Thuringia (Germany), 19:**710–712**

Thuste (Ukraine). *See* Tolstoye (Ukraine)

Thutmose III, 6:310

Thutmose IV, 2:41

Ṭibb al-Nufūs al-Salīma wa-Muʿālajat al-Nufūs al-Alīma (Aknin), 1:570

Tibbon, ibn family. *See* Ibn Tibbon family

Tibbonian Hebrew, 8:659

Tibbonids family. *See* Ibn Tibbon family

Tiberian Masorah system, 13:633–642
  accentuation, 13:637–642, 14:650
  contamination of, 13:618
  influence of, 13:631–632
  non-conventional system, 13:642–646
  pronunciation, 8:622, 628–629, 13:625–626, 628, 629

Tiberias (Jordan Valley), 1:339–340, 19:**714–716**
  Byzantine period, 10:160
  Ottoman period, 10:171, 777, 15:524
  Roman period, 10:150–151

Tiberias, Lake. *See* Kinneret, Lake

Tiberius Claudius Drusus Nero Germanicus. *See* Claudius

Tiberius Julius Alexander, 11:293, 19:**716–717**

Tibni, 19:**717**

Tibullus, Albius, 19:**717**

Tiburtinus. *See* Plato of Tivoli

Ticho, Anna, 19:**717–718**

Tidhar, David, 19:**718**

Tidhar, Lavie, 18:206

Tiempo, César, 19:**718**

Tientsin (China), 4:647, 19:**718**

Tiepolo, Giambattista, 18:762

Tietz family, 19:**718–719**

Tiferet Yisrael (Lipschutz), 13:734, 14:329, 537

Tiflis (Georgia), 19:**719**

Tiflisites, 1:336

Tigay, Jeffrey H., 19:**719**

Tigay, Jeffrey Howard. *See* Tigay, Jeffrey H.

Tiger, Theobald. *See* Tucholsky, Kurt

Tigerman, Stanley, 19:**719–720**

Tighina (Romania). *See* Bendery (Romania)

Tiglath-Pileser I, 2:404

Tiglath-Pileser II, 19:**720–721**

Tiglath-Pileser III, 1:539, 6:607
  Ammonites, 2:85

Moab, 14:402

Tigra. *See* Tigris

Tigranes, 2:473

Tigrid, Pavel, 19:**721–722**

Tigris, 19:**722**

Tikhnun ha-Mayim le-Yisrael. *See* Tahal

Tikkun (periodical), 12:659, 19:**722**

Tikkunei Shabbat (Abraham ben Eliezer ha-Levi Berukhim), 1:299

Tikkunei Zohar, 14:53, 21:650

Tikkun ha-De'ot (Albalag), 1:582, 583

Tikkun ha-Geshem. See Rain, prayer for

Tikkun Ḥazot, 19:**722–723**

Tikkun Middot ha-Nefesh (Ibn Gabirol), 6:527, 7:325, 14:372

Tikkun olam, 6:673–674

Tikkun Shelomo (London), 13:186

Tikkun Soferim, 19:**723**

Tikkun Yissakhar (Susan), 19:325

Tiktin. *See* Tykocin

Tiktin, Abraham ben Gedallah, 19:**723**

Tiktin, Gedaliah, 4:164, 19:**723**

Tiktin, Solomon, 4:164

Tiktiner, Khaym. *See* Siemiatycki, Chaim

Tiktin family, 19:**723**

Tiktinski, Abraham, 19:**724**

Tiktinski, Ḥayyim Leib, 19:**724**

Tiktinski family, 19:**723–724**

Til Eulenspiegel (Babilée), 3:21

Tillich, Paul Johannes, 19:**724**

Tilted Arc (Serra), 18:314

Tim, 19:**724**

Timagenes of Alexandria, 19:**724–725**

Timár Liza (Bródy), 4:201

Time (periodical), 1:406, 8:113

Time and eternity, 5:487, 19:**725**
  of Jerusalem, 11:208
  philosophical analysis of, 16:85

A Time For Change (Kalms), 11:747

A Time of Favor. See Ha-Hesder

The Time of Indifference (Moravia), 14:476

Time Remembered (Solomon), 18:764

Timerman, Jacobo, 11:469, 19:**725–726**

The Times. See Die Zeit (newspaper)

Time's Arrow (Amis), 18:200

"The Times They Are A-Changing" (Dylan), 6:78

Timișoara (Romania). *See* Timisoara (Romania)

Timisoara (Romania), 19:**726–727**

Timna (Israel), 6:288, 19:**727–728**

Timnah (territory of Dan), 19:**728**

Timnah (territory of Judah), 19:**728**

Timnath-Heres (territory of Ephraim), 19:**728**

Timnath-Serah (territory of Ephraim). *See* Timnath-Heres (territory of Ephraim)

Timochares, 19:**728**

Timofey. *See* Kopelson, Ẓemaḥ

Timoshin. *See* Kopelson, Ẓemaḥ

Tin, 14:126, 128

The Tin Drum, 9:443

Tingis (Morocco). *See* Tangier (Morocco)

Tinneius Rufus, 11:491, 575, 19:**728–729**

Tinshemet, 15:550

Tintoretto, 14:541

Tintori, Abraham ben Ḥayyim dei, 4:48

Tiomkin, Vladimir, 19:**729**
Bienstok, Judah Lieb, as replacement for, 3:691
Odessa Committee, 15:382

Tiomkin, Ze'ev. *See* Tiomkin, Vladimir

Ṭīra, al- (Israel), 19:**729**

Tirado, Jacob, 19:**729**
Amsterdam, 2:109

Tirān Island (Sinai Peninsula). *See* Sharm el-Sheikh (Sinai Peninsula)

Tirān Straits (Sinai Peninsula). *See* Sharm el-Sheikh (Sinai Peninsula)

Tiraspol (Moldova), 19:**729**

Tirat ha-Karmel (Israel), 19:**730**

Tirat Kesef (Luzki), 11:793

Tirat Ẓevi (Israel), 19:**730**

Tirgu-Frumos (Romania), 19:**730**

Tirgu-Mureş (Romania). *See* Targu-Mures (Romania)

Tirgu Neamt (Romania), 19:**730–731**

Tirhakah, 19:**731**

Tirpa, writ of, 6:592–593

Tirzah (Canaan), 19:**731**

Tiśma, Aleksandar, 19:**734**

Tisch, Laurence Alan, 19:**731–732**

Tisch, Preston Robert, 19:**732–733**

Tisch family, 19:**731–733**

Tischler, Hans, 19:**733**

Tischler, Max, 19:**733**

Tisha Be-Av prayer, vol. 8: color insert

Tishah Be-Av, vol. 17: color insert

Tishby, Isaiah, 11:682–683, 19:**733**

Tishman, John, 19:733

Tishman, Margaret, 19:734

Tishman, Peggy. *See* Tishman, Margaret

Tishman family, 19:**733–734**

Tishri, 19:**734**

Tishvits. *See* Tyszowce

Tiso, Josef, 19:**734–735**

Tiszaeszlar (Hungary), 3:778, 779, 4:246, 15:355, 19:**735**

Tiszaeszlár (Hungary). *See* Tiszaeszlar (Hungary)

Titans, 19:**736**

Tithes, 19:**736–739**
charity, 4:570
church, 19:**739–740**
fruit offerings, 7:49
ma'aserot, 19:652–654
ma'aser sheni, 13:314
produce, 5:547
terumot, 19:652–654

Titiev, Mischa, 19:**740**

Titkin, Solomon, 6:258

Titles, 1:677, 4:364, 19:**740–741**

Titles of nobility, 19:**741–742**

Tito, partisans under, 15:667

Titus, Arch of. *See* Arch of Titus

Titus, Flavius Vespasianus, 19:**743–745**
Jerusalem and, 11:151
Josephus and, 11:436
oak of Abraham in Hebron, 15:357

Titus Flavius Clemens. *See* Clement of Alexandria

Titus Flavius Clement. *See* Clement of Alexandria

Titus Flavius Domitianus. *See* Domitian

Titus Livius. *See* Livy

Tiv Gittin (Modai), 14:405

Tivoli, Serafino da, 19:**745–746**

Tivon (Galilee), 19:**746**

Tkatch, Meir Ziml, 19:**746**

Tkhine Imohes (Horowitz), 9:542–543

Tkhine imohos min Rosh Hodesh Elul (Serl bas Jacob ben Wolf Kranz), 18:311–312

Tkhines, 3:209, 6:21, 8:277, 13:136–137, 19:**746–748**, 21:341

Tkine shaar ha-yikhed al oyleme (Bas Tovim), 3:209

Tlass, Mustafa, on blood libel, 3:780

Tlemcen (Algeria), 19:**748–749**

Tlomats (Ukraine). *See* Tlumach (Ukraine)

Tlomatske (Segalowitch), 18:249

Tlumach (Ukraine), 19:**749–750**

Tlumacz (Ukraine). *See* Tlumach (Ukraine)

Tmeim, 2:432

Tnu'at ha-Teḥiyah, 8:457

Tnuva, 9:148, 19:**750**

Toads. *See* Frogs

Toaff, Alfredo Sabato, 20:5

Toaff, Elio, 20:5

Toaff family, 20:**5**

To'afot Re'em (Carvalho), 4:502

Tob (ancient Israel), 20:**5–6**

Tobacco trade and industries, 9:303, 20:**6–7**

Tobach, Ethel, 20:**7**

Toback, James, 20:**7–8**

Tobago, 4:472–473

Tobenkin, Elias, 20:**8**

Tobiad, Hyrcanus, 20:**9–10**

Tobiad, Joseph, 20:**8–9**

Tobiad, Tobya, 20:**8**

Tobiad, Toubias, 20:**8**

Tobiad family, 9:192–193, 20:**8–10**

Tobias, Abraham, 20:**10**

Tobias, Joseph, 20:**10**

Tobias, Moses, 20:**10**

Tobias, Phillip Vallentine, 2:187, 20:**10–11**

Tobias ben Eliezer Foa, 7:92

Tobias ben Moses ha-Avel, 20:**11–12**

Tobias the physician. *See* Cohn, Tobias ben Moses

Tobit, Book of, 20:**12–14**
marriage, 6:691

Toboggan, 19:145

Toby, Jackson, 5:302–303, 20:**14**

Toch, Ernst, 20:**14**

Toch, Maximilian, 20:**14**

Tochner, Meshullam, 20:**14**

Todat Shelamim (Benjamin), 3:208

Today's English Version (TEV) (Bible), 3:619–620, 621, 636

Todd, Mike, 20:**14–15**

Der Tod des Vergil (Broch), 4:191

Todesco, Hermann, 20:**15**

"Todesfuge" (Celan), 4:536

Todorov, Petko Yordanov, 4:275

"Todos Ish Romi". *See* Theodosius of Rome

To Do the Right and the Good (Dorff), 5:755

Toennies, Ferdinand, 18:733

Toeplitz, Otto, 20:**15**

To'evah. *See* Abomination

Tofes, 18:468

Tofteh Arukh (Zacuto), 21:436

Tog (newspaper), 15:210

A Togbikhl fun a Farfirer (Der Nister), 5:596

Tohorah, 20:**15**

Tohorat ha-Mishpaḥah. *See* Taharat ha-Mishpaḥah

Tohorot (order of the Mishnah), 20:**15–16**

Tohorot (tractate), 20:**16**

Tohorot ha-Kodesh, 20:**16–17**

Toib, Ora. *See* Namir, Ora

Tojbenfeld, Konrad, 6:33

To Jerusalem and Back (Bellow), 3:300

Tokat (Turkey), 2:130, 20:**17**

Toker, Eliahu, 20:**17–18**

Tokhaḥah. *See* Rebuke and reproof

Tokhaḥat Megullah (Ergas), 6:479

Tokheḥah, 20:**18**

Tokhehot Musar (Ezra ben Ezekiel ha-Bavli), 6:662

Tokyo (Japan), 11:82, 20:**18**

Tola, Judges, Book of, 11:564

Toland, John, 5:533–534, 16:629, 20:**18**

Tolansky, Samuel, 20:**19**

Tola oak, 15:357–358

Told. *See* Feiwel, Berthold

Toldot Yisrael (Beer), 3:**253**

Toledano, Baruch, 20:19

Toledano, Daniel, 20:20

Toledano, Daniel ben Joseph, 20:19

Toledano, Ḥayyim, 14:497, 20:**19–20**

Toledano, Ḥayyim ben Ḥabib he-Ḥasid, 20:19

Toledano, Jacob Moses, 20:**21–22**

Toledano, Joseph ben Daniel, 14:497, 20:**19–20**

Toledano, R. Baruch, 20:21

Toledano, R. Ḥabib ben Eliezer, 20:21

Toledano, R. Ḥayyim ben R. Judah, 20:21

Toledano, R. Jacob, 20:20–21

Toledano, R. Raphael Baruch ben Jacob, 20:21

Toledano family, 13:798, 20:**19–21**, 20*t*

Toledo (OH), 20:**27–28**

Toledo (Spain), 20:**22–27**

    Christian rule, 20:**23–26**

    Muslim rule, 20:23

    Ocaña, 15:375

    persecutions of 1391, 20:25–26

    Visigothic period, 20:22–23

Toledo, Abraham de, 11:411, 15:540

Toledo, Moses de, 20:28

Toledot Adam, 3:9

Toledot Adam (Adret), 1:422

Toledot Adam ve-Ḥavvah (Jeroham ben Meshullam), 11:142

Toledot Aharon (Aaron of Pesaro), 1:220

Toledot Ahavah Aḥat (Smilansky), 18:687

Toledot Anshei Shem (Ephrati), 6:461

Toledot ha-Arez (Schoenhack), 18:157

Toledot ha-Ari, 20:**28**

Le-Toledot ha-Ḥinnukh be-Yisrael (Charna), 4:580

Toledot ha-Ḥinnukh shel Am Yisrael (Morris), 14:511

Toledot ha-Mekubbalim, ha-Shabbeta'im ve-ha-Hasidism (Kahana-Kogan), 11:710–711

Toledot ha-Shamayim (Slonimski), 18:679

Toledot ha-Sifrut ha-Ivrit ha-Ḥadashah (Lachower), 12:424

Toledot ha-Sifrut ha-Ivrit ha-Ḥadashah (Shapira), 18:400

Toledot ha-Yehudim be-Erez Yisrael be-Tekufat ha-Mishnah ve-ha-Talmud (Allon), 1:675

Toledot Mishpaḥah Aḥat (Kabak), 11:584

Toledot Ya'akov (Alba), 1:581

Toledot Ya'akov Yosef (Jacob Joseph ben Ẓevi ha-Kohen Katz of Polonnoye), 8:394, 10:747, 11:41

Toledot Yeshu, 1:502, 2:124, 7:13, 20:**28–29**

Toledot Yisrael (Jawitz), 11:97

Toledot Yiẓḥak (Caro), 4:488

Toledo XIII council, 4:716

Toleranzpatent, 2:690, 4:39–40, 6:689–690, 20:**29**

    education, 6:159, 178–179

    emancipation, 6:375

    Joseph II, 11:414

    Pest, 4:245

Tolkowsky, Shemuel, 20:**29**

Toller, Ernst, 20:**29–30**

Tollet, Daniel, 11:326

Tolstoy, Leo, 15:684

Tolstoye (Ukraine), 20:**30**

Tolush, 20:**30**

Tolvens, Arricha de. *See* Hollaender, Victor

Toma, A., 20:**31**

Tomar (Portugal), 20:**31**

Tomashefsky, Boris. *See* Thomashefsky, Boris

Tomashpol (Ukraine), 20:**31**

Tomaszow Lubelski (Poland), 20:**31–32**

Tomaszow Mazowiecki (Poland), 20:**32**

Tomaszow Rawski. *See* Tomaszow Mazowiecki (Poland)

The Tomb of Oscar Wild in Paris (sculpture, Epstein), 6:471

Tombs and tombstones, 20:**32–37**

    Absalom, vol. 10: color insert

    Absalom, Monument of, 1:332

    Aden, 1:388

    architecture, 16:160

    David, 5:453

    decoration on, vol. 7: color insert

    epitaphs, 6:464

    Esther and Mordecai, 8:292

    glass vessels, 7:629, 630

    as holy places, 9:499–500

    photographs of, 16:129

    Rachel, 17:48

    Zechariah, vol. 10: color insert

To Mend the World (Fackenheim), 6:673–674

Tomer, Ben Zion, 8:721

Tomis. *See* Constanta

Tomsk (Siberia), 20:**37**

Tonna, Charlotte Elizabeth, 20:**37**

To No Purpose. See Be-Ein Mattarah

Tooth. *See* Avot Nezikin

Toparchy (ancient Israel), 20:**37**

Toplpunkt: Fertlyor-Shrift Far Literatur, Kunst Un Gezelschaftlekhe Frages (journal), 20:**37–38**

Topol, Chaim, 4:26, 20:**38**

Topolcany (Slovakia), 20:**38–39**

Topolevsky, Gregorio, 20:**39**

Topolski, Feliks, 20:**39**

Torah, 3:576, 8:252, 20:**39–46**

    Abbasi, Jacob ben Moses ibn and, 1:233

    alphabet, Hebrew, 1:729–730

    amoraim, 2:90–93

    amulets, 2:121

    antinomianism, 2:199–200

    biblical criticism, nineteenth century, 3:649–650

    Birkat ha-Torah, 3:712

    Book of the Covenant, incorporation of, 4:68–69

    books of, 3:577*t*

    canonization of, 3:577–578

    cantillation, 13:661

    case (18th c.), vol. 18: color insert

    case and finial (18th c.), vol. 18: color insert

    ceremonial objects, 4:547–548

    Commandments, 5:74*t*, 85–88, 20:42, 43

    creation and, 20:40–41

    Crescas analysis, 5:285, 286–287

    divine nature of, 20:42–43

    Egyptian literature, 6:225

    environmental responsibility, 6:449

    Essenes, 6:511

Torah, *continued*

extradition, 6:626–627

fear of God, 6:725

as framework for struggle for state of Israel, 16:100

gentiles, 7:488

hatred, 8:458

heavenly laws vs. laws of, 6:529

homiletical interpretation, 5:438

homosexuality, 9:516

Islam and, 11:263

Jewish philosophy, 20:85–86

Josiah's discovery of "Book of the Torah," 11:457–458

Judah Halevi on, 11:499

Judaism and, 11:511–512, 516, 16:102

Kabbalah, 11:659–661

Kai-Feng (China), vol. 19: color insert

labor, 12:409

logos, 13:175, 20:40

Maimonides, 20:40, 42–43, 45

man with covered scroll, vol. 8: color insert

Mishnah, 14:320

mishpat Ivri, 14:339, 341

Moses, 14:528–529, 535–536

Muhammad, 1:546

as name for Bible as a whole, 3:574

nature and purpose, 20:41–45

Oral law's relationship to, 15:454–456

origin, 20:40–41

Palestine (Ottoman), religious court decisions, 10:620

Pentateuch, 15:730–753, 20:39

Pharisees, 16:31

Philo, 20:44

poetry, 16:255–256

preexistence of, 20:40–41

Rav, 17:116–117

Rava, 17:118–119

reading of, 20:**46–50**, 47*t*, 48*t*–49*t*

customs surrounding, 20:49–50

Day of Atonement, 5:489

Ezra's public reading, 6:652–653, 659, 661

history, 20:45–46, 47*t*–49*t*

laws on, 2:128

mishnaic literature, 20:46

modern period, 20:49

Samaritans, 17:730–731

triennial cycle, 20:140–143, 141*t*

yad, 21:264

Yemenite cantillation, 21:310

Renassia, Yossef, 17:218–219

revelation, 17:254–257, 20:42

Saadiah Gaon, 20:40, 42, 43–44

Sadducees, 17:654

Samaritan Bible, 3:599, 652

scholars, 11:752

scroll and case (19th c.), vol. 18: color insert

Sefer Torah, 18:241–243

Spain

Abulafia, Meir, 1:341–342

Disputation of Tortosa, 20:61

study

Abbaye on, 1:235–236

Broda, Abraham ben Saul, 4:194

Council of the lands and, 5:244

Elijah ben Solomon Zalman, 6:343–345

Hadrian, Publius Aelius on, 8:194

Ḥasidism, 10:745–746, 14:24

as religious duty, 11:516

woman study issue, 21:199–200

women's exclusion from, 15:258

synagogue scroll niches, vol. 19: color insert

Tabernacle, 19:425

teaching of during Babylonian exile, 6:163

term, 20:39

Torah codes issue, 5:132

translations

ArtScroll, 2:534–535

English translations of Torah by Jews, 3:622–625

official translation, 13:621

by Society for the Promotion of Culture Among the Jews of Russia, 18:727

targumim, 3:589–592

transmission of, 13:606–611

mistakes, 18:242

oral, 13:609

scribes, 13:606, 18:213, 242

written, 13:606–609, 787

transporting a scroll, vol. 5: color insert

Zedek Veshalom (Paramaribu, Surinam), vol. 19: color insert

See also Mount Sinai; Pentateuch

The Torah: A Modern Commentary (Plaut), 3:625, 16:228

Torah and Labor. *See* Torah va-Avodah

Toraḥ Ark curtain and valance. *See* Parokhet and Kapporet

Torah breastplates, 20:52

Torah crowns, 4:547, 20:52

Torah ha-Sifrut (Barash), 3:136

Torah min ha-Shamayim be-Aspaklaryah shel ha-Dorot (Heschel), 9:71

Torah ornaments, 20:**50–53**

Torah pointers, 20:52–53

Torah Scroll. *See* Sefer Torah

Torah service

Haftarah, 8:198–200

hagbaha, gelilah, 8:207

hakkafot, 8:250

Ḥazak, 8:486

ḥazzanim, 8:502–505

Torah she-be-al Peh. *See* Oral Law

Torah she-bi-Khetav. *See* Bible; Torah

Torah Shelemah (Kasher), 11:821

Torah Temimah (Epstein), 6:468

Torah Umesorah, 6:197, 198, 11:755–756, 20:**53**

Torah va-Avodah, 8:338, 20:**53**

Toras Emes, 13:199

Torat Avot, 12:425

Torat Elohim Meforash (Heidenheim), 8:763

Torat Emet (Baer), 13:653

Torat ha-Adam (Naḥmanides), 14:742

Torat ha-Bayit (Adret), 1:215, 423, 4:774

Torat ha-Ḥattat (Isserles), 10:770–771

Torat haMinḥah (Sikili), 18:574

Torat Ḥattat (Ḥayyim), 8:480

Torat Ḥayyim (Edrehi), 6:158

Torat Ḥayyim (Schorr), 18:162

Torat Kohanim. *See* Sifra

Torat Moshe (Alshekh), 2:10

Torat Moshe ve-ha-Nevi'im (Shapiro), 18:404

Torberg, Friedrich, 20:**53–54**

Torchin (Ukraine), 20:**54**

Torczyn. *See* Torchin (Ukraine)

Torczyner, Harry. *See* Tur-Sinai, Naphtali Herz

Torczyner, Jacques, 20:**54**

Torda. *See* Turda (Romania)

Toref, 18:468

To Remember and To Forget. See Lizkor ve-Lishko'aḥ

Torentul (Banus), 3:121

Torgov, Morley, 20:**54–55**

Torino (Italy). *See* Turin (Italy)

Torme, Mel, 20:**55**

Tormenta de Dios (Eichelbaum), 6:245

Tornimparte, Alessandra. *See* Ginzburg, Natalia

Toronto (ON), 15:435, 20:**55–58**
  community spokespersons, 11:52
  education, 6:210
  government officials, Philips, Nathan, 16:57
  Holy Blossom Temple, 11:51–52
  Jewish history, 4:398
  Jewish population, 4:411
  Lastman, Melvin Douglas, 12:503–504
  Reform Judaism, 6:737
  See also Graubart, Y.L.

Toronto Hebrew Daily Journal (newspaper), 17:274–275

Torquemada, Tomás de, 12:438, 18:44, 45, 20:**58–59**

Torre, Alfonso de la, 20:**59**

Torre de Moncorvo (Portugal). *See* Moncorvo (Portugal)

The Torrent. See Torentul

Torrès, Henry, 20:**59**

Torres, Luis de, 2:41, 20:**59**

Torrey, Charles Cutler, 20:**59–60**

Tortoises, 20:**60**

Tortosa (Spain), 20:**60–61**
  apologetics, 2:266–267
  disputation of, 18:43–45, 20:61, **62–63**
    Bonafed, Solomon ben Reuben, 4:53, 54
    Juan de Espagña, conversion of, 11:472

Tortosa, Disputation of, 18:43–45, 20:61, **62–63**
  Bonafed, Solomon ben Reuben, 4:53, 54
  Juan de Espagña, conversion of, 11:472

Torts, 12:773, 20:**63–67**
  commandments concerning, 5:78t
  nuisance law as related to, 15:328–329
  obligations arising from, 12:814, 15:369, 372

Torture. *See* Ordeal

Torun (Poland), 16:308, 20:**67**

Tosafists
  Aḥerim, 1:541
  aliyah and, 10:329
  Baruch ben Isaac of Worms, 3:189
  Bekhor Shor, Joseph ben Isaac, 3:276–277
  Elhanan ben Isaac of Dampierre, 6:315–316
  Eliezer ben Samuel of Metz, 6:329

Eliezer ben Samuel of Verona, 6:329
Eliezer of Toul, 6:330–331
Eliezer of Touques, 6:331
Ḥayyim ben Hananel ha-Kohen, 8:481
Hezekiah ben Jacob, 9:92
Isaac ben Abraham, 10:38
Isaac ben Asher ha-Levi, 10:39–40
Isaac ben Jacob ha-Lavan of Prague, 10:42
Isaac ben Meir, 10:44
Isaac ben Mordecai, 10:45
Isaac ben Samuel of Dampierre, 10:48
Israel of Bamberg, 10:758
Lieberman, Saul, 12:806
Meir ben Baruch of Rothenburg, 13:780–783
Meir ben Samuel of Ramerupt, 13:784–785
Mordacai ben Hillel ha-Kohen, 14:480–481
Perez ben Elijah of Corbeil, 15:**769–770**
Petter ben Joseph, 16:22
Solomon ben Judah of Dreux, 18:772

Tosafot, 20:**67–70**

Tosefet. *See* Tosefta

Tosefet Rishonim (Lieberman), 12:806

Tosefot Yom Tov (Heller), 1:390, 8:797–798, 14:329

Tosefta, 20:**70–72**
  Ahilot, 15:394
  Arakhin, 2:336
  Baal-Meon, 3:8
  baraita, 3:124–125, 127
  Eleazar ben Simeon, 6:308
  Ephraim ben Isaac, 6:459
  Eruvin (tractate), 6:485–486
  Halakhah, 13:90
  Hebrew manuscripts, 13:490
  Kiddushin, 12:145–146
  Kilayim, 12:154
  Megillah, 13:768
  Me'ilah, 13:**775**
  Menaḥ, 14:**27–28**
  moneylending, 11:44
  Nezikin, 15:247
  Niddah, 15:259
  obligations to poor people, 15:705
  Orlah, 15:475
  Parah, 15:630
  Shevi'it, 18:473
  Shevu'ot, 18:473
  Simeon ben Lakish, 14:413

To Take Place: Toward Theory in Ritual (Smith), 18:688

Totality and Infinity (Levinas), 12:715–716

Total Solution. *See* Final Solution

To the Bird. See El ha-Zippor

To the Six Million (Feldman), 9:407

Touati, Charles, 11:324, 20:**72–73**

Toubin, Isaac, 2:47

Touching Evil (Rosen), 17:429

Toul (France), 20:**73**

Toulon (France), 20:**73**

Toulouse (France), 20:**73–74**

Touraine (France), 20:**74–75**

Tourel, Jennie, 20:**75**

Touro, Judah, 13:223, 20:**75**

Touro College, 20:**75–76**

Touroff, Nissan, 20:**76–77**

Touro Synagogue (Newport, RI), 8:370, 15:153–154

Tours (France), 3:675, 20:**77**

Toussenel, Alphonse, 20:**77**

Tov Elem, Joseph ben Eliezer. *See* Bonfils, Joseph ben Eliezer

Tov Elem, Joseph ben Samuel. *See* Bonfils, Joseph ben Samuel

Tovey, D'Bloissiers, 20:**77**

Toward a New Yiddish (Ozick), 20:291

Toward the God of the Desert (Molodowsky), 14:430

Towarzystwo Ochrony Zdrowia Ludnosci Zydowskiej. *See* TOZ

The Tower and the Abyss (Kahler), 11:718

Tower of Babel. *See* Babel, Tower of

Tower of Babel (painting, Brueghel), 3:21

Towers, agricultural, 1:482–483

The Town Beyond the Wall (Wiesel), 9:409–410

Towne, Charles, 20:**78**

Towns. *See* Cities

Townshend Acts, 15:197

Toyanbee Hall (London, England), 18:320

Der Toyber (Bergelson), 3:419

Toys, 5:410

Toytn-Tants (Agnon), 1:466

TOZ, 2:59, 15:556, 20:**78**

Toẓa'ot Ḥayyim (Açan), 1:354

Trabot, Perez, 11:547

Trabot family, 20:**78**

Trabotto family. *See* Trabot family

Trachonitis (Palestine), 4:115, 20:**78–79**

Trachtenberg, Beba. *See* Idelsohn, Beba

Trachtenberg, Herman, 12:553
Trachtenberg, Joshua, 20:**79**
Track and field, 1:328–329, 5:211, 19:148–149
Tractado de las drogas y medicinas de las Indias Orientales con sus Plantas debuscadas al vivo (Acosta), 1:358
Tractates. *See* Mishnah
Tractatus (Wittgenstein), 21:126–127
Tractatus de Intellectus Emendatione (Spinoza), 19:112–113
Tractatus Theologico-Politicus (Spinoza), 2:531–532, 19:115–118
Tract on Contemplation. See Kuntres ha-Hitbonenut
Tract on Ecstasy. See Kuntres ha-Hitpa'alut
Tradai (Lithuania). *See* Troki (Lithuania)
Trade and commerce, 3:112, 20:**79–88**
    Aaron ben David Cohen of Ragusa, 1:212
    Abbasid dynasty, 1:234
    Abraham, Samuel, 1:291
    Agadir, 1:444
    Ahwaz, 1:548
    Alaska, 1:577
    Ballmer, Steve, 3:93
    Bally, Davicon, 3:94
    Bamberger, Louis, 3:103
    Behrends, Leffmann, 3:264
    Belisha family, 3:296
    Benaim family, 3:315
    Bensusan family, 3:379
    Ben Zaqen family, 3:390
    Bergh, Van Den family, 3:427–427
    Bernstein, Aryeh Leib, 3:477
    biblical, 20:79–81
    Bloomingdale family, 3:783–784
    brokers, 4:203–204
    Caceres, Simon de, 4:331
    California, 4:361, 362
    Canada, 4:394–395, 396
    capitulations, 4:452–454
    Caribbean, 4:469, 477
    Chambers of Commerce, 12:690
    Colmar (France), 5:58–59
    competition, restriction of, 8:450–451
    contracts, 12:412–414
    De Pass, Aaron, 5:589
    economic doctrines and, 6:115–116
    economic history, 3:251, 6:95–138
    employees, 12:410, 412, 413, 415
    employers, 12:410, 412–415
    fifteenth century reestablishment, 20:84–85

Fonseca, Alvaro De, 7:115
Franks, David, 7:217–218
Franks, David Salisbury, 7:218
Franks, Jacob (1688-1769), 7:218
Franks, Jacob (c.1766-c.1823), 7:218
Gibraltar, Cardozo, Aaron Nuñez, 4:464
Hart, Isaac, 8:370
Hart, Meyer, 8:372
Hart, Samuel, 8:372
Hatry, Clarence Charles, 8:459
Hirsch, Solomon, 9:133
Hirschmann, Ira Arthur, 9:140–141
Hirszowicz, Abraham, 9:143–144
Hoffman, Philip E., 9:309–310
Horodischtsch, Leon, 9:528
Iberia, 20:83
Ibn Fadanj family, 9:675
Ibn Khalfun, Isaac, 9:685
Israel (ancient), 9:185
    leather industry, 12:574–577
    letters and letter writers, 12:672
    livestock, 13:144–145
    Marrano, 20:83–85
    Mediterannean, 3:143
    mercantilist absolutism, 9:229–230
    Middle Ages, 1:495–497, 20:81–85
    monopolies, 8:450
    nineteenth and twentieth centuries, 20:85–86
    Phoenicia, 16:121, 122–123
    Provence (France), 16:637–638
    Rachman, Peter, 17:50
    Rée, Hartvig Philip, 17:16
    Rehine, Zalma, 17:191
    Reisman, Heather, 17:212
    Rice, Abraham Joseph, 17:284
    Rich, Marc, 17:286–287
    Rich family, 17:285
    Rivera Jacob Rodriguez, 17:346
    Robles, Antonio Rodrigues, 17:356
    Rodrigues, Bartholomew, 17:366
    Rosales, Jacob, 17:420–421
    Rosenbloom, Carrol, 17:442
    Rosensaft, Josef, 17:449–450
    Rothberg, Samuel, 17:485
    Rothschild, Kurt, 17:494
    Rothschild, Walter N., 17:495
    Russia, 4:525
    in Sarajevo, 18:48
    silk, 3:27
    U.S., 3:179, 20:86–87
    See also Labor
Trade unions, 4:608–609, 12:411
    Canada, 6:728

    communism and, 5:95
    England, Bevin, Ernest, 3:556
    Ha-Po'el ha-Mizrachi, 10:607–608
    Histadrut, 9:146–150
        Israel (state), 10:600–605, 618
        Israeli Arab integration, 10:727–728
        Palestine (Mandate), 10:594–600
    Histadrut ha-Ovedim ha-Le'ummit, 9:150–151
    Jewish
        France, 11:816
        leaders, 6:743
    leaders, 9:299–300
        Dubinsky, David, 13:708–709
        Dyche, John Alexander, 6:75–76
        Herstein, Lillian, 9:47
        Hos, Dov, 9:547
        Lozovski, Solomon Abramovich, 13:238
        Mazur, Jay, 13:708–709
        Polak, Henri, 16:286–287
        Rose, Alex, 17:424
        Sapir, Pinhas, 18:38–39
        Schlossberg, Joseph, 18:144
        Schneiderman, Rose, 18:151
        Segal, Louis, 18:247
    Palestine (Ottoman), 10:594
    Poland, 12:640
    Rosemblum, Frank, 17:443
    Rosenberg, Abraham, 17:434
    Rosenberg, Ludwig, 17:438
    study, Perlman, Selig, 15:779
    U.S., 6:734
        Cleveland, 4:756–757
        Detroit, 5:611
        education, 6:747–748
        Hillman, Sidney, 9:118
    women as leaders, 6:753, 9:117
    workers' committees, 10:609
    See also specific trade unions
Tradition and Culture (Ellenson), 6:360
Tradition and Tradenten in den Schulen Palaestinas und Babyloniens (Bacher), 3:37
Tradition Concerning Prayer, According to R. Abraham. See Kabbalah me-Inyan ha-Tefillah le-Rabbi Avraham
Die traditionelle Aussprache des Aethiopischen (Mittwoch), 14:371
Tradition in Transition (Ellenson), 6:360
Traditions, 20:**88–90**
    captives, ransoming of, 4:457

death, 5:511–512

Traenen um Modesta Zamboni (Hermann), 9:24

Tragacanth, 20:**90**

Tragédies des temps volages (Hertz), 9:48

The Tragedy of Anti-Semitism (Leftwich/Chesterton), 12:603

La Trahison des cle (Benda), 3:324

Traianus, Marcus Ulpius. *See* Trajan, Marcus Ulpius

Traina, Anthony, 15:299

The Training of American Rabbis (Liebman), 17:24–25

Trains. *See* Railroads

Traité de chimie minérale (Moissan), 14:422

Traité de la circulation et du crédit (Pinto), 16:179

Trajan, Marcus Ulpius, 9:201–202, 20:**90**

    on Christians in Bithynia, 3:729

    Pappus and Julianus, 15:619

Traken. *See* Troki

Trakishik (Lithuania). *See* Rokiskis (Lithuania)

Tralles (Turkey). *See* Aydin (Turkey)

Tramer, Moritz, 20:**90–91**

Trance. *See* Ecstasy

Trani (Italy), 20:**91**

Trani, Joseph ben Moses, 20:**91**

Trani, Joshua Boaz ben Simon Baruch, 11:455

Trani, Moses ben Joseph, 20:**91–92**

Trani the Elder, Isaiah ben Mali di. *See* Isaiah ben Mali di Trani

Trani the Younger, Isaiah ben Elijah di. *See* Isaiah ben Elijah di Trani

Transactions, mistaken, 5:186–188, 14:367–369

Transcarpathian oblast. *See* Subcarpathian Ruthenia

Transcendence of God. *See* God

Transcontinental orthodromic itineraries, 11:722

"Transfer." *See* Haavara

Transfer of property. *See* Acquisition

The Transformation of the School: Progressivism in American Education, 1876-1957 (Cremin), 5:283

Transforming Madness: New Lives for People Living with Mental Illness (Neugeborgen), 15:119

Transgression. *See* Sin

Transhumance, 15:294, 296

Transislanus, Johannes van. *See* Campen, Johannes van

The Transit Camp. See Ha-Ma'abarah

Transit camps

    Dutch Jewry, 9:*473*

    Kistarca, 12:205

    See also Camps, concentration and extermination

Transjordan (Palestine), 10:197–198, 11:404, 20:**92–94**

    Abdullah ibn Hussein, 1:243–244

    Aggadah, Edom, 6:156–157

    Bible, Edom, 6:152–153

    Edrei, 6:158–159

    Jordan, Hashemite kingdom of, 11:404

    in Joshua, 11:448–449

    Moab, 14:399–404

    Second Temple period, Edom, 6:155–156

Translation and translators

    Al-Ḥarizi, Judah ben Solomon, 1:655–657

    Baal-Makhshoves, 3:8

    Bacher, Simon, 3:36

    Balmes, Abraham ben Meir de, 3:94–95

    Bánóczi, József, 3:120

    Beilenson, Anthony Charles, 3:265–266

    Belov, A, 3:305–306

    Ben Eleizer, Moshe, 3:340

    Benjamin, Walter, 3:359

    Benveniste, Samuel, 3:385

    Benveniste ibn Benveniste, 3:382

    Ben-Zion, S., 3:392–393

    Berdyczewski, Immanuel bin Gorion, 3:406

    Berechiah Berakh ben Eliakim Getzel, 3:406–407

    Berkowitz, Yitzḥak Dov, 3:440–442

    Bialik, Ḥayyim Naḥman, 3:561–565

    Bible translated into German, 13:272

    Birnbaum, Philip, 3:716

    children's literature, 4:624, 625, 628, 629, 8:734

    Chouraqui, André, 4:672–673

    Dalven, Rachel, 5:384

    Del Medico, Henri E., 5:542

    Delmedigo, Elijah ben Moses Abba, 5:542–543

    Dor, Moshe, 5:754–755

    Dukes, Leopold, 6:44

    Dykman, Shlomo, 6:78

    Fraenkel, Issac Seckel, 7:144

    Herder, Johann Gottfried, 9:9–10

    Herschele, 9:44–45

Herxheimer, Saloman, 9:51

Hessel, Franz, 9:78

Hevesi, András, 9:79

Hevesi, Sandor, 9:79

Hillel ben Samuel, 9:113–114

Hoffmann, Camill, 9:310

Hoga, Stanislav, 9:314

Ibn Bilia, David ben Yom Tov, 9:662

Ibn Ḥasdai, Abraham ben Samuel ha-Levi, 9:679

Ibn Motot, Samuel ben Saadiah, 9:686–687

Kafaḥ, Yosef, 11:703

Kalonymus ben Kalonymus, 11:749–750

Kaminka, 11:756

Kardos, Laszlo, 11:805

Kariv, Avraham, 11:808

Kármán, Mór, 11:811

Karu, Baruch, 11:819

Kassel, David, 11:827

la'az, 12:405–406

Labi, Solomon, 12:407

La Boétie, Etienne de, 12:408

Lara, David Ben Isaac Cohen de, 12:492–493

Laza of Frankfurt, 12:558

Levin, Menahem Mendel, 12:711–712

Loeb, James, 13:159–160

Ludwig, Emil, 13:251

Luther, Martin, 13:272

medieval, 20:**94–102**

Meek, Theophile, 3:622

Mithridates, Flavius, 14:370

Mittwoch, Eugen, 14:371–372

Mohácsi, Jenö, 14:418

Pinto, Isaac, 16:178–179

poetry, 16:270, 277

Polak, Gabriel Isaac, 16:286

Radó, Antal, 17:56

Rajpurkar, Joseph Ezekiel, 17:75

Rakovsky, Puah, 17:76

Rall, Yisrael, 17:77

Ratosh, Yonathan, 17:113–114

Ravikovitch, Dalia, 17:122

Regelson, Abraham, 17:187

Reichard, Piroska, 17:199

Reicherson, Moses, 17:199

Resnick, Solomon, 17:227–228

Ricius, Paulus, 17:292

Romano, Judah ben Moses ben Daniel, 17:404

Romano, Samuel, 17:405

Rosenbaum, Morris, 17:432

Translation and translators, *continued*
    Rosenfeld, Abraham Isaac Jacob,
      17:445
    Rottová, Inna, 17:496
    Simeon, Jacob b., 11:791
    Simon, Sir Leon, 18:613–614
Translations, Bible. *See* Bible
Transliteration. *See* La'az
Transmigration of the soul. *See* Gilgul
The Transmigration of Timothy Archer
    (Dick), 18:200
Transnistria (Ukraine), 3:96, 7:19,
    12:594, 20:**102–106**, *103*
Transoxiana, 20:**106**
Transplants, 20:**106–108**
Transportation
    carts and chariots, 4:497
    railroads, 17:69–70
Transylvania (Romania), 4:762,
    20:**108–111**
    Alba Iulia, 1:581–582
    Carmilly-Weinberger, Moshe,
      4:485
    Holocaust, 20:110
    Sabbatarian sect, 15:708
Trapani (Sicily), 20:**111**
Traske, John, 11:520, 20:**111**
Traub, Marvin S., 20:**111–112**
Traube, Isidor, 20:**112**
Traube, Ludwig (paleographer),
    20:**112**
Traube, Ludwig (pathologist), 20:**112**
Traube, Moritz, 20:**112**
Traube, Wilhelm, 20:**112**
Travel, prayer for, 20:**112–113**
Travelers and explorers, 20:**113–116**
    Africa, Isaacs, Nathaniel, 10:56
    Benjamin of Tudela, 3:362–363
    Burchardt, Hermann, 4:285–286
    Burckhardt, Johann Ludwig, 4:286
    Columbus, Christopher, 5:70
    Eldad ha-Dani, 6:293
    Elias, Ney, 6:318–319
    Elijah of Pesaro, 6:347
    Elisha Ḥayyim ben Jacob
      Ashkenazi, 6:354
    Emin Pasha, 6:394
    Franchetti, Raimond, 7:172
    Hayes, Isaac Israel, 8:475
    Ibrahim ibn Ya'qūb of Tortosa,
      9:701–702
    Montezinos, Antonio de, 14:460
    Phoenicians, 16:122–123
    Saphir, Jacob, 18:35–36
    Seetzen, Ultrich Jasper, 18:239
Travelers and travels to Erez Israel,
    20:**116–121**

Traveler's Prayer (Pauker), vol. 4:
    color insert
Travel literature, 7:13, 9:133
Travel writers, 18:613
Travnik (Bosnia-Herzegovina),
    20:**121–122**
Treasure, Cave of, 11:524
Treasure, treasury, 20:**122–123**
*Treasure of Kings. See Segullat
Melakhim*
*Treasury of Secret Wisdom. See Oẓar
Razei*
Treaties
    capitulations, 4:452–454
    covenants and, 5:250–253
    minority rights, 14:289
The Treatise of the Dream (Falaquera).
    See Iggeret ha-Ḥalomi (Falaquera)
*Treatise on Logic. See Sefer ha-
Higgayon*
Treatise on Logic (Maimonides), 1:546
*Treatise on Mensuration and
Calculation* (Abraham bar Ḥiyya).
    *See Ḥibbur ha-Meshiḥah ve-ha-
Tishboret* (Abraham bar Ḥiyya)
*Treatise on Prophetic Kabbalah. See
Keter Shem Tov*
Treatise on the Intellect (Alexander of
    Aphrodisias), 1:628
Treatise on the Jews in England
    (Selden), 18:258
*A Treatise on the Uses of the Tenses in
Hebrew* (Driver), 6:22
Trebic (Czech Republic), 20:**123–124**
Třebíč. See Trebic (Czech Republic)
Trebitsch. See Trebic (Czech Republic)
Trebitsch, Abraham, 2:38, 20:**124**
Trebitsch, Arthur, 20:**124–125**
Trebitsch, Moses Loeb ben Wolf,
    20:**124**
Trebitsch, Nehemiah, 20:**124**
Trebitsch, Siegfried, 20:**124**
Treblinka (Cohen), 5:21
Treblinka concentration camp, 9:336,
    11:751, 755, 20:**125–129**
    Holocaust memorial, 9:430, vol. 9:
      color insert
Trecento novelle (Sacchetti), 10:789
Tree of Knowledge, 1:374
Tree of Life, 1:374
    Oil of Life and, 15:394
    Tree of Knowledge and paradise
      in Eden narrative, 15:624–626
Tree of Life (Aaron ben Elijah). *See Eẓ
Ḥayyim*
*The Tree of Life. See Der Boym fun
Lebn*
Tree of Life Congregation (Newark),
    8:238

Trees, 1:347, 654, 683, 14:386–387
    planting during Tu Bi-Shevat, vol.
      6: color insert
Trefousse, Hans Louis, 20:**129**
Treitschke, Heinrich von, 20:**129–130**
    on Jewish identity, 11:297
Tremellius, John Immanuel, 3:613,
    20:**130**
*The Tremendum: A Theological
Interpretation of the Holocaust*
    (Cohen), 9:396
Trencin (Slovakia), 20:**130–131**
Trent (Italy), 3:776, 15:566, 20:**131**
    Council of Trent, Latin
      translations of Bible, 3:612
Trent, Council of, 4:94, 11:380
Trenton (NJ), 20:**131–132**
Trepman, Paul, 20:**132–133**
Trepp, Leo, 15:401
Trepper, Leopold, 20:**133–134**
Trespass
    business ethics and, 4:313
    on land, 8:449
    visual, nuisance law and, 15:329
Trest (Czech Republic), 20:**134**
Trets (France), 20:**134**
Treuenberg, Jacob Bassevi von. *See*
    Bassevi of Treuenberg, Jacob
Treuhandstelle, 16:453
Treumann, Otto, 4:368
Treves (Germany). *See* Trier
    (Germany)
Treves, Abraham ben Gershon
    Ẓarefati, 20:**135**
Treves, Claudio, 16:345
Treves, Emilio, 20:**135**
Treves, Isaac B. Mordecai Gershon,
    20:**135**
Treves, Johanan ben Joseph, 2:87,
    20:**135**
Treves, Johanan ben Mattathias,
    20:**135–136**
Treves, Matthias, 20:**134**
Treves, Naphtali Hertz, 20:**134**
Treves family, 20:**134–135**
Trevet, Nicholas. *See* Triveth, Nicholas
Treviño de Sobremonte, Tomás,
    20:**136**
Treviso (Italy), 20:**136–137**
Trévoux (France), 20:**137**
Trial by ordeal, 15:462
Trial marriage, 4:7
Trials, war crimes. *See* War crimes
    trials
Triangle Shirtwaist Factory fire (NYC),
    15:205
Tribadism, 12:660

Tribe, Laurence H., 20:**137**

The Tribe of Joseph (Chagall), vol. 4: color insert

Tribe of Simeon, 18:591

Tribes

the Twelve (*See* The Twelve Tribes)

See specific tribes

Tribes, Ten Lost. *See* Ten Lost Tribes

Tribes of Israel. *See specific tribes*

Tribune (NY), 1:380

Triennial cycle, 20:**140–143**, 141*t*

Trier (Germany), 20:**143–144**

Trier, Ernst, 6:161

Trier, Walter, 20:**144**

Triesch (Czech Republic). *See* Trest (Czech Republic)

Trieste (Italy), 20:**144–146**

Trietsch, Davis, 6:286, 20:**146**

Trigano, Shmuel, 11:324, 325, 20:**147**

Trigere, Pauline, 20:**147**

Trigland, Jacob, 11:425

Trikkala (Greece), 20:**147–149**

Trilby (du Maurier), 6:436

Trillin, Calvin, 20:**149**

Trilling, Diana, 20:**149**

Trilling, Lionel, 20:**149–150**

Trinitarians, 4:249–250, 11:43

Trinity, 7:670, 18:455

Triolet, Elsa, 20:**150**

Tripartite Canon, 3:576–579

Tripoli (Lebanon), 20:**150–151**

community, nature of, 5:106

Tripoli (Libya), 1:370, 3:343, 12:790–791, 795, 20:**151–152**

Tristram, Henry Baker, 20:**152–153**

Tritel, Harvey, 12:599

Trithemius, Johannes, 20:**153**

Trito-Isaiah, 6:494

Triumpho del govierno popular y de la antigüedad holandesa (Barrios), 3:176

Triumph of Will (Riefenstahl), 9:440

El Triunpho de la virtud y Paciencia de Job (Enríquez Basurto), 6:446

Trivale, Ion, 20:**153**

Triveth, Nicholas, 20:**153**

Triwosch, Joseph Elijah, 20:**153**

Trnava (Slovakia), 3:776, 20:**153–154**

Trocmé, André, 4:564, 565

Trocmé, Daniel, 4:564, 565

Troeltsch, Ernst, 9:246

Trogianus. *See* Trajan, Marcus Ulpius

Troiki, Isaac ben Abraham

apologetics, 2:268

disputations and polemics, 5:695

Hizzuk Emunah, 5:695

Troki. *See* Malinowski, Joseph ben Mordecai

Troki (Lithuania), 20:**154–155**

Troki, Abraham ben Josiah. *See* Abraham ben Josiah Troki

Troki, Isaac ben Abraham, 4:250, 11:792, 20:**155–156**

Troki, Joseph ben Mordecai. *See* Malinowski, Joseph ben Mordecai

Troki, Solomon ben Aaron, 11:792

Trommel Kaddish (song), 11:697

Troper, Morris, 2:61

Tropic of Venus (Adelman), 1:386

Troppau (Czech Republic). *See* Opava

Tropplowitz, Joseph. *See* Ha-Efrati, Joseph

Trotsky, Leon. *See* Trotsky, Lev Davidovich

Trotsky, Lev Davidovich, 11:367, 18:705, 729, 20:**156–157**

The Trouble Air (Shaw), 18:424

Trouble in Utopia: The Overburdened Polity of Israel (Lissak), 13:82

The Trouble with Translation (Singer), 18:640

Troyes (France), 20:**157–158**

The True Word (Celsus), 4:537, 538

Truffaut, Francois, 4:23

Trujillo (Spain), 20:**158**

Truman, Harry S., 20:**158–159**

Anglo-American Committee of Enquiry, 15:584–585

Bisgyer, Maurice, 3:725

Jewish organizations and, 4:16

Niles, David K., 15:267

Trumpeldor, Berit. *See* Betar

Trumpeldor, Joseph, 3:344, 9:249, 15:694, 20:**159–160**

He-Halutz (movement), 8:757, 13:277–278

Jewish Legion, 11:303

Trunk, Isaiah, 11:527, 20:**160–161**

Trunk, Israel Joshua, 20:**161**

Trunk, Yehiel Yeshaia, 11:441, 20:**161–162**

Trust, 15:425

Trust (Ozick), 15:557

Trustees. *See* Shalish

Trustin, Harry, 15:415–416

Truth, 20:**162**

in business ethics, 4:308–310

focal point of Simḥah Bunem's religiosity, 18:604

source

acceptance regardless of, 16:68–69

historical experience as, 16:83

revelation as, 16:96

types of, 16:87

The Truth About the Dreyfuss Affair (Lazare), 6:18

Truth and Power (Morgenthau), 14:490

Truth from Erez Yisrael. See Emet, me-Erez Yisrael

Trypho, Dialogue with (Justin Martyr), 11:580

Tryphon

disputations and polemics, 5:688–689

Jonathan the Hasmonean, 11:399

Jonathan son of Absolom, 11:399

Tryphon (2nd century B.C.E.). *See* Diodotus-Tryphon

Trzcianka (Poland), 20:**162**

To T.S. Eliot (Litvinoff), 13:141

Tsaban, Ya'ir, 20:**162–163**

The Tsaddik of Seven Wonders (Haiblum), 18:199

Tsalka, Dan, 20:**163**

Tsanin, Mordkhe, 20:**163–164**

Tsar-Balekhayim (Shalom Aleichem), 18:387

Tsavoe (Shalom Aleichem), 18:388

Tsaytike Troybn (Segalowitch), 18:249

Tsaytung (newspaper), 14:420

Tschernichowsky, Saul. *See* Tchernichowsky, Saul

Tschlenow, Jehiel, 20:**164**

Tsederbaum, Iulii Osipovich. *See* Martov, Julius

Tsekhanov, Abraham ben Raphael Landau of. *See* Ciechanow, Abraham ben Raphael Landau of

Tsenerene (Jacob b. Isaac), 21:340

Tsereteli, Konstantin, 11:322

Tsevat, Job, Book of, 11:355

Der Tseylem (Shapiro), 18:407

Tseytlin, A., 21:351

Tsfassman, Alexander Naumovich, 20:**165**

Tsharny, Daniel, 15:262

Tsharny, Shmuel. *See* Niger, Shmuel

Tsharny Vladek, Boruch, 15:262

Tshebiner Rav. *See* Wiedenfeld, Dov

Tshemeriski, Alexander, 20:**165**

Tsholnt. *See* Cholent

Tsidekel. *See* Tallit katan

Tsik, Yudis. *See* Yudika

Tsolner. *See* Volchko

Tsomet, 20:**165**

Tsoyzmir (Poland). *See* Sandomierz (Poland)

Tsu a Yidishe Tokhter (Einhorn), 6:259

Tsu der Yidnfrage in Poiln (Alter), 2:18

Tsukunft (journal), 12:782, 18:708, 20:**165–166**

Tsur, Jacob, 20:**166**

Tsur-Rotenstreich Committee, 16:358

Tsuzmir (Poland). *See* Sandomierz (Poland)

Tsvey Shprakhn – Eyneyntsike Literatur (Baal-Makhshoves), 3:8

Tsvey Shteyner (Shalom Aleichem), 18:380

Tsvey Veltn (Hirschkahn), 9:139

The Tsvi Family. See Di Familye Tsvi

Tsvishn Tsvey Veltn. See Between Two Worlds (weekly column)

Tuat (North Africa), 20:**166**

Tubal, 3:729

Tubal-Cain, 20:**166**

Ṭūbās (Samaria). *See* Ṭubas (Samaria)

Ṭubas (Samaria), 19:686

Tu be-Av. *See* Av, the fifteenth of

Tubelski, Leonid Davydovich., 20:192

Tubelski, Peter Lvovich Ryzhey, 20:192

Tu bi-Shevat, 20:**167**
    biblical literature, 20:167
    boy planting a sapling, vol. 6: color insert
    food, 7:121

Tubutsch (Ehrenstein), 6:241

Tucacas (Venezuela), 20:**167**

Tuchin (Ukraine), 20:**167–168**

Tuchman, Barbara Wertheim, 20:**168**

Tucholsky, Kurt, 20:**168–169**

Tuck, Raphael, 20:**169**

Tuckachinsky, Yosef. *See* Tekoah, Yosef

Tucker, Richard, 20:**169**

Tucker, Sophie, 20:**169**

Tuckum (Latvia). *See* Tukums (Latvia)

Tucson (AZ), 20:**169–171**

Tuczyn (Ukraine). *See* Tuchin (Ukraine)

Tudela (Spain), 20:**171–172**
    elite families, 6:679

Tudḥaliya IV, 9:292

The Tudor Revolution in Government (Elton), 6:370

Tuebingen (Germany), 20:**172–173**

Tugal, Pierre, 20:**173**

Tugendhold, Jacob, 20:**173**
    apologetics, 2:269

Tugendhold, Wolf, 20:173

Tuka, Vojtech, 20:**174**

Tukulti-apil-Esharra the Third. *See* Tiglath-Pileser II

Tukulti-Ninurta I, 3:23

Tukums (Latvia), 20:**174**

Tulchin (Ukraine), 20:**174**

Tulchiner, Baruch. *See* Baruch ben Jehiel of Medzibezh

Ṭūl Karm (Ereẓ Israel), 20:**174–175**

Tumarkin, Igael, 10:699, 20:**175**

Tumin, Melvin Marvin, 18:733, 20:**175**

Tunisia, 2:323–324, 20:**175–191**, *176*
    Alḥayk, Uzziel ben Mordecai, 1:657
    Arab rule, 20:177–179
    community, nature of, 5:105–106, 111
    community organization and structures, 5:108, 110, 118*t*
    crime, 5:291, 292
    French protectorate, 20:184–185
    Hasfid rule, 20:179–181
    Holocaust, Tunis, 20:188–189
    Holocaust period, 20:188–189
    immigration to Israel from, 10:523
    Jewish dress, 6:14–15
    Jewish music, 1:439–440, 14:393
    Kairouan, 11:726–727
    musical traditions, 1:439–440
    Muslim-Jewish relations, 20:186–187, 189
    newspapers, 16:497
    Ottoman rule, 20:181–185
    pilgrims going to synagogue, vol. 5: color insert
    politics, 3:498–499, 16:346
    post-WW II, 20:189–190
    Second Temple period, 20:175–177
    since Six-Day War, 20:190–191
    WW II, 20:188–189
    Zionism and political activity, 20:187–188
    See also Orientalists

Tunkel, Joseph, 20:**191–192**

Der Tunkeler. *See* Tunkel, Joseph

Tur. *See* Jacob ben Asher

Tur (Caro), 8:257

Tura (Bar-Yosef), 8:720

Tura (Smilansky), 8:720

Turba Philosophorum (Plessner), 16:237

Turbato Corde, 3:146, 4:277

Tur brothers, 20:**192**

Turda (Romania), 20:**192**

Tureck, Rosalyn, 20:**192**

Turei Zahav (David ben Samuel ha-Levi), 5:469–470, 18:338–339

Turei Zahav (Joel ben Moses Gad), 11:365–366

Turin (Italy), 15:249, 20:**193–194**

Turing Award, 5:131

Turka (Ukraine), 20:**194–195**

Turkey, 10:197*t*, 20:**195–203**, *196*
    Aaronsohn family, 1:221–223
    Abenaes, Solomon, 1:249
    Amasiya, 2:33
    Chief Rabbinate, Secular Council, 11:762
    coinage, 14:300
    communal schools, 20:197–198
    community organization and structures, 5:108, 110, 118
    Congress of Berlin, 3:453–454
    Constantinople, printing industry, 9:762
    demography, 20:196–197, 197*t*, 198
    developments, 1980s onward, 20:198–200
    economic activities, 20:195–196
    emancipation, 6:385
    Greece, Salonika, 17:700–701
    Hebrew printing industry, Edirne, 6:149
    history, Edessa, 6:146–147
    Holocaust, Sephardim, 18:301
    Israel, relations with, 20:200–201
    Istanbul, Jews in, 10:782–784
    Izmir, Jews in, 10:826–828
    Jewish dress, 6:14
    Jewish Legion, 11:303–306
    Karaites and Karitism, 11:795
    Kurdistan, 12:389
    Lapseki, 12:491–492
    literature, Levi, Mario, 12:690
    Mersin, 14:71
    museums, 14:627
    music, Edirne, 6:148–150
    newspapers, 12:772, 16:497
    Nili, 15:267–268
    Ottoman Empire, 2:147, 6:148, 149
    politics, 16:345–346
    printing, publishing, 16:536
    Quincentennial Foundation, 11:755
    responsa literature, 17:232, 233, 234
    synagogue architecture, 19:375
    synagogue musical traditions, 20:201–202
    Tokat, 2:130
    Young Turks Revolution, 2:33, 15:542–543, 544
    See also Kemal Mustafa; Ottoman empire

Turkow, Itzḥak, 20:203
Turkow, Jonas, 20:203
Turkow, Marc, 20:**203**
Turkow, Zygmunt, 20:203
Turkow family, 20:**203**
Tur Malka. *See* Greenberg, Uri Ẓevi
Turner, J.M.W., 14:542
Turner, Ya'akov, 20:**203**
Turnip and rape, 20:488–489
Turnov (Czech Republic), 20:203–**204**
Turnus Rufus. *See* Tinneius Rufus
Turóczi-Trostler, József, 20:**204**
Turok, Ben, 16:349
Turow, Scott, 20:**204**
Turrigiano, Gina, 4:125
Tur-Sinai, Naphtali Herz, 20:**204–205**
   biblical exegesis and study, 3:647
   Job, Book of, 11:343, 344, 346,
      351, 352
Turtle doves, 20:**205**
Tuscany (Italy), 20:**205–206**
Tusch-Letz, S. J. *See* Lec, Stainslaw
   Jerzy
Tushiyah, 4:622
Tuska, Simon, 20:**206**
Tussman, Malka Heifetz, 20:**206–207**
Tustar (Iran). *See* Shushtar (Iran)
Tustarī family, 7:472
Tutsi, 20:**207**
Tuvim, Judith. *See* Holliday, Judy
Tuviyyah ha-Rofe. *See* Cohn, Tobias
   ben Moses
Tuwim, Julian, 20:**207–208**
Tuzora. *See* Kalarash
"Tvoya pobeda" (Aliger), 1:659
Twelve (number), 15:336
The Twelve Chairs. *See* Dvenadtsat stul
   yev
*Twelve Lectures on the Structure of the
   Central Nervous System* (Edinger),
   6:147
Twelve tone composition technique,
   18:155, 156
The Twelve Tribes, 12:684, 20:**137–
   140**
Twenty (number), 15:336
Twenty-Five Ghetto Songs (Mlotek,
   Gottlieb), 14:396
"Twenty-four." *See* Moses Esrim ve-
   Arba
Twerski, Jacob Israel, 20:**208**
Twersky, Atarah, 18:780
Twersky, David, 15:230, 20:209
Twersky, David ben Mordecai. *See*
   David of Talna
Twersky, Isadore, 18:780, 20:**209**
Twersky, Menahem Nahum ben Ẓevi,
   20:208

Twersky, Mordecai of Chernobyl,
   20:208
Twersky, Yoḥanan, 8:736, 20:**209**
Twersky dynasty, 20:**208–209**
Twersky family, 8:420
Twilight, 20:**209–210**
The Twilight Zone (television show),
   18:312
Two (number), 15:334
"Two Camps" (Israel). *See*
   Maḥanayim (Israel)
"Two-gun" Cohen. *See* Cohen, Morris
   Abraham
Two Languages – One Literature. *See*
   *Tsvey Shprakhn - Eyneyntsike
   Literatur*
Two Men and a Wardrobe (Polanski),
   16:326
Tworkov, Jack, 20:**210**
Two Types of Faith (Buber), 4:234
Two Women (Moravia), 14:477
Two Worlds. *See* Tsvey Veltn
Tychsen, Olaus Gerhard, 20:**210**
Tykocin (Poland), 3:567, 20:**211**
Tykocinski, Ḥayyim, 20:**211**
Tykocinski, Jehiel Michel, 20:**211–212**
Tykotsin (Poland). *See* Tykocin
   (Poland)
Tyndale, William, 3:611, 612, 619,
   20:**212**
Tynyanov, Yuri Nikolayevich, 20:**212**
Typographers, 12:663, 20:**212–213**
Typography, 12:589, 20:**213–218**, *214,
   215*
Tyre (Lebanon), 1:522, 524, 9:123–
   124, 11:112, 16:120–122, 20:**218–
   219**
Tyre, Ladder of. *See* Ladder of Tyre
Tyre of the Tobiads, 20:**219**
Tyrnau, Isaac, 4:133, 20:**219–220**
Tyrol (Austria), 20:**220**
Tyrolean-Vorarlberg Insurrection. *See*
   Hofer, Andreas
Tysmenitsa (Ukraine), 20:**220–221**
Tyszka, Jan. *See* Jogiches, Leon
Tyszko, Jan. *See* Jogiches, Leon
Tyszowce (Poland), 20:**221**
Tzara, Tristan, 20:**221**
Tzedakah
   Eleazar ben Judah of Bartota,
      6:303
   ḥalukkah, 8:287–290
   pletten, 16:237
   poor, provision for, 16:371–372
Tzelniker, Meir, 20:**221**
Tzentral Veltlech Yiddishe Shul
   Organizatzie (TZVISHO), 7:33

Tziperman, Eli, 6:450
Tzomet political party, 6:279
Tzvi Migdal traffic network (Brazil),
   4:147–148

U

U (letter), 20:*223*
UAHC. *See* Union of Reform Judaism
U.A.R. *See* Egypt
Ubiquitin, 4:725
Uceda, Samuel ben Isaac, 20:**223**
Ucko, Siegfried, 20:**223–224**
UCLA (University of California, Los
   Angeles), 11:776
Udakov, Solomon, 4:264
Udenfriend, Sidney, 13:10
Udim (Israel), 20:**224**
Udin, Sophie A., 20:**224**
Udlice (Czech Republic), 20:**224**
Ueberall, Ehud. *See* Avriel, Ehud
Ueber das Altern (Améry), 2:65
Ueber den Prozess der Zivilisation. *See*
   The Civilizing Process
*Ueber die Autonomie der Rabbinen und
   das Prinzip der juedischen Ehe*
   (Holdheim), 9:316
*Ueber die buergerliche Verbesserung der
   Juden* (Dohm), 4:550, 5:733–734
Ueberlingen (Germany), 3:43, 20:**224–
   225**
Ufa (Russia), 20:**225**
Uganda
   Bayudaya, 3:233, 11:521
   Mbale community, vol. 20: color
      insert
   plane hijacking, 6:447–448
Uganda scheme, 4:88, 8:497, 9:63–66,
   13:148, 20:**225**
   Abramowitz, Grigori, 1:325
   Ben-Yehuda, Eliezer, 3:388
   Chamberlain, Joseph, 4:564
   Herzl, Theodor, 9:63–66
   Levin, Shmarya, 12:713
   Nordau, Max, 15:298
   See also Kharkov Conference
Ugarit (ancient city), 4:511, 20:**225–
   228**
   Anath, 2:131
   archives, 2:403
   Ashtoreth, 2:131
   biblical criticism and archaeology,
      3:652
   Emar, 6:386–390
   Kamish, 6:86
   Ras Shamra, 18:103
Ugaritic language, 3:652, 8:621, 622,
   623, 18:281, 284, 285, 20:**228–230**

Ugaritic myths, 3:10, 11, 12, 6:22
Ugav Raḥel: Shirim ve-Iggerot (Morpurgo), 14:509
U.G.I.F. *See* Union Générale des Israélites de France
Ugiyot ha-Melah shel Savta Sultana (Seri), 18:301
Ugoda, 20:**230**
UHC (United Hebrew Congregation), 5:317
Uhde, Milan, 20:**230–231**
Uherske Hradiste (Czech Republic), 20:**231**
Uhersky Brod (Czech Republic), 20:**231–232**
Uhlman, Fred, 20:**232**
UIA. *See* United Israel Appeal
U.I.W.U. *See* United Israel World Union
UJA. *See* United Jewish Appeal (UJA)
Ujejski, Kornel, 18:761
Ujhely (Hungary). *See* Satoraljaujhely (Hungary)
Uj Kelet (newspaper), 20:**232**
Ujpest (Hungary), 13:**172**
UJPO (United Jewish People's Order), 4:406
Ujvári, Péter, 20:**232**
Ujvidék. *See* Novi Sad
Ukba, Mar (Amora), 20:**232–233**
Ukba, Mar (Exilarch), 11:726–727, 20:**233**
'Ukbarā (Babylon), 20:**233**
Ukhmani, Azriel, 20:**233–234**
Uklein, Simeon, 11:521
Ukmerge (Lithuania), 20:**234**
Ukraine, 20:**234–239**
  agriculture, Jewish, 1:497–498, 11:735
  Ananyev, 2:130
  antisemitism, 19:174, 20:235–236, 238, 244–245
    Aleksandriya, 1:610
    Bratslav, 4:134
    Cherkassy, 4:594–595
    Chernigov, 4:596
    Chernobyl, 4:597
    Chernovtsy, 4:597–599
    Chudnov, 4:708
    Haller's Army, 8:281
    Yekaterinoslav, 5:724–725
  Babi Yar memorial, 9:430
  Berdyansk, 3:404
  Birzula, 3:724
  Bobrovy Kut, 4:24
  Boguslav, 4:37
  Bojan, 4:42–43

  Bolekhov, 4:44–45
  Borislav, 4:85–86
  Brailov, 4:118–119
  Briceva, 4:177–178
  Brody, 4:198–200
  camps, concentration and internment, Lvov, 13:291–292
  Chmielnicki, Bogdan, 4:654–656
  community organization, Lvov, 13:288–290
  Drogobych, 6:23–24
  early Jewish settlement, 11:754
  economic situation, 20:235
  Feodosiya, 6:758
  Haidamacks, 8:233–234
  Holocaust, 4:86, 178, 199–200, 238, 316
    Aleksandriya, 1:610
    Bar, 3:123
    Belgorod-Dnestrovski, 3:288
    Berestechko, 3:413
    Berezhany, 3:414
    Bolekhov, 4:45
    Bratslav, 4:134
    Brody, 4:199–200
    Busk, 4:316
    Cherkassy, 4:595
    Chernigov, 4:596
    Chernobyl, 4:597
    Chernovtsy, 4:598
    Chortkov, 4:668–669
    Drogobych, 6:24
    Dubno, 6:33–34
    Dunayevtsy, 6:49
    Glinyany, 7:639
    Gorodenka, 7:782
    Gorodok, 7:782
    Kamenka-Bugskaya, 11:754
    Kazatin, 12:44
    Kerch, 12:81
    Kharkov, 12:105–106
    Kherson, 12:114
    Khmelnik, 12:115
    Khorol, 12:117
    Khust, 12:119
    Kirovograd, 12:187–188
    Kolomyya, 12:280
    Komarno, 12:282
    Konotop, 12:288
    Korets, 12:307–308
    Korosten, 12:316
    Korsun-Shevchenkovski, 12:316
    Kosov, 12:320–321
    Kovel, 12:328
    Kovno, 6:358–359

    Krasnoye, 12:339
    Kremenchug, 12:351
    Kremenets, 12:352
    Krivoi-Rog, 12:365
    Krivoye Ozero, 12:365
    Kuty, 12:399–400
    Leshnev, 12:662
    Lutsk, 13:274
    Lvov, 13:291–292
    Lyuboml, 13:301
    Medzibezh, 13:763
    Melitopol, 14:13
    Mezhirech, 14:156
    Monastyriska, 14:433
    Mostiska, 14:568
    Mukachevo, 14:607
    Nadvornaya, 14:727
    photographs, 9:475
    Piryatin, 16:184
    Podgaitsy, 16:250–251
    Podkamen, 16:252
    Podolia, 16:253
    Podvolochisk, 16:254
    Polonnoye, 16:361
    Poltava, 16:363
    Priluki, 16:527
    Proskurov, 16:595
    Radomyshl, 17:58
    Radziwillow, 17:60
    Rogatin, 17:368
    Romny, 17:418
    Rovno, 17:502
    Rozdol, 17:503
    Sadagora, 17:651
    Sambor, 17:744–745
    Sarny, 18:60
    Sasov, 18:66
    Satanov, 18:73
    Sekiryany, 18:256–257
    Sevastopol, 18:324
    Shargorod, 18:414
    Shepetovka, 18:460
    Skalat, 18:656–657
    Smela, 18:686
    Snyatyn, 18:697
    Sokal, 18:746
    Stanislav, 19:163
    Staro-Konstantinov, 19:166
    Storozhinets, 19:239
    Stry, 19:263
    Talnoye, 19:491
    Tarnopol, 19:518
    Tarutino, 19:524
    Tlumach, 19:749–750
    Tolstoye, 20:30

Tomashpol, 20:31
Torchin, 20:54
Tuchin, 20:167–168
Tulchin, 20:174
Turka, 20:195
Tysmenitsa, 20:221
Uman, 20:245
Uzhgorod, 20:448
Vasilkov, 20:479
Vinnitsa, 20:538
Vishnevets, 20:543
Vizhnitsa, 20:564
Vladimir Volynsk, 20:565
Vladimir Volynski, 20:565
Volhynia, 20:573
Voznesensk, 20:586
Yavorov, 21:291
Yefingar, 21:293–294
Yevpatoriya, 21:325
Zabolotov, 21:432
Zaleshchiki, 21:448
Zaporozhe, 21:457
Zastavna, 21:462
Zbarazh, 21:465
Zbarzh, 21:465
Zborov, 21:466
Zhdanov, 21:521
Zhidachov, 21:521
Zhitomir, 21:524
Zhmerinka, 21:525
Zholkva, 21:526
Zhuravno, 21:526
Zlatopol, 21:643
Zolochev, 21:667
Zolotonosha, 21:667
Zvenigorodka, 21:693
independent, 20:236, 237–238
judges, Ehrlich, Eugen, 6:243
Kamenka, hasidic dynasty, 11:754
Kazatin, 12:44
Kerch, 12:81
Kharkov, 12:105–106
Kherson, 12:114–115
Khorol, 12:117–118
Kiev, 12:148–153
Kirovograd, 12:187–188
language, Bible translated into, 3:634–635
Lyuboml, 13:300–301
Mezhirech, 14:155–156
Nazi occupation, 11:735
Nezhin, 15:246
Nikolayev, 15:265–266
Novaya Ushitsa, 15:317
Novgorod-Seversk, 15:319–320

Novy Oleksiniec, 15:324
Odessa, 15:377–382
Olesko, 15:402
Olgopol, 15:403–404
Olyka, 15:412
orphans and orphanages, 15:486
Ostrog, 15:510–512
Ovruch, 15:549
Pavlograd, 15:699
Pavoloch, 15:699
poetry, 11:808, 12:443–444
    Kaminer, Isaac, 11:755
pogroms of 1919, 16:17
printing, Hebrew
    Bratslav, 4:134
    Dubno, 6:34
    Lawat, Abraham David Ben
      Judah Leib, 12:541
    Lvov, 13:291
Skvira, 18:662–663
Slavuta, 18:672–673
Smela, 18:686
Snyatyn, 18:**697–698**
Sokal, 18:745–746
synagogues, 4:598
Transnistria, 20:102–106, *103*
Uman massacre, 20:244–245
United Jewish Socialist Worker's
  Party, 20:258–259
WW I, 12:443
post WW II, 20:236–237
WW II, Yekaterinoslav, 5:724–725
Yiddish education, 6:188
See also Kiev
Ukraine (Europe), museums, 14:630
Ukva, Mar. *See* Ukba, Mar
Ukẓin, 20:**239**
Ulaan Bataar (Mongolia), 14:443
Ulam, Stanislaw Marcin, 20:**239–240**
Ulan Bator (Mongolia). *See* Ulaan
  Bataar (Mongolia)
Ulan-Ude (Russia). *See* Verkhneudinsk
  (Russia)
Ulfilas, Bible translations of, 3:629–630
Ulianover, Miriam, 20:**240**
Ulif, Gershon. *See* Ashkenazi, Gershon
Ulla I, 20:**240**
Ullendorf, Edward, 20:**240**
Ullman, Micha, 10:699, 20:**240–241**
Ullman, Samuel, 3:713
Ullman, Tracey, 20:**241**
Ullman, Viktor, 20:**241**
Ullmann, Adolph, 20:**241–242**
Ullmann, Ernest, 20:**242**
Ullmann, Salomon, 20:**242**

Ulloa, Alberto, 15:585
Ullstein, Hermann, 20:242
Ullstein, Leopold, 20:242
Ullstein family, 20:**242**
Ulm (Germany), 20:**242–243**
Ulman, Abraham, 20:**243**
Ulman, Joseph N., 20:**243**
Ulpan, 20:**243–244**
Ulpian, 20:**244**
Ulrich, Johann Caspar, 9:158, 20:**244**
Ulster (Ireland). *See* Ireland
Ultima Hora, 11:469–470
Ultima Oră (Sebastian), 18:231
Ultra-Orthodox. *See* Ḥaredim
Ultra-orthodox Judism. *See* Orthodox
  Judaism
Ulyalayevschina (Selvinski), 18:272
Ulyanov, Vladimir Ilyich. *See* Lenin,
  Vladimir Ilyich
Ulysses (Joyce), 6:33, 436
Uman (Ukraine), 14:752, 20:**244–245**
Umano, Felice. *See* Anau, Phinehas
  Ḥai ben Menahem
'Umāra ibn Wathīma, 3:669
Umayyad dynasty, 10:14, 20:**245–247**
    Abbasids and, 1:233
    Jerusalem and, 11:154–155
Umayya ibn Abī al-Salt, 14:538–539,
  20:**247**
UMEJ. *See* World Union of Jewish
  Students
U-mi-ẓur Devash (Ben Simeon),
  3:374–375
In Umru (Litvakov), 13:140
*Die Umsiedlung und Umschichtung des
  juedischen volkes im Laufe des letzten
  Jahrhundert* (Lestschinsky), 12:666
UN. *See* United Nations
Un air de famille (Bacri), 3:42
Unavoidable causes, 15:427, 429–431
Uncertain Poetries (Heller), 20:299–300
Unclean Jerusalem oracle, 6:639
Uncle Mike. *See* Jacobs, Michael
  Strauss
Unction. *See* Anointing
Under a Fence. See Unter a Ployt
Under Camouflage. See Sub camuflaj
Undercharging. *See* Ona'ah
Under Copper Skies (Elberg), 6:291
Underground (Sobol), 18:702
Underground organizations
    Israel (state), Loḥamei Ḥerut
      Israel, 13:175–176
    Polish, 16:315–316
      Karski, Jan, 11:817–818
      Plotnicka, Frumka, 16:241
    WW II
      Beriḥah, 3:434–435

Underground organizations, *continued*
Berit ha-Biryonim, 3:436

Underground Town. See Podzemní město

Under Plum Cake (Davidson), 18:204

Under the Domim Tree (Almagor), 1:678

Under the Yoke (Esselin), 6:509

Underwater Exploration Society of Israel, 17:6

Undoing Gender (Butler), 4:317

UNESCO, 14:453, 20:272

U-Netanneh Tokef, 20:**247–248**
Amnon of Mainz, 2:87

Unfailing Light (Drachman), 6:6

Unfinished Sentence. See Befejezetlen mondat

Ungar, Benjamin, 20:**248**

Ungar, Joel of Rechnitz, 20:**248**

Ungarische Brod (Czech Republic). *See* Uhersky Brod (Czech Republic)

Ungarische-Hradisch. *See* Uherske Hradiste

Der Ungarisch Israelit (Einhorn), 6:259

Unger, Irwin, 20:**248**

Unger, Josef, 12:549, 20:**248**

Unger, Joseph. *See* Unger, Josef

Unger, Max, 20:**248–249**

Ungerfeld, Moshe, 20:**249**

Ungerman, Irving, 20:**249**

Ungvár. *See* Uzhgorod

Uniformity, criterion of, 8:388–389

Union, Oesterreichische-Israelitische. *See* Oesterreichische-Israelitische Union

Union Catalog of Hebrew Manuscipts and Their Location (Freimann), 7:237

Union County (NJ), 20:**249–250**

Union Democracy (Lipset), 13:75

Union for Liberal Judaism in Germany. *See* Vereinigung Fuer das Liberale Judentum in Deutschland

Union for Progressive Jewish Education, 6:211

Union for Traditional Judaism, 17:26

Union Générale des Israélites de France, 12:443, 20:**250–251**

Union Hymnal (Kaiser), 11:728

Union of American Hebrew Congregations (UAHC). *See* Union of Reform Judaism

Union of Councils for Jews in the Former Soviet Union, 20:**251–253**

Union of Czech Jews. *See* Svaz čechů-Židů

Union of Israel. *See* Agudat Israel

Union of Italian Jewish Communities, 10:806, 809, 811–812

Union of Needletrades, Industrial and Textile Employees (UNITE), leaders
Mazur, Jay, 13:708–709
Sheinkman, Jacob, 18:438

Union of Orthodox Jewish Congregations of America, 3:6, 6:6, 197, 20:**253**

Union of Orthodox Rabbis of the United States and Canada, 3:758, 18:585, 20:**253**

Union of Reform Judaism, 3:13, 4:545, 20:**254–255**
Board of Delegates of American Israelites, 4:19–20
education, Jewish, 6:192, 196, 198
Schindler, Alexander M., 18:135

Union of Sephardic Congregations, 18:303, 20:**256**

Union of Soviet Socialist Republics (USSR), 9:245, 246, 17:542–546, 546t
agricultural projects, 17:544–545
Agursky, Samuel, 1:520
aliyah and absorption
Israel (state), 1:661
post-Six Day War to 1970s, 10:345–349, 349t
American Joint Distribution Committee, 2:59–60, 62, 63, 64
annexation of territories, 17:546–547, 546t
An-Ski collections, 2:182–183
anti-Fascism, 6:634
Anti-Fascist Committee, Jewish, 2:196–197
antisemitism, 2:217, 221–222, 235–236, 236, 4:65, 16:320–321, 17:543
authors, 5:427
Brodsky, Joseph, trial, 4:198
dance, 5:415
doctors' plot, 5:728–729
Ovruch, arrests of attendees at Jewish worship service in, 15:549
anti-zionism, 2:236
army, 17:550
assimilation, 17:544
ba'alei tesuvah, 3:6–7
Babi Yar, 3:22–23
Birobidzhan, 3:717–720, 718, 719
Blumel, André, 4:10
Bobrovy Kut, 4:24
Bukhara under, 4:261–262
caricatures of Jews, 4:479
communism, 5:91–96, 679–680
Crimea, 5:299–300, 301
criticism of, 5:90

dance, 5:412, 415–416
demography, 17:545–546, 545t, 546t
discrimination and, 5:679–680
Dymshyts, Veniamin E., 6:79
economic history, 6:136, 12:493–494, 781–782, 17:542, 544, 546, 546t
education, general, contributions to, 6:161
education, Jewish, 6:186, 188
effect of disintegration of, 10:264
emancipation, 6:384–385
foreign policy and relations with Israel, 5:96, 10:219, 228, 234, 262, 263, 264
Madrid Peace Conference, 10:243
Six-Day War, 10:229–232
gulags, Dykman, Shlomo, 6:78
Hebrew language, 17:543
Holocaust memorials, 9:430
Holocaust rescue efforts, 9:491–492
immigration to Israel from, 10:235, 243, 263, 264, 346, 348–349, 350, 352–353, 453, 523–524, 631–632, 636
Jewish communities in, 10:348
Jewish identity in, 11:298–299
Jewish studies in, 11:319–324
Judeo-Tat language, 11:561
Karaites, 11:795
Komzet, 12:285
labor movement, 5:96–97
Lebanon War, 12:581–582
Lenin, Vladimir Ilyich, 12:639–640
Lithuania, 13:124–125
military service
Dragunski, David Abramovich, 6:7
Jewish participation in, 14:242, 242t
Mekhlis, Lev Zakharovich, 13:797
minority rights, 14:290–291
motion pictures, 14:577
newspapers, 16:500–501
New York City, modern Russian Jewish immigrants to, 15:229–231
numerus clausus in, 15:340–341
ORT, 15:488–489
parody, Hebrew, 15:661
partisans, 15:666–667
politics, 12:775, 16:348
population, 16:399, 17:545t
post-WW II
demography, 12:523, 17:555t, 571–572

population statistics, 17:555t, 571–572
Red Army
    Jewish officers, 5:682, 11:8–9
    pogroms, 16:281
Refuseniks, 11:299
Russian literature, 12:774–775, 17:589–591
Soviet Jewry, 4:492, 493, 20:270
space program, 1:430
Stalin, Joseph, 19:157–158
Trotsky, Leon, 20:156–157
Uzbekistan, 4:261–262
WW II
    army, 17:550
    Bereza, 3:413
    Dragunski, David Abramovich, 6:7
    Einsatzgruppen massacres, 9:334–336
    German retreat, 9:342
    Ribbentrop-Molotov Pact, 9:331
    underground organizations, 3:435
    war crimes trials, 20:644
Yevreyski Komissariat, 21:325–326
Yevsektsiya, 5:95, 8:757, 21:326–327
Yiddish language, 17:543–544
Yiddish publishing, 17:543
Zinoviev, Grigori, 21:537–538
Union of the Communities, 17:389–390
Union of the Russian People, 20:**255–256**
Union of Zionists-Revisionists. See Revisionists movement
The Union Prayer Book for Jewish Worship, 4:545, 13:137–138, 16:465–466, 17:171
Unions. See *specific organizations*
Unión Sionista de Cuba, 5:322
United Arab Republic. See Egypt
United Auto Workers, 12:411
United Cloth, Hat, Cap and Millinery Workers Union, 18:151
United Council of Working Women, 18:422
United Federation of Teachers, 18:396
United Garment Workers of America, 12:411, 18:144
United Hebrew Congregation (UHC), 5:317
United Hebrew Trades, 6:743, 12:411
United Israel Appeal (UIA), 20:257
United Israel World Union, 16:593
United Jewish Appeal (UJA), 16:41–42, 20:256, 257–258
    education, 6:209

Montor, Henry, 14:461
New Israel Fund, 15:138–139
organizational structure, 7:136–137
United Jewish Charities of Cincinnati, 18:289
United Jewish Choral Societies of America and Canada, 4:663
United Jewish Communities, 20:**256–258**
United Jewish People's Order (UJPO), 4:406
United Jewish Social Agencies, 18:289
United Jewish Socialist Workers' Party, 18:576, 20:**258–259**
United Kingdom, 12:548
    Abdullah ibn Hussein, 1:243–244
    advertising, 1:428
    antisemitism, 2:233, 237
        Aden, 1:388, 389
        Aliens Act of 1905, 1:659
        Samuel Commission, 17:775
    architecture and architects, 5:481, 12:494
    arts and artists, 12:479, 545
    Barbados, 4:473
    Birmingham, 3:713–714
    Board of Deputies of British Jews, 4:20
    Bradford, 4:116
    Brighton, 4:181
    Bristol, 4:185
    Canada, 4:394, 406
    Cyprus, administration of, 5:349
    divorce statistics, 5:720
    Don Pacifico affair, 15:564
    education, Jewish, 6:204–207, 12:458
    emancipation, 6:377
    foreign policy and relations with Israel (state), 12:546
        borders guarantees, 10:217
        Sinai Campaign, 10:220
        Six-Day War, 10:230
    gems industry, Paiva, Jacques, 15:571
    Guianas, 4:470–471
    Hebrew publishing, 16:722–723
    Holocaust
        Channel Islands, 4:566
        refugees, 9:368–369
    Iraq
        Mandate period, 10:17–18
        occupation, 10:17–18
    Irgun attacks against, 10:27–28
    Jamaica, 4:473–474
    Jewish artists, 2:504, 506, 507

Jewish Historical Society of England, 11:292
Jewish Legion, 11:304, 306
Jewish participation in military service, 14:240–241
Jews' Temporary Shelter, 11:333
journalism in, 11:467, 12:457, 546–547, 707, 764–765
Kochi (India), 12:248–249
liberalism, 12:776–777
libraries, 12:787
Libya occupation, 12:792
Mandate period
    Iraq, 10:17–18
    White Paper policy, 3:345–346
migrations, 1:659
Neo-Nazism, 15:81–82
Nevis, 4:474
Nili, 15:267–268
Northampton, 15:301
Norwich, 15:312
Nottingham, 15:**316**
Orthodox Judaism, 1:328, 405, 15:495
Oxford, 15:552–554, *553*
philosophy, 12:440
politicians
    Barnett, Joel, Baron, 3:169
    Chamberlain, Joseph, 4:564
    Churchill, Winston, 4:722–723
    Edelman, Maurice, 6:142–143
    Eden, Anthony, 6:145
    Hore-Belisha, Leslie, Lord, 9:524
    Howard, Michael, 9:572
    Laski, Neville Jonas, 12:498–499
    Lever, Harold, Baron Lever of Manchester, 12:680
    Lever, Leslie, Baron Lever, 12:680
    Segal, Samuel, 18:248
    Selden, John, 18:258
publishing, 16:718–719
Scotland, 3:636, 18:**207–208**
scouting, 18:209
sheḥitah protection, 18:435
socialism, 12:499, 18:704, 706
St. Eustatius, 4:472
textiles, 19:664
Wales, 20:606–607
youth movements, 9:717t, 718
Zionism
    Aaronsohn family, 1:221–223
    Brodetsky, Selig, 4:196

United Kingdom, *continued*
    Cowen, Joseph, 5:255
    See also England; Mandate for
        Palestine
United Nations, 20:**259–274**
    antisemitism, 20:268–269
    Arab refugees and, 10:267, 268–
        271, 20:262–264
    Bloom, Sol, 3:782
    B'nai B'rith, 4:16
    Cassin, René Samuel, 4:509
    Department of Social Affairs,
        11:720
    Economic Commission (Europe),
        11:723
    foreign policy and relations with
        Israel, 10:239, 254–255, 258,
        266
        anti-Israel campaign, 20:273–
            274
        holy places in Israel and,
            9:503
        internationalization of
            Jerusalem, 10:214–215
        Israel admitted, 10:214
        Israel-Arab negotiations,
            2:475–476, 20:262–267
        Israel War of Independence,
            20:260–265
    International Council of Jewish
        Women, 9:812
    Jerusalem and, 10:255, 11:177,
        178, 20:261–262
    Jewish communities in Arab lands,
        20:269–270
    partition plans, 11:177
        Mandate for Palestine, 10:207
        Partition Resolution of 1947,
            20:259–260
    Resolution 181, 15:588, 594
    Resolution 242, 11:235, 15:594
    Sinai Campaign, 10:220, 20:265–
        266
    Six-Day War, 10:229–232, 20:267–
        268
    Soviet Jewry, 20:270
    Special Committee on Palestine,
        15:585, *587*, 588
    specialized agencies, 20:271–273
    Statement on Race (UNESCO
        report), 14:453
    UNESCO, 14:453, 20:272
    UNRRA, 20:417
    UNSCOP, 20:417
    Waldheim Affair, 20:602–604
    War Crimes Commission, 20:635
    See also League of Nations
United Palestine Appeal, 14:461

United Restitution Organization
    (URO), 20:**274–275**
United Soviet Socialist Republic. *See*
    Union of Soviet Socialist Republics
    (USSR)
United States, 9:275*t*, 20:**302–404**, *323,*
    361
    1980 to 2000, 20:359–362
        Conservative Judaism,
            20:365–366
        economic history, 6:136–137
        education and culture, 20:369
        Ginzburg appointment,
            20:374–375
        homosexuality, 20:368
        identity, changes in, 20:362–
            365
        intermarriage, 20:363–364
        Judaism, 6:265
        Orthodox Judaism, 20:366
        philanthropy, 20:368–369
        politics, 20:373
        Reconstuctionist Judaism,
            20:366
        Reform Judaism, 20:365
        religion, 20:365–367
        women's roles, 20:367–368
        Zionism and Israel, 20:382–
            386
    antisemitism, 2:44, 46, 223, 229–
        233, 237, 238, 20:387–394
        1900 to WW II, 20:388–390
        1920s-1930s, 6:697
        contemporary period,
            20:390–394
        dance, 5:414
        efforts to combat, 15:716
        eighteenth, nineteenth
            centuries, 20:387–388
    Civil War, 2:44–45, 465
        antisemitism, 8:34–35
        Louisiana, 13:223–224
        Saint Louis (MO), 17:671
    Cold War era, 20:342–359
        1960s, 20:352–353
        1970s, 20:353–354
        anti-communist red scare,
            20:343
        Conservative Judaism, 20:350
        education and culture,
            20:350–351
        feminism, 20:347–348
        Nazi war criminals, 20:357–
            358
        Orthodox Judaism, 20:349,
            350
        politics, 20:354–355
        population, demography,
            20:343–345

        Reform Judaism, 20:348,
            349–350
        religion, 20:348–349
        reverse discrimination,
            20:355–356
        social, cultural life, 20:345–
            347
        Soviet and Ethiopian Jewry,
            20:358–359
        Zionism and Israel, 20:356–
            357
    colonial era, 20:303–309
        communalism, 20:308–309
        English colonies, 20:305–309
        Jewish life, 20:305–306
        New Amsterdam, 20:304–305
    cultural and social life
        acculturation of Jewish
            immigrants, 2:608–611
        age and the aged, 1:448
        architects and architecture,
            2:400–401
        archives, 2:409–413
        art and artists, 2:513–516
        artisans, 5:269–271
        assimilation, 2:608–611,
            6:695–696, 698–700
        bar mitzvah, 3:166
        Beta Israel immigration to
            Israel, 3:507
        black Jews in, 11:520, 521
        calligraphy, Hebrew, 4:371–
            372
        cemeteries, 4:539
        charitable organizations,
            4:573–574
        choral singing, 4:661, 662–
            663
        community organization and
            structures, 5:112–113, 115*t,*
            116*t,* 119*t,* 9:236, 13:196–
            197
        cookbooks, 5:201
        cooperatives, 5:206–207
        dance, 5:412, 414, 12:492, 770
        divorce statistics, 5:720–721
        embalming, 6:390
        families, 6:**695–707**, 702–706
        Freemasons, 7:228
        "Great Society" programs,
            11:385
        hakhsharah farms, 8:760–761
        hospitals, 9:563–565
        humor and, 9:594–595
        Iranian Jews in, 10:13
        Jewish alcohol consumption,
            6:27–28
        journalism, 11:466, 468–469,
            16:503–505

Karaites and Karitism, 11:795

libraries, 12:784–785, 787–788

medicine, 12:596, 758, 13:734–735, 15:708–720

museums, 14:631–634

music, 14:687, *688*

orphans and orphanages, 15:485, 487

parody, Hebrew, 15:660–661

Southern Jewry, 6:571

television and radio, 19:594–595

theater, 19:674–675

United States Holocaust Memorial Museum, 20:275–277

welfare organizations, 13:210–211

demography, 5:563–564

early national period

abolition, 16:170, 20:316–317

Civil War, 20:316–317, 316–318

German Jewish period, 20:313–322, *319*

homesteaders, 4:375–376

post-Civil War, 20:318

Reform Judaism, 20:315–316

Revolutionary era, 20:309–313, *311*

social exclusion, 20:320–321

women's profile, 20:321–322

Eastern European Jewish period, 20:322–337

communal structure and education, 20:332

garment industry, 20:327–328

Great Depression, 20:336–337

greenhorn, native clash, 20:330–332

immigration waves, 20:322–324

Johnson-Reed Act of 1924, 20:335

labor movement, 20:328–329

social and cultural life, 20:324–325

theater and film industries, 20:335–336

women, 20:329–330

WW I and Zionism, 20:333

Yiddish literature, 20:324–326

Yiddish theater, films, 20:326

economic affairs, 6:670

agriculture, Jewish, 1:499–500

bankers, moneylenders, 3:117–119, 12:558, 613–614

boycott, anti-Nazi, 4:110–111, 111*t*

building and construction, 5:183–184, 12:602–603

cooperatives, 5:206–207

department stores, 5:588

fur trade, 7:313, 314

glassmaking, 7:632

history, 6:136–137

labor in, 12:411

labor unions, 12:411

loan guarantees to Israel, 4:304

oil industry development, 16:20

peddling, 13:665, 15:710–711

printing, publishing, 16:538

publishing, 16:719–721

space program, 11:66–67

tailoring, 19:437–438

textiles, 19:664

tobacco trade, 20:6

trade and commerce, 20:86–87

trade unionism, 9:117, 118, 16:420–421, 19:275

typographers, 12:663, 20:213

wine and liquor trade, 21:83–85

education, 6:189–204

colonial and national period, 6:189–190

Colorado, 5:68

congregational education 1960s and 1970s, 6:199

contributions to, 6:161

day schools, growth of, 6:198–199

Eastern Europe immigration 1881-1910, 6:192–195

Facing History and Ourselves Program, 9:451–452

German-Jewish immigration 1840-1880, 6:191–192

Hebrew College, 8:553–554

Holocaust, 9:422–423, 447–454

innovations in settings for, 6:199–201

institutional development 1910-1945, 6:195

institutions of higher learning, 6:196–197

Los Angeles (CA), 13:207–208

medical, 15:780

national organizations, 6:196–197

non-formal education, 6:195–196

post-WW II 1945-1975, 6:198

scholarly societies, 18:723

sunday schools, 6:190–191

twentieth century, 6:201–202, 12:469

foreign policy and affairs

American Judaism and Israel, 4:93

Bitburg Controversy, 3:727–728

Conference of Presidents of Major American Jewish Organizations, 5:141

German refugees, Evian Conference, 6:576

Iran hostage crisis, 15:571

Palestine Inquiry Commissions, 15:582, 584–585

Palestine Liberation Organization and, 10:241–242

Palestinian Authority and, 15:599–600

Saudi Arabia, 18:77

Soviet Union, 5:90

St. Louis, voyage of the, 19:229

Holocaust

documentation, resource centers, 9:424–425

education, 9:422–423, 447–454

Facing History and Ourselves Program, 9:451–452

films and cinema, 9:440–441, 442–444

impact on American Judaism of, 4:93

memorials, 3:409, 9:431

rescue efforts, 9:490–491

response to, 9:364–368, 402

United States Holocaust Memorial Museum, 20:275–277

War Refugee Board Holocaust rescue efforts, 9:490–491

Israel relations, 10:258–260, 262, 263, 266–267, 20:394–400

1950s, 20:395–397

1950s, Eisenhower Doctrine, 10:434

1970s-1980s, 10:259–260

armaments, 10:235

arms purchases, 10:470, 471

borders guarantees, 10:217

United States, *continued*

    Declaration of Independence, 5:529

    economic aid, 10:550, 578

    Eisenhower Doctrine, 10:221

    Israel (state), 10:258–260, 262, 263, 266–267

    Madrid Peace Conference, 10:243

    Oslo Accords, 10:245–246

    peace proposals, 10:235

    Pollard Affair, 16:357–359

    Reagan, Clinton years, 20:398–400

    Reagan, Ronald, 17:135–136

    strategic cooperation understanding, 10:239

    War of Independence, 20:394–395

  Jewish movements and organizations

    Am Olam, 2:87–88

    Galveston Plan for immigration, 7:363–364

    He-Ḥalutz, 8:760

    Hillel, 9:111–112, 19:267

    Industrial Removal movement, 9:779

    Jewish Legion, enlistment in, 11:304–306

    Jewish Volunteer Corps, 20:369–370

    Maccabi Youth Games, 20:372

    settlement house movement, 18:320

    student movements, 19:266–268

    United Jewish Communities, 20:256–257

    Young Israel movement, 4:284

    youth movements, Iḥud Habonim, 9:717t, 718

  laws and legal systems, 6:677, 12:555–557, 614

    alcoholism and drunkenness, 6:27–28

    crime and criminology, 5:291, 292, 303, 12:504

    Demanjuk case, 20:644–645

    discrimination and, 5:680

    emancipation, 6:376, 9:231

    Frayheyt trial, 19:175

    government investigations, 5:438–439

    Haggadot, 8:213

    intermarriage, 14:377–382

    Jerusalem and legal aspects of, 11:234

    Johnson-Reed Act of 1924, 20:335

    Naturalization Act of 1740, 20:305–306

    numerus clausus in, 15:343

    Office of Special Investigations, 15:**388**

    prostitution, 16:627–628

    rabbis, 17:17–18

    religious freedom, 11:102–103

    sheḥitah protection, 18:435

    Social Security program, 6:466–467

    Southern Jewry, 6:571

    WW II war crimes trials, 20:645

  migrations, 6:558–559

    family units, 6:696–698

    Jewish arrival, 20:304–305

    Jewish Colonization Association, 11:287

    Landsmannschaften, 12:477

  New Deal to Israel independence, 20:337–342

    communal organization and education, 20:338–339

    Nazism and antisemitism impact, 20:338

    parody, Hebrew, 15:661

    political activity, 20:337–338

    WW II and Zionism, 20:339–342

  political theories, parties and organizations

    Agudat Israel, 1:508

    anarchism, 18:710

    communism, 5:98

    Ha-Shomer ha-Ẓa'ir, 8:385

    Jewish Agency and, 11:259–260

    Jewish socialism in, 18:718–719, 721

    liberalism, 12:779–780

    Mizrachi, 14:392

    neo-Nazism, 15:78–80

    Po'alei Agudat Israel, 16:244

    Po'alei Zion, 16:245–246

    political participation, 16:338, 339

    Progressive Jewish Alliance, 16:544

    Republican Jewish Coalition, 17:225

    socialism, 7:619, 687–688, 9:118, 18:706, 708–709, 21:214–215

    Workmen's Circle, 21:**214–215**

    Zionism, 2:610, 12:419–420, 563–564, 21:605–615

  politicians

    ambassadors, 9:779

    Congresspersons, 9:497, 10:742, 12:614, 710, 713

    governors, 12:613, 796

    mayors, 12:437–438, 766

    senators, 6:739–740, 740, 11:97, 12:528–529, 707, 804–805

    vice presidents, 9:599–600

  population, 2:*42–45*, 5:562, 16:392–394, 395, 397t, 399, 20:*319*

  religious life and scholarship

    bar mitzvah, 3:166

    Borowitz, distinctively American theology of, 4:93

    Catholicism, 4:713–715

    conferences, 5:146–147

    Conservative Judaism, 5:171–175, 6:698

    gender equality in religion, 6:753

    Haggadot, 8:214

    Ḥaredim, 8:350

    Ḥasidism, 8:397

    Hasidism in, 15:495

    havurot, 8:471–472

    ḥazzanim, 8:504–505

    Hebraist movement, 15:792

    historiography, 9:161–163

    homiletic literature and, 9:515

    Jewish studies, 11:316–319, 13:665, 666

    Orientalists, 12:696

    Orthodox Judaism, 3:6, 6:141–142, 696, 698, 15:495

    Pittsburgh Platform, 16:190–191

    prayer, women's role in, 16:461

    proselytism, 16:593–594

    Protestant-Jewish relationship, 16:633

    Reform Judaism, 17:166–181

    responsa literature, 12:529, 17:236–237

    scholarly societies, 18:723

    Sephardim, 18:302–303

    sheḥitah protection, 18:435

    synagogues, 6:700–701, 19:357, 360–361, 379–381

    Washington Haggadah, 8:214

yeshivot, 21:321
Yiddish education, 6:188–189
Yom ha-Shoah, 9:495
twenty-first century
Black-Jewish relations,
20:377–378
Catholic-Jewish relations,
20:379
Christian-Jewish relations,
20:378–379
Crown Heights afair, 20:377–
378
Holocaust related matters,
20:379–380
Homeland Security, Iraq war,
20:376–377
Soviet Jewry immigration,
20:382
WW II
Army chaplains, 9:564–565
Jewish participation in
military service, 12:746,
756, 14:238–240
War Refugee Board, 20:665
See also Civil rights movement;
specific cities and states
United States Committee for Refugees,
17:7
United States Conference of Major
Jewish Organizations. *See*
Conference of Presidents of Major
American Jewish Organizations
United States Holocaust Memorial
Council, 12:656
United States Holocaust Memorial
Museum, 2:412–413, 9:389, 425–
426, 432–433, 451, 20:**275–277**
architecture, 7:224
Benjamin and Vladka Meed
Registry of Jewish Holocaust
Survivors, 2:49
Eizenstat, Stuart, 6:280
Summer Seminar Program on
Holocaust and Jewish
Resistance, 2:49
Tower of Faces, vol. 9: color insert
United States literature, 20:**277–301**
anthologies, 20:291–292
Bellow, Saul, 20:293–294
Bible and Hebrew culture
influence, 20:277–278
biblical influence, 3:672
Broner, Esther M., 4:204
Bukiet, Melvin Jules, 4:265
children's, 4:628, 629, 632–633,
20:372–373
Coleman, Edward Davidson, 5:57
contemporary, 20:284–301
criticism, 8:728
Dahlberg, Edward, 5:379

Fadiman, Clifton, 6:675
Daniel in, 5:418
De Casseres, Benjamin, 5:528
De Leon, Thomas Cooper, 5:538
Douglas, Kirk, 5:764–765
editors, Phillips, William, 16:58
Elkin, Stanley, 6:359
encyclopedias, 6:400, 401
graphic novels, 6:277–278
Hindus, Maurice Gerschon, 9:123
Hobson, Laura Z., 9:299
Holocaust inspired, 20:288
humor, 9:595–596, 20:289–290
Levenson, Sam, 12:680
Perelman, Sidney Joseph,
15:761
Rosten, Leo Calvin, 17:474
Hurst, Fanni, 9:630
Isaacs, Susan, 10:56
Jew, image of, 20:278–280
Jewish contribution, 20:280–281
Laurents, Arthur, 12:527–528
Lawson, John Howard, 12:547
Lengyel, Emil, 12:638
Lerner, Max, 12:658
Levin, Ira, 12:709
Levinger, Lee Joseph, 12:720
"little magazines," 16:58
Malamud, 20:294–295
Neugeboren, Jay, 15:119
novelists
Brinig, Myron, 4:184
Calisher, Hortense, 4:365
Chabon, Michael, 4:555
Cournos, John, 5:246
Davenport, Marcia, 5:443–
444
Doctorow, Edgar Lawrence,
5:728
Epstein, Leslie, 6:475
Harris, Mark, 8:363
Heller, Joseph, 8:795
Leviant, Curt, 12:696
Levin, Meyer, 12:711–712
Lewisohn, Ludwig, 12:768
Liebling, A. J., 12:809
Plain, Belva, 16:214
Shaw, Irwin, 18:424
Sheldon, Sidney, 18:445
Ozick, 20:295
playwrights
Heller, Joseph, 8:795
Horovitz, Israel, 9:528
Podhoretz, Norman, 16:251
poets
Brody, Alter, 4:200

Deutsch, Babette, 5:621
Dine, Jim, 5:669–670
Efros, Israel Isaac, 6:216
Ignatow, David, 9:715–716
Landau, Zishe, 12:466
Lazarus, Emma, 12:560–561
Lieberman, Elias, 12:804
Pinsky, Robert, 16:176
playwrights, 9:528, 20:283,
297–301
Rich, Adrienne, 17:285–286
Rukeyser, Muriel, 17:528
Schwartz, Delmore, 18:183
Shapiro, Karl Jay, 18:406–407
twentieth century, 6:724–725,
746
popular, 11:68–69
post-WW II, 20:281–284
Raisin, Max, 17:74–75
Rand, Ayn, 17:89–90
Robbins, Harold, 17:353
Rosen, Norma, 17:429–430
Rosenberg, James Naumburg,
17:437
Rosenfeld, Isaac, 17:445–446
Rosenfeld, Paul, 17:447
Roth, Henry, 17:481–482
Roth, Philip Milton, 17:484–485,
20:295–297
Schwarz, Leo Walder, 18:189–190
Segal, Erich, 18:245
Seid, Ruth, 18:253
Sklarew, Myra, 18:660–661
twentieth century, 5:443–444
United Synagogue, 6:196, 198, 415,
418, 420, 425, 427–428, 13:197,
18:764, 20:*404*, **404–405**
United Synagogue of Conservative
Judaism, 18:244, 20:**405–406**
United Zionists of America, 4:5
Unity (periodical). *See Eynikeyt*
(periodical)
Unity of God. *See* God
Unity of Labor-Workers of Zion. *See*
Aḥdut ha-Avodah-Po'alei Zion
The Unity of the Family (Ackerman),
1:357
Universal dogmas of faith, 2:532
Universal Film Manufacturing
Company. *See* Universal Studios
Universalism
in Bible, 11:514–515
Kook, Abraham Isaac, 12:292
Universal Jewish Encyclopedia, 6:400
Universal Studios, 12:436, 14:570
*De universa mulierum morborum
medicina* (de Castro), 4:518

Universe, cosmological models, 5:231–232

Univers Israélite (journal), 20:**406**

Universities, 12:550, 20:**406–411**
Brandeis University, 4:124–125
Brazil, 18:33
Enlightenment era, 20:408
Gratz College, 8:38–39
Hebrew University of Jerusalem, 8:740–744
Jewish quotas, 7:225
Jewish studies, 20:411
Laura and Alving Siegal College of Judaic Studies, 12:526
Middle Ages, 20:406–407
modern era, 20:408–409
seventeenth-eighteenth centuries, 20:407–408
U.S., 20:409–411
See also specific colleges and universities for additional page locations

Universities: American, English, German (Flexner), 7:78

University in Exile, New York City (U.S.), 15:219

University of California, Berkeley, 15:358

University of California, Los Angeles (UCLA), 11:776, 13:206

University of California, Santa Cruz, 18:27

University of Haifa, 8:**238**, 11:773

University of Judaism, 5:173, 12:803, 13:197, 206–207, 20:**411–413**

University of Pennsylvania Center for Judaic Studies, 6:25–26

Unjust enrichment, 14:360, 20:**413–416**

Unleavened bread. See Manna

Unleavened Bread, Feast of, 15:680–681

Unmeisterliche Wanderjahre (Améry), 2:65

Unna, Paul Gerson, 20:**416–417**

UNO. See United Nations

UNRRA, 20:**417**

UNSCOP, 20:**417**

Unser Verkehr (Sessa), 18:318

Der unsterbliche Mensch; Ein religioeses Gespraech (Doeblin), 5:729–730

Un tal Servando Gómez (Eichelbaum), 6:245

Unter a Ployt (Der Nister), 5:597

Unterberg, Israel, 15:205

Unter der Last (Esselin). See Under the Yoke (Esselin)

Unter Kuperne Himlen (Elberg). See Under Copper Skies (Elberg)

Unterman, Isser Yehuda, 20:**417**

Untermeyer, Jean Starr, 20:418

Untermeyer, Louis, 20:**418**

Untermyer, Samuel, 4:111, 20:**418**

Untersuchungen zur Redaction der Mishna (Albeck), 3:126, 14:326

Untier of Knots. See Mashreh Kitrin

Untitled (Rothko), vol. 2: color insert

Unug. See Erech

U.O.J.C.A. See Union of Orthodox Jewish Congregations of America

U.P.A. See United Palestine Appeal

Uplanim, 10:343

The Uplifting of the Torah (Menkes), 14:49

Upper Galilee (Israel). See Galilee (Israel)

Upper Silesia. See Silesia (region)

Upper West Side (NYC), 15:201, 223, 232–234

Ur (ancient city), 14:83–84, 20:**418–419**

Ur al-Ẓalam (Nethanel ben Isaiah), 15:93

Uranograph, 13:70

Urbach, Ephraim Elimelech, 1:462, 20:**419–420**

Urban II (pope), 16:372

Urban VI (pope), 4:63

Urban VIII (pope), 16:376

Urban Civilization in Pre-Crusade Europe (Agus), 1:521

Urbanization
Abbasid dynasty, 1:234
demography and, 5:565–568
ecology, and open spaces in, 6:95
economic doctrines and, 6:115
See also Cities

Urbino (Italy), 20:**420**

Urfa (Turkey). See Edessa (Turkey)

Urfali, communities of Jews, Israel (state), 10:298

Urhai (Mesopotamia). See Osroene

Uri, Pierre Emmanuel, 20:**420**

Uriah, 20:**420–421**

Uri ben Aaron ha-Levi, 20:**421**

Uri ben Phinehas of Strelisk. See Strelisk, Uri ben Phinehas of

Uri ben Simeon of Biala, 20:**421**

Uriel, 20:**421–422**

Uriel Shelah. See Ratosh, Yonathan

Uriel Weinreich Program, 21:362

Urijah. See Uriah

Urim (Israel), 20:**422**

Urim and Thummim, 5:703–704, 20:**422–423**

Urim ve-Tummim (Serero), 18:310

Uri Phoebus, printing industry in Amsterdam, 2:108

Uris, Leon, 8:465, 20:**423**

Uris family, 20:**423**

Das Urkundenwesen im Talmud (Beyer), 18:470

Urman, Dan, 20:**423–424**

Urmia. See Razaieh (Iran); Rizaieh

URO. See United Restitution Organization

Urschrift und Uebersetzungen der Bibel (Geiger), 7:413

Ursicinus, 11:387

Ursinus, 2:37

Urspruenge des israelitischen Rechts (Alt), 14:436–437

Uruguay, 20:**424–428**
education, Jewish, 6:212–213
Zionism, 21:595

Uruk (Mesopotamia). See Erech (Mesopotamia)

Uruk incantation text, Aramaic, 2:348

Ury, Else, 20:**428**

Ury, Lesser, 15:290, 20:**428–429**

U.S. Army and the Holocaust, 3:435, 20:**429–431**

Usage. See Minhag

The Uses of Philosophy (Edman), 6:150

Usha (Israel), 20:**431**

Usha, Synod of, 20:**431–432**

Ushpizin, 19:301, 20:**432**

’Usifiyyā (Israel), 20:**432–433**

Usov (Czech Republic), 20:**433**

Uspekhi petrografii v Rossii (Loewinson-Lessing), 13:171

Usque, Abraham, 3:636, 20:**433**

Usque, Samuel, 9:225, 11:429, 20:**433–434**

Usque, Solomon, 20:**434**

Ussishkin, Abraham Menaḥem Mendel, 4:88, 20:**434–436**
Dubrovno, 6:39
Ha-Ḥalutz (movement), 8:756
Odessa Committee, 15:382

Ussishkin, David, 20:**436**

USSR. See Union of Soviet Socialist Republics (USSR)

The USSR and Finland (Brody), 4:200

Ustaše, 15:698

Ustek (Czech Republic), 20:**436–437**

Usti nad Labem (Czech Republic), 20:**437**

Usury, 2:554, 3:112, 20:**437–443**
in Alsace, 2:6
antichresis, 2:193
Calvin, John, 4:376
heter iskah, 20:441–442

legal aspects, 11:264

linked loans, inflation, 20:441–442

pledges and, 16:234–235

Rabbinic period, 12:606, 20:440–441

Talmudic literature, 20:438–441

See Also Moneylending

Utah (U.S.), 3:105, 4:214, 20:*443*, **443–444**

Utena (Lithuania), 20:**444**

Utensils, cooking, 5:203

Utica (NY), 20:**444–445**

Utilidades del agua y de la nieve (Cardozo), 4:467

Utin, Nicolai, 18:707

Utitz, Emil, 20:**445**

Utkin, Joseph Pavlovich, 20:**445**

Utnapishtim, 7:82, 15:287

Utopianism

Bloch, Ernst, on, 3:760

Buber, Martin, 4:235

Utrecht Psalter, 3:675

Utsyany (Lithuania). *See* Utena (Lithuania)

Utyana (Lithuania). *See* Utena (Lithuania)

Uvarov, Sergey Semyonovich, 13:16, 20:**445–446**

U-Vikashtem mi-Sham (Soloveitchik), 18:779

Uviller, Harry, 20:**446**

Uxor Ebraica (Selden), 18:258

Uz (ancient Israel), 20:**446**

Uzal (ancient Israel), 20:**446–447**

Uzan, Aharon, 20:**447**

Uzan family, 20:**447**

Uzbekistan, 4:259–261, 20:**447–448**

Anusim, 4:259

Bukharan Jews in Israel, 10:297

costumes, 4:263–264

dance, 4:264

dowries, 4:264

Jewish man at synagogue entrance, vol. 5: color insert

Khorezm, 12:116–117

relations with, Israel (state), 4:263

Russia, 4:259–261

Soviet Union, 4:261–262

Uzedah, Samuel ben Isaac. *See* Uceda, Samuel ben Isaac

Uzhgorod (Ukraine), 20:**448**

Uziel, Abraham, 4:199

Uziel, Baruch, 20:**449**

Uziel, Isaac ben Abraham, 6:668, 20:**449–450**

Uziel, Judah, 20:**449**

Uziel family, 20:**449**

Uzza and Aza'el, 20:**450**

Uzzah, 1:258, 259, 20:**450**

Uzziah (King of Judah), 9:178–179, 20:**450–451**

Ahaz, 1:539

Ammonites, 2:85

Edom, 6:155

Jotham and, 11:465

V

V (letter), 20:*453*

Va'ad Arba Arazot. *See* Councils of the Lands

Vaad ha-Hatzalah, 3:411, 9:490–491, 20:**453–455**

Va'ad ha-Haẓẓalah. *See* Vaad ha-Hatzalah

Va'ad Ha'ir, 14:465

Va'ad ha-Kehillot (Argentina), 2:445, 6:211, 11:754

Va'ad Halakhah, 5:174–175

Va'ad ha-Lashon, 8:673, 678–679

Va'ad ha-Lashon ha-Ivrit. *See* Academy of the Hebrew Language

Va'ad ha-Pekidim ve-ha-Amarkalim, 20:**455**

Va'ad ha-Yam, 20:**449**

Va'ad Haẓẓalah, 18:585

Va'ad Le'ummi, 10:393, 654–656, 11:695, 20:**455–456**

Va'ad Medinat Lita, 2:422

Va'ad Pekidei Erez Israel be-Kushta, 20:**456–457**

Vabalathus, 15:**377**

Vac (Hungary), 20:**457**

Vadász, Lipót, 20:**457**

Vaderland (Herzberg), 9:52

Vad Rashkov (Moldova), 20:**457**

Vadum Jacob (Israel). *See* Gesher Benot Ya'akov (Israel)

Vaez, Abraham, 20:**457**

Vagenshtajn, Anjel, 4:277

Vágó, József, 20:**457**

Vágó, László, 20:**457**

Vágúhely. *See* Nove Mesto Nad Vahom

Vaida-Voevod, A., numerus clausus in Romania, 15:342

Vaillant, A., 6:444

Vajda, Georges, 11:324, 20:**457–458**

Vajs, Albert, 20:**458**

Vakhalaklakoys (Shalom Aleichem), 18:385, 386

Vakhnakht. *See* Sholem Zokhor

Vakhtangov, Yevgeni, 8:179

Vakhtnakht, 4:734

Valabrega, Cesare, 20:**458**

Valabrègue, Mardochée, Georges, 20:**458–459**

Valance of Torah Ark. *See* Parokhet and Kapporet

Valansi, Isaac ben David. *See* Balansi, Isaac ben David

Valea-Lui-Vlad (Bessarabia), 20:**459**

Valeanu, I. H. *See* Wechsler, Max

Văleanu, I. H.. *See* Wechsler, Max

Valenca family. *See* Valensi family

Valence (France), 20:**459**

Valencia (Spain), 11:94–95, 20:**459–462**

Valencia family. *See* Valensi family

Valenciano family. *See* Valensi family

Valensi, Alfred, 20:463

Valensi, Gabriel, 20:462

Valensi, Joseph, 20:462

Valensi, Samuel, 20:462

Valensi, Samuel ben Abraham, 20:462

Valensi family, 16:346, 20:**462–463**

Valenstein, Lawrence, 1:428

Valentin, Gabriel Gustav, 20:**463**

Valentin, Hugo Maurice, 20:**463**

Valentini, Pietro, 18:762

The Vale of Cedars (Aguilar), 1:509

Valerius Gratus, 2:128, 20:**463**

Valerius Maximus, 20:**463**

Valero, Ḥayyim Aaron, 20:463–464

Valero, Jacob, 20:463

Valero family, 20:**463–464**

Valladolid (Spain), 3:42, 20:**464–465**

Valladolid, Alfonso de. *See* Abner of Burgos

Vallat, Xavier, 20:**465**

Valle, Moses David ben Samuel, 20:**465**

Valley of Hinnom (Israel). *See* Gehinnom (Israel)

The Valley of Vision (Jagel). *See* Gei Ḥizzayon

Valmaseda (Spain), 20:**465–466**

Valona (Albania), 20:**466**

Valréas (France), 20:**466**

Values of a Jewish and democratic state, 20:**466–469**

Valvrojenski, Bernard. *See* Berenson, Bernard

Valyi, Peter, 20:**469–470**

Vambery, Arminius, 6:46, 9:62, 20:**470**

Van Buren, Abigail. *See* Friedman, Pauline Esther

Van Buren, Paul, 4:684, 687

Vance, Zebulon Baird, 20:**470**

Vancouver (Canada), 4:187, 188, 20:**470–472**

Van Dam, Hendrik George, 20:**472–473**

Van Der Driesche, J. C. *See* Drusius, Johann Clemens

Van Der Driesche, Johann Clemens. *See* Drusius, Johann Clemens

Van der Hoeden, Jacob, 20:**473**

Van Diemen's Land. *See* Australia

Vándor, Lajos, 20:**473**

A vándor katona (Emöd). *See The Wandering Soldier* (Emöd)

Van Dyck, Anthony, 14:542

Vane, John R. *See* Vane, Sir John R.

Vane, Sir John R., 13:10, 20:**473**

Van Erpe, Thomas. *See* Erpenius, Thomas

Van Geldern family. *See* Geldern, Van, family

Van Gogh, Vincent, 4:139

Van Heusen, Jimmy, 4:338

Van Hoddis, Jakob, 20:**473**

Vanik, Charles, 2:51

"Vanishing American Jew" (article), 14:377

Van Leer, Lia, 20:**473–474**

Van Leeuwen, C., 3:658

Van Leeuwen, Denys. *See* Dionysius van Ryckel

Van Limborch, Philipp, disputations and polemics, 5:695

Van Nierop family. *See* Nierop, Van, family

Van Oven, Abraham, 20:**474**

Van Oven, Joshua, 20:**474**

Van Oven family, 20:**474**

Van Paassen, Pierre, 20:**474**

Van Praagh, William, 20:**474**

Van Raalte, Eduard Ellis, 12:553, 16:345, 20:**474–475**

Di Vant (Segalowitch), 18:249

Vanunu, Mordecai, 9:44

Vanunu affair, 20:**475**

Van Vriesland, Siegfried Adolf, 20:**475**

Van Vriesland, Victor Emanuel, 6:70, 20:**475**

Várad (Romania). *See* Oradea

Varaždin (Croatia), 20:**475–476**

Vardi, Arie, 20:**476**

Vardi, Moshe, 20:**476**

Varga, Yevgeni Samoilovich, 20:**476–477**

Die Varheit (Adler), 1:393

Varia (Seeligmann), 18:239

Variations (Seter), 18:319

Variations sur le destin (Loewenson), 13:167

Variety (periodical), 18:588

Varley, Frederick, 15:252

Varlin, 20:**477**

Varmus, Harold Eliot, 20:**477**

Varmus, Harold Elliot, 13:9

Varna (Bulgaria), 20:**477**

Várnai, Zseni, 20:**477**

Varnhagen, Rahel Levin, 20:**477–478**

Varonca, Ilarie, 15:609

Varro, Marcus Terentius, 20:**478**

Varshavski, Abraham, 20:**478**

Varshavski, Y. *See* Singer, Isaac Bashevis

Varshavsky, Oser. *See* Warszawski, Oser

Varssano, Mario. *See* Arbell, Mordecai

Vas, István, 20:**478**

Vašek, Anton, 20:**478**

Vashti, 18:215, 333, 20:**478–479**

Vasilkov (Ukraine), 20:**479**

Vaslui (Romania), 20:**479**

Vatican, 20:**479–486**
   foreign policy and relations with, Israel (state), 10:266
   foreign policy and relations with Israel, 10:265, 20:**482–486**
   Zionism and, 20:**479–481**
   See also Catholic Church; Popes

Vatican Council I, 4:717–718

Vatican Council II, 4:714–715, 718, 11:380, 384, 15:695

Vatican councils, 4:687–690, 717–718

Vatke, Wilhelm, 3:649, 20:**486**

Vatra Dornei (Romania), 20:**486**

Vaudeville theater, 17:126
   See also Theater

Vaughan, Frankie, 20:**486–487**

Vaurien (D'Israeli), 5:702

Vauvert (France). *See* Posquières (France)

Vaux, Roland de, 20:**487**

Vav, 20:**487**

Va-Yakhel Moshe (Alfalas), 1:636

Va-Yedabber Rabbah. See Numbers Rabbah

Va-Yehi ha-Yom (Bialik). *See And It Came to Pass* (Bialik)

Va-Yiggash Yehudah (Ḥanneles, 8:326

Vayol, Hans, 4:222

Va-Yomer Shemu'el (Elbaz), 6:290

Dos Vayse Hoyz (Shtern), 4:426

Vazov, Ivan, 4:276

Vázsonyi, Vilmos, 12:552, 20:**487**

V dremuchikh lesakh (Byadulya-Yasakar), 4:323

Vecchietti, Giambattista
   Akbar the Great, 1:555
   Judeo-Persian manuscripts collected by, 11:558

Vecinho, Joseph, 20:**487–488**

Veeck, Bill, 15:688

Vega, Joseph Penso del la. *See* Penso del la Vega, Joseph

Vega, Lope de, 11:256

Vegetables, 20:**488–489**
   cabbage, 4:329
   leek, 12:600
   legumes, 12:610–611
   lettuce, 12:675

Vegetarianism, 5:165–166, 13:711

Vegn a Yidishn Akademishn Institut (Shtif), 18:527

Ve-Hu Aḥer (Ballas), 3:92

Veigelsberg, Hugó. *See* Ignotus, Hugó

Veigelsberg, Leo, 20:**489**

Veil, 20:**489**

Veil, Charles-Marie de, 4:99

Veil, Lewis Compiègne de, 4:99, 20:**489**

Veil, Simone, 2:28, 16:343, 18:615, 20:**489–490**

The Veiled Room (Singer), 18:640

Veinberg, Moissey Samuilovich, 20:**490**

Veiner, Harry, 20:**490**

Veinger, Mordecai, 20:**490–491**

Veinstein, Nathan. *See* Tertulian, Nicolae

Veit, Moritz, 16:344, 20:**491**

Veit, Phillipp, 2:502, 504, 20:**491**

Veit, Simon, 20:**491**

Veit family, 20:**491**

Veith, Johann Emanuel, 20:**491–492**

Veksler, Vladimir, 20:**492**

Velhartice (Germany), 3:778

Velizh (Russia), 3:779, 14:483, 20:**492–493**

Veltmann, Henrique, 11:469

Veltwyck, Gerard, 20:**493**

Velvel (Rabbi). *See* Soloveichik, Isaac Ze'ev Ha-Levi

"Velvele Khersoner". *See* Shestapol, Wolf

Velvel Zbarazher. *See* Ehrenkranz, Benjamin Zeeb

Velvet Revolution of 1989, 13:248

The Velvet Underground, 17:162

Velvl Zbarzher. *See* Ehrenkranz, ben jamin Zeeb

Velyun (Poland). *See* Wielun (Poland)

Vendrell, Francisca, 14:251

Vendrovsky, Zalman. *See* Wendroff, Zalman

Venetianer, Lajos, 20:**493**

The Venetian Painters of the Renaissance (Berenson), 3:411

Venetus, F. G. *See* Giorgio, Francesco

Veneziani, Emmanuel Felix, 20:**493**
Venezky, Julian, 4:58
Venezuela, 20:**493–498**, *494*
    antisemitism, 20:497–498
    Brenner, Pynchas, 4:158
    Caribbean, Spanish-Portuguese
        Nation of the: La Nacion,
        4:474–475
    Chocrón, Isaac, 4:657
    colonial period, 20:494–495
    contemporary period, 20:497–498
    early independence, 20:495–496
    immigration, communal
        organization, 20:496
    Israel relations, 20:498
    Zionism, 21:595
    See also New Granada
Vengeance, 20:**498–499**
Vengeroff, Semyon. *See* Wengeroff,
    Semyon Afanasyevich
Vengrove (Poland). *See* Wegrow
    (Poland)
Venice (Italy), 16:390, 532–533,
    20:**499–504**
    Haggadah, 8:214–215
    Hebrew printing, 20:502–503
    Holocaust period, 20:503–504
    Lattes. Abraham ben Isaac, 12:518
    medieval, 20:*499*, 499–500
    Modena, Leon, 14:408–409
    Parenzo family, 15:641
    printing, publishing, 16:536
Ven Ikh Bin Roytshild (Shalom
    Aleichem), 18:383
Venosa (Italy), 4:522, 20:**504**
Ventianer, Lajos, 20:**493**
Ventidius, Publius, 20:**504–505**
Ventspils (Latvia), 20:**505**
Ventura, Michon, 20:**505**
Ventura, Moïse, 20:**505**
Ventura, Rubino, 20:**505**
Venture, Mardochée, French Bible
    translation by, 3:629
Veprik, Alexander Moiseyevitch,
    20:**505–506**
Vera y Alarcon, Lope de, 20:**506**
Verbal. *See* entries at Oral
Verband der Deutschen Juden, 20:**506**
Verband der Vereine Fuer Juedische
    Geschichte und Literatur, 20:**506**
Verband Nationaldeutscher Juden,
    20:**507**
Verbitsky, Bernardo, 11:469, 20:**507**
Verbitsky, Horacio, 11:469
Verblovski, Gregori, 12:553
Der Verbrecher und seine Richter
    (Alexander), 1:622

Verbs, Hebrew. *See under* Hebrew
    grammar
Vercelli (Italy), 20:**507–508**
Vercors, 20:**508**
Verdun (France), 20:**508**
Verdun-sur-Garonne (France), 20:**508**
Verea, Adrian, 20:**508**
Verein Fuer Kultur und Wissenschaft
    des Judentums, 14:522, 20:**509**
Vereinigung Fuer das Liberale
    Judentum in Deutschland, 20:**509**
Verein zur Abwehr des
    Antisemitismus, 20:**509–510**
Verga, Solomon. *See* Ibn Verga,
    Solomon
Vergelis, Aaron, 14:519, 20:**510**
La vergine a 18 carati (Pitigrilli),
    16:188
Veria. *See* Veroia
Veria (Greece). *See* Veroia (Greece)
Veritas, 1:247
La Verité (newspaper), 4:396
Verkhneudinsk (Russia), 20:**510**
Verkuyl, Gerritt, *Modern Language
    Bible (MLB)* and, 3:616
Vermes, Geza, 20:**510–511**
Vermont (U.S.), 20:**511**, *511*
Vernichtungslager. *See* Camps,
    concentration and extermination
Vernon, Florida (motion picture),
    14:510
Veroia (Greece), 20:**511–513**
Verona (Italy), 16:391, 20:**513–514**
Verratenes Volk (Doeblin), 5:729–730
Versailles Peace Conference
    Jewish delegation, 3:173
    Minority Rights, 14:288–291
*Versions of Survival: The Holocaust and
    the Human Spirit* (Langer), 9:352
The Vertical Mosaic (Porter), 4:413
Vertov, Dziga, 20:**514**
Verus. *See* Marcus, Aaron
Verwandlungen (Silbermann), 18:577
Die Verzauberung (Broch), 4:191
Verzhboloro. *See* Virbalis (Lithuania)
*Der Verzweiflungskampf der arischen
    Voelker mit dem Judentum*
    (Ahlwardt), 1:547
Veselovsky, Aleksandr, 6:246
Vesoul (France), 20:**514**
Vespasian, Titus Flavius, 9:200, 20:**514**
    Agrippa II, 1:503
    Fiscus Judaicus, 7:57
    Jaffa and, 11:61
    Josephus' prophecy regarding,
        11:435–436
    Josippon on, 11:462

    Justus of Tiberias and, 11:581–582
Vessels, breaking of, 11:644–646
Vessillo Israelitico (journal), 18:317,
    20:**514–515**
Vestnik evreskogo universiteta v Moskve
    (periodical). *See Bulletin of the
    Jewish University of Moscow
    (periodical)*
Vestnik sovetso-evreiskoi kul'tury
    (newspaper), 14:520
Vészi, Endre, 20:**515**
Vészi, Jozsef, 20:**515**
Veszprem (Hungary), 20:**515**
La Veuve de Sarepta (de Genlis), 6:336
Veysberg, Julia. *See* Weissberg, Julia
    Lazarevna
Ve-Zivvah ha-Kohen (Aaron Samuel
    ben Naphtali Herz ha-Kohen),
    1:220
Ve-Zot li-Yhudah (Poki), 16:284–285
Viacom-CBS, 11:812, 14:469
Via de Salvación (Acosta), 1:359
Viaţa lui Cilibi Moïse Vestitul (Cilibi
    Moïse), 4:726
Vibert of Nogent, 20:**515**
Vicenza (Italy), 20:**515**
Vices eius nos (papal bull), 18:313
Vich (Spain), 20:**515–516**
Vichniac, Jacques. *See* Givet, Jacques
Vicky. *See* Weisz, Victor
Vicol, Adrian, 20:**516**
The Victim (Bellow), 3:300, 301
Victor Emanuel III, 9:65
Victoria (Canada), 4:186
    Franklin, Lumley, 7:216
Victorine School, modern biblical
    criticism, as precursor of, 3:648
Victor Porchetto Salvatici. *See*
    Porchetus Salvagus
Victory (Kabak). *See NizzahonI*
Victory at Entebbe, 6:21
Victory dance, 5:409
Vidal, Crescas, 20:**516**
Vidal, Salomon, 4:299
Vidal, Solomon, 4:299
Vidal Bellsom. *See* Moses ben Joshua
    of Narbonne
Vidal ben Benvenist ibn Lavi de la
    Cavalleria., 4:53, 54
Vidal ben Solomon ben Israel Jacob
    Saferty, 18:55
Vidal et les siens (Morin), 14:492
Vidal-Naquet, Pierre, 20:**516–517**
Vidal Yom Tov of Tolosa, 20:**517**
Vidas, Elijah ben Moses de, 20:**517–
518**
En Vidas de Gerona. *See* De Piera,
    Meshullam ben Solomon

Viddui. *See* Confession of sins

Videla, Gabriel González, 4:643

Vidin (Bulgaria), 20:**518**

Vidvilt, 20:**518**

Vieira, Antonio, 20:**518**

El Viejo. *See* Juan de Espagña

Viejos. *See* Adelantados

La Vie mode d'emploi (Perec), 15:758

Vienna (Austria), 20:**518–523**

  archives, 2:408

  expulsion of Jews from, 15:450

  Hebrew printing, 20:523

  Holocaust, 6:244, 20:521–522

  Kadimah, 11:699

  Middle Ages, 20:518–520

  Oesterreichische
    Nationalbibliothek, 15:384

  seventeenth-nineteenth centuries,
    20:519–520

  taxation, 7:172

  Wiener Gesera, 21:**50**

  Zionist Socialism in, 18:718

Vienna, Congress of. *See* Congress of
  Vienna

Vienna Circle. *See* Logical positivism

Vienna Genesis, 1:463, 3:674, 9:726

Vienne (France), 20:**524**

Viertel, Berthold, 20:**524–525**

*Vierteljahrsschrift fuer
Musikwissenschaft* (publication),
1:397

Vies imaginaires (Schwob), 18:197

Vietnam War, 1:327, 6:362

Vigée, Claude, 20:**525**

Vigenère, Blaise de, 20:**525**

Vigny, Alfred de, 14:540

Vigoda, Samuel, 20:**525–526**

Vigvammim Shotekim (Efros), 8:736

Vihar, Bella, 20:**526**

Vijnita (Ukraine). *See* Vizhnitsa
  (Ukraine)

Vikku'ah Mayim Hayyim (Hayyim ben
  Bezalel), 8:480

Vikku'ah Mayim Hayyim (Isserles),
  10:771

Vikku'ah Yosef ve-ha-Shevatim (Enoch
  ben Abraham), 6:445

Vikkuha Rabbah (Bachrach), 3:39

Vilenkin, N.M. *See* Minski, Nikolai
  Maximovich

Vilensky, Zevi. *See* Vilnay, Zev

Vilkaviškis (Lithuania), 20:**526–527**

Vilkomir (Lithuania). *See* Ukmerge
  (Lithuania)

Villadiego (Spain), 20:**527**

Villafranca del Panadés (Spain),
  20:**527**

Villaraigosa, Antonio, 13:198

Villa Real (Portugal), 20:**526**

Villa Real (Spain). *See* Ciudad Real
  (Spain)

Villareal, Isaac, 20:527

Villareal, José da Costa, 20:527

Villareal family, 20:**527–528**

Villaroel, Isaac. *See* Villareal, Isaac

Villa triste (Modiano). *See* Sad Villa
  (Modiano)

Villefranche-de-Conflent (France),
  20:**528**

Villimpenta, Marquis of. *See* Fano,
  Joseph da

Villingen (Germany), 20:**528**

Vilna (Lithuania), 14:630, 20:**528–534**

  early settlement, 20:528–529

  Elijah ben Solomon Zalman,
    6:341–343

  ghetto, 7:576

  ghetto uprising, 21:125

  halukkah, 8:287

  Hebrew printing, 20:530–531

  Holocaust period, 20:532–533

  Karaism, 11:794

  partisans, 15:666, 667

  scholarship, communal affairs,
    20:529–530

  writings by Karpinovitsh, 11:816

  yeshivot, 11:747

Vilna Gaon. *See* Elijah ben Solomon
  Zalman

Vilna Troupe, 20:**534**

Vilnay, Zev, 20:**534**

Vilnius (Lithuania). *See* Vilna
  (Lithuania)

Vilsker, Leyb, 11:323

Vinaver, Chemjo, 20:**534**

Vinawer, Maxim, 12:554, 16:348,
  20:**534–535**

  Society for the Attainment of Full
    Civil Rights for the Jewish
    People in Russia, 18:724

Vincent, A., Joshua, Book of, 11:447

Vincent, Louis Hugues, 20:**535**

Vinchevsky, Morris, 4:108, 18:718,
  20:**535**

Vincze, Paul, 20:**535–536**

Vindava (Latvia). *See* Ventspils
  (Latvia)

Vineam sorce, 15:259

Vineam soreth, 4:277

Vineland (NJ), 20:**537**

Viner, Jacob, 20:**537–538**

Viner, Meir. *See* Wiener, Meir

Di Viner Karete (Altman), 2:21

Vines, 20:**536–537**

Vine wood parable, 6:638

Vinitski, M. *See* Medem, Vladimir

Vinkovci (Croatia), 20:**538**

Vinnikov, Isaac N., 11:321, 20:**538**

Vinnitsa (Ukraine), 9:475, 20:**538**

Vinogradov, Konstantin. *See* Sobol,
  Andrey Mikhailovich

Dos Vintshfingerl (Abramovitsh), 1:321

La violence du monde (Morin), 14:492

Vipers. *See* Snakes

Virbalis (Lithuania), 20:**538–539**

Virgil, 20:**539**

Virgily, P. *See* Kahan, Baruch
  Mordecai

Virginia (U.S.), 15:300–301, 20:*541,*
  541–542

Virginia Bill for Establishing Religious
  Freedom of 1785, 2:42

Virgin Islands, 4:474, 20:**542–543**

Virginity, 15:255, 20:**539–541**

Virgins. *See* Virginity

Virinea (Slonimsky), 18:680

Virology. *See* Medicine

Viseul-de-Sus (Romania), 20:**543**

Vishegrod (Poland). *See* Wyszogrod
  (Poland)

Vishnevets (Ukraine), 20:**543**

Vishniac, Roman, 16:126, 128, 131,
  20:**543**

Vishniak, Mark, 16:348

Vishniets (Ukraine). *See* Vishnevets
  (Ukraine)

Vishnits (Ukraine). *See* Vizhnitsa
  (Ukraine)

Visigoths, 1:575, 4:716

*Vision deleytable y sumario de todas las
sciencias* (Caceres), 4:330, 331

A Vision of Love Revealed in Sleep
(Solomon), 18:767

Vision of Seventy Shepherds, 18:324

Visions, 20:**543–545**

  Daniel, 5:421, 423–424, 426

  in literature, 11:71

  prophets, 16:573–574

  Rabbah bar bar Hana, 17:8

Visions of Jewish Education (report),
6:203

Visitações, 3:64

*A Visit to Freeland, or the New
Paradise Regained. See Eine Reise
nach Freiland*

A Visit to the Valley of Sheuli (Elias),
6:319

Visser, Lodewijk Ernst, 12:553,
  20:**545–546**

Visual trespass, nuisance law and,
15:329

*Vita Adae et Evae. See Book of the Life
of Adam and Eve*

La Vita è bella (Benigni), 9:445–446, 10:813

La Vita e le opere del Manzoni (Momigliano), 14:431

Vita ipsa (Altenberg), 2:17

Vital, David ben Solomon, 20:**546**

Vital, Ḥayyim ben Joseph, 1:254, 2:10, 20:**546–549**
  Abraham ben Eliezer ha-Levi Berukhim, 1:299
  Abulafia, Jacob ben Solomon, 1:341
  angels, 2:158
  disciple of Isaac Luria, 13:262–265
  Jonah, Moses, 11:392
  Joseph della Raina legend, 11:428
  Joseph Ibn Ṭabūl, 11:430
  Joshua ben Nun, 11:456
  Sefer ha-Ḥezyonot, 7:15

Vital, Joseph, 20:546

Vital, Moses ben Joseph, 20:546

Vital, Samuel ben Ḥayyim, 2:130, 13:264, 20:**549–550**

Vitale, Benjamin. *See* Benjamin ben Eliezer ha-Kohen Vitale of Reggio

Vitale family, 1:617–618

Vital family, 20:**546**

Vitali, Isaiah. *See* Eisenstadt, Isaiah

Vital statistics, 20:**550–559**
  21st century, 20:558–559
  births, 20:556–557
  increase, natural, 20:557–558
  marriage and divorce, 20:554–556, 554t, 555t, 558–559
  measurement, sources, 20:550–551
  mortality, 20:551, 551t–552t, 553t, 554t

Vitebsk (Belarus), 3:778, 20:**559–560**

Vitellius, 11:396

Viterbo (Italy), 20:**560**

Viterbo, Aegidius da. *See* Egidio da Viterbo

Viterbo, Carlo Alberto, 20:**560**

Viterbo, Jehiel Ḥayyim, 20:**560–561**

Vítězslav. *See* Kapper, Siegfried

Vitkin, Jacob. *See* Zerubavel, Jacob

Vitkin, Joseph, 20:**561**

Vitoria (Spain), 20:**561**

Vitoria, Francisco de, 20:**561**

Vitruvius, Pollo, 20:**561**

Vitry (France), 20:**562**

Vitry-en-Pertois (France). *See* Vitry (France)

Vitta, Cino, 12:552, 20:**562**

Vittorio Veneto (Italy), 20:**562**

Vivante, Cesare, 12:552, 20:**562–563**

Vivante, David Abraham, 20:**563**

Vivante, Vita, 16:345

Vivante Chartres, Annie, 20:**563**

Vivas, Solomon. *See* Solomon ben Judah of Lunel

Vives, Juan Luis, 20:**563–564**

Vives ben Joseph ibn Vives, 1:253

Vives family. *See* Abenvives family

Vivian Grey (Disraeli), 5:699

Vixhnievietski family, 13:246

Vizhnitsa (Ukraine), 20:**564**

Vizhnitz dynasty, 8:421, 20:**564**

Viziers
  Aaron ben Batash, 1:212
  etymology of, 1:211

Vladek, Baruch Charney, 20:**564**

Vladikavkaz (Russia). *See* Ordzhonikidze (Russia)

Vladikavkaz (Russia and Soviet Union). *See* Ordzhonikidze

Vladimir Volynski (Ukraine), 20:**564–565**

Vladivostok (Russia), 20:**566**

Vlodavi (Poland). *See* Wlodawa (Poland)

Vlyudjakh (Donskoy), 5:752

Vne zakona (Lunts), 13:260

Vocalization (nekuddot), 4:101

Vocational Service Bureau, 4:15

Vocational training
  ancient, 6:165
  ORT, 15:488–492
  See also Education; Jewish education

Vodnář (Dostál), 5:762

Voelker, Rassen, Sprachen (Von Luschan), 13:270

Voet, Andries, 20:**566**

Vogel, Arthur Israel, 20:**566**

Vogel, David, 20:**566–567**

Vogel, Julius. *See* Vogel, Sir Julius

Vogel, Karel, 20:**567**

Vogel, Simon, 20:**567**

Vogel, Sir Julius, 15:243, 20:**567**

Vogel, Wladimir, 12:809, 20:**567**

Vogelsang, Karl von, 13:252, 20:**567–568**

Vogelstein, Heinemann, 20:568

Vogelstein, Hermann, 20:568

Vogelstein, Ludwig, 20:**568**

Vogelstein family, 20:**568**

Vogüé, Charles Eugene Melchior, Comte de, 20:**568**

Vohryzek, Josef, 20:**568–569**

Voiage (Mandeville), 6:436

The Voice of Happiness—or of Simḥah—or the Victory of Wisdom. See Kol Simḥah o Nizu'aḥ ha-Hokhmah

Voice of Jacob, 7:214–215

The Voice of Jacob (newspaper), 3:353, 16:488

The Voice of Jerusalem (Zangwill), 21:455–456

Voice of the People. See Kol ha-Am

Voices of Masada (Kossoff), 6:438

The Voice which Brings Tidings (periodical). *See Kol Mevasser* (periodical)

La Voix des Communautés (newspaper), 14:504

Volcani, Raanan, 6:290

Volchko, 20:**569**

Volcker, Paul A., 20:**569–570**

Volfenson, Leonid. *See* Leonidov, Leonid Mironovich

Volgare. *See* Judeo-Italian language

Volhynia (Ukraine), 2:423, 16:314, 20:**570–573**

Volkovyshki. *See* Vilkaviškis

Volkovysk (Belarus), 20:**573–574**

Volkspartei, Juedische (Austria). *See* Juedische Volkspartei (Austria)

Volkstuemliche Geschichte der Juden (Graetz). *See Jewish History* (Graetz)

Volleyball, 19:149

Volli, Gemma, 20:**574**

Volo (Greece). *See* Volos (Greece)

Volos (Greece), 20:**574–575**

Volovelski, Yehuda. *See* Karni, Yehuda

Volozhin (Belarus), 3:457–458, 561, 20:**575–577**

Volozhiner, Ḥayyim ben Isaac, 20:**577–578**

Volozhiner, Ḥayyim Isaac, 8:415–416

Volozhiner, Isaac ben Ḥayyim, 20:**578**

Volp. *See* Volpa (Belarus)

Volpa (Belarus), 20:**578**

Volpe. *See* Volpa (Belarus)

Volpe, Arnold, 20:**578**

Voltaire, 20:**578–579**
  Adams, John, 1:380
  antisemitism of, 11:297

Volterra, Bonaventura, 20:579

Volterra, Edoardo, 12:552, 20:**579**

Volterra, Lazzaro, 20:579

Volterra, Meshullam ben Menahem, da, 20:**579–580**

Volterra, Vito, 20:**580**

Volterra family, 20:**579**

Voluntarism, 10:824–825

Volyn (Ukraine). *See* Volhynia (Ukraine)

Volynski, Akim Levovich, 20:**580**

Volz, Paul, 20:**580**

Vom Geist der hebraeischen Poesie (Herder), 9:10, 13:57

Von Buelow. *See* Buelow, Bernhard von

Von Furstenberg, Diane, 20:**580–581**

Von Hoenigstein, Adam Albert. *See* Hoenig, Adam Albert

Von Joelson, Raphael. *See* Joel, Raphael

von Kármán, Theodore. *See* Kármán, Theodore von

Von Laemel, Simon. *See* Laemel, Simon von

Von Material zu Architektur (Moholy-Nagy). *See The New Vision: From Material to Architecture* (Moholy-Nagy)

Von Neuwall, Albert, 12:**626**

Von Rad, Gerhard
  biblical theology of, 3:651
  form criticism and, 3:651
  Wisdom literature, modern critical interest in, 3:654

Von Spiegel, Herman, 15:565

Von Weisl, Ze'ev, 20:**581**

Von Welsenburg. *See* Bloch, Iwan

Voorsanger, Jacob, 20:**581**

Vopl docheri iudeyskoy (Nevakhovich), 8:441

Voprosy yevreyskoy zhizni (Morgulis), 14:491

Vorarlberg (Austria), 20:**581–582**

Die Voraussetzungen des Sozialismus und die Aufgaben der Sozialdemokratie (Bernstein), 3:478

Vorenberg, James, 20:**582**

Vorlesungen ueber die juedische Philosophie des Mittelalters (Eisler). *See Lectures on Jewish Philosophy in the Middle Ages* (Eisler)

Vorlesungen ueber die neuere Geschichte der Juden in Vienna (Loewisohn), 8:440

Vorlesungen ueber Geschichte der Mathematik (Cantor), 4:440

Voronca, Ilarie, 20:**582**

Voronezh (Russia), 20:**582–583**

Voronoff, Serge, 20:**583**

Voroshilovgrad (Ukraine). *See* Lugansk (Ukraine)

Vorsheimer, Johann. *See* Forster, Johann

Vorspan, Al, 20:**583**

Vorspan, Max, 20:**583**

Vorst, Louis J., 20:**584**

Vorsteimer, Johann. *See* Forster, Johann

Vorster, Johann. *See* Forster, Johann

Vos, Isidor H.J., 20:**584**

Voskhod (journal), 20:**584–585**

Voskhod (Morgulis), 14:491

Voskovec, George, 20:**585**

Votadio. *See* Wandering Jew

Votice (Czech Republic), 20:**585**

Votslavsk (Poland). *See* Wloclawek (Poland)

Vovsi, Solomon. *See* Mikhoels, Solomon

Vowels in Hebrew, 8:565–569, 570–573

Vows and vowing, 20:**585–586**
  commandments concerning, 5:75*t*
  women's asceticism, 2:549
  See also Oaths

Voznesensk (Ukraine), 20:**586**

Voznitsyn, Alexander Artemyevich, 20:**586**

Vozrozhdeniye, 12:524, 20:**586–587**

Vrata (Dostál), 5:762

Vrchlický, Jaroslav, 20:**587–588**

Vries, Leonard de, 6:72

Vriesland, Siegfried Adolf van. *See* Van Vriesland, Siegfried Adolf

Vriezen, Theodorus Christiaan, 20:**588**

Vroman, Akiva, 20:**588**

Vroman, Leo, 20:**588**

Vronik (Poland). *See* Wronki (Poland)

Vronsky, Victoria, 3:21

Vu Bistu Khaver Sidorov? (Smolar), 18:690

Vught concentration camp, 20:**588–589**

Vulgate, 3:598, 666, 20:**589**

Vultures, 20:**589**

Vvedeniye v filosofiyu dialekticheskogo materializma (Deborin), 5:520

Vygotski, Lev Semyonovich, 20:**589–590**

Vyprodáno (Poláček), 16:285

Vysokoye (Belarus), 20:**590**

W

W (letter), 20:*591*, 21:5

Wachenheimer, Fred. *See* Friendly, Fred W.

Wachnacht. *See* Sholem Zokhor

Wachner, Linda Joy, 20:**591**

Wachstein, Bernhard, 20:**591–592**

Wachtler, Sol, 2:18, 20:**592**

Waddington, Miriam, 4:424, 20:**592–593**

Wadi al-Naṭṭūf, 20:**593**

Wadi Dāliya, 20:**593**

Waffen-SS, Bitburg Controversy, 3:727–728

Wagenaar, Lion, 20:**593**

Wageningen, J. van. *See* Presser, Jacob

Wagenseil, Johann Christoph, 9:228, 20:**593–594**

Wagenstein, Angel Raymond, 20:**594**

Wages for services, 5:185–186, 12:409, 410, 412–413, 419, 569

Wagg, Abraham, 15:197, 20:**594**

Wagg family, 20:**594**

Waghalter, Ignatz, 20:**594**

Wagman, Adam. *See* Ważyk, Adam

Wagner, Gerhard, 15:349

Wagner, Richard, 20:**594–595**
  Levi, Hermann, 12:688
  Nietzsche, Friedrich Wilhelm, 15:262

Wagner, Siegfried, 20:**595**

Wagner, Stanley M., 20:**595–596**

Wagner-Rogers Bill, 9:365–366

Waharan (Algeria). *See* Oran

Wahb ibn Jiyath. *See* Nethanel ben Isaiah

Wahb ibn Munabbih, 20:**596**

Wahhabism, 18:77

Wahl, Isaak, 20:**596–597**

Wahl, Jacques Henri, 20:**597**

Wahl, Jean, 20:**597**

Wahl, Saul ben Judah, 20:**597**

Wahle, Richard, 20:**597**

Der Wahrheit (newspaper), 14:254

Wahrmann, Abraham David ben Asher Anschel, 20:**598**

Wahrmann, Israel, 20:**598**

Wahrmann, Moritz, 20:**598**

Waife, Benjamin. *See* Goldberg, Ben Zion

Wailing Wall. *See* Western Wall (Jerusalem)

Wainer, Samuel, 11:470

Waismann, Friedrich, 20:**598**

Waiting for Godot (Beckett), 3:742, 6:467

Waitzen (Hungary). *See* Vac (Hungary)

Wakefield, Robert, 20:**598–599**

Wakfeldus, Robert. *See* Wakefield, Robert

Waksman, Selman Abraham, 6:451, 20:**599**

Walbrook, Anton, 20:**599**

Walch family. *See* Wallich family

Wald, Arnold, 20:**599–600**

Wald, George, 13:10, 20:**600**

Wald, Henri, 20:**600**

Wald, Herman, 20:**600**

Wald, Jerry, 20:**600**

Wald, Lillian, 6:161, 12:661, 15:205, 207, 18:320, 20:**600–601**

Wald, Meir. *See* Ya'ari, Me'ir

Wald, Me'ir. *See* Ya'ari, Me'ir

Wald, S., 11:505

Walden, Aaron ben Isaiah Nathan, 3:682, 20:**601**

Walden, Henry W., 15:240

Walden, Herwarth, 20:**601**

Waldenberg, Eliezer Judah, 1:272–273, 20:**601–602**

Waldenses, 3:629, 633

Waldheim, Kurt, 15:388, 18:461, 20:**602–604**

 Entebbe Raid, 6:448

 John Paul II and, 11:384

Waldheim Affair, 20:**602–604**

Waldinger, Ernst, 20:**604–605**

Waldman, Leibele, 20:**605**

Waldman, Leon, 4:180

Waldman, Morris David, 20:**605**

Waldman, Moshe, 20:**605–606**

Waldmann, Israel, 20:**606**

Waldteufel, Emil, 20:**606**

Wales (United Kingdom), 20:**606–607**

Waletsky, Josh, 20:**607**

Waley, Alfred Joseph, 20:607

Waley, Arthur, 20:**608**

Waley, David, 20:607

Waley, Elizabeth, 20:607

Waley, Jacob, 20:607

Waley family, 20:**607–608**

Walinsky, Adam, 20:608

Walinsky, Anna Walinska, 20:608

Walinsky, Louis Joseph, 20:608

Walinsky, Ossip Joseph, 20:608

Walinsky family, 20:**608**

Walkin, Aaron, 20:**609**

The Walking (sculpture), 6:357

Walking etiquette, 6:539

The Walking Stick of the Old (Brudo). *See* ʾAsā ʿ-i Pīrān

Walkomitz, Simḥah Ḥayyim, 20:**609**

Walk on Water, 7:140

Walkowitz, Abraham, 20:**609**

The Wall (Hersey), 9:406

Wall, Hilde, 15:439

Wallace, Irving, 20:**609**

Wallace, Mike, 20:**610**

Wallach, Eli, 20:**610**

Wallach, Meir-Henokh Moiseevitch. *See* Litvinov, Maxim Maximovich

Wallach, Meir MoiSee vitch. *See* Litvinov, Maxim Maximovich

Wallach, Moshe, 20:**610**

Wallach, Otto, 4:592, 20:**610–611**

Wallach, Yona, 8:706, 20:**611**

Wallage, Jacques, 16:345

Wallant, Edward Lewis, 20:**611**

Wallenberg: A Hero's Story, 9:444–445

Wallenberg, Raoul, 11:379, 12:486–487, 13:275, 18:619, 20:**611–612**

Wallenrod, Reuben, 20:**612**

Wallenstein (Doeblin), 5:729–730

Wallenstein, Alfred, 20:**612**

Wallenstein, Meir, 20:**612**

Wallenstein, William Francis, 4:267

Wallerstein, Immanuel, 18:732, 733

Wallich, Abraham, 20:**613**

Wallich, Joseph ben Meir, 20:**613**

Wallich, Nathaniel, 20:**613**

Wallich family, 20:**613**

Wall of Death, 9:430

Wall of Silence (motion picture), 6:429

Wall Street Journal, 11:765–766

Walnuts, 15:354

Walser, Martin, 4:237

Walston, Charles. *See* Walston, Sir Charles

Walston, Sir Charles, 20:**613**

Walt, Abraham. *See* Liessin, Abraham

Walt Disney Co., 6:277

Walter, Bruno, 20:**613**

Walters, Barbara, 20:**613–614**

Walton, Bryan, 13:56, 20:**614**

Walzer, Michael, 20:**614–615**

Walzer, Richard Rudolf, 20:**615**

Wanamaker, Sam, 20:**615**

Wandering Jew, 6:434, 14:509, 18:199, 20:**615–617**

Wanderings. *See* Migrations

The Wandering Soldier (Emöd), 6:396

Wandering Stars (anthology), 18:199

Wandsbeck (Germany), 8:296, 20:**617**

Wanneh, Isaac ben Abraham, 20:**617**

Wannfried, Menahem. *See* Katz, Menahem

Wannsee Conference, 2:665, 9:336, 20:**617–619**

 Bormann, Martin, 4:87

 Heydrich, Reinhard Tristan, 9:85

 See also Final Solution

The Want Bone (Pinsky), 16:176–177

The Wanting of Levine (Halberstam), 18:200

Waqāsa family. *See* Waqqāṣa family

Waqqāṣa, Khalīfa al-Ṣaghīr, 20:619

Waqqāṣa, Khalifa ben Ḥayun ben, 20:619

Waqqāṣa family, 16:346, 20:**619**

The War against the Jews 1933–1945 (Dawidowicz), 9:416

War and Peace in Finland (Brody), 4:200

War and warfare, 20:**619–629**

 agunah, 1:511, 512, 513

 Ahab, 1:523

 bow, 20:622

Bronze age, 20:619–622, 623–625

chariot, 20:623

commandments concerning, 5:77t

disinterment and, 5:682

eschatological, 6:498–499

Falklands War, 2:441

fortifications, 20:623–625

Iron age, 20:622–623, 625

Kingdoms of Judah and Israel, 20:623

laws of, 15:739

photography of, 16:126

Second Temple, 20:626–628

weapons, 20:619–623

Yom Kippur War of 1973, 2:51

See also Military law; World War I; World War II; *specific wars*

Warbeck, Perkin, 4:120

Warberg, Frieda Schiff, 11:307

Warburg, Aby Moritz, 2:370, 20:**631**

Warburg, Edward Mortimer Morris, 2:61, 20:630–631

Warburg, Felix M., 20:629

 American Jewish Archives, 2:53

 American Joint Distribution Committee, 2:59

 New York City and, 15:217

Warburg, Frederick, 20:**631**

Warburg, Frederick Marcus, 20:630

Warburg, Frieda, 20:630

Warburg, Gavriel Reuben, 20:**631–632**

Warburg, James Paul, 20:629

Warburg, Karl Johan, 12:453, 20:**632**

Warburg, Max M., 20:**632**

Warburg, Otto, 20:**632–633**

Warburg, Otto Heinrich, 20:**633**

Warburg, Paul Felix, 20:630–631

Warburg, Paul Moritz, 20:629

Warburg, Siegmund. *See* Warburg, Sir Siegmund

Warburg, Sir Siegmund, 20:**633–634**

Warburg family, 20:**629–631**, 630t

Warburg Institute, 2:525

War crimes trials, 20:**634–649**

 Auschwitz, 2:676

 Austria, 20:642–643

 Barbie, Nikolaus, 3:141

 Demjanjuk, John, 5:551–552

  case, 20:644–645

 England, 6:424

 impact of, 20:647

 International Military Tribunal, 9:381, 20:634–635

 Latvia, 12:523

 legal principles, history of, 20:634–635

War crimes trials, *continued*
    Lithuania, 13:127
    Nuremberg, 4:128, 11:828–829, 12:553, 20:637–638
    other liberated countries, 20:643–645
    precedents, implications of, 20:648–649
    Romania, 3:133
    West German, 20:638–642
    witnesses issue, 20:640–641
War Criminal on Trial (Littman), 13:129
War criminals. *See* Holocaust
Ward. *See* Apotropos
Warden. *See* Gabbai
Warendorf (Germany), 20:**649–650**
Warfield, David, 20:**650**
Warhaftig, Zerah, 20:**650**
Warka. *See* Erech
Warka, Isaac of, 20:650–651
Warka, Menahem Mendel of, 20:651
Warka dynasty, 20:**650–651**
Warnenczyk, Wladislaw, 15:403
Warner Brothers, 13:198, 14:571
Warner family, 20:**651–652**
War of Deborah, 5:517–518, 9:170
War of Independence (Israel), 3:**346,** 10:209–212, 20:**652–665,** *653, 654, 655*
    Altalena, 20:660
    Armistice Agreement, 10:214
    arms purchases, 10:470
    Ben-Gurion, David, 3:346–347
    Dayan in, 5:485
    demarcation lines, 10:190–191, 521
    demographic effects, 10:521–522
    Egyptian front, 20:660
    Ein Gev, 6:256
    Ein Kerem, 6:260
    Ein Zurim, 6:264–265
    El-Arish, 6:286
    Elazar, David, 6:289
    first phase, 20:652–656
        Arab offensive, 20:652–653
        Jewish forces, 20:652, 653–656
    Haganah role, 8:204–205
    Hammat Gader, 8:306
    Laskov, Hayyim, 12:500
    Latrun, 12:517–518
    Mishmar ha-Negev, 14:316
    Mishmar ha-Yarden, 14:317
    Nizzanah, 15:283–284
    Nizzanim, 15:284

    Partition Resolution of 1947, 20:259–260
    second phase, 20:656
        Arab forces, 20:656–660, 662–663
        Jerusalem, fight for, 20:658, 662
        truces, 20:660–662
    United Nations, 20:260–265
War of Quietus, 10:148
The War of Remembrances (Duda), 6:40
War Refugee Board (WRB), 2:61, 9:141, 367, 490, 14:489, 20:341, **665**
Warren, Charles. *See* Warren, Sir Charles
Warren, Earl, 3:685
Warren, Sir Charles, 2:377, 15:589, 20:**665–666**
Warrens, Rosa, 20:**666**
Warrenton Female Academy, 14:480
Warsaw (Poland), 16:301*t,* 20:**666–675**
    community leaders, 5:483–484
        Dawidsohn, Hayyim, 5:483–484
        Mayzel, Maurycy, 13:704
    Congress Poland, 20:667–668
    Dutchy of Warsaw, 20:667
    education, 20:668, 669
    emancipation, 6:382
    ghetto, 7:576, 9:333, 338, *467–469, 472, 480,* 20:669–674, *671*
        American Joint Distribution Committee, 2:61
        Anielewicz, Mordecai, 2:164
        archives, 2:657
        Brandt, Willy, 4:128
        Czerniakow, Adam, 5:371–372
        diary of Chaim Aron Kaplan, 11:774–775
        Jewish armbands, 9:*464*
        Leszno Street exhibit (Yad Vashem), vol. 9: color insert
        Shapira, Kalonymous Kalman, 18:401
        street scene, 9:*467*
        uprising, 9:253, 338, 13:240–241, 20:672, 673–674, 21:676
    Holocaust period, 16:309–310, 20:670–674, *671*
    museums, 14:630
    partisans, 15:666–667
    post-WW II, 20:674
    WW I, 20:669
The Warsaw Ghetto (Gutman), 9:419

The Warsaw Ghetto Diary of Adam Czerniakow (Czerniakow), 5:372
Warsaw Ghetto Monument (Rapoport), 9:430
Warsaw Jewish Community Council, 5:371
Warsaw Jewish Fighting Organization, 3:569
Warschawski, Max, 20:**675**
War Scroll, 20:**675–676**
Warshavsky, Jakir. *See* Warshavsky, Yakir
Warshavsky, Jawnieli. *See* Yavne'eli, Shemuel
Warshavsky, Shemuel. *See* Yavne'eli, Shemuel
Warshavsky, Yakir, 20:**676**
Warshawski, Mark, 20:**676**
Warshawsky, Isaac, 20:**676**
Warski-Warszawski, Adolf, 16:347, 18:707, 20:**676–677**
Wars of the Jews (Sobol), 18:702
The Wars of the Jews (Josephus), 13:88
Wars of the Lord (Gersonides), 16:584
Wars of the Lord, Book of. See Book of the Wars of the Lord
Warszawa (Poland). *See* Warsaw (Poland)
Warszawski, Oser, 20:**677**
Warta statute of 1423 (Poland), 15:403
Warwick (England), 20:**677**
Wase (Egypt). *See* Thebes (Egypt)
Was hat Mohammed aus dem Judenthume aufgenommen? (Geiger), 1:463
Washing the hands and feet. *See* Ablution
Washington (U.S.), 20:*677,* **677–678**
Washington, George, 20:**682**
    Josephson, Manuel, 11:434
    Seixas, Moses, correspondence with, 4:18
Washington Bullets. *See* Washington Wizards
Washington D.C. (U.S.), 20:**678–682**
    21st century, 20:681
    federal city and the Jews, 20:681–682
    first congregations, 20:678–679
    immigrant generation, 20:678–679
    suburbanization, 20:680–681
    wartime, 20:679–680
Washington Declaration, 10:246
Washington Hebrew Congregation, 12:751, 18:608
Washington Heights (NYC), 15:202, 203, 230, 234–236

Washington Principles on Art, 6:281
Washington Wizards, 16:359
Washofsky, Mark E., 20:**682**
Wasit (Iraq), 20:**682–683**
Waskow, Arthur, 20:**683**
Wasser, Dennis M., 20:**683**
Wasserman, Bryna, 20:**684**
Wasserman, Dale, 20:**683–684**
Wasserman, Dora, 20:**684**
Wasserman, Elhanan Bunim, 20:**684**
Wasserman, Isaac, 6:33
Wasserman, Lew, 20:**684–685**
Wassermann, August von, 20:**685**
Wassermann, Jakob, 20:**685–686**
Wassermann, Oscar, 20:**686**
Wassermann Schultz, Debbie, 20:**686**
Wasserstein, Bernard, 20:**687**
Wasserstein, Bruce, 20:**687**
Wasserstein, Wendy, 15:227, 20:**687**
Wasserzug, Ḥayyim, 20:**687**
Waste disposal laws, 5:167, 6:93–94
Wasteland (Seid), 12:661, 18:253
Wat, Alexander, 20:**687–688**
Watchers, 20:**688**
The Watchman of the House of Israel (Erter), 6:483–484
Watchmen, Jewish Association of. *See* Ha-Shomer
Watchtower and stockade. *See* Stockade and watchtower
Waten, Judah, 20:**688**
Watergate, 11:468
    Nixon, Richard Milhaus, 15:283
    Pakula, Alan Jay, and *All the Presidents' Men*, 15:572
Waterman, Leroy, 18:307
Watermelon, 14:14
Water of bitterness, 11:374, 15:462
Water Planning for Israel. *See* Tahal
Water pollution, 5:168
Water polo, 19:146–147
Water skiing, 19:149
Water supply
    amenities, communal, 2:40
    Elath, 6:287–288
    Israel (state)
        Arab diversion of Jordan River, 10:228–229
        border skirmishes with Syria, 6:506, 10:218
        constraints, 10:531–532
        rural planning, 10:368
    Jerusalem, 11:169–170, 174, 177, 179, 182, 194, 205–207
    Palestine (Mandate), irrigation drive, 10:509–510

Wattasid dynasty, 20:**688**
Watters, Leo Laizer, 20:**688–689**
Watzinger, Carl, 20:**689**
Wawelberg, Hipolit, 20:**689**
Waxman, Al, 20:**689–690**
Waxman, Franz, 11:444
Waxman, Meyer, 20:**690**
Waxman, Mordecai, 20:**690–691**
Way, Lewis, 16:630, 20:**691**
The Wayfarer (Menahem Boraisha). *See Der Geyer*
Wayfarers. *See* Travelers and explorers; Travelers and travels to Erez Israel
Wayne, Johnny, 20:**691**
Wayne and Shuster, 20:**691**
The Way of Holiness. See Derekh ha-Kodesh
The Way of Reason. See Derekh Tevunot (Luzzatto)
Ważyk, Adam, 20:**691**
Wdowinski, David, 20:**692**
Wealth
    business ethics and, 4:306–307
    closeness to God and, 11:42
Weapons contracting, 5:198–200
Weather
    gods, 3:9–10
    prayers, 13:601
Webb, Jack, 20:**692**
Weber, Koloman, 20:**692**
Weber, Max, 15:221, 20:**692–693**
    on Jewish identity, 11:297
    on socioeconomics, 18:733
    sociology of Bible and, 3:658–659
Wechler, Adrian. *See* Verea, Adrian
Wechsler, Adrian. *See* Verea, Adrian
Wechsler, David, 20:**693**
Wechsler, Elina, 20:**693**
Wechsler, Herbert, 20:**693–694**
Wechsler, Israel, 20:**694**
Wechsler, James Arthur, 15:222, 20:**694**
Wechsler, Joseph, 1:288
Wechsler, Judah, 20:**694**
Wechsler, Max, 20:**694–695**
Wedding rings (17th c.), vol. 3: color insert
Weddings
    badḥan, 3:48
    dance, 5:409–410, 411
    games at, 7:371
    hakhnasat kallah, 8:247–248
    music at, 14:647
    photographs of, 16:128, vol. 5: color insert
    Yemenite bride and groom, vol. 3: color insert

See also Marriage
Wedgewood, Josiah Clement, First Baron, 20:**695**
We Don't Need Another Hero (Kruger), vol. 4: color insert
Weeds, 20:**695**, vol. 16: color insert
Weegee, 20:**695–696**
Weeks, Feast of. *See* Shavuot
Wege in Judentum (Baeck), 3:51
Wegrow (Poland), 20:**696–697**
We Have Sinned (prayer). *See* Ashamnu
Wehemibre Neko. *See* Neco
Wehemibre Neko II. *See* Neco
Das Weib des Akiba (Heimann), 8:769
Weichert, Michael, 18:370, 20:**697**
Weichmann, Herbert, 16:344, 20:**697**
Weidenfeld, George, Baron, 20:**697**
Weidenreich, Franz, 20:**697–698**
Weider, Ben, 20:**698**
Weidman, Hiram, 20:**698**
Weidman, Jerome, 20:**698–699**
Weidman, Mordecai S., 20:**698**
Weidner, Paulus, 20:**699**
Weigand, Theodor, 20:**699**
Weigel, Catherine, 20:**699**
Weigel, Helene, 20:**699–700**
Weigert, Carl, 20:**700**
Weigert, Fritz, 20:**700**
Weightlifting, 3:424–425, 19:149
Weights and measures, 3:83, 20:**700–709**
    agoranomos, 1:469–470
    agricultural fields, 1:476–479
    archeological finds, 20:705–706
    area, 20:703
    biblical measures, 20:700–701
    Business ethics, 4:309
    eggs, 6:220
    linear measure, 20:701–702, 701t, 702t
    shekel and talent, 20:703–705, 703t, 704t
    Talmudic, 20:706–709, 707t, 708t
    volume, 20:702–703, 702t
    weight, 20:703–705, 703t, 704t
Weil, A. Leo, 20:**709–710**
Weil, André, 20:**710**
Weil, Eric, 20:**710**
Weil, Federico, 11:364
Weil, Frank Leopold, 20:**710**
Weil, Gertrude, 15:303
Weil, Gotthold, 20:**711**
Weil, Gustav, 20:**711**
Weil, Herman, 15:302
Weil, Jacob ben Judah, 12:462, 14:26, 15:347, 20:**711–712**

Weil, Jiři, 20:**712**

Weil, Joseph, 20:**712**

Weil, Lionel, 15:303

Weil, Meir. *See* Weyl, Meir ben Simḥah

Weil, Nethanel ben Naphtali Ẓevi, 20:**712–713**

Weil, R. Adrienne, 20:**713**

Weil, Simone, 20:**713**

Weiler, Gershon, 16:104

Weiler, Jack D., 20:**713**

Weiler, Samuel, 4:200

Weill, Alexandre Abraham, 2:8, 20:**713–714**

Weill, Kurt, 18:138–139, 20:**714**

Weill, Michel Aaron, 20:**714**

Weill, Raymond, 20:**714**

Weill, Sanford G., 15:226

Weill, Sanford I., 20:**714–715**

Weill, Shraga, 20:**715**

Wein, George, 20:**715–716**

Weinbaum, Mark Efimovich, 20:**716**

Weinberg, Abraham, II, 18:677

Weinberg, Abraham, III, 18:677

Weinberg, Abraham ben Isaac Mattathias, 18:676, 677

Weinberg, Dvora. *See* Lapson, Dvora

Weinberg, Gladys Davidson, 20:**716**

Weinberg, Harry, 18:211, 20:**716–717**

Weinberg, Issachar Aryeh, 18:677

Weinberg, Jacob, 20:**717**

Weinberg, Jehiel Jacob, 15:495, 20:**717**

Weinberg, Joel, 11:321

Weinberg, Moissey. *See* Veinberg, Moissey Samuilovich

Weinberg, Noah, 18:677

Weinberg, Samuel, 18:677

Weinberg, Saul S., 20:**717–718**

Weinberg, Sidney J., 20:**718**

Weinberg, Solomon, 18:677

Weinberg, Steven, 20:**718**

Weinberg, Ẓevi Zebulun, 20:**718–719**

Weinberger, Caspar, 16:357

Weinberger, Jaromir, 4:193, 20:**719**

Weinberger, Joshua Aaron Ẓevi, 4:186

Weinberger, Moshe, 15:207, 20:**719**

Weiner, Aloys. *See* Sonnenfels, Aloys von

Weiner, Anthony, 20:**719–720**

Weiner, D., 15:224

Weiner, Dan, 16:126

Weiner, Lazar, 20:**720**

Weiner, Leo, 20:**720**

Weiner, Mattityahu. *See* Shelem, Mattityahu

Weiner, Richard, 20:**720**

Weinfeld, Edward, 20:**720–721**

Weingarten, Joab Joshua, 20:**721**

Weingarten, Johnny. *See* Wayne, Johnny

Weinger, Mordecai. *See* Veinger, Mordecai

Weingreen, Jacob, 20:**721**

Weinheim (Germany), 20:**721**

Weinhouse, Sidney, 20:**722**

Weininger, Otto, 20:**722**

Weininger's Night (Sobol), 18:702

Weinman. *See* Ben-Zion

Weinmann, Eduard J. *See* Weinmann, Jacob

Weinmann, Jacob, 20:**722**

Weinper, Zishe, 20:**722–723**

Weinperlech, Zise. *See* Weinper, Zishe

Weinreb, Friedrich, 20:**723**

Weinrebe, Boruch Abraham. *See* Rivkin, Boruch

Weinreich, Max, 14:396, 20:**723–724**, 21:363–364

Weinreich, Uriel, 20:**724**

Weinrub, Matvey, 20:**724–725**

Weinryb, Bernard Dov Sucher, 20:**725**

Weinryb, Boruch Abraham. *See* Rivkin, Boruch

Weinshall, Abraham, 20:**725**

Weinshall, Ben Zion Ze'ev, 20:**725**

Weinshall, Jacob, 20:**725**

Weinshall family, 20:**725**

Weinstein, Aaron, 20:**725–726**

Weinstein, Baruch, 11:315, 316

Weinstein, Berish, 20:**726**

Weinstein, Bob, 20:**726**

Weinstein, Harvey, 20:**726**

Weinstein, Jack B., 20:**726–727**

Weinstein, Jacob, 20:**727–728**

Weinstein, Lewis H., 20:**728**

Weinstein, Miksa. *See* Szabolcsi, Miksa

Weinstein, Nathan. *See* West, Nathanael

Weinstein, Nathan Wallenstein. *See* West, Nathanael

Weinstock, Arnold, Baron. *See* Weinstock, Sir Arnold, Baron

Weinstock, Harris, 20:**728**

Weinstock, Herbert, 20:**728–729**

Weinstock, Sir Arnold, Baron, 20:**728**

Weinthrop, Bud. *See* Flanagan, Bud

Weintraub, Aaron. *See* Aescoly, Aaron Ze'ev

Weintraub, Aaron Ze'ev. *See* Aescoly, Aaron Ze'ev

Weintraub, Dov, 18:735

Weintraub, Solomon, 20:**729**

Weinzweig, Helen, 20:**729**

Weinzweig, John, 20:**729–730**

Weisberger, Bernard Allen, 20:**730**

Weisel (statesman). *See* Magnus, Marcus

Weisel, Naphtali Hirsch. *See* Wessely, Naphtali Herz

Weisenburg, Theodore H., 20:**730**

Weisenfreund, Muni. *See* Muni, Paul

Weiser-Varon, Benno, 20:**730–731**

Der Weise und der Narr; Koenig Salomo und der Schuster (Gronemann). *See The King and the Cobbler* (Gronemann)

Weisgal, Abba Joseph, 20:**731**

Weisgal, Meyer Wolf, 14:462, 20:**731**

Weisgall, Hugo, 20:**731**

Weisglas, Frans, 16:345

Weisman, Adele. *See* Wiseman, Adele

Weiss, Abraham, 20:**731**

Weiss, Albert Paul, 20:**732**

Weiss, Andre. *See* Vészi, Endre

Weiss, Aureliu, 20:**732**

Weiss, Avi, 20:**732**

Weiss, Ernst, 20:**732–733**

Weiss, Isaac Eizik, 19:111

Weiss, Isaac Hirsch, 20:**733–734**

Weiss, Isaac Jacob, 20:**734**

Weiss, Jiří, 20:**734**

Weiss, Joseph G., 20:**734**

Weiss, Joseph Joshua, 20:**734**

Weiss, Joseph Meir, 20:**734–735**

Weiss, Joseph Zevi, 6:217

Weiss, Manfréd, 20:**735**

Weiss, Meir, 20:**735**

Weiss, Melvyn I., 20:**735**

Weiss, Morry, 18:39

Weiss, Paul, 20:**735–736**

Weiss, Peter, 20:**736**

Weiss, Samson, 20:**736**

Weiss, Samuel Arthur, 20:**736**

Weiss, Slavko. *See* Livni, Hillel

Weiss, Yaakov, 20:**736–737**

Weissberg, Isaac Jacob, 20:**737**

Weissberg, Julia Lazarevna, 20:**737**

Weissberg, Meir, 20:**737**

Weisse Liebe, ein Roman aus dem Quartier (Holitscher), 9:321

Weissenberg, Alexis, 20:**737**

Weissenberg, Isaac Meir, 12:654, 20:**737–738**

Weissenberg, Samuel Abramovich, 20:**738**

Weisser, Albert, 20:**738**

Weisser, Joshua, 20:**738**

Weiss family. *See* Sapirstein-Stone-Weiss family

Weisskopf, Victor F., 20:**738–739**

Weissler, Barry, 20:**739**

Weissler, Fran, 20:**739**

Weissman, Baruch Mordecai, 20:**739–740**

Weissman, Irving, 13:10

Weissmandel, Michael, 6:553

Weissmandel, Michael Dov, 20:**740**

Weissmann, Adolf, 20:**740**

Weiss-Rosmarin, Trude, 20:**740–741**

    American Jewish Archives, 2:53

Weisz, Dezsö. *See* Szomory, Dezsö

Weisz, Eric. *See* Houdini, Harry

Weisz, Max, 20:**741**

Weisz, Victor, 20:**741**

Weiter, A., 20:**741–742**

Weitz, Joseph, 20:**742**

Weitz, Naphtali, 20:**742**

Weitz, Ra'anan, 10:363, 364, 20:742

Weitz, Yeḥiam, 20:742

Weitzmann, Chaim, 6:417

Wei-Yang. *See* Yang-Chou

Weizel, Mordecai. *See* Rosenblatt, Mordecai ben Menahem

Weizel, Mordecau ben Menahem. *See* Rosenblatt, Mordecai ben Menahem

Weizman, Ezer, 20:**742–743**

Weizmann, Chaim, 20:**744–752**

    1920s, 1930s, 20:747

    American Jewish Committee, 2:55

    Balfour Declaration, 3:85–87, 89

    Bevin period, 20:750–751

    Biltmore Program, 3:699

    Bisgyer, Maurice, 3:725

    Brandeis, Louis Dembitz, 4:122–123

    Brodetsky, Selig, 4:196

    chemist, 20:751–752

    early Zionism, 20:744–746

    Einstein, Albert, 6:262

    Hebrew University, 8:740

    Israel's first President, 20:751

    Jabotinsky, Vladimir and, 11:11, 12

    Jewish legion and, 11:303, 306

    Morgenthau, Henry, Sr., 14:488

    Nili, 15:267, 268

    WW I, 20:746–747

    WW II, 20:749–750

Weizmann, Ḥaya, 20:743–744

Weizmann, Mikhail, 20:744

Weizmann, Vera, 20:752

Weizmann family, 20:**743–744**

Weizmann Institute, 13:12

Weizmann Institute of Science, 18:611, 20:751, **752–753**

Welensky, Roy. *See* Welensky, Sir Roy

Welensky, Sir Roy, 21:**5**

Welfare organizations

    Berlin (Germany), 1:409

    Los Angeles (CA), 13:210–211

    Pest (Hungary), 4:246

Weller, Michael, 21:**5**

Weller, Moses Cyrus, 11:378

Wellesz, Egon Joseph, 21:**5–6**

Wellesz, Julius, 21:**6**

Wellhausen, Julius, 16:630, 21:**6–7**

    Eissfeldt, Otto, 6:278

    on incense altar, 2:14

    modern biblical criticism and, 3:648, 649–650

Well-poisoning libels

    Black Death and, 3:732–733

    in Opava, 15:438

    See also Blood libel

Wells, 21:**7**

Wells, Charles Jeremiah, 6:433

Wellstone, Paul, 4:95, 21:**7–8**

Welner, Pinches, 21:**8**

Welsh, Arthur L., 21:**8**

Welsh language, 3:636

Die Welt (newspaper), 1:247, 6:744, 12:465, 21:**8–9**

Die Weltgeschichte des juedischen Volkes (Dubnow), 6:34

Weltsch, Felix, 21:**9**

Weltsch, Robert, 21:**9–10**

    Juedische Rundschau, 11:571

Weltsh, Felix, 21:9

Weltsh, Robert, 21:9–10

Wenceslaus IV, 21:**10**

Wendish language, 3:635–636

Wendland, Paul, 21:**10**

Wendroff, Zalman, 21:**10**

Wengeroff, Pauline Epstein, 21:**10–11**

Wengeroff, Semyon Afanasyevich, 21:**11**

Weni (ancient Egyptian official), 6:223

Weniger Maersdorf. *See* Eisenstadt

Werba, Dorit. *See* Beinisch, Dorit

Werbel, Eliahu Mordecai, 21:**11**

Werber, Baruch, 4:199, 21:**11–12**

Werber, Jack, 9:496

Werber, Jacob, 4:199

Werbermacher, Hannah Rachel. *See* Ludomir, Maid of

Werbermacher, Hannah Rochel. *See* Ludomir, Maid of

Werblowsky, Raphael Juda Zwi, 21:**12**

Were We Our Brothers' Keepers? The Public Response of American Jews to the Holocaust 1938-1944 (Lookstein), 13:188

Werewolves in their Youth (Chabon), 4:555

Werfel, Franz, 21:**12–13**

Werfel, Yitzhak. *See* Raphael, Yitzhak

Wergeland, Henrik Arnold, 15:305, 21:**13**

Wergelands Barn, 15:311

Werner, Eric, 21:**13–14**

Werner, Heinz, 21:**14**

Werner, Michael, 21:**14**

Werner, Sidonie, Juedischer Frauenbund, 11:570

Werner Herzog Eats His Shoes (motion picture), 14:510

Werner, Siegmund, 21:**14**

Werses, Samuel, 21:**14**

Werth, Alexander, 21:**14–15**

Wertheim, Abraham Carel, 16:345, 21:**15**

    Rabbinical Seminary of Amsterdam and, 2:114

Wertheim, George, 21:**15**

Wertheim, Maurice, 21:**15**

Wertheim, Naphtali Ḥerz, 15:566

Wertheim, Rosalie Marie, 21:**15–16**

Wertheim, Wolff, 21:15

Wertheimer, Asher, 21:**16**

Wertheimer, Chaim Ernst, 21:**16**

Wertheimer, Eduard von, 21:**16**

Wertheimer, Joseph Ritter von, 21:**16–17**

Wertheimer, Leopold. *See* Brunner, Constantin

Wertheimer, Max, 21:**17**

Wertheimer, Samson, 6:269, 11:765, 21:**17–18**

Wertheimer, Simon, 8:747

Wertheimer, Solomon Aaron, 21:**18**

Wertheimer, Stef, 21:**18**

Wertheim family, 21:**15**

Wesel, Baruch Bendet ben Reuben, 4:164, 21:**18–19**

Wesen des Judentums (Baeck), 3:51

Wesker, Arnold, 21:**19**

Wessely, Naphtali Hartwig. *See* Wessely, Naphtali Herz

Wessely, Naphtali Herz, 5:468, 8:299, 436, 437, 687, 724, 21:**19–21**

    Berlin, Saul ben Ẓevi Hirsch Levin, 3:459

    biblical exegesis and study of, 3:646

    Exodus, 14:540

    Hebrew literature, 8:686

    Hurwitz, Judah ben Mordecai ha-Levi, 9:632

    Landau, Ezekiel Ben Judah, 12:460

Wessely, Naphtali Herz, *continued*
  Levin, Zevi Hirsch ben Aryeh
    Loeb, 12:714
  prosody, 16:614
  Shirei Tiferet, 8:687, 14:540, 21:20
Wessely, Wolfgang, 12:549, 21:**21**
West, Mae, 21:**21**
West, Nathanael, 21:**22**
West Bank, 2:333
  American Joint Distribution
    Committee, 2:64
  Arab population
    1948-1967, 10:715–717
    after Six-Day war, 10:717–718
  feminist organizations, 6:754
  Gush Etzyon, 8:145–147
  Gush Katif, 8:147–148
  security lockout, 10:726
  See also Gaza Strip; Gush Emunim
Westchester County (NY), 21:**22–24**
Westerbork (Holland), 21:**24**
Western Europe
  Blitzkrieg invasion, 9:332–333
  economic and social development
    eighteenth-early nineteenth
      century, 9:233–234
    modern, 6:134–135
  education, Jewish, 6:181, 186
  emancipation, 6:375–380
  encyclopedias, 6:400
  epitaphs, 6:464–465
  foreign policy and relations with
    Israel, 10:260, 263, 265–266
  Hebrew literature, publishing,
    16:721–722
  Holocaust studies, 9:423
  Jewish artists, 2:504–507
  Jewish settlement, 9:207–208
  Middle Ages, Jewish expulsion in,
    9:216–217, 221–222
  museums, 14:625–627
  women, dress, 6:15
  Yiddish theater, 19:679
*Western European Socialism and the
  Jewish Problem. See Ha-Sozyalism
  ha-Ma'aravi u-She'elat ha-Yehudim*
  (Silberner)
Western Palatinate (Germany). *See*
  Palatinate (Germany)
Western Synagogue archives, 2:408
Western Wall (Jerusalem), 9:499,
  15:583, 21:**24–27**
  Av, Ninth of, 2:716
  bar mitzvah at, vol. 3: color insert
  Behar, Nissim, 3:263
  commission of inquiry, 15:583
  holy places in Israel, 9:499, 500

  kissing of, 12:202
  Madaba mosaic map, 13:329
  pilgrimages, 16:155, 156
  plaza and pilgrims at, vol. 11:
    color insert
  praying the kaddish at, vol. 3:
    color insert
  psalms recitation, 16:667
  religious life, 10:626
  seal motif, 18:228
  Simeon the Just, 18:602
  Sukkot blessing, vol. 17: color
    insert
  surrounding neighborhood of, vol.
    11: color insert
  women praying, vol. 20: color
    insert
  Yemenite Jew with shofar, vol. 17:
    color insert
Westerweel, Johan, 21:**27**
Westheimer, Frank Henry, 21:**27–28**
Westheimer, Ruth, 21:**28**
Westminster Synagogue (England),
  5:352–353
Westmoreland, William, 1:406
Westphalia (Germany), 11:54, 21:**28–
  29**
Westport (CT), 15:**304–305**
West Side Story (musical), 15:220
West Virginia (U.S.), 21:*29*, **29–30**
Wettach, Charles Adrien. *See* Grock
Wette, de, Wilhelm Martin Leberecht,
  21:**30**
Wettstein, Feivel Hirsch, 21:**30**
Wetzlar (Germany), 21:**30–31**
Wetzlar von Plankenstern, Abraham,
  21:**31**
Wetzlar von Plankenstern family,
  21:**31**
Wetzler, Gustave, 6:83
WEVD (Yiddish radio station in New
  York City), 15:221
Wexler, Harry, 21:**31**
Wexler, Robert, 15:605, 20:412–413
Wexler, Robert D., 21:**32**
Wexler, William Abe, 21:**32**
Wexner, Abigail, 21:33
Wexner, Leslie H., 5:588, 21:**32–34**
Wexner Foundation, 21:32–33
Weyl, Meir ben Simḥah, 4:165, 21:**34**
Weyssenburg (Transylvania). *See* Alba
  Iulia (Transylvania)
"What is different?". *See* Mah
  Nishtannah
What is Man (Buber), 4:232
What Makes Sammy Run? (Schulberg),
  18:171

What Will Happen to the Jews?
  (Leftwich), 12:603
Wheat, 21:**34–35**
Wheel of Fortune (Moravia), 14:477
When Love Passed By (Solis-Cohen),
  18:754
When Memory Comes (Friedlaender),
  9:414
Whentthe State of Israel Broke (Ben
  Yehuda), 3:389
Where Am I?. See Heykhan Ani Nimzet
Whippings. *See* Floggings
Whisky ze beseder (Sobol), 18:702
White, Harry D., 21:**35**
White, Katherine Elkus, 14:445
White, Morton Gabriel, 21:**35**
White, Robert Mayer, 21:**35–36**
White, Theodore H., 21:**36**
White, Walter, 3:736
White Barn Theater, 13:195
White Chistmas (motion picture),
  14:571–572
White Goods Workers Union, 18:151
Whitehall Ferry Terminal (NYC),
  18:184
The White House. See Dos Vayse Hoyz
White magic. *See* Magic
White Papers, 9:490, 21:**36–38**
  1939, 4:722
  Attlee, Clement Richard, Earl,
    2:647
  Ben-Gurion, David, 3:345, 346
  Bevin, Ernest, 3:556
  Chamberlain, Neville, 4:564
  Churchill White Paper, 9:250,
    21:36–37
  Haganah, 8:203, 204
  illegal immigration, 9:722, 723
  League of Nations, 12:564–565
  Malcolm MacDonald Paper, 21:38
  Passfield White Paper, 13:148,
    21:37
  policy, 3:345–346
  Rothschild, James Armand de,
    17:493
  Zionism, 4:722, 21:555, 569, 570–
    571
  Zionist Congress (21st), 21:632
White poplars, vol. 16: color insert
White Rabbi (artwork), 1:407
White Revolution, Iran, 15:569
White slave trade, 4:400, 15:477,
  16:627–628
Whither? (Feierberg). *See Le'an?*
  (Feierberg)
Whittengehame College, 6:206
*Who Gave the Order. See Mi Natan
  Ha-Hora'ah*

Who Has Allowed Us to Suffer? (composition, Morawetz), 14:478

The Whole Land Brimstone (Langfus), 9:408

The Whole World in a Clover Leaf (Bunting), vol. 13: color insert

Whose Little Boy are You?. See Shel Mi Attah Yeled?

Why a Jewish State? (Feuer), 6:773

Wiat (Libya). *See* Tripoli (Libya)

Wichmann, Malkah. *See* Esther (1880-1943)

Wickedness, 11:109, 12:537–540

Wicked Priest, 21:**38–39**

Wickes, W., printed editions of Hebrew Bible, 3:588

Widal, Fernand, 21:**39**

Widder, Dávid. *See* Giszkalay, János

Widmanstetter, Johann Albrecht, 21:**39–40**

Widows, 21:**40–45**
    Bene Israel, 3:338
    B'nai B'rith, 4:13–14
    Levirate marriage and ḥaliẓah, 12:725–726
    pledge of debts, 16:232–233
    See also Agunah

Wiedenfeld, Dov, 21:**45**

Wieder, N., 11:796

Wie ich es sehe (Altenberg), 2:17

Wieizel, Mordecai ben Menahem. *See* Rosenblatt, Mordecai ben Menahem

Wieliczka (Poland), 21:**45**

Wielki, Kazimierz. *See* Casimir III

Wielun (Poland), 21:**45–46**

Wiener, Alexander S., 21:**46**

Wiener, Alfred, 21:**46**

Wiener, Charles, 21:46

Wiener, Ernest Edouard, 21:**47**

Wiener, Franz. *See* Croisset, Francis de

Wiener, Harold Marcus, 21:**47**

Wiener, Jacques, 21:46

Wiéner, Jean, 21:**47**

Wiener, Leo, 21:**47–48**

Wiener, Leopold, 21:46

Wiener, Max, 21:**48**

Wiener, Meir, 21:**48–49**

Wiener, Norbert, 13:679, 21:**49**

Wiener, Philip Paul, 21:**49**

Wiener, Samuel, 21:**49–50**

Wiener family, 21:46

Wiener Gesera, 21:50

Wiener Library, 18:723, 21:**50–51**

Wiener Morgenzeitung, 1:247

Wiener Neustadt (Austria), 21:51

Wienlawski, Henri, 21:51

Wierblowski, Stefan, 16:347

Wiernik, Peter, 21:**51**

Wiernikorski, Judah, 21:**51–52**

Wieruszowski, Helene, 21:**52**

Wierzbolow. *See* Virbalis (Lithuania)

Wiesbaden (Germany), 21:**52**

Wiesel, Elie, 9:388, 401, 409–410, 11:818, 21:**52–54**
    Bitburg Controversy, 3:728
    children's literature, 4:630–631
    Halivni, David Weiss, 8:275
    in New York City, 15:221
    Soviet Jewry, 15:20
    on TV miniseries *The Holocaust*, 9:473

Wieseltier, Meir, 21:**54**

Wiesenthal, Simon, 4:631, 21:**54–55**

Wieslander, Rose. *See* Stokes, Rose Pastor

Wiesner, Jerome Bert, 21:**55**

Wiesner, Julius von, 21:**55–56**

Wieviorka, Annette, 11:326, 21:**56**

Wife. *See* Husband and wife

Wiggen, Henry W. *See* Harris, Mark

Wigner, Eugene Paul, 21:**56–57**

Wigoder, Basil Thomas, Baron, 21:**57**

Wigoder, Geoffrey, 21:**57**

Wigs, 8:507
    See also Head, covering of

Wihl, Ludwig, 21:**57**

Wijnkoop, David, 16:345, 21:**57–58**

Wilbuschewitz, Gedaliah, 21:58

Wilbuschewitz, Moshe, 21:58

Wilbuschewitz, Naḥum Wilbush, 21:58

Wilbuschewitz family, 21:58

Wilchek, Meir, 21:58

Wild Animals. See Animales feroces

Wild Bull, 21:58

The Wild Coast. *See* The Guianas

Wildenstein, Georges, 21:**59**

Wildenstein, Nathan, 21:**58–59**

Wildenstein family, 21:**58–59**

Wilder, Billy, 14:450, 571, 21:**59**

Wilder, Gene, 21:**59**

Wilder, Hertz Emanuel, 21:**59–60**

Wilderness, 21:**60–61**

Wilderness of Ziph (ancient Israel). *See* Ziph (ancient Israel)

Wildmann, Isaac Eisik, 21:**61**

Wilensky, Michael, 21:**61**

Wilensky, Miriam. *See* Yalan-Stekelis, Miriam

Wilensky, Moshe, 21:**61**

Wilensky, Yehudah Leib Nisan, 21:**61–62**

Wilentz, David, 21:62

Wilentz, Robert N., 21:**62**

Wilhelm, Kurt, 21:**62**

Wilhelm II, Kaiser, 3:93, 9:56, 58, 59, 60–61

Wilkansky, Meir, 6:290

Wilkansky, Yiẓḥak. *See* Elazari-Volcani, Yiẓḥak

Wilkenfeld, Ḥaim Joseph. *See* Zadok, Ḥaim Joseph

Wilkes-Barre and Kingston (PA), 21:**62–63**

Wilkomierz. *See* Ukmerge (Lithuania)

Wilkomitz, Simḥah Ḥayyim. *See* Walkomitz, Simḥah Ḥayyim

Will
    freedom of (*See* Free will).
    See Wills

Will, Divine. *See* God

Will Elder: The Mad Playboy of Art (Elder), 6:296–297

Willen, Joseph, 21:**63–64**

Willen, Pearl Larner, 21:63–64

William, Mitchell. *See* Miller, Mitch

William I (Netherlands), 2:111

William IV (Netherlands), 2:108

William Morris Agency, 14:511

William of Auvergne, 21:**64**

William of Norwich, 3:775, 15:312

Williams, Charles, 21:**64**

Williams, Roger, 9:227–228

Williamsburg (NYC)
    1870-1920, 15:202–203, 207, 212
    1920-1970, 15:212–213, 217
    1970-2006, 15:224, 231, 234–238

William the Conqueror, 6:410

Willner, Itamar, 21:**64**

Will of God. *See* God

Willow, 21:**65**, vol. 16: color insert

Willowski, Jacob David ben Ze'ev, 1:597, 21:**65**

Wills, 5:156, 21:**65–74**
    acquisition, 1:363
    child maintenance, 15:636
    deceased wishes, 21:67
    Eliezer ben Samuel ha-Levi, 6:329
    enforcing a defective will, 21:72–73
    ethical, 13:106–107, 21:**74–75**
    form and wording, 21:69
    interpretation of, 21:69–70
    in Israel, 21:72, 73–74
    rights accrual, renunciation, 21:70
    takkanot, 21:71–72

Willstaetter, Richard, 4:592, 21:**75–76**

Wilmington (DE), 21:**76**

Wilna, Jacob ben Benjamin Wolf, 18:355, 21:**77**

Wilno (Lithuania). *See* Vilna (Lithuania)

Wilofski, Jacob. *See* Willowski, Jacob David ben Ze'ev

Wilozni v. Rabbinical Court of Appeals, 12:607–608, 14:361

Wilpon, Fred, 21:**77**

Wilshire Boulevard Temple, 13:197

Wilson, Charles William. *See* Wilson, Sir Charles William

Wilson, Harold, Baron Wilson of Rievaulx, 21:**77–78**

Wilson, "Scottie," 21:**78**

Wilson, Sir Charles William, 2:377, 15:589, 21:**77**

Wilson, Sol, 21:**78**

Wilson, Woodrow, 21:**78**
    Brandeis, Louis Dembitz, 4:122
    King-Crane Palestine Inquiry Commission, 15:582
    Morgenthau, Henry, Sr., 14:488–489, 490

Winawer, Bruno, 21:**79**

Winawer, Chemjo. *See* Vinaver, Chemjo

Wincenty. *See* Brauner, Isaac

Winchell, Walter, 21:**79**

Winchester (England), 21:**79**

Winchevsky, Morris. *See* Vinchevsky, Morris

Winckler, Hugo, 3:651, 21:**79–80**

Windau (Latvia). *See* Ventspils (Latvia)

Winder, Ludwig, 21:**80**

Windsor School (Vermont), 4:60

Windsurfing, 19:149

Wine, 7:117, 21:**80–81**

Wine, Sherwin, 21:**81–82**

Wine and liquor trade, 21:**82–86**
    Israel, 21:85–86
    kosher winery, vol. 20: color insert
    Middle Ages, 21:82–83
    sixteenth century to modern times, 21:83–85
    Talmudic period, 21:82

Wine of Choice (Behrman), 3:264

Wing, Bendit ben Ayzek, 2:38

Wingate, Orde, 21:**86–87**

Winger, Debra, 21:**87**

Winik, Meir, 21:**87**

Winkler, Henry, 21:**87**

Winkler, Irwin, 21:**87–88**

Winkler, Leo, 21:**88**

Winnik, Henry Zvi, 21:**88**

Winninger, Solomon, 21:**88**

Winnipeg (Canada), 6:210, 11:716–717, 20:**698**, 21:**88–90**
    aid societies, 4:399–400
    Canadian literature, 4:424
    Jewish nursing home, 11:762

Winnowing, 1:485–486

Winogrand, Garry, 21:**90**

Winsberg, Jacques, 15:650

Winstein, Saul, 21:**90**

Winston, Robert, Baron, 21:**90**

Winston, Stan, 21:**90–91**

Winter, Gustav, 21:**91**

Winter, Jacob, 6:11, 21:**91**

Winter, Leon de, 6:71

Winter, Lev, 21:91

Winter, Paul, 21:**91**

Winternitz, Emanuel, 21:**91–92**

Winternitz, Moritz, 21:**92**

Winters, Shelley, 21:**92**

Winter Sports, 19:149–150

Winterstein, Alfred, 21:**92**

Winterstein, Simon, 16:340

Winthrop, Bud. *See* Flanagan, Bud

Wintrobe, Maxwell Myer, 21:**92**

Wirballen. *See* Virbalis (Lithuania)

Wirszubski, Chaim, 21:**92–93**

Wirth, Christian, 21:**93**

Wirth, Louis, 18:731, 734, 21:**93**

Wirths, Eduard, 8:464

Wiśniowiecki, Jeremi, 21:**105**

Wischnitzer, Mark, 21:**93–94**

Wischnitzer, Rachel, 2:526, 21:**94**

Wisconsin (WI), 21:**94**, 94–95

Wisdom, Divine. *See* God

Wisdom and wisdom literature, 21:**95–99**
    Abaddon, 1:224
    divine, 11:589
    on drunkenness, 6:26–27
    Egypt, 6:225, 226
    feminization of, 16:105
    modern critical interest in, 3:654
    sacrifices, 17:644
    Solomon, 18:758–759
    Wisdom of Solomon, 6:497, 18:768

Wisdom of Ben Sira Apocrypha, 3:**376–378**

Wisdom of Solomon, 6:497, 18:**768–769**

Wise, George Schneiweis, 21:**99**

Wise, Isaac Mayer, 15:392, 17:167–168, 21:**99–100**
    Albany, 1:585
    American Israelite, 2:50
    American Jewish Archives, 2:53
    cantors, 8:503
    Central Conference of American Rabbis, 4:545

Cincinnati, 4:727
    Die Deborah, 5:648
    education, Jewish, 6:192
    Einhorn, David (Rabbi), 6:258
    Hebrew Union College, 8:739
    Jewish Institute for Religion, 8:739
    Leeser, Isaac, 12:601
    Morais, Sabato, 14:471
    in New York State, 15:239
    Reform Judaism, 2:43

Wise, Jonah, 2:50

Wise, Jonah Bondi, 21:**100**

Wise, Justine. *See* Polier, Justine Wise

Wise, Leo, 2:50

Wise, Louis Elsberg, 21:**100**

Wise, Louise Waterman, 21:102

Wise, Robert Earl, 21:**100**

Wise, Stephen Samuel, 21:**100–103**
    American Jewish Congress, 2:57
    Brandeis, Louis Dembitz, 4:123
    cable to, 9:366
    New York City and, 15:206, 217
    quotas, 15:343

Wiseman, Adele, 4:424, 21:**103**

Wiseman, Frederick, 21:**103**

Wiseman, Shloime, 21:**103–104**

The Wishing-Ring. See Dos Vintshfingerl

Wislica (Poland), 21:**104**

Wisliceny, Dieter, 6:553, 21:**104–105**

Wisniowiec (Ukraine). *See* Vishnevets (Ukraine)

Wisse, Ruth R., 21:**105**

Wissenschaft des Judentums, 21:**105–114**
    biography and autobiography, 3:707
    Breslau seminary, 21:108–109
    building momentum, 21:108
    Cassel, David, 4:507
    Elbogen, Ismar, 6:291
    first generation, 21:107–108
    historiography, 9:158–159, 21:109–113
    Jewish nationalism, 6:37
    Jewish studies and, 11:316, 325
    Krochmal, Nachman, 12:368
    Leopold Zunz, 21:107
    motives, factors, 21:106–107
    origin, definition, 21:105–106
    periodicals, 21:109
    Zunz, Leopold, 18:722

Wissotzky, Kalonymus Ze'ev, 14:517, 21:**114**

Wistrich, Robert S., 21:**114**

Witchcraft. *See* Sorcery

Witch of En-Dor, 6:404, **405**, 18:80, 81

With God in Hell: Judaism in the Ghettos and Death Camps (Berkovits), 3:439

Within the City's Wall. See Lifnim min ha-Ḥomah

With the Trade Winds (Morris), 14:511

With the Turks in Palestine (Aaronsohn), 1:222

Witkon, Alfred, 21:**114–115**

Witkowski, Felix Ernst. *See* Harden, Maximillian

Witkowski, Georg, 8:347

Witmund, Uri. *See* Uri ben Aaron ha-Levi

Witnesses, 21:**115–125**
    apostasy, 2:276
    competency, 21:115–117
    duty to testify, 21:117–118, 122–123
    examination, 21:117, 123–124
    oaths of, 15:363–364
    perjury by, 15:772–773
    recorded testimony, 21:119–120
    wicked, disqualification, 21:121–122
    women as, 21:115–116, 120–121
    See also Evidence

Witness from the Pulpit: Topical Sermons 1933-1980 (Saperstein), 18:35

Witte, Sergey Yulyevich, Count, 4:128, 21:**125**

Wittenberg, Yiẓhak, 20:532–533, 21:**125–126**

Wittgenstein, Ludwig, 21:**126–127**

Wittgenstein, Paul, 21:**127**

Wittkower, Rudolf J., 21:**127–128**

Wittkowsky, Samuel, 15:302

Wittlin, Józef, 21:**128**

Witz, Chaim. *See* Simmons, Gene

Witzenhausen, Josef, 3:610, 631

Witzenhausen, Uri. *See* Uri ben Aaron ha-Levi

Witztum, Doron, 3:679

Wives. *See* Husband and wife

Wizards (Bakshi), 3:74

Wizen, Moshe Aharon, 21:**128**

Wiznitzer, Arnold, 4:143, 144

WIZO (Women International Zionist Organization), 21:**128–130**
    Amsterdam, 2:118
    women leaders, 11:72

W.J.C. *See* World Jewish Congress

Wloclawek (Poland), 3:47, 21:**130**

Wlodawa (Poland), 21:**130–131**

Wlodmierz (Ukraine). *See* Vladimir Volynski (Ukraine)

WMO. *See* World Meteorological Organization

Wodzislaw (Poland), 21:**131**

Wodzislaw Ślawski. *See* Wodzislaw (Poland)

Woelfflein of Schnaittach, 15:503

Woerterbuch der aegyptischen Sprache (Erman), 6:482

Wogue, Lazare Eliezer, 3:629, 21:**131**

Wohl, Henryk, 16:347, 21:**131**

Wohlberg, Moshe, 21:**131–132**

Wohlbruek, Anton. *See* Walbrook, Anton

Wohlgemuth, Joseph, 21:**132**

Wohlgemuth, Judah Ari, 21:132

Wojda, Carol Frederick, 21:**132**

Wojslawski, Zevi. *See* Woyslawski, Zevi

Wojtyla, Karol. *See* John Paul II

Wolberg, Lewis Robert, 21:**132–133**

Wolborz dynasty, 8:424–425

Wolbrom (Poland), 21:**133**

Wólczko. *See* Volchko

Wold, Lucien, 3:694

Wolf (animal). *See* Wolves

Wolf, Abner, 21:**134**

Wolf, Abraham, 21:**134**

Wolf, Adolf Grant, 21:139

Wolf, Alfred, 13:204, 21:**134–135**

Wolf, Arnold Jacob, 4:92, 21:**135**

Wolf, Aron. *See* Berlijn, Anton

Wolf, Edwin, II, 21:134

Wolf, Egon, 4:144

Wolf, Elias, 21:133

Wolf, Eric Robert, 21:**135–136**

Wolf, Francisca. *See* Wolf, Frumet

Wolf, Frieda, 4:144

Wolf, Friedrich, 21:**136**

Wolf, Friedrich Augustus, 15:191

Wolf, Frumet, 21:**137**

Wolf, Gerson, 21:**137**

Wolf, Gustav, 21:**137**

Wolf, Johann Christoph, 21:**137–138**
    bibliography of, 3:681
    Jonathan ben Joseph of Ruzhany, 11:398

Wolf, Leyzer, 21:**138**

Wolf, Lucien, 3:86, 11:292, 21:**138–139**

Wolf, Maurice, 14:446

Wolf, Morris, 21:134

Wolf, Moses, 11:114

Wolf, Øystein Wingaard, 18:96

Wolf, Richard Riegel, 21:**139**

Wolf, Simon, 4:14, 21:**139–140**

Wolf, Ze'ev. *See* Bermann, Vasili

Wolfe, Alan S., 21:**140–141**

Wolfe, Bertram David, 21:**141**

Wolfe, Humbert, 4:116, 21:**141**

Wolfe, Isobel, 3:183

Wolfe, Ray D., 21:140

Wolfe, Rose, 21:140

Wolfe, Umberto. *See* Wolfe, Humbert

Wolfe family, 21:140

Wolfenbuettel (Germany), 21:**141–142**

Wolfensohn, James David, 21:**142**

Wolfenstein, Alfred, 21:**142**

Wolfert, Ira, 21:**142**

Wolff, A. A., 3:627

Wolff, Abraham Alexander, 21:**142–143**

Wolff, Albert Louis, 21:**143**

Wolff, Bernhard, 21:**143**

Wolff, Charlotte, 21:**143–144**

Wolff, Gustav, 21:**144**

Wolff, Hermann, 21:**144**

Wolff, Jeanette, 21:**144**

Wolff, Joseph, 21:**144–145**

Wolff, Louis. *See* Wolff, Albert Louis

Wolff, Theodore, 21:**145**

Wolff, Werner, 21:**145**

Wolf family, 6:269, 21:**133–134**

Wolff-Benda, Bernhard. *See* Wolff, Bernhard

Wolffsohn, David, 4:27, 15:291, 21:**145–147**

Wolffsohn, Julius, 11:441

Wolfowski, Menahem Zalman, 21:**147**

Wolfsberg (Austria), 21:**148**

Wolfsberg, Oscar. *See* Aviad, Yeshayahu

Wolfskehl, Karl, 21:**148**

Wolfsohn, Juliusz, 21:**148**

Wolfsohn-Halle, Aaron, 8:688, 21:**148**

Wolfson, Arthur, 15:507

Wolfson, Elliot, 21:**148–149**

Wolfson, Harry Austryn, 11:317, 18:211, 21:**149–150**

Wolfson, Isaac. *See* Wolfson, Sir Isaac

Wolfson, Madeline Gail. *See* Kahn, Madeline

Wolfson, Sir Isaac, 5:588, 21:**150**

Wolfson, Theresa, 21:**150–151**

Wolfson family, 15:554

Wolfsthal, Chune, 21:**151**

Wolkers, Jan, 6:68

Wolkowiski, Jehiel Ber, 21:**151**

Wolkowysk. *See* Volkovysk (Belarus)

Wollenborg, Leone, 16:345, 21:**151**

Wollheim, Gert H., 21:**151–152**

Wollheim, Norbert, 2:48

Wolman, Abel, 21:**152**

Wolmark, Alfred, 21:**152**

Wolofsky, Hirsh, 21:**152**

Wolomin (Poland), 21:**152–153**

Wolowski, Elisha, 21:153

Wolowski, Franciszek, 21:153

Wolowski, Jan Kanty, 21:153

Wolowski family, 21:**153**

Wolpa (Belarus). *See* Volpa (Belarus)

Wolpe, Berthold L., 4:368

Wolpe, David E., 21:**153–154**

Wolpe, David J., 21:**154**

Wolpe, Howard Eliot III, 21:**154–155**

Wolpe, Stefan, 21:**155**

Wolper, David Lloyd, 21:**155**

Wolpert, Ludwig Yehuda, 21:**155**

Wolsey, Louis, 21:**156**

Wolves, 21:**133**

Wolyá (Ukraine). *See* Volhynia (Ukraine)

"The Woman Hater." See "Sone ha-Nashim" (Abraham of Sarteano)

Woman of Valor (Fineman), 7:26

Women, 21:**156–209**

    ablution and, 1:263

    abortion, 1:270–273

    aggadah, 1:459–460

    agunah, 1:510–520, 19:452

    agunot, 21:206–207

    Alliance Israelite Universelle, 1:674

    Ammonite, 2:84

    Amsterdam, 2:108

    amulets, 2:122

    anthropology, 2:186, 187

    artisans, 5:268

    asceticism, 2:549

    bankers, 3:115

    bat mitzvah, 3:165–166, 21:205–206

    biblical exegesis and study by, 3:663

    biblical stereotypes of, 16:105–106

    bigamy and polygamy, 3:691

    birth of female children, 3:721–723

    in Black

        Amsterdam, 2:119

        in Israel, 6:754

    Blumenthal, Aaron H., 4:12

    B'nai B'rith Women, 4:14, 17

    breadmaking, 4:155

    Bukhara music-dance, 4:264

    Canada, 4:400, 401, 406, 409, 417

    candles, rituals using, 4:429–430

    cantors, 15:507

    child marriage, 4:616–617

circumcision, 4:733

civil rights, 4:409, 5:771–772

common law wives, 13:683

Conservative Judaism, 5:174

crime and, 5:297

Crypto-Judaism, 2:253

custody, 15:636–637

daughters

    custody of, 15:636–637

    parental maintenance of, 15:635

deportations, 9:*478, 479*

dietary laws and, 5:658–659

divorce and rights of, 5:712–713, 714, 17:7–8

domestic violence and, 5:739–741

domiciles of wives, 5:741–742

dowries, 5:768–772

Eastern European gender models, 21:180–181

economic roles, 21:158–159, 170–172

education, Jewish, 6:168–169, 173, 176, 177, 179, 8:438

eighteenth to twentieth century

    dress, 6:16

    headdress, 6:16–17

England, 6:428–429

Enlightenment period, 16:109

equal rights, 3:177, 4:462–463

Eshet Ḥayil, 6:505

exclusion from study and worship, 15:258

female voice prohibition, 14:649

festivals, 6:771

firzogerin, 7:50

folk music, 14:692

fraternal women's organizations, 4:220

Funeral rituals, 4:293

gender and, in Jewish philosophy, 16:105–111

ghetto roles and survival, 21:183

government officials, Canada, 16:56

Hadassah, 8:185–188

hakkafot participation, 8:250

ḥallah, 8:277

ḥalukkah, 8:289–290

Ḥasidism, 8:397–398, 21:177–178, 185

Haskalah, 8:435, 438, 443, 699–700, 21:178–179, 181–182

ḥazzanim, 8:505

head covering, 8:507

head shaving, 8:507

Hebrew writers, 8:699–702

ḥevra kaddisha, 9:82

historians, 9:152–153, 12:657

historical perspective, 9:163

    biblical period, 21:156–161

    early modern period, 21:174–178

    Holocaust, 9:420

    Israel, 21:190–194

    modern Central, Western Europe, 21:178–180

    modern Eastern Europe, 21:180–183

    North America, 21:183–186

    post-biblical, Talmudic period, 21:161

inheritance rights of, 21:161–162, 169–170, 195

intermarriage, 14:384

Islamic world, 21:165–169, 186–190

    education, 21:189, 190

    gender roles, 21:186–188

    modern, 21:186–190

    poetry, 21:188–189

Israel

    kibbutz participation, 21:192, 194

    labor force participation, 21:193–194

    military service participation, 21:193

    modern, 21:192–194

    politics, 10:819–820

    post-1948, 21:192–194

    publishing, 15:792

    religion and, 10:632

    twentieth century, 21:190

    workers, 10:611

    writers, 8:710–711

    yishuv era, 21:190–192

Israel judicial system, 21:194–207

    agunot, 21:206–207

    Bat Mitzvah celebration, 21:205–206

    economic rights, 21:195–196

    husband and wife issues, 21:195

    public prayer rights, 21:200–205

    status, 21:194–195

    succession and inheritance, 21:195

    Torah study issue, 21:199–200

    Women of the Wall case, 21:204–205

Jewish scholarship, 1:409

in Jewish studies, 11:319

The Jewish Woman, 11:331–332

Judah ben Isaac Ibn Shabbetai, 11:487–488

Judges, Book of, 11:561–562

Kaddish recitation, 11:697–698

labor movement, Katznelson, Raḥel, 12:26

laws and legal systems
marriage and, 13:680–683
right of preemption and, 13:707–708
status, 21:161–163, 170–171, 194–207
takkanot, 19:451–452
Talmud, 12:660

lesbianism, 12:660–661

literature, 21:175, 178–179, 184
Adams, Hannah, 1:380
Haskalah writers, 8:699–700
letter writers, 12:673–674
Liebrecht, Savyon, 12:811–812
Morpurgo, Rachel Luzzatto, 14:509

liturgy, involvement in, 4:204

Maid of Ludomir, 13:250

marriage and children, 21:157–158, 171, 195

Matriarchs, 4:562–563

menstruation, 2:133, 135, 3:772

Middle Ages
Christian Europe, 21:170–174
dress, 6:14–15
Islam, 21:165–170
physicians, 13:727
Spain, 21:168–170

military service, 14:246, 21:193

minyans, 5:174, 14:302

misogyny, 1:313–314, 16:63–64

Mo'eẓet ha-Po'alot, 14:415

morality of, 13:787

musicians, 5:411
Iraq, 10:23
Liebling, Estelle, 12:809–810
Mendelssohn Hensel, Fanny Caecilie, 14:40–41

mystics, messianics, 21:176–177

Nazi Germany, 21:180

New Moon, 15:151

niddah, 1:263

numerus clausus in Poland and, 15:341

ordination, 5:174, 17:16, 17, 18, 18:278–279, 19:361, 20:367–368, 21:186
Jewish Theological Seminary, 11:330

Jonas, Regina, 11:394

origins of woman, 13:449

orphanages, role in, 15:486

in Ottoman empire, 15:539

parental maintenance of, 15:635

as partisans, 15:667

Passover observance and, 15:681–682

patriarchy concept, critique, 21:161

philanthropy, 16:46–47, 57

political participation, 21:182, 184–185

practice of mitzvot by, 13:787–788

prayer, 16:460–461

praying at Western Wall, vol. 20: color insert

pregnancy and childbirth, 2:122

printers, 16:539–540

psychology, 16:690–693

puberty, 16:695, 696

rabbis, 2:118, 6:753, 21:164–165, vol. 5: color insert

Ravensbrueck concentration camp, 17:120–121

Reform Judaism, 21:179

religious role, 21:159–160, 163, 172–173, 176, 188, 200–205

rights of, 8:186
Abzug, Bella Savitzky, 1:347
Cardin, Shoshana Shoubin, 4:462–463
Morgenstern, Lina, 14:487
Schmolka, Marie, 18:146

rites and rituals, involvement in, 4:204

Rosh Ḥodesh, 6:771

salons, 8:435, 17:707

scribes, 14:312

secular education, 8:438

sexuality, 6:755–756

Shabbatean view, 21:177

sheḥitah, 18:436–437

shtetl, 18:525–526

signs and symbols, Shekhinah, 18:442–443

Simḥat Torah honors, 4:180

socialism, 18:713–714

Sotah (tractate), 21:161–162

spiritual leaders
Ackerman, Paula Herskovitz, 1:357–358
Frank, Ray, 7:193–194

studies, 6:754–756

synagogues
integration into, 19:360–362
segregation of sexes, 13:771–772, 18:224

Talmud, dress, 6:13

tikhines literature, 21:176

Torah study, 19:273–275, 21:199–200

Tzvi Migdal traffic network, Brazil, 4:147–148

U.S., 21:183–186
athletes, 12:805–806
authors, 6:677
Civil War, 15:719–720
educators, 6:542, 15:714
lawyers, 6:677
middle class acculturation, 21:185
ordination, 21:186
poets, 6:686–687
post-WW II, 21:185–186
professionalization and family role, 6:704
trade union movement, 21:184–185

veils, 20:490

voting rights, 21:196–198

white slave trade, 16:627–628

witness status, 21:115–116, 120–121

wives of David, 5:448–449, 452–453

Women of the Wall case, 21:204–205

women's seder, vol. 17: color insert

working women, advancement of, 16:278–279, 18:183–184

Yiddish biography and autobiography by, 3:708

Ze'enah U-Re'enah, 21:491

See also Feminism; Hadassah, the Women's Zionist Organization of America; Misogynism; Mothers; *specific organizations*

Women International Zionist Organization. *See* WIZO (Women International Zionist Organization)

Women of Israel (Aguilar), 1:509

Women of Reform Judaism. *See* National Federation of Temple Sisterhoods

Women of the Wall case, 21:204–205

Women of valor, Bithiah, 3:729

Women's Equal Rights Law, 5711 (1951), 5:771–772

Women's groups
Brazil, 18:31
Emma Lazarus Federation of Jewish Women's Clubs, 6:395
Emunah, 6:395
National Council of Jewish Women, 15:**21–22**

Women's groups, *continued*
  National Federation of Temple
    Sisterhoods, 15:22
The Women's Haggadah, 4:204, 15:682
Women's League for Conservative
  Judaism, 18:113, 21:**209–210**
Women's Trade Union League, 9:117,
  15:147, 18:151
Wonder Boys (Chabon), 4:555
Wonders. *See* Miracles
Wonder working and prophets, 16:571
Wondrous Tale of Alroy (Disraeli), 2:6,
  18:201
Wood, 1:347, 6:88, 21:**210**
Wood, Albert J., 6:25–26
Woodhead, John, 15:584, 586
Woodhead Commission. *See* Palestine
  Partition Commission
Woodsworth, J.S., 4:396
Woodward, Robert, 11:468
Woog, Mayer, 21:**210–211**
Woolf, Bob, 21:**211**
Woolf, H. W., 11:362
Woolf, Harry, Baron. *See* Woolf, Sir
  Harry, Baron
Woolf, Leonard, 21:**211–212**
Woolf, Moshe, 21:**212**
Woolf, Sir Harry, Baron, 21:**211**
Woolin, Dr. Elias, 15:196
Woolley, Charles Leonard. *See*
  Woolley, Sir Charles Leonard
Woolley, Sir Charles Leonard, 21:**212**
Worcester (England), 21:**212**
Worcester (MA), 21:**213–214**
Worchester Account (Behrman), 3:264
Word, 21:**214**
*A Word about Tomorrow. See Solvo o
  zavtrashnem dne*
Word of God. *See* Logos
Words about Music (Babbitt), 3:17
*Work and History: An Essay on the
  Structure of Civilization* (Schrecker),
  18:167
Workers. *See* Labor
Workers' settlements. *See* Moshavim
Workers' Theater of Palestine. *See*
  Ohel
Work in Progress (Eisner), 6:277
Workmen's Circle, 13:257, 21:**214–215**
  Canada, 4:399
  creation of, 18:719
  in New York City, 15:205, 208,
    209–210
Works Progress Administration
  (WPA)
  Bolotowsky, Ilya, 4:50
  in New York City, 15:221

World, size and density of, 7:489
The World and the Book (Josipovici),
  11:461
World communist movement, 5:96–99
World Conference of Jewish
  Organizations, 21:**215–216**
World Council of Churches (WCC),
  4:684–685, 686, 11:277–278, 280–
  281
  antisemitism, 16:631
  Committee on the Church and
    the Jewish People, 16:630, 631–
    632
  Holocaust, response to, 9:376
  on Israeli-Palestinian relations,
    16:632–633
World Council of Synagogues, 5:176–
  177
*The World Dictionary of Hebrew Slang.
  See Millon Olami le-Ivrit Meduberet*
World Federation of Ha-Shomer,
  8:384
World Gathering of Jewish Holocaust
  Survivors, 2:48
World Health Organization, 6:294,
  20:271
The World Hitler Never Made
  (Rosenfeld), 9:415, 421
World Jewish Associations, 21:**216–
  221**
  contemporary period, 21:219–221
  minority rights, 21:218–219
  nineteenth century, 21:216–217
  welfare and protection, 21:217
  Zionist, 21:217–218
World Jewish Congress, 21:217–218,
  219, **221–222**
  African Jewish Congress, 1:440–
    441
  American Gathering of Jewish
    Holocaust Survivors, 2:49
  American Jewish Archives, 2:53
  American Jewish Committee, 2:55
  American Jewish Congress, 2:57
  League of Nations, 12:565
  Ravensbrueck concentration camp
    and, 17:121
  Singer, Israel, 18:636–637
World Jewish Economic Federation,
  4:111
World Jewish Relief. *See* Central
  British Fund (CBF)
World Jewish Restitution
  Organization, 2:49
World Labor Zionist movement,
  21:**222–223**
World Meteorological Organization,
  20:272
"World of Art" movement, 18:214

The World of Odysses (Finley), 7:39
World of Our Fathers (Howe), 15:227
World Over (periodical), 6:475
World Parliament of Religions, 2:47
World Religions in America (Neusner),
  15:*125*
Worlds, The Four, 21:**224–225**
World Sephardi Federation, 15:548,
  18:303, 21:**223–224**
World Series (Baseball), 6:20–21
World's Fair (Doctorow), 5:728
*The World's Greatest Restauration, or
  Calling of the Jews* (Finch), 7:24–25
World Slovak Congress, 13:162
World Socialist Union, 16:246–248
World to come. *See* Olam ha-ba
World Trade Center (WTC), 18:589
World Trade Center attacks. *See*
  September 11, 2001 terrorist attacks
World Trade Organization (WTO),
  11:771
World Union for Progressive Judaism
  Amsterdam, 2:114
  Hirsch, Richard, 3:129
World Union for the Propagation of
  Judaism, 16:593
World Union of General Zionists,
  7:439
World Union of Jewish Students,
  19:269
World Union of Jewish Studies,
  11:320
World War I
  American Jewish Committee, 2:55
  American Jewry, 2:45–46
  American Joint Distribution
    Committee, 2:59
  Bonn, Moritz Julius, and "policy
    of fulfillment," 4:64
  England, 6:417
  Filderman, Wilhelm, 7:19
  Haller's Army, 8:281
  Jewish Legion in, 11:303–306
  Jewish participation in military
    service, 14:239–240, 239*t*
  Jewish units, 11:11
  jihād proclaimed in, 11:336
  Monash, John, 14:432
  Morgenthau Commission, 14:490
  Nili, 15:267–268
  Ottoman empire, 15:543
  OZE, 15:556
  population, 6:559
  Russia, 1881-1911: Second Phase,
    11:540
  San Remo Conference, 18:26
  Sykes-Picot Agreement, 19:350–
    351, *351*

Ukraine, 12:443
World War II, 9:252–253, 11:547–549, 548, 551, 560–561, 17:546–553, 546t
American Jewish Committee, 2:55
American Joint Distribution Committee, 2:61
Ancona, 2:141
anti-zionism, 2:243–244
Bermuda Conference, 3:466
Bialystok (Poland), 3:568–570
Biltmore Program, 3:699–700
Birobidzhan, 3:719
Bitburg Controversy, 3:727–728
Blitzkreig invasion of Western Europe, 9:332–333
blood-for-trucks negotiations, 6:250
Brody, Alter, 4:200
Bulgaria, 4:271–273
Canada, 4:407–408, 423
demography, 17:546t, 551
Dresden (Germany), 6:11
Dunkelman, Benjamin, 6:50
Dutch literature and, 6:70–71
economics, 6:138
education, Jewish, 6:186–187
Eisenhower, Dwight David, 6:266–267
England, 6:418–419, 14:510–511
Europe, education, Jewish, 6:186–187
extermination activities, 17:547–548, 551–553
German invasion, 17:547, 551
German retreat, 9:342
Hungary, 4:66
"Illegal" immigration and, 9:723
Jewish Brigade Group, 11:271–272, 16:8
Jewish participation in military service, 14:239t, 240
Morocco, 14:501–502
Norway, 15:306
nuclear physics, 16:137
"Operation Mincemeat," 14:451
ORT, 15:489
partisans, 17:548, 549–550
partisans in, 15:664–668, 665
Polish invasion, 9:331–332
population statistics, 17:546t, 551–553
refugees, 5:683–686, 17:550–551
aid to, 11:271
Japan and, 11:81
Reich expansionism, 9:288–299, 330
resistance activities, 5:263, 9:574–575, 17:548–550

Ribbentrop-Molotov Pact, 9:331
Russia, 11:546–553, 546t
antisemitism, 17:560–561
demography, 11:546t, 551
extermination activities, 11:547–548, 551–553
German invasion, 11:547, 551
partisans, 11:548, 549–550
population statistics, 11:546t, 551–553
refugees, 11:550–551
resistance activities, 11:548–550, 17:548–550
Yiddish literature, 11:553
Yiddish publishing, 11:553
Saint Louis (MO), 11:672–673
Seabees, 14:483
underground organizations
Beriḥah, 3:434–435
Berit ha-Biryonim, 3:436
University in Exile, New York City, 15:219
USSR
annexation of territories, 11:546–547, 546t
army, 11:550
Bereza, 3:413
invasion of, 9:334–336
Wannsee conference, 9:336
White Papers policy, 10:277
Yiddish literature, 17:553
Yiddish publishing, 17:553
See also Antisemitism; Holocaust; Jewish resistance; specific countries and topics
Worldwar tetralogy (Stephenson), 18:200
World Zionist Organization, 9:54
aliyah machinery established, 10:336
archives, 2:407
Asociación Mutual Israelista Argentina, 2:71
as authorized agency, 10:216
Biltmore Program, 3:699
Bodenheimer, Max Isidor, 4:27, 28
Brandeis, Louis Dembitz, 4:122–123
Druyanow, Alter, 6:29
Dulzin, Arye Leib, 6:45
Holam, 8:336
Jewish Legion, 11:306
Keren Hayesod, 12:82–84
Mizrachi, 14:389–392
Mizrachi Women's Organization of America, 2:80
Mohilewer, Samuel, 14:419

Morocco, 14:506
Sokolow, Nahum, 18:748
See also Jewish Agency
Wormann, Curt, 21:225–226
Worms (animal), 21:225
Worms (Germany), 10:41, 21:226–227
Worms, Aaron, 21:227–228
Worms, Asher Anshel, 21:228
Worms, Baron George, 21:228
Worms, de, family, 9:7, 21:228
Worms, Henry, 16:342, 21:228
Worms, René, 18:730, 21:229
Worms, Solomon, 21:228
Wormser, André, 21:229
Wormser, B.H., 3:44
Wormser, Olivier Boris, 21:229
Wormser, Seckel, 21:229
Worms Mahzor, 13:366
Wormwood, 21:229
Woroszylski, Wiktor, 21:229–230
Worship, 21:230–233
See also specific religions, organizations, and topics
The Worship of the Creator. See Avodat ha-Bore
W or The Memory of Childhood (Perec), 15:758
Wortsman, Yecheskiel Charles, 21:233
Wosk, Abrasha, 21:233
Wosk, Morris, 21:233
Wosk family, 21:233
Wotitz (Czech Republic). See Votice (Czech Republic)
Wouk, Herman, 21:233–234
Woyslawski, Zevi, 21:234
WRB. See War Refugee Board
Wreaths, 5:307–309
Wreschner, Arthur, 21:234
Wrestling, 19:150
Wright, G. E.
biblical archaeology of, 3:650, 654
Joshua, Book of, 11:446, 449
Writers (Epstein), 6:466
Writers' Association in Israel, 21:234–235
Writing, 21:235–246
ancient education, 6:166–167
animal hides, leather, 21:238
clay, 21:239
equipment, 21:240–241
inscriptions, 21:241–244
ivory, 21:239
Ladino, 12:431–432
materials, for books, 4:71, 73
metals, 21:239
monumental inscriptions, 21:236–237

Writing, *continued*
　on ostraca, 15:508–509
　papyrus, 21:237–238
　pottery, 21:238
　scripts and materials, 21:235–236
　Talmud and Halakhah, 21:244–245
　tatoos, graffiti, 21:240
　wax, 21:240
　wood, 21:239
Writings on the History of Hibbat Zion and the Settlement of Palestine (Druyanow), 6:29
Written and sealed. See Escrito y sellado
Written Law. *See* Torah
Written obligations, 15:371
Wroclaw (Poland). *See* Breslau
The Wrong Way. See Lo Zeh ha-Derekh
Wronke. *See* Wronki (Poland)
Wronker, Lili Cassel, 4:372
Wronki (Poland), 21:246
Wronsky, Siddy, 21:246
Wuensche, August Karl, 21:246
Wuerttemberg (Germany), 21:246–247
　Talheim, 19:462–463
Wuerzburg (Germany), 21:248–249
Wuerzburger Rav. *See* Bamberger, Seligmann Baer
Wuhsha al-Dallala, 21:249
WUJS. *See* World Union of Jewish Students
Wulff, Cecily. *See* Eskeles, Cecily
Wulff, Moshe. *See* Woolf, Moshe
Wulfila. *See* Ulfilas
Wunderbar, Reuben Joseph, 21:249
Wunderlich, Frieda, 21:249
Wuppertal (Germany), 21:249–250
Wurman, Osias, 11:470
Wurzburger, Walter S., 21:250
Wurzweiler, Gustav, 21:250
Wycliffe, John, 3:611
Wyden, Ronald Stephen, 21:250–251
Wye Memorandum, 15:598
Wye Plantation Agreement, 10:249
Wygodzki, Stanisllaw, 21:251
Wyler, Bea, 15:401
Wyler, William, 14:571, 21:251
Wylkowyski. *See* Vilkaviškis
Wyman, David, 2:673–674
Wynn, Ed, 21:252
Wynn, Keenan, 21:252
Wynn, Samuel, 21:252
Wynn, Steve, 21:252–253
Wyoming (U.S.), 21:*253*, **253–254**
Wyschogrod, Edith, 16:111

Wysokie Litewskie (Belarus). *See* Vysokoye (Belarus)
Wyszkow (Poland), 21:254
Wyszogrod (Poland), 21:254–255
Wyzanski, Charles Edward, Jr., 21:255

X

X (letter), 21:*257*
Xabillo, Elijah ben Joseph. *See* Habillo, Elijah ben Joseph
Xanten (Germany), 3:779, 21:257
Xanthi (Greece), 21:257–259
Xátiva (Spain). *See* Játiva (Spain)
Xenophobia, 18:31–32
Xenophon of Lampsacus, 21:259
Xerox Corporation, 13:61
Xerxes I. *See* Ahasuerus-Xerxes
Ximenes, David. *See* Ximenes, Sir David
Ximenes, Morris. *See* Ximenes, Sir Morris
Ximenes, Sir David, 21:259
Ximenes, Sir Morris, 9:6, 21:259
Ximenes, Solomon Mordecai, 21:259–260
Ximenes de Cisneros, Francisco, 21:260
Xixo, Astruc Jacob. *See* Siso, Astruc Jacob
XY, lesyndrome de l'identité masculine (Badinter), 3:49

Y

Y (letter), 21:*261*
Y.A. *See* Aharonovitch, Yosef
Ya'acobi, Gad, 21:261–262
Ya'ad parliamentary group, 6:321
Ya'akoc. *See* Jacob
"Ya'akov ha-Shomer" (Feierberg), 6:731
Ya'akov Rabinowitz be-Yarmouth (Halkin), 8:276
Ya'aleh ve-Yavo, 15:151, 21:262
Ya'aleh ve-Yavo, 2:75
Ya'alon, Moshe, 21:262
Yaari, Abraham, 3:682, 21:262
Ya'ari, Me'ir, 21:262–263
Yaari, Menahem, 21:263
Yaari, Yehudah, 21:263
Yabez, Joseph. *See* Jabez, Joseph ben Hayyim
Yabin, Yitzhak, 18:362
Yachting, 19:150
　Ellison, Lawrence J., 6:362
　Mosbacher, Emil, Jr., 14:515
Yad, 21:263–264
Yad Aharon (Alfandari), 1:637

Yad Aharon (Pinto), 16:179
Yadayim, 21:264
Yad David (Sinzheim), 18:642
Yad Hannah, 21:264
Yadin, Yigael, 21:264–265
　Anglo-Israel Archaeological Society, 2:161
　biblical archaeology of, 3:650
　Hazor, 2:371, 378
　Judean Desert caves expedition, 11:524
　Masada, 2:161
　political program, 10:237–238
Yad Izhak Ben-Zvi, 3:396
Yad la-Yeled (Israel), 7:578
Yadlin, Aharon, 21:265
Yadlin, Asher, 10:237
Yad Mordekhai (Israel), 20:657, 21:265
Yad Moshe (Amarillo), 2:32
Yad Vashem, 11:818, 17:303, 21:266–268
　Arad, Yitzhak, 2:332
　archives, 2:411
　Bialystok (Poland) secret archives at, 3:569
　Carl Lutz's saving of Jews, 13:275
　genealogical resources, 7:432–433
　Hall of Names, Holocaust History Museum, vol. 9: color insert
　Lavi, Theodor, 12:531
　Leszno Street exhibit, Warsaw Ghetto, vol. 9: color insert
　Memorial to the Deportees, vol. 9: color insert
　Shalev, Avner, 18:372
Yad Vashem International Institute for Holocaust Research, 9:426
Yad Vashem Studies, 9:424
Yael Shefer, Minor by way of her mother v. State of Israel, 13:739, 740, 743, 745–746
Yaffe, Arye. *See* Koenig, Leo
Yaffe, Arye-Leyb. *See* Koenig, Leo
Yaffe, Leyb. *See* Koenig, Leo
Yaffo (Israel). *See* Jaffa (Israel)
Yafil, Edmond Nathan, 1:440
Yagdil Torah, 1:328
Yagupsky, Máximo, 21:268
Yagur (Israel), 21:268
Yagur Passover Seder Service (Sharett), 18:413
Yahad, 21:268–270
Yahalom, 16:477
YAHBI. *See* Jekuthiel ben Judah ha-Kohen
Yahdū, 6:66

Yahil, Chaim, 21:**270–271**

Yaḥiri, 8:472

Yah Ribbon Olam, 21:**271**

Yahrzeit, 21:**271**

Yahu, 6:313

Yahūd, 21:**271–272**

Yahuda, Abraham Shalom, 21:**272**

Yahuda ben David, Judeo-Persian poetry of, 11:555

Yahudi, Yusuf, 21:**273**

al-Yahudi, Isaac, 15:526

Yahvism, 13:225

Yahwism
  Baal worship, 3:12
  Elijah, 6:331–332
  seminomadism and, 15:295–296

Yahya. *See* Zuta

Yahya, Samuel. *See* Denis, Albertus

Yahya ben Abraham ben Sa'adiah al-Bashiri. *See* Bashiri, Yaḥya

Yaḥyā ben Suleiman al-Ṭabīb. *See* Zechariah ben Solomon-Rofe

Yaḥya family, 13:251–252

Ya'ir Nativ (Abbas), 1:231

Ya-ish (Hazaz), 8:493

Ya'ish, Baruch ben Isaac ibn, 21:**273**

Ya'ish, Solomon ibn. *See* Abenaes, Solomon

Yakar, Joseph, Yiddish translations of Bible, 3:610

Yakerson, Simon, 11:323

Yakhini, Abraham ben Elijah, 18:345, 352, 21:**273**

Yakhin Lashon (Baer), 3:53

Yakir, Yonah, 21:**273**

Yaknehaz (abbreviation), 21:**273–274**

Yaknehaz (Goldberg, Isaiah-Nissan Hakohen), 21:**274**

Yakobovits, Avraham Aryeh Leib. *See* Akavya, Avraham Aryeh Leib

Yakub, Hekim. *See* Pasha, Jacob

Yakum (Israel), 21:**274**

Yakutyonok Oleska (Altauzen), 2:17

Yalan-Stekelis, Miriam, 21:**274**

Yaldei ha-Ẓel (Tomer), 8:721

Yaldei Ruḥi (Pines), 16:167–168

Yaldut Kashah (Banai), 3:106

Yale Art Gallery, 11:722

Yale University, 12:712–713, 15:137
  law school, 12:555–556
  Levin, Richard C., 12:712–713

Yalkut ha-Gershuni (Stern), 19:209

Yalkut ha-Makhiri (Anthology), 21:**274–275**

Yalkut Me-Am Lo'ez (Yerushalmi), 13:710

Yalkut Moreshet (periodical), 14:484–485

Yalkut Shimoni, 7:212, 8:389, 21:**275–276**

Yalkut Shirat he-Ammim (Minski), 14:297

Yalkut Shirim (Elisheva), 6:354

Yalon, Hanoch, 8:640–641, 653, 21:**276–277**

Yalow, Rosalyn Sussman, 21:**277**

Yalta (Russia), 21:**277**

Yalta (wife of Naḥman), 21:**277**

Yamah shel Sedom (Israel). *See* Dead Sea (Israel)

Yam ha-Aravah (Israel). *See* Dead Sea (Israel)

Yam ha-Melaḥ (Israel). *See* Dead Sea (Israel)

Yamim Nora'im, 21:**277–278**

Yamim Yedabberu (Shenhar), 18:459

Yammit region (Egypt), 21:**278–279**

Yampolsky Berta, 21:**279**

Yam shel Shelomo (Luria), 13:268

Yam Suf. *See* Red Sea

Yang-Chou (China), 21:**279–280**

Yankelovich, Daniel, 18:733

Yankl der Shmid (Pinski), 16:175

Yankl the Blacksmith. See Yankl der Shmid

Yankowich, Leon Rene, 21:**280**

Yannai (Palestinian amora), 11:487, 21:**280**

Yannai (poet), 21:**280–282**

Yannai, Alexander, 2:457, 18:600, 21:*282*, **282–283**
  Ammatha, 2:81
  Obedas I, 15:367
  rebellion against, 18:238

Yannai Rabbah. *See* Yannai

Yanni, Alexander, olam ha-ba, 15:399

Yanow Lyubelski (Poland). *See* Janow Lubelski (Poland)

Yanshuf, 15:550

Yanuka (Zohar), 21:649

Ya'qūb. *See* Jacob

Yaqut, 6:5

Yarcho, Noe, 21:**283**

Yardenah (Israel), 21:**284**

Yarḥei kallah, 1:350–351, 11:715

Yarīm (Yemen), 21:**284**

Yariv, Aharon, 21:**284**

Yariv-Shem-Tov formula, 18:458–459

Yarkonah (Israel), 21:**285**

Yarkon Bridge Trio (music group), 6:263

Yarkoni, Yaffa, 21:**285**

Yarkon river (Israel), 21:**284–285**

Yarmolinsky, Avrahm, 21:**285**

Yarmuk river (Israel), 11:401, 403, 21:**285–286**

Yaron, Reuven, 21:**286–287**

Yaron, Ẓevi, 21:**287**

Yaroslavsky, Yemelyan, 21:**287**

Yarrow, Alfred, First Baronet. *See* Yarrow, Sir Alfred, First Baronet

Yarrow, Peter, 21:**287–288**

Yarrow, Sir Alfred, First Baronet, 21:**287**

Yarshater, E., 11:558

Yashar. *See* Delmedigo, Joseph Solomon

Yashar ben Ḥesed. *See* Sahl ibn Faḍl

Yashfeh, 16:478

Yaski, Avraham, 21:**288**

Yasser, Joseph, 21:**288**

Yassi. *See* Assi

Yassky, Haim, 21:**288**

Yated Neeman (newspaper), 21:**288–289**

Yates, Sidney Richard, 21:**289**

Yathrib (Arabia). *See* Medina (Saudi Arabia)

Yatom, Abraham ben Moses, 4:345

Ya'uri, Yari, 8:472

Yavets, Zvi, 21:**289**

Yaveẓ. *See* Emden, Jacob

Yavin, Ḥayyim, 21:**289**

Yavne'eli, Shemuel, 21:**290**

Yavneh (Israel), 21:**290**

Yavneh (Kibbutz), 21:**290**

Yavneh-Yam, legal document from, 21:**290–291**

Yavorov (Ukraine), 21:**291**

Yavorov, Peyo Kracholov, 4:275

Yawetz, Joseph. *See* Jabez, Joseph ben Ḥayyim

Yazep Krushinski (Byadulya-Yasakar), 4:323

Yazernitzki, Yitzhak. *See* Shamir, Yitzhak

Year, 21:**291–292**

Yearbook for Sexual Intermediate Stages (Hirschfeld), 9:138

Yearbooks. *See* Jewish yearbooks

Year of Birth. See God rozhdeniya

Yeats: The Man and the Masks (Ellmann), 6:362

Yeb (Egypt). *See* Elephantine (Egypt)

Yedidiah. *See* Theophilus (son of Hanan son of Seth)

Yedidyah (Israel), 21:**292**

Yedintsy (Moldova), 21:**292–293**

Yedioth Aharonoth (newspaper), 14:591–592, 21:**293**

Yedi'ot ha-Shi'urim (Lichtenfeld), 12:797

Yefed Nefesh (Azikiri), 3:72–73

Yefeh Einayim (Jellin), 11:119

Yefet, Sarah, 21:**293**

Yefingar (Ukraine), 21:**293–294**

Yefroykin, Israel, 21:**294**

Yeḥi'am (Israel), 21:**294**

Yeḥiel ha-Hagri (Halkin), 8:736–737

Yehiel Nahmany Sefardi. *See* Consolo, Federico

Yehoash, 3:611, 21:**294–295**

Yehoshua, Avraham B., 8:705, 11:216–217, 21:**295–296**

Yehud. *See* Judea

Yehud (Israel), 21:**296–297**

Yehudah Ish-Keriyyot (Agmon), 1:465

Yehudai ben Naḥman, 21:**297**

Yehude-Leyb, Lewis. *See* Cahan, Judah Loeb

Yehudi. *See* Jew

Yehudi, Ish. *See* Rabinovich, Yehudah Leib

Yehudi ben Sheshet, 6:48, 21:**297–298**

Yehudi ha-Kadosh. *See* Przysucha, Jacob Isaac ben Asher

Yeivi, R. *See* Jacob Joseph of Ostrog

Yeivin, Israel, 21:**298**

Yeivin, Shemuel, 21:**298**

Yeivin, Yehoshua Heschel, 21:**298**

Yekaterinodar (Russia). *See* Krasnodar (Russia)

Yekaterinoslav (Ukraine). *See* Dnepropetrovsk (Ukraine)

Yekl, a Tale of the New York Ghetto (Cahan), 4:336

YEKOPO, 18:337, 21:**298–299**, 299*t*

Yekum Purkan, 21:**299–300**

Yelizavetgrad (Ukraine). *See* Kirovograd (Ukraine)

Yellin, Avinoam, 3:699

Yellin, David, 8:673, 21:**300–301**

Yellin-Bentwich, Thelma, 21:**301**

Yellin family, 21:**300–301**, 300*t*

Yellin-Mor, Nathan, 4:393, 6:292, 21:**301–302**

Yellow badges. *See* Jewish badges

Yellow-star. *See* Jewish badges

Yemei Ẓiklag, (Yizhar), 21:378

Yemen, 7:626, 9:206, 21:**302–312**, *303*

  Abyaḍ Yiḥya ben Shalom, 1:346

  Aden, 1:387, 388, 389

  American Joint Distribution Committee, 2:62, 64

  Amran, 2:106

  antisemitism, 18:6

  Arab world (1945–2006), 2:304

  art, music, 21:309–311

  Bible cantillation, 13:663

  bride and groom in traditional clothing, vol. 3: color insert

  crime rates, 5:295

  emancipation, 6:385

  exilarchate of, 6:606

  expulsions from, seventeenth century, 13:694

  Ḥabban, 8:173–174

  Ḥabil, 8:178

  Ḥanukkah celebration, vol. 6: color insert

  history, 21:302–306

  illuminated Hebrew manuscripts from, 3:678

  Israel

    immigration to, 8:474, 10:340, 21:307

      Yemenites in, 10:296, 14:722–723

  Jewish communities, 2:106, 293, 296

  Jewish quarters, 11:312

  Jews in ancient, 6:653

  Judeo-Arabic literature in, 11:537–538

  Kawkabān, 12:40

  Levi, Said ben Shalom, 12:692

  literary, scholarly activities, 21:307–309

  liturgy, 13:136

  messianic activities, 21:306–307

  nagid leadership, 14:733

  Najrān, 14:762–763

  Niebuhr, Carston, travels of, 15:259

  Ottoman conquest of, 15:525

  responsa literature, 17:233

  Saadiah Gaon's Bible translations used in, 3:604

  Sārūm, Abraham, 18:64

  Shar'ab, 18:410

  social, economic factors, 21:306

  songs, religious and secular, 21:310–311

  supralinear punctuation in manuscripts from, 3:591

  synagogues, 2:106

  Yusūf As'ar Yath'ar Dhū Nuwās, 21:428–430

Yemin Moshe (Ventura), 4:468

Yemot ha-Mashi'aḥ (Berkowitz), 3:441

Yenuka, Rav. *See* Natronai Bar Nehemiah

Yeri'ot Shelomo (Rapoport), 17:99

Yeroḥam (Israel), 21:**312**

Yeruḥam ha-Koton. *See* Blindman, Yeruḥam

Yerushalaimer Almanakh (journal), 21:354

Yerushalayim. *See* Jerusalem

Yerushalayim (Kamson), 11:758

Yerushalayim (periodical), 14:420

Yerushalayim de-Lita (Lithuania). *See* Vilna (Lithuania)

Yerushalayim ha-Benuyah (Schatz), 18:202

Yerushalayim Lo Naflah (Elon). *See* Jerusalem Did Not Fall (Elon)

Yerushalayim shel Zahav (song), 18:457

Yerushalimchik, Nahum. *See* Yud, Nahum

Yerushalmi, Abraham ben Josiah. *See* Abraham ben Josiah Yerushalmi

Yerushalmi, Rina, 8:722, 21:**312–313**

Yerushalmi, Shmuel, 13:710

Yerushalmi, Yosef Hayim, 21:**313**

Yeshayahu-Shar'abi, Israel, 21:**313**

Yeshaye, Mordekhe. *See* Tsanin, Mordkhe

Yeshevav the Scribe, 21:**313–314**

Yeshiva. *See* Yeshivot

Yeshiva Chovevei Torah, 17:29, 20:732, 21:**314**

Yeshiva College (South Africa), 6:211

Yeshivah Kneset Israel. *See* Slobodka Yeshivah

Yeshivat Etz Chaim, 6:193

Yeshivat Ḥakhmei Lublin, 18:401–402

Yeshiva Torah Vodaath, 14:44

Yeshiva University (New York City, NY), 21:**314–315**

  Belkin, Samuel, 3:296

  Center for Jewish History, 4:542

  Edah, 6:141–142

  Joel, Richard M., 11:364, 365

  Lamm, Norman, 12:453

  Levinthal, Bernard Louis, 12:724

  Lichtenstein, Aaron, 12:798

  Saracheck, Bernard, 18:40–41

  Soloveitchik, Joseph Baer, 18:777–780

  See also Soloveichik, Joseph Baer; Soloveichik, Moses

Yeshivot, 21:**315–321**

  Babylonian, 1:347–351

  Babylon to fifteenth century, 21:315–316

  Baghdad, 3:56

  Beth Medrash Govoha, 12:441

  Bnei Akiva, 4:18–19

  curriculum, 21:318

  Ereẓ Israel, 1:347–351

  fifteenth to eighteenth centuries, 21:317

  Israel, 21:320–321

  Italy, 6:180

Lithuania and Russia, 21:317–318
Mizrachi, 14:391
Morocco, 14:505
organization, 21:317–318
Poland, 5:468, 6:185
Russia, 6:183, 14:519
Slobodka Yeshivah, 7:32, 18:674
twentieth century, 21:319–320
U.K., 6:206–207
U.S., 12:441, 21:321
See also Jewish education
Yesh Noḥalin (Horowitz, 9:537–538
Yesh Tikvah (Landau), 8:717
Yeshu'a haben. *See* Sholem Zokhor
Yeshu'ot. See Nezikin
Yeshurun, Avot, 21:**321–322**
Yeshurun family. *See* Jesurun family
Yesod. *See* Judah ben Eliezer
Yesodei ha-Dat ha-Universalit
(Shapiro), 18:404
Yesodei ha-Ibbur (Slonimski), 18:679
Yesodei ha-Mishpat ha-Ivri (Gulak),
8:130
*Yesodei ha-Tevunah u-Migdal ha-
Emunah* (Abraham ben Ḥiyya ha-
Nasi), 1:293, 6:399
Yesodei ha-Torah (Luzzatto), 16:96
Yesod ha-Avodah (Weinberg), 18:677
Yesod ha-Emunah (Jabez), 2:531
Yesod Mikra (Abraham ben Judah ben
Abraham), 1:304
Yesod Mishneh Torah (Albotini),
1:595, 596
Yesod Olam (Israeli), 10:751
Yesod Olam (Zacuto), 1:287, 21:436
Yesodot (Israel), 21:**322**
Yesodot ha-Maskil (Ibn Bilia), 2:530
Yesod ve-Shoresh ha-Avodah
(Alexander Susskind ben Moses of
Grodno), 1:630
Yesod Yosef (Calahora), 4:349
Yesud ha-Ma'alah (Israel), 21:**322**
Ye'ush, 21:**322–323**
Yeushzon, B. *See* Justman, Moshe
Bunem
Yev (Egypt). *See* Elephantine (Egypt)
Yevamot (tractate), 21:**323–325**
Yeven Meẓulah (Hannover), 8:327
Yevpatoriya (Ukraine), 21:**325**
Yevrei v Rossii (Leskov), 12:663
Yevreyskaya Avtonomnaya Oblast
(Russia). *See* Birobidzhan (Russia)
Yevreyskaya Biblioteka (periodical),
18:722
Yevreyskaya Entsiklopediya, 6:5, 216,
400
Yevreyskaya Starina (periodical), 6:34

Yevreyski Komissariat, 21:**325–326**
Yevreyskiy Mir (Morgulis), 14:491
Yevreyskiy student (journal), 8:761
Yevreyskoye Istoriko-
Etnograficheskoye Obshchestvo. *See*
Jewish Society for History and
Ethnography
Yevsektsiya, 1:520, 3:718, 5:95, 8:757,
9:246, 14:518, 21:**326–327**
Yevtushenko, Yevgeni Alexandrovich,
3:22, 21:**327**
Yevzerichin, Zerubavel, 18:606
Yezd (Iran), 21:**327–328**
Yezdegerd I, 3:29
Yezierska, Anzia, 21:**328**
Yeẓirah, sefer. See Sefer Yeẓirah
Yeẓiv pitgam, 21:**331–332**
YHWH, 7:675
"Yhwh Is prince". *See* Seraiah
YHWH-Nissi, altar of, 2:29
Yiddeshe Kopf (Ginsberg), 7:608
Yiddish actors
Bozyk, Max, 4:115
Buloff, Joseph, 4:278
Burstein, Pesach, 4:301
Kessler, David, 12:**91**
Lebedeff, Aaron, 12:589
Lux, Lilian, 4:301
Mikhoels, Solomon, 14:222
Yiddish American Popular Songs
(Heskes), 9:74
Yiddish culture
Canada, 4:419
Congress for Jewish Culture,
5:160–161
folk choruses, 4:663
Kaufmann, Fritz Mordecai, 12:31
Kiev (Ukraine), 12:153
motion pictures, 14:575
Romania, 4:533–534
Russia, 5:95–96
post- World War II, 5:98–99
Yiddish education, 6:187–188
Belorussia, 6:188
Canada, 6:189
Eastern Europe, 6:188
Kazdan, Ḥayyim Solomon, 12:44–
45
Kerler, Dov-Ber, 12:85–86
Latin America, 6:189
at Oxford University, 15:554
Poland, 6:188
Russia, 6:187–188
Ukraine, 6:188
U.S., 3:206, 6:188–189, 195
Yiddish-English-Hebrew Dictionary
(Harkavy), 8:357

Yiddisher Kultur Farband (YKUF),
2:439–440, 514, 21:**332**
Der Yiddishe Tog (newspaper). *See*
Jewish Day (newspaper)
Yiddish in America (Fishman), 7:65
Yiddishist camps, 11:275
Yiddishkeit. *See* Judaism
Yiddish language, 11:301–302, 21:**332–
338**, 335t
Aaron ben Samuel of
Hergerhausen, 1:217
Abelson, Paul, 1:249
Amsterdam, 2:111, 114
Arbeiter-Zeitung, 2:363
Australia, 14:8
Bergen-Belsen, 3:421
Bible, 2:108
Bible translated into, 3:610–611
Birnbaum, Nathan, 3:715
Birnbaum, Solomon Asher, 3:716
Birobidzhan, 3:719, 720
Bund aiming to revive, 4:279
Cambridge Yiddish Codex, 4:379
Czernowitz Yiddish Language
Conference, 5:372
dialects, 21:335, 335t
Dutch language, and influence of,
6:68
dysphemisms, 6:551
education in, Heilperin, Falk,
8:767–768
evolution, 9:252
Forverts newspaper, 16:503–504
Harkavy, Alexander, 8:357
Haskalah and, 8:436–437, 686–687
Hebrew and, 8:667–669, 670,
9:252, 21:336–337
homiletic literature, 9:514
Israel, 10:294
Jewish Teachers' Seminary and
People's University, 11:327–328
Joffe, Judah Achilles, 11:368
Katz, Dovid, 12:10–11
Landau, Alfred, 12:458
Levita, Elijah, 12:732
Lifshits, Shiye-Mordkhe, 13:11
modern, 21:332–333, 336
Netherlands, 15:99
orators, 13:602
Pale of Settlement, 15:579
philology, Mieses, Matthias,
14:206
prayers, 1:217
pronunciations, 16:552, 552
radio in New York City, 15:221
Russia
1881-1917: Second Phase,
17:538, 540

Yiddish language, *continued*
  1970s, 17:564, 568
  Schulmann, Eliezer, research by, 18:173
  sound, 21:333, 333*t*
  source of, 21:334–335
  Sovetish Heymland, 19:64–65
  studies, 21:337–338
  synagogues, 2:111
  U.S., 2:610
  USSR, 11:322–323, 17:543–544
  writing, grammar, 21:333–334
  Yiddish-English-Hebrew Dictionary, 8:357
  YIVO, 21:375–377
  See also Czernowitz Yiddish Language Conference; National Yiddish Book Center
Yiddish literature, 13:113–116, 17:543–544, 21:**338–372**
  14th to eighteenth centuries, 21:339–341
  1970s onward, 21:353–357
  Aaron ben Samuel of Hergerhausen, 1:217
  Abramovitsh, Sholem Yankev, 1:318–322
  Abramowicz, Dina, 1:323–324
  Abtshuk, Avraham, 1:333
  Adam Ba'al Shem, 1:378
  Agnon, Shmuel Yosef, 1:465–466
  Akavya, Avraham Aryeh Leib, 1:554
  Alfes, Benzion, 1:641–642
  Alpersohn, Marcos, 1:688
  Amsterdam, 2:108
  Beilinson, Moses Eliezer, 3:267
  Ben-Zion, S., 3:392–393
  Bergelson, David, 3:418–419
  Berger, Lili, 3:425
  Bergner, Herz, 3:430
  Berkowitz, Yitzhak Dov, 3:440–441
  Bible in, 21:339–341
  biblical influence, 3:669–670
  bibliographical survey, 21:367–372
  Biletski, Israel Hayyim, 3:698
  biography and autobiography, 3:707–708, 4:375–376
  Birstein, Yosel, 3:720
  bobe-mayse, 4:23
  Botoshansky, Jacob, 4:103–104
  Bove-Bukh (fiction), 4:107–108
  Brainin, Rudolph, 4:119
  Bresch, Judah Loeb ben Moses Naphtali, 4:163
  Briyo ve-Zimro, 4:190

Bryks, Rachmil, 4:229–230
Bund aiming to revive, 4:279
Bursztyn, Michal, 4:302
Cambridge Yiddish Codex, 4:379
Canada, 4:425–428
censorship, 4:540
Chagall, Bella Rosenfeld, 4:556
chapbooks, 4:568
Charney, Daniel, 4:580
Chatzkels, Helene, 4:583–584
children's, 4:628–629, 11:827
cookbooks, 5:201
criticism
  Baal-Makhshoves, 3:8
  Erik, Max, 6:479
  Mendelsohn, Shelomo, 14:30
  Miron, Dan, 14:313
Czechoslovakia
  journalism, 16:489
Daniel, M., 5:426
Demblin, Benjamin, 5:548
Der Nister, 5:596–598
Dik, Isaac, 5:660–661
Dineson, Jacob, 5:671
Di Yunge Society, 21:427–428
Dluzhnowsky, Moshe, 5:723
Dobrushin, Yekhezkel, 5:727–728
Dolitzki, Menahem Mendel, 5:735–736
early Yiddish language studies, 21:364–365
editors
  Liessin, Abraham, 12:819
  Mayzel, Nachman, 13:704
eighteenth century to WW I, 21:344–348
Elye Bokher, 21:343–344
encyclopedias, 6:399, 402
England
  journalism, 16:489–490
Entin, Joel, 6:448
essayists, 6:688
ethical parables, tales, 21:341–342
Ettinger, 6:545
fables, 6:669, 14:310–311
Feinberg, Leon, 6:738
Fox, Chaim-Leib, 7:140
genizah records, 7:477
ghettos, Nazi, 21:351
Grade, Chaim, 8:24–25
Hasidic, contemporary, 21:357–358
Hasidic stories, 21:345
Haskalah comedies, 21:344–345
Heilperin, Falk, 8:767–768
Hirschbein, Peretz, 9:133–134

Hirschkahn, Zevi, 9:139
historical songs, writings, 21:342–343
Hoffer, Yehiel, 9:307
Horontchik, Simon, 9:528
Horowitz, Ber, 9:533
Hurwitz, Chaim, 9:631–632
Ignatoff, David, 9:715
Israel, 10:685, 21:353
Italian, secular, 21:343–344
Izban, Shmuel, 10:823–824
journalism, 16:487–504
  Argentina, 4:253, 12:513–514
  Australia and New Zealand, 16:488
  Austria, 16:490–492
  Belgium, 16:488
  Canada, 4:402, 425–426, 16:488–489
  Dos Yidishe Folk, 8:476
  Epstein, Melech, 6:475
  Forverts, 6:696–697
  France, 16:490
  Germany, 16:490–492
  Haynt, 8:476
  Holland, 16:492–493
  Hungary, 16:493
  India, 16:493–494
  Italy, 16:494
  Jewish Daily Forward, 11:289–290
  Jewish Day, 11:290
  Katz, Moshe, 12:14–15
  Ladino, 16:494–496
  Latin America, 16:496–497
  Medres, Isael Jonah, 13:763
  Middle East and North Africa, 16:497
  Der Moment, 8:476
  Poland, 16:497–498
  Resnick, Solomon, 17:227–228
  Ressler, Benjamin, 17:239
  Rogoff, Harry, 17:369
  Romania, 16:498
  Rosenberg, Abraham Hayyim, 17:434
  Rosenfeld, Samuel, 17:447
  Russia, 16:498–501
  Scandinavia, 16:501–502
  South Africa, 16:502
  Switzerland, 16:502–503
  U.S., 16:502–503
Ki-Bukh, 12:**138**
Kipnis, Itzik, 12:179
labor movement, 21:346

Latteiner, Joseph, 12:518
Lehrer, Leibush, 12:617
Levin, Shmarya, 12:713–714
Libin, Z., 12:782
Lieberman, Chaim, 12:804
liturgy, 21:341
Litvine, M., 13:140–141
masculine bias, 6:754–755
Mastbaum, Joel, 13:**668**
Max Weinreich, 21:363–364
Melokhim-Bukh, 14:13–14
Mendele Moykher Sforim, 21:345–
    346
Miller, Shaye, 14:255
moderism, Peretz, Issac Leib,
    15:765–768
Molodowsky, Kadia, 14:429–430
moralistic storybooks, 6:526
music, Eastern European, 21:360–
    361
naturalism, Perle, Joshua, 15:775–
    776
in New York City, 15:210, 217,
    220, 222
Palestine, 21:352–353
Pariz Un Viene, 15:651
parodies, 15:659, 662–663
parody, 15:659, 662–663
Perlov, Yitskhok, 15:780
Persov, Shmuel, 15:793
Pines, Meyer Isser, 16:167
Pinski, David, 16:175
Poland, 21:353
post-Holocaust research, 21:358–
    361
postmodern, Felzenbaum, 6:751–
    752
post-WW I, 21:348–353
printing of, 2:108
Rabinovich, Ospi Aronovich,
    17:37–38
Rabon, Israel, 17:44
Raboy, Isaac, 17:44
Raisin, Max, 17:74–75
Rakovsky, Puah, 17:76
Rashkin, Leib, 17:107
Ravitch, Melech, 17:123
Razumny, Mark, 17:133
Rebecca bat Meir Tiktiner,
    17:136–137
Reisen, Abraham, 17:211
Rejzen, Kalman, 17:213–214
research, 21:358–361, 363–367
Ressler, Benjamin, 17:239
Rivkin, Boruch, 17:348–349
Roback, Abraham Aaron, 17:352

Rochman, Leib, 17:359
romances, rhymed, 16:612
Rosenberg, Moisge, 17:438
Rosenberg, Yehuda Yudel, 17:439
Rosenfarb, Chava, 17:444–445
Rosenfeld, Jonah, 17:446
Rosenthal, Pavel, 17:456–457
Rossin, Samuel, 17:474
Rubin, Ruth, 17:513
Russia
    1970s, 17:568
    Dymov, Ossip, 6:79
    Morgulis, Manasseh, 14:490–
        491
    Moscow, 14:519
Sandler, Boris, 18:15–16
Saphire, Saul, 18:37
Schaechter-Gottesman, Bella,
    18:102
science fiction and fantasy, Jewish,
    5:660–661, 18:199
Selikovitch, George, 18:269–270
seventeenth-eighteenth centuries,
    7:16
Sfard, David, 18:333
Shakespeare, William, 18:370–371
Shalom Aleichem, 18:378–389
Shapiro, Lamed, 18:407
Shekhtman, Elye, 18:444
Shneour, Zalman, 18:500
Sholem-Aleykhem, 21:346–347
Simon, Shlome, 18:616
Singer, Isaac Bashevis, 18:634–636
Singer, Israel Joshua, 18:637–638
study centers, 21:361
tkhines, 6:21, 21:341
translations, 5:426
    Germany, 6:744
    into Russian literature, 17:591
    Schwartz, Israel Jacob, 18:185
    of Shakespeare, 18:370–371
U.S., 6:734, 11:79, 21:351–352
used to propagate Haskalah ideas,
    15:773
Y. L. Perets, 21:347–348
YIVO Institute for Jewish
    Research, 21:361–362, 375–377
See also Yiddish poetry; *specific
    publications*
Yiddish National Radical Schools,
    6:188–189
Yiddish Natzionaler Arbeiter Farband.
    See Farband
Yiddish poetry, 6:729, 7:633–634,
    19:335–336, 21:346, 348–350, 351
    Adler, Jacob, 1:399–400
    Basman, Ben-Hayim, Rivke,
        3:203–204

Bassin, Moses, 3:209
Beider, Chaim, 3:265
Berinski, Lev, 3:265
Berliner, Isaac, 3:461
Bialoblotzky, Benjamin Jacob,
    3:566
Bible translations, rhymed, 3:610–
    611
Bovshover, Joseph, 4:108
Broderzon, Moyshe, 4:195–196
Canada, 4:426–427
Chmelnitzki, Melech, 4:654
Dillon, Abraham Moses, 5:662
Dropkin, Celia, 6:24
Edelstadt, David, 6:144
Ehrenkranz, Benjamin Zeeb, 6:240
Einhorn, David, 6:258
Emiot, Israel, 6:394–395
epics, 14:13–14
Esselin, Alter, 6:509
Fininberg, Ezra, 7:30
Fram, David, 7:146
Gottlober, Abraham Baer, 8:13–14
Greenberg, Eliezer, 8:68
Groper, Jacob, 8:94
Gross, Naphtali, 8:96–97
Halkin, Shemuel, 8:275
Halpern, Moyshe Leib, 8:285
Heller, Bunim, 8:794
Herschele, 9:44–45
Hofstein, David, 9:313–314
Iceland, Reubin, 9:703
Imber, Samuel Jacob, 9:737
In-Zikh, 10:5
Katz, Aleph, 12:8
Katz, Menke, 12:13–14
Katzenelson, Itzhak, 12:20–21
Kerler, Yoysef, 12:86
Khalyastre, 12:100–101
Kharik, Izi, 12:104–105
Landau, Zishe, 12:466
Lapin, Berl, 12:491
Lee, Malke, 12:597–598
Leivik, H., 12:629–630
Lerer, Yehiel, 12:654
Lev, Abraham, 12:675–676
Licht, Michael, 12:796
Liessin, Abraham, 12:819
Maze, Ida, 13:706
Mestel, Jacob, 14:123
Minkoff, Nahum Baruch, 14:281–
    282
Neugroeschel, Mendel, 15:120
Neumann, Yeḥeskel Moshe,
    15:123
Rolnick, Joseph, 17:373

Yiddish poetry, *continued*
    Rosenblatt, H., 17:440–441
    Rosenfeld, Morris, 17:446–447
    Rubin, Hadassah, 17:512
    Rubinstein, Joseph, 17:517–518
    Schanpper, Ber, 18:147
    Schwartz, Israel Jacob, 18:185
    Schwarzman, Asher, 18:193
    Segal, Esther, 18:245
    Segal, Jacob Isaac, 18:247
    Segalowitch, Zusman, 18:249
    Shamri, Arie, 18:395
    Shayevitsh, Simkha-Bunim,
        18:424–425
    sweatshop poetry, 19:335–336
    In-Zikh, 10:5
    See also Esselin, Alter
Yiddish prayers. *See* Tkhines
Yiddish Press. *See* Press
Yiddish revival. *See* Estraikh, Gennady
Yiddish School Organization. *See*
    Central Yiddish School
    Organization
Yiddish Scientific Institute. *See* YIVO
    Institute for Jewish Research
Yiddish theater, 7:703–704, 763,
    19:677–685, 21:372–373
    Adler family, 1:392–394
    Amsterdam, 2:108
    Broder Singers, 19:678
    Broder singers, 4:194, 195
    Broderzon, Moyshe, 4:195–196
    Buchwald, Nathaniel, 4:243
    C.D.E., 4:533–534
    centers of, 19:683
    comedy, 8:151
    drama, 21:340–341, 372–373
    Eastern Europe, 19:679, 681–682
    Ettinger, Solomon, 6:545
    Feinman, Sigmund, 6:740
    Goldfaden era, the, 19:678–679
    Gordin, Jacob, 1:393, 7:763–764,
        19:679–680
    Gordin era, 19:679–680
    Haskalah drama, 19:678
    Herman, David, 9:23
    Hirschbein, Peretz, 9:133–134
    humor and, 9:594
    late 20th century, 19:683–684
    Latin America, 19:681
    Moscow, 8:275
    New York City, 15:210, 220,
        19:680–681
    Peretz, Issac Leib, 15:768
    playwrights
        Ettinger, 6:545

    Harendorf, Samuel Jacob,
        8:353
    Latteiner, Joseph, 12:518
    Poland, interwar, 19:682
    premodern performances, 19:677–
        678
    purimshpil, 19:684
    Schwartz, Maurice, 18:186
    summary, 19:677, 684
    theater recordings, 17:150
    USSR, 19:682–683
    Western Europe, 19:679
Yiddish Theater, Folksbiene. *See*
    Folksbiene Yiddish theater
Der Yidesher Keing Lir (Gordin), 7:763
Yidishe Fold in Tsifern (Lestschinsky),
    12:666
Dos Yidishe Folk (newspaper), 8:476
Di Yidishe Folksbibliotek (Shalom
    Aleichem), 18:380–381
"Yidishe Folkspartei In Polyn." *See*
    Folkspartei
Yidishe Kultur Lige, 13:267
Di Yidishe Melukhe (Shapiro), 18:407
Yidishe Neshomes (Litvin), 13:140
Der Yidisher Arbeter (newspaper),
    18:176
Yidisher Arbeter, Der (newspaper). *See*
    Der Yidisher Arbeter (newspaper)
*Der Yidisher Dales in di Beste Verk fun
    Undzere Folks-Shriftshteler* (Shalom
    Aleichem), 18:380
Yidisher Folkskalender (Bader), 3:44
Yidisher Kemfer (journal), 21:**373**
Der Yidisher Kenig Lir (Gordin),
    18:370
Der Yidisher Kongres in Bazl (Shalom
    Aleichem), 18:382
Yidisher Visnshaftlekher Institut. *See*
    YIVO Institute for Jewish Research
Yidishe Shtime (newspaper), 21:**373**
Yidishes Tagblat, 7:36
Yidishes Tageblat (newspaper), 12:804,
    18:50, 21:**373**
Der Yidishe Tog. *See* Jewish Day
    (newspaper)
Yidishkeyt. *See* Judaism
Yidn in Polyn (Shulman), 18:532
Yidn on Gele Lates (Smolar), 18:690
Yigdal, 21:**373–374**
Yiḥus, 21:**374**
Yiḥye, Isaac ha-Levi, 21:**374–375**
Yikrav Ish (Elyashar), 6:372
Yinchwan (China). *See* Ningsia
    (China)
Yinnon, Moshe, 21:**375**
Yishtabbaḥ, 21:**375**
Yishuv, 9:249–250, 377–379
    aliyahs and, 10:194

    economic affairs, 10:511–512
    ḥalukkah, 8:287–290
    Lapin, Israel Moses Fischel, 12:491
Yismaḥ Moshe, 14:543
Yismaḥ Yisrael (Calahorra), 4:350
Yisrael bein ha-Amim (Ehrenreich).
    See Israel Among the Nations
    (Ehrenreich)
Yisraeli, Shaul, 6:630
Yisrael Shenat 2000 (Goldfluss), 18:204
Yisrail ba-Golah (Dinur), 5:672
Yisrail be Arẓo (Dinur), 5:672
Yissa Berakhah. *See* Elyashar, Jacob
    Saul ben Eliezer Jeroham
Yissurei Iyov (Levin), 8:722
Yitshok, Yankev. *See* Segal, Jacob Isaac
YIVO Bleter (journal), 11:746–747
YIVO Institute for Jewish Research,
    2:407, 9:425, 21:361–362, **375–377**
    Center for Jewish History, 4:542
    founding of, 18:723
    historiography, 9:162
    Landau, Alfred, 12:458
    Niger, Shmuel, 15:263
    Shabad, Ẓemaḥ, 18:337
Yiẓhaki, Abraham ben David, 8:477,
    21:**377**
Yiẓhaki, David, 21:**377**
Yizhar, S., 8:704, 21:**377–379**
Yizkor, 8:496–497, 21:**379**
Yizre'el (Israel), 21:**379**
YKUF. *See* Yiddisher Kultur Farband
Ylla. *See* Koffler, Camilla
YMHA (Young Men's Hebrew
    Association), 6:191
Yod, 21:**379**
Yodefat (Israel). *See* Jotapata (Israel)
Yoel. *See* Almanzi, Joseph
Yoelson, Asa. *See* Jolson, Al
Yoffe, Alter, 21:**379**
Yoffe, Mordecai, 21:**379**
Yoffey, Israel Jacob ben Abraham ha-
    Kohen, 21:**380**
Yoffey, Joseph ben Moses, 21:379–380
Yoffey, Joseph Mendel, 21:**380**
Yoffey family, 21:**379–380**
Yoffie, Eric H., 17:172, 20:254, 255,
    21:**380**
Yoke, 21:**381**
Yokne'am (Israel). *See* Jokneam
    (Israel)
Yokohama (Japan), 21:**381**
Yoma (tractate), 21:**381–382**
Yoman ba-Galil (Shalom), 18:377
Yoman Maḥteret Ivri (Weissman),
    20:739–740
Yomano she Adam Czerniakow
    (Czerniakow), 5:372

Yom ha-Kippurim. *See* Day of
Atonement
Yom ha-Kippurim (Morpurgo), 14:509
Yom ha-Shoah, 9:455–456, 495
Yom ha-Sho'ah. *See* Holocaust
Remembrance Day
Yom ha-Zikkaron, 21:**382**
Yom Kippur. *See* Day of Atonement
Yom Kippur Katan, 21:**382–383**
Yom Kippur War, 1:470, 10:236–237,
257, 21:**383–391**, *384, 386, 388, 389*
American Israel Public Affairs
Committee, 2:51
cease fire, 21:390–391
diplomacy, 6:84
Egyptian front, 21:386–390
Elazar, David, 6:289
European Economic Community,
6:565
Kabbalah and, 11:684–685
Kissinger, Henry, 12:203
Meir and, 13:778
northern front, 21:383–386
political consequences, 10:442, 443
Yom Tov (festivals). *See* Festivals
Yom Tov ben Abraham Ishbili,
15:372, 17:8, 21:**391–392**
Yom Tov Lippman, 3:70
Yom Tov of Joigny, 11:385, 406,
21:**392**
Yom Tov Sheni shel Galuyyot. *See*
Festivals
Yonath, Ada, 21:**392–393**
Yonathan, Nathan, 21:**393**
Yongman, Moshe. *See* Yungman,
Moshe
Yonkers (NY) desegregation lawsuit,
18:9–10
Yorah De'ah (Jacob ben Asher), 11:30
Yoreh De'ah (Aknin). *See Sefer ha-
Musar* (Aknin)
Yoreh De'ah (Bueno), 4:252
Yoreh De'ah (Hezekiah), 9:91
Yoreh De'ah (Joseph ben Judah Engel),
6:409
York, (England), 6:427, 21:**393**
Yorke, Annie Rothschild, 17:490
York-Steiner, Heinrich Elchanan,
21:**394**
York University, 6:209
Yose, 21:**394**
Moses, 14:534
Oholot, 15:394
Yose (amora), 11:387
Yose bar Ḥanina, 21:**394–395**
Yose ben Akavyah, 21:**395**
Yose ben Avin, 21:**395**

Yose ben Dormaskos, 21:**395**
Yose ben Eleazar. *See* Yose ha-Gelili
Yose ben Ḥafta, 3:706
Yose ben Ḥalafta, 21:**396**
Yose ben Joezer of Zeredah, 21:**396–
397**
Yose ben Johanan ha-Tanna of
Jerusalem, 21:**397**
Yose ben Judah, 21:**397**
Yose ben Kippar, 21:**397**
Yose ben Kisma, 21:**397**
Yose ben Meshullam, 21:**397–398**
Yose ben Yose, 16:192–193, 21:**398**
Yose ben Zimra, 21:**398–399**
Yosef, Bernard. *See* Joseph, Dov
Yosef, Ovadiah, 18:419, 21:**399**
Yosef, Shlomo ben, 15:402
Yosef ha-Mekanne (Joseph Official),
15:388–389
Yose ha-Gelili, 3:129, 21:**399–400**
Yose ha-Kohen, 21:**400**
Yosele Solovey (Shalom Aleichem),
18:378, 381
Yoshe Kalb (Singer), 18:637
Yosher Divrei Emet (Heller), 14:79
Yoshke Muzikant (Dymov). *See Yoshke
the Musician* (Dymov)
Yoshke the Musician (Dymov), 6:79
Yosi (amora). *See* Yose
Yosif Omez (Hahn), 7:208, 8:231
Yossi & Jagger, 7:140
Yotvatah (Israel), 21:**400**
You Can't Print That (Seldes), 18:259
You Have Seen Their Faces (Bourke-
White and Caldwell), 4:107
You Must Know Everything (Babel),
3:19
"The Young". *See* Louis (kings of
France)
Young, Alec David, 21:**400**
Young, David Ivor, Baron Young of
Graffham, 21:**400–401**
Young, James E., 21:**401**
Young, Stuart, 21:**401**
Young Bohemia group, 11:782
Young Israel, National Council of. *See*
National Council of Young Israel
Young Israel movement, 4:284
Young Judaea, 18:583, 21:**402**
The Young Lions (Shaw), 18:424
Youngman, Henny, 21:**402–403**
Youngman, Moshe. *See* Yungman,
Moshe
Young Man Luther (Erikson), 6:479
Young Men of Zion. *See* Ze'irei Zion
Young Men's Hebrew Association
(YMHA), 6:191

The Young Ones (music group), 6:263
Youngstown (OH), 21:**403**
Young Tolstoy (Eichenbaum), 6:246
Young Turks Revolution
Amateau, Albert Jean, 2:33
Carasso, Emmanuel, 4:460
Ha-Boker, 8:181–182
Jewish participation in, 15:542–
543, 544
You Oughta Be in Pictures, 7:238
"Your Victory." *See* "Tvoya pobeda"
Youth Aliyah movement, 10:338, 343–
344, 21:**403–406**
Beyth, Hans, 3:556
Freier, Recha, 7:236
Hadassah, 8:187, 188
Jacobs, Michael Strauss, 11:51
Jewish Agency, 11:257–258, 261
Lahvot Ha-Bashan, 12:439
Landauer, Georg, 12:466
Lehmann, Siegfried, 12:616
Ollendorff, Franz, 15:409
rescue, Mizrachi Women's
Organization of America, 2:80
Youth Corps. *See* Gadna
Youth movements and groups
Beriḥah, 3:434–435
Betar, 2:164, 3:510–511, 11:10–11,
315, 316, 715
B'nai B'rith Youth Organization,
4:14–15
Bnei Akiva, 4:18–19
Hadassah, 8:188, 15:208
Iḥud Habonim
Australia, 9:717t, 719
Canada, 9:717t, 718
Germany, 9:717–718, 717t
Latin America, 9:717t, 718–
719
South Africa, Republic of,
9:717t, 719
U.K., 9:717t, 718
U.S., 9:717t, 718
scouting, 18:208–210
socialism, 18:720–721
U.S., 15:199, 208
Young Israel movement, 4:284
Yugntruf, 18:102
See also names of specific
movements and groups
Youth of Zion. *See* Ze'irei Zion
Youtie, Herbert Chayyim, 21:**406**
Yovel, 6:454
Yovel, Yirmiyahu, 21:**406**
Yoysef (Shalom Aleichem), 18:383
Yoẓerot, 21:**406–407**

Yoẓer piyyut, 16:193, 194
Ysander, Torsten, 21:**407**
Der Yud (Baal-Makhshoves), 3:8
Yud, Nahum, 21:**407**
Yudan, 21:**407–408**
Yudelevitch, David. *See* Idelovitch, David
Yudelovitz, Abraham Aaron, 21:**408**
Yuden, Isaiah. *See* Eisenstadt, Isaiah
Yudghan, 11:505, 21:**408**
Yudika, 21:**408**
Der Yudisher for Pesakh (Shatzkes), 18:421
Yudkin, John, 21:**408–409**
Yudkovitch. *See* Tashrak
Yudkovsky, Dov, 21:**409**
Yudlin, Vitali. *See* Eisenstadt, Isaiah
Yudovin, S., 4:70
Yuedels, Isaac ben Judah Loeb. *See* Isaac ben Judah
Yugoslavia, 21:**409–420**, *413*
　　archives of Jewish life in, 6:575
　　　Boznia-Herzegovina, 21:410–411, 414
　　　breakup, civil war, 21:417–418
　　　　Dubrovnik, 6:39
　　　children's literature, 4:635
　　　contemporary period, 21:415–418
　　　Croatia, 21:410, 413–414, 443–444
　　　Freiberger, Miroslav/Šalom, 7:234
　　　Holocaust, 9:339, 18:49, 21:412–415
　　　　　Monastir, 14:432
　　　　　Sarajevo, 18:49
　　　　　Sephardim, 18:301
　　　　　Zemun, 21:508
　　　Israel relations, 21:418–419
　　　journalism, 12:489
　　　kingdom, post-WW I, 21:411–412
　　　music, 21:419
　　　partisans, 15:667
　　　publishing, general, 16:717
　　　Serbia, 21:409–410, 412–413
　　　Slovenia, 21:410
　　　Vojvodina, 21:414–415
　　　Zionism, 21:615–616
　　　　Albala, David, 1:582
　　　　Alkalai, David, 1:663
　　　　Licht, Alexander, 12:796
Yugoslav literature, 21:420–423, **420–423**
　　Albahari, David, 1:581
　　biblical influence, 3:671
　　Debrecenji, Jožef, 5: 520
　　encyclopedias, 6:402
　　Ivanji, Ivan, 10:820

Lebovic, Djordje, 12:592
Levi, Solomon ben Isaac (1532-1600), 12:693–694
Levi, Solomon ben Isaac (1581-1634), 12:694
Samokovlija, Isak, 17:748
Šinko, Ervin, 18:641
twentieth century, 5:444, 463
Yuḥasin, 21:**423–426**
Yukhneva, Natalia, 11:324
Yulee, David Levy, 7:87, 21:**426–427**
Yulee family. *See* Yuly family
Yuly, Elijah Levy-, 21:427
Yuly, Joseph Levy Aben-, 21:427
Yuly, Judah Aben-, 21:427
Yuly, Judah Levy-, 21:427
Yuly, Moses Levy-, 21:427
Yuly, Samuel Levy-, 21:427
Yuly, Samuel Levy Aben-, 21:427
Yuly, Solomon Levy Aben-, 21:427
Yuly family, 21:427
Yunge, Di, 12:466, 21:**427–428**
Yungen (Fininberg), 7:30
Yung-Grin-Mai (Bryks), 4:229
Yungman, Moshe, 21:**428**
Yung-Vilne, 11:694, 21:**428**
Yuryev (Estonia). *See* Tartu (Estonia)
Yūsha' ben Nūn, 14:539
Yushkevich, Semyon Solomonovich, 21:**428**
Yussel the Muscle. *See* Jacobs, Joe
Yūsuf al-Basir. *See* Baṣīr, Joseph ben Abraham ha-Kohen Haro'eh al-
Yūsuf al-Yahūdī, 11:556
Yusūf As'ar Yath'ar Dhū Nuwās, 21:**428–430**
Yūsuf ibn Ayyūb. *See* Saladin
Yuval Ensemble, 8:503
Yuzovka (Ukraine). *See* Donetsk (Ukraine)
YWHA (Young Women's Hebrew Association). *See* Jewish Community Centers
Y. Zeh. *See* Zmora, Yisrael
Yzraely, Yossi, 21:430

Z

Z (letter), 21:*431*
Zabara, Natan, 21:**431**
Zabar's, 15:234
Zabel, William D., 2:18
Zabern (France). *See* Saverne (France)
Zabludovsky, Jacobo, 11:470
Zabludow (Poland), 21:**431–432**
Zabolotov (Ukraine), 21:**432**
Zabolotów. *See* Zabolotov (Ukraine)

Zabrody (Poland), 14:395–396
Zabrze (Poland), 21:**432**
Zaccaria of Elia Pisa, 16:185
Zach, Nathan, 8:705, 21:**432–433**
Zacharais, Jerrold Reinach, 21:**433**
Zacharias, John, 21:**433**
Żmudź (Lithuania). *See* Samogitia (Lithuania)
Zacuth, Abraham. *See* Zacutus Lusitanus
Zacuto, Abraham ben Samuel, 13:675, 21:**433–435**
　　Abraham ben Solomon of Torrutiel, 1:311
　　bibliography of, 3:681
　　John II of Portugal, 11:379
　　Leon, Isaac de, 12:644
Zacuto, Moses ben Mordecai, 1:287, 12:690, 18:347, 21:**435–437**
Zacutus Lusitanus, 21:**437**
Ẓaddik, 17:308–309, 21:**437**
　　doctrine of, 6:348, 11:39–40, 41–42
　　Eger, Judah Leib of Lublin, 6:218
　　Elimelech of Lyzhansk, 6:348–349
　　fall of, 6:348–349
　　Hasidic doctrine, 10:746
　　Mordecai of Neskhiz, 14:482
Ẓaddik, Joseph ben Jacob ibn, 4:170, 16:82, 21:**437–439**
　　commandments, reasons for, 5:87
　　form and matter, 7:131
　　Judeo-Arabic literature and, 11:535
　　philosophy, microcosm, 14:179
　　soul, immortality of, 19:36–37
Zaddikim
　　descent of, 8:412
　　ethical ideal, 6:532
　　Ḥasidic, 8:399
　　　Dynow, Ẓevi Elimelech, 6:79
　　　Issachar Dov Baer ben Aryeh Leib of Zloczow, 10:768
　　　Peremyshlyany, Meir ben Aaron Leib of, 15:762–763
　　See also Righteousness
Ẓaddik of Arévalo, 1:311
Ẓade. *See* Ṣade
Zadikow, Arnold, 21:**439**
Zadkine, Ossip, 21:**439**
Zadok (1st c.), 21:**441**
Zadok (biblical figure), 1:543, 6:298, 309, 21:**439–441**
Ẓadok, Ḥaim Joseph, 21:**441–442**
Zadok bar Mar Yishi, 21:**442**
Zadok ha-Kohen Rabinowitz of Lublin, 21:**442**

Zadok II, 21:441

Zadokites, 1:218–219, 21:442–443

Zadok the Pharisee, 21:443

Zadok the Priest (Handel), 18:762

Zafenat Pane'ah (Adani), 1:381

Ẓafenat Pa'ne'an Institute, 11:821

Ẓafnat Pa'ne'aḥ (Eliezer ben Nathan of Mainz). *See Revealer of Secrets* (Eliezer ben Nathan of Mainz)

Zafrani, Haim, 11:324, 21:443

Zagare (Lithuania), 21:443

Zager (Lithuania). *See* Zagare (Lithuania)

Zagreb (Croatia), 21:443–444

Ẓahalon, Abraham ben Isaac, 21:444

Ẓahalon, Jacob ben Isaac, 6:399, 13:729, 21:444–445

Ẓahalon, Mordecai ben Jacob, 21:444–445

Ẓahalon, Yom Tov, 11:456

Ẓahalon, Yom Tov Moses, 21:444–445

Ẓahalon family, 21:444–445

Zaḥḥut Bediḥuta de-Kiddushin (Sommo), 19:8–9

Zaiẓov, Rina, 21:445–446

Zak. *See* Jacob ben Benjamin Ze'ev

Zak, Abram, 21:446

Zak, Eugen, 21:446

Zak, Eugéne, 15:650

Zak, Jacob. *See* Jacob ben Benjamin Ze'ev

Zakarpatskaya oblast. *See* Subcarpathian Ruthenia

Zaken mamre, 21:446

Zakho (Iraq), 21:446–447

Zakhor, 21:447

Zakynthos. *See* Zante

Zalcstein, Gecl, 21:447–448

Zaleshchiki (Ukraine), 21:448

Zaleszczyki. *See* Zaleshchiki (Ukraine)

Zalizky, Moshe. *See* Carmel, Moshe

Zalkind, Rozaliya. *See* Zemlayachka, Rozalita Samoylovna

Zalkind, Yankev-Meyer. *See* Salkind, Jacob Meir

Zalman, Elijah ben Solomon. *See* Elijah ben Solomon Zalman

Zalmati, Solomon, 4:75

Zalmonovitch, Shemaryahu. *See* Talmon, Shemaryahu

Zalozhtsy, Simḥah ben Joshua of. *See* Simḥah ben Joshua of Zalozhtsy

Zaludkowski, Elijah, 21:448

Zaluszowska, Catherine. *See* Weigel, Catherine

Zam, Zvi Herz, 21:448

Zamaris, 3:27, 21:448

Zambia (Africa), 21:448–449

Zambrov. *See* Zambrow (Poland)

Zambrow (Poland), 21:449–450

Zambrowski, Roman, 16:347, 21:450

Zambrowski, Ẓemaḥ, 14:391

Zamenhof, Ludwig Lazar, 21:450–451

Zamenhof, Stephen, 21:451

Zamenhof family, 3:567

Zamet (Lithuania). *See* Samogitia (Lithuania)

Zametkin, Laura. *See* Hobson, Laura Z.

Zamir. *See* Nightingales

Zamir, Itzhak, 21:451

Zamora (Spain), 21:451

Zamosc (Poland), 21:451–452

Zamosc, David, 21:452–453

Zamosc, Israel ben Moses ha-Levi, 12:461, 21:453–454

Zamut (Lithuania). *See* Samogitia (Lithuania)

Zamzummim, 21:454

Zand, Michael, 11:322, 21:454

Zandz dynasty. *See* Halberstam dynasty

Zangwill, Israel, 6:437, 14:540, 21:454–456

Zanoah (Judah), 21:456

Zante (Greece), 21:456–457

Zanz (Poland). *See* Nowy Sacz

Zanz dynasty. *See* Halberstam dynasty

Zanz Ḥasidim, 8:424, 15:326

Zaphon (ancient city), 21:457

Zapiski Grazhdanina (Lerner), 12:658

Zapiski poeta (Selvinski), 18:272

Zápisky hrbácovy (Leda), 12:595

Zaporozhe (Ukraine), 21:457

Zapruder, Alexandra, 4:631

Zaqen, Leon Ben, 14:503

Zar'a (Dustan priest), 6:66

Zaragoza (Spain). *See* Saragossa (Spain)

Zarah Ben Samuel, 12:648

Zarasai (Lithuania), 21:458

Zárato y Castronovo, Fernando de. *See* Enríquez Gómez, Antonio

Zarchi, Asher, 21:458

Zarchi, Israel, 21:458

Zarchin, Alexander, 21:458

Zarco, Judah, 21:458–459

Zardiel, Moses. *See* Abzardiel, Moses

Ẓarefati. *See* Sarfati

Ẓarefati, Isaac, 6:148

Ẓarefati, Joseph. *See* Joseph ha-Ẓarefati

Ẓarefati, Joseph ben Samuel. *See* Sarfati, Joseph

Zarephath (Mesopotamia), 21:459

Zarethan (ancient Israel), 21:459

Zaretski, Isaac, 21:459–460

Zariski, Oscar, 21:460

Zaritsky, Max, 21:460

Zaritsky, Yossef, 13:11, 21:460

Zarko, Joseph ben Judah, 21:460

Zarphatic language. *See* Judeo-French language

Zarza, Samuel ibn Seneh, 21:460–461

Zarzab, Abraham. *See* Zarzal, Abraham ibn

Zarzal, Abraham ibn, 21:461

Zaskovitzer, Samuel ben Joseph. *See* Strashun, Samuel ben Joseph

Zaslani, Reuben. *See* Shiloaḥ, Reuben

Zaslavl (Ukraine). *See* Izyaslav (Ukraine)

Zaslavsky, David, 21:461

Zaslofsky, Max, 21:461–462

Zastavna (Ukraine), 21:462

Zatec (Czech Republic), 21:462

Die Zauberfloete (Adler), 1:405

Das Zauberreich der Liebe (Brod), 4:193

Ẓava'at Ribash, 21:462–463

Zavah, 15:254

Zavertse (Poland). *See* Zawiercie (Poland)

Zavim, 21:463–464

Zavinai. *See* Natronai ben Ḥavivai

Zavl Rimer (Boraisha), 4:80

Ẓavu'a be-Korundi (Kaleve), 18:205

Ẓavu'a be-Korundi (Melamed), 18:205

Zavva'at Rabbi Eliezer. See Orḥot Ḥayyim

Ẓavva'at Rabbi Eli'ezer ha-Gadol (Eliezer ben Isaac of Worms), 6:326

Zawiercie (Poland), 21:464

Zay, Jean, 6:161, 16:343, 21:464

"Zaydl Rovner." *See* Morogowski, Jacob Samuel

Zayin, 21:464

Ẓayyaḥ, Joseph ben Abraham ibn, 21:464–465

Zbarazh (Ukraine), 21:465

Zbarzh (Ukraine), 21:465

Zbarzher, Velvl. *See* Ehrenkranz, Benjamin Zeeb

Zbitkower, Samuel, 21:465

Zborov (Ukraine), 21:465–466

Żydaczów. *See* Zhidachov (Ukraine)

Zdunska Wola (Poland), 21:466–467

Zdzięciol (Belarus). *See* Dyatlovo (Belarus)

Zeal. *See* Jealousy

Zealots, 21:467–480

Anan, son of Anan, 2:126–127

Zealots, *continued*

Athronges, 21:476

Eleazar (son of Aaron), 6:298–299

Eleazar ben Ananias, 6:298–299

Eleazar ben Dinai, 6:301

Eleazar ben Simeon, 6:307

Jerusalem zealots, 21:471–474

John of Giscala, 2:127, 11:383, 21:476–478

Josephus, 11:436

Justus of Tiberias as, 11:581

late scholarship, 21:478–479

lots, casting of, 16:117

Sicarii, fourth philosophy, 21:467–471

Simeon bar Giora, 21:474–476

suicide, 21:470

Zebah and Zalmmna, 21:**480**

Zebidah family, 21:**480**

Zebulun, 21:**480–481**, *481*

Zec, Philip, 21:**481**

Zechariah (book, prophet), 21:**482–486**

on angels, 2:151–152, 153

Deutero-Zechariah, 6:494

eschatology in, 6:493, 494

fast days, 6:719

tomb of, vol. 10: color insert

Zechariah (high priest), 21:**481–482**

Zechariah (King of Israel), 9:179, 21:**482**

Zechariah (son of Jeberechiah), 21:**482**

Zechariah al-Ḍāhiri, 21:**486**

Zechariah ben Avkilus, 21:**486**

Zechariah ben Barachel, 21:**486**

Zechariah ben ha-Kaẓẓav, 3:584

Zechariah ben Solomon-Rofe, 11:538, 21:**486–487**

Zechariah-Deutero, 6:494

Zechariah Mendel ben Aryeh Leib, 21:**487**

Ẓedakah, 4:569–571

Zedek. *See* Justice

Zedekiah (King of Judah), 6:365–366, 9:182, 15:50, 21:**487–489**

Zedekiah (son of Chenaanah), 21:**489**

Zedekiah (son of Maaseiah), 21:**489**

Zederbaum, Alexander, 8:300, 13:11, 21:**489–490**

Zedner, Joseph, 21:**490**

Zedukim. *See* Sadducees

Zeeb (Midianite prince), 15:**463–464**

Ze'eira, 21:**490–491**

Ze'enah U-Re'enah (Jacob ben Isaac), 21:340, 21:**491**

Zeepost (Herzberg). *See* Seamail (Herzberg)

Zeev, Benjamin, of Arta, 4:77

Ze'ev, Binjamin. *See* Herzl, Theodor

Ze'evi, Israel ben Azariah, 21:**492**

Ze'evi, Reḥavam, 6:367, 21:**492–493**

Ze'ev Wolf of Strykow, 4:726

Ze'ev Wolf of Zhitomir, 21:**492**

Ẓefat (Israel). *See* Safed (Israel)

Zefira, Brachah, 21:**493**

Zehavi, David, 21:**493**

Zeh Mistovev (Mundy), 8:721

Zehn Vorlesungen ueber den Bau der nervoesen Zentralorgane (Edinger). *See Twelve Lectures on the Structure of the Central Nervous System* (Edinger)

Zeichner, Oscar, 21:**493**

Zeid, Alexander, 21:**493–494**

Ẓeidah la-Derekh (Menahem ben Aaron ibn Zeraḥ), 14:21

Zeilig, Froim. *See* Aderca, Felix

Zeira. *See* Ze'eira

Zeira, Mordecai, 21:**494**

Ze'irei Zion, 9:286

Ze'irei Zion, 18:720, 21:**494–495**

Ze'irei Zion (movement), 8:756–757

Ze'iri, 21:**495**

Die Zeit (newspaper), 21:**495**

Zeitgehöf (Celan), 4:536

Zeitlin, Aaron, 8:737, 18:370, 21:**496**

Zeitlin, Hillel, 21:**496**

Zeitlin, Israel. *See* Tiempo, César

Zeitlin, Joshua, 8:441, 21:**496–497**

Zeitlin, Solomon, 11:313, 21:**497**

Zeitlin, William, 3:682, 21:**497**

Zeitschrift fuer die Wissenschaft des Judentums, 20:509

Zekan Aharon (Aaron ben David Cohen of Ragusa), 1:212

Zekan Aharon (Elijah ben Benjamin ha-Levi), 6:339

Zekenim. *See* Adelantados

Zekenim im Ne'arim (Braudes), 4:136

"Zekher Asiti le-Nifle'ot El" (Aboab), 4:144

Zekher Yiẓḥak (Shapira), 18:399

Zekhor le-Avraham (Alkalai), 1:663

Zekhor le-Avraham (Alnakar), 1:686

Zekhut avot, 15:691, 21:**497–498**

Zelaznik, Isaac. *See* Berger-Barzilai, Joseph

Zelcer, S. *See* Grosser, Bronislaw

Zelda, 21:**498–499**

Zeldin, Isaiah, 13:202–203, 21:**499–500**

Zeldovich, Yakov Borisovich, 21:**500**

Zelechow (Poland), 21:**500**

Zelenka, František, 21:**500**

Ẓeli Esh (Modena), 14:409

Zelikovitsh, Getsl. *See* Selikovitch, George

Ẓelilei Ḥanina (Karaczewski), 11:785

Zelizer, Nathan, 21:**500–501**

Zelk, Zoltan, 21:**501**

Zellerbach, Anthony, 21:**501**

Zellerbach family, 21:**501**

Zellick, Graham, 21:**501**

Zelophehad, 15:332, 21:**501–502**

Zelow (Poland), 21:**502**

Zelus Christi contra Judaeos (de la Cavalleria), 4:531–532

Zelus christi contra Judaeos, Saracenos et infideles (Cavalleria), 4:531–532, 18:45

Zeluta de-Avraham (Adler), 8:504

Zelva (Belarus), 21:**502–503**

Zelwa. *See* Zelva (Belarus)

Zemach, Benjamin, 21:**503**

Zemach, Nahum, 8:179, 21:**503**

Zemach, Shlomo, 21:**503–505**

Ẓemaḥ David (Pomis, de'), 16:367

Ẓemaḥ, Jacob. *See* Jacob ben Ẓemaḥ ben Nissim

Ẓemaḥ, R., 18:55

Ẓemaḥ ben Ḥayyim, 21:**505**

Ẓemaḥ ben Paltoi, 15:607–608, 21:**505**

Ẓemaḥ David (Gans), 6:515, 7:377, 9:157–158

Ẓemaḥ Jacob ben Ḥayyim, 2:77, 21:**505**

Ẓemaḥ Ẓaddik (Modena), 14:409

Ẓemaḥ Ẓedek ben Isaac, 21:**505**

Žemaitisa (Lithuania). *See* Samogitia (Lithuania)

Zeman, Kamil. *See* Olbracht, Ivan

Zemaraim (ancient Israel), 21:**505–506**

Zemba, Menahem, 21:**506**

Zemer, Hannah, 21:**506**

Zemirot, 21:**507**

Zemirot ha-Areẓ (Bacher), 3:36

Zemirot Yisrael (Coèn), 4:781

Zemlayachka, Rozalita Samoylovna, 21:**507**

Zemlya i Volya, 18:707

Zemun (Yugoslavia), 21:**507–508**

Zemurray, Samuel, 21:**508**

Zenata Berbers. *See* Sijilmassa (Morocco)

Zendel, Gabriel, 15:650

Zenica (Bosnia-Herzegovina), 21:**508**

Zenkevich, Lev Aleksandrovich, 21:**508–509**

Zeno, papyri of, 21:**509**

Zenobia. *See* Odenathus and Zenobia

Zenobia (Queen of Palmyra), 2:82

Zenobia Julia Aurelia Septimia, 15:**377**

Zenodorus, 21:**509**

Zenstralstelle, Zentralstelle fuer juedische Auswanderung, 17:203

Zenta (Hungary). *See* Senta (Hungary)

Zentrale Stelle der Landesjustizverwaltungen, 21:**510**

Zentralrat der Juden in Deutschland, 6:42, 21:**510**

Zentralstelle der Fuersorge Fuer Kriegsfluechtlinge, 21:**510**

Zentral-Verein deutscher Staatsbuerger juedischen Glaubens. *See* Central-Verein Deutscher Staatsbuerger Juedischen Glaubens

Zentralwohlfahrtstelle der Deutschen Juden, 21:**511**

Zenwirth, Yehoshua. *See* Bar-Josef, Yehoshua

Zephaniah, 6:492, 21:**511–512**

Zephaniah ben Mordecai, 21:**512**

Zephira, Bracha, 4:96

Zeppelin, 1:429

Zeppelin (airship), 18:189

Zerah (Edomite chief), 21:**513**

Zerah (levite), 21:**513**

Zerah (son of Judah), 15:769, 21:**512–513**

Zerah (son of Simeon), 21:**513**

Zerah ben Nathan of Troki, 21:**513**

Zerahiah ben Isaac ben Shealtiel, 21:**514–515**

Zerahiah ben Isaac ha-Levi, 1:297, 21:**515**

Zerah the Cushite, 21:**513**

Zera'im, 21:**515**

Zerbst (Germany), 21:**515**

Zered, 21:**516**

Zeredah (ancient Israel), 21:**516**

Zerimat Ḥakhamim (Moav), 18:205

Zeror ha-Ḥayyim (Ḥayyim ben Samuel ben David of Tudela), 8:482

Zer Peraḥim (Bader), 3:45

Zerubavel, Jacob, 21:**516**

Zerubbabel (biblical figure), 5:460, 11:241, 18:465–466, 19:608–610, 21:**516–517**

Zerubbabel, Book of. See Book of Zerubbabel

Zerubbavel (Levinsohn), 12:722

Zeta Beta Tau American Jewish Fraternal Organization, 6:240

Zeus Casius (Egypt). *See* Baal-Zephon (Egypt)

Zev, 15:650

Zevahim, 21:**518**

Zevi, Bruno, 16:345, 21:**519**

Zevi, Tullia, 10:812

Ẓevi, Shabbetai. *See* Shabbetai Ẓevi

Ẓevi Hirsch ben David Broda, 4:193

Ẓevi Hirsch Freidman of Lesko, 21:**519**

Ẓevi Hirsch of Nadworna, 21:**519**

Ẓevi Hirsh of Kamenka. *See* Kamenka, Ẓevi Hirsch of

Ẓevi Muddaḥ (Frances), 7:171, 18:347

Zevin, Israel Joseph. *See* Tashrak

Zevin, Solomon Joseph, 21:**519–520**

"Der Zeyde." *See* Vinchevsky, Morris

Zeyer, Julius, 11:412, 21:**520**

Der Zeyger (Shalom Aleichem), 18:382

Zgerzh. *See* Zgierz (Poland)

Zgierz (Poland), 21:**520–521**

Zgurita. *See* Zguritsa (Moldova)

Zguritsa (Moldova), 21:**521**

Zhagare (Lithuania). *See* Zagare (Lithuania)

Zhdanov (Ukraine), 21:**521**

Zhelezniak, Yokheved. *See* Bat-Miriam, Yokheved

Zhernensky, Moshe Eliyahu, 21:**521**

Zhetl (Belarus). *See* Dyatlovo (Belarus)

Zhidachov (Ukraine), 21:**521**

Zhidachov dynasty, 8:422, 21:**522**

Zhirkova, Elizaveta. *See* Elisheva

Zhirmunsky, Viktor Maksimovich, 21:**522–523**

Zhitlowsky, Chaim, 16:348, 18:707, 21:**523–524**

   An-Ski, S., 2:182

   minority rights, 14:288

   Sejmists, 11:314, 315

Zhitnitski, Mark, 21:**524**

Zhitomir (Ukraine), 18:263, 21:**524–525**

Zhitomirski, Alexander Matveyevich, 21:**525**

Zhmerinka (Ukraine), 21:**525**

Zhmud (Lithuania). *See* Samogitia (Lithuania)

Zhmud-Samogitia (Lithuania). *See* Birzai (Lithuania)

Zholkva (Ukraine), 21:**525–526**

Zhuravno (Ukraine), 21:**526**

Ziba, 21:**526–527**

Zidarov, Kamen, 4:276

Ẓidduk ha-Din, 21:**527**

Žídek, Pavel, 21:**527**

Zidon (Lebanon). *See* Sidon (Lebanon)

Židovská Strana, 21:**527–528**

Ziegfeld, Florenz, 4:177, 21:**528**

Ziegler, Archibald, 21:**528**

Ziegler, Ignaz, 21:**528**

Ziegler School of Rabbinic Studies at the Univ. of Judaism, 17:26

Ziff, Morris, 21:**528–529**

Ziffer, Mosche, 18:223

Zifroni, Israel ben Daniel, 21:**529**

Der Zigeunerprimas (Kalman), 11:745

Zikaron Zot (Jacob Isaac ha-Ḥozeh mi-Lublin), 11:40, 41

Zikhron Devarim (Shabtai), 18:359–360

Zikhronet le-Veit David (Reckendorf), 17:146

Zikhronot, 1:351, 352–353, 2:75, 21:**529**

Zikhronot shel Ḥoleh Shikheḥah (Reich), 17:196

Zikhron Shemu'el (Modern), 14:410

Zikhron Ya'akov (Israel), 1:221, 222, 223, 21:**529–530**

Zikhroynes fun Mayn Haym (Adler), 1:399–400

Zikkaron (Kimḥi). *See Sefer Zikkaron* (Kimḥi)

Zikkaron Im Eshkaḥekh, 18:450

Ziklag (ancient Israel), 21:**530**

Zikronot Wa'ad ha-Lašon, 8:675

Zikronot Wa'ad ha-Lašon II, 8:678

Zilber, Lev Aleksandrovich, 21:**530**

Zilberg, Avraham. *See* Tehomi, Avraham

Zilberg, Benjamin A. *See* Kaverin, Benjamin Aleksandrovich

Zilberman, Alexandru. *See* Sever, Alexandru

Zilbershtein, Gedalyah. *See* Silverstone, Gedalyah

Zilberts, Zavel, 21:**530**

Zilboorg, Gregory, 5:302, 21:**530–531**

Zilina (Slovakia), 21:**531–532**

Zilis, 2:419

Zilkha, Khedoury, 21:532

Zilkha, Na'im, 12:548, 21:**532**

Zilkha family, 21:**532**

Ẓilo shel Rosendrof (Shaham), 18:363

Zilpah, 1:415, 21:**532**

Zim, 21:**532–533**

Zimbabwe, 21:**533**, **533–534**

Zimbalist, Efrem, 21:**534**

Zimbalist, Efrem, Jr., 21:**534**

Zimberlin, John, 2:476, 477

Zimel Sofer, 4:367

Zimman, Harry, 15:415

Zimmels, Hirsch Jacob, 21:**534**

Zimmerli, Walther, 21:**534**

Zimmerman, Charles Sascha, 21:**534**

Zimmerman, Harry M., 21:**535**

Zimmerman, Robert. *See* Dylan, Bob

Zimmerman, Robert Allen. *See* Dylan, Bob

Zimmerman, Sheldon, 21:**535**

Zimmern, Alfred. *See* Zimmern, Sir Alfred

Zimmern, Sir Alfred, 21:**535–536**

Zimrat Yah (Dato), 5:441

Zimri. *See* Zamaris

Zimri (chariot captain), 6:282

Zimri (King), 21:**536**

Zimri (Prince), 21:**536**

Zimri-Lim of Mari, 2:96

Ẓimẓum, 11:641–644, 17:283, 18:351–352

Zinberg, Israel, 21:**536–537**

Zinnemann, Fred, 21:**537**

Zinoviev, Grigori Yevseyevich, 21:**537–538**

Zinovyevsk (Ukraine). *See* Kirovograd (Ukraine)

Zion, 21:**538**

Ẓioni (Eisenstadt), 6:270

Zioni, A. *See* Elazari-Volcani, Yiẓhak

Zionides, 11:214–215, 495–497

Ẓioni family, 13:251–252

Zionism, 9:238–239, 21:**539–627,** *602*
  1880's, 21:545–547, *547*
    Aaronsohn, Aaron and, 1:221–222
    Abeles, Otto, 1:247
    Abraham, Abrahams, 1:315
    Abrahams, Israel, 1:316
    Abramowitz, Dov Baer, 1:324
    Abramowitz, Grigori, 1:324–325
    Abzug, Bella Savitzky, 1:347
    Aden, 1:389
    Adler, Cyrus, 1:395
    Adler, Friedrich, 1:397
    Adler, Hermann, 1:398
    Agnon, Shmuel Yosef, 1:466
    agriculture, 1:497
    Agron, Gershon, 1:504
    Agudat Israel, 1:505, 506–507, 506–508, 507t, 14:15
    Aguddat Aḥim, 1:508
    Aḥad Ha-Am on biblical exegesis and study, 3:647
    Aharonovitch, Yosef, 1:537
    Aḥdut ha-Avodah, 1:540
    Aḥdut ha-Avodah-Po'alei Zion, 1:540–541
    Aḥ ha-Am, 1:525–529
    Ahwaz, 1:548
    Akedah, 1:558–559
    Albala, David, 1:582
    aliyah and absorption, 1:660–661
      Ḥibbat Zion period, 1880s, 10:330–333
      post-Six-DayWar, 10:231

    post World War I, 10:335–336
    Alkalai, David, 1:663
    Alkalai, Judah ben Solomon Ḥai, 1:663
    Allen, Isaac, 1:667
    American Israel Public Affairs Committee, 2:50
    American Jewish Committee, 2:55
    American Jewish Congress, 2:56–58
    American Zionist Committee for Public Affairs, 2:50
    American Zionist Emergency Council, 2:65, 6:773, 21:607
    American Zionist Federation, 2:65
    Amery, Leopold Charles Maurice Stennet, 2:66
    Amsterdam, 2:113
    Amusin, Joseph, 2:124
    Anglo-American Committee, 21:572
    Anglo-Jewish Association, 2:162
    anti-zionism, 2:236–237, 239–240, 244–245, 5:99–100
      anti-nationalists, 21:559–560
      Argentinian agricultural settlement, 21:560–561
      Australia, 10:54
      autonomists, 21:559–560
      religious anti-nationalists, 21:560
      Soviet Jewish culture, early, 21:561
      territorialism, 21:560
      Yiddishists, 21:559–560
    apologetics, 2:269
    Arab labor issue, 10:195
    Arab problem, 20:748
    Arab relations, 21:553–555
    Arad Program., 21:614
    Argentina, 2:430, 432, 434, 435, 437–438, 440, 445
    Australia, 14:8
    Austria
      Kadimah society, 18:151
      Scherlag, Mark, 18:123
    Bahā'ī and, 10:650
    Balfour, Arthur James, 3:85
    Balfour Declaration, 3:85–89, 21:567
    Barishansky, Raphael, 3:154
    Baruch, Joseph Marcou, 3:187
    Basle Program, 3:202–203
    Belkowsky, Ẓevi Hirsch, 3:297–298
    Benei Moshe, 3:**334–335**
    in Bialystok (Poland), 3:567

    Bibas, Judah, 3:572
    biblical exegesis and study influenced by, 3:663
    bibliographies, 21:622–625
    Bienenfeld, Franz Rudolf, 3:690
    Bienenstock, Max, 3:690
    Bierer, Rubin, 3:691
    Biltmore Program, 3:699–700
    Bilu, 3:700–701
    Biram, Arthur, 3:709
    in Birmingham, 3:713
    Birnbaum, Nathan, 3:714–716
    Birobidzhan as alternative to, 3:718
    in Bistrita, 3:727
    Blau-Weiss, 3:746–747, 11:721
    Blis, David, 3:756
    Bloch, Ernst, on, 3:760
    Bloch, Joseph Samuel, 3:763, 764
    blood libel, Arab association with, 3:780
    Bodenheimer, Max Isidor, 4:27
    Boehm, Adolf, 4:31
    Borochov, Ber, 4:88–90
    in Boston, 4:100
    Brandeis, Louis Dembitz, 4:122–123
    Brazil, 4:148, 150–151, 17:338, 18:32
    Breuer, Isaac, 4:171
    Buber, Martin, 4:231, 234–235
    Bulgaria, 4:270
    Bund on, 4:278, 279, 280, 281
    Canada, 4:400–401, 406–407, 408, 410, 421–423, 6:728, 11:716
    Central Zionist Archives, 9:427
    Chaim Weitzmann, 20:744–752
    Chajes, Hirsch Perez, 4:558–559
    Chasanowich, Joseph, 4:580–581
    children's literature, 4:624
    Chile, 4:638–639, 640, 641, 644
    China, 4:647–648
    Chomsky, Noah, 4:665
    Christian, 21:621–622
    Christian attitude, 4:685–686
    Christian millenarianism and, 3:737
    chronology, 9:273t, 275t, 277t
    Churchill support, 4:722
    Cleveland, 4:757
    Comintern and, 5:97
    Concerned Jewish Students, 21:613
    conferences, 5:147
    Cuba, 5:321–323

cultural, 10:682–684, 21:*548*, 548–550

Czech Republic, 4:192–193

Democratic Fraction, 5:552–553, 8:284

Depression era, 20:338–339

dramatic literature, 8:716–717

East Africa Uganda option, 21:560, 562–563

Egypt, 4:345, 6:235–236

Einstein support for, 6:262

England, 6:417, 418, 10:81

Erez Israel, 18:134

Europe, 6:744, 11:56, 64–66, 87–88, 89, 13:764–765

feminism in, 6:754

financial institutions, 11:285

Finkelstein, Noah, 7:36

Fischer, Jean, 7:53

flag, 7:68

forerunners of, 21:540–542

France, 4:9–10, 242, 12:489

fund raising, 16:44–45

Galicia, 4:135, 724

General Zionists, 7:439–440

Germany

Bergen-Belsen, 3:421

Berlin, 3:448

Blumenfeld, Kurt Yehudah, 4:11

Bruck, Grigori, 4:219

Hess, Moses, 9:75–76

influence on self-hate, 18:265

Juedische Rundschau, 11:570–571

Lichtheim, Richard, 12:800

Schach, Fabius, 18:98

Senator, David Werner, 18:287

goals, 21:616–619

Gordonia, 7:775–776

Gordon's philosophy, 7:765–766

Greece, 4:339–340, 18:125

Hadassah, the Women's Zionist Organization of America, 8:185–188

Halprin, Rose Luria, 8:286

halukkah, 8:287–290

halutz plays, 8:718–719

Hamizpeh, 8:305

Hantke, Arthur, 8:331

Haolam, 8:336

Harkavi, Yitzhak, 8:355–356

Hartman views on, 8:374–376

Ha-Shilo'ah, 8:381

Hebrew Committee for National Liberation, 21:606–607

He-Halutz, 8:756–761

He-Haver, 8:761

Hibbat Zion, 8:289, 9:94, 11:755, 756, 13:120, 21:542–545

Hitahadut, 9:285–286

Holocaust period, 21:571

Hungary, 4:200, 11:828–829, 18:139–140, 157

ideological evolution, 21:545–559

Iran, 1:224, 10:10

Iraq, 10:17–18, 19

Israel and, 21:556–559

Israel film critique of, 10:709–710

Italy, 4:495, 10:806–807, 12:703, 14:408

Jabotinsky, Vladimir, 11:10–14

Jewish Agency, 11:256–260, 21:218, 606–607

Jewish artists, 2:509

Jewish Chronicle and, 11:284–285

Jewish identity and, 11:297

Jewish Legion, 11:303, 305, 306, 21:550, *550*

Jewish State Party, 11:315–316

Jewish Student Movement, 21:610–615

in Johannesburg, 11:378

Joseph Trumpeldor, 20:159–160

Judaism, development of concept of, 11:518

Judeo-Persian literature and, 11:557–558

Juedischer Kulturbund, 11:570

Juedischer Verlag, 11:571

Kalischer, Zevi Hirsch, 11:737–738

Kharkov Conference, 12:106

labor movement, 21:606

Ha-Poel ha-Mizrachi, 8:338–340

Landau, Saul Raphael, 12:465

Laharanne, Ernest, 12:439

Landau, Shemuel Hayyim, 12:465–466

Language War, 12:482–483

Latin America, 12:511–512

League for Israel, The American Jewish, 12:563–564

League of Nations recognition of, 10:198

Leibowitz, Yeshayahu, 12:623–624

Leibowitz position, 12:623–624

Leo Motzkin, 14:578–579

Leon Pinsker, 16:173–174

Levin, Shmarya, 12:713–714

Libya, 12:792, 793–794

literature, 6:349, 11:66, 584

Lithuania, 13:120–121

meaning of, 21:539–540

Mexico, 6:723

Mishpat Ivri, 14:352–354

Mohilewer, Josef, 14:419

Mohilewer, Samuel, 14:418–419

Morgenthau, Henry, Sr., 14:488–489

Morocco, 4:503, 7:7–8, 14:501

Moses Hess, 21:541–542

music, 6:745

national renaissance, 9:247–249

Netherlands, 15:101, 102, 108, 18:144

new types of social organization, 9:245–246

in New Zealand, 15:243

Nietzsche, Friedrich Wilhelm, 15:262

Niger, Shmuel, 15:263

Nissenbaum, Isaac, 15:277

Nobel, Nehemiah Anton, 15:291

non-Jewish supporters, 13:600, 775

Nordau, Max, 15:297–299

Nossig, Alfred, 15:314

in Odessa, 15:380

Odessa Committee, 15:382

Oliphant, Laurence, 15:404

organization of

general council, 21:578–579

government, 21:578–580

history, 21:576–577

Israel and, 21:580

Jewish Agency, 21:579–580

structure, 21:577–578

Zionist Congress, 21:578

organizations, 15:27, 90

Palestine (Ottoman), 10:196–197, 15:542, 543–545

Palestine Inquiry Commissions, 15:582–585

Palestine Office, 15:595

Palestinian opposition, 10:272–275

Pardes, Eliyahu, 15:633

Partition Commission, 21:570

Patterson, John Henry, 15:694

Peel Commission, 20:748–749, 21:554, 569–570

Persia, 15:791

Peru, 15:796

philosophical analysis of, 16:100–103

PICA, 16:143

Pioneer Women, 16:180

Po'alei Agudat Israel, 16:244

Po'alei Zion, 16:244–249

Zionism, *continued*
  Poland, 12:466
    Lewite, Leon, 12:768–769
    Nowy Dziennik, 15:326
    Scharzbart, Isaac Ignacy,
      18:192
  policy
    Arab problem, 21:564–565
    Herzl period, 21:561–563
    internal struggles, 21:564–567
    interwar period, 21:567–571
    transition period, 21:563–564
  post-Holocaust, 21:554–556, 571–573
  post-WW I period, 21:551–553
  Prague, 16:452
  Protestants, 16:630
  protestrabbiner and, 16:633
  Rabbi Judah Alkalai, 21:540–541
  redemption, 17:155
  Reform Judaism, 17:170, 21:607
  religious courts in Palestine
    (Ottoman) and, 10:620–621
  revisionists, 17:260–267
  Romania, 11:828–829
    Braunstein, Menahem
      Mendel, 4:139
    Brociner, Joseph, 4:192
    center in, 11:91–92
    Moinesti, 14:421
  Romano, Marco, 17:405
  Rónai, János, 18:418–419
  Rosen, Pinhas, 17:430
  Rosenberg, Abraham Hayyim,
    17:433–434
  Rosenblatt, Bernard Abraham,
    17:440
  Rosensohn, Etta Lasker, 17:450
  Rotenstreich, Fischel, 17:478
  Rothenberg, Morris, 17:485
  Rothschild, James Armand de,
    17:493–494
  Rozovski, Pinhas, 17:504–505
  Rubenovitz, Herman H., 17:509–510
  Ruelf, Isaac, 17:526–527
  Rufeisen, Joseph, 17:527
  Ruppin, Arthur, 17:529–530
  Russia, 4:88, 21:601–604
    Brandt, Boris, 4:128
    Bruck, Grigori, 4:219
    leaders, 13:706
    Minsk Conference, 14:297
    Moscow, 14:518
    Petrograd Conference, 16:19
    Sheinkin, Menahem, 18:437–438

  sacrifices, 17:644
  Schalit, Isidor, 18:104–105
  Schechtman, Joseph B., 18:115–116
  Schocken, Salman, 18:154–155
  Schwadron, Abraham, 18:181–182
  science fiction and fantasy, Jewish,
    18:204–206
  Selbstemanzipation, 18:257–258
  Shapira, Avraham Elkana Kahana,
    18:399
  Shapira, Hayyim Eleazar,
    opposition to, 18:398–399
  shekel, 18:440
  Sinai Covenant, significance of,
    8:375–376
  Slánský trial, 18:665
  socialism, 4:88–90, 12:709–710,
    18:711
  South Africa, 4:444, 445, 19:49–50
  Soviet Jews, 12:493–494, 21:557–558
  students' movements, 18:261–262,
    19:265–269
  summer camps, 11:275
  Sykes-Picot Agreement, 10:185,
    19:350–351, *351*
  synthetic, 20:745
  Theodore Herzl, 9:54–66
  Torah, approach to, 20:44
  Torah va-Avodah, 8:338, 20:53
  Tunisia, 20:187–188
  U.A., Hibbat Zion movement,
    3:99
  Uganda scheme, 8:497, 20:225
  U.K., 4:196, 5:255, 18:208
  Ukraine, 1:610
  U.N. anti-Israel campaign, 20:273–274
  underground organizations WW
    II, 3:433–436
  UN involvement, 21:573–576
  U.S., 2:45, 610, 12:497, 21:185
    1960s, 20:353
    aliyah and youth movements,
      21:608–609
    The American Jewish League
      for Israel, 12:563–564
    Bublick, Gedaliah, 4:237
    Chicago, 4:611
    Federation of Zionists of
      Greater New York and
      Vicinity, 21:605–606
    fraternal orders, 6:**712–713**
    Jewish Student Movement,
      21:610–615
    Labor Zionist Alliance,
      12:419–420

  Network, 21:613
  New York City, 15:209
  opposition, 21:607–608
  orators, 13:602
  Radical Zionist Alliance,
    21:614–615
  radical Zionists, 21:610–615
  religious and ideological
    issues, 21:609–610
  Saint Louis, 17:673
  Schenk, Fay L., 18:122
  Schiff, Jacob Henry,
    opposition to, 18:131
  Schoolman, Bertha S., 18:161
  Seligsberg, Allice Lillie, 18:268
  Shapiro, Ezra Z., 18:405
  WW II period, 21:606
  WW I period, 21:605–606
  Zionist Organization of
    America, 21:636–637
  utopian visions, 18:202–203,
    21:620–622
  Vatican and, 20:479–481
  Volkspartei, Juedische, 20:574
  Die Welt, 21:**8–9**
  White Paper, 4:722, 21:569, 570–571
  women's participation, 21:185, 190
  world development
    Australia and New Zealand,
      21:580–581
    Austria, 21:581–582
    Bulgaria, 21:582–583
    Canada, 21:583–585
    France, 21:586–587
    Germany, 21:587–588
    Holland, 21:589–590
    Hungary, 21:590–592
    Italy, 21:592–593
    Latin America, 21:593–595
    North Africa, Asian
      countries, 21:595–597, *596t*
    Poland, 21:597–599
    Romania, 21:599–601
    Russia, 21:601–604, *602*
    South Africa, 21:604–605
    U.K., 21:588–589
    United States, 21:605–615
    Yugoslavia, 21:615–616
  World Jewish Congress, 21:217–218, 219, **221–222**
  World Labor Zionist movement,
    21:**222–223**
  World Zionist Organization as
    authorized agency, 10:216
  Youth Aliyah, 21:403–406
  youth movements
    Betar, 3:510

Ha-Ḥalutz, 8:**756–761**
Ha-No'ar ha-Ivri-Akiba, 8:327
Ha-No'ar ha-Oved Ve-ha-Lomed, 8:327–328
Ha-Shomer ha-Ẓa'ir, 8:382–385
He-Ḥalutz ha-Ẓa'ir, 8:759
Young Judea, 21:402
Ẓe'irei Zion, 8:756–757
Yugoslavia, 12:796
Ze'irei Zion, 21:494–495
Ẓevi Hirsch Kalischer, 21:541
Zionist Congresses, 21:627–636
zionist leaders
Kahn, Franz, 11:721
Kalef, Yehoshua, 11:733
Kallenbach, Hermann, 11:743–744
Kamhi, Leon, 11:755
Kaplan, Isaac, 11:775
Kaplan, Morcechai Menahem, 11:777–779
Kaplan, Sender Meyer, 11:780
Kaplansky, Shelomo, 11:780–781
Kasztner, Rezso Rudolf, 11:828–829
Lindheim, Irma Levy, 13:28
Neumann, Emanuel, 15:121
Rabinowitz, Samuel Jacob, 17:41
Reich, Leon, 17:197
Sapir, Joseph, 18:38
Silver, Abba, 18:583–584
Simon, Julius, 18:613
Simon, Sir Leon, 18:613–614
Sneerson, Ḥayyim Ẓevi, 18:696
zionist socialism, 18:717–718
Zionists of America, 3:758
See also Judah Halevi; specific organizations; specific Zionist organizations
Zionism from the Religious Point of View. See Ha-Ẓiyyonut mi-Nekuddat Hashkafat ha-Dat
Zionismus und Politik (Heimann), 8:769
Zionist Commission, 6:146, 12:703, 18:613–614, 21:**627**
Zionist Commission for Palestine. See Zionist Commission
Zionist Congresses, 8:740, 9:245–246, 286–287, 21:**627–636**
Zionist Federation of Great Britain, 18:587
The Zionist Idea (Hertzberg), 9:49

Zionist Organization
Antebi, Albert, 2:184
Bulgaria, 11:733
Jewish National Fund, 11:308–309
Kann, Jacobus Henricus, 11:765
Netherlands, 11:765
Russia, 13:269
Zionist Organization of America (ZOA), 21:**636–637**
Fishman, Jacob, 7:64
Jewish Legion, 11:305
Klein, Morton, 12:224
Zionist Organization of Canada, 4:406, 407, 11:716
Zionist party (Russia), 3:88
Zionist Revisionist movement, 2:21
Zionists, 5:439, 725
Austria, 16:340–341
Bentwich family, 3:381
Berman, Adolf Abraham, 3:461
Berman Berman, Natalio, 3:465
Bernstein, Louis, 3:481–482
Bernstein, Perez, 3:483
Bernstein-Kogan, Jacob, 3:486
Bettelheim, Samuel, 3:552
Cresson, Warder, 5:288–289
Deedes, Sir Wyndham, 5:530
De Lieme, Nehemia, 5:538–539
Dénes, Béla, 5:579
de Sola, Aaron David Meldola, 5:603
de Sola, Clarence Isaac, 5:603
Deutsch, Felix, 5:622–623
Diamant, Paul Joseph, 5:632
Don-Yaḥia, Yehudah Leib, 5:752
Dugdale, Blanche Elizabeth Campbell, 6:42
Dulzin, Arye Leib, 6:45
Dunant, Jean Henri, 6:47
Dunkelman, Rose, 6:50
Ebner, Meir, 6:87–88
Edelstein, Jacob, 6:145
Eder, Montague David, 6:146
Einstein, Albert, 6:262
Eisenstadt, Benzion, 6:270
Eisler, Edmund Menahem, 6:274–275
Eitingon, Max, 6:279–280
Elias, Joseph, 6:318
Fitch, Louis, 7:65
Greenberg, Hayim, 8:68
Grossman, Meir, 8:100–101
Gruenbaum, Yiẓhak, 8:106–107
Haan, Jacob Israël De, 8:163–164
Hartglas, Maximilian Meir Apolinary, 8:374

Hausdorf, Azriel Zelig, 8:462
Hausner, Bernard, 8:464
Hechler, William Henry, 8:150, 750
Hellman, Jacob, 8:800
Herbst, Karl, 9:9
Herlitz, Georg, 9:23
Hermann, Leo, 9:24–25
Hertzberg, Arthur, 9:49
Hickl, Max, 9:95
Hirsch, Richard, 3:129
Hirshenberg, Samuel, 9:142–143
Katzenelson, Nissan, 12:21–22
Katzenelson, Yosef, 12:22
Katznelson, Berl, 12:23–26
Kirshblum, Mordecai, 12:189–190
Klarman, Yosef, 12:211
Klatzkin, Jacob, 12:**213–214**
Klausner, Joseph Gedaliah, 12:215–217
Klumel, Meir, 12:**234**
Landau, Saul Raphael, 12:465
Latvian, Deinard, Ephraim, 5:532
Lipsky, Louis, 13:75–76
Mirsky, Samuel Kalman, 14:315
Molho, Isaac Raphael, 14:425–426
Mond, Alfred Moritz, 14:434
Mond, Henry, 14:434–435
Monsky, Henry, 14:451
Montefiore, Moses, 14:457
Montor, Henry, 14:461–462
Mordovtsev, Danil Lukich, 14:483
Moser, Jacob, 14:522
Pincus, Louis Arieh, 16:165
Pineles, Samuel, 16:166–167
Plotnicka, Frumka, 16:241
Polish, David, 16:333–334
Rabinowicz, Oskar K., 17:40
Raisin, Max, 17:74–75
Rakovsky, Puah, 17:76
Rapoport, Samuel, 17:98
Recanati, Abraham Samuel, 17:141
Richter, Mozés, 17:291–292
Ringel, Michael, 17:335
Singer, Ludvik, 18:639
Venezuelan, Czenstochowski, Walter, 5:370
Zionist Socialist Labor Party. See Aḥdut ha-Avodah
Zionist Socialist Party. See ZS (Zionist Socialist party)
Zionist Socialist Workers' Party, 21:**637–638**
Zion Mule Corps, 9:249, 11:303
Ziph (ancient Israel), 21:**638**
Ziphion (ancient city). See Zaphon (ancient city)

Zipper, Gershon, 21:**638**

Zipper, Jacob. *See* Zipper, Ya'akov

Zipper, Ya'akov, 4:426, 21:**638–639**

Zipporah, 14:524, 526, 532, 535, 21:**639**

Zipporei Zel (Seri), 18:310

Zippori (Galilee). *See* Sepphoris (Galilee)

Zipser, Majer, 21:**639**

Zirelson, Judah Leib, 21:**639–640**

Zirid dynasty, 21:**640**

Zirid emirs, 11:726–727

Ziryāb, 1:679

Zislin, Meir, 11:322

Zisling, Aharon, 21:**640**

Zissu, Abraham Leib, 21:**640–641**

Zissu, Theodore, 21:641

Zitnitsky, Pincas Lázaro, 21:**641**

Zitron, Samuel Leib, 21:**641**

Ziusudra, 7:81, 15:287

Ziv, Jacob, 21:**641–642**

Zivhei Shelamiim (Badihi), 3:49

Zivion, 21:**642**

Ziyanid dynasty, 21:**642**

Ziyyaḥ, Joseph ben Abraham ibn. *See* Zayyaḥ, Joseph ben Abraham ibn

Zizat Novel Zevi (Sasportas), 18:66, 67, 347

Zizit, 6:13, 14, 39, 21:**642–643**

Ziz Nezer ha-Kodesh (Kalfa), 11:733

Zlatopol (Ukraine), 21:**643**

Zlatopolsky, Hillel, 21:**643**

Zlocisti, Theodor, 21:**643**

Zloczow, Issachar of. *See* Issachar Dov Baer ben Aryeh Leib of Zloczow

Zlotnick, Yehuda Leib. *See* Avida, Yehuda Leib

Zlotnik, J.L., 7:13

Zlotowitz, Bernard M., 21:**644**

Zlotowitz, Meir, 21:**644–645**

Złow. *See* Zolochev (Ukraine)

Zmigrod Nowy (Poland), 21:**645**

Zmora, Yisrael, 21:**645**

Znaim (Czech Republic). *See* Znojmo (Czech Republic)

Znaimer, Moses, 21:**645–646**

Znojmo (Czech Republic), 21:**646**

ZOA. *See* Zionist Organization of America

Zoan (Ancient Egypt), 21:**646**

Z.O.B. (Zydowska Organizacja Bojowa), 2:164

Zodiac, 21:**646–647**

The Zodiac. See Ḥagorat Mazzalot

Zofim (ancient Israel), 21:**647**

Zofit (Israel), 21:**647**

Zohar, 11:609–610
   Aaron Selig ben Moses of Zolkiew, 1:220–221
   abortion, 1:271
   afterlife, 3:239–240
   author, 21:657–658
   biblical study in middle ages, influence of, 3:662–663
   chiromancy, 4:653
   commentaries, 21:659–660
   composition, 21:655–657
   demons, demonology, 5:576–577
   dreams, 6:9
   editions, manuscripts, 21:658–659
   Eleazar ben Simeon, 6:308
   Emden critique, 6:393
   eschatology, 6:500–502
   evil, 11:639, 640
   hagiography, 8:225
   Ḥasidei Ummot ha-Olam, 8:389
   Joseph ben Emanuel Ergas, 6:479
   Labi, Simeon, 12:408
   Landauer, Meyer Heinrich Hirsch, 12:467
   language, 21:653–655
   literary form, 21:648–650
   magical arts in practical Kabbalah, 11:666
   Moses, 14:537
   on onanism, 15:427
   parodies of, 15:658
   scholarship, research, 21:660–663
   Shema reading, 18:455
   sources, 21:652–653
   style, 21:651–652

Zohar, 2:579, 21:**647–664**

Zohar, Miriam, 21:**664**

Zohar, Uri, 21:**664**

Zohar, Zvi, 4:188

Zohar ha-Tevah (Hanau), 8:318

Zohary, Michael, 21:**664**

Zola, Émile, 6:19, 21:**664–665**

Zola, Gary Phillip, 2:54, 21:**665**

Zöld, Márton, 21:**665**

Zolf, Falek, 21:**665–666**

Zolf, Larry, 21:**666**

Zolf family, 21:**665–666**

Zoller, Israel, 21:**666**

Zollschan, Ignaz, 21:**666**

Zolochev (Ukraine), 21:**666–667**

Zolotonosha (Ukraine), 21:**667**

Zolotoy Telenok (Ilf), 9:720

Zołkiew. *See* Zholkva (Ukraine)

Zolty, Yaacov Bezalel, 21:**667**

Zomber, Dov Baer, 21:**667–668**

Zombor. *See* Sombor (Yugoslavia)

Zonana, David, 21:**668**

Zonana, Jacob, 21:**668**

Zonana, Samuel Halevy, 21:**668**

Zonana family, 21:**668**

Zondek, Bernhard, 21:**668–669**

Zondek, Hermann, 21:**668**

Zondek, Max, 21:**668**

Zondek, Samuel Georg, 21:**669**

Zondek family, 21:**668–669**

Zonenshayn, Meir. *See* Tashrak

Zon Kodashim (Schorr), 18:162

Zoology
   Aharoni, Israel, 1:531
   Bloch, Marcus Eliezer, 3:765
   Bodenheimer, Frederick Simon, 4:27
   Bresslau, Ernst, 4:167
   Enriques, Paolo, 6:445
   Haas, Fritz, 8:168–169
   Haas, Georg, 8:169
   Hyman, Libbie Henrietta, 9:650
   Mendelssohn, Heinrich, 14:33
   Semon, Richard Wolfgang, 18:286

Zopyrion, 21:**669**

Zorach, William, 21:**669**

Zorah (Israel), 21:**669–670**

Zoran (Israel), 21:**670**

Zoref, Abraham Solomon Zalman, 21:**670**

Zoref, Joshua Heshel ben Joseph, 1:378, 21:**670–671**

Zoref, Heshel, 18:354

Zori. *See* Balsam

Zori ha-Guf (Falaquera), 6:679

Zoritte-Megged, Eda, 13:766

Zorn, John, 21:**671**

Zoroastrianism
   dualism, 6:29
   Enoch, Slavonic Book of, 6:445
   Judaism, 11:515

Zor vi-Trushalayim (Shoham), 11:216

Zorzi, Franciscus Geogius. *See* Giorgio, Francesco

Zotos. *See* Izates II

Zot Zikaron (Jacob Isaac ha-Ḥozeh mi-Lublin), 11:40, 41

Zox, Ephraim, 16:340

Zrenjanin (Serbia), 21:**671–672**

ZS (Zionist Socialist party), 2:360, 21:**672–673**

A zsidók emancipatiója (Eötvös). *See Emancipation of the Jews* (Eötvös)

Zsidókérdés, asszimiláció, antiszemitizmus, 9:607

Zsigmond, Ede, 21:**673**

Zsoldos, Jenő, 21:**673**

Zsolna. *See* Zilina (Slovakia)

Zsolt, Béla, 21:**673**

Zubatovists. *See* Independent Jewish Workers Party

Zuchowicki, Abraham Moses. *See* Dillon, Abraham Moses

Zucker, Aaron. *See* Lutzky, A.

Zucker, David, 21:**673–674**

Zucker, Henry L., 21:**674**

Zucker, Jacques, 21:**674**

Zucker, Jeff, 21:**674**

Zucker, Moshe, 21:**674–675**

Zuckerkandl, Emil, 21:**675**

Zuckerman, Baruch, 21:**675**

Zuckerman, Ben, 21:**675–676**

Zuckerman, Itzhak, 21:**676**

Zuckerman, Mortimer, 15:225, 21:**676–677**

Zuckerman, Paul, 21:**677**

Zuckerman, Pinchas. *See* Zukerman, Pinchas

Zuckerman, Solly, Lord, 21:**677**

Zuckermandel, Moses Samuel, 21:**677–678**

Zuckermann, Benedict, 21:**678**

Zuckermann, Eliezer, 21:**678**

Zuckermann, Hugo, 21:**678**

Zuckmayer, Carl, 21:**678–679**

Zucrow, Maurice Joseph, 21:**679**

Zuelz (Poland), 18:578, 21:**679**

Zuelz, Aryeh Leib ben Moses. *See* Zuenz, Aryeh Leib ben Moses

Zuenz, Aryeh Leib ben Moses, 21:**679–680**

Zuf Devash (Altaras), 2:16

Zugot, 9:108–109, 14:340, 21:**680**

Zuhun Juhuri. *See* Judeo-Tat language

Zuhun Tati. *See* Judeo-Tat language

Zukerman, Jacob T., 21:**680–681**

Zukerman, Pinchas, 21:**681**

Zukertort, Johannes, 21:**681**

Zukofsky, Louis, 15:219, 442, 21:**681–682**

Zukofsky, Paul, 21:**682**

Zukor, Adolph, 12:500, 14:570, 21:**682**

Zukru (Emarite festival), 6:387, 389

Zukunft. See Tsukunft

Die Zukunft (periodical), 8:346, 21:**682–683**

Zulay, Menahem, 21:**683**

Zum Alten Testament und seiner Umwelt (Baumgartner), 3:222

Zundelevitch, Aaron, 16:348, 21:**683**

Zundel of Salant. *See* Salant, Joseph Sundel ben Benjamin Benish

Zunim. *See* Tares

Die Zunkunft (periodical), 8:346

Zunser, Eliakum, 3:48, 4:194–195, 21:**684**

Zuntz, Alexander, 21:**684**

Zuntz, Judah, 15:197

Zunz, Leopold, 16:12, 21:107, **684–688**
  aggadah, 1:460, 462
  bibliography of, 3:682
  biographical writings of, 3:707
  German translation of Bible by, 3:631
  Lebrecht, Fuerchtegott, 12:593
  on Oral Law, 15:457
  organs, use of, 15:468
  Wissenschaft des Judentums, 18:722

Zur, Menachem, 21:**688**

Zur, Zevi, 21:**688**

Zurat ha-Arez (Elijah ben Solomon Zalman), 6:343

Zurat ha-Arez ve-Tavnit Kaddurei ha Raki'a (Abraham bar Hiyya), 1:293

Zurawno (Ukraine). *See* Zhuravno (Ukraine)

Zur Entstehungsgeschichte des islamischen Gebets und Kultus (Mittwoch), 14:371

Zuri, Jacob Samuel, 21:**688–689**

Zurich (Switzerland), 21:**689–690**

Zuri-Szezak, Jacob Samuel. *See* Zuri, Jacob Samuel

Zur mi-Shello, 21:**690**

Zur Moshe (Israel), 21:**690**

Zuroff, Efraim, 21:**690–691**

Zur Yigal (Israel), 21:**691**

Zusya of Hanipoli, 21:**691–692**

Zuta, 6:231, 21:**692**

Zuta, Hayyim Aryeh, 21:**692**

Zutra, Mar I, 2:37, 21:**692**

Zutra, Mar II, 21:**692–693**

Zutra, Mar III, 21:**693**

Zutra ben Tobi, 21:693

Zvenigorodka (Ukraine), 21:**693**

Zvia, 21:**693**

Zvoleń. *See* Zwolen (Poland)

Zvolen (Poland). *See* Zwolen (Poland)

Zwartz, David, 15:246

Zwebner, Abraham. *See* Shag, Abraham

Zweifel, Eliezer, 8:416, 21:**693–694**

Zweig, Arnold, 21:**694**

Zweig, Stefan, 4:152, 17:338, 21:**694–695**

Zweihl family, 8:420

Zwick, Edward, 9:**46–47**

Zwickau (Germany), 21:**695**

Zwingli, Ulrich, 4:32

Das Zwoelfprophetenbuch (Sellin), 18:272

Zwolen (Poland), 21:**696**

Zychlin (Poland), 21:**696**

Zychlin. *See* Zychlin (Poland)

Zychlinska, Rajzel, 21:**696**

Zydowska Organizacja Bojowa (Z.O.B.), 2:164

Zydzi lwówscy na przełomie XVI–XVII wieku (Balaban), 3:82

Zygelbojm, Samuel Mordecai, 11:817–818, 21:**696–697**

Zyklon B, 7:393

Zyklon-B, 2:664–665, 9:305, *485*

Zylbercweig, Zalman, 21:**697**

Zynstein, Solomon, 2:48

Zyradów. *See* Zyrardow (Poland)

Zyrardow (Poland), 21:**697**

Zyskind, Bruno. *See* Jasieński, Bruno